February 5–9, 2018
Marina Del Rey, CA, USA

Association for
Computing Machinery

Advancing Computing as a Science & Profession

wsdm 2018

WSDM'18

Proceedings of the Eleventh ACM International Conference on
Web Search and Data Mining

Sponsored by:

ACM SIGIR, ACM SIGKDD, ACM SIGMOD, and ACM SIGWEB

Supported by:

LinkedIN, Microsoft, Huawei, Baidu, Adobe, Snap Inc., Amazon, Google, Yahoo! Research, Tencent AI Lab, JD.com, CreditX, Hulu, Appen, Pinterest, KKbox, & Kaggle

Association for
Computing Machinery

Advancing Computing as a Science & Profession

The Association for Computing Machinery
2 Penn Plaza, Suite 701
New York, New York 10121-0701

ISBN: 978-1-4503-5581-0 (Digital)

ISBN: 978-1-4503-5869-9 (Print)

Additional copies may be ordered prepaid from:

ACM Order Department
PO Box 30777
New York, NY 10087-0777, USA

Phone: 1-800-342-6626 (USA and Canada)
+1-212-626-0500 (Global)
Fax: +1-212-944-1318
E-mail: acmhelp@acm.org
Hours of Operation: 8:30 am – 4:30 pm ET

Welcome by the General Chairs

Welcome to the Eleventh ACM International Conference on Web Search and Data Mining (WSDM 2018), which is one of the top conferences in the areas of web search and web mining. WSDM 2018 will be held at The Ritz-Carlton Hotel, Marina del Rey, near Los Angeles, California from February 5 to 9, 2018.

The program for WSDM 2018 is packed with a VC & Industry Day, 8 tutorials, and a Doctoral Consortium on the first day. The VC & Industry Day focuses on the interaction of the search and data mining communities with the VC and Industry communities, and a series of invited talks by prominent speakers will be mixed with panels on the topics ranging from the role of the data science in startups to the sharing economy. The tutorial program includes tutorials on Neural Networks for Information Retrieval, A Critical Review of Online Social Data, Winning in Sports with Data, Differential Privacy for Information Retrieval, Influence Maximization in Online Social Networks, Network Science of Teams, Metrics of User Engagement, Mining Knowledge Graphs From Text.

For the main technical program, on the second, third and fourth day of the conference, we continue the single-track tradition established in previous years at WSDM, and the papers are categorized into oral papers and spotlight papers. The technical program also features keynotes by six prominent researchers: three from industry, Harry Shum (Microsoft), Igor Perisic (LinkedIn), Andrei Broder (Google), and three from academia, Shang-Hua Teng (USC), Judea Pearl (UCLA), Jiawei Han (UIUC). We would like to thank the keynote speakers for sharing their technical insights and research contributions with the conference participants.

On the final day of the conference the program includes 8 workshops and a dedicated event to WSDM CUP 2018. The workshop program includes workshops on Marketplace Optimization, Misinformation and Misbehavior Mining, Knowledge Base, Heterogeneous Networks, Disaster Management on Social Media, User Interaction Understanding, Adversarial Activity Analytics, User Modeling and Personalization.

We would like to acknowledge the key contributions by our Program Chairs, Yan Liu and Yoelle Maarek. We are also grateful to our Treasurer, Jimmy Huang; our Local Chair, Roger Jie Luo; our VC & Industry Day Chairs, Evgeniy Gabrilovich and Rong Yan; our Tutorial Chairs, David Carmel and Jaap Kamps; our Workshop Chairs, Jiliang Tang and Eugene Agichtein; our WSDM CUP Chairs, Shou-De Lin and Xing Xie; our Doctoral Consortium Chairs, Yizhou Sun and Hui Fang; our Best Paper Award Chairs, Charlie Clarke and Huan Liu; our Test of Time Award Chair, Fernando Diaz; our Sponsorship Chairs, Shipeng Yu and Dawei Yin; our Media & Publicity Chairs, Zhaochun Ren and Makoto Yamada; our Poster & Demo Chairs, Hongning Wang; our Proceedings Chairs, Qi Yu and Jianhui Chen; our Workflow Chair, Natali Ruchansky; our Web Chair, Yaguang Li. We would also like to sincerely thank ACM, our sponsors and WSDM Steering Committee for their support.

Finally, we would like to thank all Senior PC members, PC members, workshop and tutorial organizers, student volunteers and everyone who helped us in organizing WSDM 2018. We hope that you will enjoy the conference and the opportunity to share and discuss ideas in Web Search and Mining with other researchers and practitioners around the world.

Yi Chang
WSDM'18 General Chair
Jilin University & Huawei Inc.

Chengxiang Zhai
WSDM'18 General Chair
UIUC

Welcome by the Program Chairs

We are delighted to welcome you to the Eleventh ACM International Conference on Web Search and Data Mining (WSDM 2018) held in Los Angeles, California, USA, on February 5-9, 2018. Now in its eleventh year, WSDM has become a top tier conference in Web-inspired research relating to search and data mining. As in previous years, we continued observing a growth in number of submissions. The conference this year, with 514 valid submissions, maintained the major boost that was observed last year in Cambridge UK (with 505 submissions as compared to 386 in year 2016 in San Francisco). Interestingly, we saw an increase in 10% in abstract submissions with a record breaking 757 abstracts (as compared to 687 in 2017) but only 68% of those ended up as valid submissions. This is partly due to a relatively high number of invalid submissions that did not adhere to our new double-blind review policy.

The 514 valid submissions originated from 41 countries, out of which 84 (as compared to 80 in 2017) were accepted for full paper publication in the proceedings, thus reaching an acceptance rate of 16.12% (as compared to 15.94% last year) and within the range of the last 11 years (with a min of 15.5% and a max of 22.3%.) Unfortunately, three papers were withdrawn/rejected after acceptance due to their violations of WSDM guidelines. The final 81 papers that will be published in the proceedings are from 23 countries, spanning four continents, making this a truly international forum. Oral presentation slots were allocated to all papers. Yet, in order to maintain the single track model that most attendees prefer, we followed the "spotlight" short presentation plus poster approach that was introduced in 2012. Out of the 81 accepted papers, 58 were assigned such a two-minute spotlight slot, while 23 were assigned a long twenty-minute talk slot. The type of slot was chosen by the Senior PC members and Program co-chairs, mostly based on whether the topic and the content of the paper were best suited for a large group presentation or for a more focused and interactive poster style of presentation.

The double-blind flavor we adopted this year allowed the authors to indicate the source of their data set, or deployment environment (so as not to refer to "major commercial search engines" as has often been done in the past). However, we observed that several authors failed to indicate their conflict of interest (COI) adequately and we will make sure to enforce COI guidelines (through both awareness campaigns and hopefully automated tools) more rigorously now that the double-blind review policy has been adopted.

We would like to acknowledge the tremendous work of the 230 members of the international Program Committee (representing 27 countries), and in particular the effort of the 60 Senior Program Committee members. They should be credited for the high quality of the program this year. We would also like to thank the general chairs, Yi Chang and ChengXiang Zhai, who were wonderful partners in getting this program together, always looking for creative solutions to improve the quality of the conference.

Finally, we are in debt to the authors and attendees, who are the ones who make this conference possible and have allowed WSDM to become a wonderful forum to advance Web research and the premier ACM conference in the field.

We hope that you will find this program interesting and thought-provoking. Our goal was not only to give you the opportunity to share ideas with other researchers and practitioners from around the world, but also to foster new research and innovation in this fascinating Web era.

Yan Liu
WSDM'18 Program co-Chair
University of Southern California

Yoelle Maarek
WSDM'18 Program co-Chair
Amazon Research, Israel

Table of Contents

Doctoral Presentations

Demonstrations

Tutorials

Workshops

WSDM 2018 Conference Organization

General Chairs:	Yi Chang *(Jilin University & Huawei Inc.)* Chengxiang Zhai *(University of Illinois at Urbana-Champaign)*
Program Chairs:	Yan Liu *(University of Southern California)* Yoelle Maarek *(Amazon Research, Israel)*
Treasurer:	Jimmy Huang *(York University)*
Local Chair:	Roger Jie Luo *(Snapchat Inc)*
VC & Industry Chairs:	Evgeniy Gabrilovich *(Google Research)* Rong Yan *(Snapchat Inc.)*
Tutorial Chairs:	David Carmel *(Amazon)* Jaap Kamps *(University of Amsterdam)*
Workshop Chairs:	Jiliang Tang *(Michigan State University)* Eugene Agichtein *(Emory University)*
WSDM CUP Chairs:	Shou-De Lin *(National Taiwan University)* Xing Xie *(Microsoft Research)*
Doctoral Consortium Chairs:	Yizhou Sun *(University of California, Los Angeles)* Hui Fang *(University of Delaware)*
Best Paper Award Chairs:	Charlie Clarke *(University of Waterloo)* Huan Liu *(Arizona State University)*
Test of Time Award Chair:	Fernando Diaz *(Spotify)*
Sponsorship Chairs:	Shipeng Yu *(LinkedIn)* Dawei Yin *(JD.com)*
Media and Publicity Chairs:	Makoto Yamada *(RIKEN)* Zhaochun Ren *(JD.com)*
Proceedings Chairs:	Qi Yu *(Caltech)* Jianhui Chen *(Microsoft)*
Poster and Demo Chair:	Hongning Wang *(University of Virginia)*
Web Chair:	Yaguang Li *(University of Southern California)*

Senior Program Committee: Lada Adamic (Facebook Inc)
Eytan Adar (University of Washington)
Deepak Agarwal (LinkedIn)
Charu Aggarwal (IBM)
Eugene Agichtein (Emory University)
Leman Akoglu (Carnegie Mellon University)
James Allan (UMass Amherst)
Aris Anagnostopoulos (Sapienza University of Rome)
Ricardo Baeza-Yates (NTENT)
Roberto Bayardo (Google)
Paul Bennett (Microsoft Research)
Edward Bortnikov (Yahoo Research)
Jamie Callan (Carnegie Mellon University)
Ed H. Chi (Google, Inc.)
Charles Clarke (University of Waterloo)
Koby Crammer (The Technion)
Brian Davison (Lehigh University)
Maarten de Rijke (University of Amsterdam)
Arjen de Vries (Radboud University)
Fernando Diaz (Microsoft Research)
Aristides Gionis (Aalto University)
Manuel Gomez Rodriguez (MPI for Software Systems)
Jimmy Huang (York University)
Ravi Kumar (Google)
Oren Kurland (Technion, Israel Institute of Technology)
Mounia Lalmas (Yahoo Research)
Ronny Lempel (Outbrain)
Kristina Lerman (University of Southern California)
Jure Leskovec (Stanford University)
Liane Lewin-Eytan (Yahoo Research)
Hang Li (Toutiao)
Edo Liberty (Amazon)
Ee-Peng Lim (Singapore Management University)
Shou-De Lin (National Taiwan University)
Bing Liu (University of Illinois at Chicago)
Huan Liu (Arizona State University)
Qiaozhu Mei (University of Michigan)
Alistair Moffat (The University of Melbourne)
Marc Najork (Google)
Jennifer Neville (Purdue University)
Jian Pei (Simon Fraser University)
Dan Pelleg (Yahoo Research)
B. Aditya Prakash (Virginia Tech)
Kira Radinsky (eBay)
Filip Radlinski (Google)

Senior Program Committee (continued):

Dafna Shahaf (The Hebrew University of Jerusalem)
Dou Shen (Microsoft Adcenter Labs)
Fabrizio Silvestri (Facebook)
Aya Soffer (IBM)
Le Song (Georgia Tech)
Jie Tang (Tsinghua University)
Andrew Tomkins (Google)
Hongning Wang (University of Virginia)
Wei Wang (UCLA)
Ryen W. White (Microsoft Research)
Makoto Yamada (RIKEN)
Emine Yilmaz (University College London)
Dawei Yin (jd.com)
Hongyuan Zha (Georgia Institute of Technology)
Min Zhang (Tsinghua University)

WSDM 2018 Sponsors & Supports

Platinum Supports

Gold Supports

Silver Supports

Bronze Supports

WSDM Cup Gold Supports

Sponsors

A Call to Arms: Embrace Assistive AI Systems!

Andrei Broder
Google
broder@acm.org

ABSTRACT

A quarter-century ago Web search stormed the world: within a few years the Web search box became a standard tool of daily life ready to satisfy informational, transactional, and navigational queries needed for some task completion. However, two recent trends are dramatically changing the box's role: first, the explosive spread of smartphones brings significant computational resources literally into the pockets of billions of users; second, recent technological advances in machine learning and artificial intelligence, and in particular in speech processing led to the wide deployment of assistive AI systems, culminating in personal digital assistants. Along the way, the "Web search box" has become an "assistance request box" (implicit, in the case of voice-activated assistants) and likewise, many other information processing systems (e.g. e-mail, navigation, personal search, etc) have adopted assistive aspects.

Formally, the assistive systems can be viewed as a selection process within a base set of alternatives driven by some user input. The output is either one alternative or a smaller set of alternatives, maybe subject to future selection. Hence, classic IR is a particular instance of this formulation, where the input is a textual query and the selection process is relevance ranking over the corpus.

In increasing order of selection capabilities, assistive systems can be classified into three categories:

(1) *Subordinate*: systems where the selection is fully specified by the request; if this results in a singleton the system provides it, otherwise the system provides a random alternative from the result set. Therefore, the challenge for subordinate systems consists only in the correct interpretation of the user request (e.g., weather information, simple personal schedule management, a "play jazz" request).
(2) *Conducive*: systems that reduce the set of alternatives to a smaller set, possibly via an interactive process (e.g. the classic ten blue links, the three "smart replies" in Gmail, interactive recommendations, etc).
(3) *Decisive*: systems that make all necessary decisions to reach the desired goal (in other words, select a single alternative from the set of possibilities) including resolving ambiguities and other substantive decisions without further input from the user (e.g., typical translation systems, self-driving cars).

The main goal of this talk is to examine these developments and to urge the WSDM community to increase its focus on assistive AI solutions that are becoming pertinent to a wide variety of information processing problems. I will mostly present ideas and work in progress, and there will be many more open questions than definitive answers.

BIOGRAPHY

Broder is a Distinguished Scientist at Google where he leads a multidisciplinary research team located across three continents. From 2005 to 2012 he was a Fellow and VP for Computational Advertising at Yahoo. Previous positions include Distinguished Engineer at IBM and VP for Research and Chief Scientist at AltaVista. He was graduated Summa cum Laude from Technion and obtained his M.Sc. and Ph.D. in Computer Science at Stanford under Don Knuth. Broder has authored more than a hundred papers and was awarded fifty US patents. His current research interests are focused on user understanding, computational advertising, context-driven information supply, and randomized algorithms. He is a member of the US National Academy of Engineering and a Fellow of ACM and of IEEE. Other honors include the ACM Paris Kanellakis Theory and Practice Award and a doctorate Honoris Causa from Technion.

WSDM 2018, February 5–9, 2018, Marina Del Rey, CA, USA

ACM ISBN 978-1-4503-5581-0/18/02.
https://doi.org/10.1145/3159652.3160603

On the Power of Massive Text Data

Jiawei Han
University of Illinois at Urbana-Champaign
hanj@illinois.edu

ABSTRACT

The real-world big data is largely unstructured, dynamic, and interconnected, in the form of natural language text. It is highly desirable to transform such massive unstructured data into structured knowledge. Many researchers and practitioners rely on labor-intensive labeling and curation to extract knowledge from unstructured text data. However, such approaches may not be scalable to web-scale or adaptable to new domains, especially considering that a lot of text corpora are highly dynamic and domain-specific. We argue that massive text data itself contains a large body of hidden patterns, structures, and knowledge. Equipped with domain-independent and domain-specific knowledge-bases, a promising direction is to develop more systematic data mining methods to turn massive unstructured text data into structured knowledge.

We introduce a set of methods developed recently in our own group on exploration of the power of big text data, including mining quality phrases using unsupervised, weakly supervised and distantly supervised approaches, recognition and typing of entities and relations by distant supervision, meta-pattern-based entity-attribute-value extraction, set expansion and local embedding-based multi-faceted taxonomy discovery, allocation of text documents into multi-dimensional text cubes, construction of heterogeneous information networks from text cube, and eventually mining multi-dimensional structured knowledge from massive text data. We show that massive text data itself can be powerful at disclosing patterns, structures and hidden knowledge, and it is promising to explore the power of massive, interrelated text data for transforming such unstructured data into structured knowledge.

KEYWORDS

Data mining, text mining, multi-dimensional text cube, heterogeneous information networks, data to knowledge

ACM Reference format:

Jiawei Han. 2018. On the Power of Massive Text Data. In *Proceedings of WSDM 2018: The Eleventh ACM International Conference on Web Search and Data Mining , Marina Del Rey, CA, USA, February 5–9, 2018 (WSDM 2018),* 1 pages.
https://doi.org/10.1145/3159652.3160604

WSDM 2018, February 5–9, 2018, Marina Del Rey, CA, USA

ACM ISBN 978-1-4503-5581-0/18/02.
https://doi.org/10.1145/3159652.3160604

Jiawei Han is the Abel Bliss Professor of Engineering in the Department of Computer Science, the University of Illinois at Urbana-Champaign. He has been researching into data mining, information network analysis, text mining, and database systems, with over 900 publications.

He served as the founding Editor-in-Chief of ACM Transactions on Knowledge Discovery from Data (TKDD). He received ACM SIGKDD Innovation Award (2004), IEEE Computer Society Technical Achievement Award (2005), and IEEE Computer Society W. Wallace McDowell Award (2009). He is a Fellow of ACM and a Fellow of IEEE. His co-authored textbook "Data Mining: Concepts and Techniques" (Morgan Kaufmann) has been adopted worldwide. Professor Han is currently the co-Director of KnowEnG, a Center of Excellence in Big Data Computing, funded by NIH Big Data to Knowledge (BD2K) Initiative. He also served in 2009-2016 as the Director of Information Network Academic Research Center (INARC) supported by the Network Science-Collaborative Technology Alliance (NS-CTA) program of U.S. Army Research Lab.

ACKNOWLEDGMENTS

Research was sponsored in part by the U.S. Army Research Lab. under Cooperative Agreement No. W911NF-09-2-0053 (NSCTA), National Science Foundation IIS 16-18481, IIS 17-04532, and IIS-17-41317, and grant 1U54GM114838 awarded by NIGMS through funds provided by the trans-NIH Big Data to Knowledge (BD2K) initiative (www.bd2k.nih.gov). The views and conclusions contained in this talk are those of the author and should not be interpreted as representing the policies of any government agencies.

Theoretical Impediments to Machine Learning With Seven Sparks from the Causal Revolution

Judea Pearl
University of California, Los Angeles
Los Angeles, CA, USA
judea@cs.ucla.edu

ABSTRACT

Current machine learning systems operate, almost exclusively, in a statistical, or model-blind mode, which entails severe theoretical limits on their power and performance. Such systems cannot reason about interventions and retrospection and, therefore, cannot serve as the basis for strong AI. To achieve human level intelligence, learning machines need the guidance of a model of reality, similar to the ones used in causal inference. To demonstrate the essential role of such models, I will present a summary of seven tasks which are beyond reach of current machine learning systems and which have been accomplished using the tools of causal inference.

BIOGRAPHY

Judea Pearl is Chancellor's professor of computer science and statistics at UCLA, and a distinguished visiting professor at the Technion, Israel Institute of Technology. He joined the faculty of UCLA in 1970, where he currently directs the Cognitive Systems Laboratory and conducts research in artificial intelligence, human cognition and philosophy of science.

Pearl has authored numerous scientific papers and three seminal books, Heuristics (1983), Probabilistic Reasoning (1988) and Causality (2000, 2009) which won the London School of Economics Lakatos Award in 2002. A recent book, Causal Inference in Statistics (2016, with M. Glymour and N. Jewell) introduces causal analysis to undergraduate statistics education. His forthcoming "The Book of Why" (2018, with Dana Mackenzie) explains for the general public how the concept of cause and effect, the grand taboo in science, has been algorithmitized to serve in the interpretation of data.

Pearl is a member of the National Academy of Sciences and the National Academy of Engineering, a fellow of the Cognitive Science Society and a founding fellow of the Association for the Advancement of Artificial Intelligence. In 2012, he won the Technion's Harvey Prize and the ACM Alan Turing Award for the development of a calculus for probabilistic and causal reasoning.

REFERENCES

[1] http://ftp.cs.ucla.edu/pub/stat_ser/r475.pdf

WSDM'18, February 5-9, 2018, Marina Del Rey, CA, USA.

ACM ISBN 978-1-4503-5581-0/18/02.
DOI: http://dx.doi.org/10.1145/3159652.3160601

Conversations, Machine Learning and Privacy: LinkedIn's path towards Transforming Interaction with its Members

Igor Perisic
LinkedIn Corporation
iperisic@linkedin.com

ABSTRACT

At LinkedIn, we believe that having the right *conversations* with our members is key to unlocking economic opportunity for them. For us, these conversations are in a broader context than traditionally-defined dialogues. A typical dialogue usually only considers a limited time-window as context and is trying to satisfy an immediate intent. Advanced dialogue systems allow an user to take a number of turns, in that short-time window, to get clear on the user's intent. However, our members are having conversations with us over long periods of time about their long-term goals, such as staying informed, growing a professional network, advancing a career, getting a job, finding qualified leads, etc.

These conversational goals are often hierarchical. For example, getting a great job is a key part of advancing your career. Our goal at LinkedIn is to be able to have simultaneous conversations with our members on all of these levels. To do this, we have to build machine-learning systems that understand that there are multiple multi-level conversations going on. We have made strong headway in building components of this conversational vision by learning how to approximate long-term member value and defining an optimization framework that can incorporate multiple conflicting objectives. These problems consider the states of these conversations when interacting with our members and actively make decisions that optimize this ongoing dialogue. We have a challenging and interesting road ahead.

In this talk, Igor will present the current state of LinkedIn's machine-learning efforts towards building robust, long-term conversational systems. He will then discuss the potential privacy and ethical issues surrounding having these conversational interactions through an ever-increasing number of touchpoints with our members.

BIOGRAPHY

Igor Perisic is the Chief Data Officer (CDO) and Vice President (VP) of Engineering at LinkedIn. As CDO, he is responsible for all data policy issues and collaborates with our product, security, and legal teams to ensure that we are investing in technology, policies, and controls that will allow LinkedIn to continue to rapidly and safely scale our portfolio of product offerings to an ever broadening audience of members and customers.

WSDM 2018, February 5–9, 2018, Marina Del Rey, CA, USA

ACM ISBN 978-1-4503-5581-0/18/02.
https://doi.org/10.1145/3159652.3160600

In addition, he runs LinkedIn's Data engineering team which focuses on building infrastructure, search, machine learning and relevance systems. Igor joined LinkedIn in October 2007 after a brief stay at Microsoft. Through his tenure at LinkedIn, he and his team have developed LinkedIn's Search Engine, its Real-Time Graph Engine, Relevance infrastructure and worked on personalizing LinkedIn's site for its members.

Through open source technologies, he and his team have providing LinkedIn's members with data products, such as like People You May Know or Jobs You May Be Interested In. They have also contributed back to open source technologies with projects such as Kafka, Voldemort or extensions such as ml-ease and many others.

Igor is a data scientist and engineer with a passion for building infrastructure, products and actionable insights with a strong dependency on Data. At LinkedIn, he is focused on applying data science to decision making, product strategy and enhancing our Member experiences. He has also been instrumental in LinkedIn's outreach to the research community through the recent launch of the Economic Graph Research.

From Search to Research: Direct answers, Perspectives and Dialog

Harry Shum
Microsoft Corporation
hshum@microsoft.com

ABSTRACT

Advances in artificial intelligence have improved machine understanding of speech, images, and natural language. This in turn has allowed us to greatly enhance the intelligence of products such as Bing and Cortana. This keynote describes our continuing journey beyond keyword-driven systems, into dialog and intelligent agent functionality, helping our users "research more, search less".

Modern systems attempt to provide concise direct answers, which can fit on a small screen or become a spoken response. To find such answers, Microsoft can draw from a uniquely broad inventory of data sources such as the Bing Web & Knowledge graphs, the workplace graph of Office 365, and the Microsoft Academic Graph. Since these graphs contain a lot of text information, we apply machine reading and comprehension technology to extract concise answers. Microsoft has entries frequently topping the leaderboards in the community's machine reading contests.

To select the right answers, we use deep multi-task learning to develop a vector representation that is usable across multiple data sources and scenarios. This is combined with a large-scale data processing and serving infrastructure. We use this not only to find a single answer, but also to find multiple answers in cases where multiple valid perspectives exist. In the case of numeric answers, we provide some context to help users understand what the numbers mean. This is part of our effort to consider not just IQ but EQ in our conversational systems, where the chatbot Xiaoice leads the way in establishing a human connection, to develop long and sustained conversations.

These advances improve product quality, enable new user experiences and have challenged us to rethink the entire intelligent search platform at Microsoft.

BIOGRAPHY

Harry Shum is executive vice president of Microsoft's Artificial Intelligence (AI) and Research group.

He is responsible for driving the company's overall AI strategy and forward-looking research and development efforts spanning infrastructure, services, apps and agents. He oversees AI-focused product groups including Bing and Cortana. He also leads Microsoft Research, one of the world's premier computer science research organizations, and its integration with the engineering teams across the company.

Previously, Dr. Shum served as the corporate vice president responsible for Bing search product development from 2007 to 2013. Prior to his engineering leadership role at Bing and online services, he oversaw the research activities at Microsoft Research Asia and the lab's collaborations with universities in the Asia Pacific region, and was responsible for the Internet Services Research Center, an applied research organization dedicated to advanced technology investment in search and advertising at Microsoft.

Dr. Shum joined Microsoft Research in 1996 as a researcher based in Redmond, Washington. In 1998 he moved to Beijing as one of the founding members of Microsoft Research China (later renamed Microsoft Research Asia). There he began a nine-year tenure as a researcher, subsequently moving on to become research manager, assistant managing director and managing director of Microsoft Research Asia and a Distinguished Engineer.

Dr. Shum is an IEEE Fellow and an ACM Fellow for his contributions to computer vision and computer graphics. He received his Ph.D. in robotics from the School of Computer Science at Carnegie Mellon University. In 2017, he was elected to the National Academy of Engineering of the United States.

WSDM 2018, February 5–9, 2018, Marina Del Rey, CA, USA

ACM ISBN 978-1-4503-5581-0/18/02.
https://doi.org/10.1145/3159652.3160599

Scalable Algorithms in the Age of Big Data and Network Sciences: Characterization, Primitives, and Techniques*

Keynote Talk Abstract†

Shang-Hua Teng
University of Southern California
Los Angeles, California
shanghua.teng@gmail.com

ABSTRACT

In the age of network sciences and machine learning, efficient algorithms are now in higher demand more than ever before. Big Data fundamentally challenges the classical notion of efficient algorithms: Algorithms that used to be considered efficient, according to *polynomial-time characterization*, may no longer be adequate for solving today's problems. It is not just desirable, but essential, that efficient algorithms should be *scalable*. In other words, their complexity should be nearly linear or sub-linear with respect to the problem size. Thus, *scalability*, not just polynomial-time computability, should be elevated as the central complexity notion for characterizing efficient computation. Using several basic tasks in network analysis, machine learning, and optimization as examples — in this talk — I will highlight a family of fundamental algorithmic techniques for designing provably-good scalable algorithms.

CCS CONCEPTS

• **Theory of computation → Design & analysis of algorithms;** • **Mathematics of computing → Discrete mathematics; Probability and statistics;** • **Information systems → World Wide Web; Data mining;**

KEYWORDS

scalable algorithms, graph sparsification, local algorithms, advanced sampling, big data, network sciences, machine learning

ACM Reference Format:
Shang-Hua Teng. 2018. Scalable Algorithms in the Age of Big Data and Network Sciences: Characterization, Primitives, and Techniques: Keynote Talk Abstract. In *WSDM 2018: WSDM 2018: The Eleventh ACM International Conference on Web Search and Data Mining, February 5–9, 2018, Marina Del Rey, CA, USA*, Jennifer B. Sartor, Theo D'Hondt, and Wolfgang De Meuter (Eds.). ACM, New York, NY, USA, Article 4, 2 pages. https://doi.org/10.1145/3159652.3160602

*Supported in part by a Simons Investigator Award from the Simons Foundation and by NSF grant CCF-1111270.
†Based on the author's recent manuscript [7], "Scalable Algorithms for Data and Network Analysis", *Foundations and Trend in Theoretical Computer Science*: Vol 12, Issue 1-2, 2016.

WSDM 2018, February 5–9, 2018, Marina Del Rey, CA, USA

ACM ISBN 978-1-4503-5581-0/18/02.
https://doi.org/10.1145/3159652.3160602

Below, I will provide the backgrounds that motivate this talk and some basic definitions.

Asymptotic Analysis: Vision of Big Data

Half a century ago, the pioneers of Theoretical Computer Science began to use asymptotic analysis as the framework for complexity theory and algorithm analysis [3]. At the time, computers could only solve small-scale problems by today's standards. For example, linear programs of fifty variables, linear systems with a hundred variables, or graphs with a thousand vertices, were considered large scale. Even though our pioneers were mindful that constant factors did matter for practical computing, they used asymptotic notations — such as Big-O — to define complexity classes such as P and NP to characterize efficient algorithms and intractable problems [1, 2, 4, 5]. With respect to the size of practical inputs at the time, the asymptotic world seemed to belong to the distant future. Our pioneers persisted because they had a vision that one day computational problems would be massive, and therefore, the rate of complexity growth in relation to the growth of the inputs would be essential for characterizing the efficiency of an algorithm as well as the computational difficulty of a problem.

Polynomial-Time Characterization of Algorithmic Efficiency and its Modern Challenges

The asymptotic world has arrived with the rise of the Internet! Today, the Web has grown into a massive graph with trillions of nodes; social networks and social media have generated an unbounded amount of digital records; applications in data mining and machine learning as well as computational tasks of scientific and engineering simulation have created equations and mathematical programs that involve hundreds of millions of variables.

While *Big Data* has taken algorithm design into the asymptotic world envisioned by our pioneers, the explosive growth of problem size has also significantly challenged the classical notion of *efficient algorithms*, particularly the use of *polynomial time* as the characterization of *efficient computation* [2]: Algorithms that used to be considered efficient (in the world according to P) — such as an $O(n^2)$-time or $O(n^{1.5})$-time algorithm — can be too slow in the age of Big Data and network sciences.

Scalable Algorithms

The *scalability* of an algorithm measures the growth of its time complexity in relation to the growth of the problem size. It measures the capacity of an algorithm to handle *big* inputs. Formally, suppose Π is a computational problem whose input domain is Ω. For each instance $x \in \Omega$, let size(x) denote the *size* of input x. The input domain Ω can be viewed as the union of a collection of subdomains $\{..., \Omega_n, ...\}$, where Ω_n denotes the subset of Ω with input size n. Now, consider an algorithm A for solving Π. For $x \in \Omega$, let $T_A(x)$ denote the time complexity for running $A(x)$. The *scalability* of an algorithm A for solving an instance $x \in \Omega$ is given by:

$$\text{scalability}(A, x) = \frac{T_A(x)}{\text{size}(x)} \tag{1}$$

We now *summarize* the instanced-based scalability of algorithm A over all instances in Ω_n as:

$$\text{scalability}_A(n) := \sup_{x \in \Omega_n} \text{scalability}(A, x) = \frac{\sup_{x \in \Omega_n} T_A(x)}{n} \tag{2}$$

where $T_A(n) := \sup_{x \in \Omega_n} T_A(x)$ denote the (worst-case) complexity of algorithm A on inputs of size n. In other words, $\text{scalability}_A(n)$ is a function that measures the (worst-case) growth of the complexity of A in relation to the growth of the problem. Although $\text{scalability}_A(n)$ encodes no more information than $T_A(n)$ about algorithm A –- because $\text{scalability}_A(n) = T_A(n)/n$ – the scalability measure puts the emphasis not on polynomial-time algorithms, but on scalable algorithms. It highlights the *exponential* gap between $O(\log^c n)$ and n, and hence between scalable algorithms and quadratic-time algorithms.

Definition (Scalable Algorithms) An algorithm A is *scalable* if there exists a constant $c > 0$ such that, $\text{scalability}_A(n) = O(\log^c n)$.

In the special case when $c = 0$, we say A is *linearly-scalable*. We say algorithm A is *super-scalable*, if $\text{scalability}_A(n) = o(1)$. Super-scalable algorithms have a complexity sub-linear in problem size. Thus, necessarily, these algorithms must find solutions *without examining the entire input data set.*

Scalable Primitives and Techniques

In this talk, I will highlight a family of fundamental algorithmic techniques for designing provably-good scalable algorithms:

- scalable primitives and scalable reduction
- spectral approximation of graphs and matrices
- sparsification by multilevel structures
- advanced sampling
- local network exploration

For the first, I will focus on the emerging Laplacian Paradigm [6] that has led to breakthroughs in scalable algorithms for several fundamental problems in network analysis, machine learning, and scientific computing. I will then illustrate these algorithmic techniques with four recent applications: (1) sampling from graphic models (2) network centrality approximation (3) social-influence analysis (4) local clustering. Mathematical and algorithmic solutions to these problems exemplify the fusion of combinatorial, numerical, and statistical thinking in data and network analysis.

REFERENCES

[1] Stephen A. Cook. 1971. The Complexity of Theorem-proving Procedures. In *the Third Annual ACM Symposium on Theory of Computing*. ACM, 151–158.
[2] Jack Edmonds. 1965. Maximum Matching and a Polyhedron with 0, 1 Vertices. *Journal of Research at the National Bureau of Standards* 69 B (1965), 125–130.
[3] J. Hartmanis and R. Stearns. 1965. On the Computational Complexity of Algorithms. *Trans. Amer. Math. Soc.* 117 (1965), 285 – 306.
[4] R. Karp. 1972. Reducibility among combinatorial problems. In *Complexity of Computer Computations*, R. Miller and J. Thatcher (Eds.). Plenum Press, 85–103.
[5] L. Levin. 1973. Universal sorting problems. *Problems of Information Transmission* 9 (1973), 265 – 266.
[6] Daniel A. Spielman and Shang-Hua Teng. 2014. Nearly-Linear Time Algorithms for Preconditioning and Solving Symmetric, Diagonally Dominant Linear Systems. *SIAM J. Matrix Anal. Appl.* 35, 3 (2014), 835 885.
[7] Shang-Hua Teng. 2016. Scalable Algorithms for Data and Network Analysis. *Foundations and Trends in Theoretical Computer Science* 12, 1-2 (2016), 1–261.

Biography: Shang-Hua Teng is currently a University Professor and Seely Mudd Professor of Computer Science and Mathematics at the University of Southern California (USC), where he was the chair of the Computer Science Department from 2009-2012. He received his Ph.D. of Computer Science from Carnegie Mellon University. Before USC, he taught at BU, UIUC, U. Minnesota, and MIT.

Teng has twice won the prestigious Gödel Prize, first in 2008, for developing the theory of smoothed analysis, and then in 2015, for designing the groundbreaking nearly-linear time Laplacian solver for network systems. Both are joint work with Dan Spielman of Yale – his long-time collaborator. Smoothed analysis also won the 2009 Fulkerson Prize. Citing him as, "one of the most original theoretical computer scientists in the world", the Simons Foundation named Teng a 2014 Simons Investigator, for pursuing long-term curiosity-driven fundamental research. He and his collaborators also received the best paper award at ACM Symposium on Theory of Computing (STOC) for what's considered to be the "first improvement in 10 years" of a fundamental optimization problem – the computation of maximum flows and minimum cuts in a network. In addition, he is known for his joint work with Xi Chen and Xiaotie Deng that characterized the complexity for computing an approximate Nash equilibrium in game theory, and his joint papers on market equilibria in computational economics. He and his collaborators also pioneered the development of well-shaped Delaunay meshing algorithms for arbitrary three-dimensional geometric domains, which settled a long-term open problem in numerical simulation, also a fundamental problem in computer graphics. Software based on this development was used at the University of Illinois for the simulation of advanced rockets. Teng is also interested in mathematical board games. With his former Ph.D. student Kyle Burke, he designed and analyzed a game called Atropos, which is played on the Sperner's triangle and based on the beautiful, celebrated Sperner's Lemma. In 2000 at UIUC, Teng was named on the List of Teachers Ranked as Excellent by Their Students for his class, "Network Security and Cryptography". He has worked and consulted for Microsoft Research, Akamai, IBM Almaden Research Center, Intel Corporation, Xerox PARC, and NASA Ames Research Center, for which he received fifteen patents for his work on compiler optimization, Internet technology, and social networks.

WSDM Cup 2018: Music Recommendation and Churn Prediction

Yian Chen
KKBOX Inc.,
Taipei, Taiwan
annchen@kkbox.com

Xing Xie
Microsoft Research Asia
Beijing, China
xingx@microsoft.com

Shou-De Lin
National Taiwan University
Taipei, Taiwan
sdlin@csie.ntu.edu.tw

Arden Chiu
KKBOX Inc.,
Taipei, Taiwan
ardenchiu@kkbox.com

ABSTRACT

Recommendation systems facilitate users retrieving contents they might like but not aware of yet. Furthermore, an effective recommendation system can potentially increase users' retention and conversion rate. One critical challenge for building a recommender system lies in the existence of *cold start* cases when we have sparse records for certain users or items: without enough rating data about a new song or a new user, it is necessary to rely on auxiliary information to perform effective recommendation. In the first task of WSDM Cup 2018, we challenge the participants to solve the abovementioned challenges in building a music recommendation system. The 2nd task of the Cup focuses on churn prediction. For a subscription business, accurately predicting churn is critical to its long-term success as even a slight variation in churn can significantly affect the profits. In this task, participants are asked to build an algorithm that predicts whether a user will churn after their subscription expires. The competition data and award are provided by KKBOX, a leading music streaming service company from Taiwan.

CCS CONCEPTS

• Information systems → Personalization; • Computing methodologies → Ranking; Supervised learning by classification; Supervised learning by regression;

KEYWORDS

Recommendation, Personalization, Churn Prediction

ACM Reference Format:

Yian Chen, Xing Xie, Shou-De Lin, and Arden Chiu. 2018. WSDM Cup 2018: Music Recommendation and Churn Prediction. In *WSDM 2018: 11th ACM International Conference on Web Search & Data Mining, February 5–9, 2018, Marina Del Rey, CA, USA.* ACM, New York, NY, USA, 2 pages. https://doi.org/10.1145/3159652.3160605

WSDM'18, February 5–9, 2018, Marina Del Rey, CA, USA

ACM ISBN 978-1-4503-5581-0/18/02.
DOI: https://doi.org/10.1145/3159652.3160605

1 TASK ON MUSIC RECOMMENDATION SYSTEM

Not many years ago, it was inconceivable that the same person would listen to the Beatles, Vivaldi, and Lady Gaga on their morning commute. However, the glory days of Radio DJs have passed, and musical gatekeepers have been replaced with personalizing algorithms and unlimited streaming services.

While the public's now listening to all kinds of music, recommender systems still struggle in key areas such as the cold start problem[7][1] and context aware recommendation [6][8]. This challenge focuses on address such concerns for a music recommendation task.

In this task, participants are asked to predict the chances of a user listening to a song repetitively after the first observable listening event within a time window was triggered. If there are recurring listening event(s) triggered within a month after the user's very first observable listening event, its target is marked 1, and 0 otherwise in the dataset.

1.1 Data Description

KKBOX provides training data consisting information of the first observable listening event for each unique user-song pair within specific time duration. Moreover, we provide the metadata of our users and songs. What worth to mention is, participants are encouraged to use public external data in this data challenge.

The statistics of data are listed in Table 1 and file names represent the files we released on the competition platform, Kaggle.com[5][4]. The training data contains the contextual information, such as System tab, Screen name, and Source type, of listening events. What is worth to note is, within the training data, there are 17.5% of users and 83% of items have less then 10 observations, 1 illustrate cumulative probability of number of observations of each user and item, respectively. This phenomenon indicates we have cold start problem both for users and items and item cold start problem seems more severe then user cold start problem. The schema of training data is available on the competition platform [5].

1.2 Evaluation Metrics

We formulate the recommendation challenge as a ranking task. Thus, we employ Area under ROC curve as our evaluation metrics. It is a de-facto standard for highly imbalanced data.

Table 1: Overall metrics of the dataset of recommendation challenge

description	training data	metadata of songs	metadata of users
number of rows	7,377,418	2,296,320	34,403

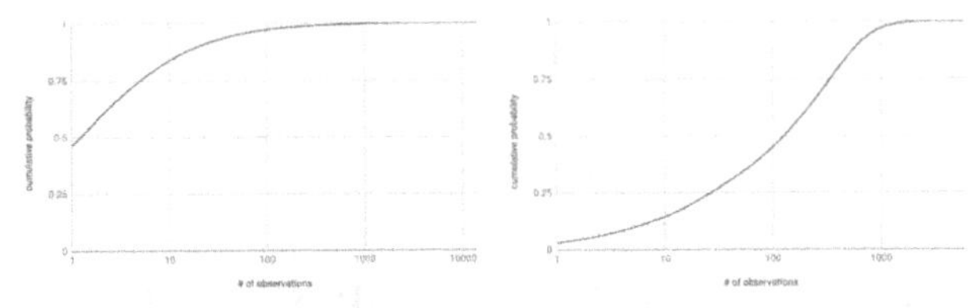

Figure 1: cumulative probablity of number of observations

2 TASK ON CHURN PREDICTION

For a subscription business, accurately predicting churn is critical to its long-term success. There have been several challenges associating with churn prediction in the past [9][3][2].

KKBOX, as the leading music streaming service in Asia, is supported by advertising and paid subscriptions. The success of such delicate business model relies heavily on accurately predicting churn of their paid users.

2.1 Data Description

In this task, participants will be predicting whether a user will churn after their subscription expires. Specifically, we want to see if a user make a new service subscription transaction within 30 days after their current membership expiration date.

As a music streaming service provider, KKBOX has members subscribe to their service. When the subscription is about to expire, the user can choose to renew, or cancel the service. They also are given the option to auto-renew, despite their membership can still be cancelled at any time.

The definition of churn/renewal can be tricky due to KKBOX's subscription model. Since the majority of the subscription length is 30 days, a lot of users re-subscribe every month. The key fields to determine churn/renewal are transaction date, membership expiration date, and is_cancel. Note that the is_cancel field indicates whether a user actively cancels a subscription. Note that a cancellation does not imply the user has churned. A user may cancel service subscription due to change of service plans or other reasons. Here we define "churn" as: no new valid service subscription within 30 days after the current membership expires. Concrete examples are listed on competition site [4]

Table 2 shows the statistics of the data released. The training and testing data are selected from users whose membership expire within a certain month. The training data consists of users whose subscription expire within the month of February 2017, and the testing data is with users whose subscription expire within the month of March 2017. This means we are looking at user churn or renewal roughly in the month of March 2017 for training set, and the user churn or renewal roughly in the month of April 2017. In this dataset, KKBOX has included a variety types of users behaviors. For example, a user could actively cancel the subscription, but renew within 30 days.

The schema of transaction log, training data, user behavioral log and user meta table is available on the competition platform [4].

Table 2: Overall metrics of the dataset of churn prediction

description	training data	user logs	transactions	members
number of rows	970961	18396363	1431010	6769474

2.2 Evaluation Metrics

The evaluation metric for this competition is Log Loss as follows

$$-\frac{1}{N}\sum_{i=1}^{N}[y_i \log p_i + (1 - y_i)\log(1 - p_i)]$$

where y_i is the actual label, i.e., is_churn, of sample i and p_i is the predicted probability of the sample's label equals to 1.

3 METRICS OF COMPETITION

Based on the data presented on competition platform, Kaggle [5][4], there are 1096 teams ,formed by 1284 individual competitors joined recommendation challenge, and 526 teams, formed by 780 individual competitors joined churn prediction on December 14, 2017.

REFERENCES

[1] Jesús Bobadilla, Fernando Ortega, Antonio Hernando, and Jesús Bernal. 2012. A collaborative filtering approach to mitigate the new user cold start problem. *Knowledge-Based Systems* 26, Supplement C (2012), 225 – 238. https://doi.org/10.1016/j.knosys.2011.07.021

[2] J. Burez and D. Van den Poel. 2009. Handling class imbalance in customer churn prediction. *Expert Systems with Applications* 36, 3, Part 1 (2009), 4626 – 4636. https://doi.org/10.1016/j.eswa.2008.05.027

[3] Kristof Coussement and Dirk Van den Poel. 2008. Churn prediction in subscription services: An application of support vector machines while comparing two parameter-selection techniques. *Expert Systems with Applications* 34, 1 (2008), 313 – 327. https://doi.org/10.1016/j.eswa.2006.09.038

[4] Kaggle. 2017. WSDM - KKBox's Churn Prediction Challenge. (2017). https://www.kaggle.com/c/kkbox-churn-prediction-challenge Accessed: 2017-12-21.

[5] Kaggle. 2017. WSDM - KKBox's Music Recommendation Challenge. (2017). https://www.kaggle.com/c/kkbox-music-recommendation-challenge Accessed: 2017-12-21.

[6] Alexandros Karatzoglou, Xavier Amatriain, Linas Baltrunas, and Nuria Oliver. 2010. Multiverse Recommendation: N-dimensional Tensor Factorization for Context-aware Collaborative Filtering. In *Proceedings of the Fourth ACM Conference on Recommender Systems (RecSys '10)*. ACM, New York, NY, USA, 79–86. https://doi.org/10.1145/1864708.1864727

[7] Blerina Lika, Kostas Kolomvatsos, and Stathes Hadjiefthymiades. 2014. Facing the cold start problem in recommender systems. *Expert Systems with Applications* 41, 4, Part 2 (2014), 2065 – 2073. https://doi.org/10.1016/j.eswa.2013.09.005

[8] Steffen Rendle, Zeno Gantner, Christoph Freudenthaler, and Lars Schmidt-Thieme. 2011. Fast Context-aware Recommendations with Factorization Machines. In *Proceedings of the 34th International ACM SIGIR Conference on Research and Development in Information Retrieval (SIGIR '11)*. ACM, New York, NY, USA, 635–644. https://doi.org/10.1145/2009916.2010002

[9] Chih-Ping Wei and I-Tang Chiu. 2002. Turning telecommunications call details to churn prediction: a data mining approach. *Expert Systems with Applications* 23, 2 (2002), 103 – 112. https://doi.org/10.1016/S0957-4174(02)00030-1

Performance Analysis of a Privacy Constrained kNN Recommendation Using Data Sketches

Armita Afsharinejad
Insight Centre for Data Analytics
University College Dublin
Dublin, Ireland
armita.afsharinejad@insight-centre.org

Neil Hurley
Insight Centre for Data Analytics
University College Dublin
Dublin, Ireland
neil.hurley@insight-centre.org

ABSTRACT

This paper evaluates two algorithms, BLIP and JLT, for creating differentially private data sketches of user profiles, in terms of their ability to protect a kNN collaborative filtering algorithm from an inference attack by third-parties. The transformed user profiles are employed in a user-based top-N collaborative filtering system. For the first time, a theoretical analysis of the BLIP is carried out, to derive expressions that relate its parameters to its performance. This allows the two techniques to be fairly compared. The impact of deploying these approaches on the utility of the system—its ability to make good recommendations, and on its privacy level—the ability of third-parties to make inferences about the underlying user preferences, is examined. An active inference attack is evaluated, that consists of the injection of a number of tailored *sybil* profiles into the system database. User profile data of targeted users is then inferred from the recommendations made to the sybils. Although the differentially private sketches are designed to allow the transformed user profiles to be published without compromising privacy, the attack we examine does not use such information and depends only on some pre-existing knowledge of some user preferences as well as the neighbourhood size of the kNN algorithm. Our analysis therefore assesses in practical terms a relatively weak privacy attack, which is extremely simple to apply in systems that allow low-cost generation of sybils. We find that, for a given differential privacy level, the BLIP injects less noise into the system, but for a given level of noise, the JLT offers a more compact representation.

KEYWORDS

Privacy Preservation; Data Sketching; Collaborative Filtering; User-based Top-N Recommneder

ACM Reference Format:
Armita Afsharinejad and Neil Hurley. 2018. Performance Analysis of a Privacy Constrained kNN Recommendation Using Data Sketches. In *Proceedings of WSDM'18.* ACM, Marina Del Rey, CA, USA, 9 pages. https://doi.org/10.1145/3159652.3159673

WSDM'18, February 5–9, 2018, Marina Del Rey, CA, USA

ACM ISBN 978-1-4503-5581-0/18/02...$15.00
https://doi.org/10.1145/3159652.3159673

1 INTRODUCTION

Recommendation systems (RS) have become an inherent part of online services as they are widely used in various fields, ranging from e-commerce to social networking. In general, such systems aggregate users' data, e.g. past purchases and item ratings, in order to make a prediction about their future preferences. The main purpose of deploying recommenders in online services is facilitating users with their decision making; however, accessing the private data of users for recommendation purposes can greatly compromise their privacy. For example, an unauthorised access to the database of a RS, which contains user profiles, can reveal users' purchase history or rating history. Recommendation algorithms such as collaborative filtering that exploit user data in making recommendations are vulnerable to attackers who use their output to make inference attacks on the underlying user data.

The differential privacy concept has been proposed as a framework in which the vulnerability of a system database to such an attack can be controlled [9]. The basic idea is to provide an implementer with a means to control the extent to which the output of computations carried out on the database differ, whether or not a row of data is present. In a setting where this difference is small, the output cannot be used to infer the presence of that row. In the context of user data in a recommender system, such a differentially private algorithm allows control over the ability to infer a row of user data, from the recommender algorithm output. However, more stringent control of the privacy level generally implies a degradation of the utility of the system; therefore, it introduces a trade-off between the desired privacy level and the accuracy of recommendations.

Differential privacy mechanisms can be categorised as either *interactive* or *non-interactive.* Interactive mechanisms require interaction between the data curator/owner and the client in order to compute each required output in a differentially private way. Essentially such strategies entail the injection of tailored noise into each computation. Their application to recommender systems has been studied in [3–5], for example. On the other hand, non-interactive mechanisms allow for a single public release of a transformed version of the dataset, such that operations can be applied on this transformed data, without further access to the private data. In order to maintain system utility, it is required that all required operations on the private data can be well approximated by a corresponding operation on the transformed data. Such transformations that allow for good approximations of particular operations on the original data are sometimes called *data sketches.* We study two such non-interactive mechanisms, referred to as BLIP (for Bloom fliter and bit flipping) and JLT (for Johnson Lindenstrass transform), that are designed to allow for good approximation of similarities using the transformed dataset.

In previous work [1, 2], a utility and privacy evaluation of the BLIP and JLT has been carried out, where utility is taken as the accuracy of the similarity computation and privacy is tested against tailored attacks that access the published data sketch. These attacks depend only on offline analysis of the public data. This work compared the utility and privacy of each method for particular, arbitrarily chosen, parameter settings. No effort was made to make an informed choice of parameters, in order to compare the algorithms at a common operating point.

In this paper, we extend this work in a number of directions. In particular, we derive for the first time, the mean squared error (MSE) of a BLIP distance estimator in terms of the parameters of the method. This expression, along with the expression for the MSE of the JLT, available in the state-of-the-art, allows the two methods to be configured under a common setting and for their efficacy to be directly compared. Moreover, we examine privacy in terms of robustness to an *active* attack that involves observation of the output of the recommendation system and modification of that output in a controlled way through the insertion of fake user profiles or *sybils* into the system database. We evaluate utility in terms of the overall accuracy of the full recommendation task, rather than just the distance or similarity computation. Precision is used to measure the performance of the top-N recommender as well as evaluating the attacker's utility in inferring private user data, for a variety of privacy levels. An effective privacy protection system should maintain high precision for the top-N task, while restricting the attacker's inference to low precision. The contributions of this paper can be categorized as follows:

Contribution 1: We provide a comprehensive analysis on how to approximate the original distance between user profiles when applying BLIP. We propose a distance estimator based on the desired privacy level and also the dataset characteristics. Then, by approximating the mean-squared error (MSE) of the distance estimator, we derive a model for an optimal sketch size. Our provided models can be used for an efficient algorithm setup, which can lead to the desired utility level.

Contribution 2: Most work on differential privacy in recommender systems [3–5], has focused on the rating prediction problem, while this paper focuses on top-N recommendation. Since user-based kNN algorithms are generally robust to some noise in neighbour selection, a reasonable hypothesis is that differentially private data sketches that preserve similarity may be good candidates for protecting such algorithms. Our work here tests this hypothesis.

Contribution 3: The differential privacy mechanism studied in this paper is designed to protect against sophisticated offline attacks that have access to the published sketches. On the other hand, simple active attacks such as profile injection, that don't exploit such published information may be more relevant to real-world contexts. It is therefore useful to relate the privacy control parameter to its effectiveness in thwarting such an attack.

The paper is structured as follows: First, the privacy preservation concept in recommender systems is described and two sketching approaches, i.e. BLIP and JLT, which can deliver such a concept are reviewed. The main expressions for MSE are summaried in the body of the paper and derived in detail in appendices. Next, an active kNN attack targeting a top-N RS is described. Following, the experimental results are provided and finally, the conclusions and future works are discussed.

Notation: Let $\mathcal{U}$ be a set of users, $n = |\mathcal{U}|$ the number of users, $\mathcal{I}$ a set of items and $m = |\mathcal{I}|$ the number of items. Given a user u, the transaction database, $\mathcal{D}$, consists of a set of items known to be relevant to user u. We write the user profile, as the set $P_u \subseteq \mathcal{I}$ or equivalently as an m-dimensional binary vector, $\mathbf{u} \in \mathcal{B}^m$, where $\mathcal{B} = \{0, 1\}$ and the ith component, u_i, is 1 if item i is relevant to user u, and 0 otherwise. A data *sketch* is the image of a transformation of $\mathbf{u}$ into an L-dimensional sketch-space, $\mathbb{R}^L$ or $\mathcal{B}^L$. In this paper we consider two transformations, referred to as BLIP and JLT and write $\mathbf{b}_u$ for the L-dimensional sketch of user u. We write $d_H(\mathbf{u}, \mathbf{v}) = \|\mathbf{u} - \mathbf{v}\|_2^2$, or simply d_H, for the Hamming distance between two profiles, equivalent to the square of the Euclidean distance, since the profiles are binary.

2 PRIVACY PRESERVATION

There exists a large volume of research work addressing the privacy risks in recommender systems. Two broad categories of approaches are as follows:

(1) Distributed Data Storage: User data is stored in several different sources, typically locally to each user. There is no single repository at which to focus an attack, and the user does not need to share even with the system providing the recommendation service. The challenge is to develop a recommendation algorithm that can work in a peer-to-peer manner without direct sharing of data. For instance, Canny et al. [8], introduced a matrix factorization technique where parameters are learned in a peer-to-peer fashion.
(2) Data Modification: the goal of data modification may be encryption or obfuscation. Generally, obfuscation methods combine user data with randomly generated noise in order to provide privacy, e.g. [3, 5, 13]. Data modification may be combined with data distribution. A use-case of the data sketches studied in this paper is to provide a safe public representation of the user data that peer-to-peer systems can share. Nikolaenko et al. [12], propose a cryptographic method for computing item profiles, while user profiles remain local to the client.

The focus in this paper is on the client-server model, where the user data resides in a trusted server and the goal is to protect against third-party attacks. The techniques we discuss employ data obfuscation in the framework of differential privacy, which we describe next.

2.1 Differential Privacy

Calandrino et al. [7] studied privacy protection in several well-known recommender systems, such as Amazon, LibraryThing and Hunch. They concluded that differential privacy techniques can overcome the shortcomings of many other proposed methods. Formally, differential privacy is defined as follows:

- ϵ-differential privacy: a randomized function $F : \mathcal{D} \rightarrow \mathcal{D}$ is ϵ-differentially private if for all neighbouring profiles $x, x' \in$

$\mathcal{D}$ and for all $t \in \mathcal{D}$:

$$Pr[F(x) = t] \leq e^{\epsilon}.Pr[F(x') = t] \quad (1)$$

where the probability is computed over all the coin tosses of F. In this definition ϵ is a public variable and, and is set to control the required level of privacy. Smaller values of ϵ offer a higher degree of privacy, however, they may compromise the overall utility of output.

A relaxed variant of ϵ-differential privacy is (ϵ, δ)-differential privacy in which the privacy holds with a probability equal to $1 - \delta$:

- (ϵ, δ)-differential privacy: a randomized function $F : \mathcal{D} \rightarrow \mathcal{D}$ is (ϵ, δ)-differentially private if for all neighbouring profiles $x, x' \in \mathcal{D}$ and for all $t \in \mathcal{D}$ [11]:

$$Pr[F(x) = t] \leq e^{\epsilon}.Pr[F(x') = t] + \delta \quad (2)$$

where the probability is taken over all the coin tosses of F; also, ϵ and δ are considered as public parameters.

McSherry et al. [11], introduced the first recommendation algorithm based on differential privacy techniques, an interactive mechanism, where the steps of matrix factorisation are made differentially private through the insertion of noise. Several other works along these lines have followed e.g. [4]. Their impact on utility has generally been assessed from the point of view of rating prediction. Our goal is to instead examine the impact on recommendation accuracy of two non-interactive mechanisms, which we describe next.

3 JOHNSON LINDENSTRAUSS TRANSFORM

The JLT offers (ϵ, δ)-differential privacy [10]. The JLT first encodes each item with a codeword consisting of a vector $\mathbf{b}_i \in \mathbb{R}^L$ generated from the Gaussian distribution i.e. $\mathbf{b}_i = (b_{i1}, \ldots, b_{iL})^T$ where $b_{i\ell} \sim \mathcal{N}(0, 1/L), \ell = 1, \ldots, L$.

The generated codewords form a $L \times m$ matrix B, where m is the number of items, in which the columns correspond to the created item codewords. Writing the original user profile as an m-dimensional binary vector $\mathbf{u}$, then $\mathbf{u}$ is mapped into a JLT representation $\mathbf{j}_u$, using the transformation: $\mathbf{j}_u = \mathrm{B}\mathbf{u}$. Finally, Gaussian noise drawn from $\mathcal{N}(0, \sigma^2)$ is added to the components of $\mathbf{j}_u$. This algorithm complies with (ϵ, δ)-differential privacy, once the following conditions are satisfied [2]:

$$L \geq 2(\log m + \log \frac{2}{\delta}), \quad \sigma \geq \frac{4}{\epsilon}\sqrt{\log \frac{1}{\delta}}, \quad \epsilon < \log \frac{1}{\delta} \quad (3)$$

Kenthapadi et al. [10] derive an unbiased estimator of the true distance between profile pairs and compute its variance (equivalent to the MSE, since the estimator is unbiased). In summary, it is shown that, given two users u and v, with original binary profiles $\mathbf{u}$ and $\mathbf{v}$ and their corresponding JLT-transformed profiles $\mathbf{b}_u$ and $\mathbf{b}_v$, the squared Euclidean distance, or Hamming distance, between the user profiles can be approximated by:

$$d_{\mathrm{JLT}}(\mathbf{b}_u, \mathbf{b}_v) = \|\mathbf{b}_u - \mathbf{b}_v\|_2^2 - 2\sigma^2 L. \quad (4)$$

The variance of this estimator is:

$$\mathrm{Var}[d_{\mathrm{JLT}}(\mathbf{b}_u, \mathbf{b}_v)] = 2d_H^2/L + 8\sigma^2 d_H + 8\sigma^4 L \quad (5)$$

and the optimal sketch size L_{opt} that minimises the MSE of this estimator is given by: $L_{\mathrm{opt}} = d_H/2\sigma^2$. By inserting the upper bound for ϵ into the second term in Eqn.(3), the standard deviation of the noise can be bounded as: $\sigma \geq \frac{4}{\sqrt{\epsilon}}$. Similarly by inserting upper bound for ϵ into the first term, we arrive at a lower bound for the sketch size:

$$L \geq 2(\log(2m) + \epsilon) \geq 2(\log(2m) + 16/\sigma^2) \quad (6)$$

and hence have a bound for the optimal L_{opt} in terms of ϵ:

$$L_{\mathrm{opt}} = \max\{2(\log m + \log 2 + \epsilon), d_H\epsilon/32\} \quad (7)$$

Inserting back into Eqn.(5), we arrive at an expression for the minimal MSE, as a function of ϵ:

$$\mathrm{MSE}(\epsilon) = \begin{cases} 256 d_H/\epsilon & L_{\mathrm{opt}} = d_H\epsilon/32 \\ \frac{((64+d_H)\epsilon + 64\log(2) + 64\log(m))^2}{\epsilon^2(\log(2m)+\epsilon)} & L_{\mathrm{opt}} = 2(\log(2m) + \epsilon) \end{cases} \quad (8)$$

4 BLOOM FILTER AND BIT FLIPPING

BLIP [1] aims to prevent the attacker from learning the presence or absence of items in a user profile through the conversion of the original profile into a corresponding Bloom filter of length L [6], with the addition of noise to attain differential privacy. Each item i in the user profile u is hashed by means of k hash functions, where each hash value corresponds to a position in an L-dimensional binary vector $\mathbf{b}_i = (b_{i1}, \ldots, b_{iL})^T$, i.e.:

$$b_{i\ell} = \begin{cases} 1 & \text{if } \exists j \in \{1, \ldots, k\} \quad \text{s.t.} \quad l = h_j(i) \\ 0 & \text{otherwise} \end{cases} \quad (9)$$

for $\ell = 1, \ldots, L$, where $h_j()$ is the jth hash function. Then, the Bloom filter related to a user u is formed as follows:

$$\mathbf{b}_u = \mathbf{b}_{i_1} \vee \ldots \vee \mathbf{b}_{i_P} \quad (10)$$

where $\{i_1, \ldots, i_P\}$ are the P items in the user profile and $\vee$ denotes the OR operator. A bit-flipping function is applied to independently flip elements of the Bloom filter with bit-flipping probability p. In order to guarantee ϵ-differential privacy, p is related to ϵ through:

$$p(\epsilon) = 1/(1 + e^{\epsilon/k}). \quad (11)$$

4.1 BLIP Distance Estimator

In Appendix A, we derive an estimator for the distance between two profiles u and v, based on their BLIP sketches $\mathbf{b}_u$ and $\mathbf{b}_v$, as follows:

$$d_{\mathrm{BLIP}}(\mathbf{b}_u, \mathbf{b}_v) \triangleq \frac{1}{k(1-2q)}\left(\|\mathbf{b}_u - \mathbf{b}_v\|_2^2 - Lq\right) \quad (12)$$

where $q = 2p(1-p)$. This estimator is unbiased in the limit as $L \rightarrow \infty$.

The variance of the BLIP distance estimator is derived in Appendix B and, for large L, is given by:

$$\lim_{L\rightarrow\infty} \mathrm{Var}[d_{\mathrm{BLIP}}(\mathbf{b}_u, \mathbf{b}_v)] = \frac{1}{k^2(1-2q)^2}\left(q(1-q)L + q(1-2q)kd_H\right). \quad (13)$$

4.2 Optimisation for fixed-sized catalogue

Given a fixed number of items m, a maximum of km positions in the sketch vector can be set by the hashes corresponding to these items and, given the catalogue, it is possible to pre-determine which positions are *not* set by *any* items. These positions can be safely ignored when computing $d_{\mathrm{BLIP}}(\mathbf{b}_u, \mathbf{b}_v)$, since a bit set at these positions can only be due to bit-flipping. The mean and variance

Algorithm 1 User-based top-N algorithm.

Input: $\mathcal{D}$=transaction database of items relevant to each user
u = active user for whom recommendation is to be made
$\mathcal{B} = \{\mathbf{b}_v | v \in \mathcal{U}\}$ set of data sketches, generated from one of the sketching methods. N = recommender set size.
Output: R_u : the top-N recommended items for user u.

for all $v \in \mathcal{U} \setminus \{u\}$ **do**
  $d_v \leftarrow d(\mathbf{b}_u, \mathbf{b}_v)$
end for
Sort: $\pi \leftarrow$ sort(d_v) in ascending order {π=sort permutation}
Select: $\mathcal{N}_u \leftarrow \{v_{\pi_1}, \ldots, v_{\pi_K}\}$ {K nearest neighbours}
for all $i \in \mathcal{I} \setminus P_u$ **do**
  $c_i \leftarrow |\{v \in \mathcal{N}_u/P_u | i \in P_v\}|$
end for
Sort: $\phi \leftarrow$ sort(c_i) in descending order {ϕ=sort permutation}
Select: $R_u = \{i_{\phi_1}, \ldots, i_{\phi_N}\}$

formulae can be modified to account for this optimisation (see Appendix B). In this case, we obtain

$$d_{\text{BLIP}}(\mathbf{b}_u, \mathbf{b}_v) \triangleq \frac{1}{k(1-2q)} \left(\|\mathbf{b}_u - \mathbf{b}_v\|_2^2 - q\bar{m} \right) \tag{14}$$

where $\bar{m} = L(1 - \exp(-km/L))$ is the expected number of positions set by some hash function applied to some item in the catalogue, and $\bar{m} \to km$ as $L \to \infty$. A good approximation to the variance is given by

$$\text{Var}[d_{\text{BLIP}}(\mathbf{b}_u, \mathbf{b}_v)] \approx \frac{1}{k^2(1-2q)^2} \left(q(1-q)\bar{m} + q(1-2q)kd_H \right) . \tag{15}$$

4.3 MSE of BLIP distance estimator

An optimal sketch-size L that minimises the MSE of $d_{\text{BLIP}}()$ can be obtained by numerically minimising the MSE using the exact expressions for the mean and variance. It is instructive, however, to obtain an approximate expression, by taking a second order approximation to the mean and, as the optimal occurs for $L \ll km$, taking $L(1 - \exp(-km/L)) \approx L$ in Eqn. (15).

We obtain (see Appendix C), the optimal sketch dimension L_{opt} given in Eqn.(26) and the resulting MSE:

$$\begin{aligned} \text{MSE}_{\text{opt}}(\epsilon) =& 3\left(\frac{\exp(\epsilon/k)(1+\exp(2\epsilon/k))}{4k(1-\exp(\epsilon/k))^4} \right)^{\frac{2}{3}} \left(d_H(4P + d_H) \right)^{\frac{2}{3}} \\ &+ 2\frac{\exp(\epsilon/k)}{k(1-\exp(\epsilon/k))^2} d_H . \end{aligned} \tag{16}$$

Note that differently to JLT, the optimal L depends on the size of the profiles as well as on the Hamming distance between the two profiles.

5 USER-BASED COLLABORATIVE FILTERING WITH PROFILE SKETCHES

Sketch vectors are used in a simple user-based kNN algorithm for top-N recommendation (Algorithm 1). A recommendation is formed for the active user u, from the set of most frequent items in the profiles of u's $K > 0$ nearest neighbours. Note that a neighbour v is chosen according to the sketch estimate $d(\mathbf{b}_u, \mathbf{b}_v)$ of its true distance, $d_H(\mathbf{u}, \mathbf{v})$ from the active profile u. Thus, we can expect the performance to depend on the accuracy of this estimate. Moreover, the computational efficiency of the distance estimator is dependent on the sketch dimension L.

Table 1: The deployed datasets and their specifications.

	#Users	#Items	Sparsity	Avg. Hamming Dist.	Avg. Profile Size
MovieLens	6040	3952	4%	236	132
Epinions	780	2315	2%	98	52

6 K-NEAREST NEIGHBOUR ATTACK

A simple active attack on the privacy of a user-based kNN algorithm is described in [7]. Assume the target of the attack is a particular user u. Assume that the attacker has prior knowledge of $s \ll P$ items in u's profile. Such an itemset may not be hard to attain in practice and due to the sparsity of typical transaction data, $s \sim O(\log m)$ is sufficient. Finally, assume that the attacker knows the neighbourhood size, K, of the nearest-neighbour algorithm. The attacker generates K fake user profiles, each replicating the s items which exist in the original targeted profile. With high probability, the K nearest neighbours of each sybil are the $K - 1$ other sybils and the targeted user. Then, a recommendation to a sybil is highly likely to consist of other items in the targeted user's profile. The targeted user's private data is inferred as the recommendations made by the system to the sybil.

7 EXPERIMENTAL RESULTS

The goal of the evaluation is to assess trade-offs between utility and privacy introduced by the two non-interactive privacy mechanisms, as well as analysing their most efficient implementation setup. There are two natural baselines against which to compare the impact of data sketching. At the upper end, we compare against the *Basic* user-based algorithm in which the Hamming distance between the raw user profiles, $d_H(\mathbf{u}, \mathbf{v})$, is used to compute user similarly. If the distance estimate is sufficiently accurate, the performance of the sketch-based algorithm will approach the performance of the *Basic* algorithm. At the lower end, we compare against a *Random* user-based algorithm in which K random neighbours are chosen to form the neighbourhood. As the noise in the distance estimator becomes larger, the sketch-based algorithm will approach the performance of the *Random* algorithm.

7.1 General Setup

We evaluate the MovieLens and Epinions datasets with the specifications provided in Table 1. Epinions is filtered by removing users who have rated fewer than 40 items and items that have been rated by fewer than 40 users. Each dataset is split into training and test sets, composed of 80% and 20% of the initial data, with the former used for the recommendation purposes and the latter only used for performance calculation. Top-N recommendations are generated for each user and compared with the user's test-set items. We evaluate using precision@N and recall@N, with $N = 20$. We use

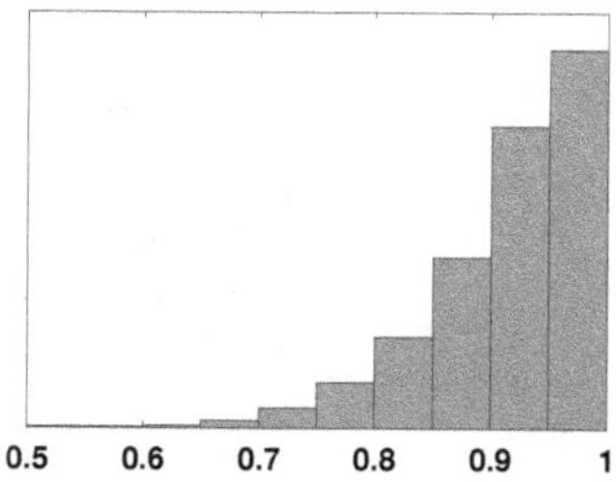

Figure 1: Movielens: Histogram of $d_H/(\|\mathbf{u}\|^2+\|\mathbf{v}\|^2)$

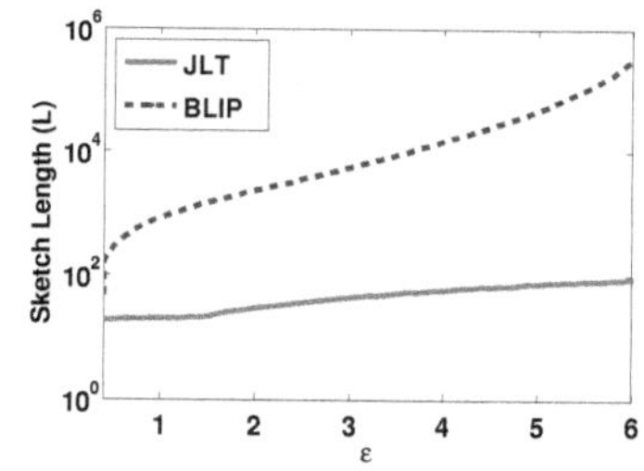

Figure 2: Movielens: Optimal Sketch size as function of ϵ

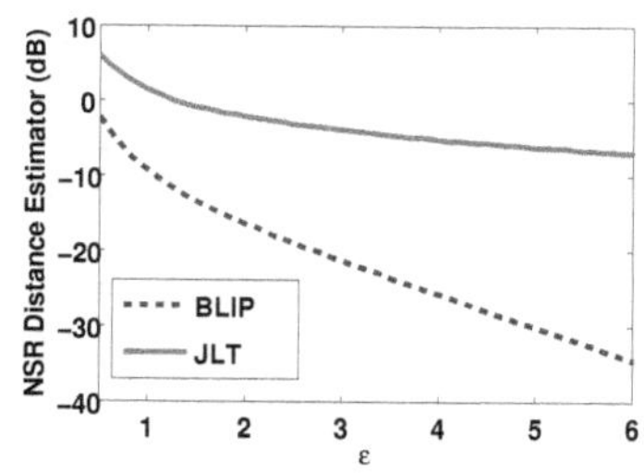

Figure 3: Movielens: Minimum Relative Error (NSR) as function of ϵ

precision plots to quantify the impact of sketching on the utility of recommendation, while setting K=100 for neighbour selection.

As the *Random* algorithm chooses the most frequent items in a set of K random neighbours, it approximates a non-personalised algorithm that recommends items according to their popularity. By definition, popular items exist in many user profiles but, equally, it is not very interesting for an attacker to successfully predict that such items are in a given profile. Hence, when we evaluate the performance of the attacker, we compute precision over those items in the test set that *are not* among some top threshold of most popular items. We take this threshold as 100. Thus, if an attacker achieves a precision of 20% on $N_{\text{attack}} = 20$ predicted items, it means 4 of the items predicted by the attacker are items that the targeted user liked that are not among the 100 most popular items in the entire dataset. We average the attack results over 500 randomly chosen users and over 5 repetitions of choosing $s = 8$ items uniformly at random as the attacker's prior knowledge.

7.2 Parameter Selection

To fairly compare the two sketching techniques, a common operating point must be chosen and the parameters of the algorithms should be set to achieve that operating point. One nature choice is ϵ, as when the parameters are set to achieve a particular value of ϵ, we expect that the sketches are providing a common level of differential privacy. In [2], the practical security of the two sketching techniques against a direct attack on the data sketches was assessed. In this analysis, on the Movielens dataset, when $\epsilon = 6$, the profile inferred by the attack had cosine similarly of ~ 0.5 to the true user profile. When $\epsilon = 60$, the attack could completely recover the profile. This suggests that we should examine the utility of the system for $0 < \epsilon \leq 6$ to operate within a range where differential privacy is achieving some practical security. On the other hand, since any noise introduced to the distance calculation provides some level of security against the active attack evaluated below, we may alternatively set the *MSE* as a common operating point, and choose the parameters to achieve a given *MSE* value. As from Eqns.(8, 16), the optional sketch size and consequent MSE are dependent on the profile lengths and true Hamming distance between them, we select parameters to meet the average case, given in Table 1, for each dataset. In Figure 1, we show a histogram of $d_H/(\|\mathbf{u}\|^2+\|\mathbf{v}\|^2)$ for all pairs of profiles in Movielens. Note that the values are concentrated in a range > 0.8. The value for the average case is $d_H/2P = 0.8939$, which is a good representative value for this dataset. As a measure of the *relative error* in the distance estimator, we use the noise-to-signal ratio (NSR) in decibels (dB), defined as

$$NSR = 10\log_{10}(\text{MSE}/d_H^2),$$

e.g., a value of $NSR = -10dB$, corresponds to a level of inaccuracy in the distance estimator of one order of magnitude less than the true distance.

7.2.1 ϵ operating point: Given ϵ, we use Eqns.(8, 16) to determine L_{opt} and MSE_{opt}. For BLIP, we take $k = 1$, since the MSE is an increasing function of k. In Figure 3, we plot the optimal NSR against ϵ for BLIP and JLT and also, in Figure 2, the optimal length L_{opt} against ϵ. Two important observations emerge from these plots. Firstly, the BLIP offers a much more accurate distance estimator for a given level of privacy, ϵ, e.g. for JLT, $NSR > -10dB$ when $\epsilon = 6$, while for BLIP, $NSR < -30dB$. However, the optimal sketch length grows much more slowly for the JLT compared to BLIP. Thus, if we are happy to accept an inaccuracy of $NSR = -7dB$ in the distance estimator, then this can be achieved in the JLT with a sketch vector of length $L = 89$ (when $\epsilon = 6$), while the BLIP requires a sketch vector of length $L = 608$ to achieve the same level of NSR (when $\epsilon = 0.8$).

7.2.2 MSE operating point: For a fixed MSE, we use Eqns. (5, 26), to write the BLIP bit flipping probability p, and, respectively, the JLT noise variance σ^2, as functions of L. Then, we choose the L that maximises the noise (solving the maximisation problem numerically), on the basis that this choice affords the greatest security, for a given MSE. As expected from Figure 2, JLT achieves a target MSE at a smaller sketch length L e.g. $NSR = -20dB$ is achieved for JLT with $L = 801$ and $\sigma^2 = 0.147$, while for BLIP, this noise level is achieved when $L = 3,378$ and $p = 0.0017$.

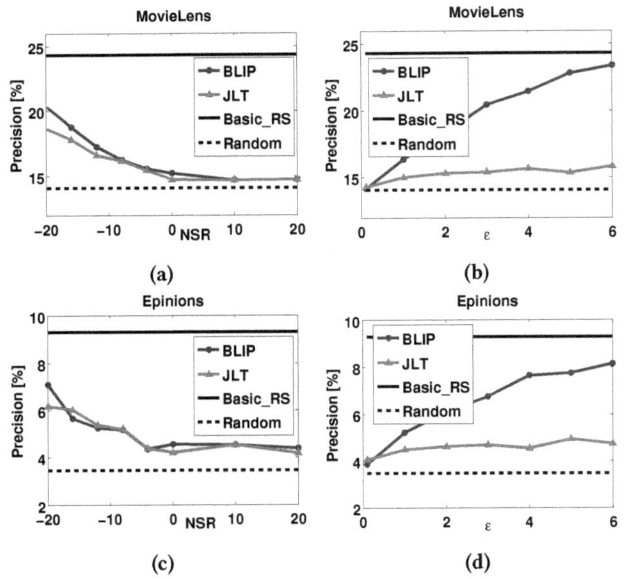

Figure 4: Utility of JLT and BLIP as function of ϵ and NSR, for both datasets, N = 20.

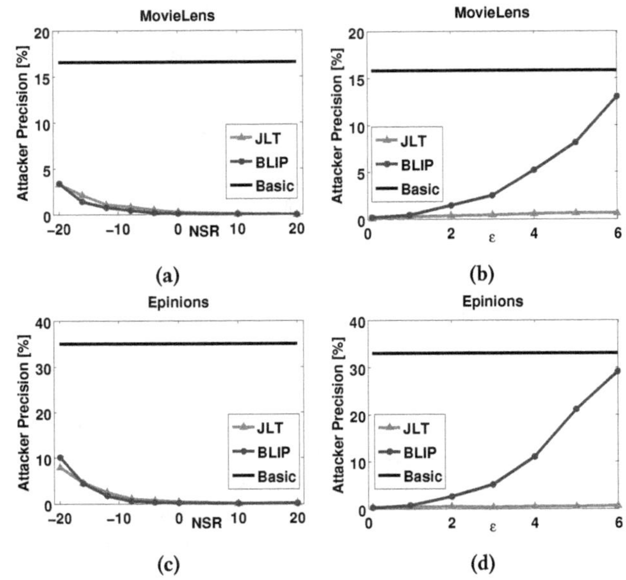

Figure 5: Attacker performance for JLT and BLIP as function of ϵ and NSR, for both datasets, N_{attack} = 20.

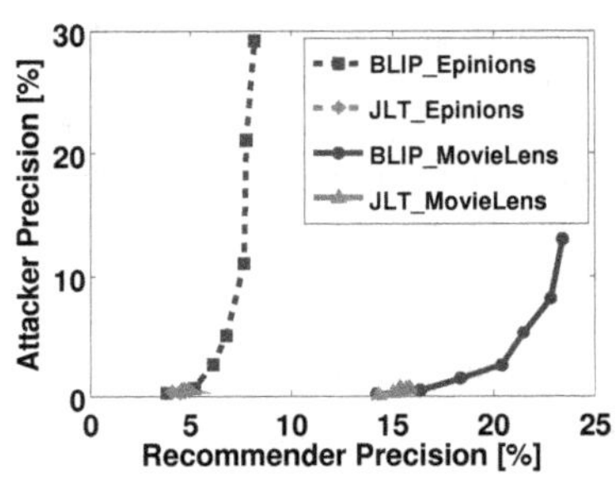

Figure 6: Attacker precision versus recommender precision for both datasets.

7.3 Recommender Utility

The effect of sketching on the utility of the recommender is presented as a function of ϵ and as a function of NSR in Figure 4 for the MovieLens and Epinions datasets. Note that for MovieLens $prec_{\text{Random}}$ = 14% and $prec_{\text{Basic}}$ = 24%, and for Epinions $prec_{\text{Random}}$ = 3.5% and $prec_{\text{Basic}}$ = 9.2% when N = 20. Within this performance range, even small amounts of noise lead to a significant performance loss over the Basic algorithm. Examining the performance wrt ϵ, we may conclude that while BLIP is clearly the preferred option, the performance loss is quite significant when ϵ is small. The plots wrt NSR show little difference between the two sketching methods, when configured to achieved a fixed amount of noise. It is important to bear in mind that the parameters have been set to achieve that level of NSR for the average case, and therefore distance calculations over different pairs of profiles will suffer larger or smaller amounts of inaccuracy. We see a small advantage for BLIP in the low-noise setting, but bear in mind that this is achieved using much larger sketch sizes L compared to JLT. Overall performance is quite sensitive to even low levels of noise. At $NSR = -20dB$, BLIP still incurs almost 15% loss in performance over the Basic algorithm, for both datasets.

7.4 Attacker Utility

The attacker utility for both sketching methods is shown in Figure 5, as a function of ϵ and NSR for the MovieLens and Epinions datasets. The attacker precision (excluding 100 popular items) when targeting the *Basic* recommender system is also shown in the plots. Just as the recommender utility is significantly compromised by small levels of noise, so too is the attacker's utility, with noise of $NSR = -20dB$ sufficient to reduce attack precision from 35% to just above 10% on Epinions. This operating point demonstrates the choice available to the system designer: is it acceptable to have a drop of 20% in recommendation precision in order to reduce an attacker's precision by 70%? This is a design choice, but it is worth noting that the headroom available to the designer is relatively small, before the performance drops to the level of a non-personalised algorithm, such as *Random*.

Finally, we summarise the overall trade-offs available to the system designer by plotting the attack precision versus the precision of recommender in Figure 6. For the parameter range of our study, BLIP explores a wider set of trade-offs. Otherwise, once configured with the correct parameters to achieve a given performance, both techniques offer similar capabilities against the active attack.

8 CONCLUSIONS AND FUTURE WORK

Data sketching techniques, such as JLT and BLIP, can offer privacy for RS implementations, through the transformation of original user profiles and addition of noise to the transformed data. For each approach, there exists a best setup which aims to minimize the MSE of the sketch-based distance estimator between two user profiles.

In this paper, we have derived some mathematical expressions to relate the parameters of the BLIP method to the MSE. When the goal of the setup is to meet a particular differential privacy level, corresponding to a particular value of the privacy parameter ϵ, the BLIP sketch can achieve this level with less cost to the MSE in comparison to the JLT. This theoretical benefit to distance estimation, translates to observed superior empirical performance of the user-based kNN recommender algorithm applied to the top-N recommendation task. One disadvantage of BLIP in comparison to JLT, is that, in order to achieve a target MSE, the size of the sketch vector is significantly larger for BLIP than for JLT and this can impact on the computational performance of the algorithm. In terms of robustness against an active attacker, as expected, JLT outperforms BLIP almost for all the range of ϵ under study, due to its great effect on increasing MSE. Recalling that such a premium comes with a cost of poor recommendation performance. In conclusion, neither method dominates the other by e.g. simultaneously achieving greater recommender utility and lower attack utility.

While in the current work, we have selected nearest neighbours on the basis of distance between user profiles, in future we will analyse data sketching using cosine similarity, rather than distance. As the cosine is bounded below 1, we can expect that the variance of the JLT estimator will be truncated, with may make it more competitive with BLIP. We also intend to examine item-based and matrix factorisation algorithms using data sketches.

A BLIP DISTANCE ESTIMATOR

We seek to approximate $d_H(\mathbf{u}, \mathbf{v})$ using the Hamming distance in sketch-space, i.e. $\|\mathbf{b}_u - \mathbf{b}_v\|_2^2$ of the binary BLIP vectors. Profiles $\mathbf{u}$ and $\mathbf{v}$ are passed through a Bloom filter with $k > 0$ hash functions, to obtain $\mathbf{b}_u, \mathbf{b}_v \in \mathcal{B}^L$, respectively. Then, the elements of the resulting vectors, i.e. $\mathbf{b}_u$ and $\mathbf{b}_v$, are flipped independently with probability p. The Hamming distance between the two BLIP vectors can be rewritten as:

$$\sum_{i=1}^{L} d_i(\mathbf{b}_u, \mathbf{b}_v) \tag{17}$$

where $d_i(\mathbf{b}_u, \mathbf{b}_v) = 1$, if the vector components are equal at position i and zero otherwise.

We define $s = \mathbf{u}^T\mathbf{v}$ as the number of items that the two profiles have in common, $r_u = \mathbf{u}^T\mathbf{u} - \mathbf{u}^T\mathbf{v}$ and $r_v = \mathbf{v}^T\mathbf{v} - \mathbf{u}^T\mathbf{v}$, as the number of items that only appear in u, and respectively v. Moreover, assuming that the k hash functions can be modelled as independent uniformly random functions, the probability that a bit in the Bloom filter is *not set* by the presence of n items in a profile is given by

$$(1 - 1/L)^{kn} \approx \exp(-kn/L)\,.$$

The s common items set the same bits in the Bloom filters generated for each profile and therefore the setting of these bits does not make a contribution to the Hamming distance, prior to the application of bit-flipping. The Hamming distance at position i changes after bit-flipping with probability $q = 2p(1 - p)$, which corresponds to a bit in only one of the profiles being flipped.

Considering for position i in the sketch vector, whether it is set by each of the $s + r_u + r_v$ items the are present across the two profiles, we can arrive at the following expression for $\Pr(d_i = 1)$:

$$q\Big(1-(1-1/L)^{sk}\Big) + (1-1/L)^{sk}\Big[q\Big((1-(1-1/L)^{r_u k})$$
$$(1-(1-1/L)^{r_v k}) + (1-1/L)^{r_u k}(1-1/L)^{r_v k}\Big) + (1-q)\Big($$
$$(1-1/L)^{r_u k}(1-(1-1/L)^{r_v k}) + (1-1/L)^{r_v k}(1-(1-1/L)^{r_u k})\Big)\Big]\,.$$

Applying the exponential approximation, inserting the expressions for r_u, r_v and s and noting that $\mathbf{u}^T\mathbf{v} = \frac{1}{2}(\|\mathbf{u}\|^2 + \|\mathbf{v}\|^2 - d_H)$, the above probability can be re-arranged as:

$$\begin{aligned}\Pr(d_i = 1) =& (1-2q)\Big(\exp(-\|\mathbf{u}\|^2 k/L) + \exp(-\|\mathbf{v}\|^2 k/L) - \\ & 2\exp(-\frac{k}{2L}[\|\mathbf{u}\|^2 + \|\mathbf{v}\|^2 + d_H])\Big) + q\,.\end{aligned} \tag{18}$$

The expected value of the distance between two sketch profiles is:

$$\mathrm{E}[\|\mathbf{b}_u - \mathbf{b}_v\|^2] = \sum_i \Pr(d_i = 1) = L\Pr(d_i = 1) \tag{19}$$

The limit as $L \to \infty$ may be found for example, by applying L'Hopital's rule, to the above expression, or more simply by noting that in the limit of large L, each item is hashed to k unique bits, so that the generated Bloom filter consists of $kd_H(\mathbf{u}, \mathbf{v})$ positions where $d_i = 1$ and $L - kd_H(\mathbf{u}, \mathbf{v})$ positions where $d_i = 0$. Then, considering bit-flipping, we have that

$$\lim_{L\to\infty} \mathrm{E}[\|\mathbf{b}_u - \mathbf{b}_v\|^2] = (1-q)kd_H + q(L - kd_H) \tag{20}$$

Therefore in the limit of large L, an unbiased estimator of d_H is obtained as Eqn. (12).

B BLIP DISTANCE ESTIMATOR VARIANCE

The variance of distances can be written as:

$$\mathrm{Var}[\sum_i d_i] = L(L-1)c_d + Lp_d - L^2 p_d^2 \tag{21}$$

where $p_d = \Pr[d_i = 1]$ as given in the previous section, and $c_d = \mathrm{E}[d_i d_j] = \Pr[d_i = 1, d_j = 1]$ for an arbitrary pair of bit positions i and j.

In order to determine c_d, we need to consider the 16 possible settings of the bits at positions i and j in the two profiles u and v, as shown in Figure 7. These bit positions are set initially by the action of the hash functions and then may be modified by bit flipping. The figure shows the possible settings of the bits after the action of the hash functions. Without bit flipping, only the blue settings on the skew diagonal correspond to $d_i = 1$ and $d_j = 1$. However, bit flipping can ultimately transform all the settings to $d_i = d_j = 1$ with the probabilities of transformation shown in the figure.

Probabilities $\Pr[u_i, u_j]$ for all 4 possible bit settings at positions i and j in profile u, after k hash functions have been applied are

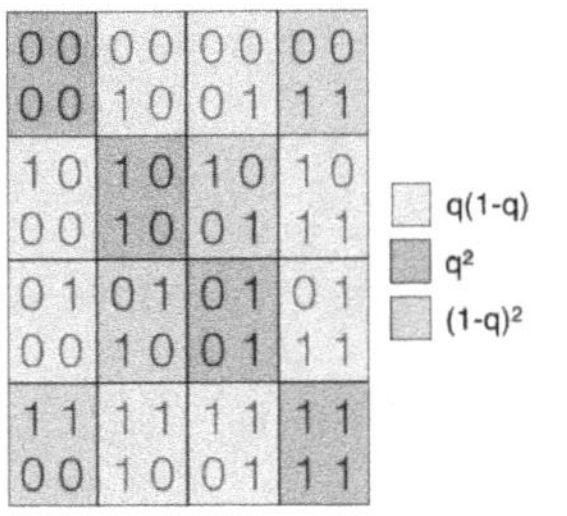

Figure 7: 16 Possible Bit Settings.

given below, along with a second-order approximation:

$$\begin{aligned}
\Pr[u_i = 0, u_j = 0] &\triangleq b_{00}(k) = (1 - 2/L)^k \approx e^{-2k/L} \\
\Pr[u_i = 0, u_j = 1] &\triangleq b_{01}(k) = (1 - 1/L)^k - (1 - 2/L)^k \\
&\approx 1/2(1 + e^{1/L})(e^{-k/L} - e^{-2k/L}) \\
\Pr[u_i = 0, u_j = 1] &\triangleq b_{01}(k) = b_{10}(k) \\
\Pr[u_i = 1, u_j = 1] &\triangleq b_{11}(k) = 1 - 2\,(1 - 1/L)^k + (1 - 2/L)^k \\
&\approx 1 + e^{-2k/L} - (1 + e^{1/L})(e^{-k/L} - e^{-2k/L})
\end{aligned} \quad (22)$$

Consider the bit settings that are obtained through the action of the hashes corresponding to the s common items, the bit settings corresponding to the r_u items in profile u and the r_v items in profile v. Each of these three independent actions result in two bit settings, for i and j giving a total of $2^6 = 64$ different possible outcomes and each of the 64 outcomes ultimately results in particular settings of u_i, u_j, v_i, v_j. Mapping the 64 outcomes of the three separate actions to the appropriate outcomes among the 16 possibilities for position i and j in u and v allows the probability to be written as a sum of products of the probabilities in Eqn.(22). For instance,

$$\Pr\left[\begin{pmatrix} 0 & 1 \\ 0 & 1 \end{pmatrix}\right] = b_{01}(ks) \times b_{00}(kr_u) \times b_{00}(kr_v) +$$
$$b_{01}(ks) \times b_{01}(kr_u) \times b_{00}(kr_v) + b_{00}(ks) \times b_{01}(kr_u) \times b_{01}(kr_v) +$$
$$b_{01}(ks) \times b_{01}(kr_u) \times b_{01}(kr_v) + b_{01}(ks) \times b_{00}(kr_u) \times b_{01}(kr_v) \text{ and}$$
$$\Pr\left[\begin{pmatrix} 0 & 0 \\ 0 & 0 \end{pmatrix}\right] = b_{00}(ks) \times b_{00}(kr_u) \times b_{00}(kr_v),$$

and similarly for the other outcomes. (Note that, for the fixed size catalogue optimisation (Section 4.2), whenever any term in these expansion of probabilities corresponds to an outcome where the bit is not set by any of the $s + r_u + r_v$ items in u and v, this term is multiplied by $1 - \exp(-k(m - s - r_u - r_v)/L)$, so that such a term only contributes if it *has been set* by some of the remaining $m - (s + r_u + r_v)$ other items in the catalogue.)

Let $c_r(L), c_b(L), c_g(L)$ be the probability of the red, green and blue outcomes, respectively, in Figure 7. Then c_d in Eqn.(21) can be written as a function of the sketch size as:

$$c_d(L) = q^2 c_r(L) + q(1 - q)c_g(L) + (1 - q)^2 c_b(L) \quad (23)$$

and $\text{Var}[\sum_i d_i]$ can be calculated by inserting c_d back to (21) and ultimately $\text{Var}[d_{\text{BLIP}}(\mathbf{b}_u, \mathbf{b}_v)]$ by dividing by $k^2(1 - 2q)^2$.

Intuitively, as $L \to \infty$, and each hash for each item maps to a different position in $\mathbf{b}_u$, we might expect the variance of the Hamming distance to converge to the sum of the variances of two Binomial processes, one with probability of success q on the $L - kd_H$ positions where the Hamming distance is 0 before bit-flipping and another with probability of success $1 - q$ on the kd_H positions where the Hamming distance is 1 before bit-flipping. However, due to the common items, the bit settings at each position are not independent and, as a result, the variance as $L \to \infty$ is slightly different:

$$\lim_{L\to\infty} \text{Var}[\sum_i d_i] = q(1 - q)L + q(1 - 2q)kd_H\,. \quad (24)$$

C MSE OF BLIP DISTANCE ESTIMATOR

Taking a second order approximation to the mean and, as the optimal occurs for $L \ll km$, taking $L(1 - \exp(-km/L)) \approx L$ in Eqn. (15), we obtain:

$$(d_H - \text{E}[d_{\text{BLIP}}]) = \frac{kd_H}{2L}\left(2\alpha_d(1 - \alpha_d)d_H + \|\mathbf{u}\|^2 + \|\mathbf{v}\|^2\right) \quad (25)$$

where α_d is defined such that $r_u = \alpha_d d_H$ and $r_v = (1 - \alpha_d)d_H$. The MSE is then:

$$\frac{q(1 - q)L + q(1 - 2q)kd_H}{k^2(1 - 2q)^2} + \frac{k^2 d_H^2}{4L^2}\left(2\alpha_d(1 - \alpha_d)d_H + \|\mathbf{u}\|^2 + \|\mathbf{v}\|^2\right)^2 \quad (26)$$

Differentiating wrt L allows the optimal L that minimises the MSE to be obtained:

$$L_{\text{opt}}^3 = \frac{(1 - 2q)^2}{q(1 - q)} \frac{k^4 d_H^2}{2}\left(2\alpha_d(1 - \alpha_d)d_H + \|\mathbf{u}\|^2 + \|\mathbf{v}\|^2\right)^2 \quad (27)$$

For a fixed size P of the largest of the two profiles, L_{opt} is largest when $\alpha_d = 1/2$, in which case

$$L_{\text{opt}}^3 = \frac{(1 - 2q)^2}{q(1 - q)} \frac{k^4 d_H^2}{8}\left(4P + d_H\right)^2 \quad (28)$$

and the resulting MSE:

$$\text{MSE}_{\text{opt}} = \frac{3}{4}\left(\frac{q(1 - q)}{(1 - 2q)^2} \frac{d_H(4P + d_H)}{k}\right)^{\frac{2}{3}} + \frac{qd_H}{k(1 - 2q)} \quad (29)$$

Inserting, from Eqn.(11), $q = 2e^{\epsilon/k}/(1 + e^{\epsilon/k})^2$, we arrive at Eqn.(16).

Note that differently to JLT, the optimal L depends on the size of the profiles as well as on the Hamming distance between the two profiles. In Figure 8, we plot the true MSE and the second-order approximation for an example value of d_H and P. Generally, the optimal L is somewhat underestimated, but as the MSE is relatively flat close to the optimal, this under-estimation does not impact strongly on the quality of the result.

ACKNOWLEDGMENTS

This project has been funded by Science Foundation Ireland under Grant No. SFI/12/RC/2289.

REFERENCES

[1] Alaggan, M., Gambs, S., and Kermarrec, A.-M. Blip: non-interactive differentially-private similarity computation on bloom filters. In *Symposium on Self-Stabilizing Systems*, Springer (2012), 202–216.

[2] Balu, R., Furon, T., and Gambs, S. Challenging differential privacy: the case of non-interactive mechanisms. In *European Symposium on Research in Computer Security*, Springer (2014), 146–164.

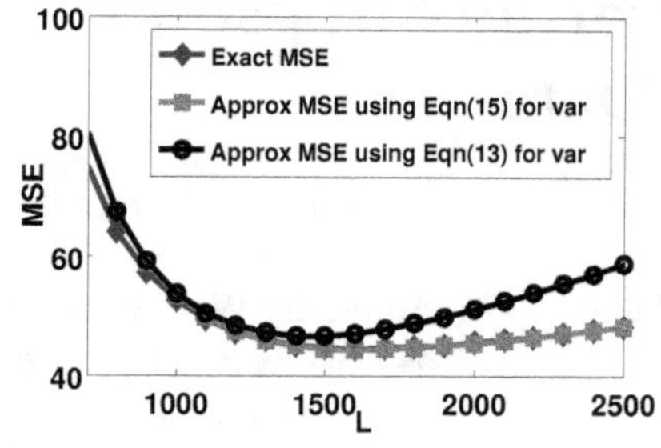

Figure 8: Approximations of MSE for $d_H = 50$ and $P = 100$

[3] Basu, A., Vaidya, J., and Kikuchi, H. Perturbation based privacy preserving slope one predictors for collaborative filtering. In *IFIP International Conference on Trust Management*, Springer (2012), 17–35.

[4] Berlioz, A., Friedman, A., Kaafar, M. A., Boreli, R., and Berkovsky, S. Applying differential privacy to matrix factorization. In *Proceedings of the 9th ACM Conference on Recommender Systems*, ACM (2015), 107–114.

[5] Bilge, A., and Polat, H. An improved privacy-preserving dwt-based collaborative filtering scheme. *Expert Systems with Applications 39*, 3 (2012), 3841–3854.

[6] Bloom, B. H. Space/time trade-offs in hash coding with allowable errors. *Communications of the ACM 13*, 7 (1970), 422–426.

[7] Calandrino, J. A., Kilzer, A., Narayanan, A., Felten, E. W., and Shmatikov, V. " you might also like:" privacy risks of collaborative filtering. In *2011 IEEE Symposium on Security and Privacy*, IEEE (2011), 231–246.

[8] Canny, J. Collaborative filtering with privacy. In *Security and Privacy, 2002. Proceedings. 2002 IEEE Symposium on*, IEEE (2002), 45–57.

[9] Dwork, C. Differential privacy: A survey of results. In *International Conference on Theory and Applications of Models of Computation*, Springer (2008), 1–19.

[10] Kenthapadi, K., Korolova, A., Mironov, I., and Mishra, N. Privacy via the johnson-lindenstrauss transform. *arXiv preprint arXiv:1204.2606* (2012).

[11] McSherry, F., and Mironov, I. Differentially private recommender systems: building privacy into the net. In *Proceedings of the 15th ACM SIGKDD international conference on Knowledge discovery and data mining*, ACM (2009), 627–636.

[12] Nikolaenko, V., Ioannidis, S., Weinsberg, U., Joye, M., Taft, N., and Boneh, D. Privacy-preserving matrix factorization. In *Proceedings of the 2013 ACM SIGSAC conference on Computer & communications security*, ACM (2013), 801–812.

[13] Parameswaran, R., and Blough, D. M. Privacy preserving collaborative filtering using data obfuscation. In *Granular Computing, 2007. GRC 2007. IEEE International Conference on*, IEEE (2007), 380–380.

Can you Trust the Trend? Discovering Simpson's Paradoxes in Social Data

Nazanin Alipourfard*
USC/ISI
4676 Admiralty Way, Marina Del Rey
Los Angeles, California 90292
nazanina@isi.edu

Peter G. Fennell
USC/ISI
4676 Admiralty Way, Marina Del Rey
Los Angeles, California 90292
pfennell@isi.edu

Kristina Lerman
USC/ISI
4676 Admiralty Way, Marina Del Rey
Los Angeles, California 90292
lerman@isi.edu

ABSTRACT

We investigate how Simpson's paradox affects analysis of trends in social data. According to the paradox, the trends observed in data that has been aggregated over an entire population may be different from, and even opposite to, those of the underlying subgroups. Failure to take this effect into account can lead analysis to wrong conclusions. We present a statistical method to automatically identify Simpson's paradox in data by comparing statistical trends in the aggregate data to those in the disaggregated subgroups. We apply the approach to data from Stack Exchange, a popular question-answering platform, to analyze factors affecting answerer performance, specifically, the likelihood that an answer written by a user will be accepted by the asker as the best answer to his or her question. Our analysis confirms a known Simpson's paradox and identifies several new instances. These paradoxes provide novel insights into user behavior on Stack Exchange.

CCS CONCEPTS

• **Mathematics of computing** → **Statistical paradigms**; **Exploratory data analysis**; *Regression analysis*; • **Information systems** → **Data mining**; *Collaborative and social computing systems and tools*; Clustering;

KEYWORDS

Simpson's Paradox, Trend Analysis

ACM Reference format:
Nazanin Alipourfard, Peter G. Fennell, and Kristina Lerman. 2018. Can you Trust the Trend? Discovering Simpson's Paradoxes in Social Data. In *Proceedings of WSDM 2018: The Eleventh ACM International Conference on Web Search and Data Mining , Marina Del Rey, CA, USA, February 5–9, 2018 (WSDM 2018)*, 9 pages.
https://doi.org/10.1145/3159652.3159684

*N. Alipourfard and P. Fennell contributed equally to this work.

WSDM 2018, February 5–9, 2018, Marina Del Rey, CA, USA

ACM ISBN 978-1-4503-5581-0/18/02...$15.00
https://doi.org/10.1145/3159652.3159684

1 INTRODUCTION

Digital traces of human activity have exposed social behavior to web and data mining algorithms. Researchers have analyzed the growing social data to understand, among other things, how information spreads in social networks [18], and the factors affecting user engagement [2] and performance [19] in online platforms. Yet social data analysis presents multi-faceted challenges that existing data mining approaches are not well-equipped to handle. Real-world data is noisy and sparse. To uncover hidden patterns, scientists aggregate data over the population, which tends to improve statistics and signal-to-noise ratio. However, real-world data is also heterogeneous, i.e., composed of subgroups that vary widely in size and behavior. This heterogeneity can severely bias analysis of social data.

One example of such bias is Simpson's paradox. According to the paradox, an association observed in data that has been aggregated over an entire population may be quite different from, and even opposite to, those of the underlying subgroups. Failure to take this effect into account can distort conclusions drawn from data. One of the better known examples of Simpson's paradox comes from a study of gender bias in graduate admissions [4]. In the aggregate admissions data there appears to be a statistically significant bias against women: a smaller fraction of female applicants is admitted for graduate studies. However, when admissions data is disaggregated by department, women have parity and even a slight advantage over men in some departments. The paradox arises because departments preferred by female applicants have lower admissions rates for both genders.

Simpson's paradox also affects analysis of trends. When measuring how an outcome changes as a function of an independent variable, the characteristics of the population over which the trend is measured may change as a function of the independent variable due to survivor bias. As a result, the data may appear to exhibit a trend, which disappears or reverses when the data is disaggregated. For example, it may appear that repeated exposures to information or hashtags on social media make an individual less likely to share it with his or her followers [18]. In fact, the opposite is true: the more people are exposed to information, the more likely they are to share it with followers [16]. However, those who follow many others (and are likely to be exposed to a meme or a hashtag multiple times) are less responsive overall, due to the high volume of information they receive [12]. Their reduced susceptibility to exposures biases the aggregate response, leading to wrong conclusions about behavior. Once disaggregated based on the volume of information received, a clearer pattern of exposure response emerges, one that is more predictive of the actual response [13]. However, despite accumulating evidence that Simpson's paradox affects inference of trends in social and behavioral data [1, 2, 15, 19], researchers do not routinely test for it in their studies.

We describe a method to identify Simpson's paradoxes in the analysis of trends in social data. Our statistical approach finds pairs of variables—that we call *Simpson's pairs*—such that a trend in some outcome as a function of the first *independent* variable observed in the aggregate data disappears or reverses itself when the data is disaggregated into distinct subgroups on the second *conditioning* variable. We perform mathematical analysis, which identifies two necessary conditions for the paradox to occur: (1) the independent and conditioning variables are correlated and (2) the value of the outcome variable differs within conditioning subgroups.

We apply the proposed approach to data collected from Stack Exchange, a popular question-answering platform. Specifically, we analyze factors affecting answerer performance, measured as the likelihood the answer provided by the answerer will be accepted by the asker as the best answer to his or her question. We construct a variety of features to describe answers and answerers, and study how the outcome—in this case answer acceptance—depends on these features. We compare results of statistical trends found in aggregated and disaggregated data to identify Simpsons's pairs. Our analysis discovers several cases of Simpson's paradox in Stack Exchange data. In addition to a known effect that describes deterioration of answerer performance over the course of a session, our method identifies several new cases of Simpson's paradox. These paradoxes yield new insights into answerer performance on Stack Exchange. For example, creating a new feature to describe answerers, which combines variables of a Simpson's pair, leads to a more robust proxy of answerer performance.

Presence of a Simpson's paradox in social data can indicate interesting patterns [8], including important behavioral differences. The paradox suggests that subgroups within the population under study systematically differ in their behavior, and these differences are large enough to affect aggregate trends. In such cases the trends discovered in disaggregated data are more likely to describe—and predict—individual behavior than the trends found in aggregated data. Thus, to build more robust models of behavior, data scientists need to identify the subgroups within their data or risk drawing wrong conclusions. The method presented in this paper provides a simple framework for identifying such interesting subgroups by systematically searching for Simpson's paradox in trend data.

The rest of the paper is organized as follows. First, we present background, including multiple observations of Simpson's paradox in a variety of disciplies (Sec. 2). Then we describe our methodology for detecting Simpson's paradox by identifying covariates in data, and analyze the paradox mathematically to gain more insight into its origins (Sec. 3). Finally, we apply our method to real-world data from the question-answering site Stack Exchange, and demonstrate its ability to automatically identify novel cases of Simpson's paradox (Sec. 4). We conclude with the discussion of implications.

2 BACKGROUND AND RELATED WORK

The goal of data analysis is to identify important associations between features, or variables, in data. However, hidden correlations between variables can lead analysis to wrong conclusions. One important manifestation of this effect is Simpson's paradox, according to which *an association that appears in different subgroups of data may disappear, and even reverse itself, when data is aggregated across subgroups.* Instances of the paradox have been documented across a variety of disciplines, including demographics, economics, political science, and clinical research, and it has been argued that the presence of Simpson's paradox implies that interesting patterns exist in data [8]. A notorious example of Simpson's paradox arose during a gender bias lawsuit against UC Berkeley. Analysis of graduate school admissions data revealed a statistically significant bias against women. However, the pattern of discrimination observed in this aggregate data disappeared when admissions data was disaggregated by department. Bickel et al. [4] attributed this effect to Simpson's paradox. They argued that the subtle correlations between the popularity of departments among the genders and their selectivity resulted in women applying to departments that were hardest to get into, which skewed analysis.

Simpson's paradox must also be considered in the analysis of trends. Vaupel and Yashin [20] give a compelling illustration of how survivor bias can shift the composition of data, distorting the conclusions drawn from it. Analysis of recidivism among convicts released from prison shows that the rate at which they return to prison declines over time. From this, policy makers may conclude that age has a pacifying effect on crime: older convicts are less likely to commit crimes. In reality, this conclusion is false. Instead, we can think of the population of ex-convicts as composed of two subgroups with constant, but very different recidivism rates. The first subgroup, let's call them "reformed," will never commit a crime once released from prison. The other subgroup, the "incorrigibles," will always commit a crime. Over time, as "incorrigibles" commit offenses and return to prison, there are fewer of them left in the population. The survivor bias changes the composition of the population under study, creating an illusion of an overall decline in recidivism rates. As Vaupel and Yashin warn, "unsuspecting researchers who are not wary of heterogeneity's ruses may fallaciously assume that observed patterns for the population as a whole also hold on the sub-population or individual level." Their paper gives numerous other examples of such *ecological fallacies.*

Similar illusions crop up in many studies of social behavior. For example, when examining how social media users respond to information from their friends (other users that they follow), it may appear that if *more* of a user's friends use a hashtag then the user will be *less* likely to use it himself or herself [18]. Similarly, the more friends share some information, the less likely the user is to share it with his or her followers [10]. From this, one may conclude the additional exposures to information in a sense "innoculate" the user and act to suppress the sharing of information. In fact, this is not the case, and instead, additional exposures monotonically increase the user's likelihood to share information with followers [16]. However, those users who follow many others, and are likely to be exposed to information or a hashtag multiple times, are less responsive overall, because they are overloaded with information they receive from all the friends they follow [12]. Calculating response as a function of the number of exposures in the aggregate data falls prey to survivor bias: the more responsive users (with fewer friends) quickly drop out of the average (since they are generally exposed fewer times), leaving the highly connected, but less responsive, users behind. The reduced susceptibility of these highly connected users biases aggregate response, leading to wrong conclusions about individual behavior. Once data is disaggregated based on the volume of information individuals receive, a clearer pattern of response emerges, one that is more predictive of behavior [13]. Multiple examples of Simpson's paradox have been identified in empirical studies of online behavior. A study [2] of Reddit found that while it may appear that average comment length on decreases over any fixed period of time, when data is disaggregated into groups based on the year user joined Reddit, comment length within each group increases during the same time period. It is only because users who joined early tend to write longer comments that the Simpson's paradox appears.

Data heterogeneity also impacts statistical analysis of data [7] and causal inference [21]. However, no general framework to recognize and mitigate Simpson's paradox exist. Current methods require that the structure of data be explicitly specified [3] or at best be guided by subject matter knowledge [11].

Despite accumulating evidence that Simpson's paradox affects inference from data [7, 21], scientists do not routinely test for the presence of this paradox in heterogeneous data. Our work addresses this knowledge gap by proposing a statistical method to systematically uncover instances of Simpson's paradox in data.

3 METHODS

We propose a method to systematically uncover Simpson's paradox for trends in data. We denote as Y the dependent variable in the data set, i.e., an outcome being measured, and as $\mathbf{X} = \{X_1, X_2, \ldots, X_m\}$ the set of m independent variables or features. The goal of the method is to identify pairs of variables (X_p, X_c)—*Simpson's pairs*— such that a trend in Y as a function of X_p disappears or reverses when the data is disaggregated by conditioning on X_c. More specifically, our method searches for pairs of variables (X_p, X_c) such that

$$\frac{d}{dx_p}\mathbb{E}[Y|X_p = x_p] > 0 \quad \forall x_p, \tag{1}$$

$$\frac{d}{dx_p}\mathbb{E}[Y|X_p = x_p, X_c = x_c] \leq 0 \quad \forall x_p, x_c. \tag{2}$$

and vice versa (i.e., $d\mathbb{E}[Y|X_p = x_p]/dx_p < 0$, $d\mathbb{E}[Y|X_p = x_p, X_c = x_c]/dx_p \geq 0$). Equations (1) and (2) hold if the expected value of Y is a monotonically increasing (or decreasing) function of X_p alone, but conditioned on X_c is a monotonically decreasing (resp. increasing) function of X_p, or is constant.

3.1 Finding Simpson's Pairs

With this goal in mind, we employ linear models to quantify the relationship between Y, an independent variable X_p, and a conditioning variable X_c upon which the data is disaggregated. Firstly, on the aggregate level, we model the relationship between Y and X_p as a linear model of the form

$$\mathbb{E}[Y|X_p = x_p] = f_p(\alpha + \beta x_p), \tag{3}$$

where $f_p(\alpha + \beta x_p)$ is a monotonically increasing function of its argument $\alpha + \beta x_p$. The parameter α in Eq. (3) is the intercept of the regression function, while the trend parameter β quantifies the effect of X_p on Y. Secondly, for the disaggregation, we fit linear models of the form of Eq. (3) but with different values of the parameters α and β depending on the value of X_c:

$$\mathbb{E}[Y|X_p = x_p, X_c = x_c] = f_{p,c}(\alpha(x_c) + \beta(x_c)x_p), \tag{4}$$

When fitting linear models $f(\alpha + \beta X)$ we have not only a fitted trend parameter β but also a p-value which gives the probability of finding an intercept β at least as extreme as the fitted value under the null hypothesis $H_0 : \beta = 0$. From this, we have three possibilities:

- β is not statistically different from zero (sgn(β) = 0),
- β is statistically different from zero and positive (sgn(β) = 1),
- β is statistically different from zero and negative (sgn(β) = -1).

This mechanism allows us to test for Simpson's paradox by comparing the sign of β from the aggregated fit (Eq. (3)) with the signs of the β's from the disaggregated fits (Eq. (4)). Although Eqs. (3) and (4) state that the signs from the disaggregated curves should all be different from the aggregated curve, in practice this is too strict, especially as human behavioral data is noisy. Thus, we compare the sign of the fit to aggregated data to the simple average of the signs of fits to disaggregated data— if the signs are different then we have uncovered an instance of Simpson's paradox. The summary of the algorithm is the following:

Trend Simpson's Paradox Algorithm

```
def trend_simpsons_pair(X, Y):
 paradox_pairs = []
 for paradox_var in vars:
  beta, pvalue =
      trend_analysis(X[paradox_var], Y)
  agg = sgn(beta, pvalue)
  for condition_var in vars:
   if paradox_var != condition_var:
    dagg = []
    for con_gr in bins_of(condition_var):
     beta, pvalue =
         trend_analysis(X[paradox_var |
         con_gr], Y)
     dagg.append(sgn(beta, pvalue))
    if agg != sgn(mean(dagg)):
     paradox_pairs.append([paradox_var,
         condition_var])
 return paradox_pairs

def sgn(beta, pvalue = 0.0):
 return (0 if (beta == 0 or pvalue > 0.05)
     else (1 if beta > 0 else -1))
```

Data Disaggregation. A critical step in our method is disaggregating data by conditioning on variable X_c. The idea behind disaggregation is to segment data into more homogeneous subgroups of similar elements. For multinomial variables X_c, disaggregation step simply involves grouping data by unique values of X_c. However, for continuous X_c or discrete variables with large range, this step is more complex. We can bin the elements according to their values of X_c, but the decision has to be made how large each bin is, whether bin sizes scale linearly or logarithmically, etc. If the bin is too small, it may not contain enough samples for a statistically significant measurement, but if it is too large, the samples may be too heterogeneous for a robust trend. In our experiments described below, bins of fixed size successfully identify Simpson's pairs, though we realize that more sophisticated binning techniques can allow us to isolate more pairs or reduce the number of false positives.

3.2 Mathematical Analysis of the Paradox

We have presented a mathematical formulation of Simpson's paradox in terms of the derivatives of conditional expectations as given by Eqs. (1) and (2), and we now examine these equations to get a better insight into the origins and causes of this paradox.

The expectation in Eq. (1) can be related to that of Eq. (2) as

$$\mathbb{E}[Y|X_p = x_p] = \int_{X_c} \mathbb{E}[Y|X_p = x_p, X_c = x_c] \Pr(X_c = x_c|X_p = x_p) dx_c, \quad (5)$$

and differentiating this expectation w.r.t. x_p allows us to compare the trends of Eqs. (1) and (2). The derivative of the right hand side of Eq. (5) with respect to x_p is

$$\int_{X_c} \left(\frac{d}{dx_p}\mathbb{E}[Y|X_p = x_p, X_c = x_c]\right) \Pr(X_c = x_c|X_p = x_p) dx_c + \int_{X_c} \mathbb{E}[Y|X_p = x_p, X_c = x_c] \left(\frac{d}{dx_p} \Pr(X_c = x_c|X_p = x_p)\right) dx_c. \quad (6)$$

If $\mathbb{E}[Y|X_p = x_p, X_c = x_c]$ is a non-increasing function of x_p—as in Eq. (2)—then the first integral in Eq. (6) will be non-positive. Thus for $\mathbb{E}[Y|X_p = x_p]$ to be an increasing function of x_p, i.e., for Eq. (6) to be positive, the second integral must be positive.

This inequality condition leads to two necessary conditions for the occurrence of Simpson's paradox. The first condition is that

$$\frac{d}{dx_p} \Pr(X_c = x_c|X_p = x_p) \neq 0, \quad (7)$$

i.e., the distribution of the conditioning variable X_c is not independent of X_p and so the two variables are correlated. As X_p changes, the distribution of the values of X_c must also change. In the case that the distribution of X_c is independent of X_p, then $d\Pr(X_c = x_c|X_p = x_p)/dx = 0$ and so the second integral of Eq. (6) will be zero resulting in no Simpson's paradox.

The second necessary condition for the occurrence of Simpson's paradox is that the expectation of Y, conditioned on X_p, must not be independent of X_c, i.e.,

$$\mathbb{E}[Y|X_p = x_p, X_c = x_c] \neq \mathbb{E}[Y|X_p = x_p]. \quad (8)$$

For any given value of X_p, the expectation of Y must vary as a function of X_c. If the condition of Eq. (8) is not met then the second integral in Eq. (6) becomes

$$\int_{X_c} \mathbb{E}[Y|X_p = x_p] \left(\frac{d}{dx_p} \Pr(X_c = x_c|X_p = x_p)\right) dx_c \quad (9)$$
$$= \mathbb{E}[Y|X_p = x_p]\frac{d}{dx_p}\left(\int_{X_c} \Pr(X_c = x_c|X_p = x_p) dx_c\right) = 0,$$

and so Simpson's paradox will not occur.

Thus, this mathematical analysis has given us an insight into causes for Simpson's paradox in data —correlations between independent variables and the fact that the distribution of the conditioning variable X_c changes at a faster rate with respect to the independent paradox variable X_p than does the expectation of Y. This point will be covered in greater detail in the next section.

4 RESULTS

We explore our approach using data from the question-answering platform called Stack Exchange. This platform, launched in 2008 to provide a forum for people to ask computer programming questions, grew over the years as a forum asking questions on a variety of technical and non-technical topics. The premise behind Stack Exchange is simple: any user can ask a question, which others may answer. Users can also *vote* for answers they find helpful, and the asker can *accept* one of the answers as the best answer to the question. In this way, the Stack Exchange community collectively curates knowledge.

4.1 Stack Exchange Data

We used anonymized data representing all questions and answers from August 2008 until September 2014.[1] The data includes 9.6M questions, of which approximately half had an accepted answer. Only the questions that received two or more answers were included [5]. Previous studies of Stack Exchange [9] and other online platforms [1, 19], identified user sessions as an important variable in understanding performance. User actions, i.e., answering questions, can be segmented into *sessions*—periods of activity without a prolonged break. Following [9] we use 100 minutes as minimum break length to define sessions. A time interval longer than 100 minutes between two answers constitutes the end of one session and the start of a new one. Note that the exact value of this threshold does not change results, but simply merge a small fraction of sessions into longer sessions.

To understand factors affecting user performance on Stack Exchange, we study the relationship between user attributes and the probability that the answer the user produces is accepted by the asker as best answer to his or her question. To this end, for each answer in the data set, we create a list of features describing the answer, as well as features of describing the user writing the answer:

- **Reputation:** Answerer's reputation at the time he or she posted the answer. This score summarizes the user's cumulative contributions to Stack Exchange.
- **Number of answers:** Cumulative number of answers written by the user at the time the current answer was posted.
- **Tenure:** Age of the user's account (in seconds) at the time the user posted the answer.
- **Percentile:** User's percentile rank based on tenure.
- **Time since previous answer:** Time interval (in seconds) since user's previous answer.
- **Session length:** The length of the session (in number of answers posted) during which the answer was posted.
- **Answer position:** Index of the answer within a session.
- **Words:** Number of words in the answer.
- **Lines of codes:** Number of lines of codes in the answer.

[1] https://archive.org/details/stackexchange

X_p: Independent Variable	X_c: Conditioning Variable
Tenure	Number of answers
Session length	Reputation
Answer position	Reputation
Answer position	Session length
Number of answers	Reputation
Time since previous answer	Answer position
Percentile	Number of answers

Table 1: Examples of Simpson's paradox in Stack Exchange data. For these variables, the trend in the outcome variable (answer acceptance) as a function of X_p in the aggregate data reverses when the data disaggregated on X_c.

URLs: Number of hyperlinks in the answer.
Readability: Answer's Flesch Reading Ease [14] score.

4.2 Simpson's Paradoxes on Stack Exchange

We apply the method described above to Stack Exchange data. Here, our dependent variable Y is binary, denoting whether or not a specific answer to a question was accepted as the best answer. In this case of binary outcomes we use the logistic regression linear model of the form

$$f(\alpha + \beta x) = \frac{1}{1 + e^{-(\alpha+\beta x)}}. \tag{10}$$

The parameters α and β are fitted using Maximum likelihood, while test of the null hypothesis $H_0 : \beta = 0$ is performed using the Likelihood Ratio Test [6].

The eleven variables in Stack Exchange data, result in 110 possible Simpson's pairs. Among these, our method identifies seven as instance of paradox. These are listed in Table 1.

Our approach reveals that the previously reported finding that acceptance probability decreases with answer position [9] is an instance of Simpson's paradox and would not have been observed had the data not been disaggregated by session length. More interestingly, our approach also identifies previously unknown instances of Simpson's paradox. We explore these in greater detail below, illustrating how it can lead to deeper insights into online behavior.

4.2.1 Answer Position & Session Length. We measure session length by the number of answers a user posts before taking an extended break. Session length was shown to be an important confounding variable in online activity. Analysis of the quality of comments posted on a social news platform Reddit showed that, once disaggregated by the length of session, the quality of comments declines over the course of a session, with each successive comment written by a user becoming shorter, less textually complex, receiving fewer responses and a lower score from others [19]. Similarly, each successive answer posted during a session by a user on Stack Exchange is shorter, less well documented with external links and code, and less likely to be accepted by the asker as the best answer [9].

Our approach automatically identifies this example as Simpson's paradox, as illustrated in Fig. 1. The figure shows average acceptance probability for an answer as a function of its position (or index) within a session. According to Fig. 1a, which reports *aggregate* acceptance probability, answers written later in a session are more likely to be accepted than earlier answers. However, once the same data is *disaggregated by session length*, the trend reverses (Fig. 1b): each successive answer within the same session is less likely to be accepted than the previous answer. For example, for sessions during which five answers were written, the first answer is more likely to be accepted than the second answer, which is more likely to be accepted than the third answer, etc., which is more likely to be accepted than the fifth answer. The lines in Fig. 1 represent fits to data using logistic regression.

This example highlights the necessity to properly disaggregate data to identify the subgroups for analysis. Unless data is disaggregated, wrong conclusions may be drawn, in this case, for example, that user performance improves during a session.

4.2.2 Number of Answers & Reputation. Experience plays an important role in the quality of answers written by users. Stack Exchange veterans, i.e., users who have been active on Stack Exchange for more than six months, post longer, better documented answers, that are also more likely to be accepted as best answers by askers [9]. There are several ways to measure experience on Stack Exchange. *Reputation*, according to Stack Exchange, gauges how much the community trusts a user to post good questions and provide useful answers. While reputation can be gained or lost with different actions, a more straightforward measure of experience is user *tenure*, which measures time since the user became active on Stack Exchange, or *Percentile*, normalized rank of a user's tenure. Alternately, experience can be measured by the *Number of Answers* a user posted during his or her tenure before writing the current answer.

Our method uncovers a novel Simpson's paradox for user experience variables *Reputation* and *Number of Answers*. In the aggregate data, acceptance probability increases as a function of the *Number of Answers* (Fig. 2a). This is consistent with our expectations that the more experienced users—who have written more answers over their tenure on Stack Exchange—produce higher quality answers. However, when data is conditioned on *Reputation*, the trend reverses (Fig. 2b). In other words, focusing on groups of users with the same reputation, those who have written more answers over their tenure are less likely to have a new answer accepted than the less active answerers.

4.3 The Origins of Simpson's paradox

To understand why Simpson's paradox occurs in Stack Exchange data, we illustrate the mathematical explanation of Section 3.2 with examples from our study. Consider the paradox for *Answer Position–Session Length* Simpson's pair, illustrated in Fig. 1a. In the disaggregated data, trend lines of acceptance probability for sessions of different length are stacked (Fig. 1b): answers produced during longer sessions are more likely to be accepted than answers

Table 2: Number of data points in each group

Session Length	1	2	3	4	5	6	7	8
Data points	7.2M	2.6M	1.3M	0.7M	0.4M	0.3M	0.2M	0.1M

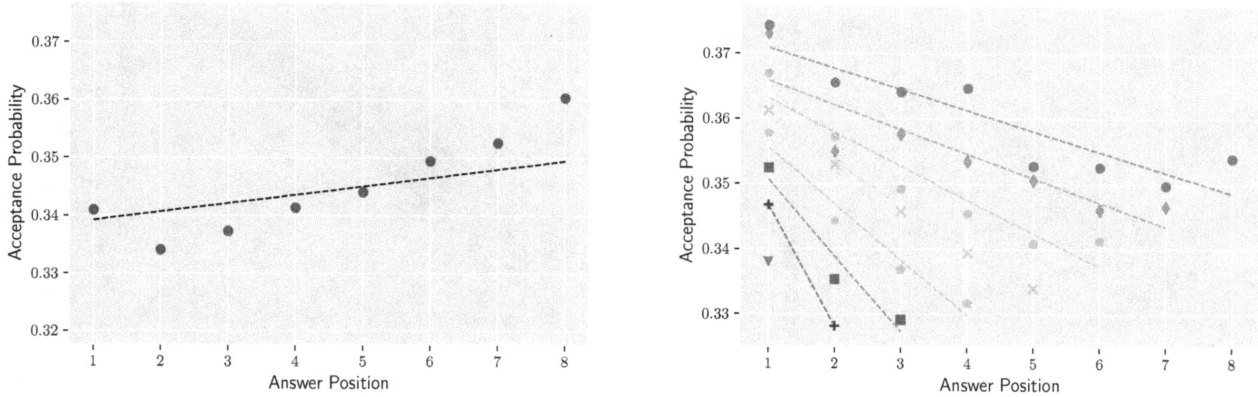

(a) Aggregated Data (b) Disaggregated Data

Figure 1: Simpson's paradox in Stack Exchange data. Both plots show the probability an answer is accepted as the best answer to a question as a function of its position within user's activity session. (a) Acceptance probability calculated over aggregated data has an upward trend, suggesting that answers written later in a session are more likely to be accepted as best answers. However, when data is disaggregated by session length (b), the trend reverses. Among answers produced during sessions of the same length (different colors represent different-length sessions), later answers are less likely to be accepted as best answers.

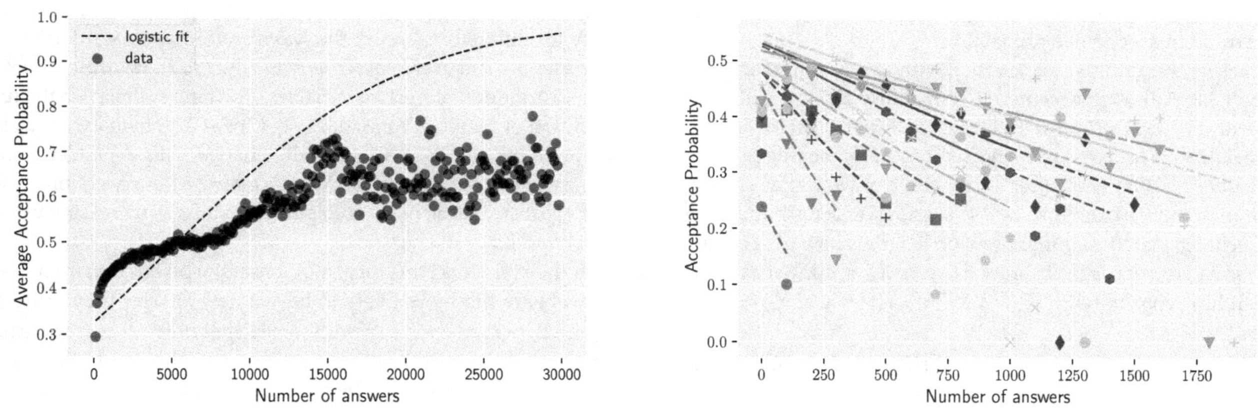

(a) Aggregated Data (b) Disaggregated Data

Figure 2: Novel Simpson's paradox discovered in Stack Exchange data. Plots show the probability an answer is accepted as best answer as a function of the number of lifetime answers written by user over his or her tenure. (a) Acceptance probability calculated over aggregated data has an upward trend, with answers written by more experienced users (who have already posted more answers) more likely to be accepted as best answers. However, when data is disaggregated by reputation (b), the trend reverses. Among answers written by users with the same reputation (different colors represent reputation bins), those posted by users who had already written more answers are less likely to be accepted as best answers.

produced during shorter sessions. In addition, there are many more shorter sessions than longer ones. Table 2 reports the number of sessions of different length. By far, the most common session has length one: users write only one answer during these sessions. Each longer session is about half as common as a session that is one answer shorter.

What happens to the trend in the aggregated data? When calculating acceptance probability as a function of answer position, all sessions contribute to acceptance probability for the first answer of a session. Sessions of length one dominate the average. When calculating acceptance probability for answers in the second position, sessions of length one do not contribute, and acceptance probability

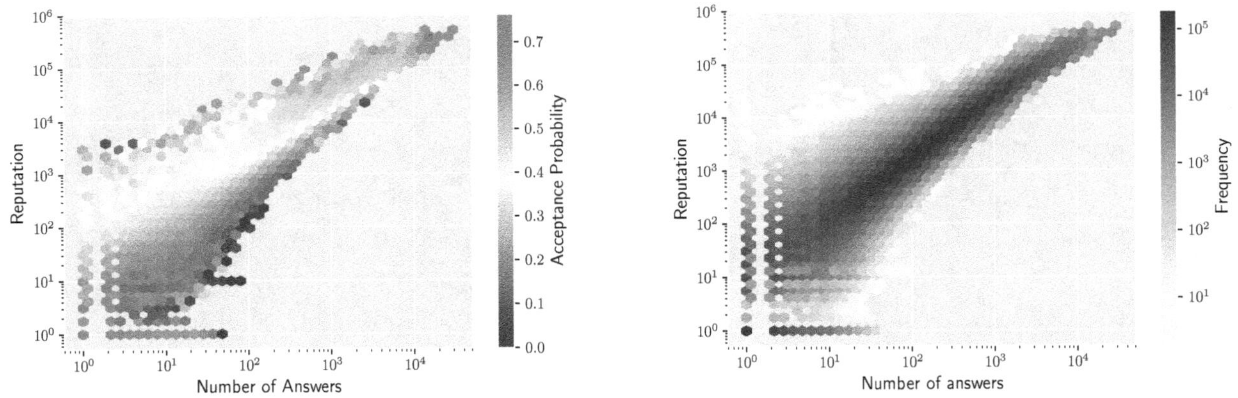

(a) Disaggregated data

(b) Joint distribution of X_c and X_p

Figure 3: Analysis of the Simpson's paradox *Reputation – Number of Answers* variable pair. (a) Average acceptance probability as a function of two variables. (b) The distribution of the number of data points contributing to the value of the outcome variable for each pair of variable values.

is dominated by data from sessions of length two. Similarly, acceptance probability of answers in the third position is dominated by sessions of length three. Survivor bias excludes data from shorter sessions, which also have lower acceptance probability, creating an upward trend in acceptance probability.

We back up this intuitive explanation with mathematical analysis of Section 3.2. Although acceptance probability is decreasing as a function of *Answer Position* for each value of *Session Length* (Fig. 1b), the probability mass of *Session Length* is constantly moving towards larger values as *Answer Position* increases. Notice that as *Answer Position* increments from a to $a + 1$, sessions of length a are no longer included (as the minimum session length is now $a + 1$). Thus, while *Session Length* has probability mass $\Pr(X_c = a|X_p = a)$ when $X_p = a$, it has probability $\Pr(X_c = a|X_p = a + 1) = 0$ at $X_p = a + 1$:

$$\frac{d}{dx_p}\Pr(X_c = a|X_p = x_p)||_{x_p=a} = -\Pr(X_c = a|X_p = a). \quad (11)$$

Meanwhile, for all other values of X_c greater than a, the probability mass at $X_p = a + 1$ is the same as that at $X_p = a$ (as the number of data points is constant along sessions of same length) but normalized to account for the sessions of length a, i.e.,

$$\Pr(X_c = x_c|X_p = a + 1) = \frac{\Pr(X_c = x_c|X_p = a)}{1 - \Pr(X_c = a|X_p = a)}. \quad (12)$$

The rate of change of these probability masses with respect to X_p is

$$\frac{d}{dx_p}\Pr(X_c = x_c|X_p = x_p)||_{x_p=a} =$$

$$\left(\frac{1}{1 - \Pr(X_c = a|X_p = a)} - 1\right)\Pr(X_c = x_c|X_p = a). \quad (13)$$

The probability mass function $\Pr(X_c = x_c|X_p = a)$ decreases for $X_c = a$ corresponding to the smallest value of acceptance probability, while increasing for all other values $X_c > a$. Moreover, the rate of increase of this probability mass is greater than the rate at which the acceptance probability decreases, resulting in an upward trend when the data is aggregated.

A similar effect plays out in the *Number of Answers–Reputation* Simpson's pair. Figure 3a shows the heatmap of acceptance probability for different values of the *Number of Answers* written over a user's tenure and user *Reputation*, while Fig. 3b shows the correlated joint distribution of the two variables. The figures illustrate the first condition of Simpson's paradox (Eq. (7)): as X_p changes, the distribution of the values of X_c must also change. This dependency can be clearly seen in Fig. 3b—as $X_p = Number\ of\ Answers$ increases then the distribution of $X_c = Reputation$ shifts to increasing values, which produces the paradox.

In the real world this means that users, who have written more answers are not more likely to have a new answer they write accepted. In fact, among users with same *Reputation*, those who earned this reputation with fewer answers are more likely to have a new answer they write accepted as best answer. This suggests that such users are simply better at answering questions, and that this can be detected early in their tenure on Stack Exchange (while they still have low reputation). Note, however, that an exception to the trend reversal occurs for users with very high reputation. In Stack Exchange, users can gain reputation by "Answer is marked accepted", "Answer is voted up", "Question is voted up", etc. It seems that, high reputation users and low reputation users are different: for high reputation users, experience (number of written answers) is important, while for low reputation users the quality of answers, which may lead to votes, is more important. Analysis of this behavior is beyond the scope of this paper.

4.4 Discussion and Implications

Presence of a Simpson's paradox in data can indicate interesting or surprising patterns [8], and for trends in social data, important behavioral differences within a population. Since social data is often generated by a mixture of subgroups, existence of Simpson's

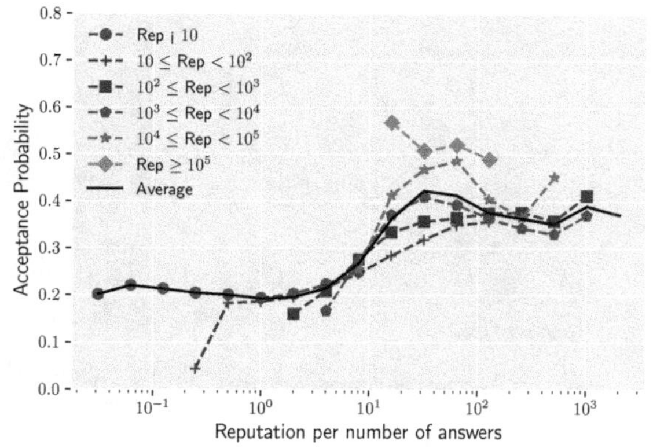

Figure 4: Relationship between acceptance probability and *Reputation Rate*, a new measure of user performance defined as reputation per number of answers users wrote over their entire tenure. Each line represents a subgroup with a different reputation score. The much smaller variance compared to Fig. 2b suggests that the new feature is a good proxy of answerer performance.

paradox suggests that these subgroups differ systematically and significantly in their behavior. By isolating important subgroups in social data, our method can yield insights into their behaviors.

For example, our method identifies *Session Length* as a conditioning variable for disaggregating data when studying trends in acceptance probability as a function of answer's position within a session. In fact, prior work has identified session length as an important parameter in studies of online performance [1, 9, 15, 19]. Unless activity data is disaggregated into individual sessions—sequences of activity without an extended break—important patterns are obscured. A pervasive pattern in online platforms is user performance deterioration, whereby the quality of a user's contribution decreases over the course of a single session. This deterioration was observed for the quality of answers written on Stack Exchange [9], comments posted on Reddit [19], and the time spent reading posts on Facebook [15]. Our method automatically identifies position of an action within a session and session length as an important pair of variables describing Stack Exchange.

We examine in detail one novel paradox discovered by our method for the *Reputation–Number of Answers* variables. The trends in Fig. 2b suggest that both variables jointly affect acceptance probability. Inspired by this observation, we construct a new variable—*Reputation / Number of Answers*—i.e., *Reputation Rate.* Figure 4 shows how acceptance probability changes with respect to *Reputation Rate* for different groups of users. There is an strong upward trend, suggesting that answers provided by users with higher *Reputation Rate* are more likely to be accepted. Moreover, while the lines span reputations of an extremely broad range—from one to 100,000—they collapse onto a single curve. This suggests that *Reputation Rate* is a good proxy of user performance. The remaining paradoxes uncovered by our method could yield similarly interesting insights into user behavior on Stack Exchange.

We also illustrate the difference between our method and linear models that model the outcome variable as a function of both X_p and X_c. For such multivariate linear models [17], we can fit a model $f_{p,c}(\alpha + \beta X_p + \beta_c X_c)$ to the disaggregated data, and compare the sign of the coefficient β to the sign of the linear coefficient of the "aggregated" model $f_p(\alpha + \beta X_p)$. In our method, we bin the values of X_c and fit separate linear models of the form of Eq. (4) in each bin of X_c, aggregating by averaging the linear coefficient signs of each model. We claim that our approach has benefits over multivariate linear models which allow it to find Simpson's pairs where multivariate linear models can not. First, in multivariate linear models, all subgroups have the same coefficient β, and intercepts $\alpha + \beta_c X_c$, which vary linearly with X_c. In our method, however, each group can have different intercept and coefficient, which makes finding paradox pairs in heterogeneous data more flexible. Indeed this flexibility is necessary — from our results (Figs. 1b and 2b) it is clear that the trend parameters $\beta(x_c)$ of the fitted lines vary significantly depending on x_c.

Secondly, our method of aggregating by simple averaging of the linear coefficient signs of the subgroups means that trends within each subgroup are weighted equally regardless of how many datapoints are in that subgroup. This is contrary to multivariate linear models, which fit the model parameters based on each datapoint (and so weigh heavily towards values of X_c with many datapoints). To illustrate, we show that our algorithm finds *Time Since Previous Answer - Answer Position* as a Simpson's pair, which a multivariate logistic regression does not. The variable *Answer Position* is the index of the answer a user has completed without an extended (>100 minute) break, and so *Answer Position* = 1 if *Time Since Previous Answer* ≥ 100 minutes and *Answer Position* > 1 if *Time Since Previous Answer* < 100 minutes. Fig. (5a) shows that, for *Answer Position* = 1, the acceptance probability decreases as a function of *Time Since Previous Answer*, possibly because better users take shorter breaks. On the other hand, for other *Answer Positions* the trend is reversed, and acceptance probability increases with *Time Since Previous Answer*, suggesting that in short term, users who take more time to answer questions or take short breaks between questions write answers of higher quality.

Clearly, *Time Since Previous Answer - Answer Position* is an important Simpson's pair, illustrating that time has a beneficial effect on answer quality ar short time scales. even though it is detrimental on the aggregate level. Multivariate logistic regression does not capture this behaviour, as 65% of the probability mass of *Time Since Previous Answer* is for values larger than 100 minutes, so when fitting $f_{p,c}(\alpha + \beta X_p + \beta_c X_c)$ to the data, it tries to fit a hyperplane, which describes the majority of the data as best as possible, in this case the decreasing trend corresponding to *Answer Position* = 1.

5 CONCLUSION

We presented a method for systematically uncovering instances of Simpson's paradox in data. The method identifies pairs of variables, such that a trend in an outcome as a function of one variable disappears or reverses itself when the same data is disaggregated by conditioning it on the second variable. The disaggregated data corresponds to subgroups within the population generating the data. Our mathematical analysis suggests that Simspon's paradox

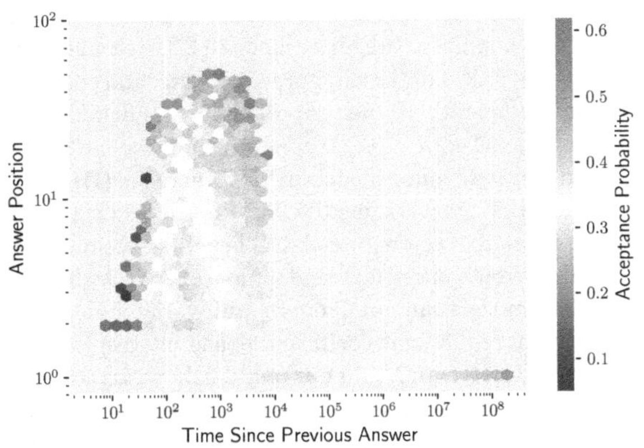

(a) Disaggregated data

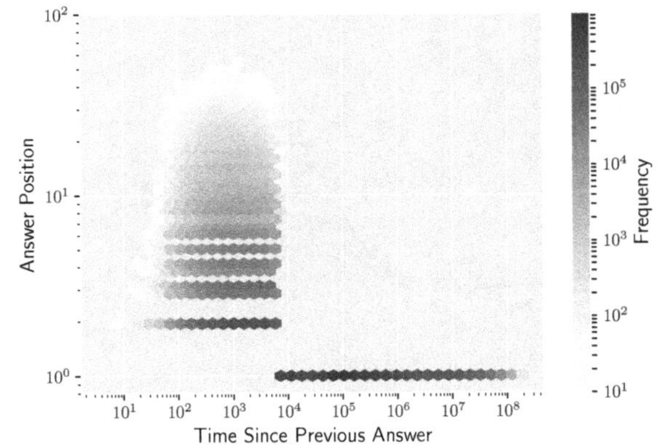

(b) Joint distribution of X_c and X_p

Figure 5: A pair which multivariate logistic regression cannot find in the data. (a) Average acceptance probability as a function of Answer Position and Time Since Previous Answer. (b) The distribution of the number of data points contributing to the value of the outcome variable for each pair of variable values.

is caused by both correlations between independent variables in data (Figs. 3b and 5b), as well as differing behaviour of the outcome variable within subgroups, illustrated here by the stacked curves of Figs. 1b and 2b. Failure to account for this effect can lead analysis to wrong conclusions about typical behavior of individuals.

We applied our method to real-world data from the question-answering site Stack Exchange. We were specifically interested in uncovering features affecting the probability that an answer written by a user will be accepted by the asker as the best answer to his or her question. We identified eleven relevant features of answers and users. Not only did the method confirm an existing paradox, but it also uncovered new instances of Simpson's paradox.

Our work opens several directions for future work. The proposed algorithm could benefit from a more principled method to bin continuous data and more sophisticated techniques for re-aggregating the intercepts of the curves fitted to disaggregated data. Also, while it appears that conditioning on X_c disaggregates the population into more homogeneous subgroups, we have not used formal methods, such as goodness of fit, to test for better fit of regression models to data. Goodness of fit may also be used to guide data disaggregation strategies. In addition, our method applies to explicitly declared variables, and not to latent variables that may affect data. While these and similar questions remain, our proposed method offers a promising tool for the analysis of heterogeneous social data.

Acknowledgments

We acknowledge funding support from the James S. McDonnell Foundation, Air Force Office of Scientific Research (FA9550-17-1-0327), and by the Army Research Office (W911NF-15-1-0142).

REFERENCES

[1] Tushar Agarwal, Keith Burghardt, and Kristina Lerman. 2017. On Quitting: Performance and Practice in Online Game Play. In *Proceedings of 11th AAAI International Conference on Web and Social Media*. AAAI.

[2] Samuel Barbosa, Dan Cosley, Amit Sharma, and Roberto M. Cesar-Jr. 2016. Averaging Gone Wrong: Using Time-Aware Analyses to Better Understand Behavior. In *WWW*. 829–841.

[3] Elias Bareinboim and Judea Pearl. 2016. Causal inference and the data-fusion problem. *PNAS* 113, 27 (2016), 7345–7352.

[4] P. J. Bickel, E. A. Hammel, and O'connell J.W. 1975. Sex bias in graduate admissions: Data from Berkeley. *Science* 187, 4175 (1975), 398–404.

[5] Keith Burghardt, Emanuel F. Alsina, Michelle Girvan, William Rand, and Kristina Lerman. 2017. The myopia of crowds: Cognitive load and collective evaluation of answers on Stack Exchange. *PLOS ONE* 12, 3 (16 March 2017), e0173610+.

[6] George Casella and Roger L Berger. 2002. *Statistical inference*. Vol. 2. Duxbury Pacific Grove, CA.

[7] William K. Estes. 1956. The problem of inference from curves based on group data. *Psychological bulletin* 53, 2 (1956), 134.

[8] Carem C Fabris and Alex A Freitas. 2000. Discovering surprising patterns by detecting occurrences of SimpsonâĂŹs paradox. In *Research and Development in Intelligent Systems XVI*. Springer, 148–160.

[9] Emilio Ferrara, Nazanin Alipoufard, Keith Burghardt, Chiranth Gopal, and Kristina Lerman. 2017. Dynamics of Content Quality in Collaborative Knowledge Production. In *ICWSM*. AAAI.

[10] Greg Ver Steeg, Rumi Ghosh, and Kristina Lerman. 2011. What stops social epidemics?. In *ICWSM*.

[11] Miguel A. Hernan, David Clayton, and Niels Keiding. 2011. Simpson's paradox unraveled. *Int J Epidemiology* 40, 3 (2011), 780–785.

[12] Nathan O. Hodas and Kristina Lerman. 2012. How Limited Visibility and Divided Attention Constrain Social Contagion. In *SocialCom*.

[13] Nathan O. Hodas and Kristina Lerman. 2014. The Simple Rules of Social Contagion. *Scientific Reports* 4 (2014).

[14] J. P. Kincaid, Jr R. P. Fishburnea, R. L. Rogers, and B. S. Chissom. 1975. *Derivation of new readability formulas (automated readability index, fog count and flesch reading ease formula) for navy enlisted personnel*. Technical Report. U.S. Navy.

[15] Farshad Kooti, Karthik Subbian, Winter Mason, Lada Adamic, and Kristina Lerman. 2017. Understanding Short-term Changes in Online Activity Sessions. In *Companion WWW2017*.

[16] Kristina Lerman. 2016. Information Is Not a Virus, and Other Consequences of Human Cognitive Limits. *Future Internet* 8, 2 (May 2016), 21+.

[17] H. James Norton and George Divine. 2015. Simpson's paradox âĂę and how to avoid it. *Significance* 12, 4 (1 Aug. 2015), 40–43.

[18] Daniel M. Romero, Brendan Meeder, and Jon Kleinberg. 2011. Differences in the Mechanics of Information Diffusion Across Topics: Idioms, Political Hashtags, and Complex Contagion on Twitter. In *WWW*.

[19] Philipp Singer, Emilio Ferrara, Farshad Kooti, Markus Strohmaier, and Kristina Lerman. 2016. Evidence of Online Performance Deterioration in User Sessions on Reddit. *PLoS ONE* 11, 8 (2016), e0161636+.

[20] J. W. Vaupel and A. I. Yashin. 1985. Heterogeneity's ruses: some surprising effects of selection on population dynamics. *Am. Stat.* 39, 3 (1985), 176–185.

[21] Yu Xie. 2013. Population heterogeneity and causal inference. *PNAS* 110, 16 (2013), 6262–6268.

Deep Neural Architecture for Multi-Modal Retrieval based on Joint Embedding Space for Text and Images

Saeid Balaneshin-kordan
Wayne State University
Detroit, MI, USA
saeid@wayne.edu

Alexander Kotov
Wayne State University
Detroit, MI, USA
kotov@wayne.edu

ABSTRACT

Recent advances in deep learning and distributed representations of images and text have resulted in the emergence of several neural architectures for cross-modal retrieval tasks, such as searching collections of images in response to textual queries and assigning textual descriptions to images. However, the multi-modal retrieval scenario, when a query can be either a text or an image and the goal is to retrieve both a textual fragment and an image, which should be considered as an atomic unit, has been significantly less studied. In this paper, we propose a gated neural architecture to project image and keyword queries as well as multi-modal retrieval units into the same low-dimensional embedding space and perform semantic matching in this space. The proposed architecture is trained to minimize structured hinge loss and can be applied to both cross- and multi-modal retrieval. Experimental results for six different cross- and multi-modal retrieval tasks obtained on publicly available datasets indicate superior retrieval accuracy of the proposed architecture in comparison to the state-of-art baselines.

CCS CONCEPTS

• **Information systems → Image search**;

KEYWORDS

Multi-Modal IR, Cross-Modal IR, Deep Neural Networks

ACM Reference Format:

Saeid Balaneshin-kordan and Alexander Kotov. 2018. Deep Neural Architecture for Multi-Modal Retrieval based on Joint Embedding Space for Text and Images. In *Proceedings of WSDM 2018: The Eleventh ACM International Conference on Web Search and Data Mining (WSDM 2018)*. ACM, New York, NY, USA, 9 pages. https://doi.org/10.1145/3159652.3159735

1 INTRODUCTION

Images and text are an integral part of the Web, from photo sharing and social media platforms to on-line encyclopedias. However, Web search systems still consider images as a separate vertical from text and provide only text-to-image (T→I) search functionality. Yet, the spectrum of information needs of Web search system users goes well beyond text-to-image searches and includes the search tasks, in which pairs of a textual fragment and an image form *atomic retrieval units*, such as in *image-to-image and text* (I→IT) and *text-to-image and text* (i.e. T→IT) retrieval scenarios. Images rarely exist without text and, as illustrated in Figure 1, often convey complementary information. Therefore, it is natural to consider both text and image as one retrieval unit.

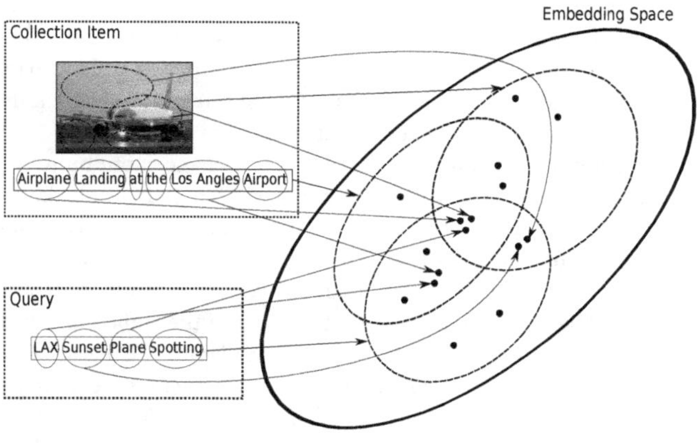

Figure 1: Projection of textual and visual components of an example query and multi-modal retrieval unit into the space of concept embeddings. The query term "plane" can be matched in both textual and visual components of a given retrieval unit, the query term "LAX" can be matched only in its textual component, while the term "sunset" can only be matched in its visual component.

These multi-modal retrieval scenarios are facing the same fundamental problem of semantic matching of queries to retrieval units, as textual information retrieval (IR). In the case of textual IR, this problem is typically addressed by projecting sparse bag-of-words representations of queries and retrieval units (e.g., documents, passages, sentences) onto dense continuous representations (i.e., embedding vectors), which capture their semantics in a low-dimensional space, and matching them in this space [7, 50]. Shallow neural architectures [37] trained with the goal of making embeddings of words that frequently appear in the same context to be close to each other have emerged as a computationally efficient way of obtaining word embeddings. At the same time, methods utilizing word embeddings for document [12] and query [2, 31] expansion as well as in pseudo-relevance feedback [9, 59] have demonstrated their effectiveness in addressing the problem of vocabulary gap

WSDM 2018, February 5–9, 2018, Marina Del Rey, CA, USA

ACM ISBN 978-1-4503-5581-0/18/02...$15.00
https://doi.org/10.1145/3159652.3159735

in textual IR. Furthermore, several neural architectures based on Convolutional Neural Network (CNN) [33] and Long-short Term Memory Network (LSTM) [20], which take word embedding based representations of queries and documents as input to estimate their relevance, have been recently proposed for Web search [38], ad-hoc document retrieval [15], microblog retrieval [41] and question answering [51].

Deep neural architectures based on CNNs [33] have also been successfully applied to unsupervised feature extraction and achieved state-of-the-art performance for many computer vision tasks, such as image classification [30, 47] and image recognition [18]. Significant progress in utilizing neural networks for image classification and learning of word embeddings led to the emergence of hybrid neural architectures for cross-modal retrieval tasks, such as generating image descriptions (i.e., captions) [10, 24–27, 36, 44, 49], some of which surpassed human performance for this task. A substantial amount of research also focused on efficient cross-modal retrieval. In particular, hashing-based methods [3, 4, 23, 34, 53, 55] apply hashing to transform different modalities into the same Hamming space and learn quantizers to convert the isomorphic latent features into compact binary codes, which provide a compromise between efficiency and accuracy of cross-modal retrieval. However, the problem of *multi-modal retrieval* (when retrieval units include different modalities) has been significantly less studied.

Drawing inspiration from the success of image captioning, we propose a *gated neural architecture* called JEMR (**J**oint-**E**mbedding for **M**ulti-modal **R**etrieval) to represent image and keyword queries as well as multi-modal retrieval units in the space of word embeddings and semantically match them in that space, as illustrated in Figure 1. The proposed architecture consists of the embedding and relevance matching layers. In the *embedding layers*, the feature vector extracted by a deep CNN for a query or a collection item image is used as the initial hidden state of LSTM to generate the embedding vectors corresponding to image descriptions, which are then used as input to the *relevance matching layers*. Both embedding and relevance matching layers are *jointly trained to minimize a structured hinge loss*. The proposed architecture also includes adaptive gating units that regulate information flow between the embedding and matching layers.

Retrieval is done based on a nearest neighbor search method to efficiently find collection items that are the most similar to a given query, as measured by the output of the matching layers. The proposed architecture is highly modular and can be easily adapted to many cross- and multi-modal retrieval scenarios.

The remainder of this paper is organized as follows. In Section 2, we provide a brief overview of the relevant prior work. The proposed deep neural architecture along with the search method are discussed in Section 3. Experimental results are presented and analyzed in Section 4. Section 5 concludes the paper.

2 RELATED WORK

Prior to discussing the details of the proposed method, we provide an overview of the recent research on neural architectures in textual IR, learning multi-modal representations and cross-modal IR.

Neural architectures in textual IR. Deep learning methods are rapidly gaining popularity in textual IR and related fields, such as question answering. As the first step of these methods, documents and queries are typically transformed into different representations, such as letter trigrams [22, 42], word embeddings [37] or matching histograms [15]. These representations are then used as input to fully connected feed-forward [15, 22], convolutional [42] or recurrent [51] neural networks for estimating relevance of documents to queries. Neural architectures for textual information retrieval tasks can also include gating units [15], which allow to directly incorporate additional relevance signals and heuristics, such as the importance weight or inverse document frequency of a query term.

Learning multi-modal representations. Similar to text retrieval, the first step of cross-modal retrieval methods typically involves obtaining dense representations for textual and visual modalities. The state-of-the-art way to obtain embedding of an image is to use activations in a penultimate layer of deep neural architectures for object recognition [30], which typically consist of several layers of convolutional filtering, local contrast normalization and max-pooling followed by several fully connected layers, after training those architectures on large image collections, such as ImageNet [40]. A variety of methods can be used to obtain dense representations for textual modality. Besides word embedding methods [37, 39], textual modality in multi-modal retrieval tasks can also be represented using a letter-trigram matrix [10]. Alternatively, hand-crafted textual features, such as bag-of-words counts and LDA topics, can be passed through several fully connected layers to obtain word embeddings [23].

Linear [57] or non-linear [11, 52] mappings can be learned to convert independently obtained embeddings of images and words into multi-modal embeddings in the same semantic space for a particular cross-model task, such as image captioning or retrieval. Alternatively, zero-shot learning methods train direct mappings of image embeddings into the space of word embeddings [43] and vice versa [6]. Image representations have also been incorporated into the skip-gram model [37] for learning word embeddings enriched with perceptual information [19, 32].

Cross-modal IR. Cross-modal (image-to-text and text-to-image) retrieval methods can be categorized into correlation-, semantic-, and hashing-based ones. Correlation-based methods utilize Canonical Correlation Analysis (CCA) [17] and its variants, such as kernel CCA [21] and normalized CCA [14], to capture linear and/or non-linear correlations between textual and visual modalities for bi-directional ranking of images and captions. Semantic methods leverage dense multi-modal representations and deep neural architectures. For example, a neural architecture for cross-modal retrieval, which combines one CNN for image representation and one CNN for calculating word-level, phrase-level and sentence-level matching scores between an image and a sentence, was proposed in [35].

A similar task to cross-modal retrieval is image captioning or associating textual descriptions (e.g. sentences [24, 44] or sentence fragments [25]) either with entire images [49] or their fragments [24, 25]. An image captioning method proposed in [10] ranks textual fragments for a given image and vice versa based on the cosine similarity between their embeddings. Captions can also be generated by sampling from a log-bilinear language model conditioned on the embeddings of already generated caption words and the image feature vector [26].

Neural network architectures proposed for image captioning are typically based on the encoder-decoder framework. For example, a deep CNN can be used as an encoder and LSTM as a decoder [49]. A combination of CNN and LSTM was used as an encoder and multiplicative neural language model incorporating linguistic structure was used as a decoder in [27]. Image feature vector obtained by a deep CNN can also be directly incorporated into an RNN [36] for caption generation.

Finally, hashing-based cross-modal retrieval methods [3, 4, 23, 34, 53, 55] learn hash functions that map images and text in the original space into a Hamming space of binary codes, such that the similarity between the objects in the original space is preserved in the Hamming space. Some hashing-based methods [3, 4, 23] also leverage deep CNNs for creating dense representations of images.

Approximate Nearest Neighbor (ANN) [1] search algorithm accompanied by a proper technique to index collection items enables fast and accurate retrieval in a Hamming space. For this reason, ANN is frequently used in cross-modal hashing methods to rank collection items in the order of their similarity to a query. For example, [23] used ANN to accelerate retrieval of binary hashes obtained using CNN, while [58] used ANN coupled with a sensitive Jaccard similarity metric to efficiently search in sparse and high-dimensional space of cross-modal codes.

3 METHOD

3.1 Proposed Neural Architecture

Without loss of generality, the proposed neural architecture is discussed for the case of text-to-image and text (T⟶IT) retrieval task (i.e., retrieving a multi-modal collection item with a textual modality d_t and a visual modality d_v given a textual keyword query q). However, we would like to emphasize that the proposed architecture is general and can be easily adapted to other cross- and multi-modal retrieval tasks (e.g. when collection items have only textual or visual modality).

The proposed neural architecture consists of two types of layers. The embedding layers (illustrated in Figure 2 for images) extract concept and topic embeddings from textual and visual modalities of queries and collection items, while the relevance matching layers (illustrated in Figure 3) calculate the relevance score of a query to a collection item.

3.1.1 Embedding layers. The goal of these layers is to create dense low-dimensional representations of a query (q) and different modalities of a collection item (d_t and d_v). The output of these layers consists of the two sets of matrices of low-dimensional representations $\mathcal{S}'$ and $\mathcal{S}''$ that are used later in estimating the relevance of a collection item to a query. Both of these matrices contain embeddings of concepts from a controlled vocabulary. In our experiments, this controlled vocabulary consists of the words in the titles of all English Wikipedia articles. Each embedding vector in these matrices is a representation of a concept, which can be a word in a query or collection item's text (textual concept) or an object in a collection item's image (visual concept).

Table 1: Summary of notation

Var.	Description
q	query
d	multi-modal collection item
d_t	textual modality of d
d_v	visual modality of d
$\mathbf{q}_i$	i^{th} concept embedding vector of q
$\mathbf{d}_{t,i}$	i^{th} concept embedding vector of d_t
$\mathbf{d}_{v,i}$	i^{th} concept embedding vector of d_v
$\mathbf{Q}'$	concept embedding matrix for q
$\mathbf{D}_t'$	concept embedding matrix for d_t
$\mathbf{D}_v'$	concept embedding matrix for d_v
$\mathbf{Q}_i''$	i^{th} topic embedding matrix for q
$\mathbf{D}_{t,i}''$	i^{th} topic embedding matrix for d_t
$\mathbf{D}_{v,i}''$	i^{th} topic embedding matrix for d_v
$p(d\|q)$	probability of d being relevant to q

The first set, $\mathcal{S}' = \{\mathbf{Q}', \mathbf{D}_t', \mathbf{D}_v'\}$, consists of *concept embedding matrices* that are used for computing the matching scores *at the concept level.* The matrices in this set contain embeddings of concepts in a query, collection item's text or collection item's image, respectively. The second set, $\mathcal{S}'' = \{\mathbf{Q}_1'', \mathbf{Q}_2'', \dots, \mathbf{D}_{t,1}'', \mathbf{D}_{t,2}'', \dots, \mathbf{D}_{v,1}'', \mathbf{D}_{v,2}'', \dots\}$, consists of *topic embedding matrices* that are used for computing the matching scores *at the topic level.* We obtain each of the matrices in this set by clustering the embedding vectors of all concepts in a given modality of a query or collection item (e.g. clustering embeddings of words in a keyword query). We use cosine similarity as a measure of semantic similarity of concept vectors. For the sake of notational simplicity, in Figure 3, we denote the matrices $\mathbf{Q}'$, $\mathbf{D}_t'$ and $\mathbf{D}_v'$ in the set $\mathcal{S}'$ as QTC (Query Text Concepts), CTC (Collection Text Concepts) and CIC (Collection Image Concepts), respectively, and the matrices $\mathbf{Q}_i''$, $\mathbf{D}_{t,i}''$ and $\mathbf{D}_{v,i}''$ in the set $\mathcal{S}''$ as QTT$_i$ (Query Text Topic i), CTT$_i$ (Collection Text Topic i) and CIT$_i$ (Collection Image Topic i).

If the number of concepts in q, d_t and d_v is $|\mathbf{Q}'|$, $|\mathbf{D}_t'|$ and $|\mathbf{D}_v'|$, and k is the size of the embedding vector representing each concept, then the dimensions of $\mathbf{Q}'$, $\mathbf{D}_t'$ and $\mathbf{D}_v'$ are $k \times |\mathbf{Q}'|$, $k \times |\mathbf{D}_t'|$ and $k \times |\mathbf{D}_v'|$, respectively. In our experiments, we set k to 300. On the other hand, if $\mathbf{Q}'$, $\mathbf{D}_t'$ and $\mathbf{D}_v'$ have $|\mathbf{Q}''|$, $|\mathbf{D}_t''|$ and $|\mathbf{D}_v''|$ clusters (topics), then $\mathbf{Q}''$, $\mathbf{D}_t''$ and $\mathbf{D}_v''$ contain embedding vectors of size k that correspond to each of the topics in q, d_t and d_v.

word2vec [37] embeddings were used to represent the concepts in textual modality of queries that exist in the adopted controlled vocabulary. Embeddings of concepts in the visual modality were obtained by adopting the neural architecture for image captioning proposed in [49] (illustrated in Figure 2), which combines a deep CNN [30] for image feature extraction and LSTM [20] for caption generation. Considering all the words in the adopted controlled vocabulary as candidate visual concepts, we use LSTM to model $p(\mathbf{d}_{v,i+1}|\mathbf{d}_{v,1}, \dots, \mathbf{d}_{v,i})$, which is the probability of the $(i+1)^{th}$ word embedding vector $\mathbf{d}_{v,i+1}$ to be used for representing a visual concept in an image of the collection item, given the word embedding

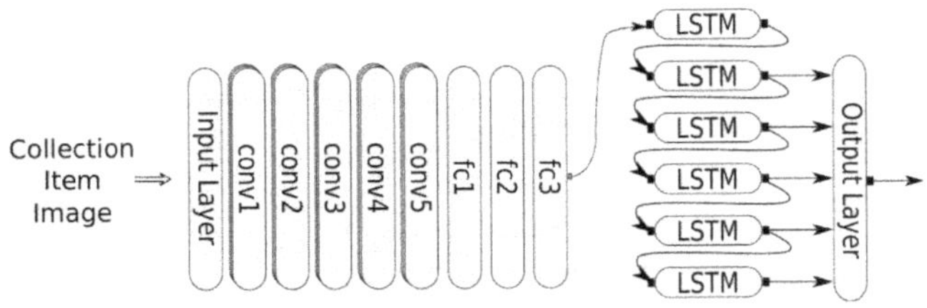

Figure 2: Image captioning layers in the proposed deep neural architecture for $T \rightarrow TI$ task. A combination of convolutional layers conv1-conv5 and fully connected layers fc1-fc3 is used for image feature extraction. LSTM is used for caption generation.

vectors $\mathbf{d}_{v,1}, \ldots, \mathbf{d}_{v,i}$ that have already been generated as visual concepts for the image, and select the word embedding $\mathbf{d}_{v,i+1}$ that maximizes the probability $p(\mathbf{d}_{v,i+1}|\mathbf{d}_{v,1}, \ldots, \mathbf{d}_{v,i})$. This criterion ensures that the selected visual concept best describes a given image in conjunction with previously selected i concepts. As can be seen from Figure 2, in this iterative approach, the first concept vector ($\mathbf{d}_{v,1}$) is generated by maximizing the probability computed directly from the feature vector obtained from the CNN layers ($\mathbf{d}_{v,0}$). We repeat this process until LSTM generates a pre-defined number of visual concept embedding vectors for a given collection item image.

Although hybrid neural architectures have been studied for image captioning [49], the objectives of these architectures are different from this component of our proposed architecture for multi-modal retrieval task. For the image captioning task, LSTM and CNN layers are trained with the goal of generating image descriptions that are the most understandable by humans, while for the multi-modal retrieval task, these layers are trained with the goal of producing the image descriptions that maximize retrieval accuracy.

3.1.2 Relevance matching layers. The goal of these layers is to calculate $p(d|q)$, the probability of a collection item d to be relevant to query q. We further decompose $p(d|q)$ into topic and concept relevance matching scores as:

$$p(d|q) \approx \rho(\mathrm{Q}', \mathrm{D}'_t)p(\mathrm{D}'_t|\mathrm{Q}') + \rho(\mathrm{Q}', \mathrm{D}'_v)p(\mathrm{D}'_v|\mathrm{Q}') + \sum_{j,k} \rho(\mathrm{Q}''_k, \mathrm{D}''_{t,j})p(\mathrm{D}''_{t,j}|\mathrm{Q}''_k) + \rho(\mathrm{Q}''_k, \mathrm{D}''_{v,j})p(\mathrm{D}''_{v,j}|\mathrm{Q}''_k) \quad (1)$$

where $\rho(\cdot, \cdot)$ computes the prior probabilities for the concept and topical relevance, which are obtained by the gating network described in Section 3.1.3. A similar idea of lexical and semantic matching has been shown to be effective in textual IR [28, 29, 54].

The probabilities $p(\mathrm{D}'_t|\mathrm{Q}')$, $p(\mathrm{D}'_v|\mathrm{Q}')$, $p(\mathrm{D}''_{t,j}|\mathrm{Q}''_k)$ and $p(\mathrm{D}''_{v,j}|\mathrm{Q}''_k)$ are computed as a combination of Bidirectional Long Short-Term Memory (BiLSTM) [48] units, max-pooling and cosine similarities, as shown in Figure 3.

3.1.3 Gating Network. To account for the semantic similarity of individual concept vectors, we use multiple gates to regulate the concept and topic relevance probabilities. In other words, similar to LSTM [20], Highway or Residual Networks [18, 45], we provide connections from the input layer of the relevance matching

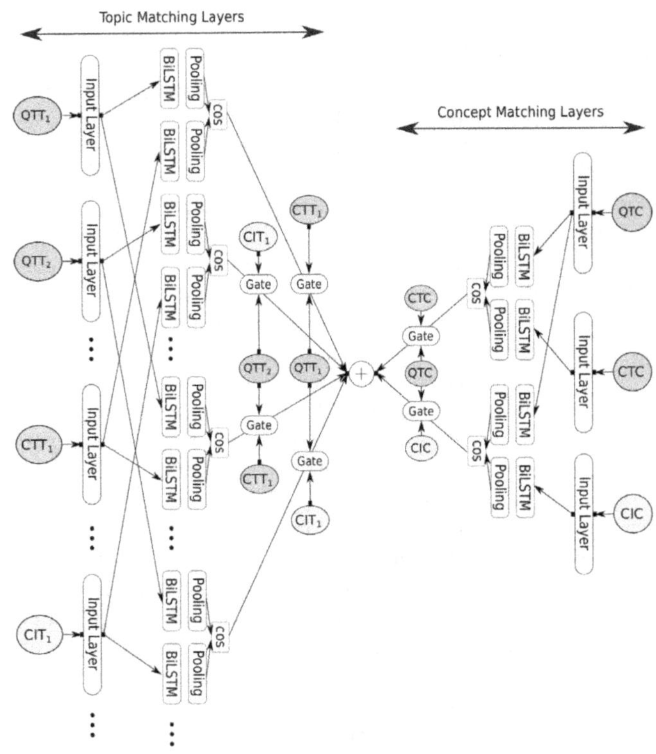

Figure 3: Projection layers in the proposed neural network architecture for $T \rightarrow TI$ task. QTT_i, CTT_i and CIT_i are low-dimensional representations of the i-th topic in the query's text, collection item's text and collection item's image, respectively. QTC, CTC and CIC are low-dimensional representations of concepts in query's text, collection item's text and collection item's image.

component to its last layer through the gating units that regulate the information flow from these layers. The gate function $\rho(\Phi, \Psi)$ depends on the sum of L^2-norms of the distances between the elements of $\Phi = [\phi_1, \phi_2, \ldots]$ and $\Psi = [\psi_1, \psi_2, \ldots]$ as:

$$\rho(\Phi, \Psi) \approx 1 - \left(\frac{\sum_l \min_i \|\phi_i - \psi_l\|_2^2}{2|\Psi|} + \frac{\sum_i \min_l \|\phi_i - \psi_l\|_2^2}{2|\Phi|} \right), \quad \Phi, \Psi \in \{\mathrm{Q}', \mathrm{D}'_t, \mathrm{D}'_v, \mathrm{Q}''_k, \mathrm{D}''_{t,j}, \mathrm{D}''_{v,j}\} \quad (2)$$

where $|\Phi|$ and $|\Psi|$ are the number of embedding vectors in Φ and Ψ. Since ϕ_i and ψ_l are normalized vectors, finding $\min_i \|\psi_i - \phi_l\|_2^2$ is equivalent to finding a concept vector in Φ that has the highest cosine similarity with ψ_j. The score $\sum_l \min_i \|\phi_i - \psi_l\|_2^2$ is the sum of distances between all embedding vectors in Ψ and their most similar embeddings in Φ. The second term in (2) accounts for the cases when $|\Psi| \neq |\Phi|$. It can be easily shown that this gate function always has values between zero and one, and it computes similarity between the most similar pairs in two sets of embedding vectors Φ and Ψ. Considering these gating units, the estimated relevance probability of two matrices of embeddings Φ and Ψ is obtained as the product of $p(\Psi|\Phi)$ calculated by the relevance matching layers and $\rho(\Phi, \Psi)$ calculated by the gating units.

3.1.4 Extensions to other Cross- and Multi-modal Retrieval Tasks. Besides T→IT (shown in Figure 3), the proposed method is evaluated in Section 4 for five other cross- and multi-modal retrieval tasks (T→I, I→T, I→I, T→T and I→TI). The architectures for these tasks can be straightforwardly obtained from the one for the T→IT task. For example, the neural architecture for the I→T task has CNN and LSTM layers associated with the query and an embedding layer associated with the collection item. Parallel projection and matching layers that share the same set of weights can be added to the proposed architecture to extend this architecture to the cases when more than one textual or visual modality is associated with a query or a collection item.

3.2 Training

The training data for the proposed architecture consists of triplets of related and unrelated collection items to a given query. If we designate one of these triplets as (q, d_i^+, d_i^-) and a vector of parameters as θ, then finding θ involves minimizing the following hinge loss:

$$\min_{\theta} \left(\frac{\lambda_o}{2} ||\theta||_2^2 + \sum_{(q,d^+,d^-)\in\mathcal{T}} \max(0, p(d^+|q) - p(d^-|q) + \beta) \right) \quad (3)$$

where $\mathcal{T}$ is the set of triplets in the training data, λ_0 is a constant, and β is a desired margin between the relevance probabilities of relevant and non-relevant collection items with respect to a query. The second term in the objective function of the above optimization problem is our training loss ($\mathcal{L}(\theta)$) which enforces $p(d_i^+|q) > p(d_i^-|q)$. The loss function can also be written in terms of the concept and topic relevance probabilities as:

$$\begin{aligned}\mathcal{L}(\theta) = \sum_{(q,d^+,d^-)\in\mathcal{T}} \Big(& \rho(Q', D'_t) \max(0, p(D'^+_t|Q') - p(D'^-_t|Q') + \beta'_t) \\ & + \rho(Q', D'_v) \max(0, p(D'^+_v|Q') - p(D'^-_v|Q') + \beta'_v) \\ & + \sum_{j,k} \rho(Q''_k, D''_{t,j}) \max(0, p(D''^+_{t,j}|Q''_k) - p(D''^-_{t,j}|Q''_k) + \beta''_t) \\ & + \sum_{j,k} \rho(Q''_k, D''_{v,j}) \max(0, p(D''^+_{v,j}|Q''_k) - p(D''^-_{v,j}|Q''_k) + \beta''_v) \Big)\end{aligned}$$

where the prior probabilities and the margin parameters β'_t, β'_v, β''_t and β''_v are independent of the neural network.

The structured loss function in the above equation can be viewed as a sum of four different loss functions. The first two loss functions depend on the probability of relevance of different modalities of a collection item and a query. The last two loss functions depend on the probability of topical relevance of a collection item and a query.

The proposed architecture is trained in several stages. In the first training stage, a shallow neural network is trained by using the skip-gram model [37] over the chosen controlled concept vocabulary. In the second training stage, the image feature extraction network is trained. In the third stage, the parameters of the LSTM layers that generate visual concept vectors are trained. Next, the parameters of the BiLSTM layers are trained, and finally, in the last training stage, the parameters of the relevance matching layers are trained.

In the first training stage, we utilize word2vec vectors pre-trained for 3 million words and phrases on a Google News corpus[1] and prune the table of word embeddings to keep the ones with a word or a phrase that exists in our controlled vocabulary. We use the pruned table as the table of concept vectors. In Stage 2, we train weights for conv1–5 and fc1–3 layers on ILSVRC-2012 dataset[2]. In Stage 3, we use the training data from 2015 MS COCO Image Captioning Challenge [49] to train LSTM layers. In Stage 4, to train the BiLSTM layers, we use the training data from Yahoo Question answering dataset, which is described in Section 4. Finally, as shown in Figure 4, in the last stage, we use the training data from multi-modal retrieval datasets, which are described in Section 4. The parameters of the fc2-fc3 and LSTM and BiLSTM layers are fine-tuned in the last training stage.

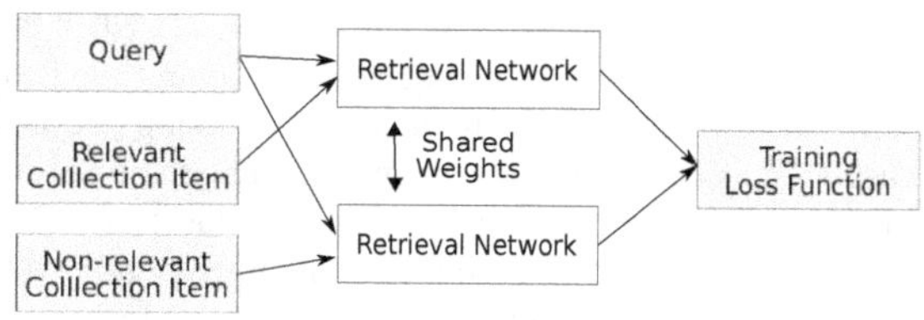

Figure 4: Procedure to train the parameters of the neural network in the last training stage. The upper and lower networks are the same as the network shown in Figure 3.

3.3 Search

We considered the inverse of the relevance matching score between a collection item and a query computed by the proposed architecture as a distance and adopted two distance-based search methods, a brute-force k-nearest neighbor search (k-NN) and approximate k-nearest neighbor (ANN) [16] to find collection items that have the maximum relevance matching scores (or minimum distance) with respect to a given query.

4 EXPERIMENTS

We evaluate our proposed architecture using two datasets, which were chosen with the goals of (1) investigating whether JEMR overfits the training data, (2) evaluating JEMR on a dataset without explicit bridge information between textual and visual modalities of collection items, and (3) evaluating JEMR on a dataset with out-of-sample images and texts. We compare the performance of our proposed method with two state-of-the-art unsupervised and three supervised baselines that leverage deep neural networks. We also investigate the effect of image feature extractors on the performance of our proposed architecture by examining the cases of using image feature extractors other than AlexNet. Finally, we examine the effect of a number of acceleration methods on the speed of the proposed method. The proposed method is compared with the baselines based on Mean Average Precision (MAP) and Precision-Recall curves.

4.1 Datasets

For all experiments in this paper, we use the two datasets based on the ones in [4] and [55]. **NUS-WIDE**[5], the first dataset, is a

[1] https://drive.google.com/file/d/0B7XkCwpI5KDYNlNUTTlSS21pQmM/

[2] https://github.com/BVLC/caffe/tree/master/models/bvlc_alexnet

multi-modal dataset with 269,648 image-tags pairs, 5,018 tags and a ground truth for 81 concept categories. Each image in the **NUS-WIDE** or ImageNet dataset [8] belongs to a category. **NUS-WIDE** and ImageNet datasets have 16 of these categories in common. We prune images from **NUS-WIDE** that do not belong to any of these common categories. **NUS-WIDE** contains one textual document for each image, which is obtained by aggregating all its corresponding tags. We obtain the query set for **NUS-WIDE** by randomly selecting 2000 textual documents and 2000 visual documents from **NUS-WIDE**.

The other dataset is **ImageNet-YahooQA** [4], which consists of 10 million images from ImageNet [8] and 300,000 texts obtained by using Yahoo Query Language API[3]. This dataset is generated by using the tags from the **NUS-WIDE** dataset, i.e., 5,018 tags in **NUS-WIDE** are used as keyword queries to obtain the set of Yahoo QAs. The relevant answers to questions in Yahoo QAs dataset are considered as the textual documents in **ImageNet-YahooQA**. The goal of multi-modal retrieval using this dataset is to find answers from Yahoo QAs dataset that are semantically related to an image query randomly chosen from the ImageNet dataset and vice versa. In other words, only T→I and I→T retrieval tasks can be examined on this dataset. Multi-modal dataset similar to **ImageNet-YahooQA** is MIRFLICKR-Yahoo Answer dataset introduced in [55]. Similar to the **NUS-WIDE**, we prune **ImageNet-YahooQA** by removing the images in ImageNet that do not have any of 5,018 tags in **NUS-WIDE**. Similar to **NUS-WIDE**, we obtain a query set by randomly selecting 2000 texts and 2000 images from **ImageNet-YahooQA**.

In the last training stage described in Section 3.2, we use the training data from **NUS-WIDE** for experiments on both **ImageNet-YahooQA** and **NUS-WIDE** datasets. To obtain the ground truth for evaluation, we assumed that any pair of query and collection items (either containing image, text or both) are relevant, if both of them belong to at least one of the 16 categories that NUS-WIDE shares with ImageNet.

4.2 Experimental Setup

We used TensorFlow version 1.0.1[4] to implement and train our deep neural architecture on a Linux server with a NVIDIA Tesla K10 GPU with batch size 32 for 100 epochs. We use back-propagation with stochastic gradient descent to train the parameters of our proposed deep neural network. To speed up mini-batch learning, RMSProp was used with a decay of 0.9, and $\epsilon = 1.0$. Hyper-parameters (e.g. ρ, β) were optimized using coordinate ascent based on three-fold cross-validation.

As mentioned earlier, besides using AlexNet as the image feature extractor, we also experimented with ResNet 152 [18], Inception V3 [47] and Inception-ResNet-v2 [46]. We use the pre-trained weights of these CNNs, which are publicly available for Tensorflow[5] and adapt the weights of AlexNet that are publicly available in Caffe[6] to Tensorflow.

4.3 Baselines

In the experiments, we consider the following two unsupervised and three supervised baselines:

CCA-MV [13]: extends canonical correlation analysis (CCA) to the case of having multiple views of visual, textual and semantic features obtained by clustering words. We use a three-view CCA ("CCA (V+T+C)" in [13]). We use the same list of features adopted in [13] to implement this method.

CCQ [34]: is an unsupervised cross-modal hashing based retrieval method that adopts a unified optimization framework to jointly learn the latent space and similarity preserving composite quantization that maximize correlation. Unlike JEMR, CCQ does not rely on neural networks.

DSM [56]: similar to JEMR provides real-valued representations for visual and textual modalities. However, DSM also uses CNN and hand-crafted features to obtain representations of visual and textual modalities. The hand-crafted features are extracted using topic models and bag-of-words.

DVSH [3]: adopts a two-sided deep CNN-LSTM network for joint representation learning and hash coding. One side applies CNN to project images and LSTM to project text into a common subspace and another LSTM network computes the matching score of these projected modalities. The other side, utilizes CNN and LSTM networks to encode the textual and visual modalities of collection items and then it computes the similarity between the generated isomorphic hash codes. The network is trained according to the computed matching score and the similarity of the generated hash codes.

THN [4]: adopts CNN and multilayer perceptrons and has a similar training process to JEMR, as both architectures utilize the training data from different datasets to train different components of the network. The main goal of using diverse training data is to enable the retrieval system to process queries in a collection that has a different distribution. For example, given a query selected from Yahoo QAs dataset, it allows the retrieval system to obtain relevant images in ImageNet dataset.

MCNN [35]: adopts one CNN to learn image representations and Skip-gram method to learn text representations, and another CNN to compute the multi-modal matching scores between a query and collection items. This method performs word-level, phrase-level and sentence-level matching using a matching CNN.

Similar to JEMR, DSM, DVSH, THN, and MCNN adopt deep neural networks to extract features from query and collection items. Specifically, DVSH is similar to JEMR in that it uses a hybrid CNN-LSTM network. However, unlike JEMR, DVSH and THN both employ hashing methods in approximating nearest neighbor search. We used 16 bits for hashes created by both DVSH and THN.

4.4 Results and Discussion

Table 2 summarizes the performance of the proposed architecture (JEMR) and six state-of-the-art baselines in terms of MAP for six multi-modal retrieval scenarios (I→T, T→I, I→IT, T→IT, I→I, and T→T) on two datasets (**NUS-WIDE** and **ImageNet-YahooQA**). In **ImageNet-YahooQA** dataset, for the tasks T→T and T→IT, we obtain the textual query from a set of related answers in Yahoo QAs dataset and the multi-modal collection items from the ImageNet

[3]https://developer.yahoo.com/yql/
[4]https://github.com/tensorflow/tensorflow/releases/tag/v1.0.1
[5]https://github.com/tensorflow/models/tree/master/slim
[6]https://github.com/BVLC/caffe/tree/master/models/bvlc_alexnet

dataset. However, since Yahoo QAs dataset does not contain any images, we do not evaluate the methods for I⟶I and I⟶IT retrieval tasks on the **ImageNet-YahooQA** dataset.

As follows from Table 2, JEMR outperforms all baselines in all of the six retrieval tasks with statistically significant difference. This table also indicates that, on average, the performance improvement of JEMR relative to DSM, DVSH, THN, and MCNN is higher for the I⟶IT, T⟶IT, I⟶I, and T⟶T, than for I⟶T and T⟶I retrieval tasks. This can be explain by the fact that DSM, DVSH, THN, and MCNN do not provide any mechanisms to create embeddings or encodings shared by both modalities for I⟶IT and T⟶IT retrieval tasks.

By experimenting with the two datasets (**NUS-WIDE** and **ImageNet-YahooQA**), we can evaluate the effect of existence of explicit relationships between query and collection items in training of the proposed network. Table 2 reveals that the methods leveraging deep neural networks, i.e., DSM, DVSH, THN, MCNN, and JEMR have higher MAP values than the unsupervised baselines, i.e., CCA-MV and CCQ. It can be also concluded that, on average, these improvements are higher on **ImageNet-YahooQA** than on **NUS-WIDE**. This is because deep neural networks can better learn from diverse training data than the shallow baselines. In particular, we can also observe that the percentage of improvement of JEMR over its best performing baselines is greater on **ImageNet-YahooQA** than on **NUS-WIDE**, which can be an indication of superior ability of JEMR to generalize to the collection items that do not exist in the multimodal retrieval training data. Although DVSH and JEMR both use hybrid deep CNN-LSTM Networks, JEMR has a higher MAP value than DVSH [3]. This can be attributed to the gated structure of JEMR, which enables computing the matching functions via considering local similarity of word embedding vectors as well as global similarity of a collection item to a query.

The results for I⟶I and T⟶T tasks were included in Table 2 in order to analyze the influence of an additional textual or visual modality (i.e., I⟶I, and T⟶T tasks) on the performance of JEMR and its baselines. Based on this table, we can conclude that the proposed architecture and baseline methods have on average 2.8% higher MAP values for the T⟶IT task than for T⟶T task on **NUS-WIDE** and **ImageNet-YahooQA** datasets. This improvement is statistically significant for all methods and we can deduce that considering additional visual modality can improve the quality of the T⟶T retrieval task. Following the same reasoning, we can conclude that with on average 4.2% higher MAP values on **NUS-WIDE** dataset, considering additional textual modality for the I⟶I task also provides statistically significant improvement for all methods.

Similar to the observations made from Table 2, the precision-recall curves in Figures 5 and 6 indicate superior performance of JEMR over its best-performing baselines for I⟶T, T⟶I, T⟶T, and T⟶IT tasks on **NUS-WIDE** and **ImageNet-YahooQA** datasets. These figures indicate that JEMR and THN have greater performance improvement in comparison to the other baselines on the **ImageNet-YahooQA** dataset than on **NUS-WIDE**, which is an indication of better generalization of these two methods to the unseen data. Figure 6 is provided to compare precision-recall curves when the retrieval method can get access to an additional visual component of the collection items, in addition to their textual components (by comparing T⟶T and T⟶IT tasks). Figure 6 indicates that JEMR demonstrates greater improvement over the baselines for T⟶IT than for T⟶T task, which is because JEMR takes into account local information between modalities of collection items.

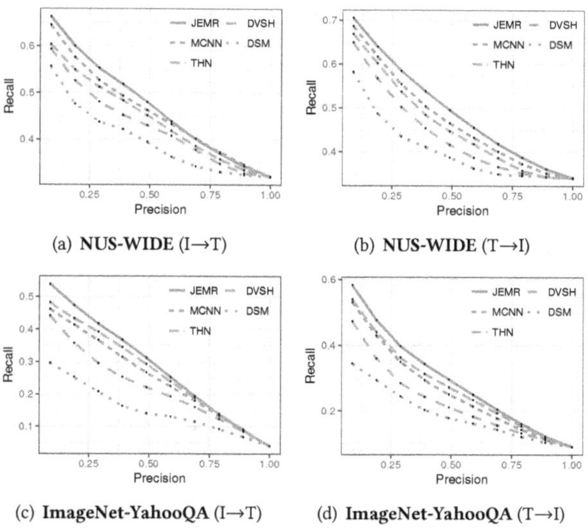

(a) **NUS-WIDE** (I⟶T) (b) **NUS-WIDE** (T⟶I)

(c) **ImageNet-YahooQA** (I⟶T) (d) **ImageNet-YahooQA** (T⟶I)

Figure 5: Precision-recall curves for the proposed method and the baselines for the NUS-WIDE and ImageNet-YahooQA datasets for I⟶T and T⟶I tasks.

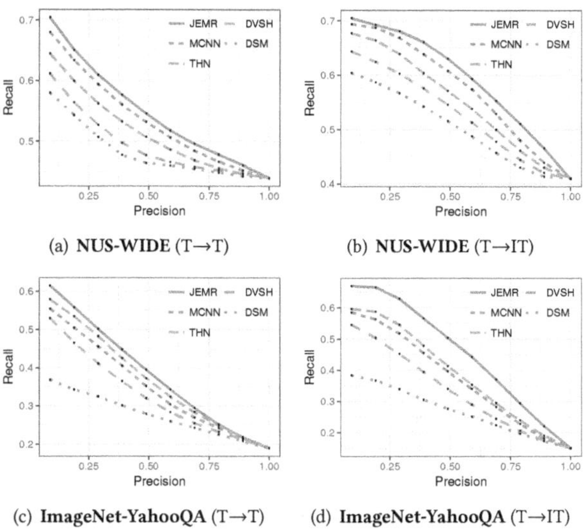

(a) **NUS-WIDE** (T⟶T) (b) **NUS-WIDE** (T⟶IT)

(c) **ImageNet-YahooQA** (T⟶T) (d) **ImageNet-YahooQA** (T⟶IT)

Figure 6: Precision-recall curves for the proposed method and the baselines for the NUS-WIDE and ImageNet-YahooQA datasets for T⟶T and T⟶IT tasks.

To investigate the effectiveness of applying accelerated search on performance of the proposed method, we combined JEMR with k-NN and approximate nearest neighbors (ANN) search methods [16] and report the results in Table 3. JEMR+KNN uses a brute-force search

Table 2: Performance of the proposed architecture (JEMR) and the baselines, as measured by MAP. ⋆ and † indicate statistically significant improvements according to Fisher's randomization test with $p < 0.05$ over the best performing baselines THN [4] and MCNN [35], respectively. The percentage improvement of JEMR over THN [4] and MCNN [35] are shown in parenthesis.

Dataset	Task	CCA-MV [13]	CCQ [34]	DSM [56]	DVSH [3]	THN [4]	MCNN [35]	JEMR
NUS-WIDE	I→T	0.4261	0.4877	0.6415	0.7236	0.7268	0.7381	**0.7538**⋆(3.71% / 2.13%)
	T→T	0.5381	0.6261	0.6801	0.7109	0.7321	0.7402	**0.7833**⋆†(6.99% / 5.82%)
	I→IT	0.4563	0.5115	0.6759	0.6983	0.7494	0.7528	**0.7984**⋆†(6.54% / 6.06%)
	T→IT	0.5449	0.6317	0.6949	0.7532	0.7649	0.7693	**0.8092**⋆†(5.79% / 5.19%)
	I→I	0.4258	0.4652	0.6568	0.6745	0.7093	0.7113	**0.7563**⋆†(6.63% / 6.33%)
	T→I	0.4481	0.5165	0.6782	0.7468	0.7572	0.7795	**0.7825**⋆(3.34% / 0.38%)
ImageNet-YahooQA	I→T	0.1145	0.2152	0.4142	0.5631	0.6132	0.6092	**0.6557**⋆†(6.93% / 7.63%)
	T→I	0.1361	0.2389	0.4209	0.5938	0.6341	0.6278	**0.6804**⋆†(7.30% / 8.38%)
	T→IT	0.2595	0.3725	0.5665	0.6102	0.6383	0.6303	**0.6929**⋆†(8.55% / 9.93%)
	T→T	0.2437	0.3571	0.4869	0.6029	0.6314	0.6282	**0.6872**⋆†(8.84% / 9.39%)

method to find all nearest neighbors, while JEMR+ANN applies approximations, which result in a smaller number of collection items than k-NN that have to be scored with the relevance matching layers of the proposed architecture. In JEMR+ANN and JEMR+KNN, the collection items are represented by a single concept vector that is an average of all of its concept vectors. In this experiment, we set the size of the neighborhood and the maximum number of iterations to be 1000 for both JEMR+ANN and JEMR+KNN.

Table 3 indicates that, although JEMR uses a brute-force search method and examines all collection items, its MAP is, on average, around 5% higher than MAP of JEMR+ANN. On the other hand, JEMR+KNN has, on average, around 5% higher MAP than JEMR+ANN. Without considering the time to locate objects of collection items in the embedding space, we observed that, on average, JEMR is around **1200** times and JEMR+KNN is around **150** times slower than JEMR+ANN. Therefore, we can conclude that using an approximate search method can substantially decrease the search time with a negligible degradation in accuracy.

Table 3: MAP of JEMR on NUS-WIDE dataset when different search methods are used.

Task	I→T	T→I	I→IT	T→IT
JEMR+ANN	0.7381	0.7303	0.7723	0.7926
JEMR+KNN	0.7477	0.7791	0.7921	0.8035
JEMR	0.7538	0.7825	0.7984	0.8092

Table 4 reflects the impact of state-of-the-art deep CNN architectures, such as ResNet 152[18], Inception V3[47] and Inception-ResNet-v2[46] on performance of JEMR, if they are utilized for image feature extraction instead of AlexNet. Similar to the training of AlexNet, the parameters of these three networks are pre-trained using the training data from ImageNet dataset with the parameters of their last two layers fine-tuned based on the training data, once using MS-COCO and once using **NUS-WIDE** datasets. Table 4 indicates that utilizing Inception-ResNet-v2, ResNet 152 and Inception V3 results in higher MAP than AlexNet, with Inception-ResNet-v2 producing a statistically significant improvement in MAP over the other networks, according to the Fisher's randomization test with $p < 0.05$.

Table 4: MAP of JEMR on NUS-WIDE dataset when different CNN networks are used in the proposed architecture.

CNN	I→T	T→I	I→IT	T→IT
AlexNet	0.7538	0.7825	0.7984	0.8092
ResNet 152	0.7932	0.8053	0.8178	0.8223
Inception V3	0.7986	0.8114	0.8250	0.8377
Inception-ResNet-v2	0.8049	0.8230	0.8287	0.8424

5 CONCLUSIONS

This paper presents a novel neural architecture for multi-modal retrieval when the query has a single modality and collection items can have multiple modalities. The proposed architecture utilizes a hybrid LSTM-CNN network to project the visual modalities and the skip-gram model to project the textual modalities into a common subspace, which contains embeddings of words in the textual modalities and embeddings of words that describe the visual modalities. The proposed architecture also includes a gating network to regulate the information flow by accounting for concept level and topic level matching scores. The experiments on heterogeneous datasets indicate that the proposed method outperforms state-of-the-art baselines. We hypothesize that the proposed architecture can also be successfully applied to multi-modal e-commerce search and leave validation of this hypothesis to future work.

REFERENCES

[1] Alexandr Andoni and Ilya Razenshteyn. 2015. Optimal data-dependent hashing for approximate near neighbors. In *Proceedings of STOC*. 793–801.

[2] Saeid Balaneshin-kordan and Alexander Kotov. 2017. Embedding-based Query Expansion for Weighted Sequential Dependence Retrieval Model. In *Proceedings of ACM SIGIR*. 1213–1216.

[3] Yue Cao, Mingsheng Long, Jianmin Wang, Qiang Yang, and Philip S Yu. 2016. Deep Visual-Semantic Hashing for Cross-Modal Retrieval. In *Proceedings of ACM SIGKDD*. 1445–1454.

[4] Zhangjie Cao, Mingsheng Long, and Qiang Yang. 2016. Transitive Hashing Network for Heterogeneous Multimedia Retrieval. *arXiv preprint arXiv:1608.04307* (2016).

[5] Tat-Seng Chua, Jinhui Tang, Richang Hong, Haojie Li, Zhiping Luo, and Yantao Zheng. 2009. NUS-WIDE: a real-world web image database from National University of Singapore. In *Proceedings of ICIVR*.
[6] Guillem Collell, Ted Zhang, and Marie-Francine Moens. 2017. Imagined Visual Representations as Multimodal Embeddings. In *Proceedings of AAAI*. 4378–4384.
[7] Scott Deerwester, Susan T Dumais, George W Furnas, Thomas K Landauer, and Richard Harshman. 1990. Indexing by latent semantic analysis. *Journal of the Association for Information Science and Technology* (1990), 391–407.
[8] Jia Deng, Wei Dong, Richard Socher, Li-Jia Li, Kai Li, and Li Fei-Fei. 2009. Imagenet: A large-scale hierarchical image database. In *Proceedings of IEEE CVPR*. 248–255.
[9] Fernando Diaz, Bhaskar Mitra, and Nick Craswell. 2016. Query expansion with locally-trained word embeddings. *arXiv preprint arXiv:1605.07891* (2016).
[10] Hao Fang, Saurabh Gupta, Forrest Iandola, Rupesh K Srivastava, Li Deng, Piotr Dollár, Jianfeng Gao, Xiaodong He, Margaret Mitchell, John C Platt, and others. 2015. From captions to visual concepts and back. In *Proceedings of IEEE CVPR*. 1473–1482.
[11] Andrea Frome, Greg S Corrado, Jonathon Shlens, Samy Bengio, Jeffrey Dean, Marc'Aurelio Ranzato, and Tomas Mikolov. 2013. DeViSE: A deep visual-semantic embedding model. In *Proceedings of NIPS*. 2121–2129.
[12] Debasis Ganguly, Dwaipayan Roy, Mandar Mitra, and Gareth JF Jones. 2015. Word embedding based generalized language model for information retrieval. In *Proceedings of ACM SIGIR*. 795–798.
[13] Yunchao Gong, Qifa Ke, Michael Isard, and Svetlana Lazebnik. 2014. A multi-view embedding space for modeling internet images, tags, and their semantics. *International Journal of Computer Vision* (2014), 210–233.
[14] Yunchao Gong, Liwei Wang, Micah Hodosh, Julia Hockenmaier, and Svetlana Lazebnik. 2014. Improving image-sentence embeddings using large weakly annotated photo collections. In *Proceedings of ECCV*. 529–545.
[15] Jiafeng Guo, Yixing Fan, Qingyao Ai, and W Bruce Croft. 2016. A Deep Relevance Matching Model for Ad-hoc Retrieval. In *Proceedings of ACM CIKM*. 55–64.
[16] Kiana Hajebi, Yasin Abbasi-Yadkori, Hossein Shahbazi, and Hong Zhang. 2011. Fast approximate nearest-neighbor search with k-nearest neighbor graph. In *Artificial Intelligence Journal*. 1312–1317.
[17] David R Hardoon, Sandor Szedmak, and John Shawe-Taylor. 2004. Canonical correlation analysis: An overview with application to learning methods. *Neural computation* (2004), 2639–2664.
[18] Kaiming He, Xiangyu Zhang, Shaoqing Ren, and Jian Sun. 2016. Deep residual learning for image recognition. In *Proceedings of IEEE CVPR*. 770–778.
[19] Felix Hill and Anna Korhonen. 2014. Learning Abstract Concept Embeddings from Multi-Modal Data: Since You Probably Can't See What I Mean. In *Proceedings of EMNLP*. 255–265.
[20] Sepp Hochreiter and Jürgen Schmidhuber. 1997. Long short-term memory. *Neural computation* 9, 8 (1997), 1735–1780.
[21] Micah Hodosh, Peter Young, and Julia Hockenmaier. 2013. Framing image description as a ranking task: Data, models and evaluation metrics. *Journal of Artificial Intelligence Research* 47 (2013), 853–899.
[22] Po-Sen Huang, Xiaodong He, Jianfeng Gao, Li Deng, Alex Acero, and Larry Heck. 2013. Learning deep structured semantic models for web search using clickthrough data. In *Proceedings of ACM CIKM*. 2333–2338.
[23] Qing-Yuan Jiang and Wu-Jun Li. 2016. Deep Cross-Modal Hashing. *arXiv preprint arXiv:1602.02255* (2016).
[24] Andrej Karpathy and Li Fei-Fei. 2015. Deep visual-semantic alignments for generating image descriptions. In *Proceedings of IEEE CVPR*. 3128–3137.
[25] Andrej Karpathy, Armand Joulin, and Fei Fei Li. 2014. Deep fragment embeddings for bidirectional image sentence mapping. In *Proceedings of NIPS*. 1889–1897.
[26] Ryan Kiros, Ruslan Salakhutdinov, and Richard Zemel. 2014. Multimodal neural language models. In *Proceedings of ICML*. 595–603.
[27] Ryan Kiros, Ruslan Salakhutdinov, and Richard Zemel. 2014. Unifying visual-semantic embeddings with multimodal neural language models. *arXiv preprint arXiv:1411.2539* (2014).
[28] Alexander Kotov, Vineeth Rakesh, Eugene Agichtein, and Chandan K Reddy. 2015. Geographical Latent Variable Models for Microblog Retrieval. In *Proceedings of ECIR*. 635–647.
[29] Alexander Kotov, Yu Wang, and Eugene Agichtein. 2013. Leveraging geographical metadata to improve search over social media. In *Proceedings of WWW*. 151–152.
[30] Alex Krizhevsky, Ilya Sutskever, and Geoffrey E Hinton. 2012. Imagenet classification with deep convolutional neural networks. In *Proceedings of NIPS*. 1097–1105.
[31] Saar Kuzi, Anna Shtok, and Oren Kurland. 2016. Query expansion using word embeddings. In *Proceedings of ACM CIKM*. 1929–1932.
[32] Angeliki Lazaridou, Nghia The Pham, and Marco Baroni. 2015. Combining Language and Vision with a Multimodal Skip-gram Model. In *Proceedings of NACL-HLT*. 153–163.
[33] Yann LeCun, Léon Bottou, Yoshua Bengio, and Patrick Haffner. 1998. Gradient-based learning applied to document recognition. *Proceedings of IEEE* (1998), 2278–2324.
[34] Mingsheng Long, Yue Cao, Jianmin Wang, and Philip S Yu. 2016. Composite Correlation Quantization for Efficient Multimodal Retrieval. In *Proceedings of ACM SIGIR*. 579–588.
[35] Lin Ma, Zhengdong Lu, Lifeng Shang, and Hang Li. 2015. Multimodal convolutional neural networks for matching image and sentence. In *Proceedings of IEEE CVPR*. 2623–2631.
[36] Junhua Mao, Wei Xu, Yi Yang, Jiang Wang, and Alan L Yuille. 2014. Explain images with multimodal recurrent neural networks. *arXiv preprint arXiv:1410.1090* (2014).
[37] Tomas Mikolov, Ilya Sutskever, Kai Chen, Greg S Corrado, and Jeff Dean. 2013. Distributed representations of words and phrases and their compositionality. In *Proceedings of NIPS*. 3111–3119.
[38] Bhaskar Mitra, Fernando Diaz, and Nick Craswell. 2017. Learning to Match using Local and Distributed Representations of Text for Web Search. In *Proceedings of WWW*. 1291–1299.
[39] Jeffrey Pennington, Richard Socher, and Christopher Manning. 2014. Glove: Global vectors for word representation. In *Proceedings of EMNLP*. 1532–1543.
[40] Olga Russakovsky, Jia Deng, Hao Su, Jonathan Krause, Sanjeev Satheesh, Sean Ma, Zhiheng Huang, Andrej Karpathy, Aditya Khosla, Michael Bernstein, and others. 2015. Imagenet large scale visual recognition challenge. *International Journal of Computer Vision* (2015), 211–252.
[41] Aliaksei Severyn and Alessandro Moschitti. 2015. Learning to rank short text pairs with convolutional deep neural networks. In *Proceedings of ACM SIGIR*. 373–382.
[42] Yelong Shen, Xiaodong He, Jianfeng Gao, Li Deng, and Grégoire Mesnil. 2014. A latent semantic model with convolutional-pooling structure for information retrieval. In *Proceedings of ACM CIKM*. 101–110.
[43] Richard Socher, Milind Ganjoo, Christopher D Manning, and Andrew Ng. 2013. Zero-shot learning through cross-modal transfer. In *Proceedings of NIPS*. 935–943.
[44] Richard Socher, Andrej Karpathy, Quoc V Le, Christopher D Manning, and Andrew Y Ng. 2014. Grounded compositional semantics for finding and describing images with sentences. *TACL* (2014), 207–218.
[45] Rupesh K Srivastava, Klaus Greff, and Jürgen Schmidhuber. 2015. Training very deep networks. In *Proceedings of NIPS*. 2377–2385.
[46] Christian Szegedy, Sergey Ioffe, and Vincent Vanhoucke. 2016. Inception-v4, inception-resnet and the impact of residual connections on learning. *arXiv preprint arXiv:1602.07261* (2016).
[47] Christian Szegedy, Vincent Vanhoucke, Sergey Ioffe, Jonathon Shlens, and Zbigniew Wojna. 2016. Rethinking the inception architecture for computer vision. In *Proceedings of IEEE CVPR*. 2818–2826.
[48] Ming Tan, Cicero dos Santos, Bing Xiang, and Bowen Zhou. 2016. LSTM-based deep learning models for non-factoid answer selection. *Proceedings of ICLR* (2016).
[49] Oriol Vinyals, Alexander Toshev, Samy Bengio, and Dumitru Erhan. 2016. Show and Tell: Lessons learned from the 2015 MSCOCO Image Captioning Challenge. *IEEE Transactions on Pattern Analysis and Machine Intelligence* (2016), 652–663.
[50] Ivan Vulić and Marie-Francine Moens. 2015. Monolingual and cross-lingual information retrieval models based on (bilingual) word embeddings. In *Proceedings of ACM SIGIR*. 363–372.
[51] Di Wang and Eric Nyberg. 2015. A long short-term memory model for answer sentence selection in question answering. In *Proceedings of ACL*. 707–712.
[52] Liwei Wang, Yin Li, and Svetlana Lazebnik. 2016. Learning deep structure-preserving image-text embeddings. In *Proceedings of IEEE CVPR*. 5005–5013.
[53] Wei Wang, Xiaoyan Yang, Beng Chin Ooi, Dongxiang Zhang, and Yueting Zhuang. 2016. Effective deep learning-based multi-modal retrieval. *VLDB* (2016), 79–101.
[54] Xing Wei and W Bruce Croft. 2006. LDA-based document models for ad-hoc retrieval. In *Proceedings of ACM SIGIR*. 178–185.
[55] Ying Wei, Yangqiu Song, Yi Zhen, Bo Liu, and Qiang Yang. 2014. Scalable heterogeneous translated hashing. In *Proceedings of ACM SIGKDD*. 791–800.
[56] Yunchao Wei, Yao Zhao, Canyi Lu, Shikui Wei, Luoqi Liu, Zhenfeng Zhu, and Shuicheng Yan. 2016. Cross-modal retrieval with cnn visual features: A new baseline. *IEEE Transactions on Cybernetics* 47, 2 (2016), 449–460.
[57] Jason Weston, Samy Bengio, and Nicolas Usunier. 2010. Large scale image annotation: learning to rank with joint word-image embeddings. *Machine learning* 81, 1 (2010), 21–35.
[58] Fei Wu, Zhou Yu, Yi Yang, Siliang Tang, Yin Zhang, and Yueting Zhuang. 2014. Sparse multi-modal hashing. *Proceedings of MM* (2014), 427–439.
[59] Hamed Zamani and W Bruce Croft. 2017. Relevance-based Word Embedding. In *Proceedings of ACM SIGIR*. 505–514.

A Discrete Choice Model for Subset Selection

Austin R. Benson*
Cornell University
Ithaca, New York
arb@cs.cornell.edu

Ravi Kumar
Google Inc.
Mountain View, California
ravi.k53@gmail.com

Andrew Tomkins
Google Inc.
Mountain View, California
atomkins@gmail.com

ABSTRACT

Multinomial logistic regression is a classical technique for modeling how individuals choose an item from a finite set of alternatives. This methodology is a workhorse in both discrete choice theory and machine learning. However, it is unclear how to generalize multinomial logistic regression to *subset selection*, allowing the choice of more than one item at a time. We present a new model for subset selection derived from the perspective of random utility maximization in discrete choice theory. In our model, the quality of a subset is determined by the quality of its elements, plus an optional correction. Given a budget on the number of subsets that may receive correction, we develop a framework for learning the quality scores for each item, the choice of subsets, and the correction for each subset. We show that, given the subsets to receive correction, we can efficiently and optimally learn the remaining model parameters jointly. We show further that learning the optimal subsets is both NP-hard and non-submodular, but there are efficient heuristics that perform well in practice. We combine these pieces to provide an overall learning solution and apply it to subset prediction tasks. We find that with reasonably-sized budgets, there are significant gains in average per-choice likelihood ranging from 7% to 8x depending on the dataset and also substantial improvements over a determinantal point process model.

ACM Reference Format:
Austin R. Benson, Ravi Kumar, and Andrew Tomkins. 2018. A Discrete Choice Model for Subset Selection. In *WSDM 2018: The Eleventh ACM International Conference on Web Search and Data Mining, February 5–9, 2018, Marina Del Rey, CA, USA.* ACM, New York, NY, USA, 9 pages. https://doi.org/10.1145/3159652.3159702

1 INTRODUCTION

Human decision making frequently falls within the classical framework of *discrete choice*, in which an individual selects a single item from an available slate of alternatives. The items might be a set of kid-safe family sedans for possible purchase, or modes of transportation to take to work. The available alternatives may differ between individuals or over time—e.g., walking to work might not be feasible for some and a carpool may only be available certain days of the week. There is a rich history in analyzing these types of choices [2, 8, 13, 32], but typical models predict the likelihood of choosing a *single* item. Often, one chooses a *subset* of the available alternatives, e.g., a subset of items to purchase from a supermarket, or a subset of songs to form a playlist.

Of course, this is a strict extension of traditional discrete choice, in which subsets are restricted to singletons. The motivation is clear, as higher-order interactions between items are well known to have a significant effect on decision making. See, for example, research on product bundling in marketing [31] or co-purchase modeling in e-commerce recommender systems [28].

Generalizing discrete choice models to subset choice brings a number of challenges. Naively, one could consider the subsets themselves to be the items and then employ the classical models of discrete choice. However, with this approach, the size of the model grows exponentially in the number of alternatives, and the underlying structure of item correlations becomes lost in the identities of the subsets. On the other hand, one might model the selection of a subset as the independent selection of individual items. While this approach is computationally feasible, it does not capture any of the higher-order interactions between items.

Here we develop a sparse model that interpolates between a "full" model that considers the available items to be subsets and a "separable" model that assumes the presence of an item in a subset has no effect on the likelihood of selecting any other item. Our model is rooted in random utility theory so that subset choice probabilities may be interpreted as the strategy of an individual trying to maximize her utility, where the utility of each subset is a random variable expressed as the sum of a utility value (a constant) and a random error. Intuitively, our model says: (i) every item has a fixed base utility, (ii) a subset's base utility is the sum of the utilities of the items in the subset, and (iii) up to k subsets may receive an additional corrective utility, either positive or negative. Corrective utility might represent complementary value, e.g., the utility of the subset {`chips`, `guacamole`} might be larger than the sum of the individual utilities. On the other hand, while the set {`milk`, `beer`} might be frequently purchased, the utility of the subset could be well-described by the utilities of the individual items. Our model can also capture negative utility corrections. For example, `pork sausage` and `vegan tofu sausage` each carry utility, but empirically individuals may be unlikely to purchase them together.

Given a budget k, our algorithmic challenge is two-fold: (i) identify k special subsets that will most benefit from corrective utility and (ii) given these subsets, find the base (item-level) and corrective (subset-level) utilities that maximize the likelihood of the data. From the utilities, we can then determine the probability that an individual will select a given subset from a given set of alternatives through discrete choice theory. We learn the utilities (and subsequently the selection probabilities) under two different assumptions. In the first, the slate of alternatives, or *choice set*, is "universal" and common to all choices. This is largely true in the case of grocery shopping or

*Most of this work was done while the author was at Google, Mountain View, CA.

WSDM 2018, February 5–9, 2018, Marina Del Rey, CA, USA

ACM ISBN 978-1-4503-5581-0/18/02.
https://doi.org/10.1145/3159652.3159702

"market basket" data—individuals may choose any subset of items from the food in the store, modulo issues of availability. In this setting, we prove that given the k subsets receiving corrective utility, the optimal selection probabilities for universal slates have a closed form. Under the second and more general assumption, the choice set is "variable" and may change with each instance of choice in the data. For example, clicks on the `youtube.com` homepage depend on the slate of options available there, which changes frequently. In this case, there is no closed form for the selection probabilities that maximize likelihood of the data, but we can compute them efficiently via a convex optimization problem formulation, after we identify the subsets that will receive corrective utility.

For both universal and variable choice sets, we show that the problem of finding the best k subsets is NP-hard, and furthermore, the optimization problem is non-submodular. Thus, we present several heuristics for identifying good subsets and evaluate them on several real-world datasets from a variety of domains. We find that using our sparse model with these heuristics provides substantial likelihood gains over the baseline separable model while maintaining the same computational feasibility. In addition, our sparse model often out-predicts determinantal point processes that have been used for modeling subset creation [15], while also taking orders of magnitude less time to train. We also find that for some universal choice sets, the corrective utilities are always positive. We show that under this condition, our discrete choice models have an alternate representation as a mixture of two independent multinomial logits. Such mixtures have been studied heavily in discrete choice [33], where the structure is typically set by the data modeler in advance, rather than learned from data, as in our model.

To summarize, our contributions are the following:
(i) We develop a new discrete choice model for subset choice from the perspective of random utility theory, where the utility of subsets is the sum of the utility of the items and some special subsets receive corrective utility. The model parameter complexity is parameterized by the number of subsets receiving corrective utility and is close to that of multinomial logistic regression. In addition, the learned values are highly interpretable.
(ii) We analyze several structural properties of the model and give algorithms to learn the model parameters. We prove that the subset selection probabilities have a closed form for universal choice sets and a convex optimization form for variable choice sets. We also prove that it is NP-hard to find the best k subsets to receive corrective utility.
(iii) We find that over a collection of six datasets with universal choice sets, introduction of the corrective utilities improves likelihood on a held out test set in all cases. Our core metric is the geometric mean likelihood of selecting each subset. Under this metric, two of our datasets show significant gains of 5x or more; three more show between between 20% and 40% lift; and the remaining one over 7%, all with just a few corrective utilities. We also see improvements of 5–8% in two datasets with variable choice set, again with just a few corrective utilities.

Implementations of our algorithms and the datasets used in our experiments are available at

https://github.com/arbenson/discrete-subset-choice.

2 SUBSET CHOICE AND RANDOM UTILITY THEORY

We now develop our model for subset selection. We begin with a quick summary of *random utility theory*, a "rational actor" model of human decision making. In this theory, an individual's value for every possible choice is drawn from some pre-specified joint distribution. The user then behaves rationally by selecting the option of highest utility. Our models (and multinomial logit) belong to the class of random utility models and hence lie within a principled framework of decision making. Stated another way, for all the models we consider, the predicted probability of selecting a particular item or subset from a set of alternatives is always the likelihood of a rational user making this choice, under an appropriate joint utility distribution from which the rational user draws values.

The remainder of this section proceeds as follows. In Section 2.1 we review the multinomial logit model from the perspective of random utility theory. We then develop our model for size-2 subsets in Section 2.2 and extend to arbitrary subsets in Section 2.3. With the model fully described, Section 3 gives the learning algorithms and results for the case in which the choice set is always the entire universe of items, and Section 4 extends to choice sets.

2.1 Background on multinomial logit

We briefly derive the classical multinomial logit model from random utility maximization (see, e.g., the book by Train [33] for a thorough treatment). In this setting, choice theory stipulates the selection of a *single* element from a set C of choices, where C is a subset of some universe $\mathcal{U}$. The utility of choice $i \in C$ is a random variable

$$U_i = V_i + \epsilon_i, \tag{1}$$

where V_i is the inherent *quality* of item i (a constant), and the ϵ_i's are i.i.d. following a Gumbel distribution.

If individuals select the highest-utility option under this random model, an algebraic manipulation shows that the probability of selecting choice i from the choice set C is

$$\Pr[\text{select } i \mid C] = \frac{e^{V_i}}{\sum_{j \in C} e^{V_j}}. \tag{2}$$

In other words, the probability of selecting an item is proportional to the exponential of the base utility of the item, e^{V_i}, *independent* of the choice set C.

In the datasets we consider in this paper, there are many instances of selections made from choice sets. If the choice sets are $C_1, \ldots, C_N$, and $i \in C_r$, then the random utility of choosing item i in choice set C_r is

$$U_i^{(r)} = V_i + \epsilon_{ir}, \tag{3}$$

where the ϵ_{ir}'s are i.i.d. Gumbel (cf. Equation (1)). In other words, the errors are i.i.d. random across different choice sets. However, the choice probability (Equation (2)) remains the same. For the remainder of the paper, we drop the notational dependence on the choice set identifier r when it is clear from context.

While this formulation comes from discrete choice theory, multinomial logistic regression is also a widespread tool in machine learning. In this domain, one usually has a fixed choice set C of classes, a coefficient vector β_i for each class i, a feature vector x for each sample, and then assumes a linear form for the quality of each class, i.e., $V_i = \beta_i^T x$. Here, the probability of labeling the sample as class i (or in our language, "choosing" class i as the appropriate choice for the context encoded by the sample's features) is proportional to $e^{\beta_i^T x}$, and the interest is in learning the regression coefficients β_i. In this paper, we focus on learning the inherent qualities V_i and not the regression coefficients, although our models can accommodate that structure.

2.2 Fixed-size subset choice models

We are interested in extending the traditional multinomial logit model to a random utility model of subset selection. Instead of a choice being an element $i \in C$, a choice will be a subset $S \subset C$. Technically, we consider S to be a multiset, so selections may be duplicated in S. This provides additional modeling flexibility for common situations in Web data such as multiple clicks on a link.

We first consider the case of $|S| = 2$ and generalize later to larger cardinalities. We begin by presenting the *full model* that captures arbitrary interactions between elements by assigning a general utility to each of the exponentially many possible subsets. We contrast this with the *separable model* in which each item has a utility, and each subset delivers the summed utilities of its members; this model is highly efficient but captures no higher-order interactions. We then present our *sparse model* that is between these two extremes.

Full model. One simple model for subset choice is to assume a multinomial logit with an expanded space of choices, i.e., the space of subsets. In this case, the random utility of selecting a subset $S = \{i, j\}$ is

$$U_{ij} = V_{ij} + \epsilon_{ij}, \tag{4}$$

where the ϵ_{ij}'s are i.i.d. from a Gumbel distribution. In the utility maximization setting,

$$\Pr[\text{select } \{i, j\} \mid C] \propto e^{V_{ij}}. \tag{5}$$

In the case when $|S| > 2$, we again specify a unique quality V_S for each subset of that size.

This model has the advantage that it captures arbitrary higher-order structure in the utilities. However, the model grows exponentially in the size of the subsets considered, and thus is impractical for modern large-scale datasets.

Separable model. An alternative model for subset choice assumes that the utilities of elements in a subset separate additively. In this model, the presence of any given item in the subset has no effect on the remainder of the subset.

Observation 2.1. *Let the random utility of the set $\{i, j\}$ be*

$$U_{ij} = V_i + V_j + \epsilon_{ij}, \tag{6}$$

where ϵ_{ij}'s are i.i.d. Gumbel-distributed. Then the probability of any item i belonging to the subset, conditioned on item j belonging to the subset, is the same for all j.

To see this, if we condition on $j \in S$ under the utility maximization framework, we get a term independent of j:

$$\Pr[\text{select } \{i, j\} \mid C,\ j] = \frac{e^{V_i + V_j}}{\sum_{k \in C} e^{V_j + V_k}} = \frac{e^{V_i}}{\sum_{k \in C} e^{V_k}}. \tag{7}$$

The model generalizes to subsets S of larger size in the same way—the inherent subset qualities just separate additively as in Equation (6). The model has the advantage that the number of parameters is linear in the number items (i.e., linear in $|\mathcal{U}|$). However, the separable assumption on the utility is quite strong as it ignores higher-order interactions between the items in the subset.

Sparse model. In this work, we focus on a new model that interpolates between the full and separable models. This is a sparse model that takes the separable model as a baseline and adds sparse corrections for several subsets. We again derive this model from random utility theory and again begin with subsets of cardinality 2. Let H be a (small) set of pairs of indices, representing subsets to receive utility correction. The random utility U_{ij} is

$$U_{ij} = \begin{cases} V_i + V_j + \epsilon_{ij} & \{i, j\} \notin H \\ V_i + V_j + W_{ij} + \epsilon_{ij} & \{i, j\} \in H, \end{cases} \tag{8}$$

where the ϵ_{ij}'s are i.i.d. Gumbel, V_i and V_j are constants representing the individual utilities of item i and j, and W_{ij} is a constant representing the additional utility of the subset $\{i, j\}$.

Intuitively, we follow the separable model for most cases but allow ourselves the flexibility to correct the utility for special pairs of indices in H. This sparse model is a special case of both the separable model (by setting H to be empty) and the full model (by setting H to be all pairs). We emphasize that this model is still a multinomial logit—the probability of choosing a set is proportional to the exponential of the constant term in the random utility. However, we have imposed a certain structure on these constants.

The subset utilities given above may be normalized to convenient probabilities as shown in the following observation. We use this representation throughout the paper.

Observation 2.2. *Under the random utility model of Equation (8) the probability of selecting $S = \{i, j\}$ is proportional to*

$$p_{ij} = \begin{cases} \gamma p_i p_j & \{i, j\} \notin H \\ \gamma p_i p_j + q_{ij} & \{i, j\} \in H, \end{cases} \tag{9}$$

for some parameters p_i, q_{ij}, and γ, where $\sum_i p_i = 1$, $p_i \geq 0$, $\gamma \geq 0$, and $\sum_{\{i,j\}} p_{ij} = 1$.

To get this representation, set $p_i = e^{V_i} / \sum_j e^{V_j}$, $q'_{ij} = e^{V_i} e^{V_j} e^{W_{ij}} - p_i p_j$ if $\{i, j\} \in H$, $q'_{ij} = 0$ if $\{i, j\} \notin H$, and $\gamma = 1/(\sum_{\{i,j\}} (p_i p_j + q'_{ij}))$. Under utility maximization,

$$\Pr[\text{select } \{i, j\} \mid C] \propto e^{V_i} e^{V_j} e^{W_{ij}} = p_i p_j + q'_{ij} \propto \gamma (p_i p_j + q'_{ij}),$$

if $\{i, j\} \in H$. Finally, set $q_{ij} = \gamma q'_{ij}$ to get Equation (9). If $|S| > 2$, then the parameterization is again a mixture of the separable and full models: $p_S = \gamma \prod_{i \in S} p_i + q_S$ for $S \in H$.

At this point, Equation (9) provides a model for the likelihood of choosing a subset if we know the size of the subset to be selected. In the next subsection, we provide a complete model that does not rely on this conditioning.

2.3 Variable-size sparse subset choice model

We now remove the restriction that choices are a fixed size. In this case, our model becomes a mixture of multinomial logits, where each component of the mixture is a model for choosing subsets of a fixed size. Importantly, the utilities from the mixture components overlap so that the utility for each subset is the sum of utilities of the individual items in the subset plus a possible corrective term.

Following this mixture intuition, we select a subset by first choosing the size of the selection (the cardinality of S) and then choosing the subset S itself, conditioned on its size. Formally, given a subset

S of cardinality k, we say that the probability of selecting S from a choice set C is

$$\frac{z_k}{z_1 + \cdots + z_{|C|}} \cdot \Pr[\text{select } S \mid C, \text{size-}k \text{ selection}], \quad (10)$$

where z_k is the probability of choosing a size-k set, $\sum_k z_k = 1$, (here, this is normalized over the possible selection size probabilities given C). Such an approach is common in other variable-size choice models such as approval voting [10, 24], and we will show in Section 3 that it makes learning model parameters simple.

Given the size of S, we model the selection using the sparse model already outlined in Section 2.2 with the crucial assumption that *the individual item qualities V_i are the same regardless of the size of S*. In other words, baseline item qualities are the same regardless of the size of the set in which they appear. However, we learn a parameter γ_k for each subset size k and H may contain multisets of various sizes. For example, if $H = \{\{i,j\}, \{i,j,k\}\}$, then

$\Pr[S = \{i,j\} \mid \text{size-2 choice}] \propto \gamma_2 p_i p_j + q_{ij}$

$\Pr[S = \{i,j,k\} \mid \text{size-3 choice}] \propto \gamma_3 p_i p_j p_k + q_{ijk}$.

Our formulation permits size-1 selections (and our datasets contain such selections), but we restrict H to contain multisets of size at least two, since the correction term is meant to model higher-order effects. Finally, we note that the variable-size sparse subset model is a random utility model as it is a mixture of logits [33].

3 UNIVERSAL CHOICE SETS

We first study the sparse model with universal choice sets, i.e., all subset selections are made from the same slate of alternatives, which is the universe of items $\mathcal{U}$. This is common in a variety of domains, including "market basket" data where individuals buy a collection of items from a store. We show that, given the set of corrections H, the maximum likelihood estimator for the sparse model has a simple closed form. However, we also show that finding the optimal set H is NP-hard. We compare several heuristics for choosing H on a variety of real-world datasets and find substantial likelihood improvements with the sparse model. These heuristics also lead to models that are better predictors on our datasets compared to more involved probabilistic models for subset selection, namely determinantal point processes.

3.1 Optimizing model parameters

We now assume that the set H is given and learn the model parameters in two parts: (i) the mixture probabilities z_k of Equation (10) and (ii) the subset selection probabilities of Observation 2.2. We assume that our data is a list of subsets $S_1, S_2, \ldots, S_m$ representing the selections from the universe of items $\mathcal{U}$ and that there are $n = |\mathcal{U}|$ items. We use maximum likelihood estimation (MLE) for optimizing the model parameters.

Mixture probabilities. It is straightforward to find the MLE for z_k, the probabilities of choosing a subset of a particular size. Since the choice set is universal, $\sum_k z_k = 1$. Let N_S be the number of times that the set S was chosen in the data. Then the log-likelihood given the data is:

$$\sum_k \sum_{|S|=k} N_S \log(z_k \Pr[S \mid \text{size-}k \text{ choice}])$$
$$= \sum_k (\sum_{|S|=k} N_S) \log z_k + \sum_k \sum_{|S|=k} N_S \log \Pr[S \mid \text{size-}k \text{ choice}].$$

Under the constraint that $\sum_k z_k = 1$, it is easy to see that the MLE for z_k is simply the fraction of times a size-k subset was selected.

Subset selection probabilities. We now seek to maximize likelihood by optimizing the probabilities of choosing a subset for a fixed-size selection. For simplicity, we derive this for the case when $|S| = 2$. Let N_{ij} be the number of times that set $S = \{i,j\}$ was selected in the data. Then, the likelihood maximization problem is

$$\underset{p,q,\gamma}{\text{maximize}} \quad \sum_{\{i,j\}\in H} N_{ij} \log(\gamma p_i p_j + q_{ij}) + \sum_{\{i,j\}\notin H} N_{ij} \log(\gamma p_i p_j) \quad (11)$$
$$\text{subject to} \quad \sum_{i=1}^n p_i = 1,\ p_i \geq 0, 1 \leq i \leq n$$
$$\sum_{\{i,j\}} \gamma p_i p_j + \sum_{\{i,j\}\in H} q_{ij} = 1,\ \gamma \geq 0.$$

Here, the likelihood formulation uses the structure of Equation (9). Theorem 3.1 below provides a simple closed-form solution for p, q, and γ that maximizes the likelihood. Essentially, using Equation (9) to codify the random utility model of Equation (8), the optimal parameters take an intuitive form: the p_i are empirical frequencies of item appearances for subset choices not in H and then γ and q_{ij} adjust the probability of subset choices in H to match their empirical frequency of selection. This generalizes the single-item logit model, where the exponentials of the maximum likelihood utilities match the empirical frequency of item selection.

Theorem 3.1. *Let $p_{ij}^D = N_{ij} / \sum_{\{k,l\}} N_{kl}$ be the empirical probability of observing set $\{i,j\}$ in the data. The MLE for Equation (11) is: (i) the p_i's are proportional to the number of times item i is selected in any set $\{i,j\} \notin H$, i.e., $p_i \propto \sum_{j:\{i,j\}\notin H} N_{ij}$; (ii) $\gamma = (1 - \sum_{\{i,j\}\in H} p_{ij}^D)/(\sum_{\{i,j\}\notin H} p_i p_j)$; and (iii) given p and γ, q is set to match the empirical distribution of $\{i,j\}$, i.e., $\gamma p_i p_j + q_{ij} = p_{ij}^D$.*

Proof. Suppose p and γ are fixed. Dividing Equation (11) by the constant $\sum_{ij} N_{ij}$, the likelihood maximization problem becomes

$$\underset{q}{\text{maximize}} \quad \sum_{\{i,j\}\in H} p_{ij}^D \log(\gamma p_i p_j + q_{ij})$$
$$\text{subject to} \quad \sum_{\{i,j\}\in H} q_{ij} = 1 - \gamma \sum_{\{i,j\}} p_i p_j.$$

Setting the gradient of the Lagrangian to zero (with Lagrange multiplier λ) gives $p_{ij}^D/(\gamma p_i p_j + q_{ij}) - \lambda = 0 \rightarrow \gamma p_i p_j + q_{ij} = p_{ij}^D/\lambda$.

Let $R = \sum_{\{i,j\}\in H} p_i p_j$, $M = \sum_{\{i,j\}\in H} p_{ij}^D$, and $C = \sum_{\{i,j\}} p_i p_j$. Then the constraints give

$$\lambda = M/(1 - \gamma(C - R)). \quad (12)$$

Now suppose p is fixed in Equation (11). Plugging Equation (12) into the objective function over γ gives (up to constant)

$$\sum_{\{i,j\}\in H} p_{ij}^D \log(1/\lambda) + \sum_{\{i,j\}\notin H} p_{ij}^D \log(\gamma) \quad (13)$$
$$= -M \log M + M \log(1 - \gamma(C - R)) + (1 - M) \log \gamma \quad (14)$$

Equation (14) is maximized for $\gamma = (1 - M)/(C - R) \geq 0$. For this value of γ, $\lambda = 1$ and $\gamma p_i p_j + q_{ij} = p_{ij}^D$. This proves parts (ii) and (iii) of the theorem.

For constants γ and q, the log-likelihood is (up to a constant)

$$\sum_{\{i,j\}\notin H} N_{ij} \log p_i p_j = \sum_i \left(\sum_{j:\{i,j\}\notin H} N_{ij}\right) \log p_i,$$

which is maximized with $p_i \propto \sum_{j:\{i,j\}\notin H} N_{ij}$.

Finally, we check that our set probabilities sum to 1:

$$\sum_{\{i,j\}} \gamma p_i p_j + \sum_{\{i,j\}\in H} q_{ij} = \sum_{\{i,j\}\notin H} \gamma p_i p_j + \sum_{\{i,j\}\in H} \gamma p_i p_j + q_{ij}$$

$= \gamma(C-R) + M = \frac{1-M}{C-R}(C-R) + M = 1.$ □

Theorem 3.1 can be generalized for choice sets with greater than two elements; the proof remains the same. For an arbitrary subset S with $|S| = k$, we set p^D_S to be the empirical probability of observing set S among all size-k choice sets. We then set γ_k and q according to the same formulas (ii) and (iii) in the statement of Theorem 3.1, but with size-k sets instead of size-2 sets.

At this point, if we are given the set H of corrections, it is straightforward to compute the MLE. Next, we deal with the issue of constructing a set H of a fixed size to maximize likelihood.

3.2 Constructing H

Theorem 3.1 says that once we know the subsets receiving probability corrections from the separable model, finding the parameters that maximize the likelihood of the data is easy. We are now interested in algorithms for finding H. Unfortunately, this problem is difficult in general.

Proposition 3.2. *Finding the set H with $|H| = k$ that maximizes the likelihood of the sparse model is NP-hard.*

Proof. We reduce from maximum 3-dimensional matching (3DM): given a subset $T \subset X \times Y \times Z$ and an integer k, the decision problem is to determine if there exists $M \subset T$, $|M| = k$, such that no two tuples in M share an element. We construct an instance of the sparse model maximum likelihood problem as follows: for every $(x, y, z) \in T$, create one subset choice of the subset $\{x, y, z\}$. Let $d = |T| + 1$ and let d_a be the number of times element a shows up in T ($a \in X \cup Y \cup Z$) and create $d - d_a$ choices of sets $\{a\}$. With this construction, each item is selected exactly d times.

Set the budget for the size of H to be k. We claim that if there is a 3DM of size k, then such a matching is the optimal H. Let c_a be the number of times element a shows up in a subset in H. For any H, applying (the generalization of) Theorem 3.1 says that the log-likelihood is

$k \log(1/|T|) + (|T| - k) \log \gamma + \sum_a (d - c_a) \log \frac{d-c_a}{W}$,

where $W = \sum_a d - c_a$ is the normalization constant and

$$\gamma = \frac{1 - k/|T|}{\sum_{\{x,y,z\}} p_x p_y p_z - \sum_{\{x,y,z\} \in H} p_x p_y p_z} \quad (15)$$

The normalization constant W and the numerator of Equation (15) are independent of H. Thus, the likelihood is maximized when the denominator of Equation (15) is minimized. We have that

$$-\sum_{\{x,y,z\} \in H} p_x p_y p_z = -\sum_{\{x,y,z\} \in H} \frac{(d-c_x)(d-c_y)(d-c_z)}{W^3},$$

which is minimized when $c_x = c_y = c_z = 1$ for all $\{x, y, z\} \in H$. This occurs if and only if the subsets in H form a 3DM.

Next, let $L = \sum_{S=\{x,y,z\}:|S|=3} p_x p_y p_z$, $K = \sum_{S=\{x,x,y\}:|S|=2} p_x^2 p_y$, and $D = \sum_{S=\{x,x,x\}} p_x^3$. Then $6L + 3K + D = \sum_x \sum_y \sum_z p_x p_y p_z = 1$, and $\sum_{\{x,y,z\}} p_i p_j p_k = L + K + D = \frac{1+3K+5D}{6}$. We claim that this term is minimized with a 3DM. Note that

$K + D = \sum_x \sum_y p_x^2 p_y = \sum_x p_x^2 \sum_y p_y = \sum_x p_x^2 = \frac{1}{W^2} \sum_x (d - c_x)^2$.

Under the constraint that k subsets are in H, this summation is minimized when H is a 3DM so that $0 \le c_x \le 1$. Next, note that $D = \sum_x p_x^3 = \frac{1}{W^3} \sum_x (d - c_x)^3$, which again is minimized with a 3DM so that $0 \le c_x \le 1$.

Finally, we account for likelihood due to the selection of subsets not in H, which is (up to constant) $\sum_x \frac{(d-c_x)}{W} \log \frac{d-c_a}{W} = E(p)$, where $p_x = (d - c_x)/W$ and E is the entropy function. Under the constraint $\sum_x c_x = 3k$, entropy is maximized when there are exactly $3k$ elements x for which $c_x = 1$. Again, this occurs if and only if H is a 3DM. □

In addition to being NP-hard, the problem is non-submodular (formalized below), which rules out easy algorithmic approaches.

Observation 3.3. *Let $L(H)$ be the log-likelihood of the MLE. The function $f: H \to L(H)$ is non-submodular.*

To see this, consider a dataset consisting of three subset selections: $\{a, b\}$, $\{a, c\}$, and $\{d, e\}$. Using Theorem 3.1, some simple calculations show that $L(\{\{a, b\}, \{a, c\}\}) + L(\emptyset) > L(\{\{a, b\}\}) + L(\{\{a, c\}\})$.

We leave the design of approximation algorithms to future work. Instead, we develop a few simple heuristics for constructing H that still lead to substantial likelihood gains in our experiments on several real-world datasets in the next section. We briefly describe the heuristics below.

Frequency heuristic. With the frequency heuristic, we put the most frequently selected sets S in H. An advantage of this heuristic is that we can use established algorithms from frequent itemset mining to find the most frequently occurring subsets [1, 20, 27].

Lift heuristic. The frequency heuristic ignores the fact that items in frequently selected subsets may already be frequently occurring and their likelihood accounted for by high utility of those items. With the lift heuristic (analogous to the lift score in association rule mining), we select the subsets S maximizing $N_S / \prod_{i \in S} N_i$, where N_S is the number of times that the set is selected, and N_i is the number of times that item i is selected in any set.

Normalized lift heuristic. With the normalized lift heuristic, we "normalize" the lift by the frequency of the subset in the data. This corresponds to selecting the subsets S maximizing $N_S^2 / \prod_{i \in S} N_i$.

Table 1: Subset choice datasets with universal choice sets. The z_k are the fraction of selections that are size-k subsets.

Dataset	#items = $\lvert\mathcal{U}\rvert$	#choices	z_1	z_2	z_3	z_4	z_5
Bakery	50	67,488	0.05	0.20	0.37	0.25	0.13
WalmartItems	183	16,698	0.51	0.45	0.03	0.01	0.00
WalmartDepts	66	120,973	0.33	0.28	0.17	0.13	0.10
Kosarak	2,605	505,217	0.27	0.30	0.23	0.14	0.07
Instacart	9,544	806,662	0.19	0.21	0.21	0.21	0.19
LastfmGenres	413	643,982	0.52	0.21	0.12	0.08	0.06

3.3 Data

We collected six universal choice set datasets from a variety of domains. We describe them below and provide summary statistics in Table 1.

Bakery. This dataset is comprised of the receipts from purchases by patrons of a bakery.[1] The items on each receipt form a selected subset. The elements of each selected subset are distinct.

WalmartItems and WalmartDepts. These datasets are constructed from individual shopping trips at Walmart.[2] For each trip,

[1] https://wiki.csc.calpoly.edu/datasets/wiki/ExtendedBakery
[2] https://www.kaggle.com/c/walmart-recruiting-trip-type-classification

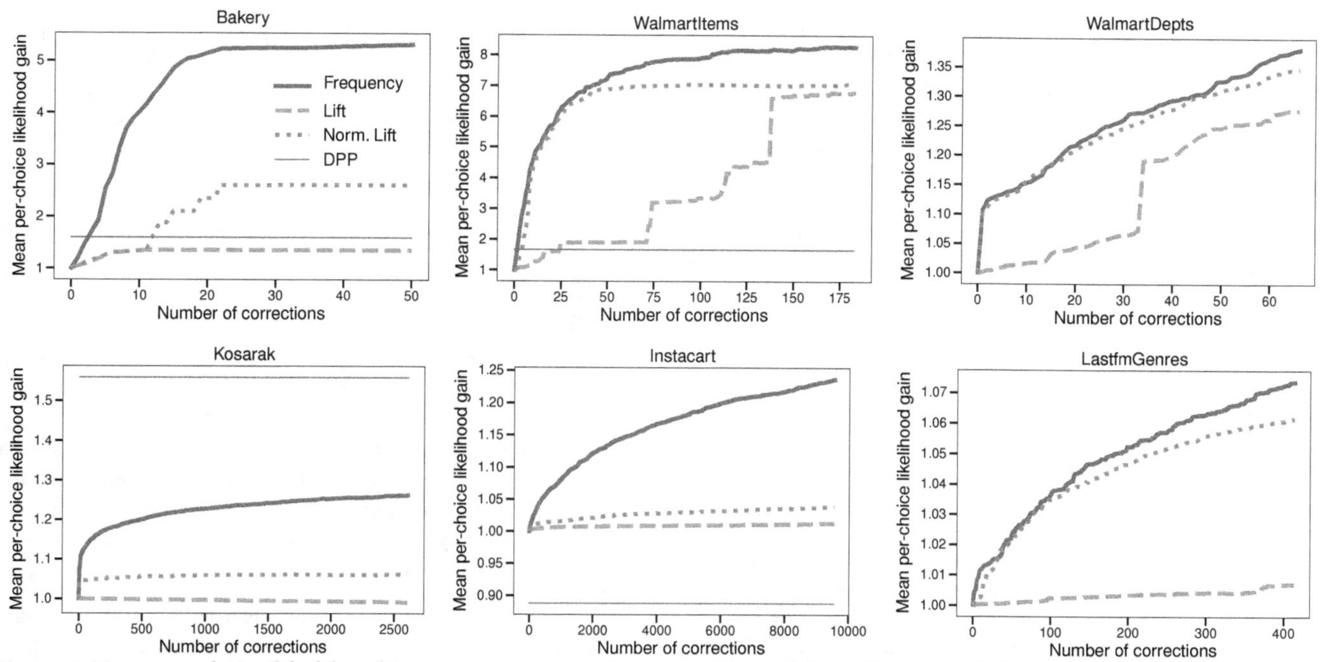

Figure 1: Mean per-choice likelihood improvements over the separable model as a function of the number of corrections in the sparse model (i.e., $|H|$) for several datasets with universal choice sets along with the relative likelihood of a determinantal point process (DPP) model. DPPs do not model subset selections with repeated items, so there are no DPP results on WALMARTDEPTS and LASTFMGENRES, which contain such multiset selections. Our sparse model (i) provides substantial improvements over the separable model with only a modest increase in the number of model parameters and (ii) out-performs DPPs with at most a few corrections on BAKERY, WALMARTITEMS, and INSTACART.

the items purchased are the selected subset. Using department identifiers for the items, we also construct a separate dataset where the selected subset consists of all departments from which the shopper made a purchase. Selections in WALMARTDEPTS may contain repeats (multiple purchases from the same department), but the elements of a subsets selected in WALMARTITEMS are distinct.

KOSARAK. The KOSARAK dataset is derived from publicly available anonymized clickstreams from a Hungarian online news portal.[3] The de-duplicated set of links visited by a user in a given session is the selected subset, so no subset selections contain repeated items.

INSTACART. Instacart is an online same-day grocery delivery service, where users order groceries through a web application. This dataset consists of a sample of orders from users living in the United States [14].[4] We consider the de-duplicated items in a user's order to be a subset choice.

LASTFMGENRES. This dataset come from the listening behavior of users from the music streaming service Last.fm [6].[5] We break user behavior into sessions, where a new session is created if the user goes 20 minutes without starting a new song (this is the same procedure from our previous work [3]). We create subset choices by the genres of music played in the session, where genres are derived from user-provided tags for artists.[6] We assign an artist to the most commonly provided tag for that artist. Many subset selections contain repeated genres, corresponding to cases when a user listens to the same genre more than once in a session.

To unify structure across our data, we filter each dataset to contain subset selections of size at most 5 and only items that are selected at least 25 times. This filtering also focuses our attention on sets that are possible candidates for corrective utility, as larger sets with more than 5 items do not tend to appear repeatedly nor frequently.

3.4 Experiments

Likelihood improvements. We used the frequency, lift, and normalized lift heuristics to find correction sets H for each dataset for $|H| = 0, 1, 2, \ldots |\mathfrak{U}|$ (see Table 1 for the values of $|\mathfrak{U}|$). The case of $|H| = 0$ corresponds to the separable model and the case of $|H| = |\mathfrak{U}|$ corresponds to the sparse model with twice the number of parameters as the separable model. Thus, all model sizes are linear in the number of items. For each value of $|H|$, we trained the model with 80% of the data and evaluated the mean per-choice likelihood gain on the remaining 20% of the data (the test data). Specifically, if LL_k is the log-likelihood on the test data when $|H| = k$, then we measured the relative improvement $r_k = e^{(LL_k - LL_0)/N}$, where N is the number of choices made in the test set.

The separable model (i.e., the case when $|H| = 0$) serves as one baseline, and we also compare against a determinantal point process (DPP) model. DPPs are probabilistic models for generating "diverse" subsets from a discrete set of objects [15]. We use the expectation maximization algorithm of Gillenwater et al. [12] to

[3]http://fimi.ua.ac.be/data
[4]https://www.instacart.com/datasets/grocery-shopping-2017
[5]http://www.dtic.upf.edu/~ocelma/MusicRecommendationDataset/lastfm-1K.html
[6]https://musicmachinery.com/2010/11/10/lastfm-artisttags2007

learn a DPP from the same training data as our sparse model. DPPs cannot model selected subsets with repeated items (i.e., multisets), and the WalmartDepts and LastfmGenres contain such subsets. Therefore, we do not evaluate DPPs for these two datasets.

Figure 1 shows r_k—the mean per-choice relative likelihood gain over the separable model—as a function of k for each of our datasets as well as the relative likelihood gain for the DPP (note that the DPP is just one model and does not depend on k). For all datasets, the likelihood gains from the frequency heuristic exhibit a sharp increase for small values of k and then gradually decay for larger values of k. In other words, a few sparse corrections can dramatically increase likelihood. In nearly all cases, the frequency heuristic outperforms the lift-based heuristics.

In all datasets, our sparse model provides substantial improvements over the separable model, often with just a few subsets in H receiving corrective probability. Our sparse model is also a much better predictor than DPPs in the Bakery, WalmartItems, and Instacart datasets, again with just a few subsets in H (the exception is Kosarak, where DPPs provide a performance gain over our sparse model). Our sparse model's performance is especially good for Bakery and WalmartItems, where we achieve 5x per-choice likelihood improvements with only a modest increase in the number of parameters in the model ($|H| < \frac{1}{2}|\mathcal{U}|$).

Running time. Using Theorem 3.1, the computational complexity of training the sparse subset choice model depends on (i) computing relative item frequencies, (ii) computing γ, and (iii) constructing H and computing the relative frequencies of subsets. Parts (i) and (ii) take linear time and space in the size of the data. The complexity of part (iii) is more involved and depends on the heuristic and distribution of subsets in the data.

Instead of a detailed complexity analysis, we report the time to train and test our sparse model with the frequency heuristic in Table 2 (times for the other heuristics were similar) as well as the time for the DPP model for our datasets. For our model, we measured the running time for the largest value of $|H|$ in Figure 1 (i.e., the biggest model). All experiments ran on a single thread of a 2.4 GHz Intel Xeon E7-4870 server. The software for learning our model was implemented in Julia,[7] and the software for DPP learning was implemented in MATLAB.[8] While the implementations are in different languages, our goal is to roughly compare the time it takes to use these models.

As shown in Table 2, training and testing our sparse model is at least two orders of magnitude faster than to train and test the DPP models. The EM algorithm for DPP training has a cubic dependence on the number of items $|\mathcal{U}|$ [12], so this performance discrepancy is not that surprising. Practically, the running times for our model are all quite modest, often completing in just a few seconds and taking fewer than 5 minutes for the largest dataset (Instacart).

Values of correction probabilities. Next, we analyze the actual values of the sparse corrections q. Specifically, we are interested in the sign of the corrections. Figure 2 shows that there are relatively few sets $S \in H$ for which $q_S < 0$, (regardless of the size of H) when using the frequency heuristic to construct H. In fact, for the Bakery, WalmartItems, and WalmartDepts datasets, the values

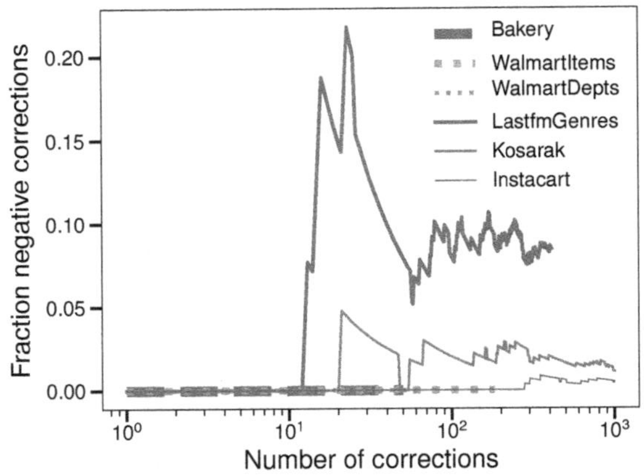

Figure 2: Fraction of subsets $S \in H$ with correction probability $q_S < 0$ as a function of the size of H when using the frequency heuristic to construct H. In many cases, the corrections are always positive, in which case our model has an alternative interpretation (Observation 3.4).

of q are always positive, and the same is true for nearly all sizes of H in the Instacart dataset. These results are consistent with prior work on supermarket purchase data showing that most co-purchase correlations are positive [9]. It turns out that our choice model has an alternative interpretation in the case when the correction values are all positive, as summarized in the following observation.

Observation 3.4. *If $q_S > 0$ for all $S \in H$, then the sparse model is a mixture of two logit models: (i) with probability $\alpha = \sum_{\{i,j\} \in H} q_{ij}$, choices follow the full model restricted to subsets in H and (ii) with probability $1 - \alpha$, choices follow the separable model.*

To see this, let $|S| = 2$ for each $S \in H$ for simplicity. Since $q_{ij}, \gamma, p_i > 0$ and $\gamma \sum_{\{i,j\}} p_i p_j + \sum_{\{i,j\} \in H} q_{ij} = 1$, $\alpha \in [0, 1]$. The probabilities for the full model are simply $\tilde{q}_{ij} = q_{ij}/\alpha$.

Thus, in many of our datasets, we can interpret user behavior as the following. First, the user decides whether or not to pick a subset from H. If the user picks from H, each set has its own utility and the user picks according to a multinomial logit. If the user does not pick from H, their set is filled with non-interacting items.

Finally, we examined the largest correction probabilities in the LastfmGenres dataset using the frequency-based algorithm. Table 3 lists the five sets with the most positive and most negative corrective values. We see that the most positive corrections account for repeat behavior—users listen to several indie, hip hop, or rock songs in the same session—whereas the negative corrections show unlikely combinations such as indie and metal.

4 VARIABLE CHOICE SETS

Next we consider datasets with subset choices where the available alternatives may change with each selection. In this setting, we no longer have the closed form of the maximum likelihood parameters provided by Theorem 3.1, but we show in Section 4.1 that the likelihood function remains concave, given the set H of subsets receiving corrective utility.

[7] https://github.com/arbenson/discrete-subset-choice
[8] https://code.google.com/archive/p/em-for-dpps

Table 2: Training and test time in seconds for (i) our sparse subset choice model with the frequency heuristic for the largest value of $|H|$ in Figure 1 and (ii) a determinantal point process (DPP) model, using EM [12]. DPPs cannot model selections with repeated items, so there are no results for WalmartDepts and LastfmGenres. In all cases, our sparse model is much faster.

	Bakery	WalmartItems	WalmartDepts	Kosarak	Instacart	LastfmGenres
Sparse subset choice	1s	0.2s	1s	26s	270s	7s
DPP	193s	12s	N/A	3,080s	67,054s	N/A

Table 3: The top five most positive and most negative correction probabilities q in LastfmGenres.

Most positive	q	Most negative	q
{indie, indie}	0.0301	{indie, metal}	-0.0015
{rock, indie}	0.0174	{indie, progressive_metal}	-0.0009
{hip_hop, hip_hop}	0.0123	{rock, rock, electronic}	-0.0007
{indie, indie, indie}	0.0119	{indie, industrial}	-0.0006
{rock, rock, rock}	0.0101	{metal, electronic}	-0.0005

4.1 Optimizing model parameters and constructing H

Again, we learn the model parameters in two parts: the mixture probabilities and the subset selection probabilities.

Mixture probabilities. There is no longer a closed form for the optimal mixture probabilities z_k that model how likely it is to choose a size-k set. The log-likelihood of choosing a size-k set S from choice set C is

$$\log \frac{z_k}{z_1+z_2+\ldots z_{|C|}} + \log \Pr[\text{select } S \mid \text{size-}k \text{ choice}]. \quad (16)$$

Since $z_k \geq 0$, we may write $z_k = e^{Y_k}$ for some Y_k, and the log-likelihood function becomes concave. We learn the z_k with a standard gradient descent algorithm.

Subset selection probabilities. With variable choice sets, it is easier to derive the optimization of model parameters from the random utility perspective of Equation (8), rather than the probabilistic formulation of Observation 2.2 used for universal choice sets. Consider some choice set C and suppose that we know that the selected subset is of size 2. The likelihood of observing a choice $S = \{i, j\} \subset C$ is $e^{V_i+V_j+W_{ij}} / \sum_{\{k,l\}\subset C} e^{V_k+V_l+W_{kl}}$ with the understanding that $W_{kl} = 0$ if $\{k, l\} \notin H$. Let $S_r = \{i_r, j_r\} \subset C_r$ be the subset selections, $r = 1, \ldots, N$, where N is the total number of selections. Given H, maximizing the log-likelihood is the following optimization problem:

$$\begin{aligned} \underset{V,W}{\text{maximize}} \quad & \textstyle\sum_{r=1}^{N} V_{i_r} + V_{j_r} + W_{i_r j_r} - \log \sum_{\{k,l\}\subset C_r} e^{V_k+V_l+W_{kl}} \\ \text{subject to} \quad & W_{ij} = 0, \text{ for } \{i, j\} \notin H. \end{aligned}$$

The optimization problem has a concave objective with trivial linear constraints. Thus, if we know the set of correction locations H, then we can efficiently find the optimal likelihood parameters (we use a simple gradient descent procedure). However, since the universal choice set data is a special case of variable choice sets, it is still NP-hard to find the optimal H by Proposition 3.2.

Constructing H. In our prior experiments, the frequency-based algorithm performed well in all cases, so we use that heuristic for our experiments here.

Table 4: Subset choice datasets with variable choice sets. Here, $|C|$ denotes the range of choice set sizes. The subset size probabilities z_k are learned from data (Section 4.1).

Dataset	#items	#choices	$\lvert C\rvert$	z_1	z_2	z_3	z_4	z_5
YcCats	20	134,057	2–10	0.26	0.31	0.23	0.12	0.08
YcItems	2,975	156,039	2–10	0.16	0.20	0.23	0.22	0.18

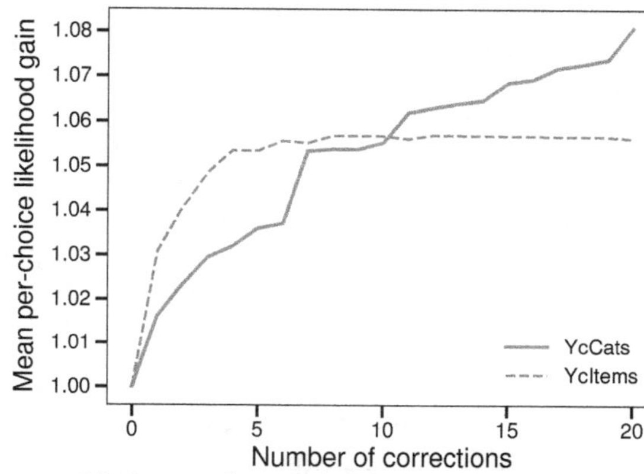

Figure 3: Mean per-choice likelihood improvements on the test set over the separable model as a function of the number of corrections in the sparse model (i.e., $|H|$) for datasets with variable choice sets.

4.2 Data

We constructed two subset choice datasets from user browsing sessions on an e-commerce Web site that contain click and purchase information (made available from YOOCHOOSE[9]). In YcItems, the variable choice set C is all items clicked on by a user in a given browsing session, and the subset selection is the set of items purchased in that session. Each item also has a category, and YcCats is constructed by considering choices at the category level. In both cases, the choice set varies for each browsing session. We filtered the datasets to consider subset selections of size at most 5 made from choice sets of size at most 10, where each item or category appears in at least 8 total choice sets and at least 4 subset selections. Table 4 provides summary statistics of the datasets.

4.3 Experiments

We used the frequency-based algorithm to find the correction sets H for each dataset for $|H| = 0, 1, 2, \ldots, 20$. Again, the case of $|H| = 0$ corresponds to the separable model. We trained the model on 80% of the data and evaluated the mean per-choice likelihood gain on the remaining 20% of the data (the same evaluation as for the datasets

[9]http://2015.recsyschallenge.com

with universal choice sets in Figure 1). There is no methodology for learning determinantal point processes with variable choice sets, so we do not compare against them here.

Figure 3 shows the mean per-choice likelihood improvements over the separable model. In both datasets, our model achieves over 5% likelihood gain with $|H| < 10$. With YcItems, we see the same pattern in likelihood gains as for the datasets with universal choice sets: a rapid increase for the first several corrections and then a leveling of the gains. For this dataset, $|H|$ is less than 1% the number of items, and we achieve substantial likelihood gains with an extremely sparse model.

5 RELATED WORK

There are variable-size choice models for universal choice sets based on pairwise interactions and conditional distributions [26], correlated random utility errors [17], or a priori knowledge of utilities [11, 35]. Our model makes no assumptions on pairwise interactions and can handle arbitrary-order interactions. Also, the datasets used in our experiments contain orders of magnitude more items than experiments for pairwise interaction models in market basket data [5, 9]. Set prediction functions in neural networks [22, 37] and mutli-label classification methods more broadly [23, 34] are also relevant to the subset prediction problem. However, these methods are designed to predict a set of labels from features (e.g., predict several tags of an image), whereas our experiments predict new subsets given previous subset selections. The recently developed set embedding model offers a statistical approach to the subset choice problem with universal choice sets [25]. Unlike our models, neural networks and the embedding models are not known to carry a random utility maximization interpretation.

Another variant of subset choice is approval voting, where an individual selects all candidates that she approves [10, 24, 29]. In this case, there is an implicit assumption that only one alternative will ultimately be selected (only one candidate will win the election), whereas we deal with subsets that give complementary utility.

Lastly, our work fits into the context of several recent analyses on effectively learning discrete choice models [4, 16, 18, 19, 21, 38] as well as applications of discrete choice models to user behavior on the Web [7, 30, 36].

6 DISCUSSION

We developed a general random utility model for how individuals choose a subset of items from a given choice set and analyzed its structure in two contexts: (i) the choice set is universal and is the same for all selections and (ii) the choice set varies. In both cases, we prove that after identifying subsets receiving corrective probability within our model, we can efficiently find the optimal model parameters. However, we also showed that finding the best set of subsets to receive corrections is NP-hard. Approximation algorithms for coping with this issue are a direction for future work. Nevertheless, our sparse model provides substantial likelihood improvements in subset prediction compared to competing baselines.

REFERENCES

[1] Rakesh Agrawal and Ramakrishnan Srikant. 1994. Fast algorithms for mining association rules. In *VLDB*.

[2] Moshe E Ben-Akiva and Steven R Lerman. 1985. *Discrete Choice Analysis: Theory and Application to Travel Demand.* MIT Press.

[3] Austin R. Benson, Ravi Kumar, and Andrew Tomkins. 2016. Modeling User Consumption Sequences. In *WWW.* 519–529.

[4] Austin R. Benson, Ravi Kumar, and Andrew Tomkins. 2016. On the Relevance of Irrelevant Alternatives. In *WWW.* 963–973.

[5] Yasemin Boztuğ and Lutz Hildebrandt. 2006. A market basket analysis conducted with a multivariate logit model. In *From Data and Information Analysis to Knowledge Engineering*. Springer, 558–565.

[6] O. Celma. 2010. *Music Recommendation and Discovery in the Long Tail.* Springer.

[7] Shuo Chen and Thorsten Joachims. 2016. Modeling intransitivity in matchup and comparison data. In *WSDM.* 227–236.

[8] David R Cox. 1958. The regression analysis of binary sequences. *Journal of the Royal Statistical Society. Series B (Methodological)* (1958), 215–242.

[9] Katrin Dippold and Harald Hruschka. 2013. Variable selection for market basket analysis. *Computational Statistics* 28, 2 (2013), 519–539.

[10] J-Cl Falmagne and Michael Regenwetter. 1996. A random utility model for approval voting. *Journal of Mathematical Psychology* 40, 2 (1996), 152–159.

[11] Peter C Fishburn and Irving H LaValle. 1996. Binary interactions and subset choice. *European Journal of Operational Research* 92, 1 (1996), 182–192.

[12] Jennifer A Gillenwater, Alex Kulesza, Emily Fox, and Ben Taskar. 2014. Expectation-maximization for learning determinantal point processes. In *NIPS*.

[13] Nick Hanley, Robert E Wright, and Vic Adamowicz. 1998. Using choice experiments to value the environment. *Environ. Resour. Econ* 11, 3-4 (1998), 413–428.

[14] Instacart. 2017. The Instacart Online Grocery Shopping Dataset. https://www.instacart.com/datasets/grocery-shopping-2017. (2017).

[15] Alex Kulesza and Ben Taskar. 2012. Determinantal point processes for machine learning. *Foundations and Trends in Machine Learning* 5, 2–3 (2012), 123–286.

[16] Ravi Kumar, Andrew Tomkins, Sergei Vassilvitskii, and Erik Vee. 2015. Inverting a steady-state. In *WSDM.* 359–368.

[17] Puneet Manchanda, Asim Ansari, and Sunil Gupta. 1999. The "shopping basket": a model for multicategory purchase incidence decisions. *Marketing Science* 18, 2 (1999), 95–114.

[18] Lucas Maystre and Matthias Grossglauser. 2015. Fast and accurate inference of Plackett–Luce models. In *NIPS*.

[19] Lucas Maystre and Matthias Grossglauser. 2017. ChoiceRank: Identifying Preferences from Node Traffic in Networks. In *ICML*.

[20] Jong Soo Park, Ming-Syan Chen, and Philip S. Yu. 1995. An Effective Hash-based Algorithm for Mining Association Rules. In *SIGMOD.* 175–186.

[21] Stephen Ragain and Johan Ugander. 2016. Pairwise Choice Markov Chains. In *NIPS*.

[22] Siamak Ravanbakhsh, Jeff Schneider, and Barnabas Poczos. 2017. Deep learning with sets and point clouds. In *ICLR Workshop Track*.

[23] Jesse Read, Bernhard Pfahringer, Geoff Holmes, and Eibe Frank. 2011. Classifier chains for multi-label classification. *Machine Learning* 85, 3 (2011), 333–359.

[24] Michel Regenwetter and Bernard Grofman. 1998. Choosing subsets: a size-independent probabilistic model and the quest for a social welfare ordering. *Social Choice and Welfare* 15, 3 (1998), 423–443.

[25] Maja Rudolph, Francisco Ruiz, Stephan Mandt, and David Blei. 2016. Exponential family embeddings. In *NIPS*.

[26] Gary J Russell and Ann Petersen. 2000. Analysis of cross category dependence in market basket selection. *Journal of Retailing* 76, 3 (2000), 367–392.

[27] Ashoka Savasere, Edward Omiecinski, and Shamkant B Navathe. 1995. An Efficient Algorithm for Mining Association Rules in Large Databases. In *VLDB*.

[28] J Ben Schafer, Joseph Konstan, and John Riedl. 1999. Recommender systems in e-commerce. In *EC.* 158–166.

[29] Nihar Shah, Dengyong Zhou, and Yuval Peres. 2015. Approval voting and incentives in crowdsourcing. In *ICML*.

[30] Or Sheffet, Nina Mishra, and Samuel Ieong. 2012. Predicting Consumer Behavior in Commerce Search. In *ICML*.

[31] Stefan Stremersch and Gerard J Tellis. 2002. Strategic bundling of products and prices: A new synthesis for marketing. *Journal of Marketing* 66, 1 (2002), 55–72.

[32] Kenneth Train. 1986. *Qualitative Choice Analysis: Theory, Econometrics, and an Application to Automobile Demand.* Vol. 10. MIT press.

[33] Kenneth E Train. 2009. *Discrete Choice Methods with Simulation.* Cambridge University Press.

[34] Grigorios Tsoumakas and Ioannis Vlahavas. 2007. Random k-labelsets: An ensemble method for multilabel classification. In *ECML.* 406–417.

[35] Iris van Rooij, Ulrike Stege, and Helena Kadlec. 2005. Sources of complexity in subset choice. *Journal of Mathematical Psychology* 49, 2 (2005), 160–187.

[36] Shuang-Hong Yang, Bo Long, Alexander J Smola, Hongyuan Zha, and Zhaohui Zheng. 2011. Collaborative competitive filtering: learning recommender using context of user choice. In *SIGIR.* 295–304.

[37] Manzil Zaheer, Satwik Kottur, Siamak Ravanbakhsh, Barnabas Poczos, Ruslan Salakhutdinov, and Alexander Smola. 2017. Deep Sets. In *NIPS*.

[38] Danqing Zhang, Kimon Fountoulakis, Junyu Cao, Mogeng Yin, Michael Mahoney, and Alexei Pozdnoukhov. 2017. Social Discrete Choice Models. *arXiv* (2017).

Latent Cross: Making Use of Context in Recurrent Recommender Systems

Alex Beutel, Paul Covington, Sagar Jain, Can Xu, Jia Li*, Vince Gatto, Ed H. Chi
Google, Inc.
Mountain View, California
{alexbeutel, pcovington, sagarj, canxu, vgatto, edchi}@google.com, vena900620@gmail.com

ABSTRACT

The success of recommender systems often depends on their ability to understand and make use of the context of the recommendation request. Significant research has focused on how time, location, interfaces, and a plethora of other contextual features affect recommendations. However, in using deep neural networks for recommender systems, researchers often ignore these contexts or incorporate them as ordinary features in the model.

In this paper, we study how to effectively treat contextual data in neural recommender systems. We begin with an empirical analysis of the conventional approach to context as features in feed-forward recommenders and demonstrate that this approach is inefficient in capturing common feature crosses. We apply this insight to design a state-of-the-art RNN recommender system. We first describe our RNN-based recommender system in use at YouTube. Next, we offer "Latent Cross," an easy-to-use technique to incorporate contextual data in the RNN by embedding the context feature first and then performing an element-wise product of the context embedding with model's hidden states. We demonstrate the improvement in performance by using this Latent Cross technique in multiple experimental settings.

ACM Reference Format:
Alex Beutel, Paul Covington, Sagar Jain, Can Xu, Jia Li, Vince Gatto, Ed H. Chi. 2018. Latent Cross: Making Use of Context in Recurrent Recommender Systems. In *WSDM 2018: The Eleventh ACM International Conference on Web Search and Data Mining , February 5–9, 2018, Marina Del Rey, CA, USA*. ACM, New York, NY, USA, 9 pages. https://doi.org/10.1145/3159652.3159727

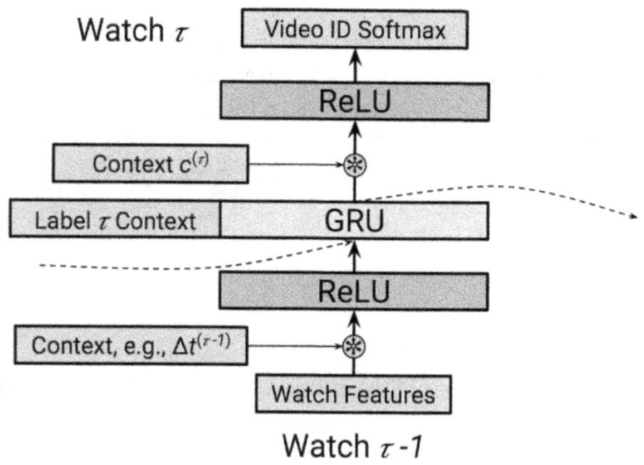

Figure 1: Overall structure of our recommender system, including "latent crosses" of context features throughout.

1 INTRODUCTION

Recommender systems have long been used for predicting what content a user would enjoy. As online services like Facebook, Netflix, YouTube, and Twitch continue to grow, having a high quality recommender system to help users sift through the expanding and increasingly diverse content becomes ever-more important.

Much of the research in recommender systems has focused on effective machine learning techniques — how to best learn from users actions, e.g., clicks, purchases, watches, and ratings. In this effort, there is a large body of research on collaborative filtering and recommendation algorithms, including matrix factorization during the Netflix Prize [24, 28, 30, 35], local focused models [5, 9, 31], and more recently deep learning [11, 36].

In parallel, and increasingly prominently, there is an understanding of the importance of modeling the *context* of a recommendation – not just the user who is looking for a video to watch, but also the time of day, the location, the user's device, etc. Many of these models have been proposed in the factorization setting, such as with tensor factorization for location [17], unfolding tensors for different types of user actions [46], or hand-crafted features about the effect of time [29].

As deep learning has grown in prominence, how to incorporate these contextual features in neural recommender systems has been less directly explored. Previous work on deep neural network (DNN) recommender systems has largely relied on modeling context as direct features in the model or having a multi-task objective [11]. One notable exception is the use of recurrent neural networks (RNNs) to model temporal patterns [25, 39, 43]. In this paper, we bridge the contextual collaborative filtering literature and neural recommender literature. We explore how to make use of contextual data in deep neural recommenders (particularly in RNN models) and demonstrate that prevailing techniques miss a significant amount of the information in these features.

We explore the ability to make use of contextual data in an RNN-based recommender system used at YouTube. As with most production settings, we have a significant amount of contextual data that is important to include: request and watch time, the type of device, and the page on the website or mobile app. In this paper, first,

[1]Jia Li is affiliated with the University of Illinois at Chicago, but worked on this project while interning at Google.

WSDM'18, February 5–9, 2018, Marina Del Rey, CA, USA

ACM ISBN 978-1-4503-5581-0/18/02.
https://doi.org/10.1145/3159652.3159727

we offer a theoretical interpretation of the limitations of modeling context as direct features, particularly using feed-forward neural networks as the example baseline DNN approach. We then offer an easy-to-use technique to incorporate these features that results in improved prediction accuracy, even within a more complicated RNN model.

Our contributions are:

- **First-Order Challenges:** We demonstrate the challenges of first-order neural networks to model low-rank relationships.
- **Production Model:** We describe how we have constructed a large-scale RNN recommender system for YouTube.
- **Latent Cross:** We offer a simple technique, called the "Latent Cross", to include contextual features more expressively in our model. Specifically, latent cross performs an element-wise product between the context embedding and the neural network hidden states.
- **Empirical Results:** We offer empirical results verifying that our approach improves recommendation accuracy.

2 RELATED WORK

We begin with a survey of the various related research. An overview can be seen in Table 1.

Contextual Recommendation. A significant amount of research has focused on using contextual data during recommendation. In particular, certain types of contextual data have been explored in depth, where as others have been treated abstractly. For example, temporal dynamics in recommendation have been explored widely [6]. During the Netflix Prize [4], Koren [29] discovered the significant long-ranging temporal dynamics in the Netflix data set and added temporal features to his Collaborative Filtering (CF) model to account for these effects. Researchers have also explored the how preferences evolve in shorter time-scales, e.g., sessions [39]. More general abstractions have been used to model preference evolution for recommendation such as point processes [15] and recurrent neural networks [43]. Similarly, modeling user actions along with geographical data has been widely explored with probabilistic models [2, 8], matrix factorization [32], and tensor factorization [17]. A variety of methods have built on matrix and tensor factorization for cross domain learning [45, 46]. Methods like factorization machines [34] and other contextual recommenders [22, 37, 48] have provided generalizations of these collaborative filtering approaches.

Neural Recommender Systems. As neural networks have grown in popularity for computer vision and natural language processing (NLP) tasks, recommender systems researchers have begun applying DNNs to recommendation. Early iterations focused on directly applying the collaborative filtering intuition to neural networks, such as through an auto-encoder [36] or joint deep and CF models [20]. More complex networks have been devised to incorporate a wider variety of input features [11]. Cheng et al. [7] handles this problem through a linear model to handle interactions among contextual features, outside the DNN portion of the model.

There has been a recent growth in using *recurrent* neural networks for recommendation [21, 25, 39, 43]. [25, 43] include temporal information as features and supervision in their models, and [41] includes general context features. However, in both cases, these features are concatenated with input, which we show provides limited benefit. Concurrent and independent research [49] improved LSTMs by multiplicatively incorporating temporal information, but did not generalize this to other context data.

Second-order Neural Networks. A major thrust of this paper is the importance of multiplicative relations in neural recommenders. These second-order units show up in a few places in neural networks. Recurrent units, e.g., LSTMs [23] and GRUs [10], are common second-order units with gating mechanisms that use an element-wise multiplication. A more complete tutorial on recurrent networks can be found in [18].

Additionally, softmax layers at the top of networks for classification are explicitly bi-linear layers between the embedding produced by the DNN and embeddings of the label classes. This technique has been extended in multiple papers to include user-item bi-linear layers on top of DNNs [20, 41, 43, 47].

Similar to the technique described in this paper is a body of work on multiplicative models [27, 44]. These multiplicative structures have most commonly been used in natural language processing as in [14, 27]. The NLP approach was applied to personalized modeling of reviews [40] (with a slightly different mathematical structure). Recently, [25] uses the multiplicative technique not over contextual data but directly over users, similar to a tensor factorization. PNN [33] and NFM [19] push this idea to an extreme, taking multiplying all pairs of features at the input and either concatenating or averaging the results before passing through a feed-forward network. The intuition of these models is similar to ours, but differ in that we focus on the relationship between contextual data and user actions, our latent crossing mechanism can be and is applied throughout the model, and we demonstrate the importance of these interactions even within an RNN recommender system.

More complex model structures like attention models [3], memory networks [38], and meta-learning [42] also rely on second-order relations and are increasingly popular. Attention models, for instance, use attention vectors that modulate the hidden states with a multiplication. However, these methods are significantly more complex structurally and are generally found to be much more difficult to train. In contrast, the latent cross technique proposed in this paper we found to be easy to train and effective in practice.

3 MODELING PRELIMINARIES

We consider a recommender system in which we we have a database $\mathcal{E}$ of events e which are k-way tuples. We consider e_ℓ to refer to the ℓth value in the tuple and $e_{\bar{\ell}}$ to refer to the other $k-1$ values in the tuple.

For example, the Netflix Prize setting would be described by tuples $e \equiv (i, j, R)$ where user i gave movie j a rating of R. We may also have context such as time and device such that $e \equiv (i, j, t, d)$ where user i watched video j at time t on device type d. Note, each value can be either discrete categorical variables, as in there are N users where $i \in \mathcal{I}$, or continuous, e.g., t is a unix timestamp. Continuous variables are not uncommonly discretized as a preprocessing step, such as to convert t to only the day on which the event took place.

With this data, we can frame recommender systems as trying to predict one value of the event given the others. For example, the Netflix Prize said for a tuple $e = (i, j, R)$, use (i, j) predict R. From a

	Latent Cross RNN	FM [22, 34]	CF [29, 32, 48]	TF [17, 37, 46]	RRN [21, 43]	YT [11]	NCF [20]	PNN [19, 33]	Conext-RNN [41]	Time-LSTM [49]
Neural Network	✓	×	×	×	✓	✓	✓	✓	✓	✓
Models Sequences	✓	×	×	×	✓	×	×	×	✓	✓
Uses Context	✓	✓	✓	✓	*time*	✓	×	✓	✓	*time*
Multiplicative User/Item	✓	✓	✓	✓	✓	×	✓	✓	✓	✓
Multiplicative Context	✓	✓	✓	✓	×	×	×	✓	×	*time*

Table 1: Relationship with related recommenders: We bridge the intuition and insights from contextual collaborative filtering with the power of recurrent recommender systems.

Symbol	Description
e	Tuple of k values describing an observed event
e_ℓ	Element ℓ in the tuple
$\mathcal{E}$	Set of all observed events
u_i, v_j	Trainable embeddings of user i and item j
$\mathcal{X}_i$	All events for user i
$\mathcal{X}_{i,t}$	All events for user i before time t
$e^{(\tau)}$	Event at step τ in a particular sequence
$\langle\cdot\rangle$	k-way inner product
$*$	Element-wise product
$f(\cdot)$	An arbitrary neural network

Table 2: Notation

machine learning perspective, we can split our tuple e into features x and label y such that $x = (i, j)$ and label $y = R$.

We could further re-frame the recommendation problem as predicting which video a user will watch at a given time by defining $x = (i, t)$ and $y = j$. Note, again, depending on if the label is categorical random value, e.g., video ID, or real value, e.g., rating, the machine learning problem is either a classification or regression problem, respectively.

In factorization models, all input values are considered to be discrete, and are embedded and multiplied. When we "embed" a discrete value, we learn a dense latent representation, e.g., user i is described by dense latent vector u_i and item j is described by dense latent vector v_j. In matrix factorization models, predictions are generally based on $u_i \cdot v_j$. In tensor factorization models, predictions are based on $\sum_r u_{i,r} v_{j,r} w_{t,r}$, where w_t would be a dense vector embedding of time or some other contextual feature. See factorization machines [34] for a clean and clear abstraction for these types of models. For notational simplicity we will consider $\langle\cdot\rangle$ to represent a multi-dimensional inner-product, i.e., $\langle u_i, v_j, w_t\rangle = \sum_r u_{i,r} v_{j,r} w_{t,r}$.

Neural networks typically also embed discrete inputs. That is, given an input (i, j) the input to the network will be $x = [u_i; v_j]$ where u_i and v_j are concatenated and as before are parameters that are trainable (in the case of neural networks, through back-propagation). Thus, we consider neural networks of the form $e_\ell = f(e_{\bar{\ell}})$, where the network takes all but one value of the tuple as the input and we train f to predict the last value of the tuple. We will later expand this definition to allow the model to take relevant previous events also as inputs to the network, as in sequence models.

4 MOTIVATION: CHALLENGES IN FIRST-ORDER DNN

In order to understand how neural recommenders make use of concatenated features, we begin by inspecting the typical building blocks of these networks. As alluded to above, neural networks, especially feed-forward DNNs, are often built on first-order operations. More precisely stated, neural networks often rely on matrix-vector products of the form Wh where W is a learned weight matrix and h is an input (either an input to the network, or the output of a previous layer). In feed-forward networks, fully-connected layers are generally of the form:

$$h_\tau = g(W_\tau h_{\tau-1} + b_\tau) \tag{1}$$

where g is an element-wise operation such as a sigmoid or ReLU, $h_{\tau-1}$ is the output of the last layer, and W_τ and b_τ are learned parameters. We consider this to be a first-order cell in that $h_{\tau-1}$, which is a k-dimensional vector, only has its different values added together, with weights based on W, but never multiplied together.

Although neural networks with layers like these have been shown to be able to approximate any function, their core computation is structurally significantly different from the past intuition on collaborative filtering. As described above, matrix factorization models take the general form $u_i \cdot v_j$, resulting in the model learning low-rank relationships between the different types of inputs, i.e., between users, items, time, etc. Given that low-rank models have been successful in recommender systems, we ask the following question: How well can neural networks with first-order cells model low-rank relations?

4.1 Modeling Low-Rank Relations

To test whether first-order neural networks can model low-rank relations, we generate synthetic low-rank data and study how well different size neural networks can fit that data. To be more precise, we consider an m-mode tensor where each dimension is of size N. For the mN discrete features we generate random vectors u_i of length r using a simple equation:

$$u_i \sim \mathcal{N}\left(0, \frac{1}{r^{1/2m}}\mathbf{I}\right) \tag{2}$$

The result is that our data is a rank r matrix or tensor with approximately the same scale (with mean of 0, and an empirical variance close to 1). As an example, with $m = 3$, we can use these embeddings to represent events of the form $(i, j, t, \langle u_i, u_j, u_t\rangle)$.

We try to fit models of different sizes using this data. In particular, we consider a model with the discrete features embedded and concatenated as inputs. The model has one hidden layer with ReLU

Hidden Layer	$r = 1, m = 2$	$r = 1, m = 3$	$r = 2, m = 3$
1	0.42601	0.27952	0.287817
2	0.601657	0.57222	0.472421
5	0.997436	0.854734	0.717233
10	0.999805	0.973214	0.805508
20	0.999938	0.996618	0.980821
30	0.999983	0.99931	0.975782
50	0.999993	0.999738	0.997821
100	0.999997	0.999928	0.99943

Table 3: Pearson correlation for different width models when fitting low-rank data.

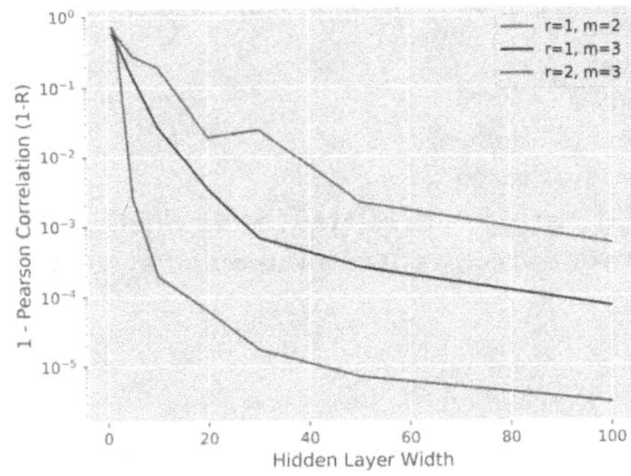

Figure 2: ReLU layers can learn to approximate low-rank relations, but are inefficient in doing so.

activation, as is common in neural recommender systems, followed by a final linear layer. The model is programmed in TensorFlow [1], trained with mean squared error loss (MSE) using the Adagrad optimizer [16], and trained to convergence. We measure and report the model's accuracy by the Pearson correlation (R) between the training data and the model's predictions. We use the Pearson correlation so that it is invariant to slight differences in variance of the data. We report the accuracy against the training data because we are testing how well these model structures fit low-rank patterns (i.e., not even whether they can generalize from it).

To model low-rank relations, we want to see how well the model can approximate individual multiplications, representing interaction between variables. All data is generated with $N = 100$. With $m = 2$, we examine how large the hidden layer must be to multiply two scalars, and with $m = 3$ we examine how large the hidden layer must be to multiply three scalars. We use $r \in \{1, 2\}$ to see how size of the model grows as more multiplications are needed. We embed each discrete feature as a 20-dimensional vector, much larger than r (but we found the model's accuracy to be independent of this size). We test with hidden layers $\in \{1, 2, 5, 10, 20, 30, 50\}$.

Empirical Findings. As can be seen in Table 3 and Figure 2, we find that the model continually approximates the data better as hidden layer size grows. Given the intuition that the network is approximating the multiplication, a wider network should give a better approximation. Second, we observe that, as we increase the rank r of the data from 1 to 2, we see the hidden layer size approximately doubles to get the same accuracy. This too matches our intuition, as increasing r means there are more interactions to add—something the network can easily do exactly.

More interestingly, we find that even for $r = 1$ and $m = 2$, it takes a hidden layer of size 5 to get a "high" accuracy estimate. Considering collaborative filtering models will often discover rank 200 relations [28], this intuitively suggests that real world models would require very wide layers for a single two-way relation to be learned.

Additionally, we find that modeling more than 2-way relations increases the difficulty of approximating the relation. That is, when we go from $m = 2$ to $m = 3$ we find that the model goes from needing a width 5 hidden layer to a width 20 hidden layer to get an MSE of approximately 0.005 or a Pearson correlation of 0.99.

In summary, we observe that ReLU layers can approximate multiplicative interactions (crosses) but are quite inefficient in doing so. This motivates the need for models that can more easily express, and deal with, multiplicative relations. We now turn our attention to using an RNN as a baseline; this is a stronger baseline in that it can better express multiplicative relations compared to feed-forward DNNs.

5 YOUTUBE'S RECURRENT RECOMMENDER

With the above analysis as motivation, we now describe the improvements to YouTube's RNN recommender system. RNNs are notable as a baseline model because they are already second-order neural networks, significantly more complex than the first-order models explored above, and are at the cutting edge of dynamic recommender systems.

We begin with an overview of the RNN recommender we built for YouTube and then in Section 6 describe how we improve it to better make use of contextual data.

5.1 Formal Description

In our setting, we observe events of the form user i has watched video j (uploaded by user $\psi(j)$) at time t. (We will later introduce additional contextual features.) In order to model the evolution of user preferences and behavior, we use a recurrent neural network (RNN) model, where the input to the model is the set of events for user $\mathcal{X}_i = \{e = (i, j, \psi(j), t) \in \mathcal{E} | e_0 = i\}$. We will use $\mathcal{X}_{i,t}$ to denote all watches before t for user $\mathcal{X}_i$:

$$\mathcal{X}_{i,t} = \{e = (i, j, t) \in \mathcal{E} | e_0 = i \wedge e_3 < t\} \subset \mathcal{X}_i. \quad (3)$$

The model is trained to produce sequential prediction $\Pr(j|i, t, \mathcal{X}_{i,t})$, i.e., the video j that user i will watch at a given time t based on all watches before t. For the sake of simplicity, we will use $e^{(\tau)}$ to denote the τth event in the sequence, $x^{(\tau)}$ to denote the transformed input for $e^{(\tau)}$, and $y^{(\tau)}$ to denote the label trying to be predicted for the τth event. In the example above, if $e^{(\tau)} = (i, j, \psi(j), t)$ and $e^{(\tau+1)} = (i, j', \psi(j'), t')$ then the input $x^{(\tau)} = [v_j; u_{\psi(j)}; w_t]$, which is used to predict $y^{(\tau+1)} = j'$, where v_j is the video embedding, $u_{\psi(j)}$ is the uploader embedding, and w_t is the context embedding.

When predicting $y^{(\tau)}$, we of course cannot use the label of the corresponding event $e^{(\tau)}$ as an input, but we can use context from $e^{(\tau)}$, which we will denote by $c^{(\tau)}$, e.g., $c^{(\tau)} = [w_t]$.

5.2 Structure of the Baseline RNN Model

A diagram of our RNN model can be seen in Figure 1, and described below. Recurrent neural networks model a sequence of actions. With each event $e^{(\tau)}$, the model takes a step forward, processing $x^{(\tau)}$ and updating a hidden state vector $z^{(\tau-1)}$. To be more precise, each event is first processed by a neural network $h_0^{(\tau)} = f_i(x^{(\tau)})$. In our setting, this will either be an identity function or fully-connected ReLU layers.

The recurrent part of the network is a function $h_1^{(\tau)}, z^{(\tau)} = f_r(h_0^{(\tau)}, z^{(\tau-1)})$. That is, we use a recurrent cell, such as an LSTM [23] or GRU [10], that takes as an input the state from the previous step and the transformed input $f_i(x^{(\tau)})$.

To predict $y^{(\tau)}$, we use $f_o(h_1^{(\tau-1)}, c^{(\tau)})$, which is another trainable neural network that produces a probability distribution over possible values of $y^{(\tau)}$. In our setting, this network takes the output of the RNN as its input and context of the upcoming prediction, and finally ends with a softmax layer over all videos. This network can include multiple fully-connected layers.

5.3 Context Features

Core to the success of this model is the incorporation of contextual data beyond just the sequence of videos watched. We discuss below how we utilize these features.

TimeDelta. In our system, incorporating time effectively was highly valuable to the accuracy of our RNN. Historically, time context has been incorporated into collaborative filtering models in a variety of ways. Here we use an approach we call *timedelta*:

$$\Delta t^{(\tau)} = \log\left(t^{(\tau+1)} - t^{(\tau)}\right) \tag{4}$$

That is, when considering event $e^{(\tau)}$ we consider how long until the next event or prediction to be made. This is essentially equivalent to time representation described in [25] and [49].

Software Client. YouTube videos can be watched on a variety of devices: in browser, iOS, Android, Roku, Chromecast, etc. Treating these contexts as equivalent misses relevant correlations. For example, users are probably less likely to watch a full-length feature film on their phone than through a Roku device. Similarly, short videos like trailers may be relatively more likely to be watched on a phone. Modeling the software client, and in particular how it interacts with the watch decisions, is important.

Page. We also record where a watch initiated from in our system. For example, we distinguish between watches that starts from the homepage (i.e. Home Page Watches) and watches that initiate as recommended follow-up watches once a user is already watching a video (i.e. Watch Next Watches). This is important as watches from the homepage may be more open to new content, whereas watches following a previous watch may be due to users wanting to dig into a topic more deeply.

Pre- and Post-Fusion. We can use these context features, which we collectively refer to as $c^{(\tau)}$, as direct inputs in two ways. As can be seen in Figure 1, we can include context as an input at the bottom of the network, or concatenated with the output of the RNN cell. We refer to the inclusion of context features before the RNN as pre-fusion, and the inclusion of context features after the RNN cell as post-fusion [12]. Although possibly a subtle point, this decision can have a significant effect on the RNN. In particular, by including a feature through pre-fusion, that feature will affect the prediction through how it modifies the state of the RNN. However, by including a feature through post-fusion, that feature can more directly have an effect on the prediction at that step.

To manage this, when predicting $y^{(\tau)}$, we generally use $c^{(\tau)}$ as a post-fusion feature, and use $c^{(\tau-1)}$ as a pre-fusion feature. This means that $c^{(\tau-1)}$ will effect the RNN state but $c^{(\tau)}$ will be used for predicting $y^{(\tau)}$. Subsequently, at the next step when predicting $y^{(\tau+1)}$, $c^{(\tau)}$ will now be a pre-fusion feature effecting the state of the RNN from that time forward.

5.4 Implementation & Training

Our model is implemented in TensorFlow [1] and trained over many distributed workers and parameter servers. The training uses one of the available back-propagated mini-batch stochastic gradient descent algorithms, either Adagrad [16] or ADAM [26]. During training we use as supervision the 100 most recent watches during the period $(t_0 - 7 \text{ days}, t_0]$, where t_0 is the time of training. This generally prioritizes recent watches because the behavior is more similar to the prediction task when the learned model will be applied to live traffic.

Due to the large number of videos available, we limit our set of possible videos to predict as well as the number of uploaders of those videos that we model. In the experiments below, these sets range in size from 500,000 to 2,000,000. The softmax layer, which covers this set of candidate videos, is trained using sampled softmax with 20,000 negative samples per batch. We use the predictions of this sampled softmax in the cross entropy loss against all labels.

6 CONTEXT MODELING WITH THE LATENT CROSS

As should be clear in the above description of our baseline model, the use of contextual features is typically done as concatenated inputs to simple fully-connected layers. However, as we explained in Section 4, neural networks are inefficient in modeling the interactions between concatenated input features. Here we propose a simple alternative.

6.1 Single Feature

We begin with the case where we have a single context feature that we want to include. For sake of clarity, we will use time as an example context feature. Rather than incorporating the feature as another input concatenated with the other relevant features, we perform an element-wise product in the middle of the network. That is, we perform:

$$h_0^{(\tau)} = (1 + w_t) * h_0^{(\tau)} \tag{5}$$

where we initialize w_t by a 0-mean Gaussian (note, $w = \mathbf{0}$ is an identity). This can be interpreted as the context providing a mask or attention mechanism over the hidden state. However, it also enables low-rank relations between the input previous watch and the time. Note, we can also apply this operation after the RNN:

$$h_1^{(\tau)} = (1 + w_t) * h_1^{(\tau)}. \tag{6}$$

The technique offered in [27] can be viewed as a special case where multiplicative relations are included at the very top of the network along with the softmax function to improve NLP tasks. In that case, this operation can be perceived as a tensor factorization where the embedding for one modality is produced by a neural network.

6.2 Using Multiple Features

In many cases we have more than one contextual feature that we want to include. When including multiple contextual features, say time t and device d, we perform:

$$h^{(\tau)} = (1 + w_t + w_d) * h^{(\tau)} \tag{7}$$

We use this form for a few different reasons: (1) By initializing both w_t and w_d by 0-mean Gaussians, the multiplicative term has a mean of 1 and thus can similarly act as a mask/attention mechanism over the hidden state. (2) By adding these terms together we can capture 2-way relations between the hidden state and each context feature. This follows the perspective taken in the design of factorization machines [34]. (3) Using a simple additive function is easy to train. A more complex function like $w_t * w_d * h^{(\tau)}$ will increase the non-convexity significantly with each additional contextual feature. Similarly we found learning a function $f([w_t; w_d])$ to be more difficult to train and to give worse results. An overview of including these features in a model can be seen in Figure 1.

Efficiency. We note that one significant benefit of using latent crosses is their simplicity and computational efficiency. With N context features and d-dimensional embeddings, the latent cross can be computed in $O(Nd)$ and does not increase the width of the subsequent layers.

7 EXPERIMENTS

We perform two sets of experiments. The first is on a restricted dataset where time is the only contextual feature, and we compare several model families. In the second set of experiments we use our production model and explore the relative improvements based on how we incorporate context features.

7.1 Comparative Analysis

7.1.1 Setup. We begin with an explanation of our experimental setup.

Dataset and Metrics. We use a dataset with sequences of watches for hundreds of millions users. The users are split into training, validation and test sets, with both validation and test sets having tens of millions of users. Watches are restricted to a set of 500,000 popular videos, and all users have at least 50 watches in their sequence. The sequence is given by a list of watched videos and the timestamp of each watch.

Method	Precision@1	MAP@20
RNN with Δt Latent Cross	**0.1621**	**0.0828**
RRN (Concatenated Δt)	0.1465	0.0753
RNN (Plain, no time)	0.1345	0.0724
Bag Of Words	0.1250	0.0707
Bag of Words with time	0.1550	0.0794
Paragraph Vectors	0.1123	0.0642
Cowatch	0.1204	0.0621

Table 4: Results for Comparative Study: RNN with a latent cross performs the best.

The task is to predict the last 5 watches in the user's sequence. To measure this, we use Mean-Average-Precision-at-k (MAP@k) for $k = 1$ and $k = 20$ on the test set.

Model. For this set of experiments we use an RNN with an LSTM recurrent unit. We have no ReLU cells before or after the recurrent unit, and use a pre-determined hierarchical softmax (HSM) to predict the videos. Here, we use all but the first watch in the sequence as supervision during training. The model is trained using back-propagation with ADAM [26].

Since time is the only contextual feature in this data set, we use the video embedding v_j as the input and perform the latent cross with the timedelta value $w_{\Delta t}$ such that the LSTM is given $v_j * w_{\Delta t}$. This is an example of a pre-fusion cross. We will call this RNNLatentCross.

Baselines. We compare the RNNLatentCross model described above to highly tuned models of alternative forms:

- RRN: Use $[v_j; w_{\Delta t}]$ as the input to the RNN; similar to [43] and [41].
- RNN: RNN directly over v_j (without time); similar to [21].
- BOW: Bag of words model over the set of videos in the user's history and user demographics.
- BOW+Time: 3-layer feed-forward model taking as input a concatenation of a bag-of-watches, each of the last three videos watched, Δt, and the time of the week of the request. The model is trained with a softmax over the 50 videos most co-watched with the last watch.
- Paragraph Vector (PV): Use [13] to learn unsupervised embeddings of each user (based on user demographics and previous watches). Use the learned embeddings as well as an embedding of the last watch as input to a 1-layer feed forward classifier trained with sampled softmax.
- Cowatch: Predict the most common co-watched videos based on the last watch in the sequence.

Unless otherwise specified, all models have a hierarchical softmax. All models and their hyperparameters are tuned over the course of a modeling competition. Note, only BagOfWords and Paragraph Vector make use of user demographic data.

7.1.2 Results. We report our results for this experiment in Table 4. As can be seen there, our model, using the RNN with Δt having a latent cross with the watch, gives the best result for both Precision@1 and MAP@20. Possibly even more interestingly, is the relative performance of the models. We observe in both the bag of words models and the RNN models the critical importance of modeling time. Further, observe that the improvement from performing a latent cross instead of just concatenating Δt is *greater* than the improvement from including Δt as an input feature at all.

7.2 YouTube's Model

Second, we study multiple variants of our production model against a larger, more unrestricted dataset.

7.2.1 Setup. Here, we use a production dataset of user watches, which is less restrictive than the above setting. Our sequences are composed of the video that was watched and who created the video (uploader). We use a larger vocabulary on the order of millions of recently popular uploaded videos and uploaders.

We split the dataset into a training and test set based jointly on users and time. First, we split users into two sets: 90% of our users are in our training set and 10% in our test set. Second, to split by time, we select a time cut-off t_0 and during training only consider watches from before t_0. During testing, we consider watches from after t_0 + 4 hours. Similarly, the vocabulary of videos is based on data from before t_0.

Our model consists of embedding and concatenating all of the features defined above as inputs, followed by a 256-dimensional ReLU layer, a 256-dimensional GRU cell, and then another 256-dimensional ReLU layer, before being fed into the softmax layer. As described previously, we use the 100 most recent watches during the period $(t_0 - 7 \text{ days}, t_0]$ as supervision. Here, we train using the Adagrad optimizer [16] over many workers and parameter servers.

To test our model, we again measure the mean-average-precision-at-k. For watches that are not in our vocabulary, we always mark the prediction as incorrect. The evaluation MAP@k scores reported here are measured using approximately 45,000 watches.

7.2.2 The Value of Page as Context. We begin analyzing the accuracy improvements by incorporating Page in different ways. In particular, we compare not using Page, using Page as an input concatenated with the other inputs, and performing a post-fusion latent cross with Page. (Note, when we include page as a concatenated feature, it is concatenated during both pre-fusion and post-fusion.)

As can be seen in Figure 3, using Page with a latent cross offers the best accuracy. Additionally, we see that using both the latent cross and the concatenated input offers no additional improvement in accuracy, suggesting that the latent cross is sufficient to capture the relevant information that would be obtained through using the feature as a direct input.

7.2.3 Total Improvement. Last, we test how adding latent crosses on top of the full production model effects the accuracy. In this case, with each watch the model knows the page, the device type, the time, how long the video was watched for (watch time), how old the watch is (watch age), and the uploader. In particular, our baseline YouTube model uses the page, device, watch time, and timedelta values as pre-fusion concatenated features, and also uses the page, device, and watch age as post-fusion concatenated features.

We test including timedelta and page as pre-fusion latent crosses, as well as device type and page as post-fusion latent crosses. As can be seen in Figure 4, although all of these features were already included through concatenation, including them as latent crosses provides an improvement in accuracy over the baseline model. This also demonstrates the ability for pre-fusion and post-fusion with multiple features to work together and provide a strong accuracy improvement.

8 DISCUSSION

We explore below a number of questions raised by this work and implications for future work.

8.1 Discrete Relations in DNNs

While much of this paper has focused on enabling multiplicative interactions between features, we found that neural networks can also approximate discrete interactions, an area where factorization models have more difficulty. As an example, in [46] the authors find that modeling when user i performs action a on item j, $\langle u_{(i,a)}, v_j \rangle$ has better accuracy than $\langle u_i, v_j, w_a \rangle$. However, discovering that indexing users and actions together performs better is difficult, requiring data insights.

Similar to the experiments in Section 4, we generate synthetic data following the pattern $X_{i,j,a} = \langle u_{(i,a)}, v_j \rangle$ and test how well different network architectures predict $X_{i,j,a}$ given i, j and a are only concatenated as independent inputs. We initialize $u \in \mathbb{R}^{10000}$ and $v \in \mathbb{R}^{100}$ as vectors, such that X is a rank-1 matrix. We follow the same general experimental procedure as in Section 4, measuring the Pearson correlation (R) for networks with varying number of hidden layers and varying width to those hidden layers. (We train these networks with a learning rate of 0.01, ten-times smaller than the learning rate used above.) As a baseline, we also measure the Pearson correlation for tensor factorization ($\langle u_i, v_j, w_a \rangle$) for different ranks.

As can be seen in Figure 5, deep models, in some cases, attain a reasonably high Pearson correlation, suggesting that they are in fact able to approximate discrete crosses. Also interestingly, learning these crosses requires deep networks with wide hidden layers, particularly large for the size of the data. Additionally, we find that these networks are difficult to train.

These numbers are interesting relative to the baseline tensor factorization performance. We observe that the factorization models can approximate the data reasonably well, but requires relatively high rank. (Note, even if the underlying tensor is full rank, a factorization of rank 100 would suffice to describe it.) However, even at this high rank, the tensor factorization models require fewer parameters than the DNNs and are easier to train. Therefore, as with our results in Section 5, DNNs can approximate these patterns, but doing so can be difficult, and including low-rank interactions can help in providing easy-to-train approximations.

8.2 Second-Order DNNs

A natural question to ask when reading this paper is why not try much wider layers, make the model deeper, or more second-order units, like GRUs and LSTMs? All of these are reasonable modeling decisions, but in our experience make training of the model significantly more difficult. One of the strengths of this approach is that it is easy to implement and train, while still offering clear performance improvements, even when applied in conjunction with other second-order units like LSTMs and GRUs.

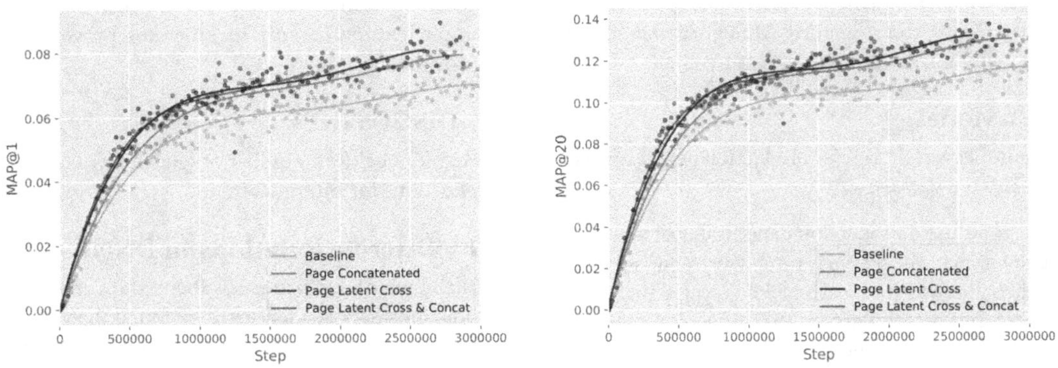

Figure 3: Accuracy from using page as either input or a latent cross feature (reported over training steps).

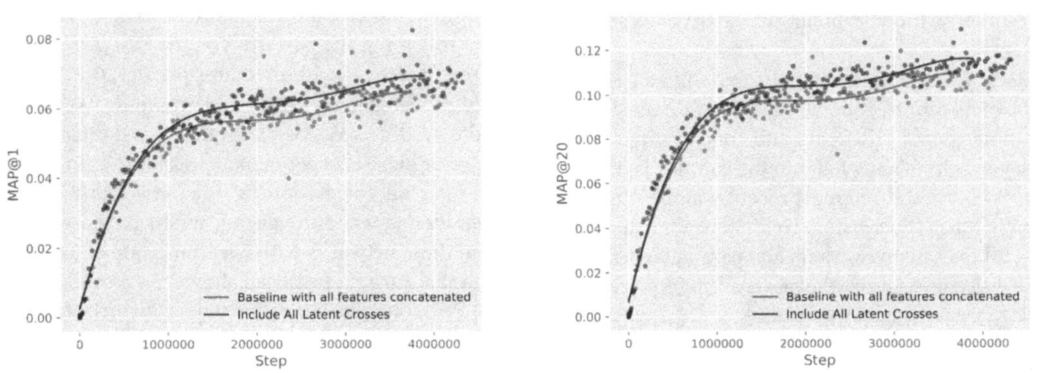

Figure 4: Accuracy from using all latent cross features against a baseline of using all possible concatenated input features.

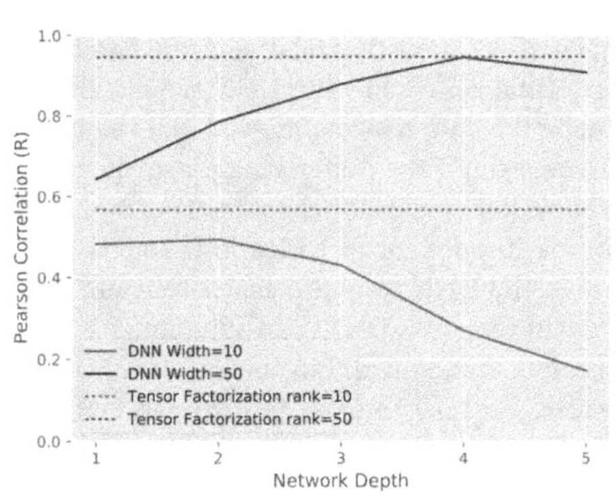

Figure 5: Sufficiently large DNNs can learn to approximate discrete interactions.

The growing trend throughout deep learning appears to be using more second-order interactions. For example, this is common in attention models and memory networks, as list above. While these are even more difficult to train, we believe this work shows the promise in that direction for neural recommender systems.

9 CONCLUSION

In this paper we have explored how to incorporate contextual data in a production recurrent recommender system at YouTube. In particular, this paper makes following contributions:

- **Challenges of First-Order DNNs:** We found feed-forward neural networks to be inefficient in modeling multiplicative relations (crosses) between features.
- **Production Model:** We offer a detailed description of our RNN-based recommender system used at YouTube.
- **Latent Cross:** We offer a simple technique for learning multiplicative relations in DNNs, including RNNs.
- **Empirical Results:** We demonstrate in multiple settings and with different context features that latent crosses improve recommendation accuracy, even on top of complex, state-of-the-art RNN recommenders.

REFERENCES

[1] Martín Abadi, Paul Barham, Jianmin Chen, Zhifeng Chen, Andy Davis, Jeffrey Dean, Matthieu Devin, Sanjay Ghemawat, Geoffrey Irving, Michael Isard, and others. 2016. TensorFlow: A system for large-scale machine learning. In *Proceedings of the 12th USENIX Symposium on Operating Systems Design and Implementation (OSDI). Savannah, Georgia, USA.*

[2] Amr Ahmed, Liangjie Hong, and Alexander J Smola. 2013. Hierarchical geographical modeling of user locations from social media posts. In *Proceedings of the 22nd international conference on World Wide Web (WWW).* ACM, 25–36.

[3] Dzmitry Bahdanau, Kyunghyun Cho, and Yoshua Bengio. 2014. Neural machine translation by jointly learning to align and translate. *arXiv preprint arXiv:1409.0473* (2014).

[4] James Bennett, Stan Lanning, and others. 2007. The netflix prize. In *Proceedings of KDD cup and workshop*, Vol. 2007. New York, NY, USA, 35.

[5] Alex Beutel, Ed H Chi, Zhiyuan Cheng, Hubert Pham, and John Anderson. 2017. Beyond Globally Optimal: Focused Learning for Improved Recommendations. In *Proceedings of the 26th International Conference on World Wide Web (WWW).* ACM.

[6] Pedro G Campos, Fernando Díez, and Iván Cantador. 2014. Time-aware recommender systems: a comprehensive survey and analysis of existing evaluation protocols. *User Modeling and User-Adapted Interaction* 24, 1-2 (2014), 67–119.

[7] Heng-Tze Cheng, Levent Koc, Jeremiah Harmsen, Tal Shaked, Tushar Chandra, Hrishi Aradhye, Glen Anderson, Greg Corrado, Wei Chai, Mustafa Ispir, and others. 2016. Wide & deep learning for recommender systems. In *Proceedings of the 1st Workshop on Deep Learning for Recommender Systems.* ACM, 7–10.

[8] Zhiyuan Cheng, James Caverlee, and Kyumin Lee. 2010. You are where you tweet: a content-based approach to geo-locating twitter users. In *Proceedings of the 19th ACM international conference on Information and knowledge management.* ACM, 759–768.

[9] Evangelia Christakopoulou and George Karypis. 2016. Local Item-Item Models For Top-N Recommendation. In *Proceedings of the 10th ACM Conference on Recommender Systems (RecSys).* ACM, 67–74.

[10] Junyoung Chung, Caglar Gülçehre, Kyunghyun Cho, and Yoshua Bengio. 2015. Gated Feedback Recurrent Neural Networks.. In *ICML.* 2067–2075.

[11] Paul Covington, Jay Adams, and Emre Sargin. 2016. Deep Neural Networks for YouTube Recommendations. In *Proceedings of the 10th ACM Conference on Recommender Systems (RecSys).* ACM, 191–198.

[12] Bin Cui, Anthony KH Tung, Ce Zhang, and Zhe Zhao. 2010. Multiple feature fusion for social media applications. In *Proceedings of the 2010 ACM SIGMOD International Conference on Management of data.* ACM, 435–446.

[13] Andrew M Dai, Christopher Olah, and Quoc V Le. 2015. Document embedding with paragraph vectors. *arXiv preprint arXiv:1507.07998* (2015).

[14] Yann N Dauphin, Angela Fan, Michael Auli, and David Grangier. 2016. Language modeling with gated convolutional networks. *arXiv preprint arXiv:1612.08083* (2016).

[15] Nan Du, Yichen Wang, Niao He, Jimeng Sun, and Le Song. 2015. Time-sensitive recommendation from recurrent user activities. In *Advances in Neural Information Processing Systems.* 3492–3500.

[16] John Duchi, Elad Hazan, and Yoram Singer. 2011. Adaptive subgradient methods for online learning and stochastic optimization. *Journal of Machine Learning Research* 12, Jul (2011), 2121–2159.

[17] Hancheng Ge, James Caverlee, and Haokai Lu. 2016. TAPER: A contextual tensor-based approach for personalized expert recommendation. (2016).

[18] Alex Graves. 2013. Generating sequences with recurrent neural networks. *arXiv preprint arXiv:1308.0850* (2013).

[19] Xiangnan He and Tat-Seng Chua. 2017. Neural Factorization Machines for Sparse Predictive Analytics. In *Proceedings of the 40th International ACM SIGIR Conference on Research and Development in Information Retrieval (SIGIR '17).* ACM, New York, NY, USA, 355–364. DOI: https://doi.org/10.1145/3077136.3080777

[20] Xiangnan He, Lizi Liao, Hanwang Zhang, Liqiang Nie, Xia Hu, and Tat-Seng Chua. 2017. Neural collaborative filtering. In *Proceedings of the 26th International Conference on World Wide Web.* International World Wide Web Conferences Steering Committee, 173–182.

[21] Balázs Hidasi, Alexandros Karatzoglou, Linas Baltrunas, and Domonkos Tikk. 2015. Session-based recommendations with recurrent neural networks. *arXiv preprint arXiv:1511.06939* (2015).

[22] Balázs Hidasi and Domonkos Tikk. 2016. General factorization framework for context-aware recommendations. *Data Mining and Knowledge Discovery* 30, 2 (2016), 342–371.

[23] Sepp Hochreiter and Jürgen Schmidhuber. 1997. Long short-term memory. *Neural computation* 9, 8 (1997), 1735–1780.

[24] Yifan Hu, Yehuda Koren, and Chris Volinsky. 2008. Collaborative filtering for implicit feedback datasets. In *ICDM.*

[25] How Jing and Alexander J. Smola. 2017. Neural Survival Recommender. In *Proceedings of the Tenth ACM International Conference on Web Search and Data Mining (WSDM).* 515–524.

[26] Diederik Kingma and Jimmy Ba. 2014. Adam: A method for stochastic optimization. *arXiv preprint arXiv:1412.6980* (2014).

[27] Ryan Kiros, Richard Zemel, and Ruslan R Salakhutdinov. 2014. A multiplicative model for learning distributed text-based attribute representations. In *Advances in neural information processing systems.* 2348–2356.

[28] Yehuda Koren. 2008. Factorization meets the neighborhood: a multifaceted collaborative filtering model. In *KDD.* ACM, 426–434.

[29] Yehuda Koren. 2010. Collaborative filtering with temporal dynamics. *Commun. ACM* 53, 4 (2010), 89–97.

[30] Yehuda Koren, Robert Bell, and Chris Volinsky. 2009. Matrix Factorization Techniques for Recommender Systems. *Computer* 42, 8 (Aug. 2009), 30–37. DOI: https://doi.org/10.1109/MC.2009.263

[31] Joonseok Lee, Seungyeon Kim, Guy Lebanon, and Yoram Singer. 2013. Local Low-Rank Matrix Approximation. In *Proceedings of the 30th International Conference on Machine Learning (ICML).* 82–90. http://jmlr.org/proceedings/papers/v28/lee13.html

[32] Haokai Lu and James Caverlee. 2015. Exploiting geo-spatial preference for personalized expert recommendation. In *Proceedings of the 9th ACM Conference on Recommender Systems (RecSys).* ACM, 67–74.

[33] Yanru Qu, Han Cai, Kan Ren, Weinan Zhang, Yong Yu, Ying Wen, and Jun Wang. 2016. Product-based neural networks for user response prediction. In *Data Mining (ICDM), 2016 IEEE 16th International Conference on.* IEEE, 1149–1154.

[34] Steffen Rendle. 2012. Factorization Machines with libFM. *ACM TIST* 3, 3, Article 57 (May 2012), 22 pages.

[35] Ruslan Salakhutdinov and Andriy Mnih. 2008. Bayesian probabilistic matrix factorization using Markov chain Monte Carlo. In *ICML.* ACM, 880–887.

[36] Suvash Sedhain, Aditya Krishna Menon, Scott Sanner, and Lexing Xie. 2015. Autorec: Autoencoders meet collaborative filtering. In *Proceedings of the 24th International Conference on World Wide Web (WWW).* ACM, 111–112.

[37] Yue Shi, Alexandros Karatzoglou, Linas Baltrunas, Martha Larson, Alan Hanjalic, and Nuria Oliver. 2012. TFMAP: optimizing MAP for top-n context-aware recommendation. In *Proceedings of the 35th international ACM SIGIR conference on Research and development in information retrieval.* ACM, 155–164.

[38] Sainbayar Sukhbaatar, Jason Weston, Rob Fergus, and others. 2015. End-to-end memory networks. In *Advances in neural information processing systems.* 2440–2448.

[39] Yong Kiam Tan, Xinxing Xu, and Yong Liu. 2016. Improved recurrent neural networks for session-based recommendations. In *Proceedings of the 1st Workshop on Deep Learning for Recommender Systems.* ACM, 17–22.

[40] Duyu Tang, Bing Qin, Ting Liu, and Yuekui Yang. 2015. User Modeling with Neural Network for Review Rating Prediction.. In *IJCAI.* 1340–1346.

[41] Bartlomiej Twardowski. 2016. Modelling Contextual Information in Session-Aware Recommender Systems with Neural Networks.. In *RecSys.* 273–276.

[42] Manasi Vartak, Hugo Larochelle, and Arvind Thiagarajan. 2017. A Meta-Learning Perspective on Cold-Start Recommendations for Items. In *Advances in Neural Information Processing Systems.* 6888–6898.

[43] Chao-Yuan Wu, Amr Ahmed, Alex Beutel, Alexander J. Smola, and How Jing. 2017. Recurrent Recommender Networks. In *Proceedings of the Tenth ACM International Conference on Web Search and Data Mining (WSDM).* 495–503.

[44] Yuhuai Wu, Saizheng Zhang, Ying Zhang, Yoshua Bengio, and Ruslan R Salakhutdinov. 2016. On multiplicative integration with recurrent neural networks. In *Advances in Neural Information Processing Systems.* 2856–2864.

[45] Chunfeng Yang, Huan Yan, Donghan Yu, Yong Li, and Dah Ming Chiu. 2017. Multi-site User Behavior Modeling and Its Application in Video Recommendation. In *Proceedings of the 40th International ACM SIGIR Conference on Research and Development in Information Retrieval.* ACM, 175–184.

[46] Zhe Zhao, Zhiyuan Cheng, Lichan Hong, and Ed H Chi. 2015. Improving User Topic Interest Profiles by Behavior Factorization. In *Proceedings of the 24th International Conference on World Wide Web (WWW).* 1406–1416.

[47] Lei Zheng, Vahid Noroozi, and Philip S Yu. 2017. Joint deep modeling of users and items using reviews for recommendation. In *Proceedings of the Tenth ACM International Conference on Web Search and Data Mining (WSDM).* ACM, 425–434.

[48] Yong Zheng, Bamshad Mobasher, and Robin Burke. 2014. CSLIM: Contextual SLIM recommendation algorithms. In *Proceedings of the 8th ACM Conference on Recommender Systems.* ACM, 301–304.

[49] Yu Zhu, Hao Li, Yikang Liao, Beidou Wang, Ziyu Guan, Haifeng Liu, and Deng Cai. 2017. What to Do Next: Modeling User Behaviors by Time-LSTM. In *Proceedings of the Twenty-Sixth International Joint Conference on Artificial Intelligence, IJCAI-17.* 3602–3608. DOI: https://doi.org/10.24963/ijcai.2017/504

Consistent Transformation of Ratio Metrics for Efficient Online Controlled Experiments

Roman Budylin
Yandex; Moscow, Russia
budylin@yandex-team.ru

Alexey Drutsa
Yandex & MSU; Moscow, Russia
adrutsa@yandex.ru

Ilya Katsev
Yandex; Moscow, Russia
bromozel@yandex-team.ru

Valeriya Tsoy
Yandex; Moscow, Russia
leratsoy@yandex-team.ru

ABSTRACT

We study ratio overall evaluation criteria (user behavior quality metrics) and, in particular, average values of non-user level metrics, that are widely used in A/B testing as an important part of modern Internet companies' evaluation instruments (e.g., abandonment rate, a user's absence time after a session). We focus on the problem of sensitivity improvement of these criteria, since there is a large gap between the variety of sensitivity improvement techniques designed for user level metrics and the variety of such techniques for ratio criteria. We propose a novel transformation of a ratio criterion to the average value of a user level (randomization-unit level, in general) metric that creates an opportunity to directly use a wide range of sensitivity improvement techniques designed for the user level that make A/B tests more *efficient*. We provide theoretical guarantees on the novel metric's *consistency* in terms of preservation of two crucial properties (*directionality* and *significance level*) w.r.t. the source ratio criteria. The experimental evaluation of the approach is done on hundreds large-scale real A/B tests run at one of the most popular global search engines, reinforces the theoretical results, and demonstrates up to +34% of sensitivity rate improvement achieved by the transformation combined with the best known regression adjustment.

KEYWORDS

linearization; online controlled experiment; A/B test; non-user level metric; ratio OEC; delta method; sensitivity; directionality

ACM Reference Format:
Roman Budylin, Alexey Drutsa, Ilya Katsev, and Valeriya Tsoy. 2018. Consistent Transformation of Ratio Metrics for Efficient Online Controlled Experiments. In *WSDM 2018: WSDM 2018: The Eleventh ACM International Conference on Web Search and Data Mining , February 5–9, 2018, Marina Del Rey, CA, USA.* ACM, New York, NY, USA, 9 pages. https://doi.org/10.1145/3159652.3159699

WSDM 2018, February 5–9, 2018, Marina Del Rey, CA, USA

ACM ISBN 978-1-4503-5581-0/18/02...$15.00
https://doi.org/10.1145/3159652.3159699

1 INTRODUCTION

A/B testing (i.e., online controlled experiments) is accepted as the state-of-the-art technique that is widely used to improve web services (e.g., search engines [11, 19, 21, 25], social networks [2, 41], media providers [40], etc.) based on data-driven decisions [6, 27, 39] in permanent manner and on a large scale, which grew considerably over the last years (e.g., reportedly, from 200 run experiments per day in 2013 [26] to more than 1000 in 2015 [19]). An A/B test compares two variants of a service at a time, usually its current version (control) and a new one (treatment), by exposing them to two groups of users. The goal of this experiment is to detect the causal (treatment) effect of the service update on its performance in terms of an *Overall Evaluation Criterion (OEC)* [29], a user behavior metric that is assumed to correlate with the quality of the service.

First, alignment of the sign of the treatment effect detected by an OEC with positive/negative impact of the treatment on user experience (the *directionality* property) allows analysts to be confident in their conclusions about the change in the system's quality, particularly, about the sign and magnitude of that change [6, 13, 32]. Second, when the treatment effect exists, the OEC has to detect the difference of the two versions of the service at a high level of statistical significance in order to distinguish the treatment effect from the noise observed when the effect does not exist (the *sensitivity* property) [29, 34]. A more sensitive OEC allows analysts to make decisions in more A/B tests with small magnitude of the treatment effect or, alternatively, use less user traffic to achieve a desired level of confidence, optimizing thus resources consumed by the experimentation platform [21–23, 27]. Leading industrial Internet companies permanently upgrade their OECs [8, 21, 27, 34] requiring both preservation of directionality and improvement of sensitivity, which is a challenging goal [6, 25, 32, 34].

In the current study, we focus, *first*, on a non-user level metric (e.g., the absence time of a user after a session [15]) when the randomization remains on the user level, while *the key metric*[1] is calculated for entities (events, a.k.a. analysis units [5]) related to a user[2]. The corresponding OEC is the average value over the metric's values (e.g., the average absence time per session [14]). Since these values are dependent (e.g., the values for sessions of the same user), the state-of-the-art t-test could not be applied to correctly measure

[1] Usually, an OEC is an aggregation of some key metric over entities (events, etc.).
[2] More generally, we consider the case when the analysis unit (i.e., the one for which the value of the key metric is calculated) is not the randomization unit [5], but since the common randomization unit is a user [2, 4, 27], for simplicity, we further use the term "user", assuming that it could be replaced by another randomization unit.

the statistical significance[3], which makes the work with this metric more complicated than with user level ones. The considered OEC is a particular case of a more general class of evaluation criteria that are ratios of the average values (or, equivalently, the sum values) of two user level metrics: for instance, the ratio of the total number of clicks to the total number of queries, i.e., the total CTR. Such ratio OECs represent thus *the second focus* of our study.

In order to detect the treatment effect in these ratio OECs, a computationally expensive statistical significance test based on Bootstrapping technique [16] is usually applied [2, 4, 14, 27]. An alternative approach is to replace the standard t-statistic's variance estimation by a more accurate one obtained via the Delta method [5, 7, 18]. This makes difficult to apply a wide range of state-of-the-art and recently proposed sensitivity improvement techniques [7, 11, 21, 34] since they rely on t-statistic (z-score) as a measure of sensitivity and mostly were thus developed for user level metrics. Of course, some of these techniques may be adapted for non-user level metrics and ratio OECs by means of the Delta method, but such an adaptation should be done individually for each technique and is able to make it too complicated[4]. Thus, there is a large gap between the variety of sensitivity improvement techniques for user level metrics and the variety of such techniques for non-user level metrics (ratio OECs, in general), while the latter ones represent an important part of web service evaluation instruments.

In contrast to the above mentioned approaches with statistical tests and sophisticated variance estimations aimed to make applicable ratio OECs, *the primary research goal of our study* is to find a transformation of a ratio OEC to a new OEC that (a) will be the average value of some new *user level metric* and (b) will be *consistent* with the source ratio OEC in terms of directionality and sensitivity. This should pave the way for direct application of known sensitivity improvement techniques developed for user level metrics to the transformed one, removing thus the identified gap between user level metrics and non-user ones. Note that there is a naive straightforward approach to construct a user level metric from a ratio OEC: calculate the ratio (which constitutes the source OEC) for each user individually[5] and consider the average value of this individual ratio over users as a new OEC. But, it is well known and shown experimentally that the OEC obtained in such a way will not preserve both directionality and sensitivity of the ratio OEC [14].

In our work, we propose a novel transformation, referred to as *linearization*, that provides a user level metric which is a special linear combination of the metrics that constitute the numerator and denominator of the ratio OEC. Under some mild assumptions, we prove that the novel OEC (the average value of the transformed user level metric): first, *preserves* both *directionality* and even the magnitude (scaled up to a nearly constant factor) of the treatment effect of the source ratio OEC; second, when used with the state-of-the-art t-test, has the achieved significance level that asymptotically equals to the one of the ratio OEC (*sensitivity preservation*). Hence, we are able to improve sensitivity of the novel OEC (e.g., by means of a regression adjustment with a linear model [7, 17] or boosted decision trees [34], a linear combination with other user level metrics [21], etc.) or, equivalently, use less data (reduce user traffic or duration of an A/B test) to achieve the same level of confidence in comparison with the source ratio OEC.

We reinforce our theoretical results by conducting experimental evaluation of our novel approach by applying it to five user engagement and satisfaction metrics [10, 12, 14, 25, 35, 36], since the ones of them that represent user loyalty (e.g., *absence time* [15]) are accepted as good predictors of long-term success of a web service [25, 27, 36] and their sensitivity improvement is a quite important and challenging task [26, 27, 34]. Additionally, we apply the best known regression adjustment based on boosted decision trees [34] to the linearized variants of the metrics and show that our approach in combination with sensitivity improvement techniques (designed for the user level) is able to detect the treatment effect in up to +34% more A/B experiments than the source OEC. In our analysis of the studied metrics, we use 390 large-scale A/B tests run on hundreds of thousands of real users of Yandex (www.yandex.com).

Summarizing, our paper focuses on the problem, which is accepted as fundamental for the *present and emerging Internet companies' needs*: to develop more sensitive A/B test metrics with a clear directional interpretation that allow to make confident data-driven decisions faster and based on less data. Specifically, the major contributions of our study include:

- A novel approach to transform a ratio OEC to the average value of a user level (randomization-unit level, in general) metric that, to the best of our knowledge, was never used in A/B testing and creates an opportunity to directly utilize a wide range of sensitivity improvement techniques designed for user level metrics and to boost thus A/B tests' efficiency.
- Theoretical guarantees on the consistency of the novel OEC with the source ratio OEC in terms of preservation of directionality and sensitivity.
- Validation of our novel approach on the basis of 5 state-of-the-art metrics of user engagement and satisfaction by means of 390 large-scale real A/B experiment run at Yandex, one of the most popular global search engines, showing, first, that the theoretically guaranteed consistency holds in practice and, second, sensitivity improvement, when our approach is combined with the best known user level regression adjustment (up to +34% more A/B tests with detected treatment effects w.r.t. the source ratio OEC).

2 RELATED WORK

Studies on A/B testing were devoted to both its theoretical aspects [28, 29, 33] and various aspects of its application in Internet companies: large-scale experimental infrastructure [22, 26, 39, 42]; evaluation of changes in various components of web services (e.g., the user interface [10, 12, 24, 32], ranking algorithms [10, 12, 32, 38], ad auctions [3], and mobile apps [41]); different facets of user experience with a web service (speed [27, 30], absence [15], abandonment [27], periodicity [9, 10, 12, 13], engagement [9–11, 14], switching to an alternative service [1], etc.). The trustworthiness

[3]It is experimentally demonstrated that utilization of Student's t-test for non-user level metrics leads to an underestimate of the false-positive rate [14, 39].

[4]For instance, Deng et al. [7] derived a closed-form solution to the linear regression adjustment of a ratio OECs by means of the Delta method. However, application of more advanced machine learned regression adjustments [34] will not be straightforward as the optimization objective obtained via the Delta method will be drastically more complex than the standard mean square error (MSE) as in [34].

[5]For instance, given a user, it is the number of *his* clicks divided by the number of *his* queries when the considered source ratio OEC is the total CTR.

of A/B test results was studied through several "rules of thumb", pitfalls, and puzzling outcomes [4–6, 25, 27]. Studies focused on the problem of sensitivity improvement, first, considered alterations of both the user groups involved in an A/B test [29, 38] and the experiment duration [11, 29]; a search for more sensitive modifications of metrics and OECs [13, 14, 27] (without a change of the analysis unit); utilization of special statistical tests (e.g., the optimal distribution decomposition approach [32] sequential testing for early stopping [23], etc.). The second group of studies proposed techniques that improve sensitivity through utilization of more data on user behavior (e.g., from the period before the experiment [7, 34] and from the experiment period by learning a linear combination of metrics [21] or by predicting a future metric value [11]).

The studies [2, 4, 5, 14, 15, 27, 39] that considered ratio OECs (and in particular, non-user level key metrics) are relevant to ours, but they were concentrated on correct calculations of statistical significance either by Bootstrapping [2, 4, 14, 27] or by accurate estimations of an OEC's variance through the Delta method [5, 7, 18] and similar techniques [5]. In contrast, we target to build a user level metric whose average value preserves sensitivity and directionality of the source ratio OEC, which, to the best of our knowledge, has not been studied. Deng et al. showed how to adapt their sensitivity improvement technique [7] to non-user level metrics. A similar adaptation may be done for other techniques, but may result in individual issues (e.g., complication of optimization objectives in [21, 34]), while our approach solves the problem of the techniques' adaptation universally since it allows to directly (without modifications) apply sensitivity improvement methods designed for user level metrics (e.g. [7, 11, 21, 34]). In our experimentation, we consider 4 non-user level engagement metrics studied in [14] and apply the sensitivity improvement technique (designed for the user level) from the study [34] as the demonstration of the profit that can be achieved through our approach, while the other known user level techniques (e.g., [7, 11, 21]) could be utilized as well.

3 PRELIMINARIES

3.1 A/B testing methodology

A typical A/B test (also known as a randomized experiment or online controlled experiment) [18, 25, 27, 29, 31] compares the performance of a new variant B (*the treatment*) of a web service and the current production variant A (*the control*) by means of randomly exposition (assignment) of users, participated in the experiment, (a user set $\mathcal{U}$) to one of the two variants of the service (i.e., $\mathcal{U} = \mathcal{U}_A \sqcup \mathcal{U}_B$). The difference between the variants is quantitatively measured by an *Overall Evaluation Criterion* $\mathfrak{C}$ (*OEC*, also known as the evaluation metric, the online service quality metric, etc. [29]), which quantifies user behavior. In the classical methodology of A/B testing, this OEC is usually an *evaluation statistic* (e.g., *the average value*) of a *key metric* $\mathsf{m}(\omega)$ over the events (entities) $\omega \in \Omega$, referred to as *analysis units* [5, 39]. More precisely, for each user group $\mathcal{U}_V, V = A, B$, we have the observations of the metric m over the analysis units Ω_V. Then, the OEC values $\mathfrak{C}_V := \mathfrak{C}(\mathcal{U}_V)$ (e.g., the average value $\mathfrak{C}(\mathcal{U}_V) = \mathrm{avg}_{\Omega_V}\mathsf{m}$), $V = A, B$, are calculated and their difference $\Delta(\mathfrak{C}) = \mathfrak{C}_B - \mathfrak{C}_A$ is used to quantify the sign and the magnitude of the change in the OEC caused by the treatment.

In order to have confidence in positive or negative consequences of the evaluated changes of the service, the difference $\Delta(\mathfrak{C})$ is controlled by a statistical significance test that calculates the probability (also known as *p-value* or the *achieved significance level*, ASL [14]) to observe this value or larger under *the null hypothesis*, which assumes that the observed difference is caused by random fluctuations, and the variants of the system are not actually different w.r.t. user experience. If the p-value is lower than the threshold $p_{\mathrm{val}} \leq \alpha$ ($\alpha = 0.05$ is commonly used [7, 11, 13, 27, 29, 34]), then the test rejects the null hypothesis, and the difference $\Delta(\mathfrak{C})$ is accepted as statistically significant. The pair of an OEC and a statistical test is referred to as an *Overall Acceptance Criterion* (*OAC*) [14]. The additional details of the A/B testing framework could be found in the survey and practical guide [29].

In a large number of cases [7, 11, 13, 21, 34, 38], the key metric is a function of users, i.e., the analysis units match the *randomization units*[6], and the OEC is simply its average value of a set of users. We denote *user level* key metrics by capital letters, e.g., $\mathsf{M} : \mathcal{U} \to \mathbb{R}$, in order to distinguish them from key metrics that are based on analysis units other than randomization ones. Since the values of the key metric over users (randomization units) are accepted to be i.i.d. in a common situation [5], *Student's two-sample t-test* [11, 14, 29] is used. This test is based on the *t-statistic*:

$$\Delta(\mathfrak{C})/\sqrt{\sigma_A^2(\mathsf{M}) \cdot |\mathcal{U}_A|^{-1} + \sigma_B^2(\mathsf{M}) \cdot |\mathcal{U}_B|^{-1}}, \tag{1}$$

where $\sigma_V(\mathsf{M})$ is the standard deviation of the key metric M over the users $\mathcal{U}_V, V = A, B$. The larger the absolute value of the t-statistic, the lower the p-value. For the average values of a metric M over the user groups, we use shorten notations: $\mathsf{M}_V := \mathrm{avg}_{\mathcal{U}_V}\mathsf{M}, V = A, B$.

3.2 Non-user level metrics and ratio OECs

Besides the case of the previous subsection, analysis units may be some events (e.g., a user session [14], a user query [27], a web page visit [7], etc.) related to users. In this case, for each user $u \in \mathcal{U}$, we denote by Ω_u the set of related analysis unit (e.g., all sessions of the user u), the key metric is referred to as a non-user level metric $\mathsf{x} : \Omega(\mathcal{U}) \to \mathbb{R}$ (we denote such a metric in lowercase letters), and the corresponding OEC $\mathfrak{R}(\mathcal{U}')$ is chosen as the average over all events $\Omega(\mathcal{U}') := \bigcup_{u \in \mathcal{U}'} \Omega_u$ observed for all users in $\mathcal{U}' \subseteq \mathcal{U}$:

$$\mathfrak{R}(\mathcal{U}') := \mathrm{avg}_{\Omega(\mathcal{U}')}\mathsf{x} \equiv \sum_{u \in \mathcal{U}'} \sum_{\omega \in \Omega_u} \mathsf{x}(\omega) / \sum_{u \in \mathcal{U}'} |\Omega_u|, \tag{2}$$

e.g., the absence-time-per-session metric [14] or the abandonment rate (the fraction of search queries with no clicks on its result page) [27, 35]. The OEC from Eq. (2), in fact, is a particular case of a more general *ratio OEC* of the following form:

$$\mathfrak{R}(\mathcal{U}') := \frac{\mathrm{avg}_{\mathcal{U}'}(\mathsf{X})}{\mathrm{avg}_{\mathcal{U}'}(\mathsf{Y})} \equiv \sum_{u \in \mathcal{U}'} \mathsf{X}(u) / \sum_{u \in \mathcal{U}'} \mathsf{Y}(u), \tag{3}$$

where X and Y are some user level metrics (we assume that Y is positive). Note that this ratio OEC trivially reduces to the OEC from Eq. (2) by setting $\mathsf{X}(u) := \sum_{\omega \in \Omega_u} \mathsf{x}(\omega)$ and $\mathsf{Y}(u) := |\Omega_u|$[7].

[6] More generally, we can consider the case when the randomization unit is not a user [5], for which our approach and reasonings will be valid as well. For simplicity, from here on we consider a user as a randomization unit since it is the most popular choice in the online industry [2, 4, 13, 19, 27, 34].

[7] The click-through-rate (CTR) is another example of a ratio OEC $\mathfrak{R}$ of the form Eq. (3), when the metric $\mathsf{X}(u)$ ($\mathsf{Y}(u)$) is the number of clicks (page views, resp.) of the user u.

Since the observations $\{\mathsf{x}(\omega) \mid \omega \in \Omega_u\}$ related to the same user u are usually dependent, Student's t-test with t-statistic Eq. (1) is no longer applicable[8], and alternative statistical tests are used.

Bootstrap test. Bootstrapping technique [16] is usually used [2, 4, 14, 27] to estimate the achieved significance level in our case of the ratio OEC, moreover, it could be, in fact, applied to any evaluation statistic $\mathfrak{C}$. This method is based on resampling of users, where for each sample the difference $\Delta(\mathfrak{R})$ is calculated (see, e.g., [16, Alg. 16.1]). The main drawback of this statistical test is its computational expensiveness[9]: it takes $\Theta(NB)$ operations, where N is the number of operations needed to calculate the OEC $\mathfrak{R}$ (e.g., $N = O(|\Omega|)$ for the mean value) and B is the number of bootstrap iterations, which are usually taken at least $B = 1000$ [14, 32, 37].

Delta method. An alternative known way to get the achieved significance level of the ratio OEC is to construct an estimator of $\mathrm{Var}(\Delta(\mathfrak{R}))$ that is aware of the dependences between the observations of the same user. This can be done by means of the Delta method [18], which is based on the following approximation for two random variables X and Y:

$$\mathrm{Var}\,\frac{X}{Y} \approx \frac{1}{\mathrm{E}[Y]^2}\,\mathrm{Var}\,X + \frac{\mathrm{E}[X]^2}{\mathrm{E}[Y]^4}\,\mathrm{Var}\,Y - 2\frac{\mathrm{E}[X]}{\mathrm{E}[Y]^3}\,\mathrm{cov}(X,Y). \quad (4)$$

Thus, if we replace the denominator of t-statistic in Eq. (1) by the square root of the estimator $\delta(\mathfrak{R}_A) + \delta(\mathfrak{R}_B)$ of $\mathrm{Var}(\Delta(\mathfrak{R}))$, where

$$\delta(\mathfrak{R}_V) = \frac{1}{|\mathcal{U}_V|}\left(\frac{1}{\mathsf{Y}_V^2}\sigma_V^2(\mathsf{X}) + \frac{\mathsf{X}_V^2}{\mathsf{Y}_V^4}\sigma_V^2(\mathsf{Y}) - 2\frac{\mathsf{X}_V}{\mathsf{Y}_V^3}\widehat{\mathrm{cov}}_V(\mathsf{X},\mathsf{Y})\right) \quad (5)$$

and $\widehat{\mathrm{cov}}_V(\mathsf{X},\mathsf{Y})$ is the sample covariance of the user level metrics X and Y over the users $\mathcal{U}_V, V = A, B$, we obtain a statistic which is asymptotically normally distributed (converges by probability to the standard normal distribution) [5, 7, 18]. The Delta method can be used to adapt some simple sensitivity improvement techniques [7], but its use in more sophisticated ones results in excessive complications (e.g., non-standard optimization objectives in [21, 34]).

Naive transformations to a user level metrics. Note that there are naive straightforward approaches to construct a user level metric from the ratio OEC $\mathfrak{R}$ in Eq. (3). The first one is the ratio $\mathsf{A}_{\mathsf{X},\mathsf{Y}}(u) := \mathsf{X}(u)/\mathsf{Y}(u)$ of the key metrics X and Y calculated for each user $u \in \mathcal{U}$ individually. For the particular case of a non-user level metric x, it is the average value of x over all events related to a user (e.g., the absence time per session of the user [11, 13, 14, 34]):

$$\mathsf{A}_{\mathsf{x}}(u) := \sum_{\omega\in\Omega_u} \mathsf{x}(\omega)/|\Omega_u|, \quad u \in \mathcal{U}. \quad (6)$$

A non-user level metric x is also mapped to the user level as the sum of values over all events related to a user $\mathsf{S}_{\mathsf{x}}(u) := \sum_{\omega\in\Omega_u}\mathsf{x}(\omega), u \in \mathcal{U}$ (e.g., the total presence time of the user [11, 13, 14, 34]), which is the second straightforward transformation. In our terms of the ratio OEC in Eq. (3), $\mathsf{S}_{\mathsf{x}}(u)$ is just exactly $\mathsf{X}(u)$. The OECs that correspond to the metrics A and S are the average values over a set of users (denoted by $\mathfrak{A}$ and $\mathfrak{S}$, resp.), e.g., the absence time per session per user and the total presence time per user [11, 13, 14, 34]). Since the observations over users are accepted to be i.i.d., p-value of changes in $\mathfrak{A}$ and $\mathfrak{S}$ could be estimated by Student's t-test. However, these transformations have a fundamental drawback: their interpretations differ from the one of the source OEC; particularly, experimental analysis [14] showed that the OECs $\mathfrak{A}$ and $\mathfrak{S}$ do not preserve directionality of the ratio OEC $\mathfrak{R}$ and its significance level.

[8] Its application results in an underestimate of the false-positive rate in this case [14].
[9] For comparison, Student's two-sample t-test requires $4N + o(N)$ operations.

3.3 Problem statement

Summarizing Sec. 3.2, all approaches that process ratio OECs $\mathfrak{R}$, as in Eq. (3), do not allow to directly apply a series of effective sensitivity improvement techniques [7, 11, 17, 21, 34] (developed for the average values of user level metrics) and to conduct thus A/B testing efficiently, since the higher the sensitivity is, the faster and with less user traffic the same significance level can be achieved [29]. Hence, the primary goal of our study, is to find a technique that:

(R1) provides an OEC which is the average value of a user level metric, that will thus allow to apply efficient approaches developed to improve sensitivity on the user level;
(R2) preserves the directionality of the source OEC $\mathfrak{R}$;
(R3) allows to calculate the achieved significance level efficiently and consistently with the one of the source OEC $\mathfrak{R}$.

Note that Bootstrapping does not satisfy the requirements (R1) and (R3), the Delta method does not align with the req. (R1), and the naive transformations do not satisfy the req. (R2) and (R3).

4 LINEARIZATION METHOD

In this section, in order to solve the problem stated in Sec. 3.3, we introduce our approach which is based on (1) a novel transformation to a user level metric (Sec. 4.1), for which we prove theoretical guarantees on preservation of (2) directionality (Sec. 4.2) and (3) significance level (Sec. 4.3). Further, we overview the methodology of our approach (Sec. 4.4) and reinforce its advantages by extensive empirical evaluation on real A/B experiments (Sec. 5).

4.1 Linearized user level metric and OEC

So, let us consider the general case of the source ratio OEC $\mathfrak{R}$ from Eq. (3), then we introduce the following user level metric:

$$\mathsf{L}_{\mathsf{X},\mathsf{Y},\kappa}(u) := \mathsf{X}(u) - \kappa\mathsf{Y}(u), \quad \forall u \in \mathcal{U}, \quad (7)$$

and the corresponding OEC (standard for user level metrics)

$$\mathfrak{L}_{\mathsf{X},\mathsf{Y},\kappa}(\mathcal{U}) = \mathrm{avg}_{\mathcal{U}}\mathsf{L}_{\mathsf{X},\mathsf{Y},\kappa}. \quad (8)$$

For the particular case of the source ratio OEC $\mathfrak{R}$, Eq. (2), which is based on a non-user level metric x, Eq. (7) and (8) take the form:

$$\mathsf{L}_{\mathsf{x},\kappa}(u) := \sum_{\omega\in\Omega_u} \mathsf{x}(\omega) - \kappa|\Omega_u|, \quad \mathfrak{L}_{\mathsf{x},\kappa}(\mathcal{U}) = \mathrm{avg}_{\mathcal{U}}\mathsf{L}_{\mathsf{x},\kappa}. \quad (9)$$

We refer to this user level metric (in Eq. (7) or (9)) and its OEC (in Eq. (8) or (9)) as the *linearized* (or, *linearization*) metric and OEC, respectively. Some constrains on the parameter κ will be introduced in order to guarantee useful properties of the linearized metric L (see Sec. 4.2). Looking forward, if κ is close to the expected value of the fraction $\sum_{\omega\in\Omega_u}\mathsf{x}(\omega)/|\Omega_u|$, then the intuition behind our transformation is the following: the key metric $\mathsf{L}_{\mathsf{x},\kappa}(u)$ is the sum of deviations of the non-user level metric x from the average for all events Ω_u of the considered user u. So, if some user has a lot of events Ω_u and the values of x on them are far from the average, then the absolute value of this sum $|\mathsf{L}_{\mathsf{x},\kappa}(u)|$ will be large (larger than for another user with only one event with the value of x of similar magnitude). For the sake of convenience, we omit designation of dependences on x, X, Y, and κ from the subscripts where it does not cause a confusion.

4.2 Theoretical guarantees on directionality

We remind that, for a user level metric M and an OEC $\mathfrak{C}$, we use the short notations: $M_V = \mathrm{avg}_{\mathcal{U}_V} M$ and $\mathfrak{C}_V = \mathfrak{C}(\mathcal{U}_V), V = A, B$.

PROPOSITION 1. *Let* X *and* Y *be user level metrics (s.t.* Y_A, Y_B *are positive),* $\mathfrak{R}$ *be the (source) ratio OEC defined by Eq. (3), and* $\mathfrak{L}$ *be the linearized OEC defined by Eq. (8). The parameter* κ *being set as* $\kappa(\eta) = (1-\eta)\mathfrak{R}_A + \eta\mathfrak{R}_B, \eta \in \mathbb{R}$, *implies the following identity on the OEC's differences between the control and treatment variants:*

$$\Delta(\mathfrak{L}_{X,Y,\kappa(\eta)}) = ((1-\eta)Y_B + \eta Y_A) \cdot \Delta(\mathfrak{R}). \tag{10}$$

PROOF. First of all, let us show that, for $\eta = 0$ (i.e., $\kappa = \mathfrak{R}_A$), $\Delta(\mathfrak{L}_{X,Y,\kappa(0)}) = Y_B \Delta(\mathfrak{R})$. One gets it straightforwardly:

$\Delta(\mathfrak{L}_{X,Y,\kappa(0)}) = \Delta(X) - \kappa(0)\Delta(Y) = (X_B - X_A) - (X_A/Y_A)(Y_B - Y_A) = X_B - X_A Y_B/Y_A = Y_B(X_B/Y_B - X_A/Y_A) = Y_B(\mathfrak{R}_B - \mathfrak{R}_A) = Y_B\Delta(\mathfrak{R})$.

Similarly, one can show that $\Delta(\mathfrak{L}_{X,Y,\kappa(1)}) = Y_A\Delta(\mathfrak{R})$ for $\eta = 1$ (i.e., $\kappa = \mathfrak{R}_B$). Finally, one represents $\mathfrak{L}_{X,Y,\kappa(\eta)}$ as a linear combination of $\mathfrak{L}_{X,Y,\kappa(0)}$ and $\mathfrak{L}_{X,Y,\kappa(1)}$ to reduce this case to the previous ones:

$\Delta(\mathfrak{L}_{X,Y,\kappa(\eta)}) = \Delta(X) - ((1-\eta)\mathfrak{R}_A + \eta\mathfrak{R}_B)\Delta(Y) =$
$= (1-\eta)\Delta(\mathfrak{L}_{X,Y,\mathfrak{R}_A}) + \eta\Delta(\mathfrak{L}_{X,Y,\mathfrak{R}_B}) = (1-\eta)Y_B\Delta(\mathfrak{R}) + \eta Y_A\Delta(\mathfrak{R})$.

Hence, Eq. (10) holds. □

First, Proposition 1 provides us with a clear sufficient condition on the parameter κ to preserve the directionality of $\mathfrak{R}$ in $\mathfrak{L}$: while κ is between $\mathfrak{R}_A$ and $\mathfrak{R}_B$ (the source OEC values for the control and the treatment versions), the utilization of the average value of the user level metric L allows an analysts to make conclusions about the sign (direction) of the system quality change *consistently* with the conclusions that are relied on the source OEC $\mathfrak{R}$. We formalize this statement in the following corollary[10]:

COROLLARY 1. *Given the user level metrics* X *and* Y *(s.t.* Y_A, Y_B *are positive), the (source) ratio OEC* $\mathfrak{R}$ *defined by Eq. (3), and the linearized OEC* $\mathfrak{L}$ *defined by Eq. (8), if* $\kappa \in [\min\{\mathfrak{R}_A, \mathfrak{R}_B\}, \max\{\mathfrak{R}_A, \mathfrak{R}_B\}]$ *(in particular, if* $\kappa = \mathfrak{R}_A$ *or* $\mathfrak{R}_B$*), then* $\operatorname{sgn}\Delta(\mathfrak{R}) = \operatorname{sgn}\Delta(\mathfrak{L})$.

Second, Prop. 1 establishes the relation between the treatment effect magnitude of the source ratio OEC and the one of the linearized OEC. For instance, let $\kappa = \mathfrak{R}_A$ for each A/B test, then Prop. 1 implies a proportion between the differences $\Delta(\mathfrak{L})$ and $\Delta(\mathfrak{R})$:

$$\Delta(\mathfrak{L}) = Y_B \cdot \Delta(\mathfrak{R}). \tag{11}$$

Note that the coefficient Y_B in this proportionality has the explicit dependence on a particular A/B experiment. However, we argue below that, in practice, this dependence may be drastically low and Eq. (11), in fact, represents a (nearly) linear relationship between the differences $\Delta(\mathfrak{L})$ and $\Delta(\mathfrak{R})$ w.r.t. a set of A/B experiments.

User engagement example. In many cases of web industry [25], ratio OECs are applied in those situations when a more important user level metric does not detect the treatment effect of an A/B test, and, moreover, the average of this user level metric is used as denominator of the ratio OECs (i.e., as $\mathrm{avg}_{\mathcal{U}} Y$). For instance, in the very important case of user engagement, the number of sessions [25, 38] represents such user level metric, which is accepted as the state-of-the-art loyalty metric to evaluate major web services like global search engines [10, 11, 26, 27, 34]. First, this metric is difficult to shift by a web service update [13, 27, 38] and, thus, the relative change of its mean value in an A/B test (i.e., $(Y_B - Y_A)/Y_A$) does not usually exceed several percents [11, 13, 14]. Second, this session-per-user OEC changes slightly between months [10, 12]. Hence, the range of its values within a set of A/B tests with the same duration (even collected over several years) is tightly bounded with deviation of several percents. The second widely used OEC of user loyalty is the absence-time-per-session [14, 15], which is more sensitive than the session-per-user and is the example of a ratio OEC based on a non-user level metric, namely, a session level metric. For this case, the key metric $Y(u)$ is the number of sessions of a user $u \in \mathcal{U}$ and, hence, the factor Y_B in Eq. (11) is nearly constant within a set of A/B tests with the same duration, that we demonstrate by our experimental analysis in Sec. 5.2.

4.3 Theoretical guarantees on significance level

First of all, in order to measure the achieved statistical significance level of the difference $\Delta(\mathfrak{L})$, one needs to construct a statistic whose distribution is known under the null hypothesis. Since the OEC $\mathfrak{L}$ is the average value of the metric L over users, that are assumed to be randomization units, one would like to utilize the state-of-the-art t-statistic, Eq. (1), and apply Student's t-test. This is valid approach, when the parameter κ being set as a constant independent of any observations. However, if we set $\kappa = \mathfrak{R}_A$[11], two key conditions of Student's t-test are violated: (a) the OEC values $\mathfrak{L}_A$ and $\mathfrak{L}_B$ calculated for the treatment and the control variants are not independent; and (b) the observations within $\{L(u) | u \in \mathcal{U}_V\}, V = A, B$, are not independent as well. Nonetheless, we argue below that Student's t-test with the t-statistic Eq. (1) is applicable for our difference $\Delta(\mathfrak{L})$ to correctly measure the achieved significance level (p-value).

THEOREM 1. *Given* X *and* Y *be user level metrics (s.t.* Y *is positive),* $\mathfrak{R}$ *be the (source) ratio OEC defined by Eq. (3), and* $\mathfrak{L}$ *be the linearized OEC defined by Eq. (8) with the parameter* $\kappa = \mathfrak{R}_A$. *Let* $T(\mathfrak{L})$ *be the t-statistic from Eq. (1) applied to the OEC* $\mathfrak{L}$ *with the metric* L *and* $D(\mathfrak{R}) = \Delta(\mathfrak{R})/\sqrt{\delta(\mathfrak{R}_A) + \delta(\mathfrak{R}_B)}$ *be the asymt. standard normal statistic of* $\mathfrak{R}$ *obtained via the Delta method with* $\delta(\mathfrak{R}_V)$ *from Eq. (5).*

(1) Then the following identity holds:

$$T(\mathfrak{L}) = D(\mathfrak{R})\sqrt{1 - \frac{\gamma}{\delta(\mathfrak{R}_A) + \delta(\mathfrak{R}_B) + \gamma}}, \tag{12}$$

where $\gamma = (Y_A^2/Y_B^2 - 1)\delta(\mathfrak{R}_A) + \beta$ *and*

$$\beta = |\mathcal{U}_B|^{-1} Y_B^{-2} \Delta(\mathfrak{R})((\mathfrak{R}_A + \mathfrak{R}_B)\sigma_B^2(Y) - 2\widehat{\mathrm{cov}}_B(X, Y)).$$

(2) If the sample correlation $\widehat{\mathrm{corr}}_B(X, Y)$ *is bounded as follows* $|\widehat{\mathrm{corr}}_B(X, Y)| < c < 1$, *then the following inequality holds*

$$|T(\mathfrak{L})/D(\mathfrak{R}) - 1| \le C_1(c)|\Delta X/X_B| + C_2(c)|\Delta Y/Y_B| \tag{13}$$

for sufficiently small relative changes, i.e., $|\Delta X/X_B| < \epsilon_1(c)$ *and* $|\Delta Y/Y_B| < \epsilon_2(c)$*; where the constants* $C_1(c), C_2(c), \epsilon_1(c)$, *and* $\epsilon_2(c)$ *depend only on the bound* c.

[10] In fact, the directionality is preserved for a wider range of κ than required in Cor. 1. Namely, an attentive reader can easily prove that if either (a) $\Delta(\mathfrak{R})\Delta(Y) > 0$ and $\kappa < \Delta(X)/\Delta(Y)$, or (b) $\Delta(\mathfrak{R})\Delta(Y) < 0$ and $\kappa > \Delta(X)/\Delta(Y)$, then $\operatorname{sgn}\Delta(\mathfrak{R}) = \operatorname{sgn}\Delta(\mathfrak{L})$.

[11] The arguments in this subsec. hold for $\kappa \in [\min\{\mathfrak{R}_A, \mathfrak{R}_B\}, \max\{\mathfrak{R}_A, \mathfrak{R}_B\}]$ as well.

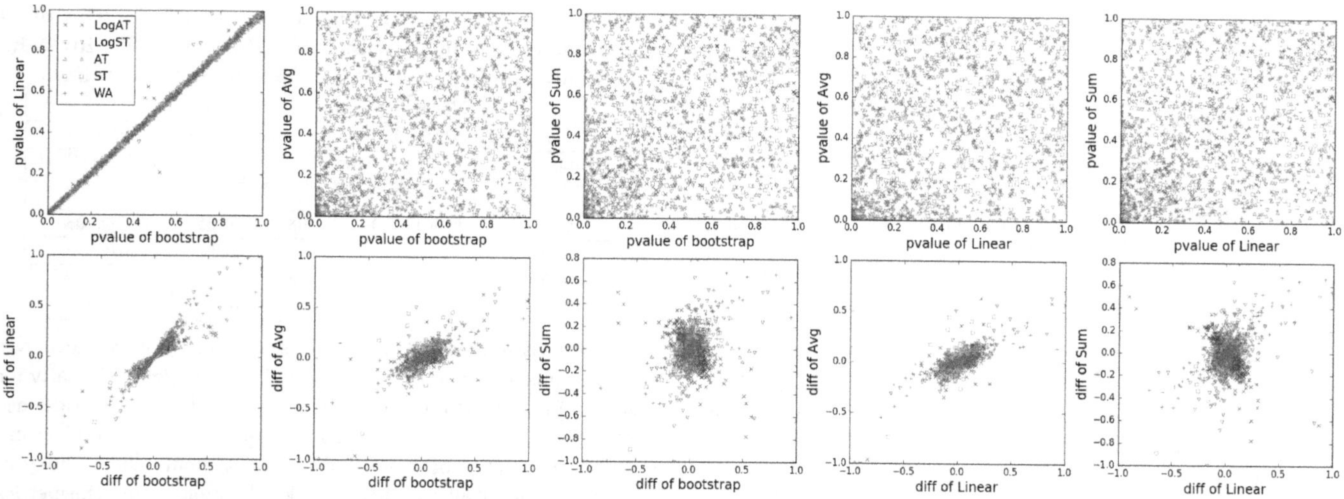

Figure 1: Joint distributions of 390 A/B tests on the plane (p-value of $\mathfrak{C}_1$, p-value of $\mathfrak{C}_2$) and the plane $(\Delta(\mathfrak{C}_1), \Delta(\mathfrak{C}_2))$, where $\mathfrak{C}_j, j = 1, 2$, are either averages of the studied transformations ("Linear": the linearized $\mathfrak{L}$, "Avg": the individual average $\mathfrak{A}$, "Sum": the individual sum $\mathfrak{S}$) with t-test or the source ratio $\mathfrak{R}$ with the Bootstrap test, for each studied non-user level metric.

(3) If $|\mathrm{corr}(\mathsf{X}, \mathsf{Y} \mid B)| < c < 1$ *and* $\mathrm{E}[\mathsf{X} \mid A] \neq 0, \mathrm{E}[\mathsf{Y} \mid A] \neq 0$, *then the t-statistics* $T(\mathfrak{L})$ *is asymptotically normal under the null hypothesis that* $\mathrm{E}[\Delta\mathsf{X}] = 0$ *and* $\mathrm{E}[\Delta\mathsf{Y}] = 0$.

Proof. The claim (1) represents, in fact, an identity that directly follows from the definitions of $T(\mathfrak{L})$ and $D(\mathfrak{R})$ by rearrangement of their components. Let us compare the denominators of $T(\mathfrak{L})$ (see Eq. (8)) and $D(\mathfrak{R})$. The one of the t-statistic $T(\mathfrak{L})$ is based on the standard deviation over the user samples $\mathcal{U}_V, V = A, B$:

$$\begin{aligned}\sigma_V^2(\mathsf{L}) &\equiv \widehat{\mathrm{cov}}_V(\mathsf{X} - \mathfrak{R}_A\mathsf{Y}, \mathsf{X} - \mathfrak{R}_A\mathsf{Y}) \\ &= \widehat{\mathrm{cov}}_V(\mathsf{X}, \mathsf{X}) + \widehat{\mathrm{cov}}_V(\mathfrak{R}_A\mathsf{Y}, \mathfrak{R}_A\mathsf{Y}) - 2\widehat{\mathrm{cov}}_V(\mathsf{X}, \mathfrak{R}_A\mathsf{Y}) \\ &= \sigma_V^2(\mathsf{X}) + \mathfrak{R}_A^2\sigma_V^2(\mathsf{Y}) - 2\mathfrak{R}_A\widehat{\mathrm{cov}}_V(\mathsf{X}, \mathsf{Y}), \quad V = A, B,\end{aligned}$$

where the last identity holds since $\mathfrak{R}_A$ is constant for all users in $\mathcal{U}_V$ (i.e., $\mathsf{L}(u) = \mathsf{X}(u) - \kappa\mathsf{Y}(u)$, $\forall u \in \mathcal{U}_V$, where $\kappa = \mathfrak{R}_A$) and can be thus factored out. Note that, for the variant $V = A$, the standard deviation $\sigma_A^2(\mathsf{L})$ is exactly $\delta(\mathfrak{R}_A) \cdot \mathsf{Y}_A^2 \cdot |\mathcal{U}_A|$ (see Eq. (5)), while, for $V = B$, the standard deviation $\sigma_B^2(\mathsf{L})$ differs from $\delta(\mathfrak{R}_B) \cdot \mathsf{Y}_B^2 \cdot |\mathcal{U}_B|$ in the presence of $\mathfrak{R}_A$ in places of $\mathfrak{R}_B$ in Eq. (5), see the definition of β. Hence, using Eq. (11), we obtain:

$$T(\mathfrak{L}) = \frac{\mathsf{Y}_B\Delta(\mathfrak{R})}{\sqrt{\mathsf{Y}_A^2\delta(\mathfrak{R}_A) + \mathsf{Y}_B^2(\delta(\mathfrak{R}_B) + \beta)}} = \frac{\Delta(\mathfrak{R})}{\sqrt{\delta(\mathfrak{R}_A) + \delta(\mathfrak{R}_B) + \gamma}},$$

where β and γ are from the claim (1). This identity together with the definition of $D(\mathfrak{R})$ implies Eq. (12).

The proof of the claim (2) is rather technical, and is thus deferred to Appendix A. The claim (3) easily follows from the claim (2). Namely, under the null hypothesis $|\Delta\mathsf{X}/\mathsf{X}_B|$ and $|\Delta\mathsf{Y}/\mathsf{Y}_B|$ tends to 0 by probability. The inequality $|\widehat{\mathrm{corr}}_B(\mathsf{X}, \mathsf{Y})| < c + \varepsilon < 1$ holds for some $\varepsilon > 0$ with probability that converges to 1. So, using the inequality in Eq. (13), we conclude that $T(\mathfrak{L})/D(\mathfrak{R})$ tends to 1 by probability. Hence, $T(\mathfrak{L})$ is asymptotically normal as $D(\mathfrak{R})$ is. □

The condition $|\widehat{\mathrm{corr}}_B(\mathsf{X}, \mathsf{Y})| < c < 1$ is necessary, because one can build an example, where the variance calculated by linearization is not zero, while the variations calculated by delta-method and bootstrap are zero for the case of $|\widehat{\mathrm{corr}}_B(\mathsf{X}, \mathsf{Y})| = 1$ and $\mathfrak{R}_B = 1$. The condition $\mathrm{E}(\Delta\mathsf{X}) = 0$ in the third claim of Theorem 1 can be replaced by $\mathrm{E}(\Delta\mathfrak{R}) = 0$, while we do not know how to relax the condition $\mathrm{E}(\Delta\mathsf{Y}) = 0$. However, in practice, we are satisfied with changes of X and Y being sufficiently small.

In practice, the mean values and variations of X and Y vary in a narrow range, and the metrics' changes are relatively small, no more than several percents (see, user engagement example in Sec. 4.2). For instance, if relative $\Delta(\mathsf{X})$ and $\Delta(\mathsf{Y})$ are no more than 2–3%, then the relative difference between $T(\mathfrak{L})$ and $D(\mathfrak{R})$ will be of the same order (according to Eq. (13)), and, further, we experimentally show that these statistics are close in terms of p-values (see Sec. 5.1). Hence, in practice, the achieved significance level of $\Delta(\mathfrak{L})$ *calculated by the state-of-the-art t-test* is *consistent* with the one of $\Delta(\mathfrak{R})$ obtained by the Delta method and, thus, by Bootstrap technique.

4.4 The methodology of the approach

To sum up the results of the previous subsections, we argued that our approach of linearization a ratio OEC satisfy all the requirement of the stated problem (see Sec. 3.3). So, the methodology of the linearization to be used in an A/B test is as follows. Given user level metrics X, Y (or a non-user level metric x) and a ratio OEC $\mathfrak{R}$ defined by Eq. (3) (or by Eq. (2), resp.),

(I) for each user participated in the A/B test, calculate the linearized metric $\mathsf{L}_{\mathsf{X},\mathsf{Y},\kappa}$ defined by Eq. (8) (or $\mathsf{L}_{\mathsf{x},\kappa}$ by Eq. (9), resp.) with the parameter $\kappa = \mathfrak{R}_A$.

(II) Optionally, upgrade the metric L to a metric $\widetilde{\mathsf{L}}$ (and its OEC $\widetilde{\mathfrak{L}}$) by one of known sensitivity improvement techniques designed for the user level (e.g., regression adjustment [7, 34], future value prediction [11], learned linear combination [21], etc.) or just left $\widetilde{\mathsf{L}} := \mathsf{L}$.

(III) Calculate the t-statistic Eq. (1) applied to $\Delta(\widetilde{\mathfrak{L}})$ and the corresponding p-value p_{val}.

(IV) Make a decision: if $p_{\mathrm{val}} > \alpha$, then there is no treatment effect, otherwise derive positiveness/negativeness of the treatment effect from $\mathrm{sgn}\,\Delta(\widetilde{\mathfrak{L}})$.

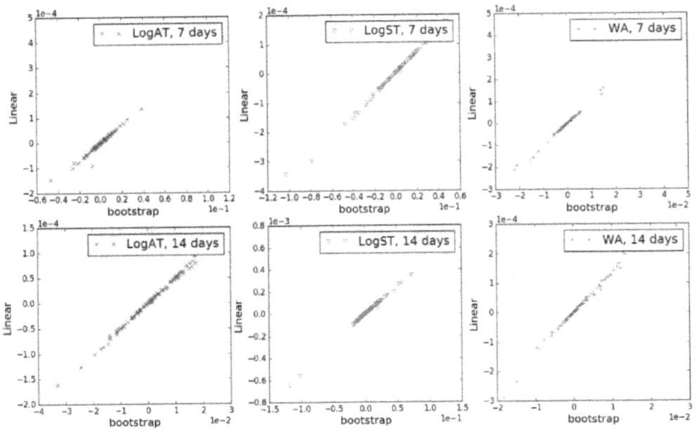

Figure 2: Joint distributions of 78 7-day A/B tests (the top row of plots) and 93 14-day A/B tests (the bottom row of plots) on the plane ($\mathrm{Diff}_1(\mathfrak{L})$, $\mathrm{Diff}_2(\mathfrak{R})$).

5 EXPERIMENTATION

Experimental setup. In order to experimentally evaluate our approach, we use 390 large-scale A/B tests[12] carried out on *the users* of one of the most popular global search engines in the period 2013–2016. The user samples used in these tests are all uniformly randomly selected, and the control and the treatment groups are approximately of the same size, according to a common practice of industrial A/B testing [13, 14, 27, 29]. Each experiment has been conducted over at least several hundreds of thousands of users (from 0.5M to 30M with the median equal to 4M users). Most of tests (90%) have duration between 7 and 30 days (the median equals to 14 days). These A/B tests evaluate changes in main components of the search engine, that include the ranking algorithm, the user interface, the server efficiency, etc. Each of those changes is either an update of a search engine component, which is evaluated before being shipped to production [6], or its artificial deterioration (e.g., a swap of the 2-nd and the 4-th results in the ranked list returned by the current ranking algorithm as in [10, 32]).

Studied key metrics. In our work, the following ratio OECs $\mathfrak{R}$ of user engagement and satisfaction are studied:

- the session time per session [14] (ST);
- the session time logarithm per session [14] (LogST);
- the absence time per absence [14] (AT);
- the absence time logarithm per absence [14] (LogAT);
- the web abandonment rate [27, 35] (WA).

These ratio OECs are based on non-user level metrics: ST, LogST, AT, LogAT are at the session level and WA is at the query one[13]. Following common practice [10, 13, 15, 20, 25, 34, 38], a session is defined as a sequence of user actions (clicks or queries) whose dwell times are less than 30 minutes. The session time ST is measured as the duration (in seconds) of a session, while the metric AT [14] is the duration of an absence (a time period between two consecutive sessions of a considered user or between the end of the last session in an A/B test and the test's end). The metrics LogST and LogAT are logarithms of corresponding durations. The ratio OEC "the session time per session" is thus the average session duration averaged over all sessions of all users in a considered sample group (similarly for AT, LogST, and LogAT). The metric WA is the indicator of the absence of clicks at the result page of a search query [27, 35], and its ratio OEC is the fraction of abandoned queries (without a click) among all search queries of all users in a considered sample group. The metrics AT and LogAT (ST, LogST) represent the user loyalty (activity, resp.) aspect of user engagement [25, 36], while the metric WA corresponds to user satisfaction [35]. Activity and satisfaction metrics are known to be more sensitive than the loyalty ones [13, 14, 21, 27].

[12] This amount of A/B tests is more than twice larger than in previously known largest experimental studies [12–14, 21, 34], which should make the results of our work more valuable for practical use in modern Internet companies.

[13] We remind that the randomization units are users. Browser cookie IDs are used to identify them as done in other studies on online A/B testing [5, 8, 14, 15, 19, 38, 39].

Table 1: Mean absolute difference between the p-value of an approach ($\mathfrak{L}$, $\mathfrak{A}$, and $\mathfrak{S}$ with Student's t-test or $\mathfrak{R}$ with Delta method) and the one of Bootstrap applied to the ratio $\mathfrak{R}$.

	Novel	Baselines		
OEC:	Linearized $\mathfrak{L}$	Average $\mathfrak{A}$	Sum $\mathfrak{S}$	Ratio $\mathfrak{R}$
Stat.test:	Student's t-test			Delta Method
AT	0.00586	0.2934	0.35	0.00586
ST	0.0061	0.2908	0.2553	0.00608
LogAT	0.00808	0.2886	0.213	0.00806
LogST	0.00634	0.2546	0.3292	0.00629
WA	0.00404	0.2222	0.2148	0.00402

Baseline approaches. We consider approaches that process ratio OECs $\mathfrak{R}$ and are listed in Sec. 3.2 as our baselines. Namely, first, we consider a source ratio OEC whose p-value is calculated by Bootstrap test and the Delta method. Since these p-values are nearly equal (that we further show in Table 1), in most result presentations, we demonstrate only one of them. Second, the naive straightforward transformations of our metrics are also considered as our baselines: (a) the individual per-user average value A and its OEC $\mathfrak{A}$ (defined in Eq. 6), e.g., $\mathsf{A}(u)$ is the session time per session of the user u; (b) the individual per-user sum S and its OEC $\mathfrak{S}$, e.g., $\mathsf{S}(u)$ is the sum session durations (i.e., the presence time [10, 11, 13, 14]) of the user u. These transformations are used with Student's t-test.

Overall, our baselines are the source ratio OEC $\mathfrak{R}$ (with Delta method and Bootstrap), the transformation OECs $\mathfrak{A}$ and $\mathfrak{S}$.

Statistical tests. In our experimentation, we utilize three most popular statistical tests in A/B testing: the two-sample Student's t-test [7, 10, 11, 38], the test based on the Delta method [5], and the Bootstrap test [16, Alg. 16.1] with $B = 10000$ iterations [14, 32, 37]. First, we remind that two latter ones provides nearly equal p-values for ratio OECs [5]. Second, Drutsa et al. have shown by the extensive empirical analysis that p-values calculated by means of t-test and Bootstrap are very close to each other for user level engagement metrics, but differ for non-user level ones (t-test underestimates the false-positive rate) [14].

In A/B testing, correctness of an experimentation is verified via A/A tests, a.k.a. control experiments, that compare two identical variants of the web service [4, 13, 14, 21, 29, 34]. They should be failed (i.e, the treatment effect is wrongly detected) in no more than $\alpha \cdot 100\%$ of cases for the p-value threshold α (e.g., 5% for $\alpha = 0.05$), since p-value should be uniformly distributed over $[0, 1]$ on A/A tests. The fraction of failed A/A tests is referred to as the *false-positive rate* (the type I error). We made thousands synthetic AA experiments [5, 21, 34] by taking some real A/B test and dividing its control user group $\mathcal{U}_A$ into two samples randomly. We find that all our approaches (both baseline and novel ones) do not fail the predefined false-positive rate threshold with confidence.

Table 2: Sensitivity comparison of the linearized metric / the linearized metric with regression adjustment in terms of the sensitivity rate and the average t-statistic over 197 A/B tests.

metric	sens.rate $\alpha = 0.05$	sens.rate $\alpha = 0.01$	avg. t-stat. (improvement in %)
AT	**10** / 6	2 / **6**	0.87 / 0.92 (+5.7%)
ST	23 / **25**	11 / **14**	0.99 / **1.08** (+9.2%*)
LogAT	**21** / 18	5 / **7**	0.95 / 0.94 (−1%)
LogST	51 / **60**	35 / **44**	1.6 / **1.78** (+11.5%**)
WA	56 / **75**	43 / **54**	1.7 / **1.95** (+14.8%**)

5.1 Comparison of significance levels

In order to empirically evaluate the consistency of our novel linearized OEC $\mathfrak{L}$, we calculate the mean absolute difference between p-values[14] of the Bootstrap test applied to the source ratio $\mathfrak{R}$ and the t-test applied to the novel OEC $\mathfrak{L}$ over our 390 A/B experiments. We also compare all our baseline approaches with the Bootstrap test in the same way and present the obtained results in Table 1 for each of 5 studied key metrics. It is easy to see that the difference is much closer to 0 for the linearized variant $\mathfrak{L}$ of studied metrics than for the other transformations $\mathfrak{A}$ and $\mathfrak{S}$, that are thus not consistent with the source ratio OEC $\mathfrak{R}$. Note that the linearization demonstrates p-value consistency with the Bootstrap test applied to the source OEC $\mathfrak{R}$ on the same level as the test based on the Delta method for $\mathfrak{R}$ (compare the left and right columns in Table 1).

We reinforce the results discussed above by presenting Fig. 1 (the top row of plots) with the joint distributions of our 390 A/B tests on the plane (p-value of $\mathfrak{C}_1$, p-value of $\mathfrak{C}_2$), where $\mathfrak{C}_j, j = 1, 2$, are either averages of the studied transformations (the linearized $\mathfrak{L}$, the individual average $\mathfrak{A}$, the individual sum $\mathfrak{S}$) with t-test or the source ratio $\mathfrak{R}$ with the Bootstrap test, for each studied non-user level metric. Overall, *the results on these comparisons of significance levels form an empirical evidence of Theorem 1 and, thus, additionally show that, in practice, an analyst can rely on p-values calculated for our novel transformation to make conclusions on statistical significance of a change in the quality of a web service.*

5.2 Comparison of directionality

Fig. 1 (the bottom row of plots) also provides us with the joint distributions of 390 A/B tests on the plane $(\Delta(\mathfrak{C}_1), \Delta(\mathfrak{C}_2))$[15], where $\mathfrak{C}_j, j = 1, 2$, are studied OECs. As we see, only for the left-bottom plot in Fig. 1 (with comparison of our novel transformation $\mathfrak{L}$ and the source ratio OEC $\mathfrak{R}$), all points (marks) belong either to the first quadrant or to the third one, which does not definitely hold for the naive transformations (the per-user average $\mathfrak{A}$ and the per-user sum $\mathfrak{S}$). In other words, the left plot in the bottom of Fig. 1 is an empirical evidence of Cor. 1 from Sec. 4.2. *We conclude that the consistency req. (R2) from Sec. 3.3 is satisfied in practice as well.*

Additionally, in order to empirically study the factor in the proportionality between the novel linearized OEC $\mathfrak{L}$ and the source ratio OEC $\mathfrak{R}$ in Eq. (11)[16], we select all 1-week and 2-week A/B experiments from our set of 390 A/B tests (obtaining 78 7-day A/B tests and 93 14-day A/B tests). The selection of A/B tests with the same duration (1 week or 2 weeks) implies that these A/B tests have nearly the same average value of Y over the treatment group (i.e., the average number of sessions for LogAT, LogST, AT, and ST; the average number of queries for WA) and thus the factor in Eq. (11). In Fig. 2, we plot the joint distributions of the 1-week and 2-week A/B experiments on the plane $(\mathrm{Diff}_1(\mathfrak{L}), \mathrm{Diff}_2(\mathfrak{R}))$, where $\mathrm{Diff}_k, k = 1, 2$, is the usual difference Δ scaled by a hidden factor $\varkappa_k$[17] (i.e., $\mathrm{Diff}_1(\mathfrak{L}) = \varkappa_1 \Delta(\mathfrak{L})$ and $\mathrm{Diff}_2(\mathfrak{R}) = \varkappa_2 \Delta(\mathfrak{R})$) for several representative non-user level metrics. We see that these plots form an empirical evidence of a (nearly) linear relationship between the differences $\Delta(\mathfrak{L})$ and $\Delta(\mathfrak{R})$ established by Eq. (11).

5.3 Sensitivity improvement

In Sec. 5.1 and 5.2, we showed that our novel OEC $\mathfrak{L}$ satisfies the consistency requirements (R2) & (R3) from Sec. 3.3 and can be thus used instead of Bootstrap and Delta method for the source OEC $\mathfrak{R}$. But, in contrast to the latter methods, our approach also satisfies the req. (R1): $\mathfrak{L}$ is the mean value of a user level metric. In order to highlight this advantage, we apply the best known regression adjustment based on boosted decision trees [34][18] to the linearized user level version L of the studied metrics. The parameters of the prediction model and features are the same as in [34], and we consider a part of our A/B tests consisting of 197 experiments[19]. Following [8–11, 14, 32, 34], we compare sensitivity in terms of the *success sensitivity rate* (the number of A/B tests where p-value of an OAC $\leq \alpha$) [14, 34] and the average t-statistic [8, 21]. In Table 2, we present the sensitivity rates at different levels and the average t-statistics in the form "value for $\mathfrak{L}$ / value for $\mathfrak{L}$ with regression adjustment"[20]. Stat. sign. differences between average t-statistics are marked with * (**) for the confidence level 0.05 (0.01, resp.). Note that regression adjustment improves sensitivity of 4 metrics from 5 and for one metric it gives statistically insignificant loss. We see that the best improvement of the sensitivity rate with $\alpha = 0.05$ is 33.9% for the metric WA, which *demonstrates the capability of our approach to effectively apply sensitivity improvement techniques and to improve thus efficiency of A/B testing.*

6 CONCLUSIONS

We focused on the problem of sensitivity improvement of ratio overall evaluation criteria and non-user level metrics. We proposed a novel transformation of a ratio OEC to the average value of a user level (randomization-unit level, in general) metric that represents an instrument-proxy for a direct use of a wide range of sensitivity improvement techniques designed for user level metrics. We provided theoretical guarantees on the novel metric's consistency in terms of preservation of directionality and significance level. We evaluated our approach on 390 large-scale A/B tests run at Yandex,

[14] i.e., $\sum_{i=1}^{N} |p_{\mathrm{val,i}} - p'_{\mathrm{val,i}}|/N$, where $p_{\mathrm{val,i}}$ and $p'_{\mathrm{val,i}}$ are p-value of two statistical tests for the i-th A/B experiment of the given set of A/B tests, $i = 1, \ldots, N$.

[15] Since the studied metrics have different magnitudes of the OECs' differences, we scale each $\Delta_{AB_i}(\mathfrak{C}_j)$, $i = 1, .., N$, by $1/|\max_i \Delta_{AB_i}(\mathfrak{C}_j)|$ in order to fit $\Delta(\mathfrak{C}_j)$ in $[-1, 1]$, $j = 1, 2$, and thus make visible distributions of 5 metrics on the same plot.

[16] We remind that we set the parameter $\kappa = \mathfrak{R}_A$ in our experimentation.

[17] The constants $\varkappa_k$, $k = 1, 2$, are randomly chosen once in our study to hide real values of $\Delta(\mathfrak{L})$ and $\Delta(\mathfrak{R})$ for confidentiality reasons. The constants $\varkappa_1$ and $\varkappa_2$ are different to hide real value of Y_B which is nearly $\Delta(\mathfrak{L})/\Delta(\mathfrak{R})$.

[18] The boosted decision tree regression adjustment outperforms the sensitivity improvement method of Deng et al. [7] by 20% in terms of the success sensitivity rate [34].

[19] Reduction of the set in comparison with the set in the previous analysis is explained by technical reasons such as increased calculation time.

[20] The results for Bootstrap and Delta method are similar to the ones of the linearized OEC $\mathfrak{L}$ without regression adjustment (due to the established consistency), and the studied regression adjustment is not applicable to them (as we earlier discussed).

one of the most popular global search engines, and showed up to +34% of sensitivity rate improvement achieved by our approach combined with the best known regression adjustment. The results of our study, first, impact on ongoing development of effective online metrics in modern Internet companies (in Yandex, in particular) and, second, will boost research studies in the area of online evaluation (e.g., on more complicated OECs than the ratio ones).

A MISSED PROOF OF THEOREM 1

Proof of the claim (2) in Th. 1. Let us suppose that $|\Delta \mathsf{X}/\mathsf{X}_B|$ and $|\Delta \mathsf{Y}/\mathsf{Y}_B| < 1/2$ (these bounds are further united with $\epsilon_1(c)$ and $\epsilon_2(c)$). Hence, the expressions $|\mathsf{X}_A/\mathsf{X}_B|$, $|\mathsf{Y}_A/\mathsf{Y}_B|$, and $|\mathsf{Y}_B/\mathsf{Y}_A|$ are < 2, that imply $|\Re_A| < 4|\Re_B|$. So, let $\Xi := \delta(\Re_A)+\delta(\Re_B)$, then:

$$|\gamma/\Xi| \leq |\mathsf{Y}_A^2/\mathsf{Y}_B^2-1| + |\beta/(\delta(\Re_A)+\delta(\Re_B))| \leq 3|\Delta(\mathsf{Y})/\mathsf{Y}_B| + |\beta/\delta(\Re_B)| \leq$$
$$\leq 3|\Delta(\mathsf{Y})/\mathsf{Y}_B| + |\Delta(\Re)/\Re_B| \cdot (5|m_1(r)| + 2|m_2(r)|),$$

where we use the following notations:

$$m_1(r) := \frac{r^2}{\rho(r)}, \quad m_2(r) := \frac{r \cdot \widehat{\mathrm{corr}}_B(\mathsf{X},\mathsf{Y})}{\rho(r)}, \quad r := \frac{\Re_B \sigma_B(\mathsf{Y})}{\sigma_B(\mathsf{X})},$$

$$\rho(r) := 1 + r^2 - 2r\widehat{\mathrm{corr}}_B(\mathsf{X},\mathsf{Y}), \quad \text{and} \quad \widehat{\mathrm{corr}}_B(\mathsf{X},\mathsf{Y}) \equiv \frac{\widehat{\mathrm{cov}}_B(\mathsf{X},\mathsf{Y})}{\sigma_B(\mathsf{X})\sigma_B(\mathsf{Y})}.$$

$m_1(r)$ and $m_2(r)$ are bounded as $r \to \pm\infty$ for any $\widehat{\mathrm{corr}}_B(\mathsf{X},\mathsf{Y}) \in [-1,1]$ and, since $\exists c \in (0,1)$ s.t. $|\widehat{\mathrm{corr}}_B(\mathsf{X},\mathsf{Y})| < c < 1$, their denominators $\rho(r)$ do not vanish to zero $\forall r \in \mathbb{R}$. Hence, m_1 and m_2 are bounded by a constant that depends on c only. Using Eq. (11):

$$\left|\frac{\Delta(\Re)}{\Re_B}\right| = \left|\frac{\Delta(\mathfrak{L})}{\mathsf{X}_B}\right| = \left|\frac{\Delta\mathsf{X}}{\mathsf{X}_B} - \frac{\mathsf{X}_A \Delta\mathsf{Y}}{\mathsf{Y}_A \mathsf{X}_B}\right| \leq \left|\frac{\Delta\mathsf{X}}{\mathsf{X}_B}\right| + 4\left|\frac{\Delta\mathsf{Y}}{\mathsf{Y}_B}\right|.$$

Therefore, continuing the chain of inequalities for $|\gamma/\Xi|$, we get

$$|\gamma/\Xi| \leq C_3(c) \cdot |\Delta\mathsf{Y}/\mathsf{Y}_B| + C_4(c) \cdot |\Delta\mathsf{X}/\mathsf{X}_B|,$$

where the constants $C_3(c)$ and $C_4(c)$ depend on c only. Taking $|\Delta\mathsf{Y}/\mathsf{Y}_B|$ and $|\Delta\mathsf{X}/\mathsf{X}_B|$ less than some $\epsilon_1(c)$ and $\epsilon_2(c)$, we can get $|\gamma/\Xi| \leq 1/2$. For the left part of Eq. (13), this inequality implies that $|T(\mathfrak{L})/D(\Re)-1| = (1+\gamma/\Xi)^{-1/2}-1 \leq |\gamma/\Xi|$. Hence, we get Eq. (13). □

REFERENCES

[1] Olga Arkhipova, Lidia Grauer, Igor Kuralenok, and Pavel Serdyukov. 2015. Search Engine Evaluation based on Search Engine Switching Prediction. In *SIGIR'2015*. ACM, 723–726.

[2] Eytan Bakshy and Dean Eckles. 2013. Uncertainty in online experiments with dependent data: An evaluation of bootstrap methods. In *KDD'2013*. 1303–1311.

[3] Shuchi Chawla, Jason Hartline, and Denis Nekipelov. 2016. A/B testing of auctions. In *EC'2016*.

[4] Thomas Crook, Brian Frasca, Ron Kohavi, and Roger Longbotham. 2009. Seven pitfalls to avoid when running controlled experiments on the web. In *KDD'2009*. 1105–1114.

[5] Alex Deng, Jiannan Lu, and Jonthan Litz. 2017. Trustworthy Analysis of Online A/B Tests: Pitfalls, challenges and solutions. In *WSDM'2017*. 641–649.

[6] Alex Deng and Xiaolin Shi. 2016. Data-Driven Metric Development for Online Controlled Experiments: Seven Lessons Learned. In *KDD'2016*.

[7] Alex Deng, Ya Xu, Ron Kohavi, and Toby Walker. 2013. Improving the sensitivity of online controlled experiments by utilizing pre-experiment data. In *WSDM'2013*. 123–132.

[8] Pavel Dmitriev and Xian Wu. 2016. Measuring Metrics. In *CIKM'2016*. 429–437.

[9] Alexey Drutsa. 2015. Sign-Aware Periodicity Metrics of User Engagement for Online Search Quality Evaluation. In *SIGIR'2015*. 779–782.

[10] Alexey Drutsa, Gleb Gusev, and Pavel Serdyukov. 2015. Engagement Periodicity in Search Engine Usage: Analysis and Its Application to Search Quality Evaluation. In *WSDM'2015*. 27–36.

[11] Alexey Drutsa, Gleb Gusev, and Pavel Serdyukov. 2015. Future User Engagement Prediction and its Application to Improve the Sensitivity of Online Experiments. In *WWW'2015*. 256–266.

[12] Alexey Drutsa, Gleb Gusev, and Pavel Serdyukov. 2017. Periodicity in User Engagement with a Search Engine and its Application to Online Controlled Experiments. *ACM Transactions on the Web (TWEB)* 11 (2017).

[13] Alexey Drutsa, Gleb Gusev, and Pavel Serdyukov. 2017. Using the Delay in a Treatment Effect to Improve Sensitivity and Preserve Directionality of Engagement Metrics in A/B Experiments. In *WWW'2017*.

[14] Alexey Drutsa, Anna Ufliand, and Gleb Gusev. 2015. Practical Aspects of Sensitivity in Online Experimentation with User Engagement Metrics. In *CIKM'2015*. 763–772.

[15] Georges Dupret and Mounia Lalmas. 2013. Absence time and user engagement: evaluating ranking functions. In *WSDM'2013*. 173–182.

[16] Bradley Efron and Robert J Tibshirani. 1994. *An introduction to the bootstrap*. CRC press.

[17] David A Freedman. 2008. On regression adjustments to experimental data. *Advances in Applied Mathematics* 40, 2 (2008), 180–193.

[18] David A Freedman, David Collier, Jasjeet S Sekhon, and Philip B Stark. 2010. *Statistical models and causal inference: a dialogue with the social sciences*. Cambridge University Press.

[19] Henning Hohnhold, Deirdre O'Brien, and Diane Tang. 2015. Focusing on the Long-term: It's Good for Users and Business. In *KDD'2015*. 1849–1858.

[20] Bernard J Jansen, Amanda Spink, and Vinish Kathuria. 2007. How to define searching sessions on web search engines. In *Advances in Web Mining and Web Usage Analysis*. Springer, 92–109.

[21] Eugene Kharitonov, Alexey Drutsa, and Pavel Serdyukov. 2017. Learning Sensitive Combinations of A/B Test Metrics. In *WSDM'2017*.

[22] Eugene Kharitonov, Craig Macdonald, Pavel Serdyukov, and Iadh Ounis. 2015. Optimised Scheduling of Online Experiments. In *SIGIR'2015*. 453–462.

[23] Eugene Kharitonov, Aleksandr Vorobev, Craig Macdonald, Pavel Serdyukov, and Iadh Ounis. 2015. Sequential Testing for Early Stopping of Online Experiments. In *SIGIR'2015*. 473–482.

[24] Ronny Kohavi, Thomas Crook, Roger Longbotham, Brian Frasca, Randy Henne, Juan Lavista Ferres, and Tamir Melamed. 2009. Online experimentation at Microsoft. *Data Mining Case Studies* (2009), 11.

[25] Ron Kohavi, Alex Deng, Brian Frasca, Roger Longbotham, Toby Walker, and Ya Xu. 2012. Trustworthy online controlled experiments: Five puzzling outcomes explained. In *KDD'2012*. 786–794.

[26] Ron Kohavi, Alex Deng, Brian Frasca, Toby Walker, Ya Xu, and Nils Pohlmann. 2013. Online controlled experiments at large scale. In *KDD'2013*. 1168–1176.

[27] R. Kohavi, A. Deng, R. Longbotham, and Y. Xu. 2014. Seven Rules of Thumb for Web Site Experimenters. In *KDD'2014*.

[28] Ron Kohavi, Randal M Henne, and Dan Sommerfield. 2007. Practical guide to controlled experiments on the web: listen to your customers not to the hippo. In *KDD'2007*. 959–967.

[29] Ron Kohavi, Roger Longbotham, Dan Sommerfield, and Randal M Henne. 2009. Controlled experiments on the web: survey and practical guide. *Data Min. Knowl. Discov.* 18, 1 (2009), 140–181.

[30] Ron Kohavi, David Messner, Seth Eliot, Juan Lavista Ferres, Randy Henne, Vignesh Kannappan, and Justin Wang. 2010. Tracking Users' Clicks and Submits: Tradeoffs between User Experience and Data Loss. (2010).

[31] Stephen L Morgan and Christopher Winship. 2014. *Counterfactuals and causal inference*. Cambridge University Press.

[32] Kirill Nikolaev, Alexey Drutsa, Ekaterina Gladkikh, Alexander Ulianov, Gleb Gusev, and Pavel Serdyukov. 2015. Extreme States Distribution Decomposition Method for Search Engine Online Evaluation. In *KDD'2015*. 845–854.

[33] Eric T Peterson. 2004. *Web analytics demystified: a marketer's guide to understanding how your web site affects your business*. Ingram.

[34] Alexey Poyarkov, Alexey Drutsa, Andrey Khalyavin, Gleb Gusev, and Pavel Serdyukov. 2016. Boosted Decision Tree Regression Adjustment for Variance Reduction in Online Controlled Experiments. In *KDD'2016*. 235–244.

[35] Filip Radlinski, Madhu Kurup, and Thorsten Joachims. 2008. How does clickthrough data reflect retrieval quality?. In *CIKM'2008*. 43–52.

[36] Kerry Rodden, Hilary Hutchinson, and Xin Fu. 2010. Measuring the user experience on a large scale: user-centered metrics for web applications. In *CHI'2010*. 2395–2398.

[37] Tetsuya Sakai. 2006. Evaluating evaluation metrics based on the bootstrap. In *SIGIR'2006*. 525–532.

[38] Yang Song, Xiaolin Shi, and Xin Fu. 2013. Evaluating and predicting user engagement change with degraded search relevance. In *WWW'2013*. 1213–1224.

[39] Diane Tang, Ashish Agarwal, Deirdre O'Brien, and Mike Meyer. 2010. Overlapping experiment infrastructure: More, better, faster experimentation. In *KDD'2010*. 17–26.

[40] Huizhi Xie and Juliette Aurisset. 2016. Improving the Sensitivity of Online Controlled Experiments: Case Studies at Netflix. In *KDD'2016*.

[41] Ya Xu and Nanyu Chen. 2016. Evaluating Mobile Apps with A/B and Quasi A/B Tests. In *KDD'2016*.

[42] Ya Xu, Nanyu Chen, Addrian Fernandez, Omar Sinno, and Anmol Bhasin. 2015. From infrastructure to culture: A/B testing challenges in large scale social networks. In *KDD'2015*.

Neural Graph Learning: Training Neural Networks Using Graphs

Thang D. Bui*
University of Cambridge
Cambridge, UK
tdb40@cam.ac.uk

Sujith Ravi
Google Research
Mountain View, California, US
sravi@google.com

Vivek Ramavajjala
Google Research
Mountain View, California, US
vramavaj@google.com

ABSTRACT

Label propagation is a powerful and flexible semi-supervised learning technique on graphs. Neural networks, on the other hand, have proven track records in many supervised learning tasks. In this work, we propose a training framework with a graph-regularised objective, namely *Neural Graph Machines*, that can combine the power of neural networks and label propagation. This work generalises previous literature on graph-augmented training of neural networks, enabling it to be applied to multiple neural architectures (Feed-forward NNs, CNNs and LSTM RNNs) and a wide range of graphs. The new objective allows the neural networks to harness both labeled and unlabeled data by: (a) allowing the network to train using labeled data as in the supervised setting, (b) biasing the network to learn similar hidden representations for neighboring nodes on a graph, in the same vein as label propagation. Such architectures with the proposed objective can be trained efficiently using stochastic gradient descent and scaled to large graphs, with a runtime that is linear in the number of edges. The proposed joint training approach convincingly outperforms many existing methods on a wide range of tasks (multi-label classification on social graphs, news categorization, document classification and semantic intent classification), with multiple forms of graph inputs (including graphs with and without node-level features) and using different types of neural networks.

CCS CONCEPTS

• **Computing methodologies** → **Neural networks**; *Semi-supervised learning settings*;

KEYWORDS

semi-supervised learning, neural network, graph

ACM Reference Format:
Thang D. Bui, Sujith Ravi, and Vivek Ramavajjala. 2018. Neural Graph Learning: Training Neural Networks Using Graphs. In *WSDM 2018: 11th ACM International Conference on Web Search and Data Mining, February 5–9, 2018, Marina Del Rey, CA, USA.* ACM, New York, NY, USA, 8 pages. https://doi.org/10.1145/3159652.3159731

*This work was done during an internship at Google.

WSDM 2018, February 5–9, 2018, Marina Del Rey, CA, USA

ACM ISBN 978-1-4503-5581-0/18/02
https://doi.org/10.1145/3159652.3159731

1 INTRODUCTION

Semi-supervised learning is a powerful machine learning paradigm that can improve the prediction performance compared to techniques that use only labeled data, by leveraging a large amount of unlabeled data. The need of semi-supervised learning arises in many problems in computer vision, natural language processing or social networks, in which getting labeled datapoints is expensive or unlabeled data is abundant and readily available.

There exist a plethora of semi-supervised learning methods. The simplest one uses bootstrapping techniques to generate pseudo-labels for unlabeled data generated from a system trained on labeled data. However, this suffers from label error feedbacks [13]. In a similar vein, autoencoder based methods often need to rely on a two-stage approach: train an autoencoder using unlabeled data to generate an embedding mapping, and use the learnt embeddings for prediction. In practice, this procedure is often costly and inaccurate. Another example is transductive SVMs [8], which is too computationally expensive to be used for large datasets. Methods that are based on generative models and amortized variational inference [10] can work well for images and videos, but it is not immediately clear on how to extend such techniques to handle sparse and multi-modal inputs or graphs over the inputs.

In contrast to the methods above, graph-based techniques such as label propagation [4, 23] often provide a versatile, scalable, and yet effective solution to a wide range of problems. These methods construct a smooth graph over the unlabeled and labeled data. Graphs are also often a natural way to describe the relationships between nodes, such as similarities between embeddings, phrases or images, or connections between entities on the web or relations in a social network. Edges in the graph connect semantically similar nodes or datapoints, and if present, edge weights reflect how strong such similarities are. By providing a set of labeled nodes, such techniques iteratively refine the node labels by aggregating information from neighbours and propagate these labels to the nodes' neighbours. In practice, these methods often converge quickly and can be scaled to large datasets with a large label space [15]. We build upon the principle behind label propagation for our method.

Another key motivation of our work is the recent advances in neural networks and their performance on a wide variety of supervised learning tasks such as image and speech recognition or sequence-to-sequence learning [7, 12, 17]. Such results are however conditioned on training very large networks on large datasets, which may need millions of labeled training input-output pairs. This begs the question: can we harness previous state-of-the-art semi-supervised learning techniques, to jointly train neural networks using limited labeled data and unlabeled data to improve its performance?

Contributions: We propose a discriminative training objective for neural networks with graph augmentation, that can be trained with stochastic gradient descent and efficiently scaled to large graphs. The new objective has a regularization term for generic neural network architectures that enforces similarity between nodes in the graphs, which is inspired by the objective function of label propagation. In particular, we show that:

- Graph-augmented neural network training can work for a wide range of neural networks, such as feed-forward, convolutional and recurrent networks. Additionally, this technique can be used in both inductive and transductive settings. It also helps learning in low-sample regime (small number of labeled nodes), which cannot be handled by vanilla neural network training.
- The framework can handle multiple forms of graphs, either naturally given or constructed based on embeddings and knowledge bases.
- As a by-product, our proposed framework provides a simple technique to finding smaller and faster neural networks that offer competitive performance with larger and slower non graph-augmented alternatives (see section 4.2).

We experimentally show that the proposed training framework outperforms state-of-the-art or perform favourably on a variety of prediction tasks and datasets, involving text features and/or graph inputs and on many different neural network architectures (see section 4).

The paper is organized as follows: we first review some background and literature, and relate them to our approach in section 2; we then detail the training objective and its properties in section 3; and finally we validate our approach on a range of experiments in section 4.

2 BACKGROUND AND RELATED WORKS

In this section, we will lay out the groundwork for our proposed training objective in section 3.

2.1 Neural network learning

Neural networks are a class of non-linear mapping from inputs to outputs and comprised of multiple layers that can potentially learn useful representations for predicting the outputs. We will view various models such as feed-forward neural networks, recurrent neural networks and convolutional networks under the same umbrella. Given a set of N training input-output pairs $\{x_n, y_n\}_{n=1}^N$, such neural networks are often trained by performing maximum likelihood learning, that is, tuning their parameters so that the networks' outputs are close to the ground truth under some criterion,

$$C_{\text{NN}}(\theta) = \sum_n c(g_\theta(x_n), y_n), \tag{1}$$

where $g_\theta(\cdot)$ denotes the overall mapping, parameterized by θ, and $c(\cdot)$ denotes a loss function such as l-2 for regression or cross entropy for classification. The cost function c and the mapping g are typically differentiable w.r.t θ, which facilitates optimisation via gradient descent. Importantly, this can be scaled to a large number of training instances by employing stochastic training using minibatches of data. However, it is not clear how unlabeled data, if available, can be treated using this objective, or if extra information about the training set, such as relational structures can be used.

2.2 Graph-based semi-supervised learning

In this section, we provide a concise introduction to graph-based semi-supervised learning using *label propagation* and its training objective. Suppose we are given a graph $G = (V, E, W)$ where V is the set of nodes, E the set of edges and W the edge weight matrix. Let V_l, V_u be the labeled and unlabeled nodes in the graph. The goal is to predict a soft assignment of labels for each node in the graph, $\hat{Y}$, given the training label distribution for the seed nodes, Y. Mathematically, label propagation performs minimization of the following convex objective function, for L labels,

$$\begin{aligned} C_{\text{LP}}(\hat{Y}) = \mu_1 & \sum_{v \in V_l} \left\| \hat{Y}_v - Y_v \right\|_2^2 \\ & + \mu_2 \sum_{v \in V, u \in \mathcal{N}(v)} w_{u,v} \left\| \hat{Y}_v - \hat{Y}_u \right\|_2^2 \\ & + \mu_3 \sum_{v \in V} \left\| \hat{Y}_v - U \right\|_2^2, \end{aligned} \tag{2}$$

subject to $\sum_{l=1}^{L} \hat{Y}_{vl} = 1$, where $\mathcal{N}(v)$ is the neighbour node set of the node v, and U is the prior distribution over all labels, $w_{u,v}$ is the edge weight between nodes u and v, and μ_1, μ_2, and μ_3 are hyperparameters that balance the contribution of individual terms in the objective. The terms in the objective function above encourage that: (a) the label distribution of seed nodes should be close to the ground truth, (b) the label distribution of neighbouring nodes should be similar, and, (c) if relevant, the label distribution should stay close to our prior belief. This objective function can be solved efficiently using iterative methods such as the Jacobi procedure. That is, in each step, each node aggregates the label distributions from its neighbours and adjusts its own distribution, which is then repeated until convergence. In practice, the iterative updates can be done in parallel or in a distributed fashion which then allows large graphs with a large number of nodes and labels to be trained efficiently. [4] and [15] provide good surveys on the topic for interested readers.

There are many variants of label propagation that could be viewed as optimising modified versions of eq. (2), and in essence balancing the *smoothness* constraint and the *fitting* constraint [22]. For example, manifold regularization [3] replaces the label distribution $\hat{Y}$ by a Reproducing Kernel Hilbert Space mapping from input features. Similarly, [18] also employs such mapping but uses a feed-forward neural network instead. Both methods can be classified as inductive learning algorithms; whereas the original label propagation algorithm is transductive [19].

These aforementioned methods are closest to our proposed approach; however, there are key differences. Our work generalizes previously proposed frameworks for graph-augmented training of neural networks (e.g., [18]) and extends it to new settings, for example, when there is only graph input and no features are available. Unlike the previous works, we show that the graph augmented training method can work with multiple neural network architectures (Feed-forward NNs, CNNs, RNNs) and on multiple prediction tasks and datasets using *natural* as well as *constructed* graphs. The experiment results (see section 4) clearly validate the effectiveness of this method in all these different settings, in both inductive and transductive learning paradigms. Besides the methodology, our study also presents an important contribution towards assessing the effectiveness of graph combined neural networks as a generic training mechanism for different architectures and problems, which was not well studied in previous work.

More recently, graph embedding techniques have been used to create node embedding that encodes local structures of the graph and the provided node labels [14, 19]. These techniques target learning better node representations to be used for other tasks such as node classification. In this work, we aim to directly learn better predictive models from the graph. We compare our method to these two-stage (embedding + classifier) techniques in several experiments in section 4

Our work is also different and orthogonal to recent works on using neural networks *on* graphs, for example: [5, 11] employ spectral graph convolution to create a neural-network like classifier. However, these approaches require many approximations to arrive at a practical implementation. Here, we advocate a training objective that *uses* graphs to augment neural network learning, and works with many forms of graphs and with any type of neural network.

3 NEURAL GRAPH MACHINES

In this section, we devise a discriminative training objective for neural networks, that is inspired by the label propagation objective and uses both labeled and unlabeled data, and can be trained by stochastic gradient descent.

First, we take a close look at the two objective functions discussed in section 2. The label propagation objective (eq. (2)) ensures the predicted label distributions of neighbouring nodes to be similar, while those of labeled nodes to be close to the ground truth. For example: if a *cat* image and a *dog* image are strongly connected in a graph, and if the *cat* node is labeled as *animal*, the predicted probability of the *dog* node being *animal* is also high. In contrast, the neural network training objective (eq. (1)) only takes into account the labeled instances, and ensure correct predictions on the training set. As a consequence, a neural network trained on the *cat* image alone will not make an accurate prediction on the *dog* image.

Such shortcoming of neural network training can be rectified by biasing the network using prior knowledge about the relationship between instances in the dataset. In particular, for the domains we are interested in, training instances (either labeled or unlabeled) that are connected in a graph, for example, *dog* and *cat* in the above example, should have similar predictions. This can be done by encouraging neighboring data points to have a similar hidden representation learnt by a neural network, resulting in a modified objective function for training neural network architectures using both labeled and unlabeled datapoints. We call architectures trained using this objective *Neural Graph Machines* (NGM), and schematically illustrate the concept in figure 1. The proposed objective function is a weighted sum of the neural network cost and the label propagation cost as follows,

$$\begin{aligned} C_{\text{NGM}}(\theta) = \alpha_1 & \sum_{(u,v)\in\mathcal{E}_{LL}} w_{uv} d(h_\theta(x_u), h_\theta(x_v)) \\ + \alpha_2 & \sum_{(u,v)\in\mathcal{E}_{LU}} w_{uv} d(h_\theta(x_u), h_\theta(x_v)) \\ + \alpha_3 & \sum_{(u,v)\in\mathcal{E}_{UU}} w_{uv} d(h_\theta(x_u), h_\theta(x_v) \\ + & \sum_{n=1}^{V_l} c(g_\theta(x_n), y_n), \end{aligned} \quad (3)$$

where $\mathcal{E}_{LL}$, $\mathcal{E}_{LU}$, and $\mathcal{E}_{UU}$ are sets of labeled-labeled, labeled-unlabeled and unlabeled-unlabeled edges correspondingly, $h(\cdot)$ represents the hidden representations of the inputs produced by the neural network, and $d(\cdot)$ is a distance metric, and $\{\alpha_1, \alpha_2, \alpha_3\}$ are hyperparameters. Note that we have separated the terms based on the edge types, as these can affect the training differently.

Our framework is general so that one can plug in either the hidden representations at any intermediate layer or the estimated soft label vector at the final layer. However, similar to any neural network regularisation scheme, it is not obvious what strategy works best in general. For example, forcing bottom layers (closer to the inputs) to be similar would have a stronger regularisation effect, and vice versa. In practice, we choose an l-1 or l-2 distance metric for $d(\cdot)$, and $h(x)$ to be the last hidden layer of the neural network, or a cross-entropy cost for the predicted label vector.

3.1 Connections to previous methods

The graph-dependent α hyperparameters control the balance of the contributions of different edge types. When $\{\alpha_i = 0\}_{i=1}^3$, the proposed objective ignores the similarity constraint and becomes a supervised-only neural network objective as in eq. (1). When only $\alpha_1 \neq 0$, the training cost has an additional term for labeled nodes, that acts as a regularizer. When $g_\theta(x) = h_\theta(x) = \hat{y}$, where $\hat{y}$ is the label distribution, the individual cost functions (c and d) are squared l-2 norm, and the objective is trained using $\hat{y}$ directly instead of θ, we arrive at the label propagation objective in eq. (2). Therefore, the proposed objective could be thought of as a *non-linear* version of the label propagation objective, and a *graph-regularized* version of the neural network training objective.

3.2 Network inputs and graph construction

Similar to graph-based label propagation, the choice of the input graphs is critical, to correctly bias the neural network's prediction. Depending on the type of the graphs and nodes in the graph, they can be readily available to use such as social networks or protein linking networks, or they can be constructed (a) using generic graphs such as Knowledge Bases, that consists of relationship links between entities, (b) using embeddings learnt by an unsupervised learning technique, or, (c) using sparse feature representations for each vertex. Additionally, the proposed training objective can be easily modified for directed graphs.

We have discussed using node-level features as inputs to the neural network. In the absence of such inputs, our training scheme can still be deployed using input features derived from the graph itself.

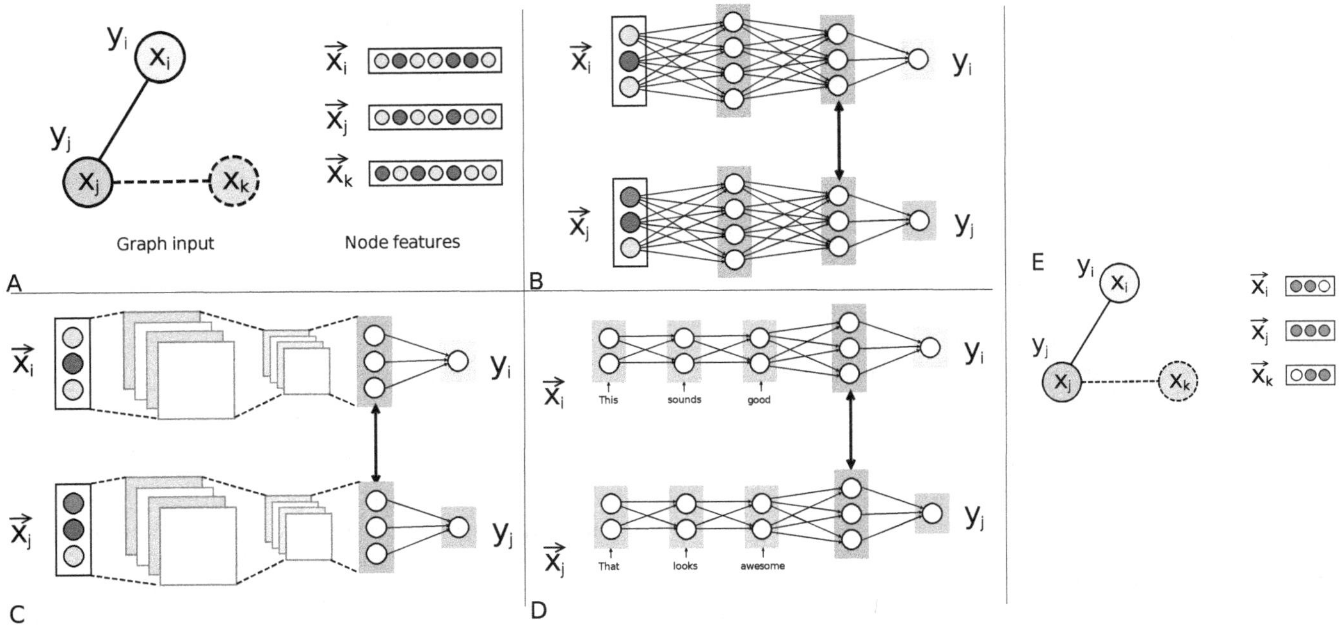

Figure 1: A: An example of a graph and feature inputs. In this case, there are two labeled nodes (x_i, x_j) and one unlabeled node (x_k), and two edges. The feature vectors, one for each node, are used as neural network inputs. B, C and D: Illustration of Neural Graph Machine for feed-forward, convolution and recurrent networks respectively: the training flow ensures the neural net to make accurate node-level predictions and biases the hidden representations/embeddings of neighbouring nodes to be similar. In this example, we force h_i and h_j to be similar as there is an edge connecting x_i and x_j nodes. E: Illustration of how we can construct inputs to the neural network using the adjacency matrix. In this example, we have three nodes and two edges. The feature vector created for each node *(shown on the right)* **has 1's at its index and indices of nodes that it's adjacent to.**

We show in figure 1 and in the experiments that the neighbourhood information such as rows in the adjacency matrix is simple to construct, yet powerful inputs to the network. These features can also be combined with existing features.

When the number of graph nodes is high, this construction can have a high complexity and result in a large number of input features. This can be avoided by several ways: (i) clustering the nodes and using the cluster assignments and similarities, (ii) learning an embedding function of nodes [14], or (iii) sampling the neighbourhood/context [19]. In practice, we observe that the input space can be bounded by a constant, even for massive graphs, with efficient scalable methods like unsupervised propagation (i.e., propagating node identity labels across the graph and selecting ones with the highest support as input features to neural graph machines).

3.3 Optimization

The proposed objective function in eq. (3) has several summations over the labeled points and edges, and can be equivalently written as follows,

$$\begin{aligned} C_{\text{NGM}}(\theta) = & \sum_{(u,v)\in\mathcal{E}_{LL}} [\alpha_1 w_{uv} d(h_\theta(x_u), h_\theta(x_v)) + c_{uv}] \\ & + \sum_{(u,v)\in\mathcal{E}_{LU}} [\alpha_2 w_{uv} d(h_\theta(x_u), h_\theta(x_v)) + c_u] \\ & + \sum_{(u,v)\in\mathcal{E}_{UU}} \alpha_3 w_{uv} d(h_\theta(x_u), h_\theta(x_v)), \end{aligned} \tag{4}$$

where

$$c_{uv} = \frac{1}{|u|} c(g_\theta(x_u), y_u) + \frac{1}{|v|} c(g_\theta(x_v), y_v); \quad c_u = \frac{1}{|u|} c(g_\theta(x_u), y_u),$$

$|u|$ and $|v|$ are the number of edges incident to vertices u and v, respectively. The objective in its new form enables stochastic training to be deployed by sampling edges. In particular, in each training iteration, we use a minibatch of edges and obtain the stochastic gradients of the objective. To further reduce noise and speedup learning, we sample edges within a neighbourhood region, that is to make sure some sampled edges have shared end nodes.

3.4 Complexity

The complexity of each epoch in training using eq. (4) is $O(M)$ where $M = |\mathcal{E}|$ is the number of edges in the graph. In the case where there is a large number of unlabeled-unlabeled edges, they potentially do not help learning and could be ignored, leading to a lower complexity. One strategy to include them is self-training, that is to grow seeds or labeled nodes as we train the networks. We experimentally demonstrate this technique in section 4.4. Predictions at inference time can be made at the same cost as that of vanilla neural networks.

4 EXPERIMENTS

In this section, we provide several experiments showing the efficacy of the proposed training objective on a wide range of tasks, datasets and network architectures. All the experiments are done using a

TensorFlow implementation [1]. Models were trained using multiple runs, each experiment was run for a fixed number of time steps and batch size (details described in each section). The observed variance across runs wrt accuracy was small, around ±0.1% Note that we did not perform any cross-validation to select the regularisation loss or which hidden layers to compare. As such, we expect even better results than ones presented below if there is a more careful selection in place.

4.1 Multi-label Classification of Nodes on Graphs

We first demonstrate our approach using a multi-label classification problem on nodes in a relationship graph. In particular, the *BlogCatalog* dataset [2], a network of social relationships between bloggers is considered. This graph has 10,312 nodes, 333,983 edges and 39 labels per node, which represent the bloggers, their social connections and the bloggers' interests, respectively. Following previous approaches in the literature [2, 6], we train and make predictions using multiple one-vs-rest classifiers.

Since there are no provided features for each node, we use the rows of the adjacency matrix as input features, as discussed in section 3.2 in the main text. Feed-forward neural networks (FFNNs) with one hidden layer of 50 units are employed to map the constructed inputs to the node labels. As we use the test set to construct the graph and augment the training objective, the training in this experiment is transductive. Critically, to combat the unbalanced training set, we employ weighted sampling during training, i.e. making sure each minibatch has both positive and negative examples. In this experiment, we fix α_i to be equal, and experiment with $\alpha = 0.1$ and use the l-2 metric to compute the distance d between the hidden representations of the networks. In addition, we create a range of train/test splits by varying the number of training points being presented to the networks.

We compare our method (NGM-FFNN) against a two-stage approach that first uses node2vec [6] to generate node embeddings and then uses a linear one-vs-rest classifier for classification. The methods are evaluated using two metrics Macro F1 and Micro F1. The average results for different train/test splits using our method and the baseline are included in table 1. In addition, we compare NGM-FFNN with a non-augmented FFNN in which $\alpha = 0$, i.e. no edge information is used during training. We observe that the graph-augmented training scheme performs better (6% relative improvement on Macro F1 when the training set size is 20% and 50% of the dataset) or comparatively (when the training size is 80%) compared to the vanilla neural networks trained with no edge information. Both methods significantly outperform the approach that uses node embeddings and linear classifiers. We observe the same improvement over node2vec on the Micro F1 metric and NGM-FFNN is comparable to vanilla FFNN ($\alpha = 0$) but outperforms other methods on the recall metric.

These results demonstrate that using the graph itself as direct inputs to the neural network and letting the network figure out a non-linear mapping directly from the raw graph is more effective

Table 1: Macro F1 results for BlogCatalog dataset averaged over 10 random splits. The higher is better. Graph regularized neural networks outperform node2vec embedding and a linear classifer in all training size settings.

|Train| / |Dataset|	NGM-FFNN	node2vec[1]
20%	**0.191**	0.168
50%	**0.242**	0.174
80%	**0.262**	0.177

than the two-stage approach considered. More importantly, the results also show that using the graph information improves the performance in the limited data regime (for example: when training set is only 20% or 50% of the dataset).

4.2 Text Classification using Character-level CNNs

We evaluate the proposed objective function on a multi-class text classification task using a character-level convolutional neural network (CNN). We use the AG news dataset from [21], where the task is to classify a news article into one of 4 categories. Each category has 30,000 examples for training and 1,900 examples for testing. In addition to the train and test sets, there are 111,469 examples that are treated as unlabeled examples.

As there is no provided graph structure linking the articles, we create such a graph based on the embeddings of the articles. We restrict the graph construction to only the train set and the unlabeled examples and keep the test set only for evaluation. We use the Google News word2vec corpus to calculate the average embedding for each news article and use the cosine similarity of document embeddings as a similarity metric. Each node is restricted to have a maximum of 5 neighbors.

We construct the CNN in the same way as [21] and pick their competitive *"small CNN"* as our baseline for a more reasonable comparison to our set-up. Our approach employs the same network, but with significantly smaller number of convolutional layers and layer sizes, as shown in table 2.

Table 2: Settings of CNNs for the text classification experiment, including the number of convolutional layers and their sizes. The baseline model is the *small CNN* from [21] and is significantly larger than our model.

Setting	Baseline	Our "tiny CNN"
# of conv. layers	6	3
Frame size in conv. layers	256	32
# of FC layers	3	3
Hidden units in FC layers	1024	256

The networks are trained with the same hyper-parameters as reported in [21]. We observed that the model converged within 20 epochs (the model loss did not change much) and hence used this as a stopping criterion for this task. Experiments also showed that running the network for longer also did not change the qualitative

[1]These results are different compared to [6], since we treat the classifiers (one per label) independently. Both methods shown here use the exact same setting and training/test data splits.

performance. We use the cross-entropy loss on the final outputs of the network, that is d = cross_entropy($g(x_u), g(x_v)$), to compute the distance between nodes on an edge. In addition, we also experiment with a data augmentation technique using an English thesaurus, as done in [21].

We compare the "tiny CNN" trained using the proposed objective function with the baseline using the accuracy on the test set in table 3. Our approach outperforms the baseline by provides a 1.8% absolute and 2.1% relative improvement in accuracy, despite using a much smaller network. In addition, our model with graph augmentation trains much faster and produces results on par or better than the performance of a significantly larger network, *"large CNN"* [21], which has an accuracy of 87.18 without using a thesaurus, and 86.61 with the thesaurus.

Table 3: Results for news article categorization using character-level CNNs. Our method gives better predictive accuracy, despite using a much smaller CNN compared to the "small CNN" baseline from [21]‡.

Network	Accuracy %
Baseline‡	84.35
Baseline with thesaurus augmentation‡	85.20
Our "tiny" CNN	85.07
Our "tiny" CNN with NGM	**86.90**

4.3 Semantic Intent Classification using LSTM RNNs

We compare the performance of our approach for training long short-term memory RNN sequence models (LSTMs) for a semantic intent classification task as described in the recent work on SmartReply [9] for automatically generating short email responses. One of the underlying tasks in SmartReply is to discover and map short response messages to semantic intent clusters.[2] We choose 20 intent classes and created a dataset comprised of 5,483 samples (3,832 for training, 560 for validation and 1,091 for testing). Each sample instance corresponds to a short response message text paired with a semantic intent category that was manually verified by human annotators. For example, *"That sounds awesome!"* and *"Sounds fabulous"* belong to the *sounds good* intent cluster.

We construct a sparse graph in a similar manner as the news categorization task using word2vec embeddings over the message text and computing similarity to generate a response message graph with fixed node degree (k=10). We use l-2 for the distance metric $d(\cdot)$ and choose α based on the development set.

We run the experiments for a fixed number of time steps and pick the best results on the development set. A multilayer LSTM architecture (2 layers, 100 dimensions) is used for the RNN sequence model. The LSTM model and its NGM variant are also compared against other baseline systems—*Random* baseline ranks the intent categories randomly and *Frequency* baseline ranks them in order of their frequency in the training corpus. To evaluate the intent prediction quality of different approaches, for each test instance, we compute the rank of the actual intent category rank_i with respect to the ranking produced by the method and use this to calculate the Mean Reciprocal Rank: MRR $= \frac{1}{N}\sum_{i=1}^{N}\frac{1}{\text{rank}_i}$ We show in table 4 that LSTM RNNs with our proposed graph-augmented training objective function outperform standard baselines by achieving a better MRR.

[2]For details regarding SmartReply and how the semantic intent clusters are generated, refer [9].

Table 4: Results for Semantic Intent Classification using graph-augmented LSTM RNNs and baselines. Higher MRR is better.

Model	Mean Reciprocal Rank (MRR)
Random	0.175
Frequency	0.258
LSTM	0.276
NGM-LSTM	**0.284**

4.4 Low-supervision Document Classification

Finally, we compare our method on a task with very limited supervision — the PubMed document classification problem [16]. The task is to classify each document into one of 3 classes, with each document being described by a TF-IDF weighted word vector. The graph is available as a citation network: two documents are connected to each other if one cites the other. The graph has 19,717 nodes and 44,338 edges, with each class having 20 seed nodes and 1000 test nodes. In our experiments we exclude the test nodes from the graph entirely, training only on the labeled and unlabeled nodes.

We train a feed-forward neural network (FFNN) with two hidden layers with 250 and 100 neurons, using the l-2 distance metric on the last hidden layer. The NGM-FFNN model is trained with $\alpha_i = 0.2$, while the baseline FFNN is trained with $\alpha_i = 0$ (i.e., a supervised-only model). We use self-training to train the model, starting with just the 60 seed nodes (20 per class) as training data. The amount of training data is iteratively increased by assigning labels to the immediate neighbors of the labeled nodes and retraining the model. For the self-trained NGM-FFNN model, this strategy results in incrementally growing the neighborhood and thereby, *LL* and *LU* edges in equation 4 objective.

We compare the final NGM-FFNN model against the FFNN baseline and other techniques reported in [19] including the Planetoid models [19], semi-supervised embedding [18], manifold regression [3], transductive SVM [8], label propagation [24], graph embeddings [14] and a linear softmax model. Full results are included in table 5. The results show that the NGM model (without any tuning) outperforms many baselines including FFNN, semi-supervised embedding, manifold regularization and Planetoid-G/Planetoid-T, and compares favorably to Planetoid-I. Most importantly, this result demonstrates the graph augmentation scheme can lead to better regularised neural networks, especially in low sample regime (20 samples per class in this case). We believe that with tuning, NGM accuracy can be improved even further.

Table 5: Results for document classification on the PubMed dataset using neural networks. The top results are taken from [19]. The bottom two rows are ours, with the NGM training outperforming all other baselines, except Planetoid-I. Please see text for relevant references.

Method	Accuracy
Linear + Softmax	0.698
Semi-supervised embedding	0.711
Manifold regularization	0.707
Transductive SVM	0.622
Label propagation	0.630
Graph embedding	0.653
Planetoid-I	0.772
Planetoid-G	0.664
Planetoid-T	0.757
Feed-forward NN	0.709
NGM-FFNN	0.759

5 CONCLUSIONS

We have revisited graph-augmentation training of neural networks and proposed Neural Graph Machines as a general framework for doing so. Its objective function encourages the neural networks to make accurate node-level predictions, as in vanilla neural network training, as well as constrains the networks to learn similar hidden representations for nodes connected by an edge in the graph. Importantly, the objective can be trained by stochastic gradient descent and scaled to large graphs.

We validated the efficacy of the graph-augmented objective on various tasks including bloggers' interest, text category and semantic intent classification problems, using a wide range of neural network architectures (FFNNs, CNNs and LSTM RNNs). The experimental results demonstrated that graph-augmented training almost always helps to find better neural networks that outperforms other techniques in predictive performance or even much smaller networks that are faster and easier to train. Additionally, the node-level input features can be combined with graph features as inputs to the neural networks. We showed that a neural network that simply takes the adjacency matrix of a graph and produces node labels, can perform better than a recently proposed two-stage approach using sophisticated graph embeddings and a linear classifier. Our framework also excels when the neural network is small, or when there is limited supervision available. We note that though overall complexity is linear in the number of edges in the graph, in practice NGM is more robust compared to the standard training method (without regularisation) and that it can converge to a better solution given a fixed time budget. We attribute this effect to the graph structure used for optimization within each mini-batch rather than individual training examples in baseline networks.

While our objective can be applied to multiple graphs which come from different domains, we have not fully explored this aspect and leave this as future work. We expect the domain-specific networks can interact with the graphs to determine the importance of each domain/graph source in prediction. We also did not explore using graph regularisation for different hidden layers of the neural networks; we expect this is key for the multi-graph transfer setting [20]. Another possible future extension is to use our objective on directed graphs, that is to control the direction of influence between nodes during training.

ACKNOWLEDGMENTS

The authors would like to thank the Google Expander team for insightful feedback.

REFERENCES

[1] Martín Abadi, Ashish Agarwal, Paul Barham, Eugene Brevdo, Zhifeng Chen, Craig Citro, Greg S. Corrado, Andy Davis, Jeffrey Dean, Matthieu Devin, Sanjay Ghemawat, Ian Goodfellow, Andrew Harp, Geoffrey Irving, Michael Isard, Yangqing Jia, Rafal Jozefowicz, Lukasz Kaiser, Manjunath Kudlur, Josh Levenberg, Dan Mané, Rajat Monga, Sherry Moore, Derek Murray, Chris Olah, Mike Schuster, Jonathon Shlens, Benoit Steiner, Ilya Sutskever, Kunal Talwar, Paul Tucker, Vincent Vanhoucke, Vijay Vasudevan, Fernanda Viégas, Oriol Vinyals, Pete Warden, Martin Wattenberg, Martin Wicke, Yuan Yu, and Xiaoqiang Zheng. 2015. TensorFlow: Large-scale machine learning on heterogeneous systems. (2015). http://tensorflow.org/ Software available from tensorflow.org.

[2] Nitin Agarwal, Huan Liu, Sudheendra Murthy, Arunabha Sen, and Xufei Wang. 2009. A social identity approach to identify familiar strangers in a social network.. In *3rd International AAAI Conference on Weblogs and Social Media (ICWSM09).*

[3] Mikhail Belkin, Partha Niyogi, and Vikas Sindhwani. 2006. Manifold regularization: A geometric framework for learning from labeled and unlabeled examples. *Journal of machine learning research* 7, Nov (2006), 2399–2434.

[4] Yoshua Bengio, Olivier Delalleau, and Nicolas Le Roux. 2006. Label propagation and quadratic criterion. In *Semi-supervised learning*, O Chapelle, B Scholkopf, and A Zien (Eds.). MIT Press, 193–216.

[5] Michaël Defferrard, Xavier Bresson, and Pierre Vandergheynst. 2016. Convolutional neural networks on graphs with fast localized spectral filtering. In *Advances in Neural Information Processing Systems.* 3837–3845.

[6] Aditya Grover and Jure Leskovec. 2016. node2vec: Scalable feature learning for networks. In *Proceedings of the 22nd ACM SIGKDD International Conference on Knowledge Discovery and Data Mining, San Francisco, CA, USA, August 13-17, 2016.* 855–864.

[7] Geoffrey Hinton, Li Deng, Dong Yu, George E Dahl, Abdel-rahman Mohamed, Navdeep Jaitly, Andrew Senior, Vincent Vanhoucke, Patrick Nguyen, Tara N Sainath, et al. 2012. Deep neural networks for acoustic modeling in speech recognition: The shared views of four research groups. *IEEE Signal Processing Magazine* 29, 6 (2012), 82–97.

[8] Thorsten Joachims. 1999. Transductive inference for text classification using support vector machines. In *International Conference on Machine Learning.*

[9] Anjuli Kannan, Karol Kurach, Sujith Ravi, Tobias Kaufmann, Andrew Tomkins, Balint Miklos, Greg Corrado, Laszlo Lukacs, Marina Ganea, Peter Young, and Vivek Ramavajjala. 2016. Smart Reply: Automated response suggestion for Email. In *Proceedings of the ACM SIGKDD Conference on Knowledge Discovery and Data Mining (KDD).*

[10] Diederik P Kingma, Shakir Mohamed, Danilo Jimenez Rezende, and Max Welling. 2014. Semi-supervised learning with deep generative models. In *Advances in Neural Information Processing Systems.* 3581–3589.

[11] Thomas N Kipf and Max Welling. 2016. Semi-supervised classification with graph convolutional networks. *arXiv preprint arXiv:1609.02907* (2016).

[12] Alex Krizhevsky, Ilya Sutskever, and Geoffrey E Hinton. 2012. Imagenet classification with deep convolutional neural networks. In *Advances in Neural Information Processing Systems.* 1097–1105.

[13] Dong-Hyun Lee. 2013. Pseudo-Label: The simple and efficient semi-supervised learning method for deep neural networks. In *ICML 2013 Workshop: Challenges in Representation Learning (WREPL).*

[14] Bryan Perozzi, Rami Al-Rfou, and Steven Skiena. 2014. Deepwalk: Online learning of social representations. In *Proceedings of the 20th ACM SIGKDD international conference on Knowledge discovery and data mining.* ACM, 701–710.

[15] Sujith Ravi and Qiming Diao. 2016. Large scale distributed semi-supervised learning using streaming approximation. In *Proceedings of the 19th International Conference on Artificial Intelligence and Statistics.* 519–528.

[16] Prithviraj Sen, Galileo Namata, Mustafa Bilgic, Lise Getoor, Brian Galligher, and Tina Eliassi-Rad. 2008. Collective classification in network data. *AI magazine* 29, 3 (2008), 93.

[17] Ilya Sutskever, Oriol Vinyals, and Quoc V Le. 2014. Sequence to sequence learning with neural networks. In *Advances in Neural Information Processing Systems.* 3104–3112.

[18] Jason Weston, Frédéric Ratle, Hossein Mobahi, and Ronan Collobert. 2012. Deep learning via semi-supervised embedding. In *Neural Networks: Tricks of the Trade.* Springer, 639–655.

[19] Zhilin Yang, William Cohen, and Ruslan Salakhudinov. 2016. Revisiting semi-supervised learning with graph embeddings. In *Proceedings of The 33rd International Conference on Machine Learning.* 40–48.

[20] Jason Yosinski, Jeff Clune, Yoshua Bengio, and Hod Lipson. 2014. How transferable are features in deep neural networks?. In *Advances in Neural Information Processing Systems.* 3320–3328.

[21] Xiang Zhang, Junbo Zhao, and Yann LeCun. 2015. Character-level convolutional networks for text classification. In *Advances in Neural Information Processing Systems.* 649–657.

[22] Denny Zhou, Olivier Bousquet, Thomas N Lal, Jason Weston, and Bernhard Schölkopf. 2004. Learning with local and global consistency. In *Advances in Neural Information Processing Systems.* 321–328.

[23] Xiaojin Zhu and Zoubin Ghahramani. [n. d.]. *Learning from labeled and unlabeled data with label propagation.* Technical Report. School of Computer Science, Canegie Mellon University.

[24] X Zhu, Z Ghahramani, and J Lafferty. 2003. Semi-supervised learning using Gaussian fields and harmonic functions. In *Proceedings of the 20th International Conference on Machine Learning (ICML-2003) Volume 2*, Vol. 2. AIAA Press, 912–919.

Sketch 'Em All: Fast Approximate Similarity Search for Dynamic Data Streams

Marc Bury
TU Dortmund
Dortmund, Germany
marc.bury@tu-dortmund.de

Chris Schwiegelshohn, Mara Sorella
Sapienza University of Rome
Rome, Italy
{schwiegelshohn,sorella}@diag.uniroma1.it

ABSTRACT

Recommender systems are an integral part of many web applications. With increasingly larger user bases, scalability has become an important issue. Many of the most scalable algorithms with respect to both space and running times are based on locality-sensitive hashing (LSH). However, a significant drawback is that these methods are only able to handle insertions to user profiles and tend to perform poorly when items may be removed. We initiate the study of scalable locality-sensitive hashing for dynamic input. Specifically, using the Jaccard index as similarity measure, we design (1) a sketching algorithm for similarity estimation via a black box reduction to ℓ_0 norm estimation and (2) a locality sensitive hashing scheme maintainable in fully dynamic data streams that quickly filters out low-similarity pairs. Our algorithms have little to no overhead in terms of running time compared to previous LSH approaches for the insertion only case, and drastically outperform previous algorithms in case of deletions.

CCS CONCEPTS

• **Information systems** → **Nearest-neighbor search**; **Data stream mining**; • **Theory of computation** → *Sketching and sampling*;

KEYWORDS

locality sensitive hashing, dynamic data streams, Jaccard index

ACM Reference Format:

Marc Bury and Chris Schwiegelshohn, Mara Sorella. 2018. Sketch 'Em All: Fast Approximate Similarity Search for Dynamic Data Streams. In *WSDM 2018: WSDM 2018: The Eleventh ACM International Conference on Web Search and Data Mining , February 5–9, 2018, Marina Del Rey, CA, USA.* ACM, New York, NY, USA, 9 pages. https://doi.org/10.1145/3159652.3159694

1 INTRODUCTION

Recommender systems are an integral part of many online applications. The aim is to suggest an item or a set of items to a user based on other her behavior compared to that of other users. *Collaborative filtering* [28] is a simple, straightforward approach to produce such an item set by basing the recommendation on the most similar users in the data set and suggesting items not contained in the intersection. To apply such an approach, one typically requires two things: (1) a measure of similarity (or dissimilarity) between users and (2) scalable algorithms for evaluating these similarities. In these contexts scalability can mean fast running times, but can also require strict space constraints.

Though it is by no means the only method employed in this line of research, locality senstive hashing (LSH) satisfies both requirements [10, 13]. For a given similarity measure, the algorithm maintains a small number of hash-values, or fingerprints that represent user behavior in a succinct way. The name implies that the fingerprints have locality properties, i.e., similar users have a higher probability of sharing the same fingerprint whereas dissimilar users have a small probability of agreeing on a fingerprint. The fingerprints themselves allow the recommendation system to quickly filter out user pairs with low similarity, leading to running times that are almost linear in input and output size.

A crucial property of LSH-families is that they are data-oblivious, that is the properties of the hash family depend only on the similarity measure but not on the data. Therefore, LSH-based filtering can be easily facilitated in online and streaming models of computation, where user attributes are added one by one in an arbitrary order. The fingerprint computation may fail, however, if certain attributes get deleted. Attribute deletion occurs frequently, for instance, if the data set evolves over time. Amazon allows user to unmark certain bought items for recommendations, Twitter users have an unfollow option, and Last.fm users may delete songs or artists from the library. A naive way to incorporate deletions within the context of LSH is to recompute any affected fingerprint, which requires scanning the entire user profile and is clearly infeasible.

1.1 Our Contribution

In this paper, we aim to initiate the study of min-hashing in the dynamic data stream model. Our input consists of a sequence of triples (i, j, k), where $i \in [n]$ is the user identifier, $j \in [|U|]$ is the item identifier and $k \in \{-1, 1\}$ signifying insertion or deletion. Instead of maintaining an $n \times [|U|]$ user/attribute matrix M, we keep a sketch of $\text{polylog}(n \cdot |U|)$ bits per user. Our first goal is to maintain a small sketch of M such that we can facilitate fast min-hashing based filtering. Specifically, given two thresholds $r_2 < r_1$, we aim to find the majority of user pairs (A, B) with similarity $S(A, B) = \frac{|A \cap B|}{|A \cup B|} \geq r_1$ and filter out the majority of user pairs (A, B) with $S(A, B) \leq r_2$. The second goal is achieve accurate similarity estimations for each pair. We can show min-hashing approach itself has reasonable guarantees in theory and is accurate in practice. We supplement this result with a black box reduction to counting algorithms.

WSDM 2018, February 5–9, 2018, Marina Del Rey, CA, USA

ACM ISBN 978-1-4503-5581-0/18/02...$15.00
https://doi.org/10.1145/3159652.3159694

1.2 Related Work

Min-Hashing. Locality-sensitive hashing (LSH) describes an algorithmic framework for fast (approximate) nearest neighbor search in metric spaces. In the seminal paper by Indyk and Motwani [18], it was proposed as a way of coping with the *curse of dimensionality* for proximity problems in high-dimensional Euclidean spaces. The later, simpler definition by Charikar [7] was used even earlier in the context of min-hashing for the Jaccard index by Broder et al. [4–6]. As mentioned above, min-hashing computes a fingerprint of a binary vector by permuting the entries and storing the first non-zero entry. When looking for item sets similar to some set A, one can arrange multiple fingerprints to filter out small similarity set pairs while retaining high similarity set pairs, see Cohen et al. [10], and Leskovec et al. [21] for details.

Instead of using multiple independent hash functions to generate k fingerprints, Cohen and Kaplan suggested using the k smallest entries after a single evaluation [11, 12] which is known as bottom k-sampling, see also Hellerstein et al. [16]. Min-hashing itself is still an active area of research. Broder et al. [6] showed that an ideal min-hash family is infeasible to store, which initiated the search for more feasible alternatives. Indyk considered families of approximate min-wise indepedence [17], i.e. the probability of an item becoming the minimum is not uniform, but close to uniform, which was further improved by Feigenblat et al [15].

Instead of basing requirements on the hash-function, other papers focus on what guarantees are achievable by simpler, easily stored and evaluated hash-functions with limited independence. Of particular interest are 2-wise independent hash functions. Dietzfelbinger [14] showed that, given two random numbers a and b, the hash of x may be computed via $(ax + b) \gg k$, where k is a power of 2 and $\gg$ denotes a bit shift operation. This construction is to the best of our knowledge the fastest available and there exists theoretical evidence which supports that it may be, in many cases, good enough. Chung et al. [9] showed that if the entropy of the input is large enough, the bias incurred by 2-wise independent hash functions becomes negligible. Thorup [29] further showed that 2-wise independent hashing may be used for a bottom k sampling with a relative error of $\frac{1}{\sqrt{fk}}$, where f is the Jaccard similarity between two items. Better bounds are possible using more involved hash functions such as twisted tabulation hashing [26], double tabulation[30], and linear probing [24, 27].

Profile Sketching. Using the index of an item as a fingerprint is immediate and requires $\log |U|$ space. For two item sets A, B, we then require roughly $\frac{\log |U|}{\varepsilon^2 \cdot S(A,B)}$ bits of space to get an $(1 \pm \varepsilon)$-approximate estimate of the similarity $S(A, B)$. It turns out that this is not optimal. Bachrach and Porat [2, 3] and Li and König [22] proposed several improvements and constant size fingerprints are now known to exist. Complementing these upper bounds are lower bounds by Pagh et al. [25] who showed that that this is essentially optimal for summarizing Jaccard similarity.

We note that one of the algorithms proposed by Bachrach and Porat in [3] use an ℓ_2 estimation algorithm as a black box. It is well known that the ℓ_2 norm of a vector can be maintained in dynamic data streams (e.g. [31]). However, their algorithm only seems to work for if the similarity is sufficiently large, i. e., $S(A, B) \geq 0.5$.

1.3 Preliminaries

We have n users. A user profile is a subset of some universe U. The symmetric difference of two sets $A, B \subseteq U$ is $A \triangle B = (A \setminus B) \cup (B \setminus A)$. The complement is denoted by $\overline{A} = U \setminus A$. A symmetric function $S : U \times U \to [0, 1]$ with $S(A, A) = 1$ for all $A \in U$ is a similarity. Given $x, y \geq 0$ and $0 \leq z \leq z'$, the *rational set similarity* $S_{x,y,z,z'}$ between two non-empty item sets A and B is

$$S_{x,y,z,z'}(A,B) = \frac{x \cdot |A \cap B| + y \cdot |\overline{A \cup B}| + z \cdot |A \triangle B|}{x \cdot |A \cap B| + y \cdot |\overline{A \cup B}| + z' \cdot |A \triangle B|}$$

if it is defined and 1 otherwise [19]. The distance function induced by a similarity $S_{x,y,z,z'}$ is defined as $D_{x,y,z,z'}(A, B) := 1 - S_{x,y,z,z'}(A, B)$. If $D_{x,y,z,z'}$ is a metric, we call $S_{x,y,z,z'}$ a metric rational set similarity. The arguably most well-known rational set similarity is the Jaccard index $S_{1,0,0,1}(A, B) = \frac{|A \cap B|}{|A \cup B|}$. We denote numerator and denominator of a rational set similarity by $Num(A, B)$ and $Den(A, B)$, respectively. For some arbitrary but fixed order of the elements, we represent A via its characteristic vector $a \in \{0, 1\}^{|U|}$ with $a_i = 1$ iff $i \in A$. The ℓ_p-norm of a vector $x \in \mathbb{R}^d$ is defined as $\ell_p(x) = \sqrt[p]{\sum_{i=1}^{d} |x_i|^p}$. Taking the limit of p to 0, $\ell_0(x)$ is exactly the number of non-zero entries, i.e. $\ell_0(x) = |\{i \mid x_i \neq 0\}|$. An LSH for a similarity measure $S : U \times U \to [0, 1]$ is a set of hash functions H on U with an associated probability distribution such that

$$\mathbf{Pr}\left[h(A) = h(B)\right] = S(A, B)$$

for h drawn from H and any two item sets $A, B \subseteq U$. We will state our results in a slightly different manner. A (r_1, r_2, p_1, p_2)-sensitive hashing scheme for a similarity measure aims to find a distribution over a family of hash functions H such that any two item sets $A, B \subseteq U$ we have $\mathbf{Pr}[h(A) = h(B)] \geq p_1$ if $S(A, B) \geq r_1$ and $\mathbf{Pr}[h(A) = h(B)] \leq p_2$ if $S(A, B) \leq r_2$. The former definition due to Charikar [7] has a number of appealing properties and is a special case of the latter definition due to Indyk and Motwani [18]. Unfortunately, it is also a very strong condition and in fact not achievable for dynamic data streams. We emphasize that the general notions behind both definitions are essentially the same.

Roadmap. Section 2 describes the black-box reduction from similarity estimation to approximate counting and Section 3 contains the LSH-based filtering algorithm. We conclude with an experimental evaluation in Section 4 where we test our filtering algorithm on both a synthetic dataset and a real dataset based on music listening habits of users from Last.FM.

2 SIMILARITY SKETCHING IN DYNAMIC STREAMS

In this section, we aim to show that the distance function of any rational set similarity with an LSH can be $(1 \pm \epsilon)$-approximated in dynamic streams. First, we require the following characterization of such similarity measures.

THEOREM 2.1. *Let $x, y, z, z' > 0$. Then the following three statements are equivalent.*

(1) *$S_{x,y,z,z'}$ has an LSH.*
(2) *$1 - S_{x,y,z,z'}$ is a metric.*
(3) *$z' \geq \max(x, y, z)$.*

(1)⇒(2) was shown by Charikar [7], (2)⇒(1) was shown by Chierichetti and Kumar [8] and (2)⇔(3) was proven by Janssens [19]. We also recall the state of the art ℓ_0 sketching in dynamic streams.

Theorem 2.2 (Th. 10 of Kane, Nelson, and Woodruff [20]). *There is a dynamic streaming algorithm for $(1 \pm \varepsilon)$-approximating $\ell_0(x)$ of a $|U|$-dimensional vector x using space $O(\frac{1}{\varepsilon^2}\log|U|)$*[1]*, with 2/3 success probability, and with $O(1)$ update and reporting times.*

Theorem 2.3. *Given a constant $0 < \varepsilon \leq 0.5$, two item sets $A, B \subseteq U$ and some rational set similarity $S_{x,y,z,z'}$ with metric distance function $1 - S_{x,y,z,z'}$, there exists a dynamic streaming algorithm that maintains a $(1 \pm \varepsilon)$ approximation to $1 - S_{x,y,z,z'}(A, B)$ with constant probability. The algorithm uses $O(\frac{1}{\varepsilon^2}\log|U|)$ space and each update and query requires $O(1)$ time.*

Proof. We start with the observation that $|A \triangle B| = \ell_0(a-b)$ and $|A \cup B| = \ell_0(a+b)$, where a and b are the characteristic vectors of A and B, respectively. Since $Den(A, B) - Num(A, B) = (z' - z) \cdot |A \triangle B|$ is always non-negative due to $z' > z$, we only have to prove that $Den(A, B)$ is always a non-negative linear combination of terms that we can approximate via sketches. First, consider the case $x \geq y$. Reformulating $Den(A, B)$, we have

$$Den(A, B) = y \cdot n + (x - y) \cdot |A \cup B| + (z' - x) \cdot |A \triangle B|.$$

Then both numerator and denominator of $1 - S_{x,y,z,z'}$ can be written as a non-negative linear combination of n, $|A \triangle B|$ and $|A \cup B|$. Given a $(1 \pm \varepsilon)$ of these terms, we have an upper bound of $\frac{1+\varepsilon}{1-\varepsilon} \leq (1 + \varepsilon) \cdot (1 + 2\varepsilon) \leq (1 + 5\varepsilon)$ and a lower bound of $\frac{1-\varepsilon}{1+\varepsilon} \geq (1 - \varepsilon)^2 \geq (1 - 2\varepsilon)$ for any $\varepsilon \leq 0.5$. The case $x < y$ may be treated analogously as $S_{x,y,z,z'}(A, B) = S_{y,x,z,z'}(\overline{A}, \overline{B})$.

By plugging in the ℓ_0 sketch of Theorem 2.2 and rescaling ε by a factor of 5, the theorem follows. □

The probability of success can be further amplified to $1 - \delta$ in the standard way by taking the median estimate of $O(\log(1/\delta))$ independent repetitions of the algorithm. For n item sets, we then get the following corollary.

Corollary 2.4. *Let S be a rational set similarity with metric distance function $1 - S$. Given an initially empty $n \times |U|$ binary matrix M, there there exists a dynamic streaming algorithm that can compute with constant probability for all pairs $(i, i') \in [n] \times [n]$*

- *a $(1 \pm \varepsilon)$ multiplicative approximation of $1 - S(M_i, M_{i'})$ and*
- *an ϵ-additive approximation of $S(M_i, M_{i'})$.*

The algorithm uses $O(n \log n \cdot \varepsilon^{-2} \cdot \log|U|)$ space and each update and query needs $O(\log n)$ time.

We would like to remark that similar statements are also achievable for the distance of root similarity functions with an LSH scheme. We provide more details in a full version of this paper.

We note that despite the characterization of LSHable rational set similarities of Theorem 2.1, the existence of the approximations of Corollary 2.4 hints at, but does not directly imply the existence of a locality-sensitive hashing scheme or even an approximate locality-sensitive hashing scheme on the sketched data matrix in dynamic streams. Our second and main contribution now lies in the design of a simple LSH scheme maintainable in dynamic data streams, albeit with weaker approximation ratios.

[1]The exact space bounds of the ℓ_0 sketch by Kane, Nelson and Woodruff depends on the magnitude of the entries of the vector. The stated space bound is sufficient for our purposes.

3 AN LSH ALGORITHM FOR DYNAMIC DATA STREAMS

In the following, we will present a simple dynamic streaming algorithm that supports Indyk and Motwani-type sensitivity. Recall that we want to find pairs of users with similarity greater than a parameter r_1, while we do not want to report pairs with similarity less than r_2. The precise statement is as follows.

Theorem 3.1. *Let $0 < \varepsilon, \delta, r_1, r_2 < 1$ be parameters. Given a dynamic data stream with n users and $|U|$ attributes, there exists an algorithm that maintains a $(r_1, r_2, (1 - \varepsilon)r_1, 6r_2/(\delta(1 - \varepsilon/5\sqrt{2r_1}))$-sensitive LSH for Jaccard similarity with probability $1 - \delta$. For each user, $O(\frac{1}{\varepsilon^4\delta^5 \cdot r_1^2}\log|U|\log n|U|)$ bits of space are sufficient. The update time is dominated by $O(\log|U|)$ evaluations of 2-wise independent hash functions.*

The proof of this theorem consists of two parts. First, we give a probabilistic lemma from which our sensitivity parameters can be derived. Second, we describe how the sampling procedure can be implemented in a streaming setting.

3.1 Sensitivity Bounds

While a black box reduction from any ℓ_0 sketch seems unlikely, we note that most ℓ_0 algorithms are based on bit-sampling techniques similar to those found in min-hashing. Our own algorithm is similarly based on sampling a sufficient number of bits or item indexes from each item set. Given a suitably filtered set of candidates, these indexes are then sufficient to infer the similarity. Let $U_k \subseteq U$ be a random set of elements where each element is included with probability 2^{-k}. Further, for any item set A, let $A_k = A \cap U_k$. Note that in $S_{x,y,z,z}(A_k, B_k)$ the value of $|U|$ is replaced by $|U_k|$. At the heart of the algorithm now lies the following technical lemma.

Lemma 3.2. *Let $0 < \varepsilon, \delta, r < 1$ be constants and $S_{x,y,z,z'}$ a rational set similarity with metric distance function. Let A and B be two item sets. Assume we sample every item uniformly at random with probability $2^{-k} \geq \frac{100 \cdot z'}{\varepsilon^2 \cdot \delta \cdot r \cdot Den_{x,y,z,z'}(A,B)}$. Then with probability at least $1 - \delta$ the following two statements hold.*

(1) *If $S_{x,y,z,z'}(A, B) \geq r$ we have*

$$(1 - \varepsilon)S_{x,y,z,z'}(A, B) \leq S(A_k, B_k) \leq (1 + \varepsilon)S_{x,y,z,z'}(A, B).$$

(2) $$S_{x,y,z,z'}(A_k, B_k) \leq \frac{2}{\delta(1 - (\varepsilon/5) \cdot \sqrt{2r})} \cdot S_{x,y,z,z'}(A, B).$$

We note that any metric distance function induced by a rational set similarity statisfies $z' \geq \max(x, y, z)$, see Theorem 2.1.

Proof. Let $Den_k = Den(A_k, B_k)$, $Num_k = Num(A_k, B_k)$, and $X_i = 1$ iff $i \in U_k$. If $S_{x,y,z,z}(A, B) \geq r$ then $|Num(A, B)| \geq r \cdot |Den(A, B)|$. Thus, we have $\mathbb{E}[Num_k] = |Num(A, B)|/2^k \geq r \cdot |Den(A, B)|/2^k$ and $\mathbb{E}[Den_k] = |Den(A, B)|/2^k$. Further, we have $\mathbf{Var}[X_i] = 2^{-k} \cdot (1 - 2^{-k}) \leq 2^{-k}$. for any X_i. We first give a variance bound on the denominator.

$$\begin{aligned} & \mathbf{Var}\left[Den_k\right] \\ = \quad & \mathbf{Var}\left[x \cdot |A_k \cap B_k| + y \cdot (|U_k| - |A_k \cup B_k|)| + z' \cdot |A_k \triangle B_k|\right] \\ = \quad & x^2 \sum_{i \in A \cap B} \mathbf{Var}\left[X_i\right] + y^2 \sum_{i \in \overline{A \cup B}} \mathbf{Var}\left[X_i\right] + z'^2 \sum_{i \in A \triangle B} \mathbf{Var}\left[X_i\right] \\ = \quad & \left((x^2 - y^2)|A \cap B| + y^2 \cdot |U| + (z'^2 - y^2)|A \triangle B|\right) \mathbf{Var}\left[X_i\right] \\ \leq \quad & \left((x^2 - y^2)|A \cap B| + y^2 \cdot |U| + (z'^2 - y^2)|A \triangle B|\right) / 2^k \\ \leq \quad & \frac{1}{2^k} \max\{x + y, z' + y, y\} \cdot ((x - y)|A \cap B| + \\ & y \cdot d + (z' - y)|A \triangle B|) \\ \leq \quad & 2z' \cdot \mathbf{E}\left[Den_k\right] \end{aligned}$$

and analogously

$$\mathbf{Var}\left[Num_k\right] \leq \max\{x + y, z + y, y\} \cdot \mathbf{E}\left[Num_k\right].$$

Combining these bounds with Chebyshev's inequality yields:

- $\mathbb{P}\left[|Den_k - \mathbf{E}\left[Den_k\right]| \geq \varepsilon/5 \cdot \mathbf{E}\left[Den_k\right]\right] \leq \frac{50z' \cdot 2^k}{\varepsilon^2 \cdot Num(A, B)}$
- $\mathbb{P}\left[|Num_k - \mathbf{E}\left[Num_k\right]| \geq \varepsilon/5 \cdot \mathbf{E}\left[Num_k\right]\right] \leq \frac{50z' \cdot 2^k}{\varepsilon^2 \cdot Num(A, B)}$.

If $k \leq \log\left(\frac{\varepsilon^2 \delta r Den(A, B)}{100z'}\right) \leq \log\left(\frac{\varepsilon^2 \delta Num(A, B)}{100z'}\right)$ then both $|Den_k| = (1 \pm \frac{\varepsilon}{5})\mathbf{E}\left[Den_k\right]$ and $|Num_k| = (1 \pm \frac{\varepsilon}{5})\mathbf{E}\left[Num_k\right]$ hold with probability at least $1 - \delta/2$. Then we can bound $S(A_k, B_k) = Num_k/Den_k$ from above by

$$\frac{Num(A, B)/2^k + \varepsilon Num(A, B}{Den(A, B)/2^k - \varepsilon Den(A, B)/2^k)/2^k} \leq (1 + \varepsilon) \cdot S_{x, y, z, z'}(A, B).$$

The lower bound on $S_{x,y,z,z'}(A_k, B_k)$ is analogous, which concludes the proof of the first statement.

For the second statement, we note that the expectation of Num_k can be very small because we have no lower bound on the similarity. Hence, we cannot use Chebyshev's inequality for an upper bound on Num_k. But it is enough to bound the probability that Num_k is greater than or equal to $(2/\delta) \cdot \mathbf{E}\left[Num_k\right]$ by $\delta/2$ using Markov's inequality. With the same arguments as above, we have that the probability of $Den_k \leq (1 - \varepsilon') \cdot \mathbf{E}\left[Den_k\right]$ is bounded by $\frac{\varepsilon^2 r \delta}{25 \cdot \varepsilon'^2}$ which is equal to $\delta/2$ if $\varepsilon' = \varepsilon/5 \cdot \sqrt{2r}$. Putting everything together we have $S_{x,y,z,z'}(A_k, B_k) \leq \frac{2}{\delta(1 - (\varepsilon/5) \cdot \sqrt{2r})} \cdot S_{x,y,z,z'}(A, B)$ with probability at least $1 - \delta$ as required. □

Applying this lemma on a few better known similarities gives us the following corollary. More examples of rational set similarities can be found in Naish, Lee, and Ramamohanarao [23].

COROLLARY 3.3. *For the following similarities, the following values of k are sufficient to apply Lemma 3.2:*

Similarity	*Parameters*	*Sampling Rate (k)*
Jaccard	$S_{1,0,0,1}$	$\log\left(\frac{\varepsilon^2 \delta r \lvert A \rvert}{100}\right)$
Hamming	$S_{1,1,0,1}$	$\log\left(\frac{\varepsilon^2 \delta r \lvert U \rvert}{100}\right)$
Anderberg	$S_{1,0,0,2}$	$\log\left(\frac{\varepsilon^2 \delta r \lvert A \rvert}{200}\right)$
Rogers-Tanimoto	$S_{1,1,0,2}$	$\log\left(\frac{\varepsilon^2 \delta r \lvert U \rvert}{200}\right)$

3.2 Streaming Implementation

When applying Lemma 3.2 to a dynamic streaming environment, we have to address a few problems. First, we may not know how to specify the number of items we are required to sample. For Hamming and Rogers-Tanimoto similarities, it is already possible to run a black box LSH algorithm (such as the one by Cohen et al. [10]) if the number of sampled items are chosen via Corollary 3.3. For Jaccard (and Anderberg), the sample sizes depend on the cardinality of A, which requires additional preprocessing steps.

Cardinality-Based Filtering. As a first filter, we limit the candidate solutions based on their respective supports. For each item, we maintain the cardinality, which can be done exactly in a dynamic stream via counting. If the sizes of two item sets A and B differ by a factor of at least r_1, i. e., $r_1|A| \geq |B|$, then the distance between these two sets has to be

$$1 - S(A, B) = \frac{|A \triangle B|}{|A \cup B|} \geq \frac{|A| - |B|}{|A|} \geq 1 - r_1.$$

We then discard any item set with cardinality not in the range of $[r_1 \cdot |A|, |A|]$.

Small Space Item Sampling. Since the cardinality of an item set may increase and decrease as the stream is processed, we have to maintain multiple samples U_k in parallel for various values of k. If a candidate k is larger than the threshold given by Corollary 3.3, we will sample only few items and still meet a small space requirement. If k is too small, $|U_k|$ might be too large to store. We circumvent this using a nested hashing approach we now describe in detail.

We first note that U_k does not have to be a fully independent randomly chosen set of items. Instead, we only require that the events X_i are pairwise independent. The only parts of the analysis of Lemma 3.2 that could be affected are the bounds on the variances, which continue to hold for pairwise independence. This allows us to emulate the sampling procedure using universal hashing. Assume that m is a power of 2 and let $h : [|U|] \to [m]$ be a 2-wise independent universal hash function, i.e. $\mathbb{P}[h(a) = j] = \frac{1}{m}$, for all $j \in [m]$. We set $U_k = \{j \in [m] \mid \text{lsb}(h(j)) = k\}$, where $\text{lsb}(x)$ denotes the first non-zero index of x when x is written in binary and $\text{lsb}(0) = \log m$. Since the image of h is uniformly distributed on $[m]$, each bit of $h(j)$ is 1 with probability $1/2$, and hence we have $\mathbb{P}[\text{lsb}(h(j)) = k] = 2^{-k}$. Moreover, for any two j, j' the events that $\text{lsb}(h(j)) = k$ and $\text{lsb}(h(j')) = k$ are independent. The value of m may be adjusted for finer (m large) or coarser (m small) sampling probabilities. In our implementation (see Section 4) as well as in the proof of Theorem 3.1, we set $m = |U|$.

To avoid storing the entire domain of h in the case of large $|U_k|$, we pick, for each $k \in [0, \ldots, \log |U|]$, another 2-wise independent

Algorithm 1: Filter-Preprocessing

input :Parameters $c \in \mathbb{N}$

output: $B_{k,l}^{(i)}$ with $i \in [n], k \in [0, \ldots, \log m], l \in [c^2]$

1 Initialize $s_i = 0$ for all $i \in [n]$, $B_{k,l}^{(i)} = 0$ for all $i \in [n], k \in [0, \ldots, \log m], l \in [c^2]$.

2 Let $h : [|U|] \to [m]$ be a 2-universal hash function.

3 Let $h_k : [m] \to [c^2]$ be independent 2-universal hash functions with $k = 0, \ldots, \log m$.

4 Let $S_k = \{i \in [n] \mid \text{lsb}(h(j)) = k\}$ with $k = 0, \ldots, \log m$.

On update (i, j, v):

5 $k = \text{lsb}(h(j))$

6 $B_{k,h_k(j)}^{(i)} = B_{k,h_k(j)}^{(i)} + v$

7 $B_{0,h_0(j)}^{(i)} = B_{0,h_0(j)}^{(i)} + v$

universal hash function $h_k : [|U|] \to [c^2]$, for some absolute constant c to be specified later. For some $j \in [|U|]$, we first check if $\text{lsb}(h(j)) = k$. If this is true, we apply $h_k(j)$.

For the ith item set, we maintain set $B_{k,\bullet}^i$ of buckets $B_{k,h_k(j)}^i$ for all $k \in \{0, \ldots \log |U|\}$ and $h_k(j) \in \{0, \ldots, c^2 - 1\}$. Each such bucket $B_{k,h_k(j)}^i$ contains the sum of the entries hashed to it. This allows us to maintain the contents of $B_{k,h_k(j)}^i$ under dynamic updates. Note that to support similarity estimation for sets that might have a low cardinality at query time, we must also maintain a bucket set $B_{0,\bullet}^i$ associated to a hash function h_0, that will receive all items seen so far for a given set i, i. e., each of them will be hashed to the bucket $B_{0,h_0(j)}^i$ with probability $2^0 = 1$ (see line 7 in Algorithm 1).

For the interesting values of k, i. e., $k \in \Theta(\log |A|)$, the number of indexes sampled by h will not exceed some constant c. This means that the sampled indexes will be perfectly hashed by h_k, i. e., the sum contained in $B_{k,h_k(j)}^i$ consists of exactly one item index. If k is too small (i.e. we sampled too many indexes), h_k has the useful effect of compressing the used space, as c^2 sums of multiple item indexes requires at most $O(\log n|U|)$ bits of space, whereas t individual item indexes require $t \log |U|$ bits of space.

We can then generate the fingerprint matrix, for instance, by performing a min-hash on the buckets $B_{k,\bullet}^i$ and storing the index of the first non zero bucket. For a pseudocode of this approach, see Algorithm 1. Algorithm 2 describes an example candidate generation as per Cohen et al. [10].

Proof of Theorem 3.1. Fix items sets P and Q and let p, q be the corresponding indexes for the sets P and Q, respectively. Without loss of generality, assume $|P| \geq |Q|$ (the other case is symmetric). Set $\alpha = \frac{\varepsilon^2 \cdot \delta}{600}$. If $S(P, Q) \geq r_1$ then $|P|/|Q| \leq 1/r_1$, then $\log(\alpha \cdot |Q|) \leq \log(\alpha \cdot |P|)$ and $\log(r_1 \cdot \alpha \cdot |Q|) \leq \log(\alpha \cdot |P|)$. Both sets will then enter line 5 of Algorithm 2 for some common values of k, and must exist at least an H_k containing min-hashes from both sets as per line 6.

Let 2^k be the largest power of 2 such that $k \leq \log(\alpha \cdot r|P \cup Q|) \leq \log(\alpha \cdot |P \cap Q|)$. Let U_k be a subset of indexes as determined by line 4 of Algorithm 1 and define $P_k := U_k \cap P$ and $Q_k := U_k \cap Q$. In expectation, $\mathbb{E}[|P_k \cup Q_k|] = |P \cup Q|/2^k$. By Markov's inequality,

Algorithm 2: Filter candidates

input :Thresholds $0 < r_1, p < 1$, $B_{k,l}^{(i)}$ from Algorithm 1 with $k \in \{0, 1, 2, \ldots, \log |U|\}$

output: Set of candidate pairs

1 Let $I = \{0, \log(1/r_1), 2\log(1/r_1), \ldots, \log |U|\}$

2 Let H_i be an empty list for $i \in I$.

3 **foreach** $i \in [n]$ **do**

4 $\quad s = \ell_0(x^{(i)})$

5 $\quad$ **foreach** $k \in [\log(r_1 \cdot \alpha \cdot s), \log(\alpha \cdot s)] \cap I$ **do**

6 $\quad\quad$ Add $(i, MinHash(B_{k,\bullet}^{(i)}))$ to H_k.

7 **return** $\{(i, i') \mid \exists k : (i, h), (i', h') \in H_k \text{ and } h = h'\}$

we have $|P_k \cup Q_k| \leq \frac{3}{\delta} \cdot |P \cup Q|/2^k \leq \frac{3600}{\varepsilon^2 \delta^2 \cdot r_1}$ with probability at least $1 - \delta/3$. By setting the number of buckets in the order of

$$c^2 = \frac{3}{\delta}|P_k \cup Q_k|^2 \in O\left(\frac{1}{\varepsilon^4 \delta^5 \cdot r_1^2}\right), \tag{1}$$

the elements of $P_k \cup Q_k$ will be perfectly hashed by h_k with probability at least $1 - \delta/3$ (line 3 of Algorithm 1). Since deleting indexes where both vector entries are zero does not change the Jaccard similarity, the probability that the smallest index in the collection of buckets $B_{k,\bullet}^{(p)}$ is equal to the smallest index in the collection of buckets $B_{k,\bullet}^{(q)}$ is equal to the similarity of P_k and Q_k. Thus we have

$$\mathbb{P}[MinHash(B_{k,\bullet}^{(p)}) = MinHash(B_{k,\bullet}^{(q)})] = S(P_k, Q_k).$$

If $S(P, Q) \geq r_1$ we have by our choice of α and due to the first part of Lemma 3.2, $S(P_k, Q_k) \geq (1 - \varepsilon) \cdot S(P, Q)$ with probability $1 - \delta/3$. If $S(P, Q) \leq r_2 < r_1$, we have due to the second part of Lemma 3.2 $S(P_k, Q_k) \leq \frac{6}{\delta(1 - (\varepsilon/5) \cdot \sqrt{2r_1})} \cdot S(P, Q) \leq \frac{6r_2}{\delta(1-(\varepsilon/5)\cdot\sqrt{2r_1})}$ with probability $1 - \delta/3$. Conditioning on all events gives us a $(r_1, r_2, (1 - \varepsilon)r_1, 6r_2/(\delta(1 - \varepsilon/5\sqrt{2r_1}))$-sensitive LSH with probability $1 - \delta$.

To bound the space requirement, observe that for each of the n item sets we have $\log |U|$ collections $B_{k,\bullet}^{(p)}$ of c^2 buckets. Each bucket contains a sum of at most n indexes in the range of $\{0, \ldots U - 1\}$. The space required for each hash function is at most $\log |U|$ due to Dietzfelbinger [14] □

4 EXPERIMENTAL EVALUATION

In this section we evaluate the practical performance of the algorithm given in Section 3. Our aim is two-fold. First, we want to show that the running time of our algorithm is competitive with more conventional min-hashing algorithms. For our use-case, i. e., , dynamic streams, we are not aware of any competitors in literature. Nevertheless, it is important to demonstrate the algorithm's viability, as in many cases a system might not even support a dynamic streaming environment. To cover all ranges of user profiles, we use a synthetic benchmark described below.

Our second goal is to be able to measure the quality of the algorithm's output. We deem our filtering mechanism to be successful if it finds most of the user pairs with high similarity, while performing a good level of filtering, returning as candidates few user pairs with low similarity. We are satisfied if our approximate computation based on sketches does not lead to high deviation with respect to exact similarities.

4.1 Implementation details

We implemented Algorithm 1, Algorithm 2, as well as other hash routines in C++ and compiled the code with gcc 4.8.4 and optimization level 3. Compared to the description of Algorithm 2, which has 5 parameters (error ε, failure probability δ, lower bound for desirable similarities r_1, upper bound for undesirable similarities r_2, and granularity of the sampling given by m), our implementation has only two parameters: (1) the inverse sampling rate α and (2) the number of buckets c^2. Recall that a higher inverse sampling rate α means selecting higher values of k in Algorithm 2, line 5, where an increasing k is associated to a decreasing sampling probability 2^{-k} of a bucket $B_{k,h_k(i)}$. The choice of c^2 influences the possible combinations of ε, δ, and r_1, see Equation 1 for an upper bound on c^2. The cardinality based filtering of Algorithm 2 is influenced by the choice of α. As long as $(1-\varepsilon)r_1 > \frac{6r_2}{\delta(1-\varepsilon/5)\sqrt{r_1}}$, we can amplify the probability of selecting highly similar items in Algorithm 2 and lower the probability in case of a small similarity (see also [21]). Let $a, b \in \mathbb{N}$. Then we repeat the hashing part of Algorithm 2 a times and only add a pair to the output set iff all a hash values are equal. This procedure is repeated b times and the final output set contains all pairs which appear at least once in an output set of the b repetitions. The probability that a pair with similarity s is in the output set is $1-(1-p^a)^b$ with $p = (1-2\delta)(1 \pm \varepsilon)s$ if $s > r_2$ and $p \le s/(\delta(1-\varepsilon/5\sqrt{r_2})$ otherwise. As a rule of thumb, r_2 is roughly of the order $r_1^{1.5}$. For example, if we aim to retain all pairs of similarity at least $\frac{1}{4}$, we can filter out pairs with similarity less than $\frac{1}{8}$. Pairs with an intermediate similarity, i.e. a similarity within the interval $[\frac{1}{8}, \frac{1}{4}]$, may or may not be detected. We view this as a minor restriction as it is rarely important for these thresholds to be sharp. All hash functions used in the implementation of both Algorithm 1, that is the functions h, h_k and the hash functions used for implementing the MinHash scheme, with amplification parameters a (functions in one band) and b (number of bands) at line 6 of Algorithm 2), are 2-wise independent hash functions. For these, we used Dietzfelbinger's multiply-add-shift method [14].

Experimental Setup. We used the following setup for all our experiments: all computations were performed on two identical machines with the same hardware configuration (2.7 GHz Intel Core i7 with 8 MB shared L3 Cache and 16 GB main memory). The implementation was done in C++ and compiled with gcc 4.8.4 and optimization level 3. Each run was repeated 10 times.

4.2 Datasets

Synthetic. To accurately measure the distortion on large datasets, for varying feature spaces, we used the synthetic benchmark by Cohen et al. [10]. Here we are given a large binary data-matrix consisting of 10,000 rows and either 10,000, 100,000 or 1,000,000 columns. The rows corresponded to item sets and the columns to items, i. e., we compared the similarities of rows. Since large binary data sets encountered in practical applications are sparse, the number of non-zero entries of each row was between 1% to 5% chosen uniformly at random. Further, for every 100th row, we added an additional row with higher Jaccard similarity in the range of $\{(0.35, 0.45), (0.45, 0.55), \ldots, (0.85, 0.95)\}$.

To obtain such a pair, we copied the preceding row (which was again uniformly chosen at random) and uniformly at random flipped an appropriate number of bits, e. g., for 10,000 items, row sparsity of 5%, and similarity range (0.45, 0.55) we deleted and added an item contained in row i with probabilities 1/3 and $\frac{1}{57}$, respectively.

In the insertion-only case, the stream consists of the sequence of 1-entries of each row. We introduced deletions by randomly removing any non-zero entry immediately after insertion with probability $\frac{1}{10}$.

Last.FM. For an evaluation of our algorithm on real data we considered a dataset from Anagnostopoulos et al. [1], containing temporal data from the popular online music recommendation system Last.fm. This dataset contains the full listening history of a set of 44,154 users, covering a period of 5 years from May 2009 to May 2014, containing 721 million listening events and around 4.6 millions genre-annotated unique tracks, To obtain a more granular feature space, we decided to map each track to the corresponding artist. To this end we queried the MusicBrainz DB [2] to obtain artist information for each track (total of $1.2M$ artists). We then processed the listening histories of each user i in chronological order to produce our event stream, emitting a triple $(i, j, +1)$ after a user has listened to at least 5 songs by an artist j, and emitting a triple$(i, j, -1)$ when no track from artist j is listened by i for a period of 6 months (expiration threshold). The initial threshold is mainly intended to mitigate the "recommendation effect": being Last.fm a recommendation system, some portions of the listening histories might be driven by recommendation sessions, where diverse artists are suggested by the system based on her interests (and not chosen by the user), and are so likely to lead to cascades of feature losses after the expiration time. Like most real world datasets that link users to bought/adopted items, this dataset is very sparse. To overcome this problem, we considered only users having at least 0.5%-dense profiles on average, obtaining a final set of $n = 15K$ users (sets), $|U| = 380K$ (items) and a stream length of $6.2M$. Table 1 shows the distibution of exact similarity values for all Last.fm user pairs.

4.3 Performance Evaluation

We evaluated the running time of our algorithm using the synthetic dataset, to understand its performance with respect to various dataset sizes, and two different scenarios, an *insertion-only stream*, and a *fully dynamic* stream, both obtained from our synthetic dataset. As a comparative benchmark, we compare our approach with an online implementation of "vanilla" minhashing scheme (later *Vanilla-MH*), where user sketches are computed online using 2-wise independent hash functions.

We tested two versions of our algorithm. The first version henceforth called *DynSymSearch Proactive* (or simply *Proactive*) maintains a set of fingerprints with every update. The second version henceforth called *DynSymSearch* maintains the sketches of Algorithm 1 and computes the fingerprints at query time. The choice of the

[2] https://musicbrainz.org/doc/MusicBrainz_Database

Similarity	0.0	0.05	0.1	0.15
Number of pairs	60432710	37947485	12031795	1938117
Similarity	0.2	0.25	0.3	0.35
Number of pairs	164246	7855	266	13
Similarity	0.4	0.45	0.5	≥ 0.55
Number of pairs	10	1	3	0

Table 1: Distribution of exact similarity values for pairs in the Last.fm dataset

first or the second implementation depends on the use case, with a trade-off between query responsiveness and update time.

Let us now focus on the two algorithms that update signatures online. When inserting item j added to set i, both *Proactive* and *Vanilla-MH* behave in the same way. When an element is added, all hash-functions are calculated on the new value, and signatures are updated in case such value is the new minimum (for a given bucket $B_k^{(i)}$ and and $B_0^{(i)}$ in the case of *Proactive*). In case of deletions, both will have to recompute signatures, *Vanilla-MH* doing so over the entire user profile and *Proactive* only considering the compressed bucket sets. A further optimization that we implemented in *Proactive*, is the *selective recomputation* of fingerprints in case of deletions. More specifically, in case of deletions of item j, we recompute fingerprints for $B_k^{(i)}$ only if the bucket is sensitive and could be subject of a query,i. e., its set cardinality and similarity threshold are such that k is the range specified by line 5 of Algorithm 2. This allows to ignore many costly recomputations.

Now we can move on to comparing the three on the various settings. We set $a = 5$, $b = 40$ as amplifying parameters for signatures of all algorithms, and further set $r_1 = 0.5$ for our two algorithms. The choice of amplification parameters a,b is not extremely important: indeed for the sake of runtime comparison it is only important that all algorithm share the same "hashing-related" overhead. Average running times of all algorithms run on 10 independent realizations of our synthetic datasets are plotted in Figure 1 where we study the impact of the parameters. The running time of our algorithms is influenced by their parameters to different extents. In particular, the number of buckets c^2 has a considerable impact (especially for *Proactive*) as higher values imply more hash function evaluations for fingerprints.

For the insertion-only stream (Figure 1a), we see that the the performances of the three algorithms are somewhat comparable, which is expected, considering that *Vanilla-MH* is to some extent naturally contained in both versions of our algorithm. In *DynSymSearch* they are computed only on query time on the sensitive sketches, rendering it the fastest option for this scenario. When considering deletions, things change dramatically. As can be seen in Figure 1b, deletions represent a problem for both *Vanilla-MH* and *Proactive*, as the fingerprint computation is not reversible, so after a deletion they must all be consistently recomputed. However, our algorithm is less affected: thanks to its compression and cardinality-based bucketing system, the updates are, to some extent, more local, as they impact only the single bucket $B_{k,h_k(j)}$. We note that *Proactive* has a range of values of α where the running time increases: these values allow for a wider range of buckets to become sensitive as

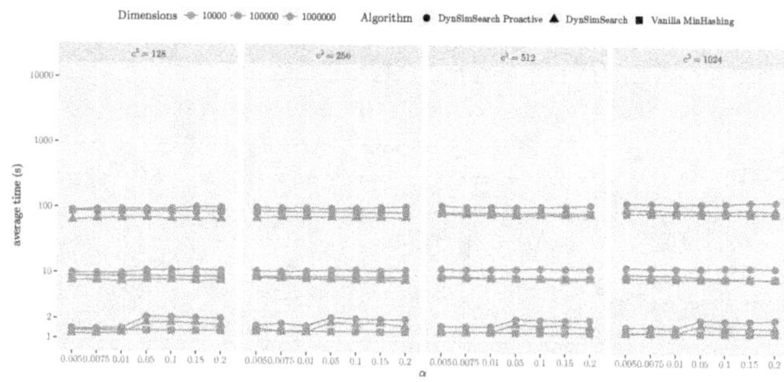

(a) Insertion only stream

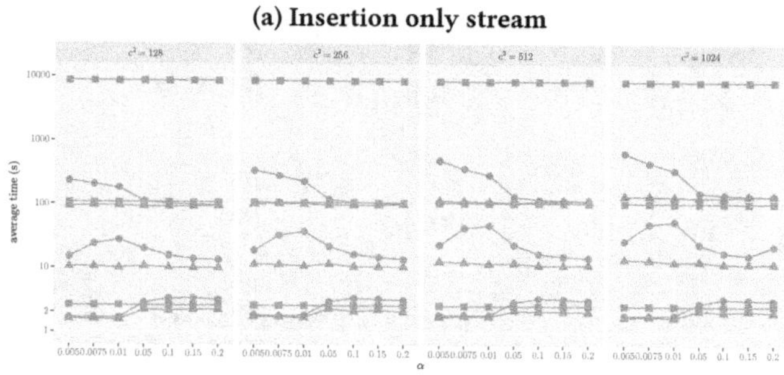

(b) Fully dynamic stream(y axis in logscale)

Figure 1: [Synthetic] Running time of our algorithm compared to a 2-wise MinHash based LSH implementation, in insertion-only or fully dynamic setting for various data scales. y-axes are in log-scale. The summary running times are the mean values of 10 repetitions.

long as the set cardinalities vary with the stream, implying more signature recomputations when each k becomes queryable. Overall, *DynSymSearch* is consistently faster then the other two options, while the performance of *Vanilla-MH* is very poor, taking from 12 to 100 times more time than *Proactive*, for $m = 1M$. We also remark that for *Vanilla-MH* to work, one is forced to store the entire data set in order to deal with deletions, to be able to recompute the fingerprints. This requirement is indeed not feasible in many settings. Furthermore, even for these comparatively sparse data sets, our algorithm has significant space savings.

Quality of approximation. We now examine the quality of approximation of our algorithm, as a function of our two main parameters, *alpha* and c^2. Concerning α, there are two opposite cases. If the inverse sampling rate is too low, we might have many collisions which decreases the approximation ratio. On the other hand if it is too high, the selected set of items might not be sensitive.

A higher bucket size instead, means always less collisions, for an increased space occupation of the sketches. Figure 2 shows the values of the average squared deviation of the sketched similiarities obtained with our algorithm and their exact Jaccard similarity, on the synthetic dataset, for different values of m, and various values of the parameters α and c^2. The goodness of a given α depends on the similarity of a pair in question. First, low pairs tend to have higher average squared deviation than high pairs, this is expected as out sketches can better approximate high similarity pairs. Also, for both kind of pairs the distortion decreases with increasing c^2,

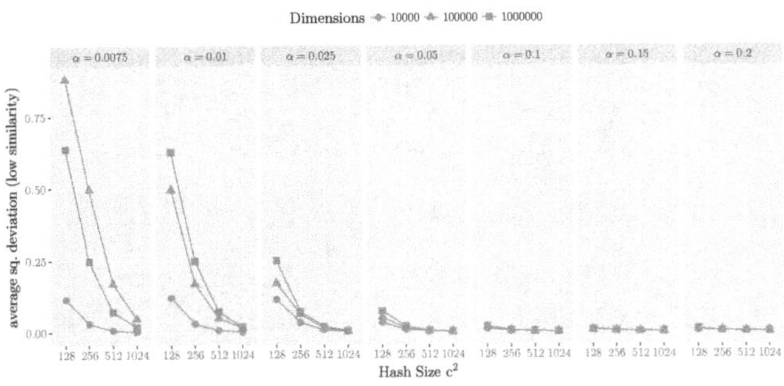

(a) Low similarity pairs

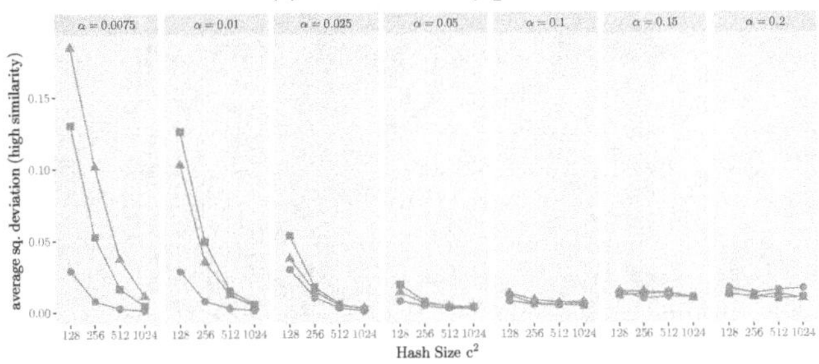

(b) High similarity pairs

Figure 2: [Synthetic] Average squared deviation for high similarity ($J \geq 0.2$) and low similarity ($J < 0.2$) pairs in the synthetic dataset, for various choices of the parameters, using *DynSymSearch*

independently of α as the number of collisions decrease monotonically. All deviations reach almost zero already at $\alpha = 0.05$ for all bucket sizes. For α above 0.1 we see that the deviation of high similarity pairs depart from the others, and especially for higher dimensional datasets tend to be slightly more distorted. Except for the lowest number of buckets, the average total deviation for these parameters was always below 0.1 and further decreased reaching to zero for larger bucket sizes. We note that these values of c^2 are below the theoretical bounds of Theorem 3.1, while having little to acceptable deviation for appropriately chosen values of α.

4.4 Analysis of the Last.fm Dataset

A realistic context like the one of Last.FM dataset, offers a valid playground to explore the performance of our similarity search, which is of primary interest in this paper. In the online music recommendation scenario where data is very sparse; even low similarities can make the difference.

For experiments on the Last.fm dataset, we use the *DynSymSearch* implementation: in Algorithm 2, we fixed $r_1 = 0.25$, therefore for each set A added a min-hash value to H_k with $k \in [s-2, s] \cap I$, with $I = \{0, log_2 \frac{1}{r_1}, \dots\} = \{0, 2, 4, \dots, log|U|\}$, where s is the actual cardinality of A at the time of the query. At the output of the filtering phase, we evaluate the similarity between the a candidate pair using $k = \log(\alpha \cdot r_1 \cdot \max(|A|, |B|)^3$ and output $S(A_k, B_k)$. Note that this dataset, as witnessed by the huge presence of very low similarity pairs (see Table 1), and very few pairs with higher similarity, is a challenge for any LSH scheme, as providing a good filtering behaviour with low similarity thresholds requires many hash functions.

We performed multiple experiments in order to choose good parameters of a and b to achieve a good filtering. We set a threshold on the maximum number of hash functions to use to 1600. Then we also set a threshold on the maximum fraction of pairs that we accept to be reported as candidate pairs, to 10%. Then we tested a number of combinations of a and b that are compatible with our choice of r_1 and meet our constraints, and report them in Table 2. The combination of $a = 5$ and $b = 300$ shows the lowest number of false negatives, and achieves a very good filtering, reporting only as low as 3.6% of pairs. We choose these values as amplification parameters for the filtering phase, and are fixed for all the experiments on this dataset.

a	b	**% candidate pairs**	**False negatives**
4	400	0.099	1393
5	50	0.016	5171
	150	0.028	2406
	300	**0.036**	**781**
	320	0.029	1587
6	200	0.0187	5415

Table 2: Fraction of pairs reported as candidates vs best number of false negatives given by our algorithm for various choices of a and b

Figure 3a shows the values of the average squared deviation of the sketched similiarities obtained with our algorithm and their exact Jaccard similarity, as function of α and c^2. Like in Figure 2, we show separate curves for pairs with Jaccard similarity below 0.2 (green curve) and high pairs (red curve). The same considerations made for the synthetic dataset hold, while we note that, for this dataset, the approximations of high similar pairs for very low bucket sizes appear slightly worse, possibly because indeed the majority of them have a similarity value is closer to the threshold, with respect to the synthetic dataset. However, for appropriate values of the parameters, all deviations tend to zero. Figure 3b shows other information regarding the detection performance of our filtering scheme. We tolerate to report pairs with similarity above $r_2 = 0.125$, and consider this range as *true positives* (**TP**), *true negatives* (**TN**) pairs below r_2 that are correctly not reported. Conversely, pairs below r_2 that are reported as candidates by our algorithm are *false positives* (**FP**), and we consider *false negatives* (**FN**) pairs that are above the real threshold $r_1 = 0.25$ but were not reported. Figure 3b shows values of $Accuracy = \frac{\text{(TP+TN)}}{\text{(TP+TN+FP+FN)}}$, $Recall = \frac{\text{(TP)}}{\text{(TP+FN)}}$ and fraction of candidate pairs reported. We can notice that the recall is approximately 1 for all values of the parameters. Accuracy instead, increases for increasing c^2, as expected, and also for increasing α, until it deteriorates for very high values, like it was for the high similarity pairs in Figure 3a. We notice that we get filtering above 90% starting from $\alpha = 0.075$, for 512 buckets. Lastly, in Figure 3c we see that we achieve very small running times for from $\alpha = 0.075$, as a consequence of the filtering. We remark that these plots show the

[3]Note that this choice of s satisfies $k \leq log_2(\alpha \cdot r \cdot |A \cup B|)$ from Lemma 3.2

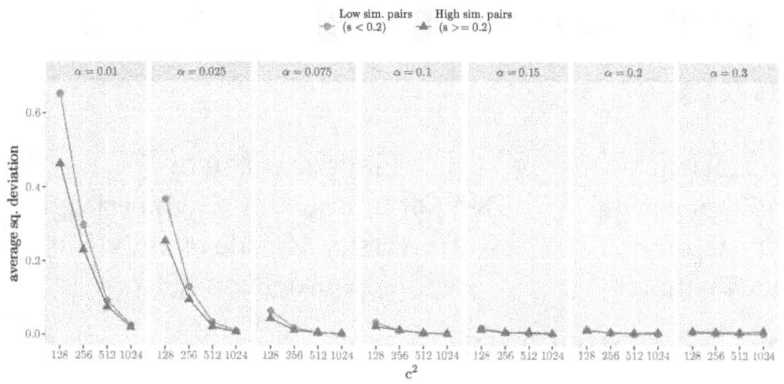

(a) Average squared deviation

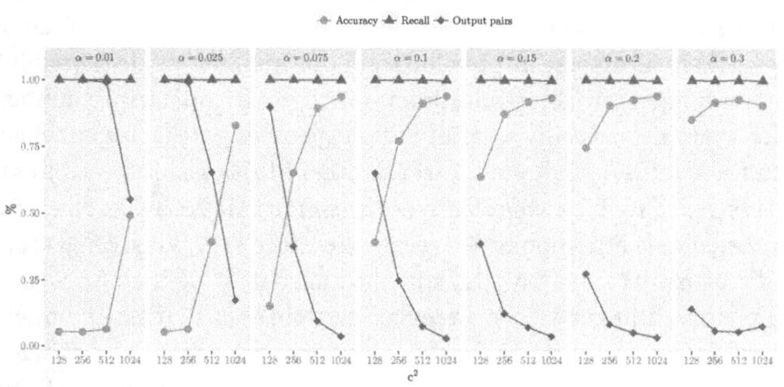

(b) Accuracy, Recall and Fraction of output pairs

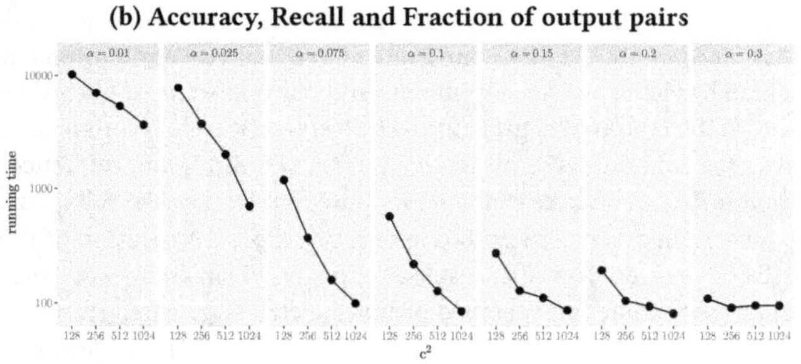

(c) Running time (log-scale)

Figure 3: [Last.fm] Approximation quality, Accuracy, Recall, Fraction of pairs found and running time, for various combinations of the parameters

performance of the filtering algorithm alone without any further pruning step. Yet, as reported by our very low deviation from actual similarities, we note that when completely avoiding false negatives is of primary concern, one can decide to choose a lower r_1 (and/or a different a, b combination) to retain more pairs in the candidate selection phase, and then perform another linear filtering using the accurate estimation given by our sketches.

ACKNOWLEDGMENTS

C.S. was supported by the Deutsche Forschungsgemeinschaft within the Collaborative Research Center SFB 876, project A2 and the Google Focused Award on Web Algorithmics for Large-scale Data Analysis. M.S. was supported by a Microsoft Azure for Research Award (*Online Event Detection and Evolution Tracking in Activity Networks*).

REFERENCES

[1] A. Anagnostopoulos and M. Sorella. 2015. Learning a Macroscopic Model of Cultural Dynamics. In *Data Mining (ICDM), 2015 IEEE International Conference on.* IEEE, 685–690.

[2] Y. Bachrach and E. Porat. 2013. Sketching for Big Data Recommender Systems Using Fast Pseudo-random Fingerprints. In *Proc. ICALP.* 459–471.

[3] Y. Bachrach and E. Porat. 2015. Fingerprints for highly similar streams. *Inf. Comput.* 244 (2015), 113–121.

[4] A. Z. Broder. 1997. On the Resemblance and Containment of Documents. In *Proc. SEQUENCES.* IEEE Computer Society, Washington, DC, USA, 21–.

[5] A. Z. Broder. 2000. Identifying and Filtering Near-Duplicate Documents. In *Proc. CPM.* 1–10.

[6] A. Z. Broder, M. Charikar, A. M. Frieze, and M. Mitzenmacher. 2000. Min-Wise Independent Permutations. *J. Comput. Syst. Sci.* 60, 3 (2000), 630–659.

[7] M. Charikar. 2002. Similarity estimation techniques from rounding algorithms. In *Proc. ACM STOC.* 380–388.

[8] F. Chierichetti and R. Kumar. 2015. LSH-Preserving Functions and Their Applications. *J. ACM* 62, 5 (2015), 33.

[9] K.-M. Chung, M. Mitzenmacher, and S. P. Vadhan. 2013. Why Simple Hash Functions Work: Exploiting the Entropy in a Data Stream. *Theory of Computing* 9 (2013), 897–945.

[10] E. Cohen, M. Datar, S. Fujiwara, A. Gionis, P. Indyk, R. Motwani, J. D. Ullman, and C. Yang. 2001. Finding Interesting Associations without Support Pruning. *IEEE Trans. Knowl. Data Eng.* 13, 1 (2001), 64–78.

[11] E. Cohen and H. Kaplan. 2007. Bottom-k sketches: better and more efficient estimation of aggregates. In *Proc. ACM SIGMETRICS.* 353–354.

[12] E. Cohen and H. Kaplan. 2007. Summarizing data using bottom-k sketches. In *Proc. PODC.* 225–234.

[13] A. Das, M. Datar, A. Garg, and S. Rajaram. 2007. Google news personalization: scalable online collaborative filtering. In *Proc. WWW.* 271–280.

[14] M. Dietzfelbinger. 1996. Universal Hashing and k-Wise Independent Random Variables via Integer Arithmetic without Primes. In *Proc. STACS.* 569–580.

[15] G. Feigenblat, E. Porat, and A. Shiftan. 2011. Exponential Time Improvement for min-wise Based Algorithms. In *Proc. ACM-SIAM SODA.* 57–66.

[16] J. M. Hellerstein, P. J. Haas, and H. J. Wang. 1997. Online Aggregation. In *Proc. ACM SIGMOD 1997.* 171–182.

[17] P. Indyk. 2001. A Small Approximately Min-Wise Independent Family of Hash Functions. *J. Algorithms* 38, 1 (2001), 84–90.

[18] P. Indyk and R. Motwani. 1998. Approximate Nearest Neighbors: Towards Removing the Curse of Dimensionality. In *Proc. ACM STOC.* 604–613.

[19] S. Janssens. 2006. *Bell inequalities in cardinality-based similarity measurement.* Ph.D. Dissertation. Ghent University.

[20] D. M. Kane, J. Nelson, and D. P. Woodruff. 2010. An optimal algorithm for the distinct elements problem. In *Proc. ACM PODS.* 41–52.

[21] J. Leskovec, A. Rajaraman, and J. D. Ullman. 2014. *Mining of Massive Datasets, 2nd Ed.* Cambridge University Press.

[22] P. Li and A. Christian König. 2011. Theory and applications of *b*-bit minwise hashing. *Commun. ACM* 54, 8 (2011), 101–109.

[23] L. Naish, H. J. Lee, and K. Ramamohanarao. 2011. A model for spectra-based software diagnosis. *ACM Trans. Softw. Eng. Methodol.* 20, 3 (2011), 11.

[24] A. Pagh, R. Pagh, and M. Ruzic. 2011. Linear Probing with 5-wise Independence. *SIAM Rev.* 53, 3 (2011), 547–558.

[25] R. Pagh, M. Stöckel, and D. P. Woodruff. 2014. Is min-wise hashing optimal for summarizing set intersection?. In *Proc. ACM PODS.* 109–120.

[26] M. Patrascu and M. Thorup. 2013. Twisted Tabulation Hashing. In *Proc ACM-SIAM SODA.* 209–228.

[27] M. Patrascu and M. Thorup. 2016. On the *k*-Independence Required by Linear Probing and Minwise Independence. *ACM Trans. Algorithms* 12, 1 (2016), 8:1–8:27.

[28] Y. Shi, M. Larson, and A. Hanjalic. 2014. Collaborative Filtering Beyond the User-Item Matrix: A Survey of the State of the Art and Future Challenges. *ACM Comput. Surv.* 47, 1, Article 3 (May 2014), 45 pages.

[29] M. Thorup. 2013. Bottom-k and priority sampling, set similarity and subset sums with minimal independence. In *Proc. ACM STOC.* 371–380.

[30] M. Thorup. 2013. Simple Tabulation, Fast Expanders, Double Tabulation, and High Independence. In *Proc. IEEE FOCS.* 90–99.

[31] M. Thorup and Y. Zhang. 2012. Tabulation-Based 5-Independent Hashing with Applications to Linear Probing and Second Moment Estimation. *SIAM J. Comput.* 41, 2 (2012), 293–331.

Fast Coreset-based Diversity Maximization under Matroid Constraints

Matteo Ceccarello
Dept. of Information Engineering
University of Padova, Italy
ceccarel@dei.unipd.it

Andrea Pietracaprina
Dept. of Information Engineering
University of Padova, Italy
andrea.pietracaprina@unipd.it

Geppino Pucci
Dept. of Information Engineering
University of Padova, Italy
geppo@dei.unipd.it

ABSTRACT

Max-sum diversity is a fundamental primitive for web search and data mining. For a given set S of n elements, it returns a subset of $k \ll n$ representatives maximizing the sum of their pairwise distances, where distance models dissimilarity. An important variant of the primitive prescribes that the desired subset of representatives satisfies an additional orthogonal requirement, which can be specified as a matroid constraint (i.e., a feasible solution must be an independent set of size k). While unconstrained max-sum diversity admits efficient coreset-based strategies, the only known approaches dealing with the additional matroid constraint are inherently sequential and are based on an expensive local search over the entire input set. We devise the first coreset constructions for max-sum diversity under various matroid constraints, together with efficient sequential, MapReduce and Streaming implementations. By running the local-search on the coreset rather than on the entire input, we obtain the first practical solutions for large instances. Technically, our coresets are subsets of S containing a feasible solution which is no more than a factor $1 - \varepsilon$ away from the optimal solution, for any fixed $\varepsilon < 1$, and, for spaces of bounded doubling dimension, they have a small size independent of n. Extensive experiments show that, with respect to full-blown local search, our coreset-based approach yields solutions of comparable quality, with improvements of up to two orders of magnitude in the running time, also for input sets of unknown dimensionality.

KEYWORDS

Diversity Maximization, Matroids, Coresets, MapReduce, Streaming, Doubling Spaces, Approximation Algorithms

ACM Reference Format:

Matteo Ceccarello, Andrea Pietracaprina, and Geppino Pucci. 2018. Fast Coreset-based Diversity Maximization under Matroid Constraints. In *Proceedings of WSDM 2018: The Eleventh ACM International Conference on Web Search and Data Mining , Marina Del Rey, CA, USA, February 5–9, 2018 (WSDM 2018),* 9 pages.
https://doi.org/10.1145/3159652.3159719

WSDM 2018, February 5–9, 2018, Marina Del Rey, CA, USA

ACM ISBN 978-1-4503-5581-0/18/02...$15.00
https://doi.org/10.1145/3159652.3159719

1 INTRODUCTION

In many application domains, data analysis often requires the extraction of a succint and significant summary of a large dataset. The summary may take the form of a small subset of elements, which are as diverse as possible from one another, while (possibly) complying with some additional orthogonal constraint such as, for example, covering a variety of prespecified categories attached to the data. The following formulation of this task, referred to as *Max-sum Diversity under Matroid Constraint* (MDMC), has received considerable attention in the recent literature [1, 7, 9]: given a set S of n elements from a metric space, a matroid $\mathcal{M}$ defined on S, and a positive integer $k \ll n$, determine a subset of S of size k which is an independent set of $\mathcal{M}$ and maximizes the sum of all pairwise distances between its elements. (A more formal definition of the problem is postponed to Section 2). MDMC is a natural generalization of the NP-Hard unconstrained max-sum diversity problem, which has been extensively studied and has important applications, e.g., in the realms of aggregator websites, web search, recommender systems, and query-result navigation (see [1, 8, 17] and references therein). As a concrete example, suppose that S is a set of Wikipedia pages, each associated with one or more topics. A solution of the MDMC problem identifies a subset of pages which are most diverse in terms of some pre-specified distance metric (e.g., cosine distance [20]) but also "well spread" among the topics. This latter property can be suitably controlled by imposing matroid constraints, such as partition or transversal matroids (defined later), depending on whether topics overlap or not.

Related work. Unconstrained max-sum diversity has been studied for over two decades within the realm of facility location (see [10] for an account of early results). More recently, efficient algorithms have been presented in [4, 8, 17] for the MapReduce and Streaming settings, based on confining the expensive computations required by standard sequential algorithms to small subsets of the input (*coresets*), cleverly extracted so to contain high-quality global solutions. On the other hand, existing approaches for solving the MDMC problem are inherently sequential and based on expensive local search over the entire set S. In particular, both [7] and [1] describe local search-based algorithms that provide (1/2)-approximate solutions to the problem, whose running times, however, are at least quadratic in the input size, hence impractical for large inputs. In fact, polynomial time can be guaranteed only at the expense of a slightly worse approximation ratio $1/2 - \varepsilon$, for any fixed $\varepsilon > 0$. Also, under the widely accepted *planted clique hypothesis*, it is hard to attain an approximation ratio larger than 1/2 [5]. Recently, an extension of the local search approach to non-metric spaces with negative-type distances has been proposed in [9].

Our contribution. The main contribution of this paper is an efficient strategy for the construction of coresets for the MDMC problem under different matroid constraints, which enable to limit the inherent computational toll of local search by confining its execution to a small subset of the input. The coresets are extracted through a suitable clustering-based approach, and embody feasible solutions to the problem, whose diversity is within a factor $(1 - \varepsilon)$ from the optimal diversity. While our coreset constructions are fully general, for the important cases of partition and transversal matroids they can be specialized so that their size becomes independent of n when the metric space has bounded doubling dimension. We provide efficient implementations of our coreset constructions in the sequential setting as well as in big-data oriented computational frameworks such as MapReduce and Streaming. Ours are the first coreset constructions for MDMC and enable dramatic performance improvements over the existing strategies, thus yielding the first practically viable approach to the solution of the problem on large instances.

Our theoretical results are complemented with extensive experiments on real-world datasets, which provide clear evidence of the superior performance of our approach with respect to pure local-search (up to two orders of magnitude), and of its scalability, obtainable through a distributed implementation.

Organization of the paper. The rest of the paper is structured as follows. A formal definition of the problem and some key concepts and notations are given in Section 2. The coresets constructions are described in Section 3, while their implementation in the various settings are presented in Section 4. Finally, the experimental results are reported in Section 5.

2 PRELIMINARIES

Let $S = \{s_1, s_2, \ldots, s_n\}$ be a set from a metric space with distance function $\mathrm{d}(\cdot,\cdot)$. Recall that d is nonnegative, symmetric, equal to 0 only on pairs of identical elements, and obeys the triangle inequality. A *matroid* [24] based on S is a pair $\mathcal{M} = (S, \mathcal{I}(S))$, where $\mathcal{I}(S)$ is a family of subsets of S, called *independent sets*, satisfying the following properties: (i) the empty set is independent; (ii) every subset of an independent set is independent (*hereditary property*); and (iii) if $A \in \mathcal{I}(S)$ and $B \in \mathcal{I}(S)$, and $|A| > |B|$, then there exist $x \in A \setminus B$ such that $B \cup \{x\} \in \mathcal{I}(S)$ (*augmentation property*). An independent set is maximal if it is not properly contained in another independent set. A basic result of matroid theory is that all maximal independent sets have the same size, which is called the *rank* of the matroid and is denoted by $\mathrm{rank}(\mathcal{M})$. In this paper we concentrate on two well-known types of matroid, namely, *partition matroids* and *transversal matroids*, which are defined as follows.

Definition 2.1 (Partition Matroid). Let $\Gamma_1 \cup \cdots \cup \Gamma_h$ be a partition of S, and let $k_i \leq |\Gamma_i|$ be a nonnegative integer, for $1 \leq i \leq h$. Define $\mathcal{I}(S)$ as the family of subsets $X \subseteq S$ with $|X \cap \Gamma_i| \leq k_i$, for $1 \leq i \leq h$. Then, $\mathcal{M} = (S, \mathcal{I}(S))$ is a *partition matroid* based on S.

Definition 2.2 (Transversal Matroid). Let $\mathcal{A} = \{A_1, \ldots, A_h\}$ be a family of (possibly non-disjoint) subsets of S, with $S = \bigcup_{i=1}^{h} A_i$, and consider the bipartite graph $(S, \mathcal{A}; E)$ where E consists of all edges $\{s_i, A_j\}$ with $s_i \in A_j$, for $1 \leq i \leq n$ and $1 \leq j \leq$. Define $\mathcal{I}(S)$ as the family of subsets $X \subseteq S$ corresponding to the left endpoints of some matching in the above graph. Then, $\mathcal{M} = (S, \mathcal{I}(S))$ is a *transversal matroid* based on S.

In the following, the sets $\Gamma_1, \ldots, \Gamma_h$ (resp., $A_1, \ldots, A_h$) in the definition of partition (resp., transversal) matroid will be referred to as *categories*. Throughout the paper, we make the reasonable assumption that for the transversal matroids each element of the input belongs to a small (i.e., constant) number of categories.

This paper focuses on the problem of *Max-sum Diversity under Matroid Constraint* (MDMC problem, for brevity), which is defined as follows: given the set S, a matroid $\mathcal{M} = (S, \mathcal{I}(S))$ and a positive integer $k \leq \mathrm{rank}(\mathcal{M})$, find an independent set $X \in I(S)$ of size k maximizing the following objective function:

$$\mathrm{div}(X) = \sum_{u,v \in X} \mathrm{d}(u, v).$$

We denote the optimal value of the objective function as

$$\mathrm{div}_{k,\mathcal{M}}(S) = \max_{X \in \mathcal{I}(S), |X|=k} \mathrm{div}(X)$$

W.l.o.g., we assume that each individual element of S makes a singleton independent set. In fact, elements for which this is not the case can be eliminated since, by the hereditary property of matroids, they cannot belong to larger independent sets.

Returning to the example mentioned in the introduction, concerning a set S of Wikipedia pages, the covering of various topics, viewed as categories, can be enforced by a partition matroid constraint when each page is labeled by a single topic, or by a transversal matroid constraint when pages may refer to multiple topics.

The algorithms presented in this paper use clustering as a subroutine. For a given positive integer τ, a *τ-clustering* of S is a pair (C, Z), where $C = \{C_1, \ldots, C_\tau\}$ is a partition of S, and $Z = \{z_1, \ldots, z_\tau\} \subset S$ is such that $z_i \in C_i$, for $1 \leq i \leq \tau$. Each z_i is said to be the *center* of its respective *cluster* C_i. We define the *radius* of the clustering as

$$r(C, Z) = \max_{1 \leq i \leq \tau} \max_{s \in C_i} \mathrm{d}(s, z_i).$$

The problem of finding a τ-clustering of minimum radius is NP-hard, as it is also NP-hard to achieve an approximation factor of $2 - \varepsilon$ in general metric spaces, for any $\varepsilon > 0$ [13]. In the paper, we will employ two well-known approximation algorithms for this problem: the 2-approximation algorithm of [13] for the sequential setting (known as GMM in the literature), and the $(2 + \delta)$-approximation algorithm of [22] (known as the *scaling algorithm*) for the streaming setting. Both algorithms work by identifying a suitable set $Z = \{z_1, \ldots, z_\tau\}$ of centers, which implicitly induce a partition $C = \{C_1, \ldots, C_\tau\}$ by defining each C_i as the set of elements which are closer to z_i than any other center.

In the paper, we will specialize our findings to metric spaces of bounded dimensionality, based on the following definition. Given an element x of the space, let the *ball of radius r centered at x* be the set of elements at distance at most r from x. The *doubling dimension* of the space is the smallest value D such that any ball of radius r centered at an element x is covered by at most 2^D suitably centered balls of radius $r/2$. Although there are metric spaces of arbitrary doubling dimension, there are notable metric spaces of constant doubling dimension. In particular, the space $\mathbb{R}^d$ paired with any ℓ_p distance (therefore including Euclidean spaces of any dimension) has doubling dimension $O(d)$ [15]. The characterization of metric spaces through their doubling dimension has been used in the literature in several contexts, including routing [19], clustering [2], nearest neighbour search [11], and machine learning [14].

3 CORESETS

The notion of *coreset* has been introduced in [3] as a tool for the development of efficient algorithms for optimization problems on large datasets. In broad terms, for a given computational objective, a coreset is a small subset of the input which embodies a feasible solution whose cost is a good approximation to the cost of an optimal solution over the entire input. Coreset constructions have been successfully developed for the uncostrained diversity maximization problem [4, 8, 17]. In fact, these constructions feature an additional *composability* property, meaning that the construction can be applied independently to the subsets of an arbitrary input partition so that the union of the coresets extracted from each subset is itself a coreset for the entire input. This additional property enables the development of scalable distributed (e.g., MapReduce) algorithms. Indeed, the coreset constructions devised in this section for the MDMC problem are also composable.

Throughout this section, we refer to an arbitrary instance of the MDMC problem, specified by an input set S of size n, a matroid $\mathcal{M} = (S, \mathcal{I}(S))$, and an integer $k \leq \text{rank}(\mathcal{M})$. The formal definition of coreset for the problem is the following.

Definition 3.1. For a positive real-valued $\beta \leq 1$, a subset $T \subseteq S$ is a *β-coreset* for the MDMC problem if $\text{div}_{k,\mathcal{M}}(T) \geq \beta\, \text{div}_{k,\mathcal{M}}(S)$.

We aim at β-coresets with β close to 1. Before describing how to construct such coresets, we need to establish some preliminary facts. Define the following two important quantities:

$$\Delta_S = \max_{a,b \in S}(\text{d}(a,b)) \quad \text{and} \quad \bar{\rho}_S = \frac{\text{div}_{k,\mathcal{M}}(S)}{\binom{k}{2}},$$

where Δ_S represents the *diameter* of S, and $\bar{\rho}_S$ the average distance between two elements in an optimal solution. We have:

Lemma 3.2. *For $k > 1$, we have that $\bar{\rho}_S \geq \Delta_S/(2 \cdot k)$.*

Proof. We first show that there is an independent set of two elements at distance at least $\Delta_S/2$ from one another. Let $a, b \in S$ be such that $\Delta_S = \text{d}(a,b)$. If $\{a,b\} \in \mathcal{I}(S)$ then the statement clearly holds. Otherwise, by the augmentation property, there must exist a point c such that $\{a,c\}, \{b,c\} \in \mathcal{I}(S)$. Clearly, by the triangle inequality we have that $\max\{\text{d}(a,c), \text{d}(b,c)\} \geq \Delta_S/2$. W.l.o.g., assume that $\text{d}(a,c) \geq \Delta_S/2$. Using again the augmentation property $k-2$ times, we can easily argue that there exists an independent set X of size k containing both a and c. By the triangle inequality, all the points of X will be at distance at least $\Delta_S/4$ from either a or c. Therefore,

$$\bar{\rho}_S = \frac{\text{div}_{k,\mathcal{M}}(S)}{\binom{k}{2}} \geq \frac{\text{div}(X)}{\binom{k}{2}} \geq \frac{(k-1)\Delta_S}{4\binom{k}{2}} \geq \frac{\Delta_S}{2k}$$

□

It is easy to argue that there are instances of the problem for which the lower bound to $\bar{\rho}_S$ is tight, up to constant factors.

Intuitively, a good coreset in our setting is a set of points such that, for each independent set in $\mathcal{I}(S)$, it contains an independent set of comparable diversity. The following lemma formalizes this intuition.

Lemma 3.3. *Let $\varepsilon < 1$ be a positive value. Consider a subset $T \subseteq S$ such that for each $X \in \mathcal{I}(S)$ of size k there is an injective proxy function $p : X \to T$ satisfying (i) $\{p(x) : x \in X\} \in \mathcal{I}(S)$; and (ii) $\text{d}(x, p(x)) \leq (\varepsilon/2)\bar{\rho}_S$, for every $x \in X$. Then, T is a $(1-\varepsilon)$-coreset.*

Proof. Let $O \subseteq S$ be the optimal solution to the MDMC problem. By the properties of the proxy function p and by the triangle inequality, it follows that $\{p(o) : o \in O\} \subseteq T$ is an independent set of size k, and that

$$\begin{aligned}\text{div}_{k,\mathcal{M}}(T) &\geq \sum_{o_1,o_2 \in O} \text{d}(p(o_1), p(o_2)) \\ &\geq \sum_{o_1,o_2 \in O} [\text{d}(o_1,o_2) - \text{d}(o_1,p(o_1)) - \text{d}(o_2,p(o_2))] \\ &\geq \sum_{o_1,o_2 \in O} \text{d}(o_1,o_2) - \binom{k}{2}\varepsilon\bar{\rho}_S = (1-\varepsilon)\,\text{div}_{k,\mathcal{M}}(S).\end{aligned}$$

□

In the next subsections, we will develop clustering-based constructions of small coresets meeting the requirements of Lemma 3.3 for partition and transversal matroids. We will also point out how to extend these constructions to the case of general matroids, at the expense of a possible blow-up in the coreset size.

3.1 Coreset construction

Fix an arbitrary positive constant $\varepsilon < 1$, and consider a *τ-clustering* (C, Z) of the input set S, where $C = \{C_1, \ldots, C_\tau\}$ and $Z = \{z_1, \ldots, z_\tau\}$, with radius

$$r(C,Z) \leq \frac{\varepsilon}{4}\bar{\rho}_S. \tag{1}$$

Observe that such a clustering surely exists, as long as τ is large enough, since the trivial n-clustering where each element of S is a singleton cluster has radius 0. Our corests are obtained by selecting a suitable subset from each cluster of C so that the properties (i) and (ii) specified in Lemma 3.3 are satisfied. In particular, the bound on the clustering radius is functional to establish property (ii).

The effectiveness of this approach relies on the existence of a clustering with suitably small τ, so that the resulting coreset size is significantly smaller than n. Although it is not easy to determine a meaningful upper bound to τ in the general case, in the next subsection we show that for the important case of metric spaces of bounded doubling dimension, τ is upper bounded by a constant w.r.t. n.

Technically, throughout this section, we work under the hypothesis that a τ-clustering (C, Z) whose radius satisfies Equation 1 is available, and postpone the description of its explicit construction to Section 4, since different constructions will be employed for the different computational settings considered in this paper.

Below, we describe how the coresets can be derived from the τ-clustering (C, Z), separately for each matroid type.

Partition matroid. We build the coreset T for S as follows. From each cluster C_i of C we select a largest independent set $T_i \subseteq C_i$ of size at most k, and let $T = \bigcup_{i=1}^{\tau} T_i$. The effectiveness of this simple strategy is stated by the following theorem.

THEOREM 3.4. *Let $\mathcal{M} = (S, \mathcal{I}(S))$ be a partition matroid with categories $\Gamma_1, \ldots, \Gamma_h$ and cardinality bounds $k_1, \ldots, k_h$, and let T be the set computed from the clustering (C, Z) by the above procedure. Then T is a $(1-\varepsilon)$-coreset of size $O(k\tau)$ for max-sum diversity on S under matroid constraint $\mathcal{M}$, .*

PROOF. First observe that the bound on the size of T is immediate by construction. As for the approximation, we now show that for any independent set $X \in \mathcal{I}(S)$ with $|X| = k$, there is an injective function $p : X \to T$ such that $\{p(x) : x \in X\} \in \mathcal{I}(S)$ and $d(x, p(x)) \leq (\varepsilon/2)\bar{\rho}_S$. The result will then follow from Lemma 3.3. Consider the set of clusters as partitioned in two families: C^ℓ includes those clusters that contain an independent set of size k, whereas $C^s = C - C^\ell$ includes the remaining clusters that contain only independent sets of size less than k. For each cluster $C_i \in C^s$, consider the independent set $T_i \subseteq C_i$ included in T by the algorithm. It is easy to see that for each category Γ_j, we have $|X \cap C_i \cap \Gamma_j| \leq |T_i \cap \Gamma_j|$, since $|T_i| < k$ and that T_i is a largest independent set in C_i. Therefore, each point $x \in X \cap C_i$ can be associated with a distinct point $p(x) \in T_i$ belonging to the same category. Let $P = \{p(x) : x \in X \cap (\cup_{C \in C^s} C)\}$ and note that P is an independent set, since $X \cap (\cup_{C \in C^s} C)$ is an independent set (by the hereditary property of matroids) and the number of elements per category is the same in X and in P. If P has size k, then X has no points in clusters of C^ℓ and the lemma is proved. If instead P has size strictly less than k, we consider the clusters in C^ℓ containing the remaining $k - |P|$ points of X. For each such C_i, we expand P to a larger independent set by adding $n_i = |X \cap C_i|$ elements from T_i using the augmentation property n_i times, exploiting the fact T_i is an independent set of size k. These n_i elements of T_i can act as distinct proxies of the elements in $X \cap C_i$ under function p. After these additions, we obtain an independent set P of k distinct proxies for the elements of X. Since, for each $x \in X$, $p(x) \in P$ is taken from the same cluster of C, we have that, by the triangle inequality and by Equation (1), $d(x, p(x)) \leq (\varepsilon/2)\bar{\rho}_S$. □

Transversal matroid. The construction of the coreset T is more involved in the case of transversal matroids. Suppose that $\mathcal{M} = (S, \mathcal{I}(S))$ is a transversal matroid defined over a set $\mathcal{A} = \{A_1, \ldots, A_h\}$ of h (not necessarily disjoint) categories. The fact that the categories can now overlap complicates the coreset construction, resulting in slightly larger coresets. For each cluster C_i of C we begin by selecting, as before, a largest independent set U_i of size at most k. If $|U_i| = k$, then we set $T_i = U_i$. Instead, if $|U_i| < k$, let $\mathcal{A}' \subseteq \mathcal{A}$ be a subfamily of $|U_i|$ categories which can be matched to the elements of U_i in the bipartite graph $(S, \mathcal{A}; E)$ associated with the matroid. We construct T_i by augmenting U_i with $\min\{|U_i| - 1, |A \cap C_i| - 1\} < k$ points taken from $A \cap C_i$, for each $A \in \mathcal{A}'$. Finally, we let $T = \bigcup_{i=1}^{\tau} T_i$.

THEOREM 3.5. *Let $\mathcal{M} = (S, \mathcal{I}(S))$ be a transversal matroid with categories $A_1, \ldots, A_h$, and let T be the set computed from the clustering (C, Z) by the above procedure. Then, T is a $(1-\varepsilon)$-coreset of size $O\left(k^2\tau\right)$ for max-sum diversity on S under matroid constraint $\mathcal{M}$.*

PROOF. The proof follows the lines of the one of Theorem 3.4. The bound on the size of T is immediate, while for the approximation guarantee of the coreset it is sufficient to show that for any independent set $X \in \mathcal{I}(S)$ with $|X| = k$, there is an injective function $p : X \to T$ such that $\{p(x) : x \in X\} \in \mathcal{I}(S)$ and $d(x, p(x)) \leq (\varepsilon/2)\bar{\rho}_S$. We split C into C^ℓ (clusters containing an independent set of size k) and C^s (remaining clusters). We first consider clusters in C^s. Fix a cluster $C_i \in C^s$ and let $\mathcal{A}' \subseteq \mathcal{A}$ be the subfamily of $|U_i|$ categories matched to elements of U_i used to augment U_i to create $|T_i|$. Let $C_i \cap X = \{x_1, x_2, \ldots, x_m\}$, and let $A_1^X, A_2^X, \ldots, A_m^X \in \mathcal{A}$ be distinct categories that can be matched to $x_1, x_2, \ldots, x_m$. Note that the maximality of U_i implies that $|U_i| \geq m$. Without loss of generality, assume that $x_1, \ldots, x_j \in T_i$ while $x_{j+1}, \ldots, x_m \notin T_i$, for some $0 \leq j \leq m$, that is, assume that exactly those j points of X are included in T_i. We initially set the proxies $p(x_1) = x_1, \ldots, p(x_j) = x_j$. Then, consider category A_{j+1}^X and observe that $A_{j+1}^X \in \mathcal{A}'$, otherwise x_{j+1} (matched to A_{j+1}^X) could be added to U_i contradicting its maximality within C_i. Since x_{j+1} was not included in T_i, there must be at least $|U_i| \geq m$ elements of A_{j+1}^X in T_i. We can thus select one such element (distinct from $p(x_1), p(x_2), \ldots, p(x_j)$) as proxy $p(x_{j+1})$, matched to A_{j+1}^X. By repeating this step for $x_{j+2}, \ldots, x_m$, we obtain an independent set of proxies for the elements of $X \cap C_i$, each matched to the same category as its corresponding element. Then, by iterating this construction over all clusters of C^s we get an independent set P of proxies for the elements of X belonging to such clusters, each matched to the same category as its corresponding element. If P has size strictly less than k, the remaining proxies for the elements of X residing in clusters of C^ℓ can be chosen by reasoning as in the proof of Theorem 3.4, using the augmentation property. Also, by the bound on the radius of (C, Z), we have $d(x, p(x)) \leq (\varepsilon/2)\bar{\rho}_S$, for each $x \in X$. □

We remark that the $O\left(k^2\tau\right)$ bound on the coreset size is a rather conservative worst-case estimate. In fact, as reported in the experimental section, it is conceivable that, in practice, much smaller sizes can be expected.

General Matroids. Consider now a constraint specified as a general matroid $\mathcal{M}(S, \mathcal{I}(S))$. We can still build a coreset T in this general scenario, using the clustering (C, Z). Specifically, for each cluster C_i of C we compute a largest independent set U_i of size at most k. If $|U_i| = k$, then we set $T_i = U_i$, otherwise we set $T_i = C_i$. Finally, we let $T = \bigcup_{i=1}^{\tau} T_i$. Note that, unlike the case of partition and transversal matroids, this coreset may potentially grow very large when clusters do not contain large enough independent sets. However, for small enough values of τ and k (hence, large cluster sizes) we expect that each cluster may reasonably contain an independent set of size k, hence an actual coreset size of $O(k\tau)$ is conceivable. We have:

THEOREM 3.6. *Let $\mathcal{M} = (S, \mathcal{I}(S))$ be a general matroid, and let T be the set computed from the clustering (C, Z) by the above procedure. Then, T is a $(1-\varepsilon)$-coreset for max-sum diversity on S under matroid constraint $\mathcal{M}$.*

PROOF. As in the proofs of Theorems 3.4 and 3.5, it is sufficient to determine a suitable proxy function p for every independent set $X \in$

$\mathcal{I}(S)$ of size k. We set function p to be the identity function for those points belonging to clusters C_i such that $T_i = C_i$. The proxies for the elements of X residing in the other clusters can then be chosen through repeated applications of the agumentation property. Also, by the bound on the radius of (C, Z), we have $d(x, p(x)) \leq (\varepsilon/2)\bar{\rho}_S$, for each $x \in X$, hence the thesis follows from Lemma 3.3. □

3.2 Spaces of bounded doubling dimension

In this subsection, we show that, for metric spaces of bounded doubling dimension, very coarse clusterings of small radius exist and can be discovered by any reasonable approximation algorithm for minimum-radius clustering. Specifically, assume that an algorithm is available which, given τ, with $1 \leq \tau \leq n$, returns a τ-clustering (C, Z) for S whose radius is a factor at most $\sigma > 1$ larger than the minimum radius attainable by any τ-clustering. We have:

THEOREM 3.7. *Let S belong to a metric space of doubling dimension D. Then, for any $\tau \geq (16\sigma k/\varepsilon)^D$, the aforementioned algorithm returns a τ-clustering (C, Z) with radius*

$$r(C, Z) \leq \varepsilon\frac{\bar{\rho}_S}{4}.$$

PROOF. Observe the whole set S is contained in the ball of radius Δ_S centered at any element of S. By iteratively applying the definition of doubling dimension starting from such a ball, we have that for any positive $\eta < 1$ (to be fixed later) we can cover S with $\tau = (1/\eta)^D$ balls of radius at most $\eta\Delta_S$, centered at elements of the metric space, which however may not belong to S. By picking, for each such ball, an arbitrary element of S as center (if any), we obtain a τ-clustering of S whose radius is at most $2\eta\Delta_S$, by virtue of the triangle inequality. This implies that the optimal τ-clustering of S has radius at most $2\eta\Delta_S$. Therefore, on input $\tau \geq (1/\eta)^D$ and S, the approximation algorithm will return a τ-clustering of radius at most

$$\sigma \cdot (2\eta\Delta_S) \leq \sigma \cdot (4\eta k\bar{\rho}_S),$$

where the inequality follows from Lemma 3.2. The theorem follows by fixing $\eta = \varepsilon/(16\sigma k)$. □

We remark that the result of the above theorem implies that on spaces of constant doubling dimension and for the partition and transversal matroids, the constructions illustrated in the previous subsection yield coresets whose size is constant w.r.t. the size n of the input set S, a crucial feature for the efficiency of our solution to the MDMC problem. However, we must observe that, in order to obtain a suitable clustering granularity τ through Theorem 3.7, the doubling dimension D of the underlying space must be known. When this is not the case, a similar granularity τ can still be obtained either by exploiting additional properties of the clustering algorithm or through guessing, as it will be made clear in the next section.

4 IMPLEMENTATIONS

Consider an instance of the MDMC problem specified by an input set S of size n, a matroid $\mathcal{M} = (S, \mathcal{I}(S))$, and an integer $k \leq \text{rank}(\mathcal{M})$. As in previous works, we assume that constant-time oracles are available to compute the distance between two elements of S and to check whether a subset of S is an independent set. In this section, we will show how to use the coreset constructions presented in the previous section to obtain efficient solutions to the problem in the sequential, MapReduce and Streaming settings. Our general approach is to extract a $(1-\varepsilon)$-coreset T from S and then run the best available sequential algorithm on T. For instance, by employing the(1/2)-approximation local search-based algorithm of [1] (which we refer to as AMT algorithm in what follows), we can get a $(1-\varepsilon)/2$ approximation ratio. Thus, for any given positive $\gamma < 1/2$, by setting $\varepsilon = 2\gamma$ this approach yields a $1/2 - \gamma$ approximation ratio. As substantiated by the experiments presented in Section 5, the fundamental advantage of our coreset-based approach is that the expensive local-search strategy, which involves a number of invocations to the distance/independent-set oracles at least quadratic in the input size, is now run on a coreset that is potentially much smaller than the original input set S.

In the following subsections, we describe an implementation of our coreset constructions in the aforementioned settings. For simplicity, we will restrict the analysis to the case of partition and transversal matroids, for which meaningful bounds on the coreset size are provable. However, a similar implementation can be developed for general matroids, and may prove to be very valuable in practice.

4.1 Sequential implementation

In order to implement the coreset constructions presented in the previous section, we resort to the well-known 2-approximate clustering algorithm GMM mentioned before [13]. For a given input S, GMM determines the set Z of cluster centers incrementally, by initializing Z with an arbitrary element of S, and iteratively adding to Z the element in $S \setminus Z$ of maximum distance from the current Z. The algorithm can be instrumented to maintain the set of clusters centered at Z, where each element of S is assigned to the cluster of its closest center, and the radius of such a clustering. It is well known that each iteration of GMM can be implemented in time linear in n and that the clustering resulting at the end of the i-th iteration has radius which is no more than twice as large as the radius of an optimal i-clustering.

Recalling that Δ_S is the diameter of S, it is easy to see that the distance δ_2 between the first two centers discovered by GMM is such that $\Delta_S/2 \leq \delta_2 \leq \Delta_S$. In order to build the $(1-\varepsilon)$-coreset T, we run GMM for a number τ of iterations sufficient to reduce the radius of the clustering to $\varepsilon\delta_2/(8k) \leq \varepsilon\Delta_S/(8k)$. Once the clustering is computed, the coreset T is obtained using one of the procedures described in the previous section to select elements from each cluster, depending on the matroid type. We have:

THEOREM 4.1. *Let $\varepsilon < 1$ be an arbitrary positive constant. The above algorithm computes a $(1-\varepsilon)$-coreset T for the MDMC problem in $O(n(\log k + \tau))$ time for both partition and transversal matroids. If the set S comes from a space with constant doubling dimension D, then $\tau = O\left((k/\varepsilon)^D\right)$. In this case, for constant k, the running time is linear in n.*

PROOF. The fact that T is $(1-\varepsilon)$-coreset for the problem follows by Theorems 3.4 and 3.5, observing that the radius of the clustering is at most $(\varepsilon/4)\bar{\rho}_S$ by Lemma 3.2. As for the running time, the cost of the GMM algorithm is $O(n\tau)$, while, the subsequent extraction of the coreset can be accomplished using a total of $O(n)$ invocations of the independent-set oracle to determine a largest independent set in each cluster, exploiting the augmentation property, and additional $O(n \log k)$ operations on suitable dictionary structures to determine the extra elements for each category (in the sole case of the transversal matroid). Finally, the bound on τ, in case the metric space has constant doubling dimension D, follows immediately from Theorem 3.7. □

We remark that thanks to the incremental nature of GMM, the coreset construction needs not know the doubling dimension D of the metric space in order to attain the desired bound on τ. This is a very desirable property, since, in general, D may not be known in advance.

4.2 MapReduce implementation

A MapReduce (MR) algorithm executes as a sequence of *rounds* where, in a round, a multiset of key-value pairs is transformed into a new multiset of pairs by applying a given reduce function, referred to as *reducer*, independently to each subset of pairs having the same key. The model is parameterized by the total memory available to the computation, denoted with M_T, and the maximum amount of memory locally available to each reducer, denoted with M_L. The typical goal for a MR algorithm is to run in as few rounds as possible while keeping M_T (resp., M_L) linear (resp., substantially sublinear) in the input size [12, 18].

To obtain MR implementations of our coreset constructions we will crucially exploit an additional property of these constructions, known as *composability* [17]. Formally, composability ensures that a $(1-\varepsilon)$-coreset for a set S can be obtained as the union of $(1-\varepsilon)$-coresets extracted from each subset of any given partition of S. Therefore, a coreset T can be built in one MR round as follows. Partition S evenly but arbitrarily into ℓ disjoint subsets $S_1, \ldots, S_\ell$, and assign each subset S_i to a distinct reducer, which builds a $(1-\varepsilon)$-coreset T_i for S_i based on a τ_i-clustering of radius at most $\varepsilon\Delta_{S_i}/(8k)$ using the sequential implementation described in the previous subsection. Coreset T is simply the union of the T_i's.

Theorem 4.2. *Let $\varepsilon < 1$ be an arbitrary positive constant. The above MR algorithm computes a $(1-\varepsilon)$-coreset T for the MDMC problem in one round, with $M_T = O(n)$ and $M_L = O(n/\ell)$, for both partition and transversal matroids.*

Proof. The coreset $T = \bigcup_{i=1,\ell} T_i$ computed by the algorithm can be regarded as being derived from a τ-clustering of S, with $\tau = \sum_{i=1}^{\ell} \tau_i$, of radius at most

$$\varepsilon\frac{\max_{i=1,\ell}\Delta_{S_i}}{8k} \le \varepsilon\frac{\Delta_S}{8k} \le \varepsilon\frac{\bar{\rho}_S}{4},$$

by virtue of Lemma 3.2. Hence, by Theorems 3.4 and 3.5, T is $(1-\varepsilon)$-coreset for S. □

We can immediately derive a 2-round MR algorithm for the MDMC problem: in the first round, we compute a coreset T, based on the above theorem; in the second round we gather T in one reducer and run the AMT algorithm on it. It easily follows that the algorithm requires $M_T = O(n)$, while the local memory requirements are $M_L = O(n/\ell + k\tau)$, for a partition matroid, and $M_L = O\left(n/\ell + k^2\tau\right)$ for a transversal matroid, where $\tau = \sum_{i=1}^{\ell}\tau_i$. If the set S is from a space with constant doubling dimension D, by Theorem 3.7, we have that $\tau_i = O\left((k/\varepsilon)^D\right)$, hence $\tau = O\left(\ell(k/\varepsilon)^D\right)$.

4.3 Streaming implementation

In the streaming setting [16] the computation is performed by a single processor with a small-size working memory, and the input is provided as a continuous stream of items which is usually too large to fit in the working memory. Typically, streaming strategies aim at a single pass on the input but in some cases few additional passes may be needed. Key performance indicators are the size of the working memory and the number of passes.

Our streaming algorithm for the coreset construction is based on the scaling algorithm for clustering mentioned before [22] which provides a $2+\delta$ approximation, for any fixed $\delta > 0$. Let $\alpha > 1$ be a parameter to be fixed later and let τ be the desired number of clusters. The algorithm runs m parallel instances of the following subroutine and every element of S is fed to each instance. For $1 \le i \le m$ the i-th instance maintains a lower bound r_i on the radius of the optimal clustering, which is initialized as the minimum distance among the first $\tau+1$ elements of S, suitably scaled depending on α and i. The elements of S are processed one at a time maintaining the following invariants: (a) a set Z_i of at most τ cluster centers is stored in the working memory; (b) the distance between any two centers in Z_i is at least $2\alpha r_i$; (c) the maximum distance between any element of S processed so far and the closest center in Z_i is at most $(2\alpha^2/(\alpha-1))r_i$. When an element s is fed to an instance, the following two rules are applied to maintain the invariants. The *update rule* first checks if invariant (c) is violated. If not, s is simply discarded. If instead the invariant is violated, s is added as a new center. If invariant (a) is now violated, the *merge rule* is invoked repeatedly until all invariants are restored. In a single invocation of this rule, the lower bound r_i is increased by a factor α and for each pair of centers violating invariant (b) one of them is discarded.

After all elements of S have been processed, each set Z_i has at most τ cluster centers stored in the working memory, which induce a clustering (C_i, Z_i) where each element of S belongs to the cluster of its closest center. Among these m clusterings, the algorithm selects the one associated with the lowest r_i. By fixing $\alpha = O(1/\delta)$ and $m = O(1/\delta \log 1/\delta)$, the authors of [22] show that the radius of this clustering is a factor at most $2+\delta$ away from that of the optimal radius.

Observe that the scaling algorithm described above provides explicitly only the set of centers but not the clusters which, however, are needed for the coreset construction. In order to compute the actual coreset T, in a second pass on S we can easily implement streamed versions of the constructions described in Section 3, by leveraging on the fact that, thanks to the augmentation property, computation of independent sets of any given size can be streamlined. In fact, the coreset construction can be embedded together with the center selection performed in the first pass, by suitably modifying the update and merge rules so to maintain, with each current center, a set of potential candidate elements to be included in the final coreset. The details of such constructions, which are tedious yet conceptually simple, are omitted for brevity and will be provided in a full version of this paper. The following theorem is an easy consequence of the above discussion, of Lemma 3.2, and of Theorems 3.4 and 3.5.

Theorem 4.3. *Let $\varepsilon, \delta < 1$ be two arbitrary positive constants, and let τ be such that the optimal τ-clustering for S has radius at*

Table 1: Datasets used in the experimental evaluation, n is the number of elements.

	n	Matroid rank	Matroid type
Wikipedia	5,315,955	100	transversal
Songs	264,681	89	partition

most $\varepsilon\Delta_S/((2+\delta)8k)$. The above streaming algorithm computes a $(1-\varepsilon)$-coreset T for the MDMC problem in one pass, using working memory of size $O(k\tau)$, for a partition matroid, and of size $O(k^2\tau)$, for a transversal matroid.

Based on the above theorem, we can immediately derive a one-pass streaming algorithm for the MDMC problem, by simply running the AMT algorithm on the coreset T stored in the working memory at the end of the coreset construction. If the set S is from a space with constant doubling dimension D, by Theorem 3.7, we have that $\tau = O\left((k/\varepsilon)^D\right)$ suffices. Unfortunately, unlike the sequential and MapReduce implementations where the value of τ that provides a suitably small cluster radius can be determined on the fly, due to the incremental nature of the GMM algorithm, in the streaming implementation such a value must be fixed *apriori*. In theory, if the doubling dimension D of the space is known, then the value of τ can be fixed analytically. Otherwise, the value τ can be guessed in a number of passes at most logarithmic in n. In practice, one can fix τ to the largest feasible tolerable value based on the size of the working memory and on the projected cost of the final local search on T. In this case, however, no bound can be easily established on the approximation quality.

5 EXPERIMENTS

In this section, we report on two sets of experiments run on a cluster of 16 machines, each equipped with a 18GB RAM and a 4-core Intel I7 processor, connected by a 10Gbit Ethernet network. The first set aims at demonstrating the superiority of our coreset-based approach to MDMC over the existing pure local search of [1], while the second set explores its applicability to very large inputs. The source code of our implementation is publicly available[1].

As testbeds, we use two real-world datasets, which are summarized in Table 1. One dataset is derived from a recent dump of the English Wikipedia[2], comprising 5,315,955 pages. Each page is associated to some *categories* out of 1,102,435 overall categories defined by the Wikipedia users, which naturally induce a transversal matroid. Observe however that due to the sheer number of categories, for any reasonable value of k, any subset of k pages would very likely be an independent set, thus making the matroid constraint immaterial. As a workaround, we applied the *Latent Dirichlet Allocation* model [6] to derive a set of 100 topics, which we use as new categories, together with a probability distribution over these categories for each page. We then assign each page to the most likely categories (probability ≥ 0.1), thus obtaining a transversal matroid of rank 100. The other dataset is a set of 264,681 songs [3], each represented by its lyrics and associated to a unique *genre*. Since genres define a partition of the dataset, they induce a partition matroid. The cardinality bounds for each genre are defined so to be proportional to the distribution of songs across genres, resulting in a partition matroid of rank 89.

For both datasets, we map each element to a 100-dimensional real-valued vector through the widely used Word2Vec model [23]. As distance metric, we use the metric version of the *cosine distance* [20]. All results reported are obtained as averages over at least 10 runs.

5.1 Sequential setting

We compare the sequential implementation of our algorithm described in Section 4.1 (dubbed SeqCoreset) against the AMT algorithm of [1]. We recall that the latter runs a local search over the entire input, and features a parameter γ to limit swaps to those providing a significant improvement to the solution quality, dependent on γ, thus exercising a tradeoff between approximation guarantee $(\frac{1}{2}-\gamma)$ and running time. Albeit polynomial for constant $\gamma > 0$, AMT is quite expensive, since it may require to check a large number of candidate swaps (possibly quadratic in the input size) where each check entails a call to the independent set oracle, which can be a costly operation, depending on the matroid type. For this reason, in order to keep the running times of AMT under a reasonable threshold, we experimented on a random sample of only 5,000 elements from each dataset.

For what concerns SeqCoreset, we control the radius of the clustering underlying the coreset construction indirectly through the number of clusters τ to be found by GMM, where larger values of τ yield smaller radii. Specifically, we set τ to powers of two from 8 to 256. For comparison, we ran two instances of AMT: one instance with $\gamma = 0$, which yields the best possible approximation, and another instance with the largest value γ yielding a diversity slightly smaller than the smallest diversity returned by our algorithm. Also, for each dataset we used two values of k, namely $k = \text{rank}(\mathcal{M})$ and $k = \text{rank}(\mathcal{M})/4$, where $\mathcal{M}$ is the associated matroid.

In Figure 1, we plot the running times of the two algorithms versus the diversity yielded by each parameter configuration, so to compare the time taken by each algorithm to compute a solution of similar quality. We also shade the area below the line relative to SeqCoreset to show the amount of time spent building the coreset (in red) and the amount of time required to run a full local search on the coreset (in green). We observe that our algorithm returns solutions of quality comparable to the ones obtained by AMT and, as emphasized by the logarithmic scale, in most cases it runs in one or two orders of magnitude less time. Note that the worst performance of SeqCoreset is on the Wikipedia dataset with $k = \text{rank}(\mathcal{M})$. In fact, due to the small dataset size used in this experiments to afford reasonable running times for AMT, for larger values of τ the coreset size becomes comparable to the input size, hence the local search on the coreset dominates the running time, bringing it closer to the one of AMT. In the next section we shall see that our coreset strategy allows to solve very large instances, which are impractical for AMT, using coresets of size substantially smaller than the input.

We observe that in all experiments, the coreset construction performed by SeqCoreset never dominates its running time. This is a consequence of both the expensive nature of the local search task

[1] https://github.com/Cecca/diversity-maximization
[2] https://dumps.wikimedia.org/backup-index.html, accessed on 2017-01-20
[3] https://www.kaggle.com/gyani95/380000-lyrics-from-metrolyrics

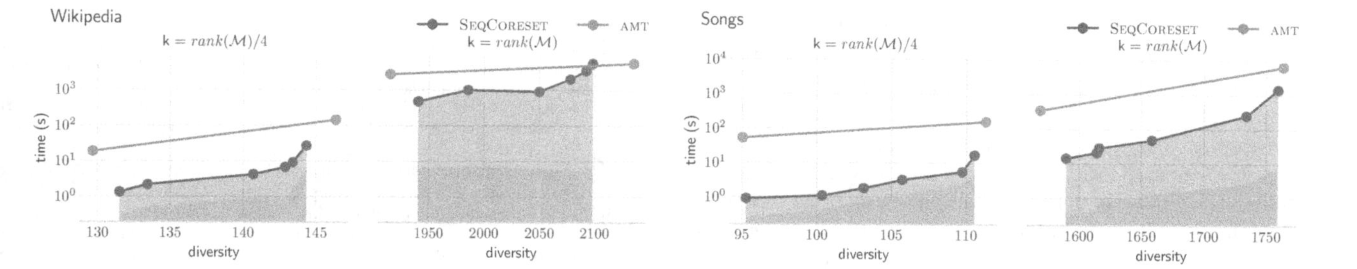

Figure 1: Time vs. diversity for AMT and SEQCORESET, for the Wikipedia (left) and the Songs (right) datasets. The area shaded in red represents the time spent by SEQCORESET in building the coreset, while the green area is the time spent computing the solution on the coreset. Blue (resp., green) points represent runs of SEQCORESET (resp., AMT) with values of τ (resp., γ) increasing (resp., decreasing) from left to right. The scale of the plots is logarithmic, and times are in seconds.

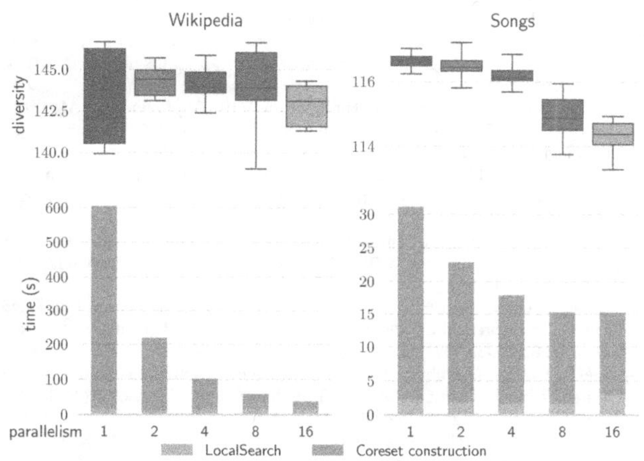

Figure 2: The top box plots report, for each level of parallelism, the distribution of the diversities found by several runs of the algorithms. The bottom bar plots report the average running times needed to compute these diversities, broken down in two components. The scale of the plots is linear, and times are in seconds.

and also of the limited input size. In fact, in the next subsection we will experiment on much larger datasets, where the coreset construction task dominates the time. Also, notice that, counterintuitively, in the case of Wikipedia with $k = \text{rank}(\mathcal{M})$, the coreset construction seems to be unrelated to τ. This is due to the fact that the oracle of the transversal matroid is rather expensive to invoke and depends on k, therefore the extraction of the coreset elements from the clustering dominates the time to compute the clustering itself, which depends on τ.

Finally, the trend of the line representing the performance of our algorithm shows that the parameter τ can be effectively used to control a tradeoff between accuracy and running time, while parameter γ of AMT seems less effective in that respect.

5.2 Distributed setting

We implemented the MapReduce version of our coreset-based strategy described in Section 4.2 (dubbed MRCORESET), using the Spark framework [25]. We ran MRCORESET on the full Wikipedia and Songs datasets so to assess the effectiveness of our approach for large instances. Conceivably, on large inputs the main bottleneck of our approach becomes the coreset construction task, which involves the whole input. Luckily, however, this task is parallelized in the MR implementation, thus yielding scalable performance. To emphasize this aspect, we fixed a cluster granularity, namely $\tau = 64$, which provides a coreset whose size is small enough to limit the impact of the local search task, but sufficient to embody a good quality solution. Then, we ran MRCORESET, on $\ell = 2, 4, 8$ and 16 machines, setting the number of clusters computed by each machine to τ/ℓ, so to extract the final coreset always from a τ-clustering. For both datasets, we fixed $k = \text{rank}(\mathcal{M})/4$.

The results of our experiments are reported in the four plots of Figure 2. In the figure, the top two plots are box plots for the diversity found by our algorithms, while the bottom pair of plots give the running time required by the algorithms, decomposed into coreset construction and local search time, under the different levels of parallelism, for the Wikipedia and the Songs dataset, respectively, In all plots, the case of parallelism 1 is obtained by running SEQCORESET. Indeed, by looking at the bars for parallelism 1, we can confirm that, on large inputs, the majority of the work goes into the coreset construction, while the bars associated to larger levels of parallelism show that such construction scales well. This scalability effect is more evident on the Wikipedia dataset which, due to its larger size, is able to take better advantage of the available parallelism. In fact, observe that on this latter dataset the coreset-construction scales more than linearly when going from 1 to 2 processors. This is due to the fact that on a single processor the clusters from which the coreset points are selected contain more points, thus there is a higher chance that a cluster contains an independent set of size k, and finding large independent sets is an expensive operation. Conversely, when the dataset is partitioned across processors, clusters are sparser and thus more likely to contain only independent sets of size smaller than k, which take considerably less to identify.

Importantly, we have that parallelizing the coreset construction, which may in theory yield coresets of worse quality, does not seem to affect the quality of the final solution: for the Wikipedia dataset, all parameter configurations find diversities in the same range; on the Songs dataset, there is a very small decrease of the quality of the solution (within 3%) when parallelism increases. These effects are the result of the complex interplay of several factors. In particular, we verified that the coreset size for both datasets remains below $\tau \cdot k$ (even in the case of Wikipedia's transversal matroid) but tends to increase with the parallelism. This may be due to the fact that, for larger values of parallelism, the clustering from which the coreset is built tends to have a larger radius, since each machine computes only τ/ℓ clusters, which in turn implies that larger independent sets can be found in each cluster. While a larger radius is detrimental for the quality of the solution, a larger coreset is beneficial. From our results, it seems that in Wikipedia's case the benefits of a larger coreset balance the disadvantages of the larger radius, whereas for the Songs dataset the negative effect of the radius slightly prevails.

We remark that the high complexity of AMT makes it impractical for such large inputs, thus ruling out a direct comparison with MRCoreset. However, by pairing the results of the comparison between AMT and SeqCoreset from the previous subsection and between SeqCoreset and MRCoreset from this subsection, we can infer that the latter holds the promise to provide solutions of similar quality as AMT but in a scalable fashion. Also, note that we ran MRCoreset with this peculiar choice of parameters so to appreciate the scalability of coreset construction. In practice, one may increase the number of clusters computed in each machine, resulting in a larger coreset, and then apply SeqCluster to this coreset to compute the final solution, yielding a two-phase approach similar in spirit to the MR clustering by [21].

6 CONCLUSIONS

Coresets provide an effective way of processing large amounts of data by building a succint summary of the input which can then be processed with the sequential algorithm of choice. In particular, we have seen how to leverage coresets to build MapReduce and streaming algorithms for the Max-Sum diversity problem under several matroid constraints that, given enough resources, exhibit a $1/2 - \varepsilon$ approximation factor. We verified experimentally that our coreset-based approach outperforms the state of the art, while attaining solutions of comparable quality.

Future avenues of research include the extension of this approach to other diversity measures. Furthermore, our streaming implementation is forced to fix the coreset size apriori. If the doubling dimension of the input space is unknown, it is harder to establish the coreset size needed to achieve a prespecified approximation ratio. A streaming approach that dynamically adjusts the coreset size to meet a given approximation requirement is a challenging open problem.

ACKNOWLEDGEMENTS

This work was supported, in part, by University of Padova under projects BIRD178792 and CPDA152255.

REFERENCES

[1] Zeinab Abbassi, Vahab S. Mirrokni, and Mayur Thakur. 2013. Diversity maximization under matroid constraints. In *Proc. KDD*. 32–40. https://doi.org/10.1145/2487575.2487636

[2] Marcel R. Ackermann, Johannes Blömer, and Christian Sohler. 2010. Clustering for metric and nonmetric distance measures. *ACM Trans. Algorithms* 6, 4 (2010), 59:1–59:26. https://doi.org/10.1145/1824777.1824779

[3] Pankaj K. Agarwal, Sariel Har-Peled, and Kasturi R. Varadarajan. 2005. Geometric approximation via coresets. *J. of Combinatorial and Computational Geometry* 52 (2005), 1–30.

[4] Sepideh Aghamolaei, Majid Farhadi, and Hamid Zarrabi-Zadeh. 2015. Diversity Maximization via Composable Coresets. In *Proc. CCCG*.

[5] Aditya Bhaskara, Mehrdad Ghadiri, Vahab S. Mirrokni, and Ola Svensson. 2016. Linear Relaxations for Finding Diverse Elements in Metric Spaces. In *Proc. NIPS*. 4098–4106. http://papers.nips.cc/paper/6500-linear-relaxations-for-finding-diverse-elements-in-metric-spaces

[6] David M. Blei, Andrew Y. Ng, and Michael I. Jordan. 2003. Latent Dirichlet Allocation. *J. of Machine Learning Research* 3 (2003), 993–1022. http://www.jmlr.org/papers/v3/blei03a.html

[7] Allan Borodin, Hyun Chul Lee, and Yuli Ye. 2012. Max-Sum diversification, monotone submodular functions and dynamic updates. In *Proc. PODS*. 155–166. https://doi.org/10.1145/2213556.2213580

[8] Matteo Ceccarello, Andrea Pietracaprina, Geppino Pucci, and Eli Upfal. 2017. MapReduce and Streaming Algorithms for Diversity Maximization in Metric Spaces of Bounded Doubling Dimension. *PVLDB* 10, 5 (2017), 469–480. http://www.vldb.org/pvldb/vol10/p469-ceccarello.pdf

[9] Alfonso Cevallos, Friedrich Eisenbrand, and Rico Zenklusen. 2017. Local Search for Max-Sum Diversification. In *Proc. SODA*. 130–142. https://doi.org/10.1137/1.9781611974782.9

[10] Barun Chandra and Magnús M. Halldórsson. 2001. Approximation Algorithms for Dispersion Problems. *J. Algorithms* 38, 2 (2001), 438–465. https://doi.org/10.1006/jagm.2000.1145

[11] Richard Cole and Lee-Ad Gottlieb. 2006. Searching dynamic point sets in spaces with bounded doubling dimension. In *Proc. STOC*. 574–583. https://doi.org/10.1145/1132516.1132599

[12] Jeffrey Dean and Sanjay Ghemawat. 2004. MapReduce: Simplified Data Processing on Large Clusters. In *Proc. OSDI*. 137–150. http://www.usenix.org/events/osdi04/tech/dean.html

[13] Teofilo F. Gonzalez. 1985. Clustering to Minimize the Maximum Intercluster Distance. *Theoretical Computer Science* 38 (1985), 293–306. https://doi.org/10.1016/0304-3975(85)90224-5

[14] Lee-Ad Gottlieb, Aryeh Kontorovich, and Robert Krauthgamer. 2014. Efficient Classification for Metric Data. *IEEE Trans. Information Theory* 60, 9 (2014), 5750–5759. https://doi.org/10.1109/TIT.2014.2339840

[15] Anupam Gupta, Robert Krauthgamer, and James R. Lee. 2003. Bounded Geometries, Fractals, and Low-Distortion Embeddings. In *Proc. FOCS*. 534–543. https://doi.org/10.1109/SFCS.2003.1238226

[16] Monika Rauch Henzinger, Prabhakar Raghavan, and Sridhar Rajagopalan. 1998. Computing on data streams. In *Proc. DIMACS*. 107–118.

[17] Piotr Indyk, Sepideh Mahabadi, Mohammad Mahdian, and Vahab S. Mirrokni. 2014. Composable core-sets for diversity and coverage maximization. In *Proc. PODS*. 100–108. https://doi.org/10.1145/2594538.2594560

[18] Howard J. Karloff, Siddharth Suri, and Sergei Vassilvitskii. 2010. A Model of Computation for MapReduce. In *Proc. SODA*. 938–948. https://doi.org/10.1137/1.9781611973075.76

[19] Goran Konjevod, Andréa W. Richa, and Donglin Xia. 2008. Dynamic Routing and Location Services in Metrics of Low Doubling Dimension. In *Proc. DISC*. 379–393. https://doi.org/10.1007/978-3-540-87779-0_26

[20] Jure Leskovec, Anand Rajaraman, and Jeffrey D. Ullman. 2014. *Mining of Massive Datasets, 2nd Ed.* Cambridge University Press.

[21] Gustavo Malkomes, Matt J. Kusner, Wenlin Chen, Kilian Q. Weinberger, and Benjamin Moseley. 2015. Fast Distributed k-Center Clustering with Outliers on Massive Data. In *Proc. NIPS*. 1063–1071. http://papers.nips.cc/paper/5997-fast-distributed-k-center-clustering-with-outliers-on-massive-data

[22] Richard Matthew McCutchen and Samir Khuller. 2008. Streaming Algorithms for k-Center Clustering with Outliers and with Anonymity. In *Proc. APPROX-RANDOM*. 165–178. https://doi.org/10.1007/978-3-540-85363-3_14

[23] Tomas Mikolov, Kai Chen, Greg Corrado, and Jeffrey Dean. 2013. Efficient Estimation of Word Representations in Vector Space. *CoRR* abs/1301.3781 (2013). http://arxiv.org/abs/1301.3781

[24] James G. Oxley. 2006. *Matroid Theory*. Oxford University Press.

[25] Matei Zaharia, Mosharaf Chowdhury, Michael J. Franklin, Scott Shenker, and Ion Stoica. 2010. Spark: Cluster Computing with Working Sets. In *Proc. HotCloud*. https://www.usenix.org/conference/hotcloud-10/spark-cluster-computing-working-sets

Putting Data in the Driver's Seat: Optimizing Earnings for On-Demand Ride-Hailing

Harshal A. Chaudhari
Boston University
harshal@cs.bu.edu

John W. Byers
Boston University
byers@cs.bu.edu

Evimaria Terzi
Boston University
evimaria@cs.bu.edu

ABSTRACT

On-demand ride-hailing platforms like Uber and Lyft are helping reshape urban transportation, by enabling car owners to become drivers for hire with minimal overhead. Although there are many studies that consider ride-hailing platforms holistically, e.g., from the perspective of supply and demand equilibria, little emphasis has been placed on optimization for the individual, self-interested drivers that currently comprise these fleets. While some individuals drive opportunistically either as their schedule allows or on a fixed schedule, we show that strategic behavior regarding when and where to drive can substantially increase driver income. In this paper, we formalize the problem of devising a driver strategy to maximize expected earnings, describe a series of dynamic programming algorithms to solve these problems under different sets of modeled actions available to the drivers, and exemplify the models and methods on a large scale simulation of driving for Uber in NYC. In our experiments, we use a newly-collected dataset that combines the NYC taxi rides dataset along with Uber API data, to build time-varying traffic and payout matrices for a representative six-month time period in greater NYC. From this input, we can reason about prospective itineraries and payoffs. Moreover, the framework enables us to rigorously reason about and analyze the sensitivity of our results to perturbations in the input data. Among our main findings is that repositioning throughout the day is key to maximizing driver earnings, whereas 'chasing surge' is typically misguided and sometimes a costly move.

ACM Reference Format:
Harshal A. Chaudhari, John W. Byers, and Evimaria Terzi. 2018. Putting Data in the Driver's Seat: Optimizing Earnings for On-Demand Ride-Hailing. In *WSDM 2018: 11th Eleventh ACM International Conference on Web Search and Data Mining, February 5–9, 2018, Marina Del Rey, CA, USA.* ACM, New York, NY, USA, 9 pages. https://doi.org/10.1145/3159652.3159721

1 INTRODUCTION

The proliferation of on-demand ride-hailing platforms like Lyft and Uber has begun to fundamentally change the nature of urban transit. In the last two years alone, the number of daily trips using ride-hailing platforms like Uber and Lyft in NYC has grown five-fold, to about 350,000 trips per day. Today, over 65,000 drivers drive on the streets of NYC as Uber or Lyft drivers. The explosive growth of these ride-hailing platforms has motivated a wide array of questions for academic research at the intersection of computer science and economics, ranging from the design of effective pricing mechanisms, to equilibrium analysis, to the design of reputation management systems for drivers, to algorithms for matching drivers with customers, as we discuss in our related work section.

While these studies consider the study of ride-hailing platforms holistically, little work has been done on optimizing strategies for individual drivers. Nevertheless, the challenge of how to maximize one's individual earnings as a driver for a ride-hailing platform like Uber or Lyft is a pressing question that millions of micro-entrepreneurs across the world now face. Anecdotally, many drivers spend a great deal of time strategizing about where and when to drive. However, drivers today are self-taught, using heuristics of their own devising or learning from one another, and employ relatively simple analytics dashboards such as SherpaShare. Indeed, rumors suggest that some drivers even collude in attempts to induce spikes in surge prices that they can then exploit. But in terms of concrete guidance, to date, there are only articles in the popular press and on blogs that offer (often contradictory) advice to ride-hailing drivers how to maximize their earnings [8, 10, 19].

In this paper, we formalize the problem of devising a driver strategy to maximize expected earnings and describe a series of dynamic programming algorithms to solve this problem under different sets of modeled actions available to the drivers. Our strategies take as input a detailed model of city-level data that constitutes a fine-grained weekly projection of forecasted demand for rides, comprising predicted spatiotemporal distributions of source-destination pairs, driver payments, transit times, and surge multipliers. The optimization framework we propose not only produces contingency plans in the form of highly optimized driving schedules and real-time in-course corrections to drivers, but also enables us to rigorously reason about and analyze the sensitivity of our output results to perturbations in the input data. Thus, we can justify the proposed strategies even under an uncertainty level in the collected data and the data model itself.

We then exemplify our results with a large-scale simulation of driving for Uber in NYC. For this simulation, we assemble a new dataset that uses both the publicly available NYC taxi rides dataset [1] as well as calls to the Uber API. From the former, we obtain information about over 200,000 taxi rides that occurred between different NYC zones. From the latter, we obtain representative pricing and traffic-time information for those trips, were they to reoccur on Uber. From this dataset, we construct a mathematical model to produce input to our algorithms. However, we view the dataset to

[1] http://www.nyc.gov/html/tlc/html/about/trip_record_data.shtml

WSDM 2018, February 5–9, 2018, Marina Del Rey, CA, USA

ACM ISBN 978-1-4503-5581-0/18/02...$15.00
https://doi.org/10.1145/3159652.3159721

be of independent interest that could subsequently be used for a multitude of other studies.

Our experiments with our methods on this dataset demonstrate the following findings. Being strategic about the areas they focus on picking up riders and the times they work, drivers can significantly increase their income, sometimes by as much as 1.5x, when compared to a naive optimization strategy. Moreover, we show that a pronounced difference between earnings holds even when there is large uncertainty in the input data. We argue that our results are therefore not purely an artifact of the NYC dataset we employ, but also have high potential to generalize. Finally, our experiments show that naively chasing surging prices does not typically lead to significant earnings gains, but it can actually introduce large opportunity costs, as drivers waste time driving to subsiding surges.

2 RELATED WORK

To the best of our knowledge, we are the first to formally address the problem of optimizing the driver's strategy in ride-hailing platforms like Uber and Lyft. Apart from some recent popular-press articles that offer, often contradictory, advice to ride-hailing drivers on how to maximize earnings, mostly via chasing surge [8, 10], the only relevant existing technical work studies other aspects of ride-hailing. Next, we discuss these works as well as some work related to optimization problems for taxi fleets.

Studies of ride-hailing platforms: Recent work has investigated the supply-side effects of specific incentives (e.g., surge pricing) that Uber and Lyft provide to drivers [20]. For example, Chen and Sheldon [7] showed a causal relationship that drivers on Uber respond to surges by driving more during high surge times, differentiating from previous work that suggests taxi drivers primarily focus on achieving earnings goals [3]. In another line of research, Chen *et al.* [6] measured many facets of Uber in NYC, including the prevalence and extent of surge pricing. Hall and Krueger [9] showed that drivers were attracted to the Uber platform due to the flexibility it offers, and the level of compensation, but that earnings per hour do not vary much with the number of hours worked. Finally, Castillo *et al.* [4] recently showed that surge pricing is responsible for effectively relocating drivers during periods of high-demand thereby preventing them from engaging in 'wild goose chases' to pick up distant customers, which only exacerbates the problem of low driver availability. These studies perform an *a posteriori* analysis of the data, but they do not focus on devising specific recommendations for drivers as we do.

In another line of work, Banerjee *et al.* [2] studied dynamic pricing strategies for ride-hailing platforms (such as Lyft) using a queuing-theoretic economic model. They showed that dynamic pricing is robust to changes in system parameters, even if it does not achieve higher performance than static pricing. More recently, Ozkan and Ward [17] looked at strategic matching between supply (individual drivers) and demand (requested rides) for Uber and Lyft. They showed that matching based on time-varying parameters like driver and customer arrival rates, and the willingness of customers to wait can achieve better performance than naively matching passengers with the closest driver. Although these works build interesting models for ride-hailing economies, they are orthogonal to ours, as they take a holistic view of such economies, while we focus on earnings of individual, self-interested drivers.

Optimization problems for taxi fleets: A considerable body of work has focused on the optimization of taxi fleets, for example building economic network models to describe demand and supply equilibria of taxi services under various tariff structures, fleet size regulations, and other policy alternatives [1, 22]. Other work seeks to optimize the allocation of taxi market resources [18]. Another direction focuses on route optimization by a centralized administrator (e.g., taxi dispatching services) [14, 16] or on maximizing occupancy and minimizing travel times in a shared-ride setting [12]. Other work has studied the supply side of the driving market from the viewpoint of behavioral economics. A seminal paper by Camerer *et al.* [3] studied cab drivers and found that inexperienced cab drivers (1) make labor supply decisions "one day at a time" instead of substituting labor and leisure across multiple days, and (2) set a loose daily income target and quit working once they reach that target. These works, however, do not focus on the design of a specific gain-optimizing strategy for drivers, as we do.

3 PROBLEM SETUP

In this section, we describe the basics of our problem setup and provide the necessary notation.

3.1 Modeling the city

Throughout the paper, we will assume that a city is divided into non-overlapping set of zones denoted by $\mathcal{X}$, and time t runs in discrete time steps. We represent a city in the form of a complete weighted directed graph $G = (\mathcal{X}, E)$ with $|\mathcal{X}| = n$ and $|E| = \binom{n}{2}$ edges, where the edge weight on edge $e(i \to j)$ corresponds to the likelihood of a driver currently at location i receiving a ride request to location j. Additionally, each edge is associated with a travel time $\tau(i, j)$, a travel cost, and a reward $r(i, j)$. In the general formulation of our problem, all of these edge attributes are time-varying, e.g., the rewards would vary with t as $r^t(i, j)$, but to avoid excess notation, we drop those superscripts in our following discussion of models and algorithms, and reintroduce them only in our experiments in Section 6. These attributes of a city, which we use as an input to our solver, are specified as follows:

Empirical transition matrix (F): Every edge $e(i \to j) \in E$ is associated with a transition probability $f(i, j) \in [0, 1]$ such that $\sum_{j \in \mathcal{X}} f(i, j) = 1, \forall i \in \mathcal{X}$.

Since the entries of F correspond to probabilities, the weights give rise to a *Markov Chain* with a transition matrix F – where each entry $f(i, j)$ denotes the probability of a passenger in zone i traveling to zone j. As we disallow trips within the same zone in our model (an assumption which could be relaxed), we let $f(i, i)$ denote the probability of a driver not finding a passenger in zone i at a given time step.

Travel time matrix (T): Every edge $e(i \to j) \in E$ is also associated with $\tau(i, j) > 0$, the travel time of a ride from zone i to zone j. These weights give us a travel time matrix T with entries $\tau(i, j)$.

Rewards matrix (R): Every edge $e(i \to j) \in E$ is also associated with a real valued reward $r(i, j)$ denoting the net reward for a driver delivering a passenger from zone i to zone j. The net rewards include the driver's share of earnings from a passenger minus the sundry costs like gas, vehicle depreciation, etc. Since these earnings and costs vary with mileage and transit time, each entry in the rewards matrix R is of the form $r(i, j)$ = earnings(i, j) - cost(i, j).

Again, in general, all of the input matrices: **F**, **T** and **R**, are time-dependent, i.e., their entries could change throughout the day

3.2 Modeling the driver

Our model assumes that each driver comes with a maximum work budget of B time units, during which the driver can pick up passengers. Depending on the specific setting, the driver can work B time units consecutively or split them over a finite horizon of N time units, where $N \geq B$. As an example, a driver seeking to optimize an 8 hour work day over a 24 hour day at a ten-minute decision granularity (at most six decisions per hour), will have $B = 48$ and $N = 144$.

Home zone (i_0): Each driver has a unique home zone denoted by $i_0 \in \mathcal{X}$. We always assume that each driver starts from their home zone and returns to it at the end of each of their shifts.

Driver actions ($\mathcal{A}$): In a driver strategy, whenever faced with a choice regarding their next decision, a driver has $n + 2$ possible actions to choose from:

- *Get Passenger* (a_0): Wait for a passenger in the current zone.
- *Go Home* (a_1): Log out of the on-demand ride service, relocate to the home zone (if needed) and stop working. This action does not consume the driver's budget.
- *Relocate* ($a_2(j)$): Relocate to city zone j. This action consumes the driver's budget.

Driver policy (π): A driver policy is a sequence of time and location-dependent actions taken by a driver at different steps of the strategy. As the total number of actions taken by a driver while exhausting the budget B depends on the actual actions, the length of a driver policy π varies.

Each time and location dependent action in π, denoted by **a**, can be expressed in form of a 3-tuple – $(\hat{i}, \hat{t}, \hat{a})$ where $\hat{a} \in \mathcal{A}$ refers to actual action, $\hat{i} \in \mathcal{X}$ is the zone at which action was taken and $\hat{t} \leq N$ is the time at which the action was taken. Finally, we use Π to denote the set of all possible policies.

3.3 Computing driver earnings

In this section, we describe the computation of the expected earnings of a driver who at a specific time t is in zone i and takes action a. We denote this by $E(i, t, a)$ and depending on the action a it is computed as follows.

- For action a_0 (*Get Passenger*), taken inside zone i at time t, the action earnings function is calculated as an expectation over possible rides,
$$E(i, t, a_0) = \mathbf{F}_i \cdot \mathbf{R}_i \tag{1}$$
where $\mathbf{F}_i$ and $\mathbf{R}_i$ denote the i-th rows of **F** and **R** respectively.
- For action a_1 (*Go Home*), taken inside zone i at time t, the action earnings function is simply
$$E(i, t, a_1) = -cost(i, i_0) \tag{2}$$
where we incur a negative reward due to the absence of a paying customer.
- Action $a_2(j)$ (*Relocate*), taken inside zone i at time t, takes the driver to zone $j \neq i$. Therefore, the action earnings function is
$$E(i, t, a_2(j)) = -cost(i, j) \tag{3}$$
where the driver again incurs a negative reward due to the absence of a paying customer.

3.4 Problem definition

Given input specification matrices **F**, **T** and **R**, as well as the driver's budget B, the *total expected earnings* of the driver with policy π is:

$$\mathcal{E}(\pi, \mathbf{F}, \mathbf{T}, \mathbf{R}, B) = \sum_{(\hat{i}, \hat{t}, \hat{a}) \in \pi} E(\hat{i}, \hat{t}, \hat{a}), \tag{4}$$

where $E(\hat{i}, \hat{t}, \hat{a})$ is computed using the Equations (1), (2) and (3).

As we seek to maximize the *total expected earnings* of the driver, we aim to solve the following optimization problem.

Problem 1 (MaxEarnings). *Given sets of time-evolving* **F**, **T** *and* **R**, *as well as the driver's budget B, find a* π^* *such that:*

$$\pi^* = \arg\max_{\pi \in \Pi} \mathcal{E}(\pi, \mathbf{F}, \mathbf{T}, \mathbf{R}, B).$$

4 DRIVER STRATEGIES AND OPTIMIZATION ALGORITHMS

We now describe the different driver strategies, which are defined based on the set of actions $\mathcal{A}$ at the driver's disposal. We also show how to optimally solve the MaxEarnings problem in polynomial time for different sets $\mathcal{A}$.

For the rest of the section, we will denote by $\Phi(i, b, t)$ the *total expected future earnings* of a driver who is in zone i at time t with budget b time units remaining. Hence, the *total expected earnings* of a driver can be expressed as $\Phi(i_0, B, N)$.

If a driver at zone i at time t with b budget units remaining either takes a passenger ride to zone j or relocates to zone j, that trip ends at time $t' = t + \tau^t(i, j)$ with remaining budget $b' = b - \tau^t(i, j)$. The total expected future earnings at that point for the driver is: $\Phi(j, b', t')$. Let $\mathbf{v}(i, b, t)$ denotes the vector of such cumulative earnings across different zones j induced when a driver takes an a_0 action i.e., $\mathbf{v}(i, b, t) = \left[\Phi(j, b', t')\right]_{j \in \mathcal{X}}$.

We now define the driver strategies as well as the solutions to the instances of the MaxEarnings problem they induce.

The *flexible-relocation* strategy: This is the most general strategy where a driver has complete freedom for choices regarding work schedule as well relocation to different zones. Specifically, a driver has a budget constraint of B time units to be consumed over a finite horizon N time units. An idle driver in zone i following this strategy has following set of available choices,

$$\mathcal{A} = \{a_0, a_1\} \cup \{a_2(j) | \forall j \in \mathcal{X}, j \neq i\} \tag{5}$$

Note that we restrict the *Relocate* actions to ones which do not result in $t \geq N$ or $b < 0$.

A driver following the *flexible-relocation* strategy chooses the action that maximizes *total expected earnings*. For this strategy, the solution to the MaxEarnings problem can be found by the following dynamic programming (DP) recurrence:

$$\Phi(i,b,t) = \max_{a\in\mathcal{A}} \begin{cases} \mathrm{F}_i(\mathrm{R}_i + \mathrm{v}(i,b,t)), & \text{if } a = a_0 \\ -cost(i,i_0) + \Phi(i_0,b,t'), & \text{if } a = a_1 \\ \max_j\{-cost(i,j) + \Phi(j,b',t')\}, & \text{if } a = a_2(j) \end{cases} \quad (6)$$

Each of the $O(nNB)$ entries in the output of this dynamic program involves consideration of at most $O(n)$ actions. Hence, the solution to the MaxEarnings problem can be found in $O(n^2NB)$ time.

Other strategies: In addition to the general *flexible-relocation* strategy, we also consider the following three special cases to model other plausible strategies of ride-hailing drivers: the *naive*, the *relocation* and the *flexible* strategies.

In the *naive* strategy, a driver performs a random walk over the city on weekdays from 9AM - 5PM, with locations dictated exclusively by the passengers picked up. At the end of every passenger ride, the driver waits in the current zone for next passenger pickup. Hence, the only allowable action is *Get Passenger.*

In the *relocation* strategy, an idle driver in zone i has two choices: *Get Passenger* and *Relocate.* Hence, the set of allowable actions for a driver contains n different actions, one of which is *Get Passenger* and $(n-1)$ *Relocate* actions, one for each different city zone. Thus: $\mathcal{A} = \{a_0\} \cup \{a_2(j) | \forall j \in \mathcal{X}, j \neq i\}$. We remove from consideration the zones where relocating exhausts the budget or where $t \geq N$.

In the *flexible* strategy, a driver has the flexibility to decide working times, modeling a driver who uses heuristics to decide the most profitable times to work. As a result, we impose an additional constraint of a working time budget B that a driver can split over a finite horizon of N time units. Thus, this strategy aims to figure out an optimal in-expectation work schedule for the driver. At any stage, a driver can log out of the on-demand ride service and return to home zone. Hence, the set of allowable actions for a driver contains 2 different actions, *Get Passenger* and *Go Home.* Thus: $\mathcal{A} = \{a_0, a_1\}$. It is common for drivers to structure their day around a desired target earning, rather than a time budget. The *flexible* strategy also naturally computes a schedule that minimizes working time required for achieving the desired target earning.

Solving MaxEarnings for the *naive*, the *relocation* and the *flexible* strategies can be done by streamlined versions of the DP presented in Eq. (6); the details are omitted due to space constraints.

5 MAXIMIZING EARNINGS UNDER UNCERTAINTY

The primary source of variability in the input of the MaxEarnings problem is the set of empirical transition matrices F. In a typical application, we expect that predictive models would be employed to generate estimates of these matrices based upon observations from historical data (as we do in our own experiments). Empirically observed transition matrices may suffer from estimation errors due to the presence of external confounding factors (e.g., weather, special events inside the city) while gathering the data. As a result, the dynamic programming solution to MaxEarnings may also be sensitive to the transition probabilities. In this section, we address the question of how the results of the solutions we described in the previous section change under the assumption that there is some uncertainty (and thus noise) in the underlying empirical transition matrices we use as part of our input.

Concretely, we now assume that the empirical transition matrix (**F**) is generated from an underlying traffic matrix, or count matrix, recording trips between locations i and j.

Count matrix (C): Every edge $e(i \to j) \in E$ is associated with an integer-valued weight $c(i,j)$ that denotes the number of requests at zone i that had node j as their destination. Then, we compute frequencies $f(i,j) = \frac{c(i,j)}{\sum_k c(i,k)}$, for all outbound trips from i.

With this, we now describe how to quantify uncertainty in the rows of F (and the underlying C, by construction). This will enable us to modify the MaxEarnings into the RobustEarnings problem following ideas developed by Nilim and El Ghaoui [15].

Modeling uncertainty: We now assume that there is an underlying *true* transition matrix P, and the question we explore is our confidence that the C we observe is actually generated by the true transition matrix P. As before, both P and C are clearly time-dependent in practice, but for ease of exposition, we ignore the time-dependency aspect of the problem here.

We consider each row of the true transition matrix and the count matrix separately; let **p** and **c** denote any particular row of P and C respectively. Following the ideas of Kullback *et al.* [13], we have a discriminatory random variable $2\hat{I}$, which follows a χ^2 distribution with $(n-1)$ degrees of freedom. Heuristically, $2\hat{I}$ can be considered as a measure of the "divergence" of **c** from **p**. Thus, for **c** to be in the $(1-\alpha)$ *(or* $100(1-\alpha)\%$*) confidence interval of* **p**, we need:

$$\mathrm{F}_{\chi^2_{n-1}}\left[2\hat{I}\right] = \mathrm{F}_{\chi^2_{n-1}}\left[2\sum_{i=1}^{n}\mathbf{c}(i)\log\mathbf{c}(i) - 2n\log n - 2\sum_{i=1}^{n}\mathbf{c}(i)\log\mathbf{p}(i)\right] = 1-\alpha,$$

where $\mathbf{p}(i)$ (resp. $\mathbf{c}(i)$) is the i-th element of vector **p** (resp. **c**). In the above equation, α quantifies the uncertainty that one can tolerate and is an upper bound on what one believes actually exists in the set of observations **p**. Thus, we call α the *input uncertainty level.*

By setting $\beta_{\max} = \sum_{i=1}^{n}\mathbf{c}(i)\log\mathbf{c}(i)$, we get

$$\sum_{i=1}^{n}\mathbf{c}(i)\log\mathbf{p}(i) = \frac{2(\beta_{\max} - n\log n) - \mathrm{F}^{-1}_{\chi^2_{n-1}}(1-\alpha)}{2}, \quad (7)$$

where $\mathrm{F}^{-1}_{\chi^2_{n-1}}$ is the inverse of the χ^2 cdf. In other words, for all vectors **p** for which Equation (7) is satisfied, **c** is within the $(1-\alpha)$-confidence interval of **p**.

Thus given C and α, we define the *α-feasible matrices $\mathcal{P}_\alpha$* to be the set of true transition matrices such that for every matrix P in $\mathcal{P}_\alpha$ and every row **p** of P, Equation (7) is satisfied.

The RobustEarnings problem: Our approach is to compute the *worst-case total expected earnings* for a driver, by finding the P among all matrices in $\mathcal{P}_\alpha$ such that the *total expected earnings* of the driver are minimized. This quantifies the worst-case difference between the earnings computed as a solution to the MaxEarnings and the worst-case earnings of the driver, given bounded uncertainty α. We formalized this as the following problem definition:

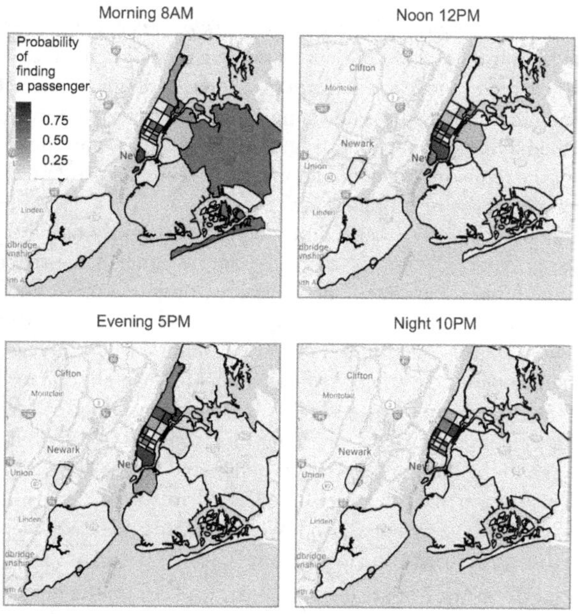

Figure 1: Probability of finding a passenger in 10 minutes across NYC zones at different times of a representative day.

Problem 2 (RobustEarnings). *Given sets of time evolving* C, T *and* R, *the driver's budget* B *and input uncertainty level* α, *find* $\widehat{\pi}$ *such that:*

$$\widehat{\pi} = \arg\max_{\pi \in \Pi} \min_{\mathrm{P} \in \mathcal{P}_\alpha} \mathcal{E}(\pi, \mathrm{P}, \mathrm{T}, \mathrm{R}, B).$$

Note that the above problem requires searching among all possible true transition matrices in $\mathcal{P}_\alpha$, which is a non-enumerable set. In fact, we can show (details omitted due to space constraints) that Problem 2 can be solved by enhancing the *total expected future earnings* associated with *Get Passenger* action in the dynamic-programming routines we described in Section 4 with an optimization problem. We use an off-the-shelf minimizer to solve this optimization problem. Alternatively, a bisection algorithm can approximate this problem within an accuracy δ in $O(\log(V_{\max}/\delta))$ time, where $V_{\max}$ is the maximum value of the value function [15].

6 DATA AND EXPERIMENTS

We now evaluate our strategies for drivers in practice. First, we discuss how we collect and combine the appropriate data from multiple data sources. Then, we perform a comprehensive experimental study that provides specific insights as to how NYC drivers can maximize their earnings.

6.1 Data collection and preparation

In order to evaluate our strategies, we need to construct time-evolving matrices F, T and R as defined in Section 3, and C as defined in Section 5. For this, we use two data sources: (1) the NYC taxi rides dataset[2] and (2) information we obtain from the Uber platform via queries to the Uber API.[3]

[2]http://www.nyc.gov/html/tlc/html/about/trip_record_data.shtml

[3]https://developer.uber.com/docs/riders/ride-requests/tutorials/api/introduction

Forming time-evolving matrices C and F: Our starting point is the NYC Taxi dataset (2015-2016), which contains yellow street-hail records of over 200,000 taxi rides per day with fields capturing pickup and dropoff times, location co-ordinates, trip distances, and fares. Each taxi record is accompanied with a taxi location ID for the pick-up and drop-off locations. Each location ID is associated with one of 29 non-overlapping city zones, as defined in the dataset. While the set of taxi rides is undoubtedly produced from a different ridership than Uber, it nonetheless provides a useful baseline that reflects many of the broader dynamics of ridership demand in NYC.

Given this data, we divide each 24-hour day of the week into 144 time-slices of duration 10 minutes each, indexed by their start time. To model traffic demand in the city at time t, the $c(i,j)$ entry of count matrix C^t is the total number of rides from zone i to zone j in a 30-minute long time window centered at time t. For example, $c(i,j)$ for the time slot [10:40, 10:50] on a Wednesday is a count of all rides from i to j that were initiated between 10:30 and 11:00 on *any* Wednesday in the dataset. Since our model disallows rides within the same zone, we ignore such rides while populating the entries of the matrix C^t, resulting in all diagonal entries of the count matrix being zero.

To populate the entries of the empirical transition matrix F^t, as defined in Section 3, we must estimate its diagonal entries, which correspond to the probability of not finding a ride, as well as the transition probabilities. We derive these from the data as follows. Assuming that the parameters do not change significantly within a single time-slice, let $N(\lambda)$ and $N(\mu)$ denote the number of passenger and driver arrivals in zone i in one time unit, with independent[4] Poisson arrival rates λ and μ respectively. Hence, the random variable $K = N(\lambda) - N(\mu)$ follows a Skellam distribution such that:

$$\Pr[K = k] = e^{-(\lambda+\mu)} \left(\frac{\lambda}{\mu}\right) I_k\left(2\sqrt{\lambda\mu}\right)$$

where $I_k(z)$ is the modified Bessel function of the first kind [21].

Whenever $K < 0$, there are more drivers than passengers. We assume a worst case scenario in which a driver (conceptually) joins the end of a FIFO queue for that zone. Hence, for $k \le 0$, the driver has to wait for $(|k|+1)$ passenger arrivals for a successful passenger pickup. Then, the probability of a successful passenger pickup is:

$$\Pr[N(\lambda) = |k| + 1] = \frac{\lambda^{\left(|k|+1\right)} e^{-\lambda}}{\left(|k| + 1\right)!}.$$

Thus, we can express a diagonal entry $f^t(i,i)$ as follows:

$$f^t(i,i) = 1 - \sum_{k \le 0} \Pr[K = k] \times \Pr[N(\lambda) \ge |k| + 1].$$

For F to be stochastic, we set every other entry $f^t(i,j)$ to:

$$f^t(i,j) = (1 - f^t(i,i)) \times \frac{c^t(i,j)}{\sum_j c^t(i,j)}.$$

The matrix F^t built in this manner satisfies all our assumptions.

Figure 1 shows an example of varying estimated probabilities of successful pickups in different zones at various times of the day derived from the NYC data using the methods above. As expected,

[4]Although we assume the independence of the passenger and driver arrival processes, we can also accommodate correlated processes with slight modification.

we see that the probability of a successful pickup is higher outside Manhattan in the morning, and this trend reverses in the evening.

Forming time-evolving matrices T and R: We obtain information regarding travel times and rewards using the `estimates/price` endpoint of the Uber API. The API takes longitude and latitude of pick-up and drop-off locations and returns price estimates for all types of Uber products – UberX, UberXL and UberBlack – together with the active surge multiplier rate at the pick-up location at the time of query. We only focus on UberX, the most popular Uber product. We also use the `/products` API endpoint to get information on the base fare, minimum fare, cost per minute and cost per unit distance for UberX. However, none of the Uber API endpoints provide information about the supply of drivers or demand of passengers; we impute this information from the NYC taxi rides dataset.

To create a representative sample of the data, we "recreated" NYC taxi rides virtually on the Uber platform. Using the Uber API, we were able to take a NYC taxi ride recorded in 2015, and capture the Uber attributes of that ride exactly one year later, collecting price estimates and other data above for that virtual ride. To respect the Uber rate limit of 1,000 API requests per hour per account, we sub-sampled one ride between each pair of zones in the city every 15 minutes. We implicitly assume that price estimates, travel times, and distance of preferred travel paths by drivers do not vary significantly in 15 minutes. Every 5 minutes, we also queried the surge multiplier active within each zone.[5] Using this approach, we collected data from the Uber API for a 6-month period (Oct. 2016–Mar 2017), recreating rides that originally occurred from Oct. 2015 to Mar 2016. Thus, we built realistic estimates for $r(i, j)$ and $\tau(i, j)$ for all pairs of zones[6]. Finally, we maintained same-day of week estimates, so that, for example, travel time estimates and rewards computed for Sunday, Oct 16, 2016, were paired with frequency estimates drawn from the NYC taxi rides dataset for Sunday, Oct. 18, 2015. In the remainder of this section, we provide results for driving during one representative week in October. Our results do not vary qualitatively across different weeks, with the exception of seasonal peak days, such as New Year's Eve.

6.2 Experimental results

For all our experiments we use a single process implementation of our algorithms on a 24-core 2.9GHz Intel Xeon E5 processor with 512GB memory. Running time for *naive* and *relocation* is less than a minute, and about 5 minutes for *flexible* and *flexible-relocation*. Uncertainty analysis (Section 6.4) with an off-the-shelf minimizer takes around 3 hours. Our code has been made publicly available in order to encourage reproducible research [5].

Comparison of strategies: First, we address the question: *what is the best driver strategy?* Intuitively, it is clear that *flexible-relocation* is the best strategy, as it takes advantage of spatial as well as temporal variations in the passenger demand across NYC. In order to verify this intuition, we compare driver earnings across different strategies. Drivers following the *naive* and the *relocation* strategies are assumed to drive from 9 AM to 5 PM, a standard 8 hour workday, while those following the *flexible* or the *flexible-relocation* strategies drive for a total of 8 hours each day with a flexible schedule.

In order to evaluate the performance of our strategies, we find the solution to MaxEarnings and simulate 100 drivers, each randomly assigned a home zone, operating on these strategies on the same day of the following week, for a total of 10 weeks. Figure 2 presents a box-plot of the resulting earnings.[7].

We observe that all "smart" strategies consistently outperform *naive*; as expected. On most days, *flexible-relocation* is the strategy with the highest earnings. The median earning of a driver following the *naive* strategy on a Sunday is \$104 while that of a driver following *flexible-relocation* is \$177, representing a 70% increase in median earnings. Averaged over all days of the week, this results in a 47% increase in median earnings per work day when following the *flexible-relocation* strategy. Thus, our strategies do exploit the spatial and the temporal variation in demand across NYC. The results also show that for a part-time Uber driver in NYC, it is more beneficial to drive midweek, from Wednesday to Friday, and Sunday than during Saturday and Monday.

Spatial dynamics of strategies: Next, we address the question - *what are the benefits of the Relocate action?* Figure 1 already shows the spatial variation in the demand across different NYC zones at different times of the day. Intuitively, this spatial variation can cause a disparity in the driver earnings based on the zone of the driver. For example, drivers based in Manhattan should be expected to earn more than those based in Brooklyn due to persistently higher demand in Manhattan. Similarly, Figure 2 shows temporal variation in earnings across days of the week. We observe that on the days of low-demand, not only are the median earnings for *relocation* consistently higher than those for *naive* but also the inter-quartile range (IQR) and the length of whiskers for *relocation* are narrower. On days with high but localized demand like Fridays, the *relocation* strategy performs on par with the *flexible-relocation* strategy and significantly outperforms *naive*.

These observations indicate that the location-based disparity in earnings for the *naive* strategy is much larger than the *relocation* strategy. Thus, we conclude that smart relocations throughout the day prevent a driver from becoming "trapped" in low-earning neighborhoods, translating into significant increases in the earnings. This may be counterintuitive to some drivers, as a *Relocate* action (essentially an empty ride) incurs a cost to the driver. Yet, the results demonstrate that these actions, when timed appropriately, lead to earnings far higher than the costs they incur.

Temporal dynamics of strategies: Intuitively, due to the periodicity of demand, we expect driver earnings to strongly depend on the time of the day they are driving. Thus, we address the question: *what is the best time of the day to drive in order to maximize earnings?* To answer this, we simulate 1000 drivers, each randomly assigned a home zone, for each of the *flexible* and *flexible-relocation* strategies. We solve the MaxEarnings problem for both strategies and create a recommended plan of action for the simulated drivers. Then, at every step of the simulation, a driver undertakes the personalized action recommended by the strategy, corresponding to their location, the time of day and their budget remaining.

[5] Chen *et al.* [6] have observed that 90% of the surges on Uber platform have durations lasting multiples of 5 minutes.

[6] We take into account the Uber fee structure in NYC as reported by the Uber API, as well as the overall *cost per mile* estimates provided by the American Automobile Association (AAA) in order to build realistic estimates for $r(i, j)$.

[7] The lower and upper edges of the boxes in Figure 2 indicate quartiles Q1 and Q3 respectively, and length of whisker is 1.5 times IQR.

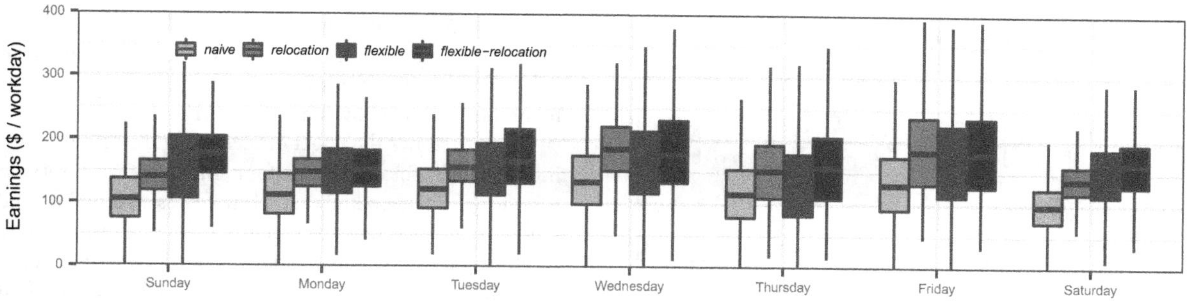

Figure 2: Daily driver earnings for different strategies averaged over different home zones on a representative day.

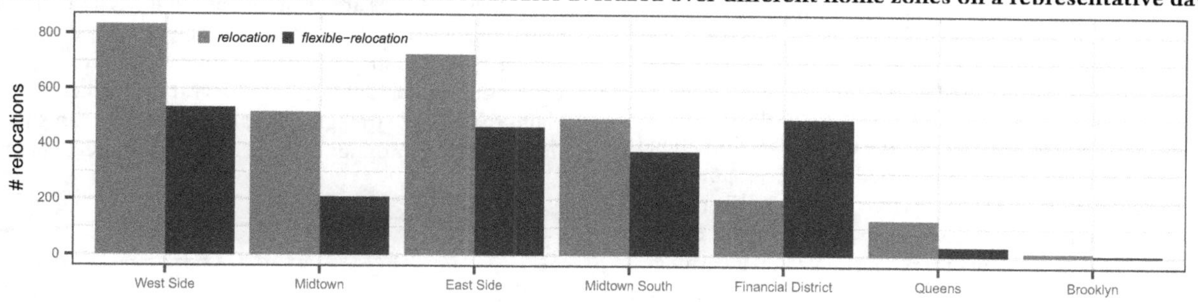

Figure 3: Contrast between preferred relocation destinations for drivers with *relocation* and *flexible-relocation* strategies on a representative day.

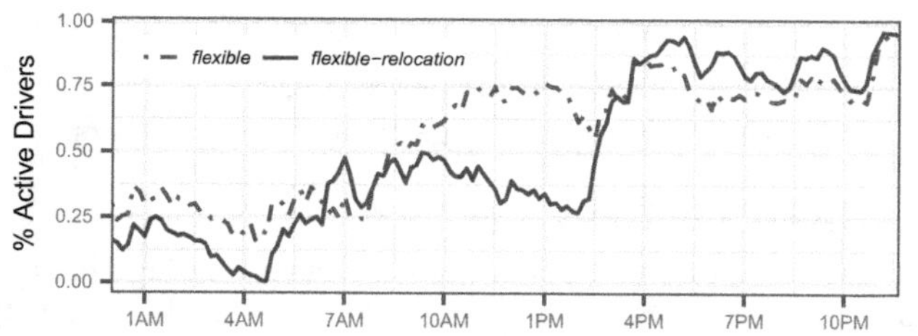

Figure 4: Active drivers with *flexible* and *flexible-relocation* strategies at different times of a representative day.

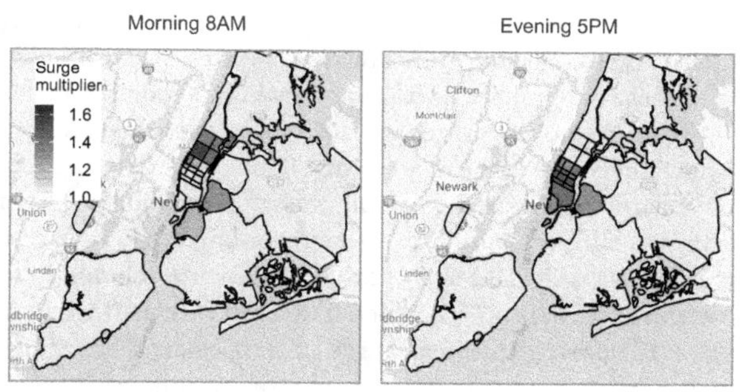

Figure 5: Active surge multiplier across NYC zones at different times of a representative day.

In Figure 4, we plot the percentage of simulated drivers driving in the city at different times of the day. We observe a noticeable difference between the "preferred" driving schedules output by *flexible* and *flexible-relocation*. In particular, a high percentage of *flexible* schedule drivers are active during the standard working hours of the day from 9AM to 6PM. This also supports our choice to evaluate fixed schedule strategies in the interval 9AM to 5PM. In contrast, the number of active drivers that follow *flexible-relocation* exhibits two distinct peaks, corresponding to the morning and the evening rush hours. Furthermore, over 50% of *flexible-relocation* drivers use their driving budget in the latter half of the day starting approximately at 3PM, continuing through until midnight. Since *flexible* and *flexible-relocation* only differ in the *Relocate* action, all observed differences are due to this action. Hence, we can conclude that the *Relocate* action is most effective in the evening hours, thereby prompting higher active percentages of *flexible-relocation* drivers at that time.

Preferred relocation zones: By simulating drivers, we can also compare the *Relocate* actions between drivers following the *relocation* strategy and those following the *flexible-relocation* strategy. The contrast between popular destinations of *Relocate* actions for drivers following the two strategies can be seen in Figure 3. Drivers following the *relocation* strategy predominantly relocate themselves to the center of Manhattan. In contrast, the drivers following the *flexible-relocation* strategy do not exhibit a clear most-preferred relocation destination. Furthermore, the *number* of relocations performed by the *relocation* strategy drivers, is, surprisingly, significantly higher than those performed by the *flexible-relocation* strategy drivers. This is due to the flexible work schedule of the latter, which allows them to drive continuously during the hours of highest demand, reducing the frequency of *Relocate* actions they take.

6.3 Surge chasing

We now turn our attention to surge pricing. Surge pricing is a feature of the Uber platform aimed at matching supply with passenger demand by increasing prices at times of high demand.According to Uber, it incentivizes drivers to start driving during the peak hours in order to efficiently meet demand with supply, albeit at a higher cost

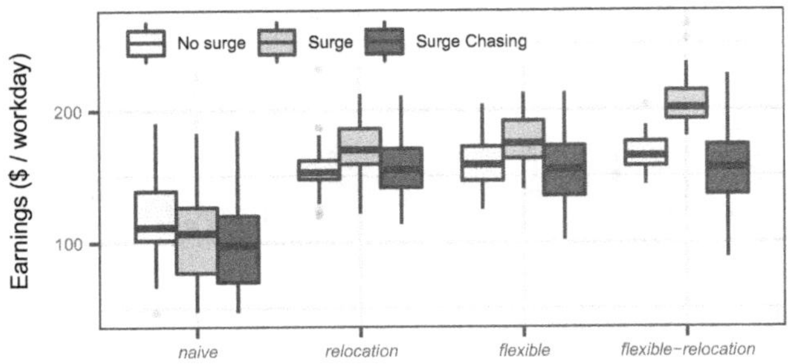

Figure 6: Exploring surge: Simulated earnings for drivers across different strategies on a representative day.

to passengers. It also decreases demand, since more price-sensitive customers drop out, as surge prices rise.

Figure 5 shows the active surge multiplier across different neighborhoods of NYC at different times of the day. This information is readily available to the drivers; however, due to uncertainty in the duration of surges as well as the proprietary nature of Uber's surge pricing algorithm, it is unclear whether drivers should relocate themselves to surging areas in order to maximize their earnings.

Next, we address the question– *Should drivers engage in surge chasing?* In order to do so, we evaluate earnings of simulated drivers in three scenarios viz., "no surge" - where we disable the surge multiplier to compute earnings; "surge" - where the multiplier is used while calculating earnings; and "surge chasing" - wherein a driver located in a non-surging zone always relocates to the zone with highest surge multiplier within a 10-minute drive radius. Simulated driver earnings in these three scenarios for each of the strategies are shown in Figure 6. We observe that blind "surge chasing" leads to lower earnings irrespective of the strategy being followed. Figure 6 reinforces our previous observation regarding the high variance of the *naive* strategy. At times, drivers following the *naive* strategy with surge multiplier enabled may earn less than when it is disabled. For other strategies, "surge chasing" consistently fails to provide any tangible benefits as compared to following the predetermined strategy. We conclude that actively and blindly chasing the surge is an ill-advised strategy and may lead to losses. Furthermore, surges last for short durations, and an unsuccessful surge chase may land a driver in a sub-optimal location with respect to longer term earnings. Note that although the NYC taxi demand data strongly correlates with active surge multipliers, we do currently model the impact of surge multiplier on consumer demand. This should be considered a limitation of our study.

6.4 Effect of uncertainty

Our experiments indicate that our strategies always outperform a *naive* strategy that is likely prevalent among Uber drivers. However, all our strategies use historical data. Consequently, our results can potentially be sensitive to perturbations of the empirically-observed transition matrices. Thus, we can only conclude that our results are robust if the drivers following one of the *relocation*, *flexible* and *flexible-relocation* strategies have higher earnings than those following *naive*, even when the input data is perturbed.

Hence, the question we have to address is the following: *Are the conclusions we drew above robust to perturbations of the empirical transition matrices?* We do so using the framework we developed in Section 5: we solve the RobustEarnings problem for each of the four strategies for increasing levels of uncertainty (α) using the Sequential Least Squares Programming (SLSQP) minimizer implementation provided by Jones *et al.* [11].

Figure 7 shows the effect of increasing uncertainty on the earnings of drivers for each of the four strategies. We observe two main takeaways. First, we find that all strategies suffer a loss under small amounts of uncertainty, even at levels of α in the range of 0.02, so all strategies are tuned closely to the empirical data. However, all strategies then remain resilient to a wide range of additional uncertainty, and we find that the *relocation*, *flexible* and *flexible-relocation* strategies are most tolerant to uncertainty in the input transition matrices. Interestingly, even with 99% uncertainty, the *flexible-relocation* strategy significantly outperforms the *naive* strategy with no uncertainty. This observation further supports our claim that being strategic using historical data can significantly improve driver earnings in on-demand ride-hailing platforms.

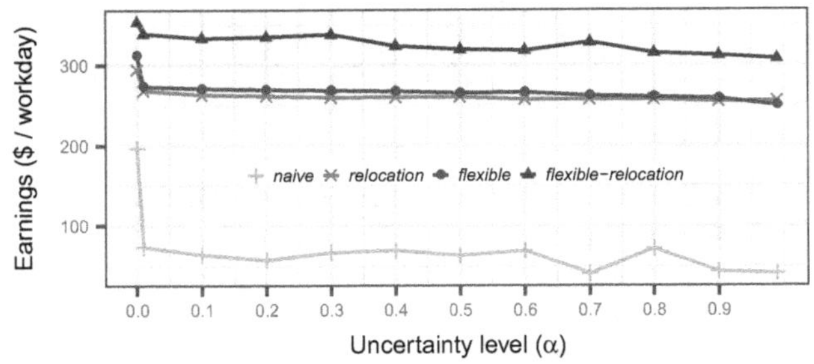

Figure 7: Sensitivity to uncertainty in parameters.

7 CONCLUSIONS

In this paper, we focused on the problem of maximizing a driver's individual earnings on ride-hailing platforms like Uber or Lyft. Our work confirms the power of strategic driving behavior using data-driven projections of ridership in the NYC area. Our first key takeaway is that a naive driver, armed with no data, and driving a 9-5 random walk schedule, is leaving roughly a 50% pay raise on the table by not driving more strategically. In contrast, a data-savvy driver armed with good historical data can build a forecast and optimal contingency driving plans with relatively little computational overhead using our dynamic programming algorithms, that have provable resilience to input uncertainty. Our experimental results yield insights into the structure of highly-optimized schedules, including relatively frequent relocation, working at specific peak periods, and taking advantage of surges when the time is ripe.

An obvious limitation of our work is that it is tailored to the setting when the methods are employed by self-interested individuals. If a significant percentage of the labor supply employs sophisticated optimization methods for driving, one would need to consider different strategies that achieve equilibria or other global objectives. Indeed, in the long run, as drivers for ride-hailing platforms like Uber and Lyft are put out of work by fleets of autonomous vehicles, the formulation and solution of new sets of optimization problems along those lines are likely to become relevant as well.

Acknowledgments: This work was supported by NSF awards: CAREER 1253393 and III 1421759. The authors also thank the anonymous reviewers for their helpful comments.

REFERENCES

[1] William A. Bailey Jr. and Thomas D. Clark Jr. 1987. A simulation analysis of demand and fleet size effects on taxicab service rates. In *Proceedings of the 19th Conference on Winter Simulation*. ACM, 838–844.

[2] Siddhartha Banerjee, Ramesh Johari, and Carlos Riquelme. 2015. Pricing in Ride-Sharing Platforms: A Queueing-Theoretic Approach. https://dl.acm.org/citation.cfm?id=2764527. Abstract appeared in ACM EC-2015.

[3] Colin Camerer, Linda Babcock, George Loewenstein, and Richard Thaler. 1997. Labor Supply of New York City Cabdrivers: One day at a Time. *The Quarterly Journal of Economics* 112, 2 (1997), 407–441.

[4] Juan Camilo Castillo, Dan Knoepfle, and Glen Weyl. 2017. Surge pricing solves the wild goose chase. In *Proceedings of the 2017 ACM Conference on Economics and Computation*. ACM, 241–242.

[5] Harshal A. Chaudhari, John W. Byers, and Evimaria Terzi. 2017. Project Webpage: Putting Data in the Driver's Seat. https://www.bu.edu/cs/groups/dblab/ride-hailing. (2017).

[6] Le Chen, Alan Mislove, and Christo Wilson. 2015. Peeking beneath the hood of Uber. In *Proceedings of the 2015 ACM Internet Measurement Conference*. ACM, 495–508.

[7] M Keith Chen and Michael Sheldon. 2016. Dynamic Pricing in a Labor Market: Surge Pricing and Flexible Work on the Uber Platform. http://www.anderson.ucla.edu/faculty_pages/keith.chen/papers/SurgeAndFlexibleWork_WorkingPaper.pdf. Working paper. Abstract appeared in ACM EC-2016.

[8] The Rideshare Guy. 2016. Advice For New Uber Drivers-Don't Chase The Surge! http://maximumridesharingprofits.com/advice-new-uber-drivers-dont-chase-surge/. (2016).

[9] Jonathan V. Hall and Alan B. Krueger. 2016. *An Analysis of the Labor Market for Uber's Driver-Partners in the United States.* Technical Report No. w22843. National Bureau of Economic Research.

[10] Waster Hudson. 2016. Chasing the Surge: 3 Tips for Maximizing Uber Earnings. https://pjmedia.com/lifestyle/2016/07/19/chasing-the-surge-3-tips-for-maximizing-uber-earnings/1/. (2016).

[11] Eric Jones, Travis Oliphant, Pearu Peterson, and others. 2001–2017. SciPy: Open source scientific tools for Python. (2001–2017). http://www.scipy.org/

[12] Jaeyoung Jung, R. Jayakrishnan, and Ji Young Park. 2013. Design and Modeling of Real-time Shared-taxi Dispatch Algorithms. In *Proc. Transportation Research Board 92nd Annual Meeting*.

[13] S. Kullback, M. Kupperman, and H. H. Ku. 1962. Tests for Contingency Tables and Markov Chains. *Technometrics* 4, 4 (1962), 573–608.

[14] Michal Maciejewski and Kai Nagel. 2013. Simulation and dynamic optimization of taxi services in MATSim. *VSP Working Paper 13-0. TU Berlin, Transport Systems Planning and Transport Telematics, 2013* (2013).

[15] Arnab Nilim and Laurent El Ghaoui. 2004. Robustness in Markov decision problems with uncertain transition matrices. In *Advances in Neural Information Processing Systems*. 839–846.

[16] Jorge Nunes, Luís Matos, and António Trigo. 2011. Taxi Pick-Ups Route Optimization Using Genetic Algorithms. *Adaptive and Natural Computing Algorithms* (2011), 410–419.

[17] Erhun Ozkan and Amy R. Ward. 2016. Dynamic Matching for Real-time Ridesharing. https://papers.ssrn.com/sol3/papers.cfm?abstract_id=2844451, (2016). Working paper.

[18] Ying Shi and Zhaotong Lian. 2016. Optimization and strategic behavior in a passenger–taxi service system. *European Journal of Operational Research* 249, 3 (2016), 1024–1032.

[19] The New York Times. 2015. An App That Helps Drivers Earn the Most From Their Trips. https://www.nytimes.com/2015/05/10/technology/a-dashboard-management-consultant.html. (2015).

[20] The New York Times. 2017. How Uber Uses Psychological Tricks to Push Its Drivers' Buttons. https://www.nytimes.com/interactive/2017/04/02/technology/uber-drivers-psychological-tricks.html. (2017).

[21] Wikipedia. 2017. Skellam distribution — Wikipedia, The Free Encyclopedia. https://en.wikipedia.org/w/index.php?title=Skellam_distribution. (2017).

[22] Hai Yang, Sze Chun Wong, and Ki Wong. 2002. Demand–supply equilibrium of taxi services in a network under competition and regulation. *Transportation Research Part B: Methodological* 36, 9 (2002), 799–819.

Improving Negative Sampling for Word Representation using Self-embedded Features

Long Chen
University of Glagow
Glasgow, UK
long.chen@glasgow.ac.uk

Fajie Yuan*
University of Glagow
Glasgow, UK
f.yuan.1@research.gla.ac.uk

Joemon M Jose
University of Glagow
Glasgow, UK
joemon.jose@glasgow.ac.uk

Weinan Zhang
Shanghai Jiao Tong University
Shang Hai, China
wnzhang@sjtu.edu.cn

ABSTRACT

Although the word-popularity based negative sampler has shown superb performance in the skip-gram model, the theoretical motivation behind oversampling popular (non-observed) words as negative samples is still not well understood. In this paper, we start from an investigation of the gradient vanishing issue in the skip-gram model without a proper negative sampler. By performing an insightful analysis from the stochastic gradient descent (SGD) learning perspective, we demonstrate that, both theoretically and intuitively, negative samples with larger inner product scores are more informative than those with lower scores for the SGD learner in terms of both convergence rate and accuracy. Understanding this, we propose an alternative sampling algorithm that dynamically selects informative negative samples during each SGD update. More importantly, the proposed sampler accounts for multi-dimensional self-embedded features during the sampling process, which essentially makes it more effective than the original popularity-based (one-dimensional) sampler. Empirical experiments further verify our observations, and show that our fine-grained samplers gain significant improvement over the existing ones without increasing computational complexity.

ACM Reference Format:

Long Chen, Fajie Yuan, Joemon M Jose, and Weinan Zhang. 2018. Improving Negative Sampling for Word Representation using Self-embedded Features. In *WSDM 2018: The Eleventh ACM International Conference on Web Search and Data Mining, February 5–9, 2018, Marina Del Rey, CA, USA.* ACM, New York, NY, USA, 9 pages. https://doi.org/10.1145/3159652.3159695

1 INTRODUCTION

In recent years, there has been a surge of work proposed to represent words as dense vectors, using various training methods inspired from neural-network language modeling [3, 5, 40]. These representations, referred to as "neural embedding" or "word embedding", have been shown to perform well in a variety of natural language processing (NLP) tasks, such as named entity recognition [15, 31], sentiment analysis [28, 37] and question answering [48].

One of the most popular word embedding techniques is the skip-gram model. Given a corpus of target words and their context, it aims to predict the probability of observing a context word conditioned on a target word by sliding a symmetric window over a subsampled training corpus. One of the major difficulties of these language models is that one needs to compute activation functions by summing over an entire vocabulary, which is often millions of words in scale. To reduce the computational cost, researchers often use two lines of methods, one is hierarchical softmax [27], another is noise contrastive estimation (or alternatively, negative sampling) [11]. While useful in general, the effectiveness of such methods largely depends on the assumption that oversampling frequent words would lead to better performance since they are more informative than less frequent ones [11]. However, in fact, infrequent words may also carry important information. In addition, a simple global and static sampling method such as popularity-based sampling strategy cannot effectively handle the cases where words are represented by a large number of embedded features.

To tackle the aforementioned problems, we first show that a not well-designed (e.g. random) sampler would easily result in the gradient vanishing problem during the parameter learning process, especially when the corpus size is very large and the words are long tail distributed. Hence, most SGD updates have no effect, which leads to slow convergence for the learning algorithm. Both theoretical and experimental analysis reveals that popularity-based negative sampling is able to alleviate the vanishing gradient issue. However, our analysis also shows that popularity-based negative sampling can only achieve suboptimal performance for two reasons: (1) non-observed context words with high popularity (frequency) are often irrelevant to the target word; (2) popular words are sampled without considering the dynamic change of parameters in the training process. Hence, in this paper we propose a non-popularity sampling strategy, termed as *Adaptive Sampler*, which makes useful of multi-dimensional semantic and syntactic information, and samples top ranked context words by considering both embedding variables and the current state of SGD learner. On two real-world corpora, the proposed algorithm can significantly outperform the

*The first two authors contributed equally to this paper and share the first authorship.

WSDM 2018, February 5–9, 2018, Marina Del Rey, CA, USA

ACM ISBN 978-1-4503-5581-0/18/02...$15.00
https://doi.org/10.1145/3159652.3159695

original word2vec baseline. Furthermore, our method has an amortized constant runtime without increasing time complexity of the original word2vec [23].

The rest of this paper is organized as follows. We firstly introduce the related work in Section 2. Section 3 formally defines the problem of word embedding with adaptive sampling. Section 4 systematically presents the proposed word-embedding sampler. The experimental results and analysis are reported in Section 5. Finally, we present our conclusion and future work in Section 6.

2 RELATED WORK

Neural network language models [22, 24, 43] have attracted a lot of attention recently given their dense and learnable representation form and generalization property, as a contrast to the traditional bag-of-words representations. Word2vec skip-gram [23] (cf. Section 3) is arguably the most widely used word embedding models today. However, the computation of output vector (softmax layer) represents the probability of the context word and is the size of the entire vocabulary [6], which is computationally prohibitive (even with the recent advance of GPU-accelerated computing). This has been a thorny problem ever since Bengio's seminal work of neural network language model [3].

There are several ways to tackle this challenge. A common way is hierarchical softmax, which was first proposed by Mnih and Hinton [25], where a hierarchical tree is constructed to index all the words in a corpus as leaves for the prediction of the normalized probability of the target class [27]. Peng recently proposed an incremental training method which is able to learn the softmax tree faster than global training [30] while the performance of this model is still comparable to the original version.

Another popular way to reduce the computational cost is simply selecting only a small fraction of the output's dimensions, which are either randomly or heuristically chosen. The reconstruction sampling of Dauphin et al. [8], the efficient use of biased importance sampling in [20], the adoption of noise contrastive estimation [11] in Mnih and Kavukcuoglu [26] all belong to this category. The most famous one in this line of work is arguable negative sampling (cf. Section 3), which is the simple version of noise contrastive estimation (NCE) that randomly samples the words not in the context to distinguish the observed data from the artificially generated noise. Empirically, negative sampling generally outperforms hierarchical softmax, especially for frequent words [23]. The reason is that hierarchical softmax builds a tree over the whole vocabulary, and the leaf nodes representing rare words will inevitably inherit their parent vector representations in the tree, as a result, they are affected by other frequent words in the corpus. Thus, we choose negative sampling as baseline in this work due to its superior performance.

Recently, the use of approximate maximum-inner-product Function has become popular [8, 41] to select a good candidate subset, which is somewhat similar to our idea. But our approach upgraded the inner product function into a rank-invariant function, and thus is computationally more efficient than these alternatives. In addition, they use the function for the task of image recognition [44] and recommender systems [33, 46, 47], while the feasibility and effectiveness of this approach for the task of word embeddings is still largely unknown.

More generally speaking, matrix factorization (MF) model is also employed to reduce the dimension of a co-occurrence matrix. Context-distribution smoothing MF [19] and global MF [31] (also known as GloVe) all belong to this category. While generally effective, MF models actually employ negative sampling implicitly [18], and thus these two techniques tend to perform quite similarly for most downstream NLP tasks [2]. To the best of our knowledge, this paper is the first attempt to investigate SGD update at a finer-grained level with embedding features, and propose to use an adaptive sampler. Furthermore, the proposed samplers can be easily adopted to other more complex factorization models, such as tensor factorization [39], even though we only implement them on word2vec in this paper.

3 PRELIMINARY

First we formally introduce several concepts and notations. Then we shortly recapitulate the skip-gram[1] model with negative sampling (SGNS). The novel contribution of this section is to show the theoretical motivation behind oversampling popular (non-observed) words as negative samples.

3.1 Continuous Skip-gram Model

In [23], words are trained with an unlabelled corpus of words $w_1, w_2, ..., w_n$ (usually n is about millions) and the context for word w_i are words surrounding it in a T-sized window $w_{i-T}, ..., w_{i-1}, w_{i+1}, ..., w_{i+T}$. The corpus of observed word and context pairs is denoted as D. We use $\#(w, c)$ to denote the frequency of pair (w, c) appears in D.

Each target word w corresponds to a vector $\vec{w} \in \mathbb{R}^d$ and similarly each context word c is represented as a vector $\vec{c} \in \mathbb{R}^d$, where d is the embedding dimension. The values in the embedding vector referred to as latent variables are the parameters to be learned. The vector $\vec{w}$ is the row in a $|V| \times d$ matrix W, and vectors $\vec{c}$ is a row in a $|V| \times d$ matrix C, where $|V|$ is the vocabulary size and is derived from the corpus D. In such cases, W_i and C_i represent vector representations of the i-th target word and context word in the vocabulary respectively.

Our starting point is the skip-gram embedding model trained with the negative sampling. Consider a word-context pair (w, c). Let $p(D = 1|w, c)$ be the probability that (w, c) is observed in D, and $p(D = 0|w, c) = 1 - p(D = 1|w, c)$ the probability that (w, c) is non-observed. The distributions can then be expressed as:

$$p(D = 1|w, c) = \sigma(\vec{w} \cdot \vec{c}) = \frac{1}{1 + e^{-\vec{w} \cdot \vec{c}}} \quad (1)$$

where $\vec{w}$ and $\vec{c}$ are d dimensional vectors, and will be learned by the model.

The word embedding learning algorithm aims to maximize $p(D = 1|w, c)$ for observed pair (w, c), meanwhile, minimize $p(D = 0|w, c)$ for randomly sampled non-observed pairs, under the intuition that randomly sampled non-observed word-context pairs are more likely to be negative pairs. For each observed (w, c) pair and a set of k negative examples $V_{w_k}^-$ that are sampled from the whole negative example set V_w^-, the SGNS objective function is defined as [23]:

[1] We merely elaborate our idea by using the skip-gram model, while it simply applies to the continuous bag-of-words (CBOW) model.

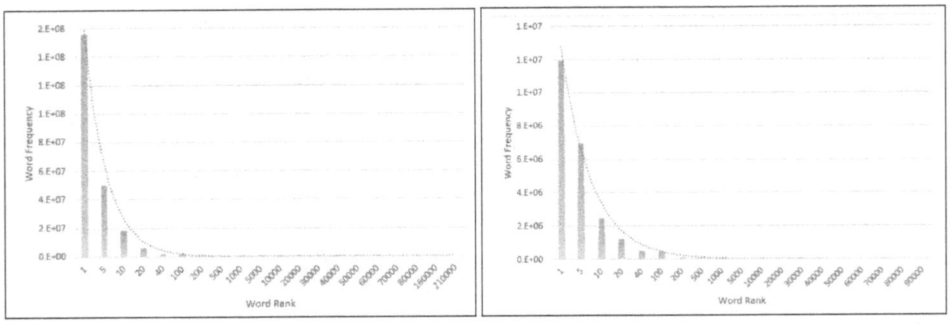

Figure 1: (a) and (b) show the word popularity distribution of Wiki2017 and NewsIR datasets respectively. Popularity in both datasets is tailed.

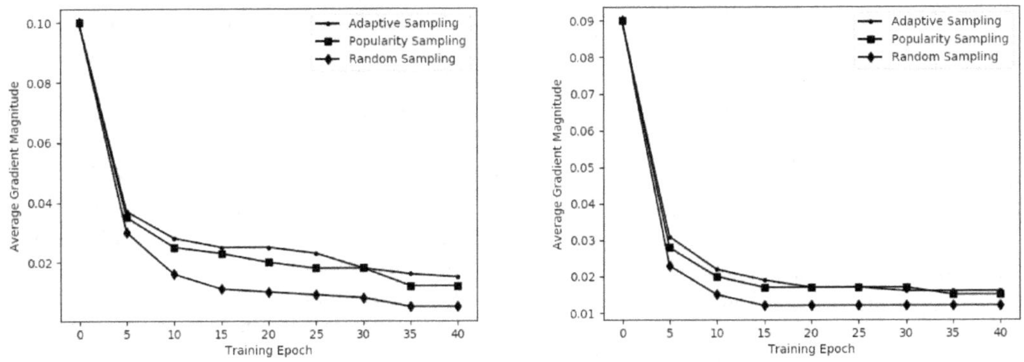

(a)

(b)

Figure 2: (a) and (b) show the probability of gradient magnitude of varying samplers with skip-gram model on Wiki2017 and NewsIR datasets respectively.

$$E = -\log\sigma(\vec{w}\cdot\vec{c}_P) - \sum_{c_N\in V^-_{w_k}} \log\sigma(-\vec{w}\cdot\vec{c}_N) \tag{2}$$

where c_P is the positive (observed) context word and c_N is the negative (non-observed) context word for w, which is selected by oversampling popular words.

$$p_D(c_N) = \frac{\#(c_N)^\alpha}{|D|} \tag{3}$$

where $\#(c_N)$ is the frequency of word c_N in the corpus D, and $|D|$ represents the number of available words. The exponent α controls the weight distribution of sampled negative words, which is experimentally shown that when $\alpha = 0.75$, the algorithm performs the best [23]. Note that the random sampling distribution is a special case by setting $\alpha = 0$.

Minimizing this objective function makes observed pair (w, c) have similar embedding representation while scattering the non-observed ones. This is intuitively correct as words appear in similar context should bear a close resemblance. Mathematically, SGNS tries to maximize the inner-product of similar words and minimize the dot-product of dissimilar ones.

3.2 Gradient Issues in Tailed Word Distribution

Even though the word-popularity based negative sampler (i.e. Eq. 3) has been successfully applied in various word embedding models, the theoretical motivation behind oversampling popular negative words is yet known. In the following, we seek to show, both theoretically and intuitively, drawing negative words with high popularity frequency is a reasonable yet suboptimal sampling method.

To begin with, we follow Mikolov et al. [23] by using stochastic gradient descent (SGD) to optimize Eq. 2. The gradient for model parameter θ is then given as:

$$\frac{\partial E}{\partial\theta} = (\sigma(\vec{w}\cdot\vec{c}_P) - 1)\frac{\partial\vec{w}\cdot\vec{c}_P}{\partial\theta} + \sum_{c_N\in V^-_{w_k}} \sigma(\vec{w}\cdot\vec{c}_N)\frac{\partial\vec{w}\cdot c_N}{\partial\theta} \tag{4}$$

Let $\theta = c_P$ or $\theta = c_N$, then we can update $\vec{c}_P$ and $\vec{c}_N$ with Eq. 4 as follows:

$$\vec{c}_P^{\,new} \leftarrow \vec{c}_P^{\,old} - \eta\underbrace{(\sigma(\vec{w}\cdot\vec{c}_P) - 1)\,\vec{w}}_{\triangle_{w,c_P}} \tag{5}$$

$$\vec{c}_N^{\,new} \leftarrow \vec{c}_N^{\,old} - \eta\underbrace{\sigma(\vec{w}\cdot\vec{c}_N)\,\vec{w}}_{\triangle_{w,c_N}} \tag{6}$$

where $\triangle_{w,c_P}$ and $\triangle_{w,c_N}$ are known as gradient magnitude. Note that since the number of observed words (i.e. c_P) is very small compared with non-observed words (i.e. c_N), it does not require to design a special sampling method. Hence, in this paper we focus only on the learning process of Eq. 6.

To provide the insight and motivation of popularity based negative sampling, we analyze the gradient update process of Eq. 6 by employing a simple random sampler (i.e. $\alpha = 0$ in Eq. 3). First, we observe that the value of the updated gradient in Eq. 6 is largely dependent on the the score function (i.e. $\vec{w} \cdot \vec{c}_N$)). The quantity of $\triangle_{w,c_N}$ is obviously a probability and is close to 0 if c_N is correctly predicted as a true negative word, because in this case $\vec{w} \cdot \vec{c}_N$ is supposed to be small. In fact, the gradient magnitude $\triangle_{w,c_N}$ can be understood as how much influence the (w, c_N) pair has for improving Θ. If it is close to 0, nothing is learned from the pair (w, c_N) because its gradient vanishes, i.e. θ cannot be changed in the updating process. It is worth noting that $\triangle_{w,c_N}$ relies on parameters Θ and is constantly changed during learning. Hence, we proceed by analyzing how the vanishing gradient occurs without a proper negative sampler and why oversampling popular words is able to address the issue.

In word-embedding tasks, word popularity (i.e. occurrence frequency) is typically non-uniform distributed and some words are in general more popular than others. Figure 1 shows word frequency distributions for Wiki2017 and NewsIR datasets respectively. Both datasets shows that the vast majority of words are low popularity and thus by random sampling, most selected negative words are those tailed words. On the other side, $\triangle_{w,c_N}$ is supposed to be small in general if c_N has lower popularity (i.e. a lower rank position) in Figure 1. The reason is straightforward because an ideal learner is expected to assign a larger score for $\triangle_{w,c}$ if c is an observed positive context word and a lower score if c is a negative word. As we know, the lower popularity c has, the fewer times it acts as a positive context word, and thus the lower score $\triangle_{w,c}$ is assigned to. If $\triangle_{w,c}$ has a very small value, then $\sigma(\vec{w} \cdot \vec{c}_P)$ is close to 0, which means the gradient vanishes. Hence, the purpose of oversampling popular words is to select more informative negative examples to overcome gradient vanishing problem and speed up the training process. Figure 2 shows the gradient magnitude of varying sampling approaches. It can be seen that after a few training epochs, almost all the negative samples, selected by the random sampler, have very small gradient magnitudes ($\triangle_{w,c_N}$), which suggests most of them are useless in the SGD learning process. On the contrary, the popularity-based sampler and our proposed adaptive sampler (cf. Section 4) can significantly increase the gradient magnitude by a large factor, and thus can alleviate the gradient vanishing issue.

3.3 Learning Optimal Ranking for Embeddings

In this subsection, we provide an intuitive example to explain the merits of popularity oversampling from ranking perspective. The reason is that training word embedding can also be naturally viewed as a ranking task that ranks an observed context word c_P higher than any non-observed context word c_N [14]. To illustrate this, we give a schematic of a ranked list for a target word w as below, where +1 and -1 denote an observed and non-observed context word respectively. We use NDCG (Normalized Discount Cumulative Gain [21]) as the ranking metric for explanation, similar to other metrics, e.g. AP (Average Precision) [21].

$$\text{Rank Order}: \overbrace{-1,\ -1,\ +1,\ -1,\quad \underbrace{-1,\ -1,\ +1}_{\triangle NDCG(w)_{75}=0.033}}^{\triangle NDCG(w)_{71}=0.409}\ , -1, \ldots, -1$$

where $\triangle NDCG_{ij}$ denotes the size of NDCG change for word w when positive context word with the position i and negative context word with the position j get swapped. As can be seen, the value of $\triangle\ NDCG(w)_{71}$ is much larger than that of $\triangle NDCG(w)_{75}$. This implies that $\triangle\ NDCG(w)$ is likely to be larger if the non-observed word c_N has a smaller rank. Hence, the new NDCG value after swapping is also larger if $\triangle NDCG(w)$ is larger[2]. This is intuitively correct as the high ranked non-observed words hurt the ranking performance more than the low ranked ones. A higher NDCG value for the rank list of target word w corresponds with better accuracy in distinguishing observed and non-observed contexts. As discussed in Section 3.2, popular words are more likely to have larger scores (or smaller rank) than non-popular words. Our idea here is similar to that used in [46, 47] for a different problem.

In fact, both Section 3.2 and 3.3 show that larger score (smaller rank) negative context words are more informative for training the embedding models, and popular words are alternative instances for larger score negative words. Empirical results in word2vec[23] have already proven that approximate sampling based on word popularity distribution usually results in both promising accuracy and faster convergence.

3.4 Issues of Popularity Sampling

Both the theoretical and intuitive motivations regarding the negative sampler have been discussed: select for a target word w, and one (or several) negative context word c such that the pair (w, c) is informative at the current state of learning. However, the original popularity oversampling does not reflect this for two reasons: (1) It is static and thus the empirical popularity distribution does not change during the learning process. However, the estimated score $\hat{y}(c|w) = \vec{w} \cdot \vec{c}$ (or rank $\hat{r}(c|w)$) of a context word c changes during learning. E.g. c might have a larger score (with w) in the beginning but after several epochs of training it is ranked low. (2) The sampler is global and does not reflect the semantic and syntactic information regarding how informative a word is. For example, a popular word is more likely to act as a context word with a group of target words, but still can be irrelevant for another one. Meanwhile, learning with popularity-based sampler can slow down after the algorithm learns to (generally) rank positive context word above popular words, and thus can be inaccurate with ranking long tail but high scoring context words. Both points can also be observed in the gradient magnitude $\triangle_{w,c}$, which depends on the inner product of self-embedded features $\vec{w}$ and $\vec{c}_N$ and changes during learning. In the next section, we will present a new adaptive sampler that select informative negative words based on the embedded features in $\vec{w}$ and $\vec{c}$, which are known as the low-dimensional representation of semantic and syntactic information.

[2] $NDCG(w)_{\text{new}}=NDCG(w)_{\text{old}}+\triangle NDCG(w)$

4 IMPROVED NEGATIVE SAMPLING

In this section, a dynamic sampler that takes account of multi-dimensional self-embedded features is proposed to replace the original popularity-based sampler.

4.1 Basic adaptive Sampler

As has been discussed in Section 3.4, we are able to propose a straightforward adaptive sampler which defines the sampling distribution directly based on the scoring function $\hat{y}(c|w) = \vec{w} \cdot \vec{c}$ instead of the popularity word distribution. Intuitively, when a negative word c_N in a given word list is sampled, the closer c_N is ranked at the the top position by $\hat{y}(c_N|w)$, the more important c_N is. This has been understood from both the gradient magnitude $\triangle_{w,c_N}$ (Section 3.2) and ranking perspective (Section 3.3). For example, if (w, c_N) is given, we should choose c_N such that $\hat{y}(c_N|w)$ is large since it will largely increase both $\triangle_{w,c_N}$ and NDCG. In the following, instead of using the notion of a large score it is better to formalize a small predicted rank $\hat{r}(c_N|w)$, since largeness of scores is only a relative value to other words but ranks will be an absolute value. This allows us to formulate a basic dynamic sampling distribution that assigns higher sampling weight for small ranked context words.

$$p_D(c_N|w) \propto \exp(\frac{-\hat{r}(c_N|w)}{\lambda}), \lambda = |V| \cdot \rho, \rho \in (0, 1] \quad (7)$$

where ρ is the hyper-parameter that controls the shape of the exponential distribution and should be tuned according to the dataset.

Properties: The context word distribution (Eq. 7) depends on $\hat{r}(c_N|w)$, and has two important properties:

(1) Feature-dependent: Remind that $\hat{r}(c_N|w)$ is the rank of word c_N among all words in the vocabulary using the inner product of self-embedded features $\vec{w}$ and $\vec{c_N}$ for ordering words, and thus it is feature-dependent and inherently can represent the semantic and syntactic relations between w and c_N.

(2) Adaptive: The sampler changes while model parameters are learned because changes in parameters lead to consequently in changes in the scoring model $\hat{y}$, the ranking $\hat{r}(c_N|w)$, and hence, the sampler.

4.2 Efficient Sampling Algorithm

So far, we have designed a trivial adaptive & self-embedded feature based sampler. However, the additional computational cost of the proposed sampler is to score all non-observed context words of w in the whole word list to obtain the rank $\hat{r}(c_N|w)$, which means before each SGD update, the rough computational complexity of $O(d|V_w^-|)$ is required[3]. As the whole training process has always millions of SGD updates, it is generally infeasible in practice. In this section, we will show how approximative sampling from Eq. 7 can be implemented efficiently in amortized time for the word embedding task.

Let the scoring model $\hat{y}$ still be the inner product of a factorized matrix.

$$\hat{y}(c|w) = \vec{w} \cdot \vec{c} = \sum_{f=1}^{d} \vec{w}_f \vec{c}_f \quad (8)$$

[3] The size of non-observed context words $|V_w^-|$ is much larger than that of observed ones $|V_w^+|$, i.e. $|V_w^-| \approx |V|$, as $|V_w^+| + |V_w^-| = |V|$.

Algorithm 1: Skip-gram model with adaptive and feature-dependent oversampling of negative words.

```
1: Random initialize the parameters Θ
2: t ← 0;
while t < MaxIteration do
    if t % |V| log |V| = 0 then
        for f ∈ {1, ..., d} do
            compute r̂(.|f)
            compute σ_f and μ_f
        end
    end
    Draw (w, c) ∈ D uniformly
    Draw r from p(r) ∝ exp(−r/λ)
    Draw f from p(f|c) ∝ |w_f|σ_f
    if sgn(w_f) = 1 then
        c_N = r^{-1}(r|f)
    end
    else
        c_N = r^{-1}(|V| − f + 1)|f)
    end
    for θ ∈ Θ do
        Update θ with Eq. 6
    end
    t ← t + 1
end
```

Now, a fast adaptive and feature-dependent sampling algorithm is presented which approximates the sampler from Eq 7. The idea is to formalize Eq 7 as a mixture of ranking distributions over normalized factors. The mixture probability is calculated by a normalized version of the scoring function Eq. 8

Rank-Invariant Normalization: First, a transformation $\hat{y}^*$ of y is defined as

$$\hat{y}^*(c|w) = \sum_{f=1}^{d} p(f|w)\mathrm{sgn}(\vec{w}_f)\vec{c'}_f \quad (9)$$

where $p(f|w)$ is a probability function as follows

$$p(f|w) \propto |\vec{w}_f|\vec{\sigma}_f \quad (10)$$

where $\vec{c'}_f$ is a standardized word factor

$$\vec{c'}_f = \frac{\vec{c}_f - \vec{\mu}_f}{\vec{\sigma}_f} \quad (11)$$

where $\vec{\mu}_f$ is the mean and $\vec{\sigma}_f$ is the variance over the factor f.

$$\vec{\mu}_f = E(\vec{c}_f), \quad \vec{\sigma}_f^2 = Var(\vec{c}_f) \quad (12)$$

Lemma 4.1 (Rank Invariance). Ranking $\hat{r}^*$ generated from scoring function $\hat{y}^*$ shares the same ranking as $\hat{r}$ from $\hat{y}$.

PROOF. First, the scoring function can be rewritten as:

$$\hat{y}(c|w) = \sum_{f=1}^{d} \vec{w}_f \vec{c}_f = \sum_{f=1}^{d} |\vec{w}_f| \text{sgn}(\vec{w}_f)(\vec{c'}_f \vec{\sigma}_f + \vec{\mu}_f) \quad (13)$$

$$= \sum_{f=1}^{d} |\vec{w}_f| \text{sgn}(\vec{w}_f) \vec{c'}_f \vec{\sigma}_f + \sum_{f=1}^{d} |\vec{w}_f| \text{sgn}(\vec{w}_f) \vec{\mu}_f \quad (14)$$

$$= \hat{y}^*(c|w) + \underbrace{\sum_{f=1}^{d} |\vec{w}_f| \text{sgn}(\vec{w}_f) \vec{\mu}_f}_{b(w)} \quad (15)$$

where the additional term $b(w)$ is independent of the context word c. Thus $\hat{y}(c|w)$ is a linear transformation of $\hat{y}^*(c|w)$ and it is rank-invariant because

$$\hat{y}(c_1|w) \geq \hat{y}(c_2|w) \Leftrightarrow \hat{y}(c_1|w) + b(w) \geq \hat{y}(c_2|w) + b(w)$$
$$\Leftrightarrow \hat{y}^*(c_1|w) \geq \hat{y}^*(c_2|w) \quad (16)$$

which means if we want the ranks generated by $\hat{y}(c|w)$, we can also work with $\hat{y}^*(c|w)$. Even if $\hat{y}(c|w) \neq \hat{y}^*(c|w)$, the generated rankings are the same, $\hat{r} = \hat{r}^*$.

Rank Mixture: The representation $\hat{y}^*$ has the advantage that $p(f|w)$ can be deemed as a mixture probability over standardized word factors, which means the larger $p(f|w)$, the more important the dimension f for the specific target word w. The sampling distribution can now be given as the mixture:

$$p(c_N|w) = \sum_{f=1}^{d} p(f|w) p(c_N|w, f) \quad (17)$$

We define $p(c_N|w, f)$ analogously to Eq. 7 by replacing the ranking function $\hat{r}^*$.

$$p(c_N|w, f) \propto \exp\left(\frac{-\widehat{r^*}(c_N|w, f)}{\lambda}\right) \quad (18)$$

where $\widehat{r^*}(c_N|w, f)$ is generated from the self-embedded feature-dependent and factor-dependent scoring function $\hat{y}^*(c_N|w, f)$. Following Eq. 9, this scoring function is given as

$$\hat{y}^*(c_N|w, f) = \text{sgn}(\vec{w}_f) \vec{c'}_{Nf} \quad (19)$$

Considering that $\hat{y}(c_N|w, f)$ is the linear transformation of $\hat{y}^*(c_N|w, f)$, we can have a simpler function:

$$\hat{y}(c_N|w, f) = \text{sgn}(\vec{w}_f) \vec{c}_{Nf} \quad (20)$$

Note that $\hat{y}^*(c_N|w, f)$ depends on the original parameters V and not on their normalization. The scoring function $\hat{y}^*(c_N|w, f)$ has a very simple relation to its rank: the entity on rank r has the $r - th$ largest factor $c_{c_N, f}$, if $sgn(w_{c,f})$ is positive otherwise it is the entity ranked at $N - r$.

Sampling from Rank Mixture: The transformation of the sampling distribution as a mixture model (Eq 17), leads to a simple sampling algorithm for negative entities, which is detailed in Algorithm 1.

(1) Draw a rank r from a Geometric distribution.
(2) Draw a factor dimension f from $p(f|e)$ (Eq. 10).
(3) Sort entities in terms of $c_{\cdot}, f$ in a descending order
(4) Return the entity c_N on position r in the sorted list when $sgn(e_{c,f})$ is positive otherwise c_N is the entity ranked at $N - r$

Steps 1 and 4 can be performed in O(1), step 2 includes the computation of $p(f|c)$ is $O(V)$. The only computational intensive step is 3, where the factors are sorted in $O(|V| log |V|)$, but this only operates for $t\%|V| \log |V|$ times for the entire training process.

As there is one sample for each gradient step, the computational complexity of the original SGD algorithm does not increase. The sampling algorithm has an amortized runtime of $O(k)$ for selecting an entity which has the same cost for a single gradient step of a Matrix Factorization model. As there is one sample for each gradient step with no additional operation, the computational complexity of the original SGD algorithm does not compromise the efficiency of the original weight-based sampling.

5 EXPERIMENTS

5.1 Experimental Setup

We evaluate the performance of the proposed adaptive sampler by using two real-world corpora. The first one is NewsIR[4] that is a collection of news articles derived from major newswires, such as Reuters, in addition to local news sources and blogs. The second one is the full Wikipedia articles[5]. Notice that these two training datasets are of varying sizes. The NewsIR dataset contains 30 million words. The Wikipedia 2017 dataset is about 2.3 billion words.

Parameter Setting We tokenize and lowercase each corpus with the Weka tokenizer. Similar to [23], the down-sampled rate is set as $1e^{-3}$, and the learning rate is set with the starting value $\eta = 0.025$ and $\eta_t = \eta(1 - t/T)$ for all experiments, where T is the total number of training samples and t is the number of trained samples. On both datasets, we train the skip-gram models with different samplers until it is converged.

For popularity-based sampler, we find that $power = 0.75$ offers the best accuracy. For comparison purpose, we set *window size* = 8, *dimension* = 200 for all methods, which are the default setting recommended in [23].

5.2 Evaluation Method

To begin with, we conduct experiments on two common tasks namely, word analogy and word similarity. The word analogy task is comprised of questions such as, "a is to b as c is to _?" The testing set has 19,544 such questions which are fallen into a semantic category and a syntactic category. The semantic questions are usually analogies about people name or locations. For instance, "London is to UK as Paris to _?". The syntactic questions are generally about verb tense or forms of adjectives, for example "Swim is to swimming as run is to _?". To resolve the question, the model has to uniquely capture the missing token, which means there is only one exact match that is considered as ground truth.

As for word similarity task, we use a word similarity benchmarks [7] to evaluate the correctness of our adaptive sampler. Specifically, we use the datasets collected by Faruqui and Dyer which include 7 datasets namely, SIMLEX-999, RW, WS353, MURK,

[4] http://research.signalmedia.co/newsir16/signal-dataset.html
[5] https://dumps.wikimedia.org/enwiki/latest/enwiki-latest-pages-articles.xml.bz2

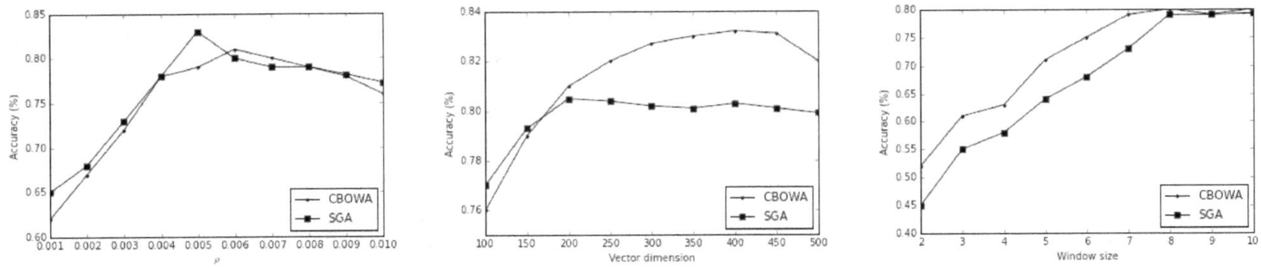

(a) (b) (c)

Figure 3: Parameters of CBOWA and SGA of varying parameter values trained on Wiki2017 dataset with adaptive samplers

WS353S, WS353R, RG65[6]. We calculate cosine value to compute the similarities between words, and then rank the similar words. The Spearman's rank correlation coefficient is adopted to measure the correlation of ranks between human annotation and computed similarities.

To demonstrate the effectiveness of our adaptive sampler, we compare it with the original popularity-based sampling method, i.e. $\rho = 0.75$. To show the effects of gradient vanishing issue, we also report results with a uniform sampler, i.e. $\rho = 0$.

- SG: The skip-gram model with the popularity-based sampler [23].
- SGU: The skip-gram model with the uniform sampler.
- SGA: The skip-gram model with the adaptive sampler described in Section 4.2.
- CBOW: Continuous bag-of-words model with the popularity-based sampler [23].
- CBOWU: Continuous bag-of-words model with the uniform sampler .
- CBOWA: Continuous bag-of-words model with the adaptive sampler.

5.3 Experimental Results

In order to make a fair comparison, the parameter ρ of SGA and CBOWA need to be properly tuned first. The performance of word embeddings were tuned on the training set (Wiki2017) and evaluated on the testing set. The results reported in Figure 3 are those on the testing set. Figure 3 (a), (b), (c) show how the performance of adaptive sampler varies given different parameter values. From Figure 3 (a), (b), one can observe that the models achieve a good result when window size is bigger than 7 and the vector dimension is larger than 200. As mentioned in Section 4.2, ρ controls the relative density of sampling distribution. From Figure 3 (c), one can see that the best performance is achieved when $\rho = 0.005$ and $\rho = 0.006$ for CBOWA and SGA, respectively.

Furthermore, [16] found that even using a small number of negative samples (e.g. $k = 5$) could achieve a respectable accuracy on large-scale datasets, although using a larger number of samples (e.g. $k = 15$) achieves considerably better performance. In Figure 5 we plot the results by increasing the number k on both datasets, which shows the similar trends with [16]. As can also be seen, the accuracy on (a) converged when k is larger than 15 for NewsIR dataset. One possible reason is that NewsIR dataset is noisier than Wiki2017 dataset, thereby as the number of negative pairs is increased beyond the minimum, overfitting tends to set in. We also observe that the SGA significantly outperforms SG irrespective of the number of negative pairs. Similarly, the CBOWA significantly outperforms CBOW (as shown in Fig 5) (c) and (d)), which indicates that our proposed sampling approach is more effective than the original word2vec [23].

Given the optimal parameter settings, the word analogies and word similarities tasks on the testing sets are reported in Table 1, 2 and Figure 4, respectively. First, it can be seen that our proposed adaptive sampler outperforms the classical popularity-based sampler for both the word analogies and word similarities tasks. Second, SGU has much worse prediction quality than SG and SGA. This further verifies the gradient vanishing issue in a uniform sampler as most SGD updates have no effect on parameter changing. It also confirms that adaptive oversampling and popularity-based sampling can effectively alleviate the vanishing gradient issue.

5.3.1 Document Classification. As a further demonstration of the utilities of our model, we experimented with document classification with a similar setup in [27]: we use 20 Newsgroups[7] as testing set, which is a collection of newsgroup documents, partitioned evenly across 20 different newsgroups. We use the full dataset with 20 categories, such as *atheism, computer graphics,* and *computer windows X.*

5.3.2 Runtime. Table 3 compares training time of different samplers. All experiments are conducted on a dual 3.5GHz Intel i5-4690 machine in a single thread. The training time depends on many factors, including embedding dimension, window size, vocabulary size, and corpus size. Due to limited space, we only report the execution time with varying embedding dimension by keeping other hyper-parameters fixed. As can be seen, our adaptive oversampling does not increases the training time much. This confirms our analysis in Section 4.2 that the sampling algorithm has an amortized runtime of $O(d)$, which is the same as the costs for a single gradient step of an inner product operation.

[6] http://www.wordvectors.org/

[7] https://qwone.com/ jason/20Newsgroups/

Table 1: The accuracy over different datasets, where $d = 200, win = 8$, and $threads = 20, neg = 5$ for both datasets (statistical significance using t-test: ** indicates p-value < 0.01 while * indicates p-value < 0.05).

Data	CBOW	CBOWU	CBOWA	SG	SGU	SGA
NewsIR (1B)	0.621	0.485	0.644	0.605	0.476	0.619
Wiki (2B)	0.760	0.592	0.788	0.782	0.648	0.793*
ALL (3B)	0.768	0.613	0.792	0.786	0.654	0.812**

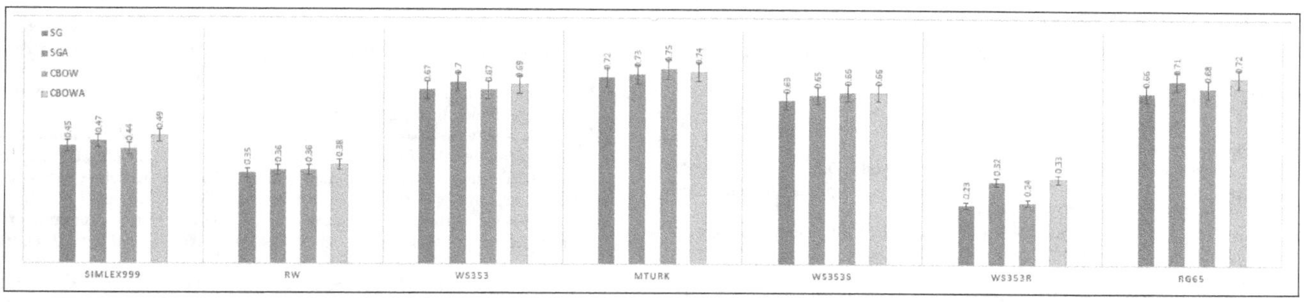

Figure 4: Comparison of word embeddings trained with Wiki2017 for word similarity tasks on benchmark datasets

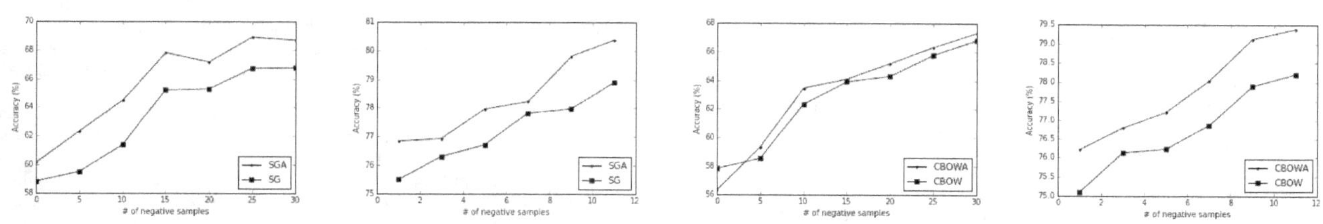

Figure 5: (a) and (b) show the accuracy of SG with varying number of negative samples on NEWSIR and WIKI2017 datasets, respectively for the word analogy task; (c) and (d) show the accuracy of CBOW with varying number of negative samples on NEWSIR and WIKI2017 datasets for the word analogy task.

Table 2: The experimental results (accuracy) trained with the whole training dataset (NEWSIR+WIKI2017), where $d = 200, win = 8$, and $threads = 20, neg = 2$.

Data	semantic	syntactic	total
CBOW	0.812	0.703	0.759
CBOWU	0.639	0.616	0.628
CBOWA	0.793	0.721	0.779*
SG	0.828	0.794	0.796
SGU	0.523	0.537	0.553
SGA	0.868	0.798	0.823*

6 CONCLUSION AND FUTURE WORK

In this paper, we first elaborated the motivation of the word popularity based oversampling in word2vec [23] from both gradient vanishing and ranking perspectives. After this, we proposed an improved negative sampler that could dynamically oversample high score negative words by leveraging embedding features. The proposed *Adaptive Sampler* superseded the existing one since the sampling process took account of multi-dimensional word information instead of only popularity. More importantly, the algorithm had an amortized constant runtime and the empirical overhead is only marginal. This makes our method highly attractive for practical use.

Table 4: The running time (minutes) of different sampling methods in the NewsIR dataset, where $win = 8$, and $threads = 20, neg = 25$.

dimension d	CBOW	CBOWA	SG	SGA
200	37.4	68.6	269.7	388.9
250	41.3	72.6	286.2	399.3
300	47.5	81.3	347.5	465.6

There are several interesting and promising directions in which this work could be extended. First, in this work we only focused on two types of applications, namely, word analogy and document classification, it will be interesting to study the performance of *Adaptive Sampler* with additional tasks, such as information retrieval and question answering. it would be also interesting to investigate the performance of our sampler by applying it to complex embedding models, such as tensor factorization [39]. Finally, most existing word embedding models rely on the negative sampling techniques with an SGD optimizer, we would like to investigate more advanced optimization techniques that could handle the entire negative samples for training embedding models, e.g. in [45].

7 ACKNOWLEDGEMENTS

We acknowledge support from the EPSRC funded project named **A Situation Aware Information Infrastructure Project** (EP/L026015). This work was also partly supported by NSF grant #61572223.

REFERENCES

[1] Eric Bailey and Shuchin Aeron. Word embeddings via tensor factorization. *arXiv preprint arXiv:1704.02686*, 2017.

[2] Marco Baroni, Georgiana Dinu, and Germán Kruszewski. Don't count, predict! a systematic comparison of context-counting vs. context-predicting semantic vectors. In *ACL (1)*, pages 238–247, 2014.

[3] Yoshua Bengio, Réjean Ducharme, Pascal Vincent, and Christian Jauvin. A neural probabilistic language model. *Journal of machine learning research*, 3(Feb):1137–1155, 2003.

[4] Long Chen, Dell Zhang, and Mark Levene. Question retrieval with user intent. In *Proceedings of the 36th international ACM SIGIR conference on Research and development in information retrieval*, pages 973–976. ACM, 2013.

[5] Ronan Collobert and Jason Weston. A unified architecture for natural language processing: Deep neural networks with multitask learning. In *Proceedings of the 25th international conference on Machine learning*, pages 160–167. ACM, 2008.

[6] Ronan Collobert, Jason Weston, Léon Bottou, Michael Karlen, Koray Kavukcuoglu, and Pavel Kuksa. Natural language processing (almost) from scratch. *Journal of Machine Learning Research*, 12(Aug):2493–2537, 2011.

[7] Manaal Faruqui and Chris Dyer. Community evaluation and exchange of word vectors at wordvectors.org. In *Proceedings of the 52nd Annual Meeting of the Association for Computational Linguistics: System Demonstrations*, Baltimore, USA, June 2014. Association for Computational Linguistics.

[8] Xavier Glorot, Yoshua Bengio, and Yann N Dauphin. Large-scale learning of embeddings with reconstruction sampling. In *Proceedings of the 28th International Conference on Machine Learning (ICML-11)*, pages 945–952, 2011.

[9] Yoav Goldberg and Omer Levy. word2vec explained: Deriving mikolov et al.'s negative-sampling word-embedding method. *arXiv preprint arXiv:1402.3722*, 2014.

[10] Michael Gutmann and Aapo Hyvärinen. Noise-contrastive estimation: A new estimation principle for unnormalized statistical models. In *AISTATS*, volume 1, page 6, 2010.

[11] Michael U Gutmann and Aapo Hyvärinen. Noise-contrastive estimation of unnormalized statistical models, with applications to natural image statistics. *Journal of Machine Learning Research*, 13(Feb):307–361, 2012.

[12] Xiangnan He, Hanwang Zhang, Min-Yen Kan, and Tat-Seng Chua. Fast matrix factorization for online recommendation with implicit feedback. In *Proceedings of the 39th International ACM SIGIR conference on Research and Development in Information Retrieval*, pages 549–558. ACM, 2016.

[13] Stanisław Jastrzebski, Damian Leśniak, and Wojciech Marian Czarnecki. How to evaluate word embeddings? on importance of data efficiency and simple supervised tasks. *arXiv preprint arXiv:1702.02170*, 2017.

[14] Shihao Ji, Hyokun Yun, Pinar Yanardag, Shin Matsushima, and SVN Vishwanathan. Wordrank: Learning word embeddings via robust ranking. *arXiv preprint arXiv:1506.02761*, 2015.

[15] Yoon Kim, Yacine Jernite, David Sontag, and Alexander M Rush. Character-aware neural language models. In *Thirtieth AAAI Conference on Artificial Intelligence*, 2016.

[16] Quoc Le and Tomas Mikolov. Distributed representations of sentences and documents. In *Proceedings of the 31st International Conference on Machine Learning (ICML-14)*, pages 1188–1196, 2014.

[17] Rémi Lebret and Ronan Collobert. Word emdeddings through hellinger pca. *arXiv preprint arXiv:1312.5542*, 2013.

[18] Omer Levy and Yoav Goldberg. Neural word embedding as implicit matrix factorization. In *Advances in neural information processing systems*, pages 2177–2185, 2014.

[19] Omer Levy, Yoav Goldberg, and Ido Dagan. Improving distributional similarity with lessons learned from word embeddings. *Transactions of the Association for Computational Linguistics*, 3:211–225, 2015.

[20] Minh-Thang Luong, Ilya Sutskever, Quoc V Le, Oriol Vinyals, and Wojciech Zaremba. Addressing the rare word problem in neural machine translation. *arXiv preprint arXiv:1410.8206*, 2014.

[21] Brian McFee and Gert R Lanckriet. Metric learning to rank. In *Proceedings of the 27th International Conference on Machine Learning (ICML-10)*, pages 775–782, 2010.

[22] Oren Melamud, Jacob Goldberger, and Ido Dagan. context2vec: Learning generic context embedding with bidirectional lstm. In *Proceedings of CONLL*, 2016.

[23] Tomas Mikolov, Ilya Sutskever, Kai Chen, Greg S Corrado, and Jeff Dean. Distributed representations of words and phrases and their compositionality. In *Advances in neural information processing systems*, pages 3111–3119, 2013.

[24] Piotr Mirowski and Andreas Vlachos. Dependency recurrent neural language models for sentence completion. *arXiv preprint arXiv:1507.01193*, 2015.

[25] Andriy Mnih and Geoffrey E Hinton. A scalable hierarchical distributed language model. In *Advances in neural information processing systems*, pages 1081–1088, 2009.

[26] Andriy Mnih and Koray Kavukcuoglu. Learning word embeddings efficiently with noise-contrastive estimation. In *Advances in neural information processing systems*, pages 2265–2273, 2013.

[27] Frederic Morin and Yoshua Bengio. Hierarchical probabilistic neural network language model. In *Aistats*, volume 5, pages 246–252. Citeseer, 2005.

[28] Preslav Nakov, Sara Rosenthal, Svetlana Kiritchenko, Saif M Mohammad, Zornitsa Kozareva, Alan Ritter, Veselin Stoyanov, and Xiaodan Zhu. Developing a successful semeval task in sentiment analysis of twitter and other social media texts. *Language Resources and Evaluation*, 50(1):35–65, 2016.

[29] Arvind Neelakantan, Quoc V Le, and Ilya Sutskever. Neural programmer: Inducing latent programs with gradient descent. *arXiv preprint arXiv:1511.04834*, 2015.

[30] Hao Peng, Jianxin Li, Yangqiu Song, and Yaopeng Liu. Incrementally learning the hierarchical softmax function for neural language models. 2016.

[31] Jeffrey Pennington, Richard Socher, and Christopher D Manning. Glove: Global vectors for word representation. In *EMNLP*, volume 14, pages 1532–1543, 2014.

[32] Steffen Rendle. Scaling factorization machines to relational data. In *Proceedings of the VLDB Endowment*, volume 6, pages 337–348. VLDB Endowment, 2013.

[33] Steffen Rendle and Christoph Freudenthaler. Improving pairwise learning for item recommendation from implicit feedback. In *Proceedings of the 7th ACM international conference on Web search and data mining*, pages 273–282. ACM, 2014.

[34] Alexandre Salle, Marco Idiart, and Aline Villavicencio. Matrix factorization using window sampling and negative sampling for improved word representations. *arXiv preprint arXiv:1606.00819*, 2016.

[35] Erik F Tjong Kim Sang and Fien De Meulder. Introduction to the conll-2003 shared task: Language-independent named entity recognition. 2003, 2014.

[36] Anshumali Shrivastava and Ping Li. Asymmetric lsh (alsh) for sublinear time maximum inner product search (mips). In *Advances in Neural Information Processing Systems*, pages 2321–2329, 2014.

[37] Duyu Tang, Furu Wei, Nan Yang, Ming Zhou, Ting Liu, and Bing Qin. Learning sentiment-specific word embedding for twitter sentiment classification. In *ACL (1)*, pages 1555–1565, 2014.

[38] Fei Tian, Hanjun Dai, Jiang Bian, Bin Gao, Rui Zhang, Enhong Chen, and Tie-Yan Liu. A probabilistic model for learning multi-prototype word embeddings. In *COLING*, pages 151–160, 2014.

[39] Ledyard R Tucker. Some mathematical notes on three-mode factor analysis. *Psychometrika*, 31(3):279–311, 1966.

[40] Peter D Turney and Patrick Pantel. From frequency to meaning: Vector space models of semantics. *Journal of artificial intelligence research*, 37:141–188, 2010.

[41] Sudheendra Vijayanarasimhan, Jonathon Shlens, Rajat Monga, and Jay Yagnik. Deep networks with large output spaces. *arXiv preprint arXiv:1412.7479*, 2014.

[42] Pascal Vincent, Alexandre de Brébisson, and Xavier Bouthillier. Efficient exact gradient update for training deep networks with very large sparse targets. In *Advances in Neural Information Processing Systems*, pages 1108–1116, 2015.

[43] Shengxian Wan, Yanyan Lan, Jiafeng Guo, Jun Xu, Liang Pang, and Xueqi Cheng. A deep architecture for semantic matching with multiple positional sentence representations. In *Thirtieth AAAI Conference on Artificial Intelligence*, 2016.

[44] Jason Weston, Samy Bengio, and Nicolas Usunier. Wsabie: Scaling up to large vocabulary image annotation.

[45] Fajie Yuan, Guibing Guo, Xiangnan He, Joemon M Jose, Long Chen, Ioannis Arapakis, and Weinan Zhang. Fast batch gradient method for implicit recommenders.

[46] Fajie Yuan, Guibing Guo, Joemon M Jose, Long Chen, Haitao Yu, and Weinan Zhang. Lambdafm: learning optimal ranking with factorization machines using lambda surrogates. In *Proceedings of the 25th ACM International on Conference on Information and Knowledge Management*, pages 227–236. ACM, 2016.

[47] Fajie Yuan, Guibing Guo, Joemon M Jose, Long Chen, Haitao Yu, and Weinan Zhang. Boostfm: Boosted factorization machines for top-n feature-based recommendation. In *Proceedings of the 22nd International Conference on Intelligent User Interfaces*, pages 45–54. ACM, 2017.

[48] Guangyou Zhou, Tingting He, Jun Zhao, and Po Hu. Learning continuous word embedding with metadata for question retrieval in community question answering. In *ACL (1)*, pages 250–259, 2015.

Sequential Recommendation with User Memory Networks

Xu Chen*
TNList, School of Software
Tsinghua University
xu-ch14@mails.tsinghua.edu.cn

Hongteng Xu
College of Computing
Georgia Institute of Technology
hxu42@gatech.edu

Yongfeng Zhang
Department of Computer Science
Rutgers University
zhangyf07@gmail.com

Jiaxi Tang
School of Computing Science
Simon Fraser University
jiaxit@sfu.ca

Yixin Cao
Department of Computer Science and Technology, Tsinghua University
caoyixin2009@163.com

Zheng Qin†
School of Software
Tsinghua University
qinzh@mails.tsinghua.edu.cn

Hongyuan Zha
College of Computing
Georgia Institute of Technology
zha@cc.gatech.edu

ABSTRACT

User preferences are usually dynamic in real-world recommender systems, and a user's historical behavior records may not be equally important when predicting his/her future interests. Existing recommendation algorithms – including both shallow and deep approaches – usually embed a user's historical records into a single latent vector/representation, which may have lost the per item- or feature-level correlations between a user's historical records and future interests. In this paper, we aim to express, store, and manipulate users' historical records in a more explicit, dynamic, and effective manner. To do so, we introduce the memory mechanism to recommender systems. Specifically, we design a memory-augmented neural network (MANN) integrated with the insights of collaborative filtering for recommendation. By leveraging the external memory matrix in MANN, we store and update users' historical records explicitly, which enhances the expressiveness of the model. We further adapt our framework to both item- and feature-level versions, and design the corresponding memory reading/writing operations according to the nature of personalized recommendation scenarios. Compared with state-of-the-art methods that consider users' sequential behavior for recommendation, e.g., sequential recommenders with recurrent neural networks (RNN) or Markov chains, our method achieves significantly and consistently better performance on four real-world datasets. Moreover, experimental analyses show that our method is able to extract the intuitive patterns of how users' future actions are affected by previous behaviors.

KEYWORDS

Sequential Recommendation; Memory Networks; Collaborative Filtering

ACM Reference Format:
Xu Chen*, Hongteng Xu, Yongfeng Zhang, Jiaxi Tang, Yixin Cao, Zheng Qin†, and Hongyuan Zha. 2018. Sequential Recommendation with User Memory Networks. In *Proceedings of WSDM'18.* ACM, New York, NY, USA, 9 pages. https://doi.org/10.1145/3159652.3159668

1 INTRODUCTION

In many real-world applications, users' current interests are influenced by their historical behaviors. For example, one may purchase accessories such as phone cases or earphones after buying a smart phone; and people may continue to buy the same brand of clothes that they had a good previous experience.

To model this phenomenon, previous methods have been proposed to make sequential recommendations with user historical records. For example, [23] adopted Markov chain to model user behavior sequences, and [19, 31] leveraged recurrent neural networks (RNNs) to embed previously purchased products for current interest prediction.

Existing methods have achieved encouraging results, however, they tend to compress all of a user's previous records into a fixed hidden representation. As exampled in Figure 1(a), the key reason for a user to buy a phone case (item E) could be that he bought a phone (item B) before, while the other prior purchases are not necessarily related to the new purchase. However, RNN (and other latent representation approaches) would forcefully summarize all of the prior items (A through D) into a vector, i.e., h_4, which is used to predict the user's next interest.

This lack of discriminating different historical records for next interest prediction leads to two unfavorable consequences: 1) it weakens the signal of highly correlated items for sequential recommendation; and 2) overlooking such signal makes it difficult for us to understand and explain the sequential recommendations.

* This work was conducted when the first author was visiting at Georgia Institute of Technology.
† Corresponding author.

WSDM'18, February 5–9, 2018, Marina Del Rey, CA, USA

ACM ISBN 978-1-4503-5581-0/18/02...$15.00
https://doi.org/10.1145/3159652.3159668

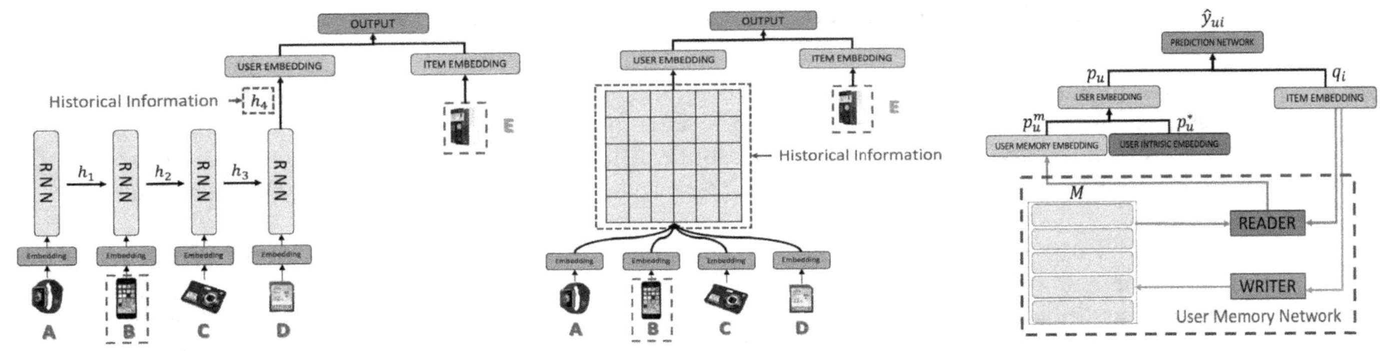

(a) Sequential recommendation based on RNN (b) General idea to adopt memory for recommendation (c) The general framework to implement our idea

Figure 1: (a) An example of leveraging user historical records for recommendation. The user bought A, B, C and D in the past orderly, these previous records (as embeddings of A, B, C and D) are summarized into h_4 for predicting E. (b) Our general idea of introducing a per user memory matrix to store user historical records. (c) A general framework to implement our idea. (best view in color)

To alleviate the problems, we view user behaviors as a decision making program described as neural turing machines [5], and propose to model user historical records with external memories. With the ability to express, store, and manipulate the records explicitly, dynamically, and effectively, external memory networks (EMN) [25, 28] have shown their promising performance for many sequential prediction tasks, such as question answering (QA) [18], natural language transduction [7], and knowledge tracking (KT) [32]. Instead of merging previous states to make predictions, EMN architecture introduces a memory matrix to store the states separately in memory slots, and then by designing proper operations on this matrix, it achieves significant improvement compared with conventional RNN/LSTM models in many tasks [28].

Inspired by EMN, we propose a novel framework integrating **R**ecommender system with external **U**ser **M**emory networks [5, 25, 28] (**RUM** for short), and further study its intuition and performance on Top-N recommendation tasks. Figure 1(b) and 1(c) illustrate the basic ideas of our proposed framework. For each user, an external user memory matrix is introduced to maintain her historical information, which enriches the representation capacity compared with traditional RNN hidden vectors. When making predictions, the memory matrix will be *attentively* read out to generate an embedding as the user representation, where the attention mechanism learns the different importance of previous records for the current recommendation. After processing each item in a sequence, the memory will be rewritten to update the user histories.

To better explore our idea, we provide two specifications of our framework, i.e., item-level and feature-level RUMs, which model user records on item- and feature-level, respectively. Compared with existing methods, our approach makes finer-grained use of user historical records based on memory networks, which improves the recommendation performance, meanwhile extracts intuitive causality of consumer behaviors based on attentive analyses.

Contributions. In summary, the main contributions of this work include:

- We propose to integrate the insights of collaborative filtering with memory-augmented neural networks for recommendation, which leverages user historical records in a more effective manner. To the best of our knowledge, this is the first attempt to introduce memory-augmented neural networks (MANNs) [5, 28] into the field of recommender systems.
- We investigate two potential memory networks (on item- and feature-level) with different representation and operation designs. We further study and compare their performance for sequential and top-N recommendation tasks.
- We also compare our model with state-of-the-art methods and verify the superiority of our model through quantitative analyses on real-world datasets, which shows that our method is able to leverage user historical records more effectively.
- We further provide empirical analyses to explain how and why an item is recommended by our model, which shows that with the attention mechanism in memory networks, our model is capable of providing intuitive explanations about how a user's historical records affect her current and future decisions.

In the following part of the paper, we first introduce the related work in section 2, and then illustrate our framework in section 3 and 4. In section 5, we verify the effectiveness of our method with experimental results, and the conclusions and outlooks of this work are presented in section 6.

2 RELATED WORK

Our work is essentially an integration of sequential recommendation and memory-augmented neural networks. In the following, we review the related work on these two research directions.

2.1 Sequential Recommendation

In the literature, many models have been proposed to leverage user historical records in a sequential manner for future behavior prediction and recommendation.

By integrating matrix factorization and Markov chains, factorized personalized Markov chains (FPMC) [23] embeds the transition information between adjacent behaviors into the item latent factors for recommendation, and the hierarchical representation model (HRM) [27] further extends the idea by leveraging representation learning as latent factors. These methods mostly model the local sequential patterns between every two adjacent records [31].

To model multiple-step sequential behaviors, [10] adopted Markov chains to provide recommendations with sparse sequences, and [31] proposed the dynamic recurrent basket model (DREAM) to capture global sequential patterns and to learn dynamic user interest representations based on recurrent neural network (RNN). In DREAM, all of a user's historical records are embedded into the final hidden state of RNN to represent her current preference, and this method has achieved significant improvement against HRM and FPMC. Similarly, [14, 26] leveraged user previous clicking and purchasing behaviors to model short-term preferences with RNN for session-based recommendation, and [9] adopted a metric space learning approach to learn additive user-item relations for sequential recommendation. Beyond e-commerce, sequential recommendation has also been applied to various application scenarios such as POI recommendation [3, 4], music recommendation [1, 8, 29], browsing recommendation [35], etc.

Existing models usually implicitly encode user's previous records into a latent factor or hidden state without distinguishing the different role that each record may play when predicting the current interest. In this work, however, we leverage user memory networks to store and manipulate each user's previous records, which helps to enhance the expressive power of user histories.

2.2 Memory-Augmented Neural Networks

With the power to process sequential data effectively, external memory network (EMN) [5, 6, 28] has been emerging in recent years. In a nutshell, it leverages a memory matrix to store historical hidden states, and by properly reading and updating this matrix, it can obtain improved performance on many sequence-oriented tasks. Following this idea, [25] designed an end-to-end memory-augmented model, which requires significantly less supervision during training, and makes it better applicable in real-world settings. Very recently, researchers have successfully adapted the idea of external memory network into several application domains, such as question answering (QA) [18], natural language transduction (NLT) [7], and knowledge tracking (KT) [32].

Typically, EMN consists of two major components: a memory matrix that maintains the states, and a controller that operates (including reading and writing) the matrix. More specifically, most methods [5, 6, 25, 28] adopt the attention mechanism to read the memory matrix, i.e., for an input $\boldsymbol{q}$, they first compute the similarity $S(\boldsymbol{q}, \boldsymbol{m}_i)$ between the input and each memory slot $\boldsymbol{m}_i$ in the memory matrix, and then the attention weights are derived by $w_i = SOFTMAX(S(\boldsymbol{q}, \boldsymbol{m}_i))$, where $SOFTMAX(x_i) = \frac{e^{x_i}}{\sum_j e^{x_j}}$, based on which the memory is attentively read out. For the writing process, [5] updated user memory by considering both content and slot location to facilitate all the locations of the memory, while [24] proposed a purely content-based writing strategy named least recently used access (LRUA) to write memories to either the least used memory location or the most recently used memory location.

In this paper, we aim to apply the idea of EMN to recommender system for leveraging user historical behaviors more effectively, which is yet to be explored in the research community.

3 RUM: RECOMMENDATION WITH USER MEMORY NETWORKS

In this section, we first present our general framework, elaborating how to integrate user memory networks with collaborative filtering. Then, we focus on designing the memory component by describing two specific implementations of the general framework, namely, the item- and feature-level user memory networks, so as to inspect our framework from different perspectives.

3.1 General Framework

For better understanding, we first re-describe the widely used matrix factorization (MF) model as a neural network. Suppose there are N users and M items, and let $\boldsymbol{p}_u$ and $\boldsymbol{q}_i$ be the embeddings of user u and item i, then the likeness score of u to i can be predicted as $\hat{y}_{ui} = \boldsymbol{p}_u^T \boldsymbol{q}_i$ in MF. In the context of neural network, the user/item IDs with one-hot format can be used as inputs fed into the architecture, then the look-up layer projects these sparse representations into dense vectors, which correspond to the user/item embeddings in MF models [13]. At last, the likeness score $\hat{y}_{ui}$ is computed as the vector inner product between $\boldsymbol{p}_u$ and $\boldsymbol{q}_i$.

Memory enhanced user embedding. To leverage user historical records in our framework, we generate a user's embedding from two parts (see Figure 1(c)): one is related to the user's memory component that encodes her previous records (named as *memory embedding* in the figure), and the other is a free vector used to encode her intrinsic preference that is not influenced by her previous actions (named as *intrinsic embedding*). The memory embedding is similar to the hidden vector in conventional RNN-based models. However, hidden vectors blindly compress all of a user's historical records into a fixed vector, while in our framework, user records are encoded, stored, and carefully updated through a more expressive structure – the personalized memory matrix $\boldsymbol{M}^u$.

Specifically, for user u, her memory embedding $\boldsymbol{p}_u^m$ is derived by reading $\boldsymbol{M}^u$ according to the current item embedding $\boldsymbol{q}_i$:

$$\boldsymbol{p}_u^m = READ(\boldsymbol{M}^u, \boldsymbol{q}_i) \tag{1}$$

And then, by merging $\boldsymbol{p}_u^m$ with the user intrinsic embedding $\boldsymbol{p}_u^*$, we get the final user embedding as:

$$\boldsymbol{p}_u = MERGE(\boldsymbol{p}_u^*, \boldsymbol{p}_u^m) \tag{2}$$

where $MERGE(\cdot)$ is a function that merges two vectors into one. The particular choice of $MERGE(\cdot)$ in our model is a simple weighted vector addition, that is:

$$MERGE(x, y) \doteq x + \alpha y = \boldsymbol{p}_u^* + \alpha \boldsymbol{p}_u^m \tag{3}$$

where α is a weighting parameter. We have also tested element-wise multiplication and concat operations, but they led to unfavorable performance. Another advantage of our choice is that we can tune the weighting parameter α to study the effect of incorporating memory mechanism for recommendation, which will be shown in the experiments.

Prediction function. When making predictions, we feed the final user embedding $\boldsymbol{p}_u$ and the item embedding $\boldsymbol{q}_i$ into a function:

$$\hat{y}_{ui} = PREDICT(\boldsymbol{p}_u, \boldsymbol{q}_i) \tag{4}$$

where $PREDICT(\cdot)$ is an arbitrary prediction function, or even a prediction neural network as in [13]. Here, we choose the sigmoid

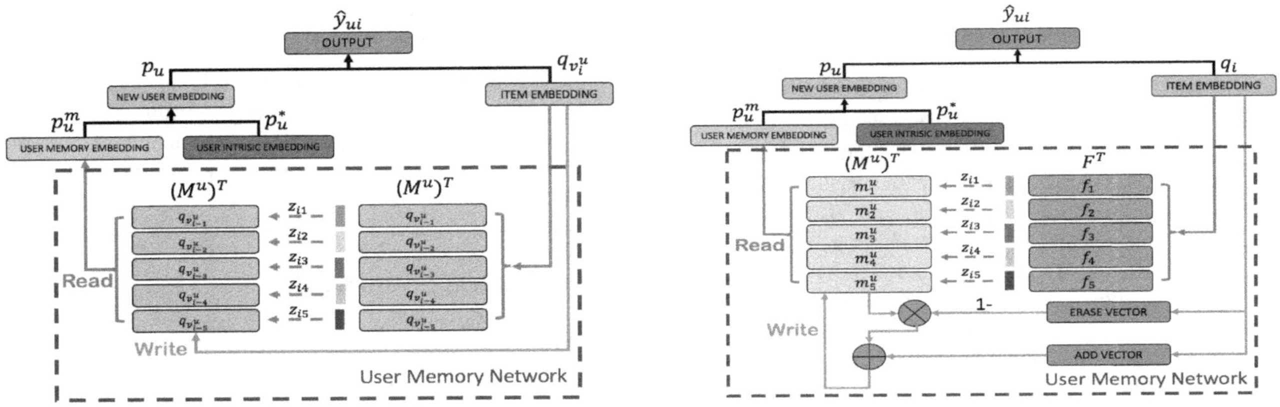

(a) Item-level RUM

(b) Feature-level RUM

Figure 2: Two specific implementations of our RUM framework. To better illustrate the model overflow, we plot $(M^u)^T$ and F^T instead of M^u and F in the figure, so that each row corresponds to a memory slot in the figure. (best view in color)

inner product $\hat{y}_{ui} = \sigma({p_u}^T \cdot q_i)$ as a specific implementation, because it gives us better training efficiency for our data. However, it is not necessarily restricted to this function and many others can be used in practice according to the specific application domain.

At last, we adapt binary cross-entropy as our loss function for model optimization, and the objective function to be maximized is:

$$\begin{aligned} l_{RUM} &= \log \prod_{(u,i)} (\hat{y}_{ui})^{y_{ui}} (1-\hat{y}_{ui})^{1-y_{ui}} - \lambda||\Theta||_F^2 \\ &= \sum_u \sum_{i \in I_u^+} \log \hat{y}_{ui} + \sum_u \sum_{i \in I/I_u^+} \log(1-\hat{y}_{ui}) - \lambda||\Theta||_F^2 \end{aligned} \quad (5)$$

where Θ is the model parameter set, y_{ui} is the ground truth that would be 1 if u has purchased i, and 0 otherwise. I is the set of all items, and I_u^+ is the set of items that u purchased arranged in purchasing order, namely, $I_u^+ = \{v_1^u, v_2^u, \cdots, v_{|I_u^+|}^u\}$, where v_j^u is the j-th item purchased by u. We uniformly sample the negative instances from unobserved item set $I_u^- = I/I_u^+$, and it should be noted that a nonuniform sampling strategy might further improve the performance, and we leave the exploration as a future work.

In this equation, we maximize the likelihood of our predicted results by the first two terms, and regularize all the model parameters to avoid over fitting by the last term. In the training phase, we learn the parameters via stochastic gradient descent (SGD).

Memory updating. After each purchasing behavior, we update the user memory matrix $\boldsymbol{M}^u$ to maintain its dynamic nature by:

$$\boldsymbol{M}^u \leftarrow WRITE(\boldsymbol{M}^u, \boldsymbol{q}_i) \quad (6)$$

In the following, we will describe how the personalized memory matrix $\boldsymbol{M}^u$ encodes user behaviors, and how to design the $READ(\cdot)$ and $WRITE(\cdot)$ operations on both item- and feature-levels.

3.2 Item-level RUM

In this section, we first implement our idea by extending previous methods in a straightforward manner (see Figure 2(a)). Similar to existing models [14, 23, 26, 27, 31], we regard each item as a unit, and model the impact of previously purchased items on the following ones. Many works [23, 27] have shown that users' recent behaviors can be more important to the current decisions. As a result, for each user u we make the memory matrix $\boldsymbol{M}^u$ store the embeddings of the u's recently purchased items, as denoted in the purple dashed box in Figure 2(a).

Suppose the set of items purchased by user u is defined as $I_u^+ = \{v_1^u, v_2^u, \cdots, v_{|I_u^+|}^u\}$ (arranged in purchasing order), where v_i^u is the i-th item purchased by u, let $\boldsymbol{p}_u \in R^D$ and $\boldsymbol{q}_{v_i^u} \in R^D$ be the embeddings of user u and item v_i^u, and suppose there are K columns (i.e., memory slots) in the memory matrix, namely, $\boldsymbol{M}^u \in R^{D \times K} = \{\boldsymbol{m}_1^u, \boldsymbol{m}_2^u, \cdots, \boldsymbol{m}_K^u\}$, where $\boldsymbol{m}_k^u \in R^D$ is the k-th column vector of $\boldsymbol{M}^u$. We design the reading and writing operations as follows.

Reading operation. Intuitively, the previous products may have different impacts on the current item, and the more influential product should be valued more in the final memory embedding. Formally, in our model, when making prediction on a user-item pair (u, v_i^u), we first adopt a similar way as FPMC [23] to compute the impacts between the items in user memory $\boldsymbol{M}^u$ and the current item by:

$$w_{ik} = (\boldsymbol{q}_{v_i^u})^T \cdot \boldsymbol{m}_k^u, \; z_{ik} = \frac{\exp(\beta w_{ik})}{\sum_j \exp(\beta w_{ij})}, \; \forall k = 1, 2, \cdots, K \quad (7)$$

where β is the strength parameter. Then, we use z_{ik}'s as the attention weights to derive u's memory embedding, which provides us with the ability to access user historical behaviors according to their influences on the current item:

$$\boldsymbol{p}_u^m = \sum_{k=1}^{K} z_{ik} \cdot \boldsymbol{m}_k^u \quad (8)$$

Different from previous models, we do not forcefully merge all the item embeddings in the reading process. On the contrary, we first store them in $\boldsymbol{M}^u$ individually, and then attentively pay more attention to some of the items, which provides us a more finer-grained method to utilize user historical records.

Writing operation. As mentioned above, users' recent behaviors usually play more important roles for current predictions. As a result, we adopt a simple first-in-first-out mechanism to maintain the latest interacted items in the user memory matrix $\boldsymbol{M}^u$. Specifically, the memory matrix $\boldsymbol{M}^u$ for user u always stores the most recent K items. Suppose the current item is $\boldsymbol{q}_{v_i^u}$, then the memory matrix is $M^u = \{q_{v^u_{i-1}}, q_{v^u_{i-2}}, ..., q_{v^u_{i-K}}\}$. When writing the memory, the earliest item would be replaced, and M^u is updated to $\{q_{v^u_i}, q_{v^u_{i-1}}, ..., q_{v^u_{i-K+1}}\}$. Note that when the memory is not full, the item is directly added without replacing any other entry.

3.3 Feature-level RUM

Inspired by the insights of classical latent factor models (LFM) [17] for recommendation, we further explore to implement the RUM framework on the feature-level. In LFM, we assume that users may consider a set of product features when making purchasing decisions, and each embedding dimension in LFM represents a latent feature in the product domain, where the features span a latent representation space. LFM then estimates a user's preference on these features as a vector in this space.

In this work, we explicitly model such latent features with the power of memory networks. Intuitively, a user's preference on these features should be dynamically reflected by his/her purchasing behaviors. For example, if a user has an excellent experience on a newly purchased iPhone, then she may continue to select Apple products on the 'brand' feature in the future.

Inspired by these intuitions, we maintain the user preference on different features in the memory matrix, which would be read to generate user memory embeddings, and be written by each item she purchased. More specifically, we formulate our method into a key-value memory neural network [21], as shown in Figure 2(b). We first design a global latent feature table (GLFT) to store the feature embeddings, and when making predictions, an item will interact with this table to identify its related features. For each user, we leverage the user memory matrix M^u to encode her likeness on the features in GLFT. Based on the above identified features, the target user will attentively merge the columns in M^u to obtain her memory embedding. Same as the global feature space in LFM, the global latent feature table here is shared across all the users, while the memory matrix is maintained per-user level in a personalized manner. At last, we update the user memory matrix M^u using the item embeddings.

Formally, we let $p_u \in R^D$ and $q_i \in R^D$ be the embeddings of user u and item i. Suppose there are K latent features in our system, and the global latent feature table is $F = \{f_1, f_2, \cdots, f_K\}$, where $f_k \in R^D$ is the embedding of feature k. For a user u, we define her memory matrix as $M^u = \{m^u_1, m^u_2, \cdots, m^u_K\}$, where $m^u_k \in R^D$ is the embedding of u's preference on the feature k.

Reading operation. To make the reading process differentiable, we adapt soft-attention mechanism to read the user memory matrix. Specifically, when making prediction for the user-item pair (u, i), we first compute i's relativeness with each feature in the global latent feature table by:

$$w_{ik} = q_i^T \cdot f_k, \; z_{ik} = \frac{\exp(\beta w_{ik})}{\sum_j \exp(\beta w_{ij})}, \; \forall k = 1, 2, \cdots, K \tag{9}$$

where β is still the strength parameter, and we also linearly merge the slots in user u's memory matrix using the derived z_{ik} attentions to compute her memory embedding:

$$p^m_u = \sum_{k=1}^{K} z_{ik} \cdot m^u_k \tag{10}$$

Writing operation. Inspired by neural turing machine (NTM) [5], when writing the user memory matrix M^u, it will be erased first before new information is added.

Specifically, we first derive a D dimensional erase vector $erase_i \in R^D$ from q_i by:

$$erase_i = \sigma(E^T q_i + b_e) \tag{11}$$

where $\sigma(\cdot)$ is the element-wise sigmoid function, and E and b are the erase parameters to be learned. Given the attention weights and the erase vector, the feature preference memory is updated by:

$$m^u_k \leftarrow m^u_k \odot (1 - z_{ik} \cdot erase_i) \tag{12}$$

where $\odot$ is element-wise product, $\mathbf{1}$ is a column-vector of all 1's. Therefore, the elements of a memory location are reset to zero only if both the weight at the location and the erase element are one. The memory vector is left unchanged if either the weight or the erase signal is zero [32].

After erasing, an add vector $add_i \in R^D$ is used to update the feature preference memory by:

$$add_i = \tanh(A^T q_i + b_a), \; m^u_k \leftarrow m^u_k + z_{ik} \cdot add_i \tag{13}$$

where A and b_a are the add parameters to be learned. This erase-add update strategy allows forgetting and strengthening user feature preference embeddings in the learning process, and the model can determine which signals to be weakened and which to be strengthened by learning the erase and add parameters automatically.

4 DISCUSSIONS AND FURTHER ANALYSIS

To provide more insights of our proposed model, we analyze the relationship between the item- and feature-level RUMs, and then further relate our method with previous ones by comparing it with matrix factorization (MF) and factorized personalized Markov chains (FPMC).

4.1 Item- v.s. Feature-level RUM

Generally speaking, both item- and feature-level RUMs are specific implementations of the same framework shown in Figure 1(c). However, they manage user historical information from different perspectives. The item-level RUM regards each item as a unit, and directly store the item embeddings in the memory matrix, which is designed to capture item-to-item transition patterns. While in the feature-level RUM, the historical information is leveraged in a feature-centered manner. The memory matrix is used to store the embeddings of user preferences on different latent features, and each item is indirectly utilized to change these embeddings.

When using these models in real-world applications, there is actually an "explanation-effectiveness" trade-off: item-level RUM can explicitly tell us which items in the past are more important for the current decision, which provides the system with certain explanatory ability. However, feature-level RUM can obtain better performance with finer-grained modeling in a "black box". We will discuss more details with experimental results in the following.

4.2 Relationship between RUM and MF

As shown in Figure 1(c), RUM will reduce to traditional MF when the user memory network is set to be unavailable, i.e., when the user memory embedding is set as an all-0 vector.

However, by enabling the user memory network, RUM can collect valuable information from the historical behaviors, which can bring improved performance in the task of Top-N recommendation as shown in our following experiments.

4.3 Relationship between RUM and FPMC

Both RUM and FPMC leverage user historical behaviors to predict the current ones. To model item-to-item transition patterns for each user, FPMC builds a tensor factorization model, and optimizes it under the Bayesian personalized ranking (BPR) criterion. The objective function is as follows [23, 27]:

$$l_{FPMC} = \sum_u \sum_{T_t^u} \sum_{i \in T_t^u} \sum_{i' \notin T_t^u} \log \sigma(\hat{x}_{u,t,i} - \hat{x}_{u,t,i'}) - \lambda ||\Theta||_F^2 \quad (14)$$

where T_t^u is u's t-th basket, Θ is the model parameter set, and $\hat{x}_{u,t,i}$ is predicted by:

$$\hat{x}_{u,t,i} = \boldsymbol{p}_u^T \cdot \boldsymbol{q}_i + \frac{1}{|T_{t-1}^u|} \sum_{l \in T_{t-1}^u} \boldsymbol{q}_l^T \cdot \boldsymbol{q}_i \quad (15)$$

When applied to the task of sequential recommendation, each basket in FPMC contains only one item, thus,

$$l_{FPMC} = \sum_u \sum_{i \in I_u^+} \sum_{i' \in I/I_u^+} \log \sigma(\hat{x}_{u,l,i} - \hat{x}_{u,l,i'}) - \lambda ||\Theta||_F^2 \quad (16)$$

and,

$$\hat{x}_{u,l,i} = \boldsymbol{p}_u^T \cdot \boldsymbol{q}_i + \boldsymbol{q}_l^T \cdot \boldsymbol{q}_i \quad (17)$$

where I_u^+ is the set of u's purchased items (arranged in purchasing orders), namely, $I_u^+ = \{v_1^u, v_2^u, \cdots, v_{|I_u^+|}^u\}$, and v_j^u is the j-th item purchased by u. I is the set of all items, and l is the item purchased just before i.

To show how our model degenerates to FPMC, we use only one memory slot in the item-level RUM (i.e., $K = 1$), and set the weighting parameter in $MERGE(\cdot)$ as 1 (i.e., $\alpha = 1$), then we have:

$$\begin{aligned} \hat{y}_{u,i} &= \sigma(\boldsymbol{p}_u^T \cdot \boldsymbol{q}_i) = \sigma(MERGE(\boldsymbol{p}_u^*, \boldsymbol{p}_u^m)^T \cdot \boldsymbol{q}_i) \\ &= \sigma((\boldsymbol{p}_u^* + \boldsymbol{p}_u^m)^T \cdot \boldsymbol{q}_i) = \sigma\Big((\boldsymbol{p}_u^* + \sum_{k=1}^{K} z_{ik} \cdot \boldsymbol{m}_k^u)^T \cdot \boldsymbol{q}_i\Big) \\ &\overset{\gamma_1}{=} \sigma((\boldsymbol{p}_u^* + \boldsymbol{m}_1^u)^T \cdot \boldsymbol{q}_i) \overset{\gamma_2}{=} \sigma((\boldsymbol{p}_u^* + \boldsymbol{q}_l)^T \cdot \boldsymbol{q}_i) \\ &= \sigma(\boldsymbol{p}_u^{*T} \cdot \boldsymbol{q}_i + \boldsymbol{q}_l^T \cdot \boldsymbol{q}_i) \end{aligned} \quad (18)$$

where step γ_1 holds because $z_{ik} = z_{i1} = 1$ when $K = 1$, and step γ_2 holds because $\boldsymbol{m}_1^u$ is exactly the embedding of the previously purchased item $\boldsymbol{q}_l$ according to our settings in item-level RUM.

By regarding the user intrinsic embedding $\boldsymbol{p}_u^*$ of RUM (in Eq.(18)) as the user embedding $\boldsymbol{p}_u$ of FPMC (in Eq.(17)), we have $\hat{y}_{u,i} = \sigma(\hat{x}_{u,l,i})$, and we can thus rewrite Eq.(5) as:

$$l_{RUM} = \sum_u \sum_{i \in I_u^+} \log \sigma(\hat{x}_{u,l,i}) + \sum_u \sum_{i \in I/I_u^+} \log(1 - \sigma(\hat{x}_{u,l,i'})) - \lambda ||\Theta||_F^2 \quad (19)$$

Comparing Eq.(16) and (19), we see that FPMC shares the same prediction function (Eq.(17)) with 1-order item-level RUM. However, their optimization methods are slightly different. For a triplet (u, i, i'), where (u, i) is an observed interaction and (u, i') is unobserved, FPMC learns the model by maximizing the margin of u's likeness between i and i', while RUM tries to maximize u's likeness on i and minimize u's likeness on i', respectively. Actually, we can also use Bayesian personalized ranking (BPR) to optimize RUM, in that way, FPMC equivalents a 1-order item-level RUM for sequential recommendation.

Based on the above analyses, we can see that RUM is a very general recommendation framework. On one hand, RUM is a generalization of many existing recommendation models, and on the other hand, RUM can provide us with the opportunity to explore other promising models by adapting the merge function, predict function, and the reading/writing strategy to other choices.

5 EXPERIMENTS

In this section we evaluate our proposed models. We begin by introducing the experimental setup, and then report and analyze the experimental results.

5.1 Experimental Setup

5.1.1 ***Datasets.*** We conduct our experiments on the Amazon dataset [1] [11, 20]. This dataset contains user-product purchasing behaviors from Amazon spanning May 1996 - July 2014. We evaluate our models on four product categories, including Instant Video, Musical Instrument, Automotive and Baby Care. To provide sequential recommendations, we select those users with at least 10 purchasing records for experiments, and the statistics of the final datasets are shown in Table 1.

Table 1: Statistics of our datasets.

Datasets	#Users	#Items	#Ratings	Density
Instant Video	1353	7786	33726	0.32%
Musical Instrument	2129	20928	55382	0.12%
Automotive	1144	24590	48706	0.17%
Baby Care	2379	14037	77198	0.23%

5.1.2 ***Evaluation methods.*** For each model, we define the generated recommendation list for user u as $R_u = \{r_u^1, r_u^2, \cdots, r_u^N\}$, where N is the number of recommended items, r_u^i is ranked at the i-th position in R_u according to the predicted score. Suppose the set of $u's$ interacted items in the test data is T_u, and there are totally M users in our system, we thus use the following measures for evaluation:

- **Precision (P), Recall (R) and F_1-score:** we adopt per-user average instead of global average for better interpretability [16]:

$$\begin{aligned} P@N &= \frac{1}{M}\sum_u P_u@N = \frac{1}{M}\sum_u \frac{|R_u \cap T_u|}{|R_u|} \\ R@N &= \frac{1}{M}\sum_u R_u@N = \frac{1}{M}\sum_u \frac{|R_u \cap T_u|}{|T_u|} \\ F_1@N &= \frac{1}{M}\sum_u F_{1u}@N = \frac{1}{M}\sum_u \frac{2 \cdot P_u@N \cdot R_u@N}{P_u@N + R_u@N} \end{aligned} \quad (20)$$

- **Hit-ratio (HR):** Hit-ratio gives the percentage of users that can receive at least one correct recommendation, which has been

[1] http://jmcauley.ucsd.edu/data/amazon/

widely used in previous work [16, 30]:

$$HR@N = \frac{1}{M}\sum_{u} I(|R_u \cap T_u|) \tag{21}$$

where $I(x)$ is an indicator function whose value is 1 when $x > 0$, and 0 otherwise.

• **NDCG:** The normalized discounted cumulative gain, which evaluates ranking performance by taking the positions of correct items into consideration [15]:

$$NDCG@N = \frac{1}{Z}DCG@N = \frac{1}{Z}\sum_{j=1}^{N}\frac{2^{I(|\{r_u^j\}\cap T_u|)}-1}{\log_2(j+1)} \tag{22}$$

where $I(x)$ is the indicator function as above, and Z is a normalization constant, which is the maximum possible value of $DCG@N$.

5.1.3 ***Baselines.*** We adopt the following representative and state-of-the-art methods as baselines for performance comparison:

• **MostPopular (MP):** This is a non-personalized static method, where the most frequently purchased items are ranked in descending order of frequency to make recommendations.

• **BPR:** Bayesian personalized ranking, which is a popular method for top-N recommendation [22]. We adopt matrix factorization as the prediction component for BPR.

• **FPMC:** Factorized personalized Markov chains, which is one of the stat-of-the-art models for sequential recommendation based on Markov chains [23]. Each purchased item in our data is regarded as a basket in this method.

• **DREAM:** The dynamic recurrent basket model, which is the stat-of-the-art sequential recommendation method based on recurrent neural networks [31].

5.1.4 ***Parameter settings.*** When implementing our method, the model parameters are first randomly initialized according to the uniform distribution, and then updated by conducting stochastic gradient descent (SGD). The learning rate of SGD is determined by grid search in the range of $\{1, 0.1, 0.01, 0.001, 0.0001\}$, and the number of memory slot K is empirically set as 20. We primarily set the weighting parameter $\alpha = 0.2$ in MERGE function, and the effect of using different α settings is also studied in the experiments.

For each purchased item (i.e., positive instance), we uniformly sample one negative instance from the uninteracted items of the user. The embedding dimension D and regularization parameters are determined by grid search in the range of $\{10, 20, 30, 40, 50\}$ and $\{0.1, 0.01, 0.001, 0.0001\}$, respectively.

In our experiments, each user's purchasing records are ordered in purchasing time, and the first 70% items of each user are used for training, while the remaining are used for testing. We recommend 5 items ($N = 5$) for each user.

5.2 Overall Performance of Our Models

We first study the performance of our item- and feature-level RUMs under default settings ($\alpha = 0.2$). Results are shown in Table 2, and we have the following observations.

The non-personalized Most Popular approach gives the most unfavorable performance in nearly all the cases. Since it does not consider user's personalized information, this observation highlights the importance of personalization in recommendation tasks.

As expected, by profiling users individually and optimizing the ranking-based objective function directly, BPR performs better than MP in most cases.

FPMC and DREAM can achieve better performance than BPR on most measures, while the difference between these two methods is not very significant. On considering that the key difference between BPR and FPMC is that the latter models user historical records in a sequential manner, this observation verifies that sequential recommendation can help to improve performance in real-world systems.

It is interesting to see that DREAM achieves better performance than FPMC on instant videos. DREAM models the multi-step behavior instead of pair-wise behavior of users, which has the ability to better capture users' long-term interests on video preference. However, on other datasets the pair-wise short-term influence between adjacent items may be more informative to predict the next behavior, but DREAM equally merges all the previous items into a single hidden vector through RNN, which may weaken the pair-wise signal for sequential recommendation. This highlights the importance of our motivation that a carefully designed mechanism is needed to automatically determine which previous item(s) are important for current interest prediction.

Encouragingly, we find that either item- or feature-level RUMs achieved better performance than the best baselines in most cases. These results indicates the effectiveness of our proposed methods for sequential recommendation, which is actually not surprising because the memory mechanism as well as the reading and writing designs in our model provide better expressive power to model user historical records.

By modeling item relations on a finer-grained level, the feature-level RUM outperforms item-level RUM on most measures. This is intuitive in that the function of two products may not be directly related, but they may share some features in common which may affect user decisions, for example, they are of the same brand.

5.3 Influence of the Weighting Parameter α

In this subsection, we are curious about whether and how the memory mechanism is helpful to sequential recommendation. To do so, we analyze the influence of the weighting parameter α, which determines the importance of the memory embedding against the intrinsic embedding in the MERGE function.

Specifically, we study the performance of our models on $F_1@5$ by tuning α in the range of $0 \sim 1$ with a step size of 0.1. Results are shown in Figure 3.

We see that when the memory component is unavailable (i.e., $\alpha = 0$), feature- and item-level RUMs reduce to the same model and share the same performance. In this case, both of them give unfavorable results across all the datasets. When memory network is incorporated, the performance increases drastically, and the best results are achieved when $\alpha \approx 0.2$. However, when the weight of memory embedding continues to rise, the performance goes down, and this observation is consistent on four datasets.

This result means that considering sequential influences from a user's recently purchased items indeed helps to provide better recommendations, but putting too much focus on this recent purchase signal may weaken a user's intrinsic preference. These results further verified the frequent observation in the research community

Table 2: Summary of the performance for baselines and our models. The first block shows the baseline performances, where starred numbers are the best baseline results; the second block shows the results of our item-level and feature-level RUM models. Bolded numbers are the best performance of each column, and all the numbers in the table are percentage numbers with '%' omitted.

Dataset	Instant Video					Musical Instrument					Automotive					Baby Care				
Measures@5(%)	P	R	F_1	HR	NDCG	P	R	F_1	HR	NDCG	P	R	F_1	HR	NDCG	P	R	F_1	HR	NDCG
MP	1.110	1.521	1.227	5.178	1.112	0.931	1.211	0.996	4.464	1.053*	0.805	0.481	0.589	3.937	0.880	0.858	0.719	0.753	4.163	0.923
BPR	1.198	1.624	1.300	5.917	1.243	0.987	1.261*	1.044*	4.699	0.930	0.822*	0.481	0.593	3.917	0.909*	0.958	0.771	0.819	4.668	1.016
FPMC	1.301	1.612	1.322	5.917	1.400	1.006*	1.170	1.014	4.793*	1.017	0.812	0.483*	0.594*	3.921*	0.873	1.009*	0.800*	0.853*	4.962*	1.026*
DREAM	1.312*	1.652*	1.342*	6.097*	1.401*	1.003	1.163	1.004	4.613	1.013	0.792	0.463	0.576	3.812	0.793	0.979	0.776	0.823	4.762	1.006
RUM (I)	1.302	1.846	1.449	6.213	1.290	1.005	1.243	1.047	4.652	**1.106**	0.823	0.485	0.591	4.022	0.921	1.051	0.878	0.918	5.088	1.025
RUM (F)	**1.405**	**1.905**	**1.491**	**6.287**	**1.448**	**1.032**	**1.308**	**1.094**	**4.734**	1.035	**0.842**	**0.501**	**0.622**	**4.111**	**0.963**	**1.070**	**0.918**	**0.951**	**5.432**	**1.103**

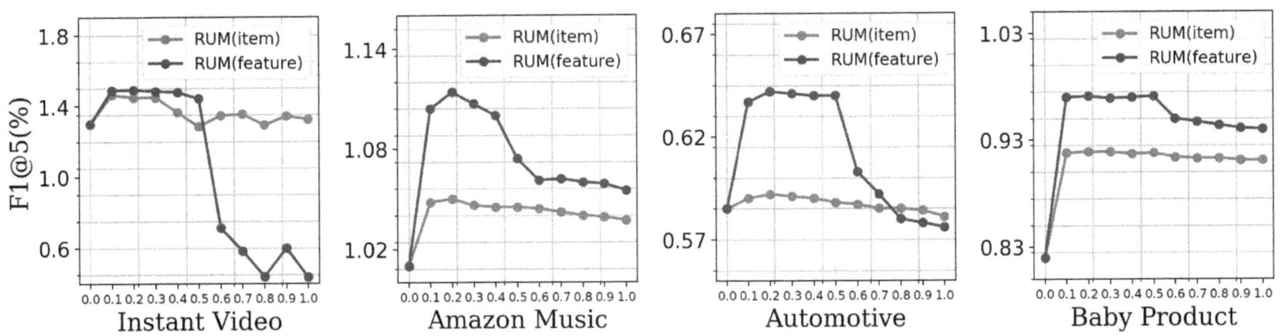

Figure 3: Performance of our item- and feature-level RUM models under difference choices of weighting parameter α.

that both short-term and long-term user preferences are important for personalized recommendation.

5.4 Intuition of Attention Weights in Item-level RUM

To illustrate intuition of item-to-item transitions, we present some example users in Figure 4, which are sampled from the results of item-level RUM with 5 memory slots ($K = 5$) on the Baby Care dataset. When a user purchased her i-th item (corresponding to the x-axis, denoted in a blue grid), we plot a length-5 column vector in her subfigure (e.g., the boxed vector in the upper-middle subfigure), and the vector element corresponding to position j on the y-axis is the attention weight z (in Eq.(7)) that this user casts on her j-th purchased item. When the user continues to purchase items, the most recently purchased 5 items are maintained in the memory, thus the column vectors shift from bottom-left to upper-right. The darker the color, the higher attention is casted on the item. Based on this figure, we have the following interesting observations.

Generally, the grids near the upper border of the diagonal strips are darker in color. This means that the most influential items in the past are usually near to the current behavior. This further confirms the assumption behind item-level RUM that recent behaviors are more important for current decisions. However, the specific position of the most influential item is not always the most recent one, which may explain why FPMC did not achieve favorable performance by only modeling the pair-wise adjacent behaviors.

Besides, we find two types of interesting user behavior patterns.

1) Some behavior sequences are continuously triggered by the most recent action (denoted in the green solid boxes), which is in line with the assumptions of FPMC [23]. We call this as the "one-to-one" behavior pattern, and a real-world example is that a user purchased some infant formula, and then bought a feeding bottle, which caused her to buy some nipples, and these nipples further made her buy a nipple cleaner.

2) Sometimes, a sequence of multiple behaviors are mostly influenced by the same previous action (denoted in the brown dotted boxes), while the relations between themselves are not so important. We call this the "one-to-multiple" pattern. A real-world example is that a mom bought a crib for her baby, after that she bought a water-proof mattress protector and a mosquito net for the crib, and further bought a bed bell to decorate the crib. In such cases, our RUM model with attention mechanism can automatically learn the importance of previous items based on large-scale user purchasing records, which is better than FPMC that assumes adjacent influence, and also better than RNN that merges all of the previous behaviors.

Based on these discovered patterns, the item-level RUM can interpret recommender system from the sequential behavior perspective, which is different from previous methods that usually leverage side information (e.g. user textual reviews [2, 12, 33, 34]) for explanations.

6 CONCLUSION

In this paper, we proposed to leverage external memory networks integrated with collaborative filtering for sequential recommendation. To do so, we designed the RUM sequential recommendation framework, and provided the item-level and feature-level specifications of the framework. Quantitative experimental analyses verified the effectiveness of our framework, and qualitative analyses verified the intuition behind our framework.

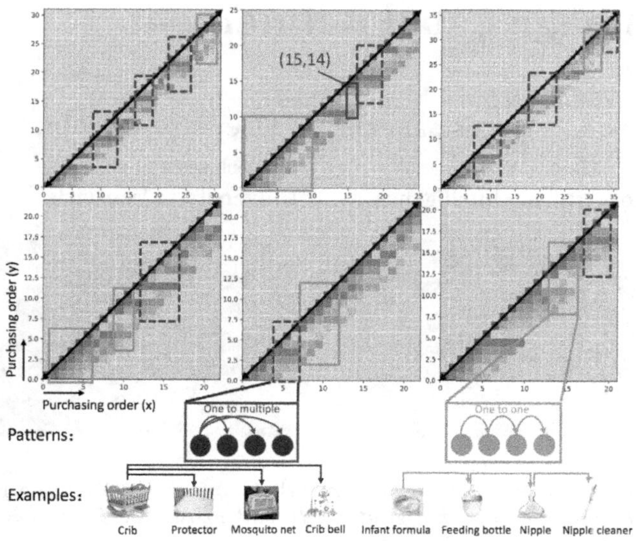

Figure 4: Illustration of item-to-item transitions. Each subplot is a sampled user, the x-axis and y-axis represent the user's purchased items orderly. The diagonal strip represents the current items. The color of an element $(i, j)(j < i)$ is proportional to the attention on previous item j when purchasing current i. For example, in the purple box of the second subplot, the darkest grid $(15, 14)$ means that the 14-th item is the most influential one among the most recent five for the 15-th purchase. Two types of user behavior patterns (one-to-one and one-to-multiple) as well as their examples are illustrated in the bottom.

This is a first step towards our goal for recommendation based on explicit user memory modeling, and there is much room for further improvements. By introducing side information such as user reviews and product images, we can align the memory units in feature-level RUM with different semantics, and thus we can build a more explainable recommender system. Besides, our RUM model is a framework with the ability of flexible generalizations, as a result, we can study other types of memory network designs to adapt our framework to different application scenarios.

ACKNOWLEDGMENT

This work was supported in part by NSF IIS-1639792, NSF IIS-1717916 and NSF CMMI-1745382. Any opinions, findings and conclusions or recommendations expressed in this material are those of the authors and do not necessarily reflect those of the sponsor.

REFERENCES

[1] Shuo Chen, Josh L Moore, Douglas Turnbull, and Thorsten Joachims. 2012. Playlist prediction via metric embedding. In *KDD*.
[2] Xu Chen, Zheng Qin, Yongfeng Zhang, and Tao Xu. 2016. Learning to rank features for recommendation over multiple categories. In *SIGIR*.
[3] Chen Cheng, Haiqin Yang, Michael R Lyu, and Irwin King. 2013. Where You Like to Go Next: Successive Point-of-Interest Recommendation.. In *IJCAI*.
[4] Shanshan Feng, Xutao Li, Yifeng Zeng, Gao Cong, Yeow Meng Chee, and Quan Yuan. 2015. Personalized Ranking Metric Embedding for Next New POI Recommendation.. In *IJCAI*.
[5] Alex Graves, Greg Wayne, and Ivo Danihelka. 2014. Neural turing machines. *arXiv preprint arXiv:1410.5401* (2014).
[6] Alex Graves, Greg Wayne, Malcolm Reynolds, Tim Harley, Ivo Danihelka, Agnieszka Grabska-Barwińska, Sergio Gómez Colmenarejo, Edward Grefenstette, Tiago Ramalho, John Agapiou, et al. 2016. Hybrid computing using a neural network with dynamic external memory. (2016).
[7] Edward Grefenstette, Karl Moritz Hermann, Mustafa Suleyman, and Phil Blunsom. 2015. Learning to transduce with unbounded memory. In *NIPS*.
[8] Negar Hariri, Bamshad Mobasher, and Robin Burke. 2012. Context-aware music recommendation based on latent topic sequential patterns. In *RecSys*.
[9] Ruining He, Wang-Cheng Kang, and Julian McAuley. 2017. Translation-based recommendation. *Recsys* (2017).
[10] Ruining He and Julian McAuley. 2016. Fusing Similarity Models with Markov Chains for Sparse Sequential Recommendation. In *ICDM*.
[11] Ruining He and Julian McAuley. 2016. Ups and downs: Modeling the visual evolution of fashion trends with one-class collaborative filtering. In *WWW*.
[12] Xiangnan He, Tao Chen, Min-Yen Kan, and Xiao Chen. 2015. Trirank: Review-aware explainable recommendation by modeling aspects. In *CIKM*.
[13] Xiangnan He, Lizi Liao, Hanwang Zhang, Liqiang Nie, Xia Hu, and Tat-Seng Chua. 2017. Neural collaborative filtering. In *WWW*.
[14] Balázs Hidasi, Alexandros Karatzoglou, Linas Baltrunas, and Domonkos Tikk. 2016. Session-based recommendations with recurrent neural networks. *ICLR* (2016).
[15] Kalervo Järvelin and Jaana Kekäläinen. 2000. IR evaluation methods for retrieving highly relevant documents. In *SIGIR*.
[16] George Karypis. 2001. Evaluation of item-based top-n recommendation algorithms. In *CIKM*.
[17] Yehuda Koren, Robert Bell, and Chris Volinsky. 2009. Matrix factorization techniques for recommender systems. *Computer* (2009).
[18] Ankit Kumar, Ozan Irsoy, Peter Ondruska, Mohit Iyyer, James Bradbury, Ishaan Gulrajani, Victor Zhong, Romain Paulus, and Richard Socher. 2016. Ask me anything: Dynamic memory networks for natural language processing. In *ICML*.
[19] Qiang Liu, Shu Wu, Diyi Wang, Zhaokang Li, and Liang Wang. 2016. Context-aware sequential recommendation. In *ICDM*.
[20] Julian McAuley, Christopher Targett, Qinfeng Shi, and Anton Van Den Hengel. 2015. Image-based recommendations on styles and substitutes. In *SIGIR*.
[21] Alexander Miller, Adam Fisch, Jesse Dodge, Amir-Hossein Karimi, Antoine Bordes, and Jason Weston. 2016. Key-value memory networks for directly reading documents. *EMNLP* (2016).
[22] Steffen Rendle, Christoph Freudenthaler, Zeno Gantner, and Lars Schmidt-Thieme. 2009. BPR: Bayesian personalized ranking from implicit feedback. In *UAI*.
[23] Steffen Rendle, Christoph Freudenthaler, and Lars Schmidt-Thieme. 2010. Factorizing personalized markov chains for next-basket recommendation. In *WWW*.
[24] Adam Santoro, Sergey Bartunov, Matthew Botvinick, Daan Wierstra, and Timothy Lillicrap. 2016. Meta-learning with memory-augmented neural networks. In *ICML*.
[25] Sainbayar Sukhbaatar, Jason Weston, Rob Fergus, et al. 2015. End-to-end memory networks. In *NIPS*.
[26] Yong Kiam Tan, Xinxing Xu, and Yong Liu. 2016. Improved recurrent neural networks for session-based recommendations. In *Proceedings of the 1st Workshop on DLRS*.
[27] Pengfei Wang, Jiafeng Guo, Yanyan Lan, Jun Xu, Shengxian Wan, and Xueqi Cheng. 2015. Learning hierarchical representation model for nextbasket recommendation. In *SIGIR*.
[28] Jason Weston, Sumit Chopra, and Antoine Bordes. 2015. Memory Networks. *ICLR* (2015).
[29] Xiang Wu, Qi Liu, Enhong Chen, Liang He, Jingsong Lv, Can Cao, and Guoping Hu. 2013. Personalized next-song recommendation in online karaokes. In *Recsys*.
[30] Liang Xiang, Quan Yuan, Shiwan Zhao, Li Chen, Xiatian Zhang, Qing Yang, and Jimeng Sun. 2010. Temporal recommendation on graphs via long-and short-term preference fusion. In *KDD*.
[31] Feng Yu, Qiang Liu, Shu Wu, Liang Wang, and Tieniu Tan. 2016. A dynamic recurrent model for next basket recommendation. In *SIGIR*.
[32] Jiani Zhang, Xingjian Shi, Irwin King, and Dit-Yan Yeung. 2017. Dynamic Key-Value Memory Networks for Knowledge Tracing. In *WWW*.
[33] Yongfeng Zhang. 2015. Incorporating phrase-level sentiment analysis on textual reviews for personalized recommendation. In *WSDM*.
[34] Yongfeng Zhang, Guokun Lai, Min Zhang, Yi Zhang, Yiqun Liu, and Shaoping Ma. 2014. Explicit factor models for explainable recommendation based on phrase-level sentiment analysis. In *SIGIR*.
[35] Yongfeng Zhang, Min Zhang, Yiqun Liu, Chua Tat-Seng, Yi Zhang, and Shaoping Ma. 2015. Task-based recommendation on a web-scale. In *BigData*.

VISIR: Visual and Semantic Image Label Refinement

Sreyasi Nag Chowdhury* Niket Tandon† Hakan Ferhatosmanoglu‡ Gerhard Weikum*

sreyasi@mpi-inf.mpg.de nikett@allenai.org hakan.f@warwick.ac.uk weikum@mpi-inf.mpg.de

*Max Planck Institute for Informatics † Allen Institute for Artificial Intelligence ‡ University of Warwick

ABSTRACT

The social media explosion has populated the Internet with a wealth of images. There are two existing paradigms for image retrieval: 1) content-based image retrieval (CBIR), which has traditionally used visual features for similarity search (e.g., SIFT features), and 2) tag-based image retrieval (TBIR), which has relied on user tagging (e.g., Flickr tags). CBIR now gains semantic expressiveness by advances in deep-learning-based detection of visual labels. TBIR benefits from query-and-click logs to automatically infer more informative labels. However, learning-based tagging still yields noisy labels and is restricted to concrete objects, missing out on generalizations and abstractions. Click-based tagging is limited to terms that appear in the textual context of an image or in queries that lead to a click. This paper addresses the above limitations by semantically refining and expanding the labels suggested by learning-based object detection. We consider the semantic coherence between the labels for different objects, leverage lexical and commonsense knowledge, and cast the label assignment into a constrained optimization problem solved by an integer linear program. Experiments show that our method, called VISIR, improves the quality of the state-of-the-art visual labeling tools like LSDA and YOLO.

ACM Reference Format:

Sreyasi Nag Chowdhury, Niket Tandon, Hakan Ferhatosmanoglu, Gerhard Weikum. 2018. VISIR: Visual and Semantic Image Label Refinement. In *Proceedings of WSDM 2018: The Eleventh ACM International Conference on Web Search and Data Mining (WSDM 2018).* ACM, New York, NY, USA, 9 pages. https://doi.org/10.1145/3159652.3159693

1 INTRODUCTION

Motivation and Problem: The enormous growth of social media has populated the Internet with a wealth of images. On one hand, this makes image search easier, as there is redundancy for many keywords with informative text surrounding the images. On the other hand, it makes search harder, as there is a huge amount of visual contents that is hardly understood by the search engine. There are two paradigms for searching images: content-based image retrieval (CBIR) and tag-based image retrieval (TBIR).

CBIR finds images similar to a query image based on visual features that are used to represent an image. These features include color, shape, texture, SIFT descriptors etc. (e.g., [2, 7, 20]). Recent

WSDM 2018, February 5–9, 2018, Marina Del Rey, CA, USA

ACM ISBN 978-1-4503-5581-0/18/02...$15.00

https://doi.org/10.1145/3159652.3159693

(a) (b)

Figure 1: Noisy and Incomplete Labels: a) from LSDA [16] - *dog, Browning machine gun, greater kudu, bird* b) from flickr.com - *happiness*

advances in deep-learning-based object detection have lifted this approach to a higher level, by assigning object labels to bounding boxes (e.g., [16, 35, 37, 42]). However, these labels are limited to concrete object classes (e.g., *truck, SUV, Toyota Yaris Hybrid 2016,*

	LSDA Labels	VISIR labels
	allosaurus loggerhead turtle person bird	person guitar *stringed instrument* *self-expression*
	bone china stove WC, loo cup or mug	food processor bowl cup or mug *utensil*
	cucumber snake green mamba	snake *reptile* *slithery* *poisonous*
	racket person bathing cap tennis ball head cabbage	tennis bat *individual* *play tennis* tennis ball

Figure 2: Images with labels from LSDA and VISIR

etc.), often trained (only) on (subsets of) the ca. 20,000 classes of ImageNet [8]. Thus, they miss out on generalizations (e.g., *vehicle*) and abstractions (e.g., *transportation, traffic jam, rush hour*). Fig 1 (a) shows the top-confidence visual labels by LSDA [16] for an example case of incorrect labels.

TBIR retrieves images by textual matches between user query and manually assigned image tags (e.g., from collaborative communities such as Flickr). While some of the semantic gap in CBIR is reduced in TBIR, the performance of TBIR often suffers from incomplete and ambiguous tags [15]. Figure 1 (b) illustrates this point: there is only a single tag *happiness* and none for the concrete objects in the image. For the big search engines, one way of overcoming this bottleneck is to exploit query-and-click logs (e.g., [6, 17, 45]). The query keyword(s) associated with a click can be treated as label(s) for the clicked image. However, this method crucially relies on the labels to appear in (sufficiently many) queries (or, traditionally, salient text surrounding the image). [22] gives a survey on TBIR and tag assignment and refinement.

Recently, the gap between the two image search paradigms is narrowing. TBIR-style tags inferred from query-and-click logs can be used to train a deep-learning network for more informative labels towards better CBIR. Also, crowdsourcing could be a way towards more semantic labels (e.g., [19]), for example, to capture human activities or emotions (e.g., [9, 13, 18, 33]). Nevertheless, there are still major shortcomings in the state-of-the-art.

This paper addresses the outlined limitations. The goal is to automatically annotate images with semantically informative tags, including generalizations and abstractions and also cleaning out noisy labels for concrete objects.

Approach and Contribution: We leverage state-of-the-art CBIR by considering the visual tags of an existing object detection tool (LSDA [16] in our experiments) as a starting point. Note that there are multiple labels for each bounding box with varying confidence scores, and our goal is to compute the most informative labels for the entire image. We impose a constrained optimization on these initial labels, in order to enforce their semantic coherence. We also consider labels that are visually similar to the detected ones, to compensate for omissions. In addition, we utilize lexical and commonsense knowledge to generate candidate labels for generalizations (hypernyms from WordNet [30]) and abstractions (concepts from ConceptNet [40]). So we both refine and expand the initial labels. The joint inference on the entire label space is modeled as an optimization problem, solved by an integer linear program (viz. using the Gurobi ILP solver). Figure 2 shows examples for the input labels from the deep-learning-based visual object detection (left column) and the output labels that VISIR computes (right column). The labels from LSDA illustrate a clear semantic incoherence for these specific examples. VISIR labels are coherent, adds generalizations (in blue) and abstractions (in green). Incorrect labels are marked red. Although our work aligns with the existing TBIR research on social tagging and tag refinement, there are key differences.

Granularity: Our starting point is labels for bounding boxes, whereas user-provided tags refer to an entire image.
Cardinality: The number of bounding boxes in one image can be quite large. Moreover, object detectors usually produce a long list of varying-confidence labels for each bounding box.
Noise: As a result, many of the visual candidate labels in our approach are of mixed quality, whereas traditional social tagging typically has few but trusted annotations per image.
For these factors, our notion of tag refinement is unlike the one in prior work. Therefore, we refer to our task as *Visual Tag Refinement.*

Visual Tag Refinement can be broken down into three sub-tasks, for which this paper provides effective solutions:
1) elimination of incoherent tags [1] among the initial visual labels,
2) expansion of the tag space by adding visually similar tags missed by object detectors, and adding candidate tags for generalization and abstraction, 3) joint inference on the enriched tag space, by integer linear program.

2 RELATED WORK

Automatic Image Annotation: Early work on this problem generated tags only for an entire image (or a single image region), but did so one class at a time (e.g., [1]). More recent methods support labeling multiple objects in the same image. One such approach, WSABIE [44], performs k-nearest-neighbor classification on embeddings of words and features to scale to many classes.

State-of-the-art work on object detection addresses both recognizing object bounding boxes and tagging them with their class labels. Such work makes heavy use of deep learning (especially convolutional neural networks or CNNs). Prominent representatives are LSDA [16], and Faster R-CNN. The latter [37] improves the speed of object detection by incorporating a Region Proposal Network (RPN). Major emphasis in this line of Computer Vision work has been on coping with small, partly occluded and poorly illuminated objects. In contrast, the emphasis of VISIR is on the semantic coherence between objects and jointly modeling the uncertainty of candidate labels. Instead of speed, we optimize for higher labeling quality. VISIR is agnostic of the underlying object detector; it is straightforward to plug in a different tool.

Context plays an important role in computer vision [10], and context-based object detectors were popular before the success of CNNs. These methods consider local context [3], global context [32] or their combination [48]. With the advent of CNNs, the focus shifted to representation learning and improving detection speed. However, contextual information is gaining renewed attention. The state-of-the-art method [43] is based on a CNN-RNN combination, where the recurrent neural network (RNN) captures label dependencies. YOLO [35, 36] unifies learning with global context into a single neural network for the entire image. It exploits a word tree derived from the WordNet whose leaf nodes appear in ImageNet. In our experiments, we use YOLO as a baseline for context-aware object detection. All learning-based methods crucially rely on extensive training data.

Social Tagging: TBIR has its origin in community-based social tagging of images (e.g., Flickr), web pages or publications (e.g., Bibsonomy). Crowdsourcing to compile large training collections can be seen as a variant of this kind of user-provided tagging. There is ample research in this area [12, 21, 28], especially on learning tag recommendations. Our task of visual tag refinement differs from social tagging substantially. The CBIR-based tags that we start with,

[1] "tag" and "label" are used interchangeably in the paper with the same meaning.

label individual objects instead of assigning tags to the overall image. Multiple candidate tags per bounding box also lead to a dense tag space in contrast to sparse user tags. Finally, the large number of varying-granularity and varying-confidence tags per image entails a much higher degree of noise in the label space, whereas social tags are usually considered trusted.

Tag Refinement: The problem of tag refinement aims at removing noisy tags from images while adding more relevant ones [22]. This line of work appears in the literature also as tag completion [11, 46] or image re-tagging [24, 25]. Most of this work uses only nouns as tags and disregards word ambiguity. Background knowledge, such as WordNet synonymy sets and other lexical relations, is rarely used. Word categories that are vital for denoting abstractions, namely, adjectives, verbs and verbal phrases, are out of scope. Moreover a common assumption is that visually similar images are semantically similar, meaning that they should have similar tags. This assumption is often invalid. This body of work employs a variety of methods, including metric learning [14], matrix completion [11, 46, 50], latent topic models [47], and more.

Commonsense Knowledge for Image Retrieval: The first work on image retrieval with commonsense knowledge (CSK) [26] exploited the Open Mind Commonsense Knowledgebase [39], a small knowledge base with simple properties of concepts for concept expansion and for activation spreading. Since then, much more comprehensive CSK knowledge bases have been constructed, most notably, ConceptNet [40] and WebChild [41]. However, such background knowledge has not been used by modern object detectors. A notable exception addresses emotions invoked by images, and tags objects with sentiment-bearing adjectives [4]. However, this work is limited to a small label space. A recent framework for image search [5] uses CSK extracted through OpenIE for query expansion.

3 MODEL AND METHODOLOGY

We define the problem of *Visual Tag Refinement* as the tasks of –
1) cleaning noisy object tags from low-level image features
2) enriching existing detections by adding additional relevant tags
3) abstracting from concrete objects towards a more conceptual space. We first present a framework for the proposed problem, followed by the description of its individual components. We then present the optimization model to solve the problem.

3.1 Framework for Visual Tag Refinement

We consider an image x with multiple bounding boxes $x_1, x_2, ...x_k$. Each bounding box x_i has labels for detected physical objects along with detection confidence scores. The values of these labels and scores are outputs of an off-the-shelf object detection tool, e.g., LSDA [16]. We define three different label spaces, candidates from which would be associated either with bounding boxes of an image or would globally add semantics to it:

- A space of all possible object labels detectable by an underlying object detection tool is denoted by CL (for Concrete-object Labels). For example, the LSDA tool [16] uses ImageNet [8] object classes, which are also leaf-level synsets of WordNet [30]. There can be two sets of such classes for a bounding box x_i of image x: cl_i constitute those labels originally detected from low-level image features, cl'_i constitute undetected labels visually similar to those in cl_i.
- A space of extended labels is denoted by XL. For each image x and bounding box x_i, a subset from this space, xl_i, contains additional label candidates that generalize the classes in cl_i and cl'_i. For example, "ant" $\in cl_i \rightarrow$ "insect" $\in xl_i$. Adding generalized terms to the label space serves a dual purpose - overcoming the training bias of the object detection tools, and broadening the label space for greater web visibility. We discuss more on the issue of training bias in section 6.

  CL and XL contain labels signifying visual objects in an image. Hence we call the super set of such labels "visual labels" VL; $VL = CL \cup XL$.
- A space of abstract labels (utilities, emotions, themes) is denoted by AL. This constitutes abstract concepts associated with visual objects derived from commonsense knowledge bases. For example, *fragrant* $\in AL$ from the ConceptNet [27] clause `hasProperty(flower, fragrant)`.

An image x can hence be described by three sets of labels - a set of deep-learning based class labels $cl \cup cl' \in CL$, a set of extended labels $xl \in XL$, and a set of abstract labels $al \in AL$. Further, we define three different scores that act as edges between nodes of the above spaces:

- Visual Similarity $vsim(l_j, l_k)$ for $l_j, l_k \in CL$
- Semantic Relatedness $srel(l_j, l_k)$ for $l_j, l_k \in VL$
- Abstraction Confidence $aconf(l_j, al_n)$ for $al_n \in AL$ and $l_j \in VL$

We present the visual tag refinement problem in terms of three sub-problems:

- The noisy tag problem - for each image x and bounding box x_i infer which of the labels in $cl_i \in CL$ should be accepted. We eliminate those labels which are not coherent with the other bounding box detections in the image. For example, in Figure 2 image 5 we eliminate the detection *cucumber* since it is not semantically related to the other labels *snake* and *green mamba*.
- The incomplete tag problem - for each image x and bounding box x_i infer which of the labels in $cl'_i \in CL$ and $xl_i \in XL$ should be additionally associated with the bounding box.
- The abstraction tag problem - infer which of $al \in AL$ should be globally associated with image x.

We solve these problems jointly and retain the most confident hypothesis for each bounding box relative to the others as well as a global hypothesis toward tag abstraction in an image. Hence, we predict a set of plausible labels $L_x \in CL \cup XL \cup AL$ for an image x.

3.2 Visual Similarity (or "Confusability")

Deep-learning based tools using low-level image features to predict the object classes can confuse one object to be another. We consider two labels to be visually similar if they occur as candidates in cl_i for the same bounding box x_i. We collect evidence of such visual similarity from low-level image features, in particular, from object detection results of LSDA [16]. We define the visual similarity between two labels l_j and l_k by a Jaccard-style similarity measure as shown in Equation 1. In this similarity measure, if labels l_j and l_k always appear together as candidates for the same bounding box, and never with any other labels, then they are considered highly visually similar, $vsim(l_j, l_k) = 1$. If labels l_j and l_k never appear together, one label is never confused by the tool to be another; in this case $vsim(l_j, l_k) = 0$, meaning l_j and l_k are not visually similar. Given that the initial object detections from low level image features are noisy in itself, this evidence would also contain noise. However, it is expected that the evidence will hold when it is computed over a large dataset.

$$vsim(l_j, l_k) = \frac{\sum\limits_{i:l_j, l_k \in cl_i} (conf_{BB}(x_i, l_j) + conf_{BB}(x_i, l_k))}{\sum\limits_{i:l_j \in cl_i} (conf_{BB}(x_i, l_j)) + \sum\limits_{i:l_k \in cl_i} (conf_{BB}(x_i, l_k))} \quad (1)$$

We can refer to this measure also as "confusability" since the object detection tool confuses one object to be another based on similar low-level visual features.

3.3 Semantic Relatedness

Semantic Relatedness between two concepts signifies their conceptual similarity. Our model uses this measure to establish the contextual coherence between labels of different bounding boxes. The relatedness between two labels l_j and l_k is defined as a weighted linear combination of their cosine similarity from word embeddings and their spatial co-location confidence.

$$srel(l_j, l_k) = \delta cosine(l_j, l_k) + (1 - \delta) coloc(l_j, l_k) \quad for\ l_j, l_k \in VL \quad (2)$$

Word Embeddings: To improve the contextual coherence between object labels in images, the context of words needs to be captured. We utilize vector space word embeddings for this purpose. A word2vec [29] model is trained from manually annotated image descriptions from a large set of image captions, as described later in more details. The cosine similarity between two labels – $cosine(.,.)$ in Equation 2 – is calculated from their respective word vectors.

Spatial Co-location: Spatial relationships between concepts carry an important evidence of relatedness. For example, an "apple" and a "table" are related concepts since they occur in close spatial proximity. Similarly, a "tennis racket" and a "lemon" are unrelated. $coloc(.,.)$ in Equation 2 is a frequency-based co-location score mined from manual annotations of image labels.

3.4 Concept Generalization

A hypernym is a superordinate of a concept. In other words, a concept is an instantiation of its hypernym. For example, *fruit* is a hypernym for *apple*, i.e., *apple* IsA *fruit*. WordNet [30] provides a hierarchy of concepts and their hypernyms which we leverage to generalize our object classes. WordNet also reports different meanings (senses) of a concept; for example a *punching bag* is (*a person on whom another person vents their anger*) or (*an inflated ball or bag that is suspended and punched for training in boxing*), leading to very different hypernymy trees. For this reason, we map our object classes from ImageNet into their correct WordNet sense number, followed by traversing their hypernymy tree up to a certain level. This yields a cleaner generalization. Further more, to avoid exotic words among the hypernyms, we use their approximate Google result counts and prune out those below a threshold. Hence for the concept *ant* we retain the hypernym *insect* and prune the hypernym *hymenopteran*. Following this heuristics, we assign 1 to 3 hypernyms per object class.

3.5 Concept Abstraction

To introduce human factors like commonsense and subjective perception, we incorporate abstract words and phrases associated with visual concepts of an image. For example an *accordion* is "used to" *make music*. We consider two relations from ConceptNet 5 [27] for assigning the abstract labels - *usedFor*, and *hasProperty*. Some example of assigned abstract labels/phrases (in green) can be found in Figure 2. Abstract concepts which are assigned to images have high abstraction confidence. Abstraction confidence of a concept/phrase is defined as the joint semantic relatedness of the phrase and the refined visual labels of the image.

3.6 Tag Refinement Modeled as an ILP

We cast the multi-label visual tag refinement problem into an Integer Linear Program (ILP) optimization with the following definitions. We choose ILP as it is a very expressive framework for modeling constrained optimization (more powerful than probabilistic graphical models), and at the same time comes with very mature and efficient solvers like Gurobi (http://gurobi.com). Some tools for probabilistic graphical models even use ILP for efficient MAP inference.

Given an image x, with bounding boxes $x_1, x_2, \ldots$, it has three sets of visual labels: cl_i (initial bounding box labels), cl'_i (labels visually similar to the original detections), and xl_i (hypernyms of labels in $cl_i \cup cl'_i$). The set $vl_i = cl_i \cup cl'_i \cup xl_i$ constitutes all visual labels which are candidates for bounding box x_i. The image would also be assigned abstract labels $al_1, al_2, \ldots$ globally. We thus introduce 0-1 decision variables:

$X_{ij} = 1$ if x_i should indeed have visual label vl_j, 0 otherwise
$Y_j = 1$ if x should indeed have abstract label al_j, 0 otherwise
$Z_{ijmk} = 1$ if $X_{ij} = 1$ and $X_{mk} = 1$, 0 otherwise
$W_{ijk} = 1$ if $X_{ij} = 1$ and $Y_k = 1$, 0 otherwise
Decision variables Z_{ijmk} and W_{ijk} emphasise pair-wise coherence between two visual labels and between a visual and an abstract label respectively.

Objective: Select labels for x and its bounding boxes which maximizes a weighted sum of evidence and coherence –

$$max \Bigg[\alpha \sum_{i,j} (vconf(x_i, l_j) + \kappa gconf(x_i, l_j)) X_{ij} + \beta \sum_{i,m} \sum_{\substack{l_j \in vl_i \\ l_k \in vl_m}} srel(l_j, l_k) Z_{ijmk} + \gamma \sum_{l_j \in VL} \sum_{k} aconf(l_j, al_k) \sum_{i} W_{ijk} \Bigg] \quad (3)$$

with hyper-parameters $\alpha, \beta, \gamma, \kappa$.

For each $l \in CL$, we define set $S(l) \subseteq CL$ of labels visually similar to l. $vsim(l, l') = 0$ if $l' \notin S(l)$. Recall the definition of $vsim(.,,)$ from Equation 1.

Visual Confidence, the confidence with which a visual label should be associated with an image is defined as:

$$vconf(x_i, l_j) = conf_{BB}(x_i, l_j) \text{ if } l_j \in cl_i \tag{4}$$

$$= \sum_{l \in cl_i} conf_{BB}(x_i, l) vsim(l, l_j) \text{ if } l_j \in cl_i'/cl_i \tag{5}$$

Here, a high confident original detection adds significant weight to the objective function, hence increasing the chances of its retention. Similarly, the weight of a label visually similar to multiple original labels is boosted. Also, labels visually similar to only one low confident original label is assigned less importance.

For $l \in CL$ we define a set $H(l) \in XL$ of hypernyms of l. The *Generalization Confidence* of a label l_j in bounding box x_i is defined in terms of the semantic relatedness between the label and its hypernym.

$$gconf(x_i, l_j) = \sum_{l: l_j \in H(l)} srel(l_j, l) \; if \; l_j \in xl_i \tag{6}$$

$$= 0 \; if \; l_j \in \{cl_i \cup cl_i'\} \tag{7}$$

Abstraction Confidence $aconf(.,.)$ of a label l_j and an abstract concept al_k is defined as their semantic relatedness, weighted by the score of the assertion containing the abstract concept in ConceptNet [27]. For example, `hasProperty(baby, newborn)` has a score of 10.17 in ConceptNet. We name this score $CNet(al_k)$.

$$aconf(l_j, al_k) = CNet(al_k) * srel(l_j, al_k) \tag{8}$$

Constraints:

$\sum_j X_{ij} <= 1$: for each bounding box x_i there can be at most one visual label ($\in VL$)

$\sum_j Y_j <= 5$: one image x can have at most five abstract labels ($\in AL$)

$$\left.\begin{aligned} (1 - Z_{ijmk}) &<= (1 - X_{ij}) + (1 - X_{mk}) \\ Z_{ijmk} &<= X_{ij} \\ Z_{ijmk} &<= X_{mk} \end{aligned}\right\} \text{Pair-wise mutual coherence between visual labels}$$

$$\left.\begin{aligned} (1 - W_{ijk}) &<= (1 - X_{ij}) + (1 - Y_k) \\ W_{ijk} &<= X_{ij} \\ W_{ijk} &<= Y_k \end{aligned}\right\} \text{Pair-wise mutual coherence between visual and abstract labels}$$

The final set of visual and abstract labels per image are expected to be highly coherent. This is validated in Section 5.

4 DATA SETS AND TOOLS

In this section, we present the image data sets as well as the criteria and heuristics we follow to mine the various background knowledge utilized in our optimization model.

ImageNet Object Classes: LSDA [16] is used to get the initial visual object labels from low-level image features. The LSDA tool has been trained on 7604 leaf-level nodes of ImageNet [8]. Most of these object classes are exotic concepts which rarely occur in everyday images. Examples include scientific names of flora and fauna – *interior live oak, Quercus wislizenii, American white oak, Quercus alba*, and obscure terms – *pannikin, reliquary, lacrosse*. We prune those exotic classes by thresholding on their Google and Flickr search result counts. Some object class names are ambiguous where two senses of the same word from WordNet have been included. We consider only the most common sense. We work with the most frequent 1000 object classes obtained after pruning [2].

WordNet Hypernyms: For the ImageNet object classes described above, we traverse the WordNet hypernymy tree of the associated sense up to level three. We restrict the traversal level to avoid too much generalization – for example, *person* generalizing to *organism*. We prune out hypernyms with Google and Flickr result counts below a threshold. By considering the hypernyms of the 1000 ImageNet object classes mentioned above, we add 800 new visual labels to the model.

The ImageNet object classes and the WordNet hypernyms together constitute the **Visual Labels** of VISIR.

Abstract Labels: Commonsense knowledge (CSK) assertions from ConceptNet [40] contribute to concept abstraction in VISIR. For example, in Figure 2, the abstract concept *poisonous* is added to the labels of the fifth image. ConceptNet is a crowd-sourced knowledge base where most assertions have the default confidence score of 1.0 (as they were stated only by one person). Only popular statements like `hasProperty(apple, red fruit)` are stated by multiple people, hence raising the confidence score significantly. Certain assertions have contradictory scores – for example, `usedFor(acne medicine, clear skin)` appears twice, with scores 1.0 and -1.0. This happens when someone down-votes a statement. Using such indistinctive scores in VISIR would be uninformative. We therefore use the joint semantic relatedness of the assertion and visual labels of an image, weighted by the ConceptNet score (only positive scores), as the abstraction confidence.

Visual Similarity: The visual similarity or "confusability" scores (Equation 1) are mined from object detection results (from low-level image features) over 1 million images from the following data sets that are popularly employed in the computer vision community: Flickr 30k [49], Pascal Sentence Dataset [34], SBU Image Dataset [31], MS-COCO [23]. All these data sets have collections of Flickr images not pertaining to any particular domain. For each detected bounding box, LSDA provides a confidence score distribution over 7604 object classes (leaf nodes in ImageNet). Only predictions with a positive confidence score are considered as candidates for a bounding box. An object class pair appearing as candidates for the same bounding box are considered as visually similar. Table 1 shows few examples of visually similar object class pairs – *mail train* and *commuter train* are confused 91% times whereas *diaper* and *plaster cast* are confused 18% times.

Spatial Co-location: Spatial co-location scores between different object classes are mined from ground truth annotations of the detection challenge (DET) of ImageNet ILSVRC 2015 [38]. We consider two objects to be spatially co-located only if they are tagged in the same image. For simplicity, we do not consider the physical distance between the bounding boxes of the tagged object classes.

[2]The full list is available at http://people.mpi-inf.mpg.de/~sreyasi/visTagRef/1000classes_names.txt

Table 1: Object class pairs and visual similarity scores

object1	object2	visual similarity
mail train	commuter train	0.91
cattle	horse	0.76
soccer ball	kite baloon	0.26
Red Delicious	bowling ball	0.21
diaper	plaster cast	0.18
bicycle pump	mascara	0.17

A frequency-based co-location score is assigned to pairs of object classes based on evidence over the train set of ILSVRC DET. We find spatial co-location data for 200 object classes (since the detection challenge only considers 200 object classes). The top few frequently co-located objects are: *(person, microphone), (table, chair), (person, sunglasses), (person, table), (person, chair).* A general observation would be that the image collection in ILSVRC DET has a high occurrence of *person*.

5 EXPERIMENTS AND RESULTS

We analyze and compare the results that VISIR produces with that of two baselines: LSDA [3] and YOLO [4]. The performances of LSDA, YOLO, and VISIR are compared on the basis of precision, recall and F1-score measures.

5.1 Setup

As discussed in Section 3.1, we operate with three kinds of labels: visual class labels from ImageNet (*CL*), their generalizations (*XL*) which consist of WordNet hypernyms of labels $\in CL$, and abstract labels (*AL*) from commonsense knowledge. We evaluate the methods with respect to three different label spaces (as the combination of three types of labels): CL, $CL + XL$, and $CL + XL + AL$. LSDA and YOLO operate only on CL, while VISIR has three variants (configuring it for the above combinations of label spaces). Each system is given a label budget of 5 tags per image. For VISIR, this is enforced by an ILP constraint; for the two baselines, we use their confidence scores to pick the top-5.

Hyper-parameter Tuning: To tune the hyper-parameters for Equation 3 we use the annotations of the training image set of ILSVRC DET. We also extend this set by adding the hypernyms of the ground-truth labels as correct labels. A randomized search is used to tune the hyperparameters.

User Evaluation: Besides establishing semantic coherence among concrete object labels, VISIR applies concept generalization and abstraction. For modern benchmark datasets like ILSVRC 2015 DET, such enriched labeling does not exist so far. Therefore, in order to evaluate VISIR and compare to baselines, we construct a labeled image dataset by collecting human judgments about correctness of labels as discussed below.

For each label space, CL, $CL+XL$, and $CL+XL+AL$, the union of the labels produced by each method forms the set of result labels for an image. This result pool is evaluated by human annotators. Judges determined whether each label is appropriate and informative for an image. Instead of a binary assessments, annotators are asked to grade each label in the pool with 0, 1, or 2 – 0 corresponding to incorrect labels, 2 corresponding to highly relevant labels. We gather user judgments for the three label pools (corresponding to the label spaces) separately. This produces three different sets of graded labels per image. Users are not informed about the nature of the label pools. For each label pool we collect responses from at least 5 judges. The final assessment is determined by the majority of the judges (e.g., at least 3 out of 5 need to assert that a label is good).

[3]http://lsda.berkeleyvision.org/
[4]https://pjreddie.com/darknet/yolo/

Selection of Test Images: A major goal of this work is to make the refined labels more coherent or semantically related. Hence, we focus on the case where the deep-learning-based object detection tools produce contextually incoherent results. For the user evaluation, we collect a set of images with a reasonable context – those that have 3-7 detected bounding boxes and with LSDA labels having a semantic relatedness score less than 0.1. Such 100 images are collected from the ILSVRC 2015 DET Val image set.

5.2 Model Performance

Precision is estimated as the fraction of "good labels" detected, where a "good label" is one considered relevant by the majority of the human judges. We assess the recall per method as the number of labels picked from the good labels in the pool of labels generated by all three methods. The recall is artificially restricted because the label pool may contain more good labels than the label budget of the method. For example, if the label budget per method is set to 5, even if all 5 labels of a method are good, the recall for a pool with 8 good labels would only be 5/8. However, it is a fair notion across the different methods.

Relaxed vs Conservative Assessments: According to the evaluation design, labels graded 1 are either inconspicuous, or less relevant to the image than labels graded 2. In order to identify the "good labels" in a label pool, we define two methods of assessment: *Relaxed Assessment* considers all labels graded 1 or 2 as correct. *Conservative Assessment* considers only those labels graded 2 as correct, resulting in a stricter setup. The three graded label pools from the user evaluations naturally have labels in common.

Performance Results: Tables 2 through 4 compare the three methods for the three different label pools – CL, $CL + XL$, $CL + XL + AL$ – with conservative assessment. For CL, there is no real improvement over LSDA, but we see that for $CL + XL$ and $CL + AL + XL$ VISIR adds a good number of semantically informative labels and improves on the two baselines in terms of both precision and recall.

We also test VISIR's performance with a tighter constraint on choosing the number of bounding boxes per image, by setting the label budget to 80% of all bounding boxes received as input. This variant, which we refer to as VISIR*, aims to filter out more noise in the output of the deep-learning-based object detections. Naturally, VISIR*-CL would have higher precision than VISIR-CL while sacrificing on recall. VISIR*-CL improves further on precision and F1-score because it is able to eliminate some of the initial noise the LSDA detections bring in. For pools $CL + XL$ and $CL + XL + AL$, VISIR* has higher precision than VISIR, but slighly loses in recall.

Table 2: Pool CL: Conservative Assessment

System	Precision	Recall	F1-score
LSDA	0.51	0.86	0.64
YOLO	0.49	0.56	0.52
VISIR-CL	0.51	0.86	0.64
VISIR*-CL	**0.57**	0.81	**0.67**

Table 3: Pool CL+XL: Conservative Assessment

System	Precision	Recall	F1-score
LSDA	0.52	0.81	0.63
YOLO	0.49	0.51	0.50
VISIR-CL+XL	**0.54**	**0.82**	**0.65**
VISIR*-CL+XL	**0.60**	0.76	**0.67**

Table 4: Pool CL+XL+AL: Conservative Assessment

System	Precision	Recall	F1-score
LSDA	0.49	0.35	0.41
YOLO	0.52	0.23	0.32
VISIR-CL+XL+AL	**0.54**	**0.91**	**0.68**
VISIR*-CL+XL+AL	**0.56**	**0.89**	**0.69**

Table 5 and Table 6 show the relaxed and conservative assessments with respect to the combined pool (i.e., for all three label spaces together) of good labels per image. It is natural that all methods perform better for the relaxed setting compared to that of the conservative assessment. However, the observation that VISIR's performance does not degrade much for the conservative assessment demonstrates its high output quality and robustness. Figure 3 illustrates this by anecdotal examples with the labels assigned by each of the competitors (with good labels in black and bad ones in red). In image 4, LSDA produces typically unrelated labels – a *monkey* and a *tennis ball.* This contextual incoherence likely arises due to low level color features. In contrast to LSDA, YOLO addresses the semantic coherence of the labels, however likely in expense of recall (for example in image 6). By necessitating semantic coherence among detected labels VISIR eliminates incoherent labels - for example, VISIR removes *motorcycle* from image 1, *tennis ball* from image 4, *hat with a wide brim* from image 5 and so on.

Table 5: Aggregate Pool: Relaxed Assessment

System	Precision	Recall	F1-score
LSDA	0.55	0.30	0.39
YOLO	0.57	0.19	0.29
VISIR-CL	**0.57**	0.28	0.38
VISIR-CL+XL	**0.62**	0.30	**0.40**
VISIR-CL+XL+AL	**0.71**	**0.90**	**0.79**

Table 7 lists the new labels introduced by VISIR, each for at least 10 images. These labels are generated via generalization (from WordNet hypernyms) and abstraction (from commonsense knowledge). As none of the baselines can produce these labels, VISIR naturally achieves a recall of 1. The precision values for the labels illustrate how VISIR addresses the problem of label incompleteness. In most cases, these labels were assessed as correct by the judges.

Table 6: Aggregate Pool: Conservative Assessment

System	Precision	Recall	F1-score
LSDA	0.49	0.35	0.41
YOLO	0.52	0.23	0.32
VISIR-CL	**0.52**	0.34	0.41
VISIR-CL+XL	**0.55**	**0.35**	**0.43**
VISIR-CL+XL+AL	**0.54**	**0.91**	**0.68**

Table 7: New labels suggested by VISIR

Label	Label frequency	Precision
individual	46	0.59
man or woman	44	0.64
animal	31	0.94
human	20	0.95
canine	18	0.94
furniture	12	0.83
barking animal	11	1.00

6 DISCUSSION OF LIMITATIONS

Training Bias in LSDA: The LSDA tool predicts only leaf-level object classes of ImageNet. The same limitation holds for most other state-of-the-art object detectors. Because of this incomplete tag space many important objects cannot be detected. For example, *giraffe* is not a leaf-level object class of ImageNet. Since LSDA did not see any training images of a giraffe, it mis-labels objects in Figure 1a according to its training. This noise propagates to our model, sometimes making it impossible to find the correct labels.

Incorrect Sense Mapping in ImageNet: LSDA trains on ImageNet images. Hence improper word sense mappings in ImageNet propagate to incorrect labels from LSDA. For example, ImageNet contains similar images for two separate synsets *Sunglass (a convex lens used to start a fire)* and *Sunglasses (shades, dark glasses).* Naturally, these two synsets have completely different WordNet hypernyms which VISIR uses, hence introducing noise. The direct hypernym of *Sunglass* is *lens,* while that of *Sunglasses* is *glasses.*

Incomplete Spatial Co-location data: Spatial co-location patterns mined from text contain noise due to linguistic variations in the form of proverbs. For example, the commonsense knowledge base WebChild [41] assigns significant confidence to the spatial co-location of *elephant* and *room* (most likely from the idiom "the elephant in the room"). To counter such linguistic bias, we have mined spatial co-location information from the manually annotated ground truth of ILSVRC [38]. Unfortunately, annotations are available for only 200 object classes, leaving us with only a small fraction of annotated visual-label pairs. If more cues of this kind were available, we would have been able to establish stronger contextual coherence.

Incomplete and Noisy Commonsense Knowledge: ConceptNet and WebChild are quite incomplete; so we cannot assign an abstract concept to every detected visual label. Also, assertions in these knowledge bases are often contradictory and noisy. We manage to reduce the noise by considering semantic relatedness with the visual labels, but this only alleviates part of the problem.

	LSDA	YOLO	VISIR-CL	VISIR-CL+XL	VISIR-CL+XL+AL
	person table motorcycle	bench person bowl	person table	person table	person table man or woman furniture
	table car	tow truck bench car chair	table chair	table chair	seat furniture chair flat dining furniture table
	monkey tennis ball	bird dog	monkey	monkey	primate monkey orangutan ape simian furry
	bird hat with a wide brim	airplane bird	bird	bird	bird avian flying animal
	helmet person watercraft smelling bottle bathing cap record sleeve impeller	person	bathing cap bib watercraft helmet person	bathing cap fabric watercraft helmet person	bathing cap cloth, fabric watercraft helmet protective hat individual person
	table baby bed swimming trunks	chair	chair table	chair table	seat furniture chair table flat

Figure 3: Images with labels from LSDA, YOLO, and different configurations of VISIR

7 CONCLUSION

We presented VISIR, a new method for refining and expanding visual labels for images. Its key strengths are cleaning out noisy labels from predictions by object detection tools and adding informative labels that capture generalizations and abstractions. Our model makes this feasible by considering the visual similarity of labels, the semantic coherence across concepts, and various kinds of background knowledge. The joint inference on an enriched label candidate space is performed by means of a judiciously designed Integer Linear Program. Our experiments show the viability of the approach, and also demonstrate significant improvements over two state-of-the-art object detection and tagging tools.

ACKNOWLEDGEMENTS

This work was partly supported by the Alexander von Humboldt Foundation.

REFERENCES

[1] Emre Akbas and Fatos T. Yarman-Vural. 2007. Automatic Image Annotation by Ensemble of Visual Descriptors. In *CVPR*. https://doi.org/10.1109/CVPR.2007.383484

[2] Relja Arandjelovic and Andrew Zisserman. 2012. Three things everyone should know to improve object retrieval. In *CVPR*. https://doi.org/10.1109/CVPR.2012.6248018

[3] João Carreira, Fuxin Li, and Cristian Sminchisescu. 2012. Object Recognition by Sequential Figure-Ground Ranking. *International Journal of Computer Vision* (2012). https://doi.org/10.1007/s11263-011-0507-2

[4] Tao Chen, Felix X. Yu, Jiawei Chen, Yin Cui, Yan-Ying Chen, and Shih-Fu Chang. 2014. Object-Based Visual Sentiment Concept Analysis and Application. In *ACM MM*. http://doi.acm.org/10.1145/2647868.2654935

[5] Sreyasi Nag Chowdhury, Niket Tandon, and Gerhard Weikum. 2016. Know2Look: Commonsense Knowledge for Visual Search. In *5th Workshop on Automated Knowledge Base Construction, AKBC@NAACL-HLT*.

[6] Nick Craswell and Martin Szummer. 2007. Random Walks on the Click Graph. In *SIGIR*. http://doi.acm.org/10.1145/1277741.1277784

[7] Ritendra Datta, Dhiraj Joshi, Jia Li, and James Ze Wang. 2008. Image retrieval: Ideas, influences, and trends of the new age. *ACM Comput. Surv.* 40, 2 (2008), 5:1–5:60. http://doi.acm.org/10.1145/1348246.1348248

[8] Jia Deng, Wei Dong, Richard Socher, Li-Jia Li, Kai Li, and Fei-Fei Li. 2009. ImageNet: A large-scale hierarchical image database. In *CVPR*. https://doi.org/10.1109/CVPRW.2009.5206848

[9] Santosh Kumar Divvala, Ali Farhadi, and Carlos Guestrin. 2014. Learning Everything about Anything: Webly-Supervised Visual Concept Learning. In *CVPR*. https://doi.org/10.1109/CVPR.2014.412

[10] Santosh Kumar Divvala, Derek Hoiem, James Hays, Alexei A. Efros, and Martial Hebert. 2009. An Empirical Study of Context in Object Detection. In *CVPR*. https://doi.org/10.1109/CVPRW.2009.5206532

[11] Zheyun Feng, Songhe Feng, Rong Jin, and Anil K. Jain. 2014. Image Tag Completion by Noisy Matrix Recovery. In *ECCV*. https://doi.org/10.1007/978-3-319-10584-0_28

[12] Yue Gao, Meng Wang, Zheng-Jun Zha, Jialie Shen, Xuelong Li, and Xindong Wu. 2013. Visual-Textual Joint Relevance Learning for Tag-Based Social Image Search. *IEEE Trans. Image Processing* 22, 1 (2013), 363–376. https://doi.org/10.1109/TIP.2012.2202676

[13] Georgia Gkioxari, Ross B. Girshick, and Jitendra Malik. 2015. Contextual Action Recognition with R*CNN. In *ICCV*. https://doi.org/10.1109/ICCV.2015.129

[14] Matthieu Guillaumin, Thomas Mensink, Jakob J. Verbeek, and Cordelia Schmid. 2009. TagProp: Discriminative metric learning in nearest neighbor models for image auto-annotation. In *ICCV*. https://doi.org/10.1109/ICCV.2009.5459266

[15] Harry Halpin, Valentin Robu, and Hana Shepherd. 2007. The complex dynamics of collaborative tagging. In *WWW*. http://doi.acm.org/10.1145/1242572.1242602

[16] Judy Hoffman, Sergio Guadarrama, Eric Tzeng, Ronghang Hu, Jeff Donahue, Ross B. Girshick, Trevor Darrell, and Kate Saenko. 2014. LSDA: Large Scale Detection through Adaptation. In *NIPS*. http://papers.nips.cc/paper/5418-lsda-large-scale-detection-through-adaptation

[17] Xian-Sheng Hua and Jin Li. 2014. Tell me what. In *ICME Workshops*. https://doi.org/10.1109/ICMEW.2014.6890616

[18] Ronak Kosti, Jose M. Alvarez, Adrià Recasens, and Àgata Lapedriza. 2017. Emotion Recognition in Context. In *CVPR*. https://doi.org/10.1109/CVPR.2017.212

[19] Adriana Kovashka, Olga Russakovsky, Li Fei-Fei, and Kristen Grauman. 2016. Crowdsourcing in Computer Vision. *Foundations and Trends in Computer Graphics and Vision* 10, 3 (2016), 177–243. https://doi.org/10.1561/0600000071

[20] Michael S. Lew, Nicu Sebe, Chabane Djeraba, and Ramesh Jain. 2006. Content-based multimedia information retrieval: State of the art and challenges. *TOMCCAP* 2, 1 (2006), 1–19. http://doi.acm.org/10.1145/1126004.1126005

[21] Xirong Li, Cees G. M. Snoek, and Marcel Worring. 2009. Learning Social Tag Relevance by Neighbor Voting. *IEEE Trans. Multimedia* 11, 7 (2009), 1310–1322. https://doi.org/10.1109/TMM.2009.2030598

[22] Xirong Li, Tiberio Uricchio, Lamberto Ballan, Marco Bertini, Cees G. M. Snoek, and Alberto Del Bimbo. 2016. Socializing the Semantic Gap: A Comparative Survey on Image Tag Assignment, Refinement, and Retrieval. *ACM Comput. Surv.* 49, 1 (2016), 14:1–14:39. http://doi.acm.org/10.1145/2906152

[23] Tsung-Yi Lin, Michael Maire, Serge J. Belongie, James Hays, Pietro Perona, Deva Ramanan, Piotr Dollár, and C. Lawrence Zitnick. 2014. Microsoft COCO: Common Objects in Context. In *ECCV*. https://doi.org/10.1007/978-3-319-10602-1_48

[24] Dong Liu, Xian-Sheng Hua, Meng Wang, and Hong-Jiang Zhang. 2010. Retagging social images based on visual and semantic consistency. In *WWW*. http://doi.acm.org/10.1145/1772690.1772848

[25] Dong Liu, Shuicheng Yan, Xian-Sheng Hua, and Hong-Jiang Zhang. 2011. Image Retagging Using Collaborative Tag Propagation. *IEEE Trans. Multimedia* 13, 4 (2011), 702–712. https://doi.org/10.1109/TMM.2011.2134078

[26] Hugo Liu and Henry Lieberman. 2002. Robust photo retrieval using world semantics. In *Proceedings of LREC2002 Workshop: Using Semantics for IR*. 15–20.

[27] Hugo Liu and Push Singh. 2004. ConceptNet - a practical commonsense reasoning tool-kit. *BT technology journal* 22, 4 (2004), 211–226.

[28] Leandro Balby Marinho, Alexandros Nanopoulos, Lars Schmidt-Thieme, Robert Jäschke, Andreas Hotho, Gerd Stumme, and Panagiotis Symeonidis. 2011. Social Tagging Recommender Systems. In *Recommender Systems Handbook*. 615–644. https://doi.org/10.1007/978-0-387-85820-3_19

[29] Tomas Mikolov, Ilya Sutskever, Kai Chen, Gregory S. Corrado, and Jeffrey Dean. 2013. Distributed Representations of Words and Phrases and their Compositionality. In *NIPS*. 3111–3119.

[30] George A. Miller. 1995. WordNet: A Lexical Database for English. *Commun. ACM* 38, 11 (1995), 39–41. http://doi.acm.org/10.1145/219717.219748

[31] Vicente Ordonez, Girish Kulkarni, and Tamara L. Berg. 2011. Im2Text: Describing Images Using 1 Million Captioned Photographs. In *NIPS*. http://papers.nips.cc/paper/4470-im2text-describing-images-using-1-million-captioned-photographs

[32] Andrew Rabinovich, Andrea Vedaldi, Carolina Galleguillos, Eric Wiewiora, and Serge J. Belongie. 2007. Objects in Context. In *ICCV*. https://doi.org/10.1109/ICCV.2007.4408986

[33] Vignesh Ramanathan, Congcong Li, Jia Deng, Wei Han, Zhen Li, Kunlong Gu, Yang Song, Samy Bengio, Chuck Rosenberg, and Fei-Fei Li. 2015. Learning semantic relationships for better action retrieval in images. In *CVPR*. https://doi.org/10.1109/CVPR.2015.7298713

[34] Cyrus Rashtchian, Peter Young, Micah Hodosh, and Julia Hockenmaier. 2010. Collecting Image Annotations Using Amazon's Mechanical Turk. In *Workshop on Creating Speech and Language Data with Amazon's Mechanical Turk*. 139–147. http://aclanthology.info/papers/W10-0721/collecting-image-annotations-using-amazon-s-mechanical-turk

[35] Joseph Redmon, Santosh Kumar Divvala, Ross B. Girshick, and Ali Farhadi. 2016. You Only Look Once: Unified, Real-Time Object Detection. In *CVPR*. https://doi.org/10.1109/CVPR.2016.91

[36] Joseph Redmon and Ali Farhadi. 2017. YOLO9000: Better, Faster, Stronger. In *CVPR*. https://doi.org/10.1109/CVPR.2017.690

[37] Shaoqing Ren, Kaiming He, Ross B. Girshick, and Jian Sun. 2015. Faster R-CNN: Towards Real-Time Object Detection with Region Proposal Networks. In *NIPS*.

[38] Olga Russakovsky, Jia Deng, Hao Su, Jonathan Krause, Sanjeev Satheesh, Sean Ma, Zhiheng Huang, Andrej Karpathy, Aditya Khosla, Michael S. Bernstein, Alexander C. Berg, and Fei-Fei Li. 2015. ImageNet Large Scale Visual Recognition Challenge. *International Journal of Computer Vision* 115, 3 (2015), 211–252. https://doi.org/10.1007/s11263-015-0816-y

[39] Push Singh, Thomas Lin, Erik T. Mueller, Grace Lim, Travell Perkins, and Wan Li Zhu. 2002. Open Mind Common Sense: Knowledge Acquisition from the General Public. In *On the Move to Meaningful Internet Systems (Lecture Notes in Computer Science)*, Vol. 2519. Springer, 1223–1237. https://doi.org/10.1007/3-540-36124-3_77

[40] Robert Speer and Catherine Havasi. 2012. Representing General Relational Knowledge in ConceptNet 5. In *LREC*. http://www.lrec-conf.org/proceedings/lrec2012/summaries/1072.html

[41] Niket Tandon, Gerard de Melo, Fabian M. Suchanek, and Gerhard Weikum. 2014. WebChild: harvesting and organizing commonsense knowledge from the web. In *WSDM*. http://doi.acm.org/10.1145/2556195.2556245

[42] Oriol Vinyals, Alexander Toshev, Samy Bengio, and Dumitru Erhan. 2017. Show and Tell: Lessons Learned from the 2015 MSCOCO Image Captioning Challenge. *IEEE Trans. Pattern Anal. Mach. Intell.* 39, 4 (2017), 652–663. https://doi.org/10.1109/TPAMI.2016.2587640

[43] Jiang Wang, Yi Yang, Junhua Mao, Zhiheng Huang, Chang Huang, and Wei Xu. 2016. CNN-RNN: A Unified Framework for Multi-label Image Classification. In *CVPR*. https://doi.org/10.1109/CVPR.2016.251

[44] Jason Weston, Samy Bengio, and Nicolas Usunier. 2011. WSABIE: Scaling Up to Large Vocabulary Image Annotation. In *IJCAI*.

[45] Fei Wu, Xinyan Lu, Jun Song, Shuicheng Yan, Zhongfei (Mark) Zhang, Yong Rui, and Yueting Zhuang. 2016. Learning of Multimodal Representations With Random Walks on the Click Graph. *IEEE Trans. Image Processing* 25, 2 (2016), 630–642. https://doi.org/10.1109/TIP.2015.2507401

[46] Lei Wu, Rong Jin, and Anil K. Jain. 2013. Tag Completion for Image Retrieval. *IEEE Trans. Pattern Anal. Mach. Intell.* 35, 3 (2013), 716–727. https://doi.org/10.1109/TPAMI.2012.124

[47] Hao Xu, Jingdong Wang, Xian-Sheng Hua, and Shipeng Li. 2009. Tag refinement by regularized LDA. In *ACM MM*. http://doi.acm.org/10.1145/1631272.1631359

[48] Jian Yao, Sanja Fidler, and Raquel Urtasun. 2012. Describing the scene as a whole: Joint object detection, scene classification and semantic segmentation. In *CVPR*. https://doi.org/10.1109/CVPR.2012.6247739

[49] Peter Young, Alice Lai, Micah Hodosh, and Julia Hockenmaier. 2014. From image descriptions to visual denotations: New similarity metrics for semantic inference over event descriptions. *Transactions of the Association for Computational Linguistics* 2 (2014), 67–78. https://tacl2013.cs.columbia.edu/ojs/index.php/tacl/article/view/229

[50] Guangyu Zhu, Shuicheng Yan, and Yi Ma. 2010. Image tag refinement towards low-rank, content-tag prior and error sparsity. In *ACM MM*. http://doi.acm.org/10.1145/1873951.1874028

Convolutional Neural Networks for Soft-Matching N-Grams in Ad-hoc Search

Zhuyun Dai
Language Technologies Institute
Carnegie Mellon University
zhuyund@cs.cmu.edu

Chenyan Xiong
Language Technologies Institute
Carnegie Mellon University
cx@cs.cmu.edu

Jamie Callan
Language Technologies Institute
Carnegie Mellon University
callan@cs.cmu.edu

Zhiyuan Liu
Department of Computer Science and Technology
Tsinghua University
liuzy@tsinghua.edu.cn

ABSTRACT

This paper presents Conv-KNRM, a Convolutional Kernel-based Neural Ranking Model that models n-gram soft matches for ad-hoc search. Instead of exact matching query and document n-grams, Conv-KNRM uses Convolutional Neural Networks to represent n-grams of various lengths and soft matches them in a unified embedding space. The n-gram soft matches are then utilized by the kernel pooling and learning-to-rank layers to generate the final ranking score. Conv-KNRM can be learned end-to-end and fully optimized from user feedback. The learned model's generalizability is investigated by testing how well it performs in a related domain with small amounts of training data. Experiments on English search logs, Chinese search logs, and TREC Web track tasks demonstrated consistent advantages of Conv-KNRM over prior neural IR methods and feature-based methods.

ACM Reference format:
Zhuyun Dai, Chenyan Xiong, Jamie Callan, and Zhiyuan Liu. 2018. Convolutional Neural Networks for Soft-Matching N-Grams in Ad-hoc Search. In *Proceedings of WSDM'18, February 5–9, 2018, Marina Del Rey, CA, USA,* 9 pages.
DOI: http://dx.doi.org/10.1145/3159652.3159659

1 INTRODUCTION

A recent success of neural methods in information retrieval (neural IR) is the development of interaction based models [13, 21, 29]. Interaction based models thrive with encoding word-word translations using word embeddings, and utilizing new pooling methods to better summarize the word translations into ranking signals [11, 13, 29]. Learned end-to-end from user feedbacks [23, 29], the word embeddings can encode soft matches tailored for relevance ranking, which has significant advantages over traditional feature-based methods [29, 30]. These initial successes of neural IR were mainly from soft matching individual words. On the other hand, the query and document often match at n-grams, such as phrases [18], concepts [2], and entities [28]; how to effectively model n-gram soft-matches remains an open question in neural IR.

This paper presents a new Convolutional Kernel-based Neural Ranking Model(Conv-KNRM). We first embed words in continuous vectors (embeddings), and then employ Convolutional Neural Networks (CNN) to compose adjacent words' embeddings to n-gram embeddings. In the n-gram embedding space, soft-matching n-grams is as simple as calculating the similarity of two n-grams' embeddings. The current state-of-the-art kernel pooling and learning-to-rank techniques are then used to combine the n-gram soft-matches to the final ranking score [29].

The CNN is the key to modeling n-grams. Typical IR approaches treat n-grams as discrete terms and use them the same as unigrams. For example, a document bigram 'white_house' is one term, has its own term frequency, and can only be matched to 'white_house' in queries. However, treating n-grams atomically in neural IR will explode the parameter space, and suffer from data sparsity. This work avoids the problem by learning a convolutional layer that forms n-grams from individual words' embeddings. The convolutional layer projects all n-grams into a unified embedding space, allowing matching n-grams of different lengths. For instance, 'white house' in the document can provide partial evidence for the query 'George Walker Bush'.

The whole Conv-KNRM model can be trained end-to-end with relevance signals such as clicks, so that the n-gram soft matches are fully optimized towards search accuracy. We also present a simple yet effective domain adaptation method for applying Conv-KNRM to search domains where large scale training data is not available. We first train the word embedding and convolutional layers in the source domain that has sufficient training labels. The trained Conv-KNRM is then adapted to a target domain with limited annotations by only re-training the learning-to-rank layer. The assumption is that the soft matching patterns learned on one domain are likely to generalize to similar domains, while the importance of each type of soft match can vary across domains.

Our experiments on an English search log from Bing and a Chinese search log from Sogou show the advantages of soft-matching n-grams. As a precision oriented method, Conv-KNRM almost doubled the NDCG@1 of standard feature-based learning-to-rank methods. On the English log, Conv-KNRM outperformed state-of-the-art neural methods by over 30%; in the Chinese log where many unigrams

WSDM'18, February 5–9, 2018, Marina Del Rey, CA, USA
© 2018 ACM. ISBN 978-1-4503-5581-0/18/02...$15.00
DOI: http://dx.doi.org/10.1145/3159652.3159659

are already compound word, soft-matching n-grams still provided significant improvements. Our further study reveals that the key to Conv-KNRM's advantages is its ability to cross-match n-grams with different lengths in a unified space.

Our domain adaptation experiment shows that the n-gram soft matches are generalizable. When adapted to the TREC Web Track task, the pre-trained Conv-KNRM from Bing's log outperformed two strong learning-to-rank baselines. A case study found that some connections between queries and their relevant documents can only be made by soft-matching n-grams, for example, 'atypical squamous cells' and 'cervical cancer'. To the best of our knowledge, this is the first time such cross-domain generalization ability has been achieved by neural methods in ad hoc search[1].

In the rest of this paper, Section 2 discusses related work; Section 3 describes our model architecture; Section 4 describes the domain adaptation method; Experimental setups and evaluation results are presented in Section 5 and Section 6. We conclude in Section 7.

2 RELATED WORK

The current neural IR methods can be categorized into two classes: *representation* based and *interaction* based [13]. The earlier attempts of neural IR research were mainly about how to learn good *representation* of the query and document, and the ranking was simply done by their representations' similarities, for example, DSSM [15] and its convolution version CDSSM [26]. A more recent example is the weakly supervised ranking model in which all word embeddings of a query or document are combined into one vector, and the match of two vectors is done by deep neural networks [9].

The *interaction* based methods, on the other hand, directly model query-document matches at the word level. They are rooted in statistical translation models, which construct a translation matrix of word pairs between query and document, and summarize it to a ranking score [4]. The main challenge of translation models is that the word-pair translations are too sparse to learn. To overcome this problem, word embeddings [20] are introduced to calculate the translation scores [12]. How to combine the word-level translation scores to generate query-document ranking scores has also been improved by neural methods such as Convolutional Neural Networks [14, 23].

A later study found that the CNN filters tend to mix the match signals in the translation matrix at various levels and are suboptimal for ad hoc search [22]. The DRMM model introduces the histogram pooling (pyramid pooling [11]) technique to summarize the translation matrix; it demonstrated that it is more effective to 'count' the word-level translation scores at different soft match levels, instead of to weight-sum them [13]. The *interaction* based model and the *representation* based model can also be combined in a duet architecture [21].

Another trend of neural IR research is to learn customized word embeddings by and for ad-hoc ranking. The surrounding text based word embeddings, e.g. word2vec [20] and GloVe [24], have been questioned about their suitability for ad hoc search [1, 25]. Diaz et al. train word embeddings using pseudo relevance feedback (PRF) documents, which are more effective than globally trained word2vec in query expansion [10]. The relevance feedback based word embeddings are then also found to be more effective in ad hoc ranking [30].

K-NRM unified the progress of IR customized embeddings and *interaction* based model [29]. It first embeds words and builds the translation matrix using the similarities between query and document words' embeddings. Then it uses kernel-pooling to summarize the word embeddings and provide soft match signals for learning to rank. The kernel-pooling shares the advantage of pyramid pooling [13] that it 'counts' the soft matches at multiple levels, while also being differentiable so that word embeddings and ranking parameters can be learned together. When trained with user feedback in a search log, K-NRM outperforms both neural IR methods and feature-based learning-to-rank by a large margin [29].

Though the soft matching of n-grams in information retrieval remains an open topic, there has been a large amount of research that utilizes n-gram exact matches. The sequential dependency model (SDM) that includes n-gram phrase matches has been a standard in many IR systems [18]. There is also much work about how to better weight n-grams in SDM, for example, by emphasizing frequent and meaningful concepts [3, 32]. A more recent trend is to use entities to introduce explicit semantics from knowledge graphs to search systems [28]. The majority of these work focuses on exact matching n-grams, because learning a good statistical translation model score for every possible n-gram pair inevitably faces data sparsity and parameter explosion.

Modeling n-grams is much easier in the embedding space. Neural methods have shown the benefits of modeling n-grams in some related text processing tasks, especially with Convolutional Neural Networks. For example, in sentence classification, CNN has been used to compose word embeddings into n-gram representations, which are then max-pooled and combined by a feed-forward neural network to classify the sentence [17]. That research demonstrated CNN's ability of composing n-gram embeddings, while its ability in relevance ranking is still being explored.

3 CONVOLUTIONAL N-GRAM RANKING

This section presents our convolutional kernel-based neural ranking Model (**Conv-KNRM**), shown in Figure 1. It first composes n-gram embeddings using CNN, and constructs translation matrices between n-grams of different lengths in the n-gram embedding space (Section 3.1). Then it ranks with the n-gram soft matches using kernel-pooling and learning to rank (Section 3.2).

3.1 N-gram Composing and Cross-matching

Given a query q and document d, Conv-KNRM embeds their words by a word embedding layer, composes n-grams with a CNN layer, and cross-matches query n-grams and document n-grams of variant lengths to the translation matrices.

The **word embedding** layer maps each word t of a text to an L-dimensional continuous vector (embedding): $t \to \vec{t}$. A query q or document d is treated as a text sequence of m words $\{t_1, ..., t_m\}$, and is modeled as an $m \times L$ matrix:

$$T = \begin{bmatrix} \vec{t}_1 \\ \dots \\ \vec{t}_m \end{bmatrix}. \quad (1)$$

[1]Trained models available at: http://boston.lti.cs.cmu.edu/appendices/WSDM2018-ConvKNRM/

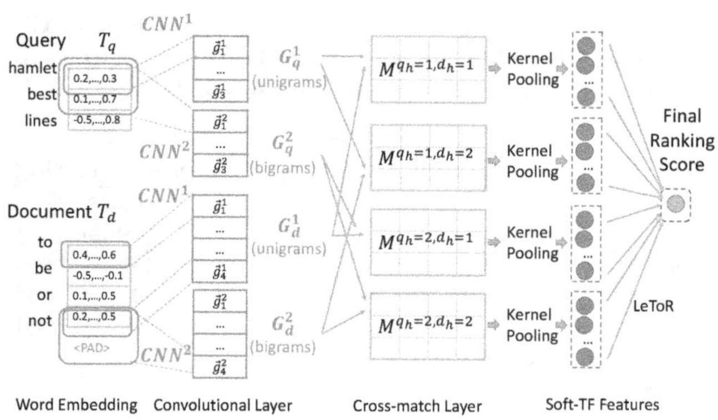

Figure 1: The Conv-KNRM Architecture. Given input query and document, the embedding layer maps their words into distributed representations, the convolutional layer generates n-gram embeddings ; the cross-match layer matches the query n-grams and document n-grams of different lengths, and forms the translation matrices; the kernel pooling layer generates soft-TF features and the learning-to-rank (LeToR) layer combines them to the ranking score. The case with Unigrams and Bigrams (h_{max} = 2) is shown.

We denote the embedding matrix of the query and the document by T_q and T_d respectively.

The **convolutional layer** applies convolution filters to compose n-grams from the text (T_q or T_d). A convolution filter slide over the text like a sliding window. For each window of h words, the filter sums up all elements in the h words' embeddings $T_{i:i+h}$, weighted by the filter weights $w \in \mathbb{R}^{hL}$,and produces a continuous score:

$$v = w \cdot T_{i:i+h}, v \in \mathbb{R}. \quad (2)$$

Using F different filters $w_1, ..., w_F$ gives F scores, each describing $T_{i:i+h}$ in a different perspective. Then we add a bias and apply a non-linear activation function, and obtain an F-dimensional embedding for the h-gram:

$$\vec{g}_i^h = \text{relu}\left(W^h \cdot T_{i:i+h} + \vec{b}^h\right), i = 1...m. \quad (3)$$

$\vec{g}_i^h \in \mathbb{R}^F$ is the embedding of the i-th h-gram. The f-th element in $\vec{g}_i^h$ is the score of the f-th filter. W^h and $\vec{b}^h$ are the weights of the F convolution filters. $|W^h| = (hL) \times F$ and $|\vec{b}^h| = F$. When a convolution filter slides across the boundary of the text, we append up to $h - 1$ '<PAD>' symbols for padding.

Thus, for each n-gram length $h \in \{1, .., h_{max}\}$, the CNN layer converts the text embedding T into h-gram embedding G^h.

$$G^h = \text{CNN}^h(T) = \begin{bmatrix} \vec{g}_1^h \\ ... \\ \vec{g}_m^h \end{bmatrix} \quad (4)$$

$|G^h| = m \times F$. Each of its rows correspond to a h-gram vector of length F. h-gram embeddings for the query and the document are denoted as G_q^h and G_d^h respectively.

The 'convolution' assumption is applied in the n-gram compositions: the same set of convolution filters is used to compose all n-grams. Thus, instead of learning an individual embedding for each n-gram in the corpus, the model only needs to learn the CNN weights for combining word-level embeddings, which have much fewer parameters.

The **cross-match layer** matches query n-grams and document n-grams of different lengths. For query n-grams of length h_q and document n-grams of length h_d, a translation matrix M^{h_q,h_d} is constructed. Its elements are the similarity scores between the corresponding query-document n-gram pairs.

$$M_{i,j}^{h_q,h_d} = \cos\left(\vec{g}_i^{h_q}, \vec{g}_j^{h_d}\right) \quad (5)$$

The unified embedding representations allow cross-matching n-grams of different lengths, e.g., the query trigram"convolutional neural networks" and the document bigram "deep learning". It generates h_{max}^2 translation matrices.

$$\mathcal{M} = \left\{M^{h_q,h_d} | 1 \le h_q \le h_{max}, 1 \le h_d \le h_{max}\right\} \quad (6)$$

3.2 Ranking with N-gram Translations

Conv-KNRM uses the kernel-pooling technique and a learning-to-rank layer to calculate the ranking score using the n-gram translations $\mathcal{M}$. This part extends K-NRM [29] to n-grams.

Kernel-pooling is a pooling technique that uses K Gaussian kernels to count the soft matches of word or n-gram pairs at K different strength levels. Each kernel K_k summarizes the translation scores as soft-TF counts in the region defined by its mean μ_k and width δ_k. As a result, a translation matrix M is pooled to a K-dimensional soft-TF feature vector $\phi(M) = \{K_1(M), ..., K_K(M)\}$. Such counting-based pooling methods have shown better performance than score-based ones like mean-pooling or max-pooling [13, 29].

Kernel-pooling is applied to each M^{h_q,h_d} matrix in $\mathcal{M}$ to generate the soft-TF feature vector $\phi\left(M^{h_q,h_d}\right)$, which describes the distribution of match scores between query h_q-grams and document h_d-grams. This leads to the ranking features as follows.

$$\Phi(\mathcal{M}) = \phi\left(M^{1,1}\right) \oplus ... \oplus \phi\left(M^{h_q,h_d}\right) \oplus ... \oplus \phi\left(M^{h_{max},h_{max}}\right)$$

$\Phi(\mathcal{M})$ has $K \times h_{max}^2$ dimensions, K soft-TF features for each of the h_{max}^2 translation matrices in $\mathcal{M}$.

The **learning-to-rank (LeToR)** layer combines the soft-TF ranking features $\Phi(\mathcal{M})$ into a ranking score:

$$f(q,d) = \tanh\left(w_r^T \Phi(\mathcal{M}) + b_r\right) \quad (7)$$

w_r and b_r are the linear ranking parameters to learn. $|w_r| = |\Phi(\mathcal{M})|$ and $|b_r| = 1$. tanh() is the activation function.

Standard pairwise learning-to-rank is used to train the model.

$$l = \sum_q \sum_{d^+,d^- \in D_q^{+,-}} \max(0, 1 - f(q,d^+) + f(q,d^-)) \quad (8)$$

$D_q^{+,-}$ are q's pairwise preferences: d^+ ranks higher than d^-.

All of Conv-KNRM layers are differentiable; the whole model, including word embeddings ($\mathcal{V}$), CNN filters (W_h, b_h), and learning-to-rank layers (w_r, b_r) can be learned end-to-end from training data. For a model with vocabulary size $|V|$, L-dimensional word embeddings, F filters, h_{max} maximum n-gram length and K kernels, the embedding layer has $|V| \times L$ parameters, the CNN layer has $O(|h_{max}|LF)$ parameters, and the learning-to-rank layer has $K \times h_{max} + 1$ parameters.

The main capacity of the model is in the word embedding and CNN filters. They are expected to learn the word embeddings and n-gram compositions from training data and provide desired multi-level n-gram soft matches. The learning-to-rank layer serves as a linear feature combiner as in standard feature-based ranking.

3.3 Summary

Conv-KNRM adds the ability of soft matching n-grams to the recent state-of-the-art K-NRM model [29] with convolutional neural networks (CNNs). Without CNNs, Conv-KNRM withdraws to K-NRM.

Matching n-grams is a well-established idea in information retrieval. However, n-grams are usually treated identically to words: they are atomic index terms, have distinct term frequencies, use the same weighting function as unigrams, and must match exactly in query and document [7]. If that approach is used by a neural ranker, the number of parameters to be learned can grow very large. The neural model has to deal with data sparsity and low efficiency problems, which are even harder for longer n-grams. Conv-KNRM avoids these problems by using CNNs to compose n-grams without dramatically enlarging the parameter space. It makes soft-matching n-grams convenient and efficient.

4 DOMAIN ADAPTATION

End-to-end training Conv-KNRM requires large-scale training data, for example, user clicks in a commercial search log [29] or industry-scale annotations [21]. However, for many search domains such as TREC benchmarks, such data are not available. We propose a domain adaption strategy that learns Conv-KNRM from a source domain that has sufficient training data, and then re-trains its learning-to-rank layer in the target domain with limited labels.

The parameters of the embedding and convolution layers are learned in the source domain to absorb the rich relevance signals in the training data. They are then used in the target domain to generate soft-TF features $\Phi(M)$. Xiong, et al. [29] showed that kernel-pooled soft-TF features reveal different types of soft match. For example, one kernel may count synonyms (e.g., 'oppor9' and 'OPPOR'); another kernel may count word pairs from the same concept class (e.g., 'son' and 'daughter', 'Java' and 'C++'). These soft match patterns are likely to be stable across related domains.

The learning-to-rank parameters indicate the importance of each kernel. They are re-trained on the target domain, because the importances of each type of soft matches can change over domains. For instance, the synonym kernel is of low importance in search logs as all candidate documents already contain the query words [29]; however, synonyms can be a strong signal in a recall-oriented domain.

Re-training the ranking layer in the target domain is a standard feature based learning-to-rank tasks. This allows one to add domain-specific features from the target domain. There is also no limitation on which learning to rank model to use in the target domain. One can leverage the power of any learning-to-rank model such as RankSVM [16] or LambdaMART [27].

Table 1: Query log datasets. Sogou-Log is a sample of Chinese query logs from Sogou.com in 2016. Bing-Log is a sample of English query logs from Bing.com in 2006

	Sogou-Log		Bing-Log	
	Training	Testing	Training	Testing
Language	Chinese		English	
Fields	Title		Title, Snippet	
Queries	95,229	1,000	99,043	1,000
Docs Per Query	12.17	30.50	50	50
Search Sessions	31M	4.1M	2.10M	0.14M
Vocabulary Size	165,877	19,079	131,225	41,940

5 EXPERIMENTAL METHODOLOGY

This section describes our datasets, how training and testing were performed, our baseline algorithms, and implementation details.

5.1 Datasets

Conv-KNRM was evaluated using two search logs in different languages (Sogou, Bing), and a TREC dataset (ClueWeb09-B).

Sogou-Log: Sogou.com is a major Chinese commercial search engine. The same settings as K-NRM were used [29]. The same sample of Sogou log and training-testing splits are used (Table 1). The testing queries were sampled from queries with more than 1000 sessions (the head); none of them were in the training set.

Documents were represented by titles. The search log did not contain document body text. Testing document's body texts were crawled, and were used by the traditional IR baselines for stronger baseline performance. Body texts of training documents were not available [29]. The Chinese text was segmented by ICTCLASS [31]; then Chinese words were treated like English words.

Bing-Log: We used a one-month sample of a 2006 Bing log from the WSDM 2009 Web Search Click Data Workshop. It contained the top 50 URLs for each query, and clicked URLs in each session. Following Sogou-Log, we split the Bing sessions into training and testing sets with no overlapping queries (Table 1). Test queries were sampled uniformly because the log contained few head queries.

Bing-Log includes documents' titles and snippets. Most snippets had 30-50 words. We can not crawl enough body texts because URLs were from 2006. All texts were tokenized and lower-cased.

ClueWeb09-B is used for domain adaptation experiments. The ClueWeb09-B corpus contains about 50 million English web documents from 2009. The TREC 2009-2012 Web Tracks created 200 queries and corresponding relevance judgments. We followed a standard re-ranking methodology in prior research [8, 28]: re-rank the top 100 candidate documents retrieved by Galago using sequential dependency model queries; the INQUERY stopword list augmented with web-specific stop words; KStemming; and spam filtering using Waterloo spam score with threshold 60. Documents were parsed by Boilerpipe using the 'KeepEverytingExtractor'. The title and the first 50 words in the body field were used to be more consistent with the source domain (Bing-Log)'s title and snippet.

5.2 In-Domain Training and Testing

Training and testing labels on Sogou-Log and Bing-Log were generated following prior research [29].

Table 2: Training and testing labels for each dataset. DCTR used the DCTR click model to infer scores that were mapped to 5 Likert scales [5]. Clicks used the sole click in a session as the binary label. TREC labels were the 5 official grades.

Dataset	Train	Test
Sogou-Log	DCTR	Testing-SAME: DCTR Testing-RAW: Clicks
Bing-Log	DCTR	Testing-SAME: DCTR Testing-RAW: Clicks
ClueWeb09-B	Embedding & CNN: Bing-Log, DCTR LeToR: TREC labels	TREC labels

Training Labels: The training labels for the Sogou and Bing logs were generated by the DCTR click model from user clicks in the training sessions [5], and training preference pairs were constructed accordingly. DCTR uses the click through rate for each query-document pair as the relevance score. DCTR is a strong baseline in click model competitions [5].

Testing-SAME: This set of testing labels was generated by DCTR, as described for training data. This setting evaluates the model's ability to fit explicit user preferences.

Testing-RAW: This set of testing labels was motivated by the cascade assumption [5]. Only the clicked document in a single-click session was considered relevant. 57% of Sogou testing sessions had only one click. 92% of Bing testing sessions had only one click. The Testing-DIFF condition was omitted due to space limits; it produced results similar to Testing-RAW.

5.3 Domain Adaptation Training and Testing

NIST provides 200 queries and corresponding relevance judgments for ClueWeb09-B. The domain adaptation experiment tests how well the n-gram soft matches trained from one domain (Bing) generalize to a similar domain (ClueWeb09-B). Both datasets contain English web documents, the timespans are somewhat similar (2006 vs. 2009), and TREC queries are similar to Bing queries[2]. However, the two datasets have different documents, different indexing methods, and different the initial rankers (Bing vs. Galago); the relevance labels are also rather different (clicks vs. manual assessments).

On ClueWeb09-B, Conv-KNRM was first trained with the Bing log (as described above). Then the embeddings and convolution filters were 'frozen' and soft TF-features $\Phi(\mathcal{M})$ were extracted using the same kernels for ClueWeb09-B. We also included the initial retrieval score from Galago with sequential dependency model (Galago-SDM) to provide whole-document information as Conv-KNRM only uses the title and the first 50 words of the body. The learning-to-rank parameters were retrained and tested using TREC relevance judgments (Table 2), 10-fold cross-validation, and RankSVM to add regularization (as discussed in Section 4).

5.4 Baselines

Traditional IR baselines included standard unsupervised retrieval models and feature-based learning-to-rank models. Unsupervised methods included BM25 and language model with Dirichlet smoothing (Lm), applied on the full text of Sogou documents, or the title plus snippet of Bing documents. Learning-to-rank baselines were RankSVM [16] and coordinate ascent (Coor-Ascent) [19] They used 20 features: Boolean AND; Boolean OR; Coordinate match; Cosine similarity of bag-of-words vectors; TF-IDF; BM25; language models with no smoothing, Dirichlet smoothing, JM smoothing, and two-way smoothing; all applied on the title and body (or snippet). Default parameters were used in feature extraction.

For ClueWeb09-B, we used state-of-the-art baselines from prior research [28] [3]. The baselines include Indri's language model (Indri), Galago with sequential dependency model queries (Galago-SDM), and learning-to-rank models: RankSVM and Coor-Ascent.

Neural IR baselines included CDSSM [26], MatchPyramid (MP) [23], DRMM [13], and K-NRM [29].

CDSSM [26] is uses CNNs to build query and document *representations* on their words' letter-tri-grams (or Chinese characters in Sogou-Log [29]). The ranking scores are calculated by the similarity between the representations.

MP [23] and DRMM [13] are both *interaction* based models built upon the embedding translation matrix. MP uses CNNs to directly combine the translation scores to the ranking score, while DRMM uses histogram pooling to count multiple levels of soft-TF, and use learning-to-rank afterwards.

K-NRM is a state-of-the-art neural model previously tested on the Sogou-Log dataset [29]. It uses kernel-pooling instead of DRMM's histogram pooling, and learns the word embeddings and the ranking layers end-to-end. It is the main baseline in our experiments.

Among these neural IR baselines, DRMM and K-NRM were compared on the ClueWeb09-B dataset. DRMM uses fixed embeddings and only learns the learning-to-rank layers, and can be trained with limited training data. K-NRM was tested the same as Conv-KNRM in the domain adaption fashion. MP and CDSSM performed worse than DRMM on TREC data in previous studies [13, 22].

It is unfair for unsupervised [30] or pseudo-supervised [9] neural IR methods to compete with Conv-KNRM, which is trained end-to-end with large amount of supervisions.

5.5 Implementation Details

Model Training: All supervised traditional IR models were trained and tested using cross-validation on the testing data. On search logs, 5-fold cross validation were used to be consistent with the previous study on Sogou-Log [29]. On ClueWeb09-B, the 10-fold cross validation splits from the provided baselines were used. All RankSVM's used the linear kernel with the hyper-parameter C selected from the range [0.0001, 10] on the development set. Recommended settings of Coor-Ascent were kept. All neural IR methods are trained on the training splits. On ClueWeb09-B, DRMM was cross-validated; K-NRM and Conv-KNRM was pretrained on Bing-Log, then used RankSVM with cross-validation to retrain the learning-to-rank layer.

Document Fields: On Sogou-Log, traditional IR methods used both title and body, and neural IR methods only used title [29], as discussed in section 5.1. On Bing-Log, all methods used the title and snippets. On ClueWeb09-B, all methods used title and body, except K-NRM and Conv-KNRM which used title and first 50 words

[2]NIST sampled the TREC queries from a Bing search log. We removed TREC queries from our Bing training data. Our training and testing data have no queries in common.

[3]https://boston.lti.cs.cmu.edu/appendices/SIGIR2017_word_entity_duet/

in the body as snippets, to be consistent with the source domain. When multiple fields were used, a separate set of features from each field was generated; the combination weights were learned as well.
Word Embeddings: DRMM used pre-trained word2vec embeddings from the candidate documents in the search log, or the ClueWeb corpus. MP, K-NRM, and Conv-KNRM embeddings were all learned end-to-end using the query logs. For Sogou-log, we set embedding dimension $L = 300$ [29] . For Bing-Log, we set $L = 100$ because our pilot study showed that $L = 100$ has similar performance with $L = 300$ but the training is 3 times faster.
Hyper Parameters: n-gram lengths were $h = 1, 2, 3$. Longer n-grams with $h > 3$ usually exceed the length of web search queries. The number of CNN filters F was 128; we found that F in the range of $(50, 300)$ give similar results. The kernel pooling layers in K-NRM and Conv-KNRM and the histogram pooling layer in DRMM all used 11 kernels/bins. The first one is the exact match kernel $\mu = 1, \sigma = 10^{-3}$, or bin $[1, 1]$. The other 10 kernels/bins equally split the cosine range $[-1, 1]$: the μ or bin centers were: $\mu_1 = 0.9, \mu_2 = 0.7, ..., \mu_{10} = -0.9$. The σ of the soft match bins were set to be 0.1 [29].
Model Implementation and Efficiency: The model was implemented with Tensorflow. The optimization used the Adam optimizer, with batch size 16, learning rate 0.001, and early stopping with the patience of 5 epochs. The training of Conv-KNRM took about 12 hours on an AWS GPU machine. The training time is similar with prior work using only unigrams [29]. Most computation time was spent on the embedding layer; the convolutional layer was very efficient.

6 EVALUATION RESULTS

Three experiments were conducted to analyze Conv-KNRM's performance: its ranking accuracy when trained end-to-end, contributions of n-gram soft match, and the effectiveness when adapted to new domain.

6.1 End-to-End Accuracy

The ranking accuracies of each ranking method on the Sogou-Log and Bing-Log datasets are shown in Table 3.

On **Testing-SAME**, Conv-KNRM outperformed all feature-based and neural IR baselines by large margin with statistical significance. The closest baseline is K-NRM, the non-convolutional version of Conv-KNRM, but the differences were still large. Conv-KNRM performed better in higher ranking positions: its NDCG@1 almost doubled Coor-Ascent . These results show Conv-KNRM's effectiveness when trained and tested on the same labeling scenario.

Testing-Raw evaluates the model's performance by raw user clicks. The same stable improvements of Conv-KNRM over all baselines were observed. Since this evaluation uses sessions with only one click, the MRR scores directly reflect the reciprocal rank of user-clicked documents. On Sogou-Log, the average rank of clicked documents of all methods except K-NRM and Conv-KNRM was below rank 5. K-NRM pulled the clicked document to rank 3, and Conv-KNRM further promoted it to rank 2.7. On Bing-Log, Conv-KNRM pulled the clicked document of all methods more than 1 position higher.

The only neural IR baselines that outperformed feature-based learning-to-rank are the two *interaction* based and *end-to-end* trained ones: MP and K-NRM. Although other neural IR methods can improve over unsupervised baselines, feature-based learning-to-rank methods are harder to beat; end-to-end learned embeddings and match-based techniques are necessary for current neural IR methods to provide additional improvements [22, 29, 30]

Comparing the two strong neural IR baselines, K-NRM outperforms MP by a large margin. Both methods use end-to-end learned word embeddings to build the translation matrix. The difference is that K-NRM uses kernel-pooling to summarize 'soft-TF' counts from the translation matrix, while MP directly applies the CNN to combine the translation scores. CNN in MP only has access to the translation scores in the translation matrix, for example, a 2×2 CNN filter sees the similarity scores between two adjacent query words and two adjacent document words, but not their embeddings. Our experiments and prior studies show that counting the frequencies of multi-level soft matches are more effective than weight-summing the similarities [13, 29]—"similarity does not necessarily mean relevance" [6].

Recall that Conv-KNRM is a richer model than K-NRM only because it leverages convolutional neural networks to learn the n-gram compositions and thus enable n-gram soft matches. The improvements of Conv-KNRM over K-NRM reveal the advantage of n-gram soft matches. The relative improvements on Sogou and Bing also correlate with our intuitions of n-gram's importance in Chinese and English. In Chinese, words are segmented by word segmentation tools. An important goal of Chinese word segmentation research is to cut meaningful phrases into one word. For example, 'information retrieval', 'deep learning', and 'The People's Republic of China' are all unigrams in Chinese. As a result, the gains are much larger on English than on Chinese.

6.2 Contribution of N-Gram Soft-match

This experiment studied the contribution of n-gram soft matches by comparing several Conv-KNRM's variations. Conv-KNRM composes n-grams with lengths up to h_{max} and cross-matches them in a unified embedding space. We started with K-NRM, which is Conv-KNRM without CNNs, and incrementally added bigram matches (+Bigram), trigram matches (+Trigram), cross unigram-bigram matches (+Uni-x-Bi), and cross all three n-grams' matches which is the Full Model. Results are shown in Table 4.

Longer n-gram were more effective in English. On the Bing-Log, trigrams were better than bigrams, and bigrams were better than unigrams. The effect was weaker in Chinese, with mixed performances on different settings. Presumably it is because many Chinese phrases were glued to one word by word segmentation.

Cross matching n-grams of different lengths boosted accuracy in both languages. +Uni-x-Bi performed significantly better than +Bigram on most metrics, and Full Model outperformed all other variants significantly. Cross matching is effective because related concepts do not necessarily have the same length, e.g. 'FIFA' and 'world cup'. Composing n-grams using CNNs makes cross matching simple: all n-grams, despite with different lengths, are represented and matched in the same embedding space.

6.3 Domain Adaption

Our third experiment examined the effectiveness of Conv-KNRM when adapted to a domain where large scale training data is not

Table 3: Ranking accuracy of Conv-KNRM and baseline methods. Relative performances compared with K-NRM are in percentages. †, ‡, §, ¶, ∗ indicate statistically significant improvements over Coor-Ast†, DRMM‡, CDSSM§, MP¶ and K-NRM*, respectively.

Method	Sogou-Log						Bing-Log					
	Testing-SAME				Testing-Raw		Testing-SAME				Testing-RAW	
	NDCG@1		NDCG@10		MRR		NDCG@1		NDCG@10		MRR	
BM25	0.142	−45%	0.287	−34%	0.228	−33%	0.043	−79%	0.123	−63%	0.102	−61%
RankSVM	0.146	−44%	0.309	−29%	0.224	−34%	0.128	−39%	$0.266^{\ddagger}$	−20%	0.207	−22%
Coor-Ascent	$0.169^{\ddagger\S}$	−34%	$0.355^{\ddagger\S}$	−16%	0.242	−29%	0.142	−32%	$0.268^{\ddagger}$	−20%	0.208	−22%
DRMM	0.137	−51%	0.315	−27%	0.234	−31%	0.137	−34%	0.247	−26%	0.200	−25%
CDSSM	0.144	−44%	$0.333^{\ddagger}$	−23%	0.232	−32%	0.156	−25%	0.273	−18%	0.212	−20%
MP	$0.218^{\dagger\ddagger\S}$	−15%	$0.379^{\dagger\ddagger\S}$	−12%	0.240	−29%	$0.182^{\dagger\ddagger\S}$	−12%	$0.301^{\dagger\ddagger\S}$	−10%	$0.244^{\dagger\ddagger\S}$	−8%
K-NRM	$0.264^{\dagger\ddagger\S\P}$	––	$0.428^{\dagger\ddagger\S\P}$	––	$0.338^{\dagger\ddagger\S\P}$	––	$0.208^{\dagger\ddagger\S\P}$	––	$0.334^{\dagger\ddagger\S\P}$	––	$0.265^{\dagger\ddagger\S\P}$	––
Conv-KNRM	$\mathbf{0.336}^{\dagger\ddagger\S\P*}$	+30%	$\mathbf{0.481}^{\dagger\ddagger\S\P*}$	+11%	$\mathbf{0.358}^{\dagger\ddagger\S\P*}$	+5%	$\mathbf{0.300}^{\dagger\ddagger\S\P*}$	+44%	$\mathbf{0.437}^{\dagger\ddagger\S\P*}$	+31%	$\mathbf{0.354}^{\dagger\ddagger\S\P*}$	+34%

Table 4: Ranking accuracy of Conv-KNRM variants. Relative performances compared with Unigram-only model (K-NRM) are in percentages. †, ‡, §, ¶ indicate statistically significant improvements over Unigram†, +Bigram‡, +Trigram§ and +Uni-x-Bi¶, respectively.

Conv-KNRM Variant	Sogou-Log						Bing-Log					
	Testing-SAME				Testing-Raw		Testing-SAME				Testing-RAW	
	NDCG@1		NDCG@10		MRR		NDCG@1		NDCG@10		MRR	
Unigram	0.264	––	0.428	––	0.338	––	0.208	––	0.334	––	0.265	––
+Bigram	$0.287^{\dagger}$	+11%	0.442	+2%	0.314	−8%	$0.235^{\dagger}$	+13%	$0.385^{\dagger}$	+15%	$0.301^{\dagger}$	+14%
+Trigram	$0.286^{\dagger}$	+11%	$0.454^{\dagger}$	+5%	$0.330^{\ddagger}$	−3%	$0.252^{\dagger}$	+21%	$0.399^{\dagger}$	+20%	$0.318^{\dagger\ddagger}$	+20%
+Uni-x-Bi	$0.308^{\dagger}$	+19%	$0.458^{\dagger\ddagger}$	+6%	$0.346^{\ddagger\S}$	+2%	$0.275^{\dagger\ddagger}$	+32%	$0.417^{\dagger\ddagger\S}$	+25%	$0.335^{\dagger\ddagger\S}$	+26%
Full Model	$0.336^{\dagger\ddagger\S\P}$	+30%	$0.481^{\dagger\ddagger\S\P}$	+11%	$0.358^{\dagger\ddagger\S}$	+5%	$\mathbf{0.300}^{\dagger\ddagger\S\P}$	+44%	$\mathbf{0.437}^{\dagger\ddagger\S\P}$	+31%	$\mathbf{0.354}^{\dagger\ddagger\S\P}$	+34%

Table 5: Performance on ClueWeb09-B using domain adaptation. Relative performance in percentages are compared to Coor-Ascent. W(in)/T(ie)/L(oss) to Coor-Ascent are compared at NDCG@20. †, ‡, §, ¶∗ indicate statistically significant improvements over Indri†, Galago SDM‡, RankSVM§, Coor-Ascent ¶ and DRMM+SDM *.

Method	ClueWeb09-B												
	NDCG@1		ERR@1		NDCG@10		ERR@10		NDCG@20		ERR@20		W/T/L
Indri	0.239	−6%	$0.062^{\ddagger*}$	−12%	0.229	−15%	0.130	−15%	0.236	−12%	0.139	−14%	68/31/101
Galago-SDM	0.219	−14%	0.053	−25%	0.238	−11%	0.130	−16%	$0.250^{\dagger}$	−7%	0.139	−14%	63/39/98
RankSVM	0.236	−7%	0.064^{*}	−10%	$0.256^{\dagger\ddagger}$	−5%	$0.146^{\dagger\ddagger}$	−5%	$0.263^{\dagger\ddagger*}$	−2%	$0.154^{\ddagger*}$	−5%	82/47/71
Coor-Ascent	$0.255^{\dagger\ddagger*}$	––	0.071	––	$0.268^{\dagger\ddagger}$	––	0.154	––	$0.268^{\dagger\ddagger}$	––	0.162	––	–/–/–
DRMM+SDM	0.215	−16%	0.049	−31%	$0.261^{\dagger\ddagger}$	−3%	0.136	−12%	0.243	−9%	0.138	−15%	66/34/100
K-NRM	0.235	−8%	0.057	−20%	$0.264^{\dagger\ddagger}$	−2%	0.140	−9%	$0.269^{\dagger\ddagger*}$	+0%	0.149	−8%	69/42/89
Conv-KNRM-exact	0.231	−10%	0.064^{*}	−10%	$0.263^{\dagger\ddagger}$	−2%	$0.146^{\dagger\ddagger*}$	−5%	$0.270^{\dagger\ddagger*}$	+1%	$0.155^{\dagger\ddagger*}$	−4%	78/42/80
Conv-KNRM	$\mathbf{0.294}^{\dagger\ddagger\S\P*}$	+15%	$0.093^{\dagger\ddagger\S\P*}$	+31%	$\mathbf{0.289}^{\dagger\ddagger\S\P*}$	+8%	$0.172^{\dagger\ddagger\S\P*}$	+12%	$0.287^{\dagger\ddagger\S\P*}$	+7%	$0.181^{\dagger\ddagger\S\P*}$	+12%	88/38/74

available. We trained Conv-KNRM's word embeddings and convolution filters in Bing-Log with a large amount of user preference labels from clicks, and re-trained the learning-to-rank part on ClueWeb09-B's TREC ranking labels. Results are shown in Table 5.

Indri and Galago-SDM are two unsupervised baselines. RankSVM, Coor-Ascent, and DRMM+SDM are supervised baselines. They used in-domain training with cross-validation, because their parameters can be learned with TREC-scale training labels. DRMM+SDM is a variant of DRMM that uses Galago-SDM score as an additional feature; it showed higher performance than the standard DRMMM. Conv-KNRM and K-NRM were both trained using domain adaption. We also examined Conv-KNRM-exact which only uses exact-matches of n-grams, e.g. 'world cup' can only be matched to 'world cup'.

As shown in Table 5, K-NRM was not able to beat DRMM+SDM, meaning that the effectiveness of unigram level soft matches was weakened by domain differences. Conv-KNRM-exact performed about the same, and was weaker than learning-to-rank approaches. It does no more than exact phrase matching as in SDM. Conv-KNRM differs from K-NRM and Conv-KNRM-exact by soft-matching n-grams; it outperformed the two strong traditional learning-to-rank models. The results demonstrate that the learned n-gram soft matches of Conv-KNRM can generate to a different domain.

Feature Weight Analysis: to further study the domain adaption, we investigated the importance of Conv-KNRM soft-TF features ($\Phi(\mathcal{M})$) in the adapted model. If the soft n-gram matching patterns learned from the Bing-Log is generalizable, their soft-TF feature

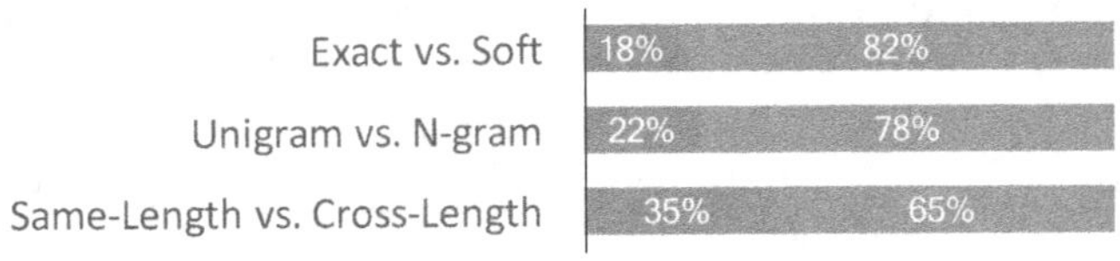

Figure 2: Learned weights of different parts of ranking features on ClueWeb09-B. The percentage is the fraction of absolute weights on each side learned by linear RankSVM.

weights would share a reasonable chunk of learning to rank weights in the adapted model.

We verified this by analyzing the weights RankSVM assigned to different groups of ranking features, as shown in Figure 2. Each analysis divides features into two groups, e.g. exact-match features and soft-match features. It then calculates the percentage of weight given to each type of features by summing up the absolute weight values of the feature set. In Figure 2, most of the weight goes to soft matches (Exact v.s. Soft); N-gram matches have more weight than unigram matches (Unigram vs. N-gram); and matching n-grams of different lengths is important compared to matching n-grams with same length (Same-length v.s. Cross-length). The high feature weights on soft n-gram match features reveals that these features do provide useful information to the learning-to-rank model—more useful than n-gram exact matches, despite that the n-gram soft matches were trained and tested on two rather different domains: different labels, different documents, and non-overlapping queries.

Case Studies: We performed case studies to better understand the soft n-gram matching. Table 6 shows examples of relevant documents that are correctly placed at rank 1 by Conv-KNRM, but not by RankSVM and KNRM. By sorting n-gram pairs according to each feature's individual performance, we can find the most important soft match that makes the document ranked highly, as highlighted in Table 6. These cases demonstrated the effectiveness in Conv-KNRM. First, Conv-KNRM overcomes the lexical mismatch, and finds query-document connections that are difficult for exact-match-based approaches, e.g. 'sewing instructions' and 'quilting 101'. Second, Conv-KNRM captures n-gram matches that are different with word matches like K-NRM. For example, ('atypical squamous', 'cervical cancer') is a strong match, but the connection between their unigram pairs, e.g. ('atypical', 'cervical'), are much weaker. These examples also illustrates Conv-KNRM's generalizability: the matchings make sense in various contexts than just in one dataset.

In summary, the domain adaptation experiment provides a thorough view of the generalization ability of Conv-KNRM. The evaluations on ClueWeb09-B shows that the cross-domain soft n-gram matching provides significant gains over in-domain feature-based learning-to-rank. Feature weight analysis demonstrates that the adapted model puts the majority of feature weights on n-gram soft match signals. Case studies prove that the learned soft-matches are intuitive and cover universally meaningful information needs. To the best of our knowledge, this is the first time we have seen such generalization ability in neural IR models.

7 CONCLUSION

This paper presents Conv-KNRM, a convolutional kernel-based neural ranking model that models n-gram soft matches for ad hoc search. Treating n-grams as discrete index terms faces the problem of dimension explosion and data sparsity. In contrast, Conv-KNRM uses Convolutional Neural Networks to compose n-gram embeddings from word embeddings, and cross-matches n-grams of various lengths in the unified embedding space. It then applies kernel pooling to extract ranking features, and uses learning-to-rank to obtain the final ranking score.

Our experiments on Chinese and English search logs demonstrate the advantages of soft-matching n-grams in relevance ranking. Gonv-GRAM almost doubled the NDCG@1 scores compared to feature-based ranking approaches, and outperformed the previous state-of-the-art model by over 30% at the top. Trained end-to-end with user feedback, Conv-KNRM learns n-gram soft match patterns tailored for matching queries and relevant documents, for example, the query 'farm' is matched to 'eat & drink'. Such IR-customized n-gram soft-match has not been seen much in previous work.

Based on our analysis, the key to Conv-KNRM's advantages is cross-matching n-grams of different lengths. Cross-matching consistently outperformed its non-cross-matching variants. On the Chinese search log, Conv-KNRM without cross-matching is about the same as its unigram competitor K-NRM, due to the phrase-like characteristics of Chinese unigrams. Cross-matching is important because related concepts do not necessarily have the same number of words, for instance, 'deep learning' and 'convolutional neural network'. But there has been little study on it due to the limitation of discrete n-gram representation. The CNN approach of modeling n-grams makes cross-matching feasible, efficient, and effective.

Beyond the good performance when trained end-to-end in domain, we show that the model trained on one domain is also generalizable to a related search domain. The model learned from Bing-log significantly outperformed strong learning-to-rank baselines when adapted to TREC Web Track task, despite important domain differences including corpus, queries and evaluation conditions. Experiments show that the embedding and CNN layers can be directly used in another related domain to generate n-gram soft-matching features. Further analysis explains the generalizability: the learned n-gram soft-matching patterns encode universal properties of language usage in ad hoc search tasks, and provide important evidences for relevance ranking even when used across domains.

8 ACKNOWLEDGMENTS

This research was supported by National Science Foundation (NSF) grant IIS-1422676. We thank Shane Culpepper and RMIT for providing the computational environment that enabled this work. Any opinions, findings, and conclusions in this paper are the authors' and do not necessarily reflect those of the sponsors.

Table 6: Examples of matched n-grams between query and snippets. Black phrases contribute more to the relevance score than gray ones.

Query	Snippet
sewing instructions	...home free resources! newsletter sewing ideas...quilting 101 what is a quilt...
atypical squamous cells	...treatment decision tools cervical cancer : prevention and early detection...
moths	... grouping of moth families commonly known as the 'smaller moths ' (micro , lepidoptera)...
fickle creek farm	.. bed & breakfast inns extended stay lodging rv parks where to eat & drink nightlife ...
university phoenix	campus locations programs : bachelor degree masters degrees account degrees business degree...
wedding budget calculator	...planning tips photographs bridal board my perfect planner tools my check lists...

REFERENCES

[1] Qingyao Ai, Liu Yang, Jiafeng Guo, and W Bruce Croft. 2016. Analysis of the paragraph vector model for information retrieval. In *Proceedings of the 2016 ACM on International Conference on the Theory of Information Retrieval (ICTIR 2016)*. ACM, 133–142.

[2] Michael Bendersky, Donald Metzler, and W. Bruce Croft. 2011. Parameterized concept weighting in verbose queries. In *Proceedings of the 34th annual international ACM SIGIR conference on Research and Development in Information Retrieval (SIGIR 2011)*. ACM.

[3] Michael Bendersky, Donald Metzler, and W Bruce Croft. 2012. Effective query formulation with multiple information sources. In *Proceedings of the Fifth ACM International Conference on Web Search and Data Mining (WSDM 2012)*. ACM, 443–452.

[4] Adam Berger and John Lafferty. 1999. Information Retrieval as statistical translation. In *Proceedings of the 22nd Annual International ACM SIGIR Conference on Research and Development in Information Retrieval (SIGIR)*. ACM, 222–229.

[5] Aleksandr Chuklin, Ilya Markov, and Maarten de Rijke. 2015. Click Models for Web Search. *Synthesis Lectures on Information Concepts, Retrieval, and Services* 7, 3 (2015), 1–115.

[6] Nick Craswell, W Bruce Croft, Jiafeng Guo, Bhaskar Mitra, and Maarten de Rijke. 2017. Report on the SIGIR 2016 Workshop on Neural Information Retrieval (Neu-IR). In *Proceedings of the 40th International ACM SIGIR Conference on Research and Development in Information Retrieval (SIGIR)*. ACM.

[7] W Bruce Croft, Donald Metzler, and Trevor Strohman. 2010. *Search Engines: Information Retrieval in Practice.* Addison-Wesley Reading.

[8] Jeffrey Dalton, Laura Dietz, and James Allan. 2014. Entity Query Feature Expansion using Knowledge Base Links. In *Proceedings of the 37th Annual International ACM SIGIR Conference on Research and Development in Information Retrieval (SIGIR 2014)*. ACM, 365–374.

[9] Mostafa Dehghani, Hamed Zamani, Aliaksei Severyn, Jaap Kamps, , and W. Crof, Bruce. 2017. Neural Ranking Models with Weak Supervision. In *Proceedings of the 40th International ACM SIGIR Conference on Research and Development in Information Retrieval (SIGIR)*. ACM.

[10] Fernando Diaz, Bhaskar Mitra, and Nick Craswell. 2016. Query Expansion with Locally-Trained Word Embeddings. In *Proceedings of the 54th Annual Meeting of the Association for Computational (ACL)*. ACL.

[11] Kristen Grauman and Trevor Darrell. 2005. The pyramid match kernel: Discriminative classification with sets of image features. In *Tenth IEEE International Conference on Computer Vision (ICCV) Volume 1*, Vol. 2. IEEE, 1458–1465.

[12] Jiafeng Guo, Yixing Fan, Qingyao Ai, and W Bruce Croft. 2016. Semantic Matching by Non-Linear Word Transportation for Information Retrieval. In *Proceedings of the 25th ACM International on Conference on Information and Knowledge Management (CIKM)*. ACM.

[13] Jiafeng Guo, Yixing Fan, Ai Qingyao, and W. Bruce Croft. 2016. A Deep Relevance Matching Model for Ad-hoc Retrieval. In *Proceedings of the 25th ACM International on Conference on Information and Knowledge Management (CIKM)*. ACM.

[14] Baotian Hu, Zhengdong Lu, Hang Li, and Qingcai Chen. 2014. Convolutional neural network architectures for matching natural language sentences. In *Advances in Neural Information Processing Systems (NIPS)*.

[15] Po-Sen Huang, Xiaodong He, Jianfeng Gao, Li Deng, Alex Acero, and Larry Heck. 2013. Learning deep structured semantic models for web search using click through data. In *Proceedings of the 22nd ACM international conference on Conference on information & knowledge management (CIKM)*. ACM, 2333–2338.

[16] Thorsten Joachims. 2002. Optimizing search engines using clickthrough Data. In *Proceedings of the 8th ACM SIGKDD International Conference on Knowledge Discovery and Data Mining (KDD 2002)*. ACM, 133–142.

[17] Yoon Kim. 2014. Convolutional neural networks for sentence classification. In *Proceedings of the 2014 Conference on Empirical Methods in Natural Language Processing (EMNLP)* (2014-10). Association for Computational Linguistics.

[18] Donald Metzler and W Bruce Croft. 2005. A Markov random field model for term dependencies. In *Proceedings of the 28th Annual International ACM SIGIR Conference on Research and Development in Information Retrieval (SIGIR 2005)*. ACM, 472–479.

[19] Donald Metzler and W Bruce Croft. 2007. Linear feature-based models for information retrieval. *Information Retrieval* (2007).

[20] Tomas Mikolov, Ilya Sutskever, Kai Chen, Greg S Corrado, and Jeff Dean. 2013. Distributed representations of words and phrases and their compositionality. In *Proceedings of the 2tth Advances in Neural Information Processing Systems 2013 (NIPS)*.

[21] Bhaskar Mitra, Fernando Diaz, and Nick Craswell. 2017. Learning to Match Using Local and Distributed Representations of Text for Web Search. In *Proceedings of the 25th International Conference on World Wide Web (WWW)*. ACM.

[22] Liang Pang, Yanyan Lan, Jiafeng Guo, Jun Xu, and Xueqi Cheng. 2016. A study of matchpyramid models on ad-hoc retrieval. *arXiv preprint arXiv:1606.04648* (2016).

[23] Liang Pang, Yanyan Lan, Jiafeng Guo, Jun Xu, Shengxian Wan, and Xueqi Cheng. Text Matching As Image Recognition. In *Proceedings of the Thirtieth AAAI Conference on Artificial Intelligence (AAAI)*.

[24] Jeffrey Pennington, Richard Socher, and Christopher D. Manning. 2014. GloVe: Global Vectors for Word Representation. In *Empirical Methods in Natural Language Processing (EMNLP)*. 1532–1543.

[25] Navid Rekabsaz, Mihai Lupu, Allan Hanbury, and Hamed Zamani. 2017. Word Embedding Causes Topic Shifting; Exploit Global Context!. In *Proceedings of the 40th International ACM SIGIR Conference on Research and Development in Information Retrieval (SIGIR)*. ACM.

[26] Yelong Shen, Xiaodong He, Jianfeng Gao, Li Deng, and Grégoire Mesnil. 2014. Learning semantic representations using convolutional neural networks for web search. In *Proceedings of the 23rd International Conference on World Wide Web (WWW)*. ACM.

[27] Qiang Wu, Christopher JC Burges, Krysta M Svore, and Jianfeng Gao. 2010. Adapting boosting for information retrieval measures. *Information Retrieval* (2010).

[28] Chenyan Xiong, Jamie Callan, and Tie-Yan Liu. 2017. Word-Entity Duet Representations for Document Ranking. In *Proceedings of the 40th annual international ACM SIGIR conference on Research and Development in Information Retrieval (SIGIR 2017)*. ACM.

[29] Chenyan Xiong, Zhuyun Dai, Jamie Callan, Zhiyuan Liu, and Russell Power. 2017. End-to-end neural ad-hoc ranking with kernel pooling. In *Proceedings of the 40th annual international ACM SIGIR conference on Research and Development in Information Retrieval (SIGIR 2017)*. ACM.

[30] Hamed Zamani and W. Croft, Bruce. 2017. Relevance-based Word Embedding. In *Proceedings of the 40th International ACM SIGIR Conference on Research and Development in Information Retrieval (SIGIR)*. ACM.

[31] Hua-Ping Zhang, Hong-Kui Yu, De-Yi Xiong, and Qun Liu. 2003. HHMM-based Chinese lexical analyzer ICTCLAS. In *Proceedings of the second SIGHAN workshop on Chinese language processing*. ACL.

[32] Guoqing Zheng and Jamie Callan. 2015. Learning to Reweight Terms with Distributed Representations. In *Proceedings of the 38th International ACM SIGIR Conference on Research and Development in Information Retrieval (SIGIR 2015)*. ACM.

Demographics and Dynamics of Mechanical Turk Workers

Djellel Difallah
New York University
New York, NY, USA
djellel@nyu.edu

Elena Filatova
City University of New York
Brooklyn, NY, USA
efilatova@citytech.cuny.edu

Panos Ipeirotis
New York University
New York, NY, USA
panos@nyu.edu

ABSTRACT

We present an analysis of the population dynamics and demographics of Amazon Mechanical Turk workers based on the results of the survey that we conducted over a period of 28 months, with more than 85K responses from 40K unique participants. The demographics survey is ongoing (as of November 2017) and the results are available at http://demographics.mturk-tracker.com: we provide an API for researchers to download the survey data.

We use techniques from the field of ecology, in particular, the capture-recapture technique, to understand the size and dynamics of the underlying population. We also demonstrate how to model and account for the inherent selection biases in such surveys. Our results indicate that there are more than 100K workers available in Amazon's crowdsourcing platform, the participation of the workers in the platform follows a heavy-tailed distribution, and at any given time there are more than 2K active workers. We also show that the half-life of a worker on the platform is around 12-18 months and that the rate of arrival of new workers balances the rate of departures, keeping the overall worker population relatively stable. Finally, we demonstrate how we can estimate the biases of different demographics to participate in the survey tasks, and show how to correct such biases. Our methodology is generic and can be applied to any platform where we are interested in understanding the dynamics and demographics of the underlying user population.

CCS CONCEPTS

• **Human-centered computing → Collaborative and social computing**;

KEYWORDS

crowdsourcing; demographics; dynamics; surveys; selection bias; Amazon Mechanical Turk; capture-recapture

ACM Reference Format:
Djellel Difallah, Elena Filatova, and Panos Ipeirotis. 2018. Demographics and Dynamics of Mechanical Turk Workers. In *Proceedings of WSDM 2018: The Eleventh ACM International Conference on Web Search and Data Mining , Marina Del Rey, CA, USA, February 5–9, 2018 (WSDM 2018),* 9 pages. https://doi.org/10.1145/3159652.3159661

WSDM 2018, February 5–9, 2018, Marina Del Rey, CA, USA

ACM ISBN 978-1-4503-5581-0/18/02...$15.00
https://doi.org/10.1145/3159652.3159661

1 INTRODUCTION

Crowdsourcing, in general, and Amazon Mechanical Turk in particular, have been extensively used over the years for a wide variety of applications that require access to a large number of humans. Many of these tasks, especially tasks around social sciences (e.g., psychology, marketing, political science, and others) are sensitive to the demographics of the underlying population. Other tasks, e.g., surveys, require access to a large number of people to ensure that the results are representative and can be generalized from the crowdsourcing platform population to the general population.

Amazon does not provide any information about the evolving demographics of the workers population. While there exist multiple demographics studies[1] of the Mechanical Turk workers population [17, 26], these studies provide only a snapshot-in-time analysis of the MTurk workers population and, thus, do not contribute to the understanding of the evolution and dynamics of the MTurk workers population. In our work, we present a comprehensive, longitudinal study of Mechanical Turk. We present data of the demographics survey that was conducted over 28 months, with more than 85K responses, and approximately 40K unique participants. We present the evolution of the MTurk demographics over time and illustrate the composition of the MTurk workers population across demographics variables such as country, gender, age, income, marital status, and household size. We contrast and compare these results against the demographics of the general population.

The second question that we address is the size of the MTurk workers population. Amazon claims that there are hundreds of thousands of workers on MTurk.[2] However, studies claim that the real number of workers available to participate in academic experiments is much smaller [34], and is closer to 7300 workers. Such conflicting messages can lead to confusion, especially for those who want to leverage Mechanical Turk for conducting studies. For example, an experimenter would like to run a survey that requires an access to 10K distinct participants. Is MTurk population size sufficient for this experiment? We answer this question by building on top of the techniques from the field of ecology, specifically the *capture-recapture* techniques. Capture-recapture techniques operate by taking sample sets of the population individuals over time, and examining the overlap among these sample sets to provide the estimate of the overall population size. Prior studies [34] use capture-recapture models for estimating the size of Mechanical Turk but rely on the assumption that all workers are equally likely to participate in the posted tasks. However, when workers have *different propensities to participate in tasks* this assumption leads to significant underestimation of the true size of the MTurk workers

[1] See http://www.mturkgrind.com/threads/demographics-of-mechanical-turk.26341/ for a comprehensive list of demographic surveys of Mechanical Turk workers.
[2] According to https://requester.mturk.com/tour, MTurk provides "*Access more than 500,000 Workers from 190 countries*", as of August 2017.

population. In fact, we demonstrate that the number of available workers on Mechanical Turk is at least 100K, with approximately 2K workers being active at any given moment. We show that the MTurk workers' half-life is 12-18 months, indicating that the population refreshes significantly over time. This is good news for anyone willing to conduct wide-reaching studies using this platform.

Finally, we address a common problem with surveys: When researchers present results from surveys, a common concern is that these results are biased as they are obtained from users who choose to participate in this particular survey. We address this issue by modeling, for each worker, the *propensity* to complete a particular task. Then, we examine how demographics are correlated with propensities to participate, and we infer the hidden selection biases. Our results indicate that most demographics variables are not affected by selection biases; the notable exception being Indian workers, that demonstrate a significantly higher propensity to participate in our survey, and are, therefore, over-represented in the raw results. However, with our presented methods, we can now adjust the over-estimates to their true values.

In summary, the contributions of the paper are:

(1) A longitudinal analysis of various demographics indicators of Mechanical Turk workers (country, gender, age, income, marital status, and household size), showing which demographics variables remain stable over time, which ones change, and comparing these to the demographics indicators of the general US population (Section 3).
(2) A capture-recapture analysis to estimate the size of the overall MTurk workers population. Our capture-recapture analysis models the expected lifetime of the workers in the marketplace and also takes into consideration the different propensities to participate in a given task. We provide theoretical and experimental proofs indicating that models that assume equal propensities of participation generate population estimates can be off by orders of magnitude (Section 4).
(3) An analysis that correlates demographics variables with participation propensities and lifetime of workers. This technique removes the selection biases from surveys and allows us to generate unbiased estimates of the demographic profiles of Mechanical Turk workers (Section 5).

For reproducibility, our code is available at https://github.com/ipeirotis/mturk_demographics and the data can be downloaded through an API at http://demographics.mturk-tracker.com.

We believe that the results reported in this paper are not only interesting as a description of the MTurk population and its dynamics, but they also provide an insight into the MTurk demographics to those who hire their study participants via MTurk. Furthermore, the techniques presented in this paper on estimating unbiased population characteristics through biased surveys can be used to study a wide variety of systems that can only be sampled through convenience samples.

2 RELATED WORK

MTurk labor marketplace is widely used by researchers in a variety of fields to recruit participants for experiments on data collection, data annotation, survey completion. Sociology, psychology, behavioral, economics, political science researchers actively recruit study participants on various crowdsourcing platforms [2, 3, 5, 23, 32, 33, 35]. Many studies show that the data collected using MTurk workers is comparable in quality to the data collected using undergraduate students or professional/commercial panels [19]. High correlation between the data collected using MTurk workers and participants recruited using other methods (e.g., college students) occurs despite the MTurk workers being significantly more socioeconomically and ethnically diverse than test participants recruited using other methods [6].

The validity of the experiments that use human subjects depends on the understanding of participants demographics. Chandler and Shapiro [8] evaluate the validity of experiments using MTurk in clinical psychological research from the point of view of sample composition and collected data quality. Other researchers are interested in getting access to experiment participants from a particular location [12], or, on the contrary, from around the world [13]. Arechar et al. [3] investigate the use of MTurk for interactive experiments in the field of economics. On the one hand, they demonstrate that MTurk can be used to replicate the results obtained in the physical laboratory, but on the other hand, they emphasize the importance of knowing the MTurk participants demographic profile.

Given that while running experiments using MTurk participants, researchers have minimal control over who volunteers to participate in the study, concerns regarding the quality of the data submitted by MTurk workers have been discussed [7, 30, 32]. According to this discussion, several methods exist that allow to filter out most of the low-quality results from MTurk workers.

Several researchers raise the concern regarding the ethics of using MTurk workers for research experiments [15, 16]. One of these concerns is considered particularly problematic, namely the low wages that MTurk workers get for their participation in the experiments. Often this issue is associated with particular locations of MTurk workers.

One work that attempts to estimate the number of MTurk workers who are ready for work at a particular moment is described in [34]. However, as mentioned in the introduction (Section 1), we believe that the presented number underestimates the MTurk workers population size. There are two reasons for this underestimation: 1) the experiment set-up where MTurk workers participate in a variety of unrelated tasks with different pay rates, that ran in irregular time intervals, and 2) insufficient calibration of the capture-recapture model. Both of these issues rely on the assumption that different MTurk workers have the same probability or propensity to participate in every experiment. This bias is a typical issue for the ecology capture-recapture models that ignore the population heterogeneity [1, 28] resulting in population size underestimation. We build on the findings from the work in the field of ecology [4, 9, 24, 25] regarding the population heterogeneity and how it affects the probability to be caught during the capture-recapture experiment.

Within the context of web-related research, Trushkowsky et al. [36] use capture-recapture models while trying to measure the cardinality of relations extracted from the web. Lu and Li [21] incorporate the heterogeneity issue into their application of the capture-recapture model for the deep web size estimation: different documents have different probabilities to be retrieved given a random query.

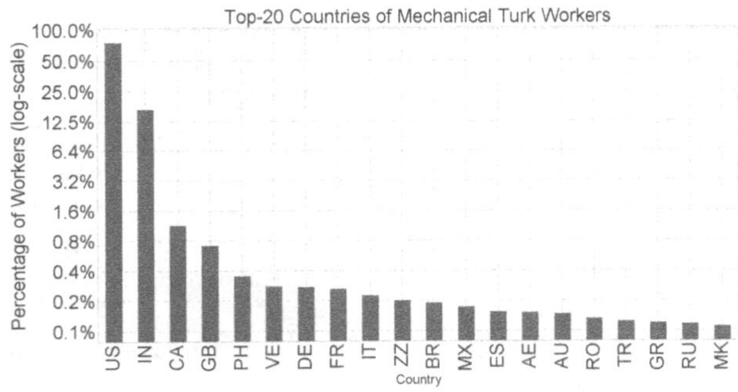

Figure 1: The top-20 countries of origin for Mechanical Turk workers. Most of the workers are from the USA (75%), with India (16%) being second, followed by Canada (1.1%), Great Britain (0.7%), Philippines (0.35%), and Germany (0.27%).

In our previous work [14], we focus on understanding the dynamics of MTurk from a market perspective, where we analyze the demand and supply on the marketplace, and examine the features that drive the speed of completion of a batch of tasks. In this work, we are interested in modeling the size and the demographics of the MTurk worker population by accounting for the workers' propensity to participate in a survey that we regularly post on the platform. We show that failing to account for the task's specific propensity leads to the underestimation of the MTurk workers population size when applying classical capture-recapture models.

3 DEMOGRAPHICS OF MTURK WORKERS

In this section, we describe our survey data collection methodology, and present the basic results for the demographics of the Mechanical Turk workers.

3.1 Data Collection

We collect basic demographics information about Mechanical Turk workers, by periodically posting a survey task asking workers to submit the following information: (a) Gender, (b) Year of Birth, (c) Marital Status, (d) Household Size, (e) Household Income, and (f) Location (City, Country). [3]

We post one survey task every 15 minutes. The survey can be completed by a single MTurk worker and takes on average 30 seconds. For every submitted survey response, we pay 5 US cents. Each worker on the platform can participate in our survey once every 30 days. As of now (August 12, 2018), the survey is continuously posted every 15 minutes, starting on March 26, 2015. For the purpose of this paper, we report the results obtained from all the surveys posted between March 26, 2015 and July 31, 2017 (859 days). In this time frame, we collected a total of 84,511 responses, submitted by 39,461 unique workers.

3.2 Survey Results Analysis

We now present the analysis of the survey results.

3.2.1 Country: Figure 1 shows the top-20 countries from which MTurk workers completed our survey. Most of the workers are from the US (75%), with India (16%) being second, followed by

[3]We also use geolocation tools to verify the location of each participating worker.

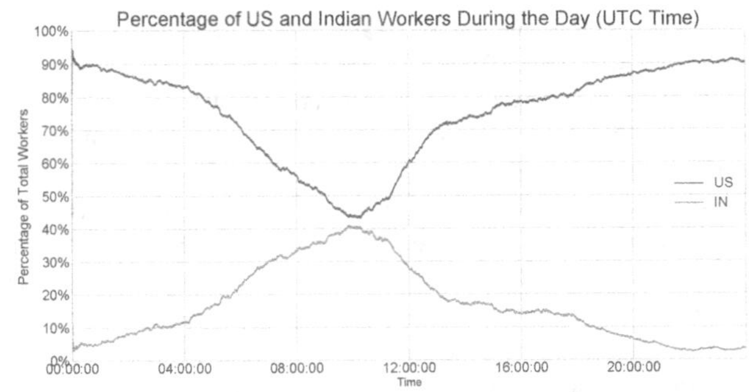

Figure 2: Percentage of US and Indian workers throughout the day.

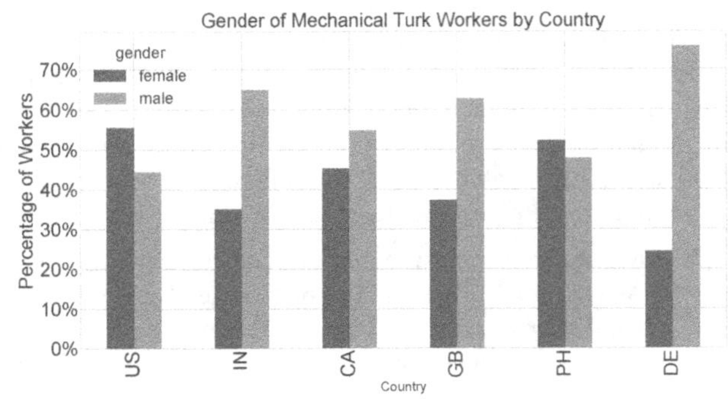

Figure 3: Gender breakdown across countries.

Canada (1.1%), Great Britain (0.7%), Philippines (0.35%), and Germany (0.27%).[4] The dominance of US and India among the worker population is well-documented in prior studies [17, 22, 26]. As expected, due to the time difference, the activity levels of US and Indian workers are different. Figure 2 shows the percentage of the US and Indian workers during the day on MTurk platform, illustrating that at 10am UTC the percentage of workers from the US is at a minimum at around 45%, while midnight UTC is at a maximum at around 90%. Our analysis did not detect any other significant periodicities in the data (e.g., day of the week, etc.)

A notable effect that we noticed in our surveys is the increase of international workers, happening around May 2016. Figure 4 shows the percentage of the MTurk workers from US, India, Canada, and Great Britain over time. Note that around May 2016 there is a sharp drop in the percentage of US workers on MTurk, and a corresponding increase in the percentage of workers from Canada, Great Britain, and other countries. We believe, this is due to the reverse of the Amazon policy from 2012, which restricted the enrollment of international workers. However, as we can see in the data, after the initial spikes in participation, the percentage of international workers has been steadily falling and is slowly converging towards April 2016 levels.

3.2.2 Gender: Our results indicate a generally balanced workforce, with 51% female workers and 49% male. However, we detected significant deviations from the average across countries. Among

[4]India is over-represented in the raw results presented here due to participation bias. We discuss this in detail in Section 5.

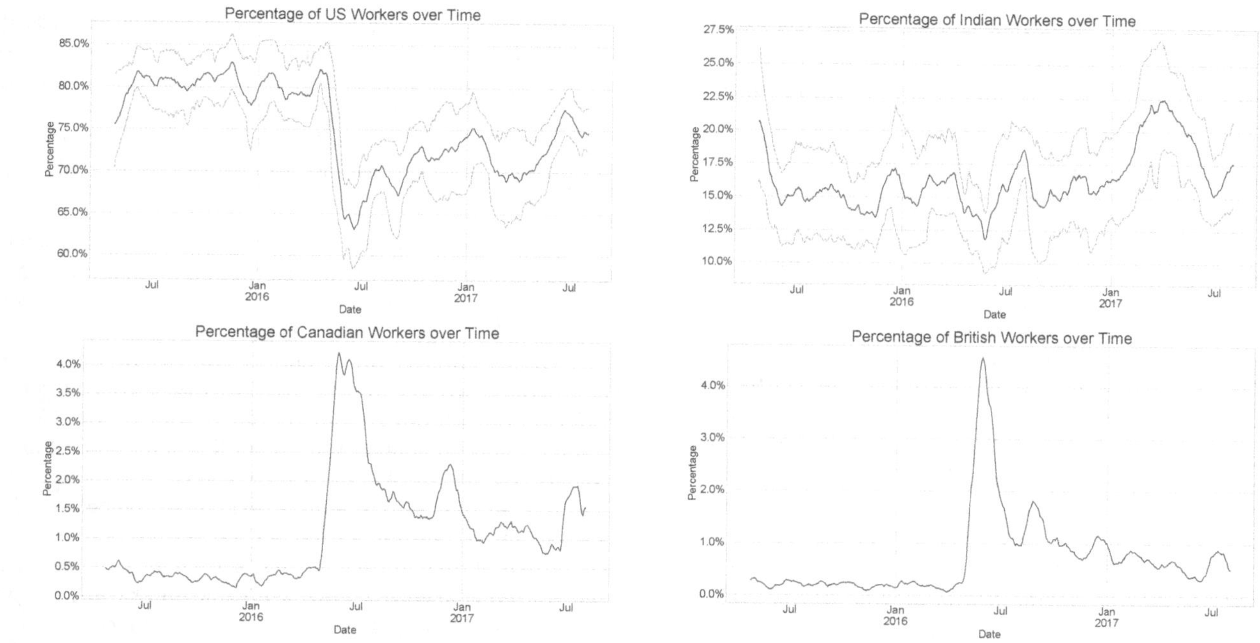

Figure 4: The average percentage of workers from various countries, over time. For US and India, we also show the the 25% and 75% percentiles to illustrate the typical noise levels in our survey measurements.

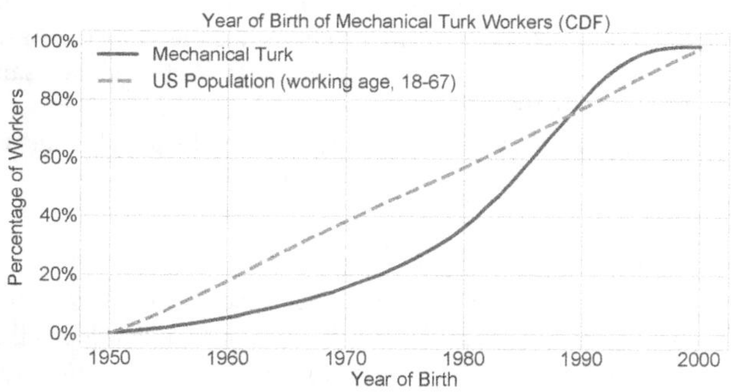

Figure 5: Year of birth.

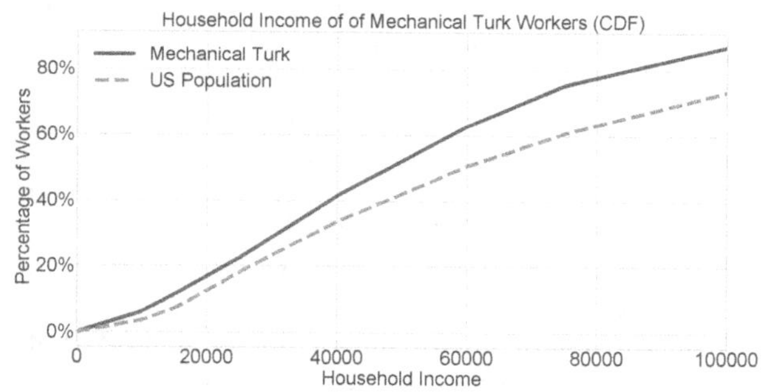

Figure 6: Household Income.

US workers, we observed that females constitute 55% of the participants, while for most other countries we observed the opposite bias. Figure 3 shows the breakdown among the top-6 countries.

3.2.3 Age: The population of MTurk workers tends to be younger than the overall population (Figure 5): 20% of the MTurk workers are born after 1990, 60% are born after 1980, and 80% are born after 1970. When compared to the *working age, adult* US population, 20% of the adult population is born after 1990, 40% are born after 1980, and 60% of the adult population is born after 1970. When comparing the population of US workers vs India, we also observe that Indian workers are a bit younger than their US counterparts.

3.2.4 Marital Status and Household Size: In terms of marital status, we observed that 40% of the workers report being single and 42% report being married; another 10% reports cohabitating, 5% being divorced, and 3% being engaged. When examining the combination of household sizes and marital status, 15% of the workers are single and live in a household of one, while the categories of singles living in household sizes of two, three, four, and five-plus account, each, for 6% of the workers. The corresponding numbers of married workers are household sizes of two (11%), three (11%), four (11%), and five-plus (8%).

3.2.5 Income: In Figure 6, we show the income distribution for workers based in the US, compared to the income distribution for the general US population. We observe that MTurk workers have household incomes that are below the average US population. For example, the median household income for the US is around \$57K, while for MTurk workers the median household income is around \$47K. Similarly, while 26.5% of US households make more than \$100K per year, for MTurk workers this percentage falls at 12.5%.

We presented raw data statistics for the MTurk worker population. This presentation is restricted to percentages of the population, as opposed to an absolute number of workers. In the next section, we show how to estimate the absolute number of workers in the marketplace by using techniques from the field of ecology. Later on, we demonstrate how to measure the selection and participation biases and explain how to ensure that our results are representative of the overall worker population, and not biased towards workers that are likely to participate in this particular task.

4 ESTIMATING POPULATION SIZE

In this section, we focus on estimating the *number* of workers on Amazon Mechanical Turk. We build on techniques from the field of ecology, specifically on a family of techniques commonly referred to as "*capture-recapture*." We start with simple techniques, and we proceed to more advanced ones, by identifying the various assumptions of the basic models that result in inconsistencies. Specifically, we highlight that for online populations some of the techniques from ecology lead to highly inaccurate results because the *MTurk worker propensity of participating in online surveys* follows a highly skewed distribution, while in ecology the probability of capturing an animal is relatively more homogeneous.

4.1 Two Occasion, Closed Population Model

The simplest capture-recapture model is the "two-occasion" model, which results in the *Lincoln estimator* [20]. In the two-occasion model there are two stages:

- The **capture** phase, in which a set of N_1 animals are captured, marked, then released. In our scenario, the capture phase is a 30-day period and we consider as "captured" the workers that participate in the survey during that period.
- The **re-capture** phase, where a set of N_2 animals are captured. Among these N_2 animals, $M = N_1 \cap N_2$ were marked in the capture phase. In our scenario, the recapture phase is a different 30-day period and we consider as "recaptured" the M workers that participate in both surveys.

Given $n_1 = |N_1|$, $n_2 = |N_2|$, and $m = |M|$, we estimate the total number of workers N. If there are N workers available during the recapture period, and n_1 among them are marked from the capture period then, when we sample a single worker, the probability that this worker was previously marked is n_1/N. When we sample n_2 workers, the expected number of marked workers is $\frac{n_1 \cdot n_2}{N}$. Since we counted m marked workers, we set $m = \frac{n_1 \cdot n_2}{N}$ and therefore we get the estimator:

$$N = \frac{n_1 \cdot n_2}{m} \tag{1}$$

Example 4.1. Consider the following simple, two-occasion measurement. During the first month of our experiment, in April 2015, our survey was completed by 2812 unique workers.[5]. During the third month of our experiment, in June 2015, our survey was completed 2828 times. Among the 2828 MTurk workers who completed the survey during June 2015, we have 593 MTurk workers who also completed the survey during April 2015. This means that approximately $593/2828 \approx 21\%$ of the recaptured workers were marked. Therefore, according to the Lincoln estimator, our population estimate is $N = \frac{2812 \cdot 2828}{593} = 13410$ workers. □

The Lincoln estimator relies on two main assumptions:

- The *closed population* assumption: None of the workers from the capture occasion have left the MTurk platform before the recapture occasion (in ecology, this corresponds to no deaths or immigration in the animal population). This ensures that, during the recapture occasion, all n_1 marked MTurk workers are present in the population and can be recaptured.
- The *equal catchability* assumption: The probability of capturing each worker is uniform across the population of MTurk workers.

In Figure 7, we present the population size estimations generated using the results of 100,000 randomly selected two-occasion measurements: each measurement takes two random 30-day periods, that have at least *diff* > 60 days between the beginning of the first and the second time periods. The *diff* > 60 ensures no "interference" between the two sample periods, as we allow a worker to participate only once every 30 days.

The results highlight a violation of the closed population assumption for the Lincoln estimator: In Figure 7a, we see that the population estimates are different as the *diff* value increases (the colors encode the *diff* value), while the population estimates remain relatively stable when the *diff* value remains fixed (e.g., follows the bands with the same color). While it would not be surprising to see an increase in population over time, such an increase should have been observed even when keeping *diff* fixed, something that we do not see in our results. Figure 7b is a variation of Figure 7a with *diff* in the x-axis, and colors encoding the beginning of the recapture period. Figure 7b makes more explicit the increase of the population estimates as the *diff* increases, for the *same* recapture period. This increase means that the overlap between two samples decreases as the time difference between samples increases, highlighting that marked workers depart from the population, and therefore violating the closed population assumption.

4.2 Open Population Model

The assumption of the closed population model was a very restrictive one in ecology, and multiple models have been developed that allow for arrivals and departures of animals in the population (e.g., see the Jolly-Seber and the Cormack-Jolly-Seber models [10, 18, 29]). In our setting, an open population model allows for the arrival of new workers on the platform, and departure of workers permanently from the platform.

To move from the closed capture-recapture model to the open one we remove the assumption of *no departure* and instead we introduce the notion of *lifetime* of MTurk workers in the platform. For simplicity, we assume that the survival probability of MTurk workers is constant over time and across the population. In this case, the survival probability $S(t)$ is defined by the survival function $S(t) = \exp(-\lambda \cdot t)$ where t is the time (in days) since the last time the survey is answered by a particular MTurk worker; and λ is the decay rate, which corresponds to the rate in which workers depart from the platform.

Given the new assumption about the MTurk population dynamics we can refine the estimator described in Section 4.1. We have a capture period at time $d - t$ and a recapture period at time d.

After the n_{d-t} workers are captured and marked during the first part of the two-occasion experiment, there is a $S(t)$ probability for each MTurk worker to survive until a recapture part of the two-occasion experiment that is t days away. On expectation, out of n_{d-t}

[5] Note that, by design, a worker can complete our survey only once every 30 days.

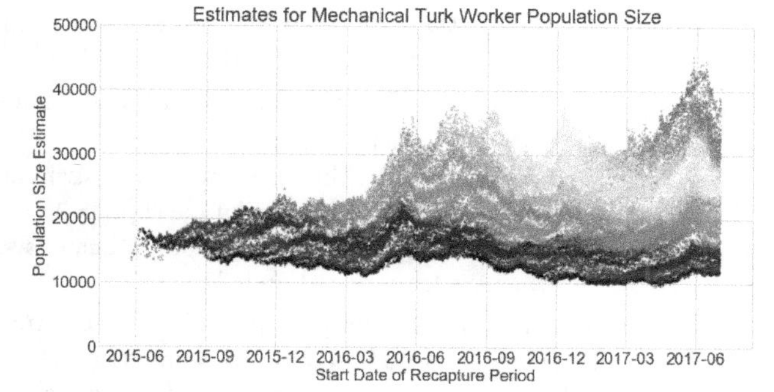

(a) Population estimates as a function of the start time of the recapture period. The colors, using a spectral colormap, encode the time distance between the two samples. Red colors correspond to large time distance and black corresponds to small time distance.

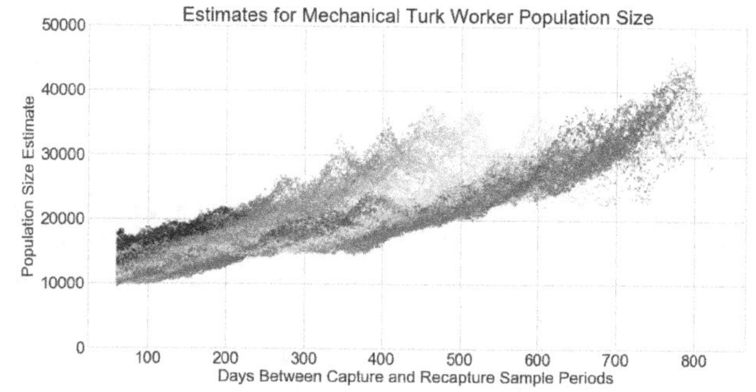

(b) Population estimates as a function of the time distance between the two samples. The colors, using a spectral colormap, encode the time corresponding to the beginning of the recapture period. Red encodes recapture periods close to July 2017 and black those close to May 2015.

Figure 7: Estimates of the size of the MTurk worker population, using the Lincoln estimator. Each data point corresponds to a comparison of two sample periods. Note that the population estimates increase as the distance between sample periods increases, signaling violation of the closed population assumption.

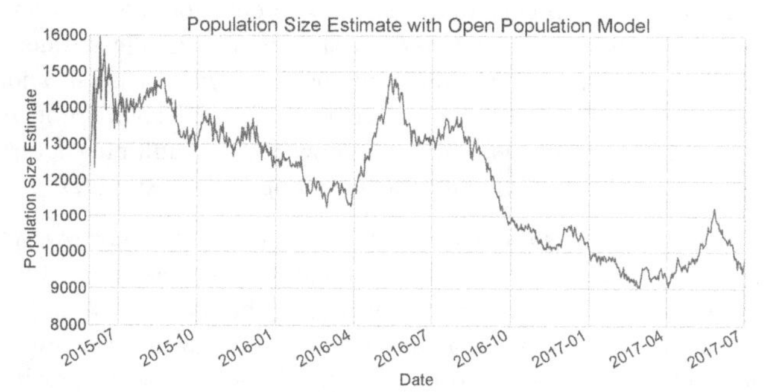

Figure 8: Estimated MTurk population using Open Population Model.

MTurk workers marked during the capture occasion, $n_{d-t} \cdot S(t)$ workers are still present in the population during the recapture occasion at time d. Therefore, the probability of picking a marked worker when picking a random MTurk worker is $\frac{n_{d-t} \cdot S(t)}{N_d}$, with N_d being the population during the recapture period. Therefore, when sampling n_d MTurk workers during the recapture, on average we expect to see $m_{d,t} = S(t) \cdot \frac{n_{d-t} \cdot n_d}{N_d}$ marker MTurk workers. Thus, estimate of population size N_d becomes:

$$N_d = \exp(-\lambda \cdot t) \cdot \frac{n_{d-t} \cdot n_d}{m_{d,t}} \quad (2)$$

In the equation above the unknowns are the N_d values and the λ, which can be estimated through a simple OLS regression after we take the logs.

Based on the model above, our estimated half-life of the MTurk worker population is 404 days, which means that roughly half of the workers leave the platform every year. Figure 8 shows the population estimates N_d over time. The results indicate that the average worker population is around 12K workers. This result is qualitatively similar with the estimate from [34], which calculates that there are around 7.3K workers available on Mechanical Turk for academic experiments.

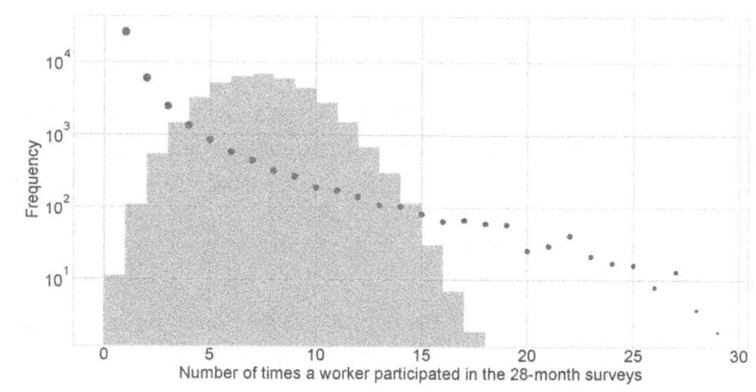

Figure 9: The dots shows the actual frequency of seeing workers in our samples during the study. The shaded histogram shows the expected distribution under the assumption of equal catchability, indicating the equal catchability assumption is violated in our data.

However, this number is a severe underestimate of the actual number of workers in the platform, due to the varying propensities of users to participate. We can detect this by analyzing the frequency of observing users in our samples. If we assume equal probability of capturing a worker in each sample, the probability of capturing a user each month is about 0.25 (3K users sampled per month, out of 12K available users). Therefore the distribution of frequencies of participation should roughly follow a binomial distribution with $p = 0.25$ and $n = 28$ samples. Figure 9 shows the observed frequencies in our study, contrasted with the expected binomial distribution. We observe that we have very significant deviations at both ends of the frequency spectrum: We see too many workers participating only one, and we also see an unusual number of workers participating "too many" times. This is a signal that the equal catchability assumption is violated, and we need to use models that account for this heterogeneity. Stewart et al. [34] dealt with the heterogeneity in participation by eliminating the heavy-hitter workers from the experiment and assuming that everyone else has an equal probability of participating. Unfortunately, this shortcut is incorrect, and leads to significant underestimates, especially in an online environment such as Amazon Mechanical Turk. We demonstrate and quantify the problem next, and we present techniques that deal with the issue.

4.3 Accounting for Propensity of Participation

An assumption of the models presented so far is that the probability of a worker participating in the survey is equal among all workers (the "equal catchability" assumption). This assumption is often incorrect in ecology (e.g., females during nesting times do not move and are unlikely to be captured) but it is a much bigger problem when applied to online environments. In many online environments, the activity levels of different users tend to follow heavy-tailed, power-law-type distributions. As we demonstrate below, when faced with such user behaviors, the estimators that assume equal catchability generate severe population underestimates.

4.3.1 Propensity in Two Occasion Model. We now take the simple two-occasion model, but allow users to have different levels of activity. Formally, we endow each user with a propensity parameter a, which captures the probability that a user will be *active and willing to participate in the survey*, at any given time. The propensity parameter is a random variable with a prior distribution $p(a)$. If we have a population of N users (not all of them *active* at the same time), each of them with a propensity a_i, then each user participates in the survey with a probability proportional to a_i and therefore the probability that we "capture" worker i in a sample of n_1 workers is:

$$P(capture|a_i) = 1 - (1 - \frac{a_i}{\sum_j^N a_j})^{n_1} \approx \frac{n_1}{N} \cdot \frac{a_i}{E[a]} \tag{3}$$

Given the propensity a_i, the probability of re-capturing in a second sample with n_2 workers is *conditionally independent given* a_i:

$$P(capture, recapture|a_i) = \frac{n_1 \cdot a_i}{N \cdot E[a]} \cdot \frac{n_2 \cdot a_i}{N \cdot E[a]} = \frac{n_1 \cdot n_2 \cdot a_i^2}{N^2 \cdot E[a]^2}$$

By integrating over the population with N workers and a distribution of propensities $p(a)$, we get that the expected intersection between two samples of size n_1 and n_2 is:

$$m = N \int \frac{n_1 n_2 a^2}{N^2 E[a]^2} p(a) da = \frac{n_1 \cdot n_2}{N} \cdot \frac{E[a^2]}{E[a]^2} = \frac{n_1 \cdot n_2}{N} \cdot \left(1 + \frac{Var[a]}{E[a]^2}\right)$$

The baseline Lincoln estimator is $\frac{n_1 \cdot n_2}{N}$, so the difference is the $\frac{Var[a]}{E[a]^2}$ factor. When the factor $\frac{Var[a]}{E[a]^2}$ is small then the Lincoln estimator is close to the true value. However, when the variance is high compared to the average propensity, the underestimates can be significant. Intuitively, this happens because the users with the highest propensity are significantly more likely to appear in both the capture and the recapture phase. Therefore the intersection of the sample tends to be dominated by the highly-returning users; the higher the variance in propensity, the more significant the effect.

Example 4.2. Consider the following three cases, where the *average* propensity to participate is $E[a] = 0.5$, i.e., workers on average have 50% probability of being active and willing to participate in the survey.

- *Constant a:* In the simplest case, where *all* workers have identical propensity, then the Lincoln estimator gives accurate results.
- *Uniformly distributed a:* Consider the case where a is uniformly distributed in the $[0, 1]$ interval ($E[a] = 0.5$). In this case, $Var[a] = 0.08$, $\frac{Var[a]}{E[a]^2} = 0.33$ and the Lincoln estimator will be $0.75 \cdot N$ when the true population is N.
- *Beta-distributed a:* Consider the case where a is distributed following the $Beta(0.001, 0.001)$ distribution ($E[a] = 0.5$). In this case $Var[a] = 0.245$, and the the Lincoln estimator will be $0.5 \cdot N$ when the true population is N.

The cased above, all with mean propensity $E[a] = 0.5$, illustrate that increased variance can lead to significant population underestimates. The underestimates are much more extreme under heavily skewed distributions that are common in online environments. For example, if propensity follows a $Beta(0.05, 20)$ distribution, then the underestimate is a factor of 20! Such degree of heterogeneity of catchability is rare in ecology, but common online; as we will see later, such a skewed Beta distribution is a good fit for the propensities observed in the MTurk population.

Our analysis for the simple two-occasion model shows that eliminating the heavy hitters from our data (as done by Stewart et al. [34]) is not a solution, as even in the simple two-occasion model (where we cannot eliminate any worker), we still observe significant underestimates. Unfortunately, simple two-occasion models are also not sufficient to estimate the characteristics of the underlying propensity distribution $p(a)$. We show next how to use a multiple-capture setting to estimate $p(a)$ and get correct population estimates.

4.3.2 Modeling Propensity with Multiple Captures. Below, we introduce a model that leverages the multiple samples of our study to measure the underlying propensity distribution.

Our model assumes that the propensity $P(capture|a_i)$ (Equation 3) follows a Beta distribution $B(\alpha, \beta)$, which is very flexible and is commonly used to model random variables that take values in a closed interval.

In addition, we assume a super-population [27] of N^* workers available over the span of the study. This assumption simplifies away the arrival and departure variables of workers and focuses on estimating an aggregated population size which can be used to derive finer-grained estimates.

We model our capture-recapture data collection by sampling n times from an underlying super-population where each worker has a capture probability $P(capture|a_i)$ that follows a $B(\alpha, \beta)$ distribution, then the probability of seeing a worker k times follows a *Beta-Binomial distribution*, with the following pdf:

$$f(k|n, \alpha, \beta) = \binom{n}{k} \frac{B(k + \alpha, n - k + \beta)}{B(\alpha, \beta)} \tag{4}$$

We can estimate the parameters of the Beta-Binomial distribution by using either the method of moments, or by using the maximum likelihood estimation approach. For our data, through MLE estimation, we obtain $\alpha = 0.29$ and $\beta = 20.9$.

The next step is to estimate the number of workers N^* from this model. As described in [9], we focus on estimating the probability a worker having frequency $k = 0$. In our data, we observe all the S sampled workers that have frequencies $k \geq 1$. We know that:

$$S = N^* \cdot \sum_{k=1}^{n} f(k|n, \alpha, \beta) = N^* (1 - f(0|n, \alpha, \beta))$$

In our experiments, we sampled a total of $S = 39,461$ distinct workers with frequencies $k \geq 1$. For $n = 28$, $\alpha = 0.29$ and $\beta = 20.9$, we have that $f(0|n, \alpha, \beta) = 0.7793$, and therefore the estimate for the super-population of workers N^* is:

$$N^* = \frac{S}{1 - f(0|n, \alpha, \beta)} = \frac{39,461}{1 - 0.7793} \approx 178,800 \ \textit{workers}$$

Similarly, we can get additional estimates by examining the number of workers that appeared once (N_1^*), twice (N_2^*), thrice, and so on:

$$N^* = \frac{N_1^*}{f(1|n, \alpha, \beta)}, \ N^* = \frac{N_2^*}{f(2|n, \alpha, \beta)}, \ N^* = \frac{N_3^*}{f(3|n, \alpha, \beta)}, \dots$$

Our technique relies on the assumption of a Beta distribution for the probabilities of capture. To check whether our technique produces population estimates that are reasonable, we also used the technique of Chao [9, Eq. 10], which yields a lower bound for the size of the population. By using our data, the Chao approach gives a *lower bound* of 97,579 workers, which is compatible with our results.

Similarly, we also experimented with a technique from Pledger et al. [25] that uses finite mixtures to model heterogeneity in an open population. The technique operates with the assumption that the population is split into a predefined set of underlying clusters, each having unique survival and capture characteristics. Our numerical estimates were sensitive to the choice of the number of clusters (the technique did not converge when we used larger number of clusters) nonetheless, it estimated the size of the super-population to 125K-130K using 3 clusters with highly heterogeneous capture probabilities across the three groups, and with a survival probability similar to the one we estimated in Section 4.2.

Having estimated the distribution of propensities, we now move to our final question: Are the demographics estimates, reported in Section 3, affected by selection bias? We address the issue next.

5 DEMOGRAPHICS AND SELECTION BIASES

A natural concern when reporting the results of a survey is that the survey answers may be biased due to the type of people that are willing to participate in the survey. Our setting, where we survey workers multiple times over a long period of time, allows us to infer the propensity of participation for the workers. This, in turn, allows us to examine whether the demographic variables that we measure are correlated with the propensity to participate, and therefore need to be adjusted.

In our model, the propensities, and hence the probability of capture, are distributed according to a Beta distribution. Therefore, to examine if there is a correlation of the propensities with the demographic variables, we use a *Beta regression* [11, 31], which is explicitly designed to handle dependent variables that are Beta distributed and exhibit heteroskedasticity and skewness.

We examined the correlation of the six demographic variables, described in Section 3.1, with the observed propensity dependent variable computed from the frequency of participation over the course of the study periods. Since the computed propensity includes values of 1.0, indicating workers who participate every month since the beginning of the study, we perform an additional transformation [31] to shift the distribution into the open interval (0,1) using $(propensity \cdot (n-1) + 0.5)/n$, where $n = 28$ is the sample size. By inspecting the distribution of the computed propensities, we note that 88% of the participants have $a < 0.1$ propensity.

	Dependent variable: Propensity		
(Intercept)	−3.44	***	(-3.53, 3.53)
Age	0.006	***	(0.005, 0.007)
Location_Country = India	0.383	***	(0.291, 0.475)
Marital_Status = Divorced	−0.064	**	(-0.121, -0.006)
Constant(ϕ)	−3.443	***	(-3.553, -3.333)
Observations	39,453		
Pseudo R^2	0.029		
Log Likelihood	208,080.100		

Table 1: Beta Regression Results for Demographic Variables that affect propensity. Note: We only include parameter estimates when: **p<0.05; ***p<0.01 (95% CI in parentheses).

We fit a mean-only beta regression model with the logit link function. Since we have a large number of categorical variables as independent regressors, and due to space constraints, we present only on variables with statistically significant effects at the $p < 0.05$ level. (See Table 1.) We did not detect any statistically significant correlation with gender, household income, and household size.

We detected a *statistically* significant effect of age (year of birth), with older workers having a slightly higher propensity to participate; while the effect was statistically significant, the magnitude of the effect was small ($\beta_{age} = 0.006$). By exponentiating the Beta coefficient of the parameter *Age* and fixing the other parameters we can obtain the rate of increase in the odds of the mean propensity for each unit change in *Age* following $\exp(\beta_{age} \cdot Age)$. Analytically, this indicates that the error in Figure 5 would be at most 10%, in *relevant* (not absolute) terms, hinting to a *slightly* younger audience on the platform. A similarly statistical significant, but weak, effect is observed for divorced workers who are slightly underrepresented by around 6%, in relative terms.

The most significant effect was detected for the independent variable *country of origin* where we observe a significant increase in propensity for workers coming from India with ($\beta_{India} = 0.38$). Here, the odds of the mean propensity are $\exp(0.38) = 1.46$ times higher if the worker is from India. This indicates that the Indian workers are over-represented in the sample and the percentage of Indian workers in Figure 1 are inflated by 46%; the real percentages are to be closer to 10%-14% and not 15%-20%.

6 DISCUSSION AND FUTURE DIRECTIONS

We presented an analysis of population estimation for Amazon Mechanical Turk using capture-recapture techniques from ecology. We demonstrated that using simple techniques, without understanding the limitations and assumptions of these models can lead to inconsistent and inaccurate results. Our analysis indicates that the population of the Mechanical Turk worker population remains relatively stable over time and it consists of at least 100K-200K workers, and possibly more. We also see that the population of the workers renews over time, with an average half-life of 400 days; this means that there are tens of thousands of new workers arriving on the platform every year.

For employers that rely on having access to a large number of workers, our study indicates that the MTurk platform *does provide access to hundreds of thousands of workers.* Out of these, and based on our empirically estimated propensity distribution, we can compute the number of available workers at any given time, which we interpret from calculating the expected propensity times the super-population size as follows: $E[a] \cdot N^* = \frac{\alpha}{\alpha+\beta} \cdot N^* = \frac{0.29}{0.29+20.9} \cdot 178,800 \approx 2,450$ *workers*. This is in sharp contrast to the conclusions of [34], which estimated that there are only 7,500 workers available to experimenters for social science research. That incorrect estimate was due to the incorrect assumption that all workers have the same degree of activity in the platform, and the same propensity to participate in a certain type of task.

In the future, we plan to consider models that allow time-varying survival and propensities. Our current models consider both to be stable over time, and our attempts to allow time-varying parameters did not indicate significant variations over time for our data. It would be also interesting to collect participation data for other long-running tasks, and examine cross-task propensities: this will allow us to understand whether propensity to participate is a global trait across tasks, or whether workers have task-specific propensities.

We would also like to use our technique to study other online environments: By monitoring user activity on various platforms (e.g., comments in threads) we can infer the total number of users in these communities, or even identify the *potential* number of users by estimating the number of users that have made no visible contribution so far. As Trushkowsky et al. [36] have shown, it is possible to use such models also in fields like information extraction and online databases, where population sizes do not necessarily correspond to humans but are important to estimate for a variety of applications. By learning the state-of-the-art from the techniques in ecology, we can adapt these models for application in domains where the behavior is different than the behavior of animals, but the fundamental ideas behind the models remain useful.

REFERENCES

[1] Steven C. Amstrup, Trent L. McDonald, and Bryan F. J. Manly. 2010. *Handbook of Capture-Recapture Analysis.* Princeton University Press, Princeton, NJ.

[2] Joanna J. Arch and Alaina L. Carr. 2016. Using Mechanical Turk for research on cancer survivors. *Psycho-Oncology* Forthcoming (2016), –. PON-15-0731.R1.

[3] Antonio A. Arechar, Simon Gächter, and Lucas Molleman. 2017. Conducting interactive experiments online. *Experimental Economics* Forthcoming (09 May 2017), 1–33.

[4] K. P. Burnham and W. S. Overton. 1978. Estimation of the Size of a Closed Population when Capture Probabilities vary Among Animals. *Biometrika* 65, 3 (1978), 625–633.

[5] Chris Callison-Burch and Mark Dredze. 2010. Creating Speech and Language Data with Amazon's Mechanical Turk. In *Proceedings of the NAACL HLT 2010 Workshop on Creating Speech and Language Data with Amazon's Mechanical Turk (CSLDAMT '10).* Association for Computational Linguistics, Stroudsburg, PA, USA, 1–12.

[6] Krista Casler, Lydia Bickel, and Elizabeth Hackett. 2013. Separate but Equal? A Comparison of Participants and Data Gathered via Amazon's MTurk, Social Media, and Face-to-Face Behavioral Testing. *Computers in Human Behavior* 29 (2013), 2156–2160.

[7] Jesse Chandler, Gabriele Paolacci, and Pam Mueller. 2013. Risks and Rewards of Crowdsourcing Marketplaces. In *Handbook of Human Computation.* Springer, New York, 377–392.

[8] Jesse Chandler and Danielle Shapiro. 2016. Conducting Clinical Research Using Crowdsourced Convenience Samples. *Annual Review of Clinical Psychology* 12 (2016), 35–81.

[9] Anne Chao. 1987. Estimating the population size for capture-recapture data with unequal catchability. *Biometrics* 43, 4 (Dec. 1987), 783–791.

[10] R. M. Cormack. 1964. Estimates of Survival From the Sighting of Marked Animals. *Biometrics* 51 (1964), 429–438.

[11] Francisco Cribari-Neto and Achim Zeileis. 2010. Beta Regression in R. *Journal of Statistical Software, Articles* 34, 2 (2010), 1–24.

[12] Damien L. Crone and Lisa A. Williams. 2017. Crowdsourcing participants for psychological research in Australia: A test of Microworkers. *Australian Psychological Society* 69 (2017), 39–47. Issue 1.

[13] Joost de Winter, Miltos Kyriakidis, Dimitra Dodou, and Riender Happee. 2015. Using CrowdFlower to Study the Relationship between Self-reported Violations and Traffic Accidents. *Procedia Manufacturing* 3 (2015), 2518–2525.

[14] Djellel Eddine Difallah, Michele Catasta, Gianluca Demartini, Panagiotis G Ipeirotis, and Philippe Cudré-Mauroux. 2015. The Dynamics of Micro-Task Crowdsourcing: The Case of Amazon MTurk. In *Proceedings of the 24th International Conference on World Wide Web.* International World Wide Web Conferences Steering Committee, ACM, New York, NY, USA, 238–247.

[15] Karën Fort, Gilles Adda, and K. Bretonnel Cohen. 2011. Amazon Mechanical Turk: Gold Mine or Coal Mine? *Computational Linguistics* 37 (2011), 413 – 420. Issue 2.

[16] Ilka H. Gleibs. 2017. Are all research fields equal? Rethinking practice for the use of data from crowd-sourcing market places. *Behavior Research Methods* 49 (August 2017), 1333–1342. Issue 4.

[17] Panagiotis Ipeirotis. 2010. *Demographics of Mechanical Turk.* Technical Report CeDER-10-01. New York University.

[18] G. M. Jolly. 1965. Explicit Estimates from Capture-Recapture Data With Both Death and Immigration- Stochastic Model. *Biometrika* 52 (1965), 225–247.

[19] Jeremy Kees, Christopher Berry, Scot Burton, and Kim Sheehan. 2017. An Analysis of Data Quality: Professional Panels, Student Subject Pools, and Amazon's Mechanical Turk. *Journal of Advertising* 46, 1 (2017), 141–155.

[20] Frederick Charles Lincoln. 1930. *Calculating waterfowl abundance on the basis of banding returns.* US Dept. of Agriculture, Washington, DC.

[21] Jianguo Lu and Dingding Li. 2010. Estimating deep web data source size by capture-recapture method. *Information Retrieval* 13, 1 (February 2010), 70–95.

[22] Winter Mason and Duncan J. Watts. 2009. Financial Incentives and the "Performance of Crowds". In *Proceedings of the ACM SIGKDD Workshop on Human Computation (HCOMP '09).* ACM, New York, NY, USA, 77–85.

[23] Joshua D. Miller, Michael Crowe, Brandon Weiss, Jessica L. Maples-Keller, and Donald R. Lynam. 2017. Using online, crowdsourcing platforms for data collection in personality disorder research: The example of Amazon's Mechanical Turk. *Personality Disorders: Theory, Research, and Treatment* 8, 1 (2017), 26–34.

[24] Shirley Pledger, Kenneth H. Pollock, and James L. Norris. 2003. Open Capture-Recapture Models with Heterogeneity: I. Cormack-Jolly-Seber Model. *Biometrics* 59, 4 (Dec. 2003), 786–794.

[25] Shirley Pledger, Kenneth H. Pollock, and James L. Norris. 2010. Open Capture-Recapture Models with Heterogeneity: II. Jolly-Seber Model. *Biometrics* 66, 3 (September 2010), 883–890.

[26] Joel Ross, Lilly Irani, M. Six Silberman, Andrew Zaldivar, and Bill Tomlinson. 2010. Who Are the Crowdworkers?: Shifting Demographics in Mechanical Turk. In *CHI '10 Extended Abstracts on Human Factors in Computing Systems (CHI EA '10).* ACM, New York, NY, USA, 2863–2872.

[27] Carl James Schwarz and A. Neil Arnason. 1996. A General Methodology for the Analysis of Capture-Recapture Experiments in Open Populations. *Biometrics* 52, 3 (1996), 860–873.

[28] George Seber. 1982. *The Estimation of Animal Abundance and Related Parameters.* Charles Griffin, London, UK.

[29] G. A. F. Seber. 1964. A Note on the Multiple Recapture Census. *Biometrika* 52 (1964), 249–259.

[30] Victor S. Sheng, Foster Provost, and Panagiotis G. Ipeirotis. 2008. Get Another Label? Improving Data Quality and Data Mining Using Multiple, Noisy Labelers. In *Proceedings of the 14th ACM SIGKDD International Conference on Knowledge Discovery and Data Mining (KDD '08).* ACM, New York, NY, USA, 614–622.

[31] Michael Smithson and Jay Verkuilen. 2006. A better lemon squeezer? Maximum-likelihood regression with beta-distributed dependent variables. *Psychological methods* 11 (2006), 54–71. Issue 1.

[32] Rion Snow, Brendan O'Connor, Daniel Jurafsky, and Andrew Y. Ng. 2008. Cheap and Fast—but is It Good?: Evaluating Non-expert Annotations for Natural Language Tasks. In *Proceedings of the Conference on Empirical Methods in Natural Language Processing (EMNLP '08).* Association for Computational Linguistics, Stroudsburg, PA, USA, 254–263.

[33] Vanessa V. Sochat, Ian W. Eisenberg, A. Zeynep Enkavi, Jamie Li, Patrick G. Bissett, and Russell A. Poldrack. 2016. The Experiment Factory: Standardizing Behavioral Experiments. *Frontiers in Psychology* 7 (2016), 610.

[34] Neil Stewart, Christoph Ungemach, Adam J. L. Harris, Daniel M. Bartels, Ben R. Newell, Gabriele Paolaccik, and Jesse Chandler. 2015. The average laboratory samples a population of 7,300 Amazon Mechanical Turk workers. *Judgment and Decision Making* 10, 5 (2015), 479–491.

[35] Keela S. Thomson and Daniel M. Oppenheimer. 2016. Investigating an alternate form of the cognitive reflection test. *Judgment and Decision Making* 11, 1 (2016), 99–113.

[36] Beth Trushkowsky, Tim Kraska, Michael J. Franklin, and Purnamrita Sarkar. 2016. Answering Enumeration Queries with the Crowd. *Commun. ACM* 59, 1 (2016), 118–127.

Joint Generative-Discriminative Aggregation Model for Multi-Option Crowd Labels

Kamran Ghasedi Dizaji
University of Pittsburgh
kag221@pitt.edu

Yanhua Yang
Xidian University
yanhyang@xidian.edu.cn

Heng Huang*
University of Pittsburgh
heng.huang@pitt.edu

ABSTRACT

Although some crowdsourcing aggregation models have been introduced to aggregate noisy crowd labels, these models mostly consider single-option (i.e. discrete) crowd labels as the input variables, and are not compatible with multi-option (i.e. non-deterministic) crowd data. In this paper, we propose a novel joint generative-discriminative aggregation model, which is able to efficiently deal with both single-option and multi-option crowd labels. Considering the confidence of workers for each option as the input data, we first introduce a new discriminative aggregation model, called Constrained Weighted Majority Voting ($CWMV_{\ell 1}$), which improves the performance of majority voting method. $CWMV_{\ell 1}$ considers flexible reliability parameters for crowd workers, employs ℓ_1-norm loss function to deal with noisy crowd data, and includes optimization constraints to have probabilistic outputs. We prove that our object is convex, and derive an efficient optimization algorithm. Moreover, we integrate the discriminative $CWMV_{\ell 1}$ model with a generative model, resulting in a powerful joint aggregation model. Combination of these sub-models is obtained in a probabilistic framework rather than a heuristic way. For our joint model, we derive an efficient optimization algorithm, which alternates between updating the parameters and estimating the potential true labels. Experimental results indicate that the proposed aggregation models achieve superior or competitive results in comparison with the state-of-the-art models on single-option and multi-option crowd datasets, while having faster convergence rates and more reliable predictions.

CCS CONCEPTS

• **Information systems** → **Crowdsourcing**; • **Computing methodologies** → *Machine learning*;

ACM Reference format:

Kamran Ghasedi Dizaji, Yanhua Yang, and Heng Huang. 2018. Joint Generative-Discriminative Aggregation Model for Multi-Option Crowd Labels. In *Proceedings of WSDM 2018: The Eleventh ACM International Conference on Web Search and Data Mining , Marina Del Rey, CA, USA, February 5–9, 2018 (WSDM 2018)*, 9 pages.
DOI: http://dx.doi.org/10.1145/3159652.3159672

*Corresponding author. This work was partially supported by NIH R01 AG049371, NSF IIS 1302675, IIS 1344152, DBI 1356628, IIS 1619308, IIS 1633753

ACM ISBN 978-1-4503-5581-0/18/02...$15.00
DOI: http://dx.doi.org/10.1145/3159652.3159672

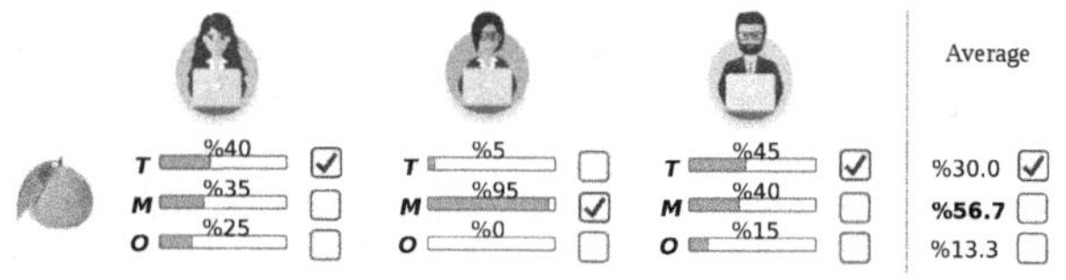

Figure 1: Three crowd workers are asked to classify a figure as tangor (T), mandarin (M) or orange (O). Their single-option and multi-option crowd labels are shown with checked boxes and confidence bars respectively. The average score of multi-option labels correctly shows higher chance for mandarin, while the majority of single-option labels incorrectly suggests tangor as the truth.

1 INTRODUCTION

Motivation: In recent years, crowdsourcing platforms, such as Amazon Mechanical Turk, have gained huge popularity due to their efficiency in collecting labels for large-scale datasets [1, 5, 10, 20, 21]. Using these platforms, a task requester can divide a large task into small micro-tasks, and then hire inexpensive crowd workers for labeling the small tasks. These crowdsourcing tasks usually consist of several questions, each one contains a set of candidate options, and crowd workers are asked to answer them only by selecting a single option for each question (i.e. single-option crowd labels). However, the collected labels from crowd workers are often noisy and unreliable, since workers are usually inexpert in the assigned tasks. To tackle this issue, each item is labeled multiple times with different workers, and these redundant crowd labels are then used to estimate the true labels.

Problem: The problem of aggregating these redundant and noisy crowd labels have been extensively explored in the literature [4, 24, 30, 34]. The previous crowdsourcing aggregation models mostly rely on generative models, which are designed for the single-option crowd labels (i.e. discrete random variables). But, recent studies have shown that crowd workers cannot completely convey their non-deterministic beliefs with the single-option crowd labels. In order to address this issue and increase the quality of collected crowd labels, they introduced more flexible data collection mechanisms, which allow crowd workers to select multiple options for a question, or report their non-deterministic confidence level for the selected options [22, 23, 36]. Fig. 1 shows an advantage of the multi-option crowd labels against the single-option crowd data with an example. *However as also mentioned in [22], the standard aggregation models are often incompatible with the multi-option crowd labels, and they are only able to handle single-option crowd data.*

Proposed aggregation models: In this paper, we propose novel crowdsourcing aggregation models, which are able to efficiently deal with both single-option and multi-option crowd data. Unlike the discrete crowd labels for the standard aggregation models, we consider the workers confidence levels for each option as the input data for our models. These confidences either are collected from crowd workers directly, or are set by assuming uniform probability for the (multiple) selected options. In order to construct our joint model, we first introduce a new discriminative aggregation model, which improves the discriminative capability of majority voting (*MV*). The proposed discriminative model, called constrained weighted majority voting ($CWMV_{\ell 1}$), considers flexible reliability parameters for crowd workers, employs ℓ_1-norm loss function to deal with noisy crowd labels, and includes optimization constraints to provide probabilistic potential true labels (called truth). We prove that the problem of $CWMV_{\ell 1}$ is jointly convex in optimization variables, hence the optimality of the estimated truth and learned parameters are guaranteed. We further derive an efficient optimization algorithm for solving the problem of $CWMV_{\ell 1}$, which alternates between estimating the truth and updating the parameters. This algorithm has fast convergence rate and empirically converge in a few iterations in our experiments.

Furthermore, we enhance the discriminative $CWMV_{\ell 1}$ model by coupling it with a generative model, resulting in a powerful joint generative-discriminative aggregation model. Combination of the generative and discriminative sub-models is obtained in a probabilistic framework rather than a heuristic way. We then employ an efficient alternating optimization algorithm, which updates the parameters when the truths are assumed to be known and estimates the truths when the parameters are fixed.

Experimental results: In our experiments, we first compare the proposed aggregation model with the state-of-the-art models on several single-option crowdsourcing datasets. Our joint model not only achieves superior results compared to the alternative models, but also shows a much faster convergence rate. Furthermore, we show that the truth obtained by our joint model is more reliable than the best alternative model, since it relatively assigns lower confidence (probability) for the mispredicted items. Finally, the proposed models outperform the alternative models with significant margins on multi-option crowdsourcing datasets, and consequently confirm their effectiveness in dealing with the multi-option crowd labels.

Contributions: Therefore, the main contributions of this paper can be summarized as follows:

- Proposing a new discriminative aggregation model with convex problem, and deriving an efficient optimization algorithm to solve it;
- Introducing a novel joint generative-discriminative aggregation model using a probabilistic framework for combination;
- Achieving superior or competitive results on single-option and multi-option crowdsourcing datasets with much faster convergence rates.

2 RELATED WORKS

There are several studies on crowdsourcing aggregation models [24, 32], which could be generally divided into two groups of generative and discriminative models.

Discriminative models: The discriminative aggregation models directly infer the truths with some aggregation rules regardless of crowd labels distribution. Majority voting (*MV*) is the simplest discriminative model, which considers equal reliability for crowd workers and simply averages their votes. An intuitive and fast extension of majority voting, called iterative weighted majority voting (*IWMV*), is introduced in [11], which improves *MV* by considering a reliability parameter for each worker. Tian and Zhu also enhanced *MV* model by adopting the notion of max-margin from support vector machines, and introduced max-margin mjority voting (M^3V) [26]. Our discriminative aggregation model employs different objective functions compared to the other weighted majority voting methods. Its constrained ℓ_1-norm problem can be seen as a variant of unsupervised least absolute methods. In addition, it achieves better results and faster convergence rate compared to M^3V, which is the state-of-the-art discriminative aggregation model.

Generative models: In contrast to the discriminative aggregation models, the generative models employ a probabilistic model to represent the distribution of noisy observations (i.e. crowd labels) given the unknown variables (i.e. true labels) and model parameters. Dawid and Skene (*DS*) introduced a well known model in [4], which considers a confusion matrix $\boldsymbol{v}_j \in \mathbb{R}^{B\times B}$ as a reliability parameter for each worker, where B is the number of classes. The (c,c) diagonal element, denoted by v_{jcc}, represents the probability of correct prediction of the c-th class items, and the off-diagonal element v_{jck} shows the probability of misprediction of the c-th class items as class k. In order to improve estimating the truths, Oyama *et al.* extended *DS* to use self-reported confidences for the single-option crowd labels. The confidence values in a range of $[0 - 100]$ are first converted to binary values using a worker specific threshold, and then they are used as the input for an aggregation model [17]. Kazai discussed the relationship between the reported confidence of workers and the quality of crowd labels [7]. Furthermore, several studies extended *DS* by assuming a prior distribution for parameters, and used Bayesian approach to compute the posterior distribution [3, 12, 19]. Another generative model, called *GLAD*, considers a scalar parameter for reliability of each worker and difficulty of each item, and calculates the probability of truths using a logistic function defined over the parameters [30]. Moreover, *GLAD* is extended in [29] such that a vector instead of a scalar is considered as the parameter of each worker and each sample. In addition to considering a confusion matrix as a worker reliability parameter, Zhou *et al.* assigned a confusion matrix as a difficulty parameter for each item, and proposed an aggregation model (*Entropy*) based on minimax conditional entropy of the crowd labels [34, 35]. In order to tackle the aggregation problem when crowd labels per worker are scarce, Venanzi *et al.* proposed CommunityBCC, which groups crowd workers into a few types (i.e. communities) and learns similar reliability parameters for each community [28].

Generative-Discriminative models: Tian and Zhu introduced a generative-discriminative model by imposing posterior regularization to a generative aggregation model using the discriminative M^3V model [26]. Our joint generative-discriminative aggregation model benefits from a variant of *DS* model, but it employs a probabilistic framework to combine the generative and discriminative sub-models. Unlike the other aggregation models, it receives the non-deterministic confidence levels as input data, and consequently is compatible with the multi-option crowd labels like approval voting data in [22]. Moreover, our joint model has superior results, faster convergence rates and more reliable predictions compared to the alternative models on several single-option and multi-option crowdsourcing datasets.

3 NEW AGGREGATION MODELS

Proposed models: In this section, we first introduce our discriminative aggregation model, called constrained weighted majority voting model. We start by formulating an objective function representing majority voting (*MV*), and then show how our model, denoted by $CWMV_{\ell 1}$, extends *MV* using reliability parameters of crowd workers, ℓ_1-norm objective function and probabilistic constraints. We later prove that the optimization problem of $CWMV_{\ell 1}$ is convex, and derive efficient optimization algorithms for solving this problem. Furthermore, we propose a joint generative-discriminative aggregation model by combining $CWMV_{\ell 1}$ with a generative model in a probabilistic framework. An efficient learning approach is also employed to solve the problem of our joint model, which alternates between estimating the truths and updating parameters.

Notations: Consider the crowdsourcing task has N items to label, where each one belongs to one of B classes. There are M crowd workers labeling a subset of items. Their labels are denoted by $\mathbf{X} = \{\mathbf{x}_{11}, ..., \mathbf{x}_{ij}, ..., \mathbf{x}_{NM}\}$, where $\mathbf{x}_{ij}$ represents the j-th worker's label for the i-th item. Note that $\mathbf{x}_{ij} = [x_{ij}^1, ..., x_{ij}^B]$ is a B dimensional column vector, where each element indicates a worker's confidence for each option. Using this notation, standard single-option crowdsourcing data has binary elements $x_{ij}^k \in \{0, 1\}$, while multi-option crowd labels could be real values $x_{ij}^k \in [0, 1]$. The crowd labels for skipped/unassigned question are shown with a zero vector. The truths are represented by $\mathbf{Y} = \{\mathbf{y}_1, ..., \mathbf{y}_N\}$, where $\mathbf{y}_i$ is a B dimensional vector with a single element set to 1 and the rest to 0 . In this paper, we represent matrix variables with uppercase bold letters, vector variables with lowercase bold letters, and scalar variables with lowercase letters.

3.1 Manhattan Norm Constrained Weighted Majority Voting

Majority voting: *MV* is the simplest discriminative aggregation model, only counting the crowd labels to compute the score of each option. The following problem can be considered as the objective of *MV*,

$$\min_{\mathbf{y}_i} \sum_{i=1}^{N} \|\mathbf{X}_i \mathbf{1} - \mathbf{y}_i\|_2^2, \tag{1}$$

where $\mathbf{X}_i = [\mathbf{x}_{i1}, ..., \mathbf{x}_{iM}]^T \in \mathbb{R}^{B \times M}$ includes crowd labels for the i-th item. *MV* assumes $\mathbf{1} \in \mathbb{R}^{M \times 1}$ as non-flexible reliability parameters for crowd workers, which can not differentiate between accurate and untruthful workers.

Constrained weighted majority voting: In order to enhance discriminative ability of *MV*, we propose $CWMV_{\ell 1}$, which benefits from flexible reliability parameters for crowd workers, robust model to noisy crowd data and probabilistic interpretation of the truths. Unlike *MV*, $CWMV_{\ell 1}$ is able to adjust its parameters, and consequently have a more flexible aggregation model. It also employs ℓ_1-norm objective function, which has shown robust performance when dealing with noisy input data. Moreover, $CWMV_{\ell 1}$ uses a constrained optimization problem to provide the probabilistic truths. The objective function of $CWMV_{\ell 1}$ is introduced with the following equation:

$$\min_{\mathbf{w}, \mathbf{y}_i \geq 0, \mathbf{1}^T \mathbf{y}_i = 1} \sum_{i=1}^{N} \|\mathbf{X}_i \mathbf{w} - \mathbf{y}_i\|_1 + \lambda_w \|\mathbf{w}\|_2^2 . \tag{2}$$

where $\mathbf{w} \in \mathbb{R}^{M \times 1}$ represents the workers reliability parameters, and λ_w is the regularization hyper-parameter. The first term in the objective function can be seen as a variant of weighted majority voting, and the second term avoids overfitting using the ℓ_2 regularization term. The constraints (under min operation) are also helpful to have the truths with probabilistic interpretation, and avoid the trivial solution $\mathbf{y}_i = \mathbf{0}$ and $\mathbf{w} = \mathbf{0}$.

Learning approach: In order to solve Problem (2) by two unknown variables ($\mathbf{y}_i$ and $\mathbf{w}$), we use an alternating learning approach, where the reliability parameters $\mathbf{w}$ are updated while the truths $\mathbf{Y}$ are fixed, and each truth $\mathbf{y}_i$ is estimated when the parameters $\mathbf{w}$ are assumed to be known. But before going further, we can rewrite Problem (2) by replacing ℓ_1-norm with trace according to the iterative reweighted optimization strategy.

$$\min_{\mathbf{w}, \mathbf{y}_i \geq 0, \mathbf{1}^T \mathbf{y}_i = 1} \sum_{i=1}^{N} Tr(\mathbf{X}_i \mathbf{w} - \mathbf{y}_i)^T \mathbf{U}_i (\mathbf{X}_i \mathbf{w} - \mathbf{y}_i) + \lambda_w \|\mathbf{w}\|_2^2 , \tag{3}$$

where $\mathbf{U}_i \in \mathbb{R}^{B \times B}$ is a diagonal matrix with element $u_{kk} = \frac{1}{2|\tilde{y}_{ik} - \mathbf{x}_{ik} \tilde{\mathbf{w}}|}$, when $\tilde{\mathbf{y}}_i$ and $\tilde{\mathbf{w}}$ are the solution from the last iteration. Previous studies showed that the optimal solution of Problem (3) iteratively converges to the optimal solution of original Problem (2) [15, 16]. We further simplify Problem (3) to:

$$\min_{\mathbf{w}, \mathbf{y}_i \geq 0, \mathbf{1}^T \mathbf{y}_i = 1} \sum_{i=1}^{N} \mathbf{w}^T (\mathbf{X}_i^T \mathbf{U}_i \mathbf{X}_i + \lambda_w \mathbf{I}) \mathbf{w} - 2\mathbf{y}_i^T \mathbf{U}_i \mathbf{X}_i \mathbf{w} + \mathbf{y}_i^T \mathbf{U}_i \mathbf{y}_i . \tag{4}$$

Now we use a learning approach, that alternates between updating the optimization variables $\mathbf{y}_i$ and $\mathbf{w}$.

Update w: When the truths $\mathbf{Y}$ is considered given, the Problem (4) is reduced to:

$$\min_{\mathbf{w}} \sum_{i=1}^{N} \mathbf{w}^T (\mathbf{X}_i^T \mathbf{U}_i \mathbf{X}_i + \lambda_w \mathbf{I}) \mathbf{w} - 2\mathbf{y}_i^T \mathbf{U}_i \mathbf{X}_i \mathbf{w} , \tag{5}$$

which has the following closed form solution:

$$\mathbf{w} = \Big(\sum_{i=1}^{N} \mathbf{X}_i^T \mathbf{U}_i \mathbf{X}_i + \lambda_w \mathbf{I} \Big)^{-1} \Big(\sum_{i=1}^{N} \mathbf{X}_i^T \mathbf{U}_i \mathbf{y}_i \Big) . \tag{6}$$

Update Y: The problem for estimating truths $\mathbf{Y}$ with the fixed parameters $\mathbf{w}$ is:

$$\min_{\mathbf{y}_i \geq 0, \mathbf{1}^T \mathbf{y}_i = 1} \sum_{i=1}^{N} \mathbf{y}_i^T \mathbf{U}_i \mathbf{y}_i - 2\mathbf{y}_i^T \mathbf{U}_i \mathbf{X}_i \mathbf{w} . \tag{7}$$

Since the objective is independent for each item $i \in \{1, ..., N\}$, the problem could be decomposed into N independent sub-problems

Algorithm 1: *$CWMV_{\ell 1}$* aggregation model

1 Initialize Y by majority voting
2 **while** *not converged* **do**
3   $\mathbf{w} = \left(\sum_{i=1}^{N} \mathbf{X}_i^T \mathbf{U}_i \mathbf{X}_i + \lambda_w \mathbf{I}\right)^{-1} \left(\sum_{i=1}^{N} \mathbf{X}_i^T \mathbf{U}_i \mathbf{y}_i\right)$
4   Solve Problem (8) to infer each $\mathbf{y}_i \quad \forall i \in \{1,...,N\}$
5 **end**

as follows:

$$\min_{\mathbf{y}_i \geq 0, \mathbf{1}^T \mathbf{y}_i = 1} \quad \mathbf{y}_i^T \mathbf{U}_i \mathbf{y}_i - 2\mathbf{y}_i^T \mathbf{U}_i \mathbf{X}_i \mathbf{w} \tag{8}$$

where each sub-problem can be seen as a quadratic programming problem with the simplex constraint. There are several first-order methods to solve this problem, such as gradient descent, subgradient descent, and Nesterov optimal method [14], which require the objective function value and its (sub) gradient at each iteration. But we derive an efficient optimization algorithm for this problem in Appendix A, that has fast convergence rate and empirically converges within one or a few iterations in our experiments.

Convexity proof: Interestingly, we can prove that the optimization problem of $CWMV_{\ell 1}$ in Eq. (2) is jointly convex in $\mathbf{w}$ and $\mathbf{y}_i$, and the optimality of the parameters and truths are guaranteed. The objective function of Problem (2) is summation of $\lambda_w \|\mathbf{w}\|_2^2$ and $f_i = \|\mathbf{X}_i \mathbf{w} - \mathbf{y}_i\|_1$ terms for every task $i \in \{1,...,N\}$. Since the inequality constraint is convex, equality constraint is affine, the regularization term is a convex function, and summation of convex functions preserves convexity, we only require to prove the convexity of f_i. The mentioned term can be reformulated as $f_i = \|[\mathbf{X}_i, -\mathbf{I}][\mathbf{w}, \mathbf{y}_i]^T\|_1$. So, we can prove convexity, since $h = \|\|_1$ is convex and $g = [\mathbf{X}_i, -\mathbf{I}][\mathbf{w}, \mathbf{y}_i]^T$ is linear *wrt* the optimization variables, then the composition $f_i = h \circ g$ is convex in $[\mathbf{w}, \mathbf{y}_i]$. Therefore, the problems in Eq. (2-5) and Eq.(7-8) are all convex over the optimization variables.

Time complexity: Algorithm 1 summarizes the steps of $CWMV_{\ell 1}$ aggregation model, in which the truths are first initialized via *MV*, and then then optimization variables $\mathbf{w}$ and $\mathbf{y}_i$ are alternatingly updated until convergence. Regarding to the time complexity of the algorithm, step 3 and step 4 take $O(NM^2B + M^3)$ and $O(NMB)$ operations in each iteration respectively. Hence, the overall time complexity in each iteration is $O(NM^2B + M^3)$.

3.2 Joint Generative-Discriminative Aggregation Models

There are several studies in different domains that showed combining generative and discriminative model improves the performance of each sub-model [9, 13, 18, 31]. However, the naive non-joint approach, in which the parameters of sub-models are learned separately, often leads to sub-optimal results. In this section, we first provide a general probabilistic framework to formulate our joint generative-discriminative aggregation models. Then, we present the corresponding algorithm for our joint aggregation model based on the discriminative $CWMV_{\ell 1}$ model.

Dawid & Skene model: In order to benefit a generative aggregation model, we employ an extended version of *DS* in our joint model. Before introducing our joint model, we briefly revisit *DS* [4]. As mentioned in Related Works Section, *DS* considers a confusion matrix $\boldsymbol{v}_j \in \mathbb{R}^{B \times B}$ for each worker, where diagonal element v_{jcc} indicates the probability of correct prediction of class c, and off-diagonal element v_{jck} shows the probability of misprediction of class c items as class k. Hence, the confusion matrix with higher diagonal elements represents a more reliable worker. *DS* maximizes the following conditional likelihood function of the parameters,

$$p(\mathbf{X}|\mathbf{Y}, \boldsymbol{v}) = \prod_{i=1}^{N} \prod_{j=1}^{M} \prod_{c,k=1}^{B} \left(v_{jck}\right)^{x_{ijk} y_{ic}}, \tag{9}$$

where the parameters have the constraint $\sum_k v_{jck} = 1$.

Coupling discriminative and generative models: Using a probabilistic framework for combination of the generative and discriminative sub-models, we compute the posterior distribution of parameters to determine the objective function for our joint model. Maximizing the logarithm of this distribution, which is called maximum a posteriori (MAP), leads the optimization of both generative and discriminative sub-models.

$$\ln P(\boldsymbol{v}, \mathbf{w}|\mathbf{X}, \mathbf{Y}) = \ln \Big(\prod_i P(\mathbf{w}|\mathbf{X}_i, \mathbf{y}_i) P(\boldsymbol{v}|\mathbf{X}_i, \mathbf{y}_i) \Big) \tag{10}$$

$$\propto \sum_i \underbrace{\ln P(\mathbf{X}_i|\mathbf{y}_i, \boldsymbol{v}) + \ln P(\boldsymbol{v})}_{\text{Gnerative Model}} + \underbrace{\ln P(\mathbf{y}_i|\mathbf{X}_i, \mathbf{w}) + \ln P(\mathbf{w})}_{\text{Discriminative Model}}$$

Following, we show how to incorporate $CWMV_{\ell 1}$ and extended *DS* as discriminative and generative sub-models into the mentioned posterior distribution, and specifically define the objective function of the proposed joint model.

Joint *DS-CWMV$_{\ell 1}$* Aggregation Model: Lets assume the discriminative model has Laplace distribution $P(\mathbf{y}_i|\mathbf{X}_i, \mathbf{w}) = \textbf{Laplace}$ $(\mathbf{y}_i|\mathbf{X}_i \mathbf{w}, \beta^{-1}\mathbf{I})$, and its parameter prior has Gaussian distribution $P(\mathbf{w}) = \mathcal{N}(\mathbf{w}|0, \alpha^{-1}\mathbf{I})$, where α and β are the precision in the distributions. It can be shown that the discriminative part of MAP objective function in Eq. (10) is equivalent of $CWMV_{\ell 1}$ loss function shown in Eq. (2), $\ln(\prod_i P(\mathbf{w}|\mathbf{X}_i, \mathbf{y}_i)) = -\beta/2 \sum_i \|\mathbf{X}_i \mathbf{w} - \mathbf{y}_i\|_1 - \alpha/2 \mathbf{w}^T \mathbf{w}$. We also assume Dirichlet prior for $\boldsymbol{v}$ and replace maximizing the logarithm of prior by minimizing the Kullback-Leibler divergence $\mathbf{KL}(p^{\boldsymbol{v}} \| p_0^{\boldsymbol{v}})$, which measures the distance between the updated confusion matrix and its prior distribution.

Moreover, the MAP objective considers same effects for discriminative and generative sub-models. But the effect of each sub-model can be tuned with different weights such as:

$$P(\boldsymbol{v}, \mathbf{w}|\mathbf{X}, \mathbf{Y}) = \prod_i P(\mathbf{w}|\mathbf{X}_i, \mathbf{y}_i)^{\gamma_D} P(\boldsymbol{v}|\mathbf{X}_i, \mathbf{y}_i)^{\gamma_G}, \tag{11}$$

where γ_D and γ_G are the weights for discriminative and generative sub-models respectively. Now, we are able reformulate the posterior distribution via the $CWMV_{\ell 1}$ and extended *DS* sub-models as follows:

$$\min_{\mathbf{w}, \mathbf{y}_i \geq 0, \mathbf{1}^T \mathbf{y}_i = 1, \boldsymbol{v}_j} \quad \mathbf{KL}(p^{\boldsymbol{v}} \| p_0^{\boldsymbol{v}}) - \sum_{ijck} x_{ijk} y_{ic} \log(v_{jck}) + \gamma \sum_i \|\mathbf{X}_i \mathbf{w} - \mathbf{y}_i\|_1 + \lambda_w \|\mathbf{w}\|_2^2, \tag{12}$$

where, $\gamma = (\gamma_D \beta)/\gamma_G$ and $\lambda_w = (\gamma_D \alpha)/\gamma_G$. We are able to further simplify the problem using iterative reweighted optimization

Algorithm 2: *DS-CWMV$_{\ell 1}$* aggregation model

```
1 Initialize Y by majority voting
2 while not converged do
3     w = ( Σ_{i=1}^{N} X_i^T U_i X_i + (λ_w/γ) I )^{-1} ( Σ_{i=1}^{N} X_i^T U_i y_i )
4     p^{ν_jck} = Dir(μ + Σ_i x_ijk y_ic)  ∀j ∈ {1,...,M}, ∀{c,k} ∈ {1,...,B}
5     Solve Problem (15) to infer y_i  ∀i ∈ {1,...,N}
6 end
```

algorithm into:

$$\min_{\mathbf{w},\mathbf{y}_i\geq 0,\mathbf{1}^T\mathbf{y}_i=1,\nu_j} \mathrm{KL}(p^{\nu}\|p_0^{\nu}) - \sum_{ijck} x_{ijk}y_{ic}\log(\nu_{jck}) \tag{13}$$
$$+\sum_i \mathbf{w}^T(\gamma\mathbf{X}_i^T\mathbf{U}_i\mathbf{X}_i + \lambda_w\mathbf{I})\mathbf{w} - 2\gamma\mathbf{y}_i^T\mathbf{U}_i\mathbf{X}_i\mathbf{w} + \gamma\mathbf{y}_i^T\mathbf{U}_i\mathbf{y}_i\,,$$

where $\mathbf{U}_i \in \mathbb{R}^{B\times B}$ is a diagonal matrix with element $u_{kk} = \frac{1}{2|\tilde{y}_{ik}-\mathbf{x}_{ik}\tilde{\mathbf{w}}|}$, when $\tilde{\mathbf{y}}_i$ and $\tilde{\mathbf{w}}$ are the solution from last iteration. Similarly, an alternating learning approach is used for the problem of *DS-CWMV$_{\ell 1}$* to update the parameters of sub-models and estimate the truths. Hence, *DS-CWMV$_{\ell 1}$* employs both generative of discriminative sub-models to estimate the truths (Y) using γ as trade off hyper-parameter, and updates the model parameters $(\mathbf{w}, \boldsymbol{\nu})$ when the other optimization variables are fixed.

Update Y: Considering $\mathbf{y}_i$ as the optimization variable, Problem (13) is reduced to:

$$\min_{\mathbf{y}_i\geq 0,\mathbf{1}^T\mathbf{y}_i=1} -\sum_{ijck} x_{ijk}y_{ic}\log(\nu_{jck}) \tag{14}$$
$$+\sum_i \mathbf{w}^T(\gamma\mathbf{X}_i^T\mathbf{U}_i\mathbf{X}_i + \lambda_w\mathbf{I})\mathbf{w} - 2\gamma\mathbf{y}_i^T\mathbf{U}_i\mathbf{X}_i\mathbf{w} + \gamma\mathbf{y}_i^T\mathbf{U}_i\mathbf{y}_i\,,$$

We further can decompose Problem (14) into N independent problem as follows:

$$\min_{\mathbf{y}_i\geq 0,\mathbf{1}^T\mathbf{y}_i=1} \mathbf{y}_i^T\mathbf{U}_i\mathbf{y}_i - 2\mathbf{y}_i^T\Big(\mathbf{U}_i\mathbf{X}_i\mathbf{w} + \frac{1}{\gamma}\sum_{jk} x_{ijk}\log(\boldsymbol{\nu}_{jk})\Big)\,, \tag{15}$$

which can be solved efficiently using the introduced optimization algorithm in Appendix.

Update $\boldsymbol{\nu}$: The following problem updates *DS* parameters:

$$\min_{\nu_j} \mathrm{KL}(p^{\nu}\|p_0^{\nu}) - \sum_{ijck} x_{ijk}y_{ic}\log(\nu_{jck})\,. \tag{16}$$

Using Bayesian approach, we derive the closed form solution $p^{\nu} \propto p_0^{\nu}p(\mathbf{X}|\mathbf{Y},\boldsymbol{\nu})$ for this problem. Considering Dirichlet distribution as the prior for confusion matrix $p_0^{\nu} = Dir(\mu)$, the updated parameters also have Dirichlet distribution as $p^{\nu_{jck}} = Dir(\mu + \sum_i x_{ijk}y_{ic})$, where μ is the prior hyper-parameter.

Update w: the problem for learning the parameters of *DS-CWMV$_{\ell 1}$* sub-model is equivalent of problem 5. solution shown in the step 3 of Algorithm 2.

Time complexity: Algorithm 2 summarizes the optimization algorithm for *DS-CWMV$_{\ell 1}$* aggregation model. Its total time complexity in each iteration is $O(NM^2B + M^3 + NMB^2)$, while steps 3, 4 and 5 take $O(NM^2B + M^3)$, $O(NMB^2)$ and $O(NMB^2)$ operations respectively.

	Datasets	# options	# questions	# workers	# labels
single-option	*Web Search*	5	2665	177	15567
	Age	7	1002	165	10020
	RTE	2	800	164	8000
	Temp	2	462	76	4620
	Flowers	2	200	36	2366
multi-option	*Flag-Approval*	4	120	60	3171
	Flag-Cumulative	4	120	60	3189
	Dog-Approval	4	256	120	7441
	Dog-Cumulative	4	256	120	7443

Table 1: Datasets Descriptions

4 EXPERIMENTAL RESULTS

In this section, we will: 1) evaluate the performance of our aggregation models on single-option crowdsourcing datasets, 2) compare the running speed of aggregation models in the biggest crowd dataset, 3) analyze the histogram of mispredicted truths, and 4) examine the effectiveness of our aggregation models on multi-option crowd datasets.

4.1 Evaluation on Single-Option Crowd Labels

In this section, we assess the proposed aggregation models using several single-option crowdsourcing datasets. The single-option crowd labels can be considered as the special case of multi-option crowd labels, where crowd workers are only allowed to select a single option as the answer for each question. Although, our aggregation models are mainly designed to deal with multi-option crowd data, they are able to accept the deterministic single-option crowd labels as the input data.

Datasets: The efficiency of our aggregation model are analyzed compared to the state-of-the-art models using the crowdsourcing benchmark datasets. We use the following five datasets, which include single-option crowd data. Their summary is presented in the first half Table 1. *Web Search*: 2665 query-URLs are labeled with 177 workers for relevance rating scale from 1 to 5 [33]. *Age*: 1002 face images are labeled with 165 workers to estimate the age of people [6]. *RTE*: 800 sentence pairs are labeled with 164 workers to check if the second sentence can be inferred from the first one [25]. *Temp*: 462 pairs of verb events are labeled with 76 workers to check if the event described in the first verb occurs before or after the second one [25]. *Flowers*: 200 flowers picture are labeled with 36 workers to check if the flower is peach or not [27].

Alternative models: We compare our models[1] with several baselines, including majority voting (*MV*), iterative weighted majority voting (*IWMV*) [11], max-margin majority voting (*M^{3}V*) [26], Dawid and Skene (*DS*) [4], Dawid and Skene with Dirichlet prior (*DS+Prior*), *GLAD* [30], multi-class minimax entropy (*Entropy (M)*), ordinal minimax entropy (*Entropy (O)*) [34], *crowdSVM*, and Gibbs crowdSVM (*G-CrowdSVM*) [26]. Note that ordinal minimax entropy model is only compatible with ordinal labels, and thus it could not be used for categorical crowd datasets. Also *G-CrowdSVM* requires Gibbs random samples, therefore its results are reported using the

[1] Our code will be available in https://github.com/KamranGhasedi/DS-CWMV_l1

	Model	*Web Search*	*Age*	*RTE*	*Temp*	*Flowers*	Average
baselines	*MV*	26.90	34.88	10.31	6.39	22.00	28.83
	IWMV	15.04	34.53	8.12	5.84	19.00	17.09
	M^3V	12.74	33.33	7.88	6.06	13.50	15.43
	DS	16.92	39.62	7.25	5.84	13.00	18.69
	DS+Prior	13.26	34.53	[7.13]	5.84	13.50	15.80
	GLAD	19.30	35.73	**7.00**	[5.63]	13.50	16.20
	Entropy (M)	11.10	**31.14**	7.50	[5.63]	13.00	14.03
	Entropy (O)	10.40	37.32	-	-	-	17.76
	CrowdSVM	9.42	33.33	7.75	[5.63]	13.50	13.65
	G-CrowdSVM	7.99±0.26	32.98±0.36	7.67±0.19	5.71±0.33	[12.10±1.07]	12.78±0.31
ours	*$CWMV_{\ell 2}$*	10.89	34.43	7.25	[5.63]	16.00	14.65
	$CWMV_{\ell 1}$	10.70	34.23	7.50	[5.63]	13.00	14.43
	$DS\text{-}CWMV_{\ell 2}$	[7.58]	32.04	[7.13]	[5.63]	13.00	[12.32]
	$DS\text{-}CWMV_{\ell 1}$	**6.78**	[31.54]	**7.00**	**5.41**	**10.00**	**11.65**

Table 2: Error rates (%) of crowdsourcing aggregation models on single-option crowdsourcing datasets. The first and second best results are shown in bold and bracket respectively. The average error rates are calculated based on the total number of questions in all datasets.

average and standard deviation of 5 runs. Moreover, we report the results for ℓ_2-norm variant of our discriminative and joint models. These models, denoted by $CWMV_{\ell 2}$ and $DS\text{-}CWMV_{\ell 2}$, differ with the proposed models in using this squared error loss function $\|\mathbf{X}_i\mathbf{w} - \mathbf{y}_i\|_2^2$ instead of ℓ_1-norm loss (See Appendix B).

Hyper-parameters selection: Because the true labels are not available in training crowdsourcing aggregation models, we are required to select the hyper-parameters $\{\mu, \lambda_w, \gamma\}$ in an unsupervised manner. Hence, we set the similar confusion matrix prior in all datasets as $\mu = 10B^2M/\sum_{ijk}\mathbf{X}$, which is proportional to #parameters / #labels. Also following [26], we select λ_w and γ using the unrelated likelihood $p(\mathbf{X}|\mathbf{Y}, \boldsymbol{\nu})$ as the criterion. In particular, we choose the hyper-parameters from $\gamma^{set} = \{0.01, 0.1, 1\}$ and $\lambda_w^{set} = \{0.01, 0.1, 1, 10\}$, such that he selected hyper-parameters have the maximum likelihood $p(\mathbf{X}|\mathbf{Y}, \boldsymbol{\nu})$. Note that for the discriminative ($CWMV_{\ell 1}$ model, we fix the truths Y after training the models, and then learn the confusion matrix $\boldsymbol{\nu}$ in one shot to calculate the likelihood. Therefore, using this approach we ensure to select the hyper-parameters without any knowledge from the original true labels.

Performance comparison: Table 2 shows the error rates of the aforementioned aggregation models on single-option crowdsourcing datasets. We also report the average error rates of each model, that are calculated based on the number of questions in all datasets. Our discriminative $CWMV_{\ell 1}$ model consistently enhances *MV* performance over all datasets, and also achieves superior or competitive results compared to M^3V , which is the state-of-the-art discriminative model. The joint $DS\text{-}CWMV_{\ell 1}$ model consistently improves the results of its base discriminative ($CWMV_{\ell 1}$) and generative (*DS+Prior*) sub-models on all datasets. $DS\text{-}CWMV_{\ell 1}$ also outperform the state-of-the-art model (*G-CrowdSVM*) with significant margin, and achieves the lowest error rate in average. Moreover, the proposed ℓ_1-norm discriminative and joint models have better results than their ℓ_2-norm variants, showing the effectiveness of ℓ_1-norm objective function in dealing with noisy crowd data.

4.2 Evaluation of Running Speed

Furthermore, we compare the running speed of our models with the state-of-the-art models on the largest crowdsourcing (*Web Search*) dataset. Figure 2 demonstrates the convergence rate of $DS\text{-}CWMV_{\ell 1}$ and $DS\text{-}CWMV_{\ell 2}$ along with some other models. Note that the discriminative models, $CWMV_{\ell 1}$ and $CWMV_{\ell 2}$, are faster than the corresponding joint models, but we do not include their results for the sake of figure clarity.

The hyper-parameters are selected from previous experiment, and we run the models until $|\mathbf{Y}^{(t)} - \mathbf{Y}^{(t-1)}|/N \leq 10^{-3}$ or the maximum iteration 100. Figure 2 shows error rate of the aggregation models after each iteration in logarithm of time scale (seconds). As it is shown, $DS\text{-}CWMV_{\ell 1}$ and $DS\text{-}CWMV_{\ell 2}$ have much faster convergence rate than the competitive models. In particular, $DS\text{-}CWMV_{\ell 1}$ not only converges the lower error rate compared to *G-CrowdSVM*, but also has 28 times faster convergence rate. This outcomes confirms that $DS\text{-}CWMV_{\ell 1}$ is a better choice for practical crowdsourcing tasks than *G-CrowdSVM*, since the former model benefits from efficient and fast optimization algorithm, but the latter model requires slow Gibbs sampling procedure.

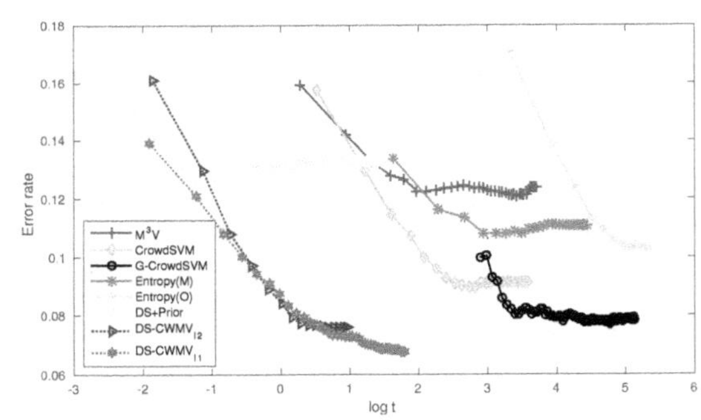

Figure 2: Convergence comparison of aggregation models on *Web Search* dataset.

4.3 Reliability Analysis of Estimated Truths

In addition to achieving lower error rates, having low confidence (probability) for the difficult samples is practically useful, because the task requesters can use this hint and collect more crowd labels for the difficult (mispredicted) items. In particular, an aggregation

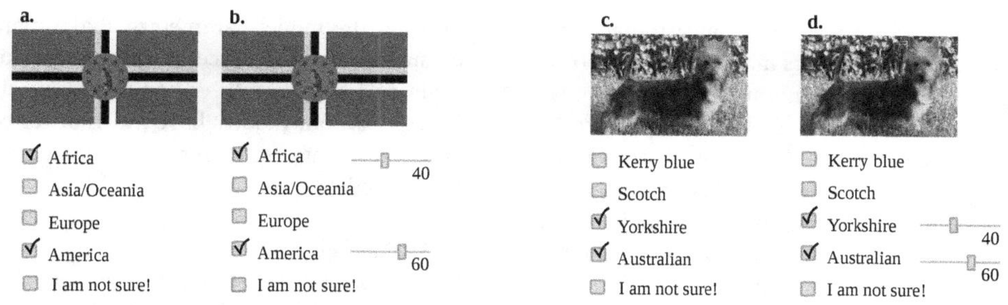

Figure 3: Four multi-option crowdsourcing datasets corresponding to the following two tasks. 1) Flag: The crowd workers are asked to mark continent of the countries whose flags are shown in the questions; 2) Dog: The crowd workers are requested to categorize four breeds of Terrier dogs. We employ two data collection mechanism, including approval voting [22] and cumulative voting systems, to collect multi-option crowd data. Figures a. and c. represent the approval voting mechanism for the flag and dog tasks. Figures b. and d. show the cumulative voting systems the for flag and dog tasks.

	Model	*Flag-Approval*	*Flag-Cumulative*	*Dog-Approval*	*Dog-Cumulative*	Average
baselines	*(soft) MV*	21.67	20.83	8.98	8.98	12.90
	(soft) DS	22.50	20.83	10.16	9.76	13.70
	(soft) DS+Prior	20.00	19.17	8.98	8.59	12.23
	(soft) Entropy (M)	17.50	16.67	12.89	12.89	14.23
ours	$CWMV_{\ell 2}$	16.67	16.67	8.98	8.59	11.30
	$CWMV_{\ell 1}$	[11.67]	[10.83]	[8.59]	[8.20]	[9.31]
	$DS\text{-}CWMV_{\ell 2}$	14.17	14.17	9.38	8.59	10.64
	$DS\text{-}CWMV_{\ell 1}$	**13.33**	**10.00**	**8.20**	**7.81**	**9.17**

Table 3: Error rates (%) of aggregation models applied on multi-option crowd datasets. The first and second best results are shown in bold and bracket respectively. The average error rates are calculated based on the total number of questions in all datasets.

model, which assigns low probability for mispredicted item, is more reliable.

Hence, we analyze the truths of wrong predictions for two competitive aggregation models, $DS\text{-}CWMV_{\ell 1}$ and *G-CrowdSVM*, on *Web Search* dataset. Figure 4 illustrates the histogram of probability of mispredicted items for the both models. As it is shown, $DS\text{-}CWMV_{\ell 1}$ tends to assign low probability for the incorrectly predicted items, while *G-CrowdSVM* makes wrong prediction with high probability. This property makes $DS\text{-}CWMV_{\ell 1}$ a more reliable aggregation model in practice, since the requester could assign more workers for low probability (i.e. difficult) items to avoid erroneous predictions.

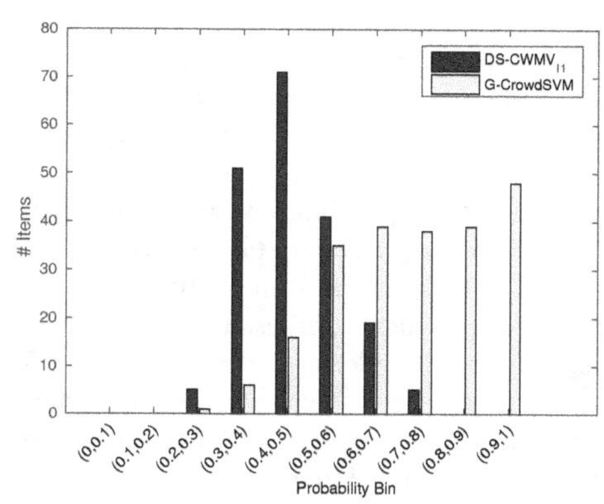

Figure 4: Histogram of the truths for mispredicted items. The results belongs to $DS\text{-}CWMV_{\ell 1}$ and *G-CrowdSVM* on *Web Search* dataset.

4.4 Evaluation on Multi-Option Crowd Labels

Multi-option data collection: To explore the effectiveness of our aggregation models on multi-option crowd data, we design two crowdsourcing tasks on Amazon Mechanical Turk platform[2]. As it is shown in figure 3, the first task asks the workers to mark continent of the countries whose flags are shown in the questions, and the second task requests the workers to categorize four breeds of Terrier dogs, including Kerry blue, Scotch, Australian and Yorkshire. The images of dogs in the second task are extracted from Stanford Dog dataset [8].

We employ two data collection mechanisms to collect the multi-option crowd data, approval voting mechanism [22] which allows the worker to select single/multiple options when they have full/partial knowledge about the question, and cumulative voting strategy that allows the workers to express their confidence level about each option. The crowd workers also could skip the questions in both data collection mechanisms, if they do not have any clue about the true option. Specifically, we hired the workers in Amazon Mechanical Turk platform with more than %85 HIT approval rate and 1000 approved HITs, located in United States.

[2] https://www.mturk.com/

In cumulative voting mechanism, there is a concern that some overconfident and underconfident workers may report their confidence in different ranges. There are some normalization preprocess techniques to balance the confidence level of crowd workers by the average of reported labels. But we do not use them in our framework, since our aggregation models penalize the incorrect high confident and correct low confident workers. Also, there is a chance that some workers label with low/high confidence level due to their poor/relevant expertise in the assigned task.

Datasets: We collect four multi-option crowd datasets: *Flag-Approval*: 120 flags are labeled with 60 workers, where each worker could select multiple options or skip the question. *Flag-Cumulative*: 120 flags are labeled with 60 workers, where each worker could select multiple options with corresponding confidence or skip the question. *Dog-Approval*: 256 dogs are categorized with 120 workers, where each worker select multiple options or skip the question. *Dog-Cumulative*: 256 dogs are categorized with 120 workers, where each worker could select multiple options with corresponding confidence or skip the question. The summary of these datasets are presented in the second half of Table 1.

Alternative models: For the sake of comparison with our aggregation models, four crowdsourcing aggregation models are applied to the multi-option crowdsourcing datasets. In order to extend the alternative models handling multi-option crowd labels, all of the selected options are considered as independent single-option crowd labels. These synthetic labels are used to estimate the truths and update the parameters by the weight corresponding to their confidence, which normalizes the effect of each multi-option crowd label. The extended models include *soft MV*, *soft DS*, *soft DS+Prior* and *soft Entropy (M)*.

Performance comparison: Table 3 reports the error rates of the aggregation models on multi-option datasets. Similar to single-option datasets, $DS\text{-}CWMV_{\ell 1}$ outperforms other models consistently on all datasets, and achieves the lowest error rate in average. Furthermore, $DS\text{-}CWMV_{\ell 1}$ has improvements over its corresponding discriminative and generative sub-models. Interestingly, our discriminative $CWMV_{\ell 1}$ model achieves the second lowest error rate in average, and provides better results compared to more sophisticated alternative models like *soft Entropy (M)* and $DS\text{-}CWMV_{\ell 2}$. The outcomes of this experiment confirm the effectiveness of our aggregation models on multi-option crowd data, and also indicate the benefits of ℓ_1-norm loss function of our models in comparison with their ℓ_2-norm counterparts when dealing with noisy multi-option crowd labels.

5 CONCLUSION

In this paper, we first proposed a new discriminative aggregation model, which extends majority voting by considering the flexible reliability parameters for crowd workers, ℓ_1-norm loss function and optimization constraints leading to probabilistic truths. After that, we enhanced the discriminative model by integrating it with a generative aggregation model. The combination of generative and discriminative sub-models was formulated using a probabilistic framework rather than a heuristic approach. We also derived an efficient optimization algorithms for solving the problem of our joint model, which alternates between estimating the truths and updating the model parameters. Experimental results validated the superior performance of our aggregation models on several single-option and multi-option crowdsourcing datasets. We also showed that our models have much faster convergence rate and more reliable aggregation score in comparison with the state-of-the-art models.

REFERENCES

[1] Yoram Bachrach, Thore Graepel, Tom Minka, and John Guiver. 2012. How to grade a test without knowing the answers, a Bayesian graphical model for adaptive crowdsourcing and aptitude testing. In *arXiv preprint arXiv:1206.6386*.

[2] Stephen Boyd and Lieven Vandenberghe. 2004. *Convex optimization*. Cambridge university press.

[3] Xi Chen, Qihang Lin, and Dengyong Zhou. 2013. Optimistic knowledge gradient policy for optimal budget allocation in crowdsourcing. In *Proceedings of the 30th International Conference on Machine Learning (ICML)*. 64–72.

[4] Alexander Philip Dawid and Allan M Skene. 1979. Maximum likelihood estimation of observer error-rates using the EM algorithm. *Applied statistics* (1979), 20–28.

[5] Tim Finin, Will Murnane, Anand Karandikar, Nicholas Keller, Justin Martineau, and Mark Dredze. 2010. Annotating named entities in Twitter data with crowdsourcing. In *Proceedings of the NAACL HLT 2010 Workshop on Creating Speech and Language Data with Amazon's Mechanical Turk*. Association for Computational Linguistics, 80–88.

[6] Hu Han, Charles Otto, Xiaoming Liu, and Anil K Jain. 2015. Demographic estimation from face images: Human vs. machine performance. *IEEE Transactions on Pattern Analysis and Machine Intelligence* 37, 6 (2015), 1148–1161.

[7] Gabriella Kazai. 2011. In search of quality in crowdsourcing for search engine evaluation. In *Advances in information retrieval*. Springer, 165–176.

[8] Aditya Khosla, Nityananda Jayadevaprakash, Bangpeng Yao, and Fei-Fei Li. 2011. Novel dataset for fine-grained image categorization: Stanford dogs. In *Proc. CVPR Workshop on Fine-Grained Visual Categorization (FGVC)*.

[9] Julia A Lasserre, Christopher M Bishop, and Thomas P Minka. 2006. Principled hybrids of generative and discriminative models. In *IEEE Computer Society Conference on Computer Vision and Pattern Recognition*, Vol. 1. IEEE, 87–94.

[10] Nolan Lawson, Kevin Eustice, Mike Perkowitz, and Meliha Yetisgen-Yildiz. 2010. Annotating large email datasets for named entity recognition with mechanical turk. In *Proceedings of the NAACL HLT 2010 workshop on creating speech and language data with Amazon's Mechanical Turk*. Association for Computational Linguistics, 71–79.

[11] Hongwei Li and Bin Yu. 2014. Error Rate Bounds and Iterative Weighted Majority Voting for Crowdsourcing. *arXiv preprint arXiv:1411.4086* (2014).

[12] Qiang Liu, Jian Peng, and Alex T Ihler. 2012. Variational inference for crowdsourcing. In *Advances in Neural Information Processing Systems (NIPS)*. 692 – 700.

[13] Andrew McCallum, Chris Pal, Gregory Druck, and Xuerui Wang. 2006. Multi-conditional learning: Generative/discriminative training for clustering and classification. In *AAAI*. 433–439.

[14] Yurii Nesterov. 2013. *Introductory lectures on convex optimization: A basic course*. Vol. 87. Springer Science & Business Media.

[15] Feiping Nie, Heng Huang, Xiao Cai, and Chris H Ding. 2010. Efficient and robust feature selection via joint l2,1-norms minimization. In *Advances in Neural Information Processing Systems (NIPS)*. 1813–1821.

[16] Feiping Nie, Xiaoqian Wang, Michael I Jordan, and Heng Huang. 2016. The Constrained Laplacian Rank Algorithm for Graph-Based Clustering. In *Thirtieth AAAI Conference on Artificial Intelligence*. Citeseer.

[17] Satoshi Oyama, Yukino Baba, Yuko Sakurai, and Hisashi Kashima. 2013. Accurate Integration of Crowdsourced Labels Using Workers' Self-reported Confidence Scores.. In *IJCAI*. Citeseer.

[18] Rajat Raina, Yirong Shen, Andrew Y Ng, and Andrew McCallum. 2003. Classification with hybrid generative/discriminative models.. In *Advances in Neural Information Processing Systems (NIPS)*, Vol. 16.

[19] Vikas C Raykar, Shipeng Yu, Linda H Zhao, Gerardo Hermosillo Valadez, Charles Florin, Luca Bogoni, and Linda Moy. 2010. Learning from crowds. *The Journal of Machine Learning Research* 11 (2010), 1297–1322.

[20] Najmeh Sadoughi and Carlos Busso. 2016. Head Motion Generation with Synthetic Speech: A Data Driven Approach.. In *INTERSPEECH*. 52–56.

[21] Najmeh Sadoughi, Yang Liu, and Carlos Busso. 2017. Meaningful head movements driven by emotional synthetic speech. *Speech Communication* (2017).

[22] Nihar Shah, Dengyong Zhou, and Yuval Peres. 2015. Approval Voting and Incentives in Crowdsourcing. In *Proceedings of the 32nd International Conference on Machine Learning (ICML)*. 10–19.

[23] Nihar Bhadresh Shah and Denny Zhou. 2015. Double or nothing: Multiplicative incentive mechanisms for crowdsourcing. In *Advances in Neural Information Processing Systems (NIPS)*. 1–9.

[24] Aashish Sheshadri and Matthew Lease. 2013. Square: A benchmark for research on computing crowd consensus. In *First AAAI Conference on Human Computation and Crowdsourcing*.

[25] Rion Snow, Brendan O'Connor, Daniel Jurafsky, and Andrew Y Ng. 2008. Cheap and fast—but is it good? evaluating non-expert annotations for natural language tasks. In *Proceedings of the conference on empirical methods in natural language processing*. 254–263.

[26] Tian Tian and Jun Zhu. 2015. Max-Margin Majority Voting for Learning from Crowds. In *Advances in Neural Information Processing Systems (NIPS)*. 1612–1620.

[27] Tian Tian and Jun Zhu. 2015. Uncovering the latent structures of crowd labeling. In *Advances in Knowledge Discovery and Data Mining*. Springer, 392–404.

[28] Matteo Venanzi, John Guiver, Gabriella Kazai, Pushmeet Kohli, and Milad Shokouhi. 2014. Community-based bayesian aggregation models for crowdsourcing. In *Proceedings of the 23rd international conference on World wide web (WWW)*. 155–164.

[29] Peter Welinder, Steve Branson, Serge J Belongie, and Pietro Perona. 2010. The Multidimensional Wisdom of Crowds.. In *Advances in Neural Information Processing Systems (NIPS)*, Vol. 23. 2424–2432.

[30] Jacob Whitehill, Ting-fan Wu, Jacob Bergsma, Javier R Movellan, and Paul L Ruvolo. 2009. Whose vote should count more: Optimal integration of labels from labelers of unknown expertise. In *Advances in Neural Information Processing Systems (NIPS)*. 2035–2043.

[31] Junbo Zhao, Michael Mathieu, Ross Goroshin, and Yann Lecun. 2015. Stacked what-where auto-encoders. *arXiv preprint arXiv:1506.02351* (2015).

[32] Yudian Zheng, Guoliang Li, Yuanbing Li, Caihua Shan, and Reynold Cheng. 2017. Truth inference in crowdsourcing: is the problem solved? *Proceedings of the VLDB Endowment* 10, 5 (2017), 541–552.

[33] Denny Zhou, Sumit Basu, Yi Mao, and John C Platt. 2012. Learning from the wisdom of crowds by minimax entropy. In *Advances in Neural Information Processing Systems (NIPS)*. 2195–2203.

[34] Dengyong Zhou, Qiang Liu, John Platt, and Christopher Meek. 2014. Aggregating ordinal labels from crowds by minimax conditional entropy. In *Proceedings of the 31st International Conference on Machine Learning (ICML)*. 262–270.

[35] Dengyong Zhou, Qiang Liu, John C Platt, Christopher Meek, and Nihar B Shah. 2015. Regularized minimax conditional entropy for crowdsourcing. *arXiv preprint arXiv:1503.07240* (2015).

[36] James Zou, Reshef Meir, and David Parkes. 2014. Approval voting behavior in doodle polls. In *The 5th Workshop on Computational Social Choice*.

A OPTIMIZATION ALGORITHM FOR ESTIMATING TRUTHS

In this section, we derive the optimization algorithm to solve the problems in Eq. (8) and (15) for estimating the truths in $CWMV_{\ell 1}$ and $DS\text{-}CWMV_{\ell 1}$. We are able to reformulate the both problems into the following one:

$$\min_{\mathbf{y}\geq 0, \mathbf{1}^T\mathbf{y}=1} \quad \mathbf{y}^T\mathbf{Q}\mathbf{y} - 2\mathbf{y}^T\mathbf{d}\,, \tag{17}$$

where $\mathbf{Q} \in \mathbb{R}^{B\times B}$ is a diagonal positive semi-definite matrix, and $\mathbf{d} \in \mathbb{R}^{B\times 1}$ is an arbitrary vector. In Problem (8), $\mathbf{Q} = \mathbf{U}_i$ is a diagonal positive semi-definite matrix and $\mathbf{d} = \mathbf{U}_i\mathbf{X}_i\mathbf{w}$ is an arbitrary B dimensional vector. In Problem (15), similarly $\mathbf{Q} = \mathbf{U}_i$ is a diagonal positive semi-definite matrix and $\mathbf{d} = \mathbf{U}_i\mathbf{X}_i\mathbf{w}+\frac{1}{\gamma}\sum_{jk} x_{ijk}\log(\boldsymbol{\nu}_{jk})$ is an arbitrary B dimensional vector.

The Lagrangian function for Problem (17) is:

$$\mathcal{L}(\mathbf{y},\lambda,\boldsymbol{\mu}) = \mathbf{y}^T\mathbf{Q}\mathbf{y} - 2\mathbf{y}^T\mathbf{d} - \lambda(\mathbf{1}^T\mathbf{y} - 1) - \boldsymbol{\mu}^T\mathbf{y}, \tag{18}$$

where λ and $\boldsymbol{\mu}$ are Lagrangian multipliers associated with the equality and inequality constraints respectively. Suppose $\mathbf{y}^*$, λ^* and $\boldsymbol{\mu}^*$ as the optimal variables, Karush-Kuhn-Tucker (KKT) conditions [2] yield the following equations,

$$\begin{cases} \mathbf{Q}\mathbf{y}^* - 2\mathbf{d} - \lambda^*\mathbf{1} - \boldsymbol{\mu}^* = 0 \\ \lambda^* \geq 0 \\ \boldsymbol{\mu}^* \geq 0 \\ \boldsymbol{\mu}^{*T}\mathbf{y}^* = 0. \end{cases}$$

Due to diagonality of $\mathbf{Q}$, the first equation in the above KKT conditions can be reformulated as $y_k^* = \frac{1}{q_{kk}}(2d_k + \lambda^* + \mu_k^*)$ for all $k \in \{1,...,B\}$. Using the inequality $\boldsymbol{\mu}^{*T}\mathbf{y}^* = 0$, we further have:

$$y_k^* = \frac{1}{q_{kk}}(2d_k + \lambda^*)_+ \tag{19}$$

where $(.)_+ = \max(0,.)$. So the optimal variable y_k^* can be computed by knowing λ^*. Using equality constraint $\mathbf{1}^T\mathbf{y} = 1$, we define the following function,

$$f(\lambda^*) = \sum_k \frac{1}{q_{kk}}(2d_k + \lambda^*)_+ - 1 \tag{20}$$

Because $f(\lambda^*) = 0$, we simply obtain λ^* as the root of this function. Note that $f(\lambda^*)$ is piece-wise linear and monotonically increasing, hence the root can be easily computed using Newton method.

B CWMV$_{L2}$ AND DS-CWMV$_{L2}$ MODELS

The objective function of $CWMV_{l2}$ is introduced as:

$$\min_{\mathbf{w},\mathbf{y}_i\geq 0,\mathbf{1}^T\mathbf{y}_i=1} \quad \sum_{i=1}^{N} ||\mathbf{X}_i\mathbf{w} - \mathbf{y}_i||_2^2 + \lambda_w||\mathbf{w}||_2^2\,, \tag{21}$$

When the truths Y is considered given, has the following closed form solution for updating $\mathbf{w}$.

$$\mathbf{w} = \Big(\sum_{i=1}^{N} \mathbf{X}_i^T\mathbf{X}_i + \lambda_w\mathbf{I}\Big)^{-1}\Big(\sum_{i=1}^{N} \mathbf{X}_i^T\mathbf{y}_i\Big)\,. \tag{22}$$

Since the objective is independent for each item $i \in \{1,...,N\}$, the problem for estimating truths with fixed parameters could be decomposed into N independent sub-problems as follows:

$$\min_{\mathbf{y}_i\geq 0,\mathbf{1}^T\mathbf{y}_i=1} \quad \mathbf{y}_i^T\mathbf{y}_i - 2\mathbf{y}_i^T\mathbf{X}_i\mathbf{w}\,, \tag{23}$$

where each sub-problem is a special case of the problem that is solved in Appendix A. Moreover, it can be proved that the problem of $CWMV_{l2}$ in Eq. (21) is jointly convex in $\mathbf{w}$ and $\mathbf{y}_i$.

The objective function for DS-CWMV$_{l2}$ has the following form:

$$\min_{\mathbf{w},\mathbf{y}_i\geq 0,\mathbf{1}^T\mathbf{y}_i=1,\boldsymbol{\nu}_j} \quad \mathrm{KL}(p^{\boldsymbol{\nu}}||p_0^{\boldsymbol{\nu}}) - \sum_{ijck} x_{ijk}y_{ic}\log(\nu_{jck})$$
$$+\gamma\sum_i ||\mathbf{X}_i\mathbf{w} - \mathbf{y}_i||_2^2 + \lambda_w||\mathbf{w}||_2^2\,, \tag{24}$$

Considering $\mathbf{y}_i$ as the optimization variable, We decompose problem (24) into N independent problems

$$\min_{\mathbf{y}_i\geq 0,\mathbf{1}^T\mathbf{y}_i=1} \quad \mathbf{y}_i^T\mathbf{y}_i - 2\mathbf{y}_i^T\Big(\mathbf{X}_i\mathbf{w} + \frac{1}{\gamma}\sum_{jk} x_{ijk}\log(\boldsymbol{\nu}_{jk})\Big)\,, \tag{25}$$

which can be efficiently solved using the introduced optimization algorithm in Appendix A.

Considering Dirichlet distribution as the prior $p_0^{\nu} = Dir(\mu)$, the updated parameter has this Dirichlet distribution $p^{\nu_{jck}} = Dir(\mu + \sum_i x_{ijk}y_{ic})$. The objective for updating $\mathbf{w}$ is equivalent to $CWMV_{l2}$ model, consequently it has the closed form solution as Eq. (22).

Predicting Audio Advertisement Quality

Samaneh Ebrahimi
Georgia Institute of Technology
samaneh.ebrahimi@gatech.edu

Hossein Vahabi
Pandora Media Inc.
puya.vahabi@gmail.com

Matthew Prockup
Pandora Media Inc.
mprockup@pandora.com

Oriol Nieto
Pandora Media Inc.
onieto@pandora.com

ABSTRACT

Online audio advertising is a particular form of advertising used abundantly in online music streaming services. In these platforms, which tend to host tens of thousands of unique audio advertisements (ads), providing high quality ads ensures a better user experience and results in longer user engagement. Therefore, the automatic assessment of these ads is an important step toward audio ads ranking and better audio ads creation.

In this paper we propose one way to measure the quality of the audio ads using a proxy metric called *Long Click Rate (LCR)*, which is defined by the amount of time a user engages with the follow-up display ad (that is shown while the audio ad is playing) divided by the impressions. We later focus on predicting the audio ad quality using only acoustic features such as harmony, rhythm, and timbre of the audio, extracted from the raw waveform. We discuss how the characteristics of the sound can be connected to concepts such as the clarity of the audio ad message, its trustworthiness, etc. Finally, we propose a new deep learning model for audio ad quality prediction, which outperforms the other discussed models trained on hand-crafted features. To the best of our knowledge, this is the first large-scale audio ad quality prediction study.

CCS CONCEPTS

• **Computing methodologies** → **Supervised learning**; *Neural networks*; • **Information systems** → *Data mining*; *Online advertising*; • **Applied computing** → *Sound and music computing*;

KEYWORDS

Ad Quality, CNN, DNN, Audio Ads, Advertising, Acoustic Features

ACM Reference Format:
Samaneh Ebrahimi, Hossein Vahabi, Matthew Prockup, and Oriol Nieto. 2018. Predicting Audio Advertisement Quality. In *WSDM 2018: WSDM 2018: The Eleventh ACM International Conference on Web Search and Data Mining , February 5–9, 2018, Marina Del Rey, CA, USA.* ACM, New York, NY, USA, 9 pages. https://doi.org/10.1145/3159652.3159701

WSDM 2018, February 5–9, 2018, Marina Del Rey, CA, USA

ACM ISBN 978-1-4503-5581-0/18/02...$15.00
https://doi.org/10.1145/3159652.3159701

1 INTRODUCTION

Audio advertising is abundantly used by online music streaming services. When users are listening to music, between two different songs, they can be exposed to audio messages from advertisers. This form of ads are called audio ads and they can have a high impact on user listening experience. Given an opportunity space for ads, typically there is an ad retrieval and bidding process. After, the eligible ads are ordered based on the amount of money the advertisers are willing to pay times the quality of the ads. The challenge is how to measure the quality of the audio ads, and what are the key acoustic components of sound composition that create an engaging audio ads.

Existing efforts toward discovering the quality of advertisements are mainly focused on visual perception: display ads and text ads [15, 41]. Therefore, the domain specific features considered in this context are text and image based features. Furthermore, in this case, there are well accepted proxy metric of ad quality, such as clicks, dwell-time [11], conversion or offensive rate [41]. However, in the context of audio ads it is not clear what kind of metric to consider as a proxy of quality as the audio ads can not be clicked. Therefore, the existing approaches are not directly applicable. Another challenge is extracting the features from sound content in order to build prediction models and understand how to create an engaging, high quality ads. To the best of our knowledge, there are no large scale audio ads quality studies that address these points.

In this paper, we aim to predict the quality of ads using the acoustic signal. The audio quality is not necessarily just the quality of the recording (clear vs. distorted), but may be implicit within the quality of an ad's overall composition. The composition of an ad includes the speaker tone and tempo, speaker gender, number of speakers, the message, music accompaniment, production effects and the overall mix of all of these sources. In the fields of *Digital Signal Processing (DSP)* and *Music Information Retrieval (Music-IR)* acoustic features are computed from the audio signal to capture elements of timbre, rhythm, and harmony, which can be used to model high-level subjective concepts (genre, mood) of sound and audio understanding [18, 32].

For the quality metric we rely on a companion display ad that is presented at the same time the ad is playing. Users are listening to music and audio ads usually using their mobile device. While they are listening to audio ads they can decide to click on the associated banner during or after the audio ad is played. Following the click they are redirected to a landing page. The user will spend an amount of time in the landing page (dwell-time). If the dwell-time is higher than a threshold we consider the interaction to be engaging and we call it *Long Click*. We use as a quality metrics *Long Click Rate (LCR)* , i.e., the number of long click divided by the number of impressions. The main reasons behind not using the simple *Click Through Rate* is that it can be very noisy because listeners may click on the banner by mistake, and because it may reflect only short-term user engagements [41].

After defining the metric (*LCR*), we propose a first acoustic based prediction model with handcrafted features. The main objective of this model is to have a prediction model that is interpretable, and that can tell us how to create a high quality audio ad. To improve the interpretation we also do a large scale user study. The results in this case shows that speech with a moderate-tempo, articulate pronunciation, and moderate yet necessary vocal animation lead to better quality ads. Finally, we also propose a deep learning model with the objective of improving the effectiveness of our prediction model, reaching an AUC of 0.79 for cold-start audio ad quality prediction using only the spectrogram of audio.

Let us resume the original contributions of this paper, where we:

- Defined a metric to measure the quality of audio ads by relying on *Long Click Rate (LCR)* on a companion display ad that appears at the same time the audio ad is playing.
- Conducted a large crowd-sourcing study to understand why an audio ad is more engaging than the other.
- Designed and implemented acoustic features to capture intuitive sonic attributes of timbre, rhythm, harmonic organization to build a prediction model for advertisement quality.
- Gave an interpretation on how low level acoustic features are connected to concepts such as speech speed, pronunciation, foreground (speech) to background sound (music and sound effects).
- Proposed different audio prediction models using only the acoustic features, reaching an AUC of 0.73.
- Proposed a deep learning model based directly on audio ad spectrograms, without using any hand-crafted features,, reaching an AUC of 0.79.

2 RELATED WORK

Computational advertising address the problem of ranking ads based on their relevance and quality. Recently, many different approaches have arisen to solve this problem, but they are all based on visual perception: display and text ads [26], native and sponsored search [30], and much more [15]. Furthermore, they are all based on well-known metrics such as clicks, offensive rate [41], and dwell-time [11]. Our contributions are proposing a new metric for the quality of *audio ads* that are not directly clickable, and a prediction model based only on acoustic signals. Next, we report the related work on classical ad quality prediction using visual perception, machine and deep learning algorithms, audio signals and music information retrieval.

Ad Quality. There are many existing approaches related to relevance of ads within sponsored search that are trying to optimize based on CTR [9], dwell-time [11], revenue [37], conversion rate [16]. Recently, Zhou et al. [41] focused on explicitly taking user ad feedback (offensive feed rate) into account to estimate ad quality. Barbieri et al. [2] presented a model on predicting the post-click user engagement using dwell-time for mobile ads. Chen [5] proposed a deep neural network (DNN) based model that directly predicts the CTR of an image ad based on raw image pixels and other basic features in one step. [40] combines deep neural networks with factorization machine and also brings an improvement.

Most of the previous predictive models on ad quality are based on viewable features: display, native, and sponsored search ads [9]. To the best of our knowledge, there is no work until now using the audio content directly to predict the user ad engagement after listening to ad.

Audio Signal Understanding and Music-IR. Many tasks in music understanding work directly with the audio signals through the computation of hand-crafted, targeted features. These features include descriptions of *timbre* to capture characteristics of the overall quality of the sound, *rhythm* to capture relationships of sound event timing, and *harmony* to capture relationships and patterns of harmonic frequency organization [18, 32]. Rhythm features can be used to model tempo, beat locations, and meter. Harmony and melody features are used to model the notes present, the key, the mode, chords, and song structure. Timbre features can be used to model instrumentation and performer expression [6, 18, 19, 23]. Audio features of many types used in combination have also proved to be useful in modeling more nebulous concepts as well. Audio feature similarity can be used to derive music similarity and drive automatic play-listing as well as song search and retrieval [14]. Supervised models using audio features can also be trained to capture very subjective concepts such as musical genre and taxonomy organization [22, 32, 34], assessing music and performer expression and sound quality [1, 38], and even the mood of the music [12]. Finally, Oord et al. proposed a deep learning approach for music recommendation [35].

In this work, we try to model the subjective concept of ad quality. Audio recording/sound quality is an important aspect of ad quality, and a well studied aspect in Music-IR (i.e., acoustical mixtures) and DSP in general (i.e., speech enhancement, synthesis) [24, 25]. However, audio ad quality refers to the quality of ad's compositional elements (message, speakers, music, sound effect). In the music domain, an analog to this work would be a quality assessment of the song and its musical composition. While it seems that is a difficult and subjective task for music, we feel that ad composition quality is a more tractable problem because ads are much shorter than most songs and are constructed to communicate a single, focused message.

3 PROBLEM DEFINITION & PRELIMINARY ANALYSIS

Defining a good or bad ad is not a trivial task. Let $A = a1, a2, ..., an$ be a set ads, where each ad has a spectrogram of audio associated to it, and a set of acoustic features, our objective is to learn a function $f : A \rightarrow R_{\geq 0}$ that indicates the quality of an ad. In order to learn a model for the audio ad quality prediction, first of all we need to define how to measure the audio ad quality, which are by their nature not clickable. After solving the measurement problem, we need to define the acoustic features in order to learn the quality prediction model. As a final step we need to define the learning model.

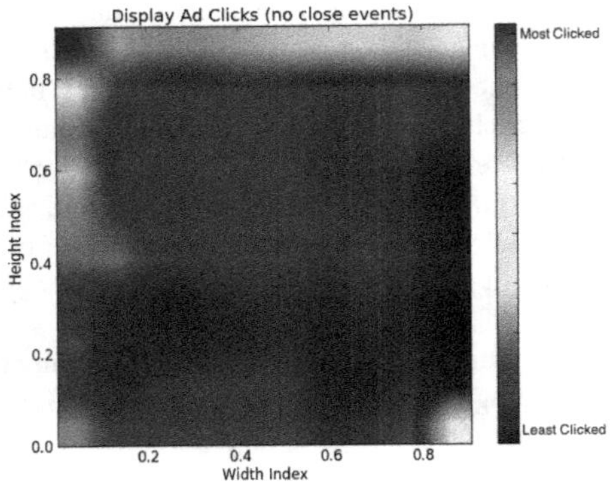

Figure 1: Heat map of the clicks (for a selected device and screen size) when a display ad of full screen size dimension is shown. Red color indicates higher number of clicks. Most of the clicks appear to be near the close button (on the top left corner). These are most likely noisy clicks.

3.1 Quality Measurement

One important step for predicting the quality of audio ad is to come up with useful quality metrics. So the major question is how one can measure the quality of an audio ad. Unfortunately, in most platforms there is no access to explicit feedback from users. However, we can gather different implicit feedback from user performance. In this case, we rely on a companion display ad that is presented at the same time the audio ad is playing. When the audio is playing the user can decide to click on the companion banner. However the clicks can be very noisy as the user might just want to close the ad or just unintentionally click. Figure 1 depicts a heat map of clicks on a mobile device. Most of the clicks are around the close button, and therefore most likely they are noisy clicks.

We use a new metric called *Long Click Rate (LCR)*, i.e., the amount of times a user clicks on the companion banner, and stay in the follow up page for more than a threshold time [1] (and its variants). In this case we discovered that more than 90% of the clicks on the top left corner clicked were resulting to user leaving in less than 5 seconds the following page. Therefore we fixed the threshold to 5 seconds.

Definition 3.1. Given an ad $a \in A$, the total number of clicks with dwell-time higher than a threshold, N_{lca}, and the total number of times the audio ad was played, N_a, we define *Long Click Rate (LCR)* as $LCR_a = (\frac{N_{lca}}{N_a})$.

We propose also a variant of the previous metric where we consider the vote for each user only once.

Definition 3.2. Given an ad $a \in A$, the total number of unique users with a long click on ad a, N_{ulca}, and the number of users the audio ad was played to, N_{ua} , we define *Robust Long Click Rate (R-LCR)* as $R - LCR_a = (\frac{N_{ulca}}{N_{ua}})$.

[1]The effectiveness of the proposed metrics is arguable, as it is the validity of CTR. However dwell-time higher than a threshold is used successfully in literature as a user engagement metric in sponsored search [11] and native ads case [15]. There might be a bias toward the images shown.

Note that our objective is not predicting LCR or R-LCR, but we want to use them as proxy to find out whether an ad is "good" or "bad". In this sense we sort the ads by these metrics, and label as "good" the top k percentile and "bad" the lower k percentile. Details will be given on 7.1.

3.2 User Preferences

We develop a user study to understand audio ad quality from users' point of view. This study can help us gain insight into the factors that affect user preferences for audio ads to inform feature engineering and the interpretation of results. To ensure a good variety in terms of audio ads quality we collect a set of ads from different *LCR* quantiles. We focus on top five categories: Retail/Mass Retail, Automotive, Education, Health Care, Financial/Insurance. The design of this study is similar to the user study in [41]. We provide evaluators with different pairs of two audio ads at a time and ask them to pick the ad they prefer. Moreover, to exclude the effect of evaluators' personal interests, at each comparison we ensure that ads are from the same category. After evaluators made the comparison, we ask them to specify the reason behind their choice from a set of given probable reasons. To define such reasons, there are several work in the literature [20, 42]. However, these studies focus on display and native advertising. Therefore, we define a set of reasons specific to audio ads. The reasons are *Clarity of Message* (clear message), *Clarity of Sound* (High Quality, with balance between background music and voice, good repetition), *Trustworthiness* (Speech matching the music, music/speech matching the product, not screaming buy), *Aesthetic* (Music background, Sound effect, Single speaker, conversation, Speakers genders), and *Brand* (Known Brand). We ensure that each pair is shown to an assessor at most once, and the order of audio ad played will be randomly chosen in each comparison. To ensure the quality of assessments, we present each pair to three people and collect three independent judgments. Moreover, we employ a gold standard check (with a known low quality audio ad created by us), and a redundancy check.

To perform the study, we collected 24 audio ads for each category randomly sampled from 6 distinctive quantiles of *LCR* distribution. Our experiment consists of 276 pairwise comparison in each category resulting in 1380 total pairs. Ensuring 3 assessments for each pair and adding the gold standard check and redundancy check, we initially collect 4968 comparisons from 414 users. Also, we ensure users' demographics have proper diversity. Users are 56% female and 44% male, with age groups of "18-25" (20.28%), "25-35" (23.19%), "35-45" (25.36%), "45-55" (16.18%), "55-65" (11.83%), and "65+" (3.14%). Among all users, 78.5% have yearly income of less than 50k, and remaining have income of 50-100k. After removing users who failed the quality checks, 286 users are verified and included in our analysis. In Table 1 the percentage of each reason selected is presented. The results show that for all categories, around 80% of time, *Audio Aesthetic* is selected as a reason with high influence. *Message clarity* and *sound quality* are the next top reasons for users to select a good ad. These results show that audio aesthetics and sound quality are important aspects for determining the quality of audio ads, and suggest that these should be included in the models to predict the audio ad quality. This motivates the later work in this paper, using acoustic features derived from the audio signal that are designed

Category	Message Clarity	Sound Quality	Trust-Worthiness	Audio Aesthetic	Brand
All	0.71	0.69	0.57	0.82	0.41
Automotive	0.67	0.74	0.52	0.83	0.40
Health Care	0.68	0.67	0.56	0.80	0.34
Education	0.78	0.68	0.62	0.82	0.43
Finance/Insurance	0.72	0.69	0.56	0.82	0.39
Retail/Mass Retail	0.69	0.69	0.56	0.81	0.47

Table 1: Users' selected reason for preferring a particular audio ad. Audio Aesthetics is selected as a reason of preference in 80% of time (for all categories).

to specifically capture elements of audio aesthetic, advertisement composition, and sound quality.

4 ACOUSTIC FEATURES

In this section, we outline a set of methods and features motivated by the user study conducted, related work *Digital Signal Processing (DSP)* and *Music Information Retrieval (Music-IR)* to obtain characteristics of the *timbre, rhythm,* and *harmony* directly from the audio signal. These are summarized in Table 2. Many of these features are high-dimensional, but are designed to capture intuitive auditory concepts in their dimensions. Because ad-quality is nebulous problem, we chose to start with these high-dimensional representations and allow the model to choose what is important. This affords the ability to gain an intuition as to what sonic attributes of an ad lead to its quality rating.

Acoustic features are computed from many sequential, fixed-length windows of audio samples and their resulting *Discrete Fourier Transform (DFT)*. The *Short-time Fourier Transform (STFT)* is many sequential DFTs computed in sliding widows across the signal. The STFT shows the magnitude of specific frequencies present at at each time step in the audio signal, and is the starting point for many hand-crafted acoustic features [18, 21]. There are a few fundamental trade-offs when computing the STFT. In this work, all audio ads start as 128kbs mp3 files. Timbre and rhythm features use a frame length of 2048 samples with a sequential overlap of 50% and 87.5% overlap respectively. Harmony features use a frame length of 16384 with a 50% overlap. These parameter values are quite common in the supporting literature [18].

4.1 Timbre Features

Timbre features capture characteristics of the overall quality of the sound. Differences in timbre can distinguish male vs. female voice, multiple speakers, music vs. speech, sound effects, etc. Many of the timbre features are computed on each spectral frame, so in order capture a compact representation for the entire signal, they are summarized with their *block statistics.* The mean and covariance (MCV) of the feature dimensions are computed on a set of fixed-length blocks of frames. The mean, variance, and the top right of the covariance matrix is vectorized to get an MCV vector for each block. All blocks are then summarized with the mean and variance of these MCV vectors [28]. This summarization is performed for TFD, SSD, MFCC, and DMFCC features.

Temporal Features and Dynamics (TFD) is a vector of the RMS energy and zero-Crossing rate (ZCR) of each audio frame. This captures a signals intensity, perceived volume, and noisiness. *Mel-frequency Cepstral Coefficients (MFCC)* are a compact representation of spectral shape motivated by how the human auditory system perceives sound. The frequency spectrum is warped with 128 perceptually motivated Mel filters. This perceptual frequency warping is linear up to 1kHz and logarithmic thereafter. Given a spectral frame X and a Mel-spaced filter-bank matrix F, each Mel-spectrum frame is computed by $X'_m = X_k F$ for each mel-frequency m. The resulting Mel-Spectrum is then log scaled and the Discrete Cosine Transform (DCT) is performed to create the *Ceptstrum* $C_c = \mathrm{DCT}\{\log(X'_m)\}$ with Cepstral frequencies c. The MFCC feature is the first 20 coefficients of that Cepstrum, starting with the second coefficient ($c \in 2 \ldots 21$). The first coefficient is often ignored because it represents scale rather than shape. This feature can be used to capture timbre, instrumentation, intonation, speaker/singer gender, number of speakers, tone, and the presence of music or sound effects. The *Delta-MFCC* is the frame-to-frame difference of MFCCs, and captures the dynamics of these attributes [18].

Mel-Spectral Patters (MSP) capture consistency, or temporal stability of the energy in the Mel-frequency bands. A coarse 32 band Mel-Spectrogram is computed from the STFT. A set of sequential 10-frame blocks is collected and activations in each band for each block are sorted. The feature is then summarized with the 60th percentile (median + 10%) of all blocks in all bands [28].

4.2 Rhythm Features

Rhythm features capture relationships of sound event timing. This can be used to model signal repetitiveness, how fast a speaker is talking, pulse/pace, and the presence of background rhythms if an the ad contains music backing tracks. Rhythm features start with the computation of an *accent-signal,* which is a summarization of the STFT that shows emphasis of where new sonic events occur in time [3]. This is also computed along three distinct frequency ranges to get sonic accents in low/bass (B: 27.5Hz-220Hz), middle/treble (T:220Hz-1.76kHz), and high (H:1.76kHz-14.08kHz) pitch accent signals [23]. The *Tempogram (TG_LIN)* feature starts with an *autocorrelation* of the accent signal a. The autocorrelation is a measure of self-similarity where $r[k]$ is the product of the two signals with respect to a time shift of lag k (Eq. 1).

$$r[k] = \sum_N a[n]a[n-k] \tag{1}$$

The tempogram is the transformation of the lag axis (time-period) to a linearly-quantized frequency axis scaled to represent beats-per-minute. This captures absolute rates of repetitiveness in the accent signal, and is also used to estimate a primary and secondary *Tempo Estimate (TEMPO).* The TG_LIN feature can be made more compact and tempo-invariant by looking at the weights in the tempogram at a set of simple fractional ratios r of the estimated tempo τ. This creates a *Tempogram Ratio (TGR)* feature of relative temporal self-similarity (Eq. 2 [23]).

$$\mathrm{TGR}_r = \{4\tau, \frac{8}{3}\tau, 3\tau, 2\tau, \frac{4}{3}\tau, \frac{3}{2}\tau, \tau, \frac{2}{3}\tau, \frac{3}{4}\tau, \frac{1}{2}\tau, \frac{1}{3}\tau, \frac{3}{8}\tau, \frac{1}{4}\tau\} \tag{2}$$

With a tempo estimate and the accent signal, musical *beat-tracking* is performed via the dynamic programming method to capture positions of a fundamental pulse [6]. The accent signal is

Type	Name	Dims	Description
	TFD	10	Temporal Features and Dynamics - Block summary of of each frame's RMS amplitude and ZCR [18, 28]
Timbre	MFCC	460	Block MFCCs - block summary of a compact snapshot of spectral shape [18, 28]
	Delta-MFCC	460	Block Delta MFCCs - Block summary of the change in spectral shape [18, 28]
	MSP	320	Block Mel-Spectral Patterns - Block summary of patterns in the activation of mel-frequency bands [28]
	TEMPO	2	A primary and secondary estimate of the beats per minute [23].
	TG_LIN	500	Tempogram TG - A histogram-like feature that shows emphasis of rhythmic repetition vs a bpm [23]
Rhythm	TGR{B,T,H}	13x3	Multi-band TG Ratios. A compact version of the tempogram at simple ratios of a tempo estimate [23]
	BPDIST{B,T,H}	36x3	Multi-band Beat Profile - Captures an snapshot of emphasis within estimated beat/pulse positions [23]
	Mellin	512	Mellin Scale transform - rhythmic self-similarity among multiple time scales [10, 23]
	SIHPCP	9	Shift-Invariant chroma histogram - 2D FFT of histogram of pitch classes (A, A#, B, etc.) present [8]
Harmony	MODE	1	Estimate of major or minor mode [8]
	SICH,SICHC,SIKC	18x3	Shift-invariant (2D-FFT) histogram of chords present and the correlations of HPCP to chord and key templates [8]

Table 2: Audio Acoustic Features Overview

summarized to create the *Beat Profile (BP)*, which is the mean of the accent signal between successive beat positions [23].

4.3 Harmony Features

Harmony features, while seemingly tangential to this mostly non-music task can still provide important information regarding frequency organization. Speech is a very dynamic and harmonically rich signal. These features can capture a person's tone as monotone vs. animated and clearly pitched vs. raspy or breathy. If the ad has background music, they will capture the harmonic organization of that as well.

Harmony features start with a *Constant-Q Transform (CQT)* performed on each STFT frame, which is a spectral filtering/warping to capture frequency emphasis at the locations of musical notes based on equal-tempered tuning. The *Harmonic Pitch Class Profile (HPCP)* $P_{p,i}$ is a circular summarization of the Constant-Q Transform that captures the emphasis of the 12 pitch classes p (A, A#, B, etc.) for all octaves $k = 0...K-1$ for each CQT frame $Q_{n,i}$ with note bins n and frames i (Eq. 3). It can be further summarized by taking the mean across all frames. This can be made shift-invariant to key (harmonic tonic, anchor point) (SIHPCP) by taking the the Fourier Transform of the HPCP to emphasize the harmonic note relationships and density][8].

$$P_{p,i} = \sum_{k=0}^{K-1} Q_{12k,i} + p \tag{3}$$

Harmony and Key specific correlation features are computed by finding the correlation of the HPCP to a set of contextual templates (chords, keys, etc.). The *chordogram* is the correlation coefficients of the HPCP at each frame to a set of 12 major and 12 minor chords. The *Chord Correlations (CHC)* feature is the mean of the chordogram. The *Chord Histogram (CH)* is a histogram of chord estimates using the max of the chordogram at each frame. The *Key Correlations (KC)* feature is the correlation coefficients of the mean of all frames of the HPCP to a set of 12 major and 12 minor key templates [8]. All of these are made shift-invariant (SICHC, SICH, SIKC) by taking the 2D-Fourier Transform (2D-FFT) of the resulting correlations/estimates. The feature becomes the Fourier Transform of the difference of the major and minor correlations/estimates concatenated to the sum of the major and minor correlations/estimates. Where $\mathbf{x}$ is the concatenated major and minor template activations,

$$\mathbf{x}_{maj} = \mathbf{x}_{i=0...12} \qquad \mathbf{x}_{min} = \mathbf{x}_{i=13...24}$$

Where $X = \mathfrak{F}(x)$ is the 16-point Discrete Fourier Transform (DFT) of x,

$$\mathbf{X}'_{sum} = \mathfrak{F}(\mathbf{x}_{maj} + \mathbf{x}_{min}) \qquad \mathbf{X}'_{diff} = \mathfrak{F}(\mathbf{x}_{maj} - \mathbf{x}_{min})$$

$$\mathbf{Y}_{shift-invariant} = \text{append}(\mathbf{X}'_{sum}, \mathbf{X}'_{diff})$$

5 MODELING USING ACOUSTIC FEATURES

In this section, we focus on predicting the quality of an audio ad, using acoustic features. We denote with $v \in R^d$ the feature vector, where d is 2440 dimension. Our goal is to predict the probability that an audio ad has high quality.

5.1 Baseline Machine Learning Methods on Acoustic Features

Due to curse of dimensionality, one important step is to reduce the number of variables or transform the features into a smaller dimension. There are total number of 2440 acoustic features extracted from audio ads which can have multi-collinearity or redundancy, and also can lead to over-fitting. We explore different dimension reduction and feature extraction techniques including PCA and Kernel PCA, feature selection based on feature importance calculated from Tree Classifiers, and L1 penalty on Logistic Regression and linear SVC.

The first baseline classification method is *Logistic Regression (LR)*. Denoting the quality as y with binary values of 0 (bad quality), and 1 (good quality), the estimated probability of ad quality is:

$$P(\hat{y} = 1|x) = \frac{1}{1 + e^{-w^T x}} \tag{4}$$

where $w \in d \times 1$ is the vector to learn. We use Logarithmic Loss (Logloss) in order to learn the previous function. Moreover, since we have many features, we use *L1 regularized logistic regression* (L1-LR) which is often used for feature selection [29, 36]. In this model, analogous to Lasso [33], penalty term is added to loss criterion, in other words we try to minimize the following function:

$$L(w) = -\frac{1}{N} \sum_i y_i log\hat{y}_i + (1 - y_i) log(1 - \hat{y}_i) + \lambda |w| \tag{5}$$

Where λ is the regularization parameter. Furthermore, we implement LR on the reduced dimension obtained with *PCA* (LR-PCA),and *Kernel PCA* (LR-KPCA). Apart from the above mentioned methods, we explore the use of *Support Vector Machines*, with linear support

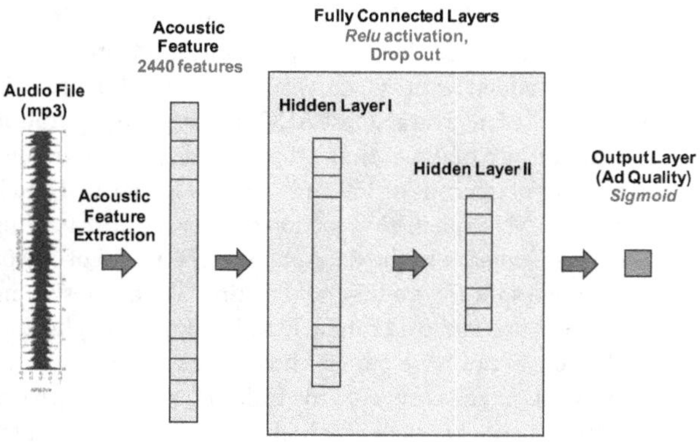

Figure 2: MLP on Acoustic Features Architecture

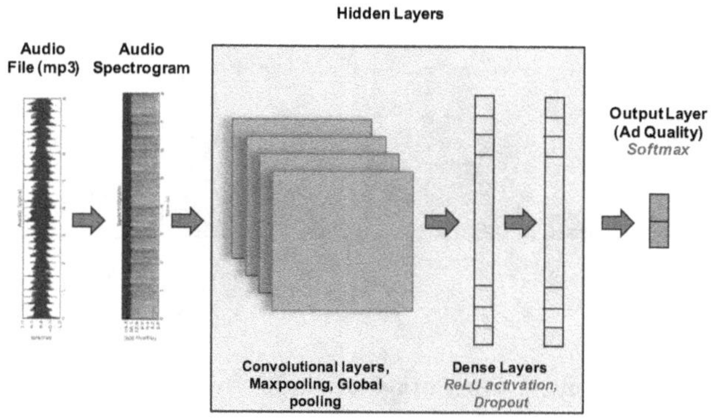

Figure 3: CNN on Spectrograms Architecture

vector classifier (Linear-SVC) and nonlinear SVC with *rbf* kernel (rbf-SVC). Furthermore, we use ensemble methods including *Random Forest classifier* (RF) [4], Ada boost with Decision Trees (Ada-DT) and Bagging Classifier with Logistic Regression (BC-LR).

5.2 Multilayer Perceptrons on Acoustic Features

The Multilayer Perceptron (MLP) [39] is one of most commonly used neural network methods for classification. MLP is a feed-forward neural networks that use standard back-propagation algorithm for training. This classifier learns how to transform input data into a desired response in a supervise manner. The MLP consists of one input layer, one or more hidden layer and one output layer.

We implement MLP on audio ad's acoustic features (as the input layer), and train the model to gain the audio quality (as the output layer). Therefore, the architecture of the MLP method has 2440 neurons of input layer, and one neuron of the output layer (representing the predicted quality as good or bad). Hidden layers are fully connected layers with Rectified Linear Units (ReLUs) activation function, which is $f(x) = max(0, x)$. ReLUs ensure faster computation, more efficient gradient propagation, and sparse structure [7]. Moreover, to prevent over-fitting and ensure regularization, Dropout is applied at the end of each layer [31]. The level of dropout, number of hidden layers, and number of neurons in each layer are tuned using cross validation in section 7.2. The output layer is one neuron with sigmoid activation function, representing the likelihood of good ad quality. The training process minimize the binary cross-entropy loss function and uses Adam as its optimizer with default parameters [13]. The MLP architecture with two hidden layer is shown in figure 2. The presented MLP network can be used for predicting the audio ad's quality. Also, the last hidden layer can be seen as a new set of learned features from audio acoustic features. This features lie in a smaller dimension, and will be useful later for representing and clustering ads in a more informative way in direction of ads' quality.

6 DEEP CONVOLUTIONAL NETWORKS ON SPECTROGRAMS

In the recent years, it is common in the field of music informatics to make use of Convolutional Neural Networks (CNNs) [35] to estimate higher-level features directly from spectrograms. These representations are typically contained in $\mathbb{R}^{F \times N}$ matrices with F frequency bins and N time frames, which become the input to the CNN.

In this work, we propose a deep learning model to predict the quality of the audio ads using spectrogram. This model is inspired by music deep learning works [35]. We compute $F = 100$ frequency bin, log-compressed constant-Q transforms (CQT) [27] for all the ads in our dataset using `librosa` [17] with these parameters: audio sampling rate at 44100Hz, hop length of 1024 samples, and 12 bins per octave. Furthermore, log-amplitude scaling is applied to the CQT spectrograms with a power law of 2 and scaling of 0.1. Even if CNNs allow for variable sized inputs due to the weight sharing nature of their convolutional filters, we need to normalize the sizes of all the spectrograms to train with minibatches of data points such that the gradients become more stable. To do so, and inspired by [35], we randomly sample three, 10-seconds long patches from each ad, resulting in a fixed-size N input to the network, which are only used for training. We need patches because we need to place them in valid tensor for mini batch gradient during training. During inference the network is able to make predictions from full (i.e., not patched and variable N) audio ads.

The network is composed of convolutional layers. All convolutions operate in the time axis only, thus having 1D convolutions instead of 2D. This is common practice when dealing with music signals [35] and it is inspired by the importance of the relation between frequency bins, whose absolute placement in the spectrum matters. After these layers of convolution and maxpooling, a layer to compute global pooling through time is placed. This layer obtains 4 different statistics: mean, max, l2-norm, and standard deviation. Due to this aggregation, the network does not need to operate on fixed-sized spectrograms, therefore audio ads of different sizes will be able to be fed into the network. Finally, two dense layers with dropout and ReLUs are added after the global pooling, and the last layer is a set of two scalars with a softmax activation that represents the likelihood of each of the two classes: good or bad quality ad. The structure of our network is shown in figure 3. The training process minimizes the binary cross-entropy loss function, and uses Adam as its optimizer with the default parameters [13].

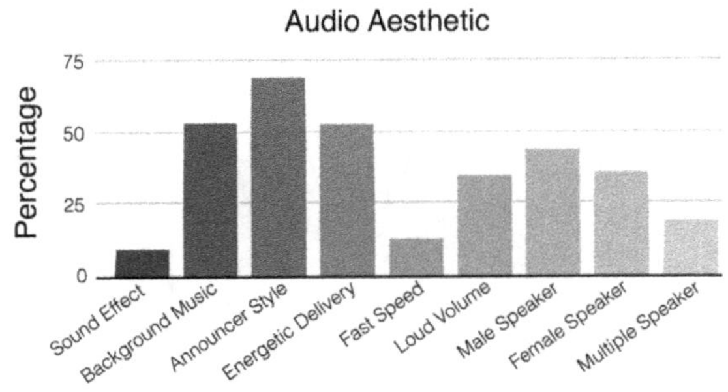

Figure 4: Percentage of Audio Aesthetics

7 EXPERIMENTS

In this section we aim to evaluate our audio ad quality prediction models. We proceed by describing our dataset, parameter tuning, and we finish by discussing our results.

7.1 Datasets

We sample a set of audio ads from Pandora.com through May and June 2017. We then collected the information about the *LCR* and *R-LCR* for the audio ads following the procedure described in Section 3.1. For both labels we applied a filter of having at least two *long clicks* or having at least two *users long clicked* over 500 impressions. The *LCR* related dataset consists of 9k unique audio ads. The *R-LCR* related dataset consists of 7k unique audio ads. The audio ads are in mp3 format with 128Kbps.

In order to have some insight about our audio datasets, we sampled a set of 500 audio ads, and asked human listeners to provide some information about their aesthetic data. The listeners determined the gender of speaker (female, male or more than one person), the speed of speaker, the existence of background music or sound effect in the ad, and the ad's volume. Figure 4 show the percentage of aesthetic characteristics. Audio ads in our dataset seems to have a good diversity in terms of audio aesthetics. Our final dataset is made of one row per each audio ads with the acoustic features extracted and the audio spectrogram, and a binary label. In order to have a binary label based on *LCR* and *R-LCR*, we sort our dataset based on each quality metric and take the upper percentile as "good", and the lower percentile as "bad". To define which percentiles should be selected, we considered different scenarios and chose the percentiles with highest prediction accuracy. The scenarios we tried are [top 50, lower 50], [top 70, lower 30], [top 30, lower 30], and [top 10, lower 10] percentile as ["good", "bad"]. The best result was gained by labeling "good" the top 30 percentile and "bad" the lower 30 percentile.

7.2 Implementation and Parameter tuning

To tune the parameters for each method and choose the best set of parameters, we implement 10-fold stratified cross validation on training data. In each fold, we use 9 fold to train the model and the remaining 1 fold for testing, and calculate the average test AUC. The average test AUC over all folds is used to select the best set of parameters. For the MLP network explained in section 5.2, batches of size 50 and total number 200 epochs are used for training, training takes around 110 seconds to finish on a 2.6 GHz Inter Core i7 processor with 16 GB 1600 MHz DDR3 memory. we implement the network with different dropout rate (None,20,40, and 50 percent), number of hidden layers (1,2,3,4), and number of neurons in each layer, and calculate average test AUC. The best configuration gained is dropout rate of 0.4 at the end of each layer, two hidden layer, and number of neurons of 150 and 75 in hidden layers I and II respectively. For CNN explained in section 6, since we are sampling 3 patches from each audio in the dataset, we have a total of 32,406 patches, which we split for training and testing. We make sure no patches from the same audio ad can be found in different splits (i.e., a given audio ad can not have patches both in, e.g., train and test). Minibatches of 64 patches are used for training, and the network converges after 14 epochs, each of which takes around 6 minutes to finish on a Tesla M40 GPU. Once the network is trained, it takes 1.09 seconds in average to do inference on full ad spectrograms. After trying different parameters (including different number of convolutional layers), the best network is gained by using 4 convolutional layers (with 1024, 1024, 2048, 2048 filters, respectively) with length in time of the filters as 4, 4, 4, and 3, respectively. Maxpool layers are placed after each convolution, which aggregate through time with the following shapes: 8, 2, 2, 1. Also, two dense layers have 2048 neurons with 50% dropout.

7.3 Performance Analysis

In this section, we compare the effectiveness of proposed methods with best configuration. For this comparison, the baseline methods are the top 5 machine learning approaches (in terms of test AUC) explained in Sec. 5.1. The results are presented in table 3. As the results shows, among the baseline methods, logistic regression with L1 regularization gives the highest AUC for both labels. Moving to MLP network on acoustic features, the AUC increases by 7.4% and 6.6% for *LCR*, and *R-LCR* labels respectively. Furthermore, the CNN on audio spectrograms gives the highest accuracy of 0.7492 and 0.7906 test AUC for *LCR* and *R-LCR* labeled data. In this case, in comparison to the best baseline method, the accuracy increases by 18.19% and 14.76% for *LCR* and *R-LCR* labels. This results shows that CNN method on spectrograms beats the methods based on acoustic features, and audio spectrograms itself can be used as a sufficient input to obtain the quality of audio ad.

Another comparison, is based on the runtime of different methods. Test and training time (in seconds) for each method is recorded in Table 4. The results show that CNN methods have much higher training time in comparison to other methods. Therefore, if the size of data increases, the run time can be hindering in comparison with other methods.

7.4 Intuition and Discussion

One good property of ML-based methods is their easy interpretation. Among ML methods, the best AUC accuracy was obtained using LR-L1 method. In this method, L1 regularization is used for variable selection. The list of selected variables and their corresponding coefficients are presented in Figure 5 for *LCR* and *R-LCR* data respectively. From the selected features and their value we can get insight about some general characteristics in favor of a better audio ad.

Method		Dataset	
		Pandora LCR	Pandora R-LCR
ML	LR	0.5960(±0.01815)	0.6582(±0.0175)
	LR+L1	**0.6338**(±0.0172)	**0.6889**(±0.0157)
	rbf-SVC	0.5801(±0.0195)	0.6238(±0.0273)
	Ada-DT	0.5641(±0.0117)	0.6105(±0.0186)
	RF	0.579(±0.018)	0.6080(±0.0233)
MLP	MLP_2layer	**0.6808**(±0.0237)	**0.7342**(±0.0146)
	MLP_3layer	0.6657(±0.0173)	0.7299(±0.0141)
CNN	CNN_4layer	**0.7491**(±0.0224)	**0.7906**(±0.0207)

Table 3: Average test AUC (and its 95% confidence interval)

Method	Training Time (sec)	Prediction Time (sec)
LR	118.1302	0.0017
LR_L1	12.4626	0.0022
rbf-SVC	54.3700	6.0630
Ada_DT	61.9137	0.0352
RF	1.9384	0.0143
MLP_2layer	111.1795	0.0852
MLP_3layer	115.4068	0.1274
CNN_4layers	3,540.1200	1.0900

Table 4: Runtime comparison for different methods

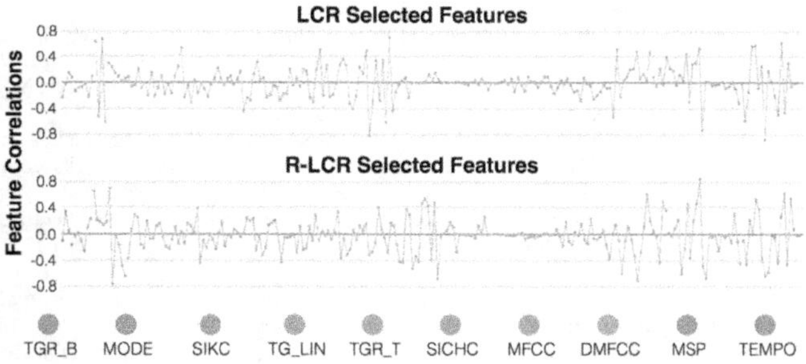

Figure 5: Features selected by L1 regularization and their corresponding coefficient in Logistic Regression.

Acoustic Feature Intuition. The *timbre features* were quite important when predicting ad-quality. Correlations in the Mel-Frequency Cepstral Coefficients (*MFCC*) and Delta MFCC (*DMFCC*), which correspond to the spectral shape of the speech and its variance, suggest that clear pronunciation is important. Furthermore, jarring sound effects and music can mask the parts of the spectrum that contain the speech, leading to poor quality. Correlations of Mel-Spectral Patterns (*MSP*) dimensions suggest that if low frequencies or high frequencies are too active, the ad is of low quality, suggesting the balance of the audio mix is bad. Furthermore high variance in low and high frequencies leads to bad quality as well, as the overall spectral range of sound is not stable. Because speech sits in the middle frequencies, the overbalance and variance of frequencies surrounding speech can be distracting.

From the *rhythm features*, specifically *TGR* and *TG_LIN*, faster relative pulse repetition was negatively correlated with quality, and slower repetition relative to a pulse was positively correlated quality. This indicates that speaking more slowly and moderate tempo music (if any) correlates to better quality.

The *harmony features* also showed some interesting correlations. Major *MODE* positively correlates with quality, suggesting the choice of music sounds (if any) in a major key. *SIKC* and *SICH*, while having little direct contextual meaning in speech signals, capture patterns and transitions in the harmonic spacing of sounds. Animated speech, where pitch shifts up and down, should be captured. These correlations show that moderately animated pitch shifts lead to good quality ads. If speech is too animated (too much shift) or too monotone (too little shift) it leads to poor quality. This suggests to speak with a slightly animated tone and to choose music (if any) with a little harmonic motion.

Qualitative Listening Analysis. Further intuition can be gained by listening to the ads that are correctly predicted as having good versus poor quality. This is done by clustering audio features as well as the last layer of the neural-network for each of the model types and listening to the ads of clusters that are primarily true-positives or true-negatives. Doing so, neural-network based methods gives much better clusters in terms of separating high and low quality audio ads. By listening to the clusters with highest and lowest quality we can gain insights about differences between these clusters. This qualitative analysis showed that *Good Ads* have clear, mid-paced, solo voice. They contain moderately varied, non-monotone speaker expression with moderate excitement. The speech is conversational between the speaker and the audience (i.e., story telling, call-to-action) or between two isolated speakers in the ad. If there is background music, it is basic. There is a good balance between background and foreground sounds, and there are almost no sound effects. *Poor quality ads* have faster paced language, long winded explanations of products, and very monotone expression. Many of them had loud backing music and jarring sound effects that sometimes obscure the speech. Finally many of these were also lower quality recordings with distortion and compression effects. These qualitative attributes were shared among the models, but were more clear to interpret in the LR-L1 method than the neural network method. It further suggests that these acoustic attribute saliences exist, echoed both in the quantitative feature correlation analysis and this qualitative analysis. However, the neural network, which has Higher AUC overall, is potentially picking up on more subtleties, which leaves room for further exploration into the additional attributes it is capturing.

8 CONCLUSIONS AND FUTURE WORK

In this work we presented the first audio ad quality prediction model. We focus on building a prediction model that is using only acoustic content. Given the fact that there is no direct feedback from users regarding audio ads, we proposed two quality metrics based on *Long Click Rate (LCR)* on the audio ad's companion display for labeling the audio files. We than conducted a user study to understand the users' reasons for prefering a particular audio ad. The results of the user study show that in 80% of the cases they prefer an audio ad due to audio aesthetics. Motivated by this, we implemented several acoustic features. We later used these features to learn a prediction model for audio ad quality. The results show that speaking slow with less jarring sound effect and only simple music (if any) can lead to better audio ad quality. Another finding is that conversational tone are usually more engaging, for instance

"Do you have a need? ... try this" is better than *"We have the best deal down at car store."*. Finally we proposed a deep convolutional network on audio spectrogram, reaching an AUC of 0.79 for the prediction task.

For future works, we plan to study further the proposed quality metrics, for instance by investigating if there is a bias toward the images shown. Furthermore, we want to include in the model the user profile features, the campaign information and historical data of ad quality. Another interesting investigation is to use the transcription of the audio ads content and perform text analysis.

REFERENCES

[1] Giuseppe Bandiera, Oriol Romani Picas, Hiroshi Tokuda, Wataru Hariya, Koji Oishi, and Xavier Serra. 2016. Good-sounds. org: A Framework to Explore Goodness in Instrumental Sounds.. In *Proc. International Society for Music Information Retrieval Conference (ISMIR)*. 414–419.

[2] Nicola Barbieri, Fabrizio Silvestri, and Mounia Lalmas. 2016. Improving Post-Click User Engagement on Native Ads via Survival Analysis. In *Proceedings of the 25th International Conference on World Wide Web (WWW '16)*. International World Wide Web Conferences Steering Committee, Republic and Canton of Geneva, Switzerland, 761–770. https://doi.org/10.1145/2872427.2883092

[3] Sebastian Böck and Gerhard Widmer. 2013. Maximum filter vibrato suppression for onset detection. In *Proc. of the Int. Conf. on Digital Audio Effects (DAFx)*.

[4] Leo Breiman. 2001. Random forests. *Machine learning* 45, 1 (2001), 5–32.

[5] Junxuan Chen, Baigui Sun, Hao Li, Hongtao Lu, and Xian-Sheng Hua. 2016. Deep ctr prediction in display advertising. In *Proceedings of the 2016 ACM on Multimedia Conference*. ACM, 811–820.

[6] Daniel PW Ellis. 2007. Beat tracking by dynamic programming. *Journal of New Music Research* 36, 1 (2007), 51–60.

[7] Xavier Glorot, Antoine Bordes, and Yoshua Bengio. 2011. Deep sparse rectifier neural networks. In *Proceedings of the Fourteenth International Conference on Artificial Intelligence and Statistics*. 315–323.

[8] Emilia Gómez. 2006. Tonal description of polyphonic audio for music content processing. *INFORMS Journal on Computing* 18, 3 (2006), 294–304.

[9] Dustin Hillard, Stefan Schroedl, Eren Manavoglu, Hema Raghavan, and Chirs Leggetter. 2010. Improving Ad Relevance in Sponsored Search. In *Proceedings of the Third ACM International Conference on Web Search and Data Mining (WSDM '10)*. ACM, New York, NY, USA, 361–370. https://doi.org/10.1145/1718487.1718532

[10] André Holzapfel and Yannis Stylianou. 2011. Scale transform in rhythmic similarity of music. *IEEE transactions on audio, speech, and language processing* 19, 1 (2011), 176–185.

[11] Youngho Kim, Ahmed Hassan, Ryen W. White, and Imed Zitouni. 2014. Modeling Dwell Time to Predict Click-level Satisfaction. In *Proceedings of the 7th ACM International Conference on Web Search and Data Mining (WSDM '14)*. ACM, New York, NY, USA, 193–202. https://doi.org/10.1145/2556195.2556220

[12] Youngmoo E Kim, Erik M Schmidt, Raymond Migneco, Brandon G Morton, Patrick Richardson, Jeffrey Scott, Jacquelin A Speck, and Douglas Turnbull. 2010. Music emotion recognition: A state of the art review. In *Proc. International Society for Music Information Retrieval Conference (ISMIR)*. 255–266.

[13] Diederik Kingma and Jimmy Ba. 2014. Adam: A method for stochastic optimization. *arXiv preprint arXiv:1412.6980* (2014).

[14] Peter Knees and Markus Schedl. 2016. Introduction to Music Similarity and Retrieval. In *Music Similarity and Retrieval*. Springer, 1–30.

[15] Mounia Lalmas, Janette Lehmann, Guy Shaked, Fabrizio Silvestri, and Gabriele Tolomei. 2015. Promoting Positive Post-Click Experience for In-Stream Yahoo Gemini Users. In *Proceedings of the 21th ACM SIGKDD International Conference on Knowledge Discovery and Data Mining (KDD '15)*. ACM, New York, NY, USA, 1929–1938. https://doi.org/10.1145/2783258.2788581

[16] Kuang-chih Lee, Burkay Orten, Ali Dasdan, and Wentong Li. 2012. Estimating Conversion Rate in Display Advertising from Past Erformance Data. In *Proceedings of the 18th ACM SIGKDD International Conference on Knowledge Discovery and Data Mining (KDD '12)*. ACM, New York, NY, USA, 768–776. https://doi.org/10.1145/2339530.2339651

[17] Brian McFee, Colin Raffel, Dawen Liang, Daniel PW Ellis, Matt McVicar, Eric Battenberg, and Oriol Nieto. 2015. librosa: Audio and music signal analysis in python. In *Proceedings of the 14th python in science conference*. 18–25.

[18] Meinard Müller. 2015. *Fundamentals of Music Processing: Audio, Analysis, Algorithms, Applications*. Springer.

[19] Oriol Nieto and Juan Pablo Bello. 2014. Music segment similarity using 2d-fourier magnitude coefficients. In *Acoustics, Speech and Signal Processing (ICASSP), IEEE International Conference on*. IEEE, 664–668.

[20] Heather L O'Brien and Elaine G Toms. 2010. The development and evaluation of a survey to measure user engagement. *Journal of the Association for Information Science and Technology* 61, 1 (2010), 50–69.

[21] Alan V. Oppenheim, Ronald W. Schafer, and John R. Buck. 1999. *Discrete-time Signal Processing (2Nd Ed.)*. Prentice-Hall, Inc., Upper Saddle River, NJ, USA.

[22] Matthew Prockup, Andreas F Ehmann, Fabien Gouyon, Erik M Schmidt, Oscar Celma, and Youngmoo E Kim. 2015. Modeling Genre with the Music Genome Project: Comparing Human-Labeled Attributes and Audio Features.. In *Proc. International Society for Music Information Retrieval Conference (ISMIR)*. 31–37.

[23] Matthew Prockup, Andreas F Ehmann, Fabien Gouyon, Erik M Schmidt, and Youngmoo E Kim. 2015. Modeling musical rhythmatscale with the music Genome project. In *IEEE Workshop on Applications of Signal Processing to Audio and Acoustics (WASPAA)*. IEEE, 1–5.

[24] Thomas F. Quatieri. 2002. *Discrete-time speech signal processing : principles and practice*. Prentice-Hall, Inc., Upper Saddle River, NJ, USA.

[25] Joshua D Reiss. 2011. Intelligent systems for mixing multichannel audio. In *Digital Signal Processing (DSP), 2011 17th International Conference on*. IEEE, 1–6.

[26] Rómer Rosales, Haibin Cheng, and Eren Manavoglu. 2012. Post-click Conversion Modeling and Analysis for Non-guaranteed Delivery Display Advertising. In *Proceedings of the Fifth ACM International Conference on Web Search and Data Mining (WSDM '12)*. ACM, New York, NY, USA, 293–302. https://doi.org/10.1145/2124295.2124333

[27] Christian Schörkhuber and Anssi Klapuri. 2010. Constant-Q transform toolbox for music processing. In *7th Sound and Music Computing Conference, Barcelona, Spain*. 3–64.

[28] Klaus Seyerlehner, Gerhard Widmer, and Tim Pohle. 2010. Fusing block-level features for music similarity estimation. In *Proc. of the Int. Conference on Digital Audio Effects (DAFx)*. 225–232.

[29] Shirish Krishnaj Shevade and S Sathiya Keerthi. 2003. A simple and efficient algorithm for gene selection using sparse logistic regression. *Bioinformatics* 19, 17 (2003), 2246–2253.

[30] Eric Sodomka, Sébastien Lahaie, and Dustin Hillard. 2013. A Predictive Model for Advertiser Value-per-click in Sponsored Search. In *Proceedings of the 22Nd International Conference on World Wide Web (WWW '13)*. ACM, New York, NY, USA, 1179–1190. https://doi.org/10.1145/2488388.2488491

[31] Nitish Srivastava, Geoffrey E Hinton, Alex Krizhevsky, Ilya Sutskever, and Ruslan Salakhutdinov. 2014. Dropout: a simple way to prevent neural networks from overfitting. *Journal of Machine Learning Research* 15, 1 (2014), 1929–1958.

[32] Bob L Sturm. 2014. The state of the art ten years after a state of the art: Future research in music information retrieval. *Journal of New Music Research* 43, 2 (2014), 147–172.

[33] Robert Tibshirani. 1996. Regression shrinkage and selection via the lasso. *Journal of the Royal Statistical Society. Series B (Methodological)* (1996), 267–288.

[34] George Tzanetakis and Perry Cook. 2002. Musical genre classification of audio signals. *IEEE Transactions on speech and audio processing* 10, 5 (2002), 293–302.

[35] Aaron Van den Oord, Sander Dieleman, and Benjamin Schrauwen. 2013. Deep content-based music recommendation. In *Advances in neural information processing systems*. 2643–2651.

[36] Martin J Wainwright, John D Lafferty, and Pradeep K Ravikumar. 2007. High-dimensional graphical model selection using l1-regularized logistic regression. In *Advances in neural information processing systems*. 1465–1472.

[37] Chong Wang, Achir Kalra, Cristian Borcea, and Yi Chen. 2015. Viewability Prediction for Online Display Ads. In *Proceedings of the 24th ACM International on Conference on Information and Knowledge Management (CIKM '15)*. ACM, New York, NY, USA, 413–422. https://doi.org/10.1145/2806416.2806536

[38] Alex Wilson and Bruno M. Fazenda. 2016. Perception of Audio Quality in Productions of Popular Music. *Journal of the Audio Engineering Society* 64, 1/2 (2016), 23–34. http://www.aes.org/e-lib/browse.cfm?elib=18102

[39] Ian H Witten, Eibe Frank, Mark A Hall, and Christopher J Pal. 2016. *Data Mining: Practical machine learning tools and techniques*. Morgan Kaufmann.

[40] Weinan Zhang, Tianming Du, and Jun Wang. 2016. Deep learning over multi-field categorical data. In *European conference on information retrieval*. Springer, 45–57.

[41] Ke Zhou, Miriam Redi, Andrew Haines, and Mounia Lalmas. 2016. Predicting Pre-click Quality for Native Advertisements. In *Proceedings of the 25th International Conference on World Wide Web (WWW '16)*. International World Wide Web Conferences Steering Committee, Republic and Canton of Geneva, Switzerland, 299–310. https://doi.org/10.1145/2872427.2883053

[42] Ke Zhou, Miriam Redi, Andrew Haines, and Mounia Lalmas. 2016. Predicting pre-click quality for native advertisements. In *Proceedings of the 25th International Conference on World Wide Web*. International World Wide Web Conferences Steering Committee, 299–310.

Cognitive Biases in Crowdsourcing

Carsten Eickhoff
Dept. of Computer Science
Zurich, Switzerland
ecarsten@inf.ethz.ch

ABSTRACT

Crowdsourcing has become a popular paradigm in data curation, annotation and evaluation for many artificial intelligence and information retrieval applications. Considerable efforts have gone into devising effective quality control mechanisms that identify or discourage cheat submissions in an attempt to improve the quality of noisy crowd judgments. Besides purposeful cheating, there is another source of noise that is often alluded to but insufficiently studied: Cognitive biases.

This paper investigates the prevalence and effect size of a range of common cognitive biases on a standard relevance judgment task. Our experiments are based on three sizable publicly available document collections and note significant detrimental effects on annotation quality, system ranking and the performance of derived rankers when task design does not account for such biases.

CCS CONCEPTS

• Information systems → Crowdsourcing; Relevance assessment; • Social and professional topics → Quality assurance;

KEYWORDS

Crowdsourcing, Human Computation, Relevance Assessment, Cognitive Biases

ACM Reference Format:

Carsten Eickhoff. 2018. Cognitive Biases in Crowdsourcing. In *Proceedings of WSDM 2018: The Eleventh ACM International Conference on Web Search and Data Mining (WSDM 2018).* ACM, New York, NY, USA, 9 pages. https://doi.org/10.1145/3159652.3159654

1 INTRODUCTION

Over the past decade, crowdsourcing has been established as a popular method for data collection, annotation and consolidation as well as conducting user studies and evaluating system performance. Instead of relying on local annotators contributing labor in controlled lab environments, human intelligence tasks, so-called HITs, are outsourced to a large anonymous crowd of workers. Academics and industrial practitioners alike praise this alternative paradigm's cost-efficiency, quick response times and access to workers of more diverse backgrounds than were commonly included in most lab-based studies. As a consequence of this distributed weakly supervised approach, quality control remains a key challenge [17].

The literature commonly assumes low label quality to stem from three possible reasons: **(1)** Unethical spammers submit imprecise or even arbitrary labels in order to maximize their financial efficiency [18] or due to external distractions. **(2)** Unqualified workers are, despite their best efforts, unable to produce an acceptable annotation quality [15]. **(3)** Malicious workers purposefully aim to undermine or influence the labelling effort [53][1].

While there certainly is strong evidence for all of the above reasons, we argue that there is a fourth fundamental reason for noisy label submissions. Cognitive biases are systematic patterns of deviation from norm or rationality in judgment, whereby inferences about other people and situations may be drawn in an illogical fashion [27]. Individuals create their own "subjective social reality" from their perception of the input. An individual's construction of social reality, instead of the objective input, may dictate their behaviour and lead to perceptual distortion, inaccurate judgment, illogical interpretation, or irrationality [5]. Recognizing systematic biases in data collection efforts is an important step towards countering their effect on those systems that are trained on the basis of this data and is a key enabling factor for algorithmic fairness [25].

In a series of document relevance assessment experiments, this paper strives to demonstrate that cognitive bias can indeed affect crowdsourced labor and leads to significantly reduced result quality. This performance detriment is subsequently propagated into system ranking robustness and machine-learned ranker efficacy. The common strategies of controlling the crowd by means of qualification tests, demographic filters, incentives, gold standards and sophisticated worker models may not be enough to overcome this new source of noise which is inherently caused by the HIT setup. Instead, we would like to advocate careful task and study design that takes into account cognitive biases to reduce the interface's susceptibility to this kind of label noise.

The remainder of this document is structured as follows: Section 2 gives an overview of related work on crowdsourced data collection and annotation, quality control, worker models and biases. Section 3 follows up with an overview of frequently encountered cognitive biases that can take effect in crowdsourced relevance assessment tasks. Our experimental evluation in Section 4 strives to answer three main research questions:

RQ1 What is the effect of cognitive biases on the quality of crowdsourced relevance labels?

RQ2 To what degree do such effects influence retrieval system evaluation?

RQ3 To which extent do cognitive biases influence the quality of machine-learned rankers?

WSDM 2018, February 5–9, 2018, Marina Del Rey, CA, USA

ACM ISBN 978-1-4503-5581-0/18/02...$15.00
https://doi.org/10.1145/3159652.3159654

[1] While we do not believe that truly malicious workers are a frequently-encountered class of workers, we include them in this overview for completeness.

Finally, Section 5 closes with a summary of our findings as well as an outlook on future directions of inquiry.

2 RELATED WORK

Beginning with the Cranfield experiments [8], test collections have been one of the pillars of IR system evaluation. Traditionally, such collections are created by trained professionals in controlled lab environments. In the IR community, the Text Retrieval Conference (TREC) [50] supports one of the most widely known efforts to creating such collections.

The emerging crowdsourcing paradigm [30] has inspired an extensive line of research dedicated to using this new channel for the creation and annotation of IR test collections. An early set of experiments [1, 22, 38, 39] note that aggregated labels of multiple untrained crowd workers can reach a quality comparable to that of a single highly trained NIST assessor.

While this alternative labour market has been shown to be time and cost efficient [18], researchers have less control over the circumstances under which relevance judgments are created. Traditionally, inaccurate judgments as well as spam submissions have been a major challenge in the crowdsourcing process. As a consequence, quality control is one of the most deeply researched question in crowdsourcing [40] with solutions ranging from aggregating the results of independent workers to the use of honey pot questions [17, 28, 32]. Marshall *et al.* [41] highlight the importance of engaging HIT design on result quality while Yan *et al.* [57] demonstrate the ability of active learning techniques to greatly improve the worker-task allocation step. Bansal *et al.* [2] exploit this notion for task selection in highly efficiency-driven crowdsourcing scenarios.

Significant effort has been made into estimating worker reliability based on various behavioural and demographic traits. Tang and Lease [48] introduce a semi-supervised method for reliability estimation based both on labeled as well as unlabeled examples. Kazai *et al.* [36, 37] organize workers in 5 different classes and study their respective judgment reliability and behaviour. Based on social media profiles, Difallah *et al.* [14] model worker topic affinities, enabling them to assign tasks to workers with matching interest, resulting in significantly improved result quality. However, as the authors further note [13], it can be hard to have the necessary degree of control over the ephemeral crowd workforce in applied crowdsourcing scenarios that involve online platforms such as Amazon Mechanical Turk and CrowdFlower. Karger *et al.* [34] propose a joint model for iteratively learning worker reliability and aggregating votes by means of approximate belief propagation. Recently, Davtyan *et al.* [11] show the use of inter-document similarities for the goal of label aggregation. They intuit that, given the same query, similar documents should show similar relevance labels. Blanco *et al.* [4] study the robustness of crowdsourced relevance assessments over time, finding that repeated labeling efforts produce stable results even as longer periods of time elapse.

Another prominent source of evidence can be found in the analysis of systematic judgment behaviour. Following Dawid and Skene [12], who investigate disagreements between diagnoses posed by multiple individual medical doctors, there have been several successful attempts at harnessing similar methods for crowdsourcing quality assurance [29, 51]. In this way, reliable workers that make occasional mistakes can be accurately separated from spammers that select answers at random or follow other, more sophisticated, cheating strategies.

While some examples were known previously, the systematic study of cognitive biases was first established by Tversky and Kahnemann [49] and has since seen many realizations in decision theory and advertisement. Recently, there have been a number of studies tying observed user behavior in Web search [55] and general information systems [21] to cognitive biases. The body of existing crowdsourcing work acknowledges the importance of task and interface design [33, 35, 46], as well as execution parameters such as batch sizes [52]. There are several articles that mention presentation and order effects [7, 16] or irrational aesthetically-motivated annotator behavior [42]. In addition, a number of scholars, without a dedicated study of the reason for biased crowd labor, present potential solutions in the form of tailored incentive schemes [20], Bayesian bias mitigation [54] or active learning [60].

While several pieces of related work have alluded to the impact of cognitive biases on crowdsourced data collection and annotation efforts, to the best of our knowledge, there exists no dedicated study that systematically describes and quantifies such effects. This paper aims to close this gap in the literature.

3 COGNITIVE BIASES

This section begins with a brief description of our experimental corpora as well as an unbiased baseline setup for crowdsourced relevance label collection. Subsequently, we propose four experimental crowdsourcing conditions in which a range of prominent cognitive biases are likely to occur.

3.1 Datasets

Our experiments are based on three well-known document collections that were selected to span different domains, document types and collection sizes. As an example of a large-scale Web collection, we include the widely-used ClueWeb12 corpus[2], containing approximately 733M Websites. Corresponding test topics are taken from the 2013 and 2014 editions of the TREC Web Track [9, 10]. The TIPSTER collection [26] compiles newswire documents from a number of major outlets across the years 1987 – 1992 and represents an example of a traditional pre-Web retrieval task on a smaller set of individually well-curated documents. We include the corresponding 4 years of TREC adhoc topics (1992 – 1995) into our experiments. Finally, the TREC Clinical Decision Support track (CDS) investigates patient-centric literature retrieval. The documents are a subset of the PubMed repository of bio-medical journal articles. While the previous collections contained rather accessible information from the Web and news domains, this corpus heavily relies on technical jargon and significantly higher reading levels. Queries in this setting stem from the highly condensed patient summaries of all three editions (2014 – 2016) of TREC CDS [43, 44, 47]. Table 1 gives an overview of key statistics such as the number of documents, topics and official NIST-provided relevance judgments.

[2]http://lemurproject.org/clueweb12/

Table 1: Details of the three experimental corpora. For each corpus, we report the domain of origin, its size, the number of topics and the amount of official NIST-provided relevance judgments.

Corpus	Domain	# Documents	# Topics	# Qrels
ClueWeb12	Web	733M	100	91k
TREC CDS	Medical	1.3M	90	114k
TIPSTER 1–3	Newswire	1M	200	336k

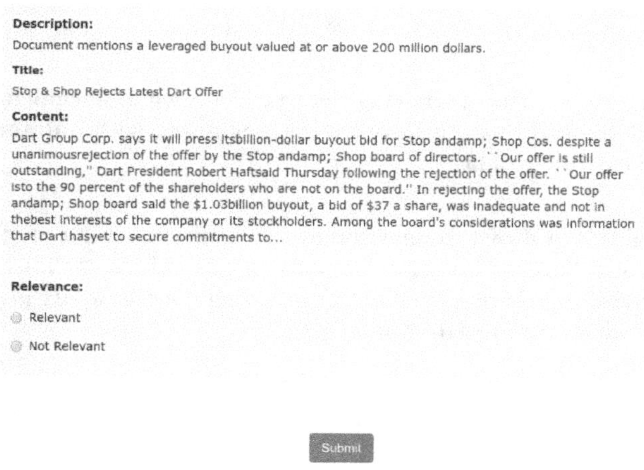

Figure 1: The baseline annotation interface presents workers with a brief topic description as well as document title and content and asks for binary relevance labels.

3.2 Baseline Setup

Let us consider a standard document relevance assessment task in which workers are first primed by a set of relevance guidelines before being presented with a brief topic description and a structured document representation. We include only the document title and main text content, with all remaining meta information hidden in this setup. Relevance assessment is made in binary fashion, distinguishing between relevant and non-relevant pairs of topics and documents. In order to prevent further sequence effects and presentation biases, we publish tasks in batches of one. Figure 1 gives an example of the judgment interface as seen by our workers. In an initial set of experiments, this baseline shows an encouraging individual accuracy of approximately 80% at matching NIST labels. In the further course of this document, we will discuss a number of interface variants used to demonstrate the effect of cognitive biases. To ensure legibility of the interface screenshots, here we truncate the, sometimes lengthy, document content field. This was exclusively done in the screenshots for this paper. Workers were always presented with the full document content.

3.3 Ambiguity Effect

The Ambiguity Effect occurs when missing information makes decisions appear more difficult and consequently less attractive [19]. While our baseline scenario includes only the title and main content fields, we further include a number of additional properties for each document: the document's age in days calculated from its publication date, its length in number of words and a random number sampled from the interval [0, 5] that we dub the "k-Index" and the origin or meaning of which is never explained to the workers. It is intuitive that neither of these properties should have a strong implication on a document's relevance towards a given topic. We confirm this assumption by means of a Pearson product-moment correlation test. The only property that shows even mild correlation with the NIST relevance label is document length[3].

We randomly sample 50 relevant and 50 non-relevant pairs from each of our three collections. To test for traces of the Ambiguity Effect, we compare two conditions: The baseline setup in which no additional fields are shown, and an alternative including the additional fields. For 50% of the pairs in this second group, the values of all additional fields are present. For the remainder, we declare them as "unknown". The document title and content are always available.

In the baseline setting, the observed likelihood of a worker assigning a label of 'relevant' is 58%. When showing additional fields with complete information, we observe a comparable likelihood of relevancy of 59%. When, however, these additional values are missing, the likelihood of a positive vote plummets to 44%, irrespective of true document relevance. Despite the fact that the potentially missing information has, at best, a weak connection to document relevance, and even though it can in some cases be inferred (*i.e.*, document length is observable from the displayed main content.), the missing values create an illusion of uncertainty and lets workers doubt the quality of a document.

Let us, in a second experiment assume a gradual occurrence of missing data that is more representative of real-life missing-value scenarios. Instead of hiding either all or none of the additional values per document, we are introducing a masking probability $p_m \in [0, 1]$ that is applied to each of the additional fields independently, allowing some values to be missing while others are present. Figure 2 shows the judgment interface for this setup.

As we plot the overall likelihood of document relevance in response to p_m (Figure 3), we note a considerable decline in the likelihood of relevance up to $p_m \approx 0.6$. At this point the likelihood of relevance stabilizes and eventually partially recovers. We believe that this final trend is due to training effects under which workers learn that hardly any of the documents exhibit complete values, making the perceived uncertainty appear less severe. It is furthermore interesting to note that at $p_m = 1.0$ when none of the additional fields are ever shown, there is still a significantly lower likelihood of arbitrary document relevance than at $p_m = 0.0$, indicating that even uniformly missing information may make workers more hesitant to assign positive labels.

In summary, we see a clear negative impact of showing missing values to workers, even if these missing properties were uninformative to start with. This observation should serve as a word of caution when designing crowdsourcing experiments. In settings that can experience missing values it may be beneficial to omit a property altogether.

[3] Age: $r = -0.16$, Length: $r = 0.23$, K-Index: $r = -0.07$

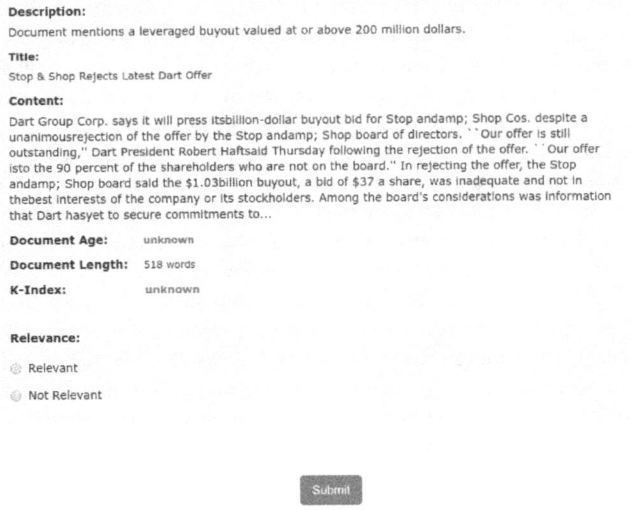

Figure 2: The ambiguity interface additionally presents workers with three uninformative meta attributes. Some of these attributes are declared "unknown" to create the impression of incomplete information.

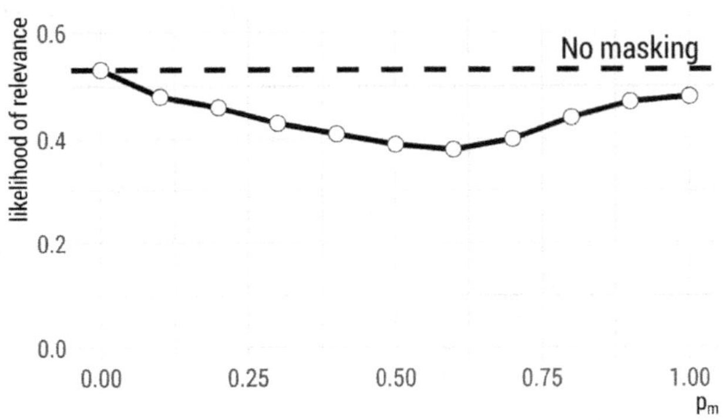

Figure 3: The masking probability p_m controls the amount of missing field values. The overall likelihood of relevance drops as p_m approaches 0.6. After this point it stabilizes and eventually recovers.

In the further course of this document, when referring to the Ambiguity Effect, we will use the above fields and individually declare their values unknown with $p_m = 0.5$.

3.4 Anchoring

Anchoring or Focalism describes situations in which workers disproportionately focus on one piece of information (often the first one presented to them) even as additional contradicting evidence becomes apparent [49]. In organic crowdsourcing experiments such effects are likely to take place as information is revealed to the user in subsequent stages. We simulate this situation by structuring the judgment process in two phases. At first, the worker is presented

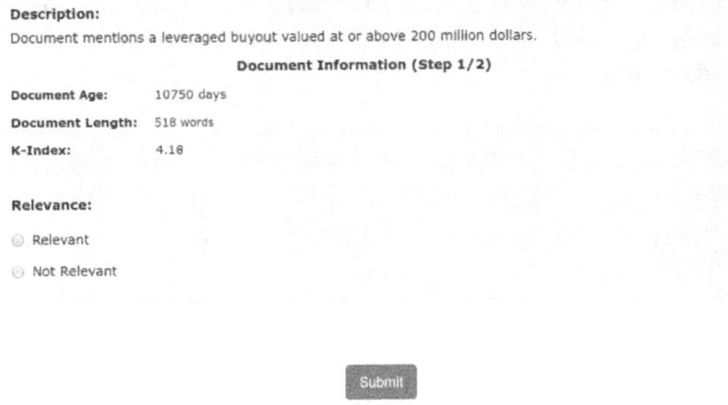

Figure 4: The anchoring interface presents document-related information in two steps, beginning with uninformative meta data.

Table 2: A direct comparison of two-stage and single-stage crowdsourcing processes demonstrates significantly lower overall label accuracy due to Anchoring when initially presenting uninformative data.

	Stage-1	Stage-2	Single-Stage
Relevant	0.42	0.43	0.54
Non-Relevant	0.58	0.57	0.46
Accuracy	0.49	0.67	0.81

exclusively with the topic description and the three additional information fields described in the previous section (document age, document length and a random number introduced as the "k-Index"). Note that this time all information is present at all times and there are no missing values. The worker is asked to assign a relevance label solely based on these three properties which, as we showed earlier have no systematic association with the true relevance label. In the second stage of the experiment we additionally reveal the document title and content to the worker and ask them to update their relevance vote. Figure 4 shows an example of the corresponding judgment interface.

Let us now consider an experiment under which we randomly draw 50 relevant and 50 non-relevant pairs from each of the three corpora and request crowd labels via the process described above. In a separate control group we request labels for the same data in a single-stage fashion, presenting the same information at once, rather than sequentially.

In expectation, a rational worker would have to blindly guess at stage one of the judgment process and would be correct 50% of the time[4]. In the next stage, when document title and content are revealed, this same rational worker would be expected to disagree with their earlier vote in 50% of the cases. Instead of such unbiased behavior, Table 2 notes significant evidence of anchoring.

[4]A highly informed worker that is privy to the mild systematic connection between document length/age and relevancy could do somewhat better. Such effects would be very subtle and are disregarded here.

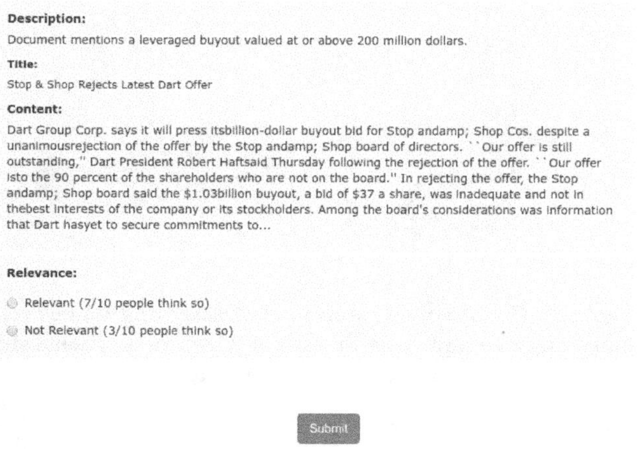

Figure 5: The bandwagon interface additionally presents workers with the historic distribution of relevance labels assigned to this topic-document pair by their peers.

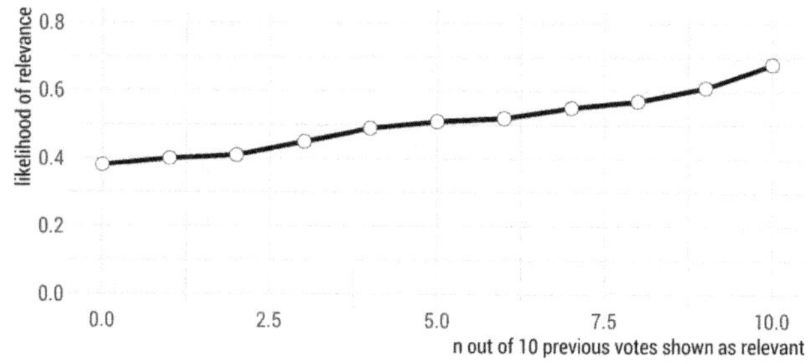

Figure 6: The likelihood of relevance monotonically follows the number of artificially reported previous positive judgments irrespective of true document relevance.

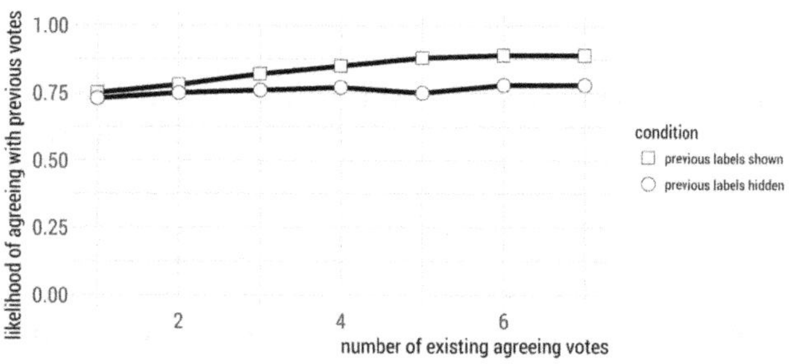

Figure 7: The likelihood of agreeing with an existing majority gently increases when votes are hidden from workers but sharply rises with the amount of existing votes when revealed prior to assessment.

While the single-stage annotators perform at the same level of accuracy of approximately 80% that was earlier observed in the baseline setting, workers under the two-stage condition updated their prior arbitrary beliefs too infrequently, resulting in a considerably reduced stage-2 accuracy. To exclude outside experimental effects, we conduct the same experiment in inverse temporal order, *i.e.*, first revealing title and content and subsequently showing the additional fields. In this experimental condition, workers show the same accuracy rates as in the single-stage case, suggesting that the detrimental effect was indeed induced by anchoring on conclusions drawn from uninformative data.

3.5 Bandwagon Effect

The Bandwagon Effect (sometimes referred to as Groupthink or Herd Behavior) occurs when workers forego their own reasoning in favor of following an existing group's behavior [3]. In crowdsourced relevance assessment tasks, we can easily simulate this effect by disclosing to workers how their peers judged a given topic-document pair. The assessment interface is identical to the baseline with the only exception of binary relevance choices additionally displaying the number of previous users who made this choice for this pair. A screenshot of the resulting interface can be found in Figure 5.

In our first experiment, instead of using actual historic votes, we show the user artificial statistics according to which n out of 10 previous users judged this pair relevant. From each of our three collections, we randomly draw 50 relevant and 50 non-relevant pairs and have crowd workers judge them once more. Figure 6 plots the likelihood of workers assigning a label of 'relevant' to an arbitrary pair as n ranges from 0 to 10.

We can observe a balanced tendency of workers following perceived herd behavior. Irrespective of the true relevance label, topic-document pairs were more likely to be judged relevant when we claim a high number of prior votes indicating relevance. Similarly, although somewhat less strongly expressed, we note the probability of relevance decreasing as the perceived prior consensus becomes more negative. In the center of the plot, for choices of n between 4-6, we do not find considerable bias in either direction.

While one might argue that such strong Bandwagon Effects are artificial and may not often occur unintentionally in organic crowdsourcing efforts, let us consider a second experiment. This time, we do not introduce false information but, instead, truthfully disclose the prior vote distribution. While the baseline experiment shows a good accuracy of 80%, the same setup significantly drops in accuracy (to a level of 76%) when disclosing prior vote statistics. Further analysis suggests that this error is introduced by early incorrect votes that are subsequently followed by other workers.

This assumption is confirmed when we inspect the distribution of likelihood of workers disagreeing with existing majority votes. Figure 7 plots the observed likelihood of disagreement with current majority vote[5]. While consensus is generally high, we note that in the baseline case, where vote distributions are not shown, agreement ratios only gently rise, reflecting the general degree of controversy in each pair while, for the exact same pairs, they sharply increase in case of disclosed vote statistics.

To summarize, the Bandwagon Effect shows clear expression in crowdsourced relevance assessment efforts both when artificially

[5]Ties are not broken in this analysis and are simply excluded from likelihood computation.

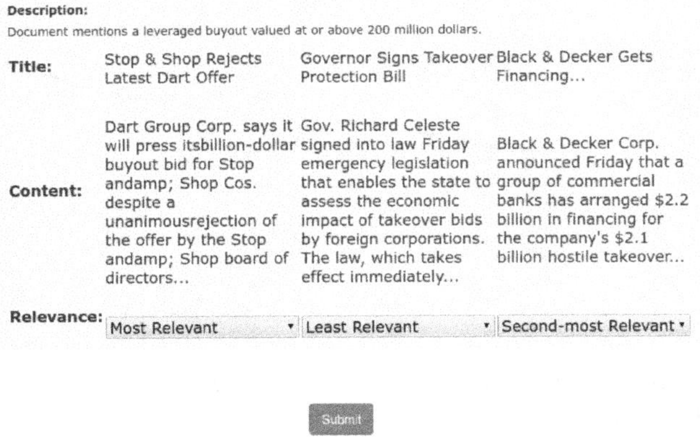

Figure 8: The decoy interface asks workers to assign relative preference labels for three documents.

primed but also when merely revealing true previous votes. In the further course of this document we will only consider this second, more realistic realization of the Bandwagon Effect.

3.6 Decoy Effect

The Decoy Effect (sometimes also referred to as the Asymmetric Dominance Effect) occurs when workers' preference between options A and B changes in favor of option B when an option C is presented, which is similar but clearly inferior to option B [31]. It is a well-known and frequently exploited bias studied in marketing and advertising where decoy products are introduced to seemingly increase the actual product's viability in comparison to actual market alternatives. We simulate this situation by asking workers rank ("most relevant", "second-most relevant", "least relevant") three documents with respect to the same topic. A screenshot of the resulting interface can be found in Figure 8.

From each of the three corpora, we randomly draw 50 relevant topic-document pairs that will serve as our choice A. For each such pair, we draw a non-relevant document B and additionally select an additional document C that is similar to B ($cos(B, C) \geq 0.7$) but less relevant ($BM25(B) > BM25(C)$). Finally, for the same topic, we draw another non-relevant document D that shares no considerable similarity with either A or B ($max(cos(A, D), cos(B, D)) \leq 0.3$). If, for a given topic these requirements cannot be fulfilled, we reject the current pair and draw another one until our pool of 50 unique tuples $\langle A, B, C, D\rangle$ per corpus is filled.

We now compare two experimental conditions: First, we present workers with options A, B, C, a setup in which we expect to see some expression of the Decoy Effect. In our control group, workers see options A,B,D, where no such effect should occur. The relative ordering of options A, B, C, and D is chosen randomly for every task and does not reflect relevance in any way. Figure 9 plots the various likelihoods of being assigned a given relevance rank across options and experimental conditions. As expected, the single relevant option, A, shows the highest probability of receiving the "most relevant" rank in both settings. If we, however, compare the observed likelihood of option B being "most relevant", we note a considerable increase in likelihood when displaying A and B alongside decoy

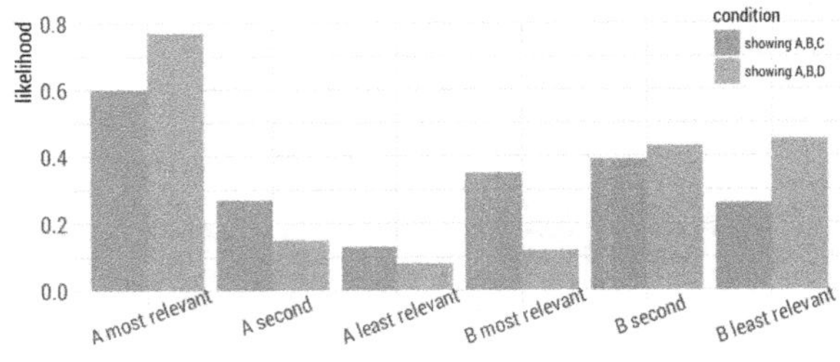

Figure 9: The observed likelihood of assigning higher relevance ranks to non-relevant option B increases when a similar but less relevant option C is presented.

option C ($p(B) = 0.35$) rather than the unrelated D ($p(B) = 0.12$). This trend shows that there is a considerable risk of suffering from Decoy Effects in real-world crowdsourcing scenarios when multiple options are shown for relative ranking. This becomes especially relevant since several studies (*e.g.*, [6, 58, 59]) find human assessors to be more reliable when assigning relative preferences rather than absolute relevance levels to documents.

For the remainder of this paper, to ensure consistency with the labels collected under the other biased processes, we translate preference ranks into binary relevance labels. To do so, we use the fact that in each tuple $\langle A, B, C, D\rangle$, only a single document A is in fact relevant. In consequence, the rank "most relevant" will be assigned a relevant vote and all remaining ones receive a non-relevance vote.

4 EXPERIMENTS

Building on the initial evidence presented in the previous section, we conduct a series of experiments in which the effect of cognitive biases is quantified in terms of label accuracy, retrieval system evaluation and machine-learned ranker effectiveness.

4.1 Label Accuracy

Let us begin by establishing a side-by-side quality comparison of relevance labels contributed by biased and unbiased crowd labeling processes. In this section, we measure the accuracy of the various crowdsourcing methods at reproducing NIST expert judgments. To this end, we consider 6 crowdsourced relevance label collection processes:

AE
: Crowd labels obtained under influence of the Ambiguity Effect with likelihood p_m of hiding additional uninformative fields of 0.5.

A
: Crowd labels obtained under influence of Anchoring when using a two-stage judging process.

BE
: Crowd labels obtained under potential influence of the Bandwagon Effect by revealing the true distribution of previous workers' votes.

DE
: Crowd labels obtained under influence of the Decoy Effect

Table 3: Accuracy of crowdsourced relevance votes at matching the existing NIST expert labels.

Collection	Year	BC	AE	A	BE	DE	UC
CW'12	2013	0.67*	0.68*	0.65*	0.70*	0.69*	0.83
	2014	0.77*	0.66*	0.63*	0.75*	0.67*	0.85
CDS	2014	0.58*	0.65*	0.52*	0.70	0.66*	0.71
	2015	0.75	0.71*	0.71*	0.60*	0.68*	0.79
	2016	0.65	0.58*	0.59*	0.67	0.65	0.68
TIPSTER	1992	0.78	0.78	0.66*	0.65*	0.67*	0.82
	1993	0.69*	0.68*	0.61*	0.71*	0.79	0.84
	1994	0.66*	0.78	0.59*	0.78	0.81	0.81
	1995	0.68*	0.80	0.68*	0.60*	0.77	0.82
Overall		0.69*	0.70*	0.63*	0.69*	0.71*	0.79

when consdering only the single most highly ranked document relevant.

BC
General biased crowd labels obtained via aggregation of all previously listed processes.

UC
A baseline crowdsourcing process designed to trigger none of the previously discussed biases.

We randomly sample 500 topic-document pairs from the NIST qrels of each TREC task edition (4500 pairs in total). For each of these pairs we collect a crowd label using the five organic crowdsourcing processes (AE, A, BE, DE, UC), giving our experimental dataset for this stage an overall volume of 9 tasks × 5 crowd processes × 500 labels × 3 workers = 135k labels. BC, finally, is merely the aggregation of all biased crowd collections (AE, A, BE, DE) in which final labels are determined via uniform majority voting with coin tosses as tie breaker.

All labels were collected on the Amazon Mechanical Turk crowdsourcing platform[6] at a rate of 0.03 US$ per label. Table 3 lists per-task and overall accuracies for the various crowdsourcing processes. Ground truth labels are given by NIST expert annotations. Statistically significant performance losses between biased crowd processes and the bias-free reference process (UC) are indicated by an asterisk. Statistical significance is determined using a Wilcoxon signed-rank test at $\alpha < 0.05$-level.

We note that, while news and Web topics can be reliably answered by UC crowd judges, the biomedical topics seem to be considerably more difficult to solve due to the high degree of medical jargon as well as the required domain-specific training. An exception to this general trend is the 2015 edition of the CDS track, the topics of which seem to be easier to solve. This observation has been previously made by CDS participants [23]. Despite some local variance, we note significant and substantial overall performance losses when considering biased crowdsourcing processes. Most notably, Anchoring shows dramatic effects with relative accuracy losses of up to 28%. In case of the already difficult CDS topics, for example, this lowers worker accuracy to a level that barely surpasses random guessing.

[6]https://www.mturk.com/

Table 4: Historic runs submitted to TREC tracks are ranked by descending nDCG according to the various crowdsourced label collection processes. Spearman's ρ describes their correlation to the original NIST ranking.

Collection	Year	# runs	# qrels	ρ_{BC}	ρ_{AE}	ρ_{A}	ρ_{BE}	ρ_{DE}	ρ_{UC}
CW'12	2013	61	47k	0.71	0.76	0.69	0.76	0.73	0.85
	2014	30	44k	0.84	0.71	0.64	0.83	0.74	0.93
CDS	2014	102	38k	0.61	0.70	0.53	0.79	0.70	0.79
	2015	178	38k	0.84	0.75	0.72	0.67	0.69	0.88
	2016	115	38k	0.71	0.65	0.61	0.70	0.66	0.74
TIPSTER	1993	38	63k	0.78	0.70	0.63	0.73	0.82	0.90
	1994	40	97k	0.73	0.81	0.64	0.82	0.86	0.89
	1995	39	87k	0.70	0.87	0.70	0.65	0.84	0.86

With respect to **RQ1**, we conclude that all investigated forms of cognitive bias show significant negative impact on the quality of crowdsourced relevance assessments.

4.2 Consequences for System Evaluation

Aside from the previously studied effect of cognitive biases on the immediate quality of crowdsourced relevance assessments, it is conceivable that such quality differences should influence retrieval system evaluation. To test for this hypothesis, we use the relevance judgments produced by the various biased crowdsourcing processes discussed earlier to rank a wide range of retrieval systems according to their retrieval performance. In a second step, we compare these system rankings to the one induced by the labels that were obtained from NIST experts (NE) and measure degree to which the relative ordering of retrieval systems is perturbed by cognitive label collection biases.

For this comparison, we consider all historic submissions to the relevant TREC adhoc, Web and CDS tracks and rank them in terms of nDCG. We can now compute the Spearman rank correlation coefficient ρ between system orderings induced by the various crowdsourced label collections and the ground truth NIST ordering. Values of ρ close to 1[7] show robust rankings in which no major differences to the original NIST ranking can be found. The further ρ's value differs from 1, the stronger the ranking perturbation, leading to faulty relative performance comparisons between retrieval systems. As ρ approaches 0, there is no systematic association between original and crowdsourced rankings any more.

Table 4 lists, for all three corpora and their respective editions, the number of historic runs, the amount of available NIST relevance assessments and the resulting values of ρ. Note that we were unable to obtain TREC-1 results from the NIST archive and therefore only include the 1993–1995 editions.

We notice that unbiased crowd labels (UC) show only minor perturbations from the original NIST rankings and generally yield robust system orderings. Again, for the 2014 and 2016 editions

[7]Values close to -1 are similarly desirable as they would reflect a near-perfect inverse system ranking that would, again, allow correct interpretation. In practice, however, we do not expect to observe such dramatic perturbations.

of CDS, the previously noted low crowd accuracy translates into somewhat reduced ranking coherency. As we turn towards the various biased crowd processes, we can observe varying degrees of perturbation, reaching, in the most severe case, a ρ of 0.53, signifying considerably different system rankings based on NIST and biased crowd judges. The various bias types appear to equally affect ranking robustness with Anchoring, again being a negative outlier.

With respect to **RQ2**, we note considerable differences in relative system orderings when using biased crowdsourcing labels as ground truth relevance indicators. In contrast, unbiased crowdsourced labels result in rankings that are largely identical to original NIST rankings.

4.3 Consequences for Derived Systems

In the previous sections, we discussed the impact of cognitive biases on relevance label accuracy as well as its propagated influence on retrieval system evaluation. In this final experimentation section, we are interested in the impact that such biases have on the quality of derived systems such as machine-learned rankers. To this end, we use the collected relevance assessments to train a range of data-driven rankers and compare three experimental conditions: Rankers based on biased crowds (BC), rankers based on unbiased crowds (UC) and rankers based on NIST expert labels (NE). As before, the biased condition is subdivided into its four constituent biases.

In each condition, we train a LambdaMART classifier [56] using a range of standard learning-to-rank features[8] and a neural network-based ranker [24]. As an additional point of reference, we include a static BM25 retrieval model [45] that does not require any training data[9]. The available topics are split into 10 non-overlapping folds and each model is trained on 9 varying folds and evaluated on the remaining one in cross-validation fashion. Performance evaluation is always based on the NIST-provided expert judgments. Table 5 shows the results of this experiment in terms of nDCG. Statistically significant differences between a biased run and its corresponding UC counterpart are indicated by an asterisk. Statistical significance is determined using a Wilcoxon signed-rank test at $\alpha < 0.05$-level.

The general trend is for both machine-learned systems to outperform simple BM25 rankers trained on NIST or UC labels. In this comparison LambdaMART is in most cases superior to DRMM. Systems trained on biased crowd labels, however, deteriorate rapidly in performance and often reach a level of ranking quality that is below that of non-parametric exact-matching models such as BM25. Again, this tendency is observed to be most severe for labels produced under the influence of Anchoring or the Bandwagon Effect.

With respect to **RQ3**, we find that cognitive biases as modelled in this paper have a significant negative effect on the performance of derived systems such as machine-learned rankers.

5 CONCLUSION

This paper investigates the effect of cognitive biases on the quality of submissions to standard document relevance assessment tasks.

[8]We use all non-proprietary features (1–130) described at https://www.microsoft.com/en-us/research/project/mslr/. For newswire and medical domains, we omit Web-based features such as PageRank.

[9]While one can use training data to tune the model's parameters, we refrain from doing so and use robust common choices of $k_1 = 1.5$ and $b = 0.75$ throughout all experiments.

Table 5: Retrieval performance of rankers trained on biased (BC) or unbiased crowd data (UC) as well as NIST expert labels (NE) in terms of nDCG. BC aggregates the various individual bias types.

Collection	Model	BC	AE	A	BE	DE	UC	NE
CW'12	LambdaMART	0.27	0.25*	0.22*	0.25*	0.23*	0.28	0.34
	DRMM	0.22*	0.25*	0.24*	0.20*	0.24*	0.30	0.32
	BM25	0.24	0.24	0.24	0.24	0.24	0.24	0.24
CDS	LambdaMART	0.18*	0.21*	0.16*	0.23	0.22	0.24	0.32
	DRMM	0.15*	0.19	0.17*	0.15*	0.18	0.21	0.24
	BM25	0.21	0.21	0.21	0.21	0.21	0.21	0.21
TIPSTER	LambdaMART	0.24*	0.26*	0.21*	0.28*	0.26*	0.32	0.38
	DRMM	0.20*	0.27	0.22*	0.23*	0.24*	0.28	0.32
	BM25	0.25	0.25	0.25	0.25	0.25	0.25	0.25

We concentrate on four common types of bias and, in a series of experiments on well-known TREC research corpora, demonstrate the significant detrimental influence that biased label collection can have on label quality, retrieval system evaluation and ranker training. Especially the more subtle forms of bias, *e.g.*, the Bandwagon or Decoy effects can occur unintentionally in crowdsourcing experiment protocols and should be carefully checked for in order to avoid label degradation.

There are several exciting direction for future inquiry. In this paper, we focus on a range of newly conducted crowdsourcing initiatives that are instrumented to induce cognitive bias and demonstrate its effect on result quality. In the future, instead, it would be interesting to devise formal tests to analyze existing historic labeling efforts such as done in the course of the TREC Crowdsourcing track in terms of their susceptibility to bias. While this paper concentrates on crowd judges, a class of human laborers that has previously been shown to be prone to distraction and noisy submissions, there is no reason why test subjects in controlled lab environments should not suffer from the same effects. In the future, we suggest further confirming this assumption with a comparable lab study.

REFERENCES

[1] Omar Alonso, Daniel E Rose, and Benjamin Stewart. 2008. Crowdsourcing for relevance evaluation. In *ACM SigIR Forum*, Vol. 42. ACM, 9–15.
[2] Piyush Bansal, Carsten Eickhoff, and Thomas Hofmann. 2016. Active Content-Based Crowdsourcing Task Selection. In *Proceedings of the 25th ACM International on Conference on Information and Knowledge Management.* ACM, 529–538.
[3] Sushil Bikhchandani, David Hirshleifer, and Ivo Welch. 1992. A theory of fads, fashion, custom, and cultural change as informational cascades. *Journal of political Economy* 100, 5 (1992), 992–1026.
[4] Roi Blanco, Harry Halpin, Daniel M Herzig, Peter Mika, Jeffrey Pound, Henry S Thompson, and Thanh Tran Duc. 2011. Repeatable and reliable search system evaluation using crowdsourcing. In *Proceedings of the 34th international ACM SIGIR conference on Research and development in Information Retrieval.* ACM, 923–932.
[5] Herbert Bless, Klaus Fiedler, and Fritz Strack. 2004. *Social cognition: How individuals construct social reality.* Psychology Press.
[6] Ben Carterette, Paul Bennett, David Chickering, and Susan Dumais. 2008. Here or there. *Advances in Information Retrieval* (2008), 16–27.
[7] Dana Chandler and John Joseph Horton. 2011. Labor allocation in paid crowdsourcing: Experimental evidence on positioning, nudges and prices. *Human Computation* 11 (2011), 11.
[8] Cyril Cleverdon. 1997. Readings in Information Retrieval. In *Readings in Information Retrieval*, Karen Sparck Jones and Peter Willett (Eds.). Morgan Kaufmann Publishers Inc., San Francisco, CA, USA, Chapter The Cranfield Tests on Index Language Devices, 47–59. http://dl.acm.org/citation.cfm?id=275537.275544

[9] Kevyn Collins-Thompson, Paul Bennett, Charles LA Clarke, and Ellen M Voorhees. 2014. *TREC 2013 web track overview.* Technical Report. MICHIGAN UNIV ANN ARBOR.

[10] Kevyn Collins-Thompson, Craig Macdonald, Paul Bennett, Fernando Diaz, and Ellen M Voorhees. 2015. *TREC 2014 web track overview.* Technical Report. MICHIGAN UNIV ANN ARBOR.

[11] Martin Davtyan, Carsten Eickhoff, and Thomas Hofmann. 2015. Exploiting Document Content for Efficient Aggregation of Crowdsourcing Votes. In *Proceedings of the 24th ACM International on Conference on Information and Knowledge Management.* ACM, 783–790.

[12] Alexander Philip Dawid and Allan M Skene. 1979. Maximum likelihood estimation of observer error-rates using the EM algorithm. *Applied statistics* (1979), 20–28.

[13] Djellel Eddine Difallah, Michele Catasta, Gianluca Demartini, and Philippe Cudré-Mauroux. 2014. Scaling-up the Crowd: Micro-Task Pricing Schemes for Worker Retention and Latency Improvement. In *Second AAAI Conference on Human Computation and Crowdsourcing.*

[14] Djellel Eddine Difallah, Gianluca Demartini, and Philippe Cudré-Mauroux. 2013. Pick-a-crowd: tell me what you like, and i'll tell you what to do. In *Proceedings of the 22nd international conference on World Wide Web.* International World Wide Web Conferences Steering Committee, 367–374.

[15] Carsten Eickhoff. 2014. Crowd-powered experts: Helping surgeons interpret breast cancer images. In *Proceedings of the First International Workshop on Gamification for Information Retrieval.* ACM, 53–56.

[16] Carsten Eickhoff and Arjen de Vries. 2011. How crowdsourcable is your task. In *Proceedings of the workshop on crowdsourcing for search and data mining (CSDM) at the fourth ACM international conference on web search and data mining (WSDM).* 11–14.

[17] Carsten Eickhoff and Arjen P de Vries. 2013. Increasing cheat robustness of crowdsourcing tasks. *Information retrieval* 16, 2 (2013), 121–137.

[18] Carsten Eickhoff, Christopher G Harris, Arjen P de Vries, and Padmini Srinivasan. 2012. Quality through flow and immersion: gamifying crowdsourced relevance assessments. In *Proceedings of the 35th international ACM SIGIR conference on Research and development in information retrieval.* ACM, 871–880.

[19] Daniel Ellsberg. 1961. Risk, ambiguity, and the Savage axioms. *The quarterly journal of economics* (1961), 643–669.

[20] Boi Faltings, Radu Jurca, Pearl Pu, and Bao Duy Tran. 2014. Incentives to counter bias in human computation. In *Second AAAI conference on human computation and crowdsourcing.*

[21] Marvin Fleischmann, Miglena Amirpur, Alexander Benlian, and Thomas Hess. 2014. Cognitive biases in information systems research: a scientometric analysis. (2014).

[22] Catherine Grady and Matthew Lease. 2010. Crowdsourcing document relevance assessment with mechanical turk. In *Proceedings of the NAACL HLT 2010 workshop on creating speech and language data with Amazon's mechanical turk.* Association for Computational Linguistics, 172–179.

[23] Simon Greuter, Philip Junker, Lorenz Kuhn, Felix Mance, Virgile Mermet, Angela Rellstab, and Carsten Eickhoff. 2016. ETH Zurich at TREC Clinical Decision Support 2016.. In *TREC.*

[24] Jiafeng Guo, Yixing Fan, Qingyao Ai, and W Bruce Croft. 2016. A deep relevance matching model for ad-hoc retrieval. In *Proceedings of the 25th ACM International on Conference on Information and Knowledge Management.* ACM, 55–64.

[25] Sara Hajian, Francesco Bonchi, and Carlos Castillo. 2016. Algorithmic bias: from discrimination discovery to fairness-aware data mining. In *Proceedings of the 22nd ACM SIGKDD International Conference on Knowledge Discovery and Data Mining.* ACM, 2125–2126.

[26] Donna Harman. 1992. The DARPA tipster project. In *ACM SIGIR Forum*, Vol. 26. ACM, 26–28.

[27] Martie G Haselton, Daniel Nettle, and Damian R Murray. 2005. The evolution of cognitive bias. *The handbook of evolutionary psychology* (2005).

[28] Matthias Hirth, Tobias Hoßfeld, and Phuoc Tran-Gia. 2010. Cheat-detection mechanisms for crowdsourcing. *University of Würzburg, Tech. Rep* 4 (2010).

[29] Mehdi Hosseini, Ingemar J Cox, Nataša Milić-Frayling, Gabriella Kazai, and Vishwa Vinay. 2012. On aggregating labels from multiple crowd workers to infer relevance of documents. In *Advances in information retrieval.* Springer, 182–194.

[30] Jeff Howe. 2008. *Crowdsourcing: Why the Power of the Crowd Is Driving the Future of Business* (1 ed.). Crown Publishing Group, New York, NY, USA.

[31] Joel Huber, John W Payne, and Christopher Puto. 1982. Adding asymmetrically dominated alternatives: Violations of regularity and the similarity hypothesis. *Journal of consumer research* 9, 1 (1982), 90–98.

[32] Panos Ipeirotis. 2011. Crowdsourcing using mechanical turk: quality management and scalability. In *Proceedings of the 8th International Workshop on Information Integration on the Web: in conjunction with WWW 2011.* ACM, 1.

[33] Panagiotis G Ipeirotis and Praveen K Paritosh. 2011. Managing crowdsourced human computation: a tutorial. In *Proceedings of the 20th international conference companion on World wide web.* ACM, 287–288.

[34] David R Karger, Sewoong Oh, and Devavrat Shah. 2014. Budget-optimal task allocation for reliable crowdsourcing systems. *Operations Research* 62, 1 (2014), 1–24.

[35] Gabriella Kazai, Jaap Kamps, Marijn Koolen, and Natasa Milic-Frayling. 2011. Crowdsourcing for book search evaluation: impact of hit design on comparative system ranking. In *Proceedings of the 34th international ACM SIGIR conference on Research and development in Information Retrieval.* ACM, 205–214.

[36] Gabriella Kazai, Jaap Kamps, and Natasa Milic-Frayling. 2011. Worker types and personality traits in crowdsourcing relevance labels. In *Proceedings of the 20th ACM international conference on Information and knowledge management.* ACM, 1941–1944.

[37] Gabriella Kazai, Jaap Kamps, and Natasa Milic-Frayling. 2013. An analysis of human factors and label accuracy in crowdsourcing relevance judgments. *Information retrieval* 16, 2 (2013), 138–178.

[38] Gabriella Kazai and Natasa Milic-Frayling. 2009. On the evaluation of the quality of relevance assessments collected through crowdsourcing. In *SIGIR 2009 Workshop on the Future of IR Evaluation.* 21.

[39] Aniket Kittur, Ed H Chi, and Bongwon Suh. 2008. Crowdsourcing user studies with Mechanical Turk. In *Proceedings of the SIGCHI conference on human factors in computing systems.* ACM, 453–456.

[40] Matthew Lease. 2011. On Quality Control and Machine Learning in Crowdsourcing. *Human Computation* 11 (2011), 11.

[41] Catherine C Marshall and Frank M Shipman. 2011. The ownership and reuse of visual media. In *Proceedings of the 11th annual international ACM/IEEE joint conference on Digital libraries.* ACM, 157–166.

[42] Rohan Ramanath, Monojit Choudhury, Kalika Bali, and Rishiraj Saha Roy. 2013. Crowd Prefers the Middle Path: A New IAA Metric for Crowdsourcing Reveals Turker Biases in Query Segmentation.. In *ACL (1).* 1713–1722.

[43] Kirk Roberts, Dina Demner-Fushman, Ellen M Voorhees, and William R Hersh. 2016. Overview of the TREC 2016 Clinical Decision Support Track.. In *TREC.*

[44] Kirk Roberts, Matthew S Simpson, Ellen M Voorhees, and William R Hersh. 2015. Overview of the TREC 2015 Clinical Decision Support Track.. In *TREC.*

[45] Stephen E Robertson, Steve Walker, Susan Jones, Micheline M Hancock-Beaulieu, Mike Gatford, and others. 1995. Okapi at TREC-3. *Nist Special Publication Sp* 109 (1995), 109.

[46] Marta Sabou, Kalina Bontcheva, Leon Derczynski, and Arno Scharl. 2014. Corpus Annotation through Crowdsourcing: Towards Best Practice Guidelines.. In *LREC.* 859–866.

[47] Matthew S Simpson, Ellen M Voorhees, and William Hersh. 2014. *Overview of the trec 2014 clinical decision support track.* Technical Report. LISTER HILL NATIONAL CENTER FOR BIOMEDICAL COMMUNICATIONS BETHESDA MD.

[48] Wei Tang and Matthew Lease. 2011. Semi-supervised consensus labeling for crowdsourcing. In *SIGIR 2011 workshop on crowdsourcing for information retrieval (CIR).*

[49] Amos Tversky and Daniel Kahneman. 1975. Judgment under uncertainty: Heuristics and biases. In *Utility, probability, and human decision making.* Springer, 141–162.

[50] Ellen M Voorhees, Donna K Harman, and others. 2005. *TREC: Experiment and evaluation in information retrieval.* Vol. 1. MIT press Cambridge.

[51] Jeroen Vuurens, Arjen P de Vries, and Carsten Eickhoff. 2011. How much spam can you take? an analysis of crowdsourcing results to increase accuracy. In *Proc. ACM SIGIR Workshop on Crowdsourcing for Information Retrieval (CIR'11).* 21–26.

[52] Jing Wang, Siamak Faridani, and Panagiotis G Ipeirotis. 2011. Estimating the Completion Time of Crowdsourced Tasks Using Survival Analysis Models. *Crowdsourcing for Search and Data Mining (CSDM 2011)* (2011), 31.

[53] Tianyi Wang, Gang Wang, Xing Li, Haitao Zheng, and Ben Y Zhao. 2013. Characterizing and detecting malicious crowdsourcing. *ACM SIGCOMM Computer Communication Review* 43, 4 (2013), 537–538.

[54] Fabian L Wauthier and Michael I Jordan. 2011. Bayesian bias mitigation for crowdsourcing. In *Advances in neural information processing systems.* 1800–1808.

[55] Ryen White. 2013. Beliefs and biases in web search. In *Proceedings of the 36th international ACM SIGIR conference on Research and development in information retrieval.* ACM, 3–12.

[56] Qiang Wu, Christopher JC Burges, Krysta M Svore, and Jianfeng Gao. 2010. Adapting boosting for information retrieval measures. *Information Retrieval* 13, 3 (2010), 254–270.

[57] Yan Yan, Glenn M Fung, Rómer Rosales, and Jennifer G Dy. 2011. Active learning from crowds. In *Proceedings of the 28th international conference on machine learning (ICML-11).* 1161–1168.

[58] Peng Ye and David Doermann. 2013. Combining preference and absolute judgements in a crowd-sourced setting. In *Proc. of Intl. Conf. on Machine Learning.* 1–7.

[59] Dongqing Zhu and Ben Carterette. 2010. An analysis of assessor behavior in crowdsourced preference judgments. In *SIGIR 2010 workshop on crowdsourcing for search evaluation.* 17–20.

[60] Honglei Zhuang and Joel Young. 2015. Leveraging in-batch annotation bias for crowdsourced active learning. In *Proceedings of the Eighth ACM International Conference on Web Search and Data Mining.* ACM, 243–252.

User Profiling through Deep Multimodal Fusion

Golnoosh Farnadi
University of California, Santa Cruz and Ghent University
gfarnadi@ucsc.edu

Jie Tang
Tsinghua University
jietang@tsinghua.edu.cn

Martine De Cock
University of Washington, Tacoma and Ghent University
mdecock@uw.edu

Marie-Francine Moens
KU Leuven
sien.moens@cs.kuleuven.be

ABSTRACT

User profiling in social media has gained a lot of attention due to its varied set of applications in advertising, marketing, recruiting, and law enforcement. Among the various techniques for user modeling, there is fairly limited work on how to merge multiple sources or modalities of user data – such as text, images, and relations – to arrive at more accurate user profiles. In this paper, we propose a deep learning approach that extracts and fuses information across different modalities. Our hybrid user profiling framework utilizes a shared representation between modalities to integrate three sources of data at the feature level, and combines the decision of separate networks that operate on each combination of data sources at the decision level. Our experimental results on more than 5K Facebook users demonstrate that our approach outperforms competing approaches for inferring age, gender and personality traits of social media users. We get highly accurate results with AUC values of more than 0.9 for the task of age prediction and 0.95 for the task of gender prediction.

CCS CONCEPTS

• **Information systems** → *Web mining*; *Data extraction and integration*;

ACM Reference Format:
Golnoosh Farnadi, Jie Tang, Martine De Cock, and Marie-Francine Moens. 2018. User Profiling through Deep Multimodal Fusion. In *Proceedings of WSDM'18.* ACM, New York, NY, USA, 9 pages. https://doi.org/10.1145/3159652.3159691

1 INTRODUCTION

Nowadays users actively generate content in many online social media platforms. User profiling by inferring users' age, gender and personality traits plays an important role in providing personalized services, viral marketing, recommender systems and tailored advertisements [17]. Previous work in the field of psychology has highlighted the value of identifying the personality traits of users as an aid in building adaptive and personalized systems to provide rich and improved user experiences [18, 27].

Various computational approaches of user profiling based on user-generated content (UGC) have been proposed in recent years [5, 22, 23]; more details on related works are presented in Section 2. Much of these efforts are aimed at finding novel techniques to infer user profiles using only one type of information, such as the user's textual posts. However, in many social media platforms, users generate content in different modalities, such as textual content (e.g., status updates, blog posts, tweets, comments, etc.) and visual content (e.g., photo and video), while also connecting with each other, i.e., creating relational content. A framework that leverages all available information about users can learn more accurate user profiles. This is especially useful for platforms where not every user generates the same type of information, and models trained based on one source of information fail to produce accurate user profiles. Examples include users who write status updates but never upload pictures, or users who join social media platforms only to consume knowledge and to relate with each other, rather than producing any textual or visual content themselves.

Neural networks lend themselves well for integrating multiple data sources, as they allow a non-linear combination of data sources to be trained to solve the problem. An early example is the use of a time-delay neural network (TDNN) to handle temporal multimodal data [28]. In general, neural networks are considered as a suitable technique to learn non-linear mappings in high-dimensional settings, however due to their slow training, they did not immediately take off as a popular technique for modeling multiple data sources. Recently, deep neural networks (DNNs), with the help of Graphics Processing Units (GPUs) which reduce the training time, gained a lot of attention. DNNs are arguably the best known method for most pattern recognition problems involving perception. They already perform on a human level on many important tasks such as handwritten digit recognition, pedestrian tracking, etc. One of the main advantages of DNN methods is that they do not need to rely on human designed features. Instead, DNNs learn their features from raw inputs. As a general reference to deep neural networks, we refer to [8].

In this paper, we make several contributions. First, we present a novel hybrid DNN based framework which we call "User Profiling through Deep Multimodal Fusion (UDMF)" that integrates multiple sources of user data for user profiling. We introduce a mechanism of stacking to leverage the dependency among target variables to more accurately infer user attributes. Second, we design a hybrid level of modeling multiple data sources with power-set combination. Using power-set combination, UDMF incorporates shared and non-shared representations among the data sources and integrates them both at the feature level and at the decision level. We perform user profiling using three modalities, namely textual data (i.e., users' posts), visual data (i.e., profile pictures) and relational data (i.e., users' page likes). For the social relational content in social media, our third contribution is that we propose to leverage a relational embedding approach called Node2Vec, in which we extract relational features from the social graph by performing a random walk through the graph. To the best of our knowledge this paper is the first paper that uses a Node2Vec embedding for extracting features from social relational content to infer users' age, gender and personality traits of social media users. Forth, we empirically evaluate UDMF for the task of user profiling in social media and

WSDM'18, , February 5–9, 2018, Marina Del Rey, CA, USA

ACM ISBN 978-1-4503-5581-0/18/02...$15.00
https://doi.org/10.1145/3159652.3159691

compare its performance with that of state-of-the-art methods on a sample dataset with 5K users from Facebook.

2 RELATED WORK

Recently, modeling heterogeneous data sources has gathered significant interest. Integrating two or more sources of data to form a unified picture or make a better decision are the main goals of data integration frameworks. Modeling of different data sources and modalities provides a benefit for various multimedia tasks in sensor networks, robotics, and video and image processing. In addition, integrating multiple media such as textual data with audio and video content has been successful in various applications such as emotion detection [21], detecting events from sports videos [33], and wearable robotics by sensor data [16]. In this paper, we design a hybrid model for user profiling which incorporates both feature level and decision level of combining users' data in social media.

Many techniques have been proposed for modeling multimodal data sources. For an overview, we refer to [1]. In this section, we first discuss related work in user profiling in social media and then discuss existing work in modeling multiple data sources using deep neural networks.

User Profiling: There is a substantial body of existing work on automatically inferring a user's characteristics from the user's digital footprint in social media platforms. Existing single-source models usually leverage either only text, images, or relations.

Machine learning models have been trained to infer the age, gender, and personality traits of users based on the *textual context* they produce, including blog posts and status updates [5, 22, 24]. Author profiling has gained a lot of attention in the past few years. Workshops and competitions such as PAN[1] that focus on various features and techniques to predict age and gender of authors, or shared tasks such as WCPR[2] for personality prediction are a few examples of recent efforts.

Independently of this, recently important progress has been made on age and gender identification from *visual content* using deep neural networks. Rothe et al. for instance successfully used a Convolutional Neural Network (CNN) framework to detect the age and gender of users from their face [23]. There are competitions concentrating on this task as well, such as the LAP Challenge 2016 on predicting apparent age estimation and gender classification of images[3]. Less work has been done on inferring personality traits from visual content. In [2], Biel and Gatica-Perez predict the personality of Vloggers (YouTube bloggers) based on their visual and audio content. Identifying personality traits from a static image such as a profile picture is mostly uncharted territory. Recently, in [12], facial features (i.e., Face++ features) are extracted from Twitter profile pictures to predict users' personality. In this paper we use a similar approach, based on the Oxford project features (see Section 4.1) which is consumed by our heterogeneous user profiling model as one of the users' data sources.

Existing work on inferring user characteristics from *relational content* focuses typically either on using homophily or heterophily relations among friends [4, 14], or indirect relations among users such as shared Facebook page likes [11]. In this paper, we use a novel embedding called Node2Vec, in which we extract relational features from the graph using a deep neural network architecture.

Although much progress has been made in the area of user profiling, leveraging multimodal information to this end is a largely unexplored area of research. Most of the related work integrates data sources at the feature level [34]. The closest work to ours is the research by Wei et al. [29], who used a framework to integrate textual data, avatars (i.e., visual data) and responsive patterns of social media users using an ensemble method. They leveraged neural networks in their work by extracting features using a CNN architecture. The work presented in this paper is different in the following ways: (1) we propose a hybrid framework which outperforms an ensemble method such as the one proposed in [29]; and (2) we infer age and gender of users in addition to predicting personality traits of all users. Wei et al. only predict personality traits of the extreme users and remove more than 70% of the users with neutral personality from the inference.

Multimodal Modeling in Deep Neural Networks: There is a large body of work on integrating multimodal data sources in deep neural networks. Our framework utilizes stacking and power-set combination for a hybrid integration of user data in social media (see Section 3). In contrast, most of the related works either combine the data sources at the feature level or at the decision level. For instance in [15], the authors propose a deep autoencoder network to learn a multimodal feature representation for the task of audio-visual speech recognition. They pre-trained their deep autoencoder network using sparse Restricted Boltzmann Machines (RBM). Hybrid integration of data sources has been studied as well, however without exploring every combination of the data sources. For instance in [31], the authors propose a hybrid deep learning framework for video classification, in which they combine CNN features with a Long Short Term Memory (LSTM) network. The features extracted from CNNs are combined using a regularized feature level integration network, and LSTM is used on the temporal modality. A hybrid architecture automatically combines the LSTM and CNN features.

The idea of stacking in deep neural networks has been used in various ways. For instance, in [30], the authors proposed to stack so-called bottleneck features (i.e., vectors consisting of the activations at a bottleneck layer with a small number of hidden units compared to the other hidden layers in the network) for the task of speech recognition. In [13], the authors use stacking to stack two deep neural networks. The first network is an unsupervised network to extract features and the second network is a supervised network for the prediction task. In this paper, we use stacking for multi-label prediction, in which we stack the output of the networks which are trained per each target label (see Section 3). In addition, we also stack two deep neural networks (i.e., supervised and unsupervised) similar to [13] to extract features from a relational graph with the novel deep neural network architecture "Node2Vec" for the task of user profiling (see Section 4). A recent related work in combining features at the feature level is [32] in which the authors propose attentional factorization machines to learn the weight of feature interactions. The authors consider a pair-wise interaction layer to learn the interaction between features after the embedding layer, while in this paper we propose a power-set combination of the data sources at the embedding layer which considers all the possible combinations of features.

3 UDMF: USER PROFILING THROUGH DEEP MULTIMODAL FUSION

The main goal of modeling multiple data sources is to integrate two or more sources of data/knowledge and create a single representation that provides a more accurate description of the data sources than any of the individual ones. To design such a framework, one of the main considerations is the level where the integration of data sources happens. There are two widely known strategies, namely the *early approach* and the *late approach*. Figure 1 sketches the early and late approaches in a deep neural network architecture.

[1] http://pan.webis.de/
[2] https://sites.google.com/site/wcprst/home/wcpr14
[3] http://gesture.chalearn.org/

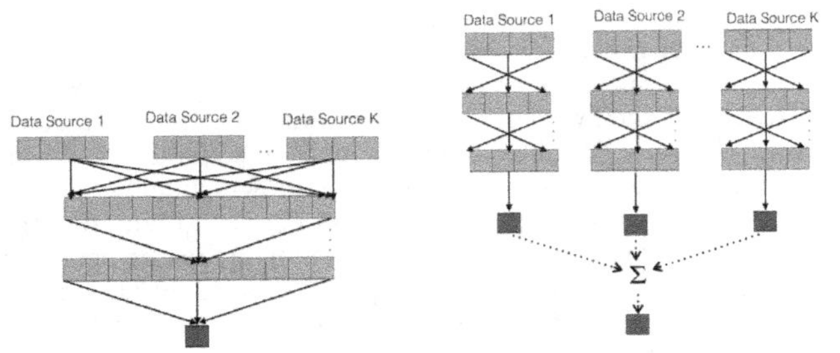

Figure 1: Early and late approaches of integrating multiple data sources in a deep neural network architecture.

The early approach is the strategy of integrating the data sources at the feature level. One of the main advantages of using the early approach is that correlation among different data sources and modalities are taken into account. The correlation among different modalities represents how different sources of knowledge co-vary with the other one. These types of correlation between data sources can provide additional cues in the integration process. But, different data sources and modalities do not necessarily correlate with each other. Therefore, in addition to using the dependency among data sources, it is often useful to fuse independent modalities to obtain a better decision. Let us consider the case of user profiling in social media. In this case, multiple modalities such as users' post and pictures can be used as a means of interaction with the platform. It is sometimes very hard to fuse these modalities at the feature level due to a lack of direct correspondence between their features.

The other popular approach of modeling multiple data sources is the late approach, where integration happens at the decision level. For instance, a linear weighted combination is the simplest decision (late) integration technique used. The widely used majority voting ensemble approach is a special case of this.

By incorporating both levels of modeling multiple data sources in our user profiling framework, we are able to take advantage of both approaches. Our hybrid model has two main properties. First, it leverages all sources of users' data and incorporates the correlation between modalities by mapping all combinations of data sources into shared representations. Second, in our model, integration of data sources also happens at the decision level when we combine the decision of all combinations of data sources. Moreover, to integrate the correlation among the target variables in a multi-task learning setup, we iteratively utilize the decision of our data integration framework for dependent tasks in the learning process.

We choose deep neural networks to implement our user profiling model for several reasons. First, it is easy to combine various data sources by using a shared representation between modalities. Second, we are able to combine data sources with non-linear functions which has been proved to enhance the learning process. Third, we are able to use neural networks on raw data sources and extract features using unsupervised approaches, i.e., the Node2Vec embedding that we use in Section 4. In the rest of this section, we introduce the structure for connecting data sources to the neurons in our proposed user profiling model, UDMF. To integrate data sources in UDMF, we design two mechanisms: *stacking* and *power-set combination.* To present them, we start from a general setting for a multilayer feedforward network described by an acyclic graph. We begin with a single data source D as input. The degree of activation of unit i on layer h is computed as:

$$U_i^h(D) = f(\sum_j w_{ij}^{hl} \cdot U_j^l(D)) \tag{1}$$

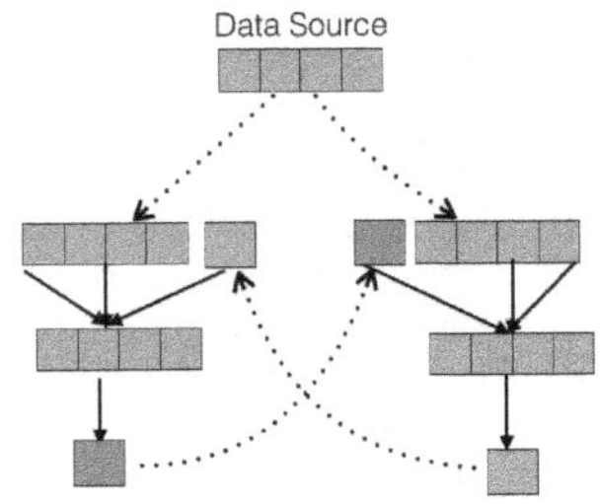

Figure 2: Stacking of 2 target variables given one data source.

where l is the layer that proceeds layer h, and j ranges over all the neurons on the layer l connected to layer h. w_{ij}^{hl} is the weight of the connection between neuron j on layer l and neuron i on layer h. f is an activation function which can be a non-linear function such as sigmoid function $\sigma(x) = 1/(1+e^{-x})$ for the output layer or ReLU ($ReLU(x) = \max(x, 0)$) for the hidden layers.

The degree of activation of unit i on layer 0, i.e., the layer connected to the input data source, is defined as follows (where $h = 0$):

$$U_i^0(D) = f(\sum_j w_{ij} \cdot D_j) \tag{2}$$

with w_{ij} representing the weight on the edge from input neuron j to neuron i on layer 0, and D_j denoting the input neuron j of the data source D, where j ranges over all values from 0 to the size of the input data source D, $|D|$.

Stacking. The stacking mechanism that we introduce in this paper makes the UDMF framework suitable for multi-task learning where target variables are correlated with each other. In a user profiling set up – which is the main focus of this paper – user attributes are correlated with each other: for instance inferring users' age becomes easier if we know their gender, and similarly, as users' demographics and personality traits are correlated, predicting one helps in predicting the other one. Farnadi et al. in [5] discuss the advantage of using multi-task learning in predicting users' personality traits using three social media data sets.

Figure 2 demonstrates stacking of two target variables given one data source in which two similar networks are trained per each target variable, but the input of each network consists of the input data source and the predicted output of the other target variable.

Assuming multiple epochs in learning the neural networks, Equation 2 is replaced with Equation 3, in which z ranges over the target variables. The degree of activation of unit i on layer 0 at epoch q is of the form:

$$U_i^{0q}(D) = f(\sum_j w_{ij} \cdot D_j + \sum_z w_{iz} \cdot \alpha_z \cdot t_z^{q-1}) \tag{3}$$

where α_z is a gating 0-1 variable. If z is equal to the target variable of the network, the value of $\alpha_z = 0$, otherwise $\alpha_z = 1$. In this way, the network for a specific target variable takes the predicted values t_z^{q-1} of the target variables of the other networks made during epoch $q-1$ as input. We initialize the value of the target neurons where $q = 0$ with zero, hence:

$$U_i^{00}(D) = f(\sum_j w_{ij} \cdot D_j) \tag{4}$$

At each epoch the predicted values of the target variables are updated based on the previously predicted values of the other target variables. As shown in Figure 2, for a sample configuration with two target variables, for each target variable, we create a network with a similar architecture. At each epoch, the predicted value of each target variable is stacked as an input for the other network. This configuration can easily be extended to more than two networks, i.e., more than two target variables. We can also update the predicted values of the target variables at every ten epochs instead of every epoch. In the experiments presented in section 4, we update the predicted values every 10 epochs and iterate 10 times to get 100 epochs.

Power-set Combination. Let $DS = \{D_1, D_2, \ldots, D_k\}$ be the finite set of k data sources that we want to integrate. Note that k is a small number as k represents the number of data sources that we have per each user. In social media k is typically between two to at most five sources of user data (i.e., textual, visual, relational, temporal, geo location). In our proposed power-set combination approach, we incorporate correlations among features and data sources by an early integration approach of all subsets of DS. We then combine their predicted outcome as a late integration approach with an ensemble method. Therefore, the UDMF model is a hybrid data integration model. The input layer of the UDMF framework consists of inputs originating from 1 to k data sources. Each neuron in the first hidden layer connected to the input layer can potentially be connected to the input neurons of any subset of these data sources. Precisely, given the set DS of the k data sources, we calculate the power-set of DS, i.e. the set of all subsets of DS. We exclude the empty set and therefore the number of subsets of DS under consideration is $2^k - 1$. Per each non-empty subset $\mathcal{D}$ in the power-set of DS we build a mini-DNN. The activation level of neuron i on layer 0 of each mini-DNN which combines $|\mathcal{D}|$ data sources at epoch q is computed as:

$$U_i^{0q}(\mathcal{D}) = f(\sum_{D \in \mathcal{D}} \sum_j w_{ij} \cdot D_j + \sum_z w_{iz} \cdot \alpha_z \cdot t_z^{q-1}) \quad (5)$$

where $\mathcal{D} \in \mathcal{P}(DS)$ is the subset of the input data sources leveraged in the mini-DNN. Equation (5) is the counterpart of Equation (2) in the UDMF framework.

As an example of power-set combination of the data sources in UDMF, we assume two available data sources A and B, $DS = \{A, B\}$, so the power-set $\mathcal{P}(DS)$ is $\{\{A\}, \{B\}, \{A, B\}, \{\}\}$. Therefore, we can make three mini-DNNs where A, B and combined A and B make up the respective input layers. We present the UDMF network for these two data sources and two target variables in Figure 3. As shown in the figure, we train three mini-DNNs for each target variable, therefore in total we train six mini-DNNs. The output of each mini-DNN is stacked as input to the sister mini-DNNs at the end of each epoch for the training at the next epoch.

If we have three data sources. i.e., textual, visual and relational, and p target variables (e.g., $p = 7$, see Section 4), we need to train $(2^3 - 1) \cdot 7 = 49$ mini-DNNs. As we stacked the target variables, we have an inter-connected network of seven mini-DNNs per each data source combination from the power-set of the data sources $\mathcal{P}(DS)$. Hence, we have seven DNN models that combine the data sources in various ways and each one of them includes seven mini-DNNs which are inter-connected to each other. Since modeling multiple data sources at the decision level of these seven DNN models happens in UDMF by majority voting as a late integration step, each multi-target network can be trained separately from each other. Training each power-set combination multi-target network in parallel reduces the time to train the UDMF to a great extent.

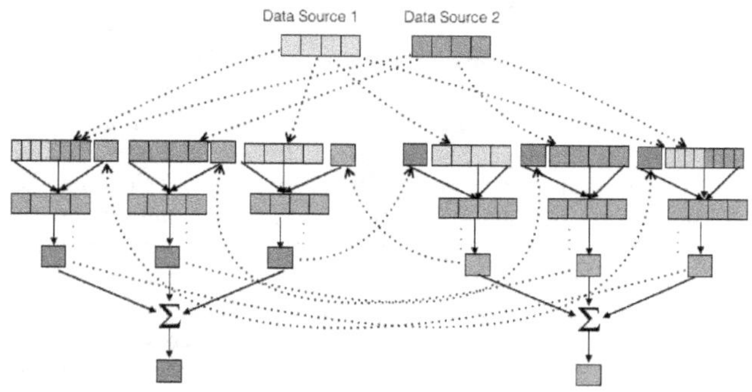

Figure 3: The architecture of UDMF with stacking of 2 target variables and power-set combination of two data sources.

4 EVALUATION

We train and test the UDMF framework with a subset of the MyPersonality project dataset[4]. MyPersonality was a popular Facebook application introduced in 2007 in which users took a standard Big Five Factor Model psychometric questionnaire [6] and gave consent to record their responses and Facebook profile. The dataset contains information about each user's demographics, friendship links, Facebook activities (e.g., number of group affiliations, page likes, education and work history), status updates, profile picture and Big Five Personality scores. However, not all of this information is available for all users. We selected users who mention English as their language, and who provide age, gender, personality, status updates, page likes and a profile picture. To increase the chance that the image depicts the profile owner, we first selected profile pictures with only one face using the Project Oxford Face detector API[5]. By removing the Facebook pages with less than 3 likes by users in this dataset, our final dataset includes 49,372 pages, and 724,948 page like relations for 5,670 users.

Personality traits are commonly described using five dimensions (known as the Big Five), i.e., Extraversion (Ext), Agreeableness (Agr), Conscientiousness (Con), Neuroticism (Neu), and Openness (Opn). The range of the personality scores in this dataset is between $[1, 5]$. We use the median value to create binary classes for each characteristic, where the median value for age = 23, Opn = 4, Con = 3.5, Ext = 3.5, Agr = 3.65, and Neu = 2.75. We evaluate the proposed user profiling model for the tasks of predicting age, gender and personality traits of Facebook users using their textual (status updates), visual (profile picture) and relational data (page likes).

We systematically perform 10-fold cross-validation. Since all the characteristics that we aim to predict are binary (i.e., positive class vs. negative class), to evaluate the results, we use AUC scores. AUC is the area under the ROC curve (i.e., receiver operating characteristic), which is created by plotting the true positive rate (i.e., portion of positives that are correctly predicted as such) against the false positive rate (i.e., portion of negatives that are wrongly predicted as positive). The natural language processing, machine learning and deep learning techniques in the following subsections are implemented using the scikit-learn[6] and keras[7] libraries in Python.

[4] http://mypersonality.org/
[5] https://www.microsoft.com/cognitive-services/en-us/face-api
[6] http://scikit-learn.org/
[7] https://keras.io/

To be able to correctly measure the effect of UDMF in integrating various data sources, as the basic building blocks of our configurations, we design simple DNNs consisting of three layers, where the first layer is the input layer, the second layer is a hidden layer which has 100 neurons per each data source as input and the last layer is a sigmoid layer that represents the result. For all the DNNs, the hidden layer of all the networks that we compare leverage ReLU as the activation function to model a non-linear combination of the inputs. We used Adam as the optimization algorithm, and we train all DNN models in this paper for 100 epochs, with a batch size set to 128. The other parameters of the DNN models are set by default values. We compare the performance of the models with the simple majority baseline algorithm that assigns the majority class from the training instances to the test instances. In addition, we compare with baseline methods that best learns combinations of modality features (early fusion)/decisions (late fusion) with the training data to show the power of the UDMF approach.

4.1 Data Source Embeddings

In practice, data always contain noise and we cannot expect to arrive at a good data representation without data cleaning and preprocessing. Which data processing to use under which constraints depends very much on the type of application. Before showing how UDMF fuses users' data, in this section we discuss how we represent each data source for the task of user profiling in social media. We define three data source embeddings: a data source embedding from the textual content, a data source embedding from the visual content, and a data source embedding from the relational content. We obtain the data source embeddings using the dataset described above.

Textual data source embedding: To build the textual data source embedding, we combine the status updates of each user in the dataset into one document per user. We represent each user with 88 Linguistic Inquiry and Word Count (LIWC) [19] features extracted from her/his status updates, consisting of features related to (a) standard counts (e.g., word count), (b) psychological processes (e.g., the number of anger words such as *hate, annoyed, ...* in the text), (c) relativity (e.g., the number of verbs in the future tense), (d) personal concerns (e.g., the number of words that refer to occupation such as *job, majors, ...*), and (e) linguistic dimensions (e.g., the number of swear words). For a complete overview, we refer to [26]. We compared the performance of using various feature sets, namely, LIWC, n-grams (n=1, 2, 3), a 300-dimensional pre-trained GloVe [20] vector based on Twitter data, and a 300-dimensional pre-trained fastText [10] vector based on English Wikipedia data with default parameters. The DNN models with LIWC features as the input layer significantly outperform similar DNN models with other feature sets and embeddings as the input layer, therefore in the rest of the paper we use LIWC features as our textual data source embedding. Results of the LIWC-based DNN models are presented in Table 1 as "Text". Due to the space restriction, we omit the results of DNN models based on other representations of the text from the paper.

Visual data source embedding: For each user we use his/her profile picture and extract 64 facial features using the Oxford Face API [3]. The extracted features are face rectangle features to capture the location of the face in the image, face landmark features which include 27-point face landmarks pointing to the important positions of face components, face characteristics including age, gender, facial hair, smile, head position and glasses type. We compared the performance of the Oxford features as the input layer, with a 128-dimensional activation vector extracted from the last layer (before the softmax) of the pre-trained VGG-16 and VGG-19 models [25] on ImageNet. The DNNs with the Oxford features as the input layer significantly outperform the VGG-based models specifically for the task of age and gender prediction. Results of the Oxford-based DNN models are presented in Table 1 as "Image". Due to the space restriction, we omit the results of DNN models based on other embeddings of the profile pictures from the paper.

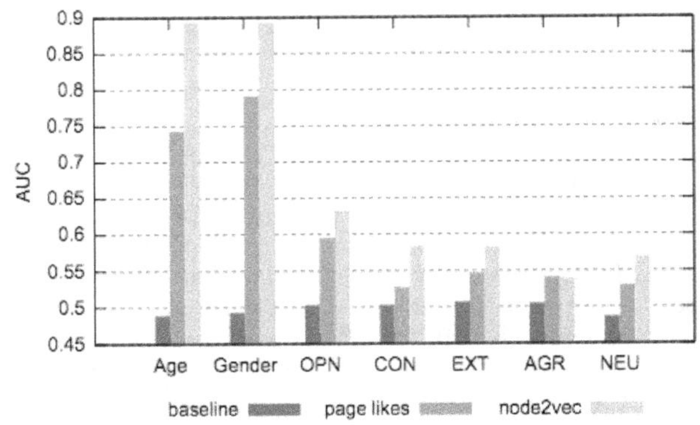

Figure 4: Node2Vec features extracted from users' page likes outperform using only pages that users like as features for the tasks of inferring gender, age, and Big Five personality traits.

Relational data source embedding: To represent users with pages that they like, we train an unsupervised deep neural network approach called Node2Vec on our relational graph [9]. Node2Vec is extending the Skip-gram architecture [7] to networks. Let $G = (V, E)$ be our relational graph, and f be the mapping function to represent nodes with features (i.e., $f : V \rightarrow \mathbb{R}^d$). The Node2Vec model optimizes the following objective function that maximizes the log-probability of observing a network neighborhood $NS(u)$ for a node u conditioned on its feature representation, given by f:

$$\max_f \sum_{u \in V} \log Pr(NS(u)|f) \tag{6}$$

We learn a mapping of users to a low-dimensional space of features that maximizes the likelihood of preserving network neighborhoods of users and pages. To this end, we train a Node2Vec model using our page like relations. Using features extracted from the Node2Vec model, we not only represent users with pages that they like (i.e., their neighbors), but also we find similar users by a flexible biased random walk procedure (Node2Vec walks) to produce $NS(u)$ that can explore neighborhoods in both a Breadth-First Sampling (BFS) as well as a Depth-First Sampling (DFS) fashion. BFS samples nodes which are immediate neighbors of the source, while DFS samples nodes at increasing distances from the source node. We iteratively perform the random Node2Vec walk on the graph to sample nearest neighbors for each node and then train a Skip-gram architecture to find embeddings for each node. We set the number of dimensions d to 127. From the output embedding, we select embeddings of the nodes which represent users in our domain and ignore the representation of the pages. The models using the Node2Vec features have outperformed state-of-the-art techniques on multi-label classification and link prediction in several real-world networks [9]. To the best of our knowledge, we are the first to use the Node2Vec embedding for user profiling using social relational content in social media.

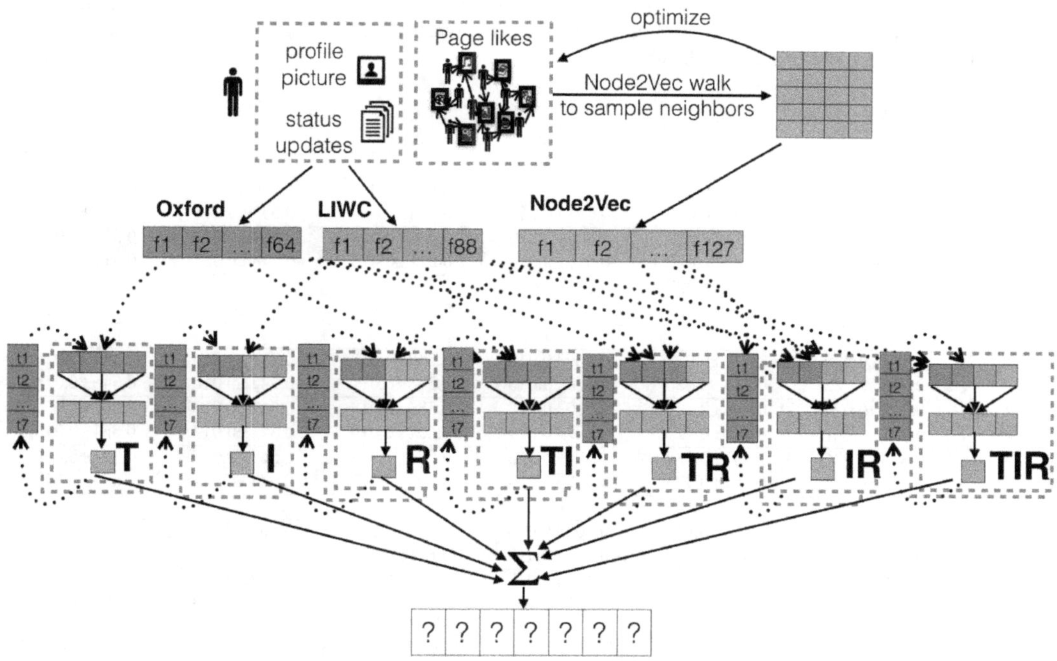

Figure 5: The architecture of user profiling with UDMF

This new representation of users and pages in a new space, allows us to gain additional knowledge compared to an adjacency matrix where users (i.e., rows) are represented by pages that they like (i.e., columns). To investigate the performance of a model using the Node2Vec embeddings for the user profiling task, we compared the performance of using the Node2Vec feature representation with the model proposed in [11]. We call the latter model the *page likes model* in the rest of this paper. In the page likes model, each row represents a user in the dataset and columns represent pages. The value of each matrix entry is one if the user likes that page in the dataset, otherwise it is zero. In [11], Lasso is used to predict the Big Five personality traits, however since our labels are binary, we use ridge regression which is a linear least squares classifier with $l2$ regularization. We set all parameters to their default values from the scikit-learn library.

The results are presented in Figure 4. We compared the Node2Vec model (shown with green bars as Node2Vec) with the majority baseline (shown with grey bars as baseline) and the page likes model (shown with orange bars as page likes) where both the Node2Vec and page likes models outperform the majority baseline and the Node2Vec models outperform the page like models in predicting all labels. Specifically, the Node2Vec models for age and gender predictions yield an AUC score which is close to 0.9. Note that we use very simple DNN models with only three layers to collect these results, however using more layers, and/or using a regularizer may further increase the accuracy of the prediction and improve these results, but this is out of the scope of this paper.

4.2 Data Source Integration

To integrate data sources in UDMF, we design a mini-DNNs architecture, with one layer for the input neurons, one hidden layer which is fully connected to the input neurons and one output layer which has the output of the learning task using the sigmoid activation function. We make similar mini-DNNs per each target variable that are integrated in the stacking process. In this way, for each subset of data sources, we have p mini-DNNs of this type which are getting updated at each epoch from the output of $p-1$ other mini-DNNs. To fuse the final result, we apply majority voting to determine the label.

In a user profiling setting, each unlabeled user is assigned labels from a finite set of labels, e.g., in our case $l = \{$ *female, young, Opn, Con, Ext, Agr, Neu*$\}$. The architecture of our user profiling framework with UDMF is shown in Figure 5. We stack $p = 7$ similar mini-DNNs where each network is trained for one target variable from a set of labels l. The parameters of each network can be tuned for the task and can possibly be different from the other networks. In this paper, however, for the sake of simplicity, we choose a common neural network architecture representation with the same choices across all the target variables to fairly compare the results with each other.

The different sources of information (profile picture, status updates, page likes) can all contribute to the construction of an accurate user profile. With regard to text, we observe that older users post more greetings in their status updates (e.g., "Happy birthday, happy christmas"), Neurotic users use more swear words, and Conscientious users utilize more terms related to time. The presence or absence of facial hair, such as a beard or mustache, is the best indicator for users' gender, and head position is a good indicator for Extraversion. Pages that users like provide useful clues as well, e.g. "I Love Being A Mum!" is a good indicator of a user's age and gender[8].

5 EXPERIMENTAL RESULTS

In this section, we evaluate the UDMF for the task of inferring users' age, gender and personality traits in Facebook. UDMF involves two main strategies: stacking and power-set combination. We first

[8]Note that in this paper, we only use the user-page like relations, and not the actual titles of the pages that users like on Facebook.

Table 1: Mean and standard deviation of area under the curve (AUC) scores in inferring age, gender and personality traits with one, two and three data source embeddings using mini-DNNs. For each category, results of using stacking (Equation 3) are shown with ✓, and results of not using stacking (Equation 2) are shown with ✗. All results are averaged over a 10-fold CV. In each column, the highest results are typeset in bold.

Model	Stack	Age	Gender	Opn	Con	Ext	Agr	Neu
Baseline		0.488	0.492	0.502	0.502	0.506	0.506	0.486
One source								
Text	✗	0.741±0.022	0.668±0.020	0.550±0.016	0.575±0.017	0.536±0.016	0.547±0.016	0.523±0.016
	✓	0.748±0.022	0.668±0.020	0.553±0.017	0.574±0.017	0.545±0.016	0.550±0.016	0.524±0.016
Image	✗	0.552±0.016	0.915±0.027	0.502±0.015	0.500±0.015	0.504±0.015	0.512±0.015	0.520±0.016
	✓	0.550±0.016	0.897±0.027	0.516±0.015	0.511±0.015	0.518±0.015	0.519±0.015	0.541±0.016
Relation	✗	0.875±0.026	0.886±0.027	0.601±0.018	0.571±0.017	0.567±0.017	0.525±0.016	0.558±0.017
	✓	0.893±0.027	0.898±0.027	0.622±0.018	0.589±0.018	0.573±0.017	0.533±0.016	0.563±0.016
Two sources								
Early approach	✗	0.734±0.022	0.873±0.026	0.569±0.017	0.588±0.018	0.536±0.016	0.545±0.016	0.547±0.016
TI	✓	0.746±0.022	0.864±0.026	0.546±0.016	0.568±0.017	0.542±0.016	0.546±0.016	0.536±0.016
Early approach	✗	0.878±0.026	0.896±0.027	0.610±0.018	0.586±0.018	0.567±0.017	0.535±0.016	0.554±0.017
TR	✓	0.891±0.027	0.899±0.027	0.627±0.019	0.601±0.019	0.572±0.017	0.551±0.016	**0.574±0.017**
Early approach	✗	0.878±0.026	0.951±0.028	0.606±0.018	0.574±0.017	0.569±0.017	0.524±0.016	0.562±0.017
IR	✓	0.895±0.027	0.951±0.028	0.633±0.019	0.592±0.018	0.577±0.017	0.537±0.016	0.564±0.017
Three sources								
Ensemble	✗	0.876±0.026	**0.952±0.028**	0.603±0.018	0.587±0.018	0.569±0.017	0.537±0.016	0.562±0.017
(Late approach)	✓	0.893±0.027	0.949±0.028	0.626±0.019	0.606±0.018	**0.582±0.017**	0.549±0.016	0.570±0.017
Early approach	✗	0.887±0.027	0.947±0.028	0.617±0.018	0.577±0.017	0.567±0.017	0.541±0.016	0.566±0.017
TIR	✓	**0.899±0.027**	0.934±0.028	**0.635±0.019**	**0.607±0.018**	0.560±0.018	**0.551±0.016**	0.572±0.017

examine the output of the UDMF framework using only stacking with a single source, a combination of two sources, and finally all three sources (Table 1). Then, we examine the capabilities of our hybrid UDMF framework with both stacking and power-set combination of two and three data sources in modeling multiple data sources (Table 2). Except for the parameter being tested, all other parameters assume default values for all the models. The learning curve of training the mini-DNNs with three data sources (i.e., shown as TIR in Figure 5) for the case of age prediction has been shown in Figure 6. As shown in the figure, all networks converge after 100 epochs. We omit the learning curve of other mini-DNNs networks, and other traits due to their similar behavior.

Unimodal baselines: To evaluate UDMF, we first get results using only one of the data sources with the basic DNN structure that we presented above (using Equation 2). These results are presented in the first rows for Text, Image, and Relation in Table 1. As expected, using Oxford features extracted from the profile picture of users to build the image model outperforms the majority baseline in predicting age and gender, however for personality traits these

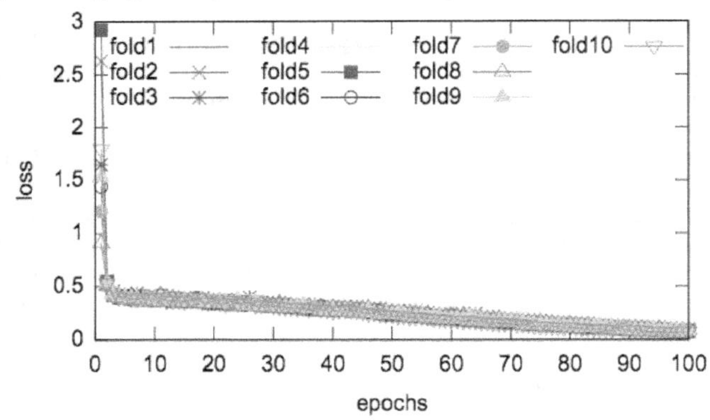

Figure 6: The training learning curve of infering age in all folds in mini-DNNs called TIR, where all three data sources are combined

features perform poorly. The text model using the LIWC features on the other hand outperforms the majority baseline for predicting all the labels, and the model using the Node2Vec features performs reasonably well in inferring all the traits. The best performing model which uses only a single source of data is the relation model using data source embeddings with Node2Vec features.

Multimodal baselines: We then combine the data sources both at feature level and decision level. We fuse all combinations of two sources and three sources of data. The results of combining two sources at the feature level are presented in the odd rows of the second section (i.e., Two sources) in Table 1, where *TI* is the combination of the textual and visual data sources, *TR* indicates the combination of the textual and relational data sources and *IR* refers to the combination of the visual and relational data sources. As expected, integrating data sources at the feature level (i.e., in an early integration manner) tends to performs better than the single source models in the first section of the table. The results of the early and late integration approach in combining three sources of data are close to each other but the early fusion approach works slightly better than the late integration approach (i.e., majority voting). These results are presented in the odd rows of the last section (i.e., Three sources) of Table 1.

To examine the stacking property, we train all networks with one, two and three data sources with stacking enabled (using Equation 3). The results are presented in the even rows of the Table 1 below the results of not using stacking per each category, where the "Stack" option is marked as enabled with ✓. It is interesting that training a network with stacking outperforms a similar network without stacking for most of the DNN networks that we examined either with single source DNNs and multi-source DNNs. Similarly, the networks trained with stacking outperform the networks without stacking both at the feature level and at the decision level. This indeed indicates the correlation among the target variables (i.e., age, gender and personality traits).

We then evaluate the UDMF architecture with both power-set combination and stacking while integrating two and three data sources (using Equation 5). As shown in Table 2 the AUC scores of

Table 2: Mean and standard deviation of AUC scores in inferring age, gender and personality traits by fusing two and three data sources in UDMF (Equation 5). All results are averaged over a 10-fold CV. In each column, the highest results are typeset in bold.

Model	Age	Gender	Opn	Con	Ext	Agr	Neu
			One/Two sources				
Page likes	0.743±0.020	0.699±0.022	0.605±0.017	0.516±0.016	0.555±0.016	0.540±0.0161	0.527±0.016
LR (T)	0.711±0.021	0.654±0.020	0.564±0.017	0.568±0.017	0.551±0.016	0.548±0.016	0.530±0.016
LR (I)	0.584±0.017	0.858 ±0.026	0.514±0.015	0.520±0.015	0.528±0.016	0.528±0.016	0.525±0.016
LR(T,I)	0.711±0.017	0.852 ±0.025	0.555±0.017	0.564±0.017	0.551±0.016	0.550±0.016	0.542±0.016
UDMF(T,I)	0.756±0.023	0.886±0.027	0.569±0.017	0.575±0.017	0.552±0.017	0.552±0.016	0.539±0.016
UDMF(T,R)	0.879±0.026	0.943±0.028	0.628±0.019	0.607±0.018	0.580±0.017	**0.564±0.017**	0.575±0.017
UDMF(I,R)	0.892±0.027	0.955±0.029	0.630±0.019	0.607±0.018	0.587±0.018	0.551±0.016	0.571±0.017
			Three sources				
Weighted Soft Voting	0.656±0.019	0.861±0.026	0.523±0.016	0.0523±0.016	0.508±0.015	0.507±0.015	0.518±0.015
Random Forest (100)(T,I,R)	0.786 ±0.023	0.900±0.027	0.588±0.018	0.564 ±0.017	0.544±0.016	0.549±0.016	0.538±0.016
LR(T,I,R)	0.808 ±0.024	0.888±0.027	0.603±0.018	0.585 ±0.018	0.550±0.017	0.550±0.016	0.572±0.017
UDMF(T,I,R)	**0.903±0.027**	**0.956±0.029**	**0.647±0.019**	**0.615±0.018**	**0.592±0.018**	0.556±0.017	**0.580±0.017**

the UDMF models are better than those obtained with early integration and late integration of the data sources as presented in Table 1. The UDMF framework in which we combined all three sources of data for user profiling outperforms all the competing networks presented in this paper for all tasks except for the Agreeableness class. In the case of Agreeableness, the UDMF model which integrates the textual and relational content outperforms the UDMF of all three sources of data. This result may be due to the poor performance of visual content in inferring the Agreeableness trait, producing noise instead of providing any additional evidence to fuse the information. We get highly accurate results in predicting age and gender of users with an AUC score of more than 0.90 in the case of age prediction and more than 0.95 for the task of gender prediction.

The UDMF framework outperforms state-of-the-art techniques for predicting age, gender and personality traits, as shown in the first section of Table 2. The first row corresponds to the *the page likes model* of Kosinski et al. [11]. The second row, containing results of logistic regression (LR) applied on LIWC features, is inspired by Farnadi et al. [5] who used decision trees and support vector machines. In our experiments, we found that LR outperformed these approaches, therefore we only include the results of using LIWC features with LR as a learner (shown as LR(T) in Table 2). Similarly we add the results of using Oxford features with LR (shown as LR(I)) and an early integration approach inspired by related works in combining features at the feature level to combine the textual and visual features (shown as LR(T,I)). In addition, we include an ensemble method and early integration approach using LR (shown as LR(T,I, R)), random forest with 100 estimators and a weighted soft voting approach of the results of the decision tree, support vector machine and LR. UDMF outperforms all these approaches.

We tested all the networks with various dropout parameters 0.1, 0.2, 0.3, 0.4, and 0.5. We find that the models are not very sensitive to variations of the dropout rate. The difference between using dropout and not using this procedure differs in a small amount, thus to keep the simplicity of the networks, we omit the results from this paper. Note that we chose a simple architecture for designing the mini-DNN networks, and we used a similar DNN architecture throughout this paper for fair comparison, however one could design a more sophisticated DNN for the task of user profiling to enhance the learning power of UDMF.

6 CONCLUSION AND FUTURE DIRECTIONS

In this paper, we have introduced a hybrid user profiling architecture in deep neural networks which we call UDMF. UDMF has two simple and yet effective properties, namely stacking and power-set combination strategies, to better integrate users' data in social media for multi-target learning task. UDMF combines different modalities both at the feature level and decision level to predict accurate multiple attributes of social media users given their user generated content and social relational content. We evaluated the UDMF architecture for the user modeling task on more than 5K users from Facebook. We built three data sources from users' textual, visual and relational content given their status updates, profile picture and pages that they like on Facebook. The results showed how stacking and power-set combination in UDMF enhance the learning power in combining the data sources. To make a user profile, we predicted age, gender and personality traits of users with UDMF. We obtained highly accurate results, including an AUC score of more than 0.9 for the task of age prediction and 0.95 for the task of gender prediction.

In this paper, we trained our user profiling UDMF framework on a sample of data from Facebook. Due to the small size of the textual and visual data, we could not use a neural network architecture to learn features. Another interesting direction for future work is to use larger datasets to learn features while integrating them with UDMF. Moreover, integrating other sources of users' data such as temporal data and geo-location data such as users' check-in information, remains as a future direction of this work.

With regard to the data integration part of UDMF, there are two main directions for future work. First, data integration frameworks are either exploiting overlap between modalities to "reinforce the signal", or gathering different pieces of information from different sources to obtain a full picture. An ideal user profiling framework utilizes each source of users' data/knowledge to discover part of the information, and therefore by integrating multiple sources of data, a data integration framework should put all pieces of data together and provide a descriptive and comprehensive representation of users in social media. One could extend the UDMF framework with a new objective function that learns the degree to which integrating modalities share evidences and the degree to which data sources provide complementarity of evidence that is captured in the learned representations.

Second, another important factor in modeling mutiple data sources is that different modalities may have varying capabilities of accomplishing a specific task. For example, we observed that a profile picture is not a suitable source of data to infer a user's personality traits by itself, however, combining this source with other sources of data such as textual content and relational content boost the performance of the learner. Although UDMF performs well in combining strong and poor sources of data, it is an interesting direction for future work to incorporate the confidence level of each source in the integration process. Learning a confidence level is a complex task that may change by considering various factors such as noise in the data. Designing an approach for learning this with a deep neural network is an open path to explore.

REFERENCES

[1] P. K. Atrey, M. A. Hossain, A. El Saddik, and M. S. Kankanhalli. Multimodal fusion for multimedia analysis: a survey. *Multimedia systems*, 16(6):345–379, 2010.

[2] J.-I. Biel and D. Gatica-Perez. The youtube lens: Crowdsourced personality impressions and audiovisual analysis of vlogs. *Proc. of IEEE Transactions on Multimedia*, 15(1):41–55, 2013.

[3] Z. Cao, Q. Yin, X. Tang, and J. Sun. Face recognition with learning-based descriptor. In *Proc. of IEEE Conference on Computer Vision and Pattern Recognition (CVPR)*, pages 2707–2714. IEEE, 2010.

[4] G. Farnadi, Z. Mahdavifar, I. Keller, J. Nelson, A. Teredesai, M.-F. Moens, and M. De Cock. Scalable adaptive label propagation in Grappa. In *Proc. of IEEE International Conference on Big Data*, pages 1485–1491, 2015.

[5] G. Farnadi, G. Sitaraman, S. Sushmita, F. Celli, M. Kosinski, D. Stillwell, S. Davalos, M.-F. Moens, and M. De Cock. Computational personality recognition in social media. *User Modeling and User Adapted Interaction*, pages 1–34, 2016.

[6] L.-R. Goldberg, J.-A. Johnson, H.-W. Eber, R. Hogan, M.-C. Ashton, C.-R. Cloninger, and H.-G. Gough. The international personality item pool and the future of public-domain personality measures. *Journal of Research in Personality*, 40(1):84–96, 2006.

[7] Y. Goldberg and O. Levy. Word2vec explained: Deriving mikolov et al.'s negative-sampling word-embedding method. *arXiv preprint arXiv:1402.3722*, 2014.

[8] I. Goodfellow, Y. Bengio, and A. Courville. *Deep Learning*. MIT Press, 2016. http://www.deeplearningbook.org.

[9] A. Grover and J. Leskovec. Node2Vec: Scalable feature learning for networks. In *Proc. of the 22nd ACM SIGKDD International Conference on Knowledge Discovery and Data Mining*, pages 855–864. ACM, 2016.

[10] A. Joulin, E. Grave, P. Bojanowski, and T. Mikolov. Bag of tricks for efficient text classification. *arXiv preprint arXiv:1607.01759*, 2016.

[11] M. Kosinski, D. J. Stillwell, and T. Graepel. Private traits and attributes are predictable from digital records of human behavior. *Proc. of the National Academy Of Sciences (PNAS)*, 110:5802–5805, 2013.

[12] L. Liu, D. Preotiuc-Pietro, Z. Riahi Samani, M. E. Moghaddam, and L. Ungar. Analyzing personality through social media profile picture choice. In *Proc. of the International AAAI Conference on Web and Social Media*, 2016.

[13] A. B.-J. Low, C-Y.and Teoh. Stacking-based deep neural network: Deep analytic network on convolutional spectral histogram features. *arXiv preprint arXiv:1703.01396*, 2017.

[14] M. McPherson, L. Smith-Lovin, and J. M. Cook. Birds of a feather: Homophily in social networks. *Annual Review of Sociology*, pages 415–444, 2001.

[15] J. Ngiam, A. Khosla, M. Kim, J. Nam, H. Lee, and A. Y. Ng. Multimodal deep learning. In *Proc. of the 28th International Conference on Machine Learning (ICML-11)*, pages 689–696, 2011.

[16] D. Novak and R. Riener. A survey of sensor fusion methods in wearable robotics. *Robotics and Autonomous Systems*, 73:155–170, 2015.

[17] S. Nowson and J. Oberlander. The identity of bloggers: Openness and gender in personal weblogs. In *Proc. of AAAI Spring Symposium: Computational Approaches to Analyzing Weblogs*, pages 163–167, 2006.

[18] R. D. Oliveira, A. Karatzoglou, P. C. Cerezo, A. A. L. D. Vicuña, and N. Oliver. Towards a psychographic user model from mobile phone usage. In *Proc. of the International Conference on Human Factors in Computing Systems, CHI*, pages 2191–2196, 2011.

[19] J.-W. Pennebaker and L.-A. King. Linguistic styles: Language use as an individual difference. *Journal of Personality and Social Psychology*, 77:1296–1312, 1999.

[20] J. Pennington, R. Socher, and C. Manning. Glove: Global vectors for word representation. In *Conference on Empirical Methods in Natural Language Processing (EMNLP)*, volume 14, pages 1532–1543, 2014.

[21] S. Poria, E. Cambria, N. Howard, G.-B. Huang, and A. Hussain. Fusing audio, visual and textual clues for sentiment analysis from multimodal content. *Neurocomputing*, 174:50–59, 2016.

[22] F. Rangel, P. Rosso, M. Potthast, B. Stein, and W. Daelemans. Overview of the 3rd Author Profiling Task at PAN 2015. In *Proc. of CLEF*, 2015.

[23] R. Rothe, R. Timofte, and L. Van Gool. Dex: Deep expectation of apparent age from a single image. In *Proc. of ICCV, ChaLearn Looking at People workshop*, 2015.

[24] H. A. Schwartz, J. C. Eichstaedt, M. L. Kern, L. Dziurzynski, S. M. Ramones, M. Agrawal, A. Shah, M. Kosinski, D. Stillwell, M. E. P. Seligman, et al. Personality, gender, and age in the language of social media: The open-vocabulary approach. *PloS one*, 8(9):e73791, 2013.

[25] K. Simonyan and A. Zisserman. Very deep convolutional networks for large-scale image recognition. *arXiv preprint arXiv:1409.1556*, 2014.

[26] Y. R. Tausczik and J. W. Pennebaker. The Psychological meaning of words: LIWC and computerized text analysis methods. *Journal of Language and Social Psychology*, 29:24–54, 2010.

[27] M. Tkalcic and L. Chen. Personality and recommender systems. In *Recommender Systems Handbook*, pages 715–739. Springer, 2015.

[28] A. Waibel, T. Hanazawa, G. Hinton, K. Shikano, and K. J. Lang. Phoneme recognition using time-delay neural networks. *IEEE Transactions on Acoustics, Speech and Signal Processing*, 37(3):328–339, 1989.

[29] H. Wei, F. Zhang, N. J. Yuan, C. Cao, H. Fu, X. Xie, Y. Rui, and W.-Y. Ma. Beyond the words: Predicting user personality from heterogeneous information. In *Proc. of the Tenth ACM International Conference on Web Search and Data Mining*, pages 305–314, 2017.

[30] Z. Wu, C. Valentini-Botinhao, O. Watts, and S. King. Deep neural networks employing multi-task learning and stacked bottleneck features for speech synthesis. In *IEEE International Conference on Acoustics, Speech and Signal Processing (ICASSP)*, pages 4460–4464, 2015.

[31] Z. Wu, X. Wang, Y.-G. Jiang, H. Ye, and X. Xue. Modeling spatial-temporal clues in a hybrid deep learning framework for video classification. In *Proc. of the 23rd ACM international conference on Multimedia*, pages 461–470, 2015.

[32] J. Xiao, H. Ye, X. He, H. Zhang, F. Wu, and T.-S. Chua. Attentional factorization machines: Learning the weight of feature interactions via attention networks. In *Proc. of the International Joint Conference on Artificial Intelligence (IJCAI)*, 2017.

[33] C. Xu, Y.-F. Zhang, G. Zhu, Y. Rui, H. Lu, and Q. Huang. Using webcast text for semantic event detection in broadcast sports video. *IEEE Transactions on Multimedia*, 10(7):1342–1355, 2008.

[34] Q. Zhu, M.-C. Yeh, and K.-T. Cheng. Multimodal fusion using learned text concepts for image categorization. In *Proceedings of the 14th ACM international conference on Multimedia*, pages 211–220. ACM, 2006.

Orienteering Algorithms for Generating Travel Itineraries

Zachary Friggstad
University of Alberta
zacharyf@ualberta.ca

Sreenivas Gollapudi
Google Research
sgollapu@google.com

Kostas Kollias
Google Research
kostaskollias@google.com

Tamas Sarlos
Google Research
stamas@google.com

Chaitanya Swamy
University of Waterloo
cswamy@uwaterloo.ca

Andrew Tomkins
Google Research
tomkins@google.com

Abstract

We study the problem of automatically and efficiently generating itineraries for users who are on vacation. We focus on the common case, wherein the trip duration is more than a single day. Previous efficient algorithms based on greedy heuristics suffer from two problems. First, the itineraries are often unbalanced, with excellent days visiting top attractions followed by days of exclusively lower-quality alternatives. Second, the trips often re-visit neighborhoods repeatedly in order to cover increasingly low-tier points of interest. Our primary technical contribution is an algorithm that addresses both these problems by maximizing the quality of the worst day. We give theoretical results showing that this algorithm's competitive factor is within a factor two of the guarantee of the best available algorithm for a single day, across many variations of the problem. We also give detailed empirical evaluations using two distinct datasets: (a) anonymized Google historical visit data and (b) Foursquare public check-in data. We show first that the overall utility of our itineraries is almost identical to that of algorithms specifically designed to maximize total utility, while the utility of the worst day of our itineraries is roughly twice that obtained from other approaches. We then turn to evaluation based on human raters who score our itineraries only slightly below the itineraries created by human travel experts with deep knowledge of the area.

ACM Reference Format:
Zachary Friggstad, Sreenivas Gollapudi, Kostas Kollias, Tamas Sarlos, Chaitanya Swamy, and Andrew Tomkins. 2018. Orienteering Algorithms for Generating Travel Itineraries. In *WSDM 2018: WSDM 2018: The Eleventh ACM International Conference on Web Search and Data Mining , February 5–9, 2018, Marina Del Rey, CA, USA.* ACM, New York, NY, USA, 9 pages. https://doi.org/10.1145/3159652.3159697

1 Introduction

Google aims to produce high-quality collections of information responsive to user needs. In the context of travel planning, it is often important to organize information about specific points of interest at a destination into a useful form such as an itinerary for a visit. We have developed and launched such a capability, which is used at various places in Google's product offerings. In one setting, the itinerary is pre-computed for hundreds of cities, which is then shown to users searching for travel in a particular city as an aid to jump-start the travel planning process. In another setting, users who have "saved" points of interest will see itineraries generated on the fly to feature the specific places they have saved. And in yet a third setting, users who have downloaded the Google Trips app will see dynamic editable itineraries which may be edited and reconfigured in real time to suit the user's needs. In this last setting, the algorithm must be sufficiently responsive to compute new itineraries in real time even running locally on a mobile device. Hence, the algorithmic generation of high-quality itineraries under various constraints is an important problem for Google, and one that we continue to explore.

The problem of generating tourist itineraries has been studied before, often in the guise of a combinatorial problem called the *Orienteering problem*: given a graph with costs on the edges and benefits on the vertices, find a max-benefit tour subject to a cost budget. This formulation easily captures, for example, finding a ten-hour tour of London that visits the best spots, even if the notion of "best" is personal and complex.

However, most trips range from 3–8 days, and many are even longer. The orienteering problem must therefore be extended to cover multiple days. This seemingly innocuous extension in fact raises a host of new issues. First, the problem tends to be larger in scale, as one can visit many more places during a longer trip. Second, standard greedy approaches perform well from a worst-case algorithmic standpoint in some settings, but do not yield good user experience for multi-day trips. For example, the first day of a visit might cover all the best destinations, then each subsequent day might visit places one tier more boring than the day before. Worse yet, each of these days may revisit the same neighborhoods along the same routes, simply replacing high-quality stops with lower-quality ones. Some heuristics may be employed to re-order days, encourage good balance, and penalize re-visits, but as our experience has shown, these heuristics are difficult to tune appropriately across the wide range of cities that human civilization has produced.

A better approach is to re-formulate the problem to make all days of the tour good, by maximizing the benefit of the worst day rather than maximizing the sum of benefits of all days. This will avoid the issue of good versus bad days, and will also naturally encourage the algorithm to spend time one day focusing on a range of good and bad places within a particular neighborhood, moving on tomorrow to a fresh new area.

We present a simple algorithm and a proof showing its competitive factor is not much worse than the factor of whatever algorithm

WSDM 2018, February 5–9, 2018, Marina Del Rey, CA, USA

ACM ISBN 978-1-4503-5581-0/18/02.
https://doi.org/10.1145/3159652.3159697

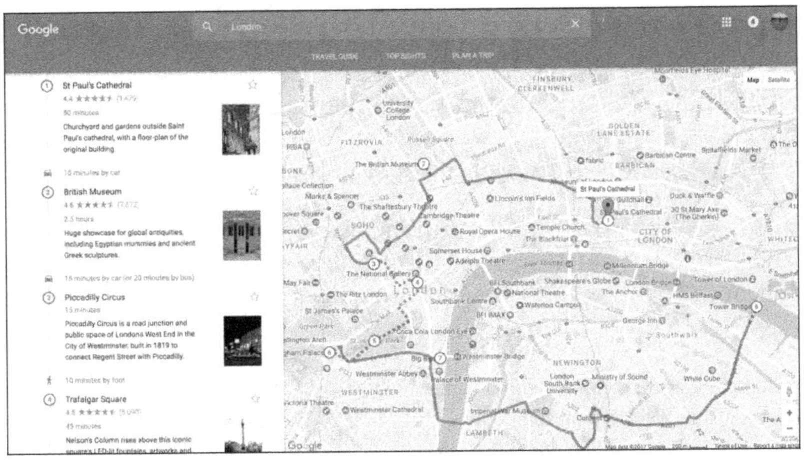

Figure 1: A precomputed tour of London.

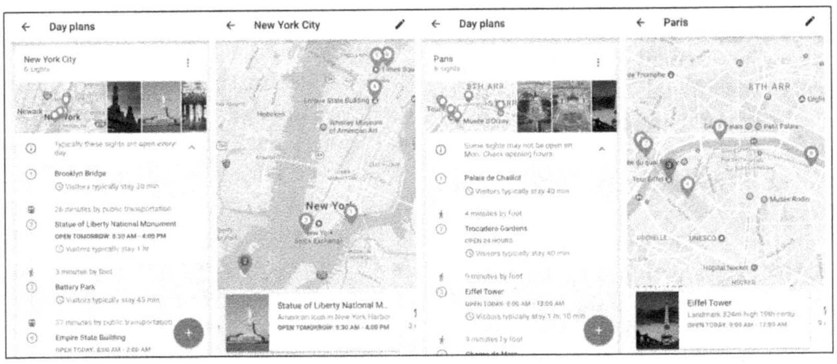

Figure 2: Tours of New York City and Paris generated on mobile.

is available to optimize a single-day visit. In particular, we show that, given an α approximation algorithm for various single-day orienteering models, our algorithm achieves an $\alpha+2$ approximation for maximizing the value of the worst day. The models covered by this result include the simplest orienteering model where the graph is undirected and there are no restrictions on obtaining the reward of a node (where we achieve a $4+\epsilon$ approximation) as well as extensions to orienteering with deadlines, or more generally, time-windows for the nodes and extensions to directed graphs (for which we achieve polylog approximations).

In response to the criticism that, while the greedy algorithm may perform well in some worst-case settings, this does not guarantee that users will enjoy the results, we provide extensive empirical verification of the performance of our algorithm and a benchmark set of alternatives. Our analysis selects two families of measures to apply to the algorithms. The first are computable measures of quality based on the objective: number of places visited, total benefit from those places, and so forth. We also add a second class of measures based on human evaluation: we employed a pool of raters tasked to assess the quality of the algorithms generated by the different algorithms. Our experimental analysis exhibits that our algorithm manages to improve the value of the worst day to a significant extent compared to a well established multi-day orienteering algorithm that maximizes the total reward obtained (on average our algorithm more than doubles the value of the worst day for 5-day itineraries across 200 cities) while at the same time sacrificing no value with respect to the total reward. In the human rater evaluation, our algorithm nearly matches the ratings of a set of multi-day itineraries curated by travel experts.

2 Related Work

Algorithmically, the orienteering problem is an excellent model for the application of planning a tourist itinerary in a city. In orienteering, the goal is to maximize the reward extracted by visiting nodes in a graph, starting and ending at a given node, subject to a budget constraint on the length of the tour. The best known approximation algorithms for orienteering and orienteering with time windows (i.e., when the reward of a node is extracted if and only if its time of visit is within a prescribed time window) are given in [7]. These algorithms follow work in [2] and [1], where the orienteering problem is solved by a dynamic program that uses the k-path algorithm from [6] as a subroutine. In the k-path problem, the goal is to minimize the cost of a path that visits at least k nodes. In turn, the work in [6] relies on a primal-dual algorithm for k-MST [15], which is the problem of constructing a tree of minimum cost that spans k nodes. The algorithm for the undirected case with no time windows is a $2+\epsilon$ approximation, while the algorithms for the other models are poly-logarithmic approximations. We discuss the best known approximation factors for various orienteering models in more detail in Section 3. A different approach to orienteering on undirected graphs without time windows was given very recently by Friggstad and Swamy [14]. The idea is to define a linear program that encodes orienteering and use a rounding algorithm to come up with a solution that is a 3 approximation to the optimal. On multi-tour orienteering, the work in [2] presents a simple greedy algorithm that uses a single-tour algorithm as a subroutine and approximates the total reward across days almost without any loss to the approximation factor of the single-day case. An extension to submodular rewards has been studied in [8], where a quasipolynomial log factor approximation is described.

As far as the application domain is concerned, various approaches to the tourist itinerary planning problem have been proposed. The authors in [3, 16, 17, 29] present comprehensive surveys of heuristic and algorithmic approaches to the problem. The work most closely related to ours is presented in [9]. The authors there focus on generating tourist itineraries based on data extracted from social media, in particular Flickr photos. They also model the problem as an orienteering instance and use the photos dataset to extract the popularity of a place, the duration of visits, and the transit time between different points of interest. We now explain the main differences of our work to the one in [9]. First, we work with a fundamentally different dataset, specifically, the work in [9] seeks to extract the number of visits to an attraction, the visit durations and the transit times from Flickr data, whereas our dataset explicitly includes this information. Secondly, the authors in [9] focus primarily on single day itineraries and mention the multi-day case as an interesting extension, whereas our main focus is on multi-day itineraries: we propose an extension of orienteering to the multi-tour case where the objective is to optimize for the value of the worst tour and present original algorithmic work for that problem, as well as experimentally evaluate it in a large number of cities world wide.

Other interesting papers in the domain of itinerary planning include [34], where the authors use GPS data to build an itinerary recommendation engine and evaluate it using Beijing as an example, [26], which focuses on suggesting routes in a city that also offer some utility to the user as opposed to just being the shortest source-destination paths, as well as various approaches that use geo-tagged social media, e.g., [4, 21, 24, 25, 30, 32, 33, 35], and approaches based on personalization [5, 11, 12, 18–20, 22, 23, 27, 28]. A final interesting piece of related work is [31] where the authors study the orienteering problem in a tourist application from a game-theoretic view-point. They consider settings such as large amusement parks where many travelers visit the same attractions and there are congestion effects at the attractions and on the travel routes from one attraction to another. The objective of the work in [31] is to compute good equilibrium solutions to the problem.

3 Orienteering Model and Preliminaries

Consider a complete (either directed or undirected) graph $G = (V, E)$ with a designated start and end node s, visit duration costs d_v for every $v \in V$, and travel time costs c_e for every $e \in E$. We assume the edge costs satisfy the triangle inequality. For any given path P, we write $V(P)$ for the set of nodes in P and $E(P)$ for the set of edges in P. We say that a vector of node visit times τ^P is admissible if for every edge $(u, v) \in E(P)$, with $v \neq s$, it is the case that

$$\tau_v^P \geq \tau_u^P + d_u + c_{(u,v)}.$$

In *multi-tour orienteering*, our input consists of a graph G with a designated start and end node s, a number k (the number of requested tours), and a (per-tour) cost budget B. For the start/end node s, we prescribe (for simplification and without loss of generality) that the duration cost d_s and the visit time τ_s^P is always 0.

A feasible output is a set of k tours $\mathcal{P}$ and a set of corresponding admissible visit time vectors τ, such that each pair of tours intersect only at s, i.e., for all $P_1 \neq P_2 \in \mathcal{P}$,

$$V(P_1) \cap V(P_2) = \{s\},$$

and, for each tour $P \in \mathcal{P}$, the budget constraint is satisfied i.e., if $t(P)$ is the last node of P before returning to s, then,

$$\tau_{t(P)}^P + d_{t(P)} + c_{(t^P,s)} \leq B.$$

For a tour P and corresponding admissible visit time vector τ^P, the *utility function* $U\left(P, \tau^P\right)$ outputs the induced utility, which is given as follows. The utility of any node $v \in V$ is a fixed number u_v, which is obtained if and only if the visit time of the node τ_v^P is within a prescribed non empty time window w_v, i.e.,

$$U\left(P, \tau^P\right) = \sum_{v \in V(P)} u_v \cdot 1_{\{\tau_v^P \in w_v\}}.$$

In *sum* orienteering, the objective is to maximize

$$SUM(\mathcal{P}, \tau) = \sum_{P \in \mathcal{P}} U\left(P, \tau^P\right),$$

while in *max-min* orienteering the objective is to maximize

$$MIN(\mathcal{P}, \tau) = \min_{P \in \mathcal{P}} U\left(P, \tau^P\right).$$

Mapping the model to our application, the graph represents a city that a traveler visits, with the nodes being the various points of interest (POIs) of the city and the edges being the travel routes between them. The utility of a node is determined by the corresponding POI's tourist popularity and the duration cost is the expected time one should spend there to enjoy what the POI has to offer. The cost of an edge is the transit time required to move from the POI corresponding to its first endpoint to the POI corresponding to its second endpoint. The start node corresponds to the traveler's hotel (or other accommodation) where the tour needs to begin and end, and the number of paths k corresponds to the number of days spent in the city. Time 0 corresponds to the time the tour may start at each day (e.g. 9am or 10am) and time B (the budget) corresponds to the time the user needs to return to the hotel.

Single-Tour Orienteering. The sum and max-min models obviously coincide when $k = 1$, i.e, for single-tour orienteering. The multi-tour algorithms we will discuss in Section 4 make use of a single-tour oracle and for this reason, we next survey the best known single-tour algorithms.

For the case when the graph is undirected and there are no time windows, i.e., $w_v = [0, \infty)$ for all $v \in V$, the best known algorithm achieves a $2 + \epsilon$ approximation, for any $\epsilon > 0$ [7]. For undirected graphs with deadline constraints on the nodes, i.e., $w_v = [0, t_v]$ for every $v \in V$, the best known is an $O(\log OPT)$ approximation, with OPT the value of the optimal solution [2]. For undirected graphs with time windows, [7] presents an $O(\max\{\log OPT, \log L\})$ approximation, with L the length of the largest time window.

Moving to directed graphs, [7] presents an $O\left(\log^2 OPT\right)$ approximation for the case with no time windows, an $O\left(\log^3 OPT\right)$ approximation for the case with deadlines, and for the case with general time windows an $O\left(\log^2 OPT \cdot \max\{\log OPT, \log L\}\right)$ approximation.

All these algorithms rely on large dynamic programs and, hence, are complicated and slow, with running times of $O(n^8)$ or worse, where $n = |V|$. Alternatively, a simpler linear-programming based algorithm of [14] for the undirected model without time windows achieves a 3 approximation.

We note that all these algorithms assume there are no node costs, which is in contrast to our setting. However, we observe that a simple transformation can convert any instance with node costs to an equivalent instance with zero node costs. Namely, for both undirected and directed graphs, increase the cost of each edge adjacent to a node by half of the node's cost. Then the cost of any tour remains the same as before the transformation. It is not hard to see that the triangle inequality property is preserved under this transformation.

Before wrapping up the section on single-tour orienteering, we describe an algorithm specifically tailored for use in practical settings, which means the algorithm is very fast (with run-times of 50ms or less) and performs well in real world instances. The algorithm greedily builds a tour by recalculating the traveling salesman tour of the so-far selected nodes plus each possible candidate node and picking the candidate that is the most cost-effective. We term this algorithm GreedyTSPCost and evaluate its quality in Section 5.2.

GreedyTSPCost Algorithm. We conclude our discussion of single tour orienteering with the description of our GreedyTSPCost algorithm, which is in fact the one we use as the single tour subroutine in the experimental evaluation of our multi-tour algorithms in Section 5.2. The algorithm is very efficient and useful in practice, even though it can't provide good worst case guarantees. The algorithm proves useful in scenarios where orienteering needs to be solved with very limited computational resources, for instance on mobile devices with no connectivity. The algorithm's behavior is reminiscent of greedy knapsack algorithms, always adding the node that offers us the biggest bang for the buck, i.e., yields the highest marginal increase to the utility of the tour, normalized by the marginal increase to the cost of the tour. We provide the details in Algorithm 1.

Algorithm 1: GreedyTSPCost

```
Input: Graph G, budget B, start/end node s
Output: Tour P, visit times τ^P
P* ←MakeSingleNodeTour(s)
do
    P ← P*
    best_margin← 0
    P* ← null
    for ∀v ∈ V do
        P' ← TSP(V(P) ∪ {v}) // Use heuristic, e.g. 2-OPT
        margin ← (U(P') − U(P))/(Cost(P') − Cost(P))
        if margin > best_margin and Cost(P') < B then
            best_margin ← margin
            P* ← P'
while P* ≠ null
τ_s^P ← 0
for e = (u, v) ∈ E(P) do
    τ_v^P ← τ_u^P + d_u + c_e
return (P, τ^P)
```

Theorem 3.1. *Algorithm 1 is an $\Omega(OPT)$ approximation, with OPT the optimal utility.*

Proof. Consider a simple instance such that all nodes have unit utilities and zero duration costs. In such instances, Algorithm 1 will pick, in each iteration, the node that has the smallest distance from the set of already selected nodes. Suppose the start/end has two outgoing edges of unit cost. One leads to a single node and the other leads to a clique of n nodes with 0 distances. The rest of the edge costs are the shortest tour distances on the graph we described so far. Let the budget be $B = 2$. Algorithm 1 might spend this budget to move to the isolated single node as opposed to the zero cost clique and extract utility 2 as opposed to $n + 1$. □

Such adversarial instances are very unlikely in real world cities. In fact, the specific structure of real world instances (which include very skewed utility distributions and where the visit times at nodes dominate the transit times through the city) is such that a greedy knapsack-style algorithm is expected to perform well. We point to the experimental evaluation of Section 5.2 and the positive results therein as further support of this intuition. With respect to the algorithm's running time, we observe that, assuming the size of the induced itinerary is always small in comparison to the size of the graph, GreedyTSPCost is linear in the number of nodes.

4 Multi-Tour Orienteering Algorithms

In this section we will present algorithms for solving sum and max-min orienteering. The algorithm for sum orienteering was described in [2]. We present it in Section 4.1 for completeness and then we proceed with our algorithm for max-min orienteering, which we present and analyze in Section 4.2. Both algorithms rely on access to an algorithm for the special case with $k = 1$, i.e., single-tour orienteering, which they use as a subroutine. We discussed the best known approximation factors for several models of single-tour orienteering in Section 3.

4.1 Sum Orienteering

A simple greedy algorithm (see Algorithm 2) solves the sum version of the multi-tour orienteering problem almost without any loss to the approximation factor from the single-tour case. More specifically, given an α approximation for the $k = 1$ case, the work in [2] shows that Algorithm 2 achieves a $\beta = 1/\left(1 - e^{-1/\alpha}\right) \approx \alpha + 1/2$ approximation to the optimal solution for the sum objective.

Algorithm 2: GreedySumOrienteering [2]

```
Input: Graph G = (V, E), budget per tour B, number of
       required tours k, start/end node s
Output: Set of tours 𝒫, visit times τ
𝒫 ← ∅
τ ← ∅
for i = 1, 2, ..., k do
    (P, τ^P) ←SingleTourOrienteering(G, B, s)
    𝒫 ← 𝒫 ∪ {P}
    τ ← τ ∪ {τ^P}
    G ←RemoveNodesFromGraph(G, V(P))
return (𝒫, τ)
```

Theorem 4.1. *[2] Given an α approximation algorithm for single-tour orienteering, Algorithm 2 achieves a $\beta = 1/\left(1 - e^{-1/\alpha}\right)$ approximation to $SUM(\mathcal{P}, \tau)$.*

Algorithm 2 does very well with respect to the sum objective, however, the output can be considered poor for a practical travel-planning setting. The reason is that itineraries tend to be front-loaded with the first few days visiting all important attractions, whereas the remaining days are poor in quality. A bad experience on one of the days can have a big impact on the perception of the quality of the entire trip, as a traveler may feel that a whole day of travel was wasted or unnecesarry to begin with. This motivates the study of max-min orienteering, which is the focus of the next section.

4.2 Max-Min Orienteering

In this section, we describe and analyze Algorithm 3, an approximation algorithm for max-min orienteering that loses a factor $\alpha + 2$, with α the approximation factor of single-tour orienteering. The algorithm receives as input the graph G (with costs for the edges and costs, utilities, and time windows for the nodes), the start/end node s, the per-tour budget B, the required number of tours k, and a target value T which all tours should achieve. If the algorithm manages to find k tours with at least value T, it returns them, otherwise it returns an empty solution. Let $\gamma = \alpha + 2$, with α the approximation factor of the single-tour case, and let OPT be the optimal value for $MIN(\mathcal{P}, \tau)$. We will prove that when $T = OPT/\gamma$, the algorithm is guaranteed to return k tours with value at least T, and, hence, achieves a γ approximation to the $MIN(\mathcal{P}, \tau)$ objective. We may run the algorithm multiple times with different guesses for T, using standard techniques (e.g., doubling the guess every time and later running binary search to pinpoint the best achievable value). The pseudocode is given in Algorithm 3. We now summarize the main stages. We will make the simplifying assumption that every node in the graph is reachable within distance $B/2$ from s (or equivalently that any node further than $B/2$ from s is removed from the graph).

Stage 1. In the first stage, the algorithm scans all nodes in the graph and removes every node that has utility at least T. Each one of these nodes, v, gives rise to a tour (s, v, s). Suppose the algorithm finds q such nodes. If $q \geq k$, we return this set of two-node tours. Otherwise we proceed to the following stages, with the assumption that $q < k$.

Algorithm 3: MaxMinOrienteering

```
Input: Graph G = (V, E), budget per tour B, number of
       required tours k, start/end node s, target value T
Output: Set of tours 𝒫, visit times τ
// Stage 1: Extract high utility nodes into tours
𝒫 ← ∅
for ∀v ∈ V : u_v ≥ T do
    (P, τ^P) ←MakeTwoNodeTour(s, v)
    𝒫 ← 𝒫 ∪ {P}
    τ ← τ ∪ {τ^P}
    G ←RemoveNodeFromGraph(G, v)
q ← |𝒫|
if q ≥ k then
    return ({𝒫_1, ..., 𝒫_k}, {τ^{𝒫_1}, ..., τ^{𝒫_k}})
// Stage 2: Iteratively run single-tour and truncate
for i = 1, 2, ..., k − q do
    (P, τ^P) ←SingleTourOrienteering(G, B, s)
    (P, τ^P) ←TruncateTour(P, τ^P, T)
    𝒫 ← 𝒫 ∪ {P}
    τ ← τ ∪ {τ^P}
    G ←RemoveNodesFromGraph(G, V(P))
// Stage 3: Check the output and return
if ∀P ∈ 𝒫, U(P, τ^P) ≥ T then
    return ({𝒫_1, ..., 𝒫_k}, {τ^{𝒫_1}, ..., τ^{𝒫_k}})
else
    return (∅, ∅)
```

Algorithm 4: TruncateTour

```
Input: Tour P, visit times τ^P, target value T
Output: Tour P, visit times τ^P
for ∀v ∈ V(P) do
    V(P) ← V(P) \ {v}
    τ^P ← τ^P \ {τ^P_v}
    if Σ_{v∈V(P)} u_v ≤ 2 · T then
        break
return (P, τ^P)
```

Stage 2. On the remainder of the graph, we run the single-tour algorithm $k - q$ times, and after each run we do the following: (i) keep removing a node from the tour (keeping the visit times of the remaining nodes unchanged) until the tour's value is $2 \cdot T$ or less, and (ii) update the graph by removing the nodes that are ultimately in the tour. Finally, before proceeding with the next iteration, we remove from the graph every node that was picked by our current iteration.

Stage 3. If Stage 2 outputs $k - q$ tours with value at least T each, return the union of tours output by Stages 1 and 2, otherwise return the empty set.

For the remainder of the section we prove the following result.

Theorem 4.2. *Given an α approximation for single-tour orienteering, running Algorithm 3 with $T = OPT/(\alpha + 2)$ achieves an $\alpha + 2$ approximation to $MIN(\mathcal{P}, \tau)$, with OPT the optimal max-min objective value.*

Proof. Let $\gamma = \alpha + 2$. If Stage 1 results in $q \geq k$, all tours have utility at least OPT/γ and, hence, the algorithm achieves a γ approximation. Now suppose $q < k$. We prove the following statement: Let $(\mathcal{P}^*, \tau^*)$ be the solution that optimizes $MIN(\mathcal{P}, \tau)$. At the end of iteration i of Stage 2 in Algorithm 3, the utility of $(\mathcal{P}^*, \tau^*)$ not picked by Algorithm 3 is at least

$$(k-q) \cdot OPT - \frac{2}{\gamma} \cdot i \cdot OPT \geq \left(1 - \frac{2}{\gamma}\right) \cdot (k-q) \cdot OPT. \quad (1)$$

We may see this as follow. After Stage 1 of Algorithm 3, we have removed q nodes. Even if we delete all tours from $(\mathcal{P}^*, \tau^*)$ that have any of these nodes, there will still be at least $k - q$ tours left and each one of them has value at least OPT, by definition. Hence, there is at least $(k - q) \cdot OPT$ utility left. Subsequently, each iteration of Stage 2, extracts value at most $2 \cdot OPT/\gamma$. Hence, the utility left is at least as in (1). We now prove that each of the tours returned by Stage 2 have value at least OPT/γ. By the fact that the utility in $(\mathcal{P}^*, \tau^*)$ not picked by the algorithm is always at least

$$\left(1 - \frac{2}{\gamma}\right) \cdot (k-q) \cdot OPT,$$

it follows that there is always one tour in $(\mathcal{P}^*, \tau^*)$ for which the algorithm has not picked

$$\left(1 - \frac{2}{\gamma}\right) \cdot OPT$$

of its utility. Since the single-tour orienteering algorithm that is used as a subroutine is an α approximation, it follows that the tour returned by single-tour orienteering will have value at least

$$\left(1 - \frac{2}{\gamma}\right) \cdot \frac{OPT}{\alpha} = \frac{OPT}{\gamma}.$$

To complete the proof, it remains to show that the process of truncating a tour will never reduce its utility to less than OPT/γ. Truncating a tour is performed by removing a node at a time, until the utility of the tour drops below $2 \cdot OPT/\gamma$. By the fact that, due to Stage 1, Stage 2 never sees nodes with utility more than OPT/γ, it follows that the last node removal of any tour will not take it to less than OPT/γ utility. □

Corollary 4.3. *For max-min orienteering on undirected graphs with no time windows, Algorithm 3 achieves a $4 + \epsilon$ approximation, for any $\epsilon > 0$. For all other models discussed at the start of the section, it achieves the same asymptotic guarantees as the single day case.*

5 Orienteering in Practice: Planning Itineraries

In this section we focus on the challenges of applying the orienteering model in a practical setting where we wish to plan tourist itineraries for a large number of cities in the world and on evaluating our method and decisions. One of the starting issues is that one needs to define a utility and cost model where the utility and duration of a node as well as other orienteering input parameters are extracted from historical visits and transit data. In Section 5.1, we explain our utility and cost model and how we apply it in two distinct datasets: a large dataset of Google data on 200 cities across the world and a smaller public set of Foursquare check-in data in New York City. We then proceed to experimentally evaluate the performance of our multi-tour algorithms for constructing itineraries in these real world cities in Section 5.2.

5.1 Data Extracted Input: Utility, Costs, and Time Windows

Google dataset. The main dataset we have at our disposal consists of a large number of anonymized historical visits to tourist attractions. The entries to the dataset include an arrival and a departure timestamp. Given this data, we wish to extract the utility of a place of interest (POI) and the typical duration of a visit to that POI. We adopt a clean and simple approach for both.

The utility of a place is expected to be an increasing function of the number of historical visits to the POI. Setting the utility to be equal to the number of historical visits is the simplest such function, but also has a natural interpretation; it is proportional to the probability that a random tourist visits the POI: Assuming no tourist visits the same POI more than once (we may fairly assume that this is a very rare occurrence), this probability is equal to the ratio of the POI's number of visits to the total number of tourists and hence proportional to the number of visits.

Understanding the typical amount of time tourists spend at a POI reduces to picking an aggregate that is a good representative of a set of given durations to the POI. We simply set the duration of a POI to be the median time spent at the place among all historical visits.

The travel times which are used as edge costs in our input to orienteering are given by a set of transit time predictions (provided by Google Maps) between all pairs of POIs and for various forms of transportation (e.g., walking, driving, public transit, any combination of those, etc.). We may fix a specific form of travel (e.g., walking only) or allow ourselves to select the smallest possible transit time between our designated endpoints. For the purposes of our experiments we allow any form of transit and use the quickest available option.

Finally, the node time windows are obtained by available data on the vast majority of POIs around the world (and which also surface on Google Maps). We set a start time for our tours (e.g. 9am) and the start and end of each time window are the corresponding offsets in minutes from the start time.

Foursquare data. We also evaluate our algorithms on a publicly available dataset of Foursquare check-ins [10, 27]. Entries in this dataset include location, category and timestamp. The utility model follows similarly to what we described above. Extracting durations of visits from this data is not possible, so we assign uniformly random durations in $[30, 60]$ minutes to the POIs.

Nature of instances. Given that transit time $t_{i,j}$ from POI i to POI j can differ from the transit time $t_{j,i}$ from POI j to POI i, and also given the presence of opening hours, real world cities manifest as instances of orienteering in directed graphs with time windows. However, the instances are far from adversarial. Transit times $t_{i,j}$ and $t_{j,i}$ can be different but in most cases their difference is small, while opening hours usually appear closer to deadline versions of orienteering (with most POIs open at the start of the tourist's day) or even orienteering without time windows (e.g., for

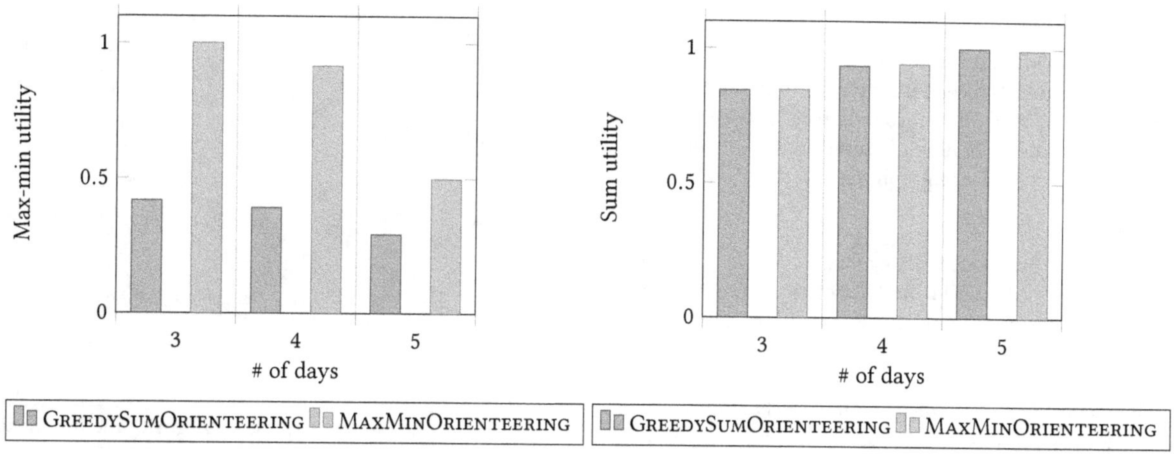

Figure 3: Max-min and sum comparison in New York City using Google data. Values have been normalized so that the largest is 1.

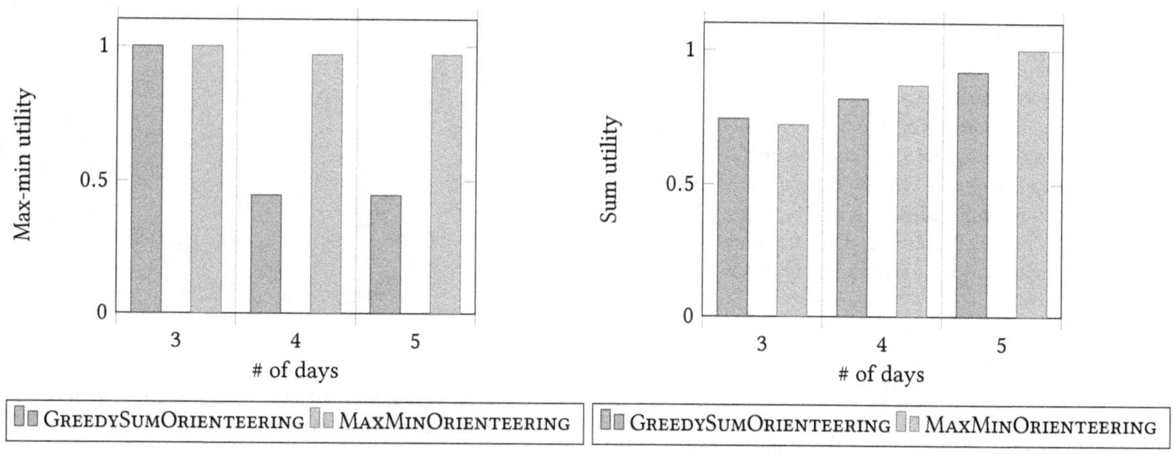

Figure 4: Max-min and sum comparison in New York City using Foursquare data. Values have been normalized so that the largest is 1.

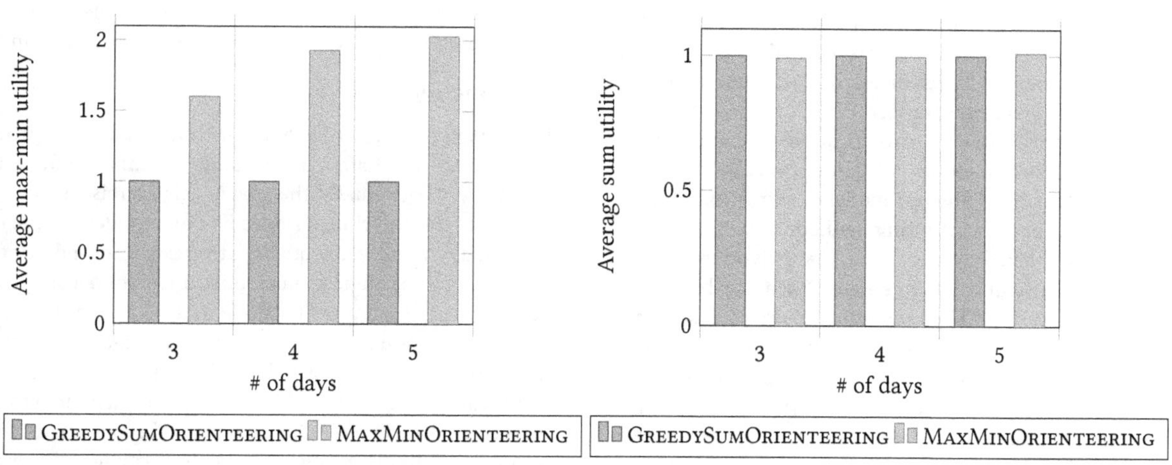

Figure 5: Average normalized max-min and sum utilities of the two algorithms across 200 cities using Google data. (By "normalized", we mean that the utilities in each city have been scaled so that GreedySumOrienteering achieves unit utility.)

10am-3pm itineraries, one would expect almost all POIs in the city to be open). In the evaluation that follows we will examine the performance of our multi-tour generating algorithms in hundreds of real world cities. As explained earlier, theoretical orienteering algorithms that are able to handle opening hours are very time consuming, especially with large graph sizes.

5.2 Evaluation

In this section we will experimentally evaluate our max-min orienteering multi-tour algorithm. Our first set of experiments shows that in real world cities under our utility and duration model, Algorithm 3 (MaxMinOrienteering) significantly improves on the performance of the literature-established multi-tour algorithm, Algorithm 2 (GreedySumOrienteering), with respect to the max-min objective, while incurring virtually no loss with respect to the sum objective. For our experiments, we generate itineraries that begin at 9am each day and have an 8 hour budget. For a starting location, we select some point near the center of the city. We note that, in our actual implementation, MaxMinOrienteering is supplemented by a post-processing stage where tours that still have enough budget left, may spend it and add more nodes via single-tour orienteering. Figures 3 and 4 present the relative performance of the two algorithms with respect to our two objectives in New York City using Google data and Foursquare [13] data respectively. Figure 5 aggregates the comparisons on Google data over 200 cities as follows: For each city, we normalize the utility values, both for max-min and for sum, so that GreedySumOrienteering achieves unit utility. The aggregate values for MaxMinOrienteering are then the averages across all cities.

We observe that our algorithm, MaxMinOrienteering, manages to improve the max-min objective to a large extent. For example, for the case with $k = 5$ days in the itinerary, the max-min solution is improved on average by a factor very close to 2, in comparison to GreedySumOrienteering, the standard multi-tour algorithm proposed in the literature. At the same time, there is virtually no loss with respect to the sum objective. In fact, the precise sum objective values for MaxMinOrienteering in Figure 5 are 0.99 for $k = 3$, 0.996 for $k = 4$, and 1.05 for $k = 5$. This suggests the performance of the two algorithms with respect to the sum objective is so close that, in some sets of instances, MaxMinOrienteering even beats GreedySumOrienteering.

Our second set of experiments consists of an evaluation of the produced itineraries by human raters. These evaluations put to the test both our algorithms and our model of extracting utilities and durations for the nodes. The rating methodology is as follows. Raters are randomly picked from a pool and are given the task of rating a multi-tour itinerary in a given city. Each city has either a two or three day itinerary. The rater has to score each separate day as *good* or *poor* and each city (i.e., multi-day itinerary) as *good*, *mediocre*, or *poor*. Each city is given to three raters. The score of each itinerary and each city is given by a majority rule. For cities, if all three scores are given, the itinerary is considered *mediocre*.

The human rater evaluation is presented in two parts. In the first part, we compare the ratings of our itineraries with two and three day itineraries that have been carefully curated by experts in 59 cities. The results exhibit that our performance is very close to that of travel experts and is presented in Figure 6. In the second part, we let raters evaluate our itineraries in a more challenging set of three day itineraries in 200 cities. The results are presented in Figure 7.

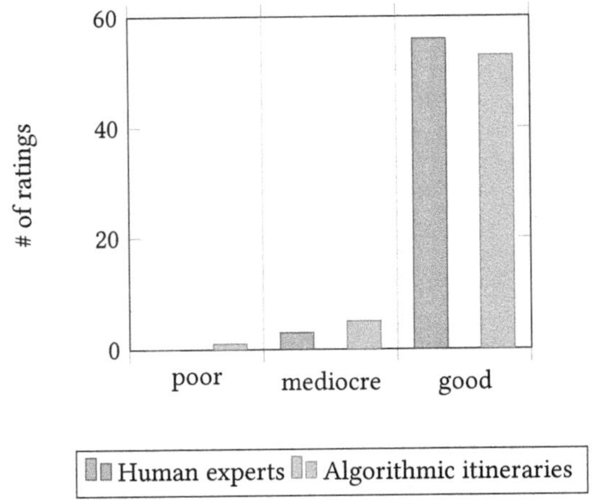

Figure 6: Evaluation by human raters for multi-day itineraries in 59 cities.

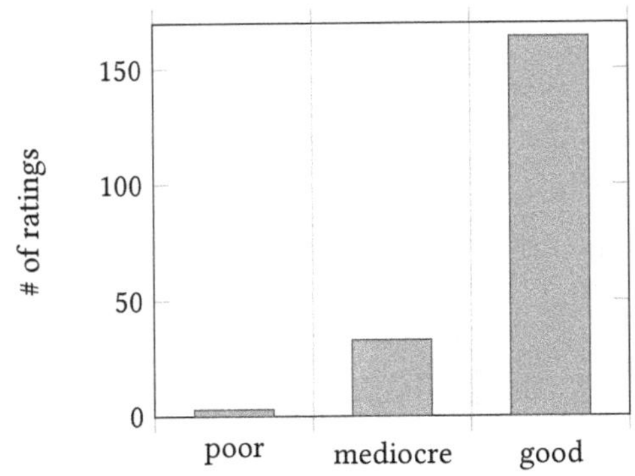

Figure 7: Evaluation of three-day algorithmic itineraries in 200 cities by human raters.

6 Conclusion

In our paper we describe an algorithm that aims to provide high quality multi-day tourist itineraries by maximizing the value of the worst day. Conceptually, the goal of this exercise is two-fold. First, do not let the travel experience be downgraded by the existence of a full day visiting low quality attractions. Second, try to impose an indirect limit on how much one can visit on a single day, thus keeping daily itineraries local and not revisiting the same neighborhoods across days. We complement the algorithm with an input model that uses real world data (Google transit time, hours, and historical visit data and public Foursquare check-ins) to construct orienteering instances. Our two sets of experiments served the purposes of, firstly, evaluating the performance of our max-min algorithm versus a standard baseline (numerical experiments) and, secondly, evaluating our overall approach of obtaining orienteering instances from data and solving them using our algorithm to produce multi-day travel itineraries (human rater evaluation).

Improving travel planning and the actual travel experience from a system perspective is still a fruitful area with many open challenges welcoming future work. On the algorithmic side, we conclude by proposing two interesting extensions. A first interesting direction is to extend our max-min algorithm to the case when the utility of a tour is a submodular function of the visited nodes. The sum algorithm is known to extend to this case but a similar extension of max-min is not straightforward. Another interesting problem is to extend both the sum and max-min algorithms to a setting where itineraries are generated for groups of people and the objective is to keep every one of them as happy as possible, by optimizing the minimum orienteering objective across all travelers.

References

[1] Nikhil Bansal, Avrim Blum, Shuchi Chawla, and Adam Meyerson. Approximation algorithms for deadline-TSP and vehicle routing with time-windows. In *Proceedings of STOC 2004*.

[2] Avrim Blum, Shuchi Chawla, David R. Karger, Terran Lane, Adam Meyerson, and Maria Minkoff. 2007. Approximation Algorithms for Orienteering and Discounted-Reward TSP. *SIAM J. Comput.* 37, 2 (2007), 653–670.

[3] Paolo Bolzoni, Sven Helmer, Kevin Wellenzohn, Johann Gamper, and Periklis Andritsos. Efficient itinerary planning with category constraints. In *Proceedings of SIGSPATIAL 2014*.

[4] Igo Brilhante, Jose Antonio Macedo, Franco Maria Nardini, Raffaele Perego, and Chiara Renso. Where shall we go today?: planning touristic tours with tripbuilder. In *Proceedings of CIKM 2013*.

[5] Igo Ramalho Brilhante, José Antônio Fernandes de Macêdo, Franco Maria Nardini, Raffaele Perego, and Chiara Renso. Where shall we go today? Planning touristic tours with TripBuilder. In *Proceedings of CIKM 2013*.

[6] Kamalika Chaudhuri, Brighten Godfrey, Satish Rao, and Kunal Talwar. Paths, Trees, and Minimum Latency Tours. In *Proceedings of FOCS 2003*.

[7] Chandra Chekuri, Nitish Korula, and Martin Pál. 2012. Improved algorithms for orienteering and related problems. *ACM Trans. Algorithms* 8, 3 (2012), 23:1–23:27.

[8] Chandra Chekuri and Martin Pál. A Recursive Greedy Algorithm for Walks in Directed Graphs. In *Proceedings of FOCS 2005*.

[9] Munmun De Choudhury, Moran Feldman, Sihem Amer-Yahia, Nadav Golbandi, Ronny Lempel, and Cong Yu. Automatic construction of travel itineraries using social breadcrumbs. In *Proceedings of Conference on Hypertext and Hypermedia 2010*.

[10] Géraud Le Falher, Aristides Gionis, and Michael Mathioudakis. Where Is the Soho of Rome? Measures and Algorithms for Finding Similar Neighborhoods in Cities. In *Proceedings of ICWSM 2015*.

[11] Shanshan Feng, Gao Cong, Bo, and Yeow Meng Chee. 2017. POI2Vec: Geographical Latent Representation for Predicting Future Visitors.

[12] Shanshan Feng, Xutao Li, Yifeng Zeng, Gao Cong, Yeow Meng Chee, and Quan Yuan. Personalized Ranking Metric Embedding for Next New POI Recommendation.. In *IJCAI 2015*.

[13] Foursquare. 2017. Foursquare Database API. https://developer.foursquare.com/. (2017).

[14] Zachary Friggstad and Chaitanya Swamy. Compact, Provably-Good LPs for Orienteering and Regret-Bounded Vehicle Routing. In *Proceedings of IPCO 2017*.

[15] Naveen Garg. Saving an epsilon: a 2-approximation for the k-MST problem in graphs. In *Proceedings of STOC 2005*.

[16] Damianos Gavalas, Vlasios Kasapakis, Charalampos Konstantopoulos, Grammati Pantziou, Nikolaos Vathis, and Christos Zaroliagis. 2015. The eCOMPASS multimodal tourist tour planner. *Expert Systems with Applications* 42, 21 (2015), 7303–7316.

[17] Damianos Gavalas, Charalampos Konstantopoulos, Konstantinos Mastakas, and Grammati E. Pantziou. 2014. A survey on algorithmic approaches for solving tourist trip design problems. *J. Heuristics* 20, 3 (2014), 291–328.

[18] Takeshi Kurashima, Tomoharu Iwata, Takahide Hoshide, Noriko Takaya, and Ko Fujimura. Geo topic model: joint modeling of user's activity area and interests for location recommendation. In *Proceedings of WSDM 2013*.

[19] Huayu Li, Yong Ge, and Hengshu Zhu. Point-of-Interest Recommendations: Learning Potential Check-ins from Friends. In *Proceedings of KDD 2016*.

[20] Defu Lian, Cong Zhao, Xing Xie, Guangzhong Sun, Enhong Chen, and Yong Rui. GeoMF: joint geographical modeling and matrix factorization for point-of-interest recommendation. In *Proceedings of KDD 2014*.

[21] Kwan Hui Lim, Jeffrey Chan, Christopher Leckie, and Shanika Karunasekera. 2015. Personalized Tour Recommendation Based on User Interests and Points of Interest Visit Durations.. In *Proceedings of IJCAI 2015*. 1778–1784.

[22] Bin Liu, Yanjie Fu, Zijun Yao, and Hui Xiong. Learning geographical preferences for point-of-interest recommendation. In *Proceedings of KDD 2013*.

[23] Yanchi Liu, Chuanren Liu, Bin Liu, Meng Qu, and Hui Xiong. Unified Point-of-Interest Recommendation with Temporal Interval Assessment. In *Proceedings of KDD 2016*.

[24] Claudio Lucchese, Raffaele Perego, Fabrizio Silvestri, Hossein Vahabi, and Rossano Venturini. How random walks can help tourism. In *Proceedings of ECIR 2012*.

[25] Cristina Ioana Muntean, Franco Maria Nardini, Fabrizio Silvestri, and Ranieri Baraglia. 2015. On learning prediction models for tourists paths. *ACM Transactions on Intelligent Systems and Technology (TIST)* 7, 1 (2015), 8.

[26] Daniele Quercia, Rossano Schifanella, and Luca Maria Aiello. The shortest path to happiness: recommending beautiful, quiet, and happy routes in the city. In *Proceedings of Conference on Hypertext and Social Media 2014*.

[27] Vineeth Rakesh, Niranjan Jadhav, Alexander Kotov, and Chandan K Reddy. Probabilistic Social Sequential Model for Tour Recommendation. In *Proceedings of WSDM 2017*.

[28] Senjuti Basu Roy, Gautam Das, Sihem Amer-Yahia, and Cong Yu. Interactive itinerary planning. In *Proceedings of ICDE 2011*.

[29] Wouter Souffriau and Pieter Vansteenwegen. Tourist trip planning functionalities: State-of-the-art and future. In *Proceedings of International Conference on Web Engineering, 2010*.

[30] Yeran Sun, Hongchao Fan, Mohamed Bakillah, and Alexander Zipf. 2015. Road-based travel recommendation using geo-tagged images. *Computers, Environment and Urban Systems* 53 (2015), 110–122.

[31] Pradeep Varakantham, Hala Mostafa, Na Fu, and Hoong Chuin Lau. DIRECT: A Scalable Approach for Route Guidance in Selfish Orienteering Problems. In *Proceedings of International Conference on Autonomous Agents and Multiagent Systems, AAMAS 2015*.

[32] Xiaoting Wang, Christopher Leckie, Jeffrey Chan, Kwan Hui Lim, and Tharshan Vaithianathan. Improving Personalized Trip Recommendation by Avoiding Crowds. In *Proceedings of CIKM 2016*.

[33] Zhijun Yin, Liangliang Cao, Jiawei Han, Jiebo Luo, and Thomas S. Huang. Diversified Trajectory Pattern Ranking in Geo-tagged Social Media. In *Proceedings of SDM 2011*.

[34] Hyoseok Yoon, Yu Zheng, Xing Xie, and Woontack Woo. 2012. Social itinerary recommendation from user-generated digital trails. *Personal and Ubiquitous Computing* 16, 5 (2012), 469–484.

[35] Yan-Tao Zheng, Zheng-Jun Zha, and Tat-Seng Chua. 2012. Mining Travel Patterns from Geotagged Photos. *ACM TIST* 3, 3 (2012), 56:1–56:18.

Unsubscription: A Simple Way to Ease Overload in Email

Iftah Gamzu
iftah.gamzu@yahoo.com
Amazon, Israel

Liane Lewin-Eytan
lliane@amazon.com
Amazon, Israel

Natalia Silberstein
natalias@oath.com
Yahoo Research, Israel

ABSTRACT

The constant growth of machine-generated mail, which today consists of more than 90% of non-spam mail traffic, is a major contributor to *information overload in email*, where users become overwhelmed with a flood of messages from commercial entities. A large part of this traffic is often junk mail that the user would prefer not to receive. Surprisingly, nearly 95% of this traffic is in fact solicited by the users themselves in the form of subscriptions to mailing services. These subscriptions are many times unintentional. Although unsubscription option from such services is enforced by commercial laws, it is hardly actually used by users.

We perform a large scale study of *unsubscribable* traffic, namely, messages that provide unsubscription option to users. We consider users behavior over such traffic in Yahoo Web mail service, and demonstrate a significant gap between users low interest in this traffic, and their lack of active behavior in decreasing its load. We conjecture that the cause of this gap is the lack of an efficient and easily accessible mechanism that would help users to unsubscribe. We validate our conjecture with an online large scale experiment, where we provide users with a novel mail feature for managing unsubscribable traffic, based on personalized recommendations. The experiment demonstrates the imminent need that exists for such a mechanism.

KEYWORDS

Machine-Generated Mail; Mail Mining; Unsubscription Recommendations

ACM Reference Format:
Iftah Gamzu, Liane Lewin-Eytan, and Natalia Silberstein. 2018. Unsubscription: A Simple Way to Ease Overload in Email. In *WSDM 2018: WSDM 2018: The Eleventh ACM International Conference on Web Search and Data Mining, February 5–9, 2018, Marina Del Rey, CA, USA.* ACM, New York, NY, USA, 9 pages. https://doi.org/10.1145/3159652.3159698

1 INTRODUCTION

Machine-generated emails, which comprise today more than 90% of non-spam Web mail traffic, have been the subject of a line of studies during the last few years [4, 16, 18]. These messages are sent at large scale across the user population, and vary in importance: from critical invoices, flight itineraries, and e-tickets, to promotions or newsletters that will remain unread by most users. Machine-generated traffic defines the nature of Web Mail today, and is the source of its growth. Indeed, email volume keeps growing, with an increase of 5% in worldwide emails during the past two years and a prediction of 4.4% increase per year up to 2021 [33, 34].

As a direct consequence, mail users are becoming overwhelmed with a flood of messages generated by organizations and commercial entities. Those are often junk mail that the user would prefer not to receive. Surprisingly, as we show in this paper, nearly 95% of the machine-generated emails are explicitly solicited by the users themselves in the form of subscription to mailing services. Importantly, the user might not even be aware of having subscribed to some of those list in the past. According to a user study from 2015 [27], nearly a quarter of all mailing list subscriptions are unintentional. For example, the result of auto-subscription of users to mailing lists. Other frequent reasons that lead to subscriptions by user interest in getting information about deals and special offers, news updates, and access to interesting articles and content.

A trivial yet important observation is that mailing lists that allow subscriptions also allow unsubscriptions. In fact, providing the user with the possibility to unsubscribe from such services is required by the *CAN-SPAM Act*, which is a law that "establishes requirements for commercial messages, gives recipients the right to have you stop emailing them, and spells out tough penalties for violations" [2]. Moreover, the unsubscribe option has also been defined and formalized in dedicated IETF RFCs [21, 23]. In particular, these RFCs define a *List Unsubscribe* header, which is an optional chunk of text that email publishers and marketers can include in the header portion of the messages they send. It is a recommendation aimed for senders to reduce complaints, improve deliverability (by avoiding spam filters that often take this header into consideration), and improve the experience of subscribers. In most cases, the unsubscribe option is presented to the user as an unsubscription link within the message body, which points to a designated unsubscription page in which unsubscription can be completed. We refer to messages of this type as *unsubscribable.*

Understanding the properties of this traffic is a major step towards devising methods and tools for easing information overload in email [13, 19, 40] caused by irrelevant messages. In the first part of the paper, we address this need by conducting a large-scale study of real mail traffic of Yahoo Web mail service. We focus on unsubscribable traffic and users' behavior over this traffic. Notably, although 85% of the entire mail traffic is unsubscribable, and despite the fact that more than 90% of this traffic remains unread, the unsubscribe option is triggered for less than 2% of all mailing lists. Our study also demonstrates that unsubscriptions are performed by only 3% of the users. One may argue that spam votes are used as proxy to mark and filter irrelevant traffic. Although the spam

---

This research was done while all authors were associated with Yahoo Research, Israel.

WSDM 2018, February 5–9, 2018, Marina Del Rey, CA, USA

ACM ISBN 978-1-4503-5581-0/18/02...$15.00
https://doi.org/10.1145/3159652.3159698

action has a higher usage, it is still triggered by only 5% of the users with respect to 3% of mailing lists.

These observations clearly show an unexplained phenomenon, demonstrating low user interest in many mailing lists without consistent active behavior to decrease the load created by those lists. This may be the result of a lack of a proper mechanism that would allow the user to efficiently stop such traffic. In contrast to popular mail actions, like read, reply, delete and mark-spam, unsubscribe is not a *mail-native* action. That is, it is not provided by the mail service, but rather by the sender of the message. Although the CAN-SPAM act requires that users are given a "clear and conspicuous explanation of how they can opt out", the unsubscribe link is often rather hard to find, appearing in small fonts in a marginal location within the message. In addition, it usually requires more steps to be performed by the user to complete the unsubscription, turning it to a cumbersome operation that users do not generally initiate.

In the second part of our work, we present a novel mail feature, providing the users with a comprehensive and convenient mechanism for managing unsubscribable traffic. Our solution is based on personalized recommendations for unsubscribing from mailing lists that are likely irrelevant for the user. We validate our solution in an online experiment conducted in Yahoo Web mail service, comprising millions of users. This experiment demonstrates that there is an imminent need for a mechanism that can help users unsubscribe from mailing lists and decrease overload in email.

The contributions of our work are thus threefold: (1) we provide an analysis of unsubscribable traffic, as well as users engagement with such traffic, (2) we develop a machine learning approach for personalized ranking of unsubscription recommendations, and (3) we perform a large-scale online experiment in Yahoo Web mail service, surfacing our unsubscription mechanism to users and validating its effectiveness. The rest of this paper is organized as follows. Section 2 covers related work in the context of mail management and overload in mail. Section 3 characterizes unsubscribable traffic and discuss its identification. Section 4 provides a study of unsubscribable traffic and related behavioral patterns of users. In Section 5, we tackle the problem of computing personalized unsubscription recommendations, while in Section 6, we discuss our online experiment. Finally, conclusions are provided in Section 7.

2 RELATED WORK

Mail has been a fertile ground for research in data science during the last two decades. A lot of work has been done, spanning a wide range of use cases, studies and applications, including mail prioritization, mail classification, mail search, analysis of mail behavioral patterns, and more. Many of these studies are related to the problem of mailbox management under overload in email [13, 19, 40].

Wang et al. [37, 38] develop a prioritization framework for broadcast emails, which are similar in nature to unsubscribable traffic. However, their approach is inherently different than our approach which makes effort to remove irrelevant traffic rather than to prioritize it. Mail prioritization and management, which study solutions for assisting users in processing their inbox, have been investigated in many papers [1, 12, 14, 15, 32, 35, 36]. The work of Aberdeen et al. [1] deals with the notion of message importance, based on the propensity that a user will perform specific actions on the message. Di Castro et al. [15] study different mail actions and devise a learning framework for predicting them. One action attracting much attention is the reply action, which has been the focus of several papers [17, 26, 31, 36, 41]. Other works such as [7, 20] consider mail as a task management resource, and study email behavior over messages that relate to tasks or events.

Classification of mail traffic as a tool to assist users has also been given a lot of attention. Multiple classification methods have been proposed for automatically assigning messages to pre-defined folders or labels [5, 18, 24, 25, 39]. One specifically important classification task is the distinctions between human and machine-generated traffic [4]. This fundamental distinction underlies our work for analyzing the largest type of machine-generated mail.

Mail search is another relevant line of research as an essential mean to efficiently access relevant information and cope with the growing volume of mail traffic. It is the default discovery paradigm for retrieving past mail, instead of exploiting organizational means such as folders, which are hardly used [9]. As such, it has attracted attention during the last few years, both in the context of ranking and of query suggestions [8–11]. The works of [3, 30] also contribute to this theme by providing a general study of mail search, activities that users perform over email, and their search behavior.

Most of the papers mentioned above attempt to alleviate the problem of information overload in email through prioritization, classification, search, and more. Yet, to the best of our knowledge, there is no work that directly considers unsubscribable traffic, or leverages the ability that users have to simply unsubscribe from superfluous mailing lists.

3 IDENTIFYING UNSUBSCRIBABLE TRAFFIC

A key concept in this paper is that of a *mailing list*. A mailing list is a collection of email addresses, also called subscribers, used for the widespread distribution of some information. As the list of subscribers is not publicly available, a natural question regards the identification of the mailing list which underlies a given email message. Although there are formal suggestions for labeling messages with a mailing list identifier [22], in practice, most guidelines are not followed, and thus identifying the underlying mailing list is a non-trivial task. There are proprietary solutions that are highly technical, but simple heuristics also provide good identification guarantees. One primary example is to associate a mailing list with its mass sender [37, 38]. This is also the approach we follow in this paper. Namely, we regard the *subscription entity* as the email address of the sender of an unsubscribable mail.

We identify a message as *unsubscribable* using two ways: we either identify unsubscription links within the message body, or establish that it has a *List Unsubscribe* header [21]. Note that this header can either contain an email address link (e.g., "mailto:..."), which can trigger an unsubscription mail message on behalf of the user, or an http link (e.g., "http://..."), which can transfer the user to a designated unsubscription page of the underlying entity. We refer to the first option as *email-based method* for unsubscription, while the latter option is referred to as *page-based method.*

While identifying the header part is easy, discovering unsubscription links in an email body is a more challenging task that requires applying classification techniques. We thus developed a classification mechanism for identifying such unsubscription links in the messages body. The classification is based on multiple features, like relevant indicative words (such as "unsub" or "optout") in the link itself as well as in the text appearing in its close proximity, link location within the message, and more. Note that it is important to achieve high precision in this task to avoid misclassification of links. Therefore, we tuned our classification mechanism such that it achieves precision of more than 0.98 with recall of 0.88. Due to space limitations, we omit the details of this mechanism.

We analyzed the entire inbound traffic of Yahoo Web mail service, and observed that about 75% of all traffic contains a List Unsubscribe header. Furthermore, more than 10% of inbound traffic that does not contain such a header, contains unsubscription links in the message body. Taking into account that about 90% of today's email traffic is machine-generated [16], and that unsubscribable messages clearly belong to this type of traffic, one can infer that almost 95% of machine-generated traffic is unsubscribable.

Figure 1 presents the overall inbound traffic with respect to the two above-mentioned types of unsubscribable traffic: messages that have a List Unsubscribe header and messages that contain only unsubscribe links in their body (no header). Note that the data was collected over a period of four weeks, from February 23, 2017 to March 22, 2017, and the values are normalized with respect to the maximum daily value of unsubscribable traffic having a List Unsubscribe header. As can be seen, the amount of unsubscribable traffic with no List Unsubscribe header is considerably smaller compared to the traffic that has such a header. This implies that such unsubscribable traffic has only a small impact on all computations, and does not change the general observed trends.

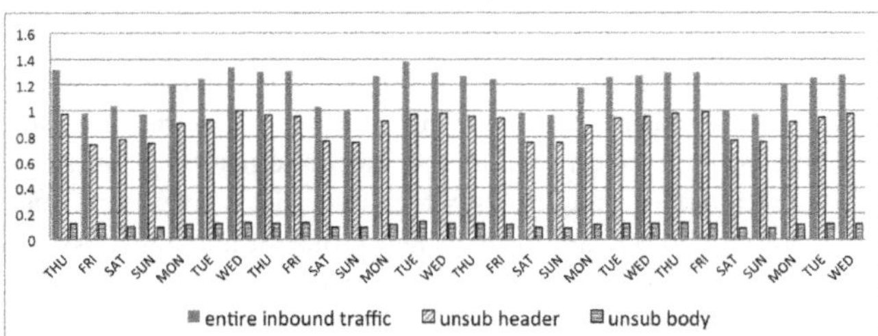

Figure 1: Normalized volume of inbound traffic, unsubscribable traffic with List Unsubscribe header, and unsubscribable traffic with only unsubscribe body links.

4 ANALYSIS OF UNSUBSCRIBABLE TRAFFIC

We provide a large-scale study of unsubscribable traffic and the behavior of users on that traffic.[1] We analyze the inbound traffic of a Yahoo Web service over a period of 28 days, from February 23, 2017 to March 22, 2017. We consider tens of millions of users that were active during this period, namely, performed at least one action over those four weeks (e.g., message read, message delete, search). The inbound traffic of those users originated in above 40M unique senders from about 3M domains.

[1]We note that all processes performed as part of our analysis were conducted under full privacy preservation in accordance with the mailing service privacy policy.

We begin by presenting a high-level analysis of unsubscribable traffic. We first focus on users subscriptions. Figure 2 exhibits the percentage of users as a function of their number of subscriptions, and the volume of unsubscribable messages they received. Note that a user that receives at least one unsubscribable message from a subscription entity is assumed to be subscribed to that entity. As expected, we observe a long-tail distribution in both cases, with 55% of users receiving emails from more than 20 subscription entities, and 50% of users receiving more than 150 emails over the analysis time period. This observation reaffirms that unsubscribable mail is a major contributor to information overload in email across the general user population.

We turn our view to the domains from which unsubscribable traffic originates. Table 1 presents the 5 domains that send unsubscribable messages to the highest number of users, as well as the 5 domains that have the highest number of users clicking on unsubscription links in their messages[2]. If unsubscription was a uniformly-random process then the top domains by number of subscribed users would have also appeared as top domains by unsubscription clicks. As can be seen, this is not true in general. This is rather expected as there are multiple factors that influence users tendency to click on unsubscription links. In what follows, we examine different user properties and actions in mail, and analyze their correlation with subscription and unsubscription behavior. This analysis establishes the basis for our unsubscription recommendations method, which is presented later on.

Subscribed users reach	Unsubscription clicks
facebookmail.com	facebookmail.com
linkedin.com	linkedin.com
twitter.com	r.groupon.com
mail.instagram.com	reply.bronto.com
explore.pinterest.com	yahoogroups.com

Table 1: Top 5 domains with respect to (1) the number of subscribed users, and (2) the number of users clicking on unsubscription links.

4.1 Unsubscribable traffic by user groups

We analyze unsubscribable traffic with respect to different user demographic sectors and activity levels. We consider four levels of activity, defined by the number of days that a user has been active during a month. A user that performed at least one action in mail during a day is regarded as active during that day. The four levels of activity are L = "Low", if the user was active between 1 and 3 days inclusive, M = "Medium" if she was active between 4 and 14 days, H = "High" for 15 to 25 days of activity, and U = "Ultra" for 26 days or more. With respect to demographics, we partition the users into seven age groups (namely, younger than 18, 18–24, 25–34, 35–44, 45–54, 55–64, and older than 65), and two gender groups (that is, men and women). Note that the sizes of groups in each partition vary. Still, as each group is large enough (consisting of millions of users), statistic differences between groups are meaningful.

[2]Note that we treat all unsubscription clicks equally since we generally cannot track the unsubscription process that follows them. In particular, we cannot know if they resulted in unsubscription or some other update in the subscription preferences.

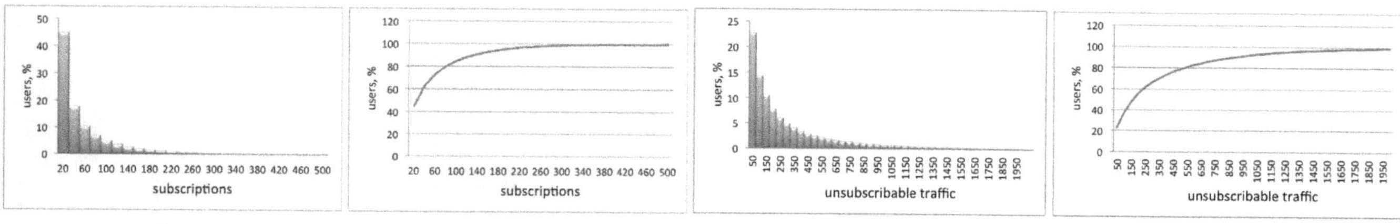

Figure 2: (a,b) PDF and CDF of users as a function of the number of unique subscriptions, (c,d) PDF and CDF of users as a function of their amount of unsubscribable traffic.

Figure 3 exhibits the mean volume of unsubscribable traffic and mean number of subscriptions for each group of users. Note that presented values are the result of normalizing the observed mean values with the corresponding means of all users, where the average user receives 328 unsubscribable emails from 50 senders. Interestingly, we observe that women receive 1.6x more unsubscribable messages from 1.4x more subscription entities, compared to men. Also, older users tend to receive more unsubscribable messages from more subscription entities. In particular, the youngest group of users receives about 4x less emails from about 5x less subscription entities than the oldest group of users. User activity level does not exhibit a clear trend with unsubscribable traffic, although there are clear differences between the different groups. All these observations indicate that different user groups have different subscription and management patterns which are of importance for the task of unsubscription recommendations.

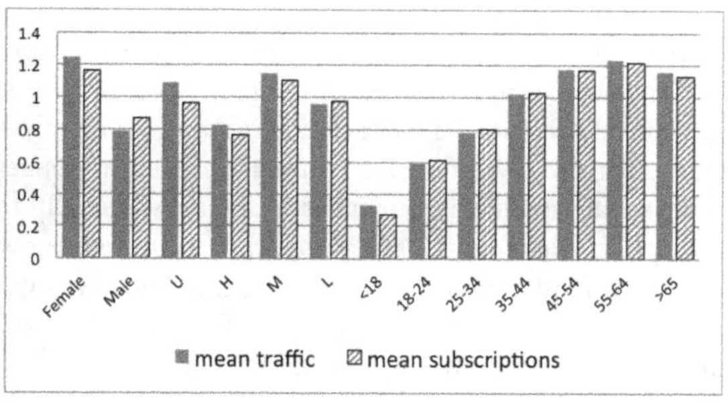

Figure 3: Normalized mean number of unsubscribable messages and subscriptions for different user groups.

To further emphasize this point, we focus on the gender group, and analyze subscriptions with respect to sender domains from few categories. Two examples of domain categories are shopping and travel. We follow Grbovic et al. [18] approach for domains categorization. Figure 4 presents the percentage of women and men that receive unsubscribable traffic from few popular domains in the *shopping* category. As can be seen, almost all domains have a significantly larger portion of subscribed women, indicating a fundamental difference in subscriptions between genders. Interestingly, a similar phenomenon occurs for popular domains in the *travel* category. For popular domains in the *social* and *career* categories, the percentage of subscribed women and men is essentially the same, with few exceptions, like `pinterest.com` and `linkedin.com` which have more tendency towards women and men subscriptions, respectively.

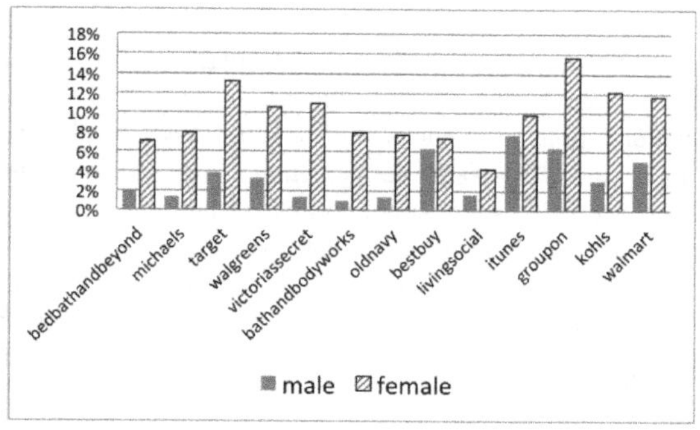

Figure 4: Percentage of women and men that are subscribed to popular shopping sites.

4.2 User actions on unsubscribable traffic

We now turn our attention to the user side. We consider unsubscriptions done by clicking on unsubscription body links as well as native mark-spam actions. Spam actions are of particular interest in our context since they could potentially reflect a similar intent of users that like to stop receiving irrelevant traffic. During the analyzed period of time, only 3% of the users clicked on unsubscription links. Those links were associated with only 2% of all subscription entities. In comparison, on the same time period, about 5% of the users used the spam action over 3% of the subscription entities.

Figure 5 exhibits a comparison between the average daily number of clicks on unsubscription body links and spam votes. Note that the values were normalized by the minimum daily number of unsubscription clicks. One can see that the daily number of spam votes is significantly higher than the number of unsubscription clicks. This difference could be explained by the ease of usage of mark-spam, which is a native mail action inherently provided by the mail service. On the contrary, unsubscription links require the user to open the email and look for an unsubscription link, which is sometimes not easy to find. This hypothesis is validated by our online experiment in Section 6.

We further compare unsubscription clicks and spam votes with respect to the different user demographic sectors and activity levels described before. Figure 6 presents the average number of unsubscription clicks and spam votes for the different user groups. The

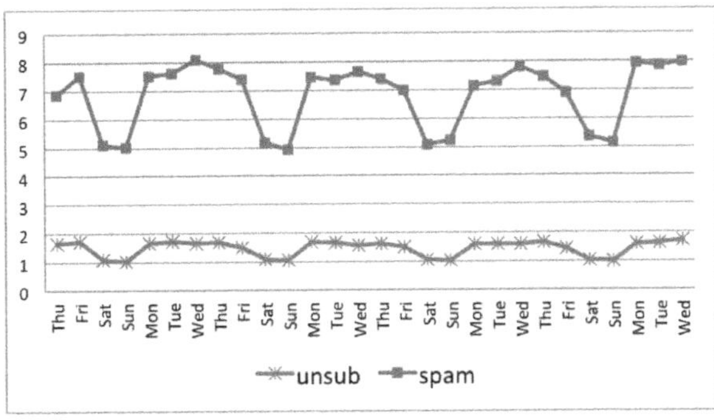

Figure 5: Normalized average daily number of unsubscription clicks and spam votes.

presented values are the result of a normalization by the mean value of unsubscription clicks for the entire user set. The difference between unsubscription clicks and spam votes can be observed for all groups. Figure 7 presents the percentage of users that performed unsubscription clicks and spam votes for each user group. Notice that more users performed spam votes than unsubscription clicks across all user groups. However, the gap here is smaller than before. This implies, in conjunction with Figure 6, that the fact that users perform more spam votes than unsubscription clicks is not only true for the entire user population but also when considering different user groups. This substantiates again that spam actions are more natural in the mail context.

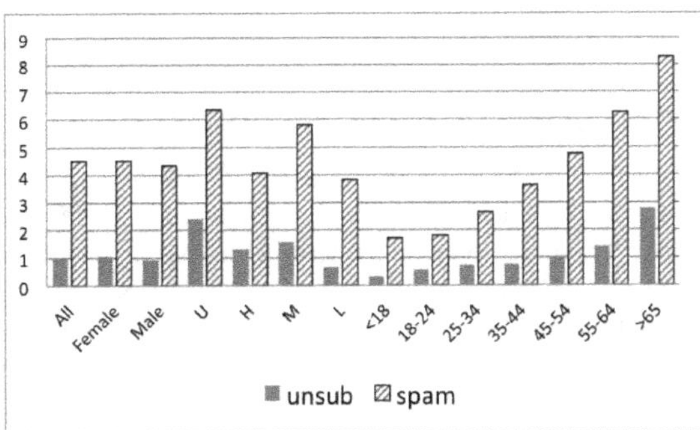

Figure 6: Normalized average number of unsubscription clicks and spam votes for different user groups.

We also consider few additional mail actions, namely, read, delete, and delete-without-read. Note that delete-without-read is simply a delete message action that was not preceded with the message being read [15]. It seems intuitive to assume that irrelevant messages should be less prone to be read and more prone to be deleted-without-read. Table 2 shows a comparison between the above-mentioned actions for unsubscribable traffic and traffic that does not contain unsubscription options. We refer to the latter traffic as "non-unsub". Remark that the table shows the percentage of messages that had each of the actions. As can be observed, only 9% of unsubscribable messages were read, while 13% of the messages were deleted without being read. Comparing this with the percentages

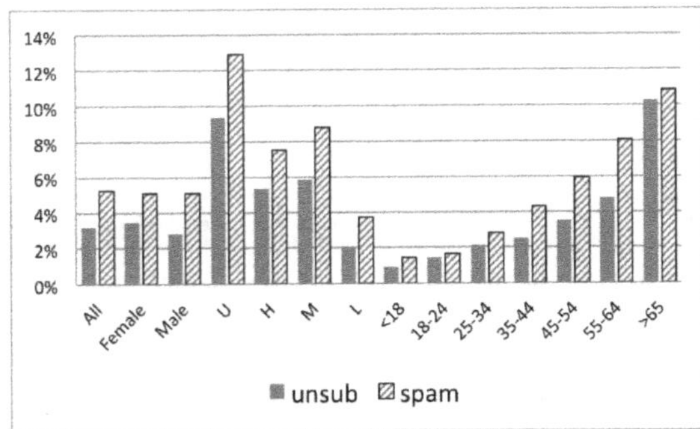

Figure 7: Percentage of users that performed unsubscription click and spam vote for different user groups.

for non-unsubscribable traffic, one can infer that unsubscribable traffic is considerably less relevant for users, thus, contributing to overload in email. In addition, those high-level statistics hint that those actions may help to identify subscriptions that are less relevant for a user.

action	unsub	non-unsub
Read	9%	23%
Delete	14%	14%
Delete-without-read	13%	11%

Table 2: Percentage of mail actions on unsubscribable and non-unsubscribable traffic.

To further emphasize the last point, we focus on several popular domains that had a high number of recipients (i.e., above 1M) in the considered time period. We selected those domains from few different categories. We decided to focus on such mass-senders to decrease the variance in our measurements, especially that of unsubscription clicks which are quite scarce. Figure 8 shows the average traffic load as well as the average number of read, delete, spam, and unsubscription actions per user for each of the selected domains. The average traffic load is defined to be the overall number of emails sent from a domain divided by its number of recipients. Note that the values in each curve line are the result of normalization with respect to the minimum (domain) value associated with that line. Also notice that the domains are sorted according to a non-increasing traffic load.

As can be seen, the traffic load and delete curves exhibit a similar trend, while the trend of the read and spam curves is also similar, but different than the former one. This is somewhat surprising since one may expect that a domain that sends more emails to users would get more reads, deletes and spam votes from the users. Perhaps the reason for this discrepancy resides in the category of the domain and its quality. For example, `facebookmail` has higher read ratio than `groupon` and `livingsocial` since its messages are social notifications while the others are of deals and coupons. We believe that this requires further investigation. Having noted that, a more important observation is that all the curves, including the unsubscription clicks, show a decreasing trend in general. This implies that the average load as well as the user actions are positively

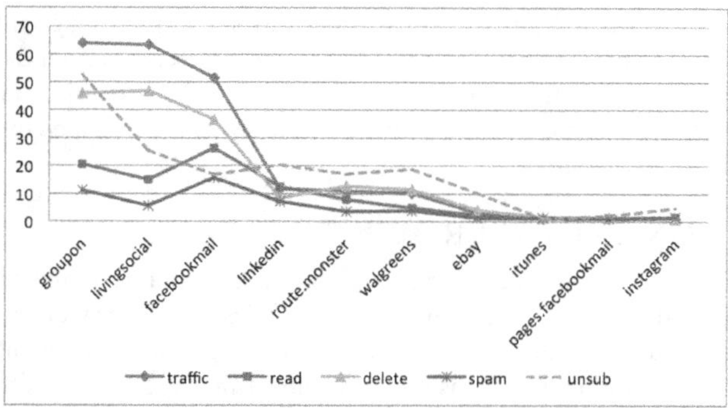

Figure 8: Normalized average traffic load and number of read, delete, spam, and unsubscribe actions. Note that we removed prefixes and suffixes from the domain names.

correlated with unsubscription clicks. Thus, they can be valuable features in predicting the tendency of a user to unsubscribe.

5 UNSUBSCRIPTION RECOMMENDATIONS

We have demonstrated through data analysis that unsubscribable mail is a major contributor to information overload in email across the general user population. Furthermore, we observed that despite the noticeable load that those emails induce, users are not inclined to actively unsubscribe from them. We conjecture that the main reason for this gap is the lack of a simple and efficient mechanism for unsubscription. To bridge this gap, we believe that one should create a native unsubscription mechanism within the mail service.

In this section, we develop a machine learning recommendation approach (backend) that can support such a native unsubscription feature in mail (frontend). This mail feature is presented in the next section. Note that the data-based insights identified in the previous section guide the development of many of the features used by our recommendation approach.

5.1 Problem and data

We formalize the unsubscription recommendation task as a ranking problem. This formalization is motivated by our mail feature from Section 6. This feature presents several unsubscription recommendations to a user. As a consequence, our objective is to provide an ordered list of all the subscription entities of a user according to the propensity of the user to unsubscribe from each of them. Notice that this task does not require to accurately predict the probability of unsubscription for each entity, but rather their relative order.

The data that is used to build and evaluate our models consist of users' inbound mail traffic, their native mail actions, and their clicks on unsubscription links within email bodies. Note that the unsubscription clicks are also the events our models need to predict, i.e., the supervision signal. Our data is collected from millions of users over approximately a month. As mail is a temporally ordered collection, we split the data into train and test by time, and not randomly. Specifically, we use the data of the first three weeks for training and tuning the models, and the remaining week for testing. This is common practice (see, e.g., [41]) to prevent an unrealistic setting in which future information is used to predict past user behavior. We like to emphasize that our test set consists of more than 50K users that clicked on unsubscription links and had more than 50 subscription entities on average. As a result, the prediction task is not trivial.

5.2 Learning and evaluation

We experiment with few machine learning algorithms. Nevertheless, since the focus of our work is on the identification and selection of features that improve the prediction, and not on the optimization of machine learning techniques, we decide to report only the experimental results of a logistic regression (LR) method. This method first predicts the probability that each user would like to unsubscribe from any of her subscription entities. Then, all the entities of each user are sorted in a non-increasing order according to the predictions. We compare this approach with a naïve random ranking method, and a manually-defined baseline heuristic that is inspired by our data analysis. Note that due to the online nature by which our data is generated and its extremely large size, we utilized the highly-scalable Vowpal Wabbit implementation [28, 29], which works well in conjunction with MapReduce architecture.

Features. Our analysis in Section 4 identified several factors that are likely to help predicting unsubscription probability. We believe it is beyond the scope of this paper to provide an exhaustive list of all the features utilized by our models as this number is in the thousands. We describe our general hierarchical design approach and identify some of the more valuable features. Those are also the features that were utilized by our strong baseline heuristic.

At the most intuitive level, we develop a *hierarchical features construction*. Namely, for each subscription entity, we collect features at several user group levels. At the lowest level of this hierarchy, we collect features that are personal for each user. These features capture properties of the traffic between the entity under consideration and the user, and the user behavior on that traffic. For example, we maintain the number of emails that were sent to the user by the entity, the implied daily load of this traffic on the user, the number of times that the user read, deleted, or performed any other action on those emails, the ratio of emails that were deleted-without-read, and more. At the highest level of the hierarchy, we collect similar aggregative features with respect to the entire user population. These features are essentially ones that capture the global properties of the subscription entity. For instance, we maintain the relative ratio of users that unsubscribed from the entity, the portion of emails that were marked spam, and more. In a similar way, we collect features at additional mid-level user groups such as demographic and activity groups. For the purpose of prediction, the features that represent the interaction between the user and subscription entity are a concatenation of all the features of the groups that include the user. For instance, if a user is a 28 years old female who visits the mail service every day then her feature vector will be the concatenation of her personal features with respect to the underlying entity, the entity features associated with the female group, the 25-34 age group, the Ultra-activity group, and finally, the global features of the entity. This approach allows us to capture the intricacies related to the different subscription, management and unsubscription patterns of different users and user groups.

The features that we collect at each level are essentially the same. For example, the feature that accounts for the relative ratio of all users that unsubscribed from an entity (at the highest level of the hierarchy) reduces to a binary feature indicating whether a user unsubscribed from an entity in the past (at the lowest level of the hierarchy). As noted before, we collect features relating to the traffic between the entity and the users, the behavior of the users on that traffic, and additional complex combinations of those features. Examples of traffic-related features are the number of emails that the entity sent to the user group, temporal features such as the days and times that those emails were sent, and content features such as statistics relating to the length of the subject line and content of the emails. Examples of behavioral-related features are the number of various actions that users in the group performed over emails of the entity, along with their temporal aspect. Examples of complex features include the ratio of emails deleted-without-read for the user group, and the ratio of users that already unsubscribed from the entity. Additional features were obtained in similar fashion to recent papers [6, 18, 41]. Overall, our hierarchical approach had several thousands of features.

Baselines. We compare our approach against two baselines:
(1) Random – This method randomly generates a ranking of all the unsubscription entities for each user.
(2) Data-driven – This manually-defined method makes a decision based on few features that have been identified by our data analysis as relatively highly-correlative with unsubscriptions. Specifically, for each user, the method first sorts the entities into the following ordered classes:

- Entities from which the user unsubscribed (or tried to) in the past.
- Entities with mail messages that the user marked as spam.
- Entities for which at least half of the messages were deleted by the user without being read.
- Entities for which any other number of messages were deleted by the user without being read.
- All remaining entities.

Then, the order inside each of those classes is defined by the global unsubscription ratio of the entities.

Experimental results. We analyze the results of our approach compared with the two baseline methods. As we are treating this problem as a ranking problem, we consider standard information retrieval ranking metrics, namely, Mean Average Precision (MAP), Mean Reciprocal Rank (MRR), Area under the ROC curve (AUC), and Normalized Discounted Cumulative Gain (NDCG). The results are presented in the following table.

Method	MAP	MRR	AUC	NDCG
Random	0.1208	0.1264	0.4958	0.2842
Data-driven	0.3562	0.3690	0.8354	0.4985
LR	**0.4426**	**0.4612**	**0.8999**	**0.5731**

As can be seen, our logistic regression-based approach outperforms both baseline methods. For example, it improves over the MRR and the AUC of the data-driven baseline by almost 25% and 8%, respectively. This is very encouraging as we applied a relatively simple learning machinery. It is also important to notice that the data-driven baseline is surprisingly strong, improving greatly over the random method. This proves the effectiveness of our data analysis and feature selection. It also reaffirms the strength of our machine learning solution, which significantly outperformed over this strong baseline.

6 ONLINE EXPERIMENT

We discuss our online experiment for unsubscription recommendations and some of its user engagement metrics. The experiment was conducted on Yahoo Web mail service over a period of one month and involved few millions of users. Our primarily focus is on the experimental setting and results. We do not discuss its internals, and in particular, the backend recommendation service. This service was based on the insights and identification methods that were presented in the previous sections with some light modifications required for matters of productization.

6.1 The setting

The online experiment ran over a period of one month from March 28, 2017 to April 28, 2017, and included few millions of users. In the experiment, users were presented with a pop-up dialog that consisted of at most 5 unsubscription recommendations from their collection of subscriptions. Figure 9 exhibits this dialog. The user could then select to unsubscribe from any number of those recommendations. For each selected recommendation, the user was prompted for approval, before additional steps for final unsubscription were made by the system. The system then sent an unsubscription email on the behalf of the user (*email-based method*) or transfered her to the designated unsubscription page of the underlying entity to complete the action (*page-based method*). The decision of which unsubscription method to use was conditioned by whether email-based unsubscription was supported or not. The dialog was presented to a user at most once a day, and was triggered only if the user performed a *batch-delete* action, which consists of deleting several emails at the same time. The batch-delete action has been identified by internal user studies as an action that indicates that the user is more inclined towards cleaning and managing her inbox.

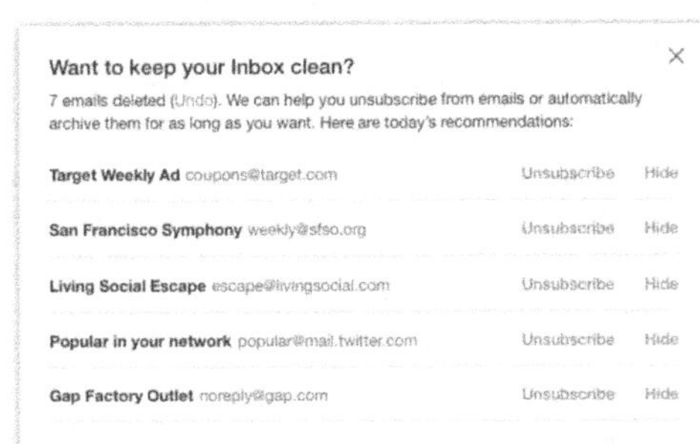

Figure 9: The unsubscription dialog.

The unsubscription recommendations were powered by a personalized recommendations service which was updated every day with respect to new inbound traffic and user actions. The service is based on the insights and techniques that were presented in the previous sections. As a general rule, top recommendations were presented, that is, the subscriptions that the service predicted as the ones that the user most likely wants to stop receiving. There were two practical adjustments applied to this general rule. First, subscriptions whose emails were part of the batch-delete action got some boost to their score. This adjustment most commonly led to the presentation of those subscriptions in the dialog. Second, subscriptions that were already presented to the user in the past got some reduction in their score. This adjustment effectively enabled rotation among recommendations, gradually showing also lower-ranked recommendations (instead of higher ranked recommendations that were not clicked by the user).

6.2 Online engagement metrics

The primary objective of the experimental feature was to mitigate the process of unsubscribing and reduce overload in email. As a result, we focus our attention on user engagement with respect to the feature. Note that we concentrated on one experimental setting and did not evaluate the influence that different components, such as the backend recommendations service or the frontend interface, have on the engagement metrics. Recall that a user had to go through two steps in the experiment. First, the user had to perform a batch-delete for the unsubscription dialog to be displayed, and second, the user had to select and approve unsubscription recommendations.

The percentage of users that performed batch-delete at least once during the time period of the experiment was 31.8%. This implies that this action was popular enough, allowing a significant portion of the users to view the unsubscription dialog. Note that batch-delete is a native mail action that also lives outside the confines of our experiment, thus, the presented statistics imply also general measurements of that action, independently of the experiment.

Considering only the users that viewed the dialog, we observe that 49.3% of those users utilized the dialog to unsubscribe at least once during the experiment, and that 34.2% of all dialogs were engaged by users. These engagement metrics are surprisingly high. They suggest few important things. First and foremost, many users have subscriptions they consider irrelevant, but so far, did not find a simple way to manage them. This is validated by the fact that nearly half of the users had at least one subscription they wanted to remove. Note that this statistics also shows that the feature along with the suggested recommendations met their management needs to unsubscribe. In addition, the fact that more than one third of the dialogs led users to unsubscribe emphasizes the usability of this feature and the quality of recommendations. These results disclose the key problem with traditional unsubscription mechanisms which users do not seem to adopt.

To better understand the usability of our new unsubscription feature, we compare unsubscriptions that were done through the feature and those done using the standard approach of clicking unsubscription links within the message body. Figure 10 presents a comparison of the unsubscription behavior of the user population participating in the experiment. The comparison encompasses the experiment time period as well as a period of ten days before its start. As can be seen in Figure 10(a), the number of unique users that utilize the feature is greater by roughly 8x compared to the number of unique users that use the standard approach. When considering the total number of unsubscriptions, as shown in Figure 10(b), the gap is even greater. The number of unsubscriptions performed using the feature is greater by about 23x the number of unsubscriptions by the standard way. These two observations further emphasize the usefulness of the feature. On one hand, it increases the number of users that perform unsubscription by about 8x, while on the other hand, each user now performs about 3x more unsubscriptions on average. This dual-effect is exactly what one can hope for.

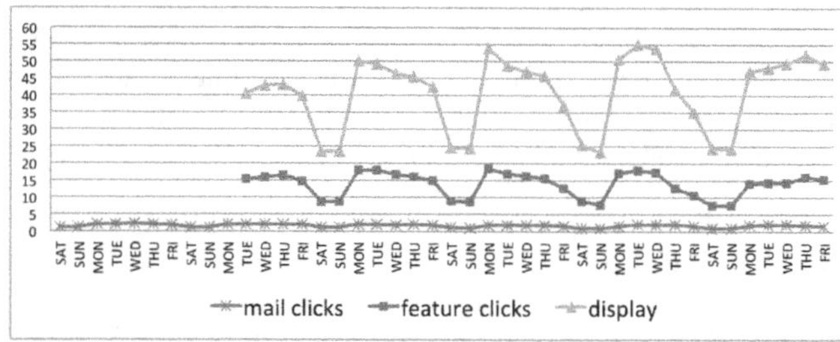

(a)

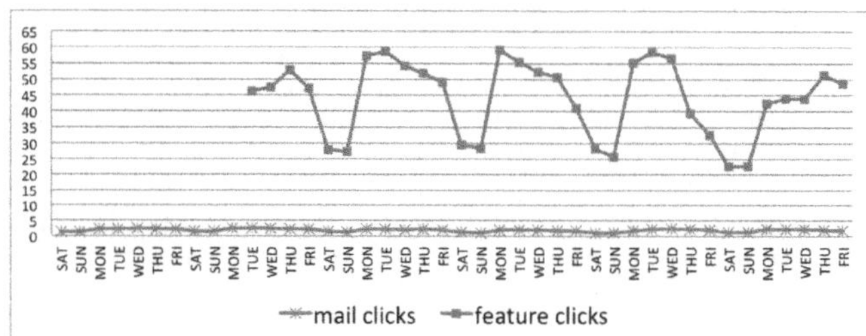

(b)

Figure 10: (a) The number of unique users that unsubscribed using the feature and the standard way, and (b) overall number of unsubscriptions done using the feature and the standard way. Values are normalized by the respective minimum value of standard unsubscription approach.

Two additional observations are worth noting. First, the number of unsubscriptions and the general trend relating to the standard approach both before and during the experiment do not change. This consistency implies that the unsubscription feature can be considered as being complimentary to the standard unsubscription mechanism. Second, the unsubscription numbers and trends seen with respect to the feature approach also stay roughly the same during the time period considered, except some slight decrease during the last week of the experiment. This consistency is encouraging, and is yet another validation of the feature usefulness.

7 CONCLUSIONS

We studied unsubscribable mail, which comprises about 95% of all machine-generated mail traffic, and as such, is the main source of information overload in email. We performed a large-scale analysis of this type of messages, based on data collected from millions of users of Yahoo Web mail service. The analysis reveals a striking gap between the low interest users are showing towards unsubscribable mail and their inactivity in decreasing the load implied by this traffic. Motivated by this gap, we developed an unsubscription recommendation service that was put into operation in an online large-scale experiment. This experiment offered users personalized unsubscription recommendations within a designated native mail feature. This feature provided the users with an efficient and easily accessible mechanism for unsubscribing from superfluous mailing lists. Our experiment resulted in an increase of 8x in the number of users that utilized the new feature, compared to the number of users that performed unsubscriptions using the standard way of clicking unsubscription links within email bodies. On the same time, the overall number of unsubscriptions that were performed using the new feature was greater by about 23x compared to that of the standard unsubscription way. These results demonstrates the imminent need for such a mechanism, which could help bridge the aforementioned gap and ease overload in email.

REFERENCES

[1] D. Aberdeen, O. Pacovsky, and A. Slater. The learning behind gmail priority inbox. In *NIPS 2010 Workshop on Learning on Cores, Clusters and Clouds*. Elsevier, 2010.

[2] C.-S. Act. Federal trade commission, 2003. https://www.ftc.gov/tips-advice/business-center/guidance/can-spam-act-compliance-guide-business.

[3] Q. Ai, S. Dumais, N. Craswell, and D. Liebling. Characterizing email search using large-scale behavioral logs and surveys. In *Proceedings of the 26th International Conference on World Wide Web*, pages 1511–1520. ACM, 2017.

[4] N. Ailon, Z. S. Karnin, E. Liberty, and Y. Maarek. Threading machine generated email. In *Proceedings of the sixth ACM international conference on Web search and data mining*, WSDM '13, pages 405–414. ACM, 2013.

[5] I. Alberts and D. Forest. Email pragmatics and automatic classification: A study in the organizational context. In *Journal of the Association for Information Science and Technology*, volume 63, pages 904–922. John Wiley & Sons, Inc., 2012.

[6] N. Avigdor-Elgrabli, M. Cwalinski, D. D. Castro, I. Gamzu, I. Grabovitch-Zuyev, L. Lewin-Eytan, and Y. Maarek. Structural clustering of machine-generated mail. In *Proceedings of the 25th ACM International Conference on Information and Knowledge Management*, pages 217–226, 2016.

[7] V. Bellotti, N. Ducheneaut, M. Howard, and I. Smith. Taking email to task: The design and evaluation of a task management centered email tool. In *Proceedings of the SIGCHI Conference on Human Factors in Computing Systems*, CHI '03, pages 345–352. ACM, 2003.

[8] M. Bendersky, X. Wang, D. Metzler, and M. Najork. Learning from user interactions in personal search via attribute parameterization. In *Proceedings of the Tenth ACM International Conference on Web Search and Data Mining*, WSDM '17, pages 791–799. ACM, 2017.

[9] D. Carmel, G. Halawi, L. Lewin-Eytan, Y. Maarek, and A. Raviv. Rank by time or by relevance?: Revisiting email search. In *Proceedings of the 24th ACM International on Conference on Information and Knowledge Management*, CIKM '15, pages 283–292. ACM, 2015.

[10] D. Carmel, L. Lewin-Eytan, A. Libov, Y. Maarek, and A. Raviv. The demographics of mail search and their application to query suggestion. In *Proceedings of the 26th International Conference on World Wide Web*, WWW '17. ACM, 2017.

[11] D. Carmel, L. Lewin-Eytan, A. Libov, Y. Maarek, and A. Raviv. Promoting relevant results in time-ranked mail search. In *Proceedings of the 26th International Conference on World Wide Web*, WWW '17. ACM, 2017.

[12] M. E. Cecchinato, A. Sellen, M. Shokouhi, and G. Smyth. Finding email in a multi-account, multi-device world. In *Proceedings of the 2016 CHI Conference on Human Factors in Computing Systems*, CHI '16, pages 1200–1210, 2016.

[13] L. A. Dabbish and R. E. Kraut. Email overload at work: An analysis of factors associated with email strain. In *Proceedings of the 2006 20th anniversary conference on Computer supported cooperative work*, CSCW '06, pages 431–440. ACM, 2016.

[14] L. A. Dabbish, R. E. Kraut, S. Fussell, and S. Kiesler. Understanding email use: Predicting action on a message. In *Proceedings of the SIGCHI Conference on Human Factors in Computing Systems*, CHI '05, pages 691–700. ACM, 2005.

[15] D. Di Castro, Z. Karnin, L. Lewin-Eytan, and Y. Maarek. You've got mail, and here is what you could do with it!: Analyzing and predicting actions on email messages. In *Proceedings of the Ninth ACM International Conference on Web Search and Data Mining*, WSDM '16, pages 307–316. ACM, 2016.

[16] D. Di Castro, L. Lewin-Eytan, Y. Maarek, R. Wolff, and E. Zohar. Enforcing k-anonymity in web mail auditing. In *Proceedings of the Ninth ACM International Conference on Web Search and Data Mining*, WSDM '16, pages 327–336. ACM, 2016.

[17] M. Dredze, T. Brooks, J. Carroll, J. Magarick, J. Blitzer, and F. Pereira. Intelligent email: Reply and attachment prediction. In *Proceedings of the 13th International Conference on Intelligent User Interfaces*, IUI '08, pages 321–324, Canary Islands, Spain, 2008.

[18] M. Grbovic, G. Halawi, Z. Karnin, and Y. Maarek. How many folders do you really need? classifying email into a handful of categories. In *Proceedings of the 23rd ACM International Conference on Conference on Information and Knowledge Management*, CIKM '14, pages 869–878. ACM, 2014.

[19] C. Grevet, D. Choi, D. Kumar, and E. Gilbert. Overload is overloaded: Email in the age of gmail. In *Proceedings of the SIGCHI Conference on Human Factors in Computing Systems*, CHI '14, pages 793–802. ACM, 2016.

[20] J. Gwizdka. Email task management styles: The cleaners and the keepers. In *CHI '04 Extended Abstracts on Human Factors in Computing Systems*, CHI EA '04, pages 1235–1238. ACM, 2004.

[21] R. . Internet Engineering Task Force. The use of urls as meta-syntax for core mail list commands and their transport through message header fields, July 1998. https://tools.ietf.org/html/rfc2369.

[22] R. . Internet Engineering Task Force. List-id: A structured field and namespace for the identification of mailing lists, March 2001. https://tools.ietf.org/html/rfc2919.

[23] R. . Internet Engineering Task Force. Signaling one-click functionality for list email headers, January 2017. https://tools.ietf.org/html/rfc8058.

[24] S. Kiritchenko and S. Matwin. Email classification with co-training. In *Center for Advanced Studies on Collaborative Research*, CASCON '11, pages 301–312, 2011.

[25] B. Klimt and Y. Yang. The enron corpus: A new dataset for email classification research. In *Machine Learning: ECML 2004: 15th European Conference on Machine Learning, Proceedings*, pages 217–226, 2004.

[26] F. Kooti, L. M. Aiello, M. Grbovic, K. Lerman, and A. Mantrach. Evolution of conversations in the age of email overload. In *Proceedings of the 24th International Conference on World Wide Web*, WWW '15, pages 603–613, 2015.

[27] G. Lab. Why do people subscribe to email newsletters?, Mars 2015. https://lab.getapp.com/new-research-getdata-why-do-people-subscribe-to-email-newsletters.

[28] J. Langford, L. Li, and A. Strehl. Vowpal wabbit online learning project, 2007. Technical report, http://hunch.net.

[29] J. Langford, L. Li, and T. Zhang. Sparse online learning via truncated gradient. *Journal of Machine Learning Research*, 10:777–801, 2009.

[30] K. Narang, S. T. Dumais, N. Craswell, D. Liebling, and Q. Ai. Large-scale analysis of email search and organizational strategies. In *Proceedings of the 2017 Conference on Conference Human Information Interaction and Retrieval*, CHIIR '17, pages 215–223. ACM, 2017.

[31] B. On, E. Lim, J. Jiang, A. Purandare, and L. Teow. Mining interaction behaviors for email reply order prediction. In *Proceedings of the 2010 International Conference on Advances in Social Networks Analysis and Mining*, ASONAM '10, pages 306–310. IEEE, 2010.

[32] A. Qadir, M. Gamon, P. Pantel, and A. H. Awadallah. Activity modeling in email. In *Proceedings of the 2016 Conference of the North American Chapter of the Association for Computational Linguistics: Human Language Technologies*, NAACL-HLT '16, pages 1452–1462, 2016.

[33] S. Radicati and J. Levenstein. Email market, 2015-2019, Nov 2015. http://www.radicati.com/wp/wp-content/uploads/2015/07/Email-Market-2015-2019-Executive-Summary.pdf.

[34] S. Radicati and J. Levenstein. Email market, 2017-2021, Nov 2017. http://www.radicati.com/wp/wp-content/uploads/2017/01/Email-Statistics-Report-2017-2021-Executive-Summary.pdf.

[35] M. Sappelli, S. Verberne, and W. Kraaij. Combining textual and non-textual features for e-mail importance estimation. In *Proceedings of the 25th Benelux Conference on Articial Intelligence*, pages 168–174. IBM Press, 2013.

[36] A. Taiwo, Z. Shikun, and K. Rinat. Applying machine learning techniques for e-mail management: solution with intelligent e-mail reply prediction. *Journal of Engineering and Technology Research*, 1(7):143–151, 10 2009.

[37] B. Wang, M. Ester, J. Bu, Y. Zhu, Z. Guan, and D. Cai. Which to view: Personalized prioritization for broadcast emails. In *Proceedings of the 25th International Conference on World Wide Web*, WWW '16, pages 1181–1190, 2016.

[38] B. Wang, M. Ester, Y. Liao, J. Bu, Y. Zhu, Z. Guan, and D. Cai. The million domain challenge: Broadcast email prioritization by cross-domain recommendation. In *Proceedings of the 22Nd ACM SIGKDD International Conference on Knowledge Discovery and Data Mining*, KDD '16, pages 1895–1904. ACM, 2016.

[39] J. B. Wendt, M. Bendersky, L. Garcia-Pueyo, V. Josifovski, B. Miklos, and I. Krka. Hierarchical label propagation and discovery for machine generated email. In *Proceedings of the Ninth ACM International Conference on Web Search and Data Mining*, WSDM '16, 2016.

[40] S. Whittaker and C. L. Sidner. Email overload: Exploring personal information management of email. In *Conference on Human Factors in Computing Systems: Common Ground, CHI*, pages 276–283, 1996.

[41] L. Yang, S. T. Dumais, P. N. Bennett, and A. H. Awadallah. Characterizing and predicting enterprise email reply behavior. In *Proceedings of the 40th International ACM SIGIR Conference on Research and Development in Information Retrieval*, SIGIR '17, pages 235–244. ACM, 2017.

Offline A/B testing for Recommender Systems

Alexandre Gilotte, Clément Calauzènes, Thomas Nedelec, Alexandre Abraham, Simon Dollé
Criteo Research
f.name@criteo.com

ABSTRACT

Online A/B testing evaluates the impact of a new technology by running it in a real production environment and testing its performance on a subset of the users of the platform. It is a well-known practice to run a preliminary offline evaluation on historical data to iterate faster on new ideas, and to detect poor policies in order to avoid losing money or breaking the system. For such offline evaluations, we are interested in methods that can compute offline an estimate of the potential uplift of performance generated by a new technology. Offline performance can be measured using estimators known as *counterfactual* or *off-policy* estimators. Traditional counterfactual estimators, such as *capped importance sampling* or *normalised importance sampling*, exhibit unsatisfying bias-variance compromises when experimenting on personalized product recommendation systems. To overcome this issue, we model the bias incurred by these estimators rather than bound it in the worst case, which leads us to propose a new counterfactual estimator. We provide a benchmark of the different estimators showing their correlation with business metrics observed by running online A/B tests on a large-scale commercial recommender system.

CCS CONCEPTS

• **Computing methodologies** → **Learning from implicit feedback**; • **Information systems** → *Evaluation of retrieval results*;

KEYWORDS

counterfactual estimation, off-policy evaluation, recommender system, importance sampling.

ACM Reference Format:
Alexandre Gilotte, Clément Calauzènes, Thomas Nedelec, Alexandre Abraham, Simon Dollé. 2018. Offline A/B testing for Recommender Systems. In *Proceedings of 11th ACM International Conf. on Web Search and Data Mining (WSDM 2018).* ACM, New York, NY, USA, 9 pages. https://doi.org/10.1145/3159652.3159687

1 INTRODUCTION

Personalized product recommendation has become a central part of most online marketing systems. Having efficient and reliable methods to evaluate recommender systems is critical in accelerating the pace of improvement of these marketing platforms.

Online A/B tests became ubiquitous in tech companies in order to make informed decisions on the rollout of a new technology such as a recommender system. Each new software implementation is tested by comparing its performance with the previous production version through randomised experiments. In practice, to compare two technologies, a pool of units (e.g. users, displays or servers) of the platform is split in two populations and each of them is exposed to one of the tested technologies. The careful choice of the unit reflects independence assumptions under which the test is run. At the end of the experiments, business metrics such as the generated revenue, the number of clicks or the time spent on the platform are compared to make a decision on the future of the new technology.

However, online A/B tests take time and cost money. Indeed, to gather a sufficient amount of data to reach statistical sufficiency and be able to study periodic behaviours (the signal can be different from one day to the other), an A/B test is usually implemented over several weeks. On top of this, prototypes need to be brought to production standard to be tested. These reasons prevent companies from iterating quickly on new ideas.

To solve these pitfalls, people historically relied on offline experiments based on some rank-based metrics, such as NDCG [13], MAP [1] or Precision@K. Such evaluations suffer from very heavy assumptions, such as independence between products or the fact that the feedback (e.g. click) can be translated into a supervised task [10, 16, 22]. To overcome these limitations, some estimators were introduced [2, 15] to estimate offline – i.e. using randomised historical data gathered under only one policy – a business comparison between two systems. In the following, we shall call the procedure of comparing offline two systems based on some business metric defining the outcome an *offline A/B test.*

This setting is called *counterfactual reasoning* or *off-policy evaluation* (OPE) (see [2] for a comprehensive study). Several estimators such as *Basic Importance Sampling* (BIS, [8, 11]), *Capped Importance Sampling* (CIS, [2]), *Normalised Importance Sampling* (NIS, [21]) and *Doubly Robust* (DR, [6]) have been introduced to compute the expected reward of the tested technology π_t based on logs collected on the current technology in production π_p.

All theses estimators achieve different trade-offs between bias and variance. After explaining why BIS (Section 3) and DR (Section 4.1) suffer from high variance in the recommendation setting, we shall focus on *capped importance sampling* (Section 4.2). [2] proposed clipping the importance weights, which leads to a biased estimator with lower variance. However, the control of the bias is very loose in the general case and [2] only advocates modifying the source probability (the current system) to further explore whether a light clipping could be sufficient.

The main caveat of such biased estimates is that a low bias is present only under unrealistic conditions (see Section 4.2). Our main contribution is to propose two variants of *capped importance*

WSDM 2018, February 5–9, 2018, Marina Del Rey, CA, USA

ACM ISBN 978-1-4503-5581-0/18/02...$15.00
https://doi.org/10.1145/3159652.3159687

sampling that achieve low bias under much more realistic conditions (Section 5.3 and Section 5.4) and show their practical interest on real personalised recommendation systems. In Section 6, we compare metrics observed during real online A/B tests with the pre-computed values of the different counterfactual estimators.

2 SETTTING AND NOTATION

We consider recommender systems in the context of online product recommendation . The task consists of displaying a set of products to a user on some e-commerce websites or on some advertising banners. These subsets of products should be personalised based on the interests of the user. This task is formalised as a ranking task, and not only a top-K retrieval, because the different product slots are not equivalent and exhibit different performance [5]. The system outputs a ranked list of products and then maps better products to better positions.

A recommendation policy is designed as a distribution over the top-K rankings. Good examples of distributions are the Bradley-Terry Luce (BTL) model [3], the Placket-Luce model [4, 7, 20] or more generally Thurstonian models [26, 28].

In the following, we will represent random variables with capital letters such as Y and realisation of random variables with lower-case letters such as y. Given a display x represented by a set of contextual features as well as a set of eligible products, the recommender system outputs a probability distribution $\pi(A|X)$ where a is a top-K ranking on the eligible products and K is the number of items that will be displayed. Taking action a in state x generates a reward $r \in [0, r_{\max}]$ that could be interpreted as a click or a purchase.

3 ONLINE AND OFFLINE A/B TESTING

In *online* A/B tests, the objective is to compare two systems *prod* and *test* to ultimately take a decision on which one performs better than the other based on their respective business value. We consider a set of n units x that are randomly assigned to either *prod* or *test* and seek to measure the average difference in value, based on the reward signal $r \in [0, r_{\max}]$ that could be the number of clicks or the generated revenue. The choice of the units, which could be internet users, recommendation opportunities or servers, heavily depends on the independence assumptions made in order to reach a statistically significant decision in a timely manner. This assumption is called the isolation assumption [2].

We will note the current production policy π_p and the test policy π_t. To compare π_p and π_t, we estimate the average difference of value $\Delta\mathcal{R}$ which is called average treatment effect and defined as

$$\Delta\mathcal{R}(\pi_p, \pi_t) = \mathbb{E}_{\pi_t}[R] - \mathbb{E}_{\pi_p}[R]$$

where $\mathbb{E}_{\pi_p}[R] = \mathbb{E}[R|A]\pi_p(A|X)\mathbb{P}(X)$. During an online A/B test, units are randomly split in two populations $\mathcal{P}_t$ and $\mathcal{P}_p$, such that we can estimate $\Delta\mathcal{R}$ using

$$\Delta\mathcal{R}(\pi_p, \pi_t) = \mathbb{E}[R|X \in \mathcal{P}_t] - \mathbb{E}[R|X \in \mathcal{P}_p]\,.$$

$\Delta\mathcal{R}$ is estimated by Monte-Carlo using the two datasets collected during the test $\mathcal{S}_p = \{(x_i, a_i, r_i) : i \in \mathcal{P}_p\}$ and $\mathcal{S}_t = \{(x_i, a_i, r_i) : i \in \mathcal{P}_t\}$. We build the empirical estimator $\Delta\hat{\mathcal{R}}$ to take the decision by performing a statistical test :

$$\Delta\hat{\mathcal{R}}(\pi_p, \pi_t) = \hat{\mathcal{R}}(\mathcal{S}_t) - \hat{\mathcal{R}}(\mathcal{S}_p)$$

where $\hat{\mathcal{R}}(\mathcal{S})$ is the empirical average of rewards over $\mathcal{S}$ gathered during the *online* AB test.

To perform an *offline* A/B test, we have only one set of n historical i.i.d. samples $\mathcal{S}_n = \{(x_i, a_i, r_i) : i \in [n]\}$ collected using a production recommender system π_p (also known as the *behaviour policy* in the RL community or *logging policy*). The goal is to compare the performance of a new technology, a test policy denoted π_t, to our current system π_p [1]. We can directly estimate $\mathbb{E}_{\pi_p}[R]$ using $\hat{\mathcal{R}}(\mathcal{S}_n)$, but for $\mathbb{E}_{\pi_t}[R]$ we cannot use a direct estimation since we do not have any data gathered under π_t. One of the main tools to estimate the expected reward under the target policy using rewards gathered under the behaviour policy is *importance sampling* or *inverse propensity score* as introduced by Hammersley and Handscomb [8] which leads to the following Monte-Carlo estimator:

$$\hat{\mathcal{R}}^{\mathrm{IS}}(\pi_t) = \frac{1}{n}\sum_{(x,a,r)\in\mathcal{S}_n} w(a,x)r \qquad \text{where } w(a,x) = \frac{\pi_t(a|x)}{\pi_p(a|x)}$$

The main advantage of such an estimator that it is unbiased, while its main pitfall is usually its high variance, which depends on how different π_t is from π_p (this variance is unbounded). All the difficulty here resides in the size of the action space. The number of top-K rankings over candidate sets of size M is extremely high ($K!\binom{M}{K}$), resulting in high variance of the importance weights W.

Several variants of importance sampling have been proposed, with different purposes, to tackle the high variance that can arise from the use of importance sampling. They use some classical variance reduction techniques, such as difference control variate or ratio control variate. However these approaches consist of using unbiased or consistent estimators and turn out to still lead to estimators suffering from high variance. An approach to trade off variance for bias is to clip the importance weights as proposed in [2]. In the next section, we detail several classic methods used in importance sampling for counterfactual reasoning.

4 REDUCING ESTIMATORS VARIANCE

4.1 Control Variates

Control variates are a popular variance reduction method in statistics. It consists of finding a second random variable with known expectation and which is correlated with the variable to estimate in order to reduce the variance of its estimation.

Doubly robust estimator. The easiest case is when we dispose of external knowledge like a reward model. We can use this as a control variate to improve our current estimator [6]. We assume we can access a model $\bar{r}(a, x)$ that estimates the expected reward of each action a at context x. We define the *doubly robust* estimator:

$$\hat{\mathcal{R}}^{\mathrm{DR}}(\pi_t) = \sum_{(x,a,r)\in\mathcal{S}_n}\Big((r - \bar{r}(a,x))\,w(a,x) + \mathbb{E}_{\pi_t}\left[\bar{r}(A,X)|X = x\right]\Big)$$

This estimator is unbiased and, if the predicted reward $\bar{r}(A, X)$ is well correlated with the actual reward R, it has lower variance than IS (see [19, §8.9] for instance).

[1] We need a stochastic policy for π_p that puts a non-zero probability on any ranking a to prevent spurious correlations from biasing the estimators we exhibit in the following sections (see [2] for details).

However, this estimator has several drawbacks in the setting of recommendation systems. First, having an accurate model of the reward given the action is challenging when the number of possible actions is very large. To overcome this problem, Williams [27] – in the context of reinforcement learning – proposed to use a model $\bar{r}$ not dependent on the action a. It has a higher variance than the initial DR model but avoid the marginalization over all the actions.

However, this approach does not solve the second and biggest drawback of this method: when the reward has a high variance even conditionally to X and A, the predicted reward cannot have a strong correlation with it. For instance, when the computed metric is the number of clicks – i.e. the reward R follows a Bernoulli with parameter close to 0 – the actual expected reward per action (typically around 10^{-3} in display advertising for instance) hardly correlates with R (0 or 1). In this particular case, DR is very close to IS: the use of the click model does not help to reduce the variance. Even if no good model is available, another control variate can be implemented to decrease the variance of IS.

Normalised importance sampling. We know that $\mathbb{E}_{\pi_p}[W] = 1$. Using the empirical average $\frac{1}{n}\sum_{(x,a,r)\in\mathcal{S}_n} w(a,x)$ as a global ratio control variate, we have the normalized importance sampling (NIS) estimator [21, 24]:

$$\hat{\mathcal{R}}^{\text{NIS}}(\pi_t) = \frac{1}{\sum_{(x,a,r)\in\mathcal{S}_n} w(a,x)} \sum_{(x,a,r)\in\mathcal{S}_n} w(a,x)r$$

The normalizing constant is equal to the sum of the importance weights and is equal in expectation to n, the number of examples in the dataset. It is a biased estimate of the expected reward but with lower variance than the *basic importance sampling* estimator. It is a consistent estimator of $\mathbb{E}_{\pi_t}[r]$ and the bias decreases in $1/n$. Thus NIS, with a certain amount of data is very close to BIS and the variance is not decreased.

The main problem of such methods aimed at reducing the variance without introducing any bias (at least asymptotically) is that if we do not dispose of a strong external knowledge, we do not reduce the variance that much.

4.2 Capping weights

Capped importance sampling. Capping weights is another way to control the variance of the IS estimator. Two forms of capping were introduced: max capping and zero capping. For some capping value $c > 0$, these estimators are respectively defined as:

$$\hat{\mathcal{R}}^{\text{maxCIS}}(\pi_t, c) = \frac{1}{n} \sum_{(x,a,r)\in\mathcal{S}_n} \min(w(a,x), c)r$$

and

$$\hat{\mathcal{R}}^{\text{zeroCIS}}(\pi_t, c) = \frac{1}{n} \sum_{(x,a,r)\in\mathcal{S}_n} \mathbf{1}_{w(a,x)<c} w(a,x)r$$

In the following, we denote the capped weights by $\overline{w}(a,x)$, for zero capping $\overline{w}(a,x) = \mathbf{1}_{w(a,x)<c}w(a,x)$ and for max capping $\overline{w}(a,x) = \min(w(a,x), c)$. All calculations presented in the following – except when explicitly specified otherwise – are valid for both zero capping and max capping. Intuitively, the behaviour of these two estimators is the same since the capped importance weights are very big compare to the capping parameter: in Fig. 1, we provide some empirical results on weights encountered when evaluating recommendation system policies. Both capping methods show very similar results and we only report max capping results in the experiments.

However, capping comes at the cost of introducing a bias: when introducing capping on the IS estimator, we only account for a sub-part of $\mathbb{E}_{\pi_t}[R]$:

$$\mathbb{E}_{\pi_t}[R] = \mathbb{E}_{\pi_t}\left[R\frac{\overline{W}}{W}\right] + \mathbb{E}_{\pi_t}\left[R\frac{W-\overline{W}}{W}\right]$$
$$= \underbrace{\mathbb{E}_{\pi_p}[\hat{\mathcal{R}}^{\text{CIS}}(\pi_t, c)]}_{\mathcal{R}^{\text{CIS}}(\pi_t, c)} + \underbrace{\mathbb{E}_{\pi_t}\left[R\frac{W-\overline{W}}{W}\middle| W > c\right]\mathbb{P}_{\pi_t}(W > c)}_{\mathcal{B}^{\text{CIS}}(\pi_t, c)}$$

One of the main issues of only estimating $\mathcal{R}^{\text{CIS}}(\pi_t, c)$ is that the bias term $\mathcal{B}^{\text{CIS}}(\pi_t, c)$ becomes low only if $\mathbb{E}_{\pi_t}(R|W > c)$ is low. It means that $\mathbb{E}[R|A, X]$ has to be low for all a such that $w(a,x) > c$ – i.e. for all actions that π_t chooses much more often than π_p. As our test policy π_t is usually a trial for improving the current system π_p, it is not really satisfying to have a estimator with a low bias only if π_t performs poorly on actions it chooses more often than the current system. More formally, as we want to take a statistically significant decision, we need to build a confidence interval around $\hat{\mathcal{R}}^{\text{CIS}}(\pi_t, c)$. We can bound $\mathcal{R}^{\text{CIS}}(\pi_t, c)$ using any concentration bound (e.g. an empirical Bernstein bound [2, 17]). However the bias term can only be controlled in the worst case: $0 \le \mathcal{B}^{\text{CIS}}(\pi_t, c) \le r_{\max}(1 - \mathbb{P}(W \le c))$. As explained right before, this inequality only gets tight when $r_{\max}$ is lower on the capped volume than elsewhere.

4.3 No good practical trade-off for CIS

In practice, no capping parameter for CIS yields confidence interval small enough to decide whether π_t is a better policy than π_p. The capping parameter used in CIS introduces a bias-variance tradeoff: Increasing its value decreases the bias and increases the variance of the estimator. However, we demonstrated in the previous section that a volume of capped weights too high will lead to an invalid bias-variance tradeoff. Based on experimental results, we show that this critical limit is often reached for recommendation systems used in production.

We consider an A/B test that was implemented in production and look at the importance weights used to compute the performance of π_t based on logs gathered with π_p. Figure 1 shows their distribution according to the test policy. Figure 2 shows the variance and the upper bound on the bias (see section 4.2 for definition) depending on the capping parameter. We clearly see the tradeoff between the two measures when the capping parameter changes. In both cases, we can determine the values of the capping parameter for which the variance and bias are lower to the uplift that we want to measure offline (usually, we consider a 1% uplift). Figure 2 shows that no value of the capping parameter satisfies both criteria: a good variance is achieved below 10^2 whereas a good value for bias requires a capping parameter above 10^{23}.

This problem led us to design new estimators that model the bias introduced by capping and achieve better bias-variance tradeoff.

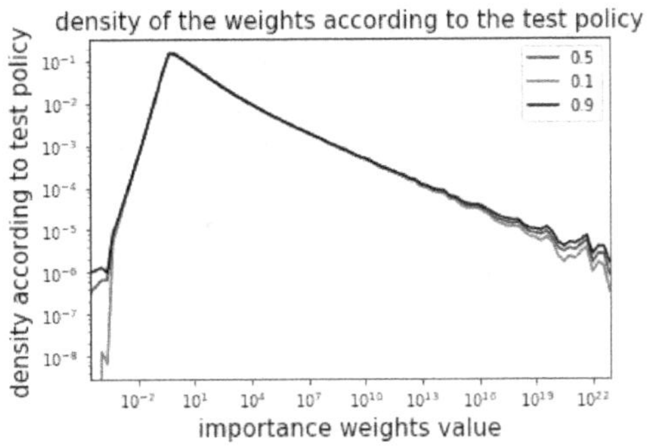

Figure 1: Distribution of the importance sampling weights when sampled according to the test policy with 80% confidence interval. (0.1 corresponds to 10th centile and 0.9 to 90th centile)

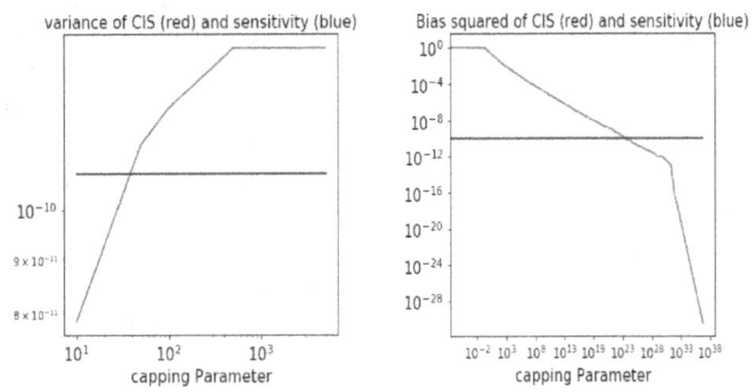

Figure 2: Variance of CIS, upper bound on the bias of CIS and sensitivity depending on the capping parameter.

5 MODELLING THE BIAS

As discussed in the previous section, CIS can not reach a tradeoff with low variance and provable low bias. In the following, we present different estimators that model the bias at different scale. We show that the well-known Normalised Capped Importance Sampling provides a model at the global level. Then, we present a new estimator that models the bias at a contextual state level.

5.1 Global bias model

Normalised Capped Importance Sampling (NCIS). A common practice in the literature (e.g. see experiments in [24]) is to use the *normalised capped importance sampling* estimator that is defined as:

$$\hat{\mathcal{R}}^{\text{NCIS}}(\pi_t, c) = \frac{\frac{1}{n}\sum_{(x,a,r)\in S_n} \overline{w}(a,x)r}{\frac{1}{n}\sum_{(x,a,r)\in S_n} \overline{w}(a,x)} \tag{1}$$

It involves in re-adjusting the expected reward proportionally to the probability mass capped. In the following, we show how this estimator models the bias introduced by capping. Asymptotically, we can compute the bias of this estimator (the proof is in the appendix):

$$\mathbb{P}\left(\lim_{n\to\infty} \hat{\mathcal{R}}^{\text{NCIS}}(\pi_t, c, S_n) = \frac{\mathbb{E}_{\pi_t}\left[\frac{\overline{W}R}{W}\right]}{\mathbb{E}_{\pi_t}\left[\frac{\overline{W}}{W}\right]}\right) = 1$$

with

$$\mathcal{R}^{\text{NCIS}}(\pi_t, c) \triangleq \frac{\mathbb{E}_{\pi_t}\left[\frac{\overline{W}R}{W}\right]}{\mathbb{E}_{\pi_t}\left[\frac{\overline{W}}{W}\right]} = \mathcal{R}^{\text{CIS}}(\pi_t, c) + \mathcal{R}^{\text{CIS}}(\pi_t, c)\frac{1 - \mathbb{E}_{\pi_t}\left[\frac{\overline{W}}{W}\right]}{\mathbb{E}_{\pi_t}\left[\frac{\overline{W}}{W}\right]} \tag{2}$$

Intuitively, if we reuse the expression of $\mathcal{B}^{\text{CIS}}(\pi_t, c)$, we see that NCIS, instead of setting $\mathcal{B}^{\text{CIS}}(\pi_t, c)$ to zero like CIS, approximates the performance on the capped volume by the performance on the non-capped volume.

In the case of zero capping, the approximation made by NCIS is even more intuitive: NCIS makes the assumption that overall,

$$\mathbb{E}_{\pi_t}[R|W > c] \approx \mathbb{E}_{\pi_t}[R|W < c] \ .$$

and approximates $\mathcal{B}^{\text{CIS}}(\pi_t, c)$ as:

$$\mathcal{B}^{\text{CIS}}[\pi_t, c] \approx \mathbb{E}_{\pi_t}[R|W < c]\,\mathbb{P}_{\pi_t}(W > c)$$

Those expectations are both on the action A and on the context X.

This approximation is exact at least in the trivial case when the reward R is independent from both the context X and the action A, and thus of the weight W. We can expect the approximation to be reasonable when the noise level is high because in this case the dependency of R on X and A is low. However we shall see in the next section why this assumption may be poor in practice.

5.2 Need for a local bias modelling

The NCIS estimator compensates the capping with a proportional rescaling. However, this rescaling is performed globally, while the underlying data may contain many sub-groups with different average rewards. For instance, the MovieLens dataset [9] exhibits a small group of frequent user and a large majority of occasional users. In the context of e-commerce, [12] reports that Prime members spend in average 4.6 times more than non-prime members on Amazon™. When operating with such different groups of customers, it is quite common to introduce changes in the recommender system that do not equally affect the different groups. For instance, one could decide to favour good deal products for registered customers, which impact both groups differently. As the new policy impact differs from registered to non-registered customers, the capping may be stronger for one of the groups (formalised by the quantity $\overline{W}/W$), thus a blind global rescaling introduces a large bias (see Table 1 for a toy counter-example).

More formally, from (2), we can directly deduce that the asymptotic bias of NCIS can be written as

$$\mathcal{B}^{\text{NCIS}}(\pi_t, c) \triangleq \mathbb{E}_{\pi_t}[R] - \mathcal{R}^{\text{NCIS}}(\pi_t, c) = -\,\text{Cov}_{\pi_t}\left(R, \frac{\overline{W}}{W}\right)\Big/\mathbb{E}_{\pi_t}\left[\frac{\overline{W}}{W}\right]$$

which makes NCIS consistent when W and R are independent. However, as we just discussed, the reward R and the capping $\overline{W}/W$ may be correlated through a third confounding variable such as the type of customer. This information is contained in the context X, which leads us to decompose the bias conditionally to X,

$$\mathcal{B}^{\text{NCIS}}(\pi_t, c) = -\frac{\text{Cov}_{\pi_t}\left(\mathbb{E}[R|X], \mathbb{E}\left[\frac{\overline{W}}{W}\Big|X\right]\right) + \mathbb{E}_{\pi_t}\left[\text{Cov}\left(R, \frac{\overline{W}}{W}\Big|X\right)\right]}{\mathbb{E}_{\pi_t}\left[\frac{\overline{W}}{W}\right]}$$

Table 1: Counter-example for NCIS. The test policy π_t proposes more good deal products to registered customers, improving the (already good) performance on them. The effect is neutral on unknown (low performing) customers. For π_t, NCIS estimates a reward of 1.8 while the (true) expected reward is 2.1. As the reward of π_p is 1.9, we would wrongly conclude that π_t is worse than π_p.

	registered customers	*unknown customers*
Proportions	0.1	0.9
Performance of π_p	10	1
Performance of π_t	12	1
$\mathbb{E}(\overline{W}/W)$	0.7	1

To improve over NCIS, we can assume the first term of the numerator to be dominant. Indeed, in practice the recommendation (the action A) itself is usually an unsolicited attempt to influence a user with a pre-existing intent (the context X). Thus, one can realistically expect the reward R to be more correlated to the initial intent than to the recommendation. Following this idea, we propose next several ways to build "local" versions of the NCIS estimator – by normalising conditionally to the context – to get rid of the first term of the bias (the biggest) and obtain estimators with a much smaller bias.

5.3 Piecewise constant model

The following estimator is the first step toward a model of the bias at a finer scale. The simplest way to build a local version of NCIS is to use stratification. In other words, to make a piecewise version of NCIS. The goal is to find a partition $\mathcal{G}$ of $\mathcal{X}$ in order to use the decomposition of the expectation over this partition,

$$\mathbb{E}_{\pi_t}[R] = \sum_{g \in \mathcal{G}} \mathbb{E}_{\pi_t}[R|X \in g]\mathbb{P}(X \in g)$$

and then estimate the expectation separately on each group of the partition with the NCIS estimator:

$$\hat{\mathcal{R}}^{\text{PieceNCIS}}(\pi_t, c) = \sum_{g \in \mathcal{G}} \alpha_g \hat{\mathcal{R}}|_g^{\text{NCIS}}(\pi_t, c)$$

where $\alpha_g = \sum_{(x,a,r) \in \mathcal{S}_n} \mathbf{1}_{x \in g}/n$ estimates $\mathbb{P}(X \in g)$ and $\hat{\mathcal{R}}|_g^{\text{NCIS}}(\pi_t, c)$ is the restriction of the NCIS estimator to the group g to estimate $\mathbb{E}_{\pi_t}[R|X \in g]$:

$$\hat{\mathcal{R}}|_g^{\text{NCIS}}(\pi_t, c) = \frac{\sum_{(x,a,r) \in \mathcal{S}_n} \mathbf{1}_{x \in g} \overline{w}(a,x) r}{\sum_{(x,a,r) \in \mathcal{S}_n} \mathbf{1}_{x \in g} \overline{w}(a,x)}$$

A desirable constraint on $\mathcal{G}$ is to be independent from the tested policy π_t. When removing the capping - i.e. $c \to \infty$ - the estimator $\hat{\mathcal{R}}^{\text{PieceNCIS}}(\pi_t, c)$ is consistent.

Apart from this constraint, the partition can be constructed from any hand-crafted splits on features of x. However, even though easy in practice, this option is not satisfying because the performance of the estimator will strongly depend on a manual choice of the partition. A more agnostic method to build an empirically "good" partition, would be to learn a value function $V(x)$ to predict the expected reward given a context x and build the partition based on the output of this model. For instance, in the experiments presented in Section 6, we use a regular partition of the output of the model in the log-space (base b):

$$\mathcal{G} = \left\{V^{-1}(I_k) : I_k = [b^k, b^{k+1}], k \in \mathbb{Z}\right\}$$

This approach provides two advantages: 1) given a group, the reward does not depend strongly on x anymore, which was the first objective of stratification, 2) the size of the partition is more controlled than with a hand-crafted one, leading to more samples per group and thus less estimation problems. However, it comes at the cost of needing to fit a value function on a separate set of data.

5.4 Pointwise model

To avoid having to learn and design a value model to perform a stratification, we push the idea further and use the decomposition:

$$\mathbb{E}_{\pi_t}[R] = \sum_{x \in \mathcal{X}} \mathbb{E}_{\pi_t}[R|X = x]\mathbb{P}(X = x)$$

However, building an estimator of $\mathbb{E}_{\pi_t}[R|X = x]$ becomes more challenging. Following the underlying idea of NCIS, we want to make the following approximation:

$$\mathbb{E}_{\pi_t}[R|X = x] \approx \frac{\mathbb{E}_{\pi_t}\left[R\frac{\overline{W}}{W}\middle|X = x\right]}{\mathbb{E}_{\pi_t}\left[\frac{\overline{W}}{W}\middle|X = x\right]}$$

Unfortunately, when conditioning on a value of x, we cannot use a simple ratio estimator such as

$$\frac{\sum_{(x',a,r) \in \mathcal{S}_n} \mathbf{1}_{x'=x} \overline{w}(a,x') r}{\sum_{(x',a,r) \in \mathcal{S}_n} \mathbf{1}_{x'=x} \overline{w}(a,x')}$$

Indeed, the number of samples in the training set exactly matching a given value of x is very low (it can even be 0 if x is continuous), so the bias of the ratio estimator is not negligible anymore. Fortunately, when conditioned on x, we can be much better at the estimation of $\mathbb{E}_{\pi_t}\left[\frac{\overline{W}}{W}\middle|X = x\right]$. In fact, we could even compute it exactly by a simple marginalisation on the actions, but the number of actions is too large in our case to perform this computation in a reasonable time. Moreover, we are not aware of any closed-form for it, even when both policies follow simple models (e.g. Plackett-Luce or Mallows).

However, we can efficiently sample from the policy π_t, and therefore compute a Monte Carlo approximation of this probability. Since we actually want an estimator of the ratio $1/\mathbb{E}_{\pi_t}\left[\frac{\overline{W}}{W}\middle|X = x\right]$, we can use a rejection sampling technique such as Lahiri's [14] or Midzuno-Sen method [18, 23] to get an unbiased estimate denoted $\hat{IP}_c(x)$. In practice to build an estimator of $1/\mathbb{E}_{\pi_t}\left[\frac{\overline{W}}{W}\middle|X = x\right]$, we use the Midzuno-Sen method. We define a random variable U uniformly distributed between 0 and 1. Then, we do successively

- sample u from the uniform distribution and w_1 from π_t until reaching $w_1 < u$
- sample $w_2, \ldots, w_n$ from π_t
- return $\frac{n}{\frac{\overline{w_1}}{w_1} + \ldots + \frac{\overline{w_n}}{w_n}})$

Through this method, the expectation of $n/(W_1/\overline{W_1} + \ldots + W_n/\overline{W_n})$ is equal to $1/\mathbb{E}_{\pi_t}\left[\frac{\overline{W}}{W}\middle|X = x\right]$. In the following, we will note it $\hat{IP}_c(x)$.

Finally, we can define the following estimator:

$$\hat{\mathcal{R}}^{\text{PointNCIS}}(\pi_t, c) = \frac{1}{n} \sum_{(x,a,r) \in \mathcal{S}_n} \hat{IP}_c(x)\overline{w}(a,x)r$$

We need to notice one pitfall of this method: if the test distribution and the prod distribution are really dissimilar, the expectation $\mathbb{E}_{\pi_t}\left[\frac{\overline{W}}{W}\middle|X=x\right]$ may become very low. It means that the effective weight by which we multiply the reward r, $\frac{w}{\mathbb{E}_{\pi_t}\left[\frac{\overline{W}}{W}\middle|X=x\right]}$ might be much bigger than the capping value, and the estimator would have a high variance. We can overcome this problem when using max capping by decreasing the capping value when the distributions do not overlap enough (see appendix for justification).

Table 2: Summary table of the different estimators. First column sum up the formulae of the estimators, second one the approximation $\tilde{\mathcal{B}}$ of the bias term $\mathcal{B}$ in the general case and the case of zero capping

	$\hat{\mathcal{R}}(\pi_t, c)$	approx $\tilde{\mathcal{B}}^{\text{CIS}}(\pi_t, c, x)$
CIS	$\frac{1}{n}\sum_{\mathcal{S}_n} r\overline{w}(a,x)$	0
NCIS	$\frac{\sum_{\mathcal{S}_n} r\overline{w}(a,x)}{\sum_{\mathcal{S}_n} \overline{w}(a,x)}$	$\mathbb{E}_{\pi_t}\left[\frac{R\overline{W}}{W}\right]\frac{1-\mathbb{E}_{\pi_t}\left[\frac{\overline{W}}{W}\right]}{\mathbb{E}_{\pi_t}\left[\frac{\overline{W}}{W}\right]}$
PieceNCIS	$\sum_{g \in \mathcal{G}} \alpha_g \hat{\mathcal{R}}\|_g^{\text{NCIS}}(\pi_t, c)$	$\mathbb{E}_{\pi_t}\left[\frac{R\overline{W}}{W}\middle\|X \in g\right]\frac{1-\mathbb{E}_{\pi_t}\left[\frac{\overline{W}}{W}\middle\|X \in g\right]}{\mathbb{E}_{\pi_t}\left[\frac{\overline{W}}{W}\middle\|X \in g\right]}$
PointNCIS	$\frac{1}{n}\sum_{\mathcal{S}_n} \hat{IP}_c(x)\overline{w}(a,x)r$	$\mathbb{E}_{\pi_t}\left[\frac{R\overline{W}}{W}\middle\|X=x\right]\frac{1-\mathbb{E}_{\pi_t}\left[\frac{\overline{W}}{W}\middle\|X=x\right]}{\mathbb{E}_{\pi_t}\left[\frac{\overline{W}}{W}\middle\|X=x\right]}$

6 EXPERIMENTS

We use the A/B test history of a commercial recommender system to compare the uplifts $\Delta\hat{R}$ estimated by our *offline A/B tests* methods with the ground truth ΔR estimated during the *online A/B tests.*

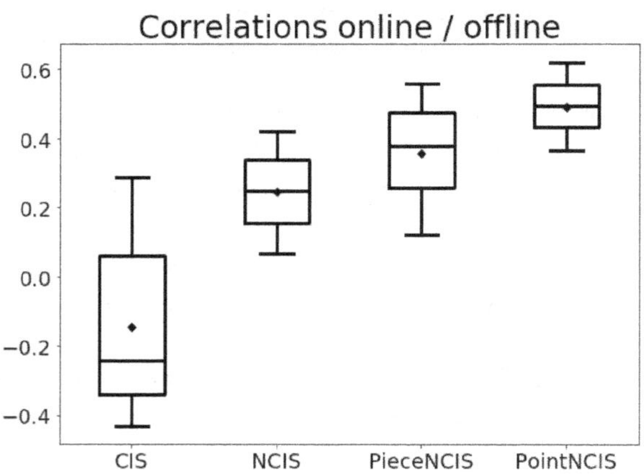

Figure 3: Correlation between online and offline uplifts. Confidence bounds are obtained using bootstraps. Whiskers are 10% and 90% quantiles and the boxes represent quartiles.

6.1 Dataset

We have access to a proprietary dataset of 39 *online A/B tests*, representing a total of few hundreds of billions of recommendations. We consider a click-based business metric. Since clicks are relatively rare, the reward signal has a high variance, even conditioned to the context and to the action. For each test, we consider:

- the two policies involved in the A/B test π_p and π_t,
- for each display (units x whose features represent the context of the display and past interactions with the user), we have access to,
  - the top-K ranking (action a) chosen along with its probability under the logging policy – $\pi_p(a|x)$ on control population A or $\pi_t(a|x)$ on test population B,
  - the set of eligible items,
  - the observed reward r.

On each A/B test, we can compute the online estimate of the uplift $\Delta\hat{\mathcal{R}}(\pi_p, \pi_t) = \hat{\mathcal{R}}(\mathcal{S}_t) - \hat{\mathcal{R}}(\mathcal{S}_p)$ – our ground truth – and for any estimator, the offline estimate of the uplift $\hat{\mathcal{R}}^{\text{EST}}(\pi_t, c, \mathcal{S}_p) - \hat{\mathcal{R}}(\mathcal{S}_p)$. We added $\mathcal{S}_p$ in the arguments of the estimator to emphasize the estimator is computed on data collected by the *prod* population.

We could run several *offline A/B tests* based on the data on a single *online A/B test* – e.g. $\Delta\hat{\mathcal{R}}(\pi_p, \pi_t)$ on the data of control population A or $\Delta\hat{\mathcal{R}}(\pi_t, \pi_p)$ on the data of test population B. We only keep one of them, because if we compare them with the same *online A/B test* result, the comparisons wouldn't be independent. In the following, we consider $\Delta\hat{\mathcal{R}}(\pi_p, \pi_t)$ on the data of control population A, which means the control (logging) policy is the production one π_p and the tested one is π_t.

6.2 Estimators

We compare here four estimators presented in the previous sections: CIS, NCIS, PieceNCIS and PointNCIS. We set the capping value to $c = 100$ based on the graph presented in Section 4.3. We discarded non-capped estimators such as IS or NIS due to their very high variance: the confidence intervals on $\Delta\hat{R}$ would never lead to a positive or negative decision, it would always be neutral. Moreover, we chose to ignore the doubly-robust estimator (DR) for two reasons. Indeed if the estimator is not capped, it suffers the same issue as IS and NIS. When it is capped [25], its performance strongly depends on the reward model such that the optimal policy under such estimator when $c \to 0$ is the deterministic policy choosing the argmax action on the reward model.

Computation time. The NCIS and PieceNCIS estimators need to be computed on the entire dataset, on both positive and negative examples. Like CIS, PointNCIS just needs to read the positive examples : it leads to a huge gain in computation time and efficiency when the reward is very sparse.

6.3 Correlation in Online / Offline Uplifts

To compare the performance of the different estimators, we first simply compute the correlations between the values of $\Delta\hat{R}$ and ΔR on the series of A/B tests. Results are presented in Fig. 3. As expected, CIS performs quite poorly, due to the strong capping. Compensating the bias only globally with NCIS already proves to

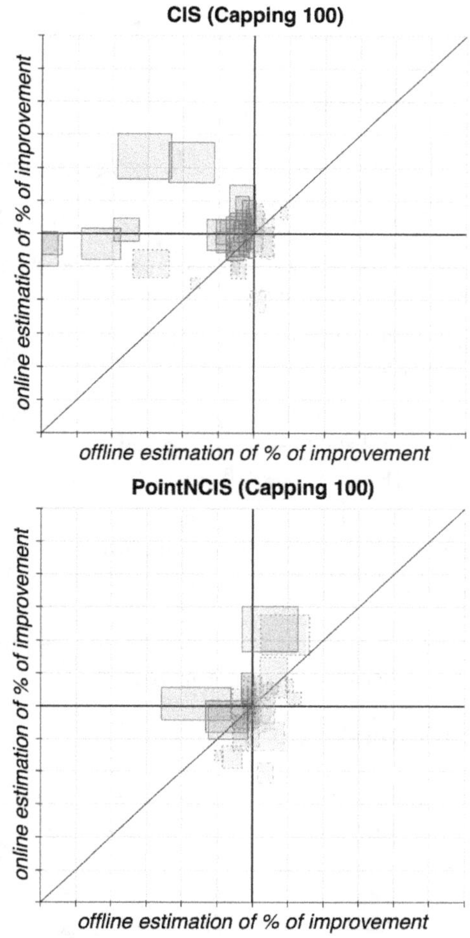

Figure 4: Comparison of online/offline decision. A box is an A/B test. The width (resp. height) of the box is a 90% confidence interval on the offline (resp. online) uplift. The scale is the same for both axis. Green/dotted: right decision. Orange/dashed: false positive). Red/plain: false negative.

be a good improvement. Then, the more local the model on the bias, the better performing the estimator: the piecewise estimator is better than the global and the pointwise is better than the piecewise.

While these first results are already satisfying, it does not reflect the fact that all types of errors are not as bad and that the different estimators do not lead to the same types of errors – which, as we will see in the following, explains why the correlation online/offline of CIS seems to be negative.

6.4 False positive VS False negative rate

From the point of view of continuously improving a production recommender system, false negatives are much worse than false positives. A false positive – predicted positive by the offline estimator and actually negative or neutral during the A/B test – has a cost limited to the A/B test duration. It slows down the pace of improvement of the system. On the contrary, a false negative is an actual improvement of the system that will never be tested online due to a mistake in the offline estimation. Such an error has a long term cost, as it is an actual improvement that won't be rolled-out.

In Figure 4, we show the comparison between online and offline decisions for our two extreme estimators CIS and PointNCIS. The number of false negatives of CIS is especially interesting: it reflects that CIS always underestimates the reward. It explains why the correlation of CIS is negative in Fig. 3, just because there are more positive decisions than negative in our dataset.

To have a clearer understanding of the quality of the different estimators, we sum up in Table 3 the uplift correlations (same data as in Fig. 3) along with metrics on the decision (positive / neutral / negative) such as the precision and the false negative rate (FNR). We can split the improvement in three. First, only using a global model of the bias – such as NCIS – is enough to drastically reduce the number of false negative errors: the FNR goes from 0.64 (CIS) to 0.33 (NCIS). This is also reflected by an improvement in precision and correlation. Then, another improvement comes from using more local approximations of the bias: precision and correlation also improves from NCIS to PieceNCIS or PointNCIS. When looking more carefully at the changes of decisions between the estimator, we actually noticed several A/B tests that include changes similar to the counter-example presented in Sec. 5.2, which support the need for more local estimators and explain the improvement the more local estimators show. Finally, we can also observe a better correlation of PointNCIS over PieceNCIS. However, as the precision is quite similar, it may only come from a better estimation of the value of the uplift and not from more aligned decisions. In the end, its performance and computation efficiency improvements make PointNCIS a better choice than the other estimators.

Table 3: Performance of the different estimators. Uncertainty is reported based on 10%/90% confidence intervals obtained by bootstrapping. *CI size* indicates the average relative width of the confidence interval compared to CIS one.

	Correlation	Precision	FNR	CI size
CIS	-0.15 ± 0.35	0.28 ± 0.10	0.64 ± 0.11	–
NCIS	0.24 ± 0.18	0.47 ± 0.11	0.33 ± 0.11	1.1
PieceNCIS	0.36 ± 0.22	0.53 ± 0.11	0.28 ± 0.08	1.5
PointNCIS	0.49 ± 0.13	0.56 ± 0.13	0.16 ± 0.09	0.8

7 CONCLUSION

Through the paper, we exhibited the different sub-optimality properties of the traditional counterfactual estimators in the setting of recommender systems. We introduced several new estimators exhibiting a better bias-variance trade-off than the traditional Normalised Capped Importance Sampling estimator. Then, we provided a benchmark of the different offline estimators with experiments conducted on a large commercial recommender system. In the future, we plan to investigate other ways to reduce the variance of the offline estimators. A simple way would be to exploit that several recommendation policies are implemented every week: combining them in order to make the mixture of policies closer to the test policy could help to reduce the variance of the different offline estimators.

A APPENDIX

A.1 Analysis of the bias of the NCIS estimator

In this section, we analyse the bias of the Normalised Capped Importance Sampling estimator in the general case (true for both max and zero capping). We also show how the formula can be simplified in the case of zero capping.

LEMMA A.1 (ASYMPTOTICAL BEHAVIOUR OF $\hat{\mathcal{R}}^{\text{NCIS}}$). *Let $\hat{\mathcal{R}}^{\text{NCIS}}$ the normalised capped importance sampling estimator defined in* (1). *Then,*

$$\mathbb{P}\left(\lim_{n\to\infty} \hat{\mathcal{R}}^{\text{NCIS}}(\pi_t, c, \mathcal{S}_n) = \hat{\mathcal{R}}^{\text{CIS}} + \hat{\mathcal{R}}^{\text{CIS}} \frac{1 - \mathbb{E}_{\pi_t}[\frac{\overline{W}}{W}]}{\mathbb{E}_{\pi_t}[\frac{\overline{W}}{W}]}\right) = 1$$

PROOF. First, we study the convergence of the numerator: It is the mean of n i.i.d. random variables. Thus, according to the strong law of large numbers, with probability one,

$$\lim_{n\to\infty} \frac{1}{n} \sum_{(x,a,r)\in\mathcal{S}_n} \overline{w}(a,x)r = \mathbb{E}_{\pi_p}\left[\overline{W}R\right] = \mathbb{E}_{\pi_t}\left[\frac{\overline{W}R}{W}\right]$$

The denominator is also the mean of n i.i.d. random variables. Then, with probability one,

$$\lim_{n\to\infty} \frac{1}{n} \sum_{(x,a,r)\in\mathcal{S}_n} \overline{w}(a,x) = \mathbb{E}_{\pi_p}\left[\overline{W}\right] = \mathbb{E}_{\pi_t}\left[\frac{\overline{W}}{W}\right]$$

Hence, we reach

$$\lim_{n\to\infty} \hat{\mathcal{R}}^{\text{NCIS}} = \frac{\mathbb{E}_{\pi_t}\left[\frac{\overline{W}R}{W}\right]}{\mathbb{E}_{\pi_t}\left[\frac{\overline{W}}{W}\right]} = \mathbb{E}_{\pi_t}\left[\frac{\overline{W}R}{W}\right] + \mathbb{E}_{\pi_t}\left[\frac{\overline{W}R}{W}\right] \frac{1 - \mathbb{E}_{\pi_t}\left[\frac{\overline{W}}{W}\right]}{\mathbb{E}_{\pi_t}\left[\frac{\overline{W}}{W}\right]}$$

$$= \hat{\mathcal{R}}^{\text{CIS}} + \hat{\mathcal{R}}^{\text{CIS}} \frac{1 - \mathbb{E}_{\pi_t}\left[\frac{\overline{W}}{W}\right]}{\mathbb{E}_{\pi_t}\left[\frac{\overline{W}}{W}\right]}$$

□

We observe that NCIS is correcting CIS by approximating the performance on the capped volume by the performance on the non-capped volume. It helps to reduce the bias of CIS. We study now the particular case of zero capping.

LEMMA A.2 (ASYMPTOTICAL BEHAVIOUR OF $\hat{\mathcal{R}}^{\text{NCIS}}_{\text{zero}}$). *: Let $\hat{\mathcal{R}}^{\text{NCIS}}_{\text{zero}}$ the capped normalised importance sampling estimator. Then,*

$$\mathbb{P}\left(\lim_{n\to\infty} \hat{\mathcal{R}}^{\text{NCIS}}_{\text{zero}}(\pi_t, c, \mathcal{S}_n) = \mathbb{E}_{\pi_t}\left[R\mathbf{1}_{W\leq c}\right]\right) = 1$$

PROOF. Straightforward application of the previous lemma □

This analysis can obviously be extended to PieceNCIS.

A.2 Analysis under varying capping parameter

To prove that we can control the variance of PointNCIS even though the value of $\tilde{w}_c(a,x) = \frac{\overline{w}(a,x)}{\mathbb{E}_{\pi_t}\left[\frac{\overline{W}}{W}\middle|X=x\right]}$ may be higher than the capping c, we need to prove that for any value of $c > 1$, we can find a $\tilde{c}$ such that $\tilde{w}_{\tilde{c}}(a,x) \leq c$. The following lemma states that it is possible to ensure this with max-capping.

LEMMA A.3 (MAX-CAPPING). *For any a and $c > 1$, there exists $\tilde{c}$ such that $\tilde{w}_{\tilde{c}}(a,x) \leq c$.*

PROOF. For any $\tilde{c}$, $\mathbb{E}_{\pi_t}\left[\frac{\overline{W}}{W}\middle|x\right] = \mathbb{E}_{\pi_p}\left[\min(W,\tilde{c})|x\right]$, thus

$$\tilde{w}_{\tilde{c}}(a,x) \leq \frac{\tilde{c}}{\mathbb{E}_{\pi_p}\left[\min(W,\tilde{c})|x\right]} \leq \frac{1}{\mathbb{P}_{\pi_p}(W \geq \tilde{c}|x)} \xrightarrow{\tilde{c}\to 0} 1$$

as $\mathbb{E}_{\pi_p}\left[\min(W,\tilde{c})|x\right] = \tilde{c}\mathbb{P}_{\pi_p}(W \geq \tilde{c}|x) + \mathbb{E}_{\pi_p}\left[W[W < \tilde{c}]|x\right]$. □

Unfortunately, we cannot ensure such property for zero-capping, which prevents us from adapting $\tilde{c}$ for PointNCIS.

LEMMA A.4 (ZERO-CAPPING). *There exists a, $c > 1$ such that for any $\tilde{c} > 0$, $\tilde{w}_{\tilde{c}}(a,x) > c$.*

PROOF. We use a counter-example where two actions a_0 and a_1 are taken with probabilities $\pi_p(a_0) = p$ and $\pi_t(a_0) = 1 - \pi_p(a_0)$ where $p > 0.5$. Then, $w(a_0) = \frac{1-p}{p} < w(a_1) = \frac{p}{1-p}$.

Case $\tilde{c} < w(a_0)$: $\tilde{w}_{\tilde{c}}(a,x)$ is undefined.

Case $\tilde{c} \in [w(a_0), w(a_1)]$: $\tilde{w}_{\tilde{c}}(a_1,x) = 0$ and $\tilde{w}_{\tilde{c}}(a_0,x) = \frac{1-p}{p^2}$.

Case $\tilde{c} \geq w(a_1)$: $\tilde{w}_{\tilde{c}}(a_1,x) = \frac{p}{1-p} > 1$ and $\tilde{w}_{\tilde{c}}(a_0,x) = \frac{1-p}{p}$.

So, if $0.5 < p < \frac{-1+\sqrt{5}}{2}$ and $1 < c < \min\left(\frac{p}{1-p}, \frac{1-p}{p^2}\right)$ then there exists an action in each case such that $\tilde{w}_{\tilde{c}} > c$. □

A.3 Additional figures

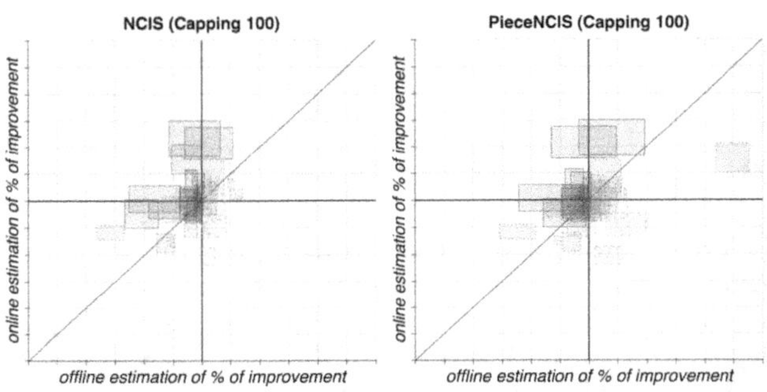

Figure 5: Comparison of online/offline decision. A box is an A/B test. The width (resp. height) of a box is a 90% confidence bound on the offline (resp. online) uplift. The scale is the same for both axis. Green/dotted: right decision. Orange/dashed: false positive. Red/plain: false negative.

REFERENCES

[1] Ricardo Baeza-Yates, Berthier Ribeiro-Neto, et al. 1999. *Modern information retrieval.*

[2] Léon Bottou and Jonas Peters. 2013. Counterfactual reasoning and learning systems: the example of computational advertising. *Proceedings of Journal of Machine Learning Research (JMLR).*

[3] Ralph Allan Bradley and Milton E. Terry. 1952. Rank Analysis of Incomplete Block Designs: The Method of Paired Comparisons. *Biometrika* (1952).

[4] Weiwei Cheng, Eyke Hüllermeier, and Krzysztof J Dembczynski. 2010. Label ranking methods based on the Plackett-Luce model. *Proceedings of the 27th International Conference on Machine Learning (ICML).*

[5] Nick Craswell, Onno Zoeter, Michael Taylor, and Bill Ramsey. 2008. An Experimental Comparison of Click Position-bias Models. *Proceedings of the International Conference on Web Search and Data Mining (WSDM).*

[6] Miroslav Dudik, John Langford, and Lihong Li. 2011. Doubly robust policy evaluation and learning. *Proceedings of the 28th International Conference on Machine Learning (ICML).*

[7] John Guiver and Edward Snelson. 2009. Bayesian inference for Plackett-Luce ranking models. *Proceedings of the 26th annual International Conference on Machine Learning (ICML).*

[8] JM Hammersley and DC Handscomb. 1964. *Monte Carlo Methods.* Chapter.

[9] F. Maxwell Harper and Joseph A. Konstan. 2015. The MovieLens Datasets: History and Context. *ACM Trans. Interact. Intell. Syst..*

[10] Jonathan L Herlocker, Joseph A Konstan, Loren G Terveen, and John T Riedl. 2004. Evaluating collaborative filtering recommender systems. *Proceedings of Transactions on Information Systems (TOIS).*

[11] Daniel G Horvitz and Donovan J Thompson. 1952. A generalization of sampling without replacement from a finite universe. *Journal of the American statistical Association.*

[12] Business Insider. 2017. Morgan Stanley puts Amazon Prime subscribers at 65M. http://www.businessinsider.fr/us/morgan-stanley-puts-amazon-prime-subscribers-at-65m-2017-2/. (2017).

[13] Kalervo Järvelin and Jaana Kekäläinen. 2000. IR evaluation methods for retrieving highly relevant documents. *Proceedings of the 23rd annual international conference on Research and development in information retrieval (SIGIR).*

[14] Deba B Lahiri. 1951. A method of sample selection providing unbiased ratio estimates. *Bulletin of the International Statistical Institute.*

[15] Lihong Li, Wei Chu, John Langford, and Xuanhui Wang. 2011. Unbiased offline evaluation of contextual-bandit-based news article recommendation algorithms. *Proceedings of the International Conference on Web Search and Data Mining (WSDM).*

[16] Benjamin M. Marlin, Richard S. Zemel, Sam Roweis, and Malcolm Slaney. 2007. Collaborative Filtering and the Missing at Random Assumption. *Proceedings of the Twenty-Third Conference on Uncertainty in Artificial Intelligence (UAI).*

[17] Andreas Maurer and Massimiliano Pontil. 2009. Empirical Bernstein bounds and sample variance penalization. *Proceedings of the 22nd Annual Conference on Learning Theory (COLT).*

[18] Hiroshi Midzuno. 1951. On the sampling system with probability proportionate to sum of sizes. *Annals of the Institute of Statistical Mathematics.*

[19] Art Owen. 2010. Monte Carlo theory, methods and examples. (2010). arXiv:arXiv:1012.5461v2

[20] R. L. Plackett. 1975. The Analysis of Permutations. *Journal of the Royal Statistical Society. Series C (Applied Statistics).*

[21] MJD Powell and J Swann. 1966. Weighted uniform sampling: a Monte Carlo technique for reducing variance. *Journal of Applied Mathematics.*

[22] Bruno Pradel, Nicolas Usunier, and Patrick Gallinari. 2012. Ranking with non-random missing ratings: influence of popularity and positivity on evaluation metrics. *Proceedings of the Sixth Conference on Recommender Systems (RecSys).*

[23] Amode Ranjan Sen. 1952. Present status of probability sampling and its use in estimation of farm characteristics. *Econometrica* (1952).

[24] Adith Swaminathan and Thorsten Joachims. 2015. The Self-Normalized Estimator for Counterfactual Learning. *Proceeding of Neural Information Processing Systems (NIPS).*

[25] Philip Thomas and Emma Brunskill. 2016. Data-efficient off-policy policy evaluation for reinforcement learning. *Proceedings of the International Conference on Machine Learning (ICML).*

[26] Louis Leon Thurstone. 1927. A Law of Comparative Judgement. *Psychological Review.*

[27] Ronald J. Williams. 1992. Simple statistical gradient-following algorithms for connectionist reinforcement learning. *Journal of Machine Learning Research (JMLR)* (1992).

[28] John I. Yellott. 1977. The relationship between Luce's Choice Axiom, Thurstone's Theory of Comparative Judgment, and the double exponential distribution. *Journal of Mathematical Psychology.*

Care to Share? Learning to Rank Personal Photos for Public Sharing

Ido Guy
Ben-Gurion University of the Negev, Beer-Sheva, Israel
eBay Research, Netanya, Israel*
idoguy@acm.org

Alexander Nus
eBay Research, Netanya, Israel*
alnus@ebay.com

Dan Pelleg
Yahoo Research, Haifa, Israel
pellegd@acm.org

Idan Szpektor
Google Research, Tel Aviv, Israel*
szpektor@google.com

ABSTRACT

With mobile devices, users are taking ever-growing numbers of photos every day. These photos are uploaded to social sites such as Facebook and Flickr, often automatically. Yet, the portion of these uploaded photos being publicly shared is low, and on a constant decline. Deciding which photo to share takes considerable time and attention, and many users would rather forfeit the social interaction and engagement than sift through their piles of uploaded photos. In this paper, we introduce a novel task of recommending socially-engaging photos to their creators for public sharing. This will turn a tedious manual chore into a quick, software-assisted process. We provide extensive analysis over a large-scale dataset from the Flickr photo sharing website, which reveals some of the traits of photo sharing in such sites. Additionally, we present a ranking algorithm for the task that comprises three steps: (a) grouping of near-duplicate photos; (b) ranking the photos in each group by their "shareability"; and (c) ranking the groups by their likelihood to contain a shareable photo. A large-scale experiment allows us to evaluate our algorithm and show its benefits compared to competitive baselines and algorithmic alternatives.

ACM Reference Format:
Ido Guy, Alexander Nus, Dan Pelleg, and Idan Szpektor. 2018. Care to Share? Learning to Rank Personal Photos for Public Sharing. In *Proceedings of 11th ACM International Conf. on Web Search and Data Mining (WSDM 2018).* ACM, New York, NY, USA, 9 pages. https://doi.org/10.1145/3159652.3159713

1 INTRODUCTION

Digital photography, as enabled by smartphones, has changed the way people take photos and interact through them. Prior to smartphones and high-quality phone cameras, people preferred looking at photos together or in person over viewing them on a computer, while e-mail was the main vehicle for digital sharing [9]. When phone cameras and image uploading and sharing became ubiquitous, users started taking many ordinary and spontaneous photos of family, friends, and travel. The phone turned into a tool for creating and maintaining social relationships, sharing experiences (either personal or collective), and self-expression and presentation [2, 27]. Specifically, automatic image uploading from mobile phones to social media, such as Facebook and Flickr, or cloud storage, such as Google Drive and Dropbox, soared in popularity. And while some use the cloud to share all their photos (i.e., set their default sharing to "public"), many others upload their photos privately, as a means for backup or limited sharing with just friends or family [2, 18, 19].

This technological change led to new challenges with respect to photo sharing. First, due to volume, many of the uploaded photos remain part of a private repository, because users do not have the time or state-of-mind to go over the photos they took and decide which should be shared. Second, when users do go over their photos, e.g., once a day, a week, or a month, they face a daunting task. And while some users overcome it with a share-all policy, even they would welcome software to help save their followers from a deluge of boring photos. To back this intuition with data, we analyzed millions of photos uploaded from smartphones to Flickr. Our analysis shows that the total number of photos has been on the expected rise, fueled by increasing popularity of mobile photos. And yet, the *portion* of public photos has been on a constant decline.

To address these challenges, we propose the novel task of automatic recommendation of photos from a private collection for the purpose of public sharing. In other words, photos would be assessed by their likelihood to be shared. The most likely ones would be recommended to the user for the actual sharing act.

This novel task is by no means a simple one. Studies revealed that human considerations when selecting photos for sharing involve concerns about social disclosure, as well as factors that traditionally influence privacy management, like family concerns or social support [1, 2, 18]. While some of these considerations are personal and difficult to model, we expect that shareable and non-shareable photos can still be distinguished using automatic analysis.

Prior work found that digital camera users often take *groups* (or "bursts") of photos on the same object or scene, which are sometimes referred to as near-duplicates [6, 17]. Our analysis shows that when users manually select photos for sharing, they typically choose at most one of the photos in each such group. In this work, we therefore propose a three-step algorithm for the photo sharing recommendation task. In the first step, the target photo collection

*Part of the research was conducted while working at Yahoo Research.

WSDM 2018, February 5–9, 2018, Marina Del Rey, CA, USA

ACM ISBN 978-1-4503-5581-0/18/02...$15.00
https://doi.org/10.1145/3159652.3159713

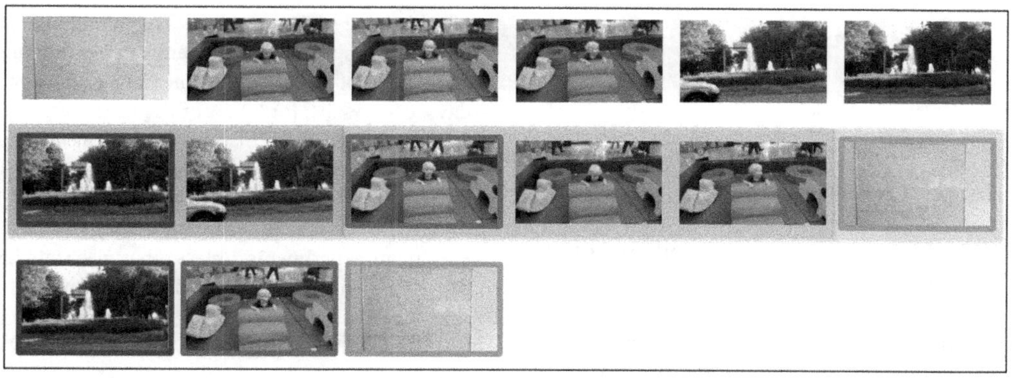

Figure 1: Photo stream, ordered from left to right in its original form (1st line), after running the three-step algorithm (2nd line), and after de-duplication (3rd line).

is segmented into near-duplicate groups. The algorithm then ranks the photos in each group by their likelihood to be shared. Finally, the groups themselves are ranked by their prospects to contain shareable photos. Following, we evaluate the final recommendation of photos for sharing under two alternative usage scenarios, in which, either: (a) de-duplication is important; or (b) duplicates are acceptable. If duplicates are unwanted, only the top-ranked photo from each group is presented to the user. Otherwise, several (or all) photos from each group are shown, ordered by the groups' ranking on top of their in-group ranking.

Figure 1 demonstrates the output of our algorithm on a daily photo stream contributed by one of the authors. First, the algorithm segments the stream into three scenes (whiteboard, child, fountain), each composed of between one and three near-duplicate photos. Then it ranks the photos in each group by their likelihood to be shared (e.g., ranking the photo of the fountain without the disrupting car first, or ranking the photo that best captures the child's face first). Then, the groups themselves are ranked by their likelihood to include a publicly shareable photo. Finally, de-duplication is performed (assuming it is desired in this case), leaving one photo per group on the final recommendation list.

We address all three steps in our approach as supervised subtasks. We consider near-duplicate grouping as a sequential segmentation of the photo collection over time and learn a threshold over similarity functions, given a training dataset. In addition, both group ranking and photo ranking within each group are treated as learning to rank (LTR) tasks. We trained our LTR models on a large dataset consisting of daily uploads of smartphone photos to Flickr, where (only some) photos are manually marked as public by the account owner. The goal in the LTR tasks is to rank the public (shared) photos and groups higher, as compared to the private ones.

We note that many works addressed the task of summarizing a photo collection [11, 17, 21, 23, 24, 26], but only a few recent studies suggested to select or recommend "interesting" photos from an album without the goal of summarizing the whole album [5, 28] (for more details, see Section 5). While we share some perspectives to these studies in terms of the algorithmic approaches and derived features, our task is inherently different: identifying private photos that are interesting for public sharing, as opposed to photos that are interesting as personal representatives of an album, or that are selected from already public collections.

To evaluate our algorithm, we conducted a large-scale experiment over hundreds of thousands of photos. We evaluated each sub-task of our algorithm, as well as the overall goal of recommending photos for sharing. We compared our three-step algorithm to a direct single-step algorithm that ranks all photos individually without the notion of groups. We also compared our algorithm to baselines such as the last photo taken or the most aesthetic photo. Our results indicate that our algorithm outperforms the respective baselines in each step, as well as in the overall recommendation task, regardless of whether de-duplication is desired or not.

To summarize, the main contributions of this paper are:

- Introducing a novel task of automatic recommendation of photos for sharing.
- Analyzing sharing behavior by Flickr users using smartphones.
- Suggesting a three-phase approach for the task, with a supervised algorithm for each stage, using a learning-to-rank framework.
- Implementing and evaluating the suggested approach using a large-scale log of selective sharing activity by Flickr users.

2 DATASET CHARACTERISTICS

To learn more about users' photo sharing behavior in social networks we analyzed Flickr, a popular social network focused on photos. Our dataset consists of basic metadata for all Flickr photos in the years 2004–2015. This metadata includes the date the photo was taken and the camera model it was taken with (available for over 80% of the photos). It also includes the sharing permissions of each photo, as set by the photo owner: at one extreme, private and accessible to the photo owner only; at the other extreme, public photos accessible to all users; and in-between, photos accessible to user-defined lists of friends, family, or both.

Our dataset indicates that the number of photos on Flickr rises every year. For example, in 2015 it was $\times 2.5$ compared to 2012 and $\times 16$ compared to 2004. This is driven by the increase in mobile photos — the portions rise from close-to-zero in 2004 to over 50% in 2015. Overall, in our dataset, 58% of the photos are private, 30% are public, and only 12% are in the middle ground for friends and family. In this work, we focus on the behavior of public sharing and leave its differences from limited sharing (with friends or family)

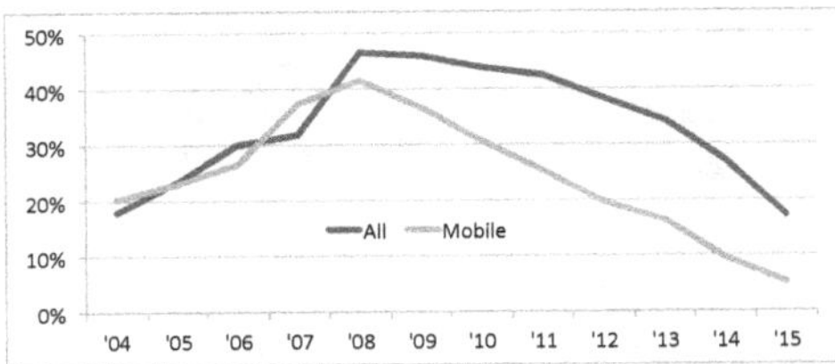

Figure 2: Portion of public photos per year for all Flickr photos and for mobile photos only.

Table 1: Characteristics of all photos and public-only photos in our experimental dataset: total counts and statistics of photos per user-day.

	Total	Avg	Std	Med	Min	Max
All photos	10.3M	58.8	110.1	31	7	7,804
Public photos	402K	2.3	4.3	1	1	191

for future work. We henceforth refer to all types of restricted access as "private" (70%).

Figure 2 shows the portion of public photos by year, for all photos and for mobile photos. From 2004 to 2008, the percentage across all photos increased, from 17.9% to a peak of 46.5%. Since then it is decreasing, down to 17.0% in 2015. One explanation to this sharp decrease is that many photos are submitted via automatic uploaders, which back up all the device photos and whose default permission is private (due to the sensitivity of this feature). Automatic uploading has become especially prevalent in mobile devices in recent years. Indeed, the percentage of public photos within all photos uploaded from mobile devices is much lower than within all photos (starting 2008). Combining this statistic with the surge in overall percentage of photos that originated from mobile devices points at the declining public photo percentage since.

Given our objective to predict which photos would be publicly shared by their owner, we constructed a more goal-oriented dataset. To this end, we focused on Flickr data from mobile devices in the years 2012–2016. We considered all unique pairs of users and calendar days, henceforth referred to as *user-days*. Each user-day consists of all photos taken by a single user in a single day, allowing us to examine sharing behavior at a one-day granularity. The average number of photos per user-day in our data is 7.9 (std: 20.3, median: 3, max: 13,231), with 30.2% of the days having one photo only. As we have seen before, most mobile photos are kept personal. Indeed, 91.8% of our user-days contain no public photos. On the other hand, in 6.9% of our user-days, all photos are public. For our experiments, however, we were interested in days for which both private and public photos exist, and in particular days for which the majority (but not all) of the photos are private, as these imply an explicit selection for sharing. After some analysis, we opted for user-days in which no more than 15% of the photos (but more than zero) are public[1].

The above selection left us with 177K user-days and 10.3M photos, to which we refer as the *experimental dataset*. Table 1 shows the characteristics of this dataset. Overall, the vast majority of the photos are private, with an average of 58.8 photos per user-day, of which only 2.3 are public. The percentage p of public photos per use-day spreads rather evenly across the range (0%, 15%], with an average of 7.8% (std: 4.1, median: 7.7%). For 30.8% of the user-days, $0\% < p \leqslant 5\%$; for 37.7% of the user-days, $5\% < p \leqslant 10\%$; and for 31.5%, $10\% < p \leqslant 15\%$. Finally, we note that the experimental dataset includes a large number of distinct users: 52.9% of them account for only one user-day in the dataset; additional 15.5% account for two user-days; and the maximum number of user-days per user is 828. In our experiments, unless otherwise stated, we randomly split the dataset into 90% training user-days and the rest for testing.

[1] Notice this implies each user-day includes at least 7 photos in total.

3 RECOMMENDING PHOTOS TO SHARE

3.1 Motivation and Overview

3.1.1 Algorithmic Approach. Our proposed algorithm consists of three steps. First, the target photo upload[2] is segmented into *groups* of near-duplicates. The algorithm then ranks the photos within each group based on their likelihood to be shared. Finally, the groups themselves are ranked by each group's likelihood to contain at least one shareable photo.

We support and experiment with two alternative recommendation scenarios: (a) the user prefers not to see near-duplicates, only a single exemplar from each scene; and (b) the user does not mind duplicates, as long as shareable photos are ranked high. Our algorithm generates the top N photos comprising the *recommendation list*, and can then be used in one of two ways. If near-duplicates are unwanted, the top-N groups that were ranked in the third step are selected. Then, the top-ranked photo from each group is considered, generating a ranked list of N photos. Alternatively, if de-duping is not essential, the recommendation list includes the top $k > 1$ photos from each group, concatenating them to a single list according to the group rankings.

3.1.2 Latent Vector Representation of Photos. Throughout the steps of our algorithm, we use a representation consisting of a 4K-dimensional vector for each photo. This *latent vector* was generated using a deep neural network model. Specifically, we utilized the YFNet-B network, which is used to power Flickr's automatic textual tags feature [10]. This network's training goal is different than ours, and its final layer performs classification over ~5,000 tags. Yet, the output of the penultimate layer can be viewed as a compressed "semantic" representation of the input photo, which is then used for inferring which tags are relevant to it. We used this output as our latent vector representation.

The full neural network includes 4 stages. In the first stage, 64 filters of size 7x7 each are applied, with stride 2. In the second stage, two layers of 128 filters are used, each factored by a 3x1 filter following by 1x3 filter, all with stride 1. The third stage consists of 256 filters, each similar to those in stage two (a 3x1 filter followed by a 1x3 filter, all with stride 1). Finally, the forth stage consists of two layers of 512 filters followed by a layer of 256 filters. All filters are similar to those in stages 2 and 3. Each convolution layer applies batch normalization and ReLU for non-linearity. The network was trained over the YFCC dataset [25], which consists of 100M photos with textual tags assigned by Flickr users. For further details see [10].

[2] In our experiments, these are daily mobile uploads.

Table 2: The different features and the steps in which they are used. Except for group-size features, group features are various aggregations over the feature score of all photos in the group: avg, std, variance, median, min, and max.

Feature Name	Step 1	Step 2	Step 3 representative	Step 3 group
color histogram diff.	×			
4K latent vector	×	×	×	
color distribution		×	×	
1,600 semantic tags		×	×	
inappropriateness		×	×	×
aesthetics		×	×	×
first in group		×	×	
last in group		×	×	
position from start		×	×	
position from end		×	×	
time delta from prev	×	×	×	×
time delta from next		×	×	
time delta from first		×	×	
time delta from last		×	×	
max photo score			×	×
group size (numeric)				×
10 group size indicators				×

We next detail the three steps in our algorithm, as well as the direct ranking algorithm. As a companion reference, Table 2 provides a summarization of all features used in each of the three steps.

3.2 Segmentation into Near-Duplicate Groups

As mentioned, we follow prior work that proposed to group photos which are considered near-duplicates [6, 17, 22]. To this end, we extracted a dataset consisting of 70 user-days[3]. Two of the authors annotated them for near-duplicate groups following three guidelines: (i) the photos in the group should capture the same scene; (ii) the photo subject stays the same within the group; and (iii) a user would not want to share more than one photo from the group.

Within each time-ordered stream of photos, we considered only consecutive photos as possible near-duplicates. Thus, annotators scanned the photo stream once, marking each photo that did not meet the guidelines for the current group as the beginning of a new group. Preliminary analysis showed that if the time gap between two photos is more than 15 seconds, they are rarely considered duplicates. We therefore automatically marked such cases (55% of all photos in our sample) as starting a new group, prior to any manual annotation, and excluded them from our gold dataset. This way, we directed the learning task to focus on the more difficult cases. In total, the two annotators labeled 1,486 photos with Cohen's kappa agreement of 0.77, measured on a shared subset of 130 photos. Overall, 70% of these photos were annotated as near-duplicates.

We constructed three features to be used as input for a classifier that determines whether a photo starts a new group (i.e., not a near-duplicate) or continues the previous one (i.e., a near-duplicate). The first two features have already been proposed in prior work on near-duplicates [17, 22]: (a) the time difference (in seconds) between the photo and its predecessor in the photo stream; and (b) the difference between the color histograms of the two photos. We computed the overall histogram difference by averaging the histogram difference for each RGB color, calculated using Hellinger distance.

Color histogram captures photo similarity at a rather low level. To compare photos at a more "semantic" level, we computed the cosine similarity between their latent vector representation, as described in Section 3.1.2. This high-level similarity was taken as a third feature, which, to the best of our knowledge, is novel for the near-duplicate task[4].

Considering the three features and our labeled gold dataset, we examined four types of classifiers for the near-duplicate task (using Weka [14]): logistic regression, support vector machine (SVM) with a Gaussian RBF kernel, C4.5 decision tree, and random forest. We used leave-one-out cross-validation to evaluate the performance of each algorithm. In each fold, we performed ten-fold cross-validation over the training set, for hyper-parameter tuning.

3.3 Ranking Photos Inside a Group

Applying group segmentation as described above on our entire experimental dataset showed that very small portions of the near-duplicate groups include more than one shared photo (full details are provided in Section 4). We therefore expect that when users share photos from such a group, they would often select the most appealing in terms of public view. Following, the second step of our algorithm selects the best "shareable" photo(s) within each group. We address this selection as a supervised ranking task, in which the goal is to rank photos that are likely to be shared above non-shareable ones.

To this end, we culled the experimental dataset to only include groups that contain at least one shared photo and one non-shared photo, since only these are useful for training and evaluating the in-group ranking task. We then trained a learning-to-rank (LTR) algorithm, where the target was to rank, in each training group, the shared photos higher than the non-shared ones. As our LTR framework we used an online variant of SVMRank [3] with AROW update [8], whose performance was found competitive for large-scale ranking [4]. The final score provided by the ranker for the top-ranked photo is denoted as the *max photo score.*

As input to the LTR algorithm, we derived from each photo a set of features (see summary in Table 2). Two types of features were considered. The first type refers to features that are extracted from each photo independently. As low-level features, we computed a distribution over a set of 16 main colors in each photo (red, blue, yellow, green, etc.). As high-level features, we included the 4K-dimensional latent vector described in Section 3.1.2. Additionally, we computed semantic features per photo, which were derived from the latent vector. These include automatically-derived semantic tags, such as '*dog*', '*baby*', and '*beach*', each with its likelihood probability [10]. We filtered out tags with likelihood smaller than 0.5, resulting in a sparse tag set of only a few tags per photo. Yet, these tags may help identify photo objects that are attractive for sharing, or vice versa. For example, we noticed that the '*child*' tag correlates negatively with shareability. We also assessed the likelihood of a photo to be inappropriate (e.g., for nudity) based on an in-house training set manually labeled for appropriateness. We expect this feature to help in demoting embarrassing photos. Finally, following prior work that found aesthetics to be useful in photo selection [21, 23], we used the approach of Zhang [30] to

[3]Since this task involved looking at personal data, we only considered photos from users who explicitly gave consent for their data to be used for research purposes.

[4]We also experimented with calculating similarity between the photos' derived tags, however this measure performed poorly, due to the low number of distinguishing tags per photo.

compute a single feature whose (continuous) value estimates the degree of aesthetics for each photo.

The second type of features for each photo refers to its relationships with other photos in the group. These include position features: (a) is the photo first in the group?; (b) is it last?; (c) its ordinal position from the group's start; and (d) its position from the end. These features assess whether group position affects photo selection for sharing. We also included features capturing the time delta (in seconds) of the photo from: (a) the previous photo in the group; (b) the next photo; (c) the first photo; and (d) the last photo. These features may help in pointing at various photography efforts as captured by different pause and activity periods.

3.4 Ranking Photo Groups

The third and final step in our algorithm, denoted by *L2RGroups*, ranks the segmented photo groups as a whole. Its goal is to place groups that are expected to contain at least one shareable photo on top of groups whose photos are expected to not be shared. We treat this ranking sub-task as a supervised ranking task, employing the same LTR framework of online SVMRank with AROW update used in step 2 (Section 3.3).

In step 2, the ranked objects were photos within a single near-duplicate group, labeled as either shared or not. Therefore, the ranker would aim to find subtle differences between photos that indicate shareability. Here, on the other hand, the objects are groups within each daily user upload, and each group is labeled as shared only if it contains at least one photo that is labeled as shared. We therefore expect the ranker to rely on more coarse differences between the groups, to distinguish between different scenes, such as a sunset versus parking cars.

As input to the ranker, we derive two types of features from each group. First, we consider all the features extracted for a single photo in step 2, as well as the max photo score provided by the ranker in step 2. To this end, a single photo is selected for each group, from which these features are extracted. Notice that this selection may not necessarily be the same as the selection of shareable photos as derived from the in-group ranking (step 2): here we aim to select a photo representative of the group that would distinguish it from other groups, while at step 2 we aimed to identify the photos in the group that are most likely to be shared. In fact, since we hypothesize that the ranker would look for more coarse-grained differences between photos for the group ranking task, we expect any photo selection rule to be useful here. We examine this hypothesis below, when analyzing group ranking results (Section 4.3).

Features of the second type are derived from the group as a whole. These include the group's size, both as a single numeric feature and as a set of 10 binary bucket features (with the last feature referring to size 10 or higher). In addition, we generated aggregate group statistics for some photo features: aesthetics, inappropriateness, max photo score, and time delta from previous photo. These statistics include the average, median, variance, standard deviation, minimum, and maximum within the group for each target feature.

3.5 Ranking Individual Photos

As already mentioned, an alternative approach that addresses the shareable group recommendation task is an algorithm that ranks all photos by inspecting each one individually, without considering the notion of a group. We implemented this algorithm, denoted as *L2RIndPhotos*, using the same LTR framework of SVMRank with AROW update, and trained the model on user-days, with the goal of ranking shared photos higher than non-shared ones. As features for each photo, we used the features extracted in step 2 (see Table 2), but ignoring any features that are derived from relationships with group members.

We note that *L2RIndPhotos* can also be applied to a scenario where de-duping is desired. This can be achieved in a post-processing step, where each photo that belongs to the same group as a higher-ranking photo is removed from the ranked list. This way, we can also adapt *L2RIndPhotos* for group ranking in a drill-down scenario (see Section 3.1). To this end, after de-duping is performed, each photo in the recommendation list, which represents a single group, can be replaced by its corresponding group.

Table 3: Classifier performance comparison for the near-duplicate grouping task.

Classifier	Accuracy (%)
Random forest	84.7
SVM (RDF kernel)	84.2
C4.5 decision tree	84.1
Logistic regression	82.6

4 EXPERIMENTS

In this section, we describe our main experimental results. These include evaluation for step 1 – near-duplicate group segmentation; step 2 – ranking photos within each group; and step 3 – group ranking. Finally, we describe our evaluation of the full-fledged pipeline for recommending individual photos for sharing, either with or without duplication.

4.1 Near-Duplicate Grouping Evaluation

Our algorithm's first step aims at grouping the stream of photos into near-duplicate groups. In Section 3.2 we defined this as a binary classification task, and set out to evaluate four types of classifiers over our manually-annotated gold dataset. Table 3 presents the accuracy of each of the four algorithms. The random forest model achieved the best performance and was therefore our final choice. Its accuracy using all three features was 84.7%. In practice, the overall accuracy of group segmentation is even higher, since photos taken over 15 seconds after their predecessors are automatically considered as non-near-duplicates, as explained in Section 3.2.

Ablation tests using the random forest model (Table 4) show the advantage of high-level similarity. Using this feature alone, the classifier achieved 83.0% accuracy. On the other hand, leaving high-level similarity out, while only considering time difference and color-histogram similarity, as in previous studies [17, 22], led to a substantively lower accuracy, at 75.1%. This shows that this task requires semantic understanding of photos, while low-level information is insufficient.

4.1.1 Grouping Statistics. As pre-processing for the next algorithmic steps, we used the random forest model, learned on the entire gold dataset with all features, to group near-duplicate pairs

Table 4: Ablation tests for near-duplicate detection using a random forest classifier. *time* stands for the time-difference feature, *colsim* for color-histogram similarity, and *highsim* for the latent-vector (high-level) similarity. Accuracy is presented both when using only the respective feature ('Only') and when using all features but the respective feature ('Exclude'). 'Exclude' for all-features (i.e., no features) reflects always selecting the majority class.

Feature Set	Acc. - Only (%)	Acc. - Exclude (%)
all features	84.7	70.0
highsim	83.0	75.1
time	73.8	84.5
colsim	69.4	84.5

Table 5: Distribution of photos in our experimental dataset by the size of their associated group ('%'), the portion of groups with at least one shared photo ('% shared (groups)'), and the likelihood of an individual photo from the group to be shared ('% shared (photos)').

Group Size	1	2	3	4 − 5	6 − 10	11+
%	43.8	20.5	9.1	9.8	8.8	8.0
% shared (groups)	4.6	7.5	10.9	12.4	14.9	21.0
% shared (photos)	4.6	4.0	4.0	3.3	2.6	1.9

with time delta of 15 seconds or less in our experimental dataset. This pre-processing resulted in an average of 35.9 groups per user-day, 9% of which containing at least one publicly shared photo.

Table 5 shows the distribution of photos by the size of the groups they belong to. The majority of the photos belong to a *non-trivial* group (i.e., size greater than 1), which indicates that near duplicates are common in mobile photography and are therefore important to consider when designing a sharing recommendation algorithm.

Another important aspect of our segmented dataset is that only 1.0% of the non-trivial groups include more than one shared photo (8.6% of these groups have exactly one shared photo), indicating that indeed users typically do not bother to share more than one photo out of a near-duplicate group. Even for groups of size greater than 5, the percentage of groups with more than one shared photo is only 3.3% (16.4% have one shared photo). Table 5 shows that as group size grows, the chances of the group to contain a shared photo increase, but the likelihood of each individual photo in the group to be shared drops.

An additional interesting statistic is shown in Table 6 – the distribution of time delta between consecutive photo pairs in groups. As seen, a substantial portion of the pairs has a time difference of zero seconds, often the result of an automatic camera feature that takes more than one photo per shooting, e.g., photos with different exposure or photos with and without high dynamic range (HDR). In addition, most other pairs are within 1 to 5 seconds from each other, indicating rapid photography in order to capture a "good" photo of a single scene.

Table 6: Distribution (percent) of consecutive photo pairs within groups by time difference (in seconds).

Time Delta	0	1 − 5	6 − 10	11 − 15
group size>1	36.6	41.4	14.6	7.4
group size>5	44.8	43.9	8.0	3.3
group size>10	50.8	42.0	5.3	1.9

Table 7: Performance of in-group ranking algorithms.

Algorithm	P@1	MRR
Chronological	0.301	0.591
Random	0.372	0.626
Distance from centroid	0.422	0.649
Reverse-chronological	0.430	0.660
Aesthetics	0.467	0.683
In-Group-LTR	0.520	0.721

4.2 In-Group Ranking Evaluation

The goal of our algorithm's second step is to learn to select the photos from a near-duplicate group, which are more likely to be shared compared to others in the group. For training and evaluation, we only considered groups with at least one public photo and at least one private photo, as explained in Section 3.3. Overall, our filtered dataset included 162K such groups across 82K different user-days, spanning a total of 684K photos. We compare our algorithmic approach, denoted further on by *In-Group-LTR*, to several baselines: (a) random order; (b) chronological – ranking by the time the photo was taken, from earliest to latest; (c) reverse-chronological; (d) distance from the centroid of the group, where the centroid is calculated over the entire feature space; and (e) aesthetics – ranking by the photo's aesthetic score, from highest to lowest. We used Precision@1 (P@1) as our main metric for this task, to reflect a selection of a single photo per group (i.e., duplication is not desired). For completeness, we also report the Mean Reciprocal Rank (MRR), which reflects the position of the highest ranking shared photo.

Table 7 reports the results. The chronological baseline yields the lowest performance, even lower than random, implying that the first attempt in a group is often a bad choice for sharing. Reverse-chronological ranking, on the other hand, is a better alternative, outperforming both a random choice, and, by a smaller margin, the distance from the centroid. We conjecture that the last photo in a group sometimes indicates user satisfaction with the outcome: after a good shot, no more are needed. Ranking by aesthetic score achieves even better performance, indicating that taking into account photo characteristics is preferable to simply considering its position within the group. Finally, our *In-Group-LTR* algorithm yields a further considerable performance enhancement, up to 52% in P@1, showing the benefit of learning to combine several high-level "semantic" and group-related features.

To further understand the contribution of the different feature categories to the task, we performed ablation tests by training the *In-Group-LTR* algorithm with each feature category by itself and, in addition, with all features excluding it. Results, presented in Table 8, indicate that the latent vector is the most valuable category, achieving high performance by itself (over 50% in P@1). It seems to encode aesthetics well enough, since the exclusion of the aesthetics score hardly has any effect. These results are consistent with

Table 8: Performance when using ('Only') or removing ('Exclude') subsets of features when training *In-Group-LTR*.

Feature Set	Only		Exclude	
	P@1	MRR	P@1	MRR
Position within group	0.394	0.638	0.520	0.721
Time delta within group	0.419	0.660	0.520	0.720
Aesthetics	0.467	0.683	0.519	0.721
Semantic tags	0.486	0.700	0.516	0.718
Latent vector	0.505	0.711	0.512	0.715
All Features	0.520	0.721		

Table 9: Performance of group ranking algorithms.

Ranking Algorithm	P@1	MRR	MAP
Random	0.090	0.242	0.218
Chronological order	0.146	0.277	0.257
Reverse-chronological order	0.164	0.300	0.279
Maximum aesthetic score	0.201	0.369	0.331
Group size	0.214	0.384	0.359
L2RIndPhotos	0.266	0.431	0.387
L2RGroups	0.310	0.470	0.427
L2RGroups – group features only	0.145	0.276	0.256
L2RGroups – no group features	0.304	0.465	0.421

the high performance achieved by high-level similarity features for the segmentation task (Section 4.1) and suggest this type of representation works well. In addition, semantic tags are useful, and combining any two of the three high-level categories (tags, aesthetics, and latent vector) results in performance similar to the full feature-set.

4.3 Group Ranking Evaluation

We next evaluate the sub-task of ranking groups by their likelihood to contain shared photos. Our training and test sets for this task are based on the experimental dataset described in Section 2. As evaluation metrics, we use Mean Average Precision (MAP) in addition to P@1 and MRR, since we are also interested in performance beyond the first hit (i.e., the first group with a shared photo). As discussed in Section 3.1, this sub-task also reflects a "drill-down" recommendation approach, in which groups are shown first and the user can then choose to view all photos of a specific group.

As mentioned in Section 3.4, the *L2RGroups* algorithm derives some of its features from a single representative photo within the group. The selection of the specific photo from which these features are derived is different in nature than the photo ranking task in step 2, which also involves the selection of photos from a near-duplicate group. Yet, here we are using the individual photo's features to derive more coarse-grained differences between groups, rather than subtle ones between individual photos within the same group. We therefore hypothesized that the selection of the specific photo from which the single-photo features are derived is not critical for the group ranking task. This hypothesis was proven correct: using different selection methods, such as first/last in group, highest aesthetic score, *In-Group-LTR*, and even random, yielded very similar performance for *L2RGroups*. For convenience, we opted to use *In-Group-LTR* as our representative selection method, yet as explained this is a rather arbitrary choice.

The direct algorithm *L2RIndPhotos*, which ranks photos individually, can be adapted to the sub-task of group ranking (Section 3.5). Following, Table 9 presents the performance of *L2RGroups* and *L2RIndPhotos* for group ranking, as well as various baselines. *L2RGroups* achieves the best performance across all metrics, by a large margin from *L2RIndPhotos* and the baselines. *L2RIndPhotos* performs better than the baselines, even though it does not include any group-related features. Among the baselines, ranking by group size, which does not consider any photo characteristics, achieves best performance. Indeed, Table 5 shows that larger groups are more likely to include a shared photo.

The bottom section of Table 9 shows the performance of *L2RGroups* with group-related features only and without them. It is clear that group features by themselves do not achieve high performance. Yet, their exclusion leads to some performance decline, indicating that they do contribute to the final model.

4.4 Photo Recommendation Evaluation

Finally, we tested the performance of different algorithms for the overall task of recommending photos to be publicly shared. We considered the following algorithms for the overall task: (a) Chronological - recommend the photos by the time they were taken (earliest first); (b) Reverse-chronological; (c) Aesthetic score – recommend the photos by their aesthetics (from highest to lowest); (d) *L2RIndPhotos*– learning to rank individual photos in a single step; and (e) *ThreeStepRanking*– our three-step algorithm, which segments into groups, ranks photos in each group (*In-Group-LTR*), and then ranks the groups (*L2RGroups*).

We evaluated two recommendation scenarios (see Section 3.1): (a) without filtering of near-duplicates; and (b) retaining only the top k photos in each near-duplicate group. When $k=1$, de-duplication yields a recommendation with only a single photo per group. For all algorithms that are unaware of groups, such as *L2RIndPhotos*, de-dupping can be performed as a post-processing step (Section 3.5). Evaluation is performed over the entire experimental dataset as described in Section 2. As evaluation metrics, we use MRR, P@K, and Recall@K (R@K), with $K \in \{1, 3, 5\}$, which enables us to inspect performance at different fixed recommendation list sizes.

Table 10 depicts the results for this experiment. Inspecting the algorithms' performance with de-duplication, both LTR algorithms significantly outperform all baselines. For example, *L2RIndPhotos* improves P@1 by 44% compared to the strongest baseline – aesthetic score. Yet, *ThreeStepRanking* performs substantially better, with an additional gain of 14.4% over *L2RIndPhotos* in MRR, and 17.5% in P@1. This gap in performance is consistent across all metrics and different recommendation list sizes, showing that splitting between group ranking and photo ranking within groups provides a leverage in ranking shareable photos high.

Interestingly, while increasing the size of the recommendation list enables the display of more shared photos (an increase of 95% in recall from R@1 to R@3, and of 29% from R@3 to R@5), precision substantially drops (a decrease of 69% from P@1 to P@3, 79% from P@3 to P@5). This shows that even for the top recommendations, it is quite difficult to identify the photos that will eventually be shared by the user. One reason may be that the choice of a single

Table 10: Performance of shareable photo ranking algorithms with de-duplication ($k=1,2$) and without it. The best result(s) in a column are boldfaced.

	Ranking Algorithm	MRR	P@1	P@3	P@5	R@1	R@3	R@5
De-dup ($k=1$)	Chronological	0.215	0.118	0.081	0.069	0.087	0.169	0.235
	Reverse-chronological	0.229	0.127	0.090	0.077	0.094	0.187	0.258
	Aesthetic score	0.272	0.143	0.110	0.095	0.105	0.234	0.323
	L2RIndPhotos	0.332	0.206	0.143	0.115	0.150	0.293	0.380
	ThreeStepRanking	0.380	**0.242**	**0.167**	0.132	**0.177**	0.345	0.445
($k=2$)	*L2RIndPhotos*	0.357	0.215	0.153	0.124	0.156	0.315	0.417
	ThreeStepRanking	**0.388**	**0.242**	**0.167**	**0.135**	**0.177**	**0.349**	**0.459**
No De-dup	Chronological	0.228	0.120	0.084	0.071	0.089	0.173	0.242
	Reverse-chronological	0.244	0.127	0.090	0.077	0.094	0.187	0.258
	Aesthetic Score	0.300	0.152	0.117	0.102	0.112	0.250	0.357
	L2RIndPhotos	0.369	0.218	0.157	0.127	0.158	0.324	0.430
	ThreeStepRanking	0.384	**0.242**	0.159	0.128	**0.177**	0.334	0.439

photo within a near-duplicate group may sometimes be arbitrary (all photos look the same) and therefore hard to reproduce.

If duplicates are allowed, the performance of *L2RIndPhotos*, which was trained for this scenario, improves by 5% to 10% in all metrics compared to the de-duplication scenario. On the other hand, the performance of *ThreeStepRanking* somewhat decreases for longer recommendation lists, yet it remains the best performing algorithm. Under the scenario where only two photos are shown per group ($k=2$), *ThreeStepRanking* performs best over all metrics, with a 3% increase in R@5 compared to full de-dupping. This scenario balances between showing a few alternatives from each group but still not over-populating the recommendation list with a single large group. Overall, these results indicate that ranking all photos is not the best option, especially when large groups are ranked high, from which only a single photo is usually shared (recall Section 4.1). We note that we also tested other values of k and found that *ThreeStepRanking* achieves its best performance when $k=2$, while *L2RIndPhotos*'s best performance is with no de-duplication.

5 RELATED WORK

The task we present in this paper – recommending private photos for public sharing – is novel. Yet, a large body of work considered related tasks in which photos are selected from a collection to represent or summarize the collection. We now describe some of these works, which influenced our algorithmic approach, the features used, such as aesthetic score, color histogram, semantic tags, and latent vectors, and the selected baselines.

Li et al. [17] created a summary of photos of a target event. They noticed that the closeness in photo acquisition time implies related image content, constituting a single *scene* within the event. Following, they segmented the photo stream into groups using timestamp and color-histogram differences. Then, the best photo in each scene was added to the summary. Their best-photo selection was based on identifying clear faces, assuming those are desired in a summary. Platt et al. [22] applied a similar approach using timestamp and color histogram similarities for segmentation. Graham et al. [11] inspected timestamp burstiness for creating clusters in a photo stream. They then selected cluster representatives, based on time differences, to form a summary, while ranking clusters by size. Chu and Lin [6] used Platt's timestamp-based clusters and then constructed a near-duplicate graph for each cluster, where edges indicated near-duplicate pairs. A representative was then selected to be the photo with the highest in-degree count. Other works examined unsupervised and supervised clustering of photo collections by events or by points of interest [7, 16, 20].

When summarizing a photo collection, different approaches considered complementing aspects, such as coverage and diversity. Singha et al. [24] summarized personal photo logs spanning several months. They introduced a framework that optimized over attractiveness, diversity, and coverage, as well as a concrete greedy algorithm. The photo factors were based on camera (EXIF, timestamp) and pixel features, as well as user-generated textual tags, face recognition, and photo location. Obardor et al. [21] composed a summary of a photo stream by splitting it into acts, i.e., long sequences of similar photos. They then selected photo representatives by combining aesthetics and narrative components. Guldogan et al. [12] automatically constructed a set of "interesting" photos by considering the view duration and the number of clicks for each photo in the user's photo collection. Tschiatschek et al. [26] summarized photo streams by evaluating each subset of the collection for coverage and diversity using a supervised mixture of sub-modular components. The components inspected how well a subset was similar to the whole collection, with similarity as a proxy to coverage and inner-subset dissimilarity as a proxy to diversity.

Several studies addressed the summarization of a collection of photos taken by several users. Jaffe et al. [15] defined collection summarization as a ranking task, in which the top K photos were selected after ranking. Their algorithm produced a hierarchical clustering of the photos based on their geo-location. Then, each cluster was scored by considering factors such as user and tag distinguishability and photo quality. Finally, the photos were recursively ranked by interleaving photos from prominent sub-clusters. Yang et al. [29] considered collections in which time settings are not calibrated. Their algorithm aligned the collections using visual and geo-location similarities. It then removed duplicates using greedy backward selection. Sadeghi et al. [23] grouped photos in multi-user collections, even when chronological boundaries were broken. They used a graphical model that considered the quality of a photo as well as pairwise similarity between all pairs in the album. The model was trained over manually-curated albums via Mechanical Turk. Photo features included face features, texture and color features, and photo aesthetics.

Recently, several works suggested to diverge from the traditional summarization approach, whose primary goal is to cover a target photo collection. Ceroni et al. [5] argued that a subset of important photos for a user need not cover all her collection. They proposed to select the top K photos deemed most important from a personal collection. They trained an SVM classifier on collections with self-labeled most important photos, and used it to rank the photos in a collection. Their features included quality-based aspects, such as contrast and blur; face recognition; high-level concept detection; and aggregate properties of the time-based clusters. Wang et al. [28] suggested that different types of albums may benefit from different types of importance prediction. They collected public photo "albums" (photos sharing many tags) from Flickr and tagged their types with Mechanical Turk. The annotators also marked the importance of each photo. They then trained a convolutional neural network in two stages, first to predict importance, then re-training the network's output stage for each album type.

6 CONCLUSIONS AND FUTURE WORK

We introduced the novel task of recommending private photos for public sharing. Such recommendation is especially helpful with the ubiquitous automatic upload, where mobile phone users need to sift dozens of photos that are uploaded daily into social networks and cloud storage services. We presented a three-step supervised ranking algorithm, which first groups together near-duplicates, then selects the best photo candidates for sharing in each group, and finally ranks groups by their likelihood to include a shareable photo. The selected photos from the top ranked groups are presented to the user as recommendations for sharing.

We conducted a large-scale experiment over a dataset of millions of photos uploaded from mobile phones, in which the owners of the photos manually selected just a few to be shared. Our algorithm outperformed other alternative algorithms and baselines, placing photos that were indeed shared higher on the recommendation list than the competitors.

To enable evaluation at large scale, we relied on a specific type of user behavior on Flickr, reflected by selective sharing of photos per-user per-day. As we showed, this data is diverse and derived from a large number of users, yet it may still limit the generalizability of our findings to some extent. Future research is needed to validate and extend our results in other settings. In addition, future work could also examine more fine-grained types of sharing, other than public, such as with family or friends only, or with communities [13], and study the differences in sharing behaviors among the various sharing types.

REFERENCES

[1] Shane Ahern, Dean Eckles, Nathaniel S Good, Simon King, Mor Naaman, and Rahul Nair. 2007. Over-exposed?: privacy patterns and considerations in online and mobile photo sharing. In *Proceedings of CHI.* 357–366.

[2] Morgan Ames, Dean Eckles, Mor Naaman, Mirjana Spasojevic, and Nancy Van House. 2010. Requirements for mobile photoware. *Personal and Ubiquitous Computing* 14, 2 (2010), 95–109.

[3] Yunbo Cao, Jun Xu, Tie-Yan Liu, Hang Li, Yalou Huang, and Hsiao-Wuen Hon. 2006. Adapting ranking SVM to document retrieval. In *Proceedings of SIGIR.* 186–193.

[4] David Carmel, Avihai Mejer, Yuval Pinter, and Idan Szpektor. 2014. Improving Term Weighting for Community Question Answering Search Using Syntactic Analysis. In *Proceedings of CIKM.* 351–360.

[5] Andrea Ceroni, Vassilios Solachidis, Claudia Niederée, Olga Papadopoulou, Nattiya Kanhabua, and Vasileios Mezaris. 2015. To Keep or Not to Keep: An Expectation-oriented Photo Selection Method for Personal Photo Collections. In *Proceedings of ICMR.* 187–194.

[6] Wei-Ta Chu and Chia-Hung Lin. 2008. Automatic selection of representative photo and smart thumbnailing using near-duplicate detection. In *Proceedings of MM.* 829–832.

[7] Matthew Cooper, Jonathan Foote, Andreas Girgensohn, and Lynn Wilcox. 2005. Temporal event clustering for digital photo collections. *ACM TOMM* 1, 3 (2005), 269–288.

[8] Koby Crammer, Alex Kulesza, and Mark Dredze. 2013. Adaptive Regularization of Weight Vectors. *MLJ* 91, 2 (2013), 155–187.

[9] David Frohlich, Allan Kuchinsky, Celine Pering, Abbe Don, and Steven Ariss. 2002. Requirements for photoware. In *Proceedings of CSCW.* 166–175.

[10] Pierre Garrigues, Sachin Farfade, Hamid Izadinia, Kofi Boakye, and Yannis Kalantidis. 2016. Tag Prediction at Flickr: a View from the Darkroom. *arXiv preprint* abs/1612.01922 (2016).

[11] Adrian Graham, Hector Garcia-Molina, Andreas Paepcke, and Terry Winograd. 2002. Time as essence for photo browsing through personal digital libraries. In *Proceedings of JCDL.* 326–335.

[12] Esin Guldogan, Jari Kangas, and Moncef Gabbouj. 2013. Personalized representative image selection for shared photo albums. In *Proceedings of ICCAT.* 1–4.

[13] Ido Guy, Inbal Ronen, Elad Kravi, and Maya Barnea. 2016. Increasing Activity in Enterprise Online Communities Using Content Recommendation. *ACM Trans. Comput.-Hum. Interact.* 23, 4 (2016), 22:1–22:28.

[14] Mark Hall, Eibe Frank, Geoffrey Holmes, Bernhard Pfahringer, Peter Reutemann, and Ian H Witten. 2009. The WEKA data mining software: an update. *ACM SIGKDD explorations newsletter* 11, 1 (2009), 10–18.

[15] Alexandar Jaffe, Mor Naaman, Tamir Tassa, and Marc Davis. 2006. Generating Summaries and Visualization for Large Collections of Geo-referenced Photographs. In *Proceedings of MIR.* 89–98.

[16] Hongzhi Li and Xian-Sheng Hua. 2010. Melog: Mobile Experience Sharing Through Automatic Multimedia Blogging. In *Proceedings of MCMC.* 19–24.

[17] Jun Li, Joo Hwee Lim, and Qi Tian. 2003. Automatic summarization for personal digital photos. In *Proceedings of ICICS-PCM*, Vol. 3. 1536–1540.

[18] Eden Litt and Eszter Hargittai. 2014. Smile, snap, and share? A nuanced approach to privacy and online photo-sharing. *Poetics* 42 (2014), 1–21.

[19] Andrew D Miller and W Keith Edwards. 2007. Give and take: a study of consumer photo-sharing culture and practice. In *Proceedings of CHI.* 347–356.

[20] Mor Naaman, Yee Jiun Song, Andreas Paepcke, and Hector Garcia-Molina. 2004. Automatic organization for digital photographs with geographic coordinates. In *Proceedings of JCDL.* 53–62.

[21] Pere Obrador, Rodrigo De Oliveira, and Nuria Oliver. 2010. Supporting personal photo storytelling for social albums. In *Proceedings of MM.* 561–570.

[22] John C. Platt, Mary Czerwinski, and Brent A Field. 2003. PhotoTOC: Automatic clustering for browsing personal photographs. In *Proceedings of ICICS-PCM.* 6–10.

[23] Fereshteh Sadeghi, J Rafael Tena, Ali Farhadi, and Leonid Sigal. 2015. Learning to select and order vacation photographs. In *Proceedings of WACV.* 510–517.

[24] Pinaki Sinha, Sharad Mehrotra, and Ramesh Jain. 2011. Summarization of Personal Photologs Using Multidimensional Content and Context. In *Proceedings of ICMR.* 4810–4819.

[25] Bart Thomee, David A. Shamma, Gerald Friedland, Benjamin Elizalde, Karl Ni, Douglas Poland, Damian Borth, and Li-Jia Li. 2015. The New Data and New Challenges in Multimedia Research. *CoRR* abs/1503.01817 (2015).

[26] Sebastian Tschiatschek, Rishabh K Iyer, Haochen Wei, and Jeff A Bilmes. 2014. Learning Mixtures of Submodular Functions for Image Collection Summarization. In *Proceedings of NIPS.* 1413–1421.

[27] Nancy Van House, Marc Davis, Morgan Ames, Megan Finn, and Vijay Viswanathan. 2005. The uses of personal networked digital imaging: an empirical study of cameraphone photos and sharing. In *CHI extended abstracts.* 1853–1856.

[28] Yufei Wang, Zhe Lin, Xiaohui Shen, Radomir Mech, Gavin Miller, and Garrison W. Cottrell. 2016. Event-Specific Image Importance. In *Proceedings of CVPR.* 4810–4819.

[29] Jianchao Yang, Jiebo Luo, Jie Yu, and Thomas S Huang. 2012. Photo stream alignment and summarization for collaborative photo collection and sharing. *IEEE Transactions on Multimedia* 14, 6 (2012), 1642–1651.

[30] Luming Zhang. 2016. Describing Human Aesthetic Perception by Deeply-learned Attributes from Flickr. *CoRR* abs/1605.07699 (2016).

Identifying Informational vs. Conversational Questions on Community Question Answering Archives

Ido Guy, Victor Makarenkov, Niva Hazon, Lior Rokach, and Bracha Shapira
Ben-Gurion University of the Negev, Beer-Sheva, Israel
idoguy@acm.org,{makarenk,nivah}@post.bgu.ac.il,{liorrk,bshapira}@bgu.ac.il

ABSTRACT

Questions on community question answering websites usually reflect one of two intents: learning information or starting a conversation. In this paper, we revisit this fundamental classification task of informational versus conversational questions, which was originally introduced and studied in 2009. We use a substantially larger dataset of archived questions from Yahoo Answers, which includes the question's title, description, answers, and votes. We replicate the original experiments over this dataset, point out the common and different from the original results, and present a broad set of characteristics that distinguish the two question types. We also develop new classifiers that make use of additional data types, advanced machine learning, and a large dataset of unlabeled data, which achieve enhanced performance.

ACM Reference Format:

Ido Guy, Victor Makarenkov, Niva Hazon, Lior Rokach, and Bracha Shapira. 2018. Identifying Informational vs. Conversational Questions on Community Question Answering Archives. In *Proceedings of 11th ACM International Conf. on Web Search and Data Mining (WSDM 2018)*. ACM, New York, NY, USA, 9 pages. https://doi.org/10.1145/3159652.3159733

1 INTRODUCTION

Community question answering (CQA) websites have experienced a great deal of success for over a decade. Questions on CQA sites span many domains and involve a variety of user needs, which generally map into two principal types, defined by Harper et al. [20]. *Informational* questions are asked with the intent of getting information that the asker hopes to learn or use via fact- or advice-oriented answers. *Conversational* questions are asked with the intent of stimulating discussion and may be aimed at getting opinions or reflect an act of self-expression [20]. While studies examined other aspects of user intent on CQA websites, such as the subjectivity orientation [3, 12, 28] or the desire to socialize [12, 35], we focus on the informational-conversational paradigm, which has been widely referenced and used since originally introduced (e.g., [32, 34, 38]).

While the original paper focused on classifying questions at posting time, in order to improve question routing and automated tagging in real time, we consider CQA archives [54], allowing us to examine additional information that accumulates after the question has been posted, such as answers and votes. Many of the uses of CQA archives suit one of the two question types and can therefore benefit from automated classification. Supporting question retrieval [25] and serving CQA-intent queries on Web search [48], perhaps the two most common practices of CQA archives, fit the informational type. On the other hand, with the recent advancements in social media mining, conversational questions on the archive can be used to support a variety of applications such as opinion mining [40], controversy detection [14], and stance identification [49], and automated debating [16].

Harper et al. [20] examined three CQA websites: Yahoo Answers, Answerbag and Ask Metfilter. The latter was found to have only 5% conversational questions, while the first two were more balanced. Answerbag, however, has decreased in popularity and eventually shut down in 2015. In this work, we opted to focus on Yahoo Answers (YA), one of the largest CQA websites. In 2008, it was reported to account for 74% of CQA traffic [20], and while somewhat decreasing in popularity since, it still enjoys tens of thousands of questions posted every day, which allows to inspect it along a decade of existence. Aside from examining a long time period, we also experiment with substantially larger data: Harper et al.'s proprietary dataset included only 151 labeled questions from YA, while we build a dataset of over 4000 labeled questions, which we publicly release. To the best of our knowledge, it is the first public CQA dataset that labels questions as informational or conversational. Additionally, we examine the use of millions of unlabeled YA questions to further enhance performance. We believe that the larger data, the use of additional textual fields, and the advancement in machine learning methods, all warrant the revisit of the informational/conversational classification challenge.

Our experiments follow the "replicate & extend" approach [53] and include three main parts. In the first, we replicate the classifiers built by Harper et al. [20], which include category-based, text-based, and social network-based classifiers, as well as as an ensemble of all three. We report both extended descriptive results and classifier performance results over our own dataset, which, in part, substantially differ from those reported by Harper et al. [20]. In the second part, we extend Harper's classifiers by using the metadata and text in additional fields: the description, answers, and votes. We enhance the text-based classifier and add a fourth classifier, which is based on different types of metadata, to the ensemble. Overall, these extensions increase AUC by 3.6%. In the third part, we experiment with recurrent neural networks that make use of unlabeled data in two ways: for pre-training word embeddings and for semi-supervised learning using label propagation. This approach yields a particularly high AUC, at 8.7% over the baseline, even when based solely on question titles and when not used as part of an ensemble.

WSDM 2018, February 5–9, 2018, Marina Del Rey, CA, USA

ACM ISBN 978-1-4503-5581-0/18/02...$15.00
https://doi.org/10.1145/3159652.3159733

2 RELATED WORK

Within CQA research, our work falls under the broad category of content modeling [45], which includes areas such as question quality estimation (e.g., [27]), answer quality ranking (e.g., [47]), question topic classification [10], and question type classification [31]. Some of the CQA research along the years has focused on specific types of questions such as factoids (e.g., [5, 18]), advice-seeking [7], how-to questions [46, 51], why questions [39], and opinion questions [30]. Some of these types have stronger association with the informational class (e.g., factoids, how-to), while others are more connected to the conversational class (e.g., opinion, why). A good summary of CQA research can be found in the recent survey by Srba and Bielikova [45].

More specifically, our work focuses on user intent classification on CQA. User intent has been extensively studied in Web information access, most prominently in Web search. The seminal work by Broder [9] distinguished between three main types of Web search queries: navigational, informational, and transactional. At a high level, all three map to the informational class in CQA, as Web search does not involve any aspect of conversation among users. Later works refined Broder's taxonomy and developed automatic classifiers to distinguish between the types (e.g., [8, 23, 55]). On the other hand, on social media, user intent typically revolves around sharing, interacting, conversing, and socializing [15, 24, 29]. To a certain extent, CQA websites combine both of these worlds, as they involve explicit user input in the form of a question, but also enable some level of user interaction.

Our work is based on the definitions of informational and conversational questions by Harper et al. [20]. Several studies examined user intent on question answering systems from other angles. Prominently, the distinction between objective and subjective questions was explored in several works [3, 12, 28]. While this distinction bears some similarity to the informational and conversational division, it is not the same: the subjective class includes, by definition [12], general advice, which is normally considered informational by Harper's definitions. For example, the question *"I am a Bangladeshi National girl and I came to USA on B1/B2 visa and now I would like to take admission pls adv?"*, given as an example for a subjective intent [12], is informational. Indeed, as reported over a YA dataset [28], only 34% of the questions were labeled as objective, while in Harper et al. [20] and our work, 61.2% and 55.6%, respectively, were labeled informational.

Mendes Rodrigues and Milic-Frayling [35] experimented with both YA and MSN QnA, a CQA website that was closed in 2009. They defined "social" intent for questions that are posted in order to informally engage and interact with other community users, as typically occurs in chatrooms. Social intent implies conversational intent, but the latter is far more comprehensive, also reflecting other needs, such as polling or discussing a topic, without socializing. Indeed, social intent was more common on MSN QnA, which enabled more intense user interaction through flexible comments and tagging, rendering a rich thread structure. A classifier deemed 6.5% of the questions on MSN QnA as social, while on YA this type's occurrence was "not sufficient to train a classifier" [35].

3 DATASET

Our dataset includes questions from Yahoo Answers, a large and diverse CQA website, which has been active for over a decade [2]. Questions on YA are spread across more than 1600 categories, in a taxonomy of up to 3 levels, with 26 categories at the top level [2]. Similarly to Harper et al. [20], we refer to the most general type of nodes in the hierarchy as "Top Level Categories" (TLCs) and to the most specific type of categories as "Low Level Categories" (LLCs).

The questions for our dataset were selected uniformly at random from the entire collection of YA non-deleted English questions, posted in the years 2006-2016. For our experiments, each question included, in addition to its title and timestamp, its description (81.5% had non-empty description), its TLC and LLC, and its list of answers with the answer's text, timestamp, and number of upvotes and downvotes per answer. In addition, each answer included a flag indicating whether it was selected as the "best answer" [2].

Questions in our dataset are manually labeled as either 'informational' or 'conversational'. In principle, as defined by Harper et al. [20], informational questions seek for facts or advice, while conversational questions pursue opinions, polling, or self-expression. As input for the labeling process, annotators were given the question's title, description, LLC, and TLC, similarly to Harper et al. [20].

At the first stage of the labeling process, two of the authors went through an iterative process to form more specific guidelines, annotating three batches of 100 questions each and carefully reviewing the disagreements. The level of agreement grew from 75% for the first batch to 93% for the third batch. The two authors then labeled a set of 1088 additional questions with a level of agreement of 93.75%, to which we refer as the *author dataset*. For our experiments, we used the 1020 questions for which there was an agreement between both annotators, similarly to Harper et al. [20]. As a few examples, the question *"Anyone knows how to get a sharpie stain off jeans?"* was labeled informational; the question *"Who thinks fur is murder?"* was labeled conversational; and for the question *"Why is Youtube so slow today?"*, there was no agreement between the two annotators.

To increase the size of our data, we asked students of the "Introduction to Information Retrieval" course to label additional questions from our random sample. Each student labeled a batch of 105 questions. The batch included a benchmark of 5 questions for which the label was rather obvious. These 5 questions were randomly shuffled together with 100 "genuine" questions. Volunteering students were graded based on their success in labeling the 5 benchmark questions, while their grade accounted for a small portion (2%) of the course's grade. The students received detailed written guidelines, based on the insights gained by the two authors during their own annotation process, with definitions and examples for both types of questions. Each question was assigned to two volunteering students. Overall, 83 students completed their annotations, with 76 (91.6%) answering correctly all 5 benchmark questions. We discarded the input from the other 7 students. The level of agreement between the student annotators was 84.7% (Harper et al. [20] reported agreement of 87.1% between their annotators), yielding a total of 2996 questions whose label was agreed between the two annotators, which make up the *student dataset*.

The portion of questions labeled as informational is very similar between the author and the student datasets, at 55.9% and 55.4%, respectively. Harper et al. [20] reported a somewhat higher portion at 61.2%. The gap can be explained, to some extent, by the mild decrease in the portion of informational questions over the years, as we will later show. The *combined dataset*[1], which includes the questions from both the author and student datasets (4016 in total), has 55.6% of the questions labeled as informational.

In addition to the labeled dataset, we created a large unlabeled dataset by sampling 20 million questions uniformly at random from the entire YA archive of non-deleted English questions in 2006-2016. We elaborate on the use of this unlabeled dataset in Section 6.

4 BASELINES

In this section, we fully replicate the experiments conducted by Harper et al. [20] (henceforth referred to as "Harper" in short) with our own dataset. Our experiments consistently showed the best performance over the combined dataset, with no principal differences between the author dataset and the student dataset. We therefore focus on the combined dataset when reporting the results, and henceforth refer to it as *the experimental dataset* or merely *our dataset*. Similarly to Harper, we used the Weka workbench [19] to build all our classifiers and 5-fold cross validation to evaluate performance. As noted in Section 1, Harper experimented with 3 CQA sites. Their models were trained and evaluated separately for each CQA site. Since we do not have access to the original dataset, we present the results they reported for their YA dataset, which consisted of 151 questions.

We use the same three principal metrics as Harper for measuring classifiers' performance: (i) sensitivity – the proportion of conversational questions that are correctly classified; (ii) specificity – the proportion of informational questions that are correctly classified; and (iii) AUC - area under the ROC curve.

4.1 Category-based Classifier

The first classifier examined by Harper deems a question as informational or conversational based on its category. Table 1 presents the sensitivity, specificity, and AUC results for different variants we experimented with, and those reported by Harper et al. [20]. Like Harper, we used a Bayesian network for all variants. The first variant included TLCs only and achieved a slightly higher AUC than Harper, with higher sensitivity and lower specificity. Using LLCs only achieved further improvement in AUC, with both specificity and sensitivity higher than Harper. Using the combination of TLCs and LLCs, as done by Harper, improved the AUC very slightly compared to LLCs only. Finally, working with a dataset of a similar size to Harper (151 questions), to which we refer as the *151-Dataset*, yielded a slightly lower AUC than they reported.

Overall, we see that with our own dataset, an enhanced performance is obtained by the category-based classifier as compared to Harper. We conjecture that the main reason is that LLCs become more effective for classification when the dataset is larger, while with a smaller dataset they might be prone to sparsity.

Table 2 presents the distribution of TLCs in our dataset by their portion of informational (or conversational) questions. Harper reported these portions only for the 3 most common TLCs, due to data sparsity. By contrast to our findings, they reported Entertainment & Music to be substantially more conversational (20 of 26 questions, i.e., 76.9%), while similarly to us they found health (16 of 22, 72.7%), and Science & Mathematics (10 of 12, 83.3%) to be more informational.

Table 3 presents the top 10 LLCs with the highest portion of informational questions and the top 10 LLCs with the highest portion of conversational questions (only LLCs that account for at least 0.5% of the questions were considered). The informational list includes different domains of science, computers/cellphones, and homework help. The conversational list is more diverse and includes the popular LLC Singles & Dating, with others ranging from psychology to politics and from baby names to mental health.

[1] http://webscope.sandbox.yahoo.com/catalog.php?datatype=l&did=82

Table 1: Performance of the category-based classifier.

	Sensitivity	Specificity	AUC
Harper et al. [20] (TLC+LLC)	0.660	0.820	0.810
Our dataset (TLC only)	0.671	0.792	0.823
Our dataset (LLC only)	0.695	0.861	0.847
Our Dataset (TLC+LLC)	0.732	0.827	**0.851**
151-Dataset (TLC+LLC)	0.768	0.732	0.798

Table 2: All 26 Top-level categories (TLCs) by the portion of informational (left, '%inf') or conversational (right, '%conv') questions, with the portion of questions of each TLC out of the total number of questions in our dataset ('%').

Top Informational TLCs			Top Conversational TLCs		
TLC	%	%inf	TLC	%	%conv
Computers & Internet	7.2%	92.7%	Family & Relationships	12.6%	95.8%
Science & Mathematics	7.1%	92.3%	Social Science	1.9%	80.0%
Home & Garden	1.3%	92.2%	News & Events	0.6%	73.1%
Yahoo! Products	2.0%	87.7%	Society & Culture	8.6%	72.8%
Cars & Transportation	2.0%	86.6%	Sports	3.2%	64.6%
Consumer Electronics	3.6%	83.9%	Politics & Government	5.4%	58.5%
Games & Recreation	3.1%	83.7%	Arts & Humanities	2.8%	55.3%
Environment	0.1%	75.0%	Beauty & Style	5.0%	50.5%
Business & Finance	2.7%	75.0%	Dining Out	0.1%	50.0%
Travel	2.1%	75.0%	Pregnancy & Parenting	4.1%	48.8%
Pets	2.8%	73.9%	Entertainment & Music	7.4%	48.3%
Health	7.8%	71.0%	Food & Drink	1.4%	36.4%
Education & Reference	4.6%	69.4%	Local Businesses	0.3%	30.8%

Table 3: Low-level categories (LLCs) with highest percentage of informational (left, '%inf') and conversational (right, '%conv') questions, with the portion of questions of each LLC out of the total number of questions in our dataset ('%').

Top Informational LLCs			Top Conversational LLCs		
LLC	%	%inf	LLC	%	%conv
Chemistry	1.2%	100.0%	Singles & Dating	8.7%	98.0%
Mathematics	2.6%	98.1%	Marriage & Divorce	0.8%	93.5%
Programming & Design	0.9%	97.1%	Psychology	0.7%	93.3%
Software	1.2%	95.8%	Friends	1.5%	91.9%
Maintenance & Repairs	0.9%	91.7%	Politics	2.1%	90.6%
Laptops & Notebooks	0.8%	90.9%	Baby Names	0.9%	89.2%
Video & Online Games	2.2%	86.7%	Religion & Spirituality	3.5%	81.7%
Homework Help	1.2%	85.7%	Other - Society & Culture	1.1%	79.1%
Cell Phones & Plans	1.1%	84.8%	Mental Health	0.8%	76.5%
Biology	1.0%	82.5%	Other - Beauty & Style	0.9%	75.0%

Table 4: Performance of the text-based classifier.

	Sensitivity	Specificity	AUC
Harper et al. [20]	0.480	0.710	0.600
Our dataset	0.667	0.845	**0.756**
151-Dataset	0.710	0.732	0.733

4.2 Text-based Classifier

The text classifier used by Harper et al. [20] was based on the 500 most common unigrams or bigrams occurring in titles of each of the two question types (in a lower-case form). For classification, Weka's sequential minimum optimization (SMO) algorithm for training support vector machines (SVM), with linear kernel, was used. In this case, they used all three datasets in conjunction for training.

Table 4 presents the classification results as reported by Harper and as obtained by applying the exact same method over our dataset and over the 151-Dataset. A substantially higher performance was achieved on our dataset. This can be associated with the larger data, since all features are sparse. Yet, even over our 151-Dataset the results are still substantially higher than the baseline. We believe this attests to the importance of training the data on YA text only, rather than a mix of questions from three different CQA sites.

In terms of prominent unigrams/bigram features, Harper reported their information gain and their occurrence portions on both informational and conversational questions, across questions words and for the pronouns "you" and "I". They also reported the four additional unigrams/bigrams with the highest information gain for the informational and for the conversational class, respectively. They did not present a specific report for YA, but rather joined the statistics across their three datasets. In Table 5, we report the same statistics on our own dataset, alongside the reported statistics by Harper, when such exist.

Observing the question words, similarly to Harper, we found that "how" and "where" were substantially more common on informational questions, while "why" was more common on conversational. Indeed, why-questions are considered more open ended [21] and may thus more often reflect a need for discussion. In addition, we also identified some signal on "who" towards conversational questions, whereas Harper found it to be slightly more common (with no information gain) on informational questions. The most common question word, "what", did not have any information gain, and so did "when" and "which".

As for "you" versus "I", like Harper we also found a strong signal in "you" for conversational questions, while "I" was more common on informational questions, albeit with a relatively small information gain.

Inspecting the top informational tokens, only one of them, "can", was also among the top four reported by Harper. The other three Harper reported were "is there", "help", and "do I". The last two were also more common on the informational class in our dataset, with a small information gain (0.002 and 0.004, respectively), while the first was not found to have any information gain. The top conversational tokens include two of the top-4 found by Harper. The word "think" had the most information gain out of all tokens in our dataset, and was far more common on conversational questions. Harper also reported "would you" and "is your" among their top

Table 5: Portions of informational and conversational question titles containing the following types of tokens, as well as the token's information gain for the text-based classifier: (i) question words; (ii) personal pronouns; and other tokens with highest information gain for predicting the (iii) informational class and (iv) conversational class.

	Our Dataset			Harper et al. [20]		
	% Inf.	% Conv.	Info Gain	% Inf.	% Conv.	Info Gain
how	19.6%	9.5%	0.014	29.8%	11.3%	0.029
where	5.0%	0.8%	0.012	15.5%	1.9%	0.033
why	3.8%	8.7%	0.007	5.6%	17.0%	0.012
who	2.0%	3.8%	0.002	13.9%	11.3%	0
what	16.9%	17.7%	0	30.2%	30.4%	0
when	3.9%	3.9%	0	17.0%	13.2%	0
which	1.9%	2.1%	0	n/a	n/a	n/a
you	8.1%	22.2%	0.024	25.8%	54.7%	0.05
I	31.3%	24.9%	0.003	68.6%	27.4%	0.124
can	14.6%	4.5%	0.02	35.1%	9.4%	0.069
what is	6.2%	1.7%	0.01	n/a	n/a	n/a
find	3.1%	0.6%	0.007	n/a	n/a	n/a
how do	6.3%	2.6%	0.006	n/a	n/a	n/a
think	0.1%	6.6%	0.031	n/a	n/a	n/a
you think	0.0%	4.8%	0.023	1.3%	8.2%	0.021
do you	2.6%	9.8%	0.017	4.9%	22.0%	0.047
what do	0.6%	4.5%	0.013	n/a	n/a	n/a

four conversational tokens. The former was also found to have a substantial information gain for the conversational class in our dataset (0.006), while the latter posed a more modest information gain for conversational questions (0.001).

4.3 Social Network-based Classifier

The third classifier used by Harper et al. [20] was based on social network (SN) properties of the question asker. Three features were used to represent the asker's social network signature [52], i.e., a representation of their egocentric network based on previous question asking and answering on the site. Specifically, they constructed a directed weighted graph based on a YA dataset that spanned a period of 49 days, with over 1.5M users and 4.3M questions[2]. The graph's vertices represented users and directed edges represented the act of one user answering another user's question. The three features that were calculated based on this graph for each question asker were: (i) *NUM_NEIGHBORS*: the number of neighbors of the asker ; (ii) *PCT_ANSWERS*: the asker's number of outgoing edges divided by the asker's total number of edges ; and (iii) *CLUST_COEFFICIENT*: the clustering coefficient [50] of the asker's ego network, reflecting its connectivity (the portion of the asker's neighbor pairs who are connected themselves).

For our own SN classier, we computed the same three features based on the entire YA repository rather than a partial dataset of 49 days. Like Harper, we calculated each feature with respect to the timestamp of the respective question, ensuring that we have an accurate snapshot of interactions up to the particular time the question was asked. Results, presented in Table 6, indicate that our own classifier did not reach the performance reported by Harper. This is in spite of the fact it was trained on a much larger dataset

[2]The dataset was not publicly released.

Table 6: Performance of the SN-based classifier, with different classifiers and feature subsets. When not otherwise stated, Bayesian network was used for classification.

	Sensitivity	Specificity	AUC
Harper et al. [20] (all features)	0.710	0.870	**0.810**
SVM (linear kernel) (all features)	0.572	0.620	0.596
Random forest (all features)	0.491	0.710	0.635
C4.5 decision tree (all features)	0.339	0.848	0.633
Logistic regression (all features)	0.412	0.796	0.653
Bayesian network (all features)	0.621	0.631	0.659
PCT_ANSWERS +CLUST_COEFFICIENT	0.658	0.553	0.639
NUM_NEIGHBORS +PCT_ANSWERS	0.551	0.674	0.645
NUM_NEIGHBORS +CLUST_COEFFICIENT	0.620	0.626	0.657
151-Dataset (all features)	0.058	0.915	0.462

and that the features were calculated over the entire YA graph[3]. To further explore this, we experimented with several other common classifiers using Weka [19], yet as Table 6 shows, they all performed worse than the Bayesian network. Inspecting the performance using each subset of two out of the three features (ablation tests) indicated that the combination of *NUM_NEIGHBORS* and *CLUST_COEFFICIENT* reached almost the same performance as all three features, i.e., *PCT_ANSWERS* did not contribute much to the overall performance. Finally, running on top of the 151-Dataset demonstrated poor performance.

Table 7 shows the statistics of the three SN features, in a similar manner as presented by Harper. The trends on our data are similar to those reported by Harper: there is a statistically significant gap in favor of conversational question askers for all three features, i.e., they tend to have more neighbors, higher ratio of answers to questions, and tighter connectivity of their neighbors. As expected, the number of neighbors is higher on our dataset, since we consider a larger time period. Statistical significance is stronger on our data, as could be expected given its size.

Overall, this analysis indicates that on a descriptive level, we observe the same differences between informational and conversational questions, validating the finding that askers of conversational questions tend to have a larger, more tightly interconnected ego network [20]. Yet, trying to use these differences as discriminative features yields a substantially weaker signal than reported by Harper[4]. The immediate suspicion that arises is that the SN model developed by Harper suffered from an overfitting issue. The small size of their dataset may help explain it, although we could not replicate the results when using our own dataset of the same size. Harper did not report the number of users in their dataset, nor the method used for creating the dataset, but it could be that multiple questions on the training and test set had the same askers, which led to memorizing their SN features in the model.

4.4 3-Way Ensemble

Under the premise that the features introduced by the three classifiers (categories, text, and SN) complement one another, at least to

[3]We also experimented with calculating the SN features based on 49 days, but the results were lower.

[4]Our experiments over the author and the student datasets separately yielded very similar performance and descriptive results. For example, the AUC for the SN-based Bayesian network classier was 0.651 and 0.643 for the two datasets, respectively

Table 7: Average and standard deviation of the three SN features for informational vs. conversational questions, as well as the p value of a two-tailed unpaired t-test.

	Our Dataset			Harper et al. [20]		
	avg inf.	avg conv.	t-test	avg inf.	avg conf.	t-test
NUM_NEIGHBORS	400	1204	$p<0.0001$	252	757	$p<0.01$
PCT_ANSWERS	0.38	0.52	$p<0.0001$	0.26	0.32	$p=0.02$
CLUST_COEFFICIENT	0.015	0.028	$p<0.0001$	0.06	0.15	$p<0.01$

Table 8: Diversity between classifier pairs.

Classifier pair	Our dataset		Harper et al. [20]
	Yule's Q	Agreement	Yule's Q
Categories–Text	0.72	71.8%	0.31
Categories–SN	0.45	61.8%	0.72
Text – SN	0.3	57.8%	0.58

Table 9: Performance of the 3-way ensemble classifier.

	Sensitivity	Specificity	AUC
Harper et al. [20]	0.780	0.950	**0.950**
Our dataset	0.754	0.866	0.886

some extent, Harper examined an ensemble classifier (meta classifier) that uses the output scores (i.e., confidence scores that the question is conversational) of the three classifiers as its features to learn one ultimate classification. To measure the diversity among the three output scores, Harper used the Yule's Q metric, which ranges from −1 to 1 [26]. Classifiers that tend to categorize the same instances correctly pose more positive values, while classifiers that tend to categorize different instances incorrectly take more negative values. Table 8 presents the Yule's Q metric for each pair of classifiers; for our own data, we also present the mere level of *agreement* between each pair, i.e., the portion of instances for which the prediction was identical.

Our results in terms of Yule's Q are quite different than Harper's. This might be attributed to the differences in performance for the text and SN classifiers. As opposed to Harper, we found a rather high agreement between the category and text classifiers. We believe this makes sense, since categories are often characterized by their own language [11]. On the other hand, we found a lower agreement between the SN classifier and the other two classifiers, likely due to the lower performance of the SN classifier.

Table 9 presents the results of the "*3-way ensemble*" classifier. Like Harper, we implemented it using JMP's neural network algorithm. It can be seen that the performance they reported could not be attained in our own settings, most probably due to the lower performance of the SN classifier. From this point onward, we refer to the 3-way ensemble result achieved on our data as our baseline, since it achieved the highest performance among all the methods reported by Harper when ran on our dataset.

5 IMPROVING THE BASELINE

In this section, we evaluate two complementary methods for improving the baseline reported in the previous section. First, we use

Table 10: Performance of n-gram SVM with linear kernel, using different combinations of the question's textual fields. Unless otherwise noted, unigram, bigram, and trigram features were used.

	Sensitivity	Specificity	AUC
Title	0.718	0.805	0.761
Description	0.600	0.826	0.713
Answers	0.533	0.716	0.625
Best answer	0.560	0.792	0.676
Title+description	0.730	0.838	0.784
Title+answers	0.657	0.786	0.721
Title+best answer	0.747	0.821	0.784
Title+description+answers	0.691	0.830	0.761
Title+description+best answer	0.743	0.844	**0.794**
Title+description+best answer (unigrams only)	0.719	0.808	0.764
Title+description+best answer (unigrams + bigrams)	0.742	0.819	0.780

lexical features from fields beyond the title, i.e., the description and the answers, assessing if their language can also help distinguish between the two classes. Second, we experiment with a set of metadata features, mostly based on description, answers, and votes, aiming to find more discriminative characteristics between the classes. For these experiments, we used the scikit-learn library [41] to run machine learning algorithms and the NLTK suite [6] for natural language processing. We continued using our combined dataset for experimentation and 5-fold cross validation for evaluation.

5.1 N-gram Classifier

Our first extension focused on the text-based classifier. As we observed good results for the title-based text classifier (Section 4.2), we set out to examine if other textual fields, specifically, the question's description and answers, can further assist in the classification task. We experimented with unigram, bigram, and trigram features, pruned based on an occurrence threshold of 2. As a classifier, we continued to use SVM with linear kernel.

The first four rows of Table 10 indicate that the title is the most useful field for classification, achieving the best AUC (similar to the baseline, up 0.6%), followed by the description, and finally the answers. Using the text of the best answer only, even though it is not selected for nearly 15% of the questions, was substantially more productive than using the text of all the answers. Apparently, all answers' text introduces a level of diversity and noise that masks the class of the question, while the best answer is more indicative.

We also experimented with combining the text from two or three fields. It can be seen that the combinations of title and description, as well as title and best answer, achieved a higher AUC compared to the tile alone (+3.0% for both). By contrast, combining title with all answers degraded the AUC (−5.3%). Using the threesome of title, description, and best answer further improved the performance (+1.3%). Following, using the n-gram classifier based on title, description, and best answer, instead of the original text-based classier, as part of the 3-way ensemble (Section 4.4), yielded an increase in performance: AUC of 0.904, up 2.0% compared to the ensemble baseline (Table 9). Throughout our experimentation, we observed that using unigrams, bigrams, and trigrams achieved higher performance than using unigrams and bigrams, which in turn was higher than unigrams only. The bottom section of Table 10 demonstrates this for the combination of title, description, and best answer.

Table 11: Performance of different n-gram classifiers based on the combination of title, description, and best answer on their own and as part of a 3-way ensemble also including category and SN classifiers.

	n-gram classifier only			3-way ensemble		
	Sensitivity	Specificity	AUC	Sensitivity	Specificity	AUC
Random forest	0.564	0.876	0.720	0.778	0.836	0.885
Gradient boosting	0.633	0.883	0.758	0.789	0.855	0.903
SVM (linear kernel)	0.743	0.844	0.794	0.796	0.861	0.904
Logistic regression	0.745	0.877	0.811	0.813	0.869	**0.914**

Thus far, we experimented with an SVM classifier, similarly to Harper. For the title, description, and best answer variant, we examined other classifiers, as reported in Table 11. It can be seen that logistic regression attained the best performance and surpassed that of SVM. Using the logistic regression version for the ensemble classifier further increased its performance to 0.914 (up 1.2%, to a total of +3.2% compared to the ensemble baseline). We also ran logistic regression with other field combinations as detailed in Table 10 and the respective results were similar to those reported in the table for SVM, with the combination of title, description, and best answer producing the best outcome.

Inspecting the n-grams with most information gain for fields other than the title (which is reported in detail in Section 4.2), we observed that for the informational class, descriptions included explicit calls for assistance, such as "does anyone know" and "please help", while best answers included verbs, such as "use", "click",or "check". For conversational questions, "think" had high information gain across all fields (titles, descriptions, and answers), while best answers included adverbs such as "really", "very", and "just".

5.2 Additional Features

As another step to improve the performance of our classifier, we set out to examine additional basic features that were not inspected by Harper. We generally refer to these features as "metadata" features.

Table 12 lists the key features and their statistics for informational versus conversational questions. Some characteristics, such as the length of the title or the portion of questions for which a best answer was selected, are similar for both classes, while other pose fundamental differences. For example, conversational questions more often include a description and when they do, it tends to be longer. Among the most distinctive features are the number of answers and number of votes (both upvotes and downvotes), which are significantly higher for conversational questions. Votes per answer are also higher for conversational questions. Interestingly, while answer length is slightly higher for informational questions, the best-answer length is somewhat higher for conversational questions. While URLs are more common on conversational titles or descriptions, they are substantially more common on informational best answers. Finally, while informational questions have substantially fewer answers and votes, the time span from question posting to the most recent answer/vote is comparable between the classes.

We also used the question's posting year as a feature. As Figure 1 indicates, the portion of informational questions slightly decreases over the years. One reason may be that Web search engines started

Table 12: Metadata feature statistics (average, standard deviation, median, maximum; or respective portions) for informational and conversational questions. Features with statistically significant average gaps, based on a two-tailed unpaired t-test, are marked with * ($p<0.01$) or ** ($p<0.001$).

	Informational				Conversational			
	Avg	Std	Med	Max	Avg	Std	Med	Max
Title length (words)	12.0	5.8	11	62	11.7	5.5	10	56
Description length (words)**	46.3	55.3	32	605	83.5	100.1	52	1016
Number of answers**	3.6	3.5	3	43	6.8	6.8	5	85
Answer length (words)*	60.3	99.5	32	3141	55.8	88.2	30	2725
Best-answer length (words)*	64.7	93.3	33	946	69.2	106.1	35	1718
Total up-votes**	1.4	4.8	0	121	5.5	15.6	1	291
Total down-votes**	1.1	4.1	0	68	4.0	11.2	0	158
Up-votes per answer**	0.43	0.82	0	14	0.73	1.14	0.33	21
Down-votes per answer*	0.30	0.62	0	5.33	0.49	0.79	0	7
Time span to last answer (days)	412	951	0.52	3768	379	920	0.51	3796
Time span to last vote (days)	86	394	0	3478	80	347	0.44	3744
Description exists	76.8%				85.6%			
No answer	2.9%				1.8%			
No votes	56.3%				39.7%			
Best answer selected	85.0%				86.2%			
Title/desc. contain URL	3.2%				5.9%			
Best answer contains URL	11.7%				4.0%			

Figure 1: Percentage of informational questions by year.

Table 13: Performance of different metadata classifiers on their own and as part of a 4-way ensemble also including category, n-gram, and SN classifiers.

	metadata classifier only			4-way ensemble		
	Sensitivity	Specificity	AUC	Sensitivity	Specificity	AUC
SVM (linear kernel)	0.369	0.769	0.569	0.815	0.861	0.912
Random forest	0.475	0.794	0.634	0.818	0.863	0.913
Logistic regression	0.504	0.848	0.676	0.811	0.871	0.915
Gradient boosting	0.545	0.814	0.680	0.818	0.872	0.918

to provide better treatment to informational queries by including direct answers on their results page [4, 17].

We used the features above to build another classifier, the *metadata classifier*, for informational versus conversational questions. Results, depicted in Table 13, indicate that the best performance was achieved by gradient boosting (with logistic regression at close second). This classifier did not reach the high performance attained by the category and text classifiers, but surpassed the performance (as we could reproduce) of the SN classifier. Using it in a *4-way ensemble* with the n-gram, category, and SN classifiers, reached a slightly higher performance than the 3-way ensemble reported in Table 11, at 0.918 (+0.44%).

Inspecting the performance of the metadata classifier when excluding different feature families (ablation tests) indicated that the description and answers metadata features were the most important, as their removal led to a decrease of 5.7% and 5.3%, respectively, in AUC. On the other hand, title, votes, and year features did not pose any substantial contribution to performance.

6 LSTM NETWORK MODEL

Thus far, we relied on n-gram features for text-based classification. In this section, we describe our experimentation with recurrent neural networks (RNNs) with long short term memory (LSTM) [22] for the classification task. RNNs with LSTM can capture more complex word relations and have recently demonstrated high performance in a variety of text processing tasks [36]. In our experiments, we lower-cased and tokenized the text and then sequentially fed it, from left to right, into the model. Similarly to Section 5.1, we experimented with title-only, title+description, title+description+answers, and title+description+best answer as our text input. To avoid overfitting, we used three dropout strategies for regularization: between the embedding layer and the recurrent LSTM layer; between the hidden layers of the LSTM recurrent layers ; and between the LSTM and the output used for classification.

We implemented all LSTM models using Tensorflow [1] with the Keras API [13]. As in Section 5, we used scikit-learn [41] with 5-fold cross validation for evaluation and NLTK [6] for text processing. We performed extensive hyper-parameter tuning, which included the number of LSTM layers, the size of the LSTM memory cell, the embedding size, the number of iterations over the entire training set , the dropout rate for each of the three types mentioned above, and the batch size of the stochastic gradient descent used for optimization. We also experimented with a bi-directional RNN with LSTM, however this model did not yield any performance gain.

As deep learning techniques typically demonstrate high performance on large data, we set out to explore the use of the large unlabeled dataset of 20M YA questions, described in Section 3. We examined two ways for leveraging the unlabeled data: pre-trained word embedding and label propagation.

6.1 Pre-trained Word Embedding

The first layer of the neural network generates a latent representation of the text in a lower-dimensional space. Instead of letting the network learn this representation in training time, based on the labeled dataset, we can learn the word embeddings in a pre-processing step [33]. Since word embedding does not require human-annotated data, it can be learned over a much larger dataset. We trained skip-gram negative sampling (SGNS) [37] word embeddings over our unlabeled dataset using the Gensim library [44], experimenting with three variants of the text used for training: titles only; titles and descriptions; and titles, descriptions, and answers. In all cases, performance differences among the three were minor, with title-only achieving slightly higher performance than the others. We therefore report only title-based embeddings, which also require less storage and computation power. To further inspect the value of the unlabeled YA dataset, we also examined the use of the popular general-purpose publicly-available GloVE [42], pre-trained on the Wikipedia 2014 and Gigaoword 5 corpora.

Table 14 summarizes the results of the LSTM model, both on its own and when used as part of a 4-way ensemble with the category, SN, and metadata classifiers, as described in Section 5.2. Inspecting the results of the LSTM model alone, it can be seen that using GloVE

Table 14: Performance of LSTM model with combinations of the question's textual fields, without pre-trained word embeddings ("No Embed") and with pre-trained word embeddings using global vectors for word representation ("GloVe") and our unlabeled YA dataset ("YA").

		LSTM classifier only			4-way ensemble		
		Sensitivity	Specificity	AUC	Sensitivity	Specificity	AUC
No Embed	Title	0.753	0.794	0.856	0.792	0.861	0.910
	Title+description	0.754	0.797	0.857	0.776	0.860	0.902
	Title+description+answers	0.470	0.609	0.562	0.741	0.849	0.871
	Title+description+best answer	0.730	0.770	0.829	0.765	0.864	0.894
GloVe	Title	0.780	0.807	0.885	0.800	0.857	0.913
	Title+description	0.780	0.821	0.880	0.795	0.856	0.909
	Title+description+answers	0.558	0.667	0.663	0.738	0.848	0.873
	Title+description+best answer	0.823	0.693	0.842	0.773	0.852	0.894
YA	Title	0.794	0.836	0.907	0.823	0.867	0.923
	Title+description	0.837	0.847	0.915	0.840	0.871	**0.926**
	Title+description+answers	0.695	0.629	0.713	0.745	0.847	0.878
	Title+description+best answer	0.866	0.793	0.906	0.817	0.855	0.918

pre-trained embeddings yielded a noticeable performance gain. Using our unlabeled YA dataset for embedding improved the results further. Across the board, title and title+description achieved the highest performance. As was the case with the n-gram models (Section 5.1), adding all answers' text to the input degraded performance, while in the case of LSTM, the best answer was again preferable to all answers, but did not improve over title or title+description. Particularly, the LSTM model based on title+description and YA pre-trained embeddings achieved the highest performance, which was substantially higher than the n-gram best classifier reported in Table 11 (+12.8% in AUC). Despite the large performance gain, using this classifier as part of a 4-way ensemble only slightly increased the AUC reported for the best performing 4-way ensemble in Table 13, bringing it to 0.926 (+0.87%).

6.2 Label Propagation

Our second attempt to leverage the unlabeled data was by using it for the complete model training, rather than for pre-trained embeddings only. Many different techniques for semi-supervised learning, which use a relatively small seed set of labeled examples and a larger set of unlabeled examples, have been proposed [43]. We opted to use *label propagation* (LP), which simply and iteratively increases the training set with examples from the unlabeled dataset, based on their predicted probability scores [56]. We started with the labeled dataset of 4016 questions and trained an initial model, using LSTM with pre-trained YA embeddings. We then selected 2000 questions uniformly at random from the unlabeled dataset and classified them using the trained model. In the next iteration, we used the questions that were classified with high confidence as part of the training set. After experimenting with various confidence thresholds, we opted to set it to 0.9, i.e., questions classified with a probability of 0.9 or higher were added to the training set in the next iteration, labeled with their predicted class. We repeated the process for 100 iterations, covering 1% of the unlabeled dataset, as performance started to converge. We experimented with title and title+description for the input text, as they yielded the best performance to begin with (Table 14).

Table 15: Performance of LSTM model with YA pre-trained embeddings after 100 iterations of label propagation.

	LSTM classifier only			4-way ensemble		
	Sensitivity	Specificity	AUC	Sensitivity	Specificity	AUC
Title	0.905	0.907	**0.963**	0.907	0.909	0.952
Title+description	0.933	0.822	0.947	0.921	0.849	0.936

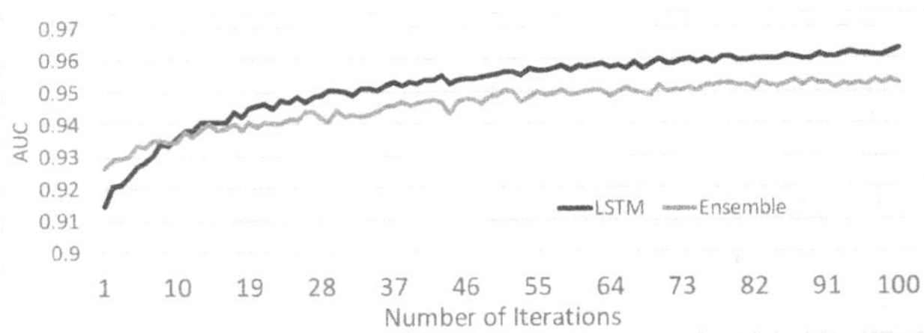

Figure 2: AUC performance of LSTM (with YA pre-trained embeddings) and 4-way ensemble by the number of label propagation iterations.

Results, presented in Table 15, show that the LP process produced a considerable performance gain. Using the results of the LP process as part of a 4-way ensemble did not yield a substantial improvement in performance and even led to a decline in AUC. Overall, running the LSTM model with LP based solely on titles yielded the best AUC, at +4.0% compared to the best performing model reported in Table 14. Figure 2 illustrates the increase in AUC with the number of LP iterations, both for the standalone LTSM model and the 4-way ensemble. After 10 iterations, the AUC of the LTSM model bypasses the ensemble.

7 CONCLUSIONS

We experimented with a variety of methods for improving the classification of questions on CQA archives as either informational or conversational. While supervised approaches achieved some performance gain relative to the baseline (up to 4.5% in AUC), semi-supervised learning using LP and a large unlabeled dataset yielded a more substantial increase (+8.7% compared to the baseline), up to an AUC of over 0.96, with both specificity and sensitivity above 90%. To the best of our knowledge, these are the highest reported results for intent classification on CQA websites. It should be noted, however, that this approach requires not only large volumes of unlabeled data, but also significant computation power[5].

The LP approach was found to work best when using only question titles as input text. Titles were also found most effective for pre-training the word embeddings. It appears that when large volumes of data are in hand, titles alone best reflect the differences between the two classes. Yet, when only relying on the labeled data, the text of the description, and in some cases the best answer, was found to be helpful for achieving better performance.

As part of our evaluation, we replicated the experiments reported by Harper et al. [20] over our larger YA dataset. For the category and text classifiers, we were able to reproduce the results and even achieve higher performance, as could be expected given the larger

[5]LP over 200K question titles ran for 48 hours on Nvidia GeForce GTX 1080 Ti GPU.

training data. For the SN classifier, however, despite observing similar descriptive differences for the features, we could not reproduce the reported performance. We therefore suggest to carefully refer to the results reported for this classifier in the original paper [20].

For future work, we intend to examine additional graph metrics that may enhance classification based on social network features. We also plan to examine additional semi-supervised learning approaches, such as co-training using text and network features.

REFERENCES

[1] Martín Abadi et al. 2016. TensorFlow: A System for Large-scale Machine Learning. In *Proc.of OSDI.* 265–283.

[2] Lada A. Adamic, Jun Zhang, Eytan Bakshy, and Mark S. Ackerman. 2008. Knowledge Sharing and Yahoo Answers: Everyone Knows Something. In *Proc. of WWW.* 665–674.

[3] Naoyoshi Aikawa, Tetsuya Sakai, and Hayato Yamana. 2011. Community QA question classification: Is the asker looking for subjective answers or not? *IPSJ Online Transactions* 4 (2011), 160–168.

[4] Michael S. Bernstein, Jaime Teevan, Susan Dumais, Daniel Liebling, and Eric Horvitz. 2012. Direct Answers for Search Queries in the Long Tail. In *Proc. of CHI.* 237–246.

[5] Jiang Bian, Yandong Liu, Eugene Agichtein, and Hongyuan Zha. 2008. Finding the Right Facts in the Crowd: Factoid Question Answering over Social Media. In *Proc. of WWW.* 467–476.

[6] Steven Bird. 2006. NLTK: The Natural Language Toolkit. In *Proc. of COLING-ACL.* 69–72.

[7] Liora Braunstain, Oren Kurland, David Carmel, Idan Szpektor, and Anna Shtok. 2016. Supporting human answers for advice-seeking questions in CQA sites. In *Proc. of ECIR.* 129–141.

[8] David J. Brenes, Daniel Gayo-Avello, and Kilian Pérez-González. 2009. Survey and Evaluation of Query Intent Detection Methods. In *Proc. of WSCD.* 1–7.

[9] Andrei Broder. 2002. A Taxonomy of Web Search. *SIGIR Forum* 36, 2 (2002), 3–10.

[10] Li Cai, Guangyou Zhou, Kang Liu, and Jun Zhao. 2011. Large-scale Question Classification in cQA by Leveraging Wikipedia Semantic Knowledge. In *Proc. of CIKM.* 1321–1330.

[11] Wen Chan, Weidong Yang, Jinhui Tang, Jintao Du, Xiangdong Zhou, and Wei Wang. 2013. Community Question Topic Categorization via Hierarchical Kernelized Classification. In *Proc. of CIKM.* 959–968.

[12] Long Chen, Dell Zhang, and Levene Mark. 2012. Understanding user intent in community question answering. In *Proc. of WWW Companion.* 823–828.

[13] François Chollet. 2015. Keras. https://github.com/fchollet/keras. (2015).

[14] Shiri Dori-Hacohen and James Allan. 2015. Automated controversy detection on the web. In *Proc. of ECIR.* 423–434.

[15] Nicole B Ellison, Charles Steinfield, and Cliff Lampe. 2007. The benefits of Facebook friends: Social capital and college students' use of online social network sites. *Journal of Computer-Mediated Communication* 12, 4 (2007), 1143–1168.

[16] Iryna Gurevych, Eduard H Hovy, Noam Slonim, and Benno Stein. 2016. Debating Technologies. In *Dagstuhl Reports*, Vol. 5.

[17] Ido Guy. 2016. Searching by Talking: Analysis of Voice Queries on Mobile Web Search. In *Proc. of SIGIR.* 35–44.

[18] Ido Guy and Dan Pelleg. 2016. The Factoid Queries Collection. In *Proc. of SIGIR.* 717–720.

[19] Mark Hall, Eibe Frank, Geoffrey Holmes, Bernhard Pfahringer, Peter Reutemann, and Ian H. Witten. 2009. The WEKA Data Mining Software: An Update. *SIGKDD Explor. Newsl.* 11, 1 (2009), 10–18.

[20] F. Maxwell Harper, Daniel Moy, and Joseph A. Konstan. 2009. Facts or Friends?: Distinguishing Informational and Conversational Questions in Social Q&A Sites. In *Proc. of CHI.* 759–768.

[21] Jaakko Hintikka and Ilpo Halonen. 1995. Semantics and pragmatics for why-questions. *The Journal of Philosophy* 92, 12 (1995), 636–657.

[22] Sepp Hochreiter and Jürgen Schmidhuber. 1997. Long Short-Term Memory. *Neural Comput.* 9, 8 (Nov. 1997), 1735–1780.

[23] Bernard J. Jansen, Danielle L. Booth, and Amanda Spink. 2007. Determining the User Intent of Web Search Engine Queries. In *Proc. of WWW.* 1149–1150.

[24] Akshay Java, Xiaodan Song, Tim Finin, and Belle Tseng. 2007. Why We Twitter: Understanding Microblogging Usage and Communities. In *Proc. of WebKDD/SNA-KDD.* 56–65.

[25] Jiwoon Jeon, W Bruce Croft, and Joon Ho Lee. 2005. Finding similar questions in large question and answer archives. In *Proc. of CIKM.* 84–90.

[26] Ludmila I. Kuncheva and Christopher J. Whitaker. 2003. Measures of Diversity in Classifier Ensembles and Their Relationship with the Ensemble Accuracy. *Machine Learning* 51, 2 (2003), 181–207.

[27] Baichuan Li, Tan Jin, Michael R. Lyu, Irwin King, and Barley Mak. 2012. Analyzing and Predicting Question Quality in Community Question Answering Services. In *Proc. of WWW Companion.* 775–782.

[28] Baoli Li, Yandong Liu, and Eugene Agichtein. 2008. CoCQA: Co-training over Questions and Answers with an Application to Predicting Question Subjectivity Orientation. In *Proc. EMNLP.* 937–946.

[29] Kuan-Yu Lin and Hsi-Peng Lu. 2011. Why people use social networking sites: An empirical study integrating network externalities and motivation theory. *Computers in human behavior* 27, 3 (2011), 1152–1161.

[30] Yandong Liu and Eugene Agichtein. 2008. On the Evolution of the Yahoo! Answers QA Community. In *Proc. of SIGIR.* 737–738.

[31] Yandong Liu, Nitya Narasimhan, Venu Vasudevan, and Eugene Agichtein. 2009. Is This Urgent?: Exploring Time-sensitive Information Needs in Collaborative Question Answering. In *Proc. of SIGIR.* 712–713.

[32] Zhe Liu and Bernard J. Jansen. 2015. A Taxonomy for Classifying Questions Asked in Social Question and Answering. In *Proc. of CHI EA '15.* 1947–1952.

[33] Denis Lukovnikov, Asja Fischer, Jens Lehmann, and Sören Auer. 2017. Neural Network-based Question Answering over Knowledge Graphs on Word and Character Level. In *Proc. of WWW.* 1211–1220.

[34] Lena Mamykina, Bella Manoim, Manas Mittal, George Hripcsak, and Björn Hartmann. 2011. Design Lessons from the Fastest Q&A Site in the West. In *Proc. of CHI.* 2857–2866.

[35] Eduarda Mendes Rodrigues and Natasa Milic-Frayling. 2009. Socializing or Knowledge Sharing?: Characterizing Social Intent in Community Question Answering. In *Proc. of CIKM.* 1127–1136.

[36] Yishu Miao, Lei Yu, and Phil Blunsom. 2016. Neural Variational Inference for Text Processing. In *Proc. of ICML.* 1727–1736.

[37] Tomas Mikolov, Kai Chen, Greg Corrado, and Jeffrey Dean. 2013. Efficient estimation of word representations in vector space. *arXiv preprint* abs/1301.3781 (2013).

[38] Liqiang Nie, Meng Wang, Yue Gao, Zheng-Jun Zha, and Tat-Seng Chua. 2013. Beyond text QA: multimedia answer generation by harvesting web information. *IEEE Transactions on Multimedia* 15, 2 (2013), 426–441.

[39] Jong-Hoon Oh, Kentaro Torisawa, Chikara Hashimoto, Takuya Kawada, Stijn De Saeger, Jun'ichi Kazama, and Yiou Wang. 2012. Why Question Answering Using Sentiment Analysis and Word Classes. In *Proc. EMNLP-CoNLL.* 368–378.

[40] Bo Pang and Lillian Lee. 2008. Opinion Mining and Sentiment Analysis. *Found. Trends Inf. Retr.* 2, 1-2 (Jan. 2008), 1–135.

[41] Fabian Pedregosa et al. 2011. Scikit-learn: Machine Learning in Python. *J. Mach. Learn. Res.* 12 (Nov. 2011), 2825–2830.

[42] Jeffrey Pennington, Richard Socher, and Christopher D Manning. 2014. Glove: Global vectors for word representation. In *Proc. of EMNLP*, Vol. 14. 1532–1543.

[43] Antti Rasmus, Harri Valpola, Mikko Honkala, Mathias Berglund, and Tapani Raiko. 2015. Semi-supervised Learning with Ladder Networks. In *Proc. of NIPS.* 3546–3554.

[44] Radim Rehurek and Petr Sojka. 2010. Software framework for topic modelling with large corpora. In *Proc. of LREC 2010 Workshop on New Challenges for NLP Frameworks.* 45–50.

[45] Ivan Srba and Maria Bielikova. 2016. A Comprehensive Survey and Classification of Approaches for Community Question Answering. *ACM Trans. Web* 10, 3 (Aug. 2016), 18:1–18:63.

[46] Mihai Surdeanu, Massimiliano Ciaramita, and Hugo Zaragoza. 2011. Learning to rank answers to non-factoid questions from web collections. *Computational linguistics* 37, 2 (2011), 351–383.

[47] Hapnes Toba, Zhao-Yan Ming, Mirna Adriani, and Tat-Seng Chua. 2014. Discovering High Quality Answers in Community Question Answering Archives Using a Hierarchy of Classifiers. *Inf. Sci.* 261 (2014), 101–115.

[48] Gilad Tsur, Yuval Pinter, Idan Szpektor, and David Carmel. 2016. Identifying Web Queries with Question Intent. In *Proc. of WWW.* 783–793.

[49] Marilyn A Walker, Pranav Anand, Robert Abbott, and Ricky Grant. 2012. Stance classification using dialogic properties of persuasion. In *Proc. of NAACL-HLT.* 592–596.

[50] Duncan J Watts and Steven H Strogatz. 1998. Collective dynamics of 'small-world' networks. *Nature* 393, 6684 (1998), 440–442.

[51] Ingmar Weber, Antti Ukkonen, and Aris Gionis. 2012. Answers, not links: extracting tips from yahoo! answers to address how-to web queries. In *Proc. of WSDM.* 613–622.

[52] Howard T Welser, Eric Gleave, Danyel Fisher, and Marc Smith. 2007. Visualizing the signatures of social roles in online discussion groups. *Journal of social structure* 8, 2 (2007), 1–32.

[53] Max L. L. Wilson, Paul Resnick, David Coyle, and Ed H. Chi. 2013. RepliCHI: The Workshop. In *Proc. of CHI EA.* 3159–3162.

[54] Xiaobing Xue, Jiwoon Jeon, and W. Bruce Croft. 2008. Retrieval Models for Question and Answer Archives. In *Proc. of SIGIR.* 475–482.

[55] Zheng-Jun Zha, Linjun Yang, Tao Mei, Meng Wang, Zengfu Wang, Tat-Seng Chua, and Xian-Sheng Hua. 2010. Visual Query Suggestion: Towards Capturing User Intent in Internet Image Search. *ACM Trans. Multimedia Comput. Commun. Appl.* 6, 3 (Aug. 2010), 13:1–13:19.

[56] Xiaojin Zhu and Zoubin Ghahramani. 2002. Learning from labeled and unlabeled data with label propagation. (2002).

Robust Transfer Learning for Cross-domain Collaborative Filtering Using Multiple Rating Patterns Approximation

Ming He
Beijing University of Technology
heming@bjut.edu.cn

Jiuling Zhang
Beijing University of Technology
zhang90@emails.bjut.edu.cn

Peng Yang
Beijing University of Technology
yangpeng@emails.bjut.edu.cn

Kaisheng Yao
Beijing University of Technology
yaokaisheng@emails.bjut.edu.cn

ABSTRACT

Collaborative filtering techniques are a common approach for building recommendations, and have been widely applied in real recommender systems. However, collaborative filtering usually suffers from limited performance due to the sparsity of user-item interaction. To address this issue, auxiliary information is usually used to improve the performance. Transfer learning provides the key idea of using knowledge from auxiliary domains. An assumption of transfer learning in collaborative filtering is that the source domain is a full rating matrix, which may not hold in many real-world applications. In this paper, we investigate how to leverage rating patterns from multiple incomplete source domains to improve the quality of recommender systems. First, by exploiting the transferred learning, we compress the knowledge from the source domain into a cluster-level rating matrix. The rating patterns in the low-level matrix can be transferred to the target domain. Specifically, we design a knowledge extraction method to enrich rating patterns by relaxing the full rating restriction on the source domain. Finally, we propose a robust multiple-rating-pattern transfer learning model for cross-domain collaborative filtering, which is called MINDTL, to accurately predict missing values in the target domain. Extensive experiments on real-world datasets demonstrate that our proposed approach is effective and outperforms several alternative methods.

ACM Reference format:
Ming He, Jiuling Zhang, Peng Yang, and Kaisheng Yao. Robust Transfer Learning for Cross-domain Collaborative Filtering Using Multiple Rating Patterns Approximation. In *WSDM '18: 11th ACM International Conference on Web Search & Data Mining*, Feb. 5–9, 2018, Marina Del Rey, CA, USA. ACM, NY, NY, USA, 9 pages.
https://doi.org/10.1145/3159652.3159675.

WSDM 2018, February 5–9, 2018, Marina Del Rey, CA, USA

ACM ISBN 978-1-4503-5581-0/18/02...$15.00 https://doi.org/10.1145/3159652.3159675

1 INTRODUCTION

Recommender systems help users faced with an overwhelming selection of items by identifying particular items that are likely to match each user's tastes or preferences. Increasingly, people are turning to recommender systems to help them find the information that is most valuable to them. One of the most successful technologies in recommender systems research and practice is collaborative filtering.

Collaborative filtering gathers user ratings and predicts what users will rate based on their similarity to other users. Collaborative filtering is known to be the most successful recommendation technique and has been used in a number of different applications such as recommending web pages [6, 23], movies, articles [31], and products. Collaborative methods can be divided into two models: the Neighborhood-Based Model (NBM) [4, 24] and the Latent Factor Model (LFM) [16]. In NBM methods, the similarity of the active user to other users is calculated. The predicted rating of an item for the active user is the weighted average of all the ratings of similar users for the item. The LFM methods transform both items and users to the same latent factor space. The latent space can be used to characterize both products and users in terms of factors.

Some of the most successful realizations of latent factor models are based on matrix factorization (MF) [2, 5, 27, 28]. In basic matrix factorization methods, both items and users are characterizes by factor vectors that have been inferred from the user-item rating matrix. These methods have become popular in recent years due to their accurate results. In addition, they offer flexible factorization for modeling various real applications [17, 19]. Recently, several MF-based approaches have been proposed, including Maximum Margin Matrix Factorization (MMMF) [15], Expectation Maximization for Matrix (EM) [26], Probabilistic Latent Semantic Analysis (PLSA) [29], Simplex Volume Maximization (SiVM) [3], Bayesian Probabilistic Matrix Factorization (BPMF) [1], and Regularized Non-Negative Matrix Factorization (RNMF) [32].

The low-rank matrix approximation is an effective model-based collaborative filtering (CF) approach. Generally, it derives a small set of latent factors from the rating matrix and characterizes both users and items on this latent factor space. The prediction for any user's rating on any item is computed with the inner product of the user and item latent factor vectors. However, in real-world recommender systems, users can rate a very limited number of items. Thus, the rating matrix is often extremely sparse. As a result, the available rating data that can be used for K-NN search, pure latent factor models, probabilistic models, or matrix factorization are radically insufficient. The sparsity problem has become a major bottleneck for most CF methods.

To alleviate the sparsity problem in collaborative filtering, one promising approach is to gather the rating data from multiple rating matrices in related domains for knowledge transfer and sharing. The cross-domain recommendation problem has been addressed from various perspectives in different research areas. The purpose of cross-domain collaborative filtering is to transform rating patterns from source domain to target domain to alleviate the sparsity problem in the target domain. Codebook-based knowledge transfer (CBT) is a widely used model in cross-domain collaborative filtering [12, 21, 22, 30]. In CBT, the codebook is a cluster-level matrix that contains rating patterns extracted from the source domain.

In earlier studies [21, 22, 25], ONMTF [8] was used to extract rating patterns. The ONMTF assumes that the source rating matrix is full. However, in practical situations, all of the available rating datasets have empty items. In fact, these datasets are extremely sparse (less than 5% rated items). The raw data matrix that is prepared as the source domain should be filtered in terms of the source rating matrix density requirement in cross-domain collaborative filtering. Beyond that, the source matrix needs to contain an appropriate number of rating items with sufficient rating patterns. We learn to get the rating pattern matrix (RPM) from the source and use the RPM to approximate the target matrix. In the real world, it is rare to have a source that is filled with an appropriate number of rating items. For example, there are 100,000 ratings of 9000 movies by 700 users in the MovieLens Latest Dataset. For one user, the maximum rating amount is 2391 and the minimum is 20. The average ratio among rated movies and unrated movies for each user is 143/8857. If we assume that 10,000 ratings (1/10 in dataset) in a 100×100 matrix (full rating) would have enough rating patterns to construct an effective RPM and that there is an equal probability event for each user-movie pair to be rated or unrated, then we can estimate the chance of getting an all-rated 100×100 matrix by data filtering. We get a probability of much less than 1% of having 100 users rate the same 100 movies in the dataset. That means we have a very small chance of getting a full rating matrix with enough rating patterns from this dataset. As for real cases, there are many features that affect the rating density, such as movie popularity and user preferences, but it is still difficult to obtain a full rating matrix with enough rating patterns in most of the real-world dataset.

The key contributions of this paper are summarized as follows:

- To the best our knowledge, this is the first work that applies the Incomplete Orthogonal Nonnegative Matrix Tri-factorizations (IONMTF) method to extract rating patterns from a source domain. This method relaxes the full rating restriction on the rating matrix of the source domain and makes the rating pattern matrix more relevant for the target matrix approximation.
- We propose a novel, robust, multiple-rating-pattern transfer learning model MINDTL for cross-domain collaborative filtering, which can be used to effectively transfer the rating patterns across domains and overcome the drawbacks of both underfitting and overfitting problems.
- Based on five real-world datasets, we conducted extensive experiments to evaluate the effectiveness of our model. The results demonstrate that our model significantly outperforms the baseline methods.

The rest of this paper is organized as follows. In Section 2 we demonstrate our model. After that, we provide optimizing formulas and related inferences in Section 3. The algorithm and implementation details are given in Section 4 and the experiment results and analysis are presented in Section 5.

2 METHODOLOGY

2.1 Source Rating Pattern Extraction

We focus on improving the process of learning rating patterns from the source domain and propose an innovative method to extract rating patterns from the source domain. This method removes the all-rating matrix restriction that the former studies

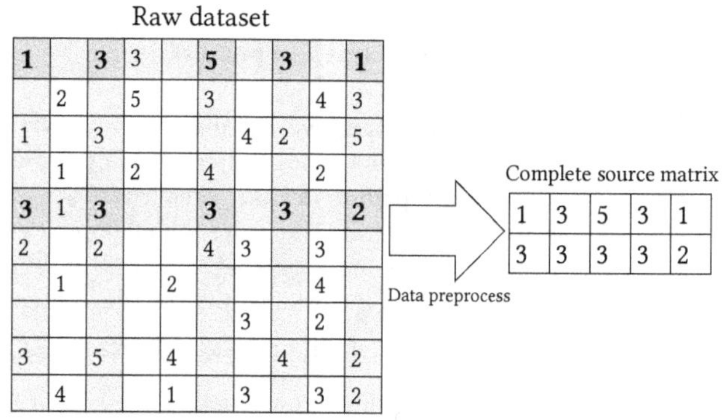

Figure 1: Raw data preprocess with full rated restriction.

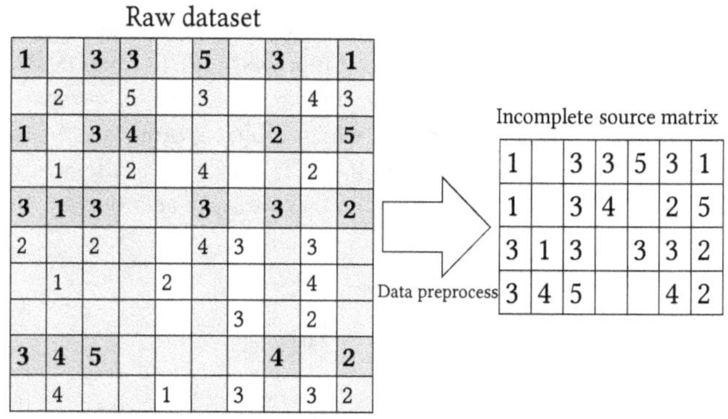

Figure 2: Raw data preprocess without full rated restriction.

imported. Therefore, we obtain more source datasets available for transfer learning. When we select a dataset as the source domain, the raw data needs to be filtered before transfer learning. We refer to the filtering process as the data preprocess. Fig. 1 and Fig. 2 show the data preprocessing in the same 10×10 toy raw data matrix with 46 rated items. The previous transfer learning required that the source domain be fully rated. There are only 10 rating items in the 2×5 filtered source matrix. Fig. 2 shows the data preprocess without full rating restriction in the toy matrix. We get a 4×7 filtered source matrix with 22 rated items and 6 empty entries. By relaxing the source matrix restriction, the rating item utilization rate in the raw dataset increases from 21% (10/46) to 48% (22/46), so we have a larger source matrix that contains many more rating items than before.

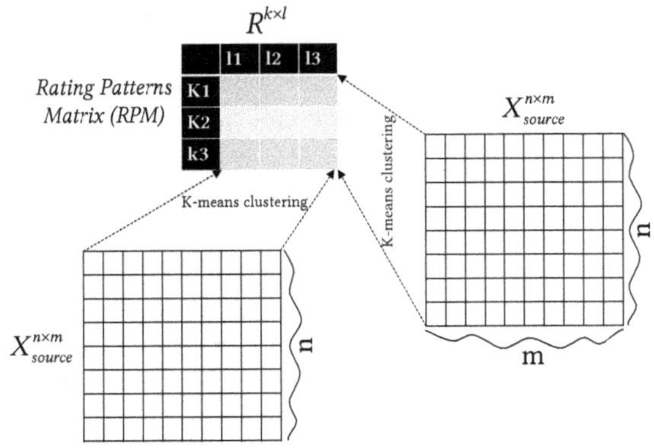

Figure 3: Rating patterns extraction process.

After raw data preprocessing, we get the source matrix. In the next step we need to extract rating patterns from the source matrix. In [22], the rating patterns matrix is called a codebook, which is defined as a $k\times l$ matrix. The codebook compresses the cluster-level user item from the $n\times m$ source matrix of k user clusters and l item clusters in the original filtered source matrix. In Fig. 3, $X_{source}^{n\times m}$ in the lower left and middle right represent the same source domain matrix. Both rows and columns of $X_{source}^{n\times m}$ are clustered in a low-level rating pattern matrix $R^{k\times l}$ (RPM).

We extend the original orthogonal nonnegative matrix tri-factorization (ONMTF) [8] to the incomplete original orthogonal nonnegative matrix tri-factorization (IONMTF). The ONMTF algorithm has been proved as equivalent to the two-way K-means clustering algorithm [8], which it also appropriate for the IONMTF. By introducing the IONMTF algorithm, the source domain rating matrix X_{source} can be tri-factorized as follows:

$$\min_{U\geq 0,\, V\geq 0,\, B\geq 0} \left\| M\circ\left(X_{source} - UBV^T\right)\right\|_F^2 \quad s.t.\ U^TU = I,\ V^TV = I \tag{1}$$

where $X_{sourc}\in R_+^{n\times m}, U\in R_+^{n\times l}, V\in R_+^{m\times l}, B\in R_+^{k\times l}$ (R_+ denotes the nonnegative real number domain). U and V are both nonnegative and orthogonal. We add the matrix M as an indicator in which M_{ij}=1 when $X_{source_{ij}}\neq 0$ and M_{ij}=0 otherwise. In Eq. 1, the $\circ$ operator denotes the Hadamard production operation between the M indicator matrix and the original ONMTF formulation. The Hadamard production ensures that the error is calculated based on the existing entries only.

2.2 Rating Patterns Approximation and Target Domain Reconstruction

After extracting rating patterns from the source domain, we can use these patterns to approximate the target rating matrix. In the CBT model, the approximation is conducted by multiplying the U_{tgt}, rating pattern matrix (RPM) and V_{tgt}^T. Fig. 4 shows the approximate process in the CBT model. The user u_1 from the target domain X_{tgt} belongs to user cluster k_2 in the RPM from the source, whereas item v_2 belongs to item cluster L_2 in the rating patterns. Thus, according to the source domain rating patterns, the missing rating of user u_1 to item v_2 is 2. After the approximate process, all unknown rates in X_{tgt} can be filled and the target matrix is reconstructed as $\tilde{X}_{tgt}$.

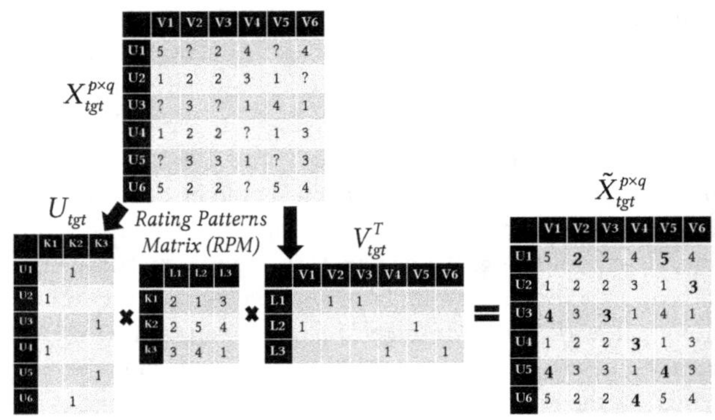

Figure 4: Decomposition of the target matrix X_{tgt} into the user membership matrix U_{tgt} and the item membership matrix V_{tgt}, and reconstruction of the $\tilde{X}_{tgt}$ by the product of U_{tgt}, R and V_{tgt}^T.

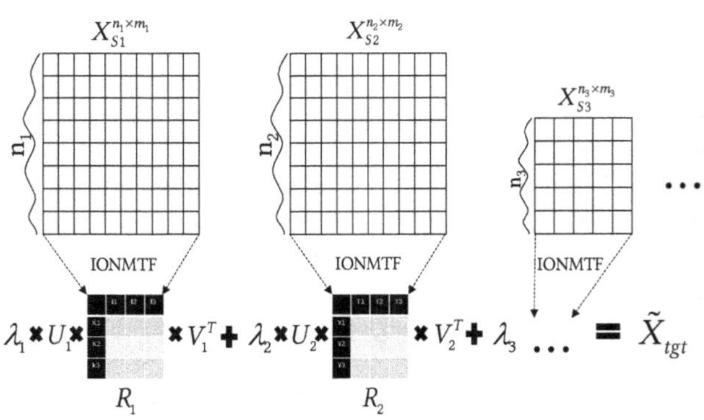

Figure 5: Multiple rating patterns approximation.

Our model MINDTL fixes the underfitting problems in the CBT by extracting rating patterns from multiple incomplete source domains. We use these rating patterns to approximate and reconstruct the sparse target matrix as shown in Fig. 5. X_{Sn} represents an incomplete source domain matrix. MINDTL uses IONMTF to extract rating patterns (R_n) from X_{Sn}. U_n refers to the users' cluster memberships with $p\times k_n$ dimension for each source n. X_{Sn} represents an incomplete source domain matrix. MINDTL uses IONMTF to extract rating patterns (R_n) from X_{Sn}. U_n refers to the users' cluster memberships with $p\times k_n$ dimension for each source n. V_n refers to the $q\times l_n$ items' cluster memberships. U_n and V_n are binary matrices, where "1" indicates a membership of the user or item in a cluster respectively. Then MINDTL linearly combines multiple rating pattern approximations to reconstruct the target matrix $\tilde{X}_{tgt}$. The MINDTL optimization formula is defined as follows:

$$\min_{\substack{U_n\in\{0,1\}^{p\times k_n}\\ V_n\in\{0,1\}^{q\times l_n}\\ a_n\in R\,\forall n\in N}} \left\| \left[X_{tgt} - \sum_{n=1}^{N} \lambda_n \left(U_{tgt_n} R_n V_{tgt_n}^T \right) \right] \circ W \right\|_F^2 \quad s.t.\ U_{tgt_n}1=1,\ V_{tgt_n}1=1,\ \sum_n \lambda_n = 1,\ \lambda_n \ge 0 \tag{2}$$

where λ_n are the linear multipliers for combining multiple rating pattern approximation. The λ_n is also regarded as relatedness values among multiple source domains in MINDTL. The λ_n are confined to [0,1] because negative relations between multiple domains in the real world are unusual. The summation of all λ_n are restrained to 1 according to the maximum correlation rate 100%.

3 OPTIMIZATION METHOD

3.1 Incomplete Orthogonal Tri-Factor NMF

We use the alternating multiplicative updating algorithm [14], which optimizes the objective function with respect to one set of parameters while fixing the others, and then, alternatively, exchanges the roles of the parameter sets. This procedure will be repeated for several iterations until convergence. The Incomplete Orthogonal Nonnegative Matrix Tri-factorization (IONMTF) loss function is defined in Eq. 1. Following the standard theory of constrained optimization, we introduce the Lagrangian multipliers δ (a symmetric matrix of size U^TU) and minimize the Lagrangian function:

$$L(U) = \left\| M \circ \left(X - UBV^T \right) \right\|_F^2 + Tr\left(\delta \left(U^TU - I \right) \right) + Tr\left(\Phi U^T \right)$$

noting that $\left\| X - UBV^T \right\|_F^2 = Tr\left(\left(X - UBV^T \right)^T \left(X - UBV^T \right) \right)$ and the $\left\| M \circ \left(X - UBV^T \right) \right\|_F^2$ can be transformed to $Tr\left(M \circ \left(X^TX - 2V^TX^TUB + U^TUBV^TVB^T \right) \right)$.

The gradient of $L(U)$ is:

$$\frac{\delta L}{\delta U} = M \circ \left(-2VXB^T + 2UBV^TVB^T \right) + 2U\delta + \Phi$$

The Φ is the nonnegative Lagrangian restraint for $U \ge 0$. The KKT complementarity condition $\Phi_{ik} U_{ik} = 0$ gives:

$$\left(\frac{\delta L}{\delta U} \right)_{ik} U_{ik} = \sum_{ik} \left(M \circ \left(-2VXB^T + 2UBV^TVB^T \right) \right)_{ik} U_{ik} = 0$$

Then we can get the following updating rule for U_{ik}:

$$U_{ik}^{n+1} = U_{ik}^{n} \sqrt{\frac{V(M \circ X)B^T}{V\left(M \circ \left(UBV^T \right) \right) B^T}} \tag{3}$$

Learning B: The latent factor B can be learned in a similar way as follows:

$$B_{ik}^{n+1} = B_{ik}^{n} \sqrt{\frac{U(M \circ X)V^T}{U^T\left(M \circ \left(UBV^T \right) \right) V}} \tag{4}$$

Learning V: The latent factor V can be learned in the similar way as follows:

$$V_{ik}^{n+1} = V_{ik}^{n} \sqrt{\frac{U(M \circ X)B^T}{U^T\left(M \circ \left(UBV^T \right) \right) B^T}} \tag{5}$$

We can prove that the learning algorithm is convergent by convergence analysis based on the above updating rules for learning different latent factors. The reader is referred to [7, 10] for more details.

3.2 Linear Multipliers Optimization

We still consider the case in which each user/item can only belong to one user/item cluster. We can alternatively update U_n and V_n in Eq. 6, which has been proved to reduce the value monotonically and converge to the local minimums in [22]. Hence, U_{tgt_n} and V_{tgt_n} are denoted U_n and V_n for each source domain. The error function denoted as F is defined as follows:

$$F = \left\| \left[X_{tgt} - \sum_{n=1}^{N} \lambda_n \left(U_n R_n V_n^T \right) \right] \circ W \right\|_F^2 \tag{6}$$

We aim to find the optimal λ_n values that minimize the MSE of F while U_n and V_n are fixed. For simplicity, we use the symbol M_n as $\left(U_n B_n V_n^T \right) \circ W$ and X as $X_{tgt} \circ W$. Practically, minimizing the value of F is equivalent to minimizing the MSE, so Eq. 6 can then be rewritten as follows:

$$F = \sum_{i,j} \left(X - \sum_{n=1}^{N} \lambda_n M_n \right)_{ij}^2 \tag{7}$$

We learn the relatedness coefficients λ_n through Stochastic Gradient Descent (SGD), which is different than least squares (LS) in TALMUD [25]. The SGD makes it easier to control updating of the values of λ_n to comply with restrictions in Eq. 2. In addition, SGD avoids the matrix inversion computation in LS, which causes an error if the matrix is singular. In addition, we reduce the computational complexity by getting around the matrix inversion computation. The gradient of F is:

$$\frac{\delta F}{\delta \lambda_n} = -2 \sum_{i,j} \left(X - \lambda_n M_n \right)_{ij} \left(M_n \right)_{ij} = 0 \tag{8}$$

Next we can update λ_n iteratively through:

$$\lambda_n^{t+1} \leftarrow \lambda_n^t - \frac{\delta L}{\delta \lambda_n^t} \times \theta \quad (9)$$

In Eq. 9, we can set the learning rate coefficient θ empirically as 0.1 to 0.01. In summary, we alternatively update a set of variables { U_n, V_n, λ_n } through each iteration until all of them converge to the local minimums.

4 ALGORITHM OVERVIEW

We use IONMTF to extract rating patterns from multiple source domains. The implementation is demonstrated in Algorithm 1. The rating pattern approximation and target matrix reconstruction in MINDTL are implemented in Algorithm 2. Both algorithms 1 and 2 are based on optimizing formulas in Section 4.

Algorithm 1 Rating Patterns Extraction

Input: The number of source matrixes N; the $p_n \times q_n$ source domain rating matrixes X_{source}; the number of user and item clusters k_n and l_n; the count of auto reboot Q; the number of maximum iterations M.

Output: $k_n \times l_n$ rating pattern matrixes R_n.

for $n \leftarrow 1......N$ **do**
  Select appropriate k_n and l_n
  Allocate U_n, V_n and B_n in Eq. 1.
  for $r \leftarrow 1......Q$ **do**
    Randomly initialize $U_n^{r(0)}$, $V_n^{r(0)}$ and $B_n^{r(0)}$
    for $t \leftarrow 1......T$ **do**
      Update $U_n^{r(t-1)}$, $V_n^{r(t-1)}$ and $B_n^{r(t-1)}$ through Eq. 3, Eq. 4 and Eq. 5, then obtain $U_n^{r(t)}$, $V_n^{r(t)}$ and $B_n^{r(t)}$
      Calculate eventual result through Eq. 6
    end for
  end for
  $U_n = \arg\min_{U_n^r} \{\text{Eq. } 1\}$, $V_n = \arg\min_{V_n^r} \{\text{Eq. } 1\}$, $B_n = \arg\min_{B_n^r} \{\text{Eq. } 1\}$ $for\ r \in \{1......R\}$
  Allocate spaces for U_n^{aux}, V_n^{aux}
  for $i \leftarrow 1......p$ **do**
    $\hat{j} = \arg\max_j \left\{ \left[U_n^{aux} \right]_{ij} \right\}$ $for\ j \in \{1......k\}$
    $\left[U_n^{aux} \right]_{i\hat{j}} \leftarrow 1$; $\left[U_n^{aux} \right]_{ij} \leftarrow 0$ $for\ j \in \{1......k\} / \hat{j}$
  end for
  for $i \leftarrow 1......q$ **do**
    $\hat{j} = \arg\max_j \left\{ \left[V_n^{aux} \right]_{ij} \right\}$ $for\ j \in \{1......k\}$
    $\left[V_n^{aux} \right]_{i\hat{j}} \leftarrow 1$; $\left[V_n^{aux} \right]_{ij} \leftarrow 0$ $for\ j \in \{1......k\} / \hat{j}$
  end for
  R_n = Get RPM by Eq. 2 in [22]
end for

Implementation details:

Because the optimizing formulas Eq. 3, Eq. 4, and Eq. 5 converge to the local minimums, we employ Random-Restart Hill Climbing (RRHC) to avoid the unfavorable local minimums. We introduce a counter Q and each U_n and V_n converge Q times. The value of Q is set empirically as 100. With each circulation, the U_n, V_n and R_n in Ep. 2 are initialized differently so that they converge to different local minimums. After Q iterations, we get Q local minimums. We select the smallest value of the minimums and set the U_n, V_n and B_n accordingly.

Algorithm 2 Rating Patterns Approximation and Target Matrix Reconstruction

Input: The number of rating pattern matrixes N; $k_n \times l_n$ rating pattern matrixes R_n; the target rating matrix X_{tgt}; maximum iteration record T.

Output: The reconstructed target matrix $\tilde{X}_{tgt}$.

for $n \leftarrow 1......N$ **do**
  Allocate $V_{tgt_n}^{(0)}$, and $U_{tgt_n}^{(0)}$
  Randomly initialize $V_{tgt_n}^{(0)}$
end for
for $n \leftarrow 1......N$ **do**
  Randomly initialize $\lambda_n^{(0)}$
end for
for $t \leftarrow 1......T$ **do**
  Fixed $V_{tgt_n}^{(t-1)}$ and $\lambda_n^{(t-1)}$, update $U_{tgt_n}^{(t)}$ according to [22]
  Fixed $U_{tgt_n}^{(t)}$ and $\lambda_n^{(t-1)}$, update $V_{tgt_n}^{(t)}$ according to [22]
  $sum \leftarrow 1$
  for $n \leftarrow 1......N$ **do**
    $\lambda_t \leftarrow$ Eq. 9
    if $\lambda_t \geq 0$ **and** $sum - \lambda_t \geq 0$ **then**
      $\lambda_n^{(t)} \leftarrow \lambda_t$
    else continue
  end for
end for
$\tilde{X}_{tgt} = W \circ X_{tgt} + [1 - W] \circ \left[\sum_{n=1}^{N} \lambda_n \left(U_{tgt_n} R_n V_{tgt_n}^T \right) \right]$

Implementation details

In algorithm 2, we solve the tri-variable set { U_{tgt}, V_{tgt}, λ_n } each time in turn and update $V_{tgt_n}^{(0)}$ and $U_{tgt_n}^{(0)}$ iteratively. We introduce a temporary correlation variable λ_t and put the new available value of λ into λ_t temporarily. For each round of iterations, the λ_t is renewed and we inspect whether the new value of λ_t complies with limits in Eq. 2 in advance. If it is satisfied, we renew λ_n as λ_t, otherwise we continue the loop without renewal λ_n.

5 EXPERIMENT

In this section, we conduct experiments to test our proposed method on several real-world datasets. We evaluate the performance on (1) the cross-domain recommendation problem, i.e., predicting missing values in a target domain using multiple domains, and (2) the overfitting and underfitting problem, i.e., a model would have poor predictive performance. The results demonstrate the robustness of our approach.

5.1 Experiment Setup

To test the performance of our work, we conducted two separate groups of experiments:

1) In the first experiment, we used Netflix and EachMovie datasets as X_{source} and BookCrossing and MovieLens datasets are used as X_{tgt}. We also carefully implemented a data preprocessing method for our test.

- For ONMTF, we first picked an 80×80 and a 30×30 full rating matrix from Netflix and EachMovie to extract rating patterns, respectively.
- For DC-ONMTF, we first used the mean value of users' ratings to fill in missing ratings in the above-mentioned incomplete Netflix and EachMovie rating matrices, respectively.
- For IONMTF, we selected a 394×400 (with 95% sparsity) and a 500×500 (with 48% sparsity) incomplete rating matrix from Netflix and EachMovie to extract rating pattern matrices, respectively.
- This experiment was executed with four different combinations of X_{source} and X_{tgt}. Each combination of X_{source} and X_{tgt} is examined (e.g., we used Netflix as X_{source} to extract rating patterns and then used these rating patterns to reconstruct the BookCrossing (X_{tgt}) rating matrix). Using this setting, we can create multiple scenarios to compare ONMTF and IONMTF. The rating pattern matrix dimensions, k and l, were set according to Li et al. [22], who state that the clusters model should be compact enough to avoid overfitting, but expressive enough to capture significant behavior patterns. We set $k= p/10$, $l= q/10$ and the X_{source} is $p\times q$ dimensions of the rating matrix.

2) In the second experiment we used the Jester, Netflix, and EachMovie datasets as the X_{source} and the MovieLens and BookCrossing datasets are used as X_{tgt}.

3) We conduct holdout experiments by randomly selecting 80% of ratings for training and the remaining for testing in the target domain.

5.2 Experimental results

In this section, we give the experimental results of applying our proposed method to our datasets.

As shown in Table 1, in the ONMTF method the size of X_{source} is smaller for the rating pattern matrix (RPM), most likely due to the fact that the X_{source} of ONMTF has a restriction on the full rating matrix. The X_{source} of ONMTF also has many fewer rated items compared to DC-ONMTF and IONMTF. Therefore, the size for ONMTF is much smaller than the other two methods as well.

Table 2 and Table 3 show that the ONMTF has the smallest RPM (R) and the highest values of MAE and RMSE, which means that the ONMTF has the lowest prediction accuracy. The possible reason behind this underperformance is that the transferred knowledge from the source domain may be insufficient. Note that IONMTF has the same RPM (R) size as DC-ONMTF, but has the highest prediction accuracy, which means that our method outperforms both ONMTF and DC-ONMTF. For the second question, we conduct our proposed MINDTL method by expanding the transfer learning algorithm to multiple source domains.

Table 1: The scale of X_{source}, *RPM (R)* and the number of rated items (*N*) among ONMTF, IONMTF and DC-ONMTF

Method	Netflix			EachMovie		
	X_{source}	N	R	X_{source}	N	R
ONMTF	80×80	6400	8×8	30×30	900	3×3
IONMTF ONMTF DC-ONMTF	394×400	149720	40×40	500×500	145000	50×50

Table 2: Learning from Netflix to BookCrossing and MovieLens

Netflix (X_{source})	RPM (R)		BookCrossing (X_{tgt})		MovieLens (X_{tgt})	
	k	l	MAE	RMSE	MAE	RMSE
ONMTF	8	8	0.9834	1.311	0.9245	1.214
DC-ONMTF	40	40	0.8651	1.105	0.8438	0.9962
IONMTF	40	40	**0.8563**	**1.084**	**0.8324**	**0.9823**

Table 3: Learning from EachMovie to BookCrossing and MovieLens

EachMovie (X_{source})	RPM (R)		BookCrossing (X_{tgt})		MovieLens (X_{tgt})	
	k	l	MAE	RMSE	MAE	RMSE
ONMTF	3	3	1.605	1.865	1.460	1.672
DC-ONMTF	50	50	0.9571	1.237	0.9237	1.196
IONMTF	50	50	**0.9146**	**1.158**	**0.8862**	**1.044**

For the second question, we conduct our proposed MINDTL method by expanding the transfer learning algorithm on multiple source domains. We evaluated the transferability of knowledge using just one of the sources or a combination of the multiple source domains and compare the performance of MINDTL with CBT and TALMUD. First, we heuristically ranked the available source domains X_{source} from the domain that is most correlated to the target domain X_{tgt} to the domain that is least correlated using the heuristic correlation (HC) estimate algorithm [25]. The larger the heuristic correlation, the larger the distance and the weaker the correlation between X_{source} and X_{tgt}. Therefore, after heuristic estimation, the X_{source} can be added to the TALMUD and MINDTL models, respectively, by increasing heuristic correlation.

In Table 4, we also observe that the MAE and RMSE values of the TALMUD model using two source domains are lower than those using three source domains according to different λ_i, which means that the TALMUD model suffers from negative transfer due to overfitting. Fig. 6 shows the changing MAE curve when available domains are sequentially added to the source domain according to their ascending relatedness coefficient.

When EachMovie is added after Netflix and Jester, we can clearly observe that the MAE values of MINDTL are 19.3% and 28.6%, significantly smaller, respectively, than the MAEs of the TALMUD model. This means that EachMovie domain is more helpful to MINDTL than to TALMUD in predictions. The reason for the underperformance is overfitting when learning is transferred from multiple sources.

Table 4: Results of our model and baselines of recommendation

Method	n	Source domains			MovieLens	
		Netflix	Jester	EachMovie	MAE	RMSE
HC	-	0.023	0.105	0.246	-	-
CBT	1	λ=1	-	-	0.9245	1.214
TALMUD	2	λ_1=1.3	λ_2=-0.50	-	0.8054	0.9517
MINDTL	2	λ_1=0.63	λ_2=0.37	-	0.8010	0.9464
TALMUD	3	λ_1=4.8	λ_2=-0.83	λ_3=-3.2	0.9736	1.298
MINDTL	3	λ_1=0.52	λ_2=0.26	λ_3=0.12	**0.7851**	**0.9131**

Method	n	Source domains			BookCrossing	
		Netflix	Jester	EachMovie	MAE	RMSE
HC	-	0.102	0.117	0.364	-	-
CBT	1	λ=1	-	-	0.9834	1.311
TALMUD	2	λ_1=1.24	λ_2=-0.28	-	0.8432	1.027
MINDTL	2	λ_1=0.59	λ_2=0.41	-	0.8509	1.038
TALMUD	3	λ_1=6.3	λ_2=-2.9	λ_3=-2.2	1.107	1.326
MINDTL	3	λ_1=0.50	λ_2=0.31	λ_3=0.19	**0.8005**	**0.9442**

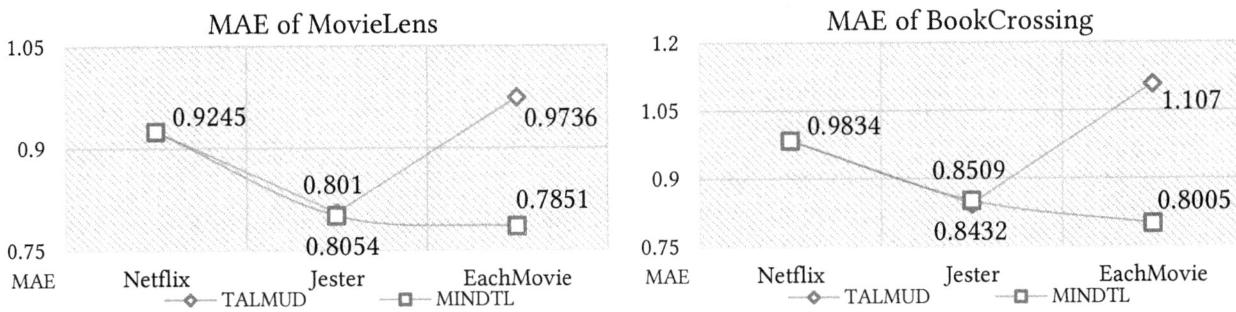

Figure 6: The MAE results of different available domains sequentially added to the source domain X_{source}.

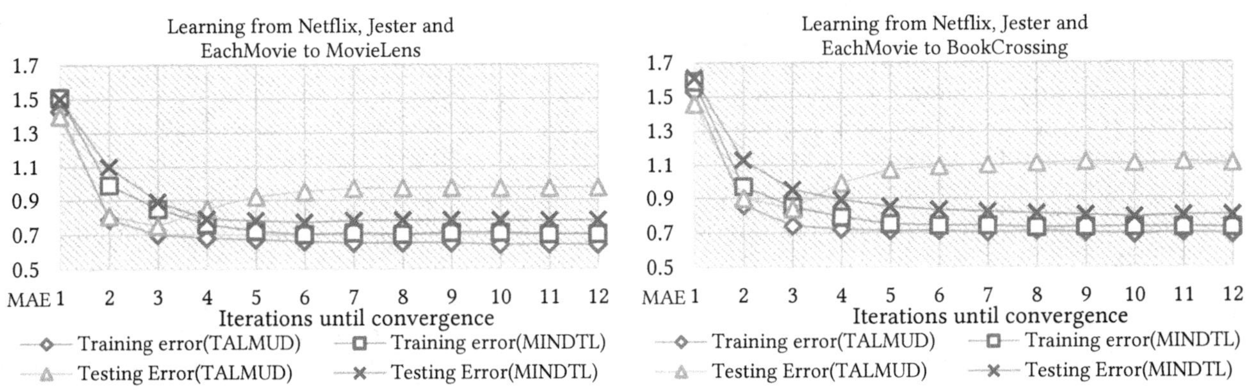

Figure 7: The learning process from multiple domains.

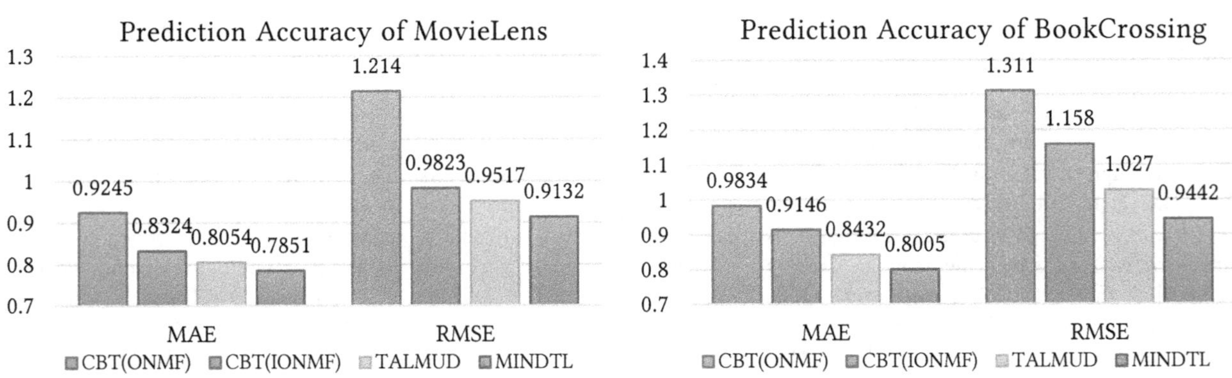

Figure 8: MAE and RMSE comparison between our model and baselines for collaborative filtering recommendation

Fig. 7 shows the MAE evaluations of our MINDTL and TALMUD models for transfer learning from multiple source domains. At the end of each round of iterations, we computed the MAE value that is achieved on the training data and on the testing data. We plotted MAE convergence curves for two models and observe that the TALMUD model has consistently smaller MAE values on the training data. However, the MAE of the TALMUD model shows an opposite trend on the testing data. In contrast, the MINDTL model shows consistently lower MAEs on both training data and testing data. From the figures, we can observe an obvious valley around the fourth round of iterations, which means our proposed model MINDTL has guaranteed convergence, achieves better performance, and overcomes the drawback of the TALMUD model, which demonstrated a positive transfer learning effect.

Fig. 8 compares the performance of our proposed MINDTL model with CBT and TALMUD in predicting missing values for collaborative recommendation. These results demonstrate that the MINDTL model has better performance than CBT and TALMUD.

6 RELATED WORK

The cluster-level rating pattern is normally called codebook, and was first proposed in [22]. Li et al. pioneered the rating patterns sharing approach in recommendation systems with their CBT algorithm. Since the advent of the CBT model, many other works have been inspired by CBT, such as the probabilistic rating-matrix generative model (RMGM) [21] and the Transfer Learning for Multiple Domains model, which alleviates the sparsity problem with multiple dense domains [25]. Ji et al. [12] have a reconstructive method for improving the accuracy of matrix approximation learned by previous matrix factorization and social recommendation models. Grolman et al. [11] extended existing transfer learning algorithms for addressing binary data and presented a collaborative filtering framework for treating data of multiple events via transfer learning. Fan et al. [9] extend the cross-domain transform into tag-based recommendation and construct a tag co-occurrence matrix transfer model to capture the user behavior patterns from different rating domains. Zhang et al. [32] improve a group-aware recommendation algorithm based on Matrix Factorization and the CBT model, which constructs the decision tree and selects top-N submatrices to approximate the rating matrix. Li et al. [20] accomplish a unified framework for cross-domain collaborative filtering over the site-time coordinate system by sharing group-level rating patterns and imposing user/item dependence across domains. Zhao et al. [33] obtain two recommendation models to solve the CCS and ICS problems for new items. Li et al. [18] introduce a privacy-preserving shared collaborative filtering problem to leverage the data from other parties (contributors) to improve its own (beneficiaries) collaborative filtering performance. Jiang et al. [13] incorporates transferable items in auxiliary domains and bridge cross-domain knowledge with the social domain to accurately predict user-item links in a target domain.

7 Conclusion

In this paper, we addressed the problem of data sparsity in recommender systems. We reconsidered the problem from the transfer learning perspective and alleviated the data sparsity problem in a target domain by transferring rating patterns from multiple incomplete source domains. We first designed an innovative IONMTF method to extract rating patterns from an incomplete source domain that relaxes the full rating restriction of the source domain and obtains richer rating patterns. Next, we proposed a new model called MINDTL for cross-domain recommendation that combines collaborative filtering and multiple rating patterns transferred to approximate the target domain and predict missing values. In particular, by considering effects of negative transfer, the weighting of information from each source to the target are automatically learned, and we obtained a robust recommendation. We conducted extensive experiments on real-world datasets and showed that the proposed method boosts the cross-domain recommendation performance, which reduced the MAE by 19.3% and 28.6% compared with baseline methods. In addition, this research indicates a promising and general way to solve the data sparsity problem.

ACKNOWLEDGMENTS

This work was partially supported by the National Natural Science Foundation of China (No. 91546111, 91646201), the Key Project of Beijing Municipal Education Commission (No.KZ201610005009), and the General Project of Beijing Municipal Education Commission (No. KM201710005023).

REFERENCES

[1] T. V. Aa, I. Chakroun, and T. Haber. Distributed Bayesian Probabilistic Matrix Factorization. *IEEE International Conference on CLUSTER Computing* IEEE Computer Society, 2016:346-349.

[2] B. Abdollahi, and O. Nasraoui. Explainable Matrix Factorization for Collaborative Filtering. *International Conference Companion on World Wide Web* International World Wide Web Conferences Steering Committee, 2016:5-6.

[3] M. Alfeld, M. Wahabzada, C. Bauckhage, K. Kersting, G. Snickt, P. Noble, K. Janssens, G. Wellenreuther and G. Falkenberg. "Simplex Volume Maximization (SiVM): A matrix factorization algorithm with non-negative constrains and low computing demands for the interpretation of full spectral X-ray fluorescence imaging data." *Microchemical Journal* 132(2017):179-184.

[4] F. Alqadah, CK. Reddy, J. Hu and HF. Alqadah. Biclustering neighborhood-based collaborative filtering method for top- n, recommender systems. *Knowledge & Information Systems* 44.2(2015):475-491.

[5] D. Bokde, S. Girase, and D. Mukhopadhyay. Matrix Factorization Model in Collaborative Filtering Algorithms: A Survey. *Icac* 2015:136-146.

[6] P. Chinnu, and S. Rani. Location-Aware and Personalized Collaborative Filtering for Web Service Recommendation : A Review. *International Journal of Computer Applications* 133(2016).

[7] C. Ding, T. Li, and M. I. Jordan. Convex and Semi-Nonnegative Matrix Factorizations. *IEEE Transactions on Pattern Analysis & Machine Intelligence* 32.1(2010):45-55.

[8] C. Ding, T. Li, W. Peng and H. Park. "Orthogonal nonnegative matrix t-factorizations for clustering." *ACM SIGKDD International Conference on Knowledge Discovery and Data Mining* ACM, 2006:126-135.

[9] Z. Fang, S. Gao, B. Li, J. Li and J. Liao. Cross-Domain Recommendation via Tag Matrix Transfer. *IEEE International Conference on Data Mining Workshop* IEEE, 2015:1235-1240.

[10] S. Gao, L. Denoyer, and P. Gallinari. Temporal link prediction by integrating content and structure information. *ACM International Conference on Information and Knowledge Management* ACM, 2011:1169-1174.

[11] E. Grolman, A. Bar, B Shapira, L Rokach and A Dayan. Utilizing transfer learning for in-domain collaborative filtering. *Knowledge-Based Systems* 107(2016):70-82.

[12] K. Ji, R. Sun X. Li and W. Shu. Improving matrix approximation for recommendation via a clustering-based reconstructive method. *Neurocomputing* 173(2016):912-920.

[13] M. Jiang, P. Cui, X. Chen, F. Wang, W. Zhu and S. Yang. Social Recommendation with Cross-Domain Transferable Knowledge. *IEEE Transactions on Knowledge & Data Engineering* 27.11(2015):3084-3097.

[14] H.A.L. Kiers. Setting up alternating least squares and iterative majorization algorithms for solving various matrix optimization problems. *Computational Statistics & Data Analysis* 41.1(2002):157-170.

[15] V. Kumar, A.K. Pujari, S.K. Sahu, V.R. Kagita and V. Padmanabhan. Collaborative filtering using multiple binary maximum margin matrix factorizations. *Information Sciences* 380(2017):1-11

[16] H. Langseth, and T. D. Nielsen. *Scalable learning of probabilistic latent models for collaborative filtering.* Elsevier Science Publishers B. V. 2015.

[17] Z. Li and J. Tang. Weakly Supervised Deep Matrix Factorization for Social Image Understanding. *IEEE Transactions on Image Processing:a Publication of the IEEE Signal Processing Society* 26.1(2017):276.

[18] J. Li, J. Yang, Y. Zhao, B. Liu, M. Zhou, J. Bi and Q. Wang. Enforcing Differential Privacy for Shared Collaborative Filtering. *IEEE Access* 5(2017):35-49.

[19] X. Li , X. Cheng, S. Su, S. Li and J. Yang. A hybrid collaborative filtering model for social influence prediction in event-based social networks. *Neurocomputing* 230(2017):197-209.

[20] B. Li, X. Zhu, R. Li and C. Zhang. Rating knowledge sharing in cross-domain collaborative filtering. *IEEE Transactions on Cybernetics* 45.5(2015):1068-1082.

[21] B. Li, Q. Yang, and X. Xue. Transfer learning for collaborative filtering via a rating-matrix generative model. *International Conference on Machine Learning, ICML 2009, Montreal, Quebec, Canada, June* DBLP, 2009:617-624.

[22] B. Li, Q. Yang and X. Xue. Can Movies and Books Collaborate? Cross-Domain Collaborative Filtering for Sparsity Reduction. *IJCAI 2009, Proceedings of the, International Joint Conference on Artificial Intelligence, Pasadena, California, Usa, July* DBLP, 2009:2052-2057.

[23] J. Liu, M. Tang, Z. Zheng, X. Liu and S. Lyu. Location-Aware and Personalized Collaborative Filtering for Web Service Recommendation. *IEEE Transactions on Services Computing* 9.5(2016):686-699.

[24] X. Liu. An improved clustering-based collaborative filtering recommendation algorithm. *Cluster Computing* (2017):1-8.s

[25] O. Moreno B, Shapira, L. Rokach and G. Shani. TALMUD:transfer learning for multiple domains. ACM International Conference on Information and Knowledge Management, Cikm'12, Maui, Hi, Usa, October 29 - November ACM, 2012:425-434.

[26] A. Santos, R. Santos, M. Silva, E. Figueiredo, C. Sales and J. C. W. A. Costa, "A Global Expectation–Maximization Approach Based on Memetic Algorithm for Vibration-Based Structural Damage Detection," in *IEEE Transactions on Instrumentation and Measurement*, vol. 66, no. 4, pp. 661-670, April 2017. *Transactions on Instrumentation & Measurement* 66.4(2017):661-670.

[27] C. Wang, C. Wang, H. Wang and Y. Gao. Attributes coupling based matrix factorization for item recommendation. *Applied Intelligence* 46.3(2017):521-533.

[28] Y. Wang and H. Xu. Stability of matrix factorization for collaborative filtering. *Computer Science - Numerical Analysis* 49.1(2012):136-146.

[29] J. Wang, and M. She. Probabilistic Latent Semantic Analysis for Multichannel Biomedical Signal Clustering. *IEEE Signal Processing Letters* PP.99(2016):1-1.

[30] G. Wen, S. Huang, and Y. Qiao. Making recommendations from top-N user-item subgroups. *Neurocomputing* 165.C(2015):228-237.

[31] X. Wu, B. Cheng, and J. Chen. Collaborative Filtering Service Recommendation Based on a Novel Similarity Computation Method. *IEEE Transactions on Services Computing* 10.3(1939):352-365.

[32] X. Zhang, L. Zhao, L. Zong, X. Liu and H. Yu. Multi-view Clustering via Multi-manifold Regularized Nonnegative Matrix Factorization. *Neural Networks* 88(2017):74.

[33] L. Zhao, S. J. Pan, and Q. Yang. A Unified Framework of Active Transfer Learning for Cross-System Recommendation. *Artificial Intelligence* 245(2017):38-55.

Ballpark Crowdsourcing: The Wisdom of Rough Group Comparisons

Tom Hope
The Hebrew University of Jerusalem
tom.hope@mail.huji.ac.il

Dafna Shahaf
The Hebrew University of Jerusalem
dshahaf@cs.huji.ac.il

ABSTRACT

Crowdsourcing has become a popular method for collecting labeled training data. However, in many practical scenarios traditional labeling can be difficult for crowdworkers (for example, if the data is high-dimensional or unintuitive, or the labels are continuous).

In this work, we develop a novel model for crowdsourcing that can complement standard practices by exploiting people's intuitions about *groups* and *relations* between them. We employ a recent machine learning setting, called *Ballpark Learning*, that can estimate individual labels given only coarse, aggregated signal over groups of data points. To address the important case of continuous labels, we extend the Ballpark setting (which focused on classification) to regression problems. We formulate the problem as a convex optimization problem and propose fast, simple methods with an innate robustness to outliers.

We evaluate our methods on real-world datasets, demonstrating how useful constraints about groups can be harnessed from a crowd of non-experts. Our methods can rival supervised models trained on many *true* labels, and can obtain considerably better results from the crowd than a standard label-collection process (for a lower price). By collecting rough guesses on groups of instances and using machine learning to infer the individual labels, our lightweight framework is able to address core crowdsourcing challenges and train machine learning models in a cost-effective way.

ACM Reference Format:
Tom Hope and Dafna Shahaf. 2018. Ballpark Crowdsourcing: The Wisdom of Rough Group Comparisons. In *WSDM 2018: WSDM 2018: The Eleventh ACM International Conference on Web Search and Data Mining , February 5–9, 2018, Marina Del Rey, CA, USA.* ACM, New York, NY, USA, 9 pages. https://doi.org/10.1145/3159652.3159670

1 INTRODUCTION

In many real-world learning scenarios, acquiring labeled training data is a challenging bottleneck for researchers and practitioners. Crowdsourcing has become a popular approach for annotating large quantities of data. Platforms such as Amazon's Mechanical Turk allow researchers to distribute labeling tasks to a large number of crowdworkers, resulting in an effective mechanism for annotating data for supervised learning models [19, 27].

WSDM 2018, February 5–9, 2018, Marina Del Rey, CA, USA

ACM ISBN 978-1-4503-5581-0/18/02...$15.00
https://doi.org/10.1145/3159652.3159670

Despite its many benefits, crowdsourcing is not a panacea for data labeling. Crowdworkers are not domain *experts*, and often are careless or make mistakes, generating unreliable labels. Since crowdworkers are error-prone, it is common to ask multiple workers to label each data point, which might make the labeling process prohibitively expensive. In particular, crowds tend to be *biased* [28], requiring special methods to de-bias their answers.

In addition, some tasks cannot be crowdsourced due to inherent *hardness* of the task. The input might not be interpretable to most people (e.g., medical EEG data), or the output might be difficult to assess (e.g., continuous targets are notoriously hard for annotators [28]). Other times one cannot show people individual data points for labeling, especially due to *privacy* considerations.

In this paper we propose a different approach to crowdsourcing, which could mitigate these problems. Rather than collecting labels for individual data points, we focus on collecting **coarse, aggregated information** over **groups of points**, and using this information to **infer individual labels**. Instead of investing resources in trying to get precise labels, we propose a lightweight framework that pools noisy crowd guesses over group averages and comparisons, and uses recent advances in machine learning to turn them into instance-level predictions.

For example, consider an advertising company. To optimize ad display, demographics are widely used to characterize customers. However, in practice such information (e.g., age, gender or richer targets like medical conditions) is usually unavailable [4].

Despite not having this information, the company might have access to millions of user-behavior mobile traces: session data, geo-location information, data derived from motion sensors, device specs, connection data, and more. These patterns are hard to interpret, rendering the data very difficult to label. Even if the company could solve the glaring privacy issues, it is left with potentially many millions of high-dimensional, complex pieces of information about users' mobile usage. Labeling this kind of data instance-by-instance is likely to be a painstaking, error-prone process [30].

Instead of trying to label individual users, it might be easier to obtain some coarse signals on *groups* of users. For example, Millennials text more and talk less [10]. People who tend to stay up and wake up late are more likely to be single [14]. Advertisers could, of course, be interested in going beyond basic demographics, wishing to learn about health issues or political leanings, which are not directly reflected in mobile usage. This renders the attempt to label individual mobile usage patterns even more problematic [30], while getting estimates on groups may be far more feasible.

We take advantage of a new machine learning setting we have proposed in [9], called **Ballpark Learning**. In the Ballpark setting we have unlabeled instances divided into bags, and we are given some aggregate information about label averages in bags in the form of loose constraints. For example, the bag of people who barely text has a higher average age than the bag of people who text often. Using only this kind of aggregate information, the goal is to predict *individual labels* – i.e., demographics of individual users.

We suggest that the Ballpark setting is particularly useful for crowdsourcing: Instead of asking the crowd to label particular users, we could construct bags of users based on some simple attributes (e.g., monthly volume of text messages) and ask people to guess which bag has older users, and by how much.

Using Ballpark learning can help address the shortcomings of crowdsourcing discussed above. Coarse guesses on simple groups require less expertise than individual labels, and fewer questions asked, as each question provides information for many datapoints. The datapoints we show the crowd are interpretable, since we can focus on a few intuitive dimensions and let the machine learning method take advantage of the other, less intuitive ones. The need to de-bias the crowd is also less pronounced, because our approach only requires wide intervals around the true average. Finally, there are no privacy concerns, as we never show crowdworkers individual datapoints. (Interestingly, estimating individual labels from group statistics does have important implications regarding privacy, as Ballpark techniques can be used on sensitive data; however, crowdworkers are only exposed to aggregated data.)

Our key contributions are:

- We propose a new model for crowdsourcing that can complement standard practices by exploiting people's intuitions about groups and relations between them. We exploit the natural human tendency for intuiting on groups and the tendency for comparison [23] to glean interesting, informative patterns. To the best of our knowledge, we are the first to focus on comparisons between groups as an important part of labeling.
- We adapt our recent machine learning setting, Ballpark Learning, to crowdsourcing, and demonstrate its effectiveness. To address the important case of continuous labels (which are notoriously hard for crowdworkers), we extend the Ballpark setting into *regression*. We formulate the Ballpark regression problem as a convex optimization problem and present fast, simple methods to solve it with a natural robustness to outliers that compares favorably to robust regression techniques.
- We demonstrate our results on real-world datasets and show that by using weak constraints harnessed from a crowd of non-experts, our methods are able to achieve results that rival supervised models based on many true labels. We discuss various ways to query the crowd for these constraints. In our experiments, we obtained better results than those reached by standard label collection – at less than a third of the price.

2 PROBLEM FORMULATION

We now present the Ballpark Learning framework. In the following sections, we will demonstrate its usefulness for crowdsourcing.

Consider a set of N training instances $\mathcal{X}_N = \{\mathbf{x}_1, \mathbf{x}_2, \ldots, \mathbf{x}_N\}$. Each $\mathbf{x}_i$ has a corresponding *unknown* label $y_i^* \in \mathcal{Y}$. We extend our previous work [9] and allow label space $\mathcal{Y}$ to be discrete or continuous, depending on the setting. Along with unlabeled instances $\mathcal{X}_N$, we could be given a (possibly empty) set of L labeled training instances $\mathcal{X}_L = \{\mathbf{x}_{N+1}, \ldots, \mathbf{x}_{N+L}\}$ with known targets y_i, where typically the vast majority of instances are unlabeled: $N \gg L$. In addition, we are given a set of K subsets of $\mathcal{X}$, which we call *bags*:

$$\mathcal{B} = \{\mathcal{B}_1, \mathcal{B}_2, \ldots \mathcal{B}_K\}, \mathcal{B}_k \subseteq \mathcal{X}_N \cup \mathcal{X}_L.$$

For example, $\mathcal{B}_1$ could be the group of mobile users who tend to wake early in the morning, while $\mathcal{B}_2$ could be those users who stay up late at night. Note that bags $\mathcal{B}$ may overlap, and do not have to cover all training instances $\mathcal{X}_N$.

Finally, we have *constraints* associated with the labels within bags ($\{y_i^* : i \in \mathcal{B}_k\}$). For example, we might have rough bounds on the label average in some bag, or know that the average in one bag is higher than in another.

We are especially interested in the case where very little information is known: constraints are *loose*, and specified only for a small subset of bags. Given this information during training, our goal is to learn a function $f(\mathbf{x})$ that predicts a label for individual instances, including instances that do not have an associated bag. In the following, we discuss the two most common settings – classification and regression.

2.1 Background: Ballpark Classification

The Ballpark setting was first proposed in [9] for *binary classification* problems. For completeness, we briefly review the classification setting here. In the next section, we extend the framework to *regression* problems with new methods and properties.

In the classification setting, label space $\mathcal{Y}$ is discrete, $y_i^* \in \{-1, 1\}$. Let p_k be the proportion of positive-labeled instances in bag $\mathcal{B}_k$:

$$p_k = |\{i : i \in \mathcal{B}_k, y_i^* = 1\}| / |\mathcal{B}_k| \quad (1)$$

(where y_i^* is replaced with y_i for instances $\mathbf{x}_i \in \mathcal{X}_L$).

Importantly, p_k is not assumed to be known (unlike related work on learning from label proportions [18]; see Section 6). Rather, the model is given weaker prior knowledge, in the form of **constraints** on proportions. In [9], constraints included:

- **Lower, upper bounds** on bag proportions: $l_k \leq p_k \leq u_k$,
- **Differences**: $l_{k_{12}} \leq p_{k_1} - p_{k_2} \leq u_{k_{12}}$.

For example, suppose we would like to predict whether a user is over age 65. We may have a bag of users $\mathcal{B}_k$ who often go out at night (based on GPS readings). From prior socio-demographic research, we could know that p_k is somewhere between $l_k = 0.1$ and $u_k = 0.3$. We may also have knowledge about the difference between users with high and low outdoor nighttime activity levels.

Our **prediction function** is $f(\mathbf{x}) = \text{sign}(\mathbf{w}^T \varphi(\mathbf{x}))$, where $\mathbf{w}$ is a weight vector we estimate and $\varphi(\cdot)$ is a feature map (to simplify notation bias term $\mathbf{b}$ is dropped by assuming a vector $\mathbf{1}_{N+L}$ is appended to the features). To attain the classification goal, we use a maximum-margin approach, formulating Ballpark classification as a *bi-convex* optimization problem and solving it with an alternating minimization algorithm. For more details, see [9].

2.2 Ballpark Regression

Many real-world problems of interest involve a continuous target, which poses a special challenge for crowdsourcing [28]. In this section, we thus extend the Ballpark setting to regression.

Denote $\bar{y}_k = \frac{\sum_{i \in \mathcal{B}_k} y_i^*}{|\mathcal{B}_k|}$, where $y_i^* \in \mathbb{R}$. Similarly to the proportion constraints in the classification scenario, our constraints are over the bag averages $\bar{y}_k$. We allow constraints of the following form:

- **Lower, upper bounds** on bag averages: $l_k \leq \bar{y}_k \leq u_k$,

- **Differences (additive):** $l_{k_{12}} \le \bar{y}_{k_1} - \bar{y}_{k_2} \le u_{k_{12}}$,
- **Differences (multiplicative):** $l_{k_{12}} \le \frac{\bar{y}_{k_1}}{\bar{y}_{k_2}} \le u_{k_{12}}$.

We extend [9] and incorporate multiplicative differences, as these often may be intuitive for crowd workers (see Section 5.1).

Our goal is to predict a target for each $\mathbf{x}_i$ using a **regression function** $f(\mathbf{x}) = \mathbf{w}^T\varphi(\mathbf{x})$. We directly model the latent variable $\mathbf{y}^*$ – the vector of unknown labels $y_i^* \in \mathbb{R}$ – in a constrained optimization problem. Let $\mathcal{R}$ be the subset of $\mathcal{B}$ for which we have upper and/or lower bounds. Let $\mathcal{D}$ be the set of tuples $(\mathcal{B}_{k_1}, \mathcal{B}_{k_2})$ for which we have difference bounds. We formulate the following convex optimization problem:

$$\begin{aligned}\operatorname*{argmin}_{\mathbf{y},\mathbf{w}} \frac{1}{2}\mathbf{w}^T\mathbf{w} &+ \frac{C_N}{N}\sum_{i=1}^{N}||y_i - \mathbf{w}^T\varphi(\mathbf{x}_i))||_2^2 \\ &+ \frac{C_L}{L}\sum_{j=N+1}^{N+L}||y_j - \mathbf{w}^T\varphi(\mathbf{x}_j))||_2^2 \\ s.t. \quad & l_k \le \hat{\bar{y}}_k \le u_k \quad \forall\{k : \mathcal{B}_k \in \mathcal{R}\} \\ & l_{k_{12}} \le \hat{\bar{y}}_{k_1} - \hat{\bar{y}}_{k_2} \le u_{k_{12}} \quad \forall\{k_1 \ne k_2 : (\mathcal{B}_{k_1}, \mathcal{B}_{k_2}) \in \mathcal{D}\}\end{aligned} \tag{2}$$

where $\hat{\bar{y}}_k = \frac{\sum_{i\in\mathcal{B}_k} y_i}{|\mathcal{B}_k|}$ is the estimated mean in bag $\mathcal{B}_k$, l_k (or u_k) can be $-\infty$ ($+\infty$) if not given as input, and analogously for difference bounds $l_{k_{12}}(u_{k_{12}})$; we omit multiplicative difference bounds for brevity. C_N and C_L are cost hyperparameters for unlabeled and labeled instances, respectively. C_L controls the weight we give to labeled instances versus prior knowledge on $\mathcal{B}$.

Importantly, unlike in Ballpark classification, this problem is convex and thus we are guaranteed to find its global minimum. We are also able to derive some insights into the regression model. Problem 2 is quadratic with respect to y, allowing the use of dedicated solvers. Furthermore, we note that with respect to w, we can write out the minimizer (as function of y) explicitly, as follows.

$$\begin{aligned}\operatorname*{argmin}_{\mathbf{w}} \frac{1}{2}\mathbf{w}^T\mathbf{w} &+ \frac{C_N}{N}\sum_{i=1}^{N}||y_i - \mathbf{w}^T\varphi(\mathbf{x}_i))||_2^2 \\ &+ \frac{C_L}{L}\sum_{j=N+1}^{N+L}||y_j - \mathbf{w}^T\varphi(\mathbf{x}_j))||_2^2\end{aligned} \tag{3}$$

Denote the solution to Problem 3 as $\mathbf{w}^*$. As is readily seen, this is essentially a (weighted) ridge regression problem. In this paper, we are interested in the case where we have no labels at all. In our experiments we do not use any labeled instances, thus at this point we set $C_L = 0$ for ease of exposition, and recover the familiar ridge solution with closed-form solution w.r.t y, $(\lambda\mathbf{I} + \mathbf{\Phi}^T\mathbf{\Phi})^{-1}\mathbf{\Phi}^T\mathbf{y}$, where $\mathbf{\Phi}$ is the feature matrix for instances $\{1, \ldots, N\}$ and λ is a regularization hyperparameter (inversely proportional to C_N). Now, we can plug the expression for $\mathbf{w}_*$ back into the objective function, and solve a quadratic program for y:

$$\begin{aligned}\operatorname*{argmin}_{\mathbf{y}} \frac{1}{N}\sum_{i=1}^{N}&||y_i - \mathbf{w}_*^T\varphi(\mathbf{x}_i))||_2^2 \\ s.t. \quad & l_k \le \hat{\bar{y}}_k \le u_k \quad \forall\{k : \mathcal{B}_k \in \mathcal{R}\} \\ & l_{k_{12}} \le \hat{\bar{y}}_{k_1} - \hat{\bar{y}}_{k_2} \le u_{k_{12}} \quad \forall\{k_1 \ne k_2 : (\mathcal{B}_{k_1}, \mathcal{B}_{k_2}) \in \mathcal{D}\},\end{aligned} \tag{4}$$

which yields our final, optimal weight vector $\mathbf{w}_*$. Intuitively, the first "step" (expressing $\mathbf{w}_*$ w.r.t y) finds a weight vector w predicting y, and linear constraints on $\hat{\bar{y}}_k$ ensure that we find an assignment to y that satisfies constraints given for bags $\mathcal{B}_k$.

In some cases we may have constraints that apply *globally* – such as that $y_i \ge 0 \forall i$, or that the global target mean is within a certain range. These constraints can easily be incorporated by setting the appropriate $\mathcal{B}_k$ (e.g., one bag consisting of the entire training set). In Section 3, we discuss how to use crowds to build constraints.

Learning as a feasibility problem. We further develop an alternative method for Ballpark regression. Here, we do not optimize for the latent y and w concurrently, but only for w in a feasibility optimization problem. Noting that our quantity of interest $\hat{\bar{y}}_k = \frac{\sum_{i\in\mathcal{B}_k} y_i}{|\mathcal{B}_k|}$ can be modeled as $\frac{\sum_{i\in\mathcal{B}_k} \mathbf{w}^T\varphi(\mathbf{x}_i)}{|\mathcal{B}_k|}$ under the standard linear regression premise that the (conditional) expected value of the target is a linear function of the input, we solve the following simple and intuitive convex program:

$$\begin{aligned}\operatorname*{argmin}_{\mathbf{w}} \frac{1}{2}\mathbf{w}^T\mathbf{w} &+ \frac{C_L}{L}\sum_{j=N+1}^{N+L}||y_j - \mathbf{w}^T\varphi(\mathbf{x}_j))||_2^2 \\ s.t. \quad & l_k \le \frac{\sum_{i\in\mathcal{B}_k}\mathbf{w}^T\varphi(\mathbf{x}_i)}{|\mathcal{B}_k|} \le u_k \quad \forall\{k : \mathcal{B}_k \in \mathcal{R}\} \\ & l_{k_{12}} \le \frac{\sum_{i\in\mathcal{B}_{k_1}}\mathbf{w}^T\varphi(\mathbf{x}_i)}{|\mathcal{B}_{k_1}|} - \frac{\sum_{i\in\mathcal{B}_{k_2}}\mathbf{w}^T\varphi(\mathbf{x}_i)}{|\mathcal{B}_{k_2}|} \le u_{k_{12}} \\ & \forall\{k_1 \ne k_2 : (\mathcal{B}_{k_1}, \mathcal{B}_{k_2}) \in \mathcal{D}\}\end{aligned} \tag{5}$$

Thus, in Problem 4 we are essentially finding an assignment $\hat{\mathbf{y}}$ to y, such that $\hat{\mathbf{y}}$ satisfies bag constraints and is at the same time close (in l_2 norm) to the ordinary (unconstrained) ridge prediction based on $\mathbf{\Phi}, \hat{\mathbf{y}}$. In contrast, in the feasibility problem, we find a regularized solution w such that *predictions themselves* satisfy the Ballpark constraints. The feasibility problem, which does not attempt to find an assignment $\hat{\mathbf{y}}$, clearly has less parameters and is thus lighter and runs blazingly fast in our experiments (less than a second for all the experiments we describe in the paper). We observed in our experiments that the two approaches led to similar results (with a slight advantage to the former that also adjusts y), and thus we focus on using the solution to Problem 2 for simplicity.[1]

PAC formulation and sample complexity bound. We briefly derive a basic sample complexity bound for Problem 5 using the general PAC (Probably Approximately Correct) framework. To simplify, we set $C_L = 0$ (no labeled data), and derive a dimension-based bound rather than norm-based by ignoring regularization term $\frac{1}{2}\mathbf{w}^T\mathbf{w}$. Keeping this term would require some slightly more technically involved analysis. Our main goal here is just to get some preliminary and intuitive theoretical grounding of the model.

LEMMA 2.1. *For* $\mathbf{w} \in \mathbb{R}^d$, *and under the modification mentioned above, Problem 5 can be cast in the general PAC learning model, and sample complexity* $m_{\mathcal{H}}$ *is bounded by* $O(\frac{d}{\epsilon^2})$, *where* $\mathcal{H}$ *is a hypothesis class* w *induces over instances* x *and bags* $\mathcal{B}$, *and* ϵ *follows the standard PAC notation (see [22]).*

Proof sketch. We incorporate the Ballpark constraints into a 0-1 loss function, taking the value 1 when constraints are violated and 0

[1] Code and more materials can be found at: https://github.com/ttthhh/ballpark.git

otherwise. Parameterizing a hypothesis class $\mathcal{H}$ over instances and bags with $\mathbf{w}$, we obtain a PAC formulation. We derive a dimension-based bound using the practical discretization trick to treat $\mathcal{H}$ as finite, applying corollary 4.6 in [22] to obtain the bound. □

Optimizing hyperparameters. In practice, we need to tune hyperparameter C_N (λ). This is typically done with cross-validation (CV) grid search. However, standard CV is impossible here as we have no labels to compute accuracy on held-out data.

We thus use a variant of CV called Constraint Violation Cross Validation (CVCV) developed in [9] for the classification case, which is readily adaptable to regression. We run K-fold CV, splitting each bag $\mathcal{B}_k$ into training and held-out subsets. The intuition is that the label average in uniformly-sampled subsets of a bag is similar to $\bar{y}_k$ in the entire bag. For each split, we solve Problem 2 on training bags, and then compute by how much constraints are violated on *held-out* bags. More formally, we compute the average deviations from bounds, $max(\hat{\bar{y}}_k - u_k, 0)$, $max(l_k - \hat{\bar{y}}_k, 0)$ for $\hat{\bar{y}}_k$ the estimated label mean in the held-out subset of bag k. We do so over a grid, and select the C_N (λ) with lowest average violation. This simple approach leads to good hyperparameter selections in practice.

3 BALLPARK WITH CROWD CONSTRAINTS

In the previous sections we presented the Ballpark formulation. Most importantly, in Ballpark learning we do not assume to be given labels, but rather weak information in the form of constraints. A natural question is how we obtain these constraints.

In [9] we assumed that constraints came from experts or some other source of domain knowledge. It was left as an open question whether the methods would still be effective using noisy information from a crowd of non-experts. Obtaining constraints from the crowd raises some interesting points which we discuss below.

Constraint aggregation. There are multiple ways to build constraints by querying the crowd. Importantly, virtually all of these methods require *aggregation* of crowd guesses. A large body of work in crowdsourcing for machine learning and "wisdom of the crowds" (WoC) deals with aggregating human guesses [7, 13, 17, 24, 25, 28]. The objective of these methods is typically to obtain accurate point estimates of some quantity. A simple and popular approach is to take the mean of guesses, potentially weighted by worker quality. More elaborate methods construct rich probabilistic models [7, 25, 28] to capture different worker properties (e.g., systematic biases). Other methods rely on multiple guesses and incentives [24] or assume labeled ground truth [28], requiring more resources and a more taxing experience for workers and practitioners. Importantly, rather than aiming to obtain a point estimate, in the Ballpark framework we only require *broad intervals* "bracketing" the true label average of bags. Instead of focusing efforts on aggregating crowd guesses "accurately", we rely on a machine learning model to use these intervals and predict accurate individual labels.

Thus, one simple method that is suitable for the Ballpark framework is to elicit crowd guesses on group label averages, and then construct bag bounds based on percentiles of the empirical guess distribution (see Section 5). An alternative, less common approach in WoC is to forgo point estimates altogether and consider the distribution of all possible values, such as assigning different probabilities to different *intervals* [8]. In [16] multiple interval guesses from a crowd are aggregated to improve predictions. Loosely inspired by this, we also consider asking people to *guess intervals* bracketing label averages in groups and simply take the means of the upper and lower bounds (see Section 5.3).

Constraint feasibility. In the Ballpark problem formulation we impose hard constraints on label means. In practice, we may face certain constraints that are infeasible. This could happen, for example, when we receive misspecified lower and upper bounds from non-experts. As we demonstrate in Section 5.2, constraints can be made soft by adding slack variables ξ to the infeasible subset.

Tasks Suitable for Crowd Constraints. We believe the intuition of crowds could be especially useful when trying to learn hidden behavioral, sociological or commercial attributes. In our experiments, we examine two predictive tasks: Predicting return to jail (complex behavioral property) and predicting rental prices (commercial intuition). Our method is less suitable for cases where the bias of crowdworkers is so extreme as to *substantially* skew even the lower or upper bounds on label averages. This could be caused by domain ignorance or deeply ingrained beliefs.

4 EVALUATION (1): SYNTHETIC CONSTRAINTS

For our first evaluation task, we wish to explore the robustness of Ballpark Learning to different constraint settings, examine the effect of constraints on prediction accuracy, and compare Ballpark to the supervised setting. We create artificial bags based on a real dataset, varying bag and constraint construction to illustrate some of the different factors that come into play. As the classification setting was evaluated in [9], we focus on regression.

Data. The Boston dataset is a well-known, small dataset (506 instances) available from the StatLib repository [26] that is popular for evaluating regression models. It contains information on Boston housing characteristics and values. The target variable is the median value of owner-occupied homes in different areas. Each area has 13 features, including crime rates, air pollution (nitric oxides concentration), average number of rooms, and more. We estimate the prices of apartments using ballpark regression with bags based on crime levels, pollution, and number of rooms.

Constraints. We construct bags based on only three variables: crime (CRIM), pollution (NOX), and average number of rooms (RM). We discretize these variables into three bags each (cutoffs at the 0.33 and 0.66 percentiles). This yields 9 bags, such as $\mathcal{B}_{\text{high crime}}$, $\mathcal{B}_{\text{medium crime}}$, $\mathcal{B}_{\text{low crime}}$. Next, we compute (true) bag averages, and construct pairwise constraints based on their partial ordering. Bounds on bag means are built by introducing a multiplicative error term multiplying the true bag means (10% in each direction, with apartment prices measured in units of \$1000). If for bag $\mathcal{B}_k$ the true bag mean is $\bar{y}_k$, then upper and lower bounds are $(1+\epsilon)\bar{y}_k$, $(1-\epsilon)\bar{y}_k$, respectively, where $\epsilon(=0.1)$ is the error term for individual bags. Bounds on bag differences are created in the same way.

We compare our method to supervised ridge regression with an increasing number of labeled examples, reporting average RMSE results (over 5-fold CV). Our goal is not to compete with the host of methods tested on this benchmark, but rather to see how far we can get using only weak information. As seen in Figure 1(a), by using weak domain knowledge on bags we are able to either

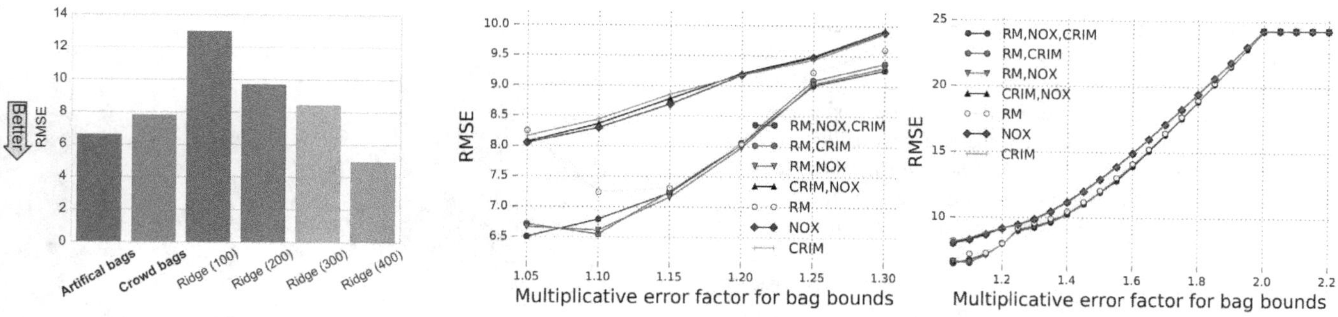

(a) (b) (c)

Figure 1: (a) Boston accuracy. Ballpark surpasses or rivals ridge regression with a considerable amount of ground-truth labels. As expected, constraints artificially constructed assuming more prior knowledge, are better than constraints aggregated from crowd guesses (Section 5.2). (b) Varying multiplicative error term on synthetically-built constraints. (c) Continuing plot (b) for extremely large error terms

surpass or rival ridge regression with a considerable amount of ground-truth labels. With 300 labels (accounting for ≈ 60% of the entire data), there is still a considerable gap in RMSE in favor of ballpark regression. We select regularization hyperparameter with the CV method described Section 2. Due to the small size of this dataset, we do so with only 3 inner training folds, which in our experiments was enough to reach good results.

Sensitivity analysis. We now explore what effect quality of constraints has on prediction quality. For the synthetic constraints described above, we vary the multiplicative factor ϵ, gradually loosening upper and lower bounds on bag means. As seen in Figures 1(b)-(c), at first error grows rather slowly with ϵ, but then picks up when constraints become broad beyond reason. Indeed, assuming for instance that a true bag mean is 20K, then $\epsilon = 0.5$ means our upper and lower bounds specify the very uncertain range [10K, 30K]. Even with such a broad set of constraints obtained with $\epsilon = 0.5$ we obtain error that is slightly better than using ridge regression with 100 labels. In real applications, constraints too weak may be dropped, or more information could be collected to tighten them.

In addition to varying ϵ, we also examine the effect of bag choice. In Figures 1(b) and 1(c), we show results for using all three bags (RM+NOX+CRIM), pairs of bags (RM+NOX, RM+CRIM,NOX+CRIM), and singletons (RM,NOX,CRIM). Results are fairly robust to this choice but, as expected, using fewer bags overall leads to inferior results. The gap is more pronounced in the range of relatively tighter constraints (up to $\epsilon = 0.2$). It is also evident that RM's (number of rooms) contribution to informative bag construction is strongest. Using only this variable for bag construction gives inferior results at first, but as ϵ grows the performance of RM-only bags rapidly gets very close to richer bag constructions based on the other variables.

5 EVALUATION (2): CROWDSOURCED CONSTRAINTS

In the previous section, we evaluated the Ballpark setting with synthetic constraints. We now set out to discover whether we can obtain good results when constraints are crowdsourced instead.

In particular, we ask: **Can crowds provide good constraints?** We are interested in both *efficiency* and *effectiveness*: Can we collect highly noisy and biased guesses from a crowd of non-experts and still obtain good instance-level predictions? Can collecting group constraints require less effort and resources than the standard practice of collecting individual labels from the crowd? How should we aggregate crowd guesses to get the best "bang for the buck"?

5.1 Classification with Crowds: Recidivism

We start by focusing on *classification* problems.

Motivation and data. In the United States, a large share of crime is committed by inmates released from prison [2]. About two-thirds of prisoners released across 30 US states in 2005 were re-arrested within 3 years [15]. Recently, statistical learning methods have been used for risk assessments attempting to predict the danger an offender would pose after release [1] to inform sentencing decisions.

We use two datasets with cohorts of inmates released in 1978 ($N = 9327$) and 1980 ($N = 9549$) from a North Carolina prison [21]. The target variable indicates whether an inmate returned to prison within a year of release. Features include race, gender, age, alcoholism, serious drug use, supervision after release, marital status, conviction due to felony/misdemeanor, and more.

Experiment design. We ask Amazon Turk workers to assess the likelihood of released inmates to return to jail, based on coarse information on groups. We build "bags" of inmates based on the following binary variables: gender, alcoholism, drug use, supervision, marital status, conviction due to felony/misdemeanor, crime

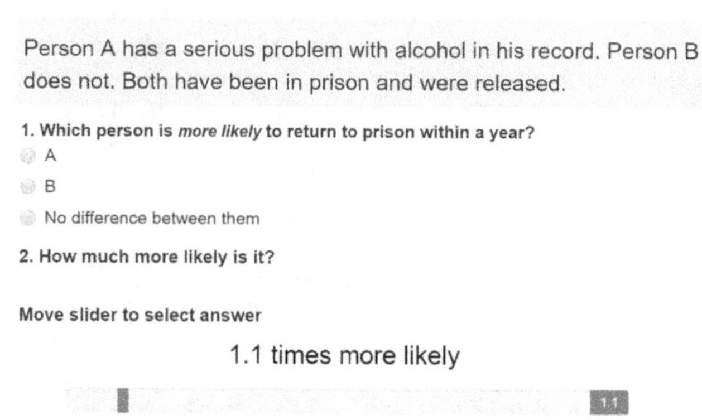

Figure 2: Recidivism AMT task example. Querying crowd workers for pairwise constraints on bags of instances.

against property/person. For each variable, we have two bags (0, 1). Workers are asked to determine which bag has higher recidivism rates, by how much, and guess the rate in one of the bags (See Figure 2 for an example; more examples are in our code repository).

We ask workers to guess which inmates are more likely to return to prison (e.g., alcoholics or not) and *how much* more likely it is. Workers are also asked to guess the rate of recidivism for groups. We have 16 groups based on 8 binary variables, but we only ask for estimates on groups corresponding to "positive" values of each variable (e.g., MARRIED = 1, MALE = 1). Our AMT task thus consists of 8 HITs, each corresponding to a feature, assigning 30 US-based workers per HIT, with approval rate greater than 97% and over 500 approved HITs, for a total cost of \$16.80 (including fees). In all our experiments we also tried downsampling the number of answers per HIT, retaining robust results.

Constraint construction. Next, we need to aggregate the crowd's replies into a set of Ballpark constraints. To construct the partial ordering $\mathcal{P}$ between pairs of bags (such as between $\mathcal{B}_{\text{male}}, \mathcal{B}_{\text{female}}$), we take the majority vote, which is unequivocal across all variables but one (crimes against property). It appears the crowd's intuition conforms with "stereotypes" on the relative likelihood of certain groups to commit crime. To build upper and lower bounds on bag proportions and differences, we take the 0.75 and 0.25 percentiles of answers and turn them into *multiplicative* constraints (other choices, such as 0.9, 0.1, led to virtually the same results; see Section 5.3 for an alternative aggregation method). We upper-bound the global proportion of recidivism at 0.4, based on the cited statistic above on general recidivism rates, which is considered common knowledge.

Results. We compare our label-free method to supervised baselines. These include results previously reported for this prediction task (1978 inmate cohort), taken from [11], all of which were obtained using all labels available during training. For the 1978 cohort data, we use the same train/test splits as the authors. We also include results we obtained ourselves by training Support Vector Machines (SVM) with different amounts of labeled examples. We vary the number of labels given to SVM to demonstrate the effect the amount of labeled data has, and compare it to our ballpark approach that uses no labeled instances. For the 1980 data, we report mean cross-validation accuracy (10 folds). BMP (Biased Minimax Probability Machine) is a method proposed in [11] for handling imbalanced classification tasks, reported for the 1978 cohort only.

As seen in Figure 3, our Ballpark method achieves results that surpass or rival supervised baselines and advanced methods exposed to all *true* labels, and SVM with an increasing number of labels. This is despite us not using even one ground-truth label, and leaving the construction of bag bounds to crowd workers with no real domain knowledge beyond commonplace intuition.[2]

A note on noise and bias. We observe the high amount of noise in the *individual* estimates, seen in Figure 4. In this figure, we see guesses for the percentage of recidivism per group, and for pairwise (multiplicative) differences between bags. There is large variability for both the rate of recidivism and group differences, despite giving workers basic background on the general rate of recidivism.

Note that a related line of work, learning from labels proportions [18], assumes that true bag proportions are known. They suggest

[2]Incidentally, one of the workers emailed us to explain she was a retired correction officer, and "that is why most, if not all, of my answers were negative".

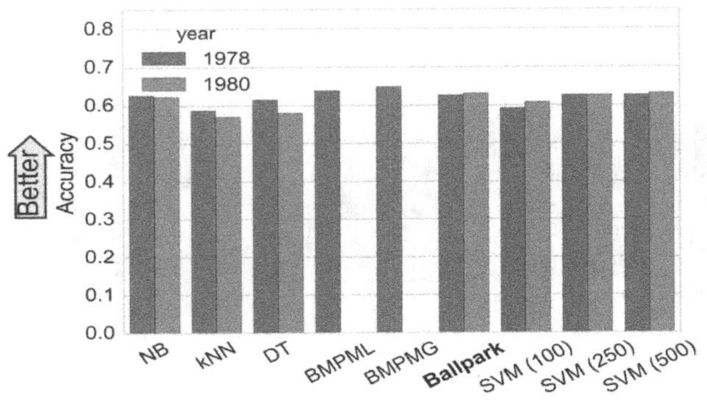

Figure 3: Recidivism results. Comparing to baseline methods reported in [11] (1978 cohort) and trained by us (1980 cohort). BN=Naive Bayes, DT=Decision Tree, kNN=k-Nearest Neighbors, BMPML/G= [11] (all using entire labeled data), SVM = Support Vector Machines trained with an increasing number of labels.

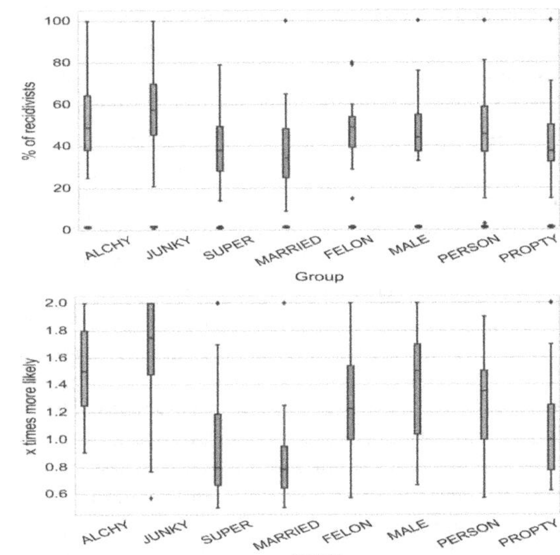

Figure 4: Recidivism AMT worker guesses on (top) bag averages per group and (bottom) pairwise constraints.

(theoretically) that sampling for bag proportions is one way to obtain accurate estimates. In practice, sampling for labels from true domain experts is typically infeasible or costly, while resorting to crowdsourcing is considered a viable option. However, while noise can potentially be averaged out, even looking at average estimates per bag leads to highly **biased** estimates, with relative errors (with respect to ground truth) of up to 60%, with most errors ranging around 30%. These render bag average proportions highly dubious. By using *broad* constraints on averages, our methods are able to exploit crowd estimates and rival supervised methods.

5.2 Regression with Crowds (1): Boston

In our second crowd experiment, we explore Ballpark regression. We return to the Boston dataset, now using *crowdsourced* constraints. We believe people should find it simpler to compare groups based on the same variable (e.g., $\mathcal{B}_{\text{medium pollution}}, \mathcal{B}_{\text{low pollution}}$).

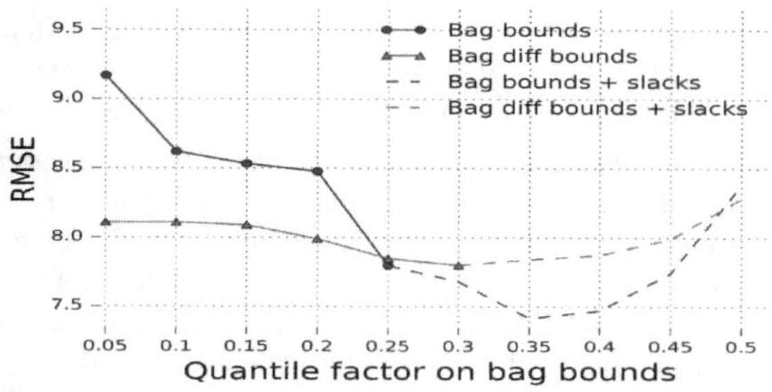

Figure 5: Constraint effects on Boston accuracy. Varying bound quantile on individual bags b_l, bag differences d_l, crowdsourced data. The graph stops abruptly when constraints are infeasible. We then add slack variables and continue increasing the bounds.

Therefore, we asked crowd workers to determine which bag has higher average apartment prices and by how much.

To make the Boston dataset relevant in 2017, we formulate questions referring to a "city somewhere in the world", and give some basic price statistics for this fictional city (average, minimum and maximum). Some things never change - common intuition nowadays still yields useful constraints, as our results below show.

Our AMT task thus consists of 9 HITs, assigning 30 US-based workers per HIT, with approval rate greater than 97% and over 500 approved HITs, for a total cost of $18.90 (including fees).

We build pairwise constraints based on (clear-cut) majority votes, and construct bounds using percentiles of answers (0.75, 0.25 as in the recidivism task). As seen in Figure 1(a), we are able to surpass supervised regression with many ground-truth labels. Unsurprisingly, synthetic constraints achieve better results due to stronger prior knowledge, but the simple bag construction from crowd constraints in this experiment still yields good results.

Sensitivity analysis. We briefly examine how the tightness of constraints could affect model performance, illustrating some of the different factors that come into play and exploring the robustness of our method. We vary tightness of upper/lower bounds for individual bags and bag differences, reporting accuracy. We denote the lower bound percentile for individual bags as b_l (e.g., 0.25 as above), and set the upper bound to $1 - b_l$. Similarly, d_l and $1 - d_l$ are lower and upper bound percentiles for bag differences. In Figure 5 we observe that after the point $b_l = 0.25$ constraints are no longer feasible, indicating badly-specified bounds. At this point we add slack variables as discussed in Section 3. The error continues to slightly drop, and then picks up when bounds are extremely loose. In the next section we show an alternative way to query crowdworkers for constraints without selecting b_l, d_l. Nonetheless, we note that even with the worst choices for parameter b_l our error is still better than supervised ridge regression with 200 labels. For parameter d_l, results are even more robust.

5.3 Regression with Crowds (2): Airbnb

In this section we continue to compare the standard practice of collecting labels to our suggested practice of collecting group constraints. We also explore another simple way to obtain constraints, asking workers to *guess intervals* directly.

Data. In this experiment we predict apartment prices again using a bigger, more modern apartment dataset. We hope workers have better intuition on apartment prices for this dataset due to its intuitive features and recency, making the evaluation more fair.

Airbnb is an online marketplace enabling people to lease or rent short-term lodging. The dataset (insideairbnb.com) consists of 5147 apartments. Our aim is to predict the price a user will enter for an apartment in Chicago in Early October 2015, based on features such as neighborhood, number of beds, amenities, and more.

Experiment design. We collect judgments via two separate tasks. First, we construct bags of apartments based solely on amenities. We look at whether or not an apartment has a *TV*, a *fireplace*, a building *doorman* and building *gym*. As in the Boston experiment, we build pairwise constraints based on majority votes by crowd workers, ask workers to guess the price difference, and construct bounds using answer percentiles. We give basic statistics on the distribution of prices in the data (average, top and bottom 5 percentiles). Our AMT task thus consists of 4 HITs, assigning 30 US-based workers per HIT, with approval rate greater than 97% and over 500 approved HITs, for a total cost of $3.6 (including fees).

Aside from collecting guesses on bags, we also collect hundreds of guesses on *individual* instances, a standard practice for collecting labeled data via crowdsourcing. We test the hypothesis that people are (often) better at reasoning about simple groups of instances and the *pairwise ordering/relation* between them, rather than about individual instances with possibly high-dimensional characteristics.

We run a parallel experiment asking workers to guess prices of 400 flats, based on the full set of features our method is trained on. We assign one US-based worker per HIT, with approval rate greater than 97% and over 500 approved HITs, for a total of $12 (including fees), 333% higher than collecting ballpark group guesses.

As we show below, the individual crowd estimations are not sufficient for training a good regression model. However, using guesses on groups in our ballpark methods achieves results comparable to a regression model based on *true* apartment prices.

Aggregating crowd guesses of intervals. In the above design, we asked workers to guess apartment prices and used percentiles of answers as bounds. While this worked well in practice, we seek an aggregation requiring less intervention by the practitioner.

As discussed in Section 3, another approach is to have the crowd directly **guess intervals**. Thus, in a separate experiment we ask people to guess lower and upper limits bracketing bag averages. To construct our constraints we then simply take the means of the upper and lower bounds, respectively. We formulate the task in simple language and encourage workers to take into account their uncertainty ("feel free to give a wide range if you are not sure").

Results and robustness to outliers. In many real-world settings, data is often "contaminated" with observations that have outlier target values. In our data set, there is a small portion of apartments with very high prices in comparison to the rest (about 0.5 percent of apartments are priced over $1000). These outlier apartments raise several points of interest. Unsurprisingly, people are not good at guessing the prices of outlier flats, rendering the labels particularly off-mark. More importantly, we find that while ridge regression suffers a considerable drop in accuracy due to these observations, our method is naturally robust since the crowd's guesses on *groups* inherently disregard extreme, non-representative behaviors.

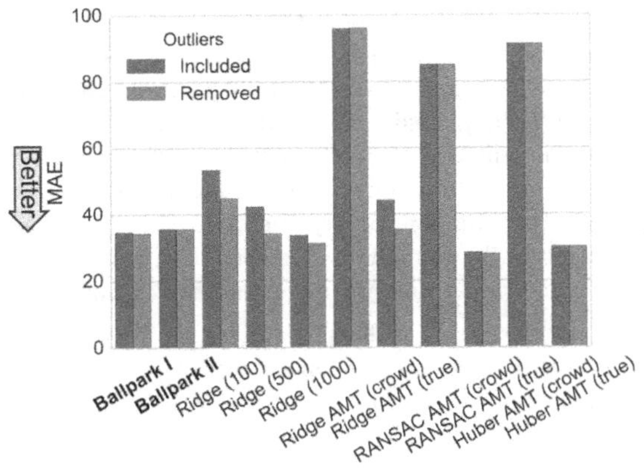

Figure 6: Airbnb results. Ballpark I denotes percentile aggregation of guesses, Ballpark II denotes eliciting interval predictions. Ridge regression is trained with an increasing number of labels. Ridge with 400 *individual* labels from crowd guesses performs poorly, as opposed to using constraints on groups in our Ballpark framework, or training ridge on the same 400 instances with *true* labels. Similar results hold for the RANSAC and Huber robust regression models.

We compare our label-free method to ridge regression with a different number of true labels, and also to ridge using 400 labels obtained from workers. To handle outliers, we use the Mean Absolute Error (MAE) metric rather than RMSE in 10-fold CV (so that the unit of error is in dollars). We compare results running on the entire data, and removing all instances with prices over $1000.

As seen in Figure 6, our method achieves MAE results comparable to ridge regression with a large number of true labels. While outliers cause a big increase in error for ridge regression with 100 labels, our method remains nearly unaffected. Our method is able to near results reached with robust regression models (RANSAC [5], Huber regression [12]) trained on ground-truth labels.

To further test the effect of outliers and the possibility that the poor baseline ridge results are due to a few large errors, we train RANSAC and Huber regression with the 400 crowd labels. These methods manage to only slightly reduce error, showing that while outliers have *some* effect, the overall quality of crowd labels is the key source of error, which our bag-based method is able to avoid.

Interestingly, both constraint aggregation approaches – using percentiles (Ballpark I in in Figure 6) and eliciting interval predictions directly (Ballpark II) – lead to nearly identical results, the latter being more hands-off. We also see that ridge regression with 400 crowd-acquired labels does rather poorly, although it does well for the exact same instances when their true labels are given.

6 RELATED WORK

Crowdsourcing for machine learning. There is a large body of work about the use of crowdsourcing for machine learning, primarily regarding label collection. In Section 3 we reviewed the most relevant work. The main focus in that field is acquiring *discrete* labels for classification. Getting *accurate* labels typically requires a lot of resources: multiple queries, worker reputation, and probabilistic models of worker patterns (e.g., biases). Our approach is different: First, we exploit the natural human tendency for intuiting on *groups* and the tendency for *comparisons*. Second, instead of focusing resources on aggregating crowd guesses accurately, we leverage a machine learning model based on rough intervals bracketing label averages, to accurately predict individual labels with *few resources*. In addition, we handle *regression* and continuous targets, which is notoriously hard for crowds and has not seen much work.

Related learning settings. The field of *Multiple Instance Learning* (MIL) is concerned with "bags" of instances, where each bag has a label associated with it. This label is modeled as a function of latent instance-level labels, which can be seen as a form of weak supervision. MIL methods vary by the assumptions made on this function [3, 6]. Most work in MIL focuses on making bag-level predictions rather than for individual instances. In a related line of work, Learning from Label Proportions, individual labels are predicted based on known label proportions for bags [18, 20, 29]. In [20], each bag is represented with its mean, showing superior performance over [18]. In [29], individual labels are explicitly modeled to counter problems with representing bags by their means (such as high variance). These approaches all assume bag proportions are known, an assumption Ballpark Learning relaxes.

To the best of our knowledge, the subject of continuous labels and regression is not discussed in this literature, let alone demonstrated on data (simulated or real). In [18] the authors mention that their framework could apply, in theory, to continuous label spaces, but their methods assume a discrete label space to be able to reconstruct class probabilities efficiently.

7 CONCLUSION AND FUTURE WORK

In this work we proposed a new method that can complement standard crowdsourcing practices when traditional labeling is difficult. People often have intuition about groups of instances and relations between them, while labeling individual instances is hard. Our framework takes advantage of this phenomenon, leveraging a recent machine learning setting called Ballpark Learning based on weak, noisy constraints over *groups* of instances. We extended Ballpark Learning to handle the useful case of continuous outputs, formulating a convex program with a simple solution. Across several real datasets, we harness constraints from a crowd of non-experts and use them to train learning models. Our results rival supervised models that use many *true* labels, at a much lower cost.

In practice it may be unclear how to construct useful bags. Interesting future work is using crowdworkers to select and build bags *themselves*, perhaps giving them a GUI to explore slices of the data.

Deriving a deeper theoretical analysis of our models is also interesting. For example, understanding what makes bags "useful" in terms of the signal they provide, depending on factors such as their size and dispersion. The Ballpark approach can also potentially be combined with deep learning models (typically requiring many labels) as a form of weak supervision. We believe our lightweight methods pose an interesting alternative to current labeling practices, and could be particularly useful when data is high-dimensional and unintuitive for crowds, when privacy concerns prevent showing individual examples, and when resources are limited.

Acknowledgments. The authors thank the anonymous reviewers for their helpful feedback. Dafna Shahaf is a Harry & Abe Sherman assistant professor. This work was supported by ISF grant 1764/15, Alon grant, and the HUJI Cyber Security Research Center in conjunction with the Israel National Cyber Bureau in the Prime Minister's Office.

REFERENCES

[1] Richard Berk, Lawrence Sherman, Geoffrey Barnes, Ellen Kurtz, and Lindsay Ahlman. 2009. Forecasting murder within a population of probationers and parolees: a high stakes application of statistical learning. *Journal of the Royal Statistical Society: Series A* (2009).

[2] M Keith Chen and Jesse M Shapiro. 2007. Do harsher prison conditions reduce recidivism? A discontinuity-based approach. *American Law and Economics Review* (2007).

[3] Veronika Cheplygina, David Tax, and Marco Loog. 2014. On classification with bags, groups and sets. *arXiv preprint arXiv:1406.0281* (2014).

[4] Yuxiao Dong, Yang Yang, Jie Tang, Yang Yang, and Nitesh V Chawla. 2014. Inferring user demographics and social strategies in mobile social networks *(KDD '14)*.

[5] Martin A Fischler and Robert C Bolles. 1981. Random sample consensus: a paradigm for model fitting with applications to image analysis and automated cartography. *Commun. ACM* (1981).

[6] James Foulds and Eibe Frank. 2010. A review of multi-instance learning assumptions. *The Knowledge Engineering Review* (2010).

[7] Jing Gao, Qi Li, Bo Zhao, Wei Fan, and Jiawei Han. 2015. Truth discovery and crowdsourcing aggregation: A unified perspective. *Proceedings of the VLDB Endowment* (2015).

[8] Uriel Haran, Don A Moore, and Carey K Morewedge. 2010. A simple remedy for overprecision in judgment. *Judgment and Decision Making* (2010).

[9] Tom Hope and Dafna Shahaf. 2016. Ballpark Learning: Estimating Labels from Rough Group Comparisons. In *ECML-PKDD*.

[10] Neil Howe. 2015. Why Millennials Are Texting More And Talking Less http://www.forbes.com/sites/neilhowe/2015/07/15/why-millennials-are-texting-more-and-talking-less/. (2015).

[11] Kaizhu Huang, Haiqin Yang, Irwin King, and Michael R Lyu. [n. d.]. Learning classifiers from imbalanced data based on biased minimax probability machine. In *Computer Vision and Pattern Recognition, 2004.*

[12] Peter J Huber. 2011. *Robust statistics.*

[13] Jan Lorenz, Heiko Rauhut, Frank Schweitzer, and Dirk Helbing. 2011. How social influence can undermine the wisdom of crowd effect. *Proceedings of the National Academy of Sciences* (2011).

[14] Dario Maestripieri. 2014. Night owl women are similar to men in their relationship orientation, risk-taking propensities, and cortisol levels: Implications for the adaptive significance and evolution of eveningness. *Evolutionary Psychology* (2014).

[15] Alexia D. Cooper Matthew R. Durose and Howard N. Snyder. 2010. Recidivism Of Prisoners Released In 30 States In 2005: Patterns From 2005 To 2010. (2010).

[16] Saemi Park and David V Budescu. 2015. Aggregating multiple probability intervals to improve calibration. *Judgment and Decision Making* (2015).

[17] Dražen Prelec, H Sebastian Seung, and John McCoy. 2017. A solution to the single-question crowd wisdom problem. *Nature* (2017).

[18] Novi Quadrianto, Alex J Smola, Tiberio S Caetano, and Quoc V Le. 2009. Estimating labels from label proportions. *JMLR* (2009).

[19] Cyrus Rashtchian, Peter Young, Micah Hodosh, and Julia Hockenmaier. 2010. Collecting image annotations using Amazon's Mechanical Turk. In *NAACL HLT.*

[20] Stefan Rueping. 2010. SVM Classifier Estimation from Group Probabilities. In *ICML '10.*

[21] Peter Schmidt and D. Ann Witte. 1984. *Predicting Recidivism In North Carolina, 1978 and 1980.* Technical Report. Michigan State University.

[22] Shai Shalev-Shwartz and Shai Ben-David. 2014. *Understanding machine learning: From theory to algorithms.* Cambridge university press.

[23] Louis L Thurstone. 1927. A law of comparative judgment. *Psychological review* (1927).

[24] Johan Ugander, Ryan Drapeau, and Carlos Guestrin. 2015. The wisdom of multiple guesses. In *Proceedings of the Sixteenth ACM Conference on Economics and Computation.*

[25] Matteo Venanzi, John Guiver, Gabriella Kazai, Pushmeet Kohli, and Milad Shokouhi. 2014. Community-based bayesian aggregation models for crowdsourcing. In *Proceedings of the 23rd international conference on World wide web.*

[26] P Vlachos. 2000. Statlib project repository. *Carnegie Mellon University* (2000).

[27] Carl Vondrick, Deva Ramanan, and Donald Patterson. 2010. Efficiently scaling up video annotation with crowdsourced marketplaces. In *European Conference on Computer Vision.*

[28] Andrew Whalen and Saiwing Yeung. 2015. Using Ground Truths to Improve Wisdom of the Crowd Estimates.. In *CogSci.*

[29] Felix Yu, Dong Liu, Sanjiv Kumar, Tony Jebara, and Shih Chang. 2013. $\propto$-SVM for learning with label proportions. In *ICML'13.*

[30] Liyue Zhao, Gita Sukthankar, and Rahul Sukthankar. 2011. Robust Active Learning Using Crowdsourced Annotations for Activity Recognition. (2011).

Collaborative Filtering via Additive Ordinal Regression

Jun Hu
Department of Computer Science
Rutgers University
jh900@cs.rutgers.edu

Ping Li
Baidu Research, and
Rutgers University
pingli98@gmail.com

ABSTRACT

Accurately predicting user preferences/ratings over items are crucial for many Internet applications, e.g., recommender systems, online advertising. In current main-stream algorithms regarding the rating prediction problem, discrete rating scores are often viewed as either numerical values or (nominal) categorical labels. Practically, viewing user rating scores as numerical values or categorical labels cannot precisely reflect the exact degree of user preferences. It is expected that for each user, the quantitative distance/scale between any pair of adjacent rating scores could be different.

In this paper, we propose a new ordinal regression approach. We view ordered preference scores in an additive way, where we are able to model users' internal rating patterns. Specifically, we model and learn the quantitative distances/scales between any pair of adjacent rating scores. In this way, we can generate a mapping from users' assigned discrete rating scores to the exact magnitude/degree of user preferences for items. In the application of rating prediction, we combine our newly proposed ordinal regression method with matrix factorization, forming a new ordinal matrix factorization method. Through extensive experiments on benchmark datasets, we show that our method significantly outperforms existing ordinal methods, as well as other popular collaborative filtering methods in terms of the rating prediction accuracy.

KEYWORDS

Ordinal regression; matrix factorization; collaborative filtering

ACM Reference Format:
Jun Hu and Ping Li. 2018. Collaborative Filtering via Additive Ordinal Regression. In *WSDM 2018: WSDM 2018: The Eleventh ACM International Conference on Web Search and Data Mining, February 5–9, 2018, Marina Del Rey, CA, USA.* ACM, New York, NY, USA, 9 pages. https://doi.org/10.1145/3159652.3159723

1 INTRODUCTION

Accurately predicting user preferences/ratings over items can be beneficial to many applications, such as recommender systems, personalized search, online advertising, etc. Generally speaking, rating prediction is the task of predicting a user's rating score for a given item based on her/his past ratings or other information [2]. Given a sparse user-item rating matrix R where observed ratings take discrete values, the rating prediction task boils down to imputing the unknown entries in R based on a small portion of observed ratings. Collaborative filtering (CF) is one of the prominent approaches for rating prediction task [24].

In most collaborative filtering algorithms, user ratings are often viewed as numerical values or (nominal) categorical labels. Such a numerical or categorical view may not precisely capture the exact magnitude/degree of user preferences. Practically it is expected that for each user, the scale between any pair of adjacent rating scores should be different. For example, assuming that rating values range from 1-star to 5-star, one user may be clear about the difference between assigning a 5-star rating or a 4-star rating, while he/she may be confused about assigning a 4-star rating or a 3-star rating. In this case, the distance between "5-star" and "4-star" should be greater than that between "4-star" and "3-star" if we quantify the star-based rating values to the real magnitude in terms of user preferences. On the other hand, different users may have distinct degrees of sensitivity over a sequence of ordered rating scores, resulting in that the distances between any pair of adjacent ratings (e.g., 5-star and 4-star) are different for individual users. Nevertheless, when user ratings are interpreted as numerical values, it equals to the assumption that the user preferences modeled by several consecutive integers (e.g., "1", "2" to "5") are equidistant. While from the viewpoint of (nominal) categorical labels, the distances between pairs of ordered scores are ignored. An example of three different views of rating scores is shown in Fig. 1. In view of aforementioned reasons, it is considered to be more natural to view user ratings as ordinal.

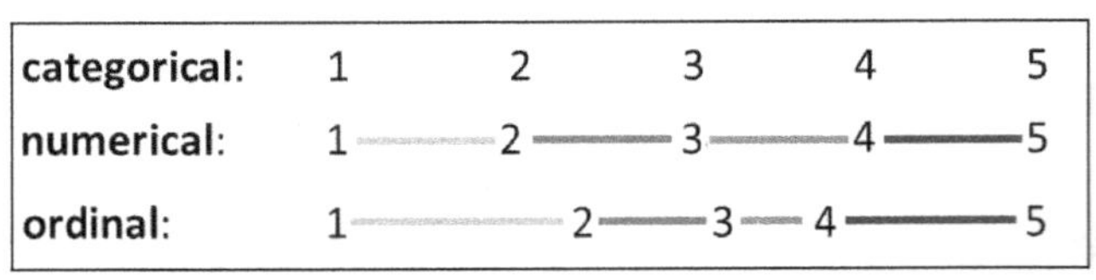

Figure 1: An example to show the difference among (nominal) categorical, numerical and ordinal values/labels. The colored (if visible) horizontal lines show the distances between pairs of adjacent rating scores.

In this work, we propose a new ordinal regression model. Most of current statistical ordinal regression methods, e.g., logistic ordinal regression [17], ordinal classification [3, 16], can be performed using a generalized linear model [3]. They view ordered scores as categorical labels and model the ordinality by transforming the cumulative probabilities of these ordered scores to their posterior probability distributions. Different from those ordinal regression models viewing preference scores as ordinal categorical labels, we introduce a new ordinal regression approach by viewing ordered

WSDM 2018, February 5–9, 2018, Marina Del Rey, CA, USA

ACM ISBN 978-1-4503-5581-0/18/02...$15.00
https://doi.org/10.1145/3159652.3159723

and discrete rating scores as *ordinal real values*. The advantage of our ordinal method is that we can learn a (quantified) mapping from discrete rating scores to the exact magnitude/degree in terms of user's internal preferences. Specifically, we view ordered scores in an additive way, and by optimizing a utility function (e.g., squared loss between observed and estimated scores) which is defined in a measurable ordinal scale, we will learn the exact magnitude between any pair of adjacent rating scores. By correctly learning the personalized mappings for individual users, it is reasonable to expect that the rating prediction can be more accurate.

We apply our newly proposed ordinal regression model in collaborative filtering by combining matrix factorization, forming a new ordinal collaborative filtering method, called "decomposed matrix factorization (DMF)". More specifically, in the first step, our ordinal regression method introduces a decomposition of a sparse rating matrix into a sequence of decomposed binary matrices and matrix factorization is then applied on each of the decomposed matrices. The final predicted rating scores are formed as a weighted sum of the predictions from each of the decomposed matrices, where the weights model the internal distances/scales between different pairs of adjacent rating values. Through extensive experiments on benchmark datasets, we demonstrate that DMF is competitive, often substantially better than existing ordinal collaborative filtering methods, as well as other popular rating prediction algorithms.

2 RELATED WORK

Rating prediction has been by far widely discussed in the literature. Collaborative filtering (CF) is the most popular approach for the rating prediction problem, which is based on the assumption that users who have expressed similar interests in the past will share common interests in the future [5, 9, 23].

There are several broad categories of collaborative filtering approaches developed for predicting ratings [4, 28]. One category of common approaches: neighborhood-based CF algorithms [1, 26, 27], also referred to as memory-based methods, predict the rating that one user gives to an item by aggregating the ratings from similar users to that item (i.e., user-based CF) or from the ratings given by that user to similar items (i.e., item-based CF). Another class of so-called model-based approaches use machine learning and data mining methods in the context of predictive models. Matrix factorization is the most popular one, which imposes a low-rank assumption on the given sparse U-I rating matrix R [6, 8, 10, 11, 15, 18, 20, 22, 25]. In general, based on the low-rank assumption, it factorizes R into UV^T, where $U \in \mathbb{R}^{m \times f}$ and $V \in \mathbb{R}^{n \times f}$ (m is the number of rows, n is the number of columns in R and f is the rank for approximation). This category of matrix factorization approaches have attracted great attention because of their scalability and high prediction accuracy, as demonstrated in the Netflix Prize competition [12].

In most of the aforementioned CF models, user ratings are considered as numerical values or (nominal) categorical labels and it is arguable that these two views of rating values may not precisely reflect the degree in terms of user's internal preferences. Thus, a small number of works propose to view rating scores as ordinal categorical labels in the rating prediction problem. For example, in [13, 14] authors apply logistic ordinal regression [17] to model the ordinality of user feedbacks. They feed a robust rating predictor (i.e., SVD++[10]) into the logistic ordinal regression model and jointly learn model parameters of SVD++ and logistic ordinal model by maximizing a likelihood, which is transformed from cumulative probabilities of ordered rating scores. Another model called "Ordinal Matrix Factorization (OMF)" [19] also combines matrix factorization with logistic ordinal regression. In that work, the ordinality of ratings is modeled as cumulative Gaussian density and then the cumulative probabilities are coupled into a hierarchical Bayesian framework. Different from OrdRec, the parameters of OMF are learned in the Bayesian framework through Gibbs sampling, while in OrdRec parameters are learned through gradient method. As shown in [14, 19], ordinal methods generally outperform other rating prediction methods.

Our proposed ordinal regression model differs with logistic ordinal regression in that we are able to learn a mapping to quantify discrete rating scores to the exact degree in terms of individual users' internal preferences. Specifically, we transfer discrete rating scores to the magnitude which is defined in the ordinal scale and learn/train model in the ordinal space. It is expected that by accurately learning individual users' internal rating patterns can generate more accurate rating predictions.

3 ADDITIVE ORDINAL REGRESSION

In this section, we introduce a new ordinal regression method called "additive ordinal regression", as we define rating scores in an additive fashion.

3.1 An Additive Way to View Ordered Values

We view discrete ordered scores in an additive way and define their magnitudes in a measurable ordinal scale. The "magnitude" in the ordinal scale can be interpreted differently in individual applications. For example, in recommender systems, it can be considered as the degree of user preferences. Without loss of generality, let's consider discrete ordered scores $\{1, 2, ..., C\}$ and let $l(c)$ represent the magnitude of a given ordered score $c \in \{1, 2, ..., C\}$. Assuming that there is a base label which can be viewed as "0" and let the magnitude of this base label be 0, i.e., $l(0) = 0$. We obtain $l(c)$ in an additive way:

$$l(c) = l(c-1) + scale(c-1, c) = \sum_{i=1}^{c} scale(i-1, i) \tag{1}$$

where $scale(c-1, c)$ is the scale/distance between ordered scores "$c-1$" and "c". If discrete ordered scores are viewed as numerical values, then it equals to the assumption that $scale(c-1, c) = 1$, $\forall c \in \{1, 2, ..., C\}$.

3.2 Mapping Numerical Scale to Ordinal Scale

In the above subsection, we compute the magnitude for all the discrete integer values $l(c)$ ($\forall c \in \{1, 2, ..., C\}$). However, we do not know the magnitudes for real values between any two consecutive integer scores, e.g., $l(1.5)$. Here we propose the mechanism to map from the whole numerical scale to the ordinal space. Without loss of generality, we consider continuous values between two discrete ordered values $c-1$ and c, and values in other intervals can be computed the same way.

Given that t locates in the interval $[c-1, c]$, we model the magnitude of t as:

$$l(t) = l(c-1) + scale(c-1, c) \cdot ratio(t, c-1)$$
$$= \sum_{i=1}^{c-1} scale(i-1, i) + scale(c-1, c) \cdot ratio(t, c-1) \quad (2)$$

where $l(c-1)$ and $scale(c-1, c)$ are defined in Eq. (1). $ratio(t, c-1)$ is a value between [0,1], formulated as follows:

$$ratio(t, c-1) = \frac{dist(c-1, t)}{dist(c-1, t) + dist(t, c)} \quad (3)$$

where $dist(\cdot, \cdot)$ is a distance measure (or kernel) (e.g., Euclidean distance). This *ratio* value tells which score (i.e., $c-1$ or c) t is closer to and how much t is closer to $c-1$ or c than the other one. For example, if $ratio = 0.5$, then t is in the middle of $c-1$ and c.

Given than $t \in [c-1, c]$, Eq. (2) can also be represented as:

$$l(t) = \sum_{i=1}^{C} scale(i-1, i) \cdot ratio(t, i-1) \quad (4)$$

if we set $ratio(t, i-1) = 1, \forall i, 1 \le i \le c-1$, and set $ratio(t, i-1) = 0$, $\forall i, c < i \le C$. This kind of setting to the *ratio* can be explained in that since we know $t \in [c-1, c]$ and the magnitude is defined in an additive way (i.e., adding from small scores), then we should add the magnitudes of all the intervals which are less than $c-1$, while ignore all the intervals which are greater than c.

Additionally, it should be mentioned that the method to calculate the *ratio* is not unique. Practitioners can develop different functions to calculate the *ratio* in different applications.

3.3 Additive Ordinal Regression

In real applications such as search and recommendation, we generally deal with problems in which we are given an observed (training) set of data and each data entry contains an input feature vector x and a response score y which takes values from a discrete set of ordered scores $\{1, 2, ..., C\}$. The task is to develop a predictive model to estimate a score $\hat{y}$ for a test input x. The estimated score $\hat{y}$ can be either discrete or continuous based on different applications. In this section, we propose a new ordinal regression model, which returns a continuous value as the response for a given input feature vector x, rather than probability distributions over ordered labels which is the general output of logistic ordinal regression.

In our model, the observed scores and estimated responses are defined in a measurable ordinal scale. We cannot directly formulate the predicted value using Eq. (2), since we are merely given input feature x and do not know which interval the estimated value $\hat{y}$ will locate in. Therefore, we formulate $\hat{y}$ as follows:

$$\hat{y} = \sum_{c=1}^{C} scale(c-1, c) \cdot ratio(f_{[c-1,c]}(x), c-1) \quad (5)$$

where $f_{[c-1,c]}(x)$ is an internal model used to generate the *ratio* for interval $[c-1, c]$. Since $\hat{y}$ has chance to be located in all intervals, every interval (i.e., $[c-1, c]$, $\forall c$) should potentially contribute to the computation of $\hat{y}$. The degree of contribution for each interval is decided by the *ratio* value.

The parameters of our proposed ordinal regression method, including $scale(c-1, c)$, $\forall c \in \{1, 2, ..., C\}$ and all the parameters in the internal model $f_{[c-1,c]}(x)$ can be jointly learned by optimizing a squared loss between observed scores and estimated scores on the training samples. It should be emphasized that in our method the objective function is defined in the ordinal scale where the distances more accurately reflect individual users' internal preferences.

Practically, the scale/distance between adjacent ordered scores models a single user's discrimination ability between these two adjacent scores. For example, if we enlarge the interval between labels "4" and "5", and shrink the interval between "3" and "4" (see the example in Fig. 1), then it can be explained in that for someone, it is much easier to discriminate between labels "4" and "5" compared with scores "4" and "3". In real applications such as personalized search and collaborative filtering, different users may have different degrees of sensitivity over a sequence of ordered scores, and thus the internal scale between a specific pair of adjacent scores can also be different for individual users.

4 DECOMPOSED MATRIX FACTORIZATION

In this section, we apply our newly proposed ordinal regression method in collaborative filtering for the task of rating prediction. In this problem, a set of ratings or preference scores are recorded by m users over n items, which are represented by an $m \times n$ user-item matrix $R \in \mathbb{R}^{m \times n}$. The ratings take discrete ordered values, e.g., 1-star to 5-star, and most of them are absent due to incomplete observations, making R a highly sparse matrix. The task of rating prediction then boils down to predicting the unknown ratings based on a small portion of observed ratings in R.

We combine matrix factorization with ordinal regression model, forming a new ordinal collaborative filtering method. In order to simplify the notations, we use w^c to replace $scale(c-1, c)$, representing the magnitude between ordered scores $c-1$ and c. We replace $\hat{y}$ with $\hat{r}$ here and use r^c to represent $ratio(f_{[c-1,c]}(x), c-1)$, where the internal model $f_{[c-1,c]}(x)$ is obtained from matrix factorization and feature vector x refers to user and item latent factors. Finally, Eq. (5) is reformulated as follows:

$$\hat{r} = \sum_{c=1}^{C} w^c \cdot r^c \quad (6)$$

Note that this formulation (6) is related to that in [16], with a distinction. For the purpose of ranking, [16] predicted rating as $\hat{r} = \sum_{c=1}^{C} cProb(r = c)$, and the task boils down to estimating the class probabilities, which was formulated both as a multi-class classification problem and as an ordinal classification problem. [16] commented that using either $\sum_{c=1}^{C} 2^c Prob(r = c)$ or $\sum_{c=1}^{C} cProb(r = c)$ does not make a noticeable difference in the ranking accuracy. In this study, however, since our goal is to accurately predict the ratings instead of rankings, we must learn the weights w^c carefully.

4.1 Decomposing User Ratings

Before discussing our proposed rating prediction model, we introduce a decomposition procedure: given a sparse rating matrix R where observed user ratings take values from a set of discrete scores $\{1, 2, ..., C\}$, we decompose the C-level rating matrix R into C binary matrices $R1$, $R2$,..., $R(C)$ ($R(c) \in \mathbb{R}^{m \times n}$, $\forall c$). Each binary matrix discriminates between observed ratings no less than a specific ordinal category c and ratings below that ordinal category ($\{\geq c\}$ vs. $\{\leq c-1\}$). For example, the entries in the c-th decomposed matrix $R(c)$ are set in the following manner: if the observed rating value $r_{u,i} \geq c$ in R, then we set "1" at the corresponding position of $R(c)$ (i.e., the intersection of u-th row and i-th column); if $r_{u,i} \leq c-1$ in R, then we set "0" at the corresponding position of $R(c)$; if an entry is missing (unobserved) in R, then its corresponding position in $R(c)$ is still missing. Therefore, the observed values in $R(c)$ discriminate rating scores $\{r \geq c\}$ and $\{r \leq c-1\}$. An example is shown below when $C = 4$, $m = n = 2$, where a "?" represents a missing entry. On the left side of the vertical line is the original rating matrix R and the right side of the vertical line are decomposed binary matrices $R1$, $R2$, $R3$, $R4$.

$$\underset{R}{\begin{bmatrix} ? & 2 \\ 4 & ? \end{bmatrix}} \;\Bigg|\; \underset{R1}{\begin{bmatrix} ? & 1 \\ 1 & ? \end{bmatrix}} \quad \underset{R2}{\begin{bmatrix} ? & 1 \\ 1 & ? \end{bmatrix}} \quad \underset{R3}{\begin{bmatrix} ? & 0 \\ 1 & ? \end{bmatrix}} \quad \underset{R4}{\begin{bmatrix} ? & 0 \\ 1 & ? \end{bmatrix}}$$

The purpose of matrix decomposition is that each binary matrix can provide information for each interval of the ordered scores. For example, the c-th decomposed binary matrix $R(c)$ captures information for the interval $[c-1, c]$, since this binary matrix discriminates ratings $\{r \geq c\}$ with $\{r \leq c-1\}$. We then apply matrix factorization on each of the decomposed sparse binary matrices. The imputed values in the entries of binary matrix to some extent model how much the estimations of rating scores are closer to $c-1$ or c, which is interpreted as the *ratio* value in Eq. (3) (or r^c in Eq. (6)). We will explain the procedures in details.

4.2 Rating Prediction on Decomposed Binary Matrices

We assume that each decomposed binary matrix has low rank and apply matrix factorization on each of them. Specifically, given any matrix $R(c)$ ($c \in \{1, 2, ..., C\}$), we formulate a rating predictor on the sparse decomposed binary matrix as follows:

$$r^c = \frac{u^c v^{cT} + 1}{2} \qquad (7)$$
$$s.t. \quad \|u^c\|^2 \leq 1, \quad \|v^c\|^2 \leq 1$$

where $u^c \in \mathbb{R}^f$ is a row vector of user latent factors and $v^c \in \mathbb{R}^f$ is a row vector of item latent factors on c-th decomposed matrix and f is the dimensionality of low-rank approximation. $r^c \in [0, 1]$ is the predicted value on $R(c)$. We set constraints $\|u^c\|^2 \leq 1$ and $\|v^c\|^2 \leq 1$ since we expect that the predicted value r^c ranges from 0 to 1. This formulation is inspired by [7].

The predicted value r^c calculated from the latent features in the c-th decomposed matrix represents the "*ratio*" for interval $[c-1, c]$ in Eq. (5). Recall that in the c-th decomposed matrix, "1" is set if the original observed rating score "$r \geq c$", and "0" is set when observed rating score "$r \leq c-1$". Thus, the estimated vale of r^c ($0 \leq r^c \leq 1$) indicates how much r is closer to c or $c-1$.

4.3 Combining Predictions from Decomposed Matrices

The task of rating prediction is to generate an estimated rating value for a user-item combination. After obtaining the predictions from each of the binary matrices through Eq. (7), we then use Eq. (6) to generate the final prediction.

In practice, it is expected that each user has distinct rating pattern or degree of sensitivity over the same set of ordered scores. Therefore, the value of w^c (i.e., scale between $c-1$ and c) in Eq. (6) should be different for individual users. Then, the prediction model becomes:

$$\hat{r}_{u,i} = \sum_{c=1}^{C} w_u^c \cdot r_{u,i}^c \qquad (8)$$

where $\hat{r}_{u,i}$ is the final predicted rating value that the u-th user gives to the i-th item and $r_{u,i}^c$ is the prediction in the corresponding entry of the c-th decomposed binary matrix. w_u^c represents that each user has distinct ordinal scale over interval $[c-1, c]$.

By combining Eq. (7) and Eq. (8), we formulate the final ordinal rating predictor as follows:

$$\hat{r}_{u,i} = \sum_{c=1}^{C} \frac{w_u^c}{2} (U_u^c V_i^{cT} + 1) = \sum_{c=1}^{C} \frac{w_u^c}{2} \Big(\sum_{j=1}^{f} U_{u,j}^c \cdot V_{i,j}^c + 1\Big) \qquad (9)$$
$$s.t. \quad \|U_u^c\|^2 \leq 1, \quad \|V_i^c\|^2 \leq 1 \quad \forall u, i, c$$

where U_u^c (the u-th row of U^c) and V_i^c (the i-th row of V^c) denote the latent factors for the u-th user and the i-th item from matrix factorization on the c-th binary matrix.

Finally, model parameters, including the latent factors from each of decomposed matrices and the scale variables between any pair of adjacent rating scores, are jointly learned through minimizing a regularized squared loss between estimated scores and observed scores, which is formulated as follows:

$$\min \sum_{(u,i)\in\Omega} \Big(r_{u,i} - \sum_{c=1}^{C} \frac{w_u^c}{2} (U_u^c V_i^{cT} + 1)\Big)^2 + \sum_{u,c} \lambda_{U,u} \|U_u^c\|^2 + \sum_{i,c} \lambda_{V,i} \|V_i^c\|^2 \qquad (10)$$
$$s.t. \quad \|U_u^c\|^2 \leq 1, \quad \|V_i^c\|^2 \leq 1 \quad \forall u, i, c$$

where Ω is the observed set of rating values, and $r_{u,i} \in \Omega$ represents one observed rating score. Shown in the above objective function, we introduce regularization terms (i.e., $\sum_{u,c} \lambda_{U,u} \|U_u^c\|^2$ and $\sum_{i,c} \lambda_{V,i} \|V_i^c\|^2$) in order to prevent from overfitting. We call this new ordinal collaborative filtering method "decomposed matrix factorization (DMF)", as our model is based on matrix factorization on a sequence of decomposed matrices.

As an extreme case of our ordinal method, if we set identical weights (i.e., $w^c = 1, \forall c$), then the ratings are still defined as numerical, since now all the ordered rating scores are equidistant (see Fig. 1 as an example). Then, our method seemingly just models "residuals" incrementally, where the "residuals" are the difference between small rating values and large rating values. If we use predefined w^c, then DMF is similar to a method called decoupled collaborative ranking proposed in [7] which also introduces the idea of decomposing R.

4.4 Comparisons with OrdRec and OMF

There are two principal differences between DMF with OrdRec and OMF, which are implemented based on the logistic ordinal regression method. Firstly, DMF factorizes C decomposed binary matrices where each one captures the insight of user assigning one pair of adjacent rating scores, while OrdRec and OMF factorize only one matrix. This property indicates that DMF essentially catches more patterns when users assign rating scores than the other two methods. Secondly, additive ordinal regression defines the full mapping from users' rating scores to unified ordinal magnitudes, allowing us to easily compare the magnitudes of the same rating score from individual users. Suppose that "4-star" from user A assigned to item i maps to 4.2 (in the ordinal scale) while "4-star" from user B assigned to item i maps to 3.7 (in the ordinal scale) and then we can conclude that user A is probably more interested in item i than user B even though they gave the same rating score to that item. Our ordinal method provides a simpler and more straightforward way to quantify this kind of difference than logistic ordinal regression.

5 PARALLEL SGD FOR LEARNING DMF

Methods based on stochastic gradient descent (SGD) have become increasingly important, especially for large-scale industrial applications. It is also fairly easy for practitioners to reproduce the SGD methods. Hence, in this paper, we develop an algorithm based on SGD to solve the optimization problem in Eq. (10). Besides, we adopt a notable share-memory parallelized algorithm, which is called HOGWILD! [21], to make the learning process of our proposed method scalable to multi-core machines.

5.1 Regularization Parameters

As shown in Eq. (10), we set different regularization parameters for different users and items. In practice, we apply a popular strategy to reduce the number of regularization parameters:

$$\lambda_{U,u} = \frac{\lambda}{\#\text{observed ratings given by user } u}$$

$$\lambda_{V,i} = \frac{\lambda}{\#\text{observed ratings gave to item } i}$$

As a result, we only have one hyper-parameter λ for all the regularization parameters.

5.2 Parallelized Stochastic Gradient Descent

In this section, we develop an EM-like SGD algorithm to learn the model parameters. We divide the model parameters of DMF into two groups: $\{U^c, V^c\}_{c=1}^C$ and $\{w^c\}_{c=1}^C$. The first set of parameters represent the user and item latent factors and the other set of parameters are the weights set for each of the decomposed matrices, modeling the different scales/distances between any pair of adjacent scores. Our SGD algorithm alternatively updates these two set of parameters. Let $e_{u,i}$ denote the predicted error, $r_{u,i} - \hat{r}_{u,i}$. We summarize the EM-like SGD algorithm as follows:

(1) Firstly, we initialize the model parameters: $\{U^c, V^c\}_{c=1}^C$ and $\{w^c\}_{c=1}^C$. In our method, we initialize $\{U^c, V^c\}_{c=1}^C$ from a normal distribution and $\{w^c\}_{c=1}^C$ are all set to 1.

Algorithm 1: Parallelized SGD for DMF

Input : observed set Ω; max round of update MAXROUND; regularization parameters λ; learning rate η_1 for user and item latent factors, η_2 for scale parameters; number of threads T; *rank* of approximation
Output: $\{w^c, U^c, V^c\}_{c=1}^C$

while stopping criteria is not met **do**
  // subroutine to update $\{U^c, V^c\}_{c=1}^C$
  while stopping criteria is not met **do**
    for each thread $t \in \{1, 2, ..., T\}$ **do**
      repeat
        choose $r_{u,i} \in \Omega$ uniformly at random;
        for each $c \in \{1, 2, ..., C\}$ **do**
          update U_u^c by Eq. (11);
          update V_i^c by Eq. (12);
          $U_u^c \leftarrow \frac{U_u^c}{\|U_u^c\|}$ and $V_i^t \leftarrow \frac{V_i^c}{\|V_i^c\|}$;
        end
      until sampling S times is done;
    end
  end
  // subroutine to update $\{w^c\}_{c=1}^C$
  while stopping criteria is not met **do**
    for each thread $t \in \{1, 2, ..., T\}$ **do**
      repeat
        choose $r_{u,i} \in \Omega$ uniformly at random;
        for each $c \in \{1, 2, ..., C\}$ **do**
          update w^c by Eq. (13);
        end
      until sampling S times is done;
    end
  end
  $\eta_1 = \frac{\eta_1}{2}, \eta_2 = \frac{\eta_2}{2}$;
end

(2) We then fix $\{w^c\}_{c=1}^C$ and estimate $\{U^c, V^c\}_{c=1}^C$ by minimizing the loss function in Eq. (10). Given an observed rating $r_{u,i}$ (i.e., $(u, i) \in \Omega$), we update the model parameters as:

$$U_u^c \leftarrow U_u^c + \eta_1 \cdot (e_{u,i} \cdot w_u^c \cdot V_i^c - 2\lambda_{U,u} \cdot U_u^c) \quad (11)$$

$$V_i^c \leftarrow V_i^c + \eta_1 \cdot (e_{u,i} \cdot w_u^c \cdot U_u^c - 2\lambda_{V,i} \cdot V_i^c) \quad (12)$$

The constraints in Eq. (10) can be satisfied by gradient projection during the update of model parameters: $U_u^c \leftarrow \frac{U_u^c}{\|U_u^c\|}$ and $V_i^t \leftarrow \frac{V_i^c}{\|V_i^c\|}$. By looping through all the training samples several iterations, we will obtain a basic estimation of the parameters $\{U^c, V^c\}_{c=1}^C$.

(3) Similar to step 2, we then fix $\{U^c, V^c\}_{c=1}^C$ and estimate $\{w^c\}_{c=1}^C$ by minimizing the same loss function in Eq. (10). The update formulation of $\{w^c\}_{c=1}^C$ is given as:

$$w_u^c \leftarrow w_u^c + \eta_2 \cdot e_{u,i} \cdot (U_u^c V_i^{cT} + 1) \quad (13)$$

By looping through all the training samples in Ω several iterations, we obtain the updated parameters of $\{w^c\}_{c=1}^C$.

Table 1: Statistics of datasets

Datasets	#Users	#Items	Rating Scale	#Ratings	Density
MovieLens-100k	943	1,682	1 - 5 (5 levels)	100,000	6.30%
MovieLens-1m	6,040	3,706	1 - 5 (5 levels)	1,000,209	4.47%
MovieLens-20m	138,493	27,278	0.5 - 5.0(10 levels)	20,000,263	5.29%
Netflix-100k	13,632	586	1 - 5 (5 levels)	112,244	1.20%
Netflix-1m	48,018	1,777	1 - 5 (5 levels)	1,020,752	1.41%
Netflix	480,189	17,770	1 - 5 (5 levels)	100,480,507	1.18%

(4) We repeat step 2 and step 3 for several rounds until meeting the stopping criteria and return $\{w^c, U^c, V^c\}_{c=1}^C$. The procedure stops when the prediction error on the validation set does not decrease or the program exceeds the number of rounds initially set.

We implement scalable DMF model based on the HOGWILD! framework. Let T be the number of threads and S be the sample size for each thread. In the paper, we take the value $S = \frac{|\Omega|}{T}$. The pseudo-code of the algorithm is described in Algorithm 1.

6 EXPERIMENTS

We empirically investigate the performance of our ordinal regression method in the context of rating prediction.

Datasets: Our algorithms are tested on four public datasets. A full statistic of datasets is described in Table 1. In each dataset, we randomly partition the data into two parts: 4/5 as training and 1/5 as test. We perform 5-fold cross validation on the training data.

Performance Metrics: Root Mean Square Error (RMSE) and Mean Absolute Error (MAE) are two popular quantified measurements used to evaluate the accuracy of rating prediction. They are defined as: RMSE $= \sqrt{\frac{\sum_i (y_i - \hat{y}_i)^2}{N}}$ and MAE $= \frac{\sum_i |y_i - \hat{y}_i|}{N}$. In our problem setting, y_i is the real rating value in the test set, $\hat{y}_i$ is the predicted rating value and N is the size of the test data.

6.1 Effectiveness of DMF

In order to study the principles in our method, we compare the performance of DMF with two baseline methods which have been discussed in the previous sections: (i) **Matrix Factorization (MF)**. In MF, an estimated rating value is represented as $\hat{r}_{u,i} = U_u V_i^T$ and these latent factors could be learned through minimizing an objective function in the form of squared loss with quadratic regularization terms. (ii) We preset $w^c = 1, \forall c$, in Eq. (9), then DMF just models the incremental "residuals" between small rating values and large rating values, where the rating values are defined as numerical values. We call this method **DMF-Res** and set it as a baseline method for comparison. The DMF-Res method is similar to applying decoupled collaborative ranking [7] for the rating prediction task.

Results are reported in different settings of *rank* (i.e., the f in Eq. (9)) for low-rank approximation. In the experiments, we choose *rank* from the set of $\{20, 50, 100\}$, and the prediction accuracy of different approaches is evaluated in terms of RMSE metric. Other parameters, e.g., learning rate, regularization parameter, are selected by cross-validation. The experimental results on some datasets are shown from Table 2 to Table 4.

Table 2: RMSE on MovieLens-100k

Methods	*rank*=20	*rank*=50	*rank*=100
MF	0.925	0.923	0.922
DMF-Res	0.920	0.919	0.917
DMF	**0.904**	**0.902**	**0.901**

Table 3: RMSE on MovieLens-1m

Methods	*rank*=20	*rank*=50	*rank*=100
MF	0.872	0.870	0.869
DMF-Res	0.867	0.865	0.864
DMF	**0.848**	**0.846**	**0.845**

Table 4: RMSE on MovieLens-20m

Methods	*rank*=20	*rank*=50	*rank*=100
MF	0.812	0.808	0.802
DMF-Res	0.790	0.787	0.786
DMF	**0.769**	**0.767**	**0.766**

MF vs. DMF-Res. The difference between MF and DMF-Res is that MF model is based on matrix factorization on the original rating matrix R, while in DMF-Res model, each binary matrix is factorized. Hence, by setting same *rank* to both methods, DMF-Res has C times more model parameters than MF. To make fair comparison between MF and DMF-Res in the setting of equal number of model parameters, we can compare MF of "$rank = 100$" with DMF-Res of "$rank = 20$" on MovieLens-100k and MovieLens-1m datasets since in both of these two datasets, there exist 5 different rating values. In such setting, Tables 2 and 3 show that DMF-Res slightly outperforms MF. In view of this, DMF-Res method in which we assume that all the ordered rating scores are equidistant (i.e., $w^c = 1$, $\forall c \in \{1, 2, ..., C\}$) is still considered as another way of matrix factorization approach to modeling user ratings as numerical.

DMF vs. DMF-Res. DMF and DMF-Res differ in that in DMF, the scales between any pair of adjacent rating scores (i.e., $\{w^c\}_{c=1}^C$) are learned, while in DMF-Res, all these variables are preset as identical values. Hence, DMF is an ordinal regression method while DMF-Res does not apply ordinal information. Through the comparisons of DMF with DMF-Res from Table 2 to Table 4, it clearly shows that the weight variables have significant impact on the rating prediction performance. In other words, modeling user ratings as ordinal is sound for rating prediction and our proposed ordinal regression method works well in this problem.

6.2 Comparing DMF with Other Ordinal Rating Prediction Algorithms

In this section, we compare our proposed DMF method with two existing ordinal matrix factorization methods: **OrdRec** [13] and **OMF** [19], which are both built on the logistic ordinal regression framework. In OrdRec, authors feed SVD++ rating predictor as an internal model. Model parameters of OrdRec are learned through gradient ascent on a likelihood. OMF is a hierarchical Bayesian model and ordinal information of ratings is coupled into the model using logistic ordinal regression by changing logistic function to the cumulative Gaussian density.

The performance comparison is shown in Table 5. All the methods are compared in the same number of latent factors. More specifically, we set $rank = 20$ for DMF and $rank = C \cdot 20$ for OrdRec and OMF. Based on the t-test results, it is noticeable that on all large-scale datasets, the improvement of our prediction algorithm against all the other ordinal approaches (i.e., OrdRec and OMF) are statistically significant at p-value< 0.01. The results show the superiority of additive ordinal regression over general logistic ordinal regression on the rating prediction problem.

Table 5: Comparing DMF with ordinal rating predictors

Datasets	Metrics	OrdRec	OMF	DMF
MovieLens-1m	MAE	0.672	0.675	**0.666**
	RMSE	0.857	0.862	**0.846**
MovieLens-20m	MAE	0.603	0.608	**0.586**
	RMSE	0.783	0.787	**0.766**
Netflix-1m	MAE	0.735	0.738	**0.722**
	RMSE	0.932	0.938	**0.914**
Netflix-Training	MAE	0.662	0.670	**0.642**
	RMSE	0.851	0.858	**0.823**

The results of performance comparison among these ordinal methods can be explained in that: logistic ordinal regression focuses on learning a correct probability distribution over a sequence of ordered rating scores, while our proposed ordinal regression method focuses more on learning the correct mapping from user assigned rating scores to the exact degree of user preference. That is, our ordinal regression model has greater power in quantifying the given rating score to a preference score. Besides, evaluation metric such as RMSE is calculated using squared distance, and it is possible that directly minimizing this loss (in our method) is more suitable than a classification loss (logistic ordinal regression). Other advantages of DMF over OrdRec and OMF are explained in Section 4.4.

6.3 More Discussions on DMF

6.3.1 ***The impact of rank for matrix approximation***. The *rank* is a tuning parameter for matrix factorization. From Table 2 to Table 4, we observe that increasing the value of *rank* can always slightly improves the prediction performance. In order to investigate the impact of *rank* more detailedly, we report the prediction performance of MF and DMF on the MovieLens-20m dataset as a function of *rank* in Fig. 2, which also shows that DMF is able to achieve a stable performance at a relative lower *rank*.

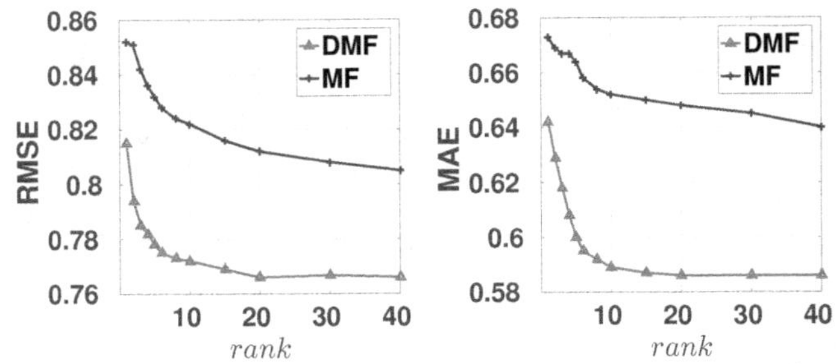

Figure 2: The impact of *rank*. Results are reported on the MovieLens-20m dataset.

6.3.2 ***Discussion on the number of decomposed matrices***. Given that observed rating scores take from a discrete set of values $\{1, 2, ..., C\}$, an interesting question concerning our ordinal regression method is that why rating values are decomposed into C different intervals, rather than less interval scales such as $\frac{C}{2}$ or more intervals such as $2C$. In order to answer this question, we conduct experiments by decomposing the original rating matrix into different number of matrices and investigate the prediction performance as a function of the number of decomposed matrices.

The performance on MovieLens-1m dataset is shown in Fig. 3. In that dataset, ratings take discrete values from $\{1, 2, 3, 4, 5\}$. We decompose the original rating matrix into different number of binary matrices in each experiment. For example, if we only obtain 1 binary matrix, then this matrix only distinguishes ratings between two groups: $\{1, 2\} \le \frac{5}{2} = 2.5$ and $\{3, 4, 5\} > \frac{5}{2} = 2.5$. Readers can also understand it as we treat C in Eq. (9) as a tuning parameter, and test this parameter here.

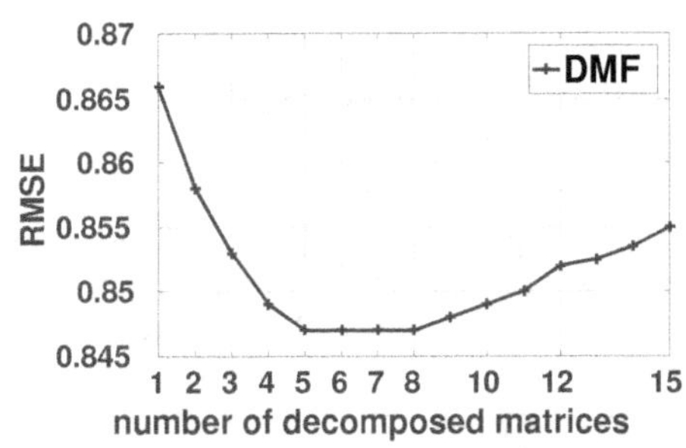

Figure 3: The performance when the original rating matrix is decomposed into different number of matrices.

The results in Fig. 3 show that: (i) when the number of decomposed matrices ≤ 5, we obtain better performance as the increasing number of decomposition; (ii) While the number of decomposed matrices ≥ 8, we obtain poorer prediction performance as the increasing number of decomposed matrices. The first observation can be explained in that as the number of decomposition increases (when this number ≤ 5), we captures more information about the distinct rating values. When we have 5 decomposed matrices (i.e., we model 5 intervals), the information of distinct ordered scores is fully used. When using more than 5 intervals, we actually capture redundant information. For example, if scores are decomposed into

10 intervals, i.e., < 1, [1,1.5), [1.5-2),..., [4.5-5.0), ≥5, some intervals (e.g., [1.5, 2), [2.5, 3)) are meaningless, since no score in the training set locates in this interval. The performance becomes poorer due to overfitting. Therefore we choose the number of decomposed matrices as the number of distinct ordered scores.

6.3.3 ***Effectiveness of parallelized SGD.*** In Fig. 4, we empirically evaluate the effectiveness of our proposed parallelized SGD algorithm on the two largest datasets in terms of RMSE metric. The prediction accuracy after each round of updating parameters is reported. As shown in Algorithm 1, in each round, we first fix $\{w^c\}_{c=1}^C$ and update $\{U^c, V^c\}_{c=1}^C$ and then fix $\{U^c, V^c\}_{c=1}^C$ and update $\{w^c\}_{c=1}^C$. Therefore, there are 2 experimental results shown within one round on the performance curve. In Fig. 4, it shows that after each update of model parameters the prediction performance can be gradually improved. We also observe that much of the improvement takes place in the first 2 rounds and after 3 rounds the performance becomes stable and thus in practice, it might be enough to update model parameters in only 2 or 3 rounds.

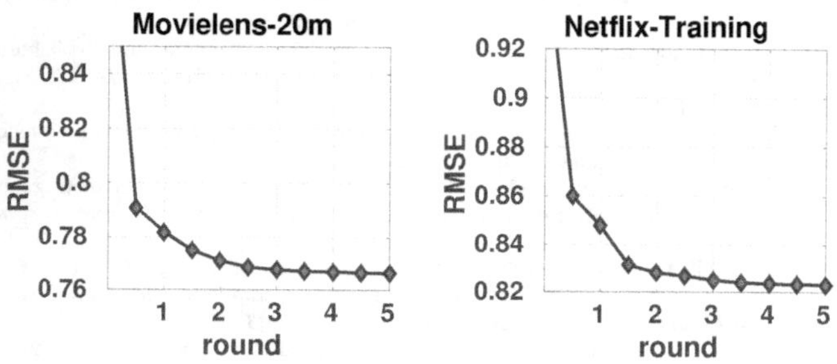

Figure 4: The effectiveness of Algorithm 1. In each round, we first report the results after updating $\{U^c, V^c\}_{c=1}^C$ and then report the results after updating $\{w^c\}_{c=1}^C$.

We also demonstrate the parallelization performance of our proposed algorithm in Fig. 5. All the experiments were conducted on a single workstation: DELL Precision T7600 with two Intel@Xeon(R) E5-2687W 3.10GHZ 16-core CPUs. Fig. 5 plots the prediction performance as a function of running time. We see that the rating prediction accuracy in terms of both RMSE and MAE metrics converges to similar results in different number of threads.

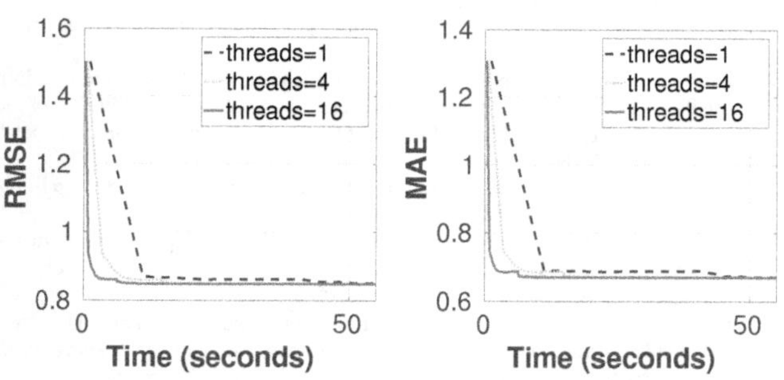

Figure 5: The accuracy of parallelized SGD measured by RMSE and MAE with respect to running time. The experiments are reported on MovieLens-1m dataset with $rank = 20$.

6.4 Comparisons with More Rating Predictors

In this section, we compare DMF with many rating prediction methods, to demonstrate the superiority of our ordinal regression method when applied to the rating prediction problem. We first compare DMF to two baseline neighborhood-based methods: **UserAvg** which predicts rating values by averaging the ratings which are given by the same active user; **ItemAvg** which predicts rating values by averaging the ratings given to the same item. We then compare DMF to model-based methods: **MF** as a baseline method. **BPMF** [25], a Bayesian probabilistic matrix factorization method; **BSVD** [20] is an improved regularized matrix factorization approach; **Factorization Machine (FM)** [22] is popular in recommender systems, which can mimic a lot of matrix factorization methods (e.g., SVD++ [10]). In the experiment, we model the feature of FM as SVD++ (see section 4.1.3 in paper [22]) since it achieves the best performance. The main purpose of this paper is to discuss our newly proposed ordinal regression approach and therefore we mainly compare DMF with other methods which also apply the same basic predictive model-matrix factorization. Practically, we can also combine other basic predictive models such as neural network in our ordinal regression method and we leave it as future work.

We report our settings used in the DMF method: the regularization parameter λ is set as 0.5; learning rates $\eta_1 = 10^{-2}$ and $\eta_2 = 10^{-3}$ are used in the first round, and updated by $\eta_1 = \eta_1/2$ and $\eta_2 = \eta_2/2$ in the following rounds. All the other matrix factorization-based methods are compared in the setting of equal number of model parameters. For example, if there are 5 distinct rating scores and we set $rank = k$ in DMF, then we will set $rank = 5k$ in other methods. This setting of comparison is fairer than the setting of comparison in same *rank*, considering both of the model complexity and performance. If we compare in the setting of same *rank*, one may still doubt that the improvement of performance results from adding more model parameters. Besides, DMF with $rank = k$ generally performs slightly worse than DMF with $rank = C \cdot k$, which demonstrates more superiority of our proposed method if it even outperforms other methods in the setting of $rank = k$. In our experiments, we set $rank = 20$ for DMF, and set $rank = C \cdot 20$ for other compared methods.

The empirical results are reported in Table 6. Observed from that table, we see that DMF outperforms all the methods for comparison in terms of both of RMSE and MAE metrics. Except for the first two neighborhood-based models, all the other compared methods apply the same basic predictive model (i.e., matrix factorization) by incorporating other understanding of the patterns when users assign rating scores. For example, they combine more elements such as mean, user's rating bias, user's rating history with basic user and item latent factors. However, all of the compared methods in this section did not introduce the ordinal interpretation of rating scores. From the performance comparisons shown in Table 6, we can conclude that modeling the ordinal nature of user preference in a correct manner can significantly improve the performance of rating prediction over methods which ignore the ordinal nature of user preference scores.

Table 6: Comparisons of rating predictors. In the experiments, we use the Netflix-Training dataset, since the ground truth of test set in the Netflix Prize dataset is not available to the public at the present time.

Datasets	Metrics	UserAvg	ItemAvg	MF	BPMF	BSVD	FM(SVD++)	DMF
MovieLens-100k	MAE	0.835	0.817	0.723	0.722	0.723	0.721	**0.710**
	RMSE	1.041	1.025	0.923	0.920	0.917	0.912	**0.901**
MovieLens-1m	MAE	0.830	0.782	0.704	0.696	0.673	0.668	**0.666**
	RMSE	1.036	0.978	0.869	0.865	0.862	0.855	**0.846**
MovieLens-20m	MAE	0.751	0.732	0.638	0.632	0.609	0.599	**0.586**
	RMSE	0.963	0.941	0.802	0.798	0.788	0.783	**0.766**
Netflix-100k	MAE	0.872	0.871	0.851	0.858	0.852	0.848	**0.826**
	RMSE	1.122	1.120	1.126	1.098	1.088	1.075	**1.035**
Netflix-1m	MAE	0.810	0.809	0.742	0.739	0.735	0.734	**0.722**
	RMSE	1.024	1.023	0.947	0.943	0.935	0.933	**0.914**
Netflix-Training	MAE	0.812	0.809	0.687	0.677	0.667	0.656	**0.642**
	RMSE	1.016	1.015	0.880	0.865	0.855	0.843	**0.823**

7 CONCLUSION

In this paper, we discussed the ordinality of user ratings: the distance/scale between any pair of adjacent scores should be different. Based on this intuition, we proposed a new ordinal regression approach to modeling the ordinal nature of user ratings. Different from current statistic ordinal regression methods which consider ordered scores as ordinal categorical labels, in our method discrete rating scores can be mapped to the exact magnitudes in terms of individual users' internal preferences. By combing matrix factorization, we applied our proposed ordinal method in collaborative filtering for the task of rating prediction. Through extensive experiments on popular datasets, we demonstrated the superiority of our proposed method over other ordinal methods in terms of the accuracy of rating prediction. We also compared our method with many notable collaborative filtering methods and show the effectiveness to model ordinal user preference scores in order to improve the rating prediction accuracy.

Acknowledgement: NSF-Bigdata-1419210 and NSF-III-1360971.

REFERENCES

[1] Gediminas Adomavicius and Alexander Tuzhilin. 2005. Toward the next generation of recommender systems: A survey of the state-of-the-art and possible extensions. *Knowledge and Data Engineering, IEEE Transactions on* 17, 6 (2005), 734–749.

[2] Charu C Aggarwal. 2016. *Recommender Systems.* Springer.

[3] Alan Agresti. 2002. Introduction to generalized linear models. *Categorical Data Analysis, Second Edition* (2002), 115–164.

[4] Michael D Ekstrand, John T Riedl, Joseph A Konstan, et al. 2011. Collaborative filtering recommender systems. *Foundations and Trends® in Human–Computer Interaction* 4, 2 (2011), 81–173.

[5] David Goldberg, David Nichols, Brian M Oki, and Douglas Terry. 1992. Using collaborative filtering to weave an information tapestry. *Commun. ACM* 35, 12 (1992), 61–70.

[6] Jun Hu and Ping Li. 2016. Improved and scalable bradley-terry model for collaborative ranking. In *Data Mining (ICDM), 2016 IEEE 16th International Conference on.* 949–954.

[7] Jun Hu and Ping Li. 2017. Decoupled Collaborative Ranking. In *Proceedings of the 26th International Conference on World Wide Web.* International World Wide Web Conferences Steering Committee, 1321–1329.

[8] Yifan Hu, Yehuda Koren, and Chris Volinsky. 2008. Collaborative filtering for implicit feedback datasets. In *Data Mining, 2008. ICDM'08. Eighth IEEE International Conference on.* 263–272.

[9] Joseph A Konstan, Bradley N Miller, David Maltz, Jonathan L Herlocker, Lee R Gordon, and John Riedl. 1997. GroupLens: applying collaborative filtering to Usenet news. *Commun. ACM* 40, 3 (1997), 77–87.

[10] Yehuda Koren. 2008. Factorization meets the neighborhood: a multifaceted collaborative filtering model. In *Proceedings of the 14th ACM SIGKDD international conference on Knowledge discovery and data mining.* 426–434.

[11] Yehuda Koren. 2010. Factor in the neighbors: Scalable and accurate collaborative filtering. *ACM Transactions on Knowledge Discovery from Data (TKDD)* 4, 1 (2010), 1.

[12] Yehuda Koren, Robert Bell, and Chris Volinsky. 2009. Matrix factorization techniques for recommender systems. *Computer* 8 (2009), 30–37.

[13] Yehuda Koren and Joe Sill. 2011. OrdRec: an ordinal model for predicting personalized item rating distributions. In *Proceedings of the fifth ACM conference on Recommender systems.* 117–124.

[14] Yehuda Koren and Joseph Sill. 2013. Collaborative Filtering on Ordinal User Feedback. In *IJCAI 2013, Proceedings of the 23rd International Joint Conference on Artificial Intelligence, Beijing, China, August 3-9, 2013.* 3022–3026.

[15] Joonseok Lee, Samy Bengio, Seungyeon Kim, Guy Lebanon, and Yoram Singer. 2014. Local collaborative ranking. In *Proceedings of the 23rd international conference on World wide web.* International World Wide Web Conferences Steering Committee, 85–96.

[16] Ping Li, Christopher J Burges, and Qiang Wu. 2007. Mcrank: Learning to rank using multiple classification and gradient boosting. In *Advances in neural information processing systems.* 897–904.

[17] Peter McCullagh. 1980. Regression models for ordinal data. *Journal of the royal statistical society. Series B (Methodological)* (1980), 109–142.

[18] Andriy Mnih and Ruslan Salakhutdinov. 2007. Probabilistic matrix factorization. In *Advances in neural information processing systems.* 1257–1264.

[19] Ulrich Paquet, Blaise Thomson, and Ole Winther. 2012. A hierarchical model for ordinal matrix factorization. *Statistics and Computing* 22, 4 (2012), 945–957.

[20] Arkadiusz Paterek. 2007. Improving regularized singular value decomposition for collaborative filtering. In *Proceedings of KDD cup and workshop*, Vol. 2007. 5–8.

[21] Benjamin Recht, Christopher Re, Stephen Wright, and Feng Niu. 2011. Hogwild: A lock-free approach to parallelizing stochastic gradient descent. In *Advances in Neural Information Processing Systems.* 693–701.

[22] Steffen Rendle. 2010. Factorization machines. In *Data Mining (ICDM), 2010 IEEE 10th International Conference on.* 995–1000.

[23] Paul Resnick, Neophytos Iacovou, Mitesh Suchak, Peter Bergstrom, and John Riedl. 1994. GroupLens: an open architecture for collaborative filtering of netnews. In *Proceedings of the 1994 ACM conference on Computer supported cooperative work.* 175–186.

[24] Francesco Ricci, Lior Rokach, and Bracha Shapira. 2011. *Introduction to recommender systems handbook.* Springer.

[25] Ruslan Salakhutdinov and Andriy Mnih. 2008. Bayesian probabilistic matrix factorization using Markov chain Monte Carlo. In *Proceedings of the 25th international conference on Machine learning.* 880–887.

[26] Badrul Sarwar, George Karypis, Joseph Konstan, and John Riedl. 2001. Item-based collaborative filtering recommendation algorithms. In *Proceedings of the 10th international conference on World Wide Web.* 285–295.

[27] Yue Shi, Martha Larson, and Alan Hanjalic. 2009. Exploiting user similarity based on rated-item pools for improved user-based collaborative filtering. In *Proceedings of the third ACM conference on Recommender systems.* 125–132.

[28] Yue Shi, Martha Larson, and Alan Hanjalic. 2014. Collaborative filtering beyond the user-item matrix: A survey of the state of the art and future challenges. *ACM Computing Surveys (CSUR)* 47, 1 (2014), 3.

Who Will Share My Image? Predicting the Content Diffusion Path in Online Social Networks

Wenjian Hu
University of California, Davis
wjhu@ucdavis.edu

Krishna Kumar Singh*
University of California, Davis
krsingh@ucdavis.edu

Fanyi Xiao*
University of California, Davis
fanyix@cs.ucdavis.edu

Jinyoung Han
Hanyang University
jinyounghan@hanyang.ac.kr

Chen-Nee Chuah
University of California, Davis
chuah@ucdavis.edu

Yong Jae Lee
University of California, Davis
yongjaelee@ucdavis.edu

ABSTRACT

Content popularity prediction has been extensively studied due to its importance and interest for both users and hosts of social media sites like Facebook, Instagram, Twitter, and Pinterest. However, existing work mainly focuses on modeling popularity using a single metric such as the total number of likes or shares. In this work, we propose Diffusion-LSTM, a memory-based deep recurrent network that learns to recursively predict the entire diffusion path of an image through a social network. By combining user social features and image features, and encoding the diffusion path taken thus far with an explicit memory cell, our model predicts the diffusion path of an image more accurately compared to alternate baselines that either encode only image or social features, or lack memory. By mapping individual users to user prototypes, our model can generalize to new users not seen during training. Finally, we demonstrate our model's capability of generating diffusion trees, and show that the generated trees closely resemble ground-truth trees.

CCS CONCEPTS

• **Networks → Online social networks**; • **Human-centered computing → Social network analysis**; • **Computing methodologies → Supervised learning by classification**; *Neural networks*; • **Information systems →** *Data mining*;

KEYWORDS

Online Social Networks; Recurrent Neural Networks; Diffusion Path Prediction

ACM Reference Format:
Wenjian Hu, Krishna Kumar Singh, Fanyi Xiao, Jinyoung Han, Chen-Nee Chuah, and Yong Jae Lee. 2018. Who Will Share My Image? Predicting the Content Diffusion Path in Online Social Networks. In *Proceedings of WSDM 2018: The Eleventh ACM International Conference on Web Search and Data Mining , Marina Del Rey, CA, USA, February 5–9, 2018 (WSDM 2018)*, 9 pages. https://doi.org/10.1145/3159652.3159705

*These two authors contributed equally.

WSDM 2018, February 5–9, 2018, Marina Del Rey, CA, USA

ACM ISBN 978-1-4503-5581-0/18/02...$15.00
https://doi.org/10.1145/3159652.3159705

1 INTRODUCTION

Online social networks (OSNs) have seen phenomenal growth: over a billion users on Facebook, and hundreds of millions on Google+, Twitter, and Pinterest. This new ecosystem of content generation and sharing enables rich data to be collected and analyzed to study individual and group behavior, as well as to study how information is diffused over social graphs. In particular, viral diffusion (also known as "word-of-mouth" diffusion) [3, 23, 37] has been shown to be an important mechanism for advertising a new idea, technology, content, or product. Unlike the mass broadcast counterpart in which a single user directly spreads information to most recipients, in viral diffusion many individuals participate in spreading information in a chain-like structure.

In this paper, we are interested in modeling how image content gets propagated through a social network. We focus on images because it has become one of the most important containers for sharing thoughts, interests, and feelings in OSNs (e.g., Pinterest, Instagram, Tumblr, Imgur). Unlike existing work [1, 5, 8, 10, 19, 22, 26], which largely focus on a single absolute metric such as the total number of users who liked/shared a content (see Figure 1 left), we are instead interested in modeling the *entire structure of the content propagation path* (see Figure 1 right). To this end, we propose Diffusion-LSTM, a novel memory-based deep network that recursively predicts each step of the image content diffusion path, using both the history of social context features of all previous users in the diffusion path as well as the image content features.

Apart from an image's content, the history of users in the diffusion path plays a key role in deciding whether the image will be further propagated, and if so, to whom next. For example, if we only know that the image was shared by a user who likes soccer, then the likelihood that the image will be shared by a soccer fan will be high. However, if we also know that the image was initially shared by a tennis fan before being shared by the soccer fan, then there is a high-likelihood that the next user will like either soccer, tennis, or sports in general. Similarly, if an image is initially shared by an influential user with lots of followers, then its likelihood to be propagated will remain high even after being shared by a user with only a few followers. Hence, we design our Diffusion-LSTM to capture the history of the social characteristics of all of the previous users who have shared the image in order to predict its future propagation path. Furthermore, in order to generalize our prediction model to new unseen users, we create prototype users by grouping individual users according to their social features.

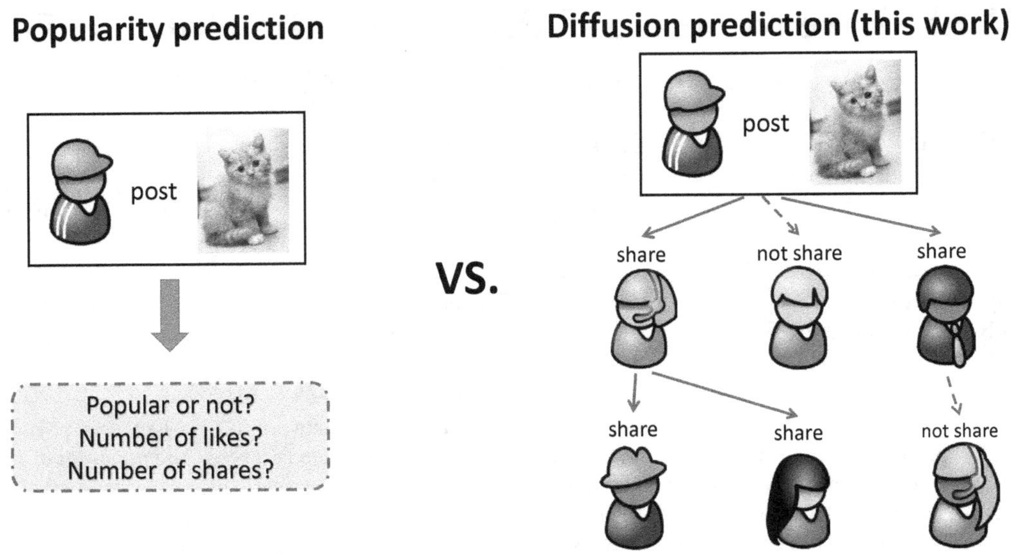

Figure 1: (Left): Prior work on popularity prediction predicts whether a user's post will become popular or not as measured by a single metric such as the total number of users who liked or shared the post. (Right): Our work on diffusion prediction predicts the entire propagation path of the user's post. Specifically, our approach recursively predicts which of the user's friends will share/re-share the post using the image features, user's social features, and the previous sharing history.

To the best of our knowledge, our work is the first attempt to generate the complete diffusion path of an image through an online social network. Our results show superior diffusion path prediction performance compared to alternative baselines that lack history information or rely only on either image or social information. Finally, while we use Pinterest data to evaluate our model, we design it to be general and applicable to other image-driven social media as well.

2 RELATED WORK

A large number of recent efforts have explored ways to predict content popularity, including for images [7, 8, 10, 14, 22, 33], videos [26], GitHub repositories [5], blogs [1], memes [36], and tweets [18, 19, 25, 28], by combing content features with user social features. In contrast to these prior work, which mainly focus on predicting a popularity score (e.g., number of shares) of the content, we aim to predict the entire content diffusion path through the social network, which is a much more challenging task. Predicting not only how many users will share a content but also the characteristics of each sharer in the diffusion sequence would enable deeper understanding of the diffusion process; e.g., one could identify the critical users in the diffusion path [3, 23] which would be useful e.g., for targeted advertisements.

Link prediction algorithms, which predict future edges between the nodes by using the current state of the graph [2, 13, 27, 30, 35] are also related. Our approach is different in that it *recursively* predicts the entire diffusion path of a content (an image) using both the content and users' social characteristics rather than predicting future edges for an existing graph.

Our Diffusion-LSTM architecture for social network tree prediction is related to Tree-LSTMs [32, 38, 39] in natural language processing (NLP). Unlike standard linear chain LSTMs, a Tree-LSTM takes the hidden vectors from multiple children to predict the next hidden state, and has shown superior performance for various NLP tasks like sentiment prediction and sentence semantic relatedness. However, due to their bottom-up structure [32, 39], they are not well suited for predicting/generating the content diffusion path in a social network, since the content diffusion path prediction has to start from the root user. Recent work by [38] predicts the tree structure in a top-down manner, but it uses techniques that are specific for language dependency tree prediction, and thus cannot be directly used for social network tree prediction. In contrast to these works, our Diffusion-LSTM generates the content diffusion path in a top-down manner for social network tree prediction. To the best of our knowledge, our work is the first attempt to generate the complete diffusion path of an image through a social network.

Finally, our work is also related to image captioning in computer vision. In image captioning (e.g., [6, 9, 20, 21, 34]), an LSTM takes the image semantic feature [24, 31] along with the history of previous words to recursively predict the next word. In contrast, in our method (Diffusion-LSTM), an LSTM takes the image semantic feature along with the history of previous users' social context features to recursively predict the image propagation path taken through the social network.

3 APPROACH

Our goal is to predict the path of diffusion of an image in an online social network. We first describe how we map individual users to a set of prototype users so that our proposed model can generalize to unseen users. We then describe our deep recurrent Diffusion-LSTM network architecture for modeling and predicting image diffusion.

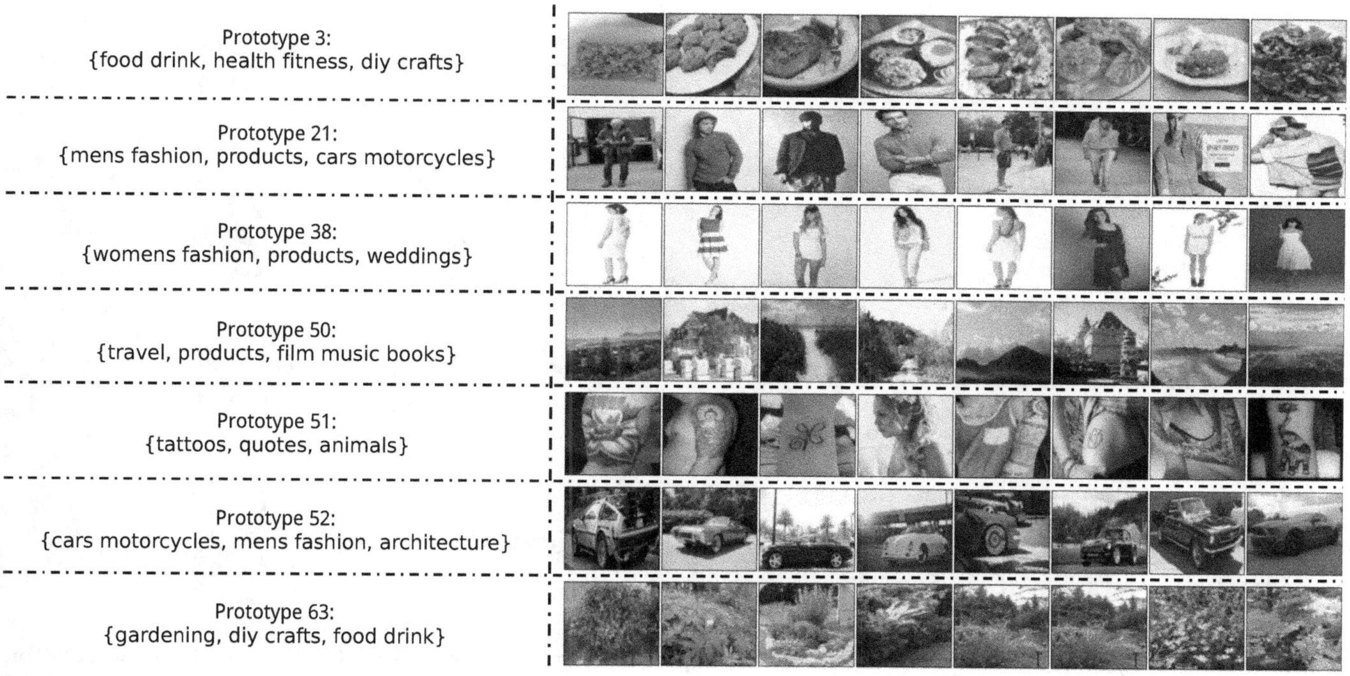

Figure 2: Examples of prototype users. The left panel shows the top three Pinterest categories that the prototype user most frequently posts images to, while the right panel shows representative images posted by individual users who are mapped to that prototype.

3.1 Mapping individual users to prototypes

A diffusion path of an image encodes the sequence of users who shared it. The set of all possible diffusion paths depends on both the users in the social network as well as the network structure (i.e., connectivity between users). Since we want our model to be able to generalize to unseen users and unseen connections (i.e., be able to train and test with a different set of users in the social network), we map individual users to a fixed set of canonical prototype users who capture the general, shared characteristics of the individual users that are mapped to them (like in which categories they post, how popular they are). In this way, we can maintain the same prototypical users during training and testing, while ignoring subtle differences between the true users. Furthermore, when there is insufficient training data for each user, combining similar individual users into a single prototype user can enlarge the training data to produce a better prediction model.

Specifically, we use k-means to cluster the social features (described in more detail below) of the users into $k = 100$ prototype groups.[1] The social feature of a prototype group is the average social feature of all of its cluster members. An unseen user is mapped to the prototype (i.e., cluster center) whose social feature is most similar based on their euclidean distance. Figure 2 shows examples of prototype users. The left panel shows the top three Pinterest categories that the prototype user most frequently posts images to, while the right panel shows representative images posted by individual users who are mapped to that prototype. For example, prototype user 38 likes to share images of women's fashion, while prototype user 52 likes to share images of cars.

[1]We set the number of prototypes to 100 to cover a broad range of users. Empirically, we find that our algorithm is robust to a wide range of k values.

3.2 Network architecture

The proposed architecture for modeling image diffusion through a social network is shown in Figure 3. The input to our model is an image I posted by a user and the user's social information S, and the output is the entire diffusion tree $\{U_1, U_2, ..., U_n\}$ (sequence of re-posters) of the image. Specifically, the initial diffusion path is conditioned on the input image and the social features of the root user. Then, in each ensuing timestep, our model takes the history of the previous posters' social features and the current poster's social features, and outputs the next re-poster (among the current poster's friends in the social network). The model stores and updates a memory that records the characteristics of the users in the diffusion path so far. The process ends when the next predicted user is "terminal".

We next describe the image and social features, our Diffusion-LSTM model, and the loss function used to optimize the model.

3.3 Image and social features

The propagation path of an image in a social network should be a function of the image content as well as the users' social features. For example, an interesting image is more likely to become viral if it is initially spread by a user who has many friends and followers.

For image features, we take the VGG 16 network [31] pretrained on ImageNet classification, and compute the FC7 activation feature

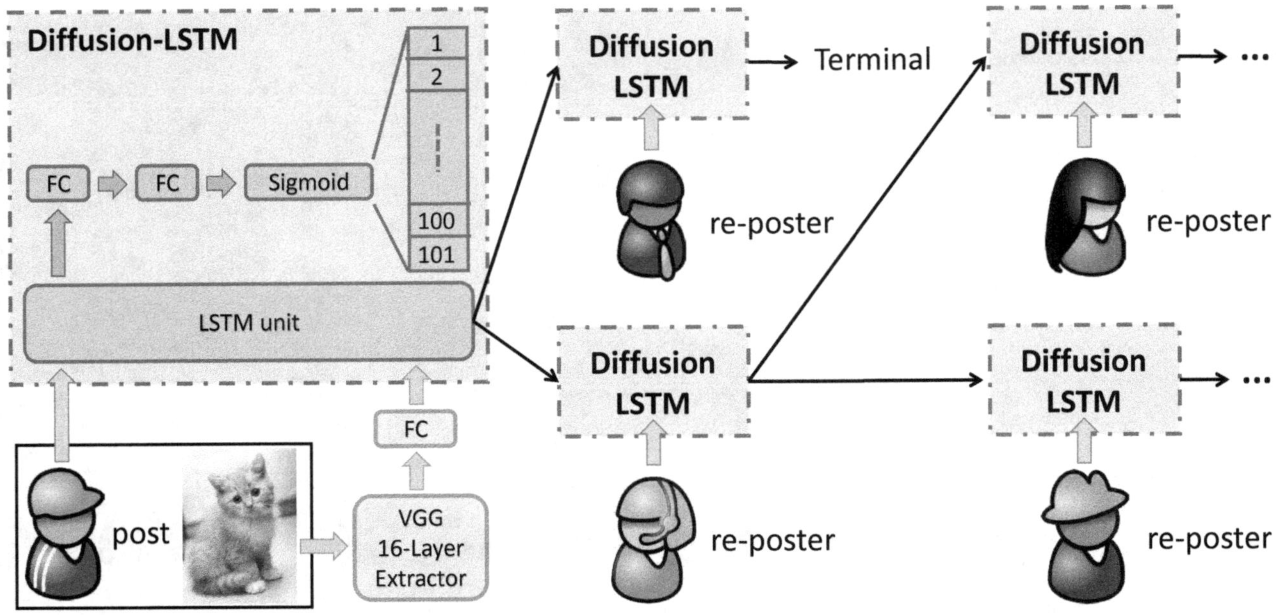

Figure 3: The architecture of the Diffusion-LSTM model. The posted image goes through the VGG 16 network and the resulting image features are fed into the Diffusion-LSTM network as the initial memory c_0 through an FC layer. In each step, the LSTM-unit takes as input the current user's social features. The hidden vector output of the LSTM-unit h goes through two FC layers and then a sigmoid function to get 101 class probabilities (100 prototype users and 1 terminal class). The Diffusion-LSTM cell in the dashed rectangle is repeated at successive tree nodes, with the only difference between the root node and children nodes being that the children nodes get the memory content c and output h from their parent node.

(4096-D) for each image. This feature encodes high-level semantics in the image (e.g., its objects/parts/attributes).

For social features, for each user, we compute the total number of followers of that user, the total number of users that the user follows, the total number of pins (shares) of all images shared by that user, and the total number of likes of all images shared by that user. We also compute the probability distribution of the 38 Pinterest categories of all images posted by the user. This captures the types of images that the user likes to share. The 4-D aggregate counts and the 38-D category distribution are concatenated to create a single 42-D social feature.[2]

3.4 Diffusion-LSTM

At any step along the diffusion path, whether an image will be further propagated will depend not only on the social influence of the current poster, but also on that of the previous posters (i.e., the history of the diffusion path taken thus far). This is an intrinsically recursive problem, and is well-suited to be modeled using Recurrent Neural Networks, which are ideal for analyzing sequences.

Since we want to model long-range dependencies across many diffusion steps, we use an LTSM network [11, 12, 17], which is more robust to the vanishing gradient problem than vanilla RNNs [4, 16]. LTSMs have been successfully used for the related problem of image captioning (e.g., [34]), where image features are combined with text features to recursively predict the next word in the image caption. In our case, the image features are combined with the current user's social features to recursively predict the next users who will share the image (recall Figure 1 right).

Our Diffusion-LSTM network for modeling image diffusion works exactly like a regular chain-structured LSTM network, with the only difference being the flow path of the memory cell c and the hidden state h following a tree. In a regular LSTM, the previous memory cell and hidden state from time step $t-1$ are passed to a single next node in time step t. However, in our Diffusion-LSTM network, the previous memory cell and hidden state of a parent node from time step $t-1$ can be passed to multiple child nodes in time step t, as shown in Figure 4. This means that during back-propagation, the gradient for a parent node will sum the gradients passed by all of its child nodes.

Formally, using the subscripts ch and p for "child" and "parent" respectively, the Diffusion-LSTM parent-child transition equations are expressed as follows:

$$\begin{aligned}
f_{ch} &= \sigma(W_x^f x_{ch} + W_h^f h_p + b^f) \\
i_{ch} &= \sigma(W_x^i x_{ch} + W_h^i h_p + b^i) \\
o_{ch} &= \sigma(W_x^o x_{ch} + W_h^o h_p + b^o) \\
c_{ch} &= f_{ch} \circ c_p + i_{ch} \circ \tanh(W_x^c x_{ch} + W_h^c h_p + b^c) \\
h_{ch} &= o_{ch} \circ \tanh(c_{ch})
\end{aligned} \tag{1}$$

where x_{ch} is the input social feature of the user at the current step, W_x, W_h and b are the weight matrices and bias vectors to be

[2]While additional social factors such as gender, geographic location, age could also be used to enrich the feature, these factors are unfortunately missing for many of the users in the Pinterest dataset collected in [15].

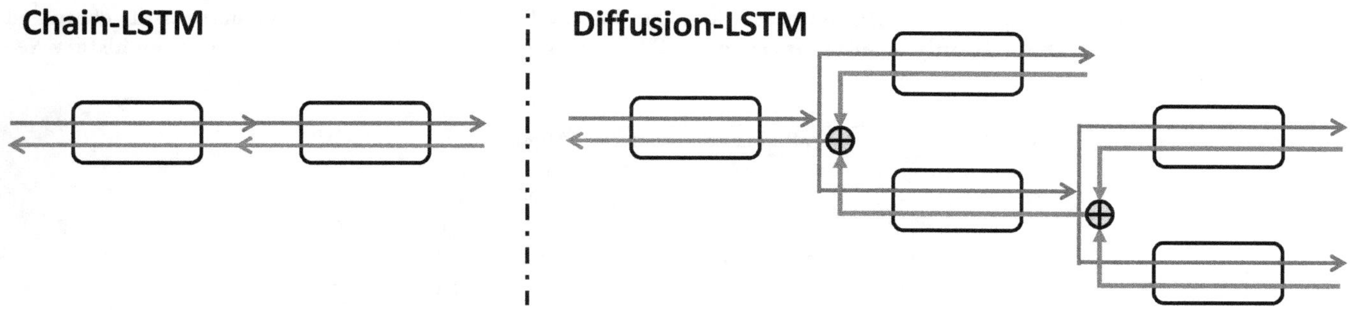

Figure 4: The blue and red lines represent forward and backpropagation, respectively. (Left): A chain-structured LSTM network. Nodes from left to right are arranged according to time step t. (Right): The Diffusion-LSTM network. Nodes are arranged according to its parent-children relationship. The *sum* of the gradients of children is passed to the parent node during backpropagation.

optimized, and $\circ$ denotes elementwise multiplication. f_{ch} denotes the forget gate vector (for remembering old information), i_{ch} denotes the input gate vector (for acquiring new information), o_{ch} denotes an output gate vector (as an output candidate), c denotes the memory cell, and h denotes the hidden state.

Our Diffusion-LSTM model consists of the regular LSTM unit followed by two FC layers and one sigmoid layer afterwards to predict one of the $k = 100$ prototypical users or the "terminal" class. To reduce overfitting and increase the nonlinearity of the model, we add one dropout layer after the LSTM unit, and one ReLU layer and one dropout layer between two FC layers.

We project the image features into the initial root parent memory c_p^{root} through an FC layer. This conditions the initial history of the propagation path with the contents of the image. Alternatively, one could concatenate a user's social features with the image features, but this produces inferior results. The initial hidden state h_0 is simply set to all zero.

3.5 Loss function for modeling image diffusion

The diffusion path of an image can be broken-down into a sequence of classification problems, where the predicted classes for a given timestep indicate the users who will reshare the image in the ensuing timestep (i.e., next depth level of the social network tree). Furthermore, since the number of users who reshare the image can range anywhere from no user (zero) to k different users, we model the diffusion prediction for a given timestep and tree node as a collection of $k + 1$ binary classification problems (where the $k+1$'th class denotes the terminal class). Thus, we use the weighted multi-class binary cross entropy loss to optimize our model:

$$L = \sum_{u=1}^{k+1} -\frac{1}{m} \sum_{i=1}^{m} (w_u^p t_{u,i} \log(o_{u,i}) + w_u^n (1 - t_{u,i}) \log(1 - o_{u,i})) \quad (2)$$

where u indexes the classes (prototype users and terminal class), i indexes the training instances (i.e., all nodes in all training trees), $o_{u,i}$ is the predicted probability of instance i being in class u, and $t_{u,i}$ is the ground-truth binary indicator indicating whether instance i is in class u.

Since the number of positive vs. negative instances in a class can be highly imbalanced, we use the weights w_u^p and w_u^n to balance their influence: $w_u^p = N_{un}/(N_{un} + N_{up})$, $w_u^n = N_{up}/(N_{un} + N_{up})$ and N_{un} (N_{up}) is the number of negative (positive) ground-truth instances for class u. Without these balancing weights, the loss function can be dominated by the dominant (positive or negative) instances.

4 EXPERIMENTS

In this section, we evaluate the accuracy of our model's image diffusion path prediction, and compare to several baselines that either use only image or social features, or lack memory. We also show qualitative examples of our model's generated diffusion trees.

4.1 Pinterest dataset

To analyze image content diffusion, we use the anonymized Pinterest data of [15], which was collected for 44 days in 2013. The dataset consists of image propagation data (pintree id, sender id, receiver id), user data (user id, number of pins (shares), number of followers, number of followings, number of likes, gender, locale, country), and image data (pintree id, Pinterest category, source, number of likes, and time stamp). For each image, its entire propagation path is available. Overall, the dataset contains more than 340K diffusion paths (Pinterest trees or "pintrees") shared by 1M users, which is randomly divided into training, validation, and test sets with size ratio $6:1:1$. The mean pintree size is 4.48 with standard deviation 11.67, the mean pintree width is 3.15 with standard deviation 6.85, and the mean pintree depth is 1.66 with standard deviation 1.05.

For social features, we use number of pins, number of followers, number of followings, and number of likes, because all other user data have more than 78% data missing, while those four social features have less than 1% data missing (which we simply fill with their mean values). As explained in Sec. 3, we expand the user social features with the 38 Pinterest category distributions, which can be summarized from all images shared by a user.

4.2 Implementation details

We train our Diffusion-LSTM model with an initial learning rate of 0.2, and then lower the learning rate to 0.02 when validation loss stops decreasing. We train both our model and all baselines until full convergence (30-60 epochs depending on the model). We

Table 1: Average Precision for per-node diffusion prediction. Our full model (last row) produces the best results compared with alternative baselines that rely only on either image or social features, or do not encode the image's posting history. See text for details.

Model	Social	Image	Memory	AP_{101}	mAP_{1-100}	mAP
Random Weights	Yes	Yes	Yes	0.803	0.005	0.013
FC	Yes	Yes	No	0.899	0.126	0.133
Diffusion-LSTM	No	Yes	Yes	0.883	0.087	0.095
Diffusion-LSTM	Yes	No	Yes	**0.932**	0.206	0.213
Diffusion-LSTM	Yes	Yes	Yes	**0.932**	**0.214**	**0.221**

optimize the weights of the model using backpropagation through time. We normalize each social feature to the range $[0, 1]$ by first applying the log function and then dividing by the maximum value. We divide each Pinterest category distribution feature by 4 to make it have roughly the same standard deviation as each non-category social features. For the VGG-16 image features, we subtract each dimension by its mean and divide by its standard deviation.

4.3 Baselines

We compare our Diffusion-LSTM model with several baselines:

Diffusion-LSTM with random weights: The same architecture as our Diffusion-LSTM model but with random weights. The initial memory c_0 is projected from image features at the beginning. This is a sanity check baseline to measure chance performance.

FC model with image and social features: This baseline consists of three fully connected (FC) layers. One ReLU layer and one dropout layer follow each of the first two FC layers. The last FC layer is followed by a sigmoid layer to convert the output values into probabilities. This baseline is chosen to study the importance of memory for content diffusion path prediction.

Diffusion-LSTM with only social features: The same architecture as our Diffusion-LSTM model but with only social features. No image features are used for this baseline, so initial memory c_0 is simply set to all zero. This baseline measures the role of social features for content diffusion path prediction.

Diffusion-LSTM with only image features: The same architecture as our Diffusion-LSTM model but with only image features. The initial memory c_0 is also set to all zero for this baseline. Since social features are not used, we instead use the (same) image features as input in each time step. This baseline measures the role of image features for content diffusion path prediction.

Note that we cannot compare with Tree-LSTMs [32, 38, 39] because it is not possible to apply them to our problem setting (i.e., top-down tree prediction/generation) due to their bottom-up nature.

4.4 Per-node diffusion prediction accuracy

We first evaluate image diffusion prediction by comparing our predicted users with the ground-truth users for each node in a tree. We evaluate per-category average precision (AP), by varying the threshold in the prediction confidences. Following the standard practice in evaluating RNNs [29], we do not generate the tree (we will do this in the next section), but instead use the ground-truth path up to timestep $t - 1$ for a tree node and evaluate whether the predicted users in timestep t match the ground-truth (and do this for all t and all nodes).

Table 1 shows the per-node prediction results. AP_{101} is the AP for the terminal class, while mAP_{1-100} is the mean AP for all prototype user classes. mAP is the mean AP computed over all 101 classes. First, we can see that all baselines outperform the random weights baseline, which produces a very low mAP showing the difficulty of the task. The reason why the AP_{101} for random weights is so high is because there are many leaf nodes (terminal class) in the database. Specifically, the terminal class has a $1 : 4$ ratio of non-leaf vs. leaf (total of $275,595$ non-leaf and $1,128,372$ leaf). On the other hand, for the 1-100 prototype user classes, the negative vs. positive instance ratio is around $200 : 1$ (an average total of $1,397,230$ negatives and $6,736$ positives). The large difference in target ratios make the prediction task for the prototype classes much more difficult than the terminal class.

Second, we see that social features alone produce better prediction results than image features alone. This corroborates many previous findings (e.g., [8, 22, 33]), which showed that social features are more important than image features for content popularity prediction. In our case, we are predicting the diffusion path, which is a much more difficult problem, and when no social features are used, it is impossible to say precisely how an image will be propagated through a social network. Third, our Diffusion-LSTM model performs much better than the FC model, indicating the crucial role of storing the image posting history in memory for predicting the next re-posting users.

Finally, combining social features and image features produces the best results, improving overall mAP by 0.8% over the baseline Diffusion-LSTM model using only social features. The main reason why the improvement is only 0.8% is because most (88.2%) users only post images in one Pinterest category instead of multiple categories. This means that those users are likely to always share similar images (e.g., of cats) to similar prototypical users (e.g., cat lovers). (Recall that we also use the probability distribution of the 38 Pinterest categories of all images posted by the user as part of the social features.) On the other hand, for users who post images of multiple Pinterest categories (e.g., cats, cars, travel, food), the image content will influence who among his/her followers will repost the image. To study this in more detail, we further break down prediction accuracy based on whether a user posts only to a single category versus multiple categories. Indeed, Figure 5 shows that image features yield only a slight improvement over social features for users who post only to a single category ($N = 1$), but

Table 2: Quantitative evaluation comparing our generated pintrees to ground-truth pintrees. Our full model (last row) generates pintrees that are closer to ground-truth than alternative baselines.

Model	Social	Image	Memory	Depth MAE	HI
Chance Performance	Yes	Yes	Yes	2.44	0.007
FC	Yes	Yes	No	2.46	0.278
Diffusion-LSTM	Yes	No	Yes	1.98	0.701
Diffusion-LSTM	Yes	Yes	Yes	**1.85**	**0.708**

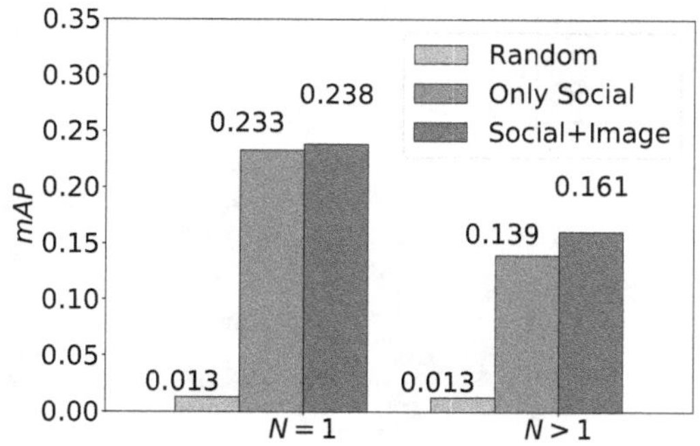

Figure 5: Single-category (left) vs. multi-category posters (right). N represents the number of categories a user post to. In each case, our full model (blue) is compared with the baseline which uses only social features (red) and the baseline which uses random weights (green). Our full model demonstrates significant improvement in prediction performance over these baselines for users who post to multiple categories.

significantly improve prediction performance for users who post to multiple categories ($N > 1$).

4.5 Tree generation accuracy

We next use our trained Diffusion-LSTM model to generate pintrees directly. We compare the generated tree with the ground-truth tree, given the same starting user and posted image. We compare the depth of the trees (which evaluates how well our model predicts the terminal class) and the user's preferred Pinterest category distributions averaged across all non-root nodes (users) in the tree (which measures how well our model predicts the prototype users). We do not consider the root node since it is already given during generation. We compute the mean absolute error (MAE) for depth, and histogram intersection for the Pinterest category distribution: $HI(\mathbf{d}_1, \mathbf{d}_2) = \sum_i min(d_{1i}, d_{2i})$, where $\mathbf{d}_1$, $\mathbf{d}_2$ are two normalized Pinterest category distributions (38-D histograms).

To generate a tree, given the features for a user and associated image, we recursively make 101 class (100 prototype users or terminal class) predictions. If a node is predicted as "terminal", we stop; otherwise, we continue generating the tree. When generating a tree, we set the terminal class prediction threshold to be 0.5, while the prototype class prediction thresholds are chosen based on validation data using depth MAE. Due to the unequal number of ground-truth pintrees per depth, we evaluate the MAE for each tree depth separately and then average across depths. We truncate any pintree if its depth > 10 or size > 150 or width > 100 to avoid degenerate trees that never stop growing (otherwise, they induce infinite error in our evaluation). 99.9% of the pintrees in the training set fall under these criteria.

Table 2 shows the results. Our generated trees are more similar to the ground-truth trees than the FC baseline, which again shows the importance of memory, and the Diffusion-LSTM baseline that lacks image features (the one that lacks social features does much worse, similar to per-node prediction). All methods outperform chance performance (sampling trees according to the training data distribution), which shows that learning is important for diffusion prediction. Figure 6 (top) shows visualizations of pintrees generated by our Diffusion-LSTM model. Our predicted pintrees are quite similar to the ground-truth pintrees. Even for the mispredicted users (red boxes), their Pinterest categories are very close to the ground-truth users' categories. Interestingly, for our top-left generated pintree, our model predicts that a user from prototype 47 will share the image from a user from prototype 10 who initially shared the image from another user from prototype 47. This shows the importance of memory as our model can remember that the image was initially shared by a user from prototype 47 and uses this to make the correct prediction.

Finally, in Figure 6 (bottom), we show how the generated pintrees change when the same prototype user posts different types of images. When a user who posts frequently to the animal category posts a gardening image (Figure 6 (bottom) right), it is shared by users who post frequently to the gardening category (indicating image plays a role). Social features still play a role, as can be seen by the common Pinterest categories between the original user and re-sharers (Diy_crafts is in common in both Figure 6 (bottom) left and right). This indicates image propagation is dependent on both image content and user social features.

5 CONCLUSION

We presented a deep recurrent network for generating the diffusion path of an image through a social network. By keeping track of the posting history of an image, our Diffusion-LSTM outperforms alternative baselines that lack memory or use only image or social features. We further demonstrated our model's capability of generating meaningful pintrees.

Although we mainly focused on Pinterest data, the proposed model is general and can be applied to different social network datasets. To further boost prediction performance, we could fine-tune the VGG 16 network, since the ImageNet dataset and Pinterest dataset may possess different characteristics (Pinterest images are more likely to be "artsy"). Finally, with sufficient training data for each user, it may also be possible to train the Diffusion-LSTM to

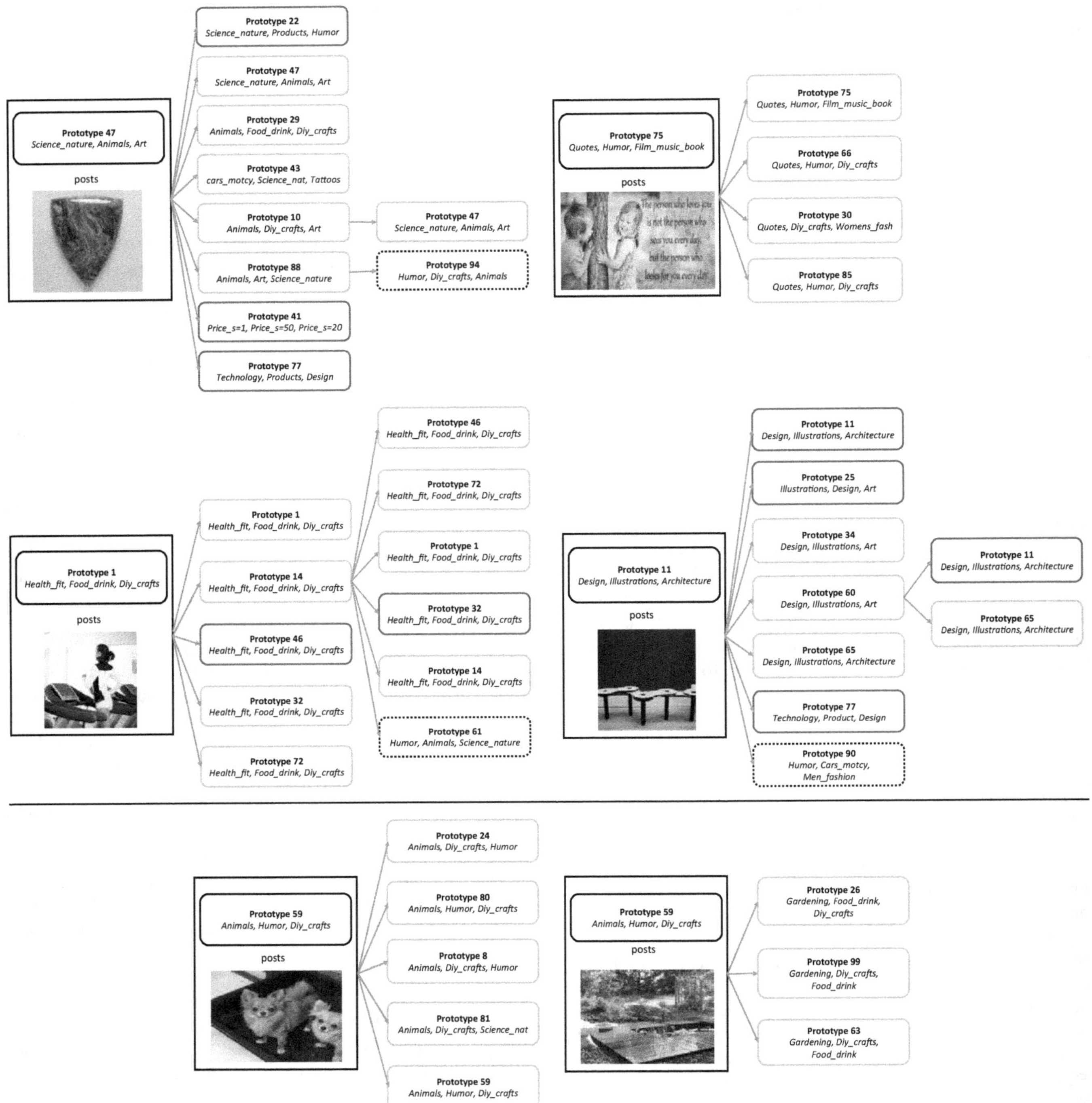

Figure 6: (Top) For a given image and its user, we generate the entire pintree showing the image propagation path through the different users. A user is shown in: 1) green box if the predicted path to that user matches the ground-truth path; 2) red box if it does not match the ground-truth; 3) dotted box if the path is present in the ground-truth pintree but not in our generated pintree. We also show the top 3 Pinterest categories for each user. Our predicted pintrees closely resemble the ground-truth pintrees. Note that while a self-loop can be observed at the prototype level (e.g., as seen in the bottom-left 'Prototype 1' social tree generation example), it still represents a mapping between different individual users since different individual users can be mapped to the same user prototype. (Bottom) Comparison of generated pintrees when the same prototype user posts different images. The generated tree depends on both the user's social features and image content.

directly predict the specific friends who will share the image, rather than predicting prototype users.

ACKNOWLEDGEMENTS

This work was supported in part by GPUs donated by NVIDIA and the research fund of Hanyang University (HY-2017-N).

REFERENCES

[1] N. Agarwal, M. Galan, H. Liu, and S. Subramanya. 2010. WisColl: Collective Wisdom Based Blog Clustering. In *Information Sciences.*

[2] L. Backstrom and J. Leskovec. 2011. Supervised Random Walks: Predicting and Recommending Links in Social Networks. In *WSDM.*

[3] E. Bakshy, I. Rosenn, C. Marlow, and L. Adamic. 2012. The Role of Social Networks in Information Diffusion. In *WWW.*

[4] Y. Bengio, P. Simard, and P. Frasconi. 1994. Learning Long-term Dependencies with Gradient Descent is Difficult. In *IEEE Transactions on Neural Networks.*

[5] H. Borges, A. Hora, and M. T. Valente. 2016. Predicting the Popularity of Github Repositories. In *PROMISE.*

[6] X. Chen and C. Lawrence Zitnicki. 2015. MindâĂŹs Eye: A Recurrent Visual Representation for Image Caption Generation. In *CVPR.*

[7] J. Cheng, L. Adamic, P. Dow, J. Kleinberg, and J. Leskovec. 2014. Can cascades be predicted?. In *WWW.*

[8] A. Deza and D. Parikh. 2015. Understanding Image Virality. In *CVPR.*

[9] J. Donahue, L. Anne Hendricks, S. Guadarrama, M. Rohrbach, S. Venugopalan, K. Saenko, and T. Darrell. 2015. Long-term Recurrent Convolutional Networks for Visual Recognition and Description. In *CVPR.*

[10] F. Gelli, T. Uricchio, M. Bertini, A. Del Bimbo, and S. F. Chang. 2015. Image Popularity Prediction in Social Media Using Sentiment and Context Features. In *ACM Multimedia.*

[11] F. A. Gers, J. Schmidhuber, and F. Cummins. 2000. Learning to Forget: Continual Prediction with LSTM. In *Neural Computation.*

[12] F. A. Gers, N. N. Schraudolph, and J. Schmidhuber. 2002. Learning Precise Timing with LSTM Recurrent Networks. In *JMLR.*

[13] A. Grover and J. Leskovec. 2016. Node2vec: Scalable Feature Learning for Networks. In *KDD.*

[14] M. Guerini, J. Staiano, and D. Albanese. 2013. Exploring image virality in google plus. In *SocialCom.*

[15] J. Han, D. Choi, A. Choi, J. Choi, T. Chung, T. T. Kwon, J. Y. Rha, and C. H. Chuah. 2015. Sharing Topics in Pinterest: Understanding Content Creation and Diffusion Behaviors. In *COSN.*

[16] S. Hochreiter. 1998. The Vanishing Gradient Problem During Learning Recurrent Neural Nets and Problem Solutions. In *IJUFKS.*

[17] S. Hochreiter and J. Schmidhuber. 1997. Long short-term memory. In *Neural Computation.*

[18] L. Hong, O. Dan, and B. D. Davison. 2011. Predicting Popular Messages in Twitter. In *WWW.*

[19] B. A. Huberman, D. M. Romero, and F. Wu. 2008. Social Networks that Matter: Twitter Under the Microscope. In *arXiv:0812.1045v1.*

[20] J. Johnson, A. Karpathy, and L. Fei-Fei. 2016. Densecap: Fully convolutional localization networks for dense captioning. In *CVPR.*

[21] A. Karpathy and L. Fei-Fei. 2015. Deep Visual-semantic Alignments for Generating Image Descriptions. In *CVPR.*

[22] A. Khosla, A. Das Sarma, and R. Hamid. 2014. What Makes an Image Popular?. In *WWW.*

[23] M. Kimura and K. Saito. 2006. Tractable Models for Information Diffusion in Social Networks. In *European Conference on Principles of Data Mining and Knowledge Discovery.*

[24] A. Krizhevsky, I. Sutskever, and G. Hinton. 2012. Imagenet Classification with Deep Convolutional Neural Networks. In *NIPS.*

[25] A. Kupavskii, A. Umnov, G. Gusev, and P. Serdyukov. 2013. Predicting the Audience Size of a Tweet. In *AAAI.*

[26] H. Li, X. Ma, F. Wang, J. Liu, and K. Xu. 2013. On Popularity Prediction of Videos Shared in Online Social Networks. In *CIKM.*

[27] D. Liben-Nowell and J. Kleinberg. 2007. The link-prediction problem for social networks. In *JASIST.*

[28] Z. Ma, A. Sun, and G. Cong. 2013. On Predicting the Popularity of Newly Emerging Hashtags in Twitter. In *JASIST.*

[29] T. Mikolov, M. KarafiÃąt, L. Burget, J. CernockÃ¡, and S. Khudanpur. 2010. Recurrent neural network based language model. In *INTERSPEECH.*

[30] S. Scellato, A. Noulas, and C. Mascolo. 2011. Exploiting place features in link prediction on location-based social networks. In *KDD.*

[31] K. Simonyan and A. Zisserman. 2015. Very Deep Convolutional Networks for Large-scale Image Recognition. In *ICLR.*

[32] K. S. Tai, R. Socher, and C. D. Manning. 2015. Improved Semantic Representations from Tree-structured Long Short-term Memory Networks. In *ACL.*

[33] L. Totti, F. Costa, S. Avila, E. Valle, W. Meira Jr, and V. Almeida. 2014. The Impact of Visual Attributes on Online Image Diffusion. In *WebSci.*

[34] O. Vinyals, A. Toshev, S. Bengio, and D. Erhan. 2015. Show and Tell: A Neural Image Caption Generator. In *CVPR.*

[35] D. Wang, D. Pedreschi, C. Song, F. Giannotti, and A. L. Barabasi. 2011. Human Mobility, Social Ties, and Link Prediction. In *KDD.*

[36] L. Weng, F. Menczer, and Y. Y. Ahn. 2013. Virality Prediction and Community Structure in Social Networks. In *Scientific Reports.*

[37] S. H. Yang and H. Zha. 2013. Mixture of Mutually Exciting Processes for Viral Diffusion. In *ICML.*

[38] X. Zhang, L. Lu, and M. Lapata. 2016. Top-down Tree Long Short-term Memory Networks. In *NAACL.*

[39] X. Zhu, P. Sobihani, and H. Guo. 2015. Long Short-term Memory Over Recursive Structures. In *ICML.*

Listening to Chaotic Whispers: A Deep Learning Framework for News-oriented Stock Trend Prediction

Ziniu Hu*
Key Lab of High-Confidence Software Technology, MoE
Peking University, China
bull@pku.edu.cn

Weiqing Liu
Microsoft Research
Beijing, China
Weiqing.Liu@microsoft.com

Jiang Bian
Microsoft Research
Beijing, China
Jiang.Bian@microsoft.com

Xuanzhe Liu
Key Lab of High-Confidence Software Technology, MoE
Peking University, China
liuxuanzhe@pku.edu.cn

Tie-Yan Liu
Microsoft Research
Beijing, China
Tie-Yan.Liu@microsoft.com

ABSTRACT

Stock trend prediction plays a critical role in seeking maximized profit from the stock investment. However, precise trend prediction is very difficult since the highly volatile and non-stationary nature of the stock market. Exploding information on the Internet together with the advancing development of natural language processing and text mining techniques have enabled investors to unveil market trends and volatility from online content. Unfortunately, the quality, trustworthiness, and comprehensiveness of online content related to stock market vary drastically, and a large portion consists of the low-quality news, comments, or even rumors. To address this challenge, we imitate the learning process of human beings facing such chaotic online news, driven by three principles: *sequential content dependency*, *diverse influence*, and *effective and efficient learning*. In this paper, to capture the first two principles, we designed a Hybrid Attention Networks (HAN) to predict the stock trend based on the sequence of recent related news. Moreover, we apply the self-paced learning mechanism to imitate the third principle. Extensive experiments on real-world stock market data demonstrate the effectiveness of our framework. A further simulation illustrates that a straightforward trading strategy based on our proposed framework can significantly increase the annualized return.

KEYWORDS

stock trend prediction; deep learning; text mining

*This work was done when the author was an intern at Microsoft Research Asia.

WSDM 2018, February 5–9, 2018, Marina Del Rey, CA, USA

ACM ISBN 978-1-4503-5581-0/18/02...$15.00
https://doi.org/10.1145/3159652.3159690

ACM Reference Format:
Ziniu Hu, Weiqing Liu, Jiang Bian, Xuanzhe Liu, and Tie-Yan Liu. 2018. Listening to Chaotic Whispers: A Deep Learning Framework for News-oriented Stock Trend Prediction. In *WSDM 2018: The Eleventh ACM International Conference on Web Search and Data Mining , February 5–9, 2018, Marina Del Rey, CA, USA.* ACM, New York, NY, USA, 9 pages. https://doi.org/10.1145/3159652.3159690

1 INTRODUCTION

In order for seeking maximized profit, stock investors continuously attempt to predict the future trends of market [20], which, however, is quite challenging due to highly volatile and non-stationary nature of the market [1]. Traditional efforts on predicting the stock trend have been carried out based on information from various fields. One of most basic ways relies on technical analysis upon recent prices and volumes on the market. Such methods yield the very limitations on unveiling the rules that govern the drastic dynamics of the market. Meanwhile, another basic method focuses on analyzing financial statements of each company, which is though incapable of catching the impact of recent trends.

With the rapid growth of the Internet, content from online media has indeed become a gold mine for investors to understand market trends and volatility. Even more, the advancing development of Natural Language Processing techniques has inspired increasing efforts on stock trend prediction by automatically analyzing stock-related articles. For instance, Tetlock et al. [24] extracts and quantifies the optimism and pessimism of Wall Street Journal reports and observes that trading volume tends to increase after pessimism reports and high pessimism scored reports tend to be followed by a downtrend and a reversion of market prices.

Not surprisingly, the effectiveness of such textual analyses depends on the quality of target articles. For instance, comparing with reading a comprehensive report of a company from Wall Street, analyzing a simple declarative news about this company is less likely to produce an accurate prediction. Unfortunately, the quality, trustworthiness, and comprehensiveness of online content related to stock market vary drastically, and a large portion of the online content consists of the low-quality news, comments, or even rumors.

To address this challenge, we imitate the learning process of human beings facing such chaotic online news, which can be summarized into three principles:

- **Sequential Context Dependency**: Even if a single piece of news is very likely to be of low-quality or not informative enough, human can comprehensively consider a sequence of related recent news as a unified context of the stock and consequently make a more reliable prediction on the subsequent stock trend. More importantly, within the unified sequential context, humans can pay different attention to various parts according to their respective importance and influence.
- **Diverse Influence**: While the influence of different online news can be diverse greatly, human beings can discriminate them based on the intrinsic content. For instance, some breaking news (e.g. air crash, military conflict) will profoundly affect the trend of related stocks, whilst some useless comments or vague rumors may cause little disturb on the stock trends. In real-world investment, people tend to consciously and comprehensively consider the estimated impact of each news at the time of predicting the subsequent stock trend.
- **Effective and Efficient Learning**: News cannot always provide obviously informative indications on stock trend, especially when the content of news contains vague information on stock trend or even there is very limited number of news about certain stocks in a period. In order for both effective and efficient learning, human beings tend to first gain knowledge by focusing on informative occasions, and then turn to disturbing evidence to obtain uneasy experience.

To capture the first two principles of human learning process, we design a Hybrid Attention Networks (HAN) to predict the stock trend based on the sequence of recent related news. First, to imitate the human cognition on sequential context with diverse attentions, we construct attention-based recurrent neural networks (RNN) at the higher level. In particular, the RNN structure enables the processing of recent related news for a stock in a unified sequence, and the attention mechanism is capable of identifying more influential time periods of the sequence. Second, to further model diverse influence of news, we propose news-level attention-based neural networks at the lower level, which aims at recognizing more important news from others at the same time point.

To imitate the effective and efficient learning of human, we employ the self-paced learning (SPL) [13] mechanism. Since the news-based stock trend prediction is more challenging in some situations, SPL enables us to automatically skip those training samples from some challenging periods in the early stage of model training, and progressively increase the complexity of training samples. Self-paced learning mechanism can automatically choose the suitable training samples for different training stage, which enhanced the final performance of our framework.

To validate the effectiveness of our approach, in this paper, we performed extensive experiments on real-world data. Comparing with traditional approaches, the experiment results show that our framework can significantly improve the performance of stock trend prediction. Furthermore, we simulated the stock investment using a simple trading strategy based on our framework, and the results illustrate that a straightforward trading strategy can achieve much better annualized return than the baseline methods.

To sum up, the contributions of our work include:

- A summarization of principles for imitating the learning process of human beings, particularly for stock trend prediction from the chaotic online news.
- A Hybrid Attention Networks with self-paced learning for stock trend prediction, driven by principles of human's learning process.
- Experimental studies on real-world data with simulated investment performance based on the real stock market.

The rest of the paper is organized as follows. We introduce related work in Section 2. We present empirical analysis to reveal principles for designing news-oriented stock prediction framework in Section 3, based on which we propose a new deep learning framework with details in Section 4. Experimental setup and results are demonstrated in Section 5. We conclude the paper and point out future directions in Section 6.

2 RELATED WORK

Stock trend prediction has attracted many research efforts due to its decisive role in stock investment. In general, traditional approaches can be categorized into two primary approaches: technical and fundamental analysis, according to the various types of information they mainly relied on.

Technical analysis deals with the time-series historic market-data, such as trading price and volume, and make predictions based on that. The main goal of this type of approach is to discover the trading patterns that can be leveraged for future prediction. One of the most widely used model in this direction is the Autoregressive (AR) model for linear and stationary time-series [15]. However, the non-linear and non-stationary nature of stock prices limits the applicability of AR models. Hence, previous studies attempted to applied non-linear learning methods [19] to catch the complex patterns underlying the market trend. With the development of deep learning, more research efforts have been paid on exploiting deep neural networks for financial prediction [2, 8, 12, 14, 21, 25]. To further model the long-term dependency in time series, recurrent neural networks (RNN), especially Long Short-Term Memory (LSTM) network, have also been employed in financial perdition [3, 7, 22]. In most recent time, Zhang *et al.* [28] proposed a new RNN, called State Frequency Memory (SFM), to discover multi-frequency trading patterns for stock price prediction.

One major limitation of technical analysis is that it is incapable of unveiling the rules that govern the dynamics of the market beyond price data. Fundamental approaches, on the contrary, seek information from outside market-historic-data, such as geopolitics, financial environment and business principles. Information explosion on the Internet has promoted online content, especially news, as one of the most important sources for fundamental analysis. There have been many attempts to mine news data for better predicting market trends. Nassirtoussi *et al.* [18] proposed a multi-layer dimension reduction algorithm with semantics and sentiment to predict intra-day directional-movements of a currency-pair in the foreign exchange market. Ding *et al.* [5] proposed a deep learning method for event-driven stock market prediction. They further augmented their approach [6] by incorporating an outside knowledge graph into the learning process for event embeddings. Wang *et al.* [26] performed a text regression task to predict the volatility of stock prices. Xie *et al.* [27] introduced a novel tree representation, and use it to train predictive models with tree kernels using support vector machines. Hagenau *et al.* [10] extract a large scale of expressive features to represent the unstructured text data and employs a robust feature selection to enhance the stock prediction.

Another major aspects for market news mining is to analyze sentiments from public news and social media, and then use it to predict market trends. Li *et al.* [16] implements a generic stock price prediction framework using sentiment analysis. Zhou*et al.* [29] studies particularly the Chinese stock market. They conduct a thorough study over 10 million stock-relevant tweets from Weibo, and find five attributes that stock market in China can be competently predicted by various online emotions. Nguyen *et al.*[23] explicitly consider the topics relating to the target stocks, and extracting topics and related sentiments from social media to make prediction.

While there have been many efforts in exploiting news for stock prediction, few of them paid enough attention to the quality, trustworthiness, and comprehensiveness of news, which highly affects the effectiveness of textual analysis. In this paper, we address the challenge of chaotic news by imitating the learning process of human beings, inspired by which we propose a Hybrid Attention Networks (HAN) to predict the stock trend based on the sequence of recent related news and employ self-paced learning for effective and efficient learning.

3 EMPIRICAL ANALYSIS

In this section, through empirical analysis, we will reveal three principles of the human learning process with respect to stock trend prediction via chaotic news. These principles can consequently provide essential guidelines in designing our learning framework.

3.1 Sequential Context Dependency

Due to the diverse quality of online financial news, human investors usually prefer not to rely on a single piece of news to make prediction due to its limited or even vague information. Instead, by broadly analyzing a sequence of news and combining them into a unified context, each news can provide complementary information and thus a more reliable assessment of stock trend can be made.

For example, Figure 1 illustrates two news sequences referring to petrol industry reforms happening in September 2014 and March 2017, respectively. The figure also displays the share price of SINOPEC, which is one of the biggest petrol companies in China.

From the figure, we can see two yellow circles with the *fluctuation* sign that represent two news declaring the initiation of two reforms, respectively. By merely referring to the two news, we can hardly tell the future trend of SINOPEC, since they revealed quite limited details about the reforms. However, the difference between these two reforms could be inferred by their previous news sequences. In particular, previous news with the *down* sign on September 2014 indicated that the reform might cause negative effects; while on March 2017, the news with the *rise* sign demonstrates quite positive signals.

In reality, human investors can naturally synthesize these analytical reports before the reforms actually began, in order to better assess the influence of these reforms on relevant stocks. Therefore, to imitate such analysis process as a human, an ideal framework should integrate and interpret each news in a sequential temporal context, rather than analyze them separately.

3.2 Diverse Influence

Significant news has more intensive and durable influence on the market than those trivial ones. For example, the third news with the *down* sign in Figure 1(b) summarizes that the share price of SINOPEC has been continuously going down, which should give a negative signal to the stock trend. However, compared with the positive news reporting the reform on petrol industry in the same period, this negative one yields much less importance. As it turns out later, after the SINOPEC's price drops down for only one day, it starts to rise up and keeps the uptrend for quite a long time, proving that the influence of the negative news is indeed weaker than the positive one.

Based on the diversity of news influence, we can conclude that when analyzing the news, an ideal framework should have the ability to distinguish the news with more intensive and durable influence, and pay more attention to them.

3.3 Effective and Efficient Learning

News cannot always provide an informative indication of the stock trend, especially when there exists only an insufficient number of news about specific stocks in a period. According to the online news we collected, Figure 2 shows the occurrence rates of the situation that there is no news about a particular stock "Jiai Technology" for consecutive l days or more. Within those 8.4% of time periods when there is no news reported for more than 10 days, it is quite tough to make any news-oriented prediction. Additionally, other situations, such as the aggregation of vague news, also introduce difficulties to the prediction.

Such diverse difficulty in news-oriented stock trend prediction task has motivated human investors to find a more effective and efficient learning process. In reality, human investors tend to first gain an overall knowledge by focusing on common occasions, and then turn to exceptional cases.

Inspired by this, an ideal learning framework for stock prediction should follow a similar process, which in particular conducts learning on more informative news at the earlier stage, and further optimized to tackle harder samples.

4 DEEP LEARNING FRAMEWORK FOR NEWS-ORIENTED TREND PREDICTION

In this section, we first formalize the problem of the stock trend prediction. Then, we present our framework based on the three design principles discussed in Empirical Analysis (Section 3). We first propose a Hybrid Attention Networks (HAN), which consists of two attention layers on news level and temporal level, respectively. Next, we incorporate a self-paced learning mechanism that enables

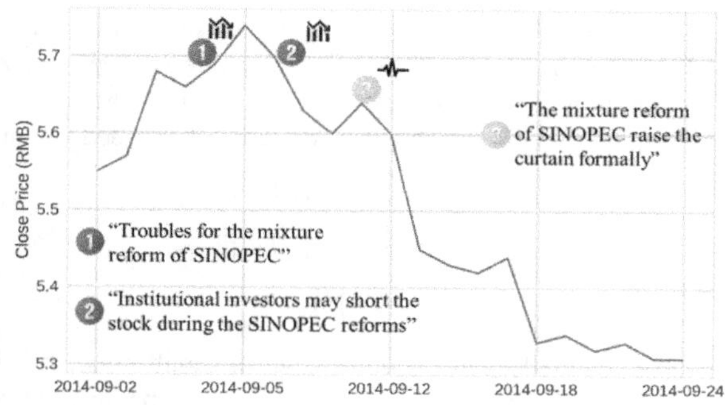

(a) Industry reform of SINOPEC on September, 2014

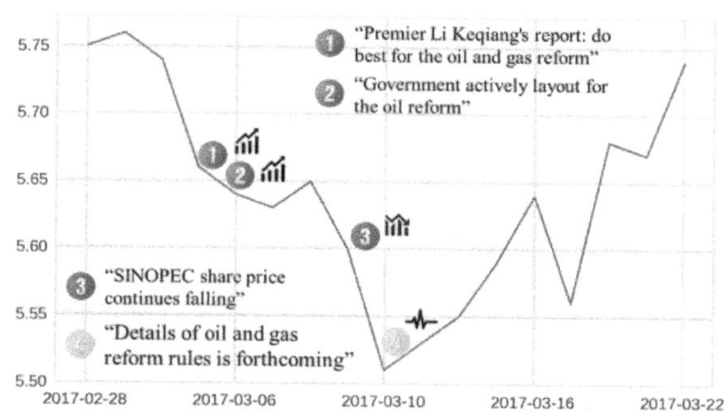

(b) Industry reform of SINOPEC on March, 2017

Figure 1: An example of two news sequences about the petrol industry reform, jointly shown with the stock price of SINOPEC that is one of the biggest petrol companies in China. In the figure, red, green and yellow circles represent negative, positive and neutral news respectively.

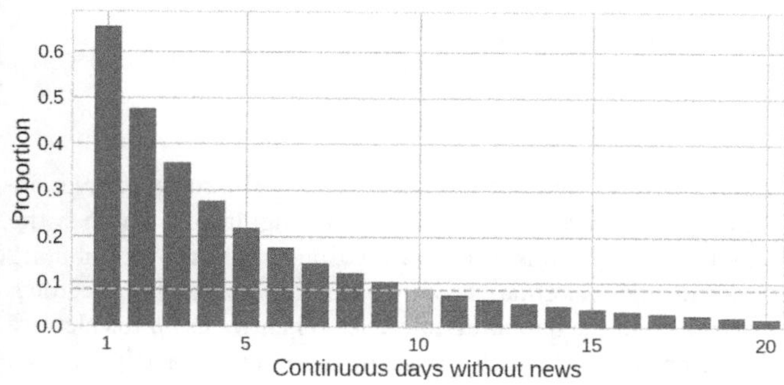

Figure 2: Proportion of the consecutive days without news.

the model to adjust the learning sequence in order to achieve better performance.

4.1 Problem Statement

We regard the problem of stock trend prediction as a classification problem. For a given date t and a given stock s, we can calculate its rise percent by:

$$Rise\_Percent(t) = \frac{Open\_Price(t+1) - Open\_Price(t)}{Open\_Price(t)}$$

Similar to many previous studies, we can divide rise percent into three classes: *DOWN*, *UP*, and *PRESERVE*, representing the significant dropping, rising, and steady stock trend on the next date, respectively.

The stock trend prediction task can be formulated as follows: given the length of a time sequence N, the stock s and date t, the goal is to use the news corpus sequence from time $t-N$ to $t-1$, denoted as $[C_{t-N}, C_{t-N+1}, ..., C_{t-1}]$, to predict the class of $Rise\_Percent(t)$, i.e. *DOWN*, *UP*, or *PRESERVE*. Note that each news corpus C_i contains a set of news with the size of L, $C_i = [n_{i1}, n_{i2}, ..., n_{iL}]$, denoting L related news on date i.

4.2 Hybrid Attention Networks

Based on the **Sequential Context Dependency** principle, our framework should interpret and analyze news in the sequential temporal context and pay more attention to critical time periods. In addition, based on the **Diverse Influence** principle, our framework should distinguish more significant news from others. To capture these two principles, we design a hybrid attention network (HAN), which incorporates attention mechanisms at both the news level and the temporal level.

We summarize the overall framework in Figure 3. Given the input of a news corpus sequence, a news embedding layer encodes each news into a news vector n_{ti}. Next, a news-level attention layer assigns an attention value to each news vector in a date, and calculate the weighted mean of these news vectors as a corpus vector for this date. Afterwards, these corpus vectors are encoded by a bi-directional Gated Recurrent Units (GRU). Then, another temporal attention layer assigns an attention value to each date, and calculate the weighted mean of these encoded corpus vectors to represent the overall sequential context information. Finally, the classification is made by a discriminative network. The details of the architecture are elaborated below.

News Embedding: For each ith news in news corpus C_t of date t, we use a word embedding layer to calculate the embedded vector for each word and then average all the words' vectors to construct a news vector n_{ti}. To reduce the complexity of the framework, we pre-train an unsupervised Word2Vec as the word embedding layer rather than tuning its parameters in the learning process.

News-level Attention: Since not all news contributes equally to predicting the stock trend, we introduce an attention mechanism to aggregate the news weighted by an assigned attention value, in order to reward the news offering critical information. Specifically,

$$u_{ti} = sigmoid(W_n n_{ti} + b_n)$$

$$\alpha_{ti} = \frac{exp(u_{ti})}{\sum_j exp(u_{tj})}$$

$$d_t = \sum_i \alpha_{ti} n_{ti}$$

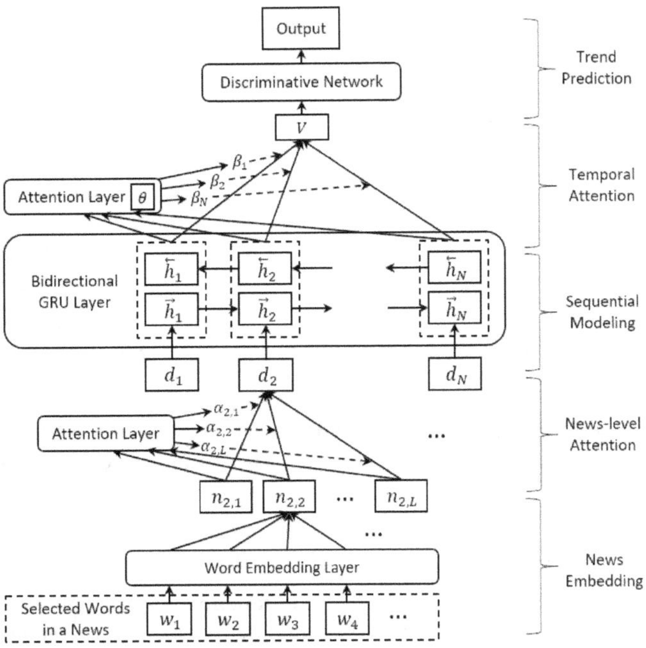

Figure 3: The overall framework of the Hybrid Attention Networks (HAN).

We first estimate attention values by feeding the news vector n_{ti} through a one-layer network to get the news-level attention value u_{ti}, and then calculate a normalized attention weight α_{ti} through a softmax function. Finally, we calculate the overall corpus vector d_t as a weighted sum of each news vector respectively, and use this vector to represent all news information for date t. Thus, we get a temporal sequence of corpus vector $D = [d_i], i \in [1, N]$. Obviously, the attention layer can be trained end-to-end and thus gradually learn to assign more attention to the reliable and informative news based on its content.

Sequential Modeling: To encode the temporal sequence of corpus vectors, we adopt Gated Recurrent Units (GRU). GRU is a variant of recurrent neural networks that uses a gating mechanism to check the state of sequences without separate memory cells. At date t, the GRU computes the news state h_t by linearly interpolating the previous state h_{t-1} and the current updated state $\tilde{h}_t$, as:

$$h_t = (1 - z_t) * h_{t-1} + z_t * \tilde{h}_t$$

The current updated state $\tilde{h}_t$ is computed by non-linearly combining the corpus vector input for this time-stamp and the previous state, as:

$$\tilde{h}_t = tanh(W_h d_t + r_t * (U_h h_{t-1}) + b_h)$$

where r_t denotes the reset gate, controlling how much past state should be used for updating the new state, and z_t is the update gate, deciding how much past information should be kept and how much new information should be added. These two gates are calculated by:

$$r_t = \sigma(W_r d_t + U_r h_{t-1} + b_r)$$
$$z_t = \sigma(W_z d_t + U_z h_{t-1} + b_z)$$

Therefore, we can get the latent vector for each date t through GRU. In order to capture the information from the past and future of a news as its context, we concatenate the latent vectors from both directions to construct a bi-directional encoded vector h_i as:

$$\overrightarrow{h_i} = \overrightarrow{GRU}(d_i), i \in [1, L]$$
$$\overleftarrow{h_i} = \overleftarrow{GRU}(d_i), i \in [L, 1]$$
$$h_i = [\overrightarrow{h_i}, \overleftarrow{h_i}]$$

The resulted h_i incorporates the information of both its surrounding context and itself. In this way, we encode the temporal sequence of corpus vectors.

Temporal Attention: Since the news published at different dates contribute to the stock trend unequally, we adopt the temporal-level attention mechanism, which incorporates both the inherent temporal pattern and the news content, to distinguish the temporal difference as:

$$o_i = sigmoid(W_h h_i + b_h)$$
$$\beta_i = \frac{exp(\theta_i o_i)}{\sum_j exp(\theta_j o_j)}$$
$$V = \sum_i \beta_i h_i$$

where θ_i is the parameter for each date in the softmax layer, indicating in general which date is more significant, and o is the latent representations of encoded corpus vectors. By combining them through a softmax layer, we can get an attention vector β to distinguish the temporal difference. Then we use β to calculate the weighted sum V, so that it can incorporate the sequential news context information with temporal attention, and will be used for classification.

Trend Prediction: The final discriminative network is a standard Multi-layer Perceptron (MLP), which takes V as input and produces the three-class classification of the future stock trend.

4.3 Self-paced Learning Mechanism

As discussed in Section 3.3, there exist some natural challenges of news-oriented stock trend prediction, such as the scarceness of news and the aggregation of vague news, which cause severe learning difficulties. To conduct an effective and efficient learning, the designed model should skip those challenging training samples at the early training stages, and progressively incorporate them into the model training.

Curriculum Learning [4] is a learning mode that can imitate such a learning process. However, the sequence of training samples in curriculum learning is fixed by predetermined heuristics (curriculum), which cannot be adjusted to the feedback from the dynamic learned models. To alleviate this issue, Kuma *et al.* [13] designed Self-Paced Learning (SPL) to embed curriculum design into the learning objective, so it can jointly optimize the curriculum and the learned model simultaneously.

Therefore, we take advantage of SPL in our framework to learn the news influence in an organized manner. Formally, given a training set $D = (x_i, y_i)_{i=1}^n$, where $x_i \in R^m$ denotes all the news inputs for the ith observed sample, and y_i represents the corresponding stock trend label. Let $L(y_i, HAN(x_i, w))$ denotes the loss function between label y_i and the output of the whole model $HAN(x_i, w)$, and w represents the model parameter to be learned. We assign each learning sample an importance weight v_i. The goal of SPL is to jointly learn the model parameter w and the latent weight $v = [v1, ..., v_n]$ by:

$$\min_{w, v \in [0,1]^n} E(w, v, \lambda) = \sum_{i=1}^{n} v_i L(y_i, HAN(x_i, w)) + f(v; \lambda) \quad (1)$$

where f denotes a self-paced regularizer which controls the learning scheme for penalizing the latent weight variables, and λ is a hyper-parameter that controls the pace at which the model learns new samples. In this paper, we choose the linear regularizer proposed in [11], which linearly discriminates samples with respect to their loss, as:

$$f(v; \lambda) = \frac{1}{2}\lambda \sum_{i=1}^{n} (v_i^2 - 2v_i) \quad (2)$$

Similar to [11] [13], we adopt Alternative Convex Search (ACS)[9] to solve Equation (1). ACS divides the variables into two disjoint blocks. In each iteration, a block of variables is optimized while fixing the other block. With the fixed w, the unconstrained close-formed solution for the linear regularizer (2) can be calculated by:

$$v_i^* = argmin_v E(w^*, v, \lambda) = \begin{cases} -\frac{1}{\lambda} l_i + 1 & l_i < \lambda \\ 0 & l_i \geq \lambda \end{cases}$$

where v_i^* denotes the ith element in the iterated optimal solution, and l_i denotes the loss for each element $L(y_i, HAN(x_i, w))$. In this way, the latent weight for samples that are different to what model has already learned will receive a linear penalty.

Algorithm 1 Self-paced Learning.

Require: Input dataset, D; linear regularizer, f; self-paced step size, μ;
Ensure: Model Parameter, w;
1: Initialize v^* evenly;
2: **while** not converged **do**
3: Update $w^* = argmin_w E(w, v^*, \lambda)$;
4: Update $v^* = argmin_v E(w^*, v, \lambda)$;
5: **if** λ is small **then**
6: increase λ by the stepsize μ;
7: **end if**
8: **end while**
9: **return** w^*;

Based on the optimization equation, the overall learning process can be abstracted as Algorithm 1. It alternates between two optimization steps described in ACS until the model finally converges: Step 3 learns the optimal model parameters with the fixed and most recent v^* by standard back-propagation mechanism; Step 4 learns the optimal weight variables with the fixed w^* by the linear regulizer. Noted that a small initial λ let only samples with rather small loss affect the learning. As the training progresses and λ increases in Step 6, samples with larger loss will be gradually incorporated, realizing the effective and efficient learning.

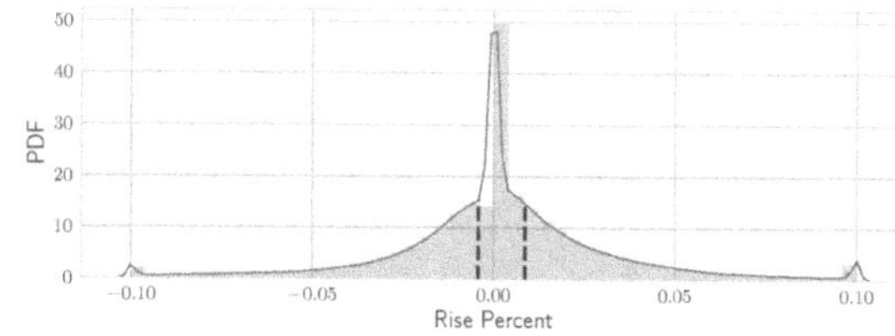

Figure 4: Distribution of the rise percent among the whole dataset.

5 EVALUATION

In this section, we first present our experimental setup. Then, we conduct comprehensive experiments to evaluate the performance of our proposed deep learning framework, followed by a systematic trading simulation to examine the effectiveness of our framework on the real-world market.

5.1 Experimental Setup

5.1.1 Data Collection. We obtained the Chinese stock data, including time series in terms of price and trading volume from 2014 to 2017 in daily frequency. There are totally 2527 stocks, covering the vast majority of Chinese stocks.

In the meantime, we collected 1, 271, 442 economic news between 2014 and 2017*. For each news, we extracted the publication timestamp, title, and its content.

Then, we correlate each of the collected news to a specific stock if the news mentioned the name of the stock in the title or content. We then filter out the news without any correlation to stocks. After such a process, the total news amount is 425, 250. For each stock, we then aggregate all the news in a certain date to construct the daily news corpus.

5.1.2 Learning Settings. To specify the label of the classification problem, we set up two particular thresholds to bin the rise percents, i.e., *DOWN* ($Rise\_Percent(t) < -0.41\%$), *UP* ($Rise\_Percent(t) > 0.87\%$), and *PRESERVE* ($-0.41\% \leq Rise\_Percent(t) \leq 0.87\%$). We define the thresholds so that the three categories are approximately even, as is shown in Figure 4.

For the following experiments, we split the dataset into a training set (66.7%) from September 2014 to May 2016, and a test set (33.3%) from May 2016 to March 2017. Then we further randomly sample a validation set from the training set with 10% size of it, in order to optimize the hyper-parameters and choose the best epoch.

In all the following experiments, we tokenize each news and remove the stop words and the words appearing less than 5 times to build the vocabulary. We then obtain the word-level embedding by training an un-supervised CBOW Word2Vec[17] model with the dimension of 500 through the whole dataset. All the models use the length of a time sequence N as 10.

5.1.3 Compared Methods. To evaluate the effectiveness of our proposed deep learning framework, we compare our result with the performance of the following methods:

*The news data are collected from two famous economic websites in China: http://www.eastmoney.com/ and http://finance.sina.com.cn/.

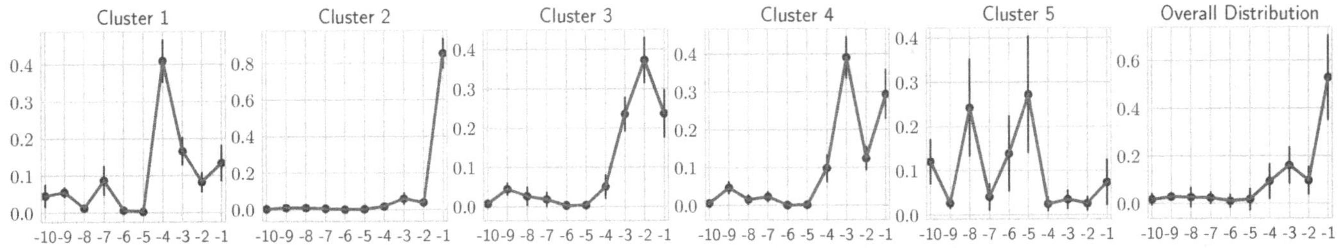

Figure 5: The five attention weight clusters for temporal attention in different context, along with an overall distribution of all the attention weights.

Figure 6: Three classes of demonstrative news in different levels of attention values.

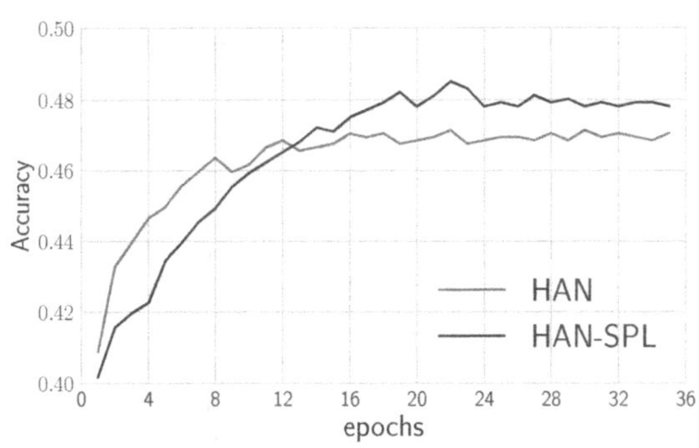

Figure 7: The learning curves of the model using self-paced learning and that without using SPL.

Random Forest: we use the Random Forest (RF) classifier, with the number of trees in the forest as 200. we define a corpus vector for one date by averaging all news vectors of a certain date, and concatenate the corpus vector in 10 days to construct the input.
Multi-layer Perceptron: we use the multilayer perceptron (MLP) classifier, with three layers of sizes as 256, 128, and 64, respectively. The input of MLP is the same as that in RF.
News-RNN: We use a bi-directional GRU-based RNN, with the dimensionality of RNN output layer as 64. The RNN model takes corpus vectors organized in a temporal sequence as the input.
One-RNN: To evaluate the effectiveness of bi-directional setting, we use a standard one-direction GRU-based RNN as a comparison with News-RNN.
Temporal-Attention-RNN: To evaluate the temporal attention layer, we use Temporal-Attention-RNN (Temp-ATT) by adding a single temporal-level attention layer on top of the News-RNN.
News-Attention-RNN: To evaluate the news attention layer, we use News-Attention-RNN (News-ATT) by adding a single news-level attention layer to process corpus vector before the News-RNN.
HAN: Our proposed hybrid attention networks with the normal learning process.
HAN-SPL: Our proposed hybrid attention networks with self-paced learning process.

5.2 Effects of Two Attention Mechanisms

5.2.1 Demonstration on News Attention. Since the news attention values are constructed by a single perception with the embedded news vector as input, we can calculate the attention values for every piece of news on the testing dataset. To validate whether our framework can select significant news and filter out those less informative ones, Figure 6 shows some detailed results of the news attention. In this figure, the number in front of the news is the attention value, and it shows demonstrative news within three classes that have the lowest, middle, and highest attention values, respectively. From the figure, we can find that the sentences with the lowest attention value merely display the price and the code of the corresponding stock, which obviously have no implication to the future trend; the news with the middle attention value records the previous market performance of the corresponding stock, which provides some information of the stock; the news with the highest value describes some prediction from official analyst or some significant events, which explicitly contain the predictive information to the market trend. These cases clearly illustrate that our news attention mechanism can indeed distinguish important news from uninformative ones, explaining why it can boost the performance.

5.2.2 Visualization of Temporal Attention. To further illustrate the effect of temporal attention, we calculate all the temporal attention vectors on the testing dataset. As is shown in Figure 5, the last plot with the title *Overall Distribution* implies that, in general, the news reported recently has more impact on the current stock trend than those reported earlier.

Next, we adopt the spectral cluster method to generate five clusters representing different patterns of temporal attention, as is

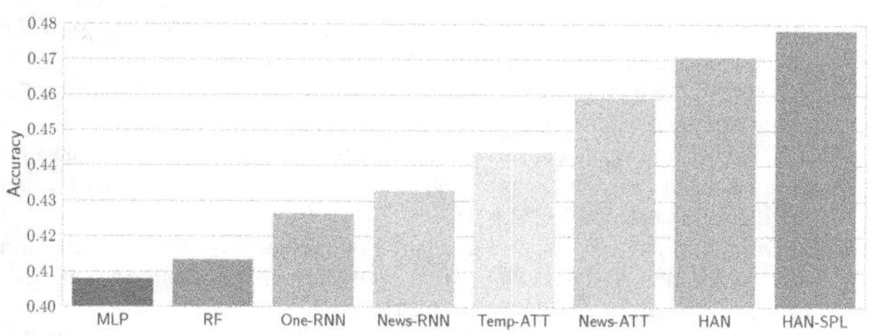

Figure 8: The accuracy result for different methods.

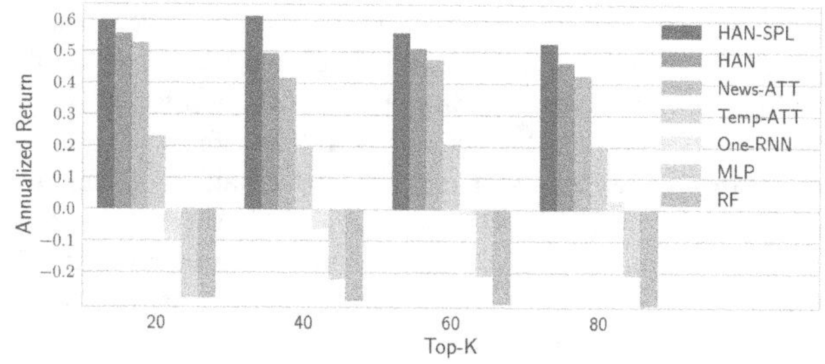

Figure 9: The annualized return for different methods.

Figure 10: The cumulative profit curve of different methods with the portfolio of choosing top 40 stocks.

shown in the first five plots in Figure 5. We can find that despite the overall distribution, in different contexts with different news contents, the attention distribution can be quite diverse as well as dynamic. The informative news even in a few days ago can also express their influences in the temporal attention layer.

5.3 Effects of Self-paced learning

To evaluate the effectiveness of the self-paced learning (SPL) in our framework, we compare the training process using the SPL with that using the standard training process. Both the convergence speed and the final result are considered as the comparison metric. As is shown in Figure 7, at the beginning, the learning speed for SPL is slower than the one without using it, probably because SPL could neglect some difficult samples at early stages. However, as the round of epochs increases, the testing accuracy of the model using SPL gradually outperforms the one without using it, and eventually converge to a better result.

5.4 Overall Performance Experiments

5.4.1 Classification Accuracy Result. In the experimental setting of a tri-label classification problem, as the three label is approximately evenly split, we choose accuracy, which means the proportion of true results among the total number of testing samples, as the evaluation metric. The final results of all the methods are shown in Figure 8, in which each bar indicates the average accuracy of the testing dataset. Our proposed framework is able to gain the best accuracy result among all the baseline methods.

5.4.2 Market Trading Simulation. To further evaluate the effectiveness of our proposed framework, we conduct a back-testing by simulating the stock trading for approximately one year, from May 2016 to March 2017.

Our estimation strategy conducts the trading in the daily frequency. At the beginning of each trading date, the model will give each stock a score based on the probability to have a rising trend minus the probability to have a declining trend. Based on these scores, a straightforward portfolio construction strategy called top-K selects K stocks with the highest scores to construct a new portfolio for the next trading day. The selected K stocks are evenly invested according to their *OpenPrices* of the next trading day. To approximate the real-world trading, we also consider a transaction cost of 0.3% for each trading. We also calculate the average return on the stock market by evenly holding every stock as the baseline, indicating the overall market trend.

To evaluate the performance of each prediction method, we use the annualized return as the metric, which is the cumulative profit per year. In reality, investors always choose multiple stocks to avoid risks. Therefore, we evenly invest on top K stocks, where k is set as 20, 40, 60 and 80, respectively, to compare the results in Figure 9. In general, the highest profits should be obtained by selecting the most top stocks. However, when the K is 20, the improvement is not that obvious. It is because that selecting few stocks is likely to cause high turnover rate, which leads to high transaction cost and offsets the profits. The detailed comparison and analysis of each algorithm will be elaborated in the next section.

We also plot a cumulative profit curve for each method with K as 40. As is illustrated in Figure 10, the cumulative profit results are consistent with the Overall Performance Analysis (section 5.4), and our proposed framework is able to gain the best profit result among all the baseline methods.

5.5 Performance Discussion

As illustrated in Figure 8 and 9, the relative comparison in terms of both the accuracy and the annualized return are consistent among different methods. Furthermore, the profit curves in Figure 10 demonstrated that the profit gaps between different methods almost do not change along the time. More importantly, our proposed framework, HAN-SPL, can achieve the best accuracy of 0.478 (Figure 8) as well as the highest profits in all different settings (Figure 9). In particular, the highest annualized return 0.611 are obtained while investing on top 40 stocks, which is a remarkable improvement compared to the Market performance of 0.04. In the following, we further analyze the results of different methods to discuss why our proposed framework can take effects:

Discussion on the RNN setting: The performances of MLP and RF are apparently worse than the others, probably because the input to these two methods are not organized in sequential contexts. To some extent, this result indicates the significance to use RNN, which processes the news in the sequential context.

Discussion on the bi-directional GRU setting: In our experiments, the News-RNN and One-RNN share the similar model structure, except that News-RNN uses a bi-directional GRU while One-RNN uses a one-directional GRU. From the figures, we can see that the News-RNN outperforms the One-RNN, which indicates that the bi-directional setting of News-RNN can utilize the information from both past and future so as to enhance the prediction.

Discussion on the attention mechanisms: As we can see from the figures, the two baseline models with one attention layer, Temp-ATT and News-ATT, can achieve a better result than that of News-RNN, which has no attention layer, indicating the effectiveness to distinguish diverse influences of different news and dates.

Discussion on our proposed HAN framework: When we combine the two attention layers, our HAN can achieve even higher performance than all above-mentioned models, indicating the effectiveness of our overall model structure. In addition, the HAN model trained by self-paced learning (HAN-SPL) outperforms HAN with the standard training process, which shows the importance of effective and efficient learning. In Figure 10, our HAN-SPL significantly outperforms all other methods for all the test time, which shows our proposed framework is indeed effective in the problem of stock trend prediction.

6 CONCLUSION AND FUTURE WORK

In this paper, we pointed out three principles for news-oriented stock trend prediction, including *sequential context dependency*, *diverse influence* and *effective and efficient learning*, by imitating the learning process of human. Based on these principles, we proposed a new learning framework, particularly a Hybrid Attention Network (HAN) with self-paced learning mechanism, for stock trend prediction from online news. Extensive experiments on real stock market data demonstrated that our proposed framework can result in significant improvement in terms of the accuracy of stock trend prediction. Meanwhile, through back-testing, our framework can produce appreciable profits, with highly increased annualized excess return, in a one-year round trading simulation.

In the future, beyond modeling the sequence of news related to one stock, we plan to further leverage the relationship between news related to different individual stocks, according to their industrial connections in real world. Moreover, we will investigate how to integrate the news-oriented approach with technical analysis for more accurate stock trend prediction.

REFERENCES

[1] K. Adam, A. Marcet, and J. P. Nicolini. Stock market volatility and learning. *The Journal of Finance*, 71(1):33–82, 2016.
[2] A. A. Adebiyi, A. O. Adewumi, and C. K. Ayo. Comparison of arima and artificial neural networks models for stock price prediction. *Journal of Applied Mathematics*, 2014.
[3] R. Akita, A. Yoshihara, T. Matsubara, and K. Uehara. Deep learning for stock prediction using numerical and textual information. In *Proceedings of the 15th International Conference on Information Systems*, pages 1–6, 2016.
[4] Y. Bengio, J. Louradour, R. Collobert, and J. Weston. Curriculum learning. *Journal of the American Podiatry Association*, 60(60):6, 2009.
[5] X. Ding, Y. Zhang, T. Liu, and J. Duan. Deep learning for event-driven stock prediction. In *Proceedings of the 24th International Joint Conference on Artificial Intelligence*, pages 2327–2333, 2015.
[6] X. Ding, Y. Zhang, T. Liu, and J. Duan. Knowledge-driven event embedding for stock prediction. In *Proceedings of the 26th International Conference on Computational Linguistics*, pages 2133–2142, 2016.
[7] Q. Gao. *Stock market forecasting using recurrent neural network*. PhD thesis, University of Missouri–Columbia, 2016.
[8] M. Göçken, M. Özçalıcı, A. Boru, and A. T. Dosdoğru. Integrating metaheuristics and artificial neural networks for improved stock price prediction. *Expert Systems with Applications*, 44:320–331, 2016.
[9] J. Gorski, F. Pfeuffer, and K. Klamroth. Biconvex sets and optimization with biconvex functions: a survey and extensions. *Mathematical Methods of Operations Research*, 66(3):373–407, 2007.
[10] M. Hagenau, M. Liebmann, and D. Neumann. Automated news reading: Stock price prediction based on financial news using context-capturing features. *Decision Support Systems*, 55(3):685–697, 2013.
[11] L. Jiang, D. Meng, Q. Zhao, S. Shan, and A. Hauptmann. Self-paced curriculum learning. In *Proceedings of the 29th AAAI Conference on Artificial Intelligence*, pages 2694–2700, 2015.
[12] K.-J. Kim and H. Ahn. Simultaneous optimization of artificial neural networks for financial forecasting. *Applied Intelligence*, pages 887–898, 2012.
[13] M. P. Kumar, B. Packer, and D. Koller. Self-paced learning for latent variable models. 1:1189–1197, 2010.
[14] L. A. Laboissiere, R. A. Fernandes, and G. G. Lage. Maximum and minimum stock price forecasting of brazilian power distribution companies based on artificial neural networks. *Applied Soft Computing*, 35:66–74, 2015.
[15] L. Li, S. Leng, J. Yang, and M. Yu. Stock market autoregressive dynamics: A multinational comparative study with quatile regression. In *Mathematical Problems in Engineering*, 2016.
[16] X. Li, H. Xie, L. Chen, J. Wang, and X. Deng. News impact on stock price return via sentiment analysis. *Knowledge-Based Systems*, 69(1):14–23, 2014.
[17] T. Mikolov, K. Chen, G. Corrado, and J. Dean. Efficient estimation of word representations in vector space. *arXiv preprint arXiv:1301.3781*, 2013.
[18] A. K. Nassirtoussi, S. Aghabozorgi, T. Y. Wah, and D. C. L. Ngo. Text mining of news-headlines for forex market prediction: A multi-layer dimension reduction algorithm with semantics and sentiment. *Expert Systems with Applications*, 42(1):306–324, 2015.
[19] R. K. Nayak, D. Mishra, and A. K. Rath. A naive svm-knn based stock market trend reversal analysis for indian benchmark indices. In *Applied Soft Computing*, 2015.
[20] W. Nuij, V. Milea, F. Hogenboom, F. Frasincar, and U. Kaymak. An automated framework for incorporating news into stock trading strategies. *IEEE Transactions on Knowledge and Data Engineering*, 2(11):823–835, 2014.
[21] J. Patel, S. Shah, P. Thakkar, and K. Kotecha. Predicting stock market index using fusion of machine learning techniques. *Expert Systems with Applications*, 42(4):2162–2172, 2015.
[22] A. M. Rather, A. Agarwal, and V. Sastry. Recurrent neural network and a hybrid model for prediction of stock returns. *Expert Systems with Applications*, 42(6):3234–3241, 2015.
[23] J. Si, A. Mukherjee, B. Liu, Q. Li, H. Li, and X. Deng. Exploiting topic based twitter sentiment for stock prediction. In *Proceedings of the 51st Annual Meeting of the Association for Computational Linguistics*, pages 24–29, 2013.
[24] P. C. Tetlock. Giving content to investor sentiment: The role of media in the stock market. *Journal of Finance*, 62(3):1139âĂŞ1168, 2007.
[25] J. L. Ticknor. A bayesian regularized artificial neural network for stock market forecasting. *Expert Systems with Applications*, 40(14):5501–5506, 2013.
[26] W. Y. Wang and Z. Hua. A semiparametric gaussian copula regression model for predicting financial risks from earnings calls. In *Proceedings of the 52nd Annual Meeting of the Association for Computational Linguistics*, pages 1155–1165, 2014.
[27] B. Xie, R. J. Passonneau, L. Wu, and G. G. Creamer. Semantic frames to predict stock price movement. In *Proceedings of the 51st Annual Meeting of the Association for Computational Linguistics*, pages 873–883, 2013.
[28] L. Zhang, C. Aggarwal, and G.-J. Qi. Stock price prediction via discovering multi-frequency trading patterns. In *Proceedings of the 23rd ACM SIGKDD International Conference on Knowledge Discovery and Data Mining*, pages 2141–2149, 2017.
[29] Z. Zhou, J. Zhao, and K. Xu. Can online emotions predict the stock market in china? In *Proceedings of the 17th International Conference on Web Information Systems Engineering*, pages 328–342. Springer, 2016.

Exploring Expert Cognition for Attributed Network Embedding

Xiao Huang,[†] Qingquan Song,[†] Jundong Li,[‡] Xia Hu[†]
[†]Department of Computer Science and Engineering, Texas A&M University, College Station, TX, USA 77843
[‡]Computer Science and Engineering, Arizona State University, Tempe, AZ, USA 85281
{xhuang,qqsong,xiahu}@tamu.edu,jundongl@asu.edu

ABSTRACT

Attributed network embedding has been widely used in modeling real-world systems. The obtained low-dimensional vector representations of nodes preserve their proximity in terms of both network topology and node attributes, upon which different analysis algorithms can be applied. Recent advances in explanation-based learning and human-in-the-loop models show that by involving experts, the performance of many learning tasks can be enhanced. It is because experts have a better cognition in the latent information such as domain knowledge, conventions, and hidden relations. It motivates us to employ experts to transform their meaningful cognition into concrete data to advance network embedding. However, learning and incorporating the expert cognition into the embedding remains a challenging task. Because expert cognition does not have a concrete form, and is difficult to be measured and laborious to obtain. Also, in a real-world network, there are various types of expert cognition such as the comprehension of word meaning and the discernment of similar nodes. It is nontrivial to identify the types that could lead to a significant improvement in the embedding. In this paper, we study a novel problem of exploring expert cognition for attributed network embedding and propose a principled framework NEEC. We formulate the process of learning expert cognition as a task of asking experts a number of concise and general queries. Guided by the exemplar theory and prototype theory in cognitive science, the queries are systematically selected and can be generalized to various real-world networks. The returned answers from the experts contain their valuable cognition. We model them as new edges and directly add into the attributed network, upon which different embedding methods can be applied towards a more informative embedding representation. Experiments on real-world datasets verify the effectiveness and efficiency of NEEC.

ACM Reference Format:
Xiao Huang, Qingquan Song, Jundong Li, Xia Hu. 2018. Exploring Expert Cognition for Attributed Network Embedding. In *Proceedings of WSDM'18.* ACM, New York, NY, USA, 9 pages. https://doi.org/10.1145/3159652.3159655

1 INTRODUCTION

Attributed networks are pervasive in real-world systems such as social media and protein-protein interaction networks, where both node dependencies and rich attribute information describing the properties of nodes are available. Attributed network embedding [14, 18] provides an efficient way to model the two information sources jointly. It aims to map each node into a low-dimensional vector representation such that its proximity in terms of both topological structure and node attributes are well preserved. The learned representations could be applied to and advance the performance of many real-world mining tasks, such as node classification [34, 49], community detection [27], and anomaly detection [22].

The helpfulness of expert cognition motivates us to investigate the potential of utilizing it to learn more informative embedding representations. We define the *expert cognition* as the intelligence-related information that experts know beyond the data, such as the understanding of domain knowledge [45], the awareness of conventions [7], and the perception of latent relations. An example would be the comprehension of bias in sampling, e.g., meteorologists know that tornadoes were more likely to be recorded in areas with more population [7]. Existing work such as explanation-based learning [8] and human-in-the-loop models [12, 17] suggest that the involvement of experts could increase the performance of many learning tasks. Expert cognition plays an essential role in advancing these data analysis. Since most existing network embedding algorithms are data-driven, we are motivated to explore how to take advantage of the expert cognition to enhance the performance of embedding. Sentiment analysis is a typical example of the utilization of expert cognition, which has been successfully applied to improve the performance of different recommendations [48]. In product review platforms such as Epinions and Slashdot, items are recommended to users based on their historical reviews. It has been shown that most reviews convey different levels of sentiment polarization [13], and the expert-created sentiment lexicons such as MPQA and SentiWordNet [37] are widely used to advance the review analysis and recommendation [9, 48].

Although some efforts have been devoted to directly learning expert cognition from the existing human-generated data [9], such concrete related data is still often limited and could be in different forms. Motivated by the success of active learning [35, 36] and interactive data mining [1, 12], in this paper, we propose to explore expert cognition via actively querying the experts. We aim to convert their abstract cognition into concrete answers, and incorporate them into attributed network embedding towards a more informative low-dimensional representation.

However, actively exploring expert cognition is a nontrivial task, with three major challenges as follows. First, expert cognition does not have a concrete format and is not easy to be measured, since it is related to the intelligence. Traditional solutions are to design specific algorithms according to the experts' understanding [8, 17]. It

WSDM'18, February 5–9, 2018, Marina Del Rey, CA, USA

ACM ISBN 978-1-4503-5581-0/18/02...$15.00
https://doi.org/10.1145/3159652.3159655

is hard to be generalized as they involve enormous engineering experimentations to transform the domain knowledge to algorithms. Second, in a real-world system, there are usually various types of expert cognition such as the comprehension of word meaning and the discernment of missing edges [12]. It is difficult to model all of them, or identify the types that can lead a significant performance gain in the embedding within a limited number of trials. It is also expensive to design specific models for different attributed networks and different embedding algorithms. A general way of modeling the expert cognition is essential. Third, the expert cognition is laborious to obtain as it involves humans in the whole process. Given a limited amount of human effort, we aim to design the queries in an effective way to maximize the total amount of learned expert cognition. Meanwhile, the returned answers from the experts could be heterogeneous with the attributed network. It is desired to have answers that could be easily incorporated into the embedding.

To bridge the gap, we formally define the problem of exploring expert cognition for attributed network embedding and study three research questions. (1) How to design effective, general, and concise format of queries to save the experts' efforts? (2) How to select the most meaningful queries to maximize the total amount of learned expert cognition, given a limited amount of human effort? (3) How to quantify the amount of expert cognition that contained in the returned answers since it is necessary when evaluating the proposed solutions? Following these research objectives, we propose a general expert cognition learning and formulating framework NEEC, and our key contributions can be summarized as follows.

- Formally define the problem of exploring expert cognition for attributed network embedding.
- Present an efficient and concise framework NEEC that could provide the experts a small number of carefully designed general and concise queries, and their answers capture expert cognition systematically and can be directly added into the network to advance the embedding.
- Develop an effective algorithm to tackle the exploration and exploitation balancing in expert cognition learning.
- Empirically evaluate the effectiveness, generalizability, and efficiency of NEEC on three real-world datasets.

2 PROBLEM STATEMENT

Notations: We use a boldface lowercase alphabet to represent a vector (e.g., $\mathbf{u}$), and a boldface uppercase alphabet to denote a matrix (e.g., U). The transpose of a matrix is displayed as $\mathbf{U}^\top$, and the ith row of the matrix U is written as $\mathbf{u}_i$. We use u_{ij} to represent the $(i, j)^{\text{th}}$ element of the matrix U. We use I to represent the identity matrix. We use $\mathbf{S}^{(\cdot)}$ to denote the node proximity defined by the rows of a matrix. In this paper, we use cosine similarity as the proximity measure, and it is straightforward to extend to other measures.

The important symbols are listed in Table 1. Let G be the adjacency matrix of n connected nodes. Edge weights in G are set to be non-negative to have physical meanings. Let A denote the node attribute matrix. Its ith row represents the node attributes of node i. Suppose the raw data of A is human-readable such as the paper abstract or the product review. For ease of presentation, in this paper, we focus on the undirected networks and propose a general framework. It can also be directly applied to the directed networks.

Table 1: Main symbols and definitions.

Notations	Definitions
n	number of nodes in the network
d	dimension of the embedding representation
B	number of prototype nodes
K	number of queries the oracle can answer
$r_{i,k}$	reward obtained from node i at iteration k
$\mathbf{G} \in \mathbb{R}_+^{n\times n}$	weighted adjacency matrix
$\mathbf{A} \in \mathbb{R}_+^{n\times m}$	node attribute information matrix
$\mathbf{H} \in \mathbb{R}^{n\times d}$	final embedding representation
$\mathbf{U}^{(G)} \in \mathbb{R}^{n\times d}$	embedding representation of the network
$\mathbf{S}^{(\cdot)} \in \mathbb{R}^{n\times n}$	node proximity defined by rows of a matrix

Definition 1 (Expert Cognition) *For real-world attributed networks, the domain experts often have a better comprehension beyond the data, such as the understanding of domain knowledge, the awareness of conventions, and the perception of latent relations. We refer their knowledge on this type of abstract, meaningful, and intelligence-related information as the expert cognition.*

The expert cognition is often valuable but hard to be modeled. For instance, humans' comprehension of word meaning is essential to the analysis of social networks, since texts in social media could be informal and fast-evolving [13]. But it is challenging to generalize and model this comprehension. Another example is the experienced doctors' discernment of similar cases of illness, which is valuable to patients but difficult to be learned and performed by computers.

Instead of directly modeling expert cognition, we propose a novel way to learn it, i.e., querying the experts a number of trials to model their abstract cognition as concrete answers. The existing related data is often limited, and it is difficult to design specific models for different systems as the given data could be in various forms. Thus, in this paper, we focus on actively learning from the experts. It is motivated by the success of active learning [36], which has been shown to be helpful in reducing the efforts of labeling. The key idea is, if we are allowed to select the nodes for training, a comparable classification accuracy could be achieved even with fewer training labels. However, existing methods cannot be applied to our problem since it is often expensive to obtain concrete labels, such as the labels in ranking systems or community detection problems. Also, it is challenging to incorporate labels into the embedding since they are heterogeneous to the attributed network.

We aim to actively explore the expert cognition in a more general way. We refer experts as the oracle and formally define the problem of exploring expert cognition for attributed network embedding as:

> Given an attributed network G associated with node attributes A and corresponding raw data, we aim to seek a d-dimensional vector representation $\mathbf{h}_i$ for each node i, such that both the topological structure and node attribute proximity could be well preserved in H. Meanwhile, the system is allowed to learn from the oracle by performing K queries one by one. Given a limited amount of effort the oracle could devote, we aim to design the queries in a general and efficient way to include as much as possible expert cognition in the K returned answers. As a result, we could incorporate the answers into the embedding towards a more informative expert cognition informed representation H.

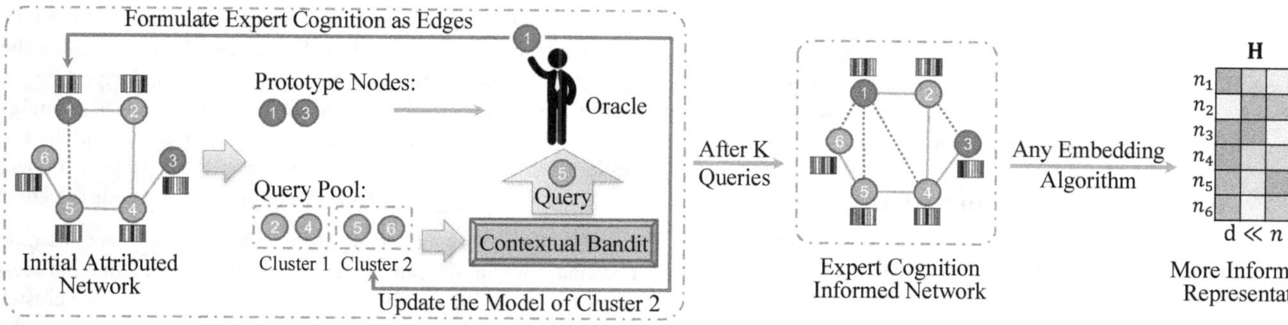

Figure 1: The overall structure of the proposed Network Embedding with Expert Cognition framework - NEEC.

3 EMBEDDING WITH EXPERT COGNITION

To efficiently model and assimilate the expert cognition actively learned from the oracle into attributed network embedding, we propose the Network Embedding with Expert Cognition framework - NEEC. It has three components as illustrated in Figure 1. (1) We design a general and concise form of queries to learn expert cognition from the oracle while greatly save his/her effort. It allows us to model the meaningful but abstract expert cognition as systematical answers. (2) We explore novel algorithms for the two steps to find the top K meaningful queries. The first step aims to find B representative and distinct nodes as prototypes, and the second step iteratively selects K nodes from the remaining nodes with the largest amount of expected learned expert cognition. (3) We formulate the returned K answers from the oracle as cognition edges and add them into the initial network structure. Figure 1 illustrates an example on a network of six nodes. We first select $B = 2$ nodes as prototypes (in red), and set the remaining nodes (in blue) as a query pool. In each query, we select a node i (e.g., $i = 5$) to query. The oracle needs to indicate a node from the prototypes (e.g., $j = 1$) that is the most similar to the queried node i. All these answers will be added into the network structure in the form of weighted edges, named as cognition edges (red dotted lines). In Figure 1, the queried nodes $i = 4, 5, 6$ are more similar to prototype node $j = 1$, so we add weighted edges between them. With these cognition edges, different attributed network embedding methods could be directly applied to the expert cognition informed network towards a more informative low-dimensional representation H.

3.1 Prototype-based Form of Queries

Given a limited amount of effort the oracle could devote, simpler queries would allow us to have a larger number of queries K. Meanwhile, we expect each query to be more effective in exploring the expert cognition from the oracle. These two aspects often contradict each other, since complex and specific queries tend to capture more information, but are both hard to design and answer.

An intuitive solution is to query the latent relations of node pairs to model the expert cognition as identified missing edges. However, it might not be efficient since the total number of queries K is quite limited compared with the total number of node pairs, i.e., $K \ll \binom{n}{2}$. It is also difficult to select the K most meaningful node pairs from all the unconnected pairs. Our proposed solution is to learn a more general type of node relations from the oracle, and in a systematical way to increase the total amount of learned expert cognition.

3.1.1 *Learning Expert Cognition with Prototypes.*

Based on the exemplar theory and prototype theory in cognitive science, we propose the prototype-based form of queries.

Theory 1 (Exemplar Theory) [28] *In psychology, humans cognize new stimuli by comparing with exemplars already have in memory, and classify objects based on their similarity to these exemplars.*

Theory 2 (Prototype Theory) [33] *For a category of stored exemplars in humans' memory, there exists an abstract average of all members called the prototype, and humans perform categorizations based on prototypes when experiencing new objects.*

Motivated by the process of humans cognizing new objects, we first select B nodes and define them as the prototypes of B categories respectively. Then we classify K other selected nodes into these B categories according to the oracle's cognition. Such classification process could capture the oracle's comprehensive comprehension of the K nodes. In the end, we formulate this valuable comprehension as cognition edges defined as follows.

Definition 2 (Prototype Node) *We select a small number (i.e., B) of representative nodes to serve as prototypes in the oracle's memory, and refer them as prototype nodes.*

Definition 3 (Cognition Edge) *In each query, we add an edge g_{ij} with a predefined weight γ between the newly selected node i and its most similar prototype node j. We refer g_{ij} as a cognition edge. If there is already an edge between nodes i and j in the initial network, we will add the weight γ into this edge.*

Figure 1 illustrates the basic idea of the prototype-based form of queries. Initially, nodes 1 and 3 are selected as prototype nodes. In each query, we select another new node i to query the oracle. He/she needs to determine node i is more similar to which prototype, based on his/her understanding of nodes' human-readable raw data and expertise. A cognition edge would be added to the network according to the returned answer. It models the category of node i in the oracle' cognition. After K queries, we could directly apply an embedding algorithm to the expert cognition informed network towards a more informative unified representation.

3.1.2 *Analysis of Prototype-based Form of Queries.*

We have proposed to learn the expert cognition with prototype nodes and model it as cognition edges. It enjoys several nice properties as follows. First, evaluating similarity takes a much smaller amount of human effort comparing to other technical tasks such as labeling. The prototype-based form of queries are general and simple with no specific similarity value required. Second, the data for some specific nodes might be limited, but domain experts' knowledge and cognition could help. For example, researchers can understand the main idea of papers by reading the abstracts, while these short paragraphs are often too limited to computers. Third, the oracle only needs to check $B + K$ nodes in total, which are selected from a pool with size n. It is much smaller than $\binom{n}{2}$.

3.2 Prototype Node Selection Algorithm

We propose two algorithms for the prototype node selection to handle different scenarios. The key idea is to make prototype nodes representative and avoid being too similar to each other, such that the oracle could easily distinguish them.

The first algorithm is k-medoids, motivated by the work of [29]. This algorithm is designed for the network with rich initial data. It aims to select B prototype nodes that cluster the entire n nodes into B distinct groups. An updating rule that similar to the k-means algorithm is employed. It first selects B nodes randomly, and then alternatively conducts the following two proceeds until no change could be made. (1) Assign nodes to their nearest prototype nodes' clusters based on node attribute similarity. (2) For each node, compute the sum of its similarities to all other nodes within the same cluster. For each cluster, set the node that has the maximum similarity sum as the new prototype node.

The second algorithm is a random strategy for networks with limited initial data or with a large number of nodes. We first select B nodes from the entire n nodes randomly, and then keep removing the prototype nodes that are too similar to each other and replacing them with new random nodes. The similarities are based on the initial attributed network.

3.3 Query Selection Algorithm

We have proposed to learn the expert cognition by linking nodes with their most similar prototype nodes. In such way, we formulate the query selection problem as a node selection task. The goal is to find K effective nodes to maximize the total amount of expert cognition contained in the learned cognition edges.

An intuitive solution is to greedily return the top K important nodes [26], aiming to make the learned cognition edges more meaningful. However, this might not end up with a good result. Because important nodes tend to have more edges included in the initial network [25], and the learned cognition edges would become less influential. It also fails to take other information into consideration, such as the feedback from the oracle and the node attributes.

3.3.1 Exploitation and Exploration Trade-off. To find the K effective nodes, we first formally define the problem. Let $r_{i,k}$ denote the amount of expert cognition contained in the kth returned answer, referred as *reward*. Here i denotes the kth node we have queried. We have no access to the reward $r_{i,k}$ before asking the kth query. The goal is to maximize the total rewards after all K queries, i.e.,

$$\underset{i \in \mathcal{P}_1}{\text{maximize}} \quad \mathcal{J}_K = \sum\nolimits_{k=1}^{K} r_{i,k}, \tag{1}$$

where $\mathcal{P}_k$ denotes the query pool in the kth iteration. In the first iteration, the initial $\mathcal{P}_1$ has $(n - B)$ nodes since we have employed B nodes as prototype nodes. For the node that is already selected previously, its reward is 0 since no new cognition edge would be added. We remove it from the pool and get the $\mathcal{P}_{k+1}$.

In the beginning, we have limited information about the relation between the node i and $r_{i,k}$. Therefore, when performing the querying, we aim to not only maximize the learned expert cognition in the current trial, but also explore the system to optimize the incoming iterations. To tackle this exploration and exploitation trade-off and maximize the total rewards $\mathcal{J}_K$, we propose a novel contextual bandit [21, 47] algorithm to perform the node selection.

3.3.2 Contextual Bandit Algorithm. Our main idea is to assume that nodes within the same cluster share the same model that measures their relations to the rewards. For nodes $i \in \mathcal{P}_1$, we cluster them into d models, and define an information vector $\mathbf{x}_i$ to describe the property of each node i. We employ a linear function to model the correlation between $\mathbf{x}_i$ and $r_{i,k}$, i.e.,

$$\mathrm{E}[r_{i,k}|\mathbf{x}_i] = \mathbf{x}_i\boldsymbol{\theta}_a + \eta_a, \tag{2}$$

where $a \in \{1, 2, \ldots, d\}$ denotes the cluster that node i belongs to, and η_a is a random noise with Gaussian distribution $\mathcal{N}(0, \sigma_a^2)$.

We aim to maximize $\mathcal{J}_K$ by conducting two processes for K iterations as follows. In iteration k: (1) We choose a node $i \in \mathcal{P}_k$ with the maximum expectation to get higher $\mathcal{J}_K$. It is based on all the learned $\boldsymbol{\theta}_a$, for $a = 1, 2, \ldots, d$. (2) After querying the selected node i, we would get a reward $r_{i,k}$ from the oracle. Based on $r_{i,k}$ and $\mathbf{x}_i$, we update the $\boldsymbol{\theta}_a$, aiming to improve the node selection strategy, where a is the cluster that node i belongs to.

We now introduce the details. There are three types of information dominate node i, i.e., network structure, node attributes, and correlations to the B prototype nodes. We define $\mathbf{x}_i \in \mathbb{R}^{1\times(d+2)}$ as,

$$\mathbf{x}_i = [\mathbf{h}_i, \mathrm{maxSimi}(i), \mathrm{Corr}(i)], \tag{3}$$

where $\mathbf{h}_i$ is the attributed network embedding representation of node i, and $\mathrm{maxSimi}(i)$ denotes the maximum similarity from node i to all B prototype nodes. $\mathrm{Corr}(i)$ denotes the average of the correlations between node i and all prototype nodes. To make the algorithm efficient, in this paper, $\mathbf{x}_i$ is fixed from the initialization. It is flexible to explore dynamic frameworks that update $\mathbf{x}_i$ in every iteration. Both the distance and correlation are based on the cosine similarities in the initial embedding representation space H_0.

We now focus on each cluster a. Let $\mathbf{Y}_a \in \mathbb{R}^{y\times(d+2)}$ be a matrix that collects the information vectors of the y queried nodes in cluster a. Let $\mathbf{y}_a \in \mathbb{R}^{y\times 1}$ denote the corresponding y rewards. By leveraging ridge regression to estimate $\boldsymbol{\theta}_a$ and adding a penalty term λ to improve the estimation performance, we have,

$$\hat{\boldsymbol{\theta}}_a = (\mathbf{Y}_a^\top\mathbf{Y}_a + \lambda\mathbf{I})^{-1}\mathbf{Y}_a^\top\mathbf{y}_a. \tag{4}$$

Then for any $\delta > 0$, with probability at lease $1 - \delta$, the expectation of the reward of selecting a node i in cluster a is bounded by [43],

$$\mathbf{x}_i\hat{\boldsymbol{\theta}}_a - \alpha f_a(i) \leq \mathrm{E}[r_{i,k}|\mathbf{x}_i] \leq \mathbf{x}_i\hat{\boldsymbol{\theta}}_a + \alpha f_a(i), \tag{5}$$

where $\alpha = 1 + \sqrt{\ln(2/\delta)/2}$ is a constant, and

$$f_a(i) \triangleq \sqrt{\mathbf{x}_i(\mathbf{Y}_a^\top\mathbf{Y}_a + \lambda\mathbf{I})^{-1}\mathbf{x}_i^\top}. \tag{6}$$

The work of [2, 3] have shown that choosing the node maximizing the upper confidence bound $\mathbf{x}_i\hat{\boldsymbol{\theta}}_a + \alpha f_a(i)$ in each iteration achieves the best performance in maximizing $\mathcal{J}_K$. The key idea is, when a node with large $\mathbf{x}_i\hat{\boldsymbol{\theta}}_a$ is chosen, a high reward is expected, and such trial is an exploitation process. When a node with large $\alpha f_a(i)$ is chosen, this high variance means that we have limited knowledge on the model for cluster a, thus, we explore it more in the current trial. Jointly maximizing $\mathbf{x}_i\hat{\theta}_a + \alpha f_a(i)$ makes a trade-off between exploitation and exploration. As a conclusion, in iteration k, the best node i for querying could be computed as follows.

$$\underset{i \in \mathcal{P}_k}{\text{maximize}} \quad g(i) = \mathbf{x}_i\hat{\theta}_a + \alpha f_a(i). \tag{7}$$

3.4 Expert Cognition Quantization

We have defined the amount of expert cognition included in the kth returned answer as $r_{i,k}$. We now introduce how to quantify it. The key idea of our proposed metric is that incorporating more expert cognition could reduce the disagreements between the network proximity and node attribute proximity. Given a new node, experts usually jointly consider different types of information to get a comprehensive understanding, including its relation network and node attributes. It matches the observation that node attributes often highly tie in with the topological structure [24, 41]. However, in the data, there always exist some disagreements between the two sources, and we quantify them as follows.

$$\mathbf{P} = |\mathbf{S}^{(\mathbf{U}^{(G)})} - \mathbf{S}^{(\mathbf{U}^{(A)})}|, \tag{8}$$

where $|\cdot|$ calculates each absolute value. $\mathbf{U}^{(G)}$ and $\mathbf{U}^{(A)}$ are the embedding representations of the initial network and node attributes. We embed them to alleviate the effect of noise and missing data. Let j be the most similar prototype node of i based on the answer. Since adding a cognition edge (i, j) could alleviate the disagreement, we quantify the learned expert cognition in the kth iteration as,

$$r_{i,k} = p_{ij}. \tag{9}$$

3.5 Network Embedding with Expert Cognition

We introduce a simple attributed network embedding algorithm based on spectral embedding [25, 42]. It should be noted that NEEC can be generalized to advance different embedding algorithms.

3.5.1 Network embedding. Network embedding [10, 30, 38] aims to use a low-dimensional vector representation $\mathbf{u}_i$ to map each node i, such that all the network proximity could be preserved in $\mathbf{U}$. The main idea of the spectrum technique is to enforce nodes i and j with larger proximity s_{ij} to be closer to each other in the embedding space. It can be achieved by minimizing the loss function $\mathcal{J}_{\text{spec}}$, i.e.,

$$\mathcal{J}_{\text{spec}} = \frac{1}{2}\sum_{i,j=1}^{n} s_{ij}\|\frac{\mathbf{u}_i}{\sqrt{d_i}} - \frac{\mathbf{u}_j}{\sqrt{d_j}}\|_2^2, \tag{10}$$

where s_{ij} is the proximity in $\mathbf{S}^{(G)}$. d_i is the sum of the ith row of $\mathbf{S}^{(G)}$, and it is employed for normalization. $\mathbf{u}_i$ needs to be orthonormal to avoid being arbitrary. We could further rewrite it as a maximization problem by defining $\mathcal{J}_G = 1 - \mathcal{J}_{\text{spec}}$, i.e.,

$$\begin{aligned} &\underset{\mathbf{U}^{(G)}}{\text{maximize}} \quad \mathcal{J}_G = \text{Tr}(\mathbf{U}^{(G)\top}\mathcal{L}^{(G)}\mathbf{U}^{(G)}) \\ &\text{subject to} \quad \mathbf{U}^{(G)\top}\mathbf{U}^{(G)} = \mathbf{I}, \end{aligned} \tag{11}$$

where $\mathcal{L}^{(G)} = \mathbf{D}^{(G)-\frac{1}{2}}\mathbf{S}^{(G)}\mathbf{D}^{(G)-\frac{1}{2}}$ is the graph Laplacian [42]. $\mathbf{D}^{(G)}$ is the degree matrix of $\mathbf{S}^{(G)}$, with d_i in the diagonal.

Similarly, we apply the same technique to the node attribute information $\mathbf{A}$, and calculate its embedding representation $\mathbf{U}^{(A)}$ by maximizing $\mathcal{J}_A = \text{Tr}(\mathbf{U}^{(A)\top}\mathcal{L}^{(A)}\mathbf{U}^{(A)})$, with $\mathbf{U}^{(A)\top}\mathbf{U}^{(A)} = \mathbf{I}$.

Algorithm 1: Network Embedding with Expert Cognition

Input: $\mathbf{G}$, $\mathbf{A}$, d, B, K, β, the oracle.
Output: Cognition informed representation $\mathbf{H}$.
1 Select B prototype nodes via k-medoids or random strategy;
2 Set the remaining nodes as $\mathcal{P}_1$ and split them into d clusters;
3 Collect the information vectors of nodes in $\mathcal{P}_1$ based on Eq. (3);
4 Calculate $\mathbf{P}$ based on Eqs. (8) and (11);
5 Calculate initial representation $\mathbf{H}_0$ based on Eq. (13);
6 Set all the $\mathbf{Q}_a \leftarrow \lambda\mathbf{I}$, $\mathbf{q}_a \leftarrow \mathbf{0}$, and calculate all the $g(i)$;
7 **for** $k = 1 : K$ **do**
8   Choose node the i with maximum $g(i)$;
9   Query the oracle node i and get the answer;
10   Incorporate node i's cognition edge to $\mathbf{G}$;
11   Calculate $r_{i,k}$ based on Eq. (9);
12   Update $\mathbf{Q}_a \leftarrow \mathbf{Q}_a + \mathbf{x}_i^\top\mathbf{x}_i$ and $\mathbf{q}_a \leftarrow \mathbf{q}_a + r_{i,k}\mathbf{x}_i^\top$;
13   Remove node i from the set $\mathcal{P}_k$ and get $\mathcal{P}_{k+1}$;
14   For nodes in cluster a, set $g(i) \leftarrow \mathbf{x}_i\mathbf{Q}_a^{-1}\mathbf{q}_a + \alpha\sqrt{\mathbf{x}_i\mathbf{Q}_a^{-1}\mathbf{x}_i^\top}$;
15 Calculate cognition informed $\mathbf{H}$ based on current $\mathbf{G}$ and $\mathbf{A}$.

3.5.2 Jointly Embed Network and Node Attributes. In many real-world networks such as social media, the topological structure and node attributes influence each other and are inherently correlated. The homophily hypothesis [24] and social influence theories [41] demonstrate that similar nodes tend to bond and connect with each other. Therefore, jointly learning from the two information sources could draw towards a better embedding representation $\mathbf{H}$. We apply a simple strategy to assimilate the two heterogeneous information towards a joint node proximity as follows.

$$\mathbf{S}^{(H)} = \beta\mathbf{S}^{(G)} + (1-\beta)\mathbf{S}^{(A)}, \tag{12}$$

where β balances the contributions of network and node attributes. Similarly, we could define the Laplacian $\mathcal{L}^{(H)} = \mathbf{D}^{(H)-\frac{1}{2}}\mathbf{S}^{(H)}\mathbf{D}^{(H)-\frac{1}{2}}$, where $\mathbf{D}^{(H)}$ is the degree matrix of $\mathbf{S}^{(H)}$, and apply the normalized spectral embedding technique to learn $\mathbf{H}$ as follows,

$$\begin{aligned} &\underset{\mathbf{H}}{\text{maximize}} \quad \mathcal{J} = \text{Tr}(\mathbf{H}^\top\mathcal{L}^{(H)}\mathbf{H}) \\ &\text{subject to} \quad \mathbf{H}^\top\mathbf{H} = \mathbf{I}. \end{aligned} \tag{13}$$

3.5.3 Embed the Learned Expert Cognition. We summary the processes of NEEC in Algorithm 1. Given an attributed network with $\mathbf{G}$ and $\mathbf{A}$, we first select B prototype nodes and set the remaining nodes as the initial query pool $\mathcal{P}_1$. To choose the optimal K nodes from $\mathcal{P}_1$, we perform a contextual bandit algorithm based on Eq. (7). It has two items that are not necessary to be computed from scratch. We denote them as follows.

$$\mathbf{Q}_a = \mathbf{Y}_a^\top\mathbf{Y}_a + \lambda\mathbf{I}, \quad \text{and} \quad \mathbf{q}_a = \mathbf{Y}_a^\top\mathbf{y}_a. \tag{14}$$

Thus, in each iteration k, we update them according to the rules in line 12. Then we select the node with the maximum explanation upper confidence bound as defined in Eq. (7). After querying the oracle, we incorporate the answer into $\mathbf{G}$ as a cognition edge. When all the budget is used, we apply an attributed network embedding method to the current network $\mathbf{G}$ and $\mathbf{A}$, and jointly embed them towards a more informative cognition informed representation $\mathbf{H}$.

4 EXPERIMENTS

We apply NEEC on three real-world attributed networks to demonstrate its effectiveness and generalizability. In the experiments, we target to investigate three questions. (1) How effective are the proposed prototype-based form of queries and the query selection algorithm? (2) Could the learned expert cognition be used to improve different embedding methods? (3) What are the impacts of the parameters B, K, and d, on the expert cognition learning?

4.1 Datasets

We now introduce the three datasets. They are all publicly available, and their statistical information is listed in Table 2.

BlogCatalog [20] is a social networking service that helps people share blogs. The bloggers can interact with each other and form a network. They could also have a list of keywords to describe their blogs, which are employed as node attributes. We leverage the predefined groups that each blogger subscribed as the labels.

Flickr [20] is a photo and video sharing service. Users follower each other and form a big community. We sampled 7,575 users to construct a network. Node attributes of each user is defined as the list of tags of interest specified by him/her. Users could also join some predefined groups, thus we employ them as labels.

ACM [39] dataset collects a citation network for papers published before 2016. We select papers in nine areas as follows. Artificial Intelligence (AAAI, IJCAI, etc.), Computer Vision (TPAMI, CVPR, etc.), Computational Linguistics (ACL, EMNLP, etc.), Data Mining (KDD, WSDM, etc.), Databases (VLDB, TKDE, etc.), Human Computer Interaction (CHI, UIST, etc.), Information Retrieval (CIKM, SIGIR, etc.), Machine Learning (ICML, COLT, etc.), Robotics (ICRA, IROS, etc.). We make the network undirected since it is too sparse for spectral embedding. We apply the bag-of-words model to represent the abstracts as node attributes and employ areas as labels.

4.2 Experimental Settings

To create the oracle, for each dataset, we randomly sample a certain percentage of the entire edges and attributes as the initial attributed network. The remaining data is considered as the cognition of the oracle, so he/she answers the queries based on the entire original dataset. The oracle determines the most similar prototype nodes based on the similarity of the original node attributes. Then the expert cognition learning methods could be employed to query the oracle and enhance the initial networks. A network embedding or attributed network learning method would be applied to both the initial network and the learned network. In such way, we are able to evaluate the amount of learned expert cognition by measuring the performance improvement of the embedding representation.

To evaluate the performance of embedding representations, we follow the traditional way [30, 38] to apply it to the node classification task [34, 49]. The goal is to predict the labels of new nodes based on the training nodes that have labels. We use 5-fold cross-validation. The nodes are randomly separated into two groups, training and test groups. The labels of nodes in test group are set as ground truth. We apply the embedding method to the entire attributed network and learn an embedding representation $\mathbf{H}$. It contains the vector representations of nodes in both training and test groups, and we split it into $\mathbf{H}_{\text{train}}$ and $\mathbf{H}_{\text{test}}$. For each of the label category, we learn a binary Support Vector Machine (SVM) classifier based on $\mathbf{H}_{\text{train}}$ and labels of nodes in the training group. By using these trained classifiers and $\mathbf{H}_{\text{test}}$, we predict the labels of nodes in the test group.

Table 2: Statistical information of the datasets.

	Nodes	Edges	Density	Attributes	Label
BlogCatalog	5,196	171,743	$1.27e{-}002$	8,189	6
Flickr	7,575	239,738	$8.36e{-}003$	12,047	9
ACM	16,484	71,980	$5.30e{-}004$	8,337	9

We use two widely adopted evaluation criteria to measure the performance of a representation in the node classification task, i.e., macro-average and micro-average [16]. The former one is the arithmetic average of F-measure of all label categories. F-measure is a commonly used metric in binary classification. The latter one is the harmonic mean of precision and recall. If it is not specified, we set $d = 100$ and $B = 9$. All results are the means of ten test runs.

4.3 Effectiveness of NEEC

To study the first question proposed at the beginning of this section, we compare NEEC with three types of baselines. First, to investigate the effectiveness of the proposed prototype-based form of queries, we include RandomPair, LinkPredict, and AddKEdges. Second, to demonstrate the effectiveness of the proposed way of formulating expert cognition, we include HiddenEdge. Third, to study the effectiveness of the proposed query selection algorithm, we include a variation of NEEC, i.e., w/o_Bandit. For NEEC, we include both k-medodis and random prototype node selection algorithms. The details of them are described as follows.

- *RandomPair*: No prototype node is defined. It randomly selects $B + K$ unconnected node pairs for querying. The oracle will indicate an edge, if the two nodes are linked in the original dataset or have an original node attribute similarity that is greater than a threshold.
- *LinkPredict*: Similar to RandomPair, but the $B + K$ pairs are selected from the unconnected pairs based on the probabilities of having edges, which are based on the weighted-ℓ_1 edge features [10] in spectral embedding space.
- *HiddenEdge*: It queries the oracle based on prototype nodes, but without using the cognition edges. It adds edges between the selected node i and any prototype nodes that have latent relationships with i or are highly similar to i.
- *w/o_Bandit*: NEEC without using the proposed query selection algorithm. It chooses the top K important nodes with the maximum eigenvector centrality [26].
- *AddKEdges*: It randomly queries the oracle a large number of node pairs until K edges were added. This baseline unfairly takes much more human effort than all others.

4.3.1 Form of Queries Investigation. To study the effectiveness of querying with prototype nodes, we compare NEEC with RandomPair, LinkPredict, and AddKEdges. All these three baselines query the oracle without a prototype. For RandomPair and LinkPredict, the total number of queries is set as $B + K$, such that the oracle needs to check at least $B + K$ nodes and pay more effort than in NEEC. AddKEdges needs to make an extremely large number of queries. The

Table 3: The classification performance of different methods on the three datasets in terms of micro-average when $d = 100$.

	BlogCatalog				Flickr				ACM			
Training	10%	25%	50%	100%	10%	25%	50%	100%	10%	25%	50%	100%
Node Num	1,455	2,078	3,118	5,196	2,121	3,030	4,545	7,575	4,616	6,594	9,890	1,6484
K	242	495	1,114	3,092	338	691	1,556	4,316	348	709	1,598	4,435
Initial	0.287	0.359	0.430	0.520	0.261	0.304	0.358	0.432	0.232	0.270	0.319	0.400
RandomPair	0.286	0.358	0.431	0.520	0.261	0.306	0.365	0.435	0.231	0.267	0.317	0.412
LinkPredict	0.287	0.360	0.430	0.523	0.261	0.303	0.359	0.433	0.230	0.278	0.310	0.392
AddKEdges	0.312	0.379	0.462	0.547	0.255	0.312	0.363	0.457	**0.258**	**0.300**	**0.380**	**0.508**
HiddenEdge	0.298	0.370	0.437	0.529	0.265	0.301	0.363	0.436	0.232	0.275	0.322	0.418
w/o_Bandit	0.295	0.366	0.447	0.556	0.259	0.326	0.368	0.439	0.238	0.265	0.306	0.391
NEEC_Rand	**0.317**	**0.393**	0.463	0.558	0.277	**0.367**	0.433	0.508	0.235	0.288	0.355	0.447
NEEC_Kmed	0.313	0.389	**0.469**	**0.571**	**0.281**	0.364	**0.443**	**0.515**	0.242	0.284	0.363	0.445
RandomPair	−0.47%	−0.27%	0.07%	−0.07%	0.04%	0.87%	1.87%	0.64%	−0.59%	−1.35%	−0.63%	3.11%
LinkPredict	−0.03%	0.35%	−0.07%	0.41%	0.00%	−0.36%	0.15%	0.15%	−0.80%	2.90%	−2.92%	−2.09%
AddKEdges	8.43%	5.55%	7.36%	5.14%	−2.28%	2.79%	1.20%	5.83%	**10.85%**	**10.96%**	**19.23%**	**27.00%**
HiddenEdge	3.61%	3.06%	1.52%	1.68%	1.60%	−0.80%	1.41%	0.81%	−0.26%	1.81%	0.93%	4.56%
w/o_Bandit	2.64%	2.06%	3.82%	6.75%	−0.80%	7.43%	2.61%	1.58%	2.30%	−2.07%	−4.13%	−2.17%
NEEC_Rand	**10.41%**	**9.63%**	7.69%	7.27%	6.24%	**20.87%**	20.78%	17.43%	1.07%	6.74%	11.25%	11.66%
NEEC_Kmed	9.03%	8.34%	**9.01%**	**9.67%**	**7.64%**	19.78%	**23.60%**	**19.22%**	4.26%	5.16%	13.71%	11.30%

Table 4: The computation time of each iteration in NEEC.

Dataset	BlogCatalog	Flickr	ACM
Average Time (s)	2.97e−003	8.02e−003	2.28e−002

classification performance w.r.t. micro-average is shown in Table 3. All of them use the same embedding algorithm in Section 3.5. From the results, we observe that NEEC outperforms all the baselines on all the three datasets. For instance, on Flickr, both RandomPair and LinkPredict have almost no improvement, while NEEC_Kmed achieves 19.22% improvement comparing with the embedding of the initial attributed network. Even though AddKEdges performs a large number of queries, NEEC improves more on BlogCatalog and Flickr. On ACM, NEEC achieves less improvement. The reason is that AddKEdges needs to perform up to 9.4×10^6 queries.

To further investigate the performance of NEEC under different training percentages, i.e., the percentage of data in training group that has been used, we vary it from 10% to 100%. The results in Table 3 show that NEEC consistently achieves higher performance than all baselines except AddKEdges. For instance, when the training percentage is 25% on Flickr, NEEC_Rand achieves 20.87% improvement. It also demonstrates that the prototype-based form of queries is effective in learning expert cognition.

4.3.2 Effectiveness of Cognition Edge Investigation. To study the effectiveness of the proposed way of transforming expert cognition into concrete data, we compare NEEC with HiddenEdge, which models the expert cognition as latent edges. Their performance in items of different training percentage is summarized in Table 3. As we can see, HiddenEdge achieves limited improvement. For instance, NEEC_Kmed achieves 9.67% while HiddenEdge achieves 1.68%, when the training percentage is 100% on BlogCatalog. It demonstrates the effectiveness of the proposed cognition edges.

4.3.3 Prototype Node Selection and Query Selection Algorithms Investigation. We provide two algorithms to select the prototype nodes, i.e., NEEC_Rand and NEEC_Kmed. As shown in Table 3, NEEC_Rand might achieve slightly better performance when the training percentage is 10% or 25%. It is because when the number of nodes is small, the initial information would be too limited to perform the clustering well in NEEC_Kmed.

To study the effectiveness of our contextual bandit algorithm in query selection, we compare NEEC with w/o_Bandit. The performance with respect to different training percentage is shown in Table 3. From the results, we find that NEEC achieves more improvement. For example, on Flickr, NEEC_Rand achieves 17.43% improvement while w/o_Bandit achieves 1.58% improvement.

4.3.4 Effectiveness and Efficiency of NEEC Investigation. Up till now, we have demonstrated the effectiveness of each component of NEEC. The number of queries we performed also demonstrates the effectiveness of NEEC. We summarize the number of queries K and performance improvement in Table 3. As we can see, NEEC achieves significant improvement with a small number of queries. For example, NEEC_Kmed achieves 19.78% improvement by conducting 691 queries in a network with 3,030 nodes on Flickr.

NEEC is also an efficient interactive system that could respond the oracle immediately. The average computation time of each iteration in NEEC is shown in Table 4. For example, on Flickr, NEEC needs 8.02 milliseconds to update the system and compute a new query. It verifies the efficiency of NEEC.

4.4 Generalizability Evaluation

We now answer the second question that how general is the expert cognition learning framework NEEC. We include two network embedding methods, i.e., Spectrum and DeepWalk, and two attributed network embedding methods, i.e., AANE and LANE, as baselines.

- *Spectrum* [42]: It performs spectral embedding on the pure topological structure to evaluate the amount of information that we have learned in the network space.
- *DeepWalk* [30]: It makes an analogy between random walks on a graph and sentences in a document, and embed the paths via language modeling techniques.

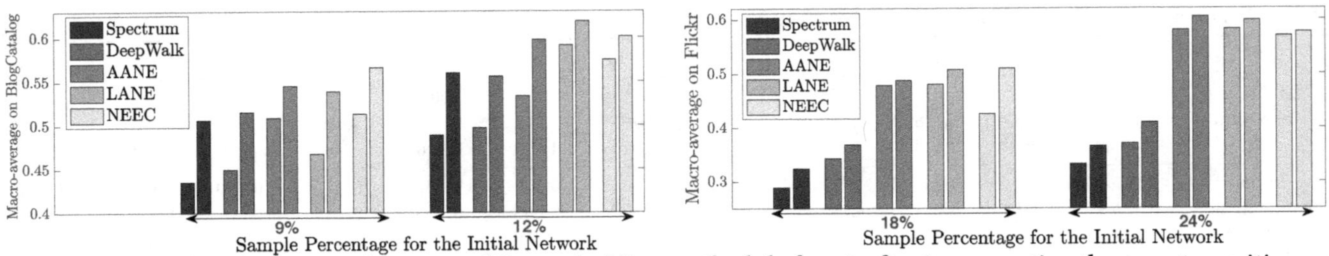

Figure 2: The classification performance of five embedding methods before & after incorporating the expert cognition.

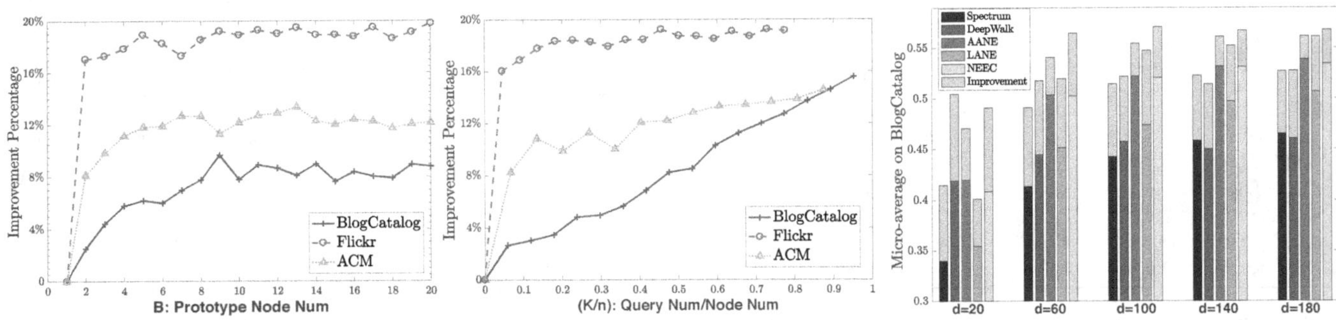

Figure 3: Performance improvement of embedding methods after incorporating the expert cognition with parameters varying.

- *AANE* [14]: It performs embedding based on the factorization of node attribute proximity and penalty of difference in the vector representations of highly correlated nodes.
- *LANE* [15]: It is used for incorporating labels into network embedding. We set the labels as zeros. It jointly embeds the network and node attributes by maximizing their correlations based on the spectral embedding.

The performance of the five embedding methods before and after incorporating the expert cognition is shown in Figure 2. We omit the result on ACM since we obtain similar observations. From the figure, we find that all the five embedding methods have significant performance improvements after incorporating the expert cognition. For example, DeepWalk achieves 14.60% improvement and LANE achieves 15.29% improvement on BlogCatalog. We further increase one-third of the sample percentage for the initial network to study its impact. From the results in Figure 2, the same observations are observed, i.e., all the five methods have significant performance improvements after incorporating the expert cognition. We also find that the amount of improvement decreased. This can be explained by the fact that, as the sample percentage increases, the amount of knowledge that the oracle obtained decreases.

4.5 Parameter Analysis

We now study the impacts of the number of prototype nodes B, the number of queries K, and the embedding representation dimension d. The performance improvement w.r.t. B and $\frac{K}{n}$ after incorporating the expert cognition is shown in Figure 3. As we can see, the performance improvement increases as B increases on all the three datasets. It is because more prototypes tend to create more accurate cognition of nodes. But it also takes more human effort. The performance improvement increases rapidly at the beginning and then increases smoothly thereafter. Similar observations are made for the parameter K. Larger query number means more expert cognition, but their correlation is not always linear. We also vary d to see the performance improvement of the five embedding methods and show the results in Figure 3. The gray bars denote the corresponding performance improvement. We see that all methods perform better after incorporating the cognition edges as d increases from 20 to 180. This also verifies the generalizability of NEEC.

5 RELATED WORK

Attributed network embedding [14, 15, 49] attracts lots of attention in recent years due to its effectiveness in modeling various information systems. Qi et al. [31] advanced the latent semantic indexing algorithm to jointly model the content similarity and context link into a low-dimensional semantic space. Le and Lauw [18] proposed to learn a joint low-dimensional representation for networked documents by incorporating a topic model into the network embedding. Chang et al. [6] considered the content as a network and embedded it along with the original network jointly via the deep learning. Several coupled matrix factorization based models [46, 49] also have been developed to assimilate these two sources of information.

Our work is also related to pool-based active learning [35, 36], which learns from the oracle by inquiring labels. It aims to select a number of unlabeled instances from a pool, such that the classification performance could be maximized by using the labels of selected instances. The typical methods are based on uncertainty sampling [19, 40], query by committee [23], expected error and variance reduction [11], or expected model change [36]. Several efforts [4, 5] also have been devoted to balancing exploration and exploitation based on the multi-armed bandit algorithms.

Multi-armed bandit algorithms [2, 3] are widely used to perform online human behavior or knowledge learning. Radlinski et al. [32] exploited a bandit algorithm to conduct an online document ranking that can learn from users behavior. Several contextual bandit based personalized recommendation frameworks [21, 44, 47] have been developed to incorporate dynamic content and user information.

6 CONCLUSIONS AND FUTURE WORK

Expert cognition is an essential type of knowledge that could advance various real-world data analysis tasks such as attributed network embedding. Learning and modeling expert cognition is promising but challenging as it is often abstract, diverse, and laborious to obtain. To fill the gap, we study a novel problem of exploring expert cognition for attributed network embedding and develop a general framework NEEC. Instead of directly modeling expert cognition, we learn it from the oracle by performing a number of concise but effective queries. The queries are carefully designed based on the exemplar theory and prototype theory, and systematically selected via a contextual bandit algorithm. Based on the returned answers from the oracle, the meaningful but abstract expect cognition is modeled as new cognition edges, which could be directly added into the network. Thus, the learned expert cognition could be incorporated into the latent representation by any embedding algorithm. Experiments on real-world datasets demonstrate the effectiveness and generalizability of NEEC. As the future work, we plan to study some open questions. (1) NEEC models the relation between queries and rewards via linear functions. How can we extend it to more general ones to improve the performance? (2) The returned answers change the network dynamically. How can we take it into consideration to advance the query selection?

ACKNOWLEDGMENTS

This work is, in part, supported by DARPA (#N66001-17-2-4031) and NSF (#IIS-1657196 and #IIS-1718840). The views, opinions, and/or findings expressed are those of the author(s) and should not be interpreted as representing the official views or policies of the Department of Defense or the U.S. Government.

REFERENCES

[1] Elke Achtert, Hans-Peter Kriegel, Erich Schubert, and Arthur Zimek. 2013. Interactive Data Mining with 3D-parallel-coordinate-trees. In *SIGMOD*. 1009–1012.

[2] Rajeev Agrawal. 1995. Sample Mean Based Index Policies by O(log n) Regret for the Multi-armed Bandit Problem. *Advances in Applied Probability* 27, 4 (1995), 1054–1078.

[3] Peter Auer. 2002. Using Confidence Bounds for Exploitation-exploration Trade-offs. *JMLR* 3 (2002), 397–422.

[4] Yoram Baram, Ran El-Yaniv, and Kobi Luz. 2004. Online Choice of Active Learning Algorithms. *JMLR* 5 (2004), 255–291.

[5] Djallel Bouneffouf, Romain Laroche, Tanguy Urvoy, Raphael Féraud, and Robin Allesiardo. 2014. Contextual Bandit for Active Learning: Active Thompson Sampling. In *ICONIP*. 405–412.

[6] Shiyu Chang, Wei Han, Jiliang Tang, Guo-Jun Qi, Charu C. Aggarwal, and Thomas S. Huang. 2015. Heterogeneous Network Embedding via Deep Architectures. In *KDD*. 119–128.

[7] Robert Davies-Jones. 2015. A review of supercell and tornado dynamics. *Atmospheric Research* 158–159 (2015), 274–291.

[8] Gerald DeJong and Shiau Hong Lim. 2011. Explanation-based Learning. *Encyclopedia of Machine Learning* (2011), 388–392.

[9] Xiaowen Ding, Bing Liu, and Philip S. Yu. 2008. A Holistic Lexicon-based Approach to Opinion Mining. In *WSDM*. 231–240.

[10] Aditya Grover and Jure Leskovec. 2016. node2vec: Scalable Feature Learning for Networks. In *KDD*. 855–864.

[11] Steven C. H. Hoi, Rong Jin, and Michael R. Lyu. 2006. Large-scale Text Categorization by Batch Mode Active Learning. In *WWW*. 633–642.

[12] Andreas Holzinger. 2016. Interactive Machine Learning for Health Informatics: When do We Need the Human-in-the-loop? *Brain Informatics* 3, 2 (2016), 119–131.

[13] Xia Hu, Jiliang Tang, Huiji Gao, and Huan Liu. 2013. Unsupervised Sentiment Analysis with Emotional Signals. In *WWW*. 607–618.

[14] Xiao Huang, Jundong Li, and Xia Hu. 2017. Accelerated Attributed Network Embedding. In *SDM*. 633–641.

[15] Xiao Huang, Jundong Li, and Xia Hu. 2017. Label Informed Attributed Network Embedding. In *WSDM*. 731–739.

[16] Ling Jian, Jundong Li, Kai Shu, and Huan Liu. 2016. Multi-label Informed Feature Selection. In *IJCAI*. 1627–1633.

[17] Waldemar Karwowski. 2001. *International Encyclopedia of Ergonomics and Human Factors*. CRC Press.

[18] Tuan M. V. Le and Hady W. Lauw. 2014. Probabilistic Latent Document Network Embedding. In *ICDM*. 270–279.

[19] David D. Lewis and William A. Gale. 1994. A Sequential Algorithm for Training Text Classifiers. In *SIGIR*. 3–12.

[20] Jundong Li, Xia Hu, Jiliang Tang, and Huan Liu. 2015. Unsupervised Streaming Feature Selection in Social Media. In *CIKM*. 1041–1050.

[21] Lihong Li, Wei Chu, John Langford, and Robert E. Schapire. 2010. A Contextual-bandit Approach to Personalized News Article Recommendation. In *WWW*. 661–670.

[22] Ninghao Liu, Xiao Huang, and Xia Hu. 2017. Accelerated Local Anomaly Detection via Resolving Attributed Networks. In *IJCAI*. 2337–2343.

[23] Andrew McCallum and Kamal Nigam. 1998. Employing EM and Pool-based Active Learning for Text Classification. In *ICML*. 350–358.

[24] Miller McPherson, Lynn Smith-Lovin, and James M. Cook. 2001. Birds of a Feather: Homophily in Social Networks. *Annual Review of Sociology* 27, 1 (2001), 415–444.

[25] Hariharan Narayanan, Mikhail Belkin, and Partha Niyogi. 2006. On the Relation Between Low Density Separation, Spectral Clustering and Graph Cuts. In *NIPS*. 1025–1032.

[26] M. E. J. Newman. 2003. The Structure and Function of Complex Networks. *SIAM Rev.* 45, 2 (2003), 167–256.

[27] M. E. J. Newman. 2006. Modularity and Community Structure in Networks. In *PNAS*, Vol. 103. 8577–8582.

[28] Robert M. Nosofsky. 1986. Attention, Similarity, and the Identification-categorization Relationship. *Journal of Experimental Psychology: General* 115, 1 (1986), 39–57.

[29] Hae-Sang Park and Chi-Hyuck Jun. 2009. A Simple and Fast Algorithm for K-medoids Clustering. *Expert Systems with Applications* 36, 2 (2009), 3336–3341.

[30] Bryan Perozzi, Rami Al-Rfou, and Steven Skiena. 2014. DeepWalk: Online Learning of Social Representations. In *KDD*. 701–710.

[31] Guo-Jun Qi, Charu Aggarwal, Qi Tian, Heng Ji, and Thomas S. Huang. 2012. Exploring Context and Content Links in Social Media: A Latent Space Method. *TPAMI* 34, 5 (2012), 850–862.

[32] Filip Radlinski, Robert Kleinberg, and Thorsten Joachims. 2008. Learning Diverse Rankings with Multi-armed Bandits. In *ICML*. 784–791.

[33] Eleanor Rosch, Carolyn B. Mervis, Wayne D. Gray, David M. Johnson, and Penny Boyes-Braem. 1976. Basic Objects in Natural Categories. *Cognitive Psychology* 8, 3 (1976), 382–439.

[34] Prithviraj Sen, Galileo Namata, Mustafa Bilgic, Lise Getoor, Brian Gallagher, and Tina Eliassi-Rad. 2008. Collective Classification in Network Data. *AI magazine* 29, 3 (2008), 93–106.

[35] Burr Settles. 2009. *Active Learning Literature Survey*. CS Technical Reports. University of Wisconsin–Madison.

[36] Burr Settles and Mark Craven. 2008. An Analysis of Active Learning Strategies for Sequence Labeling Tasks. In *EMNLP*. 1070–1079.

[37] Maite Taboada, Julian Brooke, Milan Tofiloski, Kimberly Voll, and Manfred Stede. 2011. Lexicon-based Methods for Sentiment Analysis. *Computational Linguistics* 37, 2 (2011), 267–307.

[38] Jian Tang, Meng Qu, Mingzhe Wang, Ming Zhang, Jun Yan, and Qiaozhu Mei. 2015. LINE: Large-scale Information Network Embedding. In *WWW*. 1067–1077.

[39] Jie Tang, Jing Zhang, Limin Yao, Juanzi Li, Li Zhang, and Zhong Su. 2008. Arnetminer: Extraction and Mining of Academic Social Networks. In *KDD*. 990–998.

[40] Simon Tong and Daphne Koller. 2001. Support Vector Machine Active Learning with Applications to Text Classification. *JMLR* 2 (2001), 45–66.

[41] Oren Tsur and Ari Rappoport. 2012. What's in a Hashtag? Content Based Prediction of the Spread of Ideas in Microblogging Communities. In *WSDM*. 643–652.

[42] Ulrike von Luxburg. 2007. A Tutorial on Spectral Clustering. *Statistics and Computing* 17, 4 (2007), 395–416.

[43] Thomas J. Walsh, István Szita, Carlos Diuk, and Michael L. Littman. 2009. Exploring Compact Reinforcement-learning Representations with Linear Regression. In *UAI*. 591–598.

[44] Huazheng Wang, Qingyun Wu, and Hongning Wang. 2016. Learning Hidden Features for Contextual Bandits. In *CIKM*. 1633–1642.

[45] Adam B Wilcox and George Hripcsak. 2003. The Role of Domain Knowledge in Automating Medical Text Report Classification. *JAMIA* 10, 4 (2003), 330–338.

[46] Cheng Yang, Zhiyuan Liu, Deli Zhao, Maosong Sun, and Edward Y. Chang. 2015. Network Representation Learning with Rich Text Information. In *IJCAI*. 2111–2117.

[47] Chunqiu Zeng, Qing Wang, Shekoofeh Mokhtari, and Tao Li. 2016. Online Context-aware Recommendation with Time Varying Multi-armed Bandit. In *KDD*. 2025–2034.

[48] Yongfeng Zhang. 2015. Incorporating Phrase-level Sentiment Analysis on Textual Reviews for Personalized Recommendation. In *WSDM*. 435–440.

[49] Shenghuo Zhu, Kai Yu, Yun Chi, and Yihong Gong. 2007. Combining Content and Link for Classification Using Matrix Factorization. In *SIGIR*. 487–494.

Co-PACRR: A Context-Aware Neural IR Model for Ad-hoc Retrieval

Kai Hui
Max Planck Institute for Informatics / SAP SE
kai.hui@sap.com

Andrew Yates
Max Planck Institute for Informatics
ayates@mpi-inf.mpg.de

Klaus Berberich
Max Planck Institute for Informatics / htw saar
kberberi@mpi-inf.mpg.de

Gerard de Melo
Rutgers University–New Brunswick
gdm@demelo.org

ABSTRACT

Neural IR models, such as DRMM and PACRR, have achieved strong results by successfully capturing relevance matching signals. We argue that the context of these matching signals is also important. Intuitively, when extracting, modeling, and combining matching signals, one would like to consider the surrounding text (local context) as well as other signals from the same document that can contribute to the overall relevance score. In this work, we highlight three potential shortcomings caused by not considering context information and propose three neural ingredients to address them: a disambiguation component, cascade k-max pooling, and a shuffling combination layer. Incorporating these components into the PACRR model yields Co-PACRR, a novel context-aware neural IR model. Extensive comparisons with established models on TREC Web Track data confirm that the proposed model can achieve superior search results. In addition, an ablation analysis is conducted to gain insights into the impact of and interactions between different components. We release our code to enable future comparisons[1].

ACM Reference Format:
Kai Hui, Andrew Yates, Klaus Berberich, and Gerard de Melo. 2018. Co-PACRR: A Context-Aware Neural IR Model for Ad-hoc Retrieval. In *WSDM 2018: The Eleventh ACM International Conference on Web Search and Data Mining, February 5–9, 2018, Marina Del Rey, CA, USA.* ACM, New York, NY, USA, 9 pages. https://doi.org/10.1145/3159652.3159689

1 INTRODUCTION

State-of-the-art neural models for ad-hoc information retrieval aim to model the interactions between a query and a document to produce a relevance score, which are analogous to traditional interaction signals such as BM25 scores. Guo et al. [7] pointed out that a neural IR model should capture query-document interactions in terms of *relevance matching* signals rather than capturing *semantic matching* signals as commonly used in natural language processing (NLP). Relevance matching focuses on the pertinence of local parts of the document with respect to the query (e.g., via n-gram matches), whereas semantic matching captures the overall semantic similarity between the query and the entire document. Accordingly, relevance matching over unigrams has been successfully modeled using histograms in the *DRMM* model [7], using a convolutional layer in *DUET*'s local model [15], and using a pool of kernels in the more recent *K-NRM* model [23]. In addition, position-aware relevance matching signals are further captured in *PACRR* [10] with the goal of encoding matching signals beyond unigrams, such as n-gram matches and "soft" n-gram matches, in which the order of some terms is modified.

Existing models have achieved strong results by focusing on modeling relevance matching signals. However, we argue that the context of such signals are also important but has yet to be fully accounted for in these models. Intuitively, a matching signal contributes to the final relevance score within the context of its local text window and the context of all matching signals from the whole document. Given a matching signal, a text window that embeds the signal is referred to as its *local context*, whereas all matching signals from the same document are referred to as the signal's *global context*. Inspired by past research within the IR community, we first highlight three particular shortcomings that can be addressed by incorporating context. Thereafter, we introduce novel neural components to address the shortcomings within PACRR [10], a state-of-the-art neural IR model. This ultimately leads to Co-PACRR (context-aware PACRR), a novel model as summarized in Figure 1.

To start with, when disregarding the local context, the matching signals extracted between terms from a query and a document may suffer from *ambiguity*. For example, in the query "*Jaguar SUV price*", the term "Jaguar" refers to a car brand, but "Jaguar" also happens to be the name of a species of animal. Such ambiguity can mislead a model to extract false positive matching signals. In the above example, an occurrence of the term "jaguar" referring to the animal should not contribute much to the document's relevance score.

Beyond this, accounting for the global document context may be important as well. Some such signals are desirable, while others need to be disregarded. In particular, we conjecture that the *the location of the matches* is important to better account for the level of reading effort needed to reach the relevant information. For example, consider two pseudo-documents that are both concatenations

[1] https://github.com/khui/repacrr

WSDM 2018, February 5–9, 2018, Marina Del Rey, CA, USA

ACM ISBN 978-1-4503-5581-0/18/02...$15.00
https://doi.org/10.1145/3159652.3159689

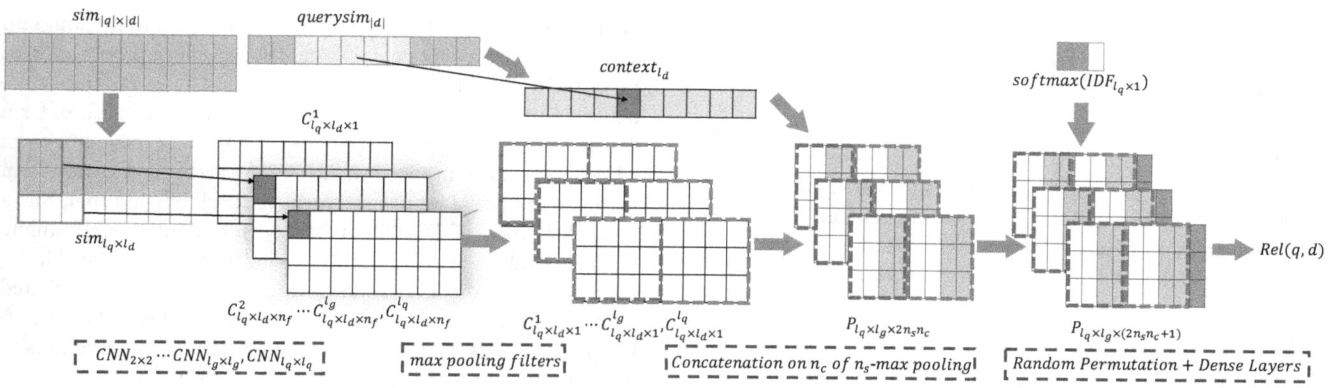

Figure 1: The pipeline of Co-PACRR. The inputs include two matrices, namely, $sim_{|q|\times|d|}$ and $querysim_{|d|}$. All these similarity matrices are truncated/zero-padded to the dimensionalities governed by l_q and l_d. Several 2D convolutional kernels are first applied to the similarity matrices, one for each $l_g \in [2, l_g]$. Next, max pooling is applied to the filters, leading to $l_g + 1$ matrices, namely, $C^1 \cdots C^{l_g}, C^{l_q}$. Following this, n_s-max pooling captures the strongest n_s signals on each C, at all n_c positions from *cpos*. At the same time, the context similarity corresponding to each term in *top-n_s* from $context_{l_d}$ is also appended, leading to $P_{l_q \times l_g \times (2n_s n_c)}$. Finally, the query terms' normalized IDFs are appended, and a feed forward network is applied, after permuting the rows in $P_{l_q \times l_g \times (2n_s n_c+1)}$, yielding a query-document relevance score $rel(q, d)$. In this plot, a setting with $l_d = 8$, $l_q = 3$, $l_g = 3$, $n_c = 2$, $n_s = 2$, and $cpos = [50\%, 100\%]$ is shown.

of one relevant and one non-relevant document, but in a different order. Although the same relevant information is present, extra effort is required when reading the pseudo-document where the non-relevant document appears first.

Not all aspects of the document context, however, are beneficial. In particular, we argue that the order in which the document matches different query terms may vary, as there can be many ways to express the same information request. When combining matching signals from different query terms, PACRR employs a recurrent layer, whereas DRMM, K-NRM, the local model in DUET, and MatchPyramid employ feedforward layers. Both kinds of models may be sensitive to the order in which query terms are matched, as the signals from individual query term matches and their associated positions in a query are jointly considered. Learning a query term order-dependent combination is particularly concerning when the query dimension is zero-padded (as in most models), because the aggregation layer may incorrectly learn to down-weight the positions that are zero-padded more often (e.g., at the end of a short query) in the training data. More generally, the aggregation layer may learn to treat matching signals differently depending on the position of a term within the query. This may hurt the model's ability to generalize to different reformulations of a given query, and it is also unnecessary because positional information is already accounted for in an earlier layer.

To close these gaps, we introduce neural components to cater to both the local and the global context. Intuitively, to avoid extracting false positive matching signals due to ambiguity, matching signals are double-checked based on their local context and penalized if there is a mismatch between the senses of words between the document and the query. To consider the global context of matching signals, the signals' strengths at different document positions are considered. To disregard the absolute positions of terms in the query, the sequential dependency over query terms is decoupled before the aggregating combination layer. While these ideas apply more generally, we incorporate them into the PACRR architecture to develop specific neural components, which leads to the Co-PACRR model that contains the following new components:

- A *disambiguation* building block to address the challenge of ambiguity by co-considering salient matching signals together with the local text window in which they occurred.
- A *cascade k-max pooling* approach in place of regular k-max pooling layers, enabling the model to benefit from information about the location of matches. These locations are jointly modeled together with the matching signals. This is inspired by the cascade model [4], which is based on the idea that relevance gains are influenced by the amount of relevant information that has already been observed.
- A *shuffling combination* layer to regularize the model so as to disregard the absolute positions of terms within the query. Removing query-dependent context before combination improves the generalization ability of the model.

Contributions. We incorporate the aforementioned building blocks into the established PACRR model, leading to the novel Co-PACRR model, jointly modeling matching signals with their local and global context. Through a comparison with multiple state-of-the-art models including DRMM, K-NRM, the local model in DUET, MatchPyramid, and the PACRR model on six years of TREC Web Track benchmarks, we demonstrate the superior performance of Co-PACRR. Remarkably, when re-ranking the search results from a naïve initial ranker, namely a query-likelihood ranking model, the re-ranked runs are ranked within the top-3 on at least five years based on

ERR@20. In addition, we also investigate the individual and joint effects of the proposed components to better understand the proposed model in an **ablation analysis**.

Organization. The rest of this paper unfolds as follows. We discuss related work in Section 2 and put our work in context. Section 3 recaps the basic neural-IR model PACRR, and thereafter Section 4 describes the proposed building components in detail. The setup, results, and analyses of our extensive experimental evaluation can be found in Section 5 and Section 6, before concluding in Section 7.

2 RELATED WORK

In ad-hoc retrieval, a system aims at creating a ranking of documents according to their relevance relative to a given query. The recent promises of deep learning methods as potential drivers for further advances in retrieval quality have attracted significant attention. Unlike learning-to-rank methods, where models are learned on top of a list of handcrafted features [13], a neural IR model aims at modeling the interactions between a query and a document directly based on their free text. Actually, the interactions being learned in a neural IR model correspond to one of the feature groups employed in learning-to-rank methods. They involve both a query and a document, as do BM25 scores. The proposed Co-PACRR belongs to this class of neural IR models and is hence compared with other neural IR models in Section 5.

As described in Section 1, neural IR approaches can be categorized as *semantic matching* and *relevance matching* models. The former follows the embedding approach adopted in many natural language processing tasks, aiming at comparing the semantic meaning of two pieces of text by mapping both into a low-dimensional representation space. Therefore, models developed for natural language processing tasks can also be used as retrieval models by assigning a similarity score to individual query-document pairs. For example, ARC-I and ARC-II [19] are two such models developed for the tasks of sentence completion, identifying the response to a microblog post, and performing paraphrase detection. In addition, Huang et al. [9] proposed Deep Structured Semantic Models (DSSM), which learn low-dimensional representations of a query and a document in a semantic space before evaluating the document according to its cosine similarity relative to the query. Similar approaches such as C-DSSM [20] further employed alternative means to learn dense representations of the documents.

In comparison, Guo et al. [7] argued that the matching required in information retrieval is different from the matching used in NLP tasks, and that *relevance matching* is better suited for retrieval tasks. Relevance matching compares two text sequences jointly, namely, a document and a query, by directly modeling their interactions. In relevance matching, local signals such as unigram matches are important. Meanwhile, semantic matching seeks to model the semantic meaning of the two text sequences independently, and the matching is considered in a semantic space. Accordingly, the Deep Relevance Matching Model (DRMM) [7] was proposed to model unigram relevance matching by encoding a query-document pair in terms of a histogram of similarities between terms from the query and the document. More recently, K-NRM [23] relied on a pool of kernels in place of the histogram, capturing the unigram relevance matching in a more smooth manner, addressing the issues of bin boundaries in generating histograms. In addition to the unigram signals, position-aware neural IR models have been proposed, such as MatchPyramid [8, 18], which is motivated by works from computer vision [21], and PACRR [10], which follows the ideas of term dependency [12, 14] and query term proximity [22] modeling from ad-hoc retrieval. Both encode matching signals beyond a single term with convolutional neural networks (CNNs). Beyond that, Mitra et al. [15] proposed DUET, a hybrid deep ranking model combining both kinds of matching, with two independent building blocks, namely, a local model for relevance matching and a distributed model for semantic matching. The proposed Co-PACRR model belongs to the class of relevance matching models, and attempts to further incorporate the context of matching signals.

3 BACKGROUND

In this section, we summarize the PACRR model [10], which we build upon by proposing novel components. When describing PACRR, we follow the notation from [10]. In general, PACRR takes a similarity matrix between a query q and a document d as input, and the output of the model is a scalar, namely, $rel(d, q)$, indicating the relevance of document d to query q. PACRR attempts to model query-document interactions based on these similarity matrices. At training time, the relevance scores for one relevant and one non-relevant document, denoted as d^+ and d^-, respectively, are fed into a max-margin loss as in Eq. 1.

$$\mathcal{L}(q, d^+, d^-; \Theta) = max(0, 1 - rel(q, d^+) + rel(q, d^-)) \quad (1)$$

In the following, PACRR is introduced component-by-component.

(1) **Input**: the similarity matrix $sim_{l_q \times l_d}$, where both l_q and l_d are hyper-parameters unifying the dimensions of the input similarity matrices. l_q is set to the longest query length, and l_d is tuned on the validation dataset. Given the settings for both l_q and l_d, a similarity matrix between a query and a document is truncated or zero-padded accordingly;

(2) **CNN kernels and max-pooling layers**: multiple CNN kernels with l_f filters capture the query-document interactions, like n-gram matching, corresponding to different text window lengths, namely $2, 3, \cdots, l_g$. The hyper-parameters l_g and l_f govern the longest text window under consideration and the number of filters, respectively. These CNN kernels are followed by a max-pooling layer on the filter dimension to retain the strongest matching signal for each kernel, leading to l_g matrices, denoted as

$$C^1_{l_q \times l_d \times 1} \cdots C^{l_g}_{l_q \times l_d \times 1};$$

(3) **k-max pooling**: subsequently, the matching signals in $C^1, \cdots, C^{l_g}$ from these kernels are further pooled with k-max pooling layers, keeping the top-n_s strongest signals for each query term and CNN kernel pair, leading to

$$P^1_{l_q \times n_s}, \cdots, P^{l_g}_{l_q \times n_s},$$

which are further concatenated for individual query terms, resulting in a matrix $P_{l_q \times (l_g n_s)}$;

(4) **combination of the signals from different query terms**: the signals in $P_{l_q \times (l_g n_s)}$, together with the inverse document frequency for individual query terms, are fed into a LSTM layer to generate the ultimate relevance score $rel(d, q)$.

Tweaks. Before moving on, we make two changes in order to ease the development of the proposed model. For simplicity, this revised model is denoted as PACRR in the following sections. First, according to our pilot experiments, the performance of the model does not change when replacing the LSTM layer with a stack of dense layers, which have been demonstrated to be able to simulate an arbitrary function [6]. Such dense layers can easily be trained in parallel, leading to faster training [6], whereas back-propagation through an LSTM layer is much more expensive due to its sequential nature. From Section 5, it can be seen that efficiency is important for this study due to the number of model variants to be trained and the limited availability of hardware at our disposal. Finally, another tweak is to switch the max-margin loss to a cross-entropy loss as in Eq. 2, following [5], where it has been demonstrated that a cross-entropy loss may lead to better results.

$$\mathcal{L}(q, d^+, d^-; \Theta) = -log \frac{\exp(rel(q, d^+))}{\exp(rel(q, d^+)) + \exp(rel(q, d^-))} \qquad (2)$$

4 METHOD

In this section, we describe the novel components in the Co-PACRR model as summarized in Figure 1.

Disambiguation: checking local context when extracting matching signals. Beyond the query-document similarity matrix $sim_{l_q \times l_d}$ used by PACRR, we introduce an input vector denoted as $querysim_{|d|}$ that encodes the similarity between document context vectors and a query vector. Document context vectors represent the meaning of text windows over the document, while the query vector represents the query's meaning. In particular, the vector of a query *queryvec* is computed by averaging the word vectors of all query terms. Similarly, given a position i in a document, its context vector of length, governed by w_c, is computed by averaging the embeddings of all the terms appeared in its surrounding context,

$$context2vec(i) = \frac{\sum_{j \in [i-w_c, i+w_c]} word2vec(\mathbf{d}[i])}{2 * w_c + 1} .$$

Thereafter, the match between the query and a document context at position i is computed by taking the cosine similarity between the query vector and context vector, that is,

$$querysim(i) = cosine(context2vec(i), queryvec) .$$

We employ pre-trained word2vec[2] embeddings due to their widespread availability. In the future, one may desire to replace this with specialized embeddings such as dual embeddings [16] or relevance-based embeddings [24].

Intuitively, to address the challenge of false positive matches stemming from ambiguity, the extracted matching signals on position i are adjusted in the model according to the corresponding similarity between its context and the query. In particular, when combining the top-n_s signals from individual query terms, the corresponding similarities for these top-n_s signals are also concatenated, making the matrices $P_{l_q \times (l_g n_s)}$ become $P_{l_q \times (2 l_g n_s)}$. This enables the aggregating layers, namely, a feed-forward network, to take any ambiguity into account when determining the ultimate score. For example, in the "jaguar" example from Section 1, if the context of "jaguar" consists of terms like "big cat" and "habitat", the context will have a low similarity with a query context containing terms such as "SUV" and "price", informing the model that such occurrences of "jaguar" actually refer to a different concept than the one in the query.

Cascade k-max pooling: encode the location of the relevance information. As discussed in Section 1, to put individual relevance signals into the context of the whole document, both the strength and the positions of match signals matter. We propose to encode such global context by conducting k-max pooling at multiple positions in a document, instead of pooling only on the entire document. For example, one could conduct multiple k-max pooling operations at 25%, 50%, 75%, and 100% of a document, ending up with $P_{l_q \times (4 l_g n_s)}$. This corresponds to when a user sifts through a document and evaluates the gained useful information after reading the first, second, third, and fourth quarters of the document. The list of offsets at which cascade k-max pooling is conducted is governed by an array *cpos*, e.g., $cpos = [25\%, 50\%, 75\%, 100\%]$ in the above example. We set the length of this array using a hyper-parameter n_c and perform pooling at equal intervals. For example, $n_c = 4$ in the previous example, and $n_c = 2$ results in $cpos = [50\%, 100\%]$.

Shuffling combination: regularizing the query-dependent information. As mentioned in Section 1, the combination of relevance signals among different query terms is supposed to be query-independent to avoid learning a dependency on query term positions. In light of this, we propose to randomly shuffle rows in $P_{l_q \times (l_g n_s)}$ before aggregating them. Note that each row contains signals for multiple n-gram lengths; shuffling the rows does not prevent the model from recognizing n-grams. We argue that, taking advantage of this independence, the shuffling regularizes the query-dependent information and effectively improves the generalization ability of the model by making the computation of the relevance scores depend solely on the importance of a query term (*idf*) and the relevance signals aggregated on it. This should be particularly helpful when training on short queries ($|q| < l_q$), where padded zeros are normally in the tail of $sim_{l_q \times l_d}$ [11]. Without shuffling, a model might remember that the relevance signals at the tail of a query (i.e., the several final rows in $sim_{l_q \times l_d}$) contribute very little and are mostly zero, leading to it mistakenly degrade the contribution from terms at tail positions when inferring relevance scores for longer queries.

5 EVALUATION

In this section, we empirically compare the proposed Co-PACRR with multiple state-of-the-art neural IR models using manual relevance judgments from six years of the TREC Web Track. Following [10], the comparison is based on three benchmarks, namely, re-ranking search results from a simple initial ranker, denoted as RERANKSIMPLE, re-ranking all runs from the TREC Web Track, denoted as RERANKALL, and further examining the classification accuracy in determining the order of document pairs, denoted as

[2] https://code.google.com/archive/p/word2vec/

PairAccuracy. We compare our model with multiple state-of-the-art neural IR models including the PACRR model [10], MatchPyramid [18], DRMM [7], the local model of DUET (DUETL) [15], and the most recent K-NRM [23] model. As discussed in Section 2, our focus is on evaluating deep relevance matching models, and hence the comparisons are limited to 1) modeling the interactions between a query and a document, excluding the learning-to-rank features for a single document or a query, e.g., PageRank scores, and 2) modeling relevance matching rather than semantic matching [7].

5.1 Experimental Setup

We rely on the 2009–2014 Trec Web Track ad-hoc task benchmarks[3]. In total, there are 300 queries and around 100k judgments (qrels). Six years (2009–14) of query-likelihood baselines (*QL*) provided by the Lemur project's online Indri services[4] [5] serve as the initial ranker in RerankSimple. In addition, the search results from runs submitted by participants from each year are employed in the RerankALL, where there are 71 (2009), 55 (2010), 62 (2011), 48 (2012), 50 (2013), and 27 (2014) runs. ERR@20 [2] is employed as evaluation measure, following the configuration in the Trec Web Track [3], which is computed with the script from Trec[6]. Note that ERR emphasizes the quality of the top-ranked documents and heavily penalizes relevant documents that are ranked lower by a model when enough relevant documents have been observed earlier [2]. This means that the improvement of the ERR for a model mainly comes from improvements on queries for which search results at the top are not good enough from an initial ranker.

Training. Models are trained and tested in a round-robin manner, using individual years as training, validation, and test data. Specifically, the available judgments are considered in accordance with the individual years of the Web Track, with 50 queries per year. Proceeding in a round-robin manner, we report test results on one year by using combinations of every four years and the two remaining years for training and validation. Model parameters and the number of training iterations are chosen by maximizing the ERR@20 on the validation set for each training/validation combination separately. Thereafter, the selected model is used to make predictions on the test data. Hence, for each test year, there are five different predictions each from a training and validation combination. Akin to the procedure in cross-validation, we report the average of these five test results as the ultimate results for individual test years, and conduct a Student's t-test over them to determine whether there is a statistically significant difference between different methods. For example, a significant difference between two evaluated methods on a particular test year is claimed if there exists a significant difference between the two vectors with five scores for individual methods. This was motivated by an observation that the closeness of the subsets for training and for validation can adversely influence the model selection. We argue that this approach minimizes the effects of the choice of training and validation data. Upper/lower-case characters are employed to indicate the significant difference under two-tailed Student's t-tests at 95% or 90% confidence levels relative to the corresponding approach, denoted as P/p for PACRR, M/m for MatchPyramid, D/d for DRMM, L/l for DUETL and K/k for K-NRM.

Variants of Co-PACRR. With the proposed components, namely, the cascade k-max pooling (C), the disambiguation component (D), and the shuffling combination (S), there are seven model variants in total by including or excluding one of the three building blocks. They are denoted as X(XX)-PACRR, where the X represents the building blocks that are turned on. For example, with cascade k-max pooling and shuffling combination turned on, the model is denoted as CS-PACRR. Meanwhile, with all three components, namely CDS-PACRR, the model is simply referred to as Co-PACRR. In evaluations based on the RerankSimple and RerankALL benchmarks, only the results for Co-PACRR are reported. Meanwhile, the results for the other six variants are reported in Section 6.1 on the PairAccuracy benchmark for an ablation test.

Choice of hyper-parameters. In this work, we focus on evaluating the effects of the proposed building blocks and their interactions, without exhaustively fine-tuning hyper-parameters due to limited computing resources. For the disambiguation building block, we fix the size of the context window as $w_c = 4$ on both sides, leading to a context vector computed over 9 terms, namely, 4+4+1. For the cascade component, we conduct k-max pooling with $cpos = [25\%, 50\%, 75\%, 100\%]$, namely, $n_c = 4$. For the combination phase, we use two fully connected layers of size 16. Apart from the two modifications mentioned in Section 3, we further fix the model choices for PACRR following the original configurations [10]. In particular, the PACRR-firstk variant is employed, fixing the unified similarity matrix dimensions $l_d = 800$ and $l_q = 16$, the k-max pooling size $n_s = 3$, the maximum n-gram size $l_g = 3$, and the number of filters used in convolutional layers is $n_f = 32$. Beyond that, we fix the batch size to 16 and we train individual models to at most 150 iterations. Note that most of the aforementioned hyper-parameters can be tuned given sufficient time and hardware, and the chosen parameters follow those in Hui et al. [10] or are based on preliminary experiments for a better focus on the proposed models. In Section 6.2 we consider the impact of the disambiguation parameter w_c and the cascade parameter n_c.

Due to the availability of training data, K-NRM is trained with a frozen word embedding layer, and with an extra fully connected middle layer including 30 neurons to partially compensate for lost strength due to the frozen word embeddings. This is slightly different from the model architecture described in Xiong et al. [23]. This setting also serves for the purpose of allowing fair model comparisons, given that all the compared models could be co-trained with the word embeddings, resulting in a better model capacity at the costs of prolonged training times and a need for much more training data [10]. Note that with the frozen embedding layer, the evaluation can focus on the model strength that comes from different model architectures, demonstrating the capacity of relatively small models in performing ad-hoc retrieval. All the models are trained with a cross-entropy loss as summarized in Eq. 2, given that different loss functions can also influence the results.

[3]http://trec.nist.gov/tracks.html
[4]http://boston.lti.cs.cmu.edu/Services/clueweb09_batch/
[5]http://boston.lti.cs.cmu.edu/Services/clueweb12_batch/
[6]http://trec.nist.gov/data/web/12/gdeval.pl

Table 1: ERR@20 on TREC Web Track 2009–14 when re-ranking search results from *QL*. The relative improvements (%) relative to QL and ranks among all runs within the respective years according to ERR@20 are also reported.

Year	Co-PACRR	PACRR	MatchPyramid	DRMM	DUETL	K-NRM
wt09	0.096 (D↑) 6% 47	0.102 (D↑) 13% 41	0.103 14% 38	0.086 (P↓) -5% 50	0.092 1% 45	0.091 1% 48
wt10	0.160 (P↑K↑D↑L↑M↑) 136% 3	0.146 (K↑D↑L↑m↑) 116% 4	0.131 (p↓L↑) 93% 9	0.131 (P↓L↑) 92% 9	0.103 (P↓K↓D↓M↓) 52% 25	0.128 (P↓L↑) 88% 10
wt11	0.167 (P↑K↑D↑L↑M↑) 52% 2	0.139 (k↑L↑M↑) 26% 15	0.114 (P↓K↓D↓) 3% 31	0.133 (L↑M↑) 21% 19	0.112 (P↓K↓D↓) 1% 35	0.129 (p↓L↑M↑) 17% 23
wt12	0.359 (K↑D↑L↑M↑) 99% 1	0.363 (K↑D↑L↑M↑) 101% 1	0.244 (P↓D↓) 35% 15	0.320 (P↓K↑L↑M↑) 77% 3	0.206 (P↓K↓D↓) 13% 22	0.269 (P↓D↓L↑) 49% 11
wt13	0.189 (K↑D↑L↑M↑) 82% 1	0.184 (K↑D↑L↑M↑) 77% 1	0.131 (P↓D↓) 26% 18	0.166 (P↓K↑L↑M↑) 60% 3	0.130 (P↓D↓) 25% 20	0.141 (P↓D↓) 36% 12
wt14	0.232 (P↑K↑D↑L↑M↑) 84% 1	0.210 (K↑d↑L↑M↑) 67% 4	0.163 (P↓D↓) 29% 19	0.191 (p↓K↑L↑M↑) 52% 10	0.159 (P↓D↓) 26% 20	0.167 (P↓D↓) 32% 17

5.2 Results for Co-PACRR

RERANKSIMPLE. We first examine how well the proposed model performs when re-ranking search results from a simple initial ranker, namely, the query-likelihood (QL) model, to put our results in context as in Guo et al. [7]. The ultimate quality of the re-ranked search results depends on both the strength of the initial ranker and the quality of the re-ranker. The query-likelihood model, as one of the most widely used retrieval models, is used due to its efficiency and practical availability, given that it is included in most retrieval toolkits like Terrier [17]. The results are summarized in Table 1. The ERR@20 of the re-ranked runs is reported, together with the improvements relative to the original QL. The ranks of the re-ranked runs are also reported when sorting the re-ranked search results together with other competing runs from the same year according to ERR@20.

It can be seen that, by simply re-ranking the search results from the query-likelihood method, Co-PACRR can already achieve the top-3 best results in 2010–14. Whereas for 2009, very limited improvements are observed. Combined with Table 3, though variants of Co-PACRR can improve different runs in TREC around 90%, the relative improvements w.r.t. QL are less than 10%, which is worse than the improvements from PACRR and MatchPyramid on 2009. This illustrates that the re-ranking model cannot work independently, as its performance highly depends on the initial ranker. Actually, in Table 1 all compared models experience difficulties in improving QL on 2009, where DRMM even receives a worse ranking. This might be partially explained by the difference of the initial ranker in terms of the recall rate. Intuitively, there should be enough relevant documents to be re-ranked in the initial ranking, otherwise the re-ranker is unable to achieve anything, no matter its quality. The recall rates of QL in different years are as follows (in parentheses): 2009 (0.35), 2010 (0.37), 2011 (0.67), 2012 (0.46), 2013 (0.61), and 2014 (0.68), where 2009 witnesses the lowest recall. However, there may also be other causes for these results.

RERANKALL. Given that the search results from QL only account for a small subset of all judged documents, and, more importantly, that the performance of a re-ranker also depends on the initial runs, we evaluate our re-ranker's performance by re-ranking all submitted runs from the TREC Web Track 2009–14. This evaluation focuses on two aspects: how many different runs we can improve upon and by how much we improve. The former aspect is about the *adaptability* of a neural IR model, investigating whether it can make improvements based on different kinds of retrieval models, while the latter aspect focuses on the *magnitude of improvements*. Table 2 summarizes the percentages of systems that see improvements based on ERR@20 out of the total number of systems in each year. In Table 3, we further report the average percentage of improvements.

Table 2 demonstrates that at least 90% of runs, and on average more than 96% of runs, can be improved by Co-PACRR, which implies a good adaptability, namely, the proposed Co-PACRR can work together with a wide range of initial rankers using different methods. Compared with other neural IR models, in terms of the absolute numbers, Co-PACRR improves the highest number of systems in all the years; when conducting significance tests, in three out of six years, the proposed Co-PACRR significantly outperforms all the baselines. Noticeably, Co-PACRR uniformly achieves good results on all six years, whereas all other methods fail to improve more than 75% of systems in at least one year. There are similar observations for the average improvements shown in Table 3, where Co-PACRR performs best in terms of the average improvements for all six years; on four out of six years Co-PACRR leads other methods with a significant difference. This table shows that Co-PACRR can improve different runs in each year by at least 34% on average.

PAIRACCURACY. Ideally, a re-ranking model should make correct decisions when ranking all kinds of documents. Therefore, we further rely on a pairwise ranking task to compare different models in this regard. Compared with the other two benchmarks, we argue that PAIRACCURACY can lead to more comprehensive and more robust comparisons, as a result of its inclusion of all the labeled ground-truth data and its removal of the effects of initial rankers.

In particular, given a query and a set of documents, different models assign a score to each document according to their inferred relevance relative to the given query. Thereafter, all pairs of documents are examined and the pairs that are ranked in concordance with the ground-truth judgments from TREC are deemed correct, based on which an aggregated accuracy is reported on all such document pairs in different years. For example, given query q and two documents d_1 and d_2, along with their ground-truth judgments $label(d_1)$ and $label(d_2)$, a re-ranking model provides their relevance scores as $rel(q, d_1)$ and $rel(q, d_2)$. The re-ranking model is correct when it predicts these two documents to be ranked in the same order as in the ranking from the ground-truth label, e.g., $rel(q, d_1) > rel(q, d_2)$ and $label(d_1) > label(d_2)$. The relevance judgments in the TREC Web Track include up to six relevance levels: junk pages (Junk), non-relevant (NRel), relevant (Rel), highly relevant (HRel), key pages (Key), and navigational pages (Nav). Note that the label Nav actually indicates that a document can satisfy a navigational intent rather than assigning a degree of relevance as Rel and HRel, which makes it difficult to compare navigational documents with other kinds of

Table 2: The percentage of runs that show improvements in terms of ERR@20 when re-ranking all runs from the TREC Web Track 2009–14.

Year	Co-PACRR	PACRR	MatchPyramid	DRMM	DUETL	K-NRM
wt09	90% (D↑L↑)	93% (D↑L↑)	88% (D↑l↑)	70% (P↓K↓M↓)	74% (P↓K↓m↓)	89% (D↑L↑)
wt10	98% (K↑D↑L↑M↑)	96% (D↑L↑M↑)	89% (P↓K↓L↑)	91% (P↓K↓L↑)	74% (P↓K↓D↓M↓)	95% (D↑L↑M↑)
wt11	98% (P↑K↑D↑L↑M↑)	71% (D↑L↑M↑)	15% (P↓K↓D↓L↓)	42% (P↓K↓L↑M↑)	21% (P↓K↓D↓M↑)	69% (D↑L↑M↑)
wt12	98% (P↑K↑d↑L↑M↑)	95% (K↑L↑M↑)	73% (P↓k↓D↓)	94% (K↑L↑M↑)	72% (P↓k↓D↓)	83% (P↓D↓l↑m↑)
wt13	93% (p↑K↑d↑L↑M↑)	86% (K↑L↑M↑)	56% (P↓D↓)	87% (K↑L↑M↑)	43% (P↓K↓D↓)	63% (P↓D↓L↑)
wt14	96% (K↑D↑L↑M↑)	84% (K↑L↑M↑)	61% (P↓K↑L↑)	69% (K↑L↑)	39% (P↓D↓M↓)	43% (P↓D↓M↓)

Table 3: The average differences of the measure score for individual runs when re-ranking all runs from the TREC Web Track 2009–14 based on ERR@20.

Year	Co-PACRR	PACRR	MatchPyramid	DRMM	DUETL	K-NRM
wt09	47% (p↑K↑D↑L↑M↑)	42% (K↑D↑L↑M↑)	29% (P↓D↑L↑)	17% (P↓K↓M↓)	16% (P↓K↓M↓)	35% (P↓D↑L↑)
wt10	93% (P↑K↑D↑L↑M↑)	76% (D↑L↑M↑)	51% (P↓K↓L↑)	48% (P↓K↓L↑)	27% (P↓K↓D↓M↓)	68% (D↑L↑M↑)
wt11	39% (P↑K↑D↑L↑M↑)	10% (D↑L↑M↑)	-22% (P↓K↓D↓l↓)	-3% (P↓K↓L↑M↑)	-17% (P↓K↓D↓m↑)	8% (D↑L↑M↑)
wt12	84% (K↑D↑L↑M↑)	74% (K↑L↑M↑)	28% (P↓D↓)	69% (K↑L↑M↑)	29% (P↓D↓)	44% (P↓D↓)
wt13	38% (K↑D↑L↑M↑)	30% (K↑L↑M↑)	4% (P↓D↓)	22% (K↑L↑M↑)	-4% (P↓K↓D↓)	11% (P↓D↓L↑)
wt14	34% (P↑K↑D↑L↑M↑)	20% (K↑d↑L↑M↑)	6% (P↓K↑L↑)	10% (p↓K↑L↑)	-4% (P↓D↓M↓)	-4% (P↓D↓M↓)

relevant documents, e.g., a navigational document versus a document labeled as HRel. Thus, documents labeled with Nav are not considered in this task. Moreover, documents labeled as Junk and NRel, and documents labeled as HRel and Key are merged into NRel and HRel, respectively, due to their limited number. After aggregating the labels as described, all pairs of documents with different labels are generated as test pairs. From the "volume" and "# queries" columns in Table 4, we can see that different label pairs actually account for quite different volumes in the ground truth, making their respective degrees of influence different. On the other hand, different label pairs actually also represent different difficulties in making a correct prediction, as the closeness of two documents in terms of their relevance determines the difficulty of the predictions. Intuitively, it is easier to distinguish between HRel and NRel documents than to compare a HRel document with a Rel document. Actually, human assessors tend to also disagree more when dealing with document pairs that are very close with each other in terms of their relevance [1]. It can also be seen that these three label pairs being considered account for 95% of all document pairs from Table 4.

From the upper part of Table 4, for the label pair HRel-NRel, Co-PACRR achieves the highest accuracy in terms of the absolute number, and significantly outperforms all baselines on three years. We have similar observations for Rel-NRel, where, however, Co-PACRR performs worse than PACRR in 2014. As for the label pair HRel-Rel, however, Co-PACRR performs very close to the other models, and on 2011, it performs worse than DUETL. Therefore, we can conclude that Co-PACRR outperforms the other baseline results when comparing documents that are far away in terms of relevance, while performing similarly in dealing with harder pairs. In terms of the absolute accuracy, on average, Co-PACRR yields correct predictions on 78.7%, 73.6%, and 58.7% of document pairs for the label pairs HRel–NRel, Rel–NRel, and HRel–Rel, respectively, where the decreasing accuracy confirms the different difficulties in making predictions for different kinds of pairs.

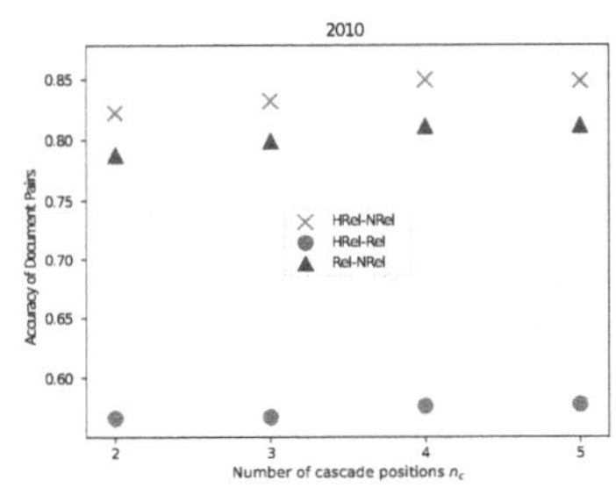

Figure 2: The accuracy on document pairs when using different number of cascade positions n_c for the cascade k-max pooling layer.

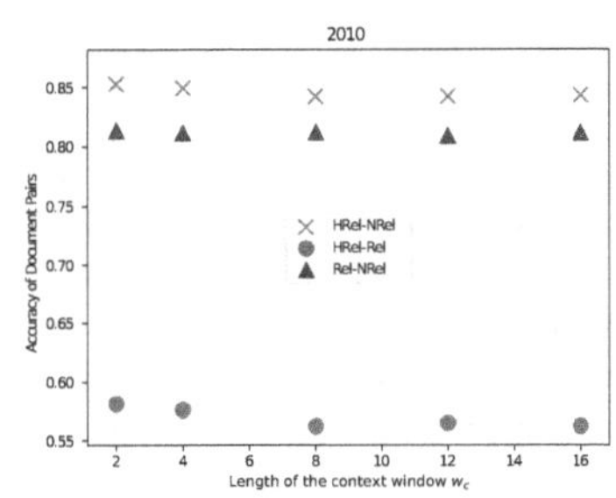

Figure 3: The accuracy on document pairs when varying the size of the context window w_c for the disambiguation component.

Table 4: Comparisons among tested methods in terms of accuracy in ranking document pairs with different label pairs. The columns "volume" and "# queries" record the occurrences of each label combination out of the total pairs, and the number of queries that include a particular label combination among all six years, respectively.

Label Pair	volume (%)	# queries	Year	Co-PACRR	PACRR	MatchPyramid	DRMM	DUETL	K-NRM
HRel-NRel	23.1%	262	wt09	0.720 (P↑K↑D↑L↑M↑)	0.695 (D↑L↑M↑)	0.654 (P↓K↓D↑L↑)	0.597 (P↓K↓M↓)	0.593 (P↓K↓M↓)	0.689 (D↑L↑M↑)
			wt10	0.850 (P↑K↑D↑L↑M↑)	0.831 (k↑D↑L↑M↑)	0.768 (P↓D↑L↑)	0.740 (P↓K↓L↑M↓)	0.677 (P↓K↓D↓M↓)	0.797 (p↓D↑L↑)
			wt11	0.829 (P↑K↑D↑L↑M↑)	0.778 (K↑D↑L↑M↑)	0.693 (P↓K↓D↓L↑)	0.728 (P↓k↓L↑M↑)	0.638 (P↓K↓D↓M↓)	0.749 (P↓d↑L↑M↑)
			wt12	0.801 (K↑D↑L↑M↑)	0.790 (K↑D↑L↑M↑)	0.703 (P↓)	0.672 (P↓K↓)	0.683 (P↓)	0.728 (P↓D↑)
			wt13	0.752 (K↑D↑L↑M↑)	0.744 (K↑D↑L↑M↑)	0.654 (P↓L↑)	0.648 (P↓l↑)	0.636 (P↓K↓d↓M↓)	0.663 (P↓L↑)
			wt14	0.772 (K↑D↑L↑M↑)	0.770 (K↑D↑L↑M↑)	0.670 (P↓K↑D↑L↑)	0.653 (P↓M↓)	0.639 (P↓M↓)	0.640 (P↓M↓)
HRel-Rel	8.4%	257	wt09	0.545 (L↑)	0.534	0.537	0.543 (L↑)	0.529 (K↓D↓)	0.542 (L↑)
			wt10	0.576 (D↑L↑)	0.577 (D↑L↑)	0.591 (D↑L↑)	0.542 (P↓M↓)	0.545 (P↓M↓)	0.572
			wt11	0.576 (P↑K↑D↓L↑m↓)	0.522 (D↓M↓)	0.589 (P↑K↑D↓L↑)	0.615 (P↑K↑L↑M↑)	0.507 (D↓M↓)	0.518 (D↓M↓)
			wt12	0.645 (K↑D↑L↑M↑)	0.644 (K↑D↑L↑M↑)	0.575 (P↓D↑)	0.528 (P↓K↓L↓M↓)	0.583 (P↓D↑)	0.583 (P↓D↑)
			wt13	0.575 (K↑D↑L↑M↑)	0.579 (m↑)	0.551 (p↓)	0.560	0.558	0.551
			wt14	0.602 (P↑K↑D↑L↑M↑)	0.575 (K↑d↑)	0.569 (K↑D↑)	0.558 (p↓K↑M↓)	0.560 (K↑)	0.507 (P↓D↓L↓M↓)
Rel-NRel	63.5%	290	wt09	0.676 (P↑K↑D↑L↑M↑)	0.663 (K↑D↑L↑M↑)	0.619 (P↓K↓D↑L↑)	0.555 (P↓K↓M↓)	0.563 (P↓K↓M↓)	0.650 (P↓D↑L↑M↑)
			wt10	0.811 (P↑K↑D↑L↑M↑)	0.791 (K↑D↑L↑M↑)	0.708 (P↓K↓L↑)	0.710 (P↓K↓L↑)	0.639 (P↓K↓D↓M↓)	0.751 (P↓D↑L↑M↑)
			wt11	0.787 (P↑K↑D↑L↑M↑)	0.770 (K↑D↑L↑M↑)	0.616 (P↓K↓)	0.607 (P↓K↓)	0.621 (P↓K↓)	0.711 (P↓D↑L↑M↑)
			wt12	0.735 (p↑K↑D↑L↑M↑)	0.721 (K↑D↑L↑M↑)	0.640 (P↓K↓L↑)	0.651 (P↓k↓L↑)	0.616 (P↓K↓D↓M↓)	0.673 (P↓d↑L↑M↑)
			wt13	0.700 (K↑D↑L↑M↑)	0.689 (K↑D↑L↑M↑)	0.612 (P↓D↑L↑)	0.589 (P↓K↓M↓)	0.579 (P↓K↓M↓)	0.623 (P↓D↑L↑)
			wt14	0.708 (p↓K↑D↑L↑M↑)	0.717 (K↑D↑L↑M↑)	0.620 (P↓K↓D↑L↑)	0.597 (P↓K↓M↓)	0.586 (P↓K↓M↓)	0.647 (P↓D↑L↑M↑)
Label Pair	**volume (%)**	**# queries**	**Year**	**C-PACRR**	**D-PACRR**	**S-PACRR**	**CD-PACRR**	**CS-PACRR**	**DS-PACRR**
HRel-NRel	23.1%	262	wt09	0.702 (K↑D↑L↑M↑)	0.701 (K↑D↑L↑M↑)	0.704 (p↑K↑D↑L↑M↑)	0.704 (K↑D↑L↑M↑)	0.716 (P↑K↑D↑L↑M↑)	0.713 (P↑K↑D↑L↑M↑)
			wt10	0.839 (p↑K↑D↑L↑M↑)	0.842 (P↑K↑D↑L↑M↑)	0.843 (P↑K↑D↑L↑M↑)	0.842 (p↑K↑D↑L↑M↑)	0.848 (P↑K↑D↑L↑M↑)	0.843 (p↑K↑D↑L↑M↑)
			wt11	0.808 (K↑D↑L↑M↑)	0.820 (P↑K↑D↑L↑M↑)	0.824 (P↑K↑D↑L↑M↑)	0.810 (p↑K↑D↑L↑M↑)	0.821 (P↑K↑D↑L↑M↑)	0.836 (P↑K↑D↑L↑M↑)
			wt12	0.812 (P↑K↑D↑L↑M↑)	0.785 (K↑D↑L↑M↑)	0.794 (K↑D↑L↑M↑)	0.786 (K↑D↑L↑M↑)	0.819 (P↑K↑D↑L↑M↑)	0.786 (K↑D↑L↑M↑)
			wt13	0.749 (K↑D↑L↑M↑)	0.745 (K↑D↑L↑M↑)	0.755 (K↑D↑L↑M↑)	0.736 (K↑D↑L↑M↑)	0.766 (P↑K↑D↑L↑M↑)	0.751 (K↑D↑L↑M↑)
			wt14	0.773 (K↑D↑L↑M↑)	0.767 (K↑D↑L↑M↑)	0.766 (K↑D↑L↑M↑)	0.768 (K↑D↑L↑M↑)	0.785 (P↑K↑D↑L↑M↑)	0.777 (K↑D↑L↑M↑)
HRel-Rel	8.4%	257	wt09	0.535 (D↓l↑)	0.539 (L↑)	0.543 (L↑)	0.541 (L↑)	0.539 (L↑)	0.546 (p↑L↑)
			wt10	0.585 (D↑L↑)	0.575 (D↑L↑)	0.580 (D↑L↑)	0.568 (p↓d↑L↑M↓)	0.581 (D↑L↑)	0.571 (d↑L↑)
			wt11	0.533 (D↓M↓)	0.565 (P↑K↑D↓L↑M↓)	0.570 (P↑K↑D↓L↑M↓)	0.548 (k↑D↓L↑M↓)	0.552 (P↑K↑D↓L↑M↓)	0.584 (P↑K↑D↓L↑)
			wt12	0.680 (P↑K↑D↑L↑M↑)	0.637 (K↑D↑L↑M↑)	0.658 (P↑K↑D↑L↑M↑)	0.651 (K↑D↑L↑M↑)	0.675 (P↑K↑D↑L↑M↑)	0.641 (K↑D↑L↑M↑)
			wt13	0.553	0.581 (K↑d↑L↑M↑)	0.580 (K↑D↑L↑M↑)	0.557	0.572 (k↑M↑)	0.587 (K↑D↑L↑M↑)
			wt14	0.598 (p↑K↑D↑L↑M↑)	0.589 (K↑D↑L↑M↑)	0.570 (K↑)	0.599 (K↑D↑L↑M↑)	0.596 (P↑K↑D↑L↑M↑)	0.584 (K↑D↑L↑m↑)
Rel-NRel	63.5%	290	wt09	0.672 (p↑K↑D↑L↑M↑)	0.665 (K↑D↑L↑M↑)	0.667 (K↑D↑L↑M↑)	0.670 (p↑K↑D↑L↑M↑)	0.679 (P↑K↑D↑L↑M↑)	0.671 (P↑K↑D↑L↑M↑)
			wt10	0.795 (K↑D↑L↑M↑)	0.802 (K↑D↑L↑M↑)	0.806 (P↑K↑D↑L↑M↑)	0.805 (p↑K↑D↑L↑M↑)	0.807 (P↑K↑D↑L↑M↑)	0.807 (P↑K↑D↑L↑M↑)
			wt11	0.778 (K↑D↑L↑M↑)	0.779 (K↑D↑L↑M↑)	0.788 (P↑K↑D↑L↑M↑)	0.775 (K↑D↑L↑M↑)	0.792 (P↑K↑D↑L↑M↑)	0.787 (P↑K↑D↑L↑M↑)
			wt12	0.728 (K↑D↑L↑M↑)	0.730 (K↑D↑L↑M↑)	0.724 (K↑D↑L↑M↑)	0.726 (K↑D↑L↑M↑)	0.737 (P↑K↑D↑L↑M↑)	0.729 (K↑D↑L↑M↑)
			wt13	0.705 (P↑K↑D↑L↑M↑)	0.685 (K↑D↑L↑M↑)	0.696 (P↑K↑D↑L↑M↑)	0.693 (K↑D↑L↑M↑)	0.714 (P↑K↑D↑L↑M↑)	0.697 (P↑K↑D↑L↑M↑)
			wt14	0.707 (P↓K↑D↑L↑M↑)	0.705 (P↓K↑D↑L↑M↑)	0.717 (K↑D↑L↑M↑)	0.698 (P↓K↑D↑L↑M↑)	0.715 (K↑D↑L↑M↑)	0.717 (K↑D↑L↑M↑)

6 DISCUSSION

6.1 Ablation Analysis

In this section, we attempt to gain further insights about the usefulness of the proposed model components, namely, the cascade k-max pooling (C), the disambiguation (D) and the shuffling combination (S) layer, by drawing comparisons among different model variants. As mentioned, the PairAccuracy benchmark is the most comprehensive due to its inclusion of all document pairs and its removal of the effects of an initial ranker, making the analysis based solely on the proposed neural models. Therefore, our analysis in this section mainly considers PairAccuracy.

Effects of the individual building blocks. We first incorporate the proposed components into PACRR one at time, leading to the C-PACRR, D-PACRR, and S-PACRR model variants, which we use to examine the effects of these building blocks separately. Table 4 demonstrates that the shuffling combination (S-PACRR) alone can boost the performance on three different label pairs, significantly outperforming PACRR on two to three years out of six years for all three label combinations, and performing at least as well as PACRR on the remaining years. As mentioned in Section 1, the shuffling combination performs regularization by preventing the model from learning query-dependent patterns. On the other hand, adding the C-PACRR or D-PACRR component to PACRR actually hurts the performance on 2014 over the Rel-NRel label pair, and only occasionally improves PACRR on other years. Intuitively, both building blocks introduce extra weights into PACRR, increasing the number of nodes for combination by adding the context vectors or by using multiple pooling layers, making the model more prone to overfitting. Such changes might be an issue when only limited training data is available.

Joint effects of different components. To resolve the extra complexity introduced by the cascade pooling layers and the disambiguation building blocks, we further combine these two with the shuffling component, leading to CS-PACRR and DS-PACRR. Meanwhile, we also investigate the joint effects between them by examining CD-PACRR. From Table 4, compared with the PACRR model, both CS-PACRR and DS-PACRR achieve better results not only relative to C-PACRR and D-PACRR, but also to S-PACRR. This is especially true for CS-PACRR, which significantly outperforms

PACRR on all years for HRel-NRel pairs, and on five years for Rel-NRel pairs. This demonstrates that both the cascade pooling and the disambiguation components can help only after introducing extra regularization to offset the extra complexity being introduced. As for CD-PACRR, not surprisingly, it performs on a par with C-PACRR and D-PACRR, and worse than the CS-PACRR and DS-PACRR. Finally, we put all components together and end up with the Co-PACRR model discussed in Section 5, which performs better than C-PACRR and D-PACRR, and similar to S-PACRR, but occasionally worse than CS-PACRR on 2012–14. We argue that this is due to the joint usage of the cascade k-max pooling and the disambiguation, making the model much more complex and thereby expensive to train like CD-PACRR, therefore requiring more training data to work well. We note that DS-PACRR performs better than the S-PACRR variant, supporting our argument that the full model's decreased performance is caused by the added complexity, and not by adding the disambiguation component itself, and this also applies to the cascade k-max pooling layer. In short, we conclude that all three components can lead to improved results. Moreover, we suggest that, when limited training data is available, either CS-PACRR or DS-PACRR could be employed in place of Co-PACRR, since they are less data-hungry compared with Co-PACRR.

6.2 Tuning of Hyper-parameters

Finally, we further investigate the effects of the two hyper-parameters introduced by our proposed components, namely, the number of cascade positions n_c and the size of the context window w_c, which govern the cascade k-max pooling component and the disambiguation component, respectively. Figures 2 and 3 show the effects of applying different n_c and w_c on 2010, where the x-axis represents the configurations of the hyper-parameter, and the y-axis represents the corresponding accuracy on document pairs. In the case of cascade k-max pooling, we uniformly divide $[0\%, 100\%]$ into n_c parts, e.g., with $n_c = 5$ we have $cpos = [20\%, 40\%, 60\%, 80\%, and 100\%]$. Owing to space constraints, we omit the plots for other years. From Figures 2 and 3, we observe that the model is robust against different choices of n_c and w_c within the investigated ranges, and the trend of the accuracy relative to different choices of hyper-parameters is consistent among the three kinds of label pairs. Furthermore, increasing the number of cascade positions slightly increases the accuracy, whereas increasing the context window size past $w_c = 4$ reduces the accuracy.

7 CONCLUSION

In this work we proposed the novel Co-PACRR neural IR model that incorporates the local and global context of matching signals into the PACRR model through the use of a disambiguation building block, a cascade k-max pooling layer, and a shuffling combination layer. Extensive experiments on TREC Web Track data demonstrated the superior performance of the proposed Co-PACRR model. Notably, the model is trained using TREC data consisting of about 100k training instances, illustrating that models performing ad-hoc retrieval can greatly benefit from architectural improvements as well as an increase in training data. As for future work, one potential direction is the combination of handcrafted learning-to-rank features with the interactions learned by Co-PACRR, where an effective way to learn such features (e.g., PageRank scores) inside the neural model appears non-trivial.

REFERENCES

[1] Omar Alonso and Stefano Mizzaro. 2012. Using crowdsourcing for TREC relevance assessment. *Information Processing & Management* 48, 6 (2012), 1053–1066.

[2] Olivier Chapelle, Donald Metlzer, Ya Zhang, and Pierre Grinspan. 2009. Expected reciprocal rank for graded relevance. In *Proceedings of the 18th ACM conference on Information and knowledge management (CIKM '09)*. ACM, New York, NY, USA, 621–630. https://doi.org/10.1145/1645953.1646033

[3] Kevyn Collins-Thompson, Craig Macdonald, Paul Bennett, Fernando Diaz, and Ellen M Voorhees. 2015. *TREC 2014 web track overview*. Technical Report. DTIC Document.

[4] Nick Craswell, Onno Zoeter, Michael Taylor, and Bill Ramsey. 2008. An experimental comparison of click position-bias models. In *Proceedings of the 2008 International Conference on Web Search and Data Mining*. ACM, 87–94.

[5] Mostafa Dehghani, Hamed Zamani, Aliaksei Severyn, Jaap Kamps, and W Bruce Croft. 2017. Neural Ranking Models with Weak Supervision. *arXiv preprint arXiv:1704.08803* (2017).

[6] Ian Goodfellow, Yoshua Bengio, and Aaron Courville. 2016. *Deep Learning*. MIT Press. http://www.deeplearningbook.org.

[7] Jiafeng Guo, Yixing Fan, Qingyao Ai, and W Bruce Croft. 2016. A deep relevance matching model for ad-hoc retrieval. In *Proceedings of the 25th ACM International on Conference on Information and Knowledge Management*. ACM, 55–64.

[8] Baotian Hu, Zhengdong Lu, Hang Li, and Qingcai Chen. 2014. Convolutional Neural Network Architectures for Matching Natural Language Sentences. In *Advances in Neural Information Processing Systems 27*. 2042–2050.

[9] Po-Sen Huang, Xiaodong He, Jianfeng Gao, Li Deng, Alex Acero, and Larry Heck. 2013. Learning Deep Structured Semantic Models for Web Search Using Clickthrough Data. In *Proceedings of the 22nd ACM International Conference on Information & Knowledge Management (CIKM '13)*. 2333–2338.

[10] Kai Hui, Andrew Yates, Klaus Berberich, and Gerard de Melo. 2017. A Position-Aware Deep Model for Relevance Matching in Information Retrieval. In *EMNLP '17*.

[11] Kai Hui, Andrew Yates, Klaus Berberich, and Gerard de Melo. 2017. Position-Aware Representations for Relevance Matching in Neural Information Retrieval. In *Proceedings of the 26th International Conference on World Wide Web Companion*. International World Wide Web Conferences Steering Committee, 799–800.

[12] Samuel Huston and W. Bruce Croft. 2014. A Comparison of Retrieval Models using Term Dependencies. In *Proceedings of the 23rd ACM International Conference on Conference on Information and Knowledge Management (CIKM'14)*. 111–120.

[13] Tie-Yan Liu et al. 2009. Learning to rank for information retrieval. *Foundations and Trends® in Information Retrieval* 3, 3 (2009), 225–331.

[14] Donald Metzler and W Bruce Croft. 2005. A Markov random field model for term dependencies. In *Proceedings of the 28th annual international ACM SIGIR conference on Research and development in information retrieval*. ACM, 472–479.

[15] Bhaskar Mitra, Fernando Diaz, and Nick Craswell. 2017. Learning to Match Using Local and Distributed Representations of Text for Web Search. In *Proceedings of WWW 2017*. ACM.

[16] Bhaskar Mitra, Eric Nalisnick, Nick Craswell, and Rich Caruana. 2016. A dual embedding space model for document ranking. *arXiv preprint arXiv:1602.01137* (2016).

[17] I. Ounis, G. Amati, V. Plachouras, B. He, C. Macdonald, and C. Lioma. 2006. Terrier: A High Performance and Scalable Information Retrieval Platform. In *Proceedings of ACM SIGIR'06 Workshop on Open Source Information Retrieval (OSIR 2006)*.

[18] Liang Pang, Yanyan Lan, Jiafeng Guo, Jun Xu, and Xueqi Cheng. 2016. A Study of MatchPyramid Models on Ad-hoc Retrieval. *CoRR* abs/1606.04648 (2016). http://arxiv.org/abs/1606.04648

[19] Liang Pang, Yanyan Lan, Jiafeng Guo, Jun Xu, Shengxian Wan, and Xueqi Cheng. 2016. Text Matching As Image Recognition. In *Proceedings of the Thirtieth AAAI Conference on Artificial Intelligence (AAAI'16)*. 2793–2799.

[20] Yelong Shen, Xiaodong He, Jianfeng Gao, Li Deng, and Grégoire Mesnil. 2014. Learning Semantic Representations Using Convolutional Neural Networks for Web Search. In *Proceedings of the 23rd International Conference on World Wide Web (WWW '14 Companion)*.

[21] Karen Simonyan and Andrew Zisserman. 2014. Very deep convolutional networks for large-scale image recognition. *arXiv preprint arXiv:1409.1556* (2014).

[22] Tao Tao and ChengXiang Zhai. 2007. An exploration of proximity measures in information retrieval. In *Proceedings of the 30th annual international ACM SIGIR conference on Research and development in information retrieval*. ACM, 295–302.

[23] Chenyan Xiong, Zhuyun Dai, Jamie Callan, Zhiyuan Liu, and Russell Power. 2017. End-to-End Neural Ad-hoc Ranking with Kernel Pooling. In *Proceedings of the 40th International ACM SIGIR Conference (SIGIR '17)*. ACM.

[24] Hamed Zamani and W Bruce Croft. 2017. Relevance-based Word Embedding. *arXiv preprint arXiv:1705.03556* (2017).

Recommendation in Heterogeneous Information Networks Based on Generalized Random Walk Model and Bayesian Personalized Ranking

Zhengshen Jiang
Peking University
Beijing, China
jiangzhengshen@pku.edu.cn

Hongzhi Liu*
Peking University
Beijing, China
liuhz@pku.edu.cn

Bin Fu
Peking University
Beijing, China
fubin1990@pku.edu.cn

Zhonghai Wu*
Peking University
Beijing, China
wuzh@pku.edu.cn

Tao Zhang
Beijing Huapinborui Network Technology Company
Beijing, China
kylen.zhang@kanzhun.com

ABSTRACT

Recommendation based on heterogeneous information network (HIN) is attracting more and more attention due to its ability to emulate collaborative filtering, content-based filtering, context-aware recommendation and combinations of any of these recommendation semantics. Random walk based methods are usually used to mine the paths, weigh the paths, and compute the closeness or relevance between two nodes in a HIN. A key for the success of these methods is how to properly set the weights of links in a HIN. In existing methods, the weights of links are mostly set heuristically. In this paper, we propose a Bayesian Personalized Ranking (BPR) based machine learning method, called HeteLearn, to learn the weights of links in a HIN. In order to model user preferences for personalized recommendation, we also propose a generalized random walk with restart model on HINs. We evaluate the proposed method in a personalized recommendation task and a tag recommendation task. Experimental results show that our method performs significantly better than both the traditional collaborative filtering and the state-of-the-art HIN-based recommendation methods.

CCS CONCEPTS

• **Information systems → Recommender systems**; *Personalization*; • **Computing methodologies → Ranking**;

KEYWORDS

recommender systems; Bayesian Personalized Ranking; heterogeneous information network; random walk

*Corresponding author.

WSDM 2018, February 5–9, 2018, Marina Del Rey, CA, USA

ACM ISBN 978-1-4503-5581-0/18/02...$15.00
https://doi.org/10.1145/3159652.3159715

ACM Reference Format:
Zhengshen Jiang, Hongzhi Liu, Bin Fu, Zhonghai Wu*, and Tao Zhang. 2018. Recommendation in Heterogeneous Information Networks Based on Generalized Random Walk Model and Bayesian Personalized Ranking. In *WSDM 2018: WSDM 2018: The Eleventh ACM International Conference on Web Search and Data Mining , February 5–9, 2018, Marina Del Rey, CA, USA.* ACM, New York, NY, USA, 9 pages. https://doi.org/10.1145/3159652.3159715

1 INTRODUCTION

1.1 Background

Recommender systems have been used to provide users with recommendations for products or services in various domains, such as e-commerce platforms and social networks [28]. Traditional recommendation approaches include [16]:

- Content-based filtering (CB): These approaches utilize the content information to recommend items that are similar to those previously preferred by the target user.
- Collaborative filtering (CF): These approaches recommend items to users based on the preferences that other users have expressed for those items [5].
- Hybrid approaches: These approaches combine collaborative with content-based methods or with different variants of other collaborative methods.

As a kind of hybrid approach, recommendations based on heterogeneous information networks (HINs) provide a new perspective to design recommendation systems. HINs are logical networks involving multiple-typed objects and multiple-typed links denoting different relations [8].

For instance, Figure 1 illustrates an example of a heterogeneous information network, which contains five types of entities: users, movies, genres, actors and directors, together with their relations.

Since these approaches combine user feedback data with additional information such as items or users attributes and relationships, they could emulate collaborative-filtering, content-based filtering, context-aware recommendation and combinations of any of these recommendation semantics [13].

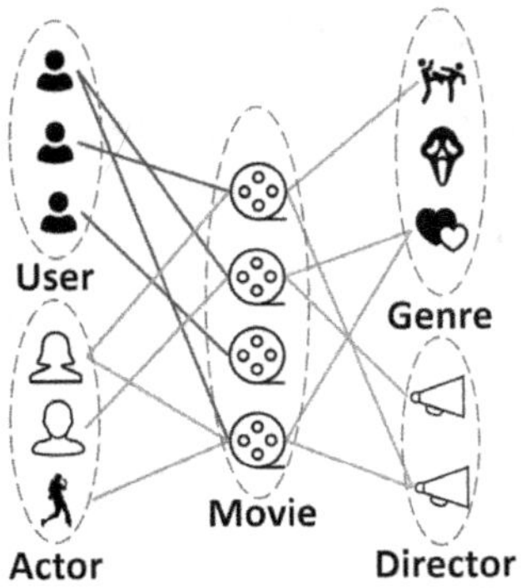

Figure 1: An example of a heterogeneous information network

1.2 Related Work

In this paper, we focus on recommendation based on HINs. Several algorithms have been presented in this field, and most of them are random walk based methods. In this subsection, we will first introduce the random walk model briefly, and then give a review on related work.

Consider a random walker that recursively moves to a random neighbour in a network. Denoting by $r_i^{(t)}$ the probability that the walker is located at node i at time t, and $r_i^{(t)}$ of all the nodes form a vector $\mathbf{r}^{(t)}$, we can write

$$\mathbf{r}^{(t+1)} = \mathbf{P} \cdot \mathbf{r}^{(t)}$$

where $\mathbf{P}$ is the transition probability matrix. The stationary probability $\mathbf{r}$ could be given by the equation $\mathbf{r} = \mathbf{P} \cdot \mathbf{r}$.

A lot of work is in close relationship with this model, such as the Local Random Walk [15], the Path-constrained random walk [11], HeteSim [23] and PathMining [12].

One important variant of random walk is the random walk with restart model. Considering a random walker starting from node i that recursively moves to a random neighbour with probability α and returns to node i with probability $1-\alpha$, we can write the iterative equation as following

$$\mathbf{r}^{(t+1)} = \alpha \mathbf{P} \cdot \mathbf{r}^{(t)} + (1-\alpha)\mathbf{t} \quad (1)$$

where $\mathbf{t}$ is called the "teleport vector", and it is usually set as $\mathbf{t} = \mathbf{r}^{(0)}$, i.e., the elements of $\mathbf{t}$ are all zero except that $t_i = 1$.

This kind of model was traditionally used in PageRank [18], and was introduced to recommender systems by Personalized PageRank [9]. Typical work include ObjectRank [1], ItemRank[7] and the HIN-based method PathRank [13].

As a representative recommendation method based on HINs, the PathRank model introduced the meta-paths on HINs into random walk with restart model. The authors proved that the PageRank, Personalized PageRank and Path-constrained Random Walk model are all special cases of PathRank.

One key problem in random walk is the setting of the transition matrix $\mathbf{P}$. In traditional random walk models, $\mathbf{P} = \mathbf{A}\mathbf{D}^{-1}$, where $\mathbf{A}$ is the adjacency matrix, and $\mathbf{D}$ is the degree matrix defined as $\mathbf{D} = \text{diag}(d_i)$ with d_i being the degree of the node i. According to physical models like resistance distance [10] and average commute time [6], the transition matrix could also be set by $\mathbf{P} = \mathbf{D}^{-1}\mathbf{A}$. In the work of [27], models using $\mathbf{P} = \mathbf{A}\mathbf{D}^{-1}$ are called "probabilistic spreading", and those using $\mathbf{P} = \mathbf{D}^{-1}\mathbf{A}$ are called "heat spreading".

In previous work, the transition matrix was mostly set heuristically, and recommendation results could only be provided by the topological relations of the network. As a result, the transition matrix could not adapt to different datasets automatically. In this work, we use a machine learning method to learn the transition matrix. We use a generalized random walk with restart method to model user preferences, and use a Bayesian Personalized Ranking (BPR) based machine learning method to learn the link weights of HINs. Experimental results show that the proposed method performs significantly better than both the traditional collaborative filtering and HIN-based recommendation methods.

1.3 Contributions

In this paper, we contribute to the field of recommender system both theoretically and empirically.

Firstly, we propose a new personalized recommendation method, called HeteLearn, on heterogeneous information networks. In this method, we use a BPR-based machine learning method to learn the weights of links in the networks. Instead of setting the weights of links or path-guides heuristically as in previous work, the proposed method could automatically learn them from the HINs. Therefore, the proposed method has a wider range of applications.

Secondly, we propose a generalized random walk with restart model to model user preferences on HINs. We also prove that, the result of random walk with restart is the accumulation of a series of random walks that consist of different random steps, and longer random walks have less impacts on the final results. In addition, the semantics of longer paths are less clear than short paths. Thus, we propose to use k-step random walk with restart model in our recommendation method.

Lastly, empirically, we demonstrate the effectiveness of our method in both item recommendation and tag recommendation tasks. According to the experimental results, the proposed method performs significantly better than both the traditional collaborative filtering and the state-of-the-art HIN-based recommendation methods.

2 PRELIMINARIES AND NOTATIONS

2.1 Heterogeneous Information Network

Following is the definition of heterogeneous information network given by Sun et al. [24].

Definition 2.1. **(Heterogeneous Information Network [24])** An information network is a directed graph $G = (V, E)$ with an object type mapping function $\phi : V \longrightarrow \mathcal{A}$ and a link type mapping function $\psi : E \longrightarrow \mathcal{R}$, where each object $v \in V$ belongs to one particular object type $\phi(v) \in \mathcal{A}$, and each link $e \in E$ belongs to a particular relation $\psi(e) \in \mathcal{R}$. When the types of objects satisfy $|\mathcal{A}| > 1$ or the types of relations satisfy $|\mathcal{R}| > 1$, the network is a **heterogeneous information network**; otherwise, it is a **homogeneous information network**.

In an information network, heterogeneous or homogeneous, each node $v_i \in V$ may have a set of attribute-value pairs which describe the properties of the node, and each edge $e(v_i, v_j) \in E$ has a corresponding weight w.

The network schema or meta-graph provides meta level description of a HIN. The definition is as follows.

Definition 2.2. **(Network Schema [24])** The network schema is a meta template for a heterogeneous network $G = (V, E)$ with the object type mapping $\phi : V \longrightarrow \mathcal{A}$ and the link mapping $\psi : E \longrightarrow \mathcal{R}$, which is a directed graph defined over object types $\mathcal{A}$, with edges as relations from $\mathcal{R}$, denoted as $T_G = (\mathcal{A}, \mathcal{R})$.

2.2 Implicit Feedback

With u and i denoting a user and an item, respectively, we define the user implicit feedback matrix R as following:

$$R_{ui} = \begin{cases} 1, & \text{if } (u,i) \text{ interaction is observed;} \\ 0, & \text{otherwise.} \end{cases}$$

We use U and I to denote the set of users and items, respectively. For each user $u \in U$, the items that satisfy $R_{ui} = 1$ are called positive items, and we denote the set of positive items by $I_u^+ \subset I$. And items in $I \backslash I_u^+$ are called negative items.

The goal is to recommend each user a personalized ranking list of items from $I \backslash I_u^+$. This problem is usually called one-class recommendation problem [19] or recommendation with implicit feedback [20, 22].

2.3 Bayesian Personalized Ranking (BPR)

In the BPR method, Rendle et al. [22] used a binary random variable $\delta((u,i) \succ (u,j))$ to denote whether user u prefers item i to item j or not. The function $\delta(z)$ equals 1 if z is true, and equals 0 otherwise. This representation is called a user's pairwise preference [20].

For a given user u, in order to calculate the overall likelihood of pairwise preferences among all the items, Rendle et al. [22] used the Bernoulli distribution over the binary random variable $\delta((u,i) \succ (u,j))$, as following

$$\begin{aligned} \text{BPR} &= \ln\{ \prod_{(u,i,j) \in U \times I \times I} p(\hat{r}_{ui} > \hat{r}_{uj})^{\delta((u,i) \succ (u,j))} \\ &\quad \times [1 - p(\hat{r}_{ui} > \hat{r}_{uj})]^{[1-\delta((u,i) \succ (u,j))]} \} \\ &= \ln\{ \prod_{(u,i) \succ (u,j)} p(\hat{r}_{ui} > \hat{r}_{uj})[1 - p(\hat{r}_{uj} > \hat{r}_{ui})] \} \\ &\propto \sum_{(u,i) \succ (u,j)} \ln p(\hat{r}_{ui} > \hat{r}_{uj}) \end{aligned}$$

where the summation is computed over all the pairs that satisfy $(u,i) \succ (u,j)$ in the training set, and $\hat{r}_{ui}$ represents the preference of user u for item i.

In the BPR method, it was defined that

$$\hat{x}_{uij} = \hat{r}_{ui} - \hat{r}_{uj}$$

and

$$p(\hat{r}_{ui} > \hat{r}_{uj}) = \frac{1}{1 + e^{-\hat{x}_{uij}}}.$$

Therefore, the gradient of BPR is

$$\frac{\partial \text{BPR}}{\partial \Theta} \propto \sum_{(u,i) \succ (u,j)} \frac{1}{1 + e^{\hat{x}_{uij}}} \cdot \frac{\partial}{\partial \Theta} \hat{x}_{uij}$$

BPR could be maximized using gradient descent as following:

$$\Theta \leftarrow \Theta + \eta \frac{\partial \text{BPR}}{\partial \Theta}$$

where η is the learning rate. When using stochastic gradient descent, Θ is updated as following:

$$\Theta \leftarrow \Theta + \eta \cdot \frac{1}{1 + e^{\hat{x}_{uij}}} \cdot \frac{\partial}{\partial \Theta} \hat{x}_{uij} \tag{2}$$

3 RECOMMENDATION ON HINS

In conventional random walk models, the transition matrix is set by $\mathbf{P} = \mathbf{A}\mathbf{D}^{-1}$. However, when using machine learning methods to learn the link weights in a network, such models will result in a non-convex target function, which could not be optimized using common methods like gradient descent.

In this section, we will propose a generalized random walk with restart model on HINs to model user preferences and facilitate the optimization. The learning method will be detailed in Section 4.

3.1 The Heterogeneous Random Walk with Restart Model

Following is the mathematical definition of our model.

Definition 3.1. **(Heterogeneous Random Walk with Restart)** Given a heterogeneous information network $G = (V, E)$ and its meta-graph $T_G = (\mathcal{A}, \mathcal{R})$, consider a random walker starting from node i that recursively moves to a random neighbour with probability α and returns to node i with probability $1 - \alpha$. Denote $\mathbf{P}$ to be the transition probability matrix, and $\mathbf{r}^{(t)}$ to be the distribution probability vectors representing the probabilities that the nodes are visited at time t. And denote the initial value of $\mathbf{r}$ to be $\mathbf{r}^{(0)}$, and satisfies that $r_i^{(0)} \geq 0$ and $\sum_i r_i^{(0)} = 1$. During each iteration, the vector $\mathbf{r}$ is updated according to the following equation

$$\mathbf{r}^{(t+1)} = \alpha \mathbf{P} \mathbf{r}^{(t)} + (1 - \alpha)\mathbf{t} \tag{3}$$

where $\mathbf{t}$ is called the "teleport vector" and is typically set to be $\mathbf{t} = \mathbf{r}^{(0)}$.

In this paper, we model the transition matrix $\mathbf{P}$ as

$$\mathbf{P}_{ij} = p(v_i | v_j) = p(\phi(v_i) | v_j) \cdot p(v_i | v_j, \phi(v_i))$$

where $\phi(v_i)$ is the type of v_i.

Further, we define

$$p(v_i | v_j, \phi(v_i)) = \frac{1}{|D_j^{\phi_i}|}$$

where

$$D_j^{\phi_i} \stackrel{def}{=} \{v_k | e(v_j, v_k) \in E \wedge \phi(v_k) = \phi(v_i)\}$$

denotes the set of nodes that is connected to node v_j and the type is $\phi(v_i)$. According to this definition, the probability that node v_j goes to node v_i is inversely proportional to the number of neighbours of v_j that are of the same type as node v_i. In other words, node v_j transfers to all the nodes of type $\phi(v_i)$ with equal probability.

To model the distribution $p(\phi(v_i)|v_j)$, we assume that

$$p(\phi(v_i)|v_j) = p(\phi(v_i)|\phi(v_j)) \tag{4}$$

In other words, we assume that all the nodes of type $\phi(v_j)$ transfer to type $\phi(v_i)$ with equal probabilities. Since the parameters $p(\phi(v_i)|\phi(v_j))$ should be learned from the training data, such assumption greatly reduces the number of parameters to be learned, and makes the learning procedure more robust. Detailed learning procedure will be given in Section 4.

In this paper, we set the initial distribution $\mathbf{r}^{(0)}$ to be different for different user u as following

$$\mathbf{r}_i^{(0)} = \begin{cases} 1, & \text{node } v_i \text{ corresponds to user } u, \\ 0, & \text{otherwise.} \end{cases}$$

Therefore, our model could make personalized recommendations.

3.2 Finite Step Random Walk with Restart

The random walk with restart model can be proved to have a stable solution. However, in practice, it is usually costly to compute the stable solution. In this subsection, we will give some analysis on the random walk with restart model, and prove that it is usually not necessary to iterate the model until convergence. Thus, in this paper, finite step random walk with restart model is used instead.

Using the iterative equation in Equation 3, after substituting $\mathbf{t} = \mathbf{r}^{(0)}$, we get

$$\begin{aligned} \mathbf{r}^{(1)} &= \alpha \mathbf{P}\mathbf{r}^{(0)} + (1-\alpha)\mathbf{r}^{(0)} \\ \mathbf{r}^{(2)} &= \alpha^2 \mathbf{P}^2\mathbf{r}^{(0)} + \alpha(1-\alpha)\mathbf{P}\mathbf{r}^{(0)} + (1-\alpha)\mathbf{r}^{(0)} \\ &\dots \\ \mathbf{r}^{(k)} &= \alpha^k \mathbf{P}^k\mathbf{r}^{(0)} + \sum_{i=0}^{k-1} \alpha^i(1-\alpha)\mathbf{P}^i\mathbf{r}^{(0)} \end{aligned} \tag{5}$$

Note that $\mathbf{P}^i\mathbf{r}^{(0)}$ corresponds to a random walk that consists of i random steps. Therefore, the result of k-step random walk with restart is the accumulation of a series of random walks that consist of different random steps, and the weights of these random walks decrease exponentially with the increasing of random steps. So the random walks with more random steps have less impacts on the results.

In addition, the semantics of longer paths are less clear than short paths, and the correlation between the nodes connected through longer paths are also less reliable. Thus, using long paths in the learning procedure may result in bad generalization performance.

Therefore, in this paper, we use k-step random walk with restart model in both the training and recommendation procedure.

4 LEARNING OF THE WEIGHT MATRIX

In this section, we will propose a BPR-based algorithm (HeteLearn) to learn the transition matrix $\mathbf{P}$ on HINs.

4.1 Objective Function

According to the assumption in Equation 4, the parameters to be learned are the probabilities $p(\phi(v_i)|\phi(v_j))$, and the total number of the parameters equals the number of link types in network G, i.e., the number of edges in the network schema T_G. Hence, in this subsection, we also use p_τ to denote the parameters, where $\tau \in \mathcal{R}$ is an edge type in network G.

We follow the BPR optimization framework to construct our objective function. The idea is that the model with appropriate parameters should rank the positive items higher than negative items, i.e., positive items should have higher probabilities than negative ones. To achieve this, we design the following objective function to be maximized

$$\underset{\Theta}{\text{argmax}} \quad Obj = \sum_{(u,i,j)\in D_S} \ln \sigma(\hat{r}_{ui} - \hat{r}_{uj}) \tag{6}$$

where

$$D_S \overset{def}{=} \{(u,i,j)|i \in I_u^+ \wedge j \in I \backslash I_u^+\}$$

and

$$\sigma(x) = \frac{1}{1+e^{-x}}$$

is the sigmoid function.

4.2 Updating Rule

The objective function could be optimized using stochastic gradient descent, and the update rule is:

$$\Theta \leftarrow \Theta + \eta \cdot \frac{1}{1+e^{\hat{r}_{ui}-\hat{r}_{uj}}} \cdot \left(\frac{\partial}{\partial \Theta}\hat{r}_{ui} - \frac{\partial}{\partial \Theta}\hat{r}_{uj}\right) \tag{7}$$

where η is the learning rate.

We use the heterogeneous random walk with restart model to estimate $\hat{r}$. Using Equation 5, taking $k = 3$ as an example, we could get

$$\hat{r}_{ui} = \alpha^3(\mathbf{P}^3)_{iu} + \alpha^2(1-\alpha)(\mathbf{P}^2)_{iu} + \alpha(1-\alpha)\mathbf{P}_{iu}$$

and

$$\begin{aligned} (\mathbf{P}^3)_{iu} &= \sum_{v_p, v_q \in V} p(v_i|v_p) \cdot p(v_p|v_q) \cdot p(v_q|v_u) \\ (\mathbf{P}^2)_{iu} &= \sum_{v_p \in V} p(v_i|v_p) \cdot p(v_p|v_u). \end{aligned}$$

Considering our model of the transition matrix and our assumption, we get

$$\mathbf{P}_{ij} = p(v_i|v_j) = p(\phi(v_i)|\phi(v_j)) \cdot \frac{1}{|D_j^{\phi_i}|}$$

We use $\psi(e(v_j, v_i))$ to denote the type of the edge from v_j to v_i. Taking all these equations into consideration, the gradient with respect to an edge type τ is

$$\begin{aligned} \frac{\partial \hat{r}_{ui}}{\partial p_\tau} &= \alpha^3 \cdot \Big(\sum_{\psi(ip)=\tau} \frac{w_{pq}w_{qu}}{|D_p^{\phi_i}|} + \sum_{\psi(pq)=\tau} \frac{w_{ip}w_{qu}}{|D_q^{\phi_p}|} \\ &+ \sum_{\psi(qu)=\tau} \frac{w_{ip}w_{pq}}{|D_u^{\phi_q}|} \Big) + \alpha^2(1-\alpha) \cdot \Big(\sum_{\psi(ip)=\tau} \frac{w_{pu}}{|D_p^{\phi_i}|} \\ &+ \sum_{\psi(pu)=\tau} \frac{w_{ip}}{|D_u^{\phi_p}|} \Big) + \alpha(1-\alpha) \cdot \frac{\delta(\psi(iu)=\tau)}{|D_u^{\phi_i}|} \end{aligned} \tag{8}$$

where we abbreviate $p(v_i|v_j)$ to w_{ij} for simplicity, and $\psi(ip) = \tau$ is short for $\psi(e(v_p, v_i)) = \tau$.

After computing the gradients of $\hat{r}_{ui}$ and $\hat{r}_{uj}$, we could update the learning parameters p_τ using Equation 7. And the learning scheme is summarized in Algorithm 1. During the learning process, if any of the parameters becomes below zero after update, the learning rate is halved (lines 5-7). At the end of each iteration, the parameters are normalized so that the sum of all the parameters is 1 (line 9).

Algorithm 1 HeteLearn

Input: the heterogeneous information network $G = (V, E)$, the network schema $T_G = (\mathcal{A}, \mathcal{R})$, the training set D_S, the parameters α and k in Equation 5, the initial learning rate η

Output: the learned parameters $\Theta \overset{def}{=} (p_{\tau_1}, p_{\tau_2}, ..., p_{\tau_{|\mathcal{R}|}})^T$

1: randomly initialize Θ
2: **repeat**
3: randomly draw (u, i, j) from D_S
4: $grad_{\tau_\alpha} \leftarrow$ using Equation 7 to compute the gradients of p_{τ_α}, $\forall \alpha \in \{1, 2, ..., |\mathcal{R}|\}$
5: **while** exists τ_α that satisfies $p_{\tau_\alpha} + \eta \cdot grad_{\tau_\alpha} < 0$ **do**
6: $\eta \leftarrow \eta/2$
7: **end while**
8: $p_{\tau_\alpha} \leftarrow p_{\tau_\alpha} + \eta \cdot grad_{\tau_\alpha}, \forall \alpha \in \{1, 2, ..., |\mathcal{R}|\}$
9: $p_{\tau_\alpha} \leftarrow p_{\tau_\alpha} / \sum_\alpha p_{\tau_\alpha}$
10: **until** convergence
11: **return** $p_{\tau_1}, p_{\tau_2}, ..., p_{\tau_{|\mathcal{R}|}}$

5 EXPERIMENTS AND RESULTS

In this section, we demonstrate the effectiveness of our method on two kinds of recommendation tasks, i.e., the item recommendation task and the tag recommendation task. We use the the Restaurant & Consumer dataset and the HetRec 2011 MovieLens dataset on the item recommendation task, and use a variant of the HetRec 2011 MovieLens dataset on the tag recommendation task.

Following we will first introduce the used datasets in Section 5.1, and then give a brief description of the compared methods in Section 5.2. In section 5.3 we will show the effects of the parameters in HeteLearn. After that, the results of the compared methods on item recommendation and tag recommendation task are shown in section 5.4 and 5.5, respectively.

5.1 Datasets

We validated the proposed method using two datasets. The smaller one is the Restaurant & Consumer dataset from the UCI Machine Learning Repository [14]. And the bigger one is the HetRec 2011 MovieLens dataset published by GroupLens research group [1].

The Restaurant & Consumer dataset was collected during a seven months period. It contains the ratings of the restaurants from the users and information about the users and restaurants. Table 1 shows the statistics of this dataset.

The HetRec 2011 MovieLens dataset is an extension of MovieLens10M dataset, and it links the movies of MovieLens dataset with their corresponding web pages at Internet Movie Database (IMDb) [2] and Rotten Tomatoes movie review systems [3]. Table 2 is the statistics of the dataset.

[1]http://www.grouplens.org
[2]http://www.imdb.com
[3]http://www.rottentomatoes.com

Table 1: Statistics of the Restaurant & Consumer dataset.

Types	Total No.	Average No. (per Restaurant)	Average No. (per User)
User	138	-	-
Restaurant	934	-	-
Parking Lot	7	-	-
Payment	11	2.14	1.33
Cuisine	59	1.19	2.39
Rating	1161	8.93	8.41

Table 2: Statistics of the HetRec 2011 MovieLens dataset.

Types	Total No.	Average No. (per Movie)	Average No. (per User)
User	2113	-	-
Movie	10197	-	-
Genre	20	2.040	-
Director	4060	1.0	-
Actor	95321	22.778	-
Country	72	1.0	-
Tag	13222	8.117	22.696
Rating	855598	84.637	404.921

5.2 Baselines

We compared the performance of our method with the following state-of-the-art methods.

5.2.1 User-Based Collaborative Filtering (User CF). These approaches predict a user's interest in an item based on rating information from similar user profiles [26]. In our experiment, we took the non-normalized neighborhood collaborative filtering approach as representative. It is a modification of traditional k-nearest neighborhood collaborative filtering (KNN CF), and it is known to perform better than traditional KNN CF for top-k recommendation [13]. For a given user and a given item, the rating $r_{u,i}$ is defined as $r_{u,i} = \sum_{u' \in \hat{U}} sim(u, u') \times r_{u',i}$ where $\hat{U}$ is the set of n_k most similar users, and the $sim(u, u')$ is the similarity between two users [3]. In our experiments, the parameter n_k was selected by grid search, and the cosine coefficient was selected as the similarity measure.

5.2.2 Item-Based Collaborative Filtering (Item CF). These approaches apply the same idea with User CF, but use similarity between items instead of users. For a given user and a given item, the rating $r_{u,i}$ is defined as $r_{u,i} = \sum_{i' \in \hat{I}} sim(i, i') \times r_{u,i'}$ where $\hat{I}$ is the set of n_k most similar items. Similar to User CF, n_k was selected by grid search, and the cosine similarity was used.

5.2.3 Non-negative Matrix Factorization (NMF). As a representative matrix factorization method, NMF tries to find two non-negative matrix factors where the product of the two matrices is an approximation of the original matrix. This method was originally proposed for image analysis. However, it has been widely used in collaborative filtering recently [2, 17].

5.2.4 Latent Factor Model (LFM). Also known as SVD (Singular Value Decomposition) models. The key idea of these models is to factorize the user-item rating matrix to a product of two lower rank matrices, one containing the so-called "user factors", while the other containing the so-called "item-factors" [3].

5.2.5 Personalized PageRank (PRank). A graph-based node ranking method [9] based on the classic PageRank algorithm [18]. In this method, the stable solution of Equation 1 is used as the ratings of a given user for the nodes in a graph. And the stable solution could be achieved by iterating Equation 1 until convergence.

5.2.6 Path-constrained Random Walk (PCRW). Such methods are based on single paths in the heterogeneous information network. They are also called semantic recommendation since each path has its corresponding semantic [23]. For instance, the paths *UMUM* and *UMTM* can be interpreted as results of user-based collaborative filtering and content(tag)-based filtering, respectively. According to the semantics of the paths and previous work, 3-step paths are the most common and important. In our experiments, the paths with their length less than or equal to 3 were considered.

5.2.7 PathRank. A state-of-the-art heterogeneous information network based method [13]. In our experiments, we took the same settings as in [13]: $w_{restart} = 0.1, w_{trans} = 0.25, w_{path} = 0.65$. For the HetRec 2011 MovieLens dataset, the path-guide *UMTM +UMU(20)M +UMUM(20)* was used since it showed the best performance in the original paper of PathRank. For the Restaurant & Consumer dataset, since no tag information is available, the path-guide *UMU(20)M+UMUM(20)* was used instead.

5.2.8 HeteRS. A state-of-the-art HIN-based method [21]. The most significant difference between our method and HeteRS is the user preference model. HeteRS uses multivariate Markov chain to model user preferences, and uses the stable solution of the model.

As for the proposed method, HeteLearn, the initial learning rate η was set to be 0.5. The parameters k and α in the generalized random walk with restart model will be discussed in section 5.3.

In the following experiments, all of the not mentioned parameters of the compared methods were decided by grid search.

5.3 Effects of the Parameters

In this section, we will show the effects of two key parameters k and α in HeteLearn.

The performances with different k and α values in Equation 5 are plotted in Figure 2. The best performance is achieved at $k = 3$ or $k = 5$, and after that the performance decreases slightly with the increase of k, which confirmed the assumption that longer random walks have less impacts on the results, as is discussed in Section 3.2.

In the following experiments, we set k to be 3. Since the performance varies with different datasets and different values of α, we choose α to be 0.8 in the HeteLearn algorithm.

5.4 Task 1: Item Recommendation

In this section, we validate our proposed method on the item recommendation task using two datasets. The used datasets and the compared methods have been shown and discussed in section 5.1 and 5.2, respectively.

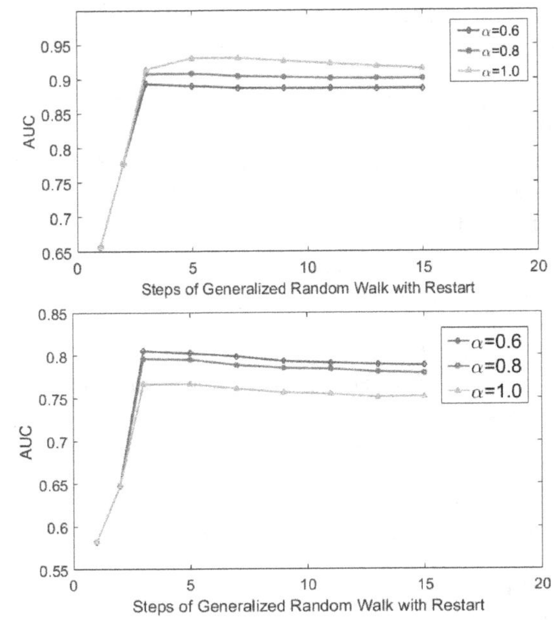

Figure 2: Performances of the generalized random walk with restart model with different steps k and different α values on the Restaurant & Consumer dataset (the upper plot) and the HetRec 2011 MovieLens dataset (the lower plot).

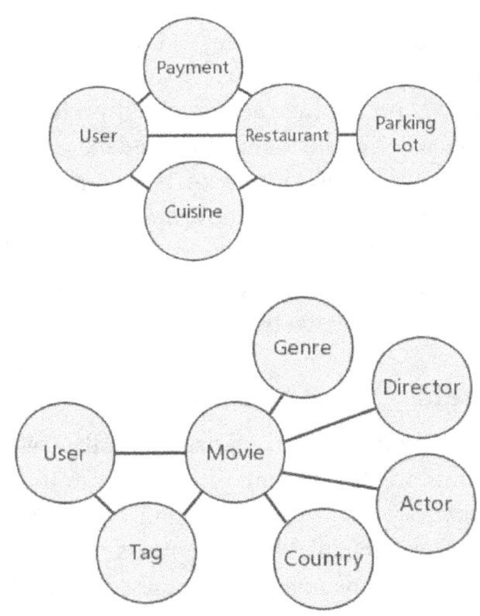

Figure 3: The network schemas of the HINs used in the item recommendation experiment. The upper network is constructed using the Restaurant & Consumer dataset and the lower network is constructed using the HetRec 2011 MovieLens dataset.

5.4.1 Experimental Setup. For each dataset, we create a heterogeneous information network based on the training set and the meta-data.

Using the Restaurant & Consumer dataset, we construct 5 types of nodes, and we abbreviate them as **U**: USER, **R**: RESTAURANT, **P**: PAYMENT, **C**: CUISINE, and **L**: PARKING LOT. We also construct 6 types of links. In this dataset, possible rating values are 0, 1 and 2, where 0 indicates that the user does not like the restaurant, and 2 denotes a high preference. We create a link between a user and a restaurant if the user rated 2 for the restaurant. That is to say, we treat these restaurants as the positive feedback to simulate the one-class feedback problem. The network schema is shown in the upper plot in Figure 3.

Using the HetRec 2011 MovieLens dataset, we construct 7 types of nodes, and use the capital of the first letter of each node type name as its abbreviation (**U**: USER, **M**: MOVIE, **T**: TAG, **G**: GENRE, **D**: DIRECTOR, **A**: ACTOR, **C**: COUNTRY). We also construct 7 types of links. For every rating on a movie m by a user u, we create a link between u and m, if and only if the rating is greater or equal to the average rating of the user u. In other words, we treat the movies whose ratings are larger than the user's personal average rating as the positive feedback. The network schema is shown in the lower plot in Figure 3.

We use the AUC (Area Under Curve of the receiver operating characteristic) criterion as the evaluation metric. We first evaluate AUC for each user from the test data, and then obtain the averaged AUC results over all users. For the Restaurant & Consumer dataset, in order to simulate sparse data, we use 50% of the dataset as the training data and the other 50% as the testing data. For the HetRec 2011 MovieLens dataset, we sort the ratings by their timestamps and use 80% as the training set and the rest 20% as the testing set.

5.4.2 Results. The experimental results of the compared methods on the two datasets are shown in Table 3. The best result on each dataset is displayed in bold. An entry is marked with '∗' (or '∗∗') if HeteLearn is significantly better than the compared method based on paired t-test at the significance level 0.05 (or 0.01).

Among all the compared methods, the proposed method, HeteLearn, achieves the best results on both datasets. And in most cases, the improvements of our method are significant at the level of 0.01.

The traditional user and item based collaborative filtering methods perform quite poor on the Restaurant & Consumer dataset. This is mainly because of the sparsity of the user-item rating matrix of this dataset.

Despite of the sparsity of the Restaurant & Consumer dataset, the matrix factorization (MF) methods, NMF and LFM, still perform quite well, which demonstrates the effectiveness of matrix factorization methods.

On both datasets, the performances of semantic recommendations using a single path (also known as the Path-constrained Random Walk method) vary greatly with the paths. The best path on the Restaurant & Consumer dataset is *UPUR*, which could be seen as a kind of user-based collaborative filtering. The best path on the HetRec 2011 MovieLens dataset is *UMGM*, which corresponds to genre-based filtering.

Both PathRank and Personalized PageRank could be seen as hybrid recommendation methods based on HINs. In our experimental results, these methods achieve better results than any of the single path methods, which demonstrates the effectiveness of HIN-based hybrid recommendation methods.

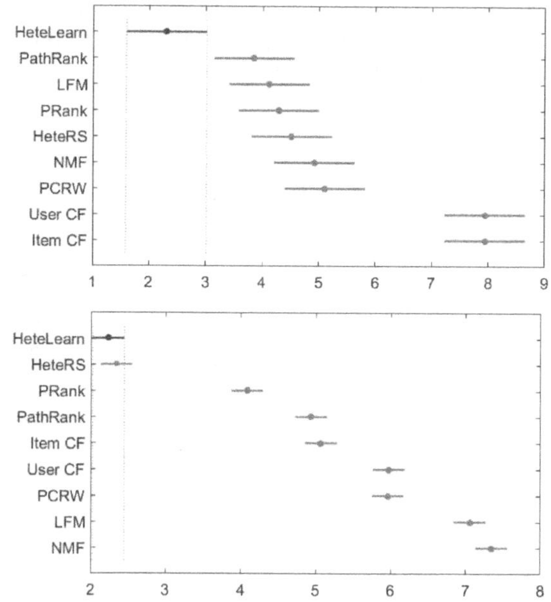

Figure 4: Freidman test results on the Restaurant & Consumer dataset (the upper plot) and the HetRec 2011 MovieLens dataset (the lower plot) on the item recommendation task.

To better compare the performance of the compared recommendation methods, we perform the Freidman test in conjunction with the Bonferroni-Dunn test [4] at significance level 0.05. The results are shown in Figure 4. The dots indicate the average ranks, the bars indicate the critical difference with the Bonferroni-Dunn test at significance level 0.05, and compared methods having non-overlapped bars are significantly different. For every kind of recommendation method, the best result is used to perform the test. On the Restaurant & Consumer dataset, HeteLearn shows significantly better result than all the other methods. And on the HetRec 2011 MovieLens dataset, HeteLearn is significantly better than all the other methods except HeteRS. Thus, the results confirm the effectiveness of our method.

It should be noticed that HeteLearn and PathRank perform better than all the traditional collaborative filtering methods. That is because of the heterogeneous information added to the user-item rating matrix, and both HeteLearn and PathRank could get use of such information effectively. Instead of setting the path-guides manually in PathRank, the proposed method, HeteLearn, could automatically learn them from the HINs. Therefore, the HeteLearn method has a broader range of potential applications.

5.5 Task 2: Tag Recommendation

We also compare our proposed method with other methods on the tag recommendation task, the goal of which is to find the set of proper words (tags) to describe the resources. Existing tag recommendation methods include content-based methods and co-occurrence based methods [25]. Content-based methods directly adopt the content of items, such as genre of movies, to perform tag recommendation. Co-occurrence based methods use the co-occurrence of

Table 3: AUC results of the compared methods on the item recommendation task. The best result on each dataset is displayed in bold. An entry is marked with '∗' (or '∗∗') if HeteLearn is significantly better than the compared method based on paired t-test at the significance level 0.05 (or 0.01).

Method	AUC (RCdata)		AUC (HetRec MovieLens)	
User CF	0.7241**		0.7004**	
Item CF	0.7241**		0.7190**	
NMF	0.8953**		0.6528**	
LFM	0.9147**		0.6587**	
Personalized PageRank	$\alpha = 0.6$	0.8932**	$\alpha = 0.6$	0.7551**
	$\alpha = 0.8$	0.9080**	$\alpha = 0.8$	0.7462**
	$\alpha = 1.0$	0.9139**	$\alpha = 1.0$	0.7163**
Path-constrained Random Walk	UR	0.6571**	UM	0.5212**
	UCR	0.6662**	UTM	0.5098**
	UPR	0.7941**	UMCM	0.5110**
	URCR	0.6745**	UTUM	0.5600**
	URUR	0.7242**	UMDM	0.6107**
	URLR	0.7563**	UMUM	0.6525**
	UCUR	0.8202**	UMAM	0.6619**
	URPR	0.8238**	UMTM	0.6648**
	UPUR	0.8684**	UMGM	0.6865**
PathRank	UMU(20)M+ UMUM(20)	0.9164**	UMTM+ UMU(20)M+ UMUM(20)	0.7127**
HeteRS	-	0.9154**	-	0.8152*
HeteLearn	$\alpha = 0.8$	**0.9396**	$\alpha = 0.8$	**0.8217**

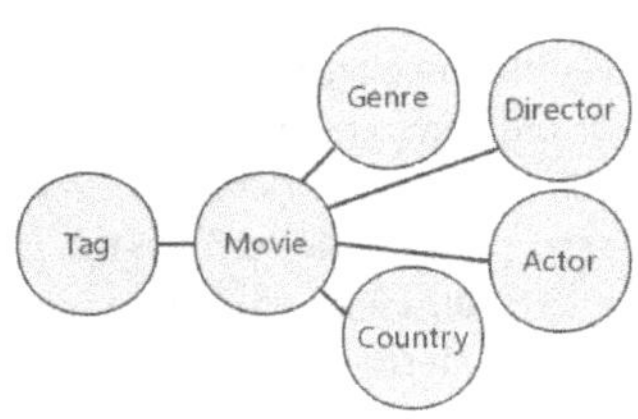

Figure 5: The network schema of the HIN used in the tag recommendation experiment. This network is constructed using the HetRec 2011 MovieLens dataset.

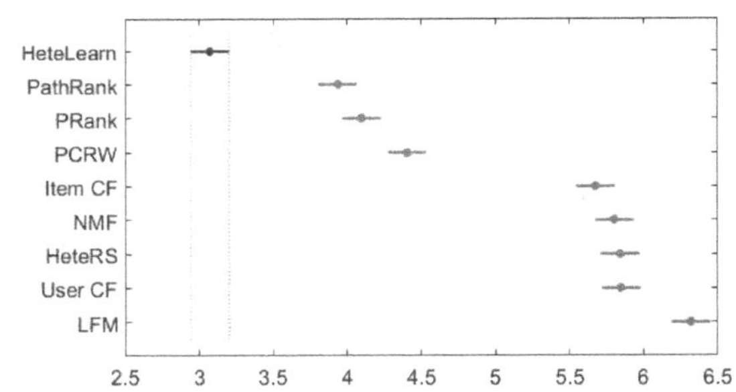

Figure 6: Freidman test result on the HetRec 2011 MovieLens dataset on the tag recommendation task.

tags among items (i.e., the item-tag matrix) for tagging. Our method, HeteLearn, is a hybrid method which combines both content-based methods and co-occurrence methods.

5.5.1 Experimental Setup. We test our method using the HetRec 2011 MovieLens dataset. We construct 6 types of nodes and used the capital of the first letter of each node type name as its abbreviation (**M**: MOVIE, **T**: TAG, **G**: GENRE, **D**: DIRECTOR, **A**: ACTOR, **C**: COUNTRY). We also construct 5 types of links. For every tag t assigned to a movie m, we create a link between t and m, if and only if the tag weight is greater or equal to the average tag weight assigned to the movie. The network schema is shown in Figure 5.

Similar to the item recommendation task, we also use the AUC criterion as the evaluation metric, and we sort the tag assignments by their timestamps and use 80% as the training set and the rest 20% as the testing set.

5.5.2 Results. The performances of the compared methods and the Friedman test result are shown in Table 4 and Figure 6.

Among the all the compared methods, HeteLearn achieves the best results, which again confirms the effectiveness of our method.

The co-occurrence methods, including User CF, Item CF, NMF and LFM, perform worse than the HIN-based methods, which coincides with the fact that hybrid methods usually achieve better performance than co-occurrence methods. Note that although NMF and LFM achieve higher average AUC results than User CF and Item CF, they do not show significantly better results according to

Table 4: AUC results of the compared methods on the tag recommendation task. The best result is in bold. An entry is marked with '*' (or '') if HeteLearn is significantly better than the compared method based on paired t-test at the significance level 0.05 (or 0.01).**

Method	AUC	
User CF	0.7128**	
Item CF	0.7115**	
NMF	0.8195**	
LFM	0.8180**	
Personalized PageRank	$\alpha = 0.6$	0.8924**
	$\alpha = 0.8$	0.8908**
	$\alpha = 1.0$	0.8423**
Path-constrained Random Walk	MT	0.5149**
	MDMT	0.5715**
	MTMT	0.7188**
	MAMT	0.7229**
	MCMT	0.8063**
	MGMT	0.8668**
PathRank	MTM(20)T+ MTMT(20)	0.8902**
HeteRS	-	0.8029**
HeteLearn	$\alpha = 0.8$	**0.9017**

Friedman test. This means that they only achieve good AUC results in a few individual cases, while in most cases they perform worse than User CF and Item CF.

6 CONCLUSION

In this paper, we proposed a new personalized recommendation method in heterogeneous information networks. In this method, we used a generalized random walk with restart model to model the user preferences, and used a BPR-based learning method to learn the weights of the links in the network. Our experimental results confirmed the effectiveness of the proposed method and provided several useful insights for the field of recommender systems. Both our theoretical and empirical results indicate that learning on heterogeneous information networks is feasible and worthwhile. And the proposed method, HeteLearn, provides a successful case for the important tasks of personalized recommendation and tag recommendation.

ACKNOWLEDGMENTS

The work is supported by the National 863 Program of China under Grant No.: 2015AA016009, the National Natural Science Fund of China under Grant No.: 61232005 and the National Key R&D Program of China under Grant No.: 2017YFB1002002.

REFERENCES

[1] Andrey Balmin, Vagelis Hristidis, and Yannis Papakonstantinou. 2004. Objectrank: Authority-based keyword search in databases. In *Proceedings of the Thirtieth international conference on Very large data bases-Volume 30*. VLDB Endowment, 564–575.

[2] Yang Bao, Hui Fang, and Jie Zhang. 2014. TopicMF: Simultaneously Exploiting Ratings and Reviews for Recommendation.. In *AAAI*, Vol. 14. 2–8.

[3] Paolo Cremonesi, Yehuda Koren, and Roberto Turrin. 2010. Performance of recommender algorithms on top-n recommendation tasks. In *Proceedings of the fourth ACM conference on Recommender systems*. ACM, 39–46.

[4] Janez Demšar. 2006. Statistical comparisons of classifiers over multiple data sets. *Journal of Machine learning research* 7, Jan (2006), 1–30.

[5] Michael D Ekstrand, John T Riedl, Joseph A Konstan, et al. 2011. Collaborative filtering recommender systems. *Foundations and Trends® in Human–Computer Interaction* 4, 2 (2011), 81–173.

[6] Francois Fouss, Alain Pirotte, Jean-Michel Renders, and Marco Saerens. 2007. Random-walk computation of similarities between nodes of a graph with application to collaborative recommendation. *IEEE Transactions on knowledge and data engineering* 19, 3 (2007).

[7] Marco Gori, Augusto Pucci, V Roma, and I Siena. 2007. ItemRank: A Random-Walk Based Scoring Algorithm for Recommender Engines.. In *International Joint Conference on Artificial Intelligence*, Vol. 7. 2766–2771.

[8] Jiawei Han. 2009. Mining heterogeneous information networks by exploring the power of links. In *International Conference on Algorithmic Learning Theory*. 20–28.

[9] Taher H Haveliwala. 2003. Topic-sensitive pagerank: A context-sensitive ranking algorithm for web search. *IEEE transactions on knowledge and data engineering* 15, 4 (2003), 784–796.

[10] Douglas J Klein and Milan Randić. 1993. Resistance distance. *Journal of Mathematical Chemistry* 12, 1 (1993), 81–95.

[11] Ni Lao and William W Cohen. 2010. Fast query execution for retrieval models based on path-constrained random walks. In *Proceedings of the 16th ACM SIGKDD international conference on Knowledge discovery and data mining*. ACM, 881–888.

[12] Sangkeun Lee, Sanghyeb Lee, and Byoung-Hoon Park. 2015. PathMining: A Path-Based User Profiling Algorithm for Heterogeneous Graph-Based Recommender Systems.. In *FLAIRS Conference*. 519–523.

[13] Sangkeun Lee, Sungchan Park, Minsuk Kahng, and Sanggoo Lee. 2013. PathRank: Ranking nodes on a heterogeneous graph for flexible hybrid recommender systems. *Expert Systems With Applications* 40, 2 (2013), 684–697.

[14] M. Lichman. 2013. UCI Machine Learning Repository. (2013). http://archive.ics.uci.edu/ml

[15] Weiping Liu and Linyuan Lü. 2010. Link prediction based on local random walk. *EPL (Europhysics Letters)* 89, 5 (2010), 58007.

[16] Linyuan Lu, Matus Medo, Ho Yeung Chi, Yi Cheng Zhang, Zi Ke Zhang, and Tao Zhou. 2012. Recommender systems. *Physics Reports* 519, 1 (2012), 1–49.

[17] Hendri Murfi and Klaus Obermayer. 2009. A Two-Level Learning Hierarchy of Concept Based Keyword Extraction for Tag Recommendations.. In *DC@ PKDD/ECML*.

[18] Lawrence Page, Sergey Brin, Rajeev Motwani, and Terry Winograd. 1999. *The PageRank citation ranking: Bringing order to the web*. Technical Report. Stanford InfoLab.

[19] Rong Pan, Yunhong Zhou, Bin Cao, Nathan N Liu, Rajan Lukose, Martin Scholz, and Qiang Yang. 2008. One-Class Collaborative Filtering. In *IEEE International Conference on Data Mining*. 502–511.

[20] Weike Pan and Li Chen. 2013. GBPR: group preference based Bayesian personalized ranking for one-class collaborative filtering. In *International Joint Conference on Artificial Intelligence*. 2691–2697.

[21] Tuan-Anh Nguyen Pham, Xutao Li, Gao Cong, and Zhenjie Zhang. 2016. A general recommendation model for heterogeneous networks. *IEEE Transactions on Knowledge and Data Engineering* 28, 12 (2016), 3140–3153.

[22] Steffen Rendle, Christoph Freudenthaler, Zeno Gantner, and Lars Schmidt-Thieme. 2009. BPR: Bayesian personalized ranking from implicit feedback. In *Proceedings of the twenty-fifth conference on uncertainty in artificial intelligence*. AUAI Press, 452–461.

[23] Chuan Shi, Xiangnan Kong, Yue Huang, and P. S Yu. 2014. HeteSim: A General Framework for Relevance Measure in Heterogeneous Networks. *Knowledge & Data Engineering IEEE Transactions on* 26, 10 (2014), 2479–2492.

[24] Yizhou Sun, Jiawei Han, Xifeng Yan, Philip S. Yu, and Tianyi Wu. 2011. PathSim: Meta Path-Based Top-K Similarity Search in Heterogeneous Information Networks. *Proceedings of the Vldb Endowment* 4, 11 (2011), 992–1003.

[25] Hao Wang, Binyi Chen, and Wu-Jun Li. 2013. Collaborative Topic Regression with Social Regularization for Tag Recommendation.. In *IJCAI*.

[26] Jun Wang, Arjen P De Vries, and Marcel JT Reinders. 2006. Unifying user-based and item-based collaborative filtering approaches by similarity fusion. In *Proceedings of the 29th annual international ACM SIGIR conference on Research and development in information retrieval*. ACM, 501–508.

[27] Fei Yu, An Zeng, Sébastien Gillard, and Matúš Medo. 2016. Network-based recommendation algorithms: A review. *Physica A: Statistical Mechanics and its Applications* 452 (2016), 192–208.

[28] Xiao Yu, Xiang Ren, Yizhou Sun, Bradley Sturt, Urvashi Khandelwal, Quanquan Gu, Brandon Norick, and Jiawei Han. 2013. Recommendation in heterogeneous information networks with implicit user feedback. In *ACM Conference on Recommender Systems*. 347–350.

Fast and Scalable Distributed Loopy Belief Propagation on Real-World Graphs

Saehan Jo
Seoul National University
naheas@snu.ac.kr

Jaemin Yoo
Seoul National University
jaeminyoo@snu.ac.kr

U Kang
Seoul National University
ukang@snu.ac.kr

ABSTRACT

Given graphs with millions or billions of vertices and edges, how can we efficiently make inferences based on partial knowledge? Loopy Belief Propagation (LBP) is a graph inference algorithm widely used in various applications including social network analysis, malware detection, recommendation, and image restoration. The algorithm calculates approximate marginal probabilities of vertices in a graph within a linear running time proportional to the number of edges. However, when it comes to real-world graphs with millions or billions of vertices and edges, this cost overwhelms the computing power of a single machine. Moreover, this kind of large-scale graphs does not fit into the memory of a single machine. Although several distributed LBP methods have been proposed, previous works do not consider the properties of real-world graphs, especially the effect of power-law degree distribution on LBP. Therefore, our work focuses on developing a fast and scalable LBP for such large real-world graphs on distributed environment.

In this paper, we propose DLBP, a Distributed Loopy Belief Propagation algorithm which efficiently computes LBP in a distributed manner across multiple machines. By setting the correct convergence criterion and carefully scheduling the computations, DLBP provides up to 10.7× speed up compared to standard distributed LBP. We show that DLBP demonstrates near-linear scalability with respect to the number of machines as well as the number of edges.

ACM Reference Format:

Saehan Jo, Jaemin Yoo, and U Kang. 2018. Fast and Scalable Distributed Loopy Belief Propagation on Real-World Graphs. In *WSDM 2018: WSDM 2018: The Eleventh ACM International Conference on Web Search and Data Mining , February 5–9, 2018, Marina Del Rey, CA, USA.* ACM, New York, NY, USA, 9 pages. https://doi.org/10.1145/3159652.3159722

1 INTRODUCTION

Given large graphs that do not fit in a single machine, how can we make inference on unobserved vertices? Loopy Belief Propagation (LBP) is an inference algorithm which calculates approximate marginal probabilities of vertices based on partial information. It has been widely used in various fields including social network analysis [15, 16, 27, 31, 35], malware detection [5, 33], fraud detection [4, 28], recommendation [14, 38], and image restoration [8].

WSDM 2018, February 5–9, 2018, Marina Del Rey, CA, USA

ACM ISBN 978-1-4503-5581-0/18/02...$15.00
https://doi.org/10.1145/3159652.3159722

A nice property of LBP is that its computation complexity scales linearly with the number of edges. Since the computing of exact marginal probabilities in a Markov Random Field (MRF) is known to be computationally exorbitant, LBP has been one of the best alternatives. However, when it comes to real-world graphs whose sizes are very large, the application of LBP on these graphs is problematic in several aspects. First, the power-law degree distribution of real-world graphs disrupts a steady convergence of LBP algorithm. Second, LBP suffers from extensive computations per iteration due to the large size of graph data. Finally, the high communication overhead impedes the speed of distributed LBP algorithm since a large graph is distributed across multiple machines.

In this paper, we propose DLBP, a Distributed Loopy Belief Propagation, which solves the above challenges by 1) utilizing a convergence criterion appropriate for real-world graphs, and 2) dividing the vertices according to their degrees and carefully scheduling the iterations to minimize data communications. As shown in Figure 1, DLBP minimizes the communication cost and achieves up to 10.7× speed up on real-world graphs compared to standard LBP. Our contributions are as follows.

- **Algorithm.** We propose DLBP, a novel distributed algorithm for LBP which solves the challenges associated with the power-law degree distribution of real-world graphs.
- **Analysis.** We provide a theoretical analysis of two different convergence criteria of LBP. Moreover, we analyze DLBP in terms of the time complexity, space complexity, and the amount of shuffled data.
- **Experiment.** We provide evidence of the theoretical analysis by conducting rigorous experiments on DLBP to present empirical results on real-world graphs. DLBP shows up to 10.7× speed up on real-world graphs compared to baseline methods, as depicted in Figure 1.

The code of DLBP and the datasets are publicly available at http://datalab.snu.ac.kr/dlbp. The rest of the paper is organized as follows. In Section 2, we introduce the preliminaries and related works on LBP and distributed graph processing frameworks. Section 3 presents our proposed method DLBP in detail. After showing experimental results of DLBP on real-world graphs in Section 4, we conclude in Section 5.

2 PRELIMINARIES AND RELATED WORKS

In this section, we provide preliminaries and related works on belief propagation and graph processing. Table 1 describes the symbols used throughout the paper.

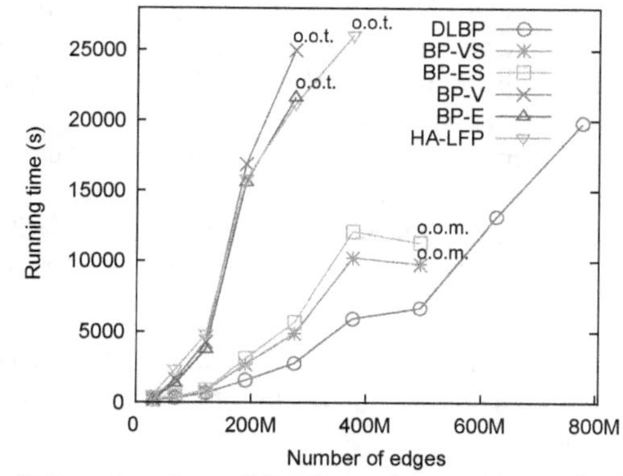

Figure 1: Running time of DLBP and competing methods on the subgraphs of YahooWeb (HA-LFP on Hadoop, rest on Spark). DLBP is up to 10.0× faster than HA-LFP, 10.7× faster than BP-E and BP-V, and 2.0× faster than BP-ES and BP-VS. o.o.t.: out of time (exceeds 8 hours). o.o.m.: out of memory (a worker node fails).

2.1 Loopy Belief Propagation

Loopy Belief Propagation (LBP) [20, 26] is an inference algorithm which approximately calculates the marginal distribution of unobserved variables in a probabilistic graphical model. We focus on LBP in a pairwise Markov Random Field (MRF) among other probabilistic graphical models to simplify the explanation. A pairwise MRF is an undirected graphical model consisting of vertices which represent random variables with a discrete number of states, and edges which represent the relationships between two variables.

To illustrate the equations of LBP, two concepts need to be introduced. A node potential $\phi_i(x_i)$ of a vertex i is the prior knowledge about the probability distribution of vertex i in the state x_i. An edge potential $\psi_{ij}(x_i, x_j)$ is the probability that vertex i has the state x_i and vertex j has the state x_j. LBP relies on the notion of iterative message passing between variables. At each iteration, all vertices send messages to their neighboring vertices. The algorithm assumes that a message m_{ij} successfully captures the influence of a vertex i on its neighboring vertex j's marginal probability. The message $m_{ij}(x_j)$ from vertex i to vertex j is updated as follows:

$$m_{ij}(x_j) \leftarrow \sum_{x_i} \phi_i(x_i)\psi_{ij}(x_i, x_j)\frac{\prod_{l\in N(i)} m_{li}(x_i)}{m_{ji}(x_i)} \tag{1}$$

where $N(i)$ is the neighbors of vertex i. The belief b_i of vertex i is computed based on the converged messages as follows:

$$b_i(x_i) = c_i\phi_i(x_i) \prod_{l\in N(i)} m_{li}(x_i) \tag{2}$$

where c_i is a normalization constant to make the beliefs of vertex i with different states x_i sum up to 1. Note that we can utilize the belief b_i of the current iteration to compute the outgoing messages m_{ij} from vertex i in the next iteration [17, 18]. Since Equation (1) uses the multiplication of the node potential $\phi_i(x_i)$ and the incoming messages $m_{li}(x_i)$ to vertex i in order to compute the next iteration messages, we can replace these terms with Equation (2) which results in:

$$m_{ij}(x_j) \leftarrow \frac{1}{c_i}\sum_{x_i} \psi_{ij}(x_i, x_j)\frac{b_i(x_i)}{m_{ji}(x_i)} \tag{3}$$

Table 1: Table of symbols.

Symbol	Definition
m_{ij}	message from vertex i to vertex j
b_i	belief of vertex i
c_i	normalization constant of vertex i
$N(i)$	set of neighboring vertices of vertex i
V	sets of vertices
E	sets of edges
V_h, V_s	sets of hub and spoke vertices
$E_{hh}, E_{ss}, E_{hs}, E_{sh}$	sets of edges from $\{V_h, V_s\}$ to $\{V_h, V_s\}$
B_h, B_s	sets of beliefs of V_h, V_s
$M_{hh}, M_{ss}, M_{hs}, M_{sh}$	sets of messages of E_{hh}, E_{ss}, E_{hs}, and E_{sh}
θ	convergence threshold
k	hub ratio
τ	maximum sub-iterations
T_h	total number of hub-to-hub iterations
T_s	total number of spoke-to-spoke iterations
T_o	total number of super-steps
T	number of iterations until standard LBP converges
n	number of machines
s	number of possible states

2.2 Distributed Graph Processing

In an attempt to solve problems in distributed graph processing, a variety of graph processing frameworks [6, 12, 19, 21, 24, 29, 30] have emerged. In those frameworks, graph data are distributed along multiple machines to promote parallel computing. However, the distribution of graph data is also a major bottleneck because of the communication cost between machines. Unfortunately, real-world graphs are known to contain little well-defined clusters [22].

Partitioning Strategies. Most of the distributed graph processing frameworks adapt either of the two graph partitioning strategies, edge-cut or vertex-cut. Edge-cut and vertex-cut mainly differ on which of the two main components of a graph, edges or vertices, are divided evenly among multiple machines. Edge-cut uniformly assigns vertices to multiple machines; hence, the edges are cut across different machines. In contrast, vertex-cut uniformly distributes edges to machines; thus, the vertices span over different machines. It is known that vertex-cut efficiently handles high-degree vertices in a real-world graph while edge-cut suffers imbalanced workloads among partitions [6, 12].

PowerLyra [6] utilizes both edge-cut and vertex-cut in parallel graph processing where one of the two partitioning methods is selected for a vertex depending on its degree. For high-degree vertices, vertex-cut is used to promote workload balancing between partitions. The low-degree vertices are partitioned using edge-cut which prevents the low-degree vertices from spanning over a large number of machines.

Parallel Belief Propagation. Different factors of parallel LBP are analyzed in [25] which still does not consider the property of real-world graphs. A parallel asynchronous LBP [10, 11, 34] uses a priority scheme in order to dynamically schedule the message updates. HA-LFP [18] formulates a MapReduce [7] version of LBP that runs in parallel on top of Apache Hadoop.

3 PROPOSED METHOD

In this section, we propose Distributed Loopy Belief Propagation (DLBP), a distributed LBP algorithm on real-world graphs. First, we give an overview of DLBP in Section 3.1 by describing the problems associated with LBP on real-world graphs. Next, we elaborate on each of the main ideas of DLBP through Section 3.2 to Section 3.4. In Section 3.5, we analyze DLBP in terms of the amount of shuffled data, time complexity, and memory usage. Section 3.6 presents the implementation details of DLBP on the Spark platform.

3.1 DLBP: Overview

DLBP is a distributed LBP algorithm that efficiently computes the beliefs of vertices in real-world graphs. When considering an efficient parallel computation of LBP in a distributed environment, there are several challenges that need to be addressed.

(1) **Setting convergence criterion.** LBP iteratively updates messages until all messages converge. However, is this "message" convergence criterion appropriate for a real-world graph with high-degree vertices?
(2) **Minimizing numerical computations.** How can we minimize the overall computations of messages and the total number of iterations until convergence?
(3) **Minimizing network communication cost.** Real-world graphs are known to have highly-skewed degree distribution. With this property in mind, how can we partition a real-world graph and arrange the message computations to minimize the data communication between machines?

We tackle the problems mentioned above with the following main ideas, which are described in detail in later subsections.

(1) **Using "belief" as convergence criterion (Section 3.2).** We show that the message-based stopping criterion is insufficient to guarantee the convergence of further iterations, especially for real-world graphs with high-degree vertices.
(2) **Skipping of converged vertices (Section 3.3).** DLBP skips the computations of outgoing messages from converged vertices due to its belief convergence criterion. As a result, we minimize redundant message computations and promote faster convergence.
(3) **Reducing full shuffling of graph data (Section 3.4).** DLBP focuses on the high-degree vertices which require more number of iterations to converge than low-degree vertices. This idea reduces the amount of data shuffling.

3.2 DLBP: Belief Convergence Criterion

DLBP checks the convergence of beliefs instead of messages as the stopping criterion to overcome the shortcoming of message-based approach on real-world graphs. It is important to note that the beliefs, not messages, are the desired output of LBP; therefore, the reliability of resulting beliefs is the most crucial factor. In this context, we show that the convergence of messages in two consecutive iterations neither guarantees 1) the convergence of beliefs nor 2) the convergence of messages in the next iteration. Then, we present the belief convergence criterion and demonstrate its superiority over its counterpart.

When the "message" convergence criterion is used, LBP iteratively computes the messages until the following inequality holds for all messages m_{ij}^{t-1} of previous iteration $t-1$ and messages m_{ij}^{t} of current iteration t:

$$\|m_{ij}^{t} - m_{ij}^{t-1}\|_{\infty} \leq \theta \quad (4)$$

where $\theta \geq 0$ is a small constant, and $\|x\|_{\infty}$ denotes the largest absolute value of a vector x. However, high-degree vertices (which we refer to as hubs) in real-world graphs impede the stability of the message convergence criterion as we show in this subsection.

We use the approximate equations of *Linearized BP* proposed in [9] to give the condition where the message convergence criterion is problematic. Using the following definitions, Linearized BP utilizes Maclaurin series expansions to replace multiplications in Equations (1), (2), and (3) with summations.

Definition 1 (Centering [9]). *We call a vector x is centered around c if the average of all elements of x is exactly c, and each element deviates from c only by a small value.*

Definition 2 (Residual Value [9]). *When there is a vector x which is centered around c, the residual value $\hat{x}_i$ of the ith element x_i is defined as the deviation of x_i from c; that is, $\hat{x}_i = x_i - c$.*

The modified equations of Linearized BP are expressed using the residual values, which are Equations (5), (6) and (7). We denote the residual values of beliefs, messages, node potentials, and edge potentials by $\hat{b}_i(x_i)$, $\hat{m}_{ij}(x_j)$, $\hat{\phi}_i(x_i)$, and $\hat{\psi}_{ij}(x_i, x_j)$, respectively.

$$\hat{m}_{ij}(x_j) \leftarrow s\sum_{x_i} \hat{\psi}_{ij}(x_i, x_j)\hat{\phi}_i(x_i) + \sum_{x_i}\sum_{l\in N(i)\setminus j} \hat{\psi}_{ij}(x_i, x_j)\hat{m}_{li}(x_i) \quad (5)$$

$$\hat{b}_i(x_i) = \hat{\phi}_i(x_i) + \frac{1}{s}\sum_{l\in N(i)} \hat{m}_{li}(x_i) \quad (6)$$

$$\hat{m}_{ij}(x_j) \leftarrow s\sum_{x_i} \hat{\psi}_{ij}(x_i, x_j)\hat{b}_i(x_i) - \sum_{x_i} \hat{\psi}_{ij}(x_i, x_j)\hat{m}_{ji}(x_i) \quad (7)$$

where s is the number of possible states x_i, and $N(i) \setminus j$ is the set of vertices neighboring vertex i except vertex j.

Using these equations, we give an upper bound to the difference of belief $b_i(x_i)$ between two consecutive iterations under the condition that all incoming messages m_{li} to vertex i have converged. The result is in Lemma 1.

Lemma 1. *The convergence of incoming messages to a high-degree vertex i **does not** guarantee the convergence of its belief.*

Proof. We compute the difference of belief $b_i(x_i)$ between two consecutive iterations using Equation (6). Since all incoming messages $m_{li}(x_i)$ have converged, we use the inequality $|\triangle\hat{m}_{li}(x_i)| \leq \theta$ to give an upper bound of the value.

$$|\triangle b_i(x_i)| = \left|\frac{1}{s}\sum_{l\in N(i)} \triangle\hat{m}_{li}(x_i)\right| \leq \frac{1}{s}\sum_{l\in N(i)} \theta = \frac{1}{s}|N(i)|\theta$$

where $|N(i)|$ is the degree of vertex i. Since $|\triangle b_i(x_i)| \leq \frac{1}{s}|N(i)|\theta$, there is no guarantee $|\triangle b_i(x_i)|$ is within a small value when $|N(i)|$ is sufficiently large. □

Next, we solve the inequality in Equation (4) for an outgoing message $m_{ij}(x_j)$ from vertex i under the same condition as above to get Lemma 2.

Lemma 2. *The convergence of incoming messages **does not** guarantee the convergence of outgoing messages when a high-degree vertex i fails to satisfy the following inequality:*

$$|N(i)| \leq \frac{1}{s \cdot \max(\hat{\psi}_{ij}(x_i, x_j))} + 1$$

Proof. We compute the difference of the outgoing message $m_{ij}(x_j)$ between previous and current iterations by substituting the message terms with Equation (5). Similar to the proof in Lemma 1, we use the inequality $|\triangle \hat{m}_{li}(x_i)| \leq \theta$ to give an upper bound of the value. We use $\max(\hat{\psi}_{ij}(x_i, x_j))$ to denote the largest absolute value among the residuals of edge potentials.

$$\begin{aligned}|\triangle m_{ij}(x_j)| &= \left|\sum_{x_i}\sum_{l\in N(i)\setminus j}\hat{\psi}_{ij}(x_i,x_j)\cdot\triangle\hat{m}_{li}(x_i)\right| \\ &\leq \sum_{x_i}\sum_{l\in N(i)\setminus j}\max(\hat{\psi}_{ij}(x_i,x_j))\cdot\theta \\ &= s(|N(i)|-1)\cdot\max(\hat{\psi}_{ij}(x_i,x_j))\cdot\theta\end{aligned}$$

Since $|\triangle m_{ij}(x_j)|$ is within the convergence threshold θ, we get the convergence criterion as:

$$|\triangle m_{ij}(x_j)| \leq s(|N(i)|-1)\cdot\max(\hat{\psi}_{ij}(x_i,x_j))\cdot\theta \leq \theta$$

By canceling out θ and rearranging the terms, we get the inequality in Lemma 2. □

Note that s is a constant value and $\max(\hat{\psi}_{ij}(x_i, x_j))$ depends on the edge potential values. Therefore, Lemma 2 indicates that if a vertex i has a degree $|N(i)|$ higher than some constant value, there is no guarantee that its outgoing messages will converge even after its incoming messages have converged.

A reasonable solution to this problem would be to introduce an alternative convergence criterion that mitigates the problem, which is to use beliefs instead of messages. When using "belief" convergence criterion, LBP stops when the following inequality holds for all beliefs b_i of two consecutive iterations:

$$\|b_i^t - b_i^{t-1}\|_\infty \leq \theta \quad (8)$$

This condition directly leads to the following lemma.

Lemma 3. *The belief convergence criterion guarantees the convergence of all beliefs.*

Next, we analyze the belief convergence criterion on the convergence of outgoing messages. By once more utilizing the Linearized BP equations, we get Lemma 4.

Lemma 4. *The convergence of the beliefs of adjacent vertices i and j restricts the difference of message between them in consecutive iterations within a small value: $|\triangle m_{ij}(x_j)| \leq \frac{s^2\cdot\max(\hat{\psi}_{ij}(x_i,x_j))}{1-s\cdot\max(\hat{\psi}_{ij}(x_i,x_j))}\theta$*

Proof. We compute the difference of the outgoing message $m_{ij}(x_j)$ by utilizing Equation (7). We give an upper bound by the inequality $|\triangle \hat{b}_i(x_i)| \leq \theta$.

$$\begin{aligned}|\triangle m_{ij}(x_j)| &= \left|s\sum_{x_i}\hat{\psi}_{ij}(x_i,x_j)\triangle\hat{b}_i(x_i) - \sum_{x_i}\hat{\psi}_{ij}(x_i,x_j)\triangle m_{ji}(x_i)\right| \\ &\leq s\sum_{x_i}\max(\hat{\psi}_{ij}(x_i,x_j))\cdot\theta + \sum_{x_i}\max(\hat{\psi}_{ij}(x_i,x_j))|\triangle m_{ji}(x_i)| \\ &= s\cdot\max(\hat{\psi}_{ij}(x_i,x_j))\cdot(s\theta + |\triangle m_{ji}(x_i)|)\end{aligned}$$

Since the same conditions apply to $|\triangle m_{ji}(x_i)|$, we get a symmetric inequality $|\triangle m_{ji}(x_i)| \leq s\cdot\max(\hat{\psi}_{ij}(x_i,x_j))\cdot(s\theta + |\triangle m_{ij}(x_j)|)$. By solving these two inequalities and rearranging the terms, we get the inequality in Lemma 4. □

We compare these two convergence criteria by introducing an example. Let's suppose there is a pairwise MRF whose vertices have two possible states, and we set edge potentials to 0.51 for the case where adjacent vertices have the same state and 0.49 for the opposite case. First, we examine the message convergence criterion by plugging the values $s = 2$ and $\max(\hat{\psi}_{ij}(x_i, x_j)) = 0.01$ to the inequality in Lemma 2:

$$|N(i)| \leq \frac{1}{2\cdot 0.01} + 1 = 51$$

For high-degree vertices with degree $|N(i)| > 51$, the convergence of their incoming messages does not guarantee the convergence of their outgoing messages. On the other hand, when we use the belief convergence criterion, the following guarantee holds on the messages between converged vertices i and j regardless of their degrees: $|\triangle m_{ij}(x_j)| \leq \frac{2^2\cdot 0.01}{1-2\cdot 0.01}\theta \approx 0.0408\cdot\theta$.

3.3 DLBP: Skipping of Converged Vertices

DLBP reuses outgoing messages m_{ij} of the previous iteration if the belief of their source vertex i satisfies the inequality in Equation (8). LBP-based algorithms using the message convergence criterion cannot safely skip the computation of outgoing messages of converged vertices because of Lemma 2. DLBP utilizes the belief convergence criterion which provides a more reliable standard for checking the convergence of a vertex. Thus, DLBP skips the computation of outgoing messages from vertices that have converged at the previous iteration with more reliability.

The obvious advantage of reusing the outgoing messages of converged vertices is that it omits the redundant computations. More importantly, skipping the computations also reduces the number of iterations required until all beliefs converge because it allows the algorithm to ignore very small errors of outgoing messages. The latter advantage contributes significantly in reducing the total running time of LBP algorithm. We easily see this by looking at the time complexity of LBP on graphs with cycles, which is given by Lemma 5.

Lemma 5 (Time Complexity of LBP [2]). *The time complexity of LBP on a graph $G = (V, E)$ with cycles is $O(|E|T)$, where V is the set of vertices, E is the set of edges, and T is the number of iterations required until all beliefs converge.*

3.4 DLBP: Hub-oriented Scheduling

We propose a hub-oriented scheduling, which DLBP uses to minimize the shuffled data when applying LBP in a distributed environment. The main idea is to focus on achieving the convergence of hubs and then propagate the messages to low-degree vertices (which we refer to as spokes). First, DLBP performs pre-processing to partition data based on hubs and spokes (Algorithm 1). Then the algorithm iterates carefully designed super-steps until all beliefs converge (Algorithm 2). Each super-step consists of four different sub-steps: hub-to-hub iteration, hub-to-spoke propagation, spoke-to-spoke iteration, and spoke-to-hub propagation. The objective of hub-oriented LBP is to minimize the full data shuffling by reducing the number of super-steps required until convergence.

3.4.1 Preprocessing Stage (Algorithm 1). In preprocessing stage, we introduce the hub ratio parameter $0 \leq k \leq 1$ to divide the

Algorithm 1: DLBP Preprocessing Stage

Input: vertex set V, edge set E, node potential set $\boldsymbol{\phi}$, and hub ratio k
Output: message sets M_{hh}, M_{sh}, M_{hs}, M_{ss}, belief sets B_h, B_s and node potential sets $\boldsymbol{\phi}_h$, $\boldsymbol{\phi}_s$

1: compute the degrees of all vertices in V
2: divide V into V_h, V_s according to vertices' degrees and k
3: divide $\boldsymbol{\phi}$ into $\boldsymbol{\phi}_h$, $\boldsymbol{\phi}_s$ with respect to V_h, V_s
4: initialize all beliefs B to $\frac{1}{s}$ where s is the number of states
5: divide B into B_h, B_s with respect to V_h, V_s
6: divide E into E_{hh}, E_{ss}, E_{hs}, E_{sh} according to their sources and destinations
7: initialize all messages M to 1
8: divide message set M into M_{hh}, M_{ss}, M_{hs}, M_{sh} with respect to E_{hh}, E_{ss}, E_{hs}, E_{sh}
9: **return** $\boldsymbol{\phi}_h$, $\boldsymbol{\phi}_s$, B_h, B_s, and M_{hh}, M_{sh}, M_{hs}, M_{ss}

vertices into hubs and spokes (lines 1 to 2). For example, if $k = 0.3$, then 30% of the vertices with the highest degrees are selected as hubs while the rest 70% become spokes. V_h and V_s represent the sets of hubs and spokes, respectively. Since each node potential ϕ_i is associated with a vertex i, the node potentials are also divided into two separate sets, $\boldsymbol{\phi}_h$ and $\boldsymbol{\phi}_s$, where boldfaced $\boldsymbol{\phi}$ denotes the set of all node potentials (line 3). In addition, we divide the beliefs into two sets, B_h and B_s (lines 4 to 5). Likewise, we divide the edges into four different sets according to their sources and destinations (line 6). E_{hh}, E_{ss}, E_{hs}, and E_{sh} denote the sets of edges whose source and destination are both hubs, both spokes, hub to spoke, and spoke to hub, respectively. M_{hh}, M_{ss}, M_{hs}, and M_{sh} are their affiliated message sets (lines 7 to 8). In the end, we have two subgraphs $G_h = (V_h, E_{hh})$ and $G_s = (V_s, E_{ss})$, and two intermediate sets of edges, E_{hs} and E_{sh}, that span over the two subgraphs (line 9).

We adapt the hybrid partitioning method from [6] and use differentiated partitioning strategies for the two subgraphs. The subgraph G_h of hubs is partitioned using vertex-cut to achieve balanced workload among machines while edge-cut is used for the subgraph G_s of spokes. For the vertex-cut, we use a 2d hash partitioner [3, 13] to limit the maximum number of machines over which a vertex spans. The intermediate edges, E_{hs} and E_{sh}, use edge-cut to group them by their destination vertices.

3.4.2 Main Stage (Algorithm 2). In main stage, DLBP carefully schedules the iterative message update steps in LBP according to the subgraphs, G_h and G_s, and intermediate edges, E_{hs} and E_{sh}. Since the subgraph of hubs is known to form a more dense graph than spokes [23], DLBP focuses on the subgraph G_h to promote the faster convergence of hubs and reduce the total number of super-steps until convergence. Each super-step of DLBP consists of two sub-iteration steps and two intermediate propagation steps: hub-to-hub iteration, hub-to-spoke propagation, spoke-to-spoke iteration, and spoke-to-hub propagation. DLBP iterates the super-steps until all beliefs satisfy the belief convergence criterion.

Hub-to-Hub Iteration (line 2 & Algorithm 3). In hub-to-hub iteration, we iteratively update M_{hh}, instead of all messages, until the belief convergence criterion holds for all beliefs in B_h. However, the naive approach to fully iterate the message updates until the convergence of B_H suffers from wasteful computations. Even though the hubs converged at current super-step, the information received

Algorithm 2: DLBP Main Stage

Input: vertex sets V_h, V_s, node potential sets $\boldsymbol{\phi}_h$, $\boldsymbol{\phi}_s$, belief sets B_h, B_s, message sets M_{hh}, M_{sh}, M_{hs}, M_{ss}, edge potentials ψ_{ij}, and maximum inner iterations τ
// Note that c_i is a normalization constant
Output: beliefs B of all vertices

1: **while** $B_h \cup B_s$ not converged **do**
2: $\quad B_h \leftarrow$ Sub-iteration(V_h, ψ_{ij}, τ, B_h, M_{hh}, $\boldsymbol{\phi}_h$, M_{sh})
3: $\quad M_{hs} \leftarrow \frac{1}{c_i}\sum_{x_i}\psi_{ij}(x_i, x_j)\frac{b_i(x_i)}{m_{ji}(x_i)}$ using M_{sh} and B_h
4: $\quad B_s \leftarrow$ Sub-iteration(V_s, ψ_{ij}, τ, B_s, M_{ss}, $\boldsymbol{\phi}_s$, M_{hs})
5: $\quad M_{sh} \leftarrow \frac{1}{c_i}\sum_{x_i}\psi_{ij}(x_i, x_j)\frac{b_i(x_i)}{m_{ji}(x_i)}$ using M_{hs} and B_s
6: **end while**
7: **return** B

Algorithm 3: Sub-iteration(·) for Main Stage

Input: vertices V, edge potentials ψ_{ij}, maximum inner iterations τ, $\forall v \in V$: beliefs B_v, messages M_{vv}, node potentials $\boldsymbol{\phi}_v$, $\forall x \notin V$ and $\forall v \in V$: messages M_{xv}
Output: beliefs B_v

1: $p_i(x_i) \leftarrow \phi_i(x_i)\prod_{l \in N(i)\setminus V} m_{li}(x_i)$ for $\forall i \in V$ using $\boldsymbol{\phi}_v$
2: **while** (B_v not converged) & (less than τ iterations) **do**
3: $\quad B_v \leftarrow c_i p_i(x_i)\prod_{l \in N(i)\cap V} m_{li}(x_i)$
4: $\quad M_{vv} \leftarrow \frac{1}{c_i}\sum_{x_i}\psi_{ij}(x_i, x_j)\frac{b_i(x_i)}{m_{ji}(x_i)}$
5: **end while**
6: **return** B_v

from spokes breaks the convergence of hubs in the next super-step. Then we need to re-compute M_{hh} until they re-converge, where some of these computations might be inefficient in terms of approaching toward a global stationary point. To alleviate the problem, we introduce a parameter τ that restricts the maximum number of sub-iterations in hub-to-hub iteration. τ controls the trade-off between the information gained by the sub-iteration and the deviation of the converged values from the global optimum.

Since $\boldsymbol{\phi}_h$ and M_{sh} have constant values at each hub-to-hub iteration, we compute the multiplication of these values in advance to avoid redundant computations. More precisely, we compute the multiplication of constant node potential and incoming messages of vertex i as $p_i(x_i) = \phi_i(x_i)\prod_{l \in N(i)\setminus V_h} m_{li}(x_i)$. $N(i) \setminus V_h$ denotes the set of neighboring vertices of vertex i, which are not hubs. Then, the belief $b_i(x_i)$ of a hub i is computed as follows:

$$b_i(x_i) = c_i\phi_i(x_i)\prod_{l \in N(i)} m_{li}(x_i) = c_i p_i(x_i)\prod_{l \in N(i)\cap V_h} m_{li}(x_i)$$

This equation resembles Equation (2), except that the term $\phi_i(x_i)$ is replaced by $p_i(x_i)$. Using this equation, only M_{hh} and the set of $p_i(x_i)$ for $i \in V_h$ are required to compute B_h.

Hub-to-Spoke Propagation (line 3). After B_h converges, we compute M_{hs} which transfer the accumulated information from hubs to spokes. Note that only one step of full computations of M_{hs} is sufficient to fully propagate the accumulated information from hubs to spokes because B_h of the last hub-to-hub iteration is used to update M_{hs}.

Spoke-to-Spoke Iteration (line 4 & Algorithm 3). In spoke-to-spoke iteration, the only two differences from the hub-to-hub iteration are that 1) M_{ss} is updated instead of M_{hh}, and 2) B_s is used to check the convergence of beliefs. Similar to that of hub-to-hub iteration, we compute the set of $p_i(x_i) = \phi_i(x_i)\prod_{l \in N(i)\setminus V_s} m_{li}(x_i)$

for $i \in V_s$ before the iteration. It is noteworthy to mention that each spoke-to-spoke iteration converges within 1-3 steps in real-world graphs, which accords with our intuition that hubs are accountable for most of the iterations until an LBP algorithm converges.

Spoke-to-Hub Propagation (line 5). We compute M_{sh} to propagate the updated information of spokes to hubs.

3.5 Analysis of DLBP

We analyze DLBP with respect to the amount of shuffled data, time complexity, and memory usage. We use the following symbols to represent each factor: n (number of machines), T_o (total number of super-step iterations), T_h (total number of hub-to-hub iterations), T_s (total number of spoke-to-spoke iterations), T (number of iterations until standard LBP converges). Note that the equation $|E_{hs}| = |E_{sh}|$ always holds since the outgoing and incoming edges are symmetric.

3.5.1 Amount of Shuffled Data. We present the main result Lemma 9 which is supported by Lemmas 6, 7, and 8.

LEMMA 6. *The amount of shuffled data in each loop of hub-to-hub iteration (lines 2 to 5 in Algorithm 3 called by line 2 in Algorithm 2) is* $O(\sqrt{n}|V_h|)$.

PROOF. DLBP partitions the subgraph $G_h = (V_h, E_{hh})$ using vertex-cut; thus, a vertex spans across at most $2\sqrt{n}$ number of machines using a 2d hash partitioner [13]. First step is to aggregate the messages in M_{hh} by their destination vertices in order to compute B_h. Since the messages are initially aggregated within each machine before shuffling, the amount of shuffled data is $O(\sqrt{n}|V_h|)$. Next step is to update M_{hh}, which requires B_h to be distributed across at most $2\sqrt{n}$ machines. This also results in $O(\sqrt{n}|V_h|)$ shuffled data. Consequently, the amount of shuffled data for one hub-to-hub iteration is $O(\sqrt{n}|V_h|)$. □

LEMMA 7. *The amount of shuffled data in each loop in spoke-to-spoke iteration (lines 2 to 5 in Algorithm 3 called by line 4 in Algorithm 2) is* $O(|E_{ss}|)$.

PROOF. DLBP partitions the subgraph $G_s = (V_s, E_{ss})$ using edge-cut which assigns edges to machines according to their destinations. Thus, no shuffling is required when computing B_s and M_{ss}. However, the directions of newly updated messages in M_{ss} are inverted (source and destination are flipped) according to Equation (3). It is necessary to re-group the edges according to their new destinations, which requires the shuffling of $O(|E_{ss}|)$ data. □

LEMMA 8. *The amount of shuffled data in each super-step except the loops in sub-iterations (line 1 in Algorithm 3, and lines 3 and 5 in Algorithm 2) is* $O(|V| + |E_{hs}|)$

PROOF. When we consider hub-to-hub iterations, we compute the multiplication of $\boldsymbol{\phi}_h$ and M_{sh} in line 1 (Algorithm 3). Since the edges in E_{sh} are partitioned by edge-cut, no shuffling happens when multiplying messages in M_{sh}. However, we still need to multiply the multiplications of messages with $\boldsymbol{\phi}_h$, where the shuffled data is $O(|V_h|)$. Note that Algorithm 3 is reused for both hubs and spokes. In line 3 (Algorithm 2), there are two parts that we need to consider. First, we distribute the beliefs in B_h according to the destinations of M_{sh} to compute M_{hs}, which require $O(|V_h|)$ data to be shuffled. Then, we need to re-partition the updated M_{hs} according to their destination vertices which requires $O(|E_{hs}|)$ of shuffled data. The computation in line 3 (Algorithm 2) is symmetric with respect to hubs and spokes; line 5 is its counterpart. Therefore, the total amount of shuffled data in each super-step except the loops in sub-iterations is $O(|V| + |E_{hs}|)$. □

LEMMA 9. *The total amount of shuffled data of DLBP until all beliefs B converge is as follows:*

$$O((|V| + |E_{hs}|)T_o + \sqrt{n}|V_h|T_h + |E_{ss}|T_s)$$

PROOF. The equation is derived by a straightforward application of Lemmas 6, 7, and 8. □

Since $T_o \le T_s < T_h \approx T$ holds in most cases (see Table 5), DLBP effectively reduces the amount of shuffled data compared to that of LBP. We easily show this by dividing the equation in Lemma 9 by the amount of shuffled data of standard LBP using vertex-cut with n machines, which is $O(\sqrt{n}|V|T)$ [13]. Under the condition that $T_o \le T_s \ll T_h \approx T$, the shuffled data of DLBP is approximately k times smaller than that of LBP as follows, where k is the hub ratio:

$$\frac{(|V| + |E_{hs}|)T_o}{\sqrt{n}|V|T} + \frac{\sqrt{n}|V_h|T_h}{\sqrt{n}|V|T} + \frac{|E_{ss}|T_s}{\sqrt{n}|V|T} \approx \frac{\sqrt{n}|V_h|T_h}{\sqrt{n}|V|T} \approx \frac{|V_h|}{|V|} = k$$

The above simplification is based on the assumption that $|V| + |E_{hs}|$ and $|E_{ss}|$ are less than or equal to $\sqrt{n}|V|$, which is reasonable when n is sufficiently large.

3.5.2 Time Complexity.

LEMMA 10. *The time complexity of DLBP is as follows:*

$$O\left(\frac{T_h|E_{hh}| + T_s|E_{ss}| + T_o|E_{hs}|}{n}\right)$$

PROOF. Since hub-to-hub iterations are identical to applying LBP on a subgraph $G_h = (V_h, E_{hh})$ where $p_i(x_i)$ resembles the node potential $\phi_i(x_i)$, the time complexity is $O(T_h|E_{hh}|)$ on a single machine according to Lemma 5. When we use n machines to synchronously compute the messages, the time complexity becomes $O(\frac{T_h|E_{hh}|}{n})$. A similar justification applies for spoke-to-spoke iterations where the time complexity is $O(\frac{T_s|E_{ss}|}{n})$. The computations of messages in M_{hs} and M_{sh} simulate LBP algorithm on a bipartite graph $G_h = (V_h \cup V_s, E_{hs} \cup E_{sh})$; thus, the time complexity is $O(\frac{T_o|E_{hs}|}{n})$. By summing up these terms, we prove the lemma. □

When compared to the time complexity of standard LBP, $O(\frac{T|E|}{n})$, DLBP reduces the complexity under the condition that $T_o \le T_s \ll T_h \approx T$. It is because $|E| = |E_{hh}| + |E_{ss}| + 2|E_{hs}|$; thus, $T_h|E_{hh}| + T_s|E_{ss}| + T_o|E_{hs}| < T|E|$ always holds true.

3.5.3 Memory Usage.

LEMMA 11. *DLBP requires at most the memory space of:*

$$O(\max(|E_{hh}| + |V_h|, |E_{hs}| + |V_h|, |E_{sh}| + |V_s|, |E_{ss}| + |V_s|))$$

PROOF. At each sub-step, we only need the memory space for the message set and the belief set associated with the sub-step. Thus, DLBP occupies up to the maximum memory space requirement among the sub-steps because unused data at current sub-step are stored in a secondary storage. □

The memory requirement of DLBP is always less than that of standard LBP since $|V| = |V_h| + |V_s|$ and $|E| = |E_{hh}| + |E_{ss}| + 2|E_{hs}|$.

Table 2: Summary of the datasets.

Dataset	Labeled	Nodes	Edges
YahooWeb-250M	13,463,596	174,577,088	776,375,840
YahooWeb-225M	11,649,829	151,082,221	627,242,209
YahooWeb-200M	9,806,416	128,663,268	494,471,965
YahooWeb-175M	8,146,152	106,656,291	376,985,487
YahooWeb-150M	6,456,257	85,309,472	275,133,522
YahooWeb-125M	4,906,727	65,829,290	190,485,192
YahooWeb-100M	3,517,351	47,141,314	121,566,975
YahooWeb-75M	2,319,233	30,731,733	68,492,600
YahooWeb-50M	1,264,080	16,402,838	30,403,395
Campaigns	12,059	23,191	877,729
PubMed	19,717	19,717	88,651
PolBlogs	991	1,224	16,716

3.6 Implementation

In this section, we present the implementation details of DLBP on Apache Spark [36, 37]. Note that DLBP can be implemented on any other distributed system which supports synchronous data processing. First, we store messages and node potentials as two separate *Resilient Distributed Datasets* (RDDs). Then, we divide RDDs according to the hub ratio k using *filter* operations. Each of the divided RDDs is partitioned by the *partitionBy* function with a customized partitioner which corresponds to either vertex-cut or edge-cut. Next, the *aggregateByKey* operation computes beliefs, and the *join* operation is used to check their convergence. Last, hub-to-hub message RDD partitioned by vertex-cut uses the *zipPartitions* function, which preserves the previous partitioning, to compute new messages while other message RDDs partitioned by edge-cut use the *join* function.

4 EXPERIMENTS

In this section, we evaluate the experimental results of DLBP. We answer the following questions:

- **Q1: Accuracy (Section 4.2).** Do the skipping technique and the hub-oriented scheduling of DLBP affect the accuracy of computed beliefs?
- **Q2: Speed (Section 4.3).** How quickly does DLBP compute the beliefs compared to baseline LBP algorithms?
- **Q3: Effect of parameters k and τ (Section 4.4).** How do the hub ratio k and the maximum sub-iterations τ affect the performance of DLBP in terms of speed?
- **Q4: Machine Scalability (Section 4.5).** How does DLBP scale up with respect to the number of machines?

4.1 Experimental Settings

Datasets. We use 4 datasets summarized in Table 2. Campaigns[1] is a graph of political committees and candidates with two possible states, where the edges represent donations. PolBlogs[2] [1] is a graph of hyperlinks where each vertex represents a web blog on US politics with two possible states. PubMed[3] is a citation graph where each vertex is a research paper with three possible categories. YahooWeb[4] is a web page hyperlink graph where labeled web pages

Table 3: Edge potential values for homophilic graphs.

(a) Two states.

State	1	2
1	**0.501**	0.499
2	0.499	**0.501**

(b) Three states.

State	1	2	3
1	**0.334**	0.333	0.333
2	0.333	**0.334**	0.333
3	0.333	0.333	**0.334**

Table 4: Classification accuracy of the algorithms using 5-fold cross validation. There is no meaningful difference between the algorithms; however, DLBP is much faster than competitors as described in Section 4.3.

Dataset	BP-E	BP-V	BP-ES	BP-VS	DLBP
Campaigns	89.36%	89.36%	89.31%	89.31%	89.31%
PolBlogs	95.62%	95.62%	95.62%	95.62%	95.62%
PubMed	82.65%	82.65%	82.79%	82.79%	82.65%

are either educational or adult pages. To make various real-world graphs with different sizes, we sample principal submatrices from the adjacency matrix of YahooWeb graph. For instance, YahooWeb-50M is the subgraph of YahooWeb where the dimensions of principal submatrix is 50M × 50M.

Note that these graphs are appropriate for LBP since they meet the homophily assumption. In particular, political groups are strongly connected to those with the same political opinion; research papers typically cite other papers within the same area; and educational web pages have links to other educational web pages, not adult web pages. The edge potential values are given by Table 3. The node potentials of labeled vertices are set to 0.9 for the correct label while other incorrect labels get a value that equally splits the remaining 0.1. Node potentials of unlabeled vertices have a uniform value $\frac{1}{s}$ for each state, where s is the number of possible states.

Methods. We evaluate our proposed DLBP compared to two baseline LBP algorithms based on edge-cut and vertex-cut (BP-E and BP-V). Moreover, we implement two additional LBP algorithms that improve BP-E and BP-V by utilizing the skipping technique introduced in Section 3.3 (BP-ES and BP-VS). The purpose of implementing BP-ES and BP-VS is to analyze the effects of the skipping technique on accuracy and speed. Lastly, DLBP uses both the skipping technique and the hub-oriented scheduling. All five algorithms are implemented on the Spark platform for a fair comparison, and use the belief convergence criterion with threshold $\theta = 10^{-4}$. The algorithms stop when the belief convergence criterion is met or total number of iterations exceeds 200.

We also evaluate DLBP compared to HA-LFP [18], a parallel LBP algorithm implemented on Apache Hadoop [7, 32]. Since HA-LFP requires users to manually choose the number of iterations, we give the number of iterations that BP-E and BP-V took to converge.

Environment Setting. We use Spark, a general data processing platform on distributed environment, to implement DLBP and four baseline algorithms mentioned above. We use the original code of HA-LFP provided by the authors of [18] and test on Apache Hadoop. The experiments were conducted on a cluster with 17 machines where each machine has a 32GB RAM and an Intel Xeon E3-1240 3.5GHz CPU with 4 cores. We configure Spark to run its application on the cluster using one machine as the driver node and the rest as the worker nodes where each node uses 24GB free memory.

[1] http://www.cs.cmu.edu/~mmcgloho/data.html
[2] http://www-personal.umich.edu/~mejn/netdata/
[3] http://linqs.cs.umd.edu/projects/projects/lbc/index.html
[4] http://webscope.sandbox.yahoo.com/

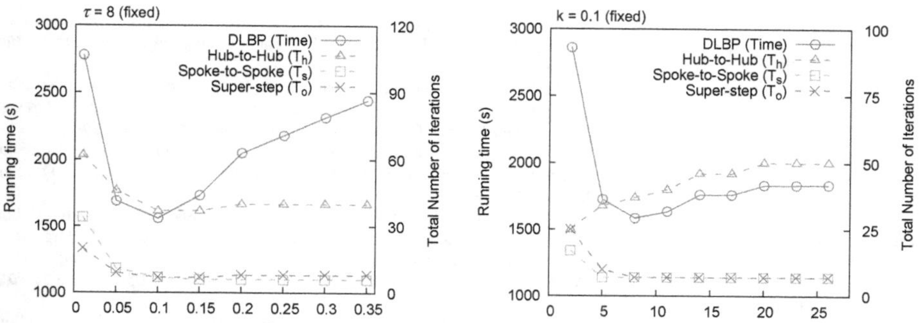

(a) Hub Ratio k. (b) Maximum Sub-iterations τ

Figure 2: Effects of the hub ratio k and the maximum sub-iterations τ on the performance of DLBP. We use YahooWeb-125M dataset to evaluate the different processing time according to the parameters. Note that the running time of DLBP is minimized when $k = 0.1$ and $\tau = 8$.

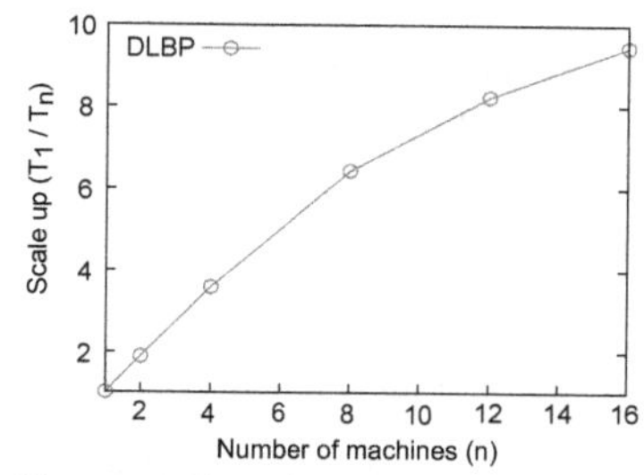

Figure 3: Running times of DLBP on YahooWeb-50M using different number of machines. DLBP demonstrates near-linear scaling with respect to the number of machines.

4.2 Accuracy (Q1)

We use vertex classification problem to measure the accuracy of the algorithms. The goal is to classify each vertex by assigning the label with the highest belief. We use 5-fold cross validation to ensure that we correctly estimate the accuracy of each algorithm. In addition, we balance the number of labeled vertices per label according to the label with the minimum number of labeled vertices.

We compare the classification accuracies of BP-ES, BP-VS, and DLBP to the baseline algorithms, BP-E and BP-V. Table 4 shows the classification results on each dataset. BP-ES, BP-VS, and DLBP show almost identical accuracies with the baseline algorithms on all the datasets. Note that the difference between the accuracies of two different methods is always less than 0.14%. Nevertheless, DLBP is much faster than competitors as we present in Section 4.3.

4.3 Speed (Q2)

We compare the running time of BP-ES, BP-VS, and DLBP with those of the baseline algorithms and HA-LFP. Since other datasets are too small to be a meaningful comparison of the speed of the algorithms, we use the subgraphs of YahooWeb to measure the running time. We measure the wall-clock time which includes the running time of the preprocessing stage of DLBP. Figure 1 presents the running time of each algorithm with regard to the number of edges. DLBP is up to 10.0× faster than HA-LFP, 10.7× faster than BP-E and BP-V, and even 2.0× faster than BP-ES and BP-VS. Table 5 demonstrates the number of sub-iterations and super-steps of DLBP until all beliefs converge. It shows that the number of super-steps of DLBP is significantly less than those of BP-ES and BP-VS.

4.4 Effects of Parameters in DLBP (Q3)

We analyze the effects of the hub ratio k and the maximum sub-iterations τ in terms of running time. Figures 2a and 2b present the running time of DLBP with varying parameters. While we evaluate the effect of one parameter, we fix the other parameters to their optimal values. Thus, $\tau = 8$ in Figure 2a and $k = 0.1$ in Figure 2b.

As shown in Figure 2a, DLBP takes more super-steps T_o until convergence when k is too small. It also causes the number of sub-iterations, T_h and T_s, to increase as well. On the other hand, large k does not affect the total number of iterations but rather increases the size of subgraph $G_h = (V_h, E_{hh})$, resulting in longer execution time. In Figure 2b, the number of super-steps until convergence increases when τ is very small, which results in longer running time. When $\tau = 1$, DLBP simulates the standard LBP where each iteration endures full shuffling of graph data. On the contrary, the number of hub-to-hub iterations increases as τ grows past the optimum value. As a result, the redundant computations in hub-to-hub iteration increase accordingly, an effect we mentioned in Section 3.4.

Table 5: Number of total sub-iterations and super-steps in DLBP on the subgraphs of YahooWeb. T denotes the number of iterations until BP-ES and BP-VS converge. The number of super-steps T_o in DLBP is much less than T on all datasets. Note that T_h has a value close to T, and T_s has a value close to T_o. k and τ are the values of hub ratio and maximum sub-iterations used in DLBP, respectively.

Dataset	k	τ	T_h	T_s	T_o	T
YahooWeb-50M	0.05	3	14	4	**4**	**12**
YahooWeb-75M	0.05	3	9	5	**5**	**13**
YahooWeb-100M	0.1	4	16	9	**7**	**16**
YahooWeb-125M	0.1	8	37	7	**7**	**39**
YahooWeb-150M	0.1	10	51	12	**8**	**50**
YahooWeb-175M	0.15	10	72	10	**10**	**77**
YahooWeb-200M	0.15	10	59	9	**9**	**54**
YahooWeb-225M	0.2	10	85	13	**13**	
YahooWeb-250M	0.25	10	86	12	**12**	

4.5 Machine Scalability (Q4)

We measure the machine scalability by measuring the running time of DLBP on YahooWeb-50M while increasing the number of machines from 1 to 16. Figure 3 illustrates the machine scalability in terms of speed up T_1/T_n where T_n is the running time using n machines. DLBP gains 9.46× speed up as the number of machines increases from 1 to 16.

5 CONCLUSION

We propose DLBP, a fast and scalable distributed loopy belief propagation method. DLBP enhances the standard LBP algorithm by overcoming the challenges associated with the skewed degree distribution of large real-world graphs. DLBP exploits a convergence criterion better suited for real-world graphs, and carefully schedules computations for better performance. Experimental results demonstrate that DLBP minimizes the communication cost of LBP and provides up to 10.7× speed up on real-world graphs without sacrificing the classification accuracy.

ACKNOWLEDGMENT

This work was supported by the National Research Foundation of Korea(NRF) funded by the Ministry of Science, ICT and Future Planning(NRF-2015K1A3A1A14021055). U Kang is the corresponding author.

REFERENCES

[1] Lada A. Adamic and Natalie Glance. 2005. The Political Blogosphere and the 2004 U.S. Election: Divided They Blog. In *Proceedings of the 3rd International Workshop on Link Discovery (LinkKDD '05)*. 36–43.

[2] Ron Bekkerman, Mikhail Bilenko, and John Langford. 2011. *Scaling up machine learning: Parallel and distributed approaches*. Cambridge University Press.

[3] Ümit V. Çatalyürek, Cevdet Aykanat, and Bora Uçar. 2010. On Two-Dimensional Sparse Matrix Partitioning: Models, Methods, and a Recipe. *SIAM J. Scientific Computing* 32, 2 (2010), 656–683.

[4] Duen Horng Chau, Shashank Pandit, and Christos Faloutsos. 2006. Detecting Fraudulent Personalities in Networks of Online Auctioneers. In *Knowledge Discovery in Databases: PKDD 2006*. Springer Berlin Heidelberg, Berlin, Heidelberg, 103–114.

[5] Duen Horng Polo Chau, Carey Nachenberg, Jeffrey Wilhelm, Adam Wright, and Christos Faloutsos. 2013. Polonium: Tera-Scale Graph Mining and Inference for Malware Detection. In *Proceedings of the 2011 SIAM International Conference on Data Mining*. Society for Industrial and Applied Mathematics, Philadelphia, PA, 131–142.

[6] Rong Chen, Jiaxin Shi, Yanzhe Chen, and Haibo Chen. 2015. PowerLyra: differentiated graph computation and partitioning on skewed graphs. In *Proceedings of the Tenth European Conference on Computer Systems, EuroSys 2015, Bordeaux, France, April 21-24, 2015*. 1:1–1:15.

[7] Jeffrey Dean and Sanjay Ghemawat. 2008. MapReduce: simplified data processing on large clusters. *Commun. ACM* 51, 1 (2008), 107–113.

[8] Pedro F. Felzenszwalb and Daniel P. Huttenlocher. 2006. Efficient Belief Propagation for Early Vision. *International Journal of Computer Vision* 70, 1 (2006), 41–54.

[9] Wolfgang Gatterbauer, Stephan Günnemann, Danai Koutra, and Christos Faloutsos. 2015. Linearized and Single-Pass Belief Propagation. *PVLDB* 8, 5 (2015), 581–592.

[10] Joseph Gonzalez, Yucheng Low, and Carlos Guestrin. 2009. Residual Splash for Optimally Parallelizing Belief Propagation. In *Proceedings of the Twelfth International Conference on Artificial Intelligence and Statistics, AISTATS 2009, Clearwater Beach, Florida, USA, April 16-18, 2009*. 177–184.

[11] Joseph Gonzalez, Yucheng Low, Carlos Guestrin, and David R. O'Hallaron. 2009. Distributed Parallel Inference on Large Factor Graphs. In *UAI 2009, Proceedings of the Twenty-Fifth Conference on Uncertainty in Artificial Intelligence, Montreal, QC, Canada, June 18-21, 2009*. 203–212.

[12] Joseph E. Gonzalez, Yucheng Low, Haijie Gu, Danny Bickson, and Carlos Guestrin. 2012. PowerGraph: Distributed Graph-Parallel Computation on Natural Graphs. In *10th USENIX Symposium on Operating Systems Design and Implementation, OSDI 2012, Hollywood, CA, USA, October 8-10, 2012*. 17–30.

[13] Joseph E. Gonzalez, Reynold S. Xin, Ankur Dave, Daniel Crankshaw, Michael J. Franklin, and Ion Stoica. 2014. GraphX: Graph Processing in a Distributed Dataflow Framework. In *Proceedings of the 11th USENIX Conference on Operating Systems Design and Implementation (OSDI'14)*. 599–613.

[14] Jiwoon Ha, Soon-Hyoung Kwon, Sang-Wook Kim, Christos Faloutsos, and Sunju Park. 2012. Top-N recommendation through belief propagation. In *21st ACM International Conference on Information and Knowledge Management, CIKM'12, Maui, HI, USA, October 29 - November 02, 2012*. 2343–2346.

[15] Min-Hee Jang, Christos Faloutsos, Sang-Wook Kim, U Kang, and Jiwoon Ha. 2016. PIN-TRUST: Fast Trust Propagation Exploiting Positive, Implicit, and Negative Information. In *Proceedings of the 25th ACM International on Conference on Information and Knowledge Management*. ACM, 629–638.

[16] Kyomin Jung, Wooram Heo, and Wei Chen. 2012. IRIE: Scalable and Robust Influence Maximization in Social Networks. In *12th IEEE International Conference on Data Mining, ICDM 2012, Brussels, Belgium, December 10-13, 2012*. 918–923.

[17] U Kang, D.H. Chau, and C. Faloutsos. 2010. Inference of Beliefs on Billion-Scale Graphs. *The 2nd Workshop on Large-scale Data Mining: Theory and Applications* (2010).

[18] U. Kang, Duen Horng Chau, and Christos Faloutsos. 2011. Mining large graphs: Algorithms, inference, and discoveries. In *Proceedings of the 27th International Conference on Data Engineering, ICDE 2011, April 11-16, 2011, Hannover, Germany*. 243–254.

[19] U. Kang, Charalampos E. Tsourakakis, and Christos Faloutsos. 2009. PEGASUS: A Peta-Scale Graph Mining System. In *ICDM 2009, The Ninth IEEE International Conference on Data Mining, Miami, Florida, USA, 6-9 December 2009*. 229–238.

[20] Danai Koutra, Tai-You Ke, U. Kang, Duen Horng Chau, Hsing-Kuo Kenneth Pao, and Christos Faloutsos. 2011. Unifying Guilt-by-Association Approaches: Theorems and Fast Algorithms. In *ECML/PKDD (2)*. 245–260.

[21] Ho Lee, Bin Shao, and U Kang. 2015. Fast graph mining with HBase. *Information Sciences* 315, 0 (2015), 56 – 66.

[22] Jure Leskovec, Kevin J. Lang, Anirban Dasgupta, and Michael W. Mahoney. 2009. Community Structure in Large Networks: Natural Cluster Sizes and the Absence of Large Well-Defined Clusters. *Internet Mathematics* 6, 1 (2009), 29–123.

[23] Yongsub Lim, U. Kang, and Christos Faloutsos. 2014. SlashBurn: Graph Compression and Mining beyond Caveman Communities. *IEEE Trans. Knowl. Data Eng.* 26, 12 (2014), 3077–3089.

[24] Grzegorz Malewicz, Matthew H. Austern, Aart J. C. Bik, James C. Dehnert, Ilan Horn, Naty Leiser, and Grzegorz Czajkowski. 2010. Pregel: a system for large-scale graph processing. In *Proceedings of the ACM SIGMOD International Conference on Management of Data, SIGMOD 2010, Indianapolis, Indiana, USA, June 6-10, 2010*. 135–146.

[25] Alexander Mendiburu, Roberto Santana, José Antonio Lozano, and Endika Bengoetxea. 2007. A parallel framework for loopy belief propagation. In *Genetic and Evolutionary Computation Conference, GECCO 2007, Proceedings, London, England, UK, July 7-11, 2007, Companion Material*. 2843–2850.

[26] Kevin P. Murphy, Yair Weiss, and Michael I. Jordan. 1999. Loopy Belief Propagation for Approximate Inference: An Empirical Study. In *UAI '99: Proceedings of the Fifteenth Conference on Uncertainty in Artificial Intelligence, Stockholm, Sweden, July 30 - August 1, 1999*. 467–475.

[27] Huy Nguyen and Rong Zheng. 2012. Influence Spread in Large-Scale Social Networks - A Belief Propagation Approach. In *Machine Learning and Knowledge Discovery in Databases - European Conference, ECML PKDD 2012, Bristol, UK, September 24-28, 2012. Proceedings, Part II*. 515–530.

[28] Shashank Pandit, Duen Horng Chau, Samuel Wang, and Christos Faloutsos. 2007. *Netprobe: a fast and scalable system for fraud detection in online auction networks*. ACM, New York, New York, USA.

[29] Chiwan Park, Ha-Myung Park, Minji Yoon, and U. Kang. 2017. PMV: Pre-partitioned Generalized Matrix-Vector Multiplication for Scalable Graph Mining. *CoRR* abs/1709.09099 (2017).

[30] Ha-Myung Park, Chiwan Park, and U Kang. 2018. PegasusN: A Scalable and Versatile Graph Mining System. In *Proceedings of the Thirty-Second AAAI Conference on Artificial Intelligence, February 2-7, 2018, New Orleans, Lousiana, USA*.

[31] Adam Sadilek, Henry A. Kautz, and Jeffrey P. Bigham. 2012. Finding your friends and following them to where you are. In *Proceedings of the Fifth International Conference on Web Search and Web Data Mining, WSDM 2012, Seattle, WA, USA, February 8-12, 2012*. 723–732.

[32] Konstantin Shvachko, Hairong Kuang, Sanjay Radia, and Robert Chansler. 2010. The Hadoop Distributed File System. In *IEEE 26th Symposium on Mass Storage Systems and Technologies, MSST 2012, Lake Tahoe, Nevada, USA, May 3-7, 2010*. 1–10.

[33] Acar Tamersoy, Kevin A. Roundy, and Duen Horng Chau. 2014. Guilt by association: large scale malware detection by mining file-relation graphs. In *The 20th ACM SIGKDD International Conference on Knowledge Discovery and Data Mining, KDD '14, New York, NY, USA - August 24 - 27, 2014*. 1524–1533.

[34] Jiangtao Yin and Lixin Gao. 2014. Scalable Distributed Belief Propagation with Prioritized Block Updates. In *Proceedings of the 23rd ACM International Conference on Conference on Information and Knowledge Management, CIKM 2014, Shanghai, China, November 3-7, 2014*. 1209–1218.

[35] Jaemin Yoo, Saehan Jo, and U. Kang. 2017. Supervised Belief Propagation: Scalable Supervised Inference on Attributed Networks. In *IEEE 17th International Conference on Data Mining, ICDM 2017, November 18-21, 2017, New Orleans, USA*.

[36] Matei Zaharia, Mosharaf Chowdhury, Tathagata Das, Ankur Dave, Justin Ma, Murphy McCauly, Michael J. Franklin, Scott Shenker, and Ion Stoica. 2012. Resilient Distributed Datasets: A Fault-Tolerant Abstraction for In-Memory Cluster Computing. In *Proceedings of the 9th USENIX Symposium on Networked Systems Design and Implementation, NSDI 2012, San Jose, CA, USA, April 25-27, 2012*. 15–28.

[37] Matei Zaharia, Mosharaf Chowdhury, Michael J. Franklin, Scott Shenker, and Ion Stoica. 2010. Spark: Cluster Computing with Working Sets. In *2nd USENIX Workshop on Hot Topics in Cloud Computing, HotCloud'10, Boston, MA, USA, June 22, 2010*.

[38] Jun Zou and Faramarz Fekri. 2013. A belief propagation approach for detecting shilling attacks in collaborative filtering. In *22nd ACM International Conference on Information and Knowledge Management, CIKM'13, San Francisco, CA, USA, October 27 - November 1, 2013*. 1837–1840.

Combating Crowdsourced Review Manipulators: A Neighborhood-Based Approach

Parisa Kaghazgaran
Texas A& M University
College Station, TX
kaghazgaran@tamu.edu

James Caverlee
Texas A& M University
College Station, TX
caverlee@tamu.edu

Anna Squicciarini
Pennsylvania State University
State College, PA
asquicciarini@ist.psu.edu

ABSTRACT

We propose a system called **TwoFace** to uncover crowdsourced review manipulators who target online review systems. A unique feature of TwoFace is its three-phase framework: (i) in the first phase, we intelligently sample actual evidence of manipulation (e.g., review manipulators) by exploiting low moderation crowdsourcing platforms that reveal evidence of strategic manipulation; (ii) we then propagate the suspiciousness of these seed users to identify similar users through a random walk over a "suspiciousness" graph; and (iii) finally, we uncover (hidden) distant users who serve structurally similar roles by mapping users into a low-dimensional embedding space that captures community structure. Altogether, the TwoFace system recovers 83% to 93% of all manipulators in a sample from Amazon of 38,590 reviewers, even when the system is seeded with only a few samples from malicious crowdsourcing sites.

ACM Reference Format:
Parisa Kaghazgaran, James Caverlee, and Anna Squicciarini. 2018. Combating Crowdsourced Review Manipulators: A Neighborhood-Based Approach. In *WSDM 2018: WSDM 2018: The Eleventh ACM International Conference on Web Search and Data Mining , February 5–9, 2018, Marina Del Rey, CA, USA.* ACM, New York, NY, USA, 9 pages. https://doi.org/10.1145/3159652.3159726

1 INTRODUCTION

User review aggregators like Amazon, Netflix, and Yelp play a central role in how we decide what movies to view, products to purchase, restaurants to patronize, and even doctors to visit. With this importance, the reviews at the heart of these aggregators are vulnerable to manipulation [32]. This manipulation – often in the form of artificial ratings and reviews – can degrade trust in these online platforms and in their products and services. Indeed, many previous efforts have explored methods to uncover this manipulation, often by applying machine learning or graph-based algorithms, e.g., [23], [31], [1], [25], [12], [34]. These methods typically are built and validated over a dataset of "known" manipulated reviews. And yet, most make one of several critical assumptions:

- *Manual labeling of fake reviews:* In the first approach, judges – often either researchers themselves or a team of labelers at a review site – assess individual reviews to determine if they are fake or not [17], [24]. These methods sometimes rely on unsupervised algorithms (e.g., the output of a proprietary company algorithm) or on manual and possibly error-prone labeling of fake reviews without access to a ground truth of the actual intent of the review writers themselves.
- *Ex post analysis of outliers:* A second approach is to validate detection algorithms through ex post analysis of suspicious reviews. Typically, an algorithm is run over a collection of reviews and the top-ranked results are examined [31], [1], [34]. This approach tends to focus on highly-visible fake behaviors (e.g., a reviewer who posts dozens of reviews in a period of minutes), but may miss more subtle behaviors.
- *Simulation of bad behavior:* A recent third approach is to *simulate* the behaviors of malicious workers [19]. In this approach, volunteers are asked to imagine themselves as fake review writers and then post fake reviews. While encouraging, this method necessarily lacks insight into the strategies and motivations of actual fake review writers.

We seek to complement these foundational studies by leveraging a large collection of *actual review manipulators.* In contrast to previous efforts where the critical knowledge of intent to deceive is missing, we collect a set of review manipulators *for whom we have strong evidence of intent to deceive.* Concretely, we monitor low moderation crowdsourcing sites like RapidWorkers, ShortTask, and Microworkers, where attacks on review sites can be launched by malicious paymasters. By tracking these workers from the crowdsourcing platform to a target review site like Amazon, we can identify deceptive review manipulators. In our analysis (see Figure 4) we find that these review manipulators engage in a deceptive mix of legitimate reviews (to build reputation and trust) and fraudulent reviews (to cash in on this trust). This two-faced behavior poses great challenges to traditional detection mechanisms since the fraudulent reviews may be masked by the large number of legitimate reviews. Indeed, through our investigation of 300 target products on Amazon and their reviewers, we find that although malicious and benign reviewers occasionally behave differently in terms of rating, burstiness of reviews, review length and so on, these traditional features do not provide strong power to distinguish between review manipulators and legitimate reviewers.

Hence, we propose in this paper the TwoFace system to uncover crowdsourced review manipulators who target online review systems. First, we intelligently sample actual evidence of manipulation (e.g., review manipulators) by exploiting low moderation crowdsourcing platforms that reveal evidence of strategic manipulation. Since we find that many traditional features do not have strong power to identify two-faced reviewers with a mix of legitimate and deceptive reviews, we propose to exploit *neighborhood-based*

WSDM 2018, February 5–9, 2018, Marina Del Rey, CA, USA

ACM ISBN 978-1-4503-5581-0/18/02...$15.00
https://doi.org/10.1145/3159652.3159726

characteristics of the reviewers themselves. The intuition is that although individual behaviors may be easy to mask, the collective campaign organization may be uncovered by exploiting the network around reviewers and products. Based on this intuition, we then propagate the suspiciousness of the original seed users to identify "similar" users through a random walk over a "suspiciousness" graph. In this way, we can identify users who may be likely to participate in deceptive review campaigns. Note, however, that users who are distant in the "suspiciousness" graph will rarely be considered as deceptive reviewers. Hence, our final step is to uncover these (hidden) distant users who serve structurally similar roles by mapping users into a low-dimensional embedding space that captures community structure. In this way, we can distinguish deceptive reviewers through their community embedding structure.

Through experiments, we evaluate the TwoFace system over a sample from Amazon of 38,590 reviewers and 580,000 reviews. We discover that social features perform much stronger in distinguishing manipulators and regular reviewers compared to behavioral features. We also find that manipulators and regular users behave relatively similar in terms of rating, review burstiness, and so on. In addition, manipulators who participate in multiple crowdsourcing campaigns play a key role in uncovering other malicious but not obviously fraudulent reviewers. We observe that many of the reviewers who write only one review on target products are more similar to actual malicious reviewers than regular users. Altogether, the TwoFace system recovers 83% to 93% of all manipulators, even when the system is seeded with only dozens of examples from malicious crowdsourcing sites, and outperforms a state-of-the-art baseline.

2 RELATED WORK

Research in review manipulation typically focuses on identifying either fake reviews or the coordinated activities of fraudulent review groups. We highlight here several major research thrusts:

In the first, the *content of the reviews* themselves may offer indicators of "spam-ness" or deception. Many works here develop text or NLP models to distinguish fake reviews from legitimate reviews, e.g., [18–20].

Complementing the review text itself, the *behavioral signals* revealed by the reviewers or the reviews may yield clues as to which are fraudulent [13]. For example, [2] detects lock-step behaviors using temporal patterns in the Facebook graph wherein users and pages are nodes and "Likes" are edges. A few works address the temporal behavior of reviews [5, 33], for example by finding burstiness or other synchronized behaviors. Bayesian approaches have been applied in rating time-series to detect anomalies [10].

In another perspective, *graph-based approaches* have become popular in fraud or anomaly detection by modeling users as nodes and their relationships as edges. Approaches include spectral methods like eigen-decomposition or singular value decomposition to cluster similar nodes in the graph [12, 23, 25]. Iterative models to label nodes as trustworthy or non-trustworthy are proposed in [6, 31]. Markov Random Fields (MRF) and belief propagation approaches have been used to identify dense and most likely suspicious subgraphs [1, 21]. In another view, malicious users are detected through graph-based measures like neighborhood diversity [34].

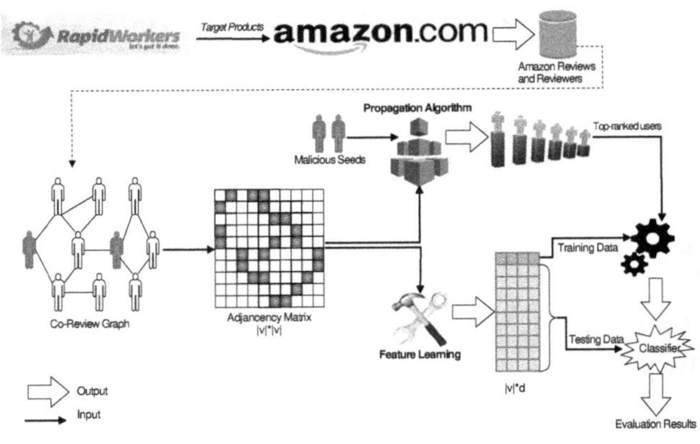

Figure 1: TwoFace overall framework.

A related direction is in *detecting dense blocks* in a review-rating matrix [11, 26, 27]. Extraordinary dense blocks correspond to groups of users with lockstep behaviors, e.g., [11]. Moreover, this method has been lately extended from matrix to tensor representation to incorporate more dimensions (e.g., temporal aspects) [26, 27]. However, these approaches may have difficulty in detecting subtle attacks where there are not such clearly defined dense block characteristics. Finally, some recent work focuses on detecting not just fake reviews but fake crowd activities, e.g., [30].

3 TWOFACE SYSTEM DESIGN

In this section, we introduce the overall system design for TwoFace (see Figure 1). TwoFace is designed to be deployed in real-world scenarios with the following characteristics:

- First, we assume there is only some *small, partial evidence of review manipulation.* In contrast to many previous efforts, we make no assumption that there is a large, curated collection of positive and negative examples of review manipulation. This corresponds to real-world scenarios of evolving and newly emerging types of review manipulation.
- Second, we target scenarios in which review manipulation engages in *difficult-to-detect behaviors.* That is, the review manipulators may engage in a mix of legitimate and deceptive reviews, so that many traditional content-based or dense-block methods may have difficulty in finding them.
- Finally, TwoFace is *recall-focused.* Our goal of uncovering review manipulators is to identify as many as possible out of the entire space of reviewers, in contrast to precision-focused approaches that may miss the vast majority of manipulators. We assume system operators can expend resources to further examine these potential manipulators.

In the following, we introduce each of the key components of TwoFace, before turning to a comprehensive evaluation in Section 4.

3.1 Identifying Suspicious Seeds

Our first task is to identify suspicious users. As we have argued, most existing methods for identifying deceptive reviews and reviewers have focused on indirect approaches, where the ground truth is necessarily an approximation. For example, previous efforts

What is expected from workers?
Read the product description before writing down a review.
Go to https://goo.gl/7QfW0h.
Leave a relevant 5-star review with at least 40 words.
Provide proof that you left the review yourself.

Figure 2: An example crowdsourcing task.

★★★★★ **Best cortisol blocker to reduce high levels of stress,** *July 24, 2017*
My stress levels have increased lately due to heavy work loads in my office and that directly impacting my life. I have gained weight and easily gets tired. I have tried many products to reduce my cortisol levels which is causing stress, but those products don't fetch any results and based on my uncle recommendation I have tried this product and it has relieved my stress and assisted in returning my cortisol levels to a more natural state. I feel more energized and active than before and the product also helped in losing body fat. Must try the product.

Figure 3: An example review written by a crowd worker.

have identified users with many reviews in a short burst of time or with a skewed rating distribution as suspicious [10, 11, 14, 27]. In contrast, many seemingly "normal" reviewers may be overlooked in practice if their deceptive reviews are blended in with legitimate ones.

Sampling Crowdsourcing Sites for Identifying Suspicious Users. Alternatively, we aim to identify users who have been tasked by a crowdsourcing site. In this way, we can identify with high confidence users who are indeed deceptive even if the majority of their reviews are legitimate. As an example, consider the task posted to RapidWorkers in Figure 2. This type of task is common on RapidWorkers and related sites like ShortTask and Microworkers. As an example of the type of review that is created by crowd worker, Figure 3 shows a sample of a crowdsourced review for a "cortisol supplement" product sold by Amazon. On examination, this review displays few (if any) clear signals of it being fraudulently written.

By monitoring such requests, we can begin to study the behaviors of fraudulent review writers. Although not representative of all types of manipulation, this approach does provide the tantalizing opportunity to study malicious behaviors in the wild. To collect suspicious users, TwoFace implements two crawlers: one for identifying crowdsourcing tasks and the other crawler has been designed to collect reviews from a target site. In this paper, we focus on tasks posted to RapidWorkers that target Amazon and simultaneously ask for fake reviews, similar to the example shown in Figure 2. Note that there are many such sites[1] and many additional targets (e.g., Yelp, App Store, Play Store).

Concretely, we crawl all such tasks from July 2016 to February 2017. In total, we identify 300 unique Amazon product IDs. By linking these IDs to Amazon, we crawl all reviews associated with each targeted product. Altogether we find 21,162 reviews that have been written by 12,212 unique reviewers. Typically, a target on these crowdsourcing sites (e.g., a product on Amazon) may be subject to dozens of fake reviews. We find that the number of required fake reviews requested by paymasters varies: the average is 13, but some paymasters ask for only 1, while the maximum requester asked for 75 reviews. Contrary to previous efforts in dense block detection or in methods that require high numbers of fake ratings, we find that 84% of the tasks require fewer than 20 fake reviews. This indicates the challenge in identifying fraudulent reviewers.

Two-Faced Reviewers. For each reviewer we encounter, we additionally collect all of their reviews (which may include products beyond those targeted by these crowdsourcing sites). Ultimately, our dataset contains the following information: product ID, review ID, reviewer ID, review title, review content, rating, and time-stamp. In total, we obtain 580,000 unique reviews in our original dataset. To investigate the behavior of fraudulent vs non-fraudulent reviewers, we sampled reviewers with at least 10 reviews. In the following, we examine their behavior in terms of rating, review burstiness, review length, self-similarity, and lexical diversity. For non-fraudulent reviewers, we sampled reviewers from the Amazon dataset introduced in [15], who co-reviewed products beyond those crowdsourcing products targeted by a crowdsourcing attack.

Ratings. We begin with Figure 4a, which shows the ratings distribution for reviews written by our two types of reviewers. Echoing previous studies, e.g., [9], we see that crowdsourcing workers tend to write 4 or 5-star reviews. While crowdsourcing efforts could be targeted at suppressing the ratings for a competitor, we see instead that most efforts focus on promotion. Compared to legitimate reviewers, the rate of 5-star reviews is 20% higher for fraudulent reviewers.

Review Length. We see in Figure 4b the distribution of the review length in terms of number of words between the two groups. We can see that reviews by fraudulent reviewers are relatively short. Even though task requestors require a minimum number of words for payment, these graphs show that all reviews written by fraudulent reviewers are not necessarily a response to crowdsourcing tasks which often require a word count minimum.

Burstiness of Reviews. Intuitively, crowd workers may seek to complete several tasks in a short time to maximize their payoff. Hence, for each reviewer we measure the standard deviation of the timestamp for that person's reviews – we consider the last 10 reviews for reviewers with more than 10 reviews. We plot the distribution for this "burstiness" as seen in Figure 4c. In this case, a small standard deviation corresponds to many reviews being posted in a short time window, whereas a higher standard deviation corresponds to reviews posted over a long time period (and hence, lacking burstiness). Contrary to our hypothesis, burstiness of reviews is not a strong indicator to distinguish fraudulent and non-fraudulent users.

Self-similarity. Finally, we measure how much a reviewer's language mimics previous reviews they have written. Perhaps fraudulent reviewers write according to a simple "template", and so new reviews tend to repeat language used in previous ones. Here, we measure the lexical overlap between each two sequential reviews (r_i, r_j) written by the same reviewer using the Jaccard similarity (JS).

[1] We also checked several other crowdsourcing websites such as ShortTask, Microworkers and Amazon Mechanical Turk (AMT); however, tasks related to promoting products in Amazon are mainly announced on RapidWorkers.

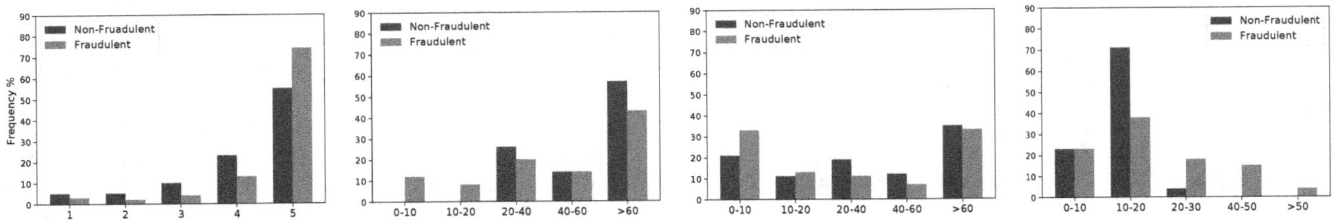

(a) Rating Distribution **(b) Review Length** **(c) Review Burstiness in Days** **(d) Self-similarity**

Figure 4: Traditional features show some differences between fraudulent and non-fraudulent reviewers, but their distinguishing power is weak.

$$JS = \frac{|r_i \cap r_j|}{|r_i \cup r_j|}$$

Figure 4d shows that non-fraudulent tend not to repeat themselves (low Jaccard score); whereas fraudulent reviewers tend to rely on repeated keywords or phrases. Intuitively, reviewers engaged in crowd-launched manipulation tend to mimic themselves over time since they are not actually experienced with the actual product.

Based on this mix of somewhat encouraging features, we evaluate a variety of classifiers (see Section 4). We find that these traditional features do a poor job of distinguishing these two-faced reviewers. Our hypothesis is that traditional signals may fail since these reviewers engage in a mix of legitimate and deceptive reviews. Motivated by these observations, we turn to how we can propagate the suspiciousness of our original seeds for uncovering unknown fraudulent reviewers.

3.2 Propagating Suspiciousness

In this and the following section, we propose two complementary perspectives on propagating the suspiciousness of a known suspicious user. The first – based on a traditional random walk over the user-user graph – exploits the locality of suspiciousness within the graph. The main intuition is that suspicious users will tend to cluster in the graph. The second – based on recent advances in network embeddings – exploits the structure of the graph around suspicious users. So even if two users are distant in the graph, they may be considered similar in terms of their malicious activities. Intuitively, the campaign network structure around fraudulent reviewers in a site like Amazon may be similar even if the specific reviewers have not been encountered before.

Reviewer-Reviewer Graph. Our approach is built on reviewer-reviewer interactions. These interactions are mapped to a co-review graph in which each reviewer is represented as a node and if two reviewers write a review on the same product, then there exists an edge between them. Formally, we model the reviewer network as a graph $G = (V, E)$ wherein V is a set of reviewers and E is a set of undirected edges that connect reviewers. In our experiments (see Section 4), we consider two scenarios: un-weighted and weighted edges. In the first setting, if two users u_i and u_j $(i \neq j)$ have written reviews on multiple common products, this connection is represented as a single edge. In the second setting, we represent the number of common products as a weight value for the edge $w(u_i, u_j)$.

The number of nodes connected to user u is its degree $D(u)$. The co-review matrix corresponding to the un-weighted graph is calculated as:

$$m(u_i, u_j) = \begin{cases} 0 & \text{if } (u_i, u_j) \notin E \\ \frac{1}{D(u_i)} & \text{if} (u_i, u_j) \in E \end{cases}$$

Accordingly, the co-review matrix corresponding to weighted graph is calculated as:

$$m(u_i, u_j) = \begin{cases} 0 & \text{if } (u_i, u_j) \notin E \\ \frac{w(u_i, u_j)}{\sum_{k \in D(u_i)} w(u_i, u_k)} & \text{if} (u_i, u_j) \in E \end{cases}$$

Note that the values in each matrix are normalized transition probabilities.

Random Walk Propagation. Our approach for propagating suspiciousness is inspired by the *TrustRank* algorithm proposed in [6]. We aim to compute a suspiciousness score for each user based on their connectivity to other users in the co-review graph. The intuition is that fraudulent users write reviews on similar products, so they may form a dense sub-graph of suspicious reviewers.

We briefly describe the algorithm and report the results in Section 4. The input to the algorithm is the co-review matrix (m), a seed set (s), teleportation parameter (α), the number of iterations (n), and the number of nodes $(|V|)$. The output is a suspiciousness vector (r).

Algorithm 1 Suspiciousness Rank

1: $e = 0_{|V|}$ //Restart Vector
2: **for** $i = 1$ to $|V|$ **do**
3:     **if** $u_i \in s$ **then**
4:         $e(i) = 1$
5: $e = \frac{e}{|e|}$
6: $r = e$
7: **for** $j = 1$ to n **do**
8:     $r = \alpha.m^T.r + (1 - \alpha).e$
9: **return** r

The restart vector e is initialized in steps 2-4 based on the seed set, i.e, the values are one in the corresponding indices of seed set items and zero in other places. Step 5 computes the $l1$ norm of vector e so that the aggregate sum of the vector is equal to 1. In step 6, the suspiciousness score vector r is initialized to e. Finally, the scores are calculated in steps 7-8 using a biased PageRank with e as a restart vector referring to the seed set of fraudulent reviewers.

In each iteration, the suspiciousness score of a node propagates among its neighbors and is dampened by the teleportation factor α. The score vector r shows the probability of reaching each node when the random walk, rooted at one of the nodes in the seed set, is traversing the graph. In other words, the final scores measure how relatively close a node is to the initial seeds. This approach ranks reviewers based on their level of suspiciousness and suggests reviewers that should be examined further by an expert.

Seed Selection. A key question is how the seeds for the random walk propagation are selected in the first place. First, we need to identify a small set of users as seeds that we certainly know are fraudulent and then propagate their suspiciousness to other users using iterative approaches. In some works, e.g., [6], initial seeds are selected based on human judgment. Here, we consider three different scenarios for seed selection that could arise in practice:

- If we find a user with tens of reviews on targeted products and notice that all of his purchase statuses are unverified, then we conclude that this user is a critical player working on behalf of crowdsourcing websites. We call such reviewers *highly malicious users.* Therefore, we pick reviewers with the maximum number of such reviews as seeds. The intuition is that such reviewers may be connected directly to other potential fraudulent reviewers in the co-review graph. Therefore, propagating their suspiciousness would lead to identifying fraudulent reviewers more accurately. We call this approach the "best" choice of seeds.
- The second approach is to pick a few number of fraudulent reviewers randomly and propagate their suspiciousness. This approach is more indicative of real-world scenarios since we are not always guaranteed to have found the best (most connected) reviewers. For example, malicious users might use different accounts to write fake reviews in order to avoid detection models. We call this approach the "random" choice of seeds.
- The third approach is to pick a few number of fraudulent reviewers randomly among reviewers with only a few reviews on target products. The intuition here is that a system operator at a user review site like Amazon may have discovered some fraudulent reviewers, but only the weakest connected ones. How well does the suspiciousness propagation work in this case? We call this approach the "worst" choice of seeds.

In practice we find that there is a great variance in the quality of seed selection approaches. To illustrate, we show in Figure 5 the Precision@k over the top-k ranked reviewers when we initialize the suspiciousness propagation algorithm with seeds from the best, random, and worst cases. In the real-world cases of random and worst, we see that the fraction of reviewers that are actually fraudulent drops precipitously with an increase in k. That is, while there may be some localness in the co-reviewer graph which helps identify nearby fraudulent reviewers, many fraudulent reviewers are not closely connected to the seeds (hence, the low precision@k as k grows). We do see that in the extreme case of picking the most prolific seeds (which we argue is rare in practice), there is good locality and good precision@k. Even so, for large choices of k, the quality drops off too.

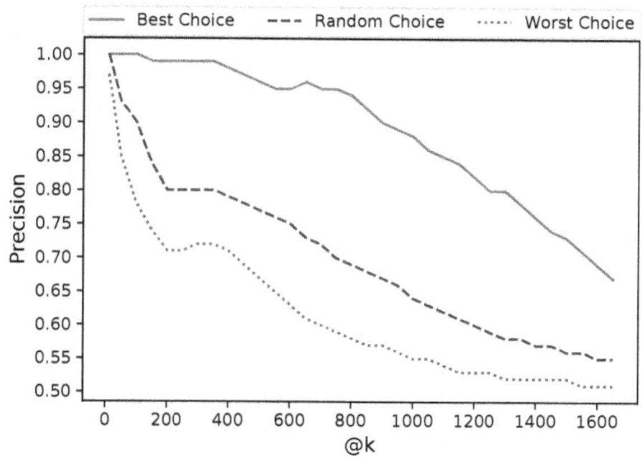

Figure 5: Precision@k for different seed selection approaches.

3.3 Uncovering Distant Users

While traditional random walk methods exploit the locality of suspiciousness within the graph, they may miss reviewers who are not closely connected to the original seeds. In particular, in crowdsourcing scenarios, different fraudulent users may participate in different crowdsourcing tasks, so there would not be a direct link between them. Therefore, we need more sophisticated models to capture this relationship. In this section, we adopt a framework for learning feature representations of nodes in the network. Concretely, we explore using network embeddings to classify similar nodes even if two users are not directly connected but may have the same structural role in the graph. For example, Figure 6 shows that even though node 5 and node 10 act in two distinct communities, they play the same structural role in their own community.

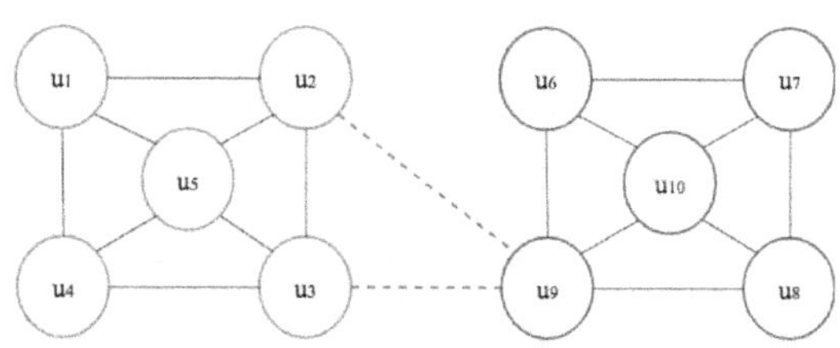

Figure 6: Same structural role in distinct communities. Here nodes 5 and 10 serve similar roles as we surmise different crowd campaigns may also be organized.

Reviewer Graph Embeddings. In node classification, the goal is to predict the most accurate labels for the nodes [29]. On the other hand, in supervised machine learning approaches, a set of informative features is required. When it comes to the problem of node classification in networks, it means feature representation of the nodes is required. The idea of network feature learning is inspired by the recent advances in natural language processing [16] such as the Skip-gram model. In summary, the Skip-gram algorithm goes over the words in a document, and builds a feature vector – the *word embedding*– for every word in the vocabulary such that it can predict its nearby words (i.e., words within a window). The continuous feature representation of words are learned by optimizing the likelihood objective function – Stochastic Gradient Descent (SGD) – and is based on the distributional hypothesis which declares words in similar contexts tend to be semantically similar [7]. In essence, similar words tend to have similar word neighborhoods.

Inspired by the Skip-gram model, a few recent works have proposed models for feature learning from networks where a network is "document" and the nodes are treated as "words" [4, 22, 28]. Similar to a document that is an ordered sequence of words, a network can be turned into an ordered sequence of nodes.

In this paper, we adopt the recent learning approach proposed in [4] in which feature learning in networks is formulated as a maximum likelihood optimization problem. Function $f :\rightarrow R^d$ maps nodes to their feature representation which are used in classification tasks later on. d indicates the number of dimensions of the feature vector, so f is a matrix of size $|V| \times d$. For each node $u \in V$, $N(u) \subset V$ is the set of its neighborhoods. Depending on the neighborhood sampling strategy, $N(u)$ includes either immediate, embedding, or mixture neighbors. The goal is to optimize the objective function given by f:

$$max_f \sum_{u \in V} log\, p_r(N(u)|f(u))$$

This function maximizes the log-probability of observing $N(u)$ as the neighborhood of node u given its feature representation $f(u)$. In our case, each node is a reviewer. Assuming the probability of observing n_i in neighborhood of u is independent from observing any other node in the neighborhood of u, the probability function can be treated as:

$$pr(N(u)|f(u)) = \prod_{n_i \in N(u)} pr(n_i|f(u))$$

Moreover, node u and its neighbors n_i have equal effect over each other in the feature space. Therefore, their conditional probability is modeled as a *softmax* function with dot product of their feature vectors:

$$pr(n_i|f(u)) = \frac{exp(f(u).f(n_i))}{\sum_{v \in V} exp(f(u).f(v))}$$

Putting it altogether, the objective function in Equation 3.3 can be re-written as follows wherein $Z_u = \sum_{v \in V} exp(f(u).f(v))$:

$$max_f \sum_{u \in V} \Big\{ - log\, Z_u + \sum_{n_i \in N(u)} f(u).f(n_i) \Big\}$$

The remainder is to wisely determine neighborhood nodes i.e., $N(u)$. The notion of neighborhood in a text document is defined by a sliding window over sequential words. However, due to the nature of networks, they do not have such a linear representation and a new notion of neighborhood is needed. Grover et. al in [4] proposed an efficient sampling strategy known as *node2vec*. Traditional neighborhood sampling approaches are Breadth-first Sampling (BFS) and Depth-first Sampling (DFS). BFS samples nodes which are in immediate neighborhood of node u, while DFS samples ones which are in increasing distance from u. *node2vec* enables interpolating between BFS and DFS. Briefly, a biased random walk explores the neighborhood of a node in a mixture of BFS and DFS ways by tuning two parameters – Return and In-out – parameters. In our case, we transform each reviewer (node) into an embedding that captures its neighborhood structure.

Putting it all Together. So far, we have suggested two complementary approaches to address the problem of uncovering fraudulent reviewers. The first one is based on traditional ranking algorithms which scores users based on their suspiciousness and is completely unsupervised. The other is to adopt an embedding feature representation of the reviewers. Here, we propose to combine these two approaches into a supervised classification framework:

- First, we take as input our seeds sampled from a crowdsourcing platform. Typically, we may have one to dozens of seeds.
- Then we propagate the suspiciousness of these reviewers via the random walk.
- After transforming every reviewer into its graph embedding representation, we then train a classifier where the positive examples (the fraudulent reviewers) are drawn from the ranked list of suspicious users. The negative examples (the legitimate reviewers) are drawn randomly from a held out set of reviewers.

4 EXPERIMENTS

In this section, we first introduce our ground truth. Then, we report the results of evaluating the complementary methods on our dataset to identify active users in review manipulation tasks. Finally, we compare our approach with a number of alternatives.

4.1 Data Preparation

As we mentioned above, there are 12,212 reviewers who wrote a review on target products. We sampled 50% of them randomly. To go one step further, considering the products those sampled reviewers are associated with – 238,000 products – we sampled their reviewers from an Amazon dataset introduced in [8, 15]. Finally, our expanded dataset contains 38,590 reviewers over whom the co-review graph is built.

Ground Truth. In total, Table 1 shows the number of reviewers who wrote a review on a specific number of target products in our dataset (which include 12,212 reviewers in total). For example, 87 reviewers wrote reviews on more than 20 products targeted by the crowdsourcing site. Our dataset naturally contains a mix of reviewers and their reviews: some are legitimate reviews, some are the result of targeted crowdsourced efforts, while others may also be fraudulent but outside the purview of our sampling method (e.g., launched via an unobservable channel like private email). Hence, we create two datasets – one based on a conservative assumption, and one that is a slight relaxation:

# Targets	1	2	3-5	6-8	9-20	>20
# Reviewers	9,096	1,669	1,093	126	141	87

Table 1: Distribution of reviewers based on number of target products they are associated with.

Conservative definition of fraudulent reviewers. We consider a reviewer to be a *fraudulent reviewer* if they have reviewed **two or more products** that have been targeted by a crowdsourcing effort.

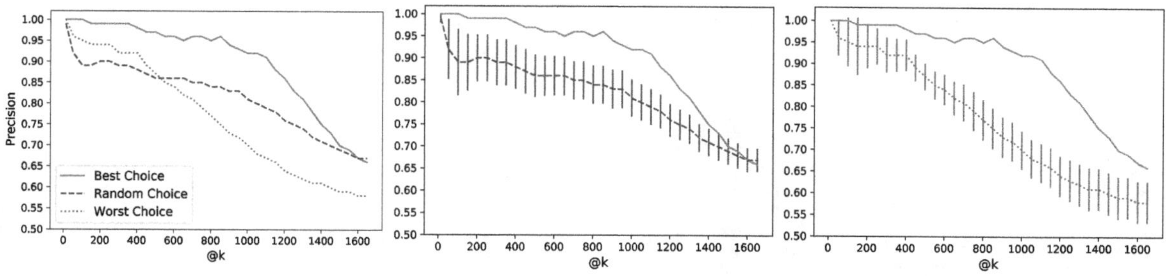

(a) All three seed selection approaches. (b) Random selection with error bars. (c) Worst selection with error bars.

Figure 7: Precision@k for un-weighted graph with different seed selection approaches and 5 initial seeds.

Intuitively, workers may aim to maximize their income by participating in many tasks (and hence, targeting many products). On the other hand, it is unlikely that a random user will write a legitimate review on two different crowdsourcing products in a short period of time, considering Amazon's selection of millions of products [3]. Making this conservative assumption, in our sampled dataset, we identify 1,650 of 38,590 reviewers as *fraudulent reviewers* and label the rest (36,940 reviewers) as *non-fraudulent.* Note that, 4,565 reviewers labeled as non-fraudulent still wrote one review on a target product. Of course, there may still be some unknown fraudulent reviewers in this set of 4,565 reviewers, but it gives us a baseline to compare against the clearly prolific fraudulent reviewers.

Relaxed definition of fraudulent reviewers. In an alternative way to identify fraudulent users, we can relax our conservative assumption and instead label all the reviewers associated with crowdsourcing products (i.e., 6,215 of 38,590) as *fraudulent reviewers* and label the rest as *non-fraudulent reviewers.* In this way, any reviewer who has reviewed a targeted product is labeled as fraudulent. While certainly overstating the number of fraudulent reviewers, this relaxed definition may give us more insights into the capability of our approach.

4.2 Propagating suspiciousness

Revisiting our initial approach to identify fraudulent reviewers by propagating suspiciousness, we report here an additional experiment where we consider five seed users. Again, we identify the best, random, and worst choice of seeds. We repeat this selection 20 times (since users are randomly chosen either from the entire set or from the least connected reviewers) and report in Figure 7 the variation of precision@k for different approaches in picking initial seeds. Here, we report all three approaches in (a), then we show the random approach with error bars in (b), and the worst approach with error bars in (c). The variability suggests that seed selection alone cannot identify fraudulent reviewers. This echoes our previous figure (see Figure 5), yet here we see that the "worst" approach can sometimes do better than random as we increase k. We attribute this result to the fact that some of the fraudulent reviewers have been more active in crowdsourcing manipulation in the past and so they are uncovered as actual fraudulent reviewers at $k <= 500$.

4.3 TwoFace detection

Given these results, we now turn to evaluating the quality of the end-to-end TwoFace system. Recall that TwoFace takes as input the seeds, the suspiciousness propagated scores, and the graph embeddings for the co-review graph.

Choice of Classifier. The first question is what classification algorithm to apply for distinguishing between fraudulent and non-fraudulent reviewers? Here, we consider six alternatives: logistic regression, SVM, Naive Bayes, Decision Tree, Random Forest, and a one-class version of SVM. One-class SVM builds a classifier using instances from only one class – fraudulent in our scenario – and then classifies new instances from both classes. We include this alternative to validate our use of legitimate reviewers in the training, even though our sample of legitimate reviewers is taken from a random sample of Amazon (and so, may erroneously include some fraudulent reviewers).

Figure 8 shows the performance of different classifiers in the presence of 10% labeled data, where the results are averaged over 20 runs. We report the Precision and Recall for the Fraudulent class as well as F1-macro for the whole dataset. It should be noted that the other class which is abundant (95% of the dataset) always has high Precision and Recall. We observe that Logistic Regression and one-class SVM give us higher Recall, 91% and 88% respectively, but Logistic Regression performs better in Precision. While Random Forest and SVM give higher Precision, 84% and 73% respectively, they have a poor Recall i.e., many of fraudulent users remain unidentified. Therefore, we do our further analysis using Logistic Regression.

How Many Seeds Do We Need? In practice, the TwoFace system may have access to only a small fraction of all fraudulent reviewers. Hence, we study here the impact of the number of fraudulent reviewers on the quality of classification. Specifically, we consider samples of our entire dataset ranging from 1% to 10% of all reviewers; in this case, 1% corresponds to about 16 fraudulent reviewers and 370 non-fraudulent ones. We additionally consider both the weighted and unweighted graph for suspiciousness propagation as input to the method. Table 2 shows their performance in the presence of 1% to 10% of labeled data. As we increase the number of seeds, Recall increases from 76% to 92% and 83% to 93% in unweighted and weighted cases respectively while Precision remains relatively constant – 30% to 35%. This encouraging result shows that TwoFace can obtain high Recall even in the presence of very

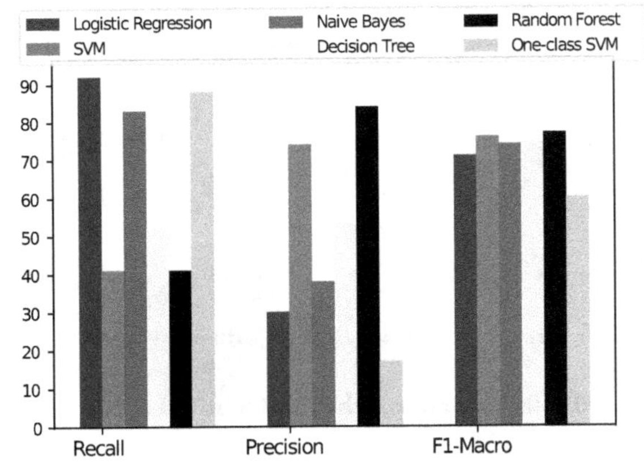

Figure 8: Comparing classifiers.

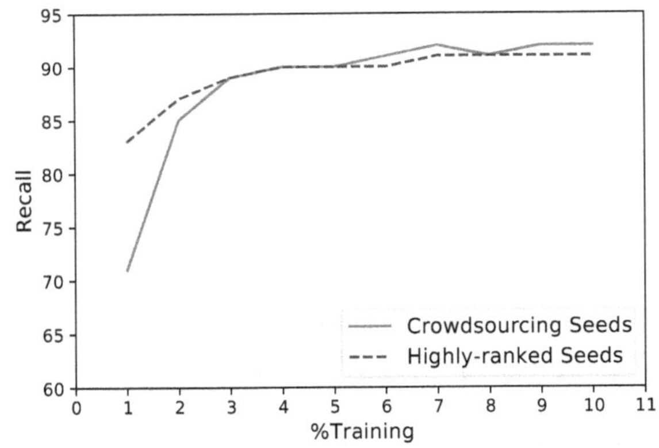

Figure 9: Impact of suspiciousness propagation in identifying fraudulent users

few seeds. Since the weighted and un-weighted cases perform relatively close, we focus our discussion on the un-weighted graph going forward.

Training	1%	2%	3%	4%	5%	6%	7%	8%	9%	10%
un-Weighted Graph										
Recall	76	85	88	90	91	91	92	92	92	92
Precision	34	33	32	30	30	30	30	30	30	30
F1-macro	72	71	70	70	70	70	70	70	70	70
Weighted Graph										
Recall	83	88	89	89	92	92	92	93	93	93
Precision	35	33	34	34	32	32	32	32	32	32
F1-macro	73	72	72	72	71	71	72	71	71	72

Table 2: Increasing the number of seed users available to TwoFace.

The Impact of Suspiciousness Propagation. In an earlier experiment, we saw that suspiciousness propagation alone is insufficient for uncovering fraudulent reviewers. Here, we investigate the impact of using the highly-ranked reviewers that are output from the suspiciousness ranking approach as input to our TwoFace classification. That is, do we really need to propagate suspiciousness? Or can we just use the initial seeds we sample from the crowdsourcing platform alone? In Figure 9, we show the impact of suspiciousness propagation on feature embedding classification. For example, if we rely only on the original seeds from the crowdsourcing platform we achieve around 71% for Recall of fraudulent reviewers; in contrast, if we feed a small number of highly-ranked users from the suspiciousness propagation algorithm into classifier, we see that Recall jumps to 83% with just 1% of seeds. This finding demonstrates the importance of propagating the suspiciousness of these seed users through the random walk over the co-review graph.

Relaxing the Ground Truth. As we can see from Table 2 Precision is in the 30% range which may seem surprising (even though Recall is quite high). This means that many of the non-fraudulent users have been misclassified as fraudulent, which could burden resources that are required to further examine these reviewers. To further explore this issue, we evaluate the TwoFace approach on the alternative "relaxed" ground truth in which every reviewer with at least one review on a target product is considered as fraudulent. In this alternative scenario, we find in Table 3 that precision jumps to 77%, while Recall increases even more to around 90%. This encouraging result suggests that many of the reviewers who only reviewed one target product historically are connected to other fraudulent reviewers and may need further examination by an expert.

	Recall	Precision	F1-macro
Conservative	83	35	72
Relaxed	91	77	89

Table 3: Relaxing the ground truth definition.

Comparing with Alternatives. Finally, we compare the proposed TwoFace system with alternative methods including classification over traditional features and the state-of-the-art D-cube method [27]. For traditional features, we adopt the standard features described in our previous analysis of fraudulent reviewers, including rating, burstiness of reviews, review length, and self-similarity. We evaluate a variety of classifiers and report the best results which are from Logistic Regression. For D-cube – a dense block detection approach – we try many different number of dense blocks and report its best results when the number of blocks is 30 and 40. For a fair comparison, we also consider the relaxed ground truth for these methods. For TwoFace, we adopt Logistic Regression and use the highly-ranked users from our suspiciousness propagation as seeds.

	Recall	Precision	F1-macro
TwoFace System	**91**	**77**	**89**
Traditional Features	61	24	54
D-cube [27]/ 30 blks	69	34	50
D-cube [27]/ 40 blks	82	24	64

Table 4: Comparison of TwoFace with alternatives.

Table 4 shows that TwoFace system outperforms the two other approaches. The low performance of traditional features – 61% Recall and 24% Precision – indicates that fraudulent reviewers do not always behave abnormally and their rating distribution or burstiness might be similar to non-fraudulent reviewers. On the other hand the D-cube approach [27] which aims to detect dense blocks, i.e., a group of reviewers who write a review on a specific number of products in a short time, is the most similar scenario to crowdsourcing manipulation. It takes number of blocks as input and returns the most dense blocks. As a result, by increasing the number of blocks it returns more fraudulent reviewers – 82% versus 69% Recall with 40 and 30 blocks respectively. However, by increasing the number of blocks, we see that many non-fraudulent reviewers will be misclassified as fraudulent – 24% and 34% Precision. Since crowdsourcing campaigns do not form dense blocks, we see that TwoFace provides the best overall performance with 91% Recall and 77% Precision.

5 CONCLUSION AND FUTURE WORK

We have explored how monitoring tasks on sites like RapidWorkers can uncover fraudulent reviewers on sites like Amazon. The proposed TwoFace framework complements previous efforts by providing a new approach for identifying these types of reviewers. The main intuition is to: (i) exploit the locality of suspiciousness within the graph through a random walk to find suspicious users who tend to cluster; and (ii) exploit the structure of the graph around suspicious users to uncover campaign network structures for identifying fraudulent reviewers who are distant in the graph. Our results are encouraging, indicating that TwoFace can indeed uncover many fraudulent reviewers. In our ongoing work, we are expanding our coverage both in terms of crowdsourcing sites and targets of manipulation (e.g., App Store, Play Store, Yelp). We are also eager to further explore how linguistic evolution may provide new insights into the strategies of review manipulation to complement our focus in this paper on the network properties of the reviewers.

Acknowledgement. This work was supported in part by AFOSR grant FA9550-15-1-0149.

REFERENCES

[1] Leman Akoglu, Rishi Chandy, and Christos Faloutsos. 2013. Opinion Fraud Detection in Online Reviews by Network Effects.. In *ICWSM*.

[2] Alex Beutel, Wanhong Xu, Venkatesan Guruswami, Christopher Palow, and Christos Faloutsos. 2013. Copycatch: stopping group attacks by spotting lockstep behavior in social networks. In *WWW*.

[3] Paul Grey. 2015. How Many Products Does Amazon Sell?, https://export-x.com, Last Access: 01/10/2017.

[4] Aditya Grover and Jure Leskovec. 2016. node2vec: Scalable feature learning for networks. In *Proceedings of the 22nd ACM SIGKDD International Conference on Knowledge Discovery and Data Mining*. ACM, 855–864.

[5] Stephan Günnemann, Nikou Günnemann, and Christos Faloutsos. 2014. Detecting anomalies in dynamic rating data: A robust probabilistic model for rating evolution. In *SIGKDD*.

[6] Zoltán Gyöngyi, Hector Garcia-Molina, and Jan Pedersen. 2004. Combating web spam with trustrank. In *Proceedings of the Thirtieth international conference on Very large data bases-Volume 30*. VLDB Endowment, 576–587.

[7] Zellig S Harris. 1954. Distributional structure. *Word* 10, 2-3 (1954), 146–162.

[8] Ruining He and Julian McAuley. 2016. Ups and downs: Modeling the visual evolution of fashion trends with one-class collaborative filtering. In *Proceedings of the 25th International Conference on World Wide Web*. International World Wide Web Conferences Steering Committee, 507–517.

[9] Bryan Hooi, Neil Shah, Alex Beutel, Stephan Gunneman, Leman Akoglu, Mohit Kumar, Disha Makhija, and Christos Faloutsos. 2015. BIRDNEST: Bayesian Inference for Ratings-Fraud Detection. *arXiv* (2015).

[10] Bryan Hooi, Neil Shah, Alex Beutel, Stephan Günnemann, Leman Akoglu, Mohit Kumar, Disha Makhija, and Christos Faloutsos. 2016. Birdnest: Bayesian inference for ratings-fraud detection. In *Proceedings of the 2016 SIAM International Conference on Data Mining*. SIAM, 495–503.

[11] Bryan Hooi, Hyun Ah Song, Alex Beutel, Neil Shah, Kijung Shin, and Christos Faloutsos. 2016. Fraudar: Bounding graph fraud in the face of camouflage. In *Proceedings of the 22nd ACM SIGKDD International Conference on Knowledge Discovery and Data Mining*. ACM, 895–904.

[12] Meng Jiang, Peng Cui, Alex Beutel, Christos Faloutsos, and Shiqiang Yang. 2014. Inferring strange behavior from connectivity pattern in social networks. In *PAKDD*.

[13] Parisa Kaghazgaran, James Caverlee, and Majid Alfifi. 2017. Behavioral Analysis of Review Fraud: Linking Malicious Crowdsourcing to Amazon and Beyond. In *ICWSM*.

[14] Huayi Li, Geli Fei, Shuai Wang, Bing Liu, Weixiang Shao, Arjun Mukherjee, and Jidong Shao. 2017. Bimodal distribution and co-bursting in review spam detection. In *Proceedings of the 26th International Conference on World Wide Web*. International World Wide Web Conferences Steering Committee, 1063–1072.

[15] Julian McAuley, Christopher Targett, Qinfeng Shi, and Anton Van Den Hengel. 2015. Image-based recommendations on styles and substitutes. In *Proceedings of the 38th International ACM SIGIR Conference on Research and Development in Information Retrieval*. ACM, 43–52.

[16] Tomas Mikolov, Ilya Sutskever, Kai Chen, Greg S Corrado, and Jeff Dean. 2013. Distributed representations of words and phrases and their compositionality. In *Advances in neural information processing systems*. 3111–3119.

[17] Arjun Mukherjee, Vivek Venkataraman, Bing Liu, and Natalie S Glance. 2013. What yelp fake review filter might be doing?. In *ICWSM*.

[18] Myle Ott, Claire Cardie, and Jeff Hancock. 2012. Estimating the prevalence of deception in online review communities. In *Proceedings of the 21st international conference on World Wide Web*. ACM, 201–210.

[19] Myle Ott, Claire Cardie, and Jeffrey T Hancock. 2013. Negative Deceptive Opinion Spam.. In *HLT-NAACL*.

[20] Myle Ott, Yejin Choi, Claire Cardie, and Jeffrey T Hancock. 2011. Finding deceptive opinion spam by any stretch of the imagination. In *ACL*.

[21] Shashank Pandit, Duen Horng Chau, Samuel Wang, and Christos Faloutsos. 2007. Netprobe: a fast and scalable system for fraud detection in online auction networks. In *WWW*.

[22] Bryan Perozzi, Rami Al-Rfou, and Steven Skiena. 2014. Deepwalk: Online learning of social representations. In *Proceedings of the 20th ACM SIGKDD international conference on Knowledge discovery and data mining*. ACM, 701–710.

[23] B Aditya Prakash, Ashwin Sridharan, Mukund Seshadri, Sridhar Machiraju, and Christos Faloutsos. 2010. Eigenspokes: Surprising patterns and scalable community chipping in large graphs. In *PAKDD*.

[24] Shebuti Rayana and Leman Akoglu. 2015. Collective opinion spam detection: Bridging review networks and metadata. In *SIGKDD*.

[25] Neil Shah, Alex Beutel, Brian Gallagher, and Christos Faloutsos. 2014. Spotting suspicious link behavior with fbox: An adversarial perspective. In *ICDM*.

[26] Kijung Shin, Bryan Hooi, and Christos Faloutsos. 2016. M-zoom: Fast dense-block detection in tensors with quality guarantees. In *Joint European Conference on Machine Learning and Knowledge Discovery in Databases*. Springer, 264–280.

[27] Kijung Shin, Bryan Hooi, Jisu Kim, and Christos Faloutsos. 2017. D-cube: Dense-block detection in terabyte-scale tensors. In *Proceedings of the Tenth ACM International Conference on Web Search and Data Mining*. ACM, 681–689.

[28] Jian Tang, Meng Qu, Mingzhe Wang, Ming Zhang, Jun Yan, and Qiaozhu Mei. 2015. Line: Large-scale information network embedding. In *Proceedings of the 24th International Conference on World Wide Web*. ACM, 1067–1077.

[29] Grigorios Tsoumakas and Ioannis Katakis. 2006. Multi-label classification: An overview. *International Journal of Data Warehousing and Mining* 3, 3 (2006).

[30] Bimal Viswanath, Muhammad Ahmad Bashir, Muhammad Bilal Zafar, Simon Bouget, Saikat Guha, Krishna P Gummadi, Aniket Kate, and Alan Mislove. 2015. Strength in numbers: Robust tamper detection in crowd computations. In *Proceedings of the 2015 ACM on Conference on Online Social Networks*. ACM, 113–124.

[31] Guan Wang, Sihong Xie, Bing Liu, and S Yu Philip. 2011. Review graph based online store review spammer detection. In *ICDM*.

[32] Elizabeth Weise. 2016. Amazon bans 'incentivized' reviews, goo.gl/K8Woqd, Last Access: 01/10/2017. *USATODAY*.

[33] Sihong Xie, Guan Wang, Shuyang Lin, and Philip S Yu. 2012. Review spam detection via temporal pattern discovery. In *SIGKDD*.

[34] Junting Ye and Leman Akoglu. 2015. Discovering opinion spammer groups by network footprints. In *ECML-PKDD*.

Topic Chronicle Forest for Topic Discovery and Tracking

Noriaki Kawamae
The University of Tokyo
Tokyo
kawamae@gmail.com

ABSTRACT

To ease the comprehension of existing time-stamped corpora, we extend topic models to handle both the specificity and temporality of topics; this is a significant advance over previous models which fail to provide both aspects simultaneously. Our proposed model combines the Topic Chronicle Forest (TCF) and Thematic Dirichlet Processes (TDP). TCF is a set of Topic Chronicle Trees, where each tree is a hierarchy of topics that becomes more specialized toward the leaves. Only one tree is defined in each time interval, a region, and is processed by TDP to generate a document. The advantage of our approach is that it provides more compact topic organization, while preserving both the semantics of the given corpus and the theme of each document. Experiments show that TCF is a useful extension for longitudinal topic discovery and tracking, and helps us to organize and digest data sets.

KEYWORDS

Time Varying Topic Models, Hierarchical Dirichlet Processes, Trend analysis, Hierarchical Bayesian Nonparametrics

ACM Reference Format:

Noriaki Kawamae. 2018. Topic Chronicle Forest for Topic Discovery and Tracking. In *Proceedings of The Eleventh ACM International Conference on Web Search and Data Mining (WSDM 2018)*. ACM, New York, NY, USA, 9 pages. https://doi.org/10.1145/3159652.3159653

1 INTRODUCTION

Our aim is to discover the topic organization of a given time-stamped corpus, and to track how this organization changes over time. This ability will help us peruse and comprehend time-stamped collections such as news, SNS, or papers, as topical mapping representing how topics evolve over time will be helpful in contextualizing information. While the notion of a "topic" is an "event" in the TDT pilot study [5], it is defined as a probability distribution over words that co-occur frequently in topic models such as Latent Dirichlet Allocation (LDA) [9] and its extensions. These term distributions can help us to understand what each topic represents. We extend these models to form a time-specific generative model that can answer the following questions: What kinds of topics are in the given data?, and How do they change over time?

WSDM 2018, February 5–9, 2018, Marina Del Rey, CA, USA

ACM ISBN 978-1-4503-5581-0/18/02...$15.00
https://doi.org/10.1145/3159652.3159653

To answer these questions, topic models are required to consider the difference between 1) specificity and temporality, 2) between temporality and periodicity of topics. For example, "LSTM" and "GRU" are new and specific terms in machine learning topics, while "LDA" and "HMM" are, in the same topics, specific and constant terms. "Neural network" and "AI" are periodic trends in the same topics, while "Web2.0" is a temporal trend of these topics. As previous models restrict themselves to either the specificity [7, 16, 18, 25, 26] or temporality [1–3, 8, 14, 34, 35] of topics, there is a need for unified models that distinguish between these differences simultaneously, and meet the two abovementioned requirements. This practical need motivates our focus on topic structures that integrate both the topic extraction task and the trend detection task.

To achieve our goal, we propose the combination of Topic Chronicle Forest (TCF) and Thematic Dirichlet Process (TDP) to create a hierarchical organization of given time-stamped corpora at different levels of granularity. TCF constructs time-interval specific topic trees, Topic Chronicle Trees (TCTs), and organizes the given corpus according to its content and trends to assist users in sifting and digesting them. These trees are based on the assumption that the difference between specificity and temporality of topics can be found by identifying topics and capturing temporal hierarchy changes instead of topic evolution. This leads TCF to identifying unique topics and constructing a set of TCTs that exhibit the temporal topic tree in each time interval, a region. In the previous example, "LSTM" and "GRU" are tagged as temporal specific topics and observed in only new trees, while "LDA" and "HMM" are tagged as long-period specific topics and observed in both new and old trees. This allows us to discover long-period specific topics and track their changes as temporal specific topics. TDP uses timestamps in selecting a TCT as a base probability measure from TCF like the hierarchical Dirichlet process (HDP) [31], and constructs a document-specific tree and generates a document via this tree to obtain thematic coherence.

Our experiments confirm the following contributions.

Theoretical contribution: (1) Unlike topic models built on either the specificity or temporality of topics, TCT handles both to create a topic hierarchy, and detects the differences between topic temporality and topic periodicity. (2) While most temporal topic models require manual selection of a fixed-width time frame (a heuristic task), TCF detects the appropriate variable-size time granularity automatically, and is purely data-driven. (3) TCF describes temporal evolution by selecting the TCT instead of topic evolution, and represents the periodicity of topics, where each topic is constant over time.

Practical contributions: (1) As TCF prevents the same topic from appearing (due to the periodicity of topics) as different topics in

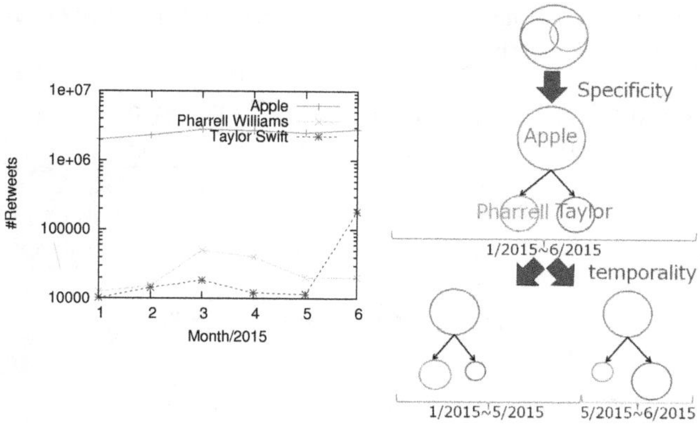

Figure 1: (left) This figure shows the number of retweets covering #apple: "Taylor Swift" was an extra hot topic after she posted a letter to "Apple" in Jun, while "Pharrell Williams" became a hot topic after wearing "Apple watch" in March. (right) The topic hierarchy constructed from the left example.

different trees, it yields more compact hierarchies than other hierarchical models. (2) TCF creates human-understandable hierarchies for topic monitoring without the need for manual intervention.

2 RELATED WORK

Topic detection is defined as generating topics from a document stream in [5], and the task of topic evolution is to discover how and what topics change over time. Topic models have been applied to both tasks. For example, Dynamic Topic Models [8] represents the evolution of topics by estimating the topic distribution at epochs. Recent models describe inter-topic correlations by applying constraints and priors to hyperparameters [27], or using a nonparametric Bayesian approach. The Chinese restaurant process (CRP) [4], a stochastic process that generates partitions of integers and is used in the Dirichlet process (DP) [23], yields the same clustering structures as created by a DP [11]. This is why our approach constructs topic trees to explain the relationship between topics using a nonparametric approach rather than non-negative matrix factorization [13, 17, 29, 32]. A DP can be considered as a distribution of random probability measure G, which we write as $G \sim DP(\gamma, H)$, where γ is a scaling parameter, and H is a base measure. We can view DP in terms of $CRP(\gamma, H)$ and compute the probability of the i-th customer sitting at table k in restaurant j as follows:

$$P(z_i = k|\mathbf{z}_{\setminus i}, \gamma) = \begin{cases} \frac{n_{jk}}{\sum_k n_{jk}+\gamma}, k \text{ is an existing table,} \\ \frac{\gamma}{\sum_k n_{jk}+\gamma}, k \text{ is a new table.} \end{cases} \quad (1)$$

where $\mathbf{z}_{\setminus i}$ is the seating arrangement of the current $i-1$ customers, and n_{jk} is the number of customers sitting at table k in restaurant j.

We show how well the relevant models meet the requirements necessary for our purpose in Table 1. As shown in this table, our proposal meets the requirements in that 1) each tree represents topic specificity, TCT, and TCF represents the temporality of topics with TCT according to continuous time instead of topic evolution, 2) each document retains thematic coherence between topics via TDP and each document specific tree as an internal structure, and 3) TCF identifies unique topics and exhibits the time-varying topic hierarchies by using birth/death/recurrence of topics via TCT.

3 TOPIC CHRONICLE FOREST, AND THEMATIC DIRICHLET PROCESS

3.1 Our motivations and Basic ideas

Why we need to consider both the specificity and temporality of topics: As shown in Figure 1, a set of timestamped data may include specific topics, temporal topics, and parent-child relationships between these topics. Since not only temporal topics but also the parent-child hierarchy could change over time, we need a set of time-specific topic trees rather than one static tree. As you can imagine, the latest IT tweets share more words with previous IT tweets than with the latest entertainment tweets, and form "IT" topics, where hot "IT" topics change over time. It is reasonable that "Apple" is associated with time-invariant "IT" topics, while "Taylor Swift" and "Pharrell Williams" are associated with hot "IT" topics assigned to "Apple", and they peak at different times. This leads us to consider that "Taylor Swift" and "Pharrell Williams" are associated with specificity and temporal topics of "IT" topics with "Apple", and thus differentiate specificity from temporality in organizing topics. Whether a certain word is a specific term or temporal term depends on the context so it can not be uniquely defined, making it difficult to include it in the dictionary beforehand. For example, although "Taylor Swift" is a specific term in a certain period, this word is likely to become a temporal term over the whole period of IT related topics. Furthermore, the period during which this change is observed varies from topic to topic, and then it is not clear how to decide the appropriate size of time window with this change automatically and discretize the timeline into periods. Our challenge is to detect the appropriate variable-size periods, capture these differences, and organize them.

How to define a hierarchical topic tree covering both specificity and temporality: Topic chronicle forest (TCF) constructs topic trees as a set of topic chronicle trees (TCTs). This structure aims to represent each document as a set of topics that are arranged over a tree-like structure whose semantics are contained in parent-child topic hierarchies, the former are more general than the latter. These hierarchies are consistent with our intuition that the root level topic is the background topic, and the child level topics are more specific or temporal than their parent level topic, and meet our requirements more thoroughly than undirected graphical models [12]; previous topic trees are founded on just one side of these aspects. In the previous example, "Taylor Swift" and "Pharrell Williams" appear in different TCTs, because they are tagged as specificity topics that peak at different times. This is why each time period needs its own TCT.

How to obtain thematic coherence with a nonparametric approach: Figure 2 shows how TCF and Thematic Dirichlet Process (TDP) employ a nonparametric approach to determine the appropriate topic tree automatically. To represent documents using the hierarchy of topics, TDP constructs a tree to reveal the thematic coherence, where this tree has a distribution over paths in a globally shared tree. To this end, TDP employs each document specific tree as an internal structure instead of a path for each document in it, so

Table 1: Only TCF/TDP meets all the requirements for topic discovery and tracking in temporal/hierarchical topic models. In this table, S, T, and P denote semantic, thematic, and periodicity of topics, respectively.

	Requirements	DTM	EvoHDP	RCRP+LDA	iDTM	sTOT	nCRP	rCRP	nHDP	TCF/TDP
	Reference	[8]	[35]	[1]	[3]	[14]	[7]	[16]	[26]	[this paper]
S	specificity	-	-	-	-	-	√	√	√	√
	temporality	√	√	√	√	√	-	-	-	√
T	topic structure	-	-	-	-	-	√	√	√	√
	internal structure	-	-	-	-	-	-	-	√	√
	topic access	node	node	node	node	node	path	path	tree	tree
P	birth/death topics	-	√	√	√	√	-	-	-	√
	recurrent topics	-	√	√	√	-	-	-	-	√
handling continuous time		-	-	-	-	√	-	-	-	√

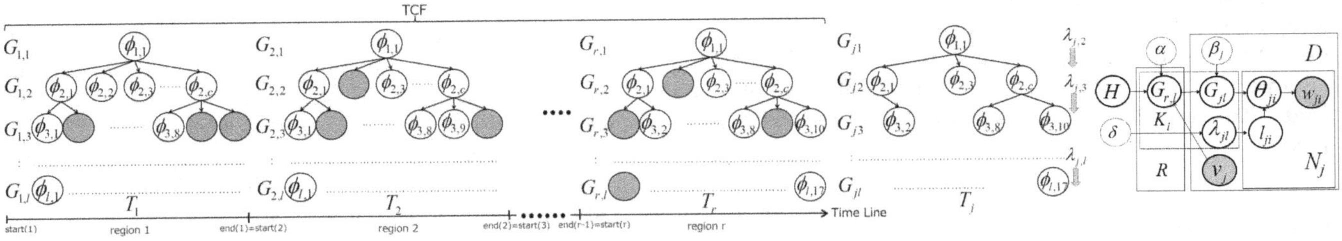

Figure 2: An example of (left) TCF (a set of TCTs, time region r specific T_r), and (center) the j-th document specific topic tree, T_j: Each node of the tree is associated with a topic, ϕ, and shaded notes are inactive in each region. Each TCT is uniquely identified by v_j with the terminating conditions of start(r) $\leq v_j <$ end(r). (right) Graphical model of TDP using TCF: Each latent variable, observed datum, and parameter are shown as nodes. An arrow indicates a conditional dependency between variables and stacked panes indicate a repeated sampling with the iteration number shown. Shaded and unshaded variables indicate observed and latent variables, respectively. Random variables R, L and K_l are finally defined as constants in the experiments/applications.

Table 2: Notations used in this paper

SYMBOL	DESCRIPTION
$D/W/R$	♯documents/♯vocabulary size/♯regions
L/K_l	♯topic levels/♯topics in l-th topic level
N_j/L_j	♯words/♯topic level in j-th document
z_{ji}/l_{ji}	the i-th topic/level variable in j-th document
w_{ji}/θ_{ji}	the i-th word/topic in j-th document
v_j	timestamp in j-th document
λ_{jl}	the l-th level random variable in j-th document
$\phi_{l,c}(\phi_k)$	the c-th topic in l-th level (shorthand of $\phi_{l,c}$)
$\alpha/\delta/\eta/\delta$	parameter: $\alpha/\delta/\eta/\delta \sim Gamma(a_1, a_2)$
β_j	the j specific parameter: $\beta_{jl} \sim Gamma(a_1, a_2)$
κ_r	the r specific parameter: $\kappa_r \sim Gamma(a_1, a_2)$
ϖ_r	the weight of dependency between the current region tree and the previous region tree

that each document can access the entire TCT; nCRP permits each word to follow its path embedded in this tree to a topic. Although rCRP enables a document to have a distribution over the entire topic tree and sample a topic at the word level, they have similar topics in many nodes of the tree, and thus fail to ensure thematic coherency. This leads TDP to share a topic distribution as a base for a second level DP for each document like nHDP, whereas HDP shares a base distribution among documents. Detecting and expressing birth/death/recurrent topics require the ability to identify the same topics as one topic. This is the reason why our approach learns TCF and TDP together; learning them individually would fail to identify topics.

3.2 Model Definition

3.2.1 Topic Chronicle Forest and Topic Chronicle Tree. Figure 2 shows an example of a topic chronicle Forest, T, which is a set of topic chronicle trees, $T_r (r \in R)$. Each T_r is constructed for a given time region (time window), r, that has a start timestamp, $start(r)$, and an end timestamp, $end(r)$, where the #TCTs equal #regions, R. We denote the DP of T_r as G_r, and represent the l-th level of G_r as $G_{r,l}$. The first level of the tree consists of only the background topic. The l-th level could have countably infinite number of children nodes, where the probability of transitioning to child node c, topic $\phi_{l,c}$, equals the probability of the c-th break of a stick-breaking construction [30]. As this construction is applied to each of these stick segments at the next level, G_r achieves coherence between topics on a path from the root to a leaf of the tree. Note that each $\phi_{l,c}$ is constant over time and is reused in other TCTs. As shown in Figure 2, TCF tells us which topics occur or disappear in each period by comparing adjacent regions. For example, $\phi_{2,2}$ is the missing topic in region 2, while $\phi_{3,9}$ is the emerging topic in the same region. This leads TCF to identify periodic topics as the same topic, which reduces the total number of topics, as a single topic cannot appear as different topics in different TCTs. To maintain the information about which topics survive or detect new topics, TCF incorporates time dependencies between adjacent topic chronicle trees.

3.2.2 Document-specific Topic Tree. TDP allows each document to have a document-specific tree, T_j, that shares the set of topics and the parent-children topic hierarchy over all documents via TCF. As shown in Figure 2, TDP selects T_r, when v_j is in region r, and uses each DP of $G_{r,l}$ as a base for a second level DP drawn independently for constructing the topic distribution of l-th level of T_j, G_{jl}. This tree contains all thematic content of a document, and allows TDP to select a thematically consistent topic path at the word level rather than the document level. For selecting this word-specific path, TDP introduces a document-specific random variable, λ_{jl}, that acts as stochastic switch; given a word at token i in document j, it decides the probability that determines whether this word uses the current topic level l in a given topic tree, or continues on down the tree. Thus, G_{jl} has the same topic as $G_{r,l}$ on the same topic level, l, in region r, but with different probability weights and topic level.

Note that TDP uses this distribution in constructing the document specific topic tree, while the nested Hierarchical Dirichlet process (nHDP) [26] extends nCRP to select a topic in a given document-specific topic tree, and then uses it on this constructed tree. This difference allows TDP to reflect the parent-child relationships more precisely than nHDP, and prevents similar topics from appearing in the global tree. Even if the transition probability from one parent topic to its child topic is the highest, T_j, nHDP might miss this relationship if the transition probability to this parent topic is lower than the others. TDP can share topics with TCT, where the probability weight on not only each topic, but also their topic level, varies with the document.

This relationship constrains the increment in the number of topics and so prevents the global topic tree from generating many similar topics that will be observed in the nCRP. Therefore, the probability of a topic level will vary with the document, even if different documents share the same topics.

3.3 Generative Process of TCF and TDP

With reference in the graphic model shown in Figure 2 and notations shown in Table 2, we can provide an overview of the generative procedure of TCF/TDP.

Topic Chronicle Forest generation: For each region $r \in R$, define G_1 using nCRP if $r = 1$; otherwise define G_r using both the previous measure G_{r-1} and DP:

$$G_{r,1} = \delta_{\phi_{1,1}}, V_{l,c} \sim GEM(\alpha), \phi_{l,c} \sim H,$$

$$G_{r,l} \begin{cases} = \sum_{c=1}^{\infty} V_{l,c}\delta_{\phi_{l,c}}, r = 1 \\ \sim DP(\kappa_r, \varpi_r G_{r-1,l} + (1-\varpi_r)H), r > 1 \end{cases} \tag{2}$$

where $GEM(\alpha)$ refers to such a process: $\tilde{V}_{l,c} \sim Beta(1,\alpha)$, $V_{l,c} = \tilde{V}_{l,c}\prod_{h=1}^{c-1}(1-\tilde{V}_{l,h})$, $\delta_{\phi_{l,c}}$ is a point measure concentrated at $\phi_{l,c}$, and the base distribution H is a symmetric Dirichlet over the vocabulary, i.e., $\phi_{\phi_{l,c}}$ are drawn independently. The sum of $V_{l,c}$ equals the stick length of their parent, as the length of the stick is divided up into an infinite number of pieces at its children topic level. Both r(start(r) and end(r)), and the set of r, R, are defined to suit the purpose.

Document-specific Topic Tree generation using TDP: For each document j ($j = 1$ to D),

1) Select T_r on the condition that $start(r) \leq v_j < end(r)$.

2) For each level l of DP in T_r, define G_{jl}:

$$G_{jl} \sim DP(\beta_j, G_{r,l}). \tag{3}$$

3) For each level l in T_j, define $\tilde{\lambda}_{jl}$:

$$\tilde{\lambda}_{jl} \sim Beta(\delta_1, \delta_2), \lambda_{jl} = \tilde{\lambda}_{jl}\prod_{h=0}^{l-1}(1-\tilde{\lambda}_{jh}). \tag{4}$$

To avoid bias toward to a specific level, we update these parameters using both the number of tokens assigned l in j and method-of-moments estimates of the parameters. **Document generation from Document-specific Topic Tree:** For the i-th ($i = 1$ to N_j) token in the j-th document,

1) Draw topic level l_{ji}: $l_{ji} \sim \lambda_{jl}$.

2) Draw topic θ_{ji}: $\theta_{ji} \sim G_{jl}$ if $l_{ji} = l$.

3) Draw word w_{ji}: $w_{ji} \sim Multinomial(\phi_k)$ if $\theta_{ji} = \phi_k$.

3.4 Posterior distribution of TCTs

We propose a Gibbs sampler for the posterior sampling of table and dish assignments in TCF/TDP. By employing a Pólya urn scheme [6] based on the marginalization of unknown infinite-dimensions [20], we gain conditional distributions by marginalizing out factors ϕ.

Topic Chronicle Forest: We use $m^r_{l,c}$ to count the #customers sitting at the table serving dish $\phi_{l,c}$ in region r, see Figure 2. Likewise, $M^r_{l,c}$ is the number of customers that are descendants of $\phi_{\acute{l},c}$ ($l < \acute{l}$) including $\phi_{l+1,c,*}$ itself. After observing draws in $T_r(r = 1)$, the customer follows one path down T_r, selects the table serving ϕ according to the following distributions using Eq (1):

$$P_r(\phi|\mathbf{S}^r) = \begin{cases} \frac{m^r_{1,1}}{M^r+\alpha}, \phi \text{ is a background topic } \phi_{1,1} \\ \frac{m^r_{l,c}}{m^r_{l,\cdot}+\alpha}, \phi \text{ is an existing topic } \phi_{l,c} \\ \frac{\alpha}{m^r_{l,\cdot}+\alpha}, \phi \text{ is a new topic } \phi_{l,c} \\ \frac{M^r_{l,c}}{m^r_{l,\cdot}+\alpha}, \phi \text{ is an existing topic } \phi_{\acute{l},c,*} \end{cases} \tag{5}$$

where $\mathbf{S}^r$ is the previous assignment in T_r, $m^r_{l,\cdot} = \sum_{c=1}^{C_l} m^r_{l,c}$, $M^r = \sum_{l=1}^{L}\sum_{c=1}^{C_{l-1}} M^r_{l,c}$.

Document specific topic tree: As illustrated in Figure 2, the i-th customer chooses an existing table with a probability proportional to the number of customers sitting at the table and shares the same topic in each document j, or selects a new table with probability β and orders a topic from G_r. This process continues until a full path is defined by descending tree T_r, which yields the construction of T_j. Combining Eq (5) and λ_{jl}, we denote $m^r_{l,c}$, ($m^r_{l,\cdot}$) in T_j by $m^j_{l,c}$ ($m^j_{l,\cdot}$) as document j-specific quantities, and gain the conditional distribution of ϕ in T_j: $P_j(\phi_k|\mathbf{S}_j) =$

$$\begin{cases} \lambda_{j1}, \text{if } \phi_k \text{ is background topic } \phi_{1,1}, \\ \lambda_{jl}\sum_{h=1}^{l-1}(1-\lambda_{jh})\left(\frac{m^j_{l,c}}{m^j_{l,\cdot}+\beta_j} + \frac{\beta_j}{m^j_{l,\cdot}+\beta_j}P_r(\phi|\mathbf{S}^r)\right), \text{otherwise,} \end{cases} \tag{6}$$

where $\mathbf{S}_j$ is the previous assignment in T_j. G_{jl} inherits the topics from $G_{r,l}$, but assigns to them document-specific weight $\lambda_{jl}\sum_{h=1}^{l-1}$ $(1-\lambda_{jh})$ at each topic level.

As w_{ji} is drawn from ϕ_k, the conditional density of w_{ji}, $f(w_{ji}|\mathbf{w}^{-ji}, z_{ji} = k)$, is gained by marginalizing out ϕ_k as

$$f(w_{ji}|\mathbf{w}^{-ji}, z_{ji} = k) = \frac{n_{kw}^{-ji} + \eta_{kw}}{\sum_w^W (n_{kw}^{-ji} + \eta_{kw})}, \tag{7}$$

where $\mathbf{w}^{-ji}$ indicates $(w_{11}, \cdots, w_{ji-1}, w_{ji+1}, \cdots, w_{DN_D})$,$\eta_k$ (η_{kw}) is the ϕ_k (word w in k) specific parameter, n_{kw}^{-ji} represents the number of w assigned to ϕ_k, except token w_{ji}.

Algorithm 1 Inference for TCF, and TDP

1: // initialization
2: zero all count variables, $m^r_{l,c}, m^r_{l,\cdot}, m^j_{l,c}, m^j_{l,\cdot}$, and set K_l
3: **for** $j = 1$ to D **do**
4:   **for** $i = 1$ to N_j **do**
5:     define region r_j according to v_j
6:     sample topic index $z_{ji} = k \sim Multinomial(1/K)$
7:     **if** $r_j = r$ **then**
8:       $m^r_{l,c}$ += 1; $m^r_{l,\cdot}$ += 1; $m^j_{l,c}$ += 1; $m^j_{l,\cdot}$ += 1
9:     **end if**
10:   **end for**
11: **end for**
12: // Gibbs sampling over burn-in and sampling period
13: **for** iteration=1 to $N_{iteration}$ **do**
14:   **for** $j = 1$ to D **do**
15:     **for** $i = 1$ to N_j **do**
16:       **if** $r_j = r$ **then**
17:         $m^r_{l,c}$ -= 1; $m^r_{l,\cdot}$ -= 1; $m^j_{l,c}$ -= 1; $m^j_{j,p,\cdot}$ -= 1
18:       **end if**
19:       draw ϕ_k using Eq (8).
20:       **if** $r_j = r$ **then**
21:         $m^r_{l,c}$ += 1; $m^r_{l,\cdot}$ += 1; $m^j_{l,c}$ += 1; $m^j_{l,\cdot}$ += 1
22:       **end if**
23:     **end for**
24:     update $\beta_{j*}, \tilde{\lambda}_{j*}$
25:   **end for**
26:   update $\alpha, \eta_{1,2}, \delta_{1,2}$
27:   **for** $k = 1$ to K **do**
28:     // Merge topic phase
29:   **end for**
30:   Call Region() (Alg 2)
31: **end for**

4 INFERENCE IN TCF/TDP

4.1 Inference algorithm of TDP

Since multinomials and distributions are marginalized out, we obtain the conditional distributions which means that a Gibbs sampler can train both TCF and TDP. Details of the inference for TCF and TDP are shown in Algorithm (1). In practice, we define $m^s_{l,c}$, $m^s_{l,\cdot}$, $M^s_{l,\cdot}$, and M^s to count the number of customers observed in each segment, s, and time-zone of s, t_s, where $m^r_{l,c} = \sum_{start(r) \le t_s < end(r)} m^s_{l,c}$. This introduction enables us to reduce the cost of calculation, when the boundaries of regions happen in this inference.

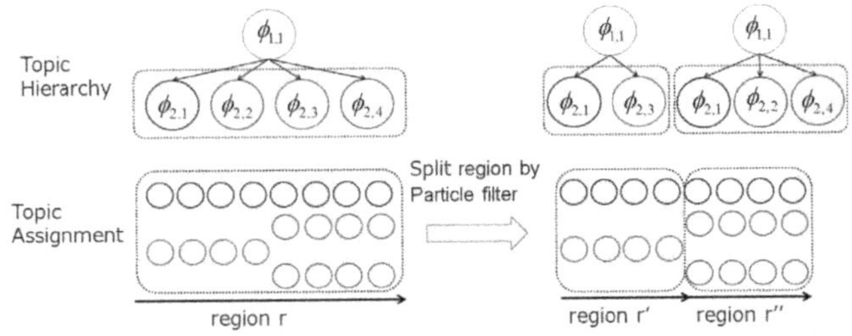

Figure 3: In this example, a l-th topic assignment, under the same parent topic located on $l-1$-th level of TCT, is sliced into two assignments on the same topic level.

At each iteration, the sampler decreases the topic assignment of the topic tree (line 17), and excludes the current customer eating w_{ji} from a table serving w_{ji} in the restaurant specified by the topic indicator k and previous word sequence u by using AddCustomer. Our sampling strategy for given token i in document j is to propose the topic assignment z_{ji}, and the seating arrangement, $S_{\setminus ji}$. It follows that we need the conditional distribution of all other given topic assignments, which is the set of seating arrangements with a customer corresponding to w_{ji}, as

$$P(z_{ji} = k|\mathbf{w}^{-ji}, S_{j\setminus ji}) \propto P_j(\phi_k|S_{\setminus ji})P(w_{ji}|\mathbf{w}^{-ji}, z_{ji} = k), \tag{8}$$

where $S_{j\setminus ji}$ denotes S_j excluding z_{ji}, $P_j(\phi_k|S_{\setminus ji})$ is given by Eq (6), and $P(w_{ji}|\mathbf{w}^{-ji}, z_{ji} = k)$ is given by Eq (7). After drawing a proposal for z_{ji}, the sampler adds a customer eating w_{ji} to a token serving w_{ji} in the restaurant specified by z_{ji}, and updates the topic assignment of TCF (line 30).

4.2 Inference algorithm of TCF

To detect the boundaries (start(r), end(r)) of region r, TCF judges the topic assignment change that the child topics assignment would persist or change over time in each topic level, where a time line consists of observed timestamps $t_1, t_2, \cdots, t_d$ in a given corpus. Here, we introduce a segment (e.g., one day, one week) as the minimum interval of a given time line. Note that discretizing the time line into bins is not practical as it is difficult to choose the optimal arrangement in advance, and global topic assignments cannot change drastically in a short interval of time. This is why TCF discretizes the time line into segments, and represents each region as a concatenation of segments. Region detection is performed over child topics of the same parent topic, since they came from their parent. As the specific or temporal topics tend to be placed on the lowest level of each tree, we decide the region on only the lowest level of TCF, and synchronize both the start and end of each region with a minimal set of segments among all possible partitions over segmentations of a given time line.

Let $b_{s,l,p}$ be a binary variable that represents whether a change in topic p's child topic assignment occurred on l-th level at s. $P_{s,l,p}(\phi)$ is topic p's child topic distribution on the l-th level from s to $s+1$, and can be calculated by using Eq (5), and $m^s_{l,c}(m^s_{l,\cdot}, M^s_{l,\cdot}, M^s)$ instead of $m^r_{l,c}(m^r_{l,\cdot}, M^r_{l,\cdot}, M^r)$. Here, the number of tables is known and fixed, as total topic assignment is given in this stage.

$$
\begin{aligned}
&P_{s,l,p}(\phi_k|S_{s,l,p}, b_{s,l,p}) = \begin{cases} P_{s-1,l,p}(\phi_k|S_{s-1,l,p}), \text{if } b_{s,l,p} = 0, \\ P_{s,l-1,p}(\phi_k|S_{s,l-1,p}), \text{if } b_{s,l,p} = 1, \end{cases} \\
&P_{s-1,l,p}(\phi_k|S_{s-1,l,p}) = P_{r,l,p}(\phi_k|S^r), \text{if start(r)} \le t_{s-1} < end(r), \\
&b_{s,l,p} \sim Bernoulli(\zeta), \zeta \sim Beta(\epsilon_1, \epsilon_2),
\end{aligned} \tag{9}
$$

where $S_{s,l,p}$ denotes topic p's child topic arrangement on the l-th level in s, and region r specific arrangement equals to the previous region arrangement, and $P_{r,l,p}(\phi_k|S^r)$ is the l-th level sub-tree of $P_r(\phi_k|S^r)$ over children topics of topic p. That is, $b_{s,l,p} = 0$ means there was no change on the l-th level of p at s ($P_{s,l,p}(\phi_k|S_{s,l,p}) = P_{s-1,l,p}(\phi_k|S_{s-1,l,p})$), and $b_{s,l,p} = 1$ means there was a change on the l-th level of p at s ($P_{s,l,p}(\phi_k|S_{s,l,p}) = P_{s,l-1,p}(\phi_k|S_{s,l-1,p})$). Figure 3 shows how appropriate TCTs can be obtained by detecting change points b_s over segments, and redefining the boundaries of regions and the corresponding topic assignments. After this synchronization, we recalculate $P_{s,l,p}(\phi)$ and construct the TCT in this region.

As TCF requires detection of the intermittent changes of hidden states, $b_{s,l,p}$, we employ particle filters, that is a family of sequential Monte Carlo sampling algorithms [10], to estimate the posterior distribution of these change points. Each particle cloud is updated recursively for each new observation using importance sampling, and is used for approximating a probability distribution over a latent variable. The particle filter for TCF is outlined in Algorithm 2, where P particles are samples of change points vector $b_s^{(p)}$. At the moment topic assignment is completed, particles form a discrete approximation of the posterior up to the previous segment. Each particle p is propagated forward by drawing change variable $b_{s,l,p}^{(p)}$ from the conditional posterior distribution $P(b_{s,l,p}^{(p)}|\mathbf{S}_{s,l,p}, b_{s-1,l,p}^{(p)})$ and scaling the particle weight by $P(\mathbf{S}_{s,l,p}|\mathbf{S}_{s-1,l,p}, b_{s-1,l,p}^{(p)})$. The conditional posterior used in this propagation step is given by

$$
\begin{aligned}
&P(b_{s,l,p}^{(p)}|\mathbf{S}_{s-1,l,p}, b_{s-1,l,p}^{(p)}) \propto \\
&P(\mathbf{S}_{s,l,p}, b_{s,l,p}^{(p)}|\mathbf{S}_{s-1,l,p}, b_{s-1,l,p}^{(p)}) = \\
&P(\mathbf{S}_{s,l,p}|\mathbf{S}_{s-1,l,p}, b_{s,l,p}^{(p)}, b_{s-1,l,p}^{(p)})P(b_{s,l,p}^{(p)}|b_{s-1,l,p}^{(p)}) = \\
&\begin{cases} P(\mathbf{S}_{s,l,p}|\mathbf{S}_{s-1,l,p}, b_{s-1,l,p}^{(p)}, b_{s,l,p}^{(p)} = 0)P(b_{s,l,p}^{(p)} = 0|b_{s-1,l,p}^{(p)}), \\ P(\mathbf{S}_{s,l,p}|\mathbf{S}_{s-1,l,p}, b_{s-1,l,p}^{(p)}, b_{s,l,p}^{(p)} = 1)P(b_{s,l,p}^{(p)} = 1|b_{s-1,l,p}^{(p)}). \end{cases}
\end{aligned} \tag{10}
$$

The first term is the likelihood of $\mathbf{S}_{s,l,p}$ when $\mathbf{S}_{s-1,l,p}$ has been fixed, and can be obtained from Eq (9) by

$$
\begin{aligned}
&P(\mathbf{S}_{s,l,p}|\mathbf{S}_{s-1,l,p}, b_{s-1,l,p}^{(p)}, b_{s,l,p}^{(p)}) \\
&\propto \prod_{c \in C_{l,p}} \begin{cases} \Gamma(m_{l,c}^s + m_{l,c}^{s-1}), \text{if } b_{s,l,p}^{(p)} = 0, \\ \Gamma(m_{l,c}^s + m_{l-1,c}^s), \text{if } b_{s,l,p}^{(p)} = 1, \end{cases}
\end{aligned} \tag{11}
$$

where Γ is the gamma function.

As a record of the history of $b_{s-1,l,p}^{(p)}$ over segments, the conditional distribution of $b_{s,l,p}^{(p)}$ is given from Eq (9) by

$$
\begin{aligned}
P(b_{s,l,p}^{(p)} = 0|b_{s-1,l,p}^{(p)}) &= \frac{\epsilon_1 + n_{s-1,l,p}^{(p)}(0)}{\epsilon_1 + \epsilon_2 + n_{s-1,l,p}^{(p)}(0) + n_{s-1,l,p}^{(p)}(1)}, \\
P(b_{s,l,p}^{(p)} = 1|b_{s-1,l,p}^{(p)}) &= \frac{\epsilon_2 + n_{s-1,l,p}^{(p)}(1)}{\epsilon_1 + \epsilon_2 + n_{s-1,l,p}^{(p)}(0) + n_{s-1,l,p}^{(p)}(1)},
\end{aligned} \tag{12}
$$

where $n_{s-1,l,p}^{(p)}(0)(n_{s-1,l,p}^{(p)}(1))$ denotes the number of topic p's children topics on the l-th level of continue (change) at s.

The particle weights are scaled by

$$
\frac{\omega_{s,l,p}^{(p)}}{\omega_{s-1,l,p}^{(p)}} \propto P(\mathbf{S}_{s,l,p}|\mathbf{S}_{s-1,l,p}, b_{s-1,l,p}^{(p)}). \tag{13}
$$

These weights are normalized so that they sum to 1, and approximate the posterior distribution over change points as

$$
P(b_{s,l,p}|S_{s,l,p}) \approx \sum_{p=1}^{P} w_{s,l,p}^{(p)} \delta_{b_{s,l,p}}(b_{s,l,p}^{(p)}), \tag{14}
$$

where $S_{s,l,p}$ is the seating arrangement in s, and $\delta_y(x)$ is a delta-mass function, which is equal to 1 when $x = y$.

Algorithm 2 Region(): Particle filter for TCF

```
// initialization
r = 0
weights ω_0^(p) = 1/P for p = 1, ···, P
for s = 1 to S do
    for p = 1 to P do
        set ω_{s,l,p}^(p) = ω_{s-1,l,p}^(p) P(S_{s,l,p}|S_{s-1,l,p}, b_{s,l,p}^(p)) using Eq (10,
        11 and 13)
        sample b_{s,l,p}^(p) w.p. P(b_{s,l,p}^(p)|b_{s-1,l,p}^(p)) using Eq (12)
    end for
    normalize ω_{s,l,p}^(p) to sum to 1
    sample b_{s,l,p} w.p. P(b_{s,l,p}|S_{s,l,p}) using Eq (14)
    if b_{s,l,p} = 1 then
        start(r)=t_s, end(r)=t_{s+1}, r = r + 1
        m_{l,c}^r = Σ_{t_s ≤ t(s) < t_{s+1}} m_{l,c}^s,
    end if
    IF ||w||^{-2} ≪ESS then resample particles
end for
```

5 EXPERIMENTS

5.1 Datasets and Experiment design

We conducted both qualitative and quantitative evaluations on the data sets noted in Table 3; we removed the stop words and rare words (appearing less than 10 times in each collection) using NLTK[1]. In experiments, Recurrent CRP [2] + LDA (RCRP+LDA) [1] and

[1]NLTK 3.2.4: http://www.nltk.org

Table 3: Data sets: ACM is a set of papers of 2001-2016 ACM CIKM, SIGIR, KDD, WWW, and WSDM. Twitter is a collection of tweets containing #apple as hashtag from 01/01/2015 to 31/06/2015 via twitter API[3], also shown in Figure 1.

	#documents	#vocabulary	time scale of v_j
ACM	6,255	29,682	publication year
Twitter	85,324	33,477	timestamp

HDP [31]+sTOT [14] are selected as benchmark temporal topic models, and recursive CRP (rCRP) [16], and nested HDP (nHDP) [26] are selected as benchmark hierarchical topic models. As rCRP, nHDP do not include a timestamp variable, we learned them by the year (ACM)/week (Twitter) scale, and compared them with the corresponding region specific TCT of TCF. We follow previous works [33] and set the topic Dirichlet parameter η to 0.1, and made the parameters of DP, α, and the Dirichlet prior, $\boldsymbol{\beta}$, using the Gamma distribution to form sparsity in models, where $\gamma \sim Gamma(0.1, 1)$, $\alpha = \gamma$, and $\boldsymbol{\beta} = \gamma\boldsymbol{\beta}$ [33]. We ran them on Spark[2] on 22 PCs with Dual Core 2.66 GHz Xeon processors.

As TCF is insensitive to the inference setting such as the size of segment (time interval), and #particles, we set #particles to 20 from pre-experiments, and evaluate how they affect the #discovered topics and TCTs extracted from the given data. Since one day is too expensive in terms of computation and not effective as a segment size, we set segment period to 1year (ACM), and 1week (Twitter). From ACM/Twitter, 211/97 topics were gained with 14/22 regions, where the average of time interval, R, was 51/1.1weeks and the average of topic level, L, was 3.2/3.1. These pre-experiments showed that the 1) difference between topics is more sensitive to region interval than the #discovered topics, and 2) the depth of topic level converges at about 3 for all data sets, although it increases in inverse proportion to region interval.

To evaluate whether TCF can discover and monitor topics in a given data and meet the our goals (See Table 1), we designed experiments to answer the following questions:

- Can TCF find the time granularity and handle both the specificity and temporality of topics?: Subsection 5.2.1
- Can TCF maintain thematic coherence, and construct more compact trees than the alternatives? Subsection 5.2.2
- Can TCF discover the periodicity of topics and track trends?: Subsection 5.3

5.2 Quantitative Evaluation

5.2.1 Comparison of specificity and temporality. We use perplexity (test set perplexity), Jensen-Shannon divergence (JS-D) [19] and Normalized Mutual Information (NMI) [21]. Perplexity is widely used to assess the predictive power of models (lower numbers are better) [15, 27, 28] in the NLP community. JS-D measures average word distribution separations between all pairs of different topics. As this allows us to quantify the difference between topics and discuss the effect of the hierarchical topic structure on distinguishing the differences between topics, we use the average JS-D to evaluate the specificity of topics. NMI is always a score between 0 and 1, where 1 means the clustering results exactly match the ground truth class (time scale of v_j) and 0 means the two sets are independent. We use NMI to evaluate the temporality of topics, where the ground truth class is year (ACM)/week (Twitter) scale of each document. This leads us to use the divergence between each document topic distribution and region (TCF)/learn unit(the others) specific topic distribution, and determine the class of each document with the minimum value as the class of cluster. The motivations of this experiment are to confirm that each TCT helps us to infer what happened at the moment in question (e.g "Taylor" in Figure 1) via temporal topics, that time-evolving models can detect trends, and that these words are representative of each trend. In this case, we used 10-fold cross-validation based on partitioning; a single subsample is retained as the validation data for testing the models, and the remaining subsamples are used as training data.

Table 4: Comparison of the specificity and temporality of topics: K(#topics), JS-D, NMI, and TSP (perplexity). JS-D is calculated by comparing 3rd level topics in the adjacent unit or region. As all models use the nonparametric setting, they learn K automatically. K of rCRP, nHDP and TCF is the average for each unit/region. Results that differ significantly, t-test $p < 0.01$, from nHDP are marked with '*'.

		RCRP +LDA	HDP +sTOT	rCRP	nHDP	TCF
ACM	K	227	233	189.3	177.5	125.7
	TSP	1487	1412	1316	1327	1215*
	JS-D	0.22	0.23	0.24	0.27	0.29
	NMI	0.35	0.31	0.45	0.51	0.82*
Twitter	K	137	138	105.7	102.2	72.5
	TSP	1231	1235	1122	1012	905*
	JS-D	0.28	0.27	0.27	0.29	0.44*
	NMI	0.41	0.43	0.52	0.58	0.86*

As shown in Table 4, TDP attains lower perplexity and higher NMI with more distinct topics than the others when identifying low dimensional components. As the trend of ACM changed more slowly than that of Twitter at the given time scale, JS-D over ACM is lower than that over Twitter. These results support our idea that 1) the coherent structure reduces # the number of similar topics and makes each topic clearer than the alternatives do, 2) this structure reduces perplexity, and 3) temporal topic models require a coherent structure. TCF detects the variable-size time granularity as regions, and constructs a time-varying tree that consists of specialized topics as in previous models and maintains the temporality of topics.

5.2.2 Topic coherence of topic trees. This experiment evaluates whether using just three topic levels is enough for distinguishing topics clearly and capturing dynamics, and how well TDP constructs the topic tree using the topic coherence measure $C(k; W^{(k)})$ [22],

$$C(k; W^{(k)}) = \sum_{m=2}^{M}\sum_{n=1}^{m-1} log\frac{D(w_m^{(k)}, w_n^{(k)}) + 1}{D(w_n^{(k)})}, \tag{15}$$

where $D(w)/D(w, w')$ means the document frequency of word w/co-document frequency of word w and w', and $W^{(k)} = (w_1^{(k)}, \cdots, w_M^{(k)})$ is a list of the M most probable words in topic k. as previously proposed metrics [24] are developed on corpora, which are dissimilar to our data sets. We compare TDP with rCRP, and nHDP as they

[2] Apache™Spark®: http://spark.apache.org/
[3] Twitter Developers: https://developer.twitter.com/en/docs

Figure 4: Word Cloud of 2-nd level/the corresponding 3-rd level topic from (upper) Twitter, and (lower) ACM: We list 20 words according to the learned probability from (left column) the 2-nd level topics, and (center and right column) corresponding 3-rd level topics under TCF. 3-rd level topics are sorted in ascending order by the start time of each region. That is, center topic (center column) is the oldest child topic of left topic (left column), and right topic (right column) is the newest child topic of the same left topic.

Table 5: Comparison on #generated topics and topic coherence score in ACM and Twitter: K_l means the average of #topics on l for each unit/region. Co means the topic coherence with M=10 and is the average for each unit/region on the same l. When l=1, this topic is the root node of all models and takes only topic. Results that differ significantly, t-test $p < 0.01$, from nHDP are marked with '*'.

l: topic level		2		3		4	
data		K_l	Co	K_l	Co	K_l	Co
ACM	rCRP	27.9	-146	102.7	-128	57.7	-117
	nHDP	29.3	-142	108.9	-121	38.3	-106
	TCF	35.3	-122*	80.6	-105*	8.8	-88*
Twitter	rCRP	27.3	-122	51.2	-118	26.2	-113
	nHDP	26.1	-112	50.1	-107	25.0	-98
	TCF	21.2	-108	44.2	-99*	6.1	-91*

are hierarchical topic models known to maintain topic coherence; the iterations of Gibbs sampler of all models was set to 2000, where the first 200 iterations were used to burn in the sampler.

Table 5 shows that TCF generated the fewest topics among all models over both data sets, and its topics became more specialized with the depth of topic level, l. As rCRP and nHDP create more topics than TCF does on the same level, their coherence score is lower than that of TDP. Although TCF yields fewer topics than the others on the same level, TCF has higher coherence score. This means that similar topics could appear in rCRP and nHDP, which lowers their scores relative to TCF, and high topic levels are not always necessary for building meaningful topic trees. Indeed, the 4-th level topics of TCF are constrained by the impact of λ_j and are much fewer in number than the other levels. That is, TCF offers a more parsimonious structure than the alternatives while matching their explanatory power.

5.3 Qualitative Evaluation

Figure 4 provides an example of the words associated with the topics learned by TCF/TDP from (upper) Twitter, and (lower) ACM. As we can see, the 2-nd level topic (left) of the first row is related to "Apple products (IT)", see Figure 1, and each 3-rd level topic (center/right) corresponds to temporal events in their parent (2-nd level) topic. For example, the number of retweets covering #apple: "Taylor Swift" indicated she became an extra hot topic after her public criticism of the royalties issue with "Apple Music service" in Jun 2015, while "Pharrell Williams" was a hot topic after wearing "Apple watch" on NBC's 'The Voice' in March 2015. This period matches the region of the 3-rd level topic in this table ($start(r) \leq v_j < end(r)$), and the corresponding words appear more intensively in this topic than the others. In the second row, the left topic is related to papers in "recommendation", center (right) topic corresponds "older topic" ("newer topic") in "recommendation". As this center topic is observed in the other regions and is not a burst topic, TCF can detect the periodicity of topics and trends in "recommendation". As another example, a topic associated with "Deep learning" appears as 2-nd level newer TCTs in TCF. That is, TCF and TDP address both the specificity and temporality of topics, and so are useful for retrospective discovery of topics; they allow trends to be tracked from timestamped corpora.

6 DISCUSSION

The advantage of TCF/TDP lies in its usage of time-varying topic structure to reduce computational cost. Pre-experiments showed that the average topic level of TCF is under 4; the alternatives yielded deeper structures. TCF generates a lot fewer 4-th level topics than the alternatives, although the appropriate level is indirectly influenced by λ_j. This is why the #topics of TCF decrease at the 4-th level in Table 5. Figure 4 shows trends similar to the results of Google trends or Scholar[4]. Since TDP yields simplified structures that constrain the possible topic assignment of each token, it achieves lower perplexity with fewer sampling iterations (more quickly) and fewer topics than the alternatives.

7 CONCLUSION

To monitor dynamics in time-stamped data, this paper presented a topic model that addresses both the specificity and temporality of topics. Our approach tackles three of the major tasks in [5]: (1) segmentation tasks are done by splitting time intervals into regions, (2) detection tasks are achieved by using the periodicity of topics in TCF, and (3) tracking tasks are performed by locating each document in each region and assigning each word a topic via the corresponding TCT. Experiments on various data sets showed that the proposed model yields time-varying topic hierarchies, and helps us comprehend time-stamped corpora. We will extend TCF/TDP for application to streaming data and thus permit the monitoring of trends in real time.

REFERENCES

[1] Amr Ahmed, Qirong Ho, Jacob Eisenstein, Eric Xing, Alexander J. Smola, and Choon Hui Teo. 2011. Unified Analysis of Streaming News. In *WWW*. 267–276.

[2] Amr Ahmed and Eric P. Xing. 2008. Dynamic Non-Parametric Mixture Models and the Recurrent Chinese Restaurant Process: with Applications to Evolutionary Clustering. In *SIAM*. 219–230.

[3] Amr Ahmed and Eric P. Xing. 2010. Timeline: A Dynamic Hierarchical Dirichlet Process Model for Recovering Birth/Death and Evolution of Topics in Text Stream. In *UAI*. 20–29.

[4] D. Aldous. 1985. *Exchangeability and related topics*. Lecture Notes in Math, Vol. 1117. Springer, Berlin. 1–198 pages.

[5] James Allan. 2002. *Topic Detection and Tracking: Event-based Information Organization*. Kluwer Academic Publishers, Norwell, MA, USA.

[6] David Blackwell and James B. MacQueen. 1973. Ferguson Distributions Via Polya Urn Schemes. *The Annals of Statistics* 1, 2 (Mar 1973), 353–355.

[7] David M. Blei, Thomas L. Griffiths, Michael I. Jordan, and Joshua B. Tenenbaum. 2004. Hierarchical topic models and the nested Chinese restaurant process. *NIPS* 16 (2004).

[8] David M. Blei and John D. Lafferty. 2006. Dynamic Topic Models. In *ICML*. 113–120.

[9] David M. Blei, Andrew Y. Ng, and Michael I. Jordan. 2003. Latent Dirichlet Allocation. *JMLR* 3 (2003), 993–1022.

[10] Arnaud Doucet, Simon Godsill, and Christophe Andrieu. 2000. On Sequential Monte Carlo Sampling Methods for Bayesian Filtering. *STATISTICS AND COMPUTING* (2000), 197–208.

[11] Thomas S. Ferguson. 1973. A Bayesian Analysis of Some Nonparametric Problems. *The Annals of Statistics* 1, 2 (Mar 1973), 209–230.

[12] Zhe Gan, Changyou Chen, Ricardo Henao, David E. Carlson, and Lawrence Carin. 2015. Scalable Deep Poisson Factor Analysis for Topic Modeling. In *ICML*. 1823–1832.

[13] Janani Kalyanam, Amin Mantrach, Diego Saez-Trumper, Hossein Vahabi, and Gert Lanckriet. 2015. Leveraging Social Context for Modeling Topic Evolution. In *KDD*. 517–526.

[14] N. Kawamae. 2011. Trend Analysis Model: Trend Consists of Temporal Words, Topics, and Timestamps. In *WSDM*. 317–326.

[15] N. Kawamae. 2014. Supervised *N*-gram topic model. In *WSDM*. 473–482.

[16] Joon Hee Kim, Dongwoo Kim, Suin Kim, and Alice Oh. 2012. Modeling topic hierarchies with the recursive chinese restaurant process. In *CIKM*. 783–792.

[17] Daniel D. Lee and H. Sebastian Seung. 1999. Learning the parts of objects by nonnegative matrix factorization. *Nature* 401, 6755 (1999), 788–791.

[18] W. Li, D. Blei, and A. McCallum. 2007. Nonparametric Bayes Pachinko allocation. In *UAI*. 243–250.

[19] J. Lin. 2006. Divergence Measures Based on the Shannon Entropy. *IEEE Trans. Inf. Theor.* 37 (2006), 145–151.

[20] S.N. MacEachern. 1994. Estimating normal means with a conjugate style Dirichlet process prio. *Communications in Statistics-Simulations* 23 (1994), 727–741.

[21] Christopher D. Manning, Prabhakar Raghavan, and Hinrich Schütze. 2008. *Introduction to Information Retrieval*. Cambridge University Press, New York.

[22] David Mimno, Hanna M. Wallach, Edmund Talley, Miriam Leenders, and Andrew McCallum. 2010. Optimizing Semantic Coherence in Topic Models. In *EMNLP*. 262–272.

[23] Radford M. Neal. 2000. Markov chain sampling methods for Dirichlet process mixture models. *JCGS* 9, 2 (2000), 249–265.

[24] David Newman, Jey Han Lau, Karl Grieser, and Timothy Baldwin. 2010. Automatic Evaluation of Topic Coherence. In *HLT*. 100–108.

[25] Viet-An Nguyen, Jordan Boyd-Graber, and Philip Resnik. 2013. Lexical and Hierarchical Topic Regression. In *NIPS*.

[26] John Paisley, Chong Wang, David M. Blei, and Michael I. Jordan. 2014. Nested hierarchical Dirichlet processes. *TPAMI* (April 2014).

[27] Michael J Paul and Mark Dredze. 2015. SPRITE: Generalizing Topic Models with Structured Priors. *Transactions of the Association for Computational Linguistics (TACL)* 3 (2015), 43–57.

[28] Md Mustafizur Rahman and Hongning Wang. 2016. Hidden Topic Sentiment Model. In *WWW*. 155–165.

[29] Ankan Saha and Vikas Sindhwani. 2012. Learning Evolving and Emerging Topics in Social Media: A Dynamic NMF approach with Temporal Regularization. In *WSDM*. 693–702.

[30] Jayaram Sethuraman. 1994. A constructive definition of Dirichlet priors. *Statistica Sinica* 4 (1994), 639–650.

[31] Yee Whye Teh, Michael I. Jordan, Matthew J. Beal, and David M. Blei. 2006. Hierarchical Dirichlet Processes. *JASA* 101, 476 (2006), 1566–1581.

[32] Carmen K. Vaca, Amin Mantrach, Alejandro Jaimes, and Marco Saerens. 2014. A Time-based Collective Factorization for Topic Discovery and Monitoring in News. In *WWW*. 527–538.

[33] H. Wallach, D. Mimno, and A. McCallum. 2009. Rethinking LDA: Why Priors Matter. In *NIPS*. 859–872.

[34] X. Wang and A. McCallum. 2006. Topics over time: a non-Markov continuous-time model of topical trends.. In *KDD*. 424–433.

[35] Jianwen Zhang, Yangqiu Song, Changshui Zhang, and Shixia Liu. 2010. Evolutionary hierarchical dirichlet processes for multiple correlated time-varying corpora. In *KDD*. 1079–1088.

[4]https://trends.google.co.jp/trends/, https://scholar.google.com

Leveraging the Crowd to Detect and Reduce the Spread of Fake News and Misinformation

Jooyeon Kim
KAIST
jooyeon.kim@kaist.ac.kr

Behzad Tabibian
MPI for Intelligent Systems
MPI for Software Systems
me@btabibian.com

Alice Oh
KAIST
alice.oh@kaist.edu

Bernhard Schölkopf
MPI for Intelligent Systems
bs@tuebingen.mpg.de

Manuel Gomez-Rodriguez
MPI for Software Systems
manuelgr@mpi-sws.org

ABSTRACT

Online social networking sites are experimenting with the following *crowd-powered* procedure to reduce the spread of fake news and misinformation: whenever a user is exposed to a story through her feed, she can flag the story as misinformation and, if the story receives *enough* flags, it is sent to a trusted third party for fact checking. If this party identifies the story as misinformation, it is marked as *disputed*. However, given the uncertain number of exposures, the high cost of fact checking, and the trade-off between flags and exposures, the above mentioned procedure requires careful reasoning and smart algorithms which, to the best of our knowledge, do not exist to date.

In this paper, we first introduce a flexible representation of the above procedure using the framework of marked temporal point processes. Then, we develop a scalable online algorithm, Curb, to select *which* stories to send for fact checking and *when* to do so to efficiently reduce the spread of misinformation with provable guarantees. In doing so, we need to solve a novel stochastic optimal control problem for stochastic differential equations with jumps, which is of independent interest. Experiments on two real-world datasets gathered from Twitter and Weibo show that our algorithm may be able to effectively reduce the spread of fake news and misinformation.

ACM Reference format:
Jooyeon Kim, Behzad Tabibian, Alice Oh, Bernhard Schölkopf, and Manuel Gomez-Rodriguez. 2018. Leveraging the Crowd to Detect and Reduce the Spread of Fake News and Misinformation. In *Proceedings of WSDM 2018: The Eleventh ACM International Conference on Web Search and Data Mining, Marina Del Rey, Ca, USA, February 5–9, 2018 (WSDM 2018)*, 9 pages.
https://doi.org/10.1145/3159652.3159734

WSDM 2018, February 5–9, 2018, Marina Del Rey, Ca, USA

ACM ISBN 978-1-4503-5581-0/18/02...$15.00
https://doi.org/10.1145/3159652.3159734

1 INTRODUCTION

In recent years, social media and online social networking sites have become a major disseminator of false facts, urban legends, fake news, or, more generally, misinformation. In this context, there are growing concerns that misinformation on these platforms has fueled the emergence of a *post-truth* society, where debate is perniciously framed by the repeated assertion of talking points to which factual rebuttals by the media or independent experts are ignored. For example, the post-truth label has been widely used to describe the presidential campaign of Donald Trump in the 2016 U.S. elections[1] and the Leave campaign in the 2016 Brexit referendum[2], whose outcomes have been then called into question.

In an effort to curb the spread of misinformation, major online social networking sites, such as Facebook, Twitter or Weibo, are (considering) resorting to the crowd[3,4,5]. In particular, they are experimenting with the following procedure to reduce the spread of misinformation: whenever users are exposed to a story through their feeds, they have a choice to flag the story as misinformation and, if the story receives *enough* flags, it is directed to a coalition of independent organizations[6], signatories of Poynter's International Fact Checking Code of Principles[7], for fact checking. If the fact checking organizations identify a story as misinformation, it gets flagged as disputed and may also appear lower in the users' feeds, reducing the number of people who are *exposed* to misinformation. In this context, online social networking sites are giving advice to its millions of users on how to spot misinformation online[8]. However, the above mentioned procedure requires careful reasoning and smart algorithms which, to the best of our knowledge, are nonexistent to date:

— *Uncertain number of exposures:* the spread of information over social networking sites is a stochastic process, which may depend on, *e.g.*, the information content, the users' influence and the network

[1] https://www.washingtonpost.com/posteverything/wp/2016/06/16/why-the-post-truth-political-era-might-be-around-for-a-while/
[2] https://www.theguardian.com/commentisfree/2016/may/13/boris-johnson-donald-trump-post-truth-politician
[3] https://newsroom.fb.com/news/2016/12/news-feed-fyi-addressing-hoaxes-and-fake-news/
[4] https://www.washingtonpost.com/news/the-switch/wp/2017/06/29/twitter-is-looking-for-ways-to-let-users-flag-fake-news/
[5] http://www.scmp.com/news/china/policies-politics/article/2055179/how-chinas-highly-censored-wechat-and-weibo-fight-fake
[6] This coalition of organizations includes, among many others, Snopes (http://www.snopes.com), FactCheck (http://www.factcheck.org) or Politifact (http://www.politifact.com).
[7] http://www.poynter.org/fact-checkers-code-of-principles/
[8] https://www.nytimes.com/2017/05/08/technology/uk-election-facebook-fake-news.html

structure. Thus, the number of users exposed to different stories varies greatly and we need to consider probabilistic exposure models to capture this uncertainty.

— *Fact checking is costly:* given the myriad of (fake) stories spreading in online social networking sites and the observation that fact checking is a costly process, we can only expect (the reviewers from) the coalition of independent organizations to fact check a small percentage of the set of stories spreading over time. Therefore, it is necessary to decide *which* stories to fact check and *when* to do so.

— *Flags vs exposures:* the more users are exposed to a story before sending it for fact checking, the greater the confidence a story may be misinformation, however, the higher the potential damage if it turns out to be misinformation. Thus, we need to find the optimal trade-off between misinformation evidence, by means of flagging data, and misinformation reduction, by means of preventing (unwarned) exposures to misinformation.

Our approach. To tackle the above challenges, we first introduce a novel representation of the above procedure using the framework of marked temporal point processes [1]. Then, we find *which* stories to send for fact checking by solving a novel stochastic optimal control problem for SDEs with jumps [16], which differs from the nascent literature on stochastic optimal control of social and information systems [41, 42, 47, 48] in two technical aspects:

I. The control signal is a multidimensional survival process (*i.e.*, a terminating temporal point process), which is defined by means of a set of conditional intensities (*i.e.*, stories to fact check), while previous work has considered nonterminating temporal point processes as control signals.

II. The SDEs with jumps depend on random variables (*i.e.*, flags) whose distributions depend on *a priori* unknown parameters (*i.e.*, flagging probability, which depends on whether a story is fake or legitimate). In this context, a posterior estimate of these parameters arises naturally in the formulation of the optimal control problem. In contrast, previous work did not consider application scenarios where posterior inference was required.

These technical aspects have implications beyond the problem of detecting and reducing misinformation since they establish an unexplored connection between stochastic online optimal control, survival analysis and Bayesian inference. Moreover, we find that the solution to the above optimal control problem is relatively simple and intuitive: the optimal intensity of fact checking is proportional to a posterior estimate of the rate of misinformation. As a consequence, we can develop a scalable online algorithm, Curb, to schedule *which* stories to send for fact checking to efficiently reduce misinformation. Finally, we experiment on two real-world datasets gathered from Twitter and Weibo and show that our algorithm is able to effectively reduce the spread of misinformation and fake news. To facilitate research in this area, we release an open source implementation of our algorithm at http://learning.mpi-sws.org/curb/.

Related work. The research areas most closely related to ours are on truth discovery and rumor detection. In terms of truth discovery, most previous work discovers the truth by assessing the trustworthiness of the information sources and they do so using link-based measures [4, 7, 15], information retrieval based measures [44], accuracy-based measures [9, 10, 19, 27, 45], content-based measures [2, 14, 35, 37, 38, 43, 51], graphical models [32, 46, 49, 50], or survival analysis [26, 36]. A recent line of work [22, 24, 31, 40] also considers scenarios in which the truth may change over time. In terms of rumor detection, previous work has typically relied on textual, network and temporal features to characterize and detect rumors [13, 20, 25, 28, 29, 33, 34]. However, our work differs from previous work in several key aspects: (i) the *crowd-powered* fact checking procedure is, to the best of our knowledge, novel; (ii) we both detect and reduce the spread of misinformation, in contrast, previous work has focused on detection and has not designed interventional strategies considering the exposure dynamics; and, (iii) we develop a principled online algorithm by solving a stochastic optimal control of SDEs with jumps, which is able to adapt to changes in the rate of exposures and flags, while previous work has developed off-line algorithms. Moreover, note that our methodology could be extended to leverage the above detection methods to further refine the posterior estimate of the rate of misinformation.

Learning from the crowd has been widely used in many different areas, *e.g.*, web security [6, 39], spam detection [5, 52], phishing detection [30] and fake online account detection [12]. Moreover, using expert knowledge, such as the one provided by fact checking organizations, has been used to improve the quality and reliability of crowd learning procedures [17, 23]. However, to the best of our knowledge, the present work is the first that leverages both the crowd and expert knowledge in the context of detecting and preventing the spread of fake news and misinformation.

Finally, there has been a paucity of work on stochastic optimal control of SDEs with jumps [41, 42, 47, 48], however, previous work has focused on steering social activity, has not considered survival processes as control signals, and has not considered SDEs with jumps depending on random variables whose distributions depend on unknown parameters.

2 PROBLEM FORMULATION

To reduce the spread of misinformation, we optimize the following fact checking procedure used by major online social networking sites. Users can flag any story in their feed as misinformation and, if a story receives *enough* flags, it is sent to a third party for fact checking. If the third-party identifies a story as misinformation, it gets flagged as disputed and may also appear lower in the users' feeds. In this procedure, since the third-party fact checking is costly, we need to decide *which* stories to fact check and *when* to do so—decide how many flags are *enough*. For ease of exposition, we assume that, if a story is sent for fact checking, the story is instantaneously verified—it is instantly revealed whether the story is fake or genuine[9].

In this section, we first leverage the framework of marked temporal point processes [1] to model the above mentioned fact checking procedure, starting from the data representation the model uses,

[9]One could easily relax this assumption by modeling the delay between the time when a story is sent for fact checking and the time when it is verified.

then define and estimate the rate of misinformation, which we will use to decide what and when to fact check, and finally state the fact checking scheduling problem.

Data representation. Given an online social networking site with a set of users $\mathcal{U}$ and a set of unverified stories $\mathcal{S}$, we define two types of user events: *exogenous* events, which correspond to the publication of stories by users on their own initiative, and *endogenous* events, which correspond to the resharing and/or flagging of stories by users who are exposed to them through their feeds, similarly as in previous work [8, 11].

Formally, we represent each exogenous event as a triplet

$$p := (\underset{\text{user}}{\underset{\uparrow}{u}}, \underset{\text{time}}{\underset{\uparrow}{t}}, \overset{\text{story}}{\overset{\downarrow}{s}}),$$

which means that user $u \in \mathcal{U}$ posted story $s \in \mathcal{S}$ at time t at her own initiative. Moreover, we denote the history of exogenous events for each story s up to time t by $\mathcal{H}_s^p(t) = \bigcup_{i:t_i<t}\{p_i \mid s_i = s\}$.

Similarly, we represent each endogenous event as a 5-tuple

$$e := (\underset{\text{user}}{\underset{\uparrow}{u}}, \underset{\text{time}}{\underset{\uparrow}{t}}, \overset{\text{story}}{\overset{\downarrow}{s}}, \underset{\text{reshare}}{\underset{\uparrow}{r}}, \overset{\text{flag}}{\overset{\downarrow}{f}}),$$

which means that user $u \in \mathcal{U}$ was exposed to story $s \in \mathcal{S}$ at time t and decided (not) to reshare it, $r = 1$ ($r = 0$), and/or (not) to flag it, $f = 1$ ($f = 0$). Then, we denote the history of endogenous events for story s up to time t by $\mathcal{H}_s^e(t) = \bigcup_{i:t_i<t}\{e_i \mid s_i = s\}$. Finally, we gather the history of exogenous and endogenous events for story s up to time t by $\mathcal{H}_s(t) = \mathcal{H}_s^p(t) \bigcup \mathcal{H}_s^e(t)$ and the overall history of exogenous and endogenous events up to time t by $\mathcal{H}(t) = \bigcup_{s\in\mathcal{S}} \mathcal{H}_s(t)$.

Fact checking generative process. We represent the times of the exogenous and endogenous events within the social networking site using two multidimensional counting processes, $\boldsymbol{N}^p(t)$ and $\boldsymbol{N}^e(t)$, in which the s-th dimension, $N_s^p(t)$ and $N_s^e(t)$, count the number of exogenous and endogenous events for story s up to time t. Following the literature on temporal point processes [1], we characterize these counting processes using their corresponding intensities, *i.e.*,

$$\mathbb{E}[d\boldsymbol{N}^p(t)|\mathcal{H}(t)] = \boldsymbol{\lambda}^p(t)dt,$$
$$\mathbb{E}[d\boldsymbol{N}^e(t)|\mathcal{H}(t)] = \boldsymbol{\lambda}^e(t)dt,$$

where $d\boldsymbol{N}^p(t)$ and $d\boldsymbol{N}^e(t)$ denote the number of exogenous and endogenous events in the window $[t, t+dt)$ and $\boldsymbol{\lambda}^p(t) := [\lambda_s^p(t)]_{s\in\mathcal{S}}$ and $\boldsymbol{\lambda}^e(t) := [\lambda_s^e(t)]_{s\in\mathcal{S}}$ denote the vector of intensities associated to all stories. Every time a user is exposed to a story s, the binary indicators r and f are sampled from two Bernoulli distributions, $\mathbb{P}(r = 1) = r_s$ and $\mathbb{P}(f = 1) = f_s$, where r_s and f_s are story specific parameters which may depend on many complex factors, *e.g.*, content, source.

Moreover, we represent the times when stories are sent to a trusted third-party for fact checking using a multidimensional binary counting process, $\boldsymbol{M}(t)$, in which the s-th dimension, $M_s(t)$, becomes one when story s is sent for fact checking. Here, we characterize this process using a vector of intensities $\boldsymbol{u}(t) := [u_s(t)]_{s\in\mathcal{S}}$ associated to all stories, *i.e.*, $\mathbb{E}[d\boldsymbol{M}(t)|\mathcal{H}(t)] = \boldsymbol{u}(t) \odot (1 - \boldsymbol{M}(t))dt$, where $\odot$ denotes pairwise product and the term $(1 - \boldsymbol{M}(t))$ ensures each story is sent for fact checking only once. Whenever story s is sent for fact checking, we assume it gets instantly verified—it gets revealed whether s is fake or genuine. Under this characterization, deciding *which* stories to fact check and *when* to do so becomes a problem of finding the vector of intensities $\boldsymbol{u}(t)$ of fact checking events.

Endogenous and exogenous intensities. We model exogenous events for each unverified story $s \in \mathcal{S}$ as:

$$\lambda_s^p(t) := h_s(t)(1 - M_s(t)), \quad (1)$$

where $h_s(t) \geq 0$ is a time-varying (differentiable) function and $(1 - M_s(t))$ ensures the intensity of endogenous events becomes zero if the story is verified (*i.e.*, fact checked).

For endogenous events, we consider the following form for the intensity functions:

$$\lambda_s^e(t) = \Big[\overbrace{\int_0^t r_s(\tau)g(t-\tau)dN_s^e(\tau)}^{\text{Reshares}} + \overbrace{\int_0^t g(t-\tau)dN_s^p(\tau)}^{\text{Posts}} \Big] \overbrace{(1 - M_s(t))}^{\text{Fact check}}, \quad (2)$$

where the first term, with $r_s(\tau) \sim \text{Bernoulli}(r_s)$, models the exposures due to reshares of story s by the previous users, the second term models the exposures due to previous posts of story s by users on their own initiative (*i.e.*, exogenous events). In the first two terms, $g_s(t)$ denotes an exponential triggering kernel, $g(t) := \gamma \exp(-\omega t)\mathbb{I}(t \geq 0)$, which models the decay of *influence* of previous reshares and posts over time. By making the intensity dependent on the history of reshares and posts, it becomes a stochastic process by itself.

Given the above functional form for the intensity of endogenous events, the following alternative representation based on stochastic differential equations (SDEs) with jumps, which can be derived using Ito's calculus [16], will be useful to design our algorithm:

Proposition 2.1. *Let $N_s^e(t)$ be a counting process with associated intensity $\lambda_s^e(t)$, given by Eq. 2. The tuple $(N_s^e(t), \lambda_s^e(t))$ is a doubly stochastic Markov process whose dynamics can be represented by the following SDE with jumps:*

$$d\lambda_s^e(t) = -\omega\lambda_s^e(t)dt - \lambda_s^e(t)dM_s(t) + \gamma\Big[r_s(t)dN_s^e(t) + (1 - M(t))dN_s^p(t)\Big] \quad (3)$$

Estimated rate of misinformation. If one cannot send all stories for fact checking, ideally, one may like to send only fake stories and favor those which, if not fact checked, would reach the greatest number of users. However, we cannot directly observe whether a story is fake (that is why we send it for fact checking!) and we do not know the total number of users who will be exposed to the story if not fact checked. Instead, for each story, we will leverage the users' flags and exposures to compute a running estimate of the rate of misinformation due to that story. Then, we will find the optimal fact checking intensities $\boldsymbol{u}(t)$ that minimize a nondecreasing function of the estimated misinformation rates over time.

Given a story $s \in \mathcal{S}$, the number of users $N_s^f(t)$ who flagged the story up to time t can be formally defined as

$$N_s^f(t) := \int_0^t f_s(\tau)dN_s^e(\tau),$$

where $N_s^e(t)$ counts the number of users exposed to story s by time t, $f_s(\tau) \sim f_s$, and it readily follows that $dN_s^f(t) = f_s(t)dN_s^e(t)$. Then, we can estimate the average number of users $\bar{N}_s^m(t)$ exposed to misinformation by time t, conditioned on the number of exposed users and flags, as

$$\begin{aligned}\bar{N}_s^m(t) &:= p_{m|s,f=1}N_s^f(t) + p_{m|s,f=0}(N_s^e(t) - N_s^f(t)) \\ &= p_{m|f=1}N_s^f(t) + p_{m|f=0}(N_s^e(t) - N_s^f(t)),\end{aligned}$$

where we assume that the probability that a story is misinformation given that a user did or did not flag it is equal for all stories, *i.e.*, $p_{m|s,f} = p_{m|f}$, and one can estimate $p_{m|f}$ from historical flag and exposure data about fact checked stories. Here, the probability $p_{m|f}$ characterizes how *good* the crowd is at spotting misinformation[10].

Next, we can compute the differential $d\bar{N}_s^m(t)$ as

$$d\bar{N}_s^m(t) = \left[(p_{m|f=1} - p_{m|f=0})f_s(t) + p_{m|f=0}\right]dN_s^e(t)$$

and define the rate of misinformation as

$$\begin{aligned}\lambda_s^m(t)dt &= \mathbb{E}[d\bar{N}_s^m(t)] \\ &= \left[(p_{m|f=1} - p_{m|f=0})f_s + p_{m|f=0}\right]\lambda_s^e(t)dt. \quad (4)\end{aligned}$$

Unfortunately, the flagging probability f_s may depend on many complex factors, *e.g.*, content, source, and is generally unknown. To overcome this challenge, we assume a Beta prior on f_s, *i.e.*, $f_s \sim Beta(\alpha, \beta)$, and compute instead a posterior estimate of the rate of misinformation, which leverages both the number of exposures $N_s^e(t)$ and flags $N_s^f(t)$ by time t, *i.e.*,

$$\begin{aligned}\hat{\lambda}_s^m(t)dt &= \mathbb{E}_{f_s(t),f_s}[d\bar{N}_s^m(t)] \\ &= \Big[(p_{m|f=1} - p_{m|f=0})\frac{\alpha + N_s^f(t)}{\alpha + \beta + N_s^e(t)} \\ &\quad + p_{m|f=0}\Big]\lambda_s^e(t)dt, \quad (5)\end{aligned}$$

where we used the conjugacy between the Bernoulli and the Beta distributions, *i.e.*,

$$f_s|N_s^f, N_s^e \sim Beta\left(\alpha + N_s^f(t), \beta + N_s^e(t) - N_s^f(t)\right).$$

Finally, given a set of stories $\mathcal{S}$, we denote the vector of posterior estimates of their associated rate of misinformation as $\hat{\boldsymbol{\lambda}}^m(t) = [\hat{\lambda}_s^m(t)]_{s\in\mathcal{S}}$.

The fact checking scheduling problem. Given a set of unverified stories $\mathcal{S}$, we aim to find the optimal fact checking intensities $\boldsymbol{u}(t)$ that minimize the expected value of nondecreasing convex loss function $\ell(\hat{\boldsymbol{\lambda}}^m(t), \boldsymbol{u}(t))$ of the posterior estimates of the stories rates of misinformation $\hat{\boldsymbol{\lambda}}^m(t)$ and the fact checking intensities $\boldsymbol{u}(t)$ over a time window $(t_0, t_f]$, *i.e.*,

$$\begin{aligned}&\underset{\boldsymbol{u}(t_0,t_f]}{\text{minimize}} \quad \mathbb{E}\left[\phi(\hat{\boldsymbol{\lambda}}^m(t_f)) + \int_{t_0}^{t_f} \ell(\hat{\boldsymbol{\lambda}}^m(\tau), \boldsymbol{u}(\tau))d\tau\right] \\ &\text{subject to} \quad \boldsymbol{u}(t) \geq 0 \quad \forall t \in (t_0, t_f], \quad (6)\end{aligned}$$

where $\boldsymbol{u}(t_0, t_f]$ denotes the fact checking intensities from t_0 to t_f, the expectation is taken over all possible realizations of the marked temporal point processes associated to the endogenous and exogenous events of all stories from t_0 to t_f, and $\phi(\hat{\boldsymbol{\lambda}}^m(t_f))$ is an arbitrary penalty function. Here, by considering a nondecreasing loss on both the posterior estimate of the rates of misinformation and fact checking intensities, we penalize high levels of misinformation and we limit the number of stories that are sent for fact checking.

3 PROPOSED ALGORITHM

In this section, we find the optimal fact-checking intensities $\boldsymbol{u}(t)$ that minimizes Eq. 6 from the perspective of stochastic optimal control of jump SDEs [16]. To ease the exposition, we first derive a solution for one story, introduce an efficient algorithm that implements the solution, and then generalize the solution and the efficient algorithm to multiple stories.

Optimizing for one story. Given an unverified story s with fact checking reviewing intensity $u_s(t) = u(t)$, exogenous intensity $\lambda_s^p(t) = \lambda^p(t)$, endogenous intensity $\lambda_s^e(t) = \lambda^e(t)$ and associated counting processes $M_s(t) = M(t)$, $N_s^p(t) = N^p(t)$ and $N_s^e(t) = N^e(t)$, respectively, we can rewrite the fact checking scheduling problem defined in Eq. 6 as:

$$\begin{aligned}&\underset{u(t_0,t_f]}{\text{minimize}} \quad \mathbb{E}\left[\phi(\hat{\lambda}^m(t_f)) + \int_{t_0}^{t_f} \ell(\hat{\lambda}^m(\tau), u(\tau))d\tau\right] \\ &\text{subject to} \quad u(t) \geq 0 \quad \forall t \in (t_0, t_f], \quad (7)\end{aligned}$$

where the dynamics of $N^e(t)$ are given by Eq. 3 and the posterior estimate of the misinformation rate is given by Eq. 5. Note that we are now focusing on a single story rather than on multiple stories.

Next, we define an optimal cost-to-go function J for the above problem, use Bellman's principle of optimality to derive the associated Hamilton-Jacobi-Bellman (HJB) equation [3], and exploit the structure of our problem to find a solution to the HJB equation.

Definition 3.1. The optimal cost-to-go J is defined as the minimum of the expected value of the cost of going from state $(M(t), N^e(t), N^f(t), N^p(t), \lambda^e(t))$ at time t to the final state at time t_f, *i.e.*,

$$\begin{aligned}&J(M(t), N^e(t), N^f(t), N^p(t), \lambda^e(t), t) \quad (8) \\ &= \min_{u(t,t_f]} \mathbb{E}\left[\phi(\hat{\lambda}^m(t_f)) + \int_t^{t_f} \ell(\hat{\lambda}^m(\tau), u(\tau))d\tau\right].\end{aligned}$$

Now, using the Markov property of the state variables $(M(t), N^e(t), N^f(t), N^p(t), \lambda^e(t))$, we can apply Bellman's principle of optimality to the above definition to break the problem into smaller subproblems and rewrite Eq. 8 as

$$\begin{aligned}0 = \min_{u(t,t+dt]} &\Big\{\mathbb{E}\left[dJ(M(t), N(t), N^f(t), N^p(t), \lambda^e(t), t)\right] \\ &+ \ell(\hat{\lambda}^m(t), u(t))dt\Big\}. \quad (9)\end{aligned}$$

Next, we differentiate J with respect to time t, $M(t)$, $N^e(t)$, $N^f(t)$, $N^p(t)$ and $\lambda^e(t)$ using Lemma 5.1 (in the Appendix) with $x(t) =$

[10] One could consider different false positive and false negative rates per user and per story, *e.g.*, using text analysis or domain knowledge about the website that published the story. However, for simplicity, we leave such extensions for future work.

$\lambda^e(t)$, $y(t) = \lambda^p(t) = h(t)$, $z(t) = r(t)$, $w(t) = f(t)$) and $F = J$.

$$\begin{aligned} dJ = \big[&J(M, N^e + 1, N^f + 1, N^p, \lambda^e + \gamma, t) f(t) r(t) \\ &+ J(M, N^e + 1, N^f + 1, N^p, \lambda^e, t) f(t)(1 - r(t)) \\ &+ J(M, N^e + 1, N^f, N^p, \lambda^e + \gamma, t)(1 - f(t)) r(t) \\ &+ J(M, N^e + 1, N^f, N^p, \lambda^e, t)(1 - f(t))(1 - r(t)) \\ &- J(M, N^e, N^f, N^p, \lambda^e, t)\big] dN^e(t) \\ &+ \big[J(M, N^e, N^f, N^p + 1, \lambda^e + \gamma, t) \\ &- J(M, N^e, N^f, N^p, \lambda^e, t)\big] dN^p(t) \\ &- \big[J(M, N^e, N^f, N^p, \lambda^e, t) - J(M + 1, N^e, N^f, N^p, 0, t)\big] dM(t) \\ &+ J_t - \omega \lambda^e(t) J_{\lambda^e}, \end{aligned}$$

Then, using that $\mathbb{E}[dN^e(t)] = \lambda^e(t)dt$, $\mathbb{E}[dN^p(t)] = h(t)dt$, $\mathbb{E}[dM(t)] = (1 - M(t))u(t)dt$, $\mathbb{E}[r(t)] = r_s = r$, and $\mathbb{E}[f(t)] = \frac{\alpha + N^f(t)}{\alpha + \beta + N^e(t)}$, the HJB equation follows:

$$\begin{aligned} 0 = \big[&J(M, N^e + 1, N^f + 1, N^p, \lambda^e + \gamma, t) \tfrac{\alpha + N^f(t)}{\alpha + \beta + N(t)} r \\ &+ J(M, N^e + 1, N^f + 1, N^p, \lambda^e, t) \tfrac{\alpha + N^f(t)}{\alpha + \beta + N(t)} (1 - r) \\ &+ J(M, N^e + 1, N^f, N^p, \lambda^e + \gamma, t)(1 - \tfrac{\alpha + N^f(t)}{\alpha + \beta + N(t)}) r \\ &+ J(M, N^e + 1, N^f, N^p, \lambda^e, t)(1 - \tfrac{\alpha + N^f(t)}{\alpha + \beta + N(t)})(1 - r) \\ &- J(M, N^e, N^f, N^p, \lambda^e, t)\big] \lambda^e(t) \\ &+ \big[J(M, N^e, N^f, N^p + 1, \lambda^e + \gamma, t) \\ &- J(M, N^e, N^f, N^p, \lambda^e, t)\big](1 - M(t)) h(t) \\ &+ \min_{u(t, t_f]} \Big\{ l(\hat{\lambda}^m(t), u(t)) + J_t - \omega \lambda^e(t) J_{\lambda^e} \\ &\qquad - \big[J(M, N^e, N^f, N^p, \lambda^e, t) \\ &\qquad - J(M + 1, N^e, N^f, N^p, 0, t)\big](1 - M(t)) u(t) \Big\}, \end{aligned} \tag{10}$$

with $J(M(t_f), N^e(t_f), N^f(t_f), N^p(t_f), \lambda^e(t_f), t_f) = \phi(\hat{\lambda}^e(t_f))$ as the terminal condition.

To solve the above HJB equation, we need to define the penalty function ϕ and the loss function ℓ. Following the literature on the stochastic optimal control [16], we consider the following quadratic forms, which penalize high levels of misinformation and limit the number of stories that are sent for fact checking:

$$\phi(\hat{\lambda}^m(t_f)) = \frac{1}{2}(\hat{\lambda}^m(t_f))^2$$

$$\ell(\hat{\lambda}^m(t), u(t)) = \frac{1}{2}(\hat{\lambda}^m(t))^2 + \frac{1}{2} q u^2(t),$$

where q is a tunable parameter to trade-off between the number of stories sent for fact checking and the spread of misinformation. With the loss function, we take the derivative with respect to $u(t)$ in Eq. 10 and uncover the relationship between the optimal fact checking intensity and the optimal cost J:

$$\begin{aligned} u^*(t) = q^{-1}(1 - M(t))\big[&J(M(t), N^e(t), N^f(t), N^p(t), \lambda^e(t), t), \\ &- J(M(t) + 1, N^e(t), N^f(t), N^p(t), 0, t)\big]. \end{aligned} \tag{11}$$

Then, we plug in the above expression in Eq. 10 and find a solution to the resulting nonlinear differential equation using the following Lemma:

Lemma 3.2. *The optimal cost-to-go J that satisfies the HJB equation, defined by Eq. 10, is given by:*

$$\begin{aligned} &J(M(t), N^e(t), N^f(t), N^p(t), \lambda^e(t), t) \\ &= q^{\frac{1}{2}} \big[(p_{m|f=1} - p_{m|f=0}) \tfrac{\alpha + N^f(t)}{\alpha + \beta + N(t)} + p_{m|f=0}\big] \big[\lambda^e(t) \\ &\qquad - \gamma N^p(t) - (\gamma r - \omega)(\alpha + \beta + N^e(t))\big]. \end{aligned}$$

Proof Sketch. We verify the above cost-to-go J satisfies the HJB equation, given by Eq. 10. To do so, we use that $J_t = 0$ and

$$J_{\lambda^e} = q^{\frac{1}{2}} \big[(p_{m|f=1} - p_{m|f=0}) \tfrac{\alpha + N^f(t)}{\alpha + \beta + N(t)} + p_{m|f=0}\big].$$

Here, note that the HJB equation needs to be satisfied only for $M(t) \in \{0, 1\}$, which are the only feasible values for the counting process associated to the fact checking event. Next, we use the above Lemma to recover the optimal fact checking intensity $u^*(t)$:

Theorem 3.3. *Given a story s, the optimal fact checking intensity for the fact checking scheduling problem, defined by Eq. 7, under quadratic loss is given by:*

$$\begin{aligned} u^*(t) = q^{-\frac{1}{2}}(1 - M(t)) \Big[&p_{m|f=0} \\ &+ (p_{m|f=1} - p_{m|f=0}) \left(\frac{\alpha + N^f(t)}{\alpha + \beta + N^e(t)} \right) \Big] \lambda^e(t). \end{aligned} \tag{12}$$

The above result reveals a linear relationship between the optimal fact checking intensity and the endogenous (*i.e.*, exposure) intensity $\lambda^e(t)$. Moreover, the corresponding coefficient depends on the number of user exposures $N^e(t)$ and the number of flags $N^f(t)$, and can increase and decrease over time. Remarkably, the optimal intensity does not depend on the exogenous intensity $\lambda^p(t)$, which is generally unknown.

Finally, we derive an efficient procedure to sample from the above intensity, summarized in Algorithm 1, which we name Curb. At a high level, as a story spreads through out the network, the algorithm updates its belief about the best time to fact-check based on how quickly the story is spreading as well as what is the likelihood that the story is misinformation. Within the algorithm, $Next()$ returns the next endogenous (*i.e.*, exposure) event, which occurs at time t' with resharing and flagging indicators r and f, respectively, $Update(N^e(t), N^f(t), \lambda^e(t))$ updates $u(t)$ using Eq. 12, and $Sample(\tau, u(t))$ samples from an intensity $u(t)$ starting at time τ using a standard thinning algorithm [21]. If the fact checking intensity increases, by $r = 1$ or $f = 1$, we apply the superposition theorem [18], *i.e.*, we sample a new candidate fact checking time κ and we take the minimum between κ and the previous candidate fact checking time. If the fact checking intensity decreases, by $f = 0$, we first use a thinning argument to decide whether to keep the current candidate fact checking time τ or we sample a new candidate fact checking time, greater than τ. This sampling procedure is very efficient since it only needs to sample $O(N^e(t_f))$ times from an inhomogeneous Poisson process. Finally, note that if we gather more and more evidence that a story s is not misinformation ($f = 0$ for many exposures), the candidate fact checking time τ will eventually become greater than t_f and the story will never be sent for fact checking.

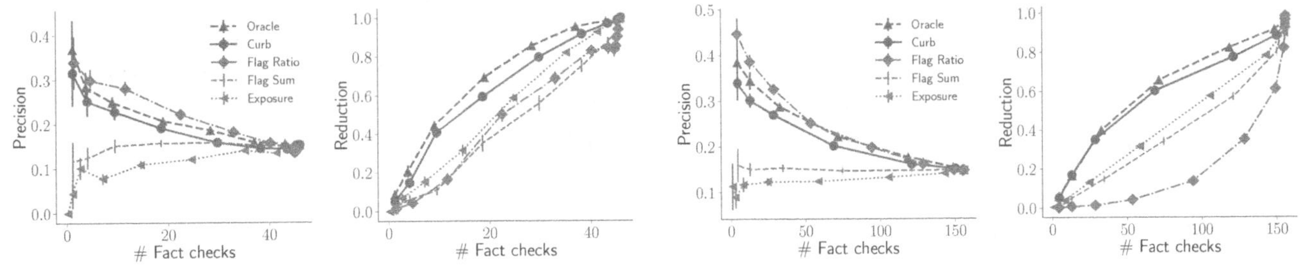

(a) Twitter (b) Weibo

Figure 1: Performance vs. number of fact checking events. We measure performance in terms of misinformation reduction, which is the fraction of unverified exposures that fact checking prevented, and precision, which is the fraction of fact checked stories that are fake. Oracle and CURB achieve a comparable performance in both datasets, beating the threshold baseline by large margins.

Algorithm 1: The CURB Algorithm

Input: Parameters $q, \alpha, \beta, p_{m|f=1}, p_{m|f=0}, t_f$
Initialization $: N(t) \leftarrow 0; N^f(t) \leftarrow 0; \lambda^e(t) \leftarrow 0;$ $Update(N^e(t), N^f(t), \lambda^e(t))$
Output: Fact checking time τ

$\tau \leftarrow t_f$
$(t', r, f) \leftarrow Next()$
while $t' < \tau$ **do**
  $u_0(t) \leftarrow u(t)$
  $N^e(t) \leftarrow N^e(t) + 1; \quad N^f(t) \leftarrow N^f(t) + f$
  $u(t) \leftarrow Update(N^e(t), N^f(t), \lambda^e(t))$
  if $f = 0$ **then**
    $x \leftarrow Uniform(0, 1)$
    if $u(t)/u_0(t) < x$ **then**
      $\tau \leftarrow Sample(\tau, u(t))$
    end
  end
  if $r = 1$ **then**
    $\lambda^e(t) \leftarrow \lambda^e(t) + g(t - t')$
    $u(t) \leftarrow Update(N^e(t), N^f(t), \lambda^e(t))$
  end
  $\kappa = Sample(t', \max(0, u(t) - u_0(t)))$
  $\tau \leftarrow min(\tau, \kappa)$
  $(t', r, f) \leftarrow Next()$
end
return τ

Optimizing for multiple stories. Given a set of unverified stories $\mathcal{S}$ with fact checking intensities $\boldsymbol{u}(t)$, exogenous intensities $\boldsymbol{\lambda}^p(t)$, endogenous intensities $\boldsymbol{\lambda}^e(t)$ and associated counting processes $\boldsymbol{M}(t)$, $\boldsymbol{N}^p(t)$ and $\boldsymbol{N}^e(t)$, we can solve the fact checking scheduling problem defined by Eq. 6 similarly as in the case of a single story. In particular, consider the following quadratic form for the penalty function ϕ and loss function ℓ:

$$\ell(\hat{\boldsymbol{\lambda}}^m(t), \boldsymbol{u}(t)) = \frac{1}{2}\sum_{s\in\mathcal{S}}(\hat{\lambda}_s^m(t))^2 + \frac{1}{2}\sum_{s\in\mathcal{S}} q_s u_s^2(t),$$

where $\{q_s\}_{s\in\mathcal{S}}$ are given parameters, which trade off the number of stories sent for fact checking and the spread of misinformation, and may favor fact checking some stories over others. Then, we can derive the optimal control signal intensity for each story, using the independence assumption between stories, proceeding similarly as in the case of a single story.

THEOREM 3.4. *Given a set of stories $\mathcal{S}$, the optimal fact checking intensity for each story $s \in \mathcal{S}$, which minimizes Eq. 6, under quadratic loss and penalty functions is given by:*

$$u_s^*(t) = q_s^{-\frac{1}{2}}(1 - M_s(t))\Big[p_{m|f=0} + (p_{m|f=1} - p_{m|f=0})\left(\frac{\alpha + N_s^f(t)}{\alpha + \beta + N_s^e(t)}\right)\Big]\lambda_s^e(t). \quad (13)$$

Finally, we can sample the fact checking times for all stories by running $|\mathcal{S}|$ instances of CURB, one per story, and the overall number of required samples is $O(\sum_{s\in\mathcal{S}} N_s^e(t_f))$. Moreover, note that the instances can be run in parallel and thus our algorithm is highly scalable.

4 EXPERIMENTS

In this section, we evaluate our algorithm on data gathered from two social networking sites, Twitter and Weibo, and compare its performance with three baselines via two metrics.

Dataset description and experimental setup. We use data gathered from Twitter and Weibo as reported in previous work [20, 28], which comprises posts and reshares for a variety of (manually annotated) genuine and fake stories[11], respectively.

More specifically, the Twitter dataset contains 192,350 posts and reshares from 117,824 users for 111 unique stories. The Weibo dataset contains 3,752,459 posts and reshares from 2,819,338 users for 4,663 unique stories. We filtered out stories posted or reshared more than 3,000 times as well as stories whose number of posts or reshares taking place after the last decile of the observation period is greater than 1%. Finally, we filtered out fake stories at random until the percentage of fake stories is less than 15%[12].

[11] In the Twitter and the Weibo datasets, stories were fact checked using snopes.com and the Sina community management center, service.account.weibo.com.

[12] We subsample the number of fake stories to resemble a more realistic scenario in which the number of fake stories is *small* in comparison with the total number of stories. We obtained qualitatively similar results without subsampling.

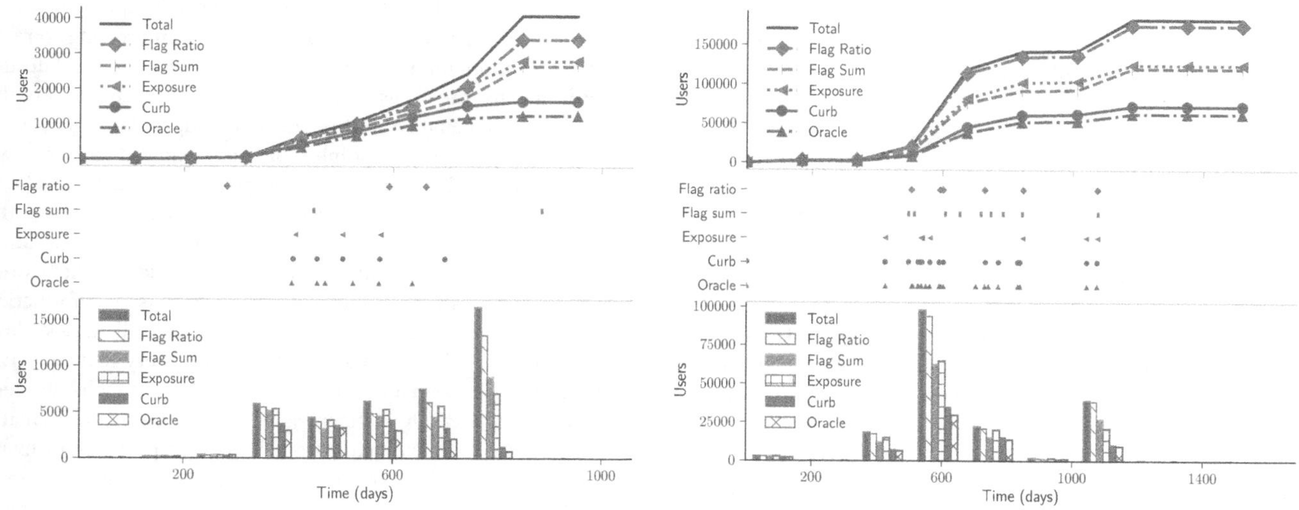

(a) Twitter

(b) Weibo

Figure 2: Misinformation reduction vs. time. For both (a) and (b), the bottom panel shows the number of users exposed to misinformation at each time period, the middle panel shows when different methods send stories for fact checking, and the top panel shows the cumulative number of users. The bars and lines show the different fact checking schedules and "Total" which shows the numbers in absence of fact checking. Both CURB and Oracle are able to prevent the spread of misinformation before it becomes viral, whereas the other baselines cannot do so. The parameters for all methods are set so that the total number of fact-checked stories is 15 ± 4 for Twitter and 64 ± 10 for Weibo.

After these preprocessing steps, our Twitter dataset consists of 28,486 posts and reshares from 18,880 users for 7 fake stories and 39 genuine stories and our Weibo dataset consists of 93,943 posts and reshares from 88,913 users for 23 fake stories and 133 genuine stories. Unfortunately, the datasets do not contain any information about the timing (or number) of exposures nor flags. To remedy the data unavailability, we generate user exposures based on user reshares and sample flags from Bernoulli distributions. We experiment with different parameter settings to ensure that our model's efficacy is robust throughout different settings. The details of the data generation steps are described in the following paragraph.

For each story, we sample exposure events using the exposure intensity defined by Eq. 2, which does depend on the observed posts and reshares. There, we set $\gamma = 10^{-4}$ and $\omega = 10^{-5}$. This choice of parameters results in approximately 10 to 20 exposures per post (or reshare) and a half-life of approximately 19 hours per post (or reshare). Under this setting, our Twitter and Weibo datasets contain 313,357 and 1,054,449 exposures respectively. Unless otherwise stated, for each exposure, we sample flags for fake and genuine stories using two bernoulli distributions with $p_{f=1|m=1} = 0.3$ and $p_{f=1|m=0} = 0.01$, respectively. Moreover, we estimate p_d using the ratio between fake and overall number of stories, compute $p_{m|f=1}$ and $p_{m|f=0}$ from $p_{f=1|m}, p_{f=0|m}$, and p_d, and set $\alpha/(\alpha + \beta) = (p_{f=1|d} + p_{f=0|d})p_d$. Finally, note that we obtained qualitatively similar results for other experimental settings.

Evaluation metrics and baselines. Throughout this section, we evaluate the performance via two metrics: precision and misinformation reduction. Precision is the fraction of fact checked stories that are fake. Misinformation reduction is the fraction of unverified exposures that fact checking prevented.

We compare the performance of CURB against an "Oracle", which is a variant of CURB and has access to the true flag probability p_f, and three baselines. The first baseline ("Flag Ratio") samples the fact checking time for each story using an intensity which is proportional to the ratio between the number of flags and the total number of exposures, *i.e.*, $u_s(t) = q_s(\alpha + N_s^f(t))/(\alpha + \beta + N_s^e(t))$. The second baseline ("Flag Sum") sends a story for fact checking as soon as it accumulates a certain number of flags. The third baseline ("Exposure") samples the fact checking time for each story using an intensity which is proportional to the exposure intensity, *i.e.*, $u_s(t) = q_s\lambda_s^e(t)$. Here, note that the Flag Sum baseline utilizes a deterministic policy while our method, the Oracle and the other baselines use a stochastic policy defined by an intensity function.

Solution quality. We first evaluate the performance of our method, the oracle and the three baselines against the number of fact checking events. Figure 1 summarizes the results, which show that: (i) the more the number of fact checking events, the higher the average misinformation reduction for all methods; and, (ii) Oracle and CURB achieve a comparable performance in both datasets, outperforming the baselines in most cases. Next, we evaluate the performance in terms of misinformation reduction over time in Figure 2. We find that both CURB and the Oracle are able to prevent the spread of

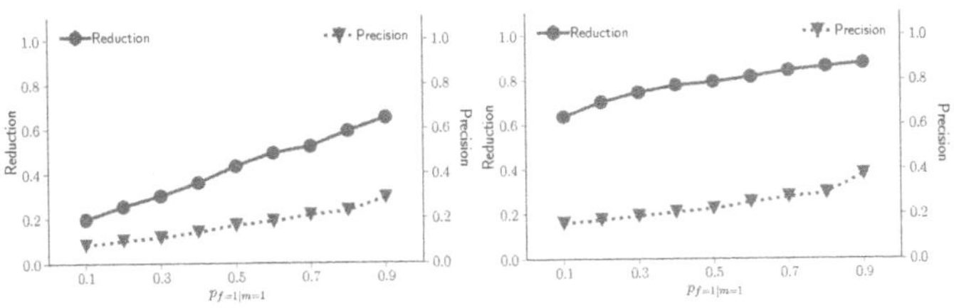

(a) Twitter (b) Weibo

Figure 3: Performance for different true positive rates, $p_{f=1|m=1}$. Here, we set the false positive rate to $p_{f=1|m=0} = 0.01$. The higher the true positive rate, the *better* the crowd is at spotting misinformation and the more effective Curb is. Total number of fact checked stories is 21 ± 2 for Twitter and 90 ± 15 for Weibo.

misinformation before it becomes viral. In contrast, the baselines are unable to spot misinformation that will become viral in time partly due to ignoring either the flags or the exposure dynamics.

Flagging behavior and misinformation evidence. In this section, we first investigate how sensitive our algorithm is to the crowd's flagging behavior and then explore the influence of the hyperparameters α and β on the posterior estimate of the misinformation rate.

Intuitively, the more (less) accurate the crowd is at spotting misinformation, the more (less) effective our algorithm will be. Figure 3 confirms this intuition by showing the performance of our algorithm for different true positive rates, $p_{f=1|m=1}$.

Next, we investigate the influence of the hyperparameter α on the posterior estimate of the misinformation rate $\lambda_s^m(t)$, which the optimal intensity $u^*(t)$ depends on, and the posterior estimate of the flagging probability $\mathbb{E}[f_s|N_s^e(t), N_s^f(t)] = \hat{f}_s$ by examining an example of a genuine and a fake story. Figure 4 summarizes the results, which show that: (i) the higher the value of α, the smaller the effect of individual exposures and flags on the posterior estimate of both the misinformation rate and the flagging probability when a story starts spreading—the lower the variance of the estimates over time; and, (ii) the posterior estimate of the misinformation rate, which the optimal intensity $u^*(t)$ depend on, changes in a more intricate way than the posterior estimate of the flagging probability since it combines the latter with the exposure intensity. This enables our algorithm to be more cautious with viral stories even if the evidence of misinformation is weak.

5 CONCLUSIONS

In this paper, we have introduced an efficient online algorithm, Curb, that leverages the crowd to detect and prevent the spread of fake news and misinformation in online social networking sites. In doing so, we establish an unexplored connection between stochastic online optimal control of SDEs with jumps, survival analysis, and Bayesian inference. We experimented with two real-world datasets gathered from Twitter and Weibo and showed that our algorithm effectively reduces the spread of misinformation, outperforms several competitive baselines and is robust to different user flagging behaviors.

There are many interesting directions for future work. For example, we assumed every person in the crowd is equally good (or bad) at flagging misinformation. It would be interesting to relax this assumption, infer each person's trustworthiness, and design algorithms that are robust to adversarial behavior from part of the crowd. Also, it would be worthwhile to investigate if one's network position affects the susceptibility of being exposed to fake news. For example, a subgroup of biased people may be the main source of misinformation. If that is the case, explicitly incorporating the network structure in the model would be beneficial in mitigating the spread of misinformation. Moreover, we considered that stories are independent and the probability that a story is misinformation given that a user did or did not flag it is equal for all stories. However, stories may be dependent and the probability that a story is misinformation given a user did or did not flag it may be different for stories supported by different sources (or domains) [36]. Finally, our algorithm optimizes a quadratic loss of the posterior estimate of the misinformation rate, however, it would be useful to derive fact checking intensities for other losses capturing more nuanced goals.

APPENDIX

Lemma 5.1. *Let $x(t)$ be a jump-diffusion process defined by the following SDE:*

$$dx(t) = f(x(t),t)dt + g(x(t),t)z(t)dN^e(t) + h(x(t),t)(1 - M(t))dN^p(t) + k(x(t),t)dM(t),$$

where $M(t)$, $N^e(t)$, $N^p(t)$ are independent jump processes, $N_f(t)$ is a jump process whose increment is defined as $dN_f(t) = w(t)dN^e(t)$, $w(t) \in \{0,1\}$, and $z(t) \in \{0,1\}$. If the function $F(M(t), N^e(t), N^f(t), N^p(t), x(t), t)$ is once continuously differentiable in $x(t)$ and t, then,

$$\begin{aligned} &dF(M(t), N(t), N^f(t), N^p(t), x(t), t) \\ &= \Big[F(M, N^e+1, N^f+1, N^p, x+g, t)w(t)z(t) \\ &\quad + F(M, N^e+1, N^f+1, N^p, x, t)w(t)(1-z(t)) \\ &\quad + F(M, N^e+1, N^f, N^p, x+g, t)(1-w(t))(z(t)) \\ &\quad + F(M, N^e+1, N^f, N^p, x, t)(1-w(t))(1-z(t)) \\ &\quad - F(M, N^e, N^f, N^p, x, t)\Big] dN^e(t) \\ &\quad + \Big[F(M, N^e, N^f, N^p+1, x+h, t) \\ &\quad - F(M, N^e, N^f, N^p, x, t)\Big] dN^p(t) \\ &\quad + \Big[F(M+1, N^e, N^f, N^p, x+k, t) \\ &\quad - F(M, N^e, N^f, N^p, x, t)\Big] dM(t) + F_t dt + f F_x dt, \end{aligned}$$

where for notational simplicity we dropped the arguments of the functions f, g, h, k.

Proof Sketch. The differential of J can be found using Ito's calculus [16]. In particular, using that the bilinear forms $dtdN^e(t) = dtdN^p(t) = dtdM(t) = 0$ and $dN^e(t)dM(t) = 0$ and $N^p(t)dM(t) = 0$ by the zero-one jump law.

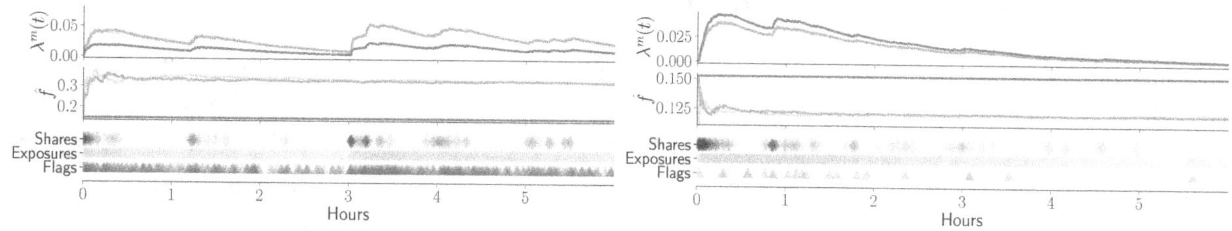

(a) Fake Story (b) Genuine Story

Figure 4: Influence of the hyperparameter α on the posterior estimate of the misinformation rate, which the optimal intensity $u_s^*(t)$ depends on, and the posterior estimate of the flagging probability. In the top and middle panels, darker shades indicate stronger prior. The higher the value of α, the smaller the effect of individual exposures and flags on the posterior estimate of both the misinformation rate and the flagging probability.

REFERENCES

[1] O. Aalen, O. Borgan, and H. K. Gjessing. 2008. *Survival and event history analysis: a process point of view.* Springer.
[2] B. T. Adler and L. De Alfaro. 2007. A content-driven reputation system for the Wikipedia. In *WWW.*
[3] D. P. Bertsekas. 1995. *Dynamic programming and optimal control.* Athena Scientific.
[4] A. Borodin, G. O. Roberts, J. S. Rosenthal, and P. Tsaparas. 2005. Link analysis ranking: algorithms, theory, and experiments. *TOIT* 5, 1 (2005), 231–297.
[5] L. Chen, Z. Yan, W. Zhang, and R. Kantola. 2015. TruSMS: a trustworthy SMS spam control system based on trust management. *Future Generation Computer Systems* 49 (2015), 77–93.
[6] P. Chia and S. Knapskog. 2011. Re-evaluating the wisdom of crowds in assessing web security. In *International Conference on Financial Cryptography and Data Security.*
[7] G. L. Ciampaglia, P. S., L. M. Rocha, J. Bollen, F. Menczer, and A. Flammini. 2015. Computational Fact Checking from Knowledge Networks. *PLOS ONE* 10, 6 (06 2015), 1–13.
[8] A. De, I. Valera, N. Ganguly, S. Bhattacharya, and M. Gomez-Rodriguez. 2016. Learning and Forecasting Opinion Dynamics in Social Networks. In *NIPS.*
[9] X. L. Dong, E. Gabrilovich, G. Heitz, W. Horn, K. Murphy, S. Sun, and W. Zhang. 2014. From data fusion to knowledge fusion. In *VLDB.*
[10] X. L. Dong, E. Gabrilovich, K. Murphy, V. Dang, W. Horn, C. Lugaresi, S. Sun, and W. Zhang. 2015. Knowledge-based trust: Estimating the trustworthiness of web sources. In *VLDB.*
[11] M. Farajtabar, N. Du, M. Gomez-Rodriguez, I. Valera, H. Zha, and L. Song. 2014. Shaping social activity by incentivizing users. In *NIPS.*
[12] D. Freeman. 2017. Can You Spot the Fakes?: On the Limitations of User Feedback in Online Social Networks. In *WWW.*
[13] A. Friggeri, L. Adamic, D. Eckles, and J. Cheng. 2014. Rumor Cascades. In *ICWSM.*
[14] A. Gupta, P. Kumaraguru, C. Castillo, and P. Meier. 2014. Tweetcred: Real-time credibility assessment of content on twitter. In *SocInfo.*
[15] Z. Gyöngyi, H. Garcia-Molina, and J. Pedersen. 2004. Combating web spam with trustrank. In *VLDB.*
[16] F. B. Hanson. 2007. *Applied stochastic processes and control for Jump-diffusions: modeling, analysis, and computation.* Society for Industrial and Applied Mathematics.
[17] N. Hung, D. Thang, M. Weidlich, and K. Aberer. 2015. Minimizing Efforts in Validating Crowd Answers. In *SIGMOD.*
[18] J. F. C. Kingman. 1993. *Poisson processes.* Wiley Online Library.
[19] S. Kumar, R. West, and J. Leskovec. 2016. Disinformation on the web: Impact, characteristics, and detection of wikipedia hoaxes. In *WWW.*
[20] S. Kwon, M. Cha, and K. Jung. 2017. Rumor detection over varying time windows. *PLOS ONE* 12, 1 (2017), e0168344.
[21] P. A. Lewis and G. S. Shedler. 1979. Simulation of nonhomogeneous Poisson processes by thinning. *Naval Research Logistics* 26, 3 (1979), 403–413.
[22] Y. Li, Q. Li, J. Gao, L. Su, B. Zhao, W. Fan, and J. Han. 2015. On the discovery of evolving truth. In *KDD.*
[23] M. Liu, L. Jiang, J. Liu, X. Wang, J. Zhu, and S. Liu. 2017. Improving Learning-from-Crowds through Expert Validation. In *IJCAI.*
[24] X. Liu, X. L. Dong, B. C. Ooi, and D. Srivastava. 2011. Online data fusion. In *VLDB.*
[25] X. Liu, A. Nourbakhsh, Q. Li, R. Fang, and S. Shah. 2015. Real-time rumor debunking on twitter. In *CIKM.*
[26] M. Lukasik, P. K. Srijith, D. Vu, K. Bontcheva, A. Zubiaga, and T. Cohn. 2016. Hawkes processes for continuous time sequence classification: an application to rumour stance classification in twitter. In *ACL.*
[27] C. Lumezanu, N. Feamster, and H. Klein. 2012. # bias: Measuring the tweeting behavior of propagandists. In *ICWSM.*
[28] J. Ma, W. Gao, P. Mitra, S. Kwon, B. Jansen, K. Wong, and M. Cha. 2016. Detecting Rumors from Microblogs with Recurrent Neural Networks. In *IJCAI.*
[29] M. Mendoza, B. Poblete, and C. Castillo. 2010. Twitter Under Crisis: Can we trust what we RT?. In *Workshop on Social Media Analytics.*
[30] T. Moore and R. Clayton. 2008. Evaluating the wisdom of crowds in assessing phishing websites. *Lecture Notes in Computer Science* 5143 (2008), 16–30.
[31] A. Pal, V. Rastogi, A. Machanavajjhala, and P. Bohannon. 2012. Information integration over time in unreliable and uncertain environments. In *WWW.*
[32] J. Pasternack and D. Roth. 2013. Latent credibility analysis. In *WWW.*
[33] V. Qazvinian, E. Rosengren, D. R. Radev, and Q. Mei. 2011. Rumor has it: Identifying misinformation in microblogs. In *EMNLP.*
[34] J. Ratkiewicz, M. Conover, M. Meiss, B. Gonçalves, S. Patil, A. Flammini, and F. Menczer. 2011. Truthy: mapping the spread of astroturf in microblog streams. In *WWW.*
[35] N. Ruchansky, S. Seo, and Y. Liu. 2017. CSI: A Hybrid Deep Model for Fake News Detection. In *CIKM.*
[36] B. Tabibian, I. Valera, M. Farajtabar, L. Song, B. Schoelkopf, and M. Gomez-Rodriguez. 2017. Distilling Information Reliability and Source Trustworthiness from Digital Traces. In *WWW.*
[37] M. Tanushree, G. Wright, and E. Gilbert. 2017. Parsimonious language model of social media credibility across disparate events. In *CSCW.*
[38] S. Volkova, K. Shaffer, J. Y. Jang, and N. Hodas. 2017. Separating facts from fiction: Linguistic models to classify suspicious and trusted news posts on twitter. In *ACL.*
[39] G. Wang, M. Mohanlal, C. Wilson, X. Wang, M. Metzger, H. Zheng, and B. Zhao. 2012. Social Turing Tests: Crowdsourcing Sybil Detection. In *arXiv.*
[40] S. Wang, D. Wang, L. Su, L. Kaplan, and T. F. Abdelzaher. 2014. Towards cyber-physical systems in social spaces: The data reliability challenge. In *RTSS.*
[41] Y. Wang, W. Grady, E. Theodorou, and L. Song. 2017. Variational Policy for Guiding Point Processes. In *ICML.*
[42] Y. Wang, G. Williams, E. Theodorou, and L. Song. 2017. Variational Policy for Guiding Point Processes. In *ICML.*
[43] W. Wei and X. Wan. 2017. Learning to Identify Ambiguous and Misleading News Headlines. In *IJCAI.*
[44] M. Wu and A. Marian. 2007. Corroborating Answers from Multiple Web Sources.. In *WebDB.*
[45] H. Xiao, J. Gao, Q. Li, F. Ma, L. Su, Y Feng., and A. Zhang. 2016. Towards Confidence in the Truth: A Bootstrapping based Truth Discovery Approach. In *KDD.*
[46] X. Yin and W. Tan. 2011. Semi-supervised truth discovery. In *WWW.*
[47] A. Zarezade, A. De, H. Rabiee, and M. Gomez-Rodriguez. 2017. Cheshire: An Online Algorithm for Activity Maximization in Social Networks. In *Allerton Conference.*
[48] A. Zarezade, U. Upadhyay, H. Rabiee, and M. Gomez-Rodriguez. 2017. RedQueen: An Online Algorithm for Smart Broadcasting in Social Networks. In *WSDM.*
[49] B. Zhao and J. Han. 2012. A probabilistic model for estimating real-valued truth from conflicting sources. In *QDB.*
[50] B. Zhao, B. I. Rubinstein, J. Gemmell, and J. Han. 2012. A bayesian approach to discovering truth from conflicting sources for data integration. In *VLDB.*
[51] Z. Zhao, P. Resnick, and Q. Mei. 2015. Enquiring minds: Early detection of rumors in social media from enquiry posts. In *WWW.*
[52] E. Zheleva, A. Kolcz, and L. Getoor. 2008. Trusting spam reporters: A reporter-based reputation system for email filtering. *TOIS* 27, 1 (2008), 3.

REV2: Fraudulent User Prediction in Rating Platforms

Srijan Kumar
Stanford University, USA
srijan@cs.stanford.edu

Bryan Hooi
Carnegie Mellon University, USA
bhooi@cs.cmu.edu

Disha Makhija
Flipkart, India
disha.makhija@flipkart.com

Mohit Kumar
Flipkart, India
k.mohit@flipkart.com

Christos Faloutsos
Carnegie Mellon University, USA
christos@cs.cmu.edu

V.S. Subrahmanian
Dartmouth College, USA
vs@dartmouth.edu

ABSTRACT

Rating platforms enable large-scale collection of user opinion about items (e.g., products or other users). However, fraudulent users give fake ratings for excessive monetary gains. In this paper, we present REV2, a system to identify such fraudulent users. We propose three interdependent intrinsic quality metrics—fairness of a user, reliability of a rating and goodness of a product. The fairness and reliability quantify the trustworthiness of a user and rating, respectively, and goodness quantifies the quality of a product. Intuitively, a user is fair if it provides reliable scores that are close to the goodness of products. We propose six axioms to establish the interdependency between the scores, and then, formulate a mutually recursive definition that satisfies these axioms. We extend the formulation to address cold start problem and incorporate behavior properties. We develop the REV2 algorithm to calculate these intrinsic scores for all users, ratings, and products *by combining network and behavior properties.* We prove that this algorithm is guaranteed to converge and has linear time complexity. By conducting extensive experiments on five rating datasets, we show that REV2 outperforms nine existing algorithms in detecting fraudulent users. We reported the 150 most unfair users in the Flipkart network to their review fraud investigators, and 127 users were identified as being fraudulent (84.6% accuracy). The REV2 algorithm is being deployed at Flipkart.

ACM Reference Format:

Srijan Kumar, Bryan Hooi, Disha Makhija, Mohit Kumar, Christos Faloutsos, and V.S. Subrahmanian. 2018. REV2: Fraudulent User Prediction in Rating Platforms. In *Proceedings of 11th ACM International Conf. on Web Search and Data Mining (WSDM 2018).* ACM, New York, NY, USA, 9 pages. https://doi.org/10.1145/3159652.3159729

1 INTRODUCTION

User generated reviews are an essential part of several online platforms. For instance, users on major online marketplaces (e.g., Flipkart, Amazon, eBay, TripAdvisor, Yelp) rate the quality of products, restaurants, hotels, and other service offerings. Users trading anonymous cryptocurrency, such as Bitcoin, rate others on their trustworthiness. Because users frequently look at these ratings and reviews before buying a product online or choosing whom to trade

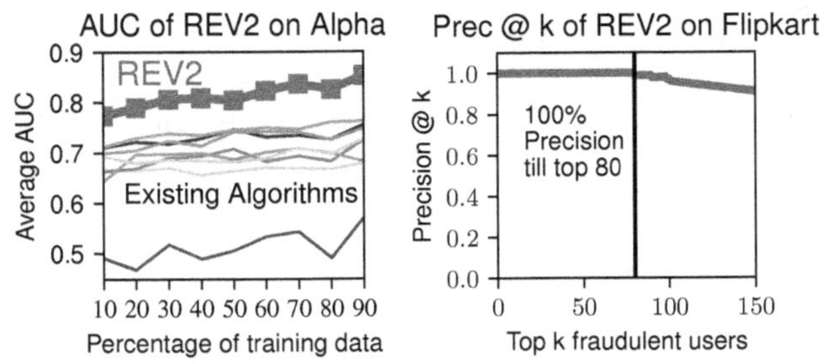

(a) (b)

Figure 1: (a) REV2 consistently performs the best, by having the highest AUC, in predicting fraudulent users with varying percentage of training labels. (b) REV2 is effective in practice, with 127 out of top 150 flagged by REV2 involved in fraud on Flipkart.

Bitcoins with, there is a huge monetary incentive for fraudulent users to give fake ratings [11, 13, 15, 34]. *The goal of this paper is to identify such fraudulent users.* This task is challenging due to the lack of training labels, disbalance in the percentage of fraudulent and non-fraudulent users, and camouflage by fraudulent users [8, 28].

In this paper, we present three metrics to quantify the trustworthiness of users and reviews, and the quality of products. We model user-to-item ratings with timestamps as a directed bipartite graph. For instance, on an online marketplace such as Amazon, a user u rates a product p with a rating (u, p). We propose that each user has an (unknown) intrinsic level of fairness $F(u)$, each product p has an (unknown) intrinsic goodness $G(p)$, and each rating (u, p) has an (unknown) intrinsic reliability $R(u, p)$. Intuitively, a fair user should give ratings that are close in score to the goodness of the product, and good products should get highly positive reliable ratings. Clearly, $F(u), G(p), R(u, p)$ are all inter-related, so we define six intuitive axioms that these intrinsic metrics should satisfy in relation to each other. We propose three mutually-recursive equations which satisfy the axioms to evaluate the values of these metrics.

However, the true trustworthiness of users that have given and true quality of products that have received only a few ratings is not certain [18, 21]. We address this *cold start problem* by adding Laplace smoothing in fairness and goodness formulations to incorporate default priors beliefs.

In addition to the rating network used so far, an entity's behavior properties are very indicative of its true quality. For instance, rapid or regular rating behavior is typical of fraudulent entities like fake accounts, sybils and bots [7, 16, 30, 31]. Similarly, fake ratings have short text [24], and bursty ratings received by a product may be indicative of fake reviews [35]. Therefore, we define an axiom that establishes the relation between the intrinsic scores and their

WSDM 2018, February 5–9, 2018, Marina Del Rey, CA, USA

ACM ISBN 978-1-4503-5581-0/18/02...$15.00
https://doi.org/10.1145/3159652.3159729

behavior properties, and propose a Bayesian technique to incorporate the behavior properites of users, ratings, and products into the formulation by penalizing for unusual behavior [7].

Combining the network, cold start treatment and behavioral properties together, we present the REV2 formulation and an iterative algorithm to find the fairness, goodness and reliability scores of all entities together. REV2 means a system to review to reviewers. REV2 works in both unsupervised, i.e., when no training labels are present, and in supervised settings. We show that REV2 formulation satisfies the six axioms, and the algorithm it is guaranteed to converge, in bounded number of iterations, and has linear time complexity.

How well does REV2 work? We conduct extensive experiments using five real-world data sets—two Bitcoin user trust networks, Epinions, Amazon, and Flipkart dataset, India's biggest online marketplace. By conducting a series of five experiments, we show that REV2 outperforms several existing methods [2, 7, 18, 22–24, 26, 32] in predicting fraudulent users. Specifically, in an unsupervised setting, REV2 has the best average precision in eight out of ten cases and second best in the remaining two, showing its effectiveness even when no training labels are present. In two supervised settings, REV2 has the highest AUC (≥ 0.85) across all five datasets. It consistently performs the best in detecting fraudulent users when percentage of training data is varied between 10 and 90, as shown for the Alpha network in Figure 1(a). Further, we experimentally show that both cold start treatment and behavior properties improve REV2 algorithm's performance.

REV2 is practically very useful as well. We reported the 150 most unfair users as predicted by REV2 in the Flipkart online marketplace. Review fraud investigators at Flipkart studied our recommendations and confirmed that 127 of them were fraudulent *(84.6% accuracy)*, presenting a validation of the utility of REV2 in identifying real-world review fraud. In fact, *REV2 is already being deployed at Flipkart.* Figure 1(b) shows the precision@k of REV2 on Flipkart dataset, showing 100% precision till top 80 unfair users.

Overall, the paper makes the following contributions:

- **Algorithm**: We propose three metrics called fairness, goodness and reliability to rank users, products and ratings, respectively. We propose Bayesian approaches to address cold start problems and incorporate behavioral properties. We propose the REV2 algorithm to iteratively compute these metrics. It works in both unsupervised and supervised settings.
- **Theoretical guarantees**: REV2 is guaranteed to converge in a bounded number of iterations, and has linear time complexity.
- **Effectiveness**: REV2 outperforms nine existing algorithms in identifying fraudulent users, conducted via five experiments on five rating networks, with AUC ≥ 0.85.

Codes of REV2 are available in the appendix [1].

2 RELATED WORK

Existing works in rating fraud detection can be categorized into network-based and behavior-based algorithms:

Network-based fraud detection algorithms are based on iterative learning, belief propagation, and node ranking techniques. Similar to the proposed REV2 algorithm, [17, 22, 32, 33] develop iterative algorithms that jointly assign scores in the rating networks based on consensus of ratings. The closest formulation is that of Wang et al. [32, 33], which also create metrics for users, ratings, and products, but their formulation is different, does not satisfy the axioms (Section 3), and is outperformed by REV2 (Section 5). FraudEagle [2] is a belief propagation model to rank users, which assumes fraudsters rate good products poorly and bad products positively, and vice-versa for honest users. Random-walk based algorithms have been developed to detect trolls [36] and link farming from collusion on Twitter [6]. [10, 17] identify group of fraudsters based on local neighborhood of the users. A survey on network-based fraud detection can be found in [3].

Table 1: Proposed REV2 algorithm satisfies all desirable properties.

	BIRDNEST[7]	Trustiness[32, 33]	BAD[22]	FraudEagle[2]	SpEagle[26]	[18, 23, 24]	REV2
Uses network information	✓	✓	✓	✓	✓		✓
Uses behavior properties	✓				✓	✓	✓
Parameter free	✓		✓			✓	✓
Theoretical Guarantees			✓				✓

Behavioral fraud detection algorithms are often feature-based. Consensus based features have been proposed in [18, 24] – our proposed goodness metric is also inspired by consensus or 'wisdom of crowds'. Commonly used features are derived from timestamps [21, 35, 37] and review text [5, 27, 29]. SpEagle [26] extends FraudEagle [2] to incorporate behavior features. BIRDNEST [7] creates a Bayesian model to estimate the belief of each user's deviation in rating behavior from global expected behavior. [4, 10, 31] study coordinated spam behavior of multiple users. A survey on behavior based algorithms can be found in [11].

The proposed REV2 algorithm combines both network and behavior components together. REV2 has theoretical guarantees of convergence and does not require any user inputs (i.e., it is prior free). Table 1 compares REV2 to the closest existing algorithms, which shows that none of them satisfy all desirable properties.

3 REV2 FORMULATION

We consider directed bipartite rating networks of user-to-product, where each rating is from a user u to an product p. We propose that users and ratings have (unknown) intrinsic scores that quantify how trustworthy they are, and products have (unknown) intrinsic scores that quantify its quality or how a layman is likely to evaluate it. Naturally, these scores are inter-dependent and unknown apriori. In this section, we describe the axioms that establish the inter-dependency between these scores, and propose an algorithm that satisfies the axioms and calculate these scores. The algorithm incorporates network properties, behavior features, and evaluates users with few reviews.

Preliminaries. A bipartite rating graph $G = (U, R, P)$ is a directed, weighted graph, where user $u \in U$ gives a rating $(u, p) \in R$ to product $p \in P$. Let the rating score be represented as $\texttt{score(u,p)}$. Let $\mathcal{U}$, $\mathcal{R}$ and $\mathcal{P}$ represent the set of all users, ratings and products, respectively, in a given bipartite network. We assume that all rating scores are scaled to be between -1 and +1, i.e. $\texttt{score(u,p)} \in [-1, 1] \forall (u, p) \in \mathcal{R}$. Let, $\texttt{Out(u)}$ be the set of ratings given by user u

and In(p) be the set of ratings received by product p. So, |Out(u)| and |In(p)| represents their respective counts. The egonetwork of a user u = Out(u) $\bigcup\{p|(u,p) \in Out(u)\}$ and that of product p = In(p) $\bigcup\{u|(u,p) \in In(p)\}$.

Definition 1 [Identical ratings egonetworks]: Two users u_1 and u_2 are said to have identical ratings egonetworks if $|\texttt{Out}(u_1)| = |\texttt{Out}(u_2)|$ and there exists a one-to-one mapping $h : Out(u_1) \rightarrow Out(u_2)$ such that score(u_1, p) = score(u_2, h(p)) $\forall(u_1,p) \in$ Out(u_1). Similarly, identical ratings egonetworks of two products p_1 and p_2 can be defined in a similar manner using ratings the products receive.

3.1 Intrinsic Properties: Fairness, Goodness and Reliability

We model the bipartite network such that users, ratings and products have (unknown) intrinsic quality scores. User and rating intrinsic scores indicates how trustworthy they are, and product intrinsic scores indicates how likable it is. Their meanings and purpose are explained below:

- Products vary in their quality, measured by a metric called ***goodness***. The goodness score is a single number indicating the most likely rating a fair user would give it. Intuitively, a good product would get several high positive ratings from fair users, and a bad product would receive high negative ratings from fair users. The goodness score $G(p)$ of a product p ranges from -1 (a very low quality product) to $+1$ (a very high quality product) $\forall p \in \mathcal{P}$. The need for incorporating the rating user's fairness arises because simple measures like a product's average or median scores can easily be manipulated by giving ratings using multiple fake accounts [12, 31].
- Users vary in terms of their ***fairness*** that indicates how trustworthy it is. Fair users rate products without bias, i.e., they give high scores to high quality products, and low scores to bad products. On the other hand, users who frequently deviate from the above behavior are 'unfair', e.g., fraudulent users that give high ratings to low quality products and low ratings to good products. Likewise, a 'strict' ('liberal', resp.) user who consistently gives negative (positive, resp.) ratings to high (low, resp.) goodness products is intuitively less fair than a user who gives negative (positive, resp.) ratings to low (high, resp.) goodness products. Fairness score $F(u)$ of a user u lies in the $[0, 1]$ interval $\forall u \in \mathcal{U}$. 0 denotes a 100% untrustworthy user, while 1 denotes a 100% trustworthy user.
- Finally, ratings vary in terms of ***reliability***, which reflects how trustworthy it is. The reliability score $R(u,p)$ of a rating (u,p) ranges from 0 (untrustworthy) to 1 (trustworthy) $\forall$(u,p) $\in \mathcal{R}$.

The reader may wonder: *isn't a rating's reliability identical to its user's fairness?* The answer is 'no'. We need separate intrinsic scores for users and ratings because a user may give ratings with different reliabilities due to their biases and perceptions. In Figure 2 we show the rating reliability distribution, measured by our REV2 algorithm (explained in Section 4), of ground truth benign and fraudulent users in the Flipkart network. Notice that while most ratings by benign users have high reliability, some of their ratings have low reliability, indicating personal opinions which disagrees with majority (see green arrow). Conversely, even fraudulent users give some high reliability ratings (red arrow), possibly to camouflage themselves as benign users. Thus, having reliability as a rating-specific metric allows us to more accurately characterize this distribution.

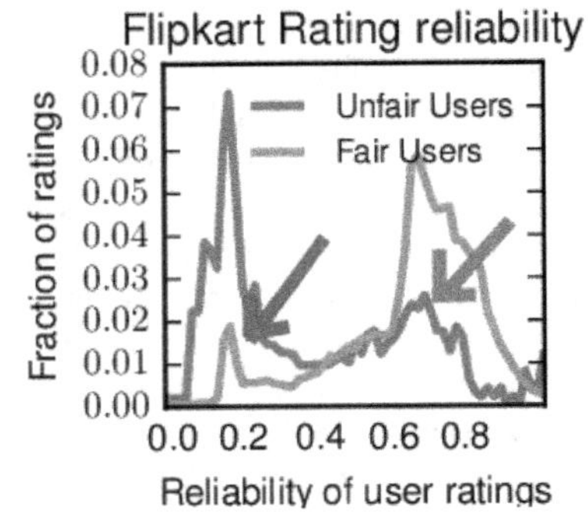

Figure 2: While most ratings by benign users have high reliability, some even have low reliability (green arrow). Conversely, fraudulent users give some highly reliability ratings (red arrow), but most of their ratings have low reliability.

Definition 2 [Identically reliable egonetworks]: We say that, two users u_1 and u_2 are said to have identically reliabile egonetworks if $|\texttt{Out}(u_1)| = |\texttt{Out}(u_2)|$ and there exists a one-to-one mapping $h : Out(u_1) \rightarrow Out(u_2)$ such that reliability(u_1, p) = reliability(u_2, h(p)) $\forall(u_1,p) \in$ Out(u_1). Simiarly, identical ratings egonetworks of two products p_1 and p_2 can be defined in a similar manner by the ratings the products receive.

Given any user-rating-product graph, all intrinsic scores are unknown apriori. Clearly, these scores are mutually interdependent. Here, we describe five intuitive axioms that establish this interdependency. The first two axioms define the relation between a product and the ratings that it receives.

AXIOM 1 (BETTER PRODUCTS GET HIGHER RATINGS). *If two products have identically reliable egonetworks and for one product, all the rating scores are higher, then quality of that product is more. Formally, for two products p_1 and p_2 have a one-to-one mapping $h : In(p_1) \rightarrow In(p_2)$ such that $R(u,p_1) = R(h(u),p_2)$ and* score(u, p_1) $\geq$ score(h(u), p_2) *$\forall(u,p_1) \in In(p_1)$, then $G(p_1) \geq G(p_2)$.*

AXIOM 2 (BETTER PRODUCTS GET MORE RELIABLE POSITIVE RATINGS). *If two products have identical rating egonetworks and for the first product, all positive ratings are more reliable and all negative ratings are less reliable than for the second product, then the first product has higher quality. Formally, if two products p_1 and p_2 have a one-to-one mapping $h : In(p_1) \rightarrow In(p_2)$ such that $R(u,p_1) \geq R(h(u),p_2) \forall(u,p_1) \in In^+(p_1)$ and $R(u,p_1) \leq R(h(u),p_2) \forall(u,p_1) \in In^-(p_1)$, then $G(p_1) \geq G(p_2)$.*

The next two axioms define the relation between a rating and the user and product it belongs to, respectively. The next axiom uses 'wisdom of crowds', by reducing the reliability of rating that deviates from a product's goodness.

AXIOM 3 (RELIABLE RATINGS ARE CLOSER TO GOODNESS SCORES). *For two ratings by equally fair users, the rating with score closer to the product's gooness has higher reliability. Formally, if two ratings (u_1,p_1) and (u_2,p_2) are such that* score(u_1,p_1) = score(u_2,p_2), *$F(u_1) = F(u_2)$, and $|score(u_1,p_1) - G(p_1)| \geq |score(u_2,p_2) - G(p_2)|$, then $R(u_1,p_1) \leq R(u_2,p_2)$.*

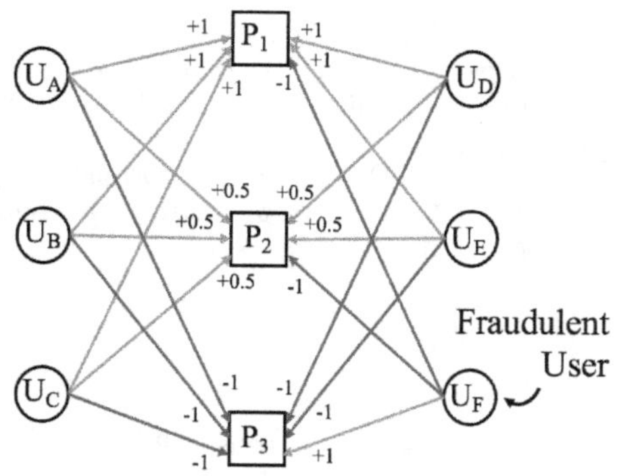

Figure 3: Toy example showing products (P_1, P_2, P_3), users (U_A, U_B, U_C, U_D, U_E and U_F), and rating scores provided by the users to the products. User U_F always disagrees with the ratings of others, so U_F is fraudulent.

One implication of this axiom is that different ratings given by the same user can have different reliability scores.

Axiom 4 (Reliable ratings are given by fairer users). *For two equal ratings to equal goodness products, the one given by more fair user has higher reliability. Formally, if two ratings (u_1, p_1) and (u_2, p_2) are such that* $\texttt{score}(u_1, p_1) = \texttt{score}(u_2, p_2)$, $F(u_1) \geq F(u_2)$, *and* $G(p_1) = G(p_2)$, *then* $R(u_1, p_1) \geq R(u_2, p_2)$.

This axiom incorporates the user's reputation in measuring reliability. This way same ratings received by a product may have different reliability scores.

The next axiom defines the relation between a user and its ratings.

Axiom 5 (Fairer users give more reliable ratings). *For two users with equal number of ratings, if one has higher reliability for all its ratings than the other, then it has higher fairness. Formally, if two users u_1 and u_2 have a one-to-one mapping $h : Out(u_1) \to Out(p_2)$ such that $|Out(u_1)| = |Out(u_2)|$ and $R(u_1, p) \geq R(u_2, h(p))$ $\forall (u_1, p) \in Out(u_1)$, then $F(u_1) \geq F(u_2)$*

Example 3.1 (Running Example). Figure 3 shows a simple example in which there are 3 products, P_1 to P_3, and 6 users, U_A to U_F. Each review is denoted as an edge from a user to a product, with rating score between −1 and +1. Note that this is a rescaled version of the traditional 5-star rating scale where a 1, 2, 3, 4 and 5 star corresponds to −1, −0.5, 0, +0.5 and +1 respectively.

One can immediately see that U_F's ratings are frequently inconsistent with those of U_A, U_B, U_C, U_D and U_E. U_F gives poor ratings to P_1 and P_2 which others all agree are very good by consensus. U_F also gives a high rating for P_3 which others agree is very bad. We will use this example to motivate our formal definitions below.

3.2 Our proposed formulation

Now that we have formally established the interdependencies between the three different metrics, below we propose one formulation that satisfies the axioms. Alternate formulations that satisfy the axioms can be developed as well, which we will explore in future work. Our proposed formulation is below. We will add cold start treatment and behavior properties to it later.

$$F(u) = \frac{\sum_{(\texttt{u,p}) \in \texttt{Out(u)}} R(u,p)}{|\texttt{Out(u)}|} \tag{1}$$

$$G(p) = \frac{\sum_{(\texttt{u,p}) \in \texttt{In(p)}} R(u,p) \cdot \texttt{score(u,p)}}{|\texttt{In(p)}|} \tag{2}$$

$$R(u,p) = \frac{(\gamma_1 \cdot F(u) + \gamma_2 \cdot (1 - \frac{|\texttt{score(u,p)} - G(p)|}{2}))}{\gamma_1 + \gamma_2} \tag{3}$$

Thus, the formulation results in ignoring low reliability ratings and giving more importance to high reliability ones. We show that the above formulation satisfies the axioms in the appendix [1].

In our *running example*, for the rating by user U_F to P_1:

$$R(U_F, P_1) = \frac{1}{2}\left(F(U_F) + (1 - \frac{|-1 - G(P_1)|}{2})\right)$$

Similar equations can be associated with every edge (rating) in the graph of Figure 3.

Addressing Cold Start Problems

In rating networks, most users give and most products receive only a few ratings [23]. For such users and products, there is little information to measure their true quality. For example, a user with few but highly accurate ratings may be a honest user or a fraudster who is camouflaging itself [8]. Conversely, a user with few and highly inaccurate ratings may be a benign novice or a throwaway fraud account [18, 24]. Due to lack of sufficient information, little can be said about their true fairness. The same happens with products that receive a few ratings. This uncertainty due to insufficient information of less active users and products is the *cold start problem.*

We address this cold start issue by adding Laplace smoothing to fairness and goodness scores as follows:

$$F(u) = \frac{\sum_{(u,p) \in \texttt{Out(u)}} R(u,p) + \alpha_1 \cdot \mu_f}{|\texttt{Out(u)}| + \alpha_1}$$

$$G(p) = \frac{\sum_{(u,p) \in \texttt{In(p)}} R(u,p) \cdot \texttt{score(u,p)} + \beta_1 \cdot \mu_g}{|\texttt{In(p)}| + \beta_1}$$

Smoothing parameters α_1 and β_1 are non-negative integer psuedocounts, and μ_f and μ_g are prior beliefs for fairness and goodness scores of new nodes, respectively. The prior is the default score each user and product has if it didn't give or get any ratings. The smoothing parameter sets the relative importance of prior – the lower (higher, resp.) the value of priors, the more (less, resp.) the fairness and goodness scores depend on the network component.

This works because if a user gives only a few ratings, then its fairness score is close to default score μ_f. The more ratings it gives, the more its fairness score moves towards the average of rating reliabilities. This way less active accounts have little impact on product goodness scores, and more importance is given to more active accounts.

The values of α_1, β_1 are set using parameter sweep (Section 4), and μ_f and μ_g are set as the mean scores of all users' fairness and all products' goodness scores, respectively.

Incorporating Behavioral Properties

In the formulation so far, we have solely used the rating graph to calculate the fairness, goodness and reliability values. But, the behavior and characteristics of users, ratings and products are very informative of their qualities as well, which may not be captured by the rating graph alone. For example, as shown in several works [7,

$$F(u) = \frac{\sum_{(u,p)\in \mathtt{Out(u)}} R(u,p) + \alpha_1 \cdot \mu_f + \alpha_2 \cdot \Pi_U(u)}{|\mathtt{Out(u)}| + \alpha_1 + \alpha_2}$$

$$R(u,p) = \frac{\gamma_1 \cdot F(u) + \gamma_2 \cdot (1 - \frac{|\mathtt{score(u,p)} - G(p)|}{2}) + \gamma_3 \cdot \Pi_R(u,p)}{\gamma_1 + \gamma_2 + \gamma_3}$$

$$G(p) = \frac{\sum_{(u,p)\in \mathtt{In(p)}} R(u,p) \cdot \mathtt{score(u,p)} + \beta_1 \cdot \mu_g + \beta_2 \cdot \Pi_P(p)}{|\mathtt{In(p)}| + \beta_1 + \beta_2}$$

Figure 4: The REV2 formulation: this is the set of mutually recursive definitions of fairness, reliability and goodness of the proposed REV2 algorithm. The yellow shaded part addresses the cold start problems and gray shaded part incorporates the behavioral properties.

16, 31], fraudulent users are bursty, i.e., they give several ratings in a very short timespan, or very regular, i.e., they give ratings after fixed intervals. Even though the rating scores themselves may be very accurate, the unusually rapid or regular behavior of the user is suspicious. Therefore, behavioral properties of the ratings that a user gives or a product receives are indicative of their true nature.

Let, $\Pi_U(u)$ represent the behavior 'normality' score of a user u, with respect to some set of behavior properties. Lower (higher, resp.) score indicates more anomalous (normal, resp.) behavior. The following axiom ties the relation between behavior properties and other components:

AXIOM 6. *For two users with identically reliable egonetworks, the one with higher behavior score has higher fairness. Formally, if two users u_1 and u_2 have a one-to-one mapping $h : Out(u_1) \rightarrow Out(p_2)$ such that $|Out(u_1)| = |Out(u_2)|$, $R(u_1, p) = R(u_2, h(p))$ $\forall (u_1, p) \in Out(u_1)$, and $\Pi_U(u_1) \geq \Pi_U(u_2)$, then $F(u_1) \geq F(u_2)$.*

Similar axioms can be defined for ratings and products as well.

Instead of developing our own algorithm to model behavior, we incorporate the state-of-the-art one in our framework. BIRDNEST [7] calculates a Bayesian estimate of how much a user's properties deviates from the global population of all users' properties, and assigns a suspicion score $0 \leq BN_U(u) \leq 1$ to each user u. Then, normality score is simply $\Pi_U(u) = 1 - BN_U(u)$. Normality score for a product $\Pi_P(p)$ and a rating $\Pi_R(u,p)$ are calculated from the properties of all products and all ratings, respectively. In our experiments, we use user's and product's inter-rating times, and a rating's text for calculating this score.

We propose a Bayesian approach to incorporate behavior properties into the formulation so far. We add Laplace smoothing to the network components, where the behavior normality scores are taken as the priors. As opposed to the global priors in cold start treatment, these priors can be different for each user, review and product based on their normality scores. The resulting equations are given in Figure 4. The smoothing parameters α_2, γ_3 and β_2 are non-negative integers.

Overall, the REV2 formulation, represented in Figure 4, is the set of three equations that define the fairness, goodness and reliability scores in terms of each other, by combining rating network and behavior properties together.

Algorithm 1 REV2 Algorithm

1: **Input**: Rating network $(\mathcal{U}, \mathcal{R}, \mathcal{P})$, $\alpha_1, \alpha_2, \beta_1, \beta_2, \gamma_1, \gamma_2, \gamma_3$
2: **Output**: Fairness, Reliability and Goodness scores, given $\alpha_1, \alpha_2, \beta_1, \beta_2, , \gamma_1, \gamma_2, \gamma_3$
3: Calculate $\Pi_U(u) \forall u \in \mathcal{U}$, $\Pi_R(u,p) \forall (u,p) \in \mathcal{R}$, and $\Pi_P(p) \forall p \in \mathcal{P}$.
4: Initialize $F^0(u) = \Pi_U(u)$, $R^0(u,p) = \Pi_R(u,p)$, and $G^0(p) = \Pi_P(p)$, $\forall u \in \mathcal{U}$, $(u,p) \in \mathcal{R}$, $p \in \mathcal{P}$.
5: $t = 0$
6: Initialize $\mu_f = \frac{\sum_{u\in\mathcal{U}} F^t(u)}{|\mathcal{U}|}$, $\mu_g = \frac{\sum_{p\in\mathcal{P}} G^t(p)}{|\mathcal{P}|}$
7: **do**
8: $t = t + 1$
9: Update goodness of products using Equation 4: $\forall p \in \mathcal{P}$, $G^t(p) = \frac{\sum_{(u,p)\in \mathtt{In(p)}} R^{t-1}(u,p).\mathtt{score(u,p)} + \beta_1 \cdot \mu_g + \beta_2 \cdot \Pi_P(p)}{|\mathtt{In(p)}| + \beta_1 + \beta_2}$.
10: Update reliability of ratings using Equation 4: $\forall (u,p) \in \mathcal{R}$, $R^t(u,p) = \frac{\gamma_1 \cdot F^{t-1}(u) + \gamma_2 \cdot (1 - \frac{|\mathtt{score(u,p)} - G^t(p)|}{2}) + \gamma_3 \cdot \Pi_R(u,p)}{\gamma_1 + \gamma_2 + \gamma_3}$.
11: Update fairness of users using Equation 4: $\forall u \in \mathcal{U}$, $F^t(u) = \frac{\sum_{(u,p)\in \mathtt{Out(u)}} R^t(u,p) + \alpha_1 \cdot \mu_f + \alpha_2 \cdot \Pi_U(u)}{|\mathtt{Out(u)}| + \alpha_1 + \alpha_2}$
12: error = $max(\sum_{u\in\mathcal{U}} |F^t(u) - F^{t-1}(u)|$,
13: $\sum_{(u,p)\in\mathcal{R}} |R^t(u,p) - R^{t-1}(u,p)|, \sum_{p\in\mathcal{P}} |G^t(p) - G^{t-1}(p)|)$
14: **while** $error > \epsilon$
15: **Return** $F^t(u)$, $R^t(u,p)$, $G^t(p)$, $\forall u \in \mathcal{U}$, $(u,p) \in \mathcal{R}$, $p \in \mathcal{P}$

4 THE REV2 ALGORITHM

Having formulated the fairness, goodness and reliability metrics in Section 3, we present the REV2 algorithm in Algorithm 1 to calculate the metrics' values for all users, products and ratings. The algorithm is iterative, so let F^t, G^t and R^t denote the fairness, goodness and reliability score at the end of iteration t. Given the rating network and non-negative integers $\alpha_1, \alpha_2, \beta_1, \beta_2, \gamma_1, \gamma_2$ and γ_3, we first initialize all scores using their respective behavior scores Π_U, Π_R, and Π_P. When behavior scores are not present (e.g., when behavior properties are unknown), then these scores are initialized to highest value 1. Then we iteratively update the scores using equations in Figure 4 until convergence (see lines 7–14). Convergence occurs when all scores change minimally (see line 14). ϵ is the acceptable error bound, which is set to a very small value, say 10^{-6}.

But how do we set the values of $\alpha_1, \alpha_2, \beta_1, \beta_2, \gamma_1, \gamma_2$ and γ_3? In an ***unsupervised*** scenario, it is not possible to find the best combination of these values apriori. Therefore, the algorithm is run for several combinations of $\alpha_1, \alpha_2, \beta_1, \beta_2, \gamma_1, \gamma_2$ and γ_3 as inputs, and the final scores of a user across all these runs are averaged to get the final REV2 score of the user. Formally, let C be the set of all parameter combinations $\{\alpha_1, \alpha_2, \beta_1, \beta_2, \gamma_1, \gamma_2, \gamma_3\}$, and $F(u|\alpha_1, \alpha_2, \beta_1, \beta_2, \gamma_1, \gamma_2, \gamma_3)$ be the fairness score of user u after running Algorithm 1 with $\alpha_1, \alpha_2, \beta_1, \beta_2, \gamma_1, \gamma_2, \gamma_3$ as inputs. So the final fairness score of user u is $F(u) = \frac{\sum_{(\alpha_1, \alpha_2, \beta_1, \beta_2, \gamma_1, \gamma_2, \gamma_3)\in C} F(u|\alpha_1, \alpha_2, \beta_1, \beta_2, \gamma_1, \gamma_2, \gamma_3)}{|C|}$. Similarly, $G(p)$ and $R(u,p)$ are calculated. In our experiments, we varied all these parameters from 0 through 2, i.e., $0 \leq \alpha_1, \alpha_2, \beta_1, \beta_2, \gamma_1, \gamma_2, \gamma_3 \leq 2$, giving $3^7 = 2187$ combinations. So, altogether, scores from 2187 different runs were averaged to get the final *unsupervised* REV2 scores. This final score is used for ranking the users.

In a ***supervised*** scenario, it is indeed possible to learn the relative importance of parameters. We represent each user u as a feature vector of its fairness scores across several runs, i.e. $F(u|\alpha_1, \alpha_2, \beta_1, \beta_2, \gamma_1,$

$\gamma_2, \gamma_3), \forall(\alpha_1, \alpha_2, \beta_1, \beta_2, \gamma_1, \gamma_2, \gamma_3) \in C$ are the features for user u. Given a set of fraudulent and benign user labels, a random forest classifier is trained that learns the appropriate weights to be given to each score. The higher the weight, the more important the particular combination of parameter values is. The learned classifier's prediction labels are then used as the *supervised* REV2 output.

Example 4.1 (Running Example). Let us revisit our running example. Let, $\alpha_1 = \alpha_2 = \beta_1 = \beta_2 = \gamma_1 = \gamma_2 = \gamma_3 = 0$. We initialize all fairness, goodness and reliability scores to 1 (line 4 in Algorithm 1). Consider the first iteration of the loop (i.e., when t is set to 1 in line 8). In line 9, we must update the goodness of all products. Let us start with product P_1. Its goodness $G^0(P_1)$ was 1, but this gets updated to

$$G^1(P_1) \quad = \quad \frac{-1(1)+1(1)+1(1)+1(1)+1(1)+1(1)}{6} = 0.67.$$

We see that the goodness of P_1 has dropped because of U_A's poor rating. The following table shows how the fairness and goodness values change over iterations (we omit reliability for brevity):

Node	Property	Fairness/Goodness in iterations				
		0	1	2	5	9 (final)
P_1	$G(P_1)$	1	0.67	0.67	0.67	0.68
P_2	$G(P_2)$	1	0.25	0.28	0.31	0.32
P_3	$G(P_3)$	1	-0.67	-0.67	-0.67	-0.68
U_A–U_E	$F(U_A)$–$F(U_E)$	1	0.92	0.89	0.86	0.86
U_F	$F(U_F)$	1	0.62	0.43	0.24	0.22

By symmetry, nodes U_A to U_E have the same fairness values throughout. After convergence, U_F has low fairness score, while U_A to U_E have close to perfect scores. Confirming our intuition, the algorithm quickly learns that U_F is a fraudulent user as all of its ratings disagree with the rest of the users. Hence, the algorithm then downweighs U_F's ratings in its estimation of the products' goodness, raising the score of P_1 and P_2 as they deserve.

4.1 Theoretical Guarantees of REV2

Here we present the theoretical properties of REV2. Let, $F^\infty(u)$, $G^\infty(p)$ and $R^\infty(u,p)$ be the final scores after convergence, for some input $\alpha_1, \alpha_2, \beta_1, \beta_2, \gamma_1, \gamma_2, \gamma_3$. Proofs are shown in appendix [1] due to lack of space.

LEMMA 4.2 (**LEMMA 1**). *The difference between a product p's final goodness score and its score after the first iteration is at most 1, i.e.* $|G^\infty(p) - G^1(p)| \le 1$. *Similarly,* $|R^\infty(u,p) - R^1(u,p)| \le 3/4$ *and* $|F^\infty(u) - F^1(u)| \le 3/4$.

THEOREM 4.3 (**CONVERGENCE THEOREM**). *The difference during iterations is bounded as* $|R^\infty(u,p) - R^t(u,p)| \le (\frac{3}{4})^t, \forall(u,p) \in \mathcal{R}$. *As t increases, the difference decreases and* $R^t(u,p)$ *converges to* $R^\infty(u,p)$. *Similarly,* $|F^\infty(u) - F^t(u)| \le (\frac{3}{4})^t, \forall u \in \mathcal{U}$ *and* $|G^\infty(p) - G^t(p)| \le (\frac{3}{4})^{(t-1)}, \forall p \in \mathcal{P}$.

As the algorithm converges for all combinations of $\alpha_1, \alpha_2, \beta_1, \beta_2, \gamma_1, \gamma_2, \gamma_3$, the entire algorithm is guaranteed to converge.

COROLLARY 4.4 (**ITERATIONS TILL CONVERGENCE**). *The number of iterations needed to reach convergence is at most* $2 + \lceil \frac{\log(\epsilon/2)}{\log(3/4)} \rceil$. *In other words, treating* ϵ *(acceptable error) as constant, the number of iterations needed to reach convergence is bounded by a constant.*

Thus, the lower the ϵ value, higher the number of iterations till convergence.

Table 2: Five rating datasets used for evaluation.

Network	# Users (% fraudulent, benign)	# Products	# Edges
OTC	4,814 (3.7%, 2.8%)	5,858	35,592
Alpha	3,286 (3.1%, 4.2%)	3,754	24,186
Amazon	256,059 (0.09%, 0.92%)	74,258	560,804
Flipkart	1,100,000 (-, -)	550,000	3,300,000
Epinions	120,486 (0.84%, 7.7%)	132,585	4,835,208

Linear algorithmic time complexity. In each iteration, the algorithm updates goodness, reliability and fairness scores of each product, rating and user, respectively. Each of these updates takes constant time. So, the complexity of each iteration is $O(|E| + |V|) = O(|E|)$. By Corollary 4.4, the algorithm converges in a constant number of iterations. Hence the time complexity is $O(k|E|)$, which is linear in the number of edges, and k is a constant equal to the product of the number of iterations till convergence and the number of runs of the algorithm.

5 EXPERIMENTAL EVALUATION

In this section, we present the results of the REV2 algorithm to identify fraudulent users. We conduct extensive experiments on five different rating networks and show five major results:
(i) We compare REV2 algorithm with five state of the art algorithms to predict fraudulent and benign users in an *unsupervised setting*. We show that REV2 performs the best in eight out of ten cases and second best in the remaining two.
(ii) In a *supervised setting* when training data is present, we show that REV2 outperforms nine algorithms across all datasets.
(iii) We show that REV2 is robust to the percentage of training data available, and consistently performs the best.
(iv) We show that both cold start treatment and behavior properties improve the performance of REV2 algorithm.
(v) We show the linear running time of REV2.

The REV2 algorithm is already being deployed at Flipkart. All codes and datasets (except Flipkart) are in the appendix [1].

5.1 Datasets: Rating Networks

Table 2 shows the properties of the five datasets used. All ratings are rescaled between -1 and +1.

- **Flipkart** is India's biggest online marketplace where users rate products. The ground truth labels are manually verified by review fraud investigators in Flipkart.
- **Bitcoin OTC** is a user-to-user trust network of Bitcoin users trading using OTC platform [14]. The network is made bipartite by splitting each user into a 'rater' with all its outgoing edges and 'product' with all incoming edges. The ground truth is defined as: benign users are the platform's founder and users he rated highly positively (≥ 0.5). Fraudulent users are the ones that these trusted users uniformly rate negatively (≤ -0.5).
- **Bitcoin Alpha** is the Bitcoin trust network of Alpha platform users [14]. Its ground truth is created similar to OTC, starting from the founder of this platform.
- **Epinions** network has two independent components—user-to-post rating network and user-to-user trust network [19]. Algorithms are run on the rating network and ground truth is defined using the separate trust network: a user is defined as benign if its total trust rating is $\geq +10$, and fraudulent if ≤ -10.
- **Amazon** is a user-to-product rating network [20]. Ground truth

Table 3: Unsupervised Predictions: The table shows the Average Precision values of all algorithms in unsupervised prediction of fraudulent and benign users across five datasets. The best algorithm in each column is colored blue and second best is light blue. Overall, REV2 performs the best or second best in 9 of the 10 cases. *nc* indicates 'no convergence'.

	Fraudulent user prediction					Benign user prediction				
	OTC	Alpha	Amazon	Epinions	Flipkart	OTC	Alpha	Amazon	Epinions	Flipkart
FraudEagle	93.67	86.08	47.21	*nc*	*nc*	86.94	71.99	96.88	*nc*	*nc*
BAD	79.75	63.29	55.92	58.31	79.96	77.41	68.31	97.19	97.09	38.07
SpEagle	74.40	68.42	12.16	*nc*	*nc*	80.91	82.23	93.42	*nc*	*nc*
BIRDNEST	61.89	53.46	19.09	37.08	85.71	46.11	77.18	93.32	98.53	62.47
Trustiness	74.11	49.40	40.05	*nc*	*nc*	84.09	78.19	97.33	*nc*	*nc*
REV2	96.30	75.29	64.89	81.56	99.65	92.85	84.85	100.0	99.81	42.83

is defined using helpfulness votes, which is indicative of malicious behavior [5]—users with at least 50 votes are benign if the fraction of helpful-to-total votes is ≥ 0.75, and fraudulent if ≤ 0.25. Experiments on Yelp dataset [26] is not done as it has all reviews for some products but not all reviews by users, leading to a sparse network.

5.2 Baselines

We compare REV2 with nine state-of-the-art unsupervised and supervised algorithms. The **unsupervised** algorithms are:

- *Bias and Deserve (BAD)* [22] assigns a bias score $bias(u)$ to each user u, which measures user's tendency to give high or low ratings. $1 - |bias(u)|$ is the prediction made by BAD.
- *Trustiness* [32, 33] algorithm assigns a trustiness, honesty and reliability score to each user, product and rating, respectively. We use the trustiness score as its prediction.
- *FraudEagle* [2] is a belief propagation based algorithm. Users are ranked according to their fraud score.
- *SpEagle* [26] incorporates behavior features (user, rating text, and product) into FraudEagle, and the final spam scores of users are used for ranking.
- *BIRDNEST* [7] ranks users by creating a Bayesian model with users' timestamp and rating distributions.

We also compare with **supervised** algorithms that need training data:

- *SpEagle+* [26] is a supervised extension of SpEagle that leverages known training labels in the ranking.
- *SpamBehavior* [18]: This technique uses user's average rating deviations as feature.
- *Spamicity* [23] is creates each user's features as its review burstiness and maximum reviews per day.
- *ICWSM'13* [24] uses user's fraction of positive reviews, maximum reviews in a day. and average rating deviation as features.

For fair comparison, all algorithms that use behavior properties, including REV2, are given users' inter-rating time distribuion, ratings' text features (e.g., number of words, LIWC category distribution [25], sentiment [9]), and products' inter-rating time distribution as the properties.

5.3 Experiment 1: Unsupervised Prediction

In this experiment, the task is to rank the users based on how fraudulent they are. We compare *unsupervised* REV2 with the suite of five unsupervised algorithms in terms of their *Average Precision scores*, which measures the relative ordering the algorithm gives to the ground truth fraudulent and benign users. These are calculated for the top and bottom 100 users, and correspond to the area under the precision-recall curve. Table 3 shows the resulting average precision scores on the five datasets.

Table 4: Supervised Predictions: AUC values of 10-fold cross validation to predict fradulent users with individual predictions as features in a Random Forest classifier. REV2 performs the best across all datasets. *nc* means 'no convergence'.

	OTC	Alpha	Amazon	Epinions	Flipkart
FraudEagle	0.89	0.76	0.81	*nc*	*nc*
BAD	0.79	0.68	0.80	0.81	0.64
SpEagle	0.69	0.57	0.63	*nc*	*nc*
BIRDNEST	0.71	0.73	0.56	0.84	0.80
Trustiness	0.82	0.75	0.72	*nc*	*nc*
SpEagle+	0.55	0.66	0.67	*nc*	*nc*
SpamBehavior	0.77	0.69	0.80	0.80	0.60
Spamicity	0.88	0.74	0.60	0.50	0.82
ICWSM'13	0.75	0.71	0.84	0.82	0.82
REV2	0.90	0.88	0.85	0.90	0.87

We see that REV2 algorithm performs the best in 4 out of 5 cases and second best in the remaining one, for identifying both fraudulent and benign users. There is no consistently well performing existing algorithm. Note that FraudEagle, SpEagle and Trustiness are not scalable and do not converge for the two largest networks, Epinions and Flipkart, as opposed to REV2 which is guaranteed to converge. We discuss scalability in Section 5.7.

We also show the precision@k curve for identifying fraudulent users by REV2 on Flipkart network in Figure 1(b). REV2 achieves 100% precision till top 80. The other networks have similar precision@k curve, shown in appendix [1]. Among the top 150 unfair users identified by REV2, Flipkart fraud investigators confirmed total of 127 as fraudulent (84.6% accuracy).

5.4 Experiment 2: Supervised Prediction

In this experiment, the task is to predict the fraudulent and benign users, given some labels from both categories. The performance is measured using *area under the ROC curve (AUC)* which is a standard measures when data is imbalanced, as is our case. For each algorithm, a feature vector is created for each user and used to train a binary classifier. As a reminder from Section 4, for each user u, supervised REV2 creates a 2187 dimensional feature vector of its fairness scores $F(u|\alpha_1, \alpha_2, \beta_1, \beta_2, \gamma_1, \gamma_2, \gamma_3)$, one for each of the 2187 combinations of $\alpha_1, \alpha_2, \beta_1, \beta_2, \gamma_1, \gamma_2, \gamma_3 \in [0, 2]$. For fair comparison, baselines are compared by using their scores as features as well. For FraudEagle, BAD, SpEagle, SpEagle+, BIRDNEST and Trustiness, the feature vector for user u is the score the baseline

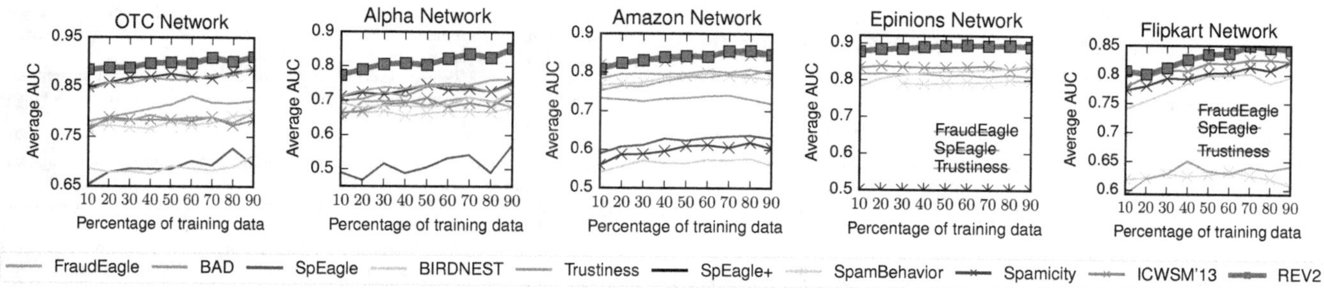

Figure 5: Variation of AUC for fraudulent user prediction with percentage of training data available for supervision. REV2 consistently performs the best across all settings, and its performance is robust to the training percentage.

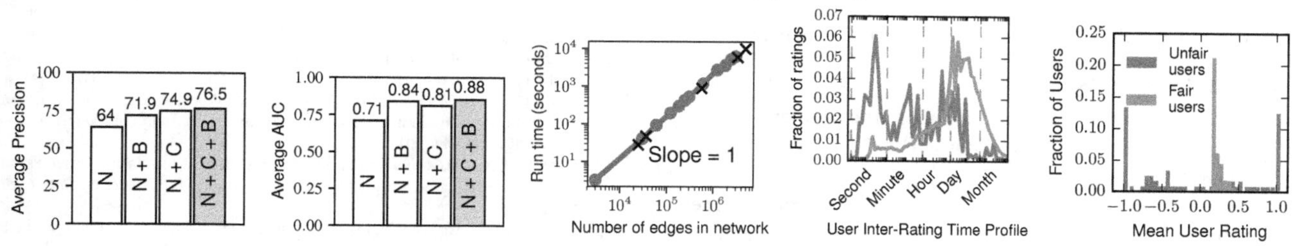

(a) Unsupervised REV2 (b) Supervised REV2 (c) Scalability of REV2 (d) (e)

Figure 6: (a-b) Change in performance of REV2 on Alpha network in (a) unsupervised and (b) supervised experiments when different components are used: network (N), cold start treatment (C) and behavioral (B). (c) REV2 scales linearly—the running time increases linearly with the number of edges. (d-e) Fraudulent users identified by REV2 in the OTC network are (d) faster in rating, and (e) give extreme ratings.

gives to u and u's outdegree. For baselines SpamBehavior, Spamicity and ICWSM'13, the feature vector for user u is their respective features explained in Section 5.2.

We perform stratified 10-fold cross-validation using random forest classifier. The resulting AUCs are reported in Table 4. We see that REV2 outperforms all existing algorithms across all datasets and consistently has an AUC ≥ 0.85.

5.5 Experiment 3: Robustness of REV2

In this experiment, we evaluate the performance of the algorithms as the percentage of training data changes. We vary the training data from 10% to 90% in steps of 10. Figure 5 shows the average AUC on test sets, averaged over 50 random iterations of training data. We make two observations. First, REV2 is robust to the amount of training data. Its performance is relatively stable (AUC ≥ 0.80 in almost all cases) as the amount of training data varies. Second, REV2 outperforms other algorithms consistently across all datasets for almost all training percentages. Together, these two show the efficiency of supervised REV2 algorithm even when a small amount of training data is available.

5.6 Experiment 4: Importance of Network, Cold Start and Behavior

In this experiment, we show the importance of the different components in the REV2 algorithm—network (given by equations 1, 2 and 3; shown as N), cold start treatment (C), and behavioral properties (B). Figure 6(a) shows the average precision in unsupervised case for the Alpha dataset, when network property is combined with the other two components, and Figure 6(b) shows the average AUC of 10-fold cross validation in the supervised case. In both cases, network properties alone has the lowest performance. Adding either the cold start treatment component or the behavioral property component to it increases this performance. To combine network properties with behavioral property component only, the cold start property is removed by setting $\alpha_2 = \beta_2 = \gamma_3 = 0$ in the REV2 algorithm. Likewise, α_1 and β_1 are set to 0 to combine with cold start treatment alone. Further, combining all three together gives the best performance. Similar observations hold for the other datasets as well, as shown in the appendix [1]. This shows that all three components are important for predicting fraudulent users.

5.7 Experiment 5: Linear scalability

We have theoretically proven in Section 4.1 that REV2 is linear in running time in the number of edges. To show this experimentally as well, we create random networks of increasing number of nodes and edges and compute the running time of the algorithm till convergence. Figure 6(c) shows that the running time increases linearly with the number of edges in the network, which shows that REV2 algorithm is indeed scalable to large size networks for practical use. The figure also shows the running time of REV2 on real networks, marked as 'x'.

5.8 Discoveries

In this part, we look at some insights and discoveries about fraudulent users found by REV2.

As seen previously in Figure 2, most ratings given by fraudulent users have low reliability, while some have high reliability, indicating camouflage to masquerade as benign users. At the same time, most ratings by benign users have high reliability, but some ratings have low reliability, indicating biases and personal opinion about products that disagrees with the 'consensus'.

We also observe in Figure 6(d-e) that fraudulent users in OTC network: (d) give ratings in quick succession of less than a few minutes, and (e) exhibit bimodal rating pattern: they either give all

-1.0 ratings (possibly, bad-mouthing a competitor) or all +1.0 ratings (possibly, over-selling their products/friends). As an example, the most fraudulent user found by REV2 had 3500 ratings, all with +0.5 score, and almost all given 15 seconds apart (apparently, a bot). On the other hand, benign users have a day to a month between consecutive ratings, and they give mildly positive ratings (between 0.1 and 0.5). These observations are coherent with existing research [16].

In summary, fraudulent users detected by REV2 exhibit strange characteristics with respect to their behavior:

- They have bimodal rating pattern—they give too low (bad-mouthing) or too high (over-selling) ratings.
- They are less active, have no daily periodicity, and post quickly, often less than a few minutes apart.
- They camouflage their behavior to masquerade as benign users.

6 CONCLUSIONS

We presented the REV2 algorithm to address the problem of identifying fraudulent users in rating networks. This paper has the following contributions:

- **Algorithm**: We defined three mutually-recursive metrics—fairness of users, goodness of products and reliability of ratings. We incorporated behavioral properties of users, ratings, and products in these metrics, and extended it to address cold start problem. We proposed the REV2 algorithm to iteratively compute the values of these metrics.
- **Theoretical guarantees**: We proved that REV2 algorithm has linear time complexity and is guaranteed to converge in a bounded number of iterations.
- **Effectiveness**: By conducting five experiments, we showed that REV2 outperforms nine existing algorithms to predict fraudulent users. In unsupervised experiment, REV2 is the best in 8 out of 10 cases and second best in the other two. In supervised experiment, REV2 performs the best with AUC $\geq$ 0.85. REV2 is practically useful, and already being deployed at Flipkart.

ACKNOWLEDGMENTS

Parts of this research is supported by the ARO Grant W911NF1610342, National Science Foundation Grants CNS-1314632, IIS-1408924, and Army Research Laboratory Cooperative Agreement Number W911NF-09-2-0053.

Any opinions, findings, and conclusions or recommendations expressed in this material are those of the author(s) and do not necessarily reflect the views of the National Science Foundation, or other funding parties. The U.S. Government is authorized to reproduce and distribute reprints for Government purposes notwithstanding any copyright notation here on.

REFERENCES

[1] Rev2 online appendix. https://cs.stanford.edu/~srijan/rev2/.
[2] L. Akoglu, R. Chandy, and C. Faloutsos. Opinion fraud detection in online reviews by network effects. In *International Conference on Web and Social Media*, 2013.
[3] L. Akoglu, H. Tong, and D. Koutra. Graph based anomaly detection and description: a survey. *ACM Transactions on Knowledge Discovery from Data*, 2015.
[4] C. Chen, K. Wu, V. Srinivasan, and X. Zhang. Battling the internet water army: Detection of hidden paid posters. In *International Conference on Advances in Social Networks Analysis and Mining*, 2013.
[5] A. Fayazi, K. Lee, J. Caverlee, and A. Squicciarini. Uncovering crowdsourced manipulation of online reviews. In *Special Interest Group on Information Retrieval*, 2015.
[6] S. Ghosh, B. Viswanath, F. Kooti, N. K. Sharma, G. Korlam, F. Benevenuto, N. Ganguly, and K. P. Gummadi. Understanding and combating link farming in the twitter social network. In *International Conference on World Wide Web*, 2012.
[7] B. Hooi, N. Shah, A. Beutel, S. Gunneman, L. Akoglu, M. Kumar, D. Makhija, and C. Faloutsos. Birdnest: Bayesian inference for ratings-fraud detection. In *SIAM International Conference on Data Mining*, 2016.
[8] B. Hooi, H. A. Song, A. Beutel, N. Shah, K. Shin, and C. Faloutsos. Fraudar: Bounding graph fraud in the face of camouflage. In *ACM International conference on Knowledge Discovery and Data Mining*, 2016.
[9] C. J. Hutto and E. Gilbert. Vader: A parsimonious rule-based model for sentiment analysis of social media text. In *Eighth international AAAI conference on weblogs and social media*, 2014.
[10] M. Jiang, P. Cui, A. Beutel, C. Faloutsos, and S. Yang. Catchsync: catching synchronized behavior in large directed graphs. In *ACM International Conference on Knowledge Discovery and Data Mining*, 2014.
[11] M. Jiang, P. Cui, and C. Faloutsos. Suspicious behavior detection: Current trends and future directions. *IEEE Intelligent Systems*, 31(1):31–39, 2016.
[12] S. Kumar, J. Cheng, J. Leskovec, and V. Subrahmanian. An army of me: Sockpuppets in online discussion communities. In *International Conference on World Wide Web*, 2017.
[13] S. Kumar and N. Shah. False information on web and social media: A survey. In *Social Media Analytics: Advances and Applications*. CRC, 2018.
[14] S. Kumar, F. Spezzano, V. Subrahmanian, and C. Faloutsos. Edge weight prediction in weighted signed networks. In *IEEE 16th International Conference on Data Mining*, 2016.
[15] T. Lappas, G. Sabnis, and G. Valkanas. The impact of fake reviews on online visibility: A vulnerability assessment of the hotel industry. *INFORMS*, 27(4), 2016.
[16] H. Li, G. Fei, S. Wang, B. Liu, W. Shao, A. Mukherjee, and J. Shao. Bimodal distribution and co-bursting in review spam detection. In *International Conference on World Wide Web*, 2017.
[17] R.-H. Li, J. Xu Yu, X. Huang, and H. Cheng. Robust reputation-based ranking on bipartite rating networks. In *SIAM International Conference on Data Mining*, 2012.
[18] E.-P. Lim, V.-A. Nguyen, N. Jindal, B. Liu, and H. W. Lauw. Detecting product review spammers using rating behaviors. In *International Conference on Information and Knowledge Management*, 2010.
[19] P. Massa and P. Avesani. Trust-aware recommender systems. In *ACM Conference on Recommender Systems*, 2007.
[20] J. J. McAuley and J. Leskovec. From amateurs to connoisseurs: modeling the evolution of user expertise through online reviews. In *International Conference on World Wide Web*, 2013.
[21] A. J. Minnich, N. Chavoshi, A. Mueen, S. Luan, and M. Faloutsos. Trueview: Harnessing the power of multiple review sites. In *International Conference on World Wide Web*, 2015.
[22] A. Mishra and A. Bhattacharya. Finding the bias and prestige of nodes in networks based on trust scores. In *International World Wide Web conference*, 2011.
[23] A. Mukherjee, A. Kumar, B. Liu, J. Wang, M. Hsu, M. Castellanos, and R. Ghosh. Spotting opinion spammers using behavioral footprints. In *ACM International conference on Knowledge Discovery and Data Mining*, 2013.
[24] A. Mukherjee, V. Venkataraman, B. Liu, and N. S. Glance. What yelp fake review filter might be doing? In *International Conference on Web and Social Media*, 2013.
[25] J. W. Pennebaker, M. E. Francis, and R. J. Booth. Linguistic inquiry and word count: Liwc 2001. *Mahway: Lawrence Erlbaum Associates*, 71(2001):2001, 2001.
[26] S. Rayana and L. Akoglu. Collective opinion spam detection: Bridging review networks and metadata. In *ACM International conference on Knowledge Discovery and Data Mining*, 2015.
[27] V. Sandulescu and M. Ester. Detecting singleton review spammers using semantic similarity. In *International Conference on World Wide Web*, 2015.
[28] V. Subrahmanian and S. Kumar. Predicting human behavior: The next frontiers. *Science*, 355(6324):489–489, 2017.
[29] H. Sun, A. Morales, and X. Yan. Synthetic review spamming and defense. In *ACM International conference on Knowledge Discovery and Data Mining*, 2013.
[30] B. Viswanath, M. A. Bashir, M. Crovella, S. Guha, K. P. Gummadi, B. Krishnamurthy, and A. Mislove. Towards detecting anomalous user behavior in online social networks. In *USENIX Security*, 2014.
[31] B. Viswanath, M. A. Bashir, M. B. Zafar, S. Bouget, S. Guha, K. P. Gummadi, A. Kate, and A. Mislove. Strength in numbers: Robust tamper detection in crowd computations. In *Conference on Online Social Networks*, 2015.
[32] G. Wang, S. Xie, B. Liu, and S. Y. Philip. Review graph based online store review spammer detection. In *IEEE International Conference on Data Mining series*, 2011.
[33] G. Wang, S. Xie, B. Liu, and P. S. Yu. Identify online store review spammers via social review graph. *ACM Transactions on Intelligent Systems and Technology*, 3(4):61, 2012.
[34] J. Wang, A. Ghose, and P. Ipeirotis. Bonus, disclosure, and choice: what motivates the creation of high-quality paid reviews? In *International Conference on Information Systems*, 2012.
[35] G. Wu, D. Greene, and P. Cunningham. Merging multiple criteria to identify suspicious reviews. In *ACM Conference on Recommender Systems*, 2010.
[36] Z. Wu, C. C. Aggarwal, and J. Sun. The troll-trust model for ranking in signed networks. In *ACM International Conference on Web Search and Data Mining*, 2016.
[37] S. Xie, G. Wang, S. Lin, and P. S. Yu. Review spam detection via temporal pattern discovery. In *ACM International Conference on Knowledge Discovery and Data Mining*, 2012.

Web Search of Fashion Items with Multimodal Querying

Katrien Laenen
KU Leuven
Human Computer Interaction
Heverlee, Belgium
katrien.laenen@kuleuven.be

Susana Zoghbi
KU Leuven
Human Computer Interaction
Heverlee, Belgium
susana.zoghbi@kuleuven.be

Marie-Francine Moens
KU Leuven
Human Computer Interaction
Heverlee, Belgium
sien.moens@kuleuven.be

ABSTRACT

In this paper, we introduce a novel multimodal fashion search paradigm where e-commerce data is searched with a multimodal query composed of both an image and text. In this setting, the query image shows a fashion product that the user likes and the query text allows to change certain product attributes to fit the product to the user's desire. Multimodal search gives users the means to clearly express what they are looking for. This is in contrast to current e-commerce search mechanisms, which are cumbersome and often fail to grasp the customer's needs. Multimodal search requires intermodal representations of visual and textual fashion attributes which can be mixed and matched to form the user's desired product, and which have a mechanism to indicate when a visual and textual fashion attribute represent the same concept. With a neural network, we induce a common, multimodal space for visual and textual fashion attributes where their inner product measures their semantic similarity. We build a multimodal retrieval model which operates on the obtained intermodal representations and which ranks images based on their relevance to a multimodal query. We demonstrate that our model is able to retrieve images that both exhibit the necessary query image attributes and satisfy the query texts. Moreover, we show that our model substantially outperforms two state-of-the-art retrieval models adapted to multimodal fashion search.

ACM Reference format:
Katrien Laenen, Susana Zoghbi, and Marie-Francine Moens. 2018. Web Search of Fashion Items with Multimodal Querying. In *Proceedings of WSDM 2018: The Eleventh ACM International Conference on Web Search and Data Mining, Marina Del Rey, CA, USA, February 5–9, 2018 (WSDM 2018),* 9 pages.
https://doi.org/10.1145/3159652.3159716

1 INTRODUCTION

Today's consumers have become very exigent. When shopping online, they have in mind a specific clothing item in a particular color and style, and they want to find it without too much effort. However, current e-commerce search mechanisms are often too limited to provide this kind of service. A common way for searching products in a webshop is to navigate through a product category hierarchy. Users end up in a subcategory which they need to search completely, which is time-consuming. They need to go through many irrelevant products, without the guarantee of actually finding the product they are looking for. To narrow down the search, users can sometimes select certain filters. However, desired product attributes might not be amongst the available filters. With a text-based search approach, users can describe the desired product by entering keywords into a search bar. The webshop then finds relevant products by matching these keywords to the words in the product descriptions. It is often difficult for users to write the right keywords that will induce the search engine to provide the products they are interested in. For example, some users might be interested in "jeans with holes", but the relevant products are described as "distressed jeans". Additionally, this approach hampers the search for product attributes which are not mentioned in the product descriptions. Alternatively but rarely, webshops offer image-based search where the user uploads an image of the desired product and receives visually similar products. Recently, there is an increasing interest of users in this kind of image-based search. One of the main reasons is the growing usage of visual social media such as Pinterest and Instagram, where users see products they want to buy. Using an image as a query allows users to convey much more information about the desired product than with a textual query. Additionally, another advantage of image-based search over text-based search is that the language of images is universal. However, the user might be interested in changing or adding attributes to the product in the query image to obtain very specific results. For example, for an image of a red dress, the user likes the sleeve length to be different.

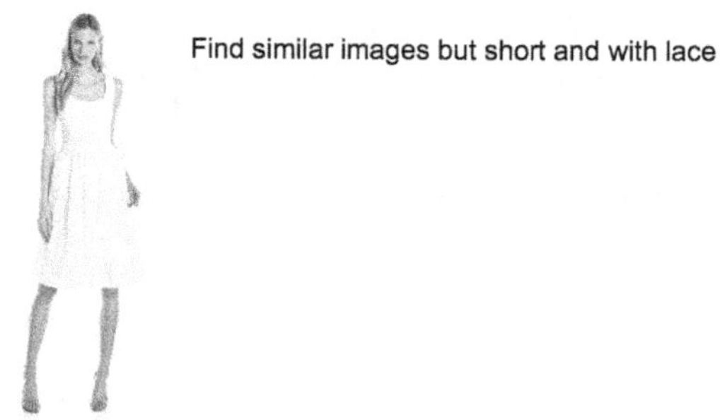

Figure 1: Example of a multimodal query [1]. It consists of a query image and a query text that alters the query image. The query text mentions two fashion attributes: short and lace. The query image is knee length and does not have a lace type appearance.

[1]Image material adapted from www.amazon.com

WSDM 2018, February 5–9, 2018, Marina Del Rey, CA, USA

ACM ISBN 978-1-4503-5581-0/18/02...$15.00
https://doi.org/10.1145/3159652.3159716

Currently, it is not possible to search for products using both an image and text, where the text is used to narrow down the search with fine-grained attributes.

We propose multimodal search where a query is composed of both an image and a text that modifies the image or adds attributes to it (Figure 1). Relevant images are those which are similar to the query image, but with the attributes that the query text changed or added. Since multimodal search allows users to search with images and uses text as a mechanism to easily manipulate image properties, it is likely to become a very popular search method. To answer a multimodal query, it should be possible to identify the fashion attributes in the query image and text to ensure the retrieval of images in which these attributes are exhibited. Hence, multimodal search requires fine-grained segmentation methods for fashion images and product descriptions, and a mechanism to determine when a visual and textual fashion attribute represent the same concept. For example, for the multimodal query in Figure 1, we need to identify the attributes of the query image, i.e., the kind of neckline, sleeve length, style, etc., and a way to know if a candidate image also displays the attributes requested by the query text, i.e., if it is short and contains lace.

In this paper, we will consider the product category of dresses. We segment fashion images and texts into image regions and phrases showing respectively visual and textual fashion attributes. We learn intermodal representations for these visual and textual attributes which capture their semantic similarity. With a neural network, we infer a common, multimodal space where a fashion image region and phrase have a large inner product if they represent the same fashion attribute. Then, we develop a multimodal retrieval model which operates on the obtained intermodal representations. Note that although this work focuses on the fashion domain, the proposed techniques are valuable for processing other product data as well (e.g., furniture, toys or food) where data consists of pairs of images and texts, with texts that describe product properties which are either shown in the corresponding image or can be inferred from it.

The contributions of our work are:

- We introduce a new search paradigm for e-commerce product retrieval constituting an improved shopping experience.
- Our model provides a mechanism to reason with both images and language, i.e., we can query a target collection using a combination of an image and text as query. The text can be used to modify specific attributes in the image, providing more fine-grained and relevant results.
- We largely improve the results of two state-of-the-art retrieval models adapted to multimodal search.
- We provide an analysis of the neural network based alignment model trained in Laenen et al. [12] to align fashion attributes in images and their textual descriptions.

The remainder of this paper is structured as follows. In Section 2 we review existing work related to the subject. Section 3 provides a detailed description of our model architecture. Section 4 describes the experiments conducted in this work. Next, the results of these experiments are presented in Section 5. Finally, section 6 gives the final conclusions and directions for future work.

2 RELATED WORK

Image search aims to retrieve relevant images to a textual or visual query. In [18], Zoghbi et al. experiment with canonical correlation analysis (CCA) and bilingual latent Dirichlet allocation (BiLDA) to realize cross-modal fashion search from a textual query to images and from an image query to text. In [12], cross-modal search of fashion items is achieved with intermodal representations for visual and textual fashion attributes inferred with a neural network alignment model. It is a short workshop paper which discusses initial experiments by the authors of this paper and which explains the objective functions used to infer the latent alignment of the visual and textual fashion attributes. Meanwhile, this work explores the capabilities of the inferred intermodal representations in a multimodal search instead of a cross-modal search setting, proposes a retrieval model for multimodal search, and reveals more details about the neural network alignment model. Opposed to textual queries, visual queries capture rich information about desired product properties. Recently, with the rise of deep convolutional neural networks, image search with visual queries or content-based image retrieval (CBIR) has attracted a lot of interest. Several systems have been developed that, given an image as a query, return products in webshops which are similar or identical to the product in the provided image [1, 7, 9, 11, 16]. In contrast to our work, these systems do not allow users to add text to change certain product properties.

Multimodal search with queries composed of an image and a text is a novel search paradigm which up until now has received little attention in the literature. In [17], an attribute manipulation network is developed which learns to construct the visual representation of the desired fashion item by properly manipulating the visual representation of the multimodal query image with the textual attributes in the multimodal query text, and retrieves images with representations similar to the constructed visual representation. In contrast, we use a neural network to infer the semantic relationship between visual and textual attributes in a joint embedding space, and propose a multimodal retrieval model which ranks images based on their semantic similarity to the query text and their visual similarity to the query image. In [6], fashion images and their corresponding product descriptions are jointly modeled in a multimodal embedding space. Then, spatial-semantic representations are derived for all fashion attributes and used to cluster the attributes (e.g., V-neck) into attribute types (e.g., neckline). Finally, the multimodal embedding space is decomposed into multiple subspaces, one for each attribute type. These subspaces are used to facilitate so-called attribute-feedback product retrieval, where a multimodal query consists of an image and a text denoting a single attribute to either add to or change in the query image, and the retrieval model is based on adding and subtracting spatial-semantic representations of attributes. In contrast, we infer only one multimodal embedding space which uncovers the latent alignment on the attribute level, where the resulting intermodal representations are used in a multimodal search paradigm that allows multimodal query texts which simultaneously change and add multiple query image attributes. In [4], multimodal queries are introduced in category-swap image-based retrieval using only three general object categories that can modify the query and exploring a retrieval model that is inspired by [13]. In [13], semantic inference is performed by adding and subtracting word embeddings. In this work, we will do the same with intermodal representations of fashion attributes in one of our multimodal search baselines.

Beyond product search, multimodal approaches have also become more popular due to the abundance of multimodal data and the recent advances in deep learning to process visual and language data. More precisely, several systems have been developed for image-text alignment where image descriptions are generated with a recurrent neural network (RNN) [3, 10, 14, 15]. In this work, our interest lies not in the generation of image annotations, but in the alignment of attributes in visual and language data, which is essential for the multimodal retrieval model.

3 METHODOLOGY

In multimodal search, a query consists of an image of a product together with text to alter or add certain product attributes. The fashion domain presents large variations of fine-grained fashion attributes: colors, shapes, patterns, textures, etc. We learn intermodal representations for these fashion attributes in images and texts, which reflect their semantic similarity.

First, we describe how we segment fashion images and product descriptions into fragments showing respectively the visual and textual fashion attributes. Next, we discuss the neural network and objective function used to obtain intermodal representations for fashion attributes. Finally, we elaborate on how multimodal search is achieved with the acquired intermodal representations.

3.1 Visual and Textual Attribute Detection

E-commerce product descriptions tend to be noisy and incomplete. To acquire the textual fashion attributes, we follow the approach of Zoghbi et al. [18] and filter the product descriptions with the glossary of the online clothing shop Zappos [2]. This process only retains fashion-related phrases and removes most noise. However, remaining phrases can still describe properties of the dress which are not displayed, e.g., all possible colors. After filtering, the remaining Zappos phrases are considered as the textual fashion attributes and form the text fragments. The text fragments are represented with word embeddings [13] trained on the Amazon Dresses dataset.

E-commerce images display clothing items straight, clearly and completely on white backgrounds, sometimes worn by a model. This tells us the approximate location of each part of a clothing item and thus of each visual fashion attribute. We implement the dress segmentation method of Laenen et al. [12] which exploits this fact to generate 7 image fragments corresponding to dress regions where visual fashion attributes are likely to be found. These 7 image fragments show respectively the full dress, the top, the full skirt, the part of the skirt above the knee, the neckline, the left sleeve and the right sleeve. The image fragments are represented with the BVLC CaffeNet CNN Model [8]. Their representations are acquired as the activation weights of the last fully connected layer before the softmax layer, which have dimension 4096 in the CNN architecture.

[2]http://www.zappos.com

3.2 Common Embedding Space for Visual and Textual Attributes

With the current image and text fragment representations, we have no way of knowing when they correspond to the same fashion attribute. Therefore, we use a neural network to induce a common, multimodal space where the inner product of an image fragment and text fragment measures their semantic similarity. A positive inner product indicates that they represent the same fashion attribute. When their inner product is negative, they are considered different. The neural network learns parameters $\theta = \{W_v, b_v, W_s, b_s\}$ to project an image fragment $\hat{v}_i$ and text fragment $\hat{s}_j$ to their intermodal representations v_i and s_j in the common, multimodal space:

$$v_i = W_v \hat{v}_i + b_v \tag{1}$$

$$s_j = f(W_s \hat{s}_j + b_s). \tag{2}$$

Activation function f is set to the rectified linear unit (ReLU) which computes $f(x) = \max(0, x)$. W_v has dimensions $h \times 4096$ and W_s has dimensions $h \times dim$, where h is the size of the common, multimodal space and dim is the dimension of the word embeddings. Parameters b_v and b_s are bias terms.

We train the neural network with objective function $C(\theta)$ composed of the fragment alignment objective $C_F(\theta)$ [10], global ranking objective $C_G(\theta)$ [10] and image cluster consistency objective $C_I(\theta)$ [12]:

$$C(\theta) = C_F(\theta) + \gamma C_I(\theta) + \beta C_G(\theta) + \alpha \|\theta\|_2^2, \tag{3}$$

where θ refers to the network parameters and α, β and γ are hyper parameters cross-validated on a validation set.

The fragment alignment objective $C_F(\theta)$ [10] uses fragment co-occurrence information to infer the semantic similarity $v_i^T s_j$ of image fragment v_i and text fragment s_j. It is formulated as:

$$C_F(\theta) = \min_{y_{ij}} C_0(\theta) \tag{4}$$

$$C_0(\theta) = \sum_i \sum_j \max(0, 1 - y_{ij} v_i^T s_j) \tag{5}$$

$$\text{subject to } \sum_{i \in p_j} \frac{y_{ij} + 1}{2} \geq 1 \; \forall j \tag{6}$$

$$y_{ij} = -1 \; \forall i, j \text{ subject to } m_v(i) \neq m_s(j) \tag{7}$$

$$\text{and } y_{ij} \in \{-1, 1\}. \tag{8}$$

Here, variable y_{ij} reflects whether v_i and s_j correspond to the same fashion attribute ($y_{ij} = 1$) or not ($y_{ij} = -1$), p_j is the bag of image fragments occurring with s_j, and $m_v(i)$ and $m_s(j)$ return the index of the image-text pair that respectively v_i and s_j belong to.

The global ranking objective $C_G(\theta)$ [10] derives semantic similarity from global image-text correspondence:

$$C_G(\theta) = \sum_k \Big[\underbrace{\sum_l \max(0, S_{kl} - S_{kk} + \Delta)}_{\text{rank images}} + \underbrace{\sum_l \max(0, S_{lk} - S_{kk} + \Delta)}_{\text{rank texts}} \Big]. \tag{9}$$

It encourages corresponding image-text pairs ($k = l$) to have a higher total semantic similarity score than non-corresponding pairs ($k \neq l$), by a margin Δ. The total semantic similarity score S_{kl} of an image k and text l is computed based on the semantic similarity scores of their respective fragments f_k and f_l:

$$S_{kl} = \frac{1}{(\mid f_l \mid + n)} \sum_{j \in f_l} \max_{i \in f_k} v_i^T s_j, \tag{10}$$

with n a smoothing term.

The image cluster consistency objective $C_I(\theta)$ [12] uses image fragment similarity information to recover semantic similarity information lost due to noise and incompleteness of product descriptions. It is given by:

$$C_I(\theta) = \sum_{m=1}^{M} \sum_i \sum_j (1 - \frac{\hat{v}_i^T \hat{c}_i}{\|\hat{v}_i\| \|\hat{c}_i\|}) |v_i^T s_j - c_i^T s_j|. \tag{11}$$

where M is the number of image-text pairs in the training set, $\hat{v}_i$ is a training image fragment, and $\hat{c}_i$ is an image fragment which is visually similar to $\hat{v}_i$.

3.3 Multimodal Search

In multimodal search, a query is composed of both an image and a text, where the query text is used to modify parts of the query image. The query text can request to change certain fashion attributes (e.g., ask for long sleeves when the dress in the query image is sleeveless) and/or to add fashion attributes to the image (e.g., ask to add rhinestones). For example, Figure 1 shows a multimodal query that both requests to change the dress length (from knee length to short) and to add ornaments (lace) to the dress. We do not support multimodal queries where the query text removes fashion attributes from the query image, as this is less in accordance with how users search.

We propose a multimodal retrieval model which ranks images i_c based on their relevance to a multimodal query q, consisting of query image i_q and query text t_q. Query image i_q and candidate image i_c are segmented with the image segmentation technique described above, producing image fragments $\hat{v}_{i,q}$ and $\hat{v}_{i,c}$ for respectively the query image and candidate image ($i = 1, \ldots, 7$). Query text t_q is filtered with the Zappos glossary to acquire one or more text fragments $\hat{s}_{j,q}$ referring to fashion attributes to be either added or interchanged with current attributes of the query image. Image and text fragments are represented with the intermodal representations $v_{i,q}$, $v_{i,c}$ and $s_{j,q}$ as inferred with the neural network. We use cosine similarity, i.e., the inner product scaled by magnitude, to measure both the visual similarity of two image fragments and the semantic similarity of an image and text fragment. The cosine similarity takes the sign of the inner product. Consequently, the cosine similarity of an image and text fragment will be positive if they represent the same fashion attribute, and will be negative otherwise. To find relevant images for a multimodal query $\{i_q, t_q\}$, we compute the similarity of $\{i_q, t_q\}$ with all candidate images i_c as follows:

$$Sim(i_q, t_q, i_c) = Sim(i_q, i_c) + Sim(t_q, i_c) \tag{12}$$

$$Sim(i_q, i_c) = \sum_i \frac{v_{i,q}^T v_{i,c}}{\|v_{i,q}\| \|v_{i,c}\|} \tag{13}$$

$$Sim(t_q, i_c) = \begin{cases} \sum_j \sum_i \max(0, w \frac{v_{i,c}^T s_{j,q}}{\|v_{i,c}\| \|s_{j,q}\|}), \\ \text{if } \sum_i \max(0, w \frac{v_{i,c}^T s_{j,q}}{\|v_{i,c}\| \|s_{j,q}\|}) > 0 \ \forall j \\ -\infty, \\ \text{otherwise.} \end{cases} \tag{14}$$

We consider an image i_c relevant if it resembles query image i_q and satisfies query text t_q (Eq. 12). Candidate image i_c resembles query image i_q if image fragments $v_{i,c}$ and $v_{i,q}$ of corresponding image parts i are visually similar (Eq. 13). Candidate image i_c satisfies query text t_q if every query text fragment $s_{j,q}$ is shown in at least one image fragment $v_{i,c}$ of the candidate image (i.e., if every $s_{j,q}$ has a positive cosine similarity with at least one $v_{i,c}$). Consequently, candidate images which are similar to the query image but which do not have (some of) the attributes requested in the query text will get a similarity of $-\infty$. The more candidate image fragments display query text fragments, the more relevant we consider the candidate image to be (Eq. 14). In Eq. 14, weighting term w regulates how strongly we want the query text to modify the query image. A smaller weight will assign a higher relevance to candidate images which are similar to the query image, while a larger weight will favor images which satisfy the query text (but which might be less similar to the query image). Hence, we should find a weight w that provides a nice balance between both.

3.4 Baseline Retrieval Models for Multimodal Search

We compare the proposed multimodal retrieval model to three baseline retrieval models for multimodal search. As a first baseline, we simply retrieve images with a high cosine similarity with the intermodal representation of the first image fragment of the query image (i.e., the image fragment showing the full dress) and ignore the query text. The second baseline is the standard multimodal retrieval model [13], which creates an intermodal representation of the desired image based on the multimodal query, and retrieves candidate images which are visually similar to the desired image. The intermodal representation of the desired image is equal to the intermodal representation of the first image fragment of the query image, plus the intermodal representations of the query text fragments, minus the intermodal representations of the attributes that the query text fragments will replace. For example, for the query in Figure 1, the standard multimodal retrieval model takes the intermodal representation of the first image fragment of the query image, adds the intermodal representations of "short" and "lace", and subtracts the intermodal representation for "knee length". Then, it retrieves candidate images with a high cosine similarity with the resulting vector. Our third baseline is the image-to-text-to-image multimodal retrieval model. The image-to-text-to-image retrieval model starts by generating a textual description l of the multimodal query. It does so by first listing for each query image fragment the 3 Zappos phrases with the highest semantic similarity score, then removing from this list the Zappos phrases referring to attributes to be replaced by the query text, and finally appending the query text fragments. Afterwards, the generated textual description l is used to search satisfying images by retrieving images k with the highest total semantic similarity S_{kl} with textual description l (Eq. 10). Note that the second and third baseline retrieval models require the user to also specify in the query text which fashion attribute(s) to replace. For example, for the multimodal query in Figure 1, the query text becomes "Find similar images but short instead of knee length and with lace".

4 EXPERIMENTAL SETUP

4.1 Dataset

We train our model on the Amazon Dresses dataset, which we obtained from Zoghbi et al. [18]. This dataset consists of 53 689 image-text pairs, where each pair consists of an image of a dress and the corresponding product description. The images show dresses for different occasions, e.g., bridesmaid, casual, wear to work, etc. Hence, they display a large variety of fine-grained fashion attributes. Their corresponding texts roughly describe the image content and can be noisy.

We use 48 689 image-text pairs for training, 4000 for validation and 1000 for testing in the same setup as in [18]. During testing, we evaluate the quality of the inferred intermodal representations in a multimodal retrieval setting. We collected 100 multimodal queries from 10 test subjects. Two men and eight women each created 10 multimodal queries reflecting real search requests encountered while browsing the dataset. The query images are images from the test set. The query texts consist of Zappos phrases denoting fashion attributes to either add to or change in the query image. In our dataset, the number of Zappos phrases in a query text ranges from one to three, but in general a query text can contain any number of Zappos phrases. The Zappos glossary consists of more than 200 phrases, 47 of which are used in the multimodal queries. As the ground truth for a multimodal query, we consider all test set images in which all query text attributes are either added or interchanged with the necessary query image attributes and all other query image attributes are preserved. However, since the test dataset only consists of 1000 images displaying a large variety of visual attributes, we can expect that for some multimodal queries there are no relevant images.

4.2 Experiments

On the image side, we detect image fragments with the image segmentation technique described above. To find visually similar image fragments, we cluster the image fragments in C clusters with k-means clustering based on cosine distance. As in [12], we take $C = 10000$. On the text side, we filter the product descriptions with the Zappos glossary. The remaining phrases function as text fragments. We represent the text fragments with 300-dimensional word embeddings which we train with the Skip-gram model on the Amazon Dresses dataset. Afterwards, the neural network induces a h-dimensional common, multimodal space, where image and text fragments have intermodal representations that capture their semantics. As in [12], we choose a common embedding space dimension h of 1000, a smoothing term n in S_{kl} of 10, a margin Δ in $C_G(\theta)$ of 40, and factors β and γ in $C(\theta)$ of 0.50 and 0.25 respectively. The neural network is trained with the proposed objective function, which we optimize with stochastic gradient descent with mini-batches of 100, a fixed learning rate of 10^{-5}, and a momentum of 0.90 during 20 epochs. Finally, we use the inferred intermodal representations in the proposed multimodal retrieval model. Here, a regulator term w of 2.5 was found to work best based on a small validation set. We investigate both the effect of including and omitting the image cluster consistency objective $C_I(\theta)$ when learning the intermodal representations on our multimodal search results. When $C_I(\theta)$ is included in the objective function, we consider both the medoid and centroid of the cluster of $\hat{v}_i$ as suitable image fragments to fulfill the role of $\hat{c}_i$.

4.3 Evaluation

In multimodal search, we retrieve for each multimodal query the top K most likely test set images. We evaluate by computing precision@K for $K = 1, 5$ and mean average precision (MAP). As the ground truth for a multimodal query, we consider all images in which all attributes requested in the query text are either added or interchanged with the necessary query image attributes and all other attributes of the query image are still present. For example, for the multimodal query in Figure 1, a relevant image has the following fashion attributes: "white", "scoop", "sleeveless", "A-line", "casual" (attributes of query image), "short" and "lace" (attributes of query text). This kind of evaluation is rather subjective and strict. It is subjective because sometimes it is unclear if a required fashion attribute is present or not. For example, the color of the retrieved image might be very similar, but not identical, to the one in the query image. Also, there are some multimodal queries which request a certain dress, but more suitable for another occasion (e.g., wear to work). The relevance of the retrieved images for such queries can be judged differently depending on the assessor. When a certain fabric is requested, the product descriptions of the retrieved images are consulted to determine the presence of the fabric, as this is often unclear from the image material. We measured annotator agreement on precision@1 with Cohen's κ which yielded a $\kappa = 0.45$. This can be considered as a fair agreement. The evaluation is also rather strict. It will consider a retrieved image irrelevant even if it has all but one of the required fashion attributes. Furthermore, we compute precision@K for $K = 5$ for each of the 47 query text attributes individually, and macro-average the obtained precision@K yielding the macro $AP@K$ for $K = 5$ across all 47 query text attributes. We compare the results of our proposed multimodal retrieval model to the three baseline retrieval models.

Since our quantitative evaluation is rather subjective and strict, we also provide a qualitative evaluation of our results. We present examples of multimodal queries and calculate precision@K for

Table 1: Multimodal search results. Comparison of performance of different retrieval models. *P@K* is precision@K and *macro AP@K* is the average attribute precision@K over all textual attributes.

Objective function	Retrieval model	P@1	P@5	MAP	Macro AP@5
$C_F(\theta), C_G(\theta), C_I(\theta)$ (centroid)	Query image similarity	3.00	2.40	1.15	13.35
$C_F(\theta), C_G(\theta), C_I(\theta)$ (centroid)	Standard	3.00	2.40	1.15	14.78
$C_F(\theta), C_G(\theta), C_I(\theta)$ (centroid)	Image-to-text-to-image	2.00	1.80	0.90	18.15
$C_F(\theta), C_G(\theta)$	Proposed	10.00	4.60	3.21	43.90
$C_F(\theta), C_G(\theta), C_I(\theta)$ (medoid)	Proposed	9.00	4.80	3.67	45.29
$C_F(\theta), C_G(\theta), C_I(\theta)$ (centroid)	Proposed	**11.00**	**6.20**	**4.06**	**50.11**

$K = 1, 5$, where we not express relevance as a yes-or-no question (0 or 1), but rather as a percentage of present required attributes.

Finally, we provide a thorough analysis of the induced common, multimodal space and the inferred intermodal representations.

5 RESULTS AND DISCUSSION

5.1 Quantitative Evaluation

Our multimodal search results are presented in Table 1. These results show that our proposed multimodal retrieval model outperforms all baseline retrieval models. Our proposed retrieval model surpasses the image-to-text-to-image retrieval model by 450% on precision@1, by 244% on precision@5, by 351% on MAP, and by 176% on macro AP@5. Compared to the standard retrieval model, our proposed retrieval model achieves an increase of 267% on precision@1, of 158% on precision@5, of 253% on MAP, and of 239% on macro AP@5.

The standard multimodal retrieval model is very intuitive and actually creates the intermodal representation of the desired image based on the multimodal query. However, it lacks a mechanism to focus on retrieving the desired fashion attributes. Only calculating an overall cosine similarity between the desired image and the candidate images is not sufficient to return relevant images exhibiting both the query image attributes and the query text attributes. The image-to-text-to-image multimodal retrieval model on the other hand, by performing image search with a textual query composed of the main query image attributes and the query text attributes, does put focus on finding candidate images exhibiting the fashion attributes requested by the multimodal query. However, Laenen et al. [12] demonstrated that both for image annotation and image search the model still has difficulties with distinguishing between visually similar fashion attributes. Consequently, these two steps, i.e., image annotation and image search, both introduce errors into the search process. Our proposed multimodal retrieval model prefers to go from the query image to the candidate image directly, and computes their visual similarity as the aggregation of the cosine similarities of corresponding query and candidate image fragments. In contrast to the image-to-text-to-image retrieval model, our proposed retrieval model avoids the introduction of noise in the search process due to the additional image annotation step, at the cost of possibly not retrieving every desired query image attribute. To satisfy the query text attributes, our proposed multimodal retrieval model uses the cosine similarity of a query text fragment and candidate image fragment to explicitly require every query text attribute to be present in the retrieved images. This approach is different from the one in the image-to-text-to-image retrieval model, which does put focus on retrieving the requested fashion attributes, but does not explicitly impose that attributes in the generated textual query are exhibited in the returned images. When comparing the macro AP@5 of the different retrieval models, it is clear that the method employed in our proposed multimodal retrieval model for returning images satisfying the multimodal query texts is the most successful one. Finally, our proposed multimodal retrieval model has the benefit of having a regulator term to steer the model to give equal importance to the query image and query text when retrieving candidate images. In contrast, the standard and image-to-text-to-image retrieval models by definition assign more importance to the query images. The standard retrieval model builds the intermodal representation

Table 2: Multimodal search results. Comparison of performance of our best model for different textual attributes. *Training set frequency* is the number of times the textual attribute occurs in the training set, *multimodal query frequency* is the number of multimodal queries containing the textual attribute and *attribute P@K* is precision@K for each individual textual attribute.

Attribute	Training set frequency	Multimodal query frequency	Attribute P@5
wedding	30 566	1	100.00
maxi	4 579	2	100.00
V-neck	6 700	7	97.14
red	2 322	2	90.00
black	5 212	8	87.50
strapless	11 441	5	84.00
applique	1 446	1	80.00
mesh	1 739	1	80.00
lace	21 658	4	80.00
floral print	682	2	80.00
sleeveless	13 306	11	78.18
short	7 658	9	77.78
short sleeves	1 158	10	74.00
wide	2 017	2	70.00
crystals	2 189	2	70.00
wear to work	129	2	70.00
white	4 171	5	68.00
knee length	3 041	5	64.00
rhinestones	1 082	2	60.00
green	754	2	60.00
scoop	2 369	2	60.00
evening	20 019	1	60.00
pink	1 248	1	60.00
summer	2 669	1	60.00
vertical stripes	8	1	60.00
⋮	⋮	⋮	⋮
winter	1 345	1	0.00
velvet	446	1	0.00
khaki	26	1	0.00
linen	553	1	0.00
cut outs	62	1	0.00
leopard print	99	1	0.00
horizontal stripes	10	2	0.00
cheetah print	340	1	0.00

of the desired image from the representation of the query image, and the image-to-text-to-image retrieval model generates a textual description which contains much more text fragments related to the query image than related to the query text.

Moreover, the results in Table 1 indicate that the intermodal representations trained with the complete objective function, i.e., including $C_I(\theta)$, and using the cluster centroids to fulfill the role of the $\hat{c_i}$ in $C_I(\theta)$ provide the best multimodal search results. Hence, our best model is the proposed multimodal retrieval model operating on the aforementioned intermodal representations.

Overall, the multimodal search results for our best model remain quite low. The method employed to evaluate the search results is rather strict. It requires that all query image and query text attributes are displayed in the candidate image for it to be relevant. However, as dresses are characterized by a multitude of fashion attributes, it might very well be that for some multimodal queries there are no relevant images in our relatively small test set. In addition, the proposed multimodal retrieval model will retrieve images which overall are as similar as possible to the query image and which satisfy the query text. However, this might be inadequate to request all necessary query image attributes to be maintained in the retrieved images.

5.2 Qualitative Evaluation

We further study our results qualitatively to assess our model's performance. Figure 2 displays the images retrieved for 6 multimodal queries. Multimodal query "Find similar images but wear to work" requests dresses which are more suitable for the office than the query image, which is more casual. The first, second and fourth dress seem appropriate to wear to work, but this is rather subjective. The second dress also preserves the query image attributes (jewel neckline, sleeveless, short, black) and is considered as the only relevant image. The first dress has the wrong neckline (notched) and sleeve length (short sleeves), the fourth dress has the wrong sleeve length (short sleeves), dress length (knee length) and color (burgundy). For multimodal query "Find similar images but with a V-neck" the first dress is relevant (V-neck, black, white, sleeveless, sheath, short, casual). All other dresses have the requested query text attribute "V-neck", but do not have all query image attributes. For multimodal query "Find similar images but red" only the fifth dress is relevant (red, V-neck, sleeveless, long, rhinestones, evening). All other dresses are red too, but do not have all required query image attributes. Multimodal query "Find similar images but shift" retrieves two dresses with this shape: the first and the fifth. None of the dresses have all requested attributes (shift, jewel neckline, short sleeves, short, pink, floral print, summer). However, each dress has some of the required attributes and can be considered similar to the query image. For multimodal query "Find similar images but with rhinestones" all dresses except the fifth one have rhinestones. None of the retrieved dresses is relevant though, as none of them have the right color (white). However, except for the color, the first dress has all requested attributes (rhinestones, strapless, sweetheart, long, A-line, pleated, bridesmaid). Multimodal query "Find similar images but strapless and short" returns three relevant dresses: the first, second and third. They are all red, strapless, short, accented with an ornament at their waist and suitable for a bridesmaid, as requested by the multimodal query. For these multimodal query results we can compute refined precision@1 and refined precision@5 scores, expressing relevance as a percentage of present required attributes. From left to right and top to bottom, refined precision@1 is respectively 60%, 100%, 66.67%, 71.43%, 87.50%, and 100%, and refined precision@5 is respectively 48%, 71.43%, 76.67%, 57.14%, 77.14% and 80%. We conclude that, although our proposed multimodal retrieval model does not have the ability to explicitly focus on retrieving all query image attributes, it is nevertheless capable of retrieving relevant candidate images for the provided multimodal queries.

5.3 Discussion of the Proposed Alignment and Retrieval Models

Our multimodal search results indicate that the neural network has learned what certain fashion attributes look like. Hence, we can analyze the 1000-dimensional intermodal representations to acquire insight in the meaning of their different components.

When we project the image fragments of the test set images and the Zappos phrases to the common, multimodal space, we clearly see two clusters: one containing all image fragments and one containing all Zappos phrases. Hence, even in the common, multimodal space the two modalities remain separated.

Within the cluster of image fragments, we observe that image fragments showing the same part of a dress are close-by, e.g., the tops are grouped together. Additionally, similar parts are closer together than dissimilar parts, e.g., necklines and tops are closer together than tops and skirts.

When looking at the intermodal representations of the Zappos phrases, both visually and semantically similar textual attributes appear to be close to each other. Textual attributes which are semantically similar but differ in appearance are further apart. For example, the colors "coral", "pink" and "orange" are very close to each other, but are further away from other colors like "brown" and "gray". Also, necklines "scoop", "square neck" and "off the shoulder" are close to each other, but further away from "sweetheart", which is very close to "strapless". In contrast, in the original word embedding space semantically similar textual attributes are close to each other, regardless of appearance.

In the intermodal representations of textual attributes a component is either zero or positive (a consequence of using the ReLU activation function). Actually, for the textual attributes in our vocabulary, we observe that only a few of the 1000 components are non-zero. This indicates that our model has learned which components of the image fragments to focus on when looking for a specific fashion attribute. For example, neckline "sweetheart" only has 7 non-zero components. Hence, image fragments in the common, multimodal space with positive values for these components will result in a positive inner product with "sweetheart" and thus are expected to show a sweetheart neckline. An interesting observation can be made regarding the number of non-zero components of fashion attribute "dress". The intermodal representation of "dress" is actually an all-zero vector. This happens because every image in the Amazon Dresses dataset is described with the text fragment "dress". Therefore, the neural network was unable to learn which components are indicators for an image fragment showing a dress. It solves this nicely by assigning the all-zero vector to "dress", which

Figure 2: Multimodal search examples [1]. Six examples of multimodal queries for which our model performs well. For each multimodal query, the top 5 retrieved images are shown.

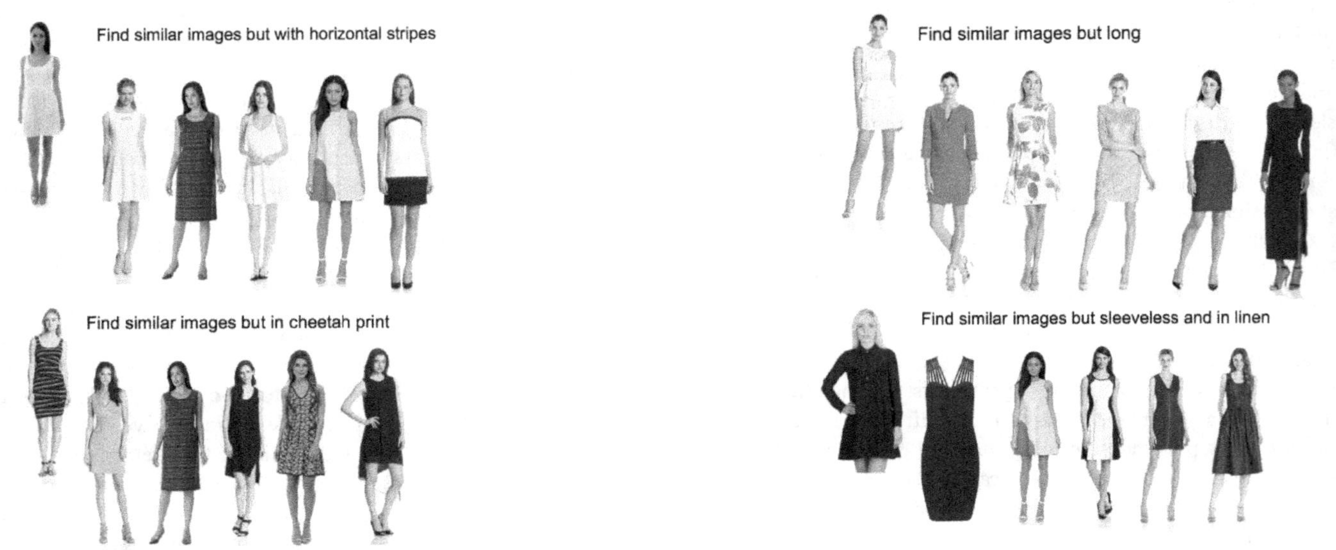

Figure 3: Multimodal search examples [1]. Four examples of multimodal queries for which our model returns bad results. For each multimodal query, the top 5 retrieved images are shown.

produces an inner product of 0 with each image fragment because everything is a dress. Additionally, we observe that there are 237 components in the intermodal representations which are zero for all textual attributes. Corresponding components in the image fragments never matter when looking for the presence of certain fashion attributes. Hence, these components represent characteristics of the image fragments which are not indicators for any fashion attributes in our current vocabulary.

Visually similar fashion attributes share some of their non-zero components. This is natural, as some of the same components matter when determining the presence of these fashion attributes. For example, "strapless" has 10 non-zero components of which 3 are also non-zero for "sweetheart". This explains why the neural network model of Laenen et al. [12] sometimes has trouble distinguishing between visually similar fashion attributes: a large value for a shared component might produce a positive inner product for an incorrect fashion attribute. Multimodal query "Find similar images but long" in Figure 3 suffers from this problem. Instead of retrieving long dresses, it retrieves dresses with longer sleeves. The intermodal representation of "long" only has 4 non-zero components, of which one is shared with "long sleeves". This shared component is probably high in the intermodal representation of the retrieved images because of their sleeve length, which produces the incorrect positive inner product regarding the dress length. Note that the opposite, i.e., mistaking "long sleeves" for "long" is less probable, as "long sleeves" has 40 non-zero components.

In other cases, our proposed multimodal retrieval model makes errors because the intermodal representations of certain fashion attributes are underdeveloped. For example, Figure 3 shows bad results for multimodal queries asking for a different print ("horizontal stripes", "cheetah print") and another fabric ("linen"). Fashion attribute "horizontal stripes" only occurs 10 times in the training set, which is not enough for the neural network to learn what this print looks like. The results for the multimodal query asking for "horizontal stripes" illustrate that the model is unable to retrieve images with a horizontally striped print. Also for other fashion attributes which occur infrequently in the training set, e.g., "khaki" and "cut outs", we observe that our retrieval model cannot find candidate images exhibiting these attributes (Table 2). Print "cheetah print" suffers from noise in the dataset. It occurs 340 times in the training set, but most of the time it is listed as another possibility for the print of the displayed dresses. This noise in the product descriptions is very obstructive and prevents the neural network from learning what a cheetah print looks like. Finally, we observe that the intermodal representations for fabrics, e.g., linen, are also of low quality. The reason for this is that in general fabrics are very difficult to identify from an image, even for humans.

6 CONCLUSION

In this paper, we have proposed a novel search paradigm to search fashion e-commerce data called multimodal search. Our multimodal queries consist of an e-commerce image of a clothing item together with text that modifies the image or adds attributes to it. We proposed a multimodal retrieval model which operates on intermodal representations of fashion attributes obtained with a neural network, and which exploits the semantic similarity information contained in their inner product. We demonstrated that the proposed multimodal retrieval model outperforms state-of-the-art models, but the retrieval of the query image attributes can still be improved. This will be the focus of our future research. Additionally, we will expand our work to allow street images as query images, i.e., images taken with a smartphone or found on social media. Moreover, it would be interesting to add additional context to this work such as co-purchase or co-click data in order to improve our image and text features [2, 5].

REFERENCES

[1] S. Bell and K. Bala. 2015. Learning Visual Similarity for Product Design with Convolutional Neural Networks. *ACM Transactions on Graphics (TOG)* 34, 4 (July 2015).

[2] N. Djuric, H. Wu, V. Radosavljevic, M. Grbovic, and N. Bhamidipati. 2015. Hierarchical Neural Language Models for Joint Representation of Streaming Documents and Their Content. In *Proceedings of the 24th International Conference on World Wide Web (WWW)*. 248–255.

[3] J. Donahue, L. A. Hendricks, S. Guadarrama, M. Rohrbach, S. Venugopalan, K. Saenko, and T. Darrell. 2015. Long-Term Recurrent Convolutional Networks for Visual Recognition and Description. In *The IEEE Conference on Computer Vision and Pattern Recognition (CVPR)*.

[4] A. Ghodrati, X. Jia, M. Pedersoli, and T. Tuytelaars. 2015. Swap Retrieval: Retrieving Images of Cats When the Query Shows a Dog. In *Proceedings of the 5th ACM International Conference on Multimedia Retrieval (ICMR)*. 395–402.

[5] M. Grbovic, V. Radosavljevic, N. Djuric, N. Bhamidipati, J. Savla, V. Bhagwan, and D. Sharp. 2015. E-commerce in Your Inbox: Product Recommendations at Scale. In *Proceedings of the 21th ACM SIGKDD International Conference on Knowledge Discovery and Data Mining*. 1809–1818.

[6] X. Han, Z. Wu, P. X. Huang, X. Zhang, M. Zhu, Y. Li, Y. Zhao, and L. S. Davis. 2017. Automatic Spatially-Aware Fashion Concept Discovery. In *The IEEE International Conference on Computer Vision (ICCV)*.

[7] J.-H. Hsiao and L.-J. Li. 2014. On Visual Similarity based Interactive Product Recommendation for Online Shopping. In *The IEEE International Conference on Image Processing (ICIP)*.

[8] Y. Jia, E. Shelhamer, J. Donahue, S. Karayev, J. Long, R. Girshick, S. Guadarrama, and T. Darrell. 2014. Caffe: Convolutional Architecture for Fast Feature Embedding. In *Proceedings of the 22nd ACM International Conference on Multimedia (ACMMM)*. 675–678.

[9] Y. Kalantidis, L. Kennedy, and L.-J. Li. 2013. Getting the Look: Clothing Recognition and Segmentation for Automatic Product Suggestions in Everyday Photos. In *Proceedings of International Conference on Multimedia Retrieval (ICMR)*.

[10] A. Karpathy and L. Fei-Fei. 2015. Deep Visual-Semantic Alignments for Generating Image Descriptions. In *The IEEE Conference on Computer Vision and Pattern Recognition (CVPR)*. 3128–3137.

[11] M. H. Kiapour, X. Han, S. Lazebnik, A. C. Berg, and T. L. Berg. 2015. Where to Buy It: Matching Street Clothing Photos in Online Shops. In *The IEEE International Conference on Computer Vision (ICCV)*. 3343–3351.

[12] K. Laenen, S. Zoghbi, and M-F. Moens. 2017. Cross-modal Search for Fashion Attributes. In *Proceedings of the KDD 2017 Workshop on Machine Learning Meets Fashion*.

[13] T. Mikolov, K. Chen, G. S. Corrado, and J. Dean. 2013. Efficient Estimation of Word Representations in Vector Space. *CoRR* abs/1301.3781 (2013).

[14] O. Vinyals, A. Toshev, S. Bengio, and D. Erhan. 2015. Show and Tell: A Neural Image Caption Generator. In *The IEEE Conference on Computer Vision and Pattern Recognition (CVPR)*.

[15] K. Xu, J. Ba, R. Kiros, K. Cho, A. Courville, R. Salakhudinov, R. Zemel, and Y. Bengio. 2015. Show, Attend and Tell: Neural Image Caption Generation with Visual Attention. In *Proceedings of the 32nd International Conference on Machine Learning (ICML)*. 2048–2057.

[16] F. Yang, A. Kale, Y. Bubnov, L. Stein, Q. Wang, H. Kiapour, and R. Piramuthu. 2017. Visual Search at eBay. In *Proceedings of the 23rd ACM SIGKDD Conference on Knowledge Discovery and Data Mining*. 2101–2110.

[17] B. Zhao, J. Feng, X. Wu, and S. Yan. 2017. Memory-Augmented Attribute Manipulation Networks for Interactive Fashion Search. In *IEEE Conference on Computer Vision and Pattern Recognition (CVPR)*. 6156–6164.

[18] S. Zoghbi, G. Heyman, J. C. Gomez, and M-F. Moens. 2016. Fashion Meets Computer Vision and NLP at e-Commerce Search. *International Journal of Computer and Electrical Engineering (IJCEE)* 8, 1 (February 2016), 31–43.

Joint Non-negative Matrix Factorization for Learning Ideological Leaning on Twitter

Preethi Lahoti*
Max Planck Institute for Informatics
Saarbruecken, Germany
plahoti@mpi-inf.mpg.de

Kiran Garimella
Aalto University
Helsinki, Finland
kiran.garimella@aalto.fi

Aristides Gionis
Aalto University
Helsinki, Finland
aristides.gionis@aalto.fi

ABSTRACT

People are shifting from traditional news sources to online news at an incredibly fast rate. However, the technology behind online news consumption promotes content that confirms the users' existing point of view. This phenomenon has led to polarization of opinions and intolerance towards opposing views. Thus, a key problem is to model information filter bubbles on social media and design methods to eliminate them. In this paper, we use a machine-learning approach to learn a *liberal-conservative* ideology space on Twitter, and show how we can use the learned latent space to tackle the filter bubble problem.

We model the problem of learning the *liberal-conservative* ideology space of social media users and media sources as a constrained non-negative matrix-factorization problem. Our model incorporates the social-network structure and content-consumption information in a joint factorization problem with shared latent factors. We validate our model and solution on a real-world Twitter dataset consisting of controversial topics, and show that we are able to separate users by ideology with over 90 % *purity*. When applied to media sources, our approach estimates ideology scores that are highly correlated (Pearson correlation 0.9) with ground-truth ideology scores. Finally, we demonstrate the utility of our model in real-world scenarios, by illustrating how the learned ideology latent space can be used to develop exploratory and interactive interfaces that can help users in diffusing their information filter bubble.

ACM Reference Format:
Preethi Lahoti, Kiran Garimella, and Aristides Gionis. 2018. Joint Non-negative Matrix Factorization for Learning Ideological Leaning on Twitter. In *Proceedings of WSDM 2018: The Eleventh ACM International Conference on Web Search and Data Mining (WSDM 2018).* ACM, New York, NY, USA, 9 pages. https://doi.org/10.1145/3159652.3159669

1 INTRODUCTION

Social media and the web have provided a foundation where users can easily access diverse information from around the world. However, over the years, various factors, such as user homophily (social network structure), and algorithmic filtering (e.g., news feeds and recommendations) have narrowed the content that a user consumes. As an example, imagine two users of opposite ideological stances (liberal and conservative). Though the two users may be looking at the same topic (e.g., a presidential debate), they might be seeing completely different viewpoints due to the diverse network surrounding and different content sources they get their information from. Consequently, users on different ends of the ideological spectrum live in their own information bubbles [30], oblivious to the views on the other side and creating their own world-view of truth. This phenomenon has led to the polarization of viewpoints, intolerance towards opposing views, and ideological segregation [34]. Many studies suggest that increasingly users live in their echo chambers [33] and polarization of the public has intensified [10].

In this paper, we propose a principled approach to infer the *ideological stances* (also known as *ideology* or *polarity* or *leaning*) of both the *users* in a social network, and the *media sources* that provide news content in the network. Our approach is based on a non-negative matrix-factorization model, which jointly decomposes the social network of users and the content they consume in a *shared latent space*. Learning the ideological stances of social media users and content sources is an important step in building useful tools that can make users aware of their informational bias and consequently, help in reducing those biases, thus mitigating the increasing polarization in the society.

Existing approaches to identifying the ideological leaning of users either (i) require large amounts of manually annotated data [9]; or (ii) consider only the structure of social ties [4] or user interactions [15, 35]; or (iii) analyze only the content shared by users [31]. Each of these families of approaches has its own limitations. First, obtaining manual annotations is both expensive and time consuming. Second, when using only the structure of social ties or interactions, it is assumed that users with the same ideology are more likely to interact with or follow each other. However, social networks are extremely sparse and noisy, and users with the same ideological leaning may never interact with or follow each other, while users with different ideological leaning may still interact due to different reasons. Last, inferring ideological leaning by using only content is a challenging task and prone to errors due to the inherent complexity of natural-language understanding.

To overcome these problems, we propose an unsupervised approach that uses simultaneously the network structure and the information about content shared by users. We are motivated by the observation that a user's ideological stance on a topic depends on both the surrounding network structure as well as the content sources that users consume their information from. Thus, we exploit the inherent connection between the two data types: Users are

*Author was at Aalto University at the time of this work.

WSDM 2018, February 5–9, 2018, Marina Del Rey, CA, USA

ACM ISBN 978-1-4503-5581-0/18/02...$15.00
https://doi.org/10.1145/3159652.3159669

not only more likely to interact with or follow like-minded users, but also to share content of aligned ideological leaning. Taking into account the full available information results in more accurate estimation of ideological leaning both for users and content sources.

In addition, we formulate the task of learning ideological leaning as a joint matrix factorization problem in which users and sources are represented in a shared latent space. This formulation allows us to identify the relationship between data points of the two types, which is particularly useful for visualizing social-media users and sources in a common space, and building applications for exploring the ideological landscape in one's media neighborhood, or making recommendations to escape the filter bubble. In fact, we demonstrate concretely how to use the learned ideology latent space to develop exploration and recommendation tools (Section 6).

Experiments comparing our approach to the state of the art show the benefit of such a principled joint approach. Our method is able to separate users into ideological clusters with over 90% purity. When applied to media sources, our approach estimates ideology scores that are highly correlated with ground-truth ideology scores.

All our analysis is done on Twitter, though the methods generalize to any other social network. In the rest of the paper, for the sake of clarity we use Twitter-specific nomenclature (e.g., retweets, follow, etc.).

In summary, our contributions are as follows:

- We present a principled approach to jointly compute the ideology scores of both users and content sources by formulating the problem as a joint constrained matrix-factorization task. This formulation allows us to jointly cluster the two data types, "user" and "source". We apply our learned ideological latent space to the problems of "who" and "what" to recommend to users so as to reduce polarization and diffuse their information filter bubble.
- To the best of our knowledge, this is the first work to compute ideological stances for *both* users and content sources, in a common latent space, based on both the network structure and the users' interaction with sources.
- We provide an extensive experimental evaluation, presenting both qualitative and quantitative results on real-world Twitter data. Our method shows promise when compared to existing state of the art approaches.

2 RELATED WORK

In this paper, we propose an approach that can identify the ideological leaning of users on Twitter. We define ideology based on the policy dimension that articulates a user's political preference. Our definition is inspired by work in political-science literature, such as work by Bafumi et al. [2], where ideology is defined as "a line whose left end is understood to reflect an extremely liberal position and whose right end corresponds to extreme conservatism."

Estimation of user ideology. Traditionally, the most common sources for estimating ideology comprised of behavioral data generated from roll call votes [32], co-sponsorship records [1], or political contributions [6]. These datasets were often only available for the political elite, like members of congress, and hence getting such estimates for a large population of ordinary citizens was difficult, if not impossible.

With the proliferation of social media platforms, behavioral data started being available at an individual level and researchers have tried to use such data for identifying political ideology for social media users at scale. Initial work started with supervised methods [9] for predicting a (binary) political alignment of users on Twitter. Though these works report accuracies over 90%, Cohen at al. [8] warns about the limitations of such approaches and their dependence on politically active users.

Unsupervised approaches have also been proposed, mainly based on the structure of user interests [22], social connections [4], and interactions [15, 35]. The main idea behind these methods is that users typically either surround themselves (follow/friend) with other users who are similar in their ideology (homophily), or interact with others (retweet/like) similar to them.

Perhaps the closest approach to this paper is the work by Lu et al. [27] (BIASWATCH), who seek to identify the *bias* of a user on a topic by combining their retweet and content networks, where a content network is obtained based on the similarity of users tweets. BIASWATCH, however, assumes the presence of a set of labeled *bias anchors* (seed hashtags), making it not completely unsupervised. Second, fusing the content and retweet networks is somewhat arbitrary, since there is no common underlying principle that holds the two networks together and hence a graph that results from such a merger contains different types of edges (multigraph) simply merged together. We compared our approach with BIASWATCH in Section 5 and show that our method outperforms their bias scores.

Estimation of source ideology. Polarization and bias of media outlets has existed long before the time of internet, however, data availability makes it easier to study and quantify nowadays. Mitchell et al. [28] study the media habits of American public using a large scale survey and show how fractured the media production and consumption have become in the recent years. Groseclosea et al. [20] propose a method to estimate the ideology of various media sources by comparing the number of citations to think tanks and policy groups to those of Congress members. For a complete survey of methods on measuring ideology of media and media bias, please refer to Groeling et al. [19].

Reducing polarization. The problem of reducing polarization and diffusing information bubbles on social media has been tackled before. Most papers approach the problem by recommending content outside a user's filter bubble. Studies have looked at what to recommend [18], how to recommend [24, 25] and to whom to recommend such content [16].

Based on the papers discussed above, we make the following observations:

a. Most existing approaches only consider one dimension (content or network) for computing user ideology. We propose a principled approach that can compute a user's ideology by taking into account *both* content and network.

b. We compute the ideology of users and sources simultaneously. No existing approach, to the best of our knowledge, proposes such a method to do it simultaneously.

c. Most approaches for reducing polarization do not take a user's *choice* into account. Our methods (in Section 6) can help users diffuse their information bubbles based on their own choices.

3 PROBLEM FORMULATION

In this section we discuss the problem setting, introduce the notation, and formally define the problem we consider.

3.1 Data model

The social graph. We consider a social graph of Twitter users $G = (U, E, w)$, where U represents the set of users, E is the set of edges representing social interactions between the users, and $w : E \rightarrow \mathbb{R}$ is a weighting function that assigns real-valued weights to each edge in G.

We also represent the graph G by its adjacency matrix $\mathbf{A} \in \mathbb{R}^{n \times n}$. In particular, it is $\mathbf{A}(u, v) = w_i$ for each edge $e_i = (u, v, w_i) \in E$, and $\mathbf{A}(u, v) = 0$ if there is no edge between u and v. Since the social graph G may not represent a symmetric relation, the matrix $\mathbf{A}$ is not necessarily symmetric.

To define the edges of the graph G one can consider social links between users based on their retweet and follow networks. Two commonly-used options are to consider an edge $e_i = (u, v, w_i)$ if (i) users u and v *follow* a common set of users, and w_i is the *number of common users*; or if (ii) user u *retweets* user v, and w_i is the *number of retweets*. In the first case the social graph is symmetric, while in the second case it is not.

Content sources. We model the presence of content in the network by considering a set of content sources S. The set S represents a set of items that are shared in the network. The number of sources is denoted by $|S| = m$. We associate with each user u the subset of sources in S that the user shares (i.e., posts) in the network. Thus the overall user activity in the network is denoted by a matrix $\mathbf{C} \in \mathbb{R}^{n \times m}$, where $\mathbf{C}(u, s)$ denotes the number of times that user $u \in U$ shares source $s \in S$.

We derive the content features (i.e., items of the set S) based on users' tweets. Specifically, we experiment with two variants of feature sets: (i) extracted urls from the tweets; and (ii) hostnames of urls extracted from the tweets. In other words, in the latter case, the content is aggregated by their source of authorship (i.e., various news media channels).

For the presentation of our method, we also need the following definitions.

Affinity matrix. Given a matrix $\mathbf{X}$, we define the *affinity matrix of the rows of* $\mathbf{X}$ to be $\mathbf{X}_{rn}\mathbf{X}_{rn}^T$, where $\mathbf{X}_{rn}$ is row normalized $\mathbf{X}$. That is, the affinity matrix of rows of $\mathbf{X}$ is formed by the cosine similarities of all pairs of rows of $\mathbf{X}$. Similarly, we define the *affinity matrix of the columns of* $\mathbf{X}$ to be $\mathbf{X}_{cn}^T\mathbf{X}_{cn}$, where $\mathbf{X}_{cn}$ is column normalized $\mathbf{X}$.

Laplacian matrix. Given a square and symmetric matrix $\mathbf{X}$, we consider its Laplacian to be the matrix $\mathbf{L} = \mathbf{D} - \mathbf{X}$, where $\mathbf{D}$ is a diagonal matrix whose (i, i) entry is the i-th row-sum of $\mathbf{X}$.

3.2 Motivation of the approach

Our goal in this paper is to learn the ideological leaning of users and content sources on Twitter. The underlying motivation is that learning the ideological leaning of Twitter users and sources is an important step in building useful tools that can help users perceive their informational bias and consequently improve their news diet.

A simple approach to identify ideological leaning of users is to consider only the social graph and apply one of the many community-detection algorithms. The intuition here is that users with the same ideological leaning are more likely to interact with each other, and thus, to form graph communities. The drawback of this simple approach is that community detection on real-world social graphs is an extremely challenging task, due to sparsity and overlapping communities. For instance, two users u and v can have the same ideological leaning even though they do not have any social interaction, or they have different topical interests.

Similarly, one simple approach to attempt identifying the ideological leaning of sources is to cluster them using deep-NLP or semantic-analysis techniques. However, this approach is again prone to errors due to the inherent complexity of the text-analysis task. Furthermore, it ignores the rich user information about how content is shared in the social network.

In contrast to these simple techniques, which rely on one-sided clustering of either users or content, with no association between them, the proposed approach seeks to *jointly* learn the ideological leaning of users and content sources.

Combining different data types in a unified learning framework has several advantages. First, we exploit the inherent connection between the two data types: users are not only more likely to interact with, or follow, like-minded users, but also to share content of aligned ideological leaning. Consequently, taking into account the full information on social structure and content will result in better clustering performance. Furthermore, considering both data types simultaneously allows us to learn the ideological leanings of users and content sources in a *shared latent space*. This means that not only do we separate users and sources into ideological clusters, but we also identify the *relationship* between the clusters of the two data types. The applications we present in the Section 6 rely heavily on the ability to represent users and content sources in a shared latent space.

3.3 Problem formulation

To learn the latent space of the input data (users and sources) we use non-negative matrix factorization (NMF) techniques. In particular, we propose a joint matrix factorization formulation, which exploits the duality between user and source clustering.

First, assume that the ideological leaning is represented by k factors (dimensions). Our model is described by two components. The first component, represented by a $n \times k$ matrix $\mathbf{U}$, captures user information. In particular, the entry (u, i) of the matrix $\mathbf{U}$ represents the degree to which user u aligns with ideology factor i.

The second component, represented by a $m \times k$ matrix $\mathbf{V}$, captures source information: the entry (s, i) of the matrix $\mathbf{V}$ represents the degree to which source item s aligns with ideology factor i.

To determine the user and source ideology clusters, we decompose the two input matrices $\mathbf{A}$ and $\mathbf{C}$, using the components $\mathbf{U}$ and $\mathbf{V}$ as latent factors. For decomposing $\mathbf{A}$ and $\mathbf{C}$ so as to capture ideology clusters we require the following constraints.

Partitioning constraints:

1. Users in a user-cluster interact with each other more often than with users outside the cluster.

2. Users in the same user-cluster post content from the same content-cluster.
3. Content in the same content-cluster is posted by users in the same user-cluster.

Co-partitioning constraints:

4. Users in a user-cluster share more articles from their corresponding content-cluster than from other content-clusters.
5. Content in a content-cluster is shared by more users from their corresponding user-cluster than from other user-clusters.

Non-negative matrix factorization for co-clustering: For a given input data matrix $\mathbf{X}$, the bi-orthogonal non-negative 3-factor decomposition (ONMTF) [12], formulated as $\mathbf{X} \approx \mathbf{W}\mathbf{H}\mathbf{Z}^T$, provides a good framework for simultaneously clustering the rows and the columns of $\mathbf{X}$. The left factor $\mathbf{W}$ provides a clustering of the rows of $\mathbf{X}$, while the right matrix $\mathbf{Z}$ provides a clustering of the columns of $\mathbf{X}$. The middle factor $\mathbf{H}$ provides association between the clusters and additional degrees of freedom.

PROBLEM 1. (ONMTF *[12]) Given an $n \times m$ matrix $\mathbf{X}$, and integer k, with $k << n, m$, find non-negative matrices $\mathbf{W}$, $\mathbf{H}$, and $\mathbf{Z}$, of respective dimensions $n \times k$, $k \times k$, and $k \times m$, so as to*

$$\begin{aligned} \textit{minimize} \quad & \|\mathbf{X} - \mathbf{W}\mathbf{H}\mathbf{Z}^T\|_F^2, \\ \textit{subject to} \quad & \mathbf{W} \geq 0, \mathbf{H} \geq 0, \mathbf{Z} \geq 0, \\ \textit{and} \quad & \mathbf{W}^T\mathbf{W} = \mathbf{Z}^T\mathbf{Z} = \mathbf{I}. \end{aligned}$$

As shown by Ding et al. [12], the bi-orthogonality constraints provide an interpretation of the ONMTF problem as a simultaneous clustering of the rows and columns of the input data matrix.

In our approach we use ONMTF to decompose the input matrices (social-graph matrix $\mathbf{A}$ and user–source matrix $\mathbf{C}$) using the latent factors $\mathbf{U}$ and $\mathbf{V}$.

First, the user–source matrix is decomposed by $\mathbf{C} \approx \mathbf{U}\mathbf{H}_s\mathbf{V}^T$, subject to orthogonality constraints for $\mathbf{U}$ and $\mathbf{V}$.

For the social-graph matrix $\mathbf{A}$, as both the rows and columns represent users, we equate the left and right factors and require $\mathbf{A} \approx \mathbf{U}\mathbf{H}_u\mathbf{U}^T$, subject to orthogonality constraints for $\mathbf{U}$.

Note that as $\mathbf{H}_u$ is not necessarily symmetric, the decomposition $\mathbf{U}\mathbf{H}_u\mathbf{U}^T$ can produce a non-symmetric matrix. Furthermore, the formulation can capture link transitivity [37]: consider a path $u_i \rightarrow u_k \rightarrow u_j$. A non-symmetric factorization $\mathbf{A} \approx \mathbf{X}\mathbf{Z}^T$ represents the values of $\mathbf{A}$ as links from set of users to a set of objects, say, $O = \{o_i\}$. Hence, it would split the path $(u_i \rightarrow u_k \rightarrow u_j)$ into two parts $u_i \rightarrow o_k$ and $u_k \rightarrow o_j$, which is a misinterpretation of the original path. Whereas, $\mathbf{A} \approx \mathbf{U}\mathbf{H}_u\mathbf{U}^T$ considers the links to be amongst the same set of objects. Hence, the transitive link $u_i \rightarrow u_k \rightarrow u_j$ is correctly captured by the latent factors in $\mathbf{U}$.

Combining link and content information is achieved by using a common latent factor $\mathbf{U}$ and formulating a joint factorization problem asking to minimize

$$\|\mathbf{A} - \mathbf{U}\mathbf{H}_u\mathbf{U}^T\|_F^2 + \|\mathbf{C} - \mathbf{U}\mathbf{H}_s\mathbf{V}^T\|_F^2, \tag{1}$$

subject to non-negativity of $\mathbf{U}$, $\mathbf{H}_u$, $\mathbf{V}$, $\mathbf{H}_s$, and orthogonality of $\mathbf{U}$ and $\mathbf{V}$. This approach is inspired by the formulation of Zhu et al. [37] for classifying web-pages by exploiting both content and link information.

Graph regularization. From a geometric perspective, a dataset can be viewed as a set of data points on a continuous manifold. The task of clustering is to find these intrinsic manifolds in the data. However, the clustering formulation of ONMTF fails to consider this geometric structure in the data. To address this problem, Cai et al. [7] introduced a graph-regularized NMF based on the *manifold assumption* that if two data points $\mathbf{x}_i$, $\mathbf{x}_j$ are close in the input data matrix $\mathbf{X}$, their projections $\mathbf{u}_i$ and $\mathbf{u}_j$ in the new basis $\mathbf{U}$ are also close. This is formulated by seeking to minimize

$$\frac{1}{2}\sum_{i,j}\|\mathbf{u}_i - \mathbf{u}_j\|^2\mathbf{W}_{ij} = tr(\mathbf{U}^T\mathbf{L}\mathbf{U}),$$

where $\mathbf{W}$ is the affinity matrix of rows of $\mathbf{X}$ (see Section 3.1), and $\mathbf{L}$ is the laplacian of $\mathbf{W}$.

Motivated by the duality between row and column manifolds, Gu et al. [21] proposed a dual-manifold regularized co-clustering method as a decomposition of an input matrix $\mathbf{X}$, by asking to minimize

$$\|\mathbf{X} - \mathbf{W}\mathbf{H}\mathbf{Z}^T\|_F^2 + \alpha \cdot tr(\mathbf{W}^T\mathbf{L}_w\mathbf{W}) + \beta \cdot tr(\mathbf{Z}^T\mathbf{L}_z\mathbf{Z}),$$

subject to non-negativity constraints of the factor matrices. Here $\mathbf{L}_w$ and $\mathbf{L}_z$ are the Laplacians on the affinity matrices of rows and columns of $\mathbf{X}$, respectively. As before, the matrix $\mathbf{H}$ captures the association between row and column clusters.

We extend our joint factorization model (Equation 1) by including dual-graph regularization constraints on users and sources. We refer to this problem by IFD, for *ideology factor decomposition.* The formal problem definition is the following.

PROBLEM 2 (IFD). *Given a user–user social matrix $\mathbf{A}$ of dimension $n \times n$, a user–source matrix $\mathbf{C}$ of dimension $n \times m$, an integer k, with $k << n, m$, and regularization parameters α and β, find factors $\mathbf{U}$, $\mathbf{H}_u$, $\mathbf{V}$, $\mathbf{H}_s$, of dimensions $n \times k$, $k \times k$, $m \times k$, $n \times k$, respectively, so as to*

$$\begin{aligned} \textit{minimize} \quad & \|\mathbf{A} - \mathbf{U}\mathbf{H}_u\mathbf{U}^T\|_F^2 + \|\mathbf{C} - \mathbf{U}\mathbf{H}_s\mathbf{V}^T\|_F^2 \\ & + \alpha \cdot tr(\mathbf{U}^T\mathbf{L}_u\mathbf{U}) + \beta \cdot tr(\mathbf{V}^T\mathbf{L}_s\mathbf{V}), \qquad (2) \\ \textit{subject to} \quad & \mathbf{U} \geq 0, \mathbf{H}_u \geq 0, \mathbf{V} \geq 0, \mathbf{H}_s \geq 0, \\ \textit{and} \quad & \mathbf{U}^T\mathbf{U} = \mathbf{V}^T\mathbf{V} = \mathbf{I}, \end{aligned}$$

where $\mathbf{L}_u$ and $\mathbf{L}_s$ are the Laplacians of the affinity matrices of rows (users) and columns (sources) of $\mathbf{C}$, respectively.

In the IFD problem we factorize $\mathbf{A}$ and $\mathbf{C}$ jointly based on the dual manifold assumption i.e., both users and content share the same latent space and the cluster labels of users are smooth with respect to the content manifold, while the cluster labels of content are smooth with respect to the user manifold. To apply these manifold constraints, we consider affinity matrices for users and content sources. While there are many ways to construct such an affinity matrices, in our experiments we consider the affinity matrices of the rows (for users) and columns (for sources) of the $\mathbf{C}$ matrix.

Finally, it is instructive to review how IFD addresses the *partitioning constraints* 1–3 and *co-partitioning constraints* 4–5: the bi-orthogonality constraints on the tri-factorization problem provide a clustering interpretation for the rows and columns of the input matrices, while the manifold constraints provide a geometric interpretation to the discovered latent space. The correspondance between the user clusters and source clusters is achieved by using a shared latent factor.

3.4 Solving the optimization problem

Following the standard theory of constrained optimization, we solve Problem 2 by introducing Lagrangian multipliers Λ (a symmetric matrix of size $k \times k$) and minimizing the Lagrangian function

$$\begin{aligned} L \;=\; & \|\mathbf{A} - \mathbf{U}\mathbf{H}_u\mathbf{U}^T\|_F^2 + \|\mathbf{C} - \mathbf{U}\mathbf{H}_s\mathbf{V}^T\|_F^2 \\ & + \alpha \cdot tr(\mathbf{U}^T\mathbf{L}_u\mathbf{U}) + \beta \cdot tr(\mathbf{V}^T\mathbf{L}_s\mathbf{V}) \\ & tr(\Lambda(\mathbf{U}^T\mathbf{U} - \mathbf{I})) + tr(\Lambda(\mathbf{V}^T\mathbf{V} - \mathbf{I})). \end{aligned} \tag{3}$$

We can compute the gradient of L with respect to $\mathbf{U}$, $\mathbf{V}$, $\mathbf{H}_u$, and $\mathbf{H}_s$. A locally-optimal solution for Problem 2 can be found using an iterative-update algorithm, similar to the one proposed by Ding et al. [12]. The multiplicative update rules are as follows:

$$U \leftarrow U \sqrt{\frac{AUH_1^T + CVH_3^T + \alpha S_u U}{UH_1U^TUH_1^T + UH_3V^TVH_3^T + \alpha D_u U + U\lambda_u}}, \tag{4}$$

$$V \leftarrow V \sqrt{\frac{C^TUH_3 + \beta S_d V}{\beta D_d V + VH_3U^TUH_3 + V\lambda_v}}, \tag{5}$$

$$H_1 \leftarrow H_1 \sqrt{\frac{U^TAU}{U^TUH_1U^TU}}, \tag{6}$$

$$H_3 \leftarrow H_3 \sqrt{\frac{U^TCV}{U^TUH_3V^TV}}, \tag{7}$$

where

$\lambda_u = U^TAUH_1^T + U^TCVH_3^T - \alpha U^TL_uU - H_1U^TUH_1^T - H_3V^TVH_3^T$ and $\lambda_v = V^TC^TUH_3 - \beta V^TL_dV - H_3U^TUH_3$.

4 ESTIMATING IDEOLOGICAL LEANING

In this section we discuss how to use the latent factors $\mathbf{U}$ and $\mathbf{V}$ computed using IFD in order to estimate ideological leaning scores for Twitter users and media channels (sources). Our approach utilizes the probabilistic model of NMF factorizations, discussed in Yoo et al. [36], to derive a probabilistic interpretation of latent factors. We also discuss how to derive a hard cross-ideological separation (hard clustering) from the latent factors.

As proposed in the literature [23, 36], the latent factors $\mathbf{U}$ and $\mathbf{V}$ have the following probabilistic interpretation:

- the entry (i, ℓ) of matrix $\mathbf{U}$ indicates the degree to which user i belongs to the user-cluster ℓ; and
- the entry (j, ℓ) of matrix $\mathbf{V}$ indicates the degree to which media source j belongs to the content-cluster ℓ.

In the context of our problem setting, we are interested in identifying two main ideologies, *liberal* and *conservative*, and thus, we set the number of latent dimensions equal to 2 ($k = 2$). It follows that each user and each media source are represented by a 2-dimensional vector (x, y) in the latent space — a row of $\mathbf{U}$ for users, and a row of $\mathbf{V}$ for media sources. Thus, user and source ideology hard clusters are derived as $\arg\max U_{ij}$ and $\arg\max V_{ij}$, respectively. To estimate a single score for users and media sources, we compute the angle of line defined by the center of origin and the latent vector (x, y), normalized to be between 0 and 1, i.e.,[1]

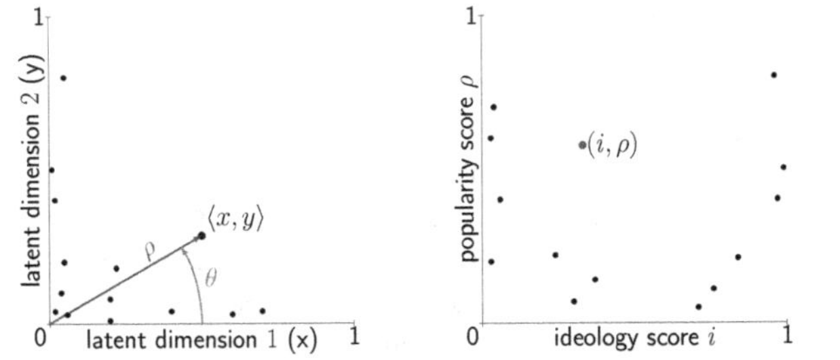

(a) original latent space (b) transformed coordinate space

Figure 1: Projection of a subset data points in the learned ideology latent space and the transformed ideology-popularity coordinate space.

$$i(x, y) = \frac{\theta}{\pi/2} = \frac{\arctan(y/x)}{\pi/2}. \tag{8}$$

We also compute the magnitude of the latent vector (x, y)

$$\rho(x, y) = \sqrt{x^2 + y^2}, \tag{9}$$

which, as can be shown easily, represents the popularity of the corresponding user or source — in particular, it is correlated with the number of re-tweets and follows of a given user, and the number of tweets containing a given source. Figure 1 visualizes a subset of real data points projected in the original latent space and their transformation to the corresponding ideology/popularity co-ordinate space according to the aforementioned computations.

In summary, given a user or media source represented by a latent vector (x, y), we can estimate a single ideological leaning score by Equation (8), as well as its popularity by Equation (9). When using more than 2 dimensions for the latent ideology space ($k > 2$) it is not possible to estimate ideology scores with a single number, but we can still handle the user and source representations by standard vector operations.

5 EXPERIMENTS

5.1 Dataset

Our dataset is collected using Twitter's streaming API from 2011 to 2016, by filtering for keywords related to three popular controversial topics: *gun control*, *abortion* and *obamacare*. We use the list of keywords proposed by Lu et al. [27] to filter the tweets related to these topics. We only consider users who tweeted about all three topics at least once, obtaining a set of $n = 6\,391$ users, and collect all their tweets, which gave us 19 million tweets.

As discussed in Section 3, we consider two variants of matrix $\mathbf{A}$ (*retweet* and *follow*) and two variants of matrix $\mathbf{C}$ (*urls* and *hostnames*). We observe that the *follow* user-user matrix $\mathbf{A}$ along with *hostname* user-content matrix $\mathbf{C}$ gives significantly superior results compared to all other variants, thus, all subsequent results use that variant. We omit results with the other variants due to lack of space.

[1] Recall that $\arctan(0) = 0$ and $\lim_{z \to \infty} \arctan(z) = \pi/2$.

5.2 Ground truth

Ideology scores for sources: We collect ground truth for news-media channels from multiple studies in the literature: (i) 500 most shared news domains on Facebook [3] (ii) 100 most visited domains in Bing toolbar [14] and (iii) 27 domains from an offline survey and webpage visit data [17]. Each of these scores roughly measures the fraction of views/shares/clicks by a conservative user. We map all scores in the [0,1] range, 1 being conservative. For the domains listed in multiple lists we compute the ideology by averaging the scores. We also remove domains that are not necessarily news sources (e.g., *wikipedia.org*, *reddit.com*, etc.). In total, we collect 559 news domains with ground-truth ideology scores. We refer to this dataset as CONTENT ground truth.

Ideology scores for Twitter users: We use two different ground-truth scores for users: (i) BARBERA: ideology score estimated by Barberá et al. [5], which applies Bayesian ideal point estimate on nearly 12 million Twitter users, and (ii) AVG_CONTENT: average ground-truth ideology scores of the sources tweeted by the user.

Popularity scores for sources: We use the aggregated number of tweets about each news media channel in the collected data set as a proxy for the popularity of the source.

Popularity scores for users: Since the collection of users is a random set of people on user, we do not have any ground truth for popularity of Twitter users.

5.3 Baseline algorithms

We compare our method with three types of methods for ideology detection: network-only, content-only, and a combination of network and content.

Network-only: We consider two types of network-only methods: (i) NMF-based methods that can provide a continuous ideology score for a user between 0 and 1; and (ii) other methods that only produce binary labels for ideology (a user is either liberal or conservative). We use symmetric NMF (NMF-SYMM) [12], a 3-factor NMF shown to be equivalent to normalized-cut spectral clustering [11], RETWEET a method based on partitioning the retweet graph [15] and FOLLOW a graph partitioning approach on the follow network. In order to construct a source-source relationship matrix, we use $C^T C$. It is noteworthy that network-only methods perform only one-side clustering – one data type at a time. Hence, we need to apply the methods separately for users and content sources. As such, network-only methods do not provide any information about the correspondence between the two clusterings. Further, RETWEET and FOLLOW return only binary labels, hence we do not use this baseline for comparing ideology scores.

Content-only: We use orthogonal NMF tri-factorization (ONMTF), a co-clustering approach [12], and dual manifold co-clustering (DMCC) [21]. In these methods the bipartite content matrix **C** is used to co-cluster the rows (users) and columns (sources) of the matrix simultaneously using bi-orthogonality and graph-regularization constraints.

Network and content: We compute ideology scores of Twitter users estimated by kulshrestha et al. [22] (KULSHRESTHA) and Lu et al. [27] (BIASWATCH).

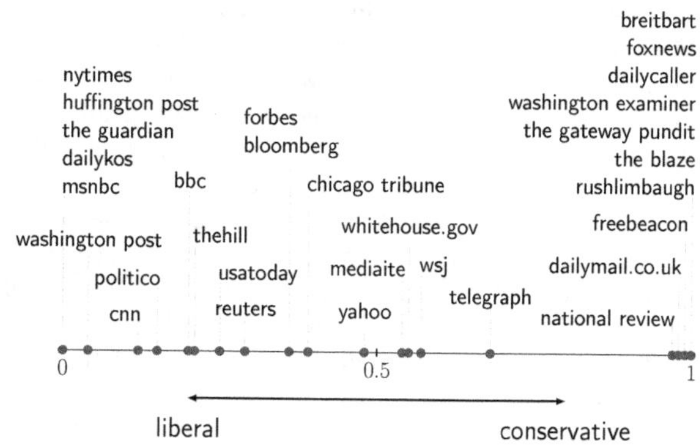

Figure 2: Popular media outlets and their ideology leaning scores computed by our method.

Proposed methods: We use the proposed method IFD, and a variant of IFD without graph-regularization constraints (IFD-NGR). We initialized **U** and **V** randomly from a uniform distribution in [0,1] and $\mathbf{H}_u$ and $\mathbf{H}_s$ as identity matrices of size k. Parameters α and β are chosen using grid search. Additional details on various approaches tried for parameter initialization, parameter tuning, and stability of the algorithms with respect to the parameters are omitted due to lack of space, and will be provided in the full version of the paper.

5.4 Experimental setup

Evaluation measures. We perform two types of qualitative evaluation tasks: (i) quality of ideological cluster separation (into *liberal* or *conservative* clusters) and (ii) correlation between the computed ideology scores and ground-truth scores. In order to evaluate cluster separation, we measure PURITY, adjusted Rand index (ARI), adjusted mutual information (AMI), and normalized mutual information (NMI) between the clusters detected by the algorithm and the set of ground-truth communities derived by separating users at ideology score threshold at 0.5. In order to measure correlation between the computed ideology scores and the ground-truth scores, we use Pearson mutual correlation coefficient (CORR).

5.5 Results

Ideology estimates for users and sources. At a first look, the user ideology scores seem intuitive with the top liberal users being @barackobama (score: 0.0), @berniesanders (0.0), @thedemocrats (0.0) and top conservative users @tedcruz (score: 0.99), @seanhannity (0.99), and @davidlimbaugh (0.9). Figure 2 shows popular news-media outlets and their ideology leaning scores computed by our method. We observe that the position of the news sources is as expected: Liberal-leaning news outlets (e.g., *nytimes, washington post, the guardian*) are on the left, and conservative news outlets (e.g., *fox news, breitbart, rushlimbaugh*) on the right. This is also consistent with the survey-based results found by [28]. While it is easy to identify the extreme left and right, it is more difficult to identify the neutral users and sources (like *yahoo, mediaite, whitehouse.gov*, etc), which, in fact, is the most important subset of users and sources to tackle the information filter-bubble issue.

Evaluation of clustering and ideology scores. We compare the proposed methods with the baselines on (i) quality of ideological cluster separation (PURITY, ARI, AMI and NMI) and (ii) correlation (CORR) between computed ideology score and ground-truth scores. The results of both evaluation tasks are listed in Table 1. Following are some noteworthy observations:

(i) IFD has the best performance among all the methods for both user as well as source clustering. We observe that combining network and content information gives consistently best results. For example, PURITY of clustering for combined methods is 20% higher than content-only methods for users and 27% higher for source clustering.

(ii) When comparing ideology scores, IFD performs better than state of the art baselines KULSHRESTHA and BIASWATCH. Note that BIASWATCH almost has no correlation with ground truth and performs poorly. This could be due to reasons mentioned in Section 2. Though KULSHRESTHA works slightly better on the clustering task, it doesn't do so well with the correlation. This indicates that our method is able to identify the fine grained ideology scores better, where as KULSHRESTHA can do better at separating users into binary clusters.

(iii) NMF-SYMM, a network-only method, performs quite well for user clustering, whereas the results are not satisfactory for source clustering. Perhaps this can be attributed to the noise in the input matrix C^TC, caused by, e.g., sparsity and topical diversity of user interests, which is mitigated in IFD because of the joint factorization. Similarly, our method performs much better than RETWEET and FOLLOW, which do not use both content and network information.

Audience of news sources. Figure 3 shows a kernel density estimate (KDE) of ideology scores computed using the proposed method (solid line) and ground truth of ideology scores (dashed line) for all 6 391 users for a selection of 5 representative news channels. The findings from our experiments are strikingly similar to the results computed using extensive user surveys [28]. We can clearly observe that there is a non-trivial association between news sources and polarization of users.

Table 1: Comparison of the proposed method with baseline methods on (i) quality of ideological cluster separation (PURITY, ARI, AMI and NMI) and (ii) correlation (CORR) between computed ideology score and ground truth. CORR for ideology is represented as CORR_i and for popularity as CORR_ρ. Since, we do not have ground truth for popularity of users we do not compute CORR_ρ for users. Best results for each measure are marked in bold.

(a) Evaluation for users using BARBERA ground truth (upper value in each row) and AVG_CONTENT ground truth (lower value in each row)

Type	Method	PURITY	ARI	AMI	NMI	CORR_i	CORR_ρ
Network Only	NMF-SYMM	**0.928** 0.861	**0.733** 0.522	**0.628** 0.418	**0.629** 0.418	**0.912** 0.744	- -
	RETWEET	0.844 0.839	0.476 0.461	0.385 0.395	0.385 0.399	- -	- -
	FOLLOW	0.867 0.845	0.538 0.476	0.454 0.382	0.456 0.382	- -	- -
Content Only	ONMTF	0.743 0.749	0.234 0.247	0.233 0.223	0.266 0.246	0.756 0.715	- -
	DMCC	0.74 0.746	0.229 0.241	0.23 0.218	0.263 0.242	0.755 0.715	- -
Network + Content	IFD	**0.925** **0.863**	**0.722** **0.528**	**0.62** **0.441**	**0.621** **0.442**	**0.904** **0.772**	- -
	IFD-NGR	**0.925** **0.863**	**0.722** **0.528**	**0.62** **0.441**	**0.621** **0.442**	**0.904** **0.772**	- -
	KULSHRESTHA	**0.931** **0.869**	**0.744** **0.547**	**0.637** **0.448**	**0.638** **0.449**	0.875 0.744	- -
	BIASWATCH	0.541 0.543	0.000 0.000	0.000 0.000	0.000 0.000	0.002 0.018	- -

(b) Evaluation for sources using CONTENT ground truth

Network Only	NMF-SYMM	0.597	0.031	0.135	0.171	0.752	0.597
	FOLLOW	0.819	0.405	0.318	0.32	-	-
Content Only	ONMTF	0.606	0.039	0.145	0.181	0.746	0.593
	DMCC	0.606	0.039	0.145	0.181	0.746	0.592
Network + Content	IFD	**0.826**	**0.424**	**0.346**	**0.348**	**0.827**	**0.929**
	IFD-NGR	**0.822**	**0.415**	**0.339**	**0.341**	**0.813**	**0.93**

6 DIFFUSING THE INFORMATION BUBBLE

In the recent years, a few papers [16] have aimed to solve the problem of echo chambers and filter bubbles on social media by connecting users with others outside of their bubble. The problem with most of these approaches is that they typically suggest technical solutions that do not take into account user biases, such as, cognitive dissonance [13] and biased assimilation [26]. In addition, in many cases, users themselves are not aware of being present in a bubble, due to the non-transparent nature of algorithmic filtering.[2]

To handle both these issues, we propose that a better solution to take users out of their bubble is to give them *information* and *choice*. We do this in two steps: (i) make a user aware of their information bubble, and (ii) provide content recommendations that can help users diffuse their bubble. In this section, we demonstrate how to use the latent space representations learned in this paper to perform both of these steps.

6.1 Visualizing the information bubble

Recent studies have shown that making users aware of their imbalance in media consumption can encourage them to make small yet significant improvements in increasing the diversity of their reading [29]. Inspired by these studies, we suggest providing to the users a visual way to explore their information filter bubble.

The way we approach this is by visualizing the user and content in the same space to allow users to explore their content consumption. To this end, we use the learned latent space to map the users and content in the same space. Using their estimated ideological positions (from Section 4), we project users as well as sources in a two dimensional ideology-popularity coordinate space with computed ideology score on x-axis and popularity score on y-axis. Since we do not have popularity score for users, we determine the position of a user on y-axis using the average popularity score of the content that the user engages with. Since all user scores are on the same scale and relative to each other, we would observe that users and

[2]E.g., the filter bubble is claimed to be a reason why many people did not predict correctly the results of Brexit or US elections
http://flamingogroup.com/trump-brexit-and-why-we-didnt-see-them-coming

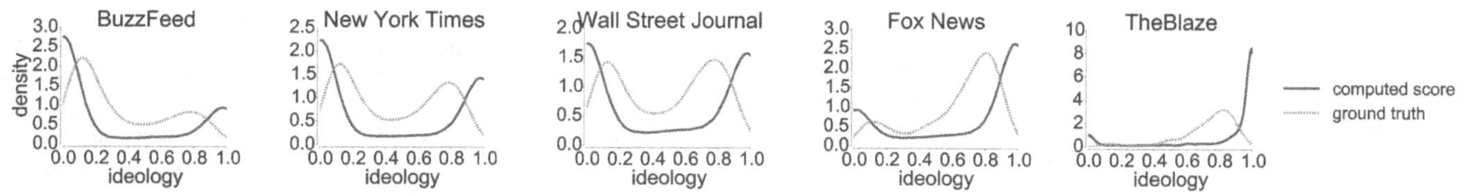

Figure 3: Polarization of the audience of news sources. Values on the x-axis represent the ideology score of users and values on the y-axis represent the kernel density estimate of the number of users at each point.

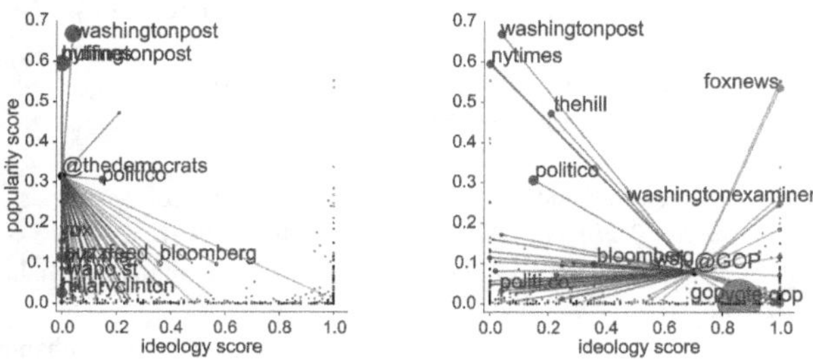

(a) Democratic Party (b) Republican Party

Figure 4: Ideological position of @thedemocrats and @gop (black dots) and their content engagement. Points in the grey are the sources that the user never interacted with.

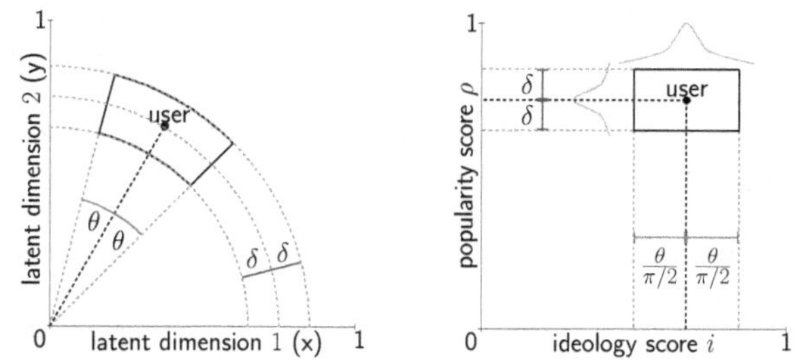

(a) original latent space (b) transformed latent space

Figure 5: Logical diagram of user content recommendation by sampling from the Gaussian over "ideology" and "popularity" positioning.

sources with similar ideology lie close to each other. Finally, we connect users to the sources that they consume by drawing a link between them. The size of a source node is proportionate to the number of times a user has consumed content from the said source. In order to increase the ease of visual interpretation, we color the content according to the ideological learning (blue: liberal, green: neutral and red: conservative). Content not consumed by the user is colored gray.

Figure 4 presents a prototype for two popular Twitter accounts from the two ends of the political spectrum: the Republican Party (@gop) and the Democratic party (@thedemocrats).[3] From this figure, one can visually observe their own ideological positioning as well as the ideology of the content that they engage with. For instance, @thedemocrats is heavily liberal in their ideology (ideology score 0.0). The content consumed by @thedemocrats is also heavily biased on the liberal side. As expected, a large fraction of the content they engage with is from the left (mainly liberal media like *nytimes.com* and *washingtonpost.com*), and negligible amount from the opposite point of view, whereas the opposite is true for @gop. It is interesting to observe that the Republican party account has a higher engagement with diverse view points than the Democrats.

6.2 Making ideologically diverse content recommendations

Garimella et al. [16] proposed an approach to diffuse a user's filter bubble by connecting him to a user outside his bubble from the opposing viewpoint. Their approach is mainly based on identifying users from opposing sides and optimizing a global function. Here, we build on top of that idea and use our computed ideology to diffuse a user's bubble by recommending him content from an opposing viewpoint, along with an *option* to choose how willing the user is to explore the other side. Recommending ideologically diverse content to a user can be controlled by the user using two parameters: ideology tolerance threshold θ and popularity threshold δ. Intuitively, a user is more likely to accept content within the region $+\theta$ and $-\theta$ on either side of the user's ideological positioning, and $+\delta$ and $-\delta$ on either side of his popularity position. Figure 5a visualizes a hypothetical user in the original ideology latent space and the transformed ideology-popularity coordinate space (detailed in Section 4). Consider that we build two Gaussian distributions around the user *box* (see Figure 5b) with their means centered at user's ideology and popularity score respectively, and variance as a function of the tolerance threshold given as input by the user. We can now sample content from these Gaussian distributions and use it for recommending content to the user. As desired, in such a sampling, the content close to the user's own ideology and popularity score has a higher probability of being selected. As we move closer to the thresholds, the probability of an article being selected gradually decreases. This "*box*" gives the space of exploration for a user and depending on the user's willingness to explore (based on parameters θ, δ), they can see content outside their bubble.

7 CONCLUSIONS

We considered the problem of identifying ideological leaning of users and news sources (content) on Twitter. The paper tackles two main challenges: (i) learning the ideological latent factors of users and content in a joint model that explores simultaneously user-to-user and user-to-content relations; and (ii) embedding the discovered factors in a common latent space so as to support visualization and exploration of the results. Our approach distinguishes itself from most existing work in the area in three major ways. First,

[3] An interactive web version of these plots can be accessed at http://resources.mpi-inf.mpg.de/d5/filterbubble.

our model aims to learn ideology on a continuous scale rather than a binary *liberal-conservative* opinion, which is a much simpler and well studied problem. Second, our model defines polarization as a multidimensional problem and allows for learning any number of dimensions (ideology, popularity, etc) rather than just one (ideology). Third, our model can identify the ideology of both the user and content simultaneously, thus making use of the interdependent structure between content and network. We also demonstrate how to use the learned latent space in an application of providing tools to visualize a users information bubble and for ideologically diverse content recommendation with the purpose of diffusing their information filter bubble.

Future work. One of the main focuses of this work was to create a strong technical foundation to understand the problem of online polarization. We believe that the methods presented in this paper provide several avenues for future work in multiple emerging interdisciplinary research areas, for instance, humanly interpretable and explanatory machine learning, transparent recommendations and a new era of social media platforms that encourage discussion and debates between users of diverse view points, thus helping to reduce the ideological segregation of users instead of reinforcing it.

Acknowledgments. This work was supported by the Academy of Finland projects "Nestor" (286211) and "Agra" (313927), and the EC H2020 RIA project "SoBigData" (654024).

8 REFERENCES

[1] Eduardo Alemán, Ernesto Calvo, Mark P Jones, and Noah Kaplan. 2009. Comparing Cosponsorship and Roll-Call Ideal Points. *Legislative Studies Quarterly* 34, 1 (2009), 87–116.

[2] Joseph Bafumi, Andrew Gelman, David K Park, and Noah Kaplan. 2005. Practical issues in implementing and understanding Bayesian ideal point estimation. *Political Analysis* 13, 2 (2005), 171–187.

[3] Eytan Bakshy, Solomon Messing, and Lada Adamic. 2015. Exposure to ideologically diverse news and opinion on Facebook. *Science* (2015).

[4] Pablo Barberá. 2015. Birds of the Same Feather Tweet Together: Bayesian Ideal Point Estimation Using Twitter Data. *Political Analysis.*

[5] Pablo Barberá, John Jost, Jonathan Nagler, Joshua Tucker, and Richard Bonneau. 2015. Tweeting from left to right: Is online political communication more than an echo chamber?. In *Psychological science.*

[6] Adam Bonica. 2013. Ideology and interests in the political marketplace. *American Journal of Political Science* 57 (2013).

[7] Deng Cai, Xiaofei He, Xiaoyun Wu, and Jiawei Han. 2008. Non-negative matrix factorization on manifold. In *ICDM.*

[8] Raviv Cohen and Derek Ruths. 2013. Classifying political orientation on Twitter: It's not easy!. In *ICWSM.*

[9] Michael Conover, Bruno Gonçalves, Jacob Ratkiewicz, Alessandro Flammini, and Filippo Menczer. 2011. Predicting the political alignment of twitter users. In *SocialCom.*

[10] Michael Dimock, Carroll Doherty, Jocelyn Kiley, and Russ Oates. 2014. Political polarization in the American public. In *Pew Research Center.*

[11] Chris Ding, Xiaofeng He, and Horst Simon. 2005. On the equivalence of nonnegative matrix factorization and spectral clustering. In *SDM.*

[12] Chris Ding, Tao Li, Wei Peng, and Haesun Park. 2006. Orthogonal nonnegative matrix tri-factorizations for clustering. In *KDD.*

[13] Leon Festinger. 1962. *A theory of cognitive dissonance.* Vol. 2. Stanford University Press.

[14] Seth Flaxman, Sharad Goel, and Justin Rao. 2016. Filter bubbles, echo chambers, and online news consumption. In *Public Opinion Quarterly.*

[15] Kiran Garimella, Gianmarco De Francisci Morales, Aristides Gionis, and Michael Mathioudakis. 2016. Quantifying controversy in social media. In *WSDM.*

[16] Kiran Garimella, Gianmarco De Francisci Morales, Aristides Gionis, and Michael Mathioudakis. 2017. Reducing controversy by connecting opposing views. In *WSDM.*

[17] Matthew Gentzkow and Jesse Shapiro. 2011. Ideological segregation online and offline. In *The Quarterly Journal of Economics.*

[18] Eduardo Graells-Garrido, Mounia Lalmas, and Daniele Quercia. 2014. People of opposing views can share common interests. In *WWW Companion.*

[19] Tim Groeling. 2013. Media bias by the numbers: Challenges and opportunities in the empirical study of partisan news. *Annual Review of Political Science* 16 (2013).

[20] Tim Groseclose and Jeffrey Milyo. 2005. A measure of media bias. *The Quarterly Journal of Economics* 120, 4 (2005), 1191–1237.

[21] Quanquan Gu and Jie Zhou. 2009. Co-clustering on manifolds. In *KDD.*

[22] Juhi Kulshrestha, Motahhare Eslami, Johnnatan Messias, Muhammad Zafar, Saptarshi Ghosh, Krishna Gummadi, and Karrie Karahalios. 2017. Quantifying Search Bias: Investigating Sources of Bias for Political Searches in Social Media. In *CSCW.*

[23] Tao Li and Chris Ding. 2006. The relationships among various nonnegative matrix factorization methods for clustering. In *ICDM.*

[24] Vera Liao and Wai-Tat Fu. 2014. Can you hear me now? mitigating the echo chamber effect by source position indicators. In *CSCW.*

[25] Vera Liao and Wai-Tat Fu. 2014. Expert voices in echo chambers: effects of source expertise indicators on exposure to diverse opinions. In *CHI.*

[26] Charles Lord, Lee Ross, and Mark Lepper. 1979. Biased assimilation and attitude polarization: The effects of prior theories on subsequently considered evidence. *Journal of personality and social psychology* 37, 11 (1979).

[27] Haokai Lu, James Caverlee, and Wei Niu. 2015. Biaswatch: A lightweight system for discovering and tracking topic-sensitive opinion bias in social media. In *CIKM.*

[28] Amy Mitchell, Jeffrey Gottfried, Jocelyn Kiley, and Katerina Matsa. 2014. Political polarization & media habits. In *Pew Research Center.*

[29] Sean Munson, Stephanie Lee, and Paul Resnick. 2013. Encouraging reading of diverse political viewpoints with a browser widget. In *ICWSM.*

[30] Eli Pariser. 2011. *The filter bubble: What the Internet is hiding from you.* Penguin UK.

[31] Ferran Pla and Lluís Hurtado. 2014. Political Tendency Identification in Twitter using Sentiment Analysis Techniques. In *COLING.*

[32] Keith Poole and Howard Rosenthal. 1997. *Ideology and congress.* Transaction Publishers.

[33] Markus Prior. 2007. *Post-broadcast democracy: How media choice increases inequality in political involvement and polarizes elections.* Cambridge University Press.

[34] Cass Sunstein. 2009. *Republic. com 2.0.* Princeton University Press.

[35] Felix Ming Fai Wong, Chee Wei Tan, Soumya Sen, and Mung Chiang. 2016. Quantifying Political Leaning from Tweets, Retweets, and Retweeters. *TKDE* 28, 8 (2016), 2158–2172.

[36] Jiho Yoo and Seungjin Choi. 2010. Orthogonal nonnegative matrix tri-factorization for co-clustering: Multiplicative updates on stiefel manifolds. *IPM* 46, 5 (2010), 559–570.

[37] Shenghuo Zhu, Kai Yu, Yun Chi, and Yihong Gong. 2007. Combining content and link for classification using matrix factorization. In *SIGIR.*

Bayesian Optimization for Optimizing Retrieval Systems

Dan Li
University of Amsterdam
Amsterdam, The Netherlands
d.li@uva.nl

Evangelos Kanoulas
University of Amsterdam
Amsterdam, The Netherlands
e.kanoulas@uva.nl

ABSTRACT

The effectiveness of information retrieval systems heavily depends on a large number of hyperparameters that need to be tuned. Hyperparameters range from the choice of different system components, e.g., stopword lists, stemming methods, or retrieval models, to model parameters, such as $k1$ and b in BM25, or the number of query expansion terms. Grid and random search, the dominant methods to search for the optimal system configuration, lack a search strategy that can guide them in the hyperparameter space. This makes them inefficient and ineffective. In this paper, we propose to use Bayesian Optimization to jointly search and optimize over the hyperparameter space. Bayesian Optimization, a sequential decision making method, suggests the next most promising configuration to be tested on the basis of the retrieval effectiveness of configurations that have been examined so far. To demonstrate the efficiency and effectiveness of Bayesian Optimization we conduct experiments on TREC collections, and show that Bayesian Optimization outperforms manual tuning, grid search and random search, both in terms of retrieval effectiveness of the configuration found, and in terms of efficiency in finding this configuration.

CCS CONCEPTS

• **Information systems → Retrieval models and ranking**;

KEYWORDS

Retrieval system; Hyperparameter optimisation; Bayesian Optimization; Covariance function

ACM Reference Format:

Dan Li and Evangelos Kanoulas. 2018. Bayesian Optimization for Optimizing Retrieval Systems. In *WSDM 2018: The Eleventh ACM International Conference on Web Search and Data Mining, February 5–9, 2018, Marina Del Rey, CA, USA.* ACM, New York, NY, USA, 9 pages. https://doi.org/10.1145/3159652.3159665

1 INTRODUCTION

The effectiveness of information retrieval (IR) systems heavily depends on a large number of hyperparameters that need to be tuned. Hyperparameters range from the choice of different system components, e.g., stopword lists, stemming methods, retrieval models, to model parameters, such as $k1$ and b values in BM25, number of top-ranked documents to consider in pseudo-relevance feedback, and number of query expansion terms.

Retrieval performance is rather sensitive to parameter (or hyperparameter) tuning. Zhai and Lafferty [37] demonstrated this sensitivity for the smoothing parameters in language models, and Trotman et al. [31] for parameters in BM25. Automatic techniques for optimizing model parameters have attracted the attention of the research community in recent years [12–15, 20, 23, 24]. However, parameters are usually optimized in isolation, while their mutual dependencies are, to a great extend, unexplored [1, 19]. Ferro and Silvello [11] recently examined this mutual dependency between choices of stopword lists, stemmers and retrieval models, and concluded that parameter interactions have a strong effect on system performance.

Grid search has been the most widely used strategy for automatic joint optimization of hyperparameters in information retrieval [33]. Grid search is easy to implement, parallelization is trivial, and it is reliable in low dimensional spaces [3]. However, grid search suffers from the *curse of dimensionality* because the number of configurations grows exponentially with the number of hyperparameters [2]. To reduce the number of candidate configurations to be explored researchers often apply grid search on one dimension/hyperparameter at a time, while fixing the values of the rest hyperparameters until all of them have been traversed. However, this approach is not guaranteed to find a global optimum. Bergstra and Bengio [3] instead propose *random search* as a more efficient search algorithm. Random search generates candidate configurations drawn uniformly from the same configuration space as would be spanned by a regular grid. Bergstra and Bengio [3] show that random search is more efficient than grid search in high-dimensional spaces because objective functions of interest often have a low effective dimensionality, i.e. they are more sensitive to changes in some dimensions than others [7]. Nevertheless, random search remains agnostic to the effect that a δ-step in the hyperparameter space that would have to the effectiveness of an IR system. Quantifying this effect could lead to more efficient search strategies.

Bayesian Optimization has risen as a promising framework for efficient and effective search in the candidate configuration space [4, 5, 17, 25, 26, 29, 36]. Under the Bayesian Optimization framework, one does not need to explicitly specify the objective function; what is only necessary is the ability to query this function and get an observation. In the case of information retrieval, one does not need to analytically express system effectiveness as a function of the hyperparameters, but only observe the effectiveness of a system configuration in terms of an evaluation measure, e.g. average precision. Bayesian Optimization uses a surrogate model to approximate system effectiveness. Taking a prior belief over this surrogate model allows Bayesian Optimization to sequentially refine it. Further, the

WSDM 2018, February 5–9, 2018, Marina Del Rey, CA, USA

ACM ISBN 978-1-4503-5581-0/18/02...$15.00
https://doi.org/10.1145/3159652.3159665

surrogate model, which indicates a probability distribution over the possible system effectiveness functions, allows designing different strategies for selecting the next configuration to be tested, exploiting hyperparameter subspaces that have shown to contain high performance configurations, or exploring hyperparameter subspaces with high potential [25].

In this paper, we use Bayesian Optimization to automatically optimize the retrieval system hyperparameters. Information retrieval effectiveness, however, as a function of the hyperparameter space exhibits high irregularity. Furthermore, hyperparameters can be continuous, or categorical [10], with the latter contributing most of the irregularity of the objective function. To tackle this we model the effect of a δ-step in the hyperparameter space to the effectiveness of the IR system, by suggesting to use different similarity functions (covariance functions) for continuous and categorical hyperparameters, and examine their ability to effectively and efficiently guide the search in the hyperparameter space. We compare Bayesian Optimization to manual tuning, grid search, and random search using TREC collections, and demonstrate that Bayesian Optimization is able to find better configurations in terms of retrieval effectiveness when all methods are granted the same computational budget. To the best of our knowledge, this is the first work that uses Bayesian Optimization to find optimal configurations of retrieval systems.

Therefore, the main contributions of this work are the following:

(1) We propose the use of Bayesian Optimization for retrieval system configuration;
(2) We decompose the components of Bayesian Optimization that affect the effectiveness of the method and suggest an instantiation of it that fits the IR hyperparameter space; and
(3) We demonstrate the effectiveness of the method in building IR systems and explain the reason in terms of optimization behaviour.

2 RELATED WORK

We first discuss prior work on hyperparameter optimization in IR. Next, we give an overview of Bayesian Optimization methods and the domains they have been applied to.

2.1 Hyperparameter optimization in IR

Optimizing the hyperparameters of a retrieval system is inevitable in order to achieve optimal performance [33]. Different methods have been proposed in the literature for automatically optimizing individual components of a retrieval system [12–15, 20, 23, 24, 30, 38]. Taylor et al. [30] use gradient descent method to optimize the parameters of ranking functions like BM25F. Their approach however makes the assumption that the cost functions must be differentiable. Bigot et al. [6] propose a method for hyperparameter optimization on a per-query basis. However, this method is hard to generalise as it only works on queries already seen in the training set. Deveaud et al. [8] cast the problem of system configuration optimization as a ranking problem and use learning to rank approaches to select the best combination of hyperparameters for IR systems. The drawback is that all the configurations to be ranked must be run in advance for training and the element number of configurations (e.g. about 10,000 in the paper) grows exponentially with the number of space dimension. The work of [6] and [8] is orthogonal to the work in this paper. In both aforementioned works all candidate configurations need to be considered and the focus lies in finding the best one of them for each query. Instead, in this paper we propose a search strategy that avoids considering all candidate configurations and focuses search in the most promising sub-spaces of hyperparameter space.

2.2 Bayesian Optimization

The problem of hyperparameter optimization appears in many machine learning applications, and lately it has attracted a wide interest in that community [4, 5, 17, 25, 26, 29, 36]. Bayesian Optimization has emerged rapidly as a promising framework for efficiently identifying effective configurations. Popular Bayesian Optimization approaches include sequential model-based optimization (SMBO) [26], sequential model-based algorithm configuration (SMAC) [17], tree-based Parzen estimator (TPE) [5] and multi-task Bayesian Optimization [29] etc. Bayesian Optimization methods have been applied successfully in many tasks [28, 34, 36]. For example, Bayesian Optimization can find better hyperparameters for deep neural networks in MNIST digit recognition and CIFAR-10 object recognition [28]. Also, by applying TPE in feature selection, basic machine learning algorithms like logistic regression and SVM are proven to outperform state-of-art neural network models in topic classification and sentiment analysis task in NLP [36]. As an important surrogate model, Gaussian process as well as its covariance functions have been also studied extensively [18, 28]. These successful applications have inspired us to use Bayesian Optimization to optimize retrieval systems.

3 PRELIMINARIES

3.1 Bayesian Optimization

The Bayesian Optimization framework provides a mechanism to sequentially search for the global optimum x of an objective function $f(x) : \mathbb{X} \rightarrow \mathbb{R}$. There are two key components in Bayesian Optimization [25]. The first is a probabilistic *surrogate model* used to predict the objective function value y given a point x. For every x, there is a random variable y, whose distribution $p(y|x)$ is given by the surrogate model. One example of the predictive distribution $p(y|x)$ can be observed in the top panels of Figure 1. In this example the surrogate model is a Gaussian Process (described in Section 3.2). The black curve depicts the original objective function (for instance mean average precision), while the x-axis in the figure represents an 1-dimensional hyperparameter space, e.g. the parameter μ of a Language Model with Dirichlet smoothing. The predictive distribution of y can then be used to construct an *acquisition function*. An acquisition function is a policy for selecting the sequence of points $\{x_1, x_2, ..., x_i, ...\}$, i.e. a mechanism to select the next configuration x_{n+1} to test given $D_{1:n} := \{(x_1, y_1), (x_2, y_2), ..., (x_n, y_n)\}$. As the acquisition function x is usually a closed-form expression of hyperparameters it is easier to be optimized than the original objective function. The bottom panel of Figure 1 demonstrates an acquisition function. The acquisition function values for different configurations (i.e. along the x-axis) dictate the potential of a certain configuration to yield a high objective function value.

The second component is the *objective function* itself, a function of the target model requiring hyperparameter optimization. In our case the objective function can be any retrieval effectiveness measure, such as average precision, normalized discount cumulative gain and so on. Computing the objective function for different system configurations is the most time-consumptive step [5].

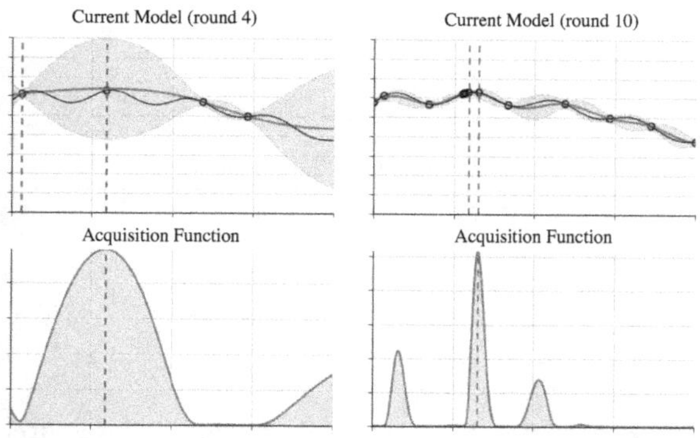

Figure 1: The optimization process of Bayesian Optimization. The upper panel describes the current model, and the bottom panel describes the acquisition function. The black curve is the actual objective function, the black dots are the observed values of the objective function. The red vertical line denotes the best value among the observed points, the green vertical line denotes the next point that Bayesian Optimization choose. The light blue line and shade are the estimated function values and variances.

The entire process of Bayesian Optimization is demonstrated in Algorithm 1. The algorithm stops when the computational budget is exhausted. Figure 1 uses an 1-dimensional continuous function to illustrate the optimization process, and demonstrates it at round 4 (i.e. after the first 3 configurations have been tests) at the left-most panels, and at round 10 at the right-most panels.

Algorithm 1 Bayesian Optimization

Require: surrogate model $\mathcal{M}$, acquisition function $\alpha_{\mathcal{M}}$, objective function f, input space X

Initially sample k points $\{x_1, x_2, \dots, x_k\}$ from X, query f to get $\{y_1, y_2, \dots, y_k\}$
Update $\mathcal{M}$
for $n = 1, 2, \dots$ **do**
  Select $x_{n+1} \leftarrow \underset{x}{\operatorname{argmax}}\, \alpha_{\mathcal{M}}(x; D_n)$
  Calculate $y_{n+1} \leftarrow f(x_{n+1})$
  Augment $D_{n+1} = \{D_n, (x_{n+1}, y_{n+1})\}$
  Update $\mathcal{M}$
end for
Select the best y from D

3.2 Gaussian Process

The Gaussian Process (GP) is the most commonly-used surrogate model in Bayesian Optimization [21]. The key hypothesis underlying GP is that any finite set of $\{y_i\}$ follows a Multivariate Gaussian Distribution. There is an analytic expression for the joint distribution $p(y_{1:n}|x_{1:n}) \sim N(0, K)$, with K being the covariance matrix,

$$K = \begin{bmatrix} k(x_1, x_1) & \cdots & k(x_1, x_n) \\ \vdots & \ddots & \vdots \\ k(x_n, x_1) & \cdots & k(x_n, x_n) \end{bmatrix}$$

and $k(x_i, x_j)$ being a covariance function. The conditional distribution of the objective function value given the sequence of past observations and a new point x_{n+1} is $p(y_{n+1}|x_{n+1}, D_{1:n}) \sim N(\mu_n(x_{n+1}), \sigma_n^2(x_{n+1}))$, where $\mu_n(x_{n+1})$, and $\sigma_n^2(x_{n+1})$ are the mean and the variance of the posterior distribution, respectively. They are defined as

$$\mu_n(x_{n+1}) = k^T K^{-1} y_{1:n}$$

$$\sigma_n^2(x_{n+1}) = k(x_{n+1}, x_{n+1}) - k^T K^{-1} k$$

and

$$k = \left[k(x_{n+1}, x_1), \quad k(x_{n+1}, x_2), \quad \cdots, \quad k(x_{n+1}, x_n)\right]^T$$

The covariance function models the effect of taking a δ-step in the hyperparameter space to the objective function. In Section 4.2 we suggest covariance functions we believe to be appropriate for the continuous, and categorical hyperparameters of a retrieval system.

3.3 Acquisition Function

A good acquisition function is the one that finds an optimal trade-off between exploration and exploitation in the hyperparameter space on the basis of the application at hand. In practice, an acquisition function balances between configurations for which the predicted function value $f(x)$ is high (exploitation) and configurations for which the predicted variance $\sigma(x)$ is high (exploration) [25]. In this work, we consider three acquisition functions: probability of improvement (PI), expected improvement (EI) [9] and upper confidence bound (UCB), defined as follows:

$$\alpha_{PI}(x|D_n) := P(y > y^*) = \Phi(\frac{\mu_n(x) - y^*}{\sigma_n(x)})$$

$$\alpha_{EI}(x|D_n) := \mathbb{E}(max(y - y^*, 0))$$

$$= (\mu_n(x) - y^*)\Phi(\frac{\mu_n(x) - y^*}{\sigma_n(x)}) + \sigma_n(x)\phi(\frac{\mu_n(x) - y^*}{\sigma_n(x)})$$

$$\alpha_{UCB}(x|D_n) := \mu_n(x) + \beta\sigma_n(x)$$

where $\alpha(\cdot)$ is the acquisition function, y^* is a target value which is often set to $\max(\{y_i\}_{i=1}^n)$ [35], and Φ and ϕ are the Cumulative Distribution Function and Probability Density Function of the standard normal distribution, respectively. β is a hyperparameter that can be set according to some theoretically motivated guidelines.

A drawback of PI, intuitively, is that it is pure exploitative. Configurations that have a high probability their effectiveness being infinitesimally greater than y^* will be drawn over configurations that offer larger gains but with less certainty. EI on the other hand considers the magnitude of the improvement a configuration can potentially yield, instead of PI. In UCB it is the parameter β that controls the trade-off between exploration and exploitation. These three acquisition functions are point-wise, that is they only care about the improvement over y^* on each single point. There are also entropy-based acquisition functions that make use of what has been observed about the objective function to pick up the most informative point, which will be left for the future study.

3.4 Initialization

The first posterior distribution of the surrogate model can be obtained by using the predefined prior distribution to draw the first hyperparameter point, i.e. the first configuration. This strategy runs the risk of getting stuck in a local optimum, since it heavily depends on the first point that will be used. A more general strategy, which we follow in this work is to sample a set of configurations randomly in the search space so that the surrogate model can observe the overall "landscape" of configurations. In this work we test three sampling methods: Latin hypercube sampling, random sampling, and sampling from Sobol sequences [16].

3.5 Selecting the Optimal Configuration

At the end of the optimization process one needs to decide which configuration is the optimal one. The natural choice is to select the configuration with the best observed effectiveness. However, this strategy runs the risk of overfitting the observed objective function values. A different strategy is to select the configuration with the highest predicted value, instead of the actual observed value, which can accommodate noisy outputs. The two strategies are called *incumbent* and *latent*, respectively [16], and we test both in this work.

4 METHODOLOGY

In this section we first elaborate the hyperparameter optimization process, then we focus on the particular characteristics of the retrieval systems hyperparameter space and discuss the covariance functions we consider appropriate for this space.

4.1 Hyperparameter Optimization Process

Following the Bayesian Optimization framework, we have two major modules in our algorithmic pipeline, the IR module and the BO module (see Figure 2). The IR module tackles the conditional hyperparameters, and computes the objective function value y_n, given a hyperparameter configuration x_n. The BO module adds (x_n, y_n) into the sample set, updates the posterior distribution of the surrogate models, selects the next hyperparameter configuration x_{n+1}, and passes it back to IR module.

4.2 Hyperparameter Structure and Covariance functions

Snoek et al. [26] suggest that it is the choice of the covariance functions that has the strongest effect on the performance of Bayesian Optimization . In this paper we only consider a simple case, *stationary covariance function*, which is defined as a function of $|\boldsymbol{x} - \boldsymbol{x}'|(= r)$. The *mean square differentiability* of a stationary covariance function around 0 determine the smoothness properties of the samples drawn from the corresponding Gaussian process [22], which essentially dictates the expected response in the objective function if a δ-step is taken in the hyperparameter space.

The *squared exponential covariance function* (SE) is a widely made choice for smooth objective functions; it is mean square differentiable at any order and thus very smooth. It is defined as:

$$K_{\text{SE}}(\boldsymbol{x}, \boldsymbol{x}') = \exp(-\frac{r^2}{2})$$

where $\boldsymbol{x}$ and $\boldsymbol{x}'$ are two points in the hyperparameter space, and r is the distance between $\boldsymbol{x}$ and $\boldsymbol{x}'$.

The *Matérn1 covariance function* (Matérn1) is appropriate to model rough objective functions, as it is only first-order mean square differentiable. Martén1 is defined as follows:

$$K_{\text{Matérn1}}(\boldsymbol{x}, \boldsymbol{x}') = \exp(-r).$$

Selecting a covariance function requires examining the hyperparameter space of an IR system. Retrieval model parameters, e.g. the smoothness parameter λ in Jelinek-Mercer Smoothing of Language Models, or the parameter b in BM25, are typically continuous. On the other hand, the choice of the retrieval model itself can be expressed with a categorical hyperparameter; the use or not of relevance feedback algorithms is also categorical, as is the choice of a stopword list, or a stemmer. The default distance used in either *SE covariance function* or *Matérn1 covariance function* is Euclidean distance, defined as

$$r_E := \sqrt{\sum_{d=1}^{N}(x_d - x_d')^2}.$$

It would treat categorical hyperparameters as ordinal, whereas this should not be the case. Therefore, considering the heterogeneity of the hyperparameters of IR systems, Euclidean distance is not a good fit. Instead, inspired by [17], we use *Hamming distance* for categorical dimensions, while *Euclidean distance* for continuous or discrete dimensions. The *Hamming distance* is defined as

$$r_H := \sum_{d=1}^{N}(1 - \delta(x_d, x_d'))$$

where δ is the Kronecker delta function (equalling one if its two arguments are identical and zero otherwise).

In order to accommodate both continuous and categorical hyperparameters, we combine the Euclidean distance and the Hamming

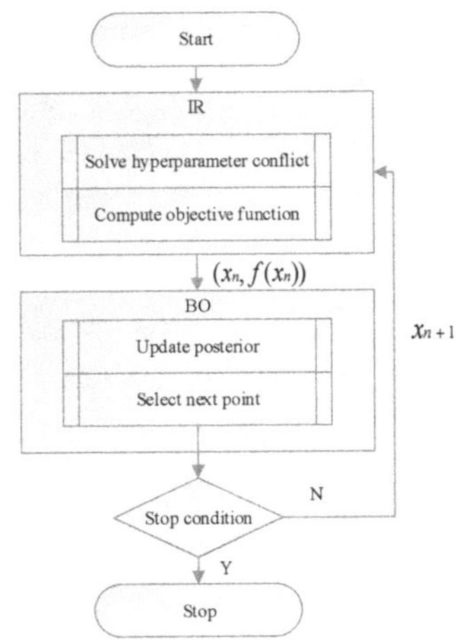

Figure 2: Hyperparameter optimization architecture.

distance into a mixture distance, the *Hamming Euclidean mixture distance* (HE distance). HE treats continuous and categorical hyperparameters differently; it is defined as

$$r_{HE} := \sqrt{\sum_{d \in \text{con}} (x_d - x_d{}')^2 + \sum_{d \in \text{cat}} (1 - \delta(x_d, x_d{}'))}$$

where *con* is the set of continuous dimensions and *cat* the set of categorical dimensions. It is easy to prove that HE is a distance (or metric). By replace the original distance function r_{SE} with r_{HE}, we get two new covariance functions,

$$K_{\text{HSE}}(\boldsymbol{x}, \boldsymbol{x}') = \exp(-\frac{r_{HE}^2}{2})$$

$$K_{\text{HMatérn1}}(\boldsymbol{x}, \boldsymbol{x}') = \exp(-r_{HE}).$$

Compared with SE and Matérn1, HSE and HMatérn1 are designed to handle heterogeneous space where the continuity property of different dimensions are not the same. To sum up, in this work, we test the performance of SE, HSE, Matérn1 and HMatérn1 as four representative covariance functions for continuous and categorical hyperparameters.

5 EXPERIMENT SETUP

5.1 Research questions

In the remainder of the paper we aim to answer the following three research questions:

RQ1 What is the most critical component of the Bayesian Optimization framework for identifying the best retrieval system configuration?

RQ2 How effective is Bayesian Optimization in searching the configuration space, and in finding configurations that generalize across queries and collections?

RQ3 How to explain the optimization behaviour of Bayesian Optimization in terms of exploration and exploitation?

5.2 Implementation of Retrieval System and Bayesian Optimization

We use Pyndri [32], a Python Interface to the *Indri* Search Engine [27], as the IR module in our pipeline, which is mainly decomposed to indexing, retrieval, and pseudo-relevance feedback. All the three modules are considered in our optimization experiments.

The objective function can be any retrieval effectiveness measure. In this work we optimize for the Mean Average Precision (MAP), Normalized Discounted Cumulative Gain (NDCG) and Mean Reciprocal Rank (MRR) and use *trec_eval* [1] for the computations.

We use *Pybo* [16] in our experiments, a Python package for Bayesian Optimization . *Pybo* supports the default version of the *SE covariance function* and the *Martén1 covariance function* which use Euclidean distance to measure the distance of two points; we implemented the *HSE covariance function* and the *HMartén1 covariance function* within *Pybo* ourselves.

[1] http://trec.nist.gov/trec_eval/

5.3 Candidate Configurations

There are two major choices to make when indexing documents: the stopword list and the stemmer. Ferro and Silvello [11] has shown that the choice of different stopword lists, like that of indri, Lucene, Smart and Terrier, has limited effect to the performance of a IR system; however, having stopword list or not makes a big difference. On the other hand, indexing document collections takes a long time. Therefore for efficiency and convenience we only set two values for the categorical hyperparameter *stopper*: TRUE means using Indri stopword list and FALSE means not using any stopword list. The situation is similar for *stemmer*: TRUE means using Krovets stemmer and FALSE means not using any stemmer.

There are three retrieval models implemented in *Indri*: TF-IDF with BM25 term weighting, Okapi BM25, and Language Models. Language Models supports three different smoothing methods, Jelinek-Mercer (JM), Dirichlet (DIR), and two-stage smoothing (TS). Let *rm* denote a categorical hyperparameter that represents the retrieval model type and takes values in [TF-IDF, BM25, LM-JM, LM-DIR, LM-TS], that is the TF-IDF model with BM25 term weighting, the Okapi BM25 model, the Language Model with JM smoothing, the Language Model with Dirichlet smoothing, and the Language Model with two-stage smoothing respectively. There is a number of hyperparameters per model: $k1$ and b for TF-IDF, $k1$, $k3$, and b for Okapi BM25, λ_{col} and λ_{doc} for the JM smoothing, μ for the Dirichlet smoothing, and λ and μ for the two stage smoothing. The parameters of these models lay in a continuous space.

Indri also supports pseudo-relevance feedback models. We consider a binary hyperparameter *prf* that takes the value TRUE if pseudo-relevance feedback is used, and FALSE otherwise. There are four hyperparameters that need to be set for the pseudo-relevance feedback models, the number of feedback documents to be considered, *fbDocs*, the number of feedback terms, *fbTerms*, the Dirichlet smoothing parameter used for the feedback document language model,*fbMu*, and the weight of the original query, *fbOrigWeight*, in the mixture model between the original query and the feedback documents. In total, we have a conditional hyperparameter space of 18 dimensions (see Figure 3).

5.4 Test collections

We conduct our experiments on the ad-hoc test collections of TREC 5-8 and TREC Robust 2004, as well as the web test collections of TREC 2010-2012 in order to thoroughly evaluate the proposed method in diversified datasets. The details can be found in Table 1. As we can see, ad-hoc tracks and web tracks are quite different test collections. Web tracks have much more documents and the average length of documents is also longer, indicating they are more challenging compared with ad-hoc tracks.

5.5 Baselines

Manual Search. The first baseline is obtained by running *Indri* with its default hyperparameters. Then we manually select the best performing model among TF-IDF/BM25/Language Models, with/without pseudo-relevance feedback.

Grid Search. The second baseline is grid search. Grid search is the most widely used method for hyperparameter tuning. For each of the five retrieval model (TF-IDF, BM25, LM-JM, LM-DIR, LM-TS)

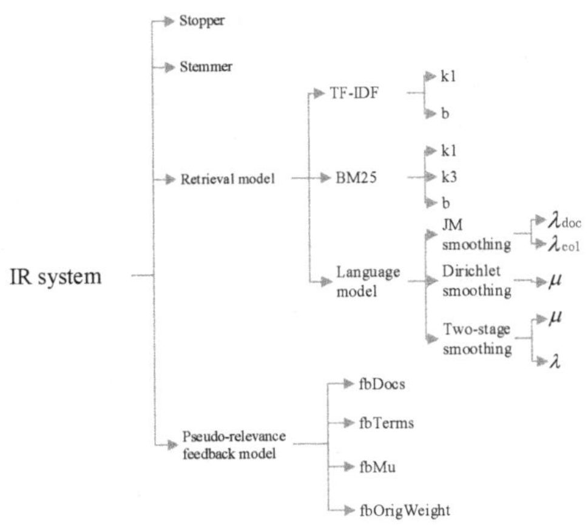

Hyperparamter	Type	Values
Stopper	Boolean	{True, False}
Stemmer	Boolean	{True, False}
rm	Integer	{TF-IDF, BM25, LM-JM, LM-DIR, LM-TS}
$k1$	Real value	[1,2]
b	Real value	[0,1]
$k1$	Real value	[1,10]
$k3$	Real value	[1,10]
b	Real value	[0,1]
λ_{doc}	Real value	[0,1]
λ_{col}	Real value	[0,1]
μ_{dir}	Real value	[0,3000]
μ_{ts}	Real value	[0,3000]
λ_{ts}	Real value	[0,1]
prf	Boolean	{True, False}
fbDocs	Integer	[1,50]
fbTerms	Integer	[1,50]
fbMu	Real value	[0,3000]
fbOrigWeight	Real value	[0,1]

Figure 3: Conditional hyperparameters and their search ranges in *Indri*

Table 1: Test collections

TREC	Document collection	No. of Doc.	Doc. Length Median	Doc. Length Mean	Topics
TREC 5	Volume 2 & 4	524,929	340	546	251-300
TREC 6	Volume 4 & 5	556,077	326	526	301-350
TREC 7	Volume 4 & 5 − CR*	528,155	328	480	351-400
TREC 8	Volume 4 & 5 − CR	528,155	328	480	401-450
TREC Robust 2004	Volume 4 & 5 − CR	528,155	328	480	301-450 601-700
TREC Web 2010	ClueWeb09	21,258,800	629	1096	51-100
TREC Web 2011	ClueWeb09	21,258,800	629	1096	101-150
TREC Web 2012	ClueWeb09	21,258,800	629	1096	151-200

* : Congressional Record documents.

in Section 5.3, we generate the grid points by evenly partitioning the search space of each parameter into 20 parts and making a complete combination of all the parameters of that retrieval model. Furthermore, based on the five sub-baselines, we easily get five more sub-baselines by setting *pfb* =TRUE and fixing *fbDocs* = 10, *fbTerms* = 10, *fbMu* = 2500, and *fbOrigWeight* = 0.5. For instance, the baseline LM-DIR + PFB contains 20 search points obtained by setting μ to the values partitioning $[0, 3000]$ into 20 parts and setting *pfb*=TRUE. For all the sub-baselines, *stopper* and *stemmer* are set to TRUE. This is a common practice in the use of grid search, and allows the reduction of the 6.6×10^{19} possible points of our hyperparameter space down to 1.8×10^4.

Random Search. The third baseline is random search [3]. For random search, we use 3 sampling designs, *Uniform*, *Latin*, *Sobol*, and we allow its number of iteration same with Bayesian Optimization .

6 RESULTS AND ANALYSIS

6.1 Decompose component effect of Bayesian Optimization

This experiment is designed to answer RQ1. In order to study which components of Bayesian Optimization has the strongest effect on the performance of Bayesian Optimization in finding optimal system configurations we run a full factorial experiment, using 54 joint strategies of Bayesian Optimization : the 3 initialization strategies × the 3 covariance functions × the 3 acquisition functions × the 2 selection strategies. The experiment was run on the Robust 2004 dataset. We measure performance on the basis of MAP and we run an analysis of variance (ANOVA) considering only the main effects of the Bayesian Optimization components (that is we ignore any interactions between them, since we do not have enough data points for a detailed analysis).

The results of the ANOVA can be seen in Table 2. The important observation lays in the last column of the table; this is the p-value that designates whether a factor has a significant effect when $p(>F)<0.05$, or there is not enough evidence to reach that conclusions otherwise. As we can observe, and in accordance to previous work [26] ANOVA suggests that the choice of the covariance function is the most important decision one needs to make when instantiating Bayesian Optimization , at least among the components we considered in this work. Therefore, we vary covariance functions and fix the rest strategies by selecting the respective best ones, that is *Sobol + EI + Incumbent* in the following sections.

Table 2: The effects of different components of Bayesian Optimization on objective function via ANOVA.

	SS	DF	F	$p(>F)$
Initialization strategy	0.000566	2.0	0.903685	0.412144
Covariance function	0.002976	2.0	4.748861	**0.013338**
Acquisition function	0.000647	2.0	1.032076	0.364368
Selection strategy	0.000543	1.0	1.734376	0.194376

6.2 Optimizing IR systems using Bayesian Optimization

This experiment is designed to answer RQ2. We first run the four methods on Robust 2004 or Web 2012 as the training set, then we tested the corresponding optimal configurations on TREC 5-8 or Web 2011-2012. In order to have a thorough study of Bayesian Optimization , we further experimented on the 2-dimensional space which is is λ and μ for the two stage smoothing, and the 18-dimensional space which includes the complete hyperparameters introduced in Section 5.3 respectively.

Table 3 shows the performance of the best configurations found by each method. As expected, there is no big difference among the four search methods in 2-dimensional space. It is because both grid search and random search are able to cover the space in low dimensional space. However, grid search needs more budget compared with Bayesian Optimization and random search. Therefore, Bayesian Optimization , grid search and random search can achieve comparable performance, but Bayesian Optimization and random search are more efficient in 2-dimensional spaces than grid search. The situation changes with the number of dimension increasing. We can see Bayesian Optimization performs slightly better than random search, grid search and manual method in 18-dimensional space. Random search is comparable with Bayesian Optimization in low (2) dimensional space, but it fails in high (18) dimensional space. However, there seems no significant difference among the four methods according to the results in Table 3 .

6.3 Optimization behaviour of Bayesian Optimization

This experiment is designed to answer RQ3. We study how Bayesian Optimization searches points in the search space and how different covariance functions affect this behaviour. For visualisation convenience we take 1-dimensional and 2-dimensional hyperparameter space as examples.

The hyperparameter considered in 1-dimensional space is μ in language model with Dirichlet smoothing. We initialised the posterior of the surrogate model with 2 points, and iteratively searched 32 points. We also recorded the predictive function predicted by the surrogate model in round 1 and 32. The result is show in Figure 4. We can see that the intensive red lines tend to appear near the global optimum for most datasets and measures, indicating that Bayesian Optimization spends more efforts and exploits much near the global optimum. It is more obvious when the objective function is highly irregular like MRR. By "irregular" we mean there are many local optimums. On the right panel of Figure 4a, we find that Bayesian Optimization prefers exploitation near these local optimums and allows exploration in other areas, and finally it spends most efforts near the global optimum. Figure 4b shows the zoomed-in result on TREC 6 + MRR. The posterior of the surrogate model in round 1 does not know much about the objective function and predicts the same value for most points except the area near the two initial points. Whereas in round 32, the predictive function can model the rough trend quite well, where several local maximums and minimums are quite consistent with the real objective function. Overall speaking, Bayesian Optimization 's performance in 1-dimensional space is as good as we expect in terms of exploration and exploitation. Its preference of exploitation near global optimum makes it a reliable optimization approach.

The hyperparameters considered in 2-dimensional space are μ and λ in language model with two-stage smoothing. We initialised the posterior of the surrogate model with 4 points, and iteratively searched 32 points. Same as 1-dimensional case, we also recorded the predictive function in round 1 and 32. In Figure 5 we ploted the results of the SE covariance function and the Matérn1 covariance function respectively. The first two panels of Figure 5a shows the effect of Matérn1 on the predictive function. In round the surrogate model predicts that the lower left corner has the potential of getting high values. In round 32 the predictive function is quite rugged

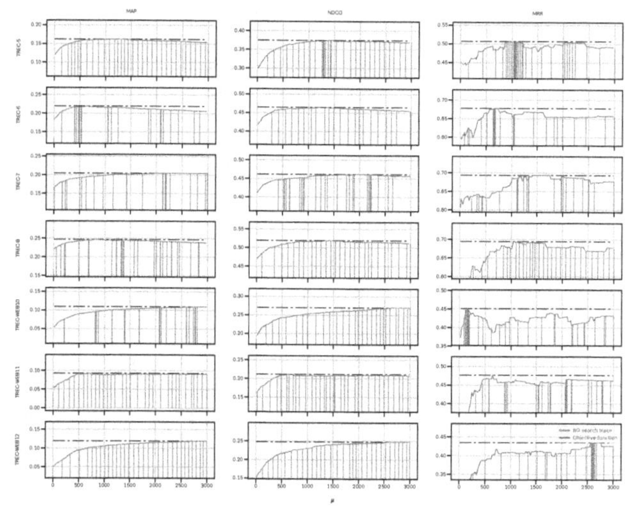

(a) **Overall optimization behaviour in a glance. Covariance function: Matérn1, objective functions: MAP, NDCG, MRR. The red vertical line associated with a number denotes Bayesian Optimization searches which point in which round. The green curve denotes the real objective function generated by 128 devisions of the interval [0, 3000]. The black dot line denotes the maximum objective function value.**

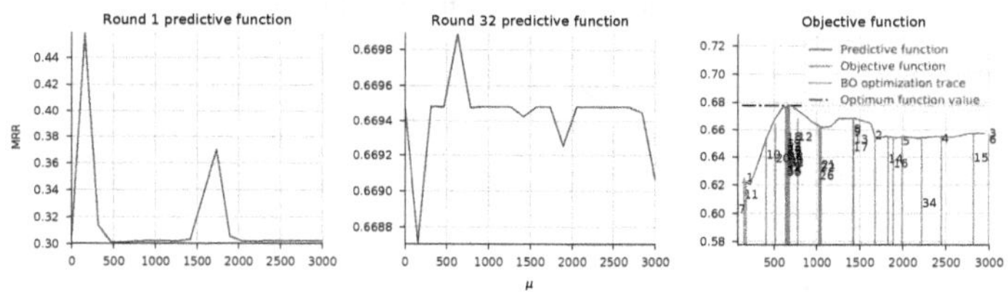

(b) **Zoomed-in result on TREC 6 + MRR. The first two panels are the predictive objective functions in round 1 and 32; the last panel is the real objective function. The red vertical line associated with a number denotes Bayesian Optimization searches which point and in which round.**

Figure 4: Optimization behaviour of Bayesian Optimization in 1-dimensional space $X = [0, 3000]$.

because multiple local optimums are observed. It predicts the area around $(2800, 0.7)$ having a global optimum, which is quite consistent with the real objective function. The right panel compares the point traces of Bayesian Optimization , random search and manual search. At the beginning, Bayesian Optimization prefers exploration and tries to cover a large area of the search space. Later it prefers exploitation as we can see it spends more efforts near the global optimum. It is also interesting to compare the way how the two covariance functions model the real objective function. We know that the smoothness of the samples generated by the two covariance functions conforms to the order: SE >Matérn1. This is consistent with Figure 5. The real objective function in this case is quite smooth and seems to have one optimum, therefore SE is enough to model its irregularity. As an evidence we can see that more points are searched within green contour line on the most right side in Figure 5b compared with Figure 5a.

Table 3: The best performing configurations for all search methods.

Method	Budget	Train A			Test A			Train B			Test B		
		MAP	NDCG	MRR	MAP	NDCG	MRR	MAP	NDCG	MRR	MAP	NDCG	MRR
2-D													
Manual	-	2415	5144	6915	1986	4446	6091	1195	2508	4084	1002	2393	4305
Grid	400	2531	5239	7028	2058	4535	6255	1216	2523	4350	1002	2395	4458
Random	4+32	2529	5239	7020	2058	4534	6341	1215	2522	4254	1000	2395	4458
BO SE	4+32	2520	5239	7022	2010	4284	6258	1212	2518	4352	998	2388	4408
BO Matérn1	4+32	2527	5239	7020	2056	4514	6314	1204	2516	4353	1003	2394	4389
18-D													
Manual	-	2755	5507	6994	2221	4817	5744	1209	2509	4242	939	2282	4019
Grid	2480	2889	5616	7248	2256	4824	6184	1404	2620	4773	922	2311	4100
Random	36+64	2692	5454	7041	2084	4776	6309	1404	2620	4773	922	2311	4100
BO SE	36+64	2908	5499	7162	2301	4705	6077	1395	2576	4860	926	2281	3933
BO HSE	36+64	2924	5549	7032	2064	4737	6273	1395	2551	5181	935	2334	3931
BO Matérn1	36+64	2925	5571	7192	2283	4781	6168	1398	2593	5268	929	2372	4140
BO HMatérn1	36+64	2747	5661	7050	2161	4864	6301	1308	2618	5502	974	2315	4160

Note: Magnitude of numbers is 10^{-4}. Train A denotes TREC Robust 2004, Test A denotes TREC 5-8, Train B denotes TREC Web 2012, Test B denotes TREC Web 2010-2011.

To sum up, Bayesian Optimization balances exploitation and exploitation by spending more search budget near the global optimum or local optimums, which makes it a reliable optimization approach. This optimization behaviour is affected by the covariance function. If the objective function is very irregular like MRR, Matérn1 is recommended; while SE is recommended if relative objective functions like MAP and NDCG.

7 CONCLUSIONS AND FUTURE WORK

In this paper we study the problem of retrieval system optimization. We propose the use of Bayesian Optimization to jointly search and optimize over the hyperparameter space. Given the heterogeneous hyperparameters in retrieval systems we suggest the use of four covariance functions that can handle both continuous and categorical hyperparameters, the SE, HSE, Matérn1 and HMatérn1 covariance function. We analyze the effect of the different components of Bayesian Optimization and reach at the same conclusion as prior research on the topic [26] that it is the choice of the covariance functions that have the strongest effect on the performance of Bayesian Optimization . To demonstrate the effectiveness and efficiency of Bayesian Optimization to identify a good system configuration, we tested it on both the ad-hoc and the web test collections of TREC. In both collections we demonstrate that Bayesian Optimization outperforms manual tuning, grid search and random search, both in terms of the retrieval effectiveness of the best configuration found, and in terms of efficiency in finding this configuration. We further examined the optimization behaviour of Bayesian Optimization in terms of exploitation and exploitation. We found it spends more search budget near the global optimum or local optimums, and this optimization behaviour is affected by covariance functions of different smoothness.

One should note that for the Gaussian Process the bounds for all dimensions of the search space are axis-aligned, i.e. the search space is a *hyper-rectangle* [25]. This is contradictory with the conditional structure of IR hyperparameters, which means that our instantiation of Bayesian Optimization wastes time in searching in inactive dimensions. We leave the study of surrogate model that can solve conditional hyperparameters as a future work.

REFERENCES

[1] Timothy G. Armstrong, Alistair Moffat, William Webber, and Justin Zobel. 2009. Improvements That Don'T Add Up: Ad-hoc Retrieval Results Since 1998. In *Proceedings of the 18th ACM Conference on Information and Knowledge Management (CIKM '09)*. ACM, New York, NY, USA, 601–610. https://doi.org/10.1145/1645953.1646031

[2] Richard E Bellman. 2015. *Adaptive control processes: a guided tour.* Princeton university press.

[3] James Bergstra and Yoshua Bengio. 2012. Random search for hyper-parameter optimization. *Journal of Machine Learning Research* 13, Feb (2012), 281–305.

[4] James Bergstra, Daniel Yamins, and David D Cox. 2013. Making a Science of Model Search: Hyperparameter Optimization in Hundreds of Dimensions for Vision Architectures. *ICML (1)* 28 (2013), 115–123.

[5] James S Bergstra, Rémi Bardenet, Yoshua Bengio, and Balázs Kégl. 2011. Algorithms for hyper-parameter optimization. In *Advances in Neural Information Processing Systems*. 2546–2554.

[6] Anthony Bigot, Sébastien Déjean, and Josiane Mothe. 2015. Learning to Choose the Best System Configuration in Information Retrieval: the Case of Repeated Queries. *Journal of Universal Computer Science* 21, 13 (2015), 1726–1745.

[7] Russel E Caflisch, William J Morokoff, and Art B Owen. 1997. *Valuation of mortgage backed securities using Brownian bridges to reduce effective dimension.* Department of Mathematics, University of California, Los Angeles.

[8] Romain Deveaud, Josiane Mothe, and Jian-Yun Nia. 2016. Learning to Rank System Configurations. In *Proceedings of the 25th ACM International on Conference on Information and Knowledge Management (CIKM '16)*. ACM, New York, NY, USA, 2001–2004. https://doi.org/10.1145/2983323.2983894

[9] Laurence Charles Ward Dixon and Giorgio Philip Szegö. 1978. *Towards global optimisation 2.* North-Holland Amsterdam.

[10] Katharina Eggensperger, Matthias Feurer, Frank Hutter, James Bergstra, Jasper Snoek, Holger Hoos, and Kevin Leyton-Brown. 2013. Towards an empirical foundation for assessing bayesian optimization of hyperparameters. In *NIPS workshop on Bayesian Optimization in Theory and Practice*. 1–5.

[11] Nicola Ferro and Gianmaria Silvello. 2016. A General Linear Mixed Models Approach to Study System Component Effects. In *Proceedings of the 39th International ACM SIGIR Conference on Research and Development in Information Retrieval (SIGIR '16)*. ACM, New York, NY, USA, 25–34. https://doi.org/10.1145/2911451.2911530

[12] Parantapa Goswami and Eric Gaussier. 2013. Estimation of the Collection Parameter of Information Models for IR. In *Proceedings of the 35th European Conference on Advances in Information Retrieval (ECIR'13)*. Springer-Verlag, Berlin, Heidelberg, 459–470. https://doi.org/10.1007/978-3-642-36973-5_39

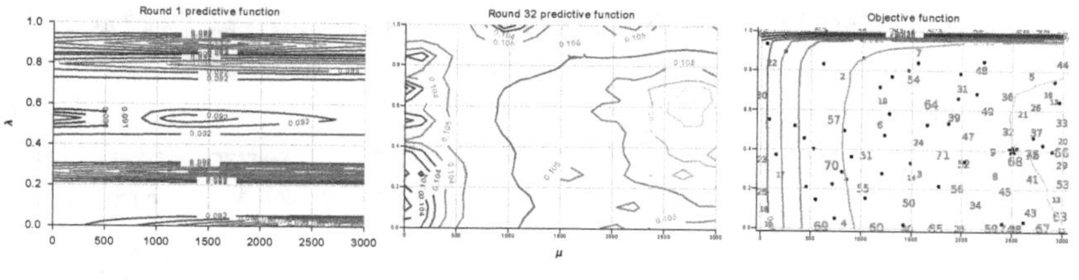

(a) Matérn1 + MAP.

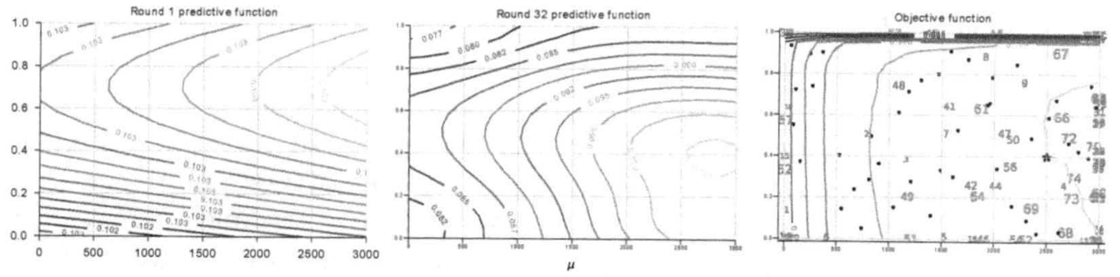

(b) SE + MAP.

Figure 5: Optimization behaviour of Bayesian Optimization in 2-dimensional space $X = \{(\mu, \lambda)|\mu \in [0, 3000], \lambda \in [0, 1]\}$. Objective function: MAP, Data set: TREC-WEB12. The contour lines depict the predictive functions in round 1 and 32 on the first two panels, and the real objective function on last panel. The red numbers denote Bayesian Optimization searches which point and in which round; the black dots denote the point trace of random search; and the star denotes the point of manual search.

[13] Ben HE and Iadh Ounis. 2003. A Study of Parameter Tuning for Term Frequency Normalization. In *Proceedings of the Twelfth International Conference on Information and Knowledge Management (CIKM '03)*. ACM, New York, NY, USA, 10–16. https://doi.org/10.1145/956863.956867

[14] Ben He and Iadh Ounis. 2007. On Setting the Hyper-parameters of Term Frequency Normalization for Information Retrieval. *ACM Trans. Inf. Syst.* 25, 3, Article 13 (July 2007). https://doi.org/10.1145/1247715.1247719

[15] Ben He and Iadh Ounis. 2007. Parameter Sensitivity in the Probabilistic Model for Ad-hoc Retrieval. In *Proceedings of the Sixteenth ACM Conference on Conference on Information and Knowledge Management (CIKM '07)*. ACM, New York, NY, USA, 263–272. https://doi.org/10.1145/1321440.1321479

[16] Matthew W Hoffman and Bobak Shahriari. 2014. Modular mechanisms for Bayesian optimization. In *NIPS Workshop on Bayesian Optimization*. Citeseer.

[17] Frank Hutter, Holger H Hoos, and Kevin Leyton-Brown. 2011. Sequential model-based optimization for general algorithm configuration. In *International Conference on Learning and Intelligent Optimization*. Springer, 507–523.

[18] Frank Hutter and Michael A Osborne. 2013. A Kernel for Hierarchical Parameter Spaces. *arXiv preprint arXiv:1310.5738* (2013).

[19] Sadegh Kharazmi, Falk Scholer, David Vallet, and Mark Sanderson. 2016. Examining Additivity and Weak Baselines. *ACM Trans. Inf. Syst.* 34, 4, Article 23 (June 2016), 18 pages. https://doi.org/10.1145/2882782

[20] Yuanhua Lv and ChengXiang Zhai. 2009. A Comparative Study of Methods for Estimating Query Language Models with Pseudo Feedback. In *Proceedings of the 18th ACM Conference on Information and Knowledge Management (CIKM '09)*. ACM, New York, NY, USA, 1895–1898. https://doi.org/10.1145/1645953.1646259

[21] Jonas Mockus. 1994. Application of Bayesian approach to numerical methods of global and stochastic optimization. *Journal of Global Optimization* 4, 4 (1994), 347–365.

[22] Carl Edward Rasmussen and Christopher K. I. Williams. 2005. *Gaussian Processes for Machine Learning (Adaptive Computation and Machine Learning)*. The MIT Press.

[23] François Rousseau and Michalis Vazirgiannis. 2013. Composition of TF Normalizations: New Insights on Scoring Functions for Ad Hoc IR. In *Proceedings of the 36th International ACM SIGIR Conference on Research and Development in Information Retrieval (SIGIR '13)*. ACM, New York, NY, USA, 917–920. https://doi.org/10.1145/2484028.2484121

[24] Jangwon Seo and W. Bruce Croft. 2010. Unsupervised Estimation of Dirichlet Smoothing Parameters. In *Proceedings of the 33rd International ACM SIGIR Conference on Research and Development in Information Retrieval (SIGIR '10)*. ACM, New York, NY, USA, 759–760. https://doi.org/10.1145/1835449.1835602

[25] Bobak Shahriari, Kevin Swersky, Ziyu Wang, Ryan P Adams, and Nando de Freitas. 2016. Taking the human out of the loop: A review of bayesian optimization. *Proc. IEEE* 104, 1 (2016), 148–175.

[26] Jasper Snoek, Hugo Larochelle, and Ryan P Adams. 2012. Practical bayesian optimization of machine learning algorithms. In *Advances in neural information processing systems*. 2951–2959.

[27] Trevor Strohman, Donald Metzler, Howard Turtle, and W. Bruce Croft. 2005. *Indri: a language-model based search engine for complex queries*. Technical Report. in Proceedings of the International Conference on Intelligent Analysis.

[28] Kevin Swersky, David Duvenaud, Jasper Snoek, Frank Hutter, and Michael A Osborne. 2014. Raiders of the lost architecture: Kernels for Bayesian optimization in conditional parameter spaces. *arXiv preprint arXiv:1409.4011* (2014).

[29] Kevin Swersky, Jasper Snoek, and Ryan P Adams. 2013. Multi-task bayesian optimization. In *Advances in neural information processing systems*. 2004–2012.

[30] Michael Taylor, Hugo Zaragoza, Nick Craswell, Stephen Robertson, and Chris Burges. 2006. Optimisation methods for ranking functions with multiple parameters. In *Proceedings of the 15th ACM international conference on Information and knowledge management*. ACM, 585–593.

[31] Andrew Trotman, Antti Puurula, and Blake Burgess. 2014. Improvements to BM25 and Language Models Examined. In *Proceedings of the 2014 Australasian Document Computing Symposium (ADCS '14)*. ACM, New York, NY, USA, Article 58, 8 pages. https://doi.org/10.1145/2682862.2682863

[32] Christophe Van Gysel, Evangelos Kanoulas, and Maarten de Rijke. 2017. Pyndri: a Python Interface to the Indri Search Engine. In *Advances in Information Retrieval: 39th European Conference on IR Research, ECIR 2017*. Springer International Publishing.

[33] Ellen M. Voorhees and Donna Harman (Eds.). 2001. *Proceedings of The REtrieval Conference (TREC 1-9)*. Vol. NIST Special Publication. National Institute of Standards and Technology (NIST). http://trec.nist.gov/pubs.html

[34] Lidan Wang, Minwei Feng, Bowen Zhou, Bing Xiang, and Sridhar Mahadevan. 2015. Efficient hyper-parameter optimization for NLP applications. In *Proceedings of EMNLP*, Vol. 15. 2112–2117.

[35] Ziyu Wang and Nando de Freitas. 2014. Theoretical analysis of bayesian optimisation with unknown gaussian process hyper-parameters. *arXiv preprint arXiv:1406.7758* (2014).

[36] Dani Yogatama and Noah A Smith. 2015. Bayesian optimization of text representations. *arXiv preprint arXiv:1503.00693* (2015).

[37] Chengxiang Zhai and John Lafferty. 2001. A Study of Smoothing Methods for Language Models Applied to Ad Hoc Information Retrieval. In *Proceedings of the 24th Annual International ACM SIGIR Conference on Research and Development in Information Retrieval (SIGIR '01)*. ACM, New York, NY, USA, 334–342. https://doi.org/10.1145/383952.384019

[38] ChengXiang Zhai and John Lafferty. 2002. Two-stage Language Models for Information Retrieval. In *Proceedings of the 25th Annual International ACM SIGIR Conference on Research and Development in Information Retrieval (SIGIR '02)*. ACM, New York, NY, USA, 49–56. https://doi.org/10.1145/564376.564387

Streaming Link Prediction on Dynamic Attributed Networks

Jundong Li
Arizona State University
jundongl@asu.edu

Kewei Cheng
Arizona State University
kcheng18@asu.edu

Liang Wu
Arizona State University
wuliang@asu.edu

Huan Liu
Arizona State University
huan.liu@asu.edu

ABSTRACT

Link prediction targets to predict the future node interactions mainly based on the current network snapshot. It is a key step in understanding the formation and evolution of the underlying networks; and has practical implications in many real-world applications, ranging from friendship recommendation, click through prediction to targeted advertising. Most existing efforts are devoted to plain networks and assume the availability of network structure in memory before link prediction takes place. However, this assumption is untenable as many real-world networks are affiliated with rich node attributes, and often, the network structure and node attributes are both dynamically evolving at an unprecedented rate. Even though recent studies show that node attributes have an added value to network structure for accurate link prediction, it still remains a daunting task to support link prediction in an online fashion on such dynamic attributed networks. As changes in the dynamic attributed networks are often transient and can be endless, link prediction algorithms need to be efficient by making only one pass of the data with limited memory overhead. To tackle these challenges, we study a novel problem of streaming link prediction on dynamic attributed networks and present a novel framework - SLIDE. Methodologically, SLIDE maintains and updates a low-rank sketching matrix to summarize all observed data, and we further leverage the sketching matrix to infer missing links on the fly. The whole procedure is theoretically guaranteed, and empirical experiments on real-world dynamic attributed networks validate the effectiveness and efficiency of the proposed framework.

ACM Reference Format:
Jundong Li, Kewei Cheng, Liang Wu, and Huan Liu. 2018. Streaming Link Prediction on Dynamic Attributed Networks. In *WSDM 2018: The Eleventh ACM International Conference on Web Search and Data Mining, February 5–9, 2018, Marina Del Rey, CA, USA.* ACM, New York, NY, USA, 9 pages. https://doi.org/10.1145/3159652.3159674

1 INTRODUCTION

The pervasiveness of myriad social media platforms significantly alters the conventional ways people interact and communicate. By performing various social activities (e.g., befriend with others, follow a celebrity, retweet a post), online social media users build different social interactions which ease the channel of information seeking and spreading. To this end, understanding and predicting the formation of social interactions will shed light on the underlying evolution mechanisms of the social networks; and also, from a microscopic perspective, it can help us gain more insights on the social behaviors of a particular user. The problem is often referred as the *link prediction problem* in the data mining and network science community [5, 37]. Formally, given a snapshot of network structure with partially observed links, link prediction aims to infer the missing links that may appear in a foreseeable future. The link prediction problem also has practical implications in many real-world applications, ranging from friend suggestion, click through prediction to targeted marketing [17].

Despite much progress has been made in the field of link prediction, existing link prediction algorithms overwhelmingly assume the availability of whole network structure. However, this assumption is untenable as real-world networks are often in large-scale and are measured in terabytes or even petabytes, making them difficult to be materialized in memory before link prediction takes place. In addition, networks are often not static but are dynamically evolving at an unprecedented rate with frequent updates (e.g., additions/deletions of nodes and edges). Furthermore, a vast majority of existing work are devoted to predicting missing links in plain networks. More often than not, nodes in the networks are affiliated with a rich set of attributes such as user profile information and user posts. Recent studies indicate that the formation of network structure highly depends on the associated node attributes and vice versa [28, 29, 34, 43]. On account of this, probing the node attributes could be potentially helpful in achieving better link prediction performance, especially when the network suffers from high sparsity. On top of that, by leveraging node attributes, it enables the prediction for those cold-start users that are otherwise intractable. In many cases, similar to the frequent updates on the network structure, node attributes also change naturally [30, 31], a typical example is the modification of online user posts. We refer such kind of networks with both topology and attribute changes as *dynamic attributed networks*.

As per the fact that node attributes are complementary for link prediction while both network structure and node attributes exhibit high dynamics, we investigate a novel problem of *streaming link prediction on dynamic attributed networks* in this paper. The following five challenges have to be addressed simultaneously.

- **Near Real-Time Prediction**: Dynamic attributed networks are characterized by streaming nodes/edges of high velocity.

WSDM 2018, February 5–9, 2018, Marina Del Rey, CA, USA

ACM ISBN 978-1-4503-5581-0/18/02...$15.00
https://doi.org/10.1145/3159652.3159674

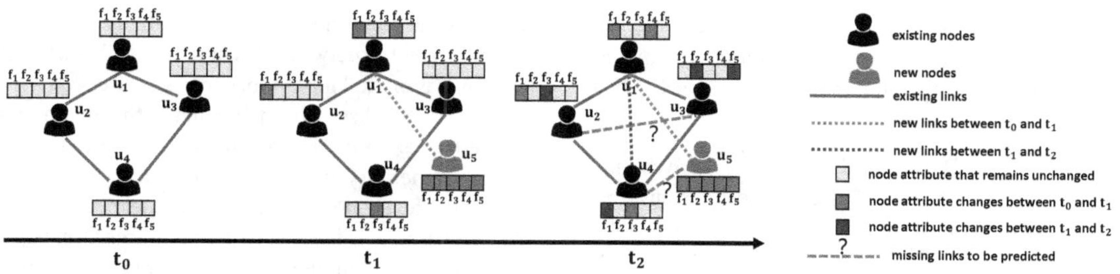

Figure 1: An illustrative example of streaming link prediction on dynamic attributed networks. As shown in the figure, at each time stamp, each node in the network is affiliated with five features ($f_1, ..., f_5$). Edges and nodes are continuously arriving in a streaming fashion. Meanwhile, the attributes of a certain number of nodes may change accordingly. Streaming link prediction attempts to infer the missing links in parallel with the rapid changes of the dynamic attributed networks. For example, given the observations at time stamp t_0, t_1 and t_2, it predicts whether there exists a link between u_2 and u_3 in the near future.

Also, the evolution of networks is often mixed with the changes of node attributes at an unsynchronized rate. As changes are essential components of the system and could occur at any time, link prediction algorithms require to be efficient and are performed in a streaming fashion to predict missing links in close to near real-time.

- **One-Pass of the Data**: The entire size of the network and affiliated node attributes are often unknown at a particular moment and could even be infinite in the worst case. Hence, the streaming link prediction algorithms need to be pass-efficient to make only one pass of the data as the further passes are either expensive or naturally impossible.
- **Space Efficiency**: Data is continuously being generated, the huge volume of data makes the dynamic attributed network hard to be materialized in memory, which necessitates the design of a cost-effective data synopsis with limited memory overhead to summarize the ever-increasing network structure and node attributes.
- **Concept Drift**: With the accumulation of new nodes/edges and the changes of node attributes, the underlying network topology and the content patterns of nodes continuously evolve over time, resulting in the emerging of unseen patterns and the fading of existing patterns, which may significantly impact the link prediction performance. This phenomenon is often referred as *concept drift* in data stream mining. In this regard, link prediction algorithms should be able to tackle the issue of concept drift.
- **Data Heterogeneity**: We examine the link prediction problem in the case of attributed networks and this kind of networks are notoriously difficult to mine due to the bewildering combination of heterogeneous data sources. Even though in the most cases that network structure and node attributes are presented in different modalities, they are often not mutually independent and could influence each other. Link prediction algorithms are supposed to seize the inherent interconnections for accurate prediction.

In this paper, we study a novel problem of *streaming link prediction on dynamic attributed networks*. An illustrative example of the studied problem is shown in Figure 1. Concretely, given a network that is characterized by fast-evolving links and node attributes, we attempt to propose an effective yet efficient (in terms of both time and space) model to enable the prediction of missing links on the fly. The main contributions of this paper are summarized as follows.

- We formally define a novel problem of streaming link prediction on dynamic attributed networks and identify its connection with many real-world applications. To our best knowledge, this is the first attempt to study link prediction in a dynamic and attributed environment.
- We propose a novel link prediction framework - SLIDE that is able to predict the missing links in an online fashion when the attributed network is characterized by both structural and attribute changes. By consuming limited memory, the proposed method leverages a cost-effective data sketch to tackle the concept drift of the underlying attributed networks with only one pass of the data.
- We theoretically prove that the proposed streaming link prediction framework SLIDE achieves similar performance as a costly offline method which stores and uses the whole historically observed data for link prediction.
- Extensive experiments on various real-world dynamic attributed networks reveal the effectiveness and efficiency of the proposed streaming link prediction framework.

2 PROBLEM STATEMENT

We use bold uppercase characters for matrices (e.g., $\mathbf{A}$), bold lowercase characters for vectors (e.g., $\mathbf{a}$), and normal lowercase characters for scalars (e.g., a). Also, we represent the i-th element of vector $\mathbf{a}$ as $\mathbf{a}_i$, the i-th row of matrix $\mathbf{A}$ as $\mathbf{A}_{i*}$, the j-th column as $\mathbf{A}_{*j}$, the (i, j)-th entry as $\mathbf{A}_{ij}$, the transpose of $\mathbf{A}$ as $\mathbf{A}^T$, the trace of $\mathbf{A}$ as $tr(\mathbf{A})$. For any vector $\mathbf{a} \in \mathbb{R}^n$, $\|\mathbf{a}\|_2 = \sqrt{\sum_i \mathbf{a}_i^2}$ denotes its Euclidean norm. For any matrix $\mathbf{A} \in \mathbb{R}^{n\times m}$, its Frobenius norm is $\|\mathbf{A}\|_F = \sqrt{\sum_{i,j} \mathbf{A}_{ij}^2}$, its spectral norm is $\|\mathbf{A}\| = \max_{\|\mathbf{x}\|_2=1} \|\mathbf{Ax}\|_2$. The *singular value decomposition* (SVD) of $\mathbf{A} \in \mathbb{R}^{n\times m}$ is denoted as $\text{svd}(\mathbf{A}) = \mathbf{U}\Sigma\mathbf{V}^T$, $\mathbf{U}$ is a $n \times n$ orthogonal matrix with the rows being left singular vectors $[\mathbf{u}_1, \mathbf{u}_2, ..., \mathbf{u}_n]$, $\mathbf{V}$ is a $m \times m$ orthogonal matrix with the columns being the right singular vectors $[\mathbf{v}_1, \mathbf{v}_2, ..., \mathbf{v}_m]$, $\Sigma = \text{diag}(\sigma_1, ..., \sigma_n)$ is a $n \times m$ diagonal matrix, where $\sigma_1 \geq \sigma_2 \geq, ..., \geq \sigma_r$ are the singular values of $\mathbf{A}$ and r is the rank of matrix $\mathbf{A}$. The best rank-k ($k \leq r$) approximation of matrix $\mathbf{A} \in \mathbb{R}^{n\times m}$ is $\mathbf{A}_k = \text{argmin}_{\text{rank}(\mathbf{X})\leq k} \|\mathbf{A} - \mathbf{X}\|_F$ and it can be computed as $\mathbf{A}_k = \mathbf{U}_k\Sigma_k\mathbf{V}_k^T = \sum_{i=1}^{k}\sigma_i\mathbf{u}_i\mathbf{v}_i^T$, where $\mathbf{U}_k$, Σ_k, $\mathbf{V}_k$ are the truncated matrices consisting of the top-k left singular vectors, singular values, and right singular vectors, respectively. $\mathbf{I}$ is an identity matrix.

Definition 2.1. **(Dynamic Attributed Networks)**: A dynamic attributed network $G = (G^{t_0}, G^{t_1}, G^{t_2}, ...)$ spans across various time stamps $\{t_0, t_1, t_2, ...\}$. At a particular time stamp t, the corresponding attributed network $G^t = (\mathcal{V}^t, \mathcal{E}^t, \mathbf{X}^t)$ consists of $\mathcal{V}^t$: the set of nodes ($n_t = |\mathcal{V}^t|$); $\mathcal{E}^t \subseteq \mathcal{V}^t \times \mathcal{V}^t$: the set of edges; and the node attributes $\mathbf{X}^t = [\mathbf{x}^1, \mathbf{x}^2, ..., \mathbf{x}^{n_t}]^T$, where $\mathbf{x}^i \in \mathbb{R}^d$ $(i = 1, ..., n_t)$ is the attribute information of the i-th node.

The problem of streaming link prediction problem on dynamic attributed networks can be formally defined as follows:

Problem 1. *Given a dynamic attributed network $G = (G^{t_0}, G^{t_1}, ...)$ with fast-evolving node/edge streams and changes of node attributes across multiple time stamps $(t_0, t_1, ...)$. At a particular time stamp t, the* ***streaming link prediction*** *problem aims to predict if there exists an edge $e = (u, v)$ for a pair of nodes (u, v) that are not connected previously before time stamp t.*

An illustration of the studied problem is shown in Figure 1. The streaming link prediction problem supports the prediction of missing links in an online fashion. For example, as shown in the figure, given a dynamic attributed network at three different time stamps t_0, t_1 and t_2 with both network structure and node attribute changes, the streaming link prediction problem predicts the missing links that may appear at time stamp t, where $t > t_2$.

3 THE PROPOSED FRAMEWORK - SLIDE

In this section, we present the proposed framework of **S**treaming **L**ink pred**I**ction for **D**ynamic attribut**E**d networks - SLIDE. The basic idea is to maintain and update a low-rank sketching matrix with limited memory overhead to summarize the currently observed links and node attributes. Then given the attributes of a pair of unconnected nodes, we leverage the low-rank sketching matrix to determine if there exists a link between these two end nodes in the future. The low-rank sketching matrix is continuously being updated when new links and new node attributes are observed. The overall workflow of the proposed streaming link prediction framework - SLIDE is shown in Figure 2. As can be observed from the figure, the proposed framework consists of three essential components: (1) maintain and update a sketching matrix to summarize the currently observed data, including all the observed links and node attributes; (2) predict missing links on the fly with the up-to-date sketching matrix; (3) calculate and update the threshold which is used to determine the existence of links.

3.1 Summarization with Matrix Sketching

On a typical dynamic attributed network, a massive amount of edges are continuously arriving at a fast pace. Meanwhile, node attributes also change naturally such that new content patterns may emerge and outdated content patterns will fade. To explicitly store such a dynamic attributed network at a particular time stamp t, we need $O(n_t^2 + n_t d)$ space in the worst case (d is often much smaller than n_t), where n_t is the number of nodes in the network until t and d is the dimensionality of node attributes. The materialization of the attributed networks becomes infeasible when n_t is very large. Hence, it is of vital importance to use cost-effective data synopsis to summarize all observed data including the links and node attributes. Nonetheless, designing a full streaming model with limited and constant memory space is a challenging problem and most of the existing efforts on graph streams are devoted to the so-called *semi-streaming* models [15, 42], which requires $O(n_t\text{polylog}(n_t))$ space. These semi-streaming models are intractable if the available memory is not proportional to the number of nodes n_t in the network. In addition, due to the heterogeneity of two information sources in attributed networks, the resulted data synopsis is expected to summarize both information sources simultaneously.

Motivated by the recent advances in full streaming models for conventional data streams, we propose to use the frequent directions algorithm [38] to maintain a low-rank sketching matrix (with limited memory overhead) to make a structural summary of the currently observed data. One major merit of the frequent directions algorithm is that it operates in a streaming fashion and makes only one pass of the data. However, the frequent directions algorithm cannot be directly applied on dynamic attributed networks for a low-rank approximation in real-time. The reason is that frequent directions algorithm is proposed to summarize conventional data streams where columns of the input matrix are added incrementally and the row of the input matrix is fixed. On dynamic attributed networks, even though the node attributes are presented as a data stream (if the number of node attributes is fixed), the changes of the underlying network structure (often encoded in an adjacency matrix), per se, cannot be simply generalized as a conventional data stream. To this end, we propose to represent the dynamic attributed networks as the feature representation based on the observed links. The similar feature representation mechanism is also widely used in many other learning tasks, such as factorization machines [46] and contextual-bandit collaborative filtering [35, 52].

Definition 3.1. **(Feature Representation of Dynamic Attributed Networks)**: Given a dynamic attributed network across multiple time stamps $G = (G^{t_0}, G^{t_1}, ...)$, its feature representation at a particular time stamp t is represented $\mathbf{F}^t \in \mathbb{R}^{2d\times|\mathcal{E}^t|}$. Each column $\mathbf{f} \in \mathbb{R}^{2d}$ in the feature representation $\mathbf{F}^t$ corresponds to an edge in G^t. Now assume that two end nodes of the edge is u_i and u_j $(i < j)$, then the corresponding feature representation, i.e., $\mathbf{f}$, can be represented as $\mathbf{f} = [\mathbf{X}_{i*}^t, \mathbf{X}_{j*}^t]^T$, where $\mathbf{X}^t$ is the node attributes of the dynamic attributed network at time stamp t.

By transforming the dynamic attributed networks into feature representations, the changes in the underlying attributed network can be presented as new columns in a conventional data stream. In particular, new columns are introduced in two scenarios: (1) the arrival of new edges; and (2) node attribute information changes. The first scenario is straightforward and easy to understand. Regarding the second scenario, if the node attributes change, then the feature representations of edges that these nodes involved in should also change, and we represent these changes as new columns in the data stream. Now we assume that we can store all the historically generated data, and the feature representation of the dynamic attributed networks until time stamp t is stored in a matrix $\mathbf{G}^t \in \mathbb{R}^{2d\times c_t}$, where c_t is the number of columns in $\mathbf{G}^t$, and $c_t \geq |\mathcal{E}^t|$. It should

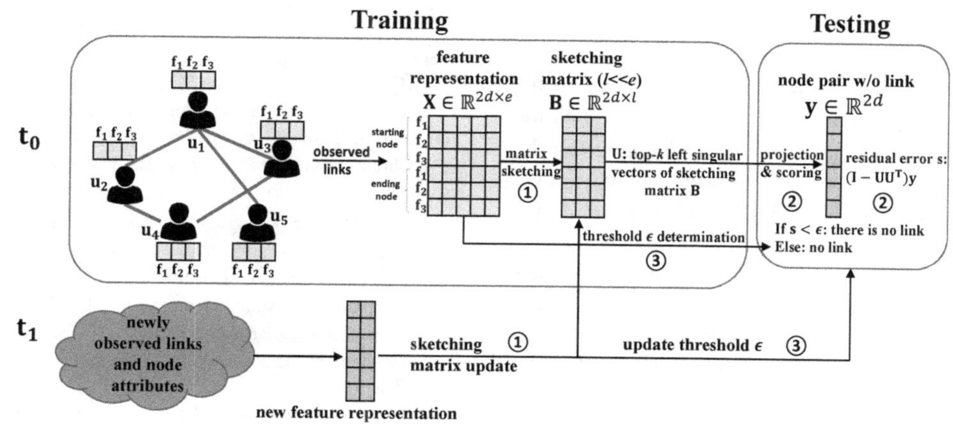

Figure 2: The workflow of the proposed streaming link prediction framework - SLIDE.

be noted that the similar technique is also applied on the dynamic recommendation problem recently [26]. However, it is different from the proposed framework as we focus on the streaming link prediction problem and consider the changes of both network structure and node attributes. While on the other hand, [26] only models the new ratings (with contextual information) as a data stream and fails to consider the changes of contextual information.

Even though we have reformulated the changes in the dynamic attributed networks as new columns in a data stream, the number of columns in $\mathbf{G}^t$ are still too large to be stored in memory, especially when the number of edges is in the scale of billion or trillion. Instead of storing the feature representations of the underlying dynamic attributed network, the frequent directions algorithm is employed to maintain a low-rank sketching matrix, and the sketching matrix can well summarize the observed data with a theoretical guarantee. Specifically, the low-rank sketching matrix $\mathbf{B}^t \in \mathbb{R}^{2d\times l}$ (l is often small) approximates the matrix $\mathbf{G}^t$ well such that $\mathbf{B}^t(\mathbf{B}^t)^T \approx \mathbf{G}^t(\mathbf{G}^t)^T$. More accurately, the approximation error is bounded by the conditions that: (1) $\mathbf{G}^t(\mathbf{G}^t)^T \succeq \mathbf{B}^t(\mathbf{B}^t)^T$; and (2) $\|\mathbf{G}^t(\mathbf{G}^t)^T - \mathbf{B}^t(\mathbf{B}^t)^T\| \leq 2\|\mathbf{G}^t\|_F^2/l$ [38].

Let $\mathbf{D}^t \in \mathbb{R}^{2d\times m_t}$ denotes the new columns generated between time stamp $t-1$ and the following time stamp t such that $\mathbf{G}^t = [\mathbf{G}^{t-1}, \mathbf{D}^t]$, where m_t is the number of new columns generated between time stamps $t-1$ and t. As mentioned above, the generation of new columns pertains to the arrival of new edges or the changes of node attributes. Here the challenges center around how to maintain and update the sketching matrix $\mathbf{B}^t$ based on the newly generated data in $\mathbf{D}^t$. At the very beginning, the sketching matrix $\mathbf{B}^t$ ($t = 0$) is set to be empty, then new columns presented in a data stream are continuously being inserted into the sketching matrix $\mathbf{B}^t$ until there are no empty columns anymore. Then frequent directions algorithm "shrinks" l orthogonal vectors by the same amount to make space for new data in the future. Concretely, a computation of singular value decomposition (SVD) is necessary each time when the sketching matrix $\mathbf{B}^t$ is full. The original frequent directions algorithm assumes that one column arrives at each time stamp, [23, 24] further extended it to tackle the case when more than one columns arrive at each time stamp. As we have more than one column in $\mathbf{D}^t$ in most cases, we leverage this

Algorithm 1 Maintain and update the sketching matrix $\mathbf{B}^t$

Input: Sketching matrix $\mathbf{B}^{t-1} \in \mathbb{R}^{2d\times l}$, new data $\mathbf{D}^t \in \mathbb{R}^{2d\times m_t}$.
Output: New sketching matrix $\mathbf{B}^t \in \mathbb{R}^{2d\times l}$, and $\tilde{\mathbf{U}}_l^t \in \mathbb{R}^{2d\times l}$.

1: $\mathbf{C}^t = [\mathbf{B}^{t-1}, \mathbf{D}^t] \in \mathbb{R}^{2d\times(l+m_t)}$;
2: $[\tilde{\mathbf{U}}_l^t, \tilde{\Sigma}_l^t, \tilde{\mathbf{V}}_l^t] = \text{svd}_l(\mathbf{C}^t)$;
3: $\hat{\Sigma}_l^t = \text{diag}(\sqrt{\tilde{\sigma}_1^2 - \tilde{\sigma}_l^2}, \sqrt{\tilde{\sigma}_2^2 - \tilde{\sigma}_l^2}, \ldots, \sqrt{\tilde{\sigma}_{l-1}^2 - \tilde{\sigma}_l^2}, 0)$;
4: $\mathbf{B}^t = \tilde{\mathbf{U}}_l^t \hat{\Sigma}_l^t$;

general solution to maintain and update the low-rank sketching matrix $\mathbf{B}^t$, upon which the patterns in the observed links and node attributes can be summarized accurately. The detailed pseudo code of the summarization phase using matrix sketching is presented in Algorithm 1. As the number of new columns m_t is much smaller than the number of columns in $\mathbf{G}^t$, we only need to perform SVD on a low-rank matrix (Line 2); its computation is efficient with a complexity of $O(2d(m_t + l)l)$. Also, it is space efficient with a maximum overhead of $O(2d(max_t\{m_t\} + l))$ across all time stamps. All in all, the summarization phase makes only one pass of the data and is both computational and space efficient.

3.2 Infer Missing Links with Sketching Matrix

The aforementioned low-rank sketching matrix $\mathbf{B}^t$ makes a structural summarization of the up-to-date observed data on dynamic attributed networks. Hence, we can leverage it to predict missing links on the fly. To show the underlying mechanism of the link prediction phase, we first assume that the feature representation $\mathbf{G}^t$ of the dynamic attributed network until time stamp t is available (which actually not). The original feature representation $\mathbf{G}^t$ could be very noisy, containing a certain amount of noisy and irrelevant attributes which may degrade the link prediction performance [32, 51]. On top of that, the link information in networks may also be noisy and even erroneous from a network analysis perspective [16]. To alleviate the negative impacts from these noisy attributes and noisy links, we propose to use principal component analysis (PCA) to reduce the noise hidden in the data stream. Formally, PCA projects the data in $\mathbf{G}^t$ onto several principal components such that the total data variance is minimized, and these principal components correspond to the top-k eigenvectors of the estimated covariance matrix

$\frac{1}{c_t}\mathbf{G}^t(\mathbf{G}^t)^T$, which is also equivalent to find the top-k left singular vectors of the matrix $\mathbf{G}^t$. Here, we denote the concatenation of the top-k eigenvectors as $\mathbf{U}_k^t \in \mathbb{R}^{2d\times k}$, and the principal components $\mathbf{U}_k^t$ is often regarded as a good rank-k basis to reconstruct all the data in the original representation $\mathbf{G}^t$. In addition, by using the linear combination of columns in $\mathbf{U}_k^t$ to represent columns in $\mathbf{G}^t$, the noisy information contained can be greatly reduced. As $\mathbf{U}_k^t$ provides a noise-resilient abstraction of patterns of connected node pairs, we can leverage the orthogonal basis to predict missing links for unconnected node pairs. In particular, let $\mathbf{y} \in \mathbb{R}^{2d}$ denotes the feature representation of an unconnected node pair for testing, if $\mathbf{y}$ is close to the space composed of columns in $\mathbf{U}_k^t$, mostly likely there will be a link between the starting node and the ending node of $\mathbf{y}$; otherwise, if $\mathbf{y}$ cannot be well reconstructed by the orthogonal basis $\mathbf{U}_k^t$, it implies that $\mathbf{y}$ deviates from the patterns of connected node pairs and the possibility that the two end nodes of $\mathbf{y}$ connected in the near future is low [23]. The residual error of the reconstruction phase is $\|\mathbf{I} - \mathbf{U}_k^t(\mathbf{U}_k^t)^T\mathbf{y}\|_2^2$. It can be observed that to obtain the residual error for each pair of unconnected nodes, only low-rank matrix multiplication operations are involved, and the computation cost is low, with a complexity of $O(2dk)$. Afterwards, we can take advantage of the residual error to predict whether there exists a link between a pair of unconnected nodes. Specifically, the smaller the residual error of a pair of unconnected nodes, the higher the chance that these two nodes will be linked in the near future.

The above phase assumes that the feature representation $\mathbf{G}^t$ is readily available before the link prediction takes place and the orthogonal basis $\mathbf{U}_k^t$ is the top-k left singular vectors of $\mathbf{G}^t$. However, as mentioned in the previous subsection that the storage of the whole feature representation $\mathbf{G}^t$ is intractable when the underlying attributed network is large; while on the other hand, the sketching matrix $\mathbf{B}^t$ is not only a low-rank matrix with light memory overhead, but also can approximate the original matrix $\mathbf{G}^t$ well. In this regard, we attempt to perform SVD on the low-rank matrix $\mathbf{B}^t$ instead of $\mathbf{G}^t$ to obtain the orthogonal basis, i.e., the top-k left singular vectors. Here, we denote these k left singular vectors of $\mathbf{B}^t$ as $\tilde{\mathbf{U}}_k^t \in \mathbb{R}^{2d\times k}$. And according to Algorithm 1, the sketching matrix $\mathbf{B}^t$ can be efficiently maintained and updated, and its top-l left singular vectors are $\tilde{\mathbf{U}}_l^t$. In this way, the approximation of the top-k left singular vectors of $\mathbf{G}^t$ can be directly obtained from $\tilde{\mathbf{U}}_l$ as long as the condition of $k \leq l$ is satisfied. And the residual error of the feature vector $\mathbf{y}$ is $\|\mathbf{I} - \tilde{\mathbf{U}}_k^t(\tilde{\mathbf{U}}_k^t)^T)\mathbf{y}\|_2^2$.

3.3 Threshold Determination

For the above phase, the potential links between unconnected nodes can be determined by verifying if the residual error is below a threshold. One simple solution to specify the threshold is to set it as a fixed value. Nonetheless, with the accumulation of new edges and new node attributes in a data stream over time, the intrinsic patterns of data change over time, and this phenomenon is often referred as concept drift in data stream mining [50]. To this end, it is more appealing to continuously update the threshold value for link prediction such that the up-to-date patterns of data can be well captured. Concretely, we propose to obtain the threshold automatically from the presented data stream instead of manually setting it up. For each observed link, i.e., a column in $\mathbf{G}^t$, we calculate its residual error, where $\tilde{\mathbf{U}}_k^t$ can be obtained by the top-k left singular vectors of the current sketching matrix $\mathbf{B}^t$ (Algorithm 1). Let us denote the collection of residual errors of links in $\mathbf{G}^t$ as $R = \{error_1, error_2, ..., error_{c_t}\}$, then the residual error threshold that is used to check the existence of new links can be determined as the largest error among R. In this way, we do not need to manually specify the threshold value and it can be automatically determined from the observed links.

Hence, the whole procedure of streaming link prediction on dynamic attributed networks is summarized in Algorithm 2.

Algorithm 2 SLIDE to predict missing links at time t

Input: Sketching matrix $\mathbf{B}^{t-1} \in \mathbb{R}^{2d\times l}$ and its top-l left singular vectors $\tilde{\mathbf{U}}_l^{t-1}$, new data $\mathbf{D}^t \in \mathbb{R}^{2d\times m_t}$, residual error threshold ϵ^{t-1}, feature representation $\mathbf{y}$ of an unconnected node pair.
Output: If there exists a link between the two end nodes of $\mathbf{y}$.
Obtain the new sketching matrix $\mathbf{B}^t$ and its top-l left singular vectors $\tilde{\mathbf{U}}_l^t$ by Algorithm 1;
Obtain the top-k singular vectors $\tilde{\mathbf{U}}_k^t$ from $\tilde{\mathbf{U}}_l^t$ ($k \leq l$);
Calculate the residual error of links in $\mathbf{D}^t$;
Update the residual error threshold ϵ^t;
Calculate the residual error of $\mathbf{y}$ by $\|\mathbf{I} - \tilde{\mathbf{U}}_k^t(\tilde{\mathbf{U}}_k^t)^T)\mathbf{y}\|_2^2$;
if error of $\mathbf{y} \leq \epsilon^t$ **then**
    There exists a future link between the two end nodes of $\mathbf{y}$;
else
    The two end nodes of $\mathbf{y}$ will not be connected;
end if

3.4 Theoretical Analysis of SLIDE

Next, we perform a theoretical analysis of the proposed streaming link prediction framework - SLIDE. In the proposed SLIDE framework, to calculate the possibility of connection between a pair of previously unconnected nodes at time stamp t, we make use of $\tilde{\mathbf{U}}_k^t$, which is the top-k left singular vectors of the sketching matrix $\mathbf{B}^t$. Now we compare the error bound of $\tilde{\mathbf{U}}_k^t$ against $\mathbf{U}_k^t$, where $\mathbf{U}_k^t$ is obtained from the original feature representation $\mathbf{G}^t$, i.e., the top-k left singular vectors of $\mathbf{G}^t$. Specifically, motivated by the analysis of the frequent directions algorithm [18] and matrix perturbation theory [47], we show that the Frobenius norm of the difference between $\tilde{\mathbf{U}}_k^t$ and $\mathbf{U}_k^t$ is bounded.

First, we define the k-conditional number of $\mathbf{G}^t$ as $\kappa = \sigma_1/\sigma_k$, where σ_i is the i-th singular value of $\mathbf{G}^t$. Next, we define α as:

$$\alpha = \frac{\kappa^2\|\mathbf{G}_k^t\|_F^2 - \|\mathbf{B}_k^t\|_F^2}{\|\mathbf{G}_k^t\|_F^2 - \|\mathbf{B}_k^t\|_F^2}. \quad (1)$$

LEMMA 3.2. *[19] For any unit vector $\mathbf{x} \in \mathbb{R}^{2d}$, the following inequality holds $\|(\mathbf{G}^t)^T\mathbf{x}\|_2^2 \geq \|(\mathbf{B}^t)^T\mathbf{x}\|_2^2$.*

LEMMA 3.3. *The inequality of $\|\mathbf{G}_k^t\|_F^2 \geq \|\mathbf{B}_k^t\|_F^2$ holds.*

PROOF. Assume that $\mathbf{a}_1, ..., \mathbf{a}_k$ are the top-k left singular vectors of $\mathbf{G}^t$, $\mathbf{b}_1, ..., \mathbf{b}_k$ are the top-k left singular vectors of $\mathbf{B}^t$. Then, we have $\|\mathbf{G}_k^t\|_F^2 = \sum_{i=1}^k \|(\mathbf{G}^t)^T\mathbf{a}_i\|_2^2 \geq \sum_{i=1}^k \|(\mathbf{G}^t)^T\mathbf{b}_i\|_2^2$. According to Lemma 3.2, $\sum_{i=1}^k \|(\mathbf{G}^t)^T\mathbf{b}_i\|_2^2 \geq \sum_{i=1}^k \|(\mathbf{B}^t)^T\mathbf{b}_i\|_2^2$. Therefore,

$||\mathbf{G}_k^t||_F^2 \geq \sum_{i=1}^k ||(\mathbf{B}^t)^T \mathbf{b}_i||_2^2 = ||\mathbf{B}_k^t||_F^2$, which completes the proof. □

As $||\mathbf{G}_k^t||_F^2 \geq ||\mathbf{B}_k^t||_F^2$, and $\kappa \geq 1$, we have $\alpha \geq 1$. In addition, as κ is a bounded number [47], we have $\alpha = O(1)$. Now, we define β as:

$$\beta = \frac{\kappa^2 - ||\mathbf{B}^t||^2/||\mathbf{G}^t||^2 + 2}{\kappa^2 - ||\mathbf{B}^t||^2/||\mathbf{G}^t||^2}. \quad (2)$$

According to the definition of the sketching matrix, we have $\mathbf{G}^t(\mathbf{G}^t)^T \geq \mathbf{B}^t(\mathbf{B}^t)^T$. Thus, $||\mathbf{G}^t||^2 \geq ||\mathbf{B}^t||^2$. Therefore, we have $\beta = O(1)$.

THEOREM 3.4. *[23] If the size of the sketching matrix l is:*

$$l = \Omega(\frac{\sqrt{2d}\kappa^2\alpha\beta k||\mathbf{G}^t||^2||\mathbf{G}^t - \mathbf{G}_k^t||_F^2}{T^2}),$$

where $T = \min_{i \neq j} |\lambda_i - \lambda_j| > 0$, and λ_i is the i-the eigenvalue of the matrix $\mathbf{G}^t(\mathbf{G}^t)^T$. Then the Frobenius norm difference between $\tilde{\mathbf{U}}_k^t$ and $\mathbf{U}_k^t$ is bounded by the following term:

$$||\tilde{\mathbf{U}}_k^t - \mathbf{U}_k^t||_F \leq \frac{\sqrt{2}T}{\sqrt{T + 8\kappa^2||\mathbf{G}^t||^2\sqrt[4]{T^2 + 16\kappa^4||\mathbf{G}^t||^4}}}.$$

The above l can further be simplified to $l = \Omega(\frac{\sqrt{2d}k||\mathbf{F}^t||^2||\mathbf{F}^t - \mathbf{F}_k^t||_F^2}{T^2})$ as $0 < \kappa \leq O(1)$, $\alpha = O(1)$ and $\beta = O(1)$.

The above theorem suggests that as long as the size of the sketching matrix l is set within a reasonable range, then the resulted orthogonal basis $\tilde{\mathbf{U}}_k^t$ from the sketching matrix $\mathbf{B}^t$ approximates the orthogonal basis $\mathbf{U}_k^t$ from the whole observed data $\mathbf{G}^t$.

4 EXPERIMENTS

In this section, we perform experiments on real-world dynamic attributed networks to validate the effectiveness and efficiency of the proposed SLIDE framework for streaming link prediction.

4.1 Datasets

We collect three real-world dynamic attributed networks for experimental validation, these datasets range from social media networks to coauthor networks. The detailed descriptions of these three dynamic attributed networks are listed below.

Epinions: Epinions is a product review site in which users build trust relationships to seek advice from others and share their reviews about products. We take each user as a node and regard his/her reviews as node attributes. In particular, we first use the bag-of-words model to extract features from user reviews and then employ state-of-the-art unsupervised feature selection methods for networked data [32] to find the top 100 important features closely hinged with the network topology. Both the network structure and the node attributes are evolving over time. In the collected dataset, there are 25 time stamps (with an interval of one month), the total number of nodes is 14,180 and the total number of edges is 308,136.

DBLP: DBLP is an extracted coauthor network for the authors who publish at least three papers from the year of 1995 to 2011. In the network, each author corresponds to a node. And similar to Epinions, we apply the bag-of-words model and feature selection on the title of their publications to find the most relevant 100 node attributes, i.e., words. As authors gradually form new coauthor relations and their research interests evolve over time, the underlying network is naturally a dynamic attributed network. The resulted dataset has 100,924 nodes and 764,392 edges over 17 time stamps.

ACM: ACM is a similar coauthor network as DBLP. We extract a subgraph consisting of the authors who publish at least three papers in the year of 1995 and 2015, and apply the same mechanism as before to extract 100 important node attributes. Therefore, we obtain a dynamic attributed network with a total amount of 122,567 nodes and 1,551,554 edges over 16 different time stamps.

4.2 Baseline Methods

To verify the effectiveness and efficiency of the proposed SLIDE framework, we compare SLIDE with the following baseline link prediction methods from three different categories: (1) with only network structure; (2) with only node attributes; and (3) with both sources of information.

- Common Neighbors (CN) [37]: CN quantifies the number of common users between node pairs for link prediction.
- Jaccard Coefficient (JC) [37]: JC calculates the similarity of pairs of nodes for link prediction with Jaccard coefficient.
- Adamic-Adar (AA) [37]: AA is an extension of CN which penalizes the common neighbors with high node degrees.
- Rooted PageRank [49]: It performs random walk with start from a root node and then determines the scores of links, i.e., node proximity, to other nodes from the root node.
- NMF [40]: It conducts non-negative matrix factorization on the adjacency matrix of the network to calculate the scores of unconnected node pairs.
- SimAttr [53]: It calculates cosine similarity on node attributes and uses the similarity score to rank links.
- FactLog [44]: It adopts matrix factorization and incorporates both network structure and node attributes in a joint framework for link prediction.
- AttriRank [22]: It performs PageRank on the attributed networks and then the score of each node pair is determined as the product of the PageRank scores of two end nodes.

Among them, CN, JC, AA, Rooted PageRank and NMF belong to the first category by using only network information; SimAttr on the other hand only takes advantage of node attribute information for link prediction; FactLog, AttriRank and the proposed SLIDE are in the third category by combining both sources of information together for link prediction.

4.3 Experimental Settings

In the experiments, we attempt to answer two research questions: (1) how accurate is the proposed SLIDE framework in predicting missing links; (2) how efficient is the proposed streaming algorithm when measured against other offline methods.

We first investigate the effectiveness of the proposed framework SLIDE. Given a dynamic attributed network with T different time stamps, for each time stamp t ($1 \leq t \leq T$), in the training phase, we first perform link prediction with the attributed network G^t, and then test the link prediction performance on G^{t+1}. It should be noted that as most of these baseline methods cannot handle cold-start nodes, we choose to predict the missing links for the nodes that appear in both G^t and G^{t+1}. More investigation on the link prediction for cold-start nodes will be presented later. As a final result, we output the average link prediction performance over $T-1$ test periods. In the experiments, we set the number of columns in the sketching matrix l according to the suggestions of [23]. Meanwhile, we specify the parameter k the same as l.

Suppose the number of new links for testing between time stamp t and $t+1$ is e_t, all these baseline methods can be regarded as a ranking model which returns the top e_t possible links from G_t and then compares with the ground truth links in G^{t+1}. To make a fair comparison between SLIDE and baseline methods, in the evaluation, we do not use the residual error threshold ϵ, instead, we rank the candidate links according to the residual errors. Three commonly used evaluation metrics are used to compare the link prediction performance of different methods. They are *area under the curve* (**AUC**) [9], *mean average precision* (**MAP**) [36], *half-life utility* (**HLU**) [45]. The higher the values of AUC, MAP and HLU are, the better the prediction performance is. Specifically, at each time stamp during the testing phase, we treat all the e_t links that will happen at the next time stamp $t+1$ as positive samples, and the other links as negative links.

Different from SLIDE that only makes one pass of the data to predict missing link on the fly, all baseline methods are offline methods that require the access of the whole historical data each time when changes occur. In other words, they need to explicitly materialize the whole attributed networks in memory before link prediction takes place. To have a fair comparison between SLIDE and the baseline methods in terms of efficiency, we allow the storage of the historical data for baseline methods in memory and compare their cumulative running time over all time stamps.

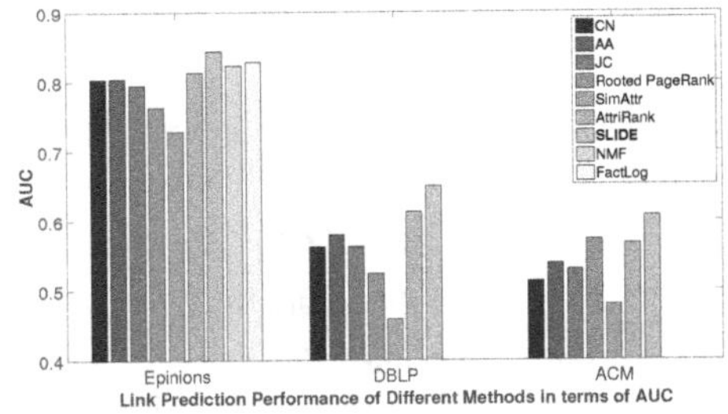

(a) AUC

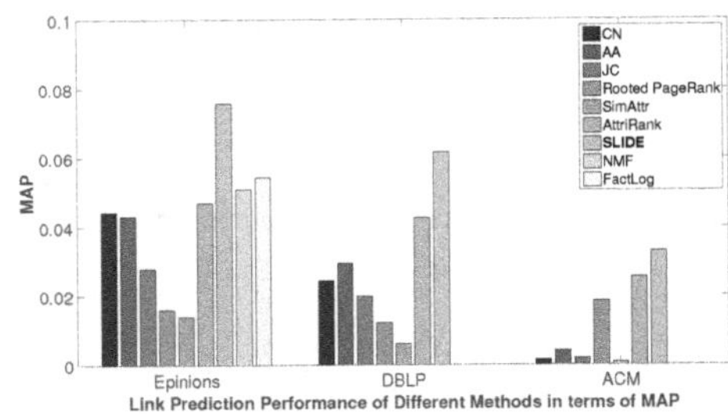

(b) MAP

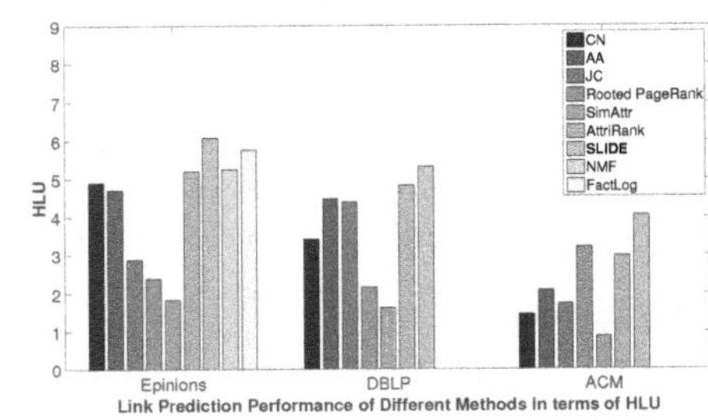

(c) HLU

Figure 3: Link prediction performance comparison.

4.4 Effectiveness of the Proposed SLIDE

First, we investigate the effectiveness of the proposed SLIDE framework by comparing its link prediction performance with the aforementioned baseline methods. The average link prediction results over multiple time stamps are presented in Figure 3. We make the following observations from the figure.

- The proposed streaming link prediction framework SLIDE outperforms all baseline methods in almost all cases. We also perform a pairwise Wilcoxon signed-rank test between SLIDE and these baseline methods. The comparison results indicate that the proposed SLIDE framework is significantly better than others, with a significance level of 0.05.
- CN, AA, JC, Rooted PageRank and NMF only leverage network structure for link prediction, and their performance is superior to SimAttr which relies on node attributes to infer missing links. It implies that the link prediction performance is influenced more by the network structure rather than the node attributes.
- The link prediction methods FactLog, AttriRank and SLIDE that leverage two sources of information achieve better link prediction performance than methods with only one source of information. The observation supports the assumption that node attribute information compliments to network structure for link prediction.
- We do not report the link prediction results of NMF and FactLog on DBLP and ACM datasets as we run out of memory for these two methods. The reason is that these two methods are both matrix factorization based methods and cannot be easily scaled to large-scale networks.

4.5 Efficiency of the Proposed SLIDE

Now we investigate the second research question about the efficiency of the proposed SLIDE framework. Specifically, we report the cumulative running time of different methods across all time stamps in Table 1. As all the baseline methods mentioned are designed for static networks by assuming the materialization of the network structure in memory, we have to rerun these baseline methods repeatedly each time when there are changes on the attributed networks. As can be observed from the table, our proposed SLIDE framework is significantly faster than all baseline methods. The overall running time of SLIDE on Epinions, DBLP and ACM are 25.67 seconds, 291.31 seconds and 689.93 seconds, respectively. Specifically, SLIDE is 49×, 243×, 58×, 12×, 30×, 10×, 278×, and 81× faster than CN, AA, JC, Rooted PageRank, NMF, SimAttr, FactLog, AttriRank, respectively in Epinions. On DBLP and ACM datasets, the cumulative running time of all baseline methods cost more than 3 hours while our method finishes within minutes. In addition to that, as our proposed SLIDE framework maintains and updates a

Table 1: Running time comparison of different methods.

	Epinions	DBLP	ACM
CN	1245.41s	> 3 hours	> 3 hours
AA	6243.32s	> 3 hours	> 3 hours
JC	1489.81s	> 3 hours	> 3 hours
Rooted PageRank	305.41s	> 3 hours	> 3 hours
NMF	774.7s	> 3 hours	> 3 hours
SimAttr	259.09s	> 3 hours	> 3 hours
FactLog	7140.18s	> 3 hours	> 3 hours
AttriRank	2081.53s	> 3 hours	> 3 hours
SLIDE	**25.67s**	**291.31s**	**689.93s**

Table 2: Link prediction results for new users in Epinions.

Metrics	AUC	MAP	HLU
SimAttr	0.6828	0.0286	3.60
AttriRank	0.7067	0.0409	4.29
SLIDE	0.7532	0.0523	4.94

low-rank sketching matrix with light memory overhead, it is also much more space efficient than most baseline methods. All in all, SLIDE achieves promising link prediction performance within a favorable amount of running time with limited memory costs.

4.6 Link Prediction of SLIDE for New Users

It has been widely known that in conventional link prediction problems, new users often suffer from the cold-start problems since we often do not have any data about newly joined users. Fortunately, the rich node attributes can help mitigate this critical issue when link information is not available. To investigate how well the proposed SLIDE framework handles new users for cold-start link prediction problem, we compare SLIDE with SimAttr and AttriRank, as these two methods can also handle the cold-start problem by leveraging node attributes. We focus on the Epinions dataset to investigate the cold-start problem as in DBLP and ACM datasets, authors create coauthor relations with other scholars the same time when they publish a paper and is therefore not suitable for cold-start problem study. In particular, in Epinions, users can first write reviews about products and then build trust relations with others, and we predict missing links for these new users by using their attribute information before they build any trust relations. The link prediction performance comparison in terms of these new users is illustrated in Table 2. It can be shown that SLIDE obtains better link prediction performance than SimAttr and AttriRank for the cold-start problem. The reason is that SLIDE summarizes the connectivity patterns of linked nodes in the sketching matrix; the orthogonal basis from the sketching matrix is noise resilient and can help us predict missing links more accurately.

5 RELATED WORK

In this work, we review related work from three perspectives: (1) link prediction on networks; and (2) mining streaming networks.

5.1 Link Prediction

The past decade has witnessed the development of a great number of link prediction methods [7, 8, 11, 13, 20, 33, 37, 44, 48, 54, 55]. The vast majority of existing link prediction methods can be broadly categorized into two classes - unsupervised methods and supervised methods. A family of unsupervised methods are heavily based on different similarity measures such as the number of common neighbors, Kartz, Jaccard coefficient and Adamic/Adar to measure the node proximity [37, 54]. Another prevalent choice of unsupervised methods is to investigate low-rank matrix techniques to approximate the initial adjacency matrix of the network structure [13, 27]. Supervised methods, on the other hand, treat link prediction as a classification task [6, 39, 44]. Typically, they first extract features from positively labeled instances (existing links) and negatively labeled instances (non-existing links), and then build a classification model to infer the missing labels of a pair of unconnected nodes. The link prediction problem on dynamic networks is also studied in [14, 57]. However, these methods have to store all historical data and cannot be supported in a streaming fashion.

Recent studies imply the existence of autocorrelation between the attributes of connected nodes. To this end, the exploitation of the autocorrelation could advance many mining tasks on attributed networks such as link prediction. For example, [20, 53] first proposed to integrate network structure and node attributes into a joint augmented network and then employ random walk based approaches. Barbieri et al. [7] presented a stochastic generative model to joint factorize social connections and node attributes. The resulted model provides accurate prediction performance and related topical explanations to support the made predictions. Wei et al. [51] further investigated the link prediction problem on networks with partially observable links and node attributes.

5.2 Mining Streaming Networks

Many real-world networks are not static but are presented in a streaming fashion such that a massive amount of interactions among nodes are continuously being received. Such high-velocity edge streams necessitate near real-time analytical methods. In many cases, the size of edge stream could be massive and cannot be easily stored, which further exacerbates the consequent learning tasks. Hence, most of the existing efforts are dedicated to designing effective data structures to summarize the observed network structure in real-time. For example, Aggarwal et al. [4] first proposed to cluster a small graph (or a collection or edges) in a streaming fashion by using the hash-based compression techniques. The similar sketching mechanism is extended to the scenario when node attributes are attached to the continuously generated nodes [56]. In [3], a reservoir sampling method is presented to maintain the structural summary of the underlying network stream for clustering and outlier detection. In terms of classification, Aggarwal [2] employed a min-hash based approach to model the dependencies between the sketched subgraphs and the class labels. Some other efforts tried to leverage the embedding or hashing techniques with kernel methods for classification in streaming networks [21, 25]. In addition, some fundamental graph mining problems such as counting triangles [12], graph matching [41] and eigen-tracking [10] are also extensively studied and a comprehensive overview of these problems could be referred to [1].

6 CONCLUSIONS

A vast majority of existing link prediction algorithms are designed for static networks and assume that the whole network structure is materialized in memory before link prediction happens. However, many real-world networks are naturally dynamic and are characterized by frequent updates. The updates are often transient and could even be infinite, which puts the applicability of conventional link prediction algorithms in jeopardy. In addition to that, rich node attributes are prevalent and often have a strong connection with the network topology, and they may also change adaptively over time. It remains a daunting task to support the link prediction on such dynamic attributed networks in an online fashion due to some unique challenges. In this paper, we study the novel problem of streaming link prediction on dynamic attributed networks and propose a sophisticated link prediction framework - SLIDE. In particular, we leverage a cost-effective matrix sketching technique to make a summarization of the current observed data by making only one pass of the data, and the sketching matrix, in turn, is used to infer the missing links. Theoretical analysis indicates that our method achieves a similar performance as a cost offline method which stores all historical data. We also perform empirical experimental evaluations on real-world datasets, the results imply that SLIDE not only can predict the missing links more accurately but also is much more computationally efficient than competitors.

ACKNOWLEDGEMENTS

This material is based upon work supported by, or in part by, the National Science Foundation (NSF) grant 1614576, and the Office of Naval Research (ONR) grant N00014-16-1-2257.

REFERENCES

- [1] Charu Aggarwal and Karthik Subbian. 2014. Evolutionary network analysis: A survey. *CSUR* (2014).
- [2] Charu C Aggarwal. 2011. On Classification of Graph Streams. In *SDM*.
- [3] Charu C Aggarwal, Yuchen Zhao, and S Yu Philip. 2011. Outlier Detection in Graph Streams. In *ICDE*.
- [4] Charu C Aggarwal, Yuchen Zhao, and Philip S Yu. 2010. On Clustering Graph Streams. In *SDM*.
- [5] Mohammad Al Hasan and Mohammed J Zaki. 2011. A Survey of Link Prediction in Social Networks. In *Social Network Data Analytics*.
- [6] Lars Backstrom and Jure Leskovec. 2011. Supervised Random Walks: Predicting and Recommending Links in Social Networks. In *WSDM*.
- [7] Nicola Barbieri, Francesco Bonchi, and Giuseppe Manco. 2014. Who to Follow and Why: Link Prediction with Explanations. In *KDD*.
- [8] Shiyu Chang, Guo-Jun Qi, Charu C Aggarwal, Jiayu Zhou, Meng Wang, and Thomas S Huang. 2014. Factorized Similarity Learning in Networks. In *ICDM*.
- [9] Shiyu Chang, Yang Zhang, Jiliang Tang, Dawei Yin, Yi Chang, Mark A Hasegawa-Johnson, and Thomas S Huang. 2016. Positive-Unlabeled Learning in Streaming Networks. In *KDD*.
- [10] Chen Chen and Hanghang Tong. 2015. Fast Eigen-Functions Tracking on Dynamic Graphs. In *SDM*.
- [11] Chen Chen, Hanghang Tong, Lei Xie, Lei Ying, and Qing He. 2016. FASCINATE: Fast Cross-Layer Dependency Inference on Multi-Layered Networks. In *KDD*.
- [12] Lorenzo De Stefani, Alessandro Epasto, Matteo Riondato, and Eli Upfal. 2016. TRIÈST: Counting Local and Global Triangles in Fully-Dynamic Streams with Fixed Memory Size. In *KDD*.
- [13] Liang Duan, Charu Aggarwal, Shuai Ma, Renjun Hu, and Jinpeng Huai. 2016. Scaling up Link Prediction with Ensembles. In *WSDM*.
- [14] Daniel M Dunlavy, Tamara G Kolda, and Evrim Acar. 2011. Temporal Link Prediction using Matrix and Tensor Factorizations. *TKDD* (2011).
- [15] Joan Feigenbaum, Sampath Kannan, Andrew McGregor, Siddharth Suri, and Jian Zhang. 2005. On Graph Problems in a Semi-Streaming Model. *TCS* (2005).
- [16] Huiji Gao, Xufei Wang, Jiliang Tang, and Huan Liu. 2013. Network Denoising in Social Media. In *ASONAM*.
- [17] Lise Getoor and Christopher P Diehl. 2005. Link Mining: A Survey. *SIGKDD Explorations* (2005).
- [18] Mina Ghashami, Amey Desai, and Jeff M Phillips. 2014. Improved Practical Matrix Sketching with Guarantees. In *ESA*.
- [19] Mina Ghashami and Jeff M Phillips. 2014. Relative Errors for Deterministic Low-Rank Matrix Approximations. In *SODA*.
- [20] Neil Zhenqiang Gong, Ameet Talwalkar, Lester Mackey, Ling Huang, Eui Chul Richard Shin, Emil Stefanov, Elaine Runting Shi, and Dawn Song. 2014. Joint Link Prediction and Attribute Inference using a Social-Attribute Network. *TIST* (2014).
- [21] Ting Guo, Lianhua Chi, and Xingquan Zhu. 2013. Graph Hashing and Factorization for Fast Graph Stream Classification. In *CIKM*.
- [22] Chin-Chi Hsu, Yi-An Lai, Wen-Hao Chen, Ming-Han Feng, and Shou-De Lin. 2017. Unsupervised Ranking using Graph Structures and Node Attributes. In *WSDM*.
- [23] Hao Huang and Shiva Prasad Kasiviswanathan. 2015. Streaming Anomaly Detection Using Randomized Matrix Sketching. *VLDB* (2015).
- [24] Hao Huang, Shinjae Yoo, and Shiva Prasad Kasiviswanathan. 2015. Unsupervised Feature Selection on Data Streams. In *CIKM*.
- [25] Ling Jian, Jundong Li, and Huan Liu. 2017. Toward Online Node Classification on Streaming Networks. *DMKD* (2017).
- [26] Takuya Kitazawa. 2017. Sketching Dynamic User-Item Interactions for Online Item Recommendation. In *CHIIR*.
- [27] Jérôme Kunegis and Andreas Lommatzsch. 2009. Learning Spectral Graph Transformations for Link Prediction. In *ICML*.
- [28] Timothy La Fond and Jennifer Neville. 2010. Randomization Tests for Distinguishing Social Influence and Homophily Effects. In *WWW*.
- [29] Jundong Li, Harsh Dani, Xia Hu, and Huan Liu. 2017. Radar: Residual Analysis for Anomaly Detection in Attributed Networks. *IJCAI* (2017).
- [30] Jundong Li, Harsh Dani, Xia Hu, Jiliang Tang, Yi Chang, and Huan Liu. 2017. Attributed Network Embedding for Learning in a Dynamic Environment. In *CIKM*.
- [31] Jundong Li, Xia Hu, Ling Jian, and Huan Liu. 2016. Toward Time-Evolving Feature Selection on Dynamic Networks. In *ICDM*.
- [32] Jundong Li, Xia Hu, Liang Wu, and Huan Liu. 2016. Robust Unsupervised Feature Selection on Networked Data. In *SDM*.
- [33] Jundong Li, Jiliang Tang, Yilin Wang, Yali Wan, Yi Chang, and Huan Liu. 2017. Understanding and Predicting Delay in Reciprocal Relations. *arXiv preprint arXiv:1703.01393* (2017).
- [34] Jundong Li, Liang Wu, Osmar R Zaïane, and Huan Liu. 2017. Toward Personalized Relational Learning. In *SDM*.
- [35] Lihong Li, Wei Chu, John Langford, and Robert E Schapire. 2010. A Contextual-Bandit Approach to Personalized News Article Recommendation. In *WWW*.
- [36] Yanen Li, Jia Hu, ChengXiang Zhai, and Ye Chen. 2010. Improving One-Class Collaborative Filtering by Incorporating Rich User Information. In *CIKM*.
- [37] David Liben-Nowell and Jon Kleinberg. 2007. The Link Prediction Problem for Social Networks. *JASIST* (2007).
- [38] Edo Liberty. 2013. Simple and Deterministic Matrix Sketching. In *KDD*.
- [39] Ryan N Lichtenwalter, Jake T Lussier, and Nitesh V Chawla. 2010. New Perspectives and Methods in Link Prediction. In *KDD*.
- [40] Chih-Jen Lin. 2007. Projected Gradient Methods for Nonnegative Matrix Factorization. *Neural Computation* (2007).
- [41] Andrew McGregor. 2005. Finding Graph Matchings in Data Streams. In *APPROX-RANDOM*.
- [42] Andrew McGregor. 2014. Graph Stream Algorithms: A Survey. *ACM SIGMOD Record* (2014).
- [43] Miller McPherson, Lynn Smith-Lovin, and James M Cook. 2001. Birds of a Feather: Homophily in Social Networks. *Annual Review of Sociology* (2001).
- [44] Aditya Menon and Charles Elkan. 2011. Link Prediction via Matrix Factorization. *ECMLPKDD* (2011).
- [45] Rong Pan, Yunhong Zhou, Bin Cao, Nathan N Liu, Rajan Lukose, Martin Scholz, and Qiang Yang. 2008. One-class Collaborative Filtering. In *ICDM*.
- [46] Steffen Rendle. 2010. Factorization Machines. In *ICDM*.
- [47] Gilbert W Stewart. 1990. Matrix Perturbation Theory. (1990).
- [48] Yizhou Sun, Jiawei Han, Charu C Aggarwal, and Nitesh V Chawla. 2012. When Will It Happen?: Relationship Prediction in Heterogeneous Information Networks. In *WWW*.
- [49] Hanghang Tong, Christos Faloutsos, and Jia-yu Pan. 2006. Fast Random Walk with Restart and Its Applications. In *ICDM*.
- [50] Alexey Tsymbal. 2004. The Problem of Concept Drift: Definitions and Related Work. *Computer Science Department, Trinity College Dublin* (2004).
- [51] Xiaokai Wei, Linchuan Xu, Bokai Cao, and Philip S Yu. 2017. Cross View Link Prediction by Learning Noise-resilient Representation Consensus. In *WWW*.
- [52] Qingyun Wu, Huazheng Wang, Quanquan Gu, and Hongning Wang. 2016. Contextual Bandits in A Collaborative Environment. In *SIGIR*.
- [53] Zhijun Yin, Manish Gupta, Tim Weninger, and Jiawei Han. 2010. A Unified Framework for Link Recommendation Using Random Walks. In *ASONAM*.
- [54] Peixiang Zhao, Charu Aggarwal, and Gewen He. 2016. Link Prediction in Graph Streams. In *ICDE*.
- [55] Tong Zhao, H Vicky Zhao, and Irwin King. 2015. Exploiting Game Theoretic Analysis for Link Recommendation in Social Networks. In *CIKM*.
- [56] Yuchen Zhao and Philip S Yu. 2013. On Graph Stream Clustering with Side Information. In *SDM*.
- [57] Linhong Zhu, Dong Guo, Junming Yin, Greg Ver Steeg, and Aram Galstyan. 2016. Scalable Temporal Latent Space Inference for Link Prediction in Dynamic Social Networks. *TKDE* (2016).

Inferring Dockless Shared Bike Distribution in New Cities

Zhaoyang Liu
Shanghai Jiao Tong University
Shanghai, China
towardsun@sjtu.edu.cn

Yanyan Shen*
Shanghai Jiao Tong University
Shanghai, China
shenyy@sjtu.edu.cn

Yanmin Zhu*
Shanghai Jiao Tong University
Shanghai, China
yzhu@sjtu.edu.cn

ABSTRACT

Recently, dockless shared bike services have achieved great success and reinvented bike sharing business in China. When expanding bike sharing business into a new city, most start-ups always wish to find out how to cover the whole city with a suitable bike distribution. In this paper, we study the problem of inferring bike distribution in new cities, which is challenging. As no dockless bikes are deployed in the new city, we propose to learn insights on bike distribution from cities populated with dockless bikes. We exploit multi-source data to identify important features that affect bike distributions and develop a novel inference model combining Factor Analysis and Convolutional Neural Network techniques. The extensive experiments on real-life datasets show that the proposed solution provides significantly more accurate inference results compared with competitive prediction methods.

CCS CONCEPTS

• **Applied computing → Transportation**; Forecasting; • **Information systems** → *Data mining*;

KEYWORDS

Dockless shared bikes; distribution inference; urban computing; GeoConv neural network

ACM Reference Format:
Zhaoyang Liu, Yanyan Shen[1], and Yanmin Zhu[1]. 2018. Inferring Dockless Shared Bike Distribution in New Cities. In *WSDM 2018: WSDM 2018: The Eleventh ACM International Conference on Web Search and Data Mining , February 5–9, 2018, Marina Del Rey, CA, USA.* ACM, New York, NY, USA, 9 pages. https://doi.org/10.1145/3159652.3159708

1 INTRODUCTION

Recent years have witnessed a worldwide prevalence of public bike sharing systems. These systems offer an environment-friendly solution to the first-and-last mile connection and help bridge the gap between existing transportation modes such as subways and bus systems [5]. In China, new dockless bike-sharing programs such as Mobike[1] and ofo[2] emerge recently, which allow users to find, ride and park bikes "anywhere" via a GPS-based smartphone app. One can locate surrounding available bikes easily on the map and unlock a bike by scanning a QR code directly. This flexibility offered by dockless bike systems brings great convenience to people and reinvents bike sharing in China.

For business purpose, every dockless bike sharing company has been devoting great effort to rapidly expanding the number of cities in which it operates. For instance, Mobike is growing popular in more than 100 cities worldwide within the past 6 months [4]. When coming into a new city, a company will encounter several practical problems among which, an essential issue should be: *how to distribute bikes over the new city in the very beginning*? Spreading bikes wisely is undoubtedly important for a company to satisfy bicycle demands from users betimes and muscle into the markets prior than its rival start-ups. Meanwhile, foreknowing possible bike distribution in advance is also of great use for local governors to renew traffic rules, plan bike lanes and prevent abuse of shared bikes. In fact, the mountains of bikes in the central areas of Shanghai are reported to take up space beside private buildings and block pedestrians on the sidewalk, while those in remote areas are dumped in rivers or even up in trees [25].

Most existing works on bike sharing systems studied the problems of station traffic/demand prediction [11, 19, 30], rebalance scheduling [21], and station site optimization [20, 22]. However, they focused on bike systems with docking stations and mainly addressed how to establish new stations or estimate bike usage demands in known stations. In [2], Bao et al. leveraged station-less bike trajectories and proposed a data-driven approach to bike lane planning. To the best of our knowledge, we are the first to infer dockless shared bike distribution in a new city where the bikes are going to be deployed in any place of the city.

The problem of inferring shared bike distribution in a new city is very challenging. First of all, an ideal bike distribution should match users' demand distribution, which is unknown in advance. Second, bike demand in each region is changing over time. Intuitively, people ride bikes from home to offices or subway stations during morning peak hours, and in a reverse direction during evening peak hours. These mobility dynamics may result in time-varying bike distributions. Finally, since new bike sharing systems have no docking stations, we have to concern every subregion in the city, where the bike demands can differ in several orders of magnitude.

Fortunately, depending on the "short-riding-distance" nature of bike routes, we observe the stability of bike distributions over time by analyzing dockless shared bike data from Mobike, the world's largest bike operator, in depth. Such stability makes bike distribution inference feasible. Furthermore, despite the unknown bike demands in a new city, we can collect bike information from the cities that are already populated with shared bikes. Data in the city occupied with dockless shared bikes typically encapsulate

*Corresponding author.
[1]https://mobike.com
[2]https://www.ofo.com

WSDM 2018, February 5–9, 2018, Marina Del Rey, CA, USA

ACM ISBN 978-1-4503-5581-0/18/02...$15.00
https://doi.org/10.1145/3159652.3159708

insights on how to distribute bikes in a new city, especially when the two cities are alike. Last but not least, various geographical information of the target city such as POI, road network, is widely available nowadays, which yields great promise in predicting bike distribution according to our intuition.

In this paper, we conduct a comprehensive study on exploring spatial-temporal characteristics of bike distributions for dockless bike sharing systems and observe the stability of bike distributions over various time slots. We propose a multi-source data-driven approach to inferring dockless shared bike distribution in a new city. Specifically, we extract important features from various data sources such as POIs, satellite light, road network, and further analyze the effects of these features over bike distribution thoroughly. Our distribution inference framework mainly consists of two components. First, we introduce a novel model, named CoFA-GeoConv, which transfers bike distribution knowledge from a given city to the new one. Our model applies Factor Analysis over features from two cities jointly to reduce the city-level difference, and then uses the CNN-based neural network to capture geographical influences on bike distribution. Second, we supply the trained model with latent features from the new city and derive its bike distribution based on model output. Different from existing transfer learning works on domain adaptations [9, 10, 23], our model leverages Factor Analysis to eliminate factors specific to the source city when adapting knowledge to a new city. The experiments show the effectiveness of our approach when the two cities are quite different in nature.

The main contributions of this paper are summarized as follows.

- To the best of our knowledge, we are the first to infer dockless shared bike distribution in new cities. We analyze spatio-temporal properties of dockless bike distribution in different cities based on massive bike data from Mobike, and discover many useful insights on how to distribute dockless shared bikes wisely. (Section 3).
- We propose a multi-source data-driven approach to predict bike distribution in new cities. We exploit information from POIs, satellite light data, subway stations, business centers, road network, and extract important features from each of them. We also analyze the correlations between the features and bike distribution in depth (Section 4).
- We propose a novel model named CoFA-GeoConv to infer bike distribution in a new city by transferring distribution knowledge from a given city. Our model applies Factor Analysis to reduce the differences between two cities and adopts CNN-based neural network to capture geographical influences on bike distribution (Section 5).
- We evaluate our inference framework extensively on Mobike data (12/06/2017 to 12/07/2017) from multiple cities in China, i.e., Shanghai, Beijing, and Ningbo. The results show that our inferred bike distributions in new cities achieve 8.1%-65.7% lower KL divergence (against truth bike distributions) compared with competitive baselines (Section 6).

2 OVERVIEW

2.1 Definitions

To compute bike distribution, we first divide a whole city area into a set G of disjoint grids.

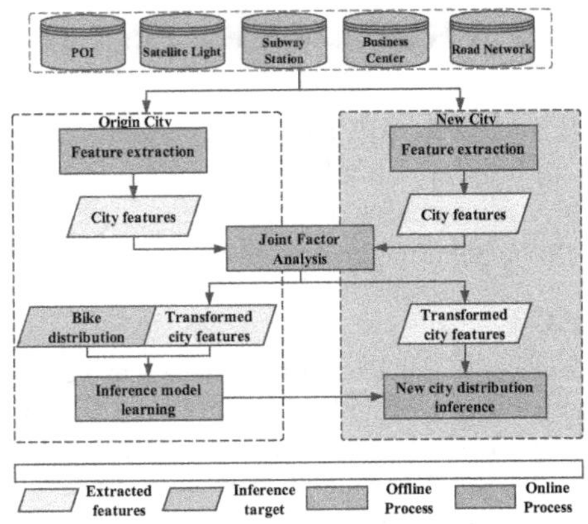

Figure 1: CoFA-GeoConv inference framework

Definition 2.1 (City Grid g and Grid Neighbors $NB_\lambda(g)$). We represent a complete city area as a two-dimensional rectangle and divide it into a set $G = \{g_{i,j} \mid i \in [1,n], j \in [1,m], i,j \in \mathbb{N}^+\}$ of grids with the same size along the longitude and latitude coordinates.

Given a window size $\lambda = 2n+1, n \in \mathbb{N}^*$, we define the neighbors of grid $g_{i,j}$ w.r.t. λ, denoted by $NB_\lambda(g_{i,j})$, as follows.

$$NB_\lambda(g_{i,j}) = \{g_{i',j'} \in G \backslash \{g_{i,j}\} \mid |i-i'| \le \frac{\lambda-1}{2} \wedge |j-j'| \le \frac{\lambda-1}{2}\}.$$

We consider a set of raw bike records, where each record contains a timestamp t, bike id, bike type, and geographic coordinates $p = (lon, lat)$, representing the existence of a bike in the point p at time t. We denote by $p \lessdot_{in} g_{i,j}$ iff p resides in the grid. Given a time period, we can map raw bike records within that period onto the grids of a city to compute bike distribution D.

Definition 2.2 (Bike Distribution D within a time period). Consider a set $\mathcal{H}_t$ of raw bike records whose timestamp belongs to the time period of $[s_t, e_t]$, and a set G of grids in a city. The bike distribution D over G during period $[s_t, e_t]$ satisfies:

$$D^t_{i,j} = \frac{|\{h \in \mathcal{H}_t \mid h.p \lessdot_{in} g_{i,j}\}|}{|\mathcal{H}_t|}, \; g_{i,j} \in G \tag{1}$$

In this paper, we try to leverage multiple data sources for bike distribution inference in new cities, as follows.

Definition 2.3 (POI Data $\mathcal{P}$). $\mathcal{P}$ contains a set of POIs in a city[3], where each POI is a city venue with attributes: name, address, coordinate, and category.

Definition 2.4 (Satellite Light Data $\mathcal{L}$). Satellite light data[4] $\mathcal{L}$ contains a set of points with light intensity, which are observed at night by remote sensing satellites. We denote by $\delta(p)$ the light intensity for a point $p = (lon, lat)$ on earth's surface.

Definition 2.5 (Transportation Data $\mathcal{T}$). Transportation data $\mathcal{T}$ contains information of subway stations in the city, including station name, line number, and the corresponding coordinates.

Definition 2.6 (Road Network Data $\mathcal{R}$). A road network[5] $\mathcal{R}$ is an undirected graph (V, E), where each vertex $r \in V$ represents a road

[3] http://map.baidu.com
[4] https://www.lightpollutionmap.info
[5] http://www.openstreetmap.org

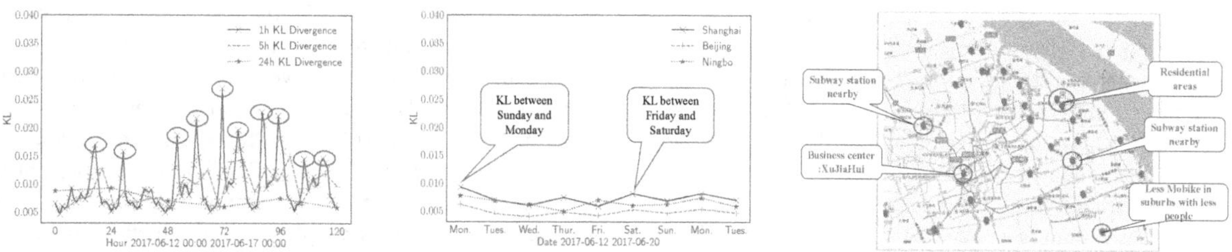

(a) KL w.r.t. different time window sizes (b) KL in three cities with 1-day time window (c) Top 30 mobike distribution locations in Shanghai

Figure 2: Properties of dockless shared bike distributions

segment in the format of $(\phi, len, type)$. ϕ contains two terminal points and a list of intermediate points in the road segment, len is the segment length, and $type \in T$ is the segment type such as motorway, trunk, pedestrian, bus guideway, etc.

Definition 2.7 (Business Center Data $\mathcal{B}$). Business center data[6] $\mathcal{B}$ contains information of city business districts specified by (loc, lev), where loc is geographical coordinates of a district and lev reflects the degree of its prosperity.

2.2 Problem Statement

We consider two cities C and C', where C contains dockless shared bikes and C' is a new city to launch shared bike business. We divide both cities into grids of the same size. Given a set of raw bike data in city C, we can compute the bike distribution D according to Definition 2.2. Our goal is to infer bike distribution in the new city C', based on the known bike distribution D from city C and multiple geo-related datasets. We formally define our problem as follows.

Definition 2.8 (Dockless Shared Bike Distribution Inference). Given bike distribution D over grids G in city C, POI data $\mathcal{P}, \mathcal{P}'$, satellite light data $\mathcal{S}, \mathcal{S}'$, transportation data $\mathcal{T}, \mathcal{T}'$, road network data $\mathcal{R}, \mathcal{R}'$, and business center $\mathcal{B}, \mathcal{B}'$ collected in two cities C and C' respectively, we try to infer bike distribution D' over grids G' in the new city C'.

2.3 Inference Framework

Figure 1 provides the framework of our proposed inference approach. It consists of two major components:

- **Distribution inference model training.** This component takes multi-source data from two cities as input and trains a distribution inference model. To do this, we first extract important features for each grid from multi-source data in two cities via clustering, entropy computation, etc. Our inference model performs Factor Analysis to transform original feature spaces into lower dimensions and generate latent features over two cities. It then leverages the CNN-based neural network to infer bike numbers for each grid based on latent features of a grid and its neighbors. We train the model using bike distribution D and multi-source data $\mathcal{P}, \mathcal{L}, \mathcal{T}, \mathcal{B}, \mathcal{R}$ from city C.
- **New city bike distribution prediction.** To infer bike distribution in the new city C', we supply the trained model with latent features from each grid in C' and the model produces the estimated number of bikes for that grid as output. We then normalize prediction results over all grids to infer bike distribution D' in C'.

[6]https://www.fliggy.com

3 DATA DESCRIPTION AND ANALYSIS

In this section, we first describe a real-world dockless shared bike dataset from Mobike, and then conduct empirical analysis to explore the spatio-temporal characteristics of bike distribution.

3.1 Data Description

We crawled Mobike data from several cities in China, including Shanghai, Beijing, and Ningbo, from 07/06/2017 to 15/07/2017. Note that Shanghai and Beijing are first-tier cities in China, while Ningbo is a third-tier city. The dataset contains location information of bikes with timestamps. We preprocess data to remove duplicates and obtain roughly $59 \times 10^4, 65 \times 10^4, 3.5 \times 10^4$ distinct bikes in Shanghai, Beijing, and Ningbo, respectively. We divide all the data into different groups based on a time window size. For each city in {Shanghai, Beijing, Ningbo}, we compute bike distribution within each time window and obtain $D^1, D^2, \cdots$. The number of grids (in the size of $1km \times 1km$) in Shanghai, Beijing, and Ningbo are 5207, 3477, and 874 respectively. By default, we set time window size to 1 hour. We also calculate the total number of distinct bikes in each hour and find the number seldom changes over time. This is because bikes have been deployed in these cities for a relatively long time and the bike volumes are approximately invariant.

3.2 Empirical Analysis

We conduct empirical analysis on dockless shared bike data and try to answer the following questions: 1) how dockless shared bike distribution varies in different time window sizes? 2) is it feasible to infer bike distribution in a city? 3) what kind of factors may affect dockless shared bike spatial distributions?

3.2.1 Temporal Properties of Dockless Shared Bike Distribution. To quantitatively measure the temporal stability of city-wide bike distributions, we adopt the Kullback-Leibler (KL) divergence to compute the closeness between two bike distributions in consecutive time windows. Formally, given two bike distributions D^t, D^{t+1} for a city in time window t and $t+1$ respectively, the KL divergence from D^{t+1} to D^t is defined as:

$$KL(D^t \| D^{t+1}) = \sum_i \sum_j D^t_{i,j} \log \frac{D^t_{i,j}}{D^{t+1}_{i,j}} \tag{2}$$

Intuitively, the smaller KL divergence is, the closer two distributions are. In our context, the closeness of every two consecutive distributions indicates the stability of bike distribution over time.

By setting time window size to 1-hour, 5-hour, 1-day, we first prepare 3 groups of bike distributions using Mobike data from Shanghai[7]. Figure 2(a) shows the KL divergences for consecutive bike distributions with different time window sizes. For illustration purpose, we only used data from 12/06/2017 to 20/06/2017. Similar results are also found in the whole crawled Mobike dataset. We summarize several key observations as follows: 1) *consecutive bike distributions have very small KL divergences with various time window sizes.* The maximum KL divergences for 1-hour, 5-hour and 1-day window sizes are 0.026, 0.015 and 0.009, respectively; 2) *the variance of KL divergences becomes larger with smaller time window size.* For 1-hour time window, the difference between maximum and minimum divergences is 0.022, while that for 1-day time window is merely 0.003. This follows the intuition that the fluctuation of the bike number in each grid can be easily canceled out using coarse-grained time windows; 3) *the trend of KL divergences in 1-hour time window exhibits periodicity.* Specifically, every weekday, the two largest divergences occur during morning peak hours and evening peak hours (highlighted in red circles). This is because that during those time periods, more bikes are in use, i.e., ridden by people from one place to another. Even for 5-hour time window, we can still observe such periodicity to a certain extent.

Figure 2(b) plots the KL divergences with 1-day time window in three cities. As we can see, KL divergences are quite stable in all three cities. On average, Shanghai has the largest KL divergence, followed by Beijing and finally Ningbo. This is reasonable as Shanghai is the first city to deploy Mobikes and achieves highest bike occupation, e.g., 17 times more bikes than Ningbo. Further, compared with Beijing and Ningbo, the road network of Shanghai is much more complex, which may cause higher variants in bike distributions. Besides, distribution difference between weekdays and weekends is relatively higher (highlighted in Figure 2(b)), which might be caused by different riding behaviors on weekdays and weekends.

Summary. All the above observations indicate temporal stability of dockless shared bike distributions using different time window sizes. Hence, inferring bike distribution in a new city is feasible. A possible explanation for such stability is the "short-riding-distance" of bike routes. Typically, bikes are used for the first-and-last-mile connection, which causes *local* variants of bike numbers in grids that cannot be easily reflected in distributions.

3.2.2 Spatial Properties of Dockless Shared Bike Distribution. Figure 2(c) plots top 30 grids in Shanghai with the highest average daily bike frequencies in the distribution from 07/06/2017 to 15/07/2017. The effective number of bikes in each of these grids exceeds 70. We observe that 1) central areas in the city and business centers surrounding are more likely to have more dockless bikes than remote areas. This is because central areas are populated with more people and lead to higher bike usage demands; 2) areas populated with more bikes have closer distances to transportation hubs such as subway stations. In particular, the average distance between the top 30 grids to their nearest subway stations is lower than 3 kilometers; 3) residential districts also involve many bikes even if they are far from central areas of the city.

Summary. From the above observations, we find that bike fractions are typically accumulated in grids near central areas, residential districts or transportation hubs. This inspires us to leverage multiple data sources such as POI, subway station, business center, and satellite light data when inferring bike distribution in new cities. In what follows, we present how to extract important features from multi-source data and discuss the correlations between these features and bike distribution in detail.

4 FEATURE EXTRACTION

We describe important features used for inference. We use Mobike data from Shanghai (07/06/2017–15/07/2017) for feature analysis.

4.1 Features from Multi-source Data

POI Features. Generally, the number of POIs and the category heterogeneity in a grid reflect its degree of prosperity, which affects bike distribution according to our observations. Hence, we extract the following POI features for each grid.

(1) *POI Category Frequency* ($\vec{p}$).

We associate each city grid g with a POI category frequency vector $\vec{p}$. $\vec{p}$ is a 17-dimensional vector and the i-th element in $\vec{p}$ is the number of venues located in grid g belonging to the i-th first-level category.

(2) *Number of POIs* (P_{num}).

Based on POI category frequency vector $\vec{p}$, we count the total number of POIs P_{num} in a grid: $P_{num}(g) = \sum_k \vec{p}_k(g)$. Figure 3(a) shows the scatter plot for (bike number, POI number) pairs in all grids. We observe that grids with more POIs have similar number of bikes (around 50), and those with fewer POIs have various number of bikes. The Pearson coefficient between bike numbers and POI numbers in all grids is 0.49.

(3) *POI Entropy* (P_{ent}). To better assess the heterogeneity of POIs, we further compute the entropy P_{ent} based on category vector $\vec{p}$.

$$P_{ent}(g) = -\sum_k \frac{\vec{p}_k(g)}{P_{num}(g)} \times \log \frac{\vec{p}_k(g)}{P_{num}(g)} \tag{3}$$

Figure 3(b) shows the scatter plot of (bike number, POI entropy). We find bike numbers are positively correlated with POI entropy (the Pearson coefficient is 0.65). This follows our intuition that location with diverse POIs such as city center typically have more bikes.

Satellite Light Features. Applying the satellite light data into our problem is a novel attempt. Not only is the satellite light data easy to acquire, but also it is a good indicator for areas with high prosperity degree or high-density residential districts [15]. We extract the following light features for each grid.

(1) *Light Intensity* (L_{int}). Let $S(g)$ be the set of light points within a city grid g. We compute the average light intensity L_{int} in g:

$$L_{int}(g) = \frac{\sum_{p \in S(g)} \delta(p)}{|S(g)|} \tag{4}$$

where $\delta(p)$ is the light intensity of the point p.

(2) *Distance to the Nearest Light Center* (L_{dist}). As light data can reflect the distribution of residential areas, we sample top $n\%$

[7]Similar results are observed from data in Beijing and Ningbo.

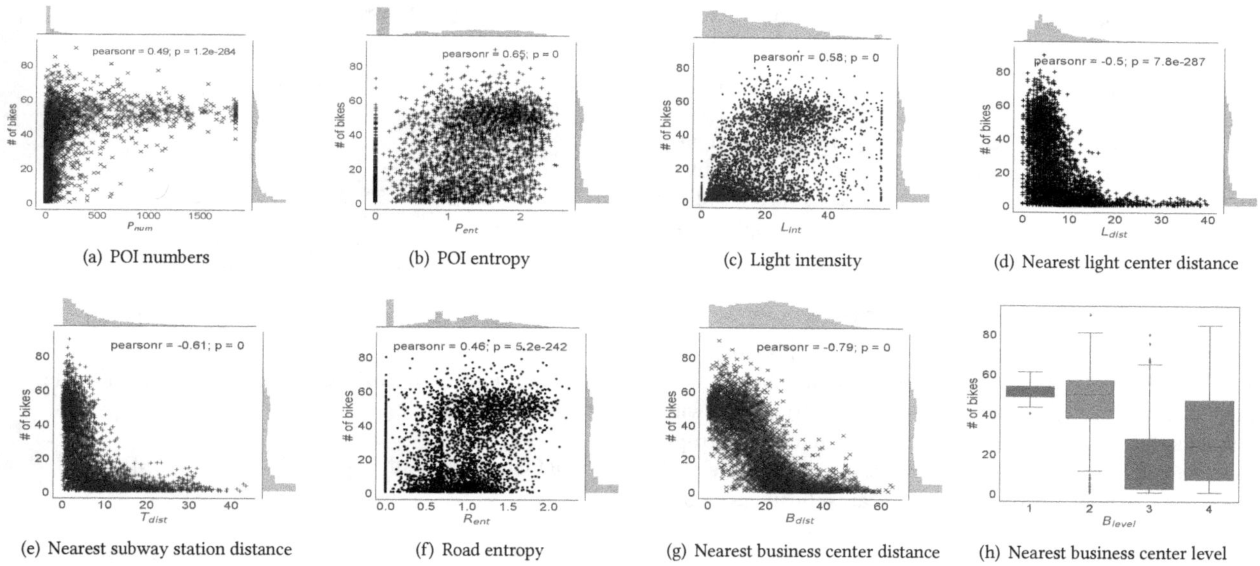

(a) POI numbers (b) POI entropy (c) Light intensity (d) Nearest light center distance

(e) Nearest subway station distance (f) Road entropy (g) Nearest business center distance (h) Nearest business center level

Figure 3: Feature analysis

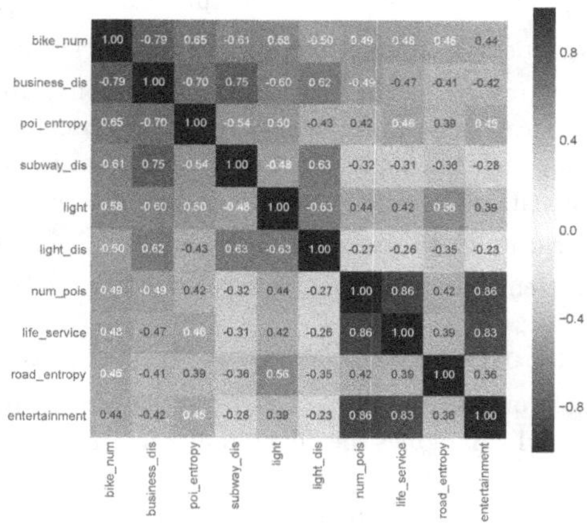

Figure 4: Correlation matrix measured by Pearson correlation coefficient between features and bike distribution

average light intensity grids and identify light centers by clustering selected grids using the Affinity Propagation algorithm [8]. Let M denotes the set of k light centers. For each grid, we measure its geographical distance to the nearest light center:

$$L_{dist}(g) = \min_k dist(g, M_k) \tag{5}$$

Figure 3(c) shows the correlation between bike number and light intensity over all grids. Few bikes are deployed in grids with low light intensity. Figure 3(d) illustrates that bike number is negatively correlated with the distance between grid to its nearest light center.

Transportation Features. We observe that nearly 60% Mobikes in Shanghai, Beijing, and Ningbo are located at maximum $1km$ away from subway stations. We thus adopt a feature T_{dist} that measures the distance between grid to its nearest subway station. Let N be the set of subway stations in the city.

$$T_{dist}(g) = \min_k dist(g, N_k) \tag{6}$$

Figure 3(e) shows that T_{dist} is negatively correlated with bike number in the grid, with the Pearson coefficient of -0.61.

Road Network Features. The Road network contains information such as traffic condition and transportation hubs in a city. We consider features that reflect road density and heterogeneity of road segment type.

(1) *Road Type Frequency* $\vec{r}$. For each grid g, we associate it with a road type frequency vector $\vec{r}$. $\vec{r}(g)$ is a $|T|$-dimensional vector, where the i-th element is the number of the i-th type road segments overlapped with g.

(2) *Number of Roads* R_{num}. Based on road type vector $\vec{r}$, we compute the total number of roads $R_{num} = \sum_k \vec{r}_k(g)$.

Intuitively, R_{num} feature reflects the degree of traffic convenience, and is positively correlated with bike numbers (the Pearson coefficient is 0.31).

(3) *Road Type Entropy* R_{ent}. We also use entropy to measure the heterogeneity of road type for each grid as follows.

$$R_{ent}(g) = -\sum_k \frac{\vec{r}_k(g)}{R_{num}(g)} \times \log \frac{\vec{r}_k(g)}{R_{num}(g)} \tag{7}$$

In general, areas with high entropy values are expected to be transportation hubs with diverse road segments. From Figure 3(f), we can see that road type entropy is positively correlated with bike distribution and the Pearson coefficient is 0.46.

Business Center Features. As discussed in Section 3.2.2, bike distribution is also affected by the locations of business centers. We collect all business centers of a city from *AliTrip* (https://www.alitrip.com), and divide them into four levels manually according to the location, people flow and per capita purchasing ability. We extract two business center features for each grid, the distance to the nearest business center (B_{dist}) and the level of the nearest business center (B_{level}). Letting O be the set of business centers, we have:

$$B_{dist}(g) = \min_k dist(g, O_k), \quad B_{level}(g) = O_{nearest}.level \tag{8}$$

Figure 3(g) and 3(h) show the effects of B_{dist} and B_{level} on bike distribution, respectively. To sum up, grids close to business centers in high levels have more bikes. This is reasonable as such locations typically involve high in/out people flow and lead to higher bike demands.

4.2 Correlation Analysis for Features

Figure 4 summarizes the Pearson correlation coefficients among the selected features and their correlations with bike numbers, where we only include 9 features that have the strongest correlations with bike numbers for illustration purpose. Features like POI entropy, POI number, light intensity, road entropy are positively correlated with bike volume, while distances to the nearest business center, to the nearest subway station and to the nearest light centers are negatively correlated.

The correlation matrix also indicates the correlations among the features. For example, the distance to the nearest business center is correlated with POI entropy, the distance to the nearest subway station and light density, in which the Pearson coefficients are all above 0.6. This inspires us to leverage multi-layer neural networks to learn deeper features that capture the correlations among the selected features, which helps to boost the prediction performance.

5 CITY-WISE NEURAL NETWORK MODEL

In this section, we introduce a novel inference model called CoFA-GeoConv, to predict dockless shared bike distribution in a new city C'. Our model mainly consists of two steps: 1) we perform joint Factor Analysis over the feature spaces of two cities C, C' and obtain latent features for city grids; 2) we take the latent features of a grid and its neighbors as an input and employ CNN-based neural network to estimate bike number in that grid. The estimated numbers over all grids are normalized to infer final bike distribution.

5.1 Co-Factor Analysis on City Feature Space

Applying an inference model learned from one city to another may suffer from poor performance because there may exist a gap between the feature distributions from two cities. That is, regarding feature vector of a city as a random variable, feature vectors from two cities may follow different distributions. Such gap is typically caused by city specificity. Intuitively, the feature vector of Shanghai, an international metropolis, can be quite different from that of Ningbo, a third-tier city in Zhejiang province of China. Hence, inferring bike distribution in Ningbo by training a model based on the data from Shanghai (or vice versa) directly may not lead to a high accuracy.

To reduce differences between feature distributions from two cities, we propose to apply Factor Analysis [16] over the extracted features of two cities jointly. The purpose of Co-Factor Analysis (or, CoFA for short) is to discover a set of latent features that help to reduce city differences and maximize variances of data from both cities in the latent feature spaces. Different from PCA [1], Factor Analysis defines the generation process of each feature x as a linear

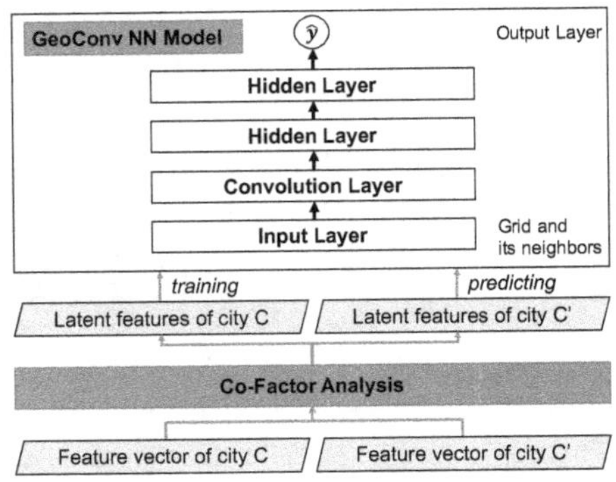

Figure 5: CoFA-GeoConv inference model

combination of latent features $H = \{h_1, \cdots, h_k\}$, i.e.,

$$x = WH + \mu + \epsilon \tag{9}$$

where W is the transform matrix between the origin and latent feature spaces, μ is the mean of x and ϵ is the Gaussian noise with zero mean and a diagonal covariance. The goal of FA is to find transform matrix W with maximum data likelihood.

In our problem, we obtain two feature matrices $X^C_{|G|\times d}$ and $X^{C'}_{|G'|\times d}$ for cities C, C', respectively, where d is the feature number. Recall that G (resp. G') is the set of grids in C (resp. C'). To perform CoFA, we concatenate two feature matrices into a combined matrix $X_{(|G|+|G'|)\times d}$ and then apply Factor Analysis to transform X into a d'-dimensional latent feature spaces $H_{(|G|+|G'|)\times d'}$. After that, we redivide the learned matrix H into two parts $H^C_{|G|\times d'}$ and $H^{C'}_{|G'|\times d'}$, which are latent feature vectors for two cities, respectively.

5.2 GeoConv Neural Network based Inference

According to our observations, more than 90% Mobike routes are under $3km$, which implies the bike number in a grid can be influenced by the situations of grid neighbors. Hence, we propose a GeoConv neural network model to encode neighbor information for bike distribution inference.

The input feature vector to our GeoConv model is the latent features learned by CoFA for a grid and its neighbors w.r.t. a given window size λ. Consider a grid g. Formally, let f_g denote the d'-dimensional latent feature vector learned by CoFA for g. The input feature vector is:

$$\phi_g = (f_g, f_{NB})$$

where $f_{NB} = (f_{g'})_{g' \in NB_\lambda(g)}$. The number of bikes $\hat{y}_g$ in grid g is predicted as output.

We organize an input feature vector ϕ_g into a $\lambda \times \lambda \times d'$ tensor T_g, which is similar to an image with d' channels. The GeoConv neural network consists of an input layer, one convolutional layer, two fully-connected layers and finally an output layer, as shown in Figure 5. While deeper layers may contain:

- In the convolutional layer, we apply convolution operation over input feature tensor, to capture the complex influence of features from grid neighbors. The convolution operation slides a kernel tensor F over tensor T_g and computes dot products to generate a convolved feature tensor, which encodes deeper features (see details in [18]). The output of the convolutional layer with a kernel F is:

$$Z_0 = \sigma(F * T_g + b_0)$$

where $*$ denotes convolutional operator, b_0 is the bias, and σ is the activation function. We apply k different filters with T_g and get new feature maps $Z = \{Z_0^1, Z_0^2, \cdots, Z_0^k\}$. We denote by z_0 the flattened vector of Z.

• Two fully-connected layers follow the convolutional layer, and perform the following operations:

$$z_1 = \sigma(W_1 z_0 + b_1), \quad z_2 = \sigma(W_2 z_1 + b_2)$$

where W_1, W_2 are weight matrices, b_1, b_2 are bias vectors.

• The output layer predicts the number of bikes $\hat{y}_g$ in grid g, which is transformed from the output of fully-connected layers z_2:

$$\hat{y}_g = h^T z_2$$

where h denotes the neuron weights of the output layer.

Finally, we derive bike distribution by normalizing the predicted values for all grids.

Learning. To estimate model parameters of GeoConv, we use *MSE* as the objective function, as defined below:

$$MSE = \frac{1}{|G|} \sum_{g \in G} (y_g - \hat{y}_g)^2 \qquad (10)$$

where $\hat{y}_g$ is the predicted bike number of grid g, and y_g is corresponding ground truth. We adopt the mini-batch Adam [17] to update parameters iteratively. To prevent overfitting in the training data, we apply dropout [27] to randomly drop neurons in the two fully-connected layers. We also perform batch normalization [14] to address the covariance shift problem and achieve faster convergence.

6 EXPERIMENTS

6.1 Experimental Settings

Datasets. We crawled Mobike data from three cities, Shanghai, Beijing and Ningbo in China during 07/06/2017 and 15/07/2017. Table 1 provides details of Mobike data we crawled and multi-source data for each city. The descriptions for Mobike data and multi-source data can also be found in Section 3.1 and 4. For the experiments, we use the average bike numbers in each grid from 12/06/2017 to 12/07/2017 with 1-day time window as target labels.

Table 1: Details of the datasets

	City		
Data Type	Shanghai	Beijing	Ningbo
# of Mobike	591,295	656,437	35,591
# of POIs	694,898	532,094	85,613
# of Satellite Light	28, 954	23,021	7,482
# of Roads	29, 398	23,021	5351
# of Subway Stations	366	334	53
# of Business Centers	28	26	17

Compared Methods. Our inference framework is quite generic. We actually consider the combinations from two sets: {joint FA, joint PCA} and {GeoConv, Gradient Boosting Regression Tree}, to get four inference methods, CoFA-GeoConv, CoFA-GBRT, CoPCA-GeoConv, CoPCA-GBRT. We compared with the following baselines and competitive inference approaches.

- $City_{mean}$: It always reports uniform bike distribution.
- *Lasso Regression.* It performs both feature selection and regularization to enhance prediction accuracy.
- *KNN.* It predicts bike numbers based on nearest neighbors in the training set using cosine similarity.
- *SVR.* SVR extends SVM to solve regression problems.
- *RandomForest.* It constructs a multitude of decision trees to boost prediction performance.
- *MLP.* This is a basic MLP neural network with two hidden layers with 32 neurons for each. All activation functions are *RELU.*
- *XGBoost.* XGBoost is an optimized distributed gradient boosting library with high efficiency [3].
- *GBRT.* GBRT is a boosting method that effectively handles data in mixed types and is robust to outliers.

Evaluation Metrics. We use KL divergence to measure the similarity between predicted bike distribution and the actual one, using Equation 2. We also adopt *RMLSE* to measure the accuracy of predicted bike distributions for new city C' against ground-truth distributions, which is defined as follows.

$$RMLSE = \sqrt{\frac{1}{|G'|} \sum_{g \in G'} (\log \frac{y_g}{\sum_{g_0 \in G'} y_{g_0}} - \log \frac{\hat{y}_g}{\sum_{g_0 \in G'} \hat{y}_{g_0}})^2} \qquad (11)$$

where $\hat{y}_g$ and y_g are predicted and truth values, respectively.

6.2 Comparison Results

We mainly consider three prediction tasks, namely Shanghai→Beijing, Shanghai→Ningbo, and Beijing→Ningbo, which is consistent with the order of dockless bike deployment in China.

For all cities, we use $1km \times 1km$ grid size distribution inference. Table 2 shows the prediction performance of various algorithms on the three cases. We find that the performances of all algorithms are consistent over two metrics: KL divergence and RMLSE. CoFA-GeoConv performs best in all the cases, i.e., reports lowest KL divergence and RMLSE values. $City_{mean}$ performs worse because it does not use any information from cities. Except for $City_{mean}$, all the other methods benefit from multi-source data for prediction and achieve at least 60% lower KL and RMLSE values. It is interesting to see the results in Shanghai→Beijing is better than Shanghai→Ningbo, followed by Beijing→Ningbo. This is because Shanghai and Beijing are more alike in nature and they both differ from Ningbo greatly. Compared with Beijing, Shanghai is closer to Ningbo geographically, i.e., the climate factors and city characteristics are more similar, and hence this similarity leads to relatively lower KL/RMLSE. Note that CoFA-GeoConv performs well when predicting distributions in Ningbo, using data from Shanghai and Beijing. KL divergences are all below 0.1 and RMLSE are lower than 0.75.

We observe that GeoConv performs better than other baselines by achieving lower KL divergence and RMLSE in all cases. For instance, GeoConv outperforms GBRT by reporting 17.79% lower KL divergence and 6.77% lower RMLSE, on average. This result verifies the effectiveness of using information from neighboring grids for prediction. In fact, we find bike riding activities mostly take place in the range of 3km. Hence, the bike number in any grid can be easily affected by the statuses of neighboring grids; and bike fractions in

Table 2: Comparison Results

Method	Shanghai → Beijing KL	Shanghai → Beijing RMLSE	Shanghai → Ningbo KL	Shanghai → Ningbo RMLSE	Beijing → Ningbo KL	Beijing → Ningbo RMLSE
$City_{mean}$	0.367	3.233	0.616	5.309	0.616	5.309
Lasso	0.122	0.890	0.214	1.031	0.283	2.054
KNN	0.13	0.776	0.172	0.873	0.187	0.924
SVR	0.109	0.802	0.164	0.932	0.226	1.533
RF	0.091	0.683	0.154	0.874	0.158	0.879
MLP	0.117	0.723	0.176	0.925	0.182	0.916
XGBoost	0.088	0.788	0.151	0.842	0.163	0.856
GBRT	0.086	0.704	0.146	0.830	0.168	0.904
GeoConv	0.082	0.675	0.114	0.757	0.123	0.837
CoPCA GBRT	0.085	0.701	0.126	0.755	0.139	0.848
CoFA GBRT	0.084	0.698	0.121	0.754	0.133	0.838
CoPCA GeoConv	0.081	0.663	0.087	0.672	0.106	0.777
CoFA GeoConv	**0.079**	**0.654**	**0.082**	**0.662**	**0.097**	**0.731**

nearby grids typically vary smoothly. Note that we leverage convolutional operation to decide the importance of different neighbor grids in various feature dimensions automatically.

Lastly, the better performance achieved by CoPCA-GBRT, CoFA-GBRT, CoPCA-GeoConv and CoFA-GeoConv compared with GBRT and GeoConv reveals the importance of reducing cross-city differences when predicting distributions in new cities. The advantages of using CoFA or CoPCA become more significant in Shanghai→Ningbo and Beijing→Ningbo cases, where the city pairs are quite different. We also observe that CoFA performs better than CoPCA in general. The reason could be that FA focuses on explaining covariances among features and PCA tries to explain variance for each feature that may not help to reduce city differences.

6.3 Effects of Joint Variable Reduction

We now evaluate the effects of joint variable reduction techniques on bike distribution inference in new cities. To do this, we apply FA/PCA on the training data from city C only and apply the learned parameters over test data from new cities. We refer to this kind of operation as *single reducer*. From Figure 6, we can see that inference models with single reducers (i.e., FA/PCA-GBRT/GeoConv) achieve lower KL divergence and RMLSE, compared with GBRT and GeoConv without reduction technique. However, they perform worse than those with joint reducers (i.e., CoFA/CoPCA-GBRT/GeoConv). The advantages of CoFA and CoPCA are more significant using GeoConv model, i.e., roughly 15.5 % and 6.2% reduction in KL divergence and RMLSE, respectively. Similar improvements are observed in Shanghai→Beijing and Beijing →Ningbo and we eliminate figures due to redundancy. While reduction techniques are useful in identifying more informative features, performing reduction over two cities jointly is beneficial to retain commonalities between cities for better prediction in the target city.

6.4 Effects of Window Size in GeoConv Model

We study the performance of various GeoConv model under different values of window size λ. We try three window sizes, 1,3 and 5. For $\lambda = 1$, no information from neighboring grids is used for prediction. Figure 7 shows the results over different λ values. For

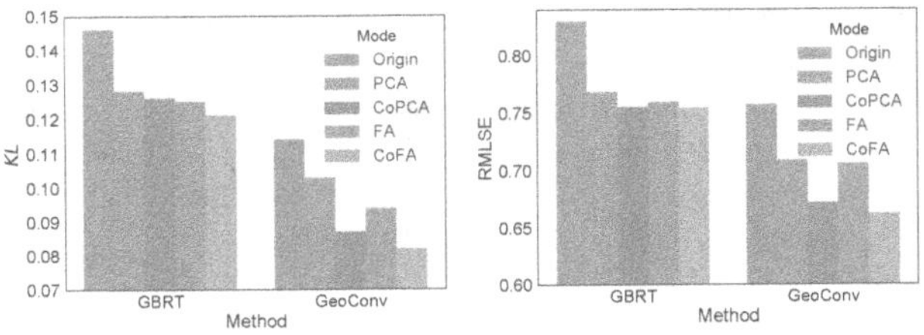

(a) KL divergence results

(b) RMLSE results

Figure 6: Single vs joint reduction (Shanghai→Ningbo)

all of the GeoConv, CoPCA-GeoConv and CoFA-GeoConv models, larger window sizes lead to lower KL divergence and RMLSE values. The performance improvement is significant when varying λ from 1 to 3. We also try window size larger than 5, but only observe slight improvement. As more parameters are involved in neural networks with larger window size, the model can be easily overfitting to the training data without performance improvements in test data.

7 RELATED WORK

Research on Bike Sharing Systems. A number of researchers have studied the problems for bike sharing systems. Some works focused on predicting traffic or bike flow based on historical bike data [13, 19, 29]. Zeng et al. [30] introduced a station-level demand prediction method. Gast et al. [11] proposed a probabilistic method to infer future availability of bikes in stations. In terms of bike distribution, several works [21, 26] studied the distribution rebalancing problem and tried to produce an optimal route for moving bikes among stations. Other works [20, 22] studied the station site optimization problem, which aims to choose best locations as bike stations from a set of candidate sites. However, none of these works consider dockless bike sharing systems, which reinvent bike sharing business recently. Moreover, the challenges they addressed are quite different from those that arise in our problem. A recent research on dockless bike sharing system studied how to plan bike lanes based on trajectories of shared bikes [2]. They only focused on a single city populated with dockless shared bikes, without applying the insights learned from a city into other cities.

Transfer Learning on urban computing. Transfer learning [24] leverages knowledge from a source domain to facilitate prediction

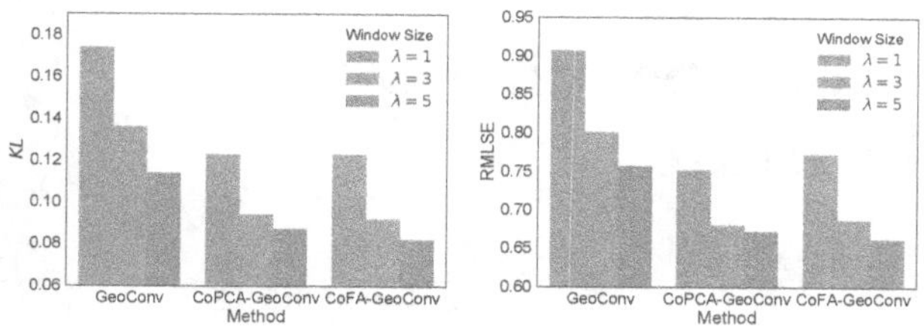

(a) KL divergence results (b) RMLSE results

Figure 7: The effect of window size λ (Shanghai→Ningbo)

or regression in a target domain. Some researchers applied transfer learning approaches for urban computing. Wei et al. [28] solved the problem of predicting air quality in a target city by transferring knowledge learned from a source city. They assumed the existence of limited air quality data in the target city, while we consider a new city without dockless shared bikes. Several approaches on domain adaptation [6, 7, 9, 10] have been proposed to adopt a model trained in the source domain to the target domain. However, these methods typically require a large amount of training data in the same source and do not consider multi-source data. Further, we propose to perform dimension reduction techniques over the source and target feature vectors jointly, which is a novel attempt and experimentally shows better inference performance.

8 CONCLUSION

In this paper, we have studied the problem on how to distribute dockless bikes in new cities, which is an important issue faced by most modern bike sharing companies. We leverage multi-source data and bike information from a source city to perform distribution inference in new cities. We analyze the effects of various data on bike distribution thoroughly and propose a novel inference model combining joint Factor Analysis and convolutional neural network techniques. Our experiments demonstrate the effectiveness of the proposed solution in inferring bike distribution in new cities, compared with competitive prediction methods. As future work, we will combine more advanced CNN models such as ResNet [12] for feature learning.

ACKNOWLEDGMENTS

We thank anonymous reviewers for their insightful and helpful comments, which improve the paper. This research is supported in part by 973 Program (no. 2014CB340303), NSFC (no. 61772341, 61472254, 61170238, 61602297 and 61472241), Singapore NRF (CREATE E2S2), and 863 Program (no. 2015AA015303). This work is also supported by the Program for Changjiang Young Scholars in University of China, and the Program for Shanghai Top Young Talents.

REFERENCES

[1] Hervé Abdi and Lynne J Williams. 2010. Principal component analysis. *Wiley interdisciplinary reviews: computational statistics* 2, 4 (2010), 433–459.
[2] Jie Bao, Tianfu He, Sijie Ruan, Yanhua Li, and Yu Zheng. 2017. Planning Bike Lanes based on Sharing-BikesâĂŹ Trajectories. (2017).
[3] Tianqi Chen and Carlos Guestrin. 2016. Xgboost: A scalable tree boosting system. In *Proceedings of the 22nd acm sigkdd international conference on knowledge discovery and data mining*. ACM, 785–794.
[4] Charlotte Cox. 2017. Mobike Manchester city bikes: How to use them, where are they and how to get the app. http://www.manchestereveningnews.co.uk/news/greater-manchester-news/mobike-manchester-city-bikes-orange-13248743. (2017).
[5] Paul DeMaio. 2009. Bike-sharing: History, impacts, models of provision, and future. *Journal of public transportation* 12, 4 (2009), 3.
[6] Chuong B Do and Andrew Y Ng. 2006. Transfer learning for text classification. In *Advances in Neural Information Processing Systems*. 299–306.
[7] Daxiang Dong, Hua Wu, Wei He, Dianhai Yu, and Haifeng Wang. 2015. Multi-Task Learning for Multiple Language Translation.. In *ACL (1)*. 1723–1732.
[8] Brendan J Frey and Delbert Dueck. 2007. Clustering by passing messages between data points. *science* 315, 5814 (2007), 972–976.
[9] Yaroslav Ganin and Victor Lempitsky. 2015. Unsupervised domain adaptation by backpropagation. In *International Conference on Machine Learning*. 1180–1189.
[10] Yaroslav Ganin, Evgeniya Ustinova, Hana Ajakan, Pascal Germain, Hugo Larochelle, François Laviolette, Mario Marchand, and Victor Lempitsky. 2016. Domain-adversarial training of neural networks. *Journal of Machine Learning Research* 17, 59 (2016), 1–35.
[11] Nicolas Gast, Guillaume Massonnet, Daniël Reijsbergen, and Mirco Tribastone. 2015. Probabilistic forecasts of bike-sharing systems for journey planning. In *Proceedings of the 24th ACM International on Conference on Information and Knowledge Management*. ACM, 703–712.
[12] Kaiming He, Xiangyu Zhang, Shaoqing Ren, and Jian Sun. 2016. Deep residual learning for image recognition. In *Proceedings of the IEEE conference on computer vision and pattern recognition*. 770–778.
[13] Minh X Hoang, Yu Zheng, and Ambuj K Singh. 2016. FCCF: forecasting citywide crowd flows based on big data. In *Proceedings of the 24th ACM SIGSPATIAL International Conference on Advances in Geographic Information Systems*. ACM, 6.
[14] Sergey Ioffe and Christian Szegedy. 2015. Batch normalization: Accelerating deep network training by reducing internal covariate shift. In *International Conference on Machine Learning*. 448–456.
[15] Neal Jean, Marshall Burke, Michael Xie, W Matthew Davis, David B Lobell, and Stefano Ermon. 2016. Combining satellite imagery and machine learning to predict poverty. *Science* 353, 6301 (2016), 790–794.
[16] Ian T Jolliffe. 1986. Principal Component Analysis and Factor Analysis. In *Principal component analysis*. Springer, 115–128.
[17] Diederik Kingma and Jimmy Ba. 2014. Adam: A method for stochastic optimization. *arXiv preprint arXiv:1412.6980* (2014).
[18] Alex Krizhevsky, Ilya Sutskever, and Geoffrey E Hinton. 2012. Imagenet classification with deep convolutional neural networks. In *Advances in neural information processing systems*. 1097–1105.
[19] Yexin Li, Yu Zheng, Huichu Zhang, and Lei Chen. 2015. Traffic prediction in a bike-sharing system. In *Proceedings of the 23rd SIGSPATIAL International Conference on Advances in Geographic Information Systems*. ACM, 33.
[20] Junming Liu, Qiao Li, Meng Qu, Weiwei Chen, Jingyuan Yang, Hui Xiong, Hao Zhong, and Yanjie Fu. 2015. Station site optimization in bike sharing systems. In *Data Mining (ICDM), 2015 IEEE International Conference on*. IEEE, 883–888.
[21] Junming Liu, Leilei Sun, Weiwei Chen, and Hui Xiong. 2016. Rebalancing Bike Sharing Systems: A Multi-source Data Smart Optimization. In *Proceedings of the 22nd ACM SIGKDD International Conference on Knowledge Discovery and Data Mining*. ACM, 1005–1014.
[22] Luis M Martinez, Luís Caetano, Tomás Eiró, and Francisco Cruz. 2012. An optimisation algorithm to establish the location of stations of a mixed fleet biking system: an application to the city of Lisbon. *Procedia-Social and Behavioral Sciences* 54 (2012), 513–524.
[23] Sinno Jialin Pan, Ivor W Tsang, James T Kwok, and Qiang Yang. 2011. Domain adaptation via transfer component analysis. *IEEE Transactions on Neural Networks* 22, 2 (2011), 199–210.
[24] Sinno Jialin Pan and Qiang Yang. 2010. A survey on transfer learning. *IEEE Transactions on knowledge and data engineering* 22, 10 (2010), 1345–1359.
[25] Sherisse Pham. 2017. China's 'dockless' bike sharing could be coming to a street near you. http://money.cnn.com/2017/07/05/technology/startups/china-bike-sharing-global/index.html. (2017).
[26] Adish Singla, Marco Santoni, Gábor Bartók, Pratik Mukerji, Moritz Meenen, and Andreas Krause. 2015. Incentivizing Users for Balancing Bike Sharing Systems.. In *AAAI*. 723–729.
[27] Nitish Srivastava, Geoffrey E Hinton, Alex Krizhevsky, Ilya Sutskever, and Ruslan Salakhutdinov. 2014. Dropout: a simple way to prevent neural networks from overfitting. *Journal of Machine Learning Research* 15, 1 (2014), 1929–1958.
[28] Ying Wei, Yu Zheng, and Qiang Yang. 2016. Transfer Knowledge between Cities.. In *KDD*. 1905–1914.
[29] Zidong Yang, Ji Hu, Yuanchao Shu, Peng Cheng, Jiming Chen, and Thomas Moscibroda. 2016. Mobility Modeling and Prediction in Bike-Sharing Systems. In *Proceedings of the 14th Annual International Conference on Mobile Systems, Applications, and Services*. ACM, 165–178.
[30] Ming Zeng, Tong Yu, Xiao Wang, Vincent Su, Le T Nguyen, et al. 2016. Improving Demand Prediction in Bike Sharing System by Learning Global Features. (2016).

Multi-Dimensional Network Embedding with Hierarchical Structure

Yao Ma*†
Data Science and Engineering Lab
Michigan State University
mayao4@msu.edu.com

Zhaochun Ren†
Data Science Lab
JD.com
renzhaochun@jd.com

Ziheng Jiang
Data Science Lab
JD.com
jiangziheng@jd.com

Jiliang Tang
Data Science and Engineering Lab
Michigan State University
tangjili@msu.edu.com

Dawei Yin‡
Data Science Lab
JD.com
yindawei@acm.org

ABSTRACT

Information networks are ubiquitous in many applications. A popular way to facilitate the information in a network is to embed the network structure into low-dimension spaces where each node is represented as a vector. The learned representations have been proven to advance various network analysis tasks such as link prediction and node classification. The majority of existing embedding algorithms are designed for the networks with one type of nodes and one dimension of relations among nodes. However, many networks in the real-world complex systems have multiple types of nodes and multiple dimensions of relations. For example, an e-commerce network can have users and items, and items can be viewed or purchased by users, corresponding to two dimensions of relations. In addition, some types of nodes can present hierarchical structure. For example, authors in publication networks are associated to affiliations; and items in e-commerce networks belong to categories. Most of existing methods cannot be naturally applicable to these networks. In this paper, we aim to learn representations for networks with multiple dimensions and hierarchical structure. In particular, we provide an approach to capture independent information from each dimension and dependent information across dimensions and propose a framework MINES, which performs **M**ulti-d**I**mension **N**etwork **E**mbedding with hierarchical **S**tructure. Experimental results on a network from a real-world e-commerce website demonstrate the effectiveness of the proposed framework.

*Work performed during an internship at Data Science Lab, JD.com.
†These two authors contributed equally.
‡Corresponding author

WSDM 2018, February 5–9, 2018, Marina Del Rey, CA, USA

ACM ISBN 978-1-4503-5581-0/18/02...$15.00
https://doi.org/10.1145/3159652.3159680

KEYWORDS

Network Embedding, Multi-dimensional Networks, Hierarchical Structure

ACM Reference Format:
Yao Ma, Zhaochun Ren, Ziheng Jiang, Jiliang Tang, and Dawei Yin. 2018. Multi-Dimensional Network Embedding with Hierarchical Structure. In *WSDM 2018: WSDM 2018: The Eleventh ACM International Conference on Web Search and Data Mining , February 5–9, 2018, Marina Del Rey, CA, USA.* ACM, New York, NY, USA, 9 pages. https://doi.org/10.1145/3159652.3159680

1 INTRODUCTION

We are living in a connected world where information networks are ubiquitous. Some examples of information networks include social networks, publication networks, the World Wide Web and e-commerce networks. Network embedding, aiming to learn vector representations for nodes, has attracted increasing attention in recent years. Many advanced network embedding algorithms have emerged such as Deepwalk [26], LINE [29] and Metapath2vec [11], which have been proven to help numerous network analysis tasks such as link prediction [18], node classification [5][33] and network visualization [21][28].

Most of existing embedding algorithms are designed for networks with one type of nodes and one dimension of relations among nodes. However, many networks in real-world complex systems contain multiple dimensions of relations among nodes. For example, in social networking sites such as Facebook, two users could be connected by friend relations, and via various social interactions; in the transportation network [3], two cities could be connected via various means of transportations such as train, highway and airplane; while in e-commerce networks, items can be viewed and purchased by users, corresponding to two dimensions of relations between users and items. In addition, some of the nodes can present certain hierarchical structure. For example, in publication networks, authors are associated to affiliations; while in e-commerce networks, items are organized by categories. A typical example of multi-dimensional networks with hierarchical structure is illustrated in Figure 1 where there are two types of nodes $\mathcal{U} = \{u_1, u_2, u_3, u_4\}$ and $\mathcal{T} = \{t_1, t_2, t_3, t_4\}$, and $C = \{c_1, c_2, c_3\}$ is the set of parent nodes. The relations of nodes in $\mathcal{U}$, nodes in $\mathcal{T}$ and nodes between $\mathcal{U}$ and $\mathcal{T}$ are two-dimensional; while each node in $\mathcal{U}$ is associated to one parent in C. The vast majority of

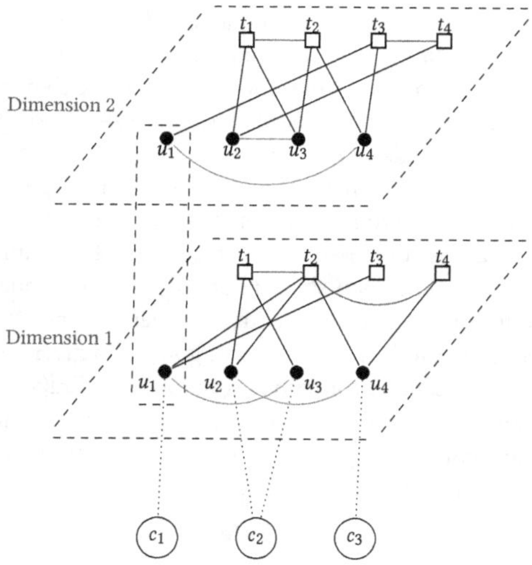

Figure 1: An illustrative example of a multi-dimensional network with hierarchical structure

existing embedding algorithms cannot be naturally applicable to multi-dimensional networks with hierarchical structure as shown in Figure 1.

In this paper, we aim to learn representations of nodes in networks with multiple dimensions and hierarchical structure. In particular, we study approaches (1) to mathematically capture multi-dimensional information and hierarchical structure; and (2) to incorporate such information simultaneously for embedding. Consequently, we propose a framework MINES for **M**ulti-d**I**mensional **N**etwork **E**mbedding with hierarchical **S**tructure. Our major contributions are summarized as follows:

- Providing a principled approach to model multi-dimensional networks, which can capture independent information from each dimension and dependent information across dimensions;
- Proposing a framework MINES, which incorporates multi-dimensional relations and hierarchical structure into a coherent model for node representation learning; and
- Validating the effectiveness of the proposed framework in a real-world e-commerce network.

The rest of this paper is arranged as follows. In Section 2, we review some works that are related to our problem. The problem of embedding networks with multiple dimensions and hierarchical structure to vector space is formally defined in Section 3. The approach to model networks with multiple dimensions and hierarchical structure and the proposed framework with an optimization method are introduced in Section 4. The experiments on a real-world e-commerce network with discussions are presented in Section 5. The conclusion and future work are presented in Section 6.

2 RELATED WORK

Our work is related to multi-dimensional network analysis and network embedding. In this section, we briefly review them.

2.1 Multi-dimensional Network Analysis

Network analysis has been extensively studied for many years [34][35][6][14][2][7]. Multidimensional networks, which are quite ubiquitous in the real-world applications, have attracted increasing attention. In [3], the authors introduced a few examples of real-world multidimensional networks, and they also defined measures such as degree, neighbors for the multidimensional networks. More measures for the multidimensional networks are introduced in [22]. The classic link prediction problem has been extended to multidimensional networks with the new problem "what is the probability that a new link between two nodes will form in a specific dimension?" [27]. Multidimensional versions of the Common Neighbors and Adamic-Adar have been introduced to solve this problem [27]. In [4], the authors studied the community discovery problem in the multidimensional network setting. In [16], the authors investigated friendship maintenance and prediction in multidimensional social networks.

2.2 Network Embedding

Networks can be represented by adjacency matrices; however, these representations are too sparse and high-dimensional. Many classic methods such as Laplacian eigenmap [1] and IsoMap [30] have been proposed to learn low-dimensional representations. These methods work fine on small size networks but cannot be scaled to very large networks. Inspired by word2vec [23][25], DeepWalk and LINE are proposed recently which can be applied to very large scale networks. DeepWalk regards the nodes in the network as the "words" of an artificial language and uses random walk to generate the "sentences" for this language. Then, following the procedure of word2vec, the representations for the nodes can be learned. LINE tries to capture both the first order and second order proximity in the representations. node2vec [13] extends DeepWalk by adding parameters to introduce the biased random walk. These network embedding methods have shown effectiveness in various tasks on many homogeneous networks. In [11], the authors extended DeepWalk method to heterogeneous networks by introducing meta-path based random walks. In [9], the authors also facilitate the meta-path to learn the heterogeneous network embedding, while they focus on the selection of the meta-path. In [8], the authors facilitate deep architectures to perform heterogeneous network embedding. In [32], a signed network embedding algorithm SiNE is proposed based on the notion that a user should be closer to their "friend" than their "enemy". In [20], the authors try to preserve both local and global information in the network for network embedding. There are also works on attributed network embedding [17][31]. Two recent surveys [10][12] give a comprehensive overview of network embedding algorithms. However, most of the existing methods cannot naturally be applicable to networks with multiple dimensions of relations and hierarchical structure. In this paper, we aim to model the multi-dimensional relations and hierarchical structure and propose a framework to embed these networks to vector space.

3 PROBLEM STATEMENT

In the multi-dimensional networks, we have different types of nodes and multiple dimensions of relations. Assume that there are K types of nodes in total and let $\mathcal{V}_i = \{v_1^{(i)}, v_2^{(i)}, \ldots, v_{N_i}^{(i)}\}$ be the set of the i-th type with N_i nodes. Let $\mathcal{V}$ denote the set of all the nodes $\mathcal{V} = \bigcup_{i=1}^{K} \mathcal{V}_i$. Some types of nodes in the network might present hierarchical structure. In other words, these nodes are associated with categories. For simplicity, we assume all the types of nodes have hierarchical structures with a depth of 2, and we name the parent nodes as categories in this case. Note that though in this work, we focus on the hierarchical structures with a depth of 2, it is straightforward to apply the proposed framework for deeper hierarchical structures. We set $C_i = \{c_1^{(i)}, c_2^{(i)}, \ldots, c_{M_i}^{(i)}\}$ as the set of M_i categories for the i-th type of nodes, and set $\mathbf{T}^{(i)} \in \mathbb{R}^{N_i \times Mi}$ as the matrix that describes the category information, for the i-th type of nodes.

Two nodes could be connected via multiple relations, and we regard each type of relations as a dimension. Thus, nodes from the same type or different types can be connected in the same dimension. These connections can be described by adjacency matrices (for the same type nodes) and the interaction matrices (for different types of nodes). Let $\mathbf{A}_{\mathbf{d}}^{(\mathbf{i})} \in \mathbb{R}^{N_i \times N_i}$ be the adjacency matrix of the i-th node type and $\mathbf{H}_{\mathbf{d}}^{(\mathbf{i},\mathbf{j})} \in \mathbb{R}^{\mathrm{N_i} \times \mathrm{N_j}}$ be the interaction matrix between the i-th and j-th types of node in the d-th dimension. We target to learn representations for each node in each dimension of the network. Let $\mathcal{U}_d{}^{(i)} = \{\mathbf{u_d}_1^{(i)}, \mathbf{u_d}_2^{(i)}, \ldots, \mathbf{u_d}_{N_i}^{(i)}\}$ denote the representations of i-th type of nodes in the dimension d ($d = 1, \ldots D$) where D is the number of dimensions.

With the aforementioned notations and definitions, our problem can be formally defined as follow:

Given

- *K different sets of nodes, i.e.,* $\mathcal{V}_i = \{v_1^{(i)}, v_2^{(i)}, \ldots, v_{N_i}^{(i)}\}$ $(i = 1, \ldots, K)$;
- *multi-dimensional relations among the nodes, i.e.,* $\mathbf{A}_d^{(i)}$ $(i = 1, \ldots, K)$ *and* $\mathbf{H}_d^{(i,j)}$ $(i, j = 1, \ldots, K; i \neq j; d = 1, \ldots, D)$;
- *the hierarchical structure information, i.e.,* $\mathbf{T_i}$ $(i = 1, \ldots, K)$.

We aim to learn a set of representations for all nodes, i.e.,

$$\mathcal{U}_d{}^{(i)} = \{\mathbf{u}_{d_1}^{(i)}, \mathbf{u}_{d_2}^{(i)}, \ldots, \mathbf{u}_{d_{N_i}}^{(i)}\} \quad (i = 1, \ldots, K)$$

in each dimension d ($d = 1, \ldots D$).

4 THE MULTI-DIMENSIONAL EMBEDDING FRAMEWORK WITH HIERARCHICAL STRUCTURE

In this section, we will first introduce how to model multi-dimensional relations and hierarchical structure; and then discuss the proposed framework with an optimization method.

4.1 Capturing Multi-Dimensional Relations

In a multi-dimensional network, all dimensions share the same set of nodes, while having their own network structures in each dimension. A straightforward way to learn representations for each dimension is to perform the network embedding for each dimension, separately. This strategy treats each dimension independently and completely ignores information across dimensions. Hence the learned representations for different dimensions are not related. However, dimensions are inherently related since they share the same set of nodes. Thus, in this subsection, we study how to model multi-dimensional relations.

Intuitively, each dimension should have its independent information individually; while all dimensions should share dependent information across dimensions. Therefore, the learned representations for each dimension should not only preserve independent information from the dimension but also keep dependent information across dimensions. To achieve this goal, for a given dimension d, the representation $\mathbf{u}_d$ for a node contains two components – (1) one component $\mathbf{u}$ for the information shared across dimensions; and (2) one component $\mathbf{e}_d$ specific to the dimension d. With these two components, we can rewrite $\mathbf{u}_d$ as:

$$\mathbf{u}_d = f(\mathbf{u}, \mathbf{e}_d), \tag{1}$$

where f is a function to combine the shared component $\mathbf{u}$ and the specific component $\mathbf{e}_d$. The shared component $\mathbf{u}$ not only captures dependent information across dimensions but also helps the learned representations of all dimensions to be related. The specific component $\mathbf{e}_d$ preserves independent information from the dimension d.

4.2 Capturing Hierarchical Structure

For these nodes which have the hierarchical structure, we also need to model its category information (or parents). The category information is actually shared by all the dimensions, hence it should be indicated in the shared component of representations. For the nodes in the same category, they should also share the similar characteristics. Therefore, to model the hierarchical structure, the shared component of the node representation should further contain two components – (1) one component $\mathbf{c}_u$ indicates category information which is shared by all the nodes in the category, and (2) one component $\mathbf{s}_u$ is specific to the node. With the defined components, we can further rewrite $\mathbf{u}$ in Eq. (1) as:

$$\mathbf{u} = g(\mathbf{c}_u, \mathbf{s}_u) \tag{2}$$

where g is the function to combine the category shared information $\mathbf{c}_u$ and the node specific information $\mathbf{s}_u$. Note that Eq. (2) can be easily extended to deeper hierarchical structure by further decomposing the category shared information $\mathbf{c}_u$.

4.3 The Proposed Framework

With approaches to capture multi-dimensional relations and hierarchical structure, in this subsection, we introduce the embedding framework MINES.

To learn the embeddings for the nodes in each dimension, we follow the idea of skip-gram model [24], which is an effective and efficient way to learn distributed representations of words. The skip-gram model predicts surrounding context given a center word, which can be formulated as follows:

$$p(N(w_c)|w_c), \tag{3}$$

where $N(w_c)$ is the set of words that surround word w_c.

Similarly, we can use the skip-gram to model the network in a given dimension d. For a node v, we define all nodes connected to

v as the "context" of v, which is formally defined as:

$$N_d(v) = \bigcup_{i=1}^{K} N_d^{(i)}(v); \tag{4}$$

where $N_d^{(i)}$ is the set of i-th type of nodes that are connected to node v in the dimension d. Note that the "context" of v consists of different types of nodes, and we treat them differently, which will be further explained later.

Then, given a center node v, we need to predict its "context" as:

$$p_d(N_d(v)|v) = \prod_{i=1}^{K} p(N_d^{(i)}(v)|v) = \prod_{i=1}^{K} \prod_{v_j^{(i)} \in N_d^{(i)}(v)} p_d(v_j^{(i)}|v); \tag{5}$$

where $p(v_j^{(i)}|v)$ can be modeled using a softmax function as:

$$p_d(v_j^{(i)}|v) = \frac{\exp(\mathbf{u}_d^T \mathbf{u}_{d_j}^{(i)})}{\sum_{v^{(i)} \in V_i} \exp(\mathbf{u}_d^T \mathbf{u}_d^{(i)})}. \tag{6}$$

In (6), the softmax function is over the i-th type nodes $\mathcal{V}_i$ instead of the whole nodes set $\mathcal{V}$.

To learn the representations for the dimension d, we model this problem as a maximum likelihood problem. In other words, we need to maximize the probability that $N_d(v)$ is the "context" of node v for all the nodes $v \in \mathcal{V}$. Hence, we need to maximize:

$$P_d = \prod_{v \in \mathcal{V}} p_d(N_d(v)|v). \tag{7}$$

With all D dimensions, we need to jointly maximize the following term:

$$P = \prod_{d=1}^{D} P_d. \tag{8}$$

Instead of maximizing Eq. (8), we equivalently minimize its negative logarithm with respect to the representations $\mathcal{U}_d^{(i)}$ as:

$$\begin{aligned} &\min_{\{\mathcal{U}_d^{(i)}\}_{i=1,\dots,K}^{d=1,\dots,D}} -\log P \\ \Leftrightarrow\ &\min_{\{\mathcal{U}_d^{(i)}\}_{i=1,\dots,K}^{d=1,\dots,D}} -\sum_{d=1}^{D} \log P_d \\ \Leftrightarrow\ &\min_{\{\mathcal{U}_d^{(i)}\}_{i=1,\dots,K}^{d=1,\dots,D}} -\sum_{d=1}^{D} \sum_{v \in \mathcal{V}} \sum_{i=1}^{K} \sum_{v_j^{(i)} \in N_d^{(i)}(v)} \log p_d(v_j^{(i)}|v). \end{aligned} \tag{9}$$

4.4 An Optimization Method

There are two challenges to address when optimizing Eq. (9). First, the minimization of Eq. (9) is computationally expensive due to summation over the whole set of nodes $\mathcal{V}_i$ when calculating each term $\log p_d(v_j^{(i)}|v)$. Second, how to choose the functions of f in Eq. (1) and g in Eq. (2).

To solve computational challenge, we adopt the negative sampling approach proposed in [25]. By using the negative sampling method, we replace each $\log p_d(v_j^{(i)}|v)$ with

$$O_d(v, v_j^{(i)}) = \log \sigma(\mathbf{u}_d^T \mathbf{u}_{d_j}^{(i)}) + \sum_{n=1}^{N_e} \log \sigma(-\mathbf{u}_d^T \mathbf{u}_{d_{(n)}}^{(i)}); \tag{10}$$

where $\sigma(x) = 1/(1 + \exp(x))$ is the sigmoid function, and N_e is the number of negative samples. The negative samples are randomly sampled from some noise distribution. For $\log p_d(v_j^{(i)}|v)$, the negative samples are sampled from node set $\mathcal{V}_i$ according to $P_{i(v)}^{(i)}(v^{(i)}) \sim d_{v^{(i)}}^{3/4}$, as proposed in [25], where $d_{v^{(i)}}$ is the in-degree of $v^{(i)}$ corresponding to the $i(v)$-th type of nodes and $i(v)$ indicates the type of node v. Note again, for i-th type of node $v_j^{(i)}$, we sample the negative samples from the i-th type of nodes set $\mathcal{V}_i$ instead of the whole nodes set $\mathcal{V}$.

We adopt mini-batch Stochastic Gradient Descent (SGD) to optimize the problem. In each step, a mini-batch of edges of the same type are sampled according to their weights. Here, by "same" type of edge, we mean, these edges have same types of nodes for source and target nodes respectively and also the relations between them is in the same dimension. For each sampled edge, the source node is treated as v and the target node is treated as $v_j^{(i)}$ in (10). The derivatives for v, $v_j^{(i)}$ and $v_{(n)}^{(i)}$ are

$$\begin{aligned} \frac{\partial O_d(v, v_j^{(i)})}{\partial u_d} &= (1 - \sigma(u_d^T u_{d_j}^{(i)}))u_{d_j}^{(i)} - \sum_{n=1}^{Ne} (1 - \sigma(-u_d^T u_{d_{(n)}}^{(i)}))u_{d_{(n)}}^{(i)}; \\ \frac{\partial O_d(v, v_j^{(i)})}{\partial u_{d_j}^{(i)}} &= (1 - \sigma(u_d^T u_{d_j}^{(i)}))u_d; \\ \frac{\partial O_d(v, v_j^{(i)})}{\partial u_{d_{(n)}}^{(i)}} &= -(1 - \sigma(-u_d^T u_{d_{(n)}}^{(i)}))u_d, n = 1, \dots, Ne. \end{aligned} \tag{11}$$

Next we discuss how to choose f and g functions. In fact, f is used to combine the dimension shared component $\mathbf{u}$ and dimension-specific component $\mathbf{c}_d$. It can be a linear function, a non-linear function (e.g., exponential functions) or even can be automatically learned (e.g., neural networks). In this work, we choose a linear function f. In other words, we define as $- f(\mathbf{u}, \mathbf{e}_d) = \mathbf{u} + \mathbf{c}_d$. We also use a similar function for g. We would like to leave the investigation of other choices of f and g as one future direction. With choices of f and g, the representations for nodes can be rewritten as:

$$\mathbf{u}_d = \mathbf{c}_u + \mathbf{s}_u + \mathbf{e}_d; \tag{12}$$

$$\mathbf{u}_{d_j}^{(i)} = \mathbf{c}_{u_j}^{(i)} + \mathbf{s}_{u_j}^{(i)} + \mathbf{e}_{d_j}^{(i)}; \tag{13}$$

$$\mathbf{u}_{d_{(n)}}^{(i)} = \mathbf{c}_{u_{(n)}}^{(i)} + \mathbf{s}_{u_{(n)}}^{(i)} + \mathbf{e}_{d_{(n)}}^{(i)}. \tag{14}$$

We need to update $\mathbf{c}_u, \mathbf{s}_u, \mathbf{e}_d, \mathbf{c}_{uj}, \mathbf{s}_{uj}, \mathbf{e}_{dj}, \mathbf{c}_{u(n)}, \mathbf{s}_{u(n)}$ and $\mathbf{e}_{d(n)}$. We update these representations using Gradient Decent (GD).

To update the representations for v, we need to update its three components $\mathbf{c}_u$, $\mathbf{s}_u$ and $\mathbf{c}_d$ according to (15).

$$c_u \leftarrow c_u + \rho \cdot \frac{\partial O_d(v, v_h^{(i)})}{\partial u_d};$$
$$s_u \leftarrow s_u + \rho \cdot \frac{\partial O_d(v, v_h^{(i)})}{\partial u_d}; \quad (15)$$
$$e_d \leftarrow e_d + \rho \cdot \frac{\partial O_d(v, v_h^{(i)})}{\partial u_d}.$$

Similarly, to update the representations for $v_j^{(i)}$, we need to update its three components $\mathbf{c}_{u_j^{(i)}}$, $\mathbf{s}_{u_j^{(i)}}$ and $\mathbf{c}_{d_j^{(i)}}$ according to (16).

$$c_{u_j^{(i)}} \leftarrow c_{u_j^{(i)}} + \rho \cdot \frac{\partial O_d(v, v_j^{(i)})}{\partial u_{d_j^{(i)}}};$$
$$s_{u_j^{(i)}} \leftarrow s_{u_j^{(i)}} + \rho \cdot \frac{\partial O_d(v, v_j^{(i)})}{\partial u_{d_j^{(i)}}}; \quad (16)$$
$$e_{d_j^{(i)}} \leftarrow e_{d_j^{(i)}} + \rho \cdot \frac{\partial O_d(v, v_j^{(i)})}{\partial u_{d_j^{(i)}}}.$$

Finally, to update the representations for $v_{(n)}^{(i)}$, $n = 1, \ldots, Ne$, we need to update their three components $\mathbf{c}_{u_{(n)}^{(i)}}$, $\mathbf{s}_{u_{(n)}^{(i)}}$ and $\mathbf{c}_{d_{(n)}^{(i)}}$ according to (17) respectively.

$$\mathbf{c}_{u_{(n)}^{(i)}} \leftarrow \mathbf{c}_{u_{(n)}^{(i)}} + \rho \cdot \frac{\partial O_d(v, v_j^{(i)})}{\partial \mathbf{u}_{d_{(n)}^{(i)}}}, n = 1, \ldots Ne;$$
$$\mathbf{s}_{u_{(n)}^{(i)}} \leftarrow \mathbf{s}_{u_{(n)}^{(i)}} + \rho \cdot \frac{\partial O_d(v, v_j^{(i)})}{\partial \mathbf{u}_{d_{(n)}^{(i)}}}, n = 1, \ldots Ne; \quad (17)$$
$$\mathbf{e}_{d_{(n)}^{(i)}} \leftarrow \mathbf{e}_{d_{(n)}^{(i)}} + \rho \cdot \frac{\partial O_d(v, v_j^{(i)})}{\partial \mathbf{u}_{d_{(n)}^{(i)}}}, n = 1, \ldots Ne.$$

We summarize the optimization procedure in Algorithm 1. In the algorithm, the input includes the number of mini-batch size m, the training size S, the dimension of representations dim, the number of negative samples Ne, the learning rate ρ and the set of all the edges $\mathcal{E}$ in the network. In line 1, we initialize all the components for all the representations. Then, we sample a set of same type edges SE from $\mathcal{E}$ in line 4. In line 6, for each edge, we sample Ne negative samples. We calculate the gradients and update the components in lines 7 and 8, respectively. Finally, we combine the components to form the representations for each node in each dimension in line 12.

To efficiently sample the edges and negatives samples, we adopt the alias methods proposed in [15], which can generate a random variable from a discrete distribution in constant time $O(1)$. The optimization with negative sampling takes $O(dim \cdot (Ne + 2) + Ne)$ time, where Ne is the number of negative samples. hence, each step of MINES takes $O(dim \cdot Ne)$ operations. If the training size is S, the overall time complexity of MINES is $O(S \cdot dim \cdot Ne)$.

Algorithm 1: Optimization procedure

Input: $Ne, m, S, \rho, dim, \mathcal{E}$
Output: $\{\mathcal{U}_d^{(i)}\}_{i=1,\ldots,K}^{d=1,\ldots,D}$

1 Initialize $\mathbf{c}_{u_j^{(i)}}$, $\mathbf{s}_{u_j^{(i)}}$ and $\mathbf{e}_{d_j^{(i)}}$, as dim dimension vectors randomly, for $d = 1, \ldots, D$, $i = 1, \ldots, K$ and $j = 1, \ldots, N_i$;
2 $s = 0$;
3 **while** $s < S$ **do**
4   Sample a set of m edges of the same type SE from $\mathcal{E}$;
5   **for** $e = (v, v_j^{(i)}) \in SE$ **do**
6   Sample a set of Ne negative samples $\{v_{(n)}^{(i)}\}_{n=1,\ldots,Ne}$;
7   Calculate the gradients according to (11);
8   Update the corresponding vectors according to (15), (16) and (17);
9   **end**
10   $s \leftarrow s + m$.
11 **end**
12 $\mathbf{u}_{d_j^{(i)}} = \mathbf{c}_{u_j^{(i)}} + \mathbf{s}_{u_j^{(i)}} + \mathbf{e}_{d_j^{(i)}}$; for $d = 1, \ldots, D$, $i = 1, \ldots, K$ and $j = 1, \ldots, N_i$;
13 **return** $\{\mathcal{U}_d^{(i)}\}_{i=1,\ldots,K}^{d=1,\ldots,D}$.

5 EXPERIMENTS

In this section, we present the experimental details to verify the effectiveness of the proposed framework. We first introduce the dataset we will use in the evaluation. Then, we describe the experimental settings. Finally, we present the experimental results with discussions and study the key parameter in the proposed framework.

5.1 Dataset

In our experiments, we sample data from JD.com, which is one of the largest e-commerce companies. In our dataset, we have two types of nodes: users and items. The items have hierarchical structure and each item belongs to some predefined categories. Users can perform various behaviors on items such as "view", "save", and "purchase". In this work, we collect two behaviors, i.e., "view" and "purchase", to construct two-dimensional relations between users and items. In addition, we collect two other relations: one is the "view session" of a user, while another is the "purchase basket" of the user.

A view session is a sequence of items that are viewed by a user within a period of time. It is intuitively to understand the items that are viewed within a short period by the same user should be similar. To incorporate these relations into the network, we construct an item-item view network by connecting the items that are viewed w items before or after a given item in a session with this item, where w is the window size. In this work, we set the window size to 5. These edges are in the "view" dimension and they are weighted where the weight is the co-occurrence frequency.

A purchase basket is a set of items that are purchased by a user at the same time. Items that are purchased in the same basket are supposed to be related to each other. To incorporate these relations, we construct an item-item purchase network. In particular, we connect two items if they are purchased in the same basket. These

# items	401,922
# users	17,806
# categories	2,788
# item-item (view)	6,402,586
# user-user (view)	13,651,206
# user-item (view)	962,362
# item-item (purchase)	3,211,660
# user-user (purchase)	6,870,510
# user-item (purchase)	485,656

Table 1: The statistics of the network

edges are weighted where the weight is the frequency of the two items presenting in the same basket. In the other way around, users that have "viewed" or "purchased" the same item also shows similarity. In each dimension, we connected users that have "viewed" or "purchased" the same items.

To sum up, in the constructed multidimensional e-commerce network, we have two types of nodes, i.e., the users and the items, and the items have hierarchical structure. There are two dimensions, i.e., the "view" dimension and the "purchase" dimension. We can conclude that the constructed network has all the characteristics of networks we want to study in this work; hence it is suitable for us to use the dataset to evaluate the proposed framework. Some statistics of the network are shown in Table 1.

5.2 Experimental Setting

Following the common way to assess network embedding algorithms [13], we choose link prediction as the evaluation task. The intuition is that a better embedding algorithm should learn better node representations, which will lead to better link prediction performance.

In the link prediction task, a certain fraction of edges are removed, and we would like to predict whether these "missing" edges exist.

In our evaluation, we perform the link prediction task on the two dimensions, separately. For each dimension, we remove the *user-item* edges and use them as parts of the testing set. We set up 3 groups of experiments, where 10%, 30% and 50% of the *user-item* edges are removed, respectively. To form the training set, we first put all the remaining *user-item* edges into the training set, and then, for each *user-item* edge in the training set, we randomly sample an item that is not connected to this user and use this user and non-connected item pair as the negative sample in the training set. We form the testing set in the same way.

After removing the edges, we use the remaining network to learn the representations for all the nodes. Then, to perform the link prediction task, the representations for the edges (or the user item pairs) should be learned. We use two different ways to combine the representations of two nodes as the representation of the edge (or user item pair) as used in [13].

- **Element-wise addition** Given two *dim* dimension representations of two nodes, we add them element-wisely and get a new *dim* dimension vector as the representation for this pair of nodes.
- **Element-wise multiplication** Given two *dim* dimension representations of two nodes, we multiply them element-wisely and get a new *dim* dimension vector as the representation for this pair of nodes.

For all the methods, we use both ways to form the representations for the pairs of nodes and report the results for each method.

After we form the representations for the pairs of the nodes in the training set and the testing set, we train a binary classifier using logistic regression on the training set and perform link prediction on the testing set. In this work, we will use Micro-F_1, Macro-F_1 and AUC as the metric to evaluate the link prediction performance.

5.3 Performance Comparison

To evaluate the performance of our algorithm, we compare the performance of our algorithm with the following representative baselines:

- **LINE** [29]: As LINE can only work for one-dimensional network, we apply LINE to the two dimensions separately and learn one set of representations for each dimension, respectively. We treat categories as nodes, and add *item-category* edges into the networks for LINE.
- **DeepWalk** [26]: We apply DeepWalk to the two dimensions separately and learn two sets of representations. We treat categories as nodes, and add *item-category* edges into the networks for DeepWalk. DeepWalk can only work for unweighted networks, hence, we convert our network to unweighted network by ignoring the weights.
- **Non-negative Matrix Factorization (NMF)** [19]: We apply it to the user-item interaction matrix and use the factorized two matrices as the embeddings for the users and items. NMF is also applied to the two dimensions, separately.
- **Co-NMF**: In Co-NMF, we perform a co-factorization on the multi-dimensional networks and learn unified user representations for all dimensions. Basically Co-NMF assumes all dimensions share the same embeddings, which completely ignores independent information from each dimension.
- **MINES(S)**: This is a variant of our framework MINES. Instead of using all three components $\mathbf{c}_u$, $\mathbf{s}_u$ and $\mathbf{e}_d$, we only use the shared components $\mathbf{c}_u$ and $\mathbf{s}_u$ to form the representation for a node v.

We summarize the experiments results for the "view" dimension and "purchase" dimension in Table 2, and Table 3, respectively. We make the following observations from Table 2:

- For all methods, using the **Element-wise multiplication** is better than **Element-wise addition**, which is consistent with the observation in [13].
- The performance of Co-NMF is worse than that of NMF, which indicates that the independent information from each dimension is very important to accurately predict links in that dimension.
- MINES shows better performance than MINES(S), which further shows the importance of the dimension specific information.
- As we remove more percent of edges, the performance of all methods decrease in all three measures when using the **Element-wise multiplication**.

		Addition			Multiplication		
	% removed edges	10%	30%	50%	10%	30%	50%
Micro-F_1(%)	MINES	**72.77**	**72.76**	**72.65**	**83.89**	**82.57**	**81.32**
	LINE	71.00	70.83	70.72	79.42	78.26	76.84
	DeepWalk	69.39	69.03	68.87	76.45	76.10	74.94
	NMF	59.80	59.79	59.86	78.16	78.16	77.98
	Co-NMF	56.66	56.83	56.93	76.96	77.00	76.87
	MINES(S)	67.22	66.78	66.82	76.98	76.28	75.78
Macro-F_1(%)	MINES	**72.74**	**72.72**	**72.58**	**83.75**	**82.35**	**80.98**
	LINE	70.94	70.82	70.78	79.17	77.95	76.44
	DeepWalk	69.28	68.92	68.79	76.22	75.79	74.63
	NMF	59.77	59.77	59.86	78.08	78.07	77.90
	Co-NMF	56.66	56.83	56.93	76.84	76.87	76.74
	MINES(S)	67.21	66.77	68.81	76.96	76.25	75.77
AUC	MINES	**0.8037**	**0.8040**	**0.8036**	**0.9261**	**0.9180**	**0.9146**
	LINE	0.7757	0.7757	0.7732	0.8879	0.8759	0.8636
	DeepWalk	0.7478	0.7434	0.7392	0.8522	0.8517	0.8351
	NMF	0.6516	0.6527	0.6529	0.8741	0.8739	0.8729
	Co-NMF	0.5912	0.5927	0.5933	0.8603	0.8605	0.8596
	MINES(S)	0.7315	0.7271	0.7278	0.8530	0.8456	0.8409

Table 2: Link Prediction Performance Comparison: The View Dimension

		Addition			Multiplication		
	% removed edges	10%	30%	50%	10%	30%	50%
Micro-F_1(%)	MINES	**78.48**	**77.94**	**77.62**	**90.93**	**89.74**	**88.57**
	LINE	71.55	70.84	70.63	87.88	86.94	85.69
	DeepWalk	67.08	67.46	67.53	82.76	82.35	80.54
	NMF	68.20	68.11	68.18	83.43	83.65	83.44
	Co-NMF	56.28	56.36	56.31	76.98	76.83	76.75
	MINES(S)	70.36	70.77	70.54	83.63	82.97	82.20
Macro-F_1(%)	MINES	**78.47**	**77.92**	**77.59**	**90.89**	**89.66**	**88.49**
	LINE	71.48	70.83	70.51	87.85	86.87	85.58
	DeepWalk	67.03	67.38	67.52	82.70	82.27	80.41
	NMF	68.19	68.10	68.18	83.36	83.59	83.36
	Co-NMF	56.24	56.33	56.27	76.84	76.67	76.60
	MINES(S)	70.34	70.75	70.52	83.61	82.96	82.19
AUC	MINES	**0.8662**	**0.8644**	**0.8623**	**0.9762**	**0.9725**	**0.9690**
	LINE	0.7892	0.7791	0.7759	0.9614	0.9518	0.9455
	DeepWalk	0.7109	0.7134	0.7128	0.9278	0.9256	0.9252
	NMF	0.7544	0.7528	0.7538	0.9346	0.9347	0.9342
	Co-NMF	0.5826	0.5834	0.5820	0.8592	0.8585	0.8568
	MINES(S)	0.7740	0.7775	0.7758	0.9146	0.9036	0.9101

Table 3: Link Prediction Performance Comparison: The Purchase Dimension

- The performance of DeepWalk is worse than LINE and NMF. This is mainly because DeepWalk can only work for unweighted networks and cannot take advantage of the edge weights.
- The proposed framework MINES obtains the best performance. For example, MINES boosts the performance 3% – 5% compared to the best baseline when 10% – 50% edges are moved. The major reason is the proposed framework has two components to capture the multi-dimensional relations and the hierarchical structure.

We have similar observations for the "purchase" dimension – (1) using the **Element-wise multiplication** is better than using

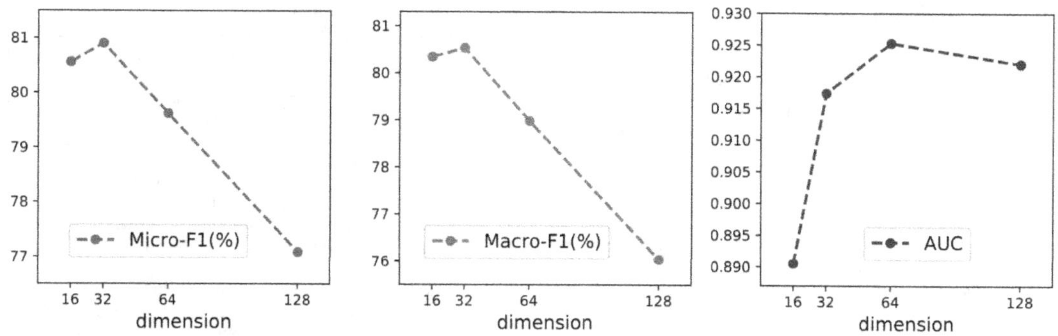

Figure 2: Parameter Analysis: The View Dimension

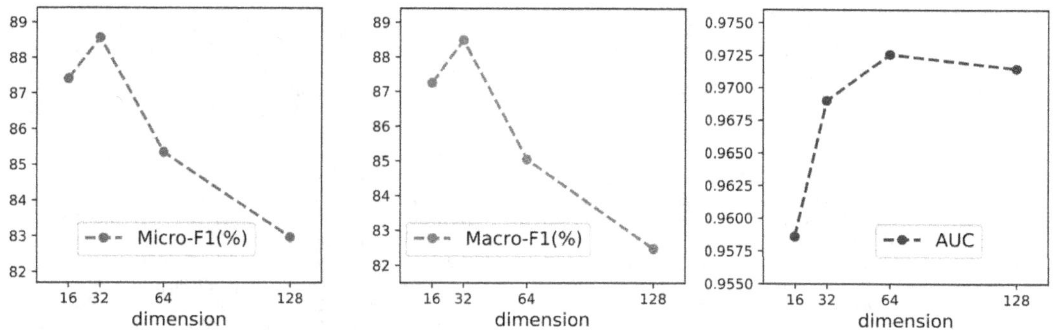

Figure 3: Parameter Analysis: The Purchase Dimension

Element-wise addition and (2) MINES outperforms all the baselines; for example, MINES obtains over 2% improvement in terms of all the measures compared to the best baseline.

5.4 Parameter Analysis

In this section, we analyze how the dimension of the learned representations in our method affects the performance of the link prediction task. In particular, we set the dimension of the representations to $\{16, 32, 64, 128\}$ with the setting of 50% edges removed. The results are reported in in Figure 2 and Figure 3 for view and purchase dimensions, separately. Note that we ignore the results with other settings since we can make similar observations.

As shown in Figure 2 and Figure 3, in both view and purchase dimensions, the Micro-F_1 and Macro-F_1 first increase as the dimension of the learned representations gets large, and then decrease. Both the Micro-F_1 and Macro-F_1 reach the maximum when the dimension of the representations is 32 in both view and purchase dimension. AUC also increases first and then decrease as the dimension of the representations gets larger. However, the AUC score reaches the maximum when the dimension of the representation is 64.

In summary, the performance first increases and then decreases as the dimension of the representations gets larger. The dimension of the representations affects the different measures differently.

6 CONCLUSION

In this paper, we propose an approach to model multi-dimensional networks, which can capture independent information from each dimension and dependent information across dimensions. Based on this approach, we propose the MINES framework which can embed multi-dimensional network with hierarchical structure to low-dimensional vector spaces. We can learn a set of node representations for each dimension using this framework. The learned representations for each dimension will contain the hierarchical information, the independent information from the specific dimension and also dependent information across dimensions. We evaluate the effectiveness of our framework on a multi-dimensional e-commerce network. The results of our experiments show the advancement of our framework.

In this work, we utilize linear functions to model the across dimension information and the hierarchical structure information. In our future work, more complicated non-linear functions such as exponential functions or even the neural networks can be used. Meanwhile, as a limitation in our work, we only focus on hierarchical structures with depth of 2 in this paper. As another direction in our future work, we would like to investigate the proposed framework with deeper hierarchical structures. Real-world networks typically evolve such as addition of new nodes and links, and deletion of old nodes and links. Therefore, multi-dimensional network embedding with dynamics should provide new insights in future.

ACKNOWLEDGEMENTS

The authors wish to thank the anonymous reviewers for their helpful comments. Yao Ma and Jiliang Tang are supported by the National Science Foundation (NSF) under grant number IIS-1714741 and IIS-1715940.

REFERENCES

[1] Mikhail Belkin and Partha Niyogi. 2002. Laplacian eigenmaps and spectral techniques for embedding and clustering. In *Advances in neural information processing systems*. 585–591.

[2] Michael GH Bell, Yasunori Iida, et al. 1997. Transportation network analysis. (1997).

[3] Michele Berlingerio, Michele Coscia, Fosca Giannotti, Anna Monreale, and Dino Pedreschi. 2013. Multidimensional networks: foundations of structural analysis. *World Wide Web* 16, 5-6 (2013), 567–593.

[4] Michele Berlingerio, Fabio Pinelli, and Francesco Calabrese. 2013. Abacus: frequent pattern mining-based community discovery in multidimensional networks. *Data Mining and Knowledge Discovery* 27, 3 (2013), 294–320.

[5] Smriti Bhagat, Graham Cormode, and S Muthukrishnan. 2011. Node classification in social networks. In *Social network data analytics*. Springer, 115–148.

[6] Ronald L Breiger, Scott A Boorman, and Phipps Arabie. 1975. An algorithm for clustering relational data with applications to social network analysis and comparison with multidimensional scaling. *Journal of mathematical psychology* 12, 3 (1975), 328–383.

[7] Carter T Butts. 2009. Revisiting the foundations of network analysis. *science* 325, 5939 (2009), 414–416.

[8] Shiyu Chang, Wei Han, Jiliang Tang, Guo-Jun Qi, Charu C Aggarwal, and Thomas S Huang. 2015. Heterogeneous network embedding via deep architectures. In *Proceedings of the 21th ACM SIGKDD International Conference on Knowledge Discovery and Data Mining*. ACM, 119–128.

[9] Ting Chen and Yizhou Sun. 2017. Task-Guided and Path-Augmented Heterogeneous Network Embedding for Author Identification. In *Proceedings of the Tenth ACM International Conference on Web Search and Data Mining, WSDM 2017, Cambridge, United Kingdom, February 6-10, 2017*, Maarten de Rijke, Milad Shokouhi, Andrew Tomkins, and Min Zhang (Eds.). ACM, 295–304.

[10] Peng Cui, Xiao Wang, Jian Pei, and Wenwu Zhu. 2017. A Survey on Network Embedding. *arXiv preprint arXiv:1711.08752* (2017).

[11] Yuxiao Dong, Nitesh V Chawla, and Ananthram Swami. 2017. metapath2vec: Scalable Representation Learning for Heterogeneous Networks. (2017).

[12] Palash Goyal and Emilio Ferrara. 2017. Graph Embedding Techniques, Applications, and Performance: A Survey. *arXiv preprint arXiv:1705.02801* (2017).

[13] Aditya Grover and Jure Leskovec. 2016. node2vec: Scalable feature learning for networks. In *Proceedings of the 22nd ACM SIGKDD international conference on Knowledge discovery and data mining*. ACM, 855–864.

[14] Gueorgi Kossinets and Duncan J Watts. 2006. Empirical analysis of an evolving social network. *science* 311, 5757 (2006), 88–90.

[15] Richard A Kronmal and Arthur V Peterson Jr. 1979. On the alias method for generating random variables from a discrete distribution. *The American Statistician* 33, 4 (1979), 214–218.

[16] Ka-Wei Roy Lee and Ee-Peng Lim. 2016. Friendship maintenance and prediction in multiple social networks. In *Proceedings of the 27th ACM Conference on Hypertext and Social Media*. ACM, 83–92.

[17] Jundong Li, Harsh Dani, Xia Hu, Jiliang Tang, Yi Chang, and Huan Liu. 2017. Attributed Network Embedding for Learning in a Dynamic Environment. *arXiv preprint arXiv:1706.01860* (2017).

[18] David Liben-Nowell and Jon M. Kleinberg. 2003. The link prediction problem for social networks. In *Proceedings of the 2003 ACM CIKM International Conference on Information and Knowledge Management, New Orleans, Louisiana, USA, November 2-8, 2003*. ACM, 556–559.

[19] Chih-Jen Lin. 2007. Projected gradient methods for nonnegative matrix factorization. *Neural computation* 19, 10 (2007), 2756–2779.

[20] Yao Ma, Suhang Wang, ZhaoChun Ren, Dawei Yin, and Jiliang Tang. 2017. Preserving Local and Global Information for Network Embedding. *arXiv preprint arXiv:1710.07266* (2017).

[21] Laurens van der Maaten and Geoffrey Hinton. 2008. Visualizing data using t-SNE. *Journal of Machine Learning Research* 9, Nov (2008), 2579–2605.

[22] MARGGF Magnani, Anna Monreale, Giulio Rossetti, and Fosca Giannotti. 2013. On multidimensional network measures. In *Italian conference on Sistemi Evoluti per le Basi di Dati (SEBD)*.

[23] Tomas Mikolov, Kai Chen, Greg Corrado, and Jeffrey Dean. 2013. Efficient estimation of word representations in vector space. *arXiv preprint arXiv:1301.3781* (2013).

[24] Tomas Mikolov, Kai Chen, Greg Corrado, and Jeffrey Dean. 2013. Efficient Estimation of Word Representations in Vector Space. *CoRR* abs/1301.3781 (2013).

[25] Tomas Mikolov, Ilya Sutskever, Kai Chen, Greg S Corrado, and Jeff Dean. 2013. Distributed representations of words and phrases and their compositionality. In *Advances in neural information processing systems*. 3111–3119.

[26] Bryan Perozzi, Rami Al-Rfou, and Steven Skiena. 2014. DeepWalk: online learning of social representations. In *The 20th ACM SIGKDD International Conference on Knowledge Discovery and Data Mining, KDD '14, New York, NY, USA - August 24 - 27, 2014*, Sofus A. Macskassy, Claudia Perlich, Jure Leskovec, Wei Wang, and Rayid Ghani (Eds.). ACM, 701–710.

[27] Giulio Rossetti, Michele Berlingerio, and Fosca Giannotti. 2011. Scalable link prediction on multidimensional networks. In *Data Mining Workshops (ICDMW), 2011 IEEE 11th International Conference on*. IEEE, 979–986.

[28] Jian Tang, Jingzhou Liu, Ming Zhang, and Qiaozhu Mei. 2016. Visualization Large-scale and High-dimensional Data. *CoRR* abs/1602.00370 (2016).

[29] Jian Tang, Meng Qu, Mingzhe Wang, Ming Zhang, Jun Yan, and Qiaozhu Mei. 2015. LINE: Large-scale Information Network Embedding. In *Proceedings of the 24th International Conference on World Wide Web, WWW 2015, Florence, Italy, May 18-22, 2015*, Aldo Gangemi, Stefano Leonardi, and Alessandro Panconesi (Eds.). ACM, 1067–1077.

[30] Joshua B Tenenbaum, Vin De Silva, and John C Langford. 2000. A global geometric framework for nonlinear dimensionality reduction. *science* 290, 5500 (2000), 2319–2323.

[31] Suhang Wang, Charu C. Aggarwal, Jiliang Tang, and Huan Liu. [n. d.]. Attributed Signed Network Embedding. In *Proceedings of CIKM*.

[32] Suhang Wang, Jiliang Tang, Charu C. Aggarwal, Yi Chang, and Huan Liu. 2017. Signed Network Embedding in Social Media. In *Proceedings of SDM*. 327–335.

[33] Suhang Wang, Jiliang Tang, Charu C. Aggarwal, and Huan Liu. 2016. Linked Document Embedding for Classification. In *Proceedings of CIKM*. 115–124.

[34] Stanley Wasserman and Katherine Faust. 1994. *Social network analysis: Methods and applications*. Vol. 8. Cambridge university press.

[35] Barry Wellman. 1983. Network analysis: Some basic principles. *Sociological theory* (1983), 155–200.

Query Driven Algorithm Selection in Early Stage Retrieval

Joel Mackenzie
RMIT University
Melbourne, Australia
joel.mackenzie@rmit.edu.au

J. Shane Culpepper
RMIT University
Melbourne, Australia
shane.culpepper@rmit.edu.au

Roi Blanco*
Amazon
Barcelona, Spain
roiblan@amazon.com

Matt Crane
University of Waterloo
Waterloo, Canada
matt.crane@uwaterloo.ca

Charles L. A. Clarke
University of Waterloo
Waterloo, Canada
claclark@gmail.com

Jimmy Lin
University of Waterloo
Waterloo, Canada
jimmylin@uwaterloo.ca

ABSTRACT

Large scale retrieval systems often employ cascaded ranking architectures, in which an initial set of candidate documents is iteratively refined and re-ranked by increasingly sophisticated and expensive ranking models. In this paper, we propose a unified framework for predicting a range of performance-sensitive parameters based on minimizing end-to-end effectiveness loss. The framework does not require relevance judgments for training, is amenable to predicting a wide range of parameters, allows for fine tuned efficiency-effectiveness trade-offs, and can be easily deployed in large scale search systems with minimal overhead. As a proof of concept, we show that the framework can accurately predict a number of performance parameters on a query-by-query basis, allowing efficient and effective retrieval, while simultaneously minimizing the tail latency of an early-stage candidate generation system. On the 50 million document ClueWeb09B collection, and across 25,000 queries, our hybrid system can achieve superior early-stage efficiency to fixed parameter systems without loss of effectiveness, and allows more finely-grained efficiency-effectiveness trade-offs across the multiple stages of the retrieval system.

ACM Reference Format:
Joel Mackenzie, J. Shane Culpepper, Roi Blanco, Matt Crane, Charles L. A. Clarke, and Jimmy Lin. 2018. Query Driven Algorithm Selection in Early Stage Retrieval. In *WSDM 2018: The Eleventh ACM International Conference on Web Search and Data Mining, February 5–9, 2018, Marina Del Rey, CA, USA.* ACM, New York, NY, USA, 9 pages. https://doi.org/10.1145/3159652.3159676

1 INTRODUCTION

The competing goals of maximizing both efficiency and effectiveness in large scale retrieval systems continue to challenge builders of search systems as the emphasis in modern architectures evolves towards multi-stage retrieval [40]. Many old efficiency problems become new again in the increasingly complex cascade of document re-ranking algorithms being developed. For example, research groups can focus on early stage retrieval efficiency [4, 16, 54], balancing feature costs [12, 53, 56], or improving the performance of the learning-to-rank algorithms [5, 26, 34, 35, 37].

While great strides have been made in all of these areas, gaps remain in our understanding of the delicate balance between efficiency and effectiveness in each "stage" of the re-ranking cascade. One of the most significant limitations preventing further progress is training data availability. While query sets to measure efficiency in various collections are plentiful, the costs of gathering relevance judgments in order to measure effectiveness limit the number of topics available for more detailed trade-off analyses.

In this work, we explore how to apply a *reference list* framework [13, 45, 46, 55] to alleviate this problem. We leverage a new labelling framework to build machine-learned models capable of predicting candidate set sizes, algorithm aggressiveness parameters, and query latency to balance efficiency and effectiveness on a query-by-query basis. In particular, we focus on using this unified framework to reduce the early-stage *tail latency* [18, 24, 25, 27], which are queries with a 95th percentile (or greater) response time in the candidate generation stage. We explore three important research questions:

Research Question 1 (RQ1): *What is the best way to use reference lists to accurately perform dynamic parameter predictions in early stage retrieval on a per-query basis?*

Research Question 2 (RQ2): *What is the relationship between tail latency and index traversal algorithms, and can our new prediction framework be used to reliably provide worst case guarantees on first-stage query efficiency?*

Research Question 3 (RQ3): *What combination of predictors will lead to efficient first-stage retrieval, minimizing the number of candidate documents returned in the first stage (and thus making later stages more efficient), while also minimizing the effectiveness loss in final stage re-ranking?*

In answering these questions, our research contributions include:

(1) A unified framework that can be used to predict a wide variety of performance-sensitive parameters in multi-stage retrieval systems, which can be trained without requiring relevance judgments.
(2) A pragmatic, yet highly tunable and easy to implement approach for parameterizing search systems on a per-query basis.

*This work was conducted while this author was at RMIT University.

WSDM 2018, February 5–9, 2018, Marina Del Rey, CA, USA

ACM ISBN 978-1-4503-5581-0/18/02...$15.00
https://doi.org/10.1145/3159652.3159676

(3) A pathway to more fine-tuned per-query optimization techniques, and the tools necessary to implement and test systems leveraging these ideas.

We achieve these goals using three ideas. First, we exploit the idea of query efficiency prediction and static pre-retrieval features to build a unified prediction framework. Next, we explore the relationship between the number of documents returned in a top-k candidate set and the efficiency of the index traversal algorithm. Finally, the efficiency predictors are integrated with an effectiveness loss minimization prediction. Together, this series of "Stage-0" pre-retrieval predictions produces a pipeline that allows fine-grained efficiency-effectiveness trade-offs in an existing multi-stage retrieval system.

2 BACKGROUND AND RELATED WORK

Efficient Query Processing. Efficient query processing can be attained through a range of index organizations and traversal strategies based on the *inverted index* data structure [59]. Document-at-a-time (DAAT) query processing relies on postings lists being sorted in ascending order of the document identifiers. At query time, a pointer is set at the beginning of each postings list. Once the current document has been evaluated, the pointers are forwarded to the next document in the lists. An efficient method for *disjunctive* DAAT processing is the *Weak-AND* (WAND) algorithm [8]. WAND is now a well understood algorithm used for a wide variety of different search tasks [4, 14, 21, 38, 41, 47].

Ding and Suel [20] (and at a similar time, Chakrabarti et al. [10]) explored an improved version of WAND named *Block-Max WAND* (BMW). The key observation in BMW is that since many index compression algorithms are block-based [30, 58], skipping can be achieved at the block level, thus saving an entire block decompression. Further enhancements to BMW have been made in the literature, usually by using additional auxiliary structures that improve the efficiency of query processing at the cost of additional space consumption [19, 42, 43].

Another entirely different method for top-k query processing is the score-at-a-time (SAAT) approach. Anh et al. [2] made the observation that the term weight for any given document could be pre-computed and stored, rather than the term frequencies. Since the term weights are typically floating point numbers, they are quantized into integer values to facilitate compression [2], the range of which impacts both effectiveness and efficiency [15]. For SAAT processing, each postings list is sorted by *decreasing* impact score, which allows the most high scoring documents for each term to be processed first, and can allow for early termination without sacrificing effectiveness. Recently, Lin and Trotman [32] introduced JASS, a modern SAAT algorithm which can be used for *anytime* retrieval, making it suitable for use in time-constrained environments and for controlling tail latency.

Tail Latency. The tail latency of a system corresponds to the response times occurring above some high percentile, such as the 95th, 99th or even the 99.99th percentile [27, 57]. As collections grow larger, systems must scale accordingly. As systems become more complex, the probability of increasing the tail latency also increases [18], particularly for distributed architectures where end-to-end latency is often bound by the slowest component. Reducing the tail latency can be addressed through either hardware or software optimizations, or both. For example, replicating and partitioning collections [18, 22, 28] allows effective load balancing which can reduce the system tail latency.

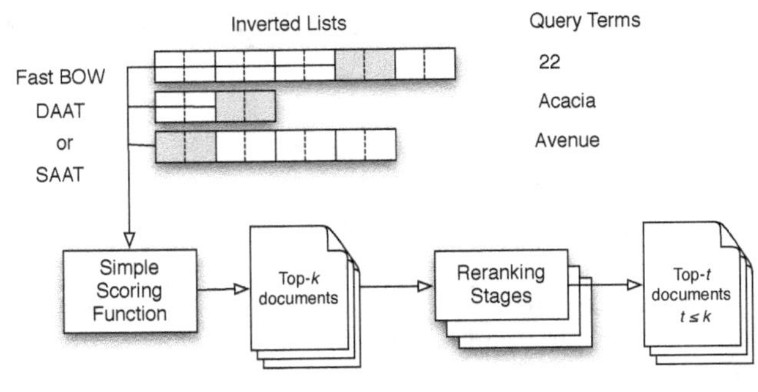

Figure 1: Architecture of a typical multi-stage retrieval system. Queries are first processed using an efficient bag-of-words retrieval algorithm. The initial candidate set of k documents then undergoes a series of re-ranking stages where the candidate pool is shrunk, and more expensive learning-to-rank algorithms are used to produce a final set of top-t documents to return to the user, where often $t \ll k$.

Previous work has attempted to reduce the tail response times in a range of different contexts. Jeon et al. [25] focus on 99th percentile tail latency at the level of a single *Index Server Node* (ISN) by predicting long running queries, and running them in parallel. Queries that are *not* predicted as long running are processed sequentially, which avoids the overhead cost of parallelization. Another recent work targets reducing the extreme tail latency (at the 99.99th percentile) [24, 27]. This target is achieved through *Dynamic, Delayed, Selective* (DDS) prediction. DDS prediction works as follows. First, a new query is processed for a short time, such as 20ms, and dynamic features are collected from this initial processing. Then, new dynamic features (and, some additional static features) are used to predict whether the query is a long running query. If so, then the query will be accelerated using parallelization. The prediction error is also estimated, and is used to improve coverage of mispredicted true long running queries.

Multi-Stage Search Architectures. Multi-stage retrieval has become the dominant model in modern web search systems [3, 4, 9, 36, 37, 40]. In this approach, a set of candidate documents is generated that is likely to be relevant to a query, and then in one or more stages, the document sample is iteratively reduced and reordered using a series of increasingly expensive machine learning techniques. Since re-ordering can be computationally expensive and is sensitive to the number of documents that must be reordered, minimizing the size of the candidate set is an important problem [9, 12, 36, 48].

Figure 1 shows a typical multi-stage retrieval architecture. A fast bag-of-words retrieval algorithm produces a top-k candidate set. This initial set of documents is then re-ranked one or more times using a learning-to-rank algorithm to produce a final output set of t documents, where $t \leq k$, and can be $t \ll k$ in some configurations.

Efficiency remains an important problem in multi-stage retrieval, with papers focused on cascaded ranking [12, 40, 56], early exit optimizations [9, 17], and efficient candidate generation [4, 54]. Recently, Wang et al. [54] proposed a fast candidate generation framework which opts to build a two-layer index. The bottom layer is the standard inverted index, and the top layer is a single or dual-term auxiliary structure which stores a subset of the bottom layer documents, sorted by impact score. At query time, a prefix of the top layer is accessed, which is then refined by accessing the lower layer of the index, which was shown to be efficient in practice. Such an approach could easily be used within our framework as it essentially attempts to improve the efficiency of the candidate generation phase of multi-stage retrieval, but we leave this as future work.

Reference List Evaluation in Multi-Stage Retrieval. One obvious question arises when trying to measure trade-offs in multi-stage retrieval systems – how can we quantify the impact on effectiveness when modifying different components of the search system? One approach is to simply make changes to the system, and re-compute a standard information retrieval metric such as average precision (AP), expected reciprocal rank (ERR), normalized discounted cumulative gain (NDCG), or rank biased precision (RBP) on the last stage result [11, 39]. However, this is unwieldy in practice, as it can be very difficult to identify exactly what changes are resulting in effectiveness differences.

A more compelling approach is to compute intermediate results at different stages of re-ranking, and measure the differences between the two. For example, in a simple two-stage system, we could generate the top-k list for both stages and somehow measure the similarity or difference between the two runs. We refer to this as a *reference list* comparison. There is now a large body of work on using reference lists for evaluation [13, 45, 46, 55]. In this work, we use *Maximized Effectiveness Difference* (MED) where the exact gain function used to compute the difference can depend on any utility-based evaluation metric, such as ERR, DCG, or RBP [46]. MED has the additional advantage that if partial judgments are available for any of the queries, the information can be used directly for the final comparison.

3 METHODOLOGY

Problem Definition. First, we define the problem we aim to solve. Given a query q, a series of re-ranking stages R, and a target evaluation metric M for the final stage, how can we predict both k and the processing algorithm A for the initial (bag-of-words) stage such that k, processing time t, and effectiveness loss L are minimized without requiring relevance judgments?

Labelling for Prediction without Relevance Annotations. We now turn to answering RQ1, by proposing a reference list model for learning efficiency parameters on a query-by-query basis. Since we wish to learn how to predict k (and other performance parameters) without relevance judgments, we employ a labelling algorithm based on the MED reference list approach. Given a *gold-standard* ranking for a query (as defined by an effective ranking model), and

Algorithm 1: Finds the smallest value of k such that effectiveness loss is minimized between a bag-of-words candidate list and a final stage re-ranked list for a given query.

Input : A bag-of-words run $\mathcal{D}^a$, a corresponding re-ranked list $\mathcal{D}^b$ (the gold-standard), and a desired MED threshold, ϵ.

Output: The smallest value of k such that $\text{MED}(\text{Top}k\text{Prefix}(\mathcal{D}^a, k), \mathcal{D}^b) < \epsilon$.

```
currentMED ← 1.0
k ← 0
candidateSet ← ∅
while currentMED > ε do
    k ← k + 1
    candidateSet.Append(DocAtRankk(D^a, k))
    currentMED ← MED(candidateSet, D^b)
end
return k
```

a corresponding bag-of-words candidate list, we iteratively measure the MED on an increasing prefix of the candidate list with respect to the gold-standard ranking. The goal is to find the shortest prefix of the candidate list that would not result in significant effectiveness loss after re-ranking. Algorithm 1 shows the psuedocode for this labelling algorithm. Once the optimal k is found, it can be used as a label for training. We note that our psuedocode is defined using a naïve (linear) approach for simplicity. In practice, a binary search can be conducted to yield the optimal k more efficiently. For our MED calculation, we use only MED_{RBP} with a small target threshold of $\epsilon = 0.001$ as we wish to aggressively minimize effectiveness loss. Clarke et al. [13] showed that other common utility-based metrics could also easily be used such as MED_{ERR} and MED_{DCG}, but we do not explore that option in this work.

Generating Gold Standard Rankings. In order to accurately label parameter values using a reference list approach, we need a ground truth which represents an idealized last stage run over a large corpus of queries. This idealized last stage represents the trusted reference list for which all comparisons can be made. In order to build a competitive "last stage" reference list, we train a Risk-Sensitive LambdaMart model using the JForests library [23, 52], and 687 queries from the 2009 Million Query Track (MQ2009) query set, which have shallow relevance judgments. A set of 400 commonly used LtR features were used in the model, and significant effectiveness improvements were observed when testing the model using the 2009 ClueWeb09 Adhoc query set.

Following Clarke et al. [13], we also tested our entire prediction framework using the `uogTRMQdph40` run as a reference list, as it was one of the top scoring systems that returned results for all of the Million Query Track topics. We found that all of the results produced are comparable independent of the reference list used. The key point is that *any* reference list can be used as long as it is consistently "better" than the first stage method being evaluated. For example, the wins/ties/losses for our URisk model compared to the Okapi BM25 baseline with NDCG@10 is 33 (0.1793)/6/10

(0.0786), where the numbers in parentheses correspond to the average differences in score. Building the best reference list is an interesting problem in its own right, but beyond the scope of this work. In the interest of succinctness, we only report results from our own end-to-end system here.

Parameter Prediction using Regression. Recently, Culpepper et al. [16] described an effective approach of dynamically predicting k while minimizing effectiveness loss. The key idea was to use the reference list methodology described above to build ground truth labels to train a classifier. However, their approach has a few drawbacks. First, the cascade classifier they described is interesting but unconventional in that it requires multiple predictions to be made, depending on the final k. Fewer predictions are required for small k, but up to 8 independent predictions are required for large k. Secondly, the problem they describe is really a regression problem in practice. Using regression allows an exact k to be predicted instead of an approximate cutoff, which translates into fewer documents being re-ranked in later stages of the retrieval system.

Commonly, regression methods estimate the conditional expectation of a target dependent variable y given the independent variables (or features) $\mathbf{x}$. This implies that the method approximates the average value of the dependent variable when the independent variables are fixed. Given training data of the form $(\mathbf{x_1}, y_1), \ldots, (\mathbf{x_n}, y_n)$ methods based on least squares try to optimize the loss function $L(\mathbf{x}, y) = \frac{1}{n}\sum_{i=1}^{n}\frac{1}{2}(\mathbf{x_i} - y_i)^2$, which results in a good estimator for the mean $E[y|\mathbf{x}]$.

So, the obvious way to reproduce their work is to use a similar feature set, and compute the exact k needed for each query that achieves a very small expected MED loss, say, $\epsilon < 0.001$, and use a random forest to produce the predictions. When we build this training set, one immediate problem becomes apparent – the ground truth labels do not follow a standard distribution, but an out-of-the-box regression algorithm *does*. Figure 2 shows three different distributions – the true distribution of k in the ground truth set (Oracle), the random forest prediction ($\text{RF}_{0.001}$), and a quantile regression prediction (QR_{τ}), which is described now.

A pitfall of standard regression methods is that they may become unstable under heavy-tailed distributions due to the dominant effects of outliers, or more precisely, when samples from the tail of the distribution have a strong influence on the mean. How to cope with this problem has been studied in the context of *robust estimation*. These estimators embody a family of methods designed to be more resilient to the data generation process by not following the underlying assumptions behind the regressor; in the context of least squares, this would be errors being uncorrelated and having the same variance.

One simple way of dealing with the outlier problem is *quantile regression*, which estimates either the conditional median or other quantiles of the response variable. If y has a cumulative distribution of $F_y(z) = p(y \leq z)$ then the τ-th quantile of y is given by $Q_y(\tau) = F_y^{-1} = \inf\{z : F_y(z) \geq \tau\}$. To learn a regressor that minimizes a τ value, we define the loss function $\xi_\tau(y) = y(\tau - I\{y < 0\})$ where $I\{\cdot\}$ is the indicator function. Therefore, τ-th quantile regression estimates the conditional τ-th quantile $F_{y|\mathbf{x}}^{-1}(\tau)$, or we want

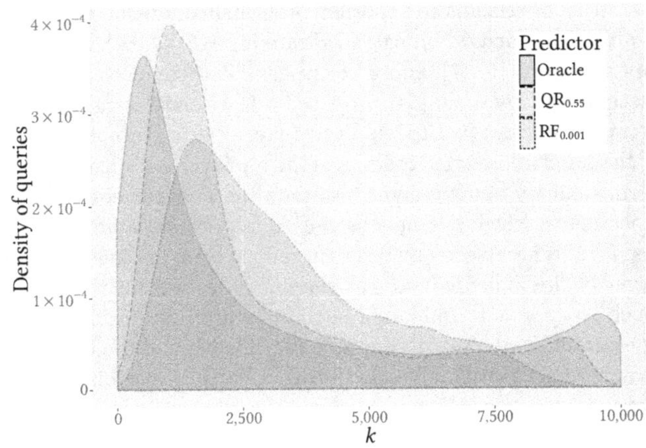

Figure 2: A comparison of the distributions of actual k versus predicted k when using a Random Forest regression and a Quantile Regression in first stage retrieval for the 26,959 queries from the MQ2009 TREC Task. Note that the Random Forest uses a training value of $\epsilon = 0.001$, whereas the best-fit distribution for the Quantile Regression was $\tau = 0.55$ for k.

an estimate $\hat{f}_\tau$ such that $p(y < \hat{f}_\tau(\mathbf{x})) = \tau$:

$$\hat{f}_\tau = \underset{f \in \mathcal{F}_\tau}{\operatorname{argmin}} \sum_{i=1}^{n} \xi_\tau(y_i - f(\mathbf{x_i})) = \quad (1)$$

$$\underset{f \in \mathcal{F}_\tau}{\operatorname{argmin}} \left[(1-\tau) \sum_{y_i < f(\mathbf{x_i})} |y_i - f(\mathbf{x_i})| + \tau \sum_{y_i \geq f(\mathbf{x_i})} |y_i - f(\mathbf{x_i})| \right], \quad (2)$$

where $\mathcal{F}_\tau$ is a predetermined class of functions.

A robust regression method is *random forests* (RF), which build several decision trees using attribute bagging. In a nutshell, the algorithm samples with replacement the training data B times and trains several decision trees f_b using only each portion of the data. The final prediction for an incoming new query is averaged from all the regressors $\hat{f} = \frac{1}{B}\sum_{i=1}^{B} f_B(\mathbf{x})$. Subsampling has the practical effect of decreasing the variance of the model, without increasing its complexity, given that even if the predictions of a single tree are highly sensitive to noise, the average of many trees is not (as long as the trees are not correlated). Bootstrapping achieves this effect by training each tree with a different randomized subsample.

When the individual trees f_b are learned, the building procedure creates tree nodes that branch data down the tree; in order to reduce the model variance, only a few features are candidates for splitting at each round. This mitigates the effect that happens when, if just a few features are very strong predictors for y, these features will be selected in many of the B trees, which become correlated.

We deploy the quantile regression within the same tree framework using gradient boosting regression trees (GBRT). In this case, each tree re-fits the training data using the residuals (gradients) of the training data with respect to the ξ_τ loss function, and a per-tree weight is calculated using line search. The final decision is a linear combination of the weighted prediction of the tree ensemble.

Parameter Prediction Features. For predicting the performance parameters, we used a similar set of features as Culpepper et al. [16].

These features are based on aggregating statistics for each postings list (such as maximum scores, harmonic/arithmetic mean/median scores, and so on) from a range of similarity functions, along with query specific features such as query length, max score of query terms, and many more. In addition to the TF·IDF, BM25 and query likelihood used by Culpepper et al. [16], we also build features using Bose-Einstein, DPH, and DFR similarity functions [1]. We also added the geometric mean as an aggregation statistic for each of these similarity functions. We used a total of 147 features for predicting parameters, and refer the reader to the work of Culpepper et al. [16] for a more detailed description of these features.

Experimental Setup. All experiments were executed on an idle 24-core Intel Xeon E5-2690 with 512 GB of RAM hosting RedHat RHEL v7.2. ATIRE [50] was used to parse and index the ClueWeb09B collection, which was stopped using the default Indri stoplist, and stemmed using an *s*-stemmer. Timings were conducted using publicly available implementations of BMW[1] and JASS,[2] which use QMX compression [49, 51] and the BM25 scoring model. Each query is processed 5 times, and the average of the 5 runs is reported. Boxplots are standard Tukey plots, and diamonds in each box denote the mean value. For the prediction tasks, we use the 2009 Million Query Track queries. Single term queries were filtered from all test, train, and validation sets, as they can be answered trivially by taking the first k documents from the relevant postings list of the impact-ordered ISN. In addition, we filtered out queries which contained out-of-vocabulary terms, and the queries which were used to train the URisk gold-standard system, resulting in a set of 26,959 unique queries. For all predictions, queries were randomly assigned to 10 folds, and standard 10 fold cross validation was performed to produce the query predictions.

4 PRELIMINARY EXPERIMENTS

The improved approach to predicting k in first stage retrieval (Figure 2) is a promising first step to achieving efficient results without sacrificing effectiveness. However, assuming that the performance of WAND-based algorithms in the first stage is a function of k may not be correct in practice [14].

Tail-Latency in DAAT Algorithms. Crane et al. [14] showed that when using WAND and BMW, outlier response times can occur at any k cutoff, making performance guarantees hard to enforce in production systems. The alternative to using WAND or BMW in the first stage retrieval is to use a SAAT algorithm such as JASS. Unfortunately, this is not an entirely satisfactory answer either as most of the performance gains in JASS come from using aggressive early termination, which can hurt effectiveness when the number of documents that must be passed to the next stage must also be minimized. So, rank safety is yet another confounding factor. DAAT and SAAT processing algorithms can sacrifice effectiveness for efficiency by relaxing the rank-safety constraint. For example, JASS allows a parameter ρ to be set which bounds the maximum number of postings to score per query, and variants of WAND can use a parameter F which induces more aggressive skipping during

[1]http://github.com/JMMackenzie/Quant-BM-WAND
[2]http://github.com/lintool/JASS/

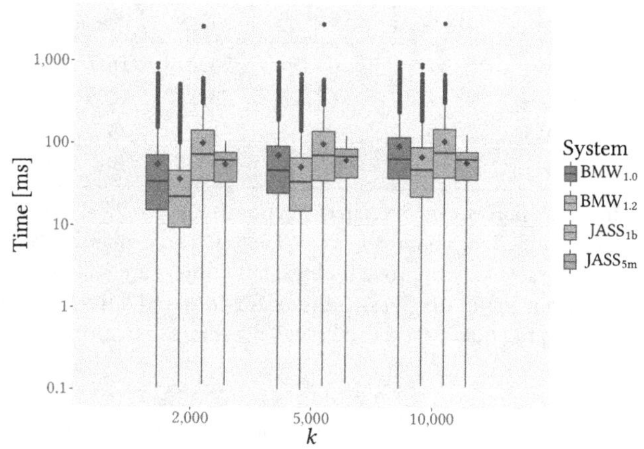

Figure 3: Efficiency comparison of the 26,959 queries from the MQ2009 TREC Task using both aggressive and rank-safe versions of BMW and JASS. Subscripts denote the aggression parameters (F for BMW and ρ for JASS).

postings list traversal. So, there is a trade-off between retrieval depth k and rank safety in a pure efficiency sense. This relationship was previously explored by Tonellotto et al. [48], who also used a query difficulty prediction framework to solve the problem. We build on this idea in this work, but also account for the fact that using only WAND-based algorithms can still result in high percentile latencies. We can see that boosting F alone does indeed make BMW faster in Figure 3, but the high tail latency remains.

Our next task is to explore the likelihood of long-running queries when using the MQ2009 topic set. Crane et al. [14] performed a comparative analysis with the UQV [6] query set and the ClueWeb12B document collection with fixed values of k. We reproduce their work here across our own query set and fixed k values. Figure 3 shows the breakdown of all 26,959 queries across a number of fixed values of k, selected as appropriate sizes for an LtR system [36]. Similar to Crane et al., we observe that the exhaustive BMW algorithm is superior to the exhaustive JASS algorithm, but the aggressive JASS traversal (with the recommended 10% heuristic) has a much lower tail latency. On the other hand, the aggressive BMW traversal does improve the mean and median times, but does not adequately reduce the high percentile latency. Note that we selected the value for the heuristic, $F = 1.2$, based on other work that shows that more aggressive approaches result in reduced effectiveness [13]. It is also noteworthy that the exhaustive BMW traversal has a faster median time than the aggressive JASS traversal when $k \leq 5{,}000$.

To further explore the relationship between the tail latency and the index traversal algorithm (RQ2), we do a simple overlap analysis on the slowest running 5% of queries for each algorithm. Table 1 shows the percentage of the tail latencies that overlap between each system, where $k = 2{,}000$. Exact JASS, exact BMW and aggressive BMW tend to share similar queries in the slowest running 5%. However, we note that the aggressive JASS traversal tends to share only a small percentage of the tail latencies that occur in the other systems.

In light of this new evidence, a pragmatic hypothesis emerges: Can we somehow combine the best properties of JASS and BMW to create a hybrid approach that captures the best of both worlds?

	BMW1.1	BMW1.2	JASS1b	JASS5m
BMW1.0	86.0	61.7	56.2	16.7
BMW1.1	-	67.4	53.1	18.3
BMW1.2	-	-	42.3	24.2
JASS1b	-	-	-	8.0

Table 1: The percentage overlap of queries that fall in $95 \le x \le 100$ percentile efficiency band for $k = 2{,}000$. Clearly, making BMW more aggressive may improve timings, but outliers are still present. On the other hand, it is less common for JASS and BMW to have overlapping tail queries, especially when a non-exhaustive ρ value is used.

Algorithm 2: Candidate generation pipeline based on predicting k

Input : A query q, a regressor $\mathcal{R}_k$ that predicts the required k for q, a regressor $\mathcal{R}_\rho$ that predicts the required ρ for JASS up to a maximum ρ value $\rho_{\max}$, and a k-threshold T_k

Output: A set of candidate documents, C

$C \leftarrow \emptyset$

$P_k \leftarrow \mathcal{R}_k(q)$

if $P_k > T_k$ **then**

  $P_\rho \leftarrow \mathcal{R}_\rho(q)$

  $C \leftarrow \text{ISN}_{\text{JASS}}(q, P_k, P_\rho)$

else

  $C \leftarrow \text{ISN}_{\text{BMW}}(q, P_k)$

end

return C

5 HYBRID ARCHITECTURE

The first major difference in our approach with respect to 'standard' systems is that we opt to build a hybrid architecture. Work on distributed IR has shown that an effective approach to scaling is to replicate popular indexes [18, 22, 28, 29]. Here, we assume that we can build ISNs that are optimized for different types of queries. In other words, when we build replicas, we may opt to build a document-ordered index (appropriate for DAAT traversal), or an impact-ordered index (appropriate for SAAT traversal). This idea is key to our novel framework: Selecting algorithm $a \in A$ actually refers to selecting an ISN to process the query which is configured to run algorithm a, and ISN selection is already a common problem in distributed search architectures [7, 27]. In practice, our "Stage-0" predictions would be performed by the resource selection process in a large scale distributed IR system.

Based on several observations about the relative performance of JASS and BMW, we are now in a position to describe a few different hybrid approaches to query processing, and to answer RQ2. Our goal is to limit the disadvantages of each traversal algorithm, and exploit the desirable properties. Several different variations were used in our preliminary experiments, and the best is shown here. The first step in the pipeline is to predict the k cutoff. If k is greater than the threshold T_k, then proceed to the JASS pipeline as outlined in Algorithm 2, If JASS is used, a prediction for ρ is made, but capped at $\rho_{\max}$, which allows us to achieve the desired performance guarantees. In our experiments, $\rho_{\max}$ = 5 million postings as this requires less than 200 ms on our current hardware configuration, and does not result in a significant loss of effectiveness for early precision metrics across ClueWeb09B [32]. The remaining queries are processed using BMW with rank-safety. We also experimented with a pipeline which predicted the run-time of the incoming query (as well as k), and used JASS if the predicted run-time was greater than 200ms, but its performance is comparable to the simpler model, so we do not report it in the interest of space.

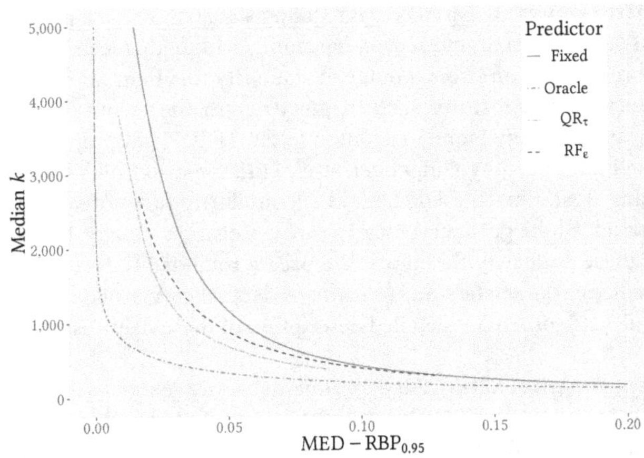

Figure 4: MED_{RBP} versus median k for all ϵ thresholds between 0.001 and 0.200 when using a Random Forest regression, and for all τ values between 0.10 and 0.75 with $\epsilon = 0.001$ for Quantile Regression, in first stage retrieval for the 26,959 queries from the MQ2009 TREC Task. Note that the Quantile Regression clearly improves the median k (compared with Random Forests) without negatively affecting the mean k.

6 EXPERIMENTS

We now look at the various predictions that are necessary to achieve our performance goals. Our performance requirement for effectiveness is a MED score that is low enough to result in no measurable effectiveness difference for the target metric. Our performance requirement for efficiency targets reducing high percentile tail latency in the candidate generation stage, while also attempting to reduce the size of both k and ρ in a query dependent way.

Predicting k. First, we validate that our new approach to k prediction using quantile regression is effective. Using our newly devised regression technique, we can compare the efficiency and effectiveness trade-offs between the size of the candidate retrieval set k, and the expected effectiveness loss MED_{RBP}. Figure 4 shows the predictive power of a random forest (RF_ϵ) and quantile regression (QR_τ) when compared to the oracle results for the MED_{RBP} target $\epsilon = [0.001, 0.20]$ and to using a fixed cutoff for all queries. Since the distribution of the true k values is skewed for the queries as shown in Figure 2, presenting the results using the median more accurately captures the trade-offs.

Predicting ρ. Based on the lessons learned when attempting to build a robust prediction framework for k, we now turn our attention to the aggressiveness parameter ρ in JASS. Previous work has

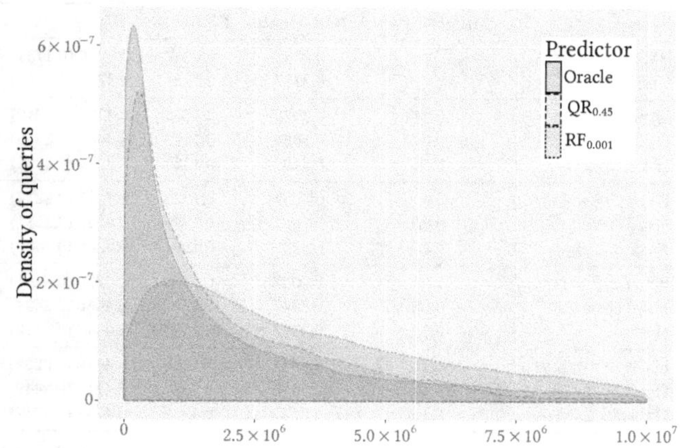

Figure 5: A comparison of the distributions the actual ρ vs the predicted ρ when using a Random Forest regression and a Quantile Regression in first stage retrieval for the 26,959 queries from the MQ2009 TREC Task. The best-fit distribution for the Quantile Regression was $\tau = 0.45$ for ρ.

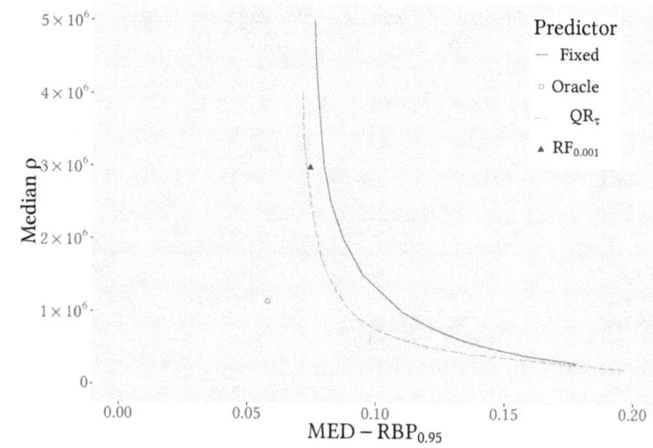

Figure 6: MED$_{RBP}$ versus median ρ. The RF model was trained to target a MED$_{RBP}$ of 0.001, and the QR model plots the various quantile points from $\tau = 0.15$ to $\tau = 0.75$. Quantile Regression and Random Forests behave similarly with respect to the median ρ, but QR is still preferred as the final predicted ρ distribution fits better with the idealized results as shown in Figure 5.

shown that using an exhaustive ρ results in effective top-k retrieval, however, using a heuristic ρ can give similar effectiveness, yet much more efficient retrieval [31, 32]. The recommended heuristic value of ρ is 10% of the size of the collection [32], which is around 5 million for the ClueWeb09B collection. Figure 5 shows the distribution of ρ values required to when targeting a MED$_{RBP}$ < 0.001, which aggressively targets no measurable difference in the results lists between exhaustive and aggressive JASS traversals. Clearly, the majority of the distribution lies well to the lower side of the 10% heuristic value. This motivates us to predict ρ on a query-by-query basis. Again, we deploy both a Random Forest and a Gradient Quantile Regression method as the distribution of ρ is skewed, and build a suitable `find_rho` algorithm, similar to `find_k` (Algorithm 1), to label the prediction training data.

Figure 6 shows the median predicted ρ values compared with the fixed and oracle. Both the QR and RF regression methods manage to improve on the fixed ρ median. Note that when measuring the MED$_{RBP}$ for this experiment (and subsequently, training the value of ρ), the k utilized was the optimal value of k from the previous experiment. The reason for using this k is that we must fix k, otherwise our effectiveness scores may change as a result of k, not just ρ. Indeed, this setting of k also allows us to find the true optimal MED$_{RBP}$ for JASS, denoted by the oracle point in Figure 6.

Putting It All Together. Here, we show that by combining all of our predictions into hybrid first-stage retrieval systems, outlined in Algorithm 2, we can achieve effectiveness equal to a fixed parameter system, while controlling various early and late-stage efficiency parameters, thus answering RQ3.

Figure 7 shows the performance for 4 different MED$_{RBP}$ cut-offs: 0.04, 0.06, 0.08, and 0.10. We present JASS$_{1b}$, JASS$_{5m}$ and BMW$_{1.0}$, which refer to using a fixed k and ρ for all queries. For these baselines, k was selected such that the mean MED value was equivalent to the target epsilon. We also report the results of the hybrid system based on Algorithm 2 (Hybrid-k-τ), which uses quantile regression

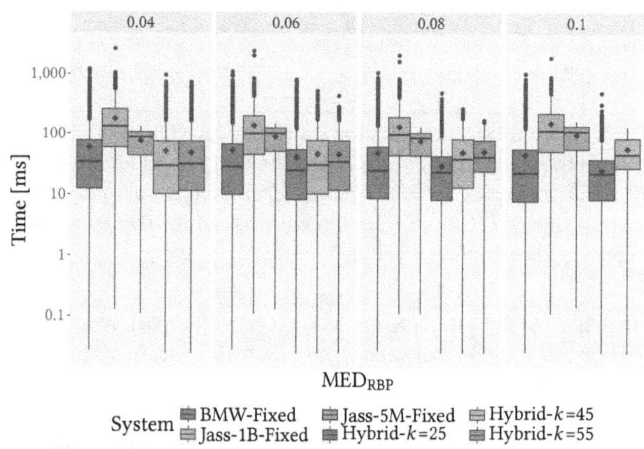

Figure 7: The response time for each system for different bands of MED$_{RBP}$ in the candidate generation stage. Different configurations of the hybrid approach can bridge the gap between the BMW and JASS systems across different MED targets, allowing for more finely-grained trade-offs.

for per-query predictions of both k and ρ. Note that the labels denote the τ value which was used to predict k using the QR predictor. For the ρ prediction, we only show results using the QR predictor with $\tau = 45$, although we can create more finely grained trade-offs by employing other values of τ. Additionally, Table 2 shows the median k, as well as the time characteristics for the systems presented in Figure 7.

Our results show that our hybrid system both outperform the equivalent fixed BMW or JASS approaches for the given MED targets. For example, with a target of MED$_{RBP}$ $= 0.02$, our hybrid systems can achieve a mean and median query response time around 10 ms, and 5 ms below the best fixed system, respectively, while also requiring a lower median k, which results in additional downstream

System	Median k	Mean time	Median time	95th perc. latency
		MED-RBP$_{0.95}$ = 0.04		
BMW	1598	60.2	34.0	205.6
JASS$_{1b}$	1598	178.7	132.7	473.0
JASS$_{5m}$	2970	75.6	87.1	**114.1**
Hybrid-k = 25	-	-	-	-
Hybrid-k = 45	**1148**	50.8	**29.3**	149.9
Hybrid-k = 55	1660	**48.1**	31.4	126.9
		MED-RBP$_{0.95}$ = 0.06		
BMW	889	52.7	28.4	183.4
JASS$_{1b}$	889	131.2	101.4	368.7
JASS$_{5m}$	1913	89.9	102.5	139.7
Hybrid-k = 25	**631**	**40.9**	**25.0**	132.8
Hybrid-k = 45	1148	46.2	30.6	121.9
Hybrid-k = 55	1659	45.6	34.5	**110.0**
		MED-RBP$_{0.95}$ = 0.08		
BMW	**578**	48.3	25.2	171.2
JASS$_{1b}$	**578**	134.1	98.1	357.4
JASS$_{5m}$	1324	75.6	86.6	119.8
Hybrid-k = 25	631	**29.3**	**23.3**	**73.4**
Hybrid-k = 45	1148	49.1	38.4	120.9
Hybrid-k = 55	1659	50.3	41.0	109.3
		MED-RBP$_{0.95}$ = 0.10		
BMW	**419**	44.3	22.6	158.2
JASS$_{1b}$	**419**	154.4	114.4	409.4
JASS$_{5m}$	959	97.7	111.5	152.2
Hybrid-k = 25	631	**25.4**	**22.1**	**59.8**
Hybrid-k = 45	1148	56.2	45.2	120.7
Hybrid-k = 55	-	-	-	-

Table 2: Summary statistics for k and time. Each sub-table corresponds to a section of Figure 7, and the best values are bold. Our Hybrid approaches generally outperform the fixed parameter systems with respect to all time dimensions, while also sometimes improving the median k value.

efficiency. Although the fixed JASS$_{5m}$ system outperforms our hybrids in reducing the tail latency, it must retrieve a larger number of documents to achieve the same effectiveness target, which has negative implications on the efficiency of the following stages. As we relax the MED target, the hybrid systems tend to require a slightly larger median k than the fixed parameter systems, but tend to perform much more efficiently in the early-stage efficiency dimensions. For example, the Hybrid-k=25 system has a mean, median and 95th percentile latency that is 18.9, 0.5, and 98.4 ms faster than the best fixed system, at the cost of requiring 212 more documents per query (based on the median) when targeting a MED$_{\text{RBP}}$ of 0.10. Note that we do not consider the time required to make our predictions, but this cost is an order of magnitude less than the run times being achieved. Recent work using similar models show a prediction overhead of < 0.75 ms per prediction [25], and this approach can be directly applied here.

Validating Robustness. As a final test of robustness, we run both our hybrid and fixed systems across the 50 (unseen) TREC 2009 Web Track queries. These queries were held out from the train and test procedures reported in earlier sections, and were used to validate the URisk model (our baseline here). Since these queries only have judgments to depth 12, we report NDCG@10, ERR@10 and

System	MED-RBP$_{0.95}$	NDCG@10	ERR@10	RBP p = 0.80
BM25	-	0.2055	0.0957	0.3070 (0.1734)
URisk-ideal	-	0.3102	0.1354	0.4250 (0.2195)
Fixed (BMW/JASS$_{1b}$)	0.04	0.3027	0.1305	0.4176 (0.2240)
Fixed (JASS$_{5m}$)	0.04	0.3028	0.1291	0.4005 (0.2503)
Hybrid	0.04	0.3107	0.1357	0.4221 (0.2220)
Fixed (BMW/JASS$_{1b}$)	0.06	0.3052	0.1320	0.4215 (0.2214)
Fixed (JASS$_{5m}$)	0.06	0.3057	0.1299	0.4028 (0.2531)
Hybrid	0.06	0.3139	0.1361	0.4265 (0.2320)
Fixed (BMW/JASS$_{1b}$)	0.08	0.3082	0.1336	0.4226 (0.2161)
Fixed (JASS$_{5m}$)	0.08	0.3047	0.1309	0.4066 (0.2484)
Hybrid	0.08	0.3137	0.1353	0.4247 (0.2312)
Fixed (BMW/JASS$_{1b}$)	0.10	0.2945	0.1270	0.4110 (0.2204)
Fixed (JASS$_{5m}$)	0.10	0.3090	0.1321	0.4114 (0.2449)
Hybrid	0.10	0.3137	0.1352	0.4247 (0.2312)

Table 3: Effectiveness measurements taken across the held-out query set. No statistical significance was measured between the hybrid systems with respect to the ideal system (URisk-ideal), using the two one-sided test with $p < 0.05$. We used the Hybrid-k = 45 system for this comparison, although the results are not significantly different to the other Hybrid parameterizations.

RBP$_{0.80}$ [33]. For the hybrid systems, we used the same prediction configuration that was used in the tasks from Figure 7 and Table 2.

Table 3 shows the effectiveness measurements. Remarkably, our hybrid systems have no loss in effectiveness when computing an complete end-to-end run. We confirm this observation using a two one-sided test [44] of equivalence (TOST). For each TOST, we set the acceptable range of inequality to ±1%. We found that the ideal system is not statistically significantly different than our hybrid systems, with $p < 0.001$. We also observe that our system outperforms the fixed-parameter equivalents across these 50 validation queries, although no statistical significance was detected.

7 CONCLUSION

We presented and validated a unified framework to predict a wide range of performance-sensitive parameters for early-stage candidate retrieval systems using MED [46] and reference lists as guides for training. Preliminary experiments show that the DAAT BMW approach is efficient but suffers from a comparatively large tail latency, while the SAAT JASS algorithm does not. A hybrid system based on this predictive framework was shown to minimize effectiveness loss while also minimizing query-latency across the candidate generation stage of the pipeline, providing improved trade-offs with respect to a standard, fixed-parameter system. Future work will involve exploring the design implications of the hybrid ISN approach, to quantify the trade-offs involved with the number of replicas required across the various hybrid parameterizations.

ACKNOWLEDGMENTS

This work was supported by the Australian Research Council's *Discovery Projects* Scheme (DP170102231), the Natural Sciences and Engineering Research Council of Canada, an Australian Government Research Training Program Scholarship, and a grant from the Mozilla Foundation. We thank Luke Gallagher for providing support with the Learning-to-Rank framework.

REFERENCES

[1] G. Amati and C. J. Van Rijsbergen. 2002. Probabilistic Models of Information Retrieval Based on Measuring the Divergence from Randomness. 20, 4 (2002), 357–389.

[2] V. N. Anh, O. de Kretser, and A. Moffat. 2001. Vector-Space Ranking with Effective Early Termination. In *Proc. SIGIR.* 35–42.

[3] N. Asadi and J. Lin. 2013. Document Vector Representations for Feature Extraction in Multi-Stage Document Ranking. *Inf. Retr.* 16, 6 (2013), 747–768.

[4] N. Asadi and J. Lin. 2013. Effectiveness/Efficiency Tradeoffs for Candidate Generation in Multi-Stage Retrieval Architectures. In *Proc. SIGIR.* 997–1000.

[5] N. Asadi, J. Lin, and A. P. De Vries. 2014. Runtime Optimizations for Tree-Based Machine Learning Models. *Trans. on Know. and Data Eng.* 26, 9 (2014), 2281–2292.

[6] P. Bailey, A. Moffat, F. Scholer, and P. Thomas. 2016. UQV100: A Test Collection with Query Variability. In *Proc. SIGIR.* 725–728.

[7] D. Broccolo, C. Macdonald, O. Salvatore, I. Ounis, R. Perego, F. Silvestri, and N. Tonellotto. 2013. Load-sensitive Selective Pruning for Distributed Search. In *Proc. CIKM.* 379–388.

[8] A. Z. Broder, D. Carmel, M. Herscovici, A. Soffer, and J. Y. Zien. 2003. Efficient Query Evaluation using a Two-Level Retrieval Process. In *Proc. CIKM.* 426–434.

[9] B. B. Cambazoglu, H. Zaragoza, O. Chapelle, J. Chen, C. Liao, Z. Zheng, and J. Degenhardt. 2010. Early Exit Optimizations for Additive Machine Learned Ranking Systems.. In *Proc. WSDM.* 411–420.

[10] K. Chakrabarti, S. Chaudhuri, and V. Ganti. 2011. Interval-based Pruning for Top-k Processing over Compressed Lists. In *Proc. ICDE.* 709–720.

[11] O. Chapelle, D. Metzler, Y. Zhang, and P. Grinspan. 2009. Expected Reciprocal Rank for Graded Relevance. In *Proc. CIKM.* 621–630.

[12] R-C. Cheng, L. Gallagher, R. Blanco, and J. S. Culpepper. 2017. Efficient Cost-Aware Cascade Ranking in Multi-Stage Retrieval. In *Proc. SIGIR.* 445–454.

[13] C. L. A. Clarke, J. S. Culpepper, and A. Moffat. 2016. Assessing Efficiency–Effectiveness Tradeoffs in Multi-Stage Retrieval Systems without using Relevance Judgments. *Inf. Retr.* 19, 4 (2016), 351–377.

[14] M. Crane, J. S. Culpepper, J. Lin, J. Mackenzie, and A. Trotman. 2017. A Comparison of Document-at-a-Time and Score-at-a-Time Query Evaluation. In *Proc. WSDM.* 201–210.

[15] M. Crane, A. Trotman, and R. O'Keefe. 2013. Maintaining Discriminatory Power in Quantized Indexes. In *Proc. CIKM.* 1221–1224.

[16] J. S. Culpepper, C. L. A. Clarke, and J. Lin. 2016. Dynamic Cutoff Prediction in Multi-Stage Retrieval Systems. In *Proc. ADCS.* 17–24.

[17] V. Dang, M. Bendersky, and W. B. Croft. 2013. Two-Stage Learning to Rank for Information Retrieval. In *Proc. ECIR.* 423–434.

[18] J. Dean and L. A. Barroso. 2013. The Tail at Scale. *Comm. ACM* 56, 2 (2013), 74–80.

[19] C. Dimopoulos, S. Nepomnyachiy, and T. Suel. 2013. Optimizing Top-k Document Retrieval Strategies for Block-Max Indexes. In *Proc. WSDM.* 113–122.

[20] S. Ding and T. Suel. 2011. Faster Top-k Document Retrieval Using Block-Max Indexes. In *Proc. SIGIR.* 993–1002.

[21] M. Fontoura, V. Josifovski, J. Liu, S. Venkatesan, X. Zhu, and J. Zien. 2011. Evaluation Strategies for Top-k Queries over Memory-resident Inverted Indexes. *Proc. VLDB* 4, 12 (2011), 1213–1224.

[22] G. Francès, X. Bai, B. B. Cambazoglu, and R. Baeza-Yates. 2014. Improving the Efficiency of Multi-site Web Search Engines. In *Proc. WSDM.* 3–12.

[23] Y. Ganjisaffar, R. Caruana, and C. Lopes. 2011. Bagging Gradient-Boosted Trees for High Precision, Low Variance Ranking Models. In *Proc. SIGIR.* 85–94.

[24] S-W. Hwang, K. Saehoon, Y. He, S. Elnikety, and S. Choi. 2016. Prediction and Predictability for Search Query Acceleration. *ACM Trans. Web* 10, 3 (Aug. 2016), 19.1–19.28.

[25] M. Jeon, S. Kim, S-W. Hwang, Y. He, S. Elnikety, A. L. Cox, and S. Rixner. 2014. Predictive Parallelization: Taming Tail Latencies in Web Search. In *Proc. SIGIR.* 253–262.

[26] X. Jin, T. Yang, and X. Tang. 2016. A Comparison of Cache Blocking Methods for Fast Execution of Ensemble-based Score Computation. In *Proc. SIGIR.* 629–638.

[27] S. Kim, Y. He, S-W. Hwang, S. Elnikety, and S. Choi. 2015. Delayed-Dynamic-Selective (DDS) Prediction for Reducing Extreme Tail Latency in Web Search. In *Proc. WSDM.* 7–16.

[28] Y. Kim, J. Callan, J. S. Culpepper, and A. Moffat. 2016. Efficient Distributed Selective Search. *Inf. Retr.* (2016), 1–32.

[29] Y. Kim, J. Callan, J. S. Culpepper, and A. Moffat. 2016. Load-Balancing in Distributed Selective Search. In *Proc. SIGIR.* 905–908.

[30] D. Lemire and L. Boytsov. 2015. Decoding Billions of Integers Per Second through Vectorization. *Soft. Prac. & Exp.* 45, 1 (2015), 1–29.

[31] J. Lin, M. Crane, A. Trotman, J. Callan, I. Chattopadhyaya, J. Foley, G. Ingersoll, C. Macdonald, and S. Vigna. 2016. Toward Reproducible Baselines: The Open-Source IR Reproducibility Challenge. In *Proc. ECIR.* 408–420.

[32] J. Lin and A. Trotman. 2015. Anytime Ranking for Impact-Ordered Indexes. In *Proc. ICTIR.* 301–304.

[33] X. Lu, A. Moffat, and J. S. Culpepper. 2016. The Effect of Pooling and Evaluation Depth on IR Metrics. *Inf. Retr.* 19, 4 (2016), 416–445.

[34] C. Lucchese, F. M. Nardini, S. Orlando, R. Perego, N. Tonellotto, and R. Venturini. 2015. QuickScorer: A Fast Algorithm to Rank Documents with Additive Ensembles of Regression Trees. In *Proc. SIGIR.* 73–82.

[35] C. Lucchese, F. M. Nardini, S. Orlando, R. Perego, N. Tonellotto, and R. Venturini. 2016. Exploiting CPU SIMD Extensions to Speed-up Document Scoring with Tree Ensembles. In *Proc. SIGIR.* 833–836.

[36] C. Macdonald, R. L. T. Santos, and I. Ounis. 2013. The Whens and Hows of Learning to Rank for Web Search. *Inf. Retr.* 16, 5 (2013), 584–628.

[37] C. Macdonald, R. L. T. Santos, I. Ounis, and B. He. 2013. About Learning Models with Multiple Query-Dependent Features. *ACM Trans. Information Systems* 31, 3 (2013), 11.

[38] J. Mackenzie, F. M. Choudhury, and J. S. Culpepper. 2015. Efficient Location-aware Web Search. In *Proc. ADCS.* 4.1–4.8.

[39] A. Moffat and J. Zobel. 2008. Rank-Biased Precision for Measurement of Retrieval Effectiveness. *ACM Trans. Information Systems* 27, 1 (2008), 2.1–2.27.

[40] J. Pedersen. 2010. Query Understanding at Bing. *Invited talk, SIGIR* (2010).

[41] M. Petri, J. S. Culpepper, and A. Moffat. 2013. Exploring the Magic of WAND. In *Proc. ADCS.* 58–65.

[42] M. Petri, A. Moffat, and J. S. Culpepper. 2014. Score-safe Term Dependency Processing with Hybrid Indexes. In *Proc. SIGIR.* 899–902.

[43] C. Rossi, E. S. de Moura, A. L. Carvalho, and A. S. da Silva. 2013. Fast Document-at-a-time Query Processing Using Two-tier Indexes. In *Proc. SIGIR.* 183–192.

[44] D. J. Schuirmann. 1987. A Comparison of the Two One-Sided Tests Procedure and the Power Approach for Assessing the Equivalence of Average Bioavailability. *J. Pharmacokinetics and Biopharmaceutics* 15, 6 (1987), 657–680.

[45] A. Shtok, O. Kurland, and D. Carmel. 2016. Query Performance Prediction Using Reference Lists. *ACM Trans. Information Systems* 34, 4 (2016), 19.1–19.34.

[46] L. Tan and C. L. A. Clarke. 2015. A Family of Rank Similarity Measures Based on Maximized Effectiveness Difference. *Trans. on Know. and Data Eng.* 27, 11 (2015), 2865–2877.

[47] N. Tonellotto, C. Macdonald, and I. Ounis. 2011. Effect of Different Docid Orderings on Dynamic Pruning Retrieval Strategies. In *Proc. SIGIR.* 1179–1180.

[48] N. Tonellotto, C. Macdonald, and I. Ounis. 2013. Efficient and Effective Retrieval using Selective Pruning. In *Proc. WSDM.* 63–72.

[49] A. Trotman. 2014. Compression, SIMD, and Postings Lists. In *Proc. ADCS.* 50.50–50.57.

[50] A. Trotman, X-F. Jia, and M. Crane. 2012. Towards an Efficient and Effective Search Engine. In *Wkshp. Open Source IR.* 40–47.

[51] A. Trotman and J. Lin. 2016. In Vacuo and In Situ Evaluation of SIMD Codecs. In *Proc. ADCS.* 1–8.

[52] L. Wang, P. N. Bennett, and K. Collins-Thompson. 2012. Robust Ranking Models via Risk-sensitive Optimization. In *Proc. SIGIR.* 761–770.

[53] L. Wang, J. Lin, and D. Metzler. 2011. A Cascade Ranking Model for Efficient Ranked Retrieval. In *Proc. SIGIR.* 105–114.

[54] Q. Wang, C. Dimpoloulos, and T. Suel. 2016. Fast First-Phase Candidate Generation for Cascading Rankers. In *Proc. SIGIR.* 295–304.

[55] W. Webber, A. Moffat, and J. Zobel. 2010. A Similarity Measure for Indefinite Rankings. *ACM Trans. Information Systems* 28, 4 (2010), 20.1–20.38.

[56] Z. Xu, M. J. Kusner, K. Q. Weinberger, M. Chen, and O. Chapelle. 2014. Classifier Cascades and Trees for Minimizing Feature Evaluation Cost. *J. of Machine Learning Research* 15 (2014), 2113–2144.

[57] J-M. Yun, Y. He, S. Elnikety, and S. Ren. 2015. Optimal Aggregation Policy for Reducing Tail Latency of Web Search. In *Proc. SIGIR.* 63–72.

[58] J. Zhang, X. Long, and T. Suel. 2008. Performance of Compressed Inverted List Caching in Search Engines. In *Proc. WWW.* 387–396.

[59] J. Zobel and A. Moffat. 2006. Inverted Files for Text Search Engines. *ACM Comp. Surv.* 38, 2 (2006), 6.1–6.56.

Index Compression Using Byte-Aligned ANS Coding and Two-Dimensional Contexts

Alistair Moffat
The University of Melbourne
Melbourne, Australia

Matthias Petri
The University of Melbourne
Melbourne, Australia

ABSTRACT

We examine approaches used for block-based inverted index compression, such as the OptPFOR mechanism, in which fixed-length blocks of postings data are compressed independently of each other. Building on previous work in which asymmetric numeral systems (ANS) entropy coding is used to represent each block, we explore a number of enhancements: (i) the use of two-dimensional conditioning contexts, with two aggregate parameters used in each block to categorize the distribution of symbol values that underlies the ANS approach, rather than just one; (ii) the use of a byte-friendly strategic mapping from symbols to ANS codeword buckets; and (iii) the use of a context merging process to combine similar probability distributions. Collectively, these improvements yield superior compression for index data, outperforming the reference point set by the Interp mechanism, and hence representing a significant step forward. We describe experiments using the 426 GiB gov2 collection and a new large collection of publicly-available news articles to demonstrate that claim, and provide query evaluation throughput rates compared to other block-based mechanisms.

KEYWORDS

Index compression; inverted index; postings list; entropy coder; asymmetric numeral systems

ACM Reference Format:
Alistair Moffat and Matthias Petri. 2018. Index Compression Using Byte-Aligned ANS Coding and Two-Dimensional Contexts. In *WSDM 2018: The Eleventh ACM International Conference on Web Search and Data Mining, February 5–9, 2018, Marina Del Rey, CA, USA.* ACM, New York, NY, USA, 9 pages. https://doi.org/10.1145/3159652.3159663

1 INTRODUCTION

The inverted index remains the primary structure used to provide fast querying to large text collections. An inverted index consists of a set of postings lists, each describing the locations and occurrences in the collection of a single term. Proposals for compactly storing postings lists include byte-aligned codes [22, 25]; word-aligned codes [2, 3, 23, 28]; and binary-packed approaches [12, 30].

The use of entropy-based approaches such as Huffman codes for index compression have also been considered in the past [6, 11, 17, 26], but have had little attention since. However the last eight years have seen reawakened interest in entropy coding as a result of the *asymmetric numeral systems* (ANS) mechanism developed by Jarek Duda [8–10], and in recent work we combined whole-of-index two-pass ANS coding with the VByte, Simple, and Packed approaches, obtaining improved compression effectiveness in each case [14].

Here we continue that investigation, focusing on packed arrangements in which fixed-length blocks of symbols are coded relative to a probability distribution identified by a *selector*. In particular, in the Packed+ANS approach we described [14], the selector was taken to be the binary magnitude of the largest value in the block. But – as was also observed in connection with the *packed frame of reference* (PFOR) mechanism [30] – using other selector values, and being willing to handle some sequence values as *exceptions*, has benefits. The flexibility provided by entropy-coding (rather than binary coding) then creates scope for improved compression, with symbol probabilities (and hence codeword lengths) fitted more closely to the underlying distribution. Entropy coding also allows further refinements, and one that we explore in detail in this work is the use of two-dimensional selectors, with two parameters (rather than one) used to summarize each block's distribution of values. We also introduce a revised mapping from symbol identifiers to ANS values that requires less memory, and provides byte-friendly output for exception values. The third area we investigate is that of context merging, with the goal of reducing the memory space required during decoding operations.

Experiments with two large document collections demonstrate the substantial compression effectiveness gains that can be achieved – consistently beating the Interp mechanism, the best-performing approach for nearly twenty years now – and as well show that query throughput speeds are relatively unaffected.

In the interests of reproducibility, all of our code is publicly available.

WSDM 2018, February 5–9, 2018, Marina Del Rey, CA, USA

ACM 978-1-4503-5581-0/18/02...$15.00
https://doi.org/10.1145/3159652.3159663

2 BACKGROUND

2.1 Index Compression

Inverted Indexing. A *postings list* is a sorted sequence of document identifiers ("docids") and corresponding within-document term frequency counts. The postings list for a term t of document frequency f_t consists of two disjoint sequences: a list $\langle d_{t,i} \mid 1 \le i \le f_t \rangle$ in which $d_{t,i}$ is the ordinal document number containing the ith occurrence of t; and a corresponding list $\langle f_{t,i} \mid 1 \le i \le f_t \rangle$ in which $f_{t,i}$ is the number of times t appears in document $d_{t,i}$. It is usual to take *gaps* within the sequence of docids, with $d_{t,1}$ stored unchanged, and then $d_{t,i+1} - d_{t,i}$ stored thereafter. This yields a distribution in which small values are common and large values are rare. The set of $f_{t,i}$ values already has the same property, without any further transformation being required.

Compression Approaches. Stored as 32-bit integers, each posting requires 64 bits. But the strong bias in favor of small values means that much more compact arrangements are possible. Traditional techniques such as Golomb, Rice, and Elias codes (see Witten et al. [26] for details) operate on a bit-by-bit basis, and are relatively slow during the decoding process. Compromises that allow faster decoding, but with reduced compression effectiveness, include the byte-based VByte mechanism [22, 25] and variants thereof [4, 5, 7]; and the word-based Simple approaches [2, 3, 23, 28]. At the other end of the scale, the Interp mechanism of Moffat and Stuiver [15] provides very good compression effectiveness, but with even slower decoding than the bit-based Golomb and Elias codes. Standard byte-oriented compression libraries can also be employed, with improved effectiveness achieved if VByte is used as a preprocessing step [20].

Packed Codes. The use of *packed* codes over fixed-length postings blocks has been a relatively recent development, with the key idea being to exploit any localized consistencies that exist. A fixed-length block of (typically) $B = 128$ consecutive values is processed as a unit, and represented as B same-width binary values, with the width indicated by a *selector* stored in the block header. In most arrangements a set of possible bit lengths is provided in advance via a set of options S. For example, the 16-element selector vector

$$S = \{0, 1, 2, 3, 4, 5, 6, 7, 8, 10, 12, 14, 16, 19, 22, 25\}, \qquad (1)$$

allows values up to 2^{25} to be represented, with (since $|S| = 16$) selectors represented in 4-bits. Each selector value $0 \leq \ell < |S|$ allows values in the range $1 \ldots 2^{S[\ell]}$ to be represented in the corresponding *payload*; overall, a block of B posting values coded via the selector ℓ requires $4 + S[\ell] \cdot B$ bits. Lemire and Boytsov [12] explore packed codes in detail and discuss implementation options. Trotman's [23] QMX approach combines the Simple and Packed approaches, using output blocks of either 128 bits or 256 bits.

Patched Frame of Reference. Zukowski et al. [30] noted that occasional larger-than-expected values are expensive with plain packed arrangements, and introduced the notion of *exceptions* – numbers bigger than $2^{S[\ell]}$ handled via a secondary mechanism. Their *patched frame of reference* (PFOR) approach chooses a bit-width $S[\ell]$ that covers most, but not all, of the B values in the block. The minority of values needing more than $S[\ell]$ bits are represented via a secondary mechanism, and "patched" into place once the rest of the block has been regenerated using the $S[\ell]$-bit codes. To determine each block's ℓ, in the Opt-PFOR variant an encode-time search is performed over likely values for ℓ, to determine the selector that yields the most compact overall package [12, 27].

Variable-Length Blocks. Ottaviano et al. [18, 19] describe techniques for partitioning the input into blocks of variable length, seeking to amortize the selector storage cost over larger input units when homogeneous data appears, and to allow smaller blocks to be constructed when the data values are more locally volatile. They employ and extend Elias-Fano codes, a mechanism with a range of properties, including the ability to provide support for fast intersection of postings lists, to carry out conjunctive "and" operations, see also Anh and Moffat [1]. Ottaviano and Venturini make their experimental code available, and we have employed their platform in some of the experimentation described in Section 4.

Other Approaches. Zhang et al. [29] and Pibiri and Venturini [21] have also recently considered two-pass index compression techniques. Our work here is complementary to those proposals.

2.2 Asymmetric Numeral Systems

The "asymmetric numeral systems" (ANS) entropy coding technique developed by Jarek Duda [8–10] is a new way of performing entropy coding. It fulfills the same role as the previous Huffman and arithmetic methods, see Moffat and Turpin [16] for descriptions, in that it assigns low bit-costs to high-probability symbols, assigns high bit-costs to low-probability symbols, and transitions between the two extremes in accordance with the *information content* of the symbol in question. With all of Huffman, arithmetic, and ANS coding, a symbol s with occurrence probability $Pr(s)$ should be assigned a codeword of length as close as is possible to $-\log_2 Pr(s)$.

Example of ANS Coding. Our initial exploration of ANS coding for index compression [14] provides a detailed example of ANS coding, pseudo-code descriptions, and an explanation that shows why ANS is an effective entropy coder. Duda provides extensive technical information about the processes he invented [8–10].

As an example, consider a three-element coding situation over an alphabet in which symbols P, Q, and R have (respectively) probabilities 1/2, 1/3, and 1/6. In a Huffman code, P gets a 1-bit codeword, and Q and R get 2-bit codewords. In an ANS-based coder for this arrangement, a *frame* of M elements is constructed in which 1/2 of the entries are labeled P; 1/3 are labeled Q; and 1/6 are labeled R. A sequence of symbols over that alphabet is represented as a *state* value relative to the corresponding frame. One frame that captures the probabilities is [P][P][P][Q][Q][R], with $n(\mathsf{P}) = 3$, $n(\mathsf{Q}) = 2$, $n(\mathsf{R}) = 1$, and $M = 6$. Other frames might also be constructed, using other permutations of the symbols, and/or larger values of M.

Once the frame has been determined, it defines an encoding transition function $T(\cdot, \cdot)$, as shown in Table 1. The consecutive integer targets of T are assigned in cycles defined by the frame, with 1/2 of them in row P; 1/3 of them in row Q; and 1/6 of them in row R. The columns of T are indexed by a *state* variable, which takes on an initial value of 0. To encode one symbol $s \in \{\mathsf{P}, \mathsf{Q}, \mathsf{R}\}$, the assignment $state' \leftarrow T(s, state)$ is applied; and to encode a whole sequence each symbol in turn is encoded, with *state* becoming larger at each step. For example, given PPQP, *state* takes on the values $0 \rightarrow 1 \rightarrow 2 \rightarrow 10 \rightarrow 20$. The final value of *state* completely encodes the whole input string, and all that is necessary is to represent it

		Current *state*															
		0	1	2	3	4	5	6	7	8	9	10	11	12	13	14	···
P	1/2	1	2	3	7	8	9	13	14	15	19	20	21	25	26	27	···
Q	1/3	4	5	10	11	16	17	22	23	28	29	34	35	40	41	46	···
R	1/6	6	12	18	24	30	36	42	48	54	60	66	72	78	84	90	···

Table 1: ANS encoding function $T(\cdot, \cdot)$ for alphabet {P, Q, R}, and probabilities 1/2, 1/3, and 1/6; and frame [P][P][P][Q][Q][R] of size $M = 6$. One cycle of the frame has been highlighted to show the regular structure within the table, covering next states 7 to 12.

as a binary number. In this case, five bits are sufficient. A Huffman code for the same input also happens to require five bits.

To decode, the inverse function $T^{-1}(\cdot)$ is used, with iterations of $(s, \mathit{state}') \leftarrow T^{-1}(\mathit{state})$ applied. For example, suppose the code 41 is received via a 6-bit binary value. It can only have arisen if the final encoding step was $\mathit{state}' \leftarrow T(\mathsf{Q}, 13)$, and hence the last symbol in the original sequence must have been Q. That previous *state* value of 13 must similarly have resulted from $\mathit{state}' \leftarrow T(\mathsf{P}, 6)$, meaning that a P must have preceded that final Q; by the same logic, an R must have come before the P. By stopping when a *state* of zero is reached, the initial sequence can always be uniquely recovered, in reverse order; in this case, it was RPQ. Note how a larger value for *state* might in fact correspond to a shorter input sequence; that difference is a direct consequence of the products of the probabilities of the symbols contained in the two sequences. In the case of PPQP, it has (among all four-symbol sequences) a probability of $1/(2\times2\times3\times2) \approx 0.0416$; whereas RPQ gives $1/(6 \times 2 \times 3) \approx 0.0277$.

As a more compelling example, the sequence QQQQQQQQQQ (ten Q's) gives rise to a *state* of 118,096, which requires 17 bits as a binary number; compared with a Huffman code of 20 bits. On the other hand, the sequence RRRRRRRRRR (ten R's) gives a *state* of 72,559,410, and needs 27 bits, ten bits more. This probability-based differential is why, over non-trivial sequences, or even short sequences in which the probabilities are highly skewed, ANS outperforms Huffman coding.

ANS Compared. Relative to Huffman and arithmetic coding, ANS offers compromises in a several dimensions, making it attractive for index compression. First, it shares with arithmetic coding the ability to closely match the ideal codeword lengths, and when amortized over a sequence of symbols, generates codes in which less than one output bit occurs for very high-probability symbols. In contrast, Huffman coding always requires at least one bit per symbol.

Second, ANS implementations are faster than arithmetic coding, and can approach the throughput rates attained by highly-engineered Huffman implementations. In each ANS decoding cycle, the integer *state* variable is modified by performing one shift, one bitwise AND, one integer multiplication and one table lookup in a relatively compact decoding table.

As a third area of compromise, ANS coding is a *static* mechanism, and requires a dedicated output stream for each *context*, where a context is one instance of a set of probabilities used to predict the symbol frequency distribution. This contrasts with adaptive arithmetic coding, which operates at throughput rates broadly comparable to static (with fixed probabilities) arithmetic coding, allowing (for example) a "q" to be transmitted using one inferred set of probabilities, and then the next symbol after it (in written English, usually a "u") to be transmitted in a fraction of a bit via a different context employing different inferred probabilities. That flexibility is not possible with ANS codes. Indeed, the ANS decoder generates output symbols in reverse order to that in which they were considered by the encoder, meaning that the symbols in each ANS message block must be regarded as being independently drawn from one context.

Fortunately, the ANS inability to be adaptive and to dynamically switch between contexts does not affect index compression.

ANS in Practice. Table 1 suggests that the mapping $T(\cdot,\cdot)$ is infinite, but that was simply to allow the general idea to be conveyed. The assignment of values based on a repeating M-element frame, means that $T(\cdot,\cdot)$ and $T^{-1}(\cdot)$ can be computed via integer arithmetic and table lookups against fixed-length arrays. In particular, fast and practical ANS encoding and decoding of sequences of symbols relative to an alphabet of m symbols and using a frame size of M requires two integer arrays of size m, and one of size M, where M is typically $8m$ or more (that is, using three or more bits of precision for each of the symbol probability estimates making up the frame), and is also usually chosen to be a power of two.

2.3 ANS for Index Compression

In our previous investigation [14] we coupled ANS with three different index compression approaches. In particular, we paired ANS entropy coding with the VByte approach to compressing postings lists; with the Simple family of codes; and with the Packed family of index representations. We showed that in each case substantially more compact storage could be attained, with only moderate decreases in decoding throughput. In each scenario, two passes over the entire index are made during encoding: one to collect symbol occurrence counts so that ANS frames can be constructed, and then a second pass to generate output relative to those frames.

Our work here extends and improves on that first description of the "Packed+ANS" mechanism. In particular, we develop the notion of "two parameter" contexts; we describe a more compact implementation that requires substantially less memory; and we add a "context merging" process. To demonstrate the utility of these techniques, we also provide detailed experimental results for compression effectiveness and query throughput using two large text collections.

3 IMPROVED PACKED INDEX COMPRESSION

3.1 Packed+ANS

In standard Packed arrangements a context identifier, or selector, is used to condition the coding arrangement for each block. When the coding step makes use of binary codes, the selector is determined by finding the maximum value in the block, determining its binary magnitude m, and then searching a vector like the one shown in Equation 1 to find the first value ℓ such that $m \leq S[l]$. The ℓth context is then used, which in traditional Packed arrangements gives rise to a payload containing $S[l]$-bit values.

In the Packed+ANS mechanism [14] these various elements are less tightly connected. The selector is again determined based on the maximum value in the block; but now identifies one of a pool of $|S|$ ANS frames. Each frame contains a different set of symbol probabilities, constructed during a first pass that processes the set of postings lists to accumulate statistics and collate the $|S|$ probability distributions. Symbol frequencies are accumulated in *binary-magnitude buckets*, and all symbols in each such bucket – for example, $5 \ldots 8$, $9 \ldots 16$, and $257 \ldots 512$ – are assumed to be equi-probable. That is, if s_k is the kth symbol in the sequence σ being coded as a set of blocks, and ℓ_k is the selector value computed from the largest binary magnitude across the symbols in the same block as s_k, then

$$L[\ell, b] = |\{s_k \in \sigma \mid \ell_k = \ell \text{ and } \lceil \log_2 s_k \rceil = b\}|$$

is a matrix of symbol magnitude counts within contexts. The probabilities used in the set of ANS frames – one for each context – are then computed from these occurrence counts. Working with equiprobable buckets avoids the need for the ANS frames to contain (potentially) $m \approx 30{,}000{,}000$ elements each.

Given this starting point, we now introduce a sequence of refinements that lead to improved compression and reduced space requirements, without compromising decoding speed.

3.2 Two-Dimensional Contexts

The first enhancement is to add further contexts. Doing so increases the cost of storing the selector, but allows more precisely-targeted probability distributions to be used. One way of adding contexts would be to employ a more fine-grained selector vector S, for example by using every power of two rather than a selected subset of them. Another option would be to alter the base of the logarithms, so that the buckets are smaller. But both of these options would continue to provide "one dimensional" conditional probabilities, in that the selector would still be completely determined by the maximum value in the block. A key benefit of using entropy coding rather than binary coding is that other options can also be considered.

In particular, we propose that "two dimensional" selectors be used, allowing two distinct observations about each block to influence the probability distribution used to code that block. The same mapping vector S (perhaps the one described by Equation 1) is used for both observations, to form a compound context identifier. For example, suppose that the first dimension is the block maximum and the second the block minimum. Then a context "*max*:*min*" implies that all of the values in the block lie in the range $\lfloor 2^{S[min-1]} \rfloor + 1 \cdots 2^{S[max]}$. Trimming probability assignment to zero for smaller values is straightforward with an entropy coder such as ANS. Zukowski et al. [30] also describe the possibility of assigning a "lower" value to each block, and then exception-coding any values smaller than that value, in the same way that values larger than the upper value of the block are handled as exceptions. None of the current PFOR implementations actually employ this flexibility, primarily because the use of binary codes makes such range-adjustment relatively ineffective unless $max = min$.

Other features might also be used as the second selector component, including the block median (denoted "med"). In Section 4.2 we describe experiments using both max:min and max:med selectors, and also selectors derived from the 90th percentile value in the block, taking inspiration from the PFOR mechanism [30]. With ANS-based coding, any value z can be coded relative to any selector ℓ provided z has been assigned a non-zero count $n_\ell(z) > 0$ in the ℓ th ANS frame, and all that is being adjusted with these alternative approaches is the size of the set of possible contexts, and the blocks that get assigned to them for processing. That is, the fact that a first pass counts frequencies and constructs the matrix $L[\cdot,\cdot]$ means that there is no need for exceptions and patching in the sense in which they are used in the PFOR and OptPFOR approaches.

Table 2 illustrates the possibilities opened up by the switch from one-dimensional contexts to two-dimensional contexts, taking as test data the term frequencies associated with the postings lists of the gov2 collection (see Section 4.1). The distribution of block counts across the "Totals" row reflects the arrangement that would have arisen via a one-dimensional categorization in which a single-component selector was derived from the maximum value in each block. The percentage breakdown above each of those totals then shows how those blocks are further sub-categorized by the addition of a secondary selector based on the median value in the block. For example, 57% of the 5,720,796 blocks for which the maximum value lies between 17 and 32 (column 5) also have a median of 1 (row 0), and should thus correspond to coding distributions in which the probability of "1" is at least 0.5. Of the same set of blocks only 8% have medians of 3 or 4 (row 2). Across the full set of 16 columns and 16 rows, 94 of the available $|S|(|S| + 1)/2 = 136$ contexts occur, and a 7-bit selector is required. In total there are 41,157,912 blocks in this data file, of which 8,697,157 contain all "1"s, and are handled in the context "0:0".

selector(*med*)	*selector*(*max*)							
	0	1	2	3	4	5	6	7
0	100	32	50	62	66	57	42	30
1		68	9	9	17	27	33	33
2			42	4	5	8	14	20
3				25	3	3	6	9
4					10	1	2	4
5						4	1	2
6							2	1
7								2
Totals ('000)	8697	3219	3319	4933	6011	5721	4336	2680

Table 2: Two dimensional contexts: percentage of blocks matching a selector for the maximum value in the block (columns), broken down by the selector for the block median (rows), for the filtered gov2.frqs file (see Section 4.1), with a blocksize of $B = 128$. Selectors are relative to the vector S shown in Equation 1; the last row gives block counts in thousands for each column. Only the first eight columns and rows are shown.

3.3 Reducing The Frame Size

One of the implementation drawbacks of the Packed+ANS arrangement described in Section 3.1 is the cost of maintaining the frames in the three-table form employed for ANS decoding (see Section 2.2). With m as large as 2^{25} in some frames, with $M \approx 8m$, and with the two-dimensional approach meaning that the number of contexts might be close to $|S|(|S| + 1)/2$, execution-time memory space is a key factor that cannot be ignored. Caching effects mean that memory space also affects decoding speed. To reduce the space required, Moffat and Petri [14] describe an additional mechanism that uses condensed tables of size $\log_2 m$ elements, but additional computation is required during the indirection. A more subtle disadvantage of the Packed+ANS arrangement arises when two-dimensional contexts are introduced: it is no longer possible to always normalize the frame counts so that M_ℓ is a power of two.

One way of addressing these issues is to use ANS for the binary magnitudes of the symbols (and not their full numeric values), in the range (say) $0 \ldots 25$, and to associate a binary offset with each coded magnitude, stored in an auxiliary bit-stream. The decoder would process the ANS stream and the auxiliary bit-stream in parallel, decoding a magnitude from the first and then fetching the indicated

```
function decode_packedANS_block(bytes[], B, ℓ):
state ← final encoding state for this block
b ← 0                                        ▹ offset within bytes
for j ← 0 to B − 1 do
    syms[j] ← decode_ANS(bytes, b, ANSframe[ℓ], state)
for j ← 0 to B − 1 do
    if syms[j] ≤ 2^8 then
        continue                             ▹ syms[j] is now final
    syms[j] ← ((syms[j] − 2^8) << 8) + bytes[b++]
    if syms[j] ≤ 2^16 then
        continue                             ▹ syms[j] is now final
    syms[j] ← ((syms[j] − 2^16) << 8) + bytes[b++]
    if syms[j] ≤ 2^24 then
        continue                             ▹ syms[j] is now final
    syms[j] ← ((syms[j] − 2^24) << 8) + bytes[b++]
return syms[0 . . . B − 1]
```

Figure 1: Decoding a block *bytes*[] of compressed data, relative to a selector ℓ, to reconstruct a block of B original values *syms*[], assuming that the encoder has processed the input block in reverse order. The function *decode_ANS*$(\cdot,\cdot,\cdot,\cdot)$ increments b as the array *bytes* is consumed, returning decoded ANS values one by one, and altering the value of *state*. The completion bytes associated with values greater than 256 are then used to adjust the decoded values, inverting the mapping shown in Equation 2.

number of bits from the second, thereby reconstructing each value. This combination is somewhat reminiscent of the Elias γ code, but with the unary "magnitude" part represented instead via an ANS code based on observed probabilities [11]. However, the auxiliary bit-stream introduces additional alignment overheads; and the bit-by-bit processing it implies is also costly.

A better arrangement is to employ an auxiliary stream that consists of whole bytes. To achieve that goal, we adapt the idea of *exceptions*, used in the PFOR and OptPFOR mechanisms, and define the following mapping between symbol values and ANS targets:

$$ANSmsb(s) = \begin{cases} s & \text{if } s \le 2^8 \\ \lfloor s/2^8 \rfloor + 256 & \text{if } 2^8 < s \le 2^{16} \\ \lfloor s/2^{16} \rfloor + 512 & \text{if } 2^{16} < s \le 2^{24} \\ \lfloor s/2^{24} \rfloor + 768 & \text{if } 2^{24} < s \le 2^{32} \end{cases} \quad (2)$$

Further stages are readily added if s can be larger than 2^{32}.

The key idea is to isolate the most significant byte of s, and map it to a unique number that captures both its value and also its position within the original word. A total of $m = 1024$ different options can be generated in this way from a 32-bit word. That is, ANS frames of at most 1024 different values are required (rather than 30,000,000), with all remaining bits provided via an auxiliary byte-stream that contains the zero, one, two, or three low-order bytes of each original value. Figure 1 describes the corresponding decoding and inverse mapping process.

Compared to the binary-magnitude ANS arrangement the space required is many orders of magnitude smaller; as well, more precise probability distributions are used across the entire range of values, potentially boosting compression effectiveness. For example, under

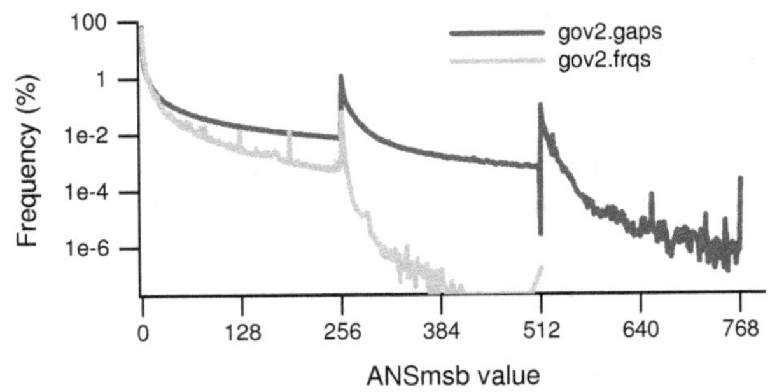

Figure 2: Probability distributions generated by *ANSmsb*$(\cdot)$ for the two sets of symbols s making up the 5,268,212,736 postings in the filtered gov2 inverted index (see Section 4.1). For the purposes of this example, a single zero-dimensional context is assumed to be used to generate each of the two symbol sequences.

the binary magnitude arrangement described in Section 3.1, symbols 17 to 32 are assigned the same estimated probability. But with the mapping shown in Equation 2, they are treated as independent symbols and receive separate probability estimates during the first pass. Small ANS frames also lead to faster execution because of caching effects.

To illustrate the usefulness of the proposed mapping, Figure 2 plots the mapped distributions for the docid gaps and frequencies associated with the gov2 text collection (see Section 4.1), assuming that a zero-dimensional context is used, that is, one ANS frame for the docid gaps and another for the frequencies. The saw-tooth pattern is a direct consequence of the definition of *ANSmsb*$(\cdot)$, with mapped value 257 representing all symbols between 257 and 512 inclusive, and accounting for more than 150 times the probability mass of symbol 256 in the docid gaps file, and 90 times in the frequencies file. Results for measured compression effectiveness when contexts constructed using the *ANSmsb*$(\cdot)$ approach are applied in two-dimensions are given in Sections 4.2 and 4.3.

3.4 Context Merging

One risk associated with adding further contexts is that the selector requires additional bits. That is, having too many contexts might be as inefficient as not having enough. Given that the context selector is being coded into a binary value as part of the metadata associated with each block, it also makes sense to ensure that the number of contexts employed is a power of two such as 32 or 64.

These targets can be achieved by pairwise *merging* of selected contexts, replacing them by a single one. Suppose that symbol s occurs $n_a(s)$ times in context a which has a total occurrence count of $N_a = \sum_{s=1}^{m} n_a(s)$ across the m different symbols being coded, and assume that a perfect entropy coder is available. Then the total cost of that context is

$$H_a = \sum_{s=1}^{m} \left(n_a(s) \log_2 \frac{N_a}{n_a(s)} \right), \quad (3)$$

with $0 \cdot \log(N_a/0)$ taken to be zero. The net cost of fusing contexts a and b and replacing them by a context v constructed via $n_v(s) = n_a(s) + n_b(s)$, for $1 \le s \le m$, is then given by $H_v - H_a - H_b$. This quantity can be computed for all possible pairs of a and b, and the least-cost pairing chosen, reducing the number of contexts by one. The compute-select-fuse sequence can then be repeated in a greedy manner (including, perhaps, further mergings on contexts formed by previous fusings) until the desired number of contexts is reached. A small mapping table from previous selector value to new fused selector value must also be constructed.

4 EXPERIMENTS

4.1 Experimental Context

Datasets. Table 3 lists the four test files used in our experiments, derived from two large test collections. The first test pair, gov2.gaps and gov2.frqs, represent a document-level inverted index for the 426 GiB gov2 collection[1], with documents in URL-sorted order. A standard processing pipeline including Apache Tika and Apache Lucene is used to build the index, covering in excess of five billion postings. The second pair of test files are derived from publicly available web-sourced news articles[2], taking English language news sources (as identified by Apache Tika) from 01/09/2016 up until and including 28/02/2017, that is, a six month crawl period that contains 7,508,082 documents. Document identifiers were again assigned in URL-sorted order. We use this second file (rather than, for example, ClueWeb data) because of its unrestricted availability, allowing other researchers to readily reproduce our experiments.

The arithmetic mean of the symbols s in each of the four files is shown in Table 3, as well as the geometric mean. The ratio between these two values (broadly) indicates the degree to which each distribution of symbols is biased in favor of small values.

Hardware and Software. All methods are implemented using c++11 and compiled with gcc 6.3.0 (using all optimizations) on a Linux server equipped with 148 GiB RAM and an Intel E5640 processor. In the interests of reproducibility, the experimental framework and all implementation details are available at http://github.com/mpetri/partitioned_ef_ans, including scripts for downloading and constructing the news collection; and we note with gratitude the previous software provided by Ottaviano and Venturini [18], which provides a foundation for our own experimental evaluation.

In terms of baselines, we have three: the OptPFOR mechanism from the FastPFor library [12]; the EF-opt approach of Ottaviano and Venturini [18]; and Interp. Zhang et al. [29] and Wang et al. [24] do not provide public implementations of their work; and while the QMX approach of Trotman [23] provides good compression effectiveness and very fast decoding, the quad-word alignment expectation of the version that we had available to us at the time we carried out our experiments was not well-suited to short sequences such as the blocks of $B = 128$ symbols considered here.

Measurement and Methodology. We measure compression effectiveness in three different ways. First, to obtain preliminary estimates of relative performance we employ Equation 3, summing over all contexts, and adding the cost of the necessary selectors. Section 4.2 gives computed effectiveness results based on this framework. Those results do not include any other block- or list-related

[1] http://ir.dcs.gla.ac.uk/test_collections/gov2-summary.htm.
[2] http://commoncrawl.org/2016/10/news-dataset-available/

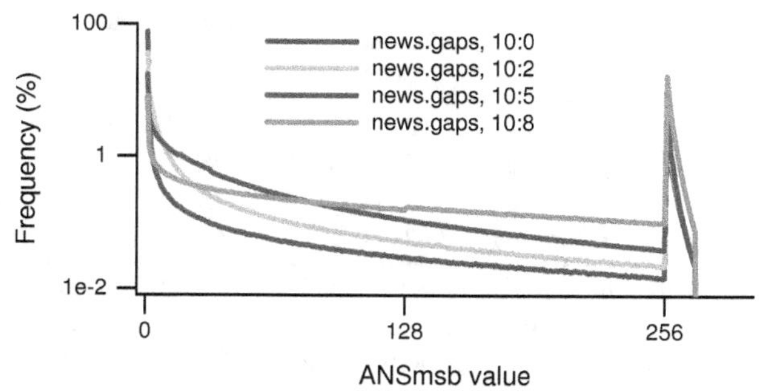

Figure 3: Probability distributions arising with the *ANSmsb* when two dimensional selectors are used on the filtered news.gaps. In each of the four plotted contexts the upper selector is 10; the lower selector is computed from the block median value. Blocks with different medians have different probability distributions.

overheads such as alignment costs, pointers, block maximum values, ANS frame storage costs, and coding inefficiency relative to entropy; that is, they are nothing more than estimates of costs relative to a set of probability distributions, and should only be compared against each other.

Having used estimation to explore the spectrum of improvements, in Section 4.3 we give confirmed compression results developed by full implementations of two Packed+ANS methods and two baseline mechanisms, all measured using the framework developed by Ottaviano and Venturini [18]. That is, in Section 4.3 the results are all-inclusive and reflect the complete cost of placing the compressed postings lists on permanent storage using demonstrably reversible compression software, including the ANS frames.

Finally, in Section 4.4, we measure the execution-time memory footprint required during querying, including all required auxiliary and metadata, term vocabulary search structures, pointers to postings lists, plus memory-mapped storage of the compressed postings lists themselves. (The measured costs do not include the block-max scores that support WAND pruning; these account for 0.19 GiB for gov2, and 0.13 GiB for news.)

Section 4.4 also reports query execution times. For these we employ the TREC 2005 Terabyte Track efficiency queries filtered such that all query terms occur in both test collections. In total, 44,368 queries (out of 50,000) were retained. Each of those queries was then executed using the BM25-based Ranked-AND and WAND top-k retrieval methods to identify $k = 10$ top-scoring documents, as described by Ottaviano and Venturini [18].

4.2 Estimated Improvement

Figure 3 plots the probability distributions associated with four of the 122 contexts generated by the max:med selectors for the file news.gaps. All contexts have 10 as the max selector, that is, blocks in which the maximum is between 1025 and 4096, as described by Equation 1, with corresponding *ANSmsb*$(\cdot)$ values as large as 272. The four different medians that are plotted give rise to four different probability distributions, and illustrate the usefulness of allowing the dispersion of the block values, represented by the block median, to influence the choice of ANS frame.

File	Unfiltered Index				Filtered Index			
	Lists	Postings	Arith.	Geom.	Lists	Postings	Arith.	Geom.
gov2.gaps	25,283,415	5,415,967,741	64,760.28	3.53	665,987	5,268,212,736	1452.78	2.90
gov2.frqs	25,283,415	5,415,967,741	4.23	1.85	665,987	5,268,212,736	4.31	1.87
news.gaps	26,240,031	4,457,492,131	24,678.69	3.14	273,978	4,375,559,040	356.50	2.74
news.frqs	26,240,031	4,457,492,131	2.17	1.48	273,978	4,375,559,040	2.19	1.49

Table 3: Test files used: number of postings lists, total number of postings n, and the arithmetic $(\sum_i s_i)/n$ and geometric $2^{(\sum_i \log_2 s_i)/n}$ means of the symbols stored in each file; for complete and filtered indexes. In the filtered indexes, postings blocks of fewer than $B = 128$ values are excluded. The filtered gov2 indexes contain 97.27% of the unfiltered postings; the filtered news indexes contain 98.16%.

	gov2.gaps	gov2.frqs	news.gaps	news.frqs
Packed+ANS	3.016	2.134	2.788	1.629
2d, max:min	3.013	1.848	2.811	1.345
2d, 90%:med	2.914	1.769	2.692	1.235
2d, max:med	2.927	1.771	2.695	1.252
ANSmsb	2.909	1.727	2.680	1.224
contexts ≤ 64	2.903	1.719	2.673	1.216
$\lvert S \rvert = 24$	2.902	1.719	2.673	1.216

Table 4: Estimated compression effectiveness derived from symbol frequency distributions (Equation 3), in bits per symbol, for four filtered test files, and (all but last row) starting with a selection vector S of length 16. In each of the final three rows the modifications of previous rows are also included, adding to the "2d, max:med" row. A blocksize of $B = 128$ is used throughout. Except for the selector, no per-block overheads are included in these estimates.

Table 4 shows the evolution of computed entropies achieved for the four data sequences associated with the two filtered indexes. All values are expressed as entropy-based (Equation 3) bits per symbol estimates, and include the cost of the binary selector required in each block. The first row reflects (in estimated terms) the Packed+ANS mechanism (Section 3.1); each row thereafter adds another of the enhancements.

The use of two-dimensional max:min contexts brings a clear improvement in compression for the two frequencies files, and also brings modest gains in the two docid gaps files. Shifting to the 90%:med contexts yields further small gains in compression for all four files; and use of the max:med selector combination also improves on the max:min ones. The max:med selectors are a better operational choice than the 90%:med ones, and are used as the basis for the remainder of Table 4. Shifting from binary-magnitude ANS coding to the *ANSmsb* approach provides small gains in effectiveness (the fifth row) as well as the space savings that were the primary motivation; and then trimming the number of contexts to 64 (the sixth row) also brings small net gains in compression effectiveness. Finally, in the seventh row, the number of selectors is increased from 16 (shown in Equation 1) to 24, prior again to the greedy reduction to 64 contexts; the absence of consistent gain demonstrates that the vector in Equation 1 is a good initial choice.

Table 4 suggests that in combination the improvements described in Section 3 give rise to effectiveness gains of around 5% in the docids, and a remarkable 25% for the frequencies. The next section gives measured compression effectiveness results for the "packed, ANS, 2d, max:med, *ANSmsb*, merged contexts" method of the sixth row, and compares that preferred combination – denoted Packed+ANS2 – with baseline methods to validate the gains.

4.3 Measured Improvement

We now describe and measure a full implementation (including reversible decompression), using the same filtered postings files.

The ANS coder implemented as part of this work uses a 63-bit internal *state* value, and emits 32-bit binary words when *state* reaches overflow point; the encoder also reverses the ordering of the input block, so that decoded symbols are generated in left-to-right order, as is supposed by Figure 1. Hence, the ANS data stream consists of a sequence of 32-bit words, and a final *state* of between 1 and 8 bytes. To accommodate this, each block of compressed data Packed+ANS2 has the following structure:

- a 16-bit word that contains packed binary values for:
  - the selector to be used for this block (6 bits);
  - the number of bytes in the final value of *state* (3 bits);
  - the number of 32-bit words in the ANS component of the output block (7 bits);
- between 1 and 8 bytes recording the decoder's initial *state*;
- a sequence of 32-bit ANS words, stored in order of decoder consumption (by function *decode_ANS*$(\cdot,\cdot,\cdot,\cdot)$ in Figure 1);
- a sequence of completion bytes in regard to the *ANSmsb* process, stored in the order required by the decoder (Figure 1).

The 10 additional bits of control data (the 6 selector bits are already accounted for in the previous subsection) represent a non-trivial overhead. The rounding of each block's final ANS state to a byte boundary also introduces some penalty. As well, slight non-perfectness in the entropy coder adds to the measured bit cost.

Table 5 shows measured compression effectiveness on the four test files using two Packed and two reference approaches, and shows the strong gains in compression effectiveness that have been achieved. As expected, the Packed+ANS and Packed+ANS2 compression rates are around 0.1 bits per symbol higher than the computed entropy values in Table 4. But even so, the sequence of improvements made to Packed+ANS result in Packed+ANS2 having compression consistently better than that of Interp, a notable achievement.

	gov2.gaps	gov2.frqs	news.gaps	news.frqs
VByte	8.519	8.021	8.455	8.002
OptPFOR	3.621	2.391	3.292	1.757
Packed+ANS	3.131	2.248	2.867	1.717
Interp	3.047	2.245	2.918	1.684
Packed+ANS2	2.979	1.830	2.734	1.323

Table 5: Measured compression effectiveness for four filtered test files, using blocks of $B = 128$ symbols. All compression rates are for reversible full-index coding, including per-block metadata and byte alignment overheads, and (for the two new methods) the cost of storing the ANS frame descriptions. The Packed+ANS2 mechanism employs 2d max:med contexts (Section 3.2), the *ANSmsb* approach (Section 3.3), and merging to 64 contexts (Section 3.4).

	gov2			news		
	GiB	msec/q	msec/q	GiB	msec/q	msec/q
VByte	11.053	5.9	11.4	9.050	4.4	8.4
OptPFOR	4.591	6.2	12.0	3.235	4.1	8.0
Packed+ANS	4.134	17.2	29.7	2.976	9.5	16.3
EF-opt	4.114	7.7	13.2	2.761	5.1	8.6
Interp	4.000	28.4	41.7	2.793	20.7	33.8
Packed+ANS2	3.678	17.1	29.4	2.596	8.8	15.1

Table 6: Execution-time memory required and measured query throughput, using the unfiltered (all postings, see Table 3) version of each index. The first column in each group shows the total space required during querying operations, including all index data and storage overheads; the middle column shows the measured query rate for top-10 conjunctive ranked queries; and the third column in each group shows the measured query rate for disjunctive WAND queries, again identifying ten documents.

4.4 Retrieval Throughput

Table 6 shows retrieval throughput (average milliseconds per query) and the complete query-time in-memory index size (in GiB, unfiltered postings lists, excluding WAND data), as measured by the framework of Ottaviano and Venturini [18], for the test queries described earlier. The relativities for existing methods reflect those reported by Ottaviano and Venturini, and we can confirm that EF-opt has slightly larger space requirements than Interp, while providing much faster retrieval performance. The OptPFOR approach slightly outperforms EF-opt in terms of query throughput, but at the cost of more space, again matching the results reported by Ottaviano and Venturini. The well-known VByte mechanism [25] is fast, but not competitive in terms of memory space.

The initial Packed+ANS mechanism is better than other fixed-block approaches, but is outperformed by the variable-block EF-opt approach. The improved Packed+ANS2 reverses that situation in terms of memory space required, but not for query throughput. It does, however, outperform Interp in both dimensions. For example, in the case of gov2, the index is 8% smaller than Interp, and query performance is up to 40% faster.

The news collection behaves somewhat differently. Of the approaches tested, Packed+ANS2 again has the smallest memory footprint, with query performance closer to that of EF-opt and OptPFOR, caused by differences in compressibility between the two collections. For gov2, 13%/3.8% of all gaps/frequencies processed at query time are in uniform blocks that get decoded without ANS steps being required. For news, it is 33%/3.5% respectively. Of the remaining postings, 31%/28% are decoded using small models ($M \leq 256$) for gov2, against 28%/70.5% for news, meaning that a greater fraction of the ANS frames being used are retained in L1/L2 cache. At 2.94 MiB, the cumulative size of the decoding models for each of the collections is non-trivial, but individual ANS frames are very small if they only encode a few unique symbols.

Finally in this section, note that ANS encoding is fast: on our test hardware constructing the EF-opt index for gov2 requires 765 seconds using 16 threads, and OptPFOR requires 566 seconds using a single thread; while the two passes of Packed+ANS2 take 350 seconds using a single thread.

5 CONCLUSIONS AND FUTURE WORK

Starting with the Packed+ANS mechanism, we have improved it in three quite different ways: two-dimensional contexts, the most-significant byte mapping, and context merging. In doing so, we have shown that the two-decade-old benchmark set by Interp can be consistently beaten, a milestone outcome for index compression.

At present the Packed+ANS2 implementation is slower than OptPFOR and EF-opt in terms of query processing speed. However, there is considerable scope to improve the decoding throughput of the ANS-based approaches. We have already observed that most postings are encoded with compact models which span only a small number of unique symbols. For these, tailored ANS coders that employ expanded decoding tables and SIMD mechanisms to decode multiple states in parallel might increase decoding speed by a factor of four or more. Open-source entropy coders employing SIMD have already been shown to attain improvements of this magnitude[3].

We also observe that use of variable-length blocks formed via a strategy similar to that employed by EF-opt [18] and in other recent work [13] might lead to further compression gains when coupled with the new Packed+ANS2 mechanism.

As a third area for future work, we note the potential for different compression mechanisms to be used for different postings lists depending on querying statistics [19], and the possibility of relatively small compression losses to be exchanged for substantial query throughput gains.

Postscript. After submitting this work for review, and with the assistance of Giulio Pibiri and Rossano Venturini, we were able to also measure the performance of their recent clustered partitioned Elias-Fano approach [21] using our test files. In particular, we built a clustered partitioned Elias-Fano index for the gov2 collection using the standard parameters $\langle 24707817, 15540, 3, 5, 5, 8, 10\rangle$ and a reference list size of 800,000, and generated an index of 2.82 GiB after 5449 seconds of computation. This index is 23% smaller than the Packed+ANS2 result shown in Table 6, somewhat muting our pleasure at having beaten the benchmark established by Interp.

[3]https://github.com/jkbonfield/rans_static

However, Pibiri and Venturini [21] show that compressing the same clustered postings list using Interp results in an index that is at most 5.6% larger than their method. Based on this result, we expect our ANS-based methods to be highly competitive when combined with the clustering approach, and we plan to examine that option next. Additionally, the complexity of the clustering process meant that construction time for the gov2 index was some 15 times greater than the Packed+ANS2 index, even though the former made use of 16 threads (rather than one in the case of Packed+ANS2).

We did not measure query performance for the clustered partitioned Elias-Fano index, but note that Pibiri and Venturini [21] report a 30–50% query performance penalty between the previous EF-opt mechanism and their clustered variant.

Software. The code related to the experiments described in this work is available at https://github.com/mpetri/partitioned_ef_ans and https://github.com/mpetri/TikaLuceneWarc. The software includes scripts to generate the news collection in ds2i format (see https://github.com/ot/ds2i). In the interests of reproducability we encourage other authors to similarly publish all of their experimental software.

Acknowledgment. This work was supported under the Australian Research Council's Discovery Projects funding scheme (project number DP140103256). We thank Giulio Pibiri and Rossano Venturini for assisting us with the use of their software.

REFERENCES

[1] V. N. Anh and A. Moffat. Compressed inverted files with reduced decoding overheads. In *Proc. SIGIR*, pages 290–297, 1998.

[2] V. N. Anh and A. Moffat. Inverted index compression using word-aligned binary codes. *Inf. Retr.*, 8(1):151–166, 2005.

[3] V. N. Anh and A. Moffat. Index compression using 64-bit words. *Soft. Prac. & Exp.*, 40(2):131–147, 2010.

[4] N. R. Brisaboa, A. Fariña, G. Navarro, and M. F. Esteller. (S, C)-Dense coding: An optimized compression code for natural language text databases. In *Proc. SPIRE*, pages 122–136, 2003.

[5] N. R. Brisaboa, A. Fariña, S. Ladra, and G. Navarro. Reorganizing compressed text. In *Proc. SIGIR*, pages 139–146, 2008.

[6] Y. Choueka, A. S. Fraenkel, and S. T. Klein. Compression of concordances in full-text retrieval systems. In *Proc. SIGIR*, pages 597–612, 1988.

[7] J. S. Culpepper and A. Moffat. Enhanced byte codes with restricted prefix properties. In *Proc. SPIRE*, pages 1–12, 2005.

[8] J. Duda. Asymmetric numeral systems. *CoRR*, abs/0902.0271, 2009.

[9] J. Duda. Asymmetric numeral systems: Entropy coding combining speed of Huffman coding with compression rate of arithmetic coding. *CoRR*, abs/1311.2540, 2013.

[10] J. Duda, K. Tahboub, N. J. Gadgil, and E. J. Delp. The use of asymmetric numeral systems as an accurate replacement for Huffman coding. In *Proc. Picture Coding Symp.*, pages 65–69, 2015.

[11] A. S. Fraenkel and S. T. Klein. Novel compression of sparse bit-strings: Preliminary report. In *Combinatorial Algorithms on Words, Volume 12*, NATO ASI Series F, pages 169–183. Springer, 1985.

[12] D. Lemire and L. Boytsov. Decoding billions of integers per second through vectorization. *Soft. Prac. & Exp.*, 45(1):1–29, 2015.

[13] A. Mallia, G. Ottaviano, E. Porciani, N. Tonellotto, and R. Venturini. Faster BlockMax WAND with variable-sized blocks. In *Proc. SIGIR*, pages 625–634, 2017.

[14] A. Moffat and M. Petri. ANS-based index compression. In *Proc. CIKM*, pages 677–686, 2017.

[15] A. Moffat and L. Stuiver. Binary interpolative coding for effective index compression. *Inf. Retr.*, 3(1):25–47, 2000.

[16] A. Moffat and A. Turpin. *Compression and Coding Algorithms*. Kluwer, Boston, 2002.

[17] A. Moffat and J. Zobel. Parameterised compression for sparse bitmaps. In *Proc. SIGIR*, pages 274–285, 1992.

[18] G. Ottaviano and R. Venturini. Partitioned Elias-Fano indexes. In *Proc. SIGIR*, pages 273–282, 2014.

[19] G. Ottaviano, N. Tonellotto, and R. Venturini. Optimal space-time tradeoffs for inverted indexes. In *Proc. WSDM*, pages 47–56, 2015.

[20] M. Petri and A. Moffat. Compact inverted index storage using general-purpose compression libraries. *Soft. Prac. & Exp.*, 2018. To appear.

[21] G. E. Pibiri and R. Venturini. Clustered Elias-Fano indexes. *ACM Trans. Inf. Sys.*, 36(1):2:1–2:33, 2017.

[22] A. Trotman. Compressing inverted files. *Inf. Retr.*, 6(1):5–19, 2003.

[23] A. Trotman. Compression, SIMD, and postings lists. In *Proc. Aust. Doc. Comp. Symp.*, pages 50–57, 2014.

[24] J. Wang, C. Lin, R. He, M. Chae, Y. Papakonstantinou, and S. Swanson. MILC: Inverted list compression in memory. *PVLDB*, 10(8):853–864, 2017.

[25] H. E. Williams and J. Zobel. Compressing integers for fast file access. *Comp. J.*, 42(3):193–201, 1999.

[26] I. H. Witten, A. Moffat, and T. C. Bell. *Managing Gigabytes: Compressing and Indexing Documents and Images*. Morgan Kaufmann, 1999.

[27] H. Yan, S. Ding, and T. Suel. Inverted index compression and query processing with optimized document ordering. In *Proc. WWW*, pages 401–410, 2009.

[28] J. Zhang, X. Long, and T. Suel. Performance of compressed inverted list caching in search engines. In *Proc. WWW*, pages 387–396, 2008.

[29] Z. Zhang, J. Tong, H. Huang, J. Liang, T. Li, R. J. Stones, G. Wang, and X. Liu. Leveraging context-free grammar for efficient inverted index compression. In *Proc. SIGIR*, pages 275–284, 2016.

[30] M. Zukowski, S. Héman, N. Nes, and P. A. Boncz. Super-scalar RAM-CPU cache compression. In *Proc. ICDE*, pages 59.1–59.12, 2006.

Fusing Diversity in Recommendations in Heterogeneous Information Networks

Sharad Nandanwar
Indian Institute of Science
sharadnandanwar@csa.iisc.ernet.in

Aayush Moroney
Indian Institute of Science
aayush.moroney@csa.iisc.ernet.in

M. N. Murty
Indian Institute of Science
mnm@csa.iisc.ernet.in

ABSTRACT

In the past, hybrid recommender systems have shown the power of exploiting relationships amongst objects which directly or indirectly effect the recommendation task. However, the effect of all relations is not equal, and choosing their right balance for a recommendation problem at hand is non-trivial. We model these interactions using a Heterogeneous Information Network, and propose a systematic framework for learning their influence weights for a given recommendation task. Further, we address the issue of redundant results, which is very much prevalent in recommender systems. To alleviate redundancy in recommendations we use Vertex Reinforced Random Walk (a non-Markovian random walk) over a heterogeneous graph. It works by boosting the transitions to the influential nodes, while simultaneously shrinking the weights of others. This helps in discouraging recommendation of multiple influential nodes which lie in close proximity of each other, thus ensuring diversity. Finally, we demonstrate the effectiveness of our approach by experimenting on real world datasets. We find that, with the weights of relations learned using the proposed non-Markovian random walk based framework, the results consistently improve over the baselines.

CCS CONCEPTS

•Information systems →Recommender systems; Social recommendation; *Semi-structured data; Social networks; Learning to rank;*

KEYWORDS

Diversity in Recommendation; Multivariate Random Walk; Vertex Reinforced Random Walk; Heterogeneous Information Network

ACM Reference format:

Sharad Nandanwar, Aayush Moroney, and M. N. Murty. 2018. Fusing Diversity in Recommendations in Heterogeneous Information Networks. In *Proceedings of WSDM'18, February 5–9, 2018, Marina Del Rey, CA, USA,* 9 pages.
DOI: http://dx.doi.org/10.1145/3159652.3159720

1 INTRODUCTION

Recommender systems deal with the task of identifying objects with which a user is likely to interact in the near future. The objects could be movies to watch in case of user-movie recommendation, products to purchase in user-product recommendation, users to friend in user-user recommendation and so on. Most of the recommender systems focus on cases where users are the recipients of recommendations. We consider a more general definition where both recommendations and recipients of recommendations could be of any type. For example, matching the responsible genes to a particular disease can be casted as a recommendation problem [7]. Formally, we define the recommendation problem as follows

Definition 1.1. Given a set of recipient objects $\mathcal{S}$ of type s, and a set of recommendation objects $\mathcal{T}$ of type t, along with the snapshot at time T of the preference matrix A_{st} encoding past preferences of objects in $\mathcal{S}$ for objects in $\mathcal{T}$, the recommendation problem is to find a subset of $\mathcal{T}$ for each object in $\mathcal{S}$ with which it is likely to interact at time $(T + 1)$.

Collaborative filtering, a key technique used in recommender systems primarily works by aggregating and ranking the preferences of users with similar past behavior. Further, in a series of works [5, 19, 25, 28] it was observed that hybrid models utilizing auxiliary information about the recommendation object and the recipient object tend to do better. This auxiliary information is generally present in the form of interactions with objects of other types, which directly or indirectly influence the recommendations under consideration. More recently, Heterogeneous Information Networks (HIN) have become popular tools for modeling such interactions. Heterogeneous Information Network models the data using a graph where nodes represent the objects and edges depict the relationships amongst objects as in the underlying data. It is to be noted that unlike homogeneous network HIN can have more than one type of object and more than one type of relationships amongst them. A more detailed and formal definition of HIN is given by Sun et al. [20]. Markovian-walk based techniques like Personalized-Page Rank, Katz similarity etc. offer a powerful way of computing similarity in a graph. However, finding this similarity becomes non-trivial when accounting for multiple types of relations. The extent to which the similarity between one type of object influences the similarity between other type varies for each relation. We explain this using a toy restaurant information network shown in Fig. 1. The figure shows a network consisting of objects of type *User, Restaurant, Locality*, and *Cuisine*. Consider the case where restaurants are to be suggested to user u_4. Conventional collaborative filtering would fail here as the restaurants preferred in the past by u_4 are not available, leading to a cold start problem. However, based on the locality of user u_4 it is possible to suggest restaurant r_3. Similarly by looking at the preferences made by friends of u_4 restaurants r_2 and r_4 can be suggested. The final set of recommendations are determined based on how these preferences from various sources are combined.

WSDM'18, February 5–9, 2018, Marina Del Rey, CA, USA
 ISBN 978-1-4503-5581-0/18/02...$15.00
DOI: http://dx.doi.org/10.1145/3159652.3159720

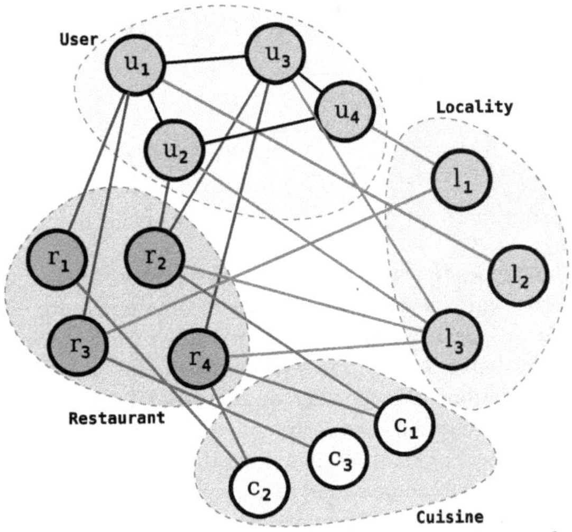

Figure 1: A toy Restaurant Information Network

One of the pressing issues in recommender systems is to do away with monotonous yet relevant recommendations. Techniques like collaborative filtering emphasize on obtaining the recommendations lying in the query proximity. However, it has been noted [27] that the utility of such recommendations is questionable. Too many of such similar results can degrade the User experience. This is easy to follow from common human psychology point of view as the system won't offer novelty for seasoned customers.

To further motivate the need of diversity in recommendation, we illustrate using our running restaurant example. In the given scenario, suppose it is chosen to recommend restaurants by exploiting the preferences expressed by friends of the user. In such a case the suggestions would be r_2 followed by r_4. However, it is worth noting that both r_2 and r_4 offer the same cuisine and share the same locality. It is very much intuitive to say that only one out of these two recommendations should be enough.

In this paper, we propose a random walk based approach for making recommendation in the underlying heterogeneous information network. To account for multiple types of relationships we create a parameterized model, where each parameter describes the role played by the corresponding relation in recommendation. For learning these parameters, we deploy a probabilistic optimization framework, wherein we systematically minimize the cross entropy loss using the available ground truth. Conventional random walk based approaches like personalized page-rank, etc. use a Markovian-random walk over the graph. And, the stationary distribution obtained as a consequence of this Markovian-random walk is used for recommendation. However, this could lead to multiple recommendations which are in close vicinity of each other. To provide diversity, it is favorable to have a non-Markovian Random walk which uses a time variant transition matrix. We propose to use vertex reinforced random walk (VRRW) for this. After each unit time interval, VRRW updates the transition probabilities using a monotonically increasing function of current arrival probabilities. This is done to further encourage the transition to nodes which currently have high arrival probabilities. We summarize our key contributions below:

- *We make use of a sublinear Vertex Reinforced Random Walk, for achieving diversity in recommendations.*
- *We describe a principled approach for learning parameters of a multivariate non-Markovian random walk over a heterogeneous graph, by minimizing the cross entropy loss.*
- *We propose a stochastic gradient descent based algorithm for the same.*
- *We show the effectiveness of the proposed approach over state-of-the-art techniques using real world datasets.*

The rest of the paper is organized as follows; we briefly survey the related work in Sec. 2. Next, we introduce the necessary background, in Sec. 3, which is helpful for understanding this paper. The vertex reinforced random walk (VRRW) is introduced in Sec. 4. In Sec. 5 we describe our framework for learning the importance of different relations in a recommendation task. We present experimental results in Sec. 6, followed by conclusion in Sec. 7. We make the source code and datasets used in our experiments publicly available at https://github.com/sharadnandanwar/DivFuse.

2 RELATED WORK

Diversity. Diversity in ranking has been studied very well in machine learning and data mining literature [17]. However, these studies have been largely concerned with the problem of ranking the web documents. Carbonell et al. [1] were first to study the interplay of relevance and novelty for ranking and summarization of text documents. They proposed to maximize marginal relevance for top ranked results. Marginal relevance is high if the document is relevant to the query, while at the same time bearing minimal similarity to other ranked results. Later Zhai et al. [26] in their work undertook the study as subtopic retrieval problem, with an aim to maximize the number of diverse subtopics amongst ranked results. Based on the definition of diversity, the subsequent works in this direction can be broadly classified into 3 paradigms namely *i)* content based, *ii)* novelty based, and *iii)* coverage based [3].

Diversity on Graphs. `Grasshopper`[29], one of the earliest works in diversified ranking on graphs, proposes a sequential algorithm to compute a diverse set of nodes. At each intermediate stage the selected nodes are switched to the absorbing state. `DivRank` [10] proposed by Mei et al. introduced a framework for diversified ranking in networks. Prior approaches like `Personalized Page-Rank` [6] considered a random walk model based on a Markovian process. Unlike this, `DivRank` considers a vertex-reinforced random walk model which is based on a non-Markovian process. The number of chances of arriving at a node increases with the number of visits to that node, in this way a single node absorbs the score of its strongly connected neighbors leading to a set of diverse nodes having high ranks. An optimization perspective to the same problem is taken in [22], wherein a goodness measure is proposed to capture relevance and diversity along with an algorithm to maximize it. Dubey et al [4] aim to find a diversified set of centers (nodes) s.t. the conductance from these centers to the rest of graph has maximum entropy. Citing to the cubic complexity of the earlier approaches, Li et al. [9] introduced an efficient greedy algorithm with liner time and space complexity.

Recommendations in Heterogeneous Networks. In homogeneous networks the problem of recommendation has been studied under various paradigms including ranking [8, 14], semi-supervised learning in graphs [11, 12] etc. Unlike homogeneous networks, each of the multiple relation types present in a heterogeneous information networks carries a different semantic meaning. In [13] it was shown that application of techniques like Page-Rank [14], HITS [8] etc. (which were developed for homogeneous networks) to HIN, yields absurd results. Sun et al. [21] proposed PathSim, a meta-path framework, for network based similarity search. However, it only considered symmetric meta-paths. In [18] a generalized framework HeteSim was proposed which allows to compute similarity between any two types of objects using any possible meta-path. Although these works studied that different meta-paths lead to different rankings, they do not provide a mechanism for choosing the meta-paths. Relationship prediction models were introduced in [19] and [25] which aim to learn the role of different meta-paths in relationship prediction task. Guerraoui et al [5] extend meta-path framework for cross domain recommendation by learning alter-ego profiles. In line with random surfer model, Pham et al. [16] proposed to use multivariate Markov chain to calculate node proximity w.r.t. a given query node along with an optimization framework for learning the influence weights between different types of objects.

3 PRELIMINARIES

3.1 Random Walk over Graph

Consider an undirected weighted graph $\mathcal{G}(\mathcal{V},\mathcal{E})$ with set of vertices $\mathcal{V} = \{v_1, v_2, \ldots, v_n\}$, and set of edges $\mathcal{E} \subset \mathcal{V}\times\mathcal{V}\times\mathbb{R}^+$; where each edge is a 3-tuple (v_i, v_j, w_{ij}) s.t. $v_i, v_j \in \mathcal{V}$ and $w_{ij} \in \mathbb{R}^+$. Then, the adjacency matrix $\mathbf{A}$ corresponding to $\mathcal{G}$ is defined as,

$$A_{ij} = \begin{cases} w_{ij} & \text{if } (v_i,v_j,w_{ij}) \in \mathcal{E} \\ 0 & \text{otherwise} \end{cases}.$$

Given a graph $\mathcal{G}(\mathcal{V},\mathcal{E})$, and an initial vertex x_0 ($\in \mathcal{V}$); a random walk over the graph makes a random choice of transition to, one of its neighboring vertices, x_1; from x_1 to, one of its neighboring vertices, x_2 and so on. The transition probabilities to the neighboring vertices are captured using a transition matrix P, which is derived from the adjacency matrix as follows,

$$P_{ij} = \frac{A_{ij}}{\sum_j A_{ij}}$$

It is worth noting here that the choice of transition to x_2 when at vertex x_1 does not depend on the initial choice x_0. Similarly, the transition made from x_2 will not depend on x_1 and so on. This tends to form a Markov Chain [2]. Given the present, future doesn't depend upon the past.

For the random walk on $\mathcal{G}$ we assume that the initial vertex x_0 is drawn from some distribution Π^0. Likewise, at time t, we denote this distribution using Π^t where $\Pi^t(v_0)$ is the probability of being at vertex v_0 at time t. We call Π^t as the state vector at time t. The distribution of the random walk is then expressed as,

$$\Pi^{t+1} = P^{\mathsf{T}}\Pi^t$$

In a limiting sense (after infinitely many iterations), the probability of being at vertex v_i does not depend on the initial choice. This limiting distribution is known as stationary distribution and is denoted by Π^*.

3.2 Heterogeneous Information Network

Very often graphs involve more than one kind of objects interacting with each other. We call such a graph having multiple types of objects and relations as Heterogeneous Information Network (HIN) which is defined [20] as follows,

Definition 3.1. An Information Network is defined as a directed graph $\mathcal{G}(\mathcal{V},\mathcal{E})$ with an object type mapping function $\tau : \mathcal{V} \to O$ and a link type mapping function $\varnothing : \mathcal{E} \to \mathcal{R}$ where each object $v \in \mathcal{V}$ belongs to one particular object type $\tau(v) \in O$, each link $e \in \mathcal{E}$ belongs to a particular relation $\varnothing(e) \in \mathcal{R}$. When the type of objects $|O| > 1$ or the type of relations $|\mathcal{R}| > 1$, then the network is called **Heterogeneous Information Network**.

If two links belong to the same relation type, the two links share the same starting object type as well as the ending object type. However, it is to be noted that the reverse is not true. Two relations can have same starting as well as ending objects and can yet be different. For example, *user*-visits-*restaurant*, and *user*-likes-*restaurant* are two different relations.

3.3 Multivariate Random Walk over HIN

In random walks over a homogeneous graph, each state is associated with a single node or vertex. However, unlike this, in HIN each state is associated with multiple objects one from each type. Hence, for a random walk over HIN each state is a tuple with the size same as that of the number of object types. For example, in restaurant information network illustrated in Fig. 1 each state during random walk consists of one object each of type *restaurant*, *user*, *locality*, and *cuisine*.

For a HIN $\mathcal{G}(\mathcal{V},\mathcal{E})$, we assume that the set of object types is $O = \{o_1, o_2, \ldots, o_k\}$. Further, for each object type, let the set of nodes be $O_1, O_2, \ldots, O_k$, such that $O_1 \bigcup O_2 \bigcup \ldots \bigcup O_k = \mathcal{V}$. Thus, each state s of the random walk belongs to $O_1 \times O_2 \times \ldots \times O_k$. We use Π_j^t (a $|O_j| \times 1$ vector) to denote the state vector of nodes, with object type o_j at time instance t. The state vector of type o_j at time $(t+1)$ is influenced by state vectors at time t of all other object types with which it shares a relation present in $\mathcal{R}$. The transition matrix for each relation is created using the corresponding adjacency matrix of relation in a manner similar to that of the homogeneous graph. We denote a relation $\mathcal{R}$ using (r, o_i, o_j) where r is the unique relation identifier, o_i is the starting object type and o_j is the ending object type. Further, to denote the transition matrix of the same we use P_r. The rule of random walk is then,

$$\Pi_j^{(t+1)} = \sum_{(r,i,j)\in\mathcal{R}_{*,j}} \alpha_r\, P_r^{\mathsf{T}}\, \Pi_i^t \qquad \text{for } j = 1,2,\ldots,k \tag{1}$$

$$\text{s.t.} \qquad \alpha_r \geq 0 \qquad \text{for all } \ r \in \mathcal{R}, \text{ and}$$

$$\sum_{(r,i,j)\in\mathcal{R}_{*,j}} \alpha_r = 1 \qquad \text{for } \ j = 1,2,\ldots,k$$

where, $\mathcal{R}_{*,j}$ ($\subset \mathcal{R}$) is set of relations having o_j as the ending object. Eqn. 1 expresses the state probability distribution at time $(t+1)$ as a weighted combination of $P_r^{\mathsf{T}}\, \Pi_i^t$ for all $(r,i,j) \in \mathcal{R}_{*,j}$. The constraints on α_r ensure that the state vector at time $(t+1)$ remains a valid probability distribution for each object type. For a given HIN, if the relations can be uniquely identified using starting and ending object (i.e. there does not exist any two relations sharing same starting and ending object) then, the Eqn. 1 can be expressed in matrix notation as follows

$$\begin{bmatrix} \Pi_1^{t+1} \\ \Pi_2^{t+1} \\ \vdots \\ \Pi_k^{t+1} \end{bmatrix} = \begin{bmatrix} \alpha_{11}P_{11}^{\mathsf{T}} & \alpha_{12}P_{12}^{\mathsf{T}} & \cdots & \alpha_{1k}P_{1k}^{\mathsf{T}} \\ \alpha_{21}P_{21}^{\mathsf{T}} & \alpha_{22}P_{22}^{\mathsf{T}} & \cdots & \alpha_{2k}P_{2k}^{\mathsf{T}} \\ \vdots & \vdots & \ddots & \vdots \\ \alpha_{k1}P_{k1}^{\mathsf{T}} & \alpha_{k2}P_{k2}^{\mathsf{T}} & \cdots & \alpha_{kk}P_{kk}^{\mathsf{T}} \end{bmatrix} \begin{bmatrix} \Pi_1^{t} \\ \Pi_1^{t} \\ \vdots \\ \Pi_k^{t} \end{bmatrix} \tag{2}$$

$$\Pi^{t+1} = \widetilde{\mathbf{P}}\,\Pi^t$$

In the above, for each relation (r,i,j) we use ij as subscript instead of r, as it can uniquely identify the relation as mentioned above. In case, where relations could not be uniquely identified using starting and ending object, each sub-matrix in $\widetilde{\mathbf{P}}$ is a weighted combination of transition matrices sharing corresponding starting and ending objects. It can be verified that Eqn. 2 has a unique solution which is a positive vector corresponding to eigenvalue of 1. For further details on this, we refer readers to the text [2]. Unlike homogeneous case, Π^t here is not a probability distribution, however, $\Pi_j^t\ \forall j$, is a probability distribution vector.

4 NON-MARKOVIAN RANDOM WALK

We now introduce the non-Markovian random walk, which we exploit in our work to ensure diversity.

Conventional random walk models like Page-Rank find a stationary distribution assuming that the transition probabilities remain constant over the entire period of time. In practice, this may not be true. For example, consider two restaurants which are open at the same time in a locality, and offer same cuisine. The first one, however offers a better deal for the price customers pay. It is quite natural, that even though on initial days both restaurants were witnessing same number of footfalls, slowly there will be a noticeable change. The first restaurant will eat away the business of the second, and there will be a significant difference in the number of footfalls. In line with this argument, it is justified to have a transition matrix which changes with time.

In order to achieve this we propose to use Vertex-Reinforced Random Walk (VRRW). First introduced by Pemantle [15], the VRRW is based on the idea that the future transition probabilities are influenced by the number of times the ending node has been visited in the past. We first explain VRRW for a homogeneous network $\mathcal{G}(\mathcal{V},\mathcal{E})$ and then generalize it to HIN. For a node $v \in \mathcal{V}$, let the number of times it has been visited by random walk $(x_0, x_1, \ldots, x_t)$ up to time t be $Z^t(v)$, then

$$\begin{aligned} Z^t(v) &= Z^{(t-1)}(v) + \mathbb{1}(x_t = v) \\ &= Z^0(v) + \sum_{i=0}^{t} \mathbb{1}(x_i = v) \end{aligned} \tag{3}$$

where, $Z^0(v)$ is the initial visit count of vertex v, before the random walk has started. In our study, we consistently take $Z^0(v)$ as zero. The transition probabilities for a vertex reinforced random walk $(x_0, x_1, \ldots, x_t)$ are then updated as follows

$$P^{t+1}(v_i, v_j) = \frac{P^0(v_i,v_j) Z^t(v_j)}{\sum_{v_k \in \mathcal{V}} P^0(v_i,v_k) Z^t(v_k)} \tag{4}$$

where P^0 is the initial reinforcement matrix at time $t = 0$. It is difficult to compute $Z^t(v_j)$ at time t based on a single instance of random walk. In [10], it was proposed to compute $Z^t(v_j)$ based on multiple instances of random walk starting with same configuration at time $(t-1)$. This amounts to using $E[Z^t(v_j)]$ in place of $Z^t(v_j)$. Taking expectation of Eqn. 3 on both sides, we have

$$\begin{aligned} E[Z^t(v)] &= E[Z^0(v)] + \sum_{i=0}^{t} \Pi^i(v) \\ &= \sum_{i=0}^{t} \Pi^i(v) \quad \{\text{putting } Z^0(v) = 0\} \end{aligned} \tag{5}$$

Then, Eqn. 4 can be accordingly expressed as,

$$P^{t+1}(v_i, v_j) = \frac{P^0(v_i,v_j) E[Z^t(v_j)]}{\sum_{v_k \in \mathcal{V}} P^0(v_i,v_k) E[Z^t(v_k)]} \tag{6}$$

Where, $E[Z^t(v)]$ is computed using Eqn. 5.

The reinforcement defined in Eqn. 4 is called as linear reinforcement. In Linear VRRW, the modified transition probabilities are linearly proportional to the number of times the vertex has been visited in the past. It was shown, in [23], that in a linear VRRW there is only a finite set of nodes which is infinitely visited with positive probability. This characteristic is not desired from a recommendation perspective as localizing on a finite set of nodes will eventually lead to lack of unseen or new recommendations.

Deviating from [10], we propose to use sublinear vetex reinforced random walks here. Transition probabilities in sublinear VRRW are defined as

$$P^{t+1}(v_i, v_j) = \frac{P^0(v_i,v_j) \left(Z^t(v_j)\right)^\rho}{\sum_{v_k \in \mathcal{V}} P^0(v_i,v_k) \left(Z^t(v_k)\right)^\rho} \tag{7}$$

where $0 < \rho < 1$. It is to be mentioned that the same is known as superlinear VRRW when $\rho > 1$. For the sublinear case, [24] shows that the random walk almost surely visits, infinitely many nodes infinitely often.

Similar to the case of linear reinforcement, for sublinear reinforcement $\left(Z^t(v_k)\right)^\rho$ can be approximated using $E[\left(Z^t(v_k)\right)^\rho]$, which can be computed as follows,

$$\begin{aligned} E\left[\left(Z^t(v)\right)^\rho\right] &= E\left[\left(Z^0(v)\right)^\rho\right] + \sum_{i=0}^{t} \left(\Pi^i(v)\right)^\rho \\ &= \sum_{i=0}^{t} \left(\Pi^i(v)\right)^\rho \quad \{\text{putting } Z^0(v) = 0\} \end{aligned} \tag{8}$$

Now that we have explained the sublinear VRRW for homogeneous network, we extend it to more general HIN. Given a HIN with set of object types $O = \{o_1, o_2, \ldots, o_k\}$ and set of relation types $\mathcal{R}$, then for each relation type $(r, o_a, o_b) \in \mathcal{R}$, the transition matrix corresponding to sublinear VRRW is defined as follows,

$$P_r^{t+1}(v_i, v_j) = \frac{P_r^0(v_i,v_j)\, E\left[\left(Z^t(v_j)\right)^\rho\right]}{\sum_{v_k \in \mathcal{V}} P_r^0(v_i,v_k)\, E\left[\left(Z^t(v_k)\right)^\rho\right]} \tag{9}$$

and, $E\left[\left(Z^t(v)\right)^\rho\right] = \sum_{i=0}^{t} \left(\Pi_b^i(v)\right)^\rho$, where b is the object type obtained using the mapping $\tau : \mathcal{V} \to O$ i.e. $\tau(v) = b$.

5 LEARNING THE PARAMETERS

Sec. 3.3 explains the multivariate random walk over HIN. However, determining the parameter α_r for each relation in $\mathcal{R}$ is a non-trivial task. In this section, we propose a principled approach to learn these parameters using the given snapshot of a HIN. Recalling our recommendation task, it is worth noting that the plain random walk model explained in Sec. 3.3 does not help here because it does not capture personalization. Random walk with restart provides a mechanism to personalize the recommendations for a given query. Random walk with restart at each step, either transitions to one of the randomly chosen neighbors, or jumps back to one of the query nodes. In a random walk over HIN $\mathcal{G}(\mathcal{V},\mathcal{E})$, with set of object types O and set of relation types $\mathcal{R}$; for object type o_j, we use β_j to denote the probability of jumping to one of the initial query nodes. The rule of random walk expressed in Eqn. 1 is then accordingly modified as

$$\begin{aligned}
\Pi_j^{(t+1)} &= \sum_{(r,i,j)\in\mathcal{R}_{*,j}} \alpha_r \left(P_r^t\right)^\top \Pi_i^t + \beta_j q_j \qquad \text{for } j = 1,2,\ldots,k \\
\text{s.t.} \quad & \alpha_r \geq 0 \qquad \text{for all } r \in \mathcal{R}, \\
& \beta_j \geq 0 \qquad \text{for } j = 1,2,\ldots,k \\
& \left(\sum_{(r,i,j)\in\mathcal{R}_{*,j}} \alpha_r\right) + \beta_j = 1 \qquad \text{for } j = 1,2,\ldots,k
\end{aligned} \tag{10}$$

where q_j is the probability vector corresponding to initial query distribution for object type o_j. The transition matrix P_r^t is for sublinear VRRW and is updated using Eqn. 9.

5.1 Cross Entropy Loss Minimization

We next focus our attention on learning the parameters α's and β's in Eqn. 10. For this, we introduce a probabilistic learning framework based on cross entropy cost function. To recall, for a given set of parameter values α's and β's there exists a stationary probability distribution Π_j^* for each object type o_j. The stationary distribution is obtained by iterative application of Eqn. 10. Although, the stationary distribution Π_j^* is obtained for all object types, at the end we are only interested in the distribution of target object type (the object type concerning the recommendations). We refer to this distribution as Π_{target}^*. However, for the sake of brevity, here in this section 5.1 we make an abuse of notation, and will write Π instead of Π_{target}^*.

For a query q = $\{q_1, q_2, \ldots, q_k\}$, we use Π_q to denote the stationary distribution, and Θ_q to denote the observed response for the target objects. It is to be mentioned here that in majority of the cases the observations are only available in the form of binary responses (whether the recommendation was useful or not) but in a few cases like movie recommendation to users, a rating on a ordinal scale is also available.

Given Π_q and Θ_q for a query q, for each pair (v_i, v_j) of target objects, we define the following

$$\begin{aligned}
\overline{p_{ij}} &= \mathbb{1}\left(\Theta_q(v_i) > \Theta_q(v_j)\right) \\
o_{ij} &= \Pi_q(v_i) - \Pi_q(v_j), \quad \textit{and} \\
p_{ij} &= \frac{e^{\lambda o_{ij}}}{1 + e^{\lambda o_{ij}}}, \qquad \text{where } \lambda \text{ is a const.} > 0
\end{aligned}$$

$\overline{p_{ij}}$ is the actual probability of node v_i being ranked higher than node v_j. However, unfortunately it is difficult to obtain this probability for each pair. To address this, we have defined $\overline{p_{ij}}$ as 1 if v_i is having higher affinity than v_j in observed response Θ_q. Similarly, the probability of recommending node v_i prior to node v_j is obtained by using the sigmoid function on the difference in corresponding values in stationary probability distribution Π_q. We then define the cross entropy cost for pair (v_i, v_j) as follows,

$$\begin{aligned}
C_{ij} &= -\overline{p_{ij}} \log p_{ij} - (1 - \overline{p_{ij}}) \log(1 - p_{ij}) \\
&= -\lambda \overline{p_{ij}} o_{ij} + \log(1 + e^{\lambda o_{ij}}) \\
& \qquad \{\text{substituting for } p_{ij}\}
\end{aligned} \tag{11}$$

The loss corresponding to a query q is then defined as the sum of C_{ij} over all possible pairs (v_i, v_j), i.e.

$$L_q = \sum_{(v_i,v_j)} C_{ij} \quad \text{s.t.} \quad \tau(v_i) = \tau(v_j) = \text{ target type}$$

We now compute the gradient of C_{ij} with respect to the parameters to be learned. Gradient of C_{ij}, w.r.t. α_r corresponding to each relation in $\mathcal{R}$ is computed as

$$\frac{\partial\, C_{ij}}{\partial \alpha_r} = \left(-\lambda\overline{p_{ij}} + \frac{\lambda e^{\lambda o_{ij}}}{1 + e^{\lambda o_{ij}}}\right)\left(\frac{\partial\, \Pi_q(v_i)}{\partial \alpha_r} - \frac{\partial\, \Pi_q(v_j)}{\partial \alpha_r}\right). \tag{12}$$

Gradient w.r.t. β_j for $j = 1,2,\ldots,k$ is also computed in a similar fashion, which we omit writing here.

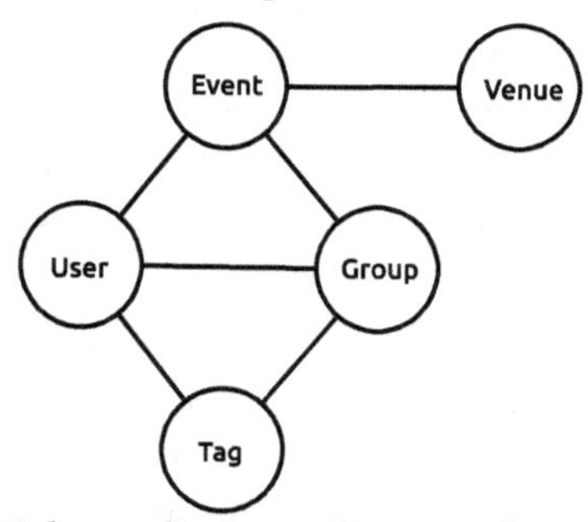

Figure 2: Schema diagram of Meetup dataset used in experiments.

5.2 Partial Derivative of Stationary Distribution

We further take a closer look at computing $\frac{\partial\, \Pi_q(v)}{\partial \alpha_r}$ $\left(\text{and } \frac{\partial\, \Pi_q(v)}{\partial \beta_j}\right)$. Although we provide a general framework for recommendation in any heterogeneous information network; for the ease of understanding, we describe computation of partial derivative of stationary probability distribution Π using Meetup schema shown in Fig. 2. We consider the task of recommend groups to the user. The stationary probability distribution corresponding to the Meetup schema is,

$$\begin{aligned}
\Pi_U^* &= \alpha_{TU}\, P_{TU}^{\mathsf{T}}\, \Pi_T^* + \alpha_{GU}\, P_{GU}^{\mathsf{T}}\, \Pi_G^* + \alpha_{EU}\, P_{EU}^{\mathsf{T}}\, \Pi_E^* + \beta_U\, q_U \\
\Pi_T^* &= \alpha_{GT}\, P_{GT}^{\mathsf{T}}\, \Pi_G^* + \alpha_{UT}\, P_{UT}^{\mathsf{T}}\, \Pi_U^* + \beta_T\, q_T \\
\Pi_G^* &= \alpha_{EG}\, P_{EG}^{\mathsf{T}}\, \Pi_E^* + \alpha_{UG}\, P_{UG}^{\mathsf{T}}\, \Pi_U^* + \alpha_{TG}\, P_{TG}^{\mathsf{T}}\, \Pi_T^* + \beta_G\, q_G \\
\Pi_E^* &= \alpha_{UE}\, P_{UE}^{\mathsf{T}}\, \Pi_U^* + \alpha_{GE}\, P_{GE}^{\mathsf{T}}\, \Pi_G^* + \alpha_{VE}\, P_{VE}^{\mathsf{T}}\, \Pi_V^* + \beta_E\, q_E \\
\Pi_V^* &= \alpha_{EV}\, P_{EV}^{\mathsf{T}}\, \Pi_E^* + \beta_V\, q_V
\end{aligned}$$

where the subscripts U, T, G, E, and V denote *user*, *tag*, *group*, *event*, and *venue* object type respectively. Likewise, the subscript TU denotes the relation *users*-associated with-*tag* and so on. By looking at Eqn. 12, it appears that only gradient of stationary distribution of object to be recommended (*group*) is of interest to us. However, from above it is easy to verify that there exists a cyclic dependency amongst all the stationary distributions and hence their gradients. Due to this, it is required to find gradients of all stationary distributions. We illustrate gradient w.r.t. one parameter α_{TU} below

$$\begin{aligned}
\frac{\partial\, \Pi_U^*}{\partial\, \alpha_{TU}} &= \alpha_{GU}\frac{\partial\, P_{GU}^{\mathsf{T}}\Pi_G^*}{\partial\, \alpha_{TU}} + \alpha_{EU}\frac{\partial\, P_{EU}^{\mathsf{T}}\Pi_E^*}{\partial\, \alpha_{TU}} + \alpha_{TU}\frac{\partial\, P_{TU}^{\mathsf{T}}\Pi_T^*}{\partial\, \alpha_{TU}} + P_{TU}^{\mathsf{T}}\Pi_T^* \\
\frac{\partial\, \Pi_T^*}{\partial\, \alpha_{TU}} &= \alpha_{GT}\frac{\partial\, P_{GT}^{\mathsf{T}}\Pi_G^*}{\partial\, \alpha_{TU}} + \alpha_{UT}\frac{\partial\, P_{UT}^{\mathsf{T}}\,\Pi_U^*}{\partial\, \alpha_{TU}} \\
\frac{\partial\, \Pi_G^*}{\partial\, \alpha_{TU}} &= \alpha_{EG}\frac{\partial\, P_{EG}^{\mathsf{T}}\Pi_E^*}{\partial\, \alpha_{TU}} + \alpha_{UG}\frac{\partial\, P_{UG}^{\mathsf{T}}\Pi_U^*}{\partial\, \alpha_{TU}} + \alpha_{TG}\frac{\partial\, P_{TG}^{\mathsf{T}}\Pi_T^*}{\partial\, \alpha_{TU}} \\
\frac{\partial\, \Pi_E^*}{\partial\, \alpha_{TU}} &= \alpha_{UE}\frac{\partial\, P_{UE}^{\mathsf{T}}\Pi_U^*}{\partial\, \alpha_{TU}} + \alpha_{GE}\frac{\partial\, P_{GE}^{\mathsf{T}}\Pi_G^*}{\partial\, \alpha_{TU}} + \alpha_{VE}\frac{\partial\, P_{VE}^{\mathsf{T}}\Pi_V^*}{\partial\, \alpha_{TU}} \\
\frac{\partial\, \Pi_V^*}{\partial\, \alpha_{TU}} &= \alpha_{EV}\frac{\partial\, P_{EV}^{\mathsf{T}}\Pi_E^*}{\partial\, \alpha_{TU}}\,,
\end{aligned} \tag{13}$$

Partial derivatives w.r.t. the other parameters can be obtained in a similar manner.

Unlike the case of conventional random walk, in VRRW the transition matrix keeps changing during the random walk, and is dependent upon the stationary probability distribution of the ending node. Hence, the computation of partial derivatives like $\frac{\partial\, P_{TU}^{\mathsf{T}}\Pi_T^*}{\partial\, \alpha_{TU}}$ is not straightforward and is computationally more involved. Using the definition of sublinear reinforced random walk, the transition matrix is modified based on the number of times the ending object has been visited. This has been specified in Eqn. 8. However, at convergence (as the length of walk tends to infinity), the same can be approximated using the stationary distribution. Thus,

$$E\left[(Z^*(v))^{\rho}\right] \approx \left(\Pi_b^*(v)\right)^{\rho} \quad \text{for all} \quad v \text{ s.t. } \tau(v) = b.$$

Without loss of generality, we consider a relation having starting object of type x and ending object of type y, with stationary distributions Π_x and Π_y respectively. We denote the initial transition matrix for this relation using $P^0 \left(= \left[P_{ij}^0\right]_{n \times m}\right)$. Then, the reinforced transition matrix P at convergence is given by

$$P = S^{-1}\, P^0\, Y^{\rho}$$

where,

$$S = diag\left(\sum_i P_{1i}^0 \left(\Pi_y(i)\right)^{\rho}, \sum_i P_{2i}^0 \left(\Pi_y(i)\right)^{\rho}, \ldots, \sum_i P_{mi}^0 \left(\Pi_y(i)\right)^{\rho}\right)$$

and $Y = diag\Big(\Pi_y(1), \Pi_y(2), \ldots, \Pi_y(n)\Big)$. We describe the partial derivative of $P^{\mathsf{T}}\Pi_x$ w.r.t. the parameter α.

$$\begin{aligned}
\frac{\partial\, P^{\mathsf{T}}\Pi_x}{\partial\, \alpha} = P^{\mathsf{T}}\,\frac{\partial\, \Pi_x}{\partial\, \alpha} &+ \rho\, Y^{\rho-1}\, P^{\mathsf{T}}\, S^{-1}\Pi_x \odot \frac{\partial\, \Pi_y}{\partial\, \alpha} \\
&- \rho\, \Pi_y^{\rho-1} \odot \Pi_x S^{-2}\, P\, Y^{\rho-1}\frac{\partial\, \Pi_y}{\partial\, \alpha}
\end{aligned}$$

where $\odot$ is the element wise product or Hadamard product. The above is used in partial derivatives specified in Eqn. 13 for Meetup schema. It is easy to follow that upon substitution, the equations in 13 form a linear system of equations. This can be efficiently solved using linear solvers. Also, there always exists a solution to this system of equations. However, due to lack of space we omit the proof of this.

5.3 Learning Algorithm

We now describe the algorithm for learning the required parameters. For a given HIN, the algorithm starts by computing the initial transition probability matrix corresponding to each relation type. Also, the parameters are initialized uniformly in the beginning. We use the projected stochastic gradient descent method for learning the optimal values of the parameters. In each epoch we pick a random subset of k queries (mini-batch of size k), and compute the stationary probability distribution corresponding to it. Next, we use these stationary probability distributions along with values of the parameters known from the previous iteration to find the gradient of stationary distribution with respect to each parameter. The gradient corresponding to k queries in a epoch are accumulated, and parameters are updated using gradient descent with step size η/c. Here, η is the specified learning rate parameter, and c is the current epoch count. To ensure the constraints in Eqn. 10, we project the obtained parameter values to $\mathbb{R}^+ \bigcup \{0\}$. Also, we normalize the new learned parameters, such that the parameters for incoming relations to an object along with the corresponding query parameter sum upto 1.

Algorithm 1 gives the pseudocode for the above described approach.

6 EXPERIMENTS

We empirically evaluate the effectiveness of the proposed approach against the state-of-the-art techniques and other baselines. On Meetup schema shown in Fig. 2, we consider the following recommendation problems:

- Recommending *Groups* to *User*.
- Recommending *Tags* to *Group*.

We specifically choose these tasks as intuitively it sounds appealing to have diversity in the first task and no diversity in the second task.

6.1 Dataset

For our experiments, we crawled the data from the Meetup website[1]. Meetup is an online social networking website, which helps users with similar interests to organize and conduct an online/offline event. Users can join the groups based on their interests and can conduct or participate in events organized by the group.

[1] www.meetup.com

Algorithm 1 Learn Parameters using Stochastic Gradient Descent.

Input:
$\mathcal{G}(\mathcal{V},\mathcal{E})$ ▷ Given HIN snapshot
Q ▷ Set of queries
d ▷ Recommendation object type
Θ ▷ Set of observed responses corresponding to queries
k ▷ Sample size for SGD
Output:
$\Lambda = [\boldsymbol{\alpha}, \boldsymbol{\beta}]$ ▷ Learned parameters

$A \leftarrow \{A_r : A_r$ is adj. matrix for each relation in $\mathcal{G}(\mathcal{V},\mathcal{E})\}$
$P \leftarrow \{P_r : P_r$ is prob. transition matrix for each $A_r\}$
$\Lambda^0 = [\alpha^0, \beta^0]^\top \leftarrow$ Init. all relations and query params.
$i \leftarrow 1$ ▷ Maintains current SGD iteration count
while not converged **do**
  $\widehat{Q} \leftarrow$ Random subset of Q of size k
  $\widehat{\Theta} \leftarrow$ subset of Θ corresponding to $\widehat{Q}$
  grad $\leftarrow$ **0**
  for each $q \in \widehat{Q}$ **do**
    $\Pi^*_q \leftarrow$ compute stationary distribution using Eqn. 10
    for each parameter α_r do
      Compute $\frac{\partial \Pi^*_q}{\partial \alpha_r}$ as in Eqn. 13
      Use $\frac{\partial \Pi^*_q}{\partial \alpha_r}$ to compute $\frac{\partial L_q}{\partial \alpha_r} = \sum_{(v_i,v_j)} \frac{\partial C_{ij}}{\partial \alpha_r}$
      $grad(\alpha_r) \leftarrow grad(\alpha_r) + \frac{\partial L_q}{\partial \alpha_r}$
  $\Lambda^i \leftarrow \Lambda^{i-1} - \frac{\eta}{i} \frac{\textbf{grad}}{\|\textbf{grad}\|}$
  $\Lambda^i \leftarrow$ Project each element in Λ^i to $\mathbb{R}^+ \bigcup \{0\}$.
  Normalize Λ^i to ensure constraints in Eqn. 10.
  $i \leftarrow i + 1$
return $\Lambda^t = [\alpha^t, \beta^t]$

City	Users	Groups	Events	Tags	Venues
Bangalore	179,415	2,304	36,525	14,939	4,213
Hyderabad	117,309	997	32,527	10,520	2,453

Table 1: Statistics of Meetup dataset for different cities.

For two cities namely Bangalore, and Hyderabad, we collected the raw data using the Meetup API. Further, we considered the time range from the day Meetup was introduced up to July 31, 2017. For each city we collected the list of Meetup groups they have. Then, for each group we collected the tags and users associated with them and information about events that the group has conducted. Next, for the events we collect the venues where they have been conducted and list of users attending the event. Using attendance of events we only crawled information about the users, who have attended at least one event. We provide the statistics of the raw dataset in Table 1.

6.2 Algorithms

In addition to the proposed technique (`Div-HeteRec`), we consider two state-of-the-art techniques and two more related baseline algorithms to show the effect of diversity. We describe these techniques below:

(1) **Random Walk with Restart (`RWR`)**: In this conventional random walk with restart model there is no distinction between various node types. All the relation types and node types are treated uniformly and a homogeneous network is created. Corresponding to the given query, it then computes a single stationary distribution which is later exploited to make recommendations.

(2) **Collaborative Filtering using NMF (`NMF`)**: Here Non-Negative Matrix Factorization is used to implement the conventional collaborative filtering model. For *Groups* to *User* and *Tags* to *Group* recommendation it takes the Group-User and Tag-Group matrices respectively and applies NMF on them. Empirically the number of dimensions (k) is fixed to be 20. After factorization, the matrix is reconstructed and the magnitude of entries which were missing earlier is used to make recommendations.

(3) **Uniform Heterogeneous Recommendation (`Uni-HeteRec`)**: This is the completely stripped off version of our proposed approach. The baseline helps in highlighting the effectiveness of introducing the diversity and learning the influence of relations. The parameters α's and β's are initialized such that for an object all its dependencies get equal importance.

(4) **Learned Heterogeneous Recommendation (`Learn-HeteRec`)**: Unlike in our proposed approach, here the transition matrix is static. However, we learn the optimal parameter values using the framework described in Sec. 5.1. It is to be noted that this approach is different from the HeteRS mentioned in [16] as the underlying loss function is different.

For sublinear reinforcement in `Div-HeteRec` we use $\rho = 1/2$. Also, with $\rho = 0$, `Div-HeteRec` is same as `Learn-HeteRec`.

6.3 Setup

Taking a glance at the data, we found the data to be highly sparse, indicating that the use of Meetup has not matured still in the cities considered. The number of users are above $100k$ for the considered cities, but surprisingly very few of these users are actively using the portal. Because of this reason, we found it helpful to filter off the not so useful objects by preprocessing the data. We remove all the users wo have attended less than 5 events over this entire duration. Similarly for groups we remove those which had conducted less than 5 events. Also, we remove events which had less than 5 people attending them.

After preprocessing the data we partition it into train, validation, and test sets. We describe the strategy adapted for partitioning next. We partition the given data into 60%, 20%, and 20% as train, validation and test dataset respectively. While partitioning we only consider the relation concerning the recommendation problem. For example, for group to user recommendation we perform the split only on user-group adjacency matrix (and correspondingly group-user). However, specifically for group to user recommendation task, after moving the groups for a user to test and validation set, we also

Algorithm	Precision@k					Recall@k					nDCG@k				
	$k=1$	$k=2$	$k=3$	$k=5$	$k=10$	$k=1$	$k=2$	$k=3$	$k=5$	$k=10$	$k=1$	$k=2$	$k=3$	$k=5$	$k=10$
RWR	.1195	.1064	.0958	.0819	.0635	.0656	.1172	.1561	.2186	.3352	.1195	.1323	.1461	.1698	.2104
NMF	.0054	.0040	.0043	.0076	.0065	.0018	.0024	.0050	.0170	.0279	.0320	.0382	.0439	.0528	.0679
Uni-HeteRec	.1150	.1120	.1045	.0854	.0651	.0634	.1238	.1745	.2376	.3516	.1150	.1366	.1562	.1797	.2196
Learn-HeteRec	.1544	.1295	.1156	.0945	.0698	.0895	.1469	.1883	.2511	.3656	.1544	.1656	.1806	.2034	.2426
Div-HeteRec	**.1600**	**.1317**	**.1177**	**.0956**	**.0713**	**.0906**	**.1471**	**.1941**	**.2601**	**.3767**	**.1600**	**.1676**	**.1843**	**.2085**	**.2494**

Table 2: *Group* to *User* Recommendation for Bangalore Meetup dataset.

Algorithm	Precision@k					Recall@k					nDCG@k				
	$k=1$	$k=2$	$k=3$	$k=5$	$k=10$	$k=1$	$k=2$	$k=3$	$k=5$	$k=10$	$k=1$	$k=2$	$k=3$	$k=5$	$k=10$
RWR	.1810	.1392	.1199	.0973	.0724	.1188	.1838	.2304	.2987	.4121	.1810	.1931	.2101	.2375	.2792
NMF	.0018	.0009	.0015	.0046	.0046	.0010	.0010	.0029	.0148	.0244	.0443	.0510	.0615	.0749	.0903
Uni-HeteRec	.1582	.1240	.1027	.0835	.0613	.1057	.1630	.2014	.2621	.3696	.1582	.1710	.1838	.2080	.2480
Learn-HeteRec	.1791	.1484	.1265	.1021	.0729	.1197	.1943	.2450	.3100	.4141	.1791	.2012	.2200	.2510	.2942
Div-HeteRec	**.2031**	**.1588**	**.1301**	**.1024**	**.0737**	**.1345**	**.2039**	**.2465**	**.3134**	**.4270**	**.2031**	**.2166**	**.2302**	**.2560**	**.2969**

Table 3: *Group* to *User* Recommendation for Hyderabad Meetup dataset.

Algorithm	Precision@k					Recall@k					nDCG@k				
	$k=1$	$k=2$	$k=3$	$k=5$	$k=10$	$k=1$	$k=2$	$k=3$	$k=5$	$k=10$	$k=1$	$k=2$	$k=3$	$k=5$	$k=10$
RWR	.0046	.0046	.0046	.0037	.0046	.0023	.0046	.0069	.0084	.0276	.0046	.0046	.0060	.0069	.0136
NMF	.0046	.0023	.0015	.0065	.0119	.0023	.0023	.0023	.0169	.0729	.0184	.0166	.0159	.0196	.0264
Uni-HeteRec	.0092	.0092	.0168	.0147	.0143	.0069	.0099	.0322	.0445	.0852	.0092	.0110	.0223	.0283	.0434
Learn-HeteRec	**.1244**	**.1037**	**.0875**	**.0654**	**.0484**	**.0883**	**.1329**	**.1651**	**.1997**	**.2887**	**.1244**	**.1349**	**.1481**	**.1648**	**.1976**
Div-HeteRec	.0552	.0483	.0399	.0350	.0253	.0399	.0637	.0791	.1059	.1444	.0553	.0629	.0693	.0829	.0981

Table 4: *Tag* to *Group* Recommendation for Bangalore Meetup dataset.

Algorithm	Precision@k					Recall@k					nDCG@k				
	$k=1$	$k=2$	$k=3$	$k=5$	$k=10$	$k=1$	$k=2$	$k=3$	$k=5$	$k=10$	$k=1$	$k=2$	$k=3$	$k=5$	$k=10$
RWR	.0000	.0000	.0034	.0031	.0015	.0000	.0000	.0077	.0098	.0098	.0000	.0000	.0041	.0052	.0052
NMF	.0000	.0000	.0000	.0000	.0018	.0000	.0000	.0000	.0000	.0077	.0128	.0095	.0122	.0154	.0207
Uni-HeteRec	.0383	.0255	.0204	.0174	.0120	.0239	.0289	.0341	.0443	.0643	.0383	.0344	.0343	.0397	.0469
Learn-HeteRec	**.2071**	**.1483**	**.1159**	**.0879**	**.0590**	**.1189**	**.1670**	**.1994**	**.2570**	**.3341**	**.2071**	**.1858**	**.1922**	**.2187**	**.2479**
Div-HeteRec	.1176	.0805	.0605	.0485	.0322	.0635	.0886	.9846	.1343	.1777	.1176	.1013	.0994	.1164	.1332

Table 5: *Tag* to *Group* Recommendation for Hyderabad Meetup dataset.

remove the events associated with a group which were attended by the user to maintain consistency. Even after preprocessing task we will be left with users associated with less than 5 groups. For performing the split we only consider the users who are members of at-least 5 groups, while the other users are retained in train set. Similar is the case with tag to group recommendation where we only consider groups with at-least 5 tags for performing the split. For evaluation, we use Precision, Recall, and Normalized Discounted Cumulative Gain as the measures for both the tasks. For a given query q with set of observed responses O_q and set of recommendations R_q. Precision is defined as $|O_q \bigcap R_q| / |R_q|$, and Recall as $|O_q \bigcap R_q| / |O_q|$. The nDCG measure is computed as

$$nDCG = \frac{1}{IDCG} \sum_{i}^{|R_q|} \frac{rel_i}{\log_2(i+1)}$$

where, $IDCG$ is the ideal discounted cumulative gain which considers the set of relevant documents only and is defined as,

$$IDCG = \sum_{i}^{|R_q|} \frac{rel_i}{\log_2(i+1)}$$

It should be noted that unlike $nDCG$ where rel_i is the relevance of ith recommendation in R_q, in $IDCG$ rel_i is the relevance of ith recommendation in O_q. For precion@k, recall@k, and nDCG@k we consider R_q as the set of top k recommendations only.

6.4 Results and Discussion

For the Meetup dataset, we present the results for *Group* to *User* recommendation in Table 2 and Table 3, and results for *Tag* to *Group* recommendation in Table 4 and Table 5 for both the cities respectively.

We first analyze the results for *Group* to *User* recommendation. To start with, conventional collaborative filtering model NMF performs worst amongst all. This reasserts the fact that exploiting axillary information helps in recommendation task. Assigning equal importance to all relations seems to perform worse than the plain random walk with restart (RWR) model. However, when the weights are learned using the proposed framework the performance improves. Further, it is easy to observe from Table 2 and Table 3, that the diverse recommendations made using Div-HeteRec outperforms all other approaches. The improvement achieved by using

Div-HeteRec over Learn-HeteRec is more pronounce in the Hyderabad Meetup dataset. This is due to the fact that, Bangalore has more of information technology (IT) culture and majority of the groups are pertaining to IT only. Hence, there is a lack of diversity amongst groups in Bangalore. As a result of this diversity in recommended groups does not make much sense for this data.
Next we analyze the results for *Tag* to *Group* recommendation. Both RWR and Collaborative Filtering using NMF fail drastically in this task. Also, the Uni-HeteRec model which was performing satisfactorily in previous task fails. The same (uniform) parameter values which were doing reasonably well in previous task do not work in this setting. This emphasizes the fact that, for different tasks, different relations carry different priorities. However, unlike the previous case where Div-HeteRec was performing best here we find that Learn-HeteRec outperforms all other approaches. This is in-line with the intuition that the tags of groups are closely related to each other and suggesting a diverse set of tags should hurt the performance.
Summarizing our observations, we find that

- Making diverse recommendations in cases where they are intuitive also improves the performance of a recommender system.
- learning the importance of relations always helps; different recommendation tasks will require different weightages to be assigned to various relations.

7 CONCLUSION

In this paper, we introduced the need for diversity in recommendations in a heterogeneous information network (HIN). We proposed a sublinear vertex reinforced random walk based mechanism for integrating diversity. This emulates rich getting richer mechanism by increasing transitions to nodes which have been visited more frequently in the past. Further, in a HIN, different relation types have significantly different priorities for a given recommendation task. In a multivariate random walk framework we proposed a cross entropy cost based learning framework for systematically learning these priorities. Finally, we demonstrated the effectiveness of our approach using real-world Meetup dataset. So, naturally for recommendations requiring diversity the proposed Div-HeteRec is performing the best and for situations where diversity is not essential, the proposed Learn-HeteRec is ideally suited. It is interesting to explore, in the future, a hybrid model that aptly combines both diverse and non-diverse requirements. We make the code and datasets used in our experiments publicly available.

REFERENCES

[1] Jaime Carbonell and Jade Goldstein. 1998. The use of MMR, diversity-based reranking for reordering documents and producing summaries. In *Proceedings of the 21st annual international ACM SIGIR conference on Research and development in information retrieval.* ACM, 335–336.
[2] Wai-Ki Ching, Ximin Huang, Michael K Ng, and Tak Kuen Siu. 2013. Markov Chains: Models, Algorithms and Applications. (2013).
[3] Marina Drosou and Evaggelia Pitoura. 2010. Search result diversification. *ACM SIGMOD Record* 39, 1 (2010), 41–47.
[4] Avinava Dubey, Soumen Chakrabarti, and Chiranjib Bhattacharyya. 2011. Diversity in ranking via resistive graph centers. In *Proceedings of the 17th ACM SIGKDD international conference on Knowledge discovery and data mining.* ACM.
[5] Rachid Guerraoui, Anne-Marie Kermarrec, Tao Lin, and Rhicheek Patra. 2017. Heterogeneous recommendations: what you might like to read after watching interstellar. *Proceedings of the VLDB Endowment* 10, 10 (2017), 1070–1081.
[6] Taher H Haveliwala. 2002. Topic-sensitive pagerank. In *Proceedings of the 11th international conference on World Wide Web.* ACM, 517–526.
[7] Daniel S Himmelstein and Sergio E Baranzini. 2015. Heterogeneous network edge prediction: a data integration approach to prioritize disease-associated genes. *PLoS computational biology* 11, 7 (2015), e1004259.
[8] Jon M Kleinberg. 1999. Hubs, authorities, and communities. *ACM computing surveys (CSUR)* 31, 4es (1999), 5.
[9] Rong-Hua Li and Jeffery Xu Yu. 2013. Scalable diversified ranking on large graphs. *IEEE Transactions on Knowledge and Data Engineering* 25, 9 (2013), 2133–2146.
[10] Qiaozhu Mei, Jian Guo, and Dragomir Radev. 2010. Divrank: the interplay of prestige and diversity in information networks. In *Proceedings of the 16th ACM SIGKDD international conference on Knowledge discovery and data mining.* Acm, 1009–1018.
[11] Sharad Nandanwar and M Narasimha Murty. 2016. Structural neighborhood based classification of nodes in a network. In *Proceedings of the 22nd ACM SIGKDD International Conference on Knowledge Discovery and Data Mining.* ACM, 1085–1094.
[12] Sharad Nandanwar and M Narasimha Murty. 2018. Overlap-Robust Decision Boundary Learning for Within-Network Classification. In *Proceedings of the 32nd AAAI Conference on Artificial Intelligence.* AAAI.
[13] Zaiqing Nie, Yuanzhi Zhang, Ji-Rong Wen, and Wei-Ying Ma. 2005. Object-level ranking: bringing order to web objects. In *Proceedings of the 14th international conference on World Wide Web.* ACM, 567–574.
[14] Lawrence Page, Sergey Brin, Rajeev Motwani, and Terry Winograd. 1999. *The PageRank citation ranking: Bringing order to the web.* Technical Report. Stanford InfoLab.
[15] Robin Pemantle. 1992. Vertex-reinforced random walk. *Probability Theory and Related Fields* 92, 1 (1992), 117–136.
[16] Tuan-Anh Nguyen Pham, Xutao Li, Gao Cong, and Zhenjie Zhang. 2015. A general graph-based model for recommendation in event-based social networks. In *Data Engineering (ICDE), 2015 IEEE 31st International Conference on.* IEEE, 567–578.
[17] Filip Radlinski, Paul N Bennett, Ben Carterette, and Thorsten Joachims. 2009. Redundancy, diversity and interdependent document relevance. In *ACM SIGIR Forum*, Vol. 43. ACM, 46–52.
[18] Chuan Shi, Xiangnan Kong, Yue Huang, S Yu Philip, and Bin Wu. 2014. Hetesim: A general framework for relevance measure in heterogeneous networks. *IEEE Transactions on Knowledge and Data Engineering* 26, 10 (2014), 2479–2492.
[19] Yizhou Sun, Rick Barber, Manish Gupta, Charu C Aggarwal, and Jiawei Han. 2011. Co-author relationship prediction in heterogeneous bibliographic networks. In *Advances in Social Networks Analysis and Mining (ASONAM), 2011 International Conference on.* IEEE, 121–128.
[20] Yizhou Sun and Jiawei Han. 2012. Mining heterogeneous information networks: principles and methodologies. *Synthesis Lectures on Data Mining and Knowledge Discovery* 3, 2 (2012), 1–159.
[21] Yizhou Sun, Jiawei Han, Xifeng Yan, Philip S Yu, and Tianyi Wu. 2011. Pathsim: Meta path-based top-k similarity search in heterogeneous information networks. *Proceedings of the VLDB Endowment* 4, 11 (2011), 992–1003.
[22] Hanghang Tong, Jingrui He, Zhen Wen, Ravi Konuru, and Ching-Yung Lin. 2011. Diversified Ranking on Large Graphs: An Optimization Viewpoint. In *Proceedings of the 17th ACM SIGKDD International Conference on Knowledge Discovery and Data Mining (KDD '11).* ACM, New York, NY, USA, 1028–1036. DOI: http://dx.doi.org/10.1145/2020408.2020573
[23] Stanislav Volkov. 2001. Vertex-reinforced random walk on arbitrary graphs. *Annals of probability* (2001), 66–91.
[24] Stanislav Volkov. 2006. Phase transition in vertex-reinforced random walks on with non-linear reinforcement. *Journal of Theoretical Probability* 19, 3 (2006), 691–700.
[25] Xiao Yu, Xiang Ren, Yizhou Sun, Quanquan Gu, Bradley Sturt, Urvashi Khandelwal, Brandon Norick, and Jiawei Han. 2014. Personalized entity recommendation: A heterogeneous information network approach. In *Proceedings of the 7th ACM international conference on Web search and data mining.* ACM, 283–292.
[26] Cheng Xiang Zhai, William W Cohen, and John Lafferty. 2003. Beyond independent relevance: methods and evaluation metrics for subtopic retrieval. In *Proceedings of the 26th annual international ACM SIGIR conference on Research and development in informaion retrieval.* ACM, 10–17.
[27] Mi Zhang and Neil Hurley. 2008. Avoiding monotony: improving the diversity of recommendation lists. In *Proceedings of the 2008 ACM conference on Recommender systems.* ACM, 123–130.
[28] Shenghuo Zhu, Kai Yu, Yun Chi, and Yihong Gong. 2007. Combining content and link for classification using matrix factorization. In *Proceedings of the 30th annual international ACM SIGIR conference on Research and development in information retrieval.* ACM, 487–494.
[29] Xiaojin Zhu, Andrew B Goldberg, Jurgen Van Gael, and David Andrzejewski. 2007. Improving Diversity in Ranking using Absorbing Random Walks.. In *HLT-NAACL.* 97–104.

Neural Personalized Ranking for Image Recommendation

Wei Niu, James Caverlee, Haokai Lu
Department of Computer Science and Engineering, Texas A&M University
{wei,caverlee,hlu}@cse.tamu.edu

ABSTRACT

We propose a new model toward improving the quality of image recommendations in social sharing communities like Pinterest, Flickr, and Instagram. Concretely, we propose *Neural Personalized Ranking (NPR)* – a personalized pairwise ranking model over implicit feedback datasets – that is inspired by Bayesian Personalized Ranking (BPR) and recent advances in neural networks. We further build an enhanced model by augmenting the basic NPR model with multiple contextual preference clues including user tags, geographic features, and visual factors. In our experiments over the Flickr YFCC100M dataset, we demonstrate the proposed NPR model is more effective than multiple baselines. Moreover, the contextual enhanced NPR model significantly outperforms the base model by 16.6% and a contextual enhanced BPR model by 4.5% in precision and recall.

ACM Reference Format:
Wei Niu, James Caverlee, Haokai Lu. 2018. Neural Personalized Ranking for Image Recommendation. In *Proceedings of 11th ACM International Conf. on Web Search and Data Mining (WSDM 2018)*. ACM, New York, NY, USA, 9 pages. https://doi.org/10.1145/3159652.3159728

1 INTRODUCTION

One of the foundations of many web and app-based communities is *image sharing*. For example, Pinterest, Facebook, Twitter, Flickr, Instagram, and Snapchat all enable communities to share, favorite, re-post, and curate images. And yet, these social actions are far outnumbered by the total number of images in the system; that is, there may be many valuable images undiscovered by each user. Hence, considerable research has focused on the challenge of *image recommendation* in these communities, e.g,. [8, 15, 19, 20, 23, 24, 31].

However, many of these works mainly leverage user profile and behavior patterns. Due to the extreme sparsity of user feedback in image sharing communities and a lack of proper representation, traditional recommendation including collaborative filtering and content-based methods face challenges. In contrast, Bayesian Personalized Ranking (BPR) has shown state-of-the-art performance for recommendation in implicit feedback datasets [30]. Yet, there exists some limitations: (i) First, user preferences in BPR are calculated as the inner product of user latent vectors and image latent vectors, which assigns equal weight to each dimension of the latent feature space, meaning the variability of user preferences may not be adequately captured; (ii) Second, the matrix factorization component of BPR is linear in nature, which has limited expressiveness when compared to nonlinear methods; and (iii) existing efforts for distributed BPR typically use partially shared memory which may limit its scalability.

To overcome these challenges, we propose *Neural Personalized Ranking (NPR)* – a new neural network based personalized pairwise ranking model for implicit feedback, which incorporates the idea of generalized matrix factorization. Neural models promise potentially more flexibility in model design, added nonlinearity through activations, and ease of parallelization. While recent work in neural methods for recommendation has focused on modeling side information [36, 40] or building pointwise learning models by directly modeling user ratings [10], a key feature of NPR is its careful modeling of users' implicit feedback via a relaxed assumption about unobserved items using pairwise ranking that builds on top of neural network based generalized matrix factorization components. Further, to alleviate the sparsity of user feedback and improve the quality of recommendation, we propose to leverage multiple categories of contextual information. Correspondingly, we augment the baseline NPR model with multiple contextual preference clues for deriving *Contextual Neural Personalized Ranking (C-NPR)* to better uncover user preferences. In particular, these preference clues include user tags, geographic features, and visual factors.

In our experiments over the Flickr YFCC100M dataset, we demonstrate the proposed NPR model's effectiveness in comparison to several state-of-the-art approaches. Moreover, the contextual enhanced NPR model significantly outperforms the baseline model by 16.6% and a contextual-BPR model by 4.5% in precision and recall. We find that NPR is more effective than BPR when there is inadequate training data.

2 RELATED WORK

Research attention on recommendation has shifted towards the common scenario where only implicit feedback is available, as is common in social imaging sharing communities. One pioneer work terms such a scenario as one-class collaborative filtering [29], where the authors proposed to weight positive and unobserved feedback differently in fitting the objective function. This idea was further improved to introduce varying confidence levels [13]. These approaches are mainly variations of pointwise approaches suitable for explicit feedback. Pairwise learning for implicit feedback, specifically Bayesian personalized ranking with matrix factorization (BPR-MF), typically outperforms pointwise learning counterparts [30].

Image Recommendation. Many works have tackled the problem of image recommendation, e.g., [8, 15, 19]. For example, Jing et al. use a weighted matrix factorization model that combines image importance and local community user rating [15]. Sang et al.

WSDM 2018, February 5–9, 2018, Marina Del Rey, CA, USA

ACM ISBN 978-1-4503-5581-0/18/02...$15.00
https://doi.org/10.1145/3159652.3159728

measure the distance of an image and a personalized query language through a graph-based topic-sensitive probabilistic model [31]. Later works begin incorporating a variety of visual features, including high-level features from deep convolutional neural networks. For example, Liu et al. introduce social embedding image distance learning that learns image similarity based on social constraints and leverages Borda Count for recommendation [23]. Lei et al. propose a comparative deep learning model that learns image and user representation jointly and identifies the nearest neighbor images of each user for recommendation [18].

Context-aware Recommendation. To overcome ratings sparsity, many recommenders have proposed to incorporate additional contextual information [1], including but not limited to social connections [14, 25], content [26, 35], and so on. Visual features have received much attention in recent work, with some methods using metrics for visual similarity according to social behavior or activity pattern to identify compatible items [23, 27] and visual enhanced recommendation [9]. With the rapid growth of location-based social networks and smart mobile devices, many applications take advantage of geographical information in modeling video watching preferences [3], Yelp ratings prediction [12], and most commonly in point of interest recommendation, where representative work includes [4, 21, 22, 39, 41]. In our work, we derive and integrate multiple categories of contextual features for image recommendation. We show that our proposed method to model user's preference is effective and adaptable to different frameworks.

Deep recommendation & ranking with implicit feedback. Recently, we have seen increasing efforts devoted to recommendation models based on deep learning [5–7, 10, 11, 18, 34, 37]; note that we neglect discussion of works that leverage deep learning for deriving features then can be integrated into traditional recommendation models. Several of these target the common scenario of implicit feedback [10, 18, 34]. For example, He and et al. introduce a pointwise neural collaborative filtering framework which includes an ensemble of multi-layer perceptron and generalized matrix factorization components that jointly contribute to better performance [10]. The work that is most relevant to ours is [34], where the authors propose a multi-layer feed forward neural network based pairwise ranking model which can be applied to personalized recommendation. Distinct from previous works, we propose a pairwise ranking based recommendation model that incorporates the idea of generalized matrix factorization for implicit feedback. We also provide a framework for explicitly modeling user's contextual preference for alleviating sparsity issues.

3 PRELIMINARIES

Our goal is to provide *personalized image recommendation*, such that each user is recommended a personalized list of images.

Problem Statement. Formally, we assume a set of M users $\mathcal{U}$={u_1, u_2,..., u_M} and a set of N images $\mathcal{I}$={i_1, i_2, ..., i_N}. We further assume some users have explicitly expressed their interest for a subset of the images in $\mathcal{I}$. This preference may be in the form of a "like" or similar social sharing function. We aim to recommend for each user a personalized list of images from the set $\mathcal{I}$.

3.1 Matrix Factorization

Toward tackling the problem of *personalized image recommendation*, we begin with a straightforward adaptation of latent factor matrix factorization (MF) [17]. The standard formulation is: the preference r_{ui} of a user u towards an image i is predicted as:

$$r_{ui} = \boldsymbol{p}_u^T \boldsymbol{q}_i + b_u + b_i + \alpha \quad (1)$$

where $\boldsymbol{p}_u$ and $\boldsymbol{q}_i$ are the K-dimensional latent factors of user preference and image characteristics, respectively. The inner product $\boldsymbol{p}_u^T \boldsymbol{q}_i$ of the user latent vector and image latent vector represents a user's preference towards an image; it measures how well the user preferences align with the properties of the image. b_u and b_i correspond to user and image bias terms while α is a global offset.

3.2 Bayesian Personalized Ranking

Since users only provide sparse one-class positive feedback (the "likes"), there is ambiguity in the interpretation of non-positive images since the negative examples and unlabeled positive examples are mixed together [29]. In this implicit feedback scenario, we may only assume users prefer the liked images to those that are not acted upon. To estimate the latent factors, instead of trying to model the matrix of "likes" directly in a pointwise setting with a least square regression formulation, we can construct the learning objective based on pairwise ranking between images. This idea is key to Bayesian Personalized Ranking [30], such that observed likes should be ranked higher than the unobserved ones. The model then tries to find latent factors that can be used to predict the expected preference of a user for an item.

Formally, we can adapt BPR to the *personalized image recommendation* task as follows. Suppose we have a user u_h and a pair of images i_j and i_k. User u_h's feedback for i_j is positive, and feedback for i_k is unobserved: we denote this relation as $j >_h k$. BPR aims to maximize the posterior probability $p(\Theta|j >_h k)$, where Θ is the set of parameters we try to estimate. According to Bayes' rule:

$$p(\Theta|j >_h k) \propto p(j >_h k|\Theta)P(\Theta)$$

and the likelihood function is defined as:

$$p(j >_h k|\Theta) = \delta(r_{hj} - r_{hk})$$

where $\delta(\cdot)$ is the sigmoid function. To simplify notation, We will use the index of a user and an image. We assume a Gaussian prior $\Theta \sim N(0, \lambda_\Theta I)$, where λ_Θ is a set of model-specific parameters and I is the identity matrix. The prior provides regularization for the parameters to prevent overfitting.

Our objective is to find Θ that maximizes the log-likelihood for all users and all images:

$$\underset{\Theta}{\arg\max} \sum_{u_h \in \mathcal{U}, i_j \in \mathcal{P}_h, i_k \in \mathcal{N}_h} \left(\ln \left(\delta(r_{hj} - r_{hk}) \right) - \lambda_\Theta \left\| \Theta_{hjk} \right\|^2 \right)$$

where $\mathcal{P}_h$, $\mathcal{N}_h$ are the sets of images for which u_h has provided positive feedback and u_h's feedback is unobserved, respectively. Θ is $\{p_u, q_i, b_i\}$ for all users and images. With this pairwise setting, the user bias and global offset in Equation 1 cancel out.

4 NEURAL PERSONALIZED RANKING

In this section, we seek to complement existing matrix factorization and BPR-based approaches to personalized image recommendation through the exploration of a new neural network based personalized pairwise ranking model. Neural recommendation models promise some exciting characteristics in comparison with BPR: (i) First, user preferences in BPR are calculated as the inner product of user latent vector and image latent vector, which assigns equal weight to each dimension of the latent feature space. In contrast, neural methods may be able to capture the variability of user preferences by relaxing this equal weight requirement. (ii) Second, the matrix factorization component of BPR is linear in nature, which has limited expressiveness. In contrast, neural methods offer more flexibility by adding nonlinearity through activations. (iii) Finally, many neural methods may be easily parallelized for scalable computation, whereas existing work on distributed BPR typically uses partially shared memory which may limit its scalability. In summary, neural models promise potentially more flexibility in model design, added nonlinearity through activations, and ease of parallelization.

4.1 Model Architecture

The NPR model structure is shown in Figure 1. There are three inputs to the model, the user and a pair of images, represented as tuple of index (h, j, k). Then user and image indexes are one-hot encoded as tuple of vectors $(\boldsymbol{u}_h, \boldsymbol{i}_j, \boldsymbol{i}_k)$. Since there are M users and N images, the dimensions of $\boldsymbol{u}_h, \boldsymbol{i}_j, \boldsymbol{i}_k$ are M, N, and N respectively. The output of the proposed model is the ground truth value which we train the model against:

$$g(h, j, k) = \begin{cases} 1 & \text{for } j >_h k \\ -1 & \text{for } j <_h k \end{cases}$$

where $j >_h k$ denotes that user u_h prefers image i_j to i_k. This definition transforms the ranking problem into a binary classification problem, which aims to check whether the pairwise preference relation holds. Following the input layer, each input is fully connected to the corresponding embedding layer for the sake of learning a compact representation of the users and images. The embedding dimension for both users and images are the same. We denote the embeddings as $\boldsymbol{p}_h, \boldsymbol{q}_j, \boldsymbol{q}_k$. Formally,

$$\boldsymbol{p}_h = \boldsymbol{W}_u \boldsymbol{u}_h, \quad \boldsymbol{q}_j = \boldsymbol{W}_i \boldsymbol{i}_j, \quad \boldsymbol{q}_k = \boldsymbol{W}_i' \boldsymbol{i}_k.$$

where $\boldsymbol{W}_u, \boldsymbol{W}_i, \boldsymbol{W}_i'$ are embedding matrices for users and images. As the model architecture is vertically symmetric, let's focus on the substructure marked inside the dotted triangle (see Figure 1). In the merge layer, user and image embedding vectors are multiplied element-wise, such that each dimension of the user preference vector and corresponding image properties are in line. This step is analogous to traditional matrix factorization. The resulting vector has the same dimension as the embeddings. More precisely:

$$\boldsymbol{m}_{hj} = \boldsymbol{p}_h \circ \boldsymbol{q}_j$$

where $\circ$ denotes the element-wise product. The merge layer is then connected to a single neuron dense layer, which computes the weighted sum of all dimensions and passes it through a ReLU nonlinear activation. Compared to traditional matrix factorization, such a design allows each latent dimension to vary in importance and supports additional expressiveness through non-linearity. We adopt ReLU here based on our exploratory experiments, where we find that alternative activation functions like *sigmoid* and *tanh* suffer from saturation, which leads to overfitting. The output is preference score r_{hj}:

$$r_{hj} = a(\boldsymbol{w}^T \boldsymbol{m}_{hj} + b_1)$$

where $a(\cdot)$ is the activation function, $\boldsymbol{w}$ is the weight vector and b_1 is the bias term. This output r_{hj} characterizes the preference of u_h to i_j. We denote the preference score from the mirror structure in Figure1 as r'_{hk}. Ultimately, the model prediction is $r_{hj} - r'_{hk}$.

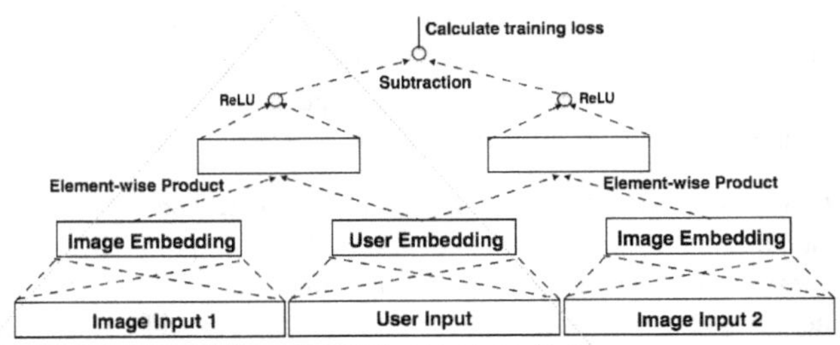

Figure 1: Neural Personalized Ranking (NPR) Structure

4.2 Objective Function

We define the objective function to maximize as:

$$\frac{1}{n} \sum_{\substack{h \in \mathcal{U}, (i_j \in \mathcal{P}_h, i_k \in \mathcal{N}_h \\ | i_j \in \mathcal{N}_h, i_k \in \mathcal{P}_h)}} \ln\left(\delta((r_{hj} - r'_{hk}) \cdot g(h, j, k))\right) - \lambda_\Theta \|\Theta\|^2$$

where n is the number of training samples and $\delta(\cdot)$ is the sigmoid function. Since we only focus on whether the sign of the output is the same as $g(h, j, k)$, we employ the product between the predicted value $r_{hj} - r'_{hk}$ and the ground truth $g(h, j, k)$ as an indicator for how the predicted value is aligned with ground truth. A larger value is acquired if their signs are the same. The regularization term is slightly different from that defined in the BPR-based model. We impose the L2-norm to the whole embedding matrix, instead of on each training sample for simpler implementation. If training samples are balanced for each user and image, such regularization will have the same effect as in the BPR model.

4.3 Model Training and Inference

We initialize the weight matrices with random values uniformly distributed in [0,1]. To train the network, we transform the objective to the equivalent minimization dual problem and adopt mini-batch gradient descent (MB-GD), which is a compromise between gradient descent (GD) and stochastic gradient descent (SGD). MB-GD converges faster than GD as it has frequent gradient updates while convergence is more stable than SGD. Besides, MB-GD allows utilization of vectorized operations from deep learning libraries, which typically results in a computational performance gain over SGD. Before each epoch, we shuffle the training dataset. Then in each step, a batch of training tuples is served to the network. The error gradient is back propagated from output to input and parameters in each layer are updated. The batch size we use in experiments is 1,024. The optimization algorithm used for gradient update is Adam's[16]. The loss generally converges within 20 epochs given the amount of training data.

Given a user u, for every image $i \in \mathcal{N}_u$, her preference score r_{ui} is predicted from the neural network. In order to obtain the preference score, we feed the tuple (u, i, i) to the neural network, and get two values r_{ui} and r'_{ui} from the parallel branches. The final preference score is calculated as $r_{ui} = \frac{1}{2}(r_{ui} + r'_{ui})$. Then the set of images with unobserved feedback are sorted according to descending predicted preference score. We pick the top ranking images for recommendation.

4.4 Implementation Details

Neural network models can easily overfit. Thus we take a few measures to prevent overfitting. First, we apply dropout to the embedding weights during training. The dropout rate is fine-tuned for each dataset. Second, if validation loss does not decrease, we reduce the learning rate to 20% of its current value, allowing for finer adjustment to gradient update. Third, early stopping is adopted to terminate training if there is no decrease on validation loss for 3 epochs. Additionally, we impose L2-regularization to the contextual preference vectors for contextual NPR model, which we will introduce in the following section, such that the preference score is not overwhelmed by large contextual feature values. Furthermore, all regularization coefficients are tuned through grid search.

5 CONTEXTUAL NPR

Although the neural personalized ranking model is promising, it faces two key challenges. The first is *sparsity* – very few images have been liked, so it is difficult to make recommendations for users who have little feedback as well as to recommend newly posted images. The second is *preference complexity* – images are diverse and there are many reasons for a user to like an image. Hence, we propose to improve NPR with an enhanced model – *contextual neural personalized ranking (C-NPR)* – by leveraging multiple categories of auxiliary information that may help overcome the sparsity issue while also providing clues to user preferences.

5.1 Geo, Topical, Visual Preference

Based on the Flickr YFCC100M dataset [33] (see Section 6.1), we begin here by highlighting evidence for the impact of three sources of contextual information on image preference, before formally defining the contextual NPR model.

Evidence of Spatial Preference. Figure 2 shows the percentage distribution of "liked" images in decreasing order across the regions where these images were taken. Here we aggregate each user's top-10 regions where their liked images come from. The kth boxplot is generated from all users who have liked images from at least k regions. We observe that the median percentage of liked images from the top region is above 33%; that is, at least half of all users have 33% of their liked images from a single region (though not necessarily the same region for each user). Suppose a user has no preference of regions, a single region would at most contain 9% of her liked images (as the largest region contains 9% of the images). Thus we conclude there is a strong tendency for a user to favor images from certain regions, especially from a few of them as the percentage decreases sharply as the region number increases.

Evidence of Topic Preference. We consider each unique user tag as a potential topic. Figure 3 shows users' liked image distribution over the tags that have been applied to those images. We list the results for the top-10 tags of each user (not necessarily the same set of tags for each user). The kth boxplot summarizes users that have more than k tags labeled to the set of liked images. We observe that ~75% of users have at least one common tag shared among more than ~35% of their liked images. Even the median ratio for the 10th tag attached to liked images is much higher than the percentage of most frequent tags in the whole dataset. Thus we conclude that users have topic preferences for the images they like. As the percentage decreases slowly with k, we ascribe this to users having multiple favored tags.

Evidence of Visual Preference. Finally, we explore clues for user's visual preference by comparing image similarity across three sampled sets, with each containing 100,000 image pairs. The sets are constructed in the following manner: (i) Randomly sample image pairs; (ii) Randomly sample a user, then sample a pair of image from her liked images; and (iii) For each image, pick its most socially alike images. Here we represent each image as a vector of user's who like it, then identify similar images with high cosine similarity score. Next, we calculate the cosine similarity of the aforementioned image pairs based on their visual feature vectors. The similarity distributions for these three sets are shown in Figure 4. We observe that image pairs liked by a user tend to be more similar in visual appearance than randomly picked image pairs, with a median similarity around 0.25 vs. 0.20. For image pairs that are liked by similar groups of users, the pairwise visual similarity is even higher, reaching 0.30. All three findings are statistically significant with p-value less than 1e-8. Hence, we conclude that users have visual preference for images that they like, and that there exists group of users that share similar preferences.

5.2 From NPR to C-NPR

This evidence of clear variation in user preference motivates our need to augment NPR. Formally, with the contextual feature vector $\bar{\boldsymbol{f}}_i$ for image i, we then seek to uncover user's preference latent vector $\boldsymbol{f_u}$ to $\bar{\boldsymbol{f}}_i$ such that the vector product $\boldsymbol{f_u} \circ \bar{\boldsymbol{f}}_i$ captures how user preference is aligned with the image's contextual features.

We modify the neural network structure of each branch in Figure 1 to accommodate for modeling contextual preference. The new architecture for a branch incorporating visual, geo, and topic contextual features and preferences is shown in Figure 5. Aside from the user and image input, each category of contextual features of image $\bar{v}_i, \bar{\boldsymbol{t}}_i, \bar{g}_i$ is served as an extra input. Each corresponding contextual preference hidden layer is fully connected above user input and is to be learned. Then the user's preference to the contextual feature is calculated with the element-wise product to measure how features and preferences are aligned. Specifically, the visual, topic, and geo latent vectors of user u_h are calculated as:

$$\boldsymbol{v}_h = \boldsymbol{W}_v \boldsymbol{u}_h, \quad \boldsymbol{t}_h = \boldsymbol{W}_t \boldsymbol{u}_h, \quad \boldsymbol{g}_h = \boldsymbol{W}_g \boldsymbol{u}_h$$

where $\boldsymbol{W}_v, \boldsymbol{W}_t, \boldsymbol{W}_g$ are the weight matrices. The visual, topic, and geo preference of user u_h to image i_j are:

$$\begin{aligned} \boldsymbol{e}^v_{hj} &= \boldsymbol{v}_h \circ \bar{\boldsymbol{v}}_j \\ \boldsymbol{e}^t_{hj} &= \boldsymbol{t}_h \circ \bar{\boldsymbol{t}}_j \\ \boldsymbol{e}^g_{hj} &= \boldsymbol{g}_h \circ \bar{\boldsymbol{g}}_j \end{aligned}$$

Then the general preference $\boldsymbol{m}_{hj}$ and contextual preferences are concatenated in the merge layer. Formally:

$$\boldsymbol{m'}_{hj} = \begin{bmatrix} \boldsymbol{m}_{hj} & \boldsymbol{e}^v_{hj} & \boldsymbol{e}^t_{hj} & \boldsymbol{e}^g_{hj} \end{bmatrix}^T$$

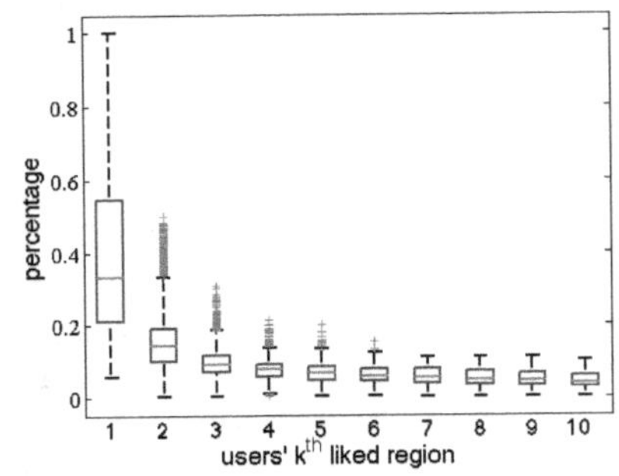

Figure 2: Geo preferences: Users tend to "like" images from only a few regions.

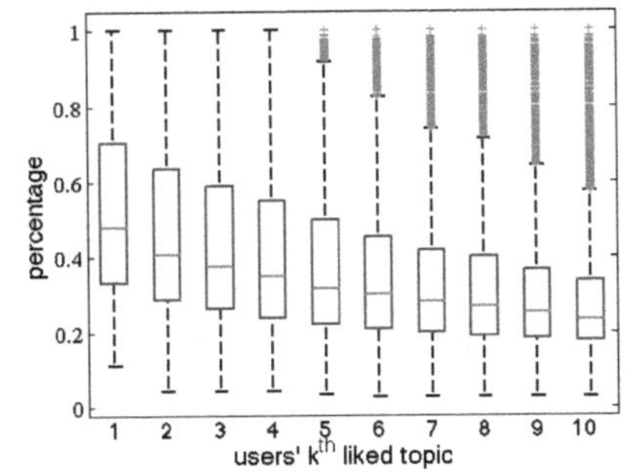

Figure 3: Topic preferences: Users tend to "like" images with similar tags.

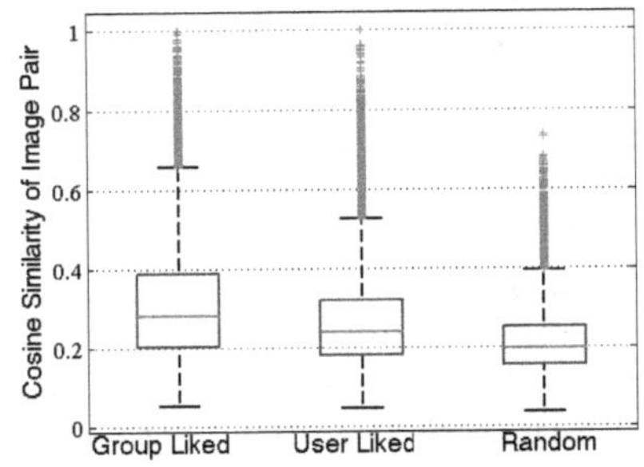

Figure 4: Visual preferences: Pairs of "liked" images tend to be more visually alike than random pairs.

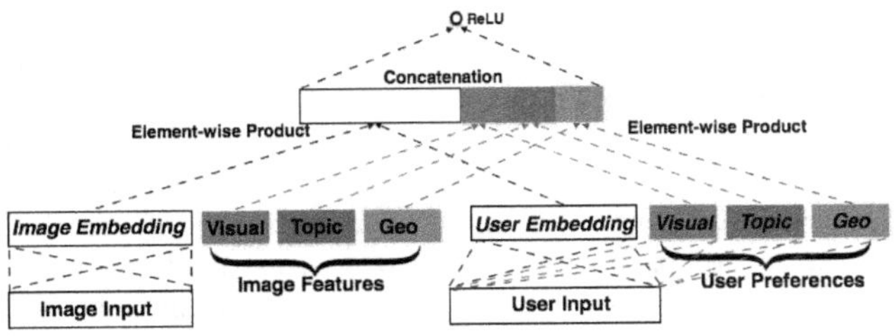

Figure 5: NPR with Contextual Information

Finally, the merge layer is further connected to a single neuron dense layer as before. The updated preference score is:

$$r_{hj} = a(\boldsymbol{w'}^T \boldsymbol{m'}_{hj} + b_1)$$

Additional contextual information about each image can be incorporated following the same steps as stated above. In summary, each new feature vector is served as an extra input to the neural network, and a corresponding preference embedding layer is augmented on top of user input. Then the element-wise product is adopted to model consistency between preferences and intrinsic properties of the image, followed by concatenation of all preference components and a weighted sum.

5.3 Modeling Geo, Topical, and Visual

Given the evidence of user preferences, we turn here to model these features for integration into the C-NPR model.

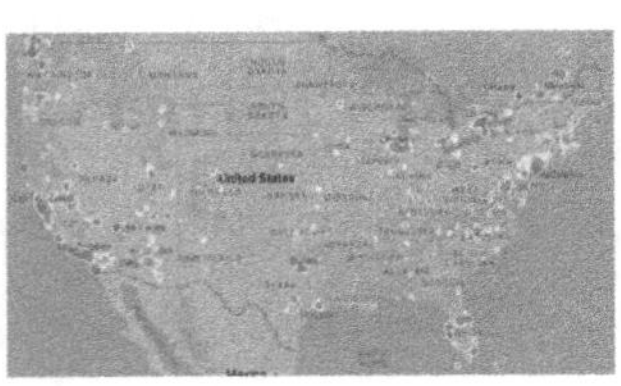

Figure 6: Image Heatmap

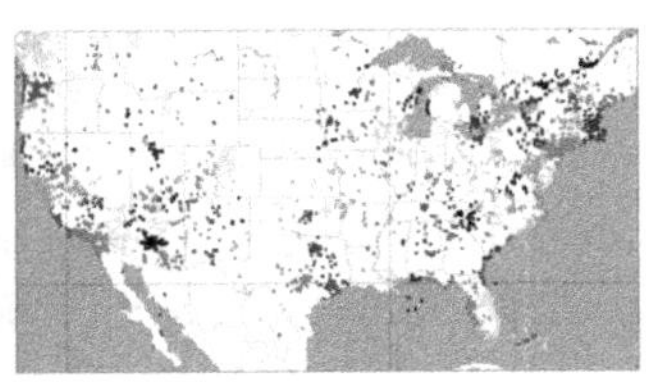

Figure 7: Geographic Regions

Deriving Spatial feature. We assume the area of interest is geographically partitioned into K regions and each image is taken from one of the regions. Instead of gridding into blocks of equal area which has been used previously [21, 28], we propose to partition areas into regions according to image density, where the shape and size of a region doesn't have to be consistent and could be irregular. The reason is images are not distributed homogeneously (generally, dense around cities and tourist attractions and sparse elsewhere). Focusing on density helps to reduce the irrelevant areas and the size of each region we drill down into, which allows for more precise modeling. We apply the mean shift clustering algorithm, which builds upon the concept of kernel density estimation (KDE), to identify geographical clusters of images. It works by placing a Gaussian kernel on each image coordinate in the dataset. Then by iteratively shifting each point in the data set until they reach the top of their nearest KDE surface peak. The only parameter to set is the bandwidth, with which it attempts to generate a reasonable number of clusters based on the density. The clustering result is shown in Figure 7, where each dot represents an image and the cluster of points represents a region. In total, there are 217 regions with a bandwidth of 100km.

We assume the probability that a user likes an image in one region is influenced by her likes status in other regions. If a user has liked images from region p, then she has a larger probability of favoring an image in a region closer to p. Previous work in POI recommendation assumes the influence distance of a POI is fixed according to a normal distribution $\mathcal{N}(0, \sigma^2)$ [21]. However, it is commonly perceived that influence for regions of the same size should be different, not to mention the diverse shape and size in our scenario. Thus we assume each region p has an influence according to a normal distribution $\mathcal{N}(0, \sigma_p^2)$, where σ_p is the standard deviation of distance from each image coordinate to the cluster center. To this end, the influence from p_i to p_j is defined as: $f_{ij} = \frac{1}{\sigma_{p_i}} K(\frac{d(i,j)}{\sigma_{p_i}})$, where p_i and p_j are the regions that image i and j belong to and the relation between image and region is many to one. $d(\cdot)$ is the Haversine distance between the center of two regions, $K(\cdot)$ is the standard normal distribution and σ_{p_i} is the standard deviation which we adopt as the bandwidth of the kernel function. Thus the influence from each region to all other regions is represented as a row vector. The advantage is it encodes the idea of kernel density estimation where the estimated geographical density of u's liked image distribution at p_j is: $d_u^j = \sum_{p_i \in P_u} \frac{n_i}{\sigma_{p_i} |P_u|} K(\frac{d(i,j)}{\sigma_{p_i}})$, where n_i is u's number of likes within p_i, P_u is the set of regions that u has likes. It can be written as the dot product of two vectors. However, different from the KDE, a user's preference vector is learned.

Deriving Topic Features. To extract the topical theme associated with each image, we aggregate the user-generated tags, title, and description (if any) for each image. This text not only acts as a descriptor of concrete objects, scenes, and weather, but also sheds light on abstract and hidden knowledge about the images like emotion and background theme, which supplements the visual appearance. We ignore tags which have occurred fewer than d times in the dataset and apply dimensionality reduction over 58k unique tags.[1]

Deriving Visual Features. Recently, high-level visual features extracted from deep convolutional neural networks have revolutionized the state-of-the-art performance in image recognition [32] and image captioning [38]. Here, the output of fc6 layer of the Places Hybrid-CNN is adopted as the image feature [42], which contains 4,096 dimensions. This CNN was trained on 1,183 categories which includes 205 scene categories from Places Database and 978 object categories from ImageNet (ILSVRC2012) images. Dimension reduction is further applied for reducing computation complexity. The existing approach for visual BPR [9], which learns an embedding kernel for visual dimension reduction while training the recommendation model, turns out to be less efficient than directly utilizing the full set of 4,096 features. Hence, we propose to reduce visual feature dimension separately from model training.[2]

6 EXPERIMENTS

In this section, we conduct a set of experiments to evaluate neural personalized image recommendation. Specifically, we first introduce the data preparation workflow and basic experimental setup. Then we compare NPR with baseline models, followed by reporting performance of contextual enhanced models. We drill down to discover the impact of each category of contextual information. We further look into the performance of the proposed model in the typical cold start scenario. Finally, we discuss the characteristics of NPR and BPR in terms of amount of training data required and convergence rate.

6.1 Data

The dataset we use for evaluation is based on the Flickr YFCC100M dataset [33]. We select images with geo-coordinates and that are located in the US mainland. We further crawl the image "likes" from the Flickr API and we select images with greater than 30 likes overall and users with more than 10 liked images.

The resulting datasets are listed in Table 1, where the sparsity for the small dataset and large dataset is 0.96% and 0.16%, respectively, which means only 0.96% and 0.16% of the possible user-image relations is available. These two datasets represent two different levels of feedback sparsity. And effective sparsity for training data is half of the reported value after train/test split. The geographical heatmap of the large dataset is shown in Figure 6; we notice the majority of images come from populated areas or famous tourist sites, as shown in red.

[1]We compare principal component analysis (PCA) and Latent Dirichlet Allocation (LDA) for carrying out this task. We report PCA-based results due to its better performance.

[2]We compare recommendation performance with reduced feature from PCA and stacked auto-encoder (AE) as well as with full set of features. Both PCA and AE perform similarly and provide a good trade-off between efficiency and accuracy, thus we only report PCA due to the space limit.

Dataset	#Users	#Images	#Feedback	Sparsity
Small	1,891	2,013	36,827	0.96%
Large	27,782	21,720	961,506	0.16%

Table 1: Post-processed Datasets Statistics

6.2 Experimental Setup

All experiments for BPR-based models were performed on a desktop machine with 60GB memory and 8 core Intel i7-4820k3.7GHz. NPR-based models are trained using Nvidia GeForce GTX Titan X GPU with 12 GB memory and 3,072 cores.

Constructing the Training Set. We randomly partition the liked images of each user into 50% for training and validation and 50% for testing. The validation set split ratio is 0.3. The loss on the validation set is used for tracking training progress. The training set consists of tuples (h, j, k) where h, j, k correspond to user index, positive image index, and negative image index, respectively. Including every pair of positive and negative combination for each user in training would be costly. Yet practically, evaluation metrics saturate even with a much smaller set of training tuples. Thus we propose to use a sampling method for generating training tuples.

To generate each training tuple, we first randomly sample a user u from user set $\mathcal{U}$, then randomly sample a positive image i_j from $\mathcal{P}_u$, and finally randomly sample k negative images i_k from $\mathcal{N}_u$ to pair with i_j. We repeat this process until generating the expected number of training data tuples. The influence of k on performance is discussed later; we set k to 10. All reported results in this paper are based on models trained over a set where the number of sampled users equals to five times the number of observed "likes".

Although it is very likely that we end up leaving part of the positive samples unused, the model based on this sampling strategy exhibits better overall performance and requires less training data to converge compared with sampling negatives for each positive sample. The model is trained in a balanced way among every user and not biased towards users that have more likes.

Evaluation Metrics. We adopt precision@k, recall@k and F1-score@k for evaluating personalized ranking. Precision measures the fraction of correctly predicted images among the retrieved images. Recall measures the fraction of relevant images that have been picked over the total relevant images. F1@k is a weighed average of Prec@k and Rec@k. All measures are averaged across all users.

$$Prec@k = \frac{1}{N}\sum_{i=1}^{N}\frac{|GT(u_i) \cap Pred(u_i)@k|}{k}$$

where $GT(u_i)$ is the ground truth liked image for u_i in test data, and $Pred(u_i)@k$ is the top k recommended images for u_i.

$$Rec@k = \frac{1}{N}\sum_{i=1}^{N}\frac{|GT(u_i) \cap Pred(u_i)@k|}{|GT(u_i)|}$$

$$F1@k = \frac{2 \cdot Prec@k \cdot Rec@k}{Prec@k + Rec@k}$$

Baselines.

- NCF. Neural collaborative filtering is a pointwise model composed of multi-layer perceptron and generalized matrix factorization components [10]. All the configurations adopted are similar according to original paper including 4 hidden layers, 64 hidden units and pre-training. We sample 5 negative examples for each positive, which was shown to be optimal in the original paper.

- Multi-layer perceptron based pairwise ranking model. A personalized pairwise ranking model based on multi-layer perceptron was introduced [34]. We adopt a setting with 3 hidden layers, with each layer containing 200, 100, and 100 units, respectively.
- BPR and its variants. We consider the basic pairwise ranking for matrix factorization model shown in Equation (1). In addition, we can also integrate the proposed contextual factors into traditional BPR. Indeed, a visual preference-enhanced version of BPR model has been previously introduced by He et al.[9]. Hence, we also consider a visual (VBPR), topic (TBPR), geo (GBPR), and combined version of BPR (C-BPR).
- NPR. This is the neural network based model for personalized pairwise ranking as shown in Figure 1.
- NPR-noact. This is the NPR model without nonlinear activation.
- Contextual NPR. This includes NPR considering only visual (VNPR), topic (TNPR), and geo (GNPR) contextual information.

Reproducibility. For all models, the user and image latent factor dimensions are set to 100 empirically for a trade-off between performance and computation complexity as well as for fair comparison. The number of visual feature dimensions is 128, the number of topic dimensions is 100 for the small dataset and 500 for the large dataset. The number of geographic dimensions is the same as the number of geo clusters which is 155 and 217 for small and large dataset, respectively.

For the NPR-based approach, we adopt mini-batch gradient descent where the batch size is set to 1,024. The dropout rate for the small dataset was set to 0.6 and for the large dataset was set to 0.45. The regularization parameters are fine-tuned. For example, on the large dataset λ_u=λ_i=1e−7, λ_v=λ_g=1e−6, and λ_t=1e−5. For BPR-based approaches, we initialize the learning rate to 0.02 and decrease it to 97% its current value in each consecutive iteration, which has been shown to be effective to help convergence in fewer iterations [12]. And generally, training converges within 80 iterations. The regularization parameters are fine-tuned and shared among all BPR baselines, concretely, λ_u=λ_i=λ_b=0.02, λ_v=λ_g=0.01 and λ_t=0.1.

6.3 NPR vs. Alternatives

We begin by investigating the quality of NPR versus each of the baselines for personalized recommendation without contextual information. We report the average precision@k, recall@k for k at 5, 10, 15 in Figure 8 for the small dataset and 9 for the large dataset. We observe that NPR and BPR are neck and neck, with BPR slightly superior (less than 1%) in precision and recall. This indicates BPR-MF is a strong baseline. Although the MF component is linear, the logistic objective function brings in nonlinearity. Both approaches consistently substantially outperform other baseline approaches in precision and recall. Moreover, the pairwise method generally yields better results. For example, NPR improves the precision and recall over the pointwise model NCF by 50% for the large dataset and improves the precision and recall. This illustrates the relaxed assumption for unobserved samples helps to reduce the recommendation bias. The nonlinear activation function lead to an average of 3.8% increase in precision and 3.3% increase in recall on the small dataset, and even larger 11.5% and 12.5% increase in precision and recall on the large dataset. By bringing in nonlinearity, the representativeness of the model is enriched. We observe the performance metrics are generally lower on the large dataset; the reason is that recommendation becomes more difficult given more images and increasing sparsity. However, the performance gap between approaches expands with increasing sparsity, indicating the great opportunity for the proposed approach when feedback is lacking.

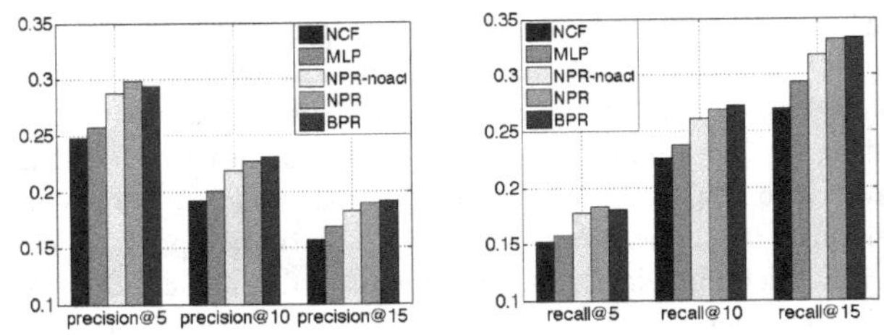

Figure 8: Average Precision and Recall for Baseline Models on the Small Dataset

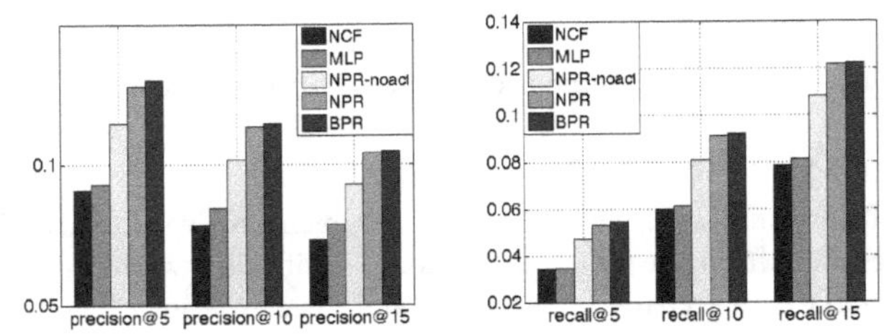

Figure 9: Average Precision and Recall for Baseline Models on the Large Dataset

6.4 Comparing Contextual Enhanced Models

To evaluate the impact of incorporating each category of contextual information in recommendation, we present precision and recall at k for each contextual enhanced NPR and BPR model over the large dataset in Tables 2 and 3. We observe that modeling additional contextual factors improves over the basic NPR and BPR method. Concretely, TNPR gives an average improvement of 10.1% in precision and 12.6% in recall over the NPR baseline on the large dataset. This indicates that rich textual side knowledge acts as an effective filter for sifting relevant images. VNPR performs slightly better than NPR, with an improvement of 4.6% and 5.4% in precision and recall. The lesson here is learning personal visual preference does help to connect users with images that have appearance agreement. Furthermore, GNPR gives an average of 3.6% percent and 5.5% percent increase in precision and recall. This confirms the importance of modeling user's geographical region which is consistent with our observation in Section 5.1, where we notice the user's strong geographical preference. Since for social image sharing sites, users do have connections focusing around their home location and places they are familiar with, we see that images in these regions may be more likely to be related with the user. Finally, we observe that C-NPR achieves an average of more than 16% increase in precision and recall. This implies that the proposed model is effective in integrating various categories of contextual information jointly to make better recommendation. We observe similar trends in C-BPR models.

Method	p@5	p@10	avg Δ	r@5	r@10	avg Δ
NPR	0.1280	0.1137	-	0.0531	0.0909	-
VNPR	0.1354	0.1177	+4.6%	0.0563	0.0952	+5.4%
TNPR	0.1411	0.1250	+10.1%	0.0599	0.1021	+12.6%
GNPR	0.1326	0.1178	+3.6%	0.0564	0.0953	+5.5%
C-NPR	0.1504	0.1317	+16.6%	0.0644	0.1081	+16.6%

Table 2: Integrating Contextual Information in NPR

Method	p@5	p@10	avg Δ	r@5	r@10	avg Δ
BPR	0.1302	0.1148	-	0.0544	0.0920	-
VBPR	0.1366	0.1188	+4.2%	0.0577	0.0961	+5.3%
TBPR	0.1384	0.1217	+8.5%	0.0588	0.0992	+8.0%
GBPR	0.1331	0.1171	+2.1%	0.0562	0.0950	+3.3%
C-BPR	0.1445	0.1255	+10.6%	0.0619	0.1034	+13.1%

Table 3: Integrating Contextual Information in BPR

6.5 NPR and BPR with Contextual Information

First, even though the NPR base model performs similarly with BPR, we observe that C-NPR leads by an average of ~4.5% higher precision and recall over C-BPR on the large dataset and ~1.5% increase on the small dataset. We ascribe this improvement to the neural network based model flexibly adjusting weights for each feature dimension and nonlinear activation enriching the expressiveness. Second, the higher increase for the large dataset indicates the C-NPR model could be more beneficial than the C-BPR model for recommendation under the real-world scenario of extreme feedback sparsity.

Method	p@5	p@10	r@15	r@5	r@10	r@15
C-NPR(S)	0.2987	0.2371	0.1977	0.1866	0.2842	0.3471
C-BPR(S)	0.3034	0.2335	0.1945	0.1874	0.2801	0.3419
C-NPR(L)	0.1504	0.1317	0.1192	0.0644	0.1081	0.1430
C-BPR(L)	0.1445	0.1255	0.1141	0.0619	0.1034	0.1363

Table 4: Compare Contextual NPR and Contextual BPR

6.6 Cold Start

In this experiment, we focus on the cold-start scenario which is commonly encountered in recommendation where we have a limited number of positive user feedbacks for training the model. Here we select users who have fewer than seven liked images to examine the performance of the proposed model on the large dataset in the cold-start setting. Interestingly we observe in Table 5 that the proposed C-NPR model outperforms the baseline NPR model by average ~21% in precision and recall. Additionally, each contextual model exhibits better performance than the NPR baseline, with TNPR taking the lead showing an average improvement of ~13% in precision and recall. This implies these contextual factors help to alleviate the sparsity in the cold-start setting. Moreover, the lager improvement compared with ordinary setting again validates our claim that contextual information is especially helpful when feedback is rare.

Method	p@5	p@10	p@15	r@5	r@10	r@15
NPR	0.0723	0.0598	0.0518	0.0643	0.1063	0.1381
VNPR	0.0775	0.0628	0.0554	0.0683	0.1131	0.1455
TNPR	0.0820	0.0678	0.0584	0.0731	0.1206	0.1558
GNPR	0.0775	0.0644	0.0563	0.0685	0.1120	0.1455
C-NPR	0.0893	0.0721	0.0626	0.0769	0.1282	0.1668

Table 5: NPR Cold-start Performance

6.7 Number of training samples

In this experiment, we explore how performance of different models is influenced by the amount of training data used as well as by the number of negative samples for each positive one. As mentioned in Section 6.2, the training data generation procedure is as follows: for NPR-1 and BPR-1, we first randomly sample a user, then sample one positive (liked) image for the user and followed by one negative (unobserved/ disliked) image of the user. For NPR-10 and BPR-10 instead, we randomly sample ten negative image for each positive image while keeping other steps the same. The total number of training tuples generated is measured in terms of the number of positive feedbacks in the original dataset. In Figure 10, the horizontal axis represents the number of times (of positive feedback) to sample and the vertical axis is the F-1 score@10. We observe that BPR-1 and NPR-1 achieve increasing F-1 score with gradual increase in training data. However, the performance of NPR-1 and BPR-1 models have disparate properties. First, the increase for the NPR-based model is relatively gentle, while steeper for the BPR-based model. Furthermore, the NPR model performs much better, for example, it gains 0.23 for F-1 score@10 at 5 times of sampling while the BPR-based model only reaches 0.17. The difference in performance is more severe when training data is lacking. Interestingly, we also notice that the neural network based model generally achieves better performance with inadequate training data. We attribute this to the linear model having less powerful expressiveness, hence incurring overfitting more easily and vice versa for nonlinear models. The performance gap doesn't decrease even after we adjust the regularization parameters to their optimal setting. To note, the same phenomenon was observed on the large dataset. After we decoupled the negative samples sampled for training, we notice better F1 score for both approaches, yet the performance curve gradually saturates as we continue serving more training data. This indicates the models would stop improving as the size of training data is no longer the bottleneck. To our best knowledge, this is the first effort to compare such differences in behavior of these two categories of models, and we hope this observation will provide some reference for further research.

7 CONCLUSION

In this paper, we tackle the problem of personalized image recommendation. We propose *Neural Personalized Ranking (NPR)* – a new neural network based personalized pairwise ranking model for implicit feedback, which incorporates the idea of generalized matrix factorization. We further build an enhanced model by augmenting the basic NPR model with users' multiple contextual preference clues and derive corresponding features that can be incorporated into both the NPR and the BPR frameworks to better uncover user

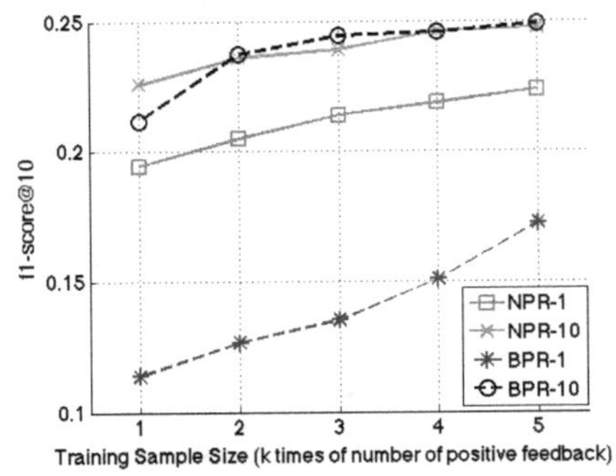

Figure 10: Performance w.r.t Training Sample Size

preferences. Through extensive experimental validation, we demonstrate the proposed NPR model significantly outperforms several state-of-the-art approaches. Moreover, we observe the superiority of contextual enhanced NPR model over the baseline model.

In future work, we are interested to incorporate user information like demographics into the framework for improving the quality of recommendation, especially for new users. Additionally, we would like to extend the current model with additional contextual information, for example, modeling the temporal evolution of preferences by revising certain model components with LSTM. Furthermore, we are eager to develop a distributed model for large scale recommendation.

Acknowledgments This work was supported in part by NSF grant IIS-1149383.

REFERENCES

[1] Gediminas Adomavicius and Alexander Tuzhilin. 2011. Context-aware recommender systems. In *Recommender systems handbook*. Springer.
[2] David M Blei, Andrew Y Ng, and Michael I Jordan. 2003. Latent dirichlet allocation. *Journal of machine Learning research* (2003).
[3] Anders Brodersen, Salvatore Scellato, and Mirjam Wattenhofer. 2012. Youtube around the world: geographic popularity of videos. In *WWW*. ACM.
[4] Chen Cheng, Haiqin Yang, Irwin King, and Michael R Lyu. 2012. Fused Matrix Factorization with Geographical and Social Influence in Location-Based Social Networks.. In *AAAI*.
[5] Heng-Tze Cheng, Levent Koc, Jeremiah Harmsen, Tal Shaked, Tushar Chandra, Hrishi Aradhye, Glen Anderson, Greg Corrado, Wei Chai, Mustafa Ispir, et al. 2016. Wide & deep learning for recommender systems. In *Proceedings of the 1st Workshop on Deep Learning for Recommender Systems*. ACM.
[6] Paul Covington, Jay Adams, and Emre Sargin. 2016. Deep neural networks for youtube recommendations. In *RecSys*. ACM.
[7] Ali Mamdouh Elkahky, Yang Song, and Xiaodong He. 2015. A multi-view deep learning approach for cross domain user modeling in recommendation systems. In *WWW*. ACM.
[8] Jianping Fan, Daniel A Keim, Yuli Gao, Hangzai Luo, and Zongmin Li. 2009. JustClick: Personalized image recommendation via exploratory search from large-scale Flickr images. *IEEE Transactions on Circuits and Systems for Video Technology* (2009).
[9] Ruining He and Julian McAuley. 2016. VBPR: visual bayesian personalized ranking from implicit feedback. In *AAAI*.
[10] Xiangnan He, Lizi Liao, Hanwang Zhang, Liqiang Nie, Xia Hu, and Tat-Seng Chua. 2017. Neural collaborative filtering. In *WWW*. ACM.
[11] Balázs Hidasi, Alexandros Karatzoglou, Linas Baltrunas, and Domonkos Tikk. 2015. Session-based recommendations with recurrent neural networks. *arXiv preprint arXiv:1511.06939* (2015).
[12] Longke Hu, Aixin Sun, and Yong Liu. 2014. Your neighbors affect your ratings: on geographical neighborhood influence to rating prediction. In *SIGIR*. ACM.
[13] Yifan Hu, Yehuda Koren, and Chris Volinsky. 2008. Collaborative filtering for implicit feedback datasets. In *ICDM*. IEEE.
[14] Mohsen Jamali and Martin Ester. 2010. A matrix factorization technique with trust propagation for recommendation in social networks. In *RecSys*. ACM.
[15] Yuchen Jing, Xiuzhen Zhang, Lifang Wu, Jinqiao Wang, Zemeng Feng, and Dan Wang. 2014. Recommendation on Flickr by combining community user ratings and item importance. In *ICME*.
[16] Diederik Kingma and Jimmy Ba. 2014. Adam: A method for stochastic optimization. *arXiv preprint arXiv:1412.6980* (2014).
[17] Yehuda Koren, Robert Bell, and Chris Volinsky. 2009. Matrix factorization techniques for recommender systems. *Computer* (2009).
[18] Chenyi Lei, Dong Liu, Weiping Li, Zheng-Jun Zha, and Houqiang Li. 2016. Comparative Deep Learning of Hybrid Representations for Image Recommendations. In *CVPR*. IEEE.
[19] Yuncheng Li, Jiebo Luo, and Tao Mei. 2014. Personalized image recommendation for web search engine users. In *Multimedia and Expo (ICME), 2014 IEEE International Conference on*. IEEE.
[20] Yuncheng Li, Tao Mei, Yang Cong, and Jiebo Luo. 2015. User-curated image collections: Modeling and recommendation. In *IEEE International Conference on Big Data*.
[21] Defu Lian, Cong Zhao, Xing Xie, Guangzhong Sun, Enhong Chen, and Yong Rui. 2014. GeoMF: joint geographical modeling and matrix factorization for point-of-interest recommendation. In *SIGKDD*. ACM.
[22] Bin Liu, Yanjie Fu, Zijun Yao, and Hui Xiong. 2013. Learning geographical preferences for point-of-interest recommendation. In *SIGKDD*. ACM.
[23] Shaowei Liu, Peng Cui, Wenwu Zhu, Shiqiang Yang, and Qi Tian. 2014. Social embedding image distance learning. In *MM*. ACM.
[24] Xianming Liu, Min-Hsuan Tsai, and Thomas Huang. 2016. Analyzing User Preference for Social Image Recommendation. *arXiv preprint arXiv:1604.07044* (2016).
[25] Hao Ma, Dengyong Zhou, Chao Liu, Michael R Lyu, and Irwin King. 2011. Recommender systems with social regularization. In *WSDM*. ACM.
[26] Augusto Q Macedo, Leandro B Marinho, and Rodrygo LT Santos. 2015. Context-aware event recommendation in event-based social networks. In *RecSys*.
[27] Julian McAuley, Christopher Targett, Qinfeng Shi, and Anton Van Den Hengel. 2015. Image-based recommendations on styles and substitutes. In *SIGIR*. ACM.
[28] Wei Niu, James Caverlee, Haokai Lu, and Krishna Kamath. 2016. Community-based geospatial tag estimation. In *ASONAM*.
[29] Rong Pan, Yunhong Zhou, Bin Cao, Nathan N Liu, Rajan Lukose, Martin Scholz, and Qiang Yang. 2008. One-class collaborative filtering. In *Data Mining, 2008. ICDM'08. Eighth IEEE International Conference on*. IEEE.
[30] Steffen Rendle, Christoph Freudenthaler, Zeno Gantner, and Lars Schmidt-Thieme. 2009. BPR: Bayesian personalized ranking from implicit feedback. In *Proceedings of the twenty-fifth conference on uncertainty in artificial intelligence*. AUAI Press.
[31] Jitao Sang and Changsheng Xu. 2012. Right buddy makes the difference: An early exploration of social relation analysis in multimedia applications. In *MM*. ACM.
[32] K. Simonyan and A. Zisserman. 2014. Very Deep Convolutional Networks for Large-Scale Image Recognition. *CoRR* abs/1409.1556 (2014).
[33] Bart Thomee, David A Shamma, Gerald Friedland, Benjamin Elizalde, Karl Ni, Douglas Poland, Damian Borth, and Li-Jia Li. 2016. Yfcc100m: The new data in multimedia research. *Commun. ACM* (2016).
[34] Mikhail Trofimov, Sumit Sidana, Oleh Horodnitskii, Charlotte Laclau, Yury Maximov, and Massih-Reza Amini. 2017. Representation Learning and Pairwise Ranking for Implicit and Explicit Feedback in Recommendation Systems. *arXiv preprint arXiv:1705.00105* (2017).
[35] Aaron Van den Oord, Sander Dieleman, and Benjamin Schrauwen. 2013. Deep content-based music recommendation. In *Advances in neural information processing systems*.
[36] Hao Wang, Naiyan Wang, and Dit-Yan Yeung. 2015. Collaborative deep learning for recommender systems. In *SIGKDD*. ACM.
[37] Yao Wu, Christopher DuBois, Alice X Zheng, and Martin Ester. 2016. Collaborative denoising auto-encoders for top-n recommender systems. In *WSDM*. ACM.
[38] Kelvin Xu, Jimmy Ba, Ryan Kiros, Kyunghyun Cho, Aaron Courville, Ruslan Salakhudinov, Rich Zemel, and Yoshua Bengio. 2015. Show, attend and tell: Neural image caption generation with visual attention. In *ICML*.
[39] Mao Ye, Peifeng Yin, Wang-Chien Lee, and Dik-Lun Lee. 2011. Exploiting geographical influence for collaborative point-of-interest recommendation. In *SIGIR*. ACM.
[40] Fuzheng Zhang, Nicholas Jing Yuan, Defu Lian, Xing Xie, and Wei-Ying Ma. 2016. Collaborative knowledge base embedding for recommender systems. In *SIGKDD*.
[41] Jia-Dong Zhang and Chi-Yin Chow. 2015. GeoSoCa: Exploiting geographical, social and categorical correlations for point-of-interest recommendations. In *SIGIR*. ACM.
[42] Bolei Zhou, Agata Lapedriza, Jianxiong Xiao, Antonio Torralba, and Aude Oliva. 2014. Learning deep features for scene recognition using places database. In *Advances in neural information processing systems*. 487–495.

Learning to Discover Domain-Specific Web Content

Kien Pham
New York University
kien.pham@nyu.edu

Aécio Santos
New York University
aecio.santos@nyu.edu

Juliana Freire
New York University
juliana.freire@nyu.edu

ABSTRACT

The ability to discover all content relevant to an information domain has many applications, from helping in the understanding of humanitarian crises to countering human and arms trafficking. In such applications, time is of essence: it is crucial to both maximize coverage and identify new content as soon as it becomes available, so that appropriate actions can be taken. In this paper, we propose new methods for efficient domain-specific re-crawling that maximize the yield for new content. By learning patterns of pages that have a high yield, our methods select a small set of pages that can be re-crawled frequently, increasing the coverage and freshness while conserving resources. Unlike previous approaches to this problem, our methods combine different factors to optimize the re-crawling strategy, do not require full snapshots for the learning step, and dynamically adapt the strategy as the crawl progresses. In an empirical evaluation, we have simulated the framework over 600 partial crawl snapshots in three different domains. The results show that our approach can achieve 150% higher coverage compared to existing, state-of-the-art techniques. In addition, it is also able to capture 80% of new relevant content within less than 4 hours of publication.

ACM Reference Format:

Kien Pham, Aécio Santos, and Juliana Freire. 2018. Learning to Discover Domain-Specific Web Content. In *WSDM 2018: The Eleventh ACM International Conference on Web Search and Data Mining, February 5–9, 2018, Marina Del Rey, CA, USA.* ACM, New York, NY, USA, 9 pages. https://doi.org/10.1145/3159652.3159724

1 INTRODUCTION

The wide availability of data on the Web has enabled many new applications in different types of organizations, from government agencies and NGOs, to research universities and tech start-ups. Consider for example, the problem of human trafficking. It is estimated that 63% of sex trafficking victims are advertised online [6]. Analysts at NGOs and law enforcement agencies continuously monitor escort ads posted online to detect traffickers and more quickly rescue the victims. At the Bureau of Alcohol, Tobacco, Firearms and Explosives (ATF), agents surveil online markets where guns and drugs are sold to generate investigation leads as well as forensic evidence to prosecute criminals. Similarly, organizations that fight against illegal trading of wildlife track online marketplaces such as ebay.com to identify illegal products and obtain evidence to prosecute traffickers [20]. As a point of reference, in 2012 one operation by the US Fish and Wildlife Service (FWS) resulted in 154 busts of illegal wildlife goods on the Web [9]. Humanitarian aid organizations need to assess the nature and magnitude of major humanitarian crises around the world in order to prioritize the responses to them. In the early stages of an emergency, they crucially rely on analysis of secondary data (i.e., primary data that is processed by local and international public institutions, non-governmental organizations and news media) collected from the Web [5].

In these applications, the goal is to find *all* pages relevant to a given domain continuously and in a *timely* fashion. But doing so is difficult. Search engines, such as Google and Bing, are the main tools for users looking for information on the Web. They make use of massive computing power to both crawl the Web and create the indexes, which currently cover hundreds of billions of documents. These systems, however, have limitations when faced with domain-specific information needs. Because they aim to maximize coverage and breadth, queries often return a very large number of results, including many that are of little relevance. For example, a law enforcement agent searching for "escort ads" will find links to escort sites but also many links to news sites, which do not contain ads. While it is possible to issue more specific queries such as "site:newyork.backpage.com/WomenSeekMen", which retrieve pages in a dating section of Backpage, there is no guarantee that all pages will be retrieved. Due to resource limitations, search engines often do not download all the pages in each site they encounter. Pruning techniques are used and pages that are important for a domain may be overlooked. In addition, to cover a given domain, a potentially large number of queries need to be issued. In the case of Backpage, to retrieve all escort ads, at least one query per city is needed; and there are many more sites that contain ads in addition to Backpage. Because of the rate limits search engines impose, users may not be able to retrieve even the ads that are in their indexes.

The ideal would be to construct an index that provides comprehensive coverage of a given domain and that is kept up to date: as new pages become available, they are automatically added to the index. Focused crawlers can be used to discover pages that are relevant to a domain [7]. These systems collect pages that satisfy a set of properties and carefully prioritize the crawl frontier to maximize the number of relevant pages discovered while minimizing the number of off-topic pages visited. But continuously crawling to discover new content is difficult and expensive. Consider again the human trafficking domain. Thorn[1] estimates that over 100,000 new escort ads are posted online everyday in a plethora of Web sites – Backpage alone has millions of ads. For users and organizations in the long tail, with limited computational resources, constantly and exhaustively re-crawling all known Web sites is not practical.

WSDM 2018, February 5–9, 2018, Marina Del Rey, CA, USA

ACM ISBN 978-1-4503-5581-0/18/02...$15.00
https://doi.org/10.1145/3159652.3159724

[1] Thorn is an international anti-human trafficking organization that works to address the sexual exploitation of children.

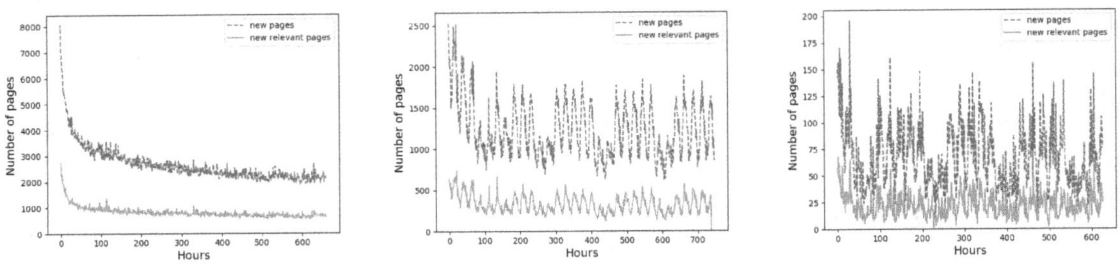

(a) Human Trafficking domain (b) Politics domain (c) Humanitarian Crisis domain

Figure 1: Number of new pages published hourly

Recognizing this problem, approaches have been proposed to make this task more efficient by reducing the number of re-crawled pages while still discovering a large percentage of new pages. Dasgupta et al. [13] estimate that 90% of all new content can be discovered by re-crawling a carefully chosen set of existing pages. They modeled the Web as graph and computed the vertex cover in order to identify a set of pages that can lead to the discovery of links to new pages over time. The selected pages are then periodically re-crawled. Unfortunately, applying this approach to discover new content in a *timely manner* creates new challenges. Re-crawling these selected pages frequently (e.g., hourly or daily) is not practical due to bandwidth limits, standard politeness constraints crawlers must adhere to, and the cost of computing resources. Also, lesser-known web crawlers (i.e., which are not associated to major search engines) are sometimes blocked when detected by sites [23], which do not have incentives to spend resources serving pages to crawlers that do not generate user traffic. Another challenge comes from the fact that pages from different domains can have very different publishing rates [25] and even within a fixed domain, these rates may change over time. This is illustrated in Figure 1 which shows how the number of new links discovered varies depending on different factors such as hour of the day, day of the week, and domain.

Timely Discovery of Domain-Specific Content. In this paper we focus on the problem of *timely discovery of new content in a domain-specific setting.* More formally, we define the content discovery problem as follows: given a set of seed pages S and we want to select the top-k pages S_k^t for every timestamp t, where $S_k^t \subset S$ and $|S_k^t| \ll |S|$, such that re-crawling every S_k^t at a timestamp t maximizes the number of new (relevant) links discovered. We assume that new content can be discovered by re-crawling previously crawled pages, but instead of crawling them periodically using a fixed schedule, we propose new algorithms that learn and leverage page change patterns to dynamically *derive efficient re-crawl schedules that optimize the new content discovery rate over time.* Unlike previous approaches which assumed the crawler has full knowledge of how pages change over time [13, 15], we dynamically learn them as the crawl proceeds and more knowlege about pages is acquired.

We propose a two-stage framework to generate dynamic re-crawl schedules. In the first phase, we predict the number of new outlinks $\hat{o}$ that the page will yield at time $t+1$ and use the prediction to select a set of candidate pages. To do so, we identify a set of useful features that are good predictors for pages that lead to a high yield (i.e., are likely to contain links to new pages) and use machine-learning based algorithms that combine these features to estimate $\hat{o}$. Because different pages may share links, selecting pages that have high yield but whose link sets overlap would negatively impact the overall performance. Thus, during the second phase, we rank the candidate pages taking into account not only the estimated number of new links, but also the estimated overlap among the sets of outlinks in the associated pages. Given a pair of pages, to efficiently estimate the overlap between their links, we propose a new algorithm that takes into account a realistic crawler scenario where only incomplete information is available, i.e., information from the top-k pages crawled in previous re-crawling cycles.

While the greedy, learning-based approach is effective, it may suffer from bias: by selecting only pages that are expected to have high-yield, it may miss new pages could lead to higher yields. A common approach to this problem is to introduce exploration: instead of just exploiting known seeds, we can explore to find (and learn the patterns from) new seeds. The challenge is how balance exploration and exploitation. We propose a method that uses the multi-armed bandits strategy [2] to automatically select an exploration threshold and to dynamically adapt the threshold as the crawl progresses.

To assess the effectiveness and efficiency of the proposed approach, we performed a detailed experimental evaluation to compare it against state-of-the-art discovery techniques using real data from different domains. The results show that the features we selected and the strategy used to combine them lead to effective predictors of page yield. By learning these features and taking the overlap into account, our algorithm outperforms all other approaches: it achieves higher coverage using less resources. In addition, by balancing exploration and exploitation, higher coverage is attained.

Contributions. Our main contributions are as follows:

- We approach content discovery as a ranking problem, where the crawling policy needs to select the top-k best seed pages to be re-crawled at every timestamp t to maximize the total number of new pages discovered. To the best of our knowledge, ours is the first attempt to consider this problem in a domain-specific setting.
- We propose a method to generate dynamic re-crawling schedules that predicts the estimated number of new outlinks $\hat{o}$ the page will yield at time $t+1$ and that also takes the estimated overlap of outlinks into account. We also show that by using

the multi-armed bandits algorithm to automatically balance the tradeoff between exploitation and exploration, our method attains improved coverage.

- We perform extensive experiments to evaluate the proposed approach and compare it against the state-of-the-art methods. The results show improvements up to 150% higher coverage compared to state-of-the-art techniques.

2 RELATED WORK

There is a significant body of work related to re-crawling web pages. Problems addressed include the characterization of the temporal dynamics and evolution of the Web [1, 3, 13, 19], maintenance of overall freshness of crawled content [11, 21, 25–27], and discovery of new links (content) [13–16]. We focus on the latter, and in particular, on *timely* content discovery in specific domains, a problem that, to the best of our knowledge, has not been tackled before. Domain-specific content discovery has been considered in the context of focused crawlers [7], where the goal is to find pages whose content is relevant to a given domain.

Temporal Dynamics and Evolution. The temporal dynamics and evolution of Web content has been studied in [1, 3, 13, 19]. Ntoulas et al. [19] observed that web pages are created and retired at a fast pace. Olston and Pandey [21] studied the longevity of information found in web pages and proposed re-crawl scheduling policies that allow crawlers to target persistent content, instead of ephemeral content that will be quickly overwritten by subsequent changes. Adar et al. [1] studied how Web content changes both with respect to time intervals (hourly and sub-hourly crawls) and the page structure (content, DOM tree and terms). Bar-Yossef [3] studied the decay of the Web and showed that not only do some web pages exhibit a rapid death but also large sub-graphs of the Web decay significantly. For applications, such as the ones discussed in Section 1, that aim to achieve large coverage of a domain over time, this underscores the importance of discovering pages fast so that they can be properly archived before they disappear.

Re-Crawling for Content Freshness. Coffman et al. [10] were one of the first to study the problem of re-crawling, and postulated that web page change events follow a Poisson process: changes occur randomly and independently. Considering the Poisson model, Cho and Garcia-Molina [8] proposed efficient change frequency estimators for various scenarios, including the web crawling scenario in which information about all change events is not available. Other works observed that features extracted from the content of web pages, web link structure, and web search logs can be used to effectively predict change patterns [4, 24, 28]. Barbosa et al. [4] were the first to exploit the use of static features extracted from the content of a page to predict its change behavior. Based on this idea, Tan and Mitra [28] proposed the use of new dynamic features, and other features extracted from the web link structure and web search logs to group pages with similar change behavior. Radinsky and Bennett [24] went a step further and proposed a change prediction framework that uses not only features from the content, but also the degree and relationship among the observed changes to a page, the relatedness to other pages, and the similarity of changes. Santos et al. [26, 27] proposed the use of ranking-based re-crawling strategies for scheduling web page updates. They described a genetic programming framework to generate ranking functions to select the top-k best pages to be re-crawled. This line of work differs from our work in the sense that their goal is to maintain overall freshness, whereas in here we aim to discover new content. We follow a ranking-based approach as in [26, 27], but with different machine learning methods and objectives.

Re-crawling for Content Discovery. Dasgupta et al. [13] studied the extent to which new pages can be efficiently discovered. They observed that by re-crawling a subset of existing pages, it is possible to discover a large portion of the newly generated content. Another important finding in their work was that a large number of page pairs share outlinks to new content: if only pages within a web site are considered, more than 20% of pages have Jaccard coefficient very close to 0 (i.e., they do not share any links) and more than 40% have a Jaccard coefficient very close to 1 (i.e., they have the same links). They proposed algorithms for selecting a small subset of pages that can be re-crawled in order to efficiently discover new content. The algorithms assume that full snapshots of the content is available. However, for scenarios where resources are limited, constructing full snapshots may not be possible. In contrast, our approach does not assume complete information is available and dynamically learns patterns as information becomes available.

Kumar et al. [15] studied the problem of discovery for pages with a high number of incoming links. They presented different policies to select pages for re-crawling based on multiple page scoring strategies such as the *yield* (number of links not present in the previous crawl of that page divided by the time since the prior crawl) and the *link score* (the number of inlinks of the discovered pages). Other policies select pages with probability proportional to the number of total inlinks, new outlinks, or both. In summary, all proposed policies try to maximize discovery of high in-degree pages and only leverage the link structure of the Web, whereas our approach aims to maximize full content coverage and does so by using additional features to learning efficient re-crawling policies.

Gupta et al. [14] proposed techniques to schedule the re-crawling of a given set of seed pages to discover news headlines. Given the crawling frequency per day as a resource constraint, they proposed a technique that monitors each news source for a particular time period to collect the news update patterns, and then analyzes them using mixed integer programming to discover the optimal crawling schedule that maximizes accuracy. In another variation of the problem, they optimized the crawling frequency and the corresponding crawling schedule for a desired accuracy level. While Gupta et al. aim to find an optimal fixed schedule for each page, our approach is adaptive. We automatically learn a crawling policy that is applied at each timestamp to select the pages that should be crawled in order to maximize coverage. We do not assume that pages are monitored during a particular time, instead, the patterns are learned dynamically as more information becomes available. Furthermore, since their seed pages were selected manually, they ignore the fact that different pages may share outlinks to new content. This overlap can negatively affect the overall performance of the crawling policy. As we discuss in Section 4, our approach takes overlap into account.

Lefortier et al. [16] studied the problem of crawling popular pages (in terms of user interest) in a timely fashion. They showed that page popularity changes over time and many pages follow a pattern where the popularity decays quickly. They propose strategies for *holistic crawling* which aim to attain a balance between crawling newly discovered links or re-crawling previously crawled pages (content sources). One of their best-performing strategies crawls content sources with priority that is proportional to the new link discovery rate, the popularity of the discovered pages, and the time since last crawl; to interleave downloads of content sources and newly discovered links, it simply crawls new links immediately after their discovery. In this work, we focus on the problem of scheduling when content sources should be re-crawled, but our approach can be easily extended to crawl all new links right after discovery. In addition, while Lefortier et al. [16] optimize discovery of popular pages based on search engine click logs, our main motivation is to obtain full coverage of a given domain.

3 PROBLEM FORMULATION

Let S be the set of n seed pages chosen for re-crawling and $T = t_0, t_1, ..., t_\infty$ be the discrete representation of timestamps for the re-crawling cycles. Let $O^t(s)$ denote a set of new pages discovered from $s \in S$ at the time $t \in T$. The set of all pages discovered from the seed pages is $O = \bigcup_{t \in T} O^t$. Let $r : O \rightarrow 0, 1$ be a function indicating the relevance of a page in O with respect to the domain D:

$$r(o) = \begin{cases} 1 \text{ if } o \in D \\ 0 \text{ if } o \notin D \end{cases}$$

At each timestamp t, let U_k^t be the set of distinct pages discovered from k seed pages $S_k^t \subset S$ for the first time:

$$U_k^t = \bigcup_{s \in S_k^t} O^t(s)$$

$R^t(S_k^t)$ denotes the number of distinct pages discovered from S_k^t that are relevant to domain D at time t:

$$R^t(S_k^t) = \sum_{p \in U^t(S_k^t)} r(p)$$

At each timestamp t, and given the information obtained from prior crawls $O^{t'}$, where $t' < t$, we would like to select S_k^t such that re-crawling S_k^t maximizes the cummulative $R^t(S_k^t)$ over time:

$$C_k = \sum_{t \in T} R^t(S_k^t)$$

We use *Coverage* to measure the efficiency of a selection strategy:

$$Coverage = \frac{C_k}{C_n}$$

where C_n is total number of relevant pages that can be discovered if all seed pages are recrawled at each timestamp. Note that *Coverage* captures the percentage of relevant pages discovered over time, and if all discovered pages are considered relevant (i.e., $O \subseteq D$ and $\forall o : r(o) = 1$), the problem is reduced to the general non-focused crawling setting, which we also consider in our evaluation.

4 ONLINE RE-CRAWLING FRAMEWORK

Unlike previously-proposed scheduling algorithms that require complete past crawls, we propose a method that learns from temporal features derived from multiple incomplete historical crawls. Below, we give an overview of the framework and then present our approach to prediction as well as how we balance exploration and exploitation during the re-crawling process to increase coverage.

4.1 Approach Overview

As outlined in Algorithm 1, our approach works in an iterative fashion. First, it builds a model (line 5) that, given a page P, predicts the number of new relevant links P will yield. Then, using this model (*Predictor*), it selects a small subset S_k^t of the seed pages S (line 6) to be crawled (in line 7) that maximizes the *Coverage* over time, i.e., S_k^t will yield a large number of new outlinks $O^t(S_k^t)$ if crawled at time t. Finally, based on the retrieved data, historical information is updated (lines 8-9) which will be used in subsequent iterations.

As discussed in Section 1, pages from different domains can have very different change rates [25]. Indeed, our experiments (see Section 5.2) confirm not only that, but also show that these rates change over time and depend on different factors. To tackle this problem, we apply learning algorithms to train a *Predictor* that uncovers such patterns from data obtained in previous re-crawling cycles (stored in *HIST*) and effectively predicts link yields. Thus, *HIST* needs to maintain the information $O^{t'}$ obtained from prior re-crawling cycles t', where $t' < t$, as well as the relevance of all discovered pages with respect to domain D (line 9). This information can then be used to generate features for the prediction (Section 4.2).

However, a significant fraction of page pairs have overlapping outlink sets [13]. Thus, if we greedly consider pages that lead to a high yield in isolation, we are likely to waste resources: if the pages selected have a large overlap, the overall yield will be low. To address this problem, we take overlap into account: if two seed pages are predicted to have a high yield but also have a high estimated overlap, only one should be selected for re-crawling. Since overlap can change over time, the overlap estimates must be updated regularly. In the previous approach [13], the overlap could be computed within a single snapshot from the most recent crawl since all seed pages are scheduled to be re-crawled at every timestamp. However, in our setting, only small subset of seed pages is re-crawled, therefore only $O(S_k)$ is available rather than $O(S)$. As a result, we need to estimate the overlap differently. To update *SIM* (line 8), we compute all pair-wise similarities between selected seed pages in S_k. Note that $|S_k| \ll |S|$ and we only need to compute the similarity between pages that are in the same web site, which significantly reduces the number of pairs to compute.

To measure the overlap between two pages p and q, we use the Jaccard similarity:

$$Jaccard(p, q) = \frac{|O(p) \cap O(q)|}{|O(p) \cup O(q)|}$$

Algorithm 2 details the page selection function. First, the predictor is applied to all pages to estimate the number of new outlinks that can be discovered from the seed pages (lines 2-5). Next, a greedy selection is performed over the candidate pages, taking into account the overlap estimate from the most recent crawls (lines 6-11).

4.2 Predicting New Outlinks

Given the information $O^0(S_k^0), O^1(S_k^1), ..., O^{t'}(S_k^{t'})$ collected during previous crawls, we need to predict the number of new pages discovered by re-crawling each seed page $s \in S$ at the timestamp t, where $t > t'$. We define the temporal prediction function as: $f : S \times T \rightarrow \mathbb{R}$ and the set of temporal training examples $X = \{x_0, x_1, ..., x_{t'}\}$, such that x_{t_i} contains set of training examples obtained by re-crawling

Algorithm 1 Online Re-Crawling

procedure Online_Recrawl(k)
  $HIST = \emptyset$
  $SIM = \emptyset$
  for $t \in T$ **do**
    $Predictor \leftarrow$ Train a model with $HIST$
    $S_k^t = Select(k, t, Predictor, SIM)$
    $O^t(S_k^t) \leftarrow$ Crawl(S_k^t) ▷ Crawl seed pages and new outlinks
    Update SIM with $O^t(S_k^t)$
    Update $HIST$ with $O^t(S_k^t)$
  end for
end procedure

Algorithm 2 Select Top-k Seed Pages

function Select(k, t, $Predictor$, SIM)
  $Candidates$ = { Seed Pages }
  for $p \in Candidates$ **do**
    $E_p = Predictor.predict(p, t)$
  end for
  $S_k = \emptyset$
  for 1 to k **do**
    Select p in $Candidates$ that has highest E_p
    Remove all q from $Candidates$, where $SIM[p, q] > \xi$
    $S_k^t \leftarrow S_k^t \cup p$
  end for
  return S_k^t
end function

selected seed pages at timestamp t_i. Each seed page s that was re-crawled is represented as one training example: $\langle F(s,t), |O^t(s)| \rangle$, where $F(s,t)$ is the featurization function that transforms a page into a single vector and $|O^t(s)|$ is the number of new relevant pages yielded by s at timestamp t.

Features. We consider features that capture temporal content creation patterns. Note, however, that other features types (e.g., content and URL, etc) can be easily integrated into our framework. We leave this for future work. Each page re-crawled at timestamp t is converted into a single vector resulting from the concatenation of the fetures described below.

avg: *Average number of new pages discovered from s in the past crawls.* In order to limit the size of the data stored and to prioritize the recent page history, we compute this feature considering only a window of size w. For example, for $w = 10$, we compute *avg* using the number of discovered pages from the last 10 previous crawls.

std: *Standard deviation of the number of new pages discovered from s in the past crawls.* This feature captures the variance of the ***avg*** value. As in *avg*, we compute *std* within a window size w.

age: *Time since the seed page s was last re-crawled.* This feature aims to prioritize *older* seeds. The intuition is that if a seed page has not been re-crawled recently, it is more likely it contains previously unseen outlinks.

tod: *Time of the day of the timestamp t.* This feature takes a value from 0 to 23. We treat this value as the categorical feature and use one-hot encoding to represent it. The rationale for this feature is that some pages may have higher probability of creating new links during speficic times of the day (e.g., day or night).

dow: *Day of the week of the timestamp of the next crawling cycle.* This feature takes value from 0 to 6, corresponding to each day of the week (Monday is 0 and Sunday is 6). As in *tod*, we use one-hot encoding to represent this feature, and the rationale is that some pages may create more links during specific days of the week (e.g., during weekends). ***aa = avg∗age***: *Reinforcement of greedy strategy.* This feature gives higher priority to pages that generate more new links on average and have not been crawled for a long time. It also introduces non-linearity that would not be possible for simple linear algorithms to learn otherwise.

Learning Algorithms. Multiple learning methods can be used to map the features into predictions. Since we are trying to predict a number (the number of new outlinks), regression algorithms are a natural choice for this task. In practice, the actual predicted number is used only for ranking the pages. Therefore, learning to rank (LTR) [17] is another class of algorithms suitable for this task. In Section 5, we present an experimental evaluation of these two classes of algorithms for our problem.

4.3 Balancing Exploitation and Exploration

Since Algorithm 2 performs a greedy selection, it naturally favors seed pages that are known to be *good*. This can introduce bias in the estimator, which by learning just from this group may end up missing other, different seed pages that have high yield in the future, and consequently, will fail to capture their patterns. To address this problem, we propose a strategy to balance exploitation and exploration using multi-armed bandits (MAB) [2], which is known to be an effective means of solving such trade-off problems. The MAB algorithm operates as follows: at each timestamp t, we choose one of a set of arms available. Then, we observe the reward obtained by choosing that arm. The goal is to select arms such that the cumulative reward over time is maximized. One intuitive way to apply this method in our setting is to model two selection methods as arms, one which favors exploitation and another that favors exploration, and then select one arm at each re-crawling cycle. However, since exploration generally yields much lower coverage than exploitation, this causes the MAB algorithm quickly coverge and therefore rarely select the explorative method. As a result, we observed that the coverage obtained by this strategy is no different than using solely exploitation. Instead, we combine exploration and exploitation using a ratio r, i.e., we select r% of the seed pages using a greedy strategy (such as Algorithm 2), and $(1 - r)$% using a strategy that favors exploration. Then, we model the arms as a finite list of ratios between 0.0 and 1.0 and apply the UCB1 algorithm [2] to choose the ratio to be used at each timestamp t. This strategy is detailed in Algorithm 3. Finally, after we crawl the selected pages we use the average number of discovered new outlinks over time by the choosen ratio as reward.

5 EXPERIMENTAL EVALUATION

We demonstrate the effectiveness of our re-crawling framework and prediction methods through extensive experiments using real-world datasets. To create a controlled environment in which we can accurately compare different strategies and avoid confounding factors that arise due to the dynamic nature of the Web, we

Algorithm 3 Balancing Exploitation and Exploration

```
function Bandit_Select(k, t, Predictor, SIM)
    ratio = UCB1.select_arm()
    k1 = ratio * k
    k2 = k − k1
    TopK1 = Select(k1, t, Predictor, SIM)
    TopK2 = Select k2 pages using exploration strategy
    TopK = TopK1 ∪ TopK2
    return TopK
end function
```

collected data from three different domains to serve as the ground truth. Using these data, we compared the coverage attained by our approach against the state of the art in re-crawling in both focused and non-focused settings. In the focused setting, we assume that the page classifier is available during the re-crawling process, while in the non-focused setting it is not. The non-focused setting reflects the scenario when the page classifier is not available and one wants to re-crawl all pages from a number of specific web sites that are considered fully relevant to the domain. We also verified the benefit of balancing exploration and exploitation, and the ability of our approach to discover new content in timely fashion.

5.1 Data Collection

To gather the ground truth data for carrying out the re-crawling experiments, we selected the following domains:

- Politics: represents news articles and blog posts that are related to politics.
- Human trafficking: represents adult ads from classified ads, escort, and related sites.
- Humanitarian crisis: contains reports about disasters that threaten human life from NGOs and news sites.

We selected these domains for two main reasons: they are very different in nature – this is confirmed in the different behaviors observed in our experimental analysis; and we had access to training examples, labeled by subject matter experts, which are critical to train a classifier required to test the relevance of the crawled pages.

For each domain, we selected the seed pages as follows. First, we fired a focused crawl using the ACHE open-source crawler[2] and retrieved between 200K to 500K pages. Note that each crawl makes use of a classifier pre-trained for the respective domain. We then sorted all pages based on the number of relevant outlinks they contain and selected pages with the highest number of outlinks, while at the same time, avoiding gathering too many pages from the same site. Besides covering a larger number of sites, we need to limit the number of pages per site so that it is possible to obtain full snapshots in hourly intervals. This also reduces the risk of the crawler being blocked by the target web sites. For our experiments, by setting the page limit to 10 in politics domain and 50 in human trafficking and humanitarian crisis domain, we can create full snapshots hourly.

The ground-truth data was obtained by crawling all seed pages and the new pages from their outlinks (i.e., ones that were not discovered in previous crawls) hourly during a 1-month period. From the crawled data, we extracted in-site outlinks from the HTML

[2]http://github.com/ViDA-NYU/ache

Table 1: Statistics of the collected data

	Human Trafficking	Politics	Hum. Crisis
# seed pages	8543	17892	3480
# seed sites	2215	3524	96
average # pages per site	2.59	5.07	36.25
# discovered pages	2,012,764	682,845	43,012
# discovered relevant pages	1,004,075	243,482	18,532

source of each seed page and ran the page classifiers to assess the relevance of pages linked by these outlinks. Table 1 summarizes the statistics of the collected data.

5.2 Discoverability Patterns

We obtained 665, 632, and 741 snapshots for human trafficking, humanitarian crisis and politics domains respectively. The total size of these data is roughly 2.7TB uncompressed. To better understand the patterns associated with the discoverability of new pages, we examined the number of new pages discovered at each re-crawling cycle. Figure 1 shows the number of new pages and new relevant pages that are directly reachable from the seed pages in the three domains. The figures clearly show that percentage of relevant pages among new pages is small, which underscores the importance of optimizing the selection strategies with respect to relevant pages. In all domains, the following pattern is observed: the number of new links starts to drop in the beginning and then stabilizes after the first 50 hours of the crawls. We initially hypothesized that the drop was due to the crawler being blocked by sites. But after inspecting the logs, we found that the number of successful requests to seed pages remains stable even at the beginning of the process. The actual reason for the drop is that this set of discovered pages already existed before the start of our crawl, and were only gradualy discovered over time after they appear in the monitored seed pages. The steeper decline in the human trafficking domain reveals that pages from the past tend to appear more often. Note that the decline for new relevant pages is less steep, suggesting that irrelevant pages (e.g., boilerplate ads) are more likely to appear repeatedly. In the plots, we also observe repeating valleys and peaks. These correspond to daily and weekly patterns, which indicate the importance of capturing the temporal features (time of the day and day of the week) described in Section 4.2.

5.3 Comparing Selection Strategies

We compare our approach with several crawling strategies. The Round Robin (*RR*) strategy selects seed pages that have the highest ***age*** (time since last crawl). It is a uniform strategy that guarantees that all pages are re-crawled once every n/k re-crawling cycles, where n is the number of seed pages. We also compare to the upper-bound greedy algorithm (*GREEDY*) from [13], which greedily selects the best pages with foreknowlege of all outlinks $O^t(S)$ and taking the overlap into account. It is unrealistic since it assumes full knowledge of $O^t(S)$ before crawling S at time t, but it serves as an approximation of the ideal upper bound coverage. The strategies *OD-WIN*, *CLIQ-WIN** and *COV** are variants of the algorithms proposed in [13]. We use * in a algorithm name to denote that the

original algorithm needed to be slightly modified to be applicable in our problem setting. In what follows, we explain each of them.
OD-WIN: This algorithm selects the top-k seed pages with the highest average of new relevant pages discovered in the past crawls.
*COV**: The original algorithm *COV* is the realistic version of *GREEDY*, which utilizes $O^{t-1}(S)$ for selecting seed pages at timestamp t. However, in our setting we only crawl k pages at each timestamp t, then only $O^{t-1}(S_k^{t-1})$ is available. One solution for this is to merge the set of outlinks from all past crawls as follows: for each page $s \in S$, let $\hat{O}^{t-1}(s) = \bigcup_{t'<t} O^{t'}(s)$, where $t' < t$. Then we apply the *GREEDY* algorithm, but using only past information $\hat{O}^{t-1}(S)$.
*CLIQ-WIN**: In its original form, the algorithm groups pages based on the overlap identified in the most recent re-crawl, and then picks one representative page from each group, starting from the one with highest estimated number of new pages. The estimation is done by computing the average number of new relevant pages discovered in the past crawls. To make this work in our setting, where all past re-crawls are incomplete, we first compute the overlap as described in Section 4. Then, we use this information to form groups and pick only one page from each group.
Prediction-Based Methods. We evaluate our framework (Section 4) using four different configurations:
REG: In this strategy we apply the Algorithms 1 and 2 described in Section 4, and use linear regression to train the $Predictor$. Note that we do not use exploration in this method.
LTR: This strategy is similar to REG, but instead of linear regression, it applies learning-to-rank. More specificaly, we represent a training example as $\langle F(s,t), log(1 + |O^t(s)|), qid \rangle$, where $log(1 + |O^t(s)|)$ is the relevance of the document and qid is the query. We set the qid to be equal to the timestamp t when the training example was created.
BANDIT: This method uses the bandit algorithm described in Section 4.3 to choose the ratio between *REG* and *RR*.
REG-RR: To evaluate the benefit of using the bandits algorithm, we also experiment with a strategy that combines *REG* and *RR* using a fixed ratio. We fix the ratio between *REG* and *RR* to be 0.9, which we empirically found to be the best in humanitarian crisis domain. We pick *REG* over *LTR* to combine with *RR* and *BANDIT* due to its better speed and coverage performance as shown later.
Implementation Details. Any available machine learning toolkit to learn the predictor described in Section 4.2; for our experiments, we used scikit-learn [22]. To learn a regression-based predictor, we considered three options: Gradient Boosting Decision Trees (GBDT), Linear Regression (LR), and Polynomial Regression (PR). However, we observed no significant improvement by using PR and GBDT over LR, therefore we only show the results obtained using LR. To construct a learning-to-rank-based predictor, we use RankLib [12] and therefore have multiple algorithm options. We picked Coordinate Ascent [18] over others to show in the final results due to its superior performance. In all re-crawl simulations using *REG*, *REG-RR*, *BANDIT* and *LTR*, we use *OD-WIN* method during the first 10 hours to bootstrap the training data. We set window size w to 168 hours (7 days) so that the predictor only learns from most recent crawls without losing the daily and hourly patterns. The predictor is re-trained every 3 hours to reduce the computation time. We set ξ in the Algorithm 2 to 0.7. We set k to 50, 400, 500 in humanitarian

Table 2: Coverage of selection methods in a focused setting

	Human Trafficking	Politics	Humanitarian Crisis
RR	0.179	0.368	0.391
OD-WIN	0.890	0.546	0.473
*COV**	0.829	0.393	0.465
*CLIQ-WIN**	0.859	0.538	0.465
REG	**0.929**	0.805	0.714
REG-RR	0.922	0.807	0.723
BANDIT	0.921	**0.808**	**0.735**
LTR	0.924	0.804	0.724

crisis, human trafficking and politics domain respectively. We pick the k close to the minimal value that the *GREEDY* method can obtain 100% coverage. For the *BANDIT* method, we choose the set of possible ratio values as $\{0.6, 0.7, 0.8, 0.9, 1.0\}$. We intentionally omit values smaller than 0.6 to force the algorithm to always favor exploitation over the exploration. Ideally, the bandit algorithm should figure this out, however this is likely to hurt coverage since it may take several re-crawling cycles to get to the optimal value.
Comparison in a Focused Setting. In this setting, we only consider a page to be relevant if it is classified as positive by the page classifier for the corresponding domain. Figure 2 shows how coverage changes over time for the different strategies, while Table 2 shows the coverage obtained at the last timestamp. We observe that our approach outperforms all the baselines. In Humanitarian Crisis and Politics, *BANDIT* attains more than 150% of the coverage obtained by all the baselines.

For Human Trafficking, the difference in coverage is smaller. As we observed in the Figure 1, this domain does not have the daily and weekly patterns present in the other domains, and the variation in the number of new pages hourly is also comparatively small. As a result, all baselines perform well in this *easy* domain. This suggests that our methods are especially effective for domains that present higher variability in the the generation of new pages. Note that for this domain, *OD-WIN*, which does not take overlap into account, is the best baseline. This can be explained by Table 1. Indeed, this domain has the smallest average number of pages per site. Therefore, it is likely that there is little overlap among the selected seed pages. Another interesting observation is that in Humanitarian Crisis domain, *COV** performs worst. One potential explanation for this is that, in this domain, the number of new relevant pages discovered per seed page in each hour is very small, which makes the estimation $\hat{O}^{t-1}(S)$ less accurate.

Comparing *REG*, *REG-RR* and *BANDIT*, their performance is comparable in Human Trafficking and Politics domain. However, in Humanitarian Crisis domain, the *BANDIT* method obtains best result and *REG* is the worst. As Figure 1 shows, this domain has the highest variability in the generation of new pages. This suggests that depending on the nature of the data to be collected, using exploration may or may not lead to improvements. However, *BANDIT* provides the best solution: by balancing exploration and exploitation in a dynamic fashion, it is able to adapt automaticall for different domains.

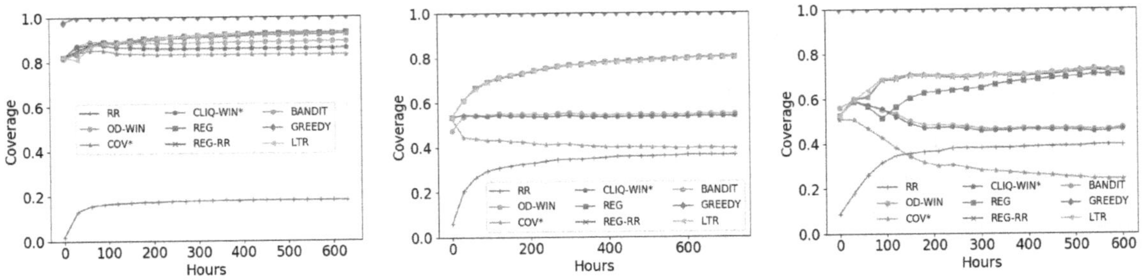

(a) Human Trafficking domain (b) Politics domain (c) Humanitarian Crisis domain

Figure 2: Comparison of coverage between baselines and prediction based methods in focused setting

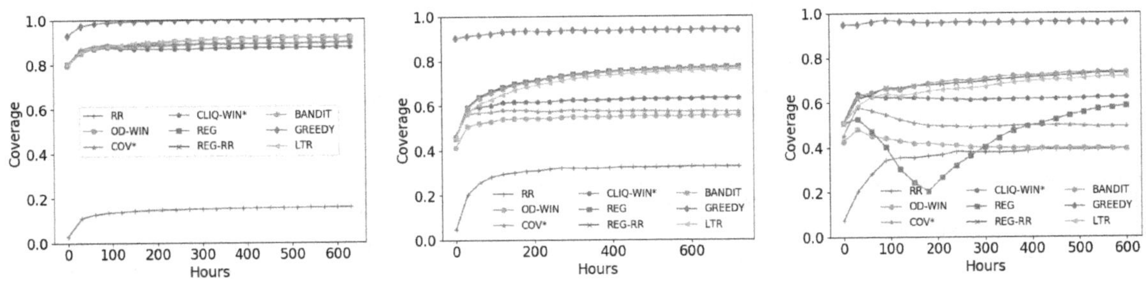

(a) Human Trafficking domain (b) Politics domain (c) Humanitarian Crisis domain

Figure 3: Comparision of coverage between baselines and prediction based methods in non-focused setting

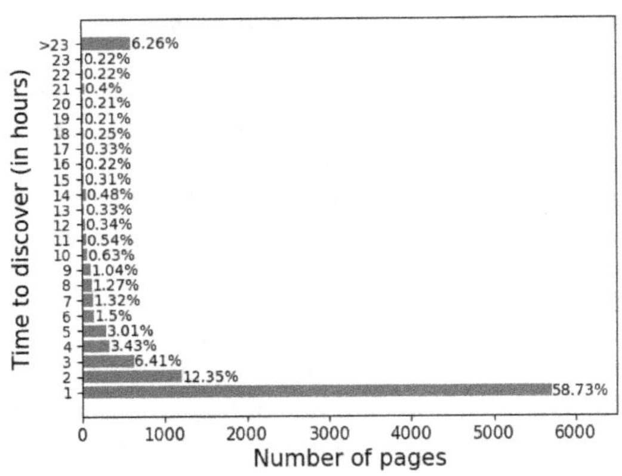

Figure 4: Age of pages discovered by the best method in focused setting from Humanitarian Crisis domain

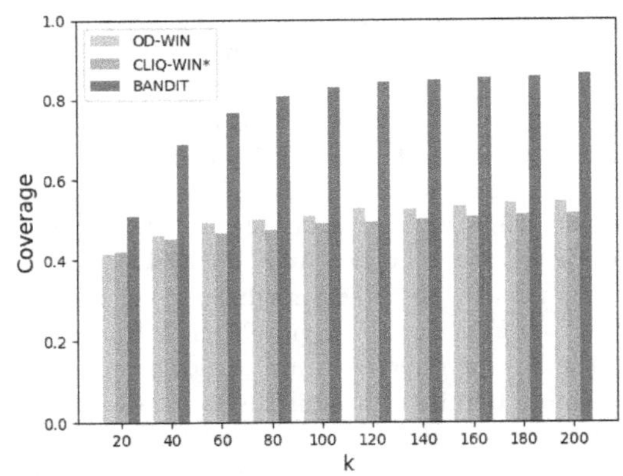

Figure 5: Coverages obtained by varing k in focused setting from Humanitarian Crisis domain

Comparison in a Non-Focused Setting. While the goal of our work is to support efficient discovery of pages in a domain, we are also interested in assessing the effectiveness of our approach for general discovery. To do so, we consider all discovered pages as relevant. Figure 3 shows how coverage varies over time for the different strategies. Although the magnitude of the difference between these methods seem to be smaller, our proposed methods still outperform all the baselines. Aside from that, we also observe that *REG* performs much worse than *BANDIT* and *REG-RR* in Humanitarian Crisis domain, which shows the effectiveness of combining exploration and exploitation. Another observation is that *CLIQ-WIN** obtains better coverage than *OD-WIN*, especially in Humanitarian Crisis domain. The reason is that the number of new pages discovered per site each hour in the non-focused setting is much higher than that in the focused one. This leads to larger overlaps between seed pages, which is considered in *CLIQ-WIN**. Note that in our data collection process, we limit the number of seed pages per site to be quite small, which likely reduces the overlaps. However, when the limit is higher, methods that eliminate the overlaps would be more effective.

5.4 Age of Discovered Pages

To demonstrate the efficiency of our method to discover relevant pages in a timely manner, we analyze the age (i.e., time interval since publication until discovery) of relevant pages when they were discovered using our best method–*BANDIT*. Figure 4 shows that in the Humanitarian Crisis domain, 58.73% of relevant pages were discovered within 1 hour of publication; and over 80% within 4 hours. Note that in this setting, we set k to 50, which is equivalent as re-crawling the entire seed pages every 2.8 days. Similar results were obtained for the other domains, which we omit due to space limitation.

5.5 Impact of k on Coverage

In the previous experiments, we fixed k in all settings for the sake of comparison. We now explore how varying values of k impacts the coverage for different selection methods. For this experiment with focused setting in Humanitarian Crisis domain, we use our best method - *BANDIT*, and the two best baselines - *OD-WIN* and *CLIQ-WIN*. As Figure 5 shows, *BANDIT* outperforms the other methods even when we vary k. We note that in a production environment, k can be set based on resource availability (i.e., maximum number of pages to be crawled in each re-crawling cycle) or politeness constraints (i.e., maximum number of pages to be crawled from single web site in each re-crawling cycle).

6 CONCLUSION AND FUTURE WORK

In this paper, we addressed the problem of efficiently discovering Web content for a given a domain of interest. We proposed a new framework whose goal is to attain high coverage for the domain while at the same time discovering new, relevant content in a timely fashion. Our framework is adaptive and updates the re-crawling schedules dynamically. At each re-crawling step, it selects the top-k seed pages that maximize the yield of new content using information collected in previous steps. Unlike previous approaches which assumed the crawler has full knowledge of how pages change over time, the framework incrementally learns the change patterns as the crawl proceeds and more knowledge about pages is acquired. In addition, to increase coverage, it also takes overlap into account and also balances exploration and exploitation. We performed a detailed experimental evaluation which shows that our approach is effective and outperforms previously-proposed, state-of-the-art methods. In future work, we plan to extend this work in several directions. First, a larger scale experiment, with a larger number of seeds and a longer data collection period, would allow a better understanding of the behavior and effectiveness of the multi-armed bandits approach over the prediction-based methods in the long run. Another direction that we would like to investigate is the effectiveness of content-based features, which were successfully employed to predict page changes in previous work [24], and may be correlated with the publication rates of new outlinks as well.

Acknowledgments. This work was supported by the DARPA MEMEX and D3M programs. Any opinions, findings, and conclusions or recommendations expressed in this material are those of the authors and do not necessarily reflect the views of DARPA.

REFERENCES

[1] Eytan Adar, Jaime Teevan, Susan T. Dumais, and Jonathan L. Elsas. The web changes everything: Understanding the dynamics of web content. In *Proceedings of the 2nd ACM International Conference on Web Search and Data Mining*, pages 282–291, 2009.

[2] Peter Auer, Nicolò Cesa-Bianchi, and Paul Fischer. Finite-time analysis of the multiarmed bandit problem. *Machine Learning*, 47(2-3):235–256, May 2002.

[3] Ziv Bar-Yossef, Andrei Z. Broder, Ravi Kumar, and Andrew Tomkins. Sic transit gloria telae: Towards an understanding of the web's decay. In *Proceedings of the 13th International Conference on World Wide Web*, pages 328–337, 2004.

[4] Luciano Barbosa, Ana Carolina Salgado, Francisco de Carvalho, Jacques Robin, and Juliana Freire. Looking at both the present and the past to efficiently update replicas of web content. In *Proceedings of the 7th Annual ACM International Workshop on Web Information and Data Management*, pages 75–80, 2005.

[5] Jeff Borland, Peter Dawkins, David Johnson, and Ross Williams. United nations disaster assessment and coordination, 2013.

[6] Vanessa Bouché. A report on the use of technology to recruit, groom and sell domestic minor sex trafficking victims. https://www.wearethorn.org/child-trafficking-statistics, January 2015.

[7] Soumen Chakrabarti. Focused web crawling. In *Encyclopedia of Database Systems*, pages 1147–1155. Springer, 2009.

[8] Junghoo Cho and Hector Garcia-Molina. Estimating frequency of change. *ACM Transactions on Internet Technology*, 3:256–290, 2003.

[9] Sandra Cleva and Gavin Shire. Global wildlife trafficking busts expose illegal internet sales in u.s., southeast asia. https://www.fws.gov/home/newsroom/operationwildwebNR07112013.html, July 2013.

[10] E. G. Coffman, Zhen Liu, and Richard R. Weber. Optimal robot scheduling for web search engines. *Journal of Scheduling*, 1(1):15–29, 1998.

[11] Ford D, Grimes C, and Tassone E. Keeping a search engine index fresh: Risk and optimality in estimating refresh rates for web pages. Technical report, 2008.

[12] Van Dang. The Lemur Project-Wiki-RankLib. https://sourceforge.net/p/lemur/wiki/RankLib/. [Online].

[13] Anirban Dasgupta, Arpita Ghosh, Ravi Kumar, Christopher Olston, Sandeep Pandey, and Andrew Tomkins. The discoverability of the web. In *Proceedings of the 16th International Conference on World Wide Web*, pages 421–430, 2007.

[14] Kanik Gupta, Vishal Mittal, Bazir Bishnoi, Siddharth Maheshwari, and Dhaval Patel. Act: Accuracy-aware crawling techniques for cloud-crawler. *World Wide Web*, 19(1):69–88, Jan 2016.

[15] Ravi Kumar, Kevin Lang, Cameron Marlow, and Andrew Tomkins. Efficient discovery of authoritative resources. In *Proceedings of the 2008 IEEE 24th International Conference on Data Engineering*, pages 1495–1497, 2008.

[16] Damien Lefortier, Liudmila Ostroumova, Egor Samosvat, and Pavel Serdyukov. Timely crawling of high-quality ephemeral new content. In *Proceedings of the 22nd ACM International Conference on Information & Knowledge Management*, pages 745–750, 2013.

[17] Tie-Yan Liu. Learning to rank for information retrieval. *Foundations and Trends in Information Retrieval*, 3(3):225–331, March 2009.

[18] Donald Metzler and W. Bruce Croft. Linear feature-based models for information retrieval. *Infomation Retrieval*, 10(3):257–274, June 2007.

[19] Alexandros Ntoulas, Junghoo Cho, and Christopher Olston. What's new on the web?: The evolution of the web from a search engine perspective. In *Proceedings of the 13th International Conference on World Wide Web*, pages 1–12, 2004.

[20] Mary Catherine O'Connor. Inside the complicated world of online wildlife trafficking. https://www.theguardian.com/vital-signs/2015/aug/03/cecil-lion-ivory-online-wildlife-trafficking-ebay, August 2015.

[21] Christopher Olston and Sandeep Pandey. Recrawl scheduling based on information longevity. In *Proceedings of the 17th International Conference on World Wide Web*, pages 437–446, 2008.

[22] Fabian Pedregosa, Gaël Varoquaux, Alexandre Gramfort, Vincent Michel, Bertrand Thirion, Olivier Grisel, Mathieu Blondel, Peter Prettenhofer, Ron Weiss, Vincent Dubourg, Jake Vanderplas, Alexandre Passos, David Cournapeau, Matthieu Brucher, Matthieu Perrot, and Édouard Duchesnay. Scikit-learn: Machine learning in python. *Journal of Machine Learning Research*, 12:2825–2830, November 2011.

[23] Kien Pham, Aécio Santos, and Juliana Freire. Understanding website behavior based on user agent. In *Proceedings of the 39th International ACM SIGIR Conference on Research and Development in Information Retrieval*, pages 1053–1056, 2016.

[24] Kira Radinsky and Paul N. Bennett. Predicting content change on the web. In *Proceedings of the 6th ACM International Conference on Web Search and Data Mining*, pages 415–424, 2013.

[25] Aécio Santos, Bruno Pasini, and Juliana Freire. A first study on temporal dynamics of topics on the web. In *Proceedings of the 25th International Conference Companion on World Wide Web*, pages 849–854, 2016.

[26] Aécio S. R. Santos, Cristiano R. Carvalho, Jussara M. Almeida, Edleno S. Moura, Altigran S. Silva, and Nivio Ziviani. A genetic programming framework to schedule webpage updates. *Infomation Retrieval*, 18(1):73–94, February 2015.

[27] Aécio S. R. Santos, Nivio Ziviani, Jussara Almeida, Cristiano R. Carvalho, Edleno Silva Moura, and Altigran Soares Silva. Learning to schedule webpage updates using genetic programming. In *Proceedings of the 20th International Symposium on String Processing and Information Retrieval - Volume 8214*, pages 271–278, 2013.

[28] Qingzhao Tan and Prasenjit Mitra. Clustering-based incremental web crawling. *ACM Transactions on Information Systems*, 28:17:1–17:27, 2010.

Extreme Multi-label Learning with Label Features for Warm-start Tagging, Ranking & Recommendation

Yashoteja Prabhu*
yashoteja.prabhu@gmail.com

Anil Kag†
anilkagak2@gmail.com

Shilpa Gopinath‡
shilpagopitvm@gmail.com

Kunal Dahiya*
kunalsdahiya@gmail.com

Shrutendra Harsola†
shharsol@microsoft.com

Rahul Agrawal†
Rahul.Agrawal@microsoft.com

Manik Varma*†
manik@microsoft.com

ABSTRACT

The objective in extreme multi-label learning is to build classifiers that can annotate a data point with the subset of relevant labels from an extremely large label set. Extreme classification has, thus far, only been studied in the context of predicting labels for novel test points. This paper formulates the extreme classification problem when predictions need to be made on training points with partially revealed labels. This allows the reformulation of warm-start tagging, ranking and recommendation problems as extreme multi-label learning with each item to be ranked/recommended being mapped onto a separate label. The SwiftXML algorithm is developed to tackle such warm-start applications by leveraging label features. SwiftXML improves upon the state-of-the-art tree based extreme classifiers by partitioning tree nodes using two hyperplanes learnt jointly in the label and data point feature spaces. Optimization is carried out via an alternating minimization algorithm allowing SwiftXML to efficiently scale to large problems.

Experiments on multiple benchmark tasks, including tagging on Wikipedia and item-to-item recommendation on Amazon, reveal that SwiftXML's predictions can be up to 14% more accurate as compared to leading extreme classifiers. SwiftXML also demonstrates the benefits of reformulating warm-start recommendation problems as extreme multi-label learning tasks by scaling beyond classical recommender systems and achieving prediction accuracy gains of up to 37%. Furthermore, in a live deployment for sponsored search on Bing, it was observed that SwiftXML could increase the relative click-through-rate by 10% while simultaneously reducing the bounce rate by 30%.

*Indian Institute of Technology Delhi
†Microsoft Research and AI
‡Samsung Research

WSDM 2018, February 5–9, 2018, Marina Del Rey, CA, USA

ACM ISBN 978-1-4503-5581-0/18/02...$15.00
https://doi.org/10.1145/3159652.3159660

KEYWORDS

Extreme multi-label learning, Sponsored search, Large scale recommender systems with user and item features

ACM Reference Format:
Yashoteja Prabhu, Anil Kag, Shilpa Gopinath, Kunal Dahiya, Shrutendra Harsola, Rahul Agrawal, and Manik Varma. 2018. Extreme Multi-label Learning with Label Features for Warm-start Tagging, Ranking & Recommendation. In *WSDM 2018: WSDM 2018: The Eleventh ACM International Conference on Web Search and Data Mining , February 5–9, 2018, Marina Del Rey, CA, USA.* ACM, New York, NY, USA, 9 pages. https://doi.org/10.1145/3159652.3159660

1 INTRODUCTION

Objective: This paper studies extreme multi-label problems where predictions need to be made on training points with partially revealed labels rather than on previously unseen test points. The SwiftXML algorithm is developed for learning in such scenarios by exploiting both label and data point features and applied to warm-start tagging, ranking and recommendation applications.

Extreme classification: Extreme multi-label learning addresses the problem of learning a classifier that can annotate a data point with the most relevant subset of labels from an extremely large label set. Note that multi-label learning is distinct from multi-class learning which aims to predict a single mutually exclusive label.

Extreme classification has opened up a new paradigm for thinking about applications such as tagging, ranking and recommendation. In general, one can reformulate these problems as extreme classification tasks by treating each item to be ranked/recommended as a separate label, learning an extreme multi-label classifier that maps a user's feature vector to a set of relevant labels, and then using the classifier to predict the subset of items that should be ranked/recommended to each user. Data points are therefore referred to as users and labels as items throughout this paper.

Unfortunately, extreme classification has thus far been studied only in the cold-start context of recommending items to new users (predicting labels for novel test points). As a result, existing extreme classification algorithms have been based on user features alone and have not exploited item features. They have therefore been unable to leverage information about the revealed item preferences of existing users available in warm-start scenarios.

Motivation and label features: This paper is motivated by the applications of tagging on Wikipedia, item-to-item recommendation on Amazon and ranking queries for a given ad-landing page for sponsored search on Bing. In the case of tagging Wikipedia articles, each Wikipedia tag is treated as a separate label and the tag's word2vec embedding is treated as its label feature vector. SwiftXML is then used to predict new tags for an existing article leveraging information about not only the article's text but also the existing tags for the article. For item-to-item recommendation on Amazon, each item is treated as a separate label and bag-of-words label features are extracted based on the product description. SwiftXML is then used to recommend other items that might be bought along with a given item leveraging not only the given item's product description but also information about existing item recommendations that had been adopted by users in the past. Finally, for sponsored search advertising, each of the top monetizable queries on Bing is treated as a separate label and label features are extracted based on CDSSM embeddings [25] for each query. SwiftXML is then used to rank the relevant queries for a given ad landing page leveraging not only the page's content but also information about existing queries that had led to clicks on the ad in the past as well as existing queries that the advertiser had bid on for that ad. This allows SwiftXML to make significantly more accurate predictions as compared to previous extreme classification algorithms which could not leverage information about existing tags, previously recommended items and relevant queries.

Limitations of current recommender systems: Warm-start recommendation is a very well studied problem and a number of algorithms have been proposed outside the extreme classification literature including those based on matrix factorization [12, 14, 16, 24], Inductive Matrix Completion [20], Local Collaborative Filtering [17], *etc.* Unfortunately, most of these algorithms cannot scale to the extreme setting as they cannot train on large item and user feature matrices involving millions of items and users in reasonable time on commodity hardware. Furthermore, some of these algorithms are unable to handle implicit ratings (where missing labels are not necessarily irrelevant) and, given millions of items, are unable to make predictions in milliseconds, both of which are critical features for deploying in real world applications. While some heuristics have been proposed to address these limitations, such as adding a tree based search over the items as a post-processing step [33], principled solutions which directly incorporate implicit ratings and logarithmic prediction costs into the learning algorithm have not been proposed for large scale recommender systems based on user and item features. Finally, many of these algorithms, with the notable exception of Local Collaborative Ranking [17], are based on the assumption that the ratings matrix is low-rank and therefore have poor prediction accuracies as this assumption is violated in the extreme setting [7].

SwiftXML: SwiftXML addresses these limitations by efficiently learning an ensemble of tree classifiers at the extreme scale. As with other extreme classification algorithms, SwiftXML can train on implicit ratings without the low-rank assumption and can make predictions in milliseconds. Unlike other extreme classification algorithms, however, SwiftXML grows its trees by recursively partitioning nodes using two hyperplanes learned jointly in the user and item feature spaces. This improves training over learning a single hyperplane based on user features alone in the following ways. First, users who were incorrectly partitioned based on user features alone might now be partitioned correctly using the additional item features. Second, users who like similar items can now be partitioned together as their item features will be similar. Predictions are made exactly as in existing tree-based extreme classifiers but for the fact that trees are now traversed based on the sign of the average prediction of both hyperplanes at a node. This improves prediction accuracy by allowing SwiftXML to recommend items that are similar to the items that are already liked by a user not just in terms of ratings similarity as in the case of existing extreme classifiers but also in terms of item feature similarity. Finally, prediction accuracy also improves over the traditional extreme classification formulation as more information is now available at test time.

Contributions: This paper extends the extreme classification formulation to handle warm-start scenarios and develops, to the best of our knowledge, the first extreme classification algorithm incorporating label features. The key technical contributions are a novel tree node splitting function based on both user and item features and a scalable algorithm for optimizing the function. Experimental results reveal that SwiftXML's predictions can be as much as 14% more accurate as compared to state-of-the-art extreme classifiers and 37% more accurate as compared to classical methods for warm-start recommendation. Another significant contribution is the live deployment of SwiftXML to real users for sponsored search on Bing. It is demonstrated that SwiftXML can increase the relative click-through-rate by 10% while simultaneously reducing the bounce rate by 30%.

2 RELATED WORK

Much progress has recently been made in developing extreme learning algorithms based on trees [5, 15, 22, 29], embeddings [7, 10, 13, 19, 27, 28, 34] and linear approaches [6, 31, 32]. While these methods might potentially be used to make warm-start recommendations, their performance degrades in this setting since they do not leverage item feature information during training and do not exploit information about a user's revealed item preferences during prediction.

Direct approaches to extreme learning, such as DiSMEC [6] learn and apply a separate linear classifier per label. As a result, they have the highest prediction accuracies but can also take months for training and prediction at extreme scales on commodity hardware. Tree-based extreme classifiers, such as PfastreXML [15] have lower prediction accuracies and larger model sizes but can train in hours on a small server and can make predictions in milliseconds per test point. Scaling to large datasets is a critical requirement for deployment in Bing and one of the major advantages that extreme classifiers enjoy over traditional warm-start recommendation algorithms based on user and item features. SwiftXML is therefore developed as an extension of PfastreXML. SwiftXML enjoys all the scaling properties of PfastreXML while having significantly higher prediction accuracies than PfastreXML, DiSMEC and state-of-the-art recommender systems.

Warm-start prediction has been well-studied in the recommender systems literature. Matrix factorization techniques such as WRMF [14], SVD++ [16], BPR [24] and WBPR [12], were specifically designed to address this scenario but factorize the ratings matrix without exploiting user or item feature information. This limitation has been addressed in IMC [20], Matchbox [26], LCR [17] and other methods [4]. Unfortunately, none of these scale to the extreme setting involving a large number of users and items with implicit ratings. Furthermore, with the exception of LCR, each of these methods assumes that the ratings matrix is low-rank, which does not hold in the extreme setting [7]. Consequently these methods have poor prediction accuracies as demonstrated in the Experiments Section. While some heuristics such as tree based post-processing search [33] have been proposed to speed-up prediction, they are not specialized for implicit rating scenarios and don't address the training time and accuracy concerns.

3 A MOTIVATING EXAMPLE

Consider the problem of tagging an existing Wikipedia article – such as that of Albert Einstein which has already been annotated with about 60 tags. State-of-the-art extreme classifiers suffer from the following three limitations. First, during training, they learn impoverished models from article text features alone and are unable to leverage features from tags such as "Recipients of the Pour le Mérite" and "Members of the Lincean Academy" which contain information not found in the article's text. SwiftXML avoids this issue by learning from word2vec features extracted from the tags in addition to the article text features. This allows SwiftXML to predict "Recipients of civil awards and decorations" for the article which could not be predicted by the traditional methods. Second, again during training, existing classifiers learn that Einstein and Newton's articles are very different as they share very few tags. However, SwiftXML learns that the two are similar as the word2vec embeddings of "American physicists" and "English physicists" as well as other corresponding tags are similar. This allows SwiftXML to annotate Einstein's article with Newton's tag "Geometers" which could not have been predicted from the article text directly. Finally, during prediction, SwiftXML can confidently annotate Einstein's article with a novel tag "Astrophysicists" by relying on its similarity to the existing tag "Cosmologists" in terms of their label features. Existing extreme classifiers are unable to leverage such label correlations.

4 SWIFTXML

This section develops the SwiftXML algorithm as an extension of PfastreXML for addressing warm start classification tasks. SwiftXML retains all the scaling properties of PfastreXML while being significantly more accurate owing to the effective use of additional information about revealed item preferences and item features. SwiftXML node partitioning optimizes a novel objective which jointly learns two separating hyperplanes in the user and item feature spaces respectively.

Classifier architecture: SwiftXML trees are grown by recursively partitioning the users into 2 child nodes. Each internal node stores 2 separating hyperplanes in the user and the item feature spaces respectively, which jointly learn the user partitioning. Since learning an optimum user partition is a computationally hard problem, SwiftXML proposes an efficient alternating minimization algorithm which converges to a locally optimal solution. The joint training allows information sharing between the 2 hyperplanes, leading to better partitions. The tree growth is terminated when all the leaf nodes contain less than a specified number of users which is a hyperparameter of the algorithm. Each leaf node stores a probability distribution over the items which are proportional to number of users in the leaf that prefer the respective items. To rectify the mistakes committed by a single, deep tree, SwiftXML trains multiple trees which differ only in the random seed values used to initialize the node partitioning algorithm. SwiftXML tree prediction involves passing the test user down each of the trees, starting from the root node until it reaches a leaf node. At each node, the test point is sent to left (right) child if the average of the scores predicted by the 2 hyperplanes is positive (negative). The probability scores of all the reached leaf nodes are averaged to obtain the label probability predictions. The SwiftXML trees are prone to predicting tail labels with low probabilities as partitioning errors in the internal nodes disproportionately reduce the support of tail labels in the leaf node distributions. SwiftXML addresses this limitation by re-ranking the tree predictions using classifiers designed specifically for tail labels. SwiftXML follows the same training and prediction procedure for tail label classifiers as [15]. SwiftXML trees were empirically observed to be well-balanced, leading to logarithmic training and prediction complexities.

Item-set features: SwiftXML nodes learn a hyperplane in the item-set feature space, jointly with a hyperplane in the user feature space. The item-set features encode semantic information about a user's revealed item preferences. The following linear formula is used for deriving the item-set features of an ith user: $\mathbf{z}_i = (\sum_j y^r_{ij}\mathbf{x}'_j)/\|\sum_j y^r_{ij}\mathbf{x}'_j\|$, where $\mathbf{y}^r_i \in \{0,1\}^L$ denotes the revealed item preference vector for the ith user, and $\mathbf{x}'_j \in \mathbb{R}^{D'}$ denotes the feature vector for the jth item. This formulation ensures that users with overlapping item preferences have similar item-set features, which helps to retain those users together in the SwiftXML trees. The item-set features provide information complementary to the user features, and allow SwiftXML to leverage correlations that exist between the revealed and the test items. To account for varying number of revealed items across users, the item-set features are normalized to unit norm.

Node partitioning objective function: SwiftXML optimizes a novel node partitioning objective which is designed to ensure both purity as well as generalizability of the learned partitions:

$$\begin{aligned}
&\textbf{Min } \|\mathbf{w}_x\|_1 + C_x \sum_i \mathcal{L}_{\text{reg}}(\delta_i \mathbf{w}_x^\top \mathbf{x}_i) + \|\mathbf{w}_z\|_1 + C_z \sum_i \mathcal{L}_{\text{reg}}(\delta_i \mathbf{w}_z^\top \mathbf{z}_i) \\
&+ C_r \sum_i \left(\frac{1+\delta_i}{2} \mathcal{L}_{\text{rank}}(\mathbf{r}^+, \mathbf{y}^r_i) + \frac{1-\delta_i}{2} \mathcal{L}_{\text{rank}}(\mathbf{r}^-, \mathbf{y}^r_i) \right) \\
&\textbf{w.r.t. } \mathbf{w}_x \in \mathcal{R}^D, \mathbf{w}_z \in \mathcal{R}^{D'}, \boldsymbol{\delta} \in \{-1,+1\}^L, \mathbf{r}^+, \mathbf{r}^- \in \Pi(1,L) \\
&\textbf{where } \mathcal{L}_{\text{reg}}(x) = \log(1+e^{-x}), \mathcal{L}_{\text{rank}}(\mathbf{r},\mathbf{y}) = -\frac{\sum_{l=1}^{L} \frac{y_l}{p_l \log(r_l+1)}}{\sum_{l=1}^{L} \frac{1}{\log(l+1)}}
\end{aligned} \tag{1}$$

Here, i enumerates the training users; $\delta_i \in \{-1,+1\}$ indicates the user assignment to either negative (right) or positive (left) partition; $\mathbf{w}_x, \mathbf{w}_z$ represent the separating hyperplanes learned in the user and item-set feature spaces; $\mathbf{r}^+$ and $\mathbf{r}^-$ represent the item ranking variables for positive and negative partitions; $\Pi(1,L)$ denotes the space of all possible rankings over the L items; C_x, C_z, C_r are SwiftXML hyper-parameters; p_l are the item propensity scores [15].

The first line in (1) promotes model sparsity as well as generalizability to test points by learning sparse logistic regressors in user and item-set feature spaces. The second line maximizes node purity by ranking the preferred items of each user as highly as possible within its partition. Concretely, this is achieved by maximizing the Propensity-scored Normalized Discounted Cumulative Gain (PSnDCG) metric. PSnDCG is unbiased to missing items and boosts accuracy over rare and informative tail labels which are also frequently missing owing to their unfamiliarity to the users. $\mathcal{L}_{\text{rank}}(\mathbf{r}^-, \mathbf{y}_i^r)$ is the loss form of PSnDCG which is minimized by (1). The tight coupling between δ_i and the two regressors as well as the ranking terms help to learn node partitions that are both pure and accurate. Upon joint optimization, the two separators bring together those users having both similar user descriptions as well as similar revealed item preferences.

The time complexity for training SwiftXML is $O(N(T\log(N) + \hat{L})(\hat{D} + \hat{D}'))$, where N, T are the number of training instances and trained trees respectively; and $\hat{L}, \hat{D}, \hat{D}'$ are the average number of revealed items, non-zero user features and non-zero item-set features of a user, respectively. The above complexity includes both tree training times as well as tail label classifier training times, and is dominated by the former. Due to small values of $\hat{L}, T$ and a tractable $\log(N) * N$ dependence on the number of users, SwiftXML training is sufficiently fast and scalable.

Optimization: The discrete objective in (1) cannot be straight forwardly optimized with usual gradient descent techniques. Therefore, an efficient, iterative, alternating minimization algorithm is adopted which alternately optimizes over one of the four classes of variables $(\boldsymbol{\delta}, \mathbf{r}^{\pm}, \mathbf{w}_x, \mathbf{w}_z)$ at a time with the others held constant. Optimization over $\boldsymbol{\delta}$ with other variables held constant reduces (1) to N separate problems over individual δ_i variables which have simple closed form solutions:

$$\delta_i = \text{Sign}\Big(C_x \mathbf{w}_x^\top \mathbf{x}_i + C_z \mathbf{w}_z^\top \mathbf{z}_i + C_r(\mathcal{L}_{\text{rank}}(\mathbf{r}^+, \mathbf{y}_i^r)) - \mathcal{L}_{\text{rank}}(\mathbf{r}^-, \mathbf{y}_i^r))\Big)$$

Optimization over $\mathbf{r}^{\pm}$ with $\boldsymbol{\delta}, \mathbf{w}_x, \mathbf{w}_z$ fixed also has a closed form solution $\mathbf{r}^{\pm} = \text{rank}\big(\sum_{i:\delta_i=\pm} I_L(\mathbf{y}_i^r)\mathbf{y}_i^r\big)$, where rank(v) returns the indices of v in their descending order, and $I_L(\mathbf{y}_i^r)$ is a user-specific constant. Optimization over $\mathbf{w}_x$ or $\mathbf{w}_z$ while fixing the remaining variables reduces to standard L1 regularized logistic regression problems which can be efficiently solved using Liblinear [11]. In practice, the algorithm alternates between $\mathbf{r}^{\pm}$,$\mathbf{w}_x$ and $\mathbf{w}_z$ variables, interleaved with efficient $\boldsymbol{\delta}$ optimizations. Early stopping with just one iteration over all variables was found to be sufficient in practice.

Optimization time is empirically dominated by learning two L1 regularized logistic regressions, which have a combined cost of $O(N_{\text{node}} t(\hat{D} + \hat{D}'))$, where N_{node} is the number of training users in the node and t (usually set to 1) is the number of iterations.

Prediction: SwiftXML tree prediction involves routing the test user down the tree, starting from the root node until it reaches a leaf. At each visited internal node, the user is sent to left (right) child if the combined scores of the two separating hyperplanes, i.e. $C_x \mathbf{w}_x^\top \mathbf{x} + C_z \mathbf{w}_z^\top \mathbf{z}$, is greater (lesser) than 0, with ties being broken randomly. When a leaf node is reached, the leaf's item distribution is used as the item preference scores. Thereupon, the individual tree scores are averaged to obtain the ensemble scores, $E_j(\mathbf{x}) = \sum_{t=1}^{T} P_j^t(\mathbf{x}, \mathbf{z})/T$ for the j item, where $P_j^t(\mathbf{x}, \mathbf{z})$ is the probability assigned by tree t to item j for the test point. These ensemble scores are further reraked by combining with the tail label classifier scores B_j as $s_j = \alpha \log E_j(\mathbf{x}) + (1-\alpha)\log B_j(\mathbf{x}) \quad \forall j \in \{1,..,L\}$. Finally the top scoring items are recommended to the test user.

The SwiftXML trees are well-balanced with $O(\log(N))$ depth. Consequently, tree prediction is efficient and its cost for a test user is $O(\log(N) * (\hat{D} + \hat{D}'))$. The overall complexity of the SwiftXML prediction algorithm is $O((T\log(N) + c) * (\hat{D} + \hat{D}'))$, where c is the number of top-scoring items being reranked by the base-classifiers.

Theoretical analysis of SwiftXML algorithm and optimization are beyond the scope of this work. Detailed derivations of the optimization steps and pseudocodes for SwiftXML training and prediction algorithms are presented in supplementary .

5 SPONSORED SEARCH ADVERTISING

Objective and motivation: Search engines generate most of their revenue via sponsored advertisements which are displayed alongside the organic search results. While creating an ad campaign, an advertiser usually provides minimalistic information such as a short description of the ad, url of the ad landing page, a few bid-phrases along with their corresponding bids. Bid-phrases are a set of search queries that are judged to be relevant to the ad, and hence bidded on by the advertisers. Since the potential monetizable queries are in the order of millions, the advertiser won't be able to provide exhaustive list of all relevant bid-phrases. To address this limitation, an ad retrieval system resorts to machine learning-based extended match techniques [9, 23] which suggest additional relevant search queries to bid on by leveraging advertiser provided information. This ad retrieval application is a natural fit for warm-start recommendations where the given bid phrases and historically known relevant search queries can be used to predict new search queries for the ad more accurately.

Ranking queries for ad retrieval: Ad retrieval task can be formulated as extreme multi-label learning problem by treating ad landing pages as data points and search queries as labels. Data point feature vectors are created by extracting bag-of-words representation from the ad landing pages. Relevant labels are generated from the historical click logs i.e. a search query is tagged to be relevant to an ad if the ad had received clicks when displayed for the query in the past. For the warm-start scenario, the advertiser provided bid-phrases as well as the queries that had led to clicks on the ad in the past are considered as revealed labels for the ad. Label features are extracted based on the CDSSM embeddings [25] of the bid-phrases or the search query phrases.

Label relevance weights: Not all ads which were clicked for a query in past are equally relevant or click-yielding to the query. One such example is the query "marco polo" which had received clicks mostly from hotel related ads along with a few clicks from book related ads. Treating all the clicked ads for this query as equally relevant results in the query "marco polo" being recommended for book related ads too, which in turn generates lower click through rates on the actual search engine traffic. To address this problem,

Table 1: Dataset statistics

Dataset	Train N	Features D	Labels L	Test M	Avg. labels per point	Avg. points per label
EURLex-4K	15,539	5,000	3,993	3,809	5.31	25.73
Wiki10-31K	14,149	101,938	30,935	6,613	17.25	11.58
AmazonCat-13K	1,186,239	203,882	13,330	306,782	5.05	566.01
CitationNetwork-36K	62,503	39,539	36,211	15,467	3.07	6.61
Amazon-79K	490,449	135,909	78,957	153,025	2.08	4.06
Wikipedia-500K	1,813,391	2,381,304	501,070	783,743	4.77	24.75

differential weights are assigned to each (query, ad) pair in the training data based on the ad's click generating potential for the query as measured by the normalized point-wise mutual information (nPMI). Let c_{ij} be number of historical clicks between ith ad and jth query. Normalized PMI is defined as $nPMI_{ij} = \frac{\log(p(i)p(j))}{\log p(i,j)} - 1$, where $p(i) = \sum_j c_{ij}/\sum_{i,j} c_{ij}$ and $p(i,j) = c_{ij}/\sum_{i,j} c_{ij}$

The nPMI values are higher for more relevant query-ad pairs in the training data and always lie between 0 and 1. SwiftXML is learned on the weighted training data, which helped to improve offline accuracy on the holdout data by 1% over the model trained on the unweighted data.

Inverted ad-index: Trained SwiftXML model was used to make recommendations for all the ads in the system. For every ad, the SwiftXML recommended queries having a score of above a threshold are inserted into an inverted ad index, to be retrieved when the corresponding query is entered in the search engine. A relatively high threshold of 0.7 was set on the SwiftXML scores to maximize precision. Additionally, the top two SwiftXML recommended queries were also inserted into the inverted ad index, since they were found to be mostly relevant despite scoring lower than the set threshold sometimes. This step improved recall, while maintaining the precision value, thus achieving 2% improvement in the offline F1-score on the holdout data, as compared to the global threshold-only approach.

Mapping onto bid-phrases: SwiftXML recommended queries need to be associated with one of the advertiser provided bid-phrases in order to choose appropriate bid value for the query, and also to allow the advertisers to track the campaign performance at the bid-phrase level. A query to bid-phrase click model is learned for this purpose, which assigns a click probability to a given (query, bid-phrase) pair. Training data of form (query, bid-phrase) is generated by considering historically clicked (query, ad) pairs and extracting the corresponding bid-phrase from the ad. A gradient boosted decision trees (GBDT) model is trained over the following features extracted for each (query, bid-phrase) pair: syntactic similarity features, historical click features (click counts at token level) and semantic similarity features (Word2vec [18] and CDSSM [25] embeddings). SwiftXML recommended query for an ad, is associated with the bid-phrase with maximum click probability, as predicted by the click model.

6 EXPERIMENTS

Experiments were carried out on benchmark datasets with up to half a million labels demonstrating that: (a) SwiftXML could be as much as 14% and 37% more accurate as compared to state-of-the-art extreme classification and warm-start recommendation algorithms, respectively; (b) SwiftXML could scale to extreme datasets beyond the scale of state-of-the-art warm-start recommendation algorithms that train on both document and label features and (c) deploying SwiftXML in a live system for sponsored search advertising on Bing led to significant gains in the click-through rate and quality of ad recommendations as well as simultaneous reductions in the bounce rate.

Table 2: SwiftXML can be up to 14% and 37% more accurate as compared to state-of-the-art extreme classifiers and warm-start recommendation algorithms respectively according to unbiased propensity-scored Precision@5 (PSP5). Results for PSP1, PSP3 and biased Precision@k are presented in the supplementary .

Dataset	Algorithm	Revealed Label Percentages 20%	40%	60%	80%
EURLex	WRMF	11.05	16.58	19.77	22.85
	SVD++	0.41	0.51	0.61	0.60
	BPR	1.13	1.01	0.86	2.24
	PfastreXML	48.21	48.64	51.13	52.46
	SLEEC	42.72	46.31	48.56	51.64
	PDSparse	43.79	45.72	46.02	49.87
	DiSMEC	47.03	48.30	50.54	51.63
	IMC	11.23	11.45	11.45	11.72
	Matchbox	0.50	–	1.00	1.09
	SwiftXML	**48.45**	**49.72**	**53.12**	**55.70**
Wiki10	WRMF	5.27	6.01	6.34	6.33
	PfastreXML	19.80	18.17	16.31	14.77
	SLEEC	12.42	12.57	12.28	12.14
	PDSparse	8.02	6.78	5.72	4.73
	DiSMEC	15.47	15.19	14.53	13.87
	IMC	2.36	3.42	3.87	3.98
	SwiftXML	**19.92**	**19.07**	**17.06**	**16.23**
AmazonCat	PfastreXML	76.32	75.80	75.17	76.30
	PDSparse	65.25	61.61	58.37	57.47
	SwiftXML	**77.17**	**81.10**	**83.77**	**87.83**
CitationNetwork	PfastreXML	15.39	15.19	15.30	15.24
	SLEEC	7.41	7.65	7.37	6.40
	PDSparse	14.65	14.48	14.05	14.21
	DiSMEC	**17.84**	17.78	18.06	18.49
	SwiftXML	16.92	**17.84**	**19.44**	**19.34**
Amazon	PfastreXML	36.39	36.14	36.61	35.40
	SLEEC	23.83	28.30	32.24	31.33
	PDSparse	34.12	33.57	33.54	32.85
	DiSMEC	**41.89**	41.94	42.54	41.86
	SwiftXML	37.69	**42.80**	**51.33**	**49.44**
Wikipedia	PfastreXML	33.34	33.35	33.22	35.22
	SwiftXML	**34.76**	**35.31**	**35.68**	**38.07**

Datasets and features: Experiments were carried out on benchmark datasets containing up to 1.8 million training points, 2.3 million dimensional features and 0.5 million labels (see Table 1 for dataset statistics). The applications considered range from tagging Wikipedia articles (Wikipedia-500K), cataloging Amazon items into multiple Amazon product categories (AmazonCat-13K), item-to-item recommendation of Amazon products (Amazon-79K), paper

Table 3: SwiftXML can be up to 14% and 4% more accurate according to unbiased propensity scored Precision@5 as compared to baseline extensions of PfastreXML incorporating label features via early and late fusion respectively. Results for other metrics, including biased Precision@k, are reported in the supplementary .

Dataset	Algorithm	Revealed Label Percentages 20%	40%	60%	80%
EURLex	PfastreXML-early	47.29	**49.82**	52.04	54.40
	PfastreXML-late	48.21	49.55	52.25	46.05
	SwiftXML	**48.45**	49.72	**53.12**	**55.70**
Wiki10	PfastreXML-early	19.59	18.17	16.31	14.94
	PfastreXML-late	19.80	18.03	16.31	14.65
	SwiftXML	**19.92**	**19.07**	**17.06**	**16.23**
AmazonCat	PfastreXML-early	74.56	78.53	79.77	81.52
	PfastreXML-late	76.23	78.20	81.43	85.40
	SwiftXML	**77.17**	**81.10**	**83.77**	**87.83**
CitationNetwork	PfastreXML-early	15.04	15.08	15.43	15.54
	PfastreXML-late	15.73	17.12	19.11	**19.86**
	SwiftXML	**16.92**	**17.84**	**19.44**	19.34
Amazon	PfastreXML-early	36.45	36.18	36.64	35.43
	PfastreXML-late	36.71	40.42	46.71	45.98
	SwiftXML	**37.69**	**42.80**	**51.33**	**49.44**
Wikipedia	PfastreXML-early	34.23	34.44	34.43	36.47
	PfastreXML-late	33.78	34.26	34.88	37.66
	SwiftXML	**34.76**	**35.31**	**35.68**	**38.07**

Table 4: SwiftXML could increase the relative click-through-rate (CTR) and relative quality of ad recommendation (QOA) by 10% while simultaneously reducing the bounce rate (BR) by 30% on sponsored search on Bing.

Algorithm	Relative CTR (%)	Relative QOA (%)	Relative BR (%)
Bing	100	100	100
PfastreXML	102	103	76
SwiftXML	110	112	69

citation recommendation (CitationNetwork-39K) and document tagging (EURLex-4K, Wiki10-31K). All the datasets can be publically downloaded from The Extreme Classification Repository [8]. Bag-of-words TF-IDF features provided on the Repository were used as the document (or user) features for each dataset. 500-dimensional word2vec embeddings [18] were used to generate the label features as these led to better results as compared to other word embedding models including glove [21] and phrase2vec [3]. Algorithms were evaluated under various warm-start conditions as more and more of a user's item preferences were revealed. This was simulated by randomly sampling 20%, 40%, 60% and 80% of the test labels and revealing them during training while the remaining labels were used for evaluation purposes as ground-truth.

Baseline algorithms: SwiftXML was compared to four types of algorithms for warm-start recommendation. First, SwiftXML was compared to WRMF [14], SVD++ [16] and BPR [24] which are collaborative filtering algorithms based on factorizing the label (ratings) matrix alone and do not leverage user or item features. Second, SwiftXML was compared to state-of-the-art extreme classifiers based on trees (PfastreXML [15]), embeddings (SLEEC [7]) and linear methods that learn a separate classifier per label (PDSparse [32] and DiSMEC [6]). The extreme classifiers improve upon the collaborative filtering methods by training on the user features along with the label (ratings) matrix. Third, SwiftXML was also compared to state-of-the-art recommender systems such as Inductive Matrix Completion (IMC) [20] and Matchbox [26] which extend collaborative filtering and extreme classification methods by leveraging user features, label (item) features and the label (ratings) matrix during both training and prediction. Finally, SwiftXML was compared to two alternate ways of extending the state-of-the-art tree based PfastreXML extreme classifier [15] to handle label features. In particular, PfastreXML-early uses early fusion to train PfastreXML on concatenated label and document features with the relative weighting of the two feature types being determined through validation. In contrast, PfastreXML-late uses late fusion to learn separate PfastreXML classifiers in the document and label feature spaces and then combines the two scores during prediction with relative weighting being again determined through validation.

Results are reported for the Mrec [2] recommender system library implementation of WRMF, the Mahout [1] implementation of SVD++ and the Matchbox implementation available on the Microsoft Azure cloud computing platform. The implementation of all the other algorithms was provided by the authors. Unfortunately, some algorithms do not scale to large datasets and results have therefore been reported for only those datasets to which an implementation scales. The relative performance of all the methods can be compared on the small scale EURLex dataset.

Hyper-parameters: In addition to the hyper-parameters of PfastreXML, SwiftXML has two extra hyper-parameters C_z, λ_z which weight the loss incurred over the label features in the node partitioning objective and the base classifiers respectively . Unfortunately, the Wikipedia-500K dataset is too large for hyper-parameter tuning through validation and therefore all algorithms were run with default values, with the default SwiftXML values kept same as in PfastreXML along with $C_z = \lambda_z = 1$. On the other datasets, the hyper-parameters for all the algorithms were tuned using fine grained validation so as to maximize the prediction accuracy on the validation set.

Evaluation metrics: Performance evaluation was done using precision@k and nDCG@k (with $k = 1,3$ and 5) which are widely used metrics for extreme classification. Performance was also evaluated using propensity scored precision@k and nDCG@k (PSPk and PSNk with $k = 1,3$ and 5) which have recently been shown to be unbiased, and more suitable, metrics [15] for extreme classification, tagging, ranking, recommendation, *etc.* The propensity model and values available on The Extreme Classification Repository were used. Results for all metrics apart from PSP5 are reported in the supplementary due to space limitations.

Results - prediction accuracy: Tables 2 and 3 compare prediction accuracy of SwiftXML to the various baseline algorithms as the percentage of labels revealed during training is varied from 20% to 80%. As can be seen in Table 2, SwiftXML's predictions can be up to 14% and 37% more accurate as compared to state-of-the-art extreme classifiers and warm-start recommendation algorithms respectively. The largest gains over existing extreme classifiers were observed for item-to-item recommendation on Amazon. This was because many Amazon products had unhelpfully brief product descriptions, translating into poor user features for existing extreme classifiers. In fact, in some extreme cases, some Amazon products had no product description whatsoever apart from the product name. However, the very same products had a number of other products that had frequently been bought together with them which contained some useful information. This was leveraged by SwiftXML as item features to make significantly better recommendations. SwiftXML was also able to make better predictions by leveraging such features even when a sufficiently verbose product description was available (see figure 1 for qualitative examples).

Table 3 also illustrates that SwiftXML can be more accurate as compared to early and late fusion methods for incorporating label features into PfastreXML by as much as 14% and 4% respectively. Early fusion has several limitations such as its tendency to overfit and an inherent bias towards the dense label features over sparse document features [30]. PfastreXML-late learns independent classifiers over the document and label features and therefore has suboptimal performance as compared to SwiftXML's which learns node separators in both spaces jointly.

Results - scaling: As Tables 2 and 3 show, SwiftXML can efficiently scale to large datasets beyond the scale of warm-start recommendation algorithms such as IMC and Matchbox which also train on both document and label features. SwiftXML's training time is comparable to that of PfastreXML-early and PfastreXML-late, other techniques for handling warm-start problems based on both document and label features, but it's prediction time and model size can be lower. As compared to PfastreXML, SwiftXML's training time is 3-4x more in general but its prediction time and model size might be sometimes lower as it learns shorter better quality trees due to the extra information available. For instance, on the AmazonCat-13K dataset with 1.1 million training points and 13.3K labels, SwiftXML, PfastreXML-early, PfastreXML-late and PfastreXML,'s trained in 25, 19, 29 and 7 hours respectively on a single core of Intel Xeon 2.6 GHz server, while their model sizes were 10, 15, 19 and 16 GB respectively with prediction times being 4.2, 6.6, 4.7 and 4.3 milliseconds respectively. Note that SwiftXML training can be easily parallelized by growing each tree on a separate core, unlike algorithms such as Matchbox whose implementations run on only a single core. More parallelization can be attained in SwiftXML training by growing each node with the same tree depth on a separate core.

Sponsored Search Advertising: SwiftXML was used to rank the queries that might lead to a click on a given ad shown on Bing. While PfastreXML could only rank the queries on the basis of the text present on the ad-landing page, SwiftXML was able to leverage information about other queries that had already led to a click on the ad as well as queries that had been bid on by the advertiser for that page. Performance is measured in terms of click-through rate (CTR), bounce rate (QBR) and quality of ad recommendations (QOA). The bounce rate is defined as the percentage of times a user returns back immediately after viewing an ad landing page, indicating user dissatisfaction. The quality of ad recommendations measures the relevance of ad recommendations to a search query and is estimated by a query-ad relevance model trained on human labelled data. Table 4 compares SwiftXML to PfastreXML as well as a large ensemble of state-of-the-art methods for query ranking which are currently in production, referred to as Bing-ensemble. As can be seen, SwiftXML leads to upto 10% higher CTR and QOA, as well as upto 10% lower QBR as compared to both PfastreXML and Bing-ensemble. The training times of SwiftXML and PfastreXML algorithms were 140 and 200 hours respectively, while their model sizes were 3.7 and 3.8 GB rspectively, with prediction times being 1.7 and 1.8 milliseconds per test point respectively.

Qualitative examples: Figure (1) illustrates the advantages of SwiftXML over PfastreXML through some representative examples. PfastreXML suffers from several limitations due to its sole reliance on user features, which are overcome by SwiftXML by leveraging revealed items and item feature information. First, the user features often fail to provide sufficient information for classification, with an extreme case being "(a) AmazonCat: Kvutzat Yavne pickles" whose web page contains limited text. In this case, PfastreXML recommends popular labels such as "Books" and "Literature & fiction" which are unfortunately irrelevant. On the other hand, SwiftXML leverages information about revealed tags such as "Pickles" and "Pickles & relishes" to recommend relevant tags such as "Dill pickles", "Grocery & gourmet food". Second, PfastreXML sometimes puts greater emphasis on the irrelevant, but frequent user features such as "language" and "Barron" in "(d) Amazon: Barron's IELTS ..." leading to irrelevant recommendations, such as "More useful french words" and "Spanish the Easy Way (Barron's E-Z)". In contrast, the information about revealed items such as "toefl" and "academic english" inform SwiftXML to emphasize more on the relevant user features such as "ielts" and "testing", resulting in useful IELTS preparation books being recommended to the customer. Third, PfastreXML is unable to disambiguate between homonyms such as "Fo" in the book title "(c) Amazon: Xsl Fo" versus "Fo" in the surname of dramatist "Dario Fo", both of which are among the user features. Hence, PfastreXML incorrectly recommends Dario Fo's plays instead of books on Xsl. SwiftXML resolves this ambiguity by using the context information from revealed books about "xsl" to recommend relevant books such as "Definitive XSL-FO" and "Learning XSLT". SwiftXML also leverages correlations between the revealed items and the relevant test items, to make accurate predictions. For example, the strong correlation between the revealed label "Marx" and novel label "Karl" in "(b) AmazonCat: Rosa Luxemburg..." is used by SwiftXML to correctly recommend "Karl". Furthermore, the revealed bid-phrases also help SwiftXML to accurately resolve advertiser intents such as selling archery items in "(e) Bing Ads: 3RiversArchery archery supplies" and selling pest bird control products in "(f) Bing Ads: Arcat pest control".

7 CONCLUSIONS

This paper extended the extreme classification formulation to handle warm-start scenarios by leveraging item features which can provide a rich, and complementary, source of information to the user features relied on by traditional extreme classifiers. The SwiftXML algorithm was developed for exploiting item features and label correlations as a simple, easy to implement and reproduce extension of the PfastreXML extreme classifier. Despite its simplicity,

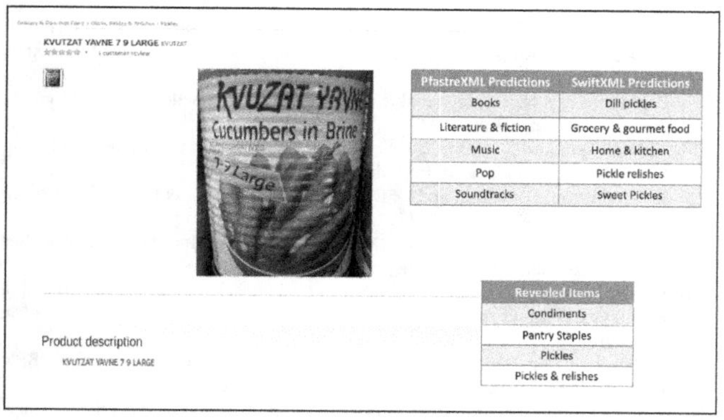

(a) AmazonCat: Kvutzat Yavne pickles

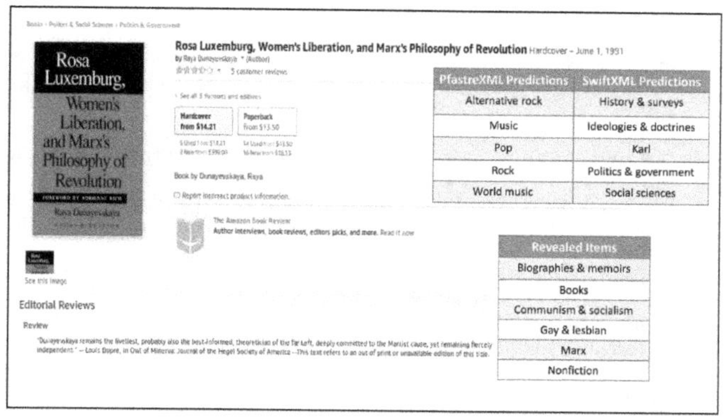

(b) AmazonCat: Rosa Luxemburg, Women's Liberation, and Marx's Philosophy of Revolution book

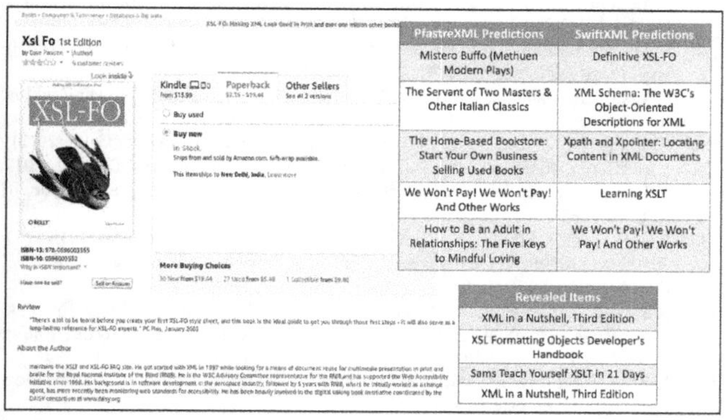

(c) Amazon: Xsl Fo book

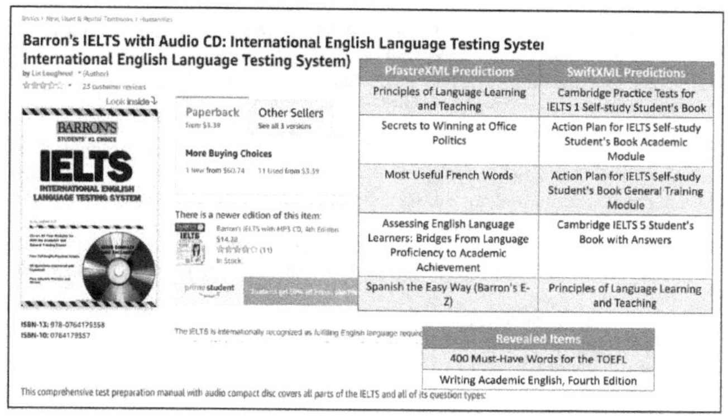

(d) Amazon: Barron's IELTS with Audio CD book

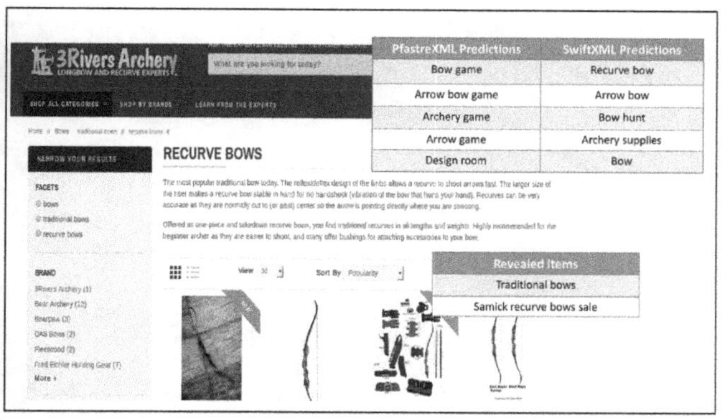

(e) Bing Ads: 3RiversArchery archery supplies

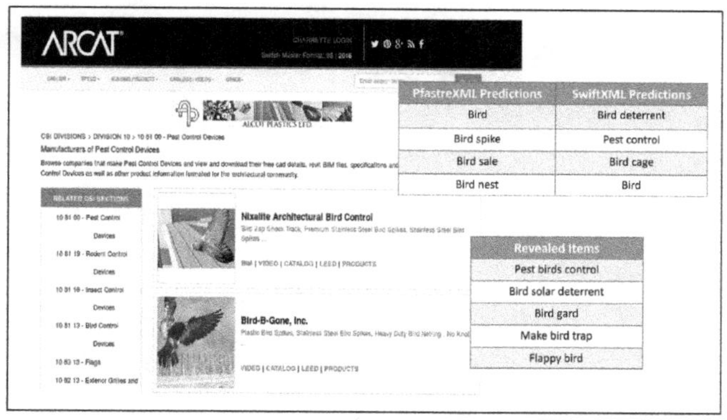

(f) Bing Ads: Arcat pest control products

Figure 1: Item recommendations by PfastreXML and SwiftXML on AmazonCat, Amazon and Bing Ads: PfastreXML predictions are frequently irrelevant due to lack of informative user features (*e.g.* (a)), emphasis on the wrong features (*e.g.* (d)) and inability to disambiguate homonyms (*e.g.* (e)). SwiftXML leverages item correlations (*e.g.* "Marx" => "Karl" in (b)) and helpful information from revealed items and their features (*e.g.* (a)-(f)) to make much more accurate predictions. See text for more details. Figure best viewed under high magnification.

SwiftXML was shown to improve prediction accuracy on the Amazon item-to-item recommendation task by as much as 37% and 14% over state-of-the-art warm start recommendation algorithms and extreme classifiers respectively. Furthermore, live deployment for sponsored search advertising on Bing revealed that SwiftXML could increase the click-through rate and quality of ad recommendations by 10%, and reduce the bounce rate by 31% as compared to a large ensemble of state-of-the-art algorithms in production. The SwiftXML code will be made publically available.

REFERENCES

[1] [n. d.]. Apache Mahout. https://mahout.apache.org. ([n. d.]).

[2] [n. d.]. Mrec recommender systems library. http://mendeley.github.io/mrec. ([n. d.]).

[3] [n. d.]. Phrase2vec. https://github.com/zseymour/phrase2vec. ([n. d.]).

[4] D. Agarwal and B. C. Chen. 2009. Regression-based Latent Factor Models. In *KDD*. 19–28.

[5] R. Agrawal, A. Gupta, Y. Prabhu, and M. Varma. 2013. Multi-label Learning with Millions of Labels: Recommending Advertiser Bid Phrases for Web Pages. In *WWW*.

[6] R. Babbar and B. Schölkopf. 2017. DiSMEC: Distributed Sparse Machines for Extreme Multi-label Classification. In *WSDM*.

[7] K. Bhatia, H. Jain, P. Kar, M. Varma, and P. Jain. 2015. Sparse Local Embeddings for Extreme Multi-label Classification. In *NIPS*.

[8] K. Bhatia, H. Jain, Y. Prabhu, and M. Varma. [n. d.]. The Extreme Classification Repository: Multi-label Datasets & Code. ([n. d.]). http://manikvarma.org/downloads/XC/XMLRepository.html

[9] Y. Choi, M. Fontoura, E. Gabrilovich, V. Josifovski, M. Mediano, and B. Pang. 2010. Using landing pages for sponsored search ad selection. In *WWW*.

[10] M. Cissé, N. Usunier, T. Artières, and P. Gallinari. 2013. Robust Bloom Filters for Large MultiLabel Classification Tasks. In *NIPS*.

[11] R. E. Fan, K. W. Chang, C. J. Hsieh, X. R. Wang, and C. J. Lin. 2008. LIBLINEAR: A library for large linear classification. *JMLR* (2008).

[12] Z. Gantner, L. Drumond, C. Freudenthaler, and L. Schmidt-Thieme. 2012. Personalized Ranking for Non-Uniformly Sampled Items. In *Proceedings of KDD Cup 2011*. 231–247.

[13] D. Hsu, S. Kakade, J. Langford, and T. Zhang. 2009. Multi-Label Prediction via Compressed Sensing. In *NIPS*.

[14] Y. Hu, Y. Koren, and C. Volinsky. 2008. Collaborative Filtering for Implicit Feedback Datasets. In *ICDM*.

[15] H. Jain, Y. Prabhu, and M. Varma. 2016. Extreme Multi-label Loss Functions for Recommendation, Tagging, Ranking & Other Missing Label Applications. In *KDD*.

[16] Y. Koren. 2008. Factorization Meets the Neighborhood: A Multifaceted Collaborative Filtering Model. In *KDD*.

[17] J. Lee, S. Bengio, S. Kim, G. Lebanon, and Y. Singer. 2014. Local collaborative ranking. In *WWW*.

[18] T. Mikolov, I. Sutskever, K. Chen, G. Corrado, and J. Dean. 2013. Distributed Representations of Words and Phrases and their Compositionality. *CoRR* abs/1310.4546 (2013).

[19] P. Mineiro and N. Karampatziakis. 2015. Fast Label Embeddings for Extremely Large Output Spaces. In *ECML*.

[20] N. Natarajan and I. Dhillon. 2014. Inductive Matrix Completion for Predicting Gene-Disease Associations. In *Bioinformatics*.

[21] J. Pennington, R. Socher, and C. D. Manning. 2014. Glove: Global Vectors for Word Representation. In *EMNLP*. 1532–1543.

[22] Y. Prabhu and M. Varma. 2014. FastXML: A fast, accurate and stable tree-classifier for extreme multi-label learning. In *KDD*.

[23] H. Raghavan and R. Iyer. 2008. Evaluating vector-space and probabilistic models for query to ad matching. In *SIGIR Workshop on Information Retrieval in Advertising*.

[24] S. Rendle, C. Freudenthaler, Z. Gantner, and L. Schmidt-Thieme. 2009. BPR: Bayesian Personalized Ranking from Implicit Feedback. In *UAI*.

[25] Y. Shen, X. He, J. Gao, L. Deng, and G. Mesnil. 2014. Learning semantic representations using convolutional neural networks for web search. In *WWW*.

[26] D. H. Stern, R. Herbrich, and T. Graepel. 2009. Matchbox: large scale online bayesian recommendations. In *WWW*.

[27] Y. Tagami. 2017. AnnexML: Approximate Nearest Neighbor Search for Extreme Multi-label Classification. In *KDD*. 455–464.

[28] J. Weston, S. Bengio, and N. Usunier. 2011. Wsabie: Scaling Up To Large Vocabulary Image Annotation. In *IJCAI*.

[29] J. Weston, A. Makadia, and H. Yee. 2013. Label Partitioning For Sublinear Ranking. In *ICML*.

[30] C. Xu, D. Tao, and C. Xu. 2013. A Survey on Multi-view Learning. *CoRR* (2013).

[31] I. E. H. Yen, X. Huang, W. Dai, P. Ravikumar, I. Dhillon, and E. Xing. 2017. PPDsparse: A Parallel Primal-Dual Sparse Method for Extreme Classification. In *KDD*. 545–553.

[32] I. E. H. Yen, X. Huang, K. Zhong, P. Ravikumar, and I. S. Dhillon. 2016. PD-Sparse: A Primal and Dual Sparse Approach to Extreme Multiclass and Multilabel Classification. In *ICML*.

[33] F. Zhang, T. Gong, Victor E. Lee, G. Zhao, C. Rong, and G. Qu. 2016. Fast Algorithms to Evaluate Collaborative Filtering Recommender Systems. *Know.-Based Syst.* (2016), 96–103.

[34] Y. Zhang and J. G. Schneider. 2011. Multi-Label Output Codes using Canonical Correlation Analysis. In *AISTATS*.

DSANLS: Accelerating Distributed Nonnegative Matrix Factorization via Sketching

Yuqiu Qian[†], Conghui Tan[‡], Nikos Mamoulis[♯], David W. Cheung[†]

[†]The University of Hong Kong [‡]The Chinese University of Hong Kong [♯]University of Ioannina

[†]{yqqian, dcheung}@cs.hku.hk [‡]chtan@se.cuhk.edu.hk [♯]nikos@cs.uoi.gr

ABSTRACT

Nonnegative matrix factorization (NMF) has been successfully applied in different fields, such as text mining, image processing, and video analysis. NMF is the problem of determining two nonnegative low rank matrices U and V, for a given input matrix M, such that $M \approx UV^\top$. There is an increasing interest in parallel and distributed NMF algorithms, due to the high cost of centralized NMF on large matrices. In this paper, we propose a *distributed sketched alternating nonnegative least squares* (DSANLS) framework for NMF, which utilizes a matrix sketching technique to reduce the size of nonnegative least squares subproblems in each iteration for U and V. We design and analyze two different random matrix generation techniques and two subproblem solvers. Our theoretical analysis shows that DSANLS converges to the stationary point of the original NMF problem and it greatly reduces the computational cost in each subproblem as well as the communication cost within the cluster. DSANLS is implemented using MPI for communication, and tested on both dense and sparse real datasets. The results demonstrate the efficiency and scalability of our framework, compared to the state-of-art distributed NMF MPI implementation.

ACM Reference Format:

Yuqiu Qian, Conghui Tan, Nikos Mamoulis, David W. Cheung. 2018. DSANLS: Accelerating Distributed Nonnegative Matrix Factorization via Sketching. In *Proceedings of WSDM'18*. ACM, New York, NY, USA, 9 pages. https://doi.org/10.1145/3159652.3159662

1 INTRODUCTION

Nonnegative matrix factorization (NMF) is a technique for discovering nonnegative latent factors and/or performing dimensionality reduction. NMF finds applications in text mining [30], image/video processing [19], and analysis of social networks [34]. Unlike general matrix factorization (MF), NMF restricts the two output matrix factors to be nonnegative. Nonnegativity is inherent in the feature space of many real-world applications, therefore the resulting factors can have a natural interpretation. Specifically, the goal of NMF is to decompose a huge matrix $M \in \mathbb{R}_+^{m\times n}$ into the product of two matrices $U \in \mathbb{R}_+^{m\times k}$ and $V \in \mathbb{R}_+^{n\times k}$ such that $M \approx UV^\top$. $\mathbb{R}_+^{m\times n}$ denotes the set of $m \times n$ matrices with nonnegative real values, and k is a user-specified dimensionality, where typically $k \ll m, n$.

Generally, NMF can be defined as an optimization problem [21] as follows:

$$\min_{U\in\mathbb{R}_+^{m\times k},\, V\in\mathbb{R}_+^{n\times k}} \left\|M - UV^\top\right\|_F, \tag{1}$$

where $\|X\|_F = \left(\sum_{ij} x_{ij}^2\right)^{1/2}$ is the Frobenius norm of X. However, Problem (1) is hard to solve directly because it is non-convex. Therefore, almost all NMF algorithms leverage two-block coordinate descent schemes: they optimize over one of the two factors, U or V, while keeping the other fixed [8]. By fixing V, we can optimize U by solving a nonnegative least squares (NLS) subproblem:

$$\min_{U\in\mathbb{R}_+^{m\times k}} \left\|M - UV^\top\right\|_F. \tag{2}$$

Modern data analysis tasks apply on big matrix data with increasing scale and dimensionality. Examples include community detection in a billion-node social network, background separation on a 4K video in which every frame has approximately 27 million rows [15], text mining on a bag-of-words matrix with millions of words. The volume of data is anticipated to increase in the 'big data' era, making it impossible to store the whole matrix in the main memory throughout NMF. Therefore, there is a need for high-performance and scalable distributed NMF algorithms.

In this paper, we propose a distributed framework for NMF. We choose Message Passing Interface using C (MPI/C) for our distributed implementation for efficiency, generality and privacy reasons. MPI/C does not require reading/writing data to/from disk or global shuffles of data matrix entries, as what Spark or MapReduce do. Nodes can collaborate without sharing their local input data, which is important for applications that involve sensitive data and have privacy considerations. Besides, high performance numerical computing routines like Intel® Math Kernel Library can be leveraged. The state-of-art implementation of distributed NMF is MPI-FAUN [15], a general framework that iteratively solves NLS subproblems for U and V. The main idea behind MPI-FAUN is to exploit the independence of local updates for rows of U and V, in order to minimize the communication requirements of matrix multiplication operations within the NMF algorithms.

Our idea is to speed up distributed NMF in a new, orthogonal direction: by reducing the problem size of each NLS subproblem within NMF, which in turn decreases the overall computation cost. In a nutshell, we reduce the size of each NLS subproblem, by employing a *matrix sketching* technique: the involved matrices in the

WSDM'18, February 5–9, 2018, Marina Del Rey, CA, USA

ACM ISBN 978-1-4503-5581-0/18/02...$15.00
https://doi.org/10.1145/3159652.3159662

subproblem are multiplied by a specially designed random matrix at each iteration, which greatly reduces their dimensionality. As a result, the computational cost of each subproblem drops.

However, applying matrix sketching comes with several issues. First, although the size of each subproblem is significantly reduced, sketching involves matrix multiplication which brings computational overhead. Second, unlike in a single machine setting, the data are distributed to different nodes, which may have to communicate extensively in a poorly designed solution. In particular, each node only retains part of both the input matrix and the generated approximate matrices, causing difficulties due to data dependencies in the computation process. Besides, the generated random matrices should be the same for all nodes in every iteration, while broadcasting the random matrix to all nodes brings severe communication overhead and can become the bottleneck of distributed NMF. Furthermore, after reducing each original subproblem to a sketched random new subproblem, it is not clear whether the algorithm still converges and whether it converges to stationary points of the original NMF problem.

Our *distributed sketched alternating nonnegative least squares* (DSANLS) overcomes these problems. First, the extra computation cost due to sketching is reduced with a proper choice of the random matrices. Second, the same random matrices used for sketching are generated independently at each node, thus there is no need for transferring them between nodes during distributed NMF. Having the complete random matrix at each node, an NMF iteration can be done locally with the help of a matrix multiplication rule with proper data partitioning. Therefore, our matrix sketching approach reduces not only the computational, but also the communication cost. Moreover, due to the fact that sketching also *shifts* the optimal solution of each original NMF subproblem, we propose subproblem solvers paired with theoretical guarantees of their convergence to a stationary point of the original subproblems.

Our contributions can be summarized as follows:

- We propose DSANLS, a novel high-performance distributed NMF algorithm. DSANLS is the first distributed NMF algorithm that leverages matrix sketching to reduce the problem size of each NLS subproblem and can be applied to both dense and sparse input matrices with a convergence guarantee.
- We propose a novel and specially designed subproblem solver (*proximal coordinate descent*), which helps DSANLS to converge faster. We also discuss the use of *projected gradient descent* as subproblem solver, showing that it is equivalent to stochastic gradient descent (SGD) on the original (non-sketched) NLS subproblem.
- We present a detailed theoretical analysis of DSANLS, and prove that DSANLS converges to a stationary point of the original NMF problem. This convergence proof is novel and non-trivial because of the involvement of matrix sketching at each iteration.
- We conduct an experimental evaluation using several (dense and sparse) real datasets, which demonstrates the efficiency and scalability of DSANLS.

The remainder of the paper is organized as follows. Section 2 briefly reviews NMF algorithms, discusses distributed NMF techniques, and introduces the matrix sketching technique. Our DSANLS algorithm is presented in Section 3. Detailed theoretical analysis of DSANLS algorithm is discussed in Section 4. Section 5 evaluates DSANLS. Finally, Section 6 concludes the paper.

2 BACKGROUND AND RELATED WORK

2.1 NMF Algorithms

Within two-block coordinate descent schemes (exact or inexact, shown as Algorithm 1), different subproblem solvers are proposed.

Algorithm 1: Two-Block Coordinate Descent: Framework of Most NMF Algorithms

```
initialize U_0 ≥ 0, V_0 ≥ 0;
for t = 0 to T − 1 do
    U_{t+1} ← update(M, U_t, V_t);
    V_{t+1} ← update(M, U_{t+1}, V_t);
end
return U_T and V_T
```

The first widely used update rule is Multiplicative Updates (MU), which was first applied for solving NLS problems in [6]. Later, MU was rediscovered and used for NMF in [21]. MU is based on the majorization-minimization framework. Its application guarantees that the objective function monotonically decreases [6, 21].

Another extensively studied method is alternating nonnegative least squares (ANLS), which represents a class of methods where the subproblems for U and V are solved exactly following the framework described in Algorithm 1. ANLS is guaranteed to converge to a stationary point [10] and has been shown to perform very well in practice with active set [16, 18], projected gradient [24], quasi-Newton [41], or accelerated gradient [12] methods as the subproblem solver.

Hierarchical alternating least squares (HALS) [4] solves each NLS subproblem using an exact coordinate descent method that updates one individual column of U at a time. The optimal solutions of the corresponding subproblems can be written in a closed form.

2.2 Distributed NMF

Parallel NMF algorithms are well studied in the literature [13, 36]. However, different from a parallel and single machine setting, data sharing and communication have considerable cost in a distributed setting. Therefore, we need specialized NMF algorithms for massive scale data handling in a distributed environment. The first method in this direction [25] is based on the MU algorithm. It mainly focuses on sparse matrices and applies a careful partitioning of the data in order to maximize data locality and parallelism. Later, CloudNMF [23], a MapReduce-based NMF algorithm similar to [25], was implemented and tested on large-scale biological datasets. Another distributed NMF algorithm [40] leverages block-wise updates for local aggregation and parallelism. It also performs frequent updates using whenever possible the most recently updated data, which is more efficient than traditional concurrent counterparts. Apart from MapReduce implementations, Spark is also attracting attention for its advantage in iterative algorithms, e.g., using MLlib [28]. Finally, there are implementations using X10 [11] and on GPU [27].

The most recent and related work in this direction is MPI-FAUN [14 15], which is the first implementation of NMF using MPI for interprocessor communication. MPI-FAUN is flexible and can be utilized for a broad class of NMF algorithms that iteratively solve NLS subproblems including MU, HALS, and ANLS/BPP. MPI-FAUN exploits the independence of local update computation for rows of U and V

to apply communication-optimal matrix multiplication. In a nutshell, the full matrix M is split across a two-dimensional grid of processors and multiple copies of both U and V are kept at different nodes, in order to reduce the communication between nodes during the iterations of NMF algorithms.

2.3 Matrix Sketching

Matrix sketching is a technique that has been previously used in numerical linear algebra [9], statistics [32] and optimization [33]. Its basic idea is described as follows. Suppose we need to find a solution x to the equation:

$$Ax = b, \quad (A \in \mathbb{R}^{m \times n},\ b \in \mathbb{R}^m). \tag{3}$$

Instead of solving this equation directly, in each iteration of matrix sketching, a random matrix $S \in \mathbb{R}^{d \times m}$ $(d \ll m)$ is generated, and we instead solve the following problem:

$$(SA)x = Sb. \tag{4}$$

Obviously, the solution of (3) is also a solution to (4), but not vice versa. However, the problem size has now decreased from $m \times n$ to $d \times n$. With a properly generated random matrix S and an appropriate method to solve subproblem (4), it can be guaranteed that we will progressively approach the solution to (3) by iteratively applying this sketching technique.

To the best of our knowledge, there is only one piece of previous work [38] which incorporates dual random projection into the NMF problem, in a centralized environment, sharing similar ideas as SANLS, the centralized version of our DSANLS algorithm. However, Wang et al. [38] did not provide an efficient subproblem solver, and their method was less effective than non-sketched methods in practical experiments. Besides, data sparsity was not taken into consideration in their work. Furthermore, no theoretical guarantee was provided for NMF with dual random projection. In short, SANLS is not same as [38] and DSANLS is much more than a distributed version of [38]. The methods that we propose in this paper are efficient in practice and have strong theoretical guarantees.

3 DSANLS: DISTRIBUTED SKETCHED ANLS

3.1 Notations

For a matrix A, we use $A_{i:j}$ to denote the entry at the i-th row and j-th column of A. Besides, either i or j can be omitted to denote a column or a row, i.e., $A_{i:}$ is the i-th row of A, and $A_{:j}$ is its j-th column. Furthermore, i or j can be replaced by a subset of indices. For example, if $I \subset \{1, 2, \dots, m\}$, $A_{I:}$ denotes the sub-matrix of A formed by all rows in I, whereas $A_{:J}$ is the sub-matrix of A formed by all columns in a subset $J \subset \{1, 2, \dots, n\}$.

3.2 Data Partitioning

Assume there are N computing nodes in the cluster. We partition the row indices $\{1, 2, \dots, m\}$ of the input matrix M into N disjoint sets $I_1, I_2, \dots, I_N$, where $I_r \subset \{1, 2, \dots, m\}$ is the subset of rows assigned to node r, as in [25]. Similarly, we partition the column indices $\{1, 2, \dots, n\}$ into disjoint sets $J_1, J_2, \dots, J_N$ and assign column set J_r to node r. The number of rows and columns in each node are near the same in order to achieve load balancing, i.e., $|I_r| \approx m/N$ and $|J_r| \approx n/N$ for each node r. The factor matrices U and V are also assigned to nodes accordingly, i.e., node r stores and updates $U_{I_r:}$ and $V_{J_r:}$ as shown in Figure 1.

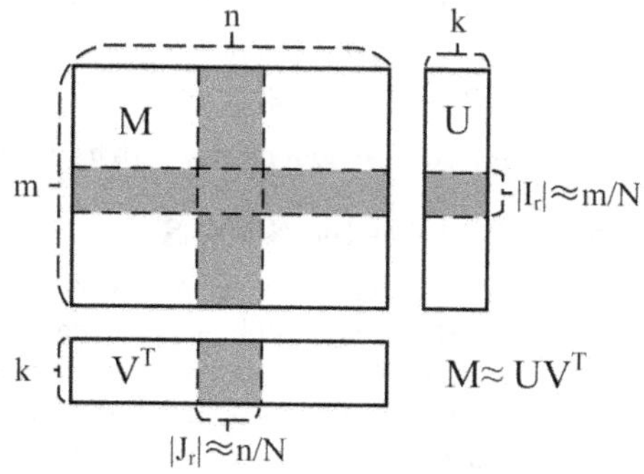

Figure 1: Data partitioning to N nodes

Data partitioning in distributed NMF differs from that in parallel NMF. Previous works on parallel NMF [13, 36] choose to partition U and V along the long dimension, but we adopt the row-partitioning of U and V as in [25]. To see why, take the U-subproblem (2) as an example and observe that it is row-independent in nature, i.e., the r-th row block of its solution $U_{I_r:}$ is given by

$$U_{I_r:} = \underset{U_{I_r:} \in \mathbb{R}_+^{|I_r| \times k}}{\arg\min} \left\| M_{I_r:} - U_{I_r:} V^\top \right\|_F^2 \tag{5}$$

and thus can be solved independently without referring to any other row blocks of U. The same holds for the V-subproblem. In addition, no communication is needed concerning M when solving (5) because $M_{I_r:}$ is already present in node r.

On the other hand, solving (5) requires the entire V of size $n \times k$, meaning that every node needs to gather V from all other nodes. This process can easily be the bottleneck of a naive distributed ANLS implementation. As we will explain shortly, our DSALNS algorithm alleviates this problem, since we use a sketched matrix of reduced size instead of the original complete matrix V.

3.3 SANLS: Sketched ANLS

To better understand DSANLS, we first introduce the Sketched ANLS (SANLS), i.e., a centralized version of our algorithm. Recall that in section 2.1, at each step of ANLS, either U or V is fixed and we solve a nonnegative least square problem (2) over the other variable. Intuitively, it is unnecessary to solve this subproblem with high accuracy, because we may not have reached the optimal solution for the fixed variable so far. Hence, when the fixed variable changes in the next step, this accurate solution from the previous step will not be optimal anymore and will have to be re-computed. Our idea is to apply matrix sketching for each subproblem, in order to obtain an approximate solution for it at a much lower computational and communication cost.

Specifically, suppose we are at the t-th iteration of ANLS, and our current estimations for U and V are U^t and V^t respectively. We must solve subproblem (2) in order to update U^t to a new matrix U^{t+1}. We apply matrix sketching to the residual term of subproblem (2). The subproblem now becomes:

$$\min_{U \in \mathbb{R}_+^{m \times k}} \left\| MS^t - U\left(V^{t\top} S^t\right) \right\|_F^2, \tag{6}$$

where $S^t \in \mathbb{R}^{n\times d}$ is a randomly-generated matrix. Hence, the problem size decreases from $n \times k$ to $d \times k$. d is chosen to be much smaller than n, in order to sufficiently reduce the computational cost[1]. Similarly, we transform the V-subproblem into

$$\min_{V\in\mathbb{R}_+^{n\times k}} \|M^\top S'^t - V\left(U^{t\top} S'^t\right)\|_F^2, \tag{7}$$

where $S'^t \in \mathbb{R}^{m\times d'}$ is also a random matrix with $d' \ll m$.

3.4 DSANLS: Distributed SANLS

Now, we come to our proposal: the distributed version of SANLS called DSANLS. Since the U-subproblem (6) is the same as the V-subproblem (7) in nature, here we restrict our attention to the U-subproblem. The first observation about subproblem (6) is that it is still row-independent, thus node r only needs to solve

$$\min_{U_{I_r:}\in\mathbb{R}_+^{|I_r|\times k}} \left\|\left(MS^t\right)_{I_r:} - U_{I_r:}\left(V^{t\top} S^t\right)\right\|_F^2.$$

For simplicity, we denote

$$A_r^t \triangleq \left(MS^t\right)_{I_r:} \quad \text{and} \quad B^t \triangleq V^{t\top} S^t, \tag{8}$$

and the above subproblem can be written as:

$$\min_{U_{I_r:}\in\mathbb{R}_+^{|I_r|\times k}} \|A_r^t - U_{I_r:}B^t\|_F^2. \tag{9}$$

Thus, node r needs to know matrices A_r^t and B^t in order to solve the subproblem.

For A_r^t, by applying matrix multiplication rules, we get

$$A_r^t = \left(MS^t\right)_{I_r:} = M_{I_r:}S^t$$

Therefore, if S^t is stored at node r, A_r^t can be computed without any communication.

On the other hand, computing $B^t = \left(V^{t\top} S^t\right)$ requires communication across the whole cluster, since the rows of V^t are distributed across different nodes. Fortunately, if we assume that S^t is stored at all nodes again, we can compute B^t in a much cheaper way. Following block matrix multiplication rules, we can rewrite B^t as:

$$\begin{aligned} B^t &= V^{t\top} S^t \\ &= \left[\left(V_{J_1:}^t\right)^\top \cdots \left(V_{J_N:}^t\right)^\top\right] \begin{bmatrix} S_{J_1:}^t \\ \vdots \\ S_{J_N:}^t \end{bmatrix} \\ &= \sum_{r=1}^N \left(V_{J_r:}^t\right)^\top S_{J_r:}^t. \end{aligned}$$

Note that the summand $\bar{B}_r^t \triangleq \left(V_{J_r:}^t\right)^\top S_{J_r:}^t$ is a matrix of size $k \times d$ and can be computed locally. As a result, communication is only needed for summing up the matrices $\bar{B}_r^t$ of size $k \times d$ by using MPI all-reduce operation, which is much cheaper than transmitting the whole V_t of size $n \times k$.

[1]However, we should not choose an extremely small d, otherwise the the size of sketched subproblem would become so small that it can hardly represent the original subproblem, preventing NMF from converging to a good result. In practice, we can set $d = 0.1n$ for medium-sized matrices and $d = 0.01n$ for large matrices if $m \approx n$. When m and n differ a lot, e.g., $m \ll n$ without loss of generality, we should not apply sketching technique to the V subproblem (since solving the U subproblem is much more expensive) and simply choose $d = m \ll n$.

Now, the only remaining problem is the transmission of S^t. Since S^t can be dense, even larger than V^t, broadcasting it across the whole cluster can be quite expensive. However, it turns out that we can avoid this. Recall that S^t is a randomly-generated matrix; each node can generate exactly the same matrix, if we use the same pseudo-random generator and the same seed. Therefore, we only need to broadcast the random seed, which is just an integer, at the beginning of the whole program. This ensures that each node generates exactly the same random number sequence and hence the same random matrices S^t at each iteration.

In short, the communication cost of each node is reduced from $O(nk)$ to $O(dk)$ by adopting our sketching technique for the U-subproblem. Likewise, the communication cost of each V-subproblem is decreased from $O(mk)$ to $O(d'k)$. The general framework of our DSANLS algorithm is listed in Algorithm 2.

Algorithm 2: Distributed SANLS on Node r

```
Initialize U^0_{I_r:}, V^0_{J_r:}
Broadcast the random seed
for t = 0 to T − 1 do
    Generate random matrix S^t ∈ R^{n×d}
    Compute A^t_r ← M_{I_r:} S^t
    Compute B̄^t_r ← (V^t_{J_r:})^⊤ S^t_{J_r:}
    All-Reduce: B^t ← Σ_{i=1}^N B̄^t_i
    Update U^{t+1}_{I_r:} by solving min_{U_{I_r:}} ||A^t_r − U_{I_r:} B^t||
    Generate random matrix S'^t ∈ R^{m×d'}
    Compute A'^t_r ← (M_{:J_r})^⊤ S'^t
    Compute B̄'^t_r ← (U^t_{I_r:})^⊤ S'^t_{I_r:}
    All-Reduce: B'^t ← Σ_{i=1}^N B̄'^t_i
    Update V^{t+1}_{J_r:} by solving min_{V_{J_r:}} ||A'^t_r − V_{J_r:} B'^t||
end
return U^T_{I_r:} and V^T_{J_r:}
```

3.5 Generation of Random Matrices

A key problem in Algorithm 2 is how to generate random matrices $S^t \in \mathbb{R}^{n\times d}$ and $S'^t \in \mathbb{R}^{m\times d'}$. Here we focus on generating a random $S^t \in \mathbb{R}^{d\times n}$ satisfying Assumption 1. The reason for choosing such a random matrix is that the corresponding sketched problem would be equivalent to the original problem on expectation; we will prove this in Section 3.6.

Assumption 1. *Assume the random matrices are normalized and have bounded variance, i.e., there exists a constant σ^2 such that*

$$\mathbb{E}\left[S^t S^{t\top}\right] = I \quad \text{and} \quad \mathbb{V}\left[S^t S^{t\top}\right] \le \sigma^2$$

for all t, where I is the identity matrix.

Different options exist for such matrices, which have different computation costs in forming sketched matrices $A_r^t = M_{I_r:}S^t$ and $\bar{B}_r^t = \left(V_{J_r:}^t\right)^\top S_{J_r:}^t$. Since $M_{I_r:}$ is much larger than $V_{J_r:}^t$ and thus computing A_r^t is more expensive, we only consider the cost of constructing A_r^t here.

The most classical choice for a random matrix is one with i.i.d. Gaussian entries having mean 0 and variance $1/d$. It is easy to show that $\mathbb{E}\left[S^t S^{t\top}\right] = I$. Besides, Gaussian random matrix has bounded variance because Gaussian distribution has finite fourth-order moment. However, since each entry of such a matrix is totally random and thus no special structure exists in S^t, matrix multiplication will be expensive. That is, when given $M_{I_r:}$ of size $|I_r|\times n$, computing its sketched matrix $A_r^t = M_{I_r:}S^t$ requires $O(|I_r|nd)$ basic operations.

A seemingly better choice for S^t would be a *subsampling* random matrix. Each column of such random matrix is uniformly sampled from $\{e_1, e_2, \ldots, e_n\}$ without replacement, where $e_i \in \mathbb{R}^n$ is the i-th canonical basis vector (i.e., a vector having its i-th element 1 and all others 0). We can easily show that such an S^t also satisfies $\mathbb{E}\left[S^t S^{t\top}\right] = I$ and the variance $\mathbb{V}\left[S^t S^{t\top}\right]$ is bounded, but this time constructing the sketched matrix $A_r^t = M_{I_r:}S^t$ only requires $O(|I_r|d)$. Besides, subsampling random matrix can preserve the sparsity of original matrix. Hence, a subsampling random matrix would be favored over a Gaussian random matrix by most applications, especially for very large-scale or sparse problems. On the other hand, we observed in our experiments that a Gaussian random matrix can result in a faster per-iteration convergence rate, because each column of the sketched matrix A_r^t contains entries from multiple columns of the original matrix and thus is more informative. Hence, it would be better to use a Gaussian matrix when the sketch size d is small and thus a $O(|I_r|nd)$ complexity is acceptable, or when the network speed of the cluster is poor, hence we should trade more local computation cost for less communication cost.

Although we only test two representative types of random matrices (i.e., Gaussian and subsampling random matrices), our framework is readily applicable for other choices, such as subsampled randomized Hadamard transform (SRHT) [1, 26] and count sketch [3, 5, 31]. The choice of random matrices is not the focus of this paper and left for future investigation.

3.6 Solving Subproblems

Before describing how to solve subproblem (9), let us make an important observation. As discussed in Section 2.3, the sketching technique has been applied in solving linear systems before. However, the situation is different in matrix factorization. Note that for the distributed matrix factorization problem we usually have

$$\min_{U_{I_r:}\in\mathbb{R}_+^{|I_r|\times k}} \left\|M_{I_r:} - U_{I_r:}V^{t\top}\right\|_F^2 \neq 0.$$

So, for the sketched subproblem (9), which can be equivalently written as

$$\min_{U_{I_r:}\in\mathbb{R}_+^{|I_r|\times k}} \left\|\left(M_{I_r:} - U_{I_r:}V^{t\top}\right) S^t\right\|_F^2,$$

the non-zero entries of the residual matrix $\left(M_{I_r:} - U_{I_r:}V^{t\top}\right)$ will be scaled by the matrix S^t at different levels. As a consequence, the optimal solution will be shifted because of sketching. This fact alerts us that for SANLS, we need to update U^{t+1} by exploiting the sketched subproblem (9) to step towards the true optimal solution and avoid convergence to the solution of the sketched subproblem.

3.6.1 Projected Gradient Descent. A natural method is to use *one step*[2] of projected gradient descent for the sketched subproblem:

$$\begin{aligned} U_{I_r:}^{t+1} &= \max\left\{U_{I_r:}^t - \eta_t \nabla_{U_{I_r:}} \left\|A_r^t - U_{I_r:}B^t\right\|_F^2\Big|_{U_{I_r:}=U_{I_r:}^t}, 0\right\} \\ &= \max\left\{U_{I_r:}^t - 2\eta_t\left[U_{I_r:}^t B^t B^{t\top} - A_r^t B^{t\top}\right], 0\right\}, \end{aligned} \tag{10}$$

where $\eta_t > 0$ is the step size and $\max\{\cdot,\cdot\}$ denotes the entry-wise maximum operation. In the gradient descent step (10), the computational cost mainly comes from two matrix multiplications: $B^t B^{t\top}$ and $A_{t,r}B^{t\top}$. Note that A_r^t and B^t are of sizes $|I_r|\times d$ and $k\times d$ respectively, thus the gradient descent step takes $O\left(kd(|I_r| + k)\right)$ in total.

To exploit the nature of this algorithm, we further expand the gradient:

$$\begin{aligned} &\nabla_{U_{I_r:}} \left\|A_r^t - U_{I_r:}B^t\right\|_F^2 = 2\left[U_{I_r:}B^t B^{t\top} - A_r^t B^{t\top}\right] \\ &\overset{(8)}{=}2\left[U_{I_r:}\left(V^{t\top}S^t\right)\left(V^{t\top}S^t\right)^\top - \left(M_{I_r:}S^t\right)\left(V^{t\top}S^t\right)^\top\right] \\ &=2\left[U_{I_r:}V^{t\top}\left(S^t S^{t\top}\right)V^t - M_{I_r:}\left(S^t S^{t\top}\right)V^t\right]. \end{aligned}$$

By taking the expectation of the above equation, and using the fact $\mathbb{E}\left[S^t S^{t\top}\right] = I$, we have:

$$\begin{aligned} &\mathbb{E}\left[\nabla_{U_{I_r:}} \left\|A_r^t - U_{I_r:}B^t\right\|_F^2\right] = 2\left[U_{I_r:}V^{t\top}V^t - M_{I_r:}V^t\right] \\ &=\nabla_{U_{I_r:}} \left\|M_{I_r:} - U_{I_r:}V^{t\top}\right\|_F^2, \end{aligned}$$

which means that the gradient of the sketched subproblem is equivalent to the gradient of the original problem on expectation. Therefore, such a step of gradient descent can be interpreted as a (generalized) *stochastic gradient descent* (SGD) [29] method on the original subproblem. Thus, according to the theory of SGD, we naturally require the step sizes $\{\eta_t\}$ to be diminishing, i.e., $\eta_t \to 0$ as t increases.

3.6.2 Proximal Coordinate Descent. However, it is well known that the gradient descent method converges slowly, while the coordinate descent method, namely the HALS method for NMF, is quite efficient [8]. Still, because of its very fast convergence, HALS should not be applied to the sketched subproblem directly because it shifts the solution away from the true optimal solution. Therefore, we would like to develop a method which resembles HALS but will not converge towards the solutions of the sketched subproblems.

To achieve this, we add a regularization term to the sketched subproblem (9). The new subproblem becomes:

$$\min_{U_{I_r:}\in\mathbb{R}_+^{|I_r|\times k}} \left\|A_r^t - U_{I_r:}B^t\right\|_F^2 + \mu_t\left\|U_{I_r:} - U_{I_r:}^t\right\|_F^2, \tag{11}$$

where $\mu_t > 0$ is a parameter. Such regularization is reminiscent to the proximal point method [37] and parameter μ_t controls the step size as $1/\eta_t$ in projected gradient descent. We therefore require $\mu_t \to +\infty$ to enforce the convergence of the algorithm, e.g., $\mu_t = t$.

At each step of proximal coordinate descent, only one column of $U_{I_r:}$, say $U_{I_r,j}$ where $j \in \{1, 2, \ldots, k\}$, is updated:

$$\min_{U_{I_r:j}\in\mathbb{R}_+^{|I_r|}} \left\|A_r^t - U_{I_r:j}B_{j:}^t - \sum_{l\neq j} U_{I_r:l}B_{l:}^t\right\|_F^2 + \mu_t\left\|U_{I_r:j} - U_{I_r:j}^t\right\|_2^2.$$

[2] Note that we only apply one step of projected gradient descent here to avoid solution shifted.

It is not hard to see that the above problem is still row-independent, which means that each entry of the row vector $U_{I_r:j}$ can be solved independently at each node. For example, for any $i \in I_r$, the solution of $U_{i:j}^{t+1}$ is given by:

$$U_{i:j}^{t+1} = \arg\min_{U_{i:j}\geq 0} \left\| (A_r^t)_{i:} - U_{i:j}B_{j:}^t - \sum_{l\neq j} U_{i:l}B_{l:}^t \right\|_2^2 + \mu_t \left\|U_{i:j} - U_{i:j}^t\right\|_2^2$$
$$= \max\left\{ \frac{\mu_t U_{i:j}^t + (A_r^t)_{i:} B_{j:}^{t\top} - \sum_{l\neq j} U_{i:l}B_{l:}^t B_{j:}^{t\top}}{B_{j:}^t B_{j:}^{t\top} + \mu_t}, 0 \right\}. \quad (12)$$

At each step of coordinate descent, we choose the column j from $\{1, 2, \ldots, k\}$ successively. When updating column j at iteration t, the columns $l < j$ have already been updated and thus $U_{I_r:l} = U_{I_r:l}^{t+1}$, while the columns $l > j$ are old so $U_{I_r:l} = U_{I_r:l}^t$.

The complete proximal coordinate descent algorithm for the U-subproblem is summarized in Algorithm 3. When updating column j, computing the matrix-vector multiplication $A_r^t B_{j:}^{t\top}$ takes $O(d|I_r|)$. The whole inner loop takes $O(k(d + |I_r|))$ because one vector dot product of length d is required for computing each summand and the summation itself needs $O(k|I_r|)$. Considering that there are k columns in total, the overall complexity of coordinate descent is $O(k((k + d)|I_r| + kd))$. Typically, we choose $d > k$, so the complexity can be simplified to $O(kd(|I_r| + k))$, which is the same as that of gradient descent.

Since proximal coordinate descent is much more efficient than projected gradient descent, we adopt it as the default subproblem solver within DSANLS.

Algorithm 3: Proximal Coordinate Descent for Local Subproblem (9) on Node r

Parameter: $\mu_t > 0$
for $j = 1$ **to** k **do**
  $T \leftarrow \mu_t U_{I_r:j}^t + A_r^t B_{j:}^{t\top}$
  for $l = 1$ **to** $j - 1$ **do**
    $T \leftarrow T - \left(B_{l:}^t B_{j:}^{t\top}\right) U_{I_r:l}^{t+1}$
  end
  for $l = j + 1$ **to** k **do**
    $T \leftarrow T - \left(B_{l:}^t B_{j:}^{t\top}\right) U_{I_r:l}^t$
  end
  $U_{I_r:j}^{t+1} \leftarrow \max\left\{T/\left(B_{j:}^t B_{j:}^{t\top} + \mu_t\right), 0\right\}$
end
return $U_{I_r:}^{t+1}$

4 THEORETICAL ANALYSIS

4.1 Complexity Analysis

We now analyze the computational and communication costs of our DSANLS algorithm, when using subsampling random sketch matrices. The computational complexity at each node is:

$$O(\overbrace{d}^{\text{generating } S^t} + \overbrace{|I_r|d}^{\text{constructing } A_r^t \text{ and } B^t} + \overbrace{kd(|I_r| + k)}^{\text{solving subproblem}})$$
$$= O(kd(|I_r| + k)) \approx O\left(kd\left(\frac{m}{N} + k\right)\right) \quad (13)$$

Moreover, as we have shown in Section 3.4, the communication cost of DSANLS is $O(kd)$.

On the other hand, for a classical implementation of distributed HALS [7], the computational cost is

$$O(kn(|I_r| + k)) \approx O\left(kn\left(\frac{m}{N} + k\right)\right) \quad (14)$$

and the communication cost is $O(kn)$ due to the all-gathering of V^t's.

Comparing the above quantities, we observe an $n/d \gg 1$ speedup of our DSANLS algorithm over HALS in both computation and communication. However, we empirically observed that DSANLS has a slower per-iteration convergence rate (i.e., it needs more iterations to converge). Still, as we will show in the next section, in practice, DSANLS is superior to alternative distributed NMF algorithms, after taking all factors into account.

4.2 Convergence Analysis

Here we provide theoretical convergence guarantees for the proposed SANLS and DSANLS algorithms. We show that SANLS and DSANLS converge to a stationary point.

To establish convergence result, Assumption 2 is needed first.

ASSUMPTION 2. *Assume all the iterates U^t and V^t have uniformly bounded norms, which means that there exists a constant R such that*

$$\|U^t\|_F \leq R \quad \textit{and} \quad \|V^t\|_F \leq R$$

for all t.

We experimentally observed that this assumption holds in practice, as long as the step sizes used are not too large. Besides, Assumption 2 can also be enforced by imposing additional constraints, e.g.:

$$U_{i:l} \leq \sqrt{2\|M\|_F} \quad \text{and} \quad V_{j:l} \leq \sqrt{2\|M\|_F} \quad \forall i, j, l, \quad (15)$$

with which we have $R = \max\{m, n\}k\sqrt{2\|M\|_F}$. Such constraints can be very easily handled by both of our projected gradient descent and regularized coordinate descent solvers. Lemma 4.1 shows that imposing such extra constraints does not prevent us from finding the global optimal solution.

LEMMA 4.1. *If the optimal solution to the original problem (1) exists, there is at least one global optimal solution in the domain (15).*

Based on Assumptions 1 (see Section 3.5) and Assumption 2, we now can formally show our main convergence result:

THEOREM 4.2. *Under Assumptions 1 and 2, if the step sizes satisfy*

$$\sum_{t=1}^{\infty} \eta_t = \infty \quad \textit{and} \quad \sum_{t=1}^{\infty} \eta_t^2 < \infty,$$

for projected gradient descent, or

$$\sum_{t=1}^{\infty} 1/\mu_t = \infty \quad \textit{and} \quad \sum_{t=1}^{\infty} 1/\mu_t^2 < \infty,$$

for regularized coordinate descent, then SANLS and DSANLS with either sub-problem solver will converge to a stationary point of problem (1) with probability 1.

The proofs of Lemma 4.1 and Theorem 4.2 can be found in our technical report [35].

Table 1: Statistics of Datasets

Task	Dataset	#Rows	#Columns	Non-zero values	Sparsity
Video analysis	BOATS	216,000	300	64,800,000	0%
Image processing	MIT CBCL FACE	2,429	361	876,869	0%
	MNIST	70,000	784	10,505,375	80.86%
	GISETTE	13,500	5,000	8,770,559	87.01%
Text mining	Reuters(RCV1)	804,414	47,236	60,915,113	99.84%
Community detection	DBLP Collaboration Network	317,080	317,080	2,416,812	99.9976%

5 EXPERIMENTAL EVALUATION

This section includes an experimental evaluation of our algorithm on both dense and sparse real data matrices. The code can be downloaded from https://github.com/qianyuqiu79/DSANLS.

5.1 Datasets

We use real public datasets corresponding to different NMF tasks in our evaluation. Their statistics are summarized in Table 1.

Video Analysis. NMF can be used on video data for background subtraction (i.e., to detect moving objects) [17]. We here use BOATS[3] video dataset [2], which includes boats moving through water. The video has 15 fps and it is saved as a sequence of png files, whose format is RGB with a frame size of 360×200. We use 'Boats2' which contains one boat close to the camera for 300 frames and reshape the matrix such that every RGB frame is a column of our matrix; the final matrix is dense with size $216,000 \times 300$.

Image Processing. The first dataset we use for this application is MIT CBCL FACE DATABASE[4] as in [20]. To form the vectorized matrix, we use all 2,429 face images (each with 19×19 pixels) in the original training set. The second dataset is MINST[5], which is a widely used handwritten digits dataset. All 70,000 samples including both training and test set are used to form the vectorized matrix. The third one is GISETTE[6], another widely used dataset in handwritten digit recognition problem. We use all 13,500 pictures in the training, validation, and test datasets and form the vectorized matrix.

Text Mining. We use the Reuters document corpora[7] as in [39]. Reuters Corpus Volume I (RCV1) [22] is an archive of 804,414 manually categorized newswire stories made available by Reuters, Ltd. for research purposes. The official LYRL2004 chronological split is utilized. Non-zero values contain cosine-normalized, log TF-IDF vectors.

Community Detection. We convert the DBLP collaboration network[8] into its adjacency matrix. It is a co-authorship graph where two authors are connected if they have published at least one paper together.

5.2 Setup

We conduct our experiments on the Linux cluster of our institute with a total of 96 nodes. Each node contains 8-core Intel® Core™ i7-3770 CPU @ 1.60GHz cores and 16 GB of memory. Our algorithm is implemented in C using the Intel® Math Kernel Library (MKL) and Message Passing Interface (MPI). We use 10 nodes by default. Since tuning the factorization rank k is outside the scope of this paper, we use 100 as default value of k. Because of the large sizes of RCV1 and DBLP, we only use subsampling random matrices for them, as the use of Gaussian random matrices is too slow.

We evaluate DSANLS with subsampling and Gaussian random matrices, denoted by DSANLS/S and DSANLS/G, respectively, using proximal coordinate descent as the default subproblem solver. As mentioned in [14, 15], it is unfair to compare with a Hadoop implementation. We only compare DSANLS with MPI-FAUN[9] (all MPI-FAUN-MU, MPI-FAUN-HALS, and MPI-FAUN-ABPP implementations), which is the first and the state-of-the-art C++/MPI implementation with MKL and Armadillo. For parameters pc and pr in MPI-FAUN, we use the optimal values for each dataset, according to the recommendations in [14, 15].

5.3 Results

5.3.1 Performance Comparison. We use the relative error of the low rank approximation compared to the original matrix to measure the effectiveness of NMF by DSANLS with MPI-FAUN. This error measure was been widely used in previous work [14, 15, 17] and is formally defined as

$$\|M - UV^\top\|_F / \|M\|_F .$$

Since the time for each iteration is significantly reduced by our proposed DSANLS compared to MPI-FAUN, in Figure 2, we show the relative error over time for DSANLS and MPI-FAUN implementations of MU, HALS, and ANLS/BPP on the 6 real public datasets. Observe that DSANLS/S performs best in all 6 datasets, although DSANLS/G has faster per-iteration convergence rate. MU converges relatively slowly and usually has a bad convergence result; on the other hand HALS may oscillate in the early rounds[10], but converges quite fast and to a good solution. Surprisingly, although ANLS/BPP is considered to be the state-of-art NMF algorithm, it does not perform well in all 6 datasets. As we will see, this is due to its high per-iteration cost.

5.3.2 Scalability Comparison. We vary the number of nodes used in the cluster from 2 to 16 and record the average time for 100 iterations of each algorithm. Figure 3 shows the reciprocal of per-iteration time as a function of the number of nodes used. All algorithms exhibit good scalability for all datasets (nearly a straight line), except for FACE (i.e., Figure 3(a)). FACE is the smallest dataset, whose number of columns is 300, while k is set to 100 by default. When n/N is smaller than k, the complexity is dominated by k, hence, increasing the number of nodes does not reduce the computational cost, but may increase the communication overhead.

[3] http://visal.cs.cityu.edu.hk/downloads/
[4] http://cbcl.mit.edu/software-datasets/FaceData2.html
[5] http://yann.lecun.com/exdb/mnist/
[6] http://clopinet.com/isabelle/Projects/NIPS2003/#challenge
[7] we use the second version RCV1-v2, which can be found in http://jmlr.csail.mit.edu/papers/volume5/lewis04a/
[8] http://snap.stanford.edu/data/com-DBLP.html
[9] public code available at https://github.com/ramkikannan/nmflibrary
[10] HALS does not guarantee the objective function to decrease monotonically.

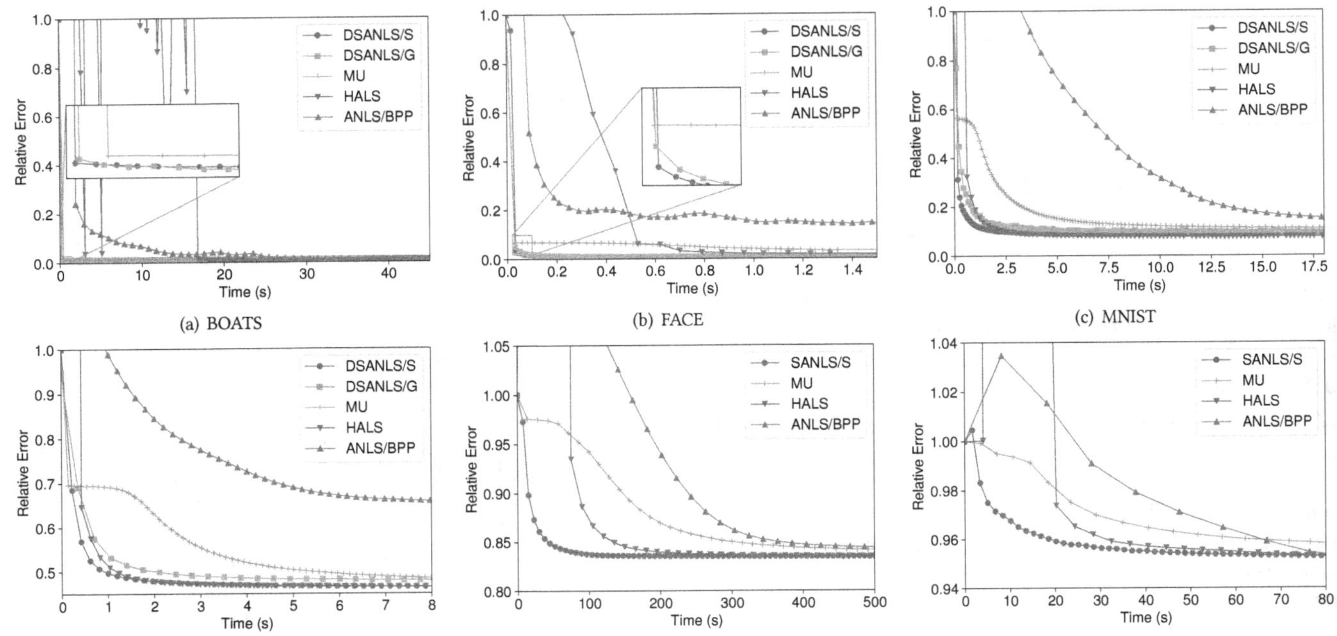

(a) BOATS (b) FACE (c) MNIST

(d) GISETTE (e) RCV1 (f) DBLP

Figure 2: Relative error over time

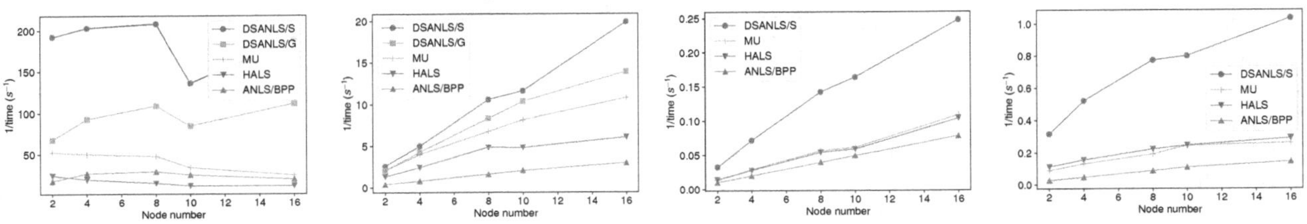

(a) FACE (b) MNIST (c) RCV1 (d) DBLP

Figure 3: Reciprocal of per-iteration time as a function of cluster size

In general, we can observe that DSANLS/Subsampling has the lowest per-iteration cost compared to all other algorithms, and DSANLS/Gaussian has similar cost to MU and HALS. ANLS/BPP has the highest per-iteration cost, explaining the bad performance of ANLS/BPP in Figure 2.

5.3.3 Performance Varying the Value of k. Although tuning the factorization rank k is outside the scope of this paper, we compare the performance of DSANLS with MPI-FAUN varying the value of k from 20 to 500 on RCV1. Observe from Figure 4 and Figure 2(e) that DSANLS outperforms the state-of-art algorithms for all values of k. Naturally, the relative error of all algorithms decreases with the increase of k, but they also take longer to converge.

5.3.4 Comparison with Projected Gradient Descent. In Section 3.6, we claimed that our proximal coordinate descent approach (denoted as DSANLS-RCD) is faster than projected gradient descent (also presented in the same section, denoted as DSANLS-PGD). Figure 5 confirms the difference in the convergence rate of the two approaches regardless of the random matrix generation approach.

6 CONCLUSION

In this paper, we presented a novel distributed NMF algorithm that can be used for scalable analytics of high dimensional matrix data. Our approach follows the general framework of ANLS, but utilizes matrix sketching to reduce the problem size of each NLS subproblem. We discussed and compared two different approaches for generating random matrices (i.e. Gaussian and subsampling random matrices). Then, we presented two subproblem solvers for our general framework, and theoretically proved that our algorithm is convergent. We analyzed the per-iteration computational and communication cost of our approach and its convergence, showing its superiority compared to the previous state-of-the-art. Our experiments on several real datasets show that our method converges fast to an accurate solution and scales well with the number of cluster nodes used. In the future, we plan to study the application of DSANLS to dense or sparse tensors.

ACKNOWLEDGEMENTS

This work is partially supported by GRF Grants 17201414 and 17205015 from Hong Kong Research Grant Council. It has also received funding from the European Union's Horizon 2020 research and innovation programme under grant agreement No 657347.

REFERENCES

[1] N. Ailon and B. Chazelle. Approximate nearest neighbors and the fast johnson-lindenstrauss transform. In *STOC*, pages 557–563. ACM, 2006.

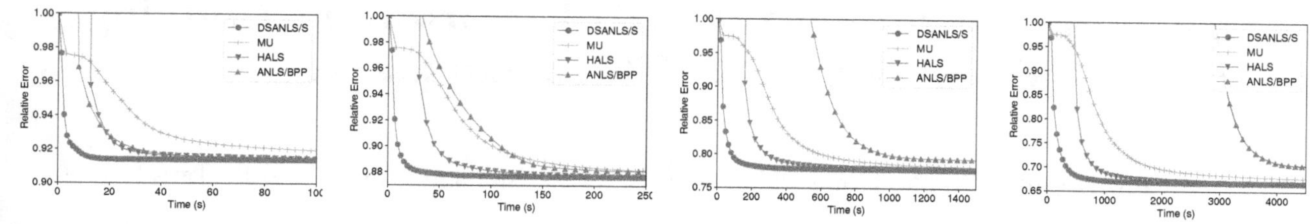

(a) k=20 (b) k=50 (c) k=200 (d) k=500

Figure 4: Relative error over time, varying k value

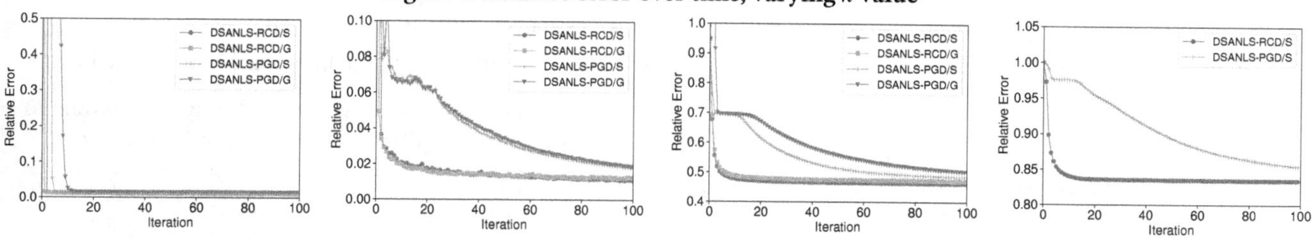

(a) BOATS (b) FACE (c) GISETTE (d) RCV1

Figure 5: Relative error per-iteration of different subproblem solvers

[2] A. B. Chan, V. Mahadevan, and N. Vasconcelos. Generalized stauffer–grimson background subtraction for dynamic scenes. *Machine Vision and Applications*, 22(5):751–766, 2011.

[3] M. Charikar, K. Chen, and M. Farach-Colton. Finding frequent items in data streams. *Theoretical Computer Science*, 312(1):3–15, 2004.

[4] A. Cichocki and P. Anh-Huy. Fast local algorithms for large scale nonnegative matrix and tensor factorizations. *IEICE transactions on fundamentals of electronics, communications and computer sciences*, 92(3):708–721, 2009.

[5] K. L. Clarkson and D. P. Woodruff. Low rank approximation and regression in input sparsity time. In *STOC*, pages 81–90. ACM, 2013.

[6] M. E. Daube-Witherspoon and G. Muehllehner. An iterative image space reconstruction algorthm suitable for volume ect. *IEEE transactions on medical imaging*, 5(2):61–66, 1986.

[7] J. P. Fairbanks, R. Kannan, H. Park, and D. A. Bader. Behavioral clusters in dynamic graphs. *Parallel Computing*, 47:38–50, 2015.

[8] N. Gillis. The why and how of nonnegative matrix factorization. *Regularization, Optimization, Kernels, and Support Vector Machines*, 12(257), 2014.

[9] R. M. Gower and P. Richtárik. Randomized iterative methods for linear systems. *SIAM Journal on Matrix Analysis and Applications*, 36(4):1660–1690, 2015.

[10] L. Grippo and M. Sciandrone. On the convergence of the block nonlinear gauss–seidel method under convex constraints. *Operations research letters*, 26(3):127–136, 2000.

[11] D. Grove, J. Milthorpe, and O. Tardieu. Supporting array programming in x10. In *ARRAY*, page 38. ACM, 2014.

[12] N. Guan, D. Tao, Z. Luo, and B. Yuan. Nenmf: an optimal gradient method for nonnegative matrix factorization. *IEEE Transactions on Signal Processing*, 60(6):2882–2898, 2012.

[13] K. Kanjani. Parallel non negative matrix factorization for document clustering. *CPSC-659 (Parallel and Distributed Numerical Algorithms) course. Texas A&M University, Tech. Rep*, 2007.

[14] R. Kannan, G. Ballard, and H. Park. A high-performance parallel algorithm for nonnegative matrix factorization. In *PPoPP*, page 9. ACM, 2016.

[15] R. Kannan, G. Ballard, and H. Park. Mpi-faun: An mpi-based framework for alternating-updating nonnegative matrix factorization. *arXiv preprint arXiv:1609.09154*, 2016.

[16] H. Kim and H. Park. Nonnegative matrix factorization based on alternating nonnegativity constrained least squares and active set method. *SIAM journal on matrix analysis and applications*, 30(2):713–730, 2008.

[17] J. Kim, Y. He, and H. Park. Algorithms for nonnegative matrix and tensor factorizations: A unified view based on block coordinate descent framework. *Journal of Global Optimization*, 58(2):285–319, 2014.

[18] J. Kim and H. Park. Fast nonnegative matrix factorization: An active-set-like method and comparisons. *SIAM Journal on Scientific Computing*, 33(6):3261–3281, 2011.

[19] I. Kotsia, S. Zafeiriou, and I. Pitas. A novel discriminant non-negative matrix factorization algorithm with applications to facial image characterization problems. *IEEE Transactions on Information Forensics and Security*, 2(3):588–595, 2007.

[20] D. D. Lee and H. S. Seung. Learning the parts of objects by non-negative matrix factorization. *Nature*, 401(6755):788–791, 1999.

[21] D. D. Lee and H. S. Seung. Algorithms for non-negative matrix factorization. In *NIPS*, pages 556–562, 2001.

[22] D. D. Lewis, Y. Yang, T. G. Rose, and F. Li. Rcv1: A new benchmark collection for text categorization research. *JMLR*, 5(Apr):361–397, 2004.

[23] R. Liao, Y. Zhang, J. Guan, and S. Zhou. Cloudnmf: a mapreduce implementation of nonnegative matrix factorization for large-scale biological datasets. *Genomics, proteomics & bioinformatics*, 12(1):48–51, 2014.

[24] C.-J. Lin. Projected gradient methods for nonnegative matrix factorization. *Neural computation*, 19(10):2756–2779, 2007.

[25] C. Liu, H.-c. Yang, J. Fan, L.-W. He, and Y.-M. Wang. Distributed nonnegative matrix factorization for web-scale dyadic data analysis on mapreduce. In *WWW*, pages 681–690. ACM, 2010.

[26] Y. Lu, P. Dhillon, D. P. Foster, and L. Ungar. Faster ridge regression via the subsampled randomized hadamard transform. In *NIPS*, pages 369–377, 2013.

[27] E. Mejía-Roa, D. Tabas-Madrid, J. Setoain, C. García, F. Tirado, and A. Pascual-Montano. Nmf-mgpu: non-negative matrix factorization on multi-gpu systems. *BMC bioinformatics*, 16(1):1, 2015.

[28] X. Meng, J. Bradley, B. Yuvaz, E. Sparks, S. Venkataraman, D. Liu, J. Freeman, D. Tsai, M. Amde, S. Owen, et al. Mllib: Machine learning in apache spark. *JMLR*, 17(34):1–7, 2016.

[29] A. Nemirovski, A. Juditsky, G. Lan, and A. Shapiro. Robust stochastic approximation approach to stochastic programming. *SIAM Journal on optimization*, 19(4):1574–1609, 2009.

[30] V. P. Pauca, F. Shahnaz, M. W. Berry, and R. J. Plemmons. Text mining using non-negative matrix factorizations. In *SDM*, pages 452–456. SIAM, 2004.

[31] N. Pham and R. Pagh. Fast and scalable polynomial kernels via explicit feature maps. In *ACM SIGKDD*, pages 239–247. ACM, 2013.

[32] M. Pilanci and M. J. Wainwright. Iterative hessian sketch: Fast and accurate solution approximation for constrained least-squares. *JMLR*, pages 1–33, 2015.

[33] M. Pilanci and M. J. Wainwright. Newton sketch: A linear-time optimization algorithm with linear-quadratic convergence. *arXiv preprint arXiv:1505.02250*, 2015.

[34] I. Psorakis, S. Roberts, M. Ebden, and B. Sheldon. Overlapping community detection using bayesian non-negative matrix factorization. *Physical Review E*, 83(6):066114, 2011.

[35] Y. Qian, C. Tan, N. Mamoulis, and D. W. Cheung. Dsanls: Accelerating distributed nonnegative matrix factorization via sketching. Technical report, HKU CS, 2017.

[36] S. A. Robila and L. G. Maciak. A parallel unmixing algorithm for hyperspectral images. In *Optics East*, pages 63840F–63840F. International Society for Optics and Photonics, 2006.

[37] R. T. Rockafellar. Monotone operators and the proximal point algorithm. *SIAM journal on control and optimization*, 14(5):877–898, 1976.

[38] F. Wang and P. Li. Efficient nonnegative matrix factorization with random projections. In *SDM*, pages 281–292. SIAM, 2010.

[39] W. Xu, X. Liu, and Y. Gong. Document clustering based on non-negative matrix factorization. In *SIGIR*, pages 267–273. ACM, 2003.

[40] J. Yin, L. Gao, and Z. M. Zhang. Scalable nonnegative matrix factorization with block-wise updates. In *ECML-PKDD*, pages 337–352. Springer, 2014.

[41] R. Zdunek and A. Cichocki. Non-negative matrix factorization with quasi-newton optimization. In *ICAISC*, pages 870–879. Springer, 2006.

Network Embedding as Matrix Factorization: Unifying DeepWalk, LINE, PTE, and node2vec

Jiezhong Qiu[†*], Yuxiao Dong[‡], Hao Ma[‡], Jian Li[♯], Kuansan Wang[‡], and Jie Tang[†]

[†]Department of Computer Science and Technology, Tsinghua University
[‡]Microsoft Research, Redmond
[♯]Institute for Interdisciplinary Information Sciences, Tsinghua University
qiujz16@mails.tsinghua.edu.cn,{yuxdong,haoma,kuansanw}@microsoft.com,{lijian83,jietang}@tsinghua.edu.cn

ABSTRACT

Since the invention of word2vec [28, 29], the skip-gram model has significantly advanced the research of network embedding, such as the recent emergence of the DeepWalk, LINE, PTE, and node2vec approaches. In this work, we show that all of the aforementioned models with negative sampling can be unified into the matrix factorization framework with closed forms. Our analysis and proofs reveal that: (1) DeepWalk [31] empirically produces a low-rank transformation of a network's normalized Laplacian matrix; (2) LINE [37], in theory, is a special case of DeepWalk when the size of vertices' context is set to one; (3) As an extension of LINE, PTE [36] can be viewed as the joint factorization of multiple networks' Laplacians; (4) node2vec [16] is factorizing a matrix related to the stationary distribution and transition probability tensor of a 2nd-order random walk. We further provide the theoretical connections between skip-gram based network embedding algorithms and the theory of graph Laplacian. Finally, we present the NetMF method[1] as well as its approximation algorithm for computing network embedding. Our method offers significant improvements over DeepWalk and LINE for conventional network mining tasks. This work lays the theoretical foundation for skip-gram based network embedding methods, leading to a better understanding of latent network representation learning.

ACM Reference Format:
Jiezhong Qiu, Yuxiao Dong, Hao Ma, Jian Li, Kuansan Wang, and Jie Tang. 2018. Network Embedding as Matrix Factorization: Unifying DeepWalk, LINE, PTE, and node2vec . In *Proceedings of WSDM'18*. ACM, New York, NY, USA, 9 pages. https://doi.org/10.1145/3159652.3159706

1 INTRODUCTION

The conventional paradigm of mining and learning with networks usually starts from the explicit exploration of their structural properties [13, 32]. But many of such properties, such as betweenness centrality, triangle count, and modularity, require extensive domain knowledge and expensive computation to handcraft. In light of these issues, as well as the opportunities offered by the recent emergence of representation learning [2], learning latent representations for networks, a.k.a., network embedding, has been extensively studied in order to automatically discover and map a network's structural properties into a latent space.

Table 1: The matrices that are implicitly approximated and factorized by DeepWalk, LINE, PTE, and node2vec.

Algorithm	Matrix
DeepWalk	$\log\left(\mathrm{vol}(G)\left(\frac{1}{T}\sum_{r=1}^{T}(D^{-1}A)^r\right)D^{-1}\right) - \log b$
LINE	$\log\left(\mathrm{vol}(G)D^{-1}AD^{-1}\right) - \log b$
PTE	$\log\left(\begin{bmatrix}\alpha\,\mathrm{vol}(G_{\mathrm{ww}})(D_{\mathrm{row}}^{\mathrm{ww}})^{-1}A_{\mathrm{ww}}(D_{\mathrm{col}}^{\mathrm{ww}})^{-1}\\ \beta\,\mathrm{vol}(G_{\mathrm{dw}})(D_{\mathrm{row}}^{\mathrm{dw}})^{-1}A_{\mathrm{dw}}(D_{\mathrm{col}}^{\mathrm{dw}})^{-1}\\ \gamma\,\mathrm{vol}(G_{\mathrm{lw}})(D_{\mathrm{row}}^{\mathrm{lw}})^{-1}A_{\mathrm{lw}}(D_{\mathrm{col}}^{\mathrm{lw}})^{-1}\end{bmatrix}\right) - \log b$
node2vec	$\log\left(\frac{\frac{1}{2T}\sum_{r=1}^{T}\left(\sum_u X_{w,u}\underline{P}_{c,w,u}^r + \sum_u X_{c,u}\underline{P}_{w,c,u}^r\right)}{(\sum_u X_{w,u})(\sum_u X_{c,u})}\right) - \log b$

Notations in DeepWalk and LINE are introduced below. See detailed notations for PTE and node2vec in Section 2.
A: $A \in \mathbb{R}_+^{|V|\times|V|}$ is G's adjacency matrix with $A_{i,j}$ as the edge weight between vertices i and j;
D_{col}: $D_{\mathrm{col}} = \mathrm{diag}(A^\top e)$ is the diagonal matrix with column sum of A;
D_{row}: $D_{\mathrm{row}} = \mathrm{diag}(Ae)$ is the diagonal matrix with row sum of A;
D: For undirected graphs ($A^\top = A$), $D_{\mathrm{col}} = D_{\mathrm{row}}$. For brevity, D represents both D_{col} & D_{row}. $D = \mathrm{diag}(d_1, \cdots, d_{|V|})$, where d_i represents generalized degree of vertex i;
$\mathrm{vol}(G)$: $\mathrm{vol}(G) = \sum_i \sum_j A_{i,j} = \sum_i d_i$ is the volume of a weighted graph G;
T & b: The context window size and the number of negative sampling in skip-gram, respectively.

Formally, the problem of network embedding is often formalized as follows: Given an undirected and weighted graph $G = (V, E, A)$ with V as the node set, E as the edge set and A as the adjacency matrix, the goal is to learn a function $V \to \mathbb{R}^d$ that maps each vertex to a d-dimensional ($d \ll |V|$) vector that captures its structural properties. The output representations can be used as the input of mining and learning algorithms for a variety of network science tasks, such as label classification and community detection.

The attempt to address this problem can date back to spectral graph theory [11] and social dimension learning [38]. Its very recent advances have been largely influenced by the skip-gram model originally proposed for word embedding [28, 29], whose input is a text corpus composed of sentences in natural language and output is the latent vector representation for each word in the corpus. Notably, inspired by this setting, DeepWalk [31] pioneers network embedding by considering the vertex paths traversed by random walks over networks as the sentences and leveraging skip-gram for learning latent vertex representations. With the advent of

*This work was partially done when Jiezhong was an intern at Microsoft Research.
[1]Code available at github.com/xptree/NetMF.

WSDM'18, , February 5–9, 2018, Marina Del Rey, CA, USA

ACM ISBN 978-1-4503-5581-0/18/02...$15.00
https://doi.org/10.1145/3159652.3159706

DeepWalk, many network embedding models have been developed, such as LINE [37], PTE [36], and node2vec [16].

The above models have thus far been demonstrated quite effective empirically. However, the theoretical mechanism behind them is much less well-understood. We note that the skip-gram model with negative sampling for word embedding has been shown to be an implicit factorization of a certain word-context matrix [24], and there is recent effort to theoretically explaining the word embedding models from geometric perspectives [1, 18]. But it is unclear what is the relation between the word-context matrix and the network structure. Moreover, there was an early attempt to theoretically analyze DeepWalk's behavior [47]. However, their main theoretical results are not fully consistent with the setting of the original DeepWalk paper. In addition, despite the superficial similarity among DeepWalk, LINE, PTE, and node2vec, there is a lack of deeper understanding of their underlying connections.

Contributions In this work, we provide theoretical results concerning several skip-gram powered network embedding methods. More concretely, we first show that the models we mentioned—DeepWalk, LINE, PTE, and node2vec—are in theory performing implicit matrix factorizations. We derive the closed form of the matrix for each model (see Table 1 for a summary). For example, DeepWalk (random walks on a graph + skip-gram) is in essence factorizing a random matrix that converges in probability to our closed-form matrix as the length of random walks goes to infinity.

Second, observed from their matrices' closed forms, we find that, interestingly, LINE can be seen as a special case of DeepWalk, when the window size T of contexts is set to 1 in skip-gram. Furthermore, we demonstrate that PTE, as an extension of LINE, is actually an implicit factorization of the joint matrix of multiple networks.

Third, we discover a theoretical connection between DeepWalk's implicit matrix and graph Laplacians. Based on the connection, we propose a new algorithm *NetMF* to approximate the closed form of DeepWalk's implicit matrix. By explicitly factorizing this matrix using SVD, our extensive experiments in four networks (used in the DeepWalk and node2vec approaches) demonstrate NetMF's outstanding performance (relative improvements by up to 50%) over DeepWalk and LINE.

2 THEORETICAL ANALYSIS AND PROOFS

In this section, we present the detailed theoretical analysis and proofs for four popular network embedding approaches: LINE, PTE, DeepWalk, and node2vec.

2.1 LINE and PTE

LINE [37] Given an undirected and weighted network $G = (V, E, A)$, LINE with the second order proximity (aka LINE (2nd)) aims to learn two representation matrices $X, Y \in \mathbb{R}^{|V|\times d}$, whose rows are denoted by x_i and y_i, $i = 1, \cdots, |V|$, respectively. The objective of LINE (2nd) is to maximize

$$\ell = \sum_{i=1}^{|V|}\sum_{j=1}^{|V|} A_{i,j}\left(\log g\left(x_i^\top y_j\right) + b\mathbb{E}_{j'\sim P_N}\left[\log g\left(-x_i^\top y_{j'}\right)\right]\right),$$

where g is the sigmoid function; b is the parameter for negative sampling; P_N is known as the noise distribution that generates negative samples. In LINE, the authors empirically set $P_N(j) \propto d_j^{3/4}$, where $d_j = \sum_{k=1}^{|V|} A_{j,k}$ is the generalized degree of vertex j. In our analysis, we assume $P_N(j) \propto d_j$ because the normalization factor has a closed form solution in graph theory, i.e., $P_N(j) = d_j/\mathrm{vol}(G)$, where $\mathrm{vol}(G) = \sum_{i=1}^{|V|}\sum_{j=1}^{|V|} A_{i,j}$.[2] Then we rewrite the objective as

$$\ell = \sum_{i=1}^{|V|}\sum_{j=1}^{|V|} A_{i,j}\log g\left(x_i^\top y_j\right) + b\sum_{i=1}^{|V|} d_i\mathbb{E}_{j'\sim P_N}\left[\log g\left(-x_i^\top y_{j'}\right)\right], \quad (1)$$

and express the expectation term $\mathbb{E}_{j'\sim P_N}\left[\log g\left(-x_i^\top y_{j'}\right)\right]$ as

$$\frac{d_j}{\mathrm{vol}(G)}\log g\left(-x_i^\top y_j\right) + \sum_{j'\neq j}\frac{d_{j'}}{\mathrm{vol}(G)}\log g\left(-x_i^\top y_{j'}\right). \quad (2)$$

By combining Eq. 1 and Eq. 2, and considering the local objective function for a specific pair of vertices (i, j), we have

$$\ell(i,j) = A_{i,j}\log g\left(x_i^\top y_j\right) + b\frac{d_i d_j}{\mathrm{vol}(G)}\log g\left(-x_i^\top y_j\right).$$

Let us define $z_{i,j} = x_i^\top y_j$. Following Levy and Goldberg [24], where the authors suggested that for a sufficient large embedding dimension, each individual $z_{i,j}$ can assume a value independence, we can take the derivative w.r.t. $z_{i,j}$ and get:

$$\frac{\partial \ell}{\partial z_{i,j}} = \frac{\partial \ell(i,j)}{\partial z_{i,j}} = A_{i,j}g(-z_{i,j}) - b\frac{d_i d_j}{\mathrm{vol}(G)}g(z_{i,j}).$$

Setting the derivative to be zero reveals

$$e^{2z_{i,j}} - \left(\frac{\mathrm{vol}(G)A_{i,j}}{bd_i d_j} - 1\right)e^{z_{i,j}} - \frac{\mathrm{vol}(G)A_{i,j}}{bd_i d_j} = 0.$$

The above quadratic equation has two solutions (1) $e^{z_{i,j}} = -1$, which is invalid; and (2) $e^{z_{i,j}} = \frac{\mathrm{vol}(G)A_{i,j}}{bd_i d_j}$, i.e.,

$$x_i^\top y_j = z_{i,j} = \log\left(\frac{\mathrm{vol}(G)A_{i,j}}{bd_i d_j}\right). \quad (3)$$

Writing Eq. 3 in matrix form, LINE (2nd) is factoring the matrix

$$\log\left(\mathrm{vol}(G)D^{-1}AD^{-1}\right) - \log b = XY^\top, \quad (4)$$

where $\log(\cdot)$ denotes the element-wise matrix logarithm, and $D = \mathrm{diag}(d_1, \cdots, d_{|V|})$.

PTE [36] PTE is an extension of LINE (2nd) in heterogeneous text networks. To examine it, we first adapt our analysis of LINE (2nd) to bipartite networks. Consider a bipartite network $G = (V_1 \cup V_2, E, A)$ where V_1, V_2 are two disjoint sets of vertices, $E \subseteq V_1 \times V_2$ is the edge set, and $A \in \mathbb{R}_+^{|V_1|\times|V_2|}$ is the bipartite adjacency matrix. The volume of G is defined to be $\mathrm{vol}(G) = \sum_{i=1}^{|V_1|}\sum_{j=1}^{|V_2|} A_{i,j}$. The goal is to learn a representation x_i for each vertex $v_i \in V_1$ and a representation y_j for each vertex $v_j \in V_2$. The objective function is

$$\ell = \sum_{i=1}^{|V_1|}\sum_{j=1}^{|V_2|} A_{i,j}\left(\log g\left(x_i^\top y_j\right) + b\mathbb{E}_{j'\sim P_N}\left[\log g\left(-x_i^\top y_{j'}\right)\right]\right).$$

Applying the same analysis procedure of LINE, we can see that maximizing ℓ is actually factorizing

$$\log\left(\mathrm{vol}(G)D_{\mathrm{row}}^{-1}AD_{\mathrm{col}}^{-1}\right) - \log b = XY^\top$$

where we denote $D_{\mathrm{row}} = \mathrm{diag}(Ae)$ and $D_{\mathrm{col}} = \mathrm{diag}(A^\top e)$.

Given the above discussion, let us consider the heterogeneous text network used in PTE, which is composed of three sub-networks

[2] A similar result could be achieved if we use $P_N(j) \propto d_j^{3/4}$.

– the word-word network G_{ww}, the document-word network G_{dw}, and the label-word network G_{lw}, where G_{dw} and G_{lw} are bipartite. Take the document-word network G_{dw} as an example, we use $A_{\text{dw}} \in \mathbb{R}^{\#\text{doc}\times\#\text{word}}$ to denote its adjacency matrix, and use $D_{\text{row}}^{\text{dw}}$ and $D_{\text{col}}^{\text{dw}}$ to denote its diagonal matrices with row and column sum, respectively. By leveraging the analysis of LINE and the above notations, we find that PTE is factorizing

$$\log\left(\begin{bmatrix} \alpha \operatorname{vol}(G_{\text{ww}})(D_{\text{row}}^{\text{ww}})^{-1}A_{\text{ww}}(D_{\text{col}}^{\text{ww}})^{-1} \\ \beta \operatorname{vol}(G_{\text{dw}})(D_{\text{row}}^{\text{dw}})^{-1}A_{\text{dw}}(D_{\text{col}}^{\text{dw}})^{-1} \\ \gamma \operatorname{vol}(G_{\text{lw}})(D_{\text{row}}^{\text{lw}})^{-1}A_{\text{lw}}(D_{\text{col}}^{\text{lw}})^{-1} \end{bmatrix}\right) - \log b, \tag{5}$$

where the factorized matrix is of shape (#word + #doc + #label) × #word, b is the parameter for negative sampling, and $\{\alpha, \beta, \gamma\}$ are non-negative hyper-parameters to balance the weights of the three sub-networks. In PTE, $\{\alpha, \beta, \gamma\}$ satisfy $\alpha \operatorname{vol}(G_{\text{ww}}) = \beta \operatorname{vol}(G_{\text{dw}}) = \gamma \operatorname{vol}(G_{\text{lw}})$. This is because the authors perform edge sampling during training wherein edges are sampled from each of three sub-networks alternatively (see Section 4.2 in [36]).

2.2 DeepWalk

In this section, we analyze DeepWalk [31] and illustrate the essence of DeepWalk is actually performing an implicit matrix factorization (See the matrix form solution in Thm. 2.3).

DeepWalk first generates a "corpus" $\mathcal{D}$ by random walks on graphs [26]. To be formal, the corpus $\mathcal{D}$ is a multiset that counts the multiplicity of vertex-context pairs. DeepWalk then trains a skip-gram model on the multiset $\mathcal{D}$. In this work, we focus on skip-gram with negative sampling (SGNS). For clarity, we summarize the DeepWalk method in Algorithm 1. The outer loop (Line 1-7) specifies the total number of times, N, for which we should run random walks. For each random walk of length L, the first vertex is sampled from a prior distribution $P(w)$. The inner loop (Line 4-7) specifies the construction of the multiset $\mathcal{D}$. Once we have $\mathcal{D}$, we run an SGNS to attain the network embedding (Line 8). Next, we introduce some necessary background about the SGNS technique, followed by our analysis of the DeepWalk method.

Preliminary on Skip-gram with Negative Sampling (SGNS) The skip-gram model assumes a corpus of words w and their context c. More concretely, the words come from a textual corpus of words $w_1, \cdots w_L$ and the contexts for word w_i are words surrounding it in a T-sized window $w_{i-T}, \cdots, w_{i-1}, w_{i+1}, \cdots, w_{i+T}$. Following the work by Levy and Goldberg [24], SGNS is implicitly factorizing

$$\log\left(\frac{\#(w,c)\,|\mathcal{D}|}{\#(w)\cdot\#(c)}\right) - \log b, \tag{6}$$

where $\#(w,c)$, $\#(w)$ and $\#(c)$ denote the number of times word-context pair (w, c), word w and context c appear in the corpus, respectively; b is the number of negative samples.

Proofs and Analysis Our analysis of DeepWalk is based on the following key assumptions. Firstly, assume the used graph is undirected, connected, and non-bipartite, making $P(w) = d_w/\operatorname{vol}(G)$ a unique stationary distribution of the random walks. Secondly, suppose the first vertex of a random walk is sampled from the stationary distribution $P(w) = d_w/\operatorname{vol}(G)$.

To characterize DeepWalk, we want to reinterpret Eq. 6 by using graph theory terminologies. Our general idea is to partition the multiset $\mathcal{D}$ into several sub-multisets according to the way in which

Algorithm 1: DeepWalk

1 **for** $n = 1, 2, \dots, N$ **do**
2 Pick w_1^n according to a probability distribution $P(w_1)$;
3 Generate a vertex sequence $(w_1^n, \cdots, w_L^n)$ of length L by a random walk on network G;
4 **for** $j = 1, 2, \dots, L - T$ **do**
5 **for** $r = 1, \dots, T$ **do**
6 Add vertex-context pair (w_j^n, w_{j+r}^n) to multiset $\mathcal{D}$;
7 Add vertex-context pair (w_{j+r}^n, w_j^n) to multiset $\mathcal{D}$;
8 Run SGNS on $\mathcal{D}$ with b negative samples.

vertex and its context appear in a random walk sequence. More formally, for $r = 1, \cdots, T$, we define

$$\mathcal{D}_{\overrightarrow{r}} = \left\{(w,c) : (w,c) \in \mathcal{D},\ w = w_j^n,\ c = w_{j+r}^n\right\},$$
$$\mathcal{D}_{\overleftarrow{r}} = \left\{(w,c) : (w,c) \in \mathcal{D},\ w = w_{j+r}^n,\ c = w_j^n\right\}.$$

That is, $\mathcal{D}_{\overrightarrow{r}}/\mathcal{D}_{\overleftarrow{r}}$ is the sub-multiset of $\mathcal{D}$ such that the context c is r steps after/before the vertex w in random walks. Moreover, we use $\#(w,c)_{\overrightarrow{r}}$ and $\#(w,c)_{\overleftarrow{r}}$ to denote the number of times vertex-context pair (w, c) appears in $\mathcal{D}_{\overrightarrow{r}}$ and $\mathcal{D}_{\overleftarrow{r}}$, respectively. The following three theorems characterize DeepWalk step by step.

Theorem 2.1. *Denote* $\mathbf{P} = \mathbf{D}^{-1}\mathbf{A}$, *when* $L \to \infty$, *we have*

$$\frac{\#(w,c)_{\overrightarrow{r}}}{|\mathcal{D}_{\overrightarrow{r}}|} \xrightarrow{p} \frac{d_w}{\operatorname{vol}(G)}(\mathbf{P}^r)_{w,c} \text{ and } \frac{\#(w,c)_{\overleftarrow{r}}}{|\mathcal{D}_{\overleftarrow{r}}|} \xrightarrow{p} \frac{d_c}{\operatorname{vol}(G)}(\mathbf{P}^r)_{c,w}.$$

Proof. See Appendix. □

Remark 1. *What if we start random walks with other distributions (e.g., the uniform distribution in the original DeepWalk work [31])? It turns out that, for a connected, undirected, and non-bipartite graph,* $P(w_j = w, w_{j+r} = c) \to \frac{d_w}{\operatorname{vol}(G)}(\mathbf{P}^r)_{w,c}$ *as* $j \to \infty$. *So when the length of random walks* $L \to \infty$, *Thm. 2.1 still holds.*

Theorem 2.2. *When* $L \to \infty$, *we have*

$$\frac{\#(w,c)}{|\mathcal{D}|} \xrightarrow{p} \frac{1}{2T}\sum_{r=1}^{T}\left(\frac{d_w}{\operatorname{vol}(G)}(\mathbf{P}^r)_{w,c} + \frac{d_c}{\operatorname{vol}(G)}(\mathbf{P}^r)_{c,w}\right).$$

Proof. Note the fact that $\frac{|\mathcal{D}_{\overrightarrow{r}}|}{|\mathcal{D}|} = \frac{|\mathcal{D}_{\overleftarrow{r}}|}{|\mathcal{D}|} = \frac{1}{2T}$. By using Thm. 2.1 and the continuous mapping theorem, we get

$$\frac{\#(w,c)}{|\mathcal{D}|} = \frac{\sum_{r=1}^{T}\left(\#(w,c)_{\overrightarrow{r}} + \#(w,c)_{\overleftarrow{r}}\right)}{\sum_{r=1}^{T}\left(|\mathcal{D}_{\overrightarrow{r}}| + |\mathcal{D}_{\overleftarrow{r}}|\right)} = \frac{1}{2T}\sum_{r=1}^{T}\left(\frac{\#(w,c)_{\overrightarrow{r}}}{|\mathcal{D}_{\overrightarrow{r}}|} + \frac{\#(w,c)_{\overleftarrow{r}}}{|\mathcal{D}_{\overleftarrow{r}}|}\right)$$
$$\xrightarrow{p} \frac{1}{2T}\sum_{r=1}^{T}\left(\frac{d_w}{\operatorname{vol}(G)}(\mathbf{P}^r)_{w,c} + \frac{d_c}{\operatorname{vol}(G)}(\mathbf{P}^r)_{c,w}\right).$$

Further, marginalizing w and c respectively reveals the fact that $\frac{\#(w)}{|\mathcal{D}|} \xrightarrow{p} \frac{d_w}{\operatorname{vol}(G)}$ and $\frac{\#(c)}{|\mathcal{D}|} \xrightarrow{p} \frac{d_c}{\operatorname{vol}(G)}$, as $L \to \infty$. □

Theorem 2.3. *For DeepWalk, when* $L \to \infty$,

$$\frac{\#(w,c)\,|\mathcal{D}|}{\#(w)\cdot\#(c)} \xrightarrow{p} \frac{\operatorname{vol}(G)}{2T}\left(\frac{1}{d_c}\sum_{r=1}^{T}(\mathbf{P}^r)_{w,c} + \frac{1}{d_w}\sum_{r=1}^{T}(\mathbf{P}^r)_{c,w}\right).$$

In matrix form, DeepWalk is equivalent to factorize

$$\log\left(\frac{\operatorname{vol}(G)}{T}\left(\sum_{r=1}^{T} \boldsymbol{P}^r\right)\boldsymbol{D}^{-1}\right) - \log(b). \tag{7}$$

Proof. Using the results in Thm. 2.2 and the continuous mapping theorem, we get

$$\frac{\#(w,c)\,|\mathcal{D}|}{\#(w)\cdot\#(c)} = \frac{\frac{\#(w,c)}{|\mathcal{D}|}}{\frac{\#(w)}{|\mathcal{D}|}\cdot\frac{\#(c)}{|\mathcal{D}|}} \xrightarrow{p} \frac{\frac{1}{2T}\sum_{r=1}^{T}\left(\frac{d_w}{\operatorname{vol}(G)}(\boldsymbol{P}^r)_{w,c} + \frac{d_c}{\operatorname{vol}(G)}(\boldsymbol{P}^r)_{c,w}\right)}{\frac{d_w}{\operatorname{vol}(G)}\cdot\frac{d_c}{\operatorname{vol}(G)}}$$

$$= \frac{\operatorname{vol}(G)}{2T}\left(\frac{1}{d_c}\sum_{r=1}^{T}(\boldsymbol{P}^r)_{w,c} + \frac{1}{d_w}\sum_{r=1}^{T}(\boldsymbol{P}^r)_{c,w}\right).$$

Write it in matrix form:

$$\frac{\operatorname{vol}(G)}{2T}\left(\sum_{r=1}^{T}\boldsymbol{P}^r\boldsymbol{D}^{-1} + \sum_{r=1}^{T}\boldsymbol{D}^{-1}(\boldsymbol{P}^r)^\top\right)$$

$$= \frac{\operatorname{vol}(G)}{2T}\left(\sum_{r=1}^{T}\underbrace{\boldsymbol{D}^{-1}\boldsymbol{A}\times\cdots\times\boldsymbol{D}^{-1}\boldsymbol{A}}_{r\text{ terms}}\boldsymbol{D}^{-1} + \sum_{r=1}^{T}\boldsymbol{D}^{-1}\underbrace{\boldsymbol{A}\boldsymbol{D}^{-1}\times\cdots\times\boldsymbol{A}\boldsymbol{D}^{-1}}_{r\text{ terms}}\right)$$

$$= \frac{\operatorname{vol}(G)}{T}\sum_{r=1}^{T}\underbrace{\boldsymbol{D}^{-1}\boldsymbol{A}\times\cdots\times\boldsymbol{D}^{-1}\boldsymbol{A}}_{r\text{ terms}}\boldsymbol{D}^{-1} = \operatorname{vol}(G)\left(\frac{1}{T}\sum_{r=1}^{T}\boldsymbol{P}^r\right)\boldsymbol{D}^{-1}.$$

□

Corollary 2.4. *Comparing Eq. 4 and Eq. 7, we can easily observe that LINE (2nd) is a special case of DeepWalk when $T = 1$.*

2.3 node2vec

node2vec [16] is a recently proposed network embedding method, which is briefly summarized in Algorithm 2. First, it defines an unnormalized transition probability tensor $\underline{\boldsymbol{T}}$ with parameters p and q, and then normalizes it to be the transition probability of a 2nd-order random walk (Line 1). Formally,

$$\underline{\boldsymbol{T}}_{u,v,w} = \begin{cases} \frac{1}{p} & (u,v)\in E,\ (v,w)\in E,\ u = w; \\ 1 & (u,v)\in E,\ (v,w)\in E,\ u \neq w,\ (w,u)\in E; \\ \frac{1}{q} & (u,v)\in E,\ (v,w)\in E,\ u\neq w,\ (w,u)\notin E; \\ 0 & \text{otherwise.}\end{cases}$$

$$\underline{\boldsymbol{P}}_{u,v,w} = \operatorname{Prob}\left(w_{j+1} = u \mid w_j = v,\ w_{j-1} = w\right) = \frac{\underline{\boldsymbol{T}}_{u,v,w}}{\sum_u \underline{\boldsymbol{T}}_{u,v,w}}.$$

Second, node2vec performs the 2nd-order random walks to generate a multiset $\mathcal{D}$ (Line 2-8) and then trains an SGNS model (Line 9) on it. To facilitate the analysis, we instead record triplets to form the multiset $\mathcal{D}$ for node2vec rather than vertex-context pairs. Take a vertex $w = w_j^n$ and its context $c = w_{j+r}^n$ as an example, we denote $u = w_{j-1}^n$ and add a triplet (w, c, u) into $\mathcal{D}$ (Line 7). Similar to our analysis of DeepWalk, we partition the multiset $\mathcal{D}$ according to the way in which the vertex and its context appear in a random walk sequence. More formally, for $r = 1, \cdots, T$, we define

$$\mathcal{D}_{\vec{r}} = \left\{(w,c,u) : (w,c,u)\in\mathcal{D},\ w_j^n = w,\ w_{j+r}^n = c,\ w_{j-1}^n = u\right\},$$

$$\mathcal{D}_{\overleftarrow{r}} = \left\{(w,c,u) : (w,c,u)\in\mathcal{D},\ w_{j+r}^n = w,\ w_j^n = c,\ w_{j-1}^n = u\right\}.$$

In addition, for a triplet (w, c, u), we use $\#(w,c,u)_{\vec{r}}$ and $\#(w,c,u)_{\overleftarrow{r}}$ to denote the number of times it appears in $\mathcal{D}_{\vec{r}}$ and $\mathcal{D}_{\overleftarrow{r}}$, respectively.

Algorithm 2: node2vec

1 Construct transition probability tensor $\underline{\boldsymbol{P}}$;
2 **for** $n = 1, 2, \ldots, N$ **do**
3 Pick w_1^n, w_2^n according to a distribution $P(w_1, w_2)$;
4 Generate a vertex sequence $(w_1^n, \cdots, w_L^n)$ of length L by the 2nd-order random walk on network G;
5 **for** $j = 2, 3, \ldots, L - T$ **do**
6 **for** $r = 1, \ldots, T$ **do**
7 Add triplet $(w_j^n, w_{j+r}^n, w_{j-1}^n)$ to multiset $\mathcal{D}$;
8 Add triplet $(w_{j+r}^n, w_j^n, w_{j-1}^n)$ to multiset $\mathcal{D}$;
9 Run SGNS on multiset $\mathcal{D}' = \{(w,c) : (w,c,u)\in\mathcal{D}\}$;

In this analysis, we assume the first two vertices of node2vec's 2nd-order random walk are sampled from its stationary distribution $\boldsymbol{X}$. The stationary distribution $\boldsymbol{X}$ of the 2nd-order random walk satisfies $\sum_w \underline{\boldsymbol{P}}_{u,v,w}\boldsymbol{X}_{v,w} = \boldsymbol{X}_{u,v}$, and the existence of such $\boldsymbol{X}$ is guaranteed by the Perron-Frobenius theorem [4]. Additionally, the higher-order transition probability tensor is defined to be $(\underline{\boldsymbol{P}}^r)_{u,v,w} = \operatorname{Prob}\left(w_{j+r} = u \mid w_j = v, w_{j-1} = w\right)$.

Main Results Limited by space, we list the main results of node2vec without proofs. The idea is similar to the analysis of DeepWalk.

- $\frac{\#(w,c,u)_{\vec{r}}}{|\mathcal{D}_{\vec{r}}|} \xrightarrow{p} \boldsymbol{X}_{w,u}(\underline{\boldsymbol{P}}^r)_{c,w,u}$ and $\frac{\#(w,c,u)_{\overleftarrow{r}}}{|\mathcal{D}_{\overleftarrow{r}}|} \xrightarrow{p} \boldsymbol{X}_{c,u}(\underline{\boldsymbol{P}}^r)_{w,c,u}$.
- $\frac{\#(w,c)_{\vec{r}}}{|\mathcal{D}_{\vec{r}}|} = \frac{\sum_u \#(w,c,u)_{\vec{r}}}{|\mathcal{D}_{\vec{r}}|} \xrightarrow{p} \sum_u \boldsymbol{X}_{w,u}(\underline{\boldsymbol{P}}^r)_{c,w,u}$.
- $\frac{\#(w,c)_{\overleftarrow{r}}}{|\mathcal{D}_{\overleftarrow{r}}|} = \frac{\sum_u \#(w,c,u)_{\overleftarrow{r}}}{|\mathcal{D}_{\overleftarrow{r}}|} \xrightarrow{p} \sum_u \boldsymbol{X}_{c,u}(\underline{\boldsymbol{P}}^r)_{w,c,u}$.
- $\frac{\#(w,c)}{|\mathcal{D}|} \xrightarrow{p} \frac{1}{2T}\sum_{r=1}^{T}\left(\sum_u \boldsymbol{X}_{w,u}(\underline{\boldsymbol{P}}^r)_{c,w,u} + \sum_u \boldsymbol{X}_{c,u}(\underline{\boldsymbol{P}}^r)_{w,c,u}\right)$.
- $\frac{\#(w)}{|\mathcal{D}|} \xrightarrow{p} \sum_u \boldsymbol{X}_{w,u}$ and $\frac{\#(c)}{|\mathcal{D}|} \xrightarrow{p} \sum_u \boldsymbol{X}_{c,u}$.

Combining all together, we conclude that, for node2vec, Eq. 6 has the form

$$\frac{\#(w,c)\,|\mathcal{D}|}{\#(w)\cdot\#(c)} \xrightarrow{p} \frac{\frac{1}{2T}\sum_{r=1}^{T}\left(\sum_u \boldsymbol{X}_{w,u}\underline{\boldsymbol{P}}^r_{c,w,u} + \sum_u \boldsymbol{X}_{c,u}\underline{\boldsymbol{P}}^r_{w,c,u}\right)}{\left(\sum_u \boldsymbol{X}_{w,u}\right)\left(\sum_u \boldsymbol{X}_{c,u}\right)}. \tag{8}$$

Though the closed form for node2vec has been achieved, we leave the formulation of its matrix form for future research.

Note that both the computation and storage of the transition probability tensor $\underline{\boldsymbol{P}}^r$ and its corresponding stationary distribution $\boldsymbol{X}$ are very expensive, making the modeling of the full 2nd-order dynamics difficult. However, we have noticed some recent progresses [3, 4, 15] that try to understand or approximate the 2nd-order random walk by assuming a rank-one factorization $\boldsymbol{X}_{u,v} = \boldsymbol{x}_u\boldsymbol{x}_v$ for its stationary distribution $\boldsymbol{X}$. Due to the page limitation, in the rest of this paper, we mainly focus on the matrix factorization framework depending on the 1st-order random walk (DeepWalk).

3 NetMF: NETWORK EMBEDDING AS MATRIX FACTORIZATION

Based on the analysis in Section 2, we unify LINE, PTE, DeepWalk, and node2vec in the framework of matrix factorization, where the factorized matrices have closed forms as showed in Eq. 4, Eq. 5, Eq. 7, and Eq. 8, respectively. In this section, we study the DeepWalk matrix (Eq. 7) because it is more general than the LINE matrix and computationally more efficient than the node2vec matrix. We first discuss the connection between the DeepWalk matrix and graph Laplacian in Section 3.1. Then in Section 3.2, we present a matrix factorization based framework—NetMF—for network embedding.

3.1 Connection between DeepWalk Matrix and Normalized Graph Laplacian

In this section, we show that the DeepWalk matrix has a close relationship with the normalized graph Laplacian. To facilitate our analysis, we introduce the following four theorems.

THEOREM 3.1. *([11]) For normalized graph Laplacian* $\mathcal{L} = I - D^{-1/2}AD^{-1/2} \in \mathbb{R}^{n\times n}$, *all its eigenvalues are real numbers and lie in* $[0,2]$, *with* $\lambda_{\min}(\mathcal{L}) = 0$. *For a connected graph with* $n > 1$, $\lambda_{\max}(\mathcal{L}) \geq n/(n-1)$.

THEOREM 3.2. *([41]) Singular values of a real symmetric matrix are the absolute values of its eigenvalues.*

THEOREM 3.3. *([19]) Let* B, C *be two* $n \times n$ *symmetric matrices. Then for the decreasingly ordered singular values* σ *of* B, C *and* BC, $\sigma_{i+j-1}(BC) \leq \sigma_i(B) \times \sigma_j(C)$ *holds for any* $1 \leq i, j \leq n$ *and* $i+j \leq n+1$.

THEOREM 3.4. *([41]) For a real symmetric matrix A, its Rayleigh Quotient* $R(A,x) = (x^\top Ax)/(x^\top x)$ *satisfies* $\lambda_{\min}(A) = \min_{x\neq 0} R(A,x)$ *and* $\lambda_{\max}(A) = \max_{x\neq 0} R(A,x)$.

By ignoring the element-wise matrix logarithm and the constant term in Eq. 7, we focus on studying the matrix $\left(\frac{1}{T}\sum_{r=1}^{T} P^r\right) D^{-1}$. By Thm. 3.1, $D^{-1/2}AD^{-1/2} = I - \mathcal{L}$ has eigen-decomposition $U\Lambda U^\top$ such that U orthonormal and $\Lambda = \operatorname{diag}(\lambda_1, \cdots, \lambda_n)$, where $1 = \lambda_1 \geq \lambda_2 \geq \cdots \geq \lambda_n \geq -1$ and $\lambda_n < 0$. Based on this eigen-decomposition, $\left(\frac{1}{T}\sum_{r=1}^{T} P^r\right) D^{-1}$ can be decomposed to be the product of there symmetric matrices:

$$\left(\frac{1}{T}\sum_{r=1}^{T} P^r\right) D^{-1} = \left(D^{-1/2}\right)\left(U\left(\frac{1}{T}\sum_{r=1}^{T}\Lambda^r\right)U^\top\right)\left(D^{-1/2}\right). \quad (9)$$

The goal here is to characterize the spectrum of $\left(\frac{1}{T}\sum_{r=1}^{T} P^r\right) D^{-1}$. To achieve this, we first analyze the second matrix at RHS of Eq. 9, and then extend our analysis to the targeted matrix at LHS.

Spectrum of $U\left(\frac{1}{T}\sum_{r=1}^{T}\Lambda^r\right)U^\top$ The matrix $U\left(\frac{1}{T}\sum_{r=1}^{T}\Lambda^r\right)U^\top$ has eigenvalues $\frac{1}{T}\sum_{r=1}^{T}\lambda_i^r, i = 1, \cdots, n$, which can be treated as the output of a transformation applied on $D^{-1/2}AD^{-1/2}$'s eigenvalue λ_i, i.e., a kind of filter! The effect of this transformation (filter) $f(x) = \frac{1}{T}\sum_{r=1}^{T} x^r$ is plotted in Figure 1(a), from which we observe the following two properties of this filter. Firstly, it prefers positive large eigenvalues; Secondly, the preference becomes stronger as the window size T increases. In other words, as T grows, this filter tries to approximate a low-rank positive semi-definite matrix by keeping large positive eigenvalues.

Spectrum of $\left(\frac{1}{T}\sum_{r=1}^{T} P^r\right) D^{-1}$ Guided by Thm. 3.2, the decreasingly ordered singular values of the matrix $U\left(\frac{1}{T}\sum_{r=1}^{T}\Lambda^r\right)U^\top$ can be constructed by sorting the absolute value of its eigenvalues in

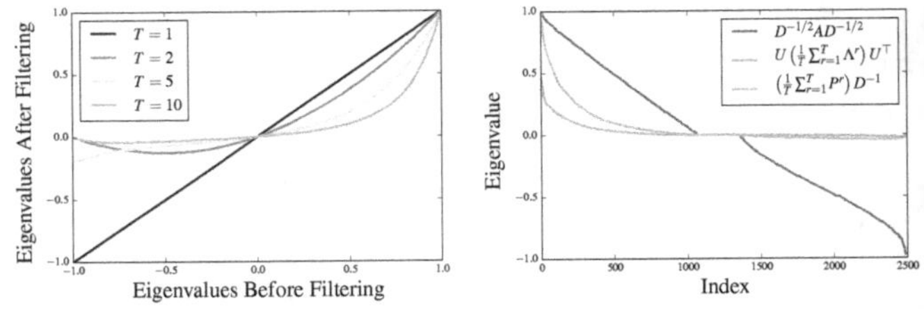

(a) (b)

Figure 1: DeepWalk Matrix as Filtering: (a) Function $f(x) = \frac{1}{T}\sum_{r=1}^{T} x^r$ **with** $\operatorname{dom} f = [-1, 1]$, **where** $T \in \{1, 2, 5, 10\}$; **(b) Eigenvalues of** $D^{-1/2}AD^{-1/2}$, $U\left(\frac{1}{T}\sum_{r=1}^{T}\Lambda^r\right)U^\top$, **and** $\left(\frac{1}{T}\sum_{r=1}^{T} P^r\right) D^{-1}$ **for Cora network** ($T = 10$).

the non-increasing order such that

$$\left|\frac{1}{T}\sum_{r=1}^{T}\lambda_{p_1}^r\right| \geq \left|\frac{1}{T}\sum_{r=1}^{T}\lambda_{p_2}^r\right| \geq \cdots \geq \left|\frac{1}{T}\sum_{r=1}^{T}\lambda_{p_n}^r\right|,$$

where $\{p_1, p_2, \cdots, p_n\}$ is a permutation of $\{1, 2, \cdots, n\}$. Similarly, since every d_i is positive, the decreasingly ordered singular values of the matrix $D^{-1/2}$ can be constructed by sorting $1/\sqrt{d_i}$ in the non-increasing order such that $1/\sqrt{d_{q_1}} \geq 1/\sqrt{d_{q_2}} \geq \cdots \geq 1/\sqrt{d_{q_n}}$ where $\{q_1, q_2, \cdots, q_n\}$ is a permutation of $\{1, 2, \cdots, n\}$. In particular, $d_{q_1} = d_{\min}$ is the smallest vertex degree. By applying Thm. 3.3 twice, we can see that the s-th singular value satisfies

$$\sigma_s\left(\left(\frac{1}{T}\sum_{r=1}^{T} P^r\right) D^{-1}\right) \leq \sigma_1\left(D^{-\frac{1}{2}}\right)\sigma_s\left(U\left(\frac{1}{T}\sum_{r=1}^{T}\Lambda^r\right)U^\top\right)\sigma_1\left(D^{-\frac{1}{2}}\right)$$
$$= \frac{1}{\sqrt{d_{q_1}}}\left|\frac{1}{T}\sum_{r=1}^{T}\lambda_{p_s}^r\right|\frac{1}{\sqrt{d_{q_1}}} = \frac{1}{d_{\min}}\left|\frac{1}{T}\sum_{r=1}^{T}\lambda_{p_s}^r\right|, \quad (10)$$

which reveals that the magnitude of $\left(\frac{1}{T}\sum_{r=1}^{T} P^r\right) D^{-1}$'s eigenvalues is always bounded by the magnitude of $U\left(\frac{1}{T}\sum_{r=1}^{T}\Lambda^r\right)U^\top$'s eigenvalues. In addition to the magnitude of eigenvalues, we also want to bound its smallest eigenvalue. Observe that the Rayleigh Quotient of $\left(\frac{1}{T}\sum_{r=1}^{T} P^r\right) D^{-1}$ has a lower bound as follows

$$R\left(\left(\frac{1}{T}\sum_{r=1}^{T} P^r\right) D^{-1}, x\right) = R\left(U\left(\frac{1}{T}\sum_{r=1}^{T}\Lambda^r\right)U^\top, D^{-1/2}x\right) R\left(D^{-1}, x\right)$$
$$\geq \lambda_{\min}\left(U\left(\frac{1}{T}\sum_{r=1}^{T}\Lambda^r\right)U^\top\right)\lambda_{\max}\left(D^{-1}\right) = \frac{1}{d_{\min}}\lambda_{\min}\left(U\left(\frac{1}{T}\sum_{r=1}^{T}\Lambda^r\right)U^\top\right).$$

By applying Thm. 3.4, we can bound the smallest eigenvalue of $\left(\frac{1}{T}\sum_{r=1}^{T} P^r\right) D^{-1}$ by the smallest eigenvalue of $U\left(\frac{1}{T}\sum_{r=1}^{T}\Lambda^r\right)U^\top$:

$$\lambda_{\min}\left(\left(\frac{1}{T}\sum_{r=1}^{T} P^r\right) D^{-1}\right) \geq \frac{1}{d_{\min}}\lambda_{\min}\left(U\left(\frac{1}{T}\sum_{r=1}^{T}\Lambda^r\right)U^\top\right).$$

Illustrative Example: Cora In order to illustrate the filtering effect we discuss above, we analyze a small citation network Cora [27]. we make the citation links undirected and choose its largest connected component. In Figure 1(b), we plot the decreasingly ordered eigenvalues of matrices $D^{-1/2}AD^{-1/2}$, $U\left(\frac{1}{T}\sum_{r=1}^{T}\Lambda^r\right)U^\top$,

Algorithm 3: NetMF for a Small Window Size T

1 Compute $P^1, \cdots, P^T$;
2 Compute $M = \frac{\text{vol}(G)}{bT}\left(\sum_{r=1}^{T} P^r\right) D^{-1}$;
3 Compute $M' = \max(M, 1)$;
4 Rank-d approximation by SVD: $\log M' = U_d \Sigma_d V_d^\top$;
5 **return** $U_d\sqrt{\Sigma_d}$ as network embedding.

Algorithm 4: NetMF for a Large Window Size T

1 Eigen-decomposition $D^{-1/2}AD^{-1/2} \approx U_h \Lambda_h U_h^\top$;
2 Approximate M with
$\hat{M} = \frac{\text{vol}(G)}{b} D^{-1/2} U_h \left(\frac{1}{T}\sum_{r=1}^{T} \Lambda_h^r\right) U_h^\top D^{-1/2}$;
3 Compute $\hat{M}' = \max(\hat{M}, 1)$;
4 Rank-d approximation by SVD: $\log \hat{M}' = U_d \Sigma_d V_d^\top$;
5 **return** $U_d\sqrt{\Sigma_d}$ as network embedding.

and $\left(\frac{1}{T}\sum_{r=1}^{T} P^r\right) D^{-1}$, respectively, with $T = 10$. For $D^{-1/2}AD^{-1/2}$, the largest eigenvalue $\lambda_1 = 1$, and the smallest eigenvalue $\lambda_n = -0.971$. For $U\left(\frac{1}{T}\sum_{r=1}^{T} \Lambda^r\right) U^\top$, we observe that all its negative eigenvalues and small positive eigenvalues are "filtered out" in spectrum. Finally, for the matrix $\left(\frac{1}{T}\sum_{r=1}^{T} P^r\right) D^{-1}$, we observe that both the magnitude of its eigenvalues and its smallest eigenvalue are bounded by those of $U\left(\frac{1}{T}\sum_{r=1}^{T} \Lambda^r\right) U^\top$.

3.2 NetMF

Built upon the theoretical analysis above, we propose a matrix factorization framework NetMF for empirical understanding of and improving on DeepWalk and LINE. For simplicity, we denote $M = \frac{\text{vol}(G)}{bT}\left(\sum_{r=1}^{T} P^r\right) D^{-1}$, and refer to $\log M$ as the DeepWalk matrix.

NetMF for a Small Window Size T NetMF for a small T is quite intuitive. The basic idea is to directly compute and factorize the DeepWalk matrix. The detail is listed in Algorithm 3. In the first step (Line 1-2), we compute the matrix power from P^1 to P^T and then get M. However, the factorization of $\log M$ presents computational challenges due to the element-wise matrix logarithm. The matrix is not only ill-defined (since $\log 0 = -\infty$), but also dense. Inspired by the *Shifted* PPMI approach [24], we define M' such that $M'_{i,j} = \max(M_{i,j}, 1)$ (Line 3). In this way, $\log M'$ is a sparse and consistent version of $\log M$. Finally, we factorize $\log M'$ by using Singular Value Decomposition (SVD) and construct network embedding by using its top-d singular values/vectors (Line 4-5).

NetMF for a Large Window Size T The direct computation of the matrix M presents computing challenges for a large window size T, mainly due to its high time complexity. Hereby we propose an approximation algorithm as listed in Algorithm 4. The general idea comes from our analysis in section 3.1, wherein we reveal M's close relationship with the normalized graph Laplacian and show its low-rank nature theoretically. In our algorithm, we first approximate $D^{-1/2}AD^{-1/2}$ with its top-h eigenpairs $U_h \Lambda_h U_h^\top$ (Line 1). Since only the top-h eigenpairs are required and the involved matrix is sparse, we can use Arnoldi method [22] to achieve significant time reduction. In step two (Line 2), we approximate M with $\hat{M} = \frac{\text{vol}(G)}{b} D^{-1/2} U_h \left(\frac{1}{T}\sum_{r=1}^{T} \Lambda_h^r\right) U_h^\top D^{-1/2}$. The final step is the same as that in Algorithm 3, in which we form $\hat{M}' = \max(\hat{M}, 1)$ (Line 3) and then perform SVD on $\log \hat{M}'$ to get network embedding (Line 4-5).

For NetMF with large window sizes, we develop the following error bound theorem for the approximation of M and the approximation of $\log M'$.

Theorem 3.5. *Let* $\|\cdot\|_F$ *be the matrix Frobenius norm. Then*

$$\left\|M - \hat{M}\right\|_F \le \frac{\text{vol}(G)}{b d_{\min}} \sqrt{\sum_{j=k+1}^{n} \left|\frac{1}{T}\sum_{r=1}^{T} \lambda_j^r\right|^2};$$

$$\left\|\log M' - \log \hat{M}'\right\|_F \le \left\|M' - \hat{M}'\right\|_F \le \left\|M - \hat{M}\right\|_F.$$

Proof. See Appendix. □

Thm. 3.5 reveals that the error for approximating $\log M'$ is bounded by the error bound for the approximation of M. Nevertheless, the major drawback of NetMF lies in this element-wise matrix logarithm. Since good tools are currently not available to analyze this operator, we have to compute it explicitly even after we have already achieved a good low-rank approximation of M.

Table 2: Statistics of Datasets.

Dataset	BlogCatalog	PPI	Wikipedia	Flickr
$\|V\|$	10,312	3,890	4,777	80,513
$\|E\|$	333,983	76,584	184,812	5,899,882
#Labels	39	50	40	195

4 EXPERIMENTS

In this section, we evaluate the proposed NetMF method on the multi-label vertex classification task, which has also been used in the works of DeepWalk, LINE, and node2vec.

Datasets We employ four widely-used datasets for this task. The statistics of these datasets are listed in Table 2.

BlogCatalog [38] is a network of social relationships of online bloggers. The vertex labels represent interests of the bloggers.

Protein-Protein Interactions (PPI) [35] is a subgraph of the PPI network for Homo Sapiens. The labels are obtained from the hallmark gene sets and represent biological states.

Wikipedia[3] is a co-occurrence network of words appearing in the first million bytes of the Wikipedia dump. The labels are the Part-of-Speech (POS) tags inferred by Stanford POS-Tagger [40].

Flickr [38] is the user contact network in Flickr. The labels represent the interest groups of the users.

Baseline Methods We compare our methods NetMF ($T = 1$) and NetMF ($T = 10$) with LINE (2nd) [37] and DeepWalk [31], which we have introduced in previous sections. For NetMF ($T = 10$), we choose $h = 1024$ for Flickr, and $h = 256$ for BlogCatelog, PPI, and

[3]http://mattmahoney.net/dc/text.html

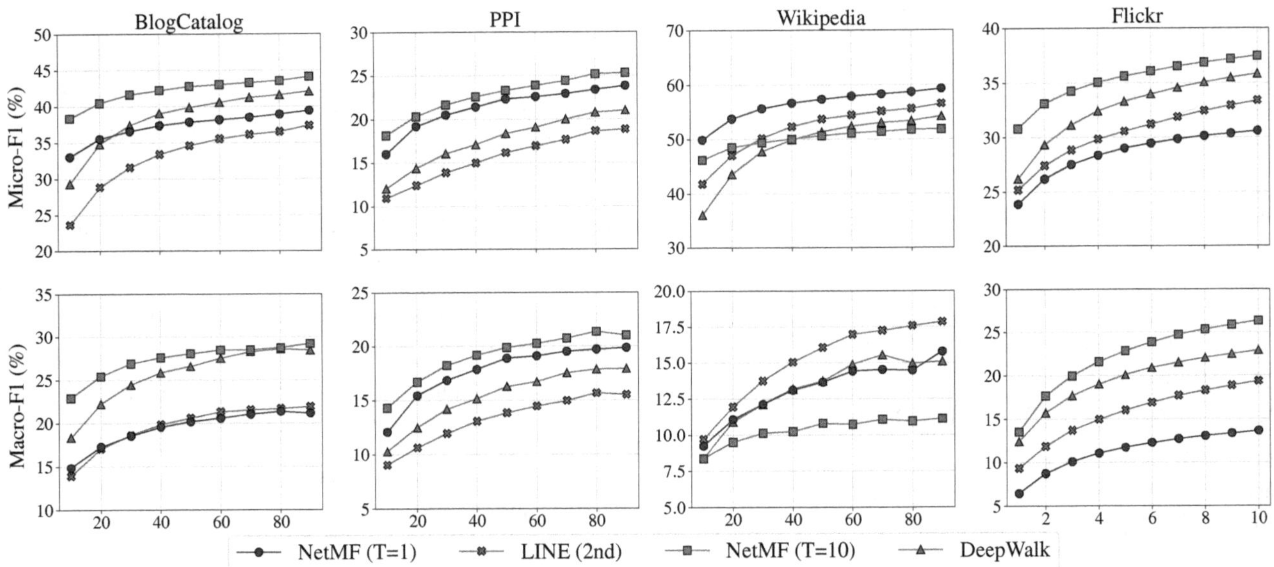

Figure 2: Predictive performance on varying the ratio of training data. The x-axis represents the ratio of labeled data (%), and the y-axis in the top and bottom rows denote the Micro-F1 and Macro-F1 scores respectively.

Wikipedia. For DeepWalk, we present its results with the authors' preferred parameters—window size 10, walk length 40, and the number of walks starting from each vertex to be 80. Finally, we set embedding dimension to be 128 for all methods.

Prediction Setting Following the same experimental procedure in DeepWalk [31], we randomly sample a portion of labeled vertices for training and use the rest for testing. For BlogCatalog, PPI, and Wikipedia datasets, the training ratio is varied from 10% to 90%. For Flickr, the training ratio is varied from 1% to 10%. We use the one-vs-rest logistic regression model implemented by LIBLINEAR [14] for the multi-label classification task. In the test phase, the one-vs-rest model yields a ranking of labels rather than an exact label assignment. To avoid the thresholding effect [39], we assume that the number of labels for test data is given [31, 39]. We repeat the prediction procedure 10 times and evaluate the performance in terms of average Micro-F1 and average Macro-F1 [42].

Experimental Results Figure 2 summarizes the prediction performance of all methods on the four datasets and Table 3 lists the quantitative and relative gaps between our methods and baselines. In specific, we show NetMF ($T = 1$)'s relative performance gain over LINE (2nd) and NetMF ($T = 10$)'s relative improvements over DeepWalk, respectively, as each pair of them share the same window size T. We have the following key observations and insights:

(1) In BlogCatalog, PPI, and Flickr, the proposed NetMF method ($T = 10$) achieves significantly better predictive performance over baseline approaches as measured by both Micro-F1 and Macro-F1, demonstrating the effectiveness of the theoretical foundation we lay out for network embedding.

(2) In Wikipedia, NetMF ($T = 1$) shows better performance than other methods in terms of Micro-F1, while LINE outperforms other methods regarding Macro-F1. This observation implies that short-term dependence is enough to model Wikipedia's network structure. This is because the used Wikipedia network is a dense word co-occurrence network with the average degree = 77.11, in which an edge between a pair of words are connected if they co-occur in a two-length window in the Wikipedia corpus.

(3) As shown in Table 3, the proposed NetMF method ($T = 10$ and $T = 1$) outperforms DeepWalk and LINE by large margins in most cases when sparsely labeled vertices are provided. Take the PPI dataset with 10% training data as an example, NetMF ($T = 1$) achieves relatively 46.34% and 33.85% gains over LINE (2nd) regarding Micro-F1 and Macro-F1 scores, respectively; More impressively, NetMF ($T = 10$) outperforms DeepWalk by 50.71% and 39.16% relatively as measured by two metrics.

(4) DeepWalk tries to approximate the exact vertex-context joint distribution with an empirical distribution through random walk sampling. Although the convergence is guaranteed by the law of large numbers, there still exist gaps between the exact and estimated distributions due to the large size of real-world networks and the relatively limited scale of random walks in practice (e.g., #walks and the walk length), negatively affecting DeepWalk's performance.

5 RELATED WORK

The story of network embedding stems from Spectral Clustering [5, 45], a data clustering technique which selects eigenvalues/eigenvectors of a data affinity matrix to obtain representations that can be clustered or embedded in a low-dimensional space. Spectral Clustering has been widely used in fields such as community detection [23] and image segmentation [33]. In recent years, there is an increasing interest in network embedding. Following a few pioneer works such as SocDim [38] and DeepWalk [31], a growing number of literature has tried to address the problem from various of perspectives, such as heterogeneous network embedding [8, 12, 20, 36], semi-supervised network embedding [17, 21, 44, 48], network embedding with rich vertex attributes [43, 47, 49], network embedding

Table 3: Micro/Macro-F1 Score(%) for Multilabel Classification on BlogCatalog, PPI, Wikipedia, and Flickr datasets. In Flickr, 1% of vertices are labeled for training [31], and in the other three datasets, 10% of vertices are labeled for training.

Algorithm	BlogCatalog (10%)		PPI (10%)		Wikipeida (10%)		Flickr (1%)	
	Micro-F1	Macro-F1	Micro-F1	Macro-F1	Micro-F1	Macro-F1	Micro-F1	Macro-F1
LINE (2nd)	23.64	13.91	10.94	9.04	41.77	**9.72**	25.18	9.32
NetMF ($T = 1$)	33.04	14.86	16.01	12.10	**49.90**	9.25	23.87	6.44
Relative Gain of NetMF ($T = 1$)	39.76	6.83%	46.34%	33.85%	19.46%	-4.84%	-5.20%	-30.90%
DeepWalk	29.32	18.38	12.05	10.29	36.08	8.38	26.21	12.43
NetMF ($T = 10$)	**38.36**	**22.90**	**18.16**	**14.32**	46.21	8.38	**30.80**	**13.54**
Relative Gain of NetMF ($T = 10$)	30.83%	24.59%	50.71%	39.16%	28.08%	0.00%	17.51%	8.93%

with high order structure [6, 16], signed network embedding [10], direct network embedding [30], network embedding via deep neural network [7, 25, 46], etc.

Among the above research, a commonly used technique is to define the "context" for each vertex, and then to train a predictive model to perform context prediction. For example, DeepWalk [31], node2vec [16], and metapath2vec [12] define vertices' context by the 1st-, 2nd-order, and meta-path based random walks, respectively; The idea of leveraging the context information are largely motivated by the skip-gram model with negative sampling (SGNS) [29]. Recently, there has been effort in understanding this model. For example, Levy and Goldberg [24] prove that SGNS is actually conducting an implicit matrix factorization, which provides us with a tool to analyze the above network embedding models; Arora et al. [1] propose a generative model RAND-WALK to explain word embedding models; and Hashimoto et al. [18] frame word embedding as a metric learning problem. Built upon the work in [24], we theoretically analyze popular skip-gram based network embedding models and connect them with spectral graph theory.

6 CONCLUSION

In this work, we provide a theoretical analysis of four impactful network embedding methods—DeepWalk, LINE, PTE, and node2vec—that were recently proposed between the years 2014 and 2016. We show that all of the four methods are essentially performing implicit matrix factorizations and the closed forms of their matrices offer not only the relationships between those methods but also their intrinsic connections with graph Laplacian. We further propose NetMF—a general framework to explicitly factorize the closed-form matrices that DeepWalk and LINE aim to implicitly approximate and factorize. Our extensive experiments suggest that NetMF's direct factorization achieves consistent performance improvements over the implicit approximation models—DeepWalk and LINE.

In the future, we would like to further explore promising directions to deepen our understanding of network embedding. It would be necessary to investigate whether and how the development in random-walk polynomials [9] can support fast approximations of the closed-form matrices. The computation and approximation of the 2nd-order random walks employed by node2vec is another interesting topic to follow. Finally, it is exciting to study the nature of skip-gram based dynamic and heterogeneous network embedding.

Acknowledgements. We thank Hou Pong Chan for his comments. Jiezhong Qiu and Jie Tang are supported by NSFC 61561130160. Jian Li is supported in part by the National Basic Research Program of China Grant 2015CB358700, and NSFC 61772297 & 61632016.

APPENDIX:

THEOREM 2.1. *Denote $\boldsymbol{P} = \boldsymbol{D}^{-1}\boldsymbol{A}$, when $L \to \infty$, we have*

$$\frac{\#(w,c)_{\overrightarrow{r}}}{|\mathcal{D}_{\overrightarrow{r}}|} \xrightarrow{p} \frac{d_w}{\operatorname{vol}(G)}(\boldsymbol{P}^r)_{w,c} \text{ and } \frac{\#(w,c)_{\overleftarrow{r}}}{|\mathcal{D}_{\overleftarrow{r}}|} \xrightarrow{p} \frac{d_c}{\operatorname{vol}(G)}(\boldsymbol{P}^r)_{c,w}.$$

LEMMA 6.1. *(S.N. Bernstein Law of Large Numbers [34]) Let $Y_1, Y_2 \cdots$ be a sequence of random variables with finite expectation $\mathbb{E}[Y_j]$ and variance $\operatorname{Var}(Y_j) < K, j \geq 1$, and covariances are s.t. $\operatorname{Cov}(Y_i, Y_j) \to 0$ as $|i-j| \to \infty$. Then the law of large numbers (LLN) holds.*

PROOF. First consider the special case when $N = 1$, thus we only have one vertex sequence $w_1, \cdots, w_L$ generated by random walk as described in Algorithm 1. Consider one certain vertex-context pair (w, c), let Y_j ($j = 1, \cdots, L-T$) be the indicator function for event that $w_j = w$ and $w_{j+r} = c$. We have the following two observations:

- The quantity $\#(w,c)_{\overrightarrow{r}}/|\mathcal{D}_{\overrightarrow{r}}|$ is the sample average of Y_j's, i.e.,

$$\frac{\#(w,c)_{\overrightarrow{r}}}{|\mathcal{D}_{\overrightarrow{r}}|} = \frac{1}{L-T}\sum_{j=1}^{L-T} Y_j.$$

- Based on our assumptions about the graph and the random walk, $\mathbb{E}[Y_j] = \frac{d_w}{\operatorname{vol}(G)}(\boldsymbol{P}^r)_{w,c}$, and when $j > i + r$,

$$\begin{aligned}\mathbb{E}(Y_iY_j) &= \operatorname{Prob}(w_i = w, w_{i+r} = c, w_j = w, w_{j+r} = c)\\ &= \frac{d_w}{\operatorname{vol}(G)}(\boldsymbol{P}^r)_{w,c}\left(\boldsymbol{P}^{j-i+r}\right)_{c,w}(\boldsymbol{P}^r)_{w,c}.\end{aligned}$$

In this way, we can evaluate the covariance $\operatorname{Cov}(Y_i, Y_j)$ when $j > i + r$ and calculate its limit when $j - i \to \infty$ by using the fact that our random walk converges to its stationary distribution:

$$\begin{aligned}\operatorname{Cov}(Y_i, Y_j) &= \mathbb{E}(Y_iY_j) - \mathbb{E}(Y_i)\mathbb{E}(Y_j)\\ &= \frac{d_w}{\operatorname{vol}(G)}(\boldsymbol{P}^r)_{w,c}\underbrace{\left(\left(\boldsymbol{P}^{j-i+r}\right)_{c,w} - \frac{d_w}{\operatorname{vol}(G)}\right)}_{\text{goes to 0 as } j-i\to\infty}(\boldsymbol{P}^r)_{w,c} \to 0.\end{aligned}$$

Then we can apply Lemma 6.1 and conclude that the sample average converges in probability towards the expected value, i.e.,

$$\frac{\#(w,c)_{\overrightarrow{r}}}{|\mathcal{D}_{\overrightarrow{r}}|} = \frac{1}{L-T}\sum_{j=1}^{L-T} Y_j \xrightarrow{p} \frac{1}{L-T}\sum_{j=1}^{L-T}\mathbb{E}(Y_j) = \frac{d_w}{\operatorname{vol}(G)}(\boldsymbol{P}^r)_{w,c}.$$

Similarly, we also have $\frac{\#(w,c)_{\overleftarrow{r}}}{|\mathcal{D}_{\overleftarrow{r}}|} \xrightarrow{p} \frac{d_c}{\operatorname{vol}(G)}(\boldsymbol{P}^r)_{c,w}$.

For the general case when $N > 1$, we define Y_j^n ($n = 1, \cdots, N$, $j = 1, \cdots, L-T$) to be the indicator function for event $w_j^n = w$ and $w_{j+r}^n = c$, and organize Y_j^n's as $Y_1^1, Y_1^2, \cdots, Y_1^N, Y_2^1, Y_2^2, \cdots, Y_2^N, \cdots$. This r.v. sequence still satisfies the condition of S.N. Bernstein LLN, so the above conclusion still holds. □

THEOREM 3.5. *Let $\|\cdot\|_F$ be the matrix Frobenius norm. Then*

$$\left\|M - \hat{M}\right\|_F \le \frac{\mathrm{vol}(G)}{bd_{\min}} \sqrt{\sum_{j=k+1}^{n} \left|\frac{1}{T}\sum_{r=1}^{T}\lambda_j^r\right|^2};$$

$$\left\|\log M' - \log \hat{M}'\right\|_F \le \left\|M' - \hat{M}'\right\|_F \le \left\|M - \hat{M}\right\|_F.$$

PROOF. The first inequality can be seen by applying the definition of Frobenius norm and Eq. 10.

For the second inequality, first to show $\left\|\log M' - \log \hat{M}'\right\|_F \le \left\|M' - \hat{M}'\right\|_F$. According to the definition of Frobenius norm, sufficient to show $\left|\log M'_{i,j} - \log \hat{M}'_{i,j}\right| \le \left|\hat{M}'_{i,j} - M'_{i,j}\right|$ for any i, j. Without loss of generality, assume $M'_{i,j} \le \hat{M}'_{i,j}$.

$$\left|\log M'_{i,j} - \log \hat{M}'_{i,j}\right| = \log \frac{\hat{M}'_{i,j}}{M'_{i,j}} = \log\left(1 + \frac{\hat{M}'_{i,j} - M'_{i,j}}{M'_{i,j}}\right)$$

$$\le \frac{\hat{M}'_{i,j} - M'_{i,j}}{M'_{i,j}} \le \hat{M}'_{i,j} - M'_{i,j} = \left|\hat{M}'_{i,j} - M'_{i,j}\right|,$$

where the first inequality is because $\log(1+x) \le x$ for $x \ge 0$, and the the second inequality is because $M'_{i,j} = \max\left(M_{i,j}, 1\right) \ge 1$. Next to show $\left\|M' - \hat{M}'\right\|_F \le \left\|M - \hat{M}\right\|_F$. Sufficient to show $\left|M'_{i,j} - \hat{M}'_{i,j}\right| \le \left|M_{i,j} - \hat{M}_{i,j}\right|$ for any i, j. Recall the definition of M' and $\hat{M}'$, we get $\left|M'_{i,j} - \hat{M}'_{i,j}\right| = \left|\max(M_{i,j}, 1) - \max(\hat{M}_{i,j}, 1)\right| \le \left|M_{i,j} - \hat{M}_{i,j}\right|$. □

REFERENCES

[1] Sanjeev Arora, Yuanzhi Li, Yingyu Liang, Tengyu Ma, and Andrej Risteski. 2016. A latent variable model approach to pmi-based word embeddings. *TACL* 4 (2016), 385–399.
[2] Yoshua Bengio, Aaron Courville, and Pierre Vincent. 2013. Representation learning: A review and new perspectives. *IEEE TPAMI* 35, 8 (2013), 1798–1828.
[3] Austin R Benson, David F Gleich, and Jure Leskovec. 2015. Tensor spectral clustering for partitioning higher-order network structures. In *SDM*. SIAM, 118–126.
[4] Austin R Benson, David F Gleich, and Lek-Heng Lim. 2017. The Spacey Random Walk: A stochastic Process for Higher-Order Data. *SIAM Rev.* 59, 2 (2017), 321–345.
[5] Matthew Brand and Kun Huang. 2003. A unifying theorem for spectral embedding and clustering.. In *AISTATS*.
[6] Shaosheng Cao, Wei Lu, and Qiongkai Xu. 2015. GraRep: Learning graph representations with global structural information. In *CIKM*. ACM, 891–900.
[7] Shaosheng Cao, Wei Lu, and Qiongkai Xu. 2016. Deep Neural Networks for Learning Graph Representations.. In *AAAI*. 1145–1152.
[8] Shiyu Chang, Wei Han, Jiliang Tang, Guo-Jun Qi, Charu C Aggarwal, and Thomas S Huang. 2015. Heterogeneous network embedding via deep architectures. In *KDD*. ACM, 119–128.
[9] Dehua Cheng, Yu Cheng, Yan Liu, Richard Peng, and Shang-Hua Teng. 2015. Efficient sampling for Gaussian graphical models via spectral sparsification. In *COLT*. 364–390.
[10] Kewei Cheng, Jundong Li, and Huan Liu. 2017. Unsupervised Feature Selection in Signed Social Networks. In *KDD*. ACM.
[11] Fan RK Chung. 1997. *Spectral graph theory*. Number 92. American Mathematical Soc.
[12] Yuxiao Dong, Nitesh V Chawla, and Ananthram Swami. 2017. metapath2vec: Scalable Representation Learning for Heterogeneous Networks. In *KDD*.
[13] David Easley and Jon Kleinberg. 2010. *Networks, Crowds, and Markets: Reasoning about a Highly Connected World*. Cambridge University Press.
[14] Rong-En Fan, Kai-Wei Chang, Cho-Jui Hsieh, Xiang-Rui Wang, and Chih-Jen Lin. 2008. LIBLINEAR: A library for large linear classification. *JMLR* 9, Aug (2008), 1871–1874.
[15] David F Gleich, Lek-Heng Lim, and Yongyang Yu. 2015. Multilinear pagerank. *SIAM J. Matrix Anal. Appl.* 36, 4 (2015), 1507–1541.
[16] Aditya Grover and Jure Leskovec. 2016. node2vec: Scalable feature learning for networks. In *KDD*. ACM, 855–864.
[17] William L. Hamilton, Rex Ying, and Jure Leskovec. 2017. Inductive Representation Learning on Large Graphs. In *NIPS*.
[18] Tatsunori B Hashimoto, David Alvarez-Melis, and Tommi S Jaakkola. 2016. Word embeddings as metric recovery in semantic spaces. *TACL* 4 (2016), 273–286.
[19] Roger A. Horn and Charles R. Johnson. 1991. *Topics in Matrix Analysis*. Cambridge University Press. https://doi.org/10.1017/CBO9780511840371
[20] Yann Jacob, Ludovic Denoyer, and Patrick Gallinari. 2014. Learning latent representations of nodes for classifying in heterogeneous social networks. In *WSDM*. ACM, 373–382.
[21] Thomas N Kipf and Max Welling. 2016. Semi-Supervised Classification with Graph Convolutional Networks. *arXiv preprint arXiv:1609.02907* (2016).
[22] Richard B Lehoucq, Danny C Sorensen, and Chao Yang. 1998. *ARPACK users' guide: solution of large-scale eigenvalue problems with implicitly restarted Arnoldi methods*. SIAM.
[23] Jure Leskovec, Kevin J Lang, and Michael Mahoney. 2010. Empirical comparison of algorithms for network community detection. In *WWW*. ACM, 631–640.
[24] Omer Levy and Yoav Goldberg. 2014. Neural Word Embedding as Implicit Matrix Factorization. In *NIPS*. 2177–2185.
[25] Hang Li, Haozheng Wang, Zhenglu Yang, and Masato Odagaki. 2017. Variation Autoencoder Based Network Representation Learning for Classification. In *ACL*. 56.
[26] László Lovász. 1993. Random walks on graphs. *Combinatorics, Paul erdos is eighty* 2 (1993), 1–46.
[27] Qing Lu and Lise Getoor. 2003. Link-based Classification. In *ICML*.
[28] Tomas Mikolov, Kai Chen, Greg Corrado, and Jeffrey Dean. 2013. Efficient estimation of word representations in vector space. *arXiv preprint arXiv:1301.3781* (2013).
[29] Tomas Mikolov, Ilya Sutskever, Kai Chen, Greg S Corrado, and Jeff Dean. 2013. Distributed Representations of Words and Phrases and their Compositionality. In *NIPS*. 3111–3119.
[30] Mingdong Ou, Peng Cui, Jian Pei, Ziwei Zhang, and Wenwu Zhu. 2016. Asymmetric Transitivity Preserving Graph Embedding.. In *KDD*. 1105–1114.
[31] Bryan Perozzi, Rami Al-Rfou, and Steven Skiena. 2014. DeepWalk: Online learning of social representations. In *KDD*. ACM, 701–710.
[32] S Yu Philip, Jiawei Han, and Christos Faloutsos. 2010. *Link mining: Models, algorithms, and applications*. Springer.
[33] Jianbo Shi and Jitendra Malik. 2000. Normalized cuts and image segmentation. *IEEE PAMI* 22, 8 (2000), 888–905.
[34] A.N. Shiryaev and A. Lyasoff. 2012. *Problems in Probability*. Springer New York.
[35] Chris Stark, Bobby-Joe Breitkreutz, Andrew Chatr-Aryamontri, Lorrie Boucher, Rose Oughtred, Michael S Livstone, Julie Nixon, Kimberly Van Auken, Xiaodong Wang, Xiaoqi Shi, et al. 2010. The BioGRID interaction database: 2011 update. *Nucleic acids research* 39, suppl_1 (2010), D698–D704.
[36] Jian Tang, Meng Qu, and Qiaozhu Mei. 2015. PTE: Predictive text embedding through large-scale heterogeneous text networks. In *KDD*. ACM, 1165–1174.
[37] Jian Tang, Meng Qu, Mingzhe Wang, Ming Zhang, Jun Yan, and Qiaozhu Mei. 2015. LINE: Large-scale information network embedding. In *WWW*. 1067–1077.
[38] Lei Tang and Huan Liu. 2009. Relational learning via latent social dimensions. In *KDD*. ACM, 817–826.
[39] Lei Tang, Suju Rajan, and Vijay K Narayanan. 2009. Large scale multi-label classification via metalabeler. In *WWW*. ACM, 211–220.
[40] Kristina Toutanova, Dan Klein, Christopher D Manning, and Yoram Singer. 2003. Feature-rich part-of-speech tagging with a cyclic dependency network. In *NAACL*. Association for Computational Linguistics, 173–180.
[41] Lloyd N Trefethen and David Bau III. 1997. *Numerical linear algebra*. Vol. 50. Siam.
[42] Grigorios Tsoumakas, Ioannis Katakis, and Ioannis Vlahavas. 2009. Mining multi-label data. In *Data mining and knowledge discovery handbook*. Springer, 667–685.
[43] Cunchao Tu, Han Liu, Zhiyuan Liu, and Maosong Sun. 2017. CANE: Context-aware network embedding for relation modeling. In *ACL*.
[44] Cunchao Tu, Weicheng Zhang, Zhiyuan Liu, and Maosong Sun. 2016. Max-Margin DeepWalk: Discriminative Learning of Network Representation.. In *IJCAI*. 3889–3895.
[45] Ulrike Von Luxburg. 2007. A tutorial on spectral clustering. *Statistics and computing* 17, 4 (2007), 395–416.
[46] Daixin Wang, Peng Cui, and Wenwu Zhu. 2016. Structural deep network embedding. In *KDD*. ACM, 1225–1234.
[47] Cheng Yang, Zhiyuan Liu, Deli Zhao, Maosong Sun, and Edward Y Chang. 2015. Network Representation Learning with Rich Text Information. In *IJCAI*. 2111–2117.
[48] Zhilin Yang, William W. Cohen, and Ruslan Salakhutdinov. 2016. Revisiting Semi-Supervised Learning with Graph Embeddings. In *ICML*. 40–48.
[49] Zhilin Yang, Jie Tang, and William W Cohen. 2016. Multi-Modal Bayesian Embeddings for Learning Social Knowledge Graphs.. In *IJCAI*. 2287–2293.

Curriculum Learning for Heterogeneous Star Network Embedding via Deep Reinforcement Learning

Meng Qu
University of Illinois
at Urbana-Champaign
mengqu2@illinois.edu

Jian Tang
HEC Montreal & Montreal
Institute for Learning Algorithms
tangjianpku@gmail.com

Jiawei Han
University of Illinois
at Urbana-Champaign
hanj@illinois.edu

ABSTRACT

Learning node representations for networks has attracted much attention recently due to its effectiveness in a variety of applications. This paper focuses on learning node representations for heterogeneous star networks, which have a center node type linked with multiple attribute node types through different types of edges. In heterogeneous star networks, we observe that the training order of different types of edges affects the learning performance significantly. Therefore we study learning curricula for node representation learning in heterogeneous star networks, i.e., learning an optimal sequence of edges of different types for the node representation learning process. We formulate the problem as a Markov decision process, with the action as selecting a specific type of edges for learning or terminating the training process, and the state as the sequence of edge types selected so far. The reward is calculated as the performance on external tasks with node representations as features, and the goal is to take a series of actions to maximize the cumulative rewards. We propose an approach based on deep reinforcement learning for this problem. Our approach leverages LSTM models to encode states and further estimate the expected cumulative reward of each state-action pair, which essentially measures the long-term performance of different actions at each state. Experimental results on real-world heterogeneous star networks demonstrate the effectiveness and efficiency of our approach over competitive baseline approaches.

ACM Reference Format:

Meng Qu, Jian Tang, and Jiawei Han. 2018. Curriculum Learning for Heterogeneous Star Network Embedding via Deep Reinforcement Learning. In *WSDM 2018: WSDM 2018: The Eleventh ACM International Conference on Web Search and Data Mining , February 5–9, 2018, Marina Del Rey, CA, USA.* ACM, New York, NY, USA, 10 pages. https://doi.org/10.1145/3159652.3159711

1 INTRODUCTION

Heterogeneous networks, which encode the relationships between different types of objects, are ubiquitous in the real world. Mining heterogeneous networks has been attracting growing attention in recent years. Among all heterogeneous networks, the star network [33] is popular and important. A star network has a center node type and multiple attribute node types, which link to the center nodes through different types of edges. Figure 1 presents an example of the bibliography star network. The center nodes are papers, linked with authors, venues, keywords and references through four types of edges. Analyzing star networks is an important problem in data mining, since a variety of real-world applications can be formulated as certain problems on star networks, such as author identification [5], predictive text embedding [37] and user attribute prediction [18].

WSDM 2018, February 5–9, 2018, Marina Del Rey, CA, USA

ACM ISBN 978-1-4503-5581-0/18/02...$15.00
https://doi.org/10.1145/3159652.3159711

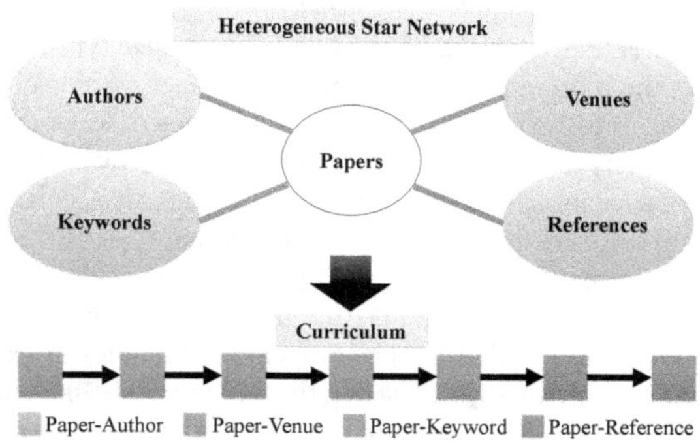

Figure 1: An example of heterogeneous star networks. Papers are the center nodes. Authors, venues, keywords, references are the attribute nodes, which connect to the papers through four types of edges. Our goal is to learn a sequence of edge types for node representation learning.

To mine heterogeneous star networks more effectively, it is helpful to learn meaningful node representations. Traditionally, nodes are represented as bag-of-neighbors, which are both high-dimensional and sparse. Recently, there is a growing trend to embed networks into low-dimensional spaces [11, 27, 38], in which each node is represented as a low-dimensional vector. The learned node representations capture the proximities between nodes, which can benefit various applications, such as node classification [27], link prediction [11] and node visualization [36]. The essential idea for node representation learning is to capture the node proximities encoded in edges. In practice, existing approaches usually sample a set of edges as training data at each learning step. To learn node representations for heterogeneous star networks, a natural solution could be applying these approaches and sampling edges of different types as training data.

Towards the goal of sampling edges in heterogeneous star networks, existing studies usually leverage the random sampling [12, 37] or weighted sampling [5, 18] strategy, without considering the relative order of edges of different types. However, each type of edges encodes a specific kind of knowledge, which may benefit the representation learning process at different training stages. In other words, the training order of edge types matters during training. For example, in Figure 1, consider learning paper representations that preserve paper semantic meanings. The venue of each paper reflects its coarse semantic domains, whereas the keywords and references capture more concrete semantic meanings. Inspired by the human learning process, the coarse meanings are easier to understand, and may benefit the learning of more concrete semantics. Based on the observation, a more reasonable strategy compared with random or weighted sampling could be first learning from the paper-venue edges, and then moving to the paper-keyword and paper-reference edges. Therefore, the training order of different edge types is likely to affect the representation learning performance significantly.

Indeed, in the machine learning literature, the order of training data has been proved to be an important factor in many applications. Learning a meaningful order of the training data (a.k.a., curriculum learning) can benefit various tasks such as shape recognition [4], handwritten text line recognition [19], word representation learning [41], sequence prediction [3] and many others. The basic idea is to start small [6], that is, selecting easier examples to learn at first, and then gradually increasing the difficulty. Though curriculum learning is widely studied, how to learn a meaningful order of training data remains unexplored for learning node representations in heterogeneous star networks.

This motivated us to study a new problem: *curriculum learning for node representation learning in heterogeneous star networks*, aiming to learn an optimal curriculum for node representation learning, in which a curriculum is defined as a sequence of edge types used for training (Figure 1). The problem is essentially a sequential decision making task, and we formulate it as a Markov decision process [2]. At each step, our action is to select a certain type of edges for node representation learning, or terminate the training process, and the state is defined as the sequence of edge types selected so far. After taking an action at a state, we will move to another state and receive a scalar reward. The goal is to learn a sequence of edge types that maximizes the total sum of the rewards. Despite its practical importance, the task is nontrivial, as the search space is exponential to the sequence length. Therefore, we are seeking an approach which can learn an effective curriculum efficiently.

In this paper, we propose such an approach based on deep reinforcement learning. Our approach learns the optimal curriculum by estimating the Q value of each state-action pair, which is defined as the expected cumulative reward after taking the action from the state. Once the Q values are learned, the optimal curriculum can be determined by sequentially selecting the action with the maximum Q value at each step. In our approach, we learn the Q value from two sources, i.e., a planning module and a learning module. Given a state, the planning module calculates Q by *looking ahead*, which explores some subsequent actions through simulations and approximates Q with the simulated rewards. On the other hand, the learning module estimates Q by *looking back* on the past experience. Specifically, it employs a deep neural network (LSTM models [13]) to learn from the past experience and further make predictions. With both modules, our approach can estimate the Q value with high accuracy and low time costs. Therefore, we are able to learn a meaningful curriculum both effectively and efficiently.

We conduct experiments on several real-world heterogeneous star networks under the task of node classification. Experimental results in both unsupervised and semi-supervised settings prove the effectiveness and efficiency of our proposed approach.

To summarize,we make the following contributions:

- We define a new problem of *curriculum learning for node representation learning in heterogeneous star networks*, aiming to learn a sequence of edge types for node representation learning.
- We formulate the problem as a Markov decision process, and propose an approach based on deep reinforcement learning.
- We conduct experiments on real-world star networks, which prove the effectiveness and efficiency of our proposed approach.

2 PROBLEM DEFINITION

Heterogeneous networks encode the relationships between different types of objects, which are widely studied recently. In this paper, we focus on a special type of heterogeneous networks, the heterogeneous star network, which is formally defined below:

Definition 2.1. **(Heterogeneous Star Network.)** *A* ***Heterogeneous Star Network*** $G = (V_0 \cup \{V_k\}_{k=1}^K, \{E_k\}_{k=1}^K)$ *contains a set of center nodes* V_0 *and different types of attribute nodes* $\{V_k\}_{k=1}^K$, *which connect to the center nodes* V_0 *through different types of edges* $E_k = (V_0, V_k)$. *Each edge is associated with a weight* $w > 0$, *indicating the strength of the relationship between the linked nodes.*

An example of heterogeneous star networks is the bibliography star network (Figure 1), in which the center nodes are papers, with the attribute nodes as authors, venues, keywords and references. There are four types of edges in the network: paper-author, paper-venue, paper-keyword and paper-reference.

For many problems of heterogeneous star network analysis, it is critical to learn meaningful node representations. To learn such representations, we can directly apply existing node representation learning algorithms [11, 27, 38] by sampling a set of edges of different types as training data. In practice, we observe that the order of the sampled edges affects the representation learning performance significantly. Therefore we study learning curricula for node representation learning in heterogeneous star networks. In other words, we aim at learning a meaningful order of different types of edges for the given node representation learning algorithm.

The problem is essentially a sequential decision making task, which can be naturally formulated as a Markov decision process. At each step, the **action** is to select a certain edge type and leverage edges of that type for node representation learning (denoted as $a = y_t$ where $y_t \in \{1, 2...K\}$ represents an edge type), or terminate the training process (denoted as $a = STOP$). The **state** is defined as the sequence of edge types selected so far (denoted as $s = (y_1, y_2...y_{t-1})$). After taking an action at a state, we will move to another state and receive a **reward**, which is calculated by a given reward function (denoted as $R(s, a)$ where s is the current state and a is the action we take). For different tasks, we may select different reward functions. For example, in the node classification task, we can define the reward as the accuracy gain after taking an action at a state, with the accuracy calculated on a held-out dataset. Given the above definition, our **goal** is to take a series of actions to maximize the cumulative rewards. In other words, we aim at learning an optimal sequence of edge types for node representation learning. Formally, we define our problem as follows:

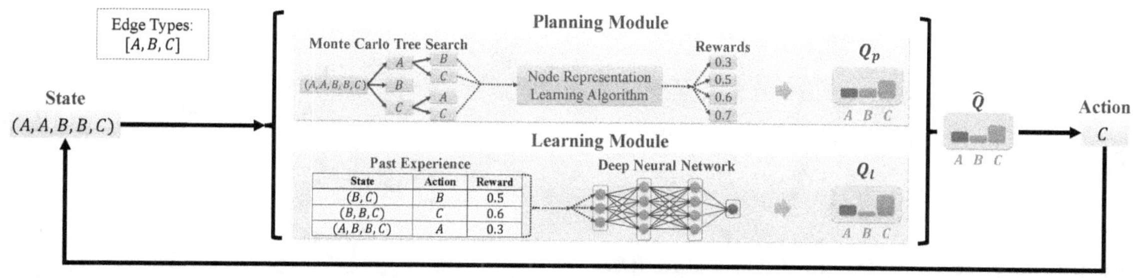

Figure 2: Framework overview. We learn curricula by sequentially selecting actions with the maximum Q values. Given a state, the action Q values are estimated from two modules. The planning module looks ahead, which simulates some actions and approximates Q with the simulated rewards, whereas the learning module looks back on the past experience for prediction.

Definition 2.2. **(Problem Definition.)** *Given a heterogeneous star network $G = (V_0 \cup \{V_k\}_{k=1}^K, \{E_k\}_{k=1}^K)$ and a reward function $R(s, a)$ for each state-action pair (s, a), we aim at taking a series of actions to maximize the total cumulative rewards. In other words, our goal is to learn a sequence of edge types for training.*

3 PRELIMINARY

In this section, we introduce LINE [38], which is a representative node representation learning algorithm. Given a network, LINE samples a number of edges from the network as training data for node representation learning.

Specifically, LINE defines the probability of a node u generated by another node v as follows:

$$p(u|v) = \frac{\exp(\mathbf{v}^T \mathbf{u})}{\sum_{u' \in V} \exp(\mathbf{v}^T \mathbf{u}')}, \quad (1)$$

where $\mathbf{x}$ is the representation of each node x, and V is the node set.

To preserve the relationships between nodes, LINE minimizes the KL-divergence between the estimated neighborhood distribution $p(\cdot|v)$ and the empirical neighborhood distribution $\hat{p}(\cdot|v)$ for every node v. The empirical distribution is defined as $\hat{p}(u|v) = w_{uv}/d_v$, where w_{uv} is the weight of the edge (u, v) and d_v is the degree of v. The final objective function of LINE can be simplified as:

$$O_{line} = - \sum_{(u,v) \in E} w_{uv} \log p(u|v). \quad (2)$$

Directly optimizing the above objective is computationally expensive because it involves traversing all nodes when computing the softmax function. Therefore LINE adopts the negative sampling techniques [20, 21], which modify the conditional probability $p(u|v)$ in Eqn. 2 as follows:

$$\log \sigma(\mathbf{u}^T \mathbf{v}) + \sum_{n=1}^{N} E_{v' \sim P_{neg}(v)}[\log \sigma(-\mathbf{u}^T \mathbf{v}')], \quad (3)$$

where $\sigma(x) = 1/(1 + \exp(-x))$ is the sigmoid function. The first term tries to maximize the probabilities of some observed edges (u, v), and the second term tries to minimize the probabilities of N noisy edges (u, v'), with v' sampled from a noisy distribution $P_{neg}(v) \propto d_v^{3/4}$ and d_v is the degree of node v in the network.

The objective function can be efficiently optimized with edge sampling [38]. In each iteration, the algorithm randomly samples an observed edge with N noisy edges, and then maximizes Eqn. 3.

Next, we take LINE as an example to introduce our approach.

4 METHODOLOGY

In this section, we introduce a deep reinforcement learning approach to the proposed curriculum learning problem. Given a heterogeneous star network, our action at each step is to select an edge type for representation learning or terminate the training process, and the state is the sequence of edge types selected so far. The reward of each action is calculated on an external task, and our goal is to take a series of actions to maximize the cumulative rewards. In other words, we aim at learning the optimal sequence of edge types for training. As the number of possible sequences is exponentially large, learning an effective sequence efficiently is very challenging.

We learn such sequence by estimating the Q value $Q(s, a)$ of each state-action pair (s, a), which is defined as the expected cumulative reward after taking action a from state s. Once the Q value is learned, the optimal series of actions can be easily determined by sequentially selecting the action with the maximum Q value.

Our approach predicts Q from two sources, i.e., a *planning* module and a *learning* module, and we denote the values calculated by them as Q_p and Q_l respectively. After Q_p and Q_l are learned, we further combine them as a more precise estimation $\widehat{Q}$. To learn Q values, given an edge type sequence as state, the planning module will simulate some actions, which either select a type of edges as training data or stop the training process, then the obtained rewards are leveraged to estimate Q_p. Different from the planning module, the learning module learns from the previous simulation results, and infers Q_l based on these past experience. With both modules, our approach can effectively predict the Q value (see Figure 7(a)). Moreover, by carefully utilizing the past experience with the learning module, we can also calculate the Q value very efficiently (see Figure 7(b)).

Even though our approach can learn a curriculum both effectively and efficiently, in practice, we may still have different emphasis on effectiveness and efficiency. To allow flexible trade-off between them, our approach tries to penalize each action. Specifically, when calculating the reward for an action, we will subtract a constant penalty from the original reward calculated by the reward function $R(s, a)$. A small penalty encourages our approach to learn a longer curriculum, which has better performance but is less efficient; whereas a large penalty leads to a shorter curriculum, with worse performance but less time costs. Overall, the two factors can be well balanced by choosing different penalties (see Figure 8).

The overall framework is summarized in Figure 2. Next, we introduce the details of our approach and analyze its time complexity.

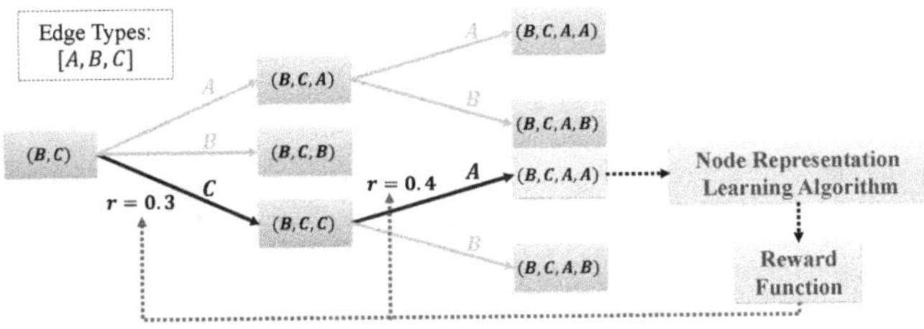

Figure 3: Illustration of the simulation. Given a state (the leftmost one), we simulate a series of actions (actions along the black path) until we reach an unvisited state (the yellow one). Then the rewards are calculated to approximate Q_t.

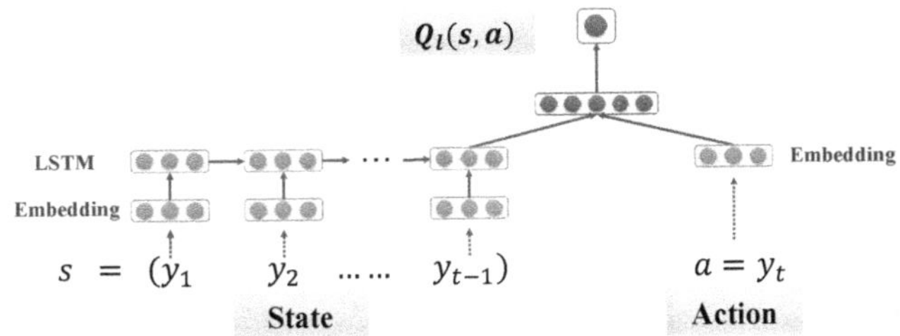

Figure 4: The network structure for the learning module.

4.1 Planning Module

The planning module of our approach estimates Q_p by looking ahead and simulating some subsequent actions starting from the given state. In each simulation, we first choose a series of actions to explore, which either select a type of edges for training or terminate the training process. Then we simulate the actions with the node representation learning algorithm and calculate the rewards, which are further utilized to approximate the expected cumulative reward Q_p. Figure 3 presents an illustration of the workflow.

Specifically, in the planning module, the $Q_p(s, a)$ value of each state-action pair (s, a) is calculated with a look-up table. Following existing studies on Monte-Carlo tree search [1, 8, 14], given a state s, in each simulation we will recursively select some actions to explore (e.g., actions along the black path in Figure 3), until we reach an unvisited state (e.g., the yellow state in Figure 3). Inspired by the UCT algorithm [8], at each state s, we select the following action a to explore:

$$a = \arg\max_a \{ \frac{Q_p(s, a)N(s, a)}{N(s, a) + 1} + \frac{Q_l(s, a)}{N(s, a) + 1} + \lambda \sqrt{\frac{\ln N(s)}{N(s, a) + 1}} \}. \quad (4)$$

For each state-action pair (s, a), $Q_p(s, a)$ and $Q_l(s, a)$ are the Q values calculated by the planning and learning modules respectively, $N(s, a)$ is the visit count and $N(s) = \sum_a N(s, a)$ is the total visit count of the state s.

Such selection rule is quite intuitive. The first term is the Q value calculated by the planning module; while the second term is calculated by the learning module, which serves as priors and decays with repeated visits. Both terms encourage the model to exploit actions with larger Q values in the past, as these actions are more likely to be the optimal ones. For the third term, it favors those actions with less visit counts, as such actions can eventually become superior than others in some cases. To balance the exploitation of the promising actions with the exploration of others, we introduce a parameter λ. A small λ will encourage the exploitation while a large one will encourage the exploration.

After reaching an unvisited state, we will simulate the selected actions with the node representation learning algorithm, that is, leveraging the corresponding types of edges to update the node representations or stop the training process. Then the rewards are calculated by applying the reward function on the learned node representations. Suppose the sequence of the visited states and the selected actions is $(s_t, a_t, ..., s_{t+l}, a_{t+l}, s_u)$, and the corresponding reward sequence is $(r_t, ..., r_{t+l})$ where $r_i = R(s_i, a_i)$. Then we update Q_p based on the temporal difference learning method [35]:

$$Q_p(s_i, a_i) = Q_p(s_i, a_i) + \alpha[r_i + Q_p(s_{i+1}, a_{i+1}) - Q_p(s_i, a_i)], \quad (5)$$

where $\alpha = \frac{1}{N(s_i, a_i)}$ is the learning rate. Basically, r_i is the immediate reward after taking a_i at s_i and $Q_p(s_{i+1}, a_{i+1})$ estimates the long-term reward, and we will use their sum to approximate the expected total reward $Q_p(s_i, a_i)$ from state s_i after taking action a_i.

4.2 Learning Module

Different from the planning module, the learning module of our approach estimates Q_l by looking back on the past experience, without look-ahead search. More specifically, we train a deep neural network to memorize the historical data, that is, the previously explored state-action pairs together with the simulated rewards. Then we infer Q_l based on the neural network.

Formally, the value $Q_l(s, a)$ of each state-action pair (s, a) is calculated by a deep neural network. In the deep neural network, we represent each edge type $y \in \{1, 2...K\}$ and action $a \in \{1, 2...K\}$ with an embedding vector. Then for a state $s = (y_1, y_2...y_t)$, we encode it using an LSTM layer [13]. After that, we concatenate the encoding vectors of state s and action a, and leverage two fully connected layers to calculate $Q_l(s, a)$. Figure 4 shows the structure of the neural network. By leveraging LSTM layers to encode states, we can effectively capture the correlations of different states, which enables us to effectively infer the Q_l values of new state-action pairs based on their similarities with the previously explored pairs.

To learn the parameters of the deep neural network, we treat the state-action pairs and the corresponding rewards explored by the planning module as training data. Formally, suppose the state-action sequence obtained in a simulation is $(s_t, a_t, ..., s_{t+l}, a_{t+l}, s_u)$, and the corresponding reward sequence is $(r_t, ..., r_{t+l})$, then we update the parameters based on the temporal difference learning method [35] as follows:

$$w_l = w_l + \alpha[r_i + Q_l(s_{i+1}, a_{i+1}) - Q_l(s_i, a_i)] \nabla_{w_l} Q_l(s_i, a_i), \quad (6)$$

where w_l is the parameter set of the neural network, α is the learning rate, which is updated with the RMSProp algorithm [40] and the initial value is set as 0.001. Basically, the immediate rewards r_i and the long-term reward $Q_l(s_{i+1}, a_{i+1})$ are leveraged to approximate the cumulative reward $Q_l(s_i, a_i)$ of the state-action pair (s_i, a_i).

4.3 Integrating Both Modules

Finally in each step, Q_p and Q_l are integrated as $\widehat{Q}$, which gives a more precise estimation of the Q value. Then we decide the optimal action with the integrated value.

Specifically, given the current state s, we calculate $\widehat{Q}(s,a)$ for each action a as follows:

$$\widehat{Q}(s,a) = \{\frac{Q_P(s,a)N(s,a)}{N(s,a)+1} + \frac{Q_l(s,a)}{N(s,a)+1}\}, \quad (7)$$

where $Q_P(s,a)$ is calculated by the planning module, $Q_l(s,a)$ is calculated by the learning module, and $N(s,a)$ is the visit count. We see that $\widehat{Q}$ is a weighted average of Q_P and Q_l. As Q_P is estimated with look-ahead search, which is more precise, we will assign larger weight to this term. For Q_l, it is learned from the past experience, which serves as priors and we will continuously decrease its weight with repeated visits.

The $\widehat{Q}$ value estimates the expected future rewards after taking a at s, and the action a^* with the maximum $\widehat{Q}$ value should be the optimal selection at the current step. Therefore, we will take action a^*, that is, either selecting a type of edges for node representation learning or terminating the training process.

The overall node representation learning process with our curriculum learning approach is summarized in Algorithm 1.

Algorithm 1 Representation learning with our approach.

Input: Star network G, reward function R, the number of simulations S.
Output: Node representations.

for each step **do**
  ⊡ ***Update the learning module:***
  Collect past experience as training data for the learning module.
  Update the learning module according to Eqn. (6).
  ⊡ ***Update the planning module:***
  while simulation $\le S$ **do**
    Select a series actions according to Eqn. (4).
    Simulate the actions with the embedding algorithm (Eqn. (2)).
    Calculate the rewards with the reward function R.
    Update the planning module according to Eqn. (5).
  end while
  ⊡ ***Integrating both modules:***
  Calculate $\widehat{Q}$ value for each action according to Eqn. (7).
  Select the optimal action a^* based on $\widehat{Q}$.
  if a^* is $STOP$ **then**
    Terminate the training process.
  end if
  Use the corresponding type of edges for training based on Eqn. (2).
  Move to the next state based on the selected action a^*.
end for

4.4 Time Complexity

Finally, we analyze the time complexity of the node representation learning process with our approach. In each step, we will simulate a series of actions, update both modules and decide the optimal action. The time costs mainly come from the simulation process. Suppose we conduct S simulations in each step, and we randomly sample E_s edges for training if an edge type is selected in an action. Then the overall time complexity is $O(ISE_s)$, where I is the number of training steps. Compared with single edge type based approaches (e.g., DeepWalk, LINE, node2vec), the time complexity of our approach ($O(ISE_s)$) is S time larger than theirs ($O(IE_s)$). In the experiment part, we will show that our approach requires very limited simulations S to achieve satisfactory results (see Figure 7). We will also show that our approach is quite efficient compared with several baseline approaches (see Figure 6).

5 EXPERIMENT

In this section, we evaluate our approach on several real-world heterogeneous star networks. We compare different approaches on the center node classification task in both the unsupervised and semi-supervised settings.

Specifically, for each compared algorithm, we treat the learned center node representations as features and train one-vs-rest linear classifiers using the LibLinear package [7] [1] for classification. In the unsupervised setting, we treat all center nodes in the training set as the held-out data, and the **reward** of an action is defined as the classification accuracy gain on the held-out dataset after taking that action. Note that in the unsupervised setting, the labeled center nodes are only used for reward calculation. In some cases, we also expect to improve node representations with the labeling information. Therefore, in the semi-supervised setting, we treat labels as an additional type of attribute nodes to guide the learning process. We use 70% center nodes in the training set to construct edges between center nodes and labels, and treat the remaining 30% as the held-out data. The **reward** of an action is defined as the classification accuracy gain on the held-out dataset after taking that action. The classification performance is evaluated using the Macro-F1 and Micro-F1 scores. Note that Micro-F1 is equal to accuracy in our setting since each node has only one label.

5.1 Experiment Setup

5.1.1 Datasets.

- **DBLP**: A bibliography star network constructed from the DBLP dataset [39][2]. The papers are the center nodes and the authors, citations, words in the titles are treated as the attribute nodes. The weights of all edges are set as 1. For the center nodes (i.e., papers), we select eight diverse research fields as labels including "machine learning", "natural language processing", "programming language", "data mining", "database", "system technology", "hardware and theory". For each research domain, several representative conferences are selected, and only papers published in these conferences are collected to construct the networks.
- **Yelp**: A business network constructed from the Yelp dataset [3], with business as the center node type, and user, word in business names, word in business reviews as attribute nodes. The weight of the edge between a business and a user is the number of reviews written by the user for the business. The weight of the edge between a business and a word is the frequency of the word in the business name/reviews. We select six categories including "Restaurants", "Hotels", "Shopping", "Health & Medical", "Beauty & Spas", "Arts & Entertainment" as labels. Businesses with multiple labels are excluded from the labeled set.
- **IMDB**: A movie network constructed from the IMDB dataset [4]. We treat the movies as the center nodes and other entities as the attribute nodes, including users, movies, keywords, actors, actresses, directors, writers. For each (movie, user) pair, the edge weight is set as 1 if the user once rated the movie. For each (movie, movie) pair, the weight is defined as the number of users who

[1] https://www.csie.ntu.edu.tw/~cjlin/liblinear/
[2] https://aminer.org/AMinerNetwork
[3] https://www.yelp.com/dataset_challenge
[4] http://files.grouplens.org/datasets/movielens/ml-10m-README.html

Table 1: Statistics of the Datasets.

Dataset	DBLP			Yelp			IMDB						
# Center Nodes	107,833			77,445			10,692						
Attribute Type	Citation	Author	Word	Review	Name	User	User	Movie	Keyword	Actor	Actress	Director	Writer
# Attribute Nodes	107,833	46,297	23,818	127,203	29,791	552,339	69,878	10,676	58,952	54,171	104,473	3,127	8,164
# Edges	655,030	117,415	346,100	20,858,371	218,034	2,225,213	10,000,054	5,318,912	564,019	90,027	206,290	6,698	15,917
# Training Nodes	13,643			17,468			1,006						
# Test Nodes	30,000			30,000			3,000						

watch one movie immediately after watching the other one. We treat the movie genres as classification labels and movies with more than one genre are excluded from the labeled set.

5.1.2 *Compared algorithms.*

- **LINE**: A node representation learning algorithm for networks with a single type of edges [38]. We report the best results of LINE with each single type of edges (**LINE**). Besides, we also apply LINE to multiple types of edges by assigning different sampling weights to different edge types, with the weights learned by grid search on the held-out dataset (**LINE-Weight**). Such weight selection strategy is widely adopted by existing methods [5, 18].
- **node2vec**: Another node representation learning approach for a single edge type [11]. Similarly, the best results on a single type of edges (**node2vec**) and the results on multiple types of edges through weight learning (**node2vec-Weight**) are reported.
- **Rand**: Randomly select a type of edges at each training step, and use LINE for node representation learning [37]. The number of training steps is set as 300 in all datasets to ensure convergence.
- **Greedy**: Greedily select the action (i.e., selecting an edge type or terminating training) with the maximum immediate reward at each step, and learn node representations with LINE.
- **DRL**: Learn curricula with our Deep Reinforcement Learning approach, and learn node representations with LINE.
- **DRL-Shuf**: Shuffle the curriculum learned by our approach, and learn node representations with LINE.
- **DRL-P**: Learn curricula with only the planning module, and keep Q_l calculated by the learning module as 0.
- **DRL-L**: Learn curricula with only the learning module, and keep Q_p calculated by the planning module as 0.

5.1.3 *Parameter Settings.* For all approaches, we set the dimension of the node representations as 100. For node2vec, we set the window size as 10, the walk length as 40, as suggested in [27]. The parameters p and q for controlling the random walk process are selected on the held-out dataset. For LINE, the number of negative samples is set as 5, and the learning rate is set as 0.015. For all the curriculum learning based approaches, if an action is to select an edge type for training, we will randomly sample 1M edges of that type as training data to update the node representations. For the learning module of our approach, the dimensions of the embedding layer and the hidden layer are set as 10. For the planning module of our approach, the parameter λ for balancing the exploitation and exploration is set as 0.2, and the penalty of each action is set as 10^{-4} by default. The number of simulations at each step is set as 12 for the DBLP and Yelp datasets, and 20 for the IMDB dataset.

5.2 Quantitative Results

In this section, we report the quantitative results on the center node classification task in both the unsupervised setting and the semi-supervised setting.

5.2.1 *Unsupervised Setting.* Table 2 presents the results in the unsupervised setting. We see that considering multiple types of edges achieves much better results compared with single type based approaches (single type). For different strategies combining multiple edge types, we observe that learning their orders (curriculum learning) consistently outperforms learning the sampling weights (weight learning), which demonstrates that curriculum learning is a more effective strategy for the node representation learning problem in star networks. For different curriculum learning approaches, the performance of random sampling (Rand) is the worst. The approach of greedily selecting the action with the maximum immediate reward (Greedy) performs much better.

With both the learning and planning modules, our deep reinforcement learning based approach (DRL) significantly improves the performance. Comparing our approach with its variants, we see that ignoring either the planning module or the learning module (DRL-P and DRL-L) leads to much worse results, which proves that the two modules can indeed mutually complement to improve the performance. Besides, if we shuffle the learned curriculum (DRL-Shuf), the results significantly drop. This shows that the training order of different edge types can indeed affect the performance. Overall, our approach can learn an effective curriculum to improve the node representation learning process.

5.2.2 *Semi-supervised Setting.* The results in the semi-supervised setting are presented in Table 3. Similar results are observed as in the unsupervised setting. The curriculum learning based approaches still outperform those weight learning based approaches. Besides, our deep reinforcement learning based approach (DRL) significantly outperforms other curriculum learning approaches with random (Rand) or greedy (Greedy) strategies.

Comparing Table 3 with Table 2, we can see that the results of our approach (DRL) are consistently improved by considering the labeled nodes during training, which shows that our approach can also effectively integrate the labeled and unlabeled information to learn more effective node representations.

5.3 Convergence Comparison

The quantitative results above show that our curriculum learning approach is able to learn an effective sequence of edge types for node representation learning. To intuitively understand how such strategy affects the training process, in this part we report the performance of different approaches at each training step. We take the DBLP dataset as an example, and the results in both settings are reported. To ensure the convergence of all approaches, we constrain the number of training steps as 50.

Figure 5 presents the results. Compared with the weight learning based approaches (LINE-Weight) and other curriculum learning based approaches (Rand and Greedy), DRL converges faster and has better performance. Therefore, our approach can both help accelerate the convergence and improve the learned representations.

Table 2: Quantitative results in the unsupervised setting. Curriculum learning based approaches outperform other approaches. Our deep reinforcement learning based approach performs the best among all compared algorithms.

Type	Algorithm	DBLP		Yelp		IMDB	
		Macro-F1	Micro-F1	Macro-F1	Micro-F1	Macro-F1	Micro-F1
Single Type	LINE	75.59	76.26	80.91	87.63	28.26	72.60
	node2vec	78.40	79.79	72.44	81.05	24.28	70.13
Weight Learning	LINE-Weight	79.76	80.99	86.78	91.32	30.63	75.60
	node2vec-Weight	80.50	81.42	85.42	90.63	26.43	74.03
Curriculum Learning	Rand	76.85	78.37	82.16	88.61	28.35	73.93
	Greedy	79.60	80.96	85.89	91.02	28.81	74.57
	DRL-P	81.04	81.95	88.87	92.85	29.55	75.93
	DRL-L	80.15	81.18	86.43	91.46	29.19	72.70
	DRL-Shuf	79.36	80.42	86.28	91.20	28.29	75.37
	DRL-MCT	**81.33**	**82.46**	**89.30**	**93.31**	**33.09**	**78.60**

Table 3: Quantitative results in the semi-supervised setting. Our deep reinforcement learning based approach outperforms all other approaches and achieves better results compared with the results in the unsupervised setting.

Type	Algorithm	DBLP		Yelp		IMDB	
		Macro-F1	Micro-F1	Macro-F1	Micro-F1	Macro-F1	Micro-F1
Single Type	LINE	75.59	76.26	80.91	87.63	28.26	72.60
	node2vec	78.40	79.79	72.44	81.05	24.28	70.13
Weight Learning	LINE-Weight	82.09	82.75	87.41	91.85	31.68	76.73
	node2vec-Weight	82.17	83.12	87.05	91.18	27.14	74.57
Curriculum Learning	Rand	79.88	80.23	88.30	89.23	28.79	74.40
	Greedy	80.26	81.49	87.42	92.17	30.08	76.33
	DRL-P	82.98	83.80	89.09	93.39	31.62	77.13
	DRL-L	82.26	83.16	88.07	92.41	29.52	73.87
	DRL-Shuf	81.73	82.22	87.06	91.74	31.09	76.07
	DRL	**83.63**	**84.49**	**89.76**	**93.97**	**35.51**	**79.67**

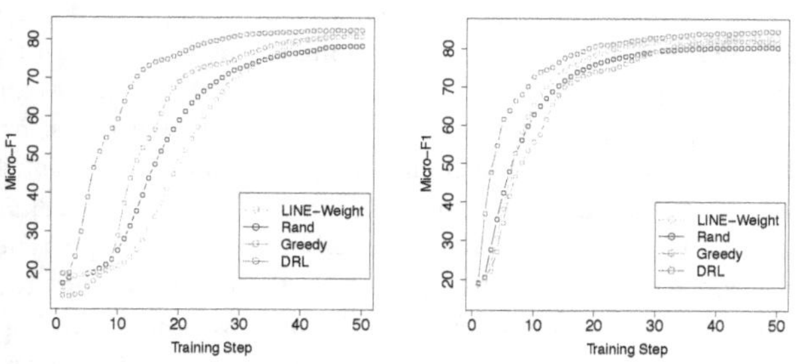

(a) DBLP (unsupervised) (b) DBLP (semi-supervised)

Figure 5: Performance w.r.t. training steps on the DBLP dataset. Our approach improves both the convergence and quality of the learned node representations.

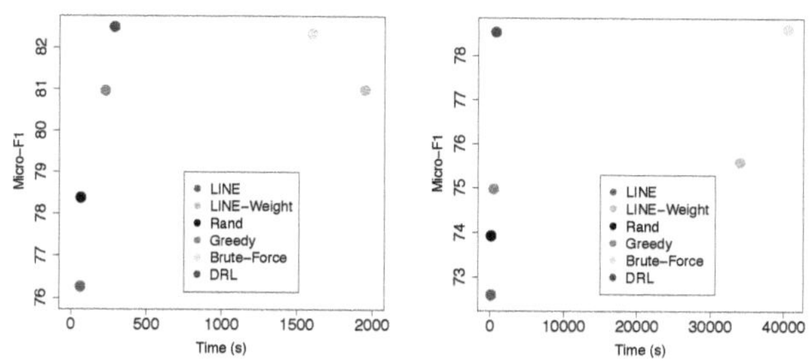

(a) DBLP (unsupervised) (b) IMDB (unsupervised)

Figure 6: Performance v.s. the running time. The upper left indicates the optimal performance. Our approach is both effective and efficient.

5.4 Efficiency Comparison

In the above sections, we have compared the effectiveness of different approaches. Next, we further evaluate their efficiency. To better illustrate the efficiency of our approach, we introduce another baseline approach Brute-Force, which learns the optimal action at each step through brute-force search based on the obtained rewards, and the maximal search depth is set as 3. We take the DBLP and the IMDB datasets as examples, and report both the performance and running time of each compared algorithm. The number of training threads is set as 16 for all approaches. For our approach, the planning module is trained on CPU with 16 threads, whereas the learning module is learned using a GPU.

Figure 6 presents the results. Comparing our approach (DRL) with the approaches based on weight learning (LINE-Weight) and brute-force search (Brute-Force), we see that our approach achieves close results but is much more efficient. On the other hand, our approach significantly outperforms other curriculum learning approaches (Rand and Greedy), and the efficiency is close. Overall, our approach can help learn more effective node representations with close efficiency.

5.5 Parameter Sensitivity

Performance w.r.t. the number of simulations. At each training step, our approach conducts several simulations to evaluate actions. Next, we study the performance of our approach under different numbers of simulations. We take the IMDB dataset in the unsupervised setting as an example. We report the Micro-F1 with

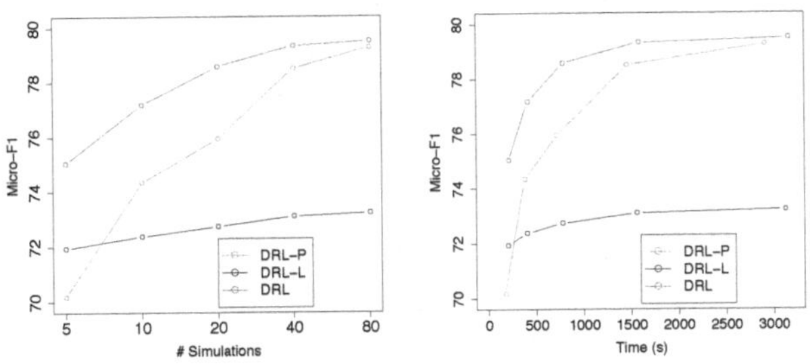

(a) Micro-F1 w.r.t. #simulations (b) Curves of Micro-F1 and time

Figure 7: Performance w.r.t. #simulations on the IMDB dataset. Our approach requires limited simulations to achieve compelling results (left). Leveraging both modules improves the effectiveness and efficiency (right).

respect to #simulations in Figure 7(a), and show the curves of Micro-F1 and running time with different #simulations in Figure 7(b) (5, 10, 20, 40, 80 simulations from left to right).

From Figure 7(a), we see that with both planning and learning strategies, our approach (DPL) requires very limited simulations to achieve compelling results, which shows that integrating them indeed improves the effectiveness. From Figure 7(b), we observe that compared with either module (DRL-L and DRL-P), our approach (DRL) achieves close results with lower time costs, demonstrating that both modules can work together to improve the efficiency.

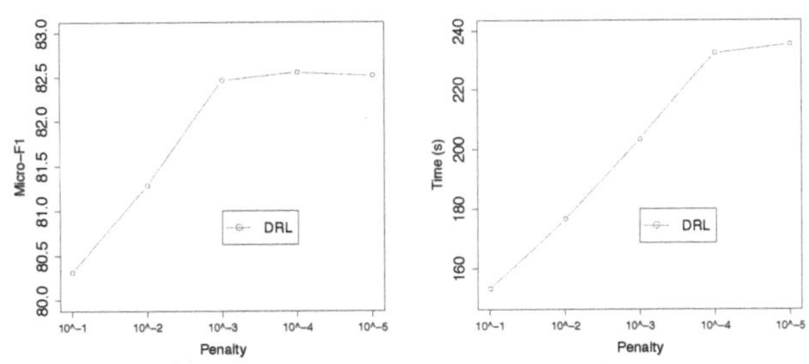

(a) Micro-F1 (b) Time

Figure 8: Performance w.r.t. penalty. We can flexibly balance the effectiveness with efficiency by adjusting penalties.

Performance w.r.t. the penalty. To balance the effectiveness with efficiency, our approach introduces a penalty for each action when calculating the rewards. A small penalty emphasizes the effectiveness while a large penalty emphasizes the efficiency. In this part, we study the performance under different penalties. We take the DBLP dataset in the unsupervised setting as an example, and report both the Micro-F1 and curriculum length (i.e., the number of training steps in the curriculum) under different penalties.

Figure 8 presents the results. When the penalty is large, we observe that the performance is quite limited but the whole training process is very efficient. As we decrease the penalty, the results are significantly improved, but the training process also takes longer time. Overall, with proper penalties, we can effectively trade off between the effectiveness and efficiency.

5.6 Case Study

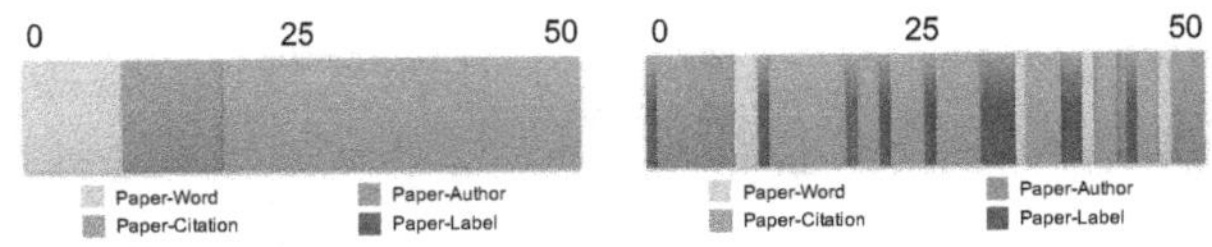

(a) DBLP (unsupervised) (b) DBLP (semi-supervised)

Figure 9: The learned curriculum on the DBLP dataset.

Finally, we present some intuitive examples to show that the curriculum learned by our approach is indeed reasonable. Taking the DBLP dataset as an example, we present the learned curriculum in Figure 9, in which we constrain the number of training steps as 50 and each color corresponds to a type of edges.

In the unsupervised setting, the edges between papers and title words are selected at the beginning steps. The reason may be that the paper titles provide the most general information, which can benefit the learning of other knowledge. In the semi-supervised setting, the learned curriculum is very interesting. At the first training step, the labeled data (i.e., edges between papers and labels) are selected, which is very intuitive. Overall, both the labeled data (red) and unlabeled data (other colors) are selected during training, showing that both information is useful for learning meaningful node representations, and our approach can effectively integrate both kinds of information.

6 RELATED WORK

Our work is related to node representation learning, which learns low-dimensional vector representations for nodes in networks. Most existing approaches including DeepWalk [27], LINE [38] and node2vec [11] aim to preserve the structure information of networks, such that nodes with similar neighbors tend to have similar representations. There are also some studies [5, 12, 16, 18, 28, 37] focusing on heterogeneous networks, which exploit multiple types of edges. However, all these approaches ignore the training order of different types of edges, while in this paper we aim at learning a meaningful training order of edges of different types to improve the representation learning performance.

Another category of related work is curriculum learning, which aims at learning a meaningful order of the training data. Bengio et al. [4] first proposed the concept of curriculum learning, and applied the idea to the tasks of shape recognition and language modeling. The strategy was then successfully applied to various research domains such as computer vision [10, 15, 19, 25] and natural language processing [3, 31, 41]. The basic idea of these approaches is to start training with easy examples to first learn some simple aspects of a given task, and then gradually increase the difficulty to learn more complex aspects. Our work shares similar intuition with these studies, but we focus on learning node representations for heterogeneous star networks, which remains unexplored yet.

Our work is also related to reinforcement learning and planning approaches, which aim to solve the sequential decision making problems by either interacting with environments or conducting simulations. These approaches have achieved impressive results in a variety of applications, including the GO game [9, 29], real-time video games [23, 26], image classification [22], dialogue generation [17] and optimization [24, 42]. All these approaches either leverage the learning strategy or the planning strategy, whereas we integrate both of them in our approach. There are also some studies combining learning and planning strategies [30, 34], which leverage linear models to approximate Q values. Different from them, we utilize deep neural networks (LSTM) to calculate Q values, and we focus on different applications from theirs.

7 CONCLUSION

In this paper, we studied the problem of curriculum learning for node representation learning in heterogeneous star networks. We proposed a deep reinforcement learning based approach, which integrates the learning and planning strategies. Experimental results proved the effectiveness and efficiency of our approach. In the future, we plan to apply our framework to general heterogeneous networks, in which a curriculum is defined as a sequence of meta-paths [32] or hyper-edges [12].

ACKNOWLEDGMENTS

Research was sponsored in part by the U.S. Army Research Lab. under Cooperative Agreement No. W911NF-09-2-0053 (NSCTA), National Science Foundation IIS-1320617 and IIS 16-18481, and grant 1U54GM114838 awarded by NIGMS through funds provided by the trans-NIH Big Data to Knowledge (BD2K) initiative (www.bd2k.nih.gov). The views and conclusions contained in this document are those of the author(s) and should not be interpreted as representing the official policies of the U.S. Army Research Laboratory or the U.S. Government. The U.S. Government is authorized to reproduce and distribute reprints for Government purposes notwithstanding any copyright notation hereon.

REFERENCES

[1] P. Auer, N. Cesa-Bianchi, and P. Fischer. Finite-time analysis of the multiarmed bandit problem. *Machine learning*, 47(2-3):235–256, 2002.
[2] R. Bellman. A markovian decision process. Technical report, DTIC Document, 1957.
[3] S. Bengio, O. Vinyals, N. Jaitly, and N. Shazeer. Scheduled sampling for sequence prediction with recurrent neural networks. In *Advances in Neural Information Processing Systems*, pages 1171–1179, 2015.
[4] Y. Bengio, J. Louradour, R. Collobert, and J. Weston. Curriculum learning. In *Proceedings of the 26th annual international conference on machine learning*, pages 41–48. ACM, 2009.
[5] T. Chen and Y. Sun. Task-guided and path-augmented heterogeneous network embedding for author identification. *arXiv preprint arXiv:1612.02814*, 2016.
[6] J. L. Elman. Learning and development in neural networks: The importance of starting small. *Cognition*, 48(1):71–99, 1993.
[7] R.-E. Fan, K.-W. Chang, C.-J. Hsieh, X.-R. Wang, and C.-J. Lin. Liblinear: A library for large linear classification. *The Journal of Machine Learning Research*, 9:1871–1874, 2008.
[8] S. Gelly and D. Silver. Combining online and offline knowledge in uct. In *Proceedings of the 24th international conference on Machine learning*, pages 273–280. ACM, 2007.
[9] S. Gelly, Y. Wang, O. Teytaud, M. U. Patterns, and P. Tao. Modification of uct with patterns in monte-carlo go. 2006.
[10] K. J. Geras and C. Sutton. Scheduled denoising autoencoders. *arXiv preprint arXiv:1406.3269*, 2014.
[11] A. Grover and J. Leskovec. node2vec: Scalable feature learning for networks. In *Proceedings of the 22nd ACM SIGKDD international conference on Knowledge discovery and data mining*, pages 855–864. ACM, 2016.
[12] H. Gui, J. Liu, F. Tao, M. Jiang, B. Norick, and J. Han. Large-scale embedding learning in heterogeneous event data. In *Data Mining (ICDM), 2016 IEEE 16th International Conference on*, pages 907–912. IEEE, 2016.
[13] S. Hochreiter and J. Schmidhuber. Long short-term memory. *Neural computation*, 9(8):1735–1780, 1997.
[14] L. Kocsis and C. Szepesvári. Bandit based monte-carlo planning. In *European conference on machine learning*, pages 282–293. Springer, 2006.
[15] Y. J. Lee and K. Grauman. Learning the easy things first: Self-paced visual category discovery. In *CVPR*, pages 1721–1728. IEEE, 2011.
[16] J. Li, H. Dani, X. Hu, J. Tang, Y. Chang, and H. Liu. Attributed network embedding for learning in a dynamic environment. *arXiv preprint arXiv:1706.01860*, 2017.
[17] J. Li, W. Monroe, A. Ritter, M. Galley, J. Gao, and D. Jurafsky. Deep reinforcement learning for dialogue generation. *arXiv preprint arXiv:1606.01541*, 2016.
[18] J. Li, A. Ritter, and D. Jurafsky. Learning multi-faceted representations of individuals from heterogeneous evidence using neural networks. *arXiv preprint arXiv:1510.05198*, 2015.
[19] J. Louradour and C. Kermorvant. Curriculum learning for handwritten text line recognition. In *Document Analysis Systems (DAS), 2014 11th IAPR International Workshop on*, pages 56–60. IEEE, 2014.
[20] T. Mikolov, I. Sutskever, K. Chen, G. S. Corrado, and J. Dean. Distributed representations of words and phrases and their compositionality. In *Advances in neural information processing systems*, pages 3111–3119, 2013.
[21] A. Mnih and Y. W. Teh. A fast and simple algorithm for training neural probabilistic language models. *arXiv preprint arXiv:1206.6426*, 2012.
[22] V. Mnih, N. Heess, A. Graves, et al. Recurrent models of visual attention. In *Advances in neural information processing systems*, pages 2204–2212, 2014.
[23] V. Mnih, K. Kavukcuoglu, D. Silver, A. Graves, I. Antonoglou, D. Wierstra, and M. Riedmiller. Playing atari with deep reinforcement learning. *arXiv preprint arXiv:1312.5602*, 2013.
[24] R. Munos. From bandits to monte-carlo tree search: The optimistic principle applied to optimization and planning. 2014.
[25] A. Pentina, V. Sharmanska, and C. H. Lampert. Curriculum learning of multiple tasks. In *Proceedings of the IEEE Conference on Computer Vision and Pattern Recognition*, pages 5492–5500, 2015.
[26] T. Pepels, M. H. Winands, and M. Lanctot. Real-time monte carlo tree search in ms pac-man. *IEEE Transactions on Computational Intelligence and AI in Games*, 6(3):245–257, 2014.
[27] B. Perozzi, R. Al-Rfou, and S. Skiena. Deepwalk: Online learning of social representations. In *Proceedings of the 20th ACM SIGKDD international conference on Knowledge discovery and data mining*, pages 701–710. ACM, 2014.
[28] M. Qu, J. Tang, J. Shang, X. Ren, M. Zhang, and J. Han. An attention-based collaboration framework for multi-view network representation learning. *arXiv preprint arXiv:1709.06636*, 2017.
[29] D. Silver, A. Huang, C. J. Maddison, A. Guez, L. Sifre, G. Van Den Driessche, J. Schrittwieser, I. Antonoglou, V. Panneershelvam, M. Lanctot, et al. Mastering the game of go with deep neural networks and tree search. *Nature*.
[30] D. Silver, R. S. Sutton, and M. Müller. Sample-based learning and search with permanent and transient memories. In *Proceedings of the 25th international conference on Machine learning*, pages 968–975. ACM, 2008.
[31] V. I. Spitkovsky, H. Alshawi, and D. Jurafsky. Baby steps: How "less is more" in unsupervised dependency parsing. *NIPS: Grammar Induction, Representation of Language and Language Learning*, pages 1–10, 2009.
[32] Y. Sun, J. Han, X. Yan, P. S. Yu, and T. Wu. Pathsim: Meta path-based top-k similarity search in heterogeneous information networks. *Proceedings of the VLDB Endowment*, 4(11):992–1003, 2011.
[33] Y. Sun, Y. Yu, and J. Han. Ranking-based clustering of heterogeneous information networks with star network schema. In *Proceedings of the 15th ACM SIGKDD international conference on Knowledge discovery and data mining*, pages 797–806. ACM, 2009.
[34] R. S. Sutton. Integrated architectures for learning, planning, and reacting based on approximating dynamic programming.
[35] R. S. Sutton and A. G. Barto. *Reinforcement learning: An introduction*, volume 1.
[36] J. Tang, J. Liu, M. Zhang, and Q. Mei. Visualizing large-scale and high-dimensional data. In *Proceedings of the 25th International Conference on World Wide Web*, pages 287–297. International World Wide Web Conferences, 2016.
[37] J. Tang, M. Qu, and Q. Mei. Pte: Predictive text embedding through large-scale heterogeneous text networks. In *Proceedings of the 21th ACM SIGKDD International Conference on Knowledge Discovery and Data Mining*, pages 1165–1174. ACM, 2015.
[38] J. Tang, M. Qu, M. Wang, M. Zhang, J. Yan, and Q. Mei. Line: Large-scale information network embedding. In *Proceedings of the 24th International Conference on World Wide Web*, pages 1067–1077. International World Wide Web Conferences Steering Committee, 2015.
[39] J. Tang, J. Zhang, L. Yao, J. Li, L. Zhang, and Z. Su. Arnetminer: extraction and mining of academic social networks. In *Proceedings of the 14th ACM SIGKDD international conference on Knowledge discovery and data mining*, pages 990–998. ACM, 2008.
[40] T. Tieleman and G. Hinton. Lecture 6.5-rmsprop: Divide the gradient by a running average of its recent magnitude. *COURSERA: Neural networks for machine learning*, 4(2):26–31, 2012.
[41] Y. Tsvetkov, M. Faruqui, W. Ling, and C. Dyer. Learning the curriculum with bayesian optimization for task-specific word representation learning. *arXiv preprint arXiv:1605.03852*, 2016.
[42] B. Zoph and Q. V. Le. Neural architecture search with reinforcement learning. *arXiv preprint arXiv:1611.01578*, 2016.

Leveraging Implicit Contribution Amounts to Facilitate Microfinancing Requests

Suhas Ranganath*
Walmart Labs
suhas.ranganath@walmartlabs.com

Ghazaleh Beigi
Arizona State University
gbeigi@asu.edu

Huan Liu
Arizona State University
huan.liu@asu.edu

ABSTRACT

The emergence of online microfinancing platforms provides new opportunities for people to seek financial assistance from a large number of potential contributors. However, these platforms deal with a huge number of requests, making it hard for the requesters to get assistance for their financial needs. Designing algorithms to identify potential contributors for a given request will assist in satisfying financial needs of requesters and improve the effectiveness of microfinancing platforms. Existing work correlates requests with contributor interests and profiles to design feature based approaches for recommending projects to prospective contributors. However, contributing money to financial requests has a cost on contributors which can affect his inclination to contribute in the future . Literature in economic behavior has investigated the manner in which memory of past contribution amounts affects user inclination to contribute to a given request. To systematically investigate whether these characteristics of economic behavior would help to facilitate requests in online microfinancing platforms, we present a novel framework to identify contributors for a given request from their past financial information. Individual contribution amounts are not publicly available, so we draw from financial modeling literature to model the implicit contribution amounts made to past requests. We evaluate the framework on two microfinancing platforms to demonstrate its effectiveness in identifying contributors.

CCS CONCEPTS

• **Information systems → Collaborative and social computing systems and tools**; *Reputation system*; • **Social and professional topics** → Information system economics;

KEYWORDS

Crowdfunding, Socioeconmics, Q&A, Information Seeking

ACM Reference Format:
Suhas Ranganath, Ghazaleh Beigi, and Huan Liu. 2018. Leveraging Implicit Contribution Amounts to Facilitate Microfinancing Requests. In *Proceedings of WSDM 2018: The Eleventh ACM International Conference on Web Search and Data Mining (WSDM 2018)*. ACM, New York, NY, USA, Article 4, 9 pages. https://doi.org/10.1145/3159652.3159679

*The paper was submitted when the author was a graduate student at Arizona State University.

WSDM 2018, February 5–9, 2018, Marina Del Rey, CA, USA

ACM ISBN 978-1-4503-5581-0/18/02...$15.00
https://doi.org/10.1145/3159652.3159679

Figure 1: Request made on the microfinance platform Kiva

1 INTRODUCTION

The rise of online financial platforms is being utilized by people to request, borrow and contribute to loans to fulfill their various financing needs. Microfinancing sites have emerged as a popular source for people to secure funding for a business venture or personal needs. Considerable interest has been shown in recent literature [1, 6, 12] regarding the use of online microfinance platforms by primarily low-income people to seek to fund for their various financial and entrepreneurial needs [4].

Fig 1 illustrates an example of a request posted in the microfinance platform Kiva seeking help for their financial needs. In the example, a request is made by a non-governmental organization in Ghana called the Nyame Tease Group. It is seeking money to finance the purchase of food and education for the children of one of their members. The funding, in turn, would enable her to use existing funds for her business. The figure also features the set of contributors who contributed to the request. This example showcases the use of microfinancing platforms by low-income individuals for requesting loans to address their financial needs.

However, microfinancing platforms receive a high frequency of requests, and this makes it difficult for requesters to get their financial needs addressed [3]. Potential contributors have many requests on their wall, and they might not notice requests. The presence of a few highly visible requests [30] can inhibit others posted during the same time from getting noticed. Automatically identifying responders for financial requests can help the people to fulfill their financial needs and also enhance the effectiveness of micro-financing platforms.

The problem of identifying suitable contributors to financial requests faces several challenges. First, fulfilling financial requests has a cost on contributors which can alter his inclination to respond to future requests. The cost of response less prominent in informational requests, hence criteria for identifying information providers like relevance, expertise may not be sufficient here. Second, the amount contributors contributed to past requests in microfinancing platforms are not publicly available, making it hard for researchers to assess future contributing decisions based on them. Third, online microfinance platforms have a high number of requests in a given time each having many candidate contributors, leading to significant issues of scalability.

Economic research on the behavior of contributors to charity [10] emphasizes the importance of previous costs to contributors, as measured by the amounts they contributed in determining their future participation. The effect of past amounts is also explored in research on consumer behavior [26] where past prices consumers pay for commodities has been shown to shape their inclinations on future purchases. Drawing concepts from the literature on the economic behavior, we propose to leverage the effect of past contribution amounts on his inclination to contribute in the future to identify suitable responders to a given micro-financing request. Specifically, we answer the following questions: How to estimate the inclination of users to contribute to a given request from the amounts they contributed in the past? How to design financial models from the implicit past contribution amounts to identify potential contributors? The major contributions of the work are

- Formally defining the problem of identifying potential contributors to a request in online microfinance platforms;
- Proposing a framework to leverage implicit past contribution amounts to identify responders to financial requests; and
- Presenting extensive experimental evaluations of the framework on real-world datasets of requests posted on two microfinance platforms.

In this paper, we propose a framework that leverages financial information from the past contribution amounts to identify potential contributors for a given request. Drawing concepts from financial modeling literature, we model the effect of past contribution amounts of the user to estimate his inclination to contribute to a given request. We then utilize the financial models to identify contributors for a given funding request in online microfinance platforms.

2 PROBLEM STATEMENT

In this section, we present the notations and formally state the problem of facilitating requests in online microfinancing platforms. We first present the set of notations used in the paper. Matrices are denoted by boldface uppercase letters (e.g. $\mathbf{X}$) , vectors by lowercase letters (e.g. $\mathbf{x}$) and sets can be denoted by $\mathcal{X}$. $\mathbf{X}_{ij}$ signifies the element in the ith row and j^{th} column of matrix $\mathbf{X}$.

The proposed framework with the input, the information we employ and the expected output is illustrated in Figure 2. Let the request for funding be denoted by r. Each request is accompanied by a description outlining the reasons the funding is being requested. We denote the description by request word vector $\mathbf{q} \in \mathbb{R}^{1\times w}$ where w is the total number of words. Each element of the vector is set to 1 if the word is present in the description and 0 if not. Let the overall set of potential contributors be denoted by C.

Each contributor in C posts a description outlining his interests. We denote the description vector of each contributor as $\mathbf{c} \in \mathbb{R}^{1\times w}$, where w are the total number of words. In addition to this, each contributor might have funded previous requests in the past, and this can be used to provide insight into his preferences. For each contributor, we denote the word vector of the previous requests he has answered by $\mathbf{p} \in \mathbb{R}^{1\times w}$, where w is the total number of words. Let us denote information from the past requests which were fulfilled as $\mathcal{P}$. The includes the requested amount vector $\mathbf{r} \in \mathbb{R}^{q\times 1}$ where q is the number of past requests, and the past request matrix $\mathbf{R} \in \mathbb{R}^{q\times C}$, where q is the number of requests and C is the number of contributors, where $\mathbf{R}_{ij} = 1$ if contributor j contributed to request i and 0 otherwise.

Having described the notations, we now formally state the problem as follows *"Given a request for funding r, the request word vector* $\mathbf{q}$, *the set of candidate contributors C, the contributor word vector* $\mathbf{c}$ *of each candidate contributor, the previous requests word vector* $\mathbf{p}$ *of each candidate contributor, information from the past requests* $\mathcal{P}$, *find the list of contributors for the given request."*

In this section, we defined the notations and came up with a detailed problem statement. We next provide a detailed description of the framework designed to address this problem.

3 THE PROPOSED FRAMEWORK

Here, we first present measures for interests of the candidate contributors to the given request using their description and the requests they responded to in the past. We draw from financial modeling literature to leverage the past implicit contribution amounts to identify contributors to a microfinance request. We finally present the complexity analysis of the algorithm to evaluate its scalability in large-scale data prevalent in online microfinancing platforms.

3.1 Measuring Contributor Interests

Research on identifying responders to online requests have proposed several measures to estimate the correlation of the candidate respondents with the request[21, 29]. We draw from these research to present metrics to estimate the contributor correlation using his interests and past response behavior. Let the word vector of the request be known as $\mathbf{q} \in \mathbb{R}^{1\times w}$ and the description word vector of the candidate contributor be given by $\mathbf{c} \in \mathbb{R}^{1\times w}$ where w is the number of words. To represent the relationship between the given request and the description of the contributor, we transform the corresponding word vectors into a common latent dimension space using $\mathrm{S} \in \mathbb{R}^{\mathrm{n}\times\mathrm{w}}$. Here n is the number of dimensions of the space ($\mathrm{n} \ll \mathrm{w}$). We can then represent the given request r and contributor interest c in the low dimensional space by $\mathbf{q}\mathrm{S}^T$ and CS^T respectively. We represent the interest of the contributor using his relationship between the request and his description by incorporating dimension correlation with $\mathbf{T} \in \mathbb{R}^{\mathrm{n}\times\mathrm{n}}$ as

$$f = \mathbf{q}\mathrm{S}^{\mathrm{T}}\mathrm{T}\mathrm{S}\mathbf{c}^{\mathrm{T}}. \quad (1)$$

The interests of the contributor can also be determined by the previous requests towards which he contributed. Let $\mathbf{p} \in \mathbb{R}^{1\times W}$ determine the previous requests answered by contributor $c \in C$, where w is the total number of words. We follow a similar procedure to model the correlation of the contributor with the given request

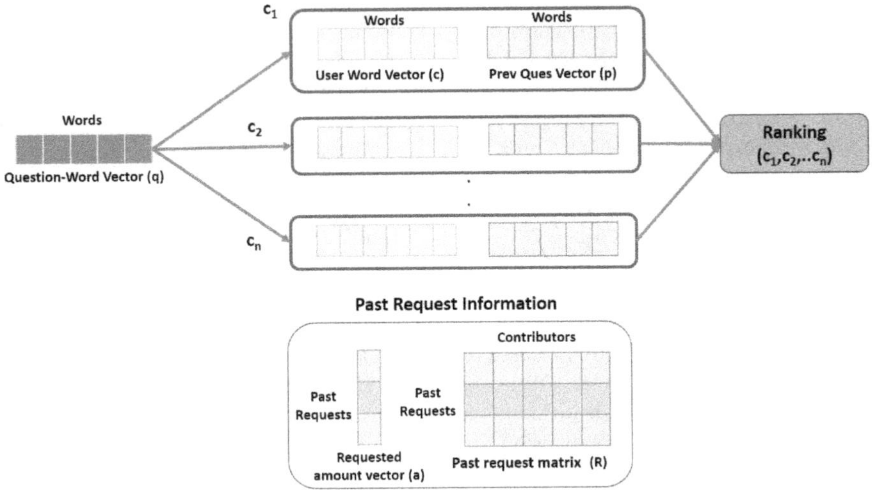

Figure 2: The proposed framework to facilitate funding requests in online microfinancing platforms

from previous requests he contributed to as

$$f_2 = \mathbf{q}\mathbf{S}^{\mathrm{T}}\mathbf{T}\mathbf{S}\mathbf{p}^{\mathrm{T}}. \tag{2}$$

We compute the overall interests of the contributor with the given request as $f = \mathbf{q}\mathbf{S}^{\mathrm{T}}\mathbf{T}\mathbf{S}\mathbf{k}^{\mathrm{T}}$, where $\mathbf{k} = \mathbf{c} + \mathbf{p}$.

3.2 Leveraging Implicit Contribution Amounts

Contributing to financial requests bears a cost to the user, and hence the inclination of the user to contribute to a given financial request is effected by his past contribution amounts. We now design financial models to estimate the user inclination from past contribution amounts and user interest measures. User inclination to contribute to a given request can be affected by a host of factors not observable in the platform [25], hence we model the variation of user inclination over time as a stochastic process.

Let the joining time of a contributor i be t_0 and the initial value he can contribute be given by s_0. We employ a stochastic variation process for modeling the user inclination. The following differential equation gives the stochastic variation of the user inclination of contributor i from the past contribution amount s_i and correlation with the request as

$$\frac{ds_i}{s_i} = \mu_i(1 + \mathbf{q}\mathbf{S}^{\mathrm{T}}\mathbf{T}\mathbf{S}\mathbf{k}^{\mathrm{T}})dt + \sigma_i dW, \tag{3}$$

where $f_i = \mathbf{q}\mathbf{S}^{\mathrm{T}}\mathbf{T}\mathbf{S}\mathbf{k}^{\mathrm{T}}$ computes the interests of the contributor to the request, μ_i is the drift which governs the deterministic component of his inclination to contribute , σ_i is the variation, and W is the Wiener process that accounts for the stochastic variation[23]. The deterministic component in the loan u_i weighted by his interest in the loan. The deterministic and stochastic component u_i and σ_i is updated for each previous transaction of the user, and models how his inclination is affected by the transaction amounts .

a Solving this differential equation, the contribution amount of contributor i for a past request that was posted at time t is

$$s_i = s_0 exp\Big((\mu_i \mathbf{n}_i - \frac{\sigma_i^2}{2})t + \sigma_i W\Big), \tag{4}$$

From the properties of the Geometric Brownian Motion [18], we get $ln(s) \sim \mathcal{N}(m, v)$. Here $\mathcal{N}$ denotes a normal distribution whose mean and variation is given by

$$m_i = ln(s_0) + (\mu_i \mathbf{n}_i - \frac{\sigma_i^2}{2})t_i, v_i = \sigma_i^2 t \tag{5}$$

$\mathbf{n}_i = 1 + \mathbf{q}\mathbf{S}^{\mathrm{T}}\mathbf{T}\mathbf{S}\mathbf{k}^{\mathrm{T}}$ The estimated mean contribution amount increases with greater interest in the question and is offset by the parameters learned from his previous transactions.

In online microfinance platforms the ground truth for the individual contribution amounts of past requests are not publicly known, but the total requested amount is known. We compute the optimal values of the parameter set $\mathcal{K} = \{\mu_i, \sigma_i, \mathbf{S}, \mathbf{T}\}$ by maximizing the log-likelihood between the real and the total implicit contribution amounts. To obtain the estimated requested amount, we follow a similar procedure for all the contributors of the past request. Combining the amounts of by all the contributors, and assuming independence, we get the estimated requested amount drawing from the normal random variable $\mathcal{N}(m, v)$, whose mean and variance is given by

$$m = \sum_{i \in C} ln(s_0) + (\mu_i \mathbf{n}_i - \frac{\sigma_i^2}{2})t_i, v = \sum_{i \in C} \sigma_i^2 t \tag{6}$$

We then equate the estimated requested amount to the actual requested amount a and compute the likelihood function as

$$\mathcal{L}(\theta) = \frac{1}{\sqrt{2\pi v^2}} exp(\frac{-(a-m)^2}{2v^2}) \tag{7}$$

Taking the natural logarithm of the likelihood, we obtain the log likelihood function as

$$ln(\mathcal{L}(\theta)) = -\frac{1}{2} ln(2\pi v^2) - \frac{(a-m)^2}{2v^2} \tag{8}$$

To obtain the optimal value of the parameters $\mathcal{K} = \{\mu_i, \sigma_i, \mathrm{S}, \mathrm{T}\}$, we minimize the negative of the log-likelihood

$$\min_{\mu_i, \sigma_i, \mathrm{S}, \mathrm{T}} \frac{1}{2} ln(2\pi v^2) + \frac{(a-m)^2}{2v^2} \tag{9}$$

We compute the parameters $\mathcal{K} = \{\mu_i, \sigma_i, \mathrm{S}, \mathrm{T}\}$ by coordinate gradient descent, keeping one parameter constant and obtaining the gradient of the other. The update equations for the parameters are given below

$$\begin{aligned} \mu_i &\leftarrow \mu_i + \eta \frac{a-m}{v} (\mathbf{q}\mathrm{S}^{\mathrm{T}}\mathrm{T}\mathbf{S}\mathbf{c}^{\mathrm{T}} t_i) \\ \sigma_i &\leftarrow \sigma_i - \eta \frac{\sigma_i}{v^2} (v(1 + \frac{a-m}{v}) - (\frac{a-m}{v})^2) \\ \mathrm{S} &\leftarrow \mathrm{S} + \eta \frac{a-m}{v} (\mathrm{T} + \mathrm{T}^T)(\mathbf{S}\mathbf{q}^T \sum_{i \in C} \mu_i t_i \mathbf{k}) \\ \mathrm{T} &\leftarrow \mathrm{T} + \eta \frac{a-m}{v} (\mathbf{S}\mathbf{q}^T \sum_{i \in C} \mu_i t_i \mathbf{u}\mathbf{S}^T), \end{aligned} \tag{10}$$

We repeat this procedure for all the past requests and obtain optimal values of the parameter set $\mathcal{K}$ for the corresponding contributors.

For each new request in the test set, we obtain the candidate set C corresponding to the request. We then compute the probable amount contributed by each contributor in the candidate set drawing from $\mathcal{N}(m_i, v_i)$ with mean m_i and variance v_i as

$$m_i = ln(s_0) + (\mu_i \mathbf{n}_i - \frac{\sigma_i^2}{2}) t_i, v_i = \sigma_i^2 t. \tag{11}$$

Here s_0 is the initial value of the contributor i is willing to contribute to the platform and t is the time elapsed since he first joined on the platform. The set $\mathcal{K} = \{\mu_i, \sigma_i, \mathrm{S}, \mathrm{T}\}$ are the optimal values of the parameters representing the financial information of the contributors computed from the past requests. We then sort the contributors in the candidate set in decreasing order of the probable contribution to the request and return to the requester as a ranked list. The procedure is summarized in Algorithm 1.

Algorithm 1: Facilitating Microfinancing Requests

Data: q, c, p, $\mathcal{K}, \mathcal{P}$
Result: Recommended list for requesters
for $l \in \mathcal{P}$ **do**
  Obtain contributor set from **R** for request l.
  Compute overall estimated m and v from Eq 6.
  Compute log likelihood of the $\mathcal{L}(\theta)$ from from Eq 8.
  Construct the optimization function from Eq 9.
  while *until convergence* **do**
    update $\mathcal{K}$ using Eq 10.
  end
end
Obtain candidate contributors $\mathcal{U}$ for test request.
Compute m_i and v_i for C from Eq 11 using optimized $\mathcal{K}$.
Sort the contributors in decreasing order of probable contribution and return to the requester.

The inputs to the algorithm are the word-vector of the given request **q**, the word-vectors of the interests of the contributor **c** and the past requests he has contributed towards **p**, the parameter set $\mathcal{K}$, and the training set of requests $\mathcal{P}$. The expected output of the algorithm is the ordered set of contributors recommended for the given request. For each request in the training set $\mathcal{P}$, we first obtain the list of contributors from the past request matrix **R**. We estimate the requested amount by adding all the means and variances of the individual contributions of the list of contributors as shown in Eq 6. We compute the log-likelihood using Eq 8. We then maximize the log likelihood and update the value of the parameters in $\mathcal{K}$ until convergence using Eq 10. We repeat this procedure for all the past requests to obtain the optimal values of the parameter set $\mathcal{K}$.

We next use the parameter set to identify contributors to the given request as follows. We obtain the candidate contributor set C for the given request. For each contributor u_i in the candidate contributor set C, we estimate their probable contribution amount using Eq 11 from the optimal values of the parameter set $\mathcal{K}$. We sort the contributors in the candidate set according to the probable contribution of each contributor to the given request in descending order to return to the as a sorted list.

$$\mathbf{e}_t(q) = \sum_{i=1}^{o} sim(\mathbf{q}\mathrm{S}^T\mathrm{T}, \mathrm{S}\mathrm{P}_i^T)\mathbf{r}t_i,$$

Until now, we described our framework to identify contributors for a given microfinancing request. We next compute the time complexity of the framework to demonstrate its scalability in large datasets usually prevalent in online microfinancing platforms.

3.3 Time Complexity Analysis

We now present the time-complexity to demonstrate the scalability of the framework for large datasets prevalent in online microfinancing platforms. The majority of the time complexity comes from the update equations in Eq 10. The complexity of $f_i = \mathbf{q}\mathrm{S}^{\mathrm{T}}\mathrm{T}\mathbf{S}\mathbf{k}^{\mathrm{T}}$ is $O(Wn)$. The complexity of $(\mathrm{T} + \mathrm{T}^T)(\mathbf{S}\mathbf{q}^T \sum_{i \in C} \mu_i t_i \mathbf{c})$ is $O(W^2 n)$. The complexity of $\mathbf{S}\mathbf{q}^T (\sum_{i \in C} \mu_i t_i \mathbf{c}\mathbf{S})$ is $O(Wn)$. Therefore the overall complexity of the proposed algorithm is low owing to the sparsity of the word vectors and the low magnitude of latent dimension n, indicating the scalability of the framework to a large dataset.

In this section, we proposed a set of measures to correlate the requests and contributors with contributor interests and past response. We utilize the proposed measures to design financial models from the past implicit contributions to previous requests. We then utilize the financial models to identify contributors for new requests in online microfinancing platforms. In the next section, we present the collected data and experiments designed to evaluate our framework.

4 EXPERIMENTAL EVALUATION

In this section, we describe the dataset and use the dataset to evaluate our framework. We use the dataset to answer the following questions: How effective is the framework in identifying prospective contributors for requests in online microfinance platforms? How does the framework perform for requests with different amounts and number of contributors? How does the framework perform with varying proportions of training data size? We first present the dataset with some relevant analysis to understand some of its salient aspects.

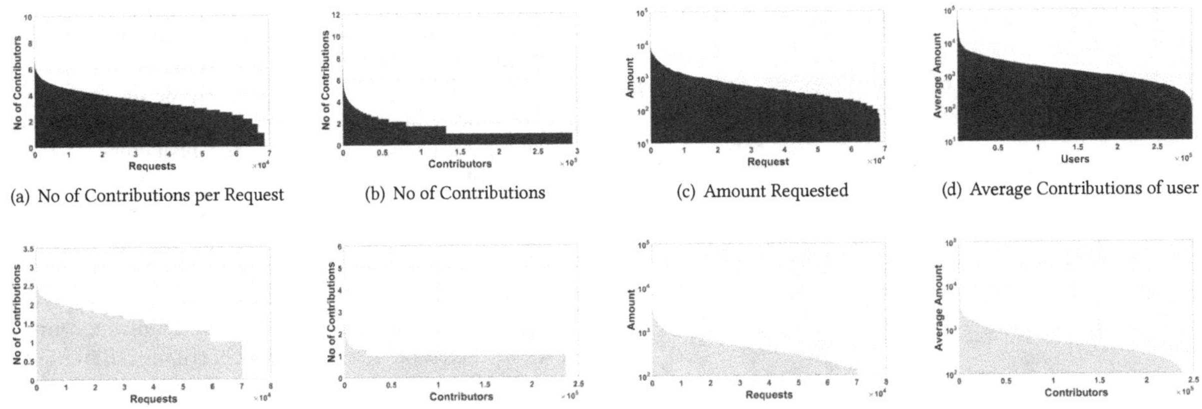

(a) No of Contributions per Request (b) No of Contributions (c) Amount Requested (d) Average Contributions of user

(e) No of Contributions per Requests (f) No of Contributions (g) Amount Asked per Request (h) Average Contributions of user

Figure 3: (a)-(d) Statistics of Kiva dataset (e)-(g) Statistics of DonorChoose dataset.

Parameter	Kiva	DonorChoose
# Requests	68,500	70,140
# Contributors	293,736	232,562
# Contributions	1,300,616	370,053
Median Contributions per request	12	4
Total amount requested	\$54,148,425	\$37,776,908
Median Amount requested	\$475	\$420

Table 1: Statistics of the datasets

4.1 Data Analysis

We collect the dataset from the microfinance platforms Kiva and DonorsChoose. Kiva provides a platform through which small entrepreneurs who are in need of funding can take the help of field partners like non-governmental organizations, while DonorsChoose focuses on asking donations to enable education infrastructure for teachers in need. The requests can be seen by potential contributors who can contribute part of the requested amount. Each request can be potentially fulfilled by a large number of individual contributors.

The statistics of the collected datasets is given in Table 1. We describe the collected statistical data in the Kiva dataset. We collect 68,500 requests which have a total of 293,736 contributors. We select only successful requests to ensure optimal training of our algorithm. The total contributions across all requests are 1,300,616 with a median of 12 contributions per request. This indicates that requests in microfinancing platforms require a lot of contributors to get fulfilled. The total amount requested for is around \$54 million with a median amount of \$475 indicating the high activity of the site. Each request is accompanied by a brief description outlining the necessity for funding. Similarly, each contributor also describes himself outlining his purpose of being on the site and his primary interests. We also collected the request, and contributor descriptions and a total of 625,243 words are used in the requests and the contributors. Comparable statistics can be seen for all the parameters can be seen for the DonorsChoose datasets.

We next characterize various aspects of the dataset from Kiva and DonorsChoose datasets. The characterizations of the dataset regarding the traits of the contributors and requested amount are plotted in Figure 3. Figure 3(a) plots the number of contributors each request in the dataset has received. We take the natural logarithm of the number of contributions each request receives. We increment the values by 1 so that requests with a single contribution to emphasize the requests having a single contributor. We sort it in the descending order and plot it on the y-axis and plot the requests on the x-axis. From the figure, we can see that a few requests obtain a large number of contributors and a large number of requests receive a lesser number of contributors. We plot the number of contributions each contributor makes in Figure 3(b). Similar to Figure 3(a), we take the natural logarithm of the number of contributions each contributor makes, increment it by 1. We plot this on the y-axis sorted in descending order and the corresponding contributors on the x-axis. From the figure, we can see that a large percentage of contributors make a single contribution and a small number of contributors make a large number of contributions. We will evaluate the performance of the framework for requests with a varying number of contributors in Sec 4.4.

We next present characteristics of the dataset related to the amount requested. Figure 3(c) plots the amount asked by each request. The amount is sorted in descending order and plotted on the y-axis, and the corresponding requests are plotted on the x-axis. This follows a power law distributions where a few requests ask for large amounts while a large number of requests asking for lesser amounts of money. Overall, from the figure, we can see that a substantial amount of money is being requested across all requests on the platform. We next examine the requests contributed by each contributor and the amount asked by request. We then plot the average of the amounts asked for all the requests the contributor has contributed in Figure 3(d). From the figure, we can see that this too follows a power-law distribution with a few contributors contributing to requests with large amounts and also provides an indication of the varying contributions of different contributors.

We will evaluate the performance of the framework for requests with a varying number of contributors in Sec 4.5.

Until now, we described the dataset and presented some analysis to understand some salient aspects of it. We now use the dataset and design experiments to evaluate our framework. We first describe the baseline we use to compare the performance of the framework.

4.2 Experimental Settings

In this work, we use the metrics Mean Average of Precision (MAP), Precision @K (Pre @K) and Mean Reciprocal Rank (MRR) to evaluate the performance of the different approaches. We compare the proposed framework against the following baselines:

- **Random Selection:** This method randomly select contributors from the dataset and the mean values of the evaluation metrics over 10 trails are taken. This is done to assess the difficulty of the problem.
- **Sulprus Maximization[33]**: The authors estimate the number of individual contributions using overall surplus maximization. We use the contributor interest to measure surplus. We use this baseline to evaluate the effectiveness of amount estimation for the proposed task.
- **Topic Match**: This baseline measures the matching between the latent representations of the contributor interests and requests as measured by Non-Negative Matrix Factorization [19]. We use the methods to assess the effectiveness of content matching to the proposed problem.
- **Promotion [7]**: The authors extract different features related to textual, contributor, requested amount, and time delay to identify useful projects for contributors. We use this work to evaluate the effectiveness of the features examined here for the proposed problem.

In the rest of the section, we describe experiments designed to evaluate the framework using the evaluation metrics. In Section 4.3, we evaluate the performance of the framework in identifying contributors for requests on microfinance platforms. We divide the dataset into ten equal time epochs. We keep the first nine epochs for training and the last time epoch for testing. Next, we evaluate the robustness of the framework for varying contributor counts in Section 4.4, and varying requested amounts in Section 4.5.

4.3 Identifying Contributors

We now evaluate the performance of the framework in identifying contributors who can contribute effectively to funding requests in micro-financing platforms. We employ the procedure described in **Algorithm 1** scoring the requests and the candidate contributors in the test set. For each request, we rank the candidate responders and employ the evaluation metrics to evaluate the performance of the framework in comparison to the baselines. The results of the experiments are presented in Table 2.

From the table, we can see that the performance of random ordering is low demonstrating the difficulty of the problem. The performance of **Sulprus Maximization**[33] improves upon the random performance showing the utility of estimating the individual contributions in identifying potential contributors. The improved performance of **TopicMatch** shows that the correlation of the contributors with the requests is a strong indicator for identifying contributors. The improved performance in **Promotion**[7] showcases the use of temporal and requested amount in identifying contributors to microfinance requests.

Our framework considerably outperforms existing baselines by a significant margin, thus demonstrating the utility of measuring the effect of past contribution amounts on user inclination for identifying contributors to online microfinance requests. This also demonstrates the effectiveness of the model in inferring implicit contribution amounts and modeling their effect on contributor inclination. We performed a paired t-test to compare the results with the baselines that showed that the improvement is significant with $p < 0.001$.

In summary, we can say from Table 2 that our framework is effective in identifying contributors for requests posted in micro-financing platforms. Next, we will examine the effect on the performance of the framework due to variation in training data size and parameter values.

4.4 Performance across Contributor Counts

As observed during analysis of the data related to the contributor counts received by requests in Section 4.1, the number of contributors varies widely for different requests in the dataset. We now evaluate the performance of the framework for requests with a different number of contributors to evaluate its robustness. We plot the performance of the framework and the nearest baseline[7] in Fig 4(a) and Fig 4(b) using the MAP and Pre@10 metrics. We order the test requests in increasing number of contributors it obtained and plotted it on the x-axis. For each contribution count, we compute the performance of the framework for requests having the same or lesser number of contributors and plot it on the y-axis. We present the results from the dataset from Kiva for the subsequent experiments to maintain better focus on the underlying concepts. We make the following observations from the two figures.

From Fig 4(a) and Fig 4(b), we notice that the framework outperforms the baselines for requests with a wide range of contributor counts. This demonstrates the robustness of the framework across requests with different counts of contributors. The framework performs relatively well with requests with a small number of contributors in both the metrics. The performance of the framework in MAP is lesser for requests with a higher number of contributors for both our framework and the baseline, showcasing the difficulty of the task when contributor count increases. From Section 4.1, we saw that the most requests have a small number of contributors, showing the effectiveness of the framework for identifying contributors for a wide range of requests.

In summary, the framework performs well for requests having a wide range of contributor counts and is robust to their variation, demonstrating its effectiveness for identifying contributors for different kinds of requests in microfinancing platforms. Next, we will examine the effect of the variation of the requested amount on the performance of the framework.

4.5 Performance across Requested Amounts

As observed during analysis of the data related to the requested amount asked by requests in Section 4.1, the requested amount

Method	Kiva MAP	Kiva P@10	Kiva MRR	DonorChoose MAP	DonorChoose P@10	DonorChoose MRR
Random	0.1253	0.0921	0.2426	0.1892	0.0908	0.2499
Sulprus Maximization [33]	0.1377	0.1602	0.3289	0.1917	0.0948	0.2724
TopicMatch	0.2129	0.2064	0.4411	0.4419	0.1243	0.5943
Promotion [7]	0.2370	0.2612	0.4332	0.6670	0.2924	0.7384
Our Method	**0.3501**	**0.4133**	**0.7489**	**0.7818**	**0.3334**	**0.8775**

Table 2: Performance evaluation of the framework. Our method outperforms baselines by a significant margin.

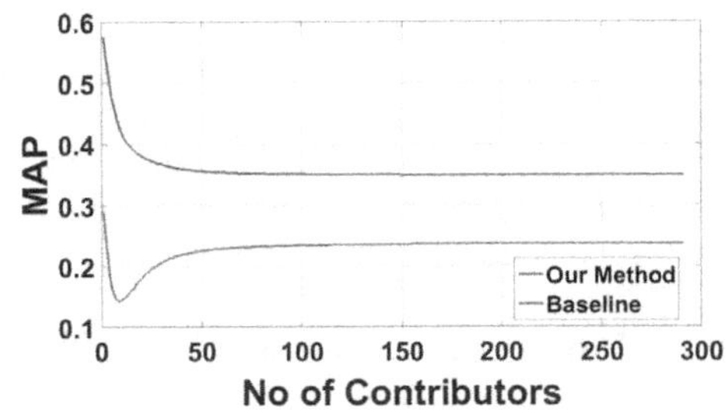

(a) MAP for Varying Amount

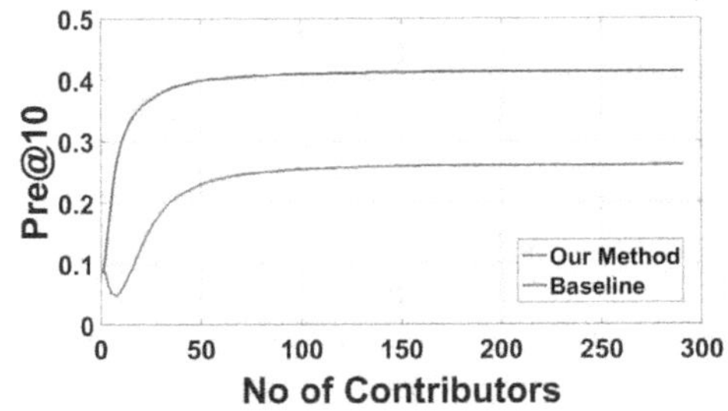

(b) Pre@10 for Varying Amount

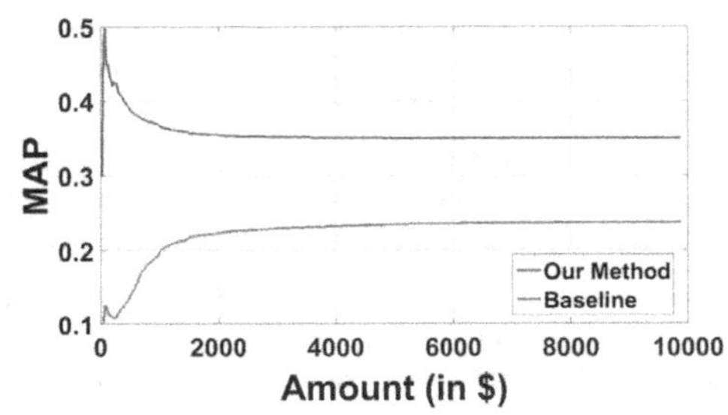

(c) MAP for Varying Contributor Count

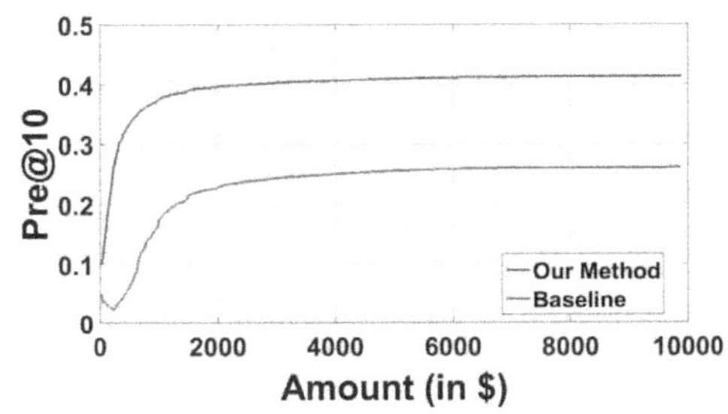

(d) Pre@10 for Varying Contributor Count

Figure 4: Performance of the framework at varying proportions of contributor count and requested amounts. The framework performs well for requests with different contributor counts and requested amounts.

varies widely across different kinds of requests. We now evaluate the performance of the framework across requests asking for various amounts. We then plot the performance of the framework and the nearest baseline[7] in Fig 4(c) and Fig 4(d) using the MAP and Pre@10 metrics. We order the test requests in increasing amount of requested contributions and plot it on the x-axis. For each requested amount on the x-axis, we compute the performance of the framework for requests asking for the same or a lesser amount and plot it on the y-axis.

From Fig 4(c) and Fig 4(d), we notice that the framework outperforms the baselines for requests asking for a broad range of amounts. This demonstrates the robustness of the framework for identifying contributors for a wide variety of requests. The framework performs relatively well with requests requesting a small number of amounts for both the metrics. From Section 4.1, we saw that the most requests request small amounts, showing the effectiveness of the framework for identifying contributors for a wide class of requests in microfinancing problems.

In summary, the framework performs well for requests having a wide range of requested amounts and is robust to their variation, demonstrating its effectiveness for identifying contributors for different kinds of requests in microfinancing platforms. Next, we will examine the effect of the variation of the training data size on the performance of the framework.

4.6 Effect of Variation in Training Data Size

We now examine the change in the performance of the framework with varying proportions of training data. This enables us to examine the performance of the framework when less amount of training information is available and also assess the robustness of the framework with varying training data size. We divide the dataset into ten equal time periods. We keep the first nine epochs for training and the last time epoch for testing. We further train the framework with different proportions of the training data and evaluate the performance using the test dataset. The different proportions of the

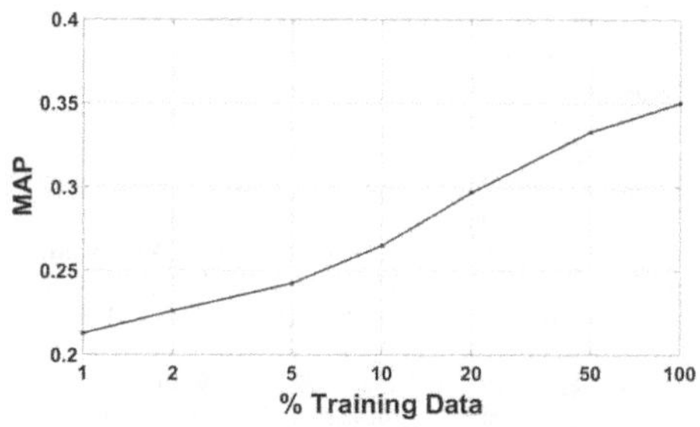

(a) MAP for Varying Training data proportion

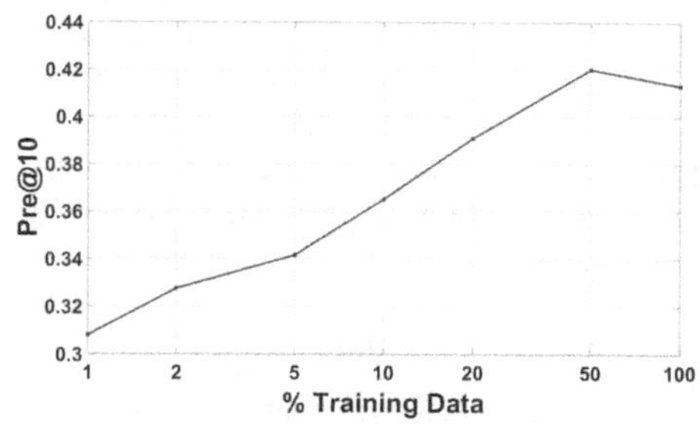

(b) Pre@10 for Varying Training data proportion

Figure 5: Performance of the framework at varying proportions of training data. The framework performs well at low proportions of training data.

training dataset we use are {1%, 2%, 5%, 10%, 20%, 50%, 100%}. We plot the results of the experiment in Fig 5(a) and 5(b) and make the following observations.

From the figure, we can say that the performance of the framework increases with increasing proportion of training data. The framework shows a good performance when 30% of the data is used for training, outperforming the nearest supervised baseline [21], demonstrating that it performs well for fairly low training data sizes. We observe a small dip in performance for higher proportions of training data, and this may be due to insufficient testing data. The performance increases with increasing training data, showing the ability of the framework to utilize the training data points effectively to identify contributors to requests posted in online microfinancing platforms.

In summary, the figure demonstrates that the framework performs well in the presence of small amount of training data and that the framework is effective in learning when more training data is available. This also demonstrates the effectiveness of the proposed framework in exploiting available financial information for identifying such contributors.

In this section, we evaluated the framework and compared it with existing baselines. We then examined the effect of variation of contributor count and requested amounts on its performance. We finally evaluated its performance in the presence of varying training data sizes. We next place our framework in the context of existing literature.

5 RELATED WORK

We present related literature in four categories: the study of resource seeking in social media, the recommendation in online microfinancing platforms, online microfinancing platforms, and Brownian motion models in online platforms.

Resource seeking in social media has received considerable attentions recently [11, 20, 32]. An analytical study of the primary motivations for information seeking and responding in Twitter is presented in [22, 24]. A study of requests and responses received in Facebook [11] presented information seeking as a tool for resource mobilization in social media. Systems have been proposed to identify responders for social media requests to match request content with profile information [14] and use crowdsourced technology [16]. A method for recommending users who can answer requests in social media [21] models temporal, behavioral and content related factors to identify suitable users. An unsupervised framework to identify users who can provide relevant answers for a given social media request is proposed in [29]. These works help social media users to find responders who can provide the information they need and do not address financial requests.

Identifying responders for online microfinancing requests have been addressed in recent literature [8, 33]. A feature based approach based on contributor interest, profile and temporal information was designed to identify appropriate projects to communities [7]. These works provide an insight to design recommender systems for microfinance platforms but do not try to estimate and leverage past contribution amounts. Estimation of individual contribution amounts has been addressed in [33] by maximizing the overall surplus for the investor. These microfinance platforms do not provide interests to the contributors, and moreover, the effect of implicit contribution amounts on user inclination is not taken into consideration. We evaluate our framework using these models proposed in the literature as baselines and the experiments demonstrate that our framework significantly outperforms them.

Increasing attention has been devoted to characterizing user behavior in crowdfunding platforms [5, 6, 13]. The authors in [12] tracks the early rise of online microfinancing and stated that the access to a large number of potential donors could unleash the entrepreneurship of the poor. The motivations of contributors to contribute money is studied in [15] and the desire to help others and be a part of a cause is stated to be a common motivator for contributors. The donor retention in online crowdfunding platforms has been studied in [2] and positive interaction and acknowledgment of their support are found to be predictive of returning donors. Algorithmic systems for crowdfunding domains proposed in the literature include connecting contributors to appropriate teams [6], using communities to identify projects for contributors [7], and identifying appropriate projects to groups of contributors [27].

The study of Brownian motion on online platforms has been investigated in [34–36]. The theoretical development for adapting Brownian motion in the network environment has been considered in [36], with applications in community discovery. Brownian motion has been used to model information propagation processes in the presence of external influence in social networks [17, 28] and the authors model the diffusion process across the propagation network to predict protest participation. Brownian motion models have been used to model financial time series data, including model movements of stock price due to its ability to model sharp changes [31] and to model variation in commodity prices due to change in contributor preferences over time [9].

6 CONCLUSIONS AND FUTURE WORK

Existing microfinancing platforms deal with a large frequency of funding requests, preventing people seeking financial assistance from getting appropriate assistance from potential contributors. Fulfilling financial requests has a cost on contributors which can affect his inclination to contribute. We draw from financial modeling literature to propose a novel framework to identify potential contributors in microfinancing platforms by modeling the effect of implicit individual contribution amounts on his inclination to contribute. We evaluate the framework on two microfinancing platforms to demonstrate its effectiveness in identifying contributors. The robustness of the framework has been shown with varying proportions of information related to contribution counts and requested amounts. We finally evaluate the ability of our framework to identify contributors in varying proportions of training data and demonstrate its effectiveness in the presence of less information.

For future work, techniques such as word-to-vec which are effective for low-dimensional representation, can be integrated into the algorithm to better address novel requests containing words not seen during training. Incorporating features like teams, contributor and request profile information to estimate amounts can further improve the performance of the framework. Estimating contribution amounts considering network effects will provide insight into how contributors are influenced by the donation behavior of their neighbors. Evaluating the privacy issues in leveraging past contribution amounts can shed lights on the characteristics of user vulnerability on microfinancing platforms. Modeling the effect of competition among requesters for identifying contributors will bring new insights on how people compete in a resource constrained environment. Predicting requesters who are prone not to repay the loan will help in increasing the satisfaction of the contributors and increase their faith in the microfinancing platform.

ACKNOWLEDGMENTS

This material is based upon work supported by, or in part by, Office of Naval Research (ONR) under grant numbers N000141410095 and N00014-16-1-2257.

REFERENCES

[1] Wei Ai, Roy Chen, Yan Chen, Qiaozhu Mei, and Webb Phillips. 2016. Recommending teams promotes prosocial lending in online microfinance. *Proceedings of the National Academy of Sciences* 113, 52 (2016), 14944–14948.
[2] Tim Althoff and Jure Leskovec. 2015. Donor retention in online crowdfunding communities: A case study of donorschoose. org. In *WWW*. ACM.
[3] Jisun An, Daniele Quercia, and Jon Crowcroft. 2014. Recommending investors for crowdfunding projects. In *WWW*. ACM.
[4] Paul N Bloom. 2009. Overcoming consumption constraints through social entrepreneurship. *Journal of Public Policy & Marketing* 28, 1 (2009), 128–134.
[5] Tillman Bruett et al. 2007. Cows, Kiva, and Prosper. Com: how disintermediation and the internet are changing microfinance. *Community Development Investment Review* 2 (2007), 44–50.
[6] Roy Chen, Yan Chen, Yang Liu, and Qiaozhu Mei. 2015. Does team competition increase pro-social lending? Evidence from online microfinance. *Games and Economic Behavior* (2015).
[7] Jaegul Choo, Changhyun Lee, Daniel Lee, Hongyuan Zha, and Haesun Park. 2014. Understanding and promoting micro-finance activities in kiva. org. In *WSDM*. ACM.
[8] Jaegul Choo, Daniel Lee, Bistra Dilkina, Hongyuan Zha, and Haesun Park. 2014. To gather together for a better world: understanding and leveraging communities in micro-lending recommendation. In *WWW*. ACM.
[9] Shijie Deng. 2000. *Stochastic models of energy commodity prices and their applications: Mean-reversion with jumps and spikes*. Berkeley: University of California Energy Institute.
[10] Merel Van Diepen, Bas Donkers, and Philip Hans Franses. 2009. Dynamic and competitive effects of direct mailings: A charitable giving application. *Journal of Marketing Research* 46, 1 (2009), 120–133.
[11] Nicole B Ellison, Rebecca Gray, Jessica Vitak, Cliff Lampe, and Andrew T Fiore. 2013. Calling All Facebook Friends: Exploring Requests for Help on Facebook.. In *International AAAI Conference on Web and Social Media*.
[12] Matt Flannery. 2007. Kiva and the birth of person-to-person microfinance. *Innovations* 2, 1-2 (2007), 31–56.
[13] Jeff Galak, Deborah Small, and Andrew T Stephen. 2011. Microfinance decision making: A field study of prosocial lending. *Journal of Marketing Research* 48, SPL (2011), S130–S137.
[14] Brent Hecht, Jaime Teevan, Meredith Morris, and Dan Liebling. 2012. SearchBuddies: Bringing Search Engines into the Conversation. In *ICWSM*.
[15] Julie S Hui, Michael D Greenberg, and Elizabeth M Gerber. 2014. Understanding the role of community in crowdfunding work. In *CSCW*. ACM.
[16] Jin-Woo Jeong, Meredith Ringel Morris, Jaime Teevan, and Dan Liebling. 2013. A Crowd-Powered Socially Embedded Search Engine. In *ICWSM*.
[17] Fang Jin, Rupinder Paul Khandpur, Nathan Self, Edward Dougherty, Sheng Guo, Feng Chen, B Aditya Prakash, and Naren Ramakrishnan. 2014. Modeling mass protest adoption in social network communities using geometric brownian motion. In *KDD*. ACM.
[18] Ioannis Karatzas and Steven Shreve. 2012. *Brownian motion and stochastic calculus*. Vol. 113. Springer Science & Business Media.
[19] Daniel D Lee and H Sebastian Seung. 2001. Algorithms for non-negative matrix factorization. In *NIPS*.
[20] Uichin Lee, Hyanghong Kang, Eunhee Yi, Mun Yi, and Jussi Kantola. 2012. Understanding mobile q&a usage: An exploratory study. In *CHI*. ACM.
[21] Jalal Mahmud, Michelle Zhou, Nimrod Megiddo, Jeffrey Nichols, and Clemens Drews. 2014. Optimizing the selection of strangers to answer questions in social media. *arXiv preprint arXiv:1404.2013* (2014).
[22] Meredith Ringel Morris, Jaime Teevan, and Katrina Panovich. 2010. What do people ask their social networks, and why?: a survey study of status message q&a behavior. In *CHI*. ACM.
[23] Bernt Oksendal. 2003. Stochastic differential equations. In *Stochastic differential equations*. Springer, 65–84.
[24] Sharoda A Paul, Lichan Hong, and Ed H Chi. 2011. Is Twitter a Good Place for Asking Questions? A Characterization Study. In *ICWSM*.
[25] Craig Pirrong. 2011. *Commodity price dynamics: A structural approach*. Cambridge University Press.
[26] Ioana Popescu and Yaozhong Wu. 2007. Dynamic pricing strategies with reference effects. *Operations Research* 55, 3 (2007), 413–429.
[27] Vineeth Rakesh, Wang-Chien Lee, and Chandan K Reddy. 2016. Probabilistic Group Recommendation Model for Crowdfunding Domains. In *WSDM*. ACM.
[28] Suhas Ranganath, Fred Morstatter, Xia Hu, Jiliang Tang, Suhang Wang, and Huan Liu. 2016. Predicting Online Protest Participation of Social Media Users. In *AAAI*.
[29] Suhas Ranganath, Jiliang Tang, Xia Hu, Hari Sundaram, and Huan Liu. 2015. Leveraging Social Foci for Information Seeking in Social Media. In *AAAI*.
[30] Jacob Solomon, Wenjuan Ma, and Rick Wash. 2016. Highly Successful Projects Inhibit Coordination on Crowdfunding Sites. In *CHI*. ACM.
[31] Peter Tankov. 2003. *Financial modelling with jump processes*. Vol. 2. CRC press.
[32] Jiang Yang, Meredith Ringel Morris, Jaime Teevan, Lada A Adamic, and Mark S Ackerman. 2011. Culture Matters: A Survey Study of Social Q&A Behavior. *ICWSM* (2011).
[33] Yongfeng Zhang, Qi Zhao, Yi Zhang, Daniel Friedman, Min Zhang, Yiqun Liu, and Shaoping Ma. 2016. Economic recommendation with surplus maximization. In *WWW*.
[34] Haijun Zhou. 2003. Distance, dissimilarity index, and network community structure. *Physical review* 67, 6 (2003), 061901.
[35] Haijun Zhou. 2003. Network landscape from a Brownian particle's perspective. *Physical Review E* 67, 4 (2003), 041908.
[36] Haijun Zhou and Reinhard Lipowsky. 2004. Network brownian motion: A new method to measure vertex-vertex proximity and to identify communities and subcommunities. In *Computational Science-ICCS 2004*. Springer, 1062–1069.

FACH: Fast Algorithm for Detecting Cohesive Hierarchies of Communities in Large Networks

Mojtaba Rezvani
Australian National University
Canberra, ACT 2601, Australia
mojtaba.rezvani@anu.edu.au

Qing Wang
Australian National University
Canberra, ACT 2601, Australia
qing.wang@anu.edu.au

Weifa Liang
Australian National University
Canberra, ACT 2601, Australia
wliang@cs.anu.edu.au

ABSTRACT

Vertices in a real-world social network can be grouped into densely connected communities that are sparsely connected to other groups. Moreover, these communities can be partitioned into successively more cohesive communities. Despite an ever-growing pile of research on hierarchical community detection, existing methods suffer from either inefficiency or inappropriate modeling. Yet, some cut-based approaches have shown to be effective in finding communities without hierarchies. In this paper, we study the hierarchical community detection problem in large networks and show that it is NP-hard. We then propose an efficient algorithm based on edge-cuts to identify the hierarchy of communities. Since communities at lower levels of the hierarchy are denser than the higher levels, we leverage a fast network sparsification technique to enhance the running time of the algorithm. We further propose a randomized approximation algorithm for information centrality of networks. We finally evaluate the performance of the proposed algorithms by conducting extensive experiments using real datasets. Our experimental results show that the proposed algorithms are promising and outperform the state-of-the-art algorithms by several orders of magnitude.

KEYWORDS

Hierarchical community detection; large-scale networks

ACM Reference Format:

Mojtaba Rezvani, Qing Wang, and Weifa Liang. 2018. FACH: Fast Algorithm for Detecting Cohesive Hierarchies of Communities in Large Networks. In *WSDM 2018: WSDM 2018: The Eleventh ACM International Conference on Web Search and Data Mining , February 5–9, 2018, Marina Del Rey, CA, USA,* Jennifer B. Sartor, Theo D'Hondt, and Wolfgang De Meuter (Eds.). ACM, New York, NY, USA, Article 4, 9 pages. https://doi.org/10.1145/3159652.3159704

1 INTRODUCTION

It is well-known that communities in a network often exhibit a hierarchical structure [9, 23, 27, 28]. For instance, metabolic networks of organisms can be decomposed into highly connected communities, where communities form a hierarchy in which communities at lower levels of the hierarchy are more cohesive, and vertices within those communities are closer to each other [23]. Researchers in a collaboration network can be grouped into communities based on their research areas, from general areas such as computer science to more specific ones such as database and data mining, where information circulates more quickly among them. Therefore, small and cohesive communities are nested into larger and less cohesive communities in a hierarchical manner. Despite the importance of the hierarchical community detection, existing approaches have their limitations. For example, they fail to reveal a cohesive hierarchical structure among communities, or they suffer from inefficiency in large-scale networks. In order to capture cohesiveness, existing approaches for flat community detection, such as k-truss [5] and k-core [3], can be adjusted to detect a hierarchical structure among communities. For instance, one can identify a hierarchy of communities by starting with $k = 1$ and increasing the value of k to obtain more cohesive communities at the lower levels of the hierarchy. Fig. 1 shows a hierarchical structure of communities detected in a real-world network Amazon, where k-core and k-truss both fail to detect the hierarchical structure of communities. It can be seen that for $k < 4$, the whole network is in a single k-core community, while k-truss is unable to detect any community for $k > 4$ or $k < 3$.

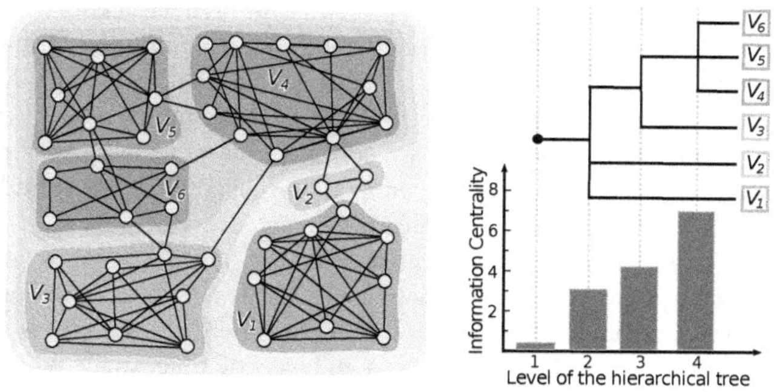

Figure 1: A hierarchical structure of communities in Amazon, where from the root to its leaves connections within communities become denser and the values of their information centrality increase.

Traditionally, hierarchical community detection methods find hierarchies by removing/merging edges and vertices of a network one by one, which can be very time consuming. For example, Girvan and Newman [11, 20] suggested starting with a given network as a community and partitioning the network by removing edges in decreasing order of their betweenness centrality. Similarly, Fortunato et al. [10] advocated to remove edges in order of impact of their removal on the information centrality (mean distance) of a network. Newman [19] proposed an approach, where communities are merged if the modularity of the resulting community can be

ACM ISBN 978-1-4503-5581-0/18/02...$15.00
https://doi.org/10.1145/3159652.3159704

increased, starting from vertices. However, repeatedly calculating modularity, difference in modularity, betweenness and information centralities in a large network is computationally infeasible.

To address the aforementioned issues, we study the problem of hierarchical community detection based on the intuitive cohesiveness among communities in a hierarchy, where communities at lower levels of a cohesive hierarchy are more densely connected with each other. We define the notion of *cohesive hierarchy* that is a rooted tree of communities, where communities at the k-th level of the hierarchy are connected to each other through weak cuts with no larger than k edges. For example in Fig. 1, communities at the second level (V_1, V_2 and $V_3 \cup \ldots \cup V_6$) are connected to each other by two edges, and communities at the third level (V_3 and $V_4 \cup V_5 \cup V_6$) are connected to each other by 3 edges. As we move towards the leaves of this hierarchy, the connectivity becomes stronger and communities become more densely connected.

We propose an efficient, yet scalable cut-based algorithm for detecting a cohesive hierarchy in a large-scale network. However, finding cuts in a network with hundreds of millions of edges is a painstaking task. Particularly at high levels of a hierarchy, when the network has not been broken into smaller subgraphs, finding cuts in the network is a challenge. Based upon this intuition, we optimize the cut detection algorithm by sparsifying the network in early iterations. Specifically, when finding communities at the k-th level of a cohesive hierarchy, we remove unnecessary edges that are not part of any edge-cut with size k. Therefore, when detecting communities at top levels of the hierarchy, the number of edges is significantly reduced, i.e. at most $\min\{m, (k+1)(n-1)\}$ at level k, where n and m are the number of edges and vertices.

One of the key ingredients of the proposed cohesive hierarchical community structure is the information centrality of communities, which is increased from communities at one level to communities at a lower level of the hierarchy. However, the information centrality can be calculated in time $O(nm)$, which is unrealistic in real-world networks. Moreover, the diameter in real-world networks is usually small, as they exhibit a small-world characteristic. Therefore, we propose a randomized approximation algorithm for calculating the information centrality whose error is no larger than a fraction ϵ of the network diameter, with high probability (at least $1 - \frac{1}{n}$), while it runs in time $\Theta(m \log n/\epsilon^2)$, where n and m are the number of vertices and the number of edges, respectively.

Our contributions in this paper are as follows,

- We first formalize the problem of cohesive hierarchical community detection, where the granularity of a community is measured using information centrality, and prove the NP-hardness of this problem.
- We then develop an efficient algorithm for the hierarchical community detection problem and enhance the algorithm by incorporating a fast sparsification for efficiently finding less granular levels of the hierarchy.
- We devise a randomized algorithm for approximating the information centrality of a network with a guaranteed approximation ratio.
- We finally evaluate the effectiveness and efficiency of our proposed algorithms by quantitatively analysing their performance using five real-world datasets.

The rest of this paper is organized as follows. Section 2 introduces preliminaries and Section 3 introduces the problem definition. Section 4 presents two novel algorithms for the hierarchical community detection problem and Section 5 presents an approximation algorithm for information centrality. Section 6 discusses the experimental results, which compare the performance of our proposed algorithms against the benchmark algorithms. Section 7 provides a literature review, and Section 8 concludes the paper.

2 PRELIMINARIES

A network can be modeled as an undirected connected graph $G = (V, E)$, where V is the set of vertices representing individuals and E is the set of edges representing relationships between individuals. Let $n = |V|$ and $m = |E|$. The *degree* of a vertex v is the number of edges incident to it, denoted by $deg(v)$. Two paths in G are called *edge-disjoint* if they do not share any edges. The number of edge-disjoint paths between two vertices u and v is the *edge-connectivity* between them, denoted by $\lambda(u, v)$. Two vertices u and v are said to be *k-edge-connected* if $\lambda(u, v) \geq k$. An *edge-cut* between two subsets V_1 and V_2 in G, denoted as $E[V_1, V_2]$, is the set of edges in G such that their removal will disconnect V_1 and V_2. For brevity, we simply write $E[V_1]$, whenever $V_1 = V_2$. Given a subset V' of V, $G[V'] = (V', E[V'])$ is the induced subgraph of G by V'.

Traditionally, communities are perceived as subsets of vertices of a graph G that the number of edges among them (density of connections) is large. Following this perception, it is possible to find hierarchical communities by recursively increasing the density threshold, and consequently finding denser communities. In this paper, we take the relationships among communities into account for finding hierarchical communities of a network, while previous studies only focused on the relationships among vertices. Specifically, we here represent the hierarchy of communities as a rooted tree of subsets of vertices in G. Given two partitions $P = \{V_1, \cdots, V_{|P|}\}$ and $P' = \{V'_1, \cdots, V_{|P'|}\}$ of V , we say that P has a higher *hierarchical order* than P', denoted by $P > P'$, if for every set $V'_i \in P'$ there is a strict superset $V_j \in P$ that includes V'_i, i.e. $V'_i \subset V_j$. However, the density of connections among communities is not uniform across different levels of a cohesive hierarchy. In fact, density of connections among communities becomes larger at lower levels of a cohesive hierarchy. Therefore, we say that P has a higher *hierarchical order at degree k* compared to P', denoted by $P >_k P'$, if for every set $V'_i \in P'$ there is a set $V_j \in P$ such that $V'_i \subset V_j$ and for every set $V'_j \in P'$, $E[V'_i, V'_j] \leq k$. A sequence of partitions of V, e.g. $\mathcal{P} = \langle P_1, \cdots, P_{|P|}\rangle$ is said to be a *hierarchy*, if $P_{i-1} > P_i$ $(1 < i \leq |\mathcal{P}|)$. We refer to $\mathcal{P}' = \langle P'_1, \cdots, P'_{|\mathcal{P}'|}\rangle$ as a *cohesive hierarchy* if $P'_{i-1} >_i P'_i$ $(1 < i \leq |\mathcal{P}'|)$. We note that every cohesive hierarchy is a hierarchy, but a hierarchy is not necessarily cohesive. Given a hierarchy $\mathcal{P}$, we refer to $P_{|\mathcal{P}|}$ the lowest level of hierarchy and we refer to P_1 as the root of the hierarchy. For every partition $P_i \in \mathcal{P}$, we say that $P_j \in \mathcal{P}$ is at a lower level if $j > i$.

Example 2.1. Let us consider the network illustrated in Fig. 1, where V is the set of vertices of the network and V_i is the set of vertices in a subgraph G_i $(1 \leq i \leq 6)$. We show that $\mathcal{P} = \langle P_1, P_2, P_3, P_4\rangle$ is a cohesive hierarchy, where $P_1 = \{V\}$, $P_2 = \{V_1, V_2, V_3 \cup V_4 \cup V_5 \cup V_6\}$, $P_3 = \{V_1, V_2, V_3, V_4 \cup V_5 \cup V_6\}$, and $P_4 = \{V_1, V_2, V_3, V_4, V_5, V_6\}$. It can be seen that $P_1 >_2 P_2$, since vertices in V_1, V_2 and $V_3 \cup V_4 \cup V_5 \cup V_6$

are connected to each other by at most 2 edges. Furthermore, $P_2 \succ_3 P_3$, since V_3 is connected to $V_4 \cup V_5 \cup V_6$ by at most 3 edges. Also $P_3 \succ_4 P_4$, as V_4, V_5 and V_6 are connected to their siblings by at most 4 edges, which means that $P_4 = \{V_1, V_2, V_3, V_4, V_5, V_6\}$. As a result, $\mathcal{P} = \langle P_1, P_2, P_3, P_4 \rangle$ is a cohesive hierarchy. It is also noted that a cohesive hierarchy such as $\mathcal{P}$ results in a decomposition tree that is illustrated in Fig. 2, where siblings at level k of the decomposition tree are connected to each other by at most k edges.

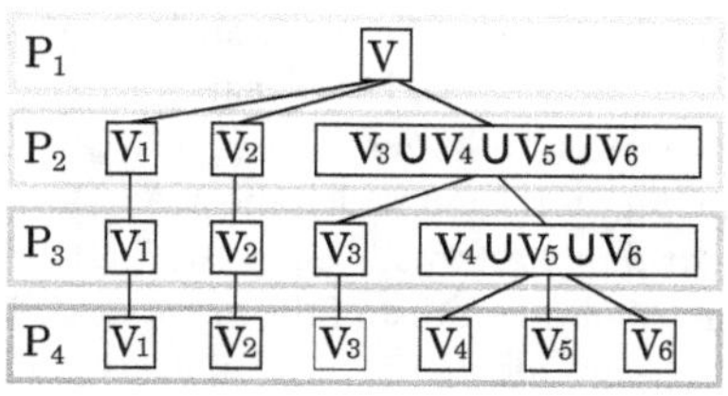

Figure 2: The cohesive hierarchy of the network in Fig. 1

The *distance* between two vertices u and v in a graph G, denoted by d^G_{uv}, is the length of the shortest path between them. We have $d^G_{vv} = 0$ for any vertex $v \in V$. The *diameter* of G is the length of the longest shortest path between any pair of vertices in G, denoted by Δ. The *information centrality* of G, denoted by $\mathcal{D}(G)$, is the inverse of mean distance between every pair of vertices u and v [10], i.e.,

$$\mathcal{D}(G) = \frac{n(n-1)}{\sum\limits_{v \in V} \sum\limits_{u \in V} d^G_{uv}}. \tag{1}$$

The measure in Eq. (1) has been widely adopted for modeling information centrality in many networks [10, 24].

3 PROBLEM DEFINITION

In this section, we formally define the problem of hierarchical community detection, based on information centrality.

Definition 3.1 (HCDP). Given a network G, the *hierarchical community detection problem* is to find a cohesive hierarchy $\mathcal{P}$ of communities, where the sum of information centralities of the subgraphs induced by all partitions in $\mathcal{P}$ is maximized, i.e.

$$\text{maximize} \sum_{P_i \in \mathcal{P}} \sum_{V' \in P_i \setminus P_{i-1}} \mathcal{D}\left(G[V']\right). \tag{2}$$

The flat community detection is a special case of this hierarchical community detection problem, when $|\mathcal{P}| = 1$. In the following, we show that the hierarchical community detection problem is NP-hard by a reduction from the maximum clique problem to its special case, i.e. the flat community detection problem. We first define the decision version of the flat community detection problem.

Definition 3.2 (CDP Decision). Given a network $G = (V, E)$, a rational number $\epsilon > 0$ and a positive integer k, the *community detection decision problem* is to determine whether there is a subset V' of vertices with size k, whose information centrality is no less than ϵ, i.e. $\mathcal{D}\left(G[V']\right) \geq \epsilon$.

The following lemma shows that the CDP Decision problem is NP-hard, using a reduction from the MaximumClique problem.

Lemma 3.3. *CDP Decision problem is NP-Complete.*

Proof. We first show that CDP Decision is in NP. Given a certificate of CDP Decision, which consists of a network G, and a set of vertices $V' \subseteq V$ with $|V'| = k$, we can use all-pairs shortest paths algorithm [6] to determine if $\mathcal{D}(G[V']) \geq \epsilon$, in polynomial time. Thus, CDP Decision is in NP.

We now show that CDP Decision is NP-hard by a reduction from the MaximumClique problem. Note that a subset of vertices V' form a clique in G, if and only if the information centrality of the induced subgraph $G[V']$ is 1, i.e. $\mathcal{D}(G[V']) = 1$. Therefore, it is implied that the MaximumClique problem is a special case of CDP Decision, where $\epsilon = 1$. Thus, given a network G and a positive integer k, one can decide the existence of a clique of the given size k by solving the CDP Decision. □

4 COHESIVE HIERARCHICAL COMMUNITY DETECTION

In this section, we propose two efficient, yet scalable algorithms for the cohesive hierarchical community detection problem: (i) CHD which is a basic cut-based algorithm to iteratively partition the network into densely connected communities, and (ii) FACH which is an optimized cut-based algorithm that relies on a sparsification technique to find sparse communities at high levels of a hierarchy.

4.1 The basic algorithm (CHD)

The CHD algorithm proceeds iteratively to identify a cohesive hierarchy $\mathcal{P}$ from a given network G. In each iteration, it finds one level of the hierarchy by creating a partition of each subset of vertices at its parent level. In iteration k, the algorithm finds a partition P_k by decomposing subsets of vertices in P_{k-1} into several subsets, where k is 1 initially, and incremented in each iteration.

Let $\mathcal{P}$ be a detected cohesive hierarchy of communities in network G, which is initialized by $\emptyset$ and let P_k be the k-th level of hierarchy $\mathcal{P}$. We assume that P_0 consists of all vertices as a community. Let k be the size of cuts detected by CHD in iteration k, which is initialized to 1 in the first iteration. In iteration k of the algorithm, for every set of vertices V' in P_{k-1}, which is currently a leaf in $\mathcal{P}$, an induced subgraph $G' = G[V']$ is constructed. Then a multi-cut of size no larger than k is detected in G' using the following procedure, called MAS-Decompose, and the result of removing this cut from G' is stored in another subgraph G''. The procedure MAS-Decompose [2] decomposes the subgraph G' into several connected components in G'', such that each connected component in G'' is connected to other vertices by at most k edges. The CHD algorithm then calculates the information centrality of G' and G'', and if the information centrality of G'' is no less than that of the initial subgraph G', it adds vertices in connected components of G'' to the k-th level of the hierarchy, i.e. P_k. Otherwise, the initial set of vertices V' is added to P_k. The CHD algorithm increments k and constructs levels of the hierarchy, until for all $V' \in P_{k-1}$, the algorithm cannot find a multi-cut of size k in G' that can increase the information centrality of G''. The detailed description of steps is given by Algorithm 1.

The rest is to show the time complexity of Algorithm 1 as follows.

Theorem 4.1. *Given a network $G = (V, E)$, the algorithm CHD delivers a feasible solution for the hierarchical community detection problem in time $O(n^2 m + n^3 \log(n))$.*

Algorithm 1 CHD(G)

Input: $G = (V, E)$
Output: A cohesive hierarchy $\mathcal{P}$

$\mathcal{P} \leftarrow \emptyset$; /* Initialize the cohesive hierarchy */
$k \leftarrow 0$;
$P_k \leftarrow \{V\}$; /* P_k is the value of k-th level of the hierarchy */
$P_{k-1} \leftarrow \emptyset$;
while $(\mathcal{D}(P_k) - \mathcal{D}(P_{k-1}) > 0)$ **do**
  $k \leftarrow k + 1$; /* Increment the value of k for this iteration */
  $P_k \leftarrow \emptyset$;
  for each $V' \in P_{k-1}$ **do**
    $G' \leftarrow G[V']$;
    $G'' \leftarrow$ MAS-Decompose(G', k); /* G'' is a graph created by removing the edges in the multi-cut of size k found by MAS from G' */
    if $\mathcal{D}(G') \leq \mathcal{D}(G'')$ **then**
      Add connected components of G'' to P_k;
    else
      $P_k \leftarrow P_k \cup \{V'\}$;
  $\mathcal{P} \leftarrow \{P_k\}$;
return $\mathcal{P}$;

Proof. The CHD algorithm proceeds iteratively. Within each iteration, for every subgraph $G[V']$ ($V' \in P_{k-1}$), a MAS-Decompose is applied in time $O(nm + n^2 \log(n))$, and the calculation of information centrality takes $O(nm)$ time.

Therefore, the time complexity of MAS-Decompose is dominant at each iteration of the CHD algorithm. It is also noted that the hierarchy $\mathcal{P}$ has at most n leaves, as the number of subgraphs is no larger than the number of vertices in the network (due to the Pigeonhole principle). Therefore, MAS-Decompose is called at most n times in each iteration of the CHD algorithm. However, in each iteration of the CHD algorithm, MAS-Decompose is run on partitions of the actual graph. Let n' and m' be the number of vertices and edges in the induced subgraph by each leaf V', i.e. $G[V']$. It is then implied that $\sum_{V' \in P_{k-1}} n'm' \leq nm$ as $\sum_{V' \in P_{k-1}} n' \leq n$ and $\sum_{V' \in P_{k-1}} m' \leq m$. This means that the overall time complexity of each iteration is no larger than $O(nm + n^2 \log(n))$. Since the edge-connectivity of a network is at most $n - 1$, the time complexity of the CHD algorithm is $O(n^2 m + n^3 \log(n))$. □

4.2 The FACH algorithm

We here propose an algorithm, called FACH, that can reduce the number of edges from m in iteration k to $\min\{m, (k+1)(n-1)\}$, where n and m are the number of vertices and edges in a network.

In the following, we describe the construction of a sparse network $G_i = (V, E_i)$ $(1 \leq i \leq m)$ from $G = (V, E)$ which is noticeably smaller than G, while it can be used to find minimum cuts of G.

Lemma 4.2. *[18] Given a network $G = (V, E)$ and an integer $k > 0$, let $F_1 = (V, E_1)$ be a spanning forest in G and $F_i = (V, E_i)$ be a spanning forest in $G \setminus E_1 \cup E_2 \cdots E_{i-1}$ $(1 < i \leq k - 1)$. For any two vertices $s \in V$ and $t \in V$, if they are k-edge-connected in G, then they must be k-edge-connected in $G_k = F_1 \cup \cdots \cup F_k$.*

Lemma 4.2 states that in the second iteration, where $k = 2$, we can find a cut with size k in a network with at most $3(n-1)$ edges, instead of the entire network with m edges. Similarly, in iteration k of the algorithm, a cut of size k can be found in a network with $\min((k+1)(n-1), m)$ edges.

Motivated by Lemma 4.2, we propose the FACH algorithm that runs significantly faster than the CHD algorithm by starting from a sparse network and gradually increasing the network size as a factor of k. Specifically, in iteration k of this algorithm, the MAS-Decompose is run on a subgraph of the initial network with at most $\min\{(k+1)(n-1), m\}$ edges. In other words, the network size in the first iteration is no larger than $2(n-1)$. In the second iteration, the network size is no larger than $3(n-1)$ and in iteration k, the network size is no larger than $(k+1)(n-1)$. Let G_k be the network in iteration k, on which the MAS-Decompose is run. The FACH algorithm starts with $G_0 = MSF(G)$, where $MSF(G)$ is the minimum spanning forest of the network G. The algorithm then constructs G_k by adding the minimum spanning forest of the residual network $G \setminus G_{k-1}$ to G_{k-1}.

Let $\mathcal{P}$ be a cohesive hierarchy, which is initially empty. The algorithm iteratively increments the value of k and finds P_k, the partition representing the k-th level of the cohesive hierarchy $\mathcal{P}$, until the information centrality of P_k cannot be increased. Let $P_0 = \{V\}$. In iteration k, the FACH algorithm finds a minimum spanning forest F_k and form $G \setminus G_{k-1}$, where G_{k-1} is the union of spanning forests found in iterations 1 to $k - 1$. For each community $V' \in P_{k-1}$, the FACH algorithm creates an induced subgraph $G_k[V']$ and finds a multi-cut in it using the MAS-Decompose procedure. If the removal of the multi-cut can increase the information centrality, the FACH algorithm applies the cut; otherwise, it proceeds to the next community in P_{k-1}. The detailed steps of the FACH algorithm is given in Algorithm 2.

Algorithm 2 FACH(G)

Input: $G = (V, E)$
Output: A cohesive hierarchy $\mathcal{P}$

$\mathcal{P} \leftarrow \emptyset$; /* Initialize the cohesive hierarchy */
$k \leftarrow 0$;
$G_k \leftarrow MSF(G)$; /* Find a Minimum Spanning Forest of G */
$P_k \leftarrow \{V\}$; /* P_k is the k-th level of the hierarchy */
$P_{k-1} \leftarrow \emptyset$;
while $(\mathcal{D}(P_k) - \mathcal{D}(P_{k-1}) > 0)$ **do**
  $k \leftarrow k + 1$; /* Increment the value of k for this iteration */
  /* Find a Minimum Spanning Forest of $G \setminus G_{k-1}$ */
  $F_k \leftarrow MSF(G \setminus G_{k-1})$;
  $G_k \leftarrow F_k \cup G_{k-1}$;
  $P_k \leftarrow \emptyset$;
  for each $V' \in P_{k-1}$ **do**
    $G' \leftarrow G_k[V']$;
    $G'' \leftarrow$ MAS-Decompose(G', k);
    if $\mathcal{D}(G') \leq \mathcal{D}(G'')$ **then**
      Add connected components of G'' to P_k;
    else
      $P_k \leftarrow P_k \cup \{V'\}$;
  $\mathcal{P} \leftarrow \{P_k\}$;
return $\mathcal{P}$;

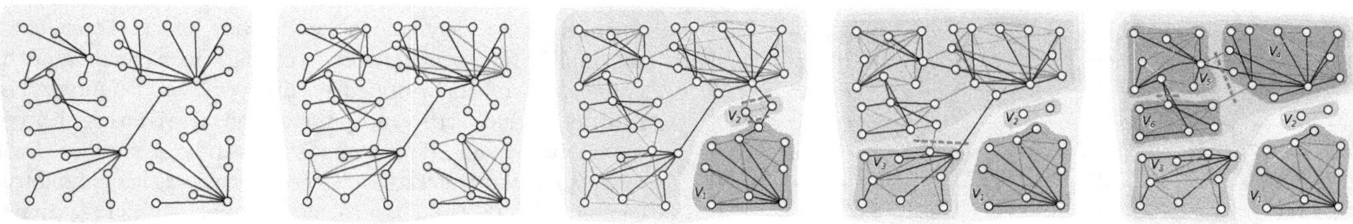

(a) $k = 0$ (b) $k = 1$ (c) $k = 2$ (d) $k = 3$ (e) $k = 4$

Figure 3: A running example of the FACH algorithm with the sparsification technique.

Example 4.3. Fig. 3 illustrates a running example of the FACH algorithm, in which network is sparsified in early iterations for finding cohesive communities. In Fig. 3b, it can be seen that in the first iteration, the edge-cuts are found in a network that has only $81 = 43 + 38$ edges, which is sparser than the original network that has 124 edges. The number of edges is increased to $105 = 77 + 28$ and $113 = 102 + 11$ in the third and fourth iterations, respectively.

We now provide the time complexity of the FACH algorithm.

THEOREM 4.4. *Given a network $G = (V, E)$, there is an algorithm for the hierarchical community detection problem, i.e. the* FACH *algorithm, which delivers a feasible solution in time $O(nm)$.*

PROOF. The FACH algorithm consists of several iterations, where in iteration k, the union of spanning forests for levels 1 to $k-1$, i.e. G_i is constructed and for every induced subgraph $G_i[V']$ ($V' \in P_{k-1}$), a MAS-Decompose is applied, and the value of the information centrality is calculated in $O(nm)$ time.

The time complexity of the MAS-Decompose is $O(nm + n^2)$ and the time complexity of information centrality estimation is $O(nm)$. Since the network is connected $m \geq n - 1$, the time complexity of the FACH algorithm is $O(nm)$. □

5 APPROXIMATING INFORMATION CENTRALITY

To efficiently detect a cohesive hierarchy of communities in a large-scale network, one challenge is to calculate the value of information centrality. One straightforward way to calculate the information centrality is to discover all-pairs shortest paths, which is very time-consuming or even infeasible for real-world networks. Thus, we devise a simple, yet scalable algorithm for approximating the information centrality in polylogarithmic time.

We here build on top of the results obtained by Eppstein et al. [8] and devise a randomized algorithm, Algorithm 3, that finds the information centrality of a network using a small number of randomly selected vertices from the network. The algorithm first selects a set S ($|S| = s$) of vertices from V, uniformly at random. It then runs the single-source shortest path algorithm (BFS), starting from each randomly selected vertex in S. Finally, it estimates the value of information centrality of the network using the following equation,

$$\hat{\mathcal{D}}(G) = \frac{s \cdot (n-1)}{\sum\limits_{u \in S} \sum\limits_{v \in V} d^G_{uv}}. \tag{3}$$

Algorithm 3 describes an overal view of the approximation algorithm for information centrality in a given network.

Algorithm 3 Estimated information centrality

Input: $G = (V, E)$, s
Output: $\hat{\mathcal{D}}(G)$

Let S be a set of s vertices selected uniformly at random;
for each vertex $u \in S$ **do**
  Calculate shortest paths d^G_{uv} from u to all $v \in V$;
for each vertex $v \in V$ **do**
  $\hat{C}(v) \leftarrow \sum_{u \in S} d^G_{uv}$;
$\hat{\mathcal{D}}(G) \leftarrow s \cdot (n-1) / \sum_{v \in V} \hat{C}(v)$;
return $\hat{\mathcal{D}}(G)$;

5.1 Theoretical analysis

We now analyse the approximation algorithm for information centrality. We first review the Hoeffding lemma [14] as follows.

LEMMA 5.1 (HOEFFDING [14]). *If $x_1, x_2, \cdots, x_n$ are independent variables, such that variable x_i ($1 \leq i \leq n$) is bounded by a_i and b_i, and $\mu = E[\sum x_i / n]$ is the expected mean, then for $\xi > 0$,*

$$\Pr\left\{ \left| \frac{\sum_{i=1}^n x_i}{n} - \mu \right| \geq \xi \right\} \leq 2e^{-2n^2\xi^2 / \sum_{i=1}^n (b_i - a_i)^2}. \tag{4}$$

Due to the small-world characteristic of complex networks [30], the diameter in such networks is usually small. Therefore, we show that the error of Algorithm 3 for approximating the information centrality of networks is no larger than $\epsilon\Delta$ with a high probability, where Δ is the diameter of network and ϵ is a given approximation ratio.

THEOREM 5.2. *Given a network $G = (V, E)$, and a set S of randomly selected vertices with size $\Theta(\log(n)/\epsilon^2)$, Algorithm 3 approximates the reciprocal of information centrality such that $|1/\hat{\mathcal{D}}(G) - 1/\mathcal{D}(G)| \leq \epsilon\Delta$, with high probability of at least $1 - 1/n$.*

PROOF. Recall that Algorithm 3 chooses $s = |S|$ random samples from vertices and the approximated value of information centrality is

$$\hat{\mathcal{D}}(G) = \frac{s \cdot (n-1)}{\sum\limits_{u \in S} \sum\limits_{v \in V} d^G_{uv}} = \frac{s \cdot n \cdot (n-1)}{n \cdot \sum\limits_{u \in S} \sum\limits_{v \in V} d^G_{uv}}. \tag{5}$$

It is noted that the expected reciprocal of estimation, i.e. $1/\hat{\mathcal{D}}(G)$, is the reciprocal of actual information centrality, i.e. $1/\mathcal{D}(G)$. Thus, in Hoeffding lemma, considering $x_i = \frac{n \sum_{v \in V} d^G_{iv}}{n(n-1)}$, we can safely assume that $\mu = 1/\mathcal{D}(G)$, $a_i = 0$ and $b_i = n\Delta/(n-1)$. Therefore, the probability that the difference between the reciprocal estimated information centrality $1/\hat{\mathcal{D}}(G)$ and the actual reciprocal information

Table 1: Real datasets with their characteristics.

Dataset	# vertices	# edges	# communities	Δ
Facebook	4,039	88,234	308	8
Amazon	334,863	925,872	14,529	44
DBLP	317,080	1,049,866	7,556	21
LiveJournal	3,997,962	34,681,189	12,115	17
Orkut	3,072,441	117,185,083	9,120	9

centrality $1/\mathcal{D}(G)$ being more than ξ is

$$\Pr\left\{|\frac{1}{\hat{\mathcal{D}}(G)} - \frac{1}{\mathcal{D}(G)}| \geq \xi\right\} \leq 2e^{-2s^2\xi^2/s(\frac{n\Delta}{n-1})^2}.$$

Considering the error being a small fraction of the diameter of G, i.e. $\xi = \epsilon\Delta \ll \Delta$, and using $s = \frac{\log n}{\epsilon^2}$ random samples, it can be seen that the probability of error is bounded above by $1/n$. Therefore, the approximation error of Algorithm 3 is smaller than $\epsilon\Delta$ with a high probability of at least $(n-1)/n$. □

The following theorem shows that the time complexity of the FACH algorithm with the proposed randomized approximation algorithm can be reduced to $O(n^2)$.

THEOREM 5.3. *Given a network $G = (V, E)$, where $m = cn$ with constant c, the* FACH *algorithm delivers a feasible solution for the hierarchical community detection problem (HCDP), in time $O(n^2)$.*

PROOF. The FACH algorithm proceeds iteratively, where in iteration k, the union of spanning forests for levels 1 to $k-1$, i.e. G_i is constructed and for every induced subgraph $G_i[V']$ ($V' \in P_{k-1}$), a MAS-Decompose is applied, and the value of the information centrality is calculated, using Algorithm 3.

As mentioned above, the time complexity of the MAS-Decompose is $O(nm+n^2)$ and the time complexity of information centrality estimation is $O(m \log n + n \log^2 n)$. It can be seen that MAS-Decompose dominates the time-complexities of each iteration of the FACH algorithm. In iteration k, the network size is $k(n-1)$. Since the number of edges in real-world social networks is usually a constant factor of the number of vertices, i.e. $m = cn$, for a constant c, the hierarchies $\mathcal{P}$ will have at most a constant number $k \leq c$ of levels. Therefore, the overall time complexity of the FACH algorithm is $O(n^2)$. □

6 EXPERIMENTAL RESULTS

In this section, we discuss the performance of the proposed algorithms, i.e. CHD and FACH, on several real datasets by comparing against several state-of-the-art algorithms. We first describe the experimental settings and then evaluate the performance of the proposed algorithms in detecting the hierarchical structure of communities. We finally investigate the performance of the CHD and FACH algorithms in finding different levels of a hierarchy.

6.1 Experimental settings

We introduce the benchmark algorithms, datasets and measures that were adopted for evaluating the proposed algorithms.

Benchmark algorithms. We compare the performance of the proposed algorithms, i.e. `CHD` and `FACH`, with the following state-of-the-art algorithms for hierarchical community detection: `LinkCluster` [1], `CNM` [4], `InfoMap` [26], and `OSLOM` [16].

Datasets. We used five real datasets that are publicly available[1], and have been widely used in the literature [32]: (1) Facebook is a subgraph of the social network facebook, where communities are groups of members identified by surveyed users, (2) Amazon is a network in which vertices are products and there is an edge between two vertices i and j if product i is frequently co-purchased with product j. Products in each category are considered as ground-truth communities, (3) DBLP is a collaboration network of researchers, where communities are defined as journals and conferences, (4) LiveJournal is a friendship network of users in the LiveJournal website. Users can create groups, and these groups are considered as the ground-truth communities. (5) Orkut is the friendship network of Orkut members. Communities in this network are groups created by users, where users can join each group.

Evaluation measures. Measuring the quality of detected communities is challenging, as different metrics lead to different interpretations of communities. We employ F-measure that is widely-adopted in the literature [12, 31–34] for quantifying the accuracy of detected communities. Let C^* be the set of ground-truth communities and let C be a detected community. The F-measure of C compared to $C^* \in \mathcal{C}^*$ is defined as follows,

$$F_k(C) = \max_{C^* \in \mathcal{C}^*} \{\frac{(k+1) \cdot p(C, C^*) \cdot r(C, C^*)}{k \cdot p(C, C^*) + r(C, C^*)}\}, \quad (6)$$

where $p(C, C^*) = |C \cap C^*|/|C|$ and $r(C, C^*) = |C \cap C^*|/|C^*|$ are the precision and recall, respectively. To calculate the accuracy of a flat community detection algorithm, one may calculate the average of F_1 and F_2-measures for all detected communities [12, 31–34]. However, the situation is different for hierarchical community detection algorithms, as communities detected at each level of a hierarchy have different characteristics and can be interpreted differently. One general rule in hierarchical community detection is that communities at the lower levels are smaller, more connected and more cohesive than the ones at the higher levels. Therefore, we suggest a weighting method in calculating the F-measure of communities at different levels of a hierarchy, which provides us with the ability to put more weight on communities at lower levels. Specifically, we incorporate a weight α_i, called the weight of level i, into F-measure of communities at level i of a hierarchy. Given a detected hierarchy $\mathcal{P} = \{P_1, \cdots, P_{|\mathcal{P}|}\}$, we define the F-measure of $\mathcal{P}$ as follows,

$$F_k(\mathcal{P}) = \sum_{1 \leq i \leq |\mathcal{P}|} \frac{1}{|\mathcal{P}|} \sum_{C \in P_i} \alpha_i \frac{F_k(C)}{|P_i|}, \quad (7)$$

$$\text{where } \alpha_i = \frac{i}{\sum_{1 \leq j \leq |\mathcal{P}|} j}.$$

Notice that the term α_i is called the weight of level i, which is used to emphasize on the accuracy of communities at the lower levels of the hierarchy. Although there are an infinite number of ways to define the weights α_i, we use a simple intuitive definition that makes both empirical and analytical sense.

All our experiments were run on a desktop computer with an Intel(R) Core(TM) i7-3770 CPU (3.40GHz) and 32GB of RAM.

[1] http://snap.stanford.edu/data/index.html

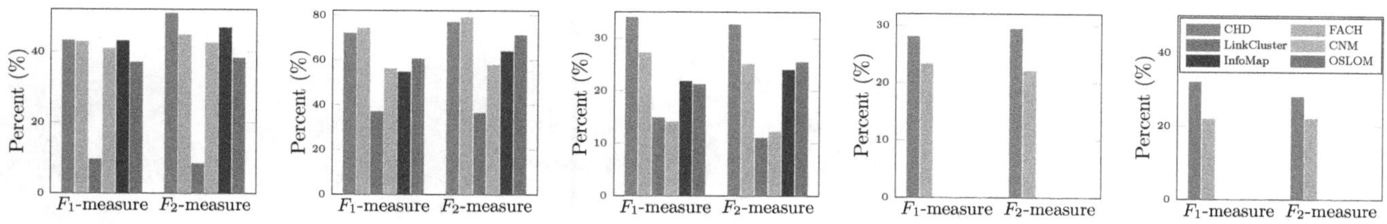

(a) Facebook (b) Amazon (c) DBLP (d) LiveJournal (e) Orkut

Figure 4: F_1 and F_2-measures of the hierarchical community detection algorithms.

6.2 Accuracy and efficiency

We study the accuracy and efficiency of our proposed algorithms CHD and FACH in hierarchical community detection by calculating the F-measures of communities found in each network and comparing them against the benchmark algorithms.

Fig. 4 shows the accuracy of different hierarchical community detection algorithms in terms of F_1 and F_2-measures. It can be seen in Fig. 4a that algorithms CHD and FACH outperform the benchmark algorithms by nearly 1% in F_1-measure for dataset Facebook. Fig. 4a also shows that algorithm CHD outperforms all other algorithms by at least 5% in F_2-measure using dataset Facebook. In Fig. 4b, it can be seen that the F_1 measures of algorithms CHD and FACH are at least 10% higher than the other algorithms in the benchmark using dataset Amazon. Similarly, F_2-measures for both CHD and FACH in this dataset are at least 5% higher than all other algorithms for dataset Amazon. Fig 4c plots the results for dataset DBLP, where it can be observed that both F_1 and F_2-measures of algorithm CHD is at least 20% higher than all other benchmark algorithms. However, the accuracy of algorithm FACH is slightly less than that of algorithm CHD for dataset DBLP. Fig. 4d presents the results for dataset LiveJournal and Fig. 4e presents the results for dataset Orkut, where due to the large size of the datasets only algorithms CHD and FACH terminated. It is noted that we waited for 150 hours for all algorithms to terminate, but only CHD and FACH found the results. Yet, the accuracy of the results is reasonable (above 20% for both datasets LiveJournal and Orkut). It is noted in Fig. 4 that the performance of algorithm CHD is better than that of algorithm FACH in datasets LiveJournal and Orkut. The reason is that algorithm CHD spends more time in finding edge-cuts in the networks.

Fig. 5 depicts the running times of different hierarchical community detection algorithms. Although dataset Facebook is small, Fig. 5 shows that the running time of algorithms CHD and FACH is only a fraction of all other benchmark algorithms. In Fig. 5, for dataset Amazon, the running time of algorithm CHD is at most 1/50 of that of all benchmark algorithms, and the running time of algorithm FACH is only 80% of the running time of algorithm CHD. Similarly, for dataset DBLP, the running time of algorithm CHD is at most 1/75 of the running time of benchmark algorithms, and the running time of algorithm FACH is only 60% of the running time of algorithm CHD. However, for datasets LiveJournal and Orkut, only algorithms CHD and FACH terminated within 150 hours, and their running time was less than 30 minutes for such a large datasets. Fig. 5 illustrates that the running time of algorithm FACH is less than that of algorithm CHD, because of the sparsification technique. However, for dataset Orkut, both algorithms CHD and FACH have similar running times, because these algorithms discovers more levels of the hierarchy.

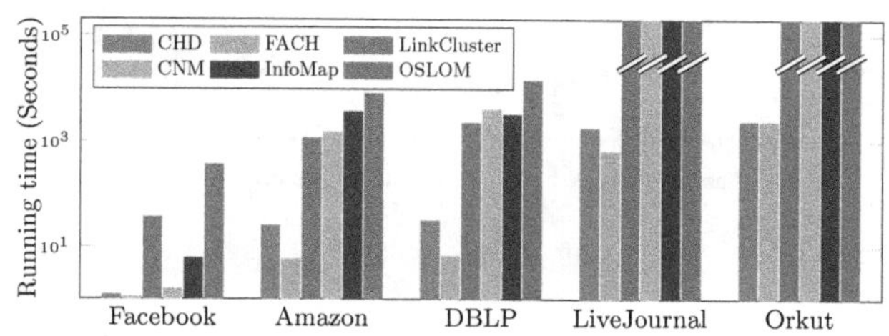

Figure 5: Running times of hierarchical community detection algorithms, where bars with parallel lines indicate that the corresponding algorithm did not terminate in 150 hours.

6.3 Hierarchies: level by level

Fig. 6 illustrates the values of F_1-measure, F_2-measure, information centrality and running times for the communities at each level of hierarchies detected by algorithms CHD and FACH. Fig. 6a shows that for dataset facebook, the value of F_1-measure increases as we move towards the lower levels of a hierarchy using algorithms CHD and FACH, with minor fluctuations. However, it can be seen in Fig. 6f that the value of $F2$-measure has a sudden drop at level 5 of the hierarchy, which indicates that the communities beyond level 5 of the hierarchy are too fine. In Fig. 6b, the values of F_1-measure of communities detected by algorithm CHD for dataset Amazon are increasing, as we move towards lower levels of hierarchy of communities. While there are some fluctuations in F_1-measure for dataset Amazon, the values are stable at the last two levels of hierarchy, i.e. levels 5 and 6. It is noted that the number of levels of the hierarchy for dataset Amazon is 6. Similarly, Fig. 6c shows that for dataset DBLP, the values of F_1-measure and F_2-measure have an increasing trend as we move towards the bottom of a hierarchy.

Fig. 6k-6o present the values of information centrality for communities at different levels of a hierarchy. Fig. 6k shows that for dataset facebook, the value of information centrality by algorithm CHD has a sudden increase and it stabilizes after that. However, in the same figure, the value of information centrality has a slower increase using algorithm FACH. It is noted in Fig. 6l that as the algorithm iterates, it finds more levels of the hierarchy and increases the values of the information centrality of communities, for dataset Amazon. Similarly for dataset DBLP, Fig. 6m shows that the information centrality of the detected communities is strictly increasing. In Fig. 6n, for dataset LiveJournal, the value of information centrality is increasing, as we move downwards in the hierarchy.

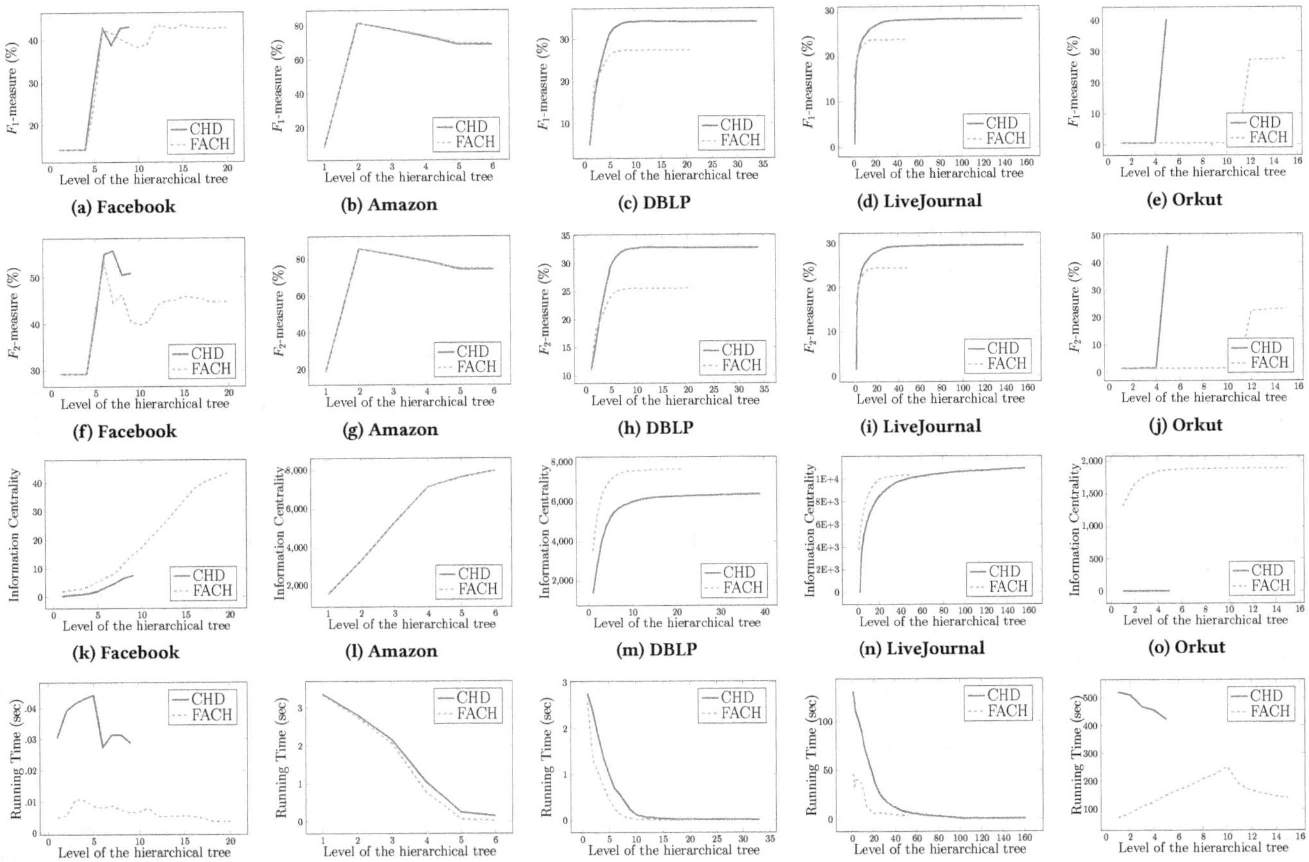

(a) Facebook (b) Amazon (c) DBLP (d) LiveJournal (e) Orkut

(f) Facebook (g) Amazon (h) DBLP (i) LiveJournal (j) Orkut

(k) Facebook (l) Amazon (m) DBLP (n) LiveJournal (o) Orkut

(p) Facebook (q) Amazon (r) DBLP (s) LiveJournal (t) Orkut

Figure 6: Running times for each level of hierarchies detected by algorithms CHD and FACH

Fig. 6p-6t plot the amounts of time that algorithms CHD and FACH need for detecting each level of a hierarchy in different datasets. Fig. 6p shows that the running time of algorithm CHD is mainly dominated by its early iterations, where k is small. However, the running time of the algorithm FACH is almost stable with minor fluctuations across different levels of the hierarchy, which is due to the fast sparsification in algorithm FACH. It can be seen in Fig. 6q that for dataset Amazon, the running time of algorithm CHD drops significantly, as the algorithm moves to lower levels of the hierarchy. The reason behind is that algorithm CHD breaks the network into smaller and smaller subgraphs at each level and therefore, the time spent for detecting lower levels of a hierarchy is much less than that of the higher one. Fig. 6r shows the running times of algorithm CHD for different levels of the hierarchy in dataset DBLP, from which it can be seen that the running time significantly drops. Similarly, Fig. 6s shows that for dataset LiveJournal, the running time drops, as we move downwards the hierarchy of communities. However algorithm FACH spends significantly less amount of time in both early and late iterations, resulting in a faster outcome. In Fig. 6t, while the running time of algorithm CHD is dominated by its early iterations, algorithm FACH performs very fast in those early iterations. The conclusion from Fig. 6p-6t is that algorithm CHD is promising in hierarchical community detection, but algorithm FACH is much more efficient, particularly in early iterations.

7 RELATED WORKS

Existing methods on hierarchical community detection can be categorized into two categories: *top-down* and *bottom-up* [28] approaches. While top-down approaches start with a given network and partition it into denser communities, bottom-up ones start with seeds, and expand those seeds gradually by merging them with each other. We here review the most influential works in each category.

Top-down approaches. Newman et al. [11, 20] proposed partitioning a network into communities by removing the edges in the order of their betweenness centralities. In order to reduce the running time of betweenness centrality calculations in [11, 20], Radicchi et al. [22] proposed to remove edges that disconnect the network, thereby, reducing the network size for the next rounds of betweenness centrality calculations. Radicchi et al. [22] also suggested replacing the betweenness centrality with the edge-clustering coefficient, which can be calculated faster. However, calculating the edge-coefficient clustering value is still very time consuming to be calculated repeatedly in a large network. Similarly, Fortunato et al. [10] used the information centrality of a network as a measure for removing edges at each iteration. Fortunato et al. [10] proposed to remove the edges, whose removal can result in the maximum decrease in the information centrality of network, where calculating the information centrality in a large-scale network is impractical.

Bottom-up approaches. Newman [19] proposed a bottom-up approach for hierarchical community detection, where communities are merged, if the modularity of the resulting community can be increased, starting from vertices as seeds. In an attempt to improve the efficiency of this algorithm [19], Clauset et al. [4] proposed several optimization techniques, which is yet unable to scale to networks with millions of vertices. Expansion of every single vertex in a network can be very time consuming and it can result in many redundant communities, therefore in LFM [15] only a randomly selected set of vertices are expanded until the value of modularity is locally maximal. Similarly, Sales-Pardo et al [27] considered a set of local maxima communities according to modularity fitness metric. However, the modularity used in [15], [19] and [27] does not allow single vertices to be a community. Haveman et al. [13] modified the fitness function to allow a single vertex to be a community. Many researchers [7, 17, 21, 29] have attempted to use small subsets of vertices as seeds. For example, in the works EAGLE [29] and COCD [7] it was proposed to start with small cliques as seeds and merge two communities with the maximum similarity into one, where the similarity between two communities is proportional to the number of edges between them. However, cliques are a very strict condition for real-world communities. Lancichinetti et al. [16] presented the algorithm OSLOM, which uses an estimated statistical significance of a community as a fitness metric and locally optimizes the statistical significance of communities. Rosvall et al. [26] proposed a method called Informap, which is a generalization of their flow-based clustering method [25] to uncover hierarchical communities. Ahn et al. [1], proposed a different approach called link clustering, where edges are partitioned via hierarchical clustering.

8 CONCLUSIONS

In this paper, we studied the hierarchical community detection problem. We formally defined the problem of hierarchical community detection, as finding a rooted tree of communities where each community is a subset of its parent in the tree, and the information centrality of communities is no less than that of their parent in the hierarchical tree. We showed that the problem of finding hierarchical communities is NP-hard and devised an efficient and scalable heuristic algorithms for this problem. We further incorporated a fast sparsification method to reduce the network size for finding global cuts. We also proposed a fast randomized algorithm to estimate the value of information centrality in large-scale networks. We finally validate the effectiveness of our proposed algorithms using extensive experiments over five large-scale real-world datasets.

9 ACKNOWLEDGEMENT

This work is supported by the grant of Australian Research Council Discovery Project No. DP120102627.

REFERENCES

[1] Yong-Yeol Ahn, James P Bagrow, and Sune Lehmann. 2010. Link communities reveal multiscale complexity in networks. *Nature* 466, 7307 (2010), 761–764.
[2] Lijun Chang, Jeffrey Xu Yu, Lu Qin, Xuemin Lin, Chengfei Liu, and Weifa Liang. 2013. Efficiently computing k-edge connected components via graph decomposition. In *SIGMOD'13*. 205–216.
[3] James Cheng, Yiping Ke, Shumo Chu, and M Tamer Özsu. 2011. Efficient core decomposition in massive networks. In *ICDE*. 51–62.
[4] Aaron Clauset, Mark EJ Newman, and Cristopher Moore. 2004. Finding community structure in very large networks. *Physical review E* 70, 6 (2004), 066111.
[5] Jonathan Cohen. 2008. Trusses: Cohesive subgraphs for social network analysis. *National Security Agency Technical Report* (2008), 16.
[6] Thomas H.. Cormen, Charles Eric Leiserson, Ronald L Rivest, and Clifford Stein. 2001. *Introduction to algorithms*. Vol. 6. MIT press Cambridge.
[7] Nan Du, Bai Wang, and Bin Wu. 2008. Overlapping community structure detection in networks. In *CIKM'08*. 1371–1372.
[8] David Eppstein and Joseph Wang. 2001. Fast approximation of centrality. In *Proc. of SODA'01*. 228–229.
[9] Santo Fortunato. 2010. Community detection in graphs. *Physics reports* 486, 3 (2010), 75–174.
[10] Santo Fortunato, Vito Latora, and Massimo Marchiori. 2004. Method to find community structures based on information centrality. *Physical review E* 70, 5 (2004), 056104.
[11] Michelle Girvan and Mark EJ Newman. 2002. Community structure in social and biological networks. *PNAS'02* 99, 12 (2002), 7821–7826.
[12] Prem K Gopalan and David M Blei. 2013. Efficient discovery of overlapping communities in massive networks. *PNAS'13* 110, 36 (2013), 14534–14539.
[13] Frank Havemann, Michael Heinz, Alexander Struck, and Jochen Gläser. 2011. Identification of overlapping communities and their hierarchy by locally calculating community-changing resolution levels. *Journal of Statistical Mechanics: Theory and Experiment* 2011, 01 (2011), P01023.
[14] Wassily Hoeffding. 1963. Probability inequalities for sums of bounded random variables. *Journal of the American statistical association* 58, 301 (1963), 13–30.
[15] Andrea Lancichinetti, Santo Fortunato, and János Kertész. 2009. Detecting the overlapping and hierarchical community structure in complex networks. *New Journal of Physics* 11, 3 (2009), 033015.
[16] Andrea Lancichinetti, Filippo Radicchi, José J Ramasco, and Santo Fortunato. 2011. Finding statistically significant communities in networks. *PloS one* 6, 4 (2011), e18961.
[17] Conrad Lee, Fergal Reid, Aaron McDaid, and Neil Hurley. 2010. Detecting highly overlapping community structure by greedy clique expansion. *SNA/KDD'10* (2010), 33–42.
[18] Hiroshi Nagamochi and Toshihide Ibaraki. 1992. Computing edge-connectivity in multigraphs and capacitated graphs. *SIAM Journal on Discrete Mathematics* 5, 1 (1992), 54–66.
[19] Mark EJ Newman. 2004. Fast algorithm for detecting community structure in networks. *Physical review E* 69, 6 (2004), 066133.
[20] Mark EJ Newman and Michelle Girvan. 2003. Mixing patterns and community structure in networks. In *Statistical mechanics of complex networks*. Springer, 66–87.
[21] Gergely Palla, Imre Derényi, Illés Farkas, and Tamás Vicsek. 2005. Uncovering the overlapping community structure of complex networks in nature and society. *Nature* 435, 7043 (2005), 814–818.
[22] Filippo Radicchi, Claudio Castellano, Federico Cecconi, Vittorio Loreto, and Domenico Parisi. 2004. Defining and identifying communities in networks. *PNAS'04* 101, 9 (2004), 2658–2663.
[23] Erzsébet Ravasz, Anna Lisa Somera, Dale A Mongru, Zoltán N Oltvai, and A-L Barabási. 2002. Hierarchical organization of modularity in metabolic networks. *Science* 297, 5586 (2002), 1551–1555.
[24] Mojtaba Rezvani, Weifa Liang, Wenzheng Xu, and Chengfei Liu. 2015. Identifying top-k structural hole spanners in large-scale social networks. In *CIKM'15*. 263–272.
[25] Martin Rosvall and Carl T Bergstrom. 2008. Maps of random walks on complex networks reveal community structure. *PNAS'08* 105, 4 (2008), 1118–1123.
[26] Martin Rosvall and Carl T Bergstrom. 2011. Multilevel compression of random walks on networks reveals hierarchical organization in large integrated systems. *PloS one* 6, 4 (2011), e18209.
[27] Marta Sales-Pardo, Roger Guimera, André A Moreira, and Luís A Nunes Amaral. 2007. Extracting the hierarchical organization of complex systems. *PNAS'07* 104, 39 (2007), 15224–15229.
[28] Satu Elisa Schaeffer. 2007. Graph clustering. *Computer science review* 1, 1 (2007), 27–64.
[29] Huawei Shen, Xueqi Cheng, Kai Cai, and Mao-Bin Hu. 2009. Detect overlapping and hierarchical community structure in networks. *Physica A: Statistical Mechanics and its Applications* 388, 8 (2009), 1706–1712.
[30] Duncan J Watts and Steven H Strogatz. 1998. Collective dynamics of 'small-world' networks. *nature* 393, 6684 (1998), 440–442.
[31] Joyce Jiyoung Whang, David F Gleich, and Inderjit S Dhillon. 2013. Overlapping community detection using seed set expansion. In *CIKM'13*. 2099–2108.
[32] Jierui Xie, Stephen Kelley, and Boleslaw K Szymanski. 2013. Overlapping community detection in networks: The state-of-the-art and comparative study. *Comput. Surveys* 45, 4 (2013), 43.
[33] Jaewon Yang and Jure Leskovec. 2013. Overlapping community detection at scale: a nonnegative matrix factorization approach. In *WSDM'13*. ACM, 587–596.
[34] Ying Zhao, George Karypis, and Usama Fayyad. 2005. Hierarchical clustering algorithms for document datasets. *Data mining and knowledge discovery* 10, 2 (2005), 141–168.

Measuring the Latency of Depression Detection in Social Media

Farig Sadeque, Dongfang Xu, Steven Bethard
School of Information, University of Arizona
1103 E 2nd St., Tucson, Arizona
{farig,dongfangxu9,bethard}@email.arizona.edu

ABSTRACT

Detecting depression is a key public health challenge, as almost 12% of all disabilities can be attributed to depression. Computational models for depression detection must prove not only that can they detect depression, but that they can do it early enough for an intervention to be plausible. However, current evaluations of depression detection are poor at measuring model latency. We identify several issues with the currently popular ERDE metric, and propose a latency-weighted F1 metric that addresses these concerns. We then apply this evaluation to several models from the recent eRisk 2017 shared task on depression detection, and show how our proposed measure can better capture system differences.

KEYWORDS

Social media; Depression; Latency; Neural networks.

ACM Reference Format:

Farig Sadeque, Dongfang Xu, Steven Bethard. 2018. Measuring the Latency of Depression Detection in Social Media. In *WSDM 2018: 11th Eleventh ACM International Conference on Web Search and Data Mining, February 5–9, 2018, Marina Del Rey, CA, USA.* ACM, New York, NY, USA, 9 pages. https://doi.org/10.1145/3159652.3159725

1 INTRODUCTION

In their Global Burden of Disease 2000 study, the World Health Organization estimated that depression is responsible for more than four percent of the Disability-Adjusted Life Years (DALYs) lost and will be the second leading cause of DALYs lost, behind ischaemic heart disease, by 2020 if the trend continues [32]. Depression also accounts for 11.9% of all years Lived with Disabilities (YLDs) - the highest among all the mental and neurological conditions - with nearly 350 million people suffering from it worldwide [31]. In 2000, depression imposed an annual economic burden of 83 billion dollars in the US - most of which was attributed to reduced productivity and increased medical expenses [22]. Depression is also a major cause of suicide: according to a study by Goodwin and Jamison [10], 15-20% of all major depressive disorder patients take their lives. This outcome is largely avoidable if there are proper interventions, and early detection of depression is the first step towards these interventions. Most studies of early detection of depression rely on diagnoses based on patients' self-reported experiences and surveys [11]. The cost of these diagnoses is extremely high, and as of 2009, 30% of world governments who provide primary health care services do not have these programs [7].

The ubiquity of social media among the world population can provide a solution to this problem. Studies have shown associations between usage of social media and depression [23, 34]. Activities in social media can be used as predictors for well-being [21] and social participation [24]. But a key aspect of detecting depression in social media is the speed of detection: the longer we wait to intervene, the greater the risk of self harm. Hence, predicting depression early in a user's lifecycle is paramount. This argues for models that don't just look at one snapshot of a user's activities, but instead track the user's activities over time. It also argues for evaluation metrics that consider not only the precision and recall of detecting depressed users, but also the speed of that detection.

The recent eRisk 2017 shared task on depression detection in social media [16] introduced the early risk detection error (ERDE) metric to incorporate speed of detection into model evaluation. ERDE penalizes the score given to true positives (e.g., depressed users that the system also identified as depressed) based on how much of the data the system observed before making a prediction. However, ERDE has several drawbacks, including that 4 different meta-parameters, which have non-obvious consequences, must be defined before its use, and that the slow-prediction penalty under-penalizes fast systems while over-penalizing slow systems.

In this work, we make the following contributions:

(1) We introduce a new metric, latency-weighted F1 or F_{latency}, for measuring the quality and speed at which a model identifies whether a user is depressed given a series of their social media posts, and show how it addresses some of the drawbacks of ERDE.
(2) We propose a general approach for improving the latency of detection models based on checking the consistency of a model's predictions over a risk window.
(3) We evaluate several different models for depression detection in social media using both ERDE and our proposed F_{latency}, and show how the latter results in a more interpretable evaluation.

2 RELATED WORK

De Choudhury et al. [6] asked Amazon Mechanical Turk users to take the CES-D depression screening test and provide their Twitter handle. They then constructed support vector machine classifiers to distinguish between depressed and non-depressed users. Their models incorporated features such as posts per day, replies per day, shared interactions with other users, use of emotion words from the Linguistic Inquiry and Word Count (LIWC) lexicon, and use of a list of depression-related words mined from Yahoo! Answers

WSDM 2018, February 5–9, 2018, Marina Del Rey, CA, USA

ACM ISBN 978-1-4503-5581-0/18/02...$15.00
https://doi.org/10.1145/3159652.3159725

Mental Health. Their model achieved almost 70% accuracy, but was not evaluated for the speed at which it could make a prediction.

Wang et al. [30] studied images posted in Flickr[1] to identify self harm contents. They started with a set of posts tagged with *selfharm* and *selfinjury*, collected tags that occur more frequently with these two tags and then collected posts tagged with one or more of these tags. They only selected those users with more than five posts with these tags, and then manually examined whether the user is tagged correctly as someone with history of self harm. They used convolutional neural networks to classify images, and took advantage of the image titles for a better prediction result. Their best model achieved a 71 F1 score on the test set. This task was mostly inclined towards identifying users with self harm history, rather than users in risk of future self harm, and early detection was not an issue with the task.

For the 2016 CLPsych shared task [20], the mental health forum ReachOut annotated a set of posts with how urgently they needed moderator attention (red/amber/green). Systems competed to take a post of interest and the user's preceding history of posts, and classify the post of interest as red, amber or green. The most successful system in the shared task used various weightings of n-grams: Mac et al. [18] used TF-IDF weightings of unigrams along with post-level and sentence level embeddings using sent2vec [15], whereas Malmasi et al. [19] went through lexical features like n-grams ranging from 1 to 8 and syntactic features like parts of speech tags and dependencies. Both of these works implemented ensemble classification over sets of simpler classification models, and in both cases the ensemble model came out as the best. While this shared task considered prediction given a series of social media posts, it did not attempt to evaluate the speed of detection.

Observational latency has been occasionally considered in fields outside of social media analysis. For example, in the field of computer vision, observational latency has been used as a parameter to facilitate early detection of events [8, 12]. Hoai and De la Torre [12] used the number of frames a model requires to detect a facial expression as a parameter for the loss function of their prediction model. Ellis et al. went in a similar direction[8], using Microsoft Kinect data to detect human movement using the minimum number of frames possible. They showed how reducing the number of frames below a certain threshold can adversely affect the accuracy of the detection model.

The eRisk 2017 shared task [16] was the first work on depression detection in social media that focused on how quickly models could detect depressed users. The goal of the shared task was to identify depressed Reddit users as early as possible using the contents they have posted. The organizers searched for specific terms like "diagnosed with depression" to identify users who have been clinically diagnosed with depression at certain point, and collected all of these users' contents (up to 2000). They also collected a control dataset of random users who never mentioned a depression diagnosis in their posts. For each user (either depressed or control), their posts were divided into 10 chunks based on their posting time, where chunk 1 contained the earliest 10% of the user's posts and chunk 10 contained the last 10%. Submitted systems were evaluated on their correctness (precision, recall and f-measure) as well as their speed of detection (Early Risk Detection Error, ERDE, described in detail in Section 3.1). Submitted models used a wide range of feature extraction methods like n-grams, paragraph vectorization, external knowledge source incorporation etc. The best performing model used an ensemble over four word level n-gram logistic regression models, with higher F-measure than models that implemented more sophisticated techniques like recurrent neural networks.

The eRisk 2017 shared task was a great venue for encouraging the research community to focus on both the speed and quality of systems. However, as discussed in the next section, the ERDE metric under-penalizes fast systems, over-penalizes slow systems, and has a number of meta-parameters that are difficult to set. At the same time, the systems that competed in eRisk 2017 all used different model architectures and different feature sets, making it difficult to understand which components of each system were the biggest contributors to their performance. In the current paper, we address both of these issues, introducing a simpler and more interpretable measure for evaluating speed of detection, and examining various features and model architectures in comparable, side-by-side evaluations.

[1] http://www.flickr.com

3 EVALUATION METRICS

3.1 Early Risk Detection Error (ERDE)

Early Risk Detection Error (ERDE) [17] aims at assessing models that take in a series of posts, and for each post, predict either '+' (depressed), '-' (not-depressed), or '?' (wait), where wait means the model wants to wait for more posts before making a prediction. Models are allowed to predict either '+' or '-' for a user only a single time, and as soon as one of these predictions is produced, the model is finished and will not be allowed to look at any more posts from that user. The goal of ERDE is to penalize models that abstain for a long time before predicting a user as depressed.

Formally, ERDE is defined as:

$$ERDE_o(U, sys) = \frac{1}{|U|} \sum_{u \in U} uERDE_o(u, sys)$$

$$uERDE_o(u, sys) = \begin{cases} c_{fp} & \text{if } ref(u){=}- \wedge sys(u){=}+ \\ c_{fn} & \text{if } ref(u){=}+ \wedge sys(u){=}- \\ c_{tp} \cdot lc_o(u, sys) & \text{if } ref(u){=}+ \wedge sys(u){=}+ \\ 0 & \text{if } ref(u){=}- \wedge sys(u){=}- \end{cases}$$

$$lc_o(u, sys) = 1 - \frac{1}{1 + e^{time(sys,u)-o}}$$

where U is the set of users, $ref(u)$ is the reference label ('+' or '-') assigned to the user, $sys(u)$ is the system's earliest non-'?' prediction, $time(sys, u)$ is the time (i.e., number of posts observed) for that earliest prediction, and where o, c_{fp}, c_{fn}, and c_{tp} are parameters of the model that must be set manually.

ERDE does penalize systems that take too long to make a prediction, but since it relies on a standard sigmoid centered at o, the transition between no penalty and 100% penalty is extreme. Figure 1 shows what the $ERDE_o$ penalty looks like for $o = 5$ and $o = 50$, the two values of o used in the eRisk 2017 evaluation. With $ERDE_5$, even a perfect system that correctly classified every user after only a single post would be penalized, since $1 - \frac{1}{1+e^{1-5}} > 0$. With $ERDE_{50}$, there is essentially no penalty for a system that takes 45 posts to

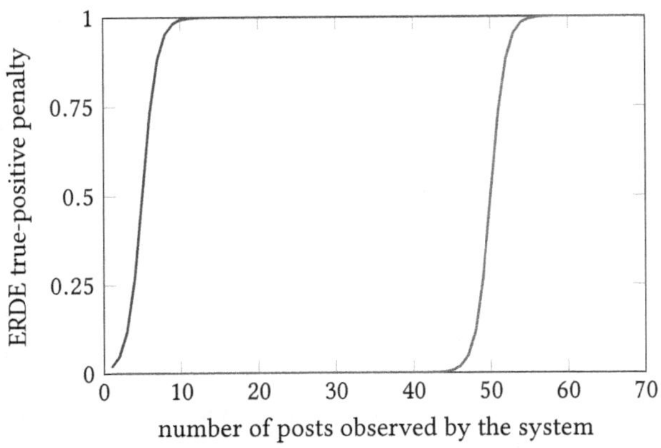

Figure 1: Plot of how the ERDE true-positive penalty increases with the number of posts observed by the system, for $o = 5$ (blue) and $o = 50$ (green)

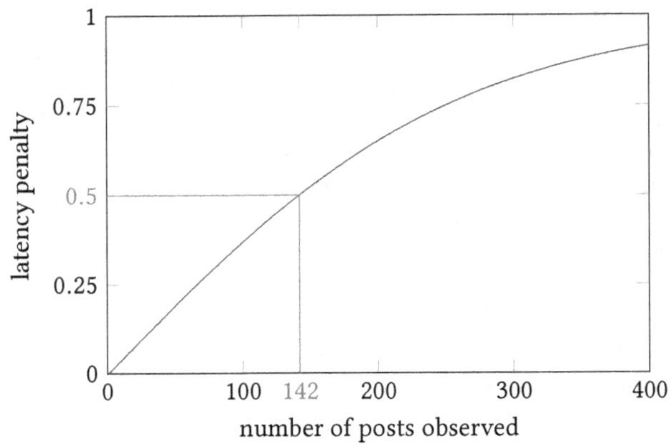

Figure 2: Plot of how the latency penalty increases with the number of posts observed by the system

predict depression, while a system that takes only 10 more posts to predict depression (55 posts) gets essentially no credit at all. We argue that such behavior is undesirable for a measure of speed of detection when, as was the case for eRisk 2017, there is no clear answer to the question "how many posts *should* it take to detect depression?"

ERDE has several additional drawbacks. Beyond the o parameter that we have just discussed, ERDE has 3 other parameters that must be manually set. In eRisk 2017, the organizers defined $c_{fn} = 1$, $c_{fp} = 0.1296$, and $c_{tp} = 1$, but these values were set heuristically, and it is not clear whether such values are appropriate or meaningful for other types of early detection tasks. ERDE is also not easily interpretable. The top system in eRisk 2017 achieved $ERDE_5 = 12.70\%$. Is that fast or slow? How many posts should one expect such a system to take to predict depression? ERDE is unable to answer such questions.

3.2 Latency and Latency-weighted F1

As an alternative to ERDE, we propose a simple, interpretable way of measuring how long it takes a system to predict a depressed user. We define the *latency* of a system to be the median number of posts that the system observes before making a prediction on a depressed user. Formally:

$$latency(U, sys) = \underset{u \in U \wedge ref(u) = +}{\text{median}} \; time(sys, u)$$

where, as above, U is the set of users, $ref(u)$ is the reference label ('+' or '-') assigned to the user, and $time(sys, u)$ is the time in number of posts observed for the system's earliest non-'?' prediction. Latency directly answers our earlier question: how many posts should one expect system sys to take to predict depression?

Latency, a measure of speed, should be coupled with measures of accuracy, like precision and recall, to give a complete picture of a system's performance. To produce a single overall measure that combines latency and accuracy, we introduce another metric *latency-weighted F1*. We define latency-weighted F1, or $F_{latency}$, as the product of a model's F1-measure (the harmonic mean of precision and recall) and the median of a set of penalties in the range [0, 1), which are determined by the model's time to predict each user. The penalty is 0 if a prediction is made after exactly 1 post is observed, and approaches 1 as the number of observed posts increases. Formally, we define:

$$P_{latency}(u, sys) = -1 + \frac{2}{1 + e^{-p \cdot (time(u, sys) - 1)}}$$

$$F_{latency}(U, sys) = F_1(U, sys) \cdot \left(1 - \underset{u \in U \wedge ref(u) = +}{\text{median}} P_{latency}(u, sys)\right)$$

where $F_1(U, sys)$ is the F-measure of the system, defined in the standard way:

$$precision(U, sys) = \frac{|u \in U : sys(u) = ref(u) = +|}{|u \in U : sys(u) = +|}$$

$$recall(U, sys) = \frac{|u \in U : sys(u) = ref(u) = +|}{|u \in U : ref(u) = +|}$$

$$F_1(U, sys) = \frac{2 \cdot precision(U, sys) \cdot recall(U, sys)}{precision(U, sys) + recall(U, sys)}$$

$F_{latency}$ has a single parameter that must be set, p, which defines how quickly the penalty should increase. We suggest that p should be set such that the latency penalty is 0.5 (i.e., 50%) at the median number of posts of a user. With this approach, p can be determined by fitting the $P_{latency}$ curve to two points: (0, 1) and (0.5, median-posts). In the eRisk 2017 data, the median number of posts of a user is 142, and fitting the $P_{latency}$ curve to (0, 1) and (0.5, 142) results in $p = 0.0078$. Figure 2 shows a plot of the resulting penalty. We argue that the shape of this penalty curve is much more appropriate than ERDE for measuring the speed of depression detection: models that predict correctly on the first post are unpenalized, and the penalty gradually increases as the number of posts observed increases. (In the early part of this curve, each post after the first that the model observes applies roughly a 0.5% penalty to F-measure.)

We believe that latency and $F_{latency}$ improve over ERDE by (1) being more interpretable, (2) having fewer parameters that must be manually tuned, and (3) using a penalty that gradually increases with the number of posts observed.

4 MODELS

Neither the models nor the model predictions from eRisk 2017 are freely available, so we re-implement some of the common approaches applied to that task. This allows us not only to evaluate the models with $F_{latency}$, but also to set up head-to-head comparisons of feature, model architectures etc. This was not possible in the shared task format because each system had its own feature set and its own model architecture, so comparing across participating systems could not reveal which sub-components were most crucial for success on the task.

The two most popular approaches to the eRisk 2017 task of predicting a user's depression status from their posts before time t were:

Non-sequential Treat each user as a bag of features, aggregated across all of the user's posts before time t. These bags of features were typically fed to linear classifiers such as a support vector machine or logistic regression [1, 25, 29].

Sequential Treat each user as a sequence of bags of features, where each bag of features corresponds to a single post by the user before time t. These sequences of bags of features were typically fed to sequential classifiers such as recurrent neural networks [9, 25, 29].

Some of the top models took advantage of ensemble approach, where results of various other classifiers were used as an input to an ensemble classifier [25, 29]. These ensembles provided better performance than the individual models.

Popular features for such models in eRisk 2017 included:

Words Words from the posts, sometimes also including bigrams and trigrams of words [1, 29].

Depression words Words commonly associated with depression, extracted from external resources such as medical webpages [25].

Medical concepts Words associated with medical symptoms, diseases, procedures, etc. extracted from external resources like the Unified Medical Language System (UMLS) or WebMD.[25, 29]

In the following sections, we describe our implementation of such models and features, following the descriptions of the task participants.

4.1 Non-sequential model

Our non-sequential model takes a feature vector summarizing all the posts of a user before time t and tries to predict whether the user is depressed or not. To aggregate post-level feature vectors into a user-level feature vector, raw counts are converted into proportions. For example, when using bag-of-words features, each feature represents the proportion of time that one word in the vocabulary appears the user's posts. We feed the user-level feature vectors to a support vector machine (SVM) classifier. Figure 3 shows the architecture of this model.

We use Weka's SVM implementation [33], with a polynomial kernel, probability estimate outputs enabled, attribute normalization enabled, complexity constant set to 1, tolerance parameter set to 0.001, and epsilon set to 1.0^{-12}. We explored a few other parameter values on the training data, but did not see any improvements.

Feature	Feature vector length
Words	9930
Depression words (DepWords)	200
Depression embeddings (DepEmbed)	64
Medical concepts (Metamap)	404

Table 1: Summary of the features

4.2 Sequential model

Our sequential model takes a sequence of feature vectors, each summarizing one of the posts of a user before time t, and tries to predict whether the user is depressed or not. We use a recurrent neural network model, in which post-level feature vectors are fed into a layer of Gated Recurrent Units (GRU) [4], the first GRU layer is followed by a second GRU layer, and the last output of the second GRU layer is fed through a sigmoid layer to produce a binary output. Figure 4 shows the architecture of this model.

We use the Keras implementation of GRUs, with 128 GRU units for all GRU layers. To avoid overfitting, dropout [26] with probability 0.3 was used on input to the the first GRU layer. We used RMSProp optimization [27] on mini-batches of size 200, and followed the standard recommendations to (1) tune the learning rate, which we set to 0.002 based on preliminary experiments, and (2) leave the other hyperparameter settings at their default values. Each model is trained for at most 800 epochs, with training time around two hours using two Graphics Processing Units (GPUs).

4.3 Features

The features we implemented, inspired by the participants in the eRisk 2017 task, are briefly summarized in Table 1 and described in detail below.

4.3.1 Word features. These are count-based features capturing the number of times that words appeared in the text. We first segmented each post into words using Stanford CoreNLP [28], and replaced all numbers, URLs, subreddits, and punctuation marks with placeholders. Then we gathered a vocabulary by analyzing the entire dataset, counting the occurrences of each unique word, and retaining as part of the vocabulary only words with frequencies equal or greater to the median, 47. We ended up with 9930 features: 9926 unique words and 4 identifiers for numbers, URLs, subreddits and punctuation marks.

4.3.2 Depression word features (DepWords). These are count-based features capturing the number of times that unigrams and bigrams commonly associated with depression, e.g., *depressed* or *anxiety*, or *my depression* or *panic attacks*, appeared in the text. We first collected two sets of texts, one representing language commonly used when talking about depression, and one representing more general language. For the depression language, we drew the most recent posts (not comments) in the "top" and "hot" section of the *depression* subreddit, resulting in 1987 posts. Posts in this subreddit are not necessarily posted by users who are depressed, but are generally topically related to depression. For the general language, we drew the most recent posts in the "top" and "hot" section of the *textventures* subreddit, resulting in 1082 posts. Posts

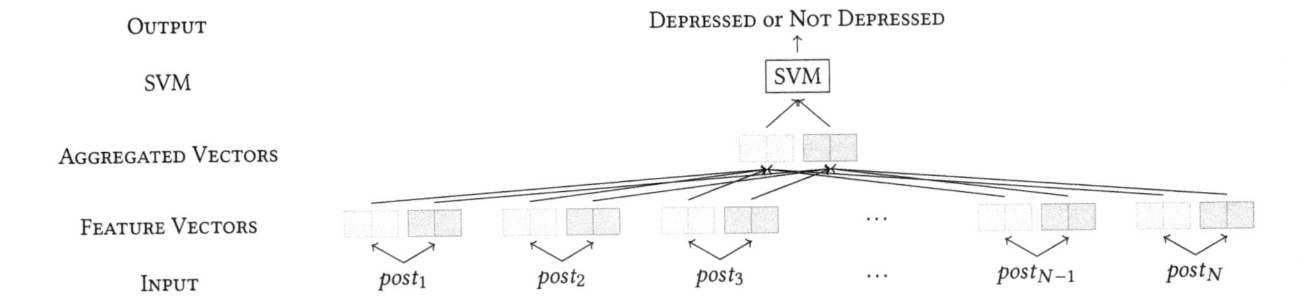

Figure 3: Architecture of the non-sequential model for predicting depression status from a user's posts.

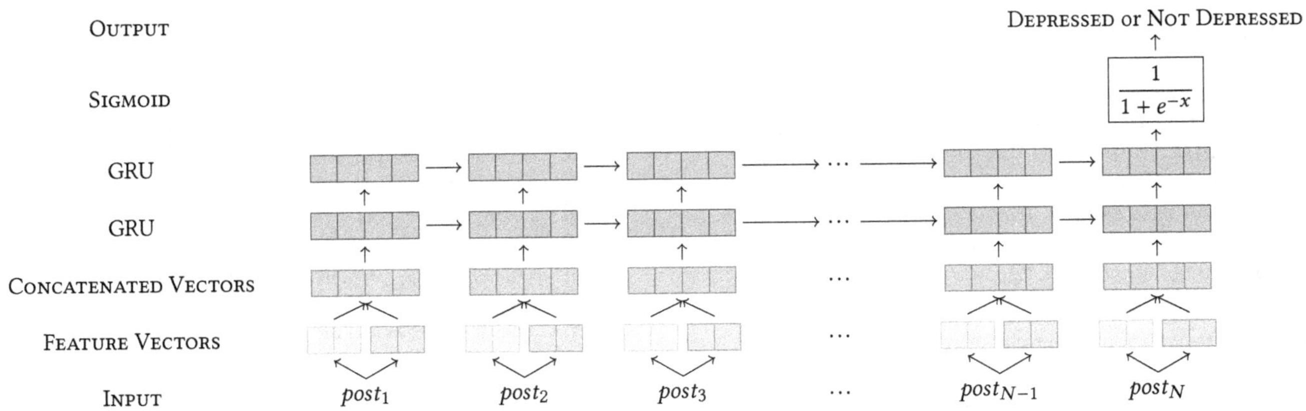

Figure 4: Architecture of the sequential model for for predicting depression status from a user's posts.

in this subreddit tell the beginning of a story (which commenters further develop), and cover a wide range of topics. We then used pointwise mutual information [5] to identify the top unigrams and bigrams most associated with the Depression subreddit. We ended up with 200 features: 100 top unigrams and 100 top bigrams.

4.3.3 Depression embedding features (DepEmbed). These are numeric features from a recurrent neural network that was trained to distinguish between depression-related language and other language. The network treats an entire post as a sequence so that it can capture linguistic phenomena that stretch over many words (e.g., *I just hit rock-bottom*), which cannot be captured by the previous features that treat a post as a bag of n-grams. We use a recurrent neural network in which the words in a post are fed into an embedding layer (128 dimensions), a Long Short-Term Memory (LSTM) [13] recurrent layer combines this sequence of embedded words into a dense vector (64 dimensions), and the result is fed through a sigmoid layer to produce a binary output. The architecture is shown in fig. 5. We train this model on the depression/textventures data from the DepWords features, asking the model to classify whether a post is from the depression subreddit or the textventures subreddit. We use an Adam optimizer [14] for training and dropout [26] with probability 0.15 to avoid overfitting. Once the model is trained, we discard the sigmoid layer, run the model on the posts from the eRisk 2017 data, and use the dense vector produced by the LSTM layer as the features. We thus ended up with 64 features: the 64 dimensions of the model's LSTM layer.

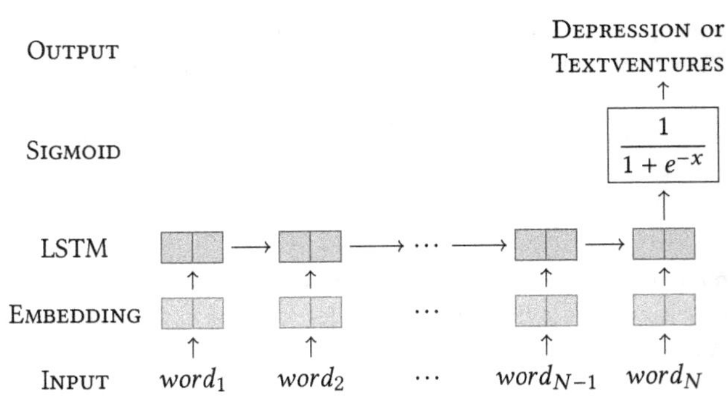

Figure 5: Architecture for training a model that can semantically summarize the contents of a post as a dense vector.

4.3.4 Medical concept features (Metamap). These are count-based features capturing the number of times concepts from the Unified Medical Language System (UMLS) [3], e.g., "Depressed mood" (C0344315), appeared in the text. We used the Metamap tool [2] to extract such concepts in the form of Concept Unique Identifiers (CUIs). We restricted Metamap to SNOMEDCT-US and to two semantic types: Mental or Behavioral Dysfunction and Clinical Drugs[2]. We passed each post through Metamap and counted the

[2]We included these restrictions because MetaMap produces a large number of spurious concept matches in social media data (e.g., the pronoun *I* is identified as IODINE; see

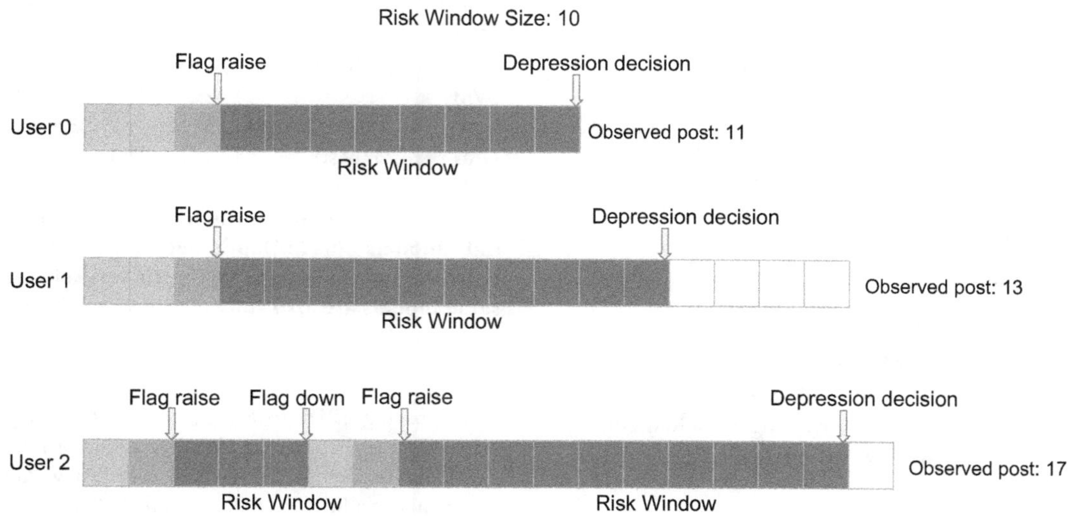

Figure 6: Example of post-by-post depression prediction with a risk window of size 10. Each block represents 1 post: gray is observed, orange is where the flag was raised, red is in the risk window, and white is unobserved. User 0 is an example where there are fewer remaining posts than the risk window, and user 2 is an example of restarting after a broken streak.

number of times each CUI occurred in the post. We ended up with 404 features: the 404 CUIs that MetaMap identified at least once in the eRisk 2017 training data.

5 PREDICTING WITH RISK WINDOWS

In preliminary analysis of the models above, we found it was common for a model to make occasional mistakes. But recall that in early depression prediction, the first "+" or "-" prediction is considered final, so occasional mistakes will force a early detection model to abort entirely, even if they have seen only a small number of posts so far. This can have a significant impact on their performance.

We thus introduce a technique, which can apply generally to any model, that trades off between latency and precision. If the model makes a prediction that the user is depressed after post p (we refer to this as *raising the flag*), we only confirm that prediction if the model continues to make the same (depressed) prediction for the next n posts (we refer to this as the *risk window*), or, if the user has fewer than n posts remaining, continues to make the same (depressed) prediction for all of their remaining posts. Figure 6 demonstrates the process with a risk window of size 10.

6 EXPERIMENTS

6.1 Data

All experiments were performed on the data published for the pilot task Early Detection of Depression in CLEF eRisk 2017 [16]. The organizers collected this data from Reddit[3], a social media and news aggregation website. Two sets of users were collected from Reddit: a depressed set and a non-depressed set. The depressed set was identified by searching the *depression* subreddit for a set of key phrases (e.g., *diagnosed with depression*), and then filtering the resulting users down to only those users for which the organizers could confirm, via a manual examination of the posts, that the user had explicitly declared that a physician had diagnosed them with depression. The non-depressed set included both random redditors from non-*depression* subreddits and random redditors who were active on the depression subreddit but had reported no depression[4]. For users from both sets, the organizers collected up to 2000 posts and comments per user, anonymized redditor ids, and then published the title, time and text of the posts. Their final collection contained 531,453 submissions from 892 unique users, but they released only part of this collection as a training dataset for the shared task; statistics for that subset are shown in Table 2.

	Train		Test	
	Depressed	Control	Depressed	Control
Subjects	83	403	52	349
Submissions	30,851	264,172	18706	217.665
Submissions/subject	371.7	655.5	359.7	623.7
Words/submission	27.6	21.3	26.9	22.5
Activity period (days)	573.23	627.17	608.8	623.7
Minutes between posts	920.99	994.08	1211.1	926.5

Table 2: Summary of the eRisk 2017 data

6.2 Model selection

Our two model architectures (non-sequential and sequential) and four feature sets (Words, DepWords, DepEmbed, and MetaMap) can be combined to create a large number of models. In this section, we use five-fold cross-validations on the training data to explore

also Appendix A). Moreover, we did not see any improvement using the 1000 most common CUIs from any semantic type in preliminary experiments.

[3]http://www.reddit.com

[4]The organizers acknowledged the possibility of having a non-depressed person in the depression group or vice versa, but suggested such events should be uncommon and the effects negligible, and pointed out that other identification strategies like questionnaires may suffer from this as well.

Model	Features	Precision	Recall	F_1
SVM	Words	53.3	38.6	44.8
SVM	DepWords	**77.3**	20.5	32.4
SVM	DepWords+Metamap	49.0	30.1	37.3
SVM	DepEmbed	69.4	30.1	42.0
SVM	DepEmbed+DepWords	66.7	45.8	54.3
SVM	DepEmbed+DepWords+Metamap	53.9	66.3	59.5
GRU	Words	72.8	51.8	60.6
GRU	DepWords	62.0	68.7	65.1
GRU	DepWords+Metamap	67.0	**75.9**	**71.2**
GRU	DepEmbed	65.8	60.2	62.9
GRU	DepEmbed+DepWords	60.0	61.4	60.7
GRU	DepEmbed+DepWords+Metamap	60.0	62.7	61.2

Table 3: Comparison of different models and feature sets in five-fold cross-validations on the training set when considering the entire posting history (window=∞).

which model/feature combinations look most promising, so that those can be evaluated on the test set. We focus for now on the simpler setup where the model observes a user's entire posting history (window=∞), and is evaluated just in terms of precision and recall.

Table 3 shows the cross-validation performance of a variety of models on the training data. The best F_1, 71.2, is achieved by the sequential (GRU) model with depression words (DepWords) and UMLS medical concept (MetaMap) features. Comparing across types of models, the sequential models are the clear winners: even the worst sequential (GRU) model had a higher F_1 than the best non-sequential (SVM) model (60.6 vs. 59.5). This finding is intuitive, given that early detection is a sequential prediction problem. Comparing across types of features, adding medical concepts (MetaMap) always improved F_1, but the results for other types of features were more mixed. Depression embeddings (DepEmbed) always improved the non-sequential (SVM) models, but always hurt the sequential (GRU) models. And using all words (Words) was better than just the depression words (DepWords) for the non-sequential (SVM) model, but the reverse was true for the sequential (GRU) model.

Looking across all the models, we selected two models for evaluation on the test set: the best non-sequential (SVM) model (DepEmbed+DepWords+ Metamap) and the best sequential (GRU) model (DepWords+Metamap). For each of these models, we apply a risk window as described in Section 5, considering all possible risk windows between 0 and the maximum number of posts, and optimizing the window size to maximize cross-validation $F_{latency}$ on the training set. For the SVM model, an 11-post risk window yields the highest $F_{latency}$ (67.1, with an F_1 of 82.0), while for the GRU model, a 23-post risk window yields the highest $F_{latency}$ (52.6, with an F_1 of 65.7).

6.3 Evaluation

Table 4 evaluates the best models on the eRisk 2017 test set. For contrast, we also show each model with a risk window of 0 (i.e., the first '+' or '-' prediction is final) and a risk window of ∞ (i.e., the model always waits for all of a user's posts and decides at the final post).

Model	Risk window	$ERDE_5$	$ERDE_{50}$	F_1	Latency	$F_{latency}$
SVM	0	13.1	9.7	51.3	63.5	38.9
SVM	11 (best)	13.6	10.1	51.4	75	36.8
SVM	∞	13.2	11.7	45.4	199	16.0
GRU	0	12.5	9.4	33.5	9	32.3
GRU	23 (best)	15.2	11.5	44.4	69.5	32.7
GRU	∞	15.0	13.6	45.0	199	15.8

Table 4: Comparison of the top non-sequential and sequential models (SVM:DepEmbed+DepWords+Metamap and GRU:DepWords+Metamap) on the test set. For contrast, the same models are also shown with risk windows of 0 and ∞.

Comparing ERDE to $F_{latency}$, we see that $F_{latency}$ is better at discriminating between models. For example, the non-sequential (SVM) and sequential (GRU) models with risk window 0 have given very similar values for ERDE, with their $ERDE_5$s differing by only 0.6 points and their $ERDE_{50}$s differing by only 0.3 points. Yet these two models have hugely different performance characteristics: the GRU is extremely fast (latency 9) at a significant cost to accuracy (F_1 of 33.5), while the SVM is much more cautious (latency 63.5) and much more accurate (F_1 of 51.3). Table 4 also shows the challenge of setting the ERDE o parameter: with $o = 5$ as in eRisk 2017, ERDE can't distinguish (only a 0.1 point difference) between a non-sequential (SVM) model that sees a median of 63.5 posts (window=0) and one that sees a median of 199 posts (window=∞), despite the latter being much, much slower to make predictions. We see these empirical results as a strong indication that $F_{latency}$ better captures the important evaluation characteristics of early detection problems.

We found that the models with risk windows optimized on the training set (SVM:window=11 and GRU:window=23) did not always outperform other simple choices of risk window (window=0 or window=∞) on the test set. While the 23-window GRU model indeed outperformed the $F_{latency}$ of the other GRUs (GRU:0 and GRU:∞), the 11-window SVM model did not have a better $F_{latency}$ than the 0-window SVM; the tiny improvement in F_1 achieved by SVM:11 over SVM:0 was outweighed by its larger jump in latency.

Despite the training set results where sequential models substantially out-performed non-sequential models, on the test set the no-risk-window non-sequential (SVM) model outperformed all sequential (GRU) models, in terms of both $F_{latency}$ and F_1. But note that on the training set, we compared systems with access to the entire posting history (window=∞), and, as can be seen in Table 4, the performance of the SVM model is much worse with such a large risk window. Probably the simple way that the non-sequential model aggregates feature vectors makes it easy to lose the signal of a single depressed post in a sea of many non-depressed posts.

7 LIMITATIONS

First, while it would have been ideal to compare ERDE to $F_{latency}$ on the actual systems submitted to eRisk 2017, since neither code nor predictions were publicly available for any of the top systems, we had to approximate such systems by exploring combinations of the most common models and features in the task. We believe this still results in a nice contribution, as the models and features can be more directly compared, but since our models are re-implementations, their performance on the task may differ somewhat from the systems submitted to the task.

Second, during model selection we first selected model architectures and feature sets under the maximal risk window, and then searched over all possible risk window sizes to select the best model in terms of F_{latency}. This two-stage procedure was not ideal for our non-sequential models, where it turned out that using no risk window, instead of the maximal one, resulted in the best models on the test set. A better approach would be to optimize risk windows simultaneously with feature sets and model architectures. There are also probably further gains to be had by directly optimizing for F_{latency} (e.g., instead of accuracy) during model training.

Third, F_{latency} combines F_1 and latency under the assumption that systems generally want to optimize F_1. However different applications may need to optimize different evaluation measures. For example, if the goal is to have a human intervene when a risk of depression is detected in a social media user, then probably a high recall even at the expense of precision would be preferred, so that the human would be able to intervene wherever possible. On the other hand, if the goal is to have an automatic intervention when a depression risk is detected, then probably a high precision is needed so that the automatic intervention is only applied when the model is very certain of the depression risk. Future work may need to extend F_{latency} to such scenarios, perhaps by including something like F_β's parameter for trading off between precision and recall.

Finally, F_{latency} is a general metric, applicable to any problem where systems must examine a sequence of items associated with an object, and make a prediction about that object's class as rapidly as possible. However, in the current paper, we only explore F_{latency} as applied to early detection of depression on social media. Future work will need to investigate the utility of F_{latency} on other kinds of problems: detecting drug discontinuation, churn prediction, etc.

8 CONCLUSION

We introduced latency and F_{latency} as evaluation metrics for early detection tasks, and showed that the theoretical behavior of these metrics is preferable to the current state-of-the-art, early risk detection error (ERDE). We replicated common models and features from the eRisk 2017 shared task on early detection of depression in social media, and showed empirically that our metrics are better than ERDE at capturing important differences between models. We also introduced the concept of risk windows for helping models find an acceptable trade-off between precision and latency, and showed that it successfully improves the performance of sequential prediction models on the eRisk 2017 test set. We believe our proposed metrics can be useful in the broad range of applications where models need to make fast user-level predictions from a sequence of the user's social media interactions.

ACKNOWLEDGEMENTS

This work was supported by National Institutes of Health grant R01GM114355 from the National Institute of General Medical Sciences (NIGMS). The computations were done in systems supported by the National Science Foundation under Grant No. 1228509. The content is solely the responsibility of the authors and does not necessarily represent the official views of the National Institutes of Health or National Science Foundation.

REFERENCES

[1] Hayda Almeida, Antoine Briand, and Marie-Jean Meurs. 2017. Detecting Early Risk of Depression from Social Media User-generated Content. In *8th International Conference of the CLEF Association, CLEF 2017, Dublin, Ireland, September 11-14, 2017.*

[2] Alan R Aronson and Francois-Michel Lang. 2010. An overview of MetaMap: historical perspective and recent advances. In *Journal of the American Medical Informatics Association 17(3).* 229–236. https://doi.org/10.1136/jamia.2009.002733

[3] Olivier Bodenreider. 2004. The Unified Medical Language System (UMLS): integrating biomedical terminology. *Nucleic Acids Research* 32, suppl_1 (2004), D267–D270. https://doi.org/10.1093/nar/gkh061

[4] Kyunghyun Cho, Bart van Merrienboer, Dzmitry Bahdanau, and Yoshua Bengio. 2014. On the Properties of Neural Machine Translation: Encoder-Decoder Approaches. In *Eighth Workshop on Syntax, Semantics and Structure in Statistical Translation (SSST-8).*

[5] Kenneth Ward Church and Patrick Hanks. 1990. Word Association Norms, Mutual Information, and Lexicography. *Computational Linguistics* 16, 1 (1990), 22–29.

[6] Munmun De Choudhury, Michael Gamon, Scott Counts, and Eric Horvitz. 2013. Predicting Depression via Social Media.. In *ICWSM.* 2.

[7] Roger Detels. 2009. *The Scope and Concerns of Public Health.* Oxford University Press Inc., New York.

[8] Chris Ellis, Syed Zain Masood, Marshall F. Tappen, Joseph J. Laviola, Jr., and Rahul Sukthankar. 2013. Exploring the Trade-off Between Accuracy and Observational Latency in Action Recognition. *Int. J. Comput. Vision* 101, 3 (Feb. 2013), 420–436. https://doi.org/10.1007/s11263-012-0550-7

[9] Marcelo L. Errecalde, Ma. Paula Villegas, Dario G. Funez, Ma. JosÃľ Garciarena Uelay, and Leticia C. Cagnina. 2017. Temporal Variation of Terms as concept space for early risk prediction. In *8th International Conference of the CLEF Association, CLEF 2017, Dublin, Ireland, September 11-14, 2017.*

[10] Frederick K. Goodwin and Kay Redfield Jamison. 1990. *Manic-Depressive Illness: Bipolar Disorder and Recurring Depression.* Oxford University Press Inc., New York.

[11] Aron Halfin. 2007. Depression: the benefits of early and appropriate treatment. *The American journal of managed care* 13, 4 Suppl (November 2007), S92âĂŤ7. http://europepmc.org/abstract/MED/18041868

[12] Minh Hoai and Fernando De la Torre. 2014. Max-Margin Early Event Detectors. *International Journal of Computer Vision* 107, 2 (01 Apr 2014), 191–202. https://doi.org/10.1007/s11263-013-0683-3

[13] Sepp Hochreiter and Jürgen Schmidhuber. 1997. Long short-term memory. *Neural computation* 9, 8 (1997), 1735–1780.

[14] Diederik Kingma and Jimmy Ba. 2015. Adam: A method for stochastic optimization. International Conference on Learning Representation.

[15] Quoc V. Le and Tomas Mikolov. 2014. Distributed Representations of Sentences and Documents. *CoRR* abs/1405.4053 (2014). http://arxiv.org/abs/1405.4053

[16] David Losada, Fabio Crestani, and Javier Parapar. 2017. CLEF 2017 eRisk Overview: Early Risk Prediction on the Internet: Experimental Foundations. In *Working Notes of CLEF 2017 - Conference and Labs of the Evaluation Forum.*

[17] David E Losada and Fabio Crestani. 2016. A Test Collection for Research on Depression and Language Use. In *International Conference of the Cross-Language Evaluation Forum for European Languages.* Springer International Publishing, 28–39.

[18] Sunghwan Mac Kim, Yufei Wang, Stephen Wan, and Cecile Paris. 2016. Data61-CSIRO systems at the CLPsych 2016 Shared Task.. In *CLPsych@ HLT-NAACL.* 128–132.

[19] Shervin Malmasi, Marcos Zampieri, and Mark Dras. 2016. Predicting Post Severity in Mental Health Forums. In *The 3rd Workshop on Computational Linguistics and Clinical Psychology.* 133–137.

[20] David N. Milne, Glen Pink, Ben Hachey, and Rafael A. Calvo. 2016. CLPsych 2016 Shared Task: Triaging content in online peer-support forums. In *Proceedings of the Third Workshop on Computational Linguistics and Clinical Psychology.* Association for Computational Linguistics, San Diego, CA, USA, 118–127. http://www.aclweb.org/anthology/W16-0312

[21] Michael J Paul and Mark Dredze. 2011. You are what you Tweet: Analyzing Twitter for public health. *Icwsm* 20 (2011), 265–272.

[22] Greenberg PE, Kessler RC, Birnbaum HG, Leong SA, Lowe SW, Berglund PA, and Corey-Lisle PK. 2003. The economic burden of depression in the United States: how did it change between 1990 and 2000?. In *J Clin Psychiatry 64(12).* 1465–1475.

[23] Brian A. Primack, Ariel Shensa, CÃľsar G. Escobar-Viera, Erica L. Barrett, Jaime E. Sidani, Jason B. Colditz, and A. Everette James. 2017. Use of multiple social media platforms and symptoms of depression and anxiety: A nationally-representative study among U.S. young adults. *Computers in Human Behavior* 69 (2017), 1 – 9. https://doi.org/10.1016/j.chb.2016.11.013

[24] Farig Sadeque, Ted Pedersen, Thamar Solorio, Prasha Shrestha, Nicolas Rey-Villamizar, and Steven Bethard. 2016. Why do they leave: Modeling participation in online depression forums. In *Proceedings of the 4th Workshop on Natural Language Processing and Social Media*. 14–19.

[25] Farig Sadeque, Dongfang Xu, and Steven Bethard. [n. d.]. UArizona at the CLEF eRisk 2017 Pilot Task: Linear and Recurrent Models for Early Depression Detection. ([n. d.]).

[26] Nitish Srivastava, Geoffrey E Hinton, Alex Krizhevsky, Ilya Sutskever, and Ruslan Salakhutdinov. 2014. Dropout: a simple way to prevent neural networks from overfitting. *Journal of Machine Learning Research* 15, 1 (2014), 1929–1958.

[27] Tijmen Tieleman and Geoffrey Hinton. 2012. Lecture 6.5-rmsprop: Divide the gradient by a running average of its recent magnitude. *COURSERA: Neural networks for machine learning* 4, 2 (2012).

[28] Kristina Toutanova, Dan Klein, Christopher D Manning, and Yoram Singer. 2003. Feature-rich part-of-speech tagging with a cyclic dependency network. In *Proceedings of the 2003 Conference of the North American Chapter of the Association for Computational Linguistics on Human Language Technology-Volume 1*. Association for Computational Linguistics, 173–180.

[29] Marcel Trotzek, Sven Koitka, and Christoph M. Friedrich. 2017. Linguistic Metadata Augmented Classifiers at the CLEF 2017 Task for Early Detection of Depression. In *8th International Conference of the CLEF Association, CLEF 2017, Dublin, Ireland, September 11-14, 2017.*

[30] Yilin Wang, Jiliang Tang, Jundong Li, Baoxin Li, Yali Wan, Clayton Mellina, Neil O'Hare, and Yi Chang. 2017. Understanding and Discovering Deliberate Self-harm Content in Social Media. In *Proceedings of the 26th International Conference on World Wide Web*. International World Wide Web Conferences Steering Committee, 93–102.

[31] World Health Organization WHO. 2001. The world health report 2001- Mental Health: New Understanding, New Hope. http://www.who.int/whr/2001/en/whr01_en.pdf?ua=1. (2001). Last Accessed: 2016-04-02.

[32] World Health Organization WHO. 2003. Global Burden of Disease (GBD) 2000: version 3 estimates. http://www.who.int/entity/healthinfo/gbdwhoregionyld2000v3.xls?ua=1. (2003). Last Accessed: 2016-04-08.

[33] Ian H Witten and Eibe Frank. 1999. Data mining: practical machine learning tools and techniques with Java implementations. (1999).

[34] Liu yi Lin, Jaime E. Sidani, Ariel Shensa, Ana Radovic, Elizabeth Miller, Jason B. Colditz, Beth L. Hoffman, Leila M. Giles, and Brian A. Primack. 2016. Association between Social Media Use and Depression among U.S. Young Adults. In *Depression and Anxiety, 33(4)*. 323–331. https://doi.org/10.1002/da.22466

A APPENDIX: METAMAP

Metamap tries to identify UMLS concepts within a text, but has been designed primarily for biomedical use and not for social media. Below is an example of MetaMap applied to the following post from the depression subreddit:

> Nobody really gives a shit how depressed you are as long as you don't kill yourself, but if you did then they wonder why you didn't ask for help. This is a messed up world.

Running Metamap on this post will produce something like:

> Nobody really [gives: PREFERRED NAME='GIVE - DOSING INSTRUCTION IMPERATIVE', CUI='C1947971', SEMTYPES='[FTCN]', TRIGGER='["GIVE - DOSING INSTRUCTION IMPERATIVE"-TX-1-"GIVES"-VERB-0]'] a shit how [depressed: PREFERRED NAME='DEPRESSED MOOD', CUI='C03443 SEMTYPES='[FNDG]', TRIGGER='["DEPRESSED MOOD"-TX-1-"DEPRESSED"-VERB-0]'] you are as [long: PREFERRED NAME='LONG', CUI='C0205166', SEMTYPES='[QLCO]', TRIGGER='["LONG"-TX-1-"LONG"-ADV-0]'] as you don't [kill: PREFERRED NAME='KILLING', CUI='C0162388', SEMTYPES='[SOCB]', TRIGGER='["KILLING"-TX-1-"KILL"-VERB-0]'] yourself, but if you did then they wonder why you didn't ask for [help: PREFERRED NAME='ASSISTED (QUALIFIER VALUE)', CUI= 'C1269765', SEMTYPES='[QLCO]', TRIGGER='["ASSI-STED (QUALIFIER VALUE)"-TX-1-"HELP"-VERB-0]']. This is a messed up world.

Metamap finds trigger words (i.e. depressed) and then maps it to a UMLS concept that has a preferred name (Depressed mood), a Concept Unique Identifier or CUI (C0344315), a semantic type (fndg or Finding) and some properties of the trigger itself.

Peeling Bipartite Networks for Dense Subgraph Discovery

Ahmet Erdem Sarıyüce
University at Buffalo
erdem@buffalo.edu

Ali Pinar
Sandia National Laboratories
apinar@sandia.gov

ABSTRACT

Finding dense bipartite subgraphs and detecting the relations among them is an important problem for affiliation networks that arise in a range of domains, such as social network analysis, word-document clustering, the science of science, internet advertising, and bioinformatics. However, most dense subgraph discovery algorithms are designed for classic, unipartite graphs. Subsequently, studies on affiliation networks are conducted on the co-occurrence graphs (e.g., co-author and co-purchase) that project the bipartite structure to a unipartite structure by connecting two entities if they share an affiliation. Despite their convenience, co-occurrence networks come at a cost of loss of information and an explosion in graph sizes, which limit the quality and the efficiency of solutions. We study the dense subgraph discovery problem on bipartite graphs. We define a framework of bipartite subgraphs based on the butterfly motif (2,2-biclique) to model the dense regions in a hierarchical structure. We introduce efficient peeling algorithms to find the dense subgraphs and build relations among them. We can identify denser structures compared to the state-of-the-art algorithms on co-occurrence graphs in real-world data. Our analyses on an author-paper network and a user-product network yield interesting subgraphs and hierarchical relations such as the groups of collaborators in the same institution and spammers that give fake ratings.

ACM Reference format:
Ahmet Erdem Sarıyüce and Ali Pinar. 2018. Peeling Bipartite Networks for Dense Subgraph Discovery. In *Proceedings of WSDM 2018: The Eleventh ACM International Conference on Web Search and Data Mining , Marina Del Rey, CA, USA, February 5–9, 2018 (WSDM 2018),* 9 pages.
https://doi.org/10.1145/3159652.3159678

1 INTRODUCTION

Many real-world systems are naturally modeled as affiliation, two-mode, or bipartite networks [9, 26]. In a bipartite network, vertices are decomposed into two disjoint sets, *primary* and *secondary*, such that edges can only connect vertices from different sets. For example authors and papers can be the primary and secondary vertex sets, with an edge representing authorship. Finding dense subgraphs in the real-world affiliation networks, and relating them to each other has been shown to be useful across different domains. Literature is rich with the examples such as spam group detection in web [21], word and document clustering [16], and sponsored search advertising on webpages [18]. Despite their representation power, bipartite graphs are underutilized, since most graph mining algorithms, including dense subgraph discovery, are studied on the traditional unipartite graphs. For this reason, affiliation networks are projected to co-occurrence graphs, such that two vertices in the primary set are connected by an edge if they share an affiliation. For instance, an author-paper network can be transformed into a co-authorship network, where two authors are connected if they co-authored a paper. However, this transformation comes at a cost of information loss and inflated graph size, as we will discuss in more detail later. Therefore, designing algorithms that can work directly on the bipartite graph, which provides an accurate representation of the underlying system, is essential.

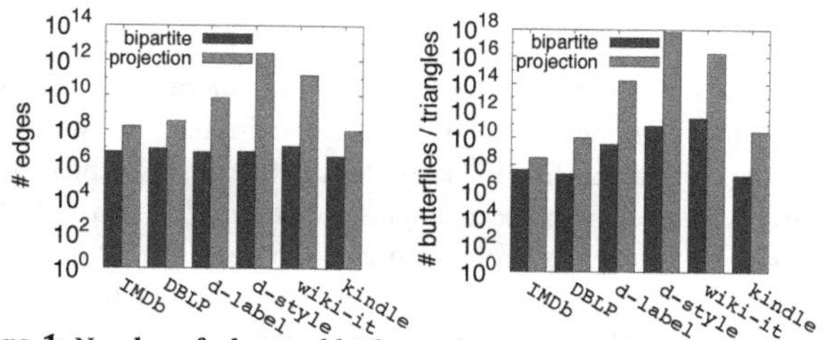

Figure 1: Number of edges and higher-order structures in bipartite graphs and their projections

This paper studies finding dense subgraphs in a *bipartite* graph and detecting the relations among them. Our approach is inspired by the k-core [30, 42] and k-truss [15, 38, 46, 48] decompositions in unipartite networks, which are instances of *peeling algorithms.* They have been shown to be effective to detect dense subgraphs with hierarchical relations [41].

1.1 Problem and Challenges

Our aim is to find many, if not all, dense regions in bipartite graphs and determine the relations among them. Despite a few successful studies that directly focus on bipartite networks [8, 13], a common practice in the literature for working with bipartite graphs has been creating co-occurrence (projection) graphs. Although the projection enables the use of well-studied unipartite graph mining algorithms [9], it has significant drawbacks:

- **Information loss and ambiguity:** Bipartite graphs comprise one-to-many relationship information, but this information is reduced to pairwise ties when projected to a weighted or unweighted unipartite form. Those pairwise ties are treated independently, which distorts the original information. In addition, projections are not bijective irrespective of the projection technique being used, which creates ambiguity.
- **Size inflation:** A secondary vertex in a bipartite network with degree d results in a d-clique in the projected graph. Thus, the number of edges in the projected graph can be as many as $\sum_{v \in V} \binom{d_v}{2}$, whereas it is only $\sum_{v \in V} d_v$ in the bipartite network, where V is the set of secondary vertices. Fig. 1 (left) shows the difference between some bipartite networks and their projections

WSDM 2018, February 5–9, 2018, Marina Del Rey, CA, USA

ACM ISBN 978-1-4503-5581-0/18/02...$15.00
https://doi.org/10.1145/3159652.3159678

Table 1: Notations

$G = (U, V, E)$	bipartite graph with vertices in U and V, and edges E
$N(u, G)$, $N(u)$	set of vertices that are connected to vertex u in G
$d(u)$	degree of vertex u, i.e., $\|N(u)\|$
(a, b)-biclique	complete bipartite graph where $\|U\| = a$ and $\|V\| = b$
$G_p = (U, E_p)$	unweighted projection of G, as in Def. 1
$G_{wp} = (U, E_{wp})$	weighted projection of G, as in Def. 1
Δ_p	number of triangles in the projected graph G_p
$\bowtie$	butterfly or (2, 2)-biclique
$\theta(u)$	tip number of vertex u, as in Def. 6
$\psi(e)$	wing number of edge e, as in Def. 8

– we observe up to 6 orders of magnitude increase in size, which degrades the performance. This also artificially boosts the clustering coefficients and the local density measures in the projected graph by creating many triangles. Regarding the smallest higher-order structures, a projection can have up to 699 quadrillion triangles whereas its original bipartite network has 77 billion butterflies (2,2-biclique), as in Fig. 1 (right).

Given the drawbacks of the projection approaches, we work directly on the bipartite graph to discover the dense structures. It has been shown that the higher-order structures (motifs, graphlets) offer deeper insights for analyzing real-world networks and detecting dense regions in a better way [7, 23, 41, 44, 45]. Peeling algorithms, k-core and k-truss decompositions, find dense regions in unipartite graphs and determine the relations among them [22, 23, 48]. Nucleus decomposition [41] is a generalization of these two approaches and can work on higher-order structures such as 4-cliques. However, none of them are applicable for the bipartite networks. k-core decomposition assumes that all vertices represent the same kind of entity, which does not hold for bipartite graphs. k-truss decomposition works on triangles, which do not exist in bipartite graphs. Nucleus decomposition uses small-cliques, which are also nonexistent in bipartite graphs. Thus, we need **higher-order structures that capture the cohesiveness in bipartite graphs**. Then the peeling algorithms can be adapted to run on these structures to find the dense regions with hierarchical relations.

1.2 Contributions

We introduce new algorithms to efficiently find dense bipartite subgraphs with hierarchy of relations. Our contributions can be summarized as follows:

- **Introducing k-tip and k-wing bipartite subgraphs:** We survey attempts to define higher-order structures in bipartite graphs, and use the *butterfly* structure (2,2-biclique) as the simplest super-edge motif. Building on that, we define the k-*tip* and k-*wing* subgraphs based on the involvements of vertices and edges in butterflies, respectively.
- **Extension of peeling algorithms:** We introduce peeling algorithms to efficiently find all the k-tip and k-wing subgraphs. Our algorithms are inspired by the degeneracy based decompositions for unipartite graphs. We present detailed psueducodes and analyze their complexities.
- **Evaluation on real-world data:** We evaluate our proposed techniques on real-world networks. Fig. 2 presents a glance of results on the IMDb movie-actor with 1.6M vertices and 5.6M edges. Our algorithms are able to extract larger and denser subgraphs of various sizes. We also examine the ratings data for the Amazon Kindle books and analyze the author-paper network of the top database conferences. We highlight the interesting subgraphs and hierarchies we detect that cannot be discovered by the existing approaches. Finally, we present the runtime performances.

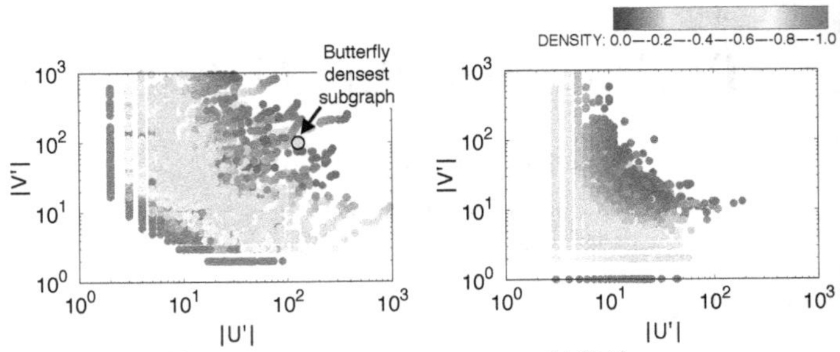

(a) WING (b) (2, 3) NUCLEUS

Figure 2: Dense subgraphs for the IMDb network. Each dot is a bipartite subgraph and edge density is color coded. U' and V' are the primary and secondary vertex sets and their sizes are given on the x- and y-axes. Wing decomposition results in 36 bipartite subgraphs with ≥ 0.9 edge density that have at least 10 vertices in each side, and perform competitive to the butterfly densest subgraph [31]. Other algorithms working on projections, on the right, cannot report any bipartite subgraphs in that quality.

2 BACKGROUND

This section reviews basics about the bipartite networks and the peeling algorithms. We present our notation in Table 1.

Let $G = (U, V, E)$ be an undirected, unweighted, simple (no loop, no multi-edge) bipartite graph. U is the set of primary vertices, V is the set of secondary vertices, and E is the set of edges s.t. $\forall(u, v) \in E, u \in U \wedge v \in V$. $N(u, G)$ denotes the neighbor set of a vertex u in the bipartite graph. We abuse the notation by using $N(u)$ when G is obvious. $d(u)$ is the degree of the vertex u and defined as $|N(u)|$. We define the density of a bipartite subgraph $G = (U, V, E)$ as the ratio of the number of existing edges over the number of all possible edges, i.e., $\frac{|E|}{|U| \cdot |V|}$. $H = (U', V', E')$ is an **induced subgraph** of the bipartite graph $G = (U, V, E)$, if $U' \subseteq U$, $V' \subseteq V$, and $V' = \cup_{u \in U'} N(u, G)$, $E' = \cup_{u \in U'} \cup_{v \in V'} (u, v)$. $G = (U, V, E)$ is an **(a,b)-biclique** if it is a complete graph between a vertices on one side and b vertices on the other.

We present two ways to convert a bipartite graph to a unipartite graph [33, 34], also illustrated in Fig. 3a. Weighted projection is built by assigning weights to the edges. Weights are computed in proportion to the number of vertices connected to each affiliation in the bipartite graph.

DEFINITION 1. *Given a bipartite graph $G = (U, V, E)$, its* ***weighted projection*** *is an edge-weighted unipartite graph $G_{wp} = (V_{wp}, E_{wp})$ s.t. $V_{wp} = U$, $E_{wp} = \{(u_1, u_2, w) \mid N(u_1) \cap N(u_2) \neq \emptyset \wedge w = \sum_{v \in (N(u_1) \cap N(u_2))} \frac{1}{|N(v)|}\}$.* ***Unweigted projection*** *is the same as weighted projection where the edge weights are* 1.

k-core [30, 42] and k-truss [15, 38, 46, 48] subgraphs, which inspire our approach, are defined as follows:

DEFINITION 2. *A connected subgraph, H, of G is a* ***k-core*** *if every vertex in H has at least degree k and no other subgraph of G that subsumes H is a k-core.* ***Core number*** *of a vertex u is the maximum k such that there is a k-core subgraph that contains u.*

To find k-cores, vertices with degree $< k$ and their edges are removed from the graph, until no such vertex remains. For a full decomposition, we increment k at each step, and assign k as the core number the removed vertex. This process is called as 'peeling', and it works in $O(|E|)$ time [6].

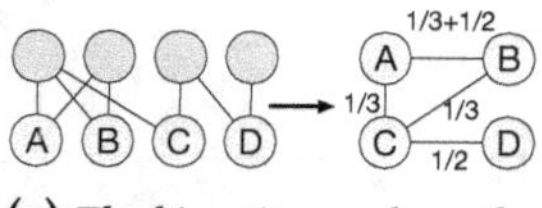

(a) The bipartite graph on the left is projected to the weighted unipartite graph on the right. A, B, and C form a triangle since they are all affiliated with the same vertex. Vertex D only connects to C in the projection since it is the only one with which it shares an affiliation. The edge between vertices A and B is assigned $1/3 + 1/2$, because one of the affiliations they share in the bipartite graph has 3 neighbors and the other affiliation has 2 neighbors.

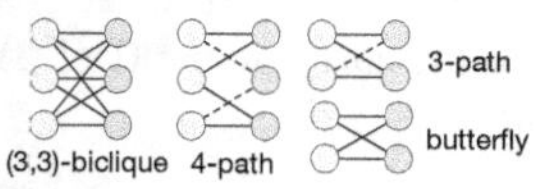

(b) Graph motifs to model cohesion in bipartite networks.

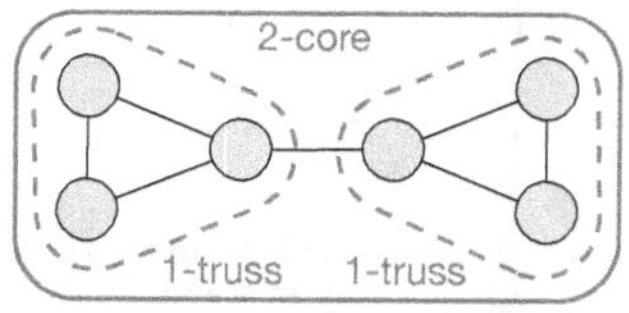

(c) The entire graph is a 2-core since each vertex have ≥ degree 2. Each triangle is a 1-truss, denoted in dashed lines, since each edge takes part in one triangle. Two 1-trusses are not merged, because the edge in the middle has no triangle.

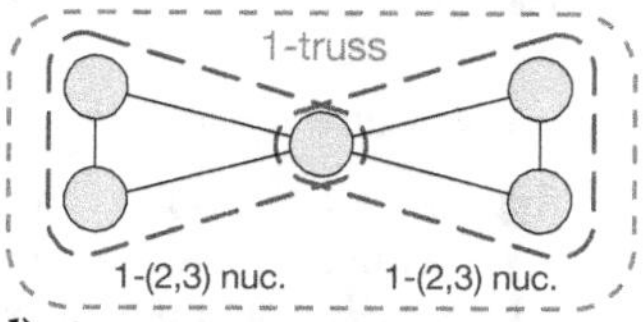

(d) The entire graph is a 1-truss since each edge has 1 triangle. There are two 1-(2,3) nucleus subgraphs, overlapping on the middle vertex. These two nuclei are not merged, because no triangle exists that contains an edge from each nucleus.

Figure 3: Examples for projections, and k-core, k-truss and k-(2,3) nucleus

DEFINITION 3. *A connected subgraph, H, of G is a **k-truss** if each edge in H takes part in ≥ k triangles and no other subgraph of G that subsumes H is a k-truss.*

Nucleus decomposition is a generalization of k-core and k-truss decompositions. Instead of vertex-edge or edge-triangle relations, nucleus decomposition works on any clique relations. The idea is described in [41], but we restrict presentation to a specific case for brevity. Here we only define k-(2,3) nucleus to highlight its stronger connectedness than the k-truss. It is also referred to as 'k-truss community' in [23].

DEFINITION 4. *A subgraph H =(V,E) of G is a **k-(2,3)-nucleus**, iff*

- *each edge takes part in at least k triangles;*
- *any pair of edges in E is connected by series of triangles;*
- *no other subgraph of G that subsumes H is a **k-(2,3)-nucleus**.*

Here $(2, 3)$ refers to the 2-clique (edge) and 3-clique (triangle) relations. Two edges e and f are connected by *series of triangles* if there exists a sequence of edges $e = e_1, e_2, \ldots, e_k = f$ such that for each i, some triangle contains e_i and e_{i+1}. In Fig. 3c, entire graph is a 2-core. Two separate 1-trusses appear since the middle edge has no triangle. In Fig. 3d, each edge takes part in 1 triangle, making the entire graph 1-truss. However, two separate 1-$(2, 3)$ nuclei exist, because there is no triangle that connect edges from each nucleus.

3 RELATED WORK

Literature on bipartite network analysis has two main thrusts: extending unipartite graph concepts to bipartite graphs and defining new projection methods to get unipartite representations. Centrality and the density metrics [9], clustering coefficients [37], matrix partitioning [10] and clustering [47] algorithms are adapted for bipartite graphs. Regarding the projections, Newman introduced the weighted projection for scientific collaboration networks [33, 34] and Everett and Borgatti proposed to use dual projections [17]. We focus on using the actual bipartite graph (without projection) to find many dense subgraphs and their relations to each other, which have not been explored thoroughly.

Bipartite graph motifs: Capturing the smallest unit of cohesion provides a structural way to find the dense regions. Various locality patterns [9, 36, 37] and density measures [26] have been proposed for bipartite graphs (see Fig. 3b). Borgatti and Everett considered the **(3, 3)-biclique** to define cohesiveness [9]. Opsahl proposed the **closed 4-path**, which is also a $(3, 3)$-biclique [36]. Robins and Alexander used the $(2, 2)$-biclique to model the cohesion [37], and looked for 3-paths, which consists of three edges with two vertices from each set. This approach is also adopted in a recent work by Aksoy *et al.* [3] to generate bipartite graphs with community structure, where $(2, 2)$-biclique is called a **butterfly**.

Bipartite dense subgraphs: Fake likes, ratings and reviews are prevalent in online social networks and can be modeled by the dense regions in the underlying bipartite network [8]. Regarding quantifying the dense regions, Borgatti and Everett proposed the biclique as a dense subgraph [9]. Kumar *et al.* used bicliques of various sizes to analyze web graphs [24]. Enumerating all the maximal bicliques and quasi-cliques is studied by Sim *et al.* [43], and Mukherjee and Tirthapura [32]. However, biclique definition is regarded as too strict, not tolerating even a single missing edge, and is also expensive to compute. More recently, Tsourakakis *et al.* [31] used sampling to find (P, Q)-biclique densest subgraph in bipartite networks. Their algorithm results in a single subgraph that has the most number of (P, Q)-bicliques in the entire network. Butterfly ($(2, 2)$-biclique) densest subgraph serves as a baseline and we check how our results compare in Sec. 6. However, we do not focus on finding a single, densest subgraph, but aim to find many dense subgraphs with hierarchical relations.

Peeling bipartite networks: There have been some attempts to adapt peeling algorithms or k-core [42] like subgraphs to bipartite graphs. Cerinsek and Batagelj [11] adapted the generalized core idea [5] to bipartite networks. However, their definition is not suitable to construct a hierarchy since it is not clear how to define a comparison function for (p, q) pairs. Giatsidis *et al.* [20] worked on the scientific collaboration networks to find dense regions. They used the weighted projections and adapted the k-core decomposition for weighted networks to detect the hierarchy. They defined the **fractional k-core** as a maximal subgraph where every vertex has at least weight k (vertex weight is the sum of edge weights that are connected). Li *et al.* [29] introduced a k-truss like definition for bipartite networks. They insert artificial edges between vertex pairs that share a neighbor and apply the peeling algorithm on those artificial edges and their triangle counts. This is actually identical to creating the projection, and applying the k-truss decomposition using the triangle counts [15]. In addition, Chen and Saad [13] proposed algorithms to find many dense structures in bipartite graphs by constructing a dendrogram of the vertices, where the subgraphs are not overlapping. *Unlike the previous work, we introduce peeling algorithms that work directly on the bipartite network and identify possible overlapping dense regions in a hierarchy.*

4 DENSE BIPARTITE SUBGRAPHS

In many real-world networks, the underlying structure that yields cohesive and close-knit subgraphs is the triangle. Triangle is the smallest unit of cohesion in uni-partite networks and butterfly can be considered as the **triangle of bipartite networks** in the sense that it is the smallest cohesive bipartite unit. Conversely, a bipartite

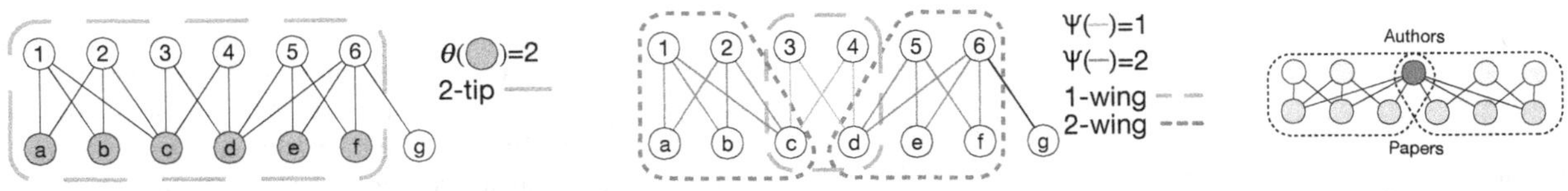

(a) We check the vertices on the bottom to find k-tips. g has no butterfly. Vertices a, b, e, and f take part in two butterflies while c and d are involved in three. But c and d cannot have a tip number of 3 since their induced subgraph has just one butterfly. Thus, vertices a to f forms a 2-tip. Each vertex gets the largest k-tip that they are part of; $\theta(a-f)$=2.

(b) k-wings on the same graph. Edge $(g, 6)$, $g6$ in short, has no butterfly. Each of the four edges in the middle, $c3, c4, d3, d4$, participate in only one butterfly, thus each edge has a wing number of 1 and they form a 1-wing. There are also two $(3, 2)$-bicliques; $abc12$ and $def56$. Each edge in those bicliques takes part in two butterflies. So, each is a 2-wing, and all the edges in those have a wing number of 2. Overall, k-wings can reveal denser regions than the k-tips on the given toy graph.

(c) In an author-paper network, the author shown in red cannot be considered in a single research community because she collaborates with different researchers on distinct sets of papers. Each affiliation of the author should be considered independently to better detect the communities she is involved in.

Figure 4: Illustrations of the k-tip and k-wing subgraphs, and tip (θ) and wing (ψ) numbers.

graph does not have a community structure without butterflies. *Motivated by that, we use the butterfly as the main higher-order structure in our bipartite subgraph models.* It is the smallest structure with multiple vertices at each side, and also cheaper to enumerate than the larger bicliques. Our aim is to discover the bipartite subgraphs with many butterflies and construct relations among them. k-core and k-truss decompositions reveal the hierarchical relations among dense regions and we follow a similar methodology in our models. We introduce two bipartite dense subgraph models that have different trade-offs between the subgraph density and the computation time to find.

4.1 Tip decomposition: the Definition

We introduce the k-tip to identify the vertex-induced subgraphs with many butterflies. Our approach enables building hierarchical relations among the subgraphs which results in a global tree structure that represents the significantly dense regions in the graph with various sizes and densities. k-tip measures the intensity of vertex participations in the butterfly structures. It is defined as follows:

Definition 5. *A bipartite subgraph $H = (U, V, E) \subseteq G$, induced on U, is a* ***k-tip*** *iff*

- *each vertex $u \in U$ takes part in at least k butterflies,*
- *each vertex pair $(u, v) \in U$ is connected by series of butterflies,*
- *H is maximal, i.e., there is no other k-tip that subsumes H.*

Two vertices a and $b \in U$ are connected by a *series of butterflies* if there exists a sequence of vertices $a = u_1, u_2, \ldots, u_k = b$ such that some butterfly contains u_i and u_{i+1}, for each i. This connectivity condition helps to separate the dense regions that are only connected by an edge, which are otherwise considered as a single combined subgraph. Butterfly density of a k-tip is obtained by ensuring a lower bound on the number of butterflies that each vertex participates. Note that a vertex with many butterflies does not imply a dense region by itself; it should also be surrounded by other vertices incident to many butterflies.

Fig. 4a illustrates k-tip examples, where U and V cover the vertices on the bottom $(a-g)$ and top $(1-6)$, respectively. There are seven butterflies in total: $ab12, ac12, bc12, cd34, de56, df56$, and $ef56$. Vertex g has no butterflies. Vertices c and d participate in three butterflies while the others in U (but g) are involved in two. Thus, vertices $a-f$ forms a 2-tip, shown with the dashed orange line. c and d cannot form a 3-tip by themselves or including any other vertex.

Storing all the k-tips is not convenient since they are in a hierarchy and have full overlaps. Instead, we define the **tip number** of a vertex, denoted as θ, in a similar spirit to the core number (Def. 2), to find any k-tip with a traversal operation.

Definition 6. ***Tip number**, $\theta(u)$, of vertex u, is the largest t such that there exists a t-tip that contains u.* ***Tip decomposition*** *of a graph $G = (U, V, E)$ is finding the tip numbers of vertices in U.*

Going back to Fig. 4a, we see that all the vertices except g has tip number of 2 (in orange). A k-tip is found by starting at a vertex with the tip number of k and doing BFS-like traversal on set U. At each step, a vertex that resides in a common butterfly is visited if its tip number is at least k. Traversal continues until no such vertex appears. Set of visited vertices forms the k-tip.

4.2 Wing decomposition: the Definition

Consider the bipartite network of authors and their papers. When an author collaborates with different groups on different topics (as in Fig. 4c), k-tip cannot handle the situation since the dense regions identified by the k-tip are defined to be disjoint. To allow the vertex overlaps, which better captures the dense regions, we introduce another generic subgraph model, **k-wing**. Its definition is similar to the k-tip with one subtle difference: focus is on the *edges*, not vertices. Distinguishing the edges that are connected to the same vertex is the key to get overlaps on the vertices. We define the **k-wing** bipartite subgraph as follows:

Definition 7. *A bipartite subgraph $H = (U, V, E) \subseteq G$ is a* ***k-wing*** *if,*

- *every edge $(u, v) \in E$ takes part in at least* ***k*** *butterflies,*
- *each edge pair $(u_1, v_1), (u_2, v_2) \in E$ is connected by series of butterflies,*
- *H is maximal, i.e., there is no other k-wing that subsumes H.*

Again we use the butterfly connectedness condition that is stronger than the traditional connectedness and helps to distinguish different regions that are traditionally connected, as shown in Fig. 4c. Two edges a and $b \in E$ are connected by a *series of butterflies* if there exists a sequence of edges $a = e_1, e_2, \ldots, e_k = b$ such that some butterfly contains e_i and e_{i+1} for each i.

Fig. 4b presents the k-wings in the same toy graph that we checked in the previous section. Edge $(g, 6)$, $g6$ in short, does not participate in any butterfly. Each of the four edges in the middle, $c3, c4, d3, d4$, participate in only one butterfly, thus each edge has a wing number of 1 and they form a 1-wing, marked by the green region. There are also two $(3, 2)$ bicliques: $abc12$ and $def56$. Each

Algorithm 1: Tip Decomposition ($G = (U, V, E)$)

```
Function D2 (u, G)
    D ← ⋃_{v∈N(u)} ( ⋃_{d∈N(v)} {d} )        // combine dist-2 neigs
    c ← multiplicities of d ∈ D               // counts of unique items
    return c, D
// find the number of ⧖ each vertex u ∈ U participates
1  D ← list, L ← list, β(·) ← 0, butterfly counts ∀ u ∈ U
2  for each u ∈ U do
3      c, D ← D2 (u, G)          // dist-2 neigs (D), multiplicity (c)
4      β(u) ← Σ_{d∈D} (c_d choose 2)                      // update u
// find the tip numbers of vertices u ∈ U by peeling
5  θ(u) ← tip numbers ∀ u ∈ U
6  for each u with minimum β(u) s.t. θ(u) is unassigned do
7      θ(u) ← β(u)                          // assign the tip number
8      c, D ← D2 (u, G)          // dist-2 neigs (D), multiplicity (c)
9      for each d ∈ D s.t. θ(d) is unassigned do
           // decrease by the num. of common ⧖, if possible
10         if β(d) − (c_d choose 2) < β(u) then β(d) ← β(u)
11         else β(d) ← β(d) − (c_d choose 2)
12 return array θ(·)
```

Algorithm 2: Wing Decomposition ($G = (U, V, E)$)

```
// find the number of ⧖ each edge e ∈ E participates
β(e) ← 0, butterfly counts ∀ e ∈ E
for each u ∈ U in order do
    for each v1, v2 pair ∈ N(u) do
        I ← N(v1) ∩ N(v2) s.t. i > u ∀i ∈ I
        for each i ∈ I do
            β(e)++, ∀e ∈ ⧖(u, i, v1, v2)            // each ⧖ visited
// find the wing numbers of edges e ∈ E by peeling
ψ(e) ← wing numbers ∀ e ∈ E
for each e with minimum β(e) s.t. ψ(e) is unassigned do
    ψ(e) ← β(e)                             // assign the wing number
    B ← set of ⧖s containing e
    for each ⧖ ∈ B do
        for each edge f in ⧖ s.t. f ≠ e do
            if β(f) > β(e) then β(f)--                // neigs updated
    E ← E \ e                        // edge is removed from the graph
return array ψ(·)
```

edge in those subgraphs participates in exactly two butterflies. So, each is a 2-wing, shown in dashed red lines. Overall, k-wings can extract denser regions that cannot be seen by the k-tips. Similar to the tip numbers, we associate each edge with a number to index the subgraphs. We define the **wing number** of an edge, denoted by ψ, as follows.

Definition 8. ***Wing number,*** $\psi(e)$, *of an edge $e \in E$ is the largest* **w** *such that there is a w-wing that contains e.* ***Wing decomposition*** *is the problem of finding the wing numbers of edges in G.*

In Fig. 4b, wing numbers of the edges are shown by the corresponding colors. $\psi(c3) = \psi(c4) = \psi(d3) = \psi(d4) = 1$, the green edges, which belong to the 1-wing, but not the 2-wing. All the other edges, except $g6$, has wing number of 2, in red. A k-wing can be found by a similar traversal operation explained for the k-tip. This time we traverse on edges. We start at an edge with the wing number of k and at each step we visit an edge that resides in a common butterfly and has a wing number of at least k. Traversal continues until no such edge remains and the set of visited edges forms the k-tip.

5 PEELING BUTTERFLIES

In this section, we present algorithms to find the tip numbers of vertices, $\theta(\cdot)$, and the wing numbers of edges, $\psi(\cdot)$. k-tips and k-wings with the hierarchical relations can be located by the $\theta(\cdot)$ and $\psi(\cdot)$ values, as explained above.

5.1 Tip decomposition: the Algorithm

We start by counting the number of butterflies that each vertex participates in, and then apply the iterative peeling process where the tip numbers are assigned in a non-decreasing order. At each step, we find the vertex that has the minimum number of butterflies, assign its current butterfly count as the tip number, say k, and decrement the butterfly counts of the vertices (if $> k$) in U that has a common butterfly.

Tip Decomposition, presented in Algorithm 1, finds the tip numbers of the vertices in U. To locate the k-tips and construct the hierarchy, we use the disjoint-set forest heuristic that is introduced in a recent work [39]. We construct the subgraphs after finding the tip numbers of vertices, and adaptation of [39] for the tip decomposition is straightforward – we do not give the details for brevity.

Algorithm 1 has two phases. First, we determine the number of butterflies that each $u \in U$ participates, in lines 1 to 4. A simple way to count the butterflies that a vertex participates is to collect its distance-2 neighbors in a multiset by using a hashmap. If a vertex d appears $c_d > 1$ times in the multiset D (except u itself), then u and d have c common neighbors, and the number of their mutual butterflies will be $\binom{c_d}{2}$, which makes $\beta(u) = \sum_{d \in D} \binom{c_d}{2}$. This phase has $O(\sum_{v \in V} d(v)^2)$ time complexity, since a vertex $v \in V$ is accessed by each of its neighbors, and each time all the vertices in $N(v)$ are accessed. In the worst case, it is $O(|U|^2)$, where the graph is a biclique. We also used an ordering heuristic which is applied in the D2 and although it does not reduce the complexity, it enables to keep the c and D smaller, in line 3, and results in less work in the following line. We omit the details for brevity.

In the peeling process (lines 5 to 11), we assign the tip numbers of the vertices, $\theta(\cdot)$, in a non-decreasing order. We leverage a bucket data structure to efficiently retrieve the vertex with the fewest butterflies at each step. Main operation at each step is to first assign the current butterfly number of u as its tip number, find the vertices that has a common butterfly with u, and decrement their butterfly numbers, if larger than the last assigned tip number. Since two vertices in U can have multiple mutual butterflies, we find those counts and decrease them at once. This again requires to collect the distance-2 neighbors in a multiset and we use D2 for that purpose in line 8. For each vertex that is not assigned a tip number yet, we decrease the butterfly number by $\binom{c}{2}$, where c is the cardinality of the common neighbors. However, the butterfly number cannot be less than the last assigned tip number, and we check that in line 10. Time complexity is again characterized by $O(\sum_{v \in V} d(v)^2)$ due to the D2 ($O(|U|^2)|$ in the worst case). All of the additional data structures in both phases are in at most $O(|U|)$ size.

Theorem 5.1. *Given a bipartite graph $G = (U, V, E)$, Algorithm 1 finds the tip numbers, $\theta(\cdot)$, of all $u \in U$* (Proof is omitted here, available in [40]).

5.2 Wing decomposition: the Algorithm

We apply a similar peeling approach to find the wing numbers of the edges in E, $\psi(\cdot)$. Instead of looking at the vertex-butterfly relations, we investigate the involvements of edges in butterflies.

There are again two phases; counting the butterflies for each edge and the peeling process to find the wing numbers. Locating the k-wings and building the hierarchy is again straightforward by the disjoint-set data structures [39] and not included here for brevity.

Algorithm 2 outlines the WING DECOMPOSITION. Butterfly counting for each edge is done in lines 1 to 6. Note that it is different than the first phase of TIP DECOMPOSITION, and also more expensive, since we need to enumerate the butterflies to find the participating edges. We compute intersections for each pair in the neighborhoods of vertices in U. We utilize a total ordering of the vertices for efficient computation. All the vertices $u \in U$ are processed in order (line 2), and in each intersection operation, we only take the vertices that succeed u (line 4). This enables to visit each butterfly only once. Total complexity is $O(\sum_{u \in U} \sum_{v_1, v_2 \in N(u)} max(d(v_1), d(v_2)))$, and it is $O(|U||V||E|)$ in the worst case where the graph is a biclique.

In the peeling phase (lines 7 to 14), wing numbers are assigned in a non-decreasing order. Bucket structure helps to get the edge with the least number of butterflies at each step. Similar to the TIP DECOMPOSITION, we assign the updated butterfly number of the edge e as its wing number, say k, find the butterflies that e participates, and decrement the butterfly counts of the other edges in those butterflies, if greater than k. Note that there are four edges in a butterfly, thus we need to check the other three edges. Lastly, we remove the edge e from the graph. Peeling phase has $O(\sum_{(u,v) \in E} \sum_{w \in N(v)} max(d(u), d(w)))$ time complexity, and $O(|U||V||E|)$ in the worst case. Additional space complexity is $O(|E|)$, since we store the butterfly and wing numbers for each edge.

THEOREM 5.2. *Given a bipartite graph $G = (U, V, E)$, Algorithm 2 finds the wing numbers, $\psi(\cdot)$, of all $e \in E$* (Proof is omitted here, available in [40]).

6 EXPERIMENTS

We evaluate our algorithms on real-world unweighted simple bipartite networks from SNAP [27], ICON [14], and Konect [25]. Table 2 shows the important statistics for our dataset. condmat is the author-paper network for the arXiv preprints about condensed matter physics, published between 1995 and 1999 [35]. dbconf is another author-paper network that we constructed with the proceedings in the three top database conferences; VLDB, SIGMOD, and ICDE [28]. github is the network between the users and repositories in the GitHub [12]. marvel is the occurrence relations between the Marvel characters and the comic books [4]. IMDb links the actors and the movies they played in [1]. DBLP is the author and paper network for all the papers in the DBLP website [28]. d-label and d-style networks are obtained from an online music database [2] and the former consists of the relations between artists and the production companies, whereas the latter is the network of the artists and the styles of their albums. wiki-it is the edit network of the Italian Wikipedia, having the users and the pages they edit. kindle is the network between the Kindle books and the users who rated those books. In Table 2, second to fourth columns show the number of primary vertices, secondary vertices, and edges in each network. We assume that the primary vertices are the ones that drive the connections, which are authors, users, characters, actors, and artists. In the fifth column, the number of edges in the projected graphs (E_p) are given. We applied the projections as described in Def. 1. Last two columns are the butterfly

Table 2: Statistics for the real-world bipartite graphs (in black) and their projections (in red). First three columns show the number of primary vertices, secondary vertices, and edges for the bipartite graphs, and the fifth column is the number of butterflies. Fourth and last columns (in red) are the number of edges and triangles in the projections, which applied on U.

network	$\|U\|$	$\|V\|$	$\|E\|$	$\|E_p\|$	$\|⧖\|$	$\|\triangle_p\|$
condmat	16.73 K	22.02 K	58.60 K	95.19 K	70.55 K	68.04 K
dbconf	11.19 K	8.92 K	30.72 K	84.79 K	34.55 K	95.66 K
github	56.56 K	123.35 K	440.24 K	44.56 M	50.89 M	962.55 M
marvel	6.49 K	12.94 K	96.66 K	336.53 K	10.71 M	3.26 M
IMDb	1.23 M	419.66 K	5.60 M	157.56 M	42.49 M	312.08 M
DBLP	4.00 M	1.43 M	8.65 M	315.89 M	21.04 M	9.99 B
d-label	1.75 M	270.77 K	5.30 M	> 7.20 B	3.26 B	> 167.99 T
d-style	1.62 M	0.38 K	5.74 M	> 2.56 T	77.38 B	> 699.01 Q
wiki-it	2.26 M	137.69 K	12.64 M	> 148.48 B	298.49 B	> 17.50 Q
kindle	430.53 K	1.41 M	3.21 M	93.19 M	15.51 M	10.14 B

(⧖) counts in each bipartite network and the triangle ($\triangle_p$) counts in the projected unipartite graph. For the d-label, d-style, and wiki-itnetworks, projections cannot be computed in 36 hours, so we give lower bounds for their edge and triangle counts, based on the degrees of the secondary vertices. Our implementation is in C++ and available [1]. We used gcc 5.2.0 at -O2 optimization level. All experiments are performed on a Linux operating system running on a machine with Intel Xeon Haswell E5-2698 2.30 GHz processor with 128GB RAM.

We compared the TIPDECOMPOSITION (TIP in short, Algorithm 1) and the WINGDECOMPOSITION (WING in short, Algorithm 2) with the previous studies that find dense subgraphs with (or without) hierarchical relations in bipartite networks and or their projections.

- For the **unweighted projection**, we use two algorithms: k-core decomposition (Def. 2) and $(2, 3)$ nucleus decomposition (Def. 4). $(2, 3)$ nuclei subgraphs have been shown to be quite effective to find dense regions with detailed hierarchical relations [23, 41].
- For the **weighted projection**, we use the fractional k-cores [20], described in Sec. 3. To the best of our knowledge, it is the only peeling adaptation that works on weighted networks. It is designed to handle the bipartite author-paper networks by using their weighted projections.
- Regarding the algorithms that directly focus on the **bipartite** data, Li *et al.* [29] proposed a k-truss adaptation, as explained at the end of Sec. 3. Although the focus is on the bipartite connections, their algorithm relies on inserting edges between the vertices in the same set, and computes the k-trusses on those new edges and new triangles, which is essentially the same as the $(2, 3)$ nucleus decomposition.
- Apart from those, we also check the **(P, Q)-biclique densest subgraphs**, proposed by Mitzenmacher et al. [31]. We obtain the $(2, 2)$-biclique (butterfly) densest region for each bipartite network in our dataset.

For each bipartite subgraph, we report the size of primary and secondary vertex sets, and the edge density, i.e. $\frac{|E|}{|U| \cdot |V|}$. For the k-core, fractional k-core, and $(2, 3)$ nucleus decompositions, we find the nuclei/cores in the projections (G_p), and then report the induced bipartite subgraphs using the vertices in those nuclei/cores.

6.1 Dense subgraph profiles

We compare the size and density of the bipartite subgraphs found by our algorithms and the previous works mentioned above. Fig. 6 (condmat), 7 (marvel), and also 2 (IMDb) (in Sec. 1) summarize the

[1] http://sariyuce.com/bnd.tar

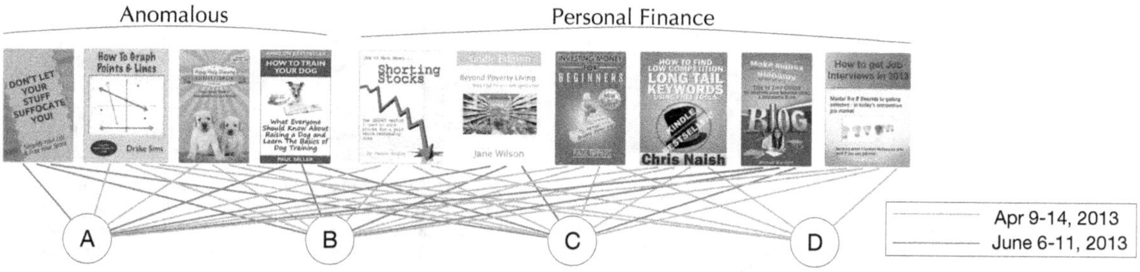

Figure 5: 10 books rated by 4 users, reported by WING. 6 books on the right are on personal finance whereas the 4 on the left are unrelated. Further investigation reveals that those 4 users rated the books in the same days and always gave 5 stars, which are strong indicators for the fake reviews.

results. In all charts, each dot is a bipartite subgraph with at least 0.1 edge density. $|U|$ and $|V|$ are given on the x- and y-axes, and the density is color coded.

Overall, we observe that many dense bipartite subgraphs with nontrivial sizes (on both sides) can be obtained with WING. For `IMDb` and `marvel` networks, those subgraphs exhibit competitive quality (high density and large size) with respect to the butterfly densest subgraphs reported by [31]. TIP also performs well on some instances with respect to other alternatives, but not as good as the WING. As we will show in Sec. 6.4, TIP is faster than the WING, and the fair quality of the TIP can be preferred for applications with strict performance requirements. We omit the results for k-cores since they consistently have lower densities and larger sizes than the $(2,3)$ NUCLEUS and we observe that the densest subgraphs reported by the previous works are concentrated on the axes, meaning that they have a single vertex in either side, which is trivial.

For `condmat` network, in Fig. 6, WING yields 416 subgraphs with at least 5 authors, 5 papers, and 0.5 density. However, it cannot find a subgraph that is as good as the butterfly densest subgraph [31], which has 11 and 13 vertices on each side with more than 0.8 density. TIP can find 59 such subgraphs, whereas the $(2,3)$ NUCLEUS and FRACTIONAL k-CORE can only detect 14 and 20, respectively. TIP and WING are also effective to find detailed hierarchical relations; respectively, they report 77 and 164 subgraphs that contain multiple other subgraphs. $(2,3)$ nucleus can yield only 30 such subgraphs and the other decompositions perform worse.

`marvel` network, as seen in Fig. 7, shows more striking differences between WING and the others; 42 subgraphs appear with more than 0.7 density and at least 5 vertices on each side by using WING, while no such subgraphs can be obtained with other algorithms, including TIP. Furthermore, WING results in pretty competitive subgraphs with respect to the butterfly densest subgraph.

6.2 Books in Amazon Kindle ratings

We analyze the ratings data for the Amazon Kindle books. The unweighted user-item bipartite graph has users on one side, items

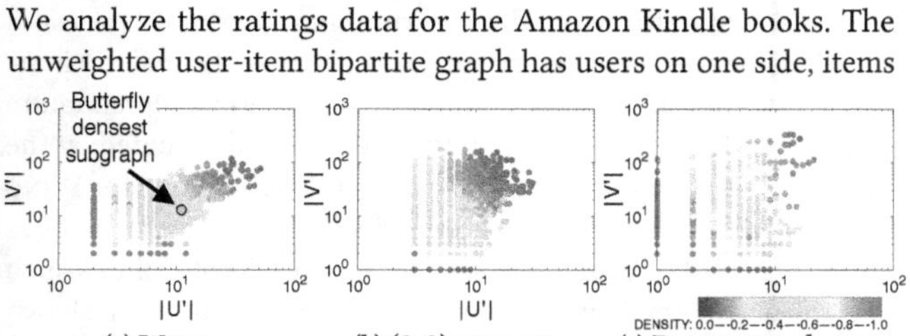

(a) WING (b) $(2,3)$ NUCLEUS (c) FRACTIONAL k-CORE

Figure 6: Dense subgraphs in `condmat`. Each dot is a bipartite subgraph, the density, $|E'|/(|U'||V'|)$, is color coded, and $|U'|$ and $|V'|$ are given on the x- and y-axes. WING results in 416 subgraphs with ≥ 0.5 density and at least 5 vertices in each side. Although it has many subgraphs with different qualities, none is as good as the butterfly densest subgraph, reported by [31].

on the other side, and edges connect the users to the items they rated. The first striking difference appears in the number of reported subgraphs: WING gives 169 distinct subgraphs that have at least 5 vertices on each side and more than 0.5 edge density. TIP reports 25 such structures whereas $(2,3)$ NUCLEUS only gives 6.

One example group that* WING *identifies while all the others cannot is a set of 38 books that are mostly on the self-improvement theme ("how to" books, guides on relationships, healthy diets and personal finance) rated by 12 users. Furthermore, there are three smaller groups within this group. The first has 6 books and all are rated by 5 users. Those books are about the relationships between spouses, like "*Finding The Ins And Outs Of Relationships*". Second group is a collection of 20 books on guides for healthy diets and self-meditation. The third group, shown in Fig. 5, reveals a different picture. There are 10 books that are rated by 4 users, and 6 of them are about the personal finance. However, the other 4 are totally unrelated; 2 on dog training, 1 on the elementary-level algebra and 1 is about creating more space at home. Checking the rating scores for those shows that that almost all the ratings are 5 stars. Furthermore, the dates those books are rated are very close: 2 books are rated between April 9 and 14 in 2013, and the other 2 are between June 6 and 11 in the same year. Bursty reviews is an important indicator for the fake reviews, as [19] notes that "*Reviewers and reviews appearing in a burst are often related in the sense that spammers tend to work with other spammers and genuine reviewers tend to appear together with other genuine reviewers*". Overall, WING can reveal the sets of books on the same theme and also point to the anomalous behaviors, like the fake reviews, in bipartite networks. It does this by using only the graph topology *without any metadata.*

6.3 Authors in the top database conferences

Here we highlight some interesting subgraphs and hierarchical structures found in the `dbconf` network. We report on what *WING and TIP can find but others cannot,* and also what *we cannot find which can be identified by other algorithms.*

Fig. 8 shows the dense subgraph profiles for the `dbconf` network. Trends are similar to the other graphs explained above. WING finds

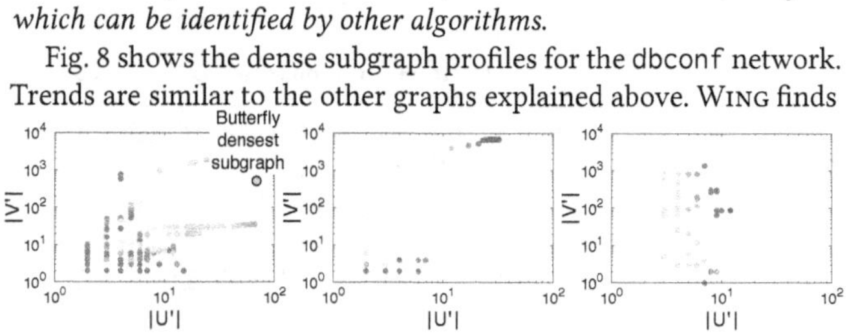

(a) WING (b) TIP (c) $(2,3)$ NUCLEUS

Figure 7: Dense subgraphs for `marvel` network. WING provides many subgraphs with ≥ 0.5 density. 57 of those have at least 5 vertices in each side and 11 have 10 vertices in each. No other algorithm can get such subgraphs.

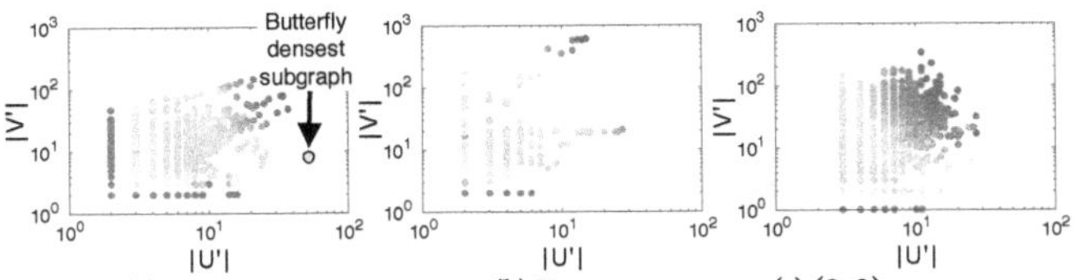

(a) WING (b) TIP (c) (2, 3) NUCLEUS

Figure 8: dbconf **network. Most dense structures in (2, 3) nuclei and fractional k-cores have only one vertex in either vertex set (the red dots along x- and y- axes). Those subgraphs represent the collaborations of many authors in a single paper. We observe that they are mostly papers on a software-product authored by a large group in a company. In most cases those authors do not have any other papers, which makes the subgraph less informative.**

dense subgraphs with non-trivial sizes and also vying with the butterfly densest subgraph, TIP cannot perform as good as the WING, and other algorithms mainly result in dense regions with a single vertex on either side, red dots along x- and y-axes. In (2, 3) NUCLEUS case, the red dots on the x-axis mostly correspond to the papers about a software product of a company and authored by a large group of researchers. In most cases those authors do not have any other papers, thus no butterfly structures exist around them and cannot be found by our WING and TIP algorithms. One example is the paper entitled *"Comdb2: Bloomberg's Highly Available Relational Database System"* in ICDE'10 is written by a large group of people in Bloomberg LP. On the other hand, in the FRACTIONAL k-CORE case, there are also red dots appearing along the y-axis. Those are the subgraphs with a single author and many papers. However, they are isolated because the fractional k-core computation assigns a large weight to this vertex and there is no other vertex around with a close weight. Divesh Srivastava[2] is one such prolific researcher appearing on the y-axis with 144 papers. But, there is no other dense subgraph in fractional k-cores that contains him, showing the weakness of the projection-based approach. ***Note that, none of those trivial subgraphs are reported by the*** TIP ***or*** WING ***algorithms, since no butterflies exist.*** We also identified some structures that can be ***only identified by the*** TIP ***and/or*** WING ***algorithms.***

Philip Yu and IBM Research: We also checked the densest subgraphs that contain a prolific researcher who is expected to participate in multiple structures. We choose Philip Yu [3] for this purpose. Tracing the hierarchical relations from his subgraph(s) in the TIP and WING results gives interesting information about the Streams group at IBM Research, denoted in Fig. 9. The bottom branch in the figure can be identified by both TIP and WING whereas all other projection-based methods fail. The densest subgraph on

[2]http://dblp.uni-trier.de/pers/hd/s/Srivastava:Divesh

[3]https://www.cs.uic.edu/PSYu

Table 3: Runtimes of all the algorithms in seconds. WING is orders of magnitude faster than the (2, 3) NUCLEUS due to the increase in the number of triangles in the projection. CORE and FRACTIONAL CORE are pretty fast, but not effective to report dense structures.

	bipartite		unipartite (projection)			densest ⧖ [31]	
(in sec.)	TIP	WING	CORE	FR. CORE	(2, 3) NUC.	enum	max flow
github	4.09	35.27	0.43	0.68	121,643	13.89	985
IMDb	11.97	72.42	3.35	3.74	8,831	21.78	668
DBLP	25.63	11.04	5.85	10.30	9,378	3.96	206
d-label	1,328	3,789	> 36*hrs*	> 36*hrs*	> 36*hrs*	1,266	1,146
d-style	22,488	25,758	> 36*hrs*	> 36*hrs*	> 36*hrs*	7,264	833
wiki-it	63,187	97,052	> 36*hrs*	> 36*hrs*	> 36*hrs*	23,564	859
kindle	7.19	33.09	1.80	2.02	29,057	10.06	165

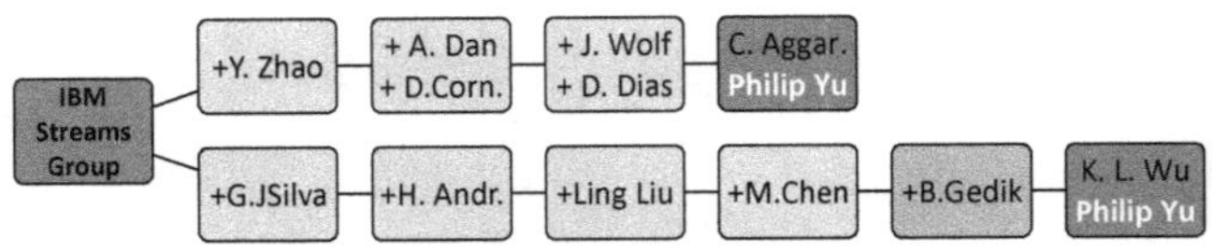

Figure 9: The subgraphs reported by WING in the dbconf **network that contains Philip Yu. Densities are color coded. Two chains show the collaborations in the IBM Research's Streams group, where the parent subgraph (left-most) contains 76 researchers that contains staff members and intern students.**

the right-most is a biclique, including Kun-Lung Wu, manager at IBM Research, and P. Yu, who used to work in the same group, and 13 papers they co-authored. They are contained in another subgraph which has 0.82 density and includes Buğra Gedik (ex-staff member) in addition to K. L. Wu and P. Yu. Looking at another parent subgraph in the chain, we find Ling Liu (B. Gedik's Ph.D. advisor) joins B. Gedik, K. L. Wu and P. Yu. The further parent subgraphs in the chain reveals other researchers, H. Andrade and G. Jacques-Silva, who used to work in the same group. WING also reports another branch that contains P. Yu. There is a biclique of Charu Aggarwal (staff member), P. Yu and their 14 papers. Its parent subgraph has two more authors, Joel Wolf and Daniel Dias (staff members), and the further parent subgraphs in the chain include other people at the same institution. This chain and the other chain described above merges in a subgraph that has 76 authors, who are the researchers and ex-interns in the Streams group.[4]

One weakness observed in the TIP ***and*** WING ***is that they tend to identify pairs of authors first, and then enlarge those pairs to larger subgraphs.*** This results in long chains in the hierarchy which needs further filtering to extract large and dense structures. Main reason for this behavior is the quadratic increase in the number butterflies for author pairs with common papers, i.e., n common neighbors gives $\binom{n}{2}$ butterflies.

6.4 Runtime performances

Lastly we check the runtimes. Table 3 presents the results. As pointed in Sec. 5, WING does more work than TIP and it is also verified by the experiments; TIP can be up to 6 times faster. (2, 3) NUCLEUS gives the most significant subgraphs among the projection based algorithms, however it has $O(|\triangle|)$ complexity *on the projected graph* and suffers from the explosion in the number of triangles. Note that, a k-clique is created for each secondary vertex with degree k, and the number of triangles increases **cubically**, for instance `d-style` network has less than 2M vertices and around 5.5M edges, but its projection has more than 699 quadrillion triangles, which is impossible to process in a reasonable time. Thus, WING is orders of magnitude faster than the (2, 3) NUCLEUS. Regarding the densest butterfly subgraph [31] runtimes, we run [31] without sampling for all the graphs, except `d-label`, `d-style`, and `wiki-it`, and show the runtimes for butterfly enumeration and maximum flow computation phases. Runtimes are mostly dominated by the maximum flow computation and significantly larger than the WING runtimes. For `d-label`, `d-style`, and `wiki-it` graphs, the ones with the most butterflies, we set the sampling probabilities such that the maximum flow operation is run on 50M butterflies (shown in red in Table 3). We observe that the butterfly enumeration, which does not depend on the sampling, takes the most time and it can be

[4]All the information is obtained from the websites of the aforementioned people.

up to 33% of the total WING time. For the `wiki-it` graph, it takes more than 24K seconds to report a single densest butterfly subgraph while 97K seconds is enough for the WING to find many in a large spectrum.

7 DISCUSSION

Our algorithms for bipartite networks can find many dense substructures with the hierarchical relations. Butterfly based definitions enable us to extract the meaningful regions in the graph and the use cases in Sec. 6.3 and 6.2 also verify this. One weakness that we observed is that, number of butterflies per vertex or edge can quadratically increase when there is a large biclique. This results in dense but smaller subgraphs focusing around a few vertices. Handling those regions is an interesting direction. Another promising direction is to find efficient heuristics to count and enumerate the butterflies and other small bicliques. There is a huge body of work on triangle counting and enumeration, but studies are immature for the bipartite structures. Indeed, butterflies can easily reach to billions in a bipartite graph with a few million edges, whereas that many triangles in unipartite networks can be observed for hundreds of millions of edges.

Acknowledgements: Sandia National Laboratories is a multimission laboratory managed and operated by National Technology and Engineering Solutions of Sandia, LLC., a wholly owned subsidiary of Honeywell International, Inc., for the U.S. Department of Energy's National Nuclear Security Administration under contract DE-NA-0003525. This research used resources of the National Energy Research Scientific Computing Center, a DOE Office of Science User Facility supported by the Office of Science of the U.S. Department of Energy under Contract No. DE-AC02-05CH11231.

REFERENCES

[1] 2016. IMDb. (2016). (`www.imdb.com/interfaces`).

[2] 2017. Konect network dataset. (2017). (`http://www.discogs.com/`).

[3] S. Aksoy, T. G. Kolda, and A. Pinar. 2017. Measuring and Modeling Bipartite Graphs with Community Structure. *Journal of Complex Networks* 5, 4 (2017), 581–603.

[4] R. Alberich, J. Miro-Julia, and F Rosselló. 2002. Marvel Universe looks almost like a real social network. *CoRR* abs/cond-mat/0202174 (2002).

[5] Vladimir Batagelj and Matjaz Zaversnik. 2002. Generalized Cores. *CoRR* cs.DS/0202039 (2002).

[6] V. Batagelj and M. Zaversnik. 2003. An O(m) Algorithm for Cores Decomposition of Networks. *CoRR* cs/0310049 (2003).

[7] A. R. Benson, D. F. Gleich, and J. Leskovec. 2016. Higher-order organization of complex networks. *Science* 353, 6295 (2016), 163–166.

[8] A. Beutel, W. Xu, V. Guruswami, C. Palow, and C. Faloutsos. 2013. CopyCatch: Stopping Group Attacks by Spotting Lockstep Behavior in Social Networks. In *Proceedings of the 22nd International Conference on World Wide Web (WWW '13)*. 119–130.

[9] S. P. Borgatti and M. G. Everett. 1997. Network analysis of 2-mode data. *Social Networks* 19, 3 (1997), 243 – 269.

[10] Ü. V. Çatalyürek and C. Aykanat. 1999. Hypergraph-partitioning-based decomposition for parallel sparse-matrix vector multiplication. *IEEE Transactions on Parallel and Distributed Systems* 10, 7 (1999), 673–693.

[11] M. Cerinsek and V. Batagelj. 2015. Generalized two-mode cores. *Social Networks* 42 (2015), 80 – 87.

[12] S. Chacon. 2009. The 2009 GitHub Contest. (2009). (`github.com/blog/466-the-2009-github-contest`).

[13] J. Chen and Y. Saad. 2012. Dense Subgraph Extraction with Application to Community Detection. *IEEE Transactions on Knowledge & Data Engineering* 24, 7 (2012), 1216–1230.

[14] A. Clauset, E. Tucker, and M. Sainz. 2016. The Colorado Index of Complex Networks. (2016). (`icon.colorado.edu`).

[15] J. Cohen. 2008. Trusses: Cohesive subgraphs for social network analysis. National Security Agency Technical Report (2008).

[16] I.S. Dhillon. 2001. Co-clustering Documents and Words Using Bipartite Spectral Graph Partitioning. In *Proceedings of the Seventh ACM SIGKDD International Conference on Knowledge Discovery and Data Mining (KDD '01)*. 269–274.

[17] M.G. Everett and S.P. Borgatti. 2013. The dual-projection approach for two-mode networks. *Social Networks* 35, 2 (2013), 204 – 210.

[18] D. C. Fain and J. O. Pedersen. 2006. Sponsored search: A brief history. *Bulletin of the American Society for Information Science and Technology* 32, 2 (2006), 12–13.

[19] G. Fei, A. Mukherjee, B. Liu, M. Hsu, M. Castellanos, and R Ghosh. 2013. Exploiting Burstiness in Reviews for Review Spammer Detection. In *ICWSM*. The AAAI Press.

[20] C. Giatsidis, D. M. Thilikos, and M. Vazirgiannis. 2011. Evaluating Cooperation in Communities with the k-Core Structure. In *ASONAM*. 87–93.

[21] D. Gibson, R. Kumar, and A. Tomkins. 2005. Discovering Large Dense Subgraphs in Massive Graphs. In *VLDB*. 721–732.

[22] E. Gregori, L. Lenzini, and C. Orsini. 2011. k-dense communities in the internet AS-level topology. In *International Conf. on Communication Systems and Networks (COMSNETS)*. 1–10.

[23] X. Huang, H. Cheng, L. Qin, W. Tian, and J. X. Yu. 2014. Querying K-truss Community in Large and Dynamic Graphs. In *Proc. of the ACM SIGMOD International Conf. on Management of Data*. 1311–1322.

[24] R. Kumar, P. Raghavan, S. Rajagopalan, and A. Tomkins. 1999. Trawling the Web for Emerging Cyber-communities. In *WWW*. 1481–1493.

[25] Jerome Kunegis. 2017. Konect network dataset. (2017). (`http://konect.uni-koblenz.de`).

[26] M. Latapy, C. Magnien, and N. Del Vecchio. 2008. Basic notions for the analysis of large two-mode networks. *Social Networks* 30, 1 (2008), 31 – 48.

[27] Jure Leskovec and Andrej Krevl. 2014. SNAP Datasets: Stanford Large Network Dataset Collection. (June 2014). (`snap.stanford.edu/data`).

[28] Michael Ley. 2016. DBLP computer science bibliography. (Sept. 2016). (`dblp.uni-trier.de`).

[29] Y. Li, T. Kuboyama, and H. Sakamoto. 2013. Truss Decomposition for Extracting Communities in Bipartite Graph. In *IMMM 2013 : The Third International Conference on Advances in Information Mining and Management*.

[30] D. Matula and L. Beck. 1983. Smallest-last ordering and clustering and graph coloring algorithms. *Journal of ACM* 30, 3 (1983), 417–427.

[31] M. Mitzenmacher, J. Pachocki, R. Peng, C. Tsourakakis, and S. C. Xu. 2015. Scalable Large Near-Clique Detection in Large-Scale Networks via Sampling. In *Proceedings of the 21th ACM SIGKDD International Conference on Knowledge Discovery and Data Mining (KDD '15)*. 815–824.

[32] A. P. Mukherjee and S. Tirthapura. 2014. Enumerating Maximal Bicliques from a Large Graph Using MapReduce. In *Proceedings of the 2014 IEEE International Congress on Big Data (BIGDATACONGRESS '14)*. 707–716.

[33] M. E. J. Newman. 2001. Scientific collaboration networks. I. Network construction and fundamental results. *Phys. Rev. E* 64 (2001), 016131. Issue 1.

[34] M. E. J. Newman. 2001. Scientific collaboration networks. II. Shortest paths, weighted networks, and centrality. *Phys. Rev. E* 64 (2001), 016132. Issue 1.

[35] M. E. J. Newman. 2001. The structure of scientific collaboration networks. *Proceedings of the National Academy of Sciences* 98, 2 (2001), 404–409.

[36] T. Opsahl. 2013. Triadic closure in two-mode networks: Redefining the global and local clustering coefficients. *Social Networks* 35, 2 (2013), 159 – 167.

[37] G. Robins and M. Alexander. 2004. Small Worlds Among Interlocking Directors: Network Structure and Distance in Bipartite Graphs. *Computational & Mathematical Organization Theory* 10, 1 (2004), 69–94.

[38] K. Saito and T. Yamada. 2006. Extracting Communities from Complex Networks by the k-dense Method. In *IEEE International Conf. on Data Mining Workshops, ICDMW*. 300–304.

[39] A. E. Sarıyüce and A. Pinar. 2016. Fast Hierarchy Construction for Dense Subgraphs. *Proc. VLDB Endow.* 10, 3 (Nov. 2016), 97–108.

[40] A. E. Sarıyüce and A. Pinar. 2017. Peeling Bipartite Networks for Dense Subgraph Discovery. *CoRR* 1611.02756 (2017). (Extended version).

[41] A. E. Sarıyüce, C. Seshadhri, A. Pınar, and Ü. V. Çatalyürek. 2015. Finding the Hierarchy of Dense Subgraphs Using Nucleus Decompositions. In *Proc. of the International Conf. on World Wide Web (WWW)*. 927–937.

[42] S. B. Seidman. 1983. Network structure and minimum degree. *Social Networks* 5, 3 (1983), 269–287.

[43] K. Sim, J. Li, V. Gopalkrishnan, and G. Liu. 2009. Mining maximal quasi-bicliques: Novel algorithm and applications in the stock market and protein networks. *Statistical Analysis and Data Mining* 2, 4 (2009), 255–273.

[44] C. Tsourakakis. 2015. The K-clique Densest Subgraph Problem. In *Proc. of the 24th International Conf. on World Wide Web (WWW '15)*. 1122–1132.

[45] C. E. Tsourakakis, J. Pachocki, and M. Mitzenmacher. 2017. Scalable Motif-aware Graph Clustering. In *Proceedings of the 26th International Conference on World Wide Web (WWW '17)*. 1451–1460.

[46] A. Verma and S. Butenko. 2012. Network clustering via clique relaxations: A community based approach. In *Graph Partitioning and Clustering, DIMACS Workshop*. 129–140.

[47] M. M. Wolf, A. M. Klinvex, and D. M. Dunlavy. 2016. Advantages to Modeling Relational Data using Hypergraphs versus Graphs. In *IEEE High Performance Extreme Computing Conference, HPEC*.

[48] Y. Zhang and S. Parthasarathy. 2012. Extracting Analyzing and Visualizing Triangle K-Core Motifs Within Networks. In *Proc. of the IEEE International Conf. on Data Engineering (ICDE)*. 1049–1060.

Short-Term Satisfaction and Long-Term Coverage: Understanding How Users Tolerate Algorithmic Exploration

Tobias Schnabel
Cornell University
Ithaca, NY, USA
tbs49@cornell.edu

Paul N. Bennett,
Susan T. Dumais
Microsoft Research
Redmond, WA, USA
[pauben,sdumais]@microsoft.com

Thorsten Joachims
Cornell University
Ithaca, NY, USA
tj@cs.cornell.edu

ABSTRACT

Any learning algorithm for recommendation faces a fundamental trade-off between exploiting partial knowledge of a user's interests to maximize satisfaction in the short term and discovering additional user interests to maximize satisfaction in the long term. To enable discovery, a machine learning algorithm typically elicits feedback on items it is uncertain about, which is termed *algorithmic exploration* in machine learning. This exploration comes with a cost to the user, since the items an algorithm chooses for exploration frequently turn out to not match the user's interests. In this paper, we study how users tolerate such exploration and how presentation strategies can mitigate the exploration cost. To this end, we conduct a behavioral study with over 600 people, where we vary how algorithmic exploration is mixed into the set of recommendations. We find that users respond non-linearly to the amount of exploration, where some exploration mixed into the set of recommendations has little effect on short-term satisfaction and behavior. For long-term satisfaction, the overall goal is to learn via exploration about the items presented. We therefore also analyze the quantity and quality of implicit feedback signals such as clicks and hovers, and how they vary with different amounts of mix-in exploration. Our findings provide insights into how to design presentation strategies for algorithmic exploration in interactive recommender systems, mitigating the short-term costs of algorithmic exploration while aiming to elicit informative feedback data for learning.

CCS CONCEPTS

• **Information systems** → **Recommender systems**; • **Human-centered computing** → *Interaction design theory, concepts and paradigms*;

KEYWORDS

recommender systems; algorithmic exploration; user experience; interactive systems; human-in-the-loop

ACM ISBN 978-1-4503-5581-0/18/02...$15.00
https://doi.org/10.1145/3159652.3159700

ACM Reference format:
Tobias Schnabel, Paul N. Bennett, Susan T. Dumais, and Thorsten Joachims. 2018. Short-Term Satisfaction and Long-Term Coverage: Understanding How Users Tolerate Algorithmic Exploration. In *Proceedings of WSDM'18, February 5–9, 2018, Marina Del Rey, CA, USA,* , 9 pages.
https://doi.org/10.1145/3159652.3159700

1 INTRODUCTION

Recommender systems are an integral component of many websites including e-commerce destinations, news content hubs, and movie streaming portals. Recommender systems help people navigate a large space of options [33] and can both increase user satisfaction as well as achieve other business goals [16]. For the continuous improvement of recommender systems, *exploration* forms a key component of how learning algorithms obtain coverage of a user's possible interests. More specifically, algorithmic exploration describes a concept in *online learning* [35], where algorithms learn sequentially, and need to try out new actions or options – explore them – to achieve good coverage of the learning domain in the long run. Algorithmic exploration not only helps with respect to a single user, but can also improve other users' recommendations, for example, through exploration of newly listed items [1, 2]. Moreover, the feedback collected through exploration can be used to counterfactually evaluate new recommender systems [4, 28, 39].

Although exploration is of great importance for many algorithmic goals, exploration has the potential to lead to user dissatisfaction, since the items chosen for exploration frequently turn out to not match the user's interests. This raises the following key question: what is the overall negative impact of exploration on user satisfaction and how can it be mitigated while ensuring a high level of quality and quantity of the resulting feedback data?

In this paper, we study the question of how to best explore from two perspectives. First, we study in a systematic way how the amount of exploration affects short-term user satisfaction. In particular, a certain number of items to explore are mixed into each impression of personalized recommendations – a process we call *mix-in exploration*. This allows us to examine different levels of exploration among the set of recommendations, starting with a base strategy that does no exploration and then gradually moving to a strategy that recommends items purely for the purpose of exploration. By conducting a user study on Amazon Mechanical Turk with over 600 participants, we find that people are able to perceive changes from different levels of exploration, but that changes affect user-reported measures in a non-linear way. In particular, we find that mixing only a few exploratory items into each personalized recommendation impression does not change reported user satisfaction significantly. However, exceeding a threshold of exploration then sharply impacts user perception. Surprisingly, we could not find any significant impact of exploration on peoples' final choices, indicating that people are quite resilient to irrelevant recommendations and that they find ways to work around them.

Second, as a step towards learning, we examine quantity and quality of feedback signals under different levels of exploration. We find that larger amounts of exploration drives down feedback quantity. Overall, we find that among the signals we studied both shortlisting events as well as hovering events provide the most informative feedback signals.

In summary, we find that people are tolerant with respect to smaller amounts of exploration, and that limiting exploration is also important for ensuring good feedback quantities. These findings indicate that for improving recommendation systems in practice, it is preferable to mix a limited amount of exploration into every impression – as opposed to having a few impressions that do pure exploration. Also, our study of feedback signals can further guide the design of learning algorithms. To the best of our knowledge, this is the first study to measure the user-centric cost of exploration in a personalized setting.

2 RELATED WORK

Our work is related to ideas from various areas, such as user-centric evaluation of recommender systems, understanding of implicit feedback, and interactive recommender systems.

We mainly follow the user-centric paradigm [26, 30, 36] for the evaluation of recommender systems in this paper. We divide user-centric evaluation into rating-based and task-based studies. Studies in the first category present a list of recommendations to users that they need to rate, whereas studies in the second category ask people to actually use a recommender system as part of a user task. The study in our paper falls into the second category.

Cosley et al. [7] conducted one of the first rating-based studies in recommendation, finding that user satisfaction decreases if a recommender shows incorrect star ratings. A study in [8] compared a number of popular recommendation algorithms. The authors found that a static popularity-based method was among the methods with highest satisfaction. Ge et al. [12] mix-in diverse items into recommendation lists. They found that inserting these diverse items did not significantly impact user satisfaction – however, the recommendations were manually created and static. Most rating-based studies, however, showed an increase in user satisfaction with an increase in diversity [10, 44]. The problem with rating-based studies is that they provide no insight into how and whether recommendations would impact users in their tasks [41], a shortcoming that is addressed by task-based studies.

One of the first task-based studies was done by Swearingen and Sinha [40]. They found users to be hesitant to purchase new items and hypothesize that having known items among the recommendations increases the chance of users adopting novel items. We were not able to see the latter effect for random mix-ins in our study. Only a few task-based studies also examine feedback signals along with user-centric measures. Cremonesi et al. [9] found different recommender algorithms to have no effect on metrics like time-to-decision or the number of examined items. Jones and Pu studied user satisfaction in music recommendation [24], and found the number of recommended items that were liked to be predictive of preference between systems, similar to shortlisting interactions in our setting.

There has been substantially more work on understanding implicit feedback signals in information retrieval (IR) [6, 11, 23, 31]. Clicks and dwell time are traditionally used as feedback signals for learning algorithms in these settings. However, we found these signals to be insufficient in quantity in our study, and recommend to consider other signals, e.g., hover time. This issue has also spurred some research in IR on alternative signals, such as cursor movements [20] or scrolling [13].

Lastly, we present a general interface useful for many interactive recommendation settings [17, 38]. In contrast, many interactive systems discussed in the literature [17] provide domain-specific controls for people, e.g., tags associated with a movie [3]. Our interface only relies on items as input, making it applicable to a wide range of domains.

In comparison to related work, ours is the first work to systematically vary the amount of exploration in a personalized recommendation setting. Because of our experimental design, we are able to study the impact of exploration on both user satisfaction and feedback signals.

3 METHODOLOGY

We conducted a randomized between-subjects study with over 600 participants on Amazon Mechanical Turk. This allowed us to collect data from a large and diverse set of people, an advantage over traditional laboratory settings [29]. The user task in this study consisted of picking a movie to watch from a large set of movies. This task is an instance of what is often referred to as the *Find Good Items* task [18], or *One-Choice* task [34]. Using movies gave us a task domain that people were already familiar with; it is also of high practical importance, and has a natural visual representation via movie posters.

We evaluate different presentation strategies through an interactive recommender interface that updates automatically while the user is browsing. This is in contrast to many other studies on user-centric evaluation of recommender studies [8, 10, 12] where users are exposed to recommendations that are only computed once. Having the ability to serve recommendations interactively has the following two benefits: (i) the recommendations are not isolated responses, but can be evaluated with respect to the user task, and (ii) we are able to observe feedback signals directly after new recommendations have been made.

3.1 Interactive recommender interface

The general idea behind our interface is to base recommendations on items that are marked as interesting during a session, similar to e-commerce settings where further items are recommended after initial items have been added to the basket. This setting is also often referred to as *session-based* recommendation [19, 34], as opposed to recommendation based on long-term preferences. To enable interactivity, we update recommendations each time a user adds items to a *shortlist* during a session, that is a temporary list of candidates that the user is currently considering [34].

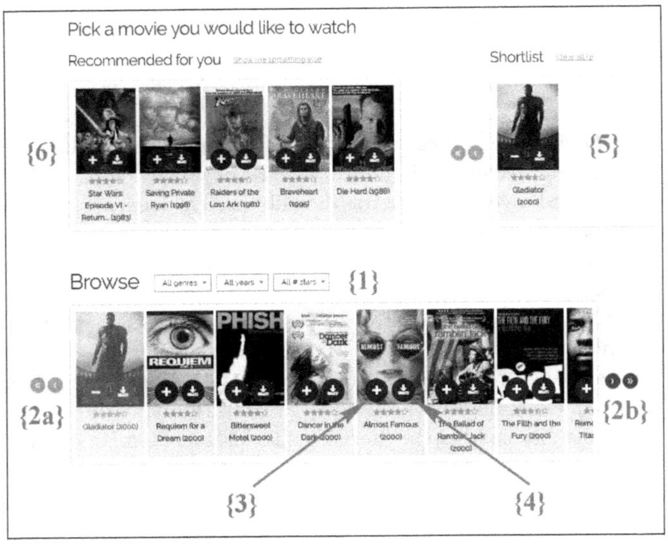

Figure 1: The interactive recommendation interface each user was presented with. The "Recommended for you" panel was updated automatically each time a user added a movie to the shortlist.

As Fig. 1 shows, there are three panels in the interface: the browsing panel (bottom), the shortlist panel {5}, and the recommendation panel {6}. The layout was motivated by the interfaces of common online movie streaming services, such as Netflix, Hulu, or Amazon. In the main panel, people can browse movies by using the paging buttons ({2a}, {2b}), and can also filter the displayed movies using facets {1}. They have the option of examining a movie further by clicking on a poster of the movie, which opens a pop-up with more information. They can add movies to the shortlist panel by clicking on the plus button {3}, and make their final choice by clicking on the download button {4}, and confirming their choice in a prompt afterwards. Every time an item is added to the shortlist, the recommendation panel {6} displays a new set of five recommendations with a brief loading animation. Once a movie is shown as a recommendation, it is blacklisted for the session and never shown again to the user to avoid repetitiveness [43]. We do not update recommendations if a user adds a recommended movie to the shortlist to avoid accidentally dismissing any other interesting recommendations.

3.2 Presentation strategies

In order to systematically test the effects of exploration on people, we created a set of controlled presentation strategies that cover the spectrum from no exploration to full exploration. We used the following strategy for presenting items to explore, which we call *mix-in exploration*: we insert a given number of items to explore from an Explore strategy into the recommendations from a personalized Base strategy. Since there were five presentation slots available, we had six different presentation strategies to cover all cases: Base (B), Mix-1 (M-1), Mix-2 (M-2), Mix-3 (M-3), Mix-4 (M-4), FullExplore (FE).

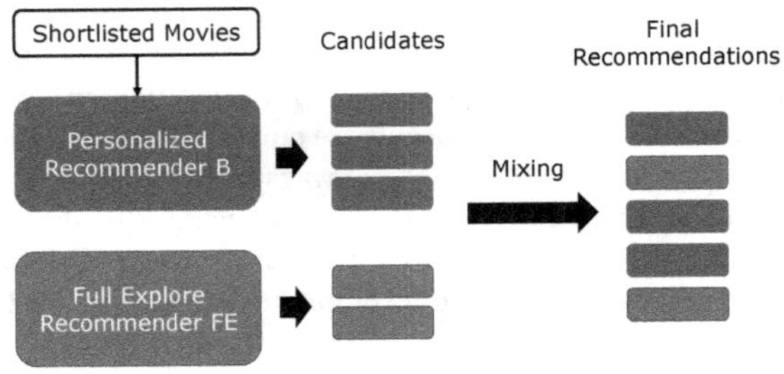

Figure 2: In mix-in exploration, items to be explored are mixed into items from a personalized recommender.

Fig. 2 shows schematically how mix-in exploration is performed in the case of Mix-2. The personalized Base recommender (B) generates a list of candidates based on the set of movies that a user has currently on her shortlist. For the final recommendation impression that is shown to the user, items generated by the FullExplore recommender (FE) are then mixed-into the items of the personalized recommender (B). The details for each strategy are provided below.

Base. This personalized content-based strategy finds the 50 most similar movies for each movie in the shortlist, and re-ranks all candidates by popularity for familiarity. We also explored collaborative filtering techniques, but found them to perform poorly for the small sample sizes available to us. To compute the content-based similarities, we project all tag vectors from the Tag Genome project [42] into a 25-dimensional space via Singular Value Decomposition for efficiency and use cosine similarities between those vectors. Popularity here is defined as the number of ratings of three or more stars for a movie in the MovieLens 1M dataset [15]. Ranking the candidates by popularity showed improved user satisfaction in our preliminary experiments over a method which did not re-rank movies by popularity, a finding that is consistent with other studies [8, 22].

FullExplore. Returns items to explore uniformly at random from the inventory. We chose this method partly because this is how many theoretically-motivated machine learning algorithms explore (e.g., [27]), and partly because it represents the worst-case for frequently missing the user's interests.

Mix-*i*. Interweaves recommendations from Base and the Random strategy, using i slots for FullExplore. It first samples i slots at random to mitigate presentation bias effects and marks them to be filled with recommendations from FullExplore. The remaining slots will be filled with recommendations from Base. The slots are then filled from left to right with the first movie from the corresponding strategy that has also not already been chosen for another slot.

3.3 Movie inventory

To make our system similar to real-world movie streaming websites, we populated it with data from OMDb[1], a free and open movie database. We only kept movies that were released after 1950 to ensure a general level of familiarity. Furthermore, we only selected movies that also appeared in the Tag Genome dataset [42], since the latter dataset was used to make recommendations. After this

[1] http://omdbapi.com/

filtering step, 3470 movies remained in our inventory. In order to have a reasonably attractive default ranking, we sorted all movies first by year in descending order, and then by review score (IMDb score), again in descending order. This means that people were shown recent and highly-rated movies first in the browsing panel by default.

3.4 Participants

We recruited 610 participants from Amazon Mechanical Turk, a crowd sourcing platform. Crowd workers were required to be from a US-based location, and to have an approval rate of at least 95% on previous tasks. Moreover, to ensure that all participants had a consistent experience and saw the same content on the screen, we tested for their browser version and screen resolution. Their median age was between 30 and 40 years as self-reported in the survey. We offered a payment of $1. With an average completion time of 8 minutes, this is an effective wage of $7.50 an hour which is above the US Federal minimum wage. Participants were randomly assigned one of the six presentation strategies as a treatment. From the 610 completed user responses, we filtered out all sessions where people reloaded the page with the interface, or shortlisted more than 15 items since we found these sessions to show overall spamming behavior. After this step, we were left with 577 sessions.

3.5 Study design

We gave participants the following instructions:

> *Imagine you are home alone and want to watch a movie. Use the interface provided next to choose a movie to watch. To make your final choice, click on the button with the download icon next to a movie.*

We chose the scenario above to keep the instructions as simple as possible since any complications were at risk of being ignored by the crowd workers.

After having read the instructions and having seen a short one-minute video about how to use the interface, the participants were taken to the recommendation interface in Fig. 1. After confirming their final choice of movie, they were asked to complete a survey that asked for their experience with the interface.

The survey questions posed to a user after they made their final choice were adapted from existing user-centric frameworks [26, 30] to the crowd sourcing setting [25]. In our survey, we chose questions focusing on the following five properties of the recommendations: quality, helpfulness, transparency, novelty, and choice satisfaction. Except for one binary question, all questions were answered on a 5-point Likert scale from strongly disagree (0) to strongly agree (4).

4 USER SATISFACTION

In this section, we study how varying the amount of exploration affects self-reported user outcome. The following research questions address different aspects of user outcome to the amount of exploration:

(1) Do people perceive differences in the amount of exploration? Besides recommendation accuracy, are any other properties perceived as different?
(2) Can exploration interfere with helpfulness?
(3) How does exploration impact perceived transparency?
(4) Is the cost of exploration linear, i.e. do linear changes in the amount of exploration also lead to linear changes in user outcome?
(5) Does introducing exploration have a significant impact on people's final choices?

Table 1 shows the aggregated results over 577 user responses (93-96 responses for each condition). The last column reports the p-value of a one-way analysis of variance (ANOVA), testing for the equivalence of means among all conditions. Furthermore, an asterisk indicates that a particular exploration strategy is significantly different from Base (t-test, $p < 0.05$, Bonferroni-correction). To test for trends, we also linearly regressed all survey responses with ANOVA significance of $p < 0.01$ against the number of mix-ins and found the slope to be significantly different from zero in all cases with $p < 0.01$. Before turning to the research questions, we will briefly discuss how people perceived their interaction with the interface. We can see from the first two questions that user responses are consistently positive across all conditions, indicating that people did indeed enjoy interacting with the interface, and did not feel stressed during the process. Participants also frequently reported that they made use of the shortlist to keep track of their current choices, independent of which exploration strategy was used (question 3). This overall positive feedback is evidence that the interface is on par with realistic settings and that our results are not biased by a poor interface design.

4.1 Do people perceive differences?

One of the key questions of this paper and of the overall design of this study is whether and how people are affected by the amount of exploration. Knowing that people are able to find differences between the conditions also indicates that our methodology is sufficiently sensitive to the differences we aim to study. Moreover, since we know the composition of each exploration strategy by design, we can formulate a set of hypotheses to test.

For example, as the amount of exploration increases, we expect people to perceive presentation strategies as less accurate and less similar to their shortlisted items. Similarly, we expect people to report an increase in novelty. As the scores of questions 4 and 5 in Table 1 show, these expectations indeed hold true – people report both decreases in recommendation accuracy ("The recommendations were a good fit for my taste") as well as decreases in recommendation similarity to the shortlist ("The recommendations were similar to the movies on the shortlist"). Moreover, people also accurately report novelty of the recommendations as shown in the responses to question 6 ("Most of the recommendations were known to me"). Also, question 6 shows that perceived novelty increases as we mix in more exploration items.

Examining the responses to each of the three questions above more closely, we can also see that user responses for Mix-4 and FullExplore are significantly different from the Base strategy. In fact, Likert scores fall off almost monotonically with an increasing number of mixed-in items. Since we know the composition of each presentation strategy by design, the findings above also serve as validation for our study design – we were to able to successfully match up the user responses with our initial hypotheses.

Question	B	M-1	M-2	M-3	M-4	FE	p
	Conditions						
Interaction adequacy							
1. I enjoyed selecting movies with this interface.	3.23	3.30	3.26	3.37	3.17	3.08	0.39
2. I was stressed out while selecting movies.	0.33	0.20	0.33	0.28	0.33	0.33	0.70
3. I used the shortlist to keep track of my current choices.	3.12	3.03	3.01	3.05	3.11	3.03	0.98
Accuracy							
4. The recommendations were a good fit for my taste.	3.05	2.90	2.93	2.77	2.35*	2.03*	<0.01
5. The recommendations were similar to the movies on the shortlist.	3.21	3.01	2.97	3.01	2.39*	2.17*	<0.01
Novelty							
6. Most of the recommendations were known to me.	2.89	2.80	2.69	2.58	2.38*	2.09*	<0.01
7. My final choice is different from the movies I usually watch.	0.85	0.96	0.91	0.89	1.09	1.20	0.31
8. I have not watched my final choice before. *[binary]*	0.28	0.30	0.30	0.25	0.33	0.24	0.76
Helpfulness							
9. I had a good idea of what I wanted to watch when I started.	1.81	1.89	2.03	1.99	2.07	1.57	0.12
10. The recommendations helped me determine what I was in the mood for.	2.76	2.69	2.64	2.62	2.08*	1.99*	<0.01
Transparency							
11. I understand why the system recommended me the movies that it did.	3.27	3.11	3.16	3.05	2.43*	2.37*	<0.01
12. I was able to steer the recommendations into the right direction.	2.95	2.75	2.82	2.92	2.42*	2.07*	<0.01
Choice Satisfaction							
13. If I were to keep browsing, I'd find a movie that I'd prefer to my final choice.	2.44	2.54	2.41	2.35	2.49	2.56	0.82
14. I would watch my finally chosen movie, given the opportunity.	3.58	3.56	3.66	3.80	3.61	3.52	0.04

Table 1: Aggregated answers for all survey questions. Answers were on a likert scale from 0 (strongly disagree) to 4 (strongly agree), except for question 8. The last column has the p-values for a one-way ANOVA.

4.2 Does exploration interfere with helpfulness?

A good recommender system should ultimately help the user with her decision. In fact, people are often not sure what to watch when they start browsing for a movie as the responses to question 9 show ("I had a good idea of what I wanted to watch when I started."). Hence, it is important to understand whether exploration can actually change how helpful people perceive a system to be. As the results for question 10 indicate ("The recommendations helped me determine what I was in the mood for"), helpfulness is negatively correlated with the amount of mixed-in exploration. Compared to the Base strategy, both Mix-4 and FullExplore produced recommendations that people perceived as significantly less useful.

4.3 Does exploration decrease transparency?

Another important property of a recommender system is transparency, i.e. why a particular recommendation was made to the user. For interactive recommendations, transparency may be even more important since people's recommendations are tied to their actions. We asked participants for transparency in two directions. In question 11, we asked for transparency in the traditional setting ("I understand why the system recommended me the movies that it did") [37], whereas in question 12 we targeted transparency in the proactive setting ("I was able to steer the recommendations into the right direction"). For both questions, we find that transparency correlates negatively with the amount of exploration. Again, Mix-4 and FullExplore were perceived to be significantly less transparent than the Base recommender.

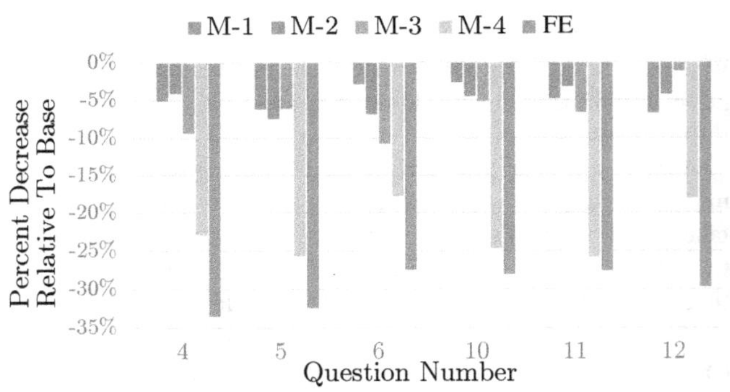

Figure 3: Likert scores fall off in a non-linear way when exploration is increased.

4.4 Are costs linear?

An interesting question is whether a linear increase in the number of mixed-in items will cause a linear change in the Likert scores of user responses. This is particularly important in order to understand *how* an algorithm should explore, i.e. how many potentially poor recommendations people are willing to tolerate. Fig. 3 gives some insight into this question. It shows the relative decrease in

Likert scores compared to Base of all questions that had significant differences under the ANOVA at $p < 0.01$, grouped together by question number, and then sorted by the number of mixed-in items within each group. The bar plot suggests that user responses partition the presentation strategies into two groups – one with Base and Mix-1, Mix-2 and Mix-3; and one with Mix-4 and FullExplore. As the statistical comparisons in Table 1 shows, this is indeed true. Strategies in the last group are significantly different from Base. In other words, scores are not statistically distinguishable from the Base recommender with up to three mixed-in items, and there is a sharp transition going to four or five items.

4.5 Does exploration affect final choices?

The goal of the user task was picking a movie that they would like to watch. A natural question therefore to ask is how much exploration impacts people's final choices. Naively, one would think that since we found decreases in helpfulness and accuracy with increased levels of exploration, these losses would also carry over to choice satisfaction. However, we did not find any significant differences between the six different conditions at the $p < 0.01$ level for choice satisfaction. Users were not more confident that they found the best option as question 13 asked ("If I were to keep browsing, I'd find a movie that I'd prefer to my final choice"). We were also unable to find a significant effect on watch intention in question 14 at the $p < 0.01$ level ("I would watch my finally chosen movie, given the opportunity").

Even though we could not find any direct effects of exploration on choice satisfaction, there could be effects on how novel the choices are. As discussed earlier, we found significant differences with respect to how novel people perceived the recommendations (cf. question 6). To the extent that people actually adopt those novel recommendations or explore more novel options themselves, we should see changes in their final choices. However, we fail to show any significant effects on the novelty of people's final choices as question 7 ("My final choice is different from the movies I usually watch") and question 8 ("I have not watched my final choice before.") show. Note that the options for question 8 were binary, with 0 (no) and 1 (yes). We can also see from question 7 that people are reluctant in general to choose something that would be outside their regular taste profile as Likert scores are consistently low. Question 8 adds even more support to this: Only 24-33% of people chose a movie that they had never seen before.

4.6 Discussion

We found that people were not only aware of the accuracy of a recommender system, but were also able to assess its degree of novelty, and whether it recommends items that are similar to the shortlist. However, even though people were able to report these properties accurately, it had little influence on their reported satisfaction with their final choices. We found neither a significant effect of exploration on overall choice satisfaction, nor on how novel people's final choices were. This implies that people still find ways to be successful at their task, even when random exploration presents less relevant items. This is similar to the finding that people are still able to perform well in information-seeking tasks, despite poorer search results [41].

Perhaps most notable for its implications for exploration cost, the cost of exploration is non-linear. In particular, for *every question* that showed a significant change with respect to the amount of exploration, there are only small statistically insignificant differences in perceived quality up to three mixed-in items. This implies that people are quite forgiving with respect to recommendation quality, as long as they can find at least multiple relevant recommendations. Practically, this suggests that when an algorithm needs to explore, there is a low cost of inserting a limited number of new options. While in our scenario, we found that people needed to have at least two good recommendations among the five, it would be interesting to see how this extends to more general cases. In the case of longer lists, another study [12] showed that inserting four items into a list of twelve recommendations for diversity also did not affect user satisfaction significantly. However, it is unclear when exactly a turning point occurs in this altered setting. Hence, future research should try to gain a better understanding of how people judge lists of recommendations, especially how the overall utility for a list is composed from its individual parts.

5 THE INFORMATIVENESS OF FEEDBACK

In the last section, we looked at how we can minimize the cost of exploration on the user side, and found that cost was minimal for few mixed-in items per recommendation impression. However, it is important to remember why we explore – we want to obtain more information about a user's preferences for future recommendations. Hence, to be effective in this step, we need to ensure a high *informativeness* of feedback signals when exploring. To facilitate a more fine-grained analysis, we define informativeness as the combination of two factors – signal quantity, i.e. how often do people give feedback of a specific type, and signal quality, i.e. how well does the feedback signal reflect the user preferences. So, when striving for highly informative feedback, we need feedback signals to be both abundant as well as indicative of user preferences.

To answer the question of how we can obtain the most informative feedback during exploration, we address the issues of signal quality and quantity in the following two sections separately with the following research questions:

(1) How does the amount of exploration affect feedback quantity? Do different types of feedback behave differently?
(2) Which type of feedback provides the highest quality, i.e. is best able to distinguish between the utility of items from Base and FullExplore?

For the remainder of this section, we will employ the following definitions for different types of feedback signals. An item was *examined* when a user clicked on it, opening a pop-up window with more details about the item. When a user added an item to the shortlist via one of the plus buttons, we refer to this item as *shortlisted*. Similarly, if the mouse cursor was inside an item card (movie poster with the gray title box) for at least 0.5 seconds, we call this item *hovered* over. Finally, if a user picked an item as his or her final choice, we refer to it as *chosen*.

5.1 Feedback quantity

In this section, we look at how the amount of feedback is influenced by exploration. As our goal is to improve learning through

Signal from rec. panel	Interactions	Availability
examined rec.	0.15	9.7%
shortlisted rec	0.94	38.1%
hovered rec.	2.60	62.4%
chosen rec.	0.30	30.0%

Table 2: Feedback quantity varies largely by signal type; with hovering being the most frequent one. Availability is defined as the fraction of sessions in which the signal occurred.

Signal from rec. panel	Conditions						
	B	M-1	M-2	M-3	M-4	FE	p
examined rec.	0.25	0.14	0.09	0.09	0.12	0.19	0.40
shortlisted rec.	1.14	1.15	1.32	1.06	0.58*	0.34*	<0.01
hovered rec.	3.04	2.72	2.90	2.62	2.46	1.87	0.25
chosen rec.	0.39	0.29	0.37	0.33	0.28	0.16*	<0.01

Table 3: Mean number of interactions with recommendations. The last column contains the p-values for a one-way ANOVA.

recommendations, we restrict our analysis to interactions with the recommendation panel. We start our analysis of feedback quantity with overall availability, averaged over all conditions. Table 2 shows the availability and the mean number of interactions with the recommendation panel across all conditions. For the interactions column, we report the average number of interactions that a user had of this type. To compute availability, we report the percentage of sessions in which people had at least one interaction of a specific type with the recommendation panel.

Disappointingly, people examined detailed information about at least one movie recommendation in less than 10% of sessions. However, in 38% of the sessions, we can observe that at least one recommendation was added to the shortlist. With an average of 0.94 interactions per session, we expect 94 shortlisting interactions with the recommendations panel in total on average for 100 sessions (since some users shortlist multiple items in a session). The signal with highest availability is hovering, which is present in 62% of all sessions. Also, the number of item interactions for it is more than twice as high as for shortlisting (2.60 vs. 0.93). One can also see the general trend that less intrusive feedback signals (i.e. hovering, shortlisting) are more common than more obtrusive signals (i.e. examining). In 30% of all sessions, people chose their final item from their recommendations as opposed to choosing it from the browsing panel as the last row shows. However, this signal obviously comes too late to influence session-based recommendation. It is important though to note that Table 2 averages across all conditions, so the fact that interaction scores are low is also due to suboptimal strategies.

We now analyze how signal quantity varies for different levels of exploration. Table 3 reports the mean number of interactions under each condition. Although not shown in the table, we did not find significant differences in average time-to-decision (session length), average total number of shortlisted movies, or in the average number of recommendations people were exposed to. Again, an asterisk indicates significance with respect to Base using a t-test ($p < 0.05$, Bonferroni correction). As Table 3 shows, the level of exploration has a significant impact on feedback quantity in two cases. There is a significant impact of exploration on both the number of shortlist interactions, and the number of chosen items that came from the recommendations. Both Mix-4 and FullExplore had significantly fewer shortlisting interactions than Base. Interestingly, this grouping is consistent with what we found in our user-centric evaluation in the last section. In the number of recommendations that were also finally chosen by people, we only were able to find significance between Base and FullExplore. However, neither the number of hover interactions nor the number of examine interactions on recommended items showed significant differences, although the number of hover interactions seems to decrease with increasing exploration.

5.2 Feedback quality

We now turn to analyze feedback quality. By construction, and also from the results in Section 4, we know that the utility of the Base strategy to people is higher on average than the utility of the FullExplore strategy which chose items at random. This controlled setting gives us the opportunity to see how this difference in average utility is reflected in implicit signals. This can help guide the design of more sensitive online experiments as well as the design of better learning algorithms. We define signal quality as the ability of a signal to distinguish between the average utility of items that came from Base and the average utility of items that came from the FullExplore strategy. Note that we know how many random items each strategy showed to a user, and also at which positions they were shown. We define the utility $U_\pi(s)$ of a strategy $\pi \in \{\text{Base, FullExplore}\}$ in session s as an average over all individual item utilities $u(i, s)$ of items i in the set $\mathcal{I}(\pi)$ of items that a strategy showed to the user:

$$U_\pi(s) = \frac{1}{|\mathcal{I}(\pi)|} \sum_{i \in \mathcal{I}(\pi)} u(i, s).$$

The individual item utilities can encode various interaction signals, for example, $u(i, s)$ could be a binary function indicating whether a user examined item i in session s. We also hope to find $U_{\text{Base}}(s)$ to be greater than $U_{\text{FullExplore}}(s)$, again, since we know it is by construction and from the user experiments. More formally, we capture this in a win score

$$\text{win}_{\text{Base}}(s) = \begin{cases} 1.0, & \text{if } U_{\text{Base}}(s) > U_{\text{FullExplore}}(s) \\ 0.5, & \text{if } U_{\text{Base}}(s) = U_{\text{FullExplore}}(s) \\ 0.0, & \text{otherwise.} \end{cases}$$

Note that this is closely related to ranking interleaving in information retrieval [31] where the utility functions capture the number of clicks each strategy obtained.

Table 4 reports the average win score for different signal types. Note that Base and FullExplore are omitted because they only showed items from one strategy. We start our discussion by looking at feedback quality in this setting only, ignoring all sessions in

Signal from rec. panel	Conditions			
	M-1	M-2	M-3	M-4
Only sessions where signal available				
examined rec.	0.80	1.00	0.86	0.55
shortlisted rec.	0.91*	0.96*	0.89*	0.70
hovered rec.	0.79*	0.82*	0.74*	0.67*
chosen rec.	0.96*	0.92*	0.87*	0.67
All sessions				
examined rec.	0.53	0.54	0.53	0.51
shortlisted rec.	0.70*	0.72*	0.65*	0.56
hovered rec.	0.72*	0.72*	0.67*	0.62*
chosen rec.	0.63*	0.65*	0.62*	0.55

Table 4: Fraction of sessions where people interacted more with Base items than with FullExplore items. An asterisk indicates significance using a two-sided Bernoulli test ($p < 0.05$, Bonferroni correction).

which no interactions were available. Looking at the upper half of Table 4, we can see that even though Base wins more in the case of examine interactions, there is not enough evidence to conclude that it is statistically different from a random preference between Base and FullExplore. The problem here is feedback quantity, and we will return to this shortly. Using hover interactions allows us to reliably tell apart the utility of Base and FullExplore for all levels of exploration. The signal quality seems lower than for shortlisting, and final choosing, with hovering being able to distinguish correctly between the utility of Base and FullExplore in around 67%-80% of sessions where a hovered recommendation existed or in 62%-72% of all sessions. There also appears to be a decay from Mix-3 to Mix-4 in signal quality; this could indicate that there are also non-linear effects on item-specific feedback signals.

We can analyze signal quality and quantity together by looking at data from all sessions in the bottom half. We can see now that examined and finally chosen items are less indicative of strategy preference (Base vs. FullExplore) since interactions of that type are only available in a fraction of sessions (cf. Table 2). The best signal types overall are shortlisting and hovering which, for conditions including up to three mixed-in items, are able to correctly order the utility of Base and FullExplore.

Although not reported in this paper, we ran a pilot experiment where we reverse the Base strategy, and inserted one mixed-in item from the reversed ranking. This ensured that the mixed-in item was from a strategy which had higher quality than FullExplore. We found the same effects as above – people still interacted more with items from Base in their sessions.

5.3 Discussion

We saw that feedback quantity, for example the number of shortlisting operations on recommended items, is affected significantly by different levels of exploration. Interestingly, looking at feedback quantity for the latter signal recovered the same grouping of presentation strategies as the user-centric evaluation in the previous section – Base, Mix-1, Mix-2, and Mix-3 were indistinguishable statistically, but different from Mix-4 and FullExplore. Limiting the amount of exploration is not only important for user satisfaction, but also for feedback quantity, as both user satisfaction and feedback quantity are affected in a similar manner. It is plausible that the reduced user satisfaction is at least partly responsible for the decreases in feedback quantity.

As a step towards learning from the collected feedback, we looked at which signals can best tell apart items from Base and FullExplore. We found that both shortlisting as well as hovering correctly rank Base over FullExplore. Clicks, as traditionally used in learning-to-rank [31], were not helpful in this scenario since there were simply too few of them available overall. Finding that shortlisting is among the most informative signals adds further support to the insight that learning algorithms can greatly benefit from improved interface design where users are offered the right incentives to interact [34].

Our results also indicate that an important but often overlooked issue when designing learning algorithms is the interplay of feedback quality and quantity. For example, we found shortlisting feedback to have higher quality than hovering, but hovering to be available in more sessions. Given these difference between feedback signals, learning algorithms could try to combine multiple signal types to further improve overall signal quality and quantity – for example, using hovering in addition to shortlisting feedback.

6 LIMITATIONS & FUTURE WORK

Our user study comes with certain limitations. First, participants were paid to participate in the study, and may had different incentives when interacting with the system, such as maximizing their hourly wage. This might influence certain measures, such as the time-to-decision. We did our best to minimize these effects, but it still would be interesting to connect our results to user behavior in the wild.

Another open question is to what extent interactivity plays a role in how people perceive recommendations. Our results mirror many findings from long-term user studies, however, there is more research needed to study the precise connections between interactive recommendations and traditional static recommendations. Understanding how these two approaches are connected could, for example, allow us to improve evaluation for static recommendation as well. As an intermediate step, future work could combine interactive recommendation with techniques for session-based recommendation [19, 21, 43].

Lastly, we only studied uninformed random exploration in this paper which does not control for concepts like novelty. There is an increasing amount of empirical evidence showing that novelty can be perceived negatively by people [5, 10] and that popular recommendations are often preferred [5]. This motivates the need for research on more constrained presentation strategies, e.g., strategies that expose people only to items they are likely to know [14, 32].

7 CONCLUSIONS

This paper explored the behavioral aspects of minimizing the cost of exploration while ensuring a high quality and quantity of feedback signals. Regarding the cost of exploration, our user study finds that small amounts of mix-in exploration are tolerated well, while larger amounts lead to a super-linear drop-off in user satisfaction as well as to a decrease the quantity of feedback. This suggests that algorithms should prefer moderate levels of exploration over longer period of time over high levels of exploration over shorter periods. We also examined different types of feedback with respect to their quality, and found both shortlisting and hovering events to provide the best overall signal. Our findings give practical advice to interface designers as well as offer starting points for designing learning algorithms using the right feedback signals.

ACKNOWLEDGMENTS

This work was supported in part through NSF Awards IIS-1513692, IIS-1615706, and a gift from Bloomberg. We thank Pantelis P. Analytis as well as the anonymous reviewers for their valuable feedback and questions.

REFERENCES

[1] Michal Aharon, Oren Anava, Noa Avigdor-Elgrabli, Dana Drachsler-Cohen, Shahar Golan, and Oren Somekh. 2015. ExcUseMe: Asking Users to Help in Item Cold-Start Recommendations. In *RecSys*. 83–90.

[2] Oren Anava, Shahar Golan, Nadav Golbandi, Zohar Karnin, Ronny Lempel, Oleg Rokhlenko, and Oren Somekh. 2015. Budget-constrained item cold-start handling in collaborative filtering recommenders via optimal design. In *WWW*. 45–54.

[3] Svetlin Bostandjiev, John O'Donovan, and Tobias Höllerer. 2012. TasteWeights: a visual interactive hybrid recommender system. In *RecSys*.

[4] Léon Bottou, Jonas Peters, Denis Xavier Charles, Max Chickering, Elon Portugaly, Dipankar Ray, Patrice Y Simard, and Ed Snelson. 2013. Counterfactual reasoning and learning systems: the example of computational advertising. *Journal of Machine Learning Research* 14, 1 (2013), 3207–3260.

[5] Òscar Celma and Perfecto Herrera. 2008. A New Approach to Evaluating Novel Recommendations. In *RecSys*.

[6] Mark Claypool, Phong Le, Makoto Wased, and David Brown. 2001. Implicit interest indicators. In *IUI*.

[7] Dan Cosley, Shyong K Lam, Istvan Albert, Joseph A Konstan, and John Riedl. 2003. Is seeing believing? How recommender system interfaces affect users' opinions. In *CHI*.

[8] Paolo Cremonesi, Franca Garzotto, Sara Negro, Alessandro Vittorio Papadopoulos, and Roberto Turrin. 2011. Looking for "good" recommendations: A comparative evaluation of recommender systems. In *INTERACT*.

[9] Paolo Cremonesi, Franca Garzotto, and Roberto Turrin. 2013. User-centric vs. system-centric evaluation of recommender systems. In *INTERACT*.

[10] Michael D Ekstrand, F Maxwell Harper, Martijn C Willemsen, and Joseph A Konstan. 2014. User perception of differences in recommender algorithms. In *RecSys*.

[11] Steve Fox, Kuldeep Karnawat, Mark Mydland, Susan Dumais, and Thomas White. 2005. Evaluating implicit measures to improve web search. *TOIS* 23, 2 (2005).

[12] Mouzhi Ge, Dietmar Jannach, Fatih Gedikli, and Martin Hepp. 2012. Effects of the Placement of Diverse Items in Recommendation Lists. In *ICEIS*.

[13] Qi Guo and Eugene Agichtein. 2012. Beyond dwell time: Estimating document relevance from cursor movements and other post-click searcher behavior. In *WWW*.

[14] Abhay S Harpale and Yiming Yang. 2008. Personalized active learning for collaborative filtering. In *SIGIR*.

[15] F Maxwell Harper and Joseph A Konstan. 2016. The MovieLens datasets: History and context. *TiiS* 5, 4 (2016).

[16] Gerald Häubl and Valerie Trifts. 2000. Consumer decision making in online shopping environments: The effects of interactive decision aids. *Marketing Science* 19, 1 (2000).

[17] Chen He, Denis Parra, and Katrien Verbert. 2016. Interactive recommender systems: A survey of the state of the art and future research challenges and opportunities. *Expert Systems with Applications* 56 (2016).

[18] Jonathan L Herlocker, Joseph A Konstan, Loren G Terveen, and John T Riedl. 2004. Evaluating collaborative filtering recommender systems. *TOIS* 22, 1 (2004).

[19] Balázs Hidasi, Massimo Quadrana, Alexandros Karatzoglou, and Domonkos Tikk. 2016. Parallel recurrent neural network architectures for feature-rich session-based recommendations. In *RecSys*.

[20] Jeff Huang, Ryen W White, and Susan Dumais. 2011. No clicks, no problem: Using cursor movements to understand and improve search. In *CHI*.

[21] Dietmar Jannach, Lukas Lerche, and Michael Jugovac. 2015. Adaptation and evaluation of recommendations for short-term shopping goals. In *RecSys*.

[22] Dietmar Jannach, Lukas Lerche, and Michael Jugovac. 2015. Item Familiarity Effects in User-Centric Evaluations of Recommender Systems. (2015).

[23] Thorsten Joachims, Laura Granka, Bing Pan, Helene Hembrooke, Filip Radlinski, and Geri Gay. 2007. Evaluating the accuracy of implicit feedback from clicks and query reformulations in web search. *TOIS* 25, 2 (2007).

[24] Nicolas Jones and Pearl Pu. 2007. User technology adoption issues in recommender systems. In *NAEC*.

[25] Aniket Kittur, Ed H Chi, and Bongwon Suh. 2008. Crowdsourcing user studies with Mechanical Turk. In *CHI*.

[26] Bart P Knijnenburg, Martijn C Willemsen, Zeno Gantner, Hakan Soncu, and Chris Newell. 2012. Explaining the user experience of recommender systems. *User Modeling and User-Adapted Interaction* 22, 4-5 (2012).

[27] Volodymyr Kuleshov and Precup Doina. 2010. Algorithms for the multi-armed bandit problem. *Journal of Machine Learning* 47, 1 (2010).

[28] Lihong Li, Wei Chu, John Langford, and Xuanhui Wang. 2011. Unbiased offline evaluation of contextual-bandit-based news article recommendation algorithms. In *Proceedings of the fourth ACM international conference on Web search and data mining*. ACM, 297–306.

[29] Winter Mason and Siddharth Suri. 2012. Conducting behavioral research on Amazon's Mechanical Turk. *Behavior Research Methods* 44, 1 (2012).

[30] Pearl Pu, Li Chen, and Rong Hu. 2011. A user-centric evaluation framework for recommender systems. In *RecSys*.

[31] Filip Radlinski, Madhu Kurup, and Thorsten Joachims. 2008. How does clickthrough data reflect retrieval quality?. In *CIKM*.

[32] Al Mamunur Rashid, Istvan Albert, Dan Cosley, Shyong K Lam, Sean M McNee, Joseph A Konstan, and John Riedl. 2002. Getting to know you: learning new user preferences in recommender systems. In *IUI*.

[33] Paul Resnick and Hal R Varian. 1997. Recommender systems. *Commun. ACM* 40, 3 (1997).

[34] Tobias Schnabel, Paul N. Bennett, Susan T. Dumais, and Thorsten Joachims. 2016. Using Shortlists to Support Decision Making and Improve Recommender System Performance. In *WWW*.

[35] Shai Shalev-Shwartz. 2012. Online Learning and Online Convex Optimization. *Found. Trends Mach. Learn.* 4, 2 (Feb. 2012).

[36] Bracha Shapira, Francesco Ricci, Paul B Kantor, and Lior Rokach. 2015. *Recommender Systems Handbook*. (2nd ed.). Springer.

[37] Rashmi Sinha and Kirsten Swearingen. 2002. The role of transparency in recommender systems. In *CHI Extended Abstracts*.

[38] Harald Steck, Roelof van Zwol, and Chris Johnson. 2015. Interactive Recommender Systems: Tutorial. In *RecSys*.

[39] Adith Swaminathan and Thorsten Joachims. 2015. Counterfactual risk minimization: Learning from logged bandit feedback. In *Proceedings of the 32nd International Conference on Machine Learning*. 814–823.

[40] K. Swearingen and R. Sinha. 2001. Beyond Algorithms: An HCI Perspective on Recommender Systems. In *SIGIR Workshops*.

[41] Andrew H Turpin and William Hersh. 2001. Why batch and user evaluations do not give the same results. In *SIGIR*.

[42] Jesse Vig, Shilad Sen, and John Riedl. 2012. The Tag Genome: Encoding community knowledge to support novel interaction. *TiiS* 2, 3 (2012).

[43] Chao-Yuan Wu, Christopher V. Alvino, Alexander J. Smola, and Justin Basilico. 2016. Using Navigation to Improve Recommendations in Real-Time. In *RecSys*.

[44] Cai-Nicolas Ziegler, Sean M McNee, Joseph A Konstan, and Georg Lausen. 2005. Improving recommendation lists through topic diversification. In *WWW*. 22–32.

CrossFire: Cross Media Joint Friend and Item Recommendations

Kai Shu
Arizona State University
kai.shu@asu.edu

Suhang Wang
Arizona State University
suhang.wang@asu.edu

Jiliang Tang
Michigan State University
tangjili@cse.msu.edu

Yilin Wang
Arizona State University
ywang370@asu.edu

Huan Liu
Arizona State University
huan.liu@asu.edu

ABSTRACT

Friend and item recommendation on a social media site is an important task, which not only brings conveniences to users but also benefits platform providers. However, recommendation for newly launched social media sites is challenging because they often lack user historical data and encounter data sparsity and cold-start problem. Thus, it is important to exploit auxiliary information to help improve recommendation performances on these sites. Existing approaches try to utilize the knowledge transferred from other mature sites, which often require overlapped users or similar items to ensure an effective knowledge transfer. However, these assumptions may not hold in practice because 1) Overlapped user set is often unavailable and costly to identify due to the heterogeneous user profile, content and network data, and 2) Different schemes to show item attributes across sites cause the attribute values inconsistent, incomplete, and noisy. Thus, how to transfer knowledge when no direct bridge is given between two social media sites remains a challenge. In addition, another auxiliary information we can exploit is the mutual benefit between social relationships and rating preferences within the platform. User-user relationships are widely used as side information to improve item recommendation, whereas how to exploit user-item interactions for friend recommendation is rather limited. To tackle these challenges, we propose a *Cross* media joint *F*riend and *I*tem *Re*commendation framework (*CrossFire*), which can capture both 1) cross-platform knowledge transfer, and 2) within-platform correlations among user-user relations and user-item interactions. Empirical results on real-world datasets demonstrate the effectiveness of the proposed framework.

KEYWORDS

Cross media recommendation; joint learning; data mining

ACM Reference format:
Kai Shu, Suhang Wang, Jiliang Tang, Yilin Wang, and Huan Liu. 2018. CrossFire: Cross Media Joint Friend and Item Recommendations. In *Proceedings of The Eleventh ACM International Conference on Web Search and Data Mining, February 5–9, 2018, Marina Del Rey, CA, USA, (WSDM'18)*, 9 pages.
DOI: http://dx.doi.org/10.1145/3159652.3159692

WSDM'18, February 5–9, 2018, Marina Del Rey, CA, USA
© 2018 ACM. ISBN 978-1-4503-5581-0/18/02...$15.00
DOI: http://dx.doi.org/10.1145/3159652.3159692

1 INTRODUCTION

Social media websites provide users with multiple services such as online reviews, networking, social publishing, etc. To improve personalized services, social media sites often attempt to suggest potential information that will match the interests of users or potential friends that users will form relationships with. Recommender systems, which aim to solve the aforementioned problems, are attracting more and more attention in recent years [20, 21, 27]. For those mature social media sites, they have abundant historical information to help build recommender system, whereas those newly launched sites often lack these information and encounter the data sparsity and cold-start challenges [22]. To build effective and practical friend and item recommendation systems for the newly launched sites, it's natural and necessary to explore *auxiliary information* from different aspects.

One popular way of exploring auxiliary information is to transfer the knowledge from the mature platform to newly created platform by assuming that either (i) there are anchor links between users across two platforms and thus knowledge can be transferred through these anchor links [3, 13]; or (ii) items attributes are consistent and thus we can directly utilize similarity between items to transfer the knowledge [11]. However, in practice, these assumptions may not hold. A typical scenario is shown in Figure 1(a), where P_1 is a mature platform and P_2 is a newly launched one. Users in P_1 can form a social network and give ratings to items in P_1. Similarly, users in P_2 can also form links and rate items in P_2. However, there are no anchor links between users in P_1 and users in P_2 and thus no information can be directly transferred between users in P_1 and P_2. In addition, directly measuring the similarity between items in P_1 and P_2 may not be applicable as different sites encode items in different schemes and result in inconsistent attribute fields and many missing values. The majority of existing work that exploits anchor links or item similarities cannot be directly applied. Therefore, it is important to study the novel and challenging problem of cross-platform recommendation when no direct bridge between users or items is given.

In addition to transferring knowledge across platforms, we can also exploit auxiliary information within a single platform. As shown in Figure 1(a), on a social media site, users can usually form relationships with others as well as express their preferences to items. For example, in GoodReads[1], people can follow and be followed by other users and also give ratings to the books they read. According to social correlation theories, users' preferences towards items and friends have inseparable correlations. Homophily [18]

[1] https://www.goodreads.com/

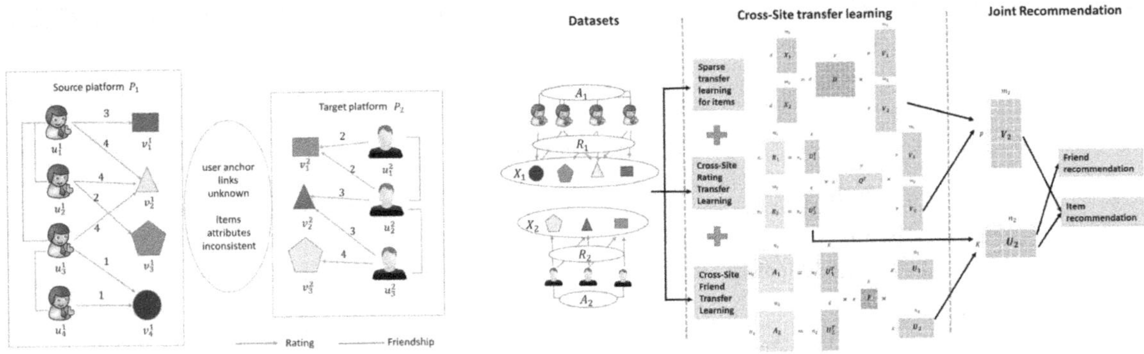

(a) An example of cross social media joint recommendations

(b) The flowchart of the proposed framework CrossFire

Figure 1: An illustration of the problem scenario for cross-media joint friend and item recommendation, and the basic idea of proposed framework integrating within-platform correlations and cross-platform information for joint recommendations.

theory shows that users who have similar attributes are more likely to become friends [18]. Likewise, social influence theory [17] suggests that users are more likely to be influenced by their friends and express similar ratings to those items visited by their friends. However, even though much efforts have been devoted to exploiting user-user relations to help item recommendations, how to exploit user-item interactions for friend recommendation remains limited [23]. Previous works also show that a positive correlation between users' interests and social relationships [26], which may indicate an added value to utilize user interests to help friend recommendations in social media. Thus, we can jointly recommend items and friends by exploiting the correlations among them. As shown in Figure 1(a), suppose u_1^2 and u_2^2 are friends, user u_1^2 is likely to be influenced by his/her friend u_2^2 and gives a similar rating to item v_1^2. Also, user u_2^2 and u_3^2 both give a rating score 3 to item v_2^2, so they are more likely to form a relationship.

Cross-platform knowledge transfer and within-platform joint learning have complementary information, which both provide new perspectives to help improve the recommendation performances for the newly launched platform. In this paper, we investigate: (1) how to transfer the information from source platform to target platform when there is no straightforward way to bridge two platforms, and (2) how to mathematically formulate joint friend and item recommendation so as to improve recommendation performance. To tackle these challenges, we propose a novel *Cross*-media joint *F*riend and *I*tem *Re*commendation framework (*CrossFire*). The framework can i) build the implicit bridge to transfer knowledge by utilizing the observation that the user behaviors share similar patterns across different networks, and the assumption that item features on two platforms share the same dictionary; ii) learn user and item latent features by exploiting the correlation between user-user relations and user-item interactions to perform joint friend and item recommendations. The main contributions are as below:

- We study a novel problem of cross-media joint friend and item recommendations when no anchor links are available;
- We propose a new framework CrossFire which integrates within-platform correlations and cross-media information into a coherent model for joint friend and item recommendations, and an optimization algorithm to solve it;
- We conduct experiments on real-world social media sites to demonstrate the effectiveness of the proposed framework CrossFire for friend and item recommendations.

2 PROBLEM FORMULATION

We first introduce the notations of this paper, and then give the formal problem definition. Let $\mathcal{U}_1 = \{u_1^1, u_2^1, \ldots, u_{n_1}^1\}$ and $\mathcal{V}_1 = \{v_1^1, v_2^1, \ldots, v_{m_1}^1\}$ be the sets of users and items in the source social media site, where n_1 and m_1 are the numbers of users and items, respectively. $\mathcal{U}_2 = \{u_1^2, u_2^2, \ldots, u_{n_2}^2\}$ and $\mathcal{V}_2 = \{v_1^2, v_2^2, \ldots, v_{m_2}^2\}$ denote the sets of users and items in the target social media site where n_2 and m_2 denote the number of users and items, respectively. We also use $\mathbf{X}_1 \in \mathbb{R}^{d \times m_1}$ and $\mathbf{X}_2 \in \mathbb{R}^{d \times m_2}$ to denote the item features in source and target domains, separately; where d is the dimension of item feature vectors. On each social media site, users can rate the items and we use $\mathbf{R}_1 \in \mathbb{R}^{n_1 \times m_1}$ and $\mathbf{R}_2 \in \mathbb{R}^{n_2 \times m_2}$ to denote the user-item rating matrices for the source domain and target domain, respectively. Users can become friend with other users and we use $\mathbf{A}_1 \in \{1,0\}^{n_1 \times n_1}$ and $\mathbf{A}_2 \in \{1,0\}^{n_2 \times n_2}$ to denote the user-user adjacency matrices on the source and target social media site, respectively. A very common situation is that the source domain is a mature source media site while the target site is newly launched. Thus, the rating matrix $\mathbf{R}_1$ and user-user adjacency matrix $\mathbf{A}_1$ in the source domain are relatively dense while $\mathbf{R}_2$ and $\mathbf{A}_2$ in the target domain are very sparse. Much work has demonstrated that we can learn better user and item latent features with dense rating and user-user matrices for friend and item recommendations while it is very difficult to make reasonable recommendations with very sparse rating matrices. Thus, we want to use $\mathbf{R}_1$ and $\mathbf{A}_1$ in the source domain to help friend and item recommendations in the target domain. We assume that there is no explicit correspondence information among users and items. With the notations given above, the problem is formally given as,

Given the rating matrix $\mathbf{R}_1$, user-user link matrix $\mathbf{A}_1$ and item-feature matrix $\mathbf{X}_1$ in the source social media site, rating matrix $\mathbf{R}_2$, user-user link matrix $\mathbf{A}_2$ and item-feature matrix $\mathbf{X}_2$ in the target social media site, we aim to make friend and item recommendations on the target social media site.

3 CROSS MEDIA JOINT RECOMMENDATIONS

In this section, we present the details of proposed framework for cross-media joint friend and item recommendations. As shown in Figure 1(b), our framework includes three major parts. We first introduce how to exploit sparse transfer learning method to model cross-media item information. Then we propose how to perform cross site rating transfer learning. Finally, we present cross site friend transfer learning followed by the proposed framework.

3.1 Sparse Transfer Learning for Items

Different online social network sites have different structures and schemes to present item detail attributes, which causes the inconsistent attribute fields and many missing values. Thus, it becomes ineffective to bridge items across sites directly using similarity metrics, such as distance-based and frequency-based [24] on these attributes. To make the bridge between items on two social network sites, we propose to utilize sparse learning based transfer learning approach. Specifically, the source feature matrix $\mathbf{X}_1$ can be reconstructed as $\mathbf{X}_1 \approx \mathbf{D}\mathbf{V}_1$ and the target matrix $\mathbf{X}_2$ is reconstructed as $\mathbf{X}_2 \approx \mathbf{D}\mathbf{V}_2$, where $\mathbf{D} \in \mathbb{R}^{d \times p}$ is the dictionary shared by source and target platforms, $\mathbf{V}_1 \in \mathbb{R}^{p \times m_1}$ and $\mathbf{V}_2 \in \mathbb{R}^{p \times m_2}$ are the sparse representations for $\mathbf{X}_1$ and $\mathbf{X}_2$, respectively. The essential idea is that $\mathbf{X}_1$ and $\mathbf{X}_2$ share a dictionary $\mathbf{D}$, which behaviors as a bridge to transfer knowledge from $\mathbf{X}_1$ to $\mathbf{X}_2$. With this assumption, the sparse learning objective is given as:

$$\min_{\mathbf{D},\mathbf{V}_1,\mathbf{V}_2} \|\mathbf{X}_1 - \mathbf{D}\mathbf{V}_1\|_F^2 + \|\mathbf{X}_2 - \mathbf{D}\mathbf{V}_2\|_F^2 + \gamma(\|\mathbf{V}_1\|_1 + \|\mathbf{V}_2\|_1) \quad s.t.\ \|\mathbf{d}_j\|_2^2 \leq 1, j = 1, \ldots, p \tag{1}$$

where $\mathbf{d}_j$ is the j_{th} column of $\mathbf{D}$.

To make the dictionary matrix $\mathbf{D}$ satisfy the intrinsic geometric structure of the item features, we incorporate a Graph Regularized Sparse Coding (GraphSC) method [38]. The basic assumption of GraphSC is that if two data points $\mathbf{x}_i$ and $\mathbf{x}_j$ are close in the intrinsic geometry of data distributions, their codings $\mathbf{v}_i$ and $\mathbf{v}_j$ are also close. Thus, given $\mathbf{X} = [\mathbf{X}_1, \mathbf{X}_2] \in \mathbb{R}^{d \times (m_1+m_2)}$, GraphSC constructs a K-nearest neighbor graph G with $(m_1 + m_2)$ nodes representing all data points. Let $\mathbf{H}$ be the weight matrix of G; if $\mathbf{x}_i$ is among the K-nearest neighbors with $\mathbf{x}_j$, then $\mathbf{H}_{ij} = \exp^{\frac{-\|\mathbf{x}_i - \mathbf{x}_j\|_2^2}{\sigma}}$, where σ is the scalar to control the bandwidth; otherwise, $\mathbf{H}_{ij} = 0$. Then the graph regularization term tries to minimize

$$\frac{1}{2} \sum_{i,j=1}^{m_1+m_2} \|\mathbf{v}_i - \mathbf{v}_j\|^2 \mathbf{H}_{ij} = Tr(\mathbf{V}\mathbf{L}\mathbf{V}^T) \tag{2}$$

where $\mathbf{V} = [\mathbf{V}_1, \mathbf{V}_2]$. $\mathbf{L} = \mathbf{S} - \mathbf{H}$ is the Laplacian matrix and $\mathbf{S}$ is a diagonal matrix with the diagonal element $\mathbf{S}_{ii} = \sum_{j=1}^{m_1+m_2} \mathbf{H}_{ij}$. Moreover, to enforce unified codings for both domains, we also regularize the model with an additional term called maximum mean discrepancy regularization [12] as follows,

$$MMD = \|\frac{1}{m_1}\mathbf{V}_1\mathbf{1} - \frac{1}{m_2}\mathbf{V}_2\mathbf{1}\|_2^2 = Tr(\mathbf{V}\mathbf{M}\mathbf{V}^T) \tag{3}$$

which is the ℓ_2-norm of the difference between mean samples of the source and target domains in the sparse coding space. $\mathbf{M}$ is the MMD matrix and is computed as $\mathbf{M}_{ij} = 1/m_1^2$ if $v_i, v_j \in \mathcal{V}_1$, $\mathbf{M}_{ij} = 1/m_2^2$ if $v_i, v_j \in \mathcal{V}_2$ and $\frac{-1}{m_1 m_2}$ otherwise.

The graph regularization term in Eq.(2) and the MMD regularization term in Eq.(3) together guide the learning process of $\mathbf{D}$ and $\mathbf{V}$ so that the probability distribution of both domains are drawn close under the new representation $\mathbf{V}$. Thus, we can formulate the sparse transfer learning for items as,

$$\min_{\mathbf{V}_1,\mathbf{V}_2,\mathbf{D}} \|\mathbf{X}_1 - \mathbf{D}\mathbf{V}_1\|_F^2 + \|\mathbf{X}_2 - \mathbf{D}\mathbf{V}_2\|_F^2 + \gamma(\|\mathbf{V}_1\|_1 + \|\mathbf{V}_2\|_1) + Tr(\mathbf{V}(\mu\mathbf{L} + \nu\mathbf{M})\mathbf{V}^T), \quad s.t. \|\mathbf{d}^i\|_2^2 \leq 1, i = 1, \ldots, p \tag{4}$$

where μ and ν are used as a trade-off for the contributions of graph regularization term and MMD, γ is to control the level of sparsity.

3.2 Cross Site Rating Transfer Learning

Following existing work that assumes users' rating behaviors share common patterns across sites [9], we propose a transfer learning model to better learn user and item latent representations. With the sparse representations of items for both the source and target domains, we introduce another projection matrix $\mathbf{Q}^{p \times K}$, which projects the sparse representations to the latent item feature representations, i.e., $\mathbf{Q}^T\mathbf{V}_1$ and $\mathbf{Q}^T\mathbf{V}_2$. Thus, we can formulate the objective function of cross-media rating transfer learning as below,

$$\min_{\mathbf{U}_1,\mathbf{V}_1\mathbf{U}_2,\mathbf{V}_2,\mathbf{Q}} \|\mathbf{W}_1 \odot (\mathbf{R}_1 - {\mathbf{U}_1}^T\mathbf{Q}^T\mathbf{V}_1)\|_F^2 + \|\mathbf{W}_2 \odot (\mathbf{R}_2 - {\mathbf{U}_2}^T\mathbf{Q}^T\mathbf{V}_2)\|_F^2 \quad s.t.\ \mathbf{Q}^T\mathbf{Q} = \mathbf{I} \tag{5}$$

where $\odot$ denotes the Hadamard product and $\mathbf{W}_1$ ($\mathbf{W}_2$) controls the contribution of $\mathbf{R}_1$ ($\mathbf{R}_2$). $\mathbf{U}_1 \in \mathbb{R}^{K \times n_1}$ ($\mathbf{U}_2 \in \mathbb{R}^{K \times n_2}$) is the user latent feature representation matrix in source (target) platform. The orthogonal constraint on $\mathbf{Q}$ is to ensure that each column of $\mathbf{Q}$ are independent.

3.3 Cross Site Friend Transfer Learning

Existing research on cross social network analysis has demonstrated that different social network platforms may have similar network structures and characteristics, e.g., the number of user relations falls into power-law distributions [2]. Following traditional setting, we decompose the user-user link matrices $\mathbf{A}_1$ and $\mathbf{A}_2$ to map them to a shared latent space and obtain user latent features $\mathbf{U}_1$ and $\mathbf{U}_2$. In order to model the latent features shared across different social media sites, we also exploit a shared interaction matrix $\mathbf{P}$. Then the modeling formulation is,

$$\min_{\mathbf{U}_1,\mathbf{U}_2,\mathbf{P}} \|\mathbf{Y}_1 \odot (\mathbf{A}_1 - {\mathbf{U}_1}^T\mathbf{P}\mathbf{U}_1)\|_F^2 + \|\mathbf{Y}_2 \odot (\mathbf{A}_2 - {\mathbf{U}_2}^T\mathbf{P}\mathbf{U}_2\|_F^2 \tag{6}$$

where $\odot$ denotes the Hadamard product and $\mathbf{Y}_1$ ($\mathbf{Y}_2$) controls the contribution of $\mathbf{A}_1$ ($\mathbf{A}_2$). The essential idea of using shared $\mathbf{P}$ is that: $\mathbf{P}$ is the interaction matrix which captures the interaction property of users, i.e., the connection status of u_s^i and u_t^i is represented via the interaction matrix $\mathbf{P}$ as $\mathbf{U}_i(s,:)^T\mathbf{P}\mathbf{U}_j(:,t)$. Since users connection behaviors are consistent in different sites, e.g., the structure of social networks are similar, $\mathbf{P}$ should also be similar across sites.

3.4 Proposed Framework

In this section, we combine the aforementioned three components together, and present the framework of cross-media joint friend and item recommendations named CrossFire. The proposed framework

CrossFire aims to solve the following optimization problem,

$$\min_{\theta} \underbrace{\sum_{i=1}^{2} ||\mathbf{X}_i - \mathbf{D}\mathbf{V}_i||_F^2 + \gamma||\mathbf{V}_i||_1 + Tr(\mathbf{V}(\mu\mathbf{L} + \nu\mathbf{M})\mathbf{V}^T)}_{\text{Item Sparse Transfer Learning}}$$
$$+\alpha \underbrace{\sum_{i=1}^{2} ||\mathbf{W}_i \odot (\mathbf{R}_i - \mathbf{U}_i^T\mathbf{Q}^T\mathbf{V}_i)||_F^2}_{\text{Cross-Media Item Recommendation}} + \lambda(||\mathbf{P}||_F^2 + ||\mathbf{Q}||_F^2) \quad (7)$$
$$+\beta \underbrace{\sum_{i=1}^{2} ||\mathbf{Y}_i \odot (\mathbf{A}_i - \mathbf{U}_i^T\mathbf{P}\mathbf{U}_i)||_F^2}_{\text{Cross-Media Friend Recommendation}} + \lambda\sum_{i=1}^{2}||\mathbf{U}_i||_F^2$$
$$s.t.\ ||\mathbf{d}_j||_2^2 \leq 1, j = 1, \ldots, p,\ \mathbf{Q}^T\mathbf{Q} = \mathbf{I}$$

where the first part is to perform item sparse transfer learning; the second part captures the cross-media rating transfer learning; the third term models the user relations transfer learning. By incorporating these components together, we are able to make joint recommendations for items and friends simultaneously with the resultant latent features.

4 AN OPTIMIZATION FRAMEWORK

In this section, we present the details of the optimization process for the proposed framework CrossFire. If we update the variables jointly, the objective function in Eq. 7 is not convex. Thus, we use alternating least square method to iteratively optimize each variable separately. Next, we will introduce the updating rules. For simplicity, we use $\mathcal{L}$ to denote the objective function in Eq. 7.

4.1 Update Rules

In this section, we will introduce the updating rules for each variable in details.

4.1.1 Update **D**. The objective function related to **D** can be rewritten as,

$$\min_{\mathbf{D}} ||\mathbf{X} - \mathbf{D}\mathbf{V}||_F^2 \quad s.t.\ ||\mathbf{d}_j||_2^2 \leq 1, j = 1, \ldots, p \quad (8)$$

where $\mathbf{X} = [\mathbf{X}_1, \mathbf{X}_2]$ and $\mathbf{V} = [\mathbf{V}_1, \mathbf{V}_2]$. Eq.(8) is a standard dictionary learning problem and can be solved using the algorithm proposed in [8].

4.1.2 Update **V**. Since updating **V** involves the l_1 norm, we propose to use Alternating Direction Method of Multiplier (ADMM) [1, 36] to update **V**. By introducing an auxiliary variable $\mathbf{Z} = \mathbf{V}$ and $\tilde{\mathbf{L}} = \mu\mathbf{L} + \nu\mathbf{M}$, we can rewrite the objective function as follows,

$$\min_{\mathbf{V}} \underbrace{||\mathbf{X} - \mathbf{D}\mathbf{V}||_F^2 + Tr(\mathbf{V}\tilde{\mathbf{L}}\mathbf{V}^T) + \alpha\sum_{i=1}^{2} ||\mathbf{W}_i \odot (\mathbf{R}_i - \mathbf{U}_i^T\mathbf{Q}^T\mathbf{V}_i)||_F^2}_{g(\mathbf{V})} + \underbrace{\gamma||\mathbf{Z}||_1}_{h(\mathbf{Z})}$$
$$s.t. \mathbf{V} - \mathbf{Z} = \mathbf{0} \quad (9)$$

This is a standard l_1 regularized ADMM problem [1]. The updating function from step t to step $t+1$ is,

$$\mathbf{V}^{t+1} := \text{argmin}(g(\mathbf{V}) + \rho/2||\mathbf{V} - \mathbf{Z}^t + \mathbf{E}^t||_F^2) \quad (10)$$
$$\mathbf{Z}^{t+1} := \mathcal{T}_{\gamma/\rho}(\mathbf{V}^{t+1} + \mathbf{E}^t) \quad (11)$$
$$\mathbf{E}^{t+1} := \mathbf{E}^t + \mathbf{V}^{t+1} - \mathbf{Z}^{t+1} \quad (12)$$

where ρ is the trade-off parameter and $\mathcal{T}_{\gamma/\rho}(\mathbf{V})$ is a the proximal function for l_1 norm (i.e., soft-thresholding operator) [19] defined as follows,

$$\left[\mathcal{T}_{\gamma/\rho}(\mathbf{V})\right]_{ij} = \text{sign}(\mathbf{V}_{ij})(|\mathbf{V}_{ij}| - \gamma/\rho)_+ \quad (13)$$

To solve Eq. 10, we use gradient descent method to update **V** as in Algorithm 1. The partial derivative of updating **V** is,

$$\frac{\partial\mathcal{L}}{\partial\mathbf{V}} = 2\mathbf{D}^T(\mathbf{D}\mathbf{V} - \mathbf{X}) + \mathbf{V}\tilde{\mathbf{L}} + \rho(\mathbf{V} - \mathbf{Z} + \mathbf{E})$$
$$+2\alpha\left[\mathbf{Q}\mathbf{U}_1[\mathbf{W}_1 \odot (\mathbf{U}_1^T\mathbf{Q}^T\mathbf{V}_1 - \mathbf{R}_1)], \mathbf{Q}\mathbf{U}_2[\mathbf{W}_2 \odot (\mathbf{U}_2^T\mathbf{Q}^T\mathbf{V}_2 - \mathbf{R}_2)]\right]$$

Algorithm 1 Update V

Require: Initial feasible V, Z, E, $\rho = 0.5$, γ, maxsteps
Ensure: Updated V

1: **for** t = 1 to maxsteps **do**
2: Update $\mathbf{V}^{t+1}$ using $\mathbf{V}^{t+1} = \mathbf{V}^t - \epsilon\frac{\partial\mathcal{L}}{\partial\mathbf{V}}$ via Eq. 14
3: Update $\mathbf{Z}^{t+1}$ via Eq. 11
4: Update $\mathbf{E}^{t+1}$ via Eq. 12
5: **end for**
6: Return V

4.1.3 Update $\mathbf{U}_i$ *and* **P**. The partial derivative of the objective function w.r.t $\mathbf{U}_i$ is given as

$$\frac{1}{2}\frac{\partial\mathcal{L}}{\partial\mathbf{U}_i} = \alpha\mathbf{Q}^T\mathbf{V}_i[\mathbf{W}_i \odot (\mathbf{U}_i^T\mathbf{Q}\mathbf{V}_i - \mathbf{R}_i)]^T + \lambda\mathbf{U}_i$$
$$+ \beta\mathbf{P}^T\mathbf{U}_i[\mathbf{Y}_i \odot (\mathbf{U}_i^T\mathbf{P}\mathbf{U}_i - \mathbf{A}_i)] + \beta\mathbf{P}\mathbf{U}_i[\mathbf{Y}_i \odot (\mathbf{U}_i^T\mathbf{P}\mathbf{U}_i - \mathbf{A}_i)]^T \quad (14)$$

and the partial derivative of the objective function w.r.t **P** is

$$\frac{1}{2}\frac{\partial\mathcal{L}}{\partial\mathbf{P}} = \beta\sum_{i=1}^{2}[\mathbf{U}_i(\mathbf{Y}_i \odot \mathbf{U}_i^T\mathbf{P}\mathbf{U}_i)\mathbf{U}_i^T - \mathbf{U}_i(\mathbf{Y}_i \odot \mathbf{A}_i)\mathbf{U}_i^T] + \lambda\mathbf{P} \quad (15)$$

4.1.4 Update **Q**. The objective with respect to **Q** is as follows,

$$\min_{\mathbf{Q}} \alpha\sum_{i=1}^{2} ||\mathbf{W}_i \odot (\mathbf{R}_i - \mathbf{U}_i^T\mathbf{Q}^T\mathbf{V}_i)||_F^2 + \lambda||\mathbf{Q}||_F^2,\ s.t.\ \mathbf{Q}^T\mathbf{Q} = \mathbf{I} \quad (16)$$

We use a gradient descent optimization procedure with curvilinear search [35] to solve it. The gradient can be calculated as,

$$\mathbf{G} = \frac{\partial\mathcal{L}}{\partial\mathbf{Q}} = 2\alpha\sum_{i=1}^{2}\mathbf{V}_i[\mathbf{W}_i \odot (\mathbf{U}_i^T\mathbf{Q}^T\mathbf{V}_i - \mathbf{R}_i)]^T\mathbf{U}_i^T + 2\lambda\mathbf{Q} \quad (17)$$

We then defined $\mathbf{F} \in \mathbb{R}^{K\times K}$ as $\mathbf{F} = \mathbf{G}\mathbf{Q}^T - \mathbf{Q}\mathbf{G}^T$. Note that $\mathbf{F}^T = -\mathbf{F}$ and thus **F** is skew-symmetric. The next new point can be searched as a curvilinear function of a step size variable τ such that,

$$\mathbf{S}(\tau) = (\mathbf{I} + \frac{\tau}{2}\mathbf{F})^{-1}(\mathbf{I} - \frac{\tau}{2}\mathbf{F})\mathbf{Q} \quad (18)$$

Algorithm 2 Update Q

```
Require: Initial feasible Q, 0 < μ < 1, 0 < ρ1 < ρ2 < 1
Ensure: Updated Q
Compute F, G, L'_τ(S(0)) respectively; set τ = 1
for s = 1 to maxsteps do
    Compute S(τ) via Eq.(18), L'_τ(S(τ)) via Eq.(20)
    if Armijio-Wolfe conditions are satisfied then break-out
    end if
    τ = μτ
end for
Update Q as Q = S
Return Q
```

Algorithm 3 The optimization process of CrossFire framework

```
Require: {X_i, R_i, A_i}_{i=1,2}, α, β, γ, λ, μ, ν
Ensure: {U_i, V_i}_{i=1,2}, P, Q, D
1: Initialize {U_i, V_i}_{i=1,2}, P, Q, D
2: Precompute L, M and L̃ = μL + νM
3: repeat
4:     Update D via algorithm proposed in [8]
5:     Update V1, V2 with Algorithm 1
6:     Update U1, U2 as U_i ← U_i − ε ∂L/∂U_i using Eq. 14
7:     Update P as P ← P − ε ∂L/∂P using Eq. 15
8:     Update Q via Algorithm 2
9: until Convergence
```

It can be proved that $S(\tau)$ is orthogonal based on Cayley transformation [6]. Thus we can stay in the feasible region along the curve defined by τ. We determine a proper step size τ satisfying the following Armijo-Wolfe conditions,

$$\mathcal{L}(S(\tau)) \leq \mathcal{L}(S(0)) + \rho_1 \tau \mathcal{L}'_\tau(S(0)), \; \mathcal{L}'_\tau(S(\tau)) \geq \rho_2 \mathcal{L}'_\tau(S(0)) \quad (19)$$

Here $\mathcal{L}'_\tau(S(\tau))$ is the derivative of $\mathcal{L}$ w.r.t τ,

$$\mathcal{L}'_\tau(S(\tau)) = -Tr(R(\tau)^T (I + \frac{\tau}{2}F)^{-1} F \frac{Q + S(\tau)}{2}) \quad (20)$$

where $R(\tau) = \nabla_{S_\tau} \mathcal{L}(S(\tau))$. Obviously, $S(0) = Q$ and thus $R(0) = \nabla_Q \mathcal{L}(Q) = G$. Therefore $\mathcal{L}'_\tau(S(0)) = -\frac{1}{2}\|F\|_F^2$. Details of updating Q is shown in Algorithm 2.

4.2 Algorithm of CrossFire

To this end, we give the detailed algorithm to learn the parameters for CrossFire in Algorithm 3. In line 1, we initialize the parameters $\{U_i, V_i\}_{i=1,2}$, P, Q and D. In line 2, we precompute graph laplacian matrix L and MMD matrix M. Next, we update these parameters sequentially from Line 4 to Line 8 until convergence. Note that ϵ is the learning rate for each iteration step. Finally, based on the resultant latent matrix representations of users and items, we can use them to perform friend and item recommendation tasks.

The convergence of the algorithm is guaranteed. The reason is that we use gradient descent to update the parameters iteratively, and the objective value will monotonically reduce. Note that the objective function in Eq. 7 is non-negative, so the proposed algorithm will converge and it will achieve a local optimal value.

Table 1: The statistics of datasets

Dataset	Book		Movie	
	Source	Target	Source	Target
Platform	GoodReads	BookLikes	Epinions	Ciao
# users	7,490	3,853	5,588	2,126
# items	6,946	5,884	8,072	2,426
# ratings	199,915	134,525	109,804	24,012
# user links	120,790	96,327	215,916	43,362

4.3 Time Complexity

For the time complexity of proposed algorithm, we mainly focus on the parameter learning process. For parameter D, we adopt the method that uses a Lagrange dual which has been shown to be much efficient [8]. The computation cost is approximately $O(d(m_1+m_2)p)$. Considering that we use ADMM to update V in Algorithm 1, the major cost is to update V and the cost is about $O(t(K(m_1+m_2)p + K(p+1)(m_1n_1+m_2n_2)+dp^2(m_1+m_2)+p(m_1+m_2)^2))$, where t is the number of iteration steps for updating V. The cost of updating U_i is $O(Kpm_i + K^2n_i + Kn_i^2 + Kn_im_i)$. Similarly, the cost of updating P is $O(K(n_1^2+n_2^2)+K^2(n_1+n_2))$. At last, Q is updated using Algorithm 8 and the computation cost is approximately $O(Kp(n_1+n_2) + (p+K)(n_1m_1+n_2m_2) + K^2(m_1+m_2))$.

5 EXPERIMENTAL EVALUATION

In this section, we will conduct experiments on real-world datasets to demonstrate the effectiveness of the proposed framework. Specifically, we aim to answer the following research questions:

- Is CrossFire able to improve friend and item recommendation by exploiting within-platform correlations and cross-platform transferring information simultaneously?
- How effective are cross-media learning and joint friend and item prediction, respectively, in improving the recommendation performance of CrossFire?

To answer the first question, we compare the performance of friend and item recommendations of CrossFire with the state-of-the-art friend and item recommender systems, respectively. We then investigate the effects of cross-media recommendation and joint prediction on the proposed framework by doing parameter analysis to answer the second question.

5.1 Datasets

We ensure that both source and target sites have the following information: *user-item interactions*, *user-user relations*, and *item features*. As shown in Table 1, we have two pairs of cross-media datasets to evaluate the proposed framework, i.e., *Book* and *Movie*. The *Book* data is collected from two book review social media sites, GoodReads[2] and BookLikes[3], using web crawlers from April 2017 to May 2017[4]. Users on GoodReads and BookLikes can rate the books they read of score 1 to 5 and they can follow and be followed by others. The *Movie* dataset includes two item review sites Epinions

[2] https://www.goodreads.com
[3] http://booklikes.com/
[4] The dataset will be publicly available in the first author's homepage

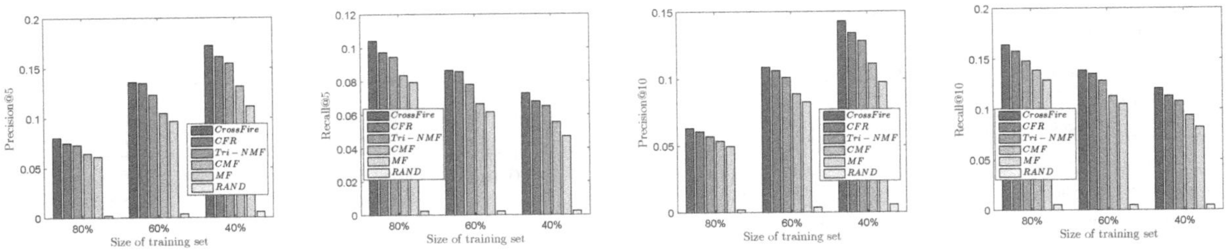

(a) Precision@5 (b) Recall@5 (c) Precision@10 (d) Recall@10

Figure 2: Precision@5, Recall@5, Precision@10 and Recall@10 on *Ciao*.

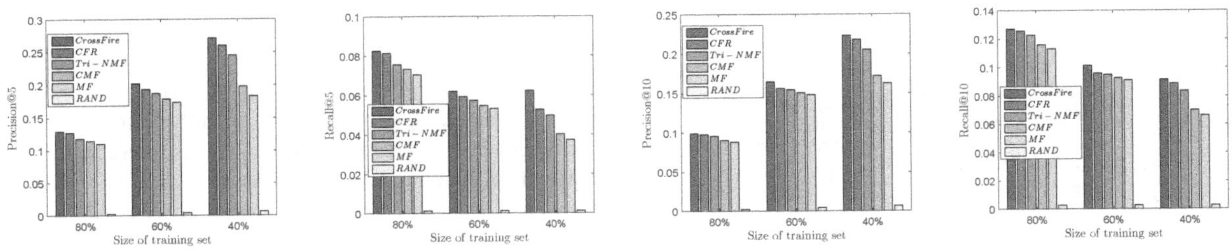

(a) Precision@5 (b) Recall@5 (c) Precision@10 (d) Recall@10

Figure 3: Precision@5, Recall@5, Precision@10 and Recall@10 on *BookLikes*.

and Ciao and public available [5]. We only keep items that belong to *movie* category. Users' ratings range from 1 to 5 and they can also establish social relations (trust relations). Since different schemes to show item attributes cause the attribute values inconsistent and incomplete, we only assume the most common text information for items, i.e., *name* and *description*, are available. Thus, Item features are represented using Bag-of-words model on the text. In the sense, it may not be applicable to directly compute similarity score on the attribute values since most of them are not available. Note that we select the source and target platform for each cross-media data based on real-world popularities of those sites.

5.2 Friend Recommendation

In this subsection, we check whether the proposed framework CrossFire can improve the performance of friend recommendation.

5.2.1 Experimental Settings. We randomly choose a fraction of $x\%$ positive user-user pairs for training and use the remaining $1-x\%$ of all links for testing, where x is varied in $\{80, 60, 40\}$. We use top-k evaluation metrics to measure the recommendation performance. Specifically, we give the definition of Precision@k and Recall@k as $Precision@k = \frac{1}{|\mathcal{U}^t|} \sum_{u_i^t \in \mathcal{U}^t} \frac{|TopK(u_i^t) \cap user(u_i^t)|}{|TopK(u_i^t)|}$ and $Recall@k = \frac{1}{|\mathcal{U}^t|} \sum_{u_i^t \in \mathcal{U}^t} \frac{|TopK(u_i^t) \cap user(u_i^t)|}{|user(u_i^t)|}$. where $TopK(u_i^t)$ is the set of friends recommended to user u_i^t on target platform that u_i^t has not yet formed links in the training set. $user(u_i^t)$ indicates the set of users that have been formed links in testing set. In our experiment, k is set to 5 and 10, respectively.

5.2.2 Performance comparison of Friend Recommendation. We compare CrossFire with several state-of-the-art friend recommendation algorithms. MF, CMF, and Tri-NMF are the friend recommendation methods for **single-platform**, and CFR is a **cross-platform** friend recommendation method. Note that CMF is also the baseline of **joint** friend and item recommendation method.

- **RAND:** This method recommends user links randomly.
- **MF:** Matrix factorization method factorizes the link matrix A into two low rank latent matrices and predicts the links by the matrix reconstructed by them.
- **CMF:** Collective matrix factorization [25] is a matrix factorization model that jointly utilizes user-user social relation matrix $\mathbf{A}_2$ and user-item preference matrix $\mathbf{R}_2$. Note that user links are predicted as $\mathbf{U}_2^T\mathbf{O}_2$.

$$\min_{\mathbf{U}_2,\mathbf{V}_2,\mathbf{O}_2} \alpha\|\mathbf{Y}_2 \odot (\mathbf{A}_2 - \mathbf{U}_2^T\mathbf{O}_2)\|_F^2 + \beta\|\mathbf{W}_2 \odot (\mathbf{R}_2 - \mathbf{U}_2^T\mathbf{V}_2)\|_F^2 + \lambda(\|\mathbf{U}_2\|_F^2 + \|\mathbf{V}_2\|_F^2 + \|\mathbf{O}_2\|_F^2) \tag{21}$$

- **Tri-NMF:** Nonnegative Matrix Tri-Factorization decomposes the link matrix **A** into two low rank matrices, i.e., user latent matrix **U** and user interaction matrix **P**. The user links are predicted as $\mathbf{U}_2^T\mathbf{P}\mathbf{U}_2$.
- **CFR:** CFR is a variant of our proposed method without item feature sparse learning and cross-site item recommendation, which has the following optimization form.

We use cross validation to determine all the model parameters. For CrossFire, we set latent dimension as $K = 10$, item sparse dimension $p = 256$. We also set $\alpha = 0.001, \beta = 1, \gamma = 0.001, \lambda = 0.01, \mu = 0.001, \nu = 1$. The experimental results are shown in Figure 2 and Figure 3. We have the following observations:

• In general, with the increase of training ratio, the recommendation performance of prec@5 and prec@10 decreases. The reason is that 1) the set of new friend relations are different for different $x\%$; 2) the difficulty of inferring new friend relations increase as the high sparsity of trust relations when training ratio is high, which can be supported by the performance of RAND. This observation is also consistent with previous work [28]. In addition, recall@5 and recall@10 increase with the increase of training ratio. The

[5]http://www.cse.msu.edu/ tangjili/trust.html

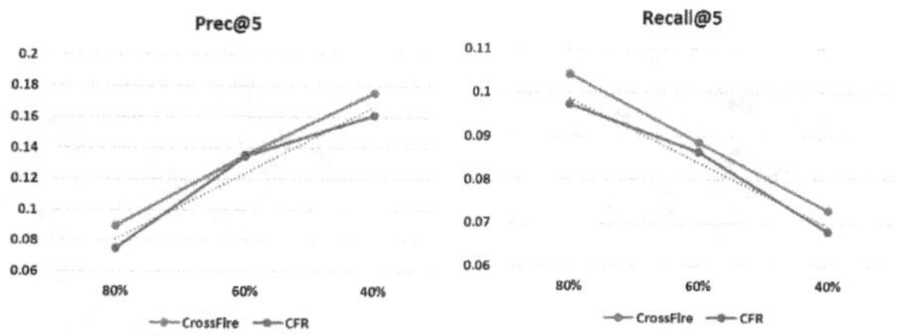

(a) Prec@5 (b) Recall@5

Figure 4: Model robustness for friend recommendation.

reason is that both truly inferred friends and remaining friends are decreasing and the latter decrease faster.

• CMF performs slightly better than MF, which shows that incorporating rating patterns to learn user latent features can help improve friend recommendation performance. In addition, Tri-NMF performs much better than MF, which indicates that factorizing user links with interaction matrix can better capture the user connection status. Moreover, cross-media friend recommendation method CFR performs better than other single-platform methods.

• CrossFire achieves the best performance comparing with other baselines. For example, CrossFire gain 54.9%, 54.9%, 46.8%,46.8% relative improvement compared with MF, in terms of *Prec@5*,*Recall@5*, *Prec@10*,*Recall@10* respectively, with 40% training size. It indicates that the combination of cross-media and joint prediction can provide complementary information for friend recommendations.

• CrossFire is more robust compared with the best baseline CFR. In Figure 4, we can see that as training ratio changes, the performance change tendencies (represented by the dotted lines) in terms of *prec@5* and *recall@5* are more flat. This indicates that CrossFire is less sensitive to training data size and thus can better handle data sparsity problems for friend recommendations.

5.3 Item Recommendation

In this subsection, we further check whether the proposed framework CrossFire can improve the performance of rating predictions.

5.3.1 Experimental Settings. We randomly choose a fraction of $x\%$ positive user-item pairs for training and use the remaining $1-x\%$ of all items for testing, where x is varied in $\{80, 60, 40\}$. We use two popular metrics, the Mean Absolute Error (MAE) and the Root Mean Square Error (RMSE), to measure the recommendation quality of our proposed approach comparing with other collaborative filtering and social recommendation methods. The metric MAE is defined as $MAE = \frac{1}{T}\sum_{i,j}|\mathbf{R}_{ij} - \hat{\mathbf{R}_{ij}}|$, where $\mathbf{R}_{ij}$ denotes the observed rating user u_i gave to item x_j, and $\hat{\mathbf{R}_{ij}}$ denotes the predicted rating, and T is the number of tested ratings. The RMSE is defined as $RMSE = \sqrt{\frac{1}{T}\sum_{i,j}(\mathbf{R}_{ij} - \hat{\mathbf{R}_{ij}})^2}$. A smaller RMSE or MAE value means better performance. Note that previous work demonstrated that *small improvement in RMSE and MAE terms can have a significant impact on the quality of top-few recommendation* [7].

5.3.2 Performance comparison of Item Recommendation. We compare the proposed framework CrossFire with the following state-of-the-art item recommendation methods, i.e. , four **single-platform** method MF, CMF, SoRec, and SoReg, and two **cross-platform** transfer learning method, RMGM [10] and CIR. CMF is also the baseline of **joint** friend and item recommendation method.

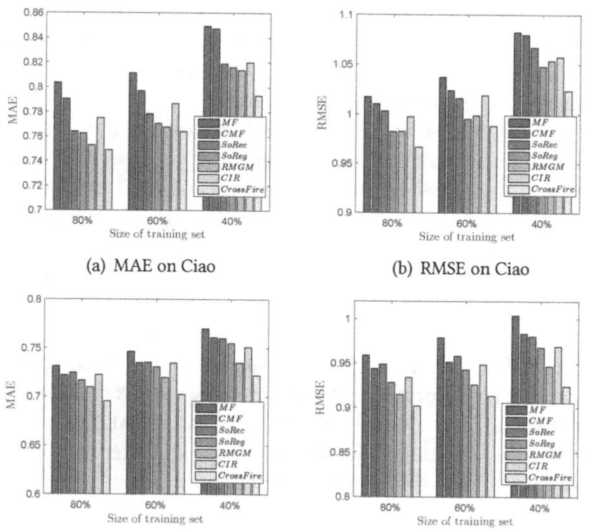

(a) MAE on Ciao (b) RMSE on Ciao

(c) MAE on BookLikes (d) RMSE on BookLikes

Figure 5: MAE, RMSE performances on *Ciao* and *BookLikes*.

- **MF:** It decomposes $\mathbf{R}$ into two low rank latent matrices and predicts the ratings by the matrix reconstructed by them. It is a variant of CrossFire without considering user relations, item attributes, and cross-platform similarities.
- **CMF:** Collective matrix factorization [25] is a matrix factorization model that jointly utilizes user-user social relation matrix $\mathbf{A}_2$ and user-item preference matrix $\mathbf{R}_2$. Note that item rating matrix is predicted as $\mathbf{U}_2^T\mathbf{V}_2$ as in Eqn 21.
- **SoRec:** This method [14] performs a co-factorization in user-rating matrix and user-user degree centrality relation confidence matrix by sharing same user latent factor through a probabilistic matrix factorization model.
- **SoReg:** This method [15] is based on matrix factorization model and add a social regularization term as constraints to encode local social relation of users.
- **RMGM**: Rating matrix generative model [10] is the state-of-the-art transfer learning method, which learns a shared cluster-level user ratings patterns by jointly modeling rating matrices on multiple domains.
- **CIR:** CIR is a variant of our proposed method without cross-site friend recommendation.

Note that we also use cross-validation to determine the parameters for all baseline methods. For CrossFire, we set the latent factor dimension as $K = 10, \alpha = 1, \beta = 0.001, \gamma = 0.001, \lambda = 0.01, \mu = 0.001, \nu = 1$. The comparison results are demonstrated in Figure 5, and we have following observations:

• Exploiting social relations as auxiliary information can help improve item recommendations. For example, CMF, SoRec, SoReg all performs better than MF. Note that the performance of CMF is worse than SoRec and SoReg. The reason is that SoRec and SoReg are both using social relation as side information to improve item recommendation performance; while CMF can perform joint friend and item recommendation and directly factorize user link matrix may not provide so much useful knowledge.

• Exploiting cross-media information can significantly improve recommendation performances. We can see that RMGM and CIR perform significantly better than MF in terms of MAE and RMSE in all cases. In addition, we can see that RMGM>CIR holds in all cases, which indicates that modeling cluster-level rating pattern help more than item-level rating patterns.

- CrossFire performs the best on both datasets in terms of MAE and RMSE on all training settings. For example, CrossFire obtains 6.55%, 5.41% relative improvement in terms of MAE and RMSE in Ciao with 40% as the training set. The major reason is that CrossFire exploits both cross-media information and joint prediction for recommendations, which have complementary information to improve item recommendations.
- CrossFire is more robust compared with the best baseline RMGM. As shown in Figure 6, we can see that as training ratio decreases, the performance decrease tendencies (represented by the dotted lines) are more flat. This indicates that CrossFire is less sensitive to training data size and thus can better handle data sparsity problems for item recommendations.

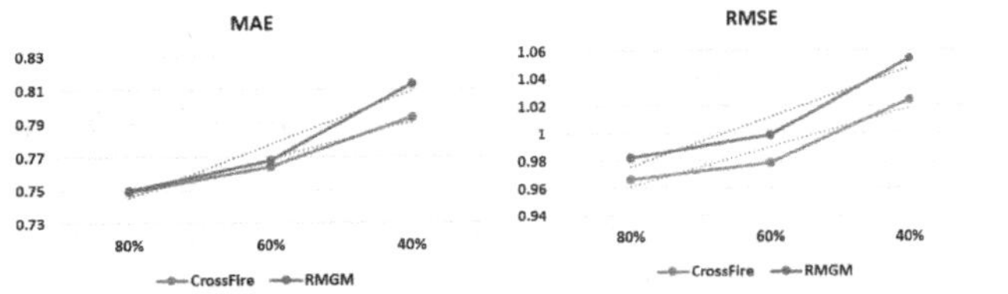

(a) MAE (b) RMSE

Figure 6: Model robustness for item recommendation.

To sum up, we conclude from the experiments that (1) the proposed framework significantly improves both friend and item recommendation performances; and (2) modeling joint prediction and cross-media recommendation simultaneously provides complementary contributions to recommendation performance improvement.

5.4 Parameter Analysis

In this section, we perform the parameter analysis for the proposed framework. We mainly focus on the parameter sensitivities for α and β, as they are controlling the joint cross friend and item recommendation components, respectively. We fix other parameters when we change the α or β. Due to the space limitation and similar observation for other settings, we only show the results when training ratio is 40% and omit the results for *prec*@10 and *recall*@10. For item recommendation, we vary the values of α as $\{1, 0.01, 0.001\}$ and β as $\{0, 0.0001, 0.001, 0.01, 0.1\}$. Similarly, for friend recommendation, we vary the values of β as $\{1, 0.01, 0.001\}$ and α as $\{0, 0.0001, 0.001, 0.01, 0.1\}$. The results for friend and item recommendations are shown in Figure 7 and Figure 8 respectively. We have the following observations: (1) When $\alpha = 1$, item recommendation has relatively good performance; however, when $\alpha = 0.01, 0.001$, the performance is much worse than MF. The reason is that $\alpha = 1$ means that the cross item recommendation part dominants the feature learning process and the resultant latent features are mainly encoded by rating information. Similarly, $\beta = 1$ ensures that latent user features are mainly encoded by user relations; (2) The performance of item recommendation is generally better when the value of β is within $[0.001, 0.01]$; similarly, for friend recommendation, α within $[0.001, 0.01]$ gives better performance. These observations ease the parameter selection process.

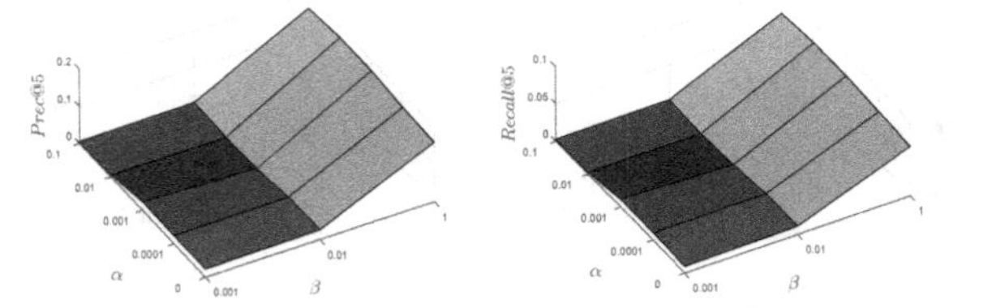

(a) Prec@5 (b) Recall@5

Figure 7: Parameter sensitivity on friend recommendation w.r.t. α and β on *prec*@5 and *recall*@5.

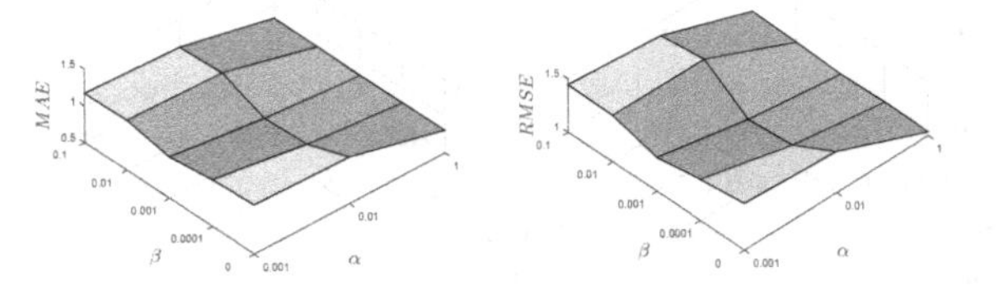

(a) MAE (b) RMSE

Figure 8: Parameter sensitivity on item recommendation w.r.t. α and β on MAE and RMSE.

6 RELATED WORK

In this section, we introduce some related work for this paper. It mainly falls into following categories: 1) Cross social media recommendations; 2) Joint friend and item recommendations.

Cross social media recommendations. Cross-domain recommendations are attracting lots of attention in recent years [4]. The underly assumption of cross-domain recommendation is that there are shared properties between user and/or item profiles across source and target domains, either *explicitly* or *implicitly*. Explicit correspondences are often costly to obtain and some user identity linkage methods are proposed to bridge the gap of user links [24, 37]. User correspondences can enrich user profiles and help improve recommendations in various applications, such as video recommendation [3], product recommendation [13], etc. Implicit correspondences can be captured by modeling item similarities or even latent rating behaviors. A third-party platform (e.g. Wikipedia) can be used to bridge links of users/hashtags between Twitter and Weibo via random walk [11]. In addition, transfer learning based on collaborative filtering has recently been proposed to capture shared rating behaviors across domains, such as codebook transfer model (CBT) [9] and rating-matrix generative model (RMGM) [10]. In this paper, we aim to capture latent shared features for items and further transfer knowledge based on rating behavior patterns.

Joint friend and item recommendations. Exploiting auxiliary information to build recommendation systems are commonly used and helpful to boost recommendation performances [31–34]. For example, the existing work that modeling user rating and user relation information aims to provide better recommendations for items, i.e., social recommendations [29, 30], which have been shown to be effective in recent years [14, 15, 28]. Social relations are modeled in different ways, such as trust ensemble [16], trust propagation [5], social regularization [28] and matrix co-factorization [14, 28]. However, how to exploit user-item interactions for user-user link predictions has remained relatively limited [23]. Even though co-factorization methods suggest that users share latent features in rating space and the social space, they can not be directly applied to user link predictions due to the indirect modeling process of social relations (e.g. social similarity matrix [15]). In this paper, we provide a collective matrix factorization [25] to directly factorize user-user and user-item matrices, which provides a novel solution to exploit the mutual benefit of rating behaviors and social relations.

7 CONCLUSION AND FUTURE WORK

Newly launched social media sites often face data sparsity challenges to perform personalized friend and item recommendations. We propose to exploit both cross-platform and within-platform information simultaneously and build a joint item and friend recommendation framework. Our framework *CrossFire* highlights three components: i) sparse coding for items, ii) matrix tri-factorization for user-user relations and user-item ratings, and iii) maintaining the factors shared across sites. Experimental results on real-world datasets demonstrate the effectiveness of proposed framework and the importance of combining cross-media recommendations and joint friend and item predictions for better recommendations.

There are several interesting future directions. First, we can consider the scenario that limited explicit user/item correspondences are given and how we can utilize this information. Second, how to perform item and friend recommendations in a streaming way for more practical use in real world cases. Third, it's also worth to explore cross-media recommendations between different domains, such as books and movies, to understand the capacity and limitations on transfer learning techniques.

8 ACKOWLEDGMENTS

This material is based upon work supported by, or in part by, the ONR grant N00014-16-1-2257.

REFERENCES

[1] Stephen Boyd, Neal Parikh, Eric Chu, Borja Peleato, and Jonathan Eckstein. 2011. Distributed optimization and statistical learning via the alternating direction method of multipliers. *Foundations and Trends® in Machine Learning* 3, 1 (2011), 1–122.

[2] Aaron Clauset, Cosma Rohilla Shalizi, and Mark EJ Newman. 2009. Power-law distributions in empirical data. *SIAM review* 51, 4 (2009), 661–703.

[3] Zhengyu Deng, Jitao Sang, and Changsheng Xu. 2013. Personalized video recommendation based on cross-platform user modeling. In *ICME'13*. IEEE, 1–6.

[4] Ignacio Fernández-Tobías, Iván Cantador, Marius Kaminskas, and Francesco Ricci. 2012. Cross-domain recommender systems: A survey of the state of the art. In *Spanish Conference on Information Retrieval*.

[5] Mohsen Jamali and Martin Ester. 2009. Trustwalker: a random walk model for combining trust-based and item-based recommendation. In *KDD'09*. ACM, 397–406.

[6] Alan Jennings and John J McKeown. 1992. *Matrix computation*. John Wiley & Sons Inc.

[7] Yehuda Koren. 2008. Factorization meets the neighborhood: a multifaceted collaborative filtering model. In *KDD'08*. ACM, 426–434.

[8] Honglak Lee, Alexis Battle, Rajat Raina, and Andrew Y Ng. 2006. Efficient sparse coding algorithms. In *NIPS*. 801–808.

[9] Bin Li, Qiang Yang, and Xiangyang Xue. 2009. Can Movies and Books Collaborate? Cross-Domain Collaborative Filtering for Sparsity Reduction.. In *IJCAI*, Vol. 9. 2052–2057.

[10] Bin Li, Qiang Yang, and Xiangyang Xue. 2009. Transfer learning for collaborative filtering via a rating-matrix generative model. In *ICML'09*. ACM, 617–624.

[11] Xiaozhong Liu, Tian Xia, Yingying Yu, Chun Guo, and Yizhou Sun. 2016. Cross Social Media Recommendation. In *ICWSM'16*.

[12] Mingsheng Long, Guiguang Ding, Jianmin Wang, Jiaguang Sun, Yuchen Guo, and Philip S Yu. 2013. Transfer sparse coding for robust image representation. In *CVPR'13*. 407–414.

[13] Chun-Ta Lu, Sihong Xie, Weixiang Shao, Lifang He, and Philip S Yu. Item recommendation for emerging online businesses.

[14] Hao Ma, Haixuan Yang, Michael R Lyu, and Irwin King. 2008. Sorec: social recommendation using probabilistic matrix factorization. In *CIKM'08*. ACM, 931–940.

[15] Hao Ma, Dengyong Zhou, Chao Liu, Michael R Lyu, and Irwin King. 2011. Recommender systems with social regularization. In *WSDM'11*. ACM, 287–296.

[16] Nan Ma, Ee-Peng Lim, Viet-An Nguyen, Aixin Sun, and Haifeng Liu. 2009. Trust relationship prediction using online product review data. In *Proceedings of the 1st ACM international workshop on Complex networks meet information & knowledge management*. ACM, 47–54.

[17] Peter V Marsden and Noah E Friedkin. 1993. Network studies of social influence. *Sociological Methods & Research* 22, 1 (1993), 127–151.

[18] Miller McPherson, Lynn Smith-Lovin, and James M Cook. 2001. Birds of a feather: Homophily in social networks. *Annual review of sociology* 27, 1 (2001), 415–444.

[19] Neal Parikh, Stephen Boyd, and others. 2014. Proximal algorithms. *Foundations and Trends® in Optimization* 1, 3 (2014), 127–239.

[20] Paul Resnick and Hal R Varian. 1997. Recommender systems. *Commun. ACM* 40, 3 (1997), 56–58.

[21] Badrul Sarwar, George Karypis, Joseph Konstan, and John Riedl. 2001. Item-based collaborative filtering recommendation algorithms. In *WWW'01*. ACM, 285–295.

[22] Andrew I Schein, Alexandrin Popescul, Lyle H Ungar, and David M Pennock. 2002. Methods and metrics for cold-start recommendations. In *SIGIR'02*. ACM, 253–260.

[23] Yue Shi, Martha Larson, and Alan Hanjalic. 2014. Collaborative filtering beyond the user-item matrix: A survey of the state of the art and future challenges. *ACM Computing Surveys (CSUR)* 47, 1 (2014), 3.

[24] Kai Shu, Suhang Wang, Jiliang Tang, Reza Zafarani, and Huan Liu. 2016. User Identity Linkage across Online Social Networks: A Review. *ACM SIGKDD Explorations Newsletter* (2016).

[25] Ajit P Singh and Geoffrey J Gordon. 2008. Relational learning via collective matrix factorization. In *KDD'08*. ACM, 650–658.

[26] Parag Singla and Matthew Richardson. 2008. Yes, there is a correlation:-from social networks to personal behavior on the web. In *WWW*. ACM, 655–664.

[27] Xiaoyuan Su and Taghi M Khoshgoftaar. 2009. A survey of collaborative filtering techniques. *AAAI* 2009 (2009), 4.

[28] Jiliang Tang, Xia Hu, Huiji Gao, and Huan Liu. 2013. Exploiting Local and Global Social Context for Recommendation.. In *IJCAI*. 264–269.

[29] Jiliang Tang, Xia Hu, and Huan Liu. 2013. Social recommendation: a review. *Social Network Analysis and Mining* 3, 4 (2013), 1113–1133.

[30] Jiliang Tang, Suhang Wang, Xia Hu, Dawei Yin, Yingzhou Bi, Yi Chang, and Huan Liu. 2016. Recommendation with Social Dimensions.. In *AAAI*. 251–257.

[31] Suhang Wang, Jiliang Tang, and Huan Liu. 2015. Toward dual roles of users in recommender systems. In *CIKM*. ACM, 1651–1660.

[32] Suhang Wang, Jiliang Tang, Yilin Wang, and Huan Liu. 2015. Exploring Implicit Hierarchical Structures for Recommender Systems.. In *IJCAI*. 1813–1819.

[33] Suhang Wang, Yilin Wang, Jiliang Tang, Kai Shu, Suhas Ranganath, and Huan Liu. 2017. What your images reveal: Exploiting visual contents for point-of-interest recommendation. In *WWW*. International World Wide Web Conferences Steering Committee, 391–400.

[34] Yilin Wang, Suhang Wang, Jiliang Tang, Guo-Jun Qi, Huan Liu, and Baoxin Li. 2017. CLARE: A Joint Approach to Label Classification and Tag Recommendation.. In *AAAI*. 210–216.

[35] Zaiwen Wen and Wotao Yin. 2013. A feasible method for optimization with orthogonality constraints. *Mathematical Programming* 142, 1-2 (2013), 397–434.

[36] Dani Yogatama and Noah A Smith. 2014. Making the Most of Bag of Words: Sentence Regularization with Alternating Direction Method of Multipliers.. In *ICML'14*. 656–664.

[37] Reza Zafarani and Huan Liu. 2013. Connecting users across social media sites: a behavioral-modeling approach. In *KDD'13*. ACM, 41–49.

[38] Miao Zheng, Jiajun Bu, Chun Chen, Can Wang, Lijun Zhang, Guang Qiu, and Deng Cai. 2011. Graph regularized sparse coding for image representation. *IEEE Transactions on Image Processing* 20, 5 (2011), 1327–1336.

Modeling Time to Open of Emails with a Latent State for User Engagement Level

Moumita Sinha
Adobe Research
mousinha@adobe.com

Vishwa Vinay
Adobe Research
vinay@adobe.com

Harvineet Singh
Adobe Research
harvines@adobe.com

ABSTRACT

Email messages have been an important mode of communication, not only for work, but also for social interactions and marketing. When messages have time sensitive information, it becomes relevant for the sender to know what is the expected time within which the email will be read by the recipient. In this paper we use a survival analysis framework to predict the time to open an email once it has been received. We use the Cox Proportional Hazards (CoxPH) model that offers a way to combine various features that might affect the event of opening an email. As an extension, we also apply a mixture model (MM) approach to CoxPH that distinguishes between recipients, based on a latent state of how prone to opening the messages each individual is. We compare our approach with standard classification and regression models. While the classification model provides predictions on the likelihood of an email being opened, the regression model provides prediction of the real-valued time to open. The use of survival analysis based methods allows us to jointly model both the open event as well as the time-to-open. We experimented on a large real-world dataset of marketing emails sent in a 3-month time duration. The mixture model achieves the best accuracy on our data where a high proportion of email messages go unopened.

KEYWORDS

Email interaction data, survival analysis, time-to-event prediction, enterprise email marketing, Cox-proportional hazards model

ACM Reference Format:
Moumita Sinha, Vishwa Vinay, and Harvineet Singh. 2018. Modeling Time to Open of Emails with a Latent State for User Engagement Level. In *WSDM 2018: WSDM 2018: The Eleventh ACM International Conference on Web Search and Data Mining , February 5–9, 2018, Marina Del Rey, CA, USA.* ACM, New York, NY, USA, 9 pages. https://doi.org/10.1145/3159652.3159683

1 INTRODUCTION

Email has a rich history of being a data source for machine learning techniques. Starting with spam filtering [9], the range of applications today covers a rich spectrum of scenarios. The Enron Corpus [24] enabled research into the modeling of users' interactions with email in a collaborative environment [8]. For email service providers, detailed understanding of consumers' interactions with the email system allows building predictive models for specific actions, e.g. if an email will be replied to or not [40] and creating rich experiences [21, 23] for the recipients. On the consumer side, given its popularity, there has been much work on different ways to handle large volumes of email effectively [39]. An early paper by Horvitz et al. [20] proposed that autonomous agents may be able to identify and prioritize emails that need attention. The authors of [14] show that historical data allows the prediction of what actions a user might take on the receipt of an email, for example, marking it for deletion [11]. Apart from being a mode of communication, email is also used as a personal information management environment [16], leading to the need to support other forms of interactions like search [31].

The domain of interest in the current paper is marketing, where the email channel ranks high in popularity [35] alongside social media, search & display advertising. Email based marketing is predicted to have a compound annual growth rate of 10% [35] and nearly every enterprise marketer uses it as a delivery channel [6, 34]. The engagement levels however are typically low, as compared to personal email messages at work or among friends. The open rates for the marketing email messages, vary by industry - ranging from 15% to 19% in the e-commerce, beauty and personal care, and gambling industries, and in the range of 20% to 28% in the hobbies, home and garden or health and fitness industries [38]. Marketers are therefore always on the lookout for techniques that might enhance the engagement levels. For example, Kumar et al. [25] modeled opt-in and opt-out behaviour and related these to transactions made by the consumer. Bonfrer et al. [3] proposed a framework that allows real-time evaluation of an email campaign.

In this submission, we propose the use of *survival analysis* for jointly modeling the open event on an email, as well as the time-to-open. The next section provides technical background to some important concepts in survival analysis that are relevant in the current scenario.

2 SURVIVAL ANALYSIS

Survival analysis refers to an area of statistical modeling where the main variable of interest is the time to an *event*. Historically, the event is assumed to be *death*. One characteristic of data that makes the use of survival models appropriate is the presence of *censoring*. This refers to the fact that not all individuals would have experienced the event within the observation window. The censoring may be because at the time of analysis the event had not yet occurred, or if the corresponding individual can no longer be tracked. Figure 1 is a pictorial representation of survival data in the context of emails. Observations are synchronized at $t = 0$, which is the time at which the individuals receive the email. If the event of

WSDM 2018, February 5–9, 2018, Marina Del Rey, CA, USA

ACM ISBN 978-1-4503-5581-0/18/02...$15.00
https://doi.org/10.1145/3159652.3159683

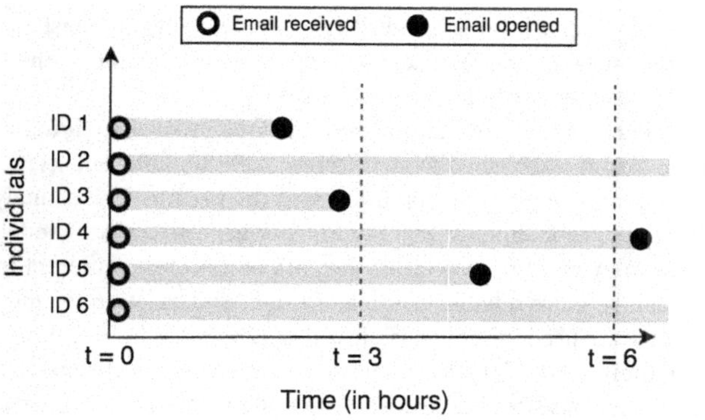

Figure 1: Example of survival data with different censoring windows. Emails are received at t=0 by all individuals. Note that at t=3 hours, outcome for individual ID 5 is censored but will be observed for t=6 hours.

the email being read is not within a chosen time interval, e.g. $t = 3$ hours, this would be a censored data point. And some recipients may of course not read the email at all.

Consider a random variable T for the time to the event of interest, with the corresponding probability density function $f(t)$ and the cumulative distribution function being $F(t)$ at a given time t. Then the survivor function is defined as

$$S(t) = P(T \geq t) = 1 - F(t) = \int_{t}^{\infty} f(u)du \tag{1}$$

It represents the probability that an individual will survive beyond time t. Equivalently, given that the individual has not yet experienced the event till time t, the hazard function $h(t)$ represents the instantaneous chance of the event occurring at time $t + dt$.

$$h(t) = \lim_{dt \to 0} \frac{P(t \leq T < t + dt | T \geq t)}{dt} \tag{2}$$

The relationship between the survivor function and the hazard function can be derived as being $S(t) = exp\{-H(t)\}$, where $H(t)$ is the cumulative hazard function corresponding to $h(t)$.

A survival analysis dataset containing N individuals is represented as $\{X_i, Y_i, \delta_i\}$, with $i = 1 \dots N$. For the ith individual, X_i is a vector of features that are believed to be predictive of the survival time. The target $Y_i = min(t_i, C_i)$ represents the survival time, where C_i represents the duration of time for which the individual was observed and is also known as the censoring window. If observed within the censoring window, t_i is the time to event for the ith individual. The indicator variable δ_i encodes if the ith individual experienced the event of interest within the censoring window.

$$\delta_i = \begin{cases} 1, & \text{if } t_i < C_i \\ 0, & \text{otherwise} \end{cases} \tag{3}$$

2.1 Cox Proportional Hazard Regression

Given a feature vector X_i for the ith individual, the hazard function for the individual at any given time t can be defined as

$$h_i(t|X_i) = h_0(t) \times \psi(X_i) \tag{4}$$

Here $h_0(t)$ is the baseline hazard function at time t, and $\psi(.)$ incorporates the dependence on the individual-specific features X_i, which are independent of time. The specific factorization of $h_i(t|X_i)$ into a global time-dependent component ($h_0(t)$) and an individual's time-independent factor ($\psi(X_i)$) is the *Proportional Hazards* assumption - Section 3.2 provides a methodology to validate this assumption on a given dataset. What has been defined above is a semi-parametric approach, in that no assumptions have been made about the shape of the baseline hazard function $h_0(t)$. The parametric alternative would be to impose a functional form, e.g. a Weibull distribution. Based on the relation between the survivor and hazard functions, the survivor function of the ith individual for Cox Proportional Hazard (CoxPH) regression is

$$\begin{aligned} S_i(t|X_i) &= exp\{-\int_{0}^{t} h_0(u)\psi(X_i)du\} \\ &= [exp\{-H_0(t)\}]^{\psi(X_i)} \\ &= S_0(t)^{\psi(X_i)} \end{aligned} \tag{5}$$

The corresponding partial likelihood function [10] is defined as

$$L(\beta) = \prod_{i:\delta_i=1} \frac{\psi(X_i;\beta)}{\sum_{l \in R(t_i)} \psi(X_l;\beta)} \tag{6}$$

where the function $\psi(.)$ has been parameterized by β that controls the combination of the features. $R(t_i)$ is the set of individuals who are *at-risk* of the event at time t_i, that is, the set of individuals for whom the event has not occurred yet. t_i is also the observed time to event of the ith individual. Note that the numerator of the likelihood is a function of only the individuals that observed the event, and censored individuals only contribute to the denominator of Equation 6. The β values are estimated by maximizing the above likelihood using a gradient based method.

The most common form of $\psi(X_i) = exp(\beta^T X_i)$, where β is a vector of parameters controlling the dependence between the features in X_i and target Y_i. Doing so assumes a linear scaling of the relative (log) hazards of different individuals with respect to the values of the features. Ridgeway [33] proposed that the likelihood in Equation 6 can alternatively be optimized directly using gradient boosting methods that might provide benefits in scenarios where the effect of the features is non-linear. Note that this is still a Proportional Hazards model, but with $\psi(X_i)$ taken to be the output of a gradient boosting machine (GBM).

2.2 Mixture Model with Cox Proportional Hazard Regression

The CoxPH model assumes that all individuals will eventually experience the event. But there may be a proportion of individuals who are not prone to the event, i.e., who are not predisposed to opening emails. The level at which an individual user is engaged with marketing messages influences his/her act of opening the email (and how quickly). The CoxPH model described earlier tries to explain all the observations using only the features (X_i) as the explanatory factors. Through the use of mixture models [4, 18], we might expect to get more discriminatory power. The ith individual is now represented as $\{X_i, Y_i, \delta_i, L_i, Z_i\}$, where L_i is a latent indicator variable such that

$$L_i = \begin{cases} 1, & \text{prone to the event} \\ 0, & \text{otherwise} \end{cases} \tag{7}$$

Z_i is a set of features that help predict if an individual is prone to the event of interest or not. The feature set Z_i can also be the same as the feature set X_i.

$$\pi(Z_i) = P(L_i = 1|Z_i) = \frac{exp(\mathbf{b}^T Z_i)}{1 + exp(\mathbf{b}^T Z_i)} \tag{8}$$

The probability $P(L_i = 1|Z_i)$ is estimated using logistic regression here, and is introduced as a mixture probability into the overall survivor function:

$$S_i(t|X_i) = \pi(Z_i)S(t_i|L = 1, X_i) + (1 - \pi(Z_i)) \tag{9}$$

If the individual is predisposed to not experiencing the event, then $\pi(Z_i) \simeq 0$, leading to a prediction of a survival probability close to 1. Conversely, a scenario with $\pi(Z_i) \simeq 1$ leads to the first term dominating, with the quantity $S(t_i|L = 1, X_i)$ representing the survival probability in the traditional sense. A proportional hazards assumption can be encoded by setting $S(t_i|L = 1, X_i) = S_0(t)^{exp(\beta^T X_i)}$ as before. The likelihood of the model is given by:

$$L(\beta, b) = \prod_{i=1}^{N} \Big([1 - \pi_i(Z_i)]^{1-L_i} \times [\pi_i(Z_i)S(t_i|L_i = 1, X_i)\{h(t_i|L_i, X_i)\}^{\delta_i}]^{L_i} \Big) \tag{10}$$

Since there are latent variables (the L_i), the optimization is an Expectation Maximization based iterative procedure that estimates the L_i, along with **b** (for calculating $\pi(Z_i)$) and β controlling how the features of an individual affect the relative hazards. In the current setting, we are interpreting $\pi_i(Z_i)$ as the engagement level of a given user i, the model however is more general. For e.g., it can be used to represent the probability that a patient has been cured, which in turn affects the chances that he/she will experience the event.

2.3 Related Work

Survival analysis has traditionally been used in the health-care domain to determine the time to 'death' in patients, but the usage of this range of techniques has recently expanded to other application areas [37]. Examples include prediction of early student dropouts [1], post-click engagement on native ads [2], query specific microblog ranking for improved retrieval [17], recommender systems in e-commerce [36], search engine evaluation via the use of "absence time" [7], and predicting time for crowd-sourced tasks [26].

By appropriately defining the event being modeled, existing marketing concepts also lend themselves survival analysis techniques. E.g. re-purchasing behavior is an indicator of high engagement [27] and a proxy for the potential value of a customer [15, 30]. Attrition modeling helps businesses identify customers who are most at-risk so that attempts can be made to keep them in the system, and [27] proposes a survival analysis based solution.

Much of the literature referred to above involve applying well-known and established models (like CoxPH) in different scenarios. But more recently, growing interest in the use of survival analysis has led to modeling improvements. For instance, when modeling time-to-event of related tasks, the parameters of the different models can be more reliably estimated using regularization techniques commonly used in multi-task learning [28]. Even in traditional application areas of survival analysis, given a large number of data points and a variety of features that potentially have a highly non-linear dependence on the time-to-event, deep latent models provide better performance [32].

The closest related work to that presented here is described in [12] where time-to-event is modelled in the email domain. Given this context, the contribution of the current paper is two-fold: (1) we describe techniques from the rich history of survival analysis to identify those models whose assumptions are better matched with the characteristics of the data (2) for the application of predicting time-to-event when the censored rows dominate, the mixture model (MM) described above is shown to not only describe the data better but also provide better predictive performance.

3 PROBLEM DEFINITION AND DATA DESCRIPTION

When emails containing time sensitive information are sent, it may be relevant for the sender to know what is the expected time within which the email will be read by the recipient. Specifically in marketing messages, if the email advertises a flash sale, the marketer will need to decide on the time window for the sale - to optimize between reaching sufficient consumers within the window and yet keep it exclusive. Prediction of time-to-open of an email by a consumer helps to determine the size of the recipient list one wants to reach.

Our dataset corresponds to email marketing campaigns that are sent out to consumers of an enterprise and we are interested in a predictive model that answers questions of two types: (a) Is a particular email likely to be opened by a given recipient? (b) Can we predict the time within which the email will be opened?

In the dataset, there is a high degree of variability amongst the marketing messages - some are sent to a large group of recipients, while others are targeted at a narrow set of consumers - e.g. a personalized birthday communication. We expect that the nature of people's interaction with these different types of emails varies drastically. In particular, we are interested in modeling how people differ in terms of their engagement with the mass marketing emails. For this reason, the analysis presented here includes only those emails that were sent to at least 50% of the total consumers. We have additionally dropped those consumers who received fewer than 10 messages during the period of interest.

The time at which an email reaches a consumer is labelled as its *start-time*. In the event that the email is read, the email has a corresponding *open-time*. The difference between the two timestamps is referred to as the *time-to-open*. The emails are divided into 3 non-overlapping buckets based on the start-time: a **Training** dataset (spanning 4 weeks) and one dataset each for **Validatation** & **Test** (spanning 3 weeks each) respectively. Table 1 shows the size of each of these datasets. Chronologically ordered, these 3 datasets cover 13 weeks of email messages with a 3 week gap between **Validatation** and **Test**. Within each group, data from the initial two weeks are used to compute features that will be used to model users' interaction with emails sent in the subsequent week(s).

Table 1: Overview of Datasets

Dataset	#Recipients (millions)	#Emails (millions)
Training	2.05	31.86
Validation	2.04	22.73
Test	2.22	19.14

3.1 Survival and Censoring

In the context of email messaging, the opening of an email is the event and the survivor function at time t provides the probability that the email will not be opened by this time. For the purposes of the results presented here, the data was gathered by monitoring the emails for 10 days after they were sent. Figure 2 shows the distribution of the time-to-open in our **Training** dataset. Note that the plot accounts for only $\sim$ 8% of the total data points.

In applications of survival models, the size of the censoring window is dictated by when the analysis needs to be performed or when information stops being available about the individuals. The choice of censoring window should include as many of the eventual opens as possible. Amongst the emails that were opened within the observed 10 days, $\sim$ 43% happened within the first 3 hours, with the corresponding numbers for 6 and 12 hours being $\sim$ 57% and $\sim$ 74% respectively. Beyond 12 hours, the opens become very rare.

With C_i = 3 hours for each individual i, over half the eventual opens would be lost - this is undesirable. On the other hand, there are practical limitations to being able to track and monitor an email campaign for extended periods of time. In addition, for time sensitive messages, the censoring window is the time within which the message needs to be opened by the recipients to ensure that the promotion is valid. Given the observations above about the data and the constraints imposed by the domain, in the current paper, we are evaluating three different censoring windows - 3, 6 and 12 hours - with a preference for the higher values. For a given choice of C_i, the emails that were not opened by their recipients within the time period are considered censored.

Given that all individuals are synchronized at $t = 0$ depending on time of receiving the email (Figure 1), the C_i's across all individuals will be the same for a given choice of censoring window. Note that when the censoring window changes, the training data provided to the survival models changes (via Equation 3). Therefore, identifying the *right* censoring window for the given application requires us to build a given model multiple times - one for each value of C_i.

Across the dataset, we can construct a histogram of the cumulative fraction of individuals that *survived* (i.e., emails that are yet to be opened) up until a given time. The Kaplan-Meier estimator [22] constructs a smooth non-parametric approximation to this histogram. In Figure 4, the curve corresponding to "Combined" represents the **Training** dataset, the significance of the other data in the plot will be explained in Section 3.2. We can see how the curve has a survival rate of 95% at around 3 hours - this represents the fact that only 5% of the users have actual time-to-open data for the censoring window of three hours (as also seen in Figure 2). This high degree of censorship is a unique characteristic of our dataset and represents one of the challenges in terms of the traditional use of survival models.

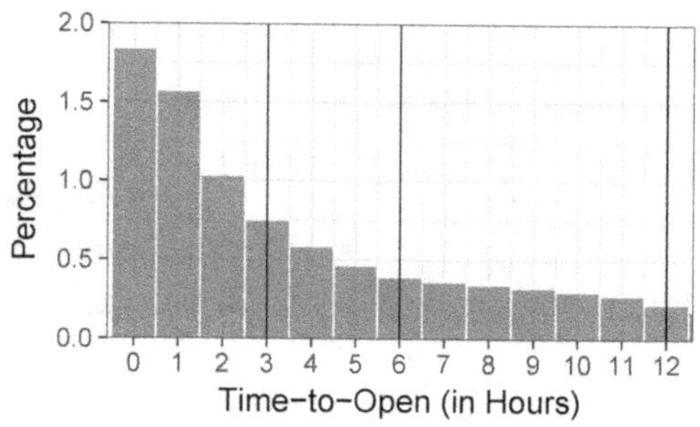

Figure 2: Distribution of time-to-open as a percentage of the number of recipients

3.1.1 Baselines: We consider the historical open rate of an individual as the baseline for predicting his/her future open events. We also include a Logistic Regression (LR) model as a classification baseline in our experiments. The auxiliary problem of predicting the time to the open event is not as straightforward. As a simplistic baseline, we consider the censoring time C as the predicted time to open for all individuals (B). Given that the majority of rows are censored, C is taken as the median of the Y_i values, with the mean being only marginally lower. We also considered a linear regression (LR) model to predict time to open, as a baseline in our experiments which excluded all individuals who had censored information from the model [5, 13]. Here, with slight abuse of notation, we denote both logistic and linear regression baselines by LR. The distinction is made clearly while presenting results.

3.2 Testing Model Assumptions

In this section, we will describe statistical analyses that validates the choice of models in our experimental section. Every model represents a corresponding set of statistical assumptions, and we need to verify that the data aligns with the assumptions of the models used.

In the original CoxPH model, the hazard of an individual at a time t is a product of two quantities - the baseline hazard and the individual's relative hazard (See Equation 4). The baseline hazard is a global quantity that incorporates the dependence on time. And the relative hazard of an individual is expressed as a parameterized function of features and is independent of time. Verifying the applicability of a proportional hazards model equates to validating that the features are independent of time. To test this independence, we take all observed (i.e., not censored) events for individual i and calculate the scaled Schoenfeld residual [19] for each feature j as

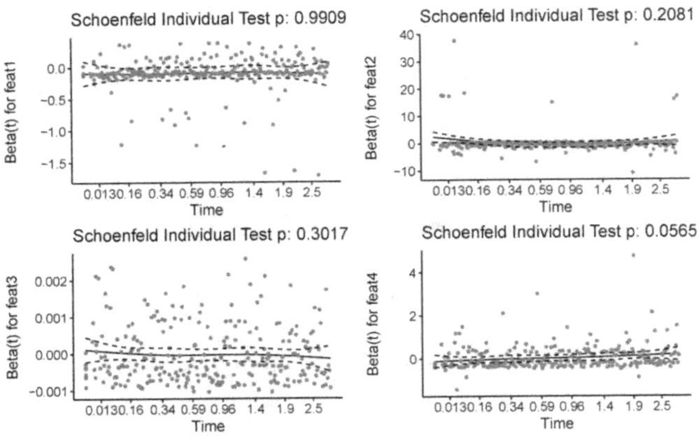

Figure 3: Test for the Proportionality Assumption in CoxPH for different features. The scaled Schoenfeld residuals do not have a trend over time

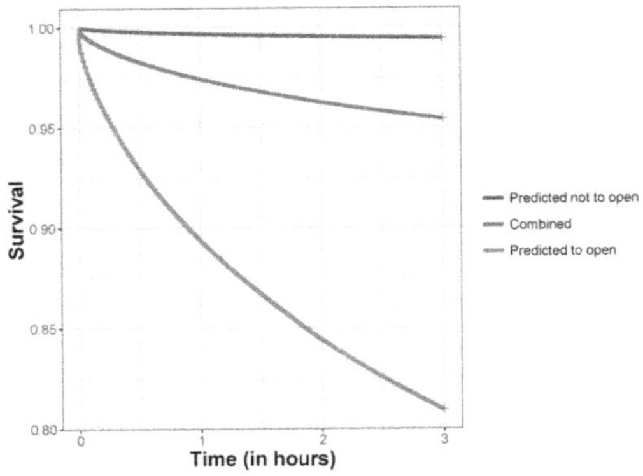

Figure 4: Survivor Functions of the Two Groups of Consumers

follows:

$$r_{ij} = X_{ij} - a_{ij} \tag{11}$$

where X_{ij} is the value of the feature and

$$a_{ij} = \frac{\sum_{k \in R(t_i)} X_{kj} exp(\beta^T X_k)}{\sum_{k \in R(t_i)} exp(\beta^T X_k)} \tag{12}$$

In the equation above, t_i represents the time at which the event occurred for individual i. And as before, the *risk set* $R(t_i)$ represents those individuals who have not yet experienced the event until t_i. Plotting the values r_{ij} as a function of the times t_i allows us to validate the proportionality assumption - the check being that the r_{ij} have no trend over time. Figure 3 plots the scaled Schoenfeld residuals calculated using the cox.zph function in the *survival* package in R. For the sake of clarity, only a sample of data points are displayed in each plot. Also included in the plot are the corresponding p-values for the null hypothesis test, that the sum of residuals for the corresponding feature across individuals is 0. This procedure allows us to ensure that the features included in the model satisfy the null hypothesis (i.e., the proportionality assumption) at a chosen significance level - the features illustrated above have p-values greater than 0.05.

Note that the above procedure utilizes the β parameters from a previously fitted CoxPH model. A similar procedure can be used for the GBM (where the dependence between the features and the hazard is non-linear) as well as the Mixture Model (*MM*). All the models considered in the current paper are based on the idea of *proportional hazards*, hence the relevance of such a test.

We note two popular extensions available from the survival analysis literature that were excluded from our experiments because they did not match the characteristics of our scenario:

(1) Parametric distributions, like the Weibull, are common choices for modeling event data. However, these were not appropriate here due to the multi-modal nature of the time-to-open, that is a large portion of the recipients are not prone to opening the message
(2) There exist extensions to the CoxPH model that are capable of utilizing time-dependent features. Given the nature of email data, where most messages that will be opened are opened within a relatively small period, obtaining updated predictions at short intervals due to changes in time-dependent feature values is not practical

Mixture models (MM) are applicable to scenarios where there are sub-populations with different characteristics. The MM estimates the probability of each individual belonging to one of the two latent states, those who will not open and those who may open the messages. The quantity $\pi(Z_i)$ in Equation 9, therefore, represents how engaged the individual is with the email messages. A proxy method to test the existence of groups with differing engagement behaviors is to use a logistic regression model to classify the recipients into two groups - prone to opening their emails versus not - and plotting their survivor functions, as done in Figure 4. Statistical differences between the two groups can then be validated by a log-rank test, where the ranks of the survival times in the two groups are compared.

3.3 Procedure for Predicting Time-to-Event

The application scenarios discussed in the *Related Work* section as well as the work described here, all utilize the main strengths of survival analysis - modeling time-to-event data as a function of features in the presence of censoring.

To predict the time-to-event for an individual (say i), we first calculate the hazard function for that individual. This is obtained by multiplying the estimate of the global baseline hazard, found using Breslow estimator [29], with the relative hazard of that individual $[h_i(t) = h_0(t) \times \psi(X_i)]$. The individual's survival curve is then constructed as $S_i(t) = exp[-H_i(t)]$ where $H_i(t)$ is the cumulative sum of $h_i(t)$ over time t. This survivor function will be similar to the one shown in Figure 5a, but instead of characterizing the population, it would be for the individual. In the survivor function, a natural estimate of time-to-open would be to use the median survival time, typically referred to as $t(50)$, which corresponds to the time when the survival probability is 0.5. Given that the observed overall survival rates are quite high in the current scenario, due to the fact that most marketing emails are never opened, the median might not be defined if the survival curve flattens above $S(t) = 0.5$ on the

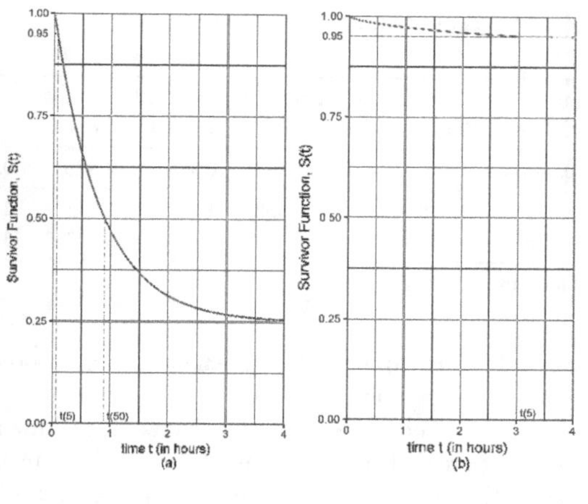

Figure 5: Two examples of survivor functions. (b) corresponds to our training data. Note that median survival time, i.e., t(50) is not defined in (b)

Y-axis, as in Figure 5b. Thus, the concept is generalized to the notion of a pth percentile such that the predicted time-to-open an email by the ith individual, is the largest t_i for which $S_i(t_i(p)) > 1 - \frac{p}{100}$ for a given percentile p. Therefore,we can have $S(t(10)) = 0.9$ and $S(t(90)) = 0.1$. Figure 5 illustrates how a time corresponding to a given survival probability threshold is identified from a survival curve. In the current paper, we evaluate a range of percentiles $p = \{5, 10, 25, 50, 75, 90\}$ as predictors of time-to-open for future emails to that recipient, and all predictions of time are made at the scale of minutes.

4 EXPERIMENTS AND RESULTS

In the earlier sections, we have described how the use case of modeling email interaction data maps to concepts in the area of survival analysis. In the current section, we evaluate the performance of a set of models on the two tasks of interest: (a) predicting the likelihood of a marketing message being opened by a recipient, and (b) estimating the time at which this event is likely to occur.

Table 2 contains the models evaluated in the current paper. The baseline for the classification task is the historical open rate of the corresponding recipient, and the corresponding time-to-open is a constant equal to the censoring window for the prediction of time-to-open. Logistic Regression is used for the "open vs not" classification task and Linear Regression is used for the time to open of emails. Models (2) – (3) were trained using an Elastic Net [41] regularization penalty to the corresponding likelihoods. Values of the hyper-parameters λ (the strength of the regularization) and α (trading off L1 vs L2) were chosen via the use of the **Validation** dataset. The equivalent parameters of the GBM - number of trees, learning rate and minimum number of observations for a leaf node - were similarly chosen.

Features: The set of features available to us are aggregates of actions that a user can take on emails, for example number of messages received, opened, clicked, and open rate in the past. We also included campaign specific information, like whether the last message was opened and/or clicked and consumer specific features like, how long the consumer has signed up for receiving these email messages. In the current paper, we primarily focused on the methodology, instead of identifying an expansive set of features. If a particular feature has good predictive signal, we expect all the models described here to benefit from it.

Table 2: List of Models

(1) **B**: Baselines
(2) **LR**: Logistic Regression (Classification)/Linear Regression (Time to Open)
(3) **CPH-L**: CoxPH Model with relative hazard, $\psi(\beta, \mathbf{X}) = exp(\beta^T X)$
(4) **CPH-G**: CoxPH Model with relative hazard, $\psi(\beta, \mathbf{X})$ from a GBM
(5) **MM**: Mixture Model with Proportional Hazards

4.1 Evaluation Metrics

For the binary prediction of whether the email will be opened within time t, we calculate the area-under-the-ROC-curve (AUC) for the probabilities calculated from the survivor function. For prediction of the time to open an email, we defined the Mean Relative Absolute Deviation (*MRAD*) between the actual value, t_i, for the time-to-open and the predicted value $\hat{t_i}$, and is given by

$$MRAD = \frac{1}{N} \sum_i \frac{|t_i - \hat{t_i}|}{t_i} \tag{13}$$

When we calculate the MRAD over all the individuals in the dataset, we refer to the resulting metric as *MRAD(A)*. We also define *MRAD(O)* as the version of the metric calculated only over the observed individuals, i.e., all the rows for which $\delta_i = 1$. For both the metrics, $\hat{t_i}$ is estimated by the value where $S_i(\hat{t_i}(p)) = 1 - \frac{p}{100}$ for a given value of p, as described in the previous section.

We compared the 5 models, as shown in Table 2 on the basis of AUC for classification of which recipients will open the messages and MRAD for time to open the messages. Higher the AUC, better the classifier, and a lower MRAD shows lesser deviance between the observed and the predicted. We now describe different sets of experiments evaluating various aspects of the models.

4.2 Comparison of Models Across Censoring Windows

We compared the different models across three different censoring windows $C_i \in \{3, 6, 12\}$ hours, using the predicted time-to-open calculated at $\hat{t_i}(5)$. Section 4.3 explores the effect of p on both AUC and MRAD for the various censoring windows. Table 3 summarizes the comparisons, and reports the results for the *best* configuration of parameters on the **Validation** set. The following observations can be made from Table 3:

(1) The separate models for each task - Logistic Regression for classification and Linear Regression for predicting time - are very compelling baselines. The benefit of jointly modeling both tasks via survival models becomes more obvious at the larger censoring windows. As discussed earlier, with $C_i = 3$ hours, ~ 57% of the actual open events are considered censored by the survival models. The noise so introduced reduces with larger choices of C_i, allowing **MM** in particular to perform well

Table 3: Comparison of the Models under AUC and MRAD across Censoring Windows

Model	Censoring Window = 3 hours					Censoring Window = 6 hours					Censoring Window = 12 hours				
	B	LR*	CPH-L	CPH-G	MM	B	LR*	CPH-L	CPH-G	MM	B	LR*	CPH-L	CPH-G	MM
AUC	0.863	0.931	0.931	**0.932**	0.929	0.870	0.939	0.939	**0.940**	0.938	0.878	0.948	0.948	**0.949**	0.948
MRAD(A)	1.226	1.332	1.085	0.941	**0.483**	2.504	1.653	1.835	1.372	**0.678**	5.079	2.332	1.707	1.572	**1.318**
MRAD(O)	26.641	**8.411**	11.953	12.217	9.499	40.602	11.706	23.245	14.788	**9.832**	62.740	17.501	19.831	28.978	**15.657**

*AUC results for LR correspond to Logistic Regression. MRAD(A) and MRAD(O) results for LR correspond to Linear Regression.

(2) Analyzing the importance of the features in our models, we find that the historical open rate is expectedly the strongest. AUC numbers when using the open rate as a predictor of a user's future open actions have also been included (**B**)
(3) **CPH-G** models non-linear relations between the features and hazard function, and as a classifier is stronger than the other models
(4) The assumptions of **MM** represent the characteristics of our data most accurately. We see that the AUC is similar to that of **CPH-L**. Note, however, that the predictions of time provided by **MM** are more accurate than the alternatives at larger C_i
(5) The MRAD(A) is much lower than the MRAD(O) as it considers the accuracy of predicting the time-to-open of the censored individuals as well, which the models do efficiently, as evidenced from the high AUC values
(6) When moving through the censoring window options ($C_i \in \{3, 6, 12\}$ hours), the classification task generally gets *easier*, as indicated by the increasing AUC values. This is because the set of observed individuals gets more complete, and separating these from the individuals that are unlikely to open the email is what the model needs to do

An additional observation from these experiments is regarding the validation metric. Across the different hyper-parameter settings, the model that had the highest AUC on the **Validation** set was chosen, instead of that with lowest MRAD. The choice of the validation metric dictates the future performance of the model - a setting chosen on the basis of higher AUC does not necessarily achieve a lower MRAD on held-out datasets compared to a parameter combination driven by MRAD. This observation indicates that there is an implicit need to pick one of the tasks as being of higher *priority* - here we have chosen the classification task to have a higher priority. Also, for the rest of the experiments in this paper, to compare models for prediction of time to open, we consider MRAD(O), instead of MRAD(A). This is because AUC already provides a comparison for classification and MRAD(O) helps to compare specifically based on those who have opened the messages.

4.3 Model Performance Across Survival Thresholds

One of the characteristics of the dataset utilized in the current paper is the high percentage of censored observations. This manifests itself in the fact that the survival curves for individuals routinely flatten well before they reach $S_i(t) = 0.5$, an illustration of this at the population level can be seen in Figure 5. Thus, across the different settings and models evaluated here, using a large value of p for $\hat{y}_i = 1 - S_i(\hat{t}_i(p))$ provides sufficient fidelity for predicting the probability of opening the email.

Table 4 describes how the MRAD(O) changes for all the models as we alter the percentile p. The column titles use the conventional notation $\hat{t}(p)$, the equivalent survival probability can be worked out readily. $\hat{t}(5)$ corresponds to the largest time when $S_i(\hat{t}_i(5)) > 0.95$. Note that the AUC values remain constant by design, and therefore are not displayed. In general, as p is reduced, since we are operating in the flatter regions of the survival curves, all $\hat{t}(p)$ become equal to the duration of the censoring window. The point at which the MRAD(O) values appear to reach the maximum is indicative of where the corresponding saturation region is in the survival plot. We would expect the corresponding MRAD(O) values to approach that of the baseline in Table 3.

In that sense, **MM** is most closely modeling the data - there is ~ 95% of the population that never opens their messages and the survival curve for **MM** arrests its drop around $p = 5$ percentile, with maximum MRAD(O) observed for all time points after that. The survival curve for **CPH-L** on the other hand seems to gradually go towards the same maximum MRAD(O), around $\hat{t}(90)$. The survival curve for **CPH-G** is in between the **MM** and **CPH-L**.

Table 4: The effect of varying the percentile p of Survivor Function on the prediction quality of the time-to-event

Censoring Window	Model	MRAD(O)					
		$\hat{t}(5)$	$\hat{t}(10)$	$\hat{t}(25)$	$\hat{t}(50)$	$\hat{t}(75)$	$\hat{t}(90)$
3 hours	CPH-L	11.952	12.608	13.929	16.744	23.462	25.716
	CPH-G	12.217	14.593	18.501	25.407	26.629	26.641
	MM	9.499	26.641	26.641	26.641	26.641	26.641
6 hours	CPH-L	23.245	17.456	18.857	19.870	27.041	34.542
	CPH-G	14.788	19.588	26.233	30.970	38.102	40.602
	MM	9.832	12.483	40.602	40.602	40.602	40.602
12 hours	CPH-L	19.831	34.632	27.229	32.510	40.356	40.750
	CPH-G	28.978	31.866	29.986	34.590	57.086	61.040
	MM	15.657	21.705	62.545	62.740	62.740	62.740

4.4 Measuring Model Stability

In this section we test the sensitivity of our models, and of the corresponding fitting processes, to variations in the data. We construct an experiment where we take bootstrap samples of the **Training** set, fit each model in turn to the datasets generated, and calculate the AUC and MRAD(O) metrics for the various models on the **Validation** set. The hyper-parameter values used were the optimal parameters for defining classification at $\hat{t}_i(5)$, same as for the results reported in Table 3. The mean and standard deviation of the metrics across the samples, for each of the four models, are shown in Table 5.

Table 5: Mean and Standard Deviation of AUC & MRAD(O) respectively on 10 boostrapped samples

Censoring Window	Model	AUC Mean	AUC StdDev	MRAD(O) Mean	MRAD(O) StdDev
3 hours	LR*	0.931	4e-5	**8.215**	0.036
	CPH-L	0.931	2e-5	13.579	1.913
	CPH-G	0.929	8e-3	13.746	0.743
	MM	0.929	3e-4	9.277	1.854
6 hours	LR*	0.939	4e-5	11.651	0.079
	CPH-L	0.939	1e-5	20.301	2.486
	CPH-G	0.939	3e-4	19.208	0.798
	MM	0.938	2e-4	**9.753**	1.194
12 hours	LR*	0.948	4e-5	17.514	0.096
	CPH-L	0.948	7e-5	38.143	3.333
	CPH-G	0.949	2e-4	29.455	1.071
	MM	0.948	2e-4	**15.444**	1.683

*AUC results for LR correspond to Logistic Regression and MRAD(O) results for LR correspond to Linear Regression.

This sampling procedure allows us to obtain proxy estimates for the confidence intervals for each metric via the standard deviation. This would be required if we were to reliably order the different models. We note that AUC in general has very low variability, and therefore, the ordering over the models on the basis of AUC is reliably stable. MRAD(O) on the other hand, shows more sensitivity to input variations. This offers another reason as to why AUC might be a more appropriate metric for validation/model-selection.

The difference between the two metrics can be attributed to the fact that AUC is a ranking metric that is an aggregate over the entire list of consumers, i.e., even if the fitted model parameters across the samples were slightly different, as long as the ordering imposed by $S_i(t)$ over the dataset does not change appreciably, AUC remains the same. In contrast, MRAD is a comparison between the individual predicted ($\hat{t_i}$) and actual (t_i) time-to-open, and is expected to be more sensitive.

When comparing across the models for a given censoring window, we find that **MM** provides the lowest mean of the MRAD values, with their standard deviations being higher than that of **CPH-G**.

4.5 Out-of-Time Model Evaluation

The final set of experiments verify if the model continues being predictive into the future. To do this, we use the **Test** dataset that has been held aside up until now. We combine the **Training** and the **Validation** sets, and use this concatenated data for building the models. The parameters that are used as input are those that have been chosen via the validation process. This not only includes the hyper-parameters of the models (e.g. the λ and α for the Elastic Net based models), but also the choice of percentile p to be used for predicting time (which is the one with least MRAD(O) in Section 4.3 for each model).

Table 6: AUC and MRAD(O) for each of the models for the out-of-time dataset

Censoring Window	Model	AUC	MRAD(O)
3 hours	LR*	0.937	7.753
	CPH-L	0.937	10.009
	CPH-G	0.934	13.787
	MM	0.935	**7.381**
6 hours	LR*	0.944	10.194
	CPH-L	0.944	23.227
	CPH-G	0.940	18.339
	MM	0.942	**9.340**
12 hours	LR*	0.952	13.409
	CPH-L	0.952	29.131
	CPH-G	0.950	21.080
	MM	0.951	**11.653**

*AUC results for LR correspond to Logistic Regression and MRAD(O) results for LR correspond to Linear Regression.

The results presented in Table 6 indicate that the performance does not degrade over time. In all the models, the AUC values are high. As was seen in Section 4.3, with the right choice of the percentile p to be used for estimating the time-to-open, the Mixture Model obtains prediction accuracy that is better than the other models. Coupled with the fact that the model assumptions of **MM** aligns more closely with the characteristics of our data, we believe that designing better optimization strategies with this model would be a fruitful avenue to explore in future work.

5 DISCUSSION AND CONCLUSION

In this paper, we proposed the use of survival models for the problems of predicting if a recipient will open an email or not, and estimating the corresponding time-to-open. We have provided a step by step procedure to check model assumptions using statistical tests. These tests help to determine whether the models that we have compared are meaningful for the data that we have. We have then performed a thorough experimental comparison of the models. Since a large proportion of emails are not opened, the median time-to-open is not defined and hence cannot be used as the estimate of future time-to-open. We therefore tested our models for various percentiles and the 5th percentile is found to be the best predictor for time-to-open.

Across our experiments, it was observed that for the task of predicting if an individual will open the email or not, a traditional classification based model (here, Logistic Regression) is a strong baseline. Survival analysis based models achieve similar accuracy to the classifier when predicting the event. While the linear regression is a strong baseline for predicting time when the censoring window is 3 hours, the proposed survival analysis performs best with the addition of new data when the censoring window is larger. Focusing on marketing email messages, we observe that a large fraction ($\sim$ 90%) of emails do not get opened (even after 10 days), owing to the fact that certain recipients are inclined to ignore such messaging. This characteristic is not commonly encountered in applications of survival analysis. Given data of this nature, a mixture model that allows for individuals to have very low predispositions to experiencing the event (here, opening the email) was explored. This differential modeling of sub-populations was done in association with a Proportional Hazards assumption and was shown to be most effective. As future extensions to our work, we plan to derive a regularization framework for the mixture model, which promises to be more effective specially when the model includes a large number of features with correlations between them.

ACKNOWLEDGMENTS

We thank Frederic Mary in Adobe Product Management for his insights, and anonymous reviewers for their constructive feedback.

REFERENCES

[1] Sattar Ameri, Mahtab J. Fard, Ratna B. Chinnam, and Chandan K. Reddy. 2016. Survival Analysis Based Framework for Early Prediction of Student Dropouts. In *Proceedings of the 25th ACM International on Conference on Information and Knowledge Management (CIKM '16)*. ACM, New York, NY, USA, 903–912. https://doi.org/10.1145/2983323.2983351

[2] Nicola Barbieri, Fabrizio Silvestri, and Mounia Lalmas. 2016. Improving post-click user engagement on native ads via survival analysis. In *Proceedings of the 25th International Conference on World Wide Web*. International World Wide Web Conferences Steering Committee, 761–770.

[3] André Bonfrer and Xavier Drèze. 2009. Real-time evaluation of e-mail campaign performance. *Marketing Science* 28, 2 (2009), 251–263.

[4] Samuel Branders, Roberto D'Ambrosio, and Pierre Dupont. 2015. A mixture Cox-Logistic model for feature selection from survival and classification data. *arXiv preprint arXiv:1502.01493* (2015).

[5] Harry B Burke, Philip H Goodman, David B Rosen, Donald E Henson, John N Weinstein, Frank E Harrell, Jeffrey R Marks, David P Winchester, and David G Bostwick. 1997. Artificial neural networks improve the accuracy of cancer survival prediction. *Cancer* 79, 4 (1997), 857–862.

[6] D Chaffey. 2009. Mint.com used StrongMail Influencer to create this viral program. http://www.strongmail.com/pdf/sm_casestudy_mint.pdf. (2009).

[7] Sunandan Chakraborty, Filip Radlinski, Milad Shokouhi, and Paul Baecke. 2014. On Correlation of Absence Time and Search Effectiveness. In *Proceedings of the 37th International ACM SIGIR Conference on Research & Development in Information Retrieval (SIGIR '14)*. ACM, New York, NY, USA, 1163–1166. https://doi.org/10.1145/2600428.2609535

[8] Anurat Chapanond, Mukkai S Krishnamoorthy, and Bülent Yener. 2005. Graph theoretic and spectral analysis of Enron email data. *Computational & Mathematical Organization Theory* 11, 3 (2005), 265–281.

[9] Gordon V. Cormack. 2008. Email Spam Filtering: A Systematic Review. In *Foundations and Trends in Information Retrieval*, Vol. 1.

[10] DR Cox. 1972. Regression models and life tables. *Journal of the Royal Statistical Society* 34 (1972), 187–220.

[11] Laura Dabbish, Gina Venolia, and JJ Cadiz. 2003. Marked for Deletion: An Analysis of Email Data. In *CHI '03 Extended Abstracts on Human Factors in Computing Systems (CHI EA '03)*. ACM, New York, NY, USA, 924–925. https://doi.org/10.1145/765891.766073

[12] Vachik S Dave, Mohammad Al Hasan, and Chandan K Reddy. 2017. How Fast Will You Get a Response? Predicting Interval Time for Reciprocal Link Creation.. In *ICWSM*. 508–511.

[13] Dursun Delen, Glenn Walker, and Amit Kadam. 2005. Predicting breast cancer survivability: a comparison of three data mining methods. *Artificial intelligence in medicine* 34, 2 (2005), 113–127.

[14] Dotan Di Castro, Zohar Karnin, Liane Lewin-Eytan, and Yoelle Maarek. 2016. You've Got Mail, and Here is What You Could Do With It!: Analyzing and Predicting Actions on Email Messages. In *Proceedings of the Ninth ACM International Conference on Web Search and Data Mining (WSDM '16)*. ACM, New York, NY, USA, 307–316. https://doi.org/10.1145/2835776.2835811

[15] Tim Drye, Graham Wetherill, and Alison Pinnock. 2001. When are customers in the market? Applying survival analysis to marketing challenges. *Journal of Targeting, Measurement and Analysis for Marketing* 10, 2 (2001), 179–188.

[16] Nicolas Ducheneaut and Victoria Bellotti. 2001. E-mail as habitat: an exploration of embedded personal information management. *interactions* 8, 5 (2001), 30–38.

[17] Miles Efron. 2012. Query-specific recency ranking: Survival analysis for improved microblog retrieval. In *Proceedings of the TAIA-12 Workshop associated to SIGIR-12*. Citeseer.

[18] Vern T Farewell. 1982. The use of mixture models for the analysis of survival data with long-term survivors. *Biometrics* (1982), 1041–1046.

[19] Patricia M Grambsch and Terry M Therneau. 1994. Proportional hazards tests and diagnostics based on weighted residuals. *Biometrika* (1994), 515–526.

[20] Eric Horvitz, Andy Jacobs, and David Hovel. 1999. Attention-sensitive Alerting. In *Proceedings of the Fifteenth Conference on Uncertainty in Artificial Intelligence (UAI'99)*. Morgan Kaufmann Publishers Inc., San Francisco, CA, USA, 305–313. http://dl.acm.org/citation.cfm?id=2073796.2073831

[21] Anjuli Kannan, Karol Kurach, Sujith Ravi, Tobias Kaufmann, Andrew Tomkins, Balint Miklos, Greg Corrado, László Lukács, Marina Ganea, Peter Young, and Vivek Ramavajjala. 2016. Smart Reply: Automated Response Suggestion for Email. *CoRR* abs/1606.04870 (2016). http://arxiv.org/abs/1606.04870

[22] Edward L Kaplan and Paul Meier. 1958. Nonparametric estimation from incomplete observations. *Journal of the American statistical association* 53, 282 (1958), 457–481.

[23] Thomas Karagiannis and Milan Vojnovic. 2009. Behavioral Profiles for Advanced Email Features. In *Proceedings of the 18th International Conference on World Wide Web (WWW '09)*. ACM, New York, NY, USA, 711–720. https://doi.org/10.1145/1526709.1526805

[24] Bryan Klimt and Yiming Yang. 2004. *The Enron Corpus: A New Dataset for Email Classification Research*. Springer Berlin Heidelberg, Berlin, Heidelberg, 217–226. https://doi.org/10.1007/978-3-540-30115-8_22

[25] V. Kumar, Xi (Alan) Zhang, and Anita Luo. 2014. Modeling Customer Opt-In and Opt-Out in a Permission-Based Marketing Context. *Journal of Marketing Research* 51, 4 (2014), 403–419. https://doi.org/10.1509/jmr.13.0169 arXiv:http://dx.doi.org/10.1509/jmr.13.0169

[26] Matthew Lease, Vitor R. Carvalho, and Emine Yilmaz. 2011. Crowdsourcing for Search and Data Mining. *SIGIR Forum* 45, 1 (May 2011), 18–24. https://doi.org/10.1145/1988852.1988856

[27] Jeong-Yoon Lee, Hang Zhang, and Valery A Petrushin. 2012. Survival Analysis for Marketing. https://pdfs.semanticscholar.org/2360/bb9ea10622c8c21595ade8f43cc237aac230.pdf. (2012). [Online; accessed 15-March-2017].

[28] Yan Li, Jie Wang, Jieping Ye, and Chandan K Reddy. 2016. A multi-task learning formulation for survival analysis. In *Proceedings of the 22nd ACM SIGKDD International Conference on Knowledge Discovery and Data Mining*. ACM, 1715–1724.

[29] DY Lin. 2007. On the Breslow estimator. *Lifetime Data Analysis* 13, 4 (2007), 471–480.

[30] Junxiang Lu and O Park. 2003. Modeling customer lifetime value using survival analysisâĂŤan application in the telecommunications industry. *Data Mining Techniques* (2003), 120–128.

[31] Kanika Narang, Susan T. Dumais, Nick Craswell, Dan Liebling, and Qingyao Ai. 2017. Large-Scale Analysis of Email Search and Organizational Strategies. In *Proceedings of the 2017 Conference on Conference Human Information Interaction and Retrieval (CHIIR '17)*. ACM, New York, NY, USA, 215–223. https://doi.org/10.1145/3020165.3020175

[32] Rajesh Ranganath, Adler Perotte, Noémie Elhadad, and David Blei. 2016. Deep Survival Analysis. In *Proceedings of the 1st Machine Learning for Healthcare Conference*. 101–114.

[33] Greg Ridgeway. 1999. The State of Boosting. (1999).

[34] G Tsirulnik. 2011. British Airways mobile email campaign garners 250K app downloads. http://www.mobilemarketer.com/ex/mobilemarketer/cms/news/email/9056.html. (2011).

[35] Shar VanBoskirk, CS Overby, and S Takvorian. 2011. US interactive marketing forecast 2011 to 2016, Forrester Research. (2011).

[36] Jian Wang and Yi Zhang. 2013. Opportunity model for e-commerce recommendation: right product; right time. In *Proceedings of the 36th international ACM SIGIR conference on Research and development in information retrieval*. ACM, 303–312.

[37] Ping Wang, Yan Li, and Chandan K Reddy. 2017. Machine Learning for Survival Analysis: A Survey. *Comput. Surveys* (2017).

[38] D Wells. 2016. Email marketing statistics 2017. http://www.smartinsights.com/email-marketing/email-communications-strategy/statistics-sources-for-email-marketing/. (2016).

[39] Steve Whittaker and Candace Sidner. 1996. Email overload: exploring personal information management of email. In *Proceedings of the SIGCHI conference on Human factors in computing systems*. ACM, 276–283.

[40] Liu Yang, Susan Dumais, Paul Bennett, and Ahmed Hassan Awadallah. 2017. Characterizing and Predicting Enterprise Email Reply Behavior. In *Proceedings of the 40th Annual International ACM SIGIR Conference on Research and Development in Information Retrieval (SIGIR 2017)*. ACM.

[41] Hui Zou and Trevor Hastie. 2005. Regularization and variable selection via the elastic net. *Journal of the Royal Statistical Society: Series B (Statistical Methodology)* 67, 2 (2005), 301–320.

Shortcutting Label Propagation for Distributed Connected Components

Stergios Stergiou*
Google
Mountain View, CA, USA
utopcell@google.com

Dipen Rughwani
Yahoo Research
Sunnyvale, CA, USA
dipen@yahoo-inc.com

Kostas Tsioutsiouliklis
Yahoo Research
Sunnyvale, CA, USA
kostas@yahoo-inc.com

ABSTRACT

Connected Components is a fundamental graph mining problem that has been studied for the PRAM, MapReduce and BSP models. We present a simple CC algorithm for BSP that does not mutate the graph, converges in $O(\log n)$ supersteps and scales to graphs of trillions of edges.

KEYWORDS

connected components, label propagation, LPSC, graph algorithms, distributed systems

ACM Reference Format:

Stergios Stergiou, Dipen Rughwani, and Kostas Tsioutsiouliklis. 2018. Shortcutting Label Propagation for Distributed Connected Components. In *WSDM 2018: WSDM 2018: The Eleventh ACM International Conference on Web Search and Data Mining , February 5–9, 2018, Marina Del Rey, CA, USA.* ACM, New York, NY, USA, 8 pages. https://doi.org/10.1145/3159652.3159696

1 INTRODUCTION

Computing connected components of a graph lies at the core of many data mining algorithms and is a fundamental operation in graph clustering. Sequentially, connectivity can be solved optimally in linear time using breadth-first or depth-first traversals. The problem has been studied extensively in the past in the parallel context [3, 5, 10, 16, 17, 19, 21, 25, 28, 30, 32, 35, 37, 39, 41, 43, 45, 46, 49]. Algorithms have been presented for shared-memory CPUs [6, 7, 29, 40, 44, 47, 54], distributed memory systems [8, 13, 14, 38] and GPUs [9, 27, 55]. Many polylogarithimic-depth parallel connectivity algorithms have also been proposed [18, 22–24, 48, 50]. In [53], a particularly efficient, albeit $O(\log^3 n)$-depth single-machine algorithm is presented that can compute CCs on graphs of 500 million edges in a few seconds. Perhaps the most influential works in parallel CCs are [4, 52]. More recently, very large-scale CC algorithms have been proposed [36, 42]. In particular, [36] reports results on graphs of up to 550 billion edges. However the reported algorithms are either presented on impractical models (such as PRAM), for single machines, or require new graphs to be generated after each iteration. In this paper we present an algorithm for the BSP model that converges in $O(\log n)$ supersteps, which is optimum and does not mutate the input graph, which allows us to scale to graphs of trillions of edges. We compare against many published algorithms [33, 34, 36, 42, 51] and report many orders of magnitude speedups while also scaling to graph sizes never before reported.

*work done while author was with Yahoo Research

WSDM 2018, February 5–9, 2018, Marina Del Rey, CA, USA

ACM ISBN 978-1-4503-5581-0/18/02...$15.00
https://doi.org/10.1145/3159652.3159696

2 GRAPH PROCESSING FRAMEWORK

The proposed algorithm is implemented on Hronos, a Yahoo proprietary in-memory / secondary-storage hybrid graph processing system, developed in C++11 on top of Hadoop MapReduce. Hronos has been used for many internal applications and has provided significant speedups for classic Machine Learning algorithms [56]. Graph nodes, and their related information including edges, are randomly placed on a set of partitions. Node-related state is maintained in memory, while the graph itself, specifically a serialization of the edges, can either be stored in memory or on disk. Messages originating from a source process are transparently buffered before being sent to target processes, with buffering occurring separately for each target partition. Each message contains an application-specific payload. The framework can optionally [de]compress buffers on-the-fly, transparently to the application. Communication across partitions is performed via a large clique of unidirectional point-to-point message queues.

The system builds on the following low-level communication primitives: clique communication for graph level computations; and one-to-all and all-to-one communication for partition-level computations. It implements loading and storing of vertex information through which it supports fault tolerance via check-pointing. Computation proceeds in supersteps. Each superstep is executed as a sequence of three primitives: a one-to-all communication primitive that sends initialization parameters to all peers, a clique communication primitive that transmits edge messages, and an all-to-one communication primitive that gathers partition-level results from the peers to the master partition. Within each superstep, each partition independently sends/receives messages to/from other partitions. Messages towards a particular node can either be unidirectional, or optionally request callback information from that node. The superstep completes when all sent messages have been processed and all partitions have signaled termination.

3 PROPOSED ALGORITHM

Let $G = (V, E)$ be an undirected graph on $n = |V|$ nodes and $m = |E|$ edges. We assume that nodes are totally ordered; for simplicity of presentation, $V = \{1, \ldots, n\}$. Let $N(v) = \{u|(v, u) \in E\}$ be the neighbors of v and $N^+(v) = N(v) \cup \{v\}$. Let Δ (diameter) be the length of the longest shortest path between any two nodes in the graph. Let $l_i : V \rightarrow V, i \in \mathbb{N}$ be functions on V, or labels associated with nodes, where $l_0(v) = v, \forall v \in V$ is the identity function. The Connected Components (CC) problem aims to assign labels $c(v)$ to each node $v \in V$ such that $c(u) = c(v)$ if and only if a path exists between u and v.

Simple graph traversal (for instance, breadth–first traversal) solves CC in $O(m)$ time in the sequential case: While there exists an unvisited node v, a breadth-first traversal starts from v and propagates its label $l_0(v)$ to all nodes reachable from v. This algorithm suggests a similar parallel algorithm called *label propagation (LP)*: At each iteration i, each node v independently and concurrently updates its label $l_i(v)$ to the minimum label among itself or its neighbors in the previous iteration: $\forall v \in V : l_i(v) = \min\{l_{i-1}(u) | u \in N^+(v)\}$.

While the sequential algorithm is optimum, LP examines every edge in the graph at each iteration and there can be up to Δ iterations before convergence. For example, consider its behavior on the following graph.

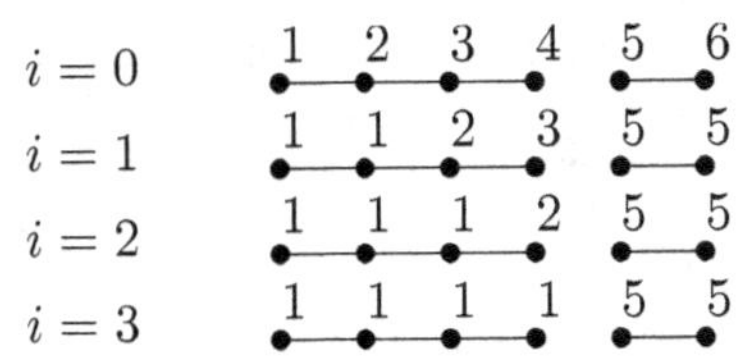

In graphs where Δ is small, LP is very efficient. However, as Δ can be $\Theta(n)$, LP is not generally a practical algorithm, especially for models of computation such as MapReduce where the startup cost for each iteration is high.

Let us consider the following graph mutating operation. At each iteration, each node v adds edges (u_1, u_2) for all nodes $u_1 \in N(v), u_2 \in N(v)$. In essence, every path (u_1, v, u_2) of length 2 is shortened to a direct edge between u_1 and u_2. Clearly the nodes in a connected component will form a clique after at most $\lceil \log n \rceil$ iterations. A single LP iteration will then suffice to label all the nodes in the connected component with the smallest label in it. This classic operation is called *path halving* or *pointer jumping* [31]. It allows us to bound the number of iterations to $O(\log n)$, which is optimum, but it does so at a significant cost: In the worst case, the resulting graph will contain $\Theta(n^2)$ edges, while iterations will become progressively slower. Moreover, even if the number of edges did not increase prohibitively, mutating the graph itself is a costly operation, because it either requires that the graph is maintained in memory (for BSP) or that a new graph is generated at every iteration (MapReduce.) For example, observe the behavior of path halving on the line graph of 8 nodes on Figure 1. While the number of required iterations for convergence reduces from 7 to 3, the resulting graph contains $\binom{8}{2}$ edges, up from 7.

Following, we will construct an algorithm that solves CC and has the following desirable properties: (1) it converges in $O(\log n)$ iterations; and (2) it only performs a single linear scan over the edges of the graph per iteration, without mutating it. The first property allows us to minimize the iterations initialization cost as well as the communication cost. The second property is more crucial: Linear scans from secondary storage are very efficient (in stark contrast to random disk accesses.) Therefore we can maintain the graph

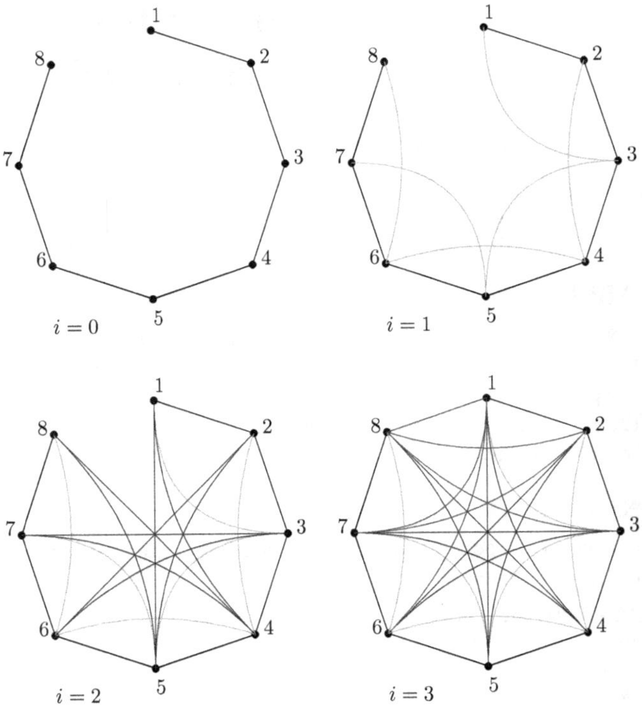

Figure 1: Path halving on a line graph.

on disk, which in turn allows us to scale CC to significantly larger graph instances than those reported in the literature.

The proposed algorithm is presented on Algorithm 1. It interleaves two supersteps until convergence. The first step is the equivalent of label propagation, executed in a manner that allows the graph edges to be processed sequentially. The second step modifies the node labels such that at most $O(\log n)$ label propagation iterations will suffice for convergence.

First, let us examine the PROPAGATE superstep which corresponds to LP. Instead of requiring that each node v queries its neighbors for their label, we simply send its current label $l(v)$ to all nodes in $N(v)$. When a node u receives a label message m from a neighbor, it updates its label to the minimum of its current value and m. Before examining the second superstep, let us show that the algorithm correctly identifies the connected components of a graph.

THEOREM 3.1. *Algorithm 1 assigns unique labels for each connected component in the graph.*

PROOF. Les us assume that graph G is comprised of k connected components $cc_j \subset V, j = 1..k$. Initially each node is assigned a unique label. Let m_j be the minimum label among all nodes in cc_j. The first superstep simulates a Breadth-First traversal starting from the nodes associated with labels m_j. For each connected component j, after at most i iterations, all nodes reachable with paths of length i from the node associated with label m_j, will update their label to m_j. Note that the second superstep never increases any of the labels. Additionally, none of the labels m used to update $l(u)$ on Line 22 correspond to a node outside the respective connected component

Algorithm 1 LABEL PROPAGATION WITH SHORT CUTTING

```
1: function LPSC(G)
2:     ∀v ∈ V : l'(v) ← v
3:     repeat
4:         l ← l'
5:         PROPAGATE(G, l, l')                    ▷ label propagation
6:         SHORTCUT(G, l, l')                     ▷ short cutting
7:     until l = l'
8:     return l
9: superstep PROPAGATE(G, l, l')
10:    for all (u, v) ∈ E do
11:        send l(u) to v
12:    for all received messages m to u do
13:        l'(u) = min(l'(u), m)
14: superstep SHORTCUT(G, l, l')
15:    for all u ∈ V do                          ▷ send messages
16:        if l'(u) < l(u) then
17:            send l'(u) to l(u)
18:        request l(l'(u)) from l'(u)            ▷ send requests
19:    for all requests from v to u do            ▷ receive requests
20:        send l(u) to v
21:    for all messages m to u do                 ▷ receive messages
22:        l'(u) = min(l'(u), m)
```

of u. Therefore their values will always be at least m_j for all nodes in cc_j. □

Let us now examine the behavior of the SHORTCUT superstep. Initially, labels $l(v) = v$. During the execution of the algorithm, $l(v)$ is either decreasing or stays the same. Therefore, at any given point, a sequence of nodes $v, l(v), l(l(v)), \cdots, u$ will never repeat itself because of the invariant $v \geq l(v)$. We formulate the directed *parent graph* $G_p = (V, E')$ where E' contains all edges of the form $(v, l(v))$. Each node has a single outgoing edge towards its "parent" node, and as shown before, the graph is cycle-free (ignoring self-loops.) Therefore G_p is a forest graph. Before convergence, the nodes of each connected component on the graph form a set of trees. After convergence, each connected component will correspond to a star (a single tree of height 1.)

The SHORTCUT superstep performs a dual role. First, it performs pointer jumping on G_p towards nodes with smaller labels (on Lines 18, 20 and 22.) In a single iteration, pointer jumping can reduce the height of a tree of height h to $\lceil h/2 \rceil$. Therefore, an individual tree will be converted into a star in at most $\lceil \log n \rceil$ iterations. Second, whenever the label of a node v gets updated to a smaller value $l'(v)$, node v informs its previous parent $l(v)$ of the new value (on Lines 17 and 22.) Trees are connected through edges on the original graph, and therefore are merged together via PROPAGATE. Specifically, for a given edge $(u, v) \in E$, the subtree rooted at $l(u)$ will be attached to $l(v)$ if $l(v) < l(u)$ at some point during the execution of the algorithm. Following, we show that $O(\log n)$ iterations suffice for converting all trees to stars in the presence of tree mergings.

THEOREM 3.2. *Algorithm 1 converges in $O(\log n)$ iterations.*

PROOF. Let us consider the path that is followed by the algorithm that connects an arbitrary node v to the root node r of its connected component. As the sequence of labels $l(v)$ of v is decreasing, the length of the path is bounded by n. Edges in E' are solid, while edges in E that are exercised by the algorithm are dashed.

All contiguous solid edges subpaths will be reduced to stars in at most $\lceil \log n \rceil$ iterations. During these iterations, dashed edges may be exercised, leading to merging of the corresponding trees. In the worst case, such tree merges will be delayed at most until all trees have been converted to stars. At that point, a single tree will be formed of depth at most n (since there can only be at most n trees.) An additional $\lceil \log n \rceil$ iterations are sufficient for converting this tree to a star. □

Following, we bound the number of messages processed by the algorithm until convergence.

THEOREM 3.3. *Algorithm 1 processes $O((m + n) \log n)$ messages until convergence.*

PROOF. Superstep PROPAGATE processes $O(m)$ messages while superstep SHORTCUT processes $O(n)$ messages and the algorithm converges in $O(\log n)$ iterations. □

Figure 2 depicts an example graph with G_p presented at the beginning of the algorithm, and after each superstep of all iterations until convergence. We observe that initially, the single connected component is represented by 9 single-node trees. After the first PROPAGATE, the same connected component is represented by two trees that include nodes $\{3, 4, 5, 6, 7, 20\}$ and $\{8, 10, 15\}$ respectively. At convergence, a single star represents the connected component.

3.1 Optimizations

3.1.1 Redundant Messages. We observe that sending label $l(u)$ from node u to node v (Line 11 on Algorithm 1) can reduce $l'(v)$ (Line 13) only if the label of node u has itself been reduced compared to the previous iteration. Otherwise, any possible effect of $l(u)$ to the label of node v has already occurred in the previous iteration. Therefore, we only send messages on Line 11 when $l(u)$ has decreased. This optimization has a significant impact on execution times, especially during the later iterations of the algorithm in which most nodes in a connected component have already detected their minimum label.

3.1.2 Label Bucketing. Let us examine the behavior of LP on a line graph of n nodes, where nodes have been assigned sequential ids.

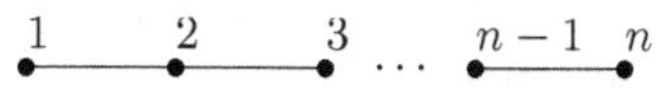

The algorithm will converge in $n - 1$ iterations. However, many redundant label updates will be performed. In our example, node i will be updated $i - 1$ times before it reaches its final value. If the algorithm knew beforehand the set S of minimum labels corresponding to each of the connected components in the graph, it would be possible to restrict propagation (i.e. message sending on Line 11 on Algorithm 1) only to nodes whose labels are in S. Although this is not possible, it would be meaningful to assume that

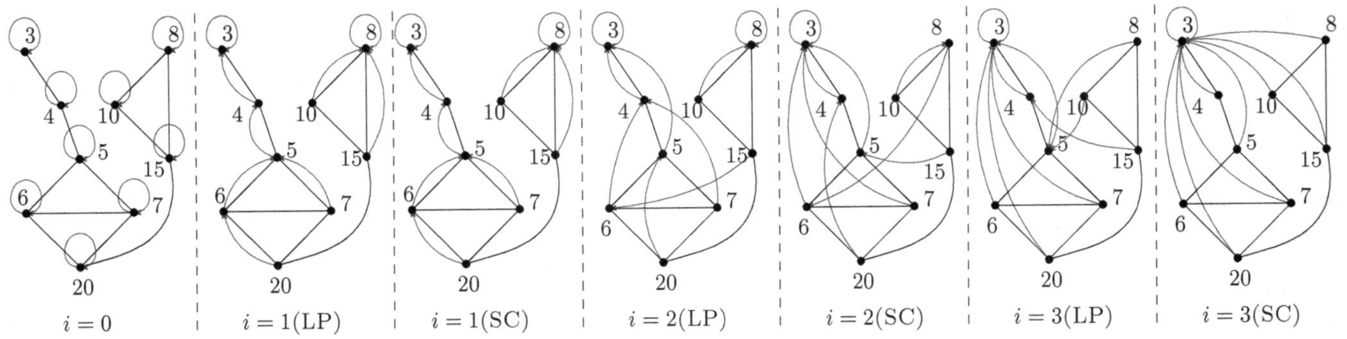

Figure 2: Supersteps of the proposed algorithm on a simple graph of 9 nodes. Initially, the single CC is covered by 9 single-node trees. After the first superstep, the trees are reduced to 2. After convergence, graph G_p is a single rooted star. Note that *SC* at $i = 1$ never alters G_p since pointer jumping occurs via l (Lines 18 and 20.) The algorithm remains valid even if l' is used instead.

S has a larger overlap with the set of k smallest labels compared with a random subset of k labels. In this optimization, we run the proposed algorithm twice: once restricting propagation to a small subset of the smallest labels B, and once afterwards without any restrictions. In our example, where $S = \{1\}$, B could be set to $\{1, 2\}$, which reduces the total number of label updates to $2n - 3$ instead of $\binom{n}{2}$.

3.1.3 Label Ordering by Node Degree. Let us examine the behavior of LP for large degree nodes (for example, node 4 on the following graph.)

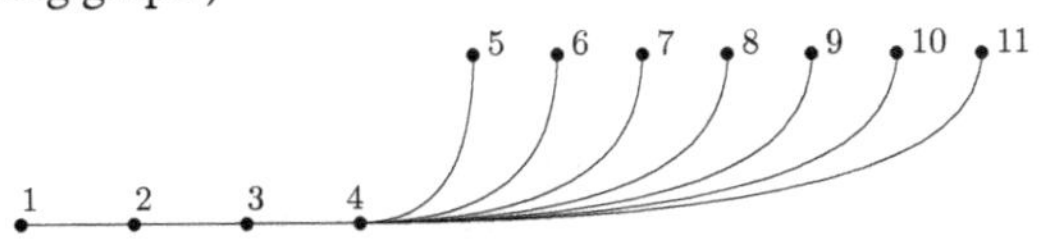

In all iterations until node 4 detects the minimum label, it will be propagating its current label to its neighbors. While this propagation happens for all nodes, it is particularly expensive for large-degree nodes. This optimization sorts nodes non-increasingly according to their degree and assigns initial labels in this order. Following is a possible assignment of labels for the example graph.

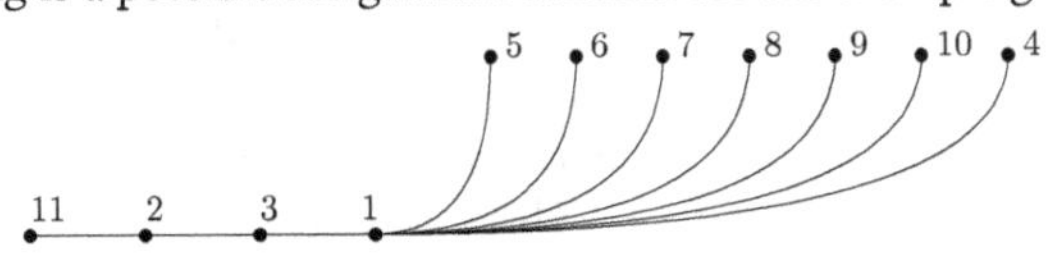

While this optimization seems promising, we have not investigated its impact on our algorithm and is presented here as future work.

3.1.4 Label Request Aggregation at Source. Algorithm 1, as presented, contains a bottleneck. Let us assume than the largest component on the input graph contains $\Theta(n)$ nodes. As the algorithm progresses, and the nodes in G_p form a star rooted at the node v with the smallest label, there will be $\Theta(n)$ request messages towards v on Line 18. Although the total number of requests is always $O(n)$, in this case the majority of these requests will be sent towards a single partition (the partition that contains node v) and thus, the algorithm is serialized at that point.

We realize that this weakness can in fact be converted to an advantage for the proposed algorithm by performing the following optimization: We modify the algorithm to only send out requests for each unique $l'(u)$ on Line 18. We also maintain a list of nodes for each unique request target, that are updated as soon as the response (sent on Line 20) arrives. Consequently, only $O(p)$ request messages will be sent towards node v instead of $\Theta(n)$, where $p \ll n$ is the number of partitions.

3.1.5 Large in-Degree Node Detection. We realize that request aggregations are only necessary for root nodes of large in-degree in G_p. Ideally we would like to apply aggregation only for those nodes. However, without global synchronization information, each partition does not know which are the large in-degree nodes on other partitions. Nevertheless, since nodes are randomly distributed across partitions, edges of the form (v, r) in G_p will also be randomly distributed among the p partitions. Therefore, it suffices to detect the most frequent targets within each partition and apply request aggregation only for those. However, computing target frequencies requires $O(|uniqueTargets|)$ memory. Instead, we detect all targets that cross a particular local frequency threshold, by adopting a heavy hitters algorithm [12, 20]. Specifically, before executing superstep SHORTCUT at each iteration, we detect the k (at most) targets whose frequency exceeds n_p/k locally in each partition, where n_p is the number of nodes in partition p, and apply request aggregation only for those. Heavy hitters is an efficient linear algorithm that requires $O(k)$ memory and $O(n_p)$ time.

4 EXPERIMENTAL RESULTS

We report experimental results for the graphs on Table 1. R-Mat graphs are synthetic power-law graphs [15] while Twitter [2], UK [11], BTC [26] and CommonCrawl [1] are publicly available real-world graphs. The Yahoo graph is a subset of Yahoo's web graph. All graphs are converted to bidirectional graphs: for every edge (u, v), edges (u, v) and (v, u) are added and duplicate edges are removed. All results are collected on a shared cluster of 128GB RAM, Intel Xeon CPU E5-2620 v2 nodes (2x 12 cores) and 10Gbps interconnect. We note that due to the large number of experiments and their long execution times, average load on the cluster may vary, affecting execution times by a small factor.

We compare with algorithms AltOpt [36], CCF [34], Cracker [42], Hash2Min [51] and Pegasus [33], as implemented in Spark by

Table 1: Graphs

graph	nodes	edges
rMat22	2,394,731	130,289,234
rMat24	8,859,723	526,329,896
rMat26	32,762,582	2,119,388,092
rMat28	121,061,651	8,515,740,646
rMat30	447,070,684	34,164,226,400
rMat32	1,642,244,247	136,975,171,827
rMat34	6,004,895,462	548,797,112,715
Twitter	52,579,682	3,228,213,000
UK	131,837,068	9,694,060,460
BTC	303,152,123	1,682,860,224
CC2012	3,443,082,320	227,193,341,978
Yahoo	272,070,468,294	5,922,604,696,718

the authors of [42]. We also compare with our own Hadoop MapReduce implementation of AltOpt [36]. Results for these algorithms are presented on Table 3. Execution times are faster than what is reported in [42]. We believe this is due to the fact that they collected their results on a small cluster with 1Gbps interconnect. We observe that Cracker is relatively faster and is the only algorithm able to complete on rMat30 within the allotted 3 hour limit. However, we can already detect their limits. None of these algorithms was able to complete on the larger rMat graphs or on the CC2012, the largest publicly available web graph.

We report results for Algorithm 1 on Table 2. In our case, we limit resources to only 100 workers for graphs with fewer than 100 billion edges, 1000 workers for graphs with up to 1 trillion edges and 5000 workers for the Yahoo web graph. To the best of our knowledge, no other algorithm has been demonstrated to work on graphs of trillions of edges. We report results without using the bucket heuristic and with using a 0.01% bucket size. We complete rMat30 in 178" and rMat34 in 537". rMat34 is the largest graph on which [36] report results. While no absolute execution times are presented in [36], they report that their algorithm completes in a couple hours using several hundreds of cluster nodes (ie thousands of workers.) Our algorithm completes in 341" for CC2012 and in 3808" for the Yahoo web graph.

Table 2: Results for Algorithm 1

graph	P	I	$T_{100\%}$ (sec)	$T_{0.01\%}$ (sec)
rMat22	100	5	1.72	1.32
rMat24	100	5	6.48	4.46
rMat26	100	5	28.26	19.66
rMat28	100	5	80.21	55.85
rMat30	100	5	328.61	177.73
rMat32	1000	6	215.01	139.87
rMat34	1000	6	784.55	536.95
Twitter	100	6	23.48	20.6
UK	100	21	108.47	94.5
BTC	100	14	89.79	42.7
CC2012	1000	13	475.89	341.44
Yahoo	5000	10	9112	3808

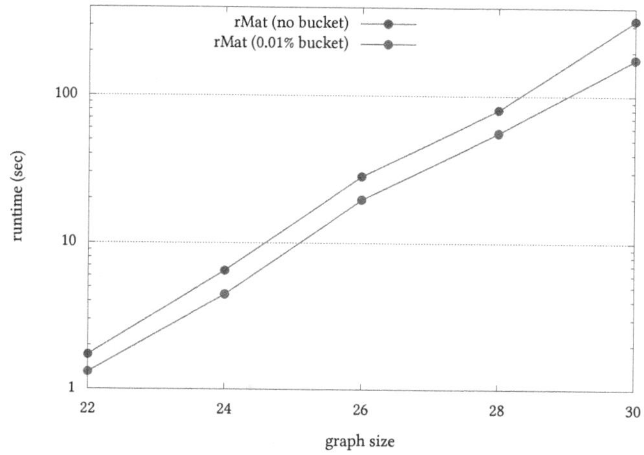

Figure 3: Log-execution times for rMat22-30

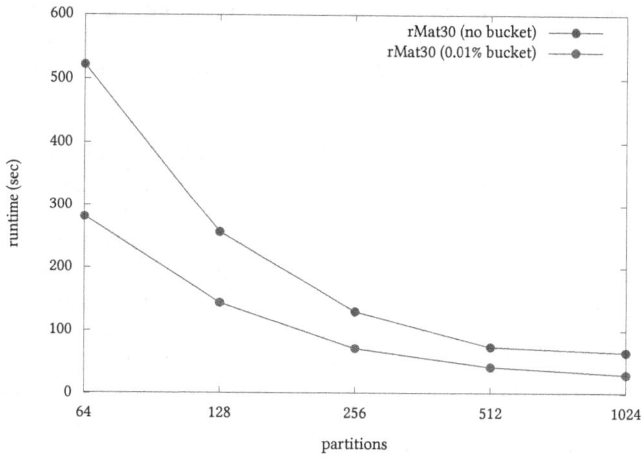

Figure 4: Runtimes for rMat30 when workers vary from 64 to 1024

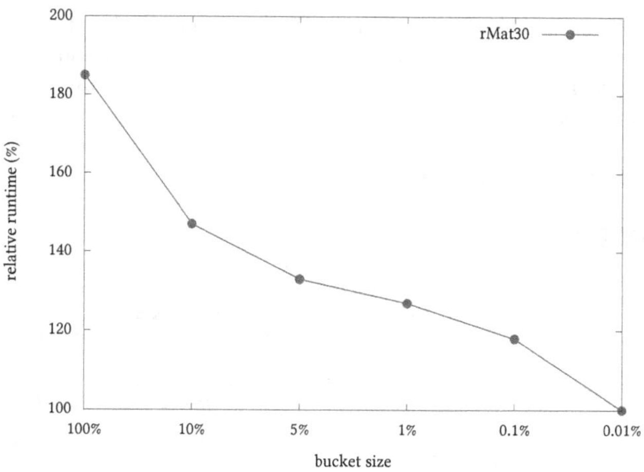

Figure 5: effect of bucket size on execution times

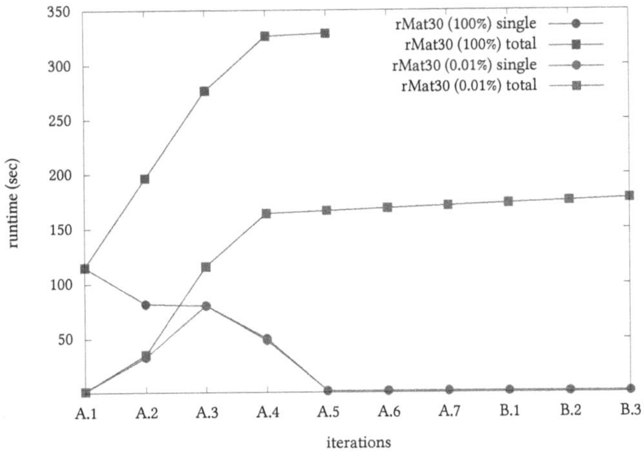

Figure 6: Individual and aggregate iteration times for rMat30, with and without the bucketing heuristic. The algorithm converges in 5 iterations without bucketing (100% bucket size) while it converges in 10 iterations split into 7 (when bucketing is used) and 3 (for the remaining nodes.)

We observe how the algorithm scales with the graph size on Figure 3. For a fixed number of 100 workers, we report execution times as the graph size increases and observe near-linear scaling. We also present results for rMat30 by varying the number of workers on Figure 4. On Figure 5, we study the effect of bucket sizing on execution times. The bucket heuristic allows for approximately 2X performance increase. On Figure 6 we present the effect of bucketing on the number of iterations. We present individual iteration times, together with aggregate times both with and without bucketing. The bucketing heuristic generally increases performance by reducing the execution times of the first few iterations, as expected. Note that the total number of iterations increases, but the later ones are typically much faster.

5 CONCLUSION

In this work, we presented a simple CC algorithm for BSP that does not mutate the graph, converges in $O(\log n)$ supersteps and scales to graphs of trillions of edges. The algorithm is practically orders of magnitude faster compared to the state of the art and is able to produce results for significantly larger graphs than previously reported in the literature.

REFERENCES

[1] 2016. Common Crawl. (2016). http://commoncrawl.org/.

[2] 2016. Twitter Graph. (2016). http://konect.uni-koblenz.de/networks/twitter_mpi.

[3] Ajit Agrawal, Lena Nekludova, and Willie Lim. 1987. *A parallel O (log N) algorithm for finding connected components in planar images.* Thinking Machines Corporation.

[4] Baruch Awerbuch and Yossi Shiloach. 1987. New connectivity and MSF algorithms for shuffle-exchange network and PRAM. *IEEE Trans. Comput.* 10, C-36 (1987), 1258–1263.

[5] Baruch Awerbuch and Tripurari Singh. 1983. New Connectivity and MSF Algorithms for Ultracomputer and PRAM.. In *ICPP*, Vol. 83. 175–179.

[6] David A Bader and Guojing Cong. 2005. A fast, parallel spanning tree algorithm for symmetric multiprocessors (SMPs). *J. Parallel and Distrib. Comput.* 65, 9 (2005), 994–1006.

[7] David A Bader, Guojing Cong, and John Feo. 2005. On the architectural requirements for efficient execution of graph algorithms. In *ICPP '05*. IEEE, 547–556.

[8] David A Bader and Joseph JáJá. 1996. Parallel algorithms for image histogramming and connected components with an experimental study. *Journal of parallel and distributed computing* 35, 2 (1996), 173–190.

[9] Dip Sankar Banerjee and Kishore Kothapalli. 2011. Hybrid algorithms for list ranking and graph connected components. In *HiPC (2011)*. IEEE, 1–10.

[10] Guy E Blelloch. 1996. Programming parallel algorithms. *Commun. ACM* 39, 3 (1996), 85–97.

[11] Paolo Boldi, Massimo Santini, and Sebastiano Vigna. 2008. A Large Time-Aware Graph. *SIGIR Forum* 42, 2 (2008), 33–38.

[12] Robert S Boyer and J Strother Moore. 1991. MJRTY-a fast majority vote algorithm. In *Automated Reasoning*. Springer, 105–117.

[13] Libor Buš and Pavel Tvrdík. 2001. A parallel algorithm for connected components on distributed memory machines. In *European Parallel Virtual Machine / Message Passing Interface Users Group Meeting*. Springer, 280–287.

[14] Edson Norberto Cáceres, Henrique Mongelli, Christiane Nishibe, and Siang Wun Song. 2010. Experimental results of a coarse-grained parallel algorithm for spanning tree and connected components. In *High Performance Computing and Simulation (HPCS), 2010*. IEEE, 631–637.

[15] Deepayan Chakrabarti, Yiping Zhan, and Christos Faloutsos. 2004. R-MAT: A recursive model for graph mining. In *Proceedings of the 2004 SIAM International Conference on Data Mining*. SIAM, 442–446.

[16] Francis Y Chin, John Lam, and I-Ngo Chen. 1982. Efficient parallel algorithms for some graph problems. *Commun. ACM* 25, 9 (1982), 659–665.

[17] Ka Wong Chong and Tak Wah Lam. 1995. Finding connected components in $O(\log n \log\log n)$ time on the EREW PRAM. *J. of Algorithms* 18, 3 (1995), 378–402.

[18] Richard Cole, Philip N Klein, and Robert E Tarjan. 1996. Finding minimum spanning forests in logarithmic time and linear work using random sampling. In *Proceedings of the eighth annual ACM symposium on Parallel algorithms and architectures*. ACM, 243–250.

[19] Richard Cole and Uzi Vishkin. 1991. Approximate parallel scheduling. II. Applications to logarithmic-time optimal parallel graph algorithms. *Information and Computation* 92, 1 (1991), 1–47.

[20] Graham Cormode and Marios Hadjieleftheriou. 2008. Finding Frequent Items in Data Streams. *Proceedings of the VLDB Endowment* 1, 2 (2008), 1530–1541.

[21] Xing Feng, Lijun Chang, Xuemin Lin, Lu Qin, and Wenjie Zhang. 2016. Computing Connected Components with linear communication cost in pregel-like systems. In *International Conference on Data Engineering (ICDE)*. IEEE, 85–96.

[22] Hillel Gazit. 1991. An optimal randomized parallel algorithm for finding connected components in a graph. *SIAM J. Comput.* 20, 6 (1991), 1046–1067.

[23] Shay Halperin and Uri Zwick. 1996. An optimal randomised logarithmic time connectivity algorithm for the EREW PRAM. *J. Comput. System Sci.* 53, 3 (1996), 395–416.

[24] Shay Halperin and Uri Zwick. 2001. Optimal randomized EREW PRAM algorithms for finding spanning forests. *Journal of Algorithms* 39, 1 (2001), 1–46.

[25] Yujie Han and Robert A Wagner. 1990. An efficient and fast parallel-connected component algorithm. *Journal of the ACM (JACM)* 37, 3 (1990), 626–642.

[26] Andreas Harth. 2009. Billion Triples Challenge data set. Downloaded from http://km.aifb.kit.edu/projects/btc-2009/. (2009).

[27] Kenneth A Hawick, Arno Leist, and Daniel P Playne. 2010. Parallel graph component labelling with GPUs and CUDA. *Parallel Comput.* 36, 12 (2010), 655–678.

[28] Daniel S. Hirschberg, Ashok K. Chandra, and Dilip V. Sarwate. 1979. Computing connected components on parallel computers. *Commun. ACM* 22, 8 (1979), 461–464.

[29] Tsan-Sheng Hsu, Vijaya Ramachandran, and Nathaniel Dean. 1997. Parallel implementation of algorithms for finding connected components in graphs. *Parallel Algorithms: Third DIMACS Implementation Challenge, October 17-19, 1994* 30 (1997), 20.

[30] Kazuo Iwama and Yahiko Kambayashi. 1994. A simpler parallel algorithm for graph connectivity. *Journal of Algorithms* 16, 2 (1994), 190–217.

[31] Joseph JáJá. 1992. *An introduction to parallel algorithms*. Addison-Wesley.

[32] Donald B Johnson and Panagiotis Metaxas. 1997. Connected components in $O(\log^{3/2} n)$ parallel time for the CREW PRAM. *J. Comput. System Sci.* 54, 2 (1997), 227–242.

[33] U Kang, Charalampos E Tsourakakis, and Christos Faloutsos. 2009. Pegasus: A peta-scale graph mining system implementation and observations. In *ICDM'09*. IEEE, 229–238.

[34] Hakan Kardes, Siddharth Agrawal, Xin Wang, and Ang Sun. 2014. Ccf: Fast and scalable connected component computation in mapreduce. In *ICNC (2014)*. IEEE, 994–998.

[35] David R Karger, Noam Nisan, and Michal Parnas. 1992. Fast connected components algorithms for the EREW PRAM. In *Proceedings of the fourth annual ACM symposium on Parallel algorithms and architectures*. ACM, 373–381.

Table 3: Experimental Results for Prior Art Algorithms

Graph	Workers	Running Time of various Algorithms											
		AltOpt		CCF		Cracker		HashToMin		Pegasus		$AltOpt_{MR}$	
		Time	Iter.*	Time	Iter.	Time	Iter.	Time	Iter.	Time	Iter.	Time	Iter.*
rMat22	10	678	4	278	5	348	4	1481	5	1887	5	454	4
	100	295	4	62	5	88	4	410	5	204	5	309	4
	256	249	4	88	5	92	4	572	5	300	5	671	4
	512	532	4	377	5	345	4	837	5	614	5	557	4
rMat24	10	1821	4	984	5	418	5	x		x		1670	4
	100	1361	4	225	5	200	5	765	5	888	5	1576	4
	256	794	4	206	5	307	5	1349	5	523	5	984	4
	512	980	4	169	5	431	5	1684	5	260	5	2014	4
	1024	1244	4	532	5	329	5	2063	5	327	5	1991	4
rMat26	100	4311	4	786	6	568	5	x		2978	6	7823	4
	256	3117	4	537	6	351	5	x		1278	6	5830	4
	512	3713	4	526	6	350	5	7231	6	1519	6	3901	4
	1024	4082	4	793	6	333	5	6865	6	393	6	5547	4
rMat28	512	x		4198	6	1487	5	x		x		x	
	1024	x		2297	6	1255	5	x		1734	6	x	
	2048	x		2311	6	1069	5	x		1176	6	x	
rMat30	2048	x		x		9915	6	x		x		x	
twitter	1024	10295	5	1195	7	487	9	9548	7	2799	13	5169	5
	2048	7544	5	2510	7	1178	9	12710	7	5593	13	4442	5
uk	1024	x		9977	20	1087	19	x		x		x	
	2048	x		9048	20	8252	19	x		x		x	
btc	100	x		x		1253	12	x		x		x	
	512	x		x		3011	12	x		x		x	
	1024	x		x		x		x		x		x	
cc2012	2048	x		x		x		x		x		x	

x – Experiment resulted in timeout (3 hours) or insufficient memory error
* – Large-Star and Small-Star are counted as one combined iteration [36]

[36] Raimondas Kiveris, Silvio Lattanzi, Vahab Mirrokni, Vibhor Rastogi, and Sergei Vassilvitskii. 2014. Connected components in mapreduce and beyond. In *Proceedings of the ACM Symposium on Cloud Computing*. ACM, 1–13.
[37] Václav Koubek and Jana Kršňáková. 1985. Parallel algorithms for connected components in a graph. In *Fund. of Computation Theory*. Springer, 208–217.
[38] Arvind Krishnamurthy, Steven Lumetta, David E Culler, and Katherine Yelick. 1997. Connected components on distributed memory machines. *Third DIMACS Implementation Challenge* 30 (1997), 1–21.
[39] Clyde P Kruskal, Larry Rudolph, and Marc Snir. 1990. Efficient parallel algorithms for graph problems. *Algorithmica* 5, 1 (1990), 43–64.
[40] Subodh Kumar, Stephen M Goddard, and Jan F Prins. 1995. Connected-Components Algorithms For Mesh-Connected Parallel Computers. In *3rd Dimacs Implementation Challenge Workshop*.
[41] Willie Lim, Ajit Agrawal, and Lena Nekludova. 1986. *A fast parallel algorithm for labeling connected components in image arrays*. Thinking Machines Corporation.
[42] Alessandro Lulli, Emanuele Carlini, Patrizio Dazzi, Claudio Lucchese, and Laura Ricci. 2017. Fast connected components computation in large graphs by vertex pruning. *IEEE Transactions on Parallel and Distributed systems* 28, 3 (2017), 760–773.
[43] Dhruva Nath and SN Maheshwari. 1982. Parallel algorithms for the connected components and minimal spanning tree problems. *Inform. Process. Lett.* 14, 1 (1982), 7–11.
[44] Donald Nguyen, Andrew Lenharth, and Keshav Pingali. 2013. A lightweight infrastructure for graph analytics. In *Proceedings of the Twenty-Fourth ACM Symposium on Operating Systems Principles*. ACM, 456–471.
[45] Noam Nisan, Endre Szemeredi, and Avi Wigderson. 1992. Undirected connectivity in $O(\log^{1.5} n)$ space. In *Foundations of Computer Science, 1992*. IEEE, 24–29.
[46] Ha-Myung Park, Namyong Park, Sung-Hyon Myaeng, and U Kang. 2016. Partition aware connected component computation in distributed systems. In *International Conference on Data Mining (2016)*. IEEE, 420–429.
[47] Md Mostofa Ali Patwary, Peder Refsnes, and Fredrik Manne. 2012. Multi-core spanning forest algorithms using the disjoint-set data structure. In *International Parallel & Distributed Processing Symposium (2012)*. IEEE, 827–835.
[48] Seth Pettie and Vijaya Ramachandran. 2002. A randomized time-work optimal parallel algorithm for finding a minimum spanning forest. *SIAM J. Comput.* 31, 6 (2002), 1879–1895.
[49] CA Philips. 1989. Parallel graph contraction. In *Proceedings of the first annual ACM symposium on Parallel algorithms and architectures*. ACM, 148–157.
[50] Chung Keung Poon and Vijaya Ramachandran. 1997. A randomized linear work EREW PRAM algorithm to find a minimum spanning forest. In *International Symposium on Algorithms and Computation*. Springer, 212–222.
[51] Vibhor Rastogi, Ashwin Machanavajjhala, Laukik Chitnis, and Anish Das Sarma. 2013. Finding connected components in map-reduce in logarithmic rounds. In *International Conference on Data Engineering (2013)*. IEEE, 50–61.
[52] Yossi Shiloach and Uzi Vishkin. 1982. An $O(\log n)$ parallel connectivity algorithm. *Journal of Algorithms* 3, 1 (1982), 57–67.
[53] Julian Shun, Laxman Dhulipala, and Guy Blelloch. 2014. A simple and practical linear-work parallel algorithm for connectivity. In *Proceedings of the 26th ACM symposium on Parallelism in algorithms and architectures*. ACM, 143–153.
[54] George M Slota, Sivasankaran Rajamanickam, and Kamesh Madduri. 2014. BFS and coloring-based parallel algorithms for strongly connected components and related problems. In *International Parallel and Distributed Processing Symposium (2014)*. IEEE, 550–559.
[55] Jyothish Soman, Kothapalli Kishore, and PJ Narayanan. 2010. A fast GPU algorithm for graph connectivity. In *International Symposium on Parallel & Distributed Processing, Workshops and PhD Forum (IPDPSW) (2010)*. IEEE, 1–8.
[56] Stergios Stergiou, Zygimantas Straznickas, Rolina Wu, and Kostas Tsioutsiouliklis. 2017. Distributed Negative Sampling for Word Embeddings. In *AAAI Conference on Artificial Intelligence (2017)*. 2569–2575.

User Intent, Behaviour, and Perceived Satisfaction in Product Search

Ning Su
DCST, Tsinghua University
Beijing, China
sn-40@163.com

Jiyin He
CWI
Amsterdam, The Netherlands
j.he@cwi.nl

Yiqun Liu*
DCST, Tsinghua University
Beijing, China
yiqunliu@tsinghua.edu.cn

Min Zhang
DCST, Tsinghua University
Beijing, China
z-m@tsinghua.edu.cn

Shaoping Ma
DCST, Tsinghua University
Beijing, China
msp@tsinghua.edu.cn

ABSTRACT

As online shopping becomes increasingly popular, users perform more product search to purchase items. Previous studies have investigated people's online shopping behaviours and ways to predict online purchases. However, from a user perspective, there still lacks an in-depth understanding of why users search, how they interact with, and perceive the product search results. In this paper, we address the following three questions: (1) what are the intents of users underlying their search activities? (2) do users behave differently under different search intents? and (3) how does user perceived satisfaction relate to their search behaviour as well as search intents, and can we predict product search satisfaction with interaction signals?

Based on an online survey and search logs collected from a major commercial product search engine, we show that user intents in product search fall into three categories: *Target Finding* (TF), *Decision Making* (DM) and *Exploration* (EP). Through a log analysis and a user study, we observe different user interaction patterns as well as perceived satisfaction under these three intents. Using a series of user interaction features, we demonstrate that we can effectively predict user satisfaction, especially for TF and DM intents.

ACM Reference Format:
Ning Su, Jiyin He, Yiqun Liu, Min Zhang, and Shaoping Ma. 2018. User Intent, Behaviour, and Perceived Satisfaction in Product Search. In *Proceedings of WSDM 2018: The Eleventh ACM International Conference on Web Search and Data Mining (WSDM 2018)*. ACM, New York, NY, USA, 9 pages. https://doi.org/10.1145/3159652.3159714

1 INTRODUCTION

Online shopping has overtaken traditional store shopping in popularity. A 2016 survey[1] shows that 54% of the shoppers worldwide buy products online weekly or monthly, and 34% agree that mobile phones have become their primary shopping devices. The search engine provided by a shopping site is one of the main entrances for its users to find specific models, brands or products to buy. In order to effectively design product search engines, it is important to understand how users interact with these systems and how this relates to their perceived system performance. Previous studies on online shopping have studied how users make online purchase decisions [30, 31]; and aimed to enhance product search engines by proposing new ranking models [25, 29]. However, there still lacks an in-depth understanding of product search from the user perspective, i.e. why users search, and how they examine and perceive the product search results.

User satisfaction, a key concept in measuring search success [21], is not yet well understood in the context of product search. Since information search is an important stage of buyer decision process [7, 32], offering result lists that satisfy users' need can increase the loyalty of users and further promote sales. While many shopping sites use purchase as a measure of user satisfaction, satisfaction is not always associated with purchase, as shown in an example search session (Table 1) below. Here user U_1 was satisfied as she found the desired product at rank 2 of the result list. Yet this did not lead to a purchase—e.g. she may decide to make the purchase later in a physical store. Further, depending on their search intents, two users issuing the same query may have very different interaction patterns and perceived satisfaction with the same search results. For instance, different from U_1 who was seeking a specific target product and satisfied after one click, U_2 wanted to investigate different price/model options, and kept exploring results while remained unsatisfied given her goal.

In summary, in the context of product search, user satisfaction depends on a variety of factors including user search intents, search result relevance, personal shopping habits, etc; and the relation between a user's perceived search satisfaction, search intent, and observable search activities can be complex and remains unclear.

Table 1: Example real world search sessions from two users who issued the query "iPhone" to a product search engine.

User	U_1	U_2
Information Need	I'm looking to buy a white iPhone 5	I'd like to investigate the most cost effective iPhone version to buy
Query	iPhone	iPhone
Rank #1 iPhone 4		click (37 sec)
Rank #2 iPhone 5	click (35 sec)	click (44 sec)
Rank #3 iPhone accessories		click (42 sec)
Satisfaction Feedback	satisfied	not satisfied
Purchase	no	no

* Corresponding author
[1] http://www.pwc.com/totalretail

WSDM 2018, February 5–9, 2018, Marina Del Rey, CA, USA

ACM ISBN 978-1-4503-5581-0/18/02...$15.00
https://doi.org/10.1145/3159652.3159714

In this paper, we focus on providing insights for the understanding of user search behaviour, and models for predicting their perceived search satisfaction in the context of product search. As mobile phones are becoming the main tools for online shopping, all the data involved is collected from mobile devices. Specifically, we aim to answer the following three research questions:

RQ1. What are the intents underlying user search activities?
RQ2. Do users behave differently under different search intents and if so, how?
RQ3. a. How does user satisfaction relate to their search behaviour and search intents? and b. Can we predict product search satisfaction with interaction signals?

With RQ1 we aim at identifying different types of user intents during product search. Based on the coding of an online survey, we propose to categorise user intents into three categories: *Target Finding* (TF), *Decision Making* (DM) and *Exploration* (EP) (discussed in Section 3). The proposed taxonomy is then verified with the survey as well as a log sample from a popular commercial product search engine. We find that the three categories cover over 95% of the search sessions from the log; and observe a similar distribution of search intents in the survey and in the log data.

By addressing RQ2 (Section 4) we study how users interact with search results under different types of search intents. From the commercial product search log we see users behave differently under different intent categories. Users with *TF* intent exhibit focused search behaviour—they use few specific queries and only browse and click a few top ranked results. In contrast, users with *DM* intent use shorter queries, browse deeper in the result list and click more results. Users with *EP* intent tend to issue many semantically dissimilar queries.

We further investigate the relation between user satisfaction, their search intent and behavioural patterns with RQ3(a) (Section 5). To do so, we carry out an in-lab user study to collect usage data of an experimental mobile product search system with designed search intents and explicit user feedback on search satisfaction. Finally, we address RQ3(b) by exploring the effectiveness of a series of classification models and interaction features in predicting user satisfaction (Section 6). Results show these models and features achieve reasonably good performance, epecially for intent categories *DM* (F1=0.808, AUC=0.760) and *TF* (F1=0.758, AUC=0.651).

Our study has the following contributions:

- We propose a novel product search intent taxonomy that is verified with both an online survey and real world search logs.
- Our analysis over the search logs from both the commercial product search engine and the in-lab study provides insights in the relation between user behavioural patterns, their underlying intents, and their perceived search satisfaction. These insights can, for instance, help search engines to personalise the search results with respect to user intents, optimising their search experience.
- We demonstrate that it is possible to effectively predict user search satisfaction using interaction features, revealing oppotunities for new evalution measures and optimisation methods for product search systems.

2 RELATED WORK

Previous research falls into three categories: taxonomy of search activities, user search satisfaction, and product search.

2.1 Taxonomy of Search Activities

In order to develop search engines satisfying diverse types of information needs, goals or intents, it is important to understand what users are searching for, why they search, and how they search. Studies have attempted to characterise search activities from various perspectives. Broder [4] proposed a taxonomy that categorises Web search into three types: navigational, informational, and transactional. Based on this, Rose and Levinson [34] created a framework for understanding user goals; and some studies proposed algorithms for automatic query type identification [24, 28]. Broder's taxonomy is rather coarse-grained, e.g. the informational category covers a diverse types of search tasks [6]. Considering information seeking from a learning perspective, studies have proposed to categorise search tasks using Anderson and Krathwohl's taxonomy of educational objectives [3], e.g. Jansen et al. [17] observed different user behaviours with respect to different task types.

While the above studies provide an overall view of Web search, the resulting taxonomies are not readily tailored to characterising product search. We focus on providing insights for the understanding of why, and how users search products and propose a novel product search intent taxonomy.

2.2 User Satisfaction

User satisfaction is widely used as a subjective measurement of search success. The concept of satisfaction was first introduced in information retrieval research in the 1970s [35], and is defined as *"the fulfillment of a specified desire or goal"* in recent literature [21]. To predict user search satisfaction, studies have focused on analysing user interactions with search engines. Guo et al. [13] employed interaction features (e.g. click-through based features), query features, and result features to predict query performance; fine-grained features such as cursor position and scrolling speed [10, 16] were considered in later studies. Unlike relevance based measures [1, 9, 11, 15], search satisfaction is based on the overall search experience, e.g. including information gained as well as the effort spent on examining SERPs and landing pages [2]. Therefore, studies have employed the cost-benefit framework that considers both document relevance and the efforts users spend [18, 19].

In the context of mobile search, studies have found interaction patterns different from those on desktops [14, 20], leading to different features for predicting user satisfaction. For example, Li et al. [26] found the good abandonment rate from mobile search is significantly higher than that from PC search. Williams et al. [36] studied different good abandonment scenarios in mobile search. Kiseleva et al. [22] found that the notion of satisfaction varies across different scenarios. Some studies (e.g. [12, 23]) analysed the viewport (the visible portion of a web page) of the mobile devices, and used it to measure user satisfaction in the absence of clicks.

Our work differs from these existing efforts in that we study user search satisfaction with respect to interaction patterns that are specific to product search.

2.3 Product Search

Research of online customer behaviour has gained much attention recently. Using page-to-page clickstream data and the general content of the pages from a given online store, Moe [31] categorized visit patterns as *buying*, *browsing*, *searching*, and *knowledge-building*. Lu et al. [30] proposed a framework for mining and predicting users' movements and purchasing transactions in the context of mobile commerce. These studies focused on the overall shopping experiences rather than the search processes. Li et al. [25] pointed out that the decision mechanism underlying a purchase process is different from that of locating relevant documents/objects. Many studies therefore focused on enhancing product search with consumption features such as consumer preferences [25] and volume of sales [29]. However, no previous work has aimed to understand users' satisfaction perception during product search. We make a first attempt to classify user intent in product search and predict user satisfaction in different search scenarios.

3 PRODUCT SEARCH INTENT TAXONOMY

In this section, we address RQ1 by proposing a product search taxonomy, followed by an empirical verification of its validity.

3.1 Establishing the Taxonomy

Human interacts with devices in response to certain intents or goals [4]. One would assume the goal of online shopping is to make a purchase. However, sometimes people only search to obtain information from the shopping site; and sometimes people simply do online window shopping to kill time. In an attempt to propose a taxonomy to characterise different types of search activities during online shopping, we designed an online survey to collect users' product search experience. Following basic demographic questions, participants were asked to answer three open-ended questions:

1. Please describe your latest product search experience with as many details as possible (target, motivation, time, place).
2. Please provide your queries. (You can view your search history to find all the queries used in this search.)
3. Please provide the name of the product you purchased (if any).

We spread the survey via a popular social software (WeChat). We received responses from 355 people with 60.56% male and 39.44% female (42% participants were between 18 and 25, 35% between 26 and 30, 20% between 31 and 50, and 3% were either above 50 or below 18). After removing replies with unclear descriptions, we obtained 295 valid replies.

Three Web search professionals reviewed the survey data and coded each response. The coding process takes a grounded theory inspired iterative process, where each iteration consists of two steps: a) conceptualizing the user descriptions, and b) clustering the concepts to form categories of user intents. A random sample of 50 responses was first coded by the researchers individually. They then discussed to resolve conflicts and established an initial coding standard. Based on this, they continued to code the remaining responses and this process repeated. The final coding scheme consists of three concepts that were used to describe user search activities.

Motivation: Why a user searches for a (type of) product(s), which includes two primary types:
a. With an immediate purchase need (e.g. to solve a problem such as replacing a broken phone, or to buy gifts for others)
b. Without immediate purchase need (e.g. to kill time, browsing new arrivals)

Target specificity: How sepcific a user's requirement of the target product(s) is—we have identified four levels of specificity from the survey descriptions:
a. Known product category (e.g. clothes, snacks)
b. Known product name/type (e.g. wind coat, chips)
c. Known product brand (e.g. Zara wind coat, Pringles chips)
d. Undetermined (unknown/multiple product categories)

Table 2: Example search scenarios from the survey.

Cat.	Examples	Query list
TF	"My phone was broken. I wanted to buy the latest iPhone."	"iPhone 7"
	"Recently I started to learn table tennis, so I needed to buy a pair of Double Happiness table tennis rackets. "	"DHS table tennis rackets"
DM	"The weather was getting cooler. I wanted to buy some long sleeves for my son."	"long sleeve T-shirt"; "autumn T-shirt"
	"I would like to buy a refrigerator in the dormitory. After comparing the different brands, I chose the Haier refrigerator."	"refrigerator"; "Haier refrigerator"
EP	"I just felt bored at class and didn't buy anything at last."	"dress"; "shoes"
	"I would like to track Nike's new products."	"Nike"

Search Strategy: How the user searches—we identified the following strategies from the survey replies:
a. Specific keyword (keyword with detailed specification)
b. Evaluate (Inspect a product's specification, price, reviews, etc);
c. Compare (two or more items—typically involves evaluation of individual items);
d. Browse (seasonal sales, new arrivals, etc);
e. Direct purchase (directly buy a targeted item);

After coding the detailed user descriptions with the above concepts, the researchers then attempted to form categories of user product search intents. Three top level categories were identified, namely *Target finding* (TF), *Decision making* (DM), and *Exploration* (EP). From TF to EP, the categories represent increasingly more explorative search strategies and less determined search target. The categories are defined as follows:

- **Target Finding (TF):** The user has a specific target in mind (target specificity is at least at level b, typically at level c). Typical search strategy includes direct purchase and specific keywords. Users normally do not need to compare different products in this category (except price comparison from different sellers); the choice of color, model and other details can often be made in the same shop after a click; evaluation may occur as users may want to check if the product is exactly as he/she expected. Search in TF is typically conducted with an immediate purchase need.
- **Decision Making (DM):** The user has an immediate purchase need. He/she has a vague idea of what to buy (i.e. target specificity is at level b) but would typically explore and compare related products of different brands/models in the result list in order to make a purchase decision.
- **Exploration (EP):** Here the user explores the search result without a specific target in mind (i.e. target specificity is at level a or d). Typical search strategy is browsing. The user may or may not have an immediate purchase need, described by the following two sub-groups:
  a. Casual exploration (e.g. kill time, exploring seasonal sales);
  b. Purposeful exploration (e.g. search for birthday gifts).

Table 2 shows some examples from the survey.

3.2 Taxonomy Verification

Having established our taxonomy, we now verify its validity using data collected from the survey as well as search logs from a commercial product search engine.

3.2.1 User Survey. Three annotators (different from the researche who established the taxonomy) were employed to examine the described search scenarios and queries, and categorize these into one of the three types of search intents as defined in our proposed taxonomy. This process examines how well our proposal can be applied in practice. We provide annotators with the definitions of

Table 3: Distribution of the three types of user intent.

	TF	DM	EP
Data from the survey	16.3%	61.8%	21.9%
Data from the search logs	15.7%	60.1%	24.2%

each user intent and asked them to select the category based on coding criteria as described in Section 3.1. They were asked to label a scenario as "others" if they could not determine which category it belongs to, or that it does not belong to any of the three.

Out of the 295 valid replies, 288 (97.6%) cases fall into one of the three categories (excluding "others") with at least two annotators agreed on the labels. The Fleiss' κ [8] is 0.756 among three annotators. This result shows that the proposed taxonomy can be understood and employed by external annotators (Fleiss' κ is 0.679 between the two sets of annotations). Additionally, we see our taxonomy has a high coverage of the search scenarios in the survey and the majority of the cases clearly belong to one of the categories. Table 3 shows the distribution of the three categories (row 1): with *DM* being the most common user intent, accounting for 61.8% of the cases, followed by *EP* (21.9%) and *TF* (16.3%).

3.2.2 Search Logs. We further verified the proposed taxonomy with the search logs of a popular commercial shopping site. We randomly sampled 1000 anonymised users and took all the queries they issued on mobile devices during one day in October 2016.

We created search sessions by setting a time-out threshold of 30 minutes [33] between consecutive queries. This resulted in 1800 search sessions. We then employed 18 assessors to annotate these sessions with our taxonomy. Every three annotators were grouped together to annotate the same 300 sessions. The annotators were shown the query list and the title of the products that users clicked/added to cart/bought on each SERP, which can be used to infer the concepts mentioned. Again, we provided them with the definitions, the coding criteria and some examples of each user intent in the taxonomy as described above (Table 2). The option of category "others" was also given.

In total, 1,713 sessions (95.2%) had at least two annotators agreeing on a user intent category other than "others", i.e. that our proposed taxonomy covers most of the real world product search sessions. Further, the distribution of the three categories among the search sessions in the log is similar to what we observed in the online survey (χ^2=0.753, p=0.686) (See Table 3). In this case, the value of Fleiss' κ among each three annotators varies between 0.492 and 0.639 (mean = 0.545), indicating a moderate agreement.

3.3 Discussion

We now briefly discuss how our taxonomy relates to some of the existing taxonomies. Both the *TF* and *DM* intents would fall into the "transactional" category of Broder's taxonomy [4], as they are both motivated by a purchase intent; while *EP* does not correspond to an existing category. Meanwhile, *DM* can also be "informational" as users explore and collect information to make purchase decisions, while *TF* is similar to "navigational". These overlaps and gaps between categories indicate that Broder's taxonomy of Web search is not directly applicable to product search and a dedicated taxonomy is needed. Moe [31]'s taxonomy, on the other hand, describes overall activities on online shopping sites, and our taxonomy essentially provides a more fine-grained description of the search activities.

Table 4: Session statistics by user intent (* indicates one-way ANOVA with Bonferroni post hoc test, significant at p<0.01)

	TF	DM	EP
Queries per Session (mean)	2.05	2.20	4.20*
Reformulation (%)	40.89	45.19	81.93
Search Depth in Pages (mean)	2.91*	5.11	4.82
Page Turning (%)	45.82	66.08	61.53
Buy (%)	10.04	10.98	8.67
Add to Cart (%)	7.06	12.83	14.22

4 USER BEHAVIOUR AND SEARCH INTENTS

In this section, we address RQ2 by exploiting the annotated search logs (see Section 3.2.2) to provide insights into user product search behaviour in relation to their search intents.

From the logs we extract user interaction data for events logged on two types of pages: the *search results pages (SERPs)* and the landing *product pages*. The product pages provide detailed product-related information, and operational options such as *add to cart* and *buy*. From each log entry we extract the following: query string, page number, result list (a set of product ids), clicked product ids, *add to cart* events and *buy* events.

4.1 Session Level Statistics

We start by examining the session level user interaction patterns in relation to their intents, providing an overview of user behaviour in product search. See Table 4.

In terms of query behaviour, *EP* sessions contain significantly more queries than *TF* and *DM* sessions. Further, 81.93% of the *EP* sessions contain more than one query—indicating that *EP* users tend to reformulate queries. *DM* sessions contain slightly more queries and query reformulations than *TF* sessions, but the difference is not significant.

In terms of search depth (defined as the number of SERPs a user browses per query), users in both *EP* and *DM* sessions browse significantly deeper than in *TF* sessions (4.82, 5.11, and 2.91 pages respectively), and tend to turn pages more often (60% of the *EP* and *DM* sessions compared to 45.8% of the *TF* sessions). It is reasonable since users seek specific products with specific queries in *TF* sessions and there is no need to explore many products as in the *DM* and *EP* sessions.

Finally, we look into purchase behaviours, i.e. the *buy* and *add to cart* events. *DM* and *TF* sessions show a higher purchase rate than *EP* sessions, which is consistent with the result collected from the online survey, based on the answers to the third question. However, *EP* sessions have the highest *add to cart* rate (14.22%), followed by *DM* and *TF*. Given the similar purchase rates, the difference in *add to cart* rates between the *TF* and *DM* sessions suggests that users tend to buy directly when they find the right product in *TF* sessions, while in *DM* sessions, they tend to add it to cart first and make decisions later.

4.2 Event Statistics

We now zoom in to examine user behaviour in terms of individual event types. This includes: click events which indicate how users interact with search results after a query is issued; and query events including query strings and query reformulations.

4.2.1 Click Event. We first measure the click-through rate (CTR) for each session type. From the search result list and the ids of the

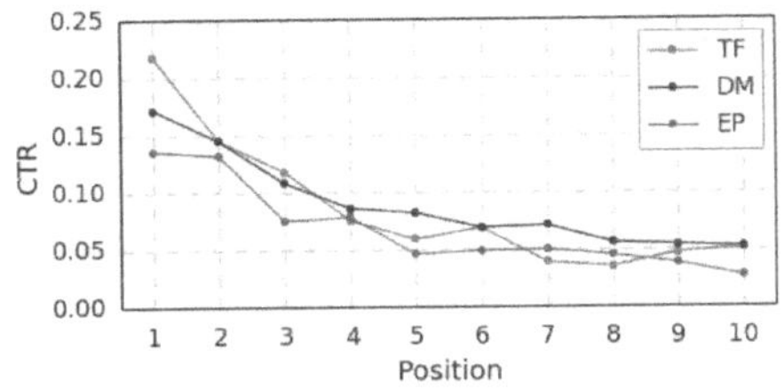

Figure 1: Click-through rate for top 10 positions

Table 5: Click statistics by user intent (* indicates one-way ANOVA with Bonferroni post hoc test, significant at p<0.01)

	TF	DM	EP
Clicks per Session (mean)	3.47*	5.51*	8.27*
Clicks per Query (mean)	1.67	2.51*	1.97
nCS (%)	43.43	29.87	36.10
nRS (%)	39.39	21.82	22.87

clicked products, we obtain the positions of each clicked product. We then calculate the average CTR as the number of clicks at each position divided by the number of queries. In Figure 1, we see the CTR for *TF* sessions is the highest at the first position, followed by a sharp decay. After the 4th position, the CTR for *DM* sessions is higher than *TF* sessions. The relatively higher position bias of the *TF* sessions suggests that users tend to find what they are looking for at top ranks in these sessions. The CTR for *EP* sessions is constantly lower than *DM* sessions suggesting that users tend to click less under the *EP* intent, perhaps because they do not have a particular target in mind.

Table 5 shows click statistics for each session type. The three types of sessions show significant difference in terms of number of clicks per session, with *EP* being the highest and *TF* the lowest, that is, from *TF* to *EP* users explore increasingly more products. Meanwhile, *DM* has a significantly higher number of clicks per query than *TF* and *EP*, suggesting users tend to spend more effort in examining the results of each query.

We also computed nCS and nRS [28], where nCS is defined as the percentage of the queries with less than n clicks (n=2) and nRS is the percentage of queries with clicks only on top n results (n=5). The higher nCS and nRS of the *TF* sessions compared to *DM* and *EP* sessions again suggests a more focused search (examining few results at the top of the list), which is consistent with what we find from the CTR analysis (Figure 1).

4.2.2 Query Strings. As shown in Table 6, *TF* sessions have significantly higher average query length (7.94) than the *DM* (6.66) and *EP* (6.46) sessions, suggesting users tend to issue more specific queries in these sessions. *TF* sessions also have the longest initial queries (7.35). From the survey we observed that users in *TF* sessions often start their search with more specific queries including the brand name and even the specific product features, suggesting that they have specific targets in their mind and therefore are able to describe it clearly. In addition, we see that for all sessions the average query lengths are higher than that of the initial query. This suggests that users tend to expand their queries.

We further investigate query reformulations by calculating the similarity between two consecutive queries, as well as that between the first and the last query, within a session. We use the Jaccard index as a measure of similarity. *EP* sessions have the lowest values

Table 6: Query string statistics by user intent (* indicates one-way ANOVA with Bonferroni post hoc test, significant at p<0.01)

	TF	DM	EP
Query Length (Chinese characters)	7.94*	6.66	6.46
Initial Query Length (Chinese characters)	7.35*	5.76	5.58
Consecutive Queries Similarity	0.42	0.43	0.29*
Head&Tail Queries Similarity	0.38	0.34	0.06*

for both statistics, suggesting that compared to *TF* and *DM* sessions, users tend to issue more diverse queries and drift between different products under this intent.

4.3 Summary

In conclusion, users tend to conduct more focused searches in *TF* sessions compared to those in the *DM* and *EP* sessions. Specifically, they use fewer but more specific queries and only browse and click a few top results. Compared to *TF* sessions, users in *DM* sessions tend to issue shorter queries, browse the result list deeper and click on more results. In *EP* sessions, users issue many more queries that are semantically diverse. They browse deep down the result lists but perform fewer clicks for each query. These findings have implications for both retrieval algorithms and interface designs. For instance, search engines may determine how the results should be displayed to users depending on their intents: e.g. in *TF* sessions accurate results may be important, while in *DM* or *EP* sessions more diverse results may be appropriate and exploratory interface elements may be useful.

5 USER BEHAVIOUR, SEARCH INTENT, AND SATISFACTION

In this section, we address RQ3(a). *How does user satisfaction relate to their search behaviour and search intents?*

5.1 Data Collection

To collect user search interaction data and their corresponding satisfaction feedback, we conducted a user study using an experimental mobile product search system. We did our best to simulate realistic product search scenarios to ensure the data we collected are credible.

Experiment procedure. The experiment consists of two steps.
Step one. Each participant was asked to complete 12 product search tasks (6 *TF* and 6 *DM* tasks). At the start of each task, the participant was shown the task description and an initial search query. After that he/she was guided to the SERP of a popular commercial shopping site. He/she can then browse the result list, click any item of his/her interests, view the details and add products to the shopping cart. We adapted the "Add to Cart" button on the product page to skip log-in. The participant can reformulate their queries if he/she was not satisfied with the current result list. Once clicked on a "Finish" button at the bottom, the participant was requested to select the most desired product he/she might eventually buy, and provide feedback of satisfaction with the search results in a 5-point scale for each query. Invalid queries caused by typing errors were discarded. He/she was then guided to step two.
Step two. After finishing the *TF* and *DM* tasks, each participant was given time to search for anything he/she liked (*EP* task). The "Finish" button appears after 10 minutes so that the participant

Table 7: A list of search tasks for TF and DM user intents

	Initial Query	Task description
TF	JanSport backpack	Your backpack is broken, and you want to buy a JanSport backpack.
	Edifier headset	You want to buy an Edifier headset to listen to music.
	3M head-wearing mask	You want to buy a 3M head-wearing mask to protect against the haze.
	Kyocera peeler	You want to buy a Kyocera peeler.
	Yonex badminton racket	You want to learn badminton, so you plan to buy a pair of Yonex badminton racket.
	Asics running shoes	You hope to lose weight by running, so you want to buy a pair of Asics running shoes.
DM	router	The router fails often recently, so you want to find a good quality router.
	rechargeable lamp	The lights out schedule will start soon, so you want to buy a long-lasting rechargeable lamp.
	tf card 64G	You want to buy a 64G TF card to expand the memory of your mobile phone.
	water cooler	You want to buy a water cooler for your dorm.
	coffee beans	Your lab ran out of coffee, so you want to find some tasty coffee beans.
	television	You want to buy a new TV for your family.

could end the session if he/she wanted to. Upon completing the task, he/she was also asked to select the products with final purchase intention and label the satisfaction scores as in step one.

Apparatus. We used a mobile phone with a 5-inch (diagonal) LCD screen and 1280-by-720-pixel resolution as the search device, similar to most modern mobile phones on the market. In the background, we ran an in-house Android application to collect user interactions and their satisfaction feedback.

Participants. We recruited 20 participants (10 female and 10 male). from our university with moderate product search engine utilization experiences. Each of them was asked to finish two example tasks to get familiar with the experiment process in a training session.

Search tasks. To cover various search intents, we selected 6 *TF* and 6 *DM* tasks from the results of the online survey (see Section 3.2.1) as shown in Table 7. We randomized the task order for each participant. The SERPs were crawled from a popular commercial shopping site with sorting and filtering functions removed as we wanted to focus on how users interact with the default result pages. We leave the investigation on more advanced SERPs for future work. The task instruction for *EP* task is: "Image yourself have ten minutes of free time to shop online before boarding an airplane/bus/train. You can search anything you like, and add products to the shopping cart or make a purchase as your like."

Data collected. We collected a total of 659 valid search queries each associated with satisfaction scores for these 13 tasks (6 *TF* tasks, 6 *DM* tasks and 1 *EP* task).

5.2 Satisfaction and Purchase

Due to the lack of user satisfaction feedback, many shopping sites use purchase as a measure of user satisfaction. However, in Table 4 we see the purchase rate is around 10% for each intent type. Users do not always make a purchase right after search: some may make the purchase later; some may buy the product offline. Hence purchase may not accurately reflect whether users are satisfied with their search experience or the performance of the search engine. It is therefore important to understand the relationship between user satisfaction and their purchase behaviour.

We consider the following two purchase scenarios: *adding to cart*, i.e. the user adds a product to the shopping cart; and *buying*, i.e. the user adds the product to cart and eventually selected to buy. We call the search sessions that contain *adding to cart/buying* actions ADD/BUY cases, and the others NOT ADD/BUY cases.

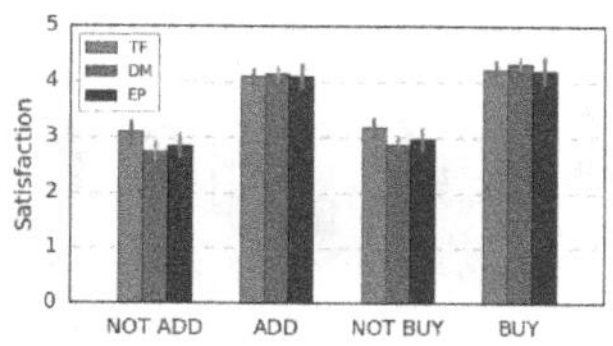

Figure 2: Average satisfaction scores of different intents.

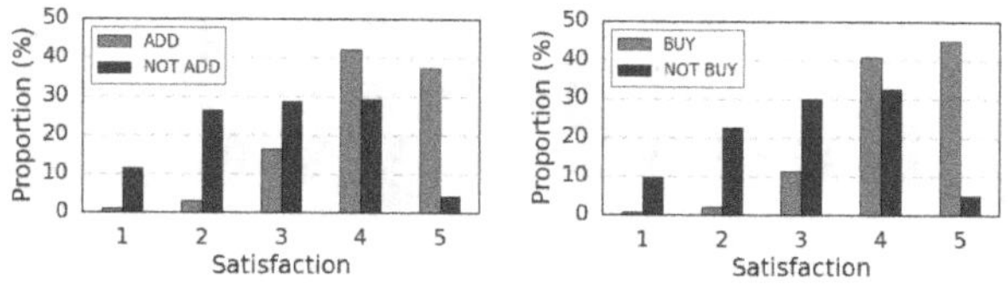

(a) ADD and NOT ADD cases (b) BUY and NOT BUY cases

Figure 3: Distribution of the satisfaction scores over different user intents.

We first compute the average satisfaction scores of the two cases. As shown in Figure 2, ADD/BUY cases have significantly higher scores than NOT ADD/BUY cases (t-test, p<0.01). This implies that users are usually more satisfied if desired products are found.

Figure 3 shows the distribution of the satisfaction scores of different cases. We see that most of the ADD and BUY cases have satisfaction scores of 4 or 5, which means users are usually satisfied in these cases. However, there are 15 (4.23%) ADD cases and 8 (2.84%) BUY cases with scores less than 3, indicating users may not be satisfied even if they find the target products, e.g. it may be that the search process took too much effort [18]. For NOT ADD/BUY cases, the distribution is more uniform: 37.8% NOT ADD cases and 32.4% NOT BUY cases have satisfaction scores less than 3; and 33.6% NOT ADD cases and 37.7% NOT BUY cases have scores of 4 or 5. This incidates users may not be dissatisfied even if they did not save or buy anything during the search process.

In summary, *adding to cart/buying* behaviour has a high correlation with user satisfaction, i.e. users usually feel satisfied if they find the desired products. However, satisfaction does not necessarily lead to purchase. On the other hand, users may be moderately satisfied even if they do not add products to the cart or make a purchase (although to a much less extent). Therefore, it is not appropriate to use buying activities as a measure of user satisfaction.

5.3 Satisfaction and Interaction Signals

Having observed that purchase behaviour alone is not an accurate indicator of user satisfaction in product search, we now investigate which other user interaction signals reflect the different levels of user satisfaction.

Query Level Statistics. We first look at the relation between user satisfaction and two query-level statistics: query duration (the time duration of a query session); browse depth (the maximum rank of results users browsed on a SERP).

In Figure 4(a), we see that satisfaction is positively correlated with query duration under each type of user intent (Spearman's ρ=0.270 (*TF*); 0.400 (*DM*); 0.336 (*EP*), p<0.01), indicating users tend to spend more time when they are satisfied with the result list; and they also tend to browse more products (Figure 4(b)). However, we observe that queries with a satisfaction score of 5 have a smaller browse depth than those with a score of 3 or 4 (t-test, p<0.01). It

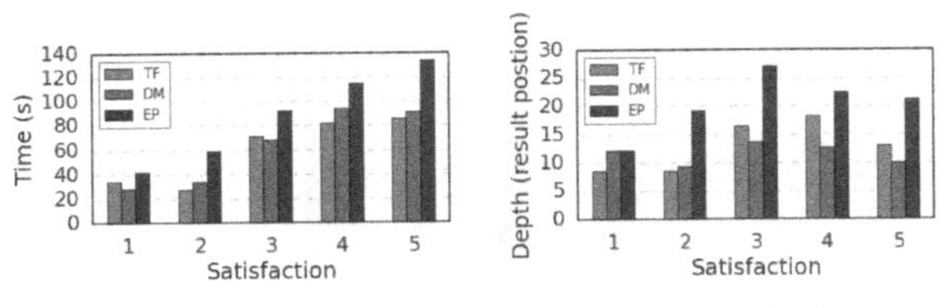

(a) Query duration (b) Browse depth

Figure 4: Query level stats w.r.t satisfaction.

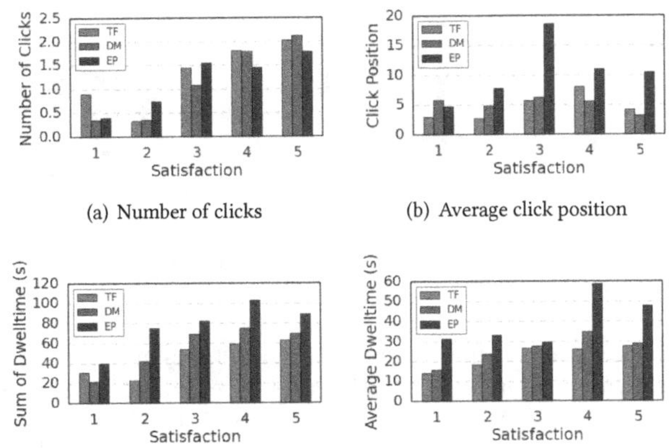

(a) Number of clicks (b) Average click position

(c) Sum of dwell time (d) Average dwell time

Figure 5: Click stats w.r.t satisfaction

suggests that users may feel more satisfied if they find the needed products in the earlier search result ranking.

Further, we find that *TF* sessions have a deeper average browse depth than *DM* sessions, which is inconsistent with previous findings in Section 4.1. This may be an artefact of the task design, e.g. some users may not be familiar with the products in the *TF* tasks and needed to browse a bit more to make sure that they find the right ones. Meanwhile, users tend to browse deeper in *EP* sessions. This may because users are more interested in this part of the experiment as they can search anything they like. However, these inconsistencies are not significant, so the current experiment data is not enough to make conclusions.

Click Statistics. Previous studies have shown that click behaviour is an important signal both for result relevance and search satisfaction for Web search [13]. Our data support this finding in the context of product search. In Figure 5(a) we see that users tend to click more products when they are satisfied with the result list (Spearman's ρ=0.334 (*TF*); 0.509 (*DM*); 0.321 (*EP*), $p<0.01$). We also compute the average position of the clicked products. In Figure 5(b), we see this statistic is small for queries with low satisfaction scores (1 and 2) in *TF* and *EP* sessions. It suggests that users tend to reformulate the query if they are not satisfied with the first few results. Meanwhile, queries with a score of 5 have a smaller average position than those with a score of 3 or 4 (t-test, $p<0.01$), which is consistent with Figure 4(b). However, this difference is not significant in *DM* sessions. It is reasonable as users need to click several products to make the comparison before they are satisfied.

Dwell time is also a strong signal for satisfaction [13, 18] in Web search. Therefore we also compute the dwell time for the clicked products. In Figure 5(c), we see users tend to spend a longer time on product pages when they feel satisfied. However, it may be due to the fact that they click more in these cases. Therefore, we also calculate the average dwell time for each query. As we see in Figure 5(d), lower satisfaction (1 and 2) is associated with shorter average

Table 8: Features for satisfaction prediction.

	Feature Description
Q1	Query duration (in second)
Q2	Browse depth
C1	Number of clicks
C2-C4	The average, max and min position of clicks
C5-C6	The sum and average of dwell time on landing pages
C7-C12	Number of clicks with dwell time of 0-5/5-10/10-15/15-30/30-60/>60 seconds

dwell time in *TF* and *DM* sessions. In *EP* sessions, this statistic is approximately the same for queries with a satisfaction score less than 4 and is significantly higher for queries with a score of 4 and 5 (t-test, $p<0.01$), suggesting users examine carefully if they are interested in the product under this intent.

Summary. To summarise, user interaction patterns are closely related to their satisfaction, while their detailed relation may vary under different intents. Next, we explore features derived from the findings of this analysis to predict user satisfaction.

6 SATISFACTION PREDICTION

We now address RQ3(b). *Can we predict product search satisfaction with interaction signals?.* In Figure 3, we see the average satisfaction score is 2.88/3.01 for NOT ADD/BUY cases and 4.12/4.27 for ADD/BUY cases. As discussed in Section 5.2, users usually feel satisfied if they find the desired products, therefore we bin the satisfaction scores, setting scores 4 and 5 as SAT and the remainder as DSAT for satisfaction prediction. This results in 384 SAT cases and 275 DSAT cases.

6.1 Feature Extraction

Based on the findings in Section 5.3 and previous studies [13, 18], we extract two types of features to predict search satisfaction in different intent scenarios: query level features (Q); and click features (C). Table 8 lists all the features. These features can all be easily collected in search logs for online shopping site.

Query Level Features. We define two query level features: query duration (Q1) and browse depth (Q2)—both are highly correlated with the user satisfaction scores (see Figure 4).

Click Features. Based on the findings in user click behaviour, we extract the following click-based features: the number of clicks that a user performed on a result list (C1); the average, maximum, and minimum position of user clicks on the result list (C2-C4). We also compute the sum and average of the dwell time on each product page (C5-C6). We further divide C1 by different dwell time intervals (C7-C12), as different users may have different product search habits. Some may read many details such as specifications, comments, and after-sales service, while others may only care about the price. Therefore we do not divide the clicks into SAT clicks and DSAT clicks with a simple threshold on dwell time [13, 18].

6.2 Prediction Results

We investigate the results of our proposed prediction models in three aspects: the performance of the classifiers; the impact of different feature groups as well as individual features; and the model performance across different user intents.

Following Cheng et al. [5], we use F1 score and AUC (area under the ROC curve) to evaluate the prediction performance. Since the relation between user satisfaction and interaction patterns varies

Table 9: Comparison of classifiers. * indicates significant difference by t-test, p<0.05.

	TF		DM		EP	
	F1	AUC	F1	AUC	F1	AUC
SVM	**0.773**	0.500	0.738	0.508	0.516	0.500
DT	0.675	0.577	0.669	0.637	0.484	0.521
NB	0.394	0.548	0.697	0.703	0.418	0.537
GBDT	0.764	**0.631***	**0.802***	**0.759***	**0.593***	**0.569***

Table 10: Comparison of different feature groups, * indicates significant difference by t-test, p<0.05

	TF		DM		EP	
	F1	AUC	F1	AUC	F1	AUC
Q	0.704	0.544	0.672	0.608	0.590	0.594
C	0.704	0.648	0.781	0.756	0.539	0.568
Q+C	**0.758***	**0.651***	**0.808***	**0.760***	**0.630***	**0.610***

Table 11: Feature importance for different intents

TF		DM		EP	
Feature	Weight	Feature	Weight	Feature	Weight
Q1	0.352	Q1	0.307	Q1	0.354
Q2	0.218	C6	0.211	Q2	0.239
C6	0.136	Q2	0.179	C6	0.110
C5	0.122	C5	0.104	C5	0.072

across different intent types, we perform the predictions for *TF*, *DM* and *EP* tasks separately.

Comparison of Classifiers. We apply Support Vector Machine with RBF kernel (SVM), Decision Tree (DT), Naive Bayes (NB) and Gradient Boosting Decision Tree (GBDT) to predict user satisfaction with 5-fold cross validation. GBDT achieves the best performance, followed by DT, NB, and SVM (Table 9). Therefore, in the rest of the investigation we continue with GBDT.

We experimented with two sampling strategies for cross-validation: (1) "random sampling" (Table 9); and (2) "sampling by user": query sessions from the same user are grouped in either the training or the test set [27]. We found that the two strategies result in very similar prediction performance, meaning the prediction model can deal with previously unseen users. Therefore, we adopt the "sampling by user" strategy to compare different feature groups next.

Comparison of Feature Groups. We first make predictions with each type of features individually (Table 10). Click features achieve better performance than query features, suggesting click behaviour provides more information about user satisfaction. After combining two type of features, we get the best performance for all tasks.

Feature Importance. We now investigate the impact of individual features on predicting user satisfaction with a more detailed feature importance analysis. Table 11 shows the top 4 features using GBDT and the Q+C feature group. We find that *query duration (Q1)* has the highest importance for all user intents. The second important feature is *average dwell time (C6)* for *DM* tasks, but *browse depth (Q2)* for *TF* and *EP* tasks. It is reasonable as users tend to focus more on a product page to compare and evaluate, which is captured by *C6*. *Sum of dwell time (C5)* is also a useful feature across user intents. Meanwhile, click position and click count features have relatively small weights in all cases, suggesting users may not be sensitive to the positions and the number of clicked results.

Comparison of Intent Groups. From both Table 9 and 10 we see that the prediction performance for *TF* and *DM* tasks is much better than *EP* tasks. We believe this is because people do not have specific purchase targets in *EP* tasks. Their perception of satisfaction may be influenced by many factors, such as the serendipity of the results, and the attractiveness of the contents; and it may vary widely among different users. We leave the research for future work on pursuing more effective satisfaction prediction for the more challenging *EP* search intent.

Summary. We conclude that, by exploiting interaction signals, we can predict product search user satisfaction reasonably well, especially for *TF* and *DM* search intents. In addition, since we collected data with mobile devices, we also experimented with gesture features (e.g. the number and direction of swipes). However, these features has limited impact. We leave the mobile specific investigation for future work.

7 DISCUSSION AND CONCLUSIONS

In this paper we investigated the relation between user intents, search behaviour, and perceived satisfaction in the context of product search. Our findings have several implications for future studies.

To characterise different types of user intents, we proposed and verified a taxonomy that identifies three types of product search intents: *Target Finding* (TF), *Decision Making* (DM) and *Exploration* (EP). This taxonomy bridges a gap between existing taxonomies that describe general Web search and online shopping activities. We found users with different intents behave differently. *TF* users tend to issue few specific queries and browse only top ranked results; *DM* users tend to issue short queries, browse deep, and click more results; and *EP* users issue many diverse queries, browse deep, but do not click often. These findings will help search engines make choices of retrieval algorithms and interface designs depending on the user intents.

Using interaction data and explicit satisfaction feedback collected from a user study, we found that user interaction patterns are closely related to satisfaction, but their detailed relation varies across different intents. Based on these findings, we demonstrate that we are able to predict user satisfaction using interaction signals with reasonable prediction performance, especially for *TF* and *DM* tasks. That is, to effectively predict user satisfaction, one need to consider not only the right interaction features but also the underlying user intent with respect to search and purchase.

One limitation of our study is that the notion of "satisfaction" is subject to users' own interpretation. While it allows users to describe an overall experience, it may also lead to variance in satisfaction due to different interpretations. We leave the investigation of more find-grained types of satisfaction for future work. As mobile phones are becoming the main tools for online shopping, we conduct log analysis and user study on mobile devices. However, user satisfaction may vary from PC to mobile. We leave the analysis on PC, and the comparison between PC and mobile product search for the future investigation.

8 ACKNOWLEDGEMENTS

We thank Dr. Ke Zhou for providing very useful suggestions for this paper. This work is supported by Natural Science Foundation of China (Grant No. 61622208, 61532011, 61672311), National Key Basic Research Program (2015CB358700), and the Netherlands Organisation for Scientific Research (NWO) under project nr. 13675.

REFERENCES

[1] Mikhail Ageev, Dmitry Lagun, and Eugene Agichtein. 2013. Improving search result summaries by using searcher behavior data. In *Proceedings of the 36th international ACM SIGIR conference on Research and development in information retrieval.* ACM, 13–22.

[2] Azzah Al-Maskari and Mark Sanderson. 2010. A review of factors influencing user satisfaction in information retrieval. *Journal of the American Society for Information Science and Technology* 61, 5 (2010), 859–868.

[3] L. W. Anderson, D. R. Krathwohl, P. W. Airasian, K. A. Cruikshank, R. E. Mayer, P. R. Pintrich, J. D. Raths, and M. C. Wittrock. 2001. *A Taxonomy for Learning, Teaching, and Assessing: A Revision of Bloom's Taxonomy of Educational Objectives.* 1013–1014 pages.

[4] Andrei Broder. 2002. A taxonomy of web search. In *ACM Sigir forum*, Vol. 36. ACM, 3–10.

[5] Justin Cheng, Caroline Lo, and Jure Leskovec. 2017. Predicting Intent Using Activity Logs: How Goal Specificity and Temporal Range Affect User Behavior. In *Proceedings of the 26th International Conference on World Wide Web Companion.* International World Wide Web Conferences Steering Committee, 593–601.

[6] Susan Dumais. 2013. Task-based search: a search engine perspective. In *NSF Workshop on Task-Based Search.* 1.

[7] James F Engel, David T Kollat, and Roger D Blackwell. 1973. Consumer behavior. (1973).

[8] Joseph L Fleiss. 1971. Measuring nominal scale agreement among many raters. *Psychological bulletin* 76, 5 (1971), 378.

[9] Qi Guo and Eugene Agichtein. 2012. Beyond dwell time: estimating document relevance from cursor movements and other post-click searcher behavior. In *Proceedings of the 21st international conference on World Wide Web.* ACM, 569–578.

[10] Qi Guo, Dmitry Lagun, and Eugene Agichtein. 2012. Predicting web search success with fine-grained interaction data. In *Proceedings of the 21st ACM international conference on Information and knowledge management.* ACM, 2050–2054.

[11] Qi Guo, Dmitry Lagun, Denis Savenkov, and Qiaoling Liu. 2012. Improving relevance prediction by addressing biases and sparsity in web search click data. In *Proc. of Int. Conf. on Web Service and Data Mining workshop on Web Search Click Data. New York: ACM.* 71–75.

[12] Qi Guo and Yang Song. 2016. Large-Scale Analysis of Viewing Behavior: Towards Measuring Satisfaction with Mobile Proactive Systems. (2016).

[13] Qi Guo, Ryen W White, Susan T Dumais, Jue Wang, and Blake Anderson. 2010. Predicting query performance using query, result, and user interaction features. In *Adaptivity, Personalization and Fusion of Heterogeneous Information.* LE CENTRE DE HAUTES ETUDES INTERNATIONALES D'INFORMATIQUE DOCUMENTAIRE, 198–201.

[14] Jeff Huang and Abdigani Diriye. 2012. Web user interaction mining from touch-enabled mobile devices. In *HCIR workshop.* Citeseer.

[15] Jeff Huang, Ryen W White, Georg Buscher, and Kuansan Wang. 2012. Improving searcher models using mouse cursor activity. In *Proceedings of the 35th international ACM SIGIR conference on Research and development in information retrieval.* ACM, 195–204.

[16] Jeff Huang, Ryen W White, and Susan Dumais. 2011. No clicks, no problem: using cursor movements to understand and improve search. In *Proceedings of the SIGCHI conference on human factors in computing systems.* ACM, 1225–1234.

[17] Bernard J. Jansen, Danielle Booth, and Brian Smith. 2009. Using the taxonomy of cognitive learning to model online searching. *Information Processing & Management* 45, 6 (2009), 643–663.

[18] Jiepu Jiang, Ahmed Hassan Awadallah, Xiaolin Shi, and Ryen W White. 2015. Understanding and predicting graded search satisfaction. In *Proceedings of the Eighth ACM International Conference on Web Search and Data Mining.* ACM, 57–66.

[19] Jiepu Jiang, Daqing He, and James Allan. 2014. Searching, browsing, and clicking in a search session: changes in user behavior by task and over time. In *Proceedings of the 37th international ACM SIGIR conference on Research & development in information retrieval.* ACM, 607–616.

[20] Maryam Kamvar and Shumeet Baluja. 2006. A large scale study of wireless search behavior: Google mobile search. In *Proceedings of the SIGCHI conference on Human Factors in computing systems.* ACM, 701–709.

[21] Diane Kelly. 2009. Methods for evaluating interactive information retrieval systems with users. *Foundations and Trends in Information Retrieval* 3, 1âĂŤ2 (2009), 1–224.

[22] Julia Kiseleva, Kyle Williams, Jiepu Jiang, Ahmed Hassan Awadallah, Aidan C Crook, Imed Zitouni, and Tasos Anastasakos. 2016. Understanding User Satisfaction with Intelligent Assistants. In *Proceedings of the 2016 ACM on Conference on Human Information Interaction and Retrieval.* ACM, 121–130.

[23] Dmitry Lagun, Chih-Hung Hsieh, Dale Webster, and Vidhya Navalpakkam. 2014. Towards better measurement of attention and satisfaction in mobile search. In *Proceedings of the 37th international ACM SIGIR conference on Research & development in information retrieval.* ACM, 113–122.

[24] Lee, Uichin, Liu, Zhenyu, and Junghoo. 2005. Automatic identification of user goals in Web search. (2005).

[25] Beibei Li, Anindya Ghose, and Panagiotis G Ipeirotis. 2011. Towards a theory model for product search. In *Proceedings of the 20th international conference on World wide web.* ACM, 327–336.

[26] Jane Li, Scott Huffman, and Akihito Tokuda. 2009. Good abandonment in mobile and PC internet search. In *Proceedings of the 32nd international ACM SIGIR conference on Research and development in information retrieval.* ACM, 43–50.

[27] Yiqun Liu, Ye Chen, Jinhui Tang, Jiashen Sun, Min Zhang, Shaoping Ma, and Xuan Zhu. 2015. Different users, different opinions: Predicting search satisfaction with mouse movement information. In *Proceedings of the 38th International ACM SIGIR Conference on Research and Development in Information Retrieval.* ACM, 493–502.

[28] Yiqun Liu, Min Zhang, Liyun Ru, and Shaoping Ma. 2006. Automatic query type identification based on click through information. In *Asia Information Retrieval Symposium.* Springer, 593–600.

[29] Bo Long, Jiang Bian, Anlei Dong, and Yi Chang. 2012. Enhancing product search by best-selling prediction in e-commerce. In *Proceedings of the 21st ACM international conference on Information and knowledge management.* ACM, 2479–2482.

[30] Eric Hsueh-Chan Lu, Wang-Chien Lee, and Vincent Shin-Mu Tseng. 2012. A framework for personal mobile commerce pattern mining and prediction. *IEEE transactions on Knowledge and Data engineering* 24, 5 (2012), 769–782.

[31] Wendy W Moe. 2003. Buying, searching, or browsing: Differentiating between online shoppers using in-store navigational clickstream. *Journal of consumer psychology* 13, 1 (2003), 29–39.

[32] Francesco M Nicosia. 1966. CONSUMER DECISION PROCESSES; MARKETING AND ADVERTISING IMPLICATIONS. (1966).

[33] Jaimie Y Park, Neil O'Hare, Rossano Schifanella, Alejandro Jaimes, and Chin-Wan Chung. 2015. A large-scale study of user image search behavior on the web. In *Proceedings of the 33rd Annual ACM Conference on Human Factors in Computing Systems.* ACM, 985–994.

[34] Daniel E Rose and Danny Levinson. 2004. Understanding user goals in web search. In *Proceedings of the 13th international conference on World Wide Web.* ACM, 13–19.

[35] Louise T Su. 1992. Evaluation measures for interactive information retrieval. *Information Processing & Management* 28, 4 (1992), 503–516.

[36] Kyle Williams, Julia Kiseleva, Aidan C Crook, Imed Zitouni, Ahmed Hassan Awadallah, and Madian Khabsa. 2016. Detecting good abandonment in mobile search. In *Proceedings of the 25th International Conference on World Wide Web.* International World Wide Web Conferences Steering Committee, 495–505.

Logician: A Unified End-to-End Neural Approach for Open-Domain Information Extraction

Mingming Sun
sunmingming01@baidu.com
Big Data Lab (BDL), Baidu Research

Xu Li
lixu13@baidu.com
Big Data Lab (BDL), Baidu Research

Xin Wang
wangxin60@baidu.com
Big Data Lab (BDL), Baidu Research

Miao Fan
fanmiao@baidu.com
Big Data Lab (BDL), Baidu Research

Yue Feng
fengyue04@baidu.com
Big Data Lab (BDL), Baidu Research

Ping Li
liping11@baidu.com
Big Data Lab (BDL), Baidu Research

Abstract

In this paper, we consider the problem of open information extraction (OIE) for extracting entity and relation level intermediate structures from sentences in open-domain. We focus on four types of valuable intermediate structures (Relation, Attribute, Description, and Concept), and propose a unified knowledge expression form, SAOKE, to express them. We publicly release a data set which contains 48,248 sentences and the corresponding facts in the SAOKE format labeled by crowdsourcing. To our knowledge, this is the largest publicly available human labeled data set for open information extraction tasks. Using this labeled SAOKE data set, we train an end-to-end neural model using the sequence-to-sequence paradigm, called Logician, to transform sentences into facts. For each sentence, different to existing algorithms which generally focus on extracting each single fact without concerning other possible facts, Logician performs a global optimization over all possible involved facts, in which facts not only compete with each other to attract the attention of words, but also cooperate to share words. An experimental study on various types of open domain relation extraction tasks reveals the consistent superiority of Logician to other states-of-the-art algorithms. The experiments verify the reasonableness of SAOKE format, the valuableness of SAOKE data set, the effectiveness of the proposed Logician model, and the feasibility of the methodology to apply end-to-end learning paradigm on supervised data sets for the challenging tasks of open information extraction.

Keywords

Knowledge expression; open information extraction; end-to-end learning; sequence-to-sequence learning; deep learning

ACM Reference Format:

Mingming Sun, Xu Li, Xin Wang, Miao Fan, Yue Feng, and Ping Li. 2018. Logician: A Unified End-to-End Neural Approach for Open-Domain Information Extraction . In *WSDM 2018: WSDM 2018: The Eleventh ACM International Conference on Web Search and Data Mining , February 5–9, 2018, Marina Del Rey, CA, USA.* ACM, New York, NY, USA, 9 pages. https://doi.org/10.1145/3159652.3159712

WSDM 2018, February 5–9, 2018, Marina Del Rey, CA, USA

ACM ISBN 978-1-4503-5581-0/18/02…$15.00
https://doi.org/10.1145/3159652.3159712

1 Introduction

Semantic applications typically work on the basis of intermediate structures derived from sentences. Traditional word-level intermediate structures, such as POS-tags, dependency trees and semantic role labels, have been widely applied. Recently, entity and relation level intermediate structures attract increasingly more attentions.

In general, knowledge based applications require entity and relation level information. For instance, in [34], the lexicalized dependency path between two entity mentions was taken as the surface pattern facts. In distant supervision [29], the word sequence and dependency path between two entity mentions were taken as evidence of certain relation. In Probase [45], candidates of taxonomies were extracted by Hearst patterns [19]. The surface patterns of relations extracted by Open Information Extraction (OIE) systems [2, 12, 13, 36, 44] worked as the source of question answering systems [14, 23]. In addition, entity and relation level intermediate structures have been proven effective in many other tasks such as text summarization [8, 9, 28], text comprehension, word similarity, word analogy [39], and more.

The task of entity/relation level mediate structure extraction studies how facts about entities and relations are expressed by natural language in sentences, and then expresses these facts in an intermediate (and convenient) format. Although entity/relation level intermediate structures have been utilized in many applications, the study of learning these structures is still in an early stage.

Firstly, the problem of extracting different types of entity/relation level intermediate structures has not been considered in a unified fashion. Applications generally need to construct their own handcrafted heuristics to extract required entity/relation level intermediate structures, rather than consulting a commonly available NLP component, as they do for word level intermediate structures. Open IE-v4 system (http://knowitall.github.io/openie/) attempted to build such components by developing two sub-systems, with each extracting one type of intermediate structures, i.e., SRLIE [7] for verb based relations, and ReNoun [31, 46] for nominal attributes. However, important information about descriptive tags for entities and concept-instance relations between entities were not considered.

Secondly, existing solutions to the task either used pattern matching technique [2, 36, 44, 45], or were trained in a self-supervised manner on the data set automatically generated by heuristic patterns or info-box matching [2, 13, 44]. It is well-understood that pattern matching typically does not generalize well and the automatically generated samples may contain lots of noises.

This paper aims at tackling some of the well-known challenging problems in OIE systems, in a supervised end-to-end deep learning paradigm. Our contribution can be summarized as three major components: **SAOKE format**, **SAOKE data set**, and **Logician**.

Symbol Aided Open Knowledge Expression (SAOKE) is a knowledge expression form with several desirable properties: (i) SAOKE is literally honest and open-domain. Following the philosophy of OIE systems, SAOKE uses words in the original sentence to express knowledge. (ii) SAOKE provides a unified view over four common types of knowledge: *relation*, *attribute*, *description* and *concept*. (iii) SAOKE is an accurate expression. With the aid of symbolic system, SAOKE is able to accurately express facts with separated relation phrases, missing information, hidden information, etc.

SAOKE Data Set is a human annotated data set containing 48,248 Chinese sentences and corresponding facts in the SAOKE form. We publish the data set for research purpose. To the best of our knowledge, this is the largest publicly available human annotated data set for open-domain information extraction tasks.

Logician is a supervised end-to-end neural learning algorithm which transforms natural language sentences into facts in the SAOKE form. Logician is trained under the attention-based sequence-to-sequence paradigm, with three mechanisms: restricted copy mechanism to ensure literally honestness, coverage mechanism to alleviate the under extraction and over extraction problem, and gated dependency attention mechanism to incorporate dependency information. Experimental results on four types of open information extraction tasks reveal the superiority of the Logician algorithm.

Our work will demonstrate that SAOKE format is suitable for expressing various types of knowledge and is friendly to end-to-end learning algorithms. Particularly, we will focus on showing that the supervised end-to-end learning is promising for OIE tasks, to extract entity and relation level intermediate structures.

The rest of this paper is organized as follows. Section 2 presents the details of SAOKE. Section 3 describes the human labeled SAOKE data set. Section 4 describes the Logician algorithm and Section 5 evaluates the Logician algorithm and compares its performance with the state-of-the-art algorithms on four OIE tasks. Section 6 discusses the related work and Section 7 concludes the paper.

2 SAOKE Format: Symbol Aided Open Knowledge Expression

When reading a sentence in natural language, humans are able to recognize the facts involved in the sentence and accurately express them. In this paper, Symbolic Aided Open Knowledge Expression (SAOKE) is proposed as the form for honestly recording these facts. SAOKE expresses the primary information of sentences in n-ary tuples $(subject, predicate, object_1, \cdots, object_N)$, and (in this paper) neglects some auxiliary information. In the design of SAOKE, we take four requirements into consideration: completeness, accurateness, atomicity and compactness.

2.1 Completeness

After having analyzed a large number of sentences, we observe that the majority of facts can be classified into the following classes:

(1) **Relation:** Verb/preposition based n-ary relations between entity mentions [7, 36];
(2) **Attribute:**Nominal attributes for entity mentions [31, 46];
(3) **Description:** Descriptive phrases of entity mentions [4];
(4) **Concept:** Hyponymy and synonym relations among concepts and instances [41].

SAOKE is designed to express all these four types of facts. Table 1 presents an example sentence and the involved facts of these four classes in the SAOKE form. We should mention that the sentences and facts in English are directly translated from the corresponding Chinese sentences and facts, and the facts in English may not be the desired outputs of OIE algorithms for those English sentences due to the differences between Chinese and English languages.

2.2 Accurateness

SAOKE adopts the ideology of "literally honest". That is, as much as possible, it uses the words in the original sentences to express the facts. SAOKE follows the philosophy of OIE systems to express various relations without relying on any predefined schema system. There are, however, exceptional situations which are beyond the expression ability of this format. Extra symbols will be introduced to handle these situations, which are explained as follows.

Separated relation phrase: In some languages such as Chinese, relation phrases may be divided into several parts residing in discontinued locations of the sentences. To accurately express these relation phrases, we add placeholders (X,Y,Z, etc) to build continuous and complete expressions. "深受X影响" ("deeply influenced by X" in English) in the example of Table 1 is an instance of relation phrase after such processing.

Abbreviated expression: We explicitly express the information in abbreviated expressions by introducing symbolic predicates. For example, the expression of "Person (birth date - death date)" is transformed into facts: (Person, BIRTH, birth date) (Person, DEATH, death date), and the synonym fact involved in "NBA (National Basketball Association)" is expressed in the form of (NBA, = , National Basketball Association) .

Hidden information: Description of an entity and hyponymy relation between entities are in general expressed implicitly in sentences, and are expressed by symbolic predicates "DESC" and "ISA" respectively, as in Table 1. Another source of hidden information is the address expression. For example, "法国巴黎" ("Paris, France" in English) implies the fact (巴黎, LOC, 法国) ((Paris, LOC, France) in English), where the symbol "LOC" means "location".

Missing information: A sentence may not tell us the exact relation between two entities, or the exact subject/objects of a relation, which are required to be inferred from the context. We use placeholders like "X, Y, Z" to denote the missing subjects/objects, and "P" to denote the missing predicates.

2.3 Atomicity

Atomicity is introduced to eliminate the ambiguity of knowledge expressions. In SAOKE format, each fact is required to be atomic, which means that: (i) it is self-contained for an accurate expression; (ii) it cannot be decomposed into multiple valid facts. We provide examples in Table 2 to help understand these two criteria.

Note that the second criterion implies that any logical connections (including nested expressions) between facts are neglected (e.g., the third case in Table 2). This problem of expression relations between facts will be considered in the future version of SAOKE.

Table 1: Expected facts of an example sentence.

	Chinese	English Translation
Sentence	李白(701年－762年)，深受庄子思想影响，爽朗大方，爱饮酒作诗，喜交友，代表作有《望庐山瀑布》等著名诗歌。	Li Bai (701 - 762), with masterpieces of famous poetries such as "Watching the Lushan Waterfall", was deeply influenced by Zhuangzi's thought, hearty and generous, loved to drink and write poetry, and liked to make friends.
Relations	(李白, 深受X影响, 庄子思想) (李白, 爱, [饮酒|作诗]) (李白, 喜, 交友)	(Li Bai, deeply influenced by, Zhuangzi's thought) (Li Bai, loved to, [drink| write poetry]) (Li Bai, liked to, make friends)
Attribute	(李白, BIRTH, 701年) (李白, DEATH, 762年) (李白, 代表作, 《望庐山瀑布》)	(Li Bai, BIRTH, 701)(Li Bai, DEATH, 762) (Li Bai, masterpiece, "Watching the Lushan Waterfall")
Description	(李白, DESC, 爽朗大方)	(Li Bai, DESC, hearty and generous)
Concept	(《望庐山瀑布》, ISA, 著名诗歌)	("Watching the Lushan Waterfall", ISA, famous poetry)

Table 2: Example sentence and corresponding wrong/correct facts.

	Sentence	Wrong Facts	Correct Facts
Chinese	山东的GDP高于所有西部的省份。	(山东的GDP, 高于, 所有省份) (所有省份, DESC, 西部的)	(山东的GDP, 高于, 西部的所有省份)
English	Shandong's GDP is higher than in all western provinces.	(Shandong's GDP, is higher than, all provinces) (all provinces, DESC, western)	(Shandong's GDP, is higher than, all western provinces)
Chinese	李白游览了雄奇灵秀的泰山。	(李白, 游览, 雄奇灵秀的泰山)	(李白, 游览, 泰山) (泰山, DESC, 雄奇灵秀)
English	Li Bai visited the magnificent Mount Tai.	(Li Bai, visited, the magnificent Mount Tai)	(Li Bai, visited, the Mount Tai)(the Mount Tai, DESC, magnificent)
Chinese	在美国的帮助下，英国抵挡住了德国的进攻。	(英国, 在X的帮助下抵挡住了Y的进攻, 美国, 德国)	(美国, 帮助, 英国)(英国, 抵挡住了X的进攻, 德国)
English	With the help of the US, the British resisted the attack from German.	(the British, resisted the attack from X with the help of Y, German, the US)	(the US, helped, the British)(the British, resisted the attack from, German)

2.4 Compactness

Natural language may express several facts in a compact form. For example, in a sentence "李白爱饮酒作诗" ("Li Bai loved to drink and write poetry" in English), according to atomicity, two facts should be extracted: (李白, 爱, 饮酒)(李白, 爱, 作诗) ((Li Bai, loved to, drink)(Li Bai, loved to, write poetry) in English). In this situation, SAOKE adopts a compact expression to merge these two facts into one expression: (李白, 爱, [饮酒|作诗]) ((Li Bai, loved to, [drink| write poetry]) in English).

The compactness of expressions is introduced to fulfill, but not to violate the rule of "literally honest". SAOKE does not allow merging facts if facts are not expressed compactly in original sentences. By this means, the differences between the sentences and the corresponding knowledge expressions are reduced, which may help reduce the complexity of learning from data in SAOKE form.

With the above designs, SAOKE is able to express various kinds of facts, with each historically considered by different open information extraction algorithms, for example, verb based relations in SRLIE [7] and nominal attributes in ReNoun [31, 46], descriptive phrases for entities in EntityTagger [4], and hypernyms in HypeNet [41]. SAOKE introduces the atomicity to eliminate the ambiguity of knowledge expressions, and achieves better accuracy and compactness with the aid of the symbolic expressions.

3 SAOKE Data Set

We randomly collect sentences from Baidu Baike (http://baike.baidu.com), and send those sentences to a crowdsourcing company to label the involved facts. The workers are trained with labeling examples and tested with exams. Then the workers with high exam scores are asked to read and understand the facts in the sentences, and express the facts in the SAOKE format. During the procedure, one sentence is only labeled by one worker. Finally, 48,248 sentences with 107,288 facts are returned to us. The manual evaluation results on 100 randomly selected sentences show that the fact level precision and recall is 89.5% and 92.2% respectively. Table 3 shows the numbers and proportions of four types of facts (described in Section 2.1) contained in the data set. Note that the facts with missing predicates represented by "P" are classified into "Unknown". We publicize the data set at http://bdl.baidu.com/dataset/SAOKE.html.

Table 3: Numbers of facts of each type in SAOKE data set.

	Relation	Attribute	Description	Concept	Unknown
Total	81,563	7,779	10,612	3,900	3,434
Ratio	76.02%	7.25%	9.89%	3.64%	3.20%

Prior to the SAOKE data set, an annotated data set for OIE tasks with 3,200 sentences in 2 domains was released in [38] to evaluate OIE algorithms, in which the data set was said [38] "13 times larger than the previous largest annotated Open IE corpus". The SAOKE data set is 16 times larger than the data set in [38]. To the best of our knowledge, SAOKE data set is the largest publicly available human labeled data set for OIE tasks. Furthermore, the data set released in [38] was generated from a QA-SRL data set [18], which indicates that the data set only contains facts that can be discovered by SRL (Semantic Role Labeling) algorithms, and thus is biased, whereas the SAOKE data set is not biased to an algorithm.

Finally, the SAOKE data set contains sentences and facts from a large number of domains.

4 Logician

Given a sentence S and a set of expected facts (with all the possible types of facts) $\mathbb{F} = \{F_1, \cdots, F_n\}$ in SAOKE form, we join all the facts in the order that annotators wrote them into a char sequence F as the expected output. We build Logician under the attention-based sequence-to-sequence learning paradigm, to transform S into F, together with the restricted copy mechanism, the coverage mechanism and the gated dependency mechanism.

4.1 Attention based Sequence-to-sequence Learning

The attention-based sequence-to-sequence learning [1] have been successfully applied to the task of generating text and patterns. Given an input sentence $S = [w_1^S, \cdots, w_{N_S}^S]$, the target sequence $F = [w_1^F, \cdots, w_{N_F}^F]$ and a vocabulary V (including the symbols introduced in Section 2 and the OOV (out of vocabulary) tag) with size N_v, the words w_i^S and w_j^F can be represented as one-hot vectors v_i^S and v_j^F with dimension N_v, and transformed into N_e-dimensional distributed representation vectors by an embedding transform $x_i = Ev_i^S$ and $y_j = Ev_j^F$ respectively, where $E \in \mathbb{R}^{(N_e \times N_v)}$. Then the sequence of $\{x_i\}_{i=1}^{N_s}$ is transformed into a sequence of N_h-dimensional hidden states $H^S = [h_1^S, \cdots, h_{N_S}^S]$ using bi-directional GRU (Gated Recurrent Units) network [6], and the sequence of $\{y_j\}_{j=1}^{N_F}$ is transformed into a sequence of N_h-dimensional hidden states $H^F = [h_1^F, \cdots, h_{N_F}^F]$ using GRU network.

For each position t in the target sequence, the decoder learns a dynamic context vector c_t to focus attention on specific location l in the input hidden states H^S, then computes the probability of generated words by $p(w_t^F | \{w_1^F, \cdots, w_{t-1}^F\}, c_t) = g(h_{t-1}^F, s_t, c_t)$, where s_t is the hidden state of the GRU decoder, g is the word selection model (details could be found in [1]), and c_t is computed as $c_t = \sum_{j=1}^{N_S} \alpha_{tj} h_j$, where $\alpha_{tj} = \frac{\exp(e_{tj})}{\sum_{k=1}^{N_S} \exp(e_{tk})}$ and $e_{tj} = a(s_{t-1}, h_j^S) = v_a^T \tanh(W_a s_{t-1} + U_a h_j^S)$ is the alignment model to measure the strength of focus on the j-th location. $W_a \in \mathbb{R}^{(N_h \times N_h)}$, $U_a \in \mathbb{R}^{(N_h \times N_h)}$, and $v_a \in \mathbb{R}^{N_h}$ are weight matrices.

4.2 Restricted Copy Mechanism

The word selection model employed in [1] selects words from the whole vocabulary V, which evidently violates the "literal honest" requirement of SAOKE. We propose a restricted version of copy mechanism [15] as the word selection model for Logician:

We collect the symbols introduced in Section 2 into a keyword set K = {"*ISA*", "*DESC*", "*LOC*", "*BIRTH*", "*DEATH*", "=", "(", ")", "$","[", "]", "|", "*X*", "*Y*", "*Z*", "*P*"} where "$" is the separator of elements of fact tuples. "*X*", "*Y*", "*Z*", "*P*" are placeholders . When the decoder is considering generating a word w_t^F, it can choose w_t^F from either S or K.

$$p(w_t^F | w_{t-1}^F, s_t, c_t) = p_X(w_t^F | w_{t-1}^F, s_t, c_t) + p_K(w_t^F | w_{t-1}^F, s_t, c_t), \tag{1}$$

where p_X is the probability of copying from S and p_K is the probability of selecting from K. Since $S \cap K = \phi$ and there are no unknown words in this problem setting, we compute p_X and p_K in a simpler way than that in [15], as follows:

$$p_X(w_t^F = w_j^S) = \frac{1}{Z}\exp(\sigma((h_j^S)^T W_c) s_t),$$
$$p_K(w_t^F = k_i) = \frac{1}{Z}\exp(v_i^T W_o s_t),$$

where the (generic) Z is the normalization term, k_i is one of keywords, v_i is the one-hot indicator vector for k_i, $W_o \in \mathbb{R}^{(|K| \times N_h)}$, $W_c \in \mathbb{R}^{(N_h \times N_h)}$, and σ is a nonlinear activation function.

4.3 Coverage Mechanism

In practice, Logician may forget to extract some facts (*under-extractio*) or extract the same fact many times (*over-extraction*). We incorporate the coverage mechanism [40] into Logician to alleviate these problems. Formally, when the decoder considers generating a word w_t^F, a coverage vector m_j^t is introduced for each word w_j^S, and updated as follows:

$$m_j^t = \mu(m_j^{t-1}, \alpha_{tj}, h_j^S, s_{t-1}) = (1 - z_i) \circ m_j^{t-1} + z_j \circ \tilde{m}_j^t,$$
$$\tilde{m}_j^t = \tanh(W_h h_j^S + u_\alpha \alpha_{tj} + W_s s_{t-1} + U_m[r_i \circ m_j^{t-1}]),$$

where $\circ$ is the element-wise multiplication operator. The update gate z_j and the reset gate r_j are defined as, respectively,

$$z_j = \sigma(W_h^z h_j^S + u_\alpha^z \alpha_{tj} + W_s^z s_{t-1} + U_m^z m_j^{t-1}),$$
$$r_j = \sigma(W_h^r h_j^S + u_\alpha^r \alpha_{tj} + W_s^r s_{t-1} + U_m^r m_j^{t-1}),$$

where σ is a logistic sigmoid function. The coverage vector m_j^t contains the information about the historical attention focused on w_j^S, and is helpful for deciding whether w_j^S should be extracted or not. The alignment model is updated as follows [40]:

$$e_{tj} = a(s_{t-1}, h_j^S, m_j^{t-1}) = v_a^T \tanh(W_a s_{t-1} + U_a h_j^S + V_a m_j^{t-1}),$$

where $V_a \in \mathbb{R}^{(N_h \times N_h)}$.

4.4 Gated Dependency Attention

The semantic relationship between candidate words and the previously decoded word is valuable to guide the decoder to select the correct word. We introduce the gated dependency attention mechanism to utilize such guidance.

For a sentence S, we extract the dependency tree using NLP tools such as CoreNLP [27] for English and LTP [5] for Chinese, and convert the tree into a graph by adding reversed edges with a revised labels (for example, adding $w_j^S \xrightarrow{-SBV} w_i^S$ for edge $w_i^S \xrightarrow{SBV} w_j^S$ in the dependency tree). Then for each pair of words (w_i^S, w_j^S), the shortest path with labels $L = [w_1^L, \cdots, w_{N_L}^L]$ in the graph is computed and mapped into a sequence of N_e-dimensional distributed representation vectors $[l_1, \cdots, l_{N_L}]$ by the embedding operation. One can employ RNN network to convert this sequence of vectors into a feature vector, but RNN operation is time-consuming. We simply concatenate vectors in short paths ($N_L \le 3$) into a $3N_e$ dimensional vector and feed the vector into a two-layer feed forward neural network to generate an N_h-dimensional feature vector n_{ij}. For long paths with $N_L > 3$, n_{ij} is set to a zero vector. We define dependency attention vector $\tilde{u}_j^t = \sum_i p^*(w_t^F = w_i^S) n_{ij}$, where p^* is the sharpened probability p defined in Equation (1). If $w_t^F \in S$, $\tilde{u}_j^t$ represents the semantic relationship between w_t^F and w_j^S. If $w_t^F \in K$, then $\tilde{u}_j^t$ is close to zero. To correctly guide the decoder, we need to gate $\tilde{u}_j^t$ to remember the previous attention vector sometimes (for example, when \$ is selected), and to forget it sometimes (for example, when a new fact is started). Finally, we define $u_j^t = g(\tilde{u}_j^t)$ as the gated dependency attention vector, where g is the GRU gated function, and update the alignment model as follows:

$$\begin{aligned} e_{tj} &= a(s_{t-1}, h_j^S, m_j^{t-1}, u_j^{t-1}) \\ &= v_a^T \tanh(W_a s_{t-1} + U_a h_j + V_a m_j^{t-1} + D_a u_j^{t-1}) \end{aligned}$$

where $D_a \in \mathbb{R}^{(N_h \times N_h)}$.

4.5 Post processing

For each sequence generated by Logician, we parse it into a set of facts, remove tuples with illegal format or duplicated tuples. The resultant set is taken as the output of the Logician.

5 Empirical Evaluation

5.1 Experimental Design

We first measure the utility of various components in Logician to select the optimal model, and then compare this model to the state-of-the-art methods in four types of information extraction tasks: verb/preposition-based relation, nominal attribute, descriptive phrase and hyponymy relation. The SAOKE data set is split into training set, validating set and testing set with ratios of 80%, 10%, 10%, respectively. For all algorithms involved in the experiments, the training set can be used to train the model, the validating set can be used to select an optimal model, and the testing set is used to evaluate the performance.

5.1.1 Evaluation Metrics For each instance pair (S, F) in the test set, where S is the input sentence and F is the formatted string of ground truth of facts, we parse F into a set of tuples $\mathbb{F} = \{F_i\}_{j=1}^M$. Given an open information extraction algorithm, it reads S and produces a set of tuples $\mathbb{G} = \{G_i\}_{j=1}^N$. To evaluate how well the $\mathbb{G}$ approximates $\mathbb{F}$, we need to match each G_i to a ground truth fact F_j and check whether G_i tells the same fact as F_j. To conduct the match, we compute the similarity between each predicted fact in $\mathbb{G}$ and each ground truth fact in $\mathbb{F}$, then find the optimal matching to maximize the sum of matched similarities by solving a linear assignment problem [43]. In the procedure, the similarity between two facts is defined as

$$Sim(G_i, F_j) = \frac{\sum_{l=1}^{\min(\mathbf{n}(G_i), \mathbf{n}(F_j))} \mathrm{g}(G_i(l), F_j(l))}{\max(\mathbf{n}(G_i), \mathbf{n}(F_j))},$$

where $G_i(l)$ and $F_j(l)$ denote the l-th element of tuple G_i and F_j respectively, $\mathrm{g}(\cdot,\cdot)$ denotes the gestalt pattern matching [33] measure for two strings and $\mathbf{n}(\cdot)$ returns the length of the tuple.

Given a matched pair of G_i and F_j, we propose an automatic approach to judge whether they tell the same fact. They are judged as telling the same fact if one of the following two conditions is satisfied:

- $\mathbf{n}(G_i) = \mathbf{n}(F_j)$, and $\mathrm{g}(G_i(l), F_j(l)) \geq 0.85, l = 1, \cdots, \mathbf{n}(G_i)$;
- $\mathbf{n}(G_i) = \mathbf{n}(F_j)$, and $\mathrm{g}(\mathcal{S}(G_i), \mathcal{S}(F_j) \geq 0.85$;

where $\mathcal{S}$ is a function formatting a fact into a string by filling the arguments into the placeholders of the predicate.

With the automatic judgement, the precision (P), recall (R) and F_1-score over a test set can be computed. By defining a confidence measure and ordering the facts by their confidences, a precision-recall curve can be drawn to illustrate the overall performance of the algorithm. For Logician, the confidence of a fact is computed as the average of log probabilities over all words in that fact.

Beyond the automatic judgement, human evaluation is also employed. Given an algorithm and the corresponding fact confidence measure, we find a threshold that produces approximately 10% recall (measured by automatic judgement) on the validation set of SAOKE data set. A certain number of sentences (200 for verb/preposition based relation extraction task, and 1000 for other three tasks) are randomly chosen from the testing set of SAOKE data set, and the facts extracted from these sentences are filtered with that threshold. Then we invite three volunteers to manually refine the labeled set of facts for each sentence and vote to decide whether each filtered fact is correctly involved in the sentence. The standard precision, recall and F_1-score are reported as the human evaluation results.

5.1.2 Training the Logician Model For each instance pair (S, F) in the training set of SAOKE data set, we split S and F into words using LTP toolset [5], and words appearing in more than 2 sentences are added to the vocabulary. By adding the OOV (out of vocabulary) tag, we finally obtain a vocabulary V with size $N_V = 65,293$. The dimension of all embedding vectors is set to $N_e = 200$, and the dimension of hidden states is set to $N_h = 256$. We use a three-layer bi-directional GRU with dimension 128 to encode $\{x_i\}_{i=1}^{N_S}$ into hidden states $\{h_i^S\}_{i=1}^{N_S}$, and a two-layer GRU with hidden-dimension 256 to encode the sequence of $\{y_j\}_{j=1}^{N_F}$ into hidden states $\{h_j^F\}_{j=1}^{N_F}$. Finally, the Logician network is constructed as stated in Section 4. The Logician is then trained using stochastic gradient descent (SGD) with RMSPROP [20] strategy for 20 epochs with batch size 10 on the training set of SAOKE data set. The model with best F_1-score by automatic judgement on the validation set is selected as the trained model. When the model is trained, given a sentence, we employ the greedy search procedure to produce the fact sequences.

5.2 Evaluating Components' Utilities

In this section, we analyze the effects of components involved in Logician: restricted copy, coverage, and gated dependency. Since the restricted copy mechanism is the essential requirement of Logician in order to achieve the goal of literally honest, we take the Logician with only copy mechanism (denoted by *Copy*) as the baseline, and analyze the effeteness of coverage mechanism (denoted by *Copy + Coverage*), gated dependency mechanism (denoted by *Copy + GatedDep*) and both (denoted by *All*). Furthermore, there is another option of whether or not to involve shallow semantic information such as POS-tag and NER-tag into the model. For models involving such information, the POS-tag and NER-tag of each word in sentence S are annotated using LTP. For each word in F that is not any keyword in K, the POS-tag and NER-tag are copied from the corresponding original word in S. For each keyword in K, a unique POS-tag and a unique NER-tag are assigned to it. Finally, for each word in S or F, the POS-tag and NER-tag are mapped into N_e-dimensional distributed representation vectors and are concatenated into x_i or y_j to attend the training.

Table 4: Analysis of Components involved in Logician.

	With Shallow Tag			No Shallow Tag		
	P	R	F_1	P	R	F_1
Copy	0.375	0.412	0.393	0.378	0.431	0.403
Copy + Coverage	0.390	0.390	0.390	0.307	0.417	0.353
Copy + GatedDep	0.427	0.371	0.397	0.335	0.419	0.372
All	0.443	0.419	**0.431**	0.373	0.435	0.402

All models are trained using the same settings described in above section, and the default output facts (without any confidence filtering) are evaluated by the automatic judgement. The results are reported in Table 4. From the results, we can see that the model involving all the components and shallow tag information archives the best performance. We use that model to attend the comparisons with existing approaches.

5.3 Comparison with Existing Approaches

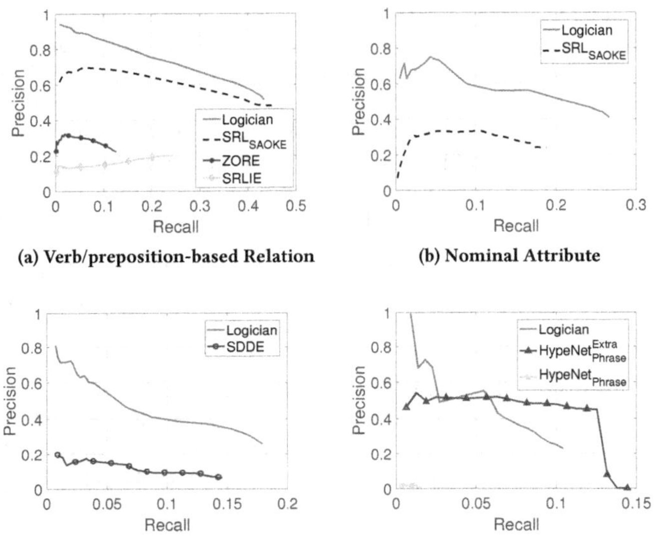

(a) Verb/preposition-based Relation (b) Nominal Attribute (c) Descriptive Phrase (d) Hyponymy

Figure 1: Performance comparison on four types of information extraction tasks.

5.3.1 Verb/preposition-Based Relation Extraction In the task of extracting verb/preposition based facts, we compare our Logician with the following state-of-the-art Chinese OIE algorithms:

SRLIE: our implementation of SRLIE [7] for the Chinese language, which first uses LTP tool set to extract the semantic role labels, and converts the results into fact tuples using heuristic rules. The confidence of each fact is computed as the ratio of the number of words in the fact to the number of words in the shortest fragment of source sentence that contains all words in the fact.

ZORE : the Chinese Open Relation Extraction system [32], which builds a set of patterns by bootstrapping based on dependency parsing results, and uses the patterns to extract relations. We used the program provided by the author of ZORE system [32] to generate the extraction results in XML format, and developed an algorithm to transform the facts into n-ary tuples, where auxiliary information extracted by ZORE is removed. The confidence measure for ZORE is the same as that for SRLIE.

SRL$_{SAOKE}$: our implementation of the states-of-the-art SRL algorithm proposed in [17] with modifications to fit OIE tasks. SRL$_{SAOKE}$ extracts facts in two steps: (i) Predicate head word detection: detects head word for predicate of each possible fact, where head word of a predicate is the last word in the predicate depending on words outside the predicate in the dependency tree. (ii) Element phrase detection: For each detected head word, detects the subject phrase, predicate phrase and object phrases by tagging the sentence with an extended BIOE tagging scheme, which tags the word neighboring the separation point of the phrase by "M" to cope with the separated phrase. We modify the code provided by the author of [17] to implement above strategy, and then train a model with the same parameter setting in [17] on the training set of SAOKE data set. The confidence measure for SRL$_{SAOKE}$ is computed as the average of log probabilities over all tags of words in facts. Note that SRL$_{SAOKE}$ can extract both verb/preposition based relation and nominal attributes, but in this section, we only evaluate the results of the former type of facts.

The precision-recall curves of Logician and above three comparison algorithms are shown in Figure 1a, and the human evaluation results are shown in the first section of Table 5.

5.3.2 Nominal Attribute Extraction The state-of-the-art nominal attribute extraction method is ReNoun [31, 46]. However, it relies on a pre-constructed English attribute schema system [16] which is not available for Chinese, so it is not an available baseline for Chinese. Since SRL$_{SAOKE}$ can extract nominal attributes, we compare Logician with SRL$_{SAOKE}$ on this task. The precision-recall curves of Logician and SRL$_{SAOKE}$ on the nominal attribute extraction task are shown in Figure 1b, and the human evaluation results are shown in the second section of Table 5.

5.3.3 Descriptive Phrase Extraction Descriptive phrase extraction has been considered in [4], in which domain names are required to develop patterns to extract candidates for descriptive phrases, so this method is not applicable to open domain tasks. We develop a baseline algorithm (called Semantic Dependency Description Extractor, SDDE) to extract descriptive phrase. It extracts semantic dependency relation between words using LTP toolset, and for each noun w_n which is the parent of some semantic "Desc" relations, identifies a noun phrase N with w_n as its heading word, assembles a descriptive phrase D containing all words with "Desc" relation to w_n, and finally outputs the fact "(N, $DESC$, D)". The confidence of fact in SDDE is computed as the ratio of the number of adverbs and adjectives in D to the number of words in D. The precision-recall curves of Logician and SDDE on the descriptive phrase extraction task are shown in Figure 1c, and the human evaluation results are shown in the third section of Table 5.

5.3.4 Hyponymy Extraction HypeNet [41] is the state-of-the-art algorithm recommended for hyponymy extraction [42], which judges whether hyponymy relation exists between two given words. To make it capable of judging hyponymy relation between two phrases, we replace the word embedding vector component in HypeNet by an LSTM network. Two modified HypeNet models are built using different training data sets: (i) HypeNet$_{Phrase}$: using the pairs of phrases with ISA relation in the training set of SAOKE data set (9,407 pairs after the compact expression expansion); (ii) $\text{HypeNet}^{\text{Extra}}_{\text{Phrase}}$: besides the training set for $\text{HypeNet}_{\text{Phrase}}$, adding two Chinese hyponymy data sets (1.4 million pair of words in total in hyponymy relation): Tongyici Cilin (Extended) (CilinE for short) [5] and cleaned Wikipedia Category data [25]. In both cases, the sentences from both Chinese Wikipedia pages and training set of SAOKE data set are taken as the background corpus for the HypeNet algorithm. In the testing phase, the trained models are used to predict whether the hyponymy relation exists for each pair of noun phrases/words in sentences of the testing set of SAOKE data set. The confidence of a judgement is the predicted probability of the existence of hyponymy relation. The precision-recall curves of Logician, $\text{HypeNet}_{\text{Phrase}}$ and $\text{HypeNet}^{\text{Extra}}_{\text{Phrase}}$ are shown in Figure 1d, and the human evaluation results in the fourth section of Table 5.

Table 5: Human evaluation results on four types of information extraction tasks.

Task	Method	P	R	F_1
1. Relation	SRLIE	0.166	0.119	0.139
	ZORE	0.300	0.136	0.187
	$\text{SRL}_{\text{SAOKE}}$	0.610	0.130	0.214
	Logician	0.883	0.147	**0.252**
2. Attribute	$\text{SRL}_{\text{SAOKE}}$	0.362	0.102	0.159
	Logician	0.603	0.126	**0.208**
3. Description	SDDE	0.135	0.146	0.140
	Logician	0.392	0.109	**0.170**
4. Hyponymy	$\text{HypeNet}_{\text{Phrase}}$	0.007	0.016	0.010
	$\text{HypeNet}^{\text{Extra}}_{\text{Phrase}}$	0.442	0.090	0.149
	Logician	0.317	0.129	**0.183**

5.4 Results Analysis

The experimental results reveal that, Logician outperforms the comparison methods with large margin in first three tasks. For hyponymy detection tasks, Logician overwhelms the $\text{HypeNet}_{\text{Phrase}}$ using the same training data, and produces comparable results to $\text{HypeNet}^{\text{Extra}}_{\text{Phrase}}$ with much less training data. Table 6 exhibits several example sentences and the facts extracted by these algorithms.

The poor performance of pattern-based methods is plausibly due to the noise in SAOKE data set. The sentences in SAOKE data set are randomly selected from a web encyclopedia, with free and casual writing style, are thus more noisy than the training data of NLP toolset used by these methods. In this situation, the NLP toolset may produce poor results, so do the pattern-based methods.

Models learned from the SAOKE data set archive much better performance. Nevertheless, $\text{SRL}_{\text{SAOKE}}$ extracts each fact without knowing whether a candidate word has been used in other facts, which results in the misleading overlap of the word "学" ("Learn" in English) between two facts in the first case of Table 6. Similarly, $\text{HypeNet}_{\text{Phrase}}$ and $\text{HypeNet}^{\text{Extra}}_{\text{Phrase}}$ focus on the semantic vectors of pairs of phrases and their dependency paths in the background corpus. They extract each fact independently from other facts and hence do not know whether there have been any other relations extracted about these two phrases. In other words, for those comparison methods, an important source of information is neglected and a global optimization for all facts involved in sentences is absent.

On the contrary, Logician performs global optimization over the facts involved in each sentence by the sequence-to-sequence learning paradigm with the help of the coverage mechanism, in which facts compete each other to attract the attention of words, but also cooperate to share words. Valuable information is shared between these multiple tasks, which makes Logician consistently superior to other algorithms in these tasks.

Furthermore, $\text{SRL}_{\text{SAOKE}}$ and HypeNet methods suffer from the OOV problem, such as unfamiliar words/phrases like the person name and school name in the last case of Table 6. In this situation they may fail to produce a reasonable result. Logician is able to cope with unfamiliar words/phrases by exploiting the context information using deep RNN network with the help of copy mechanism.

5.5 Extraction Error Analysis of Logician

We do a preliminary analysis for the results produced by the Logician model. The most notable problem is that it is unable to recall some facts for long or complex sentences. The last case in Table 6 exhibits such situation, where the fact (蔡竞,ISA,经济学博士)((Cai Jing, ISA, Ph. D. in economics) in English) is not recalled. This phenomenon indicates that the coverage mechanism may lose effectiveness in this situation. The second class of error is incomplete extraction, as exhibited in the third case in Table 6. Due to the incomplete extraction, the left parts may interfere the generation of other facts, and result in nonsense results, which is the third class of error. We believe it is helpful to introduce extra rewards into the learning procedure of Logician to overcome these problems. For example, the reward could be the amount of remaining information left after the fact extraction, or the completeness of extracted facts. Developing such rewards and reinforcement learning algorithms using those rewards to refine Logician belongs to our future works.

6 Related Works

6.1 Knowledge Expressions

Tuple is the most common knowledge expression format for OIE systems to express n-ary relation between subject and objects. Beyond such information, ClausIE [10] extracts extra information in the tuples: a complement, and one or more adverbials, and OLLIE [36] extracts additional context information. SAOKE is able to express n-ary relations, and can be easily extended to support the knowledge extracted by ClausIE, but needs to be redesigned to support context information, which belongs to our future work.

However, there is a fundamental difference between SAOKE and tuples in traditional OIE systems. In traditional OIE systems, knowledge expression is generally not directly related to the extraction algorithm. It is a tool to reorganize the extracted knowledge into a form for further easy reading/storing/computing. However, SAOKE is proposed to act as the direct learning target of the end-to-end Logician model. In such end-to-end framework, knowledge representation is the core of the system, which decides what information would be extracted and how complex the learning algorithm would be. To our knowledge, SAOKE is the first attempt to design a knowledge expression friendly to the end-to-end learning algorithm for OIE tasks. Efforts are still needed to make SAOKE more powerful in order to express more complex knowledge such as events.

Table 6: Example of extraction from a sentence for each task.

<table>
<tr><th></th><th></th><th>Chinese</th><th>English Translation</th><th>Label</th></tr>
<tr><td rowspan="5">1. Relation</td><td>Sentence</td><td>学道访仙，晚年修道于石笋山</td><td>Learn the Tao, visit the immortal, practice Taoism in the Stalagmite Hill in the old age</td><td></td></tr>
<tr><td>SRLIE</td><td>(X,学,道)(X,访,仙)</td><td>(X, learn, the Tao)(X, visit, the immortal)</td><td>✓</td></tr>
<tr><td>ZORE</td><td>(学道,访,仙)
(学道,修道于,石笋山)</td><td>(Learn the Tao, visit, the immortal)
(Learn the Tao, practice Taoism in, the Stalagmite Hill)</td><td>✗
✗</td></tr>
<tr><td>SRL_{SAOKE}</td><td>(X,学,道访)(学,修道于,石笋山)</td><td>(X, learn, Tao visit)(Learn, practice Taoism in, the Stalagmite Hill)</td><td>✗</td></tr>
<tr><td>Logician</td><td>(X,学,道)(X,访,仙)
(X,修道于,石笋山)</td><td>(X, learn, the Tao)(X, visit, the immortal)
(X, practice Taoism in, the Stalagmite Hill)</td><td>✓
✓</td></tr>
<tr><td rowspan="3">2. Attribute</td><td>Sentence</td><td>全村辖区总面积约10平方公里，其中耕地132公顷。</td><td>The whole village area of about 10 square kilometers, of which 132 hectares of arable land.</td><td></td></tr>
<tr><td>SRL_{SAOKE}</td><td>(全村辖区,总面积,约10平方公里)</td><td>(The village, whole area, about 10 square kilometers)</td><td>✓</td></tr>
<tr><td>Logician</td><td>(全村辖区,总面积,约10平方公里)
(全村,耕地,132公顷)</td><td>(The village, whole area, about 10 square kilometers)
(The village, arable land, 132 hectares)</td><td>✓
✓</td></tr>
<tr><td rowspan="3">3. Description</td><td>Sentence</td><td>硫酸钙较为常用，其性质稳定，无嗅无味，微溶于水</td><td>Calcium sulfate is commonly used, its properties are stable, odorless and tasteless, slightly soluble in water</td><td></td></tr>
<tr><td>SDDE</td><td>No Recall</td><td>No Recall</td><td></td></tr>
<tr><td>Logician</td><td>(硫酸钙,DESC,[性质稳定|无嗅无味])
(硫酸钙,DESC,稳定)</td><td>(Calcium sulfate, DESC, [properties stable | odorless and tasteless])
(Calcium sulfate, DESC, stable)</td><td>✓
✗</td></tr>
<tr><td rowspan="4">4. Hyponymy</td><td>Sentence</td><td>蔡竞，男，汉族，四川射洪人，西南财经大学经济学院毕业，经济学博士。</td><td>Cai Jing, male, Han Chinese, a Sichuan Shehong native, graduated from the economics school of Southwestern University of Finance and Economics (SUFE), and a Ph. D. in economics.</td><td></td></tr>
<tr><td>$HypeNet_{Phrase}$</td><td>(经济学博士,ISA, 蔡)</td><td>(Ph. D. in economics,ISA,Cai)</td><td>✗</td></tr>
<tr><td>$HypeNet_{Phrase}^{Extra}$</td><td>(西南财经大学经济学院,ISA,经济学博士)
(西南财经大学经济学院,ISA,四川)
(经济学博士,ISA,西南财经大学经济学院)</td><td>(the economics school of SUFE, ISA, Ph. D. in economics)
(the economics school of SUFE,ISA,Sichuan)
(Ph. D. in economics,ISA,the economics school of SUFE)</td><td>✗
✗
✗</td></tr>
<tr><td>Logician</td><td>(蔡竞,ISA,[男|汉族|四川射洪人])</td><td>(Cai Jing,ISA,[male |Han Chinese | Sichuan Shehong native])</td><td>✓</td></tr>
</table>

6.2 Relation Extraction

Relation extraction is the task to identify semantic connections between entities. Major existing relation extraction algorithms can be classified into two classes: closed-domain and open-domain. Closed-domain algorithms are learnt to identify a fixed and finite set of relations, using supervised methods [21, 30, 48, 50] or weakly supervised methods [26, 29], while the open-domain algorithms, represented by aforementioned OIE systems, discover open-domain relations without predefined schema. Beyond these two classes, methods like universal schema [35] are able to learn from both data with fixed and finite set of relations, such as relations in Freebase, and data with open-domain surface relations produced by heuristic patterns or OIE systems.

Logician can be used as an OIE system to extract open-domain relation between entities, and act as sub-systems for knowledge base construction/completion with the help of schema mapping [37]. Compared with existing OIE systems, which are pattern-based or self-supervised by labeling samples using patterns [28], to our knowledge Logician is the first model trained in a supervised end-to-end approach for OIE task, which has exhibited powerful ability in our experiments. There are some neural based end-to-end systems [26, 30, 50] proposed for relation extraction, but they all aim to solve the close-domain problem.

However, Logician is not limited to relation extraction task. First, Logician extracts more information beyond relations. Second, Logician focuses on examining how natural languages express facts [12], and producing helpful intermediate structures for high level tasks.

6.3 Language to Logic

Efforts had been made to map natural language sentences into logical form. Some approaches such as [11, 22, 47, 49] learn the mapping under the supervision of manually labeled logical forms, while others [3, 24] are indirectly supervised by distant information, system rewards, etc. However, all previous works rely on a pre-defined, domain specific logical system, which limits their ability to learn facts out of the pre-defined logical system.

Logician can be viewed as a system that maps language to *natural logic*, in which the majority of information is expressed by natural phrase. Other than systems mentioned above which aim at execution using the logical form, Logician focuses on understanding how the fact and logic are expressed by natural language. Further mapping to domain-specific logical system or even executor can be built on the basis of Logician's output, and we believe that, with the help of Logician, the work would be easier and the overall performance of the system may be improved.

7 Conclusion

In this paper, we consider the open information extraction (OIE) problem for a variety of types of facts in a unified view. Our solution consists of three components: **SAOKE format**, **SAOKE data set**, and **Logician**. SAOKE form is designed to express different types of facts in a unified manner. We publicly release the largest manually labeled data set for OIE tasks in SAOKE form. Using the labeled SAOKE data set, we train an end-to-end neural sequence-to-sequence model, called Logician, to transform sentences in natural language into facts. The experiments reveal the superiority of Logician in various open-domain information extraction tasks to the state-of-the-art algorithms.

Regarding future work, there are at least three promising directions. Firstly, one can investigate knowledge expression methods to extend SAOKE to express more complex knowledge, for tasks such as event extraction. Secondly, one can develop novel learning strategies to improve the performance of Logician and adapt the algorithm to the extended future version of SAOKE. Thirdly, one can extend SAOKE format and Logician algorithm in other languages.

References

[1] Dzmitry Bahdanau, Kyunghyun Cho, and Yoshua Bengio. 2015. Neural Machine Translation By Jointly Learning To Align and Translate. In *Proceedings of ICLR.*

[2] Michele Banko, Mj Cafarella, and Stephen Soderland. 2007. Open information extraction for the web. In *IJCAI.* 2670–2676.

[3] Qingqing Cai and Alexander Yates. 2013. Large-scale Semantic Parsing via Schema Matching and Lexicon Extension. In *Proceedings of the 51st Annual Meeting of ACL.* 423–433.

[4] Kaushik Chakrabarti, Surajit Chaudhuri, Tao Cheng, and Dong Xin. 2011. Entity-tagger: automatically tagging entities with descriptive phrases. In *Proceedings of the 20th International Conference Companion on WWW.* 19–20.

[5] Wanxiang Che, Zhenghua Li, and Ting Liu. 2010. LTP: A Chinese Language Technology Platform. In *Proceedings of COLING.* 13–16.

[6] Kyunghyun Cho, Bart van Merrienboer, Caglar Gulcehre, Dzmitry Bahdanau, Fethi Bougares, Holger Schwenk, and Yoshua Bengio. 2014. Learning Phrase Representations using RNN Encoder-Decoder for Statistical Machine Translation. In *Proceedings of the 2014 Conference on EMNLP.* 1724–1734.

[7] Janara Christensen, Mausam, Stephen Soderland, and Oren Etzioni. 2011. An analysis of open information extraction based on semantic role labeling. In *Proceedings of the sixth International Conference on Knowledge Capture.* 113–120.

[8] Janara Christensen, Mausam, Stephen Soderland, Oren Etzioni, Mausam, Stephen Soderland, and Oren Etzioni. 2013. Towards Coherent Multi-Document Summarization. In *Proceedings of the 2013 Conference of NAACL: HLT.* 1163–1173.

[9] Janara Christensen, Stephen Soderland, and Gagan Bansal. 2014. Hierarchical Summarization: Scaling Up Multi-Document Summarization. In *Proceedings of the 52nd Annual Meeting of ACL.* 902–912.

[10] Luciano Del Corro and Rainer Gemulla. 2013. ClausIE: Clause-Based Open Information Extraction. In *Proceedings of the 22nd International Conference on WWW.* 355–366.

[11] Li Dong and Mirella Lapata. 2016. Language to Logical Form with Neural Attention. In *In Proceedings of the Annual Meeting of ACL.* 33–43. arXiv:1601.01280

[12] Oren Etzioni, Anthony Fader, Janara Christensen, Stephen Soderland, and Mausam. 2011. Open information extraction: The second generation. In *Proceedings of IJCAI.* 3–10.

[13] Anthony Fader, Stephen Soderland, and Oren Etzioni. 2011. Identifying Relations for Open Information Extraction. In *Proceedings of the Conference on EMNLP.* 1535—-1545.

[14] Anthony Fader, Luke S Zettlemoyer, and Oren Etzioni. 2014. Open Question Answering Over Curated and Extracted Knowledge Bases. In *Proceedings of the 20th ACM SIGKDD.* 1156–1165.

[15] Jiatao Gu, Zhengdong Lu, Hang Li, and Victor O.K. Li. 2016. Incorporating Copying Mechanism in Sequence-to-Sequence Learning. In *Proceedings of the 54th Annual Meeting of ACL.* 1631–1640.

[16] Rahul Gupta and A Halevy. 2014. Biperpedia: An Ontology for Search Applications. In *Proceedings of the VLDB Endowment.* 505–516.

[17] Luheng He, Kenton Lee, Mike Lewis, and Luke Zettlemoyer. 2017. Deep Semantic Role Labeling: What Works and What's Next. In *Proceedings of the 55th Annual Meeting of the ACL.* 473–483.

[18] Luheng He, Mike Lewis, and Luke Zettlemoyer. 2015. Question-Answer Driven Semantic Role Labeling: Using Natural Language to Annotate Natural Language. In *Proceedings of the 2015 Conference on EMNLP.* 643–653.

[19] Marti A. Hearst. 1992. Automatic Acquisition of Hyponyms ftom Large Text Corpora. In *Proceedings of the 14th conference on Computational Linguistics.* 23–28.

[20] Geoffrey Hinton, Nitish Srivastava, and Kevin Swersky. 2012. *Overview of mini-batch gradient descent.* Technical Report.

[21] Nanda Kambhatla. 2004. Combining lexical, syntactic, and semantic features with maximum entropy models for extracting relations. In *Proceedings of the ACL: Interactive Poster and Demonstration Sessions.*

[22] Rohit J Kate, Yuk Wah, and Wong Raymond. 2005. Learning to Transform Natural to Formal Languages. In *Proceedings of the 20th AAAI.* 1062—-1068.

[23] Tushar Khot, Ashish Sabharwal, and Peter Clark. 2017. Answering Complex Questions Using Open Information Extraction. In *Proceedings of the 55th Annual Meeting of the ACL.* 311—-316. arXiv:1704.05572

[24] Tom Kwiatkowski, Eunsol Choi, Yoav Artzi, and Luke Zettlemoyer. 2013. Scaling Semantic Parsers with On-the-fly Ontology Matching. In *Proceedings of the 2013 Conference on EMNLP.* 1545–1556.

[25] Jinyang Li, Chengyu Wang, Xiaofeng He, Rong Zhang, and Ming Gao. 2015. User Generated Content Oriented Chinese Taxonomy Construction. In *Lecture Notes in Computer Science.* Vol. 9313. 623–634.

[26] Yankai Lin, Shiqi Shen, Zhiyuan Liu, Huanbo Luan, and Maosong Sun. 2016. Neural Relation Extraction with Selective Attention over Instances. In *Proceedings of the 54th Annual Meeting of ACL.* 2124–2133.

[27] Christopher D Manning, John Bauer, Jenny Finkel, Steven J Bethard, Mihai Surdeanu, and David McClosky. 2014. The Stanford CoreNLP Natural Language Processing Toolkit. In *Proceedings of 52nd Annual Meeting of ACL: System Demonstrations.* 55–60. arXiv:arXiv:1011.1669v3

[28] Mausam. 2016. Open Information Extraction Systems and Downstream Applications. In *Proceedings of the 25th IJCAI.* 4074–4077.

[29] Mike Mintz, Steven Bills, Rion Snow, and Dan Jurafsky. 2009. Distant supervision for relation extraction without labeled data. In *Proceedings of the Joint Conference of the 47th Annual Meeting of the ACL and the 4th IJCNLP,* Vol. 2. 1003.

[30] Makoto Miwa and Mohit Bansal. 2016. End-to-End Relation Extraction using LSTMs on Sequences and Tree Structures. In *Proceedings of the 54th Annual Meeting of ACL.* 1105–1116.

[31] Harinder Pal and Mausam. 2016. Demonyms and Compound Relational Nouns in Nominal Open IE. In *Proceedings of the 5th Workshop on AKBC.* 35–39.

[32] Likun Qiu and Yue Zhang. 2014. ZORE : A Syntax-based System for Chinese Open Relation Extraction. In *Proceedings of the 2014 Conference on EMNLP.* 1870–1880.

[33] John W Ratcliff and David E Metzener. 1988. Pattern Matching: The Gestalt Approach. *Dr Dobb's* 13, 7 (1988).

[34] Sebastian Riedel, Limin Yao, Andrew McCallum, and Benjamin M Marlin. 2013. Relation Extraction with Matrix Factorization and Universal Schemas. *Proceedings of the 2013 Conference of NAACL: HLT* June (2013), 74–84.

[35] Sebastian Riedel, Limin Yao, Andrew McCallum, and Benjamin M Marlin. 2013. Relation Extraction with Matrix Factorization and Universal Schemas. In *Proceedings of the 2013 Conference of NAACL: HLT.* 74–84.

[36] Michael Schmitz, Robert Bart, Stephen Soderland, and Oren Etzioni. 2012. Open language learning for information extraction. In *Proceedings of the 2012 Joint Conference on EMNLP and CoNLL.* 523–534.

[37] Stephen Soderland, Brendan Roof, Bo Qin, and Shi Xu. 2010. Adapting Open Information Extraction to Domain-Specific Relations. *AI Magazine* 31, 3 (2010), 93–102.

[38] Gabriel Stanovsky and Ido Dagan. 2016. Creating a Large Benchmark for Open Information Extraction. In *Proceedings of the 2016 Conference on EMNLP.* 2300–2305.

[39] Gabriel Stanovsky, Ido Dagan, and Mausam. 2015. Open IE as an Intermediate Structure for Semantic Tasks. In *Proceedings of the 53rd Annual Meeting of ACL and the 7th IJCNLP.* 303–308.

[40] Zhaopeng Tu, Zhengdong Lu, Yang Liu, Xiaohua Liu, and Hang Li. 2016. Modeling Coverage for Neural Machine Translation. *In Proceedings of the Annual Meeting of ACL* (2016), 76–85.

[41] Vered Shwartz, Yoav Goldberg, Ido Dagan, Vered Shwartz, Yoav Goldberg, and Ido Dagan. 2016. Improving hypernymy detection with an integrated path-based and distributional method. In *Proceedings of the 54th Annual Meeting of ACL.* 2389–2398. arXiv:1603.06076

[42] Chengyu Wang and Xiaofeng He. 2017. A Short Survey on Taxonomy Learning from Text Corpora : Issues , Resources and Recent Advances. In *Proceedings of the Conference on EMNLP.*

[43] Wikipedia. 2017. Assignment problem— Wikipedia, The Free Encyclopedia. (2017).

[44] Fei Wu and Daniel S Weld. 2010. Open Information Extraction using Wikipedia. In *Proceedings of the 48th Annual Meeting of ACL.* 118–127.

[45] Wentao Wu, Hongsong Li, Haixun Wang, and Kenny Q Zhu. 2012. Probase: A probabilistic taxonomy for text understanding. In *Proceedings of the 2012 ACM SIGMOD.* 481–492.

[46] Mohamed Yahya, Steven Euijong Whang, Rahul Gupta, and Alon Halevy. 2014. ReNoun : Fact Extraction for Nominal Attributes. In *Proceedings of the Conference on EMNLP 2014, Doha, Qatar.* 325–335.

[47] Pengcheng Yin, Zhengdong Lu, Hang Li, and Ben Kao. 2016. Neural Enquirer: Learning to Query Tables. In *In Proceedings of the Annual Meeting of ACL.* 29–35.

[48] Dmitry Zelenko, Chinatsu Aone, Anthony Richardella, Jaz Kandola, Thomas Hofmann, Tomaso Poggio, and John Shawe-Taylor. 2003. Kernel Methods for Relation Extraction. *Journal of Machine Learning Research* 3 (2003), 1083–1106.

[49] Luke S Zettlemoyer and Michael Collins. 2005. Learning to Map Sentences to Logical Form : Structured Classification with Probabilistic Categorial Grammars. In *Proceedings of the 21st Conference on UAI.* 658–666.

[50] Suncong Zheng, Feng Wang, Hongyun Bao, Yuexing Hao, Peng Zhou, and Bo Xu. 2017. Joint Extraction of Entities and Relations Based on a Novel Tagging Scheme. *Proceedings of the 55th Annual Meeting of the ACL* (2017), 1227–1236.

Personalized Top-N Sequential Recommendation via Convolutional Sequence Embedding

Jiaxi Tang
School of Computing Science
Simon Fraser University
British Columbia, Canada
jiaxit@sfu.ca

Ke Wang
School of Computing Science
Simon Fraser University
British Columbia, Canada
wangk@cs.sfu.ca

ABSTRACT

Top-N sequential recommendation models each user as a sequence of items interacted in the past and aims to predict top-N ranked items that a user will likely interact in a "near future". The order of interaction implies that sequential patterns play an important role where more recent items in a sequence have a larger impact on the next item. In this paper, we propose a Convolutional Sequence Embedding Recommendation Model (*Caser*) as a solution to address this requirement. The idea is to embed a sequence of recent items into an "image" in the time and latent spaces and learn sequential patterns as local features of the image using convolutional filters. This approach provides a unified and flexible network structure for capturing both general preferences and sequential patterns. The experiments on public data sets demonstrated that Caser consistently outperforms state-of-the-art sequential recommendation methods on a variety of common evaluation metrics.

CCS CONCEPTS

• **Information systems → Retrieval models and ranking**;

KEYWORDS

Recommender System; Sequential Prediction; Convolutional Neural Networks

ACM Reference format:
Jiaxi Tang and Ke Wang. 2018. Personalized Top-N Sequential Recommendation via Convolutional Sequence Embedding. In *Proceedings of Eleventh ACM International Conference on Web Search and Data Mining, February 5–9, 2018, Marina Del Rey, CA, USA, (WSDM 2018)*, 9 pages.
DOI: 10.1145/3159652.3159656

1 INTRODUCTION

Recommender systems have become a core technology in many applications. Most systems, e.g., *top-N recommendation* [9][19], recommend the items based on the user's *general preferences* without paying attention to the recency of items.

For example, some user always prefer Apple's products to Samsung's products. General preferences represent user's long term and static behaviors. Another type of user behaviors is *sequential patterns* where the next item or action more likely depends on the items or actions the user engaged recently. Sequential patterns represent the user's short term and dynamic behaviors and come from a certain relationship between the items within a close proximity of time. For example, a user likely buys phone accessories soon after buying an iPhone, though in general the user does not buy phone accessories. In this case, the systems that consider only general preferences will miss the opportunity of recommending phone accessories after selling an iPhone since buying phone accessories is not a long term user behavior.

1.1 Top-N Sequential Recommendation

To model user's sequential patterns, the work in [17, 21] considers *top-N sequential recommendation* that recommends N items that a user likely interacts with in a near future. This problem assumes a set of users $\mathcal{U} = \{u_1, u_2, \cdots, u_{|\mathcal{U}|}\}$ and a universe of items $\mathcal{I} = \{i_1, i_2, \cdots, i_{|\mathcal{I}|}\}$. Each user u is associated with a sequence of some items from $\mathcal{I}$, $\mathcal{S}^u = (\mathcal{S}^u_1, \cdots, \mathcal{S}^u_{|\mathcal{S}^u|})$, where $\mathcal{S}^u_i \in \mathcal{I}$. The index t for $\mathcal{S}^u_t$ denotes the order in which an action occurs in the sequence $\mathcal{S}^u$, not the absolute timestamp as in temporal recommendation like [14, 31, 34]. Given all users' sequences $\mathcal{S}^u$, the goal is to recommend each user a list of items that maximize her/his future needs, by considering both general preferences and sequential patterns. Unlike conventional top-N recommendation, top-N sequential recommendation models the user behavior as a sequence of items, instead of a set of items.

1.2 Limitations of Previous Work

The Markov chain based model [2, 6, 21, 30] is an early approach to top-N sequential recommendation, where an L-order Markov chain makes recommendations based on L previous actions. The first-order Markov chain is an item-to-item transition matrix learnt using maximum likelihood estimation. Factorized personalized Markov chains (FPMC) [21] proposed by Rendle *et al.* and its variant [2] improved this method by factorizing this transition matrix into two latent and low-rank sub-matrices. Factorized Sequential Prediction with Item Similarity ModeLs (Fossil) [6] proposed by He *et al.* generalizes this method to high-order Markov chains using a weighted sum aggregation over previous items' latent representations. However, existing approaches suffered from two major limitations:

Fail to model union-Level sequential patterns. As shown in Figure 1a, the Markov chain models only **point-level** sequential patterns where each of the previous actions (blue) influences the target action (yellow) individually, instead of collectively. FPMC

WSDM 2018, February 5–9, 2018, Marina Del Rey, CA, USA

DOI: 10.1145/3159652.3159656

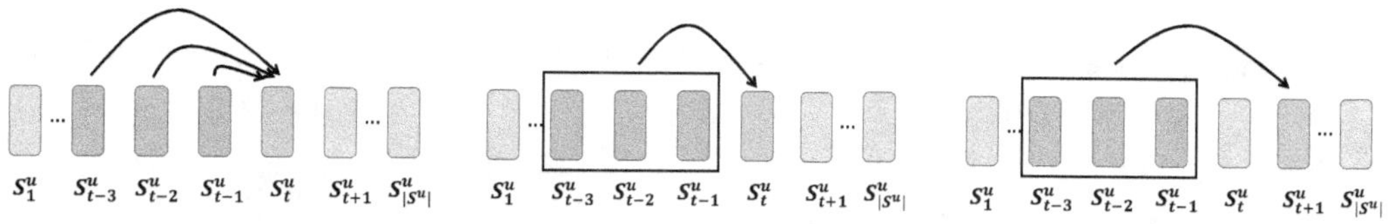

(a) point-level (b) union-level, no skip (c) union-level, skip once

Figure 1: An example of point and union level dynamic pattern influences, the order of Markov chain $L = 3$

and Fossil fall into this taxonomy. Although Fossil [6] considers a high-order Markov chain, the overall influence is a weighted sum of previous items' latent representations factorized from first-order Markov transition matrices. Such aggregation of point-level influences is not sufficient to model the **union-level** influences shown in Figure 1b where several previous actions, in that order, jointly influence the target action. For example, buying both milk and butter together leads to a higher probability of buying flour than buying milk or butter individually; buying both RAM and Hard Drive is a better indication of buying Operating System next than buying only one of the components.

Fail to allow skip behaviors. Existing models don't consider **skip behaviors** of sequential patterns as shown in Figure 1c, where the impact from past behaviors may skip a few steps and still have strength. For example, a tourist has check-ins sequentially at airport, hotel, restaurant, bar, and attraction. While the check-ins at the airport and hotel do not immediately precede the check-in of the attraction, they are strongly associated with the latter. On the other hand, the check-in at the restaurant or bar has little influence on the check-in of the attraction (because they do not necessarily occur). A L-order Markov chain does not explicitly model such skip behaviors because it assumes that the L previous steps have an influence on the immediate next step.

To provide evidences of union-level influences and skip behaviors, we mine sequential association rules [1, 4] of the following form from two real life data sets, MovieLens and Gowalla (see the details of these data sets in Section 4)

$$(\mathcal{S}^u_{t-L}, \cdots, \mathcal{S}^u_{t-2}, \mathcal{S}^u_{t-1}) \rightarrow \mathcal{S}^u_t. \tag{1}$$

For a rule $X \rightarrow Y$ of the above form, the support count $sup(XY)$ is the number of sequences in which X and Y occur in order as in the rule, and the confidence, $\frac{sup(XY)}{sup(X)}$, is the percentage of the sequences in which Y follows X among those in which X occurs. This rule represents the joint influence of all the items in X on Y. By changing the right hand side to $\mathcal{S}^u_{t+1}$ or $\mathcal{S}^u_{t+2}$, the rule also captures the influences with one or two step skips. Figure 2 summarizes the number of rules found versus the Markov order L and skip steps with the minimum support count = 5 and the minimum confidence = 50% (we also tried the minimum confidence of 10%, 20%, and 30%, these trends are similar). Most rules have the orders $L = 2$ and $L = 3$ and the confidence of rules gets higher for larger L. The figure also tells that a sizable number of rules have skip steps 1 or 2. These findings support the existence of union-level influences and skip behaviors.

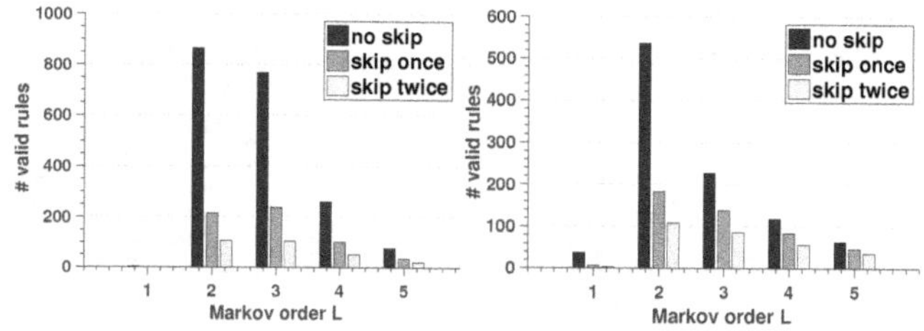

(a) MovieLens (b) Gowalla

Figure 2: The number of association rules vs L and skip steps. The minimum support count = 5 and the minimum confidence = 50%.

1.3 Contributions

To address these above limitations of existing works, we propose a *ConvolutionAl Sequence Embedding Recommendation Model*, or *Caser* for short, as a solution to top-N sequential recommendation. This model leverages the recent success of convolution filters of Convolutional Neural Network (CNN) to capture local features for image recognition [11, 16] and natural language processing [12]. The novelty of Caser is to represent the previous L items as an $L \times d$ matrix $\boldsymbol{E}$, where d is the number of latent dimensions and the rows preserve the order of the items. Similar to [12], we regard this embedding matrix as the "image" of the L items in the latent space and search for sequential patterns as local features of this "image" using various convolutional filters. Unlike image recognition, however, this "image" is not given in the input and must be learnt simultaneously with all filters.

Compared to existing methods, Caser offers several distinct advantages. (1) Caser uses horizontal and vertical convolutional filters to capture sequential patterns at point-level, union-level, and of skip behaviors. (2) Caser models both users' general preferences and sequential patterns, and generalizes several existing state-of-the-art methods in a single unified framework. (3) Caser outperforms state-of-the-art methods for top-N sequential recommendation on real life data sets. In the rest of the paper, we discuss further related work in Section 2, the Caser method in Section 3, and experimental studies in Section 4.

2 FURTHER RELATED WORK

Conventional recommendation methods, *e.g.*, collaborative filtering [24], matrix factorization [15, 22], and top-N recommendation [9][19], are not suitable for capturing sequential patterns because they do not model the order of actions. Early works on sequential pattern mining [1, 4] find explicit sequential association rules based on statistical co-occurrences [17]. This approach depends on

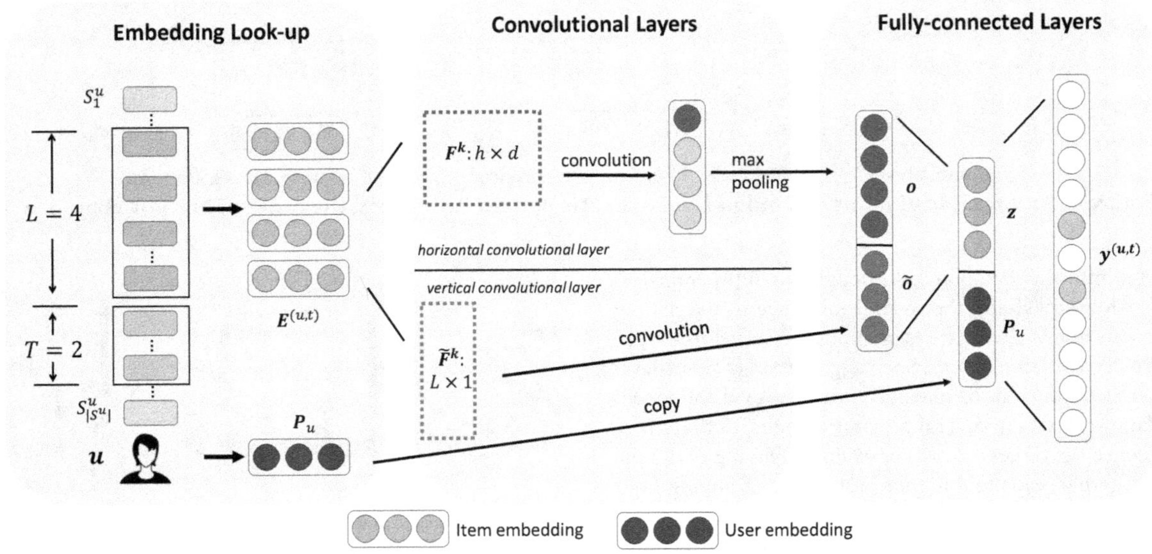

Figure 3: The network architecture of *Caser*. The rectangular boxes represent items $S_1^u, \cdots, S_{|S^u|}^u$ in user sequence, whereas a rectangular box with circles inside stands for a certain vector *e.g.*, user embedding P_u. The dash rectangular boxes are convolutional filters with different sizes. The red circles in convolutional layers stand for the max values in each of the convolution results. Here we are using previous 4 actions ($L = 4$) to predict which items this user will interact with in next 2 steps ($T = 2$).

the explicit representation of patterns, thus, could miss patterns in unobserved states. Also, it suffers from a potentially large search space, sensitivity to threshold settings, and a large number of rules, most being redundant.

Restricted Bolzmann Machine (RBM) [23] is the first successful 2-layers neural network that is applied to recommendation problems. Auto-encoder framework [25, 29] and its variant denoising auto-encoder [32] also produce a good recommendation performance. Convolutional neural network (CNN) [36] has been used to extract users' preferences from their reviews. None of these works is for sequential recommendation.

Recurrent neural networks (RNN) was used for session-based recommendation [8, 10]. While RNN has shown to have an impressive capability in modeling sequences [18], its sequentially connected network structure may not work well under sequential recommendation setting. Because in sequential recommendation problem, not all adjacent actions have dependency relationships (*e.g.* a user bought i_2 after i_1 only because she loves i_2). Our experimental results in Section 4 verify this point: RNN-based method performs better when data sets contains considerable sequential patterns. While our proposed method doesn't model sequential pattern as adjacent actions, it adopts convolutional filters from CNN and model sequential patterns as local features of the embeddings of previous items. This approach offers the flexibility of modeling sequential patterns at both point level and union level, and skip behaviors in a single unified framework. In fact, we will show that Caser generalizes several state-of-the-art methods.

A related but different problem is temporal recommendation [26, 31, 34]. For example, temporal recommendation recommends coffee in the morning, instead of evening, whereas our top-N sequential recommendation would recommend phone accessories soon after a user bought an iPhone, independently of the time. Clearly, the two problems are different and require different solutions.

3 PROPOSED METHODOLOGY

The proposed model, ConvolutionAl Sequence Embedding Recommendation (*Caser*), incorporates the Convolutional Neural Network (CNN) to learn sequential features, and Latent Factor Model (LFM) to learn user specific features. The goal of Caser's network design is multi-fold: capture both user's general preferences and sequential patterns, at both union-level and point-level, and capture skip behaviors, all in unobserved spaces. Shown in Figure 3 Caser consists of three components: Embedding Look-up, Convolutional Layers, and Fully-connected Layers. To train the CNN, for each user u, we extract every L successive items as input and their next T items as the targets from the user's sequence $\mathcal{S}^u$, shown on the left side of Figure 3. This is done by sliding a window of size $L + T$ over the user's sequence, and each window generates a training instance for u, denoted by a triplet (u, previous L items, next T items).

3.1 Embedding Look-up

Caser captures sequence features in the latent space by feeding the embeddings of previous L items into the neural network. The embedding $Q_i \in \mathbb{R}^d$ for item i is a similar concept to its latent factors. Here d is the number of latent dimensions. The embedding look-up operation retrieves the previous L items' embeddings and stacks them together, resulting in a matrix $E^{(u,t)} \in \mathbb{R}^{L \times d}$ for user u at time step t:

$$E^{(u,t)} = \begin{bmatrix} Q_{\mathcal{S}_{t-L}^u} \\ \vdots \\ Q_{\mathcal{S}_{t-2}^u} \\ Q_{\mathcal{S}_{t-1}^u} \end{bmatrix}. \qquad (2)$$

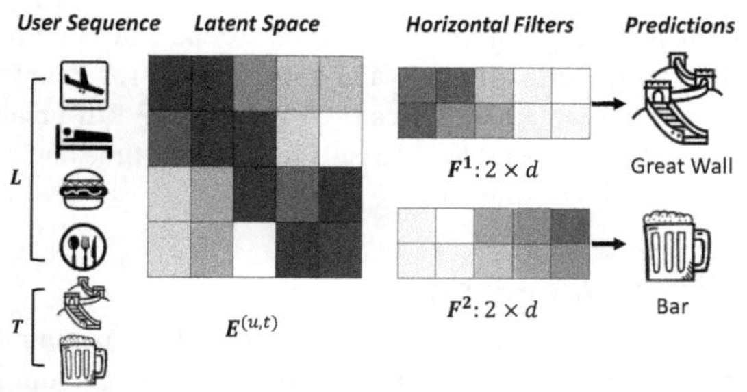

Figure 4: Darker colors mean larger values. The first filter captures "(Airport, Hotel) → Great Wall" by interacting with the embedding of airport and hotel and skipping that of fast food and restaurant. The second filter captures "(Fast Food, Restaurant) → Bar".

Along with the item embeddings, we also have an embedding $P_u \in \mathbb{R}^d$ for a user u, representing user features in latent space. These embeddings are represented by blue and purple circles in the box of Embedding Look-up in Figure 3.

3.2 Convolutional Layers

Our approach leverages the recent success of convolution filters of CNN in capturing local features for image recognition [11, 16] and natural language processing [12]. Borrows the idea of using CNN in text classification [12], our approach regards the $L \times d$ matrix E as the "image" of the previous L items in the latent space and regard sequential patterns as local features of this "image". This approach enables the use of convolution filters to search for sequential patterns. Figure 4 shows two "horizontal filters" that capture two union-level sequential patterns. These filters, represented as $h \times d$ matrices, have the height $h = 2$ and the full width equal to d. They pick up signals for sequential patterns by sliding over the rows of E. For example, the first filter picks up the sequential pattern "(Airport, Hotel) → Great Wall" by having larger values in the latent dimensions where Airport and Hotel have larger values. Similarly, a "vertical filter" is a $L \times 1$ matrix and will slide over the columns of E. More details are explained below. Unlike image recognition, the "image" E is not given because the embedding Q_i for all items i must be learnt simultaneously with all filters.

Horizontal Convolutional Layer. This layer, shown in the upper part of the second component in Figure 3, has n horizontal filters $F^k \in \mathbb{R}^{h \times d}$, $1 \le k \le n$. $h \in \{1, \cdots, L\}$ is the height of a filter. For example, if $L = 4$, one may choose to have $n = 8$ filters, two for each h in $\{1, 2, 3, 4\}$. F^k will slide from top to bottom on E and interact with all horizontal dimensions of E of the items i, $1 \le i \le L - h + 1$. The result of the interaction is the i-th convolution value given by

$$c_i^k = \phi_c(E_{i:i+h-1} \odot F^k). \tag{3}$$

where the symbol $\odot$ denotes the inner product operator and $\phi_c(\cdot)$ is the activation function for convolutional layers. This value is the inner product between F^k and the sub-matrix formed by the row i to row $i - h + 1$ of E, denoted by $E_{i:i+h-1}$. The final convolution result of F^k is the vector

$$c^k = \left[c_1^k \; c_2^k \cdots c_{L-h+1}^k\right]. \tag{4}$$

We then apply a max pooling operation to c^k to extract the maximum value from all values produced by this particular filter. The maximum value captures the most significant feature extracted by the filter. Therefore, for the n filters in this layer, the output value $o \in \mathbb{R}^n$ is

$$o = \{max(c^1), max(c^2), \cdots, max(c^n)\}. \tag{5}$$

Horizontal filters interact with every successive h items through their embeddings E. Both the embeddings and the filters are learnt to minimize an objective function that encodes the prediction error of target items (more in Section 3.4). By sliding filters of various heights, a significant signal will be picked up regardless of location. Therefore, horizontal filters can be trained to capture **union-level patterns** with multiple union sizes.

Vertical Convolutional Layer. This layer is shown in the lower part of the second component in Figure 3. We use tilde (~) for the symbols of this layer. Suppose that there are $\tilde{n}$ vertical filters $\tilde{F}^k \in \mathbb{R}^{L \times 1}$, $1 \le k \le \tilde{n}$. Each filter $\tilde{F}^k$ interacts with the columns of E by sliding d times from left to right on E, yielding the vertical convolution result $\tilde{c}^k$:

$$\tilde{c}^k = \left[\tilde{c}_1^k \; \tilde{c}_2^k \cdots \tilde{c}_d^k\right]. \tag{6}$$

For the inner product interaction, it is easy to verify that this result is equal to the weighted sum over the L rows of E with $\tilde{F}^k$ as the weights:

$$\tilde{c}^k = \sum_{l=1}^{L} \tilde{F}_l^k \cdot E_l, \tag{7}$$

where E_l is the l-th row of E. Therefore, with vertical filters we can learn to *aggregate* the embeddings of the L previous items, similar to Fossil's [6] weighted sum to aggregate the L previous items' latent representations. The difference is that each filter $\tilde{F}^k$ is acting like a different aggregator. Thus, similar to Fossil, these vertical filters are capturing **point-level sequential patterns** through weighted sums over previous items' latent representations. While Fossil uses a single weighted sum for each user, we can use $\tilde{n}$ global vertical filters to produce $\tilde{n}$ weighted sums $\tilde{o} \in \mathbb{R}^{d\tilde{n}}$ for all users:

$$\tilde{o} = \left[\tilde{c}^1 \; \tilde{c}^2 \cdots \tilde{c}^{\tilde{n}}\right]. \tag{8}$$

Since their usage is aggregation, vertical filters have some differences from horizontal ones: (1) The size of each vertical filter is fixed to be $L \times 1$. This is because each column of E is latent for us, it is meaningless to interact with multiple successive columns at one time. (2) There is no need to apply max pooling operation over the vertical convolution results, as we want to keep the aggregation for every latent dimension. Thus, the output of this layer is $\tilde{o}$.

3.3 Fully-connected Layers

We concatenate the outputs of the two convolutional layers and feed them into a fully-connected neural network layer to get more high-level and abstract features:

$$z = \phi_a(W \begin{bmatrix} o \\ \tilde{o} \end{bmatrix} + b), \tag{9}$$

where $W \in \mathbb{R}^{d \times (n + d\tilde{n})}$ is the weight matrix that projects the concatenation layer to a d-dimensional hidden layer, $b \in \mathbb{R}^d$ is the corresponding bias term and $\phi_a(\cdot)$ is the activation function for fully-connected layer. $z \in \mathbb{R}^d$ is what we called *convolutional sequence embedding*, which encodes all kinds of sequential features of the L previous items.

To capture user's general preferences, we also look-up the user embedding $\boldsymbol{P}_u$ and concatenate the two d-dimensional vectors, z and $\boldsymbol{P}_u$, together and project them to an output layer with $|\mathcal{I}|$ nodes, written as

$$y^{(u,t)} = W' \begin{bmatrix} z \\ P_u \end{bmatrix} + b', \tag{10}$$

where $b' \in \mathbb{R}^{|\mathcal{I}|}$ and $W' \in \mathbb{R}^{|\mathcal{I}| \times 2d}$ are the bias term and weight matrix for output layer, respectively. As explained in Section 3.4, the value $y_i^{(u,t)}$ in the output layer is associated with the probability of how likely user u will interact with item i at time step t. z intends to capture short term sequential patterns, whereas the user embedding $\boldsymbol{P}_u$ captures user's long-term general preferences. Here we put the user embedding Pu in the last hidden layer for several reasons: (1) As we shall see in Section 3.6, it can have the ability to generalize other models. (2) we can pre-train our model's parameters with other generalized models' parameters. As stated in [7], such pre-training is critical to model performance

3.4 Network Training

To train the network, we transform the values of the output layer, $y^{(u,t)}$, to probabilities by:

$$p(\mathcal{S}_t^u \mid \mathcal{S}_{t-1}^u, \mathcal{S}_{t-2}^u, \cdots, \mathcal{S}_{t-L}^u) = \sigma(y_{\mathcal{S}_t^u}^{(u,t)}), \tag{11}$$

where $\sigma(x) = 1/(1 + e^{-x})$ is the *sigmoid* function. Let $C^u = \{L + 1, L+2, ..., |\mathcal{S}^u|\}$ be the collection of time steps for which we would like to make predictions for user u. The likelihood of all sequences in the dataset is:

$$p(\mathcal{S}|\Theta) = \prod_u \prod_{t \in C^u} \sigma(y_{\mathcal{S}_t^u}^{(u,t)}) \prod_{j \neq \mathcal{S}_t^u} (1 - \sigma(y_j^{(u,t)})). \tag{12}$$

To further capture **skip behaviors**, we could consider the next T target items, $\mathcal{D}_t^u = \{\mathcal{S}_t^u, \mathcal{S}_{t+1}^u, ..., \mathcal{S}_{t+T}^u\}$, at once by replacing the immediate next item $\mathcal{S}_t^u$ in the above equation with $\mathcal{D}_t^u$. Taking the negative logarithm of likelihood, we get the objective function, also known as *binary cross-entropy* loss:

$$\ell = \sum_u \sum_{t \in C^u} \sum_{i \in \mathcal{D}_t^u} -\log(\sigma(y_i^{(u,t)})) + \sum_{j \neq i} -\log(1 - \sigma(y_j^{(u,t)})). \tag{13}$$

Following previous works [6, 21, 32], for each target item i, we randomly sample several (3 in our experiments) negative instances j in the second term.

The *model parameters* $\Theta = \{P, Q, F, \tilde{F}, W, W', b, b'\}$ are learned by minimizing the objective function in Eqn (13) on the training set, whereas the *hyperparameters* (*e.g.*, $d, n, \tilde{n}, L, T$) are tuned on the validation set via grid search. We adopt an variant of Stochastic Gradient Descent (SGD) called Adaptive Moment Estimation (Adam) [13] for faster convergence, with a batch size of 100. To control model complexity and avoid over-fitting, we use two kinds of regularization methods: the $L2$ Norm is applied for all model parameters and *Dropout* [27] technique with 50% drop ratio is used on fully-connected layers. We implemented Caser with MatConvNet [28]. The whole training time is proportional to the number of training instances. For example, it took around 1 hour for MovieLens data and 2 hours for Gowalla data, 2 hours for Foursquare and 1 hour for Tmall on a 4-cores i7 CPU and 32GB RAM machine. These times are comparable to Fossil's [6] running time and can be further reduced by using GPU.

3.5 Recommendation

After obtaining the trained neural network, to make recommendations for a user u at time step t, we take u's latent embedding $\boldsymbol{P}_u$ and extract his last L items' embeddings given by Eqn (2) as the neural network input. We recommend the N items that have the highest values in the output layer y. The complexity for making recommendations to all users is $O(|\mathcal{U}||\mathcal{I}|d)$, where the complexity of convolution operations is ignored. Note that the number of target items T is a hyperparameter used during the model training, whereas N is the number of items recommended after the model is trained.

3.6 Connection to Existing Models

We show that Caser is a generalization of several previous models.

Caser vs. MF. By discarding all convolutional layers and all bias terms, our model becomes a vanilla LFM with user embeddings as user latent factors and its associated weights as item latent factors. MF usually contains bias terms[1], which is b' in our model. After discarding all convolutional layers, the resulting model is the same as MF:

$$y_i^u = W_i' \begin{bmatrix} 0 \\ P_u \end{bmatrix} + b_i'. \tag{14}$$

Caser vs. FPMC. FPMC fuses factorized first-order Markov chain with LFM and is optimized by Bayesian personalized ranking (BPR). Although Caser uses a different optimization criterion, *i.e.*, the cross-entropy, it is able to generalize FPMC by copying the previous item's embedding to the hidden layer z and not using any bias terms:

$$y_i^{(u,t)} = W_i' \begin{bmatrix} Q_{\mathcal{S}_{t-1}^u} \\ P_u \end{bmatrix}. \tag{15}$$

As FPMC uses BPR as the criterion, our model is not exactly the same as FPMC. However, BPR is limited to have only 1 target and negative sample at each time step. Our cross-entropy loss does not have these limitations.

Caser vs. Fossil. By omitting the horizontal convolutional layer and using one vertical filter and copying the vertical convolution result $\tilde{c}$ to the hidden layer z, we get

$$y_i^{(u,t)} = W_i' \begin{bmatrix} \tilde{c} \\ P_u \end{bmatrix} + b_i'. \tag{16}$$

As discussed for Eqn (7), this vertical filter serves as the weighted sum of the embeddings of the L previous items, like in Fossil, though Fossil uses *Similarity Model* instead of LFM and factorizes it in the same latent space as Markov model. Another difference is that Fossil uses one local weighting for each user while we use a number of global weighting through vertical filters.

Table 1: Statistics of the datasets

Datasets	Sequential Intensity	#users	#items	avg. actions per user	Sparsity
MovieLens	0.3265	6.0k	3.4k	165.50	95.16%
Gowalla	0.0748	13.1k	14.0k	40.74	99.71%
Foursquare	0.0378	10.1k	23.4k	30.16	99.87%
Tmall	0.0104	23.8k	12.2k	13.93	99.89%

4 EXPERIMENTS

We compare *Caser* with state-of-the-art methods. The source code of Caser and processed data sets are available online[2].

4.1 Experimental Setup

Datasets. Sequential recommendation makes sense only when the data set contains sequential patterns. To identify such data sets, we applied sequential association rule mining to several public data sets and computed their sequential intensity defined by:

$$\text{Sequential Intensity } (SI) = \frac{\#\text{rules}}{\#\text{users}}. \tag{17}$$

The numerator is the total number of rules in the form of Eqn (1) found using a minimum threshold on support (*i.e.,* 5) and confidence(*i.e.,* 50%) with Markov order L range from 1 to 5. The denominator is the total number of users. We use *SI* to estimate the intensity of sequential signals in a data set.

The four data sets with their *SI* are described in Table 1. MovieLens[3] is the widely used movie rating data. Gowalla[4] constructed by [3] and Foursquare obtained from [33] contain implicit feedback through user-venue check-ins. Tmall, the largest B2C platform in China, is a user-purchase data obtained from IJCAI 2015 competition[5], which aims to forecast repeated buyers. Following previous works [6, 20, 32], we converted all numeric ratings to implicit feedback of 1. We also removed cold-start users and items of having less than n feedbacks, as dealing with cold-start recommendation is usually treated as a separate issue in the literature [6, 7, 21, 32]. n is 5,16,10,10 for MovieLens, Gowalla, Foursquare, and Tmall. The Amazon data previously used in [5, 6] was not used due to its *SI* (0.0026 for 'Office Products' category, 0.0019 for 'Clothing, Shoes, Jewelry' and 'Video Games' category), in other words, its sequential signals are much weaker than the above data sets.

Following [17, 33, 35], we hold the first 70% of actions in each user's sequence as the *training set* and use the next 10% of actions as the *validation set* to search the optimal hyperparameter settings for all models. The remaining 20% actions in each user's sequence are used as the *test set* for evaluating a model's performance.

Evaluation Metrics. As in [19, 21, 29, 32], we evaluate a model by Precision@N, Recall@N, and Mean Average Precision (MAP). Given a list of top N predicted items for a user, denoted $\hat{R}_{1:N}$, and the last 20% of actions in her/his sequence (*i.e.,* denoted R (*i.e.,* the test set), Precision@N and Recall@N are computed by

$$\text{Prec@}N = \frac{|R \bigcap \hat{R}_{1:N}|}{N}, \qquad \text{Recall@}N = \frac{|R \bigcap \hat{R}_{1:N}|}{|R|}. \tag{18}$$

We report the average of these values of all users. $N \in \{1, 5, 10\}$. The Average Precision (AP) is defined by

$$\text{AP} = \frac{\sum_{N=1}^{|\hat{R}|} \text{Prec@}N \times \text{rel}(N)}{|\hat{R}|}, \tag{19}$$

where $rel(N) = 1$ if the N-th item in $\hat{R}$ is in R. The Mean Average Precision (MAP) is the average of AP for all users.

4.2 Performance Comparison

We compare our method, Caser, proposed in Section 3 with the following baselines.

- **POP**. All items are ranked by their popularity in all users' sequences, and the popularity is determined by the number of interactions.
- **BPR**. Combined with Matrix Factorization model, Bayesian personalized ranking [20] is the state-of-the-art method for non-sequential item recommendation on implicit feedback data.
- **FMC and FPMC**. As introduced in [21], FMC factorizes the first-order Markov transition matrix into two low-dimensional sub-matrices, and FPMC is a fusion of FMC and LFM. These are the state-of-the-art sequential recommendation methods. FPMC allows a basket of several items at each step. For our sequential recommendation problem, each basket has a single item.
- **Fossil**. Fossil [6] models high-order Markov chains and uses Similarity Model instead of LFM for modeling general user preferences.
- **GRU4Rec**. This is the session-based recommendation proposed by [8]. This model uses RNN to capture sequential dependencies and make predictions.

For each method, the grid search is applied to find the optimal settings of hyperparameters using the validation set. These include latent dimensions d from $\{5, 10, 20, 30, 50, 100\}$, regularization hyperparameters, and the learning rate from $\{1, 10^{-1}, ..., 10^{-4}\}$. For Fossil, Caser and GRU4Rec, the Markov order L is from $\{1, \cdots, 9\}$. For Caser itself, the height h of horizontal filters is from $\{1, \cdots, L\}$, the target number T is from $\{1, 2, 3\}$, the activation functions ϕ_a and ϕ_c are from $\{identity, sigmoid, tanh, relu\}$. For each height h, the number of horizontal filters is from $\{4, 8, 16, 32, 64\}$. The number of vertical filters is from $\{1, 2, 4, 8, 16\}$. We report the result of each method under its optimal hyperparameter settings.

[1] Top-N recommendation ranks the items for each user individually, which is invariant to user bias and global bias.
[2] https://github.com/graytowne/caser
[3] https://grouplens.org/datasets/movielens/1m/
[4] https://snap.stanford.edu/data/loc-gowalla.html
[5] https://ijcai-15.org/index.php/repeat-buyers-prediction-competition

Table 2: Performance comparison on the four data sets.

Dataset	Metric	POP	BPR	FMC	FPMC	Fossil	GRU4Rec	Caser	Improv.
MovieLens	Prec@1	0.1280	0.1478	0.1748	0.2022	0.2306	**0.2515**	0.2502	-0.5%
	Prec@5	0.1113	0.1288	0.1505	0.1659	0.2000	0.2146	**0.2175**	1.4%
	Prec@10	0.1011	0.1193	0.1317	0.1460	0.1806	0.1916	**0.1991**	4.0%
	Recall@1	0.0050	0.0070	0.0104	0.0118	0.0144	**0.0153**	0.0148	-3.3%
	Recall@5	0.0213	0.0312	0.0432	0.0468	0.0602	0.0629	**0.0632**	0.5%
	Recall@10	0.0375	0.0560	0.0722	0.0777	0.1061	0.1093	**0.1121**	2.6%
	MAP	0.0687	0.0913	0.0949	0.1053	0.1354	0.1440	**0.1507**	4.7%
Gowalla	Prec@1	0.0517	0.1640	0.1532	0.1555	0.1736	0.1050	**0.1961**	13.0%
	Prec@5	0.0362	0.0983	0.0876	0.0936	0.1045	0.0721	**0.1129**	8.0%
	Prec@10	0.0281	0.0726	0.0657	0.0698	0.0782	0.0571	**0.0833**	6.5%
	Recall@1	0.0064	0.0250	0.0234	0.0256	0.0277	0.0155	**0.0310**	11.9%
	Recall@5	0.0257	0.0743	0.0648	0.0722	0.0793	0.0529	**0.0845**	6.6%
	Recall@10	0.0402	0.1077	0.0950	0.1059	0.1166	0.0826	**0.1223**	4.9%
	MAP	0.0229	0.0767	0.0711	0.0764	0.0848	0.0580	**0.0928**	9.4%
Foursquare	Prec@1	0.1090	0.1233	0.0875	0.1081	0.1191	0.1018	**0.1351**	13.4%
	Prec@5	0.0477	0.0543	0.0445	0.0555	0.0580	0.0475	**0.0619**	6.7%
	Prec@10	0.0304	0.0348	0.0309	0.0385	0.0399	0.0331	**0.0425**	6.5%
	Recall@1	0.0376	0.0445	0.0305	0.0440	0.0497	0.0369	**0.0565**	13.7%
	Recall@5	0.0800	0.0888	0.0689	0.0959	0.0948	0.0770	**0.1035**	7.9%
	Recall@10	0.0954	0.1061	0.0911	0.1200	0.1187	0.1011	**0.1291**	7.6%
	MAP	0.0636	0.0719	0.0571	0.0782	0.0823	0.0643	**0.0909**	10.4%
Tmall	Prec@1	0.0010	0.0111	0.0197	0.0210	0.0280	0.0139	**0.0312**	11.4%
	Prec@5	0.0009	0.0081	0.0114	0.0120	0.0149	0.0090	**0.0179**	20.1%
	Prec@10	0.0007	0.0063	0.0084	0.0090	0.0104	0.0070	**0.0132**	26.9%
	Recall@1	0.0004	0.0046	0.0079	0.0082	0.0117	0.0056	**0.0130**	11.1%
	Recall@5	0.0019	0.0169	0.0226	0.0245	0.0306	0.0180	**0.0366**	19.6%
	Recall@10	0.0026	0.0260	0.0333	0.0364	0.0425	0.0278	**0.0534**	25.6%
	MAP	0.0030	0.0145	0.0197	0.0212	0.0256	0.0164	**0.0310**	21.1%

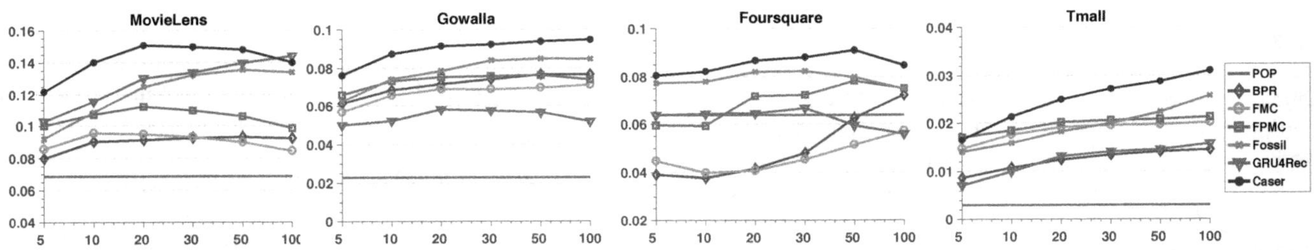

Figure 5: MAP (y-axis) vs. the number of latent dimensions d (x-axis).

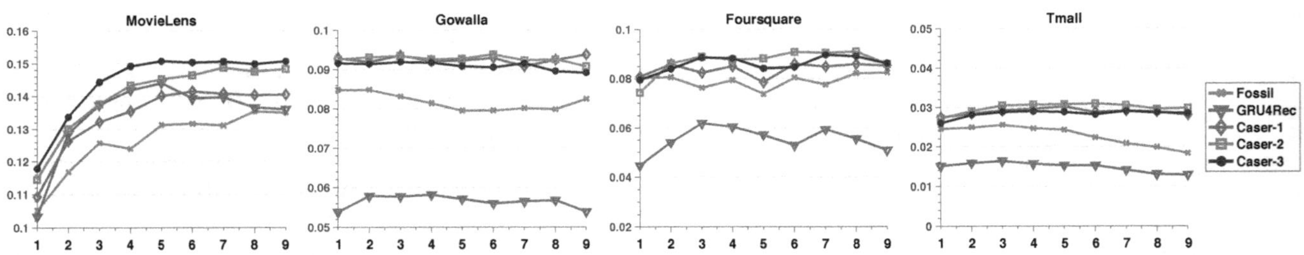

Figure 6: MAP (y-axis) vs. the Markov order L (x-axis). Caser-1, Caser-2, and Caser-3 denote Caser with the number of targets T set to 1, 2, 3.

The best results of the six baselines and Caser are summarized in Table 2. The best performer on each row is highlighted in bold face. The last column is the improvement of Caser relative to the best baseline, defined as $\frac{Caser-baseline}{baseline}$. Except for MovieLens, Caser improved the best baseline on all N tested by a large margin *w.r.t.* the three metrics. Among the baseline methods, the sequential recommenders (*e.g.*, FPMC and Fossil) usually outperform non-sequential recommenders (*i.e.*, BPR) on all data sets, suggesting the importance of considering sequential information. FPMC and Fossil outperform FMC on all data sets, suggesting the effectiveness of personalization. On MovieLens, GRU4Rec achieved a performance close to Caser's, but got a much worse performance on the other three data sets. In fact, MovieLens has more sequential signals than the other three data sets, thus, the RNN-based GRU4Rec could perform well on MovieLens but can easily get biased on training sets of the other three data sets despite the use of regularization and dropout as described in [8]. In addition, GRU4Rec's recommendation is session-based, instead of personalized, which enlarge the generalization error to some extent.

In the following studies, we examine the impact of the hyperparameters d, L, T one at a time by holding the remaining hyperparameters at their optimal settings. We focus on MAP as it is an overall performance indicator and consistent with other metrics.

4.2.1 Influence of Latent Dimensionality d. Figure 5 shows MAP for various d while keeping the other optimal hyperparameters unchanged. On the denser MovieLens, a larger d does not always lead to a better model performance. A model achieves its best performance when d is chosen properly and gets worse for a larger d because of over-fitting. But for the other three sparser data sets, each model requires more latent dimensions to achieve their best results. For all data sets, Caser beats the strongest baseline performance by using a relatively small number of latent dimensions.

4.2.2 Influence of Markov Order L and Target Number T. We vary L to explore how much of Fossil, GRU4Rec and Caser can gain from high-order information while keeping other optimal hyperparameters unchanged. Caser-1, Caser-2, and Caser-3 denote Caser with the target number T at 1, 2, 3 to study the effect of skip behaviors. The results are shown in Figure 6. On the dense MovieLens, Caser best utilizes the extra information provided by a larger L and Caser-3 performs the best, suggesting the benefits of skip steps. However, for the sparser data sets, all models do not consistently benefit from a larger L. This is reasonable, because for a sparse data set, a higher order Markov chain tends to introduce both extra information and more noises. In most cases, Caser-2 slightly outperforms the other models on these three data sets.

Table 3: MAP vs. Caser Components

	MovieLens	Gowalla
Caser-p	0.0935	0.0777
Caser-h	0.1304	0.0805
Caser-v	0.1403	0.0841
Caser-vh	0.1448	0.0856
Caser-ph	0.1372	0.0911
Caser-pv	0.1494	0.0921
Caser-pvh	0.1507	0.0928

4.2.3 Analysis of Caser Components. Finally, we evaluate the contribution of each of Caser's components, the horizontal convolutional layer (*i.e.*, o), the vertical convolutional layer (*i.e.*, $\tilde{o}$), and personalization (*i.e.*, P_u), to the overall performance while keeping all hyperparameters at their optimal settings. The result is shown in Table 3 for MovieLens and Gowalla; the results of the other two data sets are similar. For $x \in \{p, h, v, vh, ph, pv, pvh\}$, Caser-$x$ denotes Caser with the components x enabled. h denotes horizontal convolutional layer; v denotes vertical convolutional layer; p denotes personalization, which is similar to BPR and uses LFM only. Any missing component is represented by setting its corresponding o, $\tilde{o}$, and P_u to zero. For example, vh denotes both vertical convolutional layer and horizontal convolutional layer by setting P_u to all zeros, and pv denotes vertical convolutional layer and personalization by setting o to all zeros. Caser-p performs the worst whereas Caser-h, Caser-v, and Caser-vh improve the performance significantly, suggesting that treating top-N sequential recommendation as the conventional top-N recommendation will lose useful information, and that modeling both sequential patterns at the union-level and point-level is useful for improving the prediction. For both data sets, the best performance is achieved by jointly using all parts of Caser, i.e., Caser-pvh.

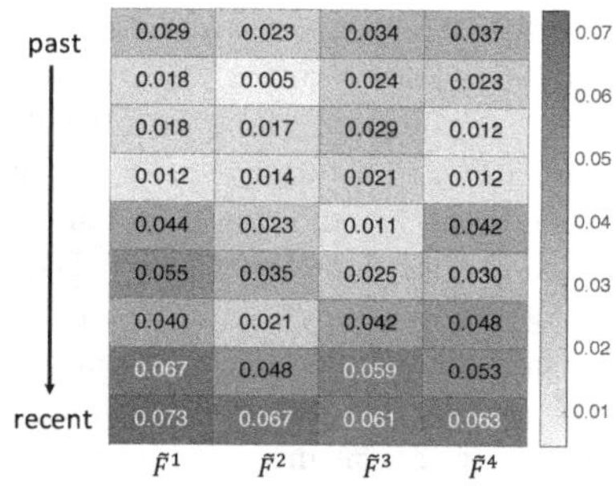

Figure 7: Visualization for four vertical convolutional filters of a trained model on MovieLens data when $L = 9$.

(a)

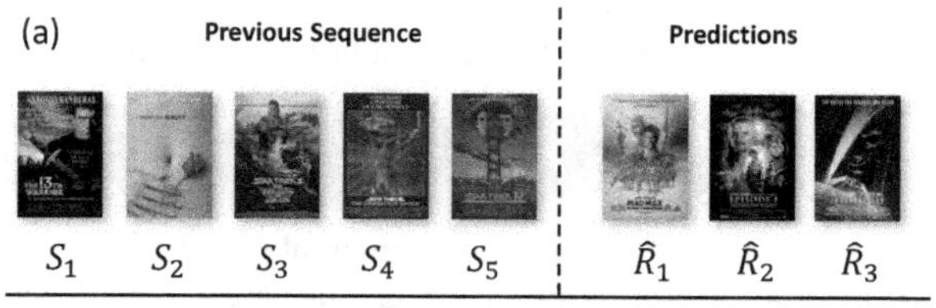

(b)

Masking Items	New Rank of $\hat{R}_3$ after masking
S_1, S_2	2
S_3	32
S_4	117
S_5	77
S_3, S_4, S_5	513

Figure 8: Horizontal convolutional filters's effectiveness of capturing union-level sequential patterns on MovieLens data.

4.3 Network Visualization

We have a closer look at some trained networks and prediction. Figure 7 shows the values of four vertical convolutional filters after training Caser on MovieLens with $L = 9$. In the micro perspective, the four filters are trained to be diverse, but in the macro perspective, they follow an ascending trend from past positions to recent positions. With each vertical filter serving as a way of weighting the embeddings of previous actions (see the related discussion in Section 3), this trend indicates that Caser puts more emphasis on recent actions, demonstrating a major difference from the conventional top-N recommendation.

To see the effectiveness of horizontal filters, Figure 8(a) shows top $N = 3$ ranked movies recommended by Caser, *i.e.*, $\hat{R}_1$ (Mad Max),

$\hat{R}_2$ (Star War), $\hat{R}_3$ (Star Trek) in that order, for a user with $L = 5$ previous movies, *i.e.*, S_1 (13th Warrior), S_2 (American Beauty), S_3 (Star Trek), S_4 (Star Trek III), and S_5 (Star Trek IV). $\hat{R}_3$ is the ground truth (*i.e.*, the next movie in the user sequence). Note that $\hat{R}_1$ and $\hat{R}_2$ are quite similar to $\hat{R}_3$, *i.e.*, all being action and science fiction movies, so are also recommended to the user. Figure 8(b) shows the new rank of $\hat{R}_3$ after masking some of the L previous movies by setting their item embeddings to zeros in the trained network. Masking S_1 and S_2 actually increases the rank of $\hat{R}_3$ to 2 (from 3); in fact, S_1 and S_2 are history or romance movies and act like noises for recommending $\hat{R}_3$. Masking each of S_3, S_4 and S_5 decreases the rank of $\hat{R}_3$ because these movies are in the same category as $\hat{R}_3$. The most decrease occurs after masking S_3, S_4 and S_5 all together. This study clearly indicates that our model correctly captures the dependence of $\hat{R}_3$ on the related $\{S_3, S_4, S_5\}$ as a union-level sequential feature for recommending $\hat{R}_3$.

5 CONCLUSION

Caser is a novel solution to top-N sequential recommendation by modeling recent actions as an "image" among time and latent dimensions and learning sequential patterns using convolutional filters. This approach provides a unified and flexible network structure for capturing many important features of sequential recommendation, *i.e.*, point-level and union-level sequential patterns, skip behaviors, and long term user preferences. Our experiments and case studies on public real life data sets suggested that Caser outperforms the state-of-the-art methods for top-N sequential recommendation.

ACKNOWLEDGEMENT

The work of the second author is partially supported by a Discovery Grant from Natural Sciences and Engineering Research Council of Canada.

REFERENCES

[1] Rakesh Agrawal and Ramakrishnan Srikant. 1995. Mining sequential patterns. In *International Conference on Data Engineering*. IEEE, 3–14.

[2] Chen Cheng, Haiqin Yang, Michael R Lyu, and Irwin King. 2013. Where You Like to Go Next: Successive Point-of-Interest Recommendation.. In *International Joint Conference on Artificial Intelligence*. 2605–2611.

[3] Eunjoon Cho, Seth A Myers, and Jure Leskovec. 2011. Friendship and mobility: user movement in location-based social networks. In *International Conference on Knowledge Discovery and Data Mining*. ACM, 1082–1090.

[4] Jiawei Han, Jian Pei, and Micheline Kamber. 2011. *Data mining: concepts and techniques*. Elsevier.

[5] R. He, W.-C. Kang, and J. McAuley. 2017. Translation-based recommendation. In *ACM Conference on Recommender systems*.

[6] R. He and J. McAuley. 2016. Fusing Similarity Models with Markov Chains for Sparse Sequential Recommendation. In *International Conference on Data Mining*. IEEE.

[7] Xiangnan He, Lizi Liao, Hanwang Zhang, Liqiang Nie, Xia Hu, and Tat-Seng Chua. 2017. Neural collaborative filtering. In *International Conference on World Wide Web*. ACM, 173–182.

[8] Balázs Hidasi, Alexandros Karatzoglou, Linas Baltrunas, and Domonkos Tikk. 2015. Session-based recommendations with recurrent neural networks. *arXiv preprint arXiv:1511.06939* (2015).

[9] Yifan Hu, Yehuda Koren, and Chris Volinsky. 2008. Collaborative filtering for implicit feedback datasets. In *International Conference on Data Mining*. IEEE, 263–272.

[10] Dietmar Jannach and Malte Ludewig. 2017. When Recurrent Neural Networks meet the Neighborhood for Session-Based Recommendation. In *ACM Conference on Recommender systems*. ACM, 306–310.

[11] Andrej Karpathy, George Toderici, Sanketh Shetty, Thomas Leung, Rahul Sukthankar, and Li Fei-Fei. 2014. Large-scale video classification with convolutional neural networks. In *IEEE conference on Computer Vision and Pattern Recognition*. 1725–1732.

[12] Yoon Kim. 2014. Convolutional Neural Networks for Sentence Classification. In *Conference on Empirical Methods on Natural Language Processing*. ACL, 1756–1751.

[13] Diederik Kingma and Jimmy Ba. 2014. Adam: A method for stochastic optimization. *arXiv preprint arXiv:1412.6980* (2014).

[14] Yehuda Koren. 2010. Collaborative filtering with temporal dynamics. *Commun. ACM* 53, 4 (2010), 89–97.

[15] Yehuda Koren, Robert Bell, and Chris Volinsky. 2009. Matrix factorization techniques for recommender systems. *Computer* 42, 8 (2009).

[16] Alex Krizhevsky, Ilya Sutskever, and Geoffrey E Hinton. 2012. Imagenet classification with deep convolutional neural networks. In *Advances in Neural Information Processing Systems*. 1097–1105.

[17] Duen-Ren Liu, Chin-Hui Lai, and Wang-Jung Lee. 2009. A hybrid of sequential rules and collaborative filtering for product recommendation. *Information Sciences* 179, 20 (2009), 3505–3519.

[18] Tomas Mikolov, Martin Karafiát, Lukas Burget, Jan Cernockỳ, and Sanjeev Khudanpur. 2010. Recurrent neural network based language model.. In *Interspeech*, Vol. 2. 3.

[19] Rong Pan, Yunhong Zhou, Bin Cao, Nathan N Liu, Rajan Lukose, Martin Scholz, and Qiang Yang. 2008. One-class collaborative filtering. In *International Conference on Data Mining*. IEEE, 502–511.

[20] Steffen Rendle, Christoph Freudenthaler, Zeno Gantner, and Lars Schmidt-Thieme. 2009. BPR: Bayesian personalized ranking from implicit feedback. In *Conference on Uncertainty in Artificial Intelligence*. AUAI Press, 452–461.

[21] Steffen Rendle, Christoph Freudenthaler, and Lars Schmidt-Thieme. 2010. Factorizing personalized markov chains for next-basket recommendation. In *International Conference on World Wide Web*. ACM, 811–820.

[22] Ruslan Salakhutdinov and Andriy Mnih. 2007. Probabilistic Matrix Factorization.. In *Advances in Neural Information Processing Systems*, Vol. 1. 2–1.

[23] Ruslan Salakhutdinov, Andriy Mnih, and Geoffrey Hinton. 2007. Restricted Boltzmann machines for collaborative filtering. In *International Conference on Machine learning*. ACM, 791–798.

[24] Badrul Sarwar, George Karypis, Joseph Konstan, and John Riedl. 2001. Item-based collaborative filtering recommendation algorithms. In *International Conference on World Wide Web*. ACM, 285–295.

[25] Suvash Sedhain, Aditya Krishna Menon, Scott Sanner, and Lexing Xie. 2015. Autorec: Autoencoders meet collaborative filtering. In *International Conference on World Wide Web*. ACM, 111–112.

[26] Yang Song, Ali Mamdouh Elkahky, and Xiaodong He. 2016. Multi-rate deep learning for temporal recommendation. In *International ACM SIGIR conference on Research and Development in Information Retrieval*. ACM, 909–912.

[27] Nitish Srivastava, Geoffrey Hinton, Alex Krizhevsky, Ilya Sutskever, and Ruslan Salakhutdinov. 2014. Dropout: A Simple Way to Prevent Neural Networks from Overfitting. *Journal of Machine Learning Research* 15, 1 (2014), 1929–1958.

[28] Andrea Vedaldi and Karel Lenc. 2015. Matconvnet: Convolutional neural networks for matlab. In *International conference on Multimedia*. ACM, 689–692.

[29] Hao Wang, Naiyan Wang, and Dit-Yan Yeung. 2015. Collaborative deep learning for recommender systems. In *International Conference on Knowledge Discovery and Data Mining*. ACM, 1235–1244.

[30] Pengfei Wang, Jiafeng Guo, Yanyan Lan, Jun Xu, Shengxian Wan, and Xueqi Cheng. 2015. Learning hierarchical representation model for nextbasket recommendation. In *International ACM SIGIR conference on Research and Development in Information Retrieval*. ACM, 403–412.

[31] Chao-Yuan Wu, Amr Ahmed, Alex Beutel, Alexander J. Smola, and How Jing. 2017. Recurrent Recommender Networks. In *International Conference on Web Search and Data Mining*. ACM, 495–503.

[32] Yao Wu, Christopher DuBois, Alice X Zheng, and Martin Ester. 2016. Collaborative denoising auto-encoders for top-n recommender systems. In *International Conference on Web Search and Data Mining*. ACM, 153–162.

[33] Quan Yuan, Gao Cong, and Aixin Sun. 2014. Graph-based point-of-interest recommendation with geographical and temporal influences. In *International Conference on Information and Knowledge Management*. ACM, 659–668.

[34] Chenyi Zhang, Ke Wang, Hongkun Yu, Jianling Sun, and Ee-Peng Lim. 2014. Latent factor transition for dynamic collaborative filtering. In *SIAM International Conference on Data Mining*. SIAM, 452–460.

[35] Shenglin Zhao, Tong Zhao, Haiqin Yang, Michael R Lyu, and Irwin King. 2016. Stellar: spatial-temporal latent ranking for successive point-of-interest recommendation. In *AAAI Conference on Artificial Intelligence*. AAAI Press, 315–321.

[36] Lei Zheng, Vahid Noroozi, and Philip S. Yu. 2017. Joint Deep Modeling of Users and Items Using Reviews for Recommendation. In *International Conference on Web Search and Data Mining*. ACM, 425–434.

sSketch: A Scalable Sketching Technique for PCA in the Cloud

Md. Mehrab Tanjim and Muhammad Abdullah Adnan
Bangladesh University of Engineering and Technology
Dhaka, Bangladesh
{mehrab.tanjim,abdullah.adnan}@gmail.com

ABSTRACT

Multidimensional data appear frequently in many web-related applications, e.g., product ratings, the bag-of-words representation of web pages, etc. Principal Component Analysis (PCA) has been widely used for discovering patterns in relationships among entities in multidimensional data. However, existing algorithms for PCA have limited scalability since they explicitly materialize intermediate data, whose size rapidly grows as the dimension increases. To avoid scalability issues, we propose sSketch, a scalable sketching technique for PCA that employs several optimization ideas, such as mean propagation, efficient sparse matrix operations, and effective job consolidation to minimize intermediate data. Using sSketch, we also provide two other scalable methods for deriving singular value and 2-norm of reconstruction error, both of which are used for data analysis purpose. We provide our implementation on popular Spark framework for distributed platform. We compare our method against state-of-the-art library functions available for distributed settings, namely MLlib-PCA and Mahout-PCA with real big datasets. Our experiments show that our method outperforms both of them by a wide margin. To encourage reproducibility, the source code of sSketch is made publicly available at https://github.com/DataMiningResearch/sSketch.

ACM Reference format:

Md. Mehrab Tanjim and Muhammad Abdullah Adnan. 2018. sSketch: A Scalable Sketching Technique for PCA in the Cloud. In *Proceedings of WSDM 2018: The Eleventh ACM International Conference on Web Search and Data Mining , Marina Del Rey, CA, USA, February 5–9, 2018 (WSDM 2018),* 9 pages. https://doi.org/10.1145/3159652.3159736

1 INTRODUCTION

Multidimensional data frequently appear in many applications [18, 28], including the following examples:

- Social Network: Dimensions are edges which represent interactions between people [21].
- Product Ratings: Dimensions are ratings from different users [27].
- Web Documents: A bag-of-words representation of web documents typically treats each word as a dimension [23].

WSDM 2018, February 5–9, 2018, Marina Del Rey, CA, USA

ACM ISBN 978-1-4503-5581-0/18/02...$15.00
https://doi.org/10.1145/3159652.3159736

As terabytes of data are being collected every day from numerous websites, multidimensional data is becoming very large. Applying a machine learning algorithm on big data is, however, a non-trivial task. Initial algorithms were designed for a single machine with limited memory, and therefore are not suitable for parallel computation. Designing a distributed machine learning algorithm is challenging because we have to divide matrix-matrix and matrix-vector computations among multiple computing nodes while preserving the accuracy and theoretical guarantees. More importantly, as we divide these computations among the nodes, they can produce several partial results and intermediate data which in turn may need to be exchanged among these nodes. The generation and exchange of intermediate data both pose a significant challenge because if they are not carefully managed, they can be the actual bottleneck of the algorithm. So, the need for designing scalable machine learning algorithms for various domains including web [31] has increased now more than ever.

In this paper, we consider the widely used technique called Principal Component Analysis (PCA). For multidimensional data, PCA is very useful for applications such as dimensionality reduction [9], lossy-data compression [10], feature extraction, and data visualization [16]. For example, in the image processing domain, PCA is used to obtain the principal facial components whose linear combination could recreate any face in the image dataset [33]. In information retrieval, the principal components explain the principal terms in a set of documents [1, 39] and can be used for web search [19]. Overall, PCA has provided meaningful results in many domains [2] as well as in web.

There are two state-of-the-art libraries that offer PCA for distributed clusters, namely: Mahout [26] and MLlib [29]. However, PCA algorithms implemented in these libraries face severe scalability issues and are not suitable for big data analysis. For example, the MLlib-PCA faced **out-of-memory error** when dealing with datasets more than 6,000 dimensions. The implementation of PCA in Mahout, too, has high memory requirement and needs to shuffle a lot of data among the cluster nodes. It finished processing a 128-dimensional dataset in about four minutes on an 8-node cluster, where each node has 8 cores. The same algorithm took **more than 5 hours** to complete when working with a 141k-dimensional dataset. Our algorithm, in contrast, finished in a **couple of minutes**. This paper addresses these issues found in current implementations of PCA and makes the following contributions:

- We analyze both state-of-the-art algorithms available for computing PCA on big data platform and identify major scalability issues. We provide both computational time and space complexities required by these methods and explain the reasons behind their failure to scale up for big data.
- We provide our own scalable algorithm for PCA. Recently various sketching methods, such as Gaussian sketch [20],

Count sketch [3], etc., have been proposed to tackle big data challenge [4, 17, 22, 32, 38]. We provide scalable implementation of the Gaussian sketch method which we refer to as sSketch and use it for PCA, referred to as sSketch-PCA. We apply our various optimization ideas, such as mean propagation, effective matrix operations, and on-the-fly computation to minimize intermediate data in order to achieve high scalability. For distributed programming platform, we consider the recent and popular Spark framework [36].

- As additional results, we provide scalable algorithms for deriving singular value and 2-norm of reconstruction error using sSketch. Singular value of a mean centered matrix is needed to determine exact low rank approximation error [15] and 2-norm of reconstruction error determines the accuracy of a given low rank approximation [30]. Both of them are used for analysis of convergence in iterative algorithms. To the best of our knowledge, we are the first to give scalable algorithms for them. We refer to the former one as sSketch-Singular and the later one as sSketch-Norm.
- We run extensive experimentation with real, large, and diverse datasets to compare the performance of our algorithms using sSketch against other distributed algorithms. Our empirical study shows that sSketch-PCA is **several orders of magnitude faster** than widely used and state-of-the-art competitors, namely MLlib-PCA and Mahout-PCA. As sSketch generates a small amount of intermediate data, it offers high scalability too. For this feature, sSketch has low network I/O and is able to run on the limited aggregated memory of the cluster. For example, on a dataset of more than 8 million text documents, sSketch-PCA generates **151 MB** of intermediate data whereas Mahout-PCA generates **3.65 GB** of intermediate data.

The rest of this paper is organized as follows. In Section 2, we discuss preliminaries on different techniques of PCA and accuracy measurement. In Section 3, we analyze state-of-the-art techniques available for PCA. We present the proposed design of sSketch in Section 4 and give the algorithm of sSketch-PCA. Later on, we present our additional results, namely sSketch-Singular and sSketch-Norm, in Section 5. We discuss the complexity in Section 6. We justify our contribution with experimental evaluation in Section 7. Finally, Section 8 concludes the paper.

2 PRELIMINARIES

In this section, we quickly go through some of the techniques for calculating PCA on a matrix. Interested readers are encouraged to read [11] which provides a detailed comparison of each of the following techniques. For all techniques, we assume that the data is Y of $N \times D$ dimensions. We also assume Y is not mean-centered and if we apply its mean of all rows, μ, to center it, then $\mathbf{Y}_c$ is the mean centered data.

2.1 Computing PCA using EVD

A simple way of computing PCA of a matrix (we will use the term 'data' and 'matrix' interchangeably) Y is to compute the Eigen Value Decomposition (EVD) of its covariance matrix. If our target dimension is k, the algorithm computes a $D \times k$ matrix V such that the columns of V are the principal components of Y. The algorithm for computing the EVD of the covariance matrix can be summarized in the following steps:

- First we have to mean center the data and get $\mathbf{Y}_c$.
- Then we have to compute its covariance matrix C, which is given by: $\mathbf{C} \equiv (\mathbf{Y_c}^T * \mathbf{Y}_c)/(N-1)$.
- As C is a symmetric square matrix, we can easily diagonalize this with the help of Eigen Value Decomposition (EVD) [34]. To put it mathematically, if V is the matrix of Eigen vectors and D is the diagonal matrix of Eigen values then for symmetric covariance matrix: $\mathbf{C} = \mathbf{VDV}^T$.

Each column of V indicates a direction or a component and each diagonal element of D indicates their respective variance [35].

2.2 Computing PCA using SVD

SVD or Singular Value Decomposition is one of the most popular techniques for matrix operations [14]. PCA of a matrix can also be found using the following steps [34, 35]:

- We have to perform SVD on mean centered matrix $\mathbf{Y}_c$. Mathematically, $\mathbf{Y}_c = \mathbf{U} * \Sigma * \mathbf{V}^T$.

SVD outputs three matrices namely U, Σ and V. Both U and V are orthonormal and Σ is a diagonal matrix. Elements of Σ are called singular values and V is the principal component.

2.3 Computing PCA using SSVD

Recently randomized sketch matrix is being used to tackle big data problem [4, 17, 22, 32]. Its main advantage is that it turns big data into small data [12]. There are different sketching techniques as well, like Gaussian sketch [20], Count sketch [3], etc. Depending on sketching techniques, theoretical guarantee about accuracy varies.

As it is very easy to implement Gaussian sketch matrix, in practice it is preferred to other sketches. If sketching parameter s is of $O(k/\epsilon)$ and Ω (dimension $D \times s$) is a Gaussian projection matrix, then $\Omega = \mathbf{G}/\sqrt{s}$, where each entry of G is sampled i.i.d. from $\mathcal{N}(0,1)$. The low rank approximation property holds for sketch $\mathbf{Z} = \mathbf{Y}_c * \Omega$ (dimension $N \times s$) in expectation [37] :

$$\min_{rank(\mathbf{A}) \leq k} ||\mathbf{Z} * \mathbf{A} - \mathbf{Y_c}||_F \leq (1+\epsilon)||\mathbf{Y}_c - \mathbf{Y}_{ck}||_F \tag{1}$$

where $\mathbf{Y}_c$ is the mean centered data matrix of dimension $N \times D$, $\mathbf{Y}_{ck}$ is the rank-k approximation of dimension $N \times k$ and ϵ is the error which satisfies $0 \leq \epsilon \leq 1$. We can find an orthonormal basis, Q, for Z by performing QR Decomposition of it. As the column space of Z is the same as the column space of Q, the minimization problem in (1) is equivalent to

$$\underset{rank(\mathbf{J}) \leq k}{argmin} ||\mathbf{Q} * \mathbf{J} - \mathbf{Y}_c||_F^2 = (\mathbf{Q}^T * \mathbf{Y}_c)_k \tag{2}$$

The matrix $\mathbf{Y}_{ck}$ can be well approximated by $\tilde{\mathbf{Y}}_{ck} \approx \mathbf{Q} * (\mathbf{Q}^T * \mathbf{Y}_c)_k$, so we only need to find the SVD of $\tilde{\mathbf{Y}}_{ck}$:

$$\tilde{\mathbf{Y}}_{ck} \approx \mathbf{Q} * (\mathbf{Q}^T * \mathbf{Y}_c)_k = \mathbf{Q} * \overline{\mathbf{U}} * \tilde{\Sigma} * \tilde{\mathbf{V}}^T = \tilde{\mathbf{U}} * \tilde{\Sigma} * \tilde{\mathbf{V}}^T \tag{3}$$

$\tilde{\mathbf{U}}$ and $\tilde{\mathbf{V}}$ are approximation of original orthonormal columns and $\tilde{\Sigma}$ is an approximate diagonal matrix. In short, the major steps for calculating PCA using these techniques are:

(1) We first start with sketching the data matrix. We will be using Gaussian sketching matrix because it is easier to implement than Count sketch. To have a Gaussian sketch matrix, Ω, we have to draw $D \times s$ numbers randomly from Gaussian distribution with 0 mean and unit variance.
(2) Then we have to multiply with $\mathbf{Y}_c$ to get sketched data matrix: $\mathbf{Z} = \mathbf{Y}_c * \Omega$. Here s is the sketching dimension which is greater than our target rank k, but much less than $D(s \ll D)$ and $p = s - k$ is called oversampling parameter. It controls how good a sketched data matrix will be in terms of approximation.
(3) After having $\mathbf{Z}$, we have to perform QR Decomposition [15] on it to get orthonormal basis $\mathbf{Q}$: $[\mathbf{Q}, \mathbf{R}] = qr(\mathbf{Z})$
(4) Then we have to perform matrix multiplication $\mathbf{Q}^T * \mathbf{Y}_c$.
(5) Finally we have to perform SVD on $\mathbf{Q}^T * \mathbf{Y}_c$ to get principal component $\mathbf{V}$: $[\sim, \sim, \mathbf{V}] = svd(\mathbf{Q}^T * \mathbf{Y}_c)$.
(6) To increase accuracy of the result we can take this $\mathbf{Q}^T * \mathbf{Y}_c$ as new Ω and repeat steps 2, 3 and 4 before performing SVD on final result. This is known as Power Iteration, and more details can be found in [17].

2.4 Accuracy Measurement

Now we present the significance of singular value of a matrix and 2-norm of reconstruction error. The reconstruction error of a principal component $\mathbf{V}_k$ for data matrix $\mathbf{Y}_c$ is defined as $\|\mathbf{Y}_c - \mathbf{Y}_c * \mathbf{V}_k * \mathbf{V}_k{}^T\|$. $(k+1)^{\text{th}}$ singular value is $(k+1)^{\text{th}}$ element of singular matrix Σ returned by SVD. There is a relationship between this reconstruction error of top k principal components $\mathbf{V}_k$ and $(k+1)^{\text{th}}$ singular value of mean centered matrix [15]. For ideal accuracy using the reconstruction error, the following is true:

$$\|\mathbf{Y}_c - \mathbf{Y}_c * \mathbf{V}_k * \mathbf{V}_k{}^T\|_2 = \Sigma(k+1, k+1)$$

In that case, $\mathbf{Y}_c * \mathbf{V}_k * \mathbf{V}_k{}^T$ is regarded as exact low rank k approximation which we refer to as $\mathbf{Y}_{ck}$. So, the reconstruction error of a principal component $\mathbf{V}_k$ is defined as follows:

$$e = \frac{\|\mathbf{Y}_c - \mathbf{Y}_c * \mathbf{V}_k * \mathbf{V}_k{}^T\|_2 - \|\mathbf{Y}_c - \mathbf{Y}_{ck}\|_2}{\|\mathbf{Y}_c - \mathbf{Y}_{ck}\|_2} \quad (4)$$

where $\|.\|_2$ denotes 2-norm. So, if we want 95% of ideal accuracy, we have to actually run iterations to reach less than 5% of this 2-norm reconstruction error ($e < 0.05$).

3 RELATED WORKS

In this section, we discuss implementation of the techniques, presented in the previous section, in state-of-the-art library functions namely MLlib [29] and Mahout [26].

3.1 MLlib PCA

MLlib is a popular library that contains many machine learning algorithms for distributed settings [29]. For PCA, MLlib implements the first technique to calculate PCA, namely computing PCA using EVD. It mainly provides distributed computation of large covariance matrix to reduce workload for one computer.

Computation Complexity: The major computation part in this method is to calculate the covariance matrix. MLlib-PCA does not leverage sparsity of the matrix, so for a data matrix with size $N \times D$, it takes $O(ND \times min(N, D))$ time to calculate covariance matrix. This is very high specially if either N or D is very large which is typically the case for big data.

Space Complexity: This method creates a large covariance matrix of size $D \times D$ which takes a lot of time to communicate. Its communication complexity thus is $O(D^2)$.

Scalability Issues: Readily from our complexity analysis we can see that MLlib PCA offers limited scalability. Its main bottleneck lies in communication which is of $O(D^2)$. As big data has higher number of dimensions, D^2 can grow very quickly and application can easily run out of memory. This is what we find in our experimentation. Specially for $141k$ and $50k$-dimensional data MLlib **fails** to compute PCA.

3.2 Mahout PCA

Mahout [26] is another popular library that provides many machine learning algorithms for distributed computing. Mahout implements both techniques 2 and 3, namely computing PCA using SVD for small data and SSVD for big data. As we are dealing with big data, we will refer Mahout's implementation of PCA using SSVD by Mahout-PCA.

Computation Complexity: In Mahout-PCA, most of the time is consumed in computing the product $\mathbf{Q}^T * \mathbf{Y}_c$, the fourth step in SSVD. Remember $\mathbf{Y}_c$ is of dimension $N \times D$ and $\mathbf{Q}$ is of dimension $N \times s$, where $s = k + p$ (p is oversampling parameter). Thus its computation complexity is $O(NDs)$.

Space Complexity: The algorithm requires storing a large intermediate matrix, namely $N \times s$ dimensional matrix $\mathbf{Q}$. So the total intermediate data can be calculated as $O(Ns)$.

Scalability Issues: In terms of computation complexity, Mahout PCA provides better scalibility than MLlib-PCA. But again its main bottleneck lies in forming and saving the intermediate data on nodes. As N is large for big data, transmitting the $N \times s$ sized intermediate data can take very long time in communication and a lot of space in memory of each node.

4 OUR OPTIMIZATION IDEAS

4.1 Mean Propagation

Most of the big data in real life are sparse and to calculate PCA on these data efficiently, we do not want to lose the sparsity. Thus we do not form mean centered data matrix explicitly, rather we propagate the mean in different calculations. For example, during the multiplication with Gaussain sketch matrix, Ω, we do the following modifications:

$$\mathbf{Y}_c * \Omega = (\mathbf{Y} - \mu) * \Omega = (\mathbf{Y} * \Omega - \mu * \Omega)$$

In this way we can leverage sparsity and calculate the first multiplication, $\mathbf{Y} * \Omega$ faster.

4.2 Effective Job Consolidation

We now present evolution of our approaches for designing sSketch. For all of these approaches, we consider **map-reduce fashion** of distributed work load [6]. In **map** operations, each row of a matrix is considered one by one in each node and used for various transformations. Map operations produce a distributed matrix as well. There is also a **blockwisemap** operation supported by various

Algorithm 1: QRModification1

```
Input: Matrix Y, Vector Ym, Vector Zm, Matrix Ω, int D, int s
Output: Matrix QtY
partR = Y.blockwisemap{Yb =>
    Zb = Yb * Ω − [Ym * Ω]          ▹ Ym * Ω is applied row-wise
    [~, Rb] = qr(Zb)}
R = partR.treeReduce{R1, R2 =>
    [~, Rb] = qr(concat(R1, R2))}
broadcast(R)
QtYSum = accumulator(newMatrix(s, D))
Y.map{Yi =>
    Zi = Yi * Ω
    Qi = Zi * R^-1 − Zm * R^-1
    (QtY)i = Qi^T * Yi − Qi^T * Ym
    QtYSum.add((QtY)i)}
QtY = QtYsum.value()
```

Algorithm 2: QRModification2

```
Input: Matrix Y, Vector Ym, Vector Zm, Matrix Ω, int D, int s
Output: Matrix QtY
ZtZSum = accumulator(newMatrix(s, s))
Y.map{Yi =>
    Zi = Yi * Ω
    (ZtZ)i = Zi^T * (Zi − Zm) − Zm^T * (Zi − Zm)}
R = chol(ZtZ)^T
broadcast(R)
QtYSum = accumulator(newMatrix(s, D))
Y.map{Yi =>
    Zi = Yi * Ω
    Qi = Zi * R^-1 − Zm * R^-1
    (QtY)i = Qi^T * Yi − Qi^T * Ym
    QtYSum.add((QtY)i)}
QtY = QtYsum.value()
```

platforms, like Spark [36], where all rows in a node is considered as matrix and operations are done on the entire block. In Spark, a block is known as a **partition**. In addition, there are special variables called **accumulators** to which each node can add values. When accumulators are used in map operation, we do not get a distributed matrix in return, rather we can get an accumulated value from all nodes. In **reduce** operation, different results from each nodes are aggregated to produce a single final result. Reduce operation can be operated in two ways: one, to accumulate all the partial results from each node in the master node and produce final result there, and two, produce results from nodes pairwise and merge them in a tree fashion. The later is known as **treereduce**. Last but not least, there is a **broadcast** operation which basically sends same copy of a data to all computing nodes. Now we present our modifications.

Straightforward Implementation: In our sketching method, all the works are done in the master node, except three, the formation of sketched matrix Z, its QR decomposition and multiplication

Algorithm 3: sSketch

```
Input: Matrix Y, Vector Ym, Vector Zm, Matrix Ω, int D, int s
Output: Matrix YtZ,Matrix ZtZ
YtZSum = accumulator(newMatrix(D, s))
ZtZSum = accumulator(newMatrix(s, s))
ZSum = accumulator(newVector(s))
Y.map{Yi =>
    Zi = Yi * Ω
    (YtZ)i = Yi^T * (Zi − Zm)
    (ZtZ)i = Zi^T * (Zi − Zm)
    YtZSum.add((YtZ)i)
    ZtZSum.add((ZtZ)i)}
    ZSum.add(Zi)}
YtZ = YtZSum.value() − Ym^T * (ZSum.value() − N * Zm)
ZtZ = ZtZSum.value() − Zm^T * (ZSum.value() − N * Zm)
```

of Q with data matrix Y. The most straightforward way to achieve this would be as follows:

- Generate and store Z first by map operation.
- Get the Q by applying QR decomposition on it. The state-of-the-art distributed QR decomposition available for distributed system is called **tallSkinnyQR** [5].
- Take each rows of Q and Y in map operation to calculate partial results of $Q^T * Y$ and use a reduce operation to sum up all partial results.

Issues: Both Z and Q are of $N{\times}s$ dimensions and so they **generate large intermediate data**. As this method stores them, it offers the least scalability.

QRModification1: We first explore the basic ideas of tallSkinnyQR [5] which are as follows:

- Perform **HouseHolder QR** [15] factorization for each block in blockwisemap operation and get the partial **R**s.
- Form full R in a treereduce operation.
- Optionally if **Q** is needed, distribute **R** to each partition and make use of map operation and $Y * R^{-1}$ formula to generate distributed **Q** matrix.

This method provides very fast QR decomposition of Tall (large number of rows) and Skinny (low dimensional) matrix. One of our first ideas was to place our computations to each of these steps to produce our results fast. Our first modified QR decomposition is shown in Algorithm 1 which includes these steps:

- Use blockwisemap operation to produce sketched matrix **Zb** from it. Then perform HouseHolder QR Factorization on it to produce partial **R**s. This way we avoid producing huge $N \times s$ matrix **Z**.
- Step 2 remains the same.
- Broadcast the full **R**.
- Each row of Z is produced again to compute each row of Q. Each row of Q is thus used to produce partial results of $Q^T * Y$. Then we use accumulators in map operations to sum up these partial results. The variable **QtY** holds the full result.

Algorithm 4: sSketch-PCA

Input: Data matrix Y of dimension $N \times D$, sketch dimension s, target rank k, max iteration q

Output: Principal Component **V**

1 $\Omega_1 = normrand(D, s)$
2 $Ym =$ **meanJob**(Y)
3 **for** $i \leftarrow 1$ **to** q **do**
4 $\quad Zm = Ym * \Omega_i$
5 $\quad \{YtZ, ZtZ\} =$ **sSketch**(Y, Ym, Zm, Ω_i)
6 $\quad R = (chol(ZtZ))^T$
7 $\quad \Omega_i = (YtZ * R^{-1})$
8 **end**
9 $[\sim, \sim, V] = svd(\Omega_q{}^T)$
10 $V = V(:, 1 : k)$

These modifications in original QR decomposition produce a significant improvement in terms of running time. Note that we do not materialize either Z or Q. And **in the last step we do not use reduce stage**, we use accumulators instead. This reduces shuffling between nodes and thus requires less communication.

Issues: We notice that there are basically **two map operations and a treereduce operation**. The treereduce portion really takes longer time to complete as there is shuffling of data.

QRModification2: For second modification, we consider Cholesky Decomposition [7] for performing QR Decomposition. Cholesky Decomposition makes use of orthonormality of Q matrix and has the following steps:

$$Z^T * Z = (Q * R)^T * (Q * R) = R^T * R$$

$$R = (chol(Z^T * Z))^T$$

We make use of this formula to replace treereduce operation. We have to consider an additional accumulator ZtZ to sum up partial results $Z^T * Z$. But as **there is no treereduce operation**, this reduces running time significantly. This modification is shown in Algorithm 2.

Issues: Still we feel that there is room for improvement. Because we need **two map operations** and Line 6 in Algorithm 2 can be considered a bridge between two. Communication time is wasted because we have to broadcast an intermediate data, namely R. Additionally, computation time is wasted because of redundant computation of Z in Line 9.

Final Modification – sSketch: If we can merge two map operations, we can obtain better performance. But to be able to do that, we need to remove dependency on **R** in the last map operation and push **R** further to the calculation. We can achieve that by making use of the following matrix operations:

$$(Q^T * Y_c)^T = ((Z * R^{-1})^T * Y_c)^T$$

$$= Y_c^T * (Z * R^{-1}) = (Y_c^T * Z) * R^{-1}$$

For calculating **R**, we need $Z^T * Z$. But we can calculate both $Z^T * Z$ and $Y_c^T * Z$ in the **same map operation**, eliminating the need for broadcasting **R** and redundantly recomputing Z. Our final modification is referred to as sSKetch and is shown in Algorithm 3. Note that we multiply only non-zero elements of Y in Line 5 and 6 in Algorithm 3. As each Y_i is sparse, it makes the intermediate data YtZ_i a sparse matrix, and we consider only its non-zero entries for addition in Line 8. We introduce another accumulator **ZSum** to sum up all Zi vectors to finally mean center our result in Line 11 and Line 12. This significantly reduces computation time and cuts previous time almost in half. Thus, sSketch achieves the most efficiency because of these optimization. The complete algorithm to derive PCA is shown in Algorithm 4.

Algorithm 5: sSketch-Norm

Input: Data matrix Y of dimension $N \times D$, sketch dimension s, target rank k, max iteration q, fixed point precision tolerance ϵ

Output: First singular value of reconstruction error, $\Sigma(1, 1)$

$\Omega_1 = normrand(D, s)$
$Ym =$ **meanJob**(Y)
for $i \leftarrow 1$ **to** q **do**
$\quad \Omega_i = \Omega_i - V * (V^T * \Omega_i)$
$\quad Zm = Ym * \Omega_i$
$\quad \{YtZ, ZtZ\} =$ **sSketch**(Y, Ym, Zm, Ω_i)
$\quad R = (chol(ZtZ))^T$
$\quad \Omega_i = YtZ * R^{-1}$
$\quad \Omega_i = \Omega_i - V * (V^T * \Omega_i)$
$\quad [\sim, \Sigma_i, \sim] = svd(\Omega_i^T)$
$\quad$ **if** $\Delta\Sigma_i(1, 1) \leq \epsilon$ **then**
$\quad\quad$ **return** $\Sigma_i(1, 1)$
$\quad$ **end**
end
return $\Sigma_q(1, 1)$

4.3 On-the-fly Computation

To avoid explicitly materializing intermediate data we compute rows of intermediate data as they are needed and discard them when their use is expired. For example, if in matrix operations $Z = Y_c * \Omega$ and $[Q, R] = qr(Z)$, we form Z explicitly and then calculate its QR Decomposition to explicitly form Q, obviously our intermediate data size will be very high. When analyzing Mahout-PCA, we find this is indeed the case, while they do not form Z, **they do materialize** Q, thus requiring high memory. **We, on the other hand, do not form either of these matrix** and generate only each rows of Z and construct partial results for $Q^T * Y_c$ on-the-fly. We do not have to consider to generate Q at all because of our effective job consolidation in Algorithm 3. Thus our method ensures minimum intermediate data.

5 ADDITIONAL RESULTS

5.1 Efficient Singular Value Derivation

We can make use of same sSketch for deriving singular value of mean centred matrix. We just need to remove Line 9 and 10, and add the following line after Line 7 in Algorithm 4 (full algorithm, sSketch-Singular, not shown due to space limitation):

$$[\sim, \Sigma_i, \sim] = svd(\Omega_i{}^T)$$

Table 1: sSketch-PCA is both time and space efficient compared to other methods.

Method	Time Complexity	Space Complexity
MLlib-PCA	$O(ND \times min(N, D))$	$O(D^2)$
Mahout-PCA	$O(NDs)$	$O(Ns)$
sSketch-PCA	$O(nnz(Y) \times s)$	$O(Ds)$

Now, if our fixed point precision tolerance is ϵ and we want to derive $(k+1)^{\text{th}}$ singular value, then we continue iterations until changes in singular value, $\Delta\Sigma_i(k+1, k+1)$, is less than ϵ.

5.2 Efficient 2-Norm of Reconstruction Error Calculation

The 2-norm of any matrix is given by its first singular value. For computing reconstruction error, we have to compute the following matrix multiplication: $Y_c - Y_c * V * V^T$. But it is a dense matrix caused by subtraction. Also, $V * V^T$ is of D^2 size, so we can face out-of-memory error. To prevent that and to leverage sparsity we do the following modification:

$$(Y_c - Y_c * V * V^T) * \Omega = ((Y - \mu) - (Y - \mu) * V * V^T) * \Omega$$
$$= Y * (\Omega - V * (V^T * \Omega)) - \mu * (\Omega - V * (V^T * \Omega))$$

We can now treat $(\Omega - V*(V^T * \Omega))$ as new Ω and apply sSketch. Note that **we do not face out of memory error** in this way because we multiply $V^T * \Omega$ first. One last modification we have to do after getting result from sSketch at i^{th} iteration is as follows: $\Omega_i = \Omega_i - V * (V^T * \Omega_i)$. This is because we are not considering only Y_c but $Y_c - Y_c * V * V^T$. We continue iteration until we get fixed point precision of the first singular value. Thus this allows us to compute 2-norm of reconstruction error for any large dataset without facing any out-of-memory error. We call this algorithm sSketch-Norm which is presented in Algorithm 5.

6 COMPLEXITY ANALYSIS

In this section we compare, complexities of all methods. Before comparison, let us quickly discuss complexities of our method.

Computation Complexity: Major calculations in each map operation in our method are the multiplication in Line 5 and 6 and addition in Line 8 in Algorithm 3. In Line 5 and 6, only sparse entries of Y_i are being considered for multiplication. Similarly, in Line 8, sparse entries of YtZ_i are considered for addition. So, the computation complexity is $O(nnz(Y) \times s)$, where $nnz(Y)$ denotes the non-zero entries of Y.

Space Complexity: In each iteration, we only have to transmit a small $Y^T * Z$ (dimension $D \times s$) and $Z^T * Z$ (dimension $s \times s$). So space complexity is $O(Ds)$.

Scalability: We present all complexities in Table 1. We can see our method offers the least space complexity of all. Also, due to our various modifications, like avoiding both reduce operation and redundant computations, use of accumulators and preservation of sparsity of both input and intermediate data, we significantly reduce the constant factors in computation time. Overall, our method offers high scalability and performance over available baseline methods.

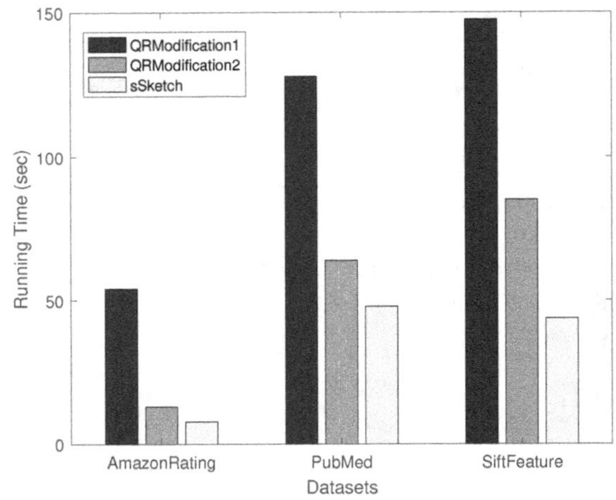

Figure 1: Comparison of running times for 1 iteration among modifications for all datasets. Our final modification, sSketch, takes least amount of time.

7 EXPERIMENTAL EVALUATION

In this section, we present a rigorous evaluation of sSketch comparing it against the closest algorithms. We have used multiple real large datasets from different domains. First, we describe our experimental settings and then we move on to detailed evaluation.

7.1 Experimental Settings

Algorithms Compared: For computing PCA we compare three methods:

- sSketch-PCA: Implementation of our method for PCA.
- Mahout-PCA: Mahout implementation of PCA [26].
- MLlib-PCA: PCA implementation in MLlib [29].

Both the Mahout-PCA and MLlib-PCA implementations are quite popular and state-of-the-art methods for computing PCA available for big data platform. For distributed framework, we consider Spark[36]. If not mentioned otherwise, we take 10 principal components ($k = 10$) for all PCA algorithms to make a uniform comparison. Also, as it is considered practical to take 5 or 10 for oversampling [25], we set oversampling parameter, p, to 10. As $s = k + p$, that makes $s = 20$ for most of our experiments.

Dataset: We use three real datasets. We consider one dense dataset and two sparse datasets. All of them are quite diverse in terms of size, dimensions, sparsity, and data values. The datasets are:

- PubMed: PubMed is a bag of word representation of medical documents from the U.S. National Library of Medicine. [23] provides a matrix from this dataset where the rows represent the documents and the columns represent the distinct words in each document. Each entry is either 1 or 0. It is a sparse matrix and its size is $8,200,000 \times 141,043$. Non-zero elements of the matrix alone occupy about 4.9 GB. We also consider a small subset of this dataset with 2000 dimension, referred to as PubMed2k.

Table 2: Comparison of running time (in sec) for sSketch-PCA on different datasets against state-of-the-art library functions MLlib-PCA and Mahout-PCA. For sSketch and Mahout-PCA the target accuracy is set to 95%.

Datasets	Size	MLlib-PCA	Mahout-PCA	sSketch-PCA
PubMed2k	$8.2M \times 2k$	94.54	57.47	18.11
PubMed	$8.2M \times 141k$	**Fail**	19491.50	235.37
AmazonRating2k	$6.6M \times 2k$	58.58	63.55	12.99
AmazonRating	$6.6M \times 50k$	**Fail**	2042.51	64.33
SiftFeature	$4.5M \times 128$	107.09	225.19	182.10

Table 3: Both sSketch-PCA and Mahout-PCA have similar convergencoxe. For all datasets, 2-norm of reconstruction error is shown after each iteration. Algorithms run until error becomes less than 0.05 (95% accuracy).

sSketch-PCA			Mahout-PCA		
PubMed	Amazon-Rating	Sift-Feature	PubMed	Amazon-Rating	Sift-Feature
0.1412	0.1968	0.1243	0.1515	0.1874	0.1435
0.05	0.0641	0.0084	0.055	0.0601	0.0143
0.019	0.0293	-	0.0162	0.0183	-

- AmazonRating: Amazon product data provided by [27] contains product reviews and meta-data from Amazon. It includes 142.8 million reviews which span from May 1996 to July 2014. We consider ratings only dataset and we take 50000 user ratings for 6594110 products from Amazon. Data entries range from 0-5. Like PubMed, it too is a sparse matrix. We also consider a small matrix with 2000 dimension which we call AmazonRating2k.
- SiftFeature: A dataset of 4455091 data vectors. We download images from ImageNet [8] and from each image, we extract SIFT [24] features, where each SIFT feature is a vector of 128 dimensions. The matrix is dense and unlike previous two datasets, the elements are not integers but real numbers. Its size is 4455091×128, where rows represent data vectors and columns represent dimensions.

Cluster Configuration: We run the experiments by creating a cluster on the Amazon EMR. Our cluster consists of 8 Amazon EC2 m3.xlarge instances/nodes, where each node has 8 vCPU, 15 GB memory, 80 SSD GB storage. The cluster runs on the latest emr-5.7.0 provided by Amazon. We install latest versions of all required software, namely Hadoop 2.7.3 for Yarn manager and file system, Spark 2.1.1 for deploying our distributed algorithm, Ganglia 3.7.2 for monitoring metrics, and Mahout 0.13.0 for Mahout-PCA. MLlib library is by default included in Spark, so we do not need any additional installment for MLlib-PCA.

7.2 Evaluation

We divide our evaluation into multiple parts. First, we compare running times of our three different techniques and justify our choice

Table 4: Comparison of running times (in sec) to complete first iteration of sSketch-PCA and Mahout-PCA.

Datasets	Size	Mahout-PCA	sSketch-PCA
PubMed	$8.2M \times 141k$	6720.30	188.09
AmazonRating	$6.6M \times 50k$	688.51	44.82
SiftFeature	$4.5M \times 128$	160.04	136.35

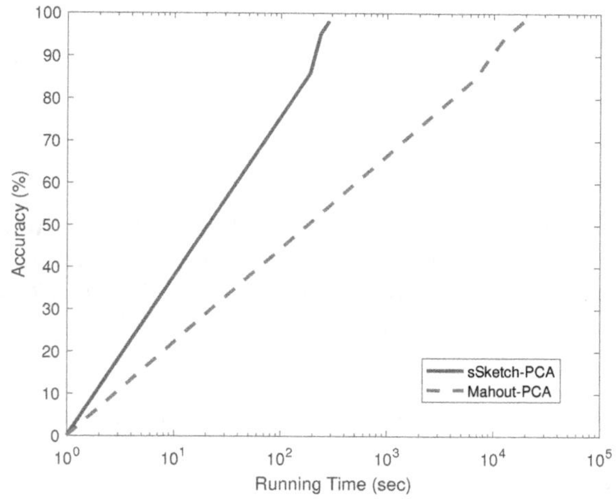

Figure 2: Accuracy vs running time for PubMed Data. The x-axis is in log scale.

of final modification, sSketch, among them. Then we compare running times of all three algorithms for computing PCA. We discuss accuracy later on. Then we show scalability of our approach by comparing memory requirements for intermediate data size.

Running Times of Modifications: To compare running times among our three modifications, we run 1 iteration of each algorithm on all three datasets. As all other parameters, like clusters, datasets, etc., are unchanged, the modification which takes the least amount of time will be chosen as our final modification. As we have discussed previously, our last modification, namely sSketch should take the least time than other two, namely QRModification1, and QRModification2. In Figure 1, we see our initial assessment is correct, as sSketch takes 47.89 seconds to finish on PubMed whereas QRModification1 and QRModification2 take 127.88 and 63.82 seconds respectively. sSketch's running times on the other datasets are less as expected. This justifies our choice of final modification, namely sSketch.

Running Times of all Methods: Now we measure the running times of all algorithms on all datasets. Our results are shown in Table 2. Before comparing running times of these algorithms, we should note that MLlib-PCA is a deterministic algorithm that finishes after completing a fixed number of matrix operations. But both sSketch-PCA and Mahout-PCA are iterative algorithms, i.e., they continue refining principal components until they reach a target accuracy. We will discuss how we measure our accuracy and what is the practical approach later on but for now we consider to

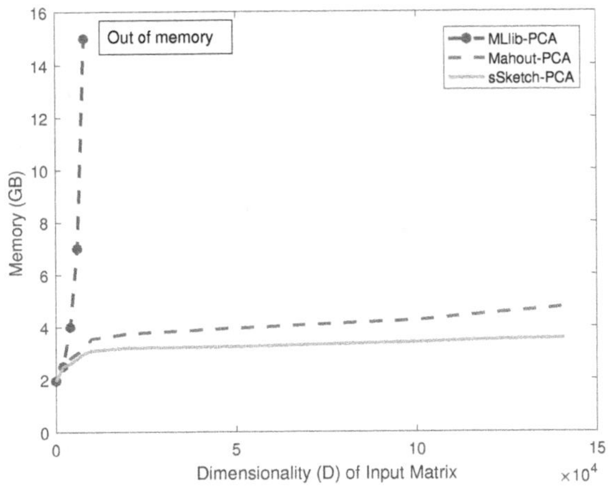

Figure 3: Memory consumption of sSketch-PCA vs. MLlib-PCA and Mahout-PCA on different input sizes for the PubMed dataset in a single node from the cluster. sSketch-PCA takes the least amount of space among all.

run both sSketch-PCA and Mahout-PCA to reach at least 95% of ideal accuracy.

From Table 2 we can make couple of observations. First, sSketch outperforms the other two algorithms by wide margins in most of the cases. For example, for 141k-dimensional data (PubMed) sSketch-PCA finishes in less than a couple of minutes (235.37 sec), while Mahout-PCA takes more than 5 hours (19491.50 sec) to finish, so Mahout-PCA is **83× slower** than sSketch-PCA. For other datasets also, sSketch-PCA **outperforms** Mahout-PCA. In our experiments, we also vary the target dimension k. For PubMed dataset, if we consider only the first iteration, the performance gain is about **31×** (9634.5s vs 312.93s) for $k = 30$ and about **20×** (9683.34s vs 492.23s) for $k = 50$ (not shown in the table due to space limitation). Results from other datasets are similar. We observe sSketch-PCA outperforms Mahout-PCA because we reduce both computation (through sparsity preserving matrix operations) and communication time (by reducing intermediate data). The second observation is when we work with high dimensional datasets, MLlib-PCA **fails to compute** the principal components. MLlib-PCA requires storing a $D \times D$ covariance matrix in the memory of each machine and the size $D \times D$ quickly becomes large as dimension increases. So the algorithm fails when the size of this matrix exceeds the available memory. Even working with much smaller dimension (2000) it can take about **5× more time than** sSketch-PCA (for cases of PubMed2k and AmazonRating2k). However, when working with low-dimensional and dense matrix as SiftFeature (dimension 128) MLlib-PCA outperforms other approaches. In this case, MLlib-PCA computes a 128×128 intermediate matrix and then does further computations on one machine, so it finishes faster than other approaches, including ours. As the dataset is dense and MLlib-PCA does not leverage sparsity, it does not become a problem. However, this is not a typical case for big data, where datasets are generally sparse and high dimensional in which case MLlib-PCA fails as shown earlier.

Table 5: sSketch is space efficient. It produces several orders of magnitude less intermediate data than state-of-the-art methods.

Technique	PubMed	AmazonRating	SiftFeature
MLlib-PCA	≥150GB	≥150GB	896KB
Mahout-PCA	3.65GB	1.05GB	0.67GB
sSketch-PCA	151MB	53MB	140KB

Accuracy: We compare sSketch-PCA and Mahout-PCA based on the time needed to reach 95% of the ideal accuracy. We derive 11th singular value of each mean centered dataset using our sSketch-Singular method for comparison with exact error as discussed in Section 2.4. Then at the end of each iteration, we calculate 2-norm of reconstruction error using sSketch-Norm to know how accurate the result has become. At this point, we need to emphasize that we need derivation of $(k+1)^{th}$ singular value and 2-norm of reconstruction error calculation both in order to analyze accuracy in results. In reality, however, a couple of iterations gives pretty good results and we need not go through all these additional tasks. It is practical to limit iterations to 2-3 as mentioned in [25].

Both algorithms reduce error according to the theory given by [17], so their nature of convergence is same as seen from Table 3. However, each algorithm takes different time to complete the first iteration (Table 4) and that is the key factor. For example, one iteration of Mahout-PCA on PubMed needed about **6720 seconds** to finish whereas our method takes only **188 seconds** (Table 4). Thus we can see from Figure 2 that sSketch-PCA reaches about 99% accuracy even before Mahout-PCA finishes its first iteration. The results for other datasets are similar and are not shown in figure for space limitation.

Intermediate Data Size: In distributed settings memory consumption depends on various factors. First and most obvious of all, if the input data matrix, on which the algorithms are run on is cached for in-memory calculation, it can consume memory in each nodes. Other way for requiring high memory will be materializing entire intermediate data generated by algorithm and load it into memory. All of the compared algorithms cache the input matrix, so this memory consumption is common to all. Depending on the approach, other intermediate data is loaded in cluster machines. For monitoring memory consumption and determining total size of intermediate data we use services provided by Ganglia [13].

Figure 3 compares the memory consumption of all algorithms for PubMed datasets in one of the machines from cluster. The results for other data are similar. We vary the dimensionality of PubMed data to show scalability of different approaches. The result shows that sSketch-PCA has almost constant memory consumption. This is because we only save input matrix and we do not materialize intermediate data. However, the memory consumption of MLlib-PCA increases drastically with increasing the number of columns. For example, MLlib-PCA consumes more than 15 GB of memory for an input matrix of 6,000 columns. This explains the results shown in Figure 3 and shows why MLlib-PCA fails to process more than 6,000 columns on a machine with 15 GB of memory. Mahout-PCA too has higher memory requirement than ours. This is because they save their intermediate data on each node and thus require higher network I/O and higher memory consumption.

Table 5 shows the size of total intermediate data for different methods for all input datasets. For MLlib-PCA the intermediate data quickly grows beyond 150 GB for high-dimensional datasets and exceeds total aggregating memory of the cluster. Mahout-PCA too generates a lot of intermediate data because Mahout-PCA's intermediate data size depends on input row size N which is typically very big. Our intermediate data, on the other hand, depends only on the number of dimensions, D, which is much less than N. For example, for the PubMed dataset, Mahout-PCA generates 3.65 GB of intermediate data, whereas sSketch generates only 151 MB, a factor of **35× reduction**. But for SiftFeature which has about 4 million entries but only 128 dimensions, we see our method offers a factor of **4785× reduction** (0.67 GB vs 140 KB).

To summarize, our results show that sSketch-PCA offers much better scalability and performance than its competitors.

8 CONCLUSIONS

In this paper, we have addressed scalability issues of state-of-the-art techniques to perform PCA and have shown how they fail as dimensions of dataset grow. We have proposed an improved algorithm, referred to as sSketch, and have shown how it can be used for different techniques as PCA, singular value derivation, and 2-norm of reconstruction error calculation. We have shown both theoretically and experimentally that compared to others, our method is highly scalable and offers better performance. For reproducibility and extensibility of our work, we make the source code of sSketch publicly available at https://github.com/DataMiningResearch/sSketch.

9 ACKNOWLEDGEMENTS

This research was conducted at the Department of Computer Science and Engineering (CSE), Bangladesh University of Engineering and Technology (BUET) and partly supported by ICT Division Innovation Fund, Grant No. 56.00.0000.028.33.080.17-214 from Government of Peoples' Republic of Bangladesh.

REFERENCES

[1] Michael W Berry, Susan T Dumais, and Gavin W O'Brien. 1995. Using linear algebra for intelligent information retrieval. *SIAM review* 37, 4 (1995), 573–595.

[2] Christopher M Bishop. 2006. Continuous Latent Variables. In *Pattern Recognition and Machine Learning*. Springer-Verlag New York, Chapter 12.

[3] Moses Charikar, Kevin Chen, and Martin Farach-Colton. 2002. Finding frequent items in data streams. In *International Colloquium on Automata, Languages, and Programming*. Springer, 693–703.

[4] Kenneth L Clarkson and David P Woodruff. 2013. Low rank approximation and regression in input sparsity time. In *Proceedings of the forty-fifth annual ACM symposium on Theory of computing*. ACM, 81–90.

[5] Paul G Constantine and David F Gleich. 2011. Tall and skinny QR factorizations in MapReduce architectures. In *Proceedings of the second international workshop on MapReduce and its applications*. ACM, 43–50.

[6] Jeffrey Dean and Sanjay Ghemawat. 2008. MapReduce: simplified data processing on large clusters. *Commun. ACM* 51, 1 (2008), 107–113.

[7] James Demmel, Laura Grigori, Mark Hoemmen, and Julien Langou. 2012. Communication-optimal parallel and sequential QR and LU factorizations. *SIAM Journal on Scientific Computing* 34, 1 (2012), A206–A239.

[8] Jia Deng, Wei Dong, Richard Socher, Li-Jia Li, Kai Li, and Li Fei-Fei. 2009. Imagenet: A large-scale hierarchical image database. In *Computer Vision and Pattern Recognition, 2009. CVPR 2009. IEEE Conference on*. IEEE, 248–255.

[9] Chris Ding and Xiaofeng He. 2004. K-means clustering via principal component analysis. In *Proceedings of the twenty-first international conference on Machine learning*. ACM, 29.

[10] Qian Du and James E Fowler. 2007. Hyperspectral image compression using JPEG2000 and principal component analysis. *IEEE Geoscience and Remote Sensing Letters* 4, 2 (2007), 201–205.

[11] Tarek Elgamal and Mohamed Hefeeda. 2015. Analysis of PCA algorithms in distributed environments. *arXiv preprint arXiv:1503.05214* (2015).

[12] Dan Feldman, Melanie Schmidt, and Christian Sohler. 2013. Turning big data into tiny data: Constant-size coresets for k-means, pca and projective clustering. In *Proceedings of the Twenty-Fourth Annual ACM-SIAM Symposium on Discrete Algorithms*. Society for Industrial and Applied Mathematics, 1434–1453.

[13] Ganglia 2001. Ganglia Monitoring System. (2001). Retrieved June 14, 2016 from http://ganglia.sourceforge.net/

[14] Gene H Golub and Christian Reinsch. 1970. Singular value decomposition and least squares solutions. *Numerische mathematik* 14, 5 (1970), 403–420.

[15] Gene H Golub and Charles F Van Loan. 2012. *Matrix computations*. Vol. 3. JHU Press.

[16] Alexander N Gorban, Balázs Kégl, Donald C Wunsch, Andrei Y Zinovyev, et al. 2008. *Principal manifolds for data visualization and dimension reduction*. Vol. 58. Springer.

[17] Nathan Halko, Per-Gunnar Martinsson, and Joel A Tropp. 2011. Finding structure with randomness: Probabilistic algorithms for constructing approximate matrix decompositions. *SIAM review* 53, 2 (2011), 217–288.

[18] Ruining He and Julian McAuley. 2016. Ups and downs: Modeling the visual evolution of fashion trends with one-class collaborative filtering. In *Proceedings of the 25th International Conference on World Wide Web*. International World Wide Web Conferences Steering Committee, 507–517.

[19] Po-Sen Huang, Xiaodong He, Jianfeng Gao, Li Deng, Alex Acero, and Larry Heck. 2013. Learning deep structured semantic models for web search using clickthrough data. In *Proceedings of the 22nd ACM international conference on Conference on information & knowledge management*. ACM, 2333–2338.

[20] William B Johnson and Joram Lindenstrauss. 1984. Extensions of Lipschitz mappings into a Hilbert space. *Contemporary mathematics* 26, 189-206 (1984), 1.

[21] Jure Leskovec and Andrej Krevl. 2014. SNAP Datasets: Stanford Large Network Dataset Collection. http://snap.stanford.edu/data. (June 2014).

[22] Yingyu Liang, Maria-Florina F Balcan, Vandana Kanchanapally, and David Woodruff. 2014. Improved distributed principal component analysis. In *Advances in Neural Information Processing Systems*. 3113–3121.

[23] M. Lichman. 2013. UCI Machine Learning Repository. (2013). http://archive.ics.uci.edu/ml

[24] David G Lowe. 1999. Object recognition from local scale-invariant features. In *Computer vision, 1999. The proceedings of the seventh IEEE international conference on*, Vol. 2. Ieee, 1150–1157.

[25] Dmitriy Lyubimov and Andrew Palumbo. 2016. *Apache Mahout: Beyond MapReduce*. CreateSpace Independent Publishing Platform.

[26] Mahout 2014. Apache Mahout Software. (2014). Retrieved 17 April 2017 from https://mahout.apache.org/

[27] Julian McAuley. 2014. Amazon Product Data. (2014). http://jmcauley.ucsd.edu/data/amazon/links.html

[28] Julian McAuley, Christopher Targett, Qinfeng Shi, and Anton Van Den Hengel. 2015. Image-based recommendations on styles and substitutes. In *Proceedings of the 38th International ACM SIGIR Conference on Research and Development in Information Retrieval*. ACM, 43–52.

[29] MLlib 2014. MLlib: Apache Spark's scalable machine learning library. (2014). Retrieved July 11, 2017 from https://spark.apache.org/mllib/

[30] Cameron Musco and Christopher Musco. 2015. Randomized block krylov methods for stronger and faster approximate singular value decomposition. In *Advances in Neural Information Processing Systems*. 1396–1404.

[31] Jinoh Oh, Kijung Shin, Evangelos E Papalexakis, Christos Faloutsos, and Hwanjo Yu. 2017. S-HOT: Scalable High-Order Tucker Decomposition. In *Proceedings of the Tenth ACM International Conference on Web Search and Data Mining*. ACM, 761–770.

[32] Ninh Pham and Rasmus Pagh. 2013. Fast and scalable polynomial kernels via explicit feature maps. In *Proceedings of the 19th ACM SIGKDD international conference on Knowledge discovery and data mining*. ACM, 239–247.

[33] Josep M Porta, Jakob J Verbeek, and Ben JA Kröse. 2005. Active appearance-based robot localization using stereo vision. *Autonomous Robots* 18, 1 (2005), 59–80.

[34] Jonathon Shlens. 2014. A tutorial on principal component analysis. *arXiv preprint arXiv:1404.1100* (2014).

[35] Lindsay I Smith et al. 2002. A tutorial on principal components analysis. *Cornell University, USA* 51, 52 (2002), 65.

[36] Spark 2014. Apache Spark: Lightning-fast Cluster Computing. (2014). Retrieved July 11, 2017 from https://spark.apache.org

[37] Shusen Wang. 2015. A Practical Guide to Randomized Matrix Computations with MATLAB Implementations. *arXiv preprint arXiv:1505.07570* (2015).

[38] David P Woodruff et al. 2014. Sketching as a tool for numerical linear algebra. *Foundations and Trends® in Theoretical Computer Science* 10, 1–2 (2014), 1–157.

[39] Hui Zou, Trevor Hastie, and Robert Tibshirani. 2006. Sparse principal component analysis. *Journal of computational and graphical statistics* 15, 2 (2006), 265–286.

Hyperbolic Representation Learning for Fast and Efficient Neural Question Answering

Yi Tay
Nanyang Technological University
ytay017@e.ntu.edu.sg

Luu Anh Tuan
Institute for Infocomm Research
at.luu@i2r.a-star.edu.sg

Siu Cheung Hui
Nanyang Technological University
asschui@ntu.edu.sg

ABSTRACT

The dominant neural architectures in question answer retrieval are based on recurrent or convolutional encoders configured with complex word matching layers. Given that recent architectural innovations are mostly new word interaction layers or attention-based matching mechanisms, it seems to be a well-established fact that these components are mandatory for good performance. Unfortunately, the memory and computation cost incurred by these complex mechanisms are undesirable for practical applications. As such, this paper tackles the question of whether it is possible to achieve competitive performance with simple neural architectures. We propose a simple but novel deep learning architecture for fast and efficient question-answer ranking and retrieval. More specifically, our proposed model, HyperQA, is a parameter efficient neural network that outperforms other parameter intensive models such as Attentive Pooling BiLSTMs and Multi-Perspective CNNs on multiple QA benchmarks. The novelty behind HyperQA is a pairwise ranking objective that models the relationship between question and answer embeddings in Hyperbolic space instead of Euclidean space. This empowers our model with a self-organizing ability and enables automatic discovery of latent hierarchies while learning embeddings of questions and answers. Our model requires no feature engineering, no similarity matrix matching, no complicated attention mechanisms nor over-parameterized layers and yet outperforms and remains competitive to many models that have these functionalities on multiple benchmarks.

KEYWORDS

Question Answering; Deep Learning; Learning to Rank

ACM Reference Format:
Yi Tay, Luu Anh Tuan, and Siu Cheung Hui. 2018. Hyperbolic Representation Learning for Fast and Efficient Neural Question Answering. In *WSDM 2018: WSDM 2018: The Eleventh ACM International Conference on Web Search and Data Mining , February 5–9, 2018, Marina Del Rey, CA, USA.* ACM, New York, NY, USA, 9 pages. https://doi.org/10.1145/3159652.3159664

1 INTRODUCTION

Neural ranking models are commonplace in many modern question answering (QA) systems [8, 23]. In these applications, the problem of question answering is concerned with learning to rank candidate answers in response to questions. Intuitively, this is reminiscent of document retrieval albeit with shorter text which aggravates the long standing problem of lexical chasm [2]. For this purpose, a wide assortment of neural ranking architectures have been proposed. The key and most basic intuition pertaining to many of these models are as follows: Firstly, representations of questions and answers are first learned via a neural encoder such as the long short-term memory (LSTM) [10] network or convolutional neural network (CNN). Secondly, these representations of questions and answers are composed by an interaction function to produce an overall matching score.

The design of the interaction function between question and answer representations lives at the heart of deep learning QA research. While it is simply possible to combine QA representations with simple feed forward neural networks or other composition functions [19, 26], a huge bulk of recent work is concerned with designing novel word interaction layers that model the relationship between the words in the QA pairs. For example, soft attention alignment [17] and attentive pooling [4] are highly popular techniques for improving the performance of neural ranking models. Apparently, it seems to be well-established that grid-based matching is essential to good performance. Notably, these new innovations come with trade-offs such as huge computational cost that lead to significantly longer training times and also a larger memory footprint. Additionally, it is good to consider that the base neural encoder employed also contributes to the computational cost of these neural ranking models, e.g., LSTM networks are known to be over-parameterized and also incur a parameter and runtime cost of quadratic scale. It also seems to be a well-established fact that a neural encoder (such as the LSTM, Gated Recurrent Unit (GRU), CNN, etc.) must be first selected for learning individual representations of questions and answers and is generally treated as mandatory for good performance.

In this paper, we propose an extremely simple neural ranking model for question answering that achieves highly competitive results on several benchmarks with only a fraction of the runtime and only 40K-90K parameters (as opposed to millions). Our neural ranking models the relationships between QA pairs in Hyperbolic space instead of Euclidean space. Hyperbolic space is an embedding space with a constant negative curvature in which the distance towards the border is increasing exponentially. Intuitively, this makes it suitable for learning embeddings that reflect a natural hierarchy (e.g., networks, text, etc.) which we believe might benefit neural ranking models for QA. Notably, our work is inspired by the recently incepted Poincaré embeddings [16] which demonstrates the effectiveness of inducing a structural (hierarchical) bias in the

WSDM 2018, February 5–9, 2018, Marina Del Rey, CA, USA

ACM ISBN 978-1-4503-5581-0/18/02...$15.00
https://doi.org/10.1145/3159652.3159664

embedding space for improved generalization. In our early empirical experiments, we discovered that a simple feed forward neural network trained in Hyperbolic space is capable of outperforming more sophisticated models on several standard benchmark datasets. We believe that this can be attributed to two reasons. Firstly, latent hierarchies are prominent in QA. Aside from the natural hierarchy of questions and answers, conceptual hierarchies also exist. Secondly, natural language is inherently hierarchical which can be traced to power law distributions such as Zipf's law [21]. The key contributions in this paper are as follows:

- We propose a new neural ranking model for ranking question answer pairs. For the first time, our proposed model, HyperQA, performs matching of questions and answers in Hyperbolic space. To the best of our knowledge, we are the first to model QA pairs in Hyperbolic space. While hyperbolic geometry and embeddings have been explored in the domains of complex networks or graphs [13], our work is the first to investigate the suitability of this metric space for question answering.
- HyperQA is an extremely fast and parameter efficient model that achieves very competitive results on multiple QA benchmarks such as TrecQA, WikiQA and YahooCQA. The efficiency and speed of HyperQA are attributed by the fact that we do not use any sophisticated neural encoder and have no complicated word interaction layer. In fact, HyperQA is a mere single layered neural network with only 90K parameters. Very surprisingly, HyperQA actually outperforms many state-of-the-art models such as Attentive Pooling BiLSTMs [4, 36] and Multi-Perspective CNNs [8]. We believe that this allows us to reconsider whether many of these complex word interaction layers are really necessary for good performance.
- We conduct extensive qualitative analysis of both the learned QA embeddings and word embeddings. We discover several interesting properties of QA embeddings in Hyperbolic space. Due to its compositional nature, we find that our model learns to self-organize not only at the QA level but also at the word-level. Our qualitative studies enable us to gain a better intuition pertaining to the good performance of our model.

2 RELATED WORK

Many prior works have established the fact that there are mainly two key ingredients to a powerful neural ranking model. First, an effective neural encoder and second, an expressive word interaction layer. The first ingredient is often treated as a given, i.e., the top performing models always use a neural encoder such as the CNN or LSTM. In fact, many top performing models adopt convolutional encoders for sentence representation [7, 8, 19, 23, 25, 36]. The usage of recurrent models is also notable [15, 23, 26, 27].

The key component in which many recent models differ at is at the interaction layer. Early works often combined QA embeddings 'as it is', i.e., representations are learned first and then combined. For example, Yu et al. [35] used CNN representations as feature inputs to a logistic regression model. The end-to-end CNN-based model of Severyn and Moschitti [23] combines the CNN encoded representations of question and answer using a multi-layered perceptron (MLP). Recently, a myriad of composition functions have been proposed as well, e.g., tensor layers in Qiu et al. [19] and holographic layers in Tay et al. [26].

It has been recently fashionable to model the relationships between question and answer using similarity matrices. Intuitively, this enables more fine-grained matching across words in question and answer sentences. The Multi-Perspective CNN (MP-CNN) [7] compared two sentences via a wide diversity of pooling functions and filter widths aiming to capture 'multi-perspectives' between two sentences. The attention based neural matching (aNMM) model of Yang et al. [31] performed soft-attention alignment by first measuring the pairwise word similarity between each word in question and answer. The attentive pooling models of Santos et al. [4] (AP-BiLSTM and AP-CNN) utilized this soft-attention alignment to learn weighted representations of question and answer that are dependent of each other. Zhang et al. [36] extended AP-CNN to 3D tensor-based attentive pooling (AI-CNN). A recent work, the Cross Temporal Recurrent Network (CTRN) [27] proposed a pairwise gating mechanism for joint learning of QA pairs.

Unfortunately, these models actually introduce a prohibitive computational cost to the model usually for a very marginal performance gain. Notably, it is easy to see that similarity matrix based matching incurs a computational cost of quadratic scale. Representation ability such as dimension size of word or CNN/RNN embeddings are naturally also quite restricted, i.e., increasing any of these dimensions can cause computation or memory requirements to explode. Moreover, it is not uncommon for models such as AI-CNN or AP-BiLSTM to spend more than 30 minutes on a single epoch on QA datasets that are only medium sized. Let us not forget that these models still have to be extensively tuned which aggravates the impracticality problem posed by some of these models.

In this paper, we seek a new paradigm for neural ranking for QA. While many recent works try to out-stack each other with new layers, we strip down our network instead. Our work is inspired by the very recent Poincarè embeddings [16] which demonstrates the superiority and efficiency of generalization in Hyperbolic space. Moreover, this alleviates many overfitting and complexity issues that Euclidean embeddings might face especially if the data has intrinsic hierarchical structure. It is good to note that power-law distributions, such as Zipf's law, have been known to be from innate hierarchical structure [21]. Specifically, the defining characteristic of Hyperbolic space is a much quicker expansion relative to that of Euclidean space which makes naturally equipped for modeling hierarchical structure. The concept of Hyperbolic spaces has been applied to domains such as complex network modeling [13], social networks [29] and geographic routing [12].

There are several key geometric intuitions regarding Hyperbolic spaces. Firstly, the concept of distance and area is *warped* in Hyperbolic spaces. Specifically, each tile in Figure 1(a) is of equal area in Hyperbolic space but diminishes towards zero in Euclidean space towards the boundary. Secondly, Hyperbolic spaces are *conformal*, i.e., angles in Hyperbolic spaces and Euclidean spaces are identical. In Figure 1(b), the arcs on the curve are parallel lines that are orthogonal to the boundary. Finally, hyperbolic spaces can be regarded as *larger* spaces relative to Euclidean spaces due to the fact that the concept of relative distance can be expressed much

(a) 'Circle Limit 1' by M.C Escher (b) Hyperbolic Parallel Lines

Figure 1: Visualizations of Hyperbolic space.

better, i.e., not only does the distance between two vectors encode information but also *where* a vector is placed in Hyperbolic space. This enables efficient representation learning.

In Nickel et al. [16], the authors applied the hyperbolic distance (specifically, the Poincarè distance) to model taxonomic entities and graph nodes. Notably, our work, to the best of our knowledge, is the only work that learns QA embeddings in Hyperbolic space. Moreover, questions and answers introduce an interesting layer of complexity to the problem since QA embeddings are in fact compositions of their constituent word embeddings. On the other hand, nodes in a graph and taxonomic entities in [16] are already at its most abstract form, i.e., symbolic objects. As such, we believe it would be interesting to investigate the impacts of QA in Hyperbolic space in lieu of the added compositional nature.

3 OUR PROPOSED APPROACH

This section outlines the overall architecture of our proposed model. Similar to many neural ranking models for QA, our network has 'two' sides with shared parameters, i.e., one for question and another for answer. However, since we optimize for a pairwise ranking loss, the model takes in a positive (correct) answer and a negative (wrong) answer and aims to maximize the margin between the scores of the correct QA pair and the negative QA pair. Figure 2 depicts the overall model architecture.

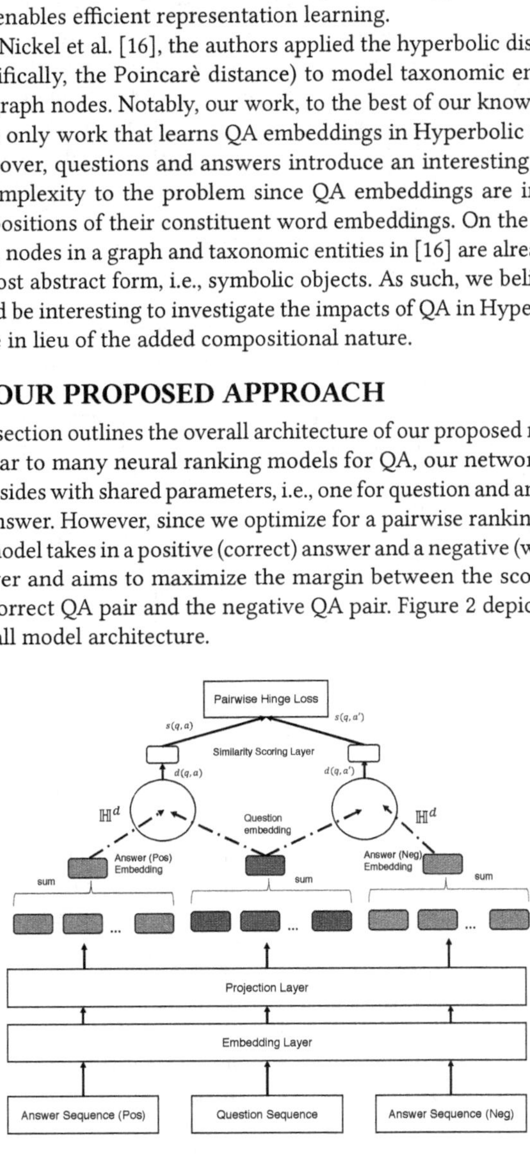

Figure 2: Our proposed model architecture.

3.1 Embedding Layer

Our model accepts three sequences as an input, i.e., the question (denoted as q), the correct answer (denoted as a) and a randomly sampled corrupted answer (denoted as a'). Each sequence consists of M words where M_q and M_a are predefined maximum sequence lengths for questions and answers respectively. Each word is represented as a one-hot vector (representing a word in the vocabulary). As such, this layer is a look-up layer that converts each word into a low-dimensional vector by indexing onto the word embedding matrix. In our implementation, we initialize this layer with pre-trained word embeddings [18]. Note that this layer is not updated during training. Instead, we utilize a projection layer that learns a task-specific projection of the embeddings.

3.2 Projection Layer

In order to learn a task-specific representation for each word, we utilize a projection layer. The projection layer is essentially a single layered neural network that is applied to **each word** in all three sequences.

$$x = \sigma(\mathbf{W}_p\, z + b_p) \tag{1}$$

where $\mathbf{W}_p \in \mathbb{R}^{d \times n}$, $z \in \mathbb{R}^n$, $x \in \mathbb{R}^d$ and σ is a non-linear function such as the rectified linear unit (ReLU). The output of this layer is a sequence of d dimensional embeddings for each sequence (question, positive answer and negative answer). Note that the parameters of this projection layer are shared for both question and answer.

3.3 Learning QA Representations

In order to learn question and answer representations, we simply take the sum of all word embeddings in the sequence.

$$y^* = \sum_{i=1}^{M_*} x_i^* \tag{2}$$

where $* = \{q, a, a'\}$. M is the predefined max sequence length (specific to question and answer) and $x_1, x_2 \ldots x_M$ are d-dimensional embeddings of the sequence. This is essentially the neural bag-of-words (NBoW) representation. Unlike popular neural encoders such as LSTM or CNN, the NBOW representation does not add any parameters and is much more efficient. Additionally, we constrain the question and answer embeddings to the unit ball before passing to the next layer, i.e., $\|y^*\| \leq 1$. This is easily done via $y^* = \frac{y^*}{\|y^*\|}$ when $\|y^*\| > 1$. Note that this projection of QA embeddings onto the unit ball is mandatory and absolutely crucial for HYPERQA to even work.

3.4 Hyperbolic Representations of QA Pairs

Neural ranking models are mainly characterized by the interaction function between question and answer representations. In our work, we mainly adopt the hyperbolic[1] distance function to model the relationships between questions and answers. Formally, let $\mathcal{B}^d = \{x \in \mathbb{R}^d \mid \|x\| < 1\}$ be the *open* d-dimensional unit ball, our model corresponds to the Riemannian manifold $(\mathcal{B}^d, g_x)$ and is equipped with the Riemannian metric tensor given as follows:

[1] While there exist multiple models of Hyperbolic geometry such as the Beltrami-Klein model or the Hyperboloid model, we adopt the Poincarè ball / disk due to its ease of differentiability and freedom from constraints [16].

$$g_x = (\frac{2}{1 - ||x||^2})^2 g^E \quad (3)$$

where g^E is the Euclidean metric tensor. The hyperbolic distance function between question and answer is defined as:

$$d(q, a) = arcosh(1 + 2\frac{||q - a||^2}{(1 - ||q||^2)(1 - ||a||^2)}) \quad (4)$$

where $||.||$ denotes the Euclidean norm and $q, a \in \mathbb{R}^d$ are the question and answer embeddings respectively. Note that $arcosh$ is the inverse hyperbolic cosine function, i.e., $arcoshx = \ln(x+\sqrt{(x^2 - 1)})$. Notably, $d(q, a)$ changes smoothly with respect to the position of q and a which enables the automatic discovery of latent hierarchies. As mentioned earlier, the distance increases exponentially as the norm of the vectors approaches 1. As such, the latent hierarchies of QA embeddings are captured through the norm of the vectors. From a geometric perspective, the origin can be seen as the root of a tree that branches out towards the boundaries of the hyperbolic ball. This self-organizing ability of the hyperbolic distance is visually and qualitatively analyzed in later sections.

3.4.1 Gradient Derivation. Amongst the other models of Hyperbolic geometry, the hyperbolic Poincarè distance is differentiable. Let The partial derivate w.r.t to θ is defined as:

$$\frac{\partial d(\theta, x)}{\partial \theta} = \frac{4}{\beta\sqrt{\gamma^2 - 1}}(\frac{||x||^2 - 2\langle\theta, x\rangle + 1}{\alpha^2}\theta - \frac{x}{\alpha}) \quad (5)$$

where $\alpha = 1 - ||\theta||^2$, $\beta = 1 - ||x||^2$ and $\gamma = 1 + \frac{2}{\alpha\beta}||\theta - x||^2$.

3.5 Similarity Scoring Layer

Finally, we pass the hyperbolic distance through a linear transformation described as follows:

$$s(q, a) = w_f \; d(q, a) + b_f \quad (6)$$

where $w_f \in \mathbb{R}^1$ and $b_f \in \mathbb{R}^1$ are scalar parameters of this layer. The performance of this layer is empirically motivated by its performance and was selected amongst other variants such as $exp(-d(q, a))$, non-linear activations such as sigmoid function or the raw hyperbolic distance.

3.6 Optimization and Learning

This section describes the optimization and learning process of HyperQA. Our model learns via a pairwise ranking loss, which is well suited for metric-based learning algorithms.

3.6.1 Pairwise Hinge Loss. Our network minimizes the pairwise hinge loss which is defined as follows:

$$L = \sum_{(q,a)\in\Delta_q} \sum_{(q,a')\notin\Delta_q} max(0, s(q, a) + \lambda - s(q, a')) \quad (7)$$

where Δ_q is the set of all QA pairs for question q, $s(q, a)$ is the score between q and a, and λ is the margin which controls the extent of discrimination between positive QA pairs and corrupted QA pairs. The adoption of the pairwise hinge loss is motivated by the good empirical results demonstrated in Rao et al. [20]. Additionally, we also adopt the *mix sampling* strategy for sampling negative samples as described in their work.

3.6.2 Gradient Conversion. Since our network learns in Hyperbolic space, parameters have to be learned via stochastic Riemannian optimization methods such as RSGD [3].

$$\theta_{t+1} = \Re_{\theta_t}(-\eta\nabla_R \, \ell(\theta_t)) \quad (8)$$

where $\Re_{\theta_t}$ denotes a retraction onto $\mathcal{B}$ at θ. η is the learning rate and $\nabla_R \, \ell(\theta_t)$ is the Riemannian gradient with respect to θ_t. Fortunately, the Riemannian gradient can be easily derived from the Euclidean gradient in this case [3]. In order to do so, we can simply scale the Euclidean gradient by the inverse of the metric tensor g_θ^{-1}. Overall, the final gradients used to update the parameters are:

$$\nabla_R = \frac{(1 - ||\theta_t||^2)^2}{4}\nabla_E \quad (9)$$

Due to the lack of space, we refer interested readers to [3, 16] for more details. For practical purposes, we simply utilize the automatic gradient feature of TensorFlow but convert the gradients with Equation (9) before updating the parameters.

4 EXPERIMENTS

This section describes our empirical evaluation and its results.

4.1 Datasets

In the spirit of experimental rigor, we conduct our empirical evaluation based on four popular and well-studied benchmark datasets for question answering.

- **YahooCQA** - This is a benchmark dataset for community-based question answering that was collected from Yahoo Answers. In this dataset, the answer lengths are relatively longer than TrecQA and WikiQA. Therefore, we filtered answers that have more than 50 words and less than 5 characters. The train-dev-test splits for this dataset are provided by [26].
- **WikiQA** - This is a recently popular benchmark dataset [32] for open-domain question answering based on factual questions from Wikipedia and Bing search logs.
- **SemEvalCQA** - This is a well-studied benchmark dataset from SemEval-2016 Task 3 Subtask A (CQA). This is a real world dataset obtained from Qatar Living Forums. In this dataset, there are ten answers in each question 'thread' which are marked as 'Good', 'Potentially Useful' or ''Bad'. We treat 'Good' as positive and anything else as negative labels.
- **TrecQA** - This is the benchmark dataset provided by Wang et al. [30]. This dataset was collected from TREC QA tracks 8-13 and is comprised of factoid based questions which mainly answer the 'who', 'what', 'where', 'when' and 'why' types of questions. There are two versions, namely clean and raw, as noted by [20] which we evaluate our models on.

Statistics pertaining to each dataset is given in Table 1.

	YahooCQA	WikiQA	SemEvalCQA	TrecQA
Train Qns	50.1K	94	4.8K	1229
Dev Qns	6.2K	65	224	82
Test Qns	6.2K	68	327	100
Train Pairs	253K	5.9K	36K	53
Dev Pairs	31.7K	1.1K	2.4K	1.1K
Test Pairs	31.7K	1.4K	3.2K	1.5K

Table 1: Statistics of datasets.

4.2 Compared Baselines

In this section, we introduce the baselines for comparison.

- **YahooCQA** - The key competitors of this dataset are the Neural Tensor LSTM (NTN-LSTM) and HD-LSTM from Tay et al. [26] along with their implementation of the Convolutional Neural Tensor Network [19], vanilla CNN model, and the Okapi BM-25 [22] benchmark. Additionally, we also report our own implementations of QA-BiLSTM, QA-CNN, AP-BiLSTM and AP-CNN on this dataset based on our experimental setup.
- **WikiQA** - The key competitors of this dataset are the Paragraph Vector (PV) and PV + Cnt models [14] of Le and Mikolv, CNN + Cnt model from Yu et al. [35] and LCLR (Yih et al.) [34]. These three baselines are reported in the original WikiQA paper [32] which also include variations that include handcrafted features. Additional strong baselines include QA-BiLSTM, QA-CNN from [4] along with AP-BiLSTM and AP-CNN which are attentive pooling improvements of the former. Finally, we also report the Pairwise Ranking MP-CNN from Rao et al. [20].
- **SemEvalCQA** - The key competitors of this dataset are the CNN-based ARC-I/II architecture by Hu et al. [11], the Attentive Pooling CNN [4], Kelp [6] a feature engineering based SVM method, ConvKN [1] a combination of convolutional tree kernels with CNN and finally AI-CNN (Attentive Interactive CNN) [36], a tensor-based attentive pooling neural model. A comparison with AI-CNN (with features) is also included.
- **TrecQA** - The key competitors on the dataset are mainly the CNN model of Severyn and Moschitti (S&M) [23], the Attention-based Neural Matching Model (aNMM) of Yang et al. [31], HD-LSTM (Tay et al.) [26] and Multi-Perspective CNN (MP-CNN) [7] proposed by He et al. Lastly, we also compare with the pairwise ranking adaption of MP-CNN (Rao et al.) [20]. Additionally and due to long standing nature of this dataset, there have been a huge number of works based on traditional feature engineering approaches [9, 24, 30, 33] which we also report. For the clean version of this dataset, we also compare with AP-CNN and QA-BiLSTM/CNN [4].

Since the training splits are standard, we are able to directly report the results from the original papers.

4.3 Evaluation Protocol

This section describes the key evaluation protocol / metrics and implementation details of our experiments.

4.3.1 Metrics. We adopt a dataset specific evaluation protocol in which we follow the prior work in their evaluation protocols. Specifically, TrecQA and WikiQA adopt the Mean Reciprocal Rank (MRR) and MAP (Mean Average Precision) metrics which are commonplace in IR research. On the other hand, YahooCQA and SemEvalCQA evaluate on MAP and Precision@1 (abbreviated P@1) which is determined based on whether the top predicted answer is the ground truth. For all competitor methods, we report the performance results from the original paper.

4.3.2 Training Time & Parameter Size. Additionally, we report the parameter size and runtime (seconds per epoch) of selected models. We selectively re-implement some of the key competitors with the best performance and benchmark their training time on our machine/GPU (a single Nvidia GTX1070). For reporting the parameter size and training time, we try our best to follow the hyperparameters stated in the original papers. As such, the same model can have different training time and parameter size on different datasets.

4.3.3 Hyperparameters. HyperQA is implemented in TensorFlow. We adopt the AdaGrad [5] optimizer with initial learning rate tuned amongst $\{0.2, 0.1, 0.05, 0.01\}$. The batch size is tuned amongst $\{50, 100, 200\}$. Models are trained for 25 epochs and the model parameters are saved each time the performance on the validation set is topped. The dimension of the projection layer is tuned amongst $\{100, 200, 300, 400\}$. L2 regularization is tuned amongst $\{0.001, 0.0001, 0.00001\}$. The negative sampling rate is tuned from 2 to 8. Finally, the margin λ is tuned amongst $\{1, 2, 5, 10, 20\}$. For TrecQA, WikiQA and YahooCQA, we initialize the embedding layer with GloVe [18] and use the version with $d = 300$ and trained on 840 billion words. For SemEvalCQA, we train our own Skipgram model using the unannotated corpus provided by the task. In this case, the embedding dimension is tuned amongst $\{100, 200, 300\}$. Embeddings are not updated during training. For the SemEvalCQA dataset, we concatenated the raw QA embeddings before passing into the final layer since we found that it improves performance.

4.4 Results and Analysis

In this section, we present our empirical results on all datasets. For all reported results, the best result is in boldface and the second best is underlined.

4.4.1 Experimental Results on WikiQA. Table 2 reports our results on the WikiQA dataset. Firstly, we observe that HyperQA outperforms a myriad of complex neural architectures. Notably, we obtain a clear performance gain of 2% – 3% in terms of MAP/MRR against models such as AP-CNN or AP-BiLSTM. Our model also outperforms MP-CNN which is severely equipped with parameterized word matching mechanisms. We achieve competitive results relative to the Rank MP-CNN. Finally, HyperQA is extremely efficient and fast, clocking 2s per epoch compared to 33s per epoch for Rank MP-CNN. The parameter cost is also 90K vs 10 million which is a significant improvement.

4.4.2 Experimental Results on YahooCQA. Table 3 reports the experimental results on YahooCQA. First, we observe that HyperQA outperforms AP-BiLSTM and AP-CNN significantly. Specifically,

Model	MAP	MRR	#Params	Time
PV	0.511	0.516	-	-
PV + Cnt	0.599	0.609	-	-
LCLR	0.599	0.609	-	-
CNN + Cnt	0.652	0.665	-	-
QA-BiLSTM (Santos et al.)	0.656	0.670	-	-
QA-CNN (Santos et al.)	0.670	0.682	-	-
AP-BiLSTM (Santos et al.)	0.671	0.684	-	-
AP-CNN (Santos et al.)	0.688	0.696	-	-
MP-CNN (He et al.)	0.693	0.709	10.0M	35s
Rank MP-CNN (Rao et al.)	0.701	0.718	10.0M	33s
HyperQA (This work)	**0.712**	**0.727**	90K	2s

Table 2: Experimental results on WikiQA.

we outperform AP-BiLSTM, the runner-up model by 6% in terms of MRR and 10% in terms of MAP. Notably, HyperQA is 32 times faster than AP-BiLSTM and has 20 times less parameters. Our approach shows that complicated attentive pooling mechanisms are not necessary for good performance.

Model	P@1	MRR	# Params	Time
Random Guess	0.200	0.457	-	-
BM-25	0.225	0.493	-	-
CNN	0.413	0.632	-	-
CNTN (Qiu et al.)	0.465	0.632	-	-
LSTM	0.465	0.669	-	-
NTN-LSTM (Tay et al.)	0.545	0.731	-	-
HD-LSTM (Tay et al.)	0.557	0.735	-	-
QA-BiLSTM (Santos et al.)	0.508	0.683	1.40M	440s
QA-CNN (Santos et al.)	0.564	0.727	90.9K	60s
AP-CNN (Santos et al.)	0.560	0.726	540K	110s
AP-BiLSTM (Santos et al.)	0.568	0.731	1.80M	640s
HyperQA (This work)	**0.683**	**0.801**	90.0K	20s

Table 3: Experimental results on YahooCQA.

4.4.3 Experimental Results on SemEvalCQA. Table 4 reports the experimental results on SemEvalCQA. Our proposed approach achieves highly competitive performance on this dataset. Specifically, we have obtained the best P@1 performance overall, outperforming the state-of-the-art AI-CNN model by 3% in terms of P@1. The performance of our model on MAP is marginally short from the best performing model. Notably, AI-CNN has benefited from external handcrafted features. As such, comparing AI-CNN (w/o features) with HyperQA shows that our proposed model is a superior neural ranking model. Next, we draw the readers attention to the time cost of AI-CNN. The training time per epoch is $\approx 3250s$ per epoch which is about 300 times longer than our model. AI-CNN is extremely cost prohibitive, i.e., attentive pooling is already very expensive and yet AI-CNN performs 3D attentive pooling. Evidently, its performance can be easily superseded in a much smaller training time and parameter cost. This raises questions about the effectiveness of the 3D attentive pooling mechanism.

4.4.4 Experimental Results on TrecQA. Table 5 reports the results on TrecQA (raw). HyperQA achieves very competitive performance on both MAP and MRR metrics. Specifically, HyperQA

Model	P@1	MAP	#Params	Time
ARC-I (Hu et al.)	0.741	0.771	-	-
ARC-II (Hu et al.)	0.753	0.780	-	-
AP-CNN (Santos et al.)	0.755	0.771	-	-
Kelp (Filice et al.)	0.751	0.792	-	-
ConvKN (Barrón-Cedeño et al.)	0.755	0.777	-	-
AI-CNN (Zhang et al.)	0.763	0.792	140K	3250s
AI-CNN + Feats (Zhang et al.)	0.769	**0.801**	140K	3250s
HyperQA (This work)	**0.809**	0.795	45K	10s

Table 4: Experimental results on SemEvalCQA.

Model	MAP	MRR	# Params	Time
Wang et al. (2007)	0.603	0.685	-	-
Heilman et al. (2010)	0.609	0.692	-	-
Wang et al. (2010)	0.595	0.695	-	-
Yao (2013)	0.631	0.748	-	-
Severyn and Moschitti (2013)	0.678	0.736	-	-
Yih et al (2014)	0.709	0.770	-	-
CNN (Yu et al)	0.711	0.785	-	-
BLSTM + BM25 (Wang & Nyberg)	0.713	0.791	-	-
CNN (Severyn & Moschitti)	0.746	0.808	-	-
aNMM (Yang et al.)	0.750	0.811	-	-
HD-LSTM (Tay et al.)	0.750	0.815	-	-
MP-CNN (He et al.)	0.762	0.822	10.0M	141s
Rank MP-CNN (Rao et al.)	**0.780**	**0.830**	10.0M	130s
HyperQA (This work)	0.770	0.825	**90K**	12s

Table 5: Experimental results on TrecQA (raw). Feature engineering and deep learning approaches are separated by the middle line.

Model	MAP	MRR	# Params	Time
QA-LSTM / CNN (Santos et al.)	0.728	0.832	-	-
AP-CNN (Santos et al.)	0.753	0.851	-	-
MP-CNN (He et al.)	0.777	0.836	10M	141
Rank MP-CNN (Rao et al.)	**0.801**	**0.877**	10M	130s
HyperQA	0.784	0.865	90K	12s

Table 6: Experimental results on TrecQA (clean)

outperforms the basic CNN model of (S&M) by 2% – 3% in terms of MAP/MRR. Moreover, the CNN (S&M) model uses handcrafted features which HyperQA does not require. Similarly, the aNMM model and HD-LSTM also benefit from additional features but are outperformed by HyperQA. HyperQA also outperforms MP-CNN but is around 10 times faster and has 100 times less parameters. MP-CNN consists of a huge number of filter banks and utilizes heavy parameterization to match multiple perspectives of questions and answers. On the other hand, our proposed HyperQA is merely a single layered neural network with 90K parameters and yet outperforms MP-CNN. Similarly, Table 6 reports the results on TrecQA (clean). Similarly, HyperQA also outperforms MP-CNN, AP-CNN and QA-CNN. On both datasets, the performance of HyperQA is competitive to Rank MP-CNN.

4.4.5 Overall analysis. Overall, we summarize the key findings of our experiments.

- It is possible to achieve very competitive performance with small parameterization, and no word matching or interaction layers. HyperQA outperforms complex models such as MP-CNN and AP-BiLSTM on multiple datasets.
- The relative performance of HyperQA is significantly better on large datasets, e.g., YahooCQA (253K training pairs) as opposed to smaller ones like WikiQA (5.9K training pairs). We believe that this is due to the fact that Hyperbolic space is *seemingly* larger than Euclidean space.
- HyperQA is extremely fast and trains at 10 – 20 times faster than complex models like MP-CNN. Note that if CPUs are used instead of GPUs (which speed convolutions up significantly), this disparity would be significantly larger.
- Our proposed approach does not require handcrafted features and yet outperforms models that benefit from them. This is evident on all datasets, i.e., HyperQA outperforms CNN model with features (TrecQA and WikiQA) and AI-CNN + features on SemEvalCQA.

Ours against	Performance	Params	Speed
AP-BiLSTM	1-7% better	20x less	32 x faster
AP-CNN	1-12% better	Same	3x faster
AI-CNN	Competitive	3x less	300x faster
MP-CNN	1-2% better	100x less	10x faster
Rank MP-CNN	Competitive	100x less	10x faster

Table 7: Overall comparison of HyperQA against other state-of-the-art models.

4.5 Effects of QA Embedding Size

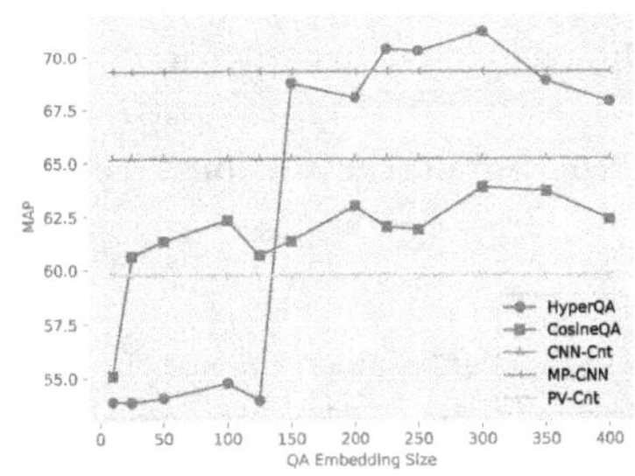

Figure 3: Effects of QA embedding size on WikiQA.

In this section, we study the effects of the QA embedding size on performance. Figure 3 describes the relationship between QA embedding size (d) and MAP on the WikiQA dataset. Additionally, we include a simple baseline (CosineQA) which is exactly the same as HyperQA but uses cosine similarity instead of hyperbolic distance. The MAP scores of three other reported models (MP-CNN, CNN-Cnt and PV-Cnt) are also reported for reference. Firstly, we notice the disparity between HyperQA and CosineQA in terms of performance. This is also observed across other datasets but is not reported due to the lack of space. While CosineQA maintains a stable performance throughout embedding size, the performance of HyperQA rapidly improves at $d > 150$. In fact, the performance of HyperQA at $d = 150$ (45K parameters) is already similar to the Multi-Perspective CNN [7] which contains 10 million parameters. Moreover, the performance of HyperQA outperforms MP-CNN with d = 250-300.

5 DISCUSSION AND ANALYSIS

This section delves into qualitative analysis of our model and aims to investigate the following research questions:

(1) **RQ1:** Is there any hierarchical structure learned in the QA embeddings? How are QA embeddings organized in the final embedding space of HyperQA?
(2) **RQ2:** What are the impacts of embedding compositional embeddings in hyperbolic space? Is there an impact on the constituent word embeddings?
(3) **RQ3:** Are we able to derive any insight about how word interaction and matching happens in HyperQA?

5.1 Analysis of QA Embeddings

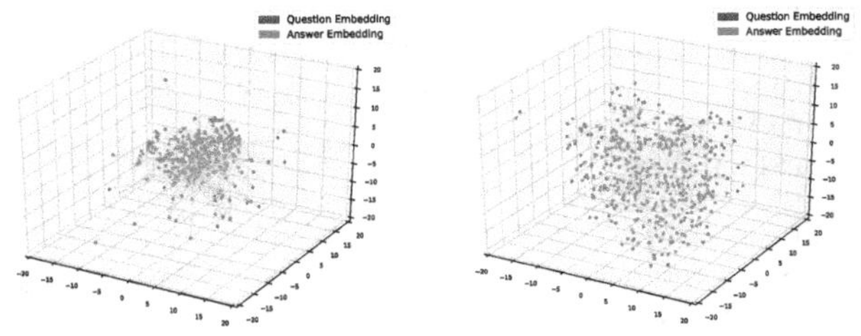

(a) HyperQA (b) CosineQA

Figure 4: Visualization of QA embeddings on the test set of TrecQA. Projected to 3 dimensions using t-SNE. Blue lines depict mapping of question embeddings to their correct answers. HyperQA learns 'sphere' shaped structure where questions embeddings surround the answer embeddings.

Figure 4(a) shows a visualization of QA embeddings on the test set TrecQA projected in 3-dimensional space using t-SNE [28]. QA embeddings are extracted from the network as discussed in Section 3.3. We observe that question embeddings form a 'sphere' over answer embeddings. Contrastingly, this is not exhibited when the cosine similarity is used as shown in Figure 4(b). It is important to note that these are embeddings from the **test** set which have not been trained and therefore the model is not explicitly told whether a particular textual input is a question or answer. This demonstrates the innate ability of HyperQA to self-organize and learn latent hierarchies which directly answers **RQ1**. Additionally, Figure 5(a) shows a histogram of the vector norms of question and answer embeddings. We can clearly see that questions in general have a higher vector norm[2] and are at a different hierarchical level from answers. In order to further understand what the model is doing, we delve deeper into the visualization at word-level.

[2]We extract QA embeddings right before the constraining / normalization layer.

Question		H1	H2	H3	H4	H5
What is the gross sale of Burger King	Q	are	**sales**, today	gross	is, what	burger, king
	A	based	sales, **14,billion**, 183	diageo	contributed	burger, corp
What is Florence Nightingale famous for	Q	in, the	for	**famous**	what	florence, nightingale
	A	of, in	was	**nursing**	founder, modern, born	nightingale, italy
Who is the founder of twitter?	Q	the, of	-	twitter, **founder**	-	who, is
	A	and, the	networking, launched	twitter, **jack dorsey**	match, social	-

Table 8: Analysis of QA pairs with respect to hierarchical level (H1-H5) based on vector norms. Self-organizing hierarchical structure facilitates better word level matching. Most informative word matches are marked in bold. Some words might be omitted from the answer due to lack of space. First two examples are from TrecQA and the third is from WikiQA.

$\|\|w\|\|$	Words (w)
0-1	to, and, an, on, in, of, its, the, had, or, go
1-2	be, a, was, up, put, said, but
2-3	judging, returning, volunteered, managing, meant, cited
3-4	responsibility, engineering, trading, prosecuting
4-5	turkish, autonomous, cowboys, warren, seven, **what**
5-6	ebay, magdalena, spielberg, watson, nova

Table 9: Examples of words in each hierarchical level of the sphere based on vector norms. Smaller norms are closer to the core/origin.

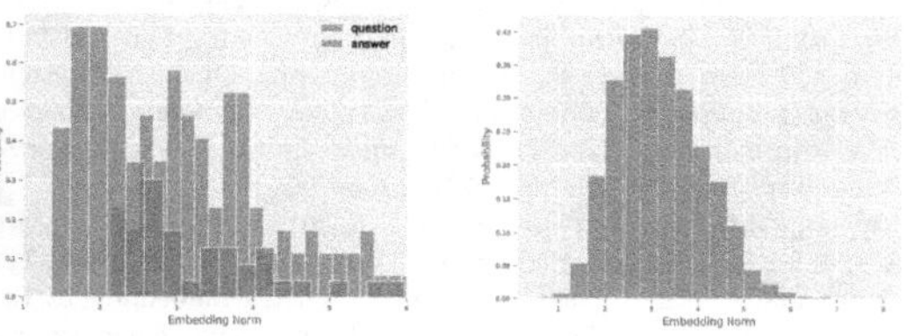

(a) QA embeddings **(b) Word embeddings**

Figure 5: Histogram plots of embedding norms.

5.2 Analysis of Word Embeddings

Table 9 shows some examples of words at each hierarchical level of the sphere on TrecQA. Recall that the vector norms[3] allow us to infer the distance of the word embedding from the origin which depicts its hierarchical level in our context. Interestingly, we found that HyperQA exhibits self-organizing ability even at word-level. Specifically, we notice that the words closer to the origin are common words such as 'to', 'and' which do not have much semantic values for QA problems. At the middle of the hierarchy ($||w|| \approx 3$), we notice that there are more verbs. Finally, as we move towards the surface of the 'sphere', the words become rarer and reflect more domain-specific words such as 'ebay' and 'spielberg'. Moreover, we also found many names and proper nouns occurring at this hierarchical level. Additionally, we also observe that words such as 'where' or 'what' have relatively high vector norms and located quite high up in the hierarchy. This is in concert with Figure 4 which shows the question embeddings form a sphere around the answer embeddings. At last, we parsed QA pairs word-by-word according to hierarchical level (based on their vector norm). Table 8 reports the outcome of this experiment where $H1 - H5$ are hierarchical levels based on vector norms. First, we find that questions often start with the overall context and drill down into more specific query words. Take the first sample in Table 8 for example, it begins at a top level with 'burger king' and then drills down progressively to 'what is gross sales?'. Similarly in the second example, it begins with 'florence nightingale' and drills down to 'famous' at H3 in which a match is being found with 'nursing' in the same hierarchical level. Overall, based on our qualitative analysis, we observe that, HyperQA builds two hierarchical structures at the **word-level** (in vector space) towards the middle which strongly facilitates word-level matching. Pertaining to answers, it seems like the model builds a hierarchy by splitting on conjunctive words ('and'), i.e., the root node of the tree starts by conjunctive words at splits sentences into semantic phrases. Overall, Figure 6 depicts our key intuitions regarding the inner workings of HyperQA which explains both **RQ2** and **RQ3**. This is also supported by Figure 5(b) which shows the majority of the word norms are clustered with $||w|| \approx 3$. This would be reasonable considering that the leaf nodes of both question and answer hierarchies would reside in the middle.

[3]Note that word embeddings are not constrained to $||x|| < 1$.

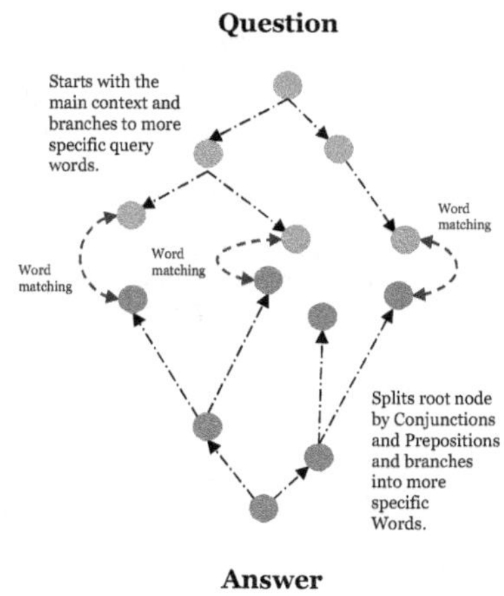

Figure 6: Dual hierarchical matching of question and answer at word-level.

6 CONCLUSION

We proposed a new neural ranking model for question answering. Our proposed HyperQA achieves very competitive performance on four well-studied benchmark datasets. Our model is light-weight, fast and efficient, outperforming many state-of-the-art models with complex word interaction layers, attentive mechanisms or rich neural encoders. Our model only has 40K-90K parameters as opposed to millions of parameters which plague many competitor models. Moreover, we derive qualitative insights pertaining to our model which enable us to further understand its inner workings. Finally, we observe that the superior generalization of our model (despite small parameters) can be attributed to self-organizing properties of not only question and answer embeddings but also word embeddings.

REFERENCES

[1] Alberto Barrón-Cedeño, Giovanni Da San Martino, Shafiq R. Joty, Alessandro Moschitti, Fahad Al-Obaidli, Salvatore Romeo, Kateryna Tymoshenko, and Antonio Uva. 2016. ConvKN at SemEval-2016 Task 3: Answer and Question Selection for Question Answering on Arabic and English Fora. In *Proceedings of the 10th International Workshop on Semantic Evaluation, SemEval@NAACL-HLT 2016, San Diego, CA, USA, June 16-17, 2016.* 896–903.

[2] Adam L. Berger, Rich Caruana, David Cohn, Dayne Freitag, and Vibhu O. Mittal. 2000. Bridging the lexical chasm: statistical approaches to answer-finding. In *SIGIR*. 192–199. https://doi.org/10.1145/345508.345576

[3] Silvere Bonnabel. 2013. Stochastic Gradient Descent on Riemannian Manifolds. *IEEE Trans. Automat. Contr.* 58, 9 (2013), 2217–2229. https://doi.org/10.1109/TAC.2013.2254619

[4] Cícero Nogueira dos Santos, Ming Tan, Bing Xiang, and Bowen Zhou. 2016. Attentive Pooling Networks. *CoRR* abs/1602.03609 (2016).

[5] John C. Duchi, Elad Hazan, and Yoram Singer. 2011. Adaptive Subgradient Methods for Online Learning and Stochastic Optimization. *Journal of Machine Learning Research* 12 (2011), 2121–2159.

[6] Simone Filice, Danilo Croce, Alessandro Moschitti, and Roberto Basili. 2016. KeLP at SemEval-2016 Task 3: Learning Semantic Relations between Questions and Answers. In *Proceedings of the 10th International Workshop on Semantic Evaluation, SemEval@NAACL-HLT 2016, San Diego, CA, USA, June 16-17, 2016.* 1116–1123.

[7] Hua He, Kevin Gimpel, and Jimmy J. Lin. 2015. Multi-Perspective Sentence Similarity Modeling with Convolutional Neural Networks. In *Proceedings of the 2015 Conference on Empirical Methods in Natural Language Processing, EMNLP 2015, Lisbon, Portugal, September 17-21, 2015.* 1576–1586.

[8] Hua He and Jimmy J. Lin. 2016. Pairwise Word Interaction Modeling with Deep Neural Networks for Semantic Similarity Measurement. In *NAACL HLT 2016, The 2016 Conference of the North American Chapter of the Association for Computational Linguistics: Human Language Technologies, San Diego California, USA, June 12-17, 2016.* 937–948.

[9] Michael Heilman and Noah A. Smith. 2010. Tree Edit Models for Recognizing Textual Entailments, Paraphrases, and Answers to Questions. In *Human Language Technologies: Conference of the North American Chapter of the Association of Computational Linguistics, Proceedings, June 2-4, 2010, Los Angeles, California, USA.* 1011–1019.

[10] Sepp Hochreiter and Jürgen Schmidhuber. 1997. Long short-term memory. *Neural computation* 9, 8 (1997), 1735–1780.

[11] Baotian Hu, Zhengdong Lu, Hang Li, and Qingcai Chen. 2014. Convolutional Neural Network Architectures for Matching Natural Language Sentences. In *Advances in Neural Information Processing Systems 27: Annual Conference on Neural Information Processing Systems 2014, December 8-13 2014, Montreal, Quebec, Canada.* 2042–2050.

[12] Robert Kleinberg. 2007. Geographic Routing Using Hyperbolic Space. In *INFOCOM 2007. 26th IEEE International Conference on Computer Communications, Joint Conference of the IEEE Computer and Communications Societies, 6-12 May 2007, Anchorage, Alaska, USA.* 1902–1909. https://doi.org/10.1109/INFCOM.2007.221

[13] Dmitri V. Krioukov, Fragkiskos Papadopoulos, Maksim Kitsak, Amin Vahdat, and Marián Boguñá. 2010. Hyperbolic Geometry of Complex Networks. *CoRR* abs/1006.5169 (2010).

[14] Quoc Le and Tomas Mikolov. 2014. Distributed representations of sentences and documents. In *Proceedings of the 31st International Conference on Machine Learning (ICML-14).* 1188–1196.

[15] Jonas Mueller and Aditya Thyagarajan. 2016. Siamese Recurrent Architectures for Learning Sentence Similarity. In *Proceedings of the Thirtieth AAAI Conference on Artificial Intelligence, February 12-17, 2016, Phoenix, Arizona, USA.* 2786–2792.

[16] Maximilian Nickel and Douwe Kiela. 2017. Poincaré Embeddings for Learning Hierarchical Representations. *CoRR* abs/1705.08039 (2017).

[17] Ankur P. Parikh, Oscar Täckström, Dipanjan Das, and Jakob Uszkoreit. 2016. A Decomposable Attention Model for Natural Language Inference. In *Proceedings of the 2016 Conference on Empirical Methods in Natural Language Processing, EMNLP 2016, Austin, Texas, USA, November 1-4, 2016.* 2249–2255.

[18] Jeffrey Pennington, Richard Socher, and Christopher D. Manning. 2014. Glove: Global Vectors for Word Representation. In *Proceedings of the 2014 Conference on Empirical Methods in Natural Language Processing, EMNLP 2014, October 25-29, 2014, Doha, Qatar, A meeting of SIGDAT, a Special Interest Group of the ACL.* 1532–1543.

[19] Xipeng Qiu and Xuanjing Huang. 2015. Convolutional Neural Tensor Network Architecture for Community-Based Question Answering. In *Proceedings of the Twenty-Fourth International Joint Conference on Artificial Intelligence, IJCAI 2015, Buenos Aires, Argentina, July 25-31, 2015.* 1305–1311.

[20] Jinfeng Rao, Hua He, and Jimmy J. Lin. 2016. Noise-Contrastive Estimation for Answer Selection with Deep Neural Networks. In *Proceedings of the 25th ACM International on Conference on Information and Knowledge Management, CIKM 2016, Indianapolis, IN, USA, October 24-28, 2016.* 1913–1916. https://doi.org/10.1145/2983323.2983872

[21] Erzsébet Ravasz and Albert-László Barabási. 2003. Hierarchical organization in complex networks. *Physical Review E* 67, 2 (2003), 026112.

[22] Stephen E. Robertson, Steve Walker, Susan Jones, Micheline Hancock-Beaulieu, and Mike Gatford. 1994. Okapi at TREC-3. In *Proceedings of The Third Text REtrieval Conference, TREC 1994, Gaithersburg, Maryland, USA, November 2-4, 1994.* 109–126.

[23] Aliaksei Severyn and Alessandro Moschitti. 2015. Learning to Rank Short Text Pairs with Convolutional Deep Neural Networks. In *Proceedings of the 38th International ACM SIGIR Conference on Research and Development in Information Retrieval, Santiago, Chile, August 9-13, 2015.* 373–382. https://doi.org/10.1145/2766462.2767738

[24] Aliaksei Severyn, Alessandro Moschitti, Manos Tsagkias, Richard Berendsen, and Maarten de Rijke. 2014. A syntax-aware re-ranker for microblog retrieval. In *The 37th International ACM SIGIR Conference on Research and Development in Information Retrieval, SIGIR '14, Gold Coast , QLD, Australia - July 06 - 11, 2014.* 1067–1070. https://doi.org/10.1145/2600428.2609511

[25] Yelong Shen, Xiaodong He, Jianfeng Gao, Li Deng, and Grégoire Mesnil. 2014. A latent semantic model with convolutional-pooling structure for information retrieval. In *Proceedings of the 23rd ACM International Conference on Conference on Information and Knowledge Management.* ACM, 101–110.

[26] Yi Tay, Minh C. Phan, Anh Tuan Luu, and Siu Cheung Hui. 2017. Learning to Rank Question Answer Pairs with Holographic Dual LSTM Architecture. In *Proceedings of the 40th International ACM SIGIR Conference on Research and Development in Information Retrieval, Shinjuku, Tokyo, Japan, August 7-11, 2017.* 695–704. https://doi.org/10.1145/3077136.3080790

[27] Yi Tay, Luu Anh Tuan, and Siu Cheung Hui. 2017. Cross Temporal Recurrent Networks for Ranking Question Answer Pairs. (2017). arXiv:arXiv:1711.07656

[28] Laurens van der Maaten. 2009. Learning a Parametric Embedding by Preserving Local Structure. In *Proceedings of the Twelfth International Conference on Artificial Intelligence and Statistics, AISTATS 2009, Clearwater Beach, Florida, USA, April 16-18, 2009.* 384–391.

[29] Kevin Verbeek and Subhash Suri. 2016. Metric embedding, hyperbolic space, and social networks. *Computational Geometry* 59 (2016), 1–12.

[30] Mengqiu Wang, Noah A. Smith, and Teruko Mitamura. 2007. What is the Jeopardy Model? A Quasi-Synchronous Grammar for QA. In *EMNLP-CoNLL 2007, Proceedings of the 2007 Joint Conference on Empirical Methods in Natural Language Processing and Computational Natural Language Learning, June 28-30, 2007, Prague, Czech Republic.* 22–32.

[31] Liu Yang, Qingyao Ai, Jiafeng Guo, and W. Bruce Croft. 2016. aNMM: Ranking Short Answer Texts with Attention-Based Neural Matching Model. In *Proceedings of the 25th ACM International on Conference on Information and Knowledge Management, CIKM 2016, Indianapolis, IN, USA, October 24-28, 2016.* 287–296. https://doi.org/10.1145/2983323.2983818

[32] Yi Yang, Wen-tau Yih, and Christopher Meek. 2015. WikiQA: A Challenge Dataset for Open-Domain Question Answering. In *Proceedings of the 2015 Conference on Empirical Methods in Natural Language Processing, EMNLP 2015, Lisbon, Portugal, September 17-21, 2015.* 2013–2018.

[33] Xuchen Yao, Benjamin Van Durme, Chris Callison-Burch, and Peter Clark. 2013. Answer Extraction as Sequence Tagging with Tree Edit Distance. In *Human Language Technologies: Conference of the North American Chapter of the Association of Computational Linguistics, Proceedings, June 9-14, 2013, Westin Peachtree Plaza Hotel, Atlanta, Georgia, USA.* 858–867.

[34] Wen-tau Yih, Ming-Wei Chang, Christopher Meek, and Andrzej Pastusiak. 2013. Question Answering Using Enhanced Lexical Semantic Models. In *Proceedings of the 51st Annual Meeting of the Association for Computational Linguistics, ACL 2013, 4-9 August 2013, Sofia, Bulgaria, Volume 1: Long Papers.* 1744–1753.

[35] Lei Yu, Karl Moritz Hermann, Phil Blunsom, and Stephen Pulman. 2014. Deep Learning for Answer Sentence Selection. *CoRR* abs/1412.1632 (2014).

[36] Xiaodong Zhang, Sujian Li, Lei Sha, and Houfeng Wang. 2017. Attentive Interactive Neural Networks for Answer Selection in Community Question Answering. In *Proceedings of the Thirty-First AAAI Conference on Artificial Intelligence, February 4-9, 2017, San Francisco, California, USA.* 3525–3531.

SHINE: Signed Heterogeneous Information Network Embedding for Sentiment Link Prediction

Hongwei Wang*
Shanghai Jiao Tong University
Shanghai, China
wanghongwei55@gmail.com

Fuzheng Zhang
Microsoft Research Asia
Beijing, China
fuzzhang@microsoft.com

Min Hou
University of Science and Technology of China, Hefei, Anhui, China
hmhoumin@gmail.com

Xing Xie
Microsoft Research Asia
Beijing, China
xingx@microsoft.com

Minyi Guo†
Shanghai Jiao Tong University
Shanghai, China
guo-my@cs.sjtu.edu.cn

Qi Liu
University of Science and Technology of China, Hefei, Anhui, China
qiliuql@ustc.edu.cn

ABSTRACT

In online social networks people often express attitudes towards others, which forms massive sentiment links among users. Predicting the sign of sentiment links is a fundamental task in many areas such as personal advertising and public opinion analysis. Previous works mainly focus on textual sentiment classification, however, text information can only disclose the "tip of the iceberg" about users' true opinions, of which the most are unobserved but implied by other sources of information such as social relation and users' profile. To address this problem, in this paper we investigate how to predict possibly existing sentiment links in the presence of heterogeneous information. First, due to the lack of explicit sentiment links in mainstream social networks, we establish a labeled heterogeneous sentiment dataset which consists of users' sentiment relation, social relation and profile knowledge by entity-level sentiment extraction method. Then we propose a novel and flexible end-to-end *Signed Heterogeneous Information Network Embedding* (SHINE) framework to extract users' latent representations from heterogeneous networks and predict the sign of unobserved sentiment links. SHINE utilizes multiple deep autoencoders to map each user into a low-dimension feature space while preserving the network structure. We demonstrate the superiority of SHINE over state-of-the-art baselines on link prediction and node recommendation in two real-world datasets. The experimental results also prove the efficacy of SHINE in cold start scenario.

ACM Reference Format:
Hongwei Wang, Fuzheng Zhang, Min Hou, Xing Xie, Minyi Guo, and Qi Liu. 2018. SHINE: Signed Heterogeneous Information Network Embedding for Sentiment Link Prediction. In *Proceedings of the 11th ACM International Conference on Web Search and Data Mining (WSDM'18)*. ACM, New York, NY, USA, 9 pages. https://doi.org/10.1145/3159652.3159666

*This work is done while H. Wang and M. Hou are visiting Microsoft Research Asia.
†M. Guo is the corresponding author.

WSDM'18, February 5–9, 2018, Marina Del Rey, CA, USA

ACM ISBN 978-1-4503-5581-0/18/02...$15.00
https://doi.org/10.1145/3159652.3159666

1 INTRODUCTION

The past decade has witnessed the proliferation of online social networks such as Facebook, Twitter and Weibo. In these social network sites, people often share feelings and express attitudes towards others, e.g., friends, movie stars or politicians, which forms *sentiment links* among these users. Different from explicit social links indicating friend or follow relationship, sentiment links are implied by the semantic content posted by users, and involve different types: *positive* sentiment links express like, trust or support attitudes, while *negative* sentiment links signify dislike or disapproval of others. For example, a tweet saying "*Vote Trump!*" shows a positive sentiment link from the poster to Donald Trump, and "*Trump is mad...*" indicates the opposite case.

For a given sentiment link, we define its *sign* to be positive or negative depending on whether its related content expresses a positive or negative attitude from the generator of the link to the recipient [14], and all such sentiment links form a new network topology called *sentiment network*. Previous work [6, 11, 15] mainly focuses on sentiment classification based on the concrete content posted by users. However, they cannot detect the existence of sentiment links without any prior content information, which greatly limits the number of possible sentiment links that could be found. For example, if a user does not post any word concerning Trump, it is impossible for traditional sentiment classifiers to extract the user's attitude towards him because "one cannot make bricks without straw". Therefore, a fundamental question is, can we predict the sign of a given sentiment link without observing its related content? The solution to this problem will benefit a great many online services such as personalized advertising, new friends recommendation, public opinion analysis, opinion polls, etc.

Despite the great importance, there is little prior work concerning predicting the sign of sentiment links among users in social networks. The challenges are two-fold. On the one hand, lack of explicit sentiment labels makes it difficult to determine the polarity of existing and potential sentiment links. On the other hand, the complexity of sentiment generation and the sparsity of sentiment links make it hard for algorithms to achieve desirable performance. Recently, several studies [12, 14, 31, 35] propose methods to solve the problem of predicting signed links. However, they rely heavily on manually designed features and cannot work well in real-world scenarios. Another promising approach called *network embedding*

[8, 17, 23, 26], which automatically learns features of users in network, seems plausible to solve the task. However, they can only apply to networks with positive-weighted (i.e., unsigned) and single-type (i.e., homogeneous) edges, which limits their power in the task of practical sentiment link prediction.

Based on the above facts, in this paper we investigate the problem of predicting sentiment links in absence of sentiment related content in online social networks. Our work is two-step. First, considering the lack of labeled data, we establish a labeled sentiment dataset from Weibo, one of the most popular social network sites in China. We leverage state-of-the-art entity-level sentiment extraction method to calculate the sentiment of the poster towards the celebrity in each tweet. Besides, to handle the sparsity problem, we collect two additional types of side information: social relationship among users and profile knowledge of users and celebrities. Our choices are enlightened by [27] and [34], respectively, in which [27] demonstrates that the structural information of social networks can greatly affect users' preference towards online items, and [34] proves that information from knowledge base could boost the performance of recommendation. The heterogeneous information networks are illustrated in Fig. 1.

To explore more possible sentiment links from the network, in the second step, we propose a novel end-to-end framework termed as *Signed Heterogeneous Information Network Embedding* (SHINE). Greatly different from existing network embedding approaches, SHINE is able to learn user representation and predict sentiment from signed heterogeneous networks. Specifically, SHINE adopts multiple deep autoencoders [20], a type of deep-learning-based embedding technique, to extract users' highly nonlinear representations from the sentiment network, social network and profile network, respectively. The learned three types of user representations are subsequently fused together by specific aggregation function for further sentiment prediction. In addition to the adaptability to signed heterogeneous networks, the superiority of SHINE also lies in its end-to-end prediction technology and high flexibility of adding or removing modules of side information (i.e., social relationship and profile knowledge), which is discuss in Section 5.

We conduct extensive experiments on two real-world datasets. The results show that SHINE achieves substantial gains compared with baselines. Specifically, SHINE outperforms other strong baselines by 8.8% to 16.8% in the task of link prediction on Accuracy, and by 17.2% to 219.4% in the task of node recommendation on Recall@100 for positive nodes. The results also prove that SHINE is able to utilize the side information efficiently, and maintains a decent performance in cold start scenario.

2 RELATED WORK

2.1 Signed Link Prediction

Our problem of predicting positive and negative sentiment links connects to a large body of work on signed social networks, including trust propagation [9], spectral analysis [13], and social media mining [22]. For the link prediction problem in signed graphs, Leskovec. *et al.* [14] adopt signed triads as features for prediction based on structural balance theory. Ye *et al.* [31] utilize transfer learning to leverage edge sign information from source network and improve prediction accuracy in target network. Tang *et al.* design NeLP framework [21] which exploits positive links in social media to predict negative links. The difference between the above work and ours is that we construct a labeled dataset by entity-level sentiment extraction method, as there is no explicit signed links in mainstream online social networks. Besides, we use state-of-the-art deep learning approach to learn the representation of links.

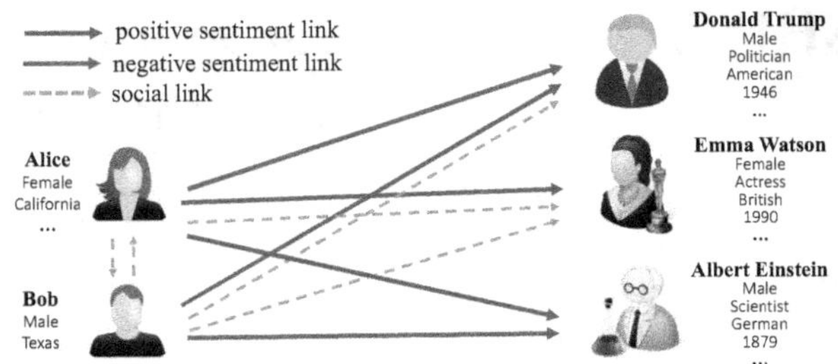

Fig. 1: Illustration of a snippet of heterogeneous networks with sentiment, social relationship and user profile.

2.2 Network Embedding

There is a long history of work on network embedding. Earlier works such as IsoMap [24] and Laplacian Eigenmap [1] first construct the affinity graph of data using the feature vectors and then embed the affinity graph into a low-dimension space. Recently, DeepWalk [17] deploys random walk to learning representations of social network. LINE [23] proposes objective functions that preserve both local and global network structures for network embedding. Node2vec [8] designs a biased random walk procedure to learn a mapping of nodes that maximizes the likelihood of preserving network neighborhoods of nodes. SDNE [26] uses autoencoder to capture first-order and second-order network structures and learn user representation. However, these methods can only address unsigned and homogeneous networks. Additionally, several studies focus on representation learning in the scenario of heterogeneous network [3, 32], attributed network [10], or signed network [29, 33]. However, these methods are specialized in only one particular type of networks, which is not applicable to the problem of sentiment prediction in real-world signed and heterogeneous networks.

3 DATASET ESTABLISHMENT

In this section we introduce the process of collecting data from online social networks, and discuss the details of how to extract sentiment towards celebrities from tweets.

3.1 Data Collection

3.1.1 Weibo Tweets. We select Weibo[1] as the online social networks studied in this work. Weibo is one of the most popular social network sites in China which is akin to a hybrid of Facebook and Twitter. We collected 2.99 billion tweets on Weibo from August 14, 2009 to May 23, 2014 as raw dataset. To filter out useful data which contains sentiment towards celebrities, we first apply Jieba[2], the most popular Chinese text segmentation tool, to tag the part of

[1] http://weibo.com
[2] https://github.com/fxsjy/jieba

Table 1: Statistics of Weibo sentiment datasets. "celebrities v." means the celebrities owning verified accounts on Weibo.

# users	12,814	# social links	71,268
# celebrities	1,723	# tweets	126,380
# celebrities v.	706	# pos. tweets	108,906
# ordinary users	11,091	# neg. tweets	17,474

speech (POS) of each word for each tweet. Then we select those tweets containing words with POS tagging as "person name" which exist in our established celebrity database (detailed in Section 3.1.4). After getting the set of candidate tweets, for each tweet we calculate its sentiment value (-1 to +1) towards the mentioned celebrities, and select those tweets with high absolute sentiment values. The final dataset consists of a set of triples (a, b, s), where a is the user who posts the tweet, b is the certain celebrity mentioned in the tweet, and $s \in \{+1, -1\}$ is the sentiment polarity of user a towards user b. The method of calculating sentiment values is detailed in Section 3.2.

3.1.2 Social Relation. In addition to the sentiment dataset, we also collect the social relation among users from Weibo. The dataset of social relation consists of tuples (a, b), where a is the follower and b is the followee.

3.1.3 Profile of Ordinary Users. The profile of ordinary users are collected from Weibo. For each ordinary user, we extract two of his attributes, *gender* and *location*, as his profile information. The attribute values are represented as one-hot vectors.

3.1.4 Profile of Celebrities. We use Microsoft Satori[3] knowledge base to extract profile of celebrities. First, we traverse the knowledge base and select terms with object type as "person". Then we filter out popular celebrities with high edit frequency in knowledge base and high appearance frequency in Weibo tweets. For each of these "hot" celebrities, we extract 9 attributes as his profile information: *place of birth, date of birth, ethnicity, nationality, specialization, gender, height, weight,* and *astrological sign*. Values of these attributes are discretized so that every celebrity's attribute values can be expressed as one-hot vectors. Furthermore, we remove celebrities with ambiguous names as well as other noises.

3.2 Sentiment Extraction

To extract users' sentiment towards celebrities in tweets, we first generate a sentiment lexicon consisting of words and their *sentiment orientation* (SO) scores. To achieve this, we manually construct a emoticon-sentiment mapping file and map each tweet to positive or negative class according to the label of emoticon appeared in the tweet. For example, *"I love Kobe! [kiss]"* is mapped to positive class if the key-value pair ([kiss], *positive*) exists in the emoticon-sentiment mapping file. Note that the class of emoticon cannot be directly regarded as the sentiment towards celebrities since we found a large number of mismatch cases, e.g., *"Miss you Taylor Swift [cry][cry]"*. Afterwards, for each word (segmented by Jieba) with occurrence frequency from 2,000 to 10,000,000 in the raw tweets datasets, similar to [2], we calculate its SO score as

$$SO(word) = PMI(word, pos) - PMI(word, neg), \quad (1)$$

[3] http://searchengineland.com/library/bing/bing-satori

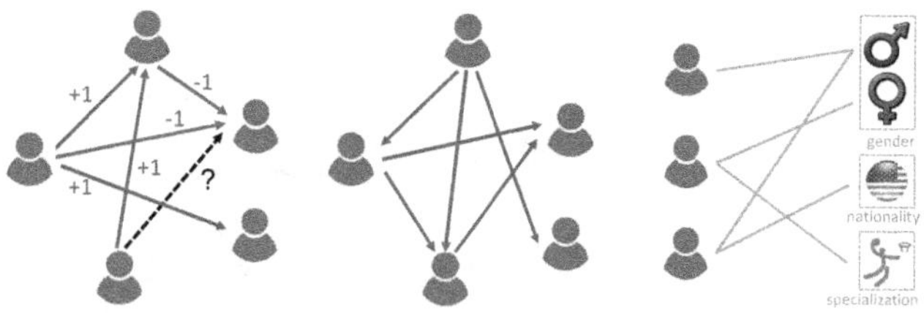

(a) Sentiment network (b) Social network (c) Profile network

Fig. 2: Illustration of the three studied networks.

where PMI is the *point-wise mutual information* [25] defined as $PMI(x, y) = \log \frac{p(x,y)}{p(x)p(y)}$, *pos* and *neg* are the tweets of positive and negative class, respectively. SO scores are subsequently normalized to $[-1, 1]$.

After getting the lexicon, we use SentiCircle [19] to calculate sentiment towards celebrities in each tweet. Given a piece of tweet as well as the mentioned celebrity, we represent the contextual semantics of the celebrity as a polar coordinate space, where the celebrity is situated in the origin and other terms in the tweet are scattered around. Specifically, for celebrity term c, the coordinate of term t_i is (r_i, θ_i), where r_i is the inverse of distance between c and t_i in syntax dependence graph generated by LTP [4], and $\theta_i = SO(t_i) \cdot \pi$. The overall sentiment towards the celebrity c is, therefore, approximated as the geometric center of all terms c_i. We take the projection of the geometric center on y-axis as final sentiment value towards the celebrity.

To validate the effectiveness of sentiment extraction, we randomly select 1,000 tweets (500 positive and 500 negative tagged by our method) in Weibo sentiment dataset, and manually label each one of them. The result shows that the precision is 95.2% for positive class and 91.0% for negative class, which we believe is accurate enough for subsequent experiments. The basic statistics of Weibo sentiment datasets is presented in Table 1.

4 PROBLEM FORMULATION

In this section we formulate the problem of predicting sentiment links in heterogeneous information networks. For better illustration, we split the original heterogeneous network into the following three single-type networks:

Sentiment network. The directed *sentiment network* is denoted as $G_s = (V, S)$, where $V = \{1, ..., |V|\}$ represents the set of users (either ordinary users or celebrities) and $S = \{s_{ij} \mid i \in V, j \in V\}$ represents sentiment links among users. Each s_{ij} can take the value of $+1$, -1 or 0, representing that user i holds a positive, negative, or unobserved sentiment towards user j, respectively.

Social network. The directed *social network* is denoted as $G_r = (V, R)$, where $R = \{r_{ij} \mid i \in V, j \in V\}$ represents social links among users. Each r_{ij} can take the value of 1 or 0, representing that user i follows user j or not in the social network.

Profile network. We denote $\mathcal{A} = \{A_1, ..., A_{|\mathcal{A}|}\}$ the set of user's attributes, and $a_{kl} \in A_k$ the l-th possible value of attribute A_k. We take the union of all possible values of attributes and renumber them as $U = \bigcup A_k = \{a_j \mid j = 1, ..., \sum_k |A_k|\}$. Then the undirected bipartite *profile network* can be denoted as $G_p = (V, U, P)$, where $P = \{p_{ij} \mid i \in V, a_j \in U\}$ represents profile links between

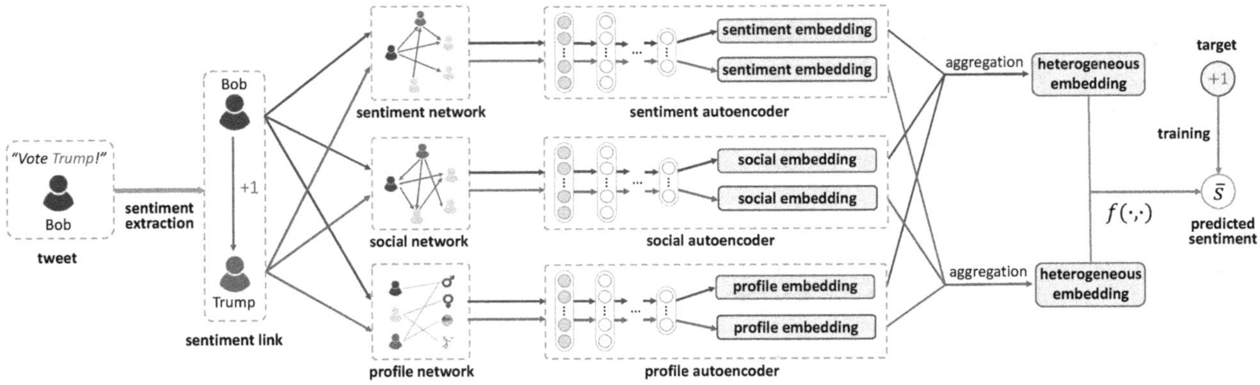

Fig. 3: Framework of the end-to-end SHINE model. To clearly demonstrate the model, we only show the encoder part of all the three autoencoders and leave out the decoder part in this figure.

users and attribute values. Each p_{ij} can take the value of 1 or 0, representing that user i possesses attribute value j or not.

The three networks are illustrated in Fig. 2.

Sentiment links prediction. We define the problem of predicting sentiment links in heterogeneous information networks as follows: Given the sentiment network G_s, social network G_r and profile network G_p, we aim to predict the sentiment of unobserved links between users in G_s.

5 SIGNED HETEROGENEOUS INFORMATION NETWORK EMBEDDING

In this section we introduce the proposed SHINE model. We first show the whole framework of SHINE. Then we present the details of the SHINE model, including how to extract user representation jointly from the three networks as well as the learning algorithm. At last we give some discussions on the model.

5.1 Framework

In this paper we propose an end-to-end SHINE model to predict sentiment links. The framework of SHINE is shown in Fig. 3. In general, the whole framework consists of three major components: sentiment extraction and heterogeneous networks construction (the left part), user representation extraction (the middle part), as well as representation aggregation and sentiment prediction (the right part). For each tweet mentioning a specific celebrity, we first calculate the associated sentiment (discussed in Section 3.1), and represent the user and the celebrity in this sentiment link by using their neighborhood information from the three constructed networks (introduced in Section 4). We then design three distinct autoencoders to extract short and dense embeddings from original sparse neighborhood-based representation respectively, and aggregate these three kinds of embeddings into final heterogeneous embedding. The predicted sentiment can thus be calculated by applying specific similarity measurement function (e.g., inner product or logistic regression) to the two heterogeneous embeddings, and the whole model can be trained based on the predicted sentiment and the target (i.e., the ground truth obtained in sentiment extraction step). In the following subsections we will introduce SHINE model in detail.

5.2 Sentiment Network Embedding

Given the sentiment graph $G_s = (V, S)$, for each user $i \in V$, we define its sentiment adjacency vector $\mathbf{x}_i = \{s_{ij} \mid j \in V\} \cup \{s_{ji} \mid j \in V\}$. Note that $\mathbf{x}_i$ fully contains the global incoming and outgoing sentiment information of user i. However, it is impractical to take $\mathbf{x}_i$ directly as the sentiment representation of user i, as the adjacency vector is too long and sparse for further processing. Recently, a lot of network embedding models [8, 17, 23, 26] are proposed, which aim to learn low-dimension representations of vertices while preserving the network structure. Among those models, deep autoencoder is proved to be one of state-of-the-art solutions, as it is able to capture highly nonlinear network structure by using deep models [26]. In general, autoencoder [20] is an unsupervised neural network model of codings aiming to learn a representation of a set of data. Autoencoder consists of two parts, the encoder and the decoder, which contains multiple nonlinear functions (layers) for mapping the input data to representation space and reconstructing original input from representation, respectively. In our SHINE model, we propose to use autoencoders for efficiently user representation learning.

Fig. 4 illustrates the autoencoder for sentiment network embedding. As shown in Fig. 4, the sentiment autoencoder maps each user to a low-dimension latent representation space and recover original information from latent representation by using multiple fully-connected layers. Given the input $\mathbf{x}_i$, the hidden representations for each layer are

$$\mathbf{x}_i^k = \sigma\left(\mathbf{W}_s^k \mathbf{x}_i^{k-1} + \mathbf{b}_s^k\right), \ k = 1, 2, ..., K_s, \tag{2}$$

where $\mathbf{W}_s^k$ and $\mathbf{b}_s^k$ are weight and bias parameters of layer k in the sentiment autoencoder, respectively, $\sigma(\cdot)$ is the nonlinear activation function, K_s is the number of layers of sentiment autoencoder, and $\mathbf{x}_i^0 = \mathbf{x}_i$. For simplicity, we denote $\mathbf{x}_i' = \mathbf{x}_i^{K_s}$ the reconstruction of $\mathbf{x}_i$.

The basic goal of the autoencoder is to minimize the reconstruction loss between input and output representations. Similar to [26], in SHINE model the reconstruction loss term of sentiment autoencoder is defined as

$$\mathcal{L}_s = \sum\nolimits_{i \in V} \left\|(\mathbf{x}_i - \mathbf{x}_i') \odot \mathbf{l}_i\right\|_2^2, \tag{3}$$

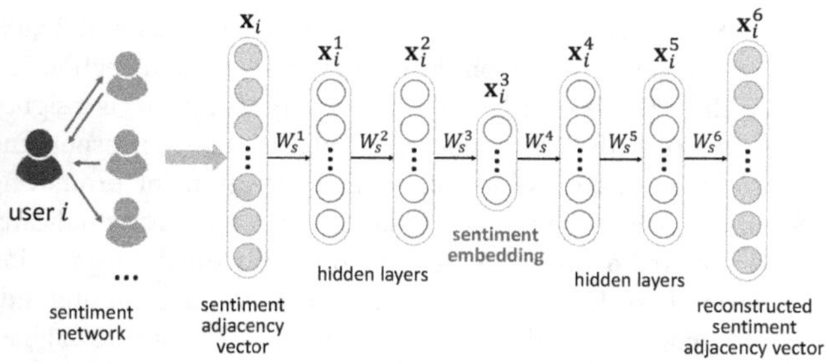

Fig. 4: Illustration of a 6-layer autoencoder for sentiment network embedding.

where $\odot$ denotes the Hadamard product, and $\mathbf{l}_i = (l_{i,1}, l_{i,2}, ..., l_{i,2|V|})$ is the sentiment reconstruction weight vector in which

$$l_{i,j} = \begin{cases} \alpha > 1, & if\ s_{ij} = \pm 1; \\ 1, & if\ s_{ij} = 0. \end{cases} \tag{4}$$

The meaning of the above loss term lies in that we impose more penalty to the reconstruction error of the non-zero elements than that of zero elements in input $\mathbf{x_i}$, as a non-zero s_{ij} carries more explicit sentiment information than an implicit zero s_{ij}. Note that the sentiment embedding of user i can be obtained from the layer $K_s/2$ in the sentiment autoencoder, and we denote $\widehat{\mathbf{x}}_i = \mathbf{x}_i^{K_s/2}$ the sentiment embedding of user i for simplicity.

5.3 Social Network Embedding

Similar to previous sentiment network embedding, we apply autoencoder to extract user representation from the social network. Given the social network $G_r = (V, R)$, for each user $i \in V$, we define its social adjacency vector $\mathbf{y}_i = \{r_{ij} \mid j \in V\} \cup \{r_{ji} \mid j \in V\}$, which fully contains the structural information of user i in the social network. The hidden representations of each layer in the social autoencoder are

$$\mathbf{y}_i^k = \sigma\left(\mathbf{W}_r^k \mathbf{y}_i^{k-1} + \mathbf{b}_r^k\right),\ k = 1, 2, ..., K_r, \tag{5}$$

where the meaning of notations are similar to those in Eq. (2). We also denote $\mathbf{y}_i' = \mathbf{y}_i^{K_r}$ the reconstruction of $\mathbf{y}_i$. Similarly, the reconstruction loss term of social autoencoder is

$$\mathcal{L}_r = \sum\nolimits_{i \in V} \left\|(\mathbf{y}_i - \mathbf{y}_i') \odot \mathbf{m}_i\right\|_2^2, \tag{6}$$

where $\mathbf{m}_i = (m_{i,1}, m_{i,2}, ..., m_{i,2|V|})$ is the social reconstruction weight vector in which if $r_{ij} = 1$, $m_{i,j} = \alpha > 1$, else $m_{i,j} = 1$. The social embedding of user i is denoted as $\widehat{\mathbf{y}}_i = \mathbf{y}_i^{K_r/2}$.

5.4 Profile Network Embedding

The profile network $G_p = (V, U, P)$ is an undirected bipartite graph which consists of two disjoint sets of users and attribute values. For each user $i \in V$, its profile adjacency vector is defined as $\mathbf{z}_i = \{p_{ij} \mid j \in U\}$. User i's hidden representations of each layer in the profile autoencoder are

$$\mathbf{z}_i^k = \sigma\left(\mathbf{W}_p^k \mathbf{z}_i^{k-1} + \mathbf{b}_p^k\right),\ k = 1, 2, ..., K_p, \tag{7}$$

where the meaning of notations are similar to those in Eq. (2). We also use the notation $\mathbf{z}_i'$ to denote the reconstruction of $\mathbf{z}_i$. Therefore, the reconstruction loss term of profile autoencoder is

$$\mathcal{L}_p = \sum\nolimits_{i \in V} \left\|(\mathbf{z}_i - \mathbf{z}_i') \odot \mathbf{n}_i\right\|_2^2, \tag{8}$$

where $\mathbf{n}_i$ is the profile reconstruction weight vector defined similarly to $\mathbf{m}_i$ in the previous subsection. The profile embedding of user i is denoted as $\widehat{\mathbf{z}}_i = \mathbf{z}_i^{K_p/2}$.

5.5 Representation Aggregation and Sentiment Prediction

Once we obtain the sentiment embedding $\widehat{\mathbf{x}}_i$, social embedding $\widehat{\mathbf{y}}_i$, and profile embedding $\widehat{\mathbf{z}}_i$ of user i, we can aggregate these embeddings into final heterogeneous embedding $\mathbf{e}_i$ by specific aggregation function $g(\cdot, \cdot, \cdot)$. We list some of the available aggregation functions as follows:

- *Summation* [34], i.e., $\mathbf{e}_i = \widehat{\mathbf{x}}_i + \widehat{\mathbf{y}}_i + \widehat{\mathbf{z}}_i$;
- *Max pooling* [28], i.e., $\mathbf{e}_i = element\text{-}wise\text{-}max(\widehat{\mathbf{x}}_i, \widehat{\mathbf{y}}_i, \widehat{\mathbf{z}}_i)$;
- *Concatenation* [23], i.e., $\mathbf{e}_i = \langle \widehat{\mathbf{x}}_i, \widehat{\mathbf{y}}_i, \widehat{\mathbf{z}}_i \rangle$.

Finally, given two users i and j as well as their heterogeneous embedding $\mathbf{e}_i$ and $\mathbf{e}_j$, the predicted sentiment $\bar{s}_{ij}$ can be calculated as $\bar{s}_{ij} = f(i, j)$, where $f(\cdot, \cdot)$ is specific similarity measurement function. For example:

- *Inner product* [3, 5], i.e., $\bar{s}_{ij} = \mathbf{e}_i^{\mathrm{T}} \mathbf{e}_j + b$, where b is a trainable bias parameter;
- *Euclidean distance* [26], i.e., $\bar{s}_{ij} = -\|\mathbf{e}_i - \mathbf{e}_j\|_2 + b$, where b is a trainable bias parameter;
- *Logistic regression* [17], i.e., $\bar{s}_{ij} = \mathbf{W}^{\mathrm{T}} \langle \mathbf{e}_i, \mathbf{e}_j \rangle + b$, where $\mathbf{W}$ and b are trainable weights and bias parameters.

We will study the choices of f and g in the experimental part.

5.6 Optimization

The complete objective function of SHINE model is as follows:

$$\mathcal{L} = \sum\nolimits_{i \in V} \left\|(\mathbf{x}_i - \mathbf{x}_i') \odot \mathbf{l}_i\right\|_2^2 + \lambda_1 \sum\nolimits_{i \in V} \left\|(\mathbf{y}_i - \mathbf{y}_i') \odot \mathbf{m}_i\right\|_2^2 + \lambda_2 \sum\nolimits_{i \in V} \left\|(\mathbf{z}_i - \mathbf{z}_i') \odot \mathbf{n}_i\right\|_2^2 + \lambda_3 \sum\nolimits_{s_{ij} = \pm 1} \left(f(\mathbf{e}_i, \mathbf{e}_j) - s_{ij}\right)^2 + \lambda_4 \mathcal{L}_{reg}, \tag{9}$$

where λ_1, λ_2, λ_3 and λ_4 are balancing parameters. The first three terms in Eq. (9) are the reconstruction loss terms of sentiment autoencoder, social autoencoder, and profile autoencoder, respectively. The fourth term in Eq. (9) is the supervised loss term for penalizing the divergence between predicted sentiment and ground truth. The last term in Eq. (9) is the regularization term that prevents over-fitting, i.e.,

$$\mathcal{L}_{reg} = \sum_{k=1}^{K_s} \|\mathbf{W}_s^k\|_2^2 + \sum_{k=1}^{K_r} \|\mathbf{W}_r^k\|_2^2 + \sum_{k=1}^{K_p} \|\mathbf{W}_p^k\|_2^2 + \|f\|_2^2, \tag{10}$$

where $\mathbf{W}_s^k$, $\mathbf{W}_r^k$, $\mathbf{W}_p^k$ are the weight parameters of layer k in the sentiment autoencoder, social autoencoder, and profile autoencoder, respectively, and $\|f\|_2^2$ is the regularization penalty for similarity measurement function $f(\cdot, \cdot)$ (if appropriate).

We employ the AdaGrad [7] algorithm to minimize the objective functions in Eq. (9). In each iteration, we randomly select a batch of sentiment links from training dataset and compute the gradient of the objective function with respect to each trainable parameter respectively. Then we update each trainable parameter according to the AdaGrad algorithm till convergence.

5.7 Discussions

5.7.1 Asymmetry. Many real-world networks are directed, which implies that for two nodes i and j in the network, edges (i, j) and (j, i) may coexist and their values are not necessarily identical. A few recent studies have focused on this asymmetry issue [16, 36]. In this work, whether the basic SHINE model can characterize asymmetry depends on the choice of similarity measurement function f. Specifically, SHINE is capable of dealing with the direction of a link if and only if $f(i, j) \neq f(j, i)$ (e.g., logistic regression). However (and fortunately), even if we choose a symmetric function (e.g., inner product or Euclidean distance) as f, we can still easily extend the basic SHINE model to asymmetry-aware version by setting two distinct sets of autoencoders to extract representation of source node and target node respectively. From this point of view, in basic SHINE model the parameters of autoencoders are actually *shared* for source node and target node to alleviate over-fitting, and we can choose to explicitly distinguish the two sets of autoencoders for asymmetry reasons.

5.7.2 Cold start problem. A practical issue for network embedding is how to learn representations for newly arrived node, which is the cold start problem. Almost all existing models cannot work well in cold start scenario because they only use the information from the target network (e.g., sentiment network in this paper), which is not applicable for the newly arrived node who has little interaction with the existing target network. However, SHINE is free of the cold start problem, as it makes full use of side information and incorporate it naturally into the target network when learning user representations. We will further study the performance of SHINE in cold start scenario in the experiment part.

5.7.3 Flexibility. It is worth noticing that SHINE is also a framework with high flexibility. For any other new available side information of users (e.g., users' browsing history), we can easily design a new parallel processing component and "plug" it in the original SHINE framework to assist learning representation. Contrarily, we can also "pull out" social autoencoder or profile autoencoder from SHINE framework if such side information is unavailable. Besides, the flexibility of SHINE also lies in that one can choose different aggregation functions g and similarity measurement functions f, as discussed in Section 5.5.

6 EXPERIMENTS

In this section, we evaluate the performance of our proposed SHINE on real-world datasets. We first introduce the datasets, baselines, and parameter settings for experiments, then present the experimental results of SHINE and baselines.

6.1 Datasets

To comprehensively demonstrate the effectiveness of SHINE framework, we use the following two datasets for experiments:

- **Weibo-STC**: Our proposed *Weibo Sentiment Towards Celebrities* dataset consists of three heterogeneous networks with 12,814 users, 126,380 tweets, 71,268 social links and 37,689 profile values, of which the detail is presented in Section 3.
- **Wiki-RfA**: *Wikipedia Requests for Adminship* [30] is a signed network with 10,835 nodes and 159,388 edges, corresponding to votes cast by Wikipedia uses in election for promoting individuals to the role of administrator. A signed link indicates a positive or negative vote by one user on the promotion of another. Note that Wiki-RfA does not contain any side information of nodes, therefore, this dataset is used to validate the efficacy of the basic sentiment autoencoder in SHINE.

6.2 Baselines

We use the following five methods as baselines, in which the first three are network embedding methods, FxG is a signed link prediction approach, and LIBFM is a generic classification model. Note that the first three methods are not directly applicable to signed heterogeneous networks, so we use them to learn user representations from positive and negative part of each network respectively, and concatenate them to form the final embeddings. For FxG on Weibo-STC dataset, we only use the sentiment network as input because the FxG model cannot utilize the side information of nodes.

- **LINE**: Large-scale Information Network Embedding [23] defines loss functions to preserve the first-order and second-order proximity and learns representations of vertices.
- **Node2vec**: Node2vec [8] designs a biased random walk procedure to learn a mapping of nodes that maximizes the likelihood of preserving network neighborhoods of nodes.
- **SDNE**: Structural Deep Network Embedding [26] is a semi-supervised network embedding model using autoencoder to capture local and global structure of target networks.
- **FxG**: Fairness and Goodness [12] predicts the weights of edges in weighted signed networks by introducing two measures of node behavior: goodness (i.e., how much the node is liked by other nodes) and fairness (i.e., how fair the node is in rating other nodes' likeability).
- **LIBFM**: LIBFM [18] is a state-of-the-art feature based factorization model. In this paper, we use the concatenated one-hot vectors of users in three networks as input to feed LIBFM.

6.3 Parameter Setttings

We design a 4-layer autoencoder in SHINE for each network, in which the hidden layer is with 1,000 units and the embedding layer is with 100 units. Deeper architectures cannot further improve the performance but incur heavier computational overhead according to our experimental results. We choose concatenation as the aggregation function g and inner product as the similarity measurement function f. Besides, we set the reconstruction weight of non-zero elements $\alpha = 10$, the balancing parameters $\lambda_1 = 1$, $\lambda_2 = 1$, $\lambda_3 = 20$, and $\lambda_4 = 0.01$ for SHINE. We will study the sensitivity of these parameters in Section 6.6. For LINE, we concatenate the first-order and second-order representations to form the final 100-dimension embeddings for each node, and the total number of samples is 100 million. For node2vec, the number of embedding dimension is set as 100. For SDNE, the reconstruction weight of non-zero elements is 10 and the weight of first-order term is 0.05. For LIBFM, the dimensionality of the factorization machine is set as $\{1, 1, 0\}$ and

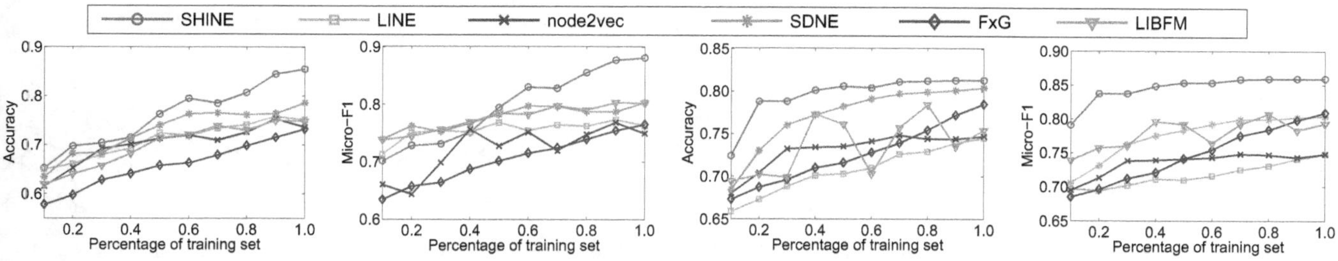

(a) Accuracy on Weibo-STC (b) Micro-F1 on Weibo-STC (c) Accuracy on Wiki-RfA (d) Micro-F1 on Wiki-RfA

Fig. 5: Accuracy and micro-F1 on Weibo-STC and Wiki-RfA for link prediction.

we use SGD method for training with learning rate of 0.5 and 200 iterations. Other parameters in these baselines are set as default.

In the following subsections, we conduct experiments on two tasks: link prediction and node recommendation.

6.4 Link Prediction

In link prediction setting, our task is to predict the sign of an unobserved link between two given nodes. As the existing links in the original network are known and can serve as the ground truth, we randomly hide 20% of links in the sentiment network and select a balanced test set (i.e., the number of positive links is the same as negative links) out of them, while use the remaining network to train SHINE as well as all baselines. We use *Accuracy* and *Micro-F1* as the evaluation metrics in link prediction task. For a more fine-grained analysis, we compare the performance while varying the percentage of training set from 10% to 100%. The result is presented in Fig. 5, from which we have the following observations:

- Fig. 5 shows that our methods SHINE achieves significant improvements in Accuracy and Micro-F1 over the baselines in both datasets. Specifically, in Weibo-STC, SHINE outperforms LINE, node2vec, and SDNE by 13.8%, 16.2%, and 8.78% respectively on Accuracy, and achieves 15.5%, 17.6%, 9.71% gains respectively on Micro-F1.
- Among the three state-of-the-art network embedding methods, SDNE performs best while LINE and node2vec show relatively poor performance. Note that SDNE also uses autoencoder to learning the embedding of nodes, which proves the superiority of autoencoder in extracting highly nonlinear representations of networks from a side.
- FxG performs much better in Wiki-RfA than in Weibo-STC. This is probably due to the following two reasons: 1) Unlike other methods, FxG cannot utilize the side information in Weibo-STC dataset. 2) Weibo-STC is sparser than Wiki-RfA, which is unfavorable to the computing of goodness and fairness of nodes in FxG model.
- Although LIBFM is not specially designed for network-structured data, it still achieves fine performance compared with other network embedding methods. However, during experiments we find that LIBFM is unstable and prone to parameters tuning. This can also be validated by the fluctuating curves of LIBFM in Fig. 5c and Fig. 5d.

To compare the performance of SHINE and baselines in cold start scenario, we construct a test set of newly arrived users for

Table 2: Comparison of models in terms of Accuracy and Micro-F1 on Weibo-STC in cold start scenario.

Model	Accuracy		Micro-F1	
	all users	new users	all users	new users
SHINE	**0.855**	**0.834**	**0.881**	**0.858**
LINE	0.751	0.664	0.763	0.739
node2vec	0.736	0.653	0.749	0.667
SDNE	0.786	0.667	0.803	0.751
FxG	0.732	0.601	0.765	0.652
LIBFM	0.748	0.639	0.802	0.746

Weibo-STC, in which the associated ordinary user of each sentiment link dose not appear in the training set. We report Accuracy and Micro-F1 for all users and new users in Table 2. From the results in Table 2 it is evident that SHINE can still maintain a decent performance in the cold start scenario, as it fully exploits the information from social network and profile network to compensate for the lack of sentiment links. By comparison, the performance of other baselines degrades significantly in cold start scenario. Specifically, the Accuracy decreases by 2.46% for SHINE and by 11.58%, 11.28%, 15.14%, 17.90%, 14.57% respectively for LINE, node2vec, SDNE, FxG and LIBFM, which proves that SHINE are more capable of effectively transferring knowledge among heterogeneous information networks, especially in cold start scenario.

6.5 Node Recommendation

In addition to link prediction, we also conduct experiments on node recommendation, in which for each user we aim to recommend a set of users who have not been explicitly expressed attitude to but may be liked by the user. The performance of node recommendation can reveal the quality of learned representations as well. Specifically, for each user, we calculate his sentiment score toward all other users, and select *K* users with largest sentiment score for recommendation. For completeness, we recommend not only the nodes that a user may like but also the nodes that he may dislike. Therefore, we use positive and negative Precision@K and Recall@K respectively for evaluation in corresponding experimental scenarios. The results are shown in Fig. 6, which provides us the following observations:

- The curve of SHINE is almost consistently above the curves of baselines, which proves that SHINE can better learn the representations of heterogeneous networks and perform recommendation than baselines.

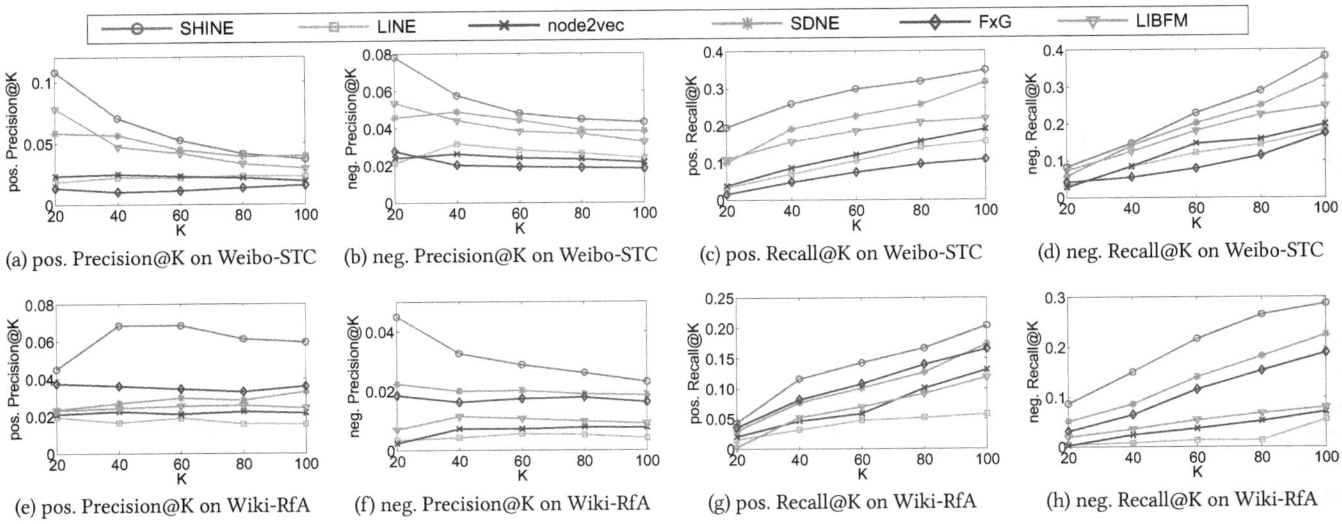

Fig. 6: Positive and negative Precision@K and Recall@K on Weibo-STC and Wiki-RfA for node recommendation.

Table 3: Accuracy on Weibo-STC w.r.t. the combinations of similarity measurement function and aggregate function.

f	g		
	Summation	Max pooling	Concatenation
Inner product	0.802	0.761	**0.855**
Euclidean distance	0.788	0.779	0.837
Logistic regression	0.816	0.782	0.842

- Negative precision is low than positive precision while negative recall is higher than positive recall for most methods. This is because negative links are far fewer than positive links in both datasets, which makes it easier to cover more negative links in the recommendation set.
- In general, the results of precision and recall on Weibo-STC is better than Wiki-RfA, which is in accordance with the results in link prediction. The reason lies in that Weibo-STC provides more side information which can greatly improve the quality of learned user representations.

6.6 Parameters Sensitivity

SHINE involves a number of hyper-parameters. In this subsection we examine how the different choices of parameters affect the Accuracy of SHINE on Weibo-STC dataset. Except for the parameter being tested, all other parameters are set as default.

Similarity measurement function f and aggregation function g. We first investigate how the similarity measurement function f and aggregation function g affect the performance by testing on all combinations of f and g, and present the results in Table 3. It is clear that the combination of inner product and concatenation achieves the best Accuracy, while max pooling performs worst, which is probably due to the reason that concatenation preserves more information out of the three types of embeddings than summation and max pooling during embedding aggregation. It should also be noted that there is no absolute advantage of all the three f functions according to the results in Table 3.

Dimension of embedding layer and reconstruction weight of non-zero elements α. We also show how the dimension of embedding layer in the three autoencoders of SHINE and the hyper-parameter α affect the performance in Fig. 7a. We have the following two observations: 1) The performance is initially improved with the increase of dimension, because more bits in embedding layer can encode more useful information. However, the performance drops when the dimension further increases, as too large number of dimensions may introduce noises which mislead the subsequent prediction. 2) α controls the reconstruction weight of non-zero elements in autoencoders. When α is too small (e.g., $\alpha = 1$), SHINE will reconstruct the zero and non-zero elements without much discrimination, which deteriorates the performance because non-zero elements are more informative than zero ones. However, the performance will decrease if α gets too large (e.g., $\alpha = 30$), because large α will lead SHINE to totally ignore the dissimilarity (i.e., zero elements) among users.

Balancing parameters λ_1, λ_2, and λ_3. λ_1, λ_2, and λ_3 balance the loss terms of the objective function in Eq. (9). We treat λ_1 and λ_2 as binary parameters and vary the value of λ_3 to study the performance of SHINE. Note that whether λ_1 or λ_2 equals 1 indicates that whether we use the additional social information or profile information in link prediction. Therefore, the study of λ_1 and λ_2 can also be seen as to validate the effectiveness of social network embedding module and profile network embedding module. The result is presented in Fig. 7b, from which we can conclude that: 1) The curve of $\lambda_1 = 1, \lambda_2 = 0$ and $\lambda_1 = 0, \lambda_2 = 1$ are both above the curve of $\lambda_1 = 0, \lambda_2 = 0$, which demonstrates the significant gain by incorporating the social information and profile information (especially the latter) into the sentiment network. Moreover, combining both additional information can further improve the performance. 2) Increasing the value of λ_3 can greatly boost the accuracy, as SHINE will concentrate more on the prediction error rather than the reconstruction error. However, similar to other hyper-parameters, too large λ_3 is not satisfactory since it breaks the trade-off among loss terms in objective function.

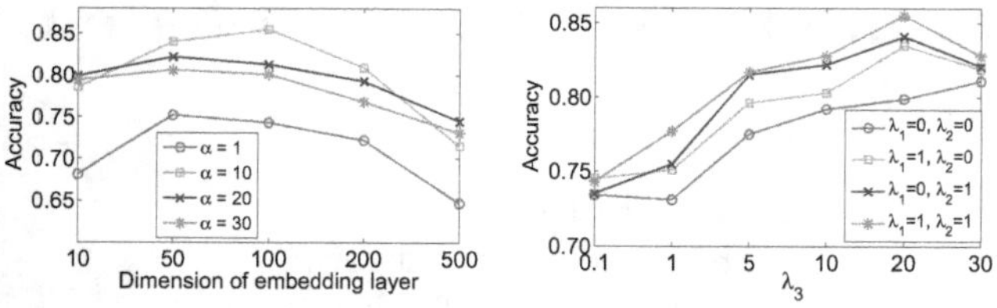

(a) dim. of embedding layer and α (b) λ_1, λ_2, and λ_3

Fig. 7: Parameter sensitivity w.r.t. the dimension of embedding layers, α, λ_1, λ_2, and λ_3.

7 CONCLUSIONS

In this paper we study the problem of predicting sentiment links in absence of sentiment related content in online social networks. We first establish a labeled, heterogeneous, and entity-level sentiment dataset from Weibo due to the lack of explicit sentiment links. To efficiently learn from these heterogeneous networks, we propose Signed Heterogeneous Information Network Embedding (SHINE), a deep-learning-based network embedding framework to extract users' highly nonlinear representations while preserving the structure of original networks. We conduct extensive experiments to evaluate the performance of SHINE. Experimental results prove the competitiveness of SHINE against several strong baselines and demonstrate the effectiveness of usage of social relation and profile information, especially in cold start scenario.

ACKNOWLEDGMENTS

We thank our anonymous reviewers for their feedback and suggestions. This work was partially sponsored by the National Basic Research 973 Program of China under Grant 2015CB352403.

REFERENCES

[1] Mikhail Belkin and Partha Niyogi. 2001. Laplacian eigenmaps and spectral techniques for embedding and clustering. In *NIPS*, Vol. 14. 585–591.

[2] Felipe Bravo-Marquez, Eibe Frank, and Bernhard Pfahringer. 2015. Positive, negative, or neutral: Learning an expanded opinion lexicon from emoticon-annotated tweets. In *IJCAI 2015*, Vol. 2015. AAAI Press, 1229–1235.

[3] Shiyu Chang, Wei Han, Jiliang Tang, Guo-Jun Qi, Charu C Aggarwal, and Thomas S Huang. 2015. Heterogeneous network embedding via deep architectures. In *Proceedings of the 21th ACM SIGKDD International Conference on Knowledge Discovery and Data Mining*. ACM, 119–128.

[4] Wanxiang Che, Zhenghua Li, and Ting Liu. 2010. Ltp: A chinese language technology platform. In *Proceedings of the 23rd International Conference on Computational Linguistics: Demonstrations*. Association for Computational Linguistics, 13–16.

[5] Xin Dong, Lei Yu, Zhonghuo Wu, Yuxia Sun, Lingfeng Yuan, and Fangxi Zhang. 2017. A Hybrid Collaborative Filtering Model with Deep Structure for Recommender Systems. In *Thirty-First AAAI Conference on Artificial Intelligence*.

[6] Cícero Nogueira Dos Santos and Maira Gatti. 2014. Deep Convolutional Neural Networks for Sentiment Analysis of Short Texts.. In *COLING*. 69–78.

[7] John Duchi, Elad Hazan, and Yoram Singer. 2011. Adaptive subgradient methods for online learning and stochastic optimization. *Journal of Machine Learning Research* 12, Jul (2011), 2121–2159.

[8] Aditya Grover and Jure Leskovec. 2016. node2vec: Scalable feature learning for networks. In *Proceedings of the 22nd ACM SIGKDD International Conference on Knowledge Discovery and Data Mining*. ACM, 855–864.

[9] Ramanthan Guha, Ravi Kumar, Prabhakar Raghavan, and Andrew Tomkins. 2004. Propagation of trust and distrust. In *Proceedings of the 13th international conference on World Wide Web*. ACM, 403–412.

[10] Xiao Huang, Jundong Li, and Xia Hu. 2017. Label informed attributed network embedding. In *Proceedings of the Tenth ACM International Conference on Web Search and Data Mining*. ACM, 731–739.

[11] Svetlana Kiritchenko, Xiaodan Zhu, Colin Cherry, and Saif Mohammad. 2014. NRC-Canada-2014: Detecting aspects and sentiment in customer reviews. In *Proceedings of the 8th International Workshop on Semantic Evaluation (SemEval 2014)*. 437–442.

[12] Srijan Kumar, Francesca Spezzano, VS Subrahmanian, and Christos Faloutsos. 2016. Edge weight prediction in weighted signed networks. In *Data Mining (ICDM), 2016 IEEE 16th International Conference on*. IEEE, 221–230.

[13] Jérôme Kunegis, Stephan Schmidt, Andreas Lommatzsch, Jürgen Lerner, Ernesto W De Luca, and Sahin Albayrak. 2010. Spectral analysis of signed graphs for clustering, prediction and visualization. In *Proceedings of the 2010 SIAM International Conference on Data Mining*. SIAM, 559–570.

[14] Jure Leskovec, Daniel Huttenlocher, and Jon Kleinberg. 2010. Predicting positive and negative links in online social networks. In *Proceedings of the 19th international conference on World wide web*. ACM, 641–650.

[15] Thien Hai Nguyen and Kiyoaki Shirai. 2015. PhraseRNN: Phrase Recursive Neural Network for Aspect-based Sentiment Analysis.. In *EMNLP*. 2509–2514.

[16] Mingdong Ou, Peng Cui, Jian Pei, Ziwei Zhang, and Wenwu Zhu. 2016. Asymmetric transitivity preserving graph embedding. In *Proc. of ACM SIGKDD*. 1105–1114.

[17] Bryan Perozzi, Rami Al-Rfou, and Steven Skiena. 2014. Deepwalk: Online learning of social representations. In *Proceedings of the 20th ACM SIGKDD international conference on Knowledge discovery and data mining*. ACM, 701–710.

[18] Steffen Rendle. 2012. Factorization machines with libfm. *ACM Transactions on Intelligent Systems and Technology (TIST)* 3, 3 (2012), 57.

[19] Hassan Saif. 2015. *Semantic Sentiment Analysis of Microblogs*. Ph.D. Dissertation. The Open University.

[20] Ruslan Salakhutdinov and Geoffrey Hinton. 2009. Semantic hashing. *International Journal of Approximate Reasoning* 50, 7 (2009), 969–978.

[21] Jiliang Tang, Shiyu Chang, Charu Aggarwal, and Huan Liu. 2015. Negative link prediction in social media. In *Proceedings of the Eighth ACM International Conference on Web Search and Data Mining*. ACM, 87–96.

[22] Jiliang Tang, Yi Chang, Charu Aggarwal, and Huan Liu. 2016. A survey of signed network mining in social media. *ACM Computing Surveys (CSUR)* 49, 3 (2016), 42.

[23] Jian Tang, Meng Qu, Mingzhe Wang, Ming Zhang, Jun Yan, and Qiaozhu Mei. 2015. Line: Large-scale information network embedding. In *Proceedings of the 24th International Conference on World Wide Web*. ACM, 1067–1077.

[24] Joshua B Tenenbaum, Vin De Silva, and John C Langford. 2000. A global geometric framework for nonlinear dimensionality reduction. *science* 290, 5500 (2000), 2319–2323.

[25] Peter D Turney. 2002. Thumbs up or thumbs down?: semantic orientation applied to unsupervised classification of reviews. In *Proceedings of the 40th annual meeting on association for computational linguistics*. Association for Computational Linguistics, 417–424.

[26] Daixin Wang, Peng Cui, and Wenwu Zhu. 2016. Structural deep network embedding. In *Proceedings of the 22nd ACM SIGKDD International Conference on Knowledge Discovery and Data Mining*. ACM, 1225–1234.

[27] Hongwei Wang, Jia Wang, Miao Zhao, Jiannong Cao, and Minyi Guo. 2017. Joint-Topic-Semantic-aware Social Recommendation for Online Voting. In *Proceedings of the 26th ACM International Conference on Conference on Information and Knowledge Management*. ACM, 347–356.

[28] Pengfei Wang, Jiafeng Guo, Yanyan Lan, Jun Xu, Shengxian Wan, and Xueqi Cheng. 2015. Learning hierarchical representation model for nextbasket recommendation. In *Proceedings of the 38th International ACM SIGIR conference on Research and Development in Information Retrieval*. ACM, 403–412.

[29] Suhang Wang, Jiliang Tang, Charu Aggarwal, Yi Chang, and Huan Liu. 2017. Signed network embedding in social media. In *Proceedings of the 2017 SIAM International Conference on Data Mining*. SIAM, 327–335.

[30] Robert West, Hristo S Paskov, Jure Leskovec, and Christopher Potts. 2014. Exploiting social network structure for person-to-person sentiment analysis. *arXiv preprint arXiv:1409.2450* (2014).

[31] Jihang Ye, Hong Cheng, Zhe Zhu, and Minghua Chen. 2013. Predicting positive and negative links in signed social networks by transfer learning. In *Proceedings of the 22nd international conference on World Wide Web*. ACM, 1477–1488.

[32] Xiao Yu, Xiang Ren, Yizhou Sun, Quanquan Gu, Bradley Sturt, Urvashi Khandelwal, Brandon Norick, and Jiawei Han. 2014. Personalized entity recommendation: A heterogeneous information network approach. In *Proceedings of the 7th ACM international conference on Web search and data mining*. ACM, 283–292.

[33] Shuhan Yuan, Xintao Wu, and Yang Xiang. 2017. SNE: Signed Network Embedding. In *Pacific-Asia Conference on Knowledge Discovery and Data Mining*. Springer, 183–195.

[34] Fuzheng Zhang, Nicholas Jing Yuan, Defu Lian, Xing Xie, and Wei-Ying Ma. 2016. Collaborative knowledge base embedding for recommender systems. In *Proceedings of the 22nd ACM SIGKDD International Conference on Knowledge Discovery and Data Mining*. ACM, 353–362.

[35] Quan Zheng and David B Skillicorn. 2015. Spectral embedding of signed networks. In *Proceedings of the 2015 SIAM International Conference on Data Mining*. SIAM, 55–63.

[36] Chang Zhou, Yuqiong Liu, Xiaofei Liu, Zhongyi Liu, and Jun Gao. 2017. Scalable Graph Embedding for Asymmetric Proximity.. In *AAAI*. 2942–2948.

A Unified Processing Paradigm for Interactive Location-based Web Search

Sheng Wang, Zhifeng Bao, Shixun Huang
RMIT University
firstname.secondname@rmit.edu.au

Rui Zhang
The University of Melbourne
rui.zhang@unimelb.edu.au

ABSTRACT

This paper studies the location-based web search and aims to build a unified processing paradigm for two purposes: (1) efficiently support each of the various types of location-based queries (kNN query, top-k spatial-textual query, etc.) on two major forms of geo-tagged data, i.e., spatial point data such as geo-tagged web documents, and spatial trajectory data such as a sequence of geo-tagged travel blogs by a user; (2) support interactive search to provide quick response for a query session, within which a user usually keeps refining her query by either issuing different query types or specifying different constraints (e.g., adding a keyword and/or location, changing the choice of k, etc.) until she finds the desired results. To achieve this goal, we first propose a general Top-k query called Monotone Aggregate Spatial Keyword query-**MASK**, which is able to cover most types of location-based web search. Next, we develop a unified indexing (called Textual-Grid-Point Inverted Index) and query processing paradigm (called ETAIL Algorithm) to answer a single **MASK** query efficiently. Furthermore, we extend ETAIL to provide interactive search for multiple queries within one query session, by exploiting the commonality of textual and/or spatial dimension among queries. Last, extensive experiments on four real datasets verify the robustness and efficiency of our approach.

ACM Reference format:
Sheng Wang, Zhifeng Bao, Shixun Huang and Rui Zhang. 2018. A Unified Processing Paradigm for Interactive Location-based Web Search. In *Proceedings of WSDM'18, February 5–9, 2018, Marina Del Rey, CA, USA, ,* 9 pages.
DOI: http://dx.doi.org/10.1145/3159652.3159667

1 INTRODUCTION

The widespread use of mobile devices with GPS enables a parade of geo-tagged web data being continually generated. Such data usually behaves in two forms: (1) a single point such as a geo-tagged document in Trip-advisor[1], (2) a trajectory which is a set or sequence of geo-tagged documents, such as a user's check-in records from Twitter[2] [42], a sequence of user's travel blogs[3], etc.

[1] https://www.tripadvisor.com/
[2] https://www.twitter.com/
[3] https://www.travelblog.org/

WSDM'18, February 5–9, 2018, Marina Del Rey, CA, USA
 ISBN 978-1-4503-5581-0/18/02...$15.00
DOI: http://dx.doi.org/10.1145/3159652.3159667

Numerous types of *location-based web search* queries [4, 8–12, 22, 23, 30, 35–37, 40, 41, 43, 47] have been proposed to retrieve such geo-tagged web data, to further support various location-aware services such as site selection, trip planning, etc, as shown in Example 1.1.

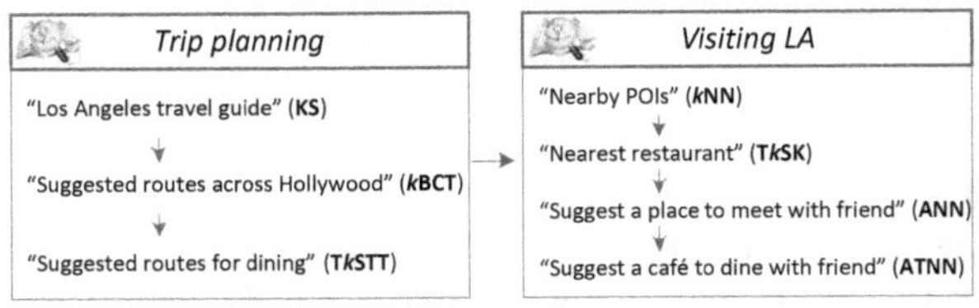

Figure 1: Exemplar queries conducted before & during a trip

Example 1.1. Grace is planning to visit *Los Angeles*, she starts her exploration by a pure keyword query (**KS**) [5] on the web to acquire initial knowledge of the famous attractions. Then she might issue a k-Best-Connected-Trajectory (k**BCT**) query [9] to find the top-k best routes (from existing travel blogs) which covers the attractions in her wish-list. Furthermore, with the Top-k Spatial-Textual Trajectory (**TkSTT**) query [30, 35, 42], she can add more keyword constraints such as preferred activities to do in the trip, to find a more personalized route to follow. After arriving in LA, Grace wants to explore the POIs around her hotel. Initially, she may do a k-Nearest Neighbor (k**NN**) query [19] search as she does not figure out which keywords to use for searching. After getting the results, she may use some keywords to add more constraints to further filter unrelated objects. It is known as Top-k Spatial Keyword (**TkSK**) query [12, 40]. Besides, she may want to find a place to meet her friends attending WSDM, which is known as Aggregate Nearest Neighbour (**ANN**) query [24] and Aggregate Textual Nearest Neighbour (**ATNN**) query [37].

It is desired to support the above queries (in Figure 1) related to location-based web data in one map-based search interface, say Google Maps (although it only supports keyword query so far). In a query session, a user may issue several queries of the same type (with different settings on textual or spatial dimension), or even different types of queries, along her exploration of the unknown data, until finding the desired objects for different purposes. Therefore, it is critical to provide quick response to various queries (probably issued in one query session), to achieve an interactive search experience [21, 43]. A straightforward approach is to adopt the above standalone work to handle each type of query; however, it is expensive in both storage and computation cost, thus failing to provide interactive search. Furthermore, an extensive literature study shows that, *no existing work can support any of the above queries over both point data and trajectory data simultaneously.*

Therefore, the first goal is to build a unified index and query processing paradigm to answer various types of location-based search queries on both spatial point data and spatial trajectory data. The second goal is to support interactive search to provide quick response for a query session consisting of different types or settings of query. We made the following contributions to achieve them:

- By studying those most common top-k queries over geo-tagged objects in academia comprehensively (Section 2), we propose the Monotone Aggregate Spatial Keyword query-**MASK** which can represent most of them (Section 3).
- We develop an efficient search framework for **MASK**, including an index called **TGP** composed by grid-index and inverted lists tightly, and an efficient search paradigm-ETAIL (Section 4).
- We highlight three common refinements of the queries over geo-tagged web data, and propose an optimized RETAIL by reusing scanned objects, to achieve an interactive search experience (Section 5).
- We conduct extensive experimental evaluations over four real datasets to verify the efficiency and generality of our approach (Section 6).

2 PRELIMINARIES & RELATED WORK

Table 1: An overview of existing top-*k* queries over geo-tagged data. The column for "Index" only lists the representative index structure.

Query	Input	Output	Similarity	Index
KS [5, 13, 16]	keywords	points	TF-IDF	Inverted list
*k*NN [3, 19, 29]	point	points	Euclidean	R-tree
T*k*SK [11, 22, 40, 41]	point, keywords	points	Aggregate	IR-tree
ANN [24, 38, 48]	points	points	Aggregate	R-tree
ATNN [23, 37]	points, keywords	points	Aggregate	IR-tree
*k*BCT [9, 25, 34]	points	trajectories	Aggregate	R-tree
T*k*STT [30, 35, 42]	points, keywords	trajectories	Aggregate	Grid index, Inverted list

2.1 Single-point Search

Spatial-only Query. A spatial-only query usually behaves in two forms: (1) a *k-nearest neighbours* (*k*NN) query, where given a spatial point p representing user's current location and a k, finding the *k*NN of p in the data repository; (2) a *range query* which finds all objects falling within a region (which could be rectangle or circle). For example, a *k*NN query can be *"find the 3 nearest ATMs around my hotel"*, and a range query can be finding all the ATMs in city.
General Methodology: R-tree [19] is one of the most popular index structures for efficient spatial searching. By judging whether the minimum distance between the query and the node of index is bigger than the distance to the current k-th result, or whether the node intersects with the query range, a batch of objects can be skipped directly.

Keyword-only Query. The keyword-only query is also an important entry to explore geo-tagged data. For example, people might want to search nearby restaurants by keywords *"tacos restaurant"* (in Google Maps) when they go to *Los Angeles*. It usually behaves in two forms: (1) a textual boolean query (*conjunctive search*), where the objects that contain all query keywords are returned as results. However, a textual boolean query is too strict when a query has multiple keywords. (2) a Top-k Keyword query (*disjunctive search*) which returns the top-k objects ranked by the similarities of objects w.r.t. the query. Here, we focus on the top-k keyword query.

General Methodology: Term-at-a-time (TAAT) and Document-at-a-time (DAAT) are two main types of search paradigm [5] in the area of information retrieval. The inverted list on each term can be used to filter those objects that do not contain any keyword of the query. In term of the similarity metric, TF-IDF [27] and Language Model [31] are two widely adopted ones.

Spatial-keyword Query. The spatial-keyword query evolves from the spatial-only query by having a further constraint on textual dimension, and can be further divided into three general groups [7]: 1) *Boolean Range Query* [20], e.g., finding all the Mexican restaurants in the CBD; 2) *Boolean kNN Query* [14], e.g., finding 3 nearest Mexican restaurants around my hotel; 3) *Top-k Spatial-keyword Query* [12, 40], e.g., finding 3 restaurants which could serve lobster, pizza or steak and are also close to my hotel.
General Methodology: Most work [7, 40] proposed to use the inverted lists on top of an existing tree-structured index (say R-tree) to deal with spatial-keyword search. The inverted list can be as simple as indicating the existence of a particular keyword to serve the boolean part of the query, or as complex as incorporating the weight of the keywords to serve the similarity computation for Top-k spatial-keyword query.

2.2 Multiple-point Search

Search over Points. Given a set of points, Papadias et al. [24] searched k Nearest Neighbour points in term of the aggregate distance of each neighbor to query points, and it is called *Aggregate Nearest Neighbour* (ANN) search. Li et al. [23], Yao et al. [37] proposed *Aggregate Textual Nearest Neighbour* (ATNN) search based on ANN by adding keywords in query. The similarity is an aggregation of the spatial proximity to the query locations and textual similarity to the query keywords.

Search over Trajectories. Given a set of points, Chen et al. [9] proposed a *k Best Connected Trajectories* (*k*BCT) query, in order to find the trajectories that are among the k-closest ones to the query points. The distance between trajectory and query is an aggregation of the shortest distance from each point (in trajectory T) to the points in query. Subsequently, *Top-k Spatial-Textual Trajectory* search evolves from the spatial-only search by incorporating keywords into the query and its search method [30, 35, 42]. In particular, a keyword could be associated with either a designated query point like [35] for a fine-grained search, or associated with the whole trajectory for a coarse-grained search like [30, 42].

2.3 Query Refinement

Query refinement originates from web search, where users have to reformulate their queries 40% to 52% of the time in order to find their desired results [32]. It can be caused by many different reasons: there do not exist matching results in the data repository that matches users' search intentions [18, 21, 39], or there is a mismatch between users' search intentions and their formulated queries (due to spelling errors, limited domain knowledge, etc.) [45]. For example, Grace is searching "3 nearest restaurants", and gets 3 results which contain Mexican food that Grace likes a lot, so she further changes the query as "3 nearest Mexican restaurants".

Query refinement applies to not only textual search, but also spatial search. One type of query refinement is the moving object query [36], where the query location keeps moving. A common methodology is to propose the concept of "safe zone", within which the up-to-date top-k results remain unchanged while it triggers a re-computation when it walks out of the safe zone. For spatial point data, the most recent work is to execute the refinement on both spatial dimension (in term of relaxing the search range) and textual dimension (via approximate string matching methods) [45].

2.4 Summary

To summarize, we observe that none of existing work can handle the single point search and multiple-point search over the point data and the trajectory data at the same time. Such limitation behaves in two-folds: a unified index to support most common query operators is missing; a unified query processing approach to handle various types of queries is missing. Moreover, it remains an open problem on how to support an interactive search where users may change the type of query or the parameters (like k, keywords) for a certain type of query.

3 PROBLEM DEFINITION

In this section, we formally define the *Top-k Monotone Aggregate Spatial Keyword Query*, which is a generalized form of most existing spatial-only and spatial-textual queries (over both the point data and trajectory data) as described in Section 2.

Definition 3.1. **(Point)** In a data repository D, a point $p = (\rho, \psi)$ is a pair consisting of the location ρ and a set of associated terms $\psi = (t_1, t_2, \ldots, t_i)$ describing ρ and/or users' activities at ρ.

Definition 3.2. **(Trajectory)** A trajectory T of length l is in the form of $\{p_1, p_2, \ldots, p_l\}$, where each p_i is a point.

As trajectory [30, 35] and point [7] are two main forms of geo-tagged data, in this paper we use object o uniformly to represent trajectory and point.

Definition 3.3. **(Query)** A query Q is a set of points in the form of $\{q_1, q_2, \ldots, q_m\}$. Specifically, $Q_s = \{\rho_1, \rho_2, \ldots, \rho_m\}$ is the query location set, and $Q_t = \bigcup_{i=1}^{m} \psi_i$ is the query keyword set, i.e., $m = |Q_s|$ and $n = |Q_t|$, m and n cannot be 0 at the same time.

By reviewing existing widely used similarity models on Top-k search [5, 9, 19, 22, 23, 27, 30, 35–37, 40, 41, 43], we can generalize them as the below definition:

Definition 3.4. **(Monotone Aggregate Similarity)** The similarity of an object o w.r.t. a query Q is defined in the below equation:

$$\hat{S}(Q, o) = \alpha \cdot \sum_{\rho \in Q_s} SProx(\rho, o.\rho) + (1 - \alpha) \cdot \sum_{\psi \in Q_t} TRel(\psi, o.\psi) \quad (1)$$

where $SProx(\rho, o.\rho)$ is the spatial proximity between $o.\rho$ and ρ, $TRel(\rho, o.\psi)$ is the textual relevance between ψ and $o.\psi$, and $\alpha \in [0, 1]$ is a query preference parameter that makes it possible to balance the spatial proximity and textual relevance, and it is always set as 0.5.

Spatial proximity. $SProx(\rho, o.\rho)$ is defined as the normalized minimum Euclidean distance from ρ to $o.\rho$, computed as:

$$SProx(\rho, o.\rho) = 1 - \frac{\min_{p_j \in o.\rho} dist(\rho, p_j)}{dist_{max}} \quad (2)$$

where $dist(\rho, p_j)$ is the *Euclidean distance* between p_j and q, and $dist_{max}$ is the maximum distance between any two objects in D. Besides the Euclidean distance, the distance function can also be the *road network distance* [38]. In this paper, we focus on the more widely used Euclidean distance function.

Textual relevance. For $TRel(\psi, o.\psi)$, similar to [5, 9, 22, 23, 30, 35–37, 40, 41, 43], we use a scoring model such as TF-IDF which is also a monotone aggregate function.

$$TRel(\psi, o.\psi) = \sum_{t \in \psi \cap o.\psi} w(t, o.\psi) \quad (3)$$

where $w(t, o.\psi)$ is a normalized similarity weight of keyword t in $o.\psi$, and the maximum value of weight is 1. In our experiment, we compute the weight of each term in an object by their occurrence numbers over the number of all keywords in the object. Beside, our framework can be modified to fit other textual similarity models that can be answered efficiently using inverted list, such as Language Model [31] and BM25 [26], we leave these details for future work.

Taking the most recent spatial-textual trajectory search work [35] for example, it combines the textual and spatial similarity at point-to-point level. It is actually also an instance of Equation 1, because for each point in the query, only the data point o that maximizes the similarity is chosen to contribute to the overall similarity $\hat{S}(Q, o)$ in Equation 1.

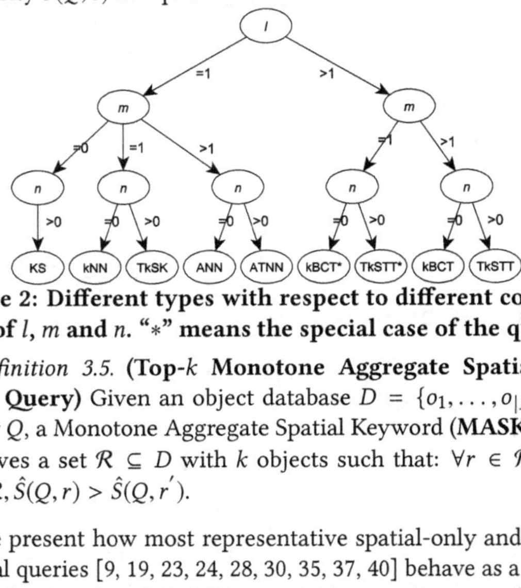

Figure 2: Different types with respect to different combination of l, m and n. "*" means the special case of the query.

Definition 3.5. **(Top-k Monotone Aggregate Spatial Keyword Query)** Given an object database $D = \{o_1, \ldots, o_{|D|}\}$ and query Q, a Monotone Aggregate Spatial Keyword (**MASK**) query retrieves a set $\mathcal{R} \subseteq D$ with k objects such that: $\forall r \in \mathcal{R}, \forall r' \in D - \mathcal{R}, \hat{S}(Q, r) > \hat{S}(Q, r')$.

We present how most representative spatial-only and spatial-textual queries [9, 19, 23, 24, 28, 30, 35, 37, 40] behave as a specific form of our proposed **MASK** query in Figure 2. For example, when $l = 1$, $m = 1$ and $n = 0$, it becomes a spatial-only kNN query over point data [19]; when $l > 1$, $m > 1$ and $n > 0$, it becomes a spatial-textual kNN query over trajectory data [35].

4 A UNIFIED PROCESSING PARADIGM

4.1 Preliminary

Threshold Algorithm. In order to avoid scanning every object $o \in D$ to get top-k results, the threshold algorithm (**TA**) of Fagin et al. [17] is used as a filtering method when accessing the ranked lists (sorted by the term weight of objects). The filtering method proceeds in three steps: **1)** for each query term, its ranking list is scanned sequentially so that objects with high similarity scores are scanned first; **2)** compute the similarity of scanned objects and update the top-k result heap; **3)** check whether the k-th result has a higher score than the upper bound of the unscanned objects (Spotted area), terminate if yes, otherwise jump to Step 1. Specifically, the upper bound is the sum of score in the current rows of each inverted list. It is worth noting that the ranked list can be divided into blocks to reduce I/Os, which is known as the *block-based early termination* [15, 16].

While in principle a similar idea can be adopted to suit search purpose, using the algorithm of Fagin et al. directly does not work because the top-k list for every point in the query is not known a priori. For example, when the query in Figure 1 comes, we can get the inverted lists for "Restaurant" and "Mexican" easily, but cannot get the inverted lists for locations. Hence, how to build a spatial inverted list for a query location is crucial to extend the threshold algorithm to handle our **MASK** query.

4.2 Index Structure-TGP

Our index is called as the Textual-Grid-Point Inverted Lists (TGP) index. The index structure consists of three components.

- Textual Inverted List (TIL). The key is a unique keyword in the database D, the value is the list which stores the ids of all points that contain this keyword in D. Similar to the impact-sorted indexes [33], it sorts the lists by a descending order of term weight, and divides the lists into blocks of fixed size. We can determine how many blocks are loaded one time based on the number of points. Let $\mathcal{I}$ denote the inverted list of ψ, each block in $\mathcal{I}$ has a maximum weight $\hat{\mathcal{I}}^{\uparrow}(\psi, it)$ and a minimum weight $\hat{\mathcal{I}}^{\downarrow}(\psi, it)$, where the it is the iteration number of loading, and every list has it_{max} blocks.
- Grid Inverted Lists (GIL). The whole space is divided into grids of equal size, and each leaf cell is assigned a unique id using the z-curve cross-coding [40] (see Figure 3). An incremental *round expansion* method [35] is adopted to access the points around the query location, from near to distant. Similar to the bounds of each block in **TIL**, the upper bound of the similarity of unscanned points (along the spatial inverted list) for ρ after it iterations, is denoted by $\hat{\mathcal{G}}^{\uparrow}(\rho, it)$, where $\mathcal{G}$ is the **GIL** for ρ.

Within each grid cell, we create its associated **TIL**, so we only need to access the objects which have at least one common textual keyword with the query.

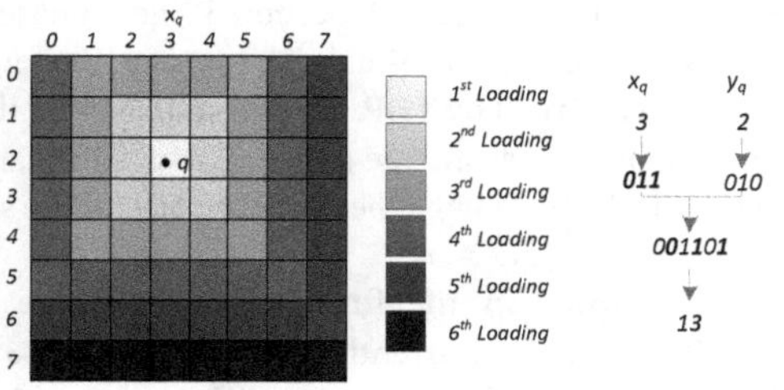

(a) Grid Inverted List (b) Cross-coding

Figure 3: (a) Incremental expansion around the query location within a Grid-index; (b) Labelling a grid cell by Z-curve cross-coding, i.e., picking bit from each binary code successively to form a new code, e.g., bold numbers are from x_q.

- Point Inverted List (PIL). Recall Section 2 all existing work such as [30, 35, 42] on top-k trajectory search model a trajectory as a set (or sequence) of points, and their proposed query processing method is built at point granularity. Therefore, we create an inverted index to store a mapping from a point to its corresponding trajectories.

Compressible Index. Our index is composed by inverted lists, each list contains equal number of blocks, and each block stores an array of object ids. Thereby, an array A can be compressed into an array B with fewer integers using the *integer compression* technology [1]. With the corresponding efficient decompression that converts B to A, the query can be conducted without much change, and the performance will not be affected.

4.3 Operators over TGP

By having **TGP** as the index for dataset D, in order to filter objects effectively, we access candidate objects in a batch-wise way from the near to the distant. To access the points and their corresponding objects, we define three main operators.

TextualIterator. Given a query keyword ψ, *TextualIterator* is invoked to get the it-th block from the beginning of textual inverted list **TIL**, as well as the upper bound of the similarity from the query to the unseen objects.

SpatialIterator. Given a query location ρ, in the it-th iteration to access the candidate points, *SpatialIterator* is invoked to get a set of grid-cells in the following way: **1)** get the grid label x_q, y_q on x and y axis of the query location; **2)** compute the x and y value of grid-cells which are going to be scanned; **3)** return the z-curve label by cross-coding as described in Figure 3(b); **4)** find those cells using the labels.

CoveredObjects. Based on the **PIL**, given a set of points, *CoveredObjects* returns all the objects that cover those points. It mainly works for the queries over trajectory data, and can be omitted when dealing with the queries over point data as the object is point itself.

The three operators above can help us achieve the first step of *Threshold Algorithm* in Section 4.1, i.e., scanning the inverted list sequentially. Based on the scanned objects, we will describe how to filter the unseen objects and return top-k result of Step 2 and 3.

4.4 Early Termination & Abandoning over Inverted Lists

As mentioned in our index structure, we expand the search of new candidates from the near to the distant in an incremental way. There are two main challenges: (1) how to stop the expansion as early as possible to reduce the search space; (2) how to efficiently compute the similarity between a candidate and the query. Since we do not store the whole object in the inverted list of a certain term, more random accesses are needed to compute the real similarity between the object and the query. To this end, we propose *early termination* and *early abandoning* on top of our **TGP** to address challenge 1 and 2 respectively. In particular, we propose an algorithm called Early Termination & Abandoning over Inverted Lists-ETAIL, as shown in Algorithm 1.

Early Termination. After several iterations of scanning candidates $R(q_i)$, we can stop expansion based on whether the best of unseen objects can beat all the current top-k result $\mathcal{R}$. More details can be found from Lines 1 to 11. Line 11 shows the condition for early termination. The bound computation can be found in Section 4.4.1.

Early Abandoning. Before computing the real similarity, we can estimate the upper bound of each candidate's similarity (see Section 4.4.2 for details on upper bound estimation), then determine whether it is bigger than the current $\mathcal{R}$. If so, we will compute the real similarity by accessing the details of each candidate; otherwise, we skip this candidate. Lines 12 to 22 show the details. The terminating condition can be found in the gray area before Line 22.

Algorithm 1: ETAIL Algorithm

Input: Object database D, query Q, k
Output: Top-k result set $\mathcal{R}$

1 $it \leftarrow 1$; $\mathcal{R} \leftarrow \emptyset$; $D_c \leftarrow \emptyset$;
2 **while** $|D_c| < |D|$ **do**
3   **foreach** $q_i \in Q$ **do**
4     $R(q_i) \leftarrow$ TextualIterator $(q_i, it-1, it, TIL)$;
5     $R(q_i) \leftarrow R(q_i) \cup$ SpatialIterator $(q_i, it-1, it, GIL)$;
6   $it \leftarrow it + 1$;
7   $D_c \leftarrow D_c \cup \bigcup_{i=1}^{|Q|}$ CoveredObjects $(R(q_i), PIL)$;
8   **if** $|D_c| > k$ **then**
9   Compute $\hat{S}^{\uparrow}(Q, D - D_c)$ (by Equation 4);
10   Compute $\hat{S}^{\downarrow}(Q, \mathcal{R})$ (by Equation 5);
11   **if** $\hat{S}^{\downarrow}(Q, \mathcal{R}) > \hat{S}^{\uparrow}(Q, D - D_c)$ **then**
12       $seen\_UB[] = \bigcup_{o \in D_c} \hat{S}^{\uparrow}(Q, o)$ (Equation 7);
13   Sort D_c by $seen\_UB[]$ in decreasing order;
14   **foreach** $o_i \in D_c$ **do**
15   Compute $\hat{S}(Q, o_i)$ (Equation 1);
16   **if** $|\mathcal{R}| < k$ **then**
17   Insert o_i in $\mathcal{R}$ and update the order;
18   **else**
19   **if** $\hat{S}(Q, o_i) > \hat{S}(Q, \mathcal{R}[k])$ **then**
20   Replace $\mathcal{R}[k]$ with o_i;
21   **if** $\hat{S}(Q, \mathcal{R}[k]) > seen\_UB[i+1]$ **then**
22   break;
23   **return** $\mathcal{R}$;

4.4.1 Bounds for Early Termination. Here we discuss how to achieve an early termination without scanning the whole database D. Based on our lower bound similarity of the k-th object in the result heap (chosen from the scanned objects D_c). The upper bound of unscanned objects in $D - D_c$ can be computed as:

$$\hat{S}^{\uparrow}(Q, D-D_c) = \alpha \cdot \sum_{\rho_i \in Q_s} \hat{\mathcal{G}}^{\uparrow}(\rho_i, it) + (1-\alpha) \cdot \sum_{\psi_j \in Q_t} \hat{\mathcal{I}}^{\uparrow}(\psi_j, it) \quad (4)$$

where $\hat{\mathcal{G}}^{\uparrow}(\rho_i, it)$ and $\hat{\mathcal{I}}^{\uparrow}(\psi_j, it)$ are the upper bound of unscanned spatial and textual inverted lists for ψ and ρ after it iterations, then the similarity of worst one in the current top-k result can be computed as:

$$\hat{S}^{\downarrow}(Q, \mathcal{R}) = \min_{o \in \mathcal{R}} \hat{S}^{\downarrow}(Q, o) \quad (5)$$

4.4.2 Bounds for Early Abandoning. For each scanned object in D_c, we will compute its upper bound similarity without randomly accessing the missing part, i.e., using less computation to estimate the best case. If the upper bound is smaller than the k-th best result, we will discard it; otherwise, we need to compute the real similarity by accessing the missing part and further check whether it can replace the current k-th result. We choose to sort the upper bounds set $seen\_UB[]$ in line 13 of Algorithm 1, as it enables potential candidates to be scanned earlier, if the current result set is better than the $(i+1)$-th candidate, and all the following candidates are worse with a smaller upper bound, so we can break in line 22.

Particularly, the lower bound for object o can be computed as:

$$\hat{S}^{\downarrow}(Q, o) = \alpha \cdot \sum_{\rho \in Q_s} SProx_{it}^{\downarrow}(\rho, o.\rho) + (1-\alpha) \cdot \sum_{\psi \in Q_t} TRel_{it}^{\downarrow}(\psi, o.\psi) \quad (6)$$

where $SProx_{it}^{\downarrow}(\rho_i, o.\rho) = 0$ if o is not scanned yet in the inverted lists of ρ_i, otherwise $SProx_{it}^{\downarrow}(\rho_i, o.\rho) = SProx(\rho_i, o.\rho)$.

Since the similarities of some terms have not been computed yet, we need to fill the gaps using the maximum similarity of each term. Then the upper bound of o can be computed as:

$$\hat{S}^{\uparrow}(Q, o) = \alpha \cdot \sum_{\rho \in Q_s} SProx_{it}^{\uparrow}(\rho, o.\rho) + (1-\alpha) \cdot \sum_{\psi \in Q_t} TRel_{it}^{\uparrow}(\psi, o.\psi) \quad (7)$$

where $SProx_{it}^{\uparrow}(\rho_i, o.\rho) = \hat{\mathcal{G}}^{\uparrow}(\rho_i, it)$ if o is not scanned yet in the inverted lists of ρ_i, otherwise $SProx_{it}^{\uparrow}(\rho_i, o.\rho) = SProx(\rho_i, o.\rho)$.

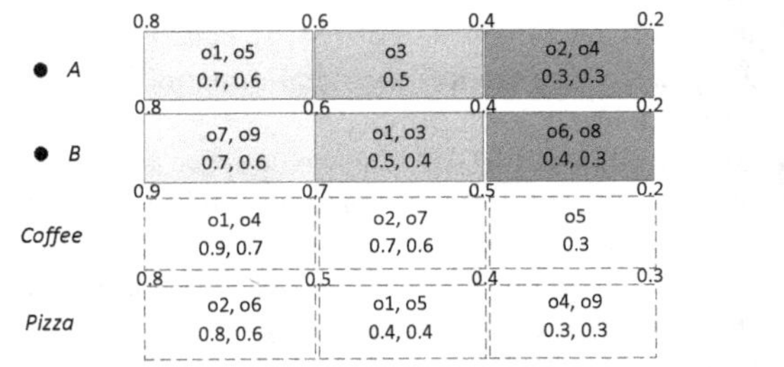

Figure 4: The loaded index structure for ATNN query $Q = \{A, B,$ "Coffee", "Pizza", $3\}$.

Example 4.1. Here we use an example to illustrate how we achieve early termination and abandoning as shown in Figure 4. Figure 4 shows an ATNN [37] search. Grace is at location A, and wants to meet with friend who is at location B. They choose "Coffee" and "Pizza" as preferences for restaurants to meet. The four partial inverted lists are returned by **TGP**. The two numbers in the upper corners of each block indicate the range of similarities among all objects in this block. The number below each object is the similarity of this object w.r.t. the query.

Early Termination: In the first iteration, we get objects $\{o1, o2, o4, o5, o6, o7, o9\}$. Currently, $\hat{S}^{\uparrow}(D - D_c) = 0.6 + 0.6 + 0.7 + 0.5 = 2.4$. For $o1$, the lower bound $0.7 + 0.9 = 1.6$ which ranks 1 in the top-3 list, another two best are $\{o2 = 0.8, o7 = 0.7\}$, so the $\hat{S}^{\downarrow}(Q, \mathcal{R}) = 0.7 < 2.4$. We keep loading more points. Until that third iteration whose upper bound reduces to $\hat{S}^{\uparrow}(D - D_c) = 0.2 + 0.2 + 0.2 + 0.3 = 0.9$, the lower bound of $o1$ are: $0.7 + 0.5 + 0.9 + 0.4 = 2.5$, then top-3 are: $\{o1 : 2.5, o2 : 1.6, o5 : 1.3\}$. Hence, $\hat{S}^{\downarrow}(Q, \mathcal{R}) = 1.3 > \hat{S}^{\uparrow}(D - D_c) = 0.9$, we terminate.

Early Abandoning: After termination, we have 9 candidate objects: $o1 - o9$. To check whether each of them can be the result, we compare it with the current top-3 results. For example, for the object $o8$ in the loaded inverted list of location B, its upper bound $\hat{S}^{\uparrow}(Q, o8) = 0.3 + 0.2 + 0.2 + 0.3 = 1 < \hat{S}^{\downarrow}(Q, \mathcal{R}) = 1.3$, thus we can skip $o8$ without further computing its real similarity by accessing the rest unloaded part in the inverted list.

4.5 Discussion on Supporting Boolean Queries

Besides top-k queries with monotone aggregate similarity function, our index TGP can also support three kinds of boolean queries which do not have the constraint of k. 1) For a range query, we can find all the grid cells that locate inside or intersect with query range, then access the objects inside the cells and refine it. 2) For a textual boolean query which finds the objects that contain all the keywords of the query, it will be easier as we can fetch the related **TIL** and conduct join operation. 3) For a boolean range query [20] that finds all the objects that contain the query keywords and locate in a query range, we can further access the node-level inverted list in a grid cell after conducting the range query.

5 OPTIMIZATION FOR QUERY REFINEMENT

In this section, we would like to discuss how to optimize the performance of processing continuous multiple queries from a user, which have many overlaps among each other.

5.1 Query Refinement

Definition 5.1. **(Query session)** A query session $\mathcal{S}$ which origins from query Q is composed by a set of queries with continuous refinements on Q.

Generally, the refinements are divided into following three types, which can be combined with each other or itself to compose $\mathcal{S}$.

Definition 5.2. **(Refinement on Keywords)** A query Q is refined to query Q' when a set of keywords $Q_t(\Delta)$ are added into or deleted from the query, denoted as $Q \xrightarrow{Q_t(\Delta)} Q'$.

Definition 5.3. **(Refinement on Points)** A query Q is refined to query Q' when a set of points $Q_s(\Delta)$ are added into or deleted from the query, denoted as $Q \xrightarrow{Q_s(\Delta)} Q'$.

Definition 5.4. **(Refinement on k)** A query Q is refined to query Q' when the user changes the expected number of returned results, denoted as $Q \xrightarrow{k(\Delta)} Q'$.

Figure 5 shows an example for each of the three types of refinements within $\mathcal{S}$. For any two *adjacent queries* Q and Q', there is a high chance that many objects can be candidates for both Q and Q' as they share query locations or (partial) keywords. Therefore, instead of simply invoking Algorithm 1 twice to process two queries independently, we propose to reuse those scanned objects of Q for Q', thereby save computation and IO costs.

5.2 Reusable Scanned Objects

To maintain the scanned objects of Q, we add a new operator called **ReuseBlock**, whose job is to maintain the intermediate inverted lists of query locations and query keywords. For the refined query Q', we can find the shared keywords $Q'_t \cap Q_t$ and locations $Q'_s \cap Q_s$ and

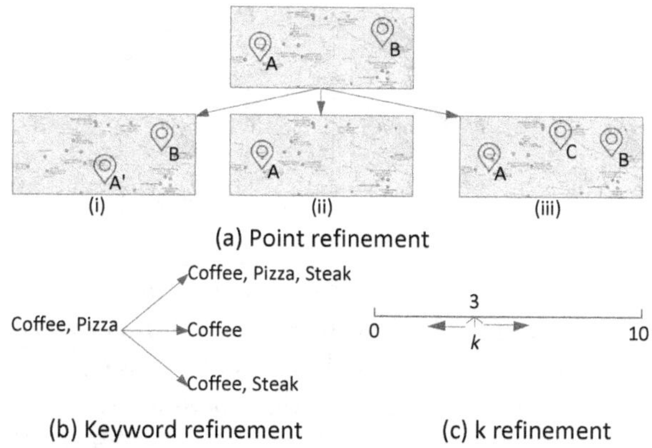

Figure 5: Three kinds of query refinements over geo-tagged data: a) refinement on points, some location(s) in the query i) move, ii) are deleted or iii) are added; b) keywords in the query are i) added, ii) deleted or iii) replaced; c) k is increased or decreased.

reuse their inverted lists without reloading it. Besides the scanned objects of the $Q_t(\Delta)$, we also record the number of iterations to get top-k result of Q, as we may need to conduct more iterations to load more new candidates. We denote the scanned objects and number of iterations as $C(Q).D_c$ and $C(Q).it$ respectively. For the new query keywords and locations $Q_t(\Delta)$ and $Q_s(\Delta)$, we also need to fill the gaps of inverted lists before conducting new expansions for more iterations. We incorporate the optimization above into ETAIL named *Reusable* ETAIL (RETAIL), which supports all three kinds of refinements. Details can be found in Algorithm 2. Next we give a running example of Algorithm 2.

Algorithm 2: RETAIL Algorithm

Input: Trajectory database D, query Q', k, maintained data of former query Q: $C(Q)$
Output: Top-k result set $\mathcal{R}$

$Q_t(\Delta) \leftarrow Q'_t - Q'_t \cap Q_t$, $Q_s(\Delta) \leftarrow Q'_s - Q'_s \cap Q_s$;
$it \leftarrow C(Q).it$, $\mathcal{R} \leftarrow \emptyset$, $D_c \leftarrow C(Q).D_c$;
while $|D_c| < |D|$ **do**
  foreach $\psi \in Q_t(\Delta)$ **do**
    $R_{it}(\psi) \leftarrow$ TextualIterator $(\psi, 0, it, TIL)$;
    $D_c \leftarrow D_c \cup$ CoveredObjects $(R_{it}(\psi), PIL)$;
  foreach $\rho \in Q_s(\Delta)$ **do**
    $R_{it}(\rho) \leftarrow$ SpatialIterator $(\rho, 0, it, GIL)$;
    $D_c \leftarrow D_c \cup$ CoveredObjects $(R_{it}(\rho), PIL)$;
  Same to Line 8 to 23 of Algorithm 1;
  $it \leftarrow it + 1$;

Example 5.5. Figure 6 shows two adjacent queries, Q and Q', for the working example of Figure 4. Q takes three iterations to find the top-3 results. Specifically, it has four inverted lists. When a new query Q' comes, since it shares two keywords and one location with Q, we can reuse the inverted lists directly, to avoid loading inverted lists again. As Q' has a new keyword "*Steak*" and a new location A', we will conduct 3 iterations separately based on $it = 3$ in Q to fill the gap of inverted lists (see the black spotted area).

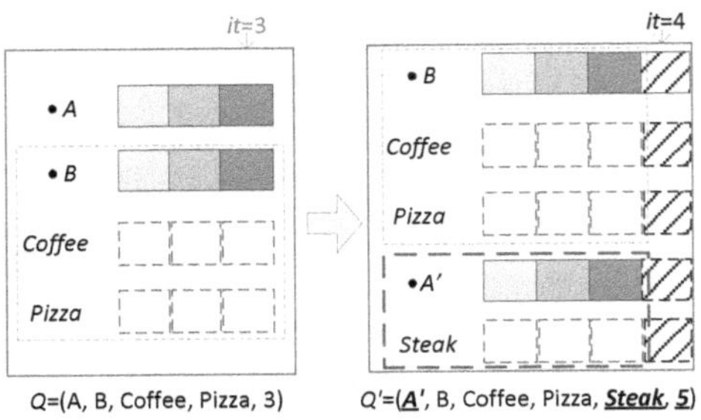

Figure 6: Making loaded objects of Q reusable for an adjacent query Q', the blocks in the red box are reused for Q'.

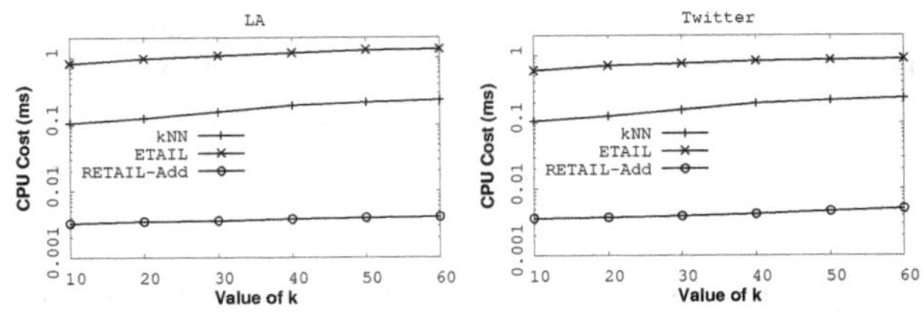

Figure 7: Comparison with [19] by increasing k.

Table 2: Four datasets for experiments.

	LA [2]	*Twitter* [6]	*GeoLife* [46]	*T-drive* [44]
#Points	215, 614	2, 267, 789	19, 476, 949	17, 511, 809
#Keywords	14.67	6.92	N/A	N/A
#Trajectories	31, 557	N/A	16, 438	10, 290
Range	Los Angeles	California & Nevada	Beijing	Beijing

Table 3: Parameter setting.

Parameter	Value
$\|Q\|$: Number of points in Q	1,2,3,4,5,6,7,8,9,10
$\|q.\psi\|$: Number of keywords in query point q	3,4,5,6,7,8,9,10
k: Number of results	10,20,30,40,50,60
α: Similarity weight in Equation 1	0.5
it_{max}: Number of blocks in **TIL** and **GIL**	150

6 EXPERIMENTS

6.1 Settings

Datasets. We take one point dataset and three trajectory datasets. Table 2 shows the statistics of these 4 datasets. Note that *LA* and *Twitter* are two check-in datasets from Foursquare and Twitter, while *LA* can be used as a trajectory dataset by linking multiple check-in points from the same user. *GeoLife* and *T-drive* are two spatial-only trajectory datasets from Beijing, which record the movements of people and taxi respectively, and have much higher sampling rate than the check-in datasets, they are mainly used to test the scalability of our algorithms for their huge amounts.

Query Generation. For each dataset, we generate a query pool randomly according to the range and vocabulary of each dataset. Each query pool contains 1, 000 lines and each line is a full query with 10 points and 10 keywords. To generate a query, we can select a full query from the pool first. Then, we reformulate it by deleting a few of last points and keywords according to the setting of parameters $|Q|$ and $|q.\psi|$ in each running. Details about the parameter setting of the query can be found in Table 3, where the default values are underlined. Moreover, all the queries reformulated from a same full query can compose a query session $\mathcal{S}$, then we can also verify our RETAIL proposed in Section 5.

Evaluation Metrics. We explored the running time of all approaches in Section 6.2 and the footprint of their index structures in Section 6.2.4. All experimental results are averaged by running all 1, 000 queries. All algorithms are implemented in Java, and run on a PC with an Intel(R) Core(TM) i7-2630QM CPU (8 CPUs) and 8GB RAM & 480GB Kingstom SSD using Windows 10, and our index **TGP** resides in the main memory.

6.2 Performance Evaluation

Before presenting the experimental results on point and trajectory data, we first show our main purposes and the observations.

6.2.1 Purposes and Overall Observations. We will verify:
1) whether our unified algorithm ETAIL has comparable performance with existing standalone methods. As our index can support multiple types of queries, we selected kNN [19], ATNN [37] which also covers ANN [24], TkSK [12], kBCT [25] and TkSTT [35] as 5 representative query types, and choose the state-of-the-art (as cited) to compare with ETAIL, R-tree [19, 29] is chosen for kNN as it is the test-of-the-time work. We observe that:

(1) Our **TGP** index can support all 5 types of queries efficiently, and it does not even occupy the largest space.
(2) For three query dependent parameters k, $|q.\psi|$ and $|Q|$, ETAIL can beat most state-of-the-art methods over all 4 datasets with a smaller index size, and by more than one order of magnitude at most, and 5 times in average.
(3) With the increase of k, $|q.\psi|$ and $|Q|$, the running time increases as more candidates need to be scanned.

2) whether our RETAIL can improve the performance of interactive search. We add two more groups of experiments for a same query session to verify RETAIL from different perspectives. Specifically, our algorithms are denoted as RETAIL-Add which starts from a simplest query to full query (keep increasing k, number of points or keywords), and RETAIL-Del which starts from a full query to a simplest query (reducing from 10). We observe that:

(1) RETAIL outperforms previous standalone solutions by more than two orders of magnitude at most.
(2) The mutations in the lines of RETAIL in ATNN, TkSK and TkSTT for query refinement is because, too many candidates are inherited from the former long query, so they need more time to check these candidates.

6.2.2 Search over Points. We use *LA* and *Twitter* to evaluate: 1) k Nearest Neighbour (kNN) search by a point. 2) Top-k Spatial Keyword (TkSK) search by a point with $|q.\psi|$ keywords. 3) Aggregate Textual Nearest Neighbour (ATNN) search by $|Q|$ points with $|q.\psi|$ keywords in each query point. We omit the Keyword search (KS) here as our framework is built on top of inverted index, which is widely adopted to answer KS efficiently.

Effect of k on the kNN query. From Figure 7, we find: (1) The running time increases w.r.t. an increasing k. (2) Although R-tree [19] beats ETAIL as we use Grid-index which should be slower than R-tree, it cannot beat our RETAIL with optimization. We do not include RETAIL-Del in the performance study for decreasing k, as we can choose them from existing top-k results directly.

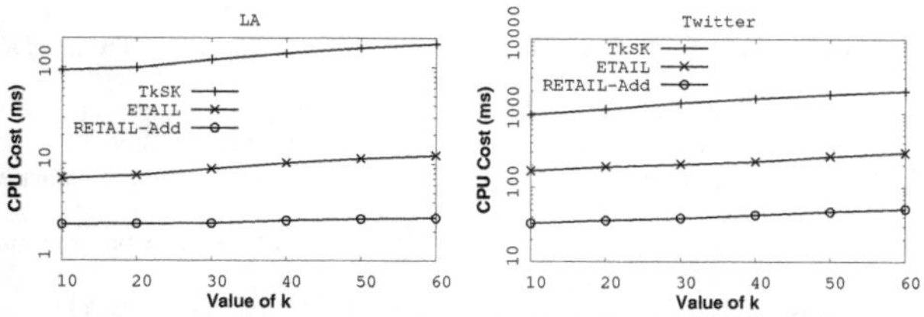

Figure 8: Comparison with [12] by increasing k.

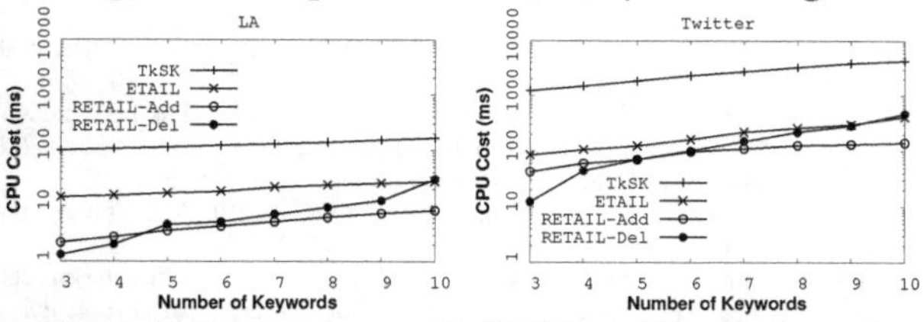

Figure 9: Comparison with [12] by adding keywords.

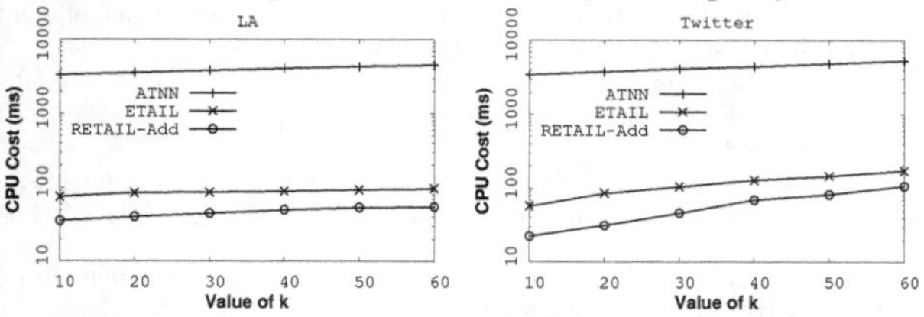

Figure 10: Comparison with [37] by increasing k.

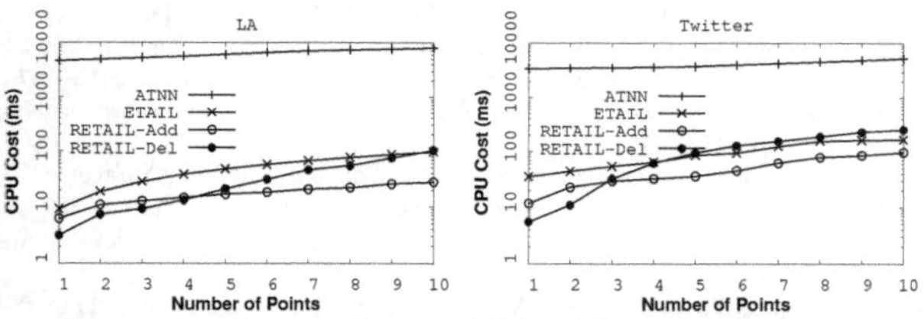

Figure 11: Comparison with [37] by adding points.

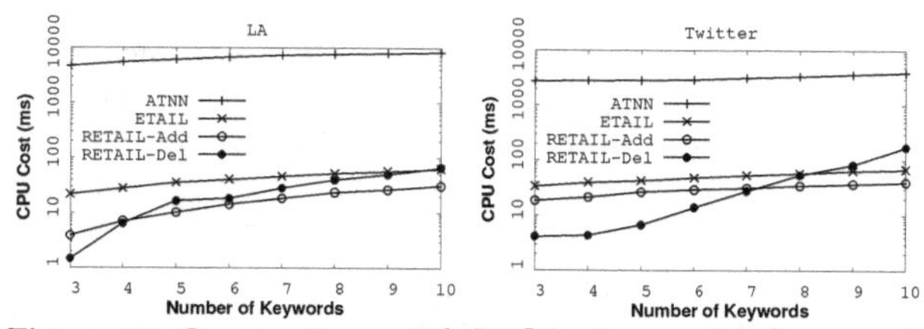

Figure 12: Comparison with [37] by increasing keywords.

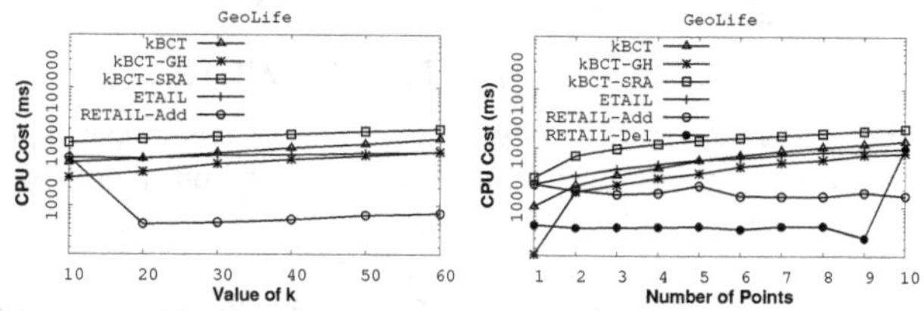

Figure 13: Comparison with [9, 25, 34] over GeoLife dataset.

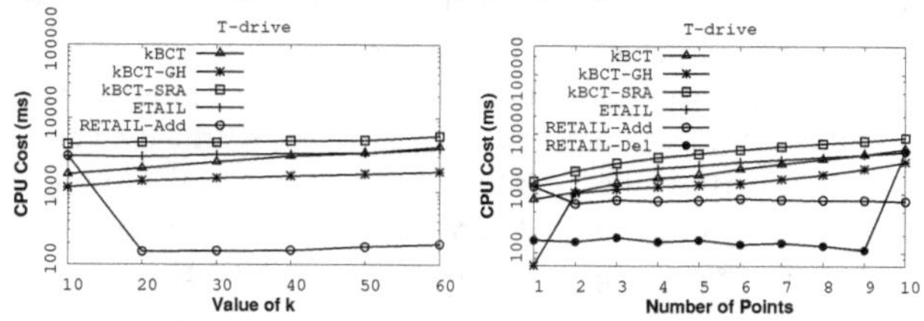

Figure 14: Comparison with [9, 25, 34] over T-drive dataset.

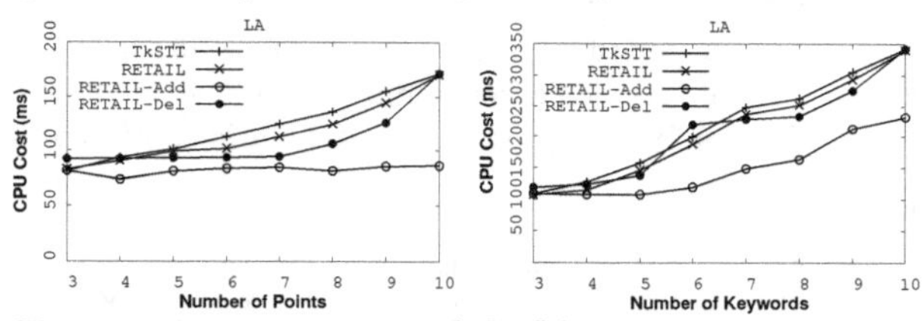

Figure 15: Comparison with [35] by increasing $|Q|$, $|q.\psi|$.

Effect of k and $|q.\psi|$ on the TkSK query. From Figures 8 and 9, we find: (1) ETAIL is faster than IR-tree [12] when we process a query without reusing the scanned objects. (2) When treating multiple queries as a query session, RETAIL is more efficient than the aggregated runtime of standalone approach over multiple queries.

Effect of k, $|Q|$ and $|q.\psi|$ on the ATNN query. Figures 10, 11 and 12 show that the running time of all algorithms keep increasing when three parameters rise.

6.2.3 Search over Trajectories. Datasets *LA*, *GeoLife* and *T-drive* are used to evaluate 2 types of queries over trajectory data: 1) k Best Connected Trajectories (kBCT) by $|Q|$ points. 2) Top-k Spatial-textual Trajectory (TkSTT) by $|Q|$ points with $|q.\psi|$ keywords.

Effect of k and $|Q|$ on the kBCT query. Figures 13 and 14 show that only kBCT-GH [34] can compete with ETAIL, while it employs R-tree which occupies more space than TGP (see Section 6.2.4). Moreover, RETAIL is 2 orders of magnitude faster than [9].

Effect of $|Q|$ and $|q.\psi|$ on the TkSTT query. Figure 15 shows: (1) the running time of all algorithms keeps increasing when parameters rise, (2) RETAIL-Add is more efficient than RETAIL-Del. We omit the figure of k here as it has a similar trend with other queries.

Statistics of Pruning. Table 4 shows the average number of scanned candidates and pruned blocks in each list over all the candidates of the queries. We focus on two most complex queries: **TkSTT** and **ATNN**. It shows that search over points terminates much earlier than trajectories (highlighted in bold).

Table 4: Statistics on the pruning power of two kinds of queries over LA dataset. (We adjust k = 10, 30, 60, $|Q|$ = 1, 5, 10 and $|q.\psi|$ = 3, 5, 10 to observe, respectively)

	Parameter	#Scanned Objects			#Pruned Blocks		
ATNN	k	8330	11450	17476	**144**	141	138
	$\|Q\|$	7534	9545	13237	145	144	140
	$\|q.\psi\|$	10004	12650	20235	143	140	135
TkSTT	k	2943	3721	4980	**78**	75	73
	$\|Q\|$	2564	3167	4249	79	75	74
	$\|q.\psi\|$	3254	4035	5132	77	74	72

6.2.4 Index Size. We employ the open-source libraries *FastPFOR*[4] to compress the inverted lists, and *Classmexer*[5] to measure the footprint of our index. From the size of indices in Table 5, we find: (1) Our **TGP** index manage to support all 5 types of queries and even does not occupy the largest space. (2) If we sum up the size of all indices for existing query types together for standalone methods, it will be more than 10 times larger than our **TGP** in *LA* and *Twitter* datasets. (3) For spatial-only datasets like *T-drive* and

[4]https://github.com/lemire/JavaFastPFOR
[5]https://www.javamex.com/classmexer/

GeoLife, **TGP** consumes at least 150MB less than other methods. (4) Our index can be compressed slightly (highlighted in bold).

Table 5: Footprint of indices for different queries.

Query	*LA* [2]	*Twitter* [6]	*GeoLife* [46]	*T-drive* [44]
T*k*STT [35]	261MB	1.5GB	N/A	N/A
T*k*SK [12], ATNN [37]	455.7MB	14.7GB	N/A	N/A
*k*BCT [9], *k*NN [19]	32MB	158MB	1.3GB	1020MB
TGP	89/**2MB**	387/**18MB**	1228.8/**71MB**	810/**52MB**

7 CONCLUSION AND FUTURE WORK

In this paper, we studied how to support various query types over geo-tagged data using a unified indexing and query paradigm. We first concluded the *Monotone Aggregate Spatial Keyword* **MASK** which can represent most existing top-*k* queries. Then we proposed an index structure called **TGP**, which is composed by grid inverted list, textual inverted list and point inverted list. On top of **TGP** we proposed an Early Termination & Abandoning method over Inverted List (ETAIL) Algorithm which can support multiple query types efficiently. Moreover, RETAIL reuses the scanned objects to improve the performance of interactive searches. In the future, we will further explore a unified paradigm which can support more similarity measures in spatial and textual dimensions.

8 ACKNOWLEDGMENT

This work was supported by ARC DP170102726, DP180102050, and National Natural Science Foundation of China (NSFC) 61728204, 91646204. Zhifeng Bao is supported by a Google Faculty Award.

REFERENCES

[1] Vo Ngoc Anh and Alistair Moffat. 2005. Inverted index compression using word-aligned binary codes. *Information Retrieval* 8, 1 (2005), 151–166.

[2] Jie Bao, Yu Zheng, and Mohamed F Mokbel. 2012. Location-based and preference-aware recommendation using sparse geo-social networking data. In *SIGSPATIAL*. 199–208.

[3] Norbert Beckmann, Hans-Peter Kriegel, Ralf Schneider, and Bernhard Seeger. 1990. The R*-tree: an efficient and robust access method for points and rectangles. In *SIGMOD*. 322–331.

[4] Paul N. Bennett, Filip Radlinski, Ryen W. White, and Emine Yilmaz. 2011. Inferring and using location metadata to personalize web search. In *SIGIR*. 135–144.

[5] Andrei Z Broder, David Carmel, Michael Herscovici, Aya Soffer, and Jason Zien. 2003. Efficient query evaluation using a two-level retrieval process. In *CIKM*. 426–434.

[6] Lisi Chen, Gao Cong, Xin Cao, and Kian-lee Tan. 2015. Temporal spatial-keyword top-k publish/subscribe. In *ICDE*. 255–266.

[7] Lisi Chen, Gao Cong, Christian S Jensen, and Dingming Wu. 2013. Spatial keyword query processing: an experimental evaluation. *PVLDB* 6, 3 (2013), 217–228.

[8] Yen-Yu Chen, Torsten Suel, and Alexander Markowetz. 2006. Efficient query processing in geographic web search engines. In *SIGMOD*. 277–288.

[9] Zaiben Chen, Heng Tao Shen, Xiaofang Zhou, Yu Zheng, and Xing Xie. 2010. Searching trajectories by locations-an efficiency study. In *SIGMOD*. 255–266.

[10] Zhiyuan Cheng, James Caverlee, Krishna Y Kamath, and Kyumin Lee. 2011. Toward traffic-driven location-based web search. In *CIKM*. 805–814.

[11] Maria Christoforaki, Jinru He, Constantinos Dimopoulos, Alexander Markowetz, and Torsten Suel. 2011. Text vs. space: efficient geo-search query processing. In *CIKM*. 423–432.

[12] Gao Cong, Christian S Jensen, and Dingming Wu. 2009. Efficient retrieval of the top-k most relevant spatial web objects. *PVLDB* 2, 1 (2009), 337–348.

[13] Caio Moura Daoud, Edleno Silva de Moura, Andre Carvalho, Altigran Soares da Silva, David Fernandes, and Cristian Rossi. 2016. Fast top-k preserving query processing using two-tier indexes. *Information Processing & Management* 52, 5 (2016), 855–872.

[14] Ian De Felipe, Vagelis Hristidis, and Naphtali Rishe. 2008. Keyword search on spatial databases. In *ICDE*. 656–665.

[15] Constantinos Dimopoulos, Sergey Nepomnyachiy, and Torsten Suel. 2013. Optimizing top-k document retrieval strategies for block-max indexes. In *WSDM*. 113–122.

[16] Shuai Ding and Torsten Suel. 2011. Faster top-k document retrieval using block-max indexes. In *SIGIR*. 993–1002.

[17] Ronald Fagin, Amnon Lotem, and Moni Naor. 2003. Optimal aggregation algorithms for middleware. *J. Comput. System Sci.* 66, 4 (2003), 614–656.

[18] Jiafeng Guo, Gu Xu, Hang Li, and Xueqi Cheng. 2008. A unified and discriminative model for query refinement. In *SIGIR*. 379–386.

[19] Antonin Guttman. 1984. R-trees: a dynamic index structure for spatial searching. *ACM SIGMOD Record* 14, 2 (1984), 47–57.

[20] Ramaswamy Hariharan, Bijit Hore, Li Chen, and Sharad Mehrotra. 2007. Processing spatial-keyword (SK) queries in Geographic Information Retrieval (GIR) systems. In *SSDBM*. 16–25.

[21] Jeff Huang and Efthimis Efthimiadis. 2009. Studying query reformulation strategies in search logs. In *CIKM*. 77–86.

[22] Zhisheng Li, Ken C K Lee, Baihua Zheng, Wang Chien Lee, Dik Lee, and Xufa Wang. 2011. IR-tree: An efficient index for geographic document search. *IEEE Transactions on Knowledge and Data Engineering* 23, 4 (2011), 585–599.

[23] Zhicheng Li, Hu Xu, Yansheng Lu, and Ailing Qian. 2010. Aggregate nearest keyword search in spatial databases. In *APWeb*. 15–21.

[24] Dimitris Papadias, Yufei Tao, Kyriakos Mouratidis, and Chun Kit Hui. 2005. Aggregate nearest neighbor queries in spatial databases. *ACM Transactions on Database Systems* 30, 2 (2005), 529–576.

[25] Shuyao Qi, Panagiotis Bouros, Dimitris Sacharidis, and Nikos Mamoulis. 2015. Efficient point-based trajectory search. In *SSTD*. 179–196.

[26] Stephen E Robertson, Steve Walker, Susan Jones, Micheline M Hancock-Beaulieu, Mike Gatford, and Others. 1995. Okapi at TREC-3. *Nist Special Publication Sp* 109 (1995), 109.

[27] Gerard Salton and Christopher Buckley. 1988. Term-weighting approaches in automatic text retrieval. *Information Processing and Management* 24, 5 (1988), 513–523.

[28] G Salton and M J Mcgill. 1986. *Introduction to modern information retrieval*. McGraw-Hill, Inc., New York, NY, USA.

[29] Timos K Sellis, Nick Roussopoulos, and Christos Faloutsos. 1987. The R+-tree: a dynamic index for multi-dimensional objects. In *VLDB*. 507–518.

[30] Shuo Shang, Ruogu Ding, Bo Yuan, Kexin Xie, Kai Zheng, and Panos Kalnis. 2012. User oriented trajectory search for trip recommendation. In *EDBT*. 156–167.

[31] Fei Song and W Bruce Croft. 1999. A general language model for information retrieval. In *CIKM*. 316–321.

[32] Amanda Spink, Bernard J Jansen, Dietmar Wolfram, and Tefko Saracevic. 2002. From e-sex to e-commerce: Web search changes. *Computer* 35, 3 (2002), 107–109.

[33] Trevor Strohman and W. Bruce Croft. 2007. Efficient document retrieval in main memory. In *SIGIR*. 175–182.

[34] Lu An Tang, Yu Zheng, Xing Xie, Jing Yuan, Xiao Yu, and Jiawei Han. 2011. Retrieving k-nearest neighboring trajectories by a set of point locations. In *SSTD*. 223–241.

[35] Sheng Wang, Zhifeng Bao, J Shane Culpepper, Timos Sellis, Mark Sanderson, and Xiaolin Qin. 2017. Answering top-k exemplar trajectory queries. In *ICDE*. 597–608.

[36] Dingming Wu, Man Lung Yiu, Christian S. Jensen, and Gao Cong. 2011. Efficient continuously moving top-k spatial keyword query processing. In *ICDE*. 541–552.

[37] Kai Yao, Jianjun Li, Guohui Li, and Changyin Luo. 2016. Efficient group top-k spatial keyword query processing. In *APWeb*. 153–165.

[38] Man Lung Yiu, Nikos Mamoulis, and Dimitris Papadias. 2005. Aggregate nearest neighbor queries in road networks. *IEEE Transactions on Knowledge and Data Engineering* 17, 6 (2005), 820–833.

[39] Yong Zeng, Zhifeng Bao, Tok Wang Ling, H. V. Jagadish, and Guoliang Li. 2014. Breaking out of the MisMatch trap. In *ICDE*. 940–951.

[40] Dongxiang Zhang, Chee-Yong Chan, and Kian-Lee Tan. 2014. Processing spatial keyword query as a top-k aggregation query. In *SIGIR*. 355–364.

[41] Dongxiang Zhang, Kian-Lee Tan, and Anthony K. H. Tung. 2013. Scalable top-k spatial keyword search. In *EDBT*. 359.

[42] Kai Zheng, Shuo Shang, Nicholas Jing Yuan, and Yi Yang. 2013. Towards efficient search for activity trajectories. In *ICDE*. 230–241.

[43] Kai Zheng, Han Su, Bolong Zheng, Jiajun Liu, and Xiaofang Zhou. 2015. Interactive top-k spatial keyword queries. In *ICDE*. 423–434.

[44] Yu Zheng. 2011. T-Drive: driving directions based on taxi trajectories. In *SIGSPATIAL*. 99–108.

[45] Yuxin Zheng, Zhifeng Bao, Lidan Shou, and Anthony K H Tung. 2015. INSPIRE : a framework for incremental spatial prefix query relaxation. *IEEE Transactions on Knowledge and Data Engineering* 27, 7 (2015), 1949–1963.

[46] Yu Zheng, Lizhu Zhang, Xing Xie, and Wei-Ying Ma. 2009. Mining interesting locations and travel sequences from GPS trajectories. In *WWW*. 791–800.

[47] Yinghua Zhou, Xing Xie, Chuang Wang, Yuchang Gong, and Wei-Ying Ma. 2005. Hybrid index structures for location-based web search. In *CIKM*. 155–162.

[48] Liang Zhu, Yinan Jing, Weiwei Sun, Dingding Mao, and Peng Liu. 2010. Voronoi-based aggregate nearest neighbor query processing in road networks. In *SIGSPATIAL*. 518–521.

Position Bias Estimation for Unbiased Learning to Rank in Personal Search

Xuanhui Wang, Nadav Golbandi, Michael Bendersky,
Donald Metzler, Marc Najork
Google Inc.
Mountain View, CA
{xuanhui,nadavg,bemike,metzler,najork}@google.com

ABSTRACT

A well-known challenge in learning from click data is its inherent bias and most notably position bias. Traditional click models aim to extract the ⟨query, document⟩ relevance and the estimated bias is usually discarded after relevance is extracted. In contrast, the most recent work on unbiased learning-to-rank can effectively leverage the bias and thus focuses on estimating bias rather than relevance [20, 31]. Existing approaches use search result randomization over a small percentage of production traffic to estimate the position bias. This is not desired because result randomization can negatively impact users' search experience. In this paper, we compare different schemes for result randomization (i.e., *RandTopN* and *RandPair*) and show their negative effect in personal search. Then we study how to infer such bias from regular click data without relying on randomization. We propose a regression-based Expectation-Maximization (EM) algorithm that is based on a position bias click model and that can handle highly sparse clicks in personal search. We evaluate our EM algorithm and the extracted bias in the learning-to-rank setting. Our results show that it is promising to extract position bias from regular clicks without result randomization. The extracted bias can improve the learning-to-rank algorithms significantly. In addition, we compare the pointwise and pairwise learning-to-rank models. Our results show that pairwise models are more effective in leveraging the estimated bias.

CCS CONCEPTS

• **Information systems → Learning to rank;**

KEYWORDS

Position bias estimation; inverse propensity weighting; expectation-maximization

ACM Reference Format:
Xuanhui Wang, Nadav Golbandi, Michael Bendersky, Donald Metzler, Marc Najork. 2018. Position Bias Estimation for Unbiased Learning to Rank in Personal Search. In *WSDM 2018: WSDM 2018: The Eleventh ACM International Conference on Web Search and Data Mining , February 5–9, 2018, Marina Del Rey, CA, USA.* ACM, New York, NY, USA, 9 pages. https://doi.org/10.1145/3159652.3159732

WSDM 2018, February 5–9, 2018, Marina Del Rey, CA, USA

ACM ISBN 978-1-4503-5581-0/18/02.
https://doi.org/10.1145/3159652.3159732

1 INTRODUCTION

Personal search is an important research topic in information retrieval that has been evolving from desktop search [13] to on-device search [21] and more recently to email search [5]. With the increasing popularity of cloud-based email and storage services, there is a large amount of personal data stored in the cloud. This large amount of data calls for effective search capabilities to improve its utility [2, 5, 6, 15]. The important difference of personal search from web search is the private content in personal search. Users can only see and search their own content. This presents an important challenge when applying learning-to-rank techniques, because collecting explicit relevance judgements becomes much harder and raters can only label their own documents with their own queries. Though possible, such an approach can be heavily biased by the selected raters and costly to maintain due to the fast-evolving nature of private content.

Click data in personal search provides implicit but abundant user feedback. It thus becomes a natural source to improve personal search quality. However, a well-known challenge in learning from click data is its inherent bias: position bias [19], presentation bias [32], and trust bias [26], etc. Among them, the position bias has a strong influence on users' clicks [20]. A prerequisite of fully leveraging the power of click data is to debias it. As a result, there has been a great deal of research on extracting reliable signals from click data.

One such effort is known as click modeling. Click models were initially proposed for web search with the goal of estimating ⟨query, document⟩ relevance by taking the click bias into account [9]. The position bias model [27] and the Cascade model [10] are the two classic click models. In the position bias model, users' clicks are determined by two factors: document positions, and the ⟨query, document⟩ relevance. The Cascade model assumes sequential user behavior: a user scans the documents one by one from the top, and the scan continues after a non-relevant document but stops after a relevant document. More sophisticated models (e.g., UBM [14], DBN [7], and CCM [17]) build upon these two classic models. In the learning-to-rank setting, the existing click models belong to the pointwise category because they estimate ⟨query, document⟩ relevance but not based on the correct *order* of documents as in pairwise and listwise approaches.

Different from click models, Joachims et al. [19] studied a few heuristics in the pairwise manner (e.g., *SkipAbove*) and found that these heuristics lead to more reliable relevance assessments. However, the data obtained by these heuristics are systematically biased and a ranking function learned from it tends to reverse the existing order [20].

Recently, Wang et al. [31] and Joachims et al. [20] introduced the unbiased learning-to-rank framework by treating the bias as a counterfactual effect. Inside the framework, the critical component is to quantify the click bias, rather than estimate the ⟨query, document⟩ relevance in click models. Due to this difference, randomizing results on a small fraction of search traffic is sufficient.

In this paper, we study different ways of position bias estimation for unbiased learning-to-rank. Result randomization intuitively degrades the users' search experience. We quantify the negative impacts of different degrees of randomization (*RandTopN* and *RandPair*) and compare their effectiveness for bias estimation. This naturally motivates us to study how to estimate the bias from regular clicks. The classical position bias model is a candidate method. A direct application of this model requires the same ⟨query, document⟩ pairs appearing at multiple positions multiple times [7], but this is not realistic in personal search. We propose a novel regression-based EM algorithm that does not need the query and document identifiers but works in a feature space. Such an approach is applicable to any ranking system where clicks and ranking features are collected. It also greatly reduces the pre-processing that is usually needed in standard click models. Furthermore, as position bias can potentially change as a ranking system evolves, our approach can be used to re-estimate position bias without any intervention like result randomization.

The contribution of this paper is summarized as follows:

- We study the problem of position bias estimation without result randomization and propose a regression-based EM [11] in personal search that can be applied to any ranking system without the need of intervention.
- We compare different degrees of result randomization based on effectiveness of bias estimation and negative impacts on an email and a file storage personal search service.
- We conduct extensive experiments and our results show that position bias estimated using EM can achieve surprisingly good results without using randomization, and that pairwise learning-to-rank algorithms can better leverage these bias estimates than pointwise ones.

The rest of this paper is organized as follows. In Section 2, we review previous related work. The unbiased learning-to-rank is set up in Section 3 and is followed by different methods of propensity estimation based on the position bias model in Section 4. We present our extensive experimental study and our evaluation methodology in Section 5. Finally, we conclude and discuss future work in Section 6.

2 RELATED WORK

Click-through data has become an indispensable resource in both web search and personal search. There is an abundance of prior work on click modeling in web search that address click bias to extract useful signals from click data. One of the seminal papers by Joachims et al. [19] evaluates a few heuristics via a user study and shows that clicks are valuable as long as certain biases, especially the position bias, are accounted for. Many click models have been proposed to model the user click behaviors based on probabilistic graphical models [7–10, 14, 17, 27, 34]. These models can account for the click bias and provide more reliable relevance estimation between queries and documents.

Unbiased learning-to-rank takes a different approach to account for click bias. Wang et al. [31] study the selection bias at the query level when click-based training data is collected in learning-to-rank. Joachims et al. [20] present a counterfactual inference framework with a principled theoretical basis. Both approaches rely on Inverse Propensity Weighting (IPW) developed in the causal inference field [28], and both rely on result randomization to estimate the propensity. Our paper is in the same unbiased learning-to-rank framework; however, we estimate the propensity without randomization.

Our work is related to recent work on personal search [2, 3, 6, 22, 33] that emphasized relevance-based over time-based ranking [6]. User behaviors in personal search show different traits compared with web search [2]. For example, repeated visits to the same results are less common in email search. Thus, applying learning-to-rank techniques is important; however, the click data is highly sparse in personal search. We use a regression-based EM algorithm that extends the standard EM algorithm to handle the highly sparse data effectively.

Inverse propensity weighting is a commonly-used technique to address the sample bias. It has been adopted for unbiased evaluation and learning (e.g., [1, 12, 23, 24, 29, 30]). Most work in this area assumes that the propensity scores are present in the logs and study how to reduce the model variance while staying unbiased. The unbiased learning-to-rank framework is different in that the propensity is not explicitly logged but buried in the user behavior data implicitly. How to estimate this propensity in a less costly manner is critical in unbiased learning-to-rank and the focus of this paper.

3 UNBIASED LEARNING-TO-RANK

For simplicity, we assume that a clicked document is relevant. Note that such an assumption can be relaxed to accommodate noisy clicks in unbiased learning-to-rank as shown in [20]. However, the reverse is not true due to the position bias: relevant documents may not get clicked all the time because the users do not go down the list to examine it. Thus, click data obtained from search logs is biased due to the unobserved feedback. Learning from it without accounting for the bias leads to less effective ranking functions. In this section, we review and discuss different ways of unbiased learning-to-rank from click data.

3.1 Inverse Propensity Weighting

In the learning-to-rank setting, there are two existing propensity-based bias correction methods. In the following, we use a Bernoulli variable O to denote whether the relevance of a document is observed. The variable O can depend on various factors such as positions or even an entire rank list. Without loss of generality, for i-th document, we use a vague notation $P(O_i = 1)$ to denote the propensity and $o_i \in \{0, 1\}$ to denote a specific value. We use $r_i \in \{0, 1\}$ to denote whether a document is relevant and use π to denote the list $[1, \cdots, n]$ of ranks of n results.

Query-level propensity. A key observation in [31] is that queries without clicks are not useful in the pairwise or listwise learning-to-rank approaches and not included in the training data. Hence, due to the position bias, queries whose relevant documents are ranked lower can be under-represented in the training data. The propensity that a query is selected in the training data depends on the highest position of its relevant documents:

$$P(O_{i_q} = 1) \text{ where } i_q = \min\{i \in \pi : r_i = 1\}.$$

The bias is corrected by using a query-level Inverse Propensity Weighting (IPW)

$$w_q = \frac{1}{P(O_{i_q} = 1)}.$$

Such an approach fits perfectly well when there is a single click per query but can be less accurate for queries with multiple relevant documents.

Document-level propensity. Document-level propensity is studied in [20]. It starts with a performance metric that measures the rank of the relevant documents (denoted as *Rank*):

$$Rank = \sum_{i \in \pi} r_i \cdot i.$$

In biased data, IPW is used to correct the bias:

$$\overline{Rank} = \sum_{i \in \pi : o_i = 1} \frac{r_i \cdot i}{P(O_i = 1)} = \sum_{i \in \pi : o_i = 1, r_i = 1} \frac{i}{P(O_i = 1)}.$$

The *Rank* metric is proven unbiased, i.e., $\mathbb{E}\{\overline{Rank}\} = Rank$ [20]. The document-level IPW is

$$w_i = \frac{1}{P(O_i = 1)}.$$

3.2 Unbiased Learning Algorithms

The *Rank* metric can be optimized by a pairwise learning-to-rank method such as SVMRank. To show this, let s_i and s_j be the scores of a ranking function for document i and j. *Rank* can be expressed as a pairwise loss using the indicator function $\mathbb{I}$:

$$\sum_{i \in \pi : o_i = 1, r_i = 1} w_i \cdot i = \sum_{i \in \pi : o_i = 1, r_i = 1} w_i \cdot (\sum_{j \in \pi} \mathbb{I}_{s_j > s_i} + 1)$$
$$= \sum_{i \in \pi : o_i = 1, r_i = 1} \sum_{j \in \pi} w_i \cdot \mathbb{I}_{s_j > s_i} + const$$

The loss above is upper-bounded by the common classification loss functions (e.g., the hinge loss or the log loss [18]) and can be optimized by pairwise learning-to-rank algorithms by constructing the following preference pairs: For each **observed** and **relevant** document i, we pair it with each of the other documents j in the given query and create a preference pair $i \rhd j$. Note that the weight for each pair is only determined by w_i, the IPW of document i.

Given a single-click training data, both query-level propensity and document-level propensity lead to the same pairwise learning algorithm. For multi-click training data, the query-level propensity can be adapted by replicating a multi-click query to multiple single-click queries with each corresponding to a click. It is easy to show that such a strategy of the query-level IPW leads to the same pairwise learning algorithm as the document-level IPW.

In addition, both *Rank* and $\overline{Rank}$ can be optimized using the λ-gradient in LambdaRank or LambdaMART [4]. Similar to *Rank*, we can define the DCG-like metric *Prec* and its IPW version $\overline{Prec}$ as follows:

$$Prec = \sum_{i \in \pi} \frac{r_i}{i} = \sum_{i \in \pi : r_i = 1} \frac{1}{i}$$
$$\overline{Prec} = \sum_{i \in \pi : o_i = 1} w_i \frac{r_i}{i} = \sum_{i \in \pi : o_i = 1, r_i = 1} w_i \frac{1}{i}$$

$\overline{Prec}$ is also provenly unbiased, i.e., $\mathbb{E}\{\overline{Prec}\} = Prec$. We use *Prec* in our paper as the optimization metric and other types of DCG-like metrics can be used easily in the current setting.

In the unbiased learning-to-rank framework, the critical part is to estimate the propensity $P(O_i = 1)$. Note that a nice property of the current metrics is that we only need the propensity of **observed** and **relevant** documents, i.e., $o_i = 1$ and $r_i = 1$, and we do not need the propensity of non-relevant documents. Such a nice property holds for pairwise learning algorithms because they are closely related to the metrics (e.g., *Rank* and *Prec*) in which non-relevant documents have no contributions to the metric values. However, it does not hold for pointwise learning algorithms because a non-relevant document usually contributes to the pointwise loss functions. We will show some attempts in our experiments; however, how to extend the IPW method to pointwise approaches is an open area of research.

4 PROPENSITY ESTIMATION

In this section, we show how to estimate the propensity from the click data based on a position bias model. The position bias model is a simple yet effective generative click model. We first set up the model and then present different methods for parameter estimation, including a novel regression-based EM algorithm.

4.1 Position Bias Model

The position bias model assumes that the observed click Bernoulli variable C depends on two other hidden Bernoulli variables E and R where E represents the event whether a user examines a document at a certain position k and R represents the event whether a document d is relevant to a query q. Specifically,

$$P(C = 1|q, d, k) = P(E = 1|k) \cdot P(R = 1|q, d),$$

where $P(C = 1|q, d, k)$ is the probability of clicking document d that is shown at position k given query q, $P(E = 1|k)$ is the probability that position k is examined, and $P(R = 1|q, d)$ is the probability that document d is relevant to query q. The model assumes that the examination only depends on the position and the relevance only depends on the query and document. We use the following shorthands for derivation:

$$\theta_k = P(E = 1|k)$$
$$\gamma_{q,d} = P(R = 1|q, d).$$

Though simple, this model has been shown to be as effective as more sophisticated click models [9]. In particular, when there is a single click per query, this model is equivalent to the User Browsing Model (UBM) [14] that achieves the state-of-the-art performance. On the other hand, more sophisticated click models can be potentially used as well for propensity estimation.

THEOREM 4.1. *In the position bias model, the* **observed** *variable O is equivalent to the* **examination** *variable E: $O \Leftrightarrow E$.*

This has been proven in [20]. When $E = 1$, the relevance R is fully observed by C and thus $O = 1$. When $E = 0$, $C = 0$ always holds and the document may or may not be relevant. In another word, we have no knowledge of R and thus $O = 0$.

With Theorem 4.1, estimating propensity $P(O = 1)$ equals to estimating the examination probability $P(E = 1)$. Also, a clicked document i means it is examined and relevant. In other words, it is relevant ($r_i = 1$) and observed ($o_i = 1$) and thus we only need to estimate and apply the propensity scores on the clicked documents.

4.2 Result Randomization

To estimate θ_k, we need a way to estimate $\gamma_{q,d}$ or eliminate it from the equation. Result randomization is a way to integrate it out. We describe two methods here.

4.2.1 Randomize TopN. In the position bias model, the relevance component $\gamma_{q,d}$ is hidden. Result randomization can be leveraged to estimate θ_k without explicitly modeling the relevance component. For a randomized data set $\mathcal{R}$ where the top N documents are randomly shuffled before showing them to users, let $\mathcal{R}_k$ be the subset of the collected logs from position k. We have

$$\begin{aligned}\mathbb{E}(C|k) &= \int_{q,d\in\mathcal{R}_k} \mathbb{E}(C|q,d,k)P(q,d)\\ &= \int_{q,d\in\mathcal{R}_k} P(C=1|q,d,k)P(q,d)\\ &= \int_{q,d\in\mathcal{R}_k} \theta_k\gamma_{q,d}P(q,d)\\ &= \theta_k\cdot\int_{q,d\in\mathcal{R}_k} \gamma_{q,d}P(q,d)\\ &\propto \theta_k\end{aligned}$$

This is the case because $\int_{q,d\in\mathcal{R}_k}\gamma_{q,d}P(q,d) = \mathbb{E}\{\gamma_{Q,D}\}$ is constant across all the positions in the randomized data $\mathcal{R}$. Thus, the position bias θ_k is proportional to the number of clicks in $\mathcal{R}_k$. We use *RandTopN* to denote this method.

4.2.2 Randomize Pair. Shuffling a few top results randomly can lower the search quality a lot and thus create undesired user experience. A relatively smaller intervention is to randomize pairs. In [20], results at rank 1 and rank k are randomly swapped half the time. In this paper, we use a simpler variant that randomly swaps adjacent pairs at position $k-1$ and k. We vary k and collect search logs for each k separately. Similarly to *RandTopN*, we can get a relative ratio $\frac{\theta_k}{\theta_{k-1}}$ for adjacent pairs based on the number of clicks at position $k-1$ and k when the results of these two positions are randomly swapped. In the position bias model, we can obtain the relative ratio between any two positions by multiplying the ratios of adjacent positions.

$$\frac{\theta_k}{\theta_1} = \frac{\theta_2}{\theta_1}\cdot\frac{\theta_3}{\theta_2}\cdots\frac{\theta_k}{\theta_{k-1}}.$$

We name this scheme *RandPair*. It is different from *RandTopN* in that the expected relevance $\mathbb{E}\{\gamma_{Q,D}\}$ for a position pair is different from another position pair. But under the assumption in the position bias model, the relative ratios between different positions should be the same as *RandTopN*, which also applies to the one used in [20] similarly.

	Email (N=3)	File Storage (N=5)
RandTopN	-13.94%*	-31.04%*
RandPair(1, 2)	-6.80%*	-12.44%*
RandPair(2, 3)	-0.56%	+3.75%
RandPair(3, 4)	+0.20%	+1.09%
RandPair(4, 5)	+0.38%	+0.36%

Table 1: The negative effect due to result randomization measured by the relative change of MRR against the production. * means statistically different.

4.2.3 Empirical Comparison. The position bias model is a simplification of real-world user click behavior and can be less precise. We empirically compare *RandTopN* and *RandPair* here to see how well they align. We use a portion of traffic for randomization on two search services: one is email search and the other is file storage search, and run multiple randomization experiments on each service. Figure 1 plots the θ_k that we got from *RandTopN* and *RandPair* experiments. For *RandTopN*, we set $N = 3$ for email search and $N = 5$ for file storage search. From this figure, we can see that *RandPair* aligns very well with *RandTopN* and this confirms that the assumption of the position bias model is reasonable.

One of the drawbacks of result randomization is its negative effect on the search experience. Reusing the randomization experiments, we quantify the impact on Mean Reciprocal Rank (MRR) of the clicked positions and compare result-randomized traffic with production traffic. Table 1 summarizes the comparison using the relative change of MRR. From this table, we can see that the search experience is dramatically decreased due to randomization on both services. *RandTopN* is worse than *RandPair* since it perturbs results more aggressively. For *RandPair*, the impact generally becomes smaller as the positions become lower. In the table, the impact becomes neutral after position 2. The fluctuation at the lower positions is mainly due to the larger variance of user buckets where fewer clicks are collected at those positions. Compared with [20], our *RandPair* is less aggressive in perturbing results per search, but may need to be run longer to get sufficient clicks for bias estimation since pairs in our method are at less visible positions. An interesting comparison is on how much traffic is necessary for bias estimation in different methods, which we leave as future work.

4.3 Estimation from Regular Clicks

Can we estimate the position bias from regular production clicks without randomization and how accurate would that be? To the best of our knowledge, there is no existing study on such a comparison. In this section, we give details of the standard EM algorithm and present a regression-based EM for personal search.

Given a regular click log $\mathcal{L} = \{(c,q,d,k)\}$, the log likelihood of generating this data is

$$\log P(\mathcal{L}) = \sum_{(c,q,d,k)\in\mathcal{L}} c\log\theta_k\gamma_{q,d} + (1-c)\log(1-\theta_k\gamma_{q,d}).$$

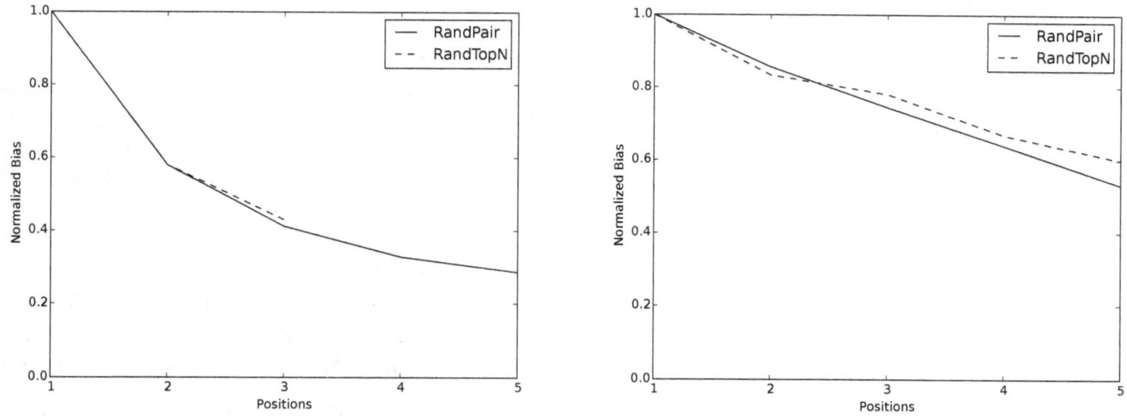

(a) Email. (b) File Storage.

Figure 1: Position bias estimated by result randomization and normalized by the top position.

The EM algorithm can find the parameters that maximize the log likelihood of the whole data.

4.3.1 Standard EM. The standard EM algorithm iterates over the Expectation and Maximization steps to update parameters $\{\theta_k\}$ and $\{\gamma_{q,d}\}$. At iteration $t+1$, the Expectation step estimates the distribution of hidden variable E and R given parameters from iteration t: $\{\theta_k^{(t)}\}$ and $\{\gamma_{q,d}^{(t)}\}$ and the observed data in $\mathcal{L}$.

$$\begin{aligned}
P(E=1,R=1|C=1,q,d,k) &= 1\\
P(E=1,R=0|C=0,q,d,k) &= \frac{\theta_k^{(t)}(1-\gamma_{q,d}^{(t)})}{1-\theta_k^{(t)}\gamma_{q,d}^{(t)}}\\
P(E=0,R=1|C=0,q,d,k) &= \frac{(1-\theta_k^{(t)})\gamma_{q,d}^{(t)}}{1-\theta_k^{(t)}\gamma_{q,d}^{(t)}}\\
P(E=0,R=0|C=0,q,d,k) &= \frac{(1-\theta_k^{(t)})(1-\gamma_{q,d}^{(t)})}{1-\theta_k^{(t)}\gamma_{q,d}^{(t)}}
\end{aligned} \tag{1}$$

From this, we can compute the marginals $P(E=1|c,q,d,k)$ and $P(R=1|c,q,d,k)$ for every data point in $\mathcal{L}$ and this can be seen as complete data where the hidden variables are estimated.

The Maximization step updates the parameters using the quantities from the Expectation step:

$$\begin{aligned}
\theta_k^{(t+1)} &= \frac{\sum_{c,q,d,k'} \mathbb{I}_{k'=k}\cdot(c+(1-c)P(E=1|c,q,d,k))}{\sum_{c,q,d,k'}\mathbb{I}_{k'=k}}\\
\gamma_{q,d}^{(t+1)} &= \frac{\sum_{c,q',d',k}\mathbb{I}_{q'=q,d'=d}\cdot(c+(1-c)P(R=1|c,q,d,k))}{\sum_{c,q',d',k,}\mathbb{I}_{q'=q,d'=d}}
\end{aligned} \tag{2}$$

4.3.2 Regression-based EM. The Maximization step in the standard EM usually works with (q,d) identifiers for $\gamma_{q,d}$. Using the exact identifiers is challenging in personal search for several reasons: (1) due to privacy concerns, these identifiers may not be accessible; (2) the click data is highly sparse and noisy since documents are private and clicks on a document may just come from a single user; (3) user corpora change quickly and a document may get very few clicks before it becomes irrelevant when a new document (e.g. email) is created. To overcome these difficulties, we propose a regression-based EM.

The regression-based EM only modifies the Maximization step in the standard EM. Instead of working with (q,d) identifiers, we assume there is a feature vector $\mathbf{x}_{q,d}$ representing them and use a function to compute the relevance $\gamma_{q,d}=f(\mathbf{x}_{q,d})$. The Maximization step is then to find a regression function $f(\mathbf{x})$ to maximize the likelihood given the estimation from the Expectation step. For any ranking system, there are usually available ranking features used in the system. The feature vector $\mathbf{x}$ in our EM can be the same as the ranking features. Thus, the proposed EM algorithm can be easily deployed to any of these systems where regular clicks and ranking features are collected. Also, as noted in [7], for the EM to work the standard EM requires that a document for a query appears in multiple positions. This is less of a concern in regression-based EM as long as similar feature vectors appear in different positions.

Specifically, for each $(c,q,d,k)\in\mathcal{L}$, the expectation step gives a probability $P(R=1|c,q,d,k)$. Intuitively, we can regress the feature vector $\mathbf{x}_{q,d}$ to the probability $P(R=1|c,q,d,k)$. In this paper, we convert such a regression problem to a classification problem based on sampling: we sample a binary relevance label $r\in\{0,1\}$ according to $P(R=1|c,q,d,k)$. This conversion allows us to use the widely available classification tools to solve our problem. After sampling, we have a training set $\{(\mathbf{x},r)\}$ for $f(\mathbf{x})$. The objective function is the log likelihood:

$$\sum_{\{(\mathbf{x},r)\}} r\log(f(\mathbf{x}))+(1-r)\log(1-f(\mathbf{x})),$$

Algorithm 1: Regression-based EM

Input: $\mathcal{L} = \{(c, q, d, k)\}, \{\mathbf{x}_{q,d}\}, \{\theta_k\}, \{\gamma_{q,d}\}$.
Output: $\{\theta_k\}$ and $f(\mathbf{x})$.

Let $F(\mathbf{x}) = 0$
repeat
  Estimate the hidden variable probability based on Eq 1.
  Let $S = \{\}$
  for all $(c, q, d, k) \in \mathcal{L}$ **do**
    Sample $r \in \{0, 1\}$ from $P(R = 1|c, q, d, k)$
    $S = S \cup (\mathbf{x}_{q,d}, r)$
  end for
  $F(\mathbf{x}) = GBDT(F(\mathbf{x}), S)$
  Update $\{\theta_k\}$ based on Eq 2.
  Update $\{\gamma_{q,d} = f(\mathbf{x}_{q,d})\}$ using Eq 3.
until Convergence.
return $\{\theta_k\}, f(\mathbf{x})$

where we use the sigmoid in the objective function

$$f(\mathbf{x}) = \frac{1}{1 + e^{-F(\mathbf{x})}} \tag{3}$$

$F(x)$ is the log odd of function $f(x)$ and can be learned by the standard logistic regression. However, the features in a ranking system are usually optimized to perform correct ordinal ranking, and may not have a linear correlation with the relevance. To account for non-linearity, we use the Gradient Boosted Decision Tree (GBDT) method [16] to learn the function $F(\mathbf{x})$.

We summarize the regression-based EM in Algorithm 1. For the GBDT, we use depth-3 trees and set the shrinkage to 0.2. A new iteration uses the GBDT trees from the previous iteration and refines them additively using the new data.

4.3.3 Embedded in Discriminative Methods. Another approach to estimate position effect is to use a discriminative method (e.g., logistic regression) by embedding positions as features. That is, we append the position of each document to the feature vector $\mathbf{x}$ and train a function to predict the click odds. We use the one-hot encoding of the positions and form a feature vector $\mathbf{k}$. Thus, for each $(c, q, d, k) \in \mathcal{L}$, we have a training instance $([\mathbf{k}, \mathbf{x}_{q,d}], c)$. A discriminative model GDBT can then be trained to optimize the likelihood of the click data. In order to separate the position effect from the ranking features, we set the split depth to be 1 in GBDT to disallow feature interaction. This is similar to the linear function used in logistic regression, but allows us to model non-linear transformation for individual features. We use $g(\mathbf{k}, \mathbf{x})$ to represent the learned function that predicts the click probability.

In the Embedded method, the positions are treated the same as the regular ranking features, so the click odds can be equally attributed to positions or to regular ranking features. When there is a high correlation between them, the attribution can be arbitrary. This also creates dependency between positions and regular click features. When positions are not present, the Embedded method cannot perform well. On the contrary, the EM algorithm is based on probabilistic graphical models and has a clear separation of a position-based bias component and a relevance component. Such a structure makes each component predictive independently. We will show this point in our experiments.

5 EVALUATIONS

In this section, we conduct a suite of experiments to compare different methods that estimate position-based propensity. We first describe our experimental setup (data sets, and metrics design), then we report our experimental results in the unbiased learning-to-rank setting.

5.1 Experimental Setup

We set up our evaluation using a standard supervised learning-to-rank framework [25]. In this section, we describe our evaluation data sets and the evaluation metrics used in our experiments.

5.1.1 Data Sets. The data sets we used in this paper are search logs from both an email and a file storage service. For each service, there is at most a single click for each query. This is because each service uses an overlay to show the results as users type and the overlay disappears when a click on the overlay happens. We discard all the queries that do not lead to clicks when we process the search logs.

For each service, we take a sample of its processed logs from a two-week period in April 2017. The first week of the data is used for training and the second is used for test. We have approximately 4M queries in each week. Each query has around 5 results. We use the existing ranking features from these services in our regression and learning-to-rank algorithms. We do not do any other pre-processing of the data.

5.1.2 Evaluation Metrics. For ranking effectiveness, the evaluation metric used in this paper is a variant of Mean Reciprocal Rank (MRR). Given a test data set with N queries, the standard MRR is defined as follows:

$$\text{MRR} = \frac{1}{N} \sum_{i=1}^{N} \frac{1}{\text{rank}_i} \tag{4}$$

where rank_i is the rank of the clicked document of the i-th query in our data set.

Due to click bias, the standard MRR is not suitable for offline evaluation. We thus define a weighted MRR using the propensity. Let w_i be the inverse propensity estimated from the *RandPair* described in Section 4.2.2 for the clicked position of the i-th query, then the weighted MRR is defined as

$$\text{MRR} = \frac{1}{\sum_{i=1}^{N} w_i} \sum_{i=1}^{N} w_i \frac{1}{\text{rank}_i}, \tag{5}$$

which is the MRR definition that we will use in the remainder of this paper. It is the same as the *Prec* in Section 3 given that we only have a single click per query in our data sets. Note that we use the propensity estimated from the *RandPair* as the ground truth in the following comparisons and this offline metric is shown to be consistent with the online experiments in [31].

We also use the average log likelihood to measure how well a model fits the click data. This can be used to compare the EM and

	EM	Embedded
Email	**-0.124**	-0.130
File Storage	-0.121	**-0.116**

Table 2: The average LogLikelihood on the test data set. A lower absolute value means a better fit.

	EM	Embedded
Email	**+0.50%***	-4.44%*
File Storage	**+0.11%**	-3.10%*

Table 3: Comparison of relevant components using the relative difference of MRR against the pointwise GBDT baseline.

the Embedded methods. Specifically,

$$\text{LogLikelihood} = \frac{1}{|\mathcal{L}|}\sum_{\mathcal{L}} c\log(p) + (1-c)\log(1-p),$$

where $p = \theta_k f(\mathbf{x})$ for the EM method and $p = g(\mathbf{k}, \mathbf{x})$ for the Embedded method. Besides fitting wellness, we also compare the relevance components estimated by these two methods using the MRR metric. In the EM method, we use the relevance component $f(\mathbf{x})$ directly. The Embedded method does not have a clearly separated relevance component. However, since the GBDT model has split depth 1, there are no interactions between features. Hence, we can remove the position feature related subtrees and use the rest as the relevance components. This is equivalent to comparing the relevance of all the documents by placing them at the same canonical position (e.g., position 1).

5.2 Experimental Results

We report our experimental results on propensity estimation and the ranking effectiveness of different learning methods.

5.2.1 Propensity Estimation. Both EM and Embedded aim to maximize the likelihood. We show the LogLikelihood results in Table 2. On the email data, EM outperforms Embedded, but Embedded fits the file storage data better. The EM method imposes a factor model to separate the effect of position while the Embedded method is limited to a split depth equal to 1 to have a separation between position and relevance features. The LogLikelihood suggests that both EM and Embedded are comparable. However, we will show that the EM method is far better in the following aspects:

- **Estimated relevance.** Table 3 shows the evaluation of relevance components of both the EM and the Embedded methods. For the baseline, we train a pointwise GBDT model over the ranking feature vector **x** directly without considering position bias. We report the relative difference over the baseline using MRR. Surprisingly, the Embedded method performs significantly worse than the baseline, while the EM method outperforms the baseline on both data sets and the improvement is statistically significant on the email data set. This confirms that the Embedded method cannot effectively attribute the click odds to the ranking features but the EM method can.

Pointwise			Pairwise
QueryLevel	DocLevel	EM	EMCorrected
-0.07%	-0.06%	+0.50%*	+1.30%*

Table 4: Comparison of unbiased pointwise learning algorithms based on relative change of MRR against the pointwise GBDT baseline without correction.

- **Estimated position bias.** Figure 2 shows the estimated position bias for both methods, together with the *RandPair* ground truth. In addition, we plot the relative empirical click rates at different positions normalized by the top position (denoted as Empirical). We can see that Empirical has more skew than *RandPair*, consistent with previous findings [7]. Both EM and Embedded differ from Empirical by taking relevance into consideration. On both data sets, EM gives much closer biases to *RandPair* than Embedded, showing that our proposed EM algorithm is effective in both relevance and position bias estimation.

5.2.2 Effects on Ranking Improvement. The position bias from the EM method is not the same as the *RandPair* method. Thus, the question is how effective the estimated propensity is to improve ranking. In this section, we leverage the estimated propensity from EM to learn a ranking function. For the baseline, we train a pairwise model on *Prec* using lambdaMART without any bias correction (denoted as NoCorrection). We use the bias estimated from *RandPair* and train a lambdaMART model to optimize IPW $\overline{Prec}$. This is the expected optimal model (denoted by RandPairCorrected). Similarly, we train a third lambdaMART ranking function to optimize the IPW $\overline{Prec}$ using EM estimated propensity scores (denoted as EMCorrected).

In Figure 3, we compare the three methods by reporting the relative MRR over the NoCorrection one. From this figure, we can see that RandPairCorrected can outperform NoCorrection significantly (+2.14% on email and +0.15% file storage). What's more important, EMCorrected achieves significant improvement over NoCorrection by +1.95% on the email data set. It performs neutrally (-0.07%) comparing with NoCorrection on the file storage data set, given that the upper bound for an improvement on file storage is very small. Overall, the EMCorrected method is shown effective in improving ranking quality without relying on randomization.

5.2.3 Unbiased Pointwise Learning. The EM method can be seen as a way to remove the bias and thus give a debiased relevance function. In this section, using the email data set, we compare it against a few other attempts for unbiased pointwise learning. As we discussed before, the IPW approach cannot be directly applied to the pointwise learning because the o_i for non-clicked documents are needed but are uncertain in click data (in contrast, $o_i = 1$ for all clicked documents). To bypass this, we use the following approximation:

- Though query-level propensity is supposed to apply to pairwise and listwise approaches, we borrow it for pointwise. In this way, all the non-clicked documents for a query will have the same IPW weights as its clicked document. We denote this by QueryLevel.

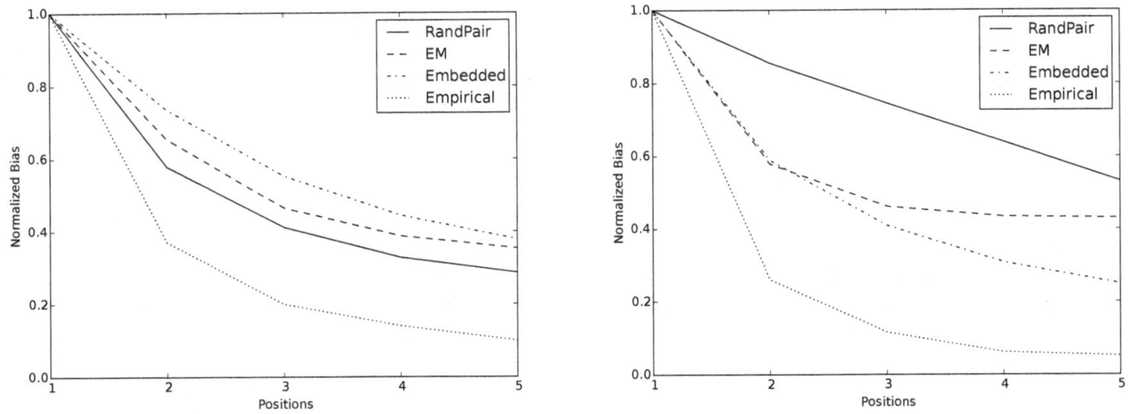

(a) Email. (b) File Storage.

Figure 2: Estimated position bias on the email and file storage services normalized by the top position.

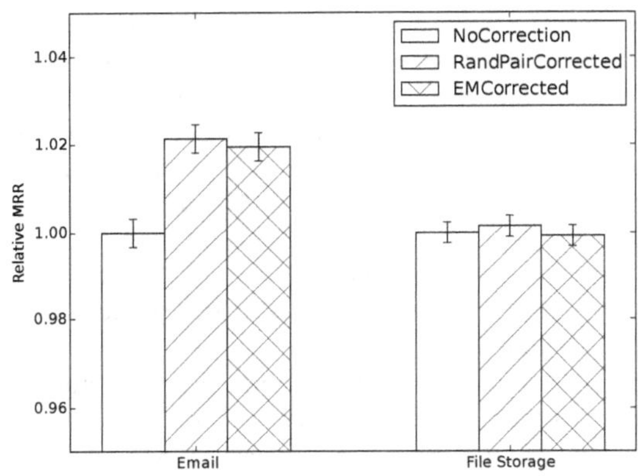

Figure 3: Ranking effectiveness comparison of pairwise approaches with different position bias correction methods.

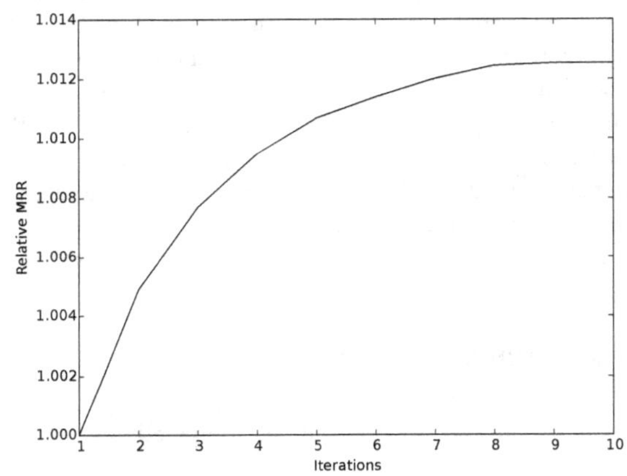

Figure 4: Convergence of EM along the iterations.

- To adapt document-level propensity, we assume $o_i = 1$ for both clicked and non-clicked documents for all the queries with clicks in our data sets. In this way, a non-clicked document has IPW weight $\frac{1}{\theta_k}$ where k is its position. We denote this by DocLevel.

In Table 4, we report the relative MRR against the pointwise model without any bias correction. As shown in the table, neither QueryLevel nor DocLevel can outperform the baseline. In contrast, the relevance function extracted from the EM algorithm is significantly better than the baseline. This shows that both QueryLevel and DocLevel have some unrealistic assumptions and are not suitable to debias the click for pointwise learning.

Furthermore, we compare the pairwise EMCorrected and the pointwise EM methods against the same baseline using the MRR metric in Table 4. Clearly, the pairwise model can leverage the estimated position bias better to improve the ranking accuracy in the learning-to-rank setting, showing the theoretical soundness of the unbiased pairwise learning-to-rank methods.

5.2.4 EM Convergence. In Figure 4, we plot the relative MRR of the relevance component against the first iteration along with the EM iterations on the email data. The results show that the EM algorithm can steadily improve the relevance function and converge quickly in about 10 iterations.

6 CONCLUSIONS

In this paper, we studied the problem of position bias estimation for unbiased learning-to-rank algorithms. We showed that the propensity estimation is equivalent to the position bias estimation in the classical position bias model. Then we compared a few estimation methods with and without result randomization. A novel regression-based EM algorithm was proposed to estimate position bias from regular production clicks. Our methods are easily applicable to any ranking system. Experimental results on email search and file storage search click data showed that our proposed EM method works well in estimating position bias and can improve ranking effectiveness significantly.

Our work inspires a few interesting future research directions. (1) The results we showed are mainly based on pairwise approaches. It is still unclear how to design an unbiased pointwise algorithm. This is worth studying given the importance of estimating pointwise CTR in applications like online advertising. (2) The current unbiased learning-to-rank is designed for binary relevance. Extending it to graded relevance with motivating applications is another interesting direction. (3) The position bias model is a simple click model; it would be interesting to study more sophisticated click models in unbiased learning-to-rank tasks.

ACKNOWLEDGMENTS

We thank Olivier Chapelle for his discussions on tradeoff among different position bias estimation methods and Roberto Bayardo for his suggestions on improving the paper presentation.

REFERENCES

[1] Aman Agarwal, Soumya Basu, Tobias Schnabel, and Thorsten Joachims. 2017. Effective Evaluation Using Logged Bandit Feedback from Multiple Loggers. In *Proc. of the 23rd ACM SIGKDD International Conference on Knowledge Discovery and Data Mining (KDD)*. 687–696.

[2] Qingyao Ai, Susan T. Dumais, Nick Craswell, and Dan Liebling. 2017. Characterizing Email Search Using Large-scale Behavioral Logs and Surveys. In *Proc. of the 26th International Conference on World Wide Web (WWW)*. 1511–1520.

[3] Michael Bendersky, Xuanhui Wang, Donald Metzler, and Marc Najork. 2017. Learning from User Interactions in Personal Search via Attribute Parameterization. In *Proc. of the 10th ACM International Conference on Web Search and Data Mining (WSDM)*. 791–799.

[4] Christopher J.C. Burges. 2010. *From RankNet to LambdaRank to LambdaMART: An Overview*. Technical Report MSR-TR-2010-82. Microsoft Research. http://research.microsoft.com/apps/pubs/default.aspx?id=132652

[5] David Carmel, Guy Halawi, Liane Lewin-Eytan, Yoelle Maarek, and Ariel Raviv. 2015. Rank by Time or by Relevance?: Revisiting Email Search. In *Proc. of the 24th ACM International Conference on Information and Knowledge Management (CIKM)*. 283–292.

[6] David Carmel, Liane Lewin-Eytan, Alex Libov, Yoelle Maarek, and Ariel Raviv. 2017. Promoting Relevant Results in Time-Ranked Mail Search. In *Proc. of the 26th International Conference on World Wide Web (WWW)*. 1551–1559.

[7] Olivier Chapelle and Ya Zhang. 2009. A dynamic bayesian network click model for web search ranking. In *Proc. of the 18th International Conference on World Wide Web (WWW)*. 1–10.

[8] Weizhu Chen, Zhanglong Ji, Si Shen, and Qiang Yang. 2011. A Whole Page Click Model to Better Interpret Search Engine Click Data.. In *Proc. of the 25th AAAI Conference on Artificial Intelligence (AAAI)*.

[9] Aleksandr Chuklin, Ilya Markov, and Maarten de Rijke. 2015. *Click Models for Web Search*. Morgan & Claypool.

[10] Nick Craswell, Onno Zoeter, Michael Taylor, and Bill Ramsey. 2008. An Experimental Comparison of Click Position-bias Models. In *Proc. of the 1st International Conference on Web Search and Data Mining (WSDM)*. 87–94.

[11] Arthur P. Dempster, Nan M. Laird, and Donald B. Rubin. 1977. Maximum Likelihood from Incomplete Data via the EM Algorithm. *Journal of the Royal Statistical Society, Series B (Methodological)* 39 (1977), 1–38. Issue 1.

[12] Miroslav Dudík, John Langford, and Lihong Li. 2011. Doubly Robust Policy Evaluation and Learning. In *Proc. of the 28th International Conference on Machine Learning (ICML)*. 1097–1104.

[13] Susan Dumais, Edward Cutrell, JJ Cadiz, Gavin Jancke, Raman Sarin, and Daniel C. Robbins. 2003. Stuff I've Seen: A System for Personal Information Retrieval and Re-Use. In *Proc. of the 26th Annual International ACM SIGIR Conference on Research and Development in Information Retrieval (SIGIR)*. 72–79.

[14] Georges E. Dupret and Benjamin Piwowarski. 2008. A User Browsing Model to Predict Search Engine Click Data from Past Observations. In *Proc. of the 31st Annual International ACM SIGIR Conference on Research and Development in Information Retrieval (SIGIR)*. 331–338.

[15] David Elsweiler, Morgan Harvey, and Martin Hacker. 2011. Understanding re-finding behavior in naturalistic email interaction logs. In *Proc. of the 34th International ACM SIGIR Conference on Research and Development in Information Retrieval (SIGIR)*. 35–44.

[16] Jerome H. Friedman. 2000. Greedy Function Approximation: A Gradient Boosting Machine. *Annals of Statistics* 29 (2000), 1189–1232.

[17] Fan Guo, Chao Liu, Anitha Kannan, Tom Minka, Michael Taylor, Yi-Min Wang, and Christos Faloutsos. 2009. Click chain model in web search. In *Proc. of the 18th International Conference on World Wide Web (WWW)*. 11–20.

[18] Trevor Hastie, Robert Tibshirani, and Jerome Friedman. 2001. *The Elements of Statistical Learning*. Springer.

[19] Thorsten Joachims, Laura Granka, Bing Pan, Helene Hembrooke, and Geri Gay. 2005. Accurately Interpreting Clickthrough Data As Implicit Feedback. In *Proc. of the 28th Annual International ACM SIGIR Conference on Research and Development in Information Retrieval (SIGIR)*. 154–161.

[20] Thorsten Joachims, Adith Swaminathan, and Tobias Schnabel. 2017. Unbiased Learning-to-Rank with Biased Feedback. In *Proc. of the 10th ACM International Conference on Web Search and Data Mining (WSDM)*. 781–789.

[21] Maryam Kamvar, Melanie Kellar, Rajan Patel, and Ya Xu. 2009. Computers and iPhones and Mobile Phones, Oh My!: A Logs-based Comparison of Search Users on Different Devices. In *Proc. of the 18th International Conference on World Wide Web (WWW)*. 801–810.

[22] Jin Young Kim, Nick Craswell, Susan Dumais, Filip Radlinski, and Fang Liu. 2017. Understanding and Modeling Success in Email Search. In *Proc. of the 40th International ACM SIGIR Conference on Research and Development in Information Retrieval (SIGIR)*. 265–274.

[23] Lihong Li, Shunbao Chen, Jim Kleban, and Ankur Gupta. 2015. Counterfactual Estimation and Optimization of Click Metrics in Search Engines: A Case Study. In *Proc. of the 24th International Conference on World Wide Web (WWW) Companion*. 929–934.

[24] Lihong Li, Wei Chu, John Langford, and Xuanhui Wang. 2011. Unbiased Offline Evaluation of Contextual-bandit-based News Article Recommendation Algorithms. In *Proc. of the 4th International Conference on Web Search and Web Data Mining (WSDM)*. 297–306.

[25] Tie-Yan Liu. 2009. Learning to rank for information retrieval. *Foundations and Trends in Information Retrieval* 3, 3 (2009), 225–331.

[26] Maeve O'Brien and Mark T Keane. 2006. Modeling result–list searching in the World Wide Web: The role of relevance topologies and trust bias. In *Proc. of the 28th Annual Conference of the Cognitive Science Society (CogSci)*. 1–881.

[27] Matthew Richardson, Ewa Dominowska, and Robert Ragno. 2007. Predicting Clicks: Estimating the Click-Through Rate for New Ads. In *Proc. of the 16th International Conference on World Wide Web (WWW)*. 521–530.

[28] Paul R Rosenbaum and Donald B Rubin. 1983. The Central Role of the Propensity Score in Observational Studies for Causal Effects. *Biometrika* 70, 1 (1983), 41–55.

[29] Tobias Schnabel, Adith Swaminathan, Ashudeep Singh, Navin Chandak, and Thorsten Joachims. 2016. Recommendations As Treatments: Debiasing Learning and Evaluation. In *Proc. of the 33rd International Conference on International Conference on Machine Learning (ICML)*. 1670–1679.

[30] Adith Swaminathan and Thorsten Joachims. 2015. Batch Learning from Logged Bandit Feedback Through Counterfactual Risk Minimization. *Journal of Machine Learning Research* 16 (2015), 1731–1755. Issue 1.

[31] Xuanhui Wang, Michael Bendersky, Donald Metzler, and Marc Najork. 2016. Learning to Rank with Selection Bias in Personal Search. In *Proc. of the 39th International ACM SIGIR Conference on Research and Development in Information Retrieval (SIGIR)*. 115–124.

[32] Yisong Yue, Rajan Patel, and Hein Roehrig. 2010. Beyond Position Bias: Examining Result Attractiveness As a Source of Presentation Bias in Clickthrough Data. In *Proc. of the 19th International Conference on World Wide Web (WWW)*. 1011–1018.

[33] Hamed Zamani, Michael Bendersky, Xuanhui Wang, and Mingyang Zhang. 2017. Situational Context for Ranking in Personal Search. In *Proc. of the 26th International Conference on World Wide Web (WWW)*. 1531–1540.

[34] Zeyuan Allen Zhu, Weizhu Chen, Tom Minka, Chenguang Zhu, and Zheng Chen. 2010. A novel click model and its applications to online advertising. In *Proc. of the 3rd ACM International Conference on Web Search and Data Mining (WSDM)*. 321–330.

A Path-constrained Framework for Discriminating Substitutable and Complementary Products in E-commerce

Zihan Wang*†
Data Science Lab, JD.com
zihanwang.jd@gmail.com

Ziheng Jiang†
Data Science Lab, JD.com
ziheng.j@gmail.com

Zhaochun Ren
Data Science Lab, JD.com
renzhaochun@jd.com

Jiliang Tang
Michigan State University
tangjili@msu.edu

Dawei Yin‡
Data Science Lab, JD.com
yindawei@acm.org

ABSTRACT

In personalized recommendation, *candidate generation* plays an infrastructural role by retrieving candidates out of billions of items. During this process, *substitutes* and *complements* constitute two main classes of retrieved candidates: substitutable products are interchangeable, whereas complementary products might be purchased together by users. Discriminating *substitutable* and *complementary* products is playing an increasingly important role in e-commerce portals by affecting the performance of candidate generation, e.g., when a user has browsed a t-shirt, it is reasonable to retrieve similar t-shirts, i.e., substitutes; whereas if the user has already purchased one, it would be better to retrieve trousers, hats or shoes, as complements of t-shirts.

In this paper, we propose a path-constrained framework (**PMSC**) for discriminating substitutes and complements. Specifically, for each product, we first learn its embedding representations in a general semantic space. Thereafter, we project the embedding vectors into two separate spaces via a novel mapping function. In the end, we incorporate each embedding with path-constraints to further boost the discriminative ability of the model. Extensive experiments conducted on two e-commerce datasets show the effectiveness of our proposed method.

ACM Reference format:
Zihan Wang, Ziheng Jiang, Zhaochun Ren, Jiliang Tang, and Dawei Yin. 2018. A Path-constrained Framework for Discriminating Substitutable and Complementary Products in E-commerce. In *Proceedings of WSDM 2018: The Eleventh ACM International Conference on Web Search and Data Mining, Marina Del Rey, CA, USA, February 5–9, 2018 (WSDM 2018),* 9 pages.
https://doi.org/10.1145/3159652.3159710

*Work performed during an internship at Data Science Lab, JD.com.
†These two authors contributed equally to the paper.
‡Corresponding author

WSDM 2018, February 5–9, 2018, Marina Del Rey, CA, USA

ACM ISBN 978-1-4503-5581-0/18/02...$15.00
https://doi.org/10.1145/3159652.3159710

1 INTRODUCTION

Personalized recommender systems (PRS) have become indispensable and ubiquitous for bridging users and items in various scenarios, e.g., multimedia recommendations [6, 7, 11, 18], news recommendations [37], and product recommendations [36], etc. In modern e-commerce portals, although billions of items exist, only a small portion of them attract users' attention. Modern e-commerce PRS usually consist of two procedures, i.e., *candidate generation* and *candidate ranking* [4, 6]: candidate generation refers to a process that retrieves personalized candidates out of billions of items [6, 17, 39]; whereas candidate ranking procedure ranks the retrieved candidates for a better conversion rate or click-through rate [4, 12, 29, 35, 40]. Thus given a user's contextual information, e-commerce PRS can be optimized by addressing these two aspects, respectively. In this paper, we address the *candidate generation* problem in e-commerce PRS.

In general, there are several strategies for retrieving personalized product candidates, among which substitutable and complementary products are of the most importance. *Substitutable* products are those that are interchangeable, while *complementary* products are those that might be purchased together [23]. Understanding substitutable and complementary products can help candidate generation. For example, when a customer is shopping for a t-shirt online, it is better to retrieve similar t-shirts, or jeans, shoes, and socks etc. rather than totally irrelevant items such as computers or movies. More importantly, apart from being general retrieval sources, substitutable and complementary products can also be used as the unique source in some specific recommendation scenarios, such as "similar products" and "recommend after purchasing", respectively.

Recently, a system named Sceptre [23] is proposed to distinguish substitutes and complements. Given two datasets called *also-view* and *also-bought* from Amazon, Sceptre is able to model and predict substitutes and complements relations by learning latent topics from textual information, such as products reviews and descriptions etc. Despite the success of Sceptre, several issues still have not been fully addressed yet: 1) Severe sparseness problem: Based on our *also-view* and *also-bought* datasets from Amazon and JD, we find there are 57.2 millions of products, with only 2.24 billion pairs. This implies that existing models may not be well trained under e-commerce circumstance, especially for those tail products in e-commerce portals. 2) Neglect of complex paths: Direct links are a kind of paths that can naturally encode products and relations as graph, where nodes are products and edges are relations. In addition to that, more complex paths exist in such a product graph, which is a sequence of relations and products, *e.g.* $i \xrightarrow{subst.} j \xrightarrow{compl.} k$. These paths represent more complex relation dependencies, which are able to further improve the performance of candidate generation.

In this paper, we propose a path-constrained method to discriminate substitutes and complements (**PMSC**). Specifically, we first predict whether there is a directed link between any pair of products, which is achieved by learning product embedding vectors in a general semantic space. Then, we define a latent vector for each relation and map the original product representations into the corresponding relation space, which can discriminate what type the directed link is, e.g. substitute or complement. Moreover, we incorporate product category constraints and multi-step path constraints to alleviate the data sparsity problem.

We conduct extensive experiments on two real-world datasets from two e-commerce portals. Experimental results show that **PMSC** significantly outperforms the baselines in various tasks in e-commerce. The embeddings of existing products can be easily generalized for new products, which helps mitigate the "cold-start" problem. The learned embeddings are visualized to understand how the proposed algorithm works. The main contributions of this paper are as follows:

- We propose a novel multi-relation learning framework, **PMSC**, which identifies substitutes and complements simultaneously.
- Two types of path constraints are incorporated, which can substantially alleviate the data sparsity problem. The visualization of the learned representations clearly shows that with path constraints, **PMSC** can effectively distinguish substitutes and complements.
- Experiments on two large-scale real world datasets show that **PMSC** significantly outperforms the baselines in various tasks in e-commerce.

2 RELATED WORK

In this section, we detail relevant previous work on collaborative filtering and neural embedding models.

2.1 Collaborative Filtering

The input of a recommendation system is often the users' demography, behaviors, and context, while the output is the relevant products. In recent years, collaborative filtering (CF) based techniques have received increased attention [10, 16, 30, 38, 41]. Unlike content-based filtering strategies [19] which predict ratings through the analysis of user profiles, collaborative filtering [31] methods, either memory-based CF or model-based CF, predict ratings using user-item ratings matrices. Early CF-based methods apply memory-based techniques. The most widely used memory-based CF methods include the nearest neighbor approach [3], user-based methods [27] and item-based methods [28]. Among the model-based CF methods, latent factor models [13] have become very popular as they show state-of-the-art performance on multiple datasets. Aimed at factorizing a rating matrix into products of a user-specific matrix and an item-specific matrix, matrix factorization based methods [13, 15] are widely used. Zhang et al. [38] propose a localized matrix factorization approach to address data sparsity and scalability by factorizing block diagonal form matrices. Ranking-oriented collaborative filtering algorithms have achieved good results: Shi et al. [30] use a list-wise learning to rank method, called CliMF. Linden et al. [17] predict user behavior links such as "Users who viewed X also viewed Y" or "Users who bought X also bought Y" . These "co-counting" methods are simple and may also produce a noisy recommendation for the rare products and has limited ability to explain results. More browsing and co-purchasing methods are proposed in [39]. Recently, He et al. [10] successfully apply neural networks to collaborative filtering. Unlike all above collaborative filtering methods, this paper is to learn the semantics of related products.

2.2 Neural Embedding Models

Recently, neural embedding methods for recommendation system and linguistic tasks have significantly improved accuracy of state-of-art models [1, 2, 5, 20, 24, 25] . In the neural embedding method, words, phrases or items are mapped into a low dimension space in order to capture semantics and correlation. For instances, motivated by word2vec [24], Barkan and Koenigstein [2] propose a modified version of the skip-gram model with negative sampling, item2vec, so as to induce a similarity measure for different items. Moreover, many recent works learn representations for relation inference with other features [9, 22, 23, 32–34]. For example, He et al. [9] learn complicated and heterogeneous relationships between items with high-level visual features.

The most similar work as ours is Sceptre [23], which learns the semantics of the substitutes and complements from data associated with products, such as the text of product reviews, ratings, specifications. However, Sceptre neglects the relations between categories and the paths of relations between two products. Our proposed method takes these two factors into consideration and formulates them as path constraints to obtain the further improvement.

3 THE PROPOSED FRAMEWORK

3.1 An Overview

Before we give a detailed description of our method, a high-level overview is presented as follows. There are four main phases: (A) directed link prediction; (B) multi-relation learning; (C) path constraints; (D) joint learning and optimization. Table 1 describes the notation we use throughout the paper.

To model plausibility of every edge between products, in phase (A), we first embed products into a general semantic space, and because of the asymmetry of relations, we utilize two types of vectors, i.e., target vector v and context vector v', to predict directed links between two products. This idea is closely related to the model of Item2vec [2]. To enable the scalability, we adopt a logistic loss function to judge the existence of the directed link between products. On top of link prediction using general semantic vectors, in phase (B) we introduce a latent vector for each relation and map the original representations into relation-specific spaces to discriminate edge types. In this way, **PMSC** enables implicit data sharing among related products and relations. Due to the data

Table 1: Glossary

Symbols	Descriptions
v_i, v'_i	target,context vector of product i
$v_{r,i}, v'_{r,i}$	projected target ,context vector of product i for r
r	product relation
β_r	projecting vector for relation r
$\mathcal{R}$	product relation set
$\mathcal{E}$	product set
$\mathcal{E}_P, \overline{\mathcal{E}}_P$	positive, negative ordered pair set
$\mathcal{E}_E, \overline{\mathcal{E}}_E$	positive, negative edge set
$\mathcal{E}_F, \overline{\mathcal{E}}_F$	positive, negative formula set
V, V'	target, context representation set
$\boldsymbol{\beta}$	projecting vector set
f, f'	positive, negative formula
N	number of negative samples

sparseness problem, embedding vectors may not be trained substantially and many products from very different categories may share indistinguishable representations. To address this problem and boost the discriminative ability of product representations, in phase (C) we incorporate two types of path constraints into the proposed model:1) The meta information such as product category is an important supplement to identify the relations between products, especially for tail products. 2) Most previous models pay much attention on learning relational data using the direct links, while multi-step paths is able to imply much more complicated patterns among the relations.

3.2 (A) Directed Link Prediction

In fact, neither substitute relation nor complement relation is necessarily symmetric. Similar to the method in [2], we use two types of vectors, *i.e.* target and context vectors, which capture the different semantics for products in directed relations. Specifically, if product i is a good substitute or a reasonable complement for products j, *i.e.* there is a substitute or complement edge from product i to product j, the probability whether this edge exists ($y_{i,j} = 1$) or not ($y_{i,j} = 0$) is calculated as:

$$P(y_{i,j}|V, V') = \sigma(v_i^T \cdot v'_j), \tag{1}$$

where v_i is the target vector of product i and v'_j is the context vector of product j. $\sigma(\cdot)$ denotes the sigmoid function. It is easy to verify that the larger $p(y_{i,j}|V, V', \boldsymbol{\beta})$ is, the more likely the edge from i to j exists.

Then, we adopt the logistic loss, which leads to the following objective function:

$$P(Y|V, V') = \prod_{(i,j)\in\mathcal{E}_P} \sigma(v_i^T \cdot v'_j)) \cdot \prod_{(i,j')\in\overline{\mathcal{E}}_P} (1 - \sigma(v_i^T \cdot v'_{j'})), \tag{2}$$

where $\mathcal{E}_P$ is the positive ordered pair set, meaning that if $(i, j) \in \mathcal{E}_P$, there exists a directed edge from product i to product j. $\overline{\mathcal{E}}_P$ is the negative ordered pair set constructed by randomly replacing the products in the corresponding positive pairs.

Since it is impractical to enumerate all the negative pairs in the training process, we adopt the efficient negative sampling strategy proposed in [24] and construct the negative instances by replacing j in the positive pair (i, j) with j' so that $(i, j') \in \overline{\mathcal{E}}_P$. Therefore, the loss function can be written as:

$$\begin{aligned} L(Y|V, V') &= -log(P(Y|V, V')) \\ &= -\sum_{(i,j)\in\mathcal{E}_P} log(\sigma(v_i^T \cdot v'_j)) \\ &\quad - N \cdot E_{j'\sim P_n(w)}[log(\sigma(-v_i^T \cdot v'_{j'}))], \end{aligned} \tag{3}$$

where N is the number of negative samples, and $P_n(w)$ is the noise distribution which is often set to the 3/4rd power of the unigram distribution $U(w) \sim 1/|\{(i, j') \in \overline{\mathcal{E}}_P\}|$. The goal of the objective function is to distinguish the positive product pairs from the noise distribution $P_n(w)$.

3.3 (B) Multi-Relation Learning

In this section, we generalize our model for the multi-relation task. Usually, when a product has multiple semantics, various relations focus on different semantics of products accordingly. We learn the product representations by projecting them from the general semantic space to corresponding relation space as follow:

$$v_{r,i} = v_i + \beta_r \odot v_i, v'_{r,i} = v'_i + \beta_r \odot v'_i, \tag{4}$$

where $v_{r,i}$ is the projected target vector for relation r and $v'_{r,i}$ is the projected context vector for relation r and β_r denotes the project vector. The difference of the product representations and projected vectors will be determined by both products and relations. In projecting operation, every entry of product representation interacts sufficiently with the relation representation in the corresponding position. In that way, we define the confidence of the directed edge (i, r, j) as $I(i, r, j)$ and calculate it as follow:

$$I(i, r, j) = P(z_{i,j,r}) = \sigma(v_{r,i}^T \cdot v'_{r,j}), \tag{5}$$

where $z_{i,j,r}$ is the label of the edge (i, r, j). The objective function for relation identification can be rewritten as:

$$\begin{aligned} L(Z|V, V', \boldsymbol{\beta}) &= -log(P(Z|V, V', \boldsymbol{\beta})) \\ &= \sum_{r\in R} \sum_{(i,r,j)\in\mathcal{E}_E} -log(I(i, r, j)) \\ &\quad - N \cdot E_{j'\sim P_n(w_0)}[log(1 - I(i, r, j'))], \end{aligned} \tag{6}$$

where $\mathcal{E}_E$ is the positive edge set. We also adopt the negative sampling strategy and $P_n(w_0) \sim 1/|\{(i, r, j') \in \overline{\mathcal{E}}_E\}|^{3/4}$, in which $\overline{\mathcal{E}}_E$ is the negative edge set.

3.4 (C) Path Constraints for Substitutes and Complements

To model path constraints in product dataset, t-norm fuzzy logics are adopted. We take a directed edge (i, r, j) as an atomic formula f_0. In that case, the probability of a complex formula f, *i.e.* $I(f)$, can be obtained by a composition of the probability of atomic formulae through specific t-norm based lattices and conjunctions in logic. We follow [8] and use the product t-norm. The compositions containing logical conjunction ($\wedge$), disjunction ($\vee$), and negation ($\neg$) are defined as follow:

$$\begin{aligned} I(f_a \wedge f_b) &= I(f_a) \cdot I(f_b), \\ I(f_a \vee f_b) &= I(f_a) + I(f_b) - I(f_a) \cdot I(f_b), \\ I(\neg f_a) &= 1 - I(f_a), \end{aligned}$$

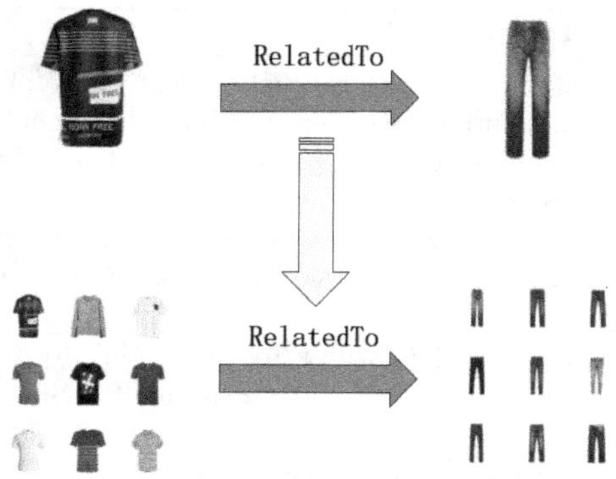

Figure 1: An Example for Category Constraints.

where f_a and f_b are two constituent formulae, either atomic or complex. Given these compositions, the confidence value of any complex formula can be calculated recursively, e.g.,

$$I(\neg f_a \wedge f_b) = I(f_b) - I(f_a)\cdot I(f_b),$$
$$I(f_a \Rightarrow f_b) = I(f_a)\cdot I(f_b) - I(f_a) + 1,$$
$$I(f_a \wedge f_b \Rightarrow f_c) = I(f_a)\cdot I(f_b)\cdot I(f_c) - I(f_a)\cdot I(f_b) + 1.$$

Product Category Constraints. Most existing data-driven approaches often suffer from the data sparsity problem in practice. To address this problem, we enhance the product representation distinctiveness by fusing information from two sources (basic structure information, *i.e.* direct links, and category feature) into a unified framework. Specifically, we take the following constraint into consideration:

$$\begin{aligned} &(Prod_A, RelatedTo, Prod_B) \\ \Rightarrow\ &(Category_A, RelatedTo, Category_B). \end{aligned} \tag{7}$$

Here $Category_A$ and $Category_B$ are respectively the product categories of $Prod_A$ and $Prod_B$. The constraint indicates that when product A and product B are related, the categories of product A and product B probably share semantic information and their representations are much closer in latent semantic space than other irrelevant product categories. For instance, in Figure 1, t-shirt and jeans are closely related to each other and so are their categories. To directly combine Eq. (7) with the original model, We consider the following constraints:

$$(Prod_A, Subst, Prod_B) \Rightarrow (Prod_A, Subst, Prod_C), \tag{8}$$

$$(Prod_A, Compl, Prod_B) \Rightarrow (Prod_A, Compl, Prod_C). \tag{9}$$

Note that $prod_C$ is in the same product category as $prod_B$. In this way, our method brings more interactions among representations of related products, which is beneficial for representation learning. Given an instance of the constraints $f_1 \triangleq (i, r_1, j) \Rightarrow (i, r_1, k)$, the confidence is obtained by:

$$\begin{aligned} I(f_1) = &I(i, r_1, j)\cdot I(i, r_1, k) \\ &- I(i, r_1, j) + 1. \end{aligned} \tag{10}$$

Multi-Step Path Constraints. In addition to the category constraints, multi-step paths between product pairs can reflect much more complex patterns than the direct links. In the graph, a multi-step path is a sequence of nodes and relations. For instance, as in Figure 2(a), a t-shirt is a substitute to a polo shirt and both of them are complements to jeans (similar ideas are shown in Figure 2). We count the frequency of instances discovered by all the reasonable two-hop relations in the Amazon dataset, and find out that four patterns, shown in Table 2, have dominated the data distribution. Therefore, to capture such information, multi-step path constraints is designed and incorporated. The form of the multi-step path constraints is $\forall i, j, k : (i, r_1, j) \wedge (j, r_2, k) \Rightarrow (i, r_3, k)$. In the product graph, we can generally represent the constraints as the following:

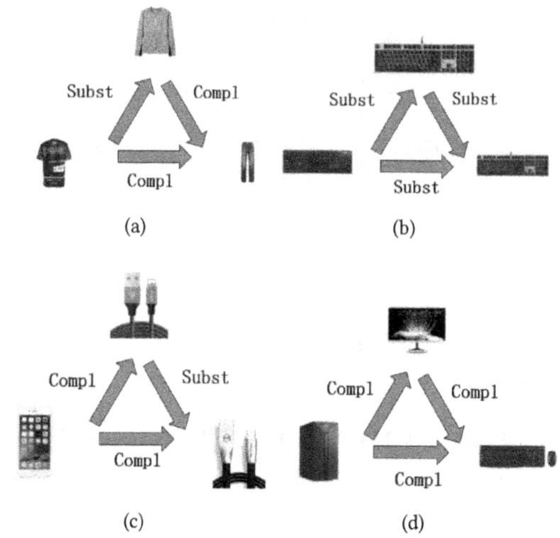

Figure 2: Examples for Multi-Step Path Constraints

$$\begin{aligned} &(Prod_A, Subst, Prod_B) \wedge (Prod_B, Subst, Prod_C) \\ &\quad \Rightarrow (Prod_A, Subst, Prod_C), \end{aligned} \tag{11}$$

$$\begin{aligned} &(Prod_A, Compl, Prod_B) \wedge (Prod_B, Subst, Prod_C) \\ &\quad \Rightarrow (Prod_A, Compl, Prod_C), \end{aligned} \tag{12}$$

$$\begin{aligned} &(Prod_A, Subst, Prod_B) \wedge (Prod_B, Compl, Prod_C) \\ &\quad \Rightarrow (Prod_A, Compl, Prod_C), \end{aligned} \tag{13}$$

$$\begin{aligned} &(Prod_A, Compl, Prod_B) \wedge (Prod_B, Compl, Prod_C) \\ &\quad \Rightarrow (Prod_A, Compl, Prod_C). \end{aligned} \tag{14}$$

Given an instance of constraints $f_2 \triangleq (i, r_1, j) \wedge (j, r_2, k) \Rightarrow (i, r_3, k)$, the confidence is obtained by:

$$\begin{aligned} I(f_2) = &I(i, r_1, j)\cdot I(j, r_2, k)\cdot I(i, r_3, k) \\ &- I(i, r_1, j)\cdot I(j, r_2, k) + 1. \end{aligned} \tag{15}$$

Note that the larger the confidence is, the better the ground rules are satisfied. Besides the rules mentioned, our framework is able to handle more general rules and paths with longer length. We might explore more types of rules in the future.

We then incorporate path constraints into our model using Eq.(10) and (15), and the negative log-likelihood loss function for the path constraint i can be rewritten as follow:

$$\begin{aligned} L(F_c|V, V', \boldsymbol{\beta}) = &- \sum\nolimits_{f_c \in \mathcal{E}_F} log(I(f_c)) \\ &- N \cdot E_{f_c' \sim P_n(w_c)}[log(1 - I(f_c'))], \end{aligned} \tag{16}$$

where F_c is the label set for the formula f_c, where f_0 represents direct edges, f_1 is a formula for the product category constraint and f_2 is a formula for the multi-step path constraint. $\mathcal{E}_F$ is the positive formula set for the formula f_c (an atomic formula or a complex

Table 2: Multi-Step Path Ratio

Multi-Step Path	Ratio	
(r_1, r_2, r_3)	Electronics	Women's Clothes
(Sub, Sub, Sub)	22.84%	66.18%
(Sub, Com, Com)	65.75%	13.64%
(Com, Sub, Com)	4.17%	7.64%
(Com, Com, Com)	3.70%	6.83%
$OtherRules$	3.54%	5.71%

formula) and $\overline{\mathcal{E}_F}$ is the negative one. The noise distribution here is $[1/|\{f_c' \in \overline{\mathcal{E}_F}\}|]^{3/4}$.

3.5 (D) Joint Learning and Optimization

After representing directed links and path constraints as atomic and complex formulae, we combine Eq. (3) and (16) and minimize a global loss to learn product and relation representations as follow:

$$\begin{aligned}\min L_{joint} &= L(Y|V,V') + \sum_{c=0}^{2} \alpha_c \cdot L(F_c|V,V',\boldsymbol{\beta}) \\ &= L(Y|V,V') + \alpha_0 \cdot L(Z|V,V',\boldsymbol{\beta}) + \alpha_1 \cdot L(F_1|V,V',\boldsymbol{\beta}) \\ &+ \alpha_2 \cdot L(F_2|V,V',\boldsymbol{\beta}),\end{aligned} \tag{17}$$

$$\text{s.t.} \quad \|\mathbf{v}_i\|_2 \le 1 \; and \; \|\mathbf{v}_i'\|_2 \le 1, \forall i \in \mathcal{E}; \; \|\mathbf{r}\|_2 \le 1, \forall r \in \mathcal{R}.$$

Before the optimization process, a training set $\mathcal{E}_F$, which contains all positive path constraints found by breadth-first search, is constructed. Next, we construct the negative set as follow: if $f \triangleq (i,r,j)$ is an observed edge in the product graph, we construct f' by replacing j with a random product j'. If $f \triangleq (i,r_1,j) \Rightarrow (i,r_1,k)$ is a positive formula for product category constraint, a possible negative instance is f' by replacing r_1 with other relation, or replacing i or k with other product. If $f \triangleq (i,r_1,j) \wedge (j,r_2,k) \Rightarrow (i,r_3,k)$ is a positive formula for multi-step path constraint, a possible negative instance is f' by replacing r_3 with other relation, or replacing i or k with other product. We filter out randomly generated formula f' appeared in the training set. Then, to optimize the loss function, stochastic gradient descent is used, where α_c is the weight for formula f_c. To satisfy the ℓ_2-constraints, $\mathbf{v}$,$\mathbf{v}'$ and $\mathbf{r}$ are projected to the unit ℓ_2-ball in every iteration. Product and relation feature vectors trained in this way are expected to fit both the directed links and path constraints. The detailed optimization procedure is described in Algorithm 1.

4 EXPERIMENTS

In this section, we first describe our datasets in §4.1. The parameters for the proposed framework are listed in §4.2. The baselines and evaluation metrics are detailed in §4.3. We evaluate **PMSC** in terms of link prediction and ranking performances in §4.4. Then we examine the impact of the cold start problem in §4.5.

4.1 Datasets

We use two real-world e-commerce datasets in our experiments:
Amazon dataset: Amazon dataset was collected on the user-product-review graph and was split into top-level categories, e.g., electronics, women's clothes, office product, etc. In this dataset, we select 5 categories from the Amazon dataset released by McAuley et al. [23],

Algorithm 1 Learning PMSC

Input: target and context representation set, V and V'; Projecting vector set, $\boldsymbol{\beta}$; formula set (atomic and complex formulas), $\mathcal{E}_F = \{f\}$; product pair set, $\mathcal{E}_P = \{(i,j)\}$; size of batch, b; the number of samples, N.

initialize: $\mathbf{v} \leftarrow$ uniform $(-0.5, 0.5)$ for each target vector $\mathbf{v} \in V$
initialize context vector $\mathbf{v}'$ and projecting vector β_p with $\mathbf{0}$
loop
  Normalize $\mathbf{v}, \mathbf{v}', \beta_p$ with $\mathbf{v}/||\mathbf{v}||, \mathbf{v}'/||\mathbf{v}'||, \beta_p/||\beta_p||$
  Sample $\mathcal{E}_{P_{batch}}, \mathcal{E}_{F_{batch}}$ of size b from $\mathcal{E}_P, \mathcal{E}_F$
  $\overline{\mathcal{E}}_{P_{batch}}, \overline{\mathcal{E}}_{F_{batch}} \leftarrow \emptyset$
  for $f \in \mathcal{E}_{F_{batch}}$ and $(i,j) \in \mathcal{E}_{P_{batch}}$ **do**
    $k = 0$
    for $k < N$ **do**
      $f_k' \leftarrow$ Sample from $\overline{\mathcal{E}}_F$
      $(i_k, j_k') \leftarrow$ Sample from $\overline{\mathcal{E}}_P$
      $\overline{\mathcal{E}}_{F_{batch}} \leftarrow \overline{\mathcal{E}}_{F_{batch}} \cup f_k'$
      $\overline{\mathcal{E}}_{batch} \leftarrow \overline{\mathcal{E}}_{batch} \cup (i_k, j_k')$
    end for
    $\mathcal{E}_{F_{batch}} \leftarrow \mathcal{E}_{F_{batch}} \cup f$
    $\mathcal{E}_{P_{batch}} \leftarrow \mathcal{E}_{P_{batch}} \cup (i,j)$
  end for
  Updating target vector v, context vector v' and projecting vector β_p w.r.t. $\nabla L_{joint}(\mathcal{E}_{P_{batch}}, \overline{\mathcal{E}}_{P_{batch}}, \mathcal{E}_{F_{batch}}, \overline{\mathcal{E}}_{F_{batch}})$
end loop

Table 3: Statistics on Amazon dataset

Category	Item	Review	Edge
Electronic	498K	11.4M	7.87M
Women's Clothes	838K	14.5M	17.5M
Home and Kitchen	437K	4.25M	12.9M
Cell Phones and Accessories	347K	3.44M	6.22M
Office Products	134K	1.24M	4.20M
All	2.26M	34.9M	48.7M

whereas four types of product pairs (x, y) are crawled to obtain ground truth of substitutes and complements, i.e., "also viewed" (users who viewed x also viewed y), "buy after viewing" (users who viewed x eventually bought y), "also bought" (users who bought x also bought y), and "bought together" (users who frequently bought x and y together). Edges of "also viewed" and "buy after viewing" are considered as substitutes and edges of "frequently buy together" and "also bought" are treated as complements. The detailed statistics of the dataset are shown in Table 3
JD dataset: we randomly sample edges of "also viewed" and "also bought" from logs of a real e-commerce site, **JD.com**. Because these edges form the majority of the dataset, we ignore the other two types of edges. The detailed statistics of the dataset are shown in Table 4.

4.2 Experimental Settings

We split our data into 80% for training, 10% for validation and 10% for test. Since it is impractical to train our model on all the negative product pairs, we randomly sample N non-links from the dataset

Table 4: Statistics on JD dataset

Category	Item	Review	Edge
Baby	707K	3.90M	35.2M
Women's Clothes	1.06M	4.20M	35.5M
Men's Clothes	734K	3.65M	18.1M
Cell Phones and Accessories	581K	3.32M	39.7M
Office Products	382K	2.88M	46.2M
All	34.7M	18.0M	175M

Given each positive instance (i, r, j), we generate N negative instances using the method proposed in [23]. We tune the dimension of our representations in $\{50, 100, 200\}$, the number of negative samples N in $\{5, 10, 20\}$, weights α_0, α_1 and α_2 in $\{0.001, 0.01, 0.1, 1.0\}$, and learning rate in $\{0.1, 0.01, 0.001\}$.

4.3 Baselines and Evaluation Metrics

We compare PMSC to several baseline methods, including Random, Matrix Factorization (MF)[13], Non-Negative Matrix Factorization (NMF)[14], and Sceptre[23].

Random. The link prediction probability $P(i, r, j)$ is replaced by random number between 0 and 1. When link prediction probability is larger than a threshold α, the edge (i, r, j) holds. The threshold α is selected on validation set.

Matrix Factorization (MF) and Non-Negative Matrix Factorization (NMF). Matrix factorization [13] and non-negative matrix factorization [14] are both developed for finding linear representation of data. In experiments, we set the entry (i, j) of original matrix as 1 for directed edge $prod_i \longrightarrow prod_j$ and 0 for non-links. We train individual model for each relation. We tune the dimension of the features in $\{200, 500, 1000, 2000, 5000\}$.

Item-to-Item Collaborative Filtering (CF). Item-to-Item Collaborative Filtering is the solution for *Amazon* recommender system reported in [17]. In our case, we evaluate the method with sets of users who review each item instead of browsing and purchasing data. Then we compute the cosine similarity between products by calculating the cosine similarity between user sets. We only test this method in ranking tasks, since it is not probabilistic.

Sceptre is proposed in [23]. The key idea of Sceptre is to combine topic modeling and supervised link prediction. In addition, Sceptre can harness additional features (such as brands, price, and rating) and predict multiple types of relations simultaneously. In the link prediction and ranking task, we follow the same experimental settings in [23]. We tune the number of products needed for a new topic in $\{200, 500, 1000, 2000, 5000\}$.

Besides, to specify performance of each component of our model, we also train **PMSC (base)** according to Eq. (3) and Eq. (6), **PMSC (base+C1)** using Eq. (17) with only product category constraints and **PMSC (base+C1+C2)** with both product category and multi-step path constraints in Eq. (17).

4.4 Link Prediction and Ranking

Link Prediction. To predict whether there is a directed edge r between the given product pair (i, j), we optimize our objective function in Eq. (17). A prediction is correct when:

- if there is a directed edge of type r from i to j: $\sigma(v_{r,i}^T \cdot v'_{r,j}) > \alpha$,

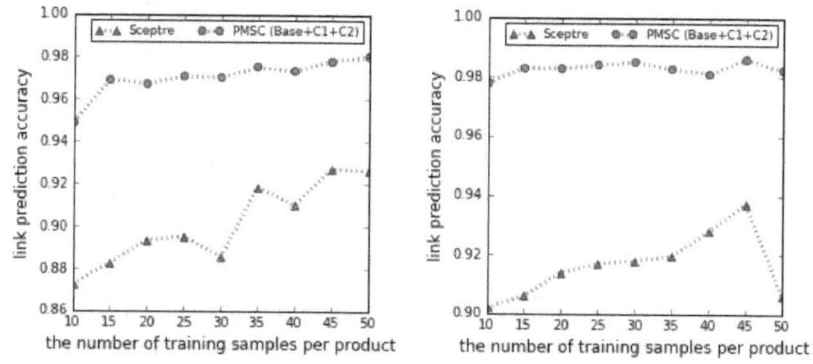

(a) Baby on JD Dataset (b) Office Product on Amazon

Figure 3: Accuracy-Training-Samples Curves

- if there is non-edge r from i to j: $\sigma(v_{r,i}^T \cdot v'_{r,j}) \leq \alpha$.

Note that the threshold α is selected between 0.1 and 0.9 on the validation set.

Results are shown in Table 5 and 6. Note that due to the different number of non-edge samples, our results of Sceptre method are different from those reported in [23]. To measure the overall predictive performance, we also demonstrate the ROC curves in Figure 4 and 5, where the AUC value of **PMSC** is coherently greater than those of the baselines. We summarize our observations as follows:

- **PMSC** is capable of accurately predicting both substitute and complement links in all categories, especially for clothes on Amazon dataset and Baby on JD dataset.
- **PMSC** significantly outperforms other baselines. MF and NMF can barely handle the substitutes and complements prediction for extremely sparse data. Comparing to Sceptre which extracts the related topics between product pairs from the review texts, product category, and multi-step path constraints uncover potential links directly. Besides, **PMSC** takes the dependencies among multiple relations into the consideration, which significantly facilitates learning the product and relation representations. Additionally, we show the performances of varying numbers of training samples per product in the link prediction task in Figure 3, where we can observe that the performance of **PMSC** is more stable than Sceptre, demonstrating that **PMSC** can address the sparsity problem well.
- **PMSC (Base+C1+C2)** consistently outperforms both **PMSC (Base+C1)** and **PMSC (Base)**, while **PMSC (Base+C1)** achieves higher accuracy on all categories comparing to **PMSC(Base)**. Thus, both product category constraints and multi-step path constraints can improve the accuracy of identifying substitutes and complements.

In summary, we are able to conclude that each component of **PMSC** contributes to the prediction accuracy. The basic **PMSC(Base)** has relatively low predictive accuracy in some product categories. The product category constraints and multi-step path constraints are helpful for both product and relation representation learning, as well as alleviating the data sparsity problem.

Ranking. In many applications, only a limited set of substitutes and complements are recommended. Thus, in addition to distinguishing links and non-links between the given product pairs, it is

Table 5: Link Prediction Accuracy on Amazon

Method	Electronics		Women's Clothes		Home and Kitchen		Cell Phones and Accessories		Office Products	
	Subst.	Compl.	Subst.	Compl.	Subst.	Compl.	Subst.	Compl.	Subst.	Compl.
Random	0.7800	0.7801	0.7803	0.7800	0.7808	0.7796	0.7809	0.7799	0.7800	0.7804
MF	0.8056	0.7916	0.7963	0.7850	0.8140	0.8094	0.7910	0.8000	0.7950	0.7927
NMF	0.8147	0.8013	0.8179	0.8023	0.8276	0.8159	0.7979	0.8269	0.8073	0.8165
Sceptre	0.9281	0.8789	0.9142	0.9091	0.8528	0.9161	0.8966	0.8895	0.9385	0.8912
PMSC (Base)	0.8698	0.8554	0.9178	0.8595	0.8483	0.8841	0.8820	0.9068	0.8688	0.8718
PMSC (Base+C1)	0.9176	0.8735	0.9284	0.9032	0.8501	0.8973	0.8923	0.9248	0.8770	0.8508
PMSC (Base+C1+C2)	**0.9790**	**0.9242**	**0.9777**	**0.9602**	**0.8631**	**0.9252**	**0.9016**	**0.9306**	**0.9778**	**0.9079**

Table 6: Link Prediction Accuracy on JD Dataset

Method	Baby		Women's Clothes		Men's clothes		Cell Phones and Accessories		Office Products	
	Subst.	Compl.	Subst.	Compl.	Subst.	Compl.	Subst.	Compl.	Subst.	Compl.
Random	0.7799	0.7802	0.7797	0.7822	0.7797	0.7790	0.7800	0.7812	0.7799	0.7798
MF	0.7993	0.8092	0.7957	0.7961	0.7960	0.7903	0.7952	0.8072	0.8013	0.8106
NMF	0.8353	0.8070	0.8164	0.8170	0.8049	0.8281	0.8078	0.8239	0.8211	0.8284
Sceptre	0.9158	0.9156	0.8974	0.9138	0.8822	0.9105	0.9135	0.9148	0.9133	0.9154
PMSC (Base)	0.8035	0.9020	0.8761	0.7778	0.8722	0.8523	0.7691	0.8987	0.7086	0.8439
PMSC (Base+C1)	0.8174	0.9075	0.8876	0.8651	0.9104	0.8588	0.7727	0.9067	0.7283	0.9180
PMSC (Base+C1+C2)	**0.9741**	**0.9457**	**0.9411**	**0.9487**	**0.9481**	**0.9488**	**0.9570**	**0.9483**	**0.9501**	**0.9405**

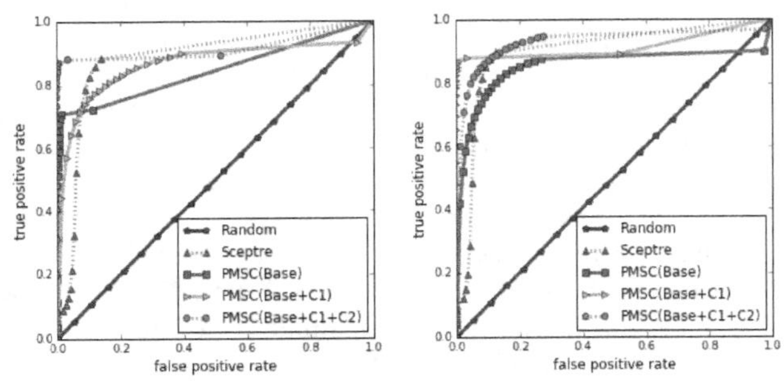

(a) Substitute (b) Complement

Figure 4: ROC Curves for Cell Phones and Accessories on Amazon

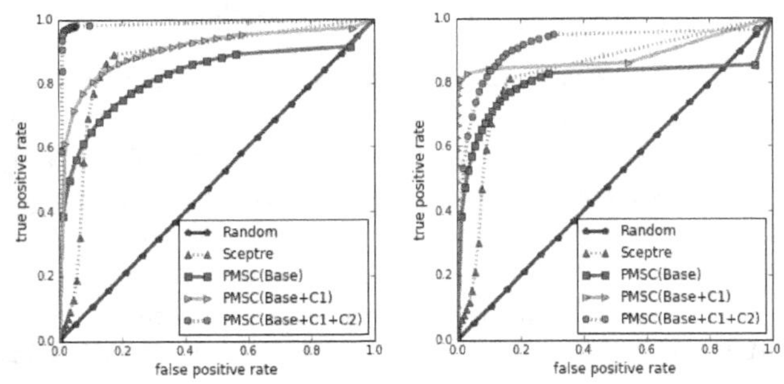

(a) Substitute (b) Complement

Figure 5: ROC Curves for Office Product on Amazon

also important that the relevant products are scored higher than the irrelevant ones.

A standard measurement for ranking methods is the precision@k. To be specific, for a given relation r, precision is the fraction of recommended products that are relevant to the query product. The precision is defined as follow:

$$precision = \frac{|\{relevant\,products\} \cap \{recommened\,products\}|}{|\{recommened\,products\}|} \tag{18}$$

Regarding to the fact that only limited results are returned by the system, precision can be evaluated at a given cut-off rank k, *i.e.* precision@k. In our experiment, we follow the setting in [23] and discard the candidate links existing in the train and validation sets.

Our ranking results are reported in Figure 6 and 7 on Cell Phones and Accessories in both Amazon dataset and JD dataset. Since we only keep the candidate links appearing in the test set, only a small number of relevant products are remain for the query products. The Random method only has the precision around 10^{-5}, meaning that Random can only recommend about 1 relevant product in 100,000 candidates, which indicates the extreme difficulty of the task.

It can be observed from the Figure 6 and 7 that MF, NMF and CF methods obtain much better performance than the Random method. The curve of **PMSC (Base+C1+C2)** is consistently above all baselines, indicating that **PMSC** is able to retrieve the most relevant products for each relation.

4.5 Cold-Start

From the previous two subsections, we can see that **PMSC** achieves the promising performance on link prediction and ranking. However, another important problem is how to predict links and recommend relevant products for new products, which are unseen in the training set. This kind of problem is notorious as "cold start" problem [26, 29, 40]. To address the "cold start" problem, we argue

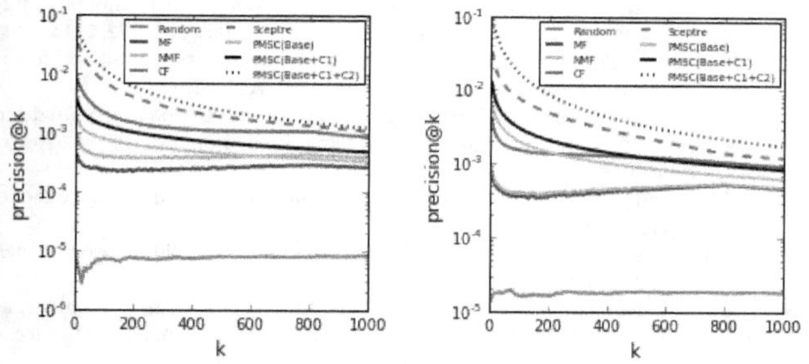

(a) Substitute (b) Complement

Figure 6: Precision@k for Cell Phones and Accessories on Amazon

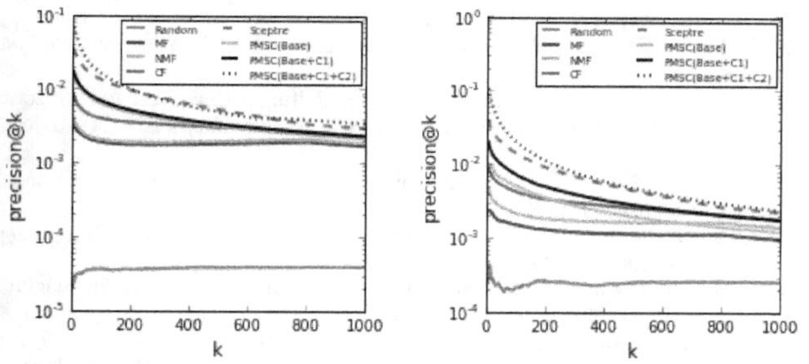

(a) Substitute (b) Complement

Figure 7: Precision@k for Cell Phones and Accessories on JD Dataset

that, as we mentioned in §3.4, when the products are related, their categories are related as well. This indicates that product category information is critical for predicting the edges between products. Thus, we represent the new product using their "category feature representations", which is defined as follow:

$$v_{c,r} = \frac{\sum_{i \in c} v_{i,r}}{N_c}, \; v'_{c,r} = \frac{\sum_{i \in c} v'_{i,r}}{N_c} \tag{19}$$

where v_c and v'_c are the target and context representations of the category c, and $v_{c,r}$ is the projected target vector of category c for r, $v'_{c,r}$ is the projected context vector of category c for r and N_c is the number of the product in category c.

To evaluate the feasibility of using category representation, we predict links between the new products and the results are shown in Table 7 and 8. **PMSC** can still make accurate predictions, especially for Baby in JD dataset with 0.9667 and 0.9335 for substitutes and complements. The results indicate that **PMSC** is able to handle the "cold start" problem with category feature representations very well.

We here visualize the product representations with t-SNE [21] in Figure 8, where points stand for products and different colors signify different product categories. We can see that in Figure 8(b), by trained with constraints, vectors of products in the same category can be gathered together, while points are more randomly distributed in Figure 8(a). It actually implies the reason why **PMSC** is able to accurately predicting "new products" with category feature representations. By further incorporating path constraints,

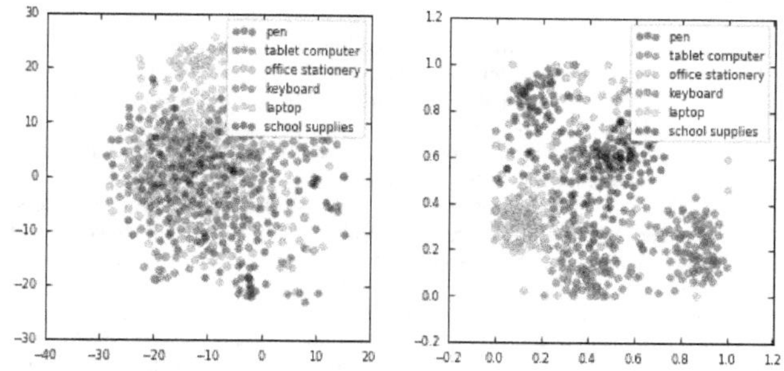

(a) Training without Constraints (b) Training with Constraints

Figure 8: Visualization for Product Representations

Table 7: Cold Start Prediction Accuracy on Amazon

Category	Method	Accuracy	
		Substitute	Complement
Electronics	cold start	0.9745	0.8733
Women's Clothes	cold start	0.9731	0.8890

Table 8: Cold Start Prediction Accuracy on JD Dataset

Category	Method	Accuracy	
		Substitute	Complement
Baby	cold start	0.9667	0.9355
Women's Clothes	cold start	0.9404	0.8331

PMSC is able to automatically capture the semantics of items and identify product categories.

In addition, the "cold start" prediction of substitutes is consistently more accurate than complements. The substitutes are easier to predict since substitute products are in the same category while the semantics of complements are more complex. This is because products in the head position may connect with products from various categories in the complement relation, which actually makes the general semantics more vague.

5 CONCLUSION

In this paper, we present a novel framework for substitutes and complements prediction, called Path-constrained Method for discriminating Substitutes and Complements (**PMSC**). The framework learns and predicts multi relations by projecting product representation to relation-specific space. We identify the useful path constraints to uncover complex data pattern, and then incorporate such path constraints into the framework through t-norm fuzzy logics. We evaluate the proposed **PMSC** on two real-world datasets. Experimental results show that **PMSC** can effectively identify links and distinguish substitutable and complementary products.

ACKNOWLEDGEMENTS

The authors wish to thank the anonymous reviewers for their helpful comments. Jiliang Tang is supported by the National Science Foundation (NSF) under grant number IIS-1714741 and IIS-1715940.

REFERENCES

[1] O. Barkan. Bayesian neural word embedding. In *AAAI*, pages 3135–3143, 2017.

[2] O. Barkan and N. Koenigstein. Item2vec: neural item embedding for collaborative filtering. In *International Workshop on Machine Learning for Signal Processing*, pages 1–6, 2016.

[3] R. M. Bell and Y. Koren. Improved neighborhood-based collaborative filtering. In *KDD Cup and Workshop at the KDD*, 2007.

[4] H.-T. Cheng, L. Koc, J. Harmsen, T. Shaked, T. Chandra, H. Aradhye, G. Anderson, G. Corrado, W. Chai, M. Ispir, et al. Wide & deep learning for recommender systems. In *Proceedings of the 1st Workshop on Deep Learning for Recommender Systems*, pages 7–10, 2016.

[5] R. Collobert and J. Weston. A unified architecture for natural language processing: Deep neural networks with multitask learning. In *ICML*, pages 160–167, 2008.

[6] P. Covington, J. Adams, and E. Sargin. Deep neural networks for youtube recommendations. In *ACM RecSys*, pages 191–198, 2016.

[7] F. Gelli, X. He, T. Chen, and T.-S. Chua. How personality affects our likes: Towards a better understanding of actionable images. In *MM*, 2017.

[8] P. Hájek. *Metamathematics of fuzzy logic*, volume 4. Springer, 1998.

[9] R. He, C. Packer, and J. Mcauley. Learning compatibility across categories for heterogeneous item recommendation. In *IEEE International Conference on Data Mining*, pages 937–942, 2017.

[10] X. He, L. Liao, H. Zhang, L. Nie, X. Hu, and T.-S. Chua. Neural collaborative filtering. In *WWW*, pages 173–182, 2017.

[11] N. Koenigstein, G. Dror, and Y. Koren. Yahoo! music recommendations: modeling music ratings with temporal dynamics and item taxonomy. In *ACM RecSys*, pages 165–172, 2011.

[12] Y. Koren and R. Bell. Advances in collaborative filtering. In *Recommender systems handbook*, pages 145–186. Springer, 2011.

[13] Y. Koren, R. Bell, and C. Volinsky. Matrix factorization techniques for recommender systems. *Computer*, 42(8):30–37, 2009.

[14] D. D. Lee and H. S. Seung. Learning the parts of objects by non-negative matrix factorization. *Nature*, 401(6755):788, 1999.

[15] D. D. Lee and H. S. Seung. Algorithms for non-negative matrix factorization. In *NIPS*, pages 556–562, 2001.

[16] J. Li, P. Ren, Z. Chen, Z. Ren, T. Lian, and J. Ma. Neural attentive session-based recommendation. In *CIKM*, 2017.

[17] G. Linden, B. Smith, and J. York. Amazon. com recommendations: Item-to-item collaborative filtering. *IEEE Internet computing*, 7(1):76–80, 2003.

[18] D. C. Liu, S. Rogers, R. Shiau, D. Kislyuk, K. C. Ma, Z. Zhong, J. Liu, and Y. Jing. Related pins at pinterest: The evolution of a real-world recommender system. In *WWW Companion*, pages 583–592, 2017.

[19] P. Lops, M. D. Gemmis, and G. Semeraro. *Content-based Recommender Systems: State of the Art and Trends*. Springer, 2011.

[20] Y. Ma, Z. Ren, Z. Jiang, J. Tang, and D. Yin. Multi-dimensional network embedding with hierarchical structures. In *WSDM*, 2018.

[21] L. v. d. Maaten and G. Hinton. Visualizing data using t-sne. *Journal of Machine Learning Research*, 9(Nov):2579–2605, 2008.

[22] J. McAuley and J. Leskovec. Hidden factors and hidden topics: understanding rating dimensions with review text. In *ACM RecSys*, pages 165–172, 2013.

[23] J. McAuley, R. Pandey, and J. Leskovec. Inferring networks of substitutable and complementary products. In *KDD*, pages 785–794. ACM, 2015.

[24] T. Mikolov, I. Sutskever, K. Chen, G. S. Corrado, and J. Dean. Distributed representations of words and phrases and their compositionality. In *NIPS*, pages 3111–3119, 2013.

[25] A. Mnih and G. E. Hinton. A scalable hierarchical distributed language model. In *NIPS*, pages 1081–1088, 2009.

[26] S.-T. Park and W. Chu. Pairwise preference regression for cold-start recommendation. In *ACM RecSys*, pages 21–28, 2009.

[27] P. Resnick, N. Iacovou, M. Suchak, P. Bergstrom, and J. Riedl. Grouplens: an open architecture for collaborative filtering of netnews. In *ACM Conference on Computer Supported Cooperative Work*, pages 175–186, 1994.

[28] B. Sarwar, G. Karypis, J. Konstan, and J. Riedl. Item-based collaborative filtering recommendation algorithms. In *WWW*, pages 285–295, 2001.

[29] A. I. Schein, A. Popescul, L. H. Ungar, and D. M. Pennock. Methods and metrics for cold-start recommendations. In *SIGIR*, pages 253–260, 2002.

[30] Y. Shi, A. Karatzoglou, L. Baltrunas, M. Larson, N. Oliver, and A. Hanjalic. Climf: learning to maximize reciprocal rank with collaborative less-is-more filtering. In *ACM RecSys*, pages 139–146, 2012.

[31] X. Su and T. M. Khoshgoftaar. *A survey of collaborative filtering techniques*. Hindawi Publishing Corp., 2009.

[32] Z. Sun, J. Yang, J. Zhang, and A. Bozzon. Exploiting both vertical and horizontal dimensions of feature hierarchy for effective recommendation. In *AAAI*, pages 189–195, 2017.

[33] I. Titov and R. McDonald. Modeling online reviews with multi-grain topic models. In *WWW*, pages 111–120, 2008.

[34] I. Titov and R. T. McDonald. A joint model of text and aspect ratings for sentiment summarization. In *ACL*, pages 308–316, 2008.

[35] C. Wang and D. M. Blei. Collaborative topic modeling for recommending scientific articles. In *KDD*, pages 448–456, 2011.

[36] P. Wang, J. Guo, Y. Lan, J. Xu, and X. Cheng. Your cart tells you: Inferring demographic attributes from purchase data. In *WSDM*, pages 173–182, 2016.

[37] X. Yi, L. Hong, E. Zhong, N. N. Liu, and S. Rajan. Beyond clicks: dwell time for personalization. In *ACM RecSys*, pages 113–120, 2014.

[38] Y. Zhang, M. Zhang, Y. Liu, S. Ma, and S. Feng. Localized matrix factorization for recommendation based on matrix block diagonal forms. In *WWW*, pages 1511–1520, 2013.

[39] J. Zheng, X. Wu, J. Niu, and A. Bolivar. Substitutes or complements: another step forward in recommendations. In *Proceedings of the 10th ACM conference on Electronic commerce*, pages 139–146, 2009.

[40] K. Zhou, S.-H. Yang, and H. Zha. Functional matrix factorizations for cold-start recommendation. In *SIGIR*, pages 315–324, 2011.

[41] M. Zhou, Z. Ding, J. Tang, and D. Yin. Micro behaviors: A new perspective in e-commerce recommender systems. In *WSDM*, 2018.

Customer Purchase Behavior Prediction from Payment Datasets

Yu-Ting Wen, Pei-Wen Yeh, Tzu-Hao Tsai, Wen-Chih Peng, Hong-Han Shuai
National Chiao Tung University
Hsinchu, Taiwan
{ytwen,pwyeh,tsuhao,wcpeng}@cs.nctu.edu.tw,hhshuai@nctu.edu.tw

ABSTRACT

With the advances in the development of mobile payments, a huge amount of payment data are collected by banks. User payment data offer a good dataset to depict customer behavior patterns. A comprehensive understanding of customers' purchase behavior is crucial to developing good marketing strategies, which may trigger much greater purchase amounts. For example, by exploring customer behavior patterns, given a target store, a set of potential customers is able to be identified. In other words, personalized campaigns at the right time and in the right place can be treated as the last stage of consumption. Here we propose a probability graphical model that exploits the payment data to discover customer purchase behavior in the spatial, temporal, payment amount and product category aspects, named STPC-PGM. As a result, the mobility behavior of an individual user could be predicted with a probabilistic graphical model that accounts for all aspects of each customer's relationship with the payment platform. To achieve real time advertising, we then develop an online framework that efficiently computes the prediction results. Our experiment results show that STPC-PGM is effective in discovering customers' profiling features, and outperforms the state-of-the-art methods in purchase behavior prediction. In addition, the prediction results are being deployed in the marketing of real-world credit card users, and have presented a significant growth in the advertising conversion rate.

KEYWORDS

financial technology, real time advertising, customer behavior prediction

ACM Reference Format:
Yu-Ting Wen, Pei-Wen Yeh, Tzu-Hao Tsai, Wen-Chih Peng, Hong-Han Shuai. 2018. Customer Purchase Behavior Prediction from Payment Datasets. In *Proceedings of WSDM 2018: The Eleventh ACM International Conference on Web Search and Data Mining (WSDM 2018).* ACM, New York, NY, USA, 9 pages. https://doi.org/10.1145/3159652.3159707

1 INTRODUCTION

With the rapid growth of data and the advances in computing power, data mining technologies have changed the world in many fields. One of the promising fields is Finance due to a wide variety of needs and the comprehensive data. For example, financial technology (FinTech) has fundamentally changed the applied marketing activities as the Internet increasingly becomes the leading advertising channel. Moreover, there are various electronic payment services available on mobile phones and smart credit cards, of which the records can serve as a medium for modeling customer behaviors. Therefore, not only e-commerce companies, such as Alibaba and Amazon, have expanded their business to provide financial services[1][2]; but finance organizations including the banking sector are also eager to innovate new business models via user modeling.

WSDM 2018, February 5–9, 2018, Marina Del Rey, CA, USA

ACM ISBN 978-1-4503-5581-0/18/02...$15.00
https://doi.org/10.1145/3159652.3159707

Table 1: Example of a payment dataset of customer '0001'.

time	week	region	category	payment
20170601	weekday	R_1	Movie	430
20160606	weekday	R_1	Gas	1000
20160612	weekday	R_3	Sport	1300
20160617	weekend	R_2	Warehouse	2200
20160620	weekday	R_1	Gas	1100
20160625	weekend	R_4	Warehouse	990
20160705	weekday	R_2	Food	599
20160705	weekday	R_1	Gas	700
20160726	weekday	R_1	Food	390
20160729	weekend	R_4	Clothes	1400

Table 1 shows a general example of the financial transactions. Each transaction record contains the customer identification id, location, purchase time, payment amount and store category. The large number of such transactions directly reflecting users' preferences in life offers an opportunity to investigate the behaviors of individuals (Who is the user?) with respect to four important aspects, namely, geographical location (Where does the customer visit?), time (When does the user perform the transaction?), payment amount (How much money does the user spend at each query time?), and category (What is the shopping preference of the user?).

To answer the above questions, one of the promising approach is to model customers' purchase behavior from the multiple aspects, such as spatial, temporal, payment, and category aspects. However, it is challenging to develop a model to capture the multiple aspects simultaneously, since 1) different data types (continuous and discrete) co-exist, and 2) the interplay between dimensions complicates the model, as well as the parameter estimation. To solve the problems of customer feature extraction and mobility prediction to identify interesting categories and regions of products for users, we propose an effective inference algorithm to derive the parameters of the probabilistic graphical model which can be

[1]https://aws.amazon.com/tw/financial-services
[2]https://www.antfin.com/index.htm

served as the different preferences of individuals. In addition, to deal with the streaming customer data in real-world applications, a framework for efficient online computation and update has been developed.

specifically, in this paper, we present a prediction model, STPC-PGM (standing for spatial, temporal, payment and product category in Probability Graphic Model), that accounts for individual customers' relationships with the financial service, and infers the latent features from other observed features with a probabilistic graphical model. We demonstrate its effectiveness in various applications such as predicting locations for customers with a given time range, predicting locations for users at a given time, and predicting users who will shop in a given location at a given time. To evaluate STPC-PGM, we conducted extensive experiments on real datasets. The experiment results show that STPC-PGM is able to retrieve effective features and efficiently perform accurate prediction, which outperforms the state-of-the-art baseline by an average of 10% – 40% in terms of accuracy.

The contributions of this paper are summarized as follows:

- By considering the unique characteristics of the payment dataset, we extract profile features from transactions into four semantic aspects: spatial, temporal, payment amount, and product category. Moreover, we extract latent features from transactions as auxiliary information to improve the prediction accuracy, such as the order of mobility patterns and purchase willingness under the credit limit. To the best of our knowledge, this is the first work to emphasize the impact of payment amount on user mobility.
- Based on the profile features, we further propose a novel framework, namely, STPC-PGM, to discover customer behavior patterns from the unique payment dataset via effectively integrating the four aspects of the features. The proposed STPC-PGM can be utilized to infer the relationship of any feature from others. In addition, an inference algorithm is provided for estimating the model parameters.
- For the purpose of real time advertising, we develop an online economical scoring framework wherein we re-score a user when any trigger events occur and apply a decay function otherwise, to enable online score updating of a large customer base with a complex model, instead of computing the value of the whole database.

2 RELATED WORK

Customer relationship management: There are a variety of methodologies that have been used to model customer behaviors in different applications. An overall literature review of various subjects related to this topic can be found in [9]. For real-world applications, [17] described the customer lifetime value problem of Groupon, and predicted the future value of an individual user with a Random Forest model. [8] dealt with the repeat buyer prediction requirement from Alibaba based on the sales data of the "Double 11 shopping event". The authors created profiles for users, merchants, brands, categories and items via extensive feature engineering. In our work, we aim to study the data from a bank, which is challenging due to the data sparsity (the lack of detailed payment information from other banks and the low frequency of the purchase actions). Another issue is to emphasize the influence on payment amount, as the most important task of the bank is to increase the value of customers' transactions.

Mobility prediction model: [21] studied individuals' mobility behaviors from user, geographic information, time, and text contents from Twitter data. However, differing from our work, location-based social network data do not consider the payment amount aspect, which is a stronger indicator than 'check-in' records [3, 4, 16]. Moreover, [21] fails to consider the interaction of two consecutive actions. Some e-commerce researchers [7, 20] adopted the *buyer decision process* [2] to model customers' behaviors from need recognition to purchase and post-purchase into five steps. However, the methods require browsing logs and user feedback comments, which the payment dataset from bank lacks. Some other existing work has focused on mining periodic behaviors to detect the future mobility. Fast Fourier Transform (FFT) and autocorrelation are common learning methods on time series data [1, 5, 18]. [3, 22] modeled the gap time by a Gaussian distribution. The authors of [6] proposed a discrepancy-based probabilistic measure for periodicity. A next location predictor was built applying the Markov Chain [14]. Also, there are approaches with tree-based probabilistic models [11, 13] and the projection-based probabilistic model [19].

In summary, our proposed STPC-PGM is distinguished from the past efforts in at least one of the following respects: 1) We consider payment amount as an important indicator to reflect behavior characteristics, which helps to separate users by their purchasing power, and determines the purchase intentions according to the credit limits. 2) We use the probabilistic approach by taking the interaction among user, location, time, payment and category entities into account, which yields more powerful prediction results for the customers. 3) We use a real bank payment dataset and conduct a marketing field trial to validate the effectiveness of our approach. ïż£

3 PROBLEM STATEMENT

In this section, we define the purchase behavior prediction problem, and analyze the bank dataset we use.

The transaction log data from banks contain five basic aspects: users, times, locations, annotated store categories and the amount of consumption.

3.1 Purchase Behavior Prediction Problem

Let D_u be the collection of transaction logs of user u, and each record $d_i = \{u, l_i, c_i, p_i, t_i\}$, where l_i, c_i, p_i and t_i represent the geographical coordinates of the store, store category, payment amount and time of d_i, respectively. We model time t as a discrete variable in $\{yy : mm : dd\}$ format, and categorize days into two classes, namely, weekdays and weekends[3].

Given D_u, current time t_{now} and specific time range ft, our goal is to find **(1) a set of categories c and regions r that u will have a purchase behavior in ft**, and **(2) how much will u pay in the predicted situation**. Note that a region r is a pre-defined geographical grid, since the advertising strategies may set a constraint region, e.g., the eastern district of Taipei city.

[3]The time of the day is not considered here due to the limitation of the log data (the scale unit is day), but our model is compatible with more detailed time information.

Table 2: User Profiling Features

Profile Type	Description
General Profile	Total / Monthly record number
	Active days
	Number of different cards
Behavior Profile	Region / Category count
	Distribution of categories / regions
	Entropy of categories / regions
	Number of days since the most recent purchase
	Interval between two records
	Weekend/Weekday probability of categories or regions
	Period (See Section 3.2.1)
	Route pattern (See Section 3.2.2)
Payment Profile	Total payment
	Average payment per transaction
	Recent 1/3/6 month payment
	Payment entropy
	Average monthly budget / payment level (See Section 3.2.3)

Formally, we estimate the probability $P(c, r)$ of u purchasing the product of category c in region r, and then $P(p|c, r)$ the probability of paying p. The inference model will be introduced in the next section after we discuss the feature engineering of the data.

3.2 User Profiling

Our model generates over 30 features based on the five aspects and their pairwise interactions, which provides a comprehensive view of an individual's demographics, general purchase behavior, and customer loyalty to the platform (i.e., the credit card service issue). In the following, we describe three types of user profiling shown in Table 2.

The user is the most important entity of the transaction dataset as each purchase record is an individual's active action. Users not only have their own identical characteristics but also have features belonging to interaction profiles, like user-category and user-payment.

Several interesting facts can be found by analyzing the profile features. For example, active credit card users can be extracted by selecting customers with large **total record number** (the total number of transaction records by the user in one year) and **active days** (the period of days from the user's first transaction to the latest record). Second, customers center on different but limited personal geographical regions. The **region count** (number of different regions visited) distribution shows that most of the customers (40%) have only two personal geographical regions, e.g., home and work. Similarly, **category count** (number of different categories purchased) presents that the average number of *categories users are interested in* is 8.5 and the maximal value is 30, while there are 173 categories in total (See Appendix A).

3.2.1 Period Detection. Sometimes users have periodic behavior in specific categories or locations. For example, a taxi driver Ben goes to the gas station every week; Jessie goes to Taipei three times a month for her internship. To detect the period V, we use the *Fast Fourier Transform* (FFT), *autocorrelation* and *segment probabilistic cut* step by step.

For each category or location, we extract its date list from all transaction data, then convert the list to a sequence. For example, ["20170501", "20170503", "20170507"] will be converted to $[1, 0, 1, 0, 0, 0, 1]$. The position is set up as one if there is at least one transaction on that date, otherwise it set to zero.

After getting the sequence, we implement *Fast Fourier Transform* (FFT) and get the spectrum. Since the higher the power of the spectrum, the more likely it is that the period will be chosen, we sort the FFT results according to the spectrum. Furthermore, we apply two filtered methods to purify these candidate periods.

To verify the detected period V, we first use *Discrete Fourier Transform* to find the periodogram and identify the range of candidate periods corresponding to the greatest power. Then we apply *circular autocorrelation* to determine whether V is the exact period in the time domain.

	1	2	3	4	5	6	7
2017/5/28~2017/6/03	1	0	1	0	0	0	0
2017/6/04~2017/6/10	1	0	0	0	0	0	0
2017/6/11~2017/6/17	0	0	0	0	0	0	0
2017/6/18~2017/6/24	1	0	1	0	0	0	0
2017/6/25~2017/7/01	0	0	1	0	0	0	0

Figure 1: An example of period segmentation.

Finally, with the expected period V detected from FFT-auto, we calculate the ratio of purchase activities in V. If the ratio is larger than the pre-defined threshold, it is determined as the real period. Suppose the observations date of category c of the user u is $t_1, t_2, ..., t_n$, and the detected potential period is V, the definition of the segment cut is:

$$\frac{\sum_{i=1}^{\lceil \frac{t_n - t_1}{V} \rceil} (1 \mid \exists j, \quad s.t. \quad \lceil \frac{t_j - t_1}{V} \rceil = i)}{\lceil \frac{t_n - t_1}{V} \rceil} > \theta \tag{1}$$

The default value of the segment threshold θ is 0.3. For example, there is a sequence $[1, 0, 1, ..., 0]$ with 35 data points and the detected period from *FFTauto* is 7 days. Figure 1 shows the sequence segmented by 7 days After cutting the sequence every 7 days, we can find that there are four out of the five segments which have transaction records. (except the third segment). The period (7 days) passes the validation because the ratio 0.8 is larger than the threshold 0.3.

Algorithm 1: Period Detection Algorithm.

```
Input: transaction data D;
Output: period of each item{category/region} V .
item_date ⇐ Divide transaction to item group ;
item_seq ⇐ Generate the sequence from date list ;
period_set ⇐ {} ;
foreach item_i do
    FFTo ⇐ FFT( item_seq_i ) ;
    FFTs ⇐ Sort FFTo by spectrum;
    foreach candidate_period ∈ FFTs do
        if Autocorrelate(candidate_period) &
           SegmentCut(candidate_period) then
            period_set.add (item, candidate_period );
return period_set.
```

Algorithm 2: Markov-Chain-based Prediction Algorithm.

Input: transaction data D, current time t_{now}, predicted time t_p, time threshold τ, category period V;
Output: probability matrix Z of next location and category.

MCTD $\Leftarrow$ Generate transition matrix with τ;
foreach *transaction*$\{u,l_i,c_i,p_i,t_i\}$ **do**
    if $\Delta(t_{now}, t_i) < \tau$ **then**
        Update Z(u);
    if t_i *in PeriodDetect*($V(c_i)$) **then**
        Update Z(u);
return Z.

3.2.2 Route Patterns. Except for the current transaction information, there are also relations between categories or regions. For example, Mary may go shopping after going to a cafe. And sometimes the potential influence needs to take longer to figure out. We build the Markov Chain Z with time range for route patterns, and calculate the probability according to recent activities.

By applying Algorithm 2, we can get the probability of categories as the next location and the expected period.

3.2.3 Monthly Budget. Generally speaking, everyone spends a limited amount of money each month since there is a fixed monthly budget. By using the **monthly record number** to determine the activity level of consumption, users are divided into five observation groups. As shown in Figure 2, we can find a dramatic decrease in all groups when the accumulated spending is larger. This shows that most customers will have less payment behavior when the total amount exceeds the monthly payment quota.

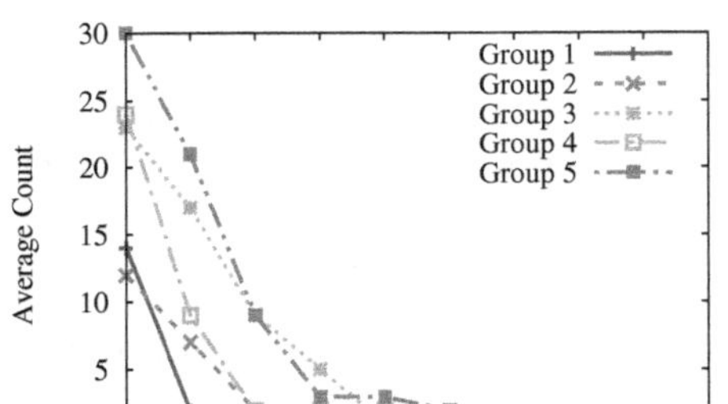

Figure 2: An illustration of monthly accumulated payment.

We define the payment with k-level and model each user with a different payment range. The closer the level value to k (reach the estimated budget of customers), the less possibility of future purchase behavior; the definition is shown as below:

$$PaymentLevel(d) = \lfloor \frac{p_d}{PaymentRange^u} \rfloor \tag{2}$$

, where $PaymentRange^u = \lfloor \frac{\sum_{\{y,m\}} \sum_j p_j |_{t_j.year=y \&\& j.month=m}}{|\{y,m\}| \cdot k} \rfloor$.

4 PREDICTION MODEL

In this section, we present the proposed approach STPC-PGM to model user mobility behavior with the discovered features. We first describe the intuitions of STPC-PGM in Section 4.1. We then describe the model and its inference process in Section 4.2, and detail the inference algorithm for prediction in Section 4.3.

4.1 Generative Intuitions

We summarize user mobility behavior based on the observations from Section 3. These observations jointly cover the five aspects of user mobility behavior, i.e., user, time, region, payment and category.

Intuition 1: the region where a user stays is influenced by the time factor, i.e., the time of the day and the day of the week. It has been reported that users often demonstrate different mobility patterns on weekdays and weekends [3]. For instance, most users have lunch at different places during weekdays and weekends, and a user is likely to stay in different regions at noon and in the evening.

Intuition 2: people usually have a monthly payment budget, so they will have different behaviors as the payments accumulate over time. For example, Angel will not buy any luxury goods if she is overdrawn this month.

Intuition 3: the purchase activities are influenced by both the user's personal category preferences and the region where the user stays. For example, suppose a user who has most of the billing fees in both eating and hiking equipment comes to a place full of restaurants; the user is more likely to be interested in the eating category. In addition, the categories of a user in her home region (e.g., entertainment and shopping) are expected to be different from the work-related categories in her work region.

Intuition 4: repeated consumption leads to the potential factor of periodicity, which is inferred from the observation in the previous section. And if the periodicity breaks, it may reflect the changes in other factors like the loss of customers and change in the range of activities.

Intuition 5: discovering regular mobility patterns in category and region, which in turn improves the prediction accuracy. Furthermore, recent activities may have more influence than earlier activities. For example, if Amy used to go to a bar for a drink every Friday night, but in the last three weeks she watched a movie instead, she will have a higher probability of buying a movie ticket than paying for a beer next Friday.

4.2 Model Description

Recall Section 3.1; we revise the transaction $d = \{u, l, c, p, t, w\}$, where w denotes the day of the week. The periodicity detected by Section 3.2.1 is denoted by V. The Markov Chain that is described in Section 3.2.2 is denoted by Z, which reflects the behavior pattern in the customer's transactions. Two variables are added to draw the influence of previous behaviors: the middle region r' and the middle category c'. For easy presentation, we use U, and D_u to denote the collection of users and her transaction logs, respectively.

Based on the aforementioned intuitions and notations, STPC-PGM generates the day, time, location and payment amount for each transaction, as shown in Figure 3. We then discuss the generative process using a go-through example.

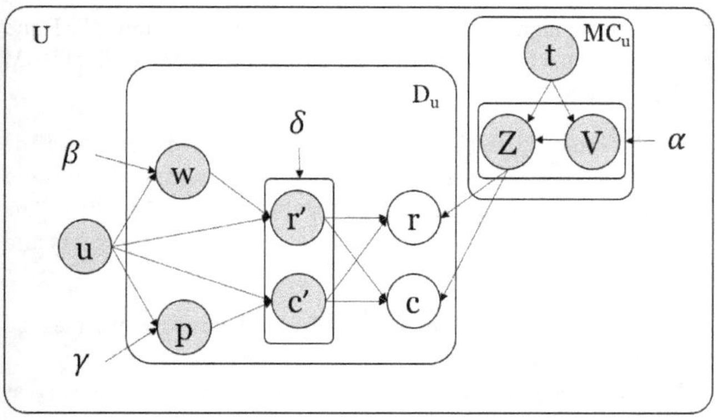

Figure 3: The graphical representation of the proposed model STPC-PGM.

- The day of week w is observed based on a *Bernoulli distribution* $P(w|u)$. (Intuition 1)
- The payment amount p is selected based on $P(p|u)$. (Intuition 2)
- After generating the day of week w and the payment amount p of user u, the middle region r' and the middle category c' are sampled based on $P(r'|u,w)$ and $P(c'|u,p)$, respectively. (Intuition 1 and 3)
- Parameterized by time t, the periodicity V is generated by $P(V|t)$. (Intuition 4)
- The route pattern Z considers the time t and the periodicity V, which is generated by $P(Z|t,V)$. (Intuition 5)

Note that the *Discrete and Dirichlet distribution* is used to describe the discrete value of each feature.

4.3 Inference Algorithm

As shown in Figure 3, there are two latent variables in STPC-PGM, namely, region r and category c. The joint probability over transaction $d = \{u, l, c, p, t, w\}$ and region r, can be written as:

$$P(r,c) = P(u,w,p,t,r',c',Z,V) = P(u)P(w|u)P(p|u)P(r'|u,w)P(c'|u,p)P(V|t)P(Z|t,V) P(r|r',c',Z)P(c|r',c',Z) \quad (3)$$

, where

$$P(r'|u,w) = \beta P(r'|w) + (1-\beta)P(r'|u)$$

$$P(c'|u,p) = \gamma P(c'|p) + (1-\gamma)P(c'|u)$$

$$P(r,c|r',c',Z) = \alpha P(Z|t,V) + (1-\alpha)[\delta P(r,c|r') + (1-\delta]P(r,c|c')$$

Considering that the more recent purchase behavior may better reflect the customer's current needs, α balances the importance between the latest two-week behaviors and overall behaviors. Usually, users show different mobility patterns at work (weekday) and at the weekend (weekend). β is the influence of the temporal feature on the user, while individuals may have different weights; γ is the influence of the monthly payment budget on the user. For example, a customer tends not to purchase expensive products or visit a high-class restaurant if she reaches the quota for this month; δ balances the importance between the region and the category, because some regions have interaction with the purchase categories, e.g., there are more department stores near the city hall.

The four parameters are initialized to $[0.5\ 0.5\ 0.5\ 0.5]$. Finally, we use the *truncated Newton algorithm* [10, 12] implemented in the *scipy.optimize.minimize* library to retrieve the optimal settings by minimizing the negative log-likelihood, which uses the gradient information.

Toy Example: We recall Table 1 that presents ten transaction logs D_{0001} of customer id '0001'. To calculate 'the probability of 0001 purchasing at R_2 on weekdays', first we select the seven records with 'weekday' and the two records with 'R_2' from the dataset. There is one record that has both 'R_2' and 'weekday'.

$P(r' = R_2)|u = \text{'}0001\text{'}, w = weekday) = \beta\frac{7}{10} \times \frac{1}{7} + (1-\beta)\frac{2}{10}$

Next we set $k = 5$, the payment amount can be discretized into levels by computing:

$PaymentRange^{0001} = \lfloor\frac{7020+3098}{2\cdot 5}\rfloor = 1010$

We then revise the continuous payment amount to $PaymentLevel$ as $[0,1,2,4,5,6,0,1,1,3]$ in order. $P(r'|u,w)$ and $P(c'|u,p)$ can be calculated similarly. With more data, the period of category 'Gas' could be detected, e.g., 15 days by using Algorithm 1. Then $P(V = \text{'}15days\text{'}|t = now)$ is computed based on the *Discrete and Dirichlet distribution*. As a result, the possibility score of 'User 0001 will fill up her car at a gas station in R_2' is calculated.

4.4 Payment Prediction

After running the STPC-PGM, we can get the potential categories and regions that the customers will go to in the future. With possible combinations of categories and regions, we can further predict the payment corresponding to them. It helps the company to provide a better marketing strategy. An example is the payment level heat map of the department store category in Taipei region.

We use the user profiling results from Section 3 to build a regression model, then predict the payment information in specific combination of categories and regions from STPC-PGM. Among several regression models like linear regression, support vector regression, and random forest regression, we finally chose the random forest regression as it has the best performance in our datasets. The detailed experiment results are shown in Section 6.2.3.

5 ONLINE FRAMEWORK

In real time transactions, the latest record is always the most important because with that record, we can discover the user's current status, e.g., where the user is at that moment. Moreover, with the intuition that nearer shops are more likely to be visited than further ones, given the instant category and location of an individual, a real time personalized recommendation that fits the user's preference might effectively increase the will of purchasing. For example, Cindy usually buys coffee after having lunch. A coupon for the Starbucks that is next to the restaurant she just left has a high possibility of being used. In summary, if we can compute and update the predicted scores of STPC-PGM immediately, it helps the design for real time marketing.

In Figure 4, all the existing (old) records run the original STPC-PGM model, and save the results in the offline part. When the online model gets the real time record, it will load the user's predicted results and match the store s according to the store's categories and

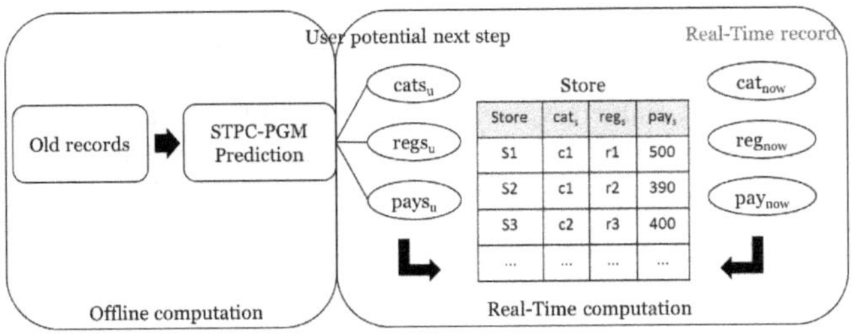

Figure 4: The framework of real time prediction of the proposed model STPC-PGM.

the user's recent category and location. For example, the online query could be set as:

$distance(r_s, r_{now}) < 5km \ \&\& \ \frac{p_s - avg(p_u)}{p_u} < 1.5 \ \&\& \ c_u[c_s] > 0$

, which only has to compute a small portion of the whole dataset.

In addition, it is inefficient to run the original model and save the new parameters every time a new record is imported. The online framework loads the user's parameters and updates the score by running the model with 1-order Markov, which assigns the largest weight to the latest record (the latest record reflects the individual's current status). Finally, the update of the whole dataset only has to be run periodically, e.g., daily.

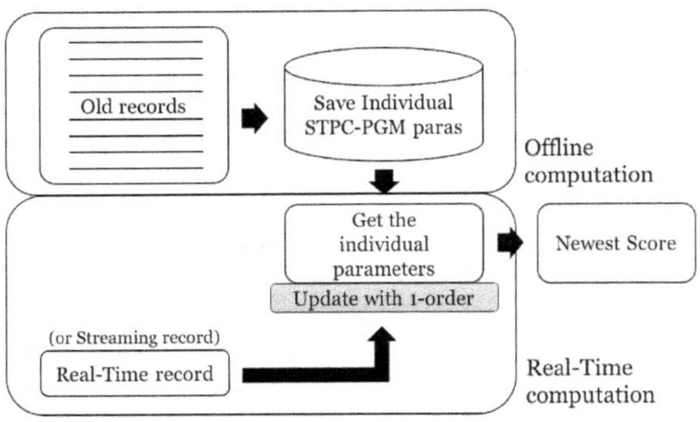

Figure 5: The online framework of updating new records.

6 EXPERIMENTS

In this section, we empirically evaluate the effectiveness and efficiency of the proposed STPC-PGM model on payment behavior prediction in regions and categories. We first introduce the datasets, baseline methods and evaluation metrics of our experiments in Section 6.1. Then we compare STPC-PGM to the state-of-the-art baseline methods in Section 6.2. The analysis of efficiency is presented in Section 6.3. Section 6.4 describes the applications in marketing with some case studies.

6.1 Experiment Settings

We evaluate different methods based on the real-world customer datasets from one Taiwanese bank. We make use of the functionality in scikit-learn[4], which is a scalable machine learning framework that supports many of the standard algorithms, including FFT and Markov Chain, etc. Models are built on a server with 66 Gb of RAM and 8 CPU cores.

[4]http://scikit-learn.org/

6.1.1 Dataset Description. For all of our model experiments, the dataset includes more than 2.5 million customers, 642 thousand merchants and 1.5 billion records for the years 2015 to 2016. The category and location information are annotated by experts and Google Places API.

6.1.2 Methods for Comparison. We will compare our method with the following methods.

TOP: The most popular locations in the training set are selected as prediction for each user. (Baseline)

MF: Based on the user-location matrix, Matrix Factorization is one of the state-of-the-art methods for conventional collaborative filtering.

MC: The Markov Chain model is a classical sequential model. It is also a component of our STPC-PGM model.

RF: Applying all user profiling results into a Random Forest model, which is a famous machine learning model.

More learning methods like Decision Tree (**DT**), Linear Regression (**LR**) and Support Vector Regression (**SVR**) are considered in Section 6.2.3.

W^4[21]: A probabilistic graphical model that considers 'Who', 'Where', 'When' and 'What' information.

STC: Our proposed probabilistic graphical model without considering payment information.

STPC: Our proposed STPC-PGM that considers spatial, temporal, payment and category features.

6.2 Performance Evaluation

In the dataset, the first 80% of elements of the behavioral history of each user are selected for training, then the remaining 20% are for testing.

6.2.1 Period Detection. To verify the effectiveness of detected period feature, here we check whether the proposed flow in Section 3.2.1 can correctly identify the periodicity of categories and the relevant repeat time. A detected periodic category of the customer u is correct if u will have at least one transaction record of that category in the next period cycle. We use accuracy (**Acc**) as the evaluation metric. The average accuracy of all kind of categories is 0.3186. Table 3 shows the accuracy among the top-10 categories, ranked by the number of transactions.

Table 3: The accuracy of category period.

	Category	Count	Acc		Category	Count	Acc
0	supermarket	6393	0.265	5	abroad	2760	0.242
1	gas station	4807	0.292	6	restaurant	2318	0.364
2	online shopping	4655	0.268	7	self refuel	2108	0.306
3	MRT5	4015	0.294	8	MRT1	2054	0.351
4	department store	3962	0.298	9	assurance	1961	0.360

First we find that even if the more data we have, the more accurate the period should be, there exists no positive correlation with the value of **Acc** and the total record number of the category. On the other hand, the extremely sparse data of only one record

Table 4: Performance comparison evaluated by precision (p), recall (r) and F1-score (f).

	$p_{0.2}$	$p_{0.4}$	$p_{0.8}$	$r_{0.2}$	$r_{0.4}$	$r_{0.8}$	$f_{0.2}$	$f_{0.4}$	$f_{0.8}$
TOP	0.478	0.478	0.478	0.395	0.395	0.395	0.431	0.431	**0.431**
MF	0.324	0.374	0.488	0.394	0.296	0.140	0.335	0.330	0.218
MC	0.562	0.625	0.651	0.569	0.365	0.140	0.563	**0.467**	0.217
RF	0.470	0.566	0.674	0.551	0.314	0.090	0.483	0.395	0.109
W^4	0.388	0.500	0.605	0.394	0.507	0.602	0.469	**0.467**	0.22
STC	0.431	0.510	0.624	**0.615**	0.412	0.142	0.500	0.460	0.244
STPC	**0.573**	**0.667**	**0.750**	0.572	**0.616**	**0.721**	**0.574**	**0.467**	0.22

results in either 0 or 1, which should be neglected. According to our inferences, additional user grouping can be applied to improve the prediction results.

6.2.2 Prediction Results. To evaluate the prediction performance of different methods, we compute a list of categories and regions ranked by probability for each customer. The performance comparison on the dataset evaluated by **precision**, **recall** and **F1-score** is illustrated in Table 4. The subscript value ρ indicates the probability score threshold; that is, if the probability score of customer u is larger than the threshold ρ, we predict that u will have a purchase behavior of category c at a store located in region r, and check whether the behavior happens in the given time.

When the predicted probability threshold is larger, we get better precision, but the recall is also worse. A higher probability means the customer is more likely to go, but only a few situations support it. For example, it is hard to say that someone has a 90% chance of going to the shopping mall because it needs strong confidence. In some cases, **MF** even has worse results than the baseline. **RF** and **W^4** achieve improvement. **MC** is similar to our proposed model because it is also a component of **STPC**. Moreover, we can observe that **STPC** outperforms the compared methods for all the metrics. We can also observe that adding the payment information really does improve the results by comparing **STPC** with **STC**.

6.2.3 Payment Prediction. Since STPC-PGM effectively predicts the latent category and location variables, the results could be used to infer more variables by applying existing regression models. In this section, we extended the experiments in Section 6.2.2 and treated category and location as the input for payment prediction. Formally, given [uid, average_payment, time, **category**, **location**, payment_this_month], the value for the next payment amount could be deduced directly by a regression model. Table 5 presents the mean absolute error (MAE) of the payment prediction results.

Table 5: Payment prediction performance by different regression models.

	DT	RF	LR	SVR
Training MAE	0.1	137	592	575
Testing MAE	365	367	589	573

With the observation of the dataset, the monthly average payment of each customer is around two thousand New Taiwan Dollars. We can find that **DT** and **RF** outperform the other two methods, and we choose **RF** to avoid the over-fitting problem.

6.2.4 Parameter Setting and Tuning. We are interested in the performance of methods on the datasets generated by different settings of parameters. For this purpose, we vary the value of a parameter, and fix the values of the others at their default values. The precision of the methods is plotted in Figure 6.

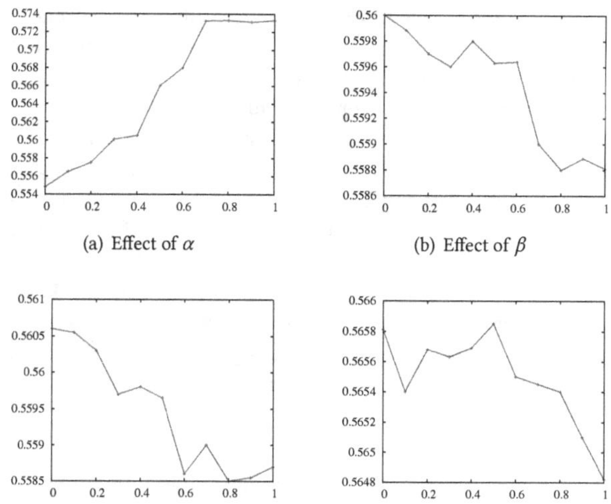

(a) Effect of α (b) Effect of β

(c) Effect of γ (d) Effect of δ

Figure 6: Precision in different parameter settings.

By tracking the training loss in the optimization process, a stable result is found after 50 iterations in Figure 7, and each customer has her own parameter setting. Figure 7(b) presents the optimized result in the subset of customers.

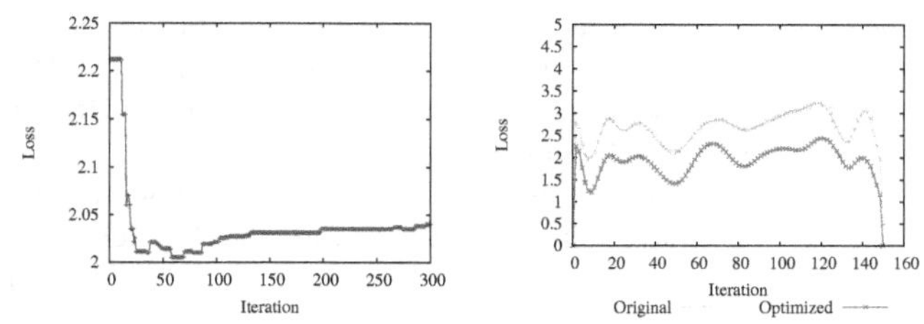

(a) Training Loss in the optimized process (b) Optimized result

Figure 7: Training loss results.

6.3 Efficiency

In this section, we present the running time for offline model training and online computation.

6.3.1 Offline Model Training. Figure 8(a) shows the running time of the different methods. We can figure out that STPC-PGM (**STPC**) has a good efficiency result. It takes around four hours to run the models of all customers one time.

Moreover, in the practical application of the company, considering that STPC-PGM is a user-based model, building a model with a parallel back-end allows the system to calculate the score more efficiently than running all data serially. Depending on the computer specifications, if we run the model with eight threads, it leads to an almost eight-fold improvement in the speed in theory. Figure 8(b) shows the running time of multiprocessing. This helps the company to get information about immediate customer changes.

6.3.2 Online Computation Time. We synthesize the real world condition by considering that (1) the server might need to deal with thousands of real time transactions in each second and (2) the response time for each customer should be less than half a second. The whole dataset except the last day (31 December) of the year 2016 is used to build the STPC-PGM model offline, and the records for 31 December are synthesized as the real time streaming data for store recommendation. The response time is the computation procedure for each streaming input to get the store with the highest purchase probability. Finally, the result is an average of **1.125** ms per streaming record, which is much less than human response time. Moreover, the online parameter update procedure only takes an average of **0.253** ms per streaming record.

6.4 Field Trails

The system has been used in one domestic bank in Taiwan since 2017/02. In this section, we present the marketing experiments and some case studies on the dataset.

6.4.1 Category marketing. The bank which cooperated with us targets two types of appointed stores[5]: supermarkets (**S**) and department stores (**D**), and compares STPC-PGM (**STPC**) to two previous marketing strategies as baseline methods: regular customers (**Reg**) and random (**Rand**). STPC-PGM extracts the users who will have purchase activity in a supermarket or a department store in less than 14 days. Regular customers are the credit card users who had transaction records at either supermarkets or department stores in the last three months. In each case, the marketing team selected about 50,000 customers to receive electronic direct mailer (EDM) advertisements, and checked the open rate of EDM (**EDM OR**) and the net increment in billing (**NIB**).

Table 6 shows the results for January, 2017. Although **STPC**, **Reg** and **Rand** have similar EDM open rates, **STPC** chooses the potential customers with higher history billing[6] (**HB**) because it considers the payment feature. It can be found that **STPC** has the best **NIB** value among other methods in supermarkets.

[5]The appointed stores are the stores that have a marketing contract with the bank.
[6]The average history billing amount in the last six months.

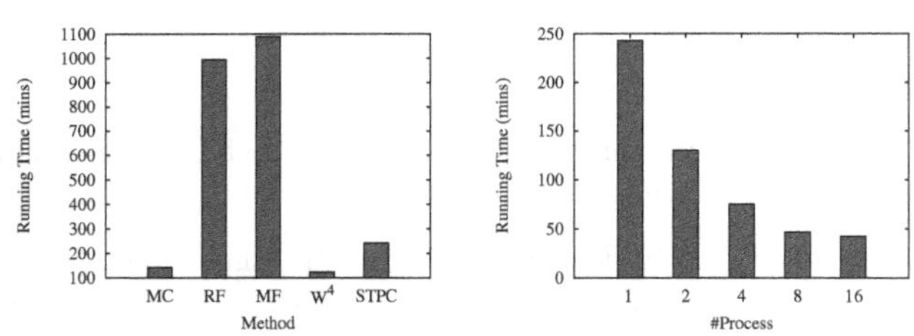

Figure 8: Running times of (a) the different methods and (b) multiprocessing of STPC-PGM.

Table 6: EDM Advertising Results of Category Marketing.

Setting	EDM OR	HB	NIB
Rand/S	2.9%	466	1,302
Rand/D	4.0%	1,850	-315
Reg/S	2.9%	1,103	3066
Reg/D	4.5%	2,002	-883
STPC/S	3.1%	3,588	**10,295**
STPC/D	4.4%	7,264	-3175

However, the marketing test was possibly influenced by the Chinese New Year vacation in Taiwan, because all the billing amounts in supermarkets increased, which somehow led to a decrement in the amounts in other stores.

6.4.2 Store Marketing. The goal of this marketing project is to guide the customers to one department store that cooperates with the bank. We compare STPC-PGM (**STPC**) to two methods that were implemented as marketing strategies: card holders[7] (**CardH**) and intent detection[8] (**Intent**). In the experiment, **STPC** extracts the users who will have purchase activity at the specific store, which is near Taipei 101. We also conduct **Period**, the method that only considers the period in the category of department store. In each case, the marketing team selected about 20,000 customers to receive EDM advertisements, and checked the open rate of EDM (EDM OR), purchase ratio[9] (**PR**) and the total billing ratio[10] (**TBR**).

Table 7: EDM Advertising Results of Store Marketing.

Setting	EDM OR	PR	TBR
CardH	12.5%	5.64%	23.79%
Intent	7.7%	0.15%	3.23%
Period	11.55%	3.40%	8.85%
STPC	**19.4%**	**48.95%**	**64.11%**

Table 7 shows the results of a promotion in April, 2017. It can be found that **STPC** has an outstanding performance in **EDM OR PR** and **TBR**. On the other hand, the performance of **Period** is unsatisfactory because it does not consider the moving distance which strongly determines the importance of the region feature.

7 CONCLUSION

In this paper, we have described the challenges faced, the observations found, and the methods chosen in building a customer purchase behavior prediction model for the FinTech marketing development of payment datasets from banks. Our STPC-probabilistic graphical model (STPC-PGM) discovers dozens of features in the spatial, temporal, payment and category aspects, giving us the ability to effectively detect patterns and changes in customer activities. Moreover, the real time framework is implemented for quick computation and new transaction updates. The experiment results outperform other mobility prediction methods, e.g., the prediction

[7]The customers who already hold the co-branded card issued by the store and the bank.
[8]The customers labeled with purchase histories in the store.
[9]The ratio of customers who have purchase records at the store.
[10]The proportion of the billing amount.

F1-score is about 40% better than the Random Forest trained baseline. This system is being run as part of a marketing strategy. The business advertising team chose users who have high probability of purchasing in target categories and regions as potential purchasers, and the results show an average 287% net increment in billing and a remarkable 48.95% conversion rate. As our next step, we aim to explore more FinTech tasks with our marketing partners, such as churn prediction, new card recommendation and personalized wealth planning.

ACKNOWLEDGMENT

Wen-Chih Peng was supported in part by MOST Taiwan, Project No. 106-3114-E-009-010 and 106-2628-E-009-008-MY3. In addition, this work is partially funded by Microsoft Research Asia.

REFERENCES

[1] Christos Berberidis, Walid G Aref, Mikhail Atallah, Ioannis Vlahavas, and Ahmed K Elmagarmid. 2002. Multiple and partial periodicity mining in time series databases. In *ECAI*. 370–374.
[2] Patrick Butler and Joe Peppard. 1998. Consumer purchasing on the Internet: Processes and prospects. *European management journal* 16, 5 (1998), 600–610.
[3] Eunjoon Cho, Seth A Myers, and Jure Leskovec. 2011. Friendship and mobility: user movement in location-based social networks. In *KDD*. 1082–1090.
[4] Marta C Gonzalez, Cesar A Hidalgo, and Albert-Laszlo Barabasi. 2008. Understanding individual human mobility patterns. *Nature* 453, 7196 (2008), 779–782.
[5] Zhenhui Li, Bolin Ding, Jiawei Han, Roland Kays, and Peter Nye. 2010. Mining periodic behaviors for moving objects. In *KDD*. 1099–1108.
[6] Zhenhui Li, Jingjing Wang, and Jiawei Han. 2012. Mining event periodicity from incomplete observations. In *KDD*. 444–452.
[7] Ying-Chun Lin, Chi-Hsuan Huang, Chu-Cheng Hsieh, Yu-Chen Shu, and Kun-Ta Chuang. 2017. Monetary Discount Strategies for Real-Time Promotion Campaign. In *WWW*. 1123–1132.
[8] Guimei Liu, Tam T Nguyen, Gang Zhao, Wei Zha, Jianbo Yang, Jianneng Cao, Min Wu, Peilin Zhao, and Wei Chen. 2016. Repeat buyer prediction for e-commerce. In *KDD*. 155–164.
[9] Tala Mirzaei and L Lyer. 2014. Application of predictive analytics in customer relationship management: a literature review and classification. In *Proceedings of the Southern Association for Information Systems Conference*. 1–7.
[10] Stephen G Nash. 1984. Newton-type minimization via the Lanczos method. *SIAM J. Numer. Anal.* 21, 4 (1984), 770–788.
[11] Manziba Akanda Nishi, Chowdhury Farhan Ahmed, Md Samiullah, and Byeong-Soo Jeong. 2013. Effective periodic pattern mining in time series databases. *Expert Systems with Applications* 40, 8 (2013), 3015–3027.
[12] Jorge Nocedal and Stephen J Wright. 2006. Numerical Optimization. (2006).
[13] Faras Rasheed, Mohammed Alshalalfa, and Reda Alhajj. 2011. Efficient periodicity mining in time series databases using suffix trees. *TKDE* 23, 1 (2011), 79–94.
[14] Steffen Rendle, Christoph Freudenthaler, and Lars Schmidt-Thieme. 2010. Factorizing personalized markov chains for next-basket recommendation. In *WWW*. 811–820.
[15] Si Si, Kai-Yang Chiang, Cho-Jui Hsieh, Nikhil Rao, and Inderjit S Dhillon. 2016. Goal-directed inductive matrix completion. In *KDD*. 1165–1174.
[16] Chaoming Song, Tal Koren, Pu Wang, and Albert-László Barabási. 2010. Modelling the scaling properties of human mobility. *Nature Physics* 6, 10 (2010), 818–823.
[17] Ali Vanderveld, Addhyan Pandey, Angela Han, and Rajesh Parekh. 2016. An Engagement-Based Customer Lifetime Value System for E-commerce. In *KDD*. 293–302.
[18] Michail Vlachos, Philip Yu, and Vittorio Castelli. 2005. On periodicity detection and structural periodic similarity. In *SDM*. 449–460.
[19] Kung-Jiuan Yang, Tzung-Pei Hong, Yuh-Min Chen, and Guo-Cheng Lan. 2013. Projection-based partial periodic pattern mining for event sequences. *Expert Systems with Applications* 40, 10 (2013), 4232–4240.
[20] Jinyoung Yeo, Sungchul Kim, Eunyee Koh, Seung-won Hwang, and Nedim Lipka. 2017. Predicting Online Purchase Conversion for Retargeting. In *WSDM*. 591–600.
[21] Quan Yuan, Gao Cong, Zongyang Ma, Aixin Sun, and Nadia Magnenat Thalmann. 2013. Who, where, when and what: discover spatio-temporal topics for twitter users. In *KDD*. 605–613.
[22] Quan Yuan, Wei Zhang, Chao Zhang, Xinhe Geng, Gao Cong, and Jiawei Han. 2017. PRED: Periodic Region Detection for Mobility Modeling of Social Media Users. In *WSDM*. 263–272.

A HIERARCHICAL CATEGORIES

For better customer management, each store is annotated by categories that represent potential customer interests. Here we describe the manually annotated categories. The hierarchy has three layers: OVERALL (10), MID (34), SMALL (173). There are ten OVERALL categories: [food, clothing, housing, transportation, education, entertainment, sales channel, service, daily living, health care]. For example, there are two MID categories [online, offline] belonging to the OVERALL category [sale channel]. [online] contains [direct sales, mail order, TV shopping] and [offline] contains [supermarket, department store, duty-free shop, second hand shop, showground, pawnshop]. Each transaction log corresponds to one store, and the category of the store reflects the intention of the purchase behavior.

B GRID RESOLUTION

In this work, we partition the area that covers Taiwan into a 3440×2000 grid map with the grid size of $100m \times 100m$. $100m$ is a proper unit of user mobility based on ground knowledge. If we set the grid size as $1km \times 1km$, there are 344×200 grids. A grid denotes to a region r. A smaller grid size leads to better resolution of different stores (low **entropy of regions**) but longer computation time.

C TIME WINDOWS

In Figure 9, we show the **precision** and **recall** for each time window: short (1 day), medium (7 days), long (30 days). For practical use by the banks, it needs some time to access the immediate payment record, so a better choice of future time windows is one or two weeks for their application. Typically, we find that the precision and recall measures tend to improve as the time windows get larger. This is because the dataset is sparse and the purchase behavior per customer is still noisy for the short time windows for this dataset.

D PERIODIC CUSTOMERS

When detecting the periodic behavior of each customer, we observe that those who have multiple credit cards show strong periodicity in Figure 10. The reason why the customers with more credit cards exhibit better periodicity is that those customers are always utilizing the specific capabilities of the different cards since they can get extra bonuses by using different cards. For example, we use a COSCO card only when we go grocery shopping; and for movies and gas stations, there are also certain cards that customers can use to get the most bonus points. According to our inferences, user grouping can be applied to improve the prediction results. The accuracy of these strongly periodic customers can be up to 0.818, while the average is 0.496.

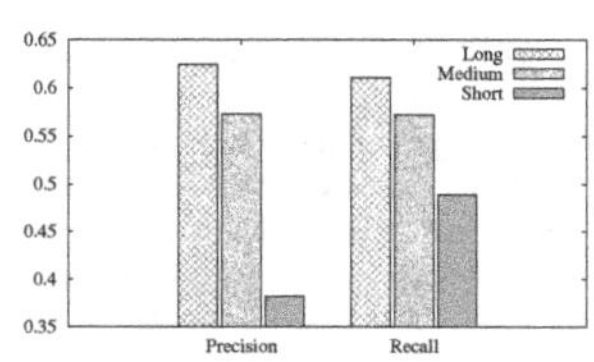

Figure 9: Time window comparison.

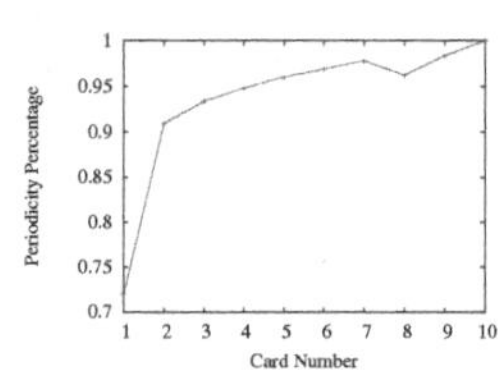

Figure 10: Periodicity percentage.

Tracing Fake-News Footprints: Characterizing Social Media Messages by How They Propagate

Liang Wu
Computer Science and Engineering
Arizona State University
Tempe, AZ
wuliang@asu.edu

Huan Liu
Computer Science and Engineering
Arizona State University
Tempe, AZ
huanliu@asu.edu

ABSTRACT

When a message, such as a piece of news, spreads in social networks, how can we classify it into categories of interests, such as genuine or fake news? Classification of social media content is a fundamental task for social media mining, and most existing methods regard it as a text categorization problem and mainly focus on using content features, such as words and hashtags. However, for many emerging applications like fake news and rumor detection, it is very challenging, if not impossible, to identify useful features from content. For example, intentional spreaders of fake news may manipulate the content to make it look like real news. To address this problem, this paper concentrates on modeling the propagation of messages in a social network. Specifically, we propose a novel approach, TraceMiner, to (1) infer embeddings of social media users with social network structures; and (2) utilize an LSTM-RNN to represent and classify propagation pathways of a message. Since content information is sparse and noisy on social media, adopting TraceMiner allows to provide a high degree of classification accuracy even in the absence of content information. Experimental results on real-world datasets show the superiority over state-of-the-art approaches on the task of fake news detection and news categorization.

KEYWORDS

Misinformation, Fake News Detection, Graph Mining, Social Network Analysis, Social Media Mining, Classification

ACM Reference Format:
Liang Wu and Huan Liu. 2018. Tracing Fake-News Footprints: Characterizing Social Media Messages by How They Propagate. In *Proceedings of WSDM 2018: The Eleventh ACM International Conference on Web Search and Data Mining (WSDM 2018).* ACM, New York, NY, USA, 9 pages. https://doi.org/10.1145/3159652.3159677

1 INTRODUCTION

As online social networks continue to pervade our culture, social networking sites have become an attractive platform to facilitate the spread of information. A recent study from Pew Research claims that 62% of adults get their news from social media in United States, with 29% among them doing so very often[1]. Concomitant with the expansive and varied sources of data are the challenges for personalizing the massive amount of information andfiltering out unwanted messages such as fake news and spam. However, the sparse and noisy social media content makes it difficult for traditional approaches, which heavily rely on content features, to tackle these challenges.

By contrast, our study aims tofi nd additional data sources to solve the problem. In this work, we focus on the diffusion of information. A key driving force behind the diffusion of information is its spreaders. People tend to spread information that caters to their interests and/orfi ts their system of belief [8]. Hence, similar messages usually leads to similar traces of information diffusion: they are more likely to be spread from similar sources, by similar people and in similar sequences. Since the diffusion information is pervasively available on social networks, in this work, we aim to investigate how the traces of information diffusion in terms of spreaders can be exploited to categorize a message. The message can be a piece of news, a story or a meme that has been posted and forwarded in social networks, and those users who post or forward it are the spreaders. Traces of a message refer to by whom and when the message is spread, *i.e.*, posted or forwarded.

We propose TraceMiner, a novel approach for classifying social media messages with diffusion network information. TraceMiner takes traces of a message as input and outputs its category. Consider the huge number of social media users and all the possible combinations of spreaders, traces will be of high dimensionality and thus may result in sparsity in the feature space. To cope with the problem, TraceMiner utilizes the proximity of nodes [34] and social dimensions [35] manifested in the social network, which have been successfully applied to capture the intrinsic characteristics of social media users in a myriad of applications.

To demonstrate TraceMiner's potential on real-world applications, we evaluate it with traditional approaches on Twitter data. TraceMiner outperforms competitors on multi-label information classification problems in large graphs. Therefore, TraceMiner provides an alternative way for modeling social media messages through learning abundant diffusion data that has not be fully utilized. Existing graph mining research mainly focuses on learning representation of graphs and nodes, while little attention has been paid to classifying information circulating between nodes. TraceMiner distances from existing graph representation methods by directly modeling information and making predictions in an

[1] http://www.journalism.org/2016/05/26/news-use-across-social-media-platforms-2016/

WSDM 2018, February 5–9, 2018, Marina Del Rey, CA, USA

ACM ISBN 978-1-4503-5581-0/18/02...$15.00
https://doi.org/10.1145/3159652.3159677

end-to-end manner other than providing only an attribute vector or embedding vector.

TraceMiner is scalable and the optimization can be easily parallelized through open-source software libraries. Hence, our method can be useful for a variety of social media mining problems where information from content is insufficient. Our contributions can be summarized as follows:

- We propose a novel approach for classifying social media messages with diffusion network information.
- We derive efficient optimization methods for TraceMiner, and provide analysis to guarantee the correctness.
- We extensively evaluate the performance on real social network data, and the experimental results demonstrate the effectiveness on different tasks.

The rest of this paper is organized as follows. In Section 2, we provide the definition for the problem. In Section 3, we introduce the proposed approaches and the optimization methods. How TraceMiner can be utilized to classify information diffusion sequences is presented in Section 4. In Section 5, we show empirical evaluation with discussions. Related work is discussed in Section 6. Conclusion and future work are presented in Section 7.

2 PROBLEM DEFINITION

We consider the problem of classifying social media messages into one or more categories. We define a graph $G \in \langle V, E \rangle$, where $v_i \in V$ with $i \in [1, |V|]$ is a node (user) and $E \subseteq V \times V$ is the set of edges. If $e_{ij} \in E$, there is an edge between v_i and v_j, otherwise there is not. Let M be the set of messages where $m_i \in M$ with $i \in [1, |M|]$. Each message m_i has a corresponding set of spreaders $\{(v_1^{m_i}, t_1^{m_i}), \{(v_2^{m_i}, t_2^{m_i}), \cdots, \{(v_n^{m_i}, t_n^{m_i})\}$, where n is the number of spreaders for m_i and $v_j^{m_i}$ is a user who spreads m_i at the time of $t_j^{m_i}$. Messages are partially labeled and thus only some of them have an associated class label. We denote the set of labels as Y, where $y_i \in Y$ indicates that m_i is labeled. Our goal is to learn a model with the social network graph G and partially labeled message M with the corresponding diffusion traces and label information Y, to predict $\hat{y}$ for the unlabeled messages.

Problem definition for traditional approaches: In order to make predictions for messages, most existing methods take the problem as a text categorization task, hence, each message m_i has a set of spreaders $\{(v_1^{m_i}, t_1^{m_i}, c_1^{m_i}), \cdots, \{(v_n^{m_i}, t_n^{m_i}, c_n^{m_i})\}$, where $c_j^{m_i}$ is the content information.

3 PROPOSED METHOD

In this section, we introduce how a diffusion trace can be used to facilitate classification. Wefi rst utilize sequential modeling methods to enable sequences to be used as attribute vectors. To alleviate the sparsity of sequences, we present a novel embedding method.

3.1 Sequence Modeling

Given the spreader information $\{(v_1^{m_i}, t_1^{m_i}), \cdots, \{(v_n^{m_i}, t_n^{m_i})\}$ and the graph G, the topology of information diffusion can be inferred by graph mining techniques [9]. The topology, which is usually a tree or forest (multiple trees) rooted with the initial spreader, contains informative patterns for characterizing a message. However, it is extremely difficult to directly deal with the tree structure. Consider two messages with similar diffusion networks, adding or removing one spreader, or changing any direction of the informationfl ow would lead to a different tree. Theoretically, there can be n^{n-2} different trees with n number of different nodes according to the Cayley's formula [7].

In order to solve this problem, we convert the tree structure into a temporal sequence. For example, given the spreaders of m_i $\{(v_1^{m_i}, t_1^{m_i}), \cdots, \{(v_n^{m_i}, t_n^{m_i})\}$, we generate a sequence $x_i = [(v_{q(1)}^{m_i}, t_{q(1)}^{m_i}), \cdots, (v_{q(n)}^{m_i}, t_{q(n)}^{m_i})]$ where for any two elements k and j in the sequence, if $k < j$, then $t_{q(k)}^{m_i} < t_{q(j)}^{m_i}$, meaning that $v_{q(k)}^{m_i}$ spread the information earlier than $v_{q(j)}^{m_i}$ did. Therefore, given n nodes, the number of all possible diffusion networks are reduced to $n!$. In order to further alleviate the sparsity, we incorporate social proximity and social dimensions in Section 3.2.

However, a possible problem of temporally sequencing spreaders is the loss of dependencies between users. Given v_i^m and v_j^m where $e_{ij} \in E$. If $t_i^m < t_j^m$, it is likely that user i spreads it to j or j is influenced by i [9]. Such direct dependency will be of vital importance in characterizing the information. For example, the informationfl ow from the controller account to the botnet followers is a key signal in detecting crowdturfing[11]. But if there is a spreader (u_k^m, t_k^m) where $< t_i^m < t_j^m$, in the sequence, i and j will be separated. Therefore, it would be appealing if the model can take advantage of dependencies between separated and distant items in a sequence. To this end, we propose to apply Recurrent Neural Networks (RNNs).

RNNs have been successfully applied in a myriad of domains for modeling sequential data [10], such as information retrieval [28], sentiment analysis [33] and machine translation [6]. We propose to use an RNN to sequentially accept each spreader of a message and recurrently project it into a latent space with the contextual information from previous spreaders in the sequence. As the RNN reaches the end of the sequence, a prediction can be made based on the embedding vector produced by the hidden activations. In order to better encode the distant and separated dependencies, we further incorporate the Long Short-Term Memory cells into the RNN model, *i.e.,* the LSTM-RNN.

In information diffusion, thefi rst spreader who initiates the diffusion process is more likely to be useful for classifying the message [1]. Hence, we feed the spread sequence in the **reverse** order, where thefi rst spreader in the sequence directly interacts with the prediction result, and thus it has more impact. Each spreader is represented by a local RNN. Parameters $\mathbf{W}$ of RNNs are shared across each replication in the sequence and h' is the previous recurrent output sent between RNNs to exploit the contextual information. In order to make the prediction, the last local RNNs are taking thefi rst spreader's attribute vector, prior recurrent output (and the label of the message) as input to predict the category of the message (or to train the RNNs model). In this work, we set the hidden node size (k) as 10. The way we obtain the attribute vector of nodes is introduced in Section 3.2.

Having chosen LSTM-RNNs as our method to classify messages, we now need a suitable way of learning attribute vectors $\mathbf{f}$, for social media users. An intuitive way is to utilize the social network

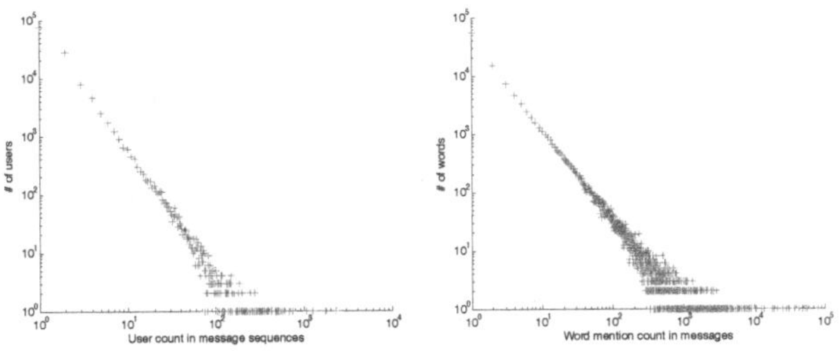

(a) Frequency of users in social media message traces. (b) Frequency of words in social media message.

Figure 1: The frequency of users appearing in traces of social media messages follows a power-law distribution, which is similar to the distribution of word frequencies in messages.

graph G to generate embedding vectors [29, 34], and feed sequences of embedding vectors to the LSTM-RNNs [28]. Such embedding-based preprocessing for sequential data has been widely used for natural language processing. We follow the practice since 1) several social graph embedding approaches have been proven useful for classification tasks, such as LINE [34] and DeepWalk [29], and 2) users appear in spread traces follow similar distribution of how words appear in the social media posts.

Figure 1 illustrates the distribution of users and words. The distribution in Figure 1(a) comes from a real-world Twitter message trace dataset showing how users appear in message traces. The distribution in Figure 1(b) comes from the same dataset showing how words appear in message content. They both follow a power-law distribution, which motivates us to embed users into low dimensional vectors, as how embedding vectors of words are used in natural language processing [16, 28]. Several graph embedding algorithms are available, we will compare their performance and provide our solution and reasons behind our choice in the next subsection. For the rest of the subsection, we will introduce the optimization for the proposed LSTM-RNNs.

We show the training of the proposed LSTM-RNNs in Algorithm 1. We input the labeled spreader sequences X and the corresponding labels Y, which are randomly split into a training and a validation set in line *2*. In addition to the maximum number of iterations Max_{iter}, we also have a function $EarlyStop()$ for controlling early termination of the training, which takes the loss on the validation set as the input. In line *1*, we initialize the model parameters randomly with Gaussian distribution. From line *3* to *7*, we update $\mathbf{W}$ with training data until the maximum epoch is reached or the early termination condition is met. The loss function used in line *4* is shown below:

$$\sum_{i=1}^{|X_{tr}|} |Y_{tr} = 0| y_i \log(\hat{y_i}) + |Y_{tr} = 1|(1 - y_i)(\log(1 - \hat{y_i})), \quad (1)$$

where y_i is the true label of i and $\hat{y}_i$ is the corresponding prediction. So Eq.(1) calculates the cross entropy between the true labels and the prediction. $|Y_{tr} = 0|$ ($|Y_{tr} = 1|$) is the number of negative (positive) instances in the training set. Since we aim to work on multi-label classification, the data is naturally imbalanced when we model one of them, introducing the weight helps the model balance the gradient of skewed data. In next subsection, we will introduce how we generate embeddings and the reason behind our choice.

Algorithm 1 Training Algorithm of LSTM-RNNs

Input: Labeled sequences and labels X, Y
Maximum number of iterations: Max_{iter}
Early termination function : $EarlyStop()$
Output: Weights of LSTM-RNNs: $\mathbf{W}$
1: Initialize $\mathbf{W}$ randomly with Gaussian distribution $VLoss[Max_{iter}]$, $i = 0$
2: Split X and Y into training and validation set, (X_{tr}, Y_{tr}) and (X_{val}, Y_{val})
3: **do**
4: Train RNNs with (X_{tr}, Y_{tr}) for 1 epoch with Eq.(1)
5: Test RNNs with (X_{val}, Y_{val}) to obtain loss $VLoss[i]$
6: $i = i + 1$
7: **while** $EarlyStop(VLoss, i) = FALSE$ AND $(i < Max_{iter})$

3.2 Embedding of Users

Given the framework of sequence modeling, the next problem is tofi nd the proper embedding method that captures the intrinsic features of social media users. As discussed previously, using embedding vectors can help alleviate the data sparsity through leveraging social proximity and social dimensions. In this work among the existing embedding methods, we will mainly focus on two state-of-the-art approaches that have been proven effective on social graphs, LINE [34] and DeepWalk [29]. Both LINE and DeepWalk aim to provide a representation for data instances that captures the inherent properties, such as social proximity.

These methods mainly focus on the microscopic structure of networks. For example,fi rst-order proximity constrains users that are connected to be similar and second-order proximity constrains users that have common friends to be similar. LINE achieves this by sampling such nodes from the network and updating their representations jointly, while DeepWalk samples a sequence of data with a random walk algorithm. Nevertheless, for a large social graph, some mesoscopic structure such as social dimensions [35] and community structures [44] are more useful in characterizing information [17]. Therefore, the ideal embedding method should be able to capture both local proximity and community structures.

Table 1 illustrates our results of using different embedding methods. We test LINE, DeepWalk and SocDim [35] on Twitter data and show the distance between neighbors with the new representation. We also detect community structures in the network and calculate the average of distances between nodes that are in the same community. The community detection algorithm is an accelerated version of Louvain method [2]. As shown in the table, LINE captures thefi rst and second-degree proximity, while SocDim best captures the community-wise proximity. Based on the random walk, DeepWalk achieves better community-wise proximity, however, it is still outperformed by SocDim, which directly models the community structure.

In order to capture both the social proximity and community wise similarity among users, we propose a principled framework that directly models both kinds of information. Given the social

Table 1: Average Euclidean distance between nodes with low dimensional representation.

Method	1st-degree	2nd-degree	Intra-group
LINE	**5.16**	**5.00**	10.76
DeepWalk	7.74	7.69	6.04
SocDim	6.87	6.12	**4.55**

graph G, we can derive an adjacency matrix $\mathbf{S} \in \mathbb{R}^{n \times n}$, where n is the number of users. Our goal is to learn a transformation matrix $\mathbf{M} \in \mathbb{R}^{n \times k}$ which converts users to a latent space with the dimensionality of k. Note that we reuse k for brevity of presentation, and the number of features and hidden nodes in the LSTM-RNNs are not necessarily the same. In order to capture the community-wise similarity, we introduce two auxiliary matrices, a community indicator matrix $\mathbf{H} \in \mathbb{R}^{n \times g}$, where g is the number of communities and $tr(\mathbf{H}\mathbf{H}^T) = n$ (only one element is 1 in each row and all the others are 0), and a community representation matrix $\mathbf{C} \in \mathbb{R}^{g \times k}$, where each row $\mathbf{c}_i$ is an embedding vector describing the community. In order to capture the community structure, we embed the problem into an attributed community detection model [44]:

$$\min_{\mathbf{M},\mathbf{H},\mathbf{C}} \sum_{i=1}^{n} ||\mathbf{s}_i\mathbf{M} - \mathbf{h}_i\mathbf{C}||_2^2 + \alpha||\mathbf{H} - \mathbf{M}\mathbf{C}^T||_F^2, \quad s.t. \quad tr(\mathbf{H}\mathbf{H}^T) = n, \tag{2}$$

where $\mathbf{s}_i\mathbf{M}$ is the embedding vector and we regularize it to be similar to the representation of its corresponding community $\mathbf{h}_i\mathbf{C}$. The second term aims to achieve the intra-group coherence by predicting the community assignment by group the embedding vectors of users and communities [44]. The objective function in Eq.(2) aims to cluster nodes with embedding vectors. In order to further regularize the clusters to be social communities, we adopt a modularity maximization-based method, which has been widely used to detect communities with network information [37]. Specifically, given the adjacency matrix S and the community membership indicator, the modularity is defined as follows [35]:

$$Q = \frac{1}{2|E|} \sum_{i,j} (S_{ij} - \frac{d_i d_j}{2|E|})(\mathbf{h}_i\mathbf{h}_j^T), \tag{3}$$

where $|E|$ is the number of edges and d_i is the degree of i. $\mathbf{h}_i$ is the community assignment vector for i, and $\mathbf{h}_i\mathbf{h}_j^T = 1$ if i and j belong to the same community, otherwise $\mathbf{h}_i\mathbf{h}_j^T = 0$. $\frac{d_i d_j}{2|E|}$ is the expected number of edges between i and j if edges are placed at random. Modularity Q measures the difference between the number of actual edges within a community and the expected number of edges placed at random. An optimal community structure H should maximize the modularity Q. By defining the modularity matrix $\mathbf{B} \in \mathbb{R}^{n \times n}$ where $B_{ij} = S_{ij} - \frac{d_i d_j}{2|E|}$ and suppressing the constant which has no effect on the modularity, we rewrite Eq.(3) as follows:

$$Q = tr(\mathbf{H}^T\mathbf{B}\mathbf{H}).$$

In order to guarantee that the embedding vectors preserve the community structure in the latent space, we propose to integrate modularity maximization into the embedding method. The objective function can be rewritten with the modularity maximization regularizer as follows:

$$\min_{\mathbf{M},\mathbf{H},\mathbf{C}} \sum_{i=1}^{n} ||\mathbf{s}_i\mathbf{M} - \mathbf{h}_i\mathbf{C}||_2^2 + \alpha||\mathbf{H} - \mathbf{M}\mathbf{C}^T||_F^2 - \beta tr(\mathbf{H}^T\mathbf{B}\mathbf{H}) \quad s.t. \quad tr(\mathbf{H}\mathbf{H}^T) = n, \tag{4}$$

where β controls the influence of community structures. As discussed previously, the microscopic structure is also of vital importance for generating embedding vectors. In order to jointly consider both mesoscopic and microscopic structures, we decompose M into a conjunction of a global model parameter $\tilde{\mathbf{M}}$ and a localized variable $\mathbf{M_i}$ for each user i ($\mathbf{M} = \tilde{\mathbf{M}} + \mathbf{M_i}$ for each user i). Therefore, $\tilde{\mathbf{M}}$ captures the community structure and $\mathbf{M_i}$ can be used to directly apprehend the microscopic structure between nodes. Motivated by recent research on network regularization, we fortify the representation of nodes with proximity by the network lasso regularization term [12]:

$$\sum_{i,j} \mathbf{A}_{ij}||\mathbf{M}_i - \mathbf{M}_j||_F^2,$$

where $\mathbf{A} \in \mathbb{R}^{n \times n}$ is the microscopic structure matrix, $A_{ij} = 1$ if we aim to preserve the proximity between i and j in the latent space. Following conventional graph embedding practices [34], we considerfi rst- and second-degree proximity, meaning that $A_{ij} = 1$ if i and j are connected or share a common friend. Note that A can be specified with particular applications. Imposing the Frobenius norm of the difference between $\mathbf{M}_i$ and $\mathbf{M}_j$ incentivizes them to be the same when $A_{ij} = 1$. By incorporating the network lasso regularizer, the objective function can be reformulated as follows:

$$\min_{\mathbf{M},\mathbf{H},\mathbf{C}} \sum_{i=1}^{n} ||\mathbf{s}_i(\tilde{\mathbf{M}} + \mathbf{M_i}) - \mathbf{h}_i\mathbf{C}||_2^2 + \alpha||\mathbf{H} - \tilde{\mathbf{M}}\mathbf{C}^T||_F^2 - \beta tr(\mathbf{H}^\mathbf{T}\mathbf{B}\mathbf{H}) + \gamma \sum_{i,j} \mathbf{A}_{ij}||\mathbf{M}_i - \mathbf{M}_j||_F^2, \quad s.t. \quad tr(\mathbf{H}\mathbf{H}^\mathbf{T}) = n, \tag{5}$$

where γ controls the influence of the network lasso. As we can see, we establish the consensus relationship between mesoscopic and microscopic network structures by jointly considering the social communities and proximity. By introducing the global parameter $\tilde{\mathbf{M}}$ and the personal variable $\mathbf{M}_i$, we force both kinds of information to be preserved in the newly-learnt embedding vectors. However, Eq.(5) is not jointly convex to all the parameters M,H and C. In order to solve the problem, we separate the optimization into four subproblems and iteratively optimize them. We will introduce details of the optimization for the rest of the section.

Update $\tilde{\mathbf{M}}$ whilefixing $\mathbf{M_i}$, H and C: By removing terms that are irrelevant to $\tilde{\mathbf{M}}$, we obtain the following optimization problem:

$$\min_{\tilde{\mathbf{M}}} \sum_{i=1}^{n} ||\mathbf{s}_i\tilde{\mathbf{M}} + \mathbf{s}_i\mathbf{M_i} - \mathbf{h}_i\mathbf{C}||_2^2 + \alpha||\mathbf{H} - \tilde{\mathbf{M}}\mathbf{C}^T||_F^2, \tag{6}$$

which is convex *w.r.t.* $\tilde{\mathbf{M}}$. In real applications, the number of users n may be huge. Hence, we adopt a gradient-based update rule as follows:

$$\tilde{\mathbf{M}} = \tilde{\mathbf{M}} - \tau\frac{\partial \epsilon_{\tilde{\mathbf{M}}}}{\partial \tilde{\mathbf{M}}}, \tag{7}$$

where τ is the step size that can be obtained through backtracking line search [27]. The derivative of $\tilde{\mathbf{M}}$ is shown as follows:

$$\frac{\partial \epsilon_{\tilde{\mathbf{M}}}}{\partial \tilde{\mathbf{M}}} = \mathbf{s}_i^T \sum_{i=1}^{n} (\mathbf{s}_i\tilde{\mathbf{M}} + \mathbf{s}_i\mathbf{M}_i - \mathbf{h}_i\mathbf{C}) + \alpha(\mathbf{H} - \tilde{\mathbf{M}}\mathbf{C}^T)\mathbf{C}. \quad (8)$$

Update $\mathbf{M}_i$ whilefixing $\tilde{\mathbf{M}}$, H and C: By removing terms that are irrelevant to $\mathbf{M}_i$, we obtain the following optimization problem:

$$\min_{\mathbf{M}_i} \sum_{i=1}^{n} ||\mathbf{s}_i\tilde{\mathbf{M}} + \mathbf{s}_i\mathbf{M}_i - \mathbf{h}_i\mathbf{C}||_2^2 + \gamma \sum_{i,j} A_{ij}||\mathbf{M}_i - \mathbf{M}_j||_F^2, \quad (9)$$

which is convex *w.r.t.* $\mathbf{M}_i$. Similarly, we derive the gradient:

$$\frac{\partial \epsilon_{\mathbf{M}_i}}{\partial \mathbf{M}_i} = \mathbf{s}_i^T \sum_{i=1}^{n} (\mathbf{s}_i\tilde{\mathbf{M}} + \mathbf{s}_i\mathbf{M}_i - \mathbf{h}_i\mathbf{C}) + \gamma \sum_{i,j} A_{ij}(\mathbf{M}_i - \mathbf{M}_j). \quad (10)$$

Update C whilefixing $\tilde{\mathbf{M}}$, $\mathbf{M}_i$, and H: By removing terms that are irrelevant to C, we obtain the following optimization problem:

$$\min_{\mathbf{C}} \sum_{i=1}^{n} ||\mathbf{s}_i(\tilde{\mathbf{M}} + \mathbf{M}_i) - \mathbf{h}_i\mathbf{C}||_2^2 + \alpha||\mathbf{H} - \tilde{\mathbf{M}}\mathbf{C}^T||_F^2, \quad (11)$$

which is convex *w.r.t.* C. Similarly, the gradient can be obtained as:

$$\frac{\partial \epsilon_{\mathbf{C}}}{\partial \mathbf{C}} = \sum_{i=1}^{n} \mathbf{h}_i^T(\mathbf{h}_i\mathbf{C} - \mathbf{s}_i\tilde{\mathbf{M}} - \mathbf{s}_i\mathbf{M}_i) + \alpha(\tilde{\mathbf{M}}\mathbf{C}^T - \mathbf{H})^T\tilde{\mathbf{M}}. \quad (12)$$

Update H whilefixing $\tilde{\mathbf{M}}$, $\mathbf{M}_i$, and C: By removing terms that are irrelevant to H, we obtain the following optimization problem:

$$\begin{aligned} &\min_{\mathbf{H}} ||\mathbf{SM} - \mathbf{HC}||_F^2 + \alpha||\mathbf{H} - \tilde{\mathbf{M}}\mathbf{C}^T||_F^2 - \beta tr(\mathbf{H}^{\mathrm{T}}(\mathbf{S} - \hat{\mathbf{B}})\mathbf{H}), \\ &s.t. \quad tr(\mathbf{H}\mathbf{H}^T) = n, \end{aligned} \quad (13)$$

where $\hat{\mathbf{B}}_{ij} = \frac{d_i d_j}{2|E|}$. Consider that H is an indicator matrix, the constraint makes the problem in Eq.(13) NP-complete, which is extremely difficult to solve. In order to cope with the problem, we relax the constraint to orthogonality $\mathbf{H}^T\mathbf{H} = \mathbf{I}$ and nonnegativity $\mathbf{H} \geq 0$ and reformulate the objective function as follows:

$$\begin{aligned} \epsilon_{\mathbf{H}} = & - \beta tr(\mathbf{H}^T\mathbf{S}\mathbf{H}) + \beta tr(\mathbf{H}^T\hat{\mathbf{B}}\mathbf{H}) \\ & + ||\mathbf{SM} - \mathbf{HC}||_F^2 + \alpha||\mathbf{H} - \hat{\mathbf{M}}\mathbf{C}^T||_F^2 \\ & + \lambda||\mathbf{H}^T\mathbf{H} - \mathbf{I}||_F^2, \end{aligned} \quad (14)$$

where $\lambda > 0$ should be a large number to guarantee the orthogonal constraint to be satisfied, and we set it as 10^8 in this work. We then utilize the property that $||\mathbf{X}||_F^2 = tr(\mathbf{X}^T\mathbf{X})$ to reformulate the loss function as follows:

$$\begin{aligned} \epsilon_{\mathbf{H}} = & - \beta tr(\mathbf{H}^T\mathbf{S}\mathbf{H}) + \beta tr(\mathbf{H}^T\hat{\mathbf{B}}\mathbf{H}) \\ & + tr(\mathbf{S}\mathbf{M}\mathbf{M}^T\mathbf{S}^T + \mathbf{H}\mathbf{C}\mathbf{C}^T\mathbf{H}^T - 2\mathbf{S}\mathbf{M}\mathbf{C}^T\mathbf{H}^T) \\ & + \alpha tr(\mathbf{H}\mathbf{H}^T + \hat{\mathbf{M}}\mathbf{C}^T\mathbf{C}\tilde{\mathbf{M}}^T - 2\mathbf{H}\mathbf{C}\tilde{\mathbf{M}}^T) \\ & + \lambda tr(\mathbf{H}^T\mathbf{H}\mathbf{H}^T\mathbf{H} - 2\mathbf{H}^T\mathbf{H} + \mathbf{I}) + tr(\Theta\mathbf{H}^T), \end{aligned} \quad (15)$$

where $\Theta = [\Theta_{ij}]$ is a Lagrange multiplier matrix to impose the nonnegative constraint. Set the derivative of $\frac{\partial \epsilon_{\mathbf{H}}}{\partial \mathbf{H}}$ to 0, we have:

$$\begin{aligned} \Theta = & \ 2\mathbf{SH} - 2\beta\tilde{\mathbf{B}}\mathbf{H} - 2\mathbf{C}\mathbf{C}^T\mathbf{H}^T + 2\mathbf{S}\mathbf{M}\mathbf{C}^T \\ & - 2\alpha\mathbf{H}^T + 2\alpha\mathbf{C}\tilde{\mathbf{M}}^T - 4\lambda\mathbf{H}\mathbf{H}^T\mathbf{H} + 4\lambda\mathbf{H}. \end{aligned} \quad (16)$$

Following the Karush-Kuhn-Tucker (KKT) condition for the nonnegativity, we have the equation as follows:

$$\begin{aligned} &(2\mathbf{SH} - 2\beta\tilde{\mathbf{B}}\mathbf{H} - 2\mathbf{C}\mathbf{C}^T\mathbf{H}^T + 2\mathbf{S}\mathbf{M}\mathbf{C}^T - 2\alpha\mathbf{H}^T \\ &+2\alpha\mathbf{C}\tilde{\mathbf{M}}^T - 4\lambda\mathbf{H}\mathbf{H}^T\mathbf{H} + 4\lambda\mathbf{H})_{ij}H_{ij} = \theta_{ij}H_{ij} = 0, \end{aligned} \quad (17)$$

which is thefi xed point equation that the solution must satisfy at convergence. The update rule for H can be written as follows:

$$\mathbf{H} = \mathbf{H} \odot \sqrt{\frac{-2\beta\tilde{\mathbf{B}}\mathbf{H} + \sqrt{\Delta}}{8\lambda\mathbf{H}\mathbf{H}^T\mathbf{H}}}, \quad (18)$$

where Δ is defined as:

$$\begin{aligned} \Delta \ = & \ 2\beta(\tilde{\mathbf{B}}\mathbf{H}) \odot (\tilde{\mathbf{B}}\mathbf{H}) + 16\lambda(\mathbf{H}\mathbf{H}^T\mathbf{H}) \\ \odot & \ (2\mathbf{SH} - 2\mathbf{C}\mathbf{C}^T\mathbf{H}^T + 2\mathbf{S}\mathbf{M}\mathbf{C}^T \\ - & \ 2\alpha\mathbf{H}^T + 2\alpha\mathbf{C}\tilde{\mathbf{M}}^T + 4\lambda\mathbf{H}). \end{aligned} \quad (19)$$

The convergence of Eq.(19) can be proven as an instance of nonnegative matrix factorization (NMF) problem [18].

3.3 Time complexity

TraceMiner consists of two components, LSTM-RNNs and the embedding method. Though LSTM-RNNs take $O(|E| + |V|)$-time for backpropagations, the scalability can be easily increased with deep learning software library like Theano[2], especially when GPU is available.

Since the number of users is usually far larger than the number of features and number of communities, the embedding method takes $O(n^2)$-time. Only matrix multiplication is used in all update rules, so the optimization can be accelerated by utilizing matrix optimization library like OpenBLAS[3].

4 ALGORITHM-TRACEMINER

In this section, we introduce the detailed procedure of TraceMiner method for network diffusion classification. The overall process consists of two steps:

- *Learning embeddings based on network connectivity.* In this work, we aim to utilize the social identity of a user to infer the information she spreads. Hence, we learn embeddings from friendships and social community memberships.
- *Construct a sequence classifier with LSTM-RNNs.* After we obtain the embeddings of social media users, we consider a social media message as a sequence of its spreaders. We employ LSTM-RNNs to model the sequence, and thefinal hidden output are aggregated using softmax to produce a predicted class label.

Thefi rst step utilizes network structures to embed social media users into space of low dimensionality, which alleviates the data sparsity of utilizing social media users as features. The second step represents user sequences of information diffusion, which allows for the classification of propagation pathways.

[2]http://deeplearning.net/software/theano/
[3]http://www.openblas.net/

Table 2: Statistics of the datasest used in this study.

	Messages	Posts	Unique Users	Class Ratio
Real News	68,892	288,591	121,211	0.27(b):0.25(t):0.37(e):0.11(m)
Fake News	3,600	17,613	9,153	0.5:0.5

5 EXPERIMENT

In this section, we introduce experiment details to validate the effectiveness of the proposed framework. Through the experiments, we aim to answer two questions:

- How well can network information be used to classify social messages compared with content information?
- How effective are the LSTM-RNNs by integrating with the proposed embedding method?

Therefore, we test the methods on two different classification tasks with real-world datasets and include both content-based and network-based baselines for comparison.

5.1 Datasets

Over 200 million posts are posted per day on Twitter[4] and the popularity has made Twitter a testbed for informationfiltering research. In this work, we aim to collect a large dataset that includes tweets about specific messages. Following [30], we leverage Twitter Search API[5] to retrieve tweets of interests by compiling queries with certain topics.

We deal with two tasks in this work, standard news classification and fake news detection. News classification is a classical multi-label text categorization problem and existing efforts have mainly focused on the content. We obtain a news dataset which was originally used for content-based classification[6] by selecting news that has at least two posts on Twitter. Queries for Twitter Search API are compiled by words in the title of the corresponding news. Based on the spreaders of news, we try to use TraceMiner to classify the news into four categories: business (b), science and technology (t), entertainment (e), medical (m). Statistics about the dataset are shown in Table 2. We sample $68,892$ pieces of news, which relate to $288,591$ posts with $121,211$ unique users. The ratio of different categories is also presented.

The other task is fake news detection. The openness of social media platforms enables timely information to be spread at a high rate. Meanwhile, it also allows for the rapid creation and dissemination of fake news. Following [30], we retrieve tweets related to fake news by compiling queries with a fact-checking website. In this work, we choose Snopes[7] to obtain ground truth, where we collect articles tagged with fake news[8]. In order to obtain non-fake news posts pertaining to the same topic, we extract keywords in regular expressions as queries to retrieve posts. Statistics of the dataset is shown in Table 2. We collect $3,600$ messages with 50% are fake news.

[4]https://blog.twitter.com/2011/200-million-tweets-per-day
[5]https://dev.twitter.com/rest/public/search
[6]https://archive.ics.uci.edu/ml/datasets/News+Aggregator
[7]http://www.snopes.com/
[8]https://www.snopes.com/tag/fake-news/

5.2 Experimental Settings

A core contribution of our work is the idea that spreaders of information can be used to predict message categories. Therefore, we try to test the effectiveness of the proposed method comparing with the state-of-the-art content-based approaches. We experiment a variety of approaches, and report the following two which achieve better results.

- **SVM** [13] trains on content information, which isfirst preprocessed with Stanford CoreNLP toolkit [24]. We adopt bigram and trigram features based on results on the validation set.
- **XGBoost** [5] is an optimized distributed gradient boosting library that implements machine learning algorithms under the Gradient Boosting framework. It has been successfully applied to various problems and competitions. We feed it with the preprocessed content produced by Stanford CoreNLP. XGBoost presents the best results among all content-based algorithms we tested.

We propose a novel embedding method to cater to TraceMiner. In order to evaluate its effectiveness, we introduce two variants of TraceMiner and present their results for comparison:

- **TM(DeepWalk)** is a variant of TraceMiner by adopting the embedding vectors from DeepWalk as input. As discussed earlier, DeepWalk captures proximity between nodes with random walk: nodes that are sampled together with one random walk are forced to preserve the similarity in the latent space. Therefore, DeepWalk does not directly model thefi rst and second-degree proximity or the community structure.
- **TM(LINE)** is a variant of TraceMiner by adopting the embedding vectors from LINE. LINE modelsfi rst and second-degree proximity while does not consider the community structure between users.

To test the prediction accuracy in terms of both precision and recall, we adopted the F_1-measure to evaluate the performance. Since there are multiple labels to be predicted, for each task t, F_1^t can be computed. In order to get the overall performance, wefirst adopt the Macro-averaged F_1-measure as:

$$Macro - F_1 = \frac{1}{|T|} \sum_{t \in T} F_1^t, \tag{20}$$

where T is the set of all identity labels and F_1^t is the F_1-measure of task t.

A possible problem of Macro-F_1 is, since the sizes of different categories are different, the task with fewer instances may be overemphasized. In order to cope with this problem, we adopted Micro-averaged F_1-measure. First, we calculate the micro averaged

Table 3: The F_1-measure of different methods on the task of social media news categorization.

	Training Ratio	10%	20%	30%	40%	50%	60%	70%	80%	90%
Micro-F_1(%)	SVM	0.6967	0.7138	0.7447	0.7577	0.7988	0.8096	0.8499	0.8787	0.8996
	XGBoost	0.7121	0.7349	0.7512	0.7794	0.8248	0.8250	0.8638	0.8951	0.9047
	TM(DeepWalk)	0.7895	0.8081	0.8149	0.8374	0.8569	0.8627	0.8852	0.8917	0.9184
	TM(LINE)	0.7691	0.7926	0.8163	0.8379	0.8467	0.8744	0.8980	0.9106	0.9253
	TraceMiner	**0.8275**	**0.8460**	**0.8658**	**0.8835**	**0.8885**	**0.9141**	**0.9218**	**0.9357**	**0.9380**
Macro-F_1(%)	SVM	0.6988	0.7260	0.7425	0.7754	0.7665	0.7872	0.8118	0.8314	0.8722
	XGBoost	0.7305	0.7438	0.7857	0.7887	0.8144	0.8344	0.8726	**0.8941**	0.9044
	TM(DeepWalk)	0.7746	0.8010	0.8156	0.8313	0.8377	0.8611	0.8646	0.8734	0.8839
	TM(LINE)	0.7561	0.7895	0.8019	0.8138	0.8235	0.8568	0.8775	0.8896	**0.9153**
	TraceMiner	**0.8181**	**0.8347**	**0.8359**	**0.8549**	**0.8635**	**0.8788**	**0.8779**	0.8882	0.9064

precision and recall:

$$Micro-precision = \frac{\#TP}{\#TP + \#FP} \quad (21)$$
$$Micro-recall = \frac{\#TP}{\#TP + \#FN},$$

where #TP is the number of true positives, #FP is the number of false positives and #FN is the number of false negatives. Micro-F_1 is the harmonic average of Micro-precision and Micro-recall.

5.3 Experimental Results

Social Media News Categorization: The performance of different methods on Twitter News data with varying training ratio, from 10% to 90%, is illustrated in Table 3. For each experiment, samples are randomly split into training and testing set. We repeat this process 10 times and report the average results. The highest performance under each setting is highlighted in bold face.

In terms of Micro-F_1, our proposed model TraceMiner outperforms all the baselines and its variations, TM(DeepWalk), TM(LINE). Diffusion-based methods perform better than content-based methods. XGBoost performs slightly better than SVM. TM(DeepWalk) is the runner-up method for 10%, 20% and 50%, and TM(LINE) is the runner-up for the rest cases. The result shows that when less network data is available, the random walk-based approach produces better embeddings of users; And a more deterministic method constraining on social proximity better apprehends user behaviors when the network information is more complete. TraceMiner achieves the best result for all tasks. By jointly modeling the microscopic and mesoscopic structures, TraceMiner is more robust to data sparsity.

In terms of Macro-F_1, XGBoost outperforms SVM for all cases. Similar pattern has again been observed: TM(DeepWalk) outperforms TM(LINE) with less training information, while TM(LINE) outperforms TM(DeepWalk) when the information is more complete. TraceMiner still performs the best among most cases until we increase the training ratio up to 80%. XGBoost and TM(LINE) achieves the best result for 80% and 90%, respectively. Two observations can be made here: with more training information becoming available, 1) the margin between proposed methods and the content-based methods becomes smaller; and 2) the margin between TraceMiner and its variants TM(LINE) and TM(DeepWalk) becomes smaller. Based on the observations we can draw conclusions that TraceMiner is more useful when less training information is available, and the proposed TraceMiner can well handle scarce data in the early phase of learning when less training information is known. XGBoost gets the best when 80% of information is available Since text-based categorization is a well-studied problem, and it is easy to solve when rich information is available, TraceMiner will be able to complement those cases that are difficult for content-based approaches to deal with, and such cases are pervasively present in social media mining tasks where content information is insufficient and noisy.

Another observation that again validates ourfi ndings is that TraceMiner performs better in terms of Micro-F_1. As shown in Eq.(20) and (21), in a multi-label classification task, the category with fewer instances is more advantageous for Macro-F_1. The results show that TraceMiner actually ends up with correctly classifying more instances.

Fake News Detection: The performance of different methods on Twitter fake news data with varying training ratio, from 10% to 90%, is illustrated in Table 4. Since the dataset is balanced Micro- and Macro-F_1 are the same, so only one set of results are presented. For the content-based approaches, XGBoost consistently outperforms SVM for all cases. For the two variants of TraceMiner, similar patterns are observed: TM(DeepWalk) outperforms TM(LINE) when less training information is available. TM(LINE) outperforms TM(DeepWalk) when more information is available for training. It again proves that random walk-based sampling is more effective for scarce data, and proximity-based regularization better captures data structures with more training information.

An interesting difference between the results for fake news and the previous experiment is the larger margin between proposed methods and content-based methods. Unlike posts related to news where the content information is more self-explanatory, content of posts about fake news is less descriptive. Intentional spreaders of fake news may manipulate the content to make it look more similar to non-rumor information. Hence, TraceMiner can be useful for many emerging tasks in social media where adversarial attacks are present, such as detecting rumors and crowdturfing The margin between content-based approaches and TraceMiner becomes smaller when more information is available for training however, in these emerging tasks, training information is usually time-consuming and labor-intensive to obtain.

Table 4: The F_1-measure of different methods on the task of fake news detection.

Training Ratio	10%	20%	30%	40%	50%	60%	70%	80%	90%
SVM	0.5825	0.5779	0.6122	0.6194	0.6658	0.7114	0.7224	0.7252	0.7581
XGBoost	0.6558	0.7004	0.7002	0.7153	0.7288	0.7703	0.7984	0.8115	0.8226
TM(DeepWalk)	0.7804	0.7810	0.8078	0.8264	0.8194	0.8491	0.8542	0.8738	0.8894
TM(LINE)	0.7542	0.7547	0.7913	0.8015	0.8083	0.8485	0.8733	0.8936	0.8971
TraceMiner	**0.7867**	**0.7935**	**0.8344**	**0.8459**	**0.8547**	**0.8751**	**0.8988**	**0.9089**	**0.9124**

Another point we would like to discuss is the performance when the training information is very insufficient. When 10% of information is available, SVM has an F_1 score of 58% which is slightly better than a random guess, while TraceMiner has an F_1 score of 78%. Although such margin is reduced when more information is available, the optimal performance with very few training information is of crucial significance for tasks which emphasize on the earliness. For example, detecting fake news at an early stage is way more meaningful than detecting it when 90% percent of its information is known [30, 31, 40]. In conclusion, TraceMiner provides an effective method for modeling messages diffused in social media with only network information, which provides a complementary tool for emerging tasks that require earliness and/or suffers from the scarcity of content information.

6 RELATED WORK

This work mainly focuses on classifying social media messages, which is a fundamental problem in social media mining. It can be useful for many classical tasks including social recommendation, personalization and targeted advertising. Accurate categorization of social media content allows for precisefi ltering of information, which helps alleviate the information overloading. A recent surge for social media platforms is the attacks of disinformation launched by malicious users. Both content and network information has been studied to detect malicious users, such as spammers [38, 39] and crowdturfers [41]. In terms of network information, traditional approaches usually derive features from the social networks and spreaders of a message. For example, Hu et al. assume that the information spread by similar users tend to share similar properties [38], and the network information mainly centers around the user instead of information itself. Our work distances from the existing work by directly studying the network information.

Our work is also related to network structure mining methods. Neural network models have been applied on network data for tasks such as classification [43] and clustering [36]. These existing methods focus on the nodes in the graph, while our work focuses on the network structure itself, which is manifested by the diffusion of messages. In addition, unlike existing graph representation methods, our goal is to provide an end-to-end system with prediction results, instead of offering only the embedding vectors. Recent research has been proposed to utilize RNNs for classification in an semi-supervised manner [25], which is also related to our work.

We present a novel graph embedding model, which is related to existing embedding methods and feature selection on networked data [20]. For example, DeepWalk [29] links a network embedding problem into a word embedding problem by showing the similar distribution of nodes appearing in random walks and words appearing in sentences. They employ a Skip-Gram model, which was originally proposed for modeling natural languages, to learn embedding of graphs. LINE [34] aims to preserve thefi rst- and second-order proximity between nodes, and provides an embedding vector by concatenating results on both levels. Our work focuses on encoding both social proximity and social community information to alleviate the data sparsity, instead of investigating only one of them [22, 23]. Recent studies also study and utilize network dynamics by observing the change of social networks over time [19, 21]. We focus on a snapshot since the newly established/withdrawn links during the study are very few.

Our work is related to information diffusion. There are various models which are designed to abstract the pattern of information diffusion, such as SIR Model [15], Tipping Model [4], Independent Cascade Model [14] and Linear Threshold Model [14]. However, traditional information diffusion models abstract the diffusion process to estimate the virality of information and ignore the interaction between multiple campaigns, which cannot be directly applied here.

Our work can be particularly helpful for identifying messages that cannot be easily detected with the content. An emerging problem that has the feature is rumor and fake news detection. For example, supervised learning approaches have been used to detect rumors [40] and the spreaders [26]. The proposed process usually consists of two stages: employing a feature engineering approach to distinguish misinformation [42] from Twitter's normal content stream and utilize a supervised learning approach to train a detector. However, supervised approaches depend on content information, which can be easily manipulated by malicious spreaders. Previous studies have explored how malicious information can be detected from node to node [3], however, the proposed systems can only help visualize and track known events and require experts to observe it and make decisions. The process requires certain domain knowledge and expertise, while TraceMiner is an end-to-end method taht directly studies the information diffusion.

7 CONCLUSION

In this work, we aim to classify messages spread in social networks, which is a fundamental problem for social media mining. We observe that for many emerging tasks, content information is usually insufficient or less descriptive, while pervasively available network information is left unused. Therefore, we propose a novel method TraceMiner that classifies social media messages with diffusion traces in social networks. To address the problem, we propose an end-to-end classification model based on LSTM-RNNs. In order to alleviate the data sparsity, we propose an embedding method that captures both social proximity and community structures.

Experimental results with real-world datasets show that TraceMiner effectively classifies social media messages and is especially useful when content information is insufficient.

Future work can be focused on two aspects. First, we would like to investigate if TraceMiner can be used to facilitate other network mining tasks, like recommendation and link prediction. Second, since content information is also readily available, we will study how content and network information can be jointly utilized.

ACKNOWLEDGMENTS

This work was supported, in part, by the Office of Naval Research grants N000141410095 and N000141310835.

REFERENCES

[1] Geoffrey Barbier, Zhuo Feng, Pritam Gundecha, and Huan Liu. 2013. Provenance data in social media. *Synthesis Lectures on Data Mining and Knowledge Discovery* 4, 1 (2013), 1–84.

[2] Vincent D Blondel, Jean-Loup Guillaume, Renaud Lambiotte, and Etienne Lefebvre. 2008. Fast unfolding of communities in large networks. *Journal of Statistical Mechanics: Theory and Experiment* 2008, 10 (2008), P10008.

[3] Nan Cao, Conglei Shi, Sabrina Lin, Jie Lu, Yu-Ru Lin, and Ching-Yung Lin. 2016. TargetVue: Visual analysis of anomalous user behaviors in online communication systems. *IEEE transactions on visualization and computer graphics* 22, 1 (2016), 280–289.

[4] Damon Centola. 2010. The spread of behavior in an online social network experiment. *science* 329, 5996 (2010), 1194–1197.

[5] Tianqi Chen and Carlos Guestrin. 2016. Xgboost: A scalable tree boosting system. In *International Conference on Knowledge Discovery and Data Mining*. ACM, 785–794.

[6] Kyunghyun Cho, Bart Van Merriënboer, Caglar Gulcehre, Dzmitry Bahdanau, Fethi Bougares, Holger Schwenk, and Yoshua Bengio. 2014. Learning phrase representations using RNN encoder-decoder for statistical machine translation. *arXiv preprint arXiv:1406.1078* (2014).

[7] LE Clarke. 1958. On Cayley's formula for counting trees. *Journal of the London Mathematical Society* 1, 4 (1958), 471–474.

[8] Michela Del Vicario, Alessandro Bessi, Fabiana Zollo, Fabio Petroni, Antonio Scala, Guido Caldarelli, H Eugene Stanley, and Walter Quattrociocchi. 2016. The spreading of misinformation online. *Proceedings of the National Academy of Sciences* 113, 3 (2016), 554–559.

[9] Manuel Gomez Rodriguez, Jure Leskovec, and Andreas Krause. 2010. Inferring networks of diffusion and influence. In *Proceedings of the 16th ACM SIGKDD international conference on Knowledge discovery and data mining*. ACM, 1019–1028.

[10] Ian Goodfellow, Yoshua Bengio, and Aaron Courville. 2016. *Deep learning*. MIT Press.

[11] Guofei Gu, Junjie Zhang, and Wenke Lee. 2008. BotSniffer: Detecting botnet command and control channels in network traffic. (2008).

[12] David Hallac, Jure Leskovec, and Stephen Boyd. 2015. Network lasso: Clustering and optimization in large graphs. In *Proceedings of the 21th ACM SIGKDD International Conference on Knowledge Discovery and Data Mining*. ACM, 387–396.

[13] Thorsten Joachims. 1998. Text categorization with support vector machines: Learning with many relevant features. In *European conference on machine learning*. Springer, 137–142.

[14] David Kempe, Jon Kleinberg, and Éva Tardos. 2003. Maximizing the spread of influence through a social network. In *Proceedings of the ninth ACM SIGKDD international conference on Knowledge discovery and data mining*. ACM, 137–146.

[15] William O Kermack and Anderson G McKendrick. 1927. A contribution to the mathematical theory of epidemics. In *Proceedings of the Royal Society of London A: Mathematical, Physical and Engineering Sciences*, Vol. 115. 700–721.

[16] Yoon Kim. 2014. Convolutional neural networks for sentence classification. *arXiv preprint arXiv:1408.5882* (2014).

[17] Edward O Laumann and Franz U Pappi. 2013. *Networks of collective action: A perspective on community influence systems*. Elsevier.

[18] Daniel D Lee and H Sebastian Seung. 2001. Algorithms for non-negative matrix factorization. In *Advances in neural information processing systems*. 556–562.

[19] Jundong Li, Harsh Dani, Xia Hu, Jiliang Tang, Yi Chang, and Huan Liu. 2017. Attributed Network Embedding for Learning in a Dynamic Environment. *arXiv preprint arXiv:1706.01860* (2017).

[20] Jundong Li, Xia Hu, Liang Wu, and Huan Liu. 2016. Robust unsupervised feature selection on networked data. In *Proceedings of the 2016 SIAM International Conference on Data Mining*. SIAM, 387–395.

[21] Jundong Li, Cheng Kewei, Liang Wu, and Huan Liu. 2018. Streaming Link Prediction on Dynamic Attributed Networks. In *Proceedings of 11th ACM International Conference on Web Search and Data Mining (WSDM 2018)*. ACM.

[22] Jundong Li, Liang Wu, Dani Harsh, and Huan Liu. 2018. Unsupervised Personalized Feature Selection. In *Proceedings of The 32nd AAAI Conference on Artificial Intelligence*. AAAI.

[23] Jundong Li, Liang Wu, Osmar R Zaïane, and Huan Liu. 2017. Toward personalized relational learning. In *Proceedings of the 2017 SIAM International Conference on Data Mining*. SIAM, 444–452.

[24] Christopher D. Manning, Mihai Surdeanu, John Bauer, Jenny Finkel, Steven J. Bethard, and David McClosky. 2014. The Stanford CoreNLP Natural Language Processing Toolkit. In *Association for Computational Linguistics (ACL) System Demonstrations*. 55–60. http://www.aclweb.org/anthology/P/P14/P14-5010

[25] John Moore and Jennifer Neville. 2017. Deep collective inference. In *Proceedings of the 31st AAAI Conference on Artificial Intelligence*.

[26] Fred Morstatter, Liang Wu, Tahora H Nazer, Kathleen M Carley, and Huan Liu. 2016. A new approach to bot detection: Striking the balance between precision and recall. In *Advances in Social Networks Analysis and Mining (ASONAM), 2016 IEEE/ACM International Conference on*. IEEE, 533–540.

[27] Jorge Nocedal and Stephen Wright. 2006. *Numerical optimization*. Springer Science & Business Media.

[28] Hamid Palangi, Li Deng, Yelong Shen, Jianfeng Gao, Xiaodong He, Jianshu Chen, Xinying Song, and Rabab Ward. 2016. Deep sentence embedding using long short-term memory networks: Analysis and application to information retrieval. *IEEE/ACM Transactions on Audio, Speech and Language Processing* 24, 4 (2016), 694–707.

[29] Bryan Perozzi, Rami Al-Rfou, and Steven Skiena. 2014. Deepwalk: Online learning of social representations. In *International Conference on Knowledge Discovery and Data Mining*. ACM, 701–710.

[30] Vahed Qazvinian, Emily Rosengren, Dragomir R Radev, and Qiaozhu Mei. 2011. Rumor has it: Identifying misinformation in microblogs. In *Proceedings of the Conference on Empirical Methods in Natural Language Processing*. Association for Computational Linguistics, 1589–1599.

[31] Justin Sampson, Fred Morstatter, Liang Wu, and Huan Liu. 2016. Leveraging the implicit structure within social media for emergent rumor detection. In *Proceedings of the 25th ACM International on Conference on Information and Knowledge Management*. ACM, 2377–2382.

[32] Kai Shu, Amy Sliva, Suhang Wang, Jiliang Tang, and Huan Liu. 2017. Fake News Detection on Social Media: A Data Mining Perspective. *ACM SIGKDD Explorations Newsletter* 19, 1 (2017), 22–36.

[33] Richard Socher, Alex Perelygin, Jean Y Wu, Jason Chuang, Christopher D Manning, Andrew Y Ng, Christopher Potts, and others. 2013. Recursive deep models for semantic compositionality over a sentiment treebank. In *Proceedings of the conference on empirical methods in natural language processing (EMNLP)*, Vol. 1631. Citeseer, 1642.

[34] Jian Tang, Meng Qu, Mingzhe Wang, Ming Zhang, Jun Yan, and Qiaozhu Mei. 2015. Line: Large-scale information network embedding. In *Proceedings of the 24th International Conference on World Wide Web*. ACM, 1067–1077.

[35] Lei Tang and Huan Liu. 2009. Relational learning via latent social dimensions. In *Proceedings of the 15th ACM SIGKDD international conference on Knowledge discovery and data mining*. ACM, 817–826.

[36] Fei Tian, Bin Gao, Qing Cui, Enhong Chen, and Tie-Yan Liu. 2014. Learning Deep Representations for Graph Clustering.. In *AAAI*. 1293–1299.

[37] Liang Wu, Xia Hu, and Huan Liu. 2016. Relational learning with social status analysis. In *Proceedings of the Ninth ACM International Conference on Web Search and Data Mining*. ACM, 513–522.

[38] Liang Wu, Xia Hu, Fred Morstatter, and Huan Liu. 2017. Adaptive Spammer Detection with Sparse Group Modeling.. In *ICWSM*. 319–326.

[39] Liang Wu, Xia Hu, Fred Morstatter, and Huan Liu. 2017. Detecting Camouflaged Content Polluters.. In *ICWSM*. 696–699.

[40] Liang Wu, Jundong Li, Xia Hu, and Huan Liu. 2017. Gleaning wisdom from the past: Early detection of emerging rumors in social media. In *Proceedings of the 2017 SIAM International Conference on Data Mining*. SIAM, 99–107.

[41] Liang Wu and Huan Liu. 2017. Detecting Crowdturfing in Social Media. (2017).

[42] Liang Wu, Fred Morstatter, Xia Hu, and Huan Liu. 2016. Mining misinformation in social media. *Big Data in Complex and Social Networks* (2016), 123–152.

[43] Pinar Yanardag and SVN Vishwanathan. 2015. Deep graph kernels. In *Proceedings of the 21th ACM SIGKDD International Conference on Knowledge Discovery and Data Mining*. ACM, 1365–1374.

[44] Jaewon Yang, Julian McAuley, and Jure Leskovec. 2013. Community detection in networks with node attributes. In *Data Mining (ICDM), 2013 IEEE 13th international conference on*. IEEE, 1151–1156.

Indirect Supervision for Relation Extraction using Question-Answer Pairs

Zeqiu Wu[1], Xiang Ren[2], Frank F. Xu[3], Ji Li[1], Jiawei Han[1]
[1]University of Illinois at Urbana-Champaign, IL, USA
[2]University of Southern California, CA, USA
[3]Shanghai Jiao Tong Univeristy, Shanghai, China
[1]{zeqiuwu1, jili3, hanj}@illinois.edu [2]xiangren@usc.edu [3]frankxu@sjtu.edu.cn

ABSTRACT

Automatic relation extraction (RE) for types of interest is of great importance for interpreting massive text corpora in an efficient manner. For example, we want to identify the relationship "president_of" between entities "*Donald Trump*" and "*United States*" in a sentence expressing such a relation. Traditional RE models have heavily relied on human-annotated corpus for training, which can be costly in generating labeled data and become obstacles when dealing with more relation types. Thus, more RE extraction systems have shifted to be built upon training data automatically acquired by linking to knowledge bases (distant supervision). However, due to the incompleteness of knowledge bases and the context-agnostic labeling, the training data collected via distant supervision (DS) can be very noisy. In recent years, as increasing attention has been brought to tackling question-answering (QA) tasks, user feedback or datasets of such tasks become more accessible. In this paper, we propose a novel framework, ReQuest, to leverage question-answer pairs as an indirect source of supervision for relation extraction, and study how to use such supervision to reduce noise induced from DS. Our model jointly embeds relation mentions, types, QA entity mention pairs and text features in two low-dimensional spaces (RE and QA), where objects with same relation types or semantically similar question-answer pairs have similar representations. Shared features connect these two spaces, carrying clearer semantic knowledge from both sources. ReQuest, then use these learned embeddings to estimate the types of test relation mentions. We formulate a global objective function and adopt a novel margin-based QA loss to reduce noise in DS by exploiting semantic evidence from the QA dataset. Our experimental results achieve an average of 11% improvement in F1 score on two public RE datasets combined with TREC QA dataset. Codes and datasets can be downloaded at https://github.com/ellenmellon/ReQuest.

ACM Reference format:
Zeqiu Wu[1], Xiang Ren[2], Frank F. Xu[3], Ji Li[1], Jiawei Han[1]. 2018. Indirect Supervision for Relation Extraction using Question-Answer Pairs. In *Proceedings of WSDM 2018: The Eleventh ACM International Conference on Web Search and Data Mining , Marina Del Rey, CA, USA, February 5–9, 2018 (WSDM 2018)*, 9 pages.
https://doi.org/10.1145/3159652.3159709

WSDM 2018, February 5–9, 2018, Marina Del Rey, CA, USA

ACM ISBN 978-1-4503-5581-0/18/02...$15.00
https://doi.org/10.1145/3159652.3159709

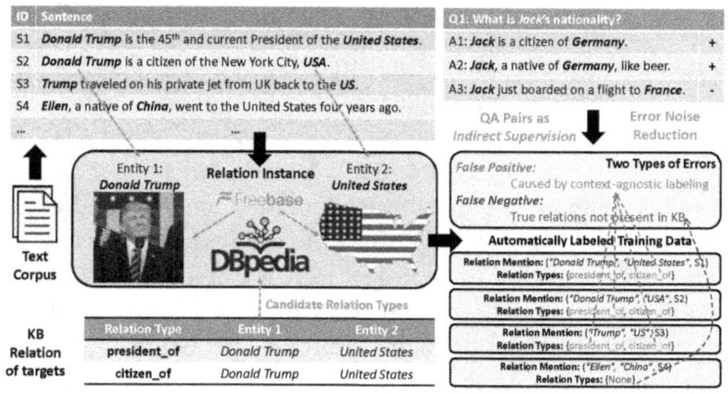

Figure 1: Distant supervision generates training data by linking relation mentions in sentences S1-S4 to KB and assigning the linkable relation types to all relation mentions. Those unlinkable entity mention pairs are treated as negative examples. This automatic labeling process may cause errors of false positives (highlighted in red) and false negatives (highlighted in purple). QA pairs provide indirect supervision for correcting such errors.

1 INTRODUCTION

Relation extraction is an important task for understanding massive text corpora by turning unstructured text data into relation triples for further analysis. For example, it detects the relationship "president_of" between entities "*Donald Trump*" and "*United States*" in a sentence. Such extracted information can be used for more downstream text analysis tasks (e.g. serving as primitives for information extraction and knowledge base (KB) completion, and assisting question answering systems).

Typically, RE systems rely on training data, primarily acquired via human annotation, to achieve satisfactory performance. However, such manual labeling process can be costly and non-scalable when adapting to other domains (e.g. biomedical domain). In addition, when the number of types of interest becomes large, the generation of handcrafted training data can be error-prone. To alleviate such an exhaustive process, the recent trend has deviated towards the adoption of distant supervision (DS). DS replaces the manual training data generation with a pipeline that automatically links texts to a knowledge base (KB). The pipeline has the following steps: (1) detect entity mentions in text; (2) map detected entity mentions to entities in KB; (3) assign, to the candidate type set of each entity mention pair, all KB relation types between their

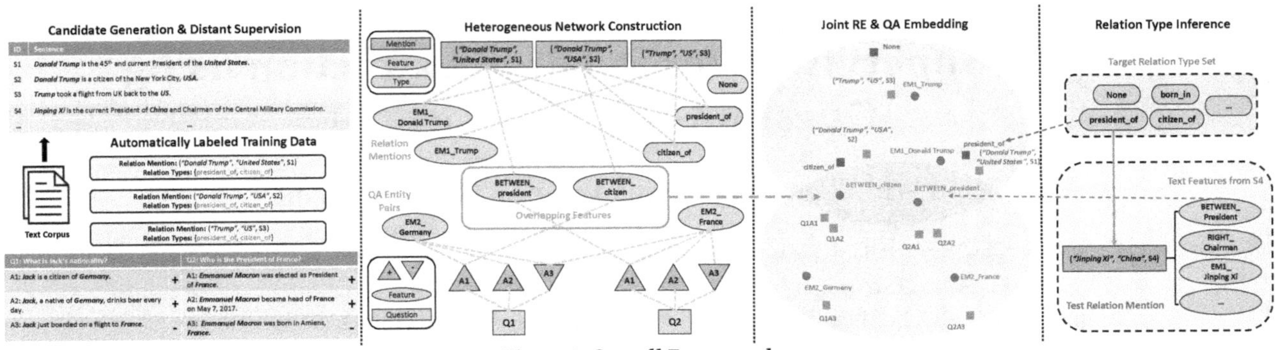

Figure 2: Overall Framework.

KB-mapped entities. However, the noise introduced to the automatically generated training data is not negligible. There are two major causes of error: incomplete KB and context-agnostic labeling process. If we treat unlinkable entity pairs as the pool of negative examples, false negatives can be commonly encountered as a result of the insufficiency of facts in KBs, where many true entity or relation mentions fail to be linked to KBs (see example in Figure 1). In this way, models counting on extensive negative instances may suffer from such misleading training data. On the other hand, context-agnostic labeling can engender false positive examples, due to the inaccuracy of the DS assumption that if a sentence contains any two entities holding a relation in the KB, the sentence must be expressing such relation between them. For example, entities "*Donald Trump*" and "*United States*" in the sentence "*Donald Trump flew back to United States*" can be labeled as "`president_of`" as well as "`born_in`", although only an out-of-interest relation type "`travel_to`" is expressed explicitly (as shown in Figure 1).

Towards the goal of diminishing the negative effects by noisy DS training data, distantly supervised RE models that deal with training noise, as well as methods that directly improve the automatic training data generation process have been proposed. These methods mostly involve designing distinct assumptions to remove redundant training information [16, 21, 26, 36]. For example, method applied in [16, 36] assumes that for each relation triple in the KB, at least one sentence might express the relation instead of all sentences. Moreover, these noise reduction systems usually only address one type of error, either false positives or false negatives. Hence, current methods handling DS noises still have the following challenges:

(1) Lack of trustworthy sources: Current de-noising methods mainly focus on recognizing labeling mistakes from the labeled data itself, assisted by pre-defined assumptions or patterns. They do not have external trustworthy sources as guidance to uncover incorrectly labeled data, while not at the expense of excessive human efforts. Without other separate information sources, the reliability of false label identification can be limited.
(2) Incomplete noise handling: Although both false negative and false positive errors are observed to be significant, most existing works only address one of them.

In this paper, to overcome the above two issues derived from relation extraction with distant supervision, we study the problem of relation extraction with indirect supervision from external sources. Recently, the rapid emergence of QA systems promotes the availability of user feedback or datasets of various QA tasks. We investigate to leverage QA, a downstream application of relation extraction, to provide additional signals for learning RE models. Specifically, we use datasets for the task of answer sentence selection to facilitate relation typing. Given a domain-specific corpus and a set of target relation types from a KB, we aim to detect relation mentions from text and categorize each in context by target types or Non-Target-Type (None) by leveraging an independent dataset of QA pairs in the same domain. We address the above two challenges as follows (1) We integrate indirect supervision from another same-domain data source in the format of QA sentence pairs, that is, each question sentence maps to several positive (where a true answer can be found) and negative (where no answer exists) answer sentences. We adopt the principle that for the same question, positive pairs of (question, answer) should be semantically similar while they should be dissimilar from negative pairs. (2) Instead of differentiating types of labeling errors at the instance level, we concentrate on how to better learn semantic representation of features. Wrongly labeled training examples essentially misguide the understanding of features. It increases the risk of having a non-representative feature learned to be close to a relation type and vice versa. Therefore, if the feature learning process is improved, potentially both types of error can be reduced. (See how QA pairs improve the feature embedding learning process in Figure 3).

To integrate all the above elements, a novel framework, ReQuest, is proposed. First, ReQuest constructs a heterogeneous graph to represent three kinds of objects: relation mentions, text features and relation types for RE training data labeled by KB linking. Then ReQuest constructs a second heterogeneous graph to represent entity mention pairs (include question, answer entity mention pairs) and features for QA dataset. These two graphs are combined into a single graph by overlapped features. We formulate a global objective to jointly embed the graph into a low-dimensional space where, in that space, RE objects whose types are semantically close also have similar representations and QA objects linked by positive (question, answer) entity mention pairs of a same question should have close representations. In particular, we design a novel margin-based loss to model the semantic similarity between QA pairs and transmit such information into feature and relation type representations via shared features. With the learned embeddings, we can efficiently estimate the types for test relation mentions. In summary, this paper makes the following contributions:

(1) We propose the novel idea of applying indirect supervision from question answering datasets to help eliminate noise from distant supervision for the task of relation extraction.
(2) We design a novel joint optimization framework, ReQuest, to extract typed relations in domain-specific corpora.

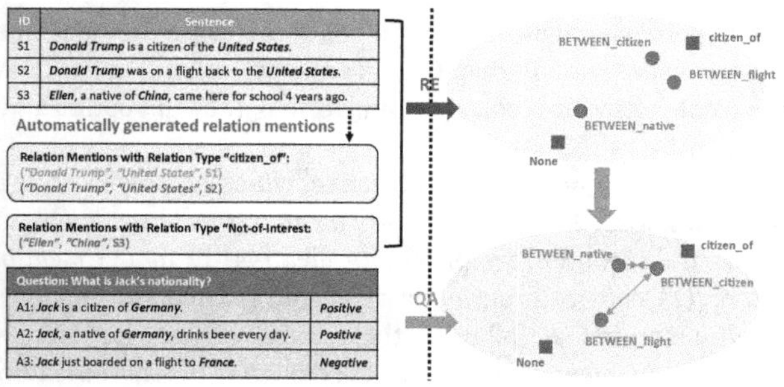

Figure 3: Due to the noise in the automatically generated RE training corpus, the associations between learned feature embeddings and relation types can be affected by the wrongly labeled training examples. However, the idea of QA pairwise interactions has the potential to correct such embedding deviations by bringing extra semantic clues from overlapped features in QA corpus.

(3) Experiments with two public RE datasets combined with TREC QA demonstrate that ReQuest improves the performance of state-of-the-art RE systems significantly.

2 DEFINITIONS AND PROBLEM

Our proposed ReQuest framework takes the following input: an automatically labeled training corpus $\mathcal{D}_L$ obtained by linking a text corpus $\mathcal{D}$ to a KB (e.g. Freebase) Ψ, a target relation type set $\mathcal{R}$ and a set of QA sentence pairs $\mathcal{D}_{QAS}$ with extract answers labeled.

Entity and Relation Mention. An *entity mention* (denoted by m) is a token span in text which represents an entity e. A *relation instance* $r(e_1, e_2, \ldots, e_n)$ denotes some type of relation $r \in \mathcal{R}$ between multiple entities. In this paper, we focus on binary relations, *i.e.*, $r(e_1, e_2)$. We define a *relation mention* (denoted by z) for some relation instance $r(e_1, e_2)$ as a (ordered) pair of entities mentions of e_1 and e_2 in a sentence s, and represent a relation mention with entity mentions m_1 and m_2 in sentence s as $z = (m_1, m_2, s)$.

Knowledge Bases and Target Types. A KB contains a set of entities $\mathcal{E}_\Psi$, entity types $\mathcal{Y}$ and relation types $\mathcal{R}$, as well as human-curated facts on both relation instances $\mathcal{I}_\Psi = \{r(e_1, e_2)\} \subset \mathcal{R}_\Psi \times \mathcal{E}_\Psi \times \mathcal{E}_\Psi$, and entity-type facts $\mathcal{T}_\Psi = \{(e, y)\} \subset \mathcal{E}_\Psi \times \mathcal{Y}_\Psi$. *Target relation type set* $\mathcal{R}$ covers a subset of relation types that the users are interested in from Ψ, *i.e.*, $\mathcal{R} \subset \mathcal{R}_\Psi$.

Automatically Labeled Training Corpora. Distant supervision maps the set of entity mentions extracted from the text corpus to KB entities $\mathcal{E}_\Psi$ with an entity disambiguation system [15, 24]. Between any two linkable entity mentions m_1 and m_2 in a sentence, a relation mention z_i is formed if there exists one or more KB relations between their KB-mapped entities e_1 and e_2. Relations between e_1 and e_2 in KB are then associated to z_i to form its candidate relation type set $\mathcal{R}_i$, *i.e.*, $\mathcal{R}_i = \{r \mid r(e_1, e_2) \in \mathcal{R}_\Psi\}$.

Let $\mathcal{Z} = \{z_i\}_{i=1}^{N_Z}$ denote the set of extracted relation mentions that can be mapped to KB. Formally, we represent the automatically labeled training corpus $\mathcal{D}_L$ for relation extraction, using a set of tuples $\mathcal{D}_L = \{(z_i, \mathcal{R}_i)\}_{i=1}^{N_Z}$. There exists publicly available automatically labeled corpora such as the NYT dataset [36] where relation mentions have already been extracted and mapped to KB.

QA Entity Mention Pairs. The set of QA sentence pairs $\mathcal{D}_{QAS}$ consists of questions Q in the same domain as the training text corpus. For each question q_i, there will be a number of positive sentences $\mathcal{A}_i^+$, each of which contains a correct answer to the question and another set of negative sentences $\mathcal{A}_i^-$ where no answer can be found. And the tokens spans of the exact answer in each positive is marked as well. For each question, we extract positive QA (ordered) entity mention pairs $\mathcal{P}_i^+$ from $\mathcal{A}_i^+$ and negative entity mention pairs $\mathcal{P}_i^-$ from $\mathcal{A}_i^-$. A positive QA entity mention pair p_k contains an entity mention being asked about (question entity mention m_1) and an entity mention serving as the answer (answer entity mention m_2) to a question. That being said, we can get one positive QA entity mention pair from each positive answer sentence if both entity mentions can be found. In contrast, A negative QA entity mention pair does not follow such pattern for the corresponding question.

Let $Q = \{q_i\}_{i=1}^{N_q}$ denote the set of questions; $\mathcal{P} = \{p_k\}_{k=1}^{N_p}$ denote all QA entity mention pairs; $\mathcal{P}_i^+ = \{p_{k^+}\}_{k^+=1}^{N_i^+}$ denote the set of positive QA entity mention pairs for q_i; $\mathcal{P}_i^- = \{p_{k^-}\}_{k^-=1}^{N_i^-}$ denote the set of negative QA entity mention pairs for q_i. Formally, the QA entity mention pairs corpus is represented as $\mathcal{D}_{QA} = \{(q_i, \mathcal{P}_i^+, \mathcal{P}_i^-)\}_{i=1}^{N_q}$.

Definition 2.1 (Problem Definition). **Given** an automatically generated training corpus $\mathcal{D}_L$, a target relation type set $\mathcal{R} \subset \mathcal{R}_\Psi$ and a set of QA sentence pairs $\mathcal{D}_{QAS}$ in the same domain, the relation extraction task **aims to** (1) extract QA entity mention pairs to generate $\mathcal{D}_{QA}$; (2) estimate a relation type $r^* \in \mathcal{R} \cup \{\text{None}\}$ for each test relation mention, using both the training corpus and the extracted QA pairs with their contexts.

3 APPROACH

Framework Overview. We propose an *embedding-based* framework with indirect supervision (illustrated in Figure 2) as follows:

(1) Generate text features for each relation mention or QA entity mention pair, and construct a heterogeneous graph using four kinds of objects in combined corpus, namely relation mentions from RE corpus, entity mention pairs from QA corpus, target relation types and text features to encode aforementioned signals in a unified form (Section 3.1).
(2) Jointly embed relation mentions, QA pairs, text features, and type labels into two low-dimensional spaces connected by shared features, where close objects tend to share the same types or questions (Section 3.2).
(3) Estimate type labels r^* for each test relation mention z from learned embeddings, by searching the target type set $\mathcal{R}$ (Section 3.3).

3.1 Heterogeneous Network Construction

Relation Mentions and Types Generation. We get the relation mentions along with their heuristically obtained relation types from the automatically labeled training corpus $\mathcal{D}_L$. And we randomly sample a set of unlinkable entity mention pairs as the negative relation mentions (*i.e.*, relation mentions assigned with type "None").

QA Entity Mention Pairs Generation. We apply Stanford NER [23] to extract entity mentions in each question or answer sentence. First, we detect the target entity being asked about in each question sentence. For example, in the question "*Who is the president of United*

Feature	Description	Example
EM head	Syntactic head token of each entity mention	"*HEAD_EM1_Trump*"
EM Token	Tokens in each entity mention	"*TKN_EM1_Donald*"
Tokens	Each token between two EMs	"*is*", "*the*", "*current*", "*President*", "*of*", "*the*"
POS tag	POS tags of tokens between two EMs	"*VBZ*", "*DT*", "*JJ*", "*NN*", "*IN*", "*DT*"
Collocations	Bigrams in 3-word window of each EM	"*NYC native*", "*native Donald*", ...
EM order	Whether EM 1 is before EM 2	"*EM1_BEFORE_EM2*"
EM distance	Number of tokens between the two EMs	"*EM_DISTANCE_6*"
EM context	Unigrams before and after each EM	"*native*", "*is*", "*the*", "."
Special pattern	Occurrence of pattern "em1_in_em2"	"*PATTERN_NULL*"
Brown cluster	Brown cluster ID for each token	"*8_1101111*", "*12_111011111111*"

Table 1: Text features for relation mentions used in this work [36, 54] (excluding dependency parse-based features and entity type features, EM = Entity Mention). ("*Donald Trump*", "*United States*") is used as an example relation mention from the sentence "*NYC native Donald Trump is the current President of the United States.*"

States", the question entity is "*United States*". In most cases, a question only contains one entity mention and for those containing multiple entity mentions, we notice the question entity is mostly mentioned at the very last. Thus, we follow this heuristic rule to assign the lastly occurred entity mention to be the question entity mention m_0 in each question sentence q_i. Then, in each positive answer sentence of q_i, we extract the entity mention with matched head token and smallest edit string distance to be the question entity mention m_1, and the entity mention matching the exact answer string to be the answer entity mention m_2. Then we form a positive QA entity mention pair with its context s, $p_k = (m_1, m_2, s) \in \mathcal{P}_i^+$ for q_i. If either m_1 or m_2 can not be found, this positive answer sentence is dropped. We randomly select pairs of entity mentions in each negative answer sentence to be negative QA entity mention pairs for q_i (*e.g.*, if a negative sentence includes 3 entity mentions, we randomly select negative examples from the $3 \cdot 2 \cdot 1 = 6$ different pairs of entity mentions in total, if we ignore the order), with each negative example marked as $p_{k'} = (m_{1'}, m_{2'}, s') \in \mathcal{P}_i^-$ for q_i.

Text Feature Extraction. We extract lexical features of various types from not only the mention itself (*e.g.*, head token), as well as the context s (*e.g.*, bigram) in a POS-tagged corpus. It is to capture the syntactic and semantic information for any given relation mentions or entity mention pairs. See Table 1 for all types of text features used, following those in [4, 26] (excluding the dependency parse-based features and entity type features).

We denote the set of M_z unique features extracted from relation mentions $\mathcal{Z}$ as $\mathcal{F}_z = \{f_j\}_{j=1}^{M_z}$ and the set of M_{QA} unique features extracted of QA entity mention pairs $\mathcal{P}$ as $\mathcal{F}_{QA} = \{f_j\}_{j=1}^{M_{QA}}$. As our embedding learning process will combine these two sets of features and their shared ones will act as the bridge of two embedding spaces, we denote the overall feature set as $\mathcal{F} = \{f_j\}_{j=1}^{M}$.

Heterogeneous Network Construction. After the nodes generation process, we construct a heterogeneous network connected by text features, relation mentions, relation types, questions, QA entity mention pairs, as shown in the second column of Figure 2.

3.2 Joint RE and QA Embedding

This section first introduces how we model different types of interactions between linkable relation mentions $\mathcal{Z}$, QA entity mention pairs $\mathcal{P}$, relation type labels $\mathcal{R}$ and text features $\mathcal{F}$ into a d-dimensional *relation vector space* and a d-dimensional *QA pair vector space.* In the relation vector space, objects whose types are close to each other should have similar representation and in the QA pair vector space, positive QA mention pairs who share the same question are close to each other. (*e.g.*, see the 3rd col. in Figure 2). We then combine multiple objectives and formulate a joint optimization problem.

We propose a novel global objective, which employs a margin-based rank loss [30] to model *noisy mention-type associations* and utilizes the second-order proximity idea [44] to model *mention-feature (QA pair-feature) co-occurrences.* In particular, we adopt a pairwise margin loss, following the intuition of pairwise rank [34] to capture the *interactions between QA pairs*, and the shared features $\mathcal{F}_z \cap \mathcal{F}_{QA}$ between relation mentions $\mathcal{Z}$ and QA pairs $\mathcal{P}$ connect the two vector spaces.

Modeling Types of Relation Mentions. We introduce the concepts of both *mention-feature co-occurrences* and *mention-type associations* in the modeling of relation types for relation mentions in set Z.

The first hypothesis involved in modeling types of relation mentions is as follows.

Hypothesis 1 (Mention-Feature Co-occurrence). *If two relation mentions share many text features, they tend to share similar types (close to each other in the embedding space). If two features co-occur with a similar set of relation mentions, they tend to have similar embedding vectors.*

This is based on the intuition that if two relation mentions share many text features, they have high distributional similarity over the set of text features $\mathcal{F}_z$ and likely they have similar relation types. On the other hand, if text features co-occur with many relation mentions in the corpus, such features tend to represent close type semantics. For example, in sentences s_1 and s_4 in the first column of Figure 2, the two relation mentions ("*Donald Trump*", "*United States*", s_1) and ("*Jinping Xi*", "*China*", s_4) share many text features including "*BETWEEN_President*" and they indeed have the same relation type "`president_of`"

Formally, let vectors $\mathbf{z}_i$, $\mathbf{c}_j \in \mathbb{R}^d$ represent relation mention $z_i \in \mathcal{Z}$ and text feature $f_j \in \mathcal{F}_z$ in the d-dimensional *relation embedding space.* Similar to the distributional hypothesis [25] in text corpora, we apply second-order proximity [44] to model the idea in Hypothesis 1 as follows.

$$\mathcal{L}_{ZF} = -\sum_{z_i \in \mathcal{Z}} \sum_{f_j \in \mathcal{F}_z} w_{ij} \cdot \log p(f_j | z_i), \tag{1}$$

where $p(f_j|z_i) = \exp(\mathbf{z}_i^T \mathbf{c}_j) / \sum_{f' \in \mathcal{F}_z} \exp(\mathbf{z}_i^T \mathbf{c}_{j'})$ denotes the probability of f_j generated by z_i, and w_{ij} is the co-occurrence frequency between (z_i, f_j) in corpus $\mathcal{D}$.

For the goal of efficient optimization, we apply negative sampling strategy [25] to sample multiple *false* features for each (z_i, f_j) based on some *noise distribution* $P_n(f) \propto D_f^{3/4}$ [25] (with D_f denotes the number of relation mentions co-occurring with f). Term $\log p(f_j|z_i)$ in Eq. (1) is replaced with the term as follows.

$$\log \sigma(\mathbf{z}_i^T \mathbf{c}_j) + \sum_{v=1}^{V} \mathbb{E}_{f_{j'} \sim P_n(f)} \left[\log \sigma(-\mathbf{z}_i^T \mathbf{c}_{j'})\right], \tag{2}$$

where $\sigma(x) = 1/(1+\exp(-x))$ is the sigmoid function. The first term in Eq. (2) models the observed co-occurrence, and the second term models the V negative feature samples.

In D_L, each relation mention z_i is associated with a set of candidate types $\mathcal{R}_i$ in a context-agnostic setting, which leads to some false associations between z_i and $r \in \mathcal{R}_i$ (*i.e.*, false positives). For example, in the first column of Figure 2, the two relation mentions ("*Donald Trump*", "*United States*", s_1) and ("*Donald Trump*", "*USA*", s_2) are assigned to the same relation types while each mention actually only has one true type. To handle such conflicts, we use the following hypothesis to model the associations between each linkable relation mention z_i (in set $\mathcal{Z}$) and its noisy candidate relation type set $\mathcal{R}_i$.

HYPOTHESIS 2 (PARTIAL-LABEL ASSOCIATION). *A relation mention's embedding vector should be more similar (closer in the low-dimensional space) to its "most relevant" candidate type, than to any other non-candidate type.*

Let vector $\mathbf{r}_k \in \mathbb{R}^d$ denote relation type $r_k \in \mathcal{R}$ in the embedding space, the similarity between (z_i, r_k) is defined as the dot product of their embedding vectors, *i.e.*, $\phi(z_i, r_k) = \mathbf{z}_i^T \mathbf{r}_k$. $\overline{\mathcal{R}}_i = \mathcal{R} \setminus \mathcal{R}_i$ denotes the set of *non-candidate types*. We extend the margin-based loss in [30] to define a partial-label loss ℓ_i for each linkable relation mention $z_i \in \mathcal{M}_L$ as follows.

$$\ell_i = \max\Big\{0,\, 1 - \Big[\max_{r \in \mathcal{R}_i} \phi(z_i, r) - \max_{r' \in \overline{\mathcal{R}}_i} \phi(z_i, r')\Big]\Big\}. \tag{3}$$

To comprehensively model the types of relation mentions, we integrate the modeling of mention-feature co-occurrences and mention-type associations by the following objective, so that feature embeddings also participate in modeling the relation type embeddings.

$$O_Z = \mathcal{L}_{ZF} + \sum_{i=1}^{N_Z} \ell_i + \frac{\lambda}{2} \sum_{i=1}^{N_Z} \|\mathbf{z}_i\|_2^2 + \frac{\lambda}{2} \sum_{k=1}^{K_r} \|\mathbf{r}_k\|_2^2, \tag{4}$$

where tuning parameter $\lambda > 0$ on the regularization terms is used to control the scale of the embedding vectors.

Modeling Associations between QA Entity Mention Pairs. We follow Hypothesis 1 to model the QA pair-feature co-occurrence in a similar way. Formally, let vectors $\mathbf{p}_i, \mathbf{c}'_j \in \mathbb{R}^d$ represent QA entity mention pair $p_i \in \mathcal{P}$ and text features (for entity mentions) $f_j \in \mathcal{F}_{QA}$ in a d-dimensional *QA entity pair embedding space*, respectively. We model the corpus-level co-occurrences between QA entity mention pairs and text features by second-order proximity as follows.

$$\mathcal{L}_{PF} = - \sum_{p_i \in \mathcal{P}} \sum_{f_j \in \mathcal{F}_{QA}} w_{ij} \cdot \log p(f_j | p_i), \tag{5}$$

where the term $\log p(f_j|p_i)$ is defined as $\log p(f_j|p_i) = \log \sigma(\mathbf{p}_i^T \mathbf{c}'_j) + \sum_{v=1}^{V} \mathbb{E}_{f_{j'} \sim P_n(f)} \big[\log \sigma(-\mathbf{p}_i^T \mathbf{c}'_{j'})\big]$.

For each QA entity mention pair, if we consider it as a relation mention with an unknown type, intuitively, positive pairs sharing a same question are relation mentions with the same relation type or more specifically, are semantically similar relation mentions. In contrast, a positive pair and a negative pair for a question should be semantically far away from each other. For example, in Figure 3, the embeddings of the entity mention pair in answer sentence A_1 should be close to the pair in A_2 while far away from the pair in A_3. To impose such idea, we model the interactions between QA entity mention pairs based on the following hypothesis.

HYPOTHESIS 3 (QA PAIRWISE INTERACTION). *A positive QA entity mention pair's embedding vector should be more similar (closer in the low-dimensional space) to any other positive QA entity mention pair, than to any negative QA entity mention pair of the same question.*

Algorithm 1: Model Learning of REQUEST

Input: labeled training corpus $\mathcal{D}_L$, text features $\{\mathcal{F}\}$, regularization parameter λ, learning rate α, number of negative samples V, dim. d
Output: relation mention/QA entity mention pair embeddings $\{\mathbf{z}_i\}/\{\mathbf{p}_k\}$, feature embeddings $\{\mathbf{c}_j\}$, $\{\mathbf{c}'_j\}$, relation type embedding $\{\mathbf{r}_k\}$

Initialize: vectors $\{\mathbf{z}_i\}, \{\mathbf{p}_k\}, \{\mathbf{c}_j\}, \{\mathbf{c}'_j\}, \{\mathbf{r}_k\}$ as random vectors
while O *in Eq. (8) not converge* **do**
  Sample one component O_{cur} from $\{O_Z,\ O_{QA}\}$
  if O_{cur} is O_Z **then**
    Sample a mention-feature co-occurrence w_{ij}; draw V negative samples; update $\{\mathbf{z}, \mathbf{c}\}$ based on $\mathcal{L}_{ZF}$
    Sample a relation mention z_i; get its candidate types $\mathcal{R}_i$; update $\mathbf{z}$ and $\{\mathbf{r}\}$ based on $O_Z - \mathcal{L}_{ZF}$
  end
  if O_{cur} is O_{QA} **then**
    Sample a pair-feature co-occurrence w_{ij}; draw V negative samples; update $\{\mathbf{p}, \mathbf{c}'\}$ based on $\mathcal{L}_{PF}$
    Sample an positive QA entity mention pair p_k of question q_i; sample one more positive pair and one negative pair of question q_i; update $\mathbf{p}$ based on $O_{QA} - \mathcal{L}_{PF}$
  end
end

Specifically, we use vector $\mathbf{p}_k \in \mathbb{R}^d$ to represent a positive QA entity mention pair p_k in the embedding space. The similarity between two QA entity mention pairs p_{k1} and p_{k2} is defined as the dot product of their embedding vectors. For a positive QA entity mention pair p_k of a question q_i (e.g. $p_k \in \mathcal{P}_i^+$), we define the pairwise margin-based loss as follows.

$$\ell_{i,k} = \sum_{p_{k_1} \in \mathcal{P}_i^+,\, p_{k_2} \in \mathcal{P}_i^-,\, k_1 \neq k} \max\Big\{0,\, 1 - \Big[\phi(p_k, p_{k_1}) - \phi(p_k, p_{k_2})\Big]\Big\}. \tag{6}$$

To integrate both the modeling of QA pair-feature co-occurrence and QA pairs interaction, we formulate the following objective.

$$O_{QA} = \mathcal{L}_{PF} + \sum_{i=1}^{N_Q} \sum_{k=1}^{N_i^+} \ell_{i,k} + \frac{\lambda}{2} \sum_{k=1}^{N_P} \|\mathbf{p}_k\|_2^2. \tag{7}$$

By doing so, we can extend the semantic relationships between QA pairs to feature embeddings, such that features of close QA pairs also have similar embeddings. Thus, the learned embeddings of text features from QA corpus carry semantic information inferred from QA pairs. The shared features can propagate such extra semantic knowledge into relation vector space and help better learn the semantic embeddings of both text features and relation types. While feature embeddings of both false positive or false negative examples in the training corpus can deviate towards unrepresentative relation types, the transmitted knowledge from QA space has the potential to adjust such semantic inconsistency. For example, as illustrated in Figure 3, the false labeled examples in s_2 and s_3 lead the features "*BETWEEN_flight*" and "*BETWEEN_native*" to be close to "`citizen_of`" and "None" type respectively. After injecting the QA pairwise interactions from the example question, these wrongly placed features are brought back towards the relation types they actually indicate. Minimizing the objective O_{QA} yields an QA pair embedding space where, in that space, positive QA mention pairs who share the same question are close to each other.

A Joint Optimization Problem. Our goal is to embed all the available information for relation mentions and relation types, QA entity mention pairs and text features into a single d-dimensional embedding space. An intuitive solution is to collectively minimize the two objectives O_Z and O_{QA} as the embedding vectors of overlapped text features are shared across relation vector space and QA pair vector space. To achieve the goal, we formulate a joint optimization problem as follows.

$$\min_{\{z_i\},\{c_j\},\{r_k\},\{p_k\},\{c'_j\}} O = O_Z + O_{QA}. \quad (8)$$

When optimizing the global objective O, the learning of RE and QA embeddings can be mutually influenced as errors in each component can be constrained and corrected by the other. This mutual enhancement also helps better learn the semantic relations between features and relation types. We apply edge sampling strategy [44] with a stochastic sub-gradient descent algorithm [40] to efficiently solve Eq. (8). In each iteration, we alternatively sample from each of the two objectives $\{O_Z, O_M\}$ a batch of edges (*e.g.*, (z_i, f_j)) and their negative samples, and update each embedding vector based on the derivatives. The detailed learning process of ReQuest can be seen in Algorithm 1. To prove convergence of this algorithm (to the local minimum), we can adopt the proof procedure in [40].

3.3 Type Inference

To predict the type for each test relation mention z, we search for nearest neighbor in the target relation type set $\mathcal{R}$, with the learned embeddings of features and relation types (*i.e.*, $\{c_i\}$, $\{c'_i\}$, $\{r_k\}$). Specifically, we represent test relation mention z in our learned relation embedding space by $z = \sum_{f_j \in \mathcal{F}_z(z)} c_j$ where $\mathcal{F}_z(z)$ is the set of text features extracted from z's local context s. We categorize z to None type if the similarity score is below a pre-defined threshold (e.g. $\eta > 0$).

4 EXPERIMENTS

4.1 Data Preparation and Experiment Setting

Our experiments consists of two different type of datasets, one for relation extraction and another answer sentence selection dataset for indirect supervision. Two public datasets are used for relation extraction: **NYT** [16, 36]and **KBP** [10, 22]. The test data are manually annotated with relation types by their respective authors. Statistics of the datasets are shown in Table 2. Automatically generated training data by distant supervision on these two training corpora have been used in [35, 36] and is accessible via public links, as well as the test data[1]. The automatic data generation process is the same as described in Section 2 by utilizing DBpedia Spotlight[2], a state-of-the-art entity disambiguation tool, and Freebase, a large entity knowledge base. As for QA dataset, we use the answer sentence selection dataset extracted from **TREC-QA** dataset [47] used by many researchers [8, 43, 48]. We obtain the compiled version of the dataset from [52, 53], which can be accessed via publicly available link[3]. Then, we parse this QA dataset to generate QA entity mention pairs following the steps described in Section 3.1. During this procedure, we drop the question or answer sentences where no valid QA entity mention pairs can be found. The statistics of this dataset is presented in Table 3.

Feature Generation. This step is run on both relation extraction dataset and preprocessed QA entity mention pairs and sentences. Table 1 lists the set of text features of both relation mentions and QA entity mention pairs used in our experiments. We use a 6-word

[1]https://github.com/shanzhenren/CoType/tree/master/data/source

[2]http://spotlight.dbpedia.org/

[3]https://github.com/xuchen/jacana/tree/master/tree-edit-data

Data sets	NYT	KBP
#Relation types	24	19
#Documents	294,977	780,549
#Sentences	1.18M	1.51M
#Training RMs	353k	148k
#Text features	2.6M	1.3M
#Test Sentences	395	289
#Ground-truth RMs	3,880	2,209

Table 2: Statistics of relation extraction datasets.

Versions of QA dataset	COMPLETE	FILTERED
#Questions	1.4K	186
#Positive Answer Sentences	6.9K	969
#Negative Answer Sentences	49K	5.5K
#Positive entity mention pairs	-	969
#Negative entity mention pairs	-	28K

Table 3: Statistics of the answer sentence selection datasets. The complete version is the raw corpus we obtain from the public link. The filtered version is the input to ReQuest after dropping sentences where no valid QA entity mention pair can be found.

Data sets	NYT	KBP
% distinct shared features with TREC QA	10.0%	11.6%
% occurrences of shared features with TREC QA	90.1%	85.6%

Table 4: Statistics of overlapped features. For example, if we have the following observations in NYT and TREC QA respectively $(f_1, f_1, f_1, f_2, f_3)$ and (f_1, f_2, f_4), then % distinct shared features with TREC QA of NYT is 66.7% (f_1, f_2) and % occurrences of shared features with TREC QA of NYT is 80.0%.

window to extract context features for each mention (3 words on the left and the right). We apply the Stanford CoreNLP tool [23] to get POS tags. Brown clusters are derived for each corpus using public implementation[4]. The same kinds of features are used in all the compared methods in our experiments. As the overlapped features in both RE and QA datasets play an important role in the optimization process, we put the statistics of the shared features in Table 4.

Evaluation Sets. The provided train/test split are used in NYT and KBP relation extraction datasets. The relation mentions in test data have been manually annotated with relation types in the released dataset (see Table 2 for the data statistics). A *validation set* is created through randomly sampling 10% of relation mentions from test data and the rest are used as *evaluation set.*

Compared Methods. We compare ReQuest with its variants which model parts of the proposed hypotheses. Several state-of-the-art relation extraction methods (*e.g.*, supervised, embedding, neural network) are also implemented (or tested using their published codes): (1) **DS+Perceptron** [22]: adopts multi-label learning on automatically labeled training data $\mathcal{D}_L$. (2) **DS+Kernel** [28]: applies bag-of-feature kernel [28] to train a SVM classifier using $\mathcal{D}_L$; (3) **DS+Logistic** [26]: trains a multi-class logistic classifier[5] on $\mathcal{D}_L$ (4) **DeepWalk** [31]: embeds mention-feature co-occurrences and mention-type associations as a homogeneous network (with binary edges); (5) **LINE** [44]: uses second-order proximity model with edge sampling on a feature-type bipartite graph (where edge weight w_{jk} is the number of relation mentions having feature f_j and type r_k); (6) **MultiR** [16]: is a state-of-the-art distant supervision method, which models noisy label in $\mathcal{D}_L$ by multi-instance multi-label learning; (7) **FCM** [12]: adopts neural language model to perform compositional embedding; (8) **DS+SDP-LSTM** [50, 51]: current state-of-the-art in SemEval 2010 Task 8 relation classification task [14], leverages a

[4]https://github.com/percyliang/brown-cluster

[5]We use liblinear package from https://github.com/cjlin1/liblinear

Relation Mention	ReQuest	CoType-RM
.. traveling to *Amman* , *Jordan* ..	/location/location/contains	None
The photograph showed **Gov.** *Ernie Fletcher* **of** *Kentucky* ..	/people/person/place_lived	None
.. **as chairman of** the *Securities and Exchange Commission* , *Christopher Cox* ..	/business/person/company	None

Table 5: Case Study.

multi-channel input along the shortest dependency path between two entities into stacked deep recurrent neural network model. We use $\mathcal{D}_L$ to train the model. (9) **DS+LSTM-ER** [27]: current state-of-the-art model on ACE2005 and ACE2004 relation classification task [7, 20]. It is a multi-layer LSTM-RNN based model that captures both word sequence and dependency tree substructure information. We use $\mathcal{D}_L$ to train the model. (10) **CoType-RM** [35]: A distant supervised model which adopts the partial-label loss to handle label noise and train the relation extractor.

Besides the proposed joint optimization model, **ReQuest-Joint**, we conduct experiments on two other variations to compare the performance (1) **ReQuest-QA_RE**: This variation optimizes objective O_{QA} first and then uses the learned feature embeddings as the initial state to optimize O_Z; and (2) **ReQuest-RE_QA**: It first optimizes O_Z, then optimizes O_{QA} to finely tune the learned feature embeddings.

Parameter Settings. In the testing of ReQuest and its variants, we set $\eta = 0.35$ and $\lambda = 10^{-4}$ and $V = 3$ based on validation sets. We stop further optimization if the relative change of O in Eq. (8) is smaller than 10^{-4}. The dimensionality of embeddings d is set to 50 for all embedding methods. For other parameters, we tune them on validation sets and picked the values which lead to the best performance.

Evaluation Metrics. We adopt standard Precision, Recall and F1 score [2, 28] for measuring the performance of relation extraction task. Note that all our evaluations are *sentence-level* or *mention-level* (*i.e.*, context-dependent), as discussed in [16].

4.2 Experiments and Performance Study

Method	NYT [16, 36] Prec	Rec	F1	Time	KBP [10, 22] Prec	Rec	F1	Time
DS+Perceptron [22]	0.068	**0.641**	0.123	15min	0.233	0.457	0.308	7.7min
DS+Kernel [28]	0.095	0.490	0.158	56hr	0.108	0.239	0.149	9.8hr
DS+Logistic [26]	0.258	0.393	0.311	25min	0.296	0.387	0.335	14min
DeepWalk [31]	0.176	0.224	0.197	1.1hr	0.101	0.296	0.150	27min
LINE [44]	0.335	0.329	0.332	2.3min	0.360	0.257	0.299	1.5min
MultiR [16]	0.338	0.327	0.333	5.8min	0.325	0.278	0.301	4.1min
FCM [12]	**0.553**	0.154	0.240	1.3hr	0.151	**0.500**	0.301	25min
DS+SDP-LSTM [51]	0.307	0.532	0.389	21hr	0.249	0.300	0.272	10hr
DS+LSTM-ER [27]	0.373	0.171	0.234	49hr	0.338	0.106	0.161	30hr
CoType-RM [35]	0.467	0.380	0.419	2.6min	0.342	0.339	0.340	1.5min
ReQuest-QA_RE	0.407	0.437	0.422	10.2min	**0.459**	0.300	0.363	5.3min
ReQuest-RE_QA	0.435	0.419	0.427	8.0min	0.356	0.352	0.354	13.2min
ReQuest-Joint	0.404	0.480	**0.439**	4.0min	0.386	0.410	**0.397**	5.9min

Table 6: Performance comparison on end-to-end relation extraction (at the highest F1 point) on the two datasets.

Performance Comparison with Baselines. To test the effectiveness of our proposed framework ReQuest, we compare with other methods on the relation extraction task. The precision, recall, F1 scores as well as the model learning time measured on two datasets are reported in Table 6. As shown in the table, ReQuest achieves superior F1 score on both datasets compared with other models. Among all these baselines, MultiR and CoType-RM handle noisy training data while the remaining ones assume the training corpus is perfectly labeled. Due to their nature of being cautious towards the noisy training data, both MultiR and CoType-RM reach relatively high results confronting with other models that blindly exploit all heuristically obtained training examples. However, as external reliable information sources are absent and only the noise from multi-label relation mentions (while none or only one assigned label is correct) is tackled in these models, MultiR and CoType-RM underperform ReQuest. Especially from the comparison with CoType-RM, which is also an embedding learning based relation extraction model with the idea of partial-label loss incorporated, we can conclude that the extra semantic inklings provided by the QA corpus do help boost the performance of relation extraction.

Performance Comparison with Ablations. We experiment with two variations of ReQuest, ReQuest-QA_RE and ReQuest-RE_QA, in order to validate the idea of joint optimization. As presented in Table 6, both ReQuest-QA_RE and ReQuest-RE_QA outperform most of the baselines, with the indirect supervision from QA corpus. However, their results still fall behind ReQuest's. Thus, separately training the two components may not capture as much information as jointly optimizing the combined objective. The idea of constraining each component in the joint optimization process proves to be effective in learning embeddings to present semantic meanings of objects (e.g. features, types and mentions).

4.3 Case Study

Example Outputs. We have done some interesting investigations regarding the type of prediction errors that can be corrected by the indirection supervision from QA corpus. We have analyzed the prediction results on NYT dataset from CoType-RM and ReQuest and find out the top three target relation types that can be corrected by ReQuest are "`contains_location`", "`work_for`", "`place_lived`". Both the issues of KB incompleteness and context-agnostic labeling are severe for these relation types. For example, there can be lots of not that well-known suburban areas belonging to a city, a state or a country while not marked in KB. And a person can has lived in tens or even hundreds places for various lengths of period. These are hard to be fully annotated into a KB. Thus, the automatically obtained training corpus may end up containing a large percentage of false negative examples for such relation types. On the other hand, there are abundant entity pairs having both "`contains_location`" and "`capital_of`", or both "`place_lived`" and "`born_in`" relation types in KB. Naturally, training examples of such entity pairs can be greatly polluted by false positives. In this case, it becomes tough to learn semantic embeddings for relevant features of these relation types. However, we notice there are quite a few answer sentences for relevant questions like "Where is *XXX* located", "Where did *XXX* live", "What company is *XXX* with" in the QA corpus, which plays an important role in adjusting vectors for features that are supposed to be the indicators for these relation types. Table 5 shows some prediction errors from CoType-RM that are fixed in ReQuest.

Study the effect of QA dataset processing on F1 scores. As stated in Section 3.1, ReQuest uses Stanford NER to extract entity mentions in QA dataset and all QA pairs consist of two entity mentions and if either question or answer entity mention is not

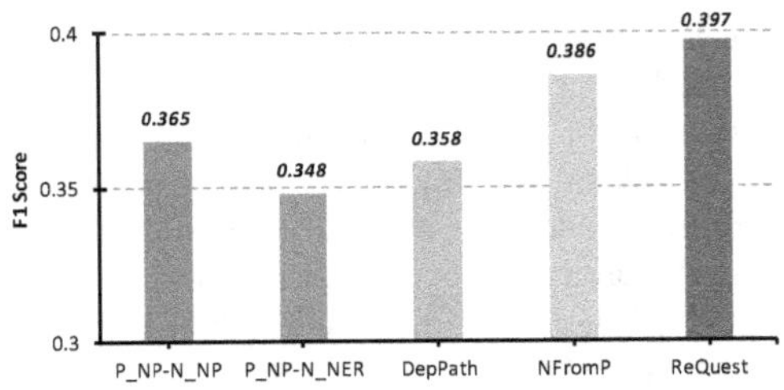

Figure 4: Effect of QA dataset processing on F1 scores. P_NP-N_NP: positive QA noun phrase pairs + negative QA noun phrase pairs, P_NP-N_NER: positive QA noun phrase pairs + negative QA named entity pairs, DepPath: convert QA sentences to dep paths, NFromP: sample negative QA pairs from both positive and negative answer sentences.

found, it drops the sentence. Beyond that, we have conducted experiments with four other ways to construct QA pairs from the raw QA sentences. As shown in Table 3, we lose many positive QA pairs if we only remain answer (or question) targets that are detected as named entities. Thus, we have tried to keep more positive pairs by relaxing the restriction from named entities to noun phrases. In addition, we have tried to evaluate the performance by 1) keeping negative pairs as named entity pairs or 2) changing them to noun phrase pairs. Besides that, inspired by [50, 51], the third processing variation we have tried is to parse the QA sentences into dependency paths and to extract features from these paths instead of the full sentences. The last one is that, we sample negative QA pairs not only from negative answer sentences, but also from positive sentence when extracting QA pairs. However, REQUEST achieves highest F1 score compared with these four processing variations (as shown in Figure 4) by filtering out all non entity mention answers, keeping full sentences and extracting only positive QA pairs from positive answer sentences.

Although by doing so, REQUEST filters out a large number of question/answer sentences and fewer QA pairs are constructed to provide semantic knowledge for RE, the remaining QA pairs provide cleaner and more consistent information with RE dataset. Thus, it still outperforms the other variations. Another interesting highlight is the comparison between using negative named entity pairs and using negative noun phrase pairs when positive QA pairs are formed by noun phrases. Although enforcing named entities is more consistent with RE datasets, a trade-off exists when the data format of positive and negative QA pairs are inconsistent. As we can see from the bar chart, the performance by using negative noun phrase pairs is better than negative named entity pairs.

5 RELATED WORK

Classifying relation types between entities in a certain sentence and automatically extracting them from large corpora plays a key role in information extraction and natural language processing applications and thus has been a hot research topic recently. Even though many existing knowledge bases are very large, they are still far from complete. A lot of information is hidden in unstructured data, such as natural language text. Most tasks focus on knowledge base completion (KBP) [42] as a goal of relation extraction from corpora like New York Times (NYT) [36]. Others extract valuable relation information from community question-answer texts, which may be unique to other sources [39].

For supervised relation extraction, feature-based methods [14] and neural network techniques [9, 41] are most common. Most of them jointly leverage both semantic and syntactic features [27], while some use multi-channel input information as well as shortest dependency path to narrow down the attention [50, 51]. Two of he aforementioned papers perform the best on the SemEval-2010 Task 8 and constitutes our neural baseline methods.

However, most of these methods require large amount of annotated data, which is time consuming and labor intensive. To address this issue, most researchers align plain text with knowledge base by *distant supervision* [26] for relation extraction. However, distant supervision inevitably accompanies with the wrong labeling problem. To alleviate the wrong labeling problem, multi-instance and multi-label learning are used [16, 36]. Others [20, 35] propose joint extraction of typed entities and relations as joint optimization problem and posing cross-constraints of entities and relations on each other. Neural models with selective attention [21] are also proposed to automatically reduce labeling noise.

The distant supervision provides one solution to the cost of massive training data. However, traditional DS methods mostly only exploit one specific kind of indirect supervision knowledge - the relations/facts in a given knowledge base, thus often suffer from the problem of lack of supervision. There exist other *indirect supervision* methods for relation extraction, where some utilize globally and cross sentence boundary supervision [13, 33], some leverage the power of passage retrieval model for providing relevance feedback on sentences [49], and others [3, 32, 45]. Recently, with the prevalence of reinforcement learning applications, many information extraction and relation extraction tasks have adopted such techniques to boost existing approaches [18, 29]. Our methodology follows the success of indirect supervision, by adding question-answering pairs as another source of supervision for relation extraction task along with knowledge base auto-labeled distant supervision as well as partial supervision.

Another indirect supervision source we use in the paper, passage retrieval, as described here, is the task of retrieving only the portions of a document that are relevant to a particular information need. It could be useful for limiting the amount of non-relevant material presented to a searcher, or for helping the searcher locate the relevant portions of documents more quickly. Passage retrieval is also often an intermediate step in other information retrieval tasks, like question answering [11, 17, 19, 38] and combining with summarization. Some passage retrieval approaches [46] include calculating query-likelihood and relevance modeling [5], others show that language model approaches used for document retrieval can be applied to answer passage retrieval [6]. Following the success of passage retrieval usage in question-answering pipelines, to the best of our knowledge, we are the first to utilize passage retrieval, or specifically, answer sentence selection from question-answer pairs to provide additional indirect feedback and supervision for relation extraction task.

6 CONCLUSION

We present a novel study on indirect supervision (from question-answering datasets) for the task of relation extraction. We propose a framework, REQUEST, that embeds information from both training data automatically generated by linking to knowledge bases and QA datasets, and captures richer semantic knowledge from both sources via shared text features so that better feature embeddings can be learned to infer relation type for test relation mentions despite the noisy training data. Our experiment results on two datasets demonstrate the effectiveness and robustness of ReQuest. Interesting future work includes identifying most relevant QA pairs for target relation types, generating most effective questions to collect feedback (or answers) via crowd-sourcing, and exploring approaches other than distant supervision [1, 37].

ACKNOWLEDGMENTS

Research was sponsored in part by the U.S. Army Research Lab. under Cooperative Agreement No. W911NF-09-2-0053 (NSCTA), National Science Foundation IIS 16-18481, IIS 17-04532, and IIS-17-41317, and grant 1U54GM114838 awarded by NIGMS through funds provided by the trans-NIH Big Data to Knowledge (BD2K) initiative (www.bd2k.nih.gov). The views and conclusions contained in this paper are those of the authors and should not be interpreted as representing any funding agencies.

REFERENCES

[1] Yoav Artzi and Luke S. Zettlemoyer. 2013. Weakly Supervised Learning of Semantic Parsers for Mapping Instructions to Actions. *TACL* 1 (2013), 49–62.

[2] Nguyen Bach and Sameer Badaskar. 2007. A Review of Relation Extraction. In *Literature review for Language and Statistics II.*

[3] Michele Banko, Michael J. Cafarella, Stephen Soderland, Matthew Broadhead, and Oren Etzioni. 2007. Open Information Extraction from the Web. In *IJCAI.*

[4] Yee Seng Chan and Dan Roth. 2010. Exploiting background knowledge for relation extraction. In *COLING.*

[5] Charles L. A. Clarke, Gordon V. Cormack, D. I. E. Kisman, and Thomas R. Lynam. 2000. Question Answering by Passage Selection (MultiText Experiments for TREC-9). In *TREC.*

[6] Andres Corrada-Emmanuel, W. Bruce Croft, and Vanessa Murdock. 2003. Answer Passage Retrieval for Question Answering. In *Tech. Reports of CIIR UMass.*

[7] George R. Doddington, Alexis Mitchell, Mark A. Przybocki, Lance A. Ramshaw, Stephanie Strassel, and Ralph M. Weischedel. 2004. The Automatic Content Extraction (ACE) Program - Tasks, Data, and Evaluation. In *LREC.*

[8] Cícero Nogueira dos Santos, Ming Tan, Bing Xiang, and Bowen Zhou. 2016. Attentive Pooling Networks. *arXiv preprint* arXiv:1602.03609.

[9] Javid Ebrahimi and Dejing Dou. 2015. Chain Based RNN for Relation Classification. In *NAACL.*

[10] Joe Ellis, Jeremy Getman, Justin Mott, Xuansong Li, Kira Griffitt, Stephanie M Strassel, and Jonathan Wright. 2014. Linguistic Resources for 2013 Knowledge Base Population Evaluations. In *TAC.*

[11] David Elworthy. 2000. Question Answering Using a Large NLP System. In *TREC.*

[12] Matthew R Gormley, Mo Yu, and Mark Dredze. 2015. Improved relation extraction with feature-rich compositional embedding models. In *EMNLP.*

[13] Xianpei Han and Le Sun. 2016. Global Distant Supervision for Relation Extraction. In *AAAI.*

[14] Iris Hendrickx, Su Nam Kim, Zornitsa Kozareva, Preslav Nakov, Diarmuid Ó Séaghdha, Sebastian Padó, Marco Pennacchiotti, Lorenza Romano, and Stan Szpakowicz. 2010. SemEval-2010 Task 8: Multi-Way Classification of Semantic Relations between Pairs of Nominals. In *SemEval@ACL.*

[15] Johannes Hoffart, Mohamed Amir Yosef, Ilaria Bordino, Hagen Fürstenau, Manfred Pinkal, Marc Spaniol, Bilyana Taneva, Stefan Thater, and Gerhard Weikum. 2011. Robust disambiguation of named entities in text. In *EMNLP.*

[16] Raphael Hoffmann, Congle Zhang, Xiao Ling, Luke S. Zettlemoyer, and Daniel S. Weld. 2011. Knowledge-Based Weak Supervision for Information Extraction of Overlapping Relations. In *ACL.*

[17] Abraham Ittycheriah, Martin Franz, Wei-Jing Zhu, Adwait Ratnaparkhi, and Richard J. Mammone. 2000. IBM's Statistical Question Answering System. In *TREC.*

[18] Pallika H. Kanani and Andrew McCallum. 2012. Selecting actions for resource-bounded information extraction using reinforcement learning. In *WSDM.*

[19] Mahboob Khalid and Suzan Verberne. 2008. Passage Retrieval for Question Answering using Sliding Windows. In *IRQA@COLING.* 26–33.

[20] Qi Li and Heng Ji. 2014. Incremental Joint Extraction of Entity Mentions and Relations. In *ACL.*

[21] Yankai Lin, Shiqi Shen, Zhiyuan Liu, Huanbo Luan, and Maosong Sun. 2016. Neural Relation Extraction with Selective Attention over Instances. In *ACL.*

[22] Xiao Ling and Daniel S Weld. 2012. Fine-Grained Entity Recognition. In *AAAI.*

[23] Christopher D Manning, Mihai Surdeanu, John Bauer, Jenny Finkel, Steven J Bethard, and David McClosky. 2014. The Stanford CoreNLP Natural Language Processing Toolkit. In *ACL.*

[24] Pablo N Mendes, Max Jakob, Andrés García-Silva, and Christian Bizer. 2011. DBpedia spotlight: shedding light on the web of documents. In *I-Semantics.*

[25] Tomas Mikolov, Ilya Sutskever, Kai Chen, Greg S Corrado, and Jeff Dean. 2013. Distributed representations of words and phrases and their compositionality. In *NIPS.*

[26] Mike Mintz, Steven Bills, Rion Snow, and Daniel Jurafsky. 2009. Distant supervision for relation extraction without labeled data. In *ACL/IJCNLP.*

[27] Makoto Miwa and Mohit Bansal. 2016. End-to-End Relation Extraction using LSTMs on Sequences and Tree Structures. *arXiv preprint* arXiv:1601.00770 (2016).

[28] Raymond J Mooney and Razvan C Bunescu. 2005. Subsequence kernels for relation extraction. In *NIPS.*

[29] Karthik Narasimhan, Adam Yala, and Regina Barzilay. 2016. Improving Information Extraction by Acquiring External Evidence with Reinforcement Learning. In *EMNLP.*

[30] Nam Nguyen and Rich Caruana. 2008. Classification with partial labels. In *KDD.*

[31] Bryan Perozzi, Rami Al-Rfou, and Steven Skiena. 2014. Deepwalk: Online learning of social representations. In *KDD.*

[32] Hoifung Poon and Pedro M. Domingos. 2008. Joint Unsupervised Coreference Resolution with Markov Logic. In *EMNLP.*

[33] Chris Quirk and Hoifung Poon. 2016. Distant Supervision for Relation Extraction beyond the Sentence Boundary. *arXiv preprint* arXiv:1609.04873 (2016).

[34] Jinfeng Rao, Hua He, and Jimmy J. Lin. 2016. Noise-Contrastive Estimation for Answer Selection with Deep Neural Networks. In *CIKM.*

[35] Xiang Ren, Zeqiu Wu, Wenqi He, Meng Qu, Clare R. Voss, Heng Ji, Tarek F. Abdelzaher, and Jiawei Han. 2017. CoType: Joint Extraction of Typed Entities and Relations with Knowledge Bases. In *WWW.*

[36] Sebastian Riedel, Limin Yao, and Andrew McCallum. 2010. Modeling Relations and Their Mentions without Labeled Text. In *ECML/PKDD.*

[37] Sebastian Riedel, Limin Yao, Andrew McCallum, and Benjamin M. Marlin. 2013. Relation Extraction with Matrix Factorization and Universal Schemas. In *NAACL.*

[38] Denis Savenkov and Eugene Agichtein. 2016. When a Knowledge Base Is Not Enough: Question Answering over Knowledge Bases with External Text Data. In *SIGIR.*

[39] Denis Savenkov, Wei-Lwun Lu, Jeff Dalton, and Eugene Agichtein. 2015. Relation Extraction from Community Generated Question-Answer Pairs. In *NAACL.*

[40] Shai Shalev-Shwartz, Yoram Singer, Nathan Srebro, and Andrew Cotter. 2011. Pegasos: Primal estimated sub-gradient solver for svm. *Mathematical programming* 127, 1 (2011), 3–30.

[41] Richard Socher, Jeffrey Pennington, Eric H Huang, Andrew Y Ng, and Christopher D Manning. 2011. Semi-supervised recursive autoencoders for predicting sentiment distributions. In *EMNLP.*

[42] Mihai Surdeanu and Heng Ji. 2014. Overview of the English Slot Filling Track at the TAC2014 Knowledge Base Population Evaluation. In *TAC.*

[43] Ming Tan, Cicero dos Santos, Bing Xiang, and Bowen Zhou. 2015. Lstm-based deep learning models for non-factoid answer selection. *arXiv preprint* arXiv:1511.04108 (2015).

[44] Jian Tang, Meng Qu, Mingzhe Wang, Ming Zhang, Jun Yan, and Qiaozhu Mei. 2015. Line: Large-scale information network embedding. In *WWW.*

[45] Kristina Toutanova, Danqi Chen, Patrick Pantel, Hoifung Poon, Pallavi Choudhury, and Michael Gamon. 2015. Representing Text for Joint Embedding of Text and Knowledge Bases. In *EMNLP.*

[46] Courtney Wade and James Allan. 2005. Passage Retrieval and Evaluation. In *Tech. Reports of DTIC.*

[47] Mengqiu Wang, Noah A. Smith, and Teruko Mitamura. 2007. What is the Jeopardy Model? A Quasi-Synchronous Grammar for QA. In *EMNLP-CoNLL.*

[48] Zhiguo Wang and Abraham Ittycheriah. 2015. FAQ-based Question Answering via Word Alignment. *arXiv preprint* arXiv:1507.02628 (2015).

[49] Wei Xu, Raphael Hoffmann, Le Zhao, and Ralph Grishman. 2013. Filling Knowledge Base Gaps for Distant Supervision of Relation Extraction. In *ACL.*

[50] Yan Xu, Ran Jia, Lili Mou, Ge Li, Yunchuan Chen, Yangyang Lu, and Zhi Jin. 2016. Improved relation classification by deep recurrent neural networks with data augmentation. *arXiv preprint* arXiv:1601.03651 (2016).

[51] Yan Xu, Lili Mou, Ge Li, Yunchuan Chen, Hao Peng, and Zhi Jin. 2015. Classifying Relations via Long Short Term Memory Networks along Shortest Dependency Paths.. In *EMNLP.*

[52] Xuchen Yao, Benjamin Van Durme, Chris Callison-Burch, and Peter Clark. 2013. Answer Extraction as Sequence Tagging with Tree Edit Distance. In *NAACL.*

[53] Xuchen Yao, Benjamin Van Durme, and Peter Clark. 2013. Automatic Coupling of Answer Extraction and Information Retrieval. In *ACL.*

[54] Guodong Zhou, Jian Su, Jie Zhang, and Min Zhang. 2005. Exploring Various Knowledge in Relation Extraction. In *ACL.*

Why People Search for Images using Web Search Engines

Xiaohui Xie
DCST, Tsinghua University
Beijing, China
xiexh_thu@163.com

Yiqun Liu
DCST, Tsinghua University
Beijing, China
yiqunliu@tsinghua.edu.cn

Maarten de Rijke
University of Amsterdam
Amsterdam, The Netherlands
derijke@uva.nl

Jiyin He
CWI
Amsterdam, The Netherlands
j.he@cwi.nl

Min Zhang
DCST, Tsinghua University
Beijing, China
z-m@tsinghua.edu.cn

Shaoping Ma
DCST, Tsinghua University
Beijing, China
msp@tsinghua.edu.cn

ABSTRACT

What are the intents or goals behind human interactions with image search engines? Knowing why people search for images is of major concern to Web image search engines because user satisfaction may vary as intent varies. Previous analyses of image search behavior have mostly been query-based, focusing on what images people search for, rather than intent-based, that is, why people search for images. To date, there is no thorough investigation of how different image search intents affect users' search behavior.

In this paper, we address the following questions: (1) Why do people search for images in text-based Web image search systems? (2) How does image search behavior change with user intent? (3) Can we predict user intent effectively from interactions during the early stages of a search session? To this end, we conduct both a lab-based user study and a commercial search log analysis.

We show that user intents in image search can be grouped into three classes: Explore/Learn, Entertain, and Locate/Acquire. Our lab-based user study reveals different user behavior patterns under these three intents, such as first click time, query reformulation, dwell time and mouse movement on the result page. Based on user interaction features during the early stages of an image search session, that is, before mouse scroll, we develop an intent classifier that is able to achieve promising results for classifying intents into our three intent classes. Given that all features can be obtained online and unobtrusively, the predicted intents can provide guidance for choosing ranking methods immediately after scrolling.

KEYWORDS

Image search; User intent; User behavior

ACM Reference Format:
Xiaohui Xie, Yiqun Liu, Maarten de Rijke, Jiyin He, Min Zhang, and Shaoping Ma. 2018. Why People Search for Images using Web Search Engines. In *Proceedings of WSDM 2018: The Eleventh ACM International Conference on Web Search and Data Mining (WSDM 2018).* ACM, New York, NY, USA, 9 pages. https://doi.org/10.1145/3159652.3159686

WSDM 2018, February 5–9, 2018, Marina Del Rey, CA, USA

ACM ISBN 978-1-4503-5581-0/18/02...$15.00
https://doi.org/10.1145/3159652.3159686

1 INTRODUCTION

Intent is assumed to be the immediate antecedent of behavior [2, 16] For any information access service, it is important to understand the underlying intent behind user behavior. A widely used Web search intent taxonomy was proposed by Broder [5], based on log-based user studies. In Broder's taxonomy, search intent of Web search users is categorized into three classes: informational, transactional and navigational.

The diversification of online information and online information services that we have seen since the introduction of Broder's search intent taxonomy creates challenges to this taxonomy. Hence, several refinements of this taxonomy have been proposed [37, 38]. However few efforts have been made towards understanding the intents of Web image search users. In image search engines, the items users search for are images instead of Web pages or online services. And the different result placement and interaction mechanisms of image search also make the search process rather different from general Web search engines [44]. Kofler and Lux [23] supported this view by conducting a user study and showing that without adaptation, user intent taxonomies applied in general web search are not applicable for image search. Similar to general purpose Web search [10, 14], we believe that a thorough understanding or even successful detection of users' image search intent helps search engines provide better image search results and improve their satisfaction. This motivates our first research question:

RQ1: ***Why do people search for images in text-based Web image search systems?***

User behavior data has been successfully adopted to improve general Web searches in result ranking [1, 45], query suggestion [6, 43] query auto completion [21, 26], etc. We therefore believe that understanding user interaction behavior in the multimedia search scenarios will also provide valuable insight into the understanding of user intent. As user behavior varies with search intent, looking into differences in behavior and how such differences relate to search intent will help to improve the performance of image search engines.

Previous work on image search intent understanding usually focuses on the query proposed by users and assumes that the query represents user intent well. However, determining users' search intents or information needs based on the queries they submitted is sometimes rather difficult, as a large proportion of keyword based queries are short, ambiguous or broad [11, 20, 35]. Compared to general (Web) search, queries used in image search on the Web tend to be even shorter [13]. As the same query may come from different search intents, previous work attempts to bridge the **intent gap** between query and the underlying intent through explicit methods, including query suggestion [46, 47] and result diversification [40, 42]. Besides work that investigates user intent based on query analysis, others look into the relationship between what people search for (query-based) and how they interact with image search engines. For example, Park et al. [33] categorize queries using two orthogonal taxonomies (subject-based and facet-based) and identify important behavioral differences across query types. Unlike previous work, we avoid analyzing query content and, instead, provide a thorough investigation into the whole interaction processes of users. As user behavior is directly affected by search intent, we propose an intent taxonomy based on the differences in user behavior patterns. This motivates our second research question:

RQ2: How does image search behavior change with user intent?

Automatically identifying search intent at an early stage of a search session helps a multimedia retrieval system to rerank its results according to the underlying user intent. Since pagination is usually not (explicitly) supported on image search SERPs, users can view results by scrolling up and down instead of clicking on the "next page" button. In this paper, we define the "early stage" of a search session as search behavior before any scrolling takes place. As user interactions with image search engines through mouse and keyboard can be captured online and unobtrusively, it will be practical to build intent recognition system based on these features if they are effective. This motivates our third research question:

RQ3: Can we effectively predict user intent from user interactions at the early stage of a search session?

To summarize, the main contributions of this work are:

- We propose a new image search intent taxonomy based on an open-coded discussion methodology [38]. The taxonomy includes three classes: Explore/Learn, Entertain, Locate/Acquire. As far as we know, ours is the first work to focus on an image search intent taxonomy in Web search engines. We verify the proposed image search intent taxonomy in two ways: through a user survey involving over 200 people and through a Web image search log analysis. Results show that the taxonomy covers a majority of user intents in Web image search.
- We design 12 tasks within the scope of the taxonomy and perform a lab-based user study to show that users interact with image search engines in different ways with different information needs. Differences are observed in temporal patterns, query reformulation patterns and mouse movement patterns.
- We build and evaluate a user intent recognition system based on the user interactions at the early stage of search sessions and achieve state-of-the-art prediction results.

The rest of the paper is organized as follows. Section 2 reviews related work. Section 3 presents our user intent taxonomy in image search. Section 4 introduces our user-study settings and reports the findings. Intent prediction and its results are given in Section 5. Finally, Section 6 discusses conclusions and future work.

2 RELATED WORK

2.1 Search intent taxonomies

In the past two decades intent taxonomies for general Web search have been investigated by several researchers. Broder [5] introduced a taxonomy of user intent in text-based Web search using both randomly selected search queries and an analysis of survey data collected from AltaVista users. The taxonomy consists of three categories: Informational, Navigational and Transactional. In [19], session characteristics of these three top-level search intents were examined and used to develop a classification algorithm. Building on Broder's taxonomy, Rose and Levinson [37] introduced a subclassification of the taxonomy to classify intent more precisely. By having humans assign task-type labels to search sessions based on Rose and Levinson's taxonomy, Russell et al. [38] found that it is hard to get sufficient inter-rater agreement on ambiguous search tasks and proposed a new search task taxonomy that contains seven categories. Taxonomies investigated in general Web search mentioned above were found to be *not* applicable in image search [23, 24].

Previous work on an intent taxonomy for image search mostly focused on *what* people search for not *why* they search. Pu [34] classified 1,000 frequent image queries based on a proprietary subject-based categorization scheme. By focusing on whether users were searching for people, location, etc., and on whether the search was about unique instances or non-unique instances, Jansen [18] classified queries based on three non subject-based image query classification schemas. Lux et al. [29] are among the first to investigate the image search intent problem. They categorized user intents into knowledge orientation, mental image, navigation, and transaction; these intents describe search activities in Flickr, a digital photo sharing platform instead of a search engine. After that, a two-dimensional taxonomy was proposed in [7]. However, this work was based on another sharing platform (Pinterest). Neither works were conducted in Web search engines which may face more complex search scenarios. Redi et al. [36] showed that Web image search must deal with images from a wide variety of sources including very poor quality images typically absent in photo sharing platforms. Thus, in this paper, we look more deeply into user intent and build a search intent taxonomy in text-based Web image search systems. As far as we know, this work is among the first to discuss the image search intents in Web search engines.

2.2 User behavior in image search

Several studies analyze the user behavior logs of image search engines [3, 13, 31, 34, 41]. Many features, such as query reformulation patterns, session length, and the number of viewed result pages are recorded and investigated. Compared to (text-based) general Web search, image search leads to shorter queries, tends to be more exploratory, and requires more interactions. Interactions with image search result pages contain abundant implicit user feedback. Previous studies on multimedia search [15, 17, 32] explored user click-through data to bridge user intent gaps for image search. O'Hare et al. [31] proposed a number of implicit relevance feedback features based on additional interactions including hover-through rate, converted-hover rate, and referral page click-through to improve image search result ranking performance. These findings help us to understand how users search for images on the Web, but do not capture variation among types of image search intent.

Although image search tends to be more exploratory, image searches can also be intent-directed [3]. Park et al. [33] analyzed a large-scale query log from Yahoo Image Search to investigate user behavior toward different query types and identified important behavioral differences across them. The major difference between their work and ours is that they tried to link query type based behavior to two of four classes of image search intent proposed by Lux et al. [29], which had been derived from user queries on a

Table 1: Age distribution of participants in our user survey and Chinese internet users according to the 38th statistical report of China internet development [8].

Age	Proportion (Survey participants)	Proportion (Chinese internet users)
(, 20)	28.4%	23.0%
[20, 30)	61.2%	30.4%
[30, 40)	5.7%	24.2%
[40, 50)	4.3%	13.4%
[50,)	0.5%	9.0%

photo sharing platform. Since user behavior in search is heavily dependent on intent [27], it is likely that behavior varies across different search intents. Understanding such differences, and how they relate to image search intent in Web search engines, is the main focus of this paper.

3 USER INTENT TAXONOMY

We start by explaining how we used an open-coded discussion methodology to arrive at our proposed image search intent taxonomy. We then verify the proposed taxonomy through a user survey involving over 200 people and through a Web image search log analysis.

3.1 Establishing an intent taxonomy for image search

To build our intent taxonomy, we conducted both an online survey and a Web search log analysis. We applied the methodology proposed in [38] to generate our criteria to categorize image search intents. In [38], an open-coded discussion was performed by Web research professionals based on 700 anonymized sessions aimed at identifying search task categories in general Web search.

3.1.1 User survey. Besides several basic demographic questions, we ask participants to answer two open-ended questions to describe their most recent image search experience. As shown in [29], interviews with search users can bring us a more comprehensive understanding of search intent.

- Please describe your most recent image search experience with as many as details as possible (e.g., time, place, motivation).
- Please provide all the queries you used in this search (you can look into your search history if necessary).

In order to make our survey more accurate, we suggest participants to check their search history to help recall the experience. We spread our survey through a widely used social platform (Wechat) and paid participants about US$0.50 if they answered the questions seriously. A total of 258 people participated in our survey; after removing noise from the answers (e.g., answers that are too short or not about text-based Web image search), 211 valid cases were kept, which are from 47.9% female users and 52.1% male users. The age distribution of our survey participants is shown in Table 1 together with the age distribution of Chinese internet users [8]. From Table 1, we can observe that the age distribution of our survey is similar to that reported in [8], except that the number of people in their 20s of our survey is much higher.

3.1.2 Search logs. From the search logs of a popular commercial image search engine, Sogou,[1] we sampled 500 search sessions during five days in April 2017. Each session contains consecutive queries produced from a single user within 30 minutes. We removed 25 pornographic search sessions and retained the other 475 sessions to avoid disturbing participants. The number of sessions examined here is similar to [38]. The minimum session length is 1 which means the user only submits one query in this session, while the maximum session length is 29. The average session length is 3.44. We show the distribution of session length in these 475 sessions in Table 2 (column 2). From Table 2, we can observe that short sessions account for a large proportion.

[1] http://sogou.com

Table 2: Distribution of session length of sampled search sessions after filtering pornographic searches and the Fleiss' Kappa [12] for sessions with different session length.

Session length	Proportion	Fleiss' Kappa
1	24.4%	0.419
2	30.1%	0.311
3	13.3%	0.317
4	9.1%	0.463
5	6.9%	0.237
> 5	16.2%	0.408
All	100%	0.375

3.1.3 Categorization criteria. After collecting the online survey data and search logs, a group of three web research professionals was recruited to review all 211 survey data cases and 475 search sessions. The researchers read each session closely and discussed to determine criteria to categorize user intent. Following [38] we performed several iterations of this open-coded discussion. In each iteration, the proposed criteria and corresponding intent taxonomy were fine-tuned to cover as many search sessions as possible and to be easy to state and understand. Based on the results of the discussion, two criteria were proposed to categorize user intent:

Criterion 1 Is the user's search behavior driven by a clear objective?

Criterion 2 Does the user need to download the image for further use after the search process?

We first divided user intent into two groups according to Criterion 1. In some cases, people regard image search as an option for entertainment. They can freely browse the image search results without prior requirements for the images. One can enjoy photos of her/his favorite stars or some humorous images without following someone's account on social media communities, which makes image search an easy way to relax. We label this kind of user intent with "*Entertain*."

In other cases, people may want to find specific images that should meet several requirements they have in mind. We further discussed intent categorization by considering Criterion 2 for such cases. In some cases, people have to download images for further use. They may already have captions for these images. For example, they may want to write a report on the 2016 US presidential elections and need to find an image that shows two presidential candidates in a television debate. We call user intent in this group "*Locate/Acquire*:" people want to find and download images for which they already have some requirements, to complete some tasks.

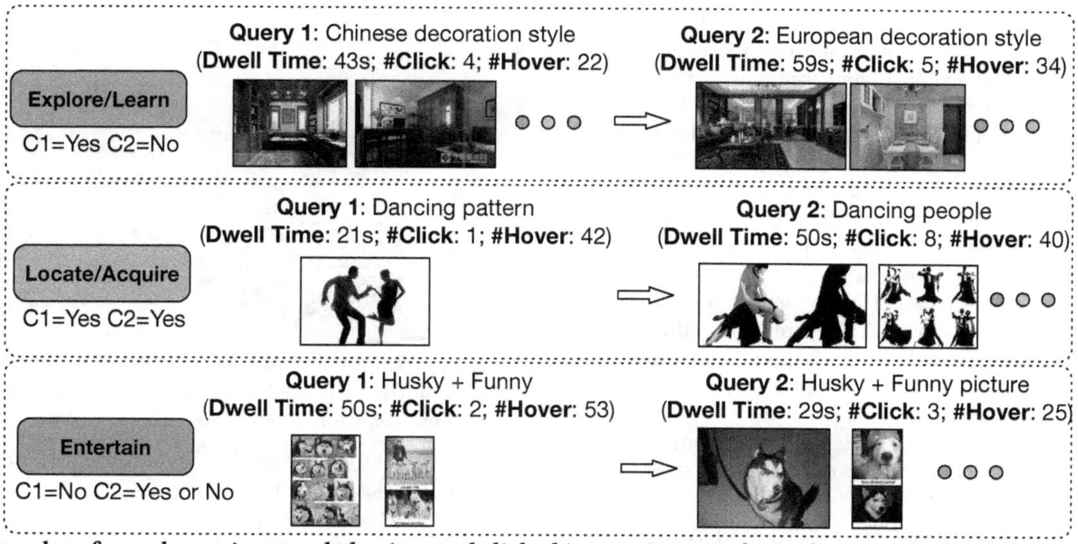

Figure 1: Examples of search queries, user behaviors and clicked images in typical search sessions with different user intents ("Explore/Learn", "Locate/Acquire", "Entertain").

For other tasks, people are capable of satisfying their information need without downloading images. Through image search engines, they can obtain, check or compare information by examining images in result pages only. To be more specific, consider three queries "New Ferrari 458," "a flower with purple stamen" and 'decoration style.". The first query may come from the need that people want to know about the appearance of the new Ferrari car. When people want to find out the name of a flower that they saw and remember its major characteristics, they may use the query "a flower with purple stamen." For the third one, people may want to compare different characteristics of different decoration style in order to find the best one for their houses. We call this kind of user intent "*Explore/Learn*:" people expect to obtain informational gain from search result pages and their need can be satisfied without downloading images.

According to Criterion 1 and 2, we group user intents into three categories as follows. We use *C*1 and *C*2 to denote the answer to Criterion 1 and 2, respectively (e.g., *C*1-YES means that the user's search behavior is driven by a clear objective):

(1) **Explore/Learn**. Users want to learn something, confirm or compare information by browsing images. (*C*1-YES, *C*2-NO)
(2) **Locate/Acquire**. Users want to find images for further use. They already have some requirements about these images. (*C*1-YES, *C*2-YES)
(3) **Entertain**. Users want to relax and kill time by freely browsing the image search results. (*C*1-NO, *C*2-YES or NO)

In Fig. 1, we show examples of search queries, user behaviors and clicked images in typical search sessions with different user intents according to the collected Web user behavior log data.

Our intent taxonomy is similar to the Web search task taxonomy proposed by Russell et al. [38]. There are important differences, however. For a start, we do not have their "Navigate" and "Meta" in our intent taxonomy, because people rarely use queries leading to a site or test web sites' capabilities in image search tasks. Furthermore, "Find-Simple" and "Find-Complex" are not in our taxonomy as they are covered by "Explore/Learn." Russell et al. [38]'s "Find-Simple" is a scenario where an information need can be satisfied with a single query and a single result; their "Find-Complex" is a scenario where a user has to search for information that requires multiple searches on related topics, inspect multiple sources, and integrate information across those sources. Finally, we rename Russell et al. [38]'s "Play" to "Entertain" in our intent taxonomy as "Play" in Russel's taxonomy focuses more on transactional needs.

3.2 Verifying the intent taxonomy

To verify our proposed intent taxonomy, we asked three annotators (who are all graduate students majored in computer science and are different from the people who proposed the categorization criteria mentioned in Section 3.1) to manually annotate the search scenarios collected in the survey into our three intent categories (Locate/Acquire, Explore/Learn, Entertain). We provided them with the definitions of each user intent specified in the proposed taxonomy mentioned in Section 3.1. We also gave our annotators two other choices: "Difficult to classify" and "Others." "Others" indicates that the user's intent cannot be fitted into any of the three intent categories and "Difficult to classify" means that the user's intent seems to belong to two or more classes in our proposed taxonomy.

For 203 out of the 211 valid online survey cases our annotators obtain a majority agreement, meaning that at least two raters assign the case into the same category. The Fleiss Kappa score [12] is 0.673 among the three annotators, which constitutes a substantial agreement [25]. The number of cases assigned to "Others" by our three annotators are 1 (0.47%), 2 (0.94%), 5 (2.37%), while the numbers for "Difficult to classify" are 3 (1.41%), 0 (0%), 2 (0.94%), respectively; a closer look at those cases reveals that the descriptions of these cases are vague. Based on these annotation results, we conclude that the proposed image search intent taxonomy covers most of users' actual intents and that the taxonomy is easy to use and apply for annotators.

We employed the same annotators to annotate our search logs. Our annotators were only shown the list of queries, i.e., they were not given hits or clicks. Again, we provided them with the definitions of each user intent in the taxonomy mentioned before. The choices of "Others" and "Difficult to classify" were also given. The Fleiss Kappa score is 0.375 among our three annotators, which constitutes a fair agreement. Also, we list the Fleiss Kappa scores for different session lengths in Table 2. We can observe that when the session length is around 4, the annotation agreement is highest, leading to moderate agreement. Compared with the substantial agreement reported in survey verification, it seems that by just examining queries, annotators cannot fully capture users' intents. This result echos similar observations by Russell et al. [38]. The result motivated us to further investigate the signals in user behavior that can be applied to distinguish search intents; see Section 4.

Through the user survey involving over 200 people and the Web search log annotations, we show that our proposed taxonomy can cover a majority of user intents and the boundary between different intents is detectable for annotators. The distribution of three intents in user survey is 27% (Explore/Learn), 66% (Locate/Acquire) and 7% (Entertain). In the search log the distribution is 56% (Explore/Learn), 39% (Locate/Acquire) and 5% (Entertain).

In summary, our answer to RQ1 is that user intents in image search on the web can be grouped into three classes: Explore/Learn, Locate/Acquire, and Entertain.

4 IMAGE SEARCH WITH DIFFERENT INTENTS

Armed with our intent taxonomy for image search, we address RQ2, "How does image search behavior change with user intents?" by conducting a lab-based user study. In this user study, we pre-design a set of tasks based on the proposed user intent taxonomy.

4.1 User behavior dataset

4.1.1 User study task. We designed 12 tasks based on the results of the user survey mentioned in Section 3.1.1. Each category of the proposed taxonomy accounts for 4 tasks. Examples of the user study tasks are shown in Table 3.

In order to simulate a realistic image search scenario, for the "Locate/Acquire" tasks, we not only ask participants to complete the search part of the tasks but also ask them to use the images they find to create some multimedia productions (e.g., a slide, a poster, a computer desktop). We provided them with frequently used software to help them make the productions, with several default settings chosen by us, including the text part and background, which guarantees that the participants only need to use the image search engine to complete their tasks. Through this setup, we want to ensure that each participant faces the same task difficulty. For example, in one of the "Locate/Acquire" tasks, participants are asked to make a slide about Harry Potter. We pre-set the theme of the slide as "The movie characters of Harry Potter" and provide the names of three characters on the slide; the participants need to find posters of these three characters and coordinate different posters and the background. For the "Explore/Learn" tasks, we ask participants to verbally answer certain questions related to the query to ensure that the task is done seriously. For example, in one of the "Explore/Learn" tasks, participants are asked to find the name of a flower that has some characteristics. As the scenario assumes that participants already saw the flower, we provide an image of the flower before they search to make sure they have a mental impression. For the "Entertain" tasks, participants can freely browse the image search results to relax. We only pre-set the theme of the task without any further constraints.

4.1.2 Data collection procedure. In the user study, each participant was asked to complete all 12 image search tasks, which were offered in a random order. Compared with collecting data from real search logs, or by browsing plugins, the laboratory user study has

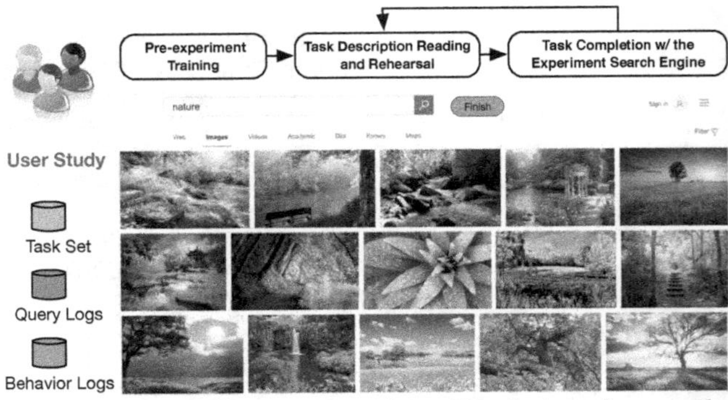

Figure 2: Data collection procedure. We designed our tasks based on the proposed user intent taxonomy. With enrolled participants, we collected query logs and behavior logs.

a smaller scale, but it does allow us to fully control the variabilities in search tasks and information needs.

We recruited 35 undergraduate students, 13 female and 22 male via email and online social networks, to take part in our user study. The ages of participants range from 18 to 25 and their majors include engineering, humanities and social science, and arts. All participants were familiar with basic usage of Web search engines. It took about an hour and a half to complete the user study. And we paid the participants about US$25 after they completed all the tasks seriously.

To make sure that every participant was familiar with the experimental procedure, an example task was used for demonstration in a Pre-experiment Training stage. In the example task, we asked participants to use the image search engine to learn how to tie a tie and they were required to describe the process in voice after searching. They could browse and click the search results, and adjust the sensitivity of the mouse to the most appropriate level as well. We did not give any further instructions on which results to click on or when to end until participants were familiar with the experimental search engine. After the Pre-experiment training stage, they were asked to complete all 12 image search tasks. For each task, the participants had to go through 2 stages, as shown in Fig. 2. Firstly, the participants should read and memorize the task description (note that the complete task description is provided to the participants). After that, they were required to describe the task in voice without viewing it. Then they can push a "Begin Task" button and will be redirected to an experimental search engine. Like Web image search scenario, they could scroll to move the page up and down, use the mouse to see hover text, and click a thumbnail to view and download the full-size image in the preview page. While no task time limits were imposed, they could stop searching and click the finish button when they thought that the task was completed or no further helpful information would be found.

We injected customized JavaScript into search result pages to log mouse activities on search pages when users perform search tasks. The search system was deployed on a 17-inch LCD monitor with a resolution of 1366 × 768. The Google Chrome browser was used to display results of search system. A database with full records of the experiments is available online for academic research.[2]

[2]https://tinyurl.com/y8pa8zk6

Table 3: Examples of user study tasks.

Category	Goal	Constraint	Success Criteria
Explore/Learn	Imagine you prepare to renovate a new house. You would like to compare different decoration styles (e.g., Chinese style, Simple European style).	–	Please introduce and compare the characteristics of different decoration styles in voice
Locate/Acquire	Please change the desktop background of this computer.	The background image should have blue sky and forest.	Change the desktop background to the required image.
Entertain	Now take a break, you can browse some posters or photos of your favorite stars.	–	–

4.2 User interaction features

From the query logs and behavior logs, we extracted 28 features that can be grouped into 6 types. We calculated all features both **globally** (i.e., using all data) and **at the early stage of a search session** (i.e., only using data captured before the first mouse scroll). Table 4 lists the complete list of 28 features.

Table 4: The list of 28 features extracted from the logged implicit user interaction with the image search engine. ("*" means that a type of feature can be extracted both in a global view and at the early stage of a search session).

Feature type	Description	#
Dwell time*	The dwell time on the SERP	1
Mouse clicks*	Number of clicks, first click time	2
Mouse hover*	First and longest hover time	2
Mouse movement*	Min, max, mean and median of the mouse movement speed at three directions(original, X-axis, Y-axis), and the mouse movement angle and radian.	20
Query reformulation	Adding and deleting terms, partially change.	3

Temporal information is a widely-used feedback feature in the setting of document relevance [4, 28], and it varies with different search tasks [22]. In this paper, we considered temporal information including dwell time on the SERP, time to first click, time to first hover and longest hover time on the images. We also examined the number of clicks on the SERP as clicks are strongly correlated with relevance and examination [9]. Temporal information is also dependent on image search query types [33].

Mouse movement features, which were explored in previous image search analyses [39], are investigated in this paper as well. Especially, as the placement of image search result is a two-dimensional grid instead of a linear result list, we considered not only the speed of mouse movement in the original direction but also in the X-axis (horizon) and Y-axis (vertical) direction.

Finally, query reformulation patterns in a search session were investigated. Previous studies show that query reformulation patterns vary with search goals [16], they occur frequently on image search platforms [3], and our data also provides evidence to support this, with approximately 76.7% of the sessions involving more than one query. Query reformulations between consecutive queries can be grouped into four categories [19]: adding terms, deleting terms, partial change, and complete change. Because the participants had to search for different items in some tasks, which was caused by the task description we provided, not by the user's cognitive processes, we only compare differences between adding terms, deleting terms, and partial change.

4.3 Statistical analysis

In this subsection, we report the relationship between the extracted features and search intents using box plots. We also perform a series of one-way ANOVA tests and pairwise t-tests to determine the significance. We show the box plots in Fig. 3. The difference in query reformulation patterns across different search intents is plotted in Fig. 4. The results of the ANOVA tests (ANOVA-p) are reported in Fig. 3 and Fig. 4. The results of the pairwise t-tests (p) are discussed in Sections 4.3.1–4.3.5.

4.3.1 Dwell time. From Fig. 3(a) and 3(b), we can observe that the mean dwell time in "Explore/Learn" tasks is longer than in "Entertain" tasks, both globally and at the early stage of a search session ($p < 0.02$ and $p < 0.07$, respectively). And the mean dwell time in "Locate/Acquire" tasks is longer than in "Entertain" tasks globally ($p < 0.05$). Before scrolling, dwell time on the SERP is significantly different between "Explore/Learn" and "Locate/Acquire" ($p < 0.05$). Recall our criteria for categorizing user intent: as users' search behavior in "Explore/Learn" and "Locate/Acquire" tasks is driven by a clear objective, there will exist more confirmation and comparison of image content, which results in more time spent on search engine result pages.

4.3.2 Mouse clicks. The number of clicks shows significant differences between the three intent classes ($p < 0.01$). The mean number of clicks in the three classes follows this relative order: "Explore/Learn" < "Locate/Acquire" < "Entertain." The first time to click is also a useful implicit feedback signal in differentiating different intents. From Fig. 3(c) and 3(d), we can observe that the average first click time of queries driven by the "Locate/Acquire" intent is longer than for queries with another intent, both globally and at the early stage of search (both have $p < 0.001$). The average first click time in "Explore/Learn" tasks is longer than in "Entertain" tasks before scrolling ($p < 0.001$) as well. When performing a "Locate/Acquire" or "Explore/Learn" task, users already have some specific requirements about the images. Image search results are self-contained, so that users do not need to click the document as in general Web search to view the landing page. Instead, they can observe several images before deciding which ones to download or to click to see a larger version. For this reason, users will spend more time on the search result page before the first click.

4.3.3 Mouse hover. Unlike the time to first click, time to first hover shows no significant differences between the three intents. However, the mean longest hover time in "Entertain" tasks is shorter than in "Locate/Acquire" and "Explore/Learn" tasks, both globally ($p < 0.001$) and at the early stage of search ($p < 0.01$), as shown in

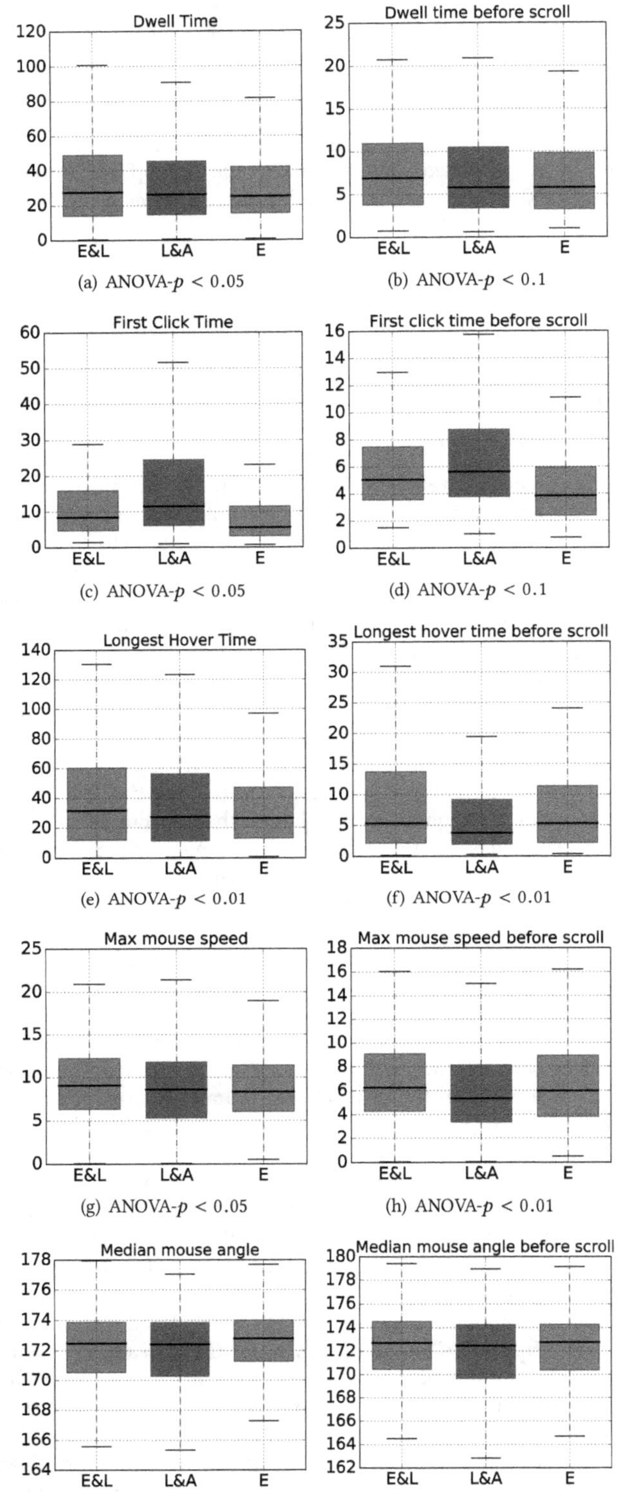

(a) ANOVA-$p < 0.05$ (b) ANOVA-$p < 0.1$ (c) ANOVA-$p < 0.05$ (d) ANOVA-$p < 0.1$ (e) ANOVA-$p < 0.01$ (f) ANOVA-$p < 0.01$ (g) ANOVA-$p < 0.05$ (h) ANOVA-$p < 0.01$ (i) ANOVA-$p < 0.01$ (j) ANOVA-$p < 0.05$

Figure 3: The extracted features on the SERP boxplots for queries with different search intents *globally* (a, c, e, g, i) and *at the early stage of search* (b, d, f, h, j). The unit on the y-axis is second for a, b, c, d, e, f; pixels per second for g, h; and number of degree for i, j. E&L denotes Explore&Learn, L&A denotes Learn&Acquire and E denotes Entertain.

Fig. 3(e) and 3(f), respectively. At the early stage of a search session, the mean longest hover time in "Locate/Acquire" is shorter than in "Explore/Learn" tasks ($p < 0.001$). As hovering on a document can be regarded as a signal that users are inspecting it; our results may be caused because "Explore/Learn" tasks require more complex cognitive processes, hence users may need to compare the image content with the background knowledge and mental impressions of their task.

4.3.4 Mouse movement. The speed of mouse movement varies between intents. As shown in Fig. 3(g) and 3(h), the average maximum speed of mouse movement in "Entertain" tasks is lower than in "Explore/Learn" tasks ($p < 0.02$) and "Locate/Acquire" tasks ($p < 0.08$), globally. And at the early stage of a search session, "Explore/Learn" tasks obtain a higher average max speed than "Locate/Acquire" tasks ($p < 0.001$). Besides in the original direction, the speed of mouse movements also shows significant differences along the X-axis and Y-axis (e.g., "Explore/Learn" tasks receive the highest average mean speed of mouse movement along the Y-axis while "Locate/Acquire" tasks receive the lowest, both globally ($p < 0.001$) and before scrolling ($p < 0.05$)). For the angle of the mouse movement, the median angle of mouse movement between the three intents is significantly different ($p < 0.01$, $p < 0.05$, and $p < 0.01$, respectively), globally. And the differences are also significant between "Locate/Acquire" and "Entertain" ($p < 0.05$), before scrolling. Thus, mouse movement patterns have the potential to help us recognizing image search intents.

4.3.5 Query reformulation. Fig. 4 shows the average number of times a query reformulation occurs, across different search intents. The numbers indicate the number of reformulations per task, on average (globally). We observe that for "Locate/Acquire" tasks, participants tend to refine queries more frequently, which serve as evidence of focused search behavior. In "Locate/Acquire" tasks, users need to find the most appropriate images to create some productions. For example, images used as materials in designing a poster should fit the background and other materials, which means that the user needs to try different styles of images until the poster looks aesthetically acceptable. Thus, "Locate/Acquire" tasks receive a larger number times for query reformulation. In contrast, in "Entertain" tasks, the users' search behavior is not driven by a clear objective. This more exploratory, browsing-like behavior results in a smaller number of query reformulations. We performed a paired two-tailed t-test to verify the significance of the observed differences: $p < 0.01$ for all comparisons except for for differences in adding terms and deleting terms between Explore/Learn and Locate/Acquire ($p < 0.05$).

In summary, through our user study, we collected query logs and behavior logs. Based on these data, we are able to answer *RQ*2 by investigating several frequently used implicit signals in general Web search. We find that temporal information and mouse movement patterns are useful in distinguishing search intents. Also, the cognitive process under different intents may result in different types and numbers of times of query reformulation.

5 IMAGE SEARCH INTENT PREDICTION USING EARLY STAGE FEATURES

The features discussed in Section 4.3 show potential in helping us identifying search intent automatically. In this paper, we utilize interaction features at the early stage of a search session to build an early stage user intent recognition system aimed at addressing *RQ*3. We aim to predict intent at the query level. If our features are

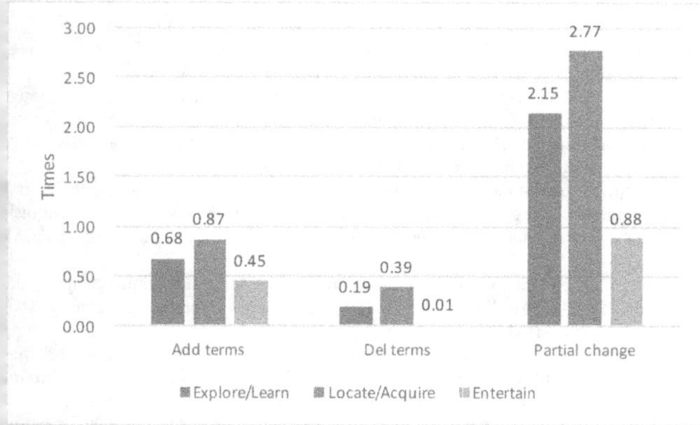

Figure 4: Average number of times of query reformulations per task, across different search intents (ANOVA-$p < 0.01$ for every type of query reformulation).

effective, this system can be practical for an image search engine to rerank its results even before users begin to scrolling, which will likely improve the satisfaction of users.

We compare different combinations of features. Due to a lack of space we do not consider all features described in Table 4 but some natural groupings only. In particular, we use "Time" to denote the combination of dwell time, time to first click and time to first hover. And as the number of clicks and first hover time show no significant difference under different intents at the early stage of a search session, we do not include it in the set of features that we consider. Also, we do not use the query reformulation patterns because we want to predict the user intents at the query level. We concatenate various features into a long feature vector to fuse all features (which is known as "early fusion" of different feature groups [39]). As this task can be treated as a multi-class classification problem, we apply a gradient boosting classifier [30] and perform 10-fold cross validation. We assign the label from the majority class to all the instances to generate a baseline.

The results are shown in Table 5. We can observe that our recognition system with user behavior features outperforms the baseline significantly ($p < 0.001$). And temporal features are more effective than the other two combinations. Fusing all features together achieves better prediction results than only using a single feature group. However, early fusion does not lead to a large increase in performance over the best single group of features. We compared another fusion method, i.e., "late fusion" in which each feature group has its own classifier and the output of all classifiers are combined to obtain a final result. We used the weighted sum of scores for "late fusion," similar to [39]. The results are also shown in Table 5. We see that "late fusion" and "early fusion" perform very similarly. It is worth pointing out that in absolute terms our performance figures are similar to other intent classification tasks considered in the literature, such as [7, 39], even though we use a much sparser signal than [7] and, unlike [39], only use features that can be collected in real-world scenarios.

Finally, concerning *RQ*3, we have found that based on interactive features at the early stages of a search session, we can recover user intents effectively through a combination of temporal features and mouse movement features.

6 CONCLUSION AND FUTURE WORK

In this paper, we proposed a new user intent taxonomy for image search and verified the taxonomy through a user survey involving over 200 people. Based on a lab-based user study, we discovered significant differences in user behavior under different intents. Finally, we used these behavioral signals to recover user intents and achieved promising results.

Table 5: Classification performance based on the user interactions features in terms of weighted average of F-1 score. Best results are in boldface. (E&L denotes Explore&Learn, L&A denotes Learn&Acquire and E denotes Entertain).

Features	All classes	E&L vs. L&A	E&L vs. E	L&A vs. E
Baseline	0.28	0.44	0.42	0.54
Time (#3)	0.42	0.56	0.56	0.64
Mouse move speed (#12)	0.40	0.55	0.54	0.60
Mouse move angle (#8)	0.38	0.55	0.54	0.61
Late fusion all features	0.44	0.57	0.56	0.64
Early fusion all features	**0.45**	**0.58**	**0.58**	**0.65**

Implications. As user intents can be different in image search scenarios, considering an evaluation metric appropriate for different intents can be beneficial. Also, recommender systems could prioritize showing specific, targeted content to users based on their search goals. Last but not the least, the optimization goal of search engines should be designed according to different search intents. For example, for users with an "Entertain" intent, the goal may be to keep them engaged with the image search engines for as long as possible. This is where our work contributes.

Future work. Interesting directions for future work include investigating the intent prediction beyond the early stage, e.g., by incorporating content features of query and images besides user interaction signals. Moreover, we plan to design strategies to rerank image search results according to different intents, with the aim to improve user satisfaction. Also, a parallel comparison between video search intents and image search intents might be interesting as both belong to multimedia search.

Acknowledgments. This work is supported by the Natural Science Foundation of China (Grant No. 61622208, 61732008, 61532011), National Key Basic Research Program (2015CB358700), Ahold Delhaize, Amsterdam Data Science, the Bloomberg Research Grant program, the Criteo Faculty Research Award program, Elsevier, the European Community's Seventh Framework Programme (FP7/2007-2013) under grant agreement nr 312827 (VOX-Pol), the Microsoft Research Ph.D. program, the Netherlands Institute for Sound and Vision, the Netherlands Organisation for Scientific Research (NWO) under project nrs. 13675, 612.001.116, CI-14-25, 652.002.001, 612.001.551, 652.001.003, and Yandex. All content represents the opinion of the authors, which is not necessarily shared or endorsed by their respective employers and/or sponsors.

REFERENCES

[1] Eugene Agichtein, Eric Brill, and Susan Dumais. 2006. Improving web search ranking by incorporating user behavior information. In *Proceedings of the 29th annual international ACM SIGIR conference on Research and development in information retrieval*. ACM, 19–26.

[2] Icek Ajzen. 2002. Perceived behavioral control, self-efficacy, locus of control, and the theory of planned behavior. *Journal of Applied Social Psychology* 32 (2002), 665–683.

[3] Paul André, Edward Cutrell, Desney Tan, and Greg Smith. 2009. Designing novel image search interfaces by understanding unique characteristics and usage. *Human-Computer Interaction–INTERACT 2009* (2009), 340–353.

[4] Alexey Borisov, Ilya Markov, Maarten de Rijke, and Pavel Serdyukov. 2016. A context-aware time model for web search. In *SIGIR 2016: 39th international ACM SIGIR conference on Research and development in information retrieval*. ACM, 205–214.

[5] Andrei Broder. 2002. A taxonomy of web search. In *ACM Sigir forum*, Vol. 36. ACM, 3–10.

[6] Huanhuan Cao, Daxin Jiang, Jian Pei, Qi He, Zhen Liao, Enhong Chen, and Hang Li. 2008. Context-aware query suggestion by mining click-through and session data. In *Proceedings of the 14th ACM SIGKDD international conference on Knowledge discovery and data mining*. ACM, 875–883.

[7] Justin Cheng, Caroline Lo, and Jure Leskovec. 2017. Predicting intent using activity logs: How goal specificity and temporal range affect user behavior. In *Proceedings of the 26th International Conference on World Wide Web Companion*. International World Wide Web Conferences Steering Committee, 593–601.

[8] I CNNIC. 2016. The 38th Statistical report on internet development in China. *China Internet Network Information Center (CNNIC), China* (2016).

[9] Nick Craswell, Onno Zoeter, Michael Taylor, and Bill Ramsey. 2008. An experimental comparison of click position-bias models. In *Proceedings of the 2008 international conference on web search and data mining*. ACM, 87–94.

[10] Honghua Kathy Dai, Lingzhi Zhao, Zaiqing Nie, Ji-Rong Wen, Lee Wang, and Ying Li. 2006. Detecting online commercial intention (OCI). In *Proceedings of the 15th international conference on World Wide Web*. ACM, 829–837.

[11] Zhicheng Dou, Ruihua Song, and Ji-Rong Wen. 2007. A large-scale evaluation and analysis of personalized search strategies. In *Proceedings of the 16th international conference on World Wide Web*. ACM, 581–590.

[12] Joseph L. Fleiss. 1971. Measuring nominal scale agreement among many raters. *Psychological bulletin* 76, 5 (1971), 378–382.

[13] Abby Goodrum and Amanda Spink. 1999. Visual information seeking: A study of image queries on the world wide web. In *Proceedings of the ASIS Annual Meeting*, Vol. 36. ERIC, 665–74.

[14] Sha Hu, Zhicheng Dou, Xiaojie Wang, Tetsuya Sakai, and Ji-Rong Wen. 2015. Search result diversification based on hierarchical intents. In *Proceedings of the 24th ACM International on Conference on Information and Knowledge Management*. ACM, 63–72.

[15] Xian-Sheng Hua, Linjun Yang, Jingdong Wang, Jing Wang, Ming Ye, Kuansan Wang, Yong Rui, and Jin Li. 2013. Clickage: Towards bridging semantic and intent gaps via mining click logs of search engines. In *Proceedings of the 21st ACM international conference on Multimedia*. ACM, 243–252.

[16] Bouke Huurnink, Laura Hollink, Wietske Van Den Heuvel, and Maarten de Rijke. 2010. Search behavior of media professionals at an audiovisual archive: A transaction log analysis. *Journal of the Association for Information Science and Technology* 61, 6 (2010), 1180–1197.

[17] Vidit Jain and Manik Varma. 2011. Learning to re-rank: query-dependent image re-ranking using click data. In *Proceedings of the 20th international conference on World wide web*. ACM, 277–286.

[18] Bernard J. Jansen. 2008. Searching for digital images on the web. *Journal of Documentation* 64, 1 (2008), 81–101.

[19] Bernard J. Jansen, Amanda Spink, and Bhuva Narayan. 2007. Query modifications patterns during web searching. In *Information Technology, 2007. ITNG'07. Fourth International Conference on*. IEEE, 439–444.

[20] Bernard J. Jansen, Amanda Spink, and Tefko Saracevic. 2000. Real life, real users, and real needs: A study and analysis of user queries on the web. *Information Processing & Management* 36, 2 (2000), 207–227.

[21] Jyun-Yu Jiang, Yen-Yu Ke, Pao-Yu Chien, and Pu-Jen Cheng. 2014. Learning user reformulation behavior for query auto-completion. In *Proceedings of the 37th international ACM SIGIR conference on Research & development in information retrieval*. ACM, 445–454.

[22] Diane Kelly, Jaime Arguello, Ashlee Edwards, and Wan-ching Wu. 2015. Development and evaluation of search tasks for IIR experiments using a cognitive complexity framework. In *Proceedings of the 2015 International Conference on The Theory of Information Retrieval*. ACM, 101–110.

[23] Christoph Kofler and Mathias Lux. 2009. Dynamic presentation adaptation based on user intent classification. In *Proceedings of the 17th ACM international conference on Multimedia*. ACM, 1117–1118.

[24] Christoph Kofler and Mathias Lux. 2009. An exploratory study on the explicitness of user intentions in digital photo retrieval. In *Proceedings of the 9th International Conference on Knowledge Management and Knowledge Technologies*.

[25] J. Richard Landis and Gary G. Koch. 1977. The measurement of observer agreement for categorical data. *Biometrics* 33, 1 (1977), 159–174.

[26] Yanen Li, Anlei Dong, Hongning Wang, Hongbo Deng, Yi Chang, and Cheng Xiang Zhai. 2014. A two-dimensional click model for query auto-completion. In *Proceedings of the 37th international ACM SIGIR conference on Research & development in information retrieval*. ACM, 455–464.

[27] Jingjing Liu, Michael J Cole, Chang Liu, Ralf Bierig, Jacek Gwizdka, Nicholas J Belkin, Jun Zhang, and Xiangmin Zhang. 2010. Search behaviors in different task types. In *Proceedings of the 10th annual joint conference on Digital libraries*. ACM 69–78.

[28] Yiqun Liu, Xiaohui Xie, Chao Wang, Jian-Yun Nie, Min Zhang, and Shaoping Ma. 2016. Time-aware click model. *ACM Transactions on Information Systems (TOIS)* 35, 3 (2016), Article 16.

[29] Mathias Lux, Christoph Kofler, and Oge Marques. 2010. A classification scheme for user intentions in image search. In *CHI'10 Extended Abstracts on Human Factors in Computing Systems*. ACM, 3913–3918.

[30] Llew Mason, Jonathan Baxter, Peter L Bartlett, and Marcus R Frean. 2000. Boosting algorithms as gradient descent. In *Advances in neural information processing systems*. 512–518.

[31] Neil O'Hare, Paloma de Juan, Rossano Schifanella, Yunlong He, Dawei Yin, and Yi Chang. 2016. Leveraging user interaction signals for web image search. In *Proceedings of the 39th International ACM SIGIR conference on Research and Development in Information Retrieval*. ACM, 559–568.

[32] Bing Pan, Helene A. Hembrooke, Geri K. Gay, Laura A. Granka, Matthew K Feusner, and Jill K. Newman. 2004. The determinants of web page viewing behavior: an eye-tracking study. In *Proceedings of the 2004 symposium on Eye tracking research & applications*. ACM, 147–154.

[33] Jaimie Y. Park, Neil O'Hare, Rossano Schifanella, Alejandro Jaimes, and Chin-Wan Chung. 2015. A large-scale study of user image search behavior on the web. In *Proceedings of the 33rd Annual ACM Conference on Human Factors in Computing Systems*. ACM, 985–994.

[34] Hsiao-Tieh Pu. 2005. A comparative analysis of web image and textual queries. *Online Information Review* 29, 5 (2005), 457–467.

[35] Davood Rafiei, Krishna Bharat, and Anand Shukla. 2010. Diversifying web search results. In *Proceedings of the 19th international conference on World wide web*. ACM, 781–790.

[36] Miriam Redi, Frank Z. Liu, and Neil O'Hare. 2017. Bridging the aesthetic gap: The wild beauty of web imagery. In *Proceedings of the 2017 ACM on International Conference on Multimedia Retrieval*. ACM, 242–250.

[37] Daniel E. Rose and Danny Levinson. 2004. Understanding user goals in web search. In *Proceedings of the 13th international conference on World Wide Web*. ACM, 13–19.

[38] Daniel M Russell, Diane Tang, Melanie Kellar, and Robin Jeffries. 2009. Task behaviors during web search: The difficulty of assigning labels. In *System Sciences, 2009. HICSS'09. 42nd Hawaii International Conference on*. IEEE, 1–5.

[39] Mohammad Soleymani, Michael Riegler, and Pål Halvorsen. 2017. Multimodal analysis of image search intent: Intent recognition in image search from user behavior and visual content. In *ACM International Conference on Multimedia Retrieval*. 251–259.

[40] Bilyana Taneva, Mouna Kacimi, and Gerhard Weikum. 2010. Gathering and ranking photos of named entities with high precision, high recall, and diversity. In *Proceedings of the third ACM international conference on Web search and data mining*. ACM, 431–440.

[41] Dian Tjondronegoro, Amanda Spink, and Bernard J. Jansen. 2009. A study and comparison of multimedia Web searching: 1997–2006. *Journal of the American Society for Information Science and Technology* 60, 9 (2009), 1756–1768.

[42] Reinier H. van Leuken, Lluis Garcia, Ximena Olivares, and Roelof van Zwol. 2009. Visual diversification of image search results. In *Proceedings of the 18th international conference on World wide web*. ACM, 341–350.

[43] Kuansan Wang, Nikolas Gloy, and Xiaolong Li. 2010. Inferring search behaviors using partially observable markov (pom) model. In *Proceedings of the third ACM international conference on Web search and data mining*. ACM, 211–220.

[44] Xiaohui Xie, Yiqun Liu, Xiaochuan Wang, Meng Wang, Zhijing Wu, Yingying Wu, Min Zhang, and Shaoping Ma. 2017. Investigating examination behavior of image search users. In *Proceedings of the 40th International ACM SIGIR conference on Research and Development in Information Retrieval*. ACM.

[45] Danqing Xu, Yiqun Liu, Min Zhang, Shaoping Ma, and Liyun Ru. 2012. Incorporating revisiting behaviors into click models. In *Proceedings of the fifth ACM international conference on Web search and data mining*. ACM, 303–312.

[46] Jinxi Xu and W. Bruce Croft. 1996. Query expansion using local and global document analysis. In *Proceedings of the 19th annual international ACM SIGIR conference on Research and development in information retrieval*. ACM, 4–11.

[47] Zheng-Jun Zha, Linjun Yang, Tao Mei, Meng Wang, Zengfu Wang, Tat-Seng Chua, and Xian-Sheng Hua. 2010. Visual query suggestion: Towards capturing user intent in internet image search. *ACM Transactions on Multimedia Computing, Communications, and Applications (TOMM)* 6, 3 (2010), 13.

OpenRec: A Modular Framework for Extensible and Adaptable Recommendation Algorithms

Longqi Yang
Cornell Tech, Cornell University
ylongqi@cs.cornell.edu

Eugene Bagdasaryan
Cornell Tech, Cornell University
eugene@cs.cornell.edu

Joshua Gruenstein
Massachusetts Institute of Technology
jgru@mit.edu

Cheng-Kang Hsieh
Cornell Tech, Cornell University
changun@cs.ucla.edu

Deborah Estrin
Cornell Tech, Cornell University
destrin@cornell.edu

ABSTRACT

With the increasing demand for deeper understanding of users' preferences, recommender systems have gone beyond simple user-item filtering and are increasingly sophisticated, comprised of multiple components for analyzing and fusing diverse information. Unfortunately, existing frameworks do not adequately support extensibility and adaptability and consequently pose significant challenges to rapid, iterative, and systematic, experimentation. In this work, we propose **OpenRec**, an open and modular Python framework that supports extensible and adaptable research in recommender systems. Each recommender is modeled as a computational graph that consists of a structured ensemble of reusable modules connected through a set of well-defined interfaces. We present the architecture of OpenRec and demonstrate that OpenRec provides adaptability, modularity and reusability while maintaining training efficiency and recommendation accuracy. Our case study illustrates how OpenRec can support an efficient design process to prototype and benchmark alternative approaches with inter-changeable modules and enable development and evaluation of new algorithms.

KEYWORDS

Recommendation; framework; modular; extensible; adaptable.

ACM Reference format:

Longqi Yang, Eugene Bagdasaryan, Joshua Gruenstein, Cheng-Kang Hsieh, and Deborah Estrin. 2018. OpenRec: A Modular Framework for Extensible and Adaptable Recommendation Algorithms. In *Proceedings of WSDM'18, February 5–9, 2018, Marina Del Rey, CA, USA*, , 9 pages.
DOI: http://dx.doi.org/10.1145/3159652.3159681

1 INTRODUCTION

Today's recommender systems have gone beyond simple collaborative or content-based filtering algorithms to become large-scale learning machines that ingest and analyze a wide range of information, e.g., diverse user feedback signals (ratings [3], click-through [17], likes [16], views [33]) and auxiliary, contextual and cross-platform traces (images [15], video [8], audio [30] and other associated metadata [25]; as well as social networks [12], software tool traces [33], and personal digital traces [16]). A state-of-the-art system [8] usually involves numerous heterogeneous and complex sub-models that analyze and fuse high-dimensional and multi-channel data streams, and each of these sub-models may have different learning architectures and a large number of hyper-parameters that need to be developed and maintained.

As a result, recommender system developers are facing an exponentially larger design space given the multiple interdependent design decisions that they need to make, such as: (1) which collaborative filtering model to use, (2) which additional data to incorporate, (3) for each additional data, which feature extraction methods to use, and (4) how to integrate the extracted features with the collaborative filtering part of the model. Moreover, researchers' design space now includes: identifying novel data sources to incorporate into the system, developing new feature extractors, and experimenting with new ways to integrate features with the user-item filtering. The software frameworks previously available for recommender systems are limited to "functional level" modularity (e.g., Librec [11] decomposes a recommender system into *inference, prediction*, and *similarity*), which does not provide the modularity needed to build and evaluate increasingly complex models. This paper addresses key challenges of **extensibility** and **adaptability**.

On the one hand, traditional frameworks, such as MyMediaLite [10] and LensKit [9], usually treat a recommendation algorithm as single and **monolithic**. As a result, in order to experiment with a new method for even a small part of the algorithm, researchers often need to re-implement the whole model from scratch or extensively patch existing code. For example, to build a recommendation algorithm that incorporates image data, a researcher needs to not only implement the neural network for image analysis, but also re-build the factorization algorithm (e.g. Probablistic Matric Factorization), because there is no interface available in the traditional frameworks to access component modules. Significant rewriting is needed even when the recommendation is a simple composition of existing models.

On the other hand, adapting traditional frameworks to diverse recommendation scenarios requires tedious re-implementations, which may significantly affect recommendation performance despite slight implementation differences (e.g., different choices of hyper-parameters and regularization terms) [9]. We argue that such re-implementations are inevitable if the frameworks are built on diverse backend and programming languages, e.g., Java [11], C# [10], and Python [18], because of the overhead and the opportunity cost

WSDM'18, February 5–9, 2018, Marina Del Rey, CA, USA

ISBN 978-1-4503-5581-0/18/02.
DOI: http://dx.doi.org/10.1145/3159652.3159681

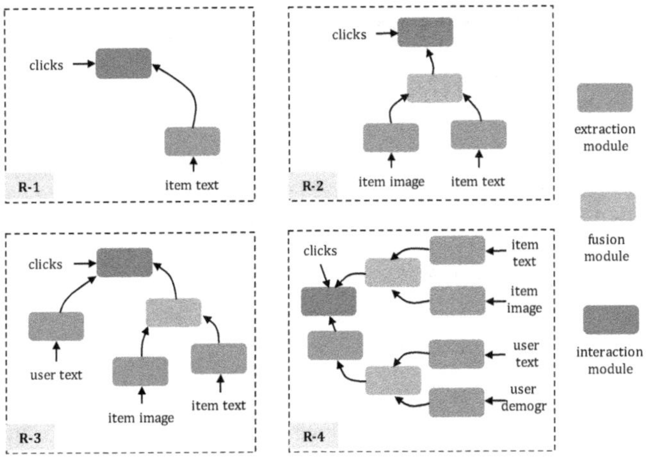

Figure 1: A modular view of recommendation algorithms. Each algorithm (R-1 to R-4) is a structured ensemble of reusable modules under three categories - extraction module, fusion module, and interaction module. The modules' color codex is shared throughout the paper. Arrows in the figure represent data flows.

of switching between different development environments. Additionally, existing frameworks typically assume a single machine environment, which can not leverage the computation power from distributed computing and modern hardware, e.g., GPU and TPU. Therefore, it is hard to be adopted when the model size increases.

To tackle these challenges, we propose a **modular** recommender-system design, where each recommender is a structured ensemble of reusable modules with standard interfaces. This allows the recommendation system innovation to be decomposed into (1) *designing new modules*, and (2) *inventing new computational graphs* that wire modules together. As demonstrated in Fig. 1, future research can readily reuse existing modules and graphs without re-implementing or modifying prior algorithms. Under such a paradigm, changes to a module or the computational graph does not affect other components, and development and testing can be more readily achieved via *plug-in and go*. Just as *modular architectures and tools* lead to rapid advances in other AI fields [5, 7, 24] and network protocol simulation [4], a modular paradigm can significantly reduce the development overhead and become fertile ground for extensible and adaptable recommender system research. In addition, we propose to use Tensorflow [1] as the standard backend for framework development. Because Tensorflow can be easily deployed in diverse computing environments (e.g., embedded devices, single machine, and distributed cloud) and is optimized for modern hardware, its use enables distributed and mini-batch (i.e., large-scale dataset) training for OpenRec and can minimize the need for language-switching re-implementations.

In this work, we present the design, implementation, and evaluation of **OpenRec**, an open and modular framework that supports extensible and adaptable research in recommender systems. Specifically, we build such a framework by (1) modularizing prior recommender systems, (2) identifying reusable modules and defining standard interfaces, and (3) iteratively implementing and developing in Tensorflow. In addition, we evaluate and demonstrate OpenRec in the following three contexts.

- **Reproducing monolithic implementations with OpenRec modular design.** We extensively compare the performance of the modular implementations to the prior implementations and demonstrate that the modularity in OpenRec does not degrade the models' performance in terms of both training efficiency and prediction accuracy. To the contrary, in many cases, OpenRec outperformed the existing implementations due to the ability to conduct large-batch training.
- **Rapid prototyping using OpenRec as a sandbox.** Using book recommendation as an example, we illustrate how developers can use OpenRec to address specific recommendation problems by efficiently prototyping and bench-marking a large number of approaches with modules that are inter-changeable.
- **Developing new recommendation algorithms by extending existing modules in OpenRec.** We use OpenRec to build a time-aware movie rating prediction algorithm for the Netflix dataset. We demonstrate that OpenRec can significantly alleviate the development burden when exploring new techniques.

The OpenRec framework (Apache-2.0) is publicly available under the URL: http://www.openrec.ai

2 EVOLUTION OF RECOMMENDER SYSTEMS

In this section we briefly review the evolution of recommender systems. We discuss how recommender systems have evolved from pure collaborative filtering approaches to hybrid and content-aware models, and discuss the design challenges that arise with such development.

2.1 Pure Collaborative Filtering Models

Early recommender system research focused on designing collaborative filtering models that process users' past user-item interaction data (e.g., ratings, click-through, etc.) to predict what users will like in the future [3, 17]. A well-known example is matrix factorization, where users' past behaviors are encoded in an incomplete user-item matrix, and the prediction is made by estimating the values of the missing cells in the matrix with a low-rank assumption. Matrix factorization and other collaborative filtering models achieved great results in the Netflix competition [3], and a great amount of work has been devoted to improving upon these original approaches. The most recent examples include Neural Collaborative Filtering [14] that utilizes a neural network to allow for non-linear interactions between users and items, and Collaborative Metric Learning [15], that approaches the collaborative filtering problem from a metric learning perspective.

2.2 Hybrid and Content-ware Models

The original use cases of collaborative filtering algorithms were for the scenarios where user-item interactions are abundant (e.g. movie recommendations on Netflix or product recommendations on Amazon [3, 21]) and the user-item interaction data alone is sufficient to make high quality recommendations. However, with digital services becoming more ubiquitous in daily life, there is a increasing demand for recommender systems to work for other scenarios where users have had little or no prior interaction with the system (i.e. the user cold start scenarios), or for the scenarios where candidate items have not received much feedback from users yet (i.e. the item cold start scenarios). Collaborative filtering algorithms work poorly in such scenarios as the amount of interaction data are too sparse for them to reliably estimate users' preferences.

This demand for more powerful and diverse recommender systems, along with the rapid advances in machine learning algorithms for content analysis, has driven a new generation of research that goes beyond the user-item matrix; in particular, new algorithms use various machine learning models to extract relevant features from additional sources [28]. For example, specific algorithms have been designed to extract item features from a large variety of signals, such as text and image data associated with items; similarly, different approaches have been proposed to extract user features from their social media traces, reviews, or other public and personal digital traces [16]. The extracted features are fused with the collaborative filtering portion of the model to allow the system to get a deeper understanding of items and users. Such hybrid models often show superior performance in cold-start scenarios, and continue to outperform the collaborative filtering solutions later on [13, 16]. Moreover, the use of content information also allows for more specific explanations to the recommendation results as compared with the generic "users like you also like this" explanations enabled by prior collaborative filtering based approaches.

3 RELATED FRAMEWORKS

The rapid evolution of recommender systems (Section 2) has posed significant challenges to the existing software frameworks. In this section, we briefly review the limitations of existing solutions, and discuss *why OpenRec is timely* and *is preferable to modularizing existing frameworks*. We show the core functions of previous frameworks and their comparisons to OpenRec in Table. 1. Existing solutions are limited in the following two aspects.

- **Lack of algorithm level modularity support.** Previous frameworks usually provide modularity at the "functional level", i.e., each recommender is divided into functionally-independent components (e.g. train, predict, and dataset). Such functionality-based modularity is convenient while developing new systems, but falls short when it comes to inventing and experimenting with complex algorithms, i.e. developers still need to build algorithms monolithically. In addition, because there is no "algorithm-level modularity", it is non-trivial to add complex auxiliary features into recommendation. Therefore, OpenRec addresses a *timely* need for the recommender system community.
- **Lack of reliable backend support.** As is shown in Table 1, previous frameworks were built on either no explicit backend or a backend that is not scalable and unfriendly to complex models, e.g. Scikit. With such backends, the recommender systems can not leverage modern hardware, such as GPUs, and is hard to scale to distributed computing environment. It is also very cumbersome for the developers to build new functions as there is little support for basic mathematical operations. Therefore, modularizing based on a legacy backend is limiting. We develop OpenRec over Tensorflow, a next generation computing engine for machine learning.

Table 1: Comparing OpenRec to existing software frameworks for recommender systems. (Sys-m: system-level modularity, Algo-m: algorithm-level modularity)

Framework	Sys-m	Auxiliary features	Backend	Algo-m
MLlib [29]	✗	✗	✗	✗
MyMediaLite [10]	✓	categorical	✗	✗
LensKit [9]	✓	✗	✗	✗
Surprise [18]	✓	✗	SciKits	✗
PredictionIO [6]	✓	categorical	✗	✗
Librec [11]	✓	categorical	✗	✗
OpenRec	✓	complex	Tensorflow	✓

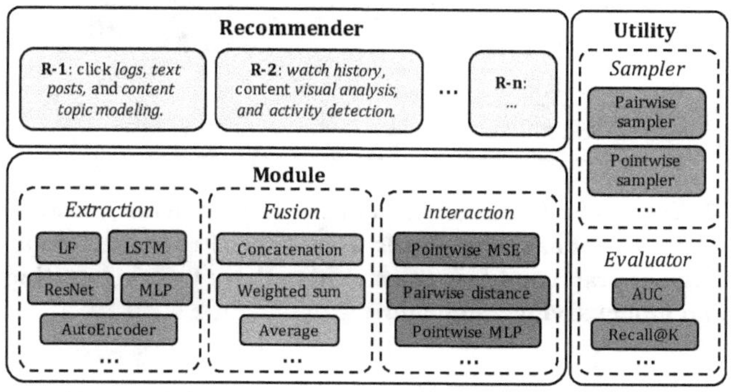

Figure 2: The architecture of OpenRec. A recommender is built out of modules. All three components (Module, Recommender, and Utility) can be used seamlessly together to conduct training, evaluation, experimentation, and serving for recommendation algorithms.

4 OPENREC FRAMEWORK

In this section, we describe the architecture of OpenRec. It views each recommendation algorithm as a computational graph that connects reusable modules together. OpenRec is comprised of two levels of abstractions - **module** and **recommender** - along with a collection of **utility** functions (Fig. 2). Under this framework, a **module** defines standard input/output interfaces for each category of algorithmic component. A **recommender** provides mechanisms to build end-to-end systems out of modules. **Utility** includes functions for efficient data sampling and model evaluation. In the rest of this section, we present the details of each abstraction. Although we illustrate OpenRec with collaborative filtering approaches, the framework is also designed for more general recommendation techniques, e.g., content-based, conversational and group recommendations. We discuss the generalization of the framework in Section 4.4.

4.1 Recommenders

The Recommender abstraction provides a standard way to construct recommendation systems with modules (Section 4.2) and to easily conduct training and testing. The design philosophy behind the recommender is to decouple the construction of a complex system

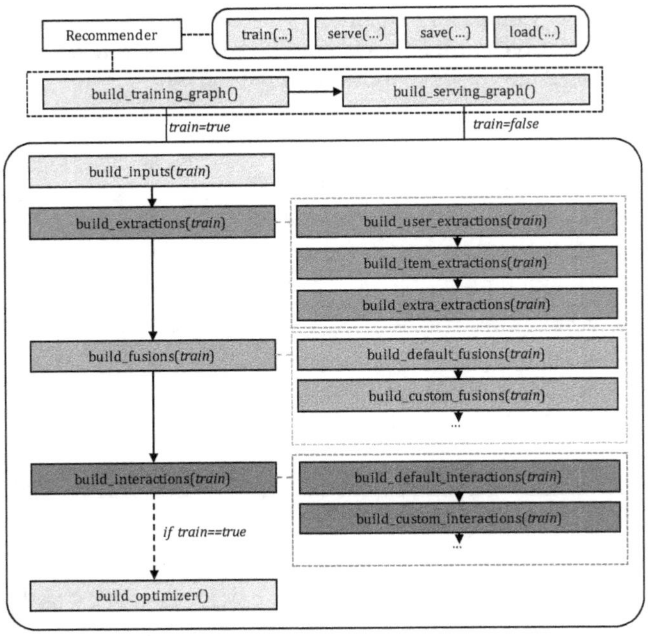

Figure 3: Standard interfaces of the Recommender abstraction. It contains procedures used to construct the computational graph and functions used to drive training, testing and model saving and loading.

into many small steps, so that the system can be easily extended to include new features. As shown in Fig. 3, it consists of two major steps - *build training graph* and *build serving graph*, each of which calls corresponding modules. When building the training graph, a sequence of functions (i.e., *build inputs*, *build extractions*, *build fusions*, *build interactions*, and *build optimizer*) is called with the flag *train* set to *True*, where the extraction, fusion, and interaction modules are built through decomposed child functions. Similarly, when building the serving graph, all of the functions above except *build optimizer* are called with the flag *train* set to *False*. During model training, the function *train* is called for each iteraction; and during testing or evaluation, the function *serve* is used to efficiently score items for a list of users. We show the flexibility and extensibility of the recommender abstraction in Section 5 with concrete examples.

4.2 Modules

Modules represent reusable components in a recommendation algorithm. As discussed in Section 2, a recommender typically contains three components that (1) model the interactions (including ratings, views, likes and thumb-ups, etc.) between users and items in the targeted recommendation context; (2) derive a user's, an item's or a context's representation from a data trace (Fig. 4), such as one-hot encoding, images, text, audio, video, location or demographic information, etc.; and (3) fuse together multiple feature representations from users, items, or environmental contexts. In OpenRec, we name components in these three categories as **interaction**, **extraction**, and **fusion** modules respectively. As shown in Fig. 4, OpenRec modules share the same conceptual architecture and outputs (i.e., a

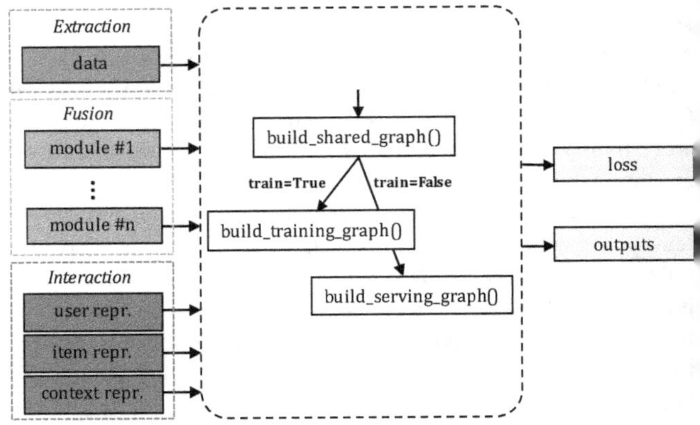

Figure 4: The structure of the Module abstraction. (Left: inputs, Right: outputs)

loss and an output list) but ingest different forms of inputs. Specifically, each module is composed of three core functions: *build shared graph*, *build training graph*, and *build testing graph*. These functions are invoked based on the value of a *train* flag that determines whether we are in training or testing mode.

- **Interaction Module.** An interaction module takes representations from users, items or interaction contexts as inputs and then calculates the loss (during training) and item rankings (during testing). The inputs to the interaction module are typically derived from one-hot encoding or auxiliary information using extraction and fusion modules. The derived loss is used to drive the end-to-end training of the recommender system, and the item rank is used for testing and real-time recommendations. For the interaction module, we do not put any restriction on the number of users and items allowed as inputs so that it is general enough to handle a wide variety of collaborative filtering and content based algorithms (e.g., Probablistic Matrix Factorization (PMF) is built on pairs of users and items, whereas Baysian Personalized Ranking (BPR) requires triplets of users and items). Our initial prototype of OpenRec includes implementations of many interaction modules using state-of-the-art algorithms, e.g., pairwise logarithm used in BPR [26], pointwise mean square error (MSE) introduced by PMF [27], pairwise euclidean distance adopted in Collaborative Metric Learning (CML) [15], and pointwise cross entropy proposed by Neural Matrix Factorization (NeuMF) [14].
- **Extraction Module.** An extraction module computes representations for a data trace from users, items, or contexts. A simple example is to compute a representation from a one-hot encoding, which performs a basic lookup operation in an embedding matrix. Such a module is leveraged by traditional recommender systems without using auxiliary information, and we refer to it as a Latent Factor module. The development of extraction modules will benefit from advancements in other machine learning fields (e.g., computer vision, natural language processing and speech processing). Models from these fields can be introduced to recommender systems to analyze multi-modal data from users and items. Because OpenRec is highly modular and implemented on Tensorflow, introducing a new content analysis model is rather straightforward and efficient. In our initial prototype we implemented two general extraction modules, Multi-layer

Perceptron (MLP) and Latent Factor (LF). We expect an open source framework like OpenRec will result in development of more sophisticated models dedicated to analyzing specific data types, such as Convolutional Neural Network (CNN) for images and Recurrent Neural Network (RNN) for sequential data.

- **Fusion Module.** In many recommendation scenarios, users, items, and environmental context may have multiple data sources. For example, in the context-aware recommendation [2] and immersive recommendation [16], a user can be modeled by many personal data traces, e.g., emails, tweets and facebook posts. To bridge the gap between multiple extraction modules and a single interaction module, an fusion module is designed to fuse multiple extraction modules together (Fig. 4). We prototype two intuitive fusion modules, i.e., concatenation and element-wise average.

4.3 Utility functions

In OpenRec, a set of utility functions are included for the ease of model training and evaluation. The model training for recommendation systems usually involves user-item sampling. For example, in BPR, (*user, positive-item, negative-item*) need to be sampled for each training batch. The samplers take the data formatted in Numpy dict as inputs and produce batches of training or validation data for a recommender. We implement popular sampling procedures (e.g. pointwise and pairwise sampling) in the OpenRec framework to drive the training process. In addition, to provide standard model testing, we implement common evaluation metrics (e.g., MSE, Recall@K and AUC) which can be seamlessly integrated with the constructed recommendation model.

4.4 Generalization

Since OpenRec makes few assumption about *users* and *items*, it can be used for a wide range of recommendation techniques and scenarios, e.g., recommendations with different forms of feedback, as well as interactive, conversational, and group recommendation.

- For **different forms of feedback signals**, researchers can customize sampling strategies and interaction modules, for example, using pointwise sampling with the pointwise MSE module for explicit feedback, and pairwise sampling with the pairwise logarithm module for implicit feedback.
- For **interactive and conversational recommender systems**, the optimizers can be designed to update user and item representations in the active-learning settings [34]. For every iteration, a recommender makes recommendations and updates model parameters according to users' and items' representations and their real-time interactions.
- For **group recommendations**, as OpenRec uses Numpy structured arrays as the input data format and does not have restrictions on the number of extraction modules. Users can be grouped based on the additional *group id* inputs to the sampler.

5 EXPERIMENTS AND USE CASES

In this section, we demonstrate the validity, efficiency and extensibility of OpenRec under the following three concrete contexts.

- **Validity.** By comparing the modular implementations with the previous ad-hoc ones, we demonstrate that modularizing recommendation algorithms does not affect the performance and efficiency. Instead, because OpenRec is built on an open-source and industry-standard deep learning tool, it can more efficiently conduct the training. (Section 5.1)
- **Efficiency.** Using OpenRec as a sandbox, developers are able to quickly and efficiently prototype and experiment with different settings of recommender systems and look for the optimal solution (Section 5.2).
- **Extensibility.** By extending and reusing existing modules, OpenRec significantly reduces the overhead of implementing **new recommendation algorithms** (Section 5.3).

For the sake of space, we show the graphical illustration of the modular implementations in the main content and a sample pseudocode snippet in the Appendix A. More examples are available online at http://www.openrec.ai.

5.1 Validity: Reproducing monolithic implementations with modular framework

In order to test whether modularization affects the accuracy and efficiency of the recommendation algorithms, we compare the OpenRec implementations with the implementations released by the original algorithm authors. We use the same model structures and parameter settings from the original papers but replace the training strategies with the standard optimization methods adopted in OpenRec, e.g.. mini-batch stochastic gradient descent. Specifically, we experiment with the following three algorithms in this paper, each of which represents recommender systems with different complexity levels.

5.1.1 *Bayesian Personalized Ranking (BPR).*

As introduced by Rendle et al. [26], Bayesian Personalized Ranking learns latent representations for users and items by using a pairwise ranking loss, as shown in eqn. 1. It is one of the most popular method used under the traditional recommendation context without considering users' and items' auxiliary information.

$$\sum_{(u,i,j)\in D_S} ln\sigma(\hat{x}_{u,i} - \hat{x}_{u,j}) - \lambda_\Theta ||\Theta|| \tag{1}$$

where $\hat{x}_{u,i} = \beta_u + \beta_i + \gamma_u^T \gamma_i$. γ represents a latent representation for an user or an item, and β denotes the corresponding bias term. D_S contains training triplets (u, i, j) where the user u likes the item i but does not indicate her preference for the item j.

To implement the vanilla version of the BPR model using OpenRec, we employ the *Latent Factor (LF)* extraction module to compute latent representations for users and items respectively and a pairwise logarithm interaction module that takes users' and items' representations and computes the loss, which is illustrated in Fig. 5. Note that we do not need to re-implement the existing modules to run the experiment. Building such a recommender system can be achieved by simply putting together the reusable modules with standard interfaces.

We compare the OpenRec modular implementation with the implementation released by He et al. [13] and MyMediaLite library [10] and evaluate them against *tradesy.com* dataset [13], where the products that users *want* and *bought* are treated as positive feedback. As a result, 19,243 users and 165,906 items are included in the experiments. For each user, we randomly sample an item that she likes for validation and another one for testing, which

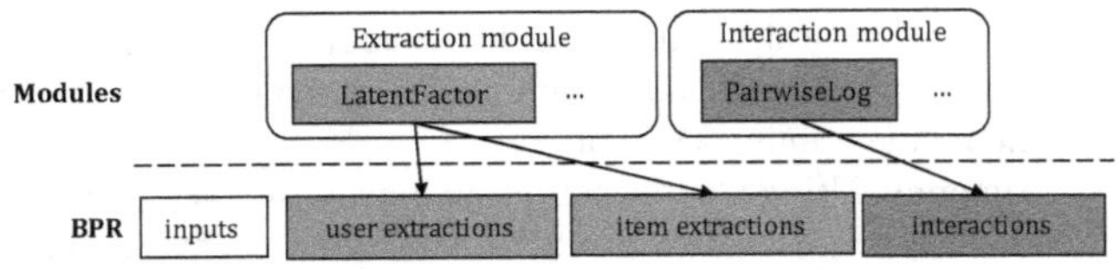

Figure 5: Implementing BPR with OpenRec (45 lines). We use rectangles to represent functions in a Recommender and shade the reusable modules and implementations. An arrow denotes an adoption or an inheritance. (Lines of code does not include blank and import lines)

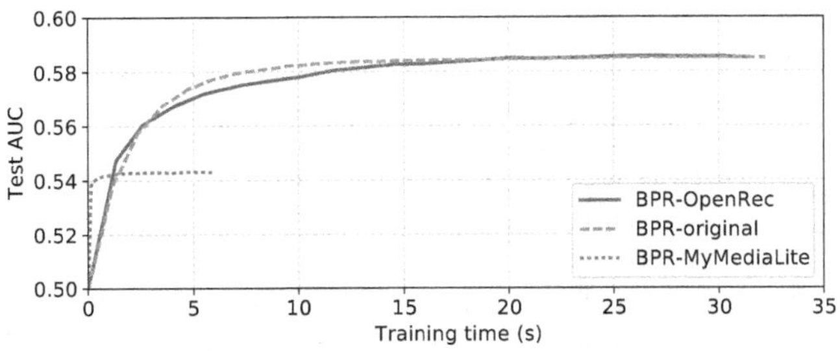

Figure 6: *tradesy.com* dataset [13] testing performance in terms of AUC (BPR-OpenRec, BPR-original, and BPR-MyMediaLite).

is consistent with the strategy used in the original paper [13]. We use the same parameter settings as [13] (λ_Θ is set to 0.1, and the dimensionality of γ is set to 20) and conduct the evaluations on an Amazon EC2 c4.4xlarge instance, which contains 16 CPU cores and 30 GB of memory.

We measure models' performance in terms of Area Under the ROC Curve (AUC), as defined in eqn. 2, against the training time.

$$\text{AUC} = \frac{1}{U}\sum_{u=1}^{U}\frac{1}{|\mathcal{P}(u)|}\frac{\sum_{(u,i)\in\mathcal{P}(u),(u,j)\in\mathcal{N}(u)}\delta(\hat{x}_{u,i} > \hat{x}_{u,j})}{|\mathcal{N}(u)|} \tag{2}$$

where $\mathcal{P}(u)$ contains items the user u likes in the validation/testing dataset, and $\mathcal{N}(u)$ contains items that did not receive any feedback signals from the user u.

The results presented in Fig. 6 show that the modular implementation achieves comparable performance to the best performed BPR implementation, and significantly outperforms the implementation from previous recommendation libraries (MyMediaLite). In other words, modularization does not affect the algorithm accuracy and efficiency for simple models such as BPR.

5.1.2 Visual Bayesian Personalized Ranking (VBPR). The vanilla BPR model does not incorporate any auxiliary information. To investigate recommendation scenarios where such information is leveraged, the second model that we experiment with is Visual Bayesian Personalized Ranking (VBPR), as proposed by [13]. VBPR incorporates visual features into recommendation by learning a transformation function f that projects visual features into the item embedding space. VBPR minimizes the same loss function as BPR but models $\hat{x}_{u,i}$ as follows.

$$\hat{x}_{u,i} = \beta_u + \beta_i + \gamma_u^T\gamma_i + \theta_u^T(\mathbf{E}f_i) \tag{3}$$

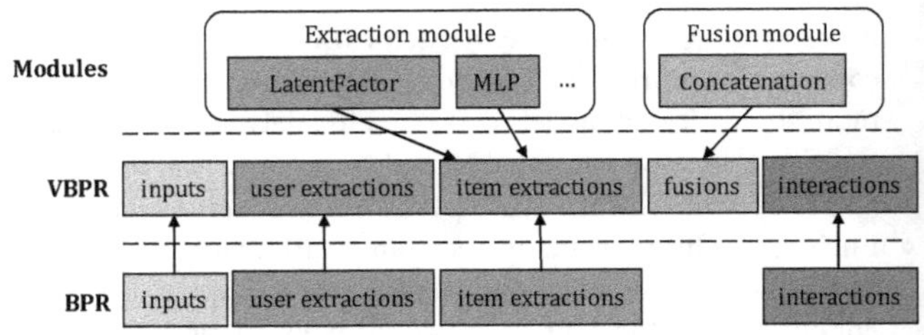

Figure 7: Implementing VBPR with OpenRec (50 lines). We use the same annotations as Fig. 5.

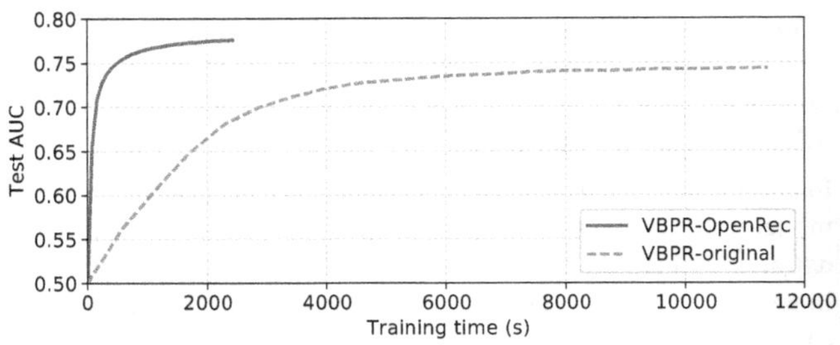

Figure 8: *tradesy.com* dataset [13] testing performance in terms of AUC (VBPR-OpenRec and VBPR-original).

where f_i is the visual feature for item i, and $\mathbf{E}$ is a learnable projection matrix[1].

To build such a model with OpenRec, we can easily extend the BPR recommender and modify the functions *build inputs*, and *build item extractions*. We change the *build item extractions* function from a LF extraction module to a concatenation fusion module that takes as inputs the representations derived from LF and MLP extraction modules, as shown in Fig. 7. At the same time, other functions can be directly reused except adding additional inputs for visual features. We evaluate the VBPR implementation with the same tradesy dataset and computing environment, but set λ_Θ to be 0.1 and the dimensionality of γ and θ to be 10. The items' visual features are extracted using the caffe reference model as released by the He et al. [13].

As shown in Fig. 8, compared to the previous implementation by He et. al. [13], the model implemented by OpenRec is significantly faster (more than 10^3 times) and yields better performance in terms of AUC. The reason for such a phenomenon is that the prior implementation uses a batch size of 1 for the training while OpenRec is able to use much larger mini-batches (batch size is set to 1000) and fully utilize the available hardware resources, e.g. multi-core and GPU, using Tensorflow (We did not use GPU in the experiments for fair comparision). Under the scenario where much auxiliary information is incorporated, the larger batch size brings significant benefits, and OpenRec makes such benefits easily available to the end developers. This example also indicates the need for a benchmarking platform like OpenRec, as directly comparing the performance reported in the literature may be problematic, especially in the cases where some ad-hoc implementation details make significant changes to the recommendation performance.

[1] Compared to the original VBPR, we did not include the visual biases

Table 2: citeulike dataset [31] testing performance in terms of AUC and Recall@K (CDL-OpenRec and CDL-Original).

Implementation	AUC	R@10	R@50	R@100
CDL-OpenRec	0.923	0.107	0.246	0.343
CDL-Original	0.918	0.099	0.248	0.349

5.1.3 Collaborative Deep Learning (CDL). The third algorithm that we explore is Collaborative Deep Learning (CDL), an algorithm built upon the framework of Probabilistic Matrix Factorization (PMF) that uses a de-noising auto-encoder to incorporate text into the recommendations [31]. We refer readers to the original paper [31] for the technical details. Similar to VBPR, CDL can be implemented by extending the PMF recommender, and the extension is analogous to the Fig. 7. We evaluate CDL implementations on the citeulike dataset [31], which contains 5,551 users and 16,980 items and extracts item features using bag-of-words approach. We leverage the same strategy as used in the original paper to split the data into training and testing. The evaluation is conducted under the optimal parameter settings suggested by [31] and on a desktop machine with 8 CPU cores and 16 GB of memory. The performance of each implementation is measured by AUC and Recall@K after convergence. As shown in Table. 2, the results stay consistent with the findings in the previous BPR and VBPR examples - the modular implementation of OpenRec does not degrade the performance and can completely reproduce the results from the original implementations.

5.2 Efficiency: OpenRec as a sandbox for quick prototyping and experimentation

In this section, we show that because of its modular nature, OpenRec can be used as a sandbox for quick designing, prototyping and evaluation in recommendation system research and development. We demonstrate this in the context of building a book recommendation system with rich context and content information, where much information is available from many different channels, including users' purchasing histories, books' content, metadata, user reviews and cover images. Therefore, developers not only need to decide what information to include in the recommender system, but also need to choose appropriate algorithms to analyze data with different modalities. In the rest of this section, we first describe the dataset for experimentation and then show the power of OpenRec in assisting and accelerating such a prototyping process.

5.2.1 Amazon book recommendation dataset. We conduct experiments using an Amazon book recommendation dataset derived from an Amazon review data dump released by [22, 23]. The goal of the system is to recommend books that users are willing to buy. In this experiment, we focus on the utilities of three data sources - users' book purchasing history, users' purchases outside of book category and books' cover images. We include users who have at least 2 purchases in the book category and 5 purchases in non-book categories, which ends up with a dataset containing 99,473 users, 450,166 books and 996,938 purchases. For each user, we derive a **user feature** by taking the bag-of-words representation of the labels for the products purchased in non-book categories. For each book, a **visual feature** is extracted based on the cover image using caffe reference model [19]. We divide the dataset into training/validation/testing by randomly sampling a purchase record for each user for validation and another one for testing.

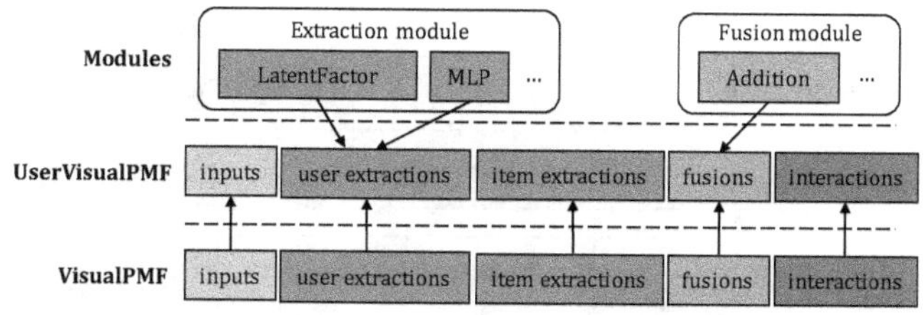

Figure 9: Implementing UserVisualPMF with OpenRec (32 lines). We use the same annotations as Fig. 5.

5.2.2 What information to include? To decide what information to include in the book recommender system, we need to experiment with combinations of the following three data sources: (A) purchasing histories, (B) user features, and (C) visual features - **PMF**(A), **UserPMF**(A+B), **VisualPMF**(A+C), and **UserVisualPMF**(A+B+C). Previously, experimenting on these models required monolithic development for each of them independently, which is a cumbersome and inefficient process. With OpenRec, the UserPMF and VisualPMF are direct extensions of PMF, and the model UserVisualPMF is an extension of UserPMF or VisualPMF. To incorporate users' or items' features, we project them into a low-dimensional embedding space with a multilayer perceptron and treat the outputs as the prior for final representations. In other words, the users' or items' representations are the element-wise addition (fusion) between the projected features and the corresponding latent factors. We implement UserVisualPMF as shown in Fig. 9 (the implementations for VisualPMF and UserPMF are likewise). As the implementation extends most of the functions from VisualPMF and builds additional functions using reusable modules, the overhead of building UserVisualPMF is significantly reduced compared to a monolithic approach. Other fusing strategies such as concatenation are also applicable here, and OpenRec is intuitive in supporting such experiments as well. To compare the performance of these recommender systems, we select the best performed L2 regularization term among $\{0.01, 0.001, 0.0001\}$ using the validation set, and then report the AUC and Recall@K on the testing set. Because of the large number of items, for each user, we randomly sample 1000 items that did not receive any feedback signals to calculate performance metrics.

As shown in Fig. 11a, in terms of AUC, adding visual features or user features significantly improves the recommendation performance, and the best performance is achieved when only visual features are incorporated. However, in terms of Recall@K, the *PMF* model performs relatively well and the *VisualPMF* is able to outperform it when $K \geq 40$. From these results, we can conclude that (1) in general, incorporating auxiliary features is helpful to book recommendations but it does not mean that more features always translate to better performance, and (2) the model selection is contingent on the metric that we want to optimize.

5.2.3 Which algorithm to use? As is studied in the previous experiment, VisualPMF significantly outperforms other systems in terms of AUC. Another interesting question is whether PMF is

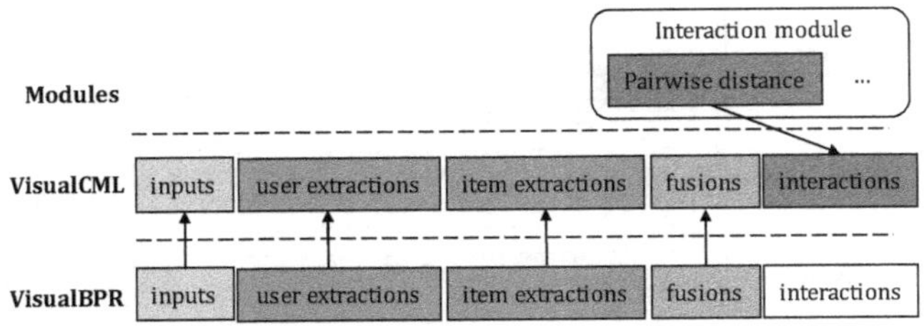

Figure 10: Implementing VisualCML with OpenRec (7 lines). We use the same annotations as Fig. 5. The model and training pseudocode is presented in the Appendix A.

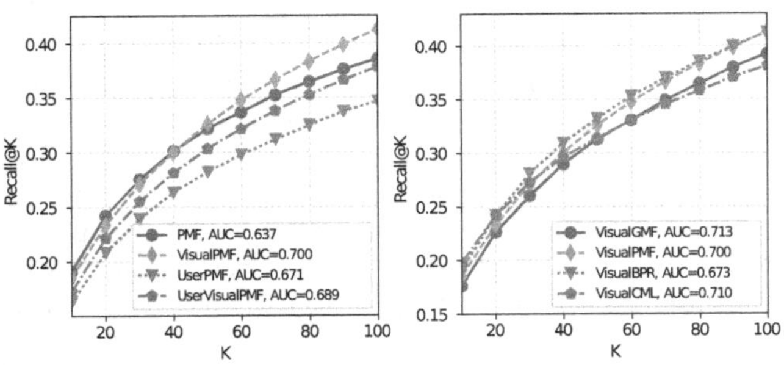

(a) Different levels of complexity. **(b) Different interaction modules.**

Figure 11: Book recommendation testing performance in terms of AUC and Recall@K.

the best collaborative filtering algorithm under such a recommendation context? We can use OpenRec to quickly investigate this question by leveraging different interaction modules and **reusing the rest of the algorithmic components**. Specifically, we show the performance of **VisualPMF**, **VisualBPR**, **VisualGMF** and **VisualCML** in Fig. 11b. The sample implementation of VisualCML is shown in Fig. 10, which demonstrates that OpenRec provides an elegant and efficient way to quickly experiment with alternative system components.

As shown in the Fig. 11b, varying the interaction module does make a difference in recommendation performance, and the best choice of the interaction module is dependent on the metric that we want to optimize. For example, VisualCML performs the best in terms of Recall@10, while VisualGMF achieves the best ranking performance, i.e. AUC.

The above examples also illustrate that there is no clear-cut solution to design a better recommender system. Design decisions involve trade-offs and require careful experimentation and benchmarking. With the modular design of OpenRec, we are able to support such a development process and allow experimentation of different designs with minimal overhead.

5.3 Extensibility: Developing new algorithms by extending existing modules in OpenRec

In this section, we demonstrate how researchers can use OpenRec to develop new recommendation algorithms by directly extending existing modules. Specifically, we develop a light-weight, iterative

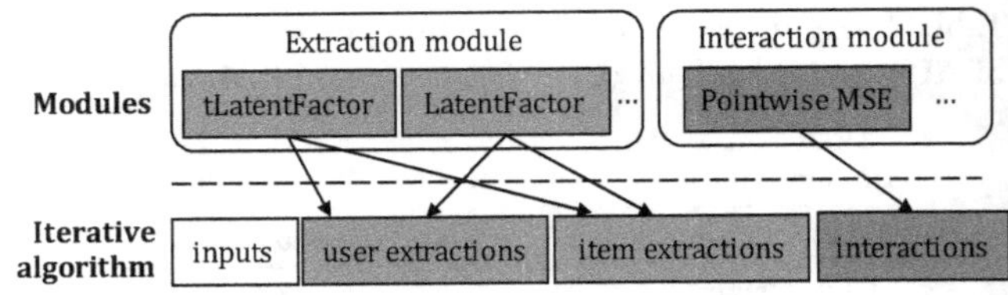

Figure 12: Implementing iterative and temporal model with OpenRec (57 lines). We use the same annotations as Fig. 5.

and temporal recommendation model for movie rating prediction (similar to recent recommendation models [20, 32] that incorporate temporal patterns). We build multi-layer deep neural networks to project user and item vectors from time $t-1$ to t, i.e. $\gamma_u^t = f(\gamma_u^{t-1})$ and $\gamma_i^t = g(\gamma_i^{t-1})$ where f and g are two separate multi-layer perceptrons, and the most recent user and item latent representations are dot-producted to predict the user-item ratings. To develop such a model with previous software frameworks, we would need to build everything from scratch even if there are many existing implementations of matrix factorization and multi-layer perceptrons available. However, using OpenRec, such a temporal model can be built by implementing a new extraction module *tLatentFactor* that executes the transition functions f and g and produces user and item vectors at time t, and directly extending the existing *Pointwise MSE* and *LatentFactor* modules, as Fig. 12 shows. This is possible because of the highly-modular nature of OpenRec. To train the model, we use traditional mean square error as the loss with L2 regularization to drive the optimization. Because OpenRec is built on a Tensorflow backend, benefits such as automatic differentiation are readily available to the developers.

We evaluate our temporal model using the Neflix dataset [3] and compare it to the traditional matrix factorization (MF) implementation from MyMediaLite. We update users' and items' representations daily[2] and validate on each batch before training (Each data point is only used once). The user and item vectors are initialized using MF over the first 3/4 of the dataset (75M ratings). We refer readers to the OpenRec online repo for additional parameter settings. The experimental results demonstrate that our model significantly outperforms the MF baseline by 6% in terms of MSE (0.066 for ours and 0.071 for MF) after only training on 3 days of rating data, which justifies the merits of temporal patterns. Note that our model is not intended to be the state-of-the-art in temporal recommendation but rather as an example of how researchers can easily use OpenRec to explore their ideas.

6 CONCLUSION AND FUTURE WORK

We introduced OpenRec, a modular framework designed to support extensible and adaptable development and research in recommender systems. Through careful experiments and case studies, we demonstrated the value of modularity and reusability. Moving forward, future work will include: standardizing interfaces; building new modules, recommenders, and utility functions (such as NDCG); evaluating models against standard datasets and criteria; and creating modularized models with non-neural network structures (such as random forest).

[2]We only make updates for users and items that have rating during that day.

A VISUALCML OPENREC IMPLEMENTATION

```
from openrec.recommenders import VisualBPR
from openrec.modules.interactions import PairwiseEuDist

class VisualCML(VisualBPR):

    def _build_default_interactions(self, train):
        if train:
            self._interaction_train = PairwiseEuDist(train=True,..)
        else:
            self._interaction_serve = PairwiseEuDist(train=False,..)
```

Listing 1: Pseudocode of an OpenRec implementation for the VisualCML recommender (Section 5.2.3).

```
from openrec import ModelTrainer
from openrec.utils import Dataset
from openrec.recommenders import VisualCML
from openrec.utils.evaluators import AUC
from openrec.utils.samplers import PairwiseSampler

raw_train_data, raw_test_data = load_raw_data()
train_dataset = Dataset(raw_train_data, .., name='Train')
test_dataset = Dataset(raw_test_data, .., name='Test')

model = VisualCML(batch_size=512, ..)
sampler = PairwiseSampler(batch_size=512, dataset=train_dataset)
model_trainer = ModelTrainer(batch_size=512, dataset=train_dataset,
                             model=model, sampler=sampler, ..)
auc_evaluator = AUC()

model_trainer.train(num_itr=1e4, eval_datasets=[test_dataset],
                    evaluators=[auc_evaluator], ..)
```

Listing 2: Pseudocode of training VisualCML with OpenRec.

ACKNOWLEDGMENTS

We would like to sincerely thank the anonymous reviewers for their insightful comments and suggestions. This research is partly funded by Oath through the Connected Experiences Laboratory at Cornel Tech. The work is further supported by the small data lab at Cornell Tech, which receives funding from NSF (#1700832), NIH, RWJF, UnitedHealth Group, Google, and Adobe.

REFERENCES

[1] Martín Abadi, Ashish Agarwal, Paul Barham, Eugene Brevdo, Zhifeng Chen, Craig Citro, Greg S Corrado, Andy Davis, Jeffrey Dean, Matthieu Devin, and others. 2016. Tensorflow: Large-scale machine learning on heterogeneous distributed systems. *arXiv preprint arXiv:1603.04467* (2016).

[2] Linas Baltrunas, Bernd Ludwig, and Francesco Ricci. 2011. Matrix factorization techniques for context aware recommendation. In *Proceedings of the fifth ACM conference on Recommender systems*. ACM, 301–304.

[3] James Bennett, Stan Lanning, and others. 2007. The netflix prize. In *Proceedings of KDD cup and workshop*, Vol. 2007. New York, NY, USA, 35.

[4] Lee Breslau, Deborah Estrin, Kevin Fall, Sally Floyd, John Heidemann, Ahmed Helmy, Polly Huang, Steven McCanne, Kannan Varadhan, Ya Xu, and others. 2000. Advances in network simulation. *Computer* 33, 5 (2000), 59–67.

[5] Denny Britz, Anna Goldie, Thang Luong, and Quoc Le. 2017. Massive Exploration of Neural Machine Translation Architectures. *ArXiv e-prints* (March 2017). arXiv:cs.CL/1703.03906

[6] Simon Chan, Thomas Stone, Kit Pang Szeto, and Ka Hou Chan. 2013. PredictionIO: a distributed machine learning server for practical software development. In *Proceedings of the 22nd ACM international conference on Information & Knowledge Management*. ACM, 2493–2496.

[7] François Chollet and others. 2015. Keras. https://github.com/fchollet/keras. (2015).

[8] Paul Covington, Jay Adams, and Emre Sargin. 2016. Deep neural networks for youtube recommendations. In *Proceedings of the 10th ACM Conference on Recommender Systems*. ACM, 191–198.

[9] Michael D Ekstrand, Michael Ludwig, Joseph A Konstan, and John T Riedl. 2011. Rethinking the recommender research ecosystem: reproducibility, openness, and LensKit. In *Proceedings of the fifth ACM conference on Recommender systems*. ACM, 133–140.

[10] Zeno Gantner, Steffen Rendle, Christoph Freudenthaler, and Lars Schmidt-Thieme. 2011. MyMediaLite: A free recommender system library. In *Proceedings of the fifth ACM conference on Recommender systems*. ACM, 305–308.

[11] Guibing Guo, Jie Zhang, Zhu Sun, and Neil Yorke-Smith. 2015. LibRec: A Java Library for Recommender Systems.. In *UMAP Workshops*.

[12] Ido Guy, Naama Zwerdling, Inbal Ronen, David Carmel, and Erel Uziel. 2010. Social media recommendation based on people and tags. In *Proceedings of the 33rd international ACM SIGIR conference on Research and development in information retrieval*. ACM, 194–201.

[13] Ruining He and Julian McAuley. 2015. VBPR: visual bayesian personalized ranking from implicit feedback. *arXiv preprint arXiv:1510.01784* (2015).

[14] Xiangnan He, Lizi Liao, Hanwang Zhang, Liqiang Nie, Xia Hu, and Tat-Seng Chua. 2017. Neural Collaborative Filtering. In *Proceedings of the 26th International Conference on World Wide Web*. International World Wide Web Conferences Steering Committee.

[15] Cheng-Kang Hsieh, Longqi Yang, Yin Cui, Tsung-Yi Lin, Serge Belongie, and Deborah Estrin. 2017. Collaborative Metric Learning. In *Proceedings of the 26th International Conference on World Wide Web*. International World Wide Web Conferences Steering Committee.

[16] Cheng-Kang Hsieh, Longqi Yang, Honghao Wei, Mor Naaman, and Deborah Estrin. 2016. Immersive Recommendation: News and Event Recommendations Using Personal Digital Traces. In *Proceedings of the 25th International Conference on World Wide Web*. International World Wide Web Conferences Steering Committee, 51–62.

[17] Yifan Hu, Yehuda Koren, and Chris Volinsky. 2008. Collaborative filtering for implicit feedback datasets. In *Data Mining, 2008. ICDM'08. Eighth IEEE International Conference on*. Ieee, 263–272.

[18] Nicolas Hug. 2017. Surprise, a Python library for recommender systems. http://surpriselib.com. (2017).

[19] Yangqing Jia, Evan Shelhamer, Jeff Donahue, Sergey Karayev, Jonathan Long, Ross Girshick, Sergio Guadarrama, and Trevor Darrell. 2014. Caffe: Convolutional architecture for fast feature embedding. In *Proceedings of the 22nd ACM international conference on Multimedia*. ACM, 675–678.

[20] Yehuda Koren. 2010. Collaborative filtering with temporal dynamics. *Commun. ACM* 53, 4 (2010), 89–97.

[21] Greg Linden, Brent Smith, and Jeremy York. 2003. Amazon. com recommendations: Item-to-item collaborative filtering. *IEEE Internet computing* 7, 1 (2003), 76–80.

[22] Julian McAuley, Rahul Pandey, and Jure Leskovec. 2015. Inferring networks of substitutable and complementary products. In *Proceedings of the 21th ACM SIGKDD International Conference on Knowledge Discovery and Data Mining*. ACM, 785–794.

[23] Julian McAuley, Christopher Targett, Qinfeng Shi, and Anton Van Den Hengel. 2015. Image-based recommendations on styles and substitutes. In *Proceedings of the 38th International ACM SIGIR Conference on Research and Development in Information Retrieval*. ACM, 43–52.

[24] Slav Petrov and others. 2016. SyntaxNet. https://github.com/tensorflow/models/tree/master/syntaxnet. (2016).

[25] István Pilászy and Domonkos Tikk. 2009. Recommending new movies: even a few ratings are more valuable than metadata. In *Proceedings of the third ACM conference on Recommender systems*. ACM, 93–100.

[26] Steffen Rendle, Christoph Freudenthaler, Zeno Gantner, and Lars Schmidt-Thieme. 2009. BPR: Bayesian personalized ranking from implicit feedback. In *Proceedings of the twenty-fifth conference on uncertainty in artificial intelligence*. AUAI Press, 452–461.

[27] Ruslan Salakhutdinov and Andriy Mnih. 2007. Probabilistic Matrix Factorization.. In *NIPS*, Vol. 1. 2–1.

[28] Yue Shi, Martha Larson, and Alan Hanjalic. 2014. Collaborative filtering beyond the user-item matrix: A survey of the state of the art and future challenges. *ACM Computing Surveys (CSUR)* 47, 1 (2014), 3.

[29] Apache Spark. 2017. MLlib. https://spark.apache.org/mllib/. (2017).

[30] Aaron Van den Oord, Sander Dieleman, and Benjamin Schrauwen. 2013. Deep content-based music recommendation. In *Advances in neural information processing systems*. 2643–2651.

[31] Hao Wang, Naiyan Wang, and Dit-Yan Yeung. 2015. Collaborative deep learning for recommender systems. In *Proceedings of the 21th ACM SIGKDD International Conference on Knowledge Discovery and Data Mining*. ACM, 1235–1244.

[32] Chao-Yuan Wu, Amr Ahmed, Alex Beutel, Alexander J Smola, and How Jing. 2017. Recurrent recommender networks. In *Proceedings of the Tenth ACM International Conference on Web Search and Data Mining*. ACM, 495–503.

[33] Longqi Yang, Chen Fang, Hailin Jin, Matt Hoffman, and Deborah Estrin. 2017. Personalizing Software and Web Services by Integrating Unstructured Application Usage Traces. In *Proceedings of the 26th International Conference on World Wide Web*. International World Wide Web Conferences Steering Committee.

[34] Longqi Yang, Cheng-Kang Hsieh, Hongjian Yang, John P Pollak, Nicola Dell, Serge Belongie, Curtis Cole, and Deborah Estrin. 2017. Yum-me: a personalized nutrient-based meal recommender system. *ACM Transactions on Information Systems (TOIS)* 36, 1 (2017), 7.

Dynamic Word Embeddings for Evolving Semantic Discovery

Zijun Yao
Rutgers University
zijun.yao@rutgers.edu

Yifan Sun
Technicolor Research
yifan.sun@technicolor.com

Weicong Ding
Amazon
20008005dwc@gmail.com

Nikhil Rao
Amazon
nikhilrao86@gmail.com

Hui Xiong
Rutgers University
hxiong@rutgers.edu

ABSTRACT

Word evolution refers to the changing meanings and associations of words throughout time, as a byproduct of human language evolution. By studying word evolution, we can infer social trends and language constructs over different periods of human history. However, traditional techniques such as word representation learning do not adequately capture the evolving language structure and vocabulary. In this paper, we develop a dynamic statistical model to learn time-aware word vector representation. We propose a model that simultaneously learns time-aware embeddings and solves the resulting "alignment problem". This model is trained on a crawled NYTimes dataset. Additionally, we develop multiple intuitive evaluation strategies of temporal word embeddings. Our qualitative and quantitative tests indicate that our method not only reliably captures this evolution over time, but also consistently outperforms state-of-the-art temporal embedding approaches on both semantic accuracy and alignment quality.

ACM Reference Format:
Zijun Yao, Yifan Sun, Weicong Ding, Nikhil Rao, and Hui Xiong. 2018. Dynamic Word Embeddings for Evolving Semantic Discovery. In *WSDM 2018: The Eleventh ACM International Conference on Web Search and Data Mining, February 5–9, 2018, Marina Del Rey, CA, USA.* ACM, New York, NY, USA, 9 pages. https://doi.org/10.1145/3159652.3159703

1 INTRODUCTION

Human language is an evolving construct, with word semantic associations changing over time. For example, `apple` which was traditionally only associated with fruits, is now also associated with a technology company. Similarly, the association of names of famous personalities (*e.g.*, `trump`) changes with a change in their roles. For this reason, understanding and tracking word evolution is useful for time-aware knowledge extraction tasks (*e.g.*, public sentiment analysis), and other applications in text mining. To this end, we aim to learn word embeddings with a temporal bent, for capturing time-aware meanings of words.

Word embeddings aim to represent words with low-dimensional vectors, where words with similar semantics are geometrically closer (*e.g.* `red` and `blue` are closer than `red` and `squirrel`). Classic word embedding techniques started in the 90s and relied on statistical approaches [9, 20]. Later, neural network approaches [5] as well as recent advances such as word2vec [24, 25] and GloVE [27] have greatly improved the performance of word representation learning. However, these techniques usually do not consider temporal factors, and assume that the word is static across time.

In this paper, we are interested in computing time-aware embedding of words. Specifically, each word in a different time frame (*e.g.* years) is represented by a different vector. From these embeddings, we have a better notion of "distance" (the cosine distance between word embedding vectors), and by looking at word "neighborhoods" (defined through this distance), we can better understand word associations as well as word meanings, as they evolve over time.

For instance, by locating the embeddings of personality names such as `trump`'s closest words, we can see that he can be associated with the trajectory : `real estate` → `television` → `republican`. Similarly, the trajectory of `apple` travels from the neighborhood of `strawberry, mango` to that of `iphone, ipad`.

A key practical issue of learning different word embeddings for different time periods is alignment. Specifically, most cost functions for training are invariant to rotations, as a byproduct, the learned embeddings across time may not be placed in the same latent space. We call this the *alignment* problem, which is an issue in general if embeddings are learned independently for each time slice.

Unlike traditional methods, literature on learning temporal word embedding is relatively short: [12, 15, 19, 40]. In general, the approaches in these works follow a similar two-step pattern: first compute static word embeddings in each time slice separately, then find a way to align the word embeddings across time slices. To achieve alignment, [15] finds a linear transformation of words between any two time slices by solving a d-dimensional least squares problem of k nearest neighbor words (where d is the embedding dimension). Additionally, [40] also use the linear transformation approach between a base and target time slices, and computes the linear transformation using anchor words, which does not change meaning between the two time slices. This method requires the prior knowledge of words that are in fact static, which involves additional expert supervision. Finally, [12] imposes the transformation to be orthogonal, and solves a d-dimensional Procrustes problem between every two adjacent time slices.

Our main novelty in this paper is to learn the word embeddings across time jointly, thus obviating the need to solve a separate alignment problem. Specifically, we propose to learn temporal embeddings in all time slices concurrently, and apply regularization

WSDM 2018, February 5–9, 2018, Marina Del Rey, CA, USA

ACM ISBN 978-1-4503-5581-0/18/02...$15.00
https://doi.org/10.1145/3159652.3159703

erms to smooth embedding changes across time. There are three nain advantages to this proposed joint modeling approach:

- First, this can be seen as an improvement over traditional, "single-time" methods such as word2vec.
- Second, our experimental results suggest that enforcing alignment through regularization yields better results than two-step methods.
- Third, we can share information across time slices for the majority of vocabulary. As a result, our method is robust against data sparsity – we can afford to have time slices where some words are rarely present, or even missing. This is a crucial practical advantage offered by our method.

Since our model requires embeddings across all time slices to be earned at the same time, it can be computationally challenging. To nitigate this, we employ a block coordinate descent method which an handle large vocabulary sizes through decomposition.

In experimental study, we learn temporal embeddings of words rom The New York Times articles between 1990 and 2016. In conrast, previous temporal word embedding works have focused on ime-stamped novels and magazine collections (such as Google J-Gram and COHA). However, news corpora are naturally advanageous to studying language evolution through the lens of current vents. In addition, it allows us to work with a corpus that mainains consistency in narrative style and grammar, as opposed to 'acebook and Twitter posts. For evaluating our embeddings, we levelop both qualitative and quantitative metrics.

Qualitatively, we illustrate the advantages of temporal embedlings for evolving semantics discovery by 1) plotting word vector rajectories to find evolving meanings and associations, 2) using lignment through time to identify associated words across time, nd 3) looking at norms as a representative of concept popularity.

Quantitatively, we first use semantic topics extracted from Secions (*e.g., Technology, World News*) of news articles as ground truth o evaluate the semantic accuracy of temporal embeddings. Addiionally, we provide two testsets to evaluate cross-time alignment uality: one consists of known changing roles (*e.g.,* U.S. presidents), letermined objectively, and one of concept replacements (*e.g.,* comact disk to mp3), determined more subjectively. The experimental esults show the effectiveness of our proposed model and demontrate substantial improvements against baseline methods.

The rest of this paper is organized as follows. In Section 2, we resent the proposed model for temporal embedding learning, and n Section 3, we describe a scalable algorithm to train it. In Secion 4, we describe the news corpus dataset and setup details of xperiments. We perform qualitative evaluations in Section 5. Fially, we quantitatively compare our embeddings against other tate-of-the-art temporal embeddings in Section 6.

2 METHODOLOGY

Ve now set up our temporal word embedding model. We consider text corpus collected across time. These kinds of corpora such s news article collections with published dates or social media liscussion with time-stamps are ubiquitous. Formally, we denote y $\mathcal{D} = (\mathcal{D}_1, \ldots, \mathcal{D}_T)$ our text corpus where each $\mathcal{D}_t$, $t = 1, \ldots T$, s the corpus of all documents in the t-th time slice. Without loss of enerality, we assume the time slices are ordered chronologically. The length of these time slices can be on the order of months, years, or decades. Moreover, the length of all the time slices could be different. We consider an overall vocabulary $\mathcal{V} = \{w_1, \ldots, w_V\}$ of size V. We note that the vocabulary $\mathcal{V}$ consists of words present in the corpus at any point in time, and thus it is possible for some $w \in \mathcal{V}$ to not appear at all in some $\mathcal{D}_t$. This includes emerging words and dying words that are typical in real-world news corpora.

Given such a time-tagged corpus, our goal is to find a dense, low-dimensional vector representation $u_w(t) \in \mathbb{R}^d$, $d \ll V$ for each word $w \in \mathcal{V}$ and each time period $t = 1, \ldots, T$. We denote by u_w the static embedding for word w (for example, learned via word2vec), and d is the embedding dimension (typically $50 \leq d \leq 200$). Compactly, we denote by $U(t)$ (of size $V \times d$) the embedding matrix of all words whose i-th row corresponds to the embedding vector of i-th word $u_{w_i}(t)$.

2.1 Time-agnostic word embeddings

A fundamental observation in static word embedding literature is that semantically similar words often have similar neighboring words in a corpus [10]. This is the idea behind learning dense low-dimensional word representations both traditionally [5, 9, 20] and recently [24, 27]. In several of these methods, the neighboring structure is captured by the frequencies by which pairs of words co-occur within a small local window.

We compute the $V \times V$ pointwise mutual information (PMI) matrix specific to a corpus $\mathcal{D}$, whose w, c-th entry is:

$$\mathrm{PMI}(\mathcal{D}, L)_{w,c} = \log \left(\frac{\#(w,c) \cdot |\mathcal{D}|}{\#(w) \cdot \#(c)} \right), \tag{1}$$

where $\#(w, c)$ counts the number of times that words w and c co-occur within a window of size L in corpus $\mathcal{D}$, and $\#(w)$, $\#(c)$ counts the number of occurrences of words w and c in $\mathcal{D}$. $|\mathcal{D}|$ is total number of word tokens in the corpus. L is typically around 5 to 10; we set $L = 5$ throughout this paper.

The key idea behind both word2vec [24] and GloVE [27] is to find embedding vectors u_w and u_c such that for any w, c combination,

$$u_w^T u_c \approx \mathrm{PMI}(\mathcal{D}, L)_{w,c}, \tag{2}$$

where each u_w has length $d \ll V$. While both [24] and [27] offer highly scalable algorithms such as negative sampling to do this implicitly, [17] shows that these are equivalent to low-rank factorization of $\mathrm{PMI}(\mathcal{D}, L)$ [1]. Our approach is primarily motivated by this observation. We note that though the PMI matrices are of size $V \times V$, in real-world datasets it is typically sparse as observed in [27], for which efficient factorization methods exist [39].

2.2 Temporal word embeddings

A natural extension of the static word embedding intuition is to use this matrix factorization technique on each time slice $\mathcal{D}_t$ separately. Specifically, for each time slice t, we define the w, c-th entry of *positive* PMI matrix ($\mathrm{PPMI}(t, L)$) as [2]

$$\mathrm{PPMI}(t, L)_{w,c} = \max\{\mathrm{PMI}(\mathcal{D}_t, L)_{w,c}, 0\}. := Y(t). \tag{3}$$

[1] with a constant shift that can be zero.

[2] We consider the PPMI rather than the PMI because when $\frac{\#(w,c)\cdot|\mathcal{D}|}{\#(w)\cdot\#(c)}$ is very small, taking the log results in large negative values and is thus extremely unstable. Since for most significantly related pairs w and c the log argument is > 1, thresholding it in this way will not affect the solution significantly, but will offer much better numerical stability. This approach is not unique to us; [17] also factorizes the PPMI.

The temporal word embeddings $U(t)$ must satisfy

$$U(t)U(t)^T \approx \text{PPMI}(t, L). \tag{4}$$

One way to find such $U(t)$ is for each t, factorizing PPMI(t, L) by either using an eigenvalue method or solving a matrix factorization problem iteratively.

The Alignment Problem: Imposing (4) is not sufficient for a unique embedding, since the solutions are invariant under rotation; that is, for any $d \times d$ orthogonal matrix R, we have the embedding $\widehat{U}(t) = U(t)R$, the approximation error in (4) is the same since

$$\widehat{U}(t)\widehat{U}(t)^T = U(t)RR^TU(t)^T = U(t)U(t)^T.$$

For this reason, it is important to enforce *alignment*; if word w did not semantically shift from t to $t+1$, then we additionally require $u_w(t) \approx u_w(t+1)$.

To do this, [12, 15] propose two-step procedures; first, they factorize each $Y(t)$ separately, and afterwards enforce alignment using local linear mapping [15] or solving an orthogonal procrustes problem [12]. Note that in these methods, aligning $U(t)$ to $U(t')$ assumes that we desire $U(t) \approx U(t')$. If we only pick $t' = t+1$ (as done in [12]), this assumption is reasonable because between any two years, only a few words experience semantic shift, emergence, or death. However, this becomes problematic if $U(t)$ was a result of a time period with extremely sparse data (and hence poorly learned); all subsequent year embeddings and previous year embeddings will be poorly aligned.

2.3 Our model

We propose finding temporal word embeddings as the solution of the following joint optimization problem:

$$\min_{U(1),\dots,U(T)} \frac{1}{2}\sum_{t=1}^{T}\|Y(t) - U(t)U(t)^T\|_F^2 + \frac{\lambda}{2}\sum_{t=1}^{T}\|U(t)\|_F^2 + \frac{\tau}{2}\sum_{t=2}^{T}\|U(t-1) - U(t)\|_F^2, \tag{5}$$

where $Y(t) = \text{PPMI}(t, L)$ and $\lambda, \tau > 0$. Here the penalty term $\|U(t)\|_F^2$ enforces the low-rank data-fidelity as widely adopted in previous literature. The key smoothing term $\|U(t-1) - U(t)\|_F^2$ encourages the word embeddings to be aligned. The parameter τ controls how fast we allow the embeddings to change; $\tau = 0$ enforces no alignment, and picking $\tau \to \infty$ converges to a static embedding with $U(1) = U(2) = \ldots = U(T)$. Note that the methods of [12, 15] can be viewed as suboptimal solutions of (5), in that they optimize for each term separately. For one, while the strategies in [15] and [12] enforce alignment pairwise, we enforce alignment across *all* time slices; that is, the final aligned solution $U(t)$ is influenced by not only $U(t-1)$ and $U(t+1)$, but every other embedding as well. This avoids the propagation of alignment errors caused by a specific time frame's subsampling. Additionally, consider an extreme case in which word w is absent from $\mathcal{D}_t$ but has similar meaning in both $t-1$ and $t+1$. Directly applying any matrix factorization technique to each time point would enforce $u_w(t) \approx \mathbf{0}$. However, for the right choice of τ, the solution $u_w(t)$ to (5) will be close to $u_w(t-1)$ and $u_w(t+1)$. Overall, our method achieves high fidelity embeddings with a much smaller corpus, and in particular, in Section 6, we demonstrate that our embeddings are robust against sudden undersampling of specific time slices.

3 OPTIMIZATION

A key challenge in solving (5) is that for large V and T, one might not be able to fit all the PPMI matrices $Y(1), \dots, Y(T)$ in memory, even though $Y(t)$ is sparse. Therefore, for scalability, an obvious solution is to first decompose the objective across time, using alternating minimization to solve for $U(t)$ at each step:

$$\min_{U(t)} \overbrace{\frac{1}{2}\|Y(t) - U(t)U(t)^T\|_F^2}^{f(U(t))} + \frac{\lambda}{2}\|U(t)\|_F^2 + \frac{\tau}{2}\left(\|U(t-1) - U(t)\|_F^2 + \|U(t) - U(t+1)\|_F^2\right) \tag{6}$$

for a specific t. Note that $f(U(t))$ is quartic in $U(t)$, and thus even if we only solve for a fixed t, (6) cannot be minimized analytically. Thus, our only option is to solve (6) iteratively using a fast first order method such as gradient descent. The gradient of the first term alone is given by

$$\nabla f(U(t)) = -2Y(t)U(t) + 2U(t)U(t)^TU(t). \tag{7}$$

Each gradient computation is of the order $O(nnz(Y(t))d + d^2V)$ (which is then nested in iteratively optimizing $U(t)$ for each t).[3] In practical applications, V is in the order of ten-thousands to hundred-thousands, and T is in the order of tens to hundreds.

Let us instead look at a slightly relaxed problem of minimizing

$$\min_{U(t),W(t)} \frac{1}{2}\sum_{t=1}^{T}\|Y(t) - U(t)W(t)^T\|_F^2 + \frac{\gamma}{2}\sum_{t=1}^{T}\|U(t) - W(t)\|_F^2 + \frac{\lambda}{2}\sum_{t=1}^{T}\|U(t)\|_F^2 + \frac{\tau}{2}\sum_{t=2}^{T}\|U(t-1) - U(t)\|_F^2 + \frac{\lambda}{2}\sum_{t=1}^{T}\|W(t)\|_F^2 + \frac{\tau}{2}\sum_{t=2}^{T}\|W(t-1) - W(t)\|_F^2, \tag{8}$$

where variables $W(t), t = 1, \dots, T$ are introduced to break the symmetry of factorizing $Y(t)$. Now, minimizing for each $U(t)$ (and equivalently $W(t)$) is just the solution of a ridge regression problem and can be solved in one step by setting the gradient of the objective of (8) to 0, *i.e.* $U(t)A = B$ where

$$A = W(t)^TW(t) + (\gamma + \lambda + 2\tau)I,$$

$$B = Y(t)W(t) + \gamma W(t) + \tau(U(t-1) + U(t+1))$$

for $t = 2, \dots, T-1$, and constants adjusted for $t = 0, T$. Forming A and B requires $O(Vd^2 + nnz(Y(t))d)$, and solving $U(t)A = B$ can be done in $O(d^3)$ computations, in one step. This can be further decomposed to row-by-row blocks of size b, by minimizing over a row block of $U(t)$ at a time, which reduces the complexity of forming A and B to $O(bd^2 + nnz(Y(t)[:b,:])d)$, *i.e.*independent of V. This allows scaling for very large V, as only one row block of $Y(t)$ must be loaded at a time.

Block coordinate descent vs. stochastic gradient descent: The method described here is commonly referred to as *block coordinate descent (BCD)* because it minimizes with respect to a single block ($U(t)$ or $W(t)$) at a time, and the block size can be made even smaller (a few rows of $U(t)$ or $W(t)$) to maintain scalability. The main appeal of BCD is scalability [39]; however, a main drawback is lack of convergence guarantees, even in the case of convex optimization [29]

[3] $nnz(\cdot)$ is the number of nonzeros in the matrix.

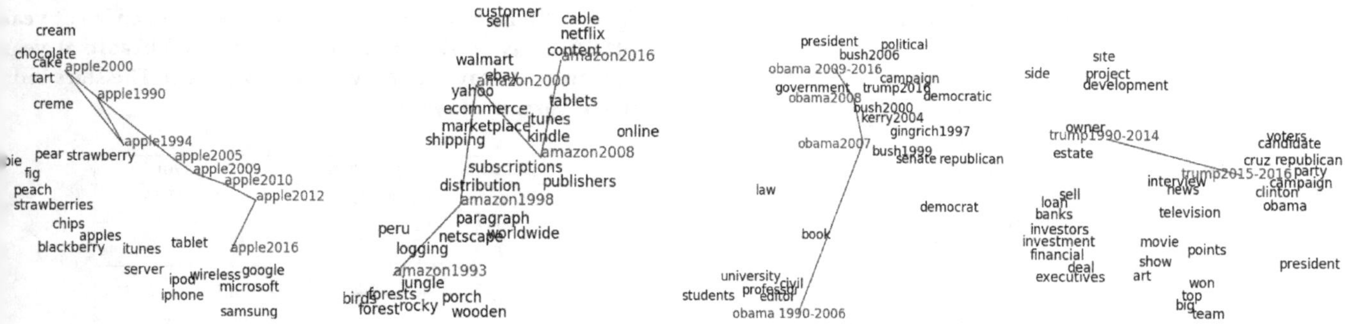

(a) apple (b) amazon (c) obama (d) trump

Figure 1: Trajectories of brand names and people through time: apple, amazon, obama, and trump.

In practice, however, BCD is highly successful and has been used in many applications [38]. Another choice of optimization is stochastic gradient descent (SGD), which decomposes the *objective* as a sum of smaller terms. For example, the first term of (8) can be written as a sum of terms, each using only one row of $Y(t)$:

$$f(U(t)) = \sum_{i=1}^{V} \|Y(t)[i,:] - u_i(t)^T W(t)\|_F^2. \tag{9}$$

The complexity at first glance is smaller than that of BCD; however, SGD comes with the well-documented issues of slow progress and hard-to-tune step sizes, and in practice, can be much slower for matrix factorization applications [30, 39]. However, we point out that the choice of the optimization method is agnostic to our model; anything that successfully solves (5) should lead to an equally successful embedding.

4 EXPERIMENTAL DATASET AND SETUP

In this section we describe the specific procedure used to generate embeddings for the next two sections.

News article dataset: First, we crawl a total of 99,872 articles from the New York Times, published between January 1990 and July 2016.[4] In addition to the text, we also collected metadata including title, author, release date, and section label (*e.g.*, Business, Sports, Technology); in total, there are 59 such sections. We use yearly time slices, dividing the corpus into $T = 27$ partitions. After removing rare words (fewer than 200 occurrences in all articles across time) and stop words, our vocabulary consists of $V = 20,936$ unique words. We then compute a co-occurrence matrix for each time slice t with a window size $L = 5$, which is then used to compute the PPMI matrix as outlined in (3). All the embedding methods that we compared against are trained on this same dataset.

Training details for our algorithm: We perform a grid search to find the best regularization and optimization parameters. As a result of our search, we obtain $\lambda = 10$, $\tau = \gamma = 50$, and run for 5 epochs (5 complete pass over all time slices, and all rows and columns of $Y(t)$). Interestingly, setting $\lambda = 0$ also yielded good results, but required more iterations to converge. The block variable is one matrix ($U(t)$ or $V(t)$ for a specific t).

Distance metric: All distances between two words are calculated by the cosine similarity between embedding vectors:

$$\text{similarity}(a, b) = \text{cosine}(u_a, u_b) = \frac{u_a^T u_b}{\|u_a\|_2 \cdot \|u_b\|_2}, \tag{10}$$

where u_a and u_b are the embeddings of words a and b.

5 QUALITATIVE EVALUATION

The embeddings we learn reveal interesting patterns in the shift of word semantics, cross-time semantic analogy, and popularity trends of concepts from the news corpus.

5.1 Trajectory visualization

The trajectory of a word in the (properly aligned) embedded space provides tools to understand the shift in meanings of words over time. This can help broader applications, such as capturing and quantifying linguistic evolution, characterizing brands and people, and analyzing emerging association between certain words.

Figure 1 shows the trajectories of a set of example words. We plot the 2-D t-SNE projection of each word's temporal embedding across time. We also plot the closest words to the target word from each time slice. We pick four words of interest: apple and amazon as emerging corporate names while originally referring to a fruit and a rainforest, and obama and trump as people with changing professional roles.

In all cases, the embeddings illustrate significant semantic shifts of the words of interest during this 27-year time frame. We see apple shift from a fruit and dessert ingredient to space of technology. Interestingly, there is a spike in 1994 in the trajectory, when Apple led a short tide of discussion because of the replacement of the CEO and a collaboration with IBM; then the association shifted back to neighborhood of fruit and dessert until the recovery by Steve Jobs in early 2000s. Similarly, amazon shifts from a forest to an e-commerce company, finally landing in 2016 as a content creation and online-streaming provider due to the popularity of its Prime Video service. The US president names, obama and trump, are most telling, shifting from their pre-presidential lives (Obama as a civil rights attorney and university professor; Trump as a real estate developer and TV celebrity) to the political sphere. Overall, Figure 1 demonstrates that first, our temporal word embeddings can well capture the semantic shifts of words across time, and second, our model provides high alignment quality in that same-meaning words across different years have geometrically close embeddings, without having to solve a separate optimization problem for alignment.

[4] The data is available at: https://sites.google.com/site/zijunyaorutgers/.

Table 1: Equivalent technologies through time: iphone, twitter, and mp3.

Query	iphone, 2012	twitter, 2012	mp3, 2000
90-94	desktop, pc, dos, macintosh, software	broadcast, cnn, bulletin, tv, radio, messages, correspondents	stereo, disk, disks, audio
95-96			mp3
97		chat, messages, emails, web	
98-02			
03	pc		napster
04			mp3
05-06	ipod	blog, posted	itunes, downloaded
07-08	iphone		
09-12		twitter	
13-16	smartphone, iphone		

5.2 Equivalence searching

Another key advantage of word alignment is the ability to find conceptually "equivalent" items or people over time. We provide examples in the field of technology, official roles, and sports professionals. In this type of test, we create a query consisting of a word-year pair that is particularly the representative of that word in that year, and look for other word-year pairs in its vicinity, for different years.

Table 1 lists the closest words (*top*-1) of each year to the query vector. For visualization purpose we lump semantically similar words together. For example, the first column shows that iphone in 2012 is closely associated with smartphones in recent years, but is close to words such as desktop and macintosh in the 90's; interestingly, telephone never appears, suggesting the iPhone serves people more as a portable computer than a calling device. As another example, by looking at the trajectory of twitter, we see the evolution of news sources, from TV & radio news broadcasts in the 90s to chatrooms, websites, and emails in the early 2000s, blogs in the late 2000s, and finally tweets today. The last example is fairly obvious; mp3 represents the main form of which music is consumed in 2000, replacing disk and stereo in 1990s (cassette also appears in *top*-3) and is later replaced by online streaming. We can see a one-year spike of Napster which was shut down because of copyright infringement[5], and later a new streaming service - iTunes.

Next, we use embeddings to identify people in political roles. Table 2 attempts to discover who is the U.S. president[6] and New York City mayor[7] of the time, using as query obama in 2016 and blasio in 2015. For president, only the closest word from each year is listed, and is always correct (accounting for the election years). For mayor, the top-1 closet word is shown unless it is mayor, in which case the second word is shown. We can see that both the roles of US president and NYC mayor have been well searched for different persons in their terms of service. We see that the embedding for the President is consistent, and for the most part, so is that of the mayor of NYC. In 2011, cuomo is also partially relevant since he was the governor of NY state. We did not find any relevant words in query NYC mayor in year 2006.

Finally, we search for equivalences in sports, repeating the experiment for the ATP rank 1 male tennis player as shown in Table 3. In the case of president and mayor, we are heavily assisted by the fact that they are commonly referred to by a title: "President Obama" and "Mayor de Blasio". Tennis champions, on the other hand, are not referred by titles. Still, a surprising number of correct champions appear as the closest words, and all the names are those of famous tennis players for the given time period. A more exhaustive empirical study of alignment quality is provided in Section 6.

[5]Napster ended its streaming service in 2001, so our equivalence is captured 2 years late; this delay could be because though the event happened in 2001, the legal ramifications were analyzed heavily in subsequent years.

[6]All data was scraped about half a year before Donald Trump was elected as U.S. president in 2016.

[7]We intentionally choose New York City because it is the most heavily discussed city in the New York Times.

Table 2: "Who governed?" The closest word to obama at year 2016 (role as president of United State) and blasio at year 2015 (role as mayor of New York City (NYC)). The stars indicate incorrect answers.

Question	US president	NYC mayor
Query	obama, 2016	blasio, 2015
90-92	bush	dinkins
93	clinton	
94-00		giuliani
01	bush	
02-05		bloomberg
06		n/a*
07		bloomberg
08		
09-10	obama	
11		cuomo*
12		bloomberg
13-16		blasio

Table 3: "Who was the ATP No.1 ranked male player?" The closest word to nadal at year 2010 for each year is listed. The correct answer is based on ATP year-end ranking and are bolded in the table.

year	1990	1991	1992	1993
word	**edberg**	lendl	sampras	**sampras**
1994	1995	1996	1997	1998
sampras	**sampras**	ivanisevic	**sampras**	**sampras**
1999	2000	2001	2002	2003
sampras	sampras	agassi	capriati	**roddick**
2004	2005	2006	2007	2008
federer	**federer**	roddick	**federer**	**nadal**
2009	2010	2011	2012	2013
federer	**nadal**	**djokovic**	federer	federer
2014	2015			
federer	**djokovic**			

5.3 Popularity determination

It has often been observed that word embeddings computed by factorizing PMI matrices have norms that grow with word frequency [2, 27]. These word vector norms across time can be viewed as a

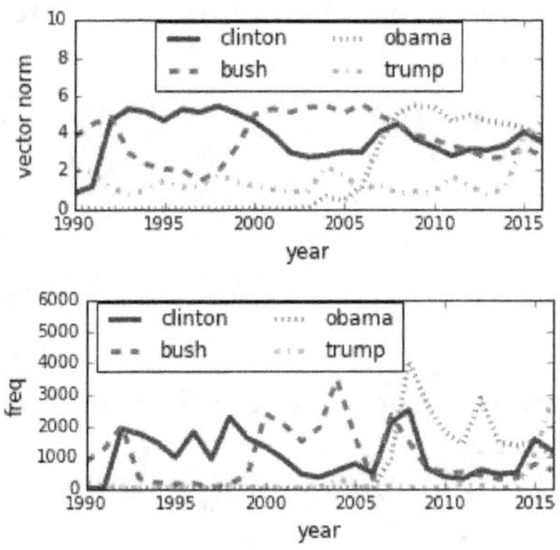

'igure 2: Norm (top) and relative frequency (bottom) hroughout years 1990-2016. We select the names of U.S presdents within this time frame - `clinton`, `bush`, `obama`, and rump. We note that `bush` could refer to George H. W. Bush 1989-1993) or George W. Bush (2001-2009). Clinton could reer to Bill Clinton (1993-2001) or Hillary Clinton (U.S. secreary of state in 2009-2013 and U.S. presidential candidate in :014-2016).

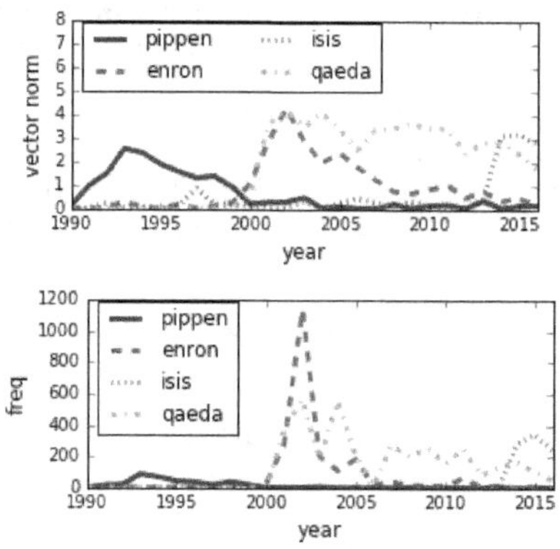

Figure 3: Norm (top) and relative frequency (bottom) per year in corpus of major event keywords: `pippen` for basketball stardom, `enron` for corporation scandal, `qaeda` and `isis` for emerging terrorism groups.

ime series for detecting the trending concepts (*e.g.*, sudden semanic shifts or emergences) behind words, with more robustness than vord frequency.

Figures 2 and 3 illustrate the comparison between embedding orm and frequency for determining *concept* popularity per year, etermined by key words in the New York Times corpus. Generally, omparing to frequencies which are much more sporadic and noisy, ve note that the norm of our embeddings encourages smoothness nd normalization while being indicative of the periods when the orresponding words were making news rounds. In Figure 2, the mbedding norms display nearly even 4-year humps corresponding o each president's term. In every term, the name of each current resident becomes a trending concept which plays an important ole in the information structure at the time. Two interesting obervations can be gleaned. First, since Hillary Clinton continuously erved as Secretary of State during 2009-2013, the popularity of `:linton` was preserved; however it was still not as popular as presdent `obama`. Second, because of the presidential campaign, `trump` n 2016 has a rising popularity that greatly surpasses that of his forner role as a business man, and eventually surpasses his opponent `.linton` in terms of news coverage.

In Figure 3, we can see smooth rises and falls of temporary phenomena (the `enron` scandal and `qaeda` rises). For `qaeda`, we see hat there is a jump in 2001, and then it remains steady with a mall decline. In contrast, `enron` shows a sharper decline, as despite ts temporal hype, it did not linger in the news long. Note also he stability of using norms to track popularity over frequency, vhich spikes for `enron` above `qaeda`, although 9/11 was far more news-prevalent than the corporation's scandalous decline. For the basketball star `pippen`, although his publicity (*e.g.*, frequency) was elatively fewer than business terms, his popularity is still recognized by the enhancement in vector norm. For another term `isis`, ve can see that it begins to replace `qaeda` as the "trending terrorist rganization" in news media.

6 QUANTITATIVE EVALUATION

In this section, we empirically evaluate our proposed Dynamic Word2Vec model (DW2V) against other temporal word embedding methods.[8] In all cases, we set the embedding dimension to $d = 50$. We have the following baselines:

- **Static-Word2Vec (SW2V)**: the standard word2vec embeddings [25], trained on the entire corpus and ignoring time information.
- **Transformed-Word2Vec (TW2V) [15]**: the embeddings $U(t)$ are first trained separately by factorizing PPMI matrix for each year t, and then transformed by optimizing a linear transformation matrix which minimizes the distance between $u_w(t)$ and $u_w(t')$ for the $k = 30$ nearest words' embeddings to the querying word w.
- **Aligned-Word2Vec (AW2V) [12]**: the embeddings $U(t)$ are first trained by factorizing the PPMI matrix for each year t, and then aligned by searching for the best othornormal transformation between $U(t)$ and $U(t+1)$.

6.1 Semantic similarity

One of the most important properties of a word embedding is how accurately it carries the meaning of words. Therefore, we develop a test to see if words can be categorized by meaning based on embeddings. The news articles we collected are tagged with their "sections" such as *Business*, *Sports*. This information can be used to determine temporal word meanings. It is important to note that this information is not used in the word embedding learning. For example, we see that `amazon` occurs 41% of the time in *World* in 1995, associating strongly with the rainforest (not part of the USA), and 50% of the time in *Technology* in 2012, associating strongly with e-commerce. We thus use this to establish a ground truth of word category, by identifying words in years that are exceptionally numerous in one particular news section. That is, if a word is extremely frequent in a particular section, we associate that word with that section and use that as ground truth. We select the 11

[8] The testsets are available at: https://sites.google.com/site/zijunyaorutgers/.

Table 4: Normailized Mutual Information (NMI).

Method	10 Clusters	15 Clusters	20 Clusters
SW2V	0.6736	0.6867	0.6713
TW2V	0.5175	0.5221	0.5130
AW2V	0.6580	0.6618	0.6386
DW2V	**0.7175**	**0.7162**	**0.6906**

Table 5: F-measure (F_β).

Method	10 Clusters	15 Clusters	20 Clusters
SW2V	0.6163	0.7147	0.7214
TW2V	0.4584	0.5072	0.5373
AW2V	0.6530	0.7115	0.7187
DW2V	**0.6949**	**0.7515**	**0.7585**

most popular and discriminative sections[9] of the New York Times, and for each section s and each word w in year t, we compute its percentage p of occurrences in each section. To avoid duplicated word-time-section $< w, t, s >$ triplets, for a particular w and s we only keep the year of the largest strength, and additionally filter away any triplet with strength less than $p = 35\%$. Note that a random uniform distribution of words would result in it appearing about 9% of the time in each section, and our threshold is about 4 times that quantity. We do this to say with sufficient confidence that such associations can be treated as ground truth.

To limit the size differences among categories, for every section s with more than 200 qualified triplets, we keep the *top*-200 words by strength. In total, this results in 1888 triplets across 11 sections, where every word-year pair is strongly associated with a section as its true category.

We then apply spherical k-means, which uses cosine similarity between embeddings as the distance function for clustering, with $K = 10$, 15, and 20 clusters. We use two metrics to evaluate the clustering results:

- *Normalized Mutual Information (NMI)*, defined as

$$NMI(L, C) = \frac{I(L; C)}{[H(L) + H(C)]/2}, \tag{11}$$

where L represents the set of labels and C the set of clusters. $I(L; C)$ denotes the sum of mutual information between any cluster c_i and any label l_j, and $H(L)$ and $H(C)$ the entropy for labels and clusters, respectively. This metric evaluates the purity of clustering results from an information-theoretic perspective.

- *F_β-measure* ($\mathbf{F}_\beta$), defined as

$$F_\beta = \frac{(\beta^2 + 1)PR}{\beta^2 P + R}, \tag{12}$$

where $P = \frac{TP}{TP+FP}$ denotes the precision and $R = \frac{TP}{TP+FN}$ denotes the recall. (TP/FP = true/false positive, TN/FN = true/false negative.) As an alternative method to evaluate clustering, we can view every pair of words as a series of decisions. Pick any two (w, t) pairs. If they are clustered together and additionally have the same section label, this is a correct decision; otherwise, the clustering performed a wrong decision. The metric F_β measures accuracy as the (β-weighted) harmonic mean of the precision and

[9] Arts, Business, Fashion & Style, Health, Home & Garden, Real Estate, Science, Sports, Technology, U.S., World.

Table 6: Mean Reciprocal Rank (MRR) and Mean Precisio (MP) for Testset 1.

Method	MRR	MP@1	MP@3	MP@5	MP@10
SW2V	0.3560	0.2664	0.4210	0.4774	0.5612
TW2V	0.0920	0.0500	0.1168	0.1482	0.1910
AW2V	0.1582	0.1066	0.1814	0.2241	0.2953
DW2V	**0.4222**	**0.3306**	**0.4854**	**0.5488**	**0.6191**

Table 7: Mean Reciprocal Rank (MRR) and Mean Precisio (MP) for Testset 2.

Method	MRR	MP@1	MP@3	MP@5	MP@10
SW2V	0.0472	0.0000	0.0787	0.0787	0.2022
TW2V	0.0664	0.0404	0.0764	0.0989	0.1438
AW2V	0.0500	0.0225	0.0517	0.0787	0.1416
DW2V	**0.1444**	**0.0764**	**0.1596**	**0.2202**	**0.3820**

recall. We set $\beta = 5$ to give more weight to recall by penalizin false negative more strongly.

Tables 4 and 5 show the clustering evaluation. We can see tha our proposed DW2V consistently outperforms other baselines fc all values of K. These results show two advantages. First, the wor semantic shift has been captured by the temporal embeddings (fc example, by correlating correctly with the section label of `amazo` which changes from *World* to *Technology*). Second, since embec dings of words of all years are used for clustering, a good clusterin result indicates good alignment across years. We can also see tha AW2V also performs well, as it also applies alignment between ac jacent time slices for all words. However, TW2V does not perforr well as others, suggesting that aligning locally (only a few words is not sufficient for high alignment quality.

6.2 Alignment quality

We now more directly evaluate alignment quality, *i.e.* the propert that the semantic distribution in temporal embedding space shoul be consistent over time. For example, if a word such as `estate` c `republican` does not change much throughout time, its embec ding should remain relatively constant for different t. By the sam logic, if a word such as `trump` does change association throughou time, its embedding should reflect this shift by moving from on position to another (*e.g.*, `estate` → `republican`). We saw this i the previous section for static words like `president` or `mayor`; the do not change meanings, though they are accompanied by name that shift to them every few years.

To examine the quality of embedding alignment, we create a tas to query equivalences across years. For example, given `obama-201` we want to query its equivalent word in 2002. As we know `obama` i the U.S. president in 2012; its equivalent in 2002 is `bush`, who wa the U.S. president at that time. In this way, we create two testsets

The first one is based on publicly recorded knowledge that fo each year lists different names for a particular role, such as U. president, U.K. prime minister, NFL superbowl champion team, an so on. For each year (*e.g.*, 2012), we put its word (*e.g.*, `obama`) int the embedding set of every other year for query its equivalence i top closest words.

The second test is human-generated, for exploring more interesting concepts like emerging technologies, brands and major events (e.g., disease outbreaks and financial crisis). For constructing the test word pairs, we first select emerging terms which have not been popularized before 1994, then query their well known precedents during 1990 to 1994 (*e.g.*, `app-2012` can correspond to `software-1990`). For emerging word (*e.g.*, app) we extract its most popular year (*e.g.*, 2012) with maximum frequency, and put its embedding into each year from 1990 to 1994 for querying its precedent (*e.g.*, software). Each word-year pair now forms a query and an answer; in total we have $N = 11028$ such pairs in the first testset, and $N = 445$ in the second one.

We use two metrics to evaluate the performance.

- For each test i, the correct answer word is identified at position rank$[i]$ for closest words. The *Mean Reciprocal Rank (MRR)* is defined as

$$MRR = \frac{1}{N}\sum_{i=1}^{N}\frac{1}{\text{rank}[i]}, \tag{13}$$

where $\frac{1}{\text{rank}[i]} = 0$ if the correct answer is not found in the *top*-10. Higher MRR means that correct answers appear more closely and unambiguously with the query embedding.

- Additionally, for test i consisting of a query and target word-year pair, consider the closest K words to the query embedding in the target year. If the target word is among these K words, then the *Precision@K* for test i (denoted P@K$[i]$) is 1; else, it is 0. Then the *Mean Precision@K* is defined as

$$MP@K = \frac{1}{N}\sum_{i=1}^{N}(P@K[i]). \tag{14}$$

Higher precision indicates a better ability to acquire correct answers using close embeddings.

Tables 6 and 7 show the evaluation of the alignment test. We can see that our proposed method outperforms others and shows good alignment quality, sometimes by an order of magnitude. Comparing to testset 1 which has a large amount of queries with considerable short range alignments (*e.g.*, from 2012 to 2013), the testset 2 mostly consists of fewer long range alignments (*e.g.*, 2012 to 1990). Therefore, we can see that the performance of SW2V is relatively good in testset 1 since the semantic distribution does not change much in short ranges which makes this test favorable to static embeddings. However, SW2V degrades sharply in testset 2, where the long range alignment is needed more. For TW2V, since it does an individual year-to-year (*e.g.*, 2012-to-1990) transformation by assuming that the local structure of target words does not shift, its overall alignment quality of whole embedding sets is not satisfied in testset 1 with many alignments. However, it does similarly to AW2V in testset 2 because its individual year-to-year transformation makes it more capable for long range alignment. AW2V, which enforces alignment for whole embedding sets between adjacent time slices, provides quite reliable performance. However, its alignment quality is still below ours, suggesting that their two-step approach is not as successful in enforcing global alignment.

Table 8: MRR and MP for alignment with every 3 years subsampling.

Method	r	MRR	MP@1	MP@3	MP@5	MP@10
AW2V	100%	0.1582	0.1066	0.1814	0.2241	0.2953
AW2V	10%	0.0884	0.0567	0.1020	0.1287	0.1727
AW2V	1%	0.0409	0.0255	0.0475	0.0605	0.0818
AW2V	0.1%	0.0362	0.0239	0.0416	0.0532	0.0690
DW2V	100%	0.4222	0.3306	0.4854	0.5488	0.6191
DW2V	10%	0.4394	0.3489	0.5036	0.5628	0.6292
DW2V	1%	0.4418	0.3522	0.5024	0.5636	0.6310
DW2V	0.1%	0.4427	0.3550	0.5006	0.5612	0.6299

6.3 Robustness

Finally, we explore the robustness of our embedding model against subsampling of words for select years. Table 8 shows the result of the alignment task (testset 1) for vectors computed from subsampled co-occurrence matrices for every three years from 1991 to 2015. To subsample, each element C_{ij} is replaced with a randomly drawn integer $\hat{C}_{ij}$ from a Binomial distribution for rate r and $n = C_{ij}$ trials; this simulates the number of co-occurrences measured if they had been missed with probability r. The new frequency $\hat{f}$ is then renormalized so that $\hat{f}_i/f_i = \sum_j \hat{C}_{ij}/\sum_j C_{ij}$. Listed are the alignment test results for $r = 1, 0.1, 0.01$, and 0.001 compared against [12], which otherwise performs comparably with our embedding. Unsurprisingly, for extreme attacks (leaving only 1% or 0.1% co-occurrences), the performance of [12] degrades sharply; however, because of our joint optimization approach, the performance of our embeddings seems to hold steady.

7 RELATED WORK

Temporal effects in natural language processing: There are several studies that investigate the temporal features of natural language. Some are using topic modeling on news corpus [1] or time-stamped scientific journals [6, 33, 36] to find spikes and emergences of themes and viewpoints. Simpler word count features are used in [7, 13, 22] to find hotly discussed concepts and cultural phenomena, in [21, 32, 34] to analyze teen behavior in chatrooms, and in [13] to discover incidents of influenza.

Word embedding learning: The idea of word embeddings has existed at least since the 90s, with vectors computed as rows of the co-occurrence [20], through matrix factorization [9], and most famously through deep neural networks [5, 8]. They have recently been repopularized with the success of low-dimensional embeddings like GloVE [27] and word2vec [24, 25], which have been shown to greatly improve the performance in key NLP tasks, like document clustering [16], LDA [28], and word similarity [3, 18]. There is a close connection between these recent methods and our proposed method, in that both word2vec and GloVE have been shown to be equivalent to matrix factorization of a shifted PMI matrix [17].

Temporal word embeddings and evaluations: While NLP tools have been used frequently to discover emerging word meanings and societal trends, many of them rely on changes in the co-occurrence or PMI matrix [11, 13, 22, 26, 37], changes in parts of speech, [23] or other statistical methods [4, 15, 35]. A few works use low-dimensional word embeddings, but either do no smoothing [31], or use two-step methods [12, 14, 15]. Semantic shift and emergence are also evaluated in many different ways. In [31], word shifts are identified by tracking the mean angle between a word and its neighbors. One of the several tests in [15] create synthetic data with injected semantic shifts, and quantifies the accuracy of capturing them using various time series metrics. In [23], the authors show the semantic meaningfulness of key lexical features by using them to predict the time-stamp of a particular phrase. And, [26] makes the connection that emergent meanings usually coexist with previous meanings, and use dynamic embeddings to discover and identify multisenses, evaluated against WordNet. Primarily, temporal word embeddings are evaluated against human-created databases of known semantically shifted words [12, 15, 35] which is our approach as well.

8 CONCLUSION

We studied the evolution of word semantics as a dynamic word embedding learning problem. We proposed a model to learn time-aware word embeddings and used it to dynamically mine text corpora. Our proposed method simultaneously learns the embeddings and aligns them across time, and has several benefits: higher interpretability for embeddings, better quality with less data, and more reliable alignment for across-time querying. We solved the resulting optimization problem using a scalable block coordinate descent method. We designed qualitative and quantitative methods to evaluate temporal embeddings for evolving word semantics, and showed that our dynamic embedding method performs favorably against other temporal embedding approaches.

REFERENCES

[1] James Allan, Rahul Gupta, and Vikas Khandelwal. 2001. Temporal summaries of new topics. In *Proceedings of the 24th annual international ACM SIGIR conference on Research and development in information retrieval.* ACM, 10–18.

[2] Sanjeev Arora, Yuanzhi Li, Yingyu Liang, Tengyu Ma, and Andrej Risteski. 2015. Rand-walk: A latent variable model approach to word embeddings. *arXiv preprint arXiv:1502.03520* (2015).

[3] Marco Baroni, Georgiana Dinu, and Germán Kruszewski. 2014. Don't count, predict! A systematic comparison of context-counting vs. context-predicting semantic vectors.. In *ACL (1).* 238–247.

[4] Pierpaolo Basile, Annalina Caputo, and Giovanni Semeraro. 2014. Analysing word meaning over time by exploiting temporal random indexing. In *First Italian Conference on Computational Linguistics CLiC-it.*

[5] Yoshua Bengio, Réjean Ducharme, Pascal Vincent, and Christian Jauvin. 2003. A Neural Probabilistic Language Model. *Journal of Machine Learning Research* 3 (2003), 1137–1155.

[6] David M Blei and John D Lafferty. 2006. Dynamic topic models. In *Proceedings of the 23rd international conference on Machine learning.* ACM, 113–120.

[7] Hyunyoung Choi and Hal Varian. 2012. Predicting the present with Google Trends. *Economic Record* 88, s1 (2012), 2–9.

[8] Ronan Collobert and Jason Weston. 2008. A unified architecture for natural language processing: Deep neural networks with multitask learning. In *Proceedings of the 25th international conference on Machine learning.* ACM, 160–167.

[9] Scott Deerwester, Susan T Dumais, George W Furnas, Thomas K Landauer, and Richard Harshman. 1990. Indexing by latent semantic analysis. *Journal of the American society for information science* 41, 6 (1990), 391.

[10] John R Firth. 1957. {A synopsis of linguistic theory, 1930-1955}. (1957).

[11] Kristina Gulordava and Marco Baroni. 2011. A distributional similarity approach to the detection of semantic change in the Google Books Ngram corpus. In *Proceedings of the GEMS 2011 Workshop on GEometrical Models of Natural Language Semantics.* Association for Computational Linguistics, 67–71.

[12] William L Hamilton, Jure Leskovec, and Dan Jurafsky. 2016. Diachronic Word Embeddings Reveal Statistical Laws of Semantic Change. *arXiv preprint arXiv:1605.09096* (2016).

[13] Gerhard Heyer, Florian Holz, and Sven Teresniak. 2009. Change of Topics over Time-Tracking Topics by their Change of Meaning. *KDIR* 9 (2009), 223–228.

[14] Yoon Kim, Yi-I Chiu, Kentaro Hanaki, Darshan Hegde, and Slav Petrov. 201 Temporal analysis of language through neural language models. *arXiv preprir arXiv:1405.3515* (2014).

[15] Vivek Kulkarni, Rami Al-Rfou, Bryan Perozzi, and Steven Skiena. 2015. Statistically significant detection of linguistic change. In *Proceedings of the 24th International Conference on World Wide Web.* ACM, 625–635.

[16] Matt J Kusner, Yu Sun, Nicholas I Kolkin, Kilian Q Weinberger, and others. 201 From Word Embeddings To Document Distances.. In *ICML*, Vol. 15. 957–966.

[17] Omer Levy and Yoav Goldberg. 2014. Neural word embedding as implicit matri factorization. In *Advances in neural information processing systems.* 2177–2185.

[18] Omer Levy, Yoav Goldberg, and Ido Dagan. 2015. Improving distributiona similarity with lessons learned from word embeddings. *Transactions of th Association for Computational Linguistics* 3 (2015), 211–225.

[19] Xuanyi Liao and Guang Cheng. 2016. Analysing the Semantic Change Based on Word Embedding. In *International Conference on Computer Processing of Orienta Languages.* Springer, 213–223.

[20] Kevin Lund and Curt Burgess. 1996. Producing high-dimensional semantic space from lexical co-occurrence. *Behavior Research Methods, Instruments, & Computer* 28, 2 (1996), 203–208.

[21] Guy Merchant. 2001. Teenagers in cyberspace: An investigation of language us and language change in internet chatrooms. *Journal of Research in Reading* 24, (2001), 293–306.

[22] Jean-Baptiste Michel, Yuan Kui Shen, Aviva Presser Aiden, Adrian Veres Matthew K Gray, Joseph P Pickett, Dale Hoiberg, Dan Clancy, Peter Norvig Jon Orwant, and others. 2011. Quantitative analysis of culture using millions o digitized books. *science* 331, 6014 (2011), 176–182.

[23] Rada Mihalcea and Vivi Nastase. 2012. Word epoch disambiguation: Finding how words change over time. In *Proceedings of the 50th Annual Meeting of th Association for Computational Linguistics: Short Papers-Volume 2.* Association fo Computational Linguistics, 259–263.

[24] Tomas Mikolov, Kai Chen, Greg Corrado, and Jeffrey Dean. 2013. Efficien estimation of word representations in vector space. *arXiv preprint arXiv:1301.378* (2013).

[25] Tomas Mikolov, Ilya Sutskever, Kai Chen, Greg S Corrado, and Jeff Dean. 201 Distributed representations of words and phrases and their compositionality. In *Advances in neural information processing systems.* 3111–3119.

[26] Sunny Mitra, Ritwik Mitra, Martin Riedl, Chris Biemann, Animesh Mukherjee and Pawan Goyal. 2014. That's sick dude!: Automatic identification of word sense change across different timescales. *arXiv preprint arXiv:1405.4392* (2014).

[27] Jeffrey Pennington, Richard Socher, and Christopher D Manning. 2014. Glove Global Vectors for Word Representation.. In *EMNLP*, Vol. 14. 1532–1543.

[28] James Petterson, Wray Buntine, Shravan M Narayanamurthy, Tibério S Caetano and Alex J Smola. 2010. Word features for latent dirichlet allocation. In *Advance in Neural Information Processing Systems.* 1921–1929.

[29] Michael JD Powell. 1973. On search directions for minimization algorithms *Mathematical Programming* 4, 1 (1973), 193–201.

[30] Nikhil Rao, Hsiang-Fu Yu, Pradeep K Ravikumar, and Inderjit S Dhillon. 201 Collaborative filtering with graph information: Consistency and scalable method In *Advances in neural information processing systems.* 2107–2115.

[31] Eyal Sagi, Stefan Kaufmann, and Brady Clark. 2011. Tracing semantic change with latent semantic analysis. *Current methods in historical semantics* (2011 161–183.

[32] Diane J Schiano, Coreena P Chen, Ellen Isaacs, Jeremy Ginsberg, Unnur Gretars dottir, and Megan Huddleston. 2002. Teen use of messaging media. In *CHI'0 extended abstracts on Human factors in computing systems.* ACM, 594–595.

[33] Ruben Sipos, Adith Swaminathan, Pannaga Shivaswamy, and Thorsten Joachims 2012. Temporal corpus summarization using submodular word coverage. In *Proceedings of the 21st ACM international conference on Information and knowledg management.* ACM, 754–763.

[34] Sali A Tagliamonte and Derek Denis. 2008. Linguistic ruin? LOL! Instant messag ing and teen language. *American speech* 83, 1 (2008), 3–34.

[35] Xuri Tang, Weiguang Qu, and Xiaohe Chen. 2016. Semantic change computatior A successive approach. *World Wide Web* 19, 3 (2016), 375–415.

[36] Xuerui Wang and Andrew McCallum. 2006. Topics over time: a non-Marko continuous-time model of topical trends. In *Proceedings of the 12th ACM SIGKDI international conference on Knowledge discovery and data mining.* ACM, 424–433.

[37] Derry Tanti Wijaya and Reyyan Yeniterzi. 2011. Understanding semantic change of words over centuries. In *Proceedings of the 2011 international workshop on DETecting and Exploiting Cultural diversiTy on the social web.* ACM, 35–40.

[38] Stephen J Wright. 2015. Coordinate descent algorithms. *Mathematical Programming* 151, 1 (2015), 3–34.

[39] Hsiang-Fu Yu, Cho-Jui Hsieh, Si Si, and Inderjit Dhillon. 2012. Scalable coordinate descent approaches to parallel matrix factorization for recommender systems. In *12th IEEE International Conference on Data Mining (ICDM).* IEEE, 765–774.

[40] Yating Zhang, Adam Jatowt, Sourav S Bhowmick, and Katsumi Tanaka. 2016. The Past is Not a Foreign Country: Detecting Semantically Similar Terms across Time *IEEE Transactions on Knowledge and Data Engineering* 28, 10 (2016), 2793–2807.

Modelling Domain Relationships for Transfer Learning on Retrieval-based Question Answering Systems in E-commerce

Jianfei Yu*
Singapore Management University
jfyu.2014@phdis.smu.edu.sg

Minghui Qiu†
Alibaba Group, China
minghui.qmh@alibaba-inc.com

Jing Jiang
Singapore Management University
jingjiang@smu.edu.sg

Jun Huang, Shuangyong Song
Alibaba Group, China
{junhuang.jh,shuangyong.ssy}@alibaba-inc.com

Wei Chu
Alibaba Group, China
weichu.cw@alibaba-inc.com

Haiqing Chen
Alibaba Group, China
haiqing.chenhq@alibaba-inc.com

ABSTRACT

Nowadays, it is a heated topic for many industries to build automatic question-answering (QA) systems. A key solution to these QA systems is to retrieve from a QA knowledge base the most similar question of a given question, which can be reformulated as a paraphrase identification (PI) or a natural language inference (NLI) problem. However, most existing models for PI and NLI have at least two problems: They rely on a large amount of labeled data, which is not always available in real scenarios, and they may not be efficient for industrial applications.

In this paper, we study transfer learning for the PI and NLI problems, aiming to propose a general framework, which can effectively and efficiently adapt the *shared* knowledge learned from a resource-rich source domain to a resource-poor target domain. Specifically, since most existing transfer learning methods only focus on learning a shared feature space across domains while ignoring the relationship between the source and target domains, we propose to simultaneously learn shared representations and domain relationships in a unified framework. Furthermore, we propose an efficient and effective hybrid model by combining a sentence encoding-based method and a sentence interaction-based method as our base model. Extensive experiments on both paraphrase identification and natural language inference demonstrate that our base model is efficient and has promising performance compared to the competing models, and our transfer learning method can help to significantly boost the performance. Further analysis shows that the *inter-domain* and *intra-domain* relationship captured by our model are insightful. Last but not least, we deploy our transfer learning model for PI into our online chatbot system, which can bring in significant improvements over our existing system.

Finally, we launch our new system on the chatbot platform Eva[1] in our E-commerce site *AliExpress*[2].

*Work done during the internship at Alibaba Group.
†Corresponding author.

WSDM 2018, February 5–9, 2018, Marina Del Rey, CA, USA

ACM ISBN 978-1-4503-5581-0/18/02...$15.00
https://doi.org/10.1145/3159652.3159685

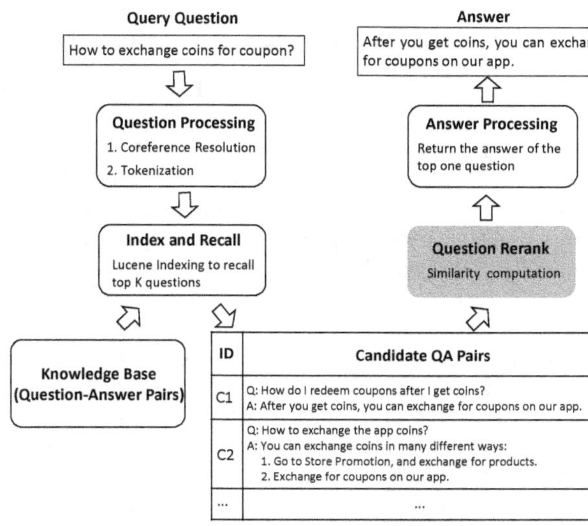

Figure 1: The workflow of IR-based QA systems.

ACM Reference format:
Jianfei Yu, Minghui Qiu, Jing Jiang, Jun Huang, Shuangyong Song, Wei Chu, and Haiqing Chen. 2018. Modelling Domain Relationships for Transfer Learning on Retrieval-based Question Answering Systems in E-commerce. In *Proceedings of WSDM 2018: The Eleventh ACM International Conference on Web Search and Data Mining, Marina Del Rey, CA, USA, February 5–9, 2018 (WSDM 2018),* 9 pages.
https://doi.org/10.1145/3159652.3159685

1 INTRODUCTION

Question Answering (QA) systems have been widely developed and used in many domains. Examples of industry applications include Alibaba's AliME [26], Microsoft's SuperAgent [7], Apple's Siri and Google's Google Assistant. Generally speaking, there are two kinds of commonly-used techniques behind most QA systems: Information Retrieval (IR)-based models [39] and generation-based models [31]. In this work, we focus on building up an IR-based QA system for automatically answering frequently asked questions (FAQs) in the E-commerce industry.

[1] https://gcx.aliexpress.com/ae/evaenglish/portal.htm?pageId=195440
[2] http://www.aliexpress.com/

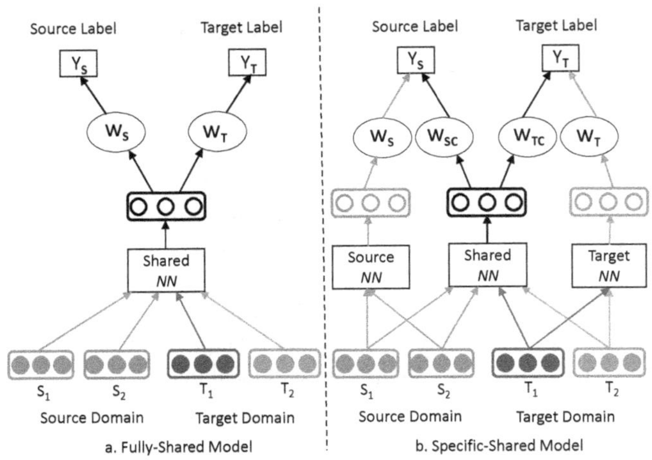

Figure 2: Existing Transfer Learning Frameworks.

Fig. 1 illustrates the workflow of IR-based QA systems, where a key component is the *Question Rerank* module which reranks candidate questions in a question-answering knowledge base (KB) to find the best matching question given a question from a user. This task can be reduced to a paraphrase identification or a natural language inference problem. Take the query question and knowledge base shown in Fig. 1 for example. If we can detect that question C1 in the KB is a paraphrase of the query question, then we can take its answer as the answer for the query. In some cases, if we allow the matching question to be more general than the query question (i.e., entailed by the query question), we can also take the answer for question C2 in the KB as the query question's answer.

In the literature, paraphrase identification (PI) and natural language inference (NLI) have been extensively studied in the last decade [3, 4, 6, 29, 42]. However, when applying existing solutions to PI and NLI in IR-based QA systems in the E-commerce industry, there are at least two major challenges we face: (1) *Lack of rich training data*: All these solutions rely on a large amount of labeled data. However, it is generally time-consuming and costly to manually annotate sufficient labeled data for each domain. For example, different product categories might need different training data. (2) *Hard to reach a high QPS*[3]. Most of the existing methods focus on improving the effectiveness or accuracy without paying much attention to efficiency. For real industry applications, when real-time responses are expected and a large number of customers are being served simultaneously, we need an efficient method to support a high QPS.

In this paper, we try to address the two challenges above. Specifically, we first make an empirical comparison of both the effectiveness and efficiency of several representative methods for modeling sentence pairs and propose an effective and efficient *hybrid model* as our base model. This ensures that we can achieve a high QPS. On top of the base model, we further design a new *transfer learning (TL) framework*, which is able to efficiently improve the performance on a resource-poor target domain by leveraging knowledge from a resource-rich source domain.

A Hybrid Base Model. Observing that LSTM-based methods [3, 6] are much more time-consuming than CNN-based methods [20, 42], we focus on CNN-based methods in this study. Meanwhil there are typically two types of CNN-based methods for the tas namely sentence encoding (SE)-based methods [21, 41] and sen tence interaction (SI)-based methods [13, 23]. We argue that thes two types of methods may highly complement each other, an thus we propose a hybrid CNN model by combining an SE-base method [42] and an SI-based method [23]. Specifically, we modif the SE-based method using two element-wise comparison function inspired by [20, 35] to match the two sentence embeddings, an then concatenate them together with sentence embeddings fro the SI-based method.

Transfer Learning Framework. Transfer learning aims to ap ply knowledge gained in a source domain to help a target do main [22]. The key issue is how to transfer the shared knowledg from the source domain to the target domain while exclude th specific knowledge in the source domain based on the *domain re lationship*. Most recent studies for TL in NLP perform *multi-tas feature learning* by exploiting different NN models to capture shared feature space across domains. As illustrated in Fig. 2a an Fig. 2b, one line of work employs a fully-shared framework t learn a shared representation followed by using two different full connected layers for each domain [21, 40], while another line c work uses a specific-shared framework to learn not only a share representation for both domains but also a domain-specific repre sentation for each domain [18].

However, the first line of work simply assumes that two domain share the same feature space but ignore the domain-specific featu space. Although the latter one is capable of capturing both th shared and the domain-specific representations, it does not conside any relationships between the weights of the final output laye Generally speaking, the weights on the output layer should captu both the *inter-domain* and the *intra-domain* relationships: (1) Fo the shared feature space across domains, since it is expected t be domain-independent, the weights corresponding to this featur space in the two domains should be positively related to each othe (2) For the shared and the domain-specific feature spaces in eac domain, since they are expected to respectively capture domai independent and domain-dependent features, their correspondin weights should be irrelevant to each other. Motivated by such a intuition, in this paper, we propose a new transfer learning metho by explicitly modeling the domain relationships via a covarianc matrix, which imposes a regularization term on the weights c the output layer to uncover both the inter-domain and the intr domain relationships. Besides, to make the shared representatio more invariant across domains, we follow some recent work o adversarial networks [11, 18] and introduce an adversarial loss o the shared feature space in our method. Fig. 3 gives an outline o our full model.

To evaluate our proposed method, we conduct both intrinsi evaluation and extrinsic evaluation.

Intrinsic Evaluation. We conduct extensive experiments o both a benchmark dataset and our own dataset. (1) The hybri CNN model is shown to be not only efficient but also effective, i comparison with several representative methods; (2) Our propose transfer learning method can bring significant improvements ove the base model without transfer learning, and outperform existin

[3]Queries Per Second

TL frameworks including the widely used fully-shared model and the recently proposed specific-shared model; (3) Further analysis on our learned correlation matrix shows that our method is able to capture the inter-domain and intra-domain relationships.

Extrinsic Evaluation. We deploy our proposed hybrid CNN-based transfer learning model into our online chatbot system, which is deployed on a real E-commerce site *AliExpress*. Both the offline and the online evaluations show that our new system can significantly outperform the existing online chatbot system. Finally, we launch our new system on Eva[4], a chatbot platform in *AliExpress*.

2 MODEL

In this section, we present our general model for paraphrase identification and natural language inference, which will be used for question reranking in our chatbot-based QA system.

2.1 Problem Formulation and Notation

Our model is designed to address the following general problem. Given a pair of sentences, we would like to identify their semantic relation. For paraphrase identification (PI), the semantic relation indicates whether or not the two sentences express the same meaning [41]; for natural language inference (NLI), it indicates whether a hypothesis sentence can be inferred from a premise sentence [3].

Formally, assume there are two sentences $\mathbf{X}_1 = (\mathbf{x}_1^1, \mathbf{x}_2^1, \ldots, \mathbf{x}_m^1)$ and $\mathbf{X}_2 = (\mathbf{x}_1^2, \mathbf{x}_2^2, \ldots, \mathbf{x}_n^2)$, where $\mathbf{x}_i^j$ denotes an l-dimensional dense embedding vector retrieved from a lookup table $\mathbf{E} \in \mathbb{R}^{l \times |\mathcal{V}|}$ for all the words in the vocabulary $\mathcal{V}$. Our task is to predict the semantic label y which indicates the relation between $\mathbf{X}_1$ and $\mathbf{X}_2$. For PI, we assume the label y to be either *paraphrase* or *not paraphrase*; for NLI, we assume y to be either *neutral*, *entailment* or *contradiction*.

We consider a transfer learning setting, where we have a set of labeled sentence pairs from a source domain and a target domain, respectively, denoted by $\mathcal{D}^{\mathrm{s}}$ and $\mathcal{D}^{\mathrm{t}}$. Note that $|\mathcal{D}^{\mathrm{s}}|$ is assumed to be much larger than $|\mathcal{D}^{\mathrm{t}}|$. We seek to use both $\mathcal{D}^{\mathrm{s}}$ and $\mathcal{D}^{\mathrm{t}}$ to train a good model so that it can work well in the target domain.

To solve such a problem, a widely used transfer learning method (as illustrated in Fig. 2a) is to use the same NN model to transform every pair of input sentences in both domains into a hidden representation $\mathbf{z_c} \in \mathbb{R}^q$, where q is the size of the hidden representations. To facilitate our discussion, let us assume $\mathbf{z_c} = f_{\Theta_c}(\mathbf{X}_1, \mathbf{X}_2)$, where f_{Θ_c} denotes the transformation function parameterized by Θ_c. Next, for the source and the target domains, we assume that two fully connected layers are separately learned to map $\mathbf{z_c}$ to label y.

$$p(y \mid \mathbf{z_c}) = \begin{cases} \mathrm{softmax}(\mathbf{W_{sc}}\mathbf{z_c} + \mathbf{b_s}) & \text{if } y \text{ is source label,} \\ \mathrm{softmax}(\mathbf{W_{tc}}\mathbf{z_c} + \mathbf{b_t}) & \text{if } y \text{ is target label,} \end{cases}$$

where $\mathbf{W_{sc}} \in \mathbb{R}^{|Y| \times q}$ and $\mathbf{W_{tc}} \in \mathbb{R}^{|Y| \times q}$ are weight matrices and $\mathbf{b_s} \in \mathbb{R}^{|Y|}$ and $\mathbf{b_t} \in \mathbb{R}^{|Y|}$ are bias vectors.

Besides, another transfer learning approach [18] was recently proposed to use a domain-shared NN model and two domain-specific NN models to obtain a shared embedding $\mathbf{z_c}$ and two domain-specific embeddings $\mathbf{z_s} = f_{\Theta_s}(\mathbf{X}_1, \mathbf{X}_2)$ and $\mathbf{z_t} = f_{\Theta_t}(\mathbf{X}_1, \mathbf{X}_2)$.

Therefore, the output layers are defined as:

$$p(y \mid \mathbf{z_c}, \mathbf{z_s}) = \begin{cases} \mathrm{softmax}(\mathbf{W_{sc}}\mathbf{z_c} + \mathbf{W_s}\mathbf{z_s} + \mathbf{b_s}) & \text{if } y \text{ is source label,} \\ \mathrm{softmax}(\mathbf{W_{tc}}\mathbf{z_c} + \mathbf{W_t}\mathbf{z_t} + \mathbf{b_t}) & \text{if } y \text{ is target label.} \end{cases}$$

The main limitation of the fully-shared framework is that it ignores source-specific or target-specific features. While for the specific-shared framework, it fails to consider any inherent correlations between the weights on the output layers. Therefore, we will introduce our proposed method that explicitly incorporates such correlations into the specific-shared framework in the next session.

2.2 Proposed Transfer Learning Method

Our goal is to model the inter-domain relationship between $\mathbf{W_{sc}}$ and $\mathbf{W_{tc}}$, and the intra-domain relationship between $\mathbf{W_s}$ and $\mathbf{W_{sc}}$ as well as $\mathbf{W_t}$ and $\mathbf{W_{tc}}$. Hence, we first reshape each weight matrix into a vector $\mathbf{w_d} \in \mathbb{R}^{q|Y|}$, followed by concatenating all the four reshaped vectors to form a new matrix $\mathbf{W} \in \mathbb{R}^{q|Y| \times 4}$, where each column corresponds to one weight matrix of the output layer.

Next, to capture the domain relationships mentioned above, we introduce a covariance matrix $\Omega \in \mathbb{R}^{4 \times 4}$. Note that each element $\Omega_{\mathbf{i},\mathbf{j}}$ indicates the correlation between $\mathbf{W_i}$ and $\mathbf{W_j}$, where **i** and **j** are one of **s**, **sc**, **t** and **tc**. Inspired by a general multi-task relationship learning framework as introduced in [45], we consider confining the output layer's weights with Ω by using $\mathbf{tr}(\mathbf{W}\Omega^{-1}\mathbf{W}^T)$, where $\mathbf{tr}(\cdot)$ is the trace of a square matrix. This means that if $\Omega_{\mathbf{i},\mathbf{j}}$ is a large positive/negative value, $\mathbf{W_i}$ and $\mathbf{W_j}$ will be positively/negatively related to each other; otherwise if $\Omega_{\mathbf{i},\mathbf{j}}$ is close to zero, $\mathbf{W_i}$ and $\mathbf{W_j}$ will be irrelevant to each other. Note that to the best of our knowledge, we are the first to apply the multi-task relationship learning framework into NN-based transfer learning methods.

In order to simultaneously learn our model parameters and the domain relationships in a unified framework, we formulate our loss function as follows:

$$\begin{aligned} \mathcal{L} = &\sum_{\mathbf{k} \in \mathbf{s},\mathbf{t}} -\frac{1}{n_\mathbf{k}} \sum_{i=1}^{n_\mathbf{k}} \log p(y_i \mid \mathbf{X}_1^i, \mathbf{X}_2^i) + \frac{\lambda_1}{2}\mathbf{tr}(\mathbf{W}\Omega^{-1}\mathbf{W}^T) \\ &+ \frac{\lambda_2}{2}||\mathbf{W}||_F^2 + \frac{\lambda_3}{2}||\Theta_c||_F^2 + \frac{\lambda_4}{2}||\Theta_s||_F^2 + \frac{\lambda_5}{2}||\Theta_t||_F^2 \\ \text{s.t.} \quad &\Omega \geq 0, \quad \mathbf{tr}(\Omega) = 1. \end{aligned} \tag{1}$$

where λ_1, λ_2, λ_3, λ_4 and λ_5 are regularization parameters, Ω is required to be positive semi-definite, and $\mathbf{tr}(\Omega)$ is required to be 1 without losing generality. In the above formulation, the first term refers to the cross-entropy loss for both domains, and the second term serves as a domain-relationship regularizer to constrain the weights on the output layer. The remaining terms are standard L2-regularization terms.

2.3 Adversarial Loss

Our above transfer learning method is based on the specific-shared framework, which is assumed to well capture the shared and domain-specific feature spaces. However, as suggested by [18], the shared representation learned in this framework may still contain noisy domain-specific features. Therefore, to eliminate the noisy features, here we also consider incorporating an adversarial loss on the shared feature space so that the trained model can not distinguish between the source and target domains on it [11].

[4]Eva can be accessed via the following link: https://gcx.aliexpress.com/ae/evaenglish/portal.htm?pageId=195440

First, we assume that the shared layer $\mathbf{z_c}$ is mapped to a binary domain label d, which indicates whether $\mathbf{z_c}$ comes from the source or the target domain:

$$p(d \mid \mathbf{z_c}) = \text{softmax}(\mathbf{W_d z_c} + \mathbf{b_d}).$$

Since the goal of adversarial training is to encourage the shared feature space indiscriminate across two domains, we define the adversarial loss as minimizing the negative entropy of the predicted domain distribution, which is different from maximizing the negative cross-entropy as in [11, 18]:

$$\ell = \sum_{\mathbf{k}\in \mathbf{s},\mathbf{t}} \Big(\frac{1}{n_\mathbf{k}} \sum_{i=1}^{n_\mathbf{k}} \sum_{j=0}^{1} p(d_{ij} \mid \mathbf{X}_1^i, \mathbf{X}_2^i) \log p(d_{ij} \mid \mathbf{X}_1^i, \mathbf{X}_2^i)\Big). \quad (2)$$

Finally, we obtain a combined objective function as follows:

$$\min_{\substack{\Omega,\mathbf{W},\mathbf{W_d},\Theta_c,\\ \Theta_s,\Theta_t,\mathbf{b_s},\mathbf{b_t},\mathbf{b_d}}} \mathcal{L} + \lambda_0 \ell$$
$$\text{s.t.} \quad \Omega \succeq 0, \quad \mathbf{tr}(\Omega) = 1,$$

where λ_0 is a hyper-parameter for tuning the importance of the adversarial loss. As suggested by [45], it is not easy to optimize such a semi-definite programming problem. We will present an alternating training approach in Section 2.5 for solving it efficiently.

2.4 Base Model

Although the proposed transfer learning method is general and any neural networks for modeling a pair of sentences can be applied to it, we further target at proposing an efficient and effective base model for encoding a pair of sentences.

On one hand, although various attention-based LSTM architectures have been proposed to achieve a superior performance on both PI and NLI [6, 24, 28, 35], these models are very time-consuming due to the computation of memory cells and attention weights in each time step, which may not satisfy the industry demand, especially when QPS is high. On the other hand, CNN-based models are proven to be efficient, hence are the focus of our study. Most existing CNN-based models can be categorized into two groups: sentence encoding (SE)-based methods and sentence interaction (SI)-based methods. The former aims to first learn good representations for each sentence, followed by using a comparison function to transform them into a single representation [21, 41], while the latter tries to directly model the interaction between two sentences at the beginning and then makes abstractions on top of the interaction output [13, 23]. Observing that the two lines of methods focus on different perspectives to model sentence pairs, we expect that a combination of them can capture both good sentence representations and rich interaction structures.

Hence, we propose a hybrid CNN (hCNN) model, which are based on some minor modifications of two existing models: a SE-based BCNN model [42] and a SI-based Pyramid model [23]. Fig. 3 depicts our full transfer learning framework, which contains one shared hCNN and two domain-specific hCNNs. Below we briefly go through the architecture of hCNN. Note that in our implementation and the model description below, we pad the two input sentences to the same length m.

Modified BCNN: Following the original BCNN [42], we first use two separate 1-D convolutional (conv) and 1-D max-pooling layers to encode the two input sentences into two sentence embeddings:

$$\mathbf{h}_1 = CNN(\mathbf{X}_1); \quad \mathbf{h}_2 = CNN(\mathbf{X}_2).$$

Furthermore, as suggested by [20, 35] that element-wise comparison can work well on the problem, we use two comparison functions to match the two sentence embeddings, and then concatenate them together with the sentence embeddings as the sentence pair representation: $\mathbf{H_b} = \mathbf{h}_1 \oplus \mathbf{h}_2 \oplus (\mathbf{h}_1 - \mathbf{h}_2) \oplus (\mathbf{h}_1 \cdot \mathbf{h}_2)$, where $-$ and $\cdot$ refer to element-wise subtraction and element-wise multiplication and $\oplus$ refers to concatenation. Note that this setting is different from the original BCNN, which yields better performance in our empirical experiments.

Pyramid: As shown in the rightmost part of Fig 3, we first produce an interaction matrix $\mathbf{M} \in \mathbb{R}^{m\times m}$, where $\mathbf{M_{i,j}}$ denotes the similarity score between the ith word in $\mathbf{X}_1$ and the jth word in $\mathbf{X}_2$. Following [23], we use dot-product to compute the similarity score.

Next, by viewing the interaction matrix as an image, we stack two 2-D convolutional layers and two 2-D max-pooling layers on it to obtain the hidden representation $\mathbf{H_p}$.

Finally, we concatenate the two hidden representations as the final representation for each input sentence pair: $\mathbf{z} = \mathbf{H_b} \oplus \mathbf{H_p}$.

2.5 Inference

In our combined objective function, we have nine parameters Ω, $\mathbf{W}$, $\mathbf{W_d}$, $\mathbf{b_s}$, $\mathbf{b_t}$, $\mathbf{b_d}$, Θ_c, Θ_s and Θ_t, and it is not easy to optimize them at the same time. Following the practice in [45], we employ an alternating stochastic method, i.e., first optimizing the other eight parameters by fixing Ω, and then alternatively optimizing Ω by fixing the others in each iteration. The details are given as below.

Updating $\mathbf{W}$, $\mathbf{W_d}$, $\mathbf{b_s}$, $\mathbf{b_t}$, $\mathbf{b_d}$, Θ_c, Θ_s and Θ_t. While fixing Ω, the optimization problem becomes:

$$\min_{\substack{\mathbf{W},\mathbf{W_d},\Theta_c,\Theta_s,\\ \Theta_t,\mathbf{b_s},\mathbf{b_t},\mathbf{b_d}}} \sum_{\mathbf{k}\in\mathbf{s},\mathbf{t}} \Big(\frac{1}{n_\mathbf{k}} \sum_{i=1}^{n_\mathbf{k}} \big(-\log p(y_i \mid \mathbf{X}_1^i, \mathbf{X}_2^i)$$
$$+ \lambda_0 \sum_{j=0}^{1} p(d_{ij} \mid \mathbf{X}_1^i, \mathbf{X}_2^i) \log p(d_{ij} \mid \mathbf{X}_1^i, \mathbf{X}_2^i)\big)\Big) + \frac{\lambda_1}{2}\mathbf{tr}(\mathbf{W}\Omega^{-1}\mathbf{W}^T)$$
$$+ \frac{\lambda_2}{2}||\mathbf{W}||_F^2 + \frac{\lambda_3}{2}||\Theta_c||_F^2 + \frac{\lambda_4}{2}||\Theta_s||_F^2 + \frac{\lambda_5}{2}||\Theta_t||_F^2$$

Since it is a smooth function, we can easily compute its partial derivatives with respect to the eight parameters.

Updating Ω. After fixing the eight parameters, the optimization problem is as follows:

$$\min_{\Omega} \quad \mathbf{tr}(\mathbf{W}\Omega^{-1}\mathbf{W}^T)$$
$$\text{s.t.} \quad \Omega \succeq 0, \quad \mathbf{tr}(\Omega) = 1.$$

As proved by [45], the above optimization problem has an analytical solution $\Omega = \frac{(\mathbf{W}^T\mathbf{W})^{\frac{1}{2}}}{\mathbf{tr}\left((\mathbf{W}^T\mathbf{W})^{\frac{1}{2}}\right)}$.

Finally, we present the whole procedure for training our full model as in Algorithm 1. Note that we only update Ω when we scan all the target training instances once.

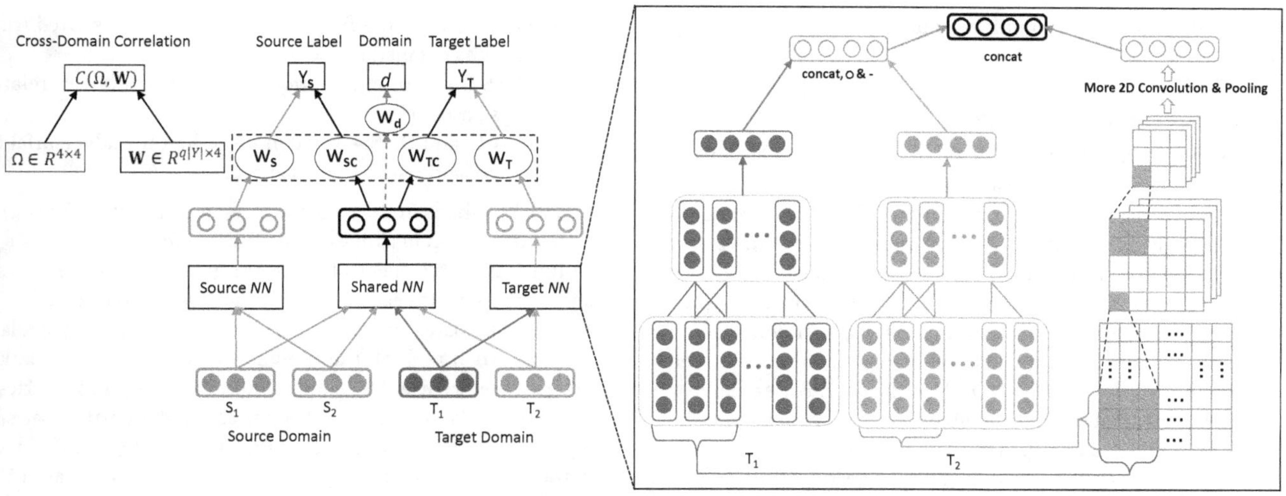

Figure 3: Our Full Transfer Learning Model for Paraphrase Identification and Natural Language Inference.

lgorithm 1 Training Procedure for our Full Model

Input: source training instances $\mathcal{D}^{\mathrm{s}}$, target training instances $\mathcal{D}^{\mathrm{t}}$ ($|\mathcal{D}^{\mathrm{s}}| \gg |\mathcal{D}^{\mathrm{t}}|$) .
Output: Ω, $\mathbf{W}$, $\mathbf{W_d}$, $\mathbf{b_s}$, $\mathbf{b_t}$, $\mathbf{b_d}$, Θ_c, Θ_s, Θ_t
Initialize $\mathbf{W}$, $\mathbf{W_d}$, $\mathbf{b_s}$, $\mathbf{b_t}$, $\mathbf{b_d}$, Θ_c, Θ_s, Θ_t with random values
Initialize $\Omega = \frac{1}{4}\mathbf{I}_4$, where $\mathbf{I}$ is an identity matrix
epoch = 0
while epoch $\leq$ MaxEpoch **do**
  $c_s, c_t = 0, 0$
  while $c_s \leq$ src_batches **do**
    read the $c_s{}^{\mathrm{th}}$ mini-batch from the source domain
    Update Θ_c, Θ_s, $\mathbf{W}$, $\mathbf{W_d}$, $\mathbf{b_s}$ and $\mathbf{b_d}$
    c_s += 1
    if c_t == tgt_batches **then**
      $c_t = 0$
      Update $\Omega = \frac{(\mathbf{W}^T\mathbf{W})^{\frac{1}{2}}}{\mathrm{tr}\left((\mathbf{W}^T\mathbf{W})^{\frac{1}{2}}\right)}$
    end if
    read the $c_t{}^{\mathrm{th}}$ mini-batch from the target domain
    Update Θ_c, Θ_t, $\mathbf{W}$, $\mathbf{W_d}$, $\mathbf{b_t}$ and $\mathbf{b_d}$
    c_t += 1
  end while
  epoch = epoch + 1
end while

.6 Implementation Details

n our full transfer learning model, we initialize the lookup table with the pre-trained vectors from *GloVe* [25] by setting l as 300. or **BCNN**, the window size and activation function are set to be and ReLU, and the feature map sizes are set to be 50 and 100 for I and NLI; for the two convolution layers of **Pyramid** in both PI nd NLI, the feature map sizes are set to be 8 and 16, the strides re set to be 1 and 3, and the kernel sizes are set to be 6×6 and $\times 4$; for the two max-pooling layers of **Pyramid**, the strides are et to be 4 and 2, and the pooling sizes are set to be 4×4 and 2×2. esides, for λ_0 and λ_1, we set them as 0.05 and 0.0008; while for λ_2, λ_3, λ_4 and λ_5, we set them as 0.0004. AdaGrad [10] is used to train our model with an initial learning rate of 0.08.

3 ONLINE SYSTEM

As introduced in Section 1, our online chatbot system is based on traditional information retrieval techniques, where the goal is to obtain the nearest question in the knowledge base for a given customer question [14]. Fig. 1 depicts the whole system architecture.

Specifically, we first build an indexing for all the questions in our knowledge base (KB) using *Apache Lucene* [5]. Next, given a query question, we employ TF-IDF ranking algorithm [38] in Lucene to compute its similarities to all the questions in the KB, and call back the top-K candidate questions. We then use a reranking algorithm to compute the similarities between the query and the K candidates, and obtain the most similar candidate. Finally we return the answer of the selected candidate to answer the query question. Note that in this paper, we only consider formulating our question rerank module as a PI task, but one can also model it as an NLI task.

Our existing reranking method is based on this ensemble method for the Answer Selection task [33]. But instead of using the output of the time-consuming LSTM model, we feed another three features, namely, Word Mover's Distance [16], keywords features [33] and the cosine distance of sentence embeddings [36] to a gradient boosted regression tree (GBDT).

To combine our model with the existing ranking method, we treat the probability of being *paraphrases* predicted by our model as an additional feature, and feed all features to GBDT for reranking.

4 EXPERIMENTS

In this section, we describe a qualitative evaluation of our proposed methods from the following perspectives: (1) From Section 4.1 to Section 4.4, we perform an **intrinsic** evaluation by utilizing a benchmark dataset and our own dataset to show the efficiency and effectiveness of our proposed base model and transfer learning framework; (2) In Section 4.5, we deploy our full model into our chatbot system, and conduct an **extrinsic** evaluation to show that

[5] https://lucene.apache.org/core/

our full model can bring in significant improvements to our existing online chatbots.

4.1 Experiment Settings

Datasets: In this section, we evaluate our methods on both Paraphrase Identification (PI) and Natural Language Inference (NLI).

For PI, we used a recently released large-scale dateset[6] by Quora as the source domain, and our E-commerce dataset as the target domain. Based on our historical data, we constructed a question answering KB, which consists of around 15,000 frequently asked QA pairs. To create labeled question pairs, we first collected all the query questions from the chat log of conversations between clients and our staff from May 22 to May 28, 2017. For each query question, we then used *Lucene* indexing to retrieve several of its similar questions, and obtained 45,075 question pairs. Finally, we asked a business analyst to annotate all the question pairs.

For NLI, we employed a large-scale multi-genre corpus [37], which contains an image captioning domain (SNLI) and another five distinct genres/domains about written and spoken English (MultiNLI).Since the number of sentence pairs in SNLI is much larger than that in the other five domains, we took SNLI as the source domain, and the others as the target domains.

Table 1 and Table 2 summarize the statistics of our datasets. Note that in Table 1, the number before and after the slash for Q-Q pairs denote respectively the total number of question pairs and the number of positive question pairs (i.e., paraphrases), while the two numbers for #Query-Q respectively denote the total number of query questions and the number of questions with paraphrasing candidates. Besides, for #Candi-Q, we refer to the average number of candidate questions for each query.

Compared Methods: For base models, we compared our hCNN model with the following models:

- **BCNN** is the left component of our hCNN model, which incorporates element-wise comparisons on top of the base model proposed in [42].
- **Pyramid** is the right component of our hCNN model based on sentence interactions as in [23].
- **ABCNN** is the attention-based CNN model by [42].
- **BiLSTM** is similar to **BCNN**, but uses LSTM instead of CNN to encode each sentence as in [3].
- **ESIM** is one of the state-of-the-art attention-based LSTM models on SNLI proposed by [6].
- **hCNN** is our hybrid CNN model as introduced in Section 2.4.

For evaluating the proposed transfer learning framework, we employed the following compared systems:

- **Tgt-Only** is the baseline trained in the target domain.
- **Src-Only** is another baseline trained in the source domain.
- **Mixed** is to simply combine the labeled data in the two domains to train the hCNN model.
- **Fine-Tune** is a widely used TL method, where we first train a model on the source data, and then use the learned parameters to initialize the model parameters for training another model on the target data.
- **FS** and **SS** are the fully-shared and specific-shared frameworks as detailed in Section 2.1.
- **DRSS** is our proposed model of learning domain relationships based on **SS** as in Section 2.2.
- **SS-Adv** and **DRSS-Adv** denote adding the adversarial loss into **SS** and **DRSS** as in Section 2.3.

All the methods in this paper are implemented with Tensorflow and are trained on machines with NVIDIA Tesla K40m GPU.

Evaluation Metrics: For PI, since our goal is to retrieve the most similar candidate for each query question, we use our model to predict each candidate's probability of being *paraphrase* as its similarity score, and then rank all the candidates. To evaluate the ranking performance, we use Precision@1, Recall@1, F_1@1 as metrics; to evaluate the classification performance for all question pairs, we employ two metrics: the Area under the Receiver Operating Characteristic curve (AUC) score [5] and the classification accuracy (ACC). For NLI, we only use ACC as the evaluation metric.

4.2 Comparisons Between Base Models

In Table 3, we compared different models for classifying sentence pairs with hCNN in both efficiency and effectiveness. Note that to fairly evaluate the efficiency of each model, we compute the total time of predicting all the test sentence pairs on CPU by setting the mini-batch size to 1, and report the average time. Also, for feature map sizes in BCNN, ABCNN and the BCNN component in hCNN, we set them as 50 for PI and 300 for NLI.

First, we can find that LSTM-based methods are generally much slower than CNN-based methods. Especially for ESIM, although it can outperform all CNN-based models, its computational time for each sentence pair is 32.2ms for our dataset and 79.5ms for SNLI, which is 6-11 times of CNN-based models. This means that most existing state-of-the-art models can only support low QPS, and therefore hard to be applied to industry. Second, clearly for both tasks, hCNN performs better than the other CNN-based methods, which indicates that BCNN and Pyramid are complementary to each other, and can work better when combined. Moreover, we verified that the improvements of hCNN over the other methods are significant with $p < 0.05$ based on McNemar's paired significance test [12]. Finally, while the computational cost of hCNN is slightly higher than BCNN and Pyramid, it can still serve 233 question pairs per second, which is able to satisfy the current demand of our industrial bot.

4.3 Comparisons Between TL Methods

We further evaluated the performance of our transfer learning method in Table 4 and Table 5.

We can observe from Table 5 that for all the five target domains, Src-Only perform much worse than Tgt-Only, and the average performance of Mixed is even worse than Tgt-Only. This implies that the source domain is quite different from all the target domains, and simply mixing the training data in two domains may lead to the model overfitting the source data since $|\mathcal{D}^s|$ is much larger than $|\mathcal{D}^t|$. In addition, it is observed that the widely used Fine-Tune method can perform slightly better than Tgt-Only in most cases, which shows that pre-training the model parameters on a related source domain is better than randomly initializing them. Moreover

[6]https://www.kaggle.com/c/quora-question-pairs

Table 1: Statistics of Paraphrase Identification Datasets

		Train	Dev	Test
AliExpress	Q-Q Pairs	29,884/8,624	7,622/1,968	7,569/2,133
	#Query-Q	3202/2414	781/578	777/584
	#Candi-Q	9.33	9.76	9.74
	#words per Query-Q	11.71	11.73	12.04
	#words per Candi-Q	8.37	8.37	8.54
Quora	Q-Q Pairs	404,290/149,265	N.A.	N.A.

Table 2: Statistics of Natural Language Inference Datesets

	SNLI	Fiction	Travel	Slate	Telephone	Government
Train	550,125	77,348	77,350	77,306	83,348	77,350
Dev	10,000	2,000	2,000	2,000	2,000	2,000
Test	10,000	2,000	2,000	2,000	2,000	2,000

Table 3: A Comparison Between Different Base Models

	E-Commerce			SNLI	
	AUC	ACC	Test Time(ms)	ACC	Test Time(ms)
BCNN	81.0	77.5	2.8	81.0	3.3
Pyramid	77.8	77.0	3.8	77.7	5.3
ABCNN	81.0	78.2	5.2	81.8	12.3
hCNN	82.2†	79.2†	4.3	83.2†	6.4
BiLSTM	79.9	77.8	7.1	80.6	19.6
ESIM	84.2	79.8	32.2	86.7	79.5

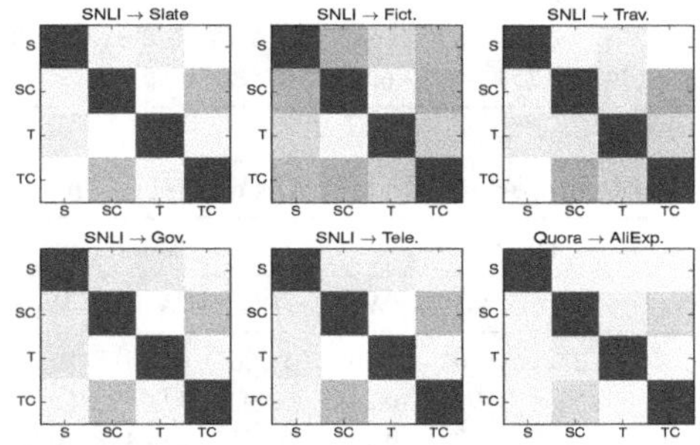

Figure 4: Learnt Correlation Matrix. A darker color means a larger entry value. S:Source, T:Target, SC:Source-shared, TC: Target-shared.

n all the five domains, the performance of two existing transfer earning frameworks FS and SS are both 1.9% better than that of Tgt-Only, which proves their usefulness. Furthermore, our proposed nethod DRSS improves the average performance of SS to 0.665, and he improvements are significant over all the tasks with $p < 0.05$ based on McNemar's paired significance test. This suggests that capturing the relationship between domains is generally useful for transfer learning. Finally, we can see that the incorporation of adversarial loss into SS and DRSS further boosts their performance, and DRSS-Adv can achieve the best accuracy across all the methods. Similar trends can be also observed for the PI task from Table 4. Interestingly, by comparing Table 3 and Table 4, we find that with the help of training data from the source domain, the performance of DRSS-Adv is even better than that of ESIM. These observations demonstrate the effectiveness of our transfer learning method.

Apart from the effectiveness, we also measure the efficiency of each method. Since the first five methods only use a single hCNN model for prediction, the computational time is the same as hCNN. As for SS, DRSS and their adversarial extensions, the computational time is 6.9ms, which is slightly longer than the other five methods but still much shorter than LSTM-based methods as in Table 3.

4.4 Domain Relationships

After obtaining the covariance matrix Ω for each source/target pair, we can derive their corresponding correlation matrices. For better comparison, here we show the square root of the correlation matrices for DRSS.

As shown in Fig. 4 that across all the six source/target pairs, $\mathbf{W}_{sc}$ and $\mathbf{W}_{tc}$ are positively related with each other. This is intuitive as the shared network is supposed to learn shared features between the source and the target domains, thus the learned $\mathbf{W}_{sc}$ and $\mathbf{W}_{tc}$ should be close to each other. This also shows the learned correlation matrix helps to capture the inter-domain relationship between $\mathbf{W}_{sc}$ and $\mathbf{W}_{tc}$.

In Fig.4, we can also see that for most source/target pairs except SNLI→Fict, the correlation between $\mathbf{W}_s$ and $\mathbf{W}_{sc}$ and that between $\mathbf{W}_t$ and $\mathbf{W}_{tc}$ learnt by our model are with small values. This indicates that in most cases, the shared feature space and the domain-specific feature space learnt by SS tend to be different from each other, and our model can help to reveal such intra-domain relationships.

Finally, to help us get a deeper insight on the helpfulness of the adversarial training, we perform comparisons on the correlation matrices learnt by DRSS and DRSS-Adv. We first show the result of SNLI→Fict. in Table 6. As we can see, for DRSS, the correlation between $\mathbf{W}_s$ (or $\mathbf{W}_t$) and $\mathbf{W}_{sc}$ (or $\mathbf{W}_{tc}$) is relatively large, while for DRSS-Adv, the correlation is relatively small. For the other subtasks, we find that the learnt matrices of DRSS-Adv are similar to those of DRSS, but we still observe that the intra-domain correlations of DRSS-Adv are generally smaller than those of DRSS. This shows that adding the adversarial loss can encourage the shared feature space to capture more domain-independent features, and further make the shared and domain-specific feature spaces more different. Therefore, the adversarial training can lead our model to better satisfy our assumption on the domain relationships, and finally improve the performance. All the above observations demonstrate that our model can capture the *inter-domain* and *intra-domain* relationship as mentioned in Section 2.2.

4.5 Extrinsic Evaluations

As mentioned in Section 3, for the online reranking algorithm, we propose to train GBDT by treating the prediction score of our DRSS model as another feature. To achieve this, we first took out the prediction scores of our DRSS model on the validation set. Then, we combined them together the other features as introduced in Section 3, and trained GBDT on the validation set. The model performance on the test set is reported in Table 7. Note that the test time here denotes the average serving time (including the Response Time), which is different from the reported test time in Table 3.

Table 4: The Result of Paraphrase Identification Task

	Prec@1	Rec@1	F1@1	ACC	AUC
Tgt-Only	0.717	0.551	0.623	0.792	0.822
Src-Only	0.619	0.368	0.461	0.719	0.686
Mixed	0.735	0.532	0.618	0.788	0.810
Fine-Tune	0.713	0.567	0.632	0.790	0.825
FS	0.734	0.595	0.657	0.797	0.831
SS	0.744	0.601	0.665	0.800	0.837
SS-Adv	0.743	0.603	0.666	0.808	0.842
DRSS	**0.757**	0.608	0.674†	**0.812**†	0.847
DRSS-Adv	0.753	**0.620**	**0.680**†	0.809	**0.849**

Table 5: The Classification Result of NLI Task

	Fict.	Trav.	Gov.	Tele.	Slate	AVG
Tgt-Only	0.647	0.658	0.692	0.644	0.579	0.644
Src-Only	0.520	0.516	0.540	0.520	0.488	0.517
Mixed	0.647	0.647	0.675	0.648	0.580	0.639
Fine-Tune	0.653	0.652	0.684	0.651	0.591	0.646
FS	0.662	0.671	0.704	0.657	0.588	0.656
SS	0.653	0.668	0.700	0.668	0.592	0.656
SS-Adv	0.666	0.666	0.701	0.664	0.597	0.659
DRSS	0.665	**0.674**†	0.706†	0.673†	0.605†	0.665
DRSS-Adv	**0.676**†	0.673	**0.707**†	**0.675**†	**0.607**†	**0.668**

Table 6: Correlation Matrices on SNLI→Fict.

	DRSS				DRSS-Adv			
	W_s	W_{sc}	W_t	W_{tc}	W_s	W_{sc}	W_t	W_{tc}
W_s	1.000	0.242	0.101	0.205	1.000	0.090	0.055	0.062
W_{sc}	0.242	1.000	0.008	0.247	0.090	1.000	0.024	0.221
W_t	0.101	0.008	1.000	0.127	0.055	0.024	1.000	0.043
W_{tc}	0.205	0.247	0.127	1.000	0.062	0.221	0.043	1.000

As we can see from the offline test, the GBDT model with the feature derived from our DRSS model (referred to as GBDT-DRSS) is respectively 26.3% and 7.1% better than our existing online model (referred to as GBDT) and the GBDT model with the feature derived from hCNN (refered to as GBDT-hCNN) in F_1@1. Although adding our DRSS feature leads to more computational time, the total prediction time is 80.7ms for each query question (i.e., QPS of 12), which is acceptable for our chatbots.

For online serving, to accelerate the computation, we set the number of candidates returned by *Lucene* as 30, and bundle the 30 candidates into a mini-batch to feed into our model for prediction. For online evaluation, we randomly sampled 2750 questions, where 1317 questions are answered by GBDT and 1433 questions are answered by GBDT-DRSS. Then, we asked one business analyst to annotate if the nearest question returned by models expresses the same meaning as the query question, and compared their precision at top-1. As shown in Table 7, the Prec@1 of GBDT-DRSS is 18.8% higher than that of GBDT.

Table 7: The Performance of Online Serving

	Offline		Online Evaluation
	F_1@1	Time(ms per query)	Prec@1
GBDT	0.539	20.1	0.614
GBDT-hCNN	0.636	69.9	-
GBDT-DRSS	**0.681**	80.7	**0.729**

5 RELATED WORK

Paraphrase Identification and Natural Language Inference: Recent years have witnessed great successes of applying different neural networks, including Recursive Neural Networks (ReNN), Reccurrent Neural Networks (RNN) and Convolutional Neural Networks (CNN), into Paraphrase Identification and Natural Language Inference [3, 29, 42]. Although all these models have been shown to significantly outperform the traditional methods without deep learning, most of them only focus on improving the performance of standard in-domain setting, and therefore require a large amount of labeled data to train a robust model. However, in practice, it will be time-consuming and costly to manually annotate much labeled data for each target domain we are interested in. Hence, in this paper, our focus is to apply an efficient and effective NN model into a transfer learning framework so that we can leverage the large amount of labeled data from a related source domain to train a robust model for a resource-poor target domain, which can benefit our chatbot-based question answering system.

Transfer Learning: Transfer learning (TL) has been extensively studied in the last decade [19]. Most existing studies for TL can be generally categorized into two groups. The first line of work assumes that we have enough labeled data from a source domain and also a little labeled data from a target domain [9], and the second line assumes that we only have labeled data from source domain but may also have some unlabeled data from a target domain [2, 44]. Our study belongs to the first line of work, which is also referred to as *supervised domain adaptation*.

For supervised domain adaptation, a majority of previous work belong to two clusters: instance-based and feature-based transfer learning. The former focuses on mining from the source labeled data to find those instances that are similar to the distribution of the target domain, and combine them together with the target labeled data [8, 15]. The core idea of the latter line of work is to find a shared feature space, which can reduce the divergence between the distribution of the source and the target domains [1, 17, 27, 32]. Our work follows the latter one, and tries to leverage NN models to learn a shared hidden representation for sentence pairs across domains.

Deep Transfer Learning: With the recent advances of deep learning, different NN-based TL frameworks have been proposed for image processing [43] and speech recognition [34] as well as NLP [18, 21, 40]. A simple but widely used framework is referred to as *fine-tuning* approaches, which first use the parameters of the well trained models on the source domain to initialize the model parameters of the target domain, and then fine tune the parameters based on labeled data in the target domain [21, 43]. Another line of work can be referred to as *multi-task feature learning* approaches, which bears the same intuition behind the feature-transfer methods as mentioned above. Among this line of work, one typical framework is to simply use a shared NN to learn a shared feature pace [21, 40], while another representative framework is to employ shared NN and two domain-specific NNs to respectively derive a hared feature space and two domain-specific feature space [18]. lotivated by the observation that both methods fail to consider ne domain relationship, in this paper, we propose to jointly learn ne shared feature representations and domain relationships in a nified model. Moreover, inspired by the recent success of applying dversarial networks into unsupervised domain adaptation [11, 30] nd multi-task learning [18], we also incorporate the adversarial aining into our transfer learning model in order to learn a more obust shared feature space across domains.

CONCLUSIONS

n this paper, we systematically evaluated different base methods nd transfer learning techniques for modelling sentence pairs, with he goal of proposing an effective and efficient transfer learning ramework for PI and NLI. Specifically, we first proposed a hyrid CNN model on the basis of two existing models, and then urther proposed a general transfer learning framework, which can imultaneously perform the shared feature learning and domain elationship learning in an end-to-end mode. Evaluations on both benchmark dataset and our own dataset showed that (1) our hyrid CNN model is both effective and efficient in comparison with everal representative models; (2) our transfer learning framework an outperform all the existing frameworks across six source/target airs. We further deployed our transfer learning model in our online hatbot system, and showed that it can improve the performance f the existing system by a large margin.

ACKNOWLEDGEMENTS

he authors would like to give great thanks to Feng Ji, Wei Zhou, Veipeng Zhao and Xu Hu for their helpfulness during the project, nd the anonymous reviewers for their constructive comments.

REFERENCES

[1] Andreas Argyriou, Theodoros Evgeniou, and Massimiliano Pontil. 2007. Multi-task feature learning. In *NIPS*.

[2] John Blitzer, Ryan McDonald, and Fernando Pereira. 2006. Domain Adaptation with Structural Correspondence Learning. In *EMNLP*.

[3] Samuel R. Bowman, Gabor Angeli, Christopher Potts, and Christopher D. Manning. 2015. A large annotated corpus for learning natural language inference. In *EMNLP*.

[4] Samuel R. Bowman, Jon Gauthier, Abhinav Rastogi, Raghav Gupta, Christopher D. Manning, and Christopher Potts. 2016. A Fast Unified Model for Parsing and Sentence Understanding. In *ACL*.

[5] Andrew P Bradley. 1997. The use of the area under the ROC curve in the evaluation of machine learning algorithms. *Pattern recognition* 30, 7 (1997), 1145–1159.

[6] Qian Chen, Xiaodan Zhu, Zhen-Hua Ling, Si Wei, Hui Jiang, and Diana Inkpen. 2017. Enhanced LSTM for Natural Language Inference. In *ACL*.

[7] Lei Cui, Shaohan Huang, Furu Wei, Chuanqi Tan, Chaoqun Duan, and Ming Zhou. 2017. SuperAgent: A Customer Service Chatbot for E-commerce Websites. In *ACL 2017, Demo*.

[8] Wenyuan Dai, Qiang Yang, Gui-Rong Xue, and Yong Yu. 2007. Boosting for transfer learning. In *ICML*.

[9] Hal Daume III. 2007. Frustratingly Easy Domain Adaptation. In *ACL*.

10] John Duchi, Elad Hazan, and Yoram Singer. 2011. Adaptive subgradient methods for online learning and stochastic optimization. *Journal of Machine Learning Research* 12, Jul (2011), 2121–2159.

11] Yaroslav Ganin, Evgeniya Ustinova, Hana Ajakan, Pascal Germain, Hugo Larochelle, François Laviolette, Mario Marchand, and Victor Lempitsky. 2016. Domain-adversarial training of neural networks. *Journal of Machine Learning Research* 17, 59 (2016), 1–35.

[12] Laurence Gillick and Stephen J Cox. 1989. Some statistical issues in the comparison of speech recognition algorithms. In *ICASSP*.

[13] Baotian Hu, Zhengdong Lu, Hang Li, and Qingcai Chen. 2014. Convolutional neural network architectures for matching natural language sentences. In *NIPS*.

[14] Jiwoon Jeon, W Bruce Croft, and Joon Ho Lee. 2005. Finding similar questions in large question and answer archives. In *CIKM*.

[15] Jing Jiang and ChengXiang Zhai. 2007. Instance Weighting for Domain Adaptation in NLP. In *ACL*.

[16] Matt Kusner, Yu Sun, Nicholas Kolkin, and Kilian Weinberger. 2015. From word embeddings to document distances. In *ICML*.

[17] Su-In Lee, Vassil Chatalbashev, David Vickrey, and Daphne Koller. 2007. Learning a meta-level prior for feature relevance from multiple related tasks. In *ICML*.

[18] Pengfei Liu, Xipeng Qiu, and Xuanjing Huang. 2017. Adversarial Multi-task Learning for Text Classification. In *ACL*.

[19] Mingsheng Long, Jianmin Wang, Guiguang Ding, Sinno Jialin Pan, and S Yu Philip. 2014. Adaptation regularization: A general framework for transfer learning. *IEEE Transactions on Knowledge and Data Engineering* 26, 5 (2014), 1076–1089.

[20] Lili Mou, Rui Men, Ge Li, Yan Xu, Lu Zhang, Rui Yan, and Zhi Jin. 2016. Natural Language Inference by Tree-Based Convolution and Heuristic Matching. In *ACL*.

[21] Lili Mou, Zhao Meng, Rui Yan, Ge Li, Yan Xu, Lu Zhang, and Zhi Jin. 2016. How Transferable are Neural Networks in NLP Applications?. In *EMNLP*.

[22] Sinno Jialin Pan and Qiang Yang. 2010. A survey on transfer learning. *IEEE Transactions on knowledge and data engineering* 22, 10 (2010), 1345–1359.

[23] Liang Pang, Yanyan Lan, Jiafeng Guo, Jun Xu, Shengxian Wan, and Xueqi Cheng. 2016. Text Matching as Image Recognition. In *AAAI*.

[24] Ankur Parikh, Oscar Täckström, Dipanjan Das, and Jakob Uszkoreit. 2016. A Decomposable Attention Model for Natural Language Inference. In *EMNLP*.

[25] Jeffrey Pennington, Richard Socher, and Christopher D. Manning. 2014. GloVe: Global Vectors for Word Representation. In *EMNLP*.

[26] Minghui Qiu, Feng-Lin Li, Siyu Wang, Xing Gao, Yan Chen, Weipeng Zhao, Haiqing Chen, Jun Huang, and Wei Chu. 2017. AliMe Chat: A Sequence to Sequence and Rerank based Chatbot Engine. In *ACL*.

[27] Minghui Qiu, Peilin Zhao, Ke Zhang, Jun Huang, Xing Shi, Xiaoguang Wang, and Wei Chu. 2017. A Short-Term Rainfall Prediction Model using Multi-Task Convolutional Neural Networks.. In *ICDM*.

[28] Tim Rocktäschel, Edward Grefenstette, Karl Moritz Hermann, Tomáš Kočiský, and Phil Blunsom. 2015. Reasoning about entailment with neural attention. *ICLR* (2015).

[29] Richard Socher, Eric H Huang, Jeffrey Pennin, Christopher D Manning, and Andrew Y Ng. 2011. Dynamic pooling and unfolding recursive autoencoders for paraphrase detection. In *NIPS*.

[30] Yaniv Taigman, Adam Polyak, and Lior Wolf. 2017. Unsupervised cross-domain image generation. *ICLR* (2017).

[31] Oriol Vinyals and Quoc Le. 2015. A neural conversational model. *arXiv preprint arXiv:1506.05869* (2015).

[32] Chang Wang and Sridhar Mahadevan. 2008. Manifold alignment using procrustes analysis. In *ICML*.

[33] Di Wang and Eric Nyberg. 2015. A Long Short-Term Memory Model for Answer Sentence Selection in Question Answering. In *ACL-IJCNLP*.

[34] Dong Wang and Thomas Fang Zheng. 2015. Transfer learning for speech and language processing. In *Signal and Information Processing Association Annual Summit and Conference (APSIPA)*.

[35] Shuohang Wang and Jing Jiang. 2017. A Compare-Aggregate Model for Matching Text Sequences. *ICLR* (2017).

[36] John Wieting, Mohit Bansal, Kevin Gimpel, and Karen Livescu. 2016. Towards universal paraphrastic sentence embeddings. *ICLR* (2016).

[37] Adina Williams, Nikita Nangia, and Samuel R Bowman. 2017. A Broad-Coverage Challenge Corpus for Sentence Understanding through Inference. *arXiv preprint arXiv:1704.05426* (2017).

[38] Ho Chung Wu, Robert Wing Pong Luk, Kam Fai Wong, and Kui Lam Kwok. 2008. Interpreting tf-idf term weights as making relevance decisions. *ACM Transactions on Information Systems (TOIS)* 26, 3 (2008), 13.

[39] Rui Yan, Yiping Song, and Hua Wu. 2016. Learning to respond with deep neural networks for retrieval-based human-computer conversation system. In *SIGIR*.

[40] Zhilin Yang, Ruslan Salakhutdinov, and William W Cohen. 2017. Transfer learning for sequence tagging with hierarchical recurrent networks. *ICLR* (2017).

[41] Wenpeng Yin and Hinrich Schütze. 2015. Convolutional Neural Network for Paraphrase Identification.. In *NAACL-HLT*.

[42] Wenpeng Yin, Hinrich Schütze, Bing Xiang, and Bowen Zhou. 2016. ABCNN: Attention-Based Convolutional Neural Network for Modeling Sentence Pairs. *Transactions of ACL* 4 (2016), 259–272.

[43] Jason Yosinski, Jeff Clune, Yoshua Bengio, and Hod Lipson. 2014. How transferable are features in deep neural networks?. In *NIPS*.

[44] Jianfei Yu and Jing Jiang. 2016. Learning Sentence Embeddings with Auxiliary Tasks for Cross-Domain Sentiment Classification. In *EMNLP*.

[45] Yu Zhang and Dit-Yan Yeung. 2010. A convex formulation for learning task relationships in multi-task learning. In *UAI*.

Review-Aware Answer Prediction for Product-Related Questions Incorporating Aspects

Qian Yu
The Chinese University of Hong Kong
yuqian@se.cuhk.edu.hk

Wai Lam
The Chinese University of Hong Kong
wlam@se.cuhk.edu.hk

ABSTRACT

In E-commerce sites, there are platforms for users to pose product-related questions and experienced customers may provide answers voluntarily. Among the questions asked by users, a large proportion of them are yes-no questions reflecting that users wish to know whether or not the product can satisfy a certain criterion or meet a certain expectation. Both Question Answering (QA) approaches and Community Question Answering methods are not suitable for answer prediction for new questions in this setting. The reasons are that questions are product-associated and many of them are concerned about user experiences and subjective opinions. In addition to existing question-answer pairs, user written reviews can provide useful clues for answer prediction. In this paper, we propose a new framework that can tackle the task of review-aware answer prediction for product-related questions. The aspect analytics model in this framework learns latent aspects as well as aspect-specific embeddings of reviews via a 3-order Autoencoder. One advantage of this learned model is that it can generate aspect-specific representations for new questions. The predictive answer model in our framework, learned jointly from existing questions, answers, and reviews, is able to predict the answers for new yes-no questions taking into consideration of aspects. Besides, our framework can provide supportive reviews grouped by relevant aspects serving as information for explainable answers. Experiment results on 15 different product categories from a large-scale benchmark E-commence QA dataset demonstrate the effectiveness of our framework.

CCS CONCEPTS

•Information systems →Question answering;

KEYWORDS

Question Answering, Aspect Detection, 3-order Autoencoder

The work described in this paper is substantially supported by a grant from the Research Grant Council of the Hong Kong Special Administrative Region, China (Project Code: 14203414).

WSDM'18, February 5–9, 2018, Marina Del Rey, CA, USA
© 2018 ACM. ISBN 978-1-4503-5581-0/18/02...$15.00
DOI: http://dx.doi.org/10.1145/3159652.3159718

ACM Reference format:
Qian Yu and Wai Lam. 2018. Review-Aware Answer Predictio for Product-Related Questions Incorporating Aspects. In *Proceedings of WSDM'18, February 5–9, 2018, Marina Del Rey, C. USA*, 9 pages.
DOI: http://dx.doi.org/10.1145/3159652.3159718

1 INTRODUCTION

Nowadays QA systems are integrated into E-commerce site such as Amazon. This kind of system provides a platfo m for users to pose questions and answers. Specifically, user can ask a question about a product, and the syster will allow some users (e.g., customers who bought this proc uct) to provide answers. Both questions and answers ar posed voluntarily, thus the user asking the question woul not be replied immediately. This is an undesirable user ex perience for potential purchasers since they would not logi the E-commerce sites frequently to check answers as commu nity sites. Automated question answering in this scenario i important for improving customers' satisfaction. One char acteristic of product-related QA in E-commerce sites is tha a large proportion of the questions are yes-no questions, i.e questions whose answer can be "*Yes*" or "*No*". Accordin to a manual analysis conducted by McAuley and Yang [16 more than 50% of the questions in Amazon, a popular E commerce site, are yes-no questions. Also, the sheer numbe of such kind of questions can be perceived from the volum of the dataset collected from the same E-commerce site a depicted in Table 1. Potential consumers who pose yes-n questions often wish to know whether or not the produc can satisfy a certain criterion or meet a certain expectatio They look for a very specific judgement which will influenc their purchase decision. In this paper, we investigate th task of automatically predicting a "*Yes*" or "*No*" answer t a new yes-no question in such setting.

Although some QA approaches [8, 14, 35] are able to gen erate answers automatically, many of them require utilizin entity knowledge graphs such as Freebase [32], or construct ing a new knowledge base. However, in E-commerce sites any two products are distinct even though they belong t the same category, and some products such as clothes an paintings do not even have proper names. Thus, buildin a factual knowledge base containing all the products is no feasible, and methods relying on entity matching or identif cation are not suitable. A lot of QA tasks are formulated a answer ranking [21, 33]. For Community QA (CQA), it typ cally consists of question retrieval and answer ranking. Can didate answers for a question are ranked via modeling th relationship between questions and answers. This approach is not effective for product-related QA. One reason is that the data is too sparse to train a product-specific model, since each question is associated with one product and any similar question or answer for other products provides no help. Another characteristic of product-related questions found in E-commerce sites is that many of them are concerned about user experiences and subjective opinions as exemplified by the questions such as "Is the padding good enough to have strong protection?". Existing user written reviews can be an informative data source. These reviews can provide clues for answer prediction regarding the corresponding product, especially when existing questions or answers are not relevant to the new question. Individual experiences and opinions covering different aspects of the product may be described in reviews from experienced customers.

Despite the fact that reviews are useful, it is not feasible to go through and analyze all the reviews of the product manually. McAuley and Yang [16, 27] proposed the state-of-the-art method for solving review-aware answer prediction, and their method is based on a machine learning model, namely, Mixture of Experts. In their model, a relevance function and a prediction function are learned. However, one shortcoming is that their model does not consider latent aspects related to the product category and the answer prediction performance will be adversely affected by the existence of reviews about irrelevant aspects with respect to the new question. We note that McAuley and Yang [16] also handled the open-ended questions via ranking answers and non-answers. But in practice this answer ranking strategy cannot provide an instant response when no candidate answer exists. For newly posed open-ended questions, the current ranking strategy can only provide relevant reviews for users to browse, but leaving the precise answer to be posed by voluntary users. For yes-no questions, we can take a further step to provide precise answer prediction as in [16]. Instant answer prediction can significantly benefit users within an E-commerce site by reducing the overall average waiting time. Therefore, we focus on yes-no questions and aim at developing a new framework achieving accurate answer prediction and providing a more explainable aspect-aware response.

In this paper, we propose a new framework that can tackle the review-aware answer prediction for product-related yes-no questions as mentioned above. Aspects of each product category are automatically detected and captured from reviews texts. Then aspects are exploited for predicting the answer for new questions. A sample output of our framework is depicted in Fig 1. It shows the answer prediction for the question about a particular car seat cover for pet. Apart from showing the predicted answer, which is "*Yes*" in this example, our framework can also display supportive reviews grouped by relevant aspects. Since the question is concerned with "coverage", "back seat" and "puppies", the two related aspects in this product category, namely "Placement, Installation" and "Cleanliness, Health" are presented to the user. The potential consumers can read the opinions shared in these aspects for obtaining more insights. For

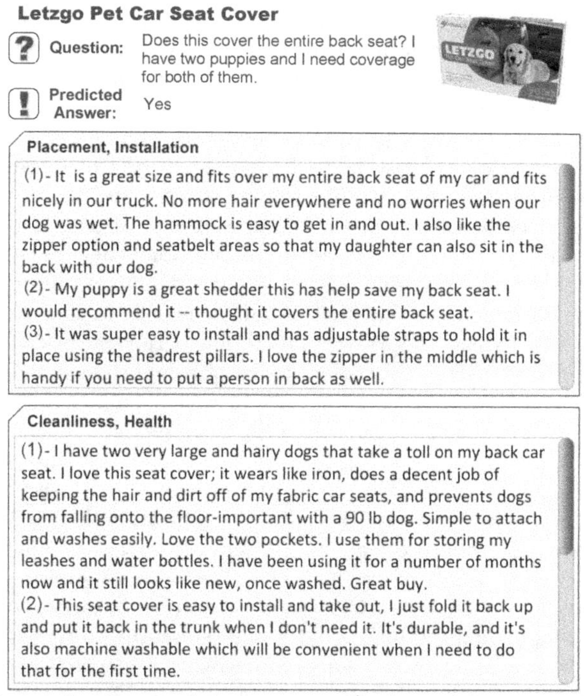

Figure 1: A sample answer prediction with supportive reviews produced by our framework.

example, Reviews (1) and (2) under the aspect "Placement, Installation" mention that this product can "cover the entire back seat", which is relevant to the question. Related user experiences and issues are also shared in the reviews shown in the other relevant aspect.

One important component in our framework is the aspect analytics model which can detect and capture latent aspects from a collection of review texts and learn aspect-specific embeddings of reviews via a 3-order Autoencoder. One advantage is that it can generate aspect-specific representations for new questions. This aspect analytics model helps to develop the predictive answer model which jointly captures intricate relationships among question texts, review texts, and yes-no answers, taking into consideration of aspects. Then, this learned model is able to predict the answers for new yes-no questions. We evaluate our answer prediction framework on 15 different product categories from a large-scale benchmark E-commerce QA dataset, and the results demonstrate the effectiveness. Besides, we also present some case studies illustrating the answer prediction as well as aspect-based explainable answers.

2 RELATED WORK

Product-related Question Answering is an emerging research topic due to the popularity of E-commerce. This QA problem setting is different from traditional QA or CQA tasks since such kind of questions/answers are product dependent and involve some extent of user experiences or subjective opinions. Therefore, user written product reviews play an important role for providing useful clues. The state-of-the-art method for this task is proposed by McAuley and Yang [16], where each associated review is utilized as an "expert" for answer prediction. Later this model is extended to handle multiple answers [27]. In their model, a relevance function and a prediction function are learned from existing questions, reviews and answers. The relevance score and the prediction of each review can be obtained based on the learned functions. Then the answer prediction for a new question is calculated via the mixture of experts paradigm. However, one shortcoming is that their model does not consider latent aspects. Thus, the answer prediction performance can be adversely affected by the existence of a large amount of irrelevant reviews since each piece of review considering any aspect is treated as an expert in their model. The model proposed by Yu et al. [36] makes use of a hierarchical organization of reviews, consisting of aspects with different granularity. However, a distinct organization structure is needed for each product, and it requires extensive domain knowledge, which makes it not feasible for large product set. Another review-aware QA model known as AQA proposed by Moghaddam and Ester [17] only supports answer ranking which is not proper for product-related question instant response. Although incorporating aspects, the above two models still suffer from the shortcomings mentioned above, and their task settings are not the same as ours.

Another QA scenario is Community Question Answering (CQA) where a collection of questions and answers previously posed by users are available. The main components for CQA include question retrieval and answer ranking [30]. Evaluation forums such as SemEval [20] have been organized to promote this research task. Toba et al. [25] proposed a generic hierarchy-of-classifiers for predicting the quality of answers in CQA. Filice et al. [10] utilized a binary kernel-based classifier to distinguish good and bad question-answer pairs. Some models exploit deep neural networks, such as Convolutional Neural Network (CNN) [3, 24], Autoencoder [1], LSTM with attention [13]. He and Golub [23] proposed a pairwise ranking strategy on a neural networks model. Semantic analysis [2, 31] is also adopted in some methods. Lexical and semantic-based similarity measures are investigated in the recent work of Franco-Salvador et al. [11]. We can observe that CQA methods commonly adopt selection or ranking models which are not feasible for our problem setting. Some CQA tasks require retrieving useful answers to produce a final Yes/No overall answer [19], but no review is exploited in that task. Unsupervised question retrieval [37] is a typical task when there are no available candidate answers, but it provides limited help for product-related questions since the answer prediction will not benefit from similar questions of other products. Fang, et al. incorporated social network modeling into a QA system [9], but social relationships in E-commerce sites are typically not available.

Knowledge bases are shown to be an effective tool for answering [4] and a lot of models require the construction of knowledge bases or the availability of entity knowledge graphs [5]. For example, Wang et al. [29] extracted a conditional knowledge base from question-answer pairs. Other QA methods make use of Freebase [7, 32, 34] or DBpedia [15, 26]. However, as mentioned before, there is no public knowledge base containing every single product, and entity matching is not feasible.

Aspect extraction for reviews is also a related area, and the state-of-the-art methods include MeLDA [38] and SERBM [28]. Compared to these methods, our proposed aspect analytics model can generate aspect-specific review embedding in addition to extracting aspects.

3 MODEL DESCRIPTION

3.1 Problem Definition

Typically there are some products under a particular product category in an E-commerce site. A set of historical product related questions are associated with each product. As mentioned before, we only focus on yes-no questions which constitute a large proportion of product-related questions. For a particular product, we denote the set of yes-no questions by Q. Each question $q \in Q$ is associated with its answer a_q which can take on only two possible answers, namely $a_q \in \{Yes, No\}$. Additionally, there is a set of reviews, denoted as R, associated with that particular product. Based on these historical questions and their answers, as well as reviews of all products in the same product category, we aim at developing an answer prediction framework for that product category. After training from the historical data, given a new yes-no question for a product in the same product category, the aim is to predict a binary answer, namely, "Yes" or "No". Moreover, supportive reviews can be presented to users for serving as information for explainable answers.

3.2 Model Overview

We develop a new answer prediction framework which consists of two components, namely, the aspect analytics model and the predictive answer model. Given a product category, the aim of the aspect analytics model is to detect and capture latent aspects from a collection of review texts in an unsupervised manner. Specifically, we employ a 3-order Autoencoder to model aspects from review texts in the same product category and learn aspect-specific embeddings for reviews. This aspect analytics model can generate aspect distributions and embeddings of reviews capturing hidden semantic features associated with certain aspects. One advantage of this learned model is that it can also generate aspect distributions as well as aspect-specific representations for new questions. The second component of our framework is the predictive answer model. This model captures intricate relationships among question texts, review texts, and yes-no answers. It incorporates aspect-based distributions, aspect specific review embeddings and question representations obtained from the aspect analytics model. Specifically, based on the aspect distributions, we can identify aspects to which the questions and reviews are relevant. Reviews with more relevant aspects can appropriately contribute more to the

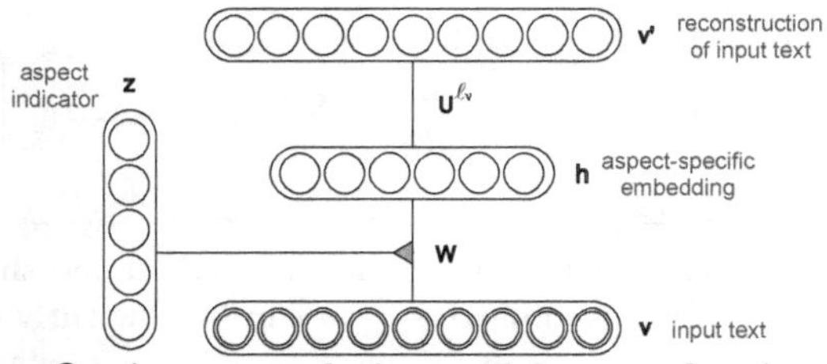

'igure 2: Aspect analytics model. v, z, h, v' are lay-rs for input, aspect, aspect-specific representation and econstruction. W, U are parameter matrices.

nswer prediction. The answer prediction model is learned rom existing historical questions, answers, and review texts n a supervised manner. Furthermore, our answer prediction ramework can offer supportive reviews grouped by relevant spects for serving as information for explainable answers.

.3 Aspect Analytics Model

3.3.1 Aspect Modeling. We propose a model for aspect nodeling in our framework based on 3-order Autoencoder. 'his model is able to detect and capture latent aspects vi- training from the set of all reviews in the same product ategory in an unsupervised manner. The model is able to apture the intricate relationships between review/question exts and aspects. Two characteristics of this model make t suitable for our problem setting. Since we would like to xtract aspects from reviews and aspect-specific embeddings or reviews and questions, a model that can jointly capture he relationships among the three elements, namely, reviews, spects and aspect-specific embeddings is desirable. Anoth-r characteristic of this model is that reconstruction-based earning for each aspect facilitates the extraction of aspect-pecific intrinsic features in an unsupervised manner.

The architecture of this aspect analytics model is shown n Fig 2. There are four inter-dependent layers. The layer lenoted by the vector **v** represents the input of the model orresponding to a piece of review or question text. To ob-ain the input vector from a piece of text, we transform the ext to a vector **v** whose dimension is the same as the size of ocabulary denoted as K. Each dimension is a binary value lenoting whether or not the corresponding word exists in his input text. The layer shown on the left of Fig 2 depict- an aspect indicator vector, denoted as **z** with dimension representing the number of aspects. The probability of ach aspect is represented by the value of the corresponding limension in the vector **z**. Given an input text, the sum of probabilities of all the aspects should be 1 meaning that ach text corresponds to an aspect distribution. The layer lenoted by **h** is the aspect-specific embedding with dimen-ion J for the input review, and $\mathbf{v}'$ is the reconstruction ayer. The dimension of $\mathbf{v}'$ is the same as the input vector , i.e., K. Conditioned on a particular aspect, the model ecomes a standard autoencoder where the hidden layer **h** s used to learn the embeddings of the input reviews and $\mathbf{v}'$ an reconstruct the input **v**. The learned features in **h** are lifferent for different aspects. Therefore this layer can be used to generate aspect-specific review embeddings. Additionally, after model training, this layer can also be used for generating aspect-specific representations for new questions in the same product category.

Let us focus on the subgraph containing the three layers, namely, **v**, **h**, and **z**. These layers in this subgraph are associated with a 3-dimensional parameter matrix **W** and this becomes an energy-based generative model similar to the model proposed in [18]. Each parameter $w^{\ell}_{kj} \in \mathbf{W}$ is associated with three nodes, namely, v_k, h_j, and z^{ℓ} from the three layers respectively. We can express the joint distribution of the input text **v**, the aspect **z** and the aspect-specific embedding **h** via energy-based formulation:

$$P(\mathbf{v},\mathbf{h},\mathbf{z}) = \frac{1}{Z}\exp[-E(\mathbf{v},\mathbf{h},\mathbf{z})] \quad (1)$$

where Z is the partition function for normalization, and $E(\mathbf{v},\mathbf{h},\mathbf{z})$ is the energy function:

$$E(\mathbf{v},\mathbf{h},\mathbf{z}) = -\sum_{k,j,\ell}^{K} W^{\ell}_{kj}\hat{v}_k h_j z_{\ell} - \sum_{k} b_k \hat{v}_k - \sum_{j}^{J} c_j h_j - \sum_{\ell}^{L} d^{\ell} z^{\ell}$$

where b_k, c_j, d^{ℓ} are the bias parameters for the corresponding nodes.

Given an input text **v**, the corresponding probability belonging to each aspect can be formulated as a softmax function:

$$P(z^{\ell}|\mathbf{v}) = \frac{\exp[-F(\mathbf{v},z^{\ell})]}{\sum_{\ell^*}\exp[-F(\mathbf{v},z^{\ell^*})]} \quad (2)$$

where $F(\mathbf{v},z^{\ell}) = -\sum_j^J \log\left[1+\exp(\sum_k^K W^{\ell}_{kj}v_k + c_j)\right] - d^{\ell}$.

For any aspect z^{ℓ} selected, we can compute the activation probability of one hidden feature node denoted as h_j based on the input **v** and the aspect z^{ℓ}:

$$P(h_j|\mathbf{v},z^{\ell}) = \sigma\left(\sum_{k}^{K} W^{\ell}_{kj}v_k + c_j\right) \quad (3)$$

where $\sigma(x) = 1/[1+\exp(-x)]$ is the sigmoid function.

Now let us take the reconstruction layer $\mathbf{v}'$ into consideration. We construct an aspect-based autoencoder which can reconstruct the input text **v** via the aspect-specific embedding. The embedding in **h** and the reconstruction in $\mathbf{v}'$ are both aspect-specific. The autoencoder corresponding to one aspect will be responsible to learn the embeddings for reviews belonging to this aspect. Thus, the extracted features focus on the dominant aspect, and the aspect-specific embeddings are more effective for answer prediction.

Based on the aspect probabilities in Eqn 2, we assign the aspect with the largest probability as the dominant aspect for **v**, denoted as $z^{\ell_{\mathbf{v}}}$. With $z^{\ell_{\mathbf{v}}}$ determined for the review **v**, we use three layers, namely, **v**, **h** and $\mathbf{v}'$ to construct an autoencoder. The encoder utilizes the parameters $W^{\ell_{\mathbf{v}}}_{kj}(\forall k, \forall j)$ to transform the input review **v** to the embedding **h** via $P(h_j|\mathbf{v},z^{\ell_{\mathbf{v}}})$ according to Eqn 3. Similarly, the decoder recovers the input review from the embedding via a parameter matrix $\mathbf{U}^{\ell_{\mathbf{v}}}$. This matrix is dependent on the dominant aspect $z^{\ell_{\mathbf{v}}}$. In other words, we need to obtain $z^{\ell_{\mathbf{v}}}$ first for a review, then the corresponding matrix $\mathbf{U}^{\ell_{\mathbf{v}}}$ is exploited for decoding. The decoding procedure is formulated as:

$$P(v'_k|\mathbf{h}, z^{\ell_\mathbf{v}}) = \sigma\left(\sum_j^J U^{\ell_\mathbf{v}}_{kj} h_j - b'_k\right) \tag{4}$$

where b'_k is the bias parameter for the k-th node in the reconstruction layer $\mathbf{v}'$.

3.3.2 Aspect Model Training. The training of our aspect analytics model can be organized as two procedures. At first, we learn the generative model which is characterized by the parameter matrix $\mathbf{W}$ described above. This procedure will automatically extract latent aspects from the reviews and also learn a set of review embeddings. Then, with the dominant aspect for each review determined, the second procedure is to train the autoencoder for each aspect to further refine the embeddings based on the reconstruction principle.

In the first procedure, the learning of the generative model is conducted in an unsupervised manner. The collection of reviews in the product category, represented as $\mathbb{R}$, is used for training. The learning objective is to maximize the likelihood of training reviews, regularized by aspect based priors:

$$L(\mathbb{R}) = \sum_{\mathbf{v}\in\mathbb{R}} P(\mathbf{v}) - \lambda L_{prior} \tag{5}$$

where $\mathbf{v}$ represents each training review in $\mathbb{R}$, and its model probability $P(\mathbf{v})$ can be formulated with the joint probability in Eqn 1 as $P(\mathbf{v}) = \sum_{\mathbf{h},\mathbf{z}} P(\mathbf{v}, \mathbf{h}, \mathbf{z})$.

Since we wish to detect the aspects and learn aspect-specific embedding via $\mathbf{z}$ and $\mathbf{h}$ respectively, we incorporate aspect-based priors to guide the learning procedure. The set of prior consists of a number of aspects and their related aspect words together with the probability of each word belonging to the corresponding aspect. The second term L_{prior} in the objective in Eqn 5 can be regarded as the regularization term incorporating the prior probabilities:

$$\sum_{k,\ell,p^\ell_k\neq 0} L^{k,\ell}_{prior} = \sum_{k,\ell,p^\ell_k\neq 0}\left[\log P(z^\ell|v_k) - \log p^\ell_k\right]^2 \tag{6}$$

where $P(z^\ell|v_k)$ is the probability that the word v_k belonging to the aspect z^ℓ in the aspect analytics model, obtained via Eqn 2.

We use p^ℓ_k to denote the prior probability that the word k belongs to the aspect denoted by the ℓ-th node in $\mathbf{z}$. This prior can be easily obtained from off-the-shelf latent topic modeling methods such as Latent Dirichlet Allocation (LDA) [6]. Optionally, one can manually scrutinize the top-ranked word list of a discovered topic generated by the topic modeling method. Generally, only a handful of words for each aspect are needed.

An adapted Contrastive Divergence (CD) training method can be adopted as the learning procedure for the first term in Eqn 5. The details of this CD method can be found in [18]. For the second term, namely, the objective term for the prior written in Eqn 6, the stochastic gradient decent method can be applied by combining with the parameter increments from the CD method. The gradient of the prior related objective term can be expressed as:

$$\frac{\partial L^{k,\ell}_{prior}}{\partial\Theta} = \log\frac{P(z^\ell|v_k)}{p^\ell_k}\left[\frac{\partial F^\ell_k}{\partial\Theta} - \sum_{\ell^*} P(z^{\ell^*}|v_k)\frac{\partial F^{\ell^*}_k}{\partial\Theta}\right] \tag{7}$$

where $\frac{\partial F^\ell_k}{\partial\Theta} = \frac{\partial F(v_k, z^\ell)}{\partial\Theta} = -\sum_j^J \sigma(W^\ell_{kj} + c_j)\frac{\partial(W^\ell_{kj}+c_j)}{\partial\Theta}$. Both the parameter increment from the CD method and the gradient from the prior objective term can be efficiently calculated.

After the generative learning, we obtain a set of values for the 3-order parameter matrix $\mathbf{W}$. The next procedure is to refine $\mathbf{W}$ via the reconstruction layer. Specifically, we construct and learn the autoencoder for each aspect. Given review as input text $\mathbf{v}$, we can obtain the aspect distribution via Eqn 2, and we select the aspect with the maximum probability as the dominant aspect denoted as $z^{\ell_\mathbf{v}}$ for this review. As described in Section 3.3.1, the parameters $W^{\ell_\mathbf{v}}_{kj}(\forall k, \forall j)$, $\mathbf{U}^{\ell_\mathbf{v}}$ and the related bias parameters make up an autoencoder for the aspect $z^{\ell_\mathbf{v}}$. This autoencoder can be trained via the back-propagation method with reconstruction error minimization as the learning objective. With reviews dominated by the same aspect as training samples, this reconstruction learning for the corresponding autoencoder is repeated until the acceptable average reconstruction error is achieved and stable embeddings are obtained for reviews. In this way, $\mathbf{W}$ is further refined for aspect-specific embeddings via considering review text reconstruction.

The trained model captures different semantics with different hidden layers. The values in the vector $\mathbf{z}$ form the distribution of aspects for the input text, and this aspect distribution can be used to indicate to which aspects the input review or question is related. When chosen one node in $\mathbf{z}$, we can obtain the hidden representation in $\mathbf{h}$ for each review as its aspect-specific embedding. Besides, $\mathbf{h}$ can also be used for generating aspect-specific representation of a given new question from the same product category when we input the new question as $\mathbf{v}$ into the learned model via Eqn 3.

3.4 Predictive Answer Model

3.4.1 Predictive Answer Modeling. In this section, we describe the predictive answer model which captures intricate relationships among questions, reviews, and the corresponding answers. Equipped with the aspect-based distributions, aspect-specific review embeddings of reviews and question representation obtained from the aspect analytics component mentioned in Section 3.3, the predictive answer model is able to predict an answer for a new yes-no question.

The main idea of the predictive answer model is to compute the predictive answer probability. The predictive answer probability, denoted as $P(a|q, R)$, is the probability of predicting the answer a for the question q given the set of reviews R of the associated product, and it is formulated as follows:

$$P(a|q, R) = \begin{cases} P(Yes|q, R) & a = Yes \\ 1 - P(Yes|q, R) & a = No \end{cases} \tag{8}$$

where

$$P(Yes|q,R) = \sum_{\ell \in L} P(z^\ell|q) \sum_{r \in R^\ell} S^\ell(q,r)P^\ell(Yes|q,r) \quad (9)$$

$P(z^\ell|q)$ is the probability that the question q belongs to each aspect z^ℓ, and it can be easily obtained via Eqn 2 treating the question text as an input to the aspect analytics model. This distribution assigns different weight for different aspect, emphasizing the influence of the most related aspects while avoiding interfering from other aspects.

To describe the formulation of $S^\ell(q,r)$ and $P^\ell(Yes|q,r)$, we first define R^ℓ. Suppose that L aspects have been discovered from the review set R based on the aspect analytics model. Each review should have one dominant aspect according to its aspect distribution. We define R^ℓ as the set of reviews whose dominant aspect is z^ℓ. Formally, this subset of reviews can be written as:

$$R^\ell = \{r \in R | \ell = \arg\max_{\ell^*} P(z^{\ell^*}|r)\} \quad (10)$$

$S^\ell(q,r)$ is the relevance score between the question q and the review r with the aspect z^ℓ. First, we obtain the aspect distribution of the question and review, denoted as $\mathbf{z}_q$ and $\mathbf{z}_r$ respectively, via Eqn 2. Then we use the cosine similarity measure to compute the relevance between them. Formally, for each review r in R^ℓ:

$$S^\ell(q,r) = \cos(\mathbf{z}_q, \mathbf{z}_r)/Z_\ell \quad (11)$$

where $Z_\ell = \sum_{r^* \in R^\ell} \cos(\mathbf{z}_q, \mathbf{z}_{r^*})$. This similarity enables the relevant reviews to obtain larger scores to influence the final answer prediction. Irrelevant reviews will provide little influence even though they belong to the same aspect.

We use different $P^\ell(Yes|q,r)$ for different review subset R^ℓ according to the aspect indicator ℓ. For reviews in R^ℓ, their embeddings in the same aspect-specific space can be readily obtained from the aspect analytics model. We denote the embedding within the aspect z^ℓ of the review r as $\mathbf{h}_r^\ell$. For the given question text q, we can obtain the aspect-specific representation $\mathbf{h}_q^\ell$ according to Eqn 3. With these aspect-specific review embeddings and question representation, the predictive answer probability given the question and a review can be formulated as:

$$P^\ell(Yes|q,r) = \sigma(\mathbf{h}_q^\ell \cdot \mathbf{M} \cdot \mathbf{h}_r^\ell) \quad (12)$$

where the matrix $\mathbf{M}$ contains the parameters for this predictive model. Each parameter value M_{ij} models the connection between the i-th feature in hidden representation of question $\mathbf{h}_q^\ell$ and the j-th feature in review embedding $\mathbf{h}_r^\ell$. The parameter matrix $\mathbf{M}$ can be learned by a supervised learning algorithm described in Section 3.4.3.

After training, the value of $P^\ell(Yes|q,r)$ is different across aspects and reviews. $P(z^\ell|q)$ and $S^\ell(q,r)$ provide the weights for aspects and individual reviews respectively. Thus, the final prediction receives more influence from related aspects and relevant reviews.

3.4.2 Providing Explanations for Answers. Related aspects for the question q can be displayed according to $P(z^\ell|q)$. Furthermore, suppose the answer prediction for q is a_q^*, namely $a_q^* = \arg\max_{a \in \{Yes,No\}} P(a|q,R)$, we design a explainability score function $S^\ell(q,r)$:

$$S^\ell_{a_q^*}(q,r) = \begin{cases} S^\ell(q,r) & P(a_q^*|q,r) > 1/2 \\ 0 & \text{otherwise} \end{cases} \quad (13)$$

to rank the reviews so that more supportive reviews for the answer prediction can be ranked higher in each aspect, served as explanations to the answer.

3.4.3 Predictive Answer Model Training. We define the training set as $T = \{(q, a_q, R)\}$, where each element in the training set is a tuple composed of a question q, its true answer a_q, and the review set of the associated product. The learning objective is to maximize an expression denoted as $O(T)$ which is the likelihood of true answers given the corresponding questions and reviews:

$$\arg\max O(T) = \arg\max_{\mathbf{M}} \sum_{(q,a_q,R) \in T} \log P(a_q|q,R) \quad (14)$$

The gradient computation of $O(T)$ is efficient, so the stochastic gradient decent method can be employed for training.

4 EXPERIMENTS

We conduct extensive experiments to evaluate our answer prediction framework, comparing with some baselines and the state-of-the-art method. A qualitative study on two sample cases are conducted illustrating the answer responses and explanations produced by our framework.

4.1 Dataset

Table 1: Number of yes-no questions, products and reviews for each product category.

product category	yes-no question	product	review
arts, crafts, sewing (arts)	10327	2739	128165
automotive (auto)	50857	12035	395872
baby	13649	3582	361095
beauty	18091	5505	499662
cell phones, accessories (phones)	48900	10165	1534094
electronics (elec)	165598	37808	4314858
health, personal care (health)	33433	9999	1162587
home, kitchen (home)	76326	22629	2012777
musical instruments (musical)	11595	2860	156888
office products (office)	20978	5357	478823
patio, lawn, garden (patio)	26347	7479	451473
pet supplies (pet sup)	15583	4437	481781
sports, outdoors (sports)	64563	17900	1013196
tools, home improvement (tools)	46521	12677	752947
toy, games (toy)	22040	6710	564835

We adopt the large-scale benchmark Amazon question/answer dataset [1] collected by McAuley and Yang [16] in our experiments. This dataset contains 1.4 million answered questions and 13 million related reviews. The product for each question can be identified, thus the associated reviews are available given a question. Yes-no questions in the dataset are labeled via a question labeling technique developed by He & Dai [12]. For each yes-no question, the ground truth answer is labeled with "*Yes*" or "*No*" via a combination of the human top-voted answer and the learned classifier. The details

[1] http://jmcauley.ucsd.edu/data/amazon/qa

of the question classification and answer labeling processes can be found in [16]. We collect all the yes-no questions from each product category and use the largest 15 product categories as shown in Table 1 for our experiments. The number of yes-no questions in each product category ranges from 10,000 to 170,000.

4.2 Experimental Setup

4.2.1 Experimental Setting. To learn the answer prediction model for each category, we use 2/3 questions and their associated answers and reviews as the training set. The remaining data is used as the test set to evaluate the answer prediction performance. 1,000 stemmed words with the highest term frequency are used as the vocabulary in a product category. Thus, for our proposed aspect analytics model, the input $\mathbf{v}$ is a 1000-dimension vector for each review. The dimension of the aspect indicator layer, namely $\mathbf{z}$, is set to 5. The dimension of the aspect-specific embedding layer, i.e., $\mathbf{h}$ is selected in $\{10, 20\}$. The parameter λ in Eqn 5 is 0.5. To evaluate the answer prediction performance, we use the commonly used prediction accuracy metric as the major evaluation metric. We note that in [16], the metric *accuracy*@50% is used. Slightly different from the ordinary accuracy metric, *accuracy*@50% only calculates the prediction accuracy of top 50% questions ranked by the prediction confidence in descending order. The details of this metric is described in [16]. In instant response scenario as indicated in our problem task, the commonly used accuracy metric is more appropriate since it considers every question. Nevertheless, we also conduct additional evaluations using *accuracy*@50% for direct comparison.

4.2.2 Comparative Methods. We make use of several baselines and the state-of-the-art method for comparison. One of the baselines is regarded as a basic CQA retrieval approach, namely, Language model (LM) [22]. We regard the given question as the query for retrieving questions in the same product category, and then use the relevance scores as weights for voting the possible answers, namely, Yes and No. The final prediction is the answer with the larger vote value. The second comparative method is recently proposed Distributed Representation based Language Model (DRLM) [37] that incorporates a distributed representation for word/question/category and becomes the state-of-the-art unsupervised method for question retrieval in CQA. Generally, CQA methods do not utilize reviews. We also consider some comparative methods that can incorporate reviews. cro-L [16] utilizes reviews for answer prediction. The relevance between a question and a review is computed via standard relevance measures from information retrieval and document summarization including cosine score, Rouge-L score and Okapi BM25 score. Then it uses the relevance scores for answer prediction. Another model called Mixture of Experts (MoE) is proposed in [16] for solving the same task and it can be considered as the state-of-the-art model. We run the programs of all the above mentioned methods as well as our framework on all the 15 product categories.

Table 2: Accuracy of answer prediction. § indicate that the performance improvement is statistically significant (0.05) over MoE.

category	LM	DRLM	cro-L	MoE	ours-10	ours-20
arts	0.644	0.657	0.667	0.689	0.713	**0.717**
auto	0.594	0.605	0.725	0.742	0.755	**0.758**
baby	0.671	0.645	0.713	0.720	**0.765**	0.759
beauty	0.627	0.624	0.676	0.698	**0.756**	0.752
phones	0.677	0.693	0.726	0.742	**0.769**	**0.769**
elec	0.675	0.682	0.721	0.734	0.767	**0.770**
health	0.565	0.589	0.655	0.685	0.706	**0.712**
home	0.621	0.664	0.676	0.689	0.711	**0.713**
musical	0.627	0.673	0.738	0.740	**0.771**	0.763
office	0.616	0.621	0.699	0.707	**0.738**	0.733
patio	0.627	0.613	0.679	0.690	0.724	**0.734**
pet sup	0.604	0.635	0.733	0.741	**0.759**	**0.759**
sports	0.643	0.633	0.704	0.721	0.746	**0.748**
tools	0.617	0.620	0.681	0.689	0.725	**0.730**
toy	0.549	0.558	0.665	0.675	0.714	**0.716**
Average	0.624	0.634	0.697	0.711	0.741§	**0.742**§

For both cro-L and MoE, we segment reviews into sentences and use each sentence as a "review" in these models since this strategy leads to slightly better performance as mentioned in [16]. For our prediction framework, we use the whole review without such preprocessing.

4.3 Experimental Results

4.3.1 Answer Prediction Performance. We present the answer prediction performance for all the product categories in Table 2. The columns "ours-10" and "ours-20" refer to our framework with the embedding dimension of $\mathbf{h}$ being 10 and 20 respectively.

The results in Table 2 demonstrate that our answer prediction framework can significantly outperform the state-of-the-art method, i.e., MoE on all product categories. Compared to MoE, our framework can improve the performance by more than 4% on average across all product categories. For each product category, our framework shows obvious advantages over other methods. It indicates that the incorporation of aspects and aspect-specific representations is helpful for predictive answer model learning. The performance improvement of our framework over the state-of-the-art method, i.e. MoE, is statistically significant at the significance level of 0.05. Besides, we can observe that question retrieval methods commonly used for CQA, i.e., LM and DRLM are not effective for this answer prediction task. Although DRLM has shown good performance in CQA, its performance for product-related questions is close to the result of LM. This result shows that, unlike CQA, answer prediction of a product-related question cannot benefit from similar questions from other products.

To directly compare our framework with the result reported by McAuley and Yang [16], we also evaluate our model using the metric *accuracy*@50%. Since only 8 product categories were done in [16], the result of these 8 categories is presented in Table 3. We find that our framework achieves better average accuracy when only evaluating the answer

Table 3: Answer prediction evaluated by accuracy@50%.

	auto	phone	elec	health	home	patio	sports	tools	Ave.
cro-L	0.766	0.763	0.797	0.755	0.646	0.754	0.728	0.690	0.737
MoE	0.784	0.794	**0.826**	0.762	0.736	**0.768**	0.741	0.732	0.768
ours	**0.788**	**0.801**	0.810	**0.772**	**0.743**	**0.768**	**0.763**	**0.749**	**0.774**

redictions with high confidence, and outperforms MoE on nost of the product categories.

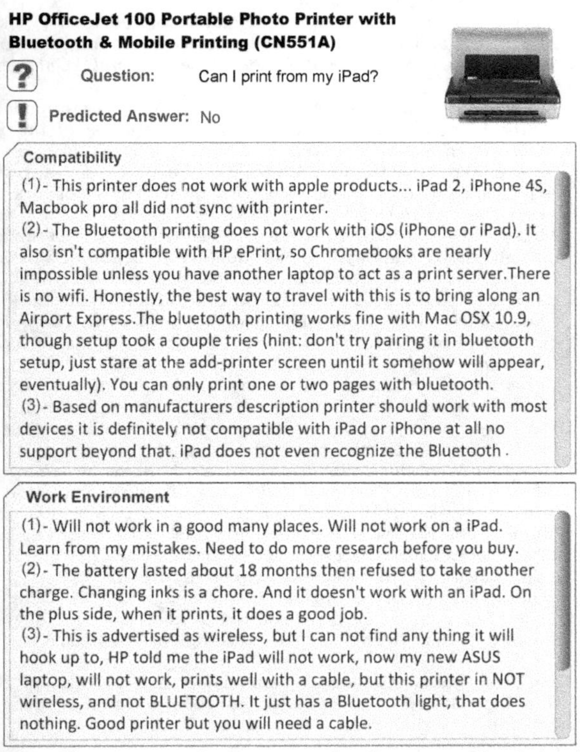

Figure 3: A sample case study for a product in the product category "Office Products".

4.3.2 Qualitative Study. We present two sample cases to llustrate the answer response and explanation quality proluced by our framework. Given a question asked by a user, our framework can immediately give the answer prediction as well as some supportive reviews grouped according to aspects providing explanations.

We study the case in Fig 1 again and describe how the esults are obtained via our framework. The question from he user is "Does this cover the entire back seat? I have wo puppies and I need coverage for both of them.". According to $P(z^\ell|q)$ from the aspect analytics model, the two most related aspects, namely "Placement, Installation" and Cleanliness, Health" are obtained and presented for the user. ntuitively, this question is indeed related to the placement of seat cover as well as the cleanliness issue. Then supportive eviews associated with a certain aspect are ranked by the score in Eqn 13, and displayed to users in scrollable panes. In he aspect "Placement, Installation", the most relevant reviews give some clues for the question. Reviews (1) and (2) n this aspect mentioning "covers entire back seat" provide an evidence for a positive answer. Review (3) considering user experiences about installation is also a helpful reference. Some reviews considering the cleanliness issues of this seat cover can be found in the next displayed aspect.

Fig 3 depicts the second case study about a question related to a portable photo printer. The question is "Can I print from my iPad?" It indicates that the user wishes to know whether or not this printer can work with an iPad. It can be observed that this question is related to the iPad and compatibility, so reviews about these aspects should be helpful for providing the answer. The ground truth answer for this question is "No" which is correctly predicted. In addition, the most relevant aspects are "Compatibility" and "Work Environment", and they are consistent with our intuition. The most related aspect is "Compatibility" according to the aspect analytics model, and some reviews supporting the answer are displayed contributing to a perception that this printer cannot work well with iPad. For example, under the aspect "Compatibility", all the top three reviews under this aspect clearly state the incompatibility between this printer and apple products including iPad. The aspect "Work Environment" is also helpful for addressing this question. For example, Reviews (1) and (2) in this aspect share user experiences with failure to work with iPad. Similar information also appears in the opinion written in Review (3).

Table 4: Top ranked words for each aspect for the product category "Cell Phones and Accessories".

Hardware	charge,battery,charger,ipad,pack,plug,cable,usb,power, port,hour,adapt,tablet,recharge,car,travel,device,trip, Anker,micro,portable,apple,dual,quickly,capacity
Appearance	protect,cover,color,OtterBox,hard,pocket,bulky,rubber, protector,case,slim,belt,drop,fit,soft,screen,slip,edge,thin, material,scratch,shell,slippery,holster,sleek,smooth,card
Software	keyboard,picture,text,android,camera,online,bubble,app, windows,video,feature,send,install,vender,instruction, get,appliation,read,open,pay,air,fix,youtube,review
Purchase	custom,ship,item,service,order,money,receive,replace, purchase,buy,month,gift,product,daughter,recommend, son,friendly,waste,seller,price,pleased,arrive,Christmas
Sound	sound,headset,ear,music,bluetooth,noise,listen,audio, mic,comfort,speaker,headphone,connect,talk,volumn, loud,call,rang,earbud,Plantron,play,earpiece,stereo,voice

4.3.3 Case Study of Aspect Learning. The aspect analytics model in our framework is able to extract aspects and learn aspect-specific embeddings of reviews, which are directly used in the predictive answer model. To facilitate further investigation of the aspect learning quality, we compute the probability of each word v_k in the vocabulary belonging to the aspect z^ℓ via Eqn 2, denoted as $P(z^\ell|v_k)$. Then we can rank the words under the aspect accordingly. Table 4 depicts the resultant aspects and word lists for the product category "Cell Phones and Accessories". We find that the aspect analytics model can detect aspects quite satisfactorily. The five aspects extracted from reviews of this product category is able to capture commonly concerned aspects when purchasing cellular phones or related accessories. In each list of an aspect, the words are quite semantically coherent to the corresponding aspect.

5 CONCLUSIONS

We propose an answer prediction framework for the product-related question, consisting of a aspect analystics model and a predictive answer model. With the 3-order Autoencoder based aspect analystics model, we discover aspects and learn aspect-specific embeddings for reviews in an unsupervised manner. Then the predictive answer model can make use of these learned representations incorporating aspect relevance and semantics into the answer prediction task. Our answer prediction model achieves better performance than the state-of-the-art method, with more explainable responses due to the aspect-based analysis capability.

REFERENCES

[1] Hadi Amiri, Philip Resnik, Jordan Boyd-Graber, and Hal Daumé III. 2016. Learning text pair similarity with context-sensitive autoencoders. In *Proceedings of the 54th ACL*. 1882–1892.

[2] Gabor Angeli, Neha Nayak, and Christopher D Manning. 2016. Combining natural logic and shallow reasoning for question answering. In *Proceedings of the 54th ACL*. 442–452.

[3] Tao Lei Hrishikesh Joshi Regina Barzilay, Tommi Jaakkola, Katerina Tymoshenko, and Alessandro Moschitti Lluıs Marquez. 2016. Semi-supervised question retrieval with gated convolutions. In *Proceedings of The 15th NAACL-HLT*. 1279–1289.

[4] Jonathan Berant, Andrew Chou, Roy Frostig, and Percy Liang. 2013. Semantic parsing on Freebase from question-answer pairs. In *Proceedings of EMNLP*. 1533–1544.

[5] Meghyn Bienvenu, Camille Bourgaux, and François Goasdoué. 2016. Explaining inconsistency-tolerant query answering over description logic knowledge bases. In *Proceedings of the Thirtieth AAAI*. 900–906.

[6] David M Blei, Andrew Y Ng, and Michael I Jordan. 2003. Latent dirichlet allocation. In *Journal of Machine Learning Research*, Vol. 3. 993–1022.

[7] Li Dong, Furu Wei, Ming Zhou, and Ke Xu. 2015. Question answering over Freebase with multi-column convolutional neural networks. In *Proceedings of ACL&IJCNLP*. 260–269.

[8] Anthony Fader, Luke Zettlemoyer, and Oren Etzioni. 2014. Open question answering over curated and extracted knowledge bases. In *Proceedings of the 20th ACM SIGKDD*. 1156–1165.

[9] Hanyin Fang, Fei Wu, Zhou Zhao, Xinyu Duan, Yueting Zhuang, and Martin Ester. 2016. Community-based question answering via heterogeneous social network learning. In *Proceedings of the Thirtieth AAAI*. 122–128.

[10] Simone Filice, Danilo Croce, Alessandro Moschitti, and Roberto Basili. 2016. KeLP at SemEval-2016 Task 3: Learning semantic relations between questions and answers. In *Proceedings of International Workshop on Semantic Evaluation*. 1116–1123.

[11] Marc Franco-Salvador, Sudipta Kar, Thamar Solorio, and Paolo Rosso. 2016. UH-PRHLT at SemEval-2016 Task 3: Combining lexical and semantic-based features for community question answering. In *Proceedings of International Workshop on Semantic Evaluation*. 814–821.

[12] Jing He and Decheng Dai. 2011. Summarization of yes/no questions using a feature function model. In *Proceedings of the 3rd ACML*. 351–366.

[13] Xiaodong He and David Golub. 2016. Character-level question answering with attention. In *Proceedings of EMNLP*. 1598–1607.

[14] Cody Kwok, Oren Etzioni, and Daniel S Weld. 2001. Scaling question answering to the web. In *ACM Transactions on Information Systems (TOIS)*, Vol. 19. ACM, 242–262.

[15] Vanessa Lopez, Andriy Nikolov, Marta Sabou, Victoria Uren, Enrico Motta, and Mathieu dAquin. 2010. Scaling up question-answering to linked data. In *Proceedings of EKAM*. 193–210.

[16] Julian McAuley and Alex Yang. 2016. Addressing complex and subjective product-related queries with customer reviews. In *Proceedings of the 25th International Conference on WWW*. 625–635.

[17] Samaneh Moghaddam and Martin Ester. 2011. AQA: aspect-based opinion question answering. In *Workshop on Sentiment Elicitation from Natural Text for Information Retrieval and Extraction (SENTIRE) in IEEE 11th ICDM*. 89–96.

[18] Vinod Nair and Geoffrey E Hinton. 2009. Implicit mixtures of restricted Boltzmann machines. In *Advances in NIPS*. 1145–1152

[19] Preslav Nakov, Llus Mrquez, Walid Magdy, Alessandro Moschitti, Jim Glass, and Bilal Randeree. 2015. SemEval-2015 Tas 3: Answer selection in community question answering. In *Proceedings of International Workshop on Semantic Evaluatio* 269–281.

[20] Preslav Nakov, Llus Mrquez, Alessandro Moschitti, Wali Magdy, Hamdy Mubarak, Abed Alhakim Freihat, Jim Glass, an Bilal Randeree. 2016. SemEval-2016 Task 3: Community que tion answering. In *Proceedings of International Workshop o Semantic Evaluation*. 525–545.

[21] Adi Omari, David Carmel, Oleg Rokhlenko, and Idan Szpekto 2016. Novelty based ranking of human answers for communit questions. In *Proceedings of the 39th International ACM SIGI* 215–224.

[22] Jay M Ponte and W Bruce Croft. 1998. A language modelin approach to information retrieval. In *Proceedings of the 21s ACM SIGIR*. ACM, 275–281.

[23] Jinfeng Rao, Hua He, and Jimmy Lin. 2016. Noise-contrastiv estimation for answer selection with deep neural networks. I *Proceedings of the 25th ACM CIKM*. 1913–1916.

[24] Aliaksei Severyn and Alessandro Moschitti. 2015. Learning t rank short text pairs with convolutional deep neural networks. I *Proceedings of the 38th International ACM SIGIR*. 373–382.

[25] Hapnes Toba, Zhao-Yan Ming, Mirna Adriani, and Tat-Sen Chua. 2014. Discovering high quality answers in communit question answering archives using a hierarchy of classifiers. I *Information Sciences*, Vol. 261. Elsevier, 101–115.

[26] Christina Unger, Lorenz Bühmann, Jens Lehmann, Axel-Cyrill Ngonga Ngomo, Daniel Gerber, and Philipp Cimiano. 201 Template-based question answering over RDF data. In *Procee ings of the 21st WWW*. 639–648.

[27] Mengting Wan and Julian McAuley. 2016. Modeling ambiguit subjectivity, and diverging viewpoints in opinion question ar swering systems. In *Proceedings of the IEEE ICDM*. 489–498.

[28] Linlin Wang, Kang Liu, Zhu Cao, Jun Zhao, and Gerard de Mel 2015. Sentiment-Aspect Extraction based on Restricted Bolt mann Machines.. In *Proceedings of ACL*. 616–625.

[29] Pengwei Wang, Lei Ji, Jun Yan, Lianwen Jin, and Wei Ying M 2016. Learning to extract conditional knowledge for questio answering using dialogue. In *Proceedings of ACM CIKM*. 277 286.

[30] Xin-Jing Wang, Xudong Tu, Dan Feng, and Lei Zhang. 200 Ranking community answers by modeling question-answer rel tionships via analogical reasoning. In *Proceedings of the 32n international ACM SIGIR*. 179–186.

[31] Kun Xu, Yansong Feng, Songfang Huang, and Dongyan Zha 2015. Question answering via phrasal semantic parsing. In *Pr ceedings of the 6th CLEF*. 414–426.

[32] Kun Xu, Siva Reddy, Yansong Feng, Songfang Huang, an Dongyan Zhao. 2016. Question answering on Freebase via rel tion extraction and textual evidence. In *Proceedings of the 54t ACL*. 2326–2336.

[33] Liu Yang, Minghui Qiu, Swapna Gottipati, Feida Zhu, Jing Jian Huiping Sun, and Zhong Chen. 2013. Cqarank: jointly mode topics and expertise in community question answering. In *Pr ceedings of the 22nd ACM CIKM*. 99–108.

[34] Xuchen Yao and Benjamin Van Durme. 2014. Information extra tion over structured data: question answering with Freebase.. I *Proceedings of the 52th ACL*. 956–966.

[35] Jun Yin, Xin Jiang, Zhengdong Lu, Lifeng Shang, Hang Li, an Xiaoming Li. 2016. Neural generative question answering. I *Proceedings of the 25th IJCAI*. 2972–2978.

[36] Jianxing Yu, Zheng-Jun Zha, and Tat-Seng Chua. 2012. Ar swering opinion questions on products by exploiting hiera chical organization of consumer reviews. In *Proceedings o EMNLP&CoNLL*. 391–401.

[37] Kai Zhang, Wei Wu, Fang Wang, Ming Zhou, and Zhoujun L 2016. Learning distributed representations of data in communit question answering for question retrieval. In *Proceedings of th Ninth ACM WSDM*. ACM, 533–542.

[38] Wayne Xin Zhao, Jing Jiang, Hongfei Yan, and Xiaoming L 2010. Jointly modeling aspects and opinions with a MaxEnt-LD hybrid. In *Proceedings of EMNLP*. Association for Computatior al Linguistics, 56–65.

Neural Ranking Models with Multiple Document Fields

Hamed Zamani*
University of Massachusetts Amherst
zamani@cs.umass.edu

Bhaskar Mitra†
Microsoft and UCL
bmitra@microsoft.com

Xia Song
Microsoft
xiaso@microsoft.com

Nick Craswell
Microsoft
nickcr@microsoft.com

Saurabh Tiwary
Microsoft
satiwary@microsoft.com

ABSTRACT

Deep neural networks have recently shown promise in the *ad-hoc retrieval* task. However, such models have often been based on one field of the document, for example considering document title only or document body only. Since in practice documents typically have multiple fields, and given that non-neural ranking models such as BM25F have been developed to take advantage of document structure, this paper investigates how neural models can deal with multiple document fields. We introduce a model that can consume short text fields such as document title and long text fields such as document body. It can also handle multi-instance fields with variable number of instances, for example where each document has zero or more instances of incoming anchor text. Since fields vary in coverage and quality, we introduce a masking method to handle missing field instances, as well as a field-level dropout method to avoid relying too much on any one field. As in the studies of non-neural field weighting, we find it is better for the ranker to score the whole document jointly, rather than generate a per-field score and aggregate. We find that different document fields may match different aspects of the query and therefore benefit from comparing with separate representations of the query text. The combination of techniques introduced here leads to a neural ranker that can take advantage of full document structure, including multiple instance and missing instance data, of variable length. The techniques significantly enhance the performance of the ranker, and outperform a learning to rank baseline with hand-crafted features.

ACM Reference Format:
Hamed Zamani, Bhaskar Mitra, Xia Song, Nick Craswell, and Saurabh Tiwary. 2018. Neural Ranking Models with Multiple Document Fields. In *WSDM 2018: The Eleventh ACM International Conference on Web Search and Data Mining, February 5–9, 2018, Marina Del Rey, CA, USA.* ACM, New York, NY, USA, 9 pages. https://doi.org/10.1145/3159652.3159730

*Work done while at Microsoft.
†The author is a part-time PhD student at UCL.

WSDM'18, February 5–9, 2018, Marina Del Rey, CA, USA

ACM ISBN 978-1-4503-5581-0/18/02...$15.00
https://doi.org/10.1145/3159652.3159730

1 INTRODUCTION

Deep neural networks have shown impressive performance in many machine learning tasks, including information retrieval models for ranking documents [5, 7, 8, 15, 23, 27]. These deep neural ranking models (NRMs) often consider a single source of document description, such as document title [8, 23] or body text [5, 15]. However, in many retrieval scenarios, additional sources of document descriptions may be available. For instance in web search, each document consists of text fields specified by the document's HTML tags, such as title and body, as well as external sources of meta-information, such as the anchor text from incoming hyperlinks or the query text for which the document has been previously viewed.

Learning a document representation suitable for retrieval tasks can be challenging when multiple document fields should be considered. These challenges primarily stem from the distinct properties of these diverse field types: (i) while the body of a web page is often long, the content of many other fields, such as title, are typically only a few terms in length, (ii) while some fields (e.g., body) contain a single instance of text, other fields may contain bags of multiple short texts (e.g., anchor text), (iii) multi-instance fields generally contain variable number of instances, e.g., zero or more instances of incoming anchor text for a given document, (iv) some fields, such as URL, may not contain natural language text, and finally (v) fields vary in coverage and accuracy, for example a field that memorizes past queries that led to a click on the document may provide a very useful (high-accuracy) ranking signal [1], but the coverage of that field may be relatively low because not every document has been clicked before. Each of these challenges increases the complexity of the representation learning task for documents with multiple fields. However, multiple fields associated with each document may contain complementary information that has motivated us to learn representation for documents by considering multiple fields in order to improve the retrieval performance.

In this paper, we propose NRM-F[1], a *general* framework for learning multiple-field document representation for ad-hoc retrieval. NRM-F is designed to address the aforementioned challenges. More specifically, NRM-F can handle multiple fields, both with single and multiple instances. In NRM-F, although the neural network parameters are shared among multiple instances of the same field, they are distinct across fields. This enables NRM-F to uniquely model the content of each field based on its specific characteristics.

[1]The naming is inspired by BM25F [21].

We employ the same topology for the sub-networks corresponding to the different fields. However, there are a number of controlling hyper-parameters that determine the exact sub-network configuration for each field. We introduce field-level masking to better cope with variable length inputs, i.e., fields with variable number of text instances. We also propose a novel field-level dropout technique that effectively regularizes the network and prevents it from over-dependence on high-accuracy fields, such as clicked queries. Given the intuition that different fields may match different aspects of the query, our model learns different query representations corresponding to different document fields.

We evaluate our models in the context of web search, using the queries sampled from the Bing's search logs. We study five fields in our experiments: title (single short text), body (single long text), URL (single short text, but not in a natural language), anchor texts (multiple short texts), and clicked queries (multiple short texts providing a ranking signal with relatively high accuracy). We consider this effective and diverse set of fields to make our findings more likely to generalize to other combinations of document fields.

In this work, we study the following research hypotheses:

H1 The ad-hoc retrieval performance of NRM-F improves as we incorporate multiple document fields.

H2 NRM-F performs better than competitive baselines, such as term matching and learning to rank.

H3 Learning a multiple-field document representation is superior to scoring based on individual field representations and summing.

H4 Learning per-field query representations performs better than learning a single query representation.

H5 The additional techniques of field-level masking and field-level dropout yield additional performance improvements.

Our experiments validate all these hypotheses, and investigate the effectiveness of our overall NRM-F framework.

2 RELATED WORK

In this section, we first review prior work on modeling structured documents for retrieval tasks. We further present a set of existing neural approaches to information retrieval.

2.1 Retrieval with Multiple Fields

Information retrieval tasks may involve semi-structured data, meaning that the text of each document is divided into sections. Given a sufficiently fine-grained structure, some past research has studied the retrieval of the particular sections that best satisfy the user's query, such as in the INEX XML retrieval initiative [6, 12]. In web search it is more typical to consider coarse-grained sections such as title and body, also referred to as *fields*, and use them to generate features in a document ranking task.

Using evidence from structure to improve document retrieval is well studied in information retrieval. Wilkinson [26] proposed a number of hypotheses about how to combine section-level and document-level evidence. For example, taking the maximum section score, or a weighted sum of section scores, and then potentially combining with a document-level score. Robertson et al. [21] further proposed BM25F, an extension to the original BM25 model [22], arguing that the linear combination of field-level scores is "dangerous", because it bypasses the careful balance across query terms in the BM25 model. The BM25F solution is to first combine frequency information across fields on a per-term basis, then compute a retrieval score using the balanced BM25 approach.

There are a number of alternative approaches to BM25F for the multiple-field document retrieval task. For instance, Piwowarski and Gallinari [19] proposed a model based on Bayesian networks for retrieving semi-structured documents. Myaeng et al. [16] extended the InQuery retrieval system to semi-structured documents. Svore and Burges [25] proposed a supervised approach, called LambdaBM25, that learns a BM25-like retrieval model based on the LambdaRank algorithm [3]. LambdaBM25 can also consider multiple document fields, without resorting to a linear combination of per-field scores. Dealing with multiple document fields without a linear combination was also studied by Ogilvie and Callan [18], who proposed and tested various combinations for a known-item search task, using a language modeling framework. Kim et al. [9] proposed a probabilistic model for the task of XML retrieval. Later on, Kim and Croft [10] introduced a model based on relevance feedback for estimating the weight of each document field.

2.2 Neural Networks for Ranking

Several recent studies have applied deep neural network methods to various information retrieval applications, including question answering [29], click models [2], ad-hoc retrieval [5, 15, 27], and context-aware ranking [30]. Neural ranking models can be partitioned into early and late combination models [5]. They can also be categorized based on whether they focus on lexical matching or learning text representations for semantic matching [15].

The early combination models are designed based on the interactions between query and document as the networks' input. For instance, the deep relevance matching model [7] gets histogram based features as input, representing the interactions between query and document. DeepMatch [13] is another example that maps the input to a sequence of terms and computes the matching score using a feed-forward network. The local component of the duet model in [15] and the neural ranking models proposed in [5, 27] are the other examples for early combination models.

The late combination models, on the other hand, separately learn a representation for query and document and then compute the relevance score using a matching function applied on the learned representations. DSSM [8] is an example of late combination models that learns representations using feed-forward networks and then uses cosine similarity as the matching function. DSSM was further extended by making use of convolutional neural networks, called C-DSSM [23]. The distributed component of the duet model [15] also uses a similar architecture for learning document representation. We refer the reader to [14] that provides an overview of various (deep) neural ranking models.

In all of the aforementioned work, each document is assumed to be a single instance of text (i.e., single field). However, documents often exist in a semi-structured format. In this paper, we focus on late combination models and propose a neural ranking model that takes multiple fields of document into account. Given the hypothesis provided in [15], our neural model can be further enriched by making use of lexical matching in addition to distributed matching.

We leave the study of lexical matching for the future and focus on document representation learning.

3 THE NRM-F FRAMEWORK

In this section, we first provide our motivation for studying the task of representation learning for documents with multiple fields, and formalize the task. We then introduce a high-level overview of our framework, and further describe how we implement each component of the proposed framework. We finally explain how we optimize our neural ranking model.

3.1 Motivation and Problem Statement

In many retrieval scenarios, there exist various sources of textual information (*fields*) associated with each document d. In web search in particular, these sources of information can be partitioned into three categories. The first category includes the information provided by the structure and the content of document d itself. Different elements of the web page specified by the HTML tags, e.g., title, header, keyword, and body, as well as the URL are examples of fields of this type. The second category includes the information provided by the other documents for representing d. For instance, when there is a hyperlink from document d' to d, the corresponding anchor text may provide useful description of d. The third category contains information that we can infer from interactions between the retrieval system and its users. For instance in web search, when a user clicks on the document d for a query q, the text of query q can be used to describe d. Svore and Burges [25] refer to these last two categories as popularity fields.

There are several previous studies showing that different fields may contain complementary information [21, 25]. Therefore, incorporating multiple fields can lead to more accurate document representation and better retrieval performance. For example, clicked queries are highly effective for the retrieval tasks [1, 25, 28]. A number of prior studies [21, 25], have also investigated the usefulness of anchor texts for web search. However, for fresh or less popular documents that may not have enough anchor or clicked query text associated with them, the body text provides important description of the document. Similarly, the URL field may be useful for matching when the query expresses an explicit or implicit intent for a specific domain. These complementary and diverse sources of textual descriptions have motivated us to study representation learning for ad-hoc retrieval by incorporating multiple fields.

The unique properties of these diverse document fields, however, make it challenging to model them within the same neural architecture. For example, the vocabulary and the language structure of clicked queries may be distinct from those of the body text, and in turn both may be distinct from the URL field. The document body text may contain thousands of terms, while the text in other fields may be only few terms in length. Finally, a key challenge also stems from the fact that a number of fields consist of multiple instances. For example, there are multiple anchor texts for each document d, and multiple queries can be found that previously led users to click on document d. A neural ranking model that considers these fields for document ranking must handle variable number of text instances per document field. To formulate the task, let $\mathcal{F}_d = \{F_1, F_2, \cdots, F_k\}$ denote a set of fields associated with the document d. Each field F_i consists of a set of instances

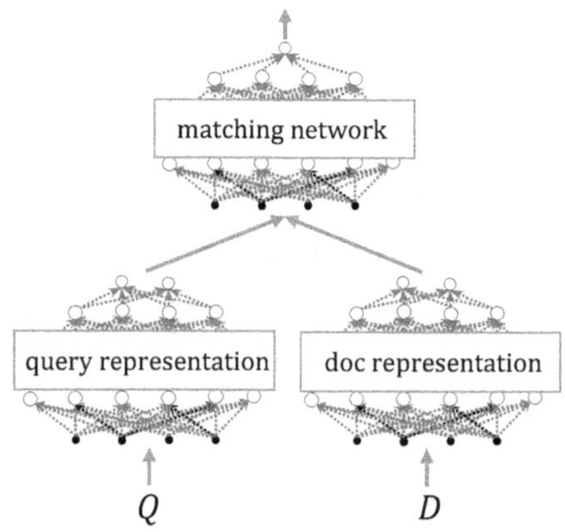

Figure 1: A neural ranking model architecture that consists of three major components: query representation, document representation, and matching network.

$\{f_{i1}, f_{i2}, \cdots, f_{im_i}\}$ where m_i denotes the number of instances in the field F_i. The task is to learn a function $\Phi_D(\mathcal{F}_d)$ whose output is a representation for document d, suitable for the ad-hoc retrieval task.

3.2 High-Level Overview of the Framework

In this paper, as shown in Figure 1, we focus on a late-combination and representation-focused neural ranking model. This architecture consists of three major components: document representation (Φ_D), query representation (Φ_Q), and the matching network (Ψ) which takes both representations and computes the retrieval score (i.e., score $= \Psi(\Phi_Q, \Phi_D)$). In this section, we describe the high-level architecture used for the document representation network, which is the focus of the paper. Sections 3.7 and 3.8 review how the query representation and matching network components are respectively implemented.

To learn multiple-field document representation (i.e., Φ_D), the framework first learns a representation for each individual instance in a field. The framework then aggregates these learned vector representations to represent the field as a whole. It finally aggregates all the field specific representations for the document. This framework is visualized in Figure 2.

To formally describe our framework, the document representation learning function Φ_D can be calculated as:

$$\Phi_D(\mathcal{F}_d) = \Lambda_D(\Phi_{F_1}(F_1), \Phi_{F_2}(F_2), \cdots, \Phi_{F_k}(F_k)) \tag{1}$$

where Φ_{F_i} denotes the representation learning function for the field F_i. Note that the representation learning functions differ for different fields, since the fields have their own unique characteristics and need their own specific functions. Λ_D aggregates representations learned for all the fields. Each Φ_{F_i} is also calculated as:

$$\Phi_{F_i}(F_i) = \Lambda_{F_i}(\Phi_{f_i}(f_{i1}), \Phi_{f_i}(f_{i2}), \cdots, \Phi_{f_i}(f_{im_i})) \tag{2}$$

where Φ_{f_i} denotes the representation learning function for each instance of the ith field (e.g., each anchor text). Note that Φ_{f_i} is the same function for all the instances of a given field. The function Λ_{F_i} aggregates the representation of all instances in the ith field.

To summarize, our document representation framework consists of three major components: learning representation for an

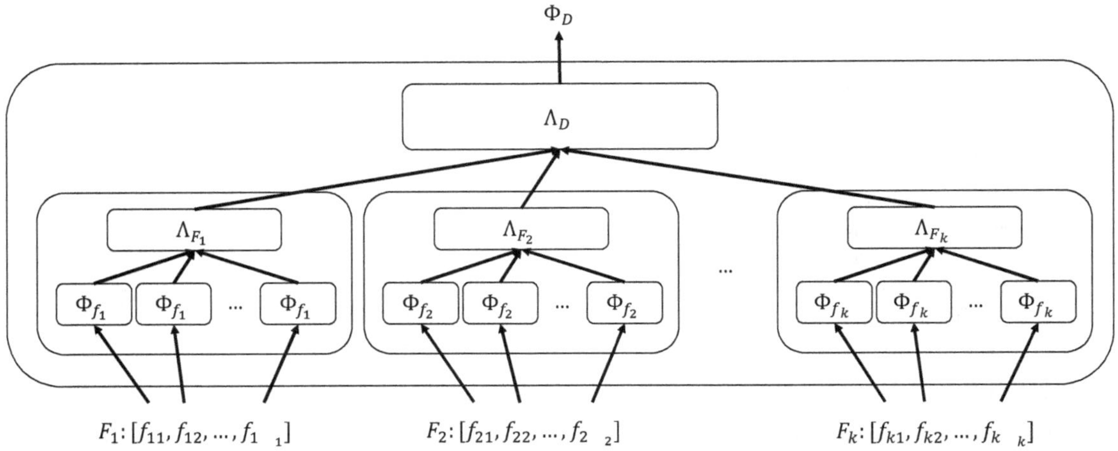

Figure 2: The high-level architecture of our document representation framework. In this architecture, aggregating field-level representations using Λ_D produces the document representation Φ_D. The representation for the ith field is computed by aggregating (Λ_{F_i}) the representations learned for the instances of the field using Φ_{f_i}.

instance of each field (i.e., Φ_{f_i}), field-level aggregation (i.e., Λ_{F_i}), and document-level aggregation (i.e., Λ_D). Sections 3.3 and 3.4 describe how we define or learn these functions.

3.3 Instance-Level Representation Learning

In this subsection, we describe our neural architecture for learning representations of individual text instances in a document field. In particular, we explain how the functions Φ_{f_i} are implemented. As pointed out in Section 3.1, each field has its own unique characteristics. One approach would be to use different neural architectures for different fields. However, in the interest of proposing a general framework, we choose an architecture that can be used for all fields, but the exact configurations are controlled by a set of hyper-parameters specified per field. These hyper-parameters are selected for each field individually based on a validation set.

Figure 3 shows the design of the per-instance model architecture. In our architecture, each term is represented using a character n-gram hashing vector, introduced by Huang et al. [8]. These are extremely sparse vectors whose dimensions correspond to all possible character n-grams. Therefore, we represent the input layer of our network using sparse tensors which is memory-efficient and also improves the efficiency of the model. Similar to [8, 23], n was set to 3 in our experiments which causes limited number of term hash collisions. We use the character n-gram representation for the following reasons: (1) it can represent out of vocabulary terms, and (2) the number of all possible tri-grams is much lower than the term-level vocabulary size which significantly reduces the number of parameters needed to be learned by the network. We use a linear embedding layer to map a character n-gram representation to a dense low-dimensional representation by multiplying the sparse input tensor for each term and an embedding matrix $\mathcal{E} \in \mathbb{R}^{N \times l}$ where N is total number of possible n-grams and l denotes the embedding dimensionality. The output of this layer for each word is normalized to prevent over-weighting long words, and represents relevance-based word embedding [32]. Inspired by C-DSSM [23] and the Duet Model [15], this layer is followed by a one-dimensional convolution layer. The aim of this layer is to capture the dependency between terms. We further use an additional convolution layer whose window size is set to be larger for the body field to

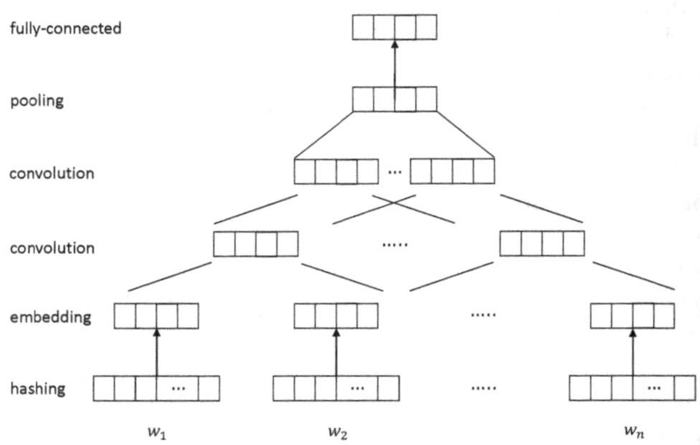

Figure 3: Instance-level representation learning network. This model embeds the character n-gram representation of each word w_i which is followed by two 1-D convolutional layers. The outputs of the second set of convolutional operations are pooled and then fed to a fully-connected layer to compute the final representation for each instance of a field.

capture sentence-level representations, and smaller for the short texts fields. We pool the output of the second convolution layer which is followed by a fully-connected layer to compute the final representation for an instance of a given field. The choice of max-pooling and average-pooling is a hyper-parameter in our model. In this network, we use dropout [24] to avoid over-fitting.

3.4 Aggregating Representations

As shown in Figure 2, NRM-F consists of two sets of aggregation components: Λ_{F_i} and Λ_D. Λ_{F_i} aggregates the representations learned for the instances of a specific field. For each multi-instance field F_i, we select a bag of at most M_i instances, and use zero padding when less than M_i instances are available. Λ_{F_i} averages the individual representations learned for the instances of the field F_i.

The component Λ_D aims at aggregating the representations learned for different fields. To be able to learn different query representations for each field, Λ_D only concatenates the input vectors to be served in the matching function explained in Section 3.8.

3.5 Field-Level Masking

The number of instances in multi-instance fields, such as anchor text, varies across documents. As shown in Table 1, a significant number of documents may not contain any anchor text or clicked queries. To deal with such cases, as mentioned in Section 3.4, we use zero padding. Although padding is a popular approach and has been previously used in neural ranking models [5, 15, 23], it suffers from a major drawback: by doing padding, the network assumes that a part of the input vector is zero; however padding represents missing values. In the extreme case, assume that there is no available anchor text for a given document; therefore, the input for the anchor text field is all zero. The gradients, however, are not zero (because of the bias parameters). This means that the back-propagation algorithm updates the weights for the sub-network corresponding to the anchor text field; which is not desirable—we do not want to update the weights when the input data is missing. This becomes crucial when there are many missing values in training data, similar to our task.

To tackle this problem, we propose a simple approach, called *field-level masking*. Let $R_i \in \mathbb{R}^{M_i \times D_i}$ denote the representation learned for the ith field (i.e., the output of Λ_{F_i}) where M_i and D_i respectively represent the maximum number of instances (fixed value) and the dimensionality for instance representation. We generate a binary masking matrix $B_i \in \mathbb{B}^{M_i \times D_i}$ whose rows are all zero or all one, showing whether each field instance exists or is missing. In masking, we use $R_i \circ B_i$ (i.e., element-wise multiplication) as the representation for F_i. We multiply the representations for existing field instances by one (means no change) and those for the missing instances by zero. This not only results in zero representation for missing values, but also forces the gradients to become zero. Therefore, the back-propagation algorithm does not update the weights for the sub-networks corresponding to missing values.

The masking matrix is also useful for computing the average in Λ_{F_i} (see Section 3.4). Averaging is a common approach for aggregating different representations, such as average word embedding for query representation [31] and neural ranking models [5]. However, in case of variable length inputs, averaging penalizes short inputs which are padded by zero. To address this issue, we can compute the exact average vector by summing the inputs and dividing them by the summation over the masking matrix. Note that the masking technique should be applied at both training and testing times.

3.6 Field-Level Dropout

As widely known and also demonstrated in our experiments, clicked queries is an effective field for representing documents in the retrieval task [1, 25]. When such a high-accuracy field is available, there is a risk that the network relies on that field, and pays less attention to learning proper representations for the other fields. This can lead to poor performance of the model when the high-accuracy field is absent (low coverage).

Although we use dropout in our neural ranking model (see Section 3.3), it is not sufficient for the task of document representation learning with multiple document fields, in particular when at least a dominant input field exists. To regularize the network in such cases, we propose a simple *field-level dropout* technique—randomly dropping all the units corresponding to a field. In other words, we may randomly drop, say, the clicked queries field or the body field at training time to prevent the neural ranking model from over-dependence on any single field. This approach is back-propagation friendly (all the proofs presented in [24] are applicable to the field-level dropout). Field-level dropout contains k hyper-parameters, where k denotes the total number of fields and each parameter controls the probability of keeping the corresponding field. Note that dropout only happens at the training time and all the units are kept at the validation and test times.

3.7 Query Representation

Since in this paper we focus on the ad-hoc retrieval task, the only available information for the query is the query text. Therefore, to represent the query (i.e., Φ_Q), we use the same network architecture as the one used for each instance of a document field (see Section 3.3). Note that different document fields may match with different aspects of a query. Therefore, the output dimensionality of the query representation network is equal to the sum of the dimensions for all fields' representations. In other words, NRM-F learns different representations of the query for each document field.

3.8 Matching Network

In this subsection, we describe how we compute the retrieval score given the output of query representation and document representation networks (i.e., the function Ψ). To do so, we compute the Hadamard product of the representations; which is the element-wise product of two matrices with the same dimensionality. We then use a fully-connected neural network with a single non-linear hidden layer to compute the final retrieval score. We avoid computing dot product or cosine similarity which would reduce the contribution of each field to a single score, forcing us to combine them linearly which is less effective as demonstrated by Robertson et al. [21] and our results in Section 4.3.

3.9 Training

We use a pairwise setting to train the designed neural ranking model. Let $T = \{(q_1, d_{11}, d_{12}, y_{11}, y_{12}), (q_2, d_{21}, d_{22}, y_{21}, y_{22}), \cdots, (q_n, d_{n1}, d_{n2}, y_{n1}, y_{n2})\}$ be a set of n training instances. Each training instance consists of a query q_i, two documents d_{i1} and d_{i2}, as well as their corresponding labels y_{i1} and y_{i2}. We consider cross entropy loss function to train neural ranking models:

$$\mathcal{L} = -\frac{1}{|T|} \sum_{i=1}^{|T|} \frac{g(y_{i1})}{g(y_{i1}) + g(y_{i2})} \log p_{i1} + \frac{g(y_{i2})}{g(y_{i1}) + g(y_{i2})} \log(1 - p_{i1})$$

where $g(\cdot)$ is a gain function. We use an exponential gain function same as the one used in calculating NDCG. p_{i1} is the estimated probability for d_{i1} being more relevant than d_{i2}. p_{i1} is calculated via softmax on the predicted labels: $p_{i1} = \exp(\hat{y}_{i1})/(\exp(\hat{y}_{i1}) + \exp(\hat{y}_{i2}))$, where $\hat{y}_{i1}$ and $\hat{y}_{i2}$ denote the estimated scores for d_{i1} and d_{i2}, respectively.

4 EXPERIMENTS

4.1 Data

To evaluate our models, we randomly sampled $\sim$140k queries from the Bing's search logs for the English United States market from a one-year period. For each query, the documents returned by the Bing's production ranker in addition to those retrieved by a

Table 1: Statistics and characteristics of the document fields used in our experiments.

Fields	Type	Coverage	Specific Feature
Title	Single Instance	100%	Short text.
URL	Single Instance	100%	Short text, but not in a natural language.
Body	Single Instance	100%	Long text.
Anchor texts	Multiple Instance	61%	Short texts with relatively low coverage.
Clicked queries	Multiple Instance	73%	Short texts with relatively low coverage. A high-accuracy field.

diverse set of experiments were labelled by human judges on a five-point scale: perfect, excellent, good, fair, and bad. In total, the data consists of ~3.8 million query-document pairs which was randomly partitioned into three sets—80% for training, 10% for validation, and 10% for testing—such that no distinct query appears in more than one set. Similar to [8, 15, 17], we evaluate all models under the *telescoping* setting by re-ranking the candidate documents for each query. Since our neural ranking model is a pairwise learning to rank model, for each query we generate all possible $< q, d_1, d_2 >$ triples such that the relevance label for d_1 and d_2 are different with respect to q. To avoid biasing towards the queries with many documents, at most 50 triples per query were sampled for training based on a uniform distribution over all possible label pairs.

The contents of web pages were retrieved from the Bing's web index and were parsed using a proprietary HTML parser. We made sure that all the documents in our data contain title and body. All texts were normalized by lower-casing and removing non-alphanumerical characters. The URLs were split using a simple proprietary approach. We set the maximum length of 20, 10, 1000, 10, and 10 for title, URL, body, anchor text, and clicked query, respectively. We used at most 5 anchor texts and at most 5 clicked queries per document.[2] They were selected based on a simple count-based functions; means that the most common anchor texts and clicked queries for each document were selected. The statistics of our data for each field is reported in Table 1.

4.2 Experimental Setup

All the models were implemented using TensorFlow[3]. We used Adam optimizer [11] to train our models. The learning rate was selected from $[1e-3, 5e-4, 1e-4, 5e-5, 1e-5]$. We set the batch size to 64 and tuned the hyper-parameters based on the loss values obtained on the validation set. We selected the layer sizes from $\{100, 300, 500\}$ and the convolution window sizes from $\{1, 3, 10, 20, 50\}$ for long texts (i.e., body) and from $\{1, 3, 5, 10\}$ for short texts (i.e., the other fields). The convolution strides were selected from $\{1, \lfloor ws/4 \rfloor, \lfloor ws/2 \rfloor, ws\}$ where ws denotes the convolution window size. The keep probability parameters for both conventional and field-level dropouts were selected from $\{0.5, 0.8, 1.0\}$.

As explained in Section 3.3, the input layer of the networks uses tri-gram hashing with ~$50k$ dimensions, i.e, all possible character tri-grams with alphanumerical characters plus a dummy character for the start and the end of each word. The tri-gram embedding dimensionality (i.e., the first layer) was set to 300. This embedding matrix is shared among all fields. Following [8, 15, 23], we used tanh as the activation function for all hidden layers.

[2]The maximum number of instances per field can be set to a much larger value. Since the network parameters for instances of each field are shared and the inputs are represented as sparse tensors, increasing the maximum number of instances would have a minor memory effect.

[3]http://tensorflow.org/

Table 2: Performance of the proposed framework with different fields. The superscript + shows significant improvements for the models with two fields compared to the ones with each of the fields, individually. The superscript * denotes significant improvements over all the other models.

Field(s)	NDCG@1	NDCG@10
Title	0.4226	0.5883
URL	0.4366	0.5865
Body	0.4115	0.5850
Anchor texts	0.4386	0.5933
Clicked queries	0.4661	0.6116
Title + URL	0.4425^+	0.6065^+
Title + Body	0.4316^+	0.6098^+
Title + Anchor texts	0.4507^+	0.6062^+
Title + Clicked queries	0.4680	0.6180^+
All	**0.4906^***	**0.6380^***

We use NDCG at two different ranking levels (NDCG@1 and NDCG@10) to evaluate the models. The significance differences between models are determined using the paired t-test at a 95% confidence level ($p\_value < 0.05$).

4.3 Experimental Results

In this subsection, we empirically address the hypotheses mentioned in Section 1.

H1: The ad-hoc retrieval performance of NRM-F improves as we incorporate multiple document fields. In this set of experiments, we address our first hypothesis (H1) by evaluating our model with each single field individually, with field pairs with title and finally with all the fields together. The results are reported in Table 2. Although title, URL, and body have much higher coverage compared to anchor texts and clicked queries (see Table 1), the performances achieved by anchor texts and clicked queries are superior to the other fields.[4] Incorporating clicked queries demonstrates the highest performance. Pairing Title with any of the other field "X" leads to a better performance compared to Title and "X", individually. These improvements are statistically significant, except for NDCG@1 in Title+Clicked queries. The reason is that clicked queries are very effective for web search, especially for the first retrieved document. Adding title to clicked queries, however, significantly improves the search quality for the top 10 documents. The NRM-F model with all fields achieves the highest performance with

[4]We randomly shuffled the documents with equal retrieval scores for a query. This process was repeated for 10 times and the average performance is reported.

Table 3: Comparison of the proposed model with baselines for a single field (Title or Body). The superscripts denote significant improvements over the models specified by the ID column.

ID	Model	Title		Body	
		NDCG@1	NDCG@10	NDCG@1	NDCG@10
1	BM25	0.4039	0.5752	0.3957	0.5693
2	LTR	0.4122	0.5861	0.3996	0.5792
3	DSSM	0.4112	0.5858	0.3961	0.5713
4	C-DSSM	0.4148	0.5874	0.3957	0.5695
5	Duet (distributed)	0.4164	0.5877	0.4066	0.5788
6	NRM-F - Single Field	**0.4226**^{12345}	**0.5883**^{123}	**0.4115**^{12345}	**0.5850**^{12345}

statistically significant margins. This suggests that the proposed framework is able to learn a more accurate document representation for the ad-hoc retrieval task by considering multiple document fields; thus the hypothesis H1 is validated.

H2: NRM-F performs better than competitive baselines, such as term matching and learning to rank. To demonstrate that the proposed instance-level representation model performs reasonably well for both short and long texts, we first evaluate our models against a set of baselines using a single field, title only and body only. We consider the following baselines: BM25 [22], a state-of-the-art learning to rank model with hand-crafted features (LTR), DSSM [8], C-DSSM [23], and the distributed part[5] of the duet model proposed by Mitra et al. [15]. The LTR baseline uses an internal advanced implementation of the LambdaMART algorithm [4] that has been used in the production. We used the features that have been typically extracted from query and document texts. Indeed, from those listed in [20], we used all the features that can be extracted from query and title/body.

To have a fair comparison, we trained all the models using the same training data and pairwise setting.[6] The hyper-parameters in all the models, including the baselines, were optimized for Title and Body, separately. Due to the memory constraints, the C-DSSM and Duet cannot use ~50k tri-grams for the word hashing phase (only for Body). Therefore, as suggested in [15], we use top 2k popular n-grams for these models. Note that since our model use sparse tensors for word hashing, it is memory-efficient and does not have the same issue.[7]

The results for Title as an example of short text and Body as an example of long text are reported in Table 3. According to this table, the proposed method outperforms all the baselines for both Title and Body. The improvements are statistically significant in nearly all cases. This demonstrates the potential of our model to be used for both short and long texts. The improvements are higher for Body, which makes our model even more suitable for long text. This experiment suggests that our instance-level representation model performs reasonably well.

Table 4: Performance of the proposed framework with all fields compared to baselines. The superscript * denotes significant improvements over all the other models.

Model	NDCG@1	NDCG@10
BM25-Field Concatenation	0.4281	0.5953
BM25F	0.4431	0.6020
LTR	0.4888	0.6341
NRM-Field Concatenation	0.4582	0.6110
NRM-Score Aggregation-Ind. Training	0.4729	0.6229
NRM-Score Aggregation-Co-training	0.4743	0.6279
NRM-F -Single Query Representation	0.4846	0.6345
NRM-F	**0.4906***	**0.6380***

To evaluate our model with multiple instances, we consider the following baselines: (1) BM25 by concatenating all the fields, (2) BM25F [21] which has been widely used for ad-hoc retrieval with multiple document fields, (3) a learning to rank (LTR) model with hand-crafted features extracted from all the fields, and (4) our neural ranking model with concatenation of all fields as a single input text (i.e., NRM - Field Concatenation). Similar to the last experiments, for LTR we consider all the typical features that can be extracted from text inputs (among those listed in [20] for the LETOR dataset). The features were extracted for all the fields. The learning algorithm for LTR is the same as the one used in the previous experiment. All models were trained on the same training set, and their hyper-parameters were tuned on the same validation set. As shown in Table 4, NRM-F significantly outperforms all the baselines. This suggests that NRM-F not only eliminates the hand-crafted feature engineering for ad-hoc retrieval, but also learns an accurate document representation that leads to higher retrieval performance. The results also validate our second hypothesis.

H3: Learning a multiple-field document representation is superior to scoring based on individual field representations and summing. A simple approach for coping with multiple document fields is to calculate the matching score for the query and each of the document fields and then aggregate the scores. We tried two score aggregation methods, one learns a neural ranking model for each document field individually and then linearly interpolates their scores. Although the other one also interpolates the scores obtained by different fields, the neural networks for different fields are co-trained together. The results in Table 4 show that co-training leads to a better performance compared to isolated training of the

[5] To have a fair comparison, we only consider the distributed part of the model. Note that all the listed neural models, including NRM-F, can be further enriched by using lexical matching, similar to the local part of the duet model.
[6] The original DSSM and C-DSSM models use binary labels (click data) and random negative sampling for training; however, as suggested by Mitra et al. [15] using explicit judgments leads to a better performance compared to random negative sampling
[7] C-DSSM and Duet perform convolution on top of word hashing layer; thus, the word hashing phase cannot be implemented using sparse tensors (at least not supported by deep learning libraries, such as TensorFlow and CNTK).

Table 5: Investigating the effectiveness of field-level masking and dropout. The superscripts denote significant improvement over the models specified by the ID column.

ID	Model	All fields		All fields except clicked queries	
		NDCG@1	NDCG@10	NDCG@1	NDCG@10
1	NRM-F (no masking, no dropout)	0.4818	0.6327	0.4577	0.6152
2	NRM-F with masking	0.4856^{1}	0.6353^{1}	0.4602^{1}	0.6174^{1}
3	NRM-F with masking & dropout	$\mathbf{0.4906}^{12}$	$\mathbf{0.6380}^{12}$	$\mathbf{0.4613}^{1}$	$\mathbf{0.6181}^{1}$

Table 6: Performance analysis based on query length, dividing the test queries into three evenly-sized groups.

Model	Short queries		Medium-length queries		Long queries	
	NDCG@1	NDCG@10	NDCG@1	NDCG@10	NDCG@1	NDCG@10
LTR	0.5040	0.6470	0.4753	0.6332	**0.4799**	0.6162
NRM-F	**0.5132**	**0.6584**	**0.4846**	**0.6355**	0.4723	**0.6186**

model for different fields, which is expected. The results also suggest that NRM-F performs better than neural ranking models with score aggregation. The improvements are statistically significant. Therefore, this experiment validates our third hypothesis.

H4: Learning per-field query representations performs better than learning a single query representation. As mentioned in Section 3.7, we believe that different aspects of the query can match different fields, and thus different query representations are needed for different fields. Our empirical results in Table 4 also validate this hypothesis by showing that NRM-F provides a superior performance in comparison with exactly the same neural ranking model, but with single query representation for different fields.

H5: The additional techniques of field-level masking and field-level dropout yield additional performance improvements. To study this hypothesis, we report the results for the following models: (1) our neural ranking model with no field-level masking and dropout, (2) our model with only field-level masking, and eventually (3) our model with both field-level masking and dropout. Note that all the models use conventional dropout [11]. Table 5 reports the results for all fields and for all fields except clicked queries. According to this table, field-level masking is useful to cope with multi-instance fields and significantly improves the performance. The model with both field-level masking and dropout achieves the highest performance; however, the field-level dropout technique is significantly helpful, when at least one of the fields is dominant (i.e., the high-accuracy fields like clicked queries).

4.4 Additional Analysis

Learning curve. It has always been important to know how much data is needed to train the model. We plot the learning curve for our NRM-F model with all fields in Figure 4. The performance is reported in terms of NDCG@10 on the test set. According to this figure, we need approximately two million training instances to have a relatively stable performance.

Analysis by query length. In this analysis, we uniformly split the test queries into three buckets based on their query length. Therefore, the number of queries in the buckets are approximately equal. The first bucket includes the shortest and the last one includes the longest queries. The results for NRM-F and the LTR baseline with all fields (the one used in Table 4) are reported in Table 6.

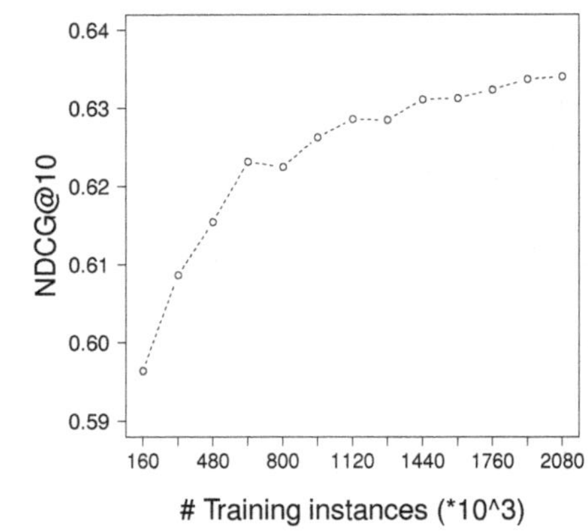

Figure 4: Learning curve demonstrating the performance of NRM-F in terms of NDCG@10 with respect to the size of training set.

According to this table, our improvements over the LTR baseline generally decrease by increasing the query length. In other words, NRM-F performs relatively better for shorter queries. The reason is that long queries are often rare and thus it is likely that the models based on representation learning work much better for shorter queries. On the other hand, the experiment is in a telescoping setting with anchor texts and clicked queries. Therefore, the additional terms and synonyms provided by, let say, clicked queries empower the LTR method that uses term matching features. In addition, for long queries in a telescoping setting, ignoring a query term is relatively likely to do not harm the results.

5 CONCLUSIONS AND FUTURE WORK

In this paper, we proposed NRM-F, a *general* framework for the task of multiple-field document representation learning for ad-hoc retrieval. NRM-F can consume both short text and long text fields. It can also handle the multi-instance fields, such as anchor text. Since fields vary in coverage, we introduced a field-level masking method to handle missing field instances. We also proposed a field-level dropout technique to prevent the model from over-dependence on high-accuracy fields, such as clicked queries. We performed extensive experiments using a large set of query-document pairs labelled by human judges. Our experiments suggested that incorporating multiple document fields significantly improves the performance of neural ranking models by a large margin. Our model also outperforms state-of-the-art traditional term matching and learning to rank models, significantly. We showed that multiple query representations are needed for different document fields, based on the intuition that different aspects of a query may be matched against different fields of a document. Our empirical results also demonstrated that learning a multiple-field document representation is superior to aggregating retrieval scores from matching the query with different fields. We further showed that field-level masking and dropout are useful for handling fields with variable number of text instances and avoiding over-dependence on high-accuracy fields, respectively.

This work smooths the path towards pursuing several research directions in the future. For instance, many retrieval tasks based on semi-structured documents, such as academic search, XML retrieval, product search, expert finding, etc. can benefit from the NRM-F framework for improving the retrieval performance. Another possible future direction is to extend the NRM-F framework by considering lexical matching of query and document fields. We can also explore incorporating query independent features, such as, PageRank score, into our framework. Finally, our findings may be applicable to non-ranking tasks, including document classification, spam detection, and document filtering.

Acknowledgements. This work was supported in part by the Center for Intelligent Information Retrieval. Any opinions, findings and conclusions or recommendations expressed in this material are those of the authors and do not necessarily reflect those of the sponsor.

REFERENCES

[1] Eugene Agichtein, Eric Brill, and Susan Dumais. 2006. Improving Web Search Ranking by Incorporating User Behavior Information. In *Proceedings of the 29th Annual International ACM SIGIR Conference on Research and Development in Information Retrieval (SIGIR '06)*. ACM, Seattle, Washington, USA, 19–26.

[2] Alexey Borisov, Ilya Markov, Maarten de Rijke, and Pavel Serdyukov. 2016. A Neural Click Model for Web Search. In *Proceedings of the 25th International Conference on World Wide Web (WWW '16)*. IW3C2, Montreal, Quebec, Canada, 531–541.

[3] Christopher J. Burges, Robert Ragno, and Quoc V. Le. 2006. Learning to Rank with Nonsmooth Cost Functions. In *Advances in Neural Information Processing Systems 19*. MIT Press, Vancouver, B.C., Canada, 193–200.

[4] Christopher J. C. Burges. 2010. *From RankNet to LambdaRank to LambdaMART: An Overview*. Technical Report. Microsoft Research.

[5] Mostafa Dehghani, Hamed Zamani, Aliaksei Severyn, Jaap Kamps, and W. Bruce Croft. 2017. Neural Ranking Models with Weak Supervision. In *Proceedings of the 40th International ACM SIGIR Conference on Research and Development in Information Retrieval (SIGIR '17)*. ACM, Shinjuku, Tokyo, Japan, 65–74.

[6] Norbert Fuhr, Mounia Lalmas, Saadia Malik, and Gabriella Kazai. 2006. *Advances in XML Information Retrieval and Evaluation: 4th International Workshop of the Initiative for the Evaluation of XML Retrieval*. Springer-Verlag New York, Inc., Secaucus, NJ, USA.

[7] Jiafeng Guo, Yixing Fan, Qingyao Ai, and W. Bruce Croft. 2016. A Deep Relevance Matching Model for Ad-hoc Retrieval. In *Proceedings of the 25th ACM International on Conference on Information and Knowledge Management (CIKM '16)*. ACM, Indianapolis, Indiana, USA, 55–64.

[8] Po-Sen Huang, Xiaodong He, Jianfeng Gao, Li Deng, Alex Acero, and Larry Heck. 2013. Learning Deep Structured Semantic Models for Web Search Using Clickthrough Data. In *Proceedings of the 22nd ACM International Conference on Information & Knowledge Management (CIKM '13)*. ACM, San Francisco, California, USA, 2333–2338.

[9] Jinyoung Kim, Xiaobing Xue, and W. Bruce Croft. 2009. A Probabilistic Retrieval Model for Semistructured Data. In *Proceedings of the 31th European Conference on IR Research on Advances in Information Retrieval (ECIR '09)*. Springer-Verlag, Toulouse, France, 228–239.

[10] Jin Young Kim and W. Bruce Croft. 2012. A Field Relevance Model for Structured Document Retrieval. In *Proceedings of the 34th European Conference on Advances in Information Retrieval (ECIR'12)*. Springer-Verlag, Barcelona, Spain, 97–108.

[11] Diederik P. Kingma and Jimmy Ba. 2014. Adam: A Method for Stochastic Optimization. In *Proceedings of the third International Conference on Learning Representations (ICLR '14)*. Banff, Canada.

[12] Mounia Lalmas and Anastasios Tombros. 2007. Evaluating XML Retrieval Effectiveness at INEX. *SIGIR Forum* 41, 1 (June 2007), 40–57.

[13] Zhengdong Lu and Hang Li. 2013. A Deep Architecture for Matching Short Texts. In *Advances in Neural Information Processing Systems 26 (NIPS '13)*. Lake Tahoe, CA, USA, 1367–1375.

[14] Bhaskar Mitra and Nick Craswell. 2018. An Introduction to Neural Information Retrieval. *Foundations and Trends® in Information Retrieval (to appear)* (2018).

[15] Bhaskar Mitra, Fernando Diaz, and Nick Craswell. 2017. Learning to Match Using Local and Distributed Representations of Text for Web Search. In *Proceedings of the 26th International Conference on World Wide Web (WWW '17)*. IW3C2, Perth, Australia, 1291–1299.

[16] Sung Hyon Myaeng, Don-Hyun Jang, Mun-Seok Kim, and Zong-Cheol Zhoo. 1998. A Flexible Model for Retrieval of SGML Documents. In *Proceedings of the 21st Annual International ACM SIGIR Conference on Research and Development in Information Retrieval (SIGIR '98)*. ACM, Melbourne, Australia, 138–145.

[17] Eric Nalisnick, Bhaskar Mitra, Nick Craswell, and Rich Caruana. 2016. Improving Document Ranking with Dual Word Embeddings. In *Proceedings of the 25th International Conference Companion on World Wide Web (WWW '16 Companion)*. IW3C2, Montreal, Quebec, Canada, 83–84.

[18] Paul Ogilvie and Jamie Callan. 2003. Combining Document Representations for Known-item Search. In *Proceedings of the 26th Annual International ACM SIGIR Conference on Research and Development in Informaion Retrieval (SIGIR '03)*. ACM, Toronto, Canada, 143–150.

[19] Benjamin Piwowarski and Patrick Gallinari. 2003. A machine learning model for information retrieval with structured documents. *Machine Learning and Data Mining in Pattern Recognition* (2003), 425–438.

[20] Tao Qin, Tie-Yan Liu, Jun Xu, and Hang Li. 2010. LETOR: A Benchmark Collection for Research on Learning to Rank for Information Retrieval. *Inf. Retr.* 13, 4 (Aug. 2010), 346–374.

[21] Stephen Robertson, Hugo Zaragoza, and Michael Taylor. 2004. Simple BM25 Extension to Multiple Weighted Fields. In *Proceedings of the Thirteenth ACM International Conference on Information and Knowledge Management (CIKM '04)*. ACM, Washington, D.C., USA, 42–49.

[22] S. E. Robertson, E. Walker, S. Jones, M. M. Hancock-Beaulieu, and M. Gatford. 1994. Okapi at TREC-3. In *Proceedings of the third Text Retrieval Conference (TREC '94)*.

[23] Yelong Shen, Xiaodong He, Jianfeng Gao, Li Deng, and Grégoire Mesnil. 2014. A Latent Semantic Model with Convolutional-Pooling Structure for Information Retrieval. In *Proceedings of the 23rd ACM International Conference on Conference on Information and Knowledge Management (CIKM '14)*. ACM, Shanghai, China, 101–110.

[24] Nitish Srivastava, Geoffrey Hinton, Alex Krizhevsky, Ilya Sutskever, and Ruslan Salakhutdinov. 2014. Dropout: A Simple Way to Prevent Neural Networks from Overfitting. *Journal of Machine Learning Research* 15 (2014), 1929–1958.

[25] Krysta M. Svore and Christopher J.C. Burges. 2009. A Machine Learning Approach for Improved BM25 Retrieval. In *Proceedings of the 18th ACM Conference on Information and Knowledge Management (CIKM '09)*. ACM, Hong Kong, China, 1811–1814.

[26] Ross Wilkinson. 1994. Effective Retrieval of Structured Documents. In *Proceedings of the 17th Annual International ACM SIGIR Conference on Research and Development in Information Retrieval (SIGIR '94)*. Springer-Verlag New York, Inc., Dublin, Ireland, 311–317.

[27] Chenyan Xiong, Zhuyun Dai, Jamie Callan, Zhiyuan Liu, and Russell Power. 2017. End-to-End Neural Ad-hoc Ranking with Kernel Pooling. In *Proceedings of the 40th International ACM SIGIR Conference on Research and Development in Information Retrieval (SIGIR '17)*. ACM, Shinjuku, Tokyo, Japan, 55–64.

[28] Gui-Rong Xue, Hua-Jun Zeng, Zheng Chen, Yong Yu, Wei-Ying Ma, WenSi Xi, and WeiGuo Fan. 2004. Optimizing Web Search Using Web Click-through Data. In *Proceedings of the Thirteenth ACM International Conference on Information and Knowledge Management (CIKM '04)*. ACM, Washington, D.C., USA, 118–126.

[29] Liu Yang, Qingyao Ai, Jiafeng Guo, and W. Bruce Croft. 2016. aNMM: Ranking Short Answer Texts with Attention-Based Neural Matching Model. In *Proceedings of the 25th ACM International on Conference on Information and Knowledge Management (CIKM '16)*. ACM, Indianapolis, Indiana, USA, 287–296.

[30] Hamed Zamani, Michael Bendersky, Xuanhui Wang, and Mingyang Zhang. 2017. Situational Context for Ranking in Personal Search. In *Proceedings of the 26th International Conference on World Wide Web (WWW '17)*. IW3C2, Perth, Australia, 1531–1540.

[31] Hamed Zamani and W. Bruce Croft. 2016. Estimating Embedding Vectors for Queries. In *Proceedings of the 2016 ACM International Conference on the Theory of Information Retrieval (ICTIR '16)*. ACM, Newark, Delaware, USA, 123–132.

[32] Hamed Zamani and W. Bruce Croft. 2017. Relevance-based Word Embedding. In *Proceedings of the 40th International ACM SIGIR Conference on Research and Development in Information Retrieval (SIGIR '17)*. ACM, Shinjuku, Tokyo, Japan, 505–514.

Discrete Deep Learning for Fast Content-Aware Recommendation

Yan Zhang, Hongzhi Yin[†]*, Zi Huang[†], Xingzhong Du[†], Guowu Yang, Defu Lian*
School of Computer Science and Engineering, University of Electronic Science and Technology of China
[†]School of Information Technology and Electrical Engineering, The University of Queensland
yixianqianzy@gmail.com,h.yin1@uq.edu.au,huang@itee.uq.edu.au,x.du@uq.edu.au,guowu@uestc.edu.cn,dove.ustc@gmail.com

ABSTRACT

Cold-start problem and recommendation efficiency have been regarded as two crucial challenges in the recommender system. In this paper, we propose a hashing based deep learning framework called Discrete Deep Learning (DDL), to map users and items to Hamming space, where a user's preference for an item can be efficiently calculated by Hamming distance, and this computation scheme significantly improves the efficiency of online recommendation. Besides, DDL unifies the user-item interaction information and the item content information to overcome the issues of data sparsity and cold-start. To be more specific, to integrate content information into our DDL framework, a deep learning model, Deep Belief Network (DBN), is applied to extract effective item representation from the item content information. Besides, the framework imposes balance and irrelevant constraints on binary codes to derive compact but informative binary codes. Due to the discrete constraints in DDL, we propose an efficient alternating optimization method consisting of iteratively solving a series of mixed-integer programming subproblems. Extensive experiments have been conducted to evaluate the performance of our DDL framework on two different Amazon datasets, and the experimental results demonstrate the superiority of DDL over the state-of-the-art methods regarding online recommendation efficiency and cold-start recommendation accuracy.

KEYWORDS

recommender system; Deep Learning; Hash code; Cold-start

ACM Reference Format:
Yan Zhang, Hongzhi Yin[†][1], Zi Huang[†], Xingzhong Du[†], Guowu Yang, Defu Lian[1]. 2018. Discrete Deep Learning for Fast Content-Aware Recommendation. In *WSDM 2018: 11th ACM International Conference on Web Search and Data Mining, February 5–9, 2018, Marina Del Rey, CA, USA.* ACM, New York, NY, USA, 9 pages. https://doi.org/10.1145/3159652.3159688

1 INTRODUCTION

In the era of information explosion, information overload becomes a challenging problem. Thus it is essential to sort out valuable information for everyone. Personalized recommender systems have been recognized as one of the most critical and effective approaches for alleviating information overload. It is a key factor for the success of many online e-commerce websites such as Taobao, Amazon, Netflix, Yelp, etc.

Collaborative filtering (CF) based recommender systems proven to be very successful. They produce top-k items that users may be interested in by exploiting the historical interaction data such as ratings, purchasing, clicking, and watching records. Among all CF-based methods, the latent factor models (e.g., matrix factorization) have been demonstrated to achieve great success in both academia and industry. Such CF methods factorize an $n \times m$ user-item interaction matrix into a low-dimensional latent vector (a.k.a. feature) space where both users and items are represented by real-valued vectors. Then the user's preference scores for items were predicted by inner products between their vector representations, and the user's top-k preferred items can be produced by ranking the scores descendingly.

However, the growing scale of users and items has made online recommendation much more challenging. Specifically, suppose there are n users and m items in an online recommender system, users and items are denoted as r-dimension real valued vectors, searching the top-k items that users may interested in is the task of online recommendation. The time complexity of online recommendation is $\mathcal{O}(nmr + nm\log k)$ [36] and it is a critical efficiency bottleneck when the size of the dataset is large. Hence a few recommendation frameworks [27-33] were proposed to speed up the online recommendation. However, the time complexity was not decreased markedly since these recommendations are still based on real-valued features.

Fortunately, hashing technique, encoding users and items into binary codes in Hamming space, is a promising approach to tackle the efficiency bottleneck. Since preference score, in this case, can be efficiently computed by bit operations, i.e. Hamming distance. One can even use a fast and accurate indexing method to find approximate top-k preferred items with sublinear or logarithmic time complexity [25]. Besides each dimension of hash codes can be stored by only one

*The corresponding authors

WSDM 2018, February 5–9, 2018, Marina Del Rey, CA, USA

ACM ISBN 978-1-4503-5581-0/18/02...$15.00
https://doi.org/10.1145/3159652.3159688

›it instead of 32/64 bits that are used for storing one di-
nension in real-valued vectors, which significantly reduces torage cost. However, many previous hashing-based recomnendation improves the recommendation efficiency at the ›rice of recommendation accuracy due to a large amount of nformation loss caused by discretization.

Existing hashing-based recommender systems were pro›osed to find some trade-off strategies between efficiency nd accuracy [35–39]. These strategies consist of two type-: two-stage hashing recommendation and hashing learning ecommendation. To learn hash codes, a discrete optimizaion problem is formulated in hashing-based recommendation rameworks. However, this discrete optimization problem s NP-hard [6], but can be resorted to a two-stage procelure, which consists of relaxed optimization via discarding he discrete constraints, and subsequent binary quantization tage. But these two-stage approaches oversimplify original liscrete optimization, so two principle hashing-based frameworks called Discrete Collaborative Filtering (DCF) [35] and)iscrete Personalized Ranking (DPR) [36], were proposed to olve the discrete optimization directly. However, hash codes ntuitively carry less information than real-valued vectors ince much fewer bits are utilized to store information, which eads to poor recommendation performance. Besides, it is videly recognized that CF-based methods suffer poor perormance when the interaction information is sparse, and an xtreme case is cold start [18], where there is no interaction nformation between new users/items and other items/users. 3ecause the above hashing recommendation frameworks are ›ased on CF, data sparsity further aggravates the poor perormance, and they cannot work in the cold-start setting.

To alleviate the above issues, we propose a hashing-based earning recommendation framework, Discrete Deep Learning DDL), which combines a deep learning framework, Deep 3elief Network (DBN), and CF framework to learn efficient ›inary representations for users and items from rating and ontent data. In order to obtain compact and informative ash codes, we add balance and irrelevant constraints on ›inary codes. Two steps solve the problem: initialize DDL nd optimize DDL. We first initialize DDL by the *pre-train* ›rocedure of DBN that will be introduced in Section 3.3. Ve then apply an efficient alternating optimization method o optimize our proposed DDL to obtain hash codes for sers and items from rating and content data. Finally, we valuate DDL on two different Amazon[1] datasets and show ts consistent superiority to the competing baselines.

The main contributions of this paper are summarized as 'ollows:

(1) We propose a hashing-based hybrid recommendation framework by combining hashing and hybrid recommendation techniques, which effectively overcome sparse and cold-start issues, and significantly speed up online recommendation.
(2) We integrate a deep learning model into our hashing based recommendation framework in a unified way, which is helpful to extract efficient binary representations. Hence DDL provides a good trade-off between recommendation efficiency and accuracy.
(3) We add balance and irrelevant constraints on hash codes and develop an alternating optimization algorithm to solve the proposed discrete mixed-integer programming problem, which is helpful to extract compact and informative hash codes and can improve the recommendation performance.

The rest of this paper is organized as follows: Section 2 and Section 3 introduce the related works and the preliminary, respectively. Section 4 introduces the model proposed in this paper in detail. Section 5 introduces the initialization and the discrete optimization algorithm to solve the proposed model. Section 6 introduces the experimental settings for DDL and other comparison methods. Section 7 analyzes the experimental results and Section 8 concludes the paper.

2 RELATED WORK

In this section, we review several major schemes closely relevant to this paper. Firstly, we introduce several real-valued hybrid recommender systems proposed to alleviate data sparsity by combining user-item interaction and content data. We then present the latest two types of hashing-based recommendation frameworks.

2.1 Real-Valued Hybrid Recommendation

2.1.1 CTR. Collaborative topic regression [23] is a state-of-the-art hybrid recommender system, which was proposed by combining topic model, collaborative filtering, and probabilistic matrix factorization (PMF) [17]. The authors developed a machine learning algorithm for recommending scientific articles to users in an online scientific community. CTR obtained real latent representations of users and items by exploiting two types of data: user's collection data and article content data. It can be used to mitigate cold start and data sparsity settings.

2.1.2 CDL. Collaborative deep learning [24] was proposed as a probabilistic model by jointly learning a probabilistic stacked denoising autoencoder (SDAE) [21] and CF. Similar to CTR, CDL exploits interaction and content data to alleviate cold start and data sparsity problems. Differ from CTR, CDL took advantage of deep learning framework to learn effective real latent representations. Thus it can be applied in cold-start and sparse settings. CDL is a tightly coupled method for recommender systems by developing a hierarchical Bayesian model.

2.1.3 CKE. Collaborative knowledge base embedding [34] is an integrated framework composed of three components: heterogeneous network embedding method, stacked denoising auto-encoders, and stacked convolutional auto-encoders. CKE extracted items semantic representations from structural content, textual content and visual content, and it was proposed to deal with cold start and data sparsity settings.

2.1.4 VBPR. Visual Bayesian Personalized Ranking [7] is a factorization model by incorporating visual features into predictors of users' preferences. By utilizing visual features

[1]https://www.amazon.com/

extracted from product images by (*pre-trained*) deep networks, VBPR is also helpful to alleviate cold start and sparse issues.

2.2 Hashing-based Recommendation

Below we mainly review recent advances of hashing-based recommendation frameworks. For comprehensive review of hashing techniques, please refer to [26].

2.2.1 Two-stage Hashing Recommendation. As discussed in Section 1, the two-stage framework consists of relaxed optimization stage and binary quantization stage. Real latent representations can be obtained by the relaxed optimization, and hash codes can be obtained by the quantization. A pioneer work [3] was proposed to exploit Locality-Sensitive Hashing [4] to generate hash codes for Google News readers based on their click history. On this basis, A. Karatzoglou et al. [10] randomly projected real latent representations learned from regularized matrix factorization into hash codes. Similar to this, K. Zhou et al.[39] followed the idea of Iterative Quantization [5] to generate binary codes from rotated real latent representations. To derive compact binary codes, the uncorrelated constraints were imposed on the real latent representations in regularized matrix factorization. However, according to the analysis in [38], hashing essentially only preserves similarity rather than preference based on inner product, since the magnitudes of the representations for users and items are discarded in the quantization stage. Thus, a constant feature norm (CFN) constraint was imposed when learning the real latent representations, and then the magnitudes and similarity are respectively quantized in [37, 38]. But the two-stage approach still suffered large information loss in the quantization procedure.

2.2.2 Hashing Learning Recommendation. Differ from two-stage hashing frameworks, hashing learning frameworks can obtain hash codes by directly solving the discrete optimization problem. Thus more information is carried by hash codes than two-stage frameworks. Zhang et al. proposed discrete collaborative filtering (DCF) [35], which is a hashing learning recommendation framework. By adding balance and uncorrelated constraints on hash codes, DCF obtained efficient binary codes. DCF was evaluated using a similar way of the conventional CF [16]. By directly optimizing a ranking evaluation metric – the Area Under ROC (Receiver Operating Characteristics) Curve (AUC), discrete personalized ranking (DPR) [36] was proposed to learn hash codes under the same constraints with DCF, and it also obtained short and informative hash codes. Since the above hashing learning frameworks are based on CF, thus they still suffer low recommendation accuracy under sparse setting, and they cannot work when new users or items present.

3 PRELIMINARY AND PROBLEM STATEMENT

In this section, we first introduce some notations used in this paper and then formulate the problem. After that, we briefly introduce the deep learning framework, DBN, used in this paper.

Table 1: Notations

Symbol	Size	Description
$\mathbf{b}_i$	$r \times 1$	hash code of user i
$\mathbf{d}_j$	$r \times 1$	hash code of user j
V	$\mathcal{S}$	the index set of observed ratings
V_i	$\mathcal{S}_i$	items set rated by user i
V_j	$\mathcal{S}_j$	users set of item j
$\mathbf{c}_j$	$P \times 1$	bag-of-words of item j
Θ	1×2	parameter of DBN
$\mathbf{W}$	$1 \times l$	weight matrices of l-layer DBN
$\mathbf{b}$	$1 \times l$	bias vectors of l-layer DBN
$\mathbf{B}$	$r \times n$	hash codes matrix of all users in I
$\mathbf{D}$	$r \times m$	hash codes matrix of all items in J
$\mathbf{X}$	$r \times n$	delegated real matrix of $\mathbf{B}$
$\mathbf{Y}$	$r \times m$	delegated real matrix of $\mathbf{D}$

3.1 Notations

Assume that there are n users and m items in a recommender system. The users set is defined as I and the items set is indicated as J. The observed rating $s_{ij} \in S$ represents the preference of user i for item j. The items content data is denoted as $\mathbf{C}$, which consists of bag-of-words vectors of all items in J. The other essential notations used in this paper are listed in Table 1.

3.2 Problem Statement

The goal of recommender system is to provide items that can match users' preferences. Preference model is formulated based on the representations of users and items, which is dependent on the recommendation framework.

Cold-Start: Cold-start problem consists of cold-start user and cold-start item. Specifically, cold-start item problem is caused by new items which have no interaction information [18]. Conducting recommendation under the two cold start settings is a challenge for recommender systems, and hence it often suffers low accuracy.

Data Sparsity: As introduced in [14], data sparsity refers to a situation where interaction data is insufficient for identifying similar users/items, and it is a major factor that affects the performance of recommendation.

Problem Definition(Discrete Deep Learning): Given a user-item rating dataset S, a content dataset $\mathbf{C}$, and a query user i, our goal is to recommend top-k items that user i would be interested in. The problem becomes a cold-start item recommendation if the predicted top-k items are not in the rating dataset S, and meanwhile in the content data C.

3.3 Deep Belief Network

To obtain effective item representations, we use DBN to extract deep hierarchical item representations from item content data. DBN [8] is a generative probabilistic model consists of one input layer and multiple hidden layers. Jointly training all layers is computationally intractable. Hinton et al. put forward an efficient algorithm to train DBN in a greedy layerwise manner [8], in which the hidden layers are trained once at a time in a bottom-up way, and the above unsupervised procedure is called *pre-train*. After adding an extra learning objective, the learned representation by *pre-train* stage is converted into a supervised learning process then *fine-tune* all the parameters of the DBN with respect to concerning the additional learning objective (in this paper, the objective in Section 5.4). The *fine-tune* process is usually implemented by Back-Propagation (BP) algorithm [9].

4 DISCRETE DEEP LEARNING

In this section, we first model users' preferences by hash codes, then we introduce the proposed DDL.

4.1 Preference Model

The preference model is a key component to formulate a recommender system. The traditional model is usually based on Matrix Factorization [12] under a low-rank assumption. Users and items are projected into a r-dimension real latent space, and the preference of user i for item j is estimated by the inner product of real-valued vectors. Similarly, the proposed hashing-based framework in this paper maps users and items into a r-dimension Hamming space, in which the preference is estimated by the Hamming distance between hash codes of users and items.

Suppose that hash codes of user i and item j are denoted by $\mathbf{b}_i \in \{\pm1\}^r$ and $\mathbf{d}_j \in \{\pm1\}^r$, respectively. The preference of user i for item j is defined as

$$\begin{aligned}\widehat{p}_{ij} &= 1 - \frac{1}{r}\sum_{k=1}^{r}\mathbb{I}\left(b_{ik} \neq d_{jk}\right)\\ &= \frac{1}{r}\sum_{k=1}^{r}\mathbb{I}\left(b_{ik} = d_{jk}\right)\\ &= \frac{1}{2} + \frac{1}{2r}\mathbf{b}_i^T\mathbf{d}_j \end{aligned} \tag{1}$$

where $\mathbb{I}(\cdot)$ is an indicator function that returns 1 if the input is true, otherwise it returns 0. $\widehat{p}_{ij}$ is in the range of 0 to 1 and that represents the predicted preference of user i over item j. From the above preference model, it can be observed that the preference model in r-dimension Hamming space is consistent with that in r-dimension real latent space.

4.2 Discrete Deep Learning

Discrete Deep Learning (DDL) is a hashing-based hybrid recommendation framework which adds hashing technique into the hybrid recommender framwork, that consists of DBN and CF by exploiting rating and item content data. Hence, DDL can obtain effective hash codes by jointly optimizing two objectives: DBN based objective and CF based objective.

For each item j, the real-valued representation $\mathbf{f}_j$ can be automatically learnt by the *pre-train* procedure of DBN from the bag-of-words $\mathbf{c}_j$:

$$\mathbf{f}_j = \mathrm{DBN}(\mathbf{c}_j, \Theta).$$

To address the issues of data sparsity and cold start item, our DDL effectively exploits the content information of items using the deep learning model DBN. Thus, one of our objectives is to minimize the difference between the learnt representation $\mathbf{f}_j$ and the binary representation (hash code) $\mathbf{d}_j$ for each item j, and it is given by

$$\arg\min_{\mathbf{D},\,\Theta} \sum_{j=1}^{m} \|\mathbf{d}_j - \mathrm{DBN}(\mathbf{c}_j,\Theta)\|_F^2, \tag{2}$$

where $\Theta = \{\mathbf{W}, \mathbf{b}\}$ is the parameters of a l-layer DBN that contains weight matrices $\mathbf{W} = \{\mathbf{W}^{(1)}, \mathbf{W}^{(2)}, \cdots, \mathbf{W}^{(l)}\}$ and bias vectors $\mathbf{b} = \{\mathbf{b}^{(1)}, \mathbf{b}^{(2)}, \cdots, \mathbf{b}^{(l)}\}$, $\mathbf{D}$ is stacked by $\mathbf{d}_j$, where $j \in J$. Therefore, by minimizing the objective function in Equation (2), we obtain effective items' hash codes by the deep hierarchical framework from content data.

The CF based objective is to minimize the difference between the observed rating s_{ij} and the predicted preference $\widehat{p}_{ij}$. We assume that $s_{ij} \in \mathbf{S}$ is in the range of 0 to 1 denoting the rating of user i to item j, and get the following objective from Equation (1):

$$\arg\min_{\mathbf{B},\mathbf{D}} \sum_{(i,j)\in V}\left(s_{ij} - \frac{1}{2} - \frac{1}{2r}\mathbf{b}_i^T\mathbf{d}_j\right)^2, \tag{3}$$

where V is the index set of S, $\mathbf{B}, \mathbf{D}$ respectively are the hash codes of users and items, and r is the hash code length. By minimizing the above objective, we can obtain effective hash codes of users and items from the observed rating data.

By combining the above two objectives of Equation (2) and Equation (3), the objective function of the proposed DDL is

$$\begin{aligned}\arg\min_{\mathbf{B},\mathbf{D},\Theta} &\sum_{(i,j)\in V}\left(2rs_{ij} - r - \mathbf{b}_i^T\mathbf{d}_j\right)^2\\ &+ \frac{\lambda}{2}\sum_{j=1}^{m}\|\mathbf{d}_j - \mathrm{DBN}(\mathbf{c}_j,\Theta)\|_F^2\\ s.t.\ \ &\mathbf{B} \in \{\pm1\}^{r\times n}, \mathbf{D} \in \{\pm1\}^{r\times m}, \end{aligned} \tag{4}$$

where $\lambda > 0$ is a tuning parameter that weights the importance of the two objectives. In order to maximize the entropy of each binary bit, it is needed to add a balance constraint, so that each bit carries as much information as possible [39]. In addition, to learn compact binary codes, irrelevant constraints also need to be imposed, that guarantees each bit is independent of others. In other words, there is no redundant information in the obtained hash codes. After adding the above two additional constraints on both $\mathbf{B}$ and $\mathbf{D}$, we can reformulate the problem Equation (4) as

$$\begin{aligned}\arg\min_{\mathbf{B},\mathbf{D},\Theta} &\sum_{(i,j)\in V}\left(2rs_{ij} - r - \mathbf{b}_i^T\mathbf{d}_j\right)^2\\ &+ \frac{\lambda}{2}\sum_{j=1}^{m}\|\mathbf{d}_j - \mathrm{DBN}(\mathbf{c}_j,\Theta)\|_F^2\\ s.t.\ \ &\mathbf{B} \in \{\pm1\}^{r\times n}, \mathbf{D} \in \{\pm1\}^{r\times m},\\ &\mathbf{B}\mathbf{1}_n = \mathbf{0}, \mathbf{D}\mathbf{1}_m = \mathbf{0}, \mathbf{B}\mathbf{B}^T{=}n\mathbf{I}_r, \mathbf{D}\mathbf{D}^T{=}m\mathbf{I}_r, \end{aligned} \tag{5}$$

where $\mathbf{1}_n$ ($\mathbf{1}_m$) present n-dimension (m-dimension) vectors that all elements are 1, and $\mathbf{I}_r$ is a $r \times r$-dimension identity matrix. As Equation (5) is a discrete optimization problem, which is proven to be an intractable NP-hard problem [6], we adopt a methodology like [35] to soften the balance and irrelevant constraints. Specifically, we add delegated real valued matrices $\mathbf{X}$ and $\mathbf{Y}$ to approximate hash codes $\mathbf{B}$ and $\mathbf{D}$, respectively. Thus Equation (5) can be rewritten as:

$$\begin{aligned}\arg\min_{\mathbf{B},\mathbf{D},\Theta} & \sum_{(i,j)\in\mathcal{V}} \left(2rs_{ij} - r - \mathbf{b}_i^T\mathbf{d}_j\right)^2 + \alpha\left\|\mathbf{B}-\mathbf{X}\right\|_F^2 \\ & + \frac{\lambda}{2}\sum_{j=1}^{m} \|\mathbf{d}_j - \mathrm{DBN}(\mathbf{c}_j,\Theta)\|_F^2 + \beta\left\|\mathbf{D}-\mathbf{Y}\right\|_F^2, \\ s.t. \;\; & \mathbf{B}\in\{\pm1\}^{r\times n}, \mathbf{D}\in\{\pm1\}^{r\times m} \\ & \mathbf{X}\mathbf{1}_n = \mathbf{0}, \mathbf{Y}\mathbf{1}_m = \mathbf{0}, \mathbf{X}\mathbf{X}^T = n\mathbf{I}_r, \mathbf{Y}\mathbf{Y}^T = m\mathbf{I}_r, \quad (6)\end{aligned}$$

where α and β are tuning parameters so that the second and last terms in Equation (6) allow certain discrepancy between $\mathbf{B}$ and $\mathbf{X}$, and between $\mathbf{D}$ and $\mathbf{Y}$. Since $tr(\mathbf{B}\mathbf{B}^T) = tr(\mathbf{X}\mathbf{X}^T) = nr$ and $tr(\mathbf{D}\mathbf{D}^T) = tr(\mathbf{Y}\mathbf{Y}^T) = mr$ are constant. Thus the objective in Equation (6) can be equivalently transformed as the following mixed integer optimization problem:

$$\begin{aligned}\arg\min_{\mathbf{B},\mathbf{D},\Theta,\mathbf{X},\mathbf{Y}} & \sum_{(i,j)\in\mathcal{V}} \left(a_{ij} - \mathbf{b}_i^T\mathbf{d}_j\right)^2 - 2\alpha tr(\mathbf{B}^T\mathbf{X}) \\ & + \frac{\lambda}{2}\sum_{j=1}^{m} \|\mathbf{d}_j - \mathrm{DBN}(\mathbf{c}_j,\Theta)\|_F^2 - 2\beta tr(\mathbf{D}^T\mathbf{Y}) \\ s.t. \;\; & \mathbf{B}\in\{\pm1\}^{r\times n}, \mathbf{D}\in\{\pm1\}^{r\times m} \\ & \mathbf{X}\mathbf{1}_n = \mathbf{0}, \mathbf{Y}\mathbf{1}_m = \mathbf{0}, \mathbf{X}\mathbf{X}^T = n\mathbf{I}_r, \mathbf{Y}\mathbf{Y}^T = m\mathbf{I}_r, \quad (7)\end{aligned}$$

where $a_{ij} = 2rs_{ij} - r$. Differ from two-stage hashing-based frameworks, we do not discard the binary constraints through the objective transformations.

4.3 Advantage of DDL for Online Recommendation

4.3.1 Time Complexity. **Real-valued space:** As discussed in Section 1, suppose there are n users and m items in a recommender system, after extracting real latent representations, predicting top-k items in real space has the time complexity of $\mathcal{O}(nmr + nm\log k)$. **Hamming space:** After hash codes have been obtained, we can make a recommendation by ranking the predicted preferences by Equation (1). For each user (denoted by hash code), ranking items by the predicted preferences is equivalent to finding the top-k nearest items (denoted by hash codes) in Hamming space. As discussed in [38], searching nearest neighbors in Hamming space is extremely fast. There are two methods to search the top-k items: one is Hamming ranking, it can be conducted by ranking Hamming distances with the query hash code (user), it has the complexity of $\mathcal{O}(m)$, which is linear with the item data size. The other one is hashing lookup. Similar hash codes are searched in a hamming ball centered at the query hash code. The time complexity is independent of the item data size. Therefore, Hashing based recommendation has evident superiority over the real-valued recommendation.

4.3.2 Storage complexity. **Real space:** At least 64 bits are needed to store a double real number. When the dimension of real latent vectors becomes large, it will cost much more space. **Hamming space:** Only one bit is needed to store a binary code. Thus the storage cost is reduced significantly. If we store m items by r-dimension real latent vectors, it will cost $64mr$ bits, while it costs mr bits by r-dimension hash codes. Moreover, if we store hash codes with sparse vectors, the storage cost will be reduced further [1, 38].

5 MODEL OPTIMIZATION

In this section, an alternating optimization strategy is developed to solve the mixed integer optimization problem shown in Equation (7). We first initialize all parameters of DDL in Section 5.1. We then introduce how to update $\mathbf{B}$, $\mathbf{D}$, Θ, $\mathbf{X}$ and $\mathbf{Y}$, respectively.

5.1 Initialization

We initialize DDL by the *pre-train* procedure of DBN. Specifically, we first learn the item representations $\mathbf{f}_j$ by the *pre-train* process of DBN. Then we initialize Θ as the result of the *pre-train*, and initialize each $\mathbf{d}_j$ as the sign of $\mathbf{f}_j$. Besides, we randomly initialize $\mathbf{X}$ and $\mathbf{Y}$ by the standard normal distribution and initialize $\mathbf{B}$ as the sign of $\mathbf{X}$.

5.2 Update B given D, X, Y, and Θ

Since the objective function in Equation (7) sums over users independently, we update $\mathbf{B}$ by updating $\mathbf{b}_i$ in parallel by minimizing the following objective function:

$$\arg\min_{\mathbf{b}_i\in\{\pm1\}^r} \sum_{j\in\mathcal{V}_i} (\mathbf{d}_j^T\mathbf{b}_i)^2 - 2\sum_{j\in\mathcal{V}_i} a_{ij}\mathbf{d}_j^T\mathbf{b}_i - 2\alpha\mathbf{x}_i^T\mathbf{b}_i, \quad (8)$$

where $\mathcal{V}_i$ is the items set rated by user i. This discrete optimization problem is NP-hard, and thus we adopt a bitwise learning strategy named Discrete Coordinate Descent (DCD) [19] to update $\mathbf{b}_i$. Particularly, let b_{ik} be the k-th bit of $\mathbf{b}_i$ and let $\mathbf{b}_{i\bar{k}}$ be the rest bits of $\mathbf{b}_i$, i.e, $\mathbf{b}_i = [\mathbf{b}_{i\bar{k}}^T, b_{ik}]^T$. Note that DCD can update b_{ik} given $\mathbf{b}_{i\bar{k}}$. Discarding the terms independent of b_{ik}, the objective function in Equation (8) is rewritten as

$$\arg\min_{b_{ik}\in\{\pm1\}} \hat{b}_{ik}b_{ik}, \quad (9)$$

where $\hat{b}_{ik} = \sum_{j\in\mathcal{V}_i} \mathbf{d}_{j\bar{k}}^T \mathbf{b}_{i\bar{k}} d_{jk} - \sum_{j\in\mathcal{V}_i} a_{ij}d_{jk} - \alpha x_{ik}$. Due to the space limit, we omit the derivation details. The above objective function reaches the minimal only if b_{ik} had the opposite sign of $\hat{b}_{ik}$. However, if $\hat{b}_{ik}$ was zero, b_{ik} would not be updated. Therefore, the update rule of b_{ik} is

$$b_{ik} = sgn\left(K\left(-\hat{b}_{ik}, b_{ik}\right)\right), \quad (10)$$

where $K(t,r) = t$ if $t \neq 0$, otherwise, $K(t,r) = r$.

5.3 Update D given B, X, Y, and Θ

Provided $\mathbf{B}$, $\mathbf{X}$, $\mathbf{Y}$, and Θ are fixed, discarding terms irrelevant to $\mathbf{d}_j$ in Equation (7), we formulate the following subproblem as:

$$\begin{aligned}\arg\min_{\mathbf{d}_j\in\{\pm1\}^r} & \sum_{i\in\mathcal{V}_j} (\mathbf{b}_i^T\mathbf{d}_j)^2 - 2\sum_{i\in\mathcal{V}_j} a_{ij}\mathbf{b}_i^T\mathbf{d}_j \\ & + \frac{\lambda}{2}\|\mathbf{d}_j - \mathrm{DBN}(\mathbf{c}_j,\Theta)\|_F^2 - 2\beta\mathbf{y}_j^T\mathbf{d}_j, \quad (11)\end{aligned}$$

where $\mathcal{V}_j$ is the users set that rated item j. Similarly, we optimize $\mathbf{d}_j$ by the bitwise learning, and the objective is rewritten as

$$\arg\min_{b_{ik}\in\{\pm1\}} \hat{d}_{jk}d_{jk}, \quad (12)$$

where $\hat{d}_{jk} = \sum_{i \in V_j} \mathbf{b}_{i\bar{k}}^T \mathbf{d}_{j\bar{k}} b_{ik} - \sum_{i \in V_j} a_{ij} b_{ik} - \frac{\lambda}{2}\mathrm{DBN}(\mathbf{v}_j, \Theta)_k +$ βy_{jk}. As discussed in Section 5.3, the update rule of d_{jk} is:

$$d_{jk} = sgn\left(K\left(-\hat{d}_{jk}, d_{jk}\right)\right). \quad (13)$$

5.4 Update Θ given B, D, X, and Y

If **B**, **D**, **X**, and **Y** are fixed, the optimization problem Equation (7) can be rewritten as

$$\arg\min_{\Theta} \sum_{j=1}^{m} \|\mathbf{d}_j - \mathrm{DBN}(\mathbf{c}_j, \Theta)\|^2. \quad (14)$$

Since **D** is fixed, Equation (14) is a supervised DBN learning framework. As introduced in Section 3.3, after initialization, all parameters need to be *fine-tuned* by using stochastic gradient descent method, where the gradient descent part is implemented by BP algorithm. As $\mathbf{d}_j \in \{\pm 1\}^r$, we choose *tanh* function as the output function of DBN since its output is in the range of -1 to 1 that has the same range with hash codes. We choose sigmoid function as the activation function for hidden layers.

5.5 Update X given B, D, Y, and Θ

Given **B**, **D**, **Y**, and Θ, the Equation (7) is transformed as

$$\underset{\mathbf{X} \in \mathbb{R}^{r \times n}}{\text{argmax}}\ tr(\mathbf{B}^T\mathbf{X}),\ s.t.\ \mathbf{X}\mathbf{1}_n = \mathbf{0}, \mathbf{X}\mathbf{X}^T = n\mathbf{I}_r. \quad (15)$$

It can be solved with the help of SVD according to [35, 36]. Specifically, **X** is updated by

$$\mathbf{X} = \sqrt{n}[\mathbf{U}_s\ \widehat{\mathbf{U}}_s][\mathbf{V}_s\ \widehat{\mathbf{V}}_s]^T, \quad (16)$$

where $\mathbf{U}_s$ and $\mathbf{V}_s$ are respectively stacked by the left and right singular vectors of the row-centered matrix $\bar{\mathbf{B}} : \bar{b}_{ij} = b_{ij} - \frac{1}{n}\sum_{i=1}^{n} b_{ij}$. $\widehat{\mathbf{U}}_s$ is stacked by the left singular vectors and $\widehat{\mathbf{V}}_s$ can be calculated by Gram-Schmidt orthogonalization, and it satisfies $[\mathbf{V}_s\ \mathbf{1}]^T\widehat{\mathbf{V}}_s = \mathbf{0}$.

5.6 Update Y with fixed B, D, X, and Θ

Given **B**, **D**, **X**, and Θ, the Equation (7) can be transformed as

$$\underset{\mathbf{Y} \in \mathbb{R}^{r \times m}}{\text{argmax}}\ tr(\mathbf{D}^T\mathbf{Y}),\ s.t.\ \mathbf{Y}\mathbf{1}_\mathbf{m} = \mathbf{0}, \mathbf{Y}\mathbf{Y}^T = m\mathbf{I}_r. \quad (17)$$

Similar to Section 5.5, **Y** can be updated by

$$\mathbf{Y} = \sqrt{m}[\mathbf{P}_s\ \widehat{\mathbf{P}}_s][\mathbf{Q}_s\ \widehat{\mathbf{Q}}_s]^T. \quad (18)$$

Similarly, $\mathbf{P}_s$, $\mathbf{Q}_s$, $\widehat{\mathbf{P}}_s$, and $\widehat{\mathbf{Q}}_s$ can be determined by the row-centered matrix of **D**.

6 EXPERIMENTAL SETTINGS

In this section, we first introduce datasets used in our experiments. Then we introduce two evaluation methods and five state-of-the-art comparison methods.

6.1 Datasets

We adopt the Amazon dataset[2] in our experiments, which is one of the biggest, most comprehensive, and publicly available datasets for the study of recommendation. It covers user interactions (such as ratings) on items as well as item content (such as item metadata and descriptions) on 24 product categories spanning May 1996 - July 2014, and each group contains a sub-dataset. We adopt two of the largest product categories Clothing, Shoes & Jewelry, and Cell Phones & Accessories for experiments, and the two datasets are briefly denoted as 'Cloth' and 'Cell' in the following. We use rating and item content data in our experiments. The rating matrix has a sparsity of 99.9%. Some statistics of the datasets are shown in Table 2.

[2] http://jmcauley.ucsd.edu/data/amazon/

Table 2: Statistics of datasets.

Dataset	#User(n)	#Item(m)	#Rating(S)	Sparsity(%)
'Cloth'	39,387	23,033	278,653	99.97%
'Cell'	27,879	10,429	194,340	99.93%

6.1.1 Data Pre-processing. For rating data, we normalize each rating into the interval of [0,1] to keep consistent with the predicted preference defined in this paper. For content data, we first remove punctuations, numbers, stop words, and words with the length smaller than two since these words usually have no discriminative meanings, we then conduct stemming on the remaining words by the Porter Stemmer [15]. Finally, similar to [23], by ranking the TF-IDF values we choose the top 8000 discriminative words from the two datasets to form dictionaries separately, then we get the bag-of-words **C** for all items.

6.1.2 Data Spliting. To simulate sparse settings, similar to [13], we take different proportions (10%, 20%) of ratings as training set D_{train} and the remaining positive ratings (i.e., original ratings ≥ 4 stars) D_{test} are used for testing. Taking 20% as an example, we randomly select 20% ratings for each item as the training data, and the remaining positive ratings are chosen for testing. The random selection is carried out 5 times independently, and we report the experimental results as the average values.

6.2 Evaluation Methods

As introduced in Section 3.2, the goal of recommendation is to find out the top-k items that users may be interested in. We adopt two common ranking evaluation methods: Accuracy@k and Mean Reciprocal Rank (MRR), to evaluate the quality of the ranking list. Accuracy@k was widely adopted by many previous ranking based recommender systems [2, 11], and MRR was also widely used as a metric for ranking tasks [20, 22].

The basic idea of Accuracy@k is to test whether a user's favorite item appears in the predicted top-k items list, we define the user's *favorite (positive) items* as the ones rated 4-stars or 5-stars (0.8 or 1 rating in this paper), and the *positive ratings* refer to ratings 0.8 or 1. For each positive rating $s_{ij} \in D_{test}$: (1) we randomly choose 1000 negative items and compute predicted rating scores for the ground-truth item j as well as the 1000 negative items; (2) we form a ranked list by ordering these items according to their predicted ratings; (3) if the ground-truth item j appears in the top-k ranked list, we have a hit; otherwise, we have a miss.

6.2.1 Accuracy@k. Accuracy@k has been widely used in evaluating recommendation accuracy by assessing the quality of the obtained top-k items list. Accuracy@k is formulated as:

$$\text{Accuracy@}k = \frac{\#hit@k}{|D_{test}|},$$

where $|D_{test}|$ is the size of the test set, and $\#hit@k$ denotes the number of hits in the test set.

6.2.2 MRR. The Mean Reciprocal Rank (MRR) [22] is to evaluate a ranking task that produces a list of responses to a query, ordered by probability of correctness. The reciprocal rank of a query response is the multiplicative inverse of the rank of the first correct answer. The mean reciprocal rank is the average of the reciprocal ranks of results for a query, MRR is defined as:

$$\text{MRR} = \frac{1}{|D_{test}|} \sum_{s_{ij} \in D_{test}} \frac{1}{rank(i,j)},$$

where $rank(i,j)$ is the position of item j in the obtained top-k items list for user i.

6.3 Comparison Methods and Settings

As introduced in Section 2.2, we choose two types of comparison methods that consist of three real-valued hybrid recommender systems (CTR, CDL, and VBPR) and two latest competing hashing-based recommender systems (DCF and DPR).

In our experiments, we use 5-fold cross validation method on randomly splits of training data, to tune the optimal hyper-parameters for our algorithm and all the compared algorithms: CTR, CDL, VBPR, DCF, and DPR. We perform grid search to find the optimal hyper-parameters.

For CTR, we set $\lambda_u = 0.1$, $\lambda_v = 10$, $a = 1$, $b = 0.01$ and $K = 50$ since it can achieve good performance. For CDL, it can achieve good performance when we set $\lambda_u = 1$, $\lambda_v = 10$, $\lambda_n = 1e^4$, $\lambda_w = 1e^{-4}$, $a = 1$ and $b = 0.01$. For aligning with the dimension of other methods, we set $K = 30$, and the layer structure of SDAE is set as $[8000, 200, 30]$. For VBPR, we set $\lambda_\Theta = 10$.

For DCF, we search α and β from $\{1e^{-4}, 1e^{-3}, \cdots, 1e^2\}$, and the optimal parameters are $\alpha = 1e^{-3}$ and $\beta = 1e^{-3}$. For DPR, we find the optimal parameters respectively are $\alpha = 1e^{-4}$ and $\beta = 1e^{-3}$.

For DDL proposed in this paper, we search α, β from $\{1e^{-4}, 1e^{-3}, \cdots, 1e^2\}$ and λ from $\{1e^{-1}, 1, \cdots, 1e^2\}$ by grid search. As a result, we set the layer structure of DBN as $[8000, 800, 30]$, and set $\alpha = 1e^{-3}$, $\beta = 1e^{-3}$ and $\lambda = 10$.

7 EXPERIMENTAL RESULTS

In this section, we first display the efficiency of hashing-based recommendation compared with real-valued hybrid recommendation frameworks on 'Cloth' and 'Cell' datasets. Then, we verify the effectiveness of our proposed DDL from three aspects: Firstly, we evaluate the accuracy in recommending cold-start items; Secondly, we explore the accuracy effectiveness in two sparse settings; Thirdly, we present the accuracy effectiveness compared with the competing hashing baselines.

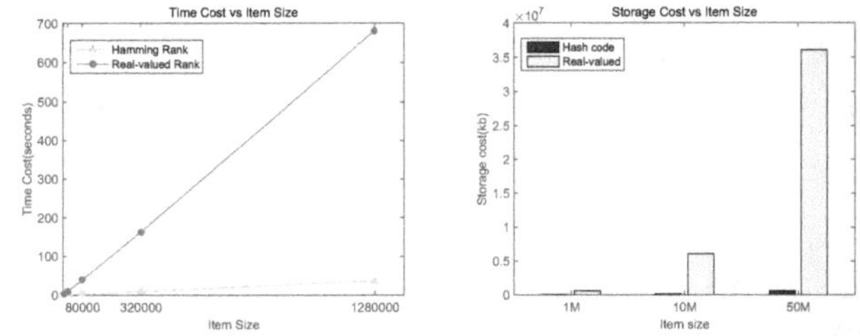

Figure 1: Efficiency comparison on artificial data Left: Time cost comparison. Right: Storage cost comparison

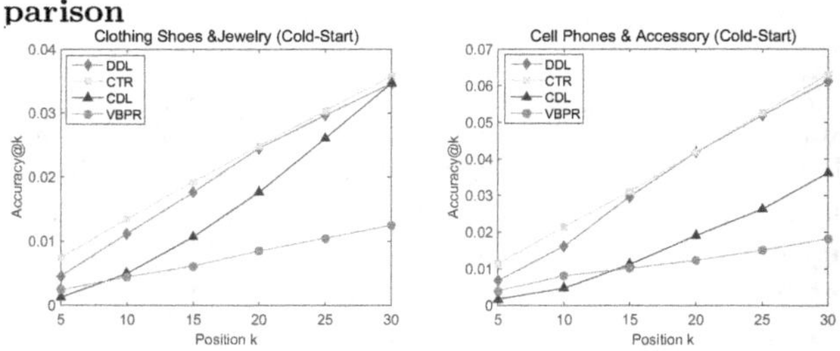

Figure 2: Accuracy@k in cold-start item setting

7.1 Efficiency Comparison

As analyzed in Section 4.3, the significant advantage of hashing recommendation over the real-valued recommendation i the efficiency of online recommendation. We separately evaluate the efficiency in terms of time and storage on synthetic data.

7.1.1 Time Complexity. We investigate the time cost of preference ranking when the item number varies. We use standard gaussian distribution to generate items' real-valued features randomly. Items hash codes are obtained from real valued vectors by the sign function. We set different sizes of items sets in the experiment: 5000, 20000, 80000, 320000, 128000, to test the time cost variation of online recommendation. The variation is shown in the left of Figure 1. We conclude that the time cost of real-valued features grows fas with item number, in comparison, the time cost of hash codes increase much slower than real-valued features. The experimental results show that hashing based recommendation has evident advantage over the real-valued recommendation for online recommendation.

7.1.2 Storage Complexity. We test the storage costs of hash codes and real-valued features on 3 different sizes of item sets: 1 million, 10 million, and 50 million. From the right of Figure 1, hash codes cost much less memory to store the same number of items, which is consistent with the analysis in Section 4.3.

7.2 Accuracy Comparison

7.2.1 Accuracy on Cold-Start Item Recommendation. This experiment studies the accuracy comparison between the existing real-valued hybrid recommender systems and DDL under the same cold-start item setting. We test the performance on the D_{test} (10%) introduced in Section6.1. Specifically, we first choose items with less than 5 positive ratings as cold-start items and then select users with at least one positive rating as test users. For each test user, we first choose his/her ratings related to cold-start items as the test set, and

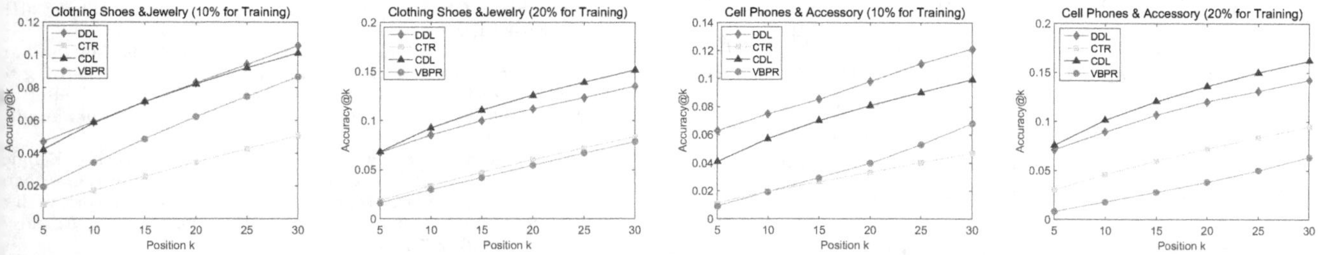

Figure 3: Comparison with Real-valued methods on 'Cloth' and 'Cell' datasets w.r.t two sparse settings.

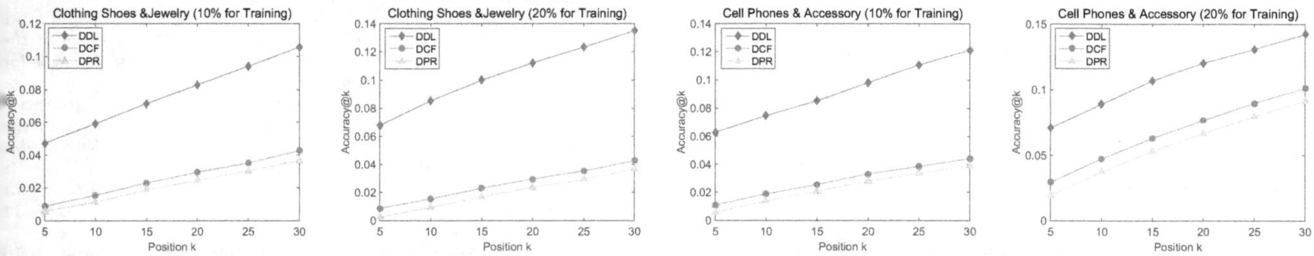

Figure 4: Comparison with Hashing methods on 'Cloth' and 'Cell' datasets w.r.t two sparse settings.

Table 3: MRR in cold-start item setting

Method	CTR	CDL	VBPR	DDL
'Cloth'	0.0082*	0.0071	0.0042	0.0077^{o}
'Cell'	0.0117*	0.0072	0.0053	0.0099^{o}

the remaining ratings as the training set. Our goal is to test whether the marked-off cold-start items can be accurately recommended to the right user.

We adopt Accuracy@k and MRR to respectively evaluate recommendation accuracy. The accuracy@k comparison of two Amazon datasets is shown in Figure 2. Our proposed DDL performs almost as well as the best result of the real-valued hybrid recommender systems. Table 3 summarizes MRR results for the four algorithms, the best result is marked as '$\star$' and the second best is marked as 'o'. We can find that the performance of DDL is very close to the best result, that is consistent with the outcome of Accuracy@k.

The real-valued hybrid recommender systems implement a recommendation by real-valued features, while DDL produces a recommendation by hash codes. As evaluated in Section 7.1, DDL has superiority in the efficiency of online recommendation over real-valued hybrid recommender systems. Due to real latent vectors intuitively carried more information than hash codes. Thus it is acceptable and reasonable to have small gaps between real-valued hybrid recommendation and hashing based DDL.

7.2.2 Accuracy on Sparse Recommendation. Our task in this section is to assess the accuracy effectiveness of DDL compared with real-valued hybrid recommendation on two sparse settings (10%, 20%) introduced in Section 6.1. The results of Accuracy@k and MRR are respectively presented in Figure 3 and Table 4. We can find that DDL performs best when the rating data is very sparse (10%). With the observed ratings becoming dense (20%), CDL performs best under Accuracy@k, and DDL performs best under MRR. In a word, the two metrics have consistent performance in sparse settings. The results indicate that DDL provides a good trade-off between efficiency and accuracy, and DDL can also make effective recommendation by hash codes in sparse settings.

Table 4: MRR on 'Cloth' and 'Cell' datasets with two spare settings (10%, 20%)

	'Cloth'		'Cell'	
	10%	20%	10%	20%
CTR	0.0102	0.0168	0.0113	0.0245
CDL	0.0311^{o}	0.0481^{o}	0.0300^{o}	0.0526^{o}
VBPR	0.0176	0.0158	0.0130	0.0123
DDL	0.0490*	0.0669*	0.0584*	0.0605*

7.2.3 Accuracy Compared with Hashing Frameworks. In this section, we evaluate the effectiveness of DDL compared with two competing hashing baselines. Figure 4 shows the results of Accuracy@k on two datasets in two sparse settings, respectively. We see that DDL outperforms DCF and DPR. DCF and DPR can not work very well in sparse settings since they are based on CF.

8 CONCLUSION

In this paper, a content-aware hashing approach called Discrete Deep Learning (DDL) is proposed to alleviate data sparsity and cold-start item problem. First, we formulate a preference model based on hash codes. Second, based on the preference model, we present the DDL recommendation framework by adding a binary constraint on the combination objective of the supervised DBN and CF-based objectives. By imposing uncorrelated and independent constraints on hash codes, compact and informative hash codes are directly learned by an alternating optimization method. Third, we evaluate the effectiveness of DDL regarding Accuracy@k and MRR on two Amazon datasets. Experiments show that DDL has an obvious advantage over the competing baselines in cold-start item and sparse settings. DDL provides a good trade-off between recommendation efficiency and accuracy.

9 ACKNOWLEDGEMENT

This work was supported by ARC Discovery Early Career Researcher Award (Grant No. DE160100308), ARC Discovery Project (Grant No. DP170103954) and New Staff Research Grant of The University of Queensland (Grant No.613134). It was also supported by National Natural Science Foundation of China (Grant No. 61572335, 61572109, 61502077, 61631005) and the Fundamental Research Funds for the Central Universities (Grant No. ZYGX2016J087).

REFERENCES

[1] Wenlin Chen, James Wilson, Stephen Tyree, Kilian Weinberger, and Yixin Chen. 2015. Compressing neural networks with the hashing trick. In *International Conference on Machine Learning*. 2285–2294.

[2] Wen-Yen Chen, Jon-Chyuan Chu, Junyi Luan, Hongjie Bai, Yi Wang, and Edward Y Chang. 2009. Collaborative filtering for orkut communities: discovery of user latent behavior. In *Proceedings of the 18th international conference on World wide web*. ACM, 681–690.

[3] Abhinandan S Das, Mayur Datar, Ashutosh Garg, and Shyam Rajaram. 2007. Google news personalization: scalable online collaborative filtering. In *Proc. of WWW*. ACM, 271–280.

[4] Mayur Datar, Nicole Immorlica, Piotr Indyk, and Vahab S Mirrokni. 2004. Locality-sensitive hashing scheme based on p-stable distributions. In *Proceedings of the twentieth annual symposium on Computational geometry*. ACM, 253–262.

[5] Yunchao Gong, Svetlana Lazebnik, Albert Gordo, and Florent Perronnin. 2013. Iterative quantization: A procrustean approach to learning binary codes for large-scale image retrieval. *IEEE Transactions on Pattern Analysis and Machine Intelligence* 35, 12 (2013), 2916–2929.

[6] Johan Håstad. 2001. Some optimal inapproximability results. *J. ACM* 48, 4 (2001), 798–859.

[7] Ruining He and Julian McAuley. 2016. VBPR: visual bayesian personalized ranking from implicit feedback. In *Thirtieth AAAI Conference on Artificial Intelligence*.

[8] Geoffrey E Hinton, Simon Osindero, and Yee-Whye Teh. 2006. A fast learning algorithm for deep belief nets. *Neural computation* 18, 7 (2006), 1527–1554.

[9] Kurt Hornik, Maxwell Stinchcombe, and Halbert White. 1989. Multilayer feedforward networks are universal approximators. *Neural networks* 2, 5 (1989), 359–366.

[10] Alexandros Karatzoglou, Markus Weimer, and Alex J Smola. 2010. Collaborative filtering on a budget. In *International Conference on Artificial Intelligence and Statistics*. 389–396.

[11] Yehuda Koren. 2008. Factorization meets the neighborhood: a multifaceted collaborative filtering model. In *Proceedings of the 14th ACM SIGKDD international conference on Knowledge discovery and data mining*. ACM, 426–434.

[12] Yehuda Koren and Robert Bell. 2011. Advances in collaborative filtering. In *Recommender systems handbook*. Springer, 145–186.

[13] Hao Ma, Haixuan Yang, Michael R Lyu, and Irwin King. 2008. Sorec: social recommendation using probabilistic matrix factorization. In *Proceedings of the 17th ACM conference on Information and knowledge management*. ACM, 931–940.

[14] Manos Papagelis, Dimitris Plexousakis, and Themistoklis Kutsuras. 2005. Alleviating the sparsity problem of collaborative filtering using trust inferences. In *International Conference on Trust Management*. Springer, 224–239.

[15] Martin F Porter. 1980. An algorithm for suffix stripping. *Program* 14, 3 (1980), 130–137.

[16] Steffen Rendle, Christoph Freudenthaler, Zeno Gantner, and Lars Schmidt-Thieme. 2009. BPR: Bayesian personalized ranking from implicit feedback. In *Proceedings of the twenty-fifth conference on uncertainty in artificial intelligence*. AUAI Press, 452–461.

[17] Ruslan Salakhutdinov and Andriy Mnih. 2007. Probabilistic Matrix Factorization.. In *Nips*, Vol. 1. 2–1.

[18] Andrew I Schein, Alexandrin Popescul, Lyle H Ungar, and David M Pennock. 2002. Methods and metrics for cold-start recommendations. In *Proceedings of the 25th annual international ACM SIGIR conference on Research and development in information retrieval*. ACM, 253–260.

[19] Fumin Shen, Chunhua Shen, Wei Liu, and Heng Tao Shen. 2015. Supervised Discrete Hashing. In *CVPR*. 37–45.

[20] Yue Shi, Alexandros Karatzoglou, Linas Baltrunas, Martha Larson, Nuria Oliver, and Alan Hanjalic. 2012. CLiMF: learning to maximize reciprocal rank with collaborative less-is-more filtering. In *Proceedings of the sixth ACM conference on Recommender systems*. ACM, 139–146.

[21] Pascal Vincent, Hugo Larochelle, Isabelle Lajoie, Yoshua Bengio, and Pierre-Antoine Manzagol. 2010. Stacked denoising autoencoders: Learning useful representations in a deep network with a local denoising criterion. *Journal of Machine Learning Research* 11, Dec (2010), 3371–3408.

[22] Ellen M Voorhees et al. 1999. The TREC-8 Question Answering Track Report. In *Trec*, Vol. 99. 77–82.

[23] Chong Wang and David M Blei. 2011. Collaborative topic modeling for recommending scientific articles. In *Proceedings of the 17th ACM SIGKDD international conference on Knowledge discovery and data mining*. ACM, 448–456.

[24] Hao Wang, Naiyan Wang, and Dit-Yan Yeung. 2015. Collaborative deep learning for recommender systems. In *Proceedings of the 21th ACM SIGKDD International Conference on Knowledge Discovery and Data Mining*. ACM, 1235–1244.

[25] Jun Wang, Sanjiv Kumar, and Shih-Fu Chang. 2012. Semi-supervised hashing for large-scale search. *IEEE TPAMI* 34, 12 (2012), 2393–2406.

[26] Jun Wang, Wei Liu, Sanjiv Kumar, and Shih-Fu Chang. 2016. Learning to hash for indexing big dataA survey. *Proc. of the IEEE* 104, 1 (2016), 34–57.

[27] Weiqing Wang, Hongzhi Yin, Shazia Sadiq, Ling Chen, Min Xie, and Xiaofang Zhou. 2016. Spore: A sequential personalized spatial item recommender system. In *Data Engineering (ICDE), 2016 IEEE 32nd International Conference on*. IEEE, 954–965.

[28] Hongzhi Yin, Bin Cui, Ling Chen, Zhiting Hu, and Xiaofang Zhou. 2015. Dynamic user modeling in social media systems. *ACM Transactions on Information Systems (TOIS)* 33, 3 (2015), 10.

[29] Hongzhi Yin, Bin Cui, Yizhou Sun, Zhiting Hu, and Ling Chen. 2014. Lcars: A spatial item recommender system. *ACM Transactions on Information Systems (TOIS)* 32, 3 (2014), 11.

[30] Hongzhi Yin, Bin Cui, Xiaofang Zhou, Weiqing Wang, Zi Huang, and Shazia Sadiq. 2016. Joint modeling of user check-in behaviors for real-time point-of-interest recommendation. *ACM Transactions on Information Systems (TOIS)* 35, 2 (2016), 11.

[31] Hongzhi Yin, Yizhou Sun, Bin Cui, Zhiting Hu, and Ling Chen. 2013. Lcars: a location-content-aware recommender system. In *Proceedings of the 19th ACM SIGKDD international conference on Knowledge discovery and data mining*. ACM, 221–229.

[32] Hongzhi Yin, Weiqing Wang, Hao Wang, Ling Chen, and Xiaofang Zhou. 2017. Spatial-Aware Hierarchical Collaborative Deep Learning for POI Recommendation. *IEEE Transactions on Knowledge and Data Engineering* 29, 11 (2017), 2537–2551.

[33] Hongzhi Yin, Xiaofang Zhou, Bin Cui, Hao Wang, Kai Zheng, and Quoc Viet Hung Nguyen. 2016. Adapting to user interest drift for poi recommendation. *IEEE Transactions on Knowledge and Data Engineering* 28, 10 (2016), 2566–2581.

[34] Fuzheng Zhang, Nicholas Jing Yuan, Defu Lian, Xing Xie, and Wei-Ying Ma. 2016. Collaborative knowledge base embedding for recommender systems. In *Proceedings of the 22nd ACM SIGKDD International Conference on Knowledge Discovery and Data Mining*. ACM, 353–362.

[35] Hanwang Zhang, Fumin Shen, Wei Liu, Xiangnan He, Huanbo Luan, and Tat-Seng Chua. 2016. Discrete collaborative filtering. In *Proceedings of the 39th International ACM SIGIR conference on Research and Development in Information Retrieval*. ACM, 325–334.

[36] Yan Zhang, Defu Lian, and Guowu Yang. 2017. Discrete Personalized Ranking for Fast Collaborative Filtering from Implicit Feedback. (2017).

[37] Yan Zhang, Guowu Yang, Lin Hu, Hong Wen, and Jinsong Wu. 2017. Dot-product based preference preserved hashing for fast collaborative filtering. In *Communications (ICC), 2017 IEEE International Conference on*. IEEE, 1–6.

[38] Zhiwei Zhang, Qifan Wang, Lingyun Ruan, and Luo Si. 2014. Preference preserving hashing for efficient recommendation. In *Proc. of SIGIR*. ACM, 183–192.

[39] Ke Zhou and Hongyuan Zha. 2012. Learning binary codes for collaborative filtering. In *Proc. of ACM SIGKDD*. ACM, 498–506.

Micro Behaviors: A New Perspective in E-commerce Recommender Systems

Meizi Zhou*
University of Minnesota
zhou0793@umn.edu

Zhuoye Ding
Data Science Lab, JD.com
dingzhuoye@jd.com

Jiliang Tang
Michigan State University
tangjili@msu.edu

Dawei Yin†
Data Science Lab, JD.com
yindawei@acm.org

ABSTRACT

The explosive popularity of e-commerce sites has reshaped users' shopping habits and an increasing number of users prefer to spend more time shopping online. This evolution allows e-commerce sites to observe rich data about users. The majority of traditional recommender systems have focused on the macro interactions between users and items, i.e., the purchase history of a customer. However, within each macro interaction between a user and an item, the user actually performs a sequence of micro behaviors, which indicate how the user locates the item, what activities the user conducts on the item (e.g., reading the comments, carting, and ordering) and how long the user stays with the item. Such micro behaviors offer fine-grained and deep understandings about users and provide tremendous opportunities to advance recommender systems in e-commerce. However, exploiting micro behaviors for recommendations is rather limited, which motivates us to investigate e-commerce recommendations from a micro-behavior perspective in this paper. Particularly, we uncover the effects of micro behaviors on recommendations and propose an interpretable **R**ecommendation framework RIB, which models inherently the sequence of m**I**cro **B**ehaviors and their effects. Experimental results on datasets from a real e-commence site demonstrate the effectiveness of the proposed framework and the importance of micro behaviors for recommendations.

CCS CONCEPTS

• **Information systems → Summarization**;

KEYWORDS

Micro behaviors, RNN, attention mechanism, e-commerce, recommendation

*This work was done, when the author was an internship at Data Science Lab of JD.com.
†Corresponding author

WSDM 2018, February 5–9, 2018, Marina Del Rey, CA, USA

ACM ISBN 978-1-4503-5581-0/18/02...$15.00
https://doi.org/10.1145/3159652.3159671

ACM Reference Format:
Meizi Zhou, Zhuoye Ding, Jiliang Tang, and Dawei Yin. 2018. Micro Behaviors: A New Perspective in E-commerce Recommender Systems. In *Proceedings of WSDM 2018: The Eleventh ACM International Conference on Web Search and Data Mining (WSDM 2018).* ACM, New York, NY, USA, 9 pages. https://doi.org/10.1145/3159652.3159671

1 INTRODUCTION

The modern e-commerce sites such as Amazon [1] and eBay [2] offer hundreds of millions of products for sale. For example, as on June 20th, 2017, Amazon has more than 372 million products [3]. It has become increasingly challenging for consumers to find their interested items. Recommender systems play a crucial role in mitigating this information overload problem by suggesting products that have potentials to fit consumers' needs. They have been proven to not only help increase customer satisfaction and create customer loyalty [34] but also boost many aspects of e-commerce services such as revenue and growth [24].

Meanwhile, the popularity of e-commerce sites has reshaped users' shopping habits and users prefer to spend more time shopping online. For example, on average, American parents spend 7 hours per week on e-commerce sites [4]. This evolution enables e-commerce sites to observe rich data about their users. Figure 1 illustrates a real example of observed data on a user from an e-commerce site in a short period. The user first enters a page of iPhone 7 from searching result page. She reads the detailed description, as well as others' comments and adds it to the cart. Then she shifts to a page of iPhone 6 from the searching result page and reads the comments. After that, she browses a page of iPhone 7 cases from the sale page and orders the case. Finally, she jumps to a page of Samsung Galaxy from the home page of the e-commerce site. From a macro perspective as shown in the top subfigure in Figure 1, the user interacted with iPhone 7, iPhone 6, iPhone 7 cases and Samsung Galaxy. While from a micro perspective as shown in the bottom subfigure, each macro interaction includes a sequence of behaviors that can indicate how the user located the product page (e.g., the search engine or the sale promotion), whether the user clicks detailed information about a product (e.g., comments, or specifications), whether a user carts or orders a product, and how long the user dwells on a product. In this work, we refer these behaviors

[1] https://www.amazon.com/
[2] https://www.ebay.com/
[3] https://www.scrapehero.com/number-of-products-sold-on-amazon-com-june-2017/
[4] https://www.bigcommerce.com/blog/ecommerce-trends/#cmtoc_anchor_id_0

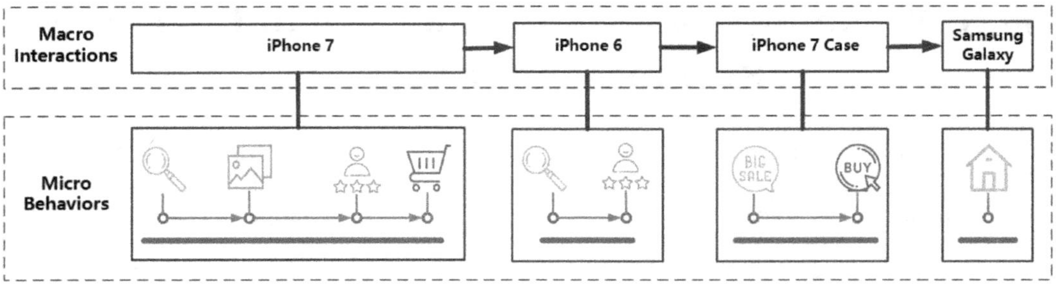

Figure 1: An illustrative example of observed data on a user from a real e-commerce site.

in macro interactions as micro-behaviors. These micro behaviors can provide fine-grained understandings about users. For example, locating a product from searching could indicate stronger intents than from the e-commerce homepage; and longer dwell time on a product suggests more interests in the product than shorter dwell time. Hence, exploiting micro behaviors has immense potential to advance recommender systems. However, such research is rather limited in the literature.

In this paper, we investigate e-commerce recommendations from the micro-behavior perspective where (a) data of a user is inherently viewed as a sequence of macro interactions between users and items; and (b) each macro interaction between a user and an item includes a sequence of micro behaviors as shown in Figure 1. One major advantage of the new perspective is – it provides a unified setting that makes various settings of existing recommender systems become its special cases:

- if we completely ignore the sequential information of macro interactions and their micro-behaviors, macro interactions can be denoted as an user-item matrix, which is the typically setting for traditional collaborative filtering [29];
- when we completely ignore the sequential information of macro interactions but consider certain micro behaviors in macro interactions, our setting is boiled down to traditional collaborative filtering with implicit feedback from certain micro behaviors such clicks [12] and dwell time [35]; and
- when we only consider the sequential information of macro interactions in a session and ignore micro-behaviors within macro interactions, the studied problem become session-based recommendations [14, 15, 31].

On the other hand, it also poses tremendous challenges including (1) how to model sequential information and (2) how to capture effects from a variety of micro behaviors. Solutions to these two challenges lead to a novel recommendation framework. Our major contributions are summarizas follows:

- We uncover the effects of micro behaviors on e-commerce recommendations;
- We provide a principled approach to capture the sequence of various micro behaviors mathematically;
- We propose an interpretable **R**ecommendation framework from the m**I**cro **B**ehavior perspective **RIB**, which incorporates the sequence of micro behaviors and their corresponding effects into a coherent model; and
- We demonstrate the effectiveness of the proposed framewor and the importance of micro behaviors on data from a rea e-commerce site.

The rest of this paper is organized as follows. In Section 2, w formally define the problem. We perform preliminary data analysi on micro behaviors in Section 3. In Section 4, we detail the propose framework RIB. Experimental results with discussions are presente in Section 5. In Section 6, we briefly review related work. Finall we conclude our work and discuss the future work in Section 7.

2 PROBLEM STATEMENT

Let $P = \{p_1, p_2, ..., p_N\}$ be the set of products where N is the numbe of products. $A = \{a_1, a_2, ..., a_M\}$ be the set of activities a user ca perform where M is the number of activities. In addition, we als consider dwell time, which indicates how long a user perform activities in A. We further assume that there are K different dwel time choices as $D = \{d_1, d_2, ..., d_K\}$. Note that dwell time is typicall continuous and in this work, we discretize it into K segments. Recal that in our studied problem, (1) data of a user is a sequence o interactions between the user and items and (2) each interactio includes a sequence of micro-behaviors. With the definitions o P, A, D, data in our study can be represented as a sequence of tuple (p_i, a_j, d_k) (or micro behaviors) where $p_i \in P$, $a_j \in A$, and $d_k \in I$ The tuple (p_i, a_j, d_k) denotes that the user performs the activity a on the product p_i with d_k dwell time.

With the notations and definitions, the problem we want to stud in this work is formally stated as: *Given their historical data of a se of users, i.e., sequences of tuples (or micro behaviors) (p_i, a_j, d_k), w aim to build a recommender system that can suggest the next produc for each user which she is interested in.*

3 UNCOVERING EFFECTS OF MICRO-BEHAVIORS

In this section, we begin by introducing the dataset we use fo this analysis and then investigate the effects of micro-behaviors o e-commerce.

3.1 Data

We collect a dataset from a real e-commerce site in a given perio It contains four types of information as:

- **Click Source.** The entrence to a product page (or clic source) can indicate why the user is interested in this prod uct. For example, if a customer enters a product page fro

Table 1: Definitions specific to the dataset

Var	Attribute	Description
p_i	Product ID	SKU (Stock Keeping Unit)
c_i	Category ID	Product category
a_1	Home2Product	Enter p_i from homepage
a_2	ShopList2Product	Enter p_i from category page
a_3	Sale2Product	Enter p_i from sale page
a_4	Cart2Product	Enter p_i from carted page
a_5	SearchList2Product	Enter p_i from searched results
a_6	Detail_comments	In p_i's comment module
a_7	Detail_specification	In p_i's specification module
a_8	Detail_bottom	At the bottom
a_9	Cart	Add p_i to cart
a_{10}	Order	Order p_i
t_1	Dwell time	0~9 seconds
t_2	Dwell time	10~24 seconds
t_3	Dwell time	25~60 seconds
t_4	Dwell time	61~120 seconds
t_5	Dwell time	>120 seconds

the home page, she may just want to look around and has no target to buy; while if a customer searches for certain products and enters one from the searching result page, he may have a strong intent to buy it. Click source includes the home page, shopping cart page, sale page, searching result page and so on.

- **Browsing Modules.** In a product page, there are several common modules, such as the brief information (name, price, thumbnail picture), comments, and specification. Browsing Modules can help us understand users' interests. For instance, if a user browses the comments and specifications instead of only browsing the brief information, he would have a higher probability of buying this product.
- **Cart and Order.** Adding to cart and ordering actions offer strong signals for recommendations. Adding to cart is usually a strong sign of buying a product. However, depending on the characteristics of products, ordering may mean interest shifting or high potential for re-purchase. For example, if a customer purchases some snacks, she may repurchase it in the near future; however, if a customer buys a TV, she is less likely to buy a TV very soon.
- **Dwell time.** Dwell time is commonly adopted to measure the importance of a webpage on a search engine [1, 18, 35]. It denotes the length of time that a visitor spends on a page before jumping to another page. Typically, the longer the dwell time, the more interesting the page. The dwell time also exits in e-commerce sites where it indicates the time a customer spends on one product.

In the dataset, each product is identified by its SKU (Stock Keeping Unit) as what is done in industry. We discretize continuous dwell time into 5 segments and each segment has a similar number of micro behaviors. The definitions of P, A and D specific to the dataset are demonstrated in Table 1.

Eventually this dataset consists of more than 2,000,000 users and 150,000 items. The total number of micro behaviors is more than 90,000,000.

3.2 Effects of Micro Behaviors

In this subsection, we investigate the correlations among micro-behaviors in the sequence. In particular, each time, we choose one micro behavior and then check how others relate to it.

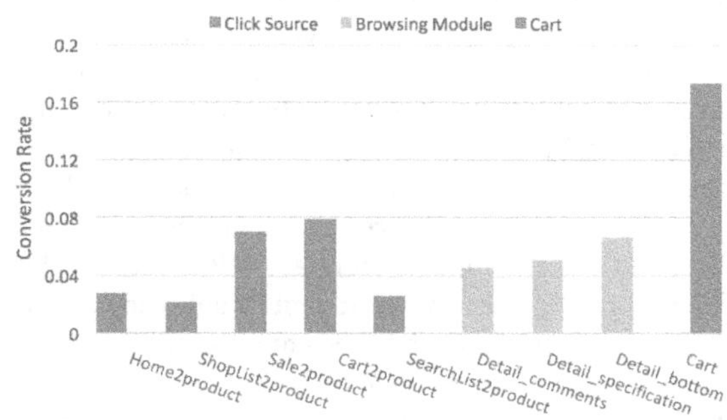

Figure 2: Ordering vs. Other micro behaviors

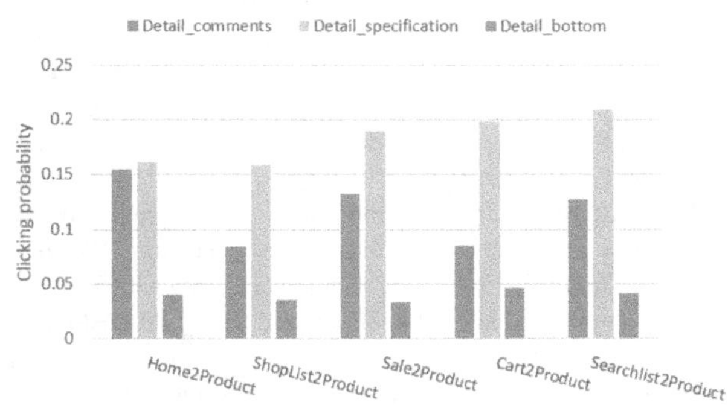

Figure 3: Click Source vs. Browsing Modules

Ordering: to study how ordering relates to other micro behaviors, we investigate the relation between certain micro behaviors and the conversion rate. The conversion rate means the percent of a given behavior that ends with ordering in a time window (or a session). The conversion rate of a micro behavior a_i can be formulated as:

$$Conversion\ rate = \frac{\#\ \text{behaviors of } a_i \text{ ended with ordering}}{\#\ \text{behaviors of } a_i} \quad (1)$$

The relations between ordering and other micro behaviors are demonstrated in Figure 2 and Figure 4. In Figure 2, the micro behavior "Cart" has the highest conversion rate, which means if a

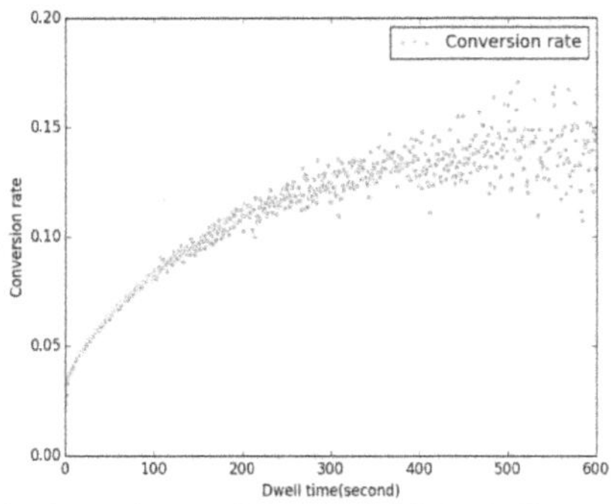

Figure 4: Ordering vs. Dwell time.

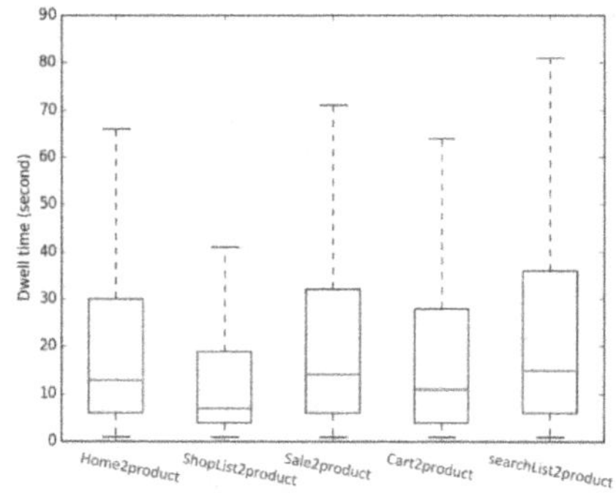

Figure 5: Dwell Time vs. Click Source

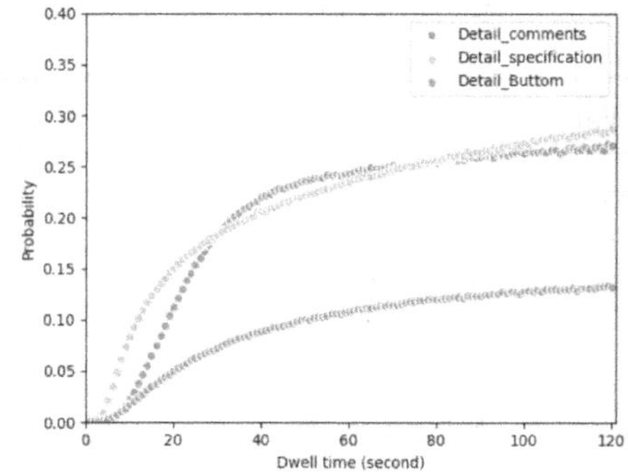

Figure 6: Dwell Time vs. Browsing Modules

user adds a product to cart, he is more likely to order it in the end. Similarly, if a user enters a product page from the cart list, he is also very likely to order it. Besides, if the user reads comments, specifications or finishes all the contents of a page, he is also very likely to order it. But if the user just enters a product page without other behaviors, he is less likely to buy the product in the end. In Figure 4, we note that within a certain range, the longer the dwell time is, the higher the conversion rate is. When the dwell time is out of a certain range, the conversion rate would drop down. If the user stays much longer than he needs to finish the page, he might have transferred his attention offline.

Dwell Time: Figure 4 has demonstrated the impact of dwell time on ordering. We further show how dwell time is related to micro-behaviors of Click Source and Browsing Modules in Figure 5 and Figure 6, respectively. In Figure 5, dwell time on a product is related to how a user locates the product. For example, from searching pages, she may spend longer time on this product; while if from the shop list, she is more likely to spend less time on this product. We also observe from Figure 6 that the longer the dwell time, the more likely a user would visit the detailed modules including reading comments and specifications.

Click Source: We have demonstrated that micro behaviors of Click Source are related to ordering and dwell time. We further show the relations between Click Source and Browsing Modules in Figure 3. We notice that the likelihood of clicking detailed modules is related to the source how a user locates the project. For example, if a customer locates a product from searching, she has a high probability to read the comments and specifications of the product.

To sum up, we make two key observations about micro behaviors via the above analysis – (1) micro behaviors are correlated; and (2) the effects of one micro-behavior on others are varied. These two observations suggest the complexity and challenges of modeling micro behaviors, however, they also offer important insights to build a meaningful model for micro behaviors in the following section.

4 E-COMMERCE RECOMMENDER SYSTEMS FROM A MICRO BEHAVIORS PERSPECTIVE

To model micro-behaviors, there are three major challenges. First, a user is a sequence of tuples (p_i, a_j, d_k) and there are in total $N \times M \times K$ tuples; thus the user representation (or input data) is very sparse and high-dimensional. Second, micro behaviors in the sequence are correlated, then how to model sequential information of micro behaviors. Third, different micro behaviors have distinct importance; hence, how to capture varied effects of micro behaviors. In this work, we propose a framework, which can tackle these three challenges simultaneously. The architecture of our framework is shown in Figure 7. It consists of five layers – an input layer, an embedding layer to solve the sparse and high-dimensional challenge, a RNN layer to model sequential information, an attention layer to capture varied effects of micro behaviors and an output layer. In the following subsections, we will detail each layer.

4.1 The Input and Embedding Layers

The input of the model is the data of a user u with a sequence of n micro behaviors. We formally define it as a sequence $S_u = \{x_1, x_2, ..., x_n\}$, where each x_i is a tuple.

$$x_t = (p_v, a_m, d_k) \tag{2}$$

$p_v \in \mathbb{R}^V$ is an one-hot indicator vector where $p_v(i) = 1$ if x_i is about the i-th product and other entities are zero. Similarly $a_m \in \mathbb{R}^M$ and $d_k \in \mathbb{R}^K$ are indicator vectors for activities and dwell time, respectively. Each of them indicates a unique element in the product set P, activity set A, dwell time set D respectively.

The vocabulary sizes of P, A, D are V, M, K respectively, and there are $V \times M \times K$ tuples in total. Therefore, the input data is extremely sparse and high-dimensional. We design an embedding layer to transform the input x_t into a low-dimensional dense vector e_t, which is formally defined as:

$$e_t = concatenate(W_P p_v, W_A a_m, W_D d_k) \tag{3}$$

where $W_P \in R^{d_P \times V}$, $W_A \in R^{d_A \times M}$, $W_D \in R^{d_D \times K}$ where $d_P \ll N$, $d_A \ll M$ and $d_D \ll K$ are the numbers of latent dimensions for products, activities and dwell time, separately. The initial weights of W_P, W_A, W_D are trained via Word2vec [25]. And the final embedding of x_t is the concatenation of three embeddings. The new representation of x_t, e_t is dense with dimension of $d_P + d_A + d_D$ which is much smaller than $V \times M \times K$.

4.2 The RNN Layer

Recurrent neural network (RNN) is a class of artificial neural network where connections between units form a directed cycle. This

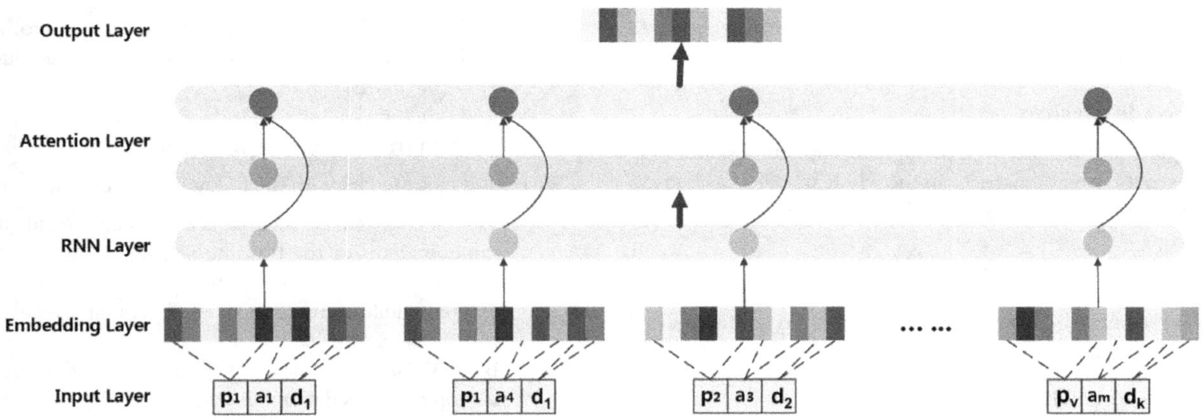

Figure 7: The architecture of the proposed framework.

reates an internal state of the network which allows it to exhibit ynamic temporal behavior. Therefore, we build a RNN layer to apture the sequential information of micro behaviors. The output f the embedding layer e_t is the input of the RNN layer. The tth idden state unit output is calculated by

$$h_t = \sigma(W_{eh}e_t + W_{hh}h_{t-1} + b_t) \quad (4)$$

where $\sigma(\cdot)$ is a nonlinear activation function, e.g. ReLU, sigmoid r tanh; $W_{eh} \in R^{d_h \times d_e}$, $W_{hh} \in R^{d_h \times d_h}$, and $b_i \in R^{d_h}$. Thus, the utput on time t is not only decided by the tth input but also by the utput of previous time h_{t-1}. Recurrently, the historical inputs in a equence are taken into consideration when making new decisions. Micro behaviors in the sequence may exist long dependencies. For xample, a customer purchased water one week ago and now she nay be interested in repurchasing the same product again. However, when the input sequence is long, RNN may have the problem f gradient vanishing. In other words, when the current micro beavior is influenced both by the recent and previous ones, RNN nay not work well. There are two possible solutions. One is the ong short-term memory model (LSTM) [16]. The LSTM updates ts hidden unit by introducing the input gate i_t, forget gate f_t and utput gate o_t as:

$$\begin{aligned}
i_t &= \sigma(W_{ei}e_t + W_{hi}h_{t-1} + b_i) \\
f_t &= \sigma(W_{ef}e_t + W_{hf}h_{t-1} + b_f) \\
o_t &= \sigma(W_{eo}e_t + W_{ho}h_{t-1} + b_o) \\
c_t &= f_t \cdot c_{t-1} + i_t \cdot tanh(W_{ec}e_t + W_{hc}h_{t-1} + b_c) \\
h_t &= o_t \cdot tanh(c_t)
\end{aligned} \quad (5)$$

The other solution is GRU, which has the gated recurrent unit[6]. The GRU is similar to the LSTM, using gates to control the hidden states. However, instead of using input gate i_t and forget gate f_t o generate a new state, GRU utilizes an update gate z_t. GRU has reset gate r_t to control the input of the former state h_{t-1}. But unlike LSTM, GRU doesn't use the output gate.

$$\begin{aligned}
r_t &= \sigma(W_{er}e_t + W_{hr}h_{t-1}) \\
z_t &= \sigma(W_{ez}e_t + W_{hz}h_{t-1}) \\
c_t &= \tanh(W_{ec}e_t + W_{hc}(r_t \cdot h_{t-1})) \\
h_t &= (1 - z_t)h_{t-1} + z_t c_t
\end{aligned} \quad (6)$$

We empirically find that LSTM and GRU achieve very similar performance in the evaluation. Given the simplified structure and faster training speed of GRU, we choose GRU for the proposed framework. In our task, each h_t means the representation of the tth product and the micro-behaviors on it. When the context changes, the representation of a product is adjusted according to the whole sequence before it.

4.3 The Attention Layer

As we shown in the last section, the micro-behaviors in the sequence have varied effects on the following micro behaviors. Therefore, it is important to capture such impacts. To achieve this goal, we introduce an attention layer [5, 36, 37] that assigns proper weight on each hidden unit. It helps get a more balanced output. The attention is formed as

$$\begin{aligned}
M_t &= \tanh(W_m h_t + b_m), M_t \in \mathbb{R}^{k \times L} \\
att_t &= \text{softmax}(W_a M_t + b_a), att_t \in \mathbb{R}^L \\
output &= \sum_{t=1}^{T} att_t h_t, output \in \mathbb{R}^k
\end{aligned} \quad (7)$$

where a_t is the attention weight on time t. The attention weight is mapped from the hidden layer vector into a real valued score by a function $\sigma(\cdot)$. In order to achieve enough expressive ability, the $\sigma(\cdot)$ is usually implemented by a neural network layer. One of the implementation is achieved by the above transformation, including tanh and softmax activation functions. Then the final output is an attention weighted pooling of the RNN layer. The significance of the attention layer has two fold. First, it models varied effects of micro-behaviors in the sequence on recommendations. Second, it increases the interpretation ability of the proposed framework since we can rely on the attention layer to understand how the proposed framework works.

4.4 Loss Function

After the output layer, we need to apply a powerful loss function to help learn the weight matrices in the whole model. We choose a pointwise loss function to compute the cross-entropy

$$L = \sum_{i} -t_i \log(o_i) \tag{8}$$

where t is the normalized target embedding and o is the normalized output embedding.

5 EXPERIMENT

In this section, we empirically evaluate our model on real world e-commerce datasets and demonstrate the effectiveness of our model. We first introduce the datasets and experimental settings. Then we compare the proposed framework with representative baselines and finally we illustrate the working of the proposed framework via a case study.

5.1 Datasets

We collect two datasets with different product categories and sizes from a real e-commerce site. They are named following their product categories, "Appliances" and "Computers". The detailed statistics of the two datasets are shown in Table 2. Both of them include 10 activities and 5 dwell time buckets as described in Table 1. Note that "TNMI" in the table denotes the total number of macro interactions and "TNMB" denotes the total number of micro behaviors.

Table 2: Statistics of Datasets.

Datasets	Appliances		Computers	
	Training	Test	Training	Test
Users	1,058,099	117,566	2,842,871	315,874
SKU	115,498	12,833	134,996	14,999
TNMI	5,290,497	587,833	11,371,485	1,263,498
TNMB	38,091,578	4,232,397	44,222,445	4,913,604

We chooses two widely used metrics to assess the recommendation performance [14, 15, 17, 22, 23, 31, 32]:

- **Recall@k**: The proportion of cases with the target among the top k predictions.
- **MRR@k**: Mean Reciprocal Rank is the average of reciprocal ranks of the target. When the rank is larger than k, the reciprocal rank is set to zero.

Note that we empirically set $k = 20$ in our experiments. To understand the effects of micro behaviors on recommendation performance, we systematically construct the following four datasets for each raw dataset:

- **SKU**: Each entity is a tuple with only a SKU, i.e. $x_t = (p_v)$.
- **SKU+Activity**: Each entity is a tuple with a SKU and an activity, i.e. $x_t = (p_v, a_m)$.
- **SKU+Dwell**: Each entity is a tuple with a SKU and a dwell time bucket, i.e. $x_t = (p_v, d_k)$.
- **SKU+Micro-behaviors**: Each entity is a micro behavic tuple with a SKU, an activity and a dwell time bucket, i. $x_t = (p_v, a_m, d_k)$.

5.2 Performance Comparison

We compare our model with the following representative method

- **POP** is a naive baseline that always recommends the mos popular items of the training set. It's a non-personalize recommendation method, however, it has been proved to b comparable to some sophisticated personalized algorithm [8].
- **BPR-MF** is one of the most commonly used matrix facto ization methods defined in [28].
- **Item-KNN** is defined as conditional probability-based sim larity in [9]. The similarity between items can be defined a $sim(i, j) = \frac{Freq(ij)}{Freq(i) \times Freq(j)}$, where $Freq(t)$ means the nun ber of sequences where an item t shows up.
- **Word2vec** [26] is a shallow, two-layer neural network tha is trained to reconstruct linguistic contexts of words. In ou work, we could regard each item as a word and train it vi Word2vec. And we only use the word vector of the last iter in a sequence for prediction.
- **Word2vec Avg.** It applies the same embeddings traine from Word2vec method. The difference is that it uses th average of all the embeddings in a sequence for predictior
- **RIB-Attention**: It is a variant of the proposed framewor RIB by removing the attention layer.

Note that in this work, we choose GRU as the RNN layer for bot RIB and RIB-Attention. We implement our model using Keras [5]. Th experiments are run on a Tesla K20 GPU. The comparison result are shown in Table 3. Note that numbers in the parentheses denot the performance improvement compared to the best baseline. Sinc the performance of Word2vec and Word2vec Avg. are different o the two datasets. For the "Appliances" dataset, we choose Word2ve as the best baseline. For the "Computers", we choose Word2ve Avg. as the best baseline. From Table 3, we made the followin observations:

- Methods capturing sequential information including Word2v Word2vec Avg, RIB and RIB-Attention outperforms thos ignoring sequential information such as POP, BPR-MF an Item-KNN.
- RIB obtains better performance than RIB-Attention. These re sults support that capturing varied effects of micro behavior can boost the performance of recommendation.
- Among SKU, SKU+Activity, SKU+Dwell and SKU + Micro behaviors, RIB consistently obtains the best performanc on SKU+Micro-behaviors. These observations suggest th importance of micro-behaviors on recommendations.

To sum up, the proposed framework achieves the best perfor mance because (1) it models sequential information; (2) it capture micro behaviors and (3) it models varied effects of micro behavior In the following subsection, we use a case study to understand wh the proposed framework works.

[5]https://keras.io

Table 3: Performance Comparison

Data type	Model	Appliances		Computers	
		Recall@20	MRR@20	Recall@20	MRR@20
SKU	POP	0.0088	0.0028	0.0149	0.0085
	BPR-MF	0.1255	0.0578	0.0747	0.0271
	Item-KNN	0.1806	0.0738	0.1101	0.0464
	Word2vec	0.3645	0.1295	0.3012	0.1044
	Word2vec Avg.	0.3668	0.1268	0.3152	0.1088
	RIB-Attention	0.4587(+25.84%)	0.1676(+29.42%)	0.3816(+21.07%)	0.1362(+25.18%)
	RIB	0.4732(+29.82%)	0.1718(+32.66%)	0.4043(+28.27%)	0.1456(+33.82%)
SKU+Activity	RIB-Attention	0.4615(+26.61%)	0.1724(+33.13%)	0.4092(+29.82%)	0.1443(+32.63%)
	RIB	0.4842(+32.82%)	0.1776(+37.14%)	0.4204(+33.38%)	0.1481(+36.12%)
SKU+Dwell	RIB-Attention	0.4673(+28.2%)	0.1745(+34.75%)	0.4108(+30.33%)	0.1482(+36.21%)
	RIB	0.4822(+32.29%)	0.1766(+36.37%)	0.4269(+35.44%)	0.149(+36.95%)
SKU+Micro-behaviors	RIB-Attention	0.474(+30.04%)	0.1784(+37.76%)	0.4227(+34.11%)	0.1516(+39.34%)
	RIB	0.4889(+34.13%)	0.1793(+38.46%)	0.4332(+37.44%)	0.1533(+40.9%)

5.3 A Case Study

In the last subsection, we demonstrate that the proposed framework outperforms various representative baselines. In this subsection, we aim to understand why the proposed framework RIB works. As discussed before, the attention layer equipped the proposed framework with the ability of interpretation. Therefore, we can understand the effects of micro behavior on recommendations via visualizing the attention layer.

Figure 8 illustrates an example from the "Appliances" dataset and we visualize the attention layers of the proposed framework on SKU, SKU+Activity, SKU+Dwell and SKU+Micro-behaviors. The left part shows a sequence of macro interactions and micro behaviors. The left bottom is what the customer actually browses in this sequence for the next time. There are 4 types of input tuples to show the influence of micro behaviors. The predicted rank of the ground truth is shown at the right bottom. From this case study, it can be observed:

- When the input tuple only consists of SKU, the attention is mainly decided by position and repetition of the product. Since Joyoung Juicer is the last of the input and shows twice in the sequence, the two Joyoung products have higher attention.
- When the activity is added to SKU, the attention becomes more fine grained. The last Joyoung still has the highest attention. But Aux Blender is getting more attention. This may be due to the activity number and the "Cart" and "Detail_specification" activities.
- When dwell time is added to SKU, the difference is that Aux Blender gets higher attention than the first Joyoung Juicer. This corresponds to the dwell time on these two products. Aux Blender has the longest dwell time which may mean the customer's deeper interests.
- When both the activity and dwell time are added to SKU, Aux Blender and Joyoung Juicer get higher attention. This may due to their "Cart" activity and long dwell time.
- From the final prediction result, we could tell the attention change corresponds to the rank precision. Micro-behaviors help understand the macro sequence and thus improve the prediction.

Via the case study, the proposed framework not only can achieve more accurate recommendations via modeling micro behaviors but also can naturally provide the interpretation for recommendations.

6 RELATED WORK

The most common and traditional methods used in item recommendation are matrix factorization models and neighborhood methods. The matrix factorization models learn a latent representation of users and items that, when decomposed, produce an approximation of the rating that a user would give to an item. There exist a lot of improved factorization-based models, such as non-negative matrix factorization, Bayesian personalized ranking[28], general factorization framework[2], hierarchical Poisson factorization[11], dynamic Poisson factorization[4], etc. Another widely used method for item recommendation is KNN[21]. The similarity between two items is decided by the co-occurrences of them in sessions. There are also some

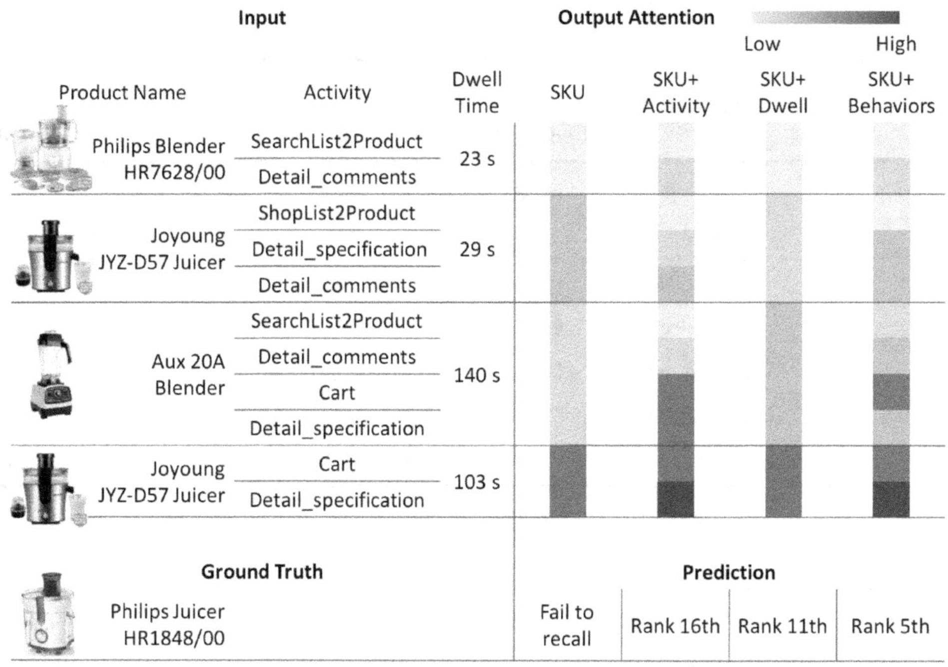

Figure 8: A case to understand the working of the proposed framework.

work combining contextual information for recommendation[20, 27]. But these methods rarely apply users' behaviors directly and capture the change of behaviors slowly. And deep learning methods perform better on these problems.

6.1 Deep Learning for Recommendation

Deep learning methods have been applied in kinds of recommendation problems. [32] achieves improved recommendation accuracy by jointly performing deep representation learning (a Bayesian model) for the item content information and collaborative filtering for the ratings matrix. [7] uses deep neural network (DNN) for recommending YouTube videos, focusing on solving candidate generation and ranking problems. [10] uses Multi-view DNN to match rich user features to item features. The proposed model is scalable to large datasets for dimensionality reduction, and it combines different domains into a single model for learning. [39] makes use of stacked convolutional auto-encoder to extract the semantic representation of visual content. And a joint model is designed by integrating collaborative filtering and visual, textual, structural knowledge to boost recommendation quality.

6.2 RNN on Sequence Data

Recurrent neural network (RNN) [33] is a deep learning model helping process sequential data. Long Short-Term Memory (LSTM) model [16] is a RNN architecture which is suitable when there are very long time lags between important events in a session. Gated Recurrent Units (GRU) [6] is a simple version of LSTM.

There exists many works using RNN to classify, process or predict sequence data. [38] proposes an attention and RNN based architecture for modeling queries and ads in online advertising. It learns to assign attention scores to words within a sequence. The scores can be successfully applied in query rewriting tasks and can also help modify BM25 metric performance. [40] introduces an RNN framework for click prediction. It models the dependency on user's sequential behaviors into click prediction through the recurrent structure in RNN. This significantly improves the prediction accuracy. And by enriching user features as input, this work fairly compares the prediction capability of different user behaviors. [13] demonstrates an RNN-based item categorization method called DeepCN. DeepCN uses multiple RNNs for generating features from text metadata and uses fully connected layers for classifying item categories from the generated features. It improves the categorization accuracy compared to the models using single RNN or using unigram-based bag-of-words. In [3], RNNs are leveraged to provide vector representations for the text content associated with items in collaborative filtering. It helps perform cold-start prediction on new items.

In recommender systems, RNN is just started to be used for session-based recommendations. In [14], Hidasi novelly applies GRU on session-based recommending problems. Comparing with item-to-item recommendations, this method proves that considering the whole session instead of one item provides more accurate recommendations. But [14] only uses item IDs as features. For a richer representation of the clicked items, in [15], Hidasi continues his work by applying parallel RNNs for processing both text and image features. [30] and [19] also solve the session-based recommendation using recurrent networks. [31] provides two new session-aware recommendation methods, matrix factorization and RNN. It concludes that the usage of RNN is considered more attractive and flexible when no session modeling assumptions is made.

17] uses LSTM to learn users' returning time prediction and item ecommendation. It shows the problem of survival analysis can be olved by RNN.

CONCLUSIONS

n this paper, we study recommender systems from the micro behavors perspective. Micro behaviors provide deeper understandings bout users, which can be utilized to advance recommender sytems. 'he new perspective provides a unified setting for several existing nes in traditional recommendations. However, modeling micro beaviors is challenging, which motivates us to develop a novel framevork RIB. Experimental results on datasets from a real e-commerce ite demonstrate the effectiveness of the proposed framework and ncover the importance of micro behaviors in recommendations.

In this work, we only consider four types of micro behaviors. Ve would like to study more types of micro behaviors and their ffects on recommendations. Meanwhile, our current focus is the lomain of e-commerce, however, micro behaviors also exist in ther domains such as movies and news. Therefore, we would like o recommender systems in more domains from the micro behavior erspective.

ACKNOWLEDGEMENTS

iliang Tang is supported by the National Science Foundation (NSF) nder grant number IIS-1714741 and IIS-1715940.

REFERENCES

[1] Eugene Agichtein, Eric Brill, and Susan Dumais. 2006. Improving Web Search Ranking by Incorporating User Behavior Information. In *Proceedings of the 29th Annual International ACM SIGIR Conference on Research and Development in Information Retrieval (SIGIR '06)*. ACM, New York, NY, USA, 19–26. https://doi.org/10.1145/1148170.1148177

[2] Hidasi Balazs and Tikk Domonkos. 2015. General factorization framework for context-aware recommendations. *Data Mining and Knowledge Discovery* (2015), 1–30.

[3] T. Bansal, D. Belanger, and A. Mccallum. 2016. Ask the GRU : Multi-task Learning for Deep Text Recommendations. *ACM Conference on Recommender Systems* (2016).

[4] L. Charlin, R. Ranganath, J. McInerney, and D. M. Blei. 2015. Dynamic poisson factorization. *CoRR* (2015).

[5] Kan Chen, Jiang Wang, Liang-Chieh Chen, Haoyuan Gao, Wei Xu, and Ram Nevatia. 2015. ABC-CNN: An Attention Based Convolutional Neural Network for Visual Question Answering. *CoRR* abs/1511.05960 (2015). http://arxiv.org/abs/1511.05960

[6] KyungHyun Cho, Bart van Merrienboer, Dzmitry Bahdanau, and Yoshua Bengio. 2014. On the Properties of Neural Machine Translation: Encoder-Decoder Approaches. *CoRR* abs/1409.1259 (2014). http://arxiv.org/abs/1409.1259

[7] P. Covington, J. Adams, and E. Sargin. 2016. Deep Neural Networks for YouTube Recommendations. *Proceedings of the 10th ACM Conference on Recommender Systems* (2016), 191–198.

[8] Paolo Cremonesi, Yehuda Koren, and Roberto Turrin. 2011. Performance of recommender algorithms on top-n recommendation tasks. *RecSys* (2011).

[9] Mukund Deshpande and George Karypis. 2004. Item-based top-N Recommendation Algorithms. *ACM Trans. Inf. Syst.* 22, 1 (Jan. 2004), 143–177. https://doi.org/10.1145/963770.963776

10] A. Elkahky, Y. Song, and X. He. 2015. A Multi-View Deep Learning Approach for Cross Domain User Modeling in Recommendation Systems. *WWW* (2015).

11] P. Gopalan, J. M. Hofman, and D. M. Blei. 2015. Scalable recommendation with hierarchical poisson factorization. *Proceedings of the Thirty-First Conference on Uncertainty in Artificial Intelligence*, (2015).

12] Linden Greg, Smith Brent, and York Jeremy. 2003. Amazon.com recommendations: item-to-item collaborative filtering. *IEEE Internet Computing* 7, 1 (Jan. 2003), 76 – 80.

13] J. W. Ha, H. Pyo, and J. Kim. 2016. Large-Scale Item Categorization in e-Commerce Using Multiple Recurrent Neural Networks. *KDD* (2016).

[14] B. Hidasi, A. Karatzoglou, L. Baltrunas, and D. Tikk. 2016. Session-based Recommendations with Recurrent Neural Networks. *ICLR* (2016).

[15] B. Hidasi, M. Quadrana, A. Karatzoglou, and D. Tikk. 2016. Parallel Recurrent Neural Network Architectures for Feature-rich Session-based Recommendations. *Proceedings of the 10th ACM Conference on Recommender Systems* (2016), 241–248.

[16] S. Hochreiter and J. Schmidhuber. 1997. Long short-term memory. *Neural computation* 9, 8 (1997), 1735–1780.

[17] How Jing and Alexander J Smola. 2017. Neural Survival Recommender. *WSDM* (2017).

[18] Youngho Kim, Ahmed Hassan, Ryen W. White, and Imed Zitouni. 2014. Modeling Dwell Time to Predict Click-level Satisfaction. In *Proceedings of the 7th ACM International Conference on Web Search and Data Mining (WSDM '14)*. ACM, New York, NY, USA, 193–202. https://doi.org/10.1145/2556195.2556220

[19] Jing Li, Pengjie Ren, Zhumin Chen, Zhaochun Ren, and Jun Ma. 2017. Neural Attentive Session-based Recommendation. *CIKM* (2017).

[20] P Li, Z Wang, Z Ren, L Bing, and W Lam. 2017. Neural Rating Regression with Abstractive Tips Generation for Recommendation. *SIGIR* (2017).

[21] G Linden, B Smith, and J York. 2003. Amazon. com recommendations: Item-to-item collaborative filtering. *Internet Computing, IEEE* 7, 1 (2003), 76–80.

[22] Qiang Liu, Shu Wu, Diyi Wang, Zhaokang Li, and Liang Wang. 2016. Context-aware Sequential Recommendation. *CoRR* abs/1609.05787 (2016). http://arxiv.org/abs/1609.05787

[23] Qiang Liu, Shu Wu, and Liang Wang. 2017. Multi-Behavioral Sequential Prediction with Recurrent Log-Bilinear Model. *IEEE Trans. on Knowl. and Data Eng.* 29, 6 (June 2017), 1254–1267. https://doi.org/10.1109/TKDE.2017.2661760

[24] Wei Lu, Shanshan Chen, Keqian Li, and Laks V. S. Lakshmanan. 2014. Show Me the Money: Dynamic Recommendations for Revenue Maximization. *Proc. VLDB Endow.* 7, 14 (Oct. 2014), 1785–1796. https://doi.org/10.14778/2733085.2733086

[25] Tomas Mikolov, Kai Chen, Greg Corrado, and Jeffrey Dean. 2013. Efficient Estimation of Word Representations in Vector Space. *CoRR* abs/1301.3781 (2013).

[26] Tomas Mikolov, Ilya Sutskever, Kai Chen, Greg S Corrado, and Jeff Dean. 2013. Distributed Representations of Words and Phrases and their Compositionality. In *Advances in Neural Information Processing Systems 26*, C. J. C. Burges, L. Bottou, M. Welling, Z. Ghahramani, and K. Q. Weinberger (Eds.). Curran Associates, Inc., 3111–3119. http://papers.nips.cc/paper/5021-distributed-representations-of-words-and-phrases-and-their-compositionality.pdf

[27] Z Ren, S Liang, P Li, S Wang, and M de Rijke. 2017. Social Collaborative Viewpoint Regression with Explainable Recommendations. *The 10th ACM International Conference on Web Search and Data Mining* (2017).

[28] Steffen Rendle, Christoph Freudenthaler, Zeno Gantner, and Lars Schmidt-Thieme. 2009. BPR: Bayesian Personalized Ranking from Implicit Feedback. (2009), 452–461. http://dl.acm.org/citation.cfm?id=1795114.1795167

[29] J. Ben Schafer, Dan Frankowski, Jon Herlocker, and Shilad Sen. 2007. *Collaborative Filtering Recommender Systems*. Springer Berlin Heidelberg, Berlin, Heidelberg, 291–324. https://doi.org/10.1007/978-3-540-72079-9_9

[30] Y. K. Tan, X. Xu, and Y. Liu. 2016. Improved recurrent neural networks for session-based recommendations. *CoRR* (2016).

[31] B. Twardowski. 2016. Modelling Contextual Information in Session-Aware Recommender Systems with Neural Networks. *ACM Conference on Recommender Systems* (2016), 273–276.

[32] H. Wang, N. Wang, and D. Yeung. 2015. Collaborative Deep Learning for Recommender Systems. *KDD* (2015).

[33] P. J. Werbos. 1990. Backpropagation through time: what it does and how to do it. *Proc. IEEE* 78, 10 (1990), 1550–1560.

[34] Chenyan Xu, Daniel Peak, and Victor Prybutok. 2015. A customer value, satisfaction, and loyalty perspective of mobile application recommendations. *Decision Support Systems* 79 (2015), 171–183.

[35] Xing Yi, Liangjie Hong, Erheng Zhong, Nanthan Nan Liu, and Suju Rajan. 2014. Beyond Clicks: Dwell Time for Personalization. In *Proceedings of the 8th ACM Conference on Recommender Systems (RecSys '14)*. ACM, New York, NY, USA, 113–120. https://doi.org/10.1145/2645710.2645724

[36] Wenpeng Yin, Sebastian Ebert, and Hinrich Schütze. 2016. Attention-Based Convolutional Neural Network for Machine Comprehension. *CoRR* abs/1602.04341 (2016). http://arxiv.org/abs/1602.04341

[37] Wenpeng Yin, Hinrich Schütze, Bing Xiang, and Bowen Zhou. 2015. ABCNN: Attention-Based Convolutional Neural Network for Modeling Sentence Pairs. *CoRR* abs/1512.05193 (2015). http://arxiv.org/abs/1512.05193

[38] S. Zhai, H. Chang, R. Zhang, and Z. Zhang. 2016. DeepIntent: learning attentions for online advertising with recurrent neural networks. *KDD* (2016).

[39] F. Zhang, N. J. Yuan, D. Lian, X. Xie, and W. Ma. 2016. Collaborative Knowledge Base Embedding for Recommender Systems. *KDD* (2016).

[40] Y. Zhang, H. Dai, C. Xu, J. Feng, T. Wang, J. Bian, B. Wang, and T. Liu. 2014. Sequential Click Prediction for Sponsored Search with Recurrent Neural Networks. *AAAI* (2014).

Predicting Multi-step Citywide Passenger Demands Using Attention-based Neural Networks

Xian Zhou, Yanyan Shen*, Yanmin Zhu, Linpeng Huang
Department of Computer Science and Engineering
Shanghai Jiao Tong University
{zhouxian, shenyy, yzhu, lphuang}@sjtu.edu.cn

ABSTRACT

Predicting passenger pickup/dropoff demands based on historical mobility trips has been of great importance towards better vehicle distribution for the emerging mobility-on-demand (MOD) services. Prior works focused on predicting next-step passenger demands at selected locations or hotspots. However, we argue that multi-step citywide passenger demands encapsulate both time-varying demand trends and global statuses, and hence are more beneficial to avoiding demand-service mismatching and developing effective vehicle distribution/scheduling strategies.

In this paper, we propose an end-to-end deep neural network solution to the prediction task. We employ the encoder-decoder framework based on convolutional and ConvLSTM units to identify complex features that capture spatiotemporal influences and pickup-dropoff interactions on citywide passenger demands. A novel attention model is incorporated to emphasize the effects of latent citywide mobility regularities. We evaluate our proposed method using real-word mobility trips (taxis and bikes) and the experimental results show that our method achieves higher prediction accuracy than the adaptations of the state-of-the-art approaches.

CCS CONCEPTS

• **Mathematics of computing → Time series analysis**; • **Computing methodologies → Neural networks**; • **Applied computing → Forecasting**;

KEYWORDS

Demands Prediction; Convolutional Neural Network; LSTM; Attention Model

ACM Reference Format:
Xian Zhou, Yanyan Shen, Yanmin Zhu, Linpeng Huang. 2018. Predicting Multi-step Citywide Passenger Demands Using Attention-based Neural Networks. In *WSDM 2018: WSDM 2018: The Eleventh ACM International Conference on Web Search and Data Mining , February 5–9, 2018, Marina Del Rey, CA, USA.* ACM, New York, NY, USA, 9 pages. https://doi.org/10.1145/3159652.3159682

WSDM 2018, February 5–9, 2018, Marina Del Rey, CA, USA

ACM ISBN 978-1-4503-5581-0/18/02...$15.00
https://doi.org/10.1145/3159652.3159682

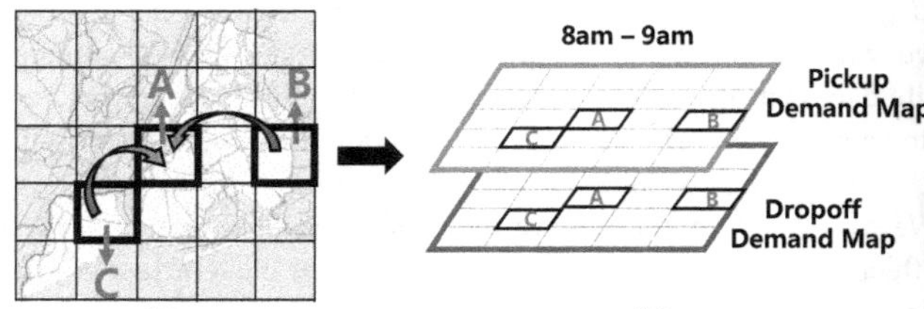

(a) (b)

time

Regions	8am – 9am	9am – 10am	10am – 11am	11am – 12am	...
A (3,3)	85/247	102/210	?	?	...
B (3,5)	164/65	145/82	?	?	...
C (4,2)	127/73	96/93	?	?	...
⋮	⋮	⋮	⋮	⋮	⋱

(c)

Figure 1: (a) Mobility trips; (b) pickup (yellow) and dropoff (blue) demand maps within a time interval; and (c) multi-step citywide passenger demands prediction problem.

1 INTRODUCTION

Recent years have witnessed the proliferation of various mobility-on-demand (MOD) services such as Uber, Didi and Mobike, which enable the evolution of passenger mobility demands towards more flexible and public vehicles, e.g., taxis, shared-use cars and bicycles. For instance, Uber doubled its gross bookings to $20 billion dollars in 2016 and now gives over one million rides a day [2]; Mobike, a bike sharing company, promoted its customers from 3 million to million in the last three months of 2016 [1].

It is vital that the mobility-on-demand systems can be further developed to predict citywide passenger mobility demands (i.e., pickup and dropoff frequencies) with high accuracy, which assists greatly in customizing effective vehicle distribution and scheduling strategies to achieve demand-resource balance. It is worth mentioning that a mismatch between the vehicle distribution and passenger demand distribution may cause severe problems including traffic congestion, wasting of resources, and more importantly, driving down customer satisfaction.

Existing methods for passenger demands prediction have been focused on anticipating next-step passenger demands for a particular set of locations such as taxi stands, bike stations and hotspots [8, 9, 16, 19]. However, we argue that *multi-step citywide passenger demands prediction* (as illustrated in Figure 1) is considerably more

*Corresponding author.

beneficial to nowadays MOD services due to the following two reasons. First, multi-step passenger demands indicate the varying demand trend, which is useful to avoid impulsive vehicle scheduling responses in the presence of temporary demand fluctuation. In contrast, short-term passenger demands prediction results are typically shortsighted and more likely to cause unnecessary vehicle scheduling back and forth. Second, the large volume of vehicles are widespread in the whole city. Citywide passenger demands are expected to encapsulate global statuses and hence are more informative in terms of achieving better vehicles distribution. Intuitively, partial passenger demands in sub-areas are insufficient to generate an effective global solution to citywide vehicle distribution or scheduling.

In this paper, we study the problem of predicting multi-step citywide passenger mobility demands (i.e., pickup and dropoff) accurately. The key technical challenge of this problem is to deal with (1) *complex spatiotemporal influences on passenger demands*, and (2) *interactions between pickups and dropoffs*. Specifically, passenger demands in a region are typically correlated with the demands in its surrounding regions. Similarly, citywide passenger demand distribution over time is often changing near-continuously, and the demands in a region could be affected by its statuses in previous time intervals. It is also very likely that demand distributions in faraway time intervals exhibit periodicity. Furthermore, pickup demands and dropoff demands themselves are often correlated. For example, a large number of dropoffs in a region will increase nearby pickups in adjacent time intervals with high probability.

Inspired by the success of deep neural networks to model complex spatiotemporal features [26, 31, 32], we propose an end-to-end deep neural network solution to the multi-step citywide passenger demand prediction problem. We organize citywide pickup and dropoff demands at certain time period into a 3D *demand tensor* and take as input a sequence of demand tensors in previous time intervals. Our prediction model follows the general encoder-decoder framework [21–23, 26]. During the encoding phase, we extract spatial features from each tensor using convolutional units, where the features capture spatial influences and interaction between pickups and dropoffs effectively. We then utilize a neural network structure combining convolutional operations and long short-term memory to disclose complex spatiotemporal influences, which leads to a high-level representation for the input sequence. The decoder behaves reversely with respect to the encoder. It generates future demand tensors step by step following the encoded citywide passenger demands tendency.

More interestingly, we observe that *citywide passenger demands present regularity and there exist representative demand tensors indicating latent citywide mobility patterns*. For example, high pickup (resp. dropoff) demands occur in residential (resp. central business) areas during morning peak hours everyday. Failure to utilize these representative demand tensors may compromise the prediction performance.

We identify representative citywide demand tensors via clustering and introduce a novel attention model to incorporate these representatives into prediction. The attention mechanism [28] has been used to identify a form of *attention* that distills information in an image down to *salient parts* when generating its caption words iteratively. In our context, the salient parts correspond to the representative demand tensors that need to be concerned for next-step passenger demands prediction. Multilayer perceptrons are adopted to learn a weight vector that indicates the relative importance of each salient part in predicting next-step passenger demand, conditioned on previous demand tendency. Our attention model can be easily incorporated into the decoder, and leads to a substantial increase in prediction accuracy according to our experiments.

The main contributions of this paper are summarized as follows.

- To the best of our knowledge, we are the first to define the problem of predicting multi-step citywide passenger demands. We propose an end-to-end deep neural network solution to this prediction task. Our method employs an encoder-decoder framework based on convolutional and ConvLSTM units, which are able to capture complex spatiotemporal influences and pickup-dropoff interactions effectively.
- We identify representative citywide demands that reflect latent mobility regularities and introduce a novel attention model to exploit the effects of these representatives on citywide distributions. The attention model is easily incorporated into the decoder, to boost the prediction performance.
- We conduct extensive experiments to evaluate the performance of our proposed approach. We consider two kinds of real-world mobility trips, i.e., taxi and bike trips in New York. The results show that our method outperforms the adaptations of state-of-the-art prediction approaches by achieving 2.85%-79.69% lower root-mean-square error.

The remainder of this paper is organized as follows. Section 2 reviews related work. Section 3 provides problem definition. We describe the details of our prediction model in Section 4. The experimental results are presented in Section 5. We conclude this paper in Section 6.

2 RELATED WORK

2.1 Predicting Passenger Demands

Single-step demands prediction. Prior works on passenger demands prediction have been focused on anticipating next-step passenger demands for locations such as taxi stands [19], hotspots [8] and bike stations [9, 16]. To achieve high prediction accuracy, different prediction models have been proposed, e.g., a hierarchical prediction model [16] and a multi-similarity-based inference model, and a data stream ensemble framework [19] that combines weighted time-varying poisson model with the traditional ARMA model. Some works addressed the problem of predicting single-step citywide passenger demands. [29] proposed a time-location-sociality model to predict the distribution of passengers over all social functional regions, based on identifying three dimensional properties of city dynamics. A few works [24, 25] have employed ensemble models that combine spatial and temporal attributes to predict passenger demands for car-hailing services in a short time horizon. Most of these methods only considered spatiotemporal influences on passenger demands, regardless of other important factors such as latent citywide mobility regularities. Moreover, they focused on single-step prediction and utilized simple regression-based methods, where time-consuming feature engineering is required to identify effective spatial and temporal features.

Prediction with spatiotemporal data in other scenarios. As predicting citywide passenger demands can be viewed as a kind of spatiotemporal data prediction problem, prediction models for spatiotemporal data are also feasible to passenger demands prediction. An increasing number of works [12, 15, 31, 32] developed deep neural networks to predict spatiotemporal data. For example, [32] and [31] proposed deep learning based prediction models for spatiotemporal data by leveraging convolutional and residual networks [13]. Their approaches exploited geographically near/distant dependencies, temporal closeness, period and trend. However, these methods aim to predict short-term spatiotemporal data and the adaptations of these methods to multi-step prediction show inferior performance experimentally (see Section 5). Recently, a novel neural network structure ConvLSTM has been proposed in [26], to perform nowcasting for local regions over a relatively short period of time. Since ConvLSTM is able to capture spatiotemporal correlations effectively, we utilize ConvLSTM to our passenger demands prediction context. However, there are some key differences between precipitation nowcasting and passenger demands prediction as the latter is affected by pickup-dropoff interactions and latent citywide mobility regularities.

2.2 Attention Mechanism in Neural Networks

Attention mechanism has been successfully incorporated into neural networks to handle a variety of tasks such as visual object classification [18], vision question answering [27], image caption generation [28, 30], machine translation [5], speech recognition [6, 10], and so on. The basic idea is to process input representation and select relevant contents iteratively.

For visual object classification, a visual attention model proposed in [18] constructs a bandwidth-limited sensor to extract retina-like representation and an environment action to decide the deployment details of next sensor. They leveraged the recurrent model inspired by human perceptron, i.e., people pay attention to selective parts of visual space, and combine information from different fixations over time to build an internal representation of the scene [20]. For vision and textual question answering, Xiong et al. [27] introduced attention-based gated recurrent units (GRU) in dynamic memory network. They used an attention gate computed by input and question representations to extract contextual information, and the attention was focused on a subset of input facts. For machine translation [5], an attention extension was introduced to encode the input sentence into several vectors and adaptively choose a subset of these vectors while performing the translation. This method automatically searches for parts of a source sentence that are relevant to the next prediction word, and is reported to outperform conventional translation models, regardless of the sentence length. Similarly, for speech recognition, [6] proposed an end-to-end system which consists of a bi-directional RNN encoder and an attention-based recurrent sequence generator. Compared with vanilla encoder-decoder models, attentive encoder-decoder models inspect alignments between the generated words and those in the source sentence, and learn which part of input sentence the model should pay attention to when generating the next word.

Inspired by the advantages of the attention mechanism in sequence prediction [5, 28, 30], in this paper, we introduce an attention model to disclose the impact of representative historical citywide demands on next-step citywide demands. Our attention model is different from existing ones as our input is a sequence of 3D demand tensors rather than a sequence of words or a single picture.

3 PROBLEM DEFINITION

To predict citywide passenger demands, we divide the complete city area into pairwise disjoint regions (i.e., grids), in the similar way as in [31].

Definition 3.1 (Grid Map). We represent a complete city area as a rectangle where $p_l = (lon_l, lat_l)$ and $p_h = (lon_h, lat_h)$ denote the lowest and the highest points in the city along longitude and latitude coordinates, respectively. Given a length λ, we divide the rectangle into $n \times m$ regions along the two coordinates, where $n = \lceil \frac{lon_h - lon_l}{\lambda} \rceil$ and $m = \lceil \frac{lat_h - lat_l}{\lambda} \rceil$.

We denote by $G_\lambda = \{g_{ij} \mid i \in [1,n], j \in [1,m]\}$ the set of all regions, which is also referred to as a grid map. For any point $p = (lon_p, lat_p)$, we say p resides in region g_{ij}, denoted by $p \in g_{ij}$ iff $lon_p \in [lon_l + (i-1)\lambda, lon_l + i\lambda)$ and $lat_p \in [lat_l + (j-1)\lambda, lat_l + j\lambda)$.

We use length λ to control the granularity of regions. Intuitively, smaller value of λ leads to a larger number of regions as well as fine-grained passenger demands, and vice versa.

We consider a set of historical mobility trips occurred in a city. Each trip is represented by a tuple of $(p_{pick}, p_{drop}, t_{pick}, t_{drop})$, which means the trip starts from point p_{pick} at time t_{pick}, and ends in point p_{drop} at time t_{drop}. We then map all trips onto the grid map of the city. Given any time interval $[s_t, e_t)$, we can obtain *pickup/dropoff demand maps* that summarize citywide pickup/dropoff passenger demand frequencies during that time period.

Definition 3.2 (Pickup/Dropoff Demand Maps). Let $\mathcal{T}$ be a set of mobility trips over grid map G_λ. Given the t-th time interval $[s_t, e_t)$, we can compute the pickup demand map $P_t = \{\delta^p_{t,ij}\}_{g_{ij} \in G_\lambda}$ within the interval that satisfies:

$$\delta^p_{t,ij} = \{|T \in \mathcal{T}| \mid T.p_{pick} \in g_{ij} \wedge T.t_{pick} \in [s_t, e_t)\}.$$

Intuitively, $\delta^p_{t,ij}$ denotes the number of trips that start from region g_{ij} during the time interval $[s_t, e_t)$. Similarly, we can obtain a dropoff demand map $D_t = \{\delta^d_{t,ij}\}_{g_{ij} \in G_\lambda}$ within the t-th interval where:

$$\delta^d_{t,ij} = \{|T \in \mathcal{T}| \mid T.p_{drop} \in g_{ij} \wedge T.t_{drop} \in [s_t, e_t)\}.$$

We organize the pickup and dropoff demand maps for the t-th time interval as a 3D demand tensor $\mathcal{M}_t \in \mathbb{R}^{n \times m \times 2}$ over the grid map G_λ. We have $(\mathcal{M}_t)_{i,j,0} = \delta^p_{t,ij}$ and $(\mathcal{M}_t)_{i,j,1} = \delta^d_{t,ij}$.

We now formalize the problem of predicting multi-step citywide passenger demands as follows.

Definition 3.3 (Multi-step Citywide Demands Prediction). Consider a grid map G_λ. Given N demand tensors $\{\mathcal{M}_i \mid i = 1, \cdots, N\}$ over the previous N time intervals, we try to predict B demand tensors $\{\mathcal{M}_i \mid i = N+1, \cdots, N+B\}$ for the next B time intervals.

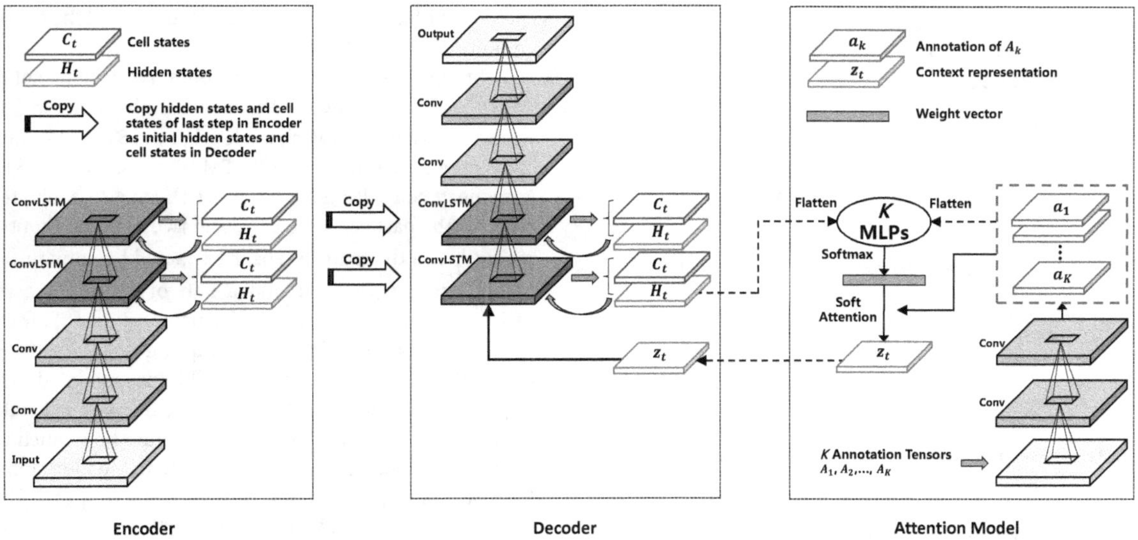

Figure 2: Overview of the Proposed Approach. The Encoder is composed of convolutional units and ConvLSTM units that encode the input sequence into fixed dimensional representations (hidden states and memory states); The Attention Model computes weights for salient parts (annotations) and identifies the attention information (context representation); The Decoder leverages the attention information (context representation) from the attention model and decodes the encoded representations from Encoder to generate future passenger demands.

4 ATTENTION BASED ENCODER-DECODER FRAMEWORK

4.1 Overview

Figure 2 provides an overview of our end-to-end deep neural network solution to the prediction task. We adopt the encoder-decoder framework which is widely used for generating target sentences [23, 28] and predicting future sequences [21, 26]. At a high-level, the idea is to first "encode" an input sequence of passenger demand tensors into fixed dimensional representations (i.e., sequence representations), and then "decode" the representations to produce the desired sequence of future demand tensors.

CNN+ConvLSTM based sequence encoding. The encoder consists of two major components: convolutional units in the lower layers and ConvLSTM units in the higher layers. Given a sequence of N demand tensors, we supply each tensor in the sequence to the stack of convolutional and ConvLSTM layers iteratively. The convolutional layers exploit the spatial influences over passenger demands and learn a latent representation I_t^e for each input demand tensor $\mathcal{M}_t$. The ConvLSTM layers absorb the sequence of latent representations $\{I_t^e\}_{t=1}^N$ produced by the last convolutional layer, and generate the sequence representations as the output. We leverage ConvLSTM, an extended version of FC-LSTM [11], to capture the temporal information flow in the sequence while retaining spatial correlations via convolutional operations. Specifically, we apply ConvLSTM to each I_t^e and the gating mechanism in ConvLSTM decides the amount of information from both I_t^e and LSTM memory state that will be propagated to enrich the final sequence representation. It is also worth mentioning that the convolutional structure in ConvLSTM is able to model the spatial information flow well. The final sequence representations are stored in the last states

Table 1: Notations

Symbol	Description
P_t/D_t	pickup/dropoff demand map at t-th step
$\mathcal{M}_t$	demand tensor comcatenating $P_t$and $D_t$at t-th step
N/B	input/output length
$I_{t,L}^e$	output of L-th CNN layer for t-th input $\mathcal{M}_t$ in encoder
i_t^e/i_t^d	input gate of encoder/decoder ConvLSTM
f_t^e/f_t^d	forget gate of encoder/decoder ConvLSTM
o_t^e/o_t^d	output gate of encoder/decoder ConvLSTM
C_t^e/C_t^d	cell state of encoder/decoder ConvLSTM for t-th input $\mathcal{M}_t$/output $\mathcal{M}_{N+t}$
H_t^e/H_t^d	hidden state of encoder/decoder ConvLSTM for t-th input $\mathcal{M}_t$/output $\mathcal{M}_{N+t}$
A_k	k-th annotation tensor
a_k	annotation of A_k
$\alpha_{t,k}^a$	weight of a_k for t-th output $\mathcal{M}_{N+t}$
z_t	context representation for t-th output $\mathcal{M}_{N+t}$ in decoder

of ConvLSTM cells, which provide a guidance for the prediction during decoding phase.

Attention-enhanced sequence decoding. The decoder predicts a sequence of next B pickup/dropoff demand tensors based on the demand tendency learnt by the encoder. The structure of decoder exhibits a symmetrical form with respect to the encoder. That is, we construct ConvLSTM units in lower layers and deconvolutional units in higher layers to predict the next B demand tensors iteratively. For ConvLSTM units, we copy hidden states and cell states of last step in encoder as initial hidden states and cell states in decoder. In each iteration, ConvLSTM layers produce a high-level representation for the next-step demand tensor by updating the

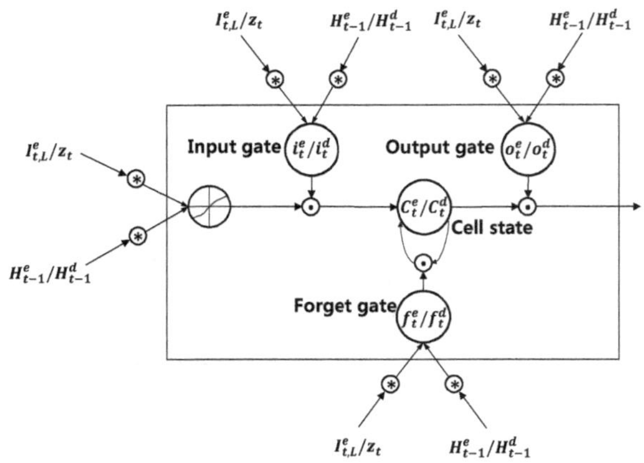

Figure 3: Structure of Encoder/Decoder ConvLSTM Cell

states accordingly. The deconvolutional layers then translate this high-level representation into the corresponding 3D demand tensor.

We find that passenger demand distributions offer certain spatiotemporal regularities, which may be caused by the latent citywide mobility patterns. For example, the demands around subway stations during weekday peak hours are always high, while those in midnight are quite low. To capture such regularities, we perform k-means clustering over historical demand tensors. The resultant K representative demand tensors are referred to as *annotation tensors*. In this paper, we leverage an attention model to incorporate these representatives into next-step demand prediction, which is a novel attempt.

Our attention model first learns high-level features, namely K *annotations*, from K annotation tensors via convolutional operation. Before decoding the next i-th demand tensor, we first put the K annotations and the current sequence representation (e.g., the encoder output if $i = 1$) into K multilayer perceptrons, and obtain a K-dimensional weight vector. The summation over weighted annotations composes a *context representation* that indicates to what degree each representative citywide demand tensor is supposed to be noticed in predicting the next-step demand tensor. This context representation is then used as an input to the decoder. With the help of attention model, we observe a substantial performance gain in predicting multi-step demand tensors (see the experiments in Section 5).

In what follows, we provide details of the encoder, attention model and the decoder, respectively. Table 1 summarizes the symbols and their meanings used throughout this paper.

4.2 Encoding Previous Passenger Demands

We construct the encoder structure based on a combination of convolutional and ConvLSTM layers. Consider a sequence $\{\mathcal{M}_1, \cdots, \mathcal{M}_N\}$ of N demand tensors as input. The convolutional layers extract spatial features from each input demand tensor. Specifically, we view each demand tensor $\mathcal{M}_t$ as a two-channel (i.e., pickups and dropoff) image and apply convolutional neural network to yield a 3D feature tensor $I^e_{t,L} = \underbrace{CNN \cdots CNN}_{L}(\mathcal{M}_t)$, where L is the number of CNN layers. The first two dimensions of $I^e_{t,L}$ correspond to spatial coordinates (i.e., rows and columns), and the third dimension contains the extracted features.

After convolutional layers, we obtain a sequence of 3D features $\{I^e_{t,L}\}_{t=1}^N$. We next encode the sequence by *encoder ConvLSTM*, Recurrent Neural Network made of ConvLSTM [26] units. Figure 3 shows the structure of ConvLSTM unit. Each ConvLSTM unit has a memory cell with a state C^e_t at t-th step. In each step, the unit receives the past cell state C^e_{t-1} and two external inputs $I^e_{t,L}$, H^e_{t-1}, where $I^e_{t,L}$ is the feature tensor extracted by convolutional layer and H^e_{t-1} is the previous hidden state of the cell. Access or modification to the cell is controlled by its input gate i^e_t, forget gate f^e_t and output gate o^e_t. That is, the input gate i^e_t decides how much information from external input will be accumulated to the cell; the forget gate f^e_t controls to what degree the past cell state C^e_{t-1} will be forgotten; the output gate o_t determines how much information the latest cell state C^e_t will be emitted to the hidden state H^e_t. When there are multiple ConvLSTM layers, the output H^e_t of previous ConvLSTM layer is taken as input for the next ConvLSTM layer.

In ConvLSTM, the inputs, outputs, hidden states, cell states and all gates are 3D tensors. To capture spatial information, when a new input $I^e_{t,L}$ in the sequence comes, the ConvLSTM determines the future cell state C^e_t and whether to activate input/forget/output gates by using a convolutional operation (see circles containing "$*$" in Figure 3). After applying ConvLSTM recursively to the input sequence, we obtain the latest hidden state H^e_t and memory state C^e_t, which will be used for our decoder. Formally, the updating equations for ConvLSTM are provided below.

$$i^e_t = \sigma(W^e_{xi} * I^e_{t,L} + W^e_{hi} * H^e_{t-1} + b^e_i) \quad (1)$$

$$f^e_t = \sigma(W^e_{xf} * I^e_{t,L} + W^e_{hf} * H^e_{t-1} + b^e_f) \quad (2)$$

$$o^e_t = \sigma(W^e_{xo} * I^e_{t,L} + W^e_{ho} * H^e_{t-1} + b^e_o) \quad (3)$$

$$C^e_t = f^e_t \circ C^e_{t-1} + i^e_t \circ tanh(W^e_{xc} * I^e_{t,L} + W^e_{hc} * H^e_{t-1} + b^e_c) \quad (4)$$

$$H^e_t = o^e_t \circ tanh(C^e_t) \quad (5)$$

where '$*$' denotes the convolutional operator (represented as a circle containing "$*$" in Figure 3), '$\circ$' is the Hadamard product (represented as a circle containing "$\cdot$" in Figure 3) and $\sigma(\cdot)$ is sigmoid function. Different kernel matrices W and biases b are parameters to be learned.

4.3 Attention Model

Figure 4 illustrates the structure of our attention model which mainly performs two steps. First, we identify K representative citywide demand tensors $\{A_k\}_{k=1}^K$, referred to as *annotation tensors*, by clustering historical demand tensors using K-means++ [4]. Intuitively, each annotation tensor A_k is a 3D tensor where the value in $(A_k)_{ij}$ indicates the pickup and dropoff demands in region g_{ij} influenced by mobility regularities of the city. While clustering all the previous demand tensors (more than N) can be expensive, the clustering is only conducted once and the results can be reused for any predictions afterwards. We then use a convolutional neural network to extract spatial features from each A_k, and obtain K *annotations* $\{a_k\}_{k=1}^K$ corresponding to the k salient parts to be concerned. We develop a two-layer CNN to retain close correspondence between a_k and A_k. Note that the *annotations* produced by CNN are also 3D tensors.

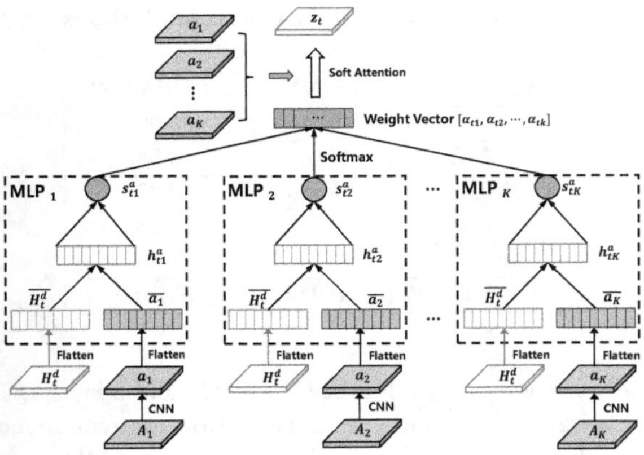

Figure 4: Structure of Attention Model

Second, we learn a weight vector $\langle \alpha_{t1}, \cdots, \alpha_{tk} \rangle$ for the K annotations, where the weight α_{tk} can be interpreted as the relative importance of a_k to the t-th output demand tensor. Each weight α_{tk} is computed by a multilayer preceptron (MLP) that takes flattened hidden state H^d_{t-1} of the previous demand tensor (denoted as $\overline{H^d_{t-1}}$) and flattened annotation a_k (denoted as $\overline{a_k}$) as input, followed by a softmax operation. Similar to the soft attention mechanism in [28], we then perform summation over weighted annotations to get a *context representation* z_t, which will be incorporated into the decoder for prediction.

The key equations to generate the context representation z_t for the t-th output demands prediction ($t \in [1, B]$) are summarized as follows.

$$h^a_{tk} = f(W^a_h \overline{H^d_{t-1}} + W_a \overline{a_k} + b^a_h), \quad \forall k \in [1, K] \tag{6}$$

$$s^a_{tk} = f(W^a_s h^a_{tk}), \quad \forall k \in [1, K] \tag{7}$$

$$\alpha_{tk} = \frac{exp(s^a_{tk})}{\sum_{k=1}^{K} exp(s^a_{tk})}, \quad \forall k \in [1, K] \tag{8}$$

$$z_t = \sum_{k=1}^{K} \alpha_{tk} a_k \tag{9}$$

where f is an activation function that could be *ReLU* or *tanh*. The context representation z_t is then fed into decoder.

4.4 Decoding Multi-step Passenger Demands

The structure of the decoder is symmetrical to that of the encoder. As shown in Figure 2, the decoder has ConvLSTM units in lower layers and deconvolutional units in higher layers. We initialize the memory states and hidden states of the *decoder ConvLSTM* by copying the last memory states and hidden states from the *encoder ConvLSTM*.

In the t-th step ($t \in [1, B]$) prediction, the external inputs to the decoder ConvLSTM are from two sources: the context representation z_t from the attention model (Equation 9) and the previous hidden state and memory state of the cell. The output is the updated hidden state H^d_t, which is a high-level representation for the next t-th step demand tensor. The key equations for the decoder ConvLSTM are the following.

$$i^d_t = \sigma(W^d_{zi} * z_t + W^d_{hi} * H^d_{t-1} + b^d_i) \tag{10}$$

$$f^d_t = \sigma(W^d_{zf} * z_t + W^d_{hf} * H^d_{t-1} + b^d_f) \tag{11}$$

$$o^d_t = \sigma(W^d_{zo} * z_t + W^d_{ho} * H^d_{t-1} + b^d_o) \tag{12}$$

$$C^d_t = f^d_t \circ C^d_{t-1} + i^d_t \circ tanh(W^d_{zc} * z_t + W^d_{hc} * H^d_{t-1} + b^d_c) \tag{13}$$

$$H^d_t = o^d_t \circ tanh(C^d_t) \tag{14}$$

where '$*$' denotes the convolutional operator and '$\circ$' denotes the Hadamard product.

Each high-level representation H^d_t will be put through deconvolutional units to compute the corresponding 3D demand tensor: $\mathcal{M}_{N+t} = \underbrace{DCNN \cdots DCNN}_{L}(H^d_t)$, where L is the number of DCNN layers, equal to the number of CNN layers in encoder.

5 EXPERIMENTS

In this section, we compare our method named **AttConvLSTM** with several state-of-the-art approaches to multi-step passenger demands prediction. We first describe the datasets used for the experiments and then list comparison methods. Finally, we present experimental results in detail.

5.1 Datasets

We conduct experiments using two real-world mobility datasets: taxi trips and bike trips in New York. The details of the two datasets are described as follows:

- **TaxiNYC**[1]: TaxiNYC consists of 1.19 billion taxicab trip records in New York from 1st January 2009 to 31st December 2015. On average, there are 170,235,925 trip records collected in each year. We use five-year records from 2009 to 2013 as training data, while the records in 2014 and 2015 are used as validation and test sets, respectively.
- **CitiBikeNYC**[2]: CitiBikeNYC contains 28,732,316 bike trips in New York from 1st July 2013 to 30th June 2016. Throughout these years, CitiBike has established over 600 stations and 10,000 bikes. An example bike trip contains: trip duration, starting and ending station IDs, start and end timestamps. We use the data from 1st July 2015 to 31st December 2015 as validation set, and the data from 1st January 2016 to 30th June 2016 as test set. The others are used as training data.

We preprocessed both datasets to generate pickup and dropoff maps as described in Section 3. By default, we set time interval to 1 hour. Regarding the relatively narrower coverage of CitiBikeNYC trips, we divided the area covered by citibikes into a 16×16 grid map, for which each grid is about $1km \times 1km$. For the larger TaxiNYC dataset, we used 64×64 grids to partition the whole area, where each grid covers $5km \times 5km$ area.

We find that the representative demand distributions exist when clustering historical demand tensors using K-means++ [4] as illustrated in Figure 5. As cluster number K increases, the distortion defined by the sum of the squared distances between each tensor and its closest centroid decreases to convergence, minimized by

[1] http://www.nyc.gov/html/tlc/html/about/trip_record_data.shtml
[2] https://www.citibikenyc.com/system-data

K-means clustering algorithm. The Silhouette value is a measure of how similar a tensor is to its own cluster compared to other clusters, where a high value indicates an appropriate match to its own cluster and poorly matched to neighboring clusters. From Figure 5, the clustering results for TaxiNYC and CitiBikeNYC justify the existence of representative demand distributions. Intuitively, an appropriate value of k with low distortion and high Silhouette strikes a balance between maximum compression of the data using a single cluster, and maximum accuracy by assigning each tensor to its own cluster. Therefore, we set the cluster number K to 16 and 32 for CitiBikeNYC and TaxiNYC, respectively.

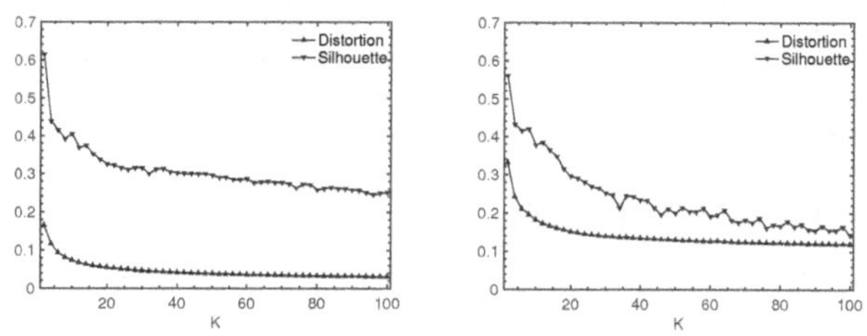

(a) TaxiNYC (b) CitiBikeNYC

Figure 5: Kmeans Results on TaxiNYC and CitiBikeNYC

5.2 Baseline Methods and Measurement

Baseline Methods. We compare our **AttConvLSTM** method with both basic and advanced methods as follows.

- **HA**: It predicts pickup and dropoff demands by averaging historical pickup and dropoff demand values for the same time interval. For example, pickup/dropoff demands at 9-10am on Monday are predicted as the average of historical pickup/dropoff demands at 9-10am on all past Mondays.
- **ARMA** [7]: Auto Regressive Moving Average (ARMA) is a widely used method for predicting future values over multiple time periods. We use this method to predict next-step passenger demands for each region.
- **VAR** [17]: Vector Auto-Regressive (VAR) is a multivariate model capable of capturing linear interdependencies among multiple time series. We implemented the prediction model by regarding the pickup/dropoff demands in different regions as variables.
- **ResNet** [31]: ResNet is a deep-learning-based approach to predicting traffic of flows based on unique properties of spatiotemporal data. It has achieved high accuracy in predicting next-step spatiotemperal data.
- **ConvLSTM**: ConvLSTM is our convolutional+ConvLSTM approach without attention model, which is used for evaluating the effectiveness of our attention model.

Experimental Settings. We now provide implementation details of **AttConvLSTM**. The encoder consists of 2-layer CNN and 2-layer ConvLSTM. The kernel size of the 2-layer CNN is set to 3×3 with a stride of 2 and the number of features is set to 8 for the lower layer and 16 for the higher layer. For the 2-layer ConvLSTM, the kernel size of all convolutional operations is 3×3 with a stride of 1, and both layers contain 64 hidden states for each grid. The

Table 2: Comparison of Different Methods

Methods	TaxiNYC	CitiBikeNYC
HA	38.675	10.095
ARMA	132.499	13.562
VAR	54.516	13.277
ResNet	43.974	10.584
ConvLSTM	34.784	7.984
AttConvLSTM	**26.912**	**7.756**

decoder is composed of 2-layer ConvLSTM and 2-layer DCNN with the same configuration as encoder. For the attention model, the number of nodes in the single hidden layer of MLP is set to 1024. The depth of AttConvLSTM makes different effects on the two datasets. Deeper model gives a better result on TaxiNYC while it predicts poorly on CitiBikeNYC, since the small grid map (i.e. 16×16) in CitiBikeNYC cannot fit deeper networks well. When training our model, we adopted mini-batch learning method with a batch size of 16 and used Adam [14] optimizer with a constant learning rate of 0.0002.

We implemented all the methods in Python and used TensorFlow [3] to implement ResNet, ConvLSTM and AttConvLSTM. For single-step prediction methods (i.e., ARMA, VAR and ResNet), we predict multi-step passenger demands by iteratively using previous prediction results as input for next-step prediction. For all methods, we used the validation set for parameter selection and test set for performance comparison. All experiments were conducted on a server with NVIDIA Tesla K80 accelerator.

Measurement. We consider previous 10-step pickup/dropoff demands as input and predict citywide pickup/dropoff demands for the next 10 steps. We evaluate all approaches using Root Mean Square Error (RMSE) as follows.

$$RMSE = \sqrt{\frac{1}{Q}\sum_t \sum_i \sum_j (x_{ij}^t - \hat{x}_{ij}^t)^2} \quad (15)$$

where $\hat{x}_{ij}^t$ and x_{ij}^t are respectively the predicted pickup/dropoff value and ground truth for region g_{ij} at t-th step; Q is the number of all the predicted values.

5.3 Results

5.3.1 Comparison of different methods. Table 2 shows the comparison results of six approaches over two datasets. As we can see, all the methods report smaller RMSE on CityBikeNYC than TaxiNYC. This is because the total number of taxi demands is about one order of magnitude larger than total bike demands. AttConvLSTM achieves the lowest RMSE values on both datasets. The incorporation of the attention model helps reduce RMSE by 22.63% on TaxiNYC and 2.36% on CityBikeNYC. This result confirms that attention model enhances decoder by exploiting intrinsic region-specific demand regularities. The larger reduction in RMSE over TaxiNYC is due to the fact that taxi demands are more easily affected by latent citywide mobility regularities than bike demands. Furthermore, both AttConvLSTM and ConvLSTM outperform ResNet, and AttConvLSTM achieves 38.80% and 26.35% lower RMSE on TaxiNYC and CitiBikeNYC datasets, respectively. ResNet focuses

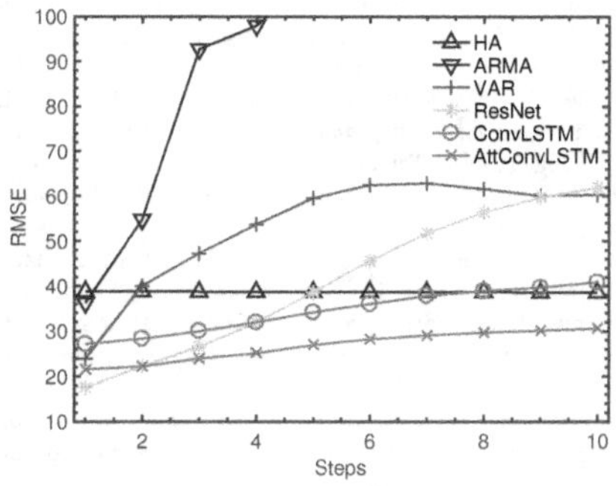

(a) TaxiNYC

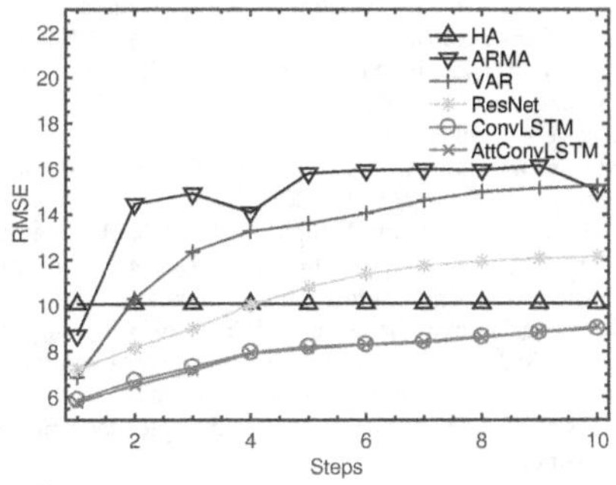

(b) CitiBikeNYC

Figure 6: Step-wise Prediction Results

on next-step prediction and benefits from historical data in the same time period and previous time intervals. However, it performs poorly for multi-step prediction when passenger demands (e.g., taxi demands) in future time intervals vary a lot.

HA leverages all historical data and achieves good prediction results, but still reports 43.71% and 29.50% higher RMSE than AttConvLSTM over the two datasets. ARMA and VAR have the largest RMSE values on both datasets. As ARMA only explores temporal dependencies and VAR captures linear spatio interdependencies, the poor prediction performance indicates the limitations of using spatiotemporal features only. The parameters of ARMA and VAR are tuned for next-step prediction, which cause the inferior performance in multi-step predictions as discussed in next part.

5.3.2 Results on step-wise prediction. For further analysis, we present the step-wise prediction results over two datasets in Figure 6. AttConvLSTM and ConvLSTM are robust as the step number varies from 1 to 10, i.e., small increase in RMSE. It performs the best for all the 10 steps except step one on TaxiNYC, and outperforms all the other approaches across all the steps on CitiBikeNYC. ARMA, VAR and ResNet perform worse for later steps. This demonstrates that for these single-step approaches, low-quality predictions from previous steps significantly degrade the accuracy of later predictions. HA performs consistently over all the steps, thanks to the availability of a large amount of historical data. From Figure 6(a) and 6(b), we see that for the first-step prediction, HA performs the worst over two datasets because other baselines adopt spatiotemporal features to improve single-step prediction accuracy effectively.

Table 3: Results on Abnormal Cases

Methods	TaxiNYC	CitiBikeNYC
HA	954.889	28.787
ARMA	1872.487	45.238
VAR	1452.385	40.330
ResNet	1161.004	32.334
ConvLSTM	817.676	19.314
AttConvLSTM	**322.537**	**14.183**

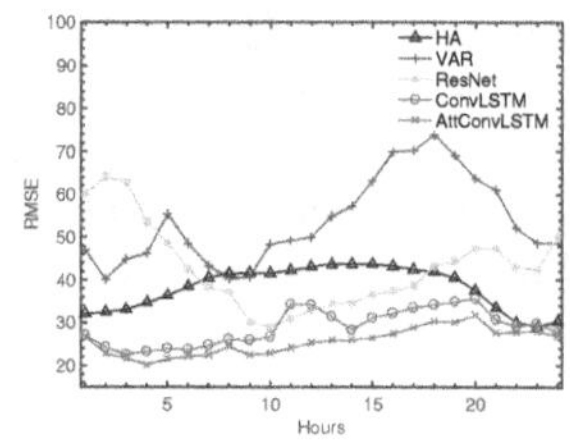

(a) TaxiNYC

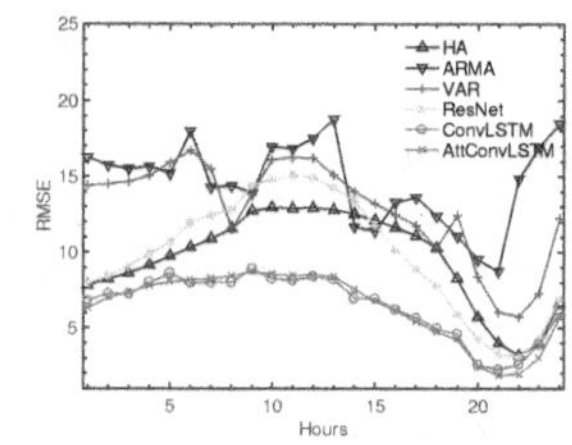

(b) CitiBikeNYC

Figure 7: RMSE Values in Different Time Intervals

ResNet achieves the smallest RMSE value for step 1 on TaxiNYC, but performs worse than AttConvLSTM and ConvLSTM on City-BikeNYC for all the steps. This may be caused by the irregular bike demands, i.e, the demands in the same hour but different days can vary greatly due to external conditions such as weather and temperature. It is worth mentioning that the inferior performance of AttConvLSTM for step 1 on TaxiNYC (compared to ResNet) is mainly caused by the different loss functions being used. The loss function used by AttConvLSTM considers prediction errors over multiple future steps while ResNet directly minimizes the prediction errors for the next step. In a nutshell, AttConvLSTM achieves higher prediction accuracy for later steps as well as over irregular mobility trips like Citibike.

5.3.3 Effects of different time intervals. In Figure 7, we present the performance of all methods over two datasets across 24 different time intervals, i.e., 0am-1am, 1am-2am, $\cdots$, 11pm-0am. That is, we try to predict demands for the next 10 intervals starting from the given time interval. To make the figures concise, we omit the results of ARMA since it gets the worst performance. AttConvLSTM achieves the best or comparable performance for all the 24 time intervals on both datasets. It performs consistently better than other approaches no matter whether the prediction starts from peak hours or off-peak hours. For TaxiNYC (in Figure 7(a)), all the methods have relatively higher RMSE values when predicting future demands from 3pm-7pm. The reason may be the uncertainty of taxi demands in the evening, when the demands can be easily influenced by people's arbitrary night activities. For CitiBikeNYC, all methods predict well for the intervals at night (8pm-11pm) but get high RMSE during daytime (5am-6pm). This is mainly because people ride bikes more often at daytime, which introduces more diversity in terms of demand distribution.

5.3.4 Analysis of abnormal cases. To further analysis on abnormal situations, we study the prediction of abnormal cases in test data where the real demands deviate historical average greatly, which are the most difficult for vehicle distribution and scheduling. Specifically, we randomly select 1,011,941 and 379,338 cases from CitiBikeNYC and TaxiNYC, in which the relative error from historical average is more than 50%. The number of abnormal cases on TaxiNYC is smaller than CitiBikeNYC since bike demands are more likely to be affected by external conditions. Table 3 shows the results on those abnormal cases. We see that all the RMSE results are greatly worse than the average error in Table 2 and AttConvLSTM achieves 60.55% and 26.57% lower RMSE than second best method ConvLSTM on TaxiNYC and CitiBikeNYC respectively. Although there are less abnormal cases on taxi demands compared to bike demands, the bad prediction on large scale could incur terrible useless dispatch and scheduling. And the results in Table 3 shows that AttConvLSTM can effectively capture human movements that are significantly deviated from the historical average compared to other methods.

6 CONCLUSION

In this paper, we study the problem of predicting multi-step citywide passenger demands. The main technical challenge is to enforce the complex spatiotemporal influences, pickup-dropoff interactions and latent citywide demand regularities into future prediction. We solve the problem by introducing a novel attention-based encoder-decoder deep learning approach. We employ convolutional and ConvLSTM units in both encoder and decoder, and learn attention to emphasize the effects of representative citywide demand patterns on each-step prediction during the decoding phase. Our experiments on two real-world datasets (taxi and bike mobility trips) demonstrate that (1) our proposed approach outperforms the state-of-the-art prediction approaches; (2) the attention model can effectively improve the accuracy for multi-step prediction. In the future work, we will consider exogenous data (e.g., weather condition data) and fuse them to predict passenger demands more accurately.

ACKNOWLEDGMENTS

We thank anonymous reviewers for their insightful and helpful comments, which improve the paper. This research is supported in part by 973 Program (no. 2014CB340303), NSFC (no. 61772341, 61472254, 61170238, 61602297 and 61472241), Singapore NRF (CREATE E2S2), and 863 Program (no. 2015AA015303). This work is also supported by the Program for Changjiang Young Scholars in University of China, and the Program for Shanghai Top Young Talents.

REFERENCES

[1] March 2, 2017. http://tech.qq.com/original/archives/a128.html. (March 2, 2017).

[2] Retrieved April 14, 2017. Uber financials 2016. (Retrieved April 14, 2017).

[3] Martín Abadi, Ashish Agarwal, Paul Barham, Eugene Brevdo, Zhifeng Chen, Craig Citro, Greg S Corrado, Andy Davis, Jeffrey Dean, Matthieu Devin, et al. 2016. Tensorflow: Large-scale machine learning on heterogeneous distributed systems. *arXiv preprint arXiv:1603.04467* (2016).

[4] David Arthur and Sergei Vassilvitskii. 2007. k-means++: The advantages of careful seeding. In *Proceedings of the eighteenth annual ACM-SIAM symposium on Discrete algorithms*. Society for Industrial and Applied Mathematics, 1027–1035.

[5] Dzmitry Bahdanau, Kyunghyun Cho, and Yoshua Bengio. 2014. Neural machine translation by jointly learning to align and translate. *arXiv preprint arXiv:1409.0473* (2014).

[6] Dzmitry Bahdanau, Jan Chorowski, Dmitriy Serdyuk, Philemon Brakel, an Yoshua Bengio. 2016. End-to-end attention-based large vocabulary speech reco nition. In *ICASSP*. IEEE, 4945–4949.

[7] George EP Box, Gwilym M Jenkins, Gregory C Reinsel, and Greta M Ljung. 201 *Time series analysis: forecasting and control*. John Wiley & Sons.

[8] Han-wen Chang, Yu-chin Tai, and Jane Yung-jen Hsu. 2009. Context-aware ta demand hotspots prediction. *International Journal of Business Intelligence an Data Mining* 5, 1 (2009), 3–18.

[9] Longbiao Chen, Daqing Zhang, Leye Wang, Dingqi Yang, Xiaojuan Ma, Shijia Li, Zhaohui Wu, Gang Pan, Thi-Mai-Trang Nguyen, and Jérémie Jakubowic 2016. Dynamic cluster-based over-demand prediction in bike sharing system In *Proceedings of the 2016 ACM International Joint Conference on Pervasive an Ubiquitous Computing*. ACM, 841–852.

[10] Jan K Chorowski, Dzmitry Bahdanau, Dmitriy Serdyuk, Kyunghyun Cho, an Yoshua Bengio. 2015. Attention-based models for speech recognition. In *Advanc in Neural Information Processing Systems*. 577–585.

[11] Alex Graves. 2013. Generating sequences with recurrent neural networks. *arX preprint arXiv:1308.0850* (2013).

[12] Aditya Grover, Ashish Kapoor, and Eric Horvitz. 2015. A deep hybrid mod for weather forecasting. In *Proceedings of the 21th ACM SIGKDD Internation Conference on Knowledge Discovery and Data Mining*. ACM, 379–386.

[13] Kaiming He, Xiangyu Zhang, Shaoqing Ren, and Jian Sun. 2016. Deep residu learning for image recognition. In *Proceedings of the IEEE Conference on Comput Vision and Pattern Recognition*. 770–778.

[14] Diederik Kingma and Jimmy Ba. 2014. Adam: A method for stochastic optimiz tion. *arXiv preprint arXiv:1412.6980* (2014).

[15] Benjamin Klein, Lior Wolf, and Yehuda Afek. 2015. A dynamic convolution layer for short range weather prediction. In *Proceedings of the IEEE Conference o Computer Vision and Pattern Recognition*. 4840–4848.

[16] Yexin Li, Yu Zheng, Huichu Zhang, and Lei Chen. 2015. Traffic prediction in a bik sharing system. In *Proceedings of the 23rd SIGSPATIAL International Conferen on Advances in Geographic Information Systems*. ACM, 33.

[17] Helmut Lütkepohl. 2005. *New introduction to multiple time series analysis*. Spring Science & Business Media.

[18] Volodymyr Mnih, Nicolas Heess, Alex Graves, et al. 2014. Recurrent models c visual attention. In *Advances in neural information processing systems*. 2204–2212

[19] Luis Moreira-Matias, Joao Gama, Michel Ferreira, Joao Mendes-Moreira, and Lu Damas. 2013. Predicting taxi–passenger demand using streaming data. *IEE Transactions on Intelligent Transportation Systems* 14, 3 (2013), 1393–1402.

[20] Ronald A Rensink. 2000. The dynamic representation of scenes. *Visual cognitio* 7, 1-3 (2000), 17–42.

[21] Nitish Srivastava, Elman Mansimov, and Ruslan Salakhudinov. 2015. Unsupe vised learning of video representations using lstms. In *International Conferenc on Machine Learning*. 843–852.

[22] Ilya Sutskever, Oriol Vinyals, and Quoc V Le. 2014. Sequence to sequence learnin with neural networks. In *Advances in neural information processing systems*. 3104 3112.

[23] Oriol Vinyals, Alexander Toshev, Samy Bengio, and Dumitru Erhan. 2015. Sho and tell: A neural image caption generator. In *Proceedings of the IEEE Conferenc on Computer Vision and Pattern Recognition*. 3156–3164.

[24] Dong Wang, Wei Cao, Jian Li, and Jieping Ye. 2017. DeepSD: Supply-Deman Prediction for Online Car-hailing Services using Deep Neural Networks. In *Dat Engineering (ICDE), 2017 IEEE 33rd International Conference on*. IEEE, 243–254.

[25] Hua Wei, Yuandong Wang, Tianyu Wo, Yaxiao Liu, and Jie Xu. 2016. ZEST: Hybrid Model on Predicting Passenger Demand for Chauffeured Car Servic In *Proceedings of the 25th ACM International on Conference on Information an Knowledge Management*. ACM, 2203–2208.

[26] SHI Xingjian, Zhourong Chen, Hao Wang, Dit-Yan Yeung, Wai-Kin Wong, an Wang-chun Woo. 2015. Convolutional LSTM network: A machine learning ap proach for precipitation nowcasting. In *Advances in Neural Information Processin Systems*. 802–810.

[27] Caiming Xiong, Stephen Merity, and Richard Socher. 2016. Dynamic memor networks for visual and textual question answering. *arXiv* 1603 (2016).

[28] Kelvin Xu, Jimmy Ba, Ryan Kiros, Kyunghyun Cho, Aaron C Courville, Rusla Salakhutdinov, Richard S Zemel, and Yoshua Bengio. 2015. Show, Attend an Tell: Neural Image Caption Generation with Visual Attention.. In *ICML*, Vol. 1 77–81.

[29] Qiuyuan Yang, Zhiqiang Gao, Xiangjie Kong, Azizur Rahim, Jinzhong Wang and Feng Xia. 2015. Taxi Operation Optimization Based on Big Traffic Data. I *UIC-ATC-ScalCom*. IEEE, 127–134.

[30] Zhilin Yang, Ye Yuan, Yuexin Wu, William W Cohen, and Ruslan R Salakhutdino 2016. Review networks for caption generation. In *Advances in Neural Informatio Processing Systems*. 2361–2369.

[31] Junbo Zhang, Yu Zheng, and Dekang Qi. 2017. Deep spatio-temporal residua networks for citywide crowd flows prediction. In *Thirty-First AAAI Conferenc on Artificial Intelligence*.

[32] Junbo Zhang, Yu Zheng, Dekang Qi, Ruiyuan Li, and Xiuwen Yi. 2016. DNN-base prediction model for spatio-temporal data. In *SIGSPATIAL*. ACM, 92.

Event Mining over Distributed Text Streams

John Calvo Martinez
School of Computer Science and Engineering
University of New South Wales
Sydney NSW 2052, Australia
j.calvomartinez@unsw.edu.au

ABSTRACT

This research presents a new set of techniques to deal with event mining from different text sources, a complex set of NLP tasks which aim to extract events of interest and their components including authors, targets, locations, and event categories. Our focus is on distributed text streams, such as tweets from different news agencies, in order to accurately retrieve events and its components by combining such sources in different ways using text stream mining. Therefore this research project aims to fill the gap between batch event mining, text stream mining and distributed data mining which have been used separately to address related learning tasks. We propose a multi-task and multi-stream mining approach to combine information from multiple text streams to accurately extract and categorise events under the assumptions of stream mining. Our approach also combines ontology matching to boost accuracy under imbalanced distributions. In addition, we plan to address two relatively unexplored event mining tasks: event coreference and event synthesis. Preliminary results show the appropriateness of our proposal, which is giving an increase of around 20% on macro prequential metrics for the event classification task.

CCS CONCEPTS

• **Computing methodologies → Natural language processing**; *Boosting*; *Distributed algorithms*; • **Information systems → Data stream mining**;

KEYWORDS

Event mining; stream mining; text mining

ACM Reference Format:
John Calvo Martinez. 2018. Event Mining over Distributed Text Streams. In *Proceedings of 11th ACM International Conference on Web Search & Data Mining, Marina Del Rey, CA, USA, February 5–9, 2018 (WSDM 2018)*, 2 pages. https://doi.org/10.1145/3159652.3170462

1 INTRODUCTION

The complex task of detecting and extracting events from unstructured text data has been heavily researched over the last decade. Event detection and extraction is a set of NLP tasks which aims to create methods and techniques to identify events, including descriptive elements such as actors, targets, locations, dates, and event types [1]. This information is extracted from unstructured texts such as news articles or social media updates as in Twitter. Researchers have devised several methods and techniques in order to extract such components transforming unstructured information into a more manageable, structured representation to be used by a human analyst e.g. social scientists could benefit by using factual, fine grained information to analyse human rights abuses in violent conflicts [6]. Nonetheless, current event extraction methods are being used on general news text corpora. This is the case for the ACE dataset, which was built to extract detailed events from general news text corpora [1]. However, a fine grained set of event categories naturally increases the imbalanced nature of the data, making it difficult to accurately classify with current state-of-the-art techniques. Pavlick *et al.* [5] recently benchmarked event extraction techniques for the gun violence dataset, a domain specific dataset for gun violence in the US, and low precision and recall results were attained using the best reported techniques in the ACE competition as in [4, 7], reaching 30.2% precision and 20.1% recall on target identification. Furthermore, given that the input can potentially change its underlying statistical distribution at any time and a text stream such as Twitter is frequently updating information near to real time, it is desirable that the learning task is able to predict at any time without losing significant accuracy.

1.1 Research questions

The following research questions are derived from the avobe mentioned challenges:

- How to efficiently categorise text streams under real time conditions and imbalanced distributions?
- How to efficiently recognise event components (actors, targets, locations) from text streams under stream mining constraints?
- How can stream mining techniques be used to find event co-references over multiple sources of information?
- Which stream mining techniques are useful for synthesising events from multiple sources of information?

2 PROPOSED APPROACH

In this section, the techniques to be applied in this research will be described. We propose several stream mining algorithms and techniques applied according to each sub-learning problem.

WSDM 2018, February 5–9, 2018, Marina Del Rey, CA, USA

ACM ISBN 978-1-4503-5581-0/18/02...$15.00
https://doi.org/10.1145/3159652.3170462

2.1 Event type classification

We propose to use a distributed ensemble stream mining approach. This learning algorithm uses the power of domain specific ontologies in order to boost accuracy compared to commonly used methods. During the pre-processing step, feature augmentation is done using the ontology by weighting the relevant words found in the text that matches any category found in the ontology. Afterwards, a stream mining algorithm classifies the incoming instance by combining two techniques, a global Naïve Bayes method and a local matching method. The local method looks at the highest weighted category calculated during the augmentation, and the global learner combines local outputs to classify the incoming instance. We found that a combination between local and global classifiers boosts prequential precision and recall under imbalanced distributions.

2.2 Event component classification

This particular task is being addressed by using a syntactic and semantic feature representation particularly useful for word classification. Contextual features based on a word's syntactic role are proposed, for instance, whether or not the observed word is on the left of the main verb of the sentence, similar to [4] but with more analysis on component selection. The use of such features into an updateable learner seems to improve results for named entities classification (actor, target, location).

2.3 Event coreference resolution

The goal of this particular learning task is to find the closest matches between event references, in order to retrieve a group of text instances reporting the same real event. To achieve this, we propose a stream clustering mechanism using a particular similarity metric we call the "eventiveness" similarity metric, combined with the cosine measure as defined in [8]. Stop words, lemmatization and Porter stemming will be applied before computing the cosine function. Finally, a stream mining model is applied to perform the binary classification task.

2.4 Event synthesis

We propose a multi-stream mining method to combine knowledge from different sources of information. For this purpose, we take all event mentions from each reported event found, including all sources. If a reported component is different across sources, then we use stream mining, using a feature representation of event components, including actors, targets and locations and the information quality measure gathered form each source. In this case, the source of information and its information quality depends only on past true label values. A majority vote algorithm is initially proposed, weighted by the credibility value of each source of information.

3 INITIAL RESULTS

A set of initial results for the event classification task is given in Table 1. Methods were tested on a dataset on the Afghanistan conflict on Twitter during 2016. This ontology was initially used in [3]. In order to compare our results, we use the prequential test-then-train methodology as defined in [2]. Prequential evaluation is complemented by using macro precision and macro recall metrics.

Table 1: Event type classification results

Method		Prequential			Macro Preq.	
		Prec.	Rec.	F1	Prec.	Rec.
TF-IDF	MC	27.8%	85.8%	42%	4.2%	3.8%
	MNB	29.7%	89.7%	55.1%	31.4%	10.1%
Ontology	MNB	42%	**90.5%**	**57.4%**	22.8%	8.8%
	HT	27.3%	88.6%	41.8%	18%	4.9%
	DE(HT)	42.4%	70.1%	53%	51.9%	25.1%
	DE(MNB)	**45.3%**	74.4%	56.5%	**52.1%**	**25.2%**

We used an initial set of existing stream mining algorithms as baselines, including majority class (MC), Multinomial Naïve Bayes (MNB), Hoeffding trees (HT), using both a TF-IDF representation of text and our ontology feature representation. Initial results show an increase in macro precision and macro recall of more than 20% using our distributed ensemble (DE). In addition, we found that very little literature has discussed macro metrics on classification tasks with skewed class distributions.

4 CONCLUSIONS

In this paper, we proposed different methods to address event mining problems under streaming conditions. We propose different techniques for each major event mining task. We focused on improving baselines by using ontology enrichment with a proposed ensemble algorithm. Preliminary results show improvements in macro precision and recall, and more specifically, we have argued that there is a research gap when dealing with imbalanced datasets. Future work will be devoted to improve results in such scenarios and also measuring the efficiency of distributed versions of our algorithms.

ACKNOWLEDGMENTS

The author would like to thank Wayne Wobcke, Alfred Krzywicki, Michael Bain and Bradford Heap for providing support and mentoring to this research and Sandeepa Kannangara for proof-reading. This work is supported by Data to Decisions CRC.

REFERENCES

[1] David Ahn. 2006. The Stages of Event Extraction. In *Proceedings of the Workshop on Annotating and Reasoning about Time and Events*. 1–8.

[2] Albert Bifet, Geoff Holmes, Richard Kirkby, and Bernhard Pfahringer. 2010. MOA: Massive Online Analysis. *Journal of Machine Learning Research* 11, 1601–1604.

[3] Bradford Heap, Alfred Krzywicki, Susanne Schmeidl, Wayne Wobcke, and Michael Bain. 2017. A Joint Human/Machine Process for Coding Events and Conflict Drivers. In *Advanced Data Mining and Applications*, G. Cong, W.-C. Peng, W.E. Zhang, C. Li, and A Sun (Eds.). Springer, Cham, 639–654.

[4] Qi Li, Heng Ji, and Liang Huang. 2013. Joint Event Extraction via Structured Prediction with Global Features.. In *Proceedings of the 51st Annual Meeting of the Association for Computational Linguistics*. 73–82.

[5] Ellie Pavlick, Heng Ji, Xiaoman Pan, and Chris Callison-Burch. 2016. The Gun Violence Database: A New Task and Data Set for NLP.. In *EMNLP*. 1018–1024.

[6] Philip A Schrodt. 2012. *CAMEO: Conflict and Mediation Event Observations Event and Actor Codebook*. Technical Report. Department of Political Science Pennsylvania State University.

[7] Lei Sha, Jing Liu, Chin-Yew Lin, Sujian Li, Baobao Chang, and Zhifang Sui. 2016. RBPB: Regularization-Based Pattern Balancing Method for Event Extraction. In *Proceedings of the 54th Annual Meeting of the Association for Computational Linguistics*. 1224–1234.

[8] Michael Steinbach, George Karypis, Vipin Kumar, et al. 2000. A Comparison of Document Clustering Techniques. In *KDD Workshop on Text Mining*. 525–526.

Connectivity in Complex Networks: Measures, Inference and Optimization

Chen Chen
Arizona State University
Tempe, Arizona
chen_chen@asu.edu

ABSTRACT

Networks are ubiquitous in many high impact domains. Among the various aspects of network studies, connectivity is the one that plays important role in many applications (e.g., information dissemination, robustness analysis, community detection, etc.). The diversified applications have spurred numerous connectivity measures. Accordingly, ad-hoc connectivity optimization methods are designed for each measure, making it hard to model and control the connectivity of the network in a uniformed framework. On the other hand, it is often impossible to maintain an accurate structure of the network due to network dynamics and noise in real applications, which would affect the accuracy of connectivity measures and the effectiveness of corresponding connectivity optimization methods.

In this work, we aim to address the challenges on network connectivity by (1) unifying a wide range of classic network connectivity measures into one uniform model; (2) proposing effective approaches to infer connectivity measures and network structures from dynamic and incomplete input data, and (3) providing a general framework to optimize the connectivity measures in the network.

CCS CONCEPTS

• **Mathematics of computing → Paths and connectivity problems;**

KEYWORDS

Graph mining; network connectivity

ACM Reference Format:
Chen Chen. 2018. Connectivity in Complex Networks: Measures, Inference and Optimization. In *WSDM 2018: The Eleventh ACM International Conference on Web Search and Data Mining, February 5–9, 2018, Marina Del Rey, CA, USA.* ACM, New York, NY, USA, 2 pages. https://doi.org/10.1145/3159652.3170460

1 INTRODUCTION

Networks are prevalent in many high-impact domains, including information dissemination, social collaboration, infrastructure constructions, and many more. The most well-studied type of networks is single-layered networks, where the nodes are collected from the same domain and the links are used to represent the same type of connections. However, as the world is becoming highly connected, cross-domain interactions are more frequently observed in numerous applications, catalyzing the emergence of a new network model–*multi-layered networks* [1, 8, 15, 16]. One typical example of such type of network is critical infrastructure network as illustrated in Figure 1. In an infrastructure network system, the full functioning of the autonomous system network (AS network) and the transportation network is dependent on the power supply from the power grid. While for the gas-fired and coal-fired generators in the power grid, their functioning is fully dependent on the gas and coal supply from the transportation network. Moreover, to keep the whole complex system working in order, extensive communications are needed between the nodes in the networks, which are supported by the AS network. Multi-layered networks also appear in many other application domains, such as organization-level collaboration platform [3] and cross-platform e-commerce [7, 12, 13, 18].

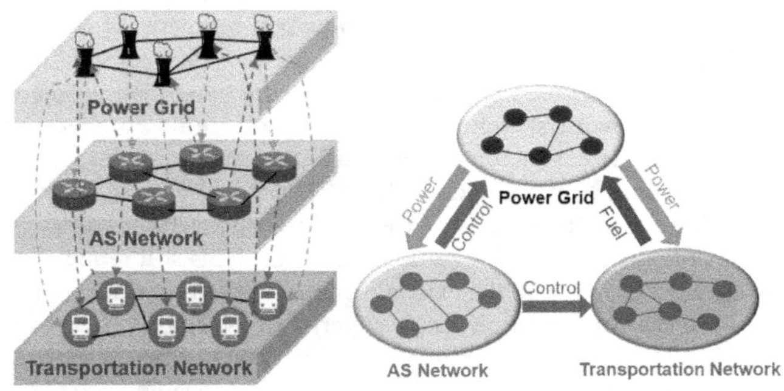

(a) Infrastructure Network (b) Dependency Relations

Figure 1: An illustrative example of multi-layered networks. In Figure 1(b), each ellipse corresponds to a critical infrastructure network in Figure 1(a). The arrows between two ellipses indicate cross-layer dependency relationships between the corresponding two networks.

Among the various network properties studied in the literature, network connectivity is the one that plays a crucial role in applications like disease control, network robustness analysis, community detection, etc. Correspondingly, different connectivity measures are designed for each of the applications. Example include epidemic threshold [2] for disease dissemination analysis, natural connectivity [11] for robustness measurement and triangle capacity for social network mining. Empirical analysis has demonstrated the effectiveness of those connectivity measures in their own tasks, but none of them can be used as a common measure across different domains. Furthermore, most, if not all, of the existing connectivity measures are defined on single-layered networks, leaving the problem of measuring multi-layered network connectivity unexplored. To address those problems, we propose two unified frameworks to evaluate the connectivity in complex network. In the first framework, we define

WSDM 2018, February 5–9, 2018, Marina Del Rey, CA, USA

ACM ISBN 978-1-4503-5581-0/18/02.
https://doi.org/10.1145/3159652.3170460

the connectivity of the network as a function of its eigen-pairs [5]. Several examples of eigen-function based connectivity measures include epidemic threshold [9], eigenvector centrality [14], triangle capacity [17], natural connectivity [11], eigen-gap [10], etc. The second connectivity model we propose is called SUBLINE connectivity family [3]. The key idea of SUBLINE is to view the connectivity of the entire network as an aggregation over the connectivity scores of its sub-networks (e.g., subgraphs). An interesting finding about SUBLINE connectivity is that it can be used to approximate a wide-range of eigen-function based connectivity measures such as epidemic threshold, triangle capacity and natural connectivity.

Existing network connectivity research predominantly assumes that the input network is static and accurate, which does not fit into the noisy and dynamic real-world settings. Real-world networks are evolving over time. In some cases, subtle changes in the network structure may lead to huge differences on some of the connectivity measures. To keep track of the connectivity measures in dynamic networks, we propose an efficient connectivity tracking framework based on matrix perturbation theory which can accurately approximate the changing connectivity measures for a fairly long period of time [5]. On the other hand, in multi-layered networks, it remains a daunting task to know the exact cross-layer dependency structure due to noise, incomplete data sources and limited accessibility. To effectively infer the cross-layer dependencies in multi-layered network, we draw an analogy from collective collaborative filtering problems and model it with an optimization problem [6].

The crucial task for network connectivity studies is to optimize (minimize/maximize) the connectivity score by adjusting the underlying network structure. Previous literature has proved that the optimization problem on epidemic threshold and triangle capacity in single-layered networks is NP-hard. However, for some complex connectivity measures (e.g. natural connectivity), the hardness of the corresponding optimization problems still remains unknown. Most importantly, existing connectivity optimization methods are mainly based on single-layered networks. Compared to single-layered networks, multi-layered networks are more sensitive to disturbance since its effect may be amplified through cross-layer dependencies in all the dependent networks, leading to a cascade failure of the entire system. To tackle the connectivity optimization problem in multi-layered networks, great efforts have been made from different research area for manipulating *two-layered* interdependent network systems [1, 8, 15, 16]. Although much progress has been made, challenges are still largely open. First, as the connectivity measures are highly diversified, the ad-hoc optimization algorithms that are effective for specific measures may not work well on other measures. Thus, the problem of how to design a generic optimization strategy that can be applied to a wide-range of network connectivity measures is in need of being investigated. Second, existing optimization strategies tailored for two-layered networks might be sub-optimal, or even misleading to arbitrarily structured multi-layered networks. Alternatively, an effective optimization algorithm should be able to unravel the nested dependency structure in the network in the first place. Thus, we propose OPERA, a generalized connectivity optimization framework that can deal with any connectivity measures that fall in the SUBLINE family with arbitrary dependency structures in [4].

To summarize, the main problems studied in our work are focused on measures, inference, and optimization of network connectivity in complex networks. The relationship between those problems are shown in Figure 2. Generally speaking, a well defined connectivity measure serves as the objective to inference and optimization tasks; The inference results in turn provide a good approximation on the connectivity measure and improve the accuracy of the input network for optimization tasks; Last, the optimization methods are used to find optimal strategies to manipulate the network structure, which can effectively change the connectivity of the network and influence the inference results from task 2.

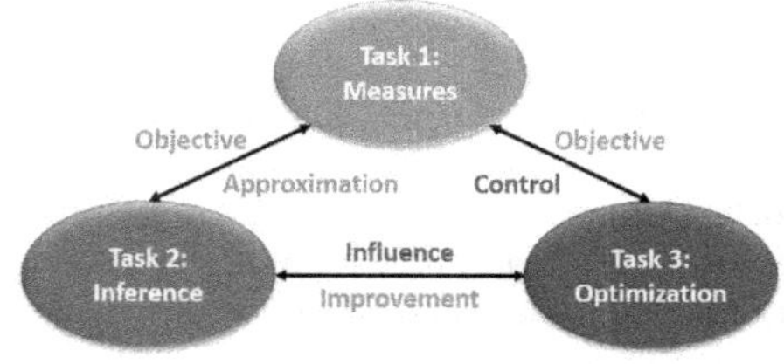

Figure 2: Problem overview.

REFERENCES

[1] Sergey V Buldyrev, Roni Parshani, Gerald Paul, H Eugene Stanley, and Shlomo Havlin. 2010. Catastrophic cascade of failures in interdependent networks. *Nature* 464, 7291 (2010), 1025–1028.

[2] Deepayan Chakrabarti, Yang Wang, Chenxi Wang, Jurij Leskovec, and Christos Faloutsos. 2008. Epidemic thresholds in real networks. *ACM Transactions on Information and System Security (TISSEC)* 10, 4 (2008), 1.

[3] Chen Chen, Jingrui He, Nadya Bliss, and Hanghang Tong. 2015. On the Connectivity of Multi-layered Networks: Models, Measures and Optimal Control. In *Data Mining (ICDM), 2015 IEEE 15th International Conference on*. IEEE, 715–720.

[4] Chen Chen, Jingrui He, Nadya Bliss, and Hanghang Tong. 2017. Towards Optimal Connectivity on Multi-Layered Networks. *IEEE Transactions on Knowledge and Data Engineering* 29, 10 (2017), 2332–2346.

[5] Chen Chen and Hanghang Tong. 2016. On the eigen-functions of dynamic graphs: Fast tracking and attribution algorithms. *Statistical Analysis and Data Mining: The ASA Data Science Journal* (2016), 121–135. https://doi.org/10.1002/sam.1131

[6] Chen Chen, Hanghang Tong, Lei Xie, Lei Ying, and Qing He. 2016. FASCINATE: Fast Cross-Layer Dependency Inference on Multi-layered Networks. In *Proceedings of the 22nd ACM SIGKDD International Conference on Knowledge Discovery and Data Mining, San Francisco, CA, USA, August 13-17, 2016*. 765–77 https://doi.org/10.1145/2939672.2939784

[7] Wei Chen, Wynne Hsu, and Mong Li Lee. 2013. Making recommendations from multiple domains. In *Proceedings of the 19th ACM SIGKDD international conference on Knowledge discovery and data mining*. ACM, 892–900.

[8] Jianxi Gao, Sergey V Buldyrev, H Eugene Stanley, and Shlomo Havlin. 2012. Networks formed from interdependent networks. *Nature physics* 8, 1 (2012) 40–48.

[9] Frank Harary and Allen Schwenk. 1979. The spectral approach to determining the number of walks in a graph. *Pacific J. Math.* 80, 2 (1979), 443–449.

[10] Shlomo Hoory, Nathan Linial, and Avi Wigderson. 2006. Expander graphs and their applications. *Bull. Amer. Math. Soc.* 43, 4 (2006), 439–561.

[11] WU Jun, Mauricio Barahona, Tan Yue-Jin, and Deng Hong-Zhong. 2010. Natural connectivity of complex networks. *Chinese Physics Letters* 27, 7 (2010), 078902.

[12] Bin Li, Qiang Yang, and Xiangyang Xue. 2009. Can Movies and Books Collaborate? Cross-Domain Collaborative Filtering for Sparsity Reduction.. In *IJCAI*, Vol. 9. 2052–2057.

[13] Zhongqi Lu, Weike Pan, Evan Wei Xiang, Qiang Yang, Lili Zhao, and ErHeng Zhong. 2013. Selective transfer learning for cross domain recommendation. In *SDM*. SIAM, 641–649.

[14] Mark EJ Newman. 2008. The mathematics of networks. *The new palgrave encyclopedia of economics* 2, 2008 (2008), 1–12.

[15] Roni Parshani, Sergey V Buldyrev, and Shlomo Havlin. 2010. Interdependent networks: Reducing the coupling strength leads to a change from a first to second order percolation transition. *Physical review letters* 105, 4 (2010), 048701.

[16] Arunabha Sen, Anisha Mazumder, Joydeep Banerjee, Arun Das, and Randy Compton. 2014. Multi-layered Network Using a New Model of Interdependency. *arXiv preprint arXiv:1401.1783* (2014).

[17] Charalampos E Tsourakakis. 2008. Fast counting of triangles in large real networks without counting: Algorithms and laws. In *Data Mining, 2008. ICDM'08. Eighth IEEE International Conference on*. IEEE, 608–617.

[18] Deqing Yang, Jingrui He, Huazheng Qin, Yanghua Xiao, and Wei Wang. 2015. A Graph-based Recommendation across Heterogeneous Domains. In *Proceedings of the 24rd ACM International Conference on Conference on Information and Knowledge Management*. ACM, 463–472.

Automatic Ranking of Information Retrieval Systems

Maram Hasanain
Qatar University, Doha, Qatar
maram.hasanain@qu.edu.qa

ABSTRACT

Typical information retrieval system evaluation requires expensive manually-collected relevance judgments of documents, which are used to rank retrieval systems. Due to the high cost associated with collecting relevance judgments and the ever-growing scale of data to be searched in practice, ranking of retrieval systems using manual judgments is becoming less feasible. Methods to automatically rank systems in absence of judgments have been proposed to tackle this challenge. However, current techniques are still far from reaching the ranking achieved using manual judgments. I propose to advance research on automatic system ranking using supervised and unsupervised techniques.

ACM Reference Format:
Maram Hasanain. 2018. Automatic Ranking of Information Retrieval Systems. In *Proceedings of 11th ACM International Conf. on Web Search and Data Mining (WSDM 2018).* ACM, New York, NY, USA, 2 pages. https://doi.org/10.1145/3159652.3170458

1 INTRODUCTION

Information retrieval (IR) evaluation typically follows the Cranfield paradigm using a test collection [12]. Many test collections were created to evaluate different retrieval tasks, especially through TREC's evaluation campaigns. However, with the growing size of data to be searched in practice (e.g., the Web), reliably evaluating systems to be used at such scale requires a sufficiently-large set of manual relevance judgments [1]. Under the Cranfield paradigm, collecting relevance judgments is considered the most time- and resource-consuming component of the process [1]. Recent years witnessed a great interest in approaches for system evaluation minimizing judgment effort [2] or even eliminating it by automatic evaluation [14]. Automatic evaluation of systems can be particularly useful in cases when the document collection is dynamically changing (e.g., the Web). Creating a test collection to reliably evaluate systems considering such dynamic change can be difficult [14].

One of the main sub-problems that stemmed from automatic evaluation is *automatic system ranking* (AR), which can be defined as follows. An evaluation setup similar to TREC is assumed with a document collection, a set of N topics each represented by a query and a set of runs retrieved by M retrieval systems. The problem aims at ranking the systems in a descending order of retrieval effectiveness and in absence of relevance judgments.

WSDM 2018, February 5–9, 2018, Marina Del Rey, CA, USA

ACM ISBN 978-1-4503-5581-0/18/02.
https://doi.org/10.1145/3159652.3170458

Existing studies on automatic ranking generally follow one of two main approaches. The first develops a set of *pseudo* relevant documents, then uses this set in evaluating and ranking the systems [4–6, 11, 14]. The other approach is based on scoring a system by comparing its ranked list to ranked lists retrieved by the other systems being ranked [15, 16].

Building on earlier work on AR, this work addresses three research questions: (1) can we learn a L2R model to automatically rank systems effectively? , (2) can automatic selection of topics from the full topic set improve automatic system ranking? , and (3) how can we *automatically* generate different representations of a topic for better automatic ranking of systems? By answering these questions, the work has the following potential contributions. First, a learning-to-rank model (L2R) is proposed to rank systems. Up to my knowledge, this is the first time L2R is employed for AR. Second, I propose to use an effective topic selection technique that predicts which topics are best for AR. Finally, I propose applying two automatic approaches for finding multiple representations of a topic for the sake of improving AR through query variations.

2 RELATED WORK

Automatic System Ranking. One of the first studies that attempted automatic ranking is the work of Soboroff et al. [14]. Authors proposed to create a set of pseudo relevance judgments (pseudo-qrels) to use in ranking of systems in place of manually-collected judgments. The set was created by pooling top documents retrieved by all systems for a topic, then a number of documents was randomly sampled from the pool. Repeating the process for all topics, the resulting set was assumed relevant and used to evaluate systems using mean average precision (MAP). The method was evaluated using a typical approach in this domain where rank correlation between the proposed ranking and ground truth ranking (TREC ranking), was computed. Results showed that system ranking using the pseudo-qrels is positively correlated with the ground truth ranking over several adhoc search TREC collections. Differently, Nuray and Can [11] proposed to rank systems by applying data fusion to per-topic result lists from systems to be ranked. Top documents in the fused list were assumed relevant.

Instead of creating pseudo-qrels, Wu and Crestani [16] proposed to compute a system ranking score. For each system, the score is first computed per query by summing the occurrences of each of the system's retrieved documents in ranked lists of other systems. The sum of the per-query scores for a system is considered its ranking score. Spoerri [15] proposed a system score that is based on comparing the system's ranked list overlap with lists retrieved by other systems. The method assumes that a poorly-performing system is that returning a lot of documents that are dissimilar from documents returned by other systems.

Gao et al. [6] proposed an Expectation- Maximization algorithm that estimates a pseudo-judgment score for each document on each topic given retrieval scores for the document from all systems. The documents per topic are ranked using the computed score; top documents are assumed relevant. Results on four TREC collections showed that the method generally outperforms the approach proposed by Soboroff et al. [14], reaching a maximum rank correlation of 0.563 for the adhoc search task over TREC-6 test collection. This indicates that existing AR techniques are still far from achieving the optimal system ranking using manual judgments.

Topic Subset Selection. An early work by Mizzaro and Robertson [10] studied the effect of topics on differentiating systems based on true effectiveness and found that some topics are more useful in distinguishing system effectiveness. Moreover, Guiver et al. [7] experimentally proved that some *subsets* of topics are better than others in predicting true system effectiveness. In a different direction, researchers worked on methods for topic subset selection for the purpose of minimizing the number of relevance judgments to collect for evaluation [9]. Topic selection was also employed for purposes such as selecting effective training data for L2R models [17].

Studies discussed earlier in this section examined the problem of topic set selection considering ranking of systems based on manual relevance judgments. However, in my work, the aim is to apply topic selection within a paradigm for *automatic* ranking of systems in lack of relevance judgments. Up to my knowledge, the only study that investigated the effect of topic subsets on AR is that of Hauff et al. [8]. Hauff et al. [8] proposed an automatic topic subset selection technique used to study the effect of using topic subsets to automatically rank systems. The study suggested that not all topics are useful in automatic ranking of systems [8].

Topic Representation Variation. Efron [4], and a later work by Efron and Winget [5], exploited the concept of using topic representation variations to collect pseudo-qrels for automatic ranking. Efron proposed to use each of a set of manually-crafted queries per topic to retrieve a set of documents using a single search system. The ranked lists retrieved for all queries are merged into a final set of pseudo-qrels. The proposed technique showed strong correlation with true system ranking reaching a rank correlation of 0.875 over TREC-8 collection. However, the method still requires manual intervention needed to create the queries. Therefore, leveraging *automatic* techniques for finding multiple topic representations (e.g., [13]) is a proposed alternative to be tested in this work.

3 PROPOSED WORK

I propose to improve AR over existing state-of-the-art techniques following three approaches:

Learning-to-rank-based AR. Although L2R was usually exclusively used for ranking documents based on relevance to a topic in the IR domain, L2R is emerging as a strong ranking model for different applications related to IR, such as ranking system configurations to select the best for a retrieval system [3]. Thus, I propose to train a L2R model to rank retrieval systems in the context of AR. Under this model, each system is represented by a set of features designed to capture its retrieval effectiveness.

Topic representation variation-based AR. Efron [4] proposed to collect pseudo-relevant documents *for system evaluation and ranking* by constructing varied representations for a topic. The proposed method notably improved AR, however, it requires human effort to create the queries for topics. I propose to replace this costly step by adopting automatic techniques (e.g., approach described in [13]) to develop variants to a topic representation.

Topic subset selection. Earlier studies showed that not all topics are useful in ranking systems [10] using manual judgments. Since similar observation was made in the context of automatic ranking [8], I extend earlier effort in this domain by adopting a L2R-based approach for topic selection that chooses a subset of topics that is better at automatically ranking systems than the full topic set [9].

Each AR technique produces a ranked list of systems. To measure the quality of a technique, rank correlation (Kendall's tau ($\tau \in [-1, 1]$)) is computed between the estimated ranking and the true ranking resulting from systems' evaluation using manual relevance judgments. In this work, experiments are focused on the adhoc retrieval task over TREC collections for the adhoc (TREC6-8) and Web (TREC9-10, and TREC 2013-2014) tracks.

ACKNOWLEDGMENTS

This work was made possible by NPRP grant# NPRP 7-1313-1-245 from the Qatar National Research Fund (a member of Qatar Foundation). The statements made herein are solely the responsibility of the authors.

REFERENCES

[1] Chris Buckley, Darrin Dimmick, Ian Soboroff, and Ellen Voorhees. 2007. Bias and the limits of pooling for large collections. *Information Retrieval* 10, 6 (2007).
[2] Ben Carterette, James Allan, and Ramesh Sitaraman. 2006. Minimal Test Collections for Retrieval Evaluation. In *SIGIR '06*.
[3] Romain Deveaud, Josiane Mothe, and Jian-Yun Nia. 2016. Learning to Rank System Configurations. In *CIKM '16*.
[4] Miles Efron. 2009. Using multiple query aspects to build test collections without human relevance judgments. In *ECIR' 09*.
[5] Miles Efron and Megan Winget. 2010. Query polyrepresentation for ranking retrieval systems without relevance judgments. *Journal of the American Society for Information Science and Technology* (2010).
[6] Ning Gao, William Webber, and Douglas W. Oard. 2014. Reducing reliance on relevance judgments for system comparison by using expectation-maximization. In *ECIR' 14*.
[7] John Guiver, Stefano Mizzaro, and Stephen Robertson. 2009. A Few Good Topics: Experiments in Topic Set Reduction for Retrieval Evaluation. *ACM Trans. Inf. Syst.* 27, 4 (2009).
[8] Claudia Hauff, Djoerd Hiemstra, Leif Azzopardi, and Franciska De Jong. 2010. A case for automatic system evaluation. In *ECIR' 10*.
[9] Mucahid Kutlu, Tamer Elsayed, and Matthew Lease. 2018. Intelligent topic selection for low-cost information retrieval evaluation: A New perspective on deep vs. shallow judging. *Information Processing & Management* 54, 1 (2018).
[10] Stefano Mizzaro and Stephen Robertson. 2007. Hits Hits TREC: Exploring IR Evaluation Results with Network Analysis. In *SIGIR '07*.
[11] Rabia Nuray and Fazli Can. 2006. Automatic ranking of information retrieval systems using data fusion. *Information Processing & Management* 42, 3 (2006).
[12] Mark Sanderson. 2010. Test Collection Based Evaluation of Information Retrieval Systems. *Foundations and TrendsÂő in Information Retrieval* 4, 4 (2010).
[13] Manmeet Singh and W Bruce Croft. 2016. Iterative Search using Query Aspects. In *CIKM' 16*.
[14] Ian Soboroff, Charles Nicholas, and Patrick Cahan. 2001. Ranking Retrieval Systems Without Relevance Judgments. In *SIGIR '01*.
[15] Anselm Spoerri. 2007. Using the structure of overlap between search results to rank retrieval systems without relevance judgments. *Information Processing & Management* 43, 4 (2007).
[16] Shengli Wu and Fabio Crestani. 2003. Methods for Ranking Information Retrieval Systems Without Relevance Judgments. In *SAC '03*.
[17] Xin Zhang, Ben He, and Tiejian Luo. 2016. Training query filtering for semi-supervised learning to rank with pseudo labels. *World Wide Web* 19, 5 (2016).

Mining Twitter for Fine-Grained Political Opinion Polarity Classification, Ideology Detection and Sarcasm Detection

Sandeepa Kannangara
School of Computer Science and Engineering
University of New South Wales
Sydney NSW 2052, Australia
s.kannangara@unsw.edu.au

ABSTRACT

In this paper, we propose three models for socio-political opinion polarity classification of microblog posts. Firstly, a novel probabilistic model, Joint-Entity-Sentiment-Topic (JEST) model, which captures opinions as a combination of the target entity, sentiment and topic, will be proposed. Secondly, a model for ideology detection called JEST-Ideology will be proposed to identify an individual's orientation towards topics/issues and target entities by extending the proposed opinion polarity classification framework. Finally, we propose a novel method to accurately detect sarcastic opinions by utilizing detected fine-grained opinion and ideology.

KEYWORDS

Fine-Grained Opinion Mining; Ideology Detection; Sarcasm Detection

ACM Reference Format:
Sandeepa Kannangara. 2018. Mining Twitter for Fine-Grained Political Opinion Polarity Classification, Ideology Detection and Sarcasm Detection. In *WSDM 2018: 11th ACM International Conference on Web Search & Data Mining, February 5–9, 2018, Marina Del Rey, CA, USA.* ACM, New York, NY, USA, 2 pages. https://doi.org/10.1145/3159652.3170461

1 INTRODUCTION

Opinions in social media platforms provide worldwide access to what people think about daily life topics/issues. Thus exploiting such a source of information to understand public opinion can be very useful in many scenarios, for example by political parties interested in monitoring attitudes towards their policies.

The opinion mining research field aims to develop automated approaches to accurately analyse such opinion data. Although there is much previous work on opinion mining, the majority of early studies analysed text documents such as product and movie reviews [5]. Only a limited number of studies have attempted to analyse public opinion in a political context [4]. The nature of political discourse which often includes sarcasm and irony makes the analysis more challenging.

Most political opinion mining studies analysed election datasets with the aim of election result prediction. The approaches employed range from lexicon based methods [8] to supervised machine learning methods using algorithms such as SVM [1] and Deep Learning approaches [11] in recent years. However, most work in this area focuses on overall sentiment classification, though Maynard and Funk [8] considered identification of the opinion target and Vijayaraghavan *et al.* [11] addressed classification of the topics along with the sentiment.

An *opinion* is defined as a tuple of four components [7]: sentiment orientation, sentiment target, opinion holder, and time. The sentiment target is defined as an entity or an entity with possibily an aspect of the entity that the sentiment has been expressed upon. As an example, if a tweet expresses a negative sentiment towards the Labor Party regarding Employment/Jobs, Labor Party is the target entity and Employment/Jobs is the aspect of the entity. However, the majority of early studies in opinion mining attempted to detect only the overall sentiment [6], regardless of the entities mentioned and their aspects. After Hu and Liu's [5] study, fine-grained opinion mining/aspect-based opinion mining became prominent. However, most of the aspect-based opinion mining studies [9] identified only aspect and sentiment by assuming a known target.

In this research, we aim to address the current challenges in socio-political opinion mining from Twitter focusing on the identification of target entity, aspect and sentiment for fine-grained opinion mining. Identifying an individual's political ideology/orientation from their reviews is also an important task for analysing political opinions. In general, opinions expressed toward the issues/topics of target entities are often indicative of political ideologies. For that, we propose a novel approach utilising the proposed opinion mining framework. Further, the presence of sarcasm is identified as a challenge for opinion polarity classification since sarcasm can potentially flip the polarity of the review. In this research, we will propose a novel method to detect sarcasm in tweets.

2 THE PROPOSED RESEARCH

Overall, the aim of this research is to develop a framework for political opinion mining focusing on fine-grained opinion mining, sarcasm detection and ideology detection. To evaluate each proposed model, we use tweets collected during the 2016 Australasian Federal Election.

2.1 Fine-Grained Political Opinion Polarity Classification

In this study, for fine-grained political opinion mining, we aim to extract the opinion target (e.g. candidates and political parties), topics discussed (e.g. Tax/Negative Gearing, Asylum Seekers/Refugees,

WSDM 2018, February 5–9, 2018, Marina Del Rey, CA, USA

ACM ISBN 978-1-4503-5581-0/18/02.
https://doi.org/10.1145/3159652.3170461

etc.) and sentiment (Positive, Negative or Neutral) towards the target from each tweet. For this, we propose a fine-grained opinion mining model, called JEST (Joint-Entity-Sentiment-Topic), to jointly model all three dimensions, based on LDA [3].

The strength of JEST is that all the component dimensions can help to improve each other during the joint modelling process. The rationale here is that it is possible to model each dimension as a latent variable in a graphical model. To distinguish the aspect and entity in the model, we utilize a knowledge base of entities which contains common names and hashtags used to represent entities in a predefined entity list. In this model, we assume that there is only one target entity and several or no topics in each tweet.

For evaluation, we use perplexity, which is the standard measure for evaluating topic models to compare the model with the selected baseline models. Furthermore, we will evaluate the document classification performance using distributions of the entity, target and sentiment generated by the model. However, since there is no prior work that models these three dimensions with similar assumptions, we need to select different baselines to evaluate each dimension. Furthermore, we can do qualitative analysis by manually inspecting the quality of the output.

2.2 Political Orientation Detection

For political orientation detection, we aim to identify a Twitter user's political alignment. However, our definition of political alignment is a user's set of political preferences over a range of policy positions of a party. For this, knowing the information such as user's opinion towards candidates or parties and topics that are discussed in his/her tweets is important. We model such evidence in our JEST model and here we propose an extension of JEST, the JEST-Ideology model, incorporating the ideology dimension.

The JEST model is capable of identifying an entity, sentiment and topics for each tweet in the corpus. The JEST-Ideology model has a top layer which can identify the favourable topics and entities for each user. However, there can be tweets that do not contain topics but generally express an opinion towards an entity. We consider such situations by modelling the general ideology of the user towards entities. The generative process runs through each user and then tweets of each user. For the evaluation of the model, we can use the same approaches proposed for the JEST model.

2.3 Sarcasm Detection in Political Tweets

Most previous approaches to sarcasm detection treat it as a purely linguistic matter, using information such as lexical cues and their corresponding sentiment as predictive features [2]. However, sarcasm has been extensively studied in the behavioural sciences and there are several theories explaining when, how and why sarcasm is expressed [10]. Those theories can be represented as contextual features by consider the user's current and previous posts.

In this research, we propose to use both linguistic and contextual features to detect sarcastic tweets. The accepted view is that sarcasm potentially flip the polarity of a review. Therefore, when we know the surface polarity of a tweet, to identify the situations where the actual polarity is different from surface polarity we can use the ideology of the author. If the ideology of the author is different from the surface polarity then we can infer that it is a sarcastic tweet. Therefore, as contextual features for the supervised model we can use the ideology of the Twitter user and surface polarity by utilizing the results of JEST and JEST-Ideology models.

The performance of the proposed approach can be measured using accuracy, recall, precision and F-measure. Further, we will compare our models with existing sarcasm detection techniques.

3 CONCLUSION AND FUTURE WORK

This paper gives a brief overview of ongoing research on political opinion mining. We have identified three main research directions to automatically analyse political opinions in Twitter: fine-grained opinion polarity classification, ideology detection and sarcasm detection. We propose novel topic models, JEST and JEST-Ideology which are capable of fine-grained opinion mining and ideology detection respectively. Finally, with the aim of improving opinion polarity classification performance, we propose a novel sarcasm detection model which uses ideology and fine-grained opinion as features with other linguistic features to classify sarcastic opinion.

In the future, it is essential to build these proposed models and evaluate model performance. A number of experiments are planned to select best performing model for each problem. Although, the models are proposed for the political domain, they are also applicable for other domain. Therefore, we are planning to conduct experiments using other datasets from different domains to evaluate the performance of the proposed models.

4 ACKNOWLEDGMENTS

I would like to sincerely thank my supervisor Wayne Wobcke and Michael Bain, Alfred Krzywicki and Bradford Heap for their continuous mentoring and constant support. The work is supported by the Data to Decisions Cooperative Research Centre.

REFERENCES

[1] Akshat Bakliwal, Jennifer Foster, Jennifer van der Puil, Ron O'Brien, Lamia Tounsi, and Mark Hughes. 2013. Sentiment Analysis of Political Tweets: Towards an Accurate Classifier. In *Proceedings of the Workshop on Language in Social Media (LASM '13)*. 49–58.

[2] David Bamman and Noah A. Smith. 2015. Contextualized Sarcasm Detection on Twitter. In *Proceedings of the Ninth International AAAI Conference on Web and Social Media (ICWSM '15)*. 574–577.

[3] David M. Blei, Andrew Y. Ng, and Michael I. Jordan. 2003. Latent Dirichlet Allocation. *Journal of Machine Learning Research* 3 (2003), 993–1022.

[4] Hsinchun Chen and David Zimbra. 2010. AI and Opinion Mining. *IEEE Intelligent Systems* 25, 3 (2010), 74–80.

[5] Minqing Hu and Bing Liu. 2004. Mining and Summarizing Customer Reviews. In *Proceedings of the Tenth ACM SIGKDD International Conference on Knowledge Discovery and Data Mining (KDD '04)*. 168–177.

[6] Farhan Hassan Khan, Saba Bashir, and Usman Qamar. 2014. TOM: Twitter Opinion Mining Framework Using Hybrid Classification Scheme. *Decision Support Systems* 57 (2014), 245–257.

[7] Bing Liu. 2012. *Sentiment Analysis and Opinion Mining*. Morgan & Claypool.

[8] Diana Maynard and Adam Funk. 2012. Automatic Detection of Political Opinions in Tweets. In *The Semantic Web: ESWC 2011 Workshops*, Raúl García-Castro, Dieter Fensel, and Grigoris Antoniou (Eds.). Springer-Verlag, Berlin, 88–99.

[9] Guang Qiu, Bing Liu, Jiajun Bu, and Chun Chen. 2011. Opinion Word Expansion and Target Extraction through Double Propagation. *Computational Linguistics* 37, 1 (2011), 9–27.

[10] Ashwin Rajadesingan, Reza Zafarani, and Huan Liu. 2015. Sarcasm Detection on Twitter: A Behavioral Modeling Approach. In *Proceedings of the Eighth ACM International Conference on Web Search and Data Mining (WSDM '15)*. 97–106.

[11] Prashanth Vijayaraghavan, Soroush Vosoughi, and Deb Roy. 2016. Automatic Detection and Categorization of Election-Related Tweets. In *Proceedings of the Tenth International Conference on Web and Social Media (ICWSM '16)*. 703–706.

Beyond Who and What: Data Driven Approaches for User Characterization

Aastha Nigam
Department of Computer Science and Engineering
Interdisciplinary Center for Network Science and Applications (iCeNSA)
University of Notre Dame, Notre Dame, IN 46556
anigam@nd.edu

ABSTRACT

Social media and technology have drastically transformed the social and information networks around us. They have impacted how we communicate with others, search for information, and even how we express our personal opinions. Further, in this era of big data, not only are the online services collecting vast variety of user data, but we, as users, are also readily divulging significant amounts of information. Together, massive datasets obtained from diverse sources such as organizations and user generated content give us the opportunity to explore and understand complex behavior of both individuals and communities. This proposal aims at designing generalizable and scalable data-driven frameworks to gain a deeper understanding of the users, explain their actions and preferences, and infer personal traits. The proposed models will enable us to move beyond asking the conventional questions of who and what, and reveal answers about how and why. Given the varying digital persona of users motivated by their personal preferences and social attributes, we characterize users in two distinct domains: online health and peace studies. The models are designed to solve various real-world challenges to maximize their broader impact.

CCS CONCEPTS

• **Information systems** → **Data mining**; **Web searching and information discovery**; • **Computing methodologies** → **Machine learning**; • **Social and professional topics** → *User characteristics*; • **Applied computing** → *Law, social and behavioral sciences*;

KEYWORDS

user behavior; computation social science; user modeling; online healthcare; peace studies

ACM Reference Format:
Aastha Nigam. 2018. Beyond Who and What: Data Driven Approaches for User Characterization. In *WSDM 2018: 11th ACM International Conference on Web Search & Data Mining, February 5–9, 2018, Marina Del Rey, CA, USA.* ACM, New York, NY, USA, Article 4, 2 pages. https://doi.org/10.1145/3159652.3170455

WSDM 2018, February 5–9, 2018, Marina Del Rey, CA, USA

ACM ISBN 978-1-4503-5581-0/18/02...$15.00
https://doi.org/10.1145/3159652.3170455

1 INTRODUCTION

With the increasing pervasive nature of technology, users today are leaving behind digital footprints and readily divulging significant amounts of information – giving rise to massive datasets with untapped potential to understand user behavior at a large scale. However, the behavior of each individual is unique and can be considered to be influenced by many confounding factors at a personal and social level – guiding their interests, preferences and consumption patterns. The nuances in these digital personas can be explained by the fundamental demographic, psychographic and geographic differences between users. Therefore, in this proposal, we focus on studying the behavior of different individuals in diverse domains and provide data-driven frameworks for understanding, modeling and predicting both individual behavior, as well as collective phenomena.

We aim to harness the power of data from diverse sources such as information collected by organizations, user generated content and census reports, to build a deeper understanding of online users, explain their actions and preferences, infer personal traits and potentially predict their next action. By modeling such diverse nuggets of data and integrating user attributes, we argue that we can move beyond asking traditional questions of "who" and "what", and instead answer integral questions about user behavior such as "how" and "why" ([2]). Such an understanding can not only unveil individual behavior, but can also reveal macroscopic properties of communities. Specifically, given the complex and multi-faceted nature of the human behavior, we formalize a set of data science problems and propose computational models to build a comprehensive understanding of users in diverse domains such as online heath and peace studies. Firstly, we focus on developing a profile for an online health seeker and examining the most informative features for understanding their health reading habits and preferences. Secondly, we propose a content driven framework to generate synthetic user profiles for user attribute inference in case of imbalanced datasets. Thirdly, we evaluate opinion and sentiment for each individual and measure the collective impact of the masses on socio-political events and finally we present a growth model to capture and predict activity trends of polarized users.

The proposed work demonstrates the significance of personal attributes such as age and gender, and social attributes, in defining the attitude, preferences, choices and behavior of a user. It also highlights diversity in information consumption/generation depending on the role an individual seeks – whether it be an online health consumer or a political tweeter. Further, the data driven frameworks designed and implemented in the research use computational models such as factorization machines and deep learning methods, which provide an effective and efficient way to characterize user behavior. Finally, the proposed problems and solutions give rise to important implications for real-world applications in user behavior understanding.

2 PROPOSED WORK

In this section, we discuss problem statements from varied user domains, present proposed data driven frameworks, and describe the results obtained for each project.

2.1 User Understanding in Online Healthcare

Various online sources including specialized websites such as WebMD[1] and Everyday Health[2] are commonly used by individuals to answer health queries about themselves. According to previous studies, many confounding factors can influence the health of an individual including demographic, socio-economic, cultural and environmental factors, which subsequently impact the health content a user would be interested in [3]. Given this close association between the factors impacting health of an individual and their subsequent health seeking behavior, we study the online health consumption of users for a large U.S. based online healthcare provider.

We firstly characterize online health consumption of users across contextual dimensions such as demographics, time and socioeconomics. Our analysis demonstrates that health interests vary substantially based on the age, gender and location attributes of an online health seeker. Further, we build a supervised model using factorization based methods to explain the topical preferences of an individual motivated by such contextual dimensions. Our analysis highlights the importance of using demographic features to understand and infer the health preferences.

2.2 Synthetic User Generation for Imbalanced Data

Given the large volumes of content being consumed by each user, the aim of this research was to predict the gender of the users given the articles they consume. Unfortunately, many real world datasets suffer from an imbalance in their user base with respect to varied attributes such as age and gender. Therefore, to address the challenge of imbalance and to infer the user attribute based on the consumed content, we proposed the URI (*User **R**epresentation and **I**nference*) framework. The framework builds a representation of users based on the content they have consumed. It consists of four main components: 1) Document vectorization, 2) Generation of user content profiles, 3) Synthetic user generation and lastly, 4) User attribute inference.

After learning representative profiles of users based on the content they have consumed, we address imbalance by building synthetic profiles for the minority user class. We use generative adversarial networks (GANs) [4] to learn a distribution of existing users. Next, we sample synthetic instances from this distribution to over-sample the minority class and create a more balanced dataset. Finally, we leverage this dataset to build a supervised model to infer the gender of the users [5].

[1] https://www.webmd.com/
[2] https://www.everydayhealth.com/

2.3 Social Signals to Inform Peace Processes Implementation and Monitoring

In the last few years, peace processes have become the dominant outcome of civil war terminations. While they have become the preferred outcome, they are protracted and contentious processes which require a significant amount of compromise and bargaining from all participants. Due to this complexity, they are subjected to a 40% chance of failure in the first 10 years of their implementation. Further, given their bureaucratic nature, they are often monitored using government and newspaper reports. As a consequence, while the peace processes are designed to bring peace to the masses, they usually lack the pulse of the nation. Therefore, we propose the use of social media to harvest key indicators such as inter-group polarization and public sentiment to study their implementation and monitor their progress.

Using 2016 Colombia final peace agreement and national referendum, we discover the Yes group (in favor) and the No group (against) and characterize the polarized groups based on their activity and content. Further, we build a predictive framework to infer the sentiment of the tweets leveraging tweet structure, content and user network features. Finally, we compare results obtained from social media analysis to compare with actual polling and referendum results. We demonstrate how social media provides large volumes of information that can be leveraged in conjunction with polls, to better understand the success or failure of a peace process. Beyond peace processes, this work also highlights how public opinion can be of key importance to other sociopolitical events such as military operations and immigration [6].

2.4 Growth Models for Polarity Change

While individuals in polarized populations behave differently, we aim to model the joint activity volume trends and predict their activity for time t_{n+1} given the trend from time $t_1,...,t_n$. In order to address this problem, we leverage the use of one of the most classic growth models in epidemiology — the Susceptible Infected (SI) model [1] as the foundation. We propose to not only leverage the growth of one group, but also study how the interaction between two differently polarized individuals affects the volume trends.

Acknowledgments: The Ph.D. study is supported in part by the Army Research Laboratory under Cooperative Agreement Number W911NF-09-2-0053 and the National Science Foundation (NSF) Grant IIS-1447795.

REFERENCES

[1] Roy M Anderson, Robert M May, and B Anderson. 1992. *Infectious diseases of humans: dynamics and control.* Vol. 28. Wiley Online Library.
[2] Alex Beutel. 2016. User Behavior Modeling with Large-Scale Graph Analysis. *Ph.D Thesis* (2016).
[3] Göran Dahlgren and Margaret Whitehead. 1991. Policies and strategies to promote social equity in health. *Stockholm: Institute for future studies* (1991).
[4] Ian Goodfellow, Jean Pouget-Abadie, Mehdi Mirza, Bing Xu, David Warde-Farley, Sherjil Ozair, Aaron Courville, and Yoshua Bengio. 2014. Generative adversarial nets. In *Advances in neural information processing systems.* 2672–2680.
[5] Aastha Nigam and Nitesh V Chawla. 2017. A Content-Driven Framework for Online User Understanding. (2017).
[6] Aastha Nigam, Henry K Dambanemuya, Madhav Joshi, and Nitesh V Chawla. 2017. Harvesting social signals to inform peace processes implementation and monitoring. *Big data* 5, 4 (2017), 1–19.

Engagement and Incentives in Online Community: Observational Data, Prediction Models, and Field Experiments

Jiezhong Qiu
Department of Computer Science and Technology, Tsinghua University
qiujz16@mails.tsinghua.edu.cn

ABSTRACT

This proposal aims to study user engagement pattern and how different incentive mechanisms influence user behavior in online communities. Work in this proposal investigates the diverse behavior patterns that different individuals follow in various online communities, and how incentive design can help increase user engagement. First, our work on MOOCs [9] leads to the discovery of behavioral heterogeneity in students' course selection as well as their learning patterns. Secondly, our work on social messaging groups [8] characterizes the formation and evolution pattern of chat groups regarding their lifecycles, structures dynamics, and underlying diffusion processes. Finally, we design and deploy a large-scale online experiment to explore how social tie, as a type of incentive, can help call back dropout users in a social game community. To the end, studying engagement and incentive offers us an opportunity to understand the fundamental principles that drive our online behaviors and activities — from individuals, to groups, to communities — and, in this way, to help design and build better online communities and organizations.

CCS CONCEPTS

• **Information systems** → **Data mining**; **Social networks**; • **Applied computing** → **Economics**; **Sociology**;

KEYWORDS

Online engagement; Incentives; Online experiment; MOOCs; Social game; Social network

ACM Reference Format:
Jiezhong Qiu. 2018. Engagement and Incentives in Online Community: Observational Data, Prediction Models, and Field Experiments. In *WSDM 2018: The Eleventh ACM International Conference on Web Search and Data Mining, February 5–9, 2018, Marina Del Rey, CA, USA.* ACM, New York, NY, USA, 2 pages. https://doi.org/10.1145/3159652.3170457

1 INTRODUCTION

The Internet offers people a variety of online communities to explore, such as MOOCs, online games, social network sites, and blogs. Characterizing and understanding the complex ways in which individuals engage with the community and respond to incentive is essential for building and maintaining online communities. In this proposal, I focus on studying the diverse behavioral patterns individuals follow within various online communities, and how to design better mechanisms for boosting user engagement.

Numerous instances of online communities created in recent years offer a rich set of user activities and interactions, including but not limited to video watching and forum discussion in MOOCs [1, 9, 16], single and group chat in social messaging services [5, 8], co-authorship and citation in academic communities [2, 10, 12], and co-play behavior in social games [3]. However, a central challenge for online communities is the low rate of user engagement, participation, and contribution. For instance, in social networks such as Facebook and Twitter, users' interactions — such as #tweets and #friends — always follow power-law distributions [4, 6, 7, 11], which indicates the phenomenon of the silent majority; In online education communities such as MOOCs, Anderson et al. [1] find that a significant number of students are bystanders — registered for the course but their total activity is below a very low threshold. In social messaging services, our previous work [8] shows that more than 40% of social groups in WeChat stop interaction within only one week. Actually, in recent years, more and more companies have realized this challenge and chosen engagement-related indicators such as MAU (monthly active users) to measure the success of their online communities [14]. Altogether, it is important to understand user engagement pattern and design effective mechanisms to motivate users to participate more in online communities. In this proposal, I aim to harness the power of data mining, social science, behavioral economics, and experimental economics to unveil, model, and understand the complex ways in which individuals involved in online communities.

In our work on MOOCS [9], we discover the significant behavioral heterogeneity in students' engagement patterns — from course selection, to forum participation, to video watching and assignment submission — in the largest Chinese MOOC platform xuetangX. For example, students who exert higher effort and ask more questions are not necessarily more likely to get certificates. Additionally, the probability that a student obtains the course certificate increases dramatically (3× higher) when she has one or more "certificate friend" in course forum.

Work on social messaging groups [8] studies the formation and evolution of groups in WeChat [15]. We discover a strong dichotomy among groups regarding their lifecycle and develop a separability model by taking into account a broad range of group-level features, showing that long-term and short-term groups are inherently distinct. In addition to modeling the growth and evolution from a group-level perspective, we investigate the individual-level attributes of group members and study the diffusion process by which groups gain new members. By considering members' historical engagement behavior as well as the local social network structure

WSDM 2018, February 5–9, 2018, Marina Del Rey, CA, USA

ACM ISBN 978-1-4503-5581-0/18/02.
https://doi.org/10.1145/3159652.3170457

that they embedded in, we develop a membership cascade model and demonstrate the effectiveness by achieving AUC of 95.31% in predicting inviter, and an AUC of 98.66% in predicting invitee.

In our ongoing work on a famous Chinese social game, King of Glory [13] (Chinese: 王者荣耀), we design and deploy a large-scale field experiment to explore how social tie increases user engagement in online game communities. In January 2017, we launched a field study of about 35 million users to test the effects of social tie theory on callback behavior. Our preliminary study shows that (1) Given a list of her dropout friends, an inviter tends to call back her intimate friends. (2) The more callback invitations one invitee received, the more likely she would come back. (3) The more callback invitations from intimate friends one invitee received, the more likely she would come back.

Collectively, the above three work offers an integral solution to understand user engagement and design better online communities through observational data, prediction models, and field experiments.

Acknowledgements. I thank Tracy Xiao Liu, Yuxiao Dong, Chenhui Zhang, and Jie Tang for their helpful comments in this Doctoral Consortium proposal.

REFERENCES

[1] Ashton Anderson, Daniel Huttenlocher, Jon Kleinberg, and Jure Leskovec. 2014. Engaging with massive online courses. In *WWW '14*. ACM, 687–698.
[2] Yuxiao Dong, Hao Ma, Zhihong Shen, and Kuansan Wang. 2017. A Century of Science: Globalization of Scientific Collaborations, Citations, and Innovations. In *KDD '17*. ACM, 1437–1446.
[3] Zhanpeng Fang, Xinyu Zhou, Jie Tang, Wei Shao, Alvis Cheuk M Fong, Longju Sun, Ying Ding, Ling Zhou, and Jarder Luo. 2014. Modeling paying behavior game social networks. In *CIKM '14*. ACM, 411–420.
[4] Haewoon Kwak, Changhyun Lee, Hosung Park, and Sue Moon. 2010. What Twitter, a social network or a news media?. In *WWW '10*. ACM, 591–600.
[5] Jure Leskovec and Eric Horvitz. 2008. Planetary-scale views on a large instar messaging network. In *WWW '08*. ACM, 915–924.
[6] Huijie Lin, Jia Jia, Jiezhong Qiu, Yongfeng Zhang, Guangyao Shen, Lexing X Jie Tang, Ling Feng, and Tat-Seng Chua. 2017. Detecting Stress Based on Soci Interactions in Social Networks. *IEEE Transactions on Knowledge and Da Engineering* (2017).
[7] Eni Mustafaraj, Samantha Finn, Carolyn Whitlock, and Panagiotis T Metaxa 2011. Vocal minority versus silent majority: Discovering the opionions of th long tail. In *PASSAT-SOCIALCOM '11*. IEEE, 103–110.
[8] Jiezhong Qiu, Yixuan Li, Jie Tang, Zheng Lu, Hao Ye, Bo Chen, Qiang Yang, ar John E Hopcroft. 2016. The lifecycle and cascade of wechat social messagin groups. In *WWW '16*. 311–320.
[9] Jiezhong Qiu, Jie Tang, Tracy Xiao Liu, Jie Gong, Chenhui Zhang, Qian Zhan and Yufei Xue. 2016. Modeling and predicting learning behavior in MOOCs. *WSDM '16*. ACM, 93–102.
[10] Jie Tang, Jing Zhang, Limin Yao, Juanzi Li, Li Zhang, and Zhong Su. 2008. A netminer: extraction and mining of academic social networks. In *KDD '08*. AC 990–998.
[11] Johan Ugander, Brian Karrer, Lars Backstrom, and Cameron Marlow. 2011. Th anatomy of the facebook social graph. *arXiv preprint arXiv:1111.4503* (2011).
[12] Chi Wang, Jiawei Han, Yuntao Jia, Jie Tang, Duo Zhang, Yintao Yu, and Jingyi Gu 2010. Mining advisor-advisee relationships from research publication network In *KDD '10*. ACM, 203–212.
[13] Wikipedia. 2017. King of Glory. (2017). en.wikipedia.org/wiki/King_of_Glory
[14] Wikipedia. 2017. List of virtual communities with more than 100 million activ users. (2017). en.wikipedia.org/wiki/List_of_virtual_communities_with_more than_100_million_active_users
[15] Wikipedia. 2017. WeChat. (2017). en.wikipedia.org/wiki/WeChat
[16] Han Zhang, Maosong Sun, Xiaochen Wang, Zhengyang Song, Jie Tang, an Jimeng Sun. 2017. Smart Jump: Automated Navigation Suggestion for Videos i MOOCs. In *WWW '17*. 331–339.

Exploiting Human Mobility Patterns for Point-of-Interest Recommendation

Zijun Yao
Rutgers University
zijun.yao@rutgers.edu

ABSTRACT

Point-of-interest (POI) recommendation, which provides personalized recommendation of places to mobile users, is an important task in location-based social networks (LBSNs). Unlike traditional interest-oriented merchandise recommendation, POI recommendation is more complex due to the *timing* effects: we need to examine whether the POI fits a user's availability. While there are some prior studies which consider temporal effects by solely using check-in timestamps for modeling, they suffer from check-in data sparsity. Recent years, the advent in positioning technology has accumulated a variety of urban data related to human mobility. There is a potential to exploit human mobility patterns from heterogeneous information sources for improving POI recommendation. To this end, we propose a novel method which incorporates the degree of temporal matching between users and POIs into personalized POI recommendations. Specifically, we profile the temporal popularity of POIs, learn the latent regularity to characterize users, and conduct comprehensive experiments with real-world data. Evaluation results demonstrate the effectiveness of the proposed method.

ACM Reference Format:
Zijun Yao. 2018. Exploiting Human Mobility Patterns for Point-of-Interest Recommendation. In *WSDM 2018: 11th ACM International Conference on Web Search & Data Mining, February 5–9, 2018, Marina Del Rey, CA, USA.* ACM, New York, NY, USA, 2 pages. https://doi.org/10.1145/3159652.3170459

1 INTRODUCTION

The rapid development of GPS equipped mobile devices (e.g., smartphones) has powered large location-based social networks (LBSNs) (e.g., Foursquare), where users share their experiences of places, also known as point-of-interests (POIs) such as restaurants or museums. POI recommendation, which suggests personalized POIs to users, becomes an important component to improve user experiences and services provided by location-based services (LBS).

Unlike traditional interest-oriented merchandise recommendation (e.g., books, films, etc.), POI recommendation is more complex and challenging due to the unique characteristics of LBS. The timing of recommended POIs should be compatible with users' personal availability. For example, if a user is usually available to explore POIs during morning hours, he would be more likely to visit POIs with morning popularity (e.g., coffee shops located in business districts); if a POI is more popular during night hours (e.g., bars located in nightlife areas), it is more rational to recommend it to users who are available at nights. To profile the changing popularity of POIs, human mobility pattern is a promising source as people concentrate to different places at different times throughout a day (e.g., work, entertainment). In Figure 1, we provide an example of New York City (NYC) to show that human mobility patterns are highly correlated with LBSN check-in behaviors. In the morning hours, we can see that people are mainly concentrated in two business regions: Midtown and Financial District. The check-ins are also around these two locations. In the night hours, people leave business regions where they work, and go to restaurant & nightlife areas where check-ins also become dense.

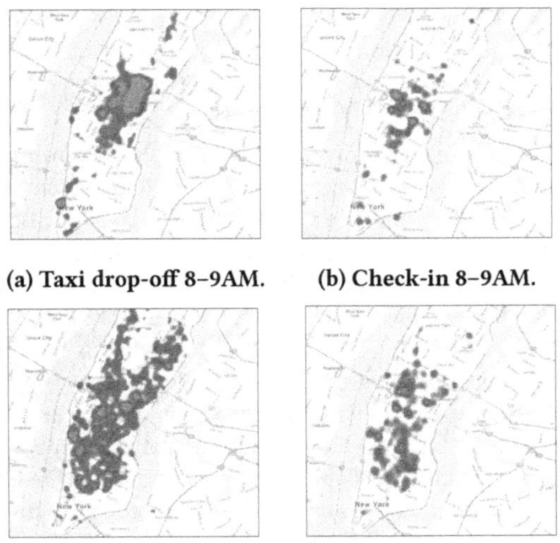

(a) Taxi drop-off 8–9AM. **(b) Check-in 8–9AM.**
(c) Taxi drop-off 8–9PM. **(d) Check-in 8–9PM.**

Figure 1: Heatmap of taxi riders and LBSN users at different time slot of weekday in New York City (NYC).

In this study, we propose a Temporal Matching Poisson Factorization Model (TM-PFM) to profile the popularity of POIs, model the regularity of users, and incorporate the temporal matching between users and POIs into overall consideration [4]. We first present a new framework to profile time-varying popularity patterns of POIs (e.g., hourly visit probability changes in a day). Previous studies [1, 5] have demonstrated that human mobility is highly regular and predictable, and human mobility data from heterogeneous sources display similar patterns. Therefore, we utilize heterogeneous human mobility data to assess POI popularity. The benefits of employing human mobility data include (i) it is more abundant and less biased than check-in data, and (ii) it reveals which areas are currently active, thus it strongly effects POI popularity. Moreover, we further analyze POIs by categories and adopt a mixture model to obtain the final POI temporal popularity pattern. Secondly, except some

WSDM 2018, February 5–9, 2018, Marina Del Rey, CA, USA

ACM ISBN 978-1-4503-5581-0/18/02.
https://doi.org/10.1145/3159652.3170459

particular events (e.g., parties, concerts), people's availability is usually determined by their routines, thus there is a predictable regularity. Therefore, we consider a temporal regularity pattern of each user which describes their regular available hours every day for POI exploration. We propose to learn the latent regularity patterns of users by finding the best match with the popularity patterns of visited POI based on check-in frequencies. Finally, with the learned user regularity, we are able to match users with POIs they have not visited yet, and consider the temporal matching score for final recommendation.

2 GENERAL FRAMEWORK

Step 1: Profiling Temporal Patterns of POI Popularity. We aim at profiling the temporal popularity of POIs which describes how the popularity of a POI varies during a day. Specifically, we split a day into S equal-sized time slots (e.g., 24 hours), and each time slot is associated with a probability describing the ratio of the time slot visit volume to the whole day visit volume. We package these S probabilities chronologically as a vector which is the temporal pattern of popularity to be profiled. To achieve this, we first extract the area activity (e.g., how many active people in the area) around POI locations by utilizing human mobility patterns. Subsequently, we extract the category popularity by aggregating the check-in frequencies at the POI category level to refine the profiling. Lastly, we use a mixture model to smooth and further characterize the temporal pattern of POI popularity.

Step 2: Modeling Temporal Matching of user-POI pairs. We aim to develop a user-POI temporal matching model to infer the temporal regularity of users. First, we consider that each user has regular available time slots every day due to personal routines, and users are more likely to visit a POI at its popular times. We associate the vector of S time slots with probabilities to show how likely a user may explore POIs during a specific time slot in a day. Then we define the inner product of a user regularity vector and a POI popularity vector as the temporal matching score for any specific user-POI pair. Finally, combining the temporal matching score and the general interest score (inferred using matrix factorization) as the overall preference for every user-POI pair, we optimize users' latent regularities by minimizing the distance between the estimated preferences and the ground-truth frequencies of history check-ins.

3 EXPERIMENT

We perform all the experiments on real-world datasets of the New York City: LSBN data from Foursquare, human mobility data from taxi trip records.

We recommend each user a list of N POIs which have the highest predicted values but are not visited in training set. Then we evaluate the lists based on the recommended POIs which are actually visited by users in testing set. F-measure is the harmonic mean of precision and recall. We adopt a unbalance F-measure F_β which puts more emphasis on precision than recall by setting $\beta = 0.5$:

$$F_\beta = (1 + \beta^2) \cdot \frac{\text{Precision} \cdot \text{Recall}}{\beta^2 \text{Precision} + \text{Recall}}. \quad (1)$$

The experimental study compares our proposed temporal matching Poisson factor model (**TM-PFM**) with state-of-the-art factor-based models. Specifically, we compare our proposed TM-PFM

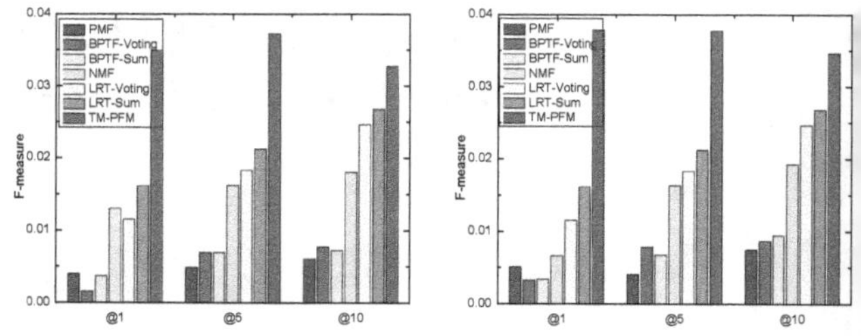

(a) F-measure, K=10. (b) F-measure, K=20.

Figure 2: F_β measure @1, @5 and @10 with two different latent dimensions K.

model with following algorithms: Probabilistic Matrix Factorization (**PMF**), Non-negative Matrix Factorization (**NMF**), Bayesian Probabilistic Tensor Factorization (**BPTF**) [3], Location Recommendation with Temporal effects (**LRT**) [2]. Since BPTF and LRT are temporal recommendation model, we obtain the overall preference for POIs by aggregating the preference at each time slot in two ways: Sum and Voting. For top-N position, we examine $N = 1, 5, 10$. For latent factor dimension, we explore $K = 10$ and $K = 20$. As shown in Figure 2, we can see that our proposed approach TM-PFM consistently outperforms baseline methods, including traditional recommendation models (PMF, NMF) as well as the temporal recommendation model (BPTF, LRT) for different N and different K.

4 CONCLUSION

In this study, we aim to developed a POI recommendation model by exploiting human mobility patterns for temporal matching between users and POIs. The open research issues are following: First, check-in data suffers from the sparsity problem that very few check-ins happen in unpopular areas and time periods. Therefore, human mobility data which is highly correlated with check-in behaviors can help to enhance POI recommendation based on two advantages: (i) it is more abundant and less biased than check-in data, and (ii) it reveals the activity of areas which is a determinant to effect POI popularity. Moreover, since human mobility data and check-in data are usually heterogeneous information sources, there is a challenge for developing ways to incorporate the knowledge of human mobility patterns into POI recommendation. In this study we propose the incorporation in terms of temporal aspect. In the future work, we aim to develop methods to exploit human mobility patterns in spatial aspect through origin-destination analysis.

REFERENCES

[1] Eunjoon Cho, Seth A Myers, and Jure Leskovec. 2011. Friendship and mobility: user movement in location-based social networks. In *Proceedings of the 17th ACM SIGKDD international conference on Knowledge discovery and data mining*. ACM, 1082–1090.

[2] Huiji Gao, Jiliang Tang, Xia Hu, and Huan Liu. 2013. Exploring temporal effects for location recommendation on location-based social networks. In *RecSys*. ACM, 93–100.

[3] Liang Xiong, Xi Chen, Tzu-Kuo Huang, Jeff G Schneider, and Jaime G Carbonell. 2010. Temporal Collaborative Filtering with Bayesian Probabilistic Tensor Factorization.. In *SDM*, Vol. 10. SIAM, 211–222.

[4] Zijun Yao, Yanjie Fu, Bin Liu, Yanchi Liu, and Hui Xiong. 2016. POI Recommendation: A Temporal Matching between POI Popularity and User Regularity. In *IEEE 16th International Conference on Data Mining (ICDM)*. IEEE, 549–558.

[5] Yu Zheng, Quannan Li, Yukun Chen, Xing Xie, and Wei-Ying Ma. 2008. Understanding mobility based on GPS data. In *Proceedings of the 10th international conference on Ubiquitous computing*. ACM, 312–321.

Percolator: Scalable Pattern Discovery in Dynamic Graphs

Sutanay Choudhury
Pacific Northwest National Laboratory, USA
sutanay.choudhury@pnnl.gov

Sumit Purohit
Pacific Northwest National Laboratory, USA
sumit.purohit@pnnl.gov

Peng Lin
Washington State University, USA
plin1@eecs.wsu.edu

Yinghui Wu
Washington State University, USA
Pacific Northwest National Laboratory, USA
yinghui@eecs.wsu.edu

Lawrence Holder
Washington State University, USA
holder@eecs.wsu.edu

Khushbu Agarwal
Pacific Northwest National Laboratory, USA
khushbu.agarwal@pnnl.gov

ABSTRACT

We demonstrate Percolator, a distributed system for graph pattern discovery in dynamic graphs. In contrast to conventional mining systems, Percolator advocates efficient pattern mining schemes that (1) support pattern detection with keywords; (2) integrate incremental and parallel pattern mining; and (3) support analytical queries such as trend analysis. The core idea of Percolator is to dynamically decide and verify a small fraction of patterns and their instances that must be inspected in response to buffered updates in dynamic graphs, with a total mining cost independent of graph size. We demonstrate a) the feasibility of incremental pattern mining by walking through each component of Percolator, b) the efficiency and scalability of Percolator over the sheer size of real-world dynamic graphs, and c) how the user-friendly GUI of Percolator interacts with users to support keyword-based queries that detect, browse and inspect trending patterns. We demonstrate how our system effectively supports event and trend analysis in social media streams and research publication, respectively.

CCS CONCEPTS

• **Information systems → Data stream mining**; • **Theory of computation → Dynamic graph algorithms**;

KEYWORDS

Graph mining; parallel system; data stream

ACM Reference Format:
Sutanay Choudhury, Sumit Purohit, Peng Lin, Yinghui Wu, Lawrence Holder, and Khushbu Agarwal. 2018. Percolator: Scalable Pattern Discovery in Dynamic Graphs. In *Proceedings of WSDM 2018: The Eleventh ACM International Conference on Web Search and Data Mining (WSDM 2018).* ACM, New York, NY, USA, 4 pages. https://doi.org/10.1145/3159652.3160589

WSDM 2018, February 5–9, 2018, Marina Del Rey, CA, USA

ACM ISBN 978-1-4503-5581-0/18/02…$15.00
https://doi.org/10.1145/3159652.3160589

1 INTRODUCTION

Discovering emerging events from massive dynamic data is a critical need in a wide range of applications. Real-world events in dynamic networks (*e.g.,* Web, social media and cyber networks) are often represented as *graph patterns.* Although desirable, discovering such patterns is more challenging than its counterpart over item streams [2]. It requires effective querying and mining over graphs that bear constant changes, while pattern mining is already expensive over static graphs [5, 8]. Moreover, it is hard to reduce the computational complexity (NP-hard). Pattern discovery should also support keyword input, *i.e.,* to discover and track patterns relevant to user-specified keywords.

One approach is to leverage incremental computation that has been applied to update query results [6]. The idea is to dynamically identify a fraction of data that must be inspected to update the patterns in response to changes. Another method is to develop parallel mining [7] to cope with the sheer amount of data. *Can we combine parallel and incremental computation to support scalable pattern discovery in massive dynamic graphs?*

Percolator. This motivates us to develop Percolator, a prototype system that combines both incremental mining and parallel mining for feasible pattern detection over graph streams. It differs from conventional systems with the following unique new features.

(1) Keyword specified patterns. Percolator supports the discovery of (general) graph patterns that pertain to user-specified keywords. It finds informative and concise patterns characterized by maximal patterns and their activeness measures. It also supports both ad-hoc top pattern detection and offline trend analysis.

(2) Incremental mining. Percolator supports *incremental* pattern mining to avoid rediscover patterns from scratch upon receiving changes. Given discovered patterns Σ over a graph, and a batch of edge updates, it incrementally updates Σ by automatically tracking and only re-verifying a set of patterns and matches. This avoids unnecessary computation from scratch, with a cost only determined by the changes of results and data, but independent of the graph size.

(3) Scale-up. Percolator is a parallel system implemented on top of Apache Spark. It parallelizes the incremental graph mining by dynamically constructing and exchanging messages that contain affected patterns and triples needed for incremental verification, in parallel and only when necessary. This reduces communication cost and ensures the scalability.

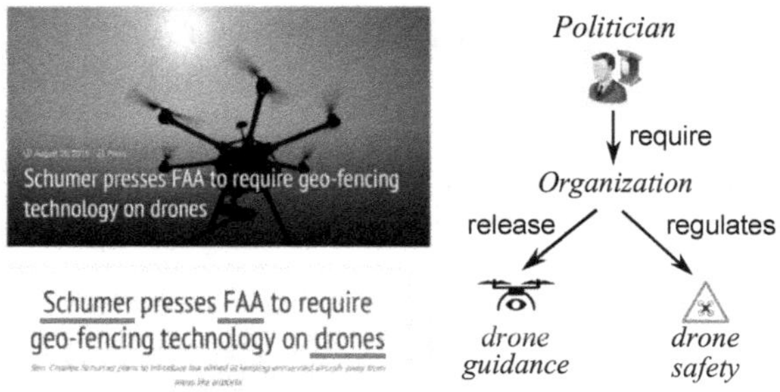

Figure 1: Emerging event pattern from News data as triples

(4) Easy-to-use. The Percolator system is easy to use. It provides a user-friendly GUI, a built-in natural-language query constructor to support keyword-based pattern discovery, a visualization component to inspect and interpret the results.

Demo overview. We next demonstrate Percolator as follows. (1) We walk through each component of Percolator from pattern models to incremental and parallel mining, to demonstrate the feasibility of Percolator over massive dynamic graphs. (2) We demonstrate the applications of Percolator with real-world event analysis scenarios in social media (news) and academic data. We demonstrate its query interface, performance analysis and visual analysis interface to demonstrate emerging events and their text interpretations.

2 PATTERN AND GRAPH STREAM MODELS

We start with the graph streams and the pattern model in Percolator.

Dynamic Graph. Percolator models a dynamic graph $\mathcal{G}_T$ as a set of triples with timestamps. Each triple e=< s, p, o > consists of a subject s, predicate p (a relation) and an object o, and each of s, p and o has a label (*e.g.*, URI). (1) A snapshot of $\mathcal{G}_T$ at time i is a graph G_i induced by triples at time i. (2) At each timestamp i, a batch of triples ΔE updates snapshot G_i to G_{i+1}.

Patterns. A pattern P is a labeled connected graph $(V_p, E_p, \bar{u})$ with a set of labeled pattern nodes V_p and a set of labeled pattern edges $E_p \subseteq V_p \times V_p$. Given a set of keywords $\mathcal{K}=\{k_1, \ldots k_n\}$, a pattern P pertains to $\mathcal{K}$ if for every keyword k_i $i \in [1, n]$, there exists a keyword node u_i in P such that $L(u_i)=k_i$.

Activeness. By default, Percolator characterizes active patterns with *minimum image support* [1]. Given a snapshot G_i, a pattern P and a set of (user-specified) keyword nodes $\bar{u}$ in P, the activeness of P in G_i (Act(P, G_i)) is quantified as min $|\{M(u)|u \in \bar{u}\}|$, where $M(u)$ refers to the matches of node u induced by all the subgraph isomorphisms from P to G_i, and u ranges over $\bar{u}$. Given an activeness threshold θ, P is active in G_i *w.r.t.* θ if Act$(P, G_i) \geq \theta$. We remark that the activeness of P preserves *anti-monotonicity* [1] *w.r.t.* a fixed $\bar{u}$: at any time i, Act$(P, G_i) \leq$ Act(P', G_i) *w.r.t.* a fixed set of keyword nodes, if P' is obtained by adding edges to P.

Maximal patterns. We are interested in detecting "informative" patterns as maximal ones. Indeed, small patterns may be active, but usually tend to be trivial ones. A pattern P is maximal in G_i *w.r.t.* threshold θ, if (1) P is active *w.r.t.* θ, and (2) there exists no active super-pattern P' of P. Percolator discovers maximal patterns that pertain to a set of user-specified keywords $\mathcal{K}$.

Example 1: Figure 1 illustrates an active pattern detected an tracked by Percolator, specified by keywords "*Politician*", "*dron* and "*organization*". It is discovered in a dynamic graph (RDF triple extracted from news articles by Nous [3], a knowledge graph co struction engine. The pattern and its matches reveal events regar ing emerging concerns of drone safety. It verifies that *politiciar* (*e.g.*, "Schumer") are pressing *organizations* (*e.g.*, "Federal Aviatio Administration (FAA)") to regulate *drones* and provide *guidance.*

Pattern discovery in dynamic graphs. Given a dynamic grap $\mathcal{G}_T$, a set of keywords $\mathcal{K}$, a set of active patterns Σ pertain to $\mathcal{T}$ (obtained by"from-scratch" discovery), Percolator updates Σ in re sponse to a set of edge transactions ΔE applied to G, without re discovery Σ from scratch, and outputs updated Σ upon request.

3 FOUNDATIONS OF PERCOLATOR

The Percolator system is built on two principles: *incremental pa tern mining* and *parallel mining.* (1) Instead of discovering pattern from scratch, each time $\mathcal{G}_T$ is updated, it performs necessary co putation that suffices to update Σ (Section 3.1). (2) To scale the pr cess over large $\mathcal{G}_T$, it performs incremental mining in parallel, an aggregates the changes to update Σ (Section 3.2).

3.1 Incremental Discovery

Percolator dynamically identifies and only verifies a set of "affecte patterns that must be inspected in order to update Σ. This nove principle is implemented by three core components: *Stream Mar ager, Affected Pattern Detector* and *Incremental Verifier.*

Stream manager. The stream manager of Percolator processe $\mathcal{G}_T$ as a triple stream and manages the built-in structures below.

Triple Buffer. Percolator uses a buffer B with a tunable size to cach the edge updates in *batches.* (1) It caches the updates ΔE in multipl batches bounded by the buffer size. It also maintains a buffer ma $B.M$, which points each triple $e \in B$ to a single-edge pattern $B.M(e$ having e as a match. A pattern P is "hit" by e if P contains a patter edge $B.M(e)$. (2) Percolator applies a novel *load shedding* strateg to prune triples in B: only triples with one end node having a key word label is cached for processing. Indeed, only these triples ma affect the activeness of patterns by the definition of activeness. Al others are applied to G directly without further processing.

Affected Pattern Detector. The manager maintains the activ events with a lattice $\mathcal{T}$ as commonly used in constrained grap mining. In addition, it tracks the activeness of the patterns. Upo receiving a batch of triples $\Delta E_B \subseteq \Delta E$, the *affected pattern detecto* of Percolator interacts with incremental verifier (to be discussed and dynamically identifies a "minimal" set $\mathcal{P}$ of patterns that ar necessary to be inspected to update Σ. (1) It initializes $\mathcal{P}$ as the pat terns "hit" by $e.M$, and sends $\mathcal{P}$ to the incremental verifier to up date their activeness. (2) For each verified pattern $P \in \mathcal{P}$, it "prop agates" $\mathcal{P}$ by taking two actions below.

Downward propagation: If Act$(P, G_i) \geq \theta$, it updates $\mathcal{P}$ as:

$$\mathcal{P} := \mathcal{P} \cup P^+,$$

where P^+ refers to the patterns obtained by adding an edge to P *i.e.*, the possible "children" of P in $\mathcal{T}$. That is, it simulates the ex ploration of larger patterns in $\mathcal{T}$ as P remains to be active.

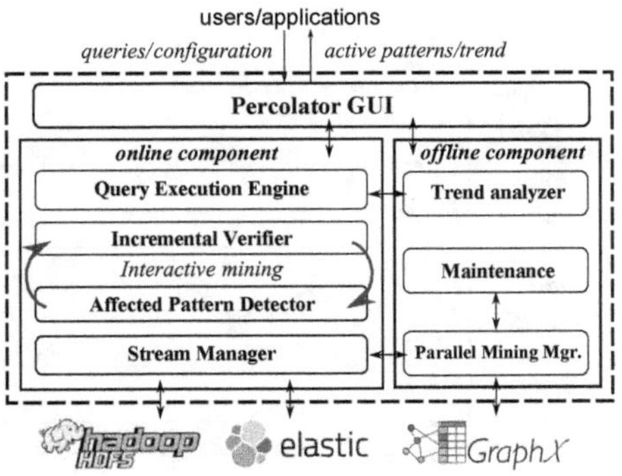

Figure 2: Architecture of Percolator

***Upward propagation**:* If $\text{Act}(P, G_i) < \theta$ (*i.e.*, becomes inactive due to *e.g.*, decrease in edge frequency), it updates $\mathcal{P}$ as:

$$\mathcal{P} := \mathcal{P} \cup P^-,$$

where P^- refers to the "parents" of P in $\mathcal{T}$, obtained by removing an edge from P. That is, it explores smaller patterns that may become new maximal ones as P becomes inactive.

Note that both P^+ and P^- (including new patterns) can be constructed without reconstructing $\mathcal{T}$ from scratch. The detector stops downward (resp. upward) propagation at pattern P if P^+ (resp. P^-) is $\emptyset$, and checks whether no child of P is active. If so, it inserts P to Σ as a newly discovered maximal pattern.

Incremental Verifier. The *Incremental Verifier* of Percolator updates the activeness of each pattern $P \in \mathcal{P}$. If P is affected, it updates $\text{Act}(P, G_i)$ by "incrementalizing" the conventional subgraph isomorphism test, which processes single-edge patterns in $\mathcal{T}$ hit by $B.M$ and "percolate-up" to P (see below). (2) Otherwise, P is obtained by either upward or downward propagation, and $\text{Act}(P, G_i)$ remains to be the same.

Percolate-up. The Incremental Verifier adopts a "*percolate-up*" strategy to reduce the processing cost of updates. Given ΔE^B, it partitions ΔE^B into groups by consulting the buffer map $B.M$, where each group hits a single-edge pattern P_0. For each pattern $P \in \mathcal{P}$, it then evaluates a sequence of patterns $\{P_0, \ldots, P_j\}$ sorted by their size, such that P_i is a sub-pattern of P_{i+1} ($i \in [0, j-1]$), and P_j=P. That is, it "*percolates*" the edges up against the affected patterns, from smaller ones to larger ones. Moreover, it never re-evaluates a pattern P_i if P_i is verified (in other sequences). This effectively reduces redundant verifications (especially for "overlapping" patterns that share sub-patterns), and early terminates at inactive patterns, guaranteed by the anti-monotonicity of the activeness.

Upon each batch of updates, Percolator interleaves Affected Pattern Detector and Incremental Verifier to "lazily" perform necessary amount of verification. The interaction repeats until no pattern can be added to $\mathcal{P}$. It then reports updated Σ upon request.

3.2 Parallel mining

To cope with large $\mathcal{G}_T$, Percolator parallelizes the incremental mining over a set of distributed, shared-nothing workers.

Parallel mining manager. This component executes the parallel computation of Percolator. It maintains the following. (1) A fragmentation $\mathcal{F}$ of dynamic graph $\mathcal{G}_T$ is a partition of the snapshot G over n workers $\{F_1, \ldots, F_n\}$, where each worker W_j manages a subgraph G_j of G. By default, Percolator applies balanced 2*D* partition. (2) The batch updates ΔE_i is fragmented as $\{\Delta E_1, \ldots, \Delta E_n\}$, where each ΔE_j changes F_i to $F_i \oplus \Delta E_j$, respectively. (3) The pattern lattice $\mathcal{T}$ is synchronized among all the workers.

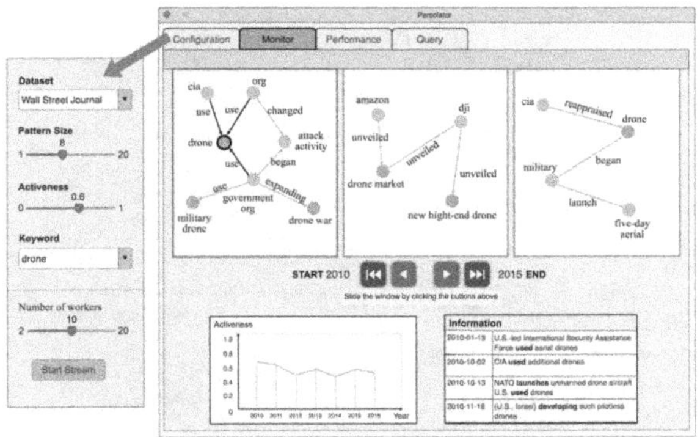

Figure 3: Percolator GUI

Parallel mining. Given $\mathcal{F}$ and a batch of updates ΔE, Percolator "parallelizes" the sequential incremental mining (Section 3.1) following a Bulk Synchronous Parallel model, and runs in supersteps.

(1) Upon receiving ΔE_j, each worker W_j invokes Affected Pattern Detector to identify a local set of affected patterns $\mathcal{P}_j$ due to local changes of F_j, and invokes Incremental Verifier to update their local activeness, in parallel. For each pattern P with diameter d that cannot be verified locally, it extends F_j with d-hop neighbors of the "border" nodes of F_j in G and performs local verification.

(2) Once all the workers complete the local verification, the coordinator W_o computes affected patterns $\mathcal{P}$=$\bigcup_{j \in [1,n]} \mathcal{P}_j$, assembles the local activeness of each pattern in $\mathcal{P}$, and updates Σ when necessary. It then broadcasts $\mathcal{P}$ to all workers.

The above two steps repeat until no new affected patterns can be added to $\mathcal{P}$, and all the affected patterns are verified. Percolator then returns Σ updated at the coordinator W_o.

4 SYSTEM OVERVIEW

Architecture. Percolator consists of three components (Figure 2).

Online pattern discovery: consists of four modules, including *Stream Manager, Affected Pattern Detector, Incremental Verification* (Section 3.1), and a *query execution engine* to evaluate ad-hoc queries.

Offline pattern analysis: consists of three modules, including a *trend analyzer* to support trend analysis, a *maintenance component* to synchronize the changes to underlying graphs, and the *parallel mining manager* to manage the distributed environment, *e.g.*, the parallel configuration, data partitioning and fault-tolerance.

GUI. The user-friendly Percolator GUI (illustrated in Figure 3) contains a *configuration panel* to receive configurations (*e.g.*, activeness threshold, number of workers). Users can browse and inspect active patterns in the *monitor panel*, which includes the activeness curve, and the details of their matches. The *performance panel* (not shown) visualizes performance analysis. Finally, a built-in *Query panel* allows users to issue natural-language style queries, supported by built-in query parsers.

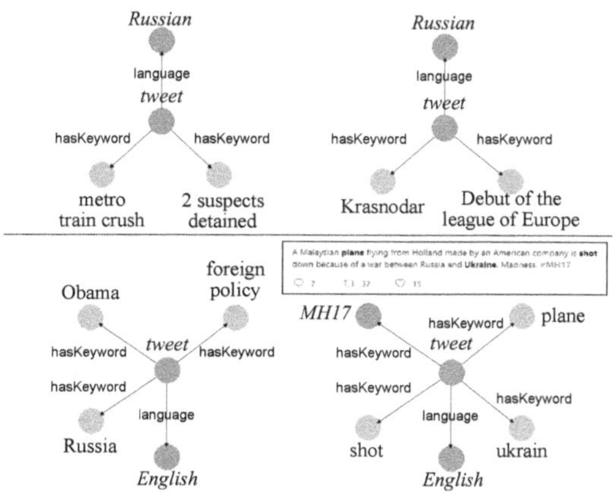

Figure 4: Top-k Twitter Patterns

Implementation. Percolator is implemented in Scala, and built on top of Apache Spark and HDFS with core functions in GraphX library. The graph stream is represented as distributed arrays (RDDs) managed by Spark. To support fast stream access, it uses in-memory Elasticsearch[1] to manage the intermediate results (*e.g.*, the mapping in Stream Manager) as key-value pairs. Percolator utilizes our prior systems for graph construction [3] and querying [4] as input and verification interfaces, respectively.

5 DEMONSTRATION OVERVIEW

The target audience of the demo includes anyone who is interested in understanding complex events and trends over data streams. Our system[2] is deployed on a cluster of 16 nodes (with one serving as the coordinator). Each node is equipped with an Intel Xeon processor (2.3 GHz) with 16 cores and 64 GB memory.

Settings. We use the following settings.

Datasets. Our real world datasets include: (1) **Twitter**, a collection of dynamic knowledge graphs with in total 5 million triples and in batches of 1.5 million triples per day. (2) **MAG**, a citation network with 153.6 million triples. Each batch of triples contains 8 million nodes and 22 million edges in one year window.

Ad-hoc queries. We invite users to inspect patterns discovered by the following two classes of ad-hoc queries: (1) Top-k active events: *"What are the current k most active patterns?"* and (2) Targeted trends: *"Tell me emerging patterns pertaining to specified keywords."*

System comparison. We compare Percolator with Arabesque [7], a state-of-the-art parallel graph mining system. Arabesque does not support mining over dynamic graphs. Thus we develop a "batch" version that interleaves buffered updates and from scratch mining.

Scenario. We invite users to experience the following scenarios. *Performance of* Percolator. Users are invited to configure Percolator and compare the performance of Percolator and Arabesque. We show that Percolator scales well. Over **MAG**, its performance is improved by 2.5 times when the number of workers varies from 2 to 8. Percolator is quite efficient: it takes 245 seconds to process 10 million updates per batch with 8 workers in parallel. In contrast, Arabesque does not run to completion using the same setting.

[1] https://www.elastic.co/products/elasticsearch

[2] available at https://github.com/streaming-graphs/NOUS

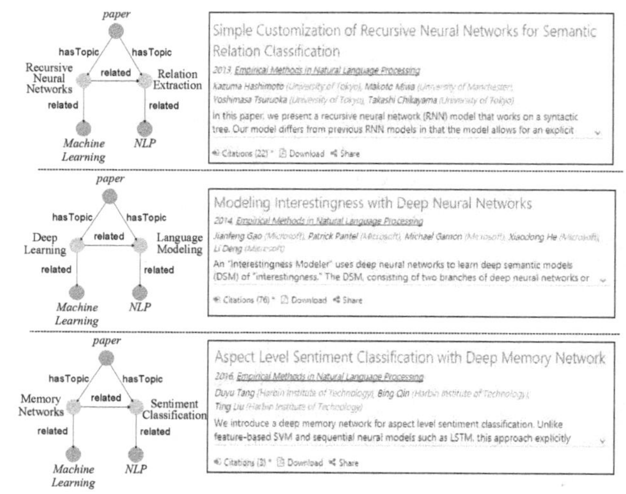

Figure 5: Trend of specified research topics (2013-2016)

Top Event Analysis. Using **Twitter**, we show that given keywords Percolator effectively tracks top events and their evolution.

Example 2: A top-1 query with three keywords "twitter", "MH17 and "English" finds the most active patterns in English tweets related to "MH17". As shown by the two patterns at bottom in Figure 4, Percolator identifies a shift of twitter topics before and after the event of MH17 plane crash in English tweets. When changing keywords "English" to "Russian", it finds that Russian tweets are less fazed by the event (shown by the two active patterns at the top).

Trend analysis. We next demonstrate that Percolator detects the trend of specified topics, with trend queries over **MAG**.

Example 3: Figure 5 illustrates a trend discovered by Percolator when user specifies trend queries with keywords "Machine Learning", "paper" and "NLP". As verified by the matched triples in **MAG** the trend shows the most active and relevant research topics change from "Recursive Neural Network" (2013-14) to "Deep learning" (2014-15) and "Memory networks" (2015-16).

REFERENCES

[1] Björn Bringmann and Siegfried Nijssen. 2008. What is frequent in a single graph? In *PAKDD*. 858–863.

[2] Yun Chi, Haixun Wang, Philip S. Yu, and Richard R. Muntz. [n. d.]. Moment Maintaining Closed Frequent Itemsets over a Stream Sliding Window *(ICDM '04)*.

[3] Sutanay Choudhury, Khushbu Agarwal, Sumit Purohit, Baichuan Zhang, Meg Pirrung, Will Smith, and Mathew Thomas. 2017. Nous: Construction and querying of dynamic knowledge graphs. In *ICDE*.

[4] Sutanay Choudhury, Lawrence Holder, George Chin, Khushbu Agarwal, and John Feo. 2015. A selectivity based approach to continuous pattern detection in streaming graphs. *EDBT* (2015).

[5] Mohammed Elseidy, Ehab Abdelhamid, Spiros Skiadopoulos, and Panos Kalnis. 2014. GRAMI: Frequent Subgraph and Pattern Mining in a Single Large Graph. *PVLDB* (2014).

[6] Wenfei Fan, Jianzhong Li, Jizhou Luo, Zijing Tan, Xin Wang, and Yinghui Wu. 2011. Incremental graph pattern matching *(SIGMOD '11)*.

[7] Carlos HC et al. Teixeira. 2015. Arabesque: a system for distributed graph mining. In *Proceedings of the 25th Symposium on Operating Systems Principles*.

[8] Xifeng Yan and Jiawei Han. 2002. gSpan: Graph-Based Substructure Pattern Mining. In *ICDM*.

Conversational Semantic Search: Looking Beyond Web Search, Q&A and Dialog Systems

Paul A. Crook, Alex Marin, Vipul Agarwal, Samantha Anderson, Ohyoung Jang, Aliasgar Lanewala, Karthik Tangirala, Imed Zitouni
Microsoft Corporation, Redmond, WA
[pacrook,alemari,vipulag,samande,ohjang,Aliasgar.Lanewala,kartang,izitouni]@microsoft.com

ABSTRACT

User expectations of web search are changing. They are expecting search engines to answer questions, to be more conversational, and to offer means to complete tasks on their behalf. At the same time, to increase the breadth of tasks that personal digital assistants (PDAs), such as Microsoft's Cortana or Amazon's Alexa, are capable of, PDAs need to better utilize information about the world, a significant amount of which is available in the knowledge bases and answers built for search engines. It thus seems likely that the underlying systems that power web search and PDAs will converge. This demonstration presents a system that merges elements of traditional multi-turn dialog systems with web based question answering. This demo focuses on the automatic composition of semantic functional units, *Botlets*, to generate responses to user's natural language (NL) queries. We show that such a system can be trained to combine information from search engine answers with PDA tasks to enable new user experiences.

ACM Reference Format:
Paul A. Crook, Alex Marin, Vipul Agarwal, Samantha Anderson, Ohyoung Jang, Aliasgar Lanewala, Karthik Tangirala, Imed Zitouni. 2018. Conversational Semantic Search: Looking Beyond Web Search, Q&A and Dialog Systems. In *Proceedings of WSDM 2018: The Eleventh ACM International Conference on Web Search and Data Mining , Marina Del Rey, CA, USA, February 5–9, 2018 (WSDM 2018),* 4 pages.
https://doi.org/10.1145/3159652.3160590

1 INTRODUCTION

An increasing number of companies are investing in personal digital assistants (PDAs) as gateways to capture and retain users in their ecosystem of services and devices, *e.g.* Microsoft's Cortana, Apple's Siri, Google Assistant, Amazon's Alexa, Samsung's Bixbi. While the range of skills and tasks that these PDAs can complete is rapidly increasing, their apparent intelligence is limited by the set of inhomogeneous back-end systems that are typically used to power such PDAs [6, 8]. The back-end systems typically exchange only limited information, if any, and the PDA engine as a whole often lacks an ability to connect or perform inference over the information they provide. Thus the PDA is often ignorant of the information shown by a particular back-end and is unable to connect it with subsequent turns in the conversation.

At the same time, web search engines are also evolving. Gone are the days where Google and Bing would show only blue links that users have to click on. Users are now presented with *entity cards e.g.* the sunrise definition in figure 1, or *answer cards, e.g.* the sunrise time answer dominating the top left of the figure 1. These cards can contain details of computed answers or the best matching well-known-entity (people, places, companies, *etc.*). Search results can also include carousels (not shown) of local restaurants or shopping opportunities related to the search query. A click, instead of leading through to a web page, can launch the user's preferred app. to complete a restaurant reservation or a purchase. This search engine richness is a significant knowledge resource that PDAs often fall-back, *e.g.* compare the left and middle panels of figure 1. Such responses are powered through both knowledge bases, and hand crafted functions. Better utilization of the rich stream of information that search engines make available could lead to a significant improvement in the usefulness and versatility of PDAs.

As search engines start to behave more like PDAs, and PDAs try to tap the knowledge built up by search engines, it seems likely that the underlying technologies will merge and a new breed of conversational-search engines will emerge. A key integration point is the semantically rich data of entities and relationships built up by search engines. With this in mind we adopt the term *Conversational Semantic Search* to broadly describe architectures such as the one presented here. We aim for an architecture that manages contextual multi-turn conversation with users. In this demo, we focus on the automatic composition of answers and PDA skills/tasks to deliver new user experience to both web search and PDA users.

The remainder of this paper is structured as follows; section 2 briefly describes related work, section 3 describes the demonstration user experience, section 4 the system operation and architecture, and section 5 concludes.

2 BACKGROUND

The authors are not aware of prior efforts to marry semantic web search (over knowledge bases that contain both knowledge entities and actions) with conversational agents (that track state information) in a single architecture.

Dipper [2] (an implementation of an information-state dialog manager (DM) [4]), and Ravenclaw [1] are among the closest DM to the demonstrated system. In Dipper and Ravenclaw, tasks are described using sets of rules and hierarchies of agents, respectively. Each rule/agent handles a sub-part of the interaction, which is akin to the function of Botlets in the current proposal. Principal differences are that in the former systems the set of rules/agents are fixed,

WSDM 2018, February 5–9, 2018, Marina Del Rey, CA, USA

ACM ISBN 978-1-4503-5581-0/18/02...$15.00
https://doi.org/10.1145/3159652.3160590

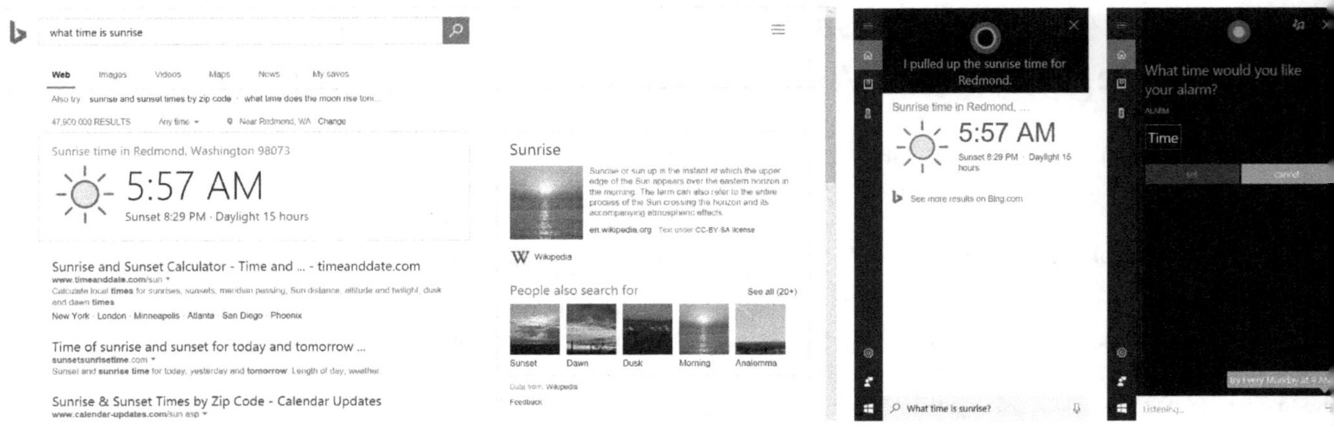

Figure 1: Left panel, Bing web search displaying an *answer card* (dominant top left) and *entity card* (right) in response to the query "what time is sunrise". Middle panel, Cortana responding to the same spoken query. Right panel, Cortana responding to "set an alarm."

they directly manipulate a shared dialog state, and dialog task developers predefine when rules/agents get executed. In the proposed platform, the state tracker builds and tracks the state over an evolving graph of entities and Botlets (the latter encoding "rules/agents" as mini-procedures with program counter and stack), where graph edges correspond to variables (both bound and unbound) and nodes represent data objects (entities) or Botlets. A Botlet's availability is dynamically determined by a search step that inserts it into the graph. A trained policy decides when or whether to execute it. A motivating factor for this architecture is that it allows extension through the addition of new Botlets via mechanisms akin to web crawling and information retrieval.

Future work considers training the system using sequential decision making. In this regard, the proposed system has similarities with sequential decision formulations of interactive information retrieval and session search approaches [5, 9]. In the proposed system, user-system dialogs can be viewed as form of query refinement.

3 DEMO EXPERIENCE

Users who type "What time is sunrise" into any of today's dominant search engines can expect their question to be immediately answered as shown in the left panel of figure 1. Similarly they can expect a PDA to understand the required information and actions that are needed in order to fulfil the request "set an alarm". Even though that same PDA is able to answer the question "What time is sunrise?", middle panel of figure 1, it is currently unlikely that the set-alarm dialog, right panel of figure 1, will have general access to functions which return the specific time of such events. Without access to the specific time it cannot successfully complete a dialogue like "Set an alarm", "For when?", "For sunrise." Or, even more challenging in terms of the additional inference required, "Set an alarm for 20 minutes before sunrise."

Although it is possible to engineer solutions to individual examples, for instance building the sunrise and sunset tables into a natural language understanding (NLU) component, our aim is to design a more general approach which will automatically scale to cover the possible combinations. An approach which, for example, also covers requests such as "Create a reminder to download the latest sales results an hour before my meeting with my boss." and "Get me driving directions to my next meeting."

Our solution is to break the problem down into functional units which we call Botlets. Botlets are transformational functions with side-effects; mini-procedures, currently hand authored, with formal input and output semantics. They both provide mappings between semantic types and capture sub-parts of procedures required to complete specific actions on behalf of the user, including requesting information from users, or booking tickets (hence the side-effects). Botlets are invoked in sequence by a policy. Learnt execution sequences of Botlets correspond to the execution of dialogue flow required to complete tasks.

Specifically, in this demo, it is possible to ask "what time is sunrise?", "when is 20 minutes before sunrise?", or even "when is 20 minutes after 1 hour before sunset" (essentially some combination of qualifiers and some event) and get an answer. Additionally, it is possible to ask the system to execute a task, for example a set an alarm task, consume that answer and complete successfully, *e.g.* ask "Set an alarm for 20 minutes before sunrise."

Internally this results in the automatic composition of Botlets to complete the required inference steps as shown in figure 3. This visualization displays a summary of the internal session state of the engine, refer to as the dynamic knowledge graph (dKG). Details of this visualization are discussed later.

4 ARCHITECTURE AND OPERATION

Figure 2 shows the system architecture. At its core is the dKG. The dKG stores the current session state which is described not only in terms of the information captured from the user, as it would be in a typical dialog system, but in addition includes Botlets and execution paths (chains of Botlets), some partially completed – see figure 3. These execution paths represent alternative analyses and hence alternate hypotheses about the user's current question/intent and how to respond. A session can span multiple dialogs, with the system carrying forward information in the dKG between dialogs.

The orange rectangles and associated arrows form an inner update-policy-execution core that can be cycled around multiple times for a single user turn (*i.e.* a query-response pair). At the start

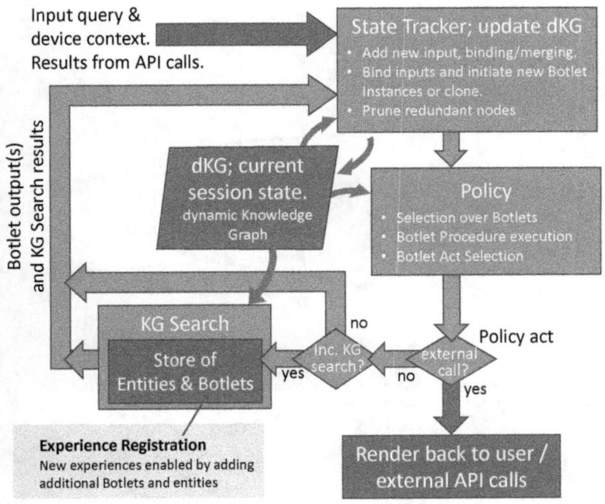

Figure 2: System architecture.

of a new conversation, a user issues a query. The user query plus context from the user's device, *e.g.* GPS coordinates, local time, *etc.* is provided to the state tracker. Input processing, such as NLU, can be applied before passing the input to the state tracker or could be treated as another Botlet and executed during the update-policy-execution cycles.

The state tracker is responsible for integrating new input into the existing dkG and pruning redundant nodes. Initially, in a brand new session, the dKG would be empty with the exception of Botlets that search the knowledge graph (KG). The state tracker is also responsible for creating executable Botlet *instances* by creating copies and binding inputs to those copies. Alternative Botlet instances represent alternative hypotheses, *e.g.* in cycle 2 of figure 3, two alternative NLU services, LuBotlet and LuisBotlet, are bound to the user input string "set an alarm for 20 minutes before sunrise."

The policy box selects the action to execute in two stages. Initially, given the state of the dKG as context, it does *Botlet Selection*, *i.e.* it selects one or more from among the Botlet instances that have not yet run. The selected Botlet instances are then executed and propose acts. Those acts may consist of writing new entities into the dKG, executing an external API call, or issuing a response to the user. The policy then considers the proposed acts and selects one or more of them. Botlet instances which were initially selected but whose acts are not chosen are reset and can be reselected by Botlet Selection in subsequent cycles.

In selecting acts, the policy has to be aware that certain acts have side effects which commit the system to a particular hypothesis. We refer to such acts as *transactional.* Transactional acts include those that present information to the user, as well as API calls that purchase goods, or tickets, *etc.* Built into the policy *Act Selection* model is the assumption that it is only safe to select one transactional act at a time. For non-transactional acts multiple can be chosen.

Initially Botlet Selection can only select the built-in KG search Botlet instances. The KG contains both knowledge entities (people, places, things), as is conventionally found in knowledge bases such as Freebase, plus a collection of Botlets. Both output entities resulting from the executed Botlets and the KG search are sent to the state tracker. The state tracker integrates these results into the session as the next cycle begins.

In the example session in figure 3 there are a total of 5 cycles (not all shown). During cycle 1, the user utterance is integrated into the dKG by the state tracker. Botlet Selection then selects the KG search Botlet instances (labelled PkgSearchBotlet and KgSearchBotlet). These return locations associated with the user, *e.g.* home and work, and a collection of Botlets that appear potentially useful in satisfying the user's request. In cycle 2 the state tracker binds the inputs of two of the returned Botlets creating two alternate NLU Botlet instances (labelled LuBotlet and LuisBotlet). The policy Botlet Selection selects both of them and Act Selection allows both to make external API calls to alternative NLU systems. The results are returned via the external API interface (blue input arrow) to the state tracker which in cycle 3 integrates them into the dKG; binding parts of the NLU analyses to EventTimeExtractorBotlet instances. The two EventTimeExtractorBotlet instances correspond to two hypothesis as to which sunrise event the user is referring to; today's or tomorrow's. The policy selects and accepts the proposed actions of both instances, which is to generate specific date-time entities. In cycle 4, the generated date-time entities are integrated and two TimeQualifierBotlet instances are bound. These Botlets handle the computation of time offsets, *e.g.* '20 minutes before'. Further EventTimeExtractorBotlet instances are also created. Botlet Selection selects only one of the TimeQualifierBotlet instances and accepts the action to generate a new specific date-time entity. Finally, in cycle 5, a number of SetAlarmBotlet instances are bound to the various date-time entities and Botlet Selection selects one to execute. The SetAlarmBotlet proposes as its act a response back to the user that an alarm has been set for 5:37 AM.

Multiple dialogs can be be represented in this system by multiple groups of Botlets and entities being stored in the dKG. These dialogs may be paused, either explicitly due to a user request, or implicitly if the user shifts focus to a different topic or unrelated request in the middle of a dialog. They maybe resumed in the future.

The architecture has multiple decision points where machine learning (ML) models can be deployed, such as state tracking, entity insertion/merging, Botlet instance creation and input binding, removal of redundant nodes, policy Botlet Selection, policy Act Selection, KG search. Future plans include casting the update of these models as a semi-Markov decision process (semi-MDP) [7] and re-train using Reinforcement Learning (RL) based on user feedback.

The immediate issue, however, is one of cold start. We have focused on first training a Botlet Selection model. For other components we adopted naïve rule based baselines. We also limited the shared-static-KG to a set of immediately useful entities and Botlets in order to simplify the implementation of the KG search.

The Botlet Selection model takes the current dKG as context and then emits decisions, one per Botlet instance that has not yet run, as to whether that instance should be selected in this cycle. As an initial approach, we used a sequence-encoder model as shown in figure 4. This approach allowed us to largely avoid the task of input feature engineering. Each sequence input (dkG and Botlet instance) consists of an embedding layer and gated recurrent units (GRUs) [3]. The output vectors of the two GRU sequences are concatenated and then fed to a single densely connected sigmoid output. The output is threshold at 0.5. The dKG is serialised as a linear sequence of tokens, where the maximum number of tokens used is truncated

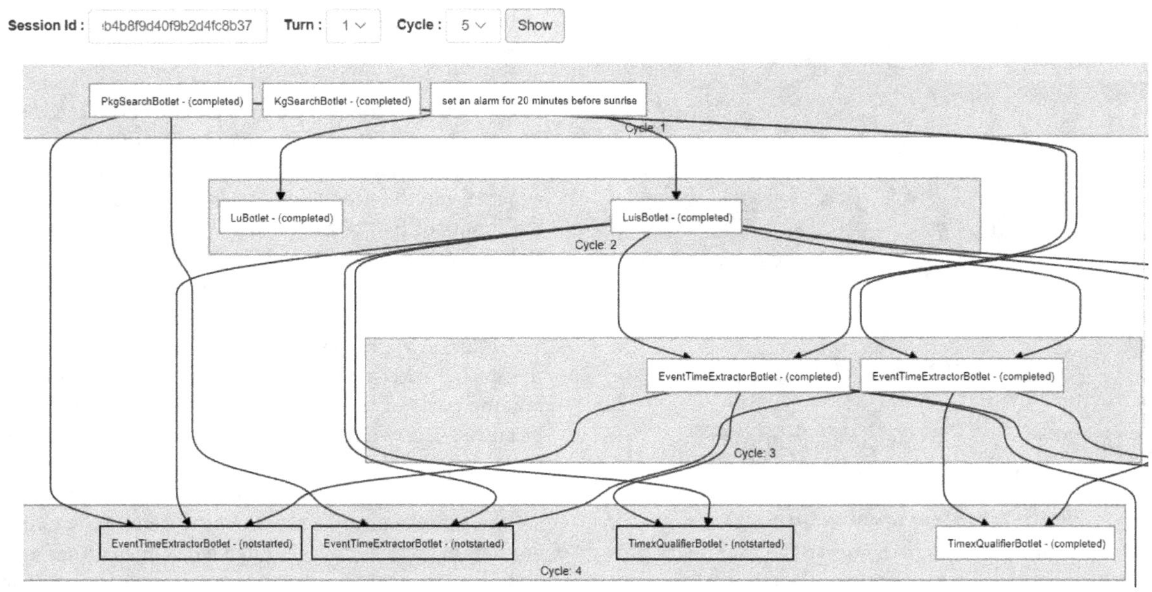

Figure 3: Screen shot from demo showing a dKG summary that illustrates information flow (arrows), *i.e.* Botlet input bindings, and selective execution. Botlets that are shown as white filled rectangles have completed execution, those shown as light grey filled rectangles have not been selected to execute by the Botlet Selection ML model.

at 12,000 retaining only the tail[1]. Botlet instances are similarly serialized to tokens but only including the instance itself and all related input entities. Maximum length of Botlet Instance tokens was limited to a few hundred.

To initially train this model we generated synthetic data by rolling out possible decision paths in response to user requests with known semantics. Each decision, from sequences that gave rise to target answers, is used a supervisory data to train the initial model. Language generation models initially trained from log data and then augment by hand generated the user requests. Using the known semantics of the requests, the exploration space for Botlet Selection could be constrained; randomized exploration within those automatically generated constraints allowed a reasonable success rate. Using this method we collected 2,860 successful single turn dialogs with an average of 6.05 cycles per dialog, and 5.87 Botlet Selection decisions per cycle, *i.e.* a total of 101,623 decisions.

This data is then used to train the seq-2-one model. All layers of the model, including the embedding layers, were jointly trained using back-propagation.

5 CONCLUSION

We demonstrate a system that merges elements of traditional multi-turn dialog systems with web based question answering. We show that such a system can be trained to combine information from search engine answers with PDA tasks to enable new user experiences. We breakdown interpretation and processing of semantic entities, along with responding to the user, into functional units, *i.e.* Botlets. The systems is trained to automatic compose the execution of Botlets in order to complete user requests. Our approach is general enough that it can automatically scale to cover new combinations of answers and PDA task. We demonstrate it answering queries such as "What time is 20 minutes before sunrise" as well as "Set an alarm for 20 minutes before sunrise."

Future work is focused on refining the system's operation and accuracy. This includes training ML models for each decision point and improving those models using user feedback and RL.

[1] Max. length 62,190 tokens, 90th percentile 18,021 tokens, 75th percentile 8,295 tokens.

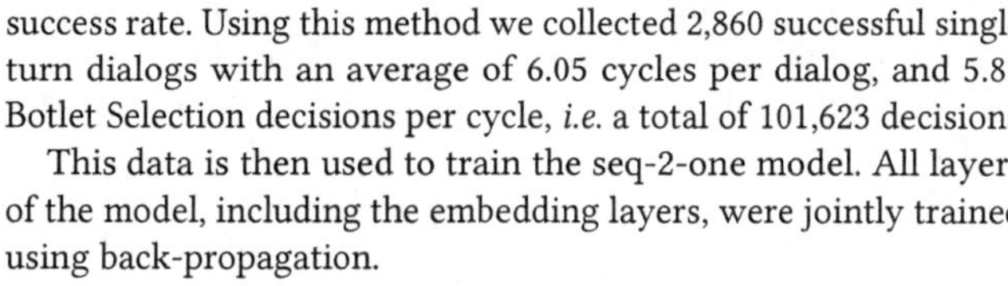

Figure 4: Seq-2-one model used for Botlet Selection.

REFERENCES

[1] D. Bohus and A. Rudnicky. 2003. RavenClaw: Dialog Management Using Hierarchical Task decomposition and an Expectation Agenda. In *Proc. Eurospeech.*

[2] J. Bos, E. Klein, O. Lemon, and T. Oka. 2003. DIPPER: Description and Formalisation of an Information-State Update Dialogue System Architecture. In *In 4th SIGdial Workshop on Discourse and Dialogue.* 115–124.

[3] J. Chung, Ç. Gülçehre, K. Cho, and Y. Bengio. 2014. Empirical Evaluation of Gated Recurrent Neural Networks on Sequence Modeling. *CoRR* abs/1412.3555 (2014). http://arxiv.org/abs/1412.3555

[4] S. Larsson and D. R. Traum. 2000. Information State and Dialogue Management in the TRINDI Dialogue Move Engine Toolkit. *Nat. Lang. Eng.* 6, 3-4 (Sept. 2000), 323–340.

[5] J. Luo, S. Zhang, and G. H. Yang. 2014. Win-win search: dual-agent stochastic game in session search. In *SIGIR 2014.* ACM.

[6] R. Sarikaya, P. A. Crook, A. Marin, M. Jeong, J. Robichaud, A. Çelikyilmaz, Y. Kim, A. Rochette, O. Z. Khan, X. Liu, D. Boies, T. Anastasakos, Z. Feizollahi, N. Ramesh, H. Suzuki, R. Holenstein, E. Krawczyk, and V. Radostev. 2016. An overview of end-to-end language understanding and dialog management for personal digital assistants. In *SLT.* IEEE, 391–397.

[7] R. S. Sutton, D. Precup, and S. Singh. 1999. Between MDPs and semi-MDPs: A framework for temporal abstraction in reinforcement learning. *Artificial Intelligence* 112, 1 (1999), 181 – 211.

[8] Z. Wang, H. Chen, G. Wang, H. Tian, H. Wu, and H. Wang. 2014. Policy Learning for Domain Selection in an Extensible Multi-domain Spoken Dialogue System. In *Proceedings of EMNLP 2014.* Association for Computational Linguistics.

[9] Y. Zhang and C. Zhai. 2016. A sequential decision formulation of the interface card model for interactive IR. In *SIGIR 2016.* ACM, 85–94.

Supporting Large-scale Geographical Visualization in a Multi-granularity Way

Mingzhao Li, Zhifeng Bao, Farhana Choudhury
RMIT University, Australia

Timos Sellis
Swinburne University of Technology, Australia

ABSTRACT

Urban data (e.g., real estate data, crime data) often have multiple attributes which are highly geography-related. With the scale of data increases, directly visualizing millions of individual data points on top of a map would overwhelm users' perceptual and cognitive capacity and lead to high latency when users interact with the data. In this demo, we present ConvexCubes, a system that supports interactive visualization of large-scale multidimensional urban data in a multi-granularity way. Comparing to state-of-the-art visualization-driven data structures, it exploits real-world geographic semantics (e.g., country, state, city) rather than using grid-based aggregation. Instead of calculating everything on demand, ConvexCubes utilizes existing visualization results to efficiently support different kinds of user interactions, such as zooming & panning, filtering and granularity control. Our system can be accessed at http://115.146.89.158/ConvexCubes/.

ACM Reference Format:
Mingzhao Li, Zhifeng Bao, Farhana Choudhury and Timos Sellis. 2018. Supporting Large-scale Geographical Visualization in a Multi-granularity Way. In *WSDM 2018: The Eleventh ACM International Conference on Web Search and Data Mining, February 5–9, 2018, Marina Del Rey, CA, USA.* ACM, New York, NY, USA, 4 pages. https://doi.org/10.1145/3159652.3160587

1 INTRODUCTION

In recent years, both the volume and the availability of urban data related to various social issues, such as real estate, crime, population, etc., are increasing rapidly. Visually analyzing such data is of practical importance: (i) the policy makers can make better informed decisions; and (ii) the residents can benefit from understanding the urban life in different areas on many occasions, for example, when selecting a property to live in.

In our previous work [4], we have designed and developed a visualization system for Australia's real estate data. In the property-level visualization, we displayed each property on top of a geographic map, where users can explore the data and compare properties in multiple dimensions. However, as the scale of data increases (e.g., over one million data points), existing information visualization methods, including directly visualizing each data point on top of a map, suffer from the following drawbacks: (i) data over-plotting, (ii) overwhelming users' perceptual and cognitive capacities(*perceptual scalability problem* [6]), and (iii) difficulties to support interactive exploration, since users' interaction with large-scale datasets would easily lead to high latency (*interactive scalability problem* [6]). It motivates us to investigate this problem.

From our literature study, we find two major types of methods that have been proposed to address the scalability issue of visualizing large-scale datasets: (i) visualization techniques, e.g., progressive visual analytics [9], predictive visual analytics, pixel-based visualization, spatial displacement, parallel data processing and rendering; and (ii) data reduction methods [6], such as filtering, sampling, and binned aggregation.

However, visualization techniques still need to scan each data item, which makes them difficult to scale. For data reduction methods, since filtering and sampling techniques fail to provide an overview of a dataset [3], one recent research trend in big data visualization is to intersect data management and visualization based on binned aggregation, and several studies [5–7, 10] have applied the idea of data cubes into visualization. They pre-compute possible data aggregations to support efficient visualization.

While their contributions are significant to the field, there exists a gap with real-life applications in terms of the following three drawbacks. **First**, existing methods (e.g., [5, 7, 10]) often partition geographic dimensions based on a grid-based hierarchical spatial data structure, such as Quadtree [2]. Such design fails to capture geographic semantics (e.g., country, state, city, etc.), thus cannot answer many real-life questions, such as *"what is the difference of house prices in different neighbourhoods?"*, or *"how many tweets have been posted for an event in different countries or states?"* **Second**, in some studies [5, 7, 10], numerical dimensions are transformed to categorical dimensions based on pre-defined binned aggregation, which results in the case that data with close-by values possibly fall into different bins. **Third**, most existing data structures are designed to support visual encoding of some specific visualization methods (e.g. heatmaps); however, they fail to support interactive visualization because all intermediate results have to be recomputed from scratch whenever the user conducts a further interaction.

To overcome the above drawbacks, we propose ConvexCubes to support the visualization of large-scale multidimensional urban data in multiple levels of granularity. The details of how we address the three problems with ConvexCubes can be found at Section 3.1, 3.3 and 4.2, respectively. The implemented demo system[1] and a demonstration video[2] are available online.

2 VIS ABSTRACTION & SYSTEM OVERVIEW

In this section, we first discuss the data and visualization tasks, followed by our visual encoding and interaction designs. Finally, we present an overview of the system.

[1]Demo system: http://115.146.89.158/ConvexCubes/
[2]Demonstration video: http://115.146.89.158/ConvexCubes/video.html

WSDM 2018, February 5–9, 2018, Marina Del Rey, CA, USA

ACM ISBN 978-1-4503-5581-0/18/02…$15.00
https://doi.org/10.1145/3159652.3160587

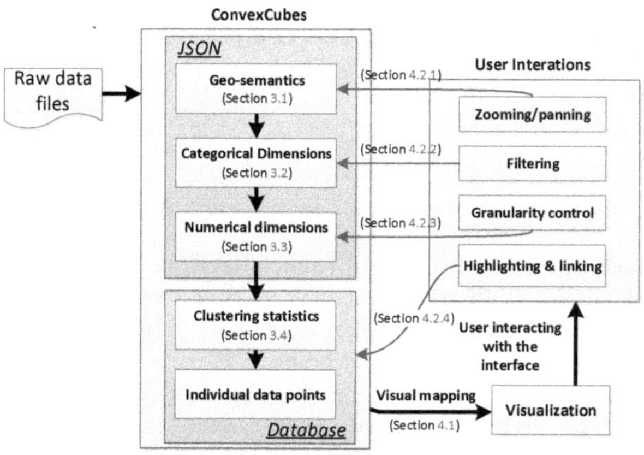

Figure 1: The system overview

2.1 Data and Task Abstraction

For the ease of explanation, we describe our work using Australia's real estate data as an example of multidimensional urban data in this paper. It includes the census profile, education profile, facility profile, transportation profile for each property and suburb (detailed in our previous work [4]). Each property is associated with its geo-spatial information (latitude and longitude), categorical dimensions (e.g., property type) and numerical dimensions (e.g., price).

We follow Shneiderman's visual information-seeking mantra [8], i.e., *overview first, zoom and filter, then details-on-demand*, to define our tasks. We illustrate the abstraction of tasks based on a series of real-life questions: *"What is the difference of property prices in different suburbs in Victoria (overview)?", "what if the user only concerns about 3-bedroom houses (filtering)?", "what is the difference between houses in the same suburb but in different blocks (zooming & granularity control)?",* and *"based on the user-defined factors, how do the houses in a block differ from houses in the rest of the suburb, or the rest of the entire state (details-on-demand, highlighting & linking)?"*

2.2 Visualization Design

To support the above visualization tasks, we design two map-based views and one linked multidimensional view. In map-based views, we cluster properties based on default settings (i.e., a selection of features of the dataset) which can also be user-specified. All properties within the same cluster share the same or similar features. When a cluster is highlighted in the map-based view, a linked multidimensional view presents the detailed information of the cluster based on user-defined dimensions.

Map-based view 1: dot maps. Comparing to [5, 7, 10] which mainly support heatmaps, we use dot maps as our basic map-based view, since it has one more retina variable (i.e., the size of the dot) to encode an extra dimension. An example is shown in Figure 3(a), where the colour and the size of each dot represent the total number and the average price of properties in each cluster, respectively.

Map-based view 2: polygons on top of the map. As locations and boundaries are important measures of the geographic information, our second map-based view draws polygons (convex hull) on top of the map to illustrate approximate positions of a group of properties in each cluster (Figure 3(b)). We use alpha blending to reduce visual cluttering.

Multidimensional view: line chart + histograms. We design linked multidimensional view to visualize the statistical informatio of a highlighted cluster. The view compares local information wit the global statistics (e.g., comparing the house prices in a subur with the house prices in the entire state). As shown in Figure 3(c for each selected dimension, we draw a vertical line chart to sho the global distribution of data, and on top of it, we draw histogram to visualize the data distribution in the highlighted cluster.

Based on our task abstraction and Shneiderman's visual informat seeking mantra, the visualization needs to support the followin interactions: (1) zooming & panning, (2) filtering, (3) granularit control, (4) other interactions, such as highlighting & linking an changing focused measures.

2.3 System Overview

Figure 1 shows an overview of our system. We construct our pro posed data structure (ConvexCubes) from the raw data files, an store them as JSON files; the statistical information for each cluste and individual data items are stored in a database (Section 3). Whe a user initializes the visualization from a browser, the JSON files ar loaded from the server, and a visualized overview is generated fo the user (Section 4.1). Different layers of ConvexCubes are affecte by different kinds of user interactions (shown with an arrow fro each interaction to a layer of the ConvexCubes). After each interac tion, only the part of the current visualization that is different fro the previous visualization will be refreshed (Section 4.2).

3 DATA MANAGEMENT AND INDEXING

In this section, we describe how we store and index the data and build the ConvexCubes. The construction of ConvexCubes re quires a multi-criteria sorting of the dataset, which is similar t Hashedcubes [7]. As shown in Figure 2, the construction of Convex Cubes starts from geo-semantic layers (Section 3.1); then categorica dimensions (Section 3.2), followed by granularity clustering of nu merical dimensions (Section 3.3). Finally, we calculate a convex hul for each cluster and store the statistical information of each cluste in the database (Section 3.4),.

3.1 Geographic Semantic Layers

The geographical layer of most state-of-the-art data cubes [5, 7, 10] are based on grid-based hierarchical spatial data structures, such as Quadtree [2] which recursively divides the space into four regions Such data structures are effective for querying on the geographical dimension, but might not preserve the geographical semantics. For example, if we partition the data based on the geo-locations of the real estate properties using Quadtree, in one of the middle layers, two properties from two different states may belong to the same grid, while they have no semantic relationship. Therefore, we design the geographical level of ConvexCubes based on real-world geographical hierarchy, such as country, state, city, etc.

For the real estate data, we apply a multi-criteria sorting based on different levels of geographic semantics. As shown in Figure 2, all properties in Victoria will be first grouped together in Level 1, then all properties in Melbourne CBD and Richmond will be grouped together, respectively. We use a 2-/3- digit number to represent each geographic semantic level.

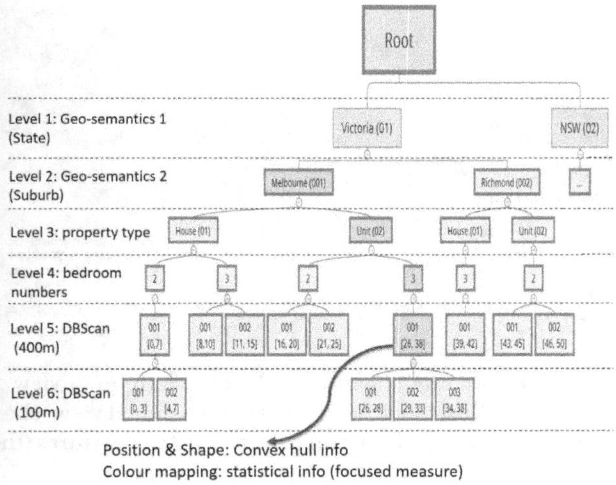

Figure 2: An example of ConvexCubes with 6 layers: 2 geo-semantic layers (Level 1 & 2), 2 categorical dimension layers (Level 3 & 4) and 2 numerical dimension layers (Level 5 & 6).

3.2 Categorical Dimensions

Categorical dimensions are often divided based on specific values or ranges. For example, Property type is a categorical dimension which has values such as *"house"* and *"apartment"*. In ConvexCubes, we use a 1-/2- digit number to represent each categorical dimension. As shown in Figure 2, two categorical dimensions (property type and bedroom number) are considered (Level 3 & 4).

3.3 Numerical Dimensions and Granularity Clustering

Existing data cubes [5, 7, 10] often transform numerical dimensions into categorical dimensions by partitioning data values into data segments. A drawback of such design is that data with close-by values may fall into different data segments. To solve the problem, we apply a granularity clustering for numerical dimensions. In our implementation, geo-spatial dimensions (latitude and longitude) are a special case of numerical dimensions. As shown in Figure 2, in Level 5, we apply DBScan [1] with a threshold of 400m to cluster the properties based on Euclidean distance. Then in Level 6, we re-apply DBScan with a smaller threshold (100m in our demonstration) to possibly divide some of the original clusters into multiple smaller clusters. Such structure allows us to visualize the clusters in a multi-granularity way, and provides better support for granularity controls in an interactive way. For each cluster, we store the pivot indices which indicate the start index number and the end index number of the sorted properties.

3.4 Convex Hull and Aggregation Functions

We calculate a convex hull for each cluster in ConvexCubes based on geo-spatial information to support our map-based visual encoding design (Map-based view 2). Instead of storing the locations for all data points, we store the convex hull (bounding polygon) of the points. If multiple clusters are required to be combined, we apply an approximate algorithm to combine the convex hulls instead of re-calculating the convex hull for the combined set of points.

We also calculate statistical information for each cluster and store them in the database. For each cluster, we store a binned statistical result based on each dimension measure to support the multidimensional view. Such information is stored as views in the database, so that when a cluster is highlighted, the information of the selected dimension measures will be loaded and visualized.

4 DEMONSTRATION

In this section, we illustrate how we use ConvexCubes to support our visualization and user interactions. Each method is followed by a demonstration scenario based on the real estate dataset. While the dataset in our previous work [4] has 50k properties, we include 1.42 million properties in Victoria and New South Wales, Australia. A detailed description of the dataset and the schema, along with demonstration scenarios on the other datasets (e.g., social network check-in datasets) can also be found in the online demo system[1].

4.1 Initializing the Visualization

The initialization of visualization requires four parameters, a default map window (i.e., maximum and minimum latitudes and longitudes), user-selected categorical dimensions (e.g., 3-bedroom houses), a default clustering granularity (e.g., 400m), and a default focused measure (e.g., price). Based on the initialization settings, the query starts from the root node of ConvexCubes and the following steps are executed: (i) the nodes in geographic semantic layers that are within the map window are accessed, (ii) the categorical dimensions are scanned, and (iii) the clusters are obtained when the right level of the clustering granularity is reached. In Fig. 2, only the highlighted clusters in level 5 will be visualized for the default initialization parameter values. Then based on the stored convex hull and the default focused measure from the database, a dot map or the corresponding polygons on the map are shown to the user.

Demonstration scenario 1: *When the user opens the webpage, a map will be initialized with a default map window and clustering granularity. After the user selects the categorical dimension (Figure 3 (a)-1), either of the two map views will be shown to the user (Figure 3 (a) or (b)) based on the stored information. For example, in Figure 3 (b), the user can observe how the prices of 3-bedroom houses are distributed in the geographical space.*

4.2 Supporting User Interactions

We illustrate how we use ConvexCubes to efficiently support different types of user interactions. The key idea is to reuse existing calculations and visualizations while updating for user interactions.

4.2.1 Zooming and panning. These are the basic operations on top of a map, which directly influences the map window. The change of the map window corresponds to the level of geographic semantics in ConvexCubes. Therefore, after the user applies zooming in/out or panning, we calculate a set subtraction between the current and previous map window, and then refresh the visualization based on the subtraction result. In contrast to a quadtree node, the boundary of a semantic geographical node often contains a lot of geo-points. Therefore, we also store the minimum bounding rectangle for each geo-boundary. If the map window covers the entire rectangle, we include all the clusters in the lower level; otherwise, the next geographic semantic level is accessed.

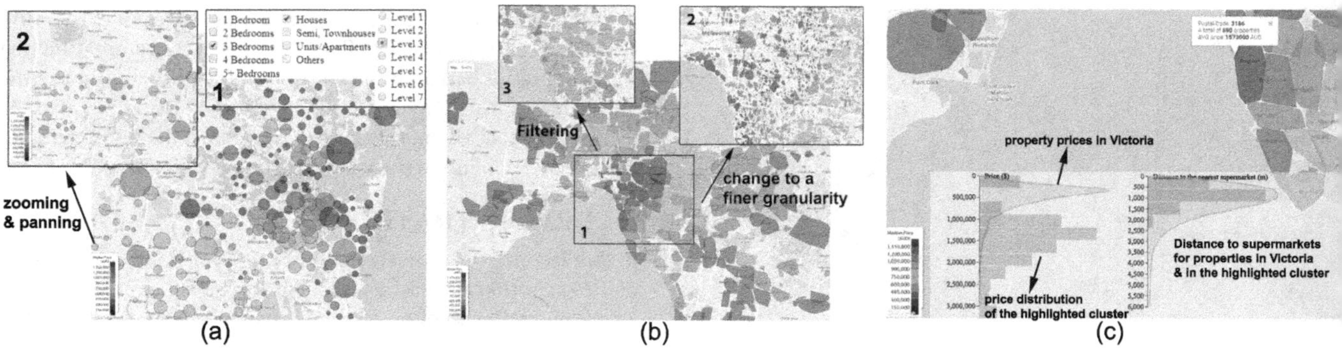

Figure 3: Demonstration examples: (a) map view 1: dot map (Sydney), with zooming & panning illustrated; (b) map view 2: polygons on top of the map (Melbourne), with filtering and granularity control illustrated; (c) the multidimensional view when a cluster is highlighted (properties in the cluster is compared to that of the entire state based on 2 user-selected measures (the price & the distance to supermarkets).

Demonstration scenario 2: *The user can zoom in or zoom out, or pan the map just as they do on Google Maps. We can illustrate how ConvexCubes re-use existing visualization results and partially refresh the interface by asking the audiences to pay attention to the borders of the map region. An example is shown in Figure 3(a).*

4.2.2 Filtering. Filtering, i.e., selections, would affect the level of categorical dimensions. For example, if previously, only 3-bedroom *units* in Melbourne are shown on the map, and the user selects to include 3-bedroom *houses* as well, then the corresponding clusters in Level 5 will be added to the visualization result while the previous result remains. Note that, having multiple selections might result in some intersecting convex hulls. To effectively detect intersections at runtime, we store the minimum bounding rectangle for each cluster along with the convex hull information, and we compute the union of the intersected convex hulls at runtime.

Demonstration scenario 3: *The user can filter on top of the pre-selected dimensions and see how properties/clusters change on top of the map. As shown in Figure 3(b)-3, we change the filtering setting from 3-bedroom houses to 2-/3- bedroom units in Melbourne.*

4.2.3 Granularity control. This will affect the level of numerical dimensions. For example, in Figure 2, if the user changes the current granularity level from Level 5 to Level 6, clusters that are not split will stay on the map, while clusters falling into multiple smaller clusters (i.e., the first and the sixth node at Level 5) will be replaced by their children clusters. To make the interaction easier, we separate zooming and granularity controls as two different operations. In our implementation, user zooming in or out will trigger the function of granularity control; users can also change to different granularities while staying at the same zooming level.

Demonstration scenario 4: *The user can change the granularity level by zooming in or zooming out, or they can directly select different levels from the selection panel (Figure 3(a)-1). As shown in Figure 3(b)-2, the user can change to a finer granularity and see how the clusters in 3(b)-1 split into multiple smaller clusters. For example, the user observing that properties in Brighton (which is closer to the coastline) is more expensive than nearby suburbs, might want to change it to a finer granularity and check whether property prices in different blocks of Brighton are also affected by the distance to the coastline.*

4.2.4 Other interactions. **Highlighting & linking** need to access the database. A row in the cluster table needs to be accessed when the user selects a cluster to highlight; while highlighting an individual property requires a row in the property table. For interactions such as **changing focused measures**, a column in the cluster table will be accessed.

Demonstration scenario 5: *The user can click to highlight a cluster, and a linked multidimensional view is generated for users to (i) check the detailed statistics of the cluster in several user-defined measures and (ii) compare properties in the cluster with properties at a higher geo-semantic level. As shown in Figure 3(c), the user highlights a cluster in Brighton, Victoria; simultaneously, in the multidimensional view, two sets of bar charts + histograms are highlighted to present a comparison of properties in the highlighted cluster and those in the entire Victoria based on two user-defined measures (the price and the distance to the nearest supermarket).*

Acknowledgements. This work was partially supported by ARC DP170102726, DP170102231, DP180102050, and National Natural Science Foundation of China (NSFC) 61728204, 91646204. Zhifeng Bao is supported by a Google Faculty Award.

REFERENCES

[1] Martin Ester, Hans-Peter Kriegel, Jörg Sander, and Xiaowei Xu. 1996. A density-based algorithm for discovering clusters in large spatial databases with noise. In *KDD*. 226–231.

[2] Raphael A Finkel and Jon Louis Bentley. 1974. Quad trees a data structure for retrieval on composite keys. *Acta Informatica* 4, 1 (1974), 1–9.

[3] Parke Godfrey, Jarek Gryz, and Piotr Lasek. 2016. Interactive visualization of large data sets. *IEEE TKDE* 28, 8 (2016), 2142–2157.

[4] Mingzhao Li, Zhifeng Bao, Timos Sellis, and Shi Yan. 2016. Visualization-aided exploration of the real estate data. In *ADC*. 435–439.

[5] Lauro Lins, James Klosowski, and Carlos Scheidegger. 2013. Nanocubes for real-time exploration of spatiotemporal datasets. *IEEE TVCG* 19, 12 (2013), 2456–2465.

[6] Zhicheng Liu, Biye Jiang, and Jeffrey Heer. 2013. imMens: real-time visual querying of big data. *Computer Graphics Forum* 32, 3 (2013), 421–430.

[7] Cicero AL Pahins, Sean A Stephens, Carlos Scheidegger, and Joao LD Comba. 2017. Hashedcubes: simple, low Memory, real-time visual exploration of big data. *IEEE TVCG* 23, 1 (2017), 671–680.

[8] Ben Shneiderman. 1996. The eyes have it: a task by data type taxonomy for information visualizations. In *IEEE Symposium on Visual Languages*. 336–343.

[9] Cagatay Turkay, Erdem Kaya, Selim Balcisoy, and Helwig Hauser. 2017. Designing progressive and interactive analytics processes for high-dimensional data analysis. *IEEE TVCG* 23, 1 (2017), 131–140.

[10] Zhe Wang, Nivan Ferreira, Youhao Wei, Aarthy Sankari Bhaskar, and Carlos Scheidegger. 2017. Gaussian cubes: real-time modeling for visual exploration of large multidimensional datasets. *IEEE TVCG* 23 (2017), 681–690.

Collabot: Personalized Group Chat Summarization

Naama Tepper, Anat Hashavit, Maya Barnea, Inbal Ronen, Lior Leiba
IBM Research AI Haifa
Haifa 31905, Israel
{naama.tepper, anath, mayab, inbal, leiba}@il.ibm.com

ABSTRACT

In recent[1] years, enterprise group chat collaboration tools, such as Slack, IBM's Watson Workspace and Microsoft Teams, have presented unprecedented growth. With all the potential benefits of these tools - productivity increase and improved group communication - come significant challenges. Specifically, the 'always on' feature that makes it hard for users to cope with the load of conversational content and get up to speed after logging off for a while. In this demo, we present Collabot - a chat assistant service that implicitly learns users interests and social ties within a chat group and provides a personalized digest of missed content. Collabot assists users in coping with chat information overload by helping them understand the main topics discussed, collaborators, links and resources. This demo has two main contributions. First, we present a novel personalized group chat summarization algorithm; second the demonstration depicts a working implementation applied on different chat groups from different domains within IBM. A video, describing the demo can be found at https://www.youtube.com/watch?v=6cVsstiJ9vk.

ACM Reference format:
N. Tepper, A. Hashavit, M. Barnea, I. Ronen, L. Leiba. 2018. Collabot: Personalized Group Chat Summarization. In *WSDM '18: 11th ACM International Conference on Web Search & Data Mining,* Feb. 5–9, 2018, Marina Del Rey, CA, USA. ACM, NY, NY, USA, 4 pages. https://doi.org/10.1145/3159652.3160588

1 GROUP CHAT IN THE WORKPLACE

Group chats have become very popular to the wide audience. Specifically, in the workplace tools such as Slack, IBM's Watson Workspace and Microsoft Teams have become an essential tool for collaboration. These tools enable asynchronous, instant communication across geographic locations and different time zones with the possibility of sharing links and content. However, their constant 'always on' nature makes it hard for users to cope with the load of conversational content and get up to speed after being offline for a while. Furthermore, chat is poor at managing interruptions and turn taking with interleaved conversations on different discussion topics [14]. An example can be seen in Figure 1 where a conversation between Vijai and Mike, marked as Conversation A, is interrupted by a message from Simone (Conversation B) and then continues. Due to such chat feed characteristics, users trying to catch up on missed content can find it difficult to focus their attention and notice issues of interest and importance to them, especially if they have been away for more than just a short time. Users could thus significantly gain from a well-organized personalized summary of the content they missed.

WSDM 2018, February 5–9, 2018, Marina Del Rey, CA, USA

ACM ISBN 978-1-4503-5581-0/18/02...$15.00
https://doi.org/10.1145/3159652.3160588

Most existing summarization systems for short text generate a uniform version of summary for different users [2, 7, 12]. On the other hand, previous work that did focus on personalized summarization, only dealt with the general domain, summarizing text documents and not chat messages. In addition, these methods usually require that users explicitly provide their interest aspects [3, 10] specify a query [6, 11], or provide additional information as tags, comments or ratings [7].

Here, we present Collabot - a personalized visual summarization system for group chat. Collabot implicitly builds a user specific profile containing users' topics and people of interest. Based on these attributes Collabot selects the most relevant conversations for the user. Conversations are then grouped in a convenient way which enables users to quickly grasp what they missed as well as to drill down and explore further.

2 PERSONALIZED SUMMARIZATION

In order to create personalized summaries, we first need to create a personalized profile for each user. We do this by implicitly learning the users' topics of interest and a representation of their social ties from chat history. Specifically, a user profile includes two weighted vectors: (i) *Topics of interest*; a normalized vector containing a weighted list of topics. For example:

$$(\langle topic1,0.2\rangle,\langle topic3,0.5\rangle,\langle topic8,0.3\rangle) .$$

and (ii) *Social ties:* a list of users' connections from a social-graph and their normalized weights. For example:

$$(\langle David,0.5\rangle,\langle Jina,0.1\rangle,\langle Mike,0.2\rangle,\langle Henry,0.2\rangle).$$

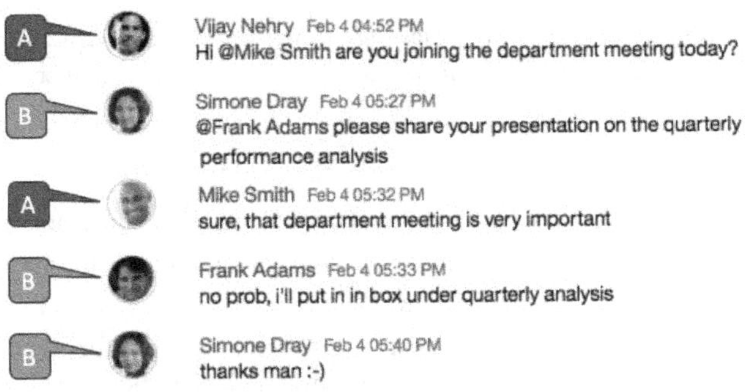

Figure 1: Chat feed example. Multiple topics are discussed between in interleaved conversations.

Summarization is done according to the stages depicted in Figure 2: First, the feed is segmented into conversations. Conversations then receive relevance scores based a user profile, and the low scored conversations are then filtered out. The remaining conversations are grouped into topical clusters, tagged, summarized and presented to the user.

2.1 Creating a User Profile

2.1.1 Topic Modeling To create the user topics of interest we utilized LDA in a unique approach which we termed *user centric LDA*. LDA is a probabilistic topic modeling algorithms [1]. It operates under an assumption that a document is composed of a mixture of topics, and each topic comprises from a probabilistic composition of words. Due to sparsity in short text word co-occurrence, a widely used strategy when using LDA is to aggregate messages into 'pseudo documents' using auxiliary contextual information such as authorship and hash-tags, and then invoke the process on those 'pseudo documents' [5, 8, 15]. In this work, we extended existing aggregation approaches by adding social and chat-specific enhancements: We define a 'user-document' as a collection of messages the user wrote or was mentioned in. After a processing phase of corpus is enhancement, the cleaned messages are aggregated to user-documents and standard LDA is invoked. User topics of interest can then be retrieved by applying the model on the user documents.

2.1.2 *Social relationships inference.* A *chat channel social graph* can be defined as a sparse weighted directional graph where the vertices represent the users and weighted edges signify the strength of their relationships with each other. We do this by examining two features that are attainable in most chat collaboration tools: Explicit referencing which we infer from mentions and implicit referencing which we infer from joint participation in conversations.

Conversations are identified using a naïve algorithm: First, we identify continuous conversational parts within the feed using a rule based decision tree heuristic relying on features such as time between messages, engaging users, discussion topics and length of the conversation. We then unify these continuous parts back together based on mentions. For example, in Figure 1 conversation B is divided into the two sequential parts. These parts are united based on the fact that Simone mentions Frank in the first part of the conversation, and Frank participated in the second part of the conversation.

We first inspect the absolute amount of communication history: Given two users, u_i and u_j, we define their absolute social score as follows:

$$soc_{i\to j} = M_{i\to j} \cdot W_{i\to j} + M_{j\to i} \cdot W_{j\to i} + \| D_{ij} \| \cdot W_{D_{ij}} \quad (1)$$

where $M_{i\to j}$ denotes the number of mentions between u_i and u_j, $\| D_{ij} \|$ denotes the number of common conversations u_i and u_j participated in and $W_{i\to j}, W_{j\to i}, W_{D_{ij}}$ signify the weight of each component respectively. Then, in order to account for users' different absolute engagement levels we normalize the scores so that all outgoing edge weights sum up to one.

2.2 Personalized Scoring of Conversations

The process for scoring conversations for a user is composed of the following steps:

2.2.1 Conversation disentanglement. The transcript is segmente into conversations according to the same heuristics described i section 2.1.2

2.2.2 *Conversation scoring.* Each conversation is compared t the user profile and a relevance score is computed. Th computation of the relevance score is given by:

$$Rel(C,U) = D_{simm}(T_u,T_c) \cdot W_{topic} + D_{simm}(S_u,S_c) \cdot W_{social} \quad (2)$$

where T_u is the user topics vector from the user profile; T_c i the conversation topic distribution vector extracted by applyin the same topic model used in the user profile to the conversatio messages; S_u is the distribution over the user's social ties; S_c is th proportion of messages users authored in the conversatior W_{social} is the weight of the social component in the relevanc function; W_{topic} is the weight of the topical component in th relevance function; and D_{simm} is the distribution relevanc function, which we chose to be cosine similarity.

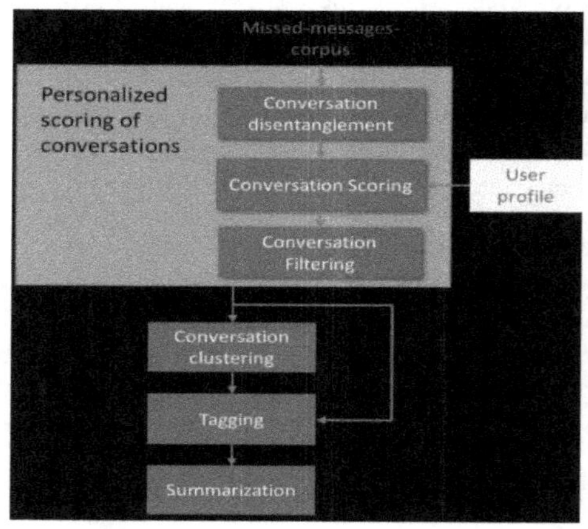

Figure 2: Personalized conversation scoring process.

2.2.3 *Conversation filtering.* Next, conversations are sorted pe their relevance score and low scored conversations, with relevance score < rel_{score} are filtered out.

2.2 Conversation Clustering

In order to present the selected conversation in a coherent way conversations discussing the same topic are clustered together The topic model is applied on each conversation and outputs a topic distribution vector. These distributions are then used tc calculate a significance score between a topic and a conversation The significance score of a topic for a given conversation is calculated as a sum of word probabilities in the topic:

$$Sig(C,T) = \sum_{w \in T \cap C} M(w,T) \quad (3)$$

where C is some conversational content (a conversation or a cluster of conversations); T is a topic; and $M(w,T)$ is the probability of word w in topic T according to model M. The topic with the highest probability and sufficient significance score sig_{score} is chosen.

2.3 Conversation and Cluster tagging

Titles (tags) are generated per each conversation and conversational cluster. The title is a short list of top-probability words from the chosen topic which are also present in the conversational content (i.e. a conversation or a conversational cluster). The words are sorted according to their probability within the topic. These probabilities, comprising a relevance score, are summed until reaching four words or exceeding a pre-defined threshold score tag_{score}.

2.4 Summarization of Conversations

Summarization is done the same for clusters and individual conversations. First, we define important messages as messages containing words from the title or messages containing actionable insights (such as questions and commitments) using the eAssistant web service [9]. For example, an important message in a conversation can either have keywords from its own title, keywords from its cluster title or contain actionable insights. Second, we sort important messages according to their length and retrieve longest messages up to $summ_{length}$ of the total number of messages.

2.5 Non-personalized Summarization

2.5.1 New topics. These are new and emerging topics that, by definition, cannot be part of the user's topics of interest. Messages not assigned to a topic in part 2.2 (without sufficient relevance score) are grouped and sorted according to their KL-divergence score compared to the entire chat corpus. Top-scored messages are presented as a 'new topics' cluster.

2.5.2 *Key users.* These are messages written by the top mentioned users in the channel. Given user profiles for all users in the group, 'influential' users can be identified [13], and conversations they participated in are clustered and summarized under the 'key users' cluster.

3 VALIDATION

We ran the personalized summarization algorithm on 17 slack channels used by employees in IBM. Each channel contained over 10,000 user generated messages ranging over a period of no less than three months. User profiles were inferred for each channel using 70% of the data and summarization done on the remaining 30%. For simplicity, W_{social}, W_{topic} were each assigned a value of 0.5. The social graph edge weights $M_{i \to j}, M_{j \to i}, \| D_{ij} \|$ were assigned equal values as well. Other settings were chosen to be: $rel_{score} = 0.25$, $sig_{score} = \frac{corpus\text{-}length}{100{,}000}$, $tag_{score} = 0.1$, $summ_{length} = 0.2$

Summary quality was tested using recall and precision metrics in which we tried to evaluate how many of the true important conversational clusters Collabot presented to the user. A true important conversation was defined as a conversation the user participated in and an important conversational cluster was a cluster that contained at least one important conversation. We received an average recall value of 0.82 and average precision value of 0.59. The high recall rate shows that Collabot successfully retrieves the vast majority of conversations that are interesting to the users, while preserving a reasonable amount of irrelevant conversation filtering, which is demonstrated in the precision rate. Note that while a conversation the user participated in is probably of interest to her, not participating in a conversation does not necessarily indicate a lack of interest.

4 COLLABOT IN AN ONLINE ENVIRONMENT

In order to accommodate for the dynamic nature of online chat tools the topic models are built periodically based on a number of accumulated messages so as to keep the topic model updated. The social graph is updated dynamically using an exponentially moving average method so that old relationships exponentially decrease. The weight parameters are assigned initial values as described in the validation section and can be updated based on metrics collected by the system in real-time.

5 DEMONSTRATION SCENARIO DETAILS

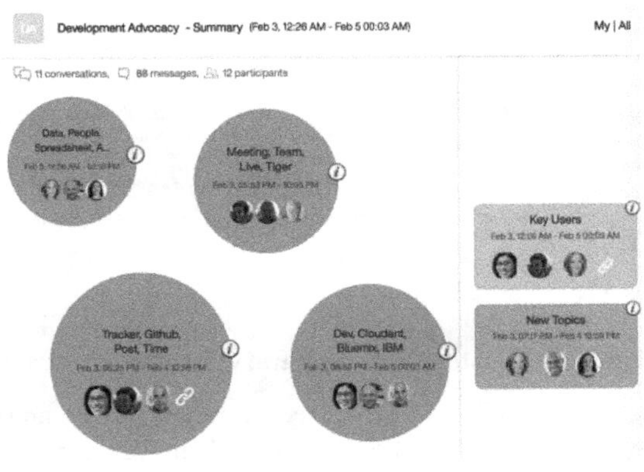

Figure 3: Personalized topical clusters view.

The demo shows how Collabot helps two different users, Helen - a team leader and Tom - an individual contributor, to quickly catch-up on the main content they missed after participating in a conference, to enable them to get back to their ongoing tasks as soon as possible.

First, we introduce the personalized summarization showing only the most relevant content. Second, we present the hierarchical structure of the summarization which enables the user to first see a high-level summary and only drill down where more information is desired. These two aspects are presented in the summary's two main views: the topics view (depicted in Figure 3) and the conversation view (Figure 5).

5.1 The Topics View

After returning from the conference, as Helen realizes that she does not have the time to go through the entire feed, she activates Collabot and is presented with the main screen (Figure 3). Most of the screen presents a personalized summary view of the main topics she missed while she was away. A topic – which is a cluster of conversations – is represented by a blue bubble where the bubble size is proportional to the magnitude of activity in this topic. Notably, the visual representation of discussions clusters was inspired by the 'chat circles' work of Donath et al. [4].

At the top of the screen, general statistics for the summary are presented to provide a notion of summary size: number of messages selected for the summary, number of corresponding conversations, number of users participating, and content that may have been shared in conversations within the topical cluster. The meta data of the topic displayed inside a bubble such as its title (section 2.3), the main participants of the selected conversations, and the time frame of the conversations provide a quick understanding of which topics of interest to her were discussed during her absence. When hovering over a bubble she can see important messages of the topic (section 2.4), and evidence helping her understand why this bubble was selected for her (Figure 4). In particular, the evidence explains the topics and people which caused the specific cluster to be part of her summary. Some conversations are selected because they contain topics she is interested in, some because people in her network are participating in them and some for both reasons.

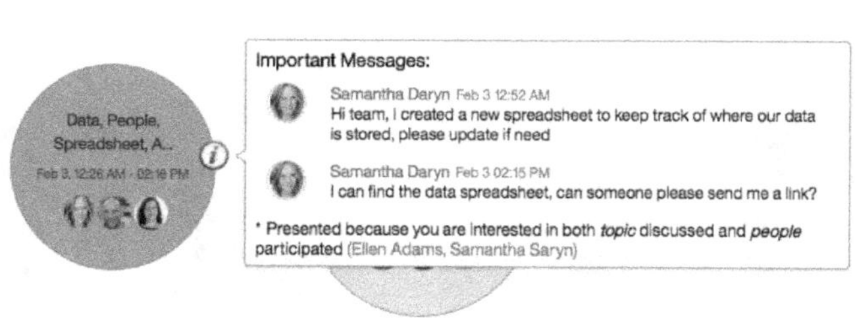

Figure 4: Cluster Summary and evidence.

The right-hand side of the screen presents two non-personalized aspects (section 2.5) - new and emerging topics bubble, and influencers box – messages that "you don't want to miss" from 'important' individuals in the group.

If Helen has time, she can view the full, non-personalized, view of the feed in the 'All' tab. This view keeps the same bubbles clustered by topics structure but creating it for the entire feed she missed and not only personally chosen sets of conversations.

5.2 The Conversations View

Helen wants to know more details on what was discussed in the 'tracker, github, post, time' topic (lower left bubble), so she clicks on its bubble and drills down into the conversations view depicted in Figure 5. This view lists the conversations that make up a topic, where long conversations are summarized (marked by yellow messages), and can be further expanded. Important keywords are highlighted to help her understand the context and content of conversations. Note that some conversations are not sequential in time, showing Collabot's capability to identify and unite disentangled conversational threads into a unified conversation.

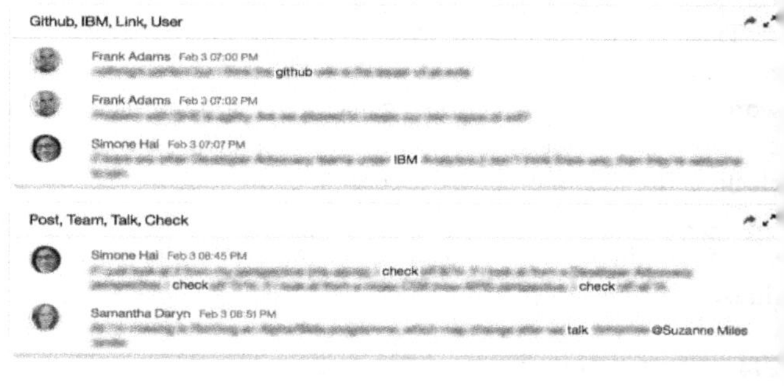

Figure 5: Conversation summaries per topic.

The demo continues to show the topics view for Tom emphasizing the fewer topics in his summary and thus the personalization aspect.

REFERENCES

[1] Blei, D. et al. 2010. Probabilistic topic models. *IEEE Signal Processing Magazine* 27, 6 (2010), 55–65.

[2] Dascalu, M. et al. 2010. A deep insight in chat analysis: Collaboration evolution and evaluation, summarization and search. *Lecture Notes in Computer Science* (2010), 191–200.

[3] Díaz, A. and Gervás, P. 2007. User-model based personalized summarization. *Information Processing and Management.* 43, 6 (2007), 1715–1734.

[4] Donath, J. and Viégas, F. 2002. The chat circles series. *Proceedings of the conference on Designing interactive systems processes, practices, methods, and techniques - DIS '02.* (2002), 359–369.

[5] Hong, L. and Davison, B. 2010. Empirical study of topic modeling in twitter. *Proceedings of the First Workshop on Social ....* (2010), 80–88.

[6] Hu, M. et al. 2008. Comments-Oriented Document Summarization: Understanding Documents with Readers' Feedback. *Proceedings of SIGIR '08.* (2008), 291–298.

[7] Hu, P. et al. 2012. Context-Enhanced Personalized Social Summarization. *In COLING.* (2012), 1223–1238.

[8] Mehrotra, R. et al. 2013. Improving LDA Topic Models for Microblogs via Tweet Pooling and Automatic Labeling. *Proc SIGIR '13.* (2013), 889–892.

[9] Nezhad, H.R.M. et al. 2017. eAssistant: Cognitive Assistance for Identification and Auto-Triage of Actionable Conversations. *Proceedings of WWW Companion.* (2017), 89–98.

[10] Nie, J. et al. 2011. Summarize What You Are Interested In: An Optimization Framework for Interactive Personalized Summarization. *Proceedings of the 2011 EMNLP'11.* (2011), 1342–1351.

[11] Ouyang, Y. et al. 2011. Applying regression models to query-focused multi-document summarization. *Information Processing and Management.* 47, 2 (2011), 227–237.

[12] Sood, A. et al. 2013. Topic-focused summarization of chat conversations. *Lecture Notes in Computer Science* (2013), 800–803.

[13] Tepper, N. et al. *Implicit User Profiling in Multiparticipant Chat.*

[14] Uthus, D.C. and Aha, D.W. 2013. Multiparticipant chat analysis: A survey. *Artificial Intelligence.* 199–200, (2013), 106–121.

[15] Zhu, Y. et al. 2013. Learning to classify short text with topic model and external knowledge. *Lecture Notes in Computer Science* (2013), 493–503.

Influence Maximization in Online Social Networks

Cigdem Aslay*
ISI Foundation
Turin, Italy
cigdem.aslay@isi.it

Laks V.S. Lakshmanan
University of British Columbia
Vancouver, B.C., Canada
laks@cs.ubc.ca

Wei Lu
Rupert Labs
Mountain View, CA
welu@cs.ubc.ca

Xiaokui Xiao
Nanyang Technological University
Singapore
xkxiao@ntu.edu.sg

ACM Reference Format:
Cigdem Aslay, Laks V.S. Lakshmanan, Wei Lu, and Xiaokui Xiao. 2018. Influence Maximization in Online Social Networks. In *WSDM 2018: WSDM 2018: The Eleventh ACM International Conference on Web Search and Data Mining , February 5–9, 2018, Marina Del Rey, CA, USA.* ACM, New York, NY, USA, 2 pages. https://doi.org/10.1145/3159652.3162007

MOTIVATION

Viral marketing, a popular concept in the business literature, has recently attracted a lot of attention also in computer science, due to its high application potential and computational challenges.The idea of viral marketing is simple yet appealing: by targeting the most influential users in a social network (*e.g.*, by giving them free or price-discounted samples), one can exploit the power of the network effect through word-of-mouth, thus delivering the marketing message to a large portion of the network analogous to the spread of a virus.

Influence maximization is the key algorithmic problem behind viral marketing. The problem, as originally defined by Kempe *et al.* [32], is as follows: given (*i*) a directed social network, (*ii*) a set of weights associated with edges, representing strengths or probabilities of influence among users, (*iii*) a stochastic influence propagation model that governs how a certain behavior would diffuse among users, and (*iv*) a cardinality constraint k, aim is to identify a set of k nodes, called the "seed set", that can be targeted to maximize the expected number of influenced nodes. Kempe *et al.* studied influence maximization as a discrete optimization problem, obtaining provable approximation guarantees under several social influence propagation models. Following this seminal work, research on the dynamics of social influence propagation and influence maximization took off in several dimensions.

In this tutorial we cover major algorithmic and theoretical developments and issues arising in this field. A good chunk of this research has been done in the data mining and databases communities. While related tutorials [2, 10, 23, 24, 35, 55] appeared in VLDB'11, KDD'11, KDD'12, WSDM'13, WWW'15, and KDD'15, our tutorial showcase recent advances in the field not covered by the previous tutorials. A tutorial like the one that we propose can allow interested researchers and practitioners to gain up-to-date knowledge on the recent theoretical and algorithmic developments and seize the opportunity to contribute to the advancement of this fast-paced field.

TUTORIAL OUTLINE

Part I: Influence maximization problem (70%)
We start the tutorial by introducing social influence propagation models and the standard influence maximization problem as defined by Kempe *et al.* We then extensively survey the algorithmic efforts for devising scalable and efficient influence maximization algorithms. We also discuss recently defined context-aware influence maximization problems, as well as closely related alternative optimization problems. The detailed outline of Part I is as follows:

- Influence maximization problem (15%)
  - Discrete- [32, 33, 43] and continuous-time [21, 51] models
  - Hardness & greedy approximation [15, 17, 32, 36]
- Improving efficiency and scalability (20%)
  - Ranking and score based heuristics [15, 17, 22, 27, 31, 47]
  - Sketches, reverse influence sampling [8, 19, 30, 46, 57, 58]
- Context-aware influence maximization (25%)
  - Topic- [3, 11, 13, 38] and time-aware [14, 39]
  - Location-aware [37, 53, 54, 61]
  - Competitive and comparative [7, 9, 40, 41, 50]
  - Dynamic influence maximization [18, 48]
- Other optimization objectives (10%)
  - Business-oriented optimization: adoption, profit, recommendation, etc [6, 42]
  - Robustness of influence maximization [12, 28, 49]

Part II: Modeling and learning social influence (15%)
In this part of the tutorial we first review the body of research that aims to learn influence weights from past propagation traces [25, 45, 52]. We then cover recent efforts that aim to directly learn the influence function [20, 26, 29, 44], thus, enabling the estimation of

*Main contact.

WSDM 2018, February 5–9, 2018, Marina Del Rey, CA, USA

ACM ISBN 978-1-4503-5581-0/18/02.
https://doi.org/10.1145/3159652.3162007

the expected influence of a given set of nodes directly from given propagation traces. We also review a recent line of work which leverages active learning and multi-armed bandits to tackle "on-line" influence maximization where influence probabilities are not known and no past propagation data is available [16, 34, 59, 60].

Part III: Broader optimization objectives (15%)
The area of computational advertising has attracted a lot of interest during the last decade. However, with the advent of social advertising, the standard interest-driven allocation of ads to users has become inadequate as it fails to leverage the potential of social influence. In comparison to computational advertising, social advertising is still in its early stage. In this part of the tutorial, we review the recent initial efforts that aim to bridge the gap between viral marketing and social advertising [1, 4, 5, 56].

REFERENCES

[1] Zeinab Abbassi, Aditya Bhaskara, and Vishal Misra. 2015. Optimizing Display Advertising in Online Social Networks. In *WWW*. 1–11.
[2] Divyakant Agrawal, Ceren Budak, and Amr El Abbadi. 2011. Information diffusion in social networks: Observing and influencing societal interests. *PVLDB* 4, 12 (2011), 1–5.
[3] Cigdem Aslay, Nicola Barbieri, Francesco Bonchi, and Ricardo A Baeza-Yates. 2014. Online Topic-aware Influence Maximization Queries.. In *EDBT*. 295–306.
[4] Cigdem Aslay, Francesco Bonchi, Laks VS Lakshmanan, and Wei Lu. 2017. Revenue maximization in incentivized social advertising. *PVLDB* 10, 11 (2017), 1238–1249.
[5] Cigdem Aslay, Wei Lu, Francesco Bonchi, Amit Goyal, and Laks VS Lakshmanan. 2015. Viral marketing meets social advertising: Ad allocation with minimum regret. *PVLDB* 8, 7 (2015), 814–825.
[6] Smriti Bhagat, Amit Goyal, and Laks VS Lakshmanan. 2012. Maximizing product adoption in social networks. In *WSDM*. 603–612.
[7] Bharathi et al., 2007. Competitive influence maximization in social networks. In *International Workshop on Web and Internet Economics*. Springer, 306–311.
[8] Christian Borgs, Michael Brautbar, Jennifer T Chayes, and Brendan Lucier. 2014. Maximizing Social Influence in Nearly Optimal Time.. In *SODA*. SIAM, 946–957.
[9] Allan Borodin, Yuval Filmus, and Joel Oren. 2010. Threshold models for competitive influence in social networks. In *WINE*. Springer, 539–550.
[10] Carlos Castillo, Wei Chen, and Laks VS Lakshmanan. 2012. Information and influence spread in social networks. In *KDD*. ACM.
[11] Shuo Chen, Ju Fan, Guoliang Li, Jianhua Feng, Kian-lee Tan, and Jinhui Tang. 2015. Online topic-aware influence maximization. *PVLDB* 8, 6 (2015), 666–677.
[12] Wei Chen, Tian Lin, Zihan Tan, Mingfei Zhao, and Xuren Zhou. 2016. Robust Influence Maximization. In *KDD (KDD '16)*. ACM, 795–804.
[13] Wei Chen, Tian Lin, and Cheng Yang. 2015. Real-time Topic-aware Influence Maximization Using Preprocessing. In *CSoNet*. Springer, 1–13.
[14] Wei Chen, Wei Lu, and Ning Zhang. 2012. Time-critical influence maximization in social networks with time-delayed diffusion process.. In *AAAI*, Vol. 2012. 1–5.
[15] Wei Chen, Chi Wang, and Yajun Wang. 2010. Scalable influence maximization for prevalent viral marketing in large-scale social networks. In *KDD*. 1029–1038.
[16] Wei Chen, Yajun Wang, and Yang Yuan. 2013. Combinatorial Multi-Armed Bandit: General Framework and Applications. In *ICML*. 151–159.
[17] Wei Chen, Yifei Yuan, and Li Zhang. 2010. Scalable Influence Maximization in Social Networks under the Linear Threshold Model. In *ICDM*. 88–97.
[18] Xiaodong Chen, Guojie Song, Xinran He, and Kunqing Xie. 2015. On influential nodes tracking in dynamic social networks. In *SDM*. SIAM, 613–621.
[19] Cohen et al., 2014. Sketch-based Influence Maximization and Computation: Scaling up with Guarantees. In *CIKM*.
[20] Nan Du, Yingyu Liang, Maria Balcan, and Le Song. 2014. Influence function learning in information diffusion networks. In *ICML*. 2016–2024.
[21] Nan Du, Le Song, Manuel Gomez-Rodriguez, and Hongyuan Zha. 2013. Scalable influence estimation in continuous-time diffusion networks. In *NIPS*. 3147–3155.
[22] Sainyam Galhotra, Akhil Arora, and Shourya Roy. 2016. Holistic influence maximization: Combining scalability and efficiency with opinion-aware models. In *SIGMOD*. ACM, 743–758.
[23] M. Gomez-Rodriguez and Le Song. 2015. Diffusion in Social and Information Metworks: Research Problems; Probabilistic Models & Machine Learning Methods. In *WWW*. ACM, 1527–1528.
[24] M. Gomez Rodriguez and Le Song. 2015. Diffusion in social and information networks: research problems, probabilistic models and machine learning methods. In *KDD*. ACM, 2315–2316.
[25] Amit Goyal, Francesco Bonchi, and Laks V. S. Lakshmanan. 2010. Learnin influence probabilities in social networks. In *WSDM*. 241–250.
[26] Amit Goyal, Francesco Bonchi, and Laks V. S. Lakshmanan. 2011. A Data-Base Approach to Social Influence Maximization. *PVLDB* 5, 1 (2011), 73–84.
[27] Amit Goyal, Wei Lu, and Laks V. S. Lakshmanan. 2011. SIMPATH: An Efficie Algorithm for Influence Maximization under the Linear Threshold Model. *ICDM*. 211–220.
[28] Xinran He and David Kempe. 2016. Robust Influence Maximization. In *KD* ACM, 885–894.
[29] Xinran He, Ke Xu, David Kempe, and Yan Liu. 2016. Learning Influence Functio from Incomplete Observations. In *NIPS*. 2065–2073.
[30] Keke Huang, Sibo Wang, Glenn Bevilacqua, Xiaokui Xiao, and Laks VS Laks manan. 2017. Revisiting the Stop-and-Stare Algorithms for Influence Maximiz tion. *PVLDB* 10, 9 (2017).
[31] Kyomin Jung, Wooram Heo, and Wei Chen. 2012. Irie: Scalable and robu influence maximization in social networks. In *ICDM*. IEEE, 918–923.
[32] David Kempe, Jon Kleinberg, and Éva Tardos. 2003. Maximizing the spread influence through a social network. In *KDD*. ACM, 137–146.
[33] David Kempe, Jon M. Kleinberg, and Éva Tardos. 2005. Influential Nodes in Diffusion Model for Social Networks. In *ICALP*. 1127–1138.
[34] Siyu Lei, Silviu Maniu, Luyi Mo, Reynold Cheng, and Pierre Senellart. 201 Online influence maximization. In *KDD*. ACM, 645–654.
[35] Jure Leskovec. 2011. Social media analytics: tracking, modeling and predictin the flow of information through networks. In *WWW*. ACM, 277–278.
[36] Leskovec et al., 2007. Cost-effective outbreak detection in networks. In *KD* ACM, 420–429.
[37] Guoliang Li, Shuo Chen, Jianhua Feng, Kian-lee Tan, and Wen-syan Li. 201 Efficient location-aware influence maximization. In *SIGMOD*. ACM, 87–98.
[38] Yuchen Li, Dongxiang Zhang, and Kian-Lee Tan. 2015. Real-time targeted infl ence maximization for online advertisements. *PVLDB* 8, 10 (2015), 1070–1081.
[39] Bo Liu, Gao Cong, Dong Xu, and Yifeng Zeng. 2012. Time constrained influenc maximization in social networks. In *ICDM*. IEEE, 439–448.
[40] Lu et al., 2013. The bang for the buck: fair competitive viral marketing from th host perspective. In *KDD*. ACM, 928–936.
[41] Wei Lu, Wei Chen, and Laks VS Lakshmanan. 2015. From competition to compl mentarity: comparative influence diffusion and maximization. *PVLDB* 9, 2 (2015 60–71.
[42] Wei Lu and Laks VS Lakshmanan. 2012. Profit maximization over social network In *ICDM*. IEEE, 479–488.
[43] Elchanan Mossel and Sebastien Roch. 2007. On the submodularity of influenc in social networks. In *STOC*. 128–134.
[44] Harikrishna Narasimhan, David C Parkes, and Yaron Singer. 2015. Learnabilit of influence in networks. In *NIPS*. 3186–3194.
[45] Praneeth Netrapalli and Sujay Sanghavi. 2012. Learning the graph of epidemi cascades. In *ACM SIGMETRICS*, Vol. 40. ACM, 211–222.
[46] Hung T. Nguyen, My T. Thai, and Thang N. Dinh. 2016. Stop-and-Stare: Optima Sampling Algorithms for Viral Marketing in Billion-scale Networks. In *SIGMOD*
[47] Ohsaka et al., 2014. Fast and Accurate Influence Maximization on Large Network with Pruned Monte-Carlo Simulations.. In *AAAI*. 138–144.
[48] Ohsaka et al., 2016. Dynamic influence analysis in evolving networks. *PVLDB* 12 (2016), 1077–1088.
[49] Naoto Ohsaka and Yuichi Yoshida. 2017. Portfolio Optimization for Influenc Spread. In *WWW*. ACM, 977–985.
[50] Pathak et al., 2010. A generalized linear threshold model for multiple cascade In *ICDM*. IEEE, 965–970.
[51] Gomez-Rodriguez et al., 2014. Uncovering the structure and temporal dynamic of information propagation. *Network Science* 2, 01 (2014), 26–65.
[52] Saito et al., 2008. Prediction of Information Diffusion Probabilities for Independen Cascade Model. In *KES*.
[53] Saleem et al., 2017. Location Influence in Location-based Social Networks. In *WSDM*. ACM, 621–630.
[54] Chonggang Song, Wynne Hsu, and Mong Li Lee. 2016. Targeted Influence Maximization in Social Networks. In *CIKM*. ACM, 1683–1692.
[55] Jimeng Sun and Jie Tang. 2013. Models and algorithms for social influence analysis. In *WSDM*. ACM, 775–776.
[56] Shaojie Tang and Jing Yuan. 2016. Optimizing Ad Allocation in Social Advertising In *CIKM*. ACM, 1383–1392.
[57] Youze Tang, Yanchen Shi, and Xiaokui Xiao. 2015. Influence maximization in near-linear time: A martingale approach. In *SIGMOD*. ACM, 1539–1554.
[58] Youze Tang, Xiaokui Xiao, and Yanchen Shi. 2014. Influence Maximization Near-Optimal Time Complexity Meets Practical Efficiency. *SIGMOD* (2014).
[59] Vaswani et al., 2017. Model-Independent Online Learning for Influence Maximization. In *ICML*. 3530–3539.
[60] Wen et al., 2017. Online Influence Maximization under Independent Cascade Model with Semi-Bandit Feedback. In *NIPS*. 3025–3035.
[61] Zhang et al., 2012. Evaluating geo-social influence in location-based social networks. In *CIKM*. ACM, 1442–1451.

Differential Privacy for Information Retrieval

Grace Hui Yang
Georgetown University
Washington, D. C.
huiyang@cs.georgetown.edu

Sicong Zhang
Georgetown University
Washington, D. C.
sz303@georgetown.edu

ABSTRACT

The concern for privacy is real for any research that uses user data. Information Retrieval (IR) is not an exception. Many IR algorithms and applications require the use of users' personal information, contextual information and other sensitive and private information. The extensive use of personalization in IR has become a double-edged sword. Sometimes, the concern becomes so overwhelming that IR research has to stop to avoid privacy leaks. The good news is that recently there have been increasing attentions paid on the joint field of privacy and IR – privacy-preserving IR. As part of the effort, this tutorial offers an introduction to differential privacy (DP), one of the most advanced techniques in privacy research, and provides necessary set of theoretical knowledge for applying privacy techniques in IR. Differential privacy is a technique that provides strong privacy guarantees for data protection. Theoretically, it aims to maximize the data utility in statistical datasets while minimizing the risk of exposing individual data entries to any adversary. Differential privacy has been successfully applied to a wide range of applications in database (DB) and data mining (DM). The research in privacy-preserving IR is relatively new, however, research has shown that DP is also effective in supporting multiple IR tasks. This tutorial aims to lay a theoretical foundation of DP and explains how it can be applied to IR. It highlights the differences in IR tasks and DB and DM tasks and how DP connects to IR. We hope the attendees of this tutorial will have a good understanding of DP and other necessary knowledge to work on the newly minted joint research field of privacy and IR.

ACM Reference Format:

Grace Hui Yang and Sicong Zhang. 2018. Differential Privacy for Information Retrieval. In *WSDM 2018: WSDM 2018: The Eleventh ACM International Conference on Web Search and Data Mining , February 5–9, 2018, Marina Del Rey, CA, USA.* ACM, New York, NY, USA, 2 pages. https://doi.org/10.1145/3159652.3162006

1 MOTIVATION

The rapid development of big data, social networks, mobile services and the growing popularity of digital communications have profoundly changed Information Retrieval (IR). Many recent advances in IR research rely on sensitive and private data such as large-scale query logs, users' search history, and location information. It is understandable that the sensitive and private data is kept within commercial companies without being shared with the research community. However, the concern of privacy sometimes became so overwhelming that it hurt IR research in the past. For instance, the TREC Medical Record Retrieval Tracks [21] were halted because of the privacy issue and the TREC Microblog Tracks [10] could not provide participants with a standard testbed of tweets for a fair comparison. The proper use of privacy techniques to empower privacy-preserving IR [25] need to be studied at a timely manner.

Differential privacy (DP) [4] is the state-of-the-art approach which provides a strong privacy notion and has been widely used in the database (DB) and data mining (DM) [2, 5, 8, 15, 17, 22] communities. Recent research has shown that differential privacy provides the strongest privacy guarantees among all other privacy techniques.

Differential privacy is mostly used to protect statistical database, or more generally, for data frequencies. A major challenge of using DP in IR research is the involvement of natural language corpora. Those natural language corpora contain open domains of words, queries, and web documents. Another challenge in applying DP to IR is related to the long-tail effect of the zipf's law. The effect produces very sparse frequency distributions, both at the term level and the document level, which makes many differentially private algorithms in data mining cannot be directly applied to IR research due to very high computational complexity. We will highlight the unique IR challenges in using DP, with comparisons to similar applications in DB and DM.

The major concerns of privacy in IR include how to properly use personalized data for IR research and how to preserve privacy when releasing them. For instance, web query logs and medical records should not be shared without privacy enhancement. During the recent years, researchers have shown that DP is effective in supporting a few IR topics such as query log anonymization [19] and Geographic IR [13]. In this tutorial, we cover successful examples of using DP to support IR tasks such as web search, query suggestion, and geological information retrieval. We hope that this tutorial could be a milestone in the development of privacy-preserving IR and enable more valuable research in this promising new joint field.

2 TOPICS TO BE COVERED

Theme 1 Privacy-Preserving IR and Early Attempts - 60 mins

(1) Background: Privacy concerns in IR. [28]
(2) Privacy-Preserving Information Retrieval (PPIR).
(3) Naive privacy techniques [3].
(4) K-Anonymity [16], T-Closeness [9], L-Diversity [12].
(5) Privacy in Search [1, 11] and recent research topics in Privacy-Preserving IR [14, 23, 25].

Theme 2 Differential Privacy - 50 mins

(1) Background knowledge in probability.

WSDM 2018, February 5–9, 2018, Marina Del Rey, CA, USA

ACM ISBN 978-1-4503-5581-0/18/02.
https://doi.org/10.1145/3159652.3162006

(2) Mathematical definitions of DP [4].
(3) Discussions about DP.

Theme 3 IR applications using Differential Privacy - 70 mins

(1) Why differential privacy is applicable to IR.
(2) Query Log Anonymization [6, 7, 26, 27, 29].
(3) Geographic IR [13, 18–20].
(4) Other applications that use DP.
(5) Wrap Up and Discussions.

3 LEARNING OBJECTIVES

The objective of this tutorial is to provide a comprehensive and up-to-date introduction to differential privacy for IR research. We also present a handful of recent IR and mining applications utilizing DP. By the end of this tutorial, the attendees are able to:

- Master DP's mathematical foundation.
- Have a sound understanding of how DP connects to IR.
- Have knowledge of how DP is used in the state-of-the-art research in IR and data mining.
- Be able to generalize the use of DP in other privacy-preserving IR scenarios.

4 LINKS TO RELATED RESOURCES

A website to related resources is located at *https://privacypreservingir.org/*. It contains related publications and

- An early version of this tutorial [24] given in the 3rd ACM International Conference on the Theory of Information Retrieval (ICTIR 2017), Amsterdam, Netherlands. Oct 1, 2017.
- The first, second, and third "Privacy-Preserving IR: When Information Retrieval Meets Privacy and Security" Workshops PPIR'14 [14], PPIR'15 [23] and PPIR'16 [25] organized by the authors during the 37-39th International ACM SIGIR Conferences (SIGIR 2014 - 2016).

5 SUPPORT MATERIALS

Attendees will be given printed handouts and a copy of slides.

6 CONCLUSION

Privacy in IR is an emerging field of research. This tutorial highlights the differences of IR applications and other applications in DB and DM and introduces a state-of-the-art privacy technique – differential privacy – to the WSDM community. The purpose of this tutorial is to provide necessary background knowledge to solve the privacy issues in IR related research. Differential privacy is a theoretical framework that requires good mathematical skills and deep understanding to master it. It is not trivial to learn this subject however due to serious privacy concerns in IR and the strong privacy guarantee provided by this latest technique, we think it is necessary for anyone who would like to pursue research in privacy-preserving IR to master this subject. We hope the tutorial to help lay a solid foundation for using DP to solve many privacy problems in IR.

7 ACKNOWLEDGMENTS

This research was supported by NSF grant IIS-145374 and DARPA grant FA8750-14-2-0226. Any opinions, findings, conclusions, or recommendations expressed in this paper are of the authors, and do not necessarily reflect those of the sponsor.

REFERENCES

[1] N. Cao, C. Wang, M. Li, K. Ren, and W. Lou. 2014. Privacy-Preserving Multi-Keyword Ranked Search over Encrypted Cloud Data. *IEEE Transactions on Parallel and Distributed Systems* 25, 1 (Jan 2014), 222–233.
[2] Rui Chen, Gergely Acs, and Claude Castelluccia. 2012. Differentially Private Sequential Data Publication via Variable-length N-grams. In *Proceedings of the 2012 ACM Conference on Computer and Communications Security (CCS '12)*.
[3] Alissa Cooper. 2008. A Survey of Query Log Privacy-enhancing Techniques from a Policy Perspective. *ACM Trans. Web* 2, 4, Article 19 (Oct. 2008), 27 pages.
[4] Cynthia Dwork, Frank McSherry, Kobbi Nissim, and Adam Smith. Calibrating Noise to Sensitivity in Private Data Analysis. In *Proceedings of the Third Conference on Theory of Cryptography (TCC'06)*.
[5] Arik Friedman and Assaf Schuster. 2010. Data mining with differential privacy. In *KDDâĂŽ10*. ACM, 493–502.
[6] Michaela Gotz, Ashwin Machanavajjhala, Guozhang Wang, Xiaokui Xiao, and Johannes Gehrke. 2012. Publishing Search Logs – A Comparative Study of Privacy Guarantees. *IEEE Trans. on Knowl. and Data Eng.* 24, 3 (March 2012).
[7] Aleksandra Korolova, Krishnaram Kenthapadi, Nina Mishra, and Alexandros Ntoulas. Releasing Search Queries and Clicks Privately. In *WWW '09*.
[8] Haoran Li, Li Xiong, Xiaoqian Jiang, and Jinfei Liu. 2015. Differentially Private Histogram Publication for Dynamic Datasets: an Adaptive Sampling Approach. In *CIKM '15*.
[9] N. Li, T. Li, and S. Venkatasubramanian. t-Closeness: Privacy Beyond k-Anonymity and l-Diversity. In *ICDE 2007*.
[10] Jimmy Lin, Miles Efron, Yulu Wang, and Garrick Sherman. 2014. *Overview of the TREC-2014 Microblog track*. Technical Report. DTIC Document.
[11] W. Lu, A. L. Varna, and M. Wu. 2010. Security analysis for privacy preserving search of multimedia. In *2010 IEEE International Conference on Image Processing*.
[12] Ashwin Machanavajjhala, Daniel Kifer, Johannes Gehrke, and Muthuramakrishnan Venkitasubramaniam. 2007. L-diversity: Privacy Beyond K-anonymity. *ACM Trans. Knowl. Discov. Data* 1, 1, Article 3 (March 2007).
[13] Cyrus Shahabi, Liyue Fan, Luciano Nocera, Li Xiong, and Ming Li. Privacy-preserving Inference of Social Relationships from Location Data: A Vision Paper. In *SIGSPATIAL '15*. Article 9, 4 pages.
[14] Luo Si, Grace Hui Yang, Sicong Zhang, and Lei Cen. 2014. Proceeding of the 1st International Workshop on Privacy-Preserving IR: When Information Retrieval Meets Privacy and Security. *PIR* (2014).
[15] S. Su, S. Xu, X. Cheng, Z. Li, and F. Yang. 2015. Differentially Private Frequent Itemset Mining via Transaction Splitting. *IEEE Transactions on Knowledge and Data Engineering* 27, 7 (July 2015).
[16] Latanya Sweeney. 2002. k-anonymity: A model for protecting privacy. *International Journal of Uncertainty, Fuzziness and Knowledge-Based Systems* 10, 05 (2002).
[17] Christine Task and Chris Clifton. 2012. A Guide to Differential Privacy Theory in Social Network Analysis. In *ASONAM '12*.
[18] Hien To, Liyue Fan, and Cyrus Shahabi. 2015. Differentially Private H-Tree. In *GeoPrivacy'15*. Article 3, 8 pages.
[19] H. To, G. Ghinita, L. Fan, and C. Shahabi. 2017. Differentially Private Location Protection for Worker Datasets in Spatial Crowdsourcing. *IEEE Transactions on Mobile Computing* 16, 4 (April 2017), 934–949.
[20] Hien To, Kien Nguyen, and Cyrus Shahabi. 2016. Differentially Private Publication of Location Entropy. In *GIS '16*. Article 35, 10 pages.
[21] Ellen M Voorhees and William R Hersh. 2012. Overview of the TREC 2012 Medical Records Track. In *TREC'12*.
[22] S. Xu, S. Su, X. Cheng, Z. Li, and L. Xiong. 2015. Differentially private frequent sequence mining via sampling-based candidate pruning. In *ICDE 2015*.
[23] Grace Hui Yang and Ian Soboroff. 2015. Privacy Preserving IR 2015: A SIGIR 2015 Workshop.. In *SIGIR Forum*, Vol. 49. 98–101.
[24] Grace Hui Yang and Sicong Zhang. 2017. Tutorial: Differential Privacy for Information Retrieval. In *the 3rd ACM International Conference on the Theory of Information Retrieval, ICTIR'17. Amsterdam, Netherlands.*
[25] Hui Yang, Ian Soboroff, Li Xiong, Charles L.A. Clarke, and Simson L. Garfinkel. 2016. Privacy-Preserving IR 2016: Differential Privacy, Search, and Social Media. In *SIGIR '16*.
[26] Sicong Zhang and Grace Hui Yang. 2017. Deriving Differentially Private Session Logs for Query Suggestion. In *ICTIR'17*.
[27] Sicong Zhang, Grace Hui Yang, Lisa Singh, and Li Xiong. 2016. Safelog: Supporting Web Search and Mining by Differentially-Private Query Logs. In *2016 AAAI Fall Symposium Series*.
[28] Sicong Zhang, Hui Yang, and Lisa Singh. 2014. Increased Information Leakage from Text.. In *PIR 2014@ SIGIR*. 41–42.
[29] Sicong Zhang, Hui Yang, and Lisa Singh. 2016. Anonymizing Query Logs by Differential Privacy. In *SIGIR '16*.

Neural Networks for Information Retrieval*

Tom Kenter†
Booking.com
Amsterdam, The Netherlands
tom.kenter@gmail.com

Alexey Borisov
Yandex
Moscow, Russia
alborisov@yandex-team.ru

Christophe Van Gysel
University of Amsterdam
Amsterdam, The Netherlands
cvangysel@uva.nl

Mostafa Dehghani
University of Amsterdam
Amsterdam, The Netherlands
dehghani@uva.nl

Maarten de Rijke
University of Amsterdam
Amsterdam, The Netherlands
derijke@uva.nl

Bhaskar Mitra
Microsoft, University College London
Cambridge, UK
bmitra@microsoft.com

CM Reference Format:
om Kenter, Alexey Borisov, Christophe Van Gysel, Mostafa Dehghani, Aaarten de Rijke, and Bhaskar Mitra. 2018. Neural Networks for Information Retrieval. In *WSDM 2018: WSDM 2018: The Eleventh ACM International Conference on Web Search and Data Mining , February 5–9, 2018, Marina Del Rey, CA, USA.* ACM, New York, NY, USA, 2 pages. https://doi.org/10.1145/3159652.3162009

bstract

Aachine learning plays a role in many aspects of modern IR systems, and deep learning is applied in all of them. The fast pace of nodern-day research has given rise to many approaches to many R problems. The amount of information available can be overwhelming both for junior students and for experienced researchers ooking for new research topics and directions. The aim of this full-lay tutorial is to give a clear overview of current tried-and-trusted neural methods in IR and how they benefit IR.

Motivation

Prompted by advances of deep learning in computer vision, neural networks (NNs) have resurfaced as a popular machine learning paradigm in many other directions of research, including IR. Recent years have seen NNs being applied to all key parts of the typical modern IR pipeline, such as click models, core ranking algorithms, dialogue systems, entity retrieval, knowledge graphs, language modeling, question answering, and text similarity.

An advantage that sets NNs apart from many learning strategies employed earlier, is their ability to work from raw input data. Where designing features used to be a crucial aspect of newly proposed IR approaches, the focus has shifted to designing network architectures instead. Hence, many architectures and paradigms have been proposed, such as auto-encoders, recursive networks, recurrent networks, convolutional networks, various embedding methods, and deep reinforcement learning. This tutorial aims to provide an overview of the main network architectures currently applied in IR and to show how they relate to previous work.

*Slides and other materials will be made available online at http://nnn4ir.com.
†Corresponding author.

WSDM 2018, February 5–9, 2018, Marina Del Rey, CA, USA

ACM ISBN 978-1-4503-5581-0/18/02.
https://doi.org/10.1145/3159652.3162009

We expect the tutorial to be useful both for academic and industrial researchers and practitioners who either want to develop new neural models, use them in their own research in other areas or apply the models described here to improve actual IR systems.

Brief outline of the topics to be covered

Table 1 gives an overview of the time schedule of the tutorial. The total time is 6 hours, plus breaks. We bring a team of six lecturers,

Table 1: Time schedule for NN4IR tutorial

Morning		Afternoon	
Preliminaries	45 min.	Recommender systems	45 min.
Semantic matching	45 min.	Modeling user behavior	45 min.
Learning to rank	45 min.	Generating responses	45 min.
Entities	45 min.	Industry insights	45 min.

all with their specific areas of specialization. Each session will have two expert lecturers (indicated by their initials below) who will together present the session.

Preliminaries *[TK, MdR].* The recent surge of interest in deep learning has given rise to a myriad of model architectures. Different though the inner structures of NNs can be, many building blocks are shared. In this preliminary session, we focus on key concepts, all of which will be referred to multiple times in subsequent sessions. In particular we will cover distributed representations/embeddings [37], fully-connect layers, convolutional layers [27], recurrent networks [36] and sequence-to-sequence models [45].

Semantic matching *[CVG, BM].* The problem of matching based on textual descriptions arises in many retrieval systems. The traditional IR approach involves computing lexical term overlap between query and document [42]. However, a vocabulary gap occurs when query and documents use different terms to describe the same concepts [31]. Semantic matching methods bridge the vocabulary gap by matching concepts rather than exact word occurrences. We cover neural network-based methods that learn to provide a semantic matching signal supervised fashion [21, 33, 38, 39], semi-supervised [12, 13], and unsupervised [2, 15, 23, 25, 29, 47–49, 53, 58].

Learning to rank *[AB, MD].* Capturing the notion of relevance for ranking needs to account for different aspects of the query, the document, and their relationship. Neural methods for ranking can use manually crafted query and document features, and combine them with regards to a ranking objective. Moreover, latent representations of the query and document can be learned in situ. We cover scenarios with different levels of supervision—unsupervised [43, 47, 48], semi/weakly-supervised [12, 13, 46], or fully-supervised using labeled data [38] or interaction data [21].

***Entities** [CVG, TK].* Entities play a central role in modern IR systems [14]. We cover neural approaches to solving the basic task of named entity recognition [8, 10, 28], as well learning representations in an end-to-end neural model for learning a specific task like entity ranking for expert finding [48], product search [47] or email attachment retrieval [50]. Furthermore, work related to knowledge graphs will be covered, such as graph embeddings [5, 55, 57].

***Recommender systems** [MdR, BM].* Deep learning has also found its way into recommender systems. We cover learning of item (products, users) embeddings [4, 17, 51], as well as deep collaborative filtering using different deep learning techniques and architectures [7, 54]. Furthermore, NN-based feature extraction from content (such as images, music, text) [3, 34, 40], and session-based recommendations with RNNs [11, 20, 41] will be covered.

***Modeling user behavior** [AB, MdR].* Modeling user browsing behavior plays an important role in modern IR systems. Accurately interpreting user clicks is difficult due to various types of bias. Many click models based on Probabilistic Graphical Models (PGMs) have been proposed [9]. Recently, it was shown that recurrent neural networks can learn to account for biases in user clicks directly from click-through, i.e., without the need for a predefined set of rules as is customary for PGM-based click models [6].

***Generating responses** [TK, MD].* Recent inventions such as smart home devices, voice search, and virtual assistants provide new ways of accessing information. They require a different response format than the classic ten blue links. Examples are conversational and dialog systems [32, 52] or machine reading and question answering tasks, where the model either infers the answer from unstructured text [18, 19, 24, 26, 44, 56] or generates natural language given structured data, like data from knowledge graphs or from external memories [1, 16, 30, 35].

***Industry insights** [AB, BM].* Where the focus of academic papers can be on a specific subtask, industry approaches have to ensure that a system works from start to end. As a result, extra challenges are involved concerning the user experience. For example in Google's SmartReply system [22] the neural model at the core of the system is embedded in a much larger framework of non-neural methods to make sure quality and efficiency requirements are met.

REFERENCES

[1] S. Ahn et al. A neural knowledge language model. *arXiv preprint arXiv:1608.00318*, 2016.
[2] Q. Ai et al. Improving language estimation with the paragraph vector model for ad-hoc retrieval. In *SIGIR*, 2016.
[3] T. Bansal, D. Belanger, and M. A. Ask the GRU: Multi-task learning for deep text recommendations. In *RecSys*, 2016.
[4] O. Barkan and N. Koenigstein. ITEM2VEC: Neural item embedding for collaborative filtering. In *MLSP*, 2016.
[5] A. Bordes, J. Weston, R. Collobert, and Y. Bengio. Learning structured embeddings of knowledge bases. In *Conference on artificial intelligence*, 2011.
[6] A. Borisov et al. A neural click model for web search. In *WWW*, 2016.
[7] H. Cheng et al. Wide & deep learning for recommender systems. In *DLRS*, 2016.
[8] J. P. Chiu and E. Nichols. Named entity recognition with bidirectional LSTM-CNNs. *TACL*, 2015.
[9] A. Chuklin, I. Markov, and M. de Rijke. *Click Models for Web Search*. Morgan & Claypool, 2015.
[10] R. Collobert and J. Weston. A unified architecture for natural language processing: Deep neural networks with multitask learning. In *ICML*, 2008.
[11] M. Dehghani, S. Rothe, E. Alfonseca, and P. Fleury. Learning to attend, copy, and generate for session-based query suggestion. In *CIKM*, 2017.
[12] M. Dehghani, A. Severyn, S. Rothe, and J. Kamps. Avoiding your teacher's mistakes: Training neural networks with controlled weak supervision. *arXiv preprint arXiv:1711.00313*, 2017.
[13] M. Dehghani et al. Neural ranking models with weak supervision. In *SIGIR*, 2017.
[14] L. Dietz, A. Kotov, and E. Meij. Utilizing knowledge bases in text-centric information retrieval. In *ICTIR*, 2016.
[15] D. Ganguly et al. Word embedding based generalized language model for information retrieval. In *SIGIR*, 2015.
[16] A. Graves, G. Wayne, and I. Danihelka. Neural turing machines. *arXiv preprint arXiv:1410.5401*, 2014.
[17] M. Grbovic et al. E-commerce in your inbox: Product recommendations at sca In *KDD*, 2015.
[18] K. M. Hermann et al. Teaching machines to read and comprehend. In *NIPS*, 20
[19] D. Hewlett et al. WIKIREADING: A novel large-scale language understandir task over Wikipedia. In *Proc. ACL*, 2016.
[20] B. Hidasi et al. Session-based recommendations with recurrent neural networ In *ICLR*, 2016.
[21] P.-S. Huang et al. Learning deep structured semantic models for web searc using clickthrough data. In *CIKM*, 2013.
[22] A. Kannan et al. Smart Reply: Automated response suggestion for email. In *KD* 2016.
[23] T. Kenter and M. de Rijke. Short text similarity with word embeddings. In *CIK* 2015.
[24] T. Kenter and M. de Rijke. Attentive memory networks: Efficient machir reading for conversational search. In *Workshop on Conversational Approaches Information Retrieval (CAIR'17) at SIGIR 2017*, 2017.
[25] T. Kenter, A. Borisov, and M. de Rijke. Siamese CBOW: Optimizing word embe dings for sentence representations. In *Proc. ACL*, 2016.
[26] T. Kenter, L. Jones, and D. Hewlett. Byte-level machine reading across morph logically varied languages. In *Proc. AAAI*, 2018.
[27] A. Krizhevsky, I. Sutskever, and G. E. Hinton. ImageNet classification with dee convolutional neural networks. In *NIPS*, 2012.
[28] G. Lample, M. Ballesteros, S. Subramanian, K. Kawakami, and C. Dyer. Neur architectures for named entity recognition. In *NAACL-HLT*, 2016.
[29] Q. V. Le and T. Mikolov. Distributed representations of sentences and documen *arXiv preprint arXiv:1405.4053*, 2014.
[30] R. Lebret, D. Grangier, and M. Auli. Neural text generation from structured dat with application to the biography domain. *arXiv preprint arXiv:1603.07771*, 201
[31] H. Li, J. Xu, et al. Semantic matching in search. *FnTIR*, 2014.
[32] J. Li et al. Deep reinforcement learning for dialogue generation. In *EMNLP*, 201
[33] Z. Lu and H. Li. A deep architecture for matching short texts. In *NIPS*, 2013.
[34] J. McAuley et al. Image-based recommendations on styles and substitutes. I *SIGIR*, 2015.
[35] H. Mei, M. Bansal, and M. R. Walter. What to talk about and how? Selective gene ation using LSTMs with coarse-to-fine alignment. *arXiv preprint arXiv:1509.008* 2015.
[36] T. Mikolov et al. Recurrent neural network based language model. In *Interspeec* 2010.
[37] T. Mikolov et al. Efficient estimation of word representations in vector spac *arXiv preprint arXiv:1301.3781*, 2013.
[38] B. Mitra, F. Diaz, and N. Craswell. Learning to match using local and distribute representations of text for web search. In *WWW '17*, 2017.
[39] B. Mitra et al. A dual embedding space model for document ranking. *arXi preprint arXiv:1602.01137*, 2016.
[40] A. Oord, S. Dieleman, and B. Schrauwen. Deep content-based music recommer dation. In *NIPS*, 2013.
[41] M. Quadrana et al. Personalizing session-based recommendations with hiera chical recurrent neural networks. In *RecSys*, 2017.
[42] S. E. Robertson et al. Okapi at TREC-3. *Nist Special Publication Sp*, 1995.
[43] R. Salakhutdinov and G. Hinton. Semantic hashing. *International Journal o Approximate Reasoning*, 2009.
[44] I. V. Serban et al. Generating factoid questions with recurrent neural network The 30m factoid question-answer corpus. *arXiv preprint arXiv:1603.06807*, 201
[45] I. Sutskever, O. Vinyals, and Q. V. Le. Sequence to sequence learning with neura networks. In *NIPS*, 2014.
[46] M. Szummer and E. Yilmaz. Semi-supervised learning to rank with preferenc regularization. In *CIKM*, 2011.
[47] C. Van Gysel, M. de Rijke, and E. Kanoulas. Learning latent vector spaces fo product search. In *CIKM*, 2016.
[48] C. Van Gysel, M. de Rijke, and M. Worring. Unsupervised, efficient and semanti expertise retrieval. In *WWW*, 2016.
[49] C. Van Gysel, M. de Rijke, and E. Kanoulas. Neural vector spaces for unsupervise information retrieval. *arXiv preprint arXiv:1708.02702*, 2017.
[50] C. Van Gysel et al. Reply with: Proactive recommendation of email attachment In *CIKM*, 2017.
[51] F. Vasile et al. Meta-Prod2Vec – product embeddings using side-information fo recommendations. In *RecSys*, 2016.
[52] O. Vinyals and Q. Le. A neural conversational model. In *ICML*, 2015.
[53] I. Vulić and M.-F. Moens. Monolingual and cross-lingual information retrieva models based on (bilingual) word embeddings. In *Proc. SIGIR*, 2015.
[54] H. Wang et al. Collaborative deep learning for recommender systems. In *KDD* 2015.
[55] Z. Wang, J. Zhang, J. Feng, and Z. Chen. Knowledge graph embedding by translating on hyperplanes. In *Proc. AAAI*, 2014.
[56] J. Weston et al. Towards AI-complete question answering: A set of prerequisite toy tasks. In *ICLR*, 2016.
[57] Y. Zhao, L. Zhiyuan, and M. Sun. Representation learning for measuring entity relatedness with rich information. In *IJCAI*, 2015.
[58] G. Zuccon, B. Koopman, P. Bruza, and L. Azzopardi. Integrating and evaluating neural word embeddings in information retrieval. In *ADCS*, 2015.

Tutorial on Metrics of User Engagement: Applications to News, Search and E-Commerce

Extended Abstract

Mounia Lalmas
Spotify
mounia@acm.org

Liangjie Hong
Etsy Inc.
lhong@etsy.com

ABSTRACT

User engagement plays a central role in companies operating online services, such as search engines, news portals, e-commerce sites, and social networks. A main challenge is to leverage collected knowledge about the daily online behavior of millions of users to understand what engage them short-term and more importantly long-term. The most common way that engagement is measured is through various online metrics, acting as proxy measures of user engagement. This tutorial will review these metrics, their advantages and drawbacks, and their appropriateness to various types of online services. As case studies, we will focus on three types of services, news, search and e-commerce. We will also briefly discuss how to develop better machine learning models to optimize online metrics, and design experiments to test these models.

KEYWORDS

User Engagement; Metrics; Optimisation

ACM Reference Format:
Mounia Lalmas and Liangjie Hong. 2018. Tutorial on Metrics of User Engagement: Applications to News, Search and E-Commerce: Extended Abstract. In *WSDM 2018: WSDM 2018: The Eleventh ACM International Conference on Web Search and Data Mining , February 5–9, 2018, Marina Del Rey, CA, USA.* ACM, New York, NY, USA, 2 pages. https://doi.org/10.1145/3159652.3162010

1 MOTIVATION

In the online world, user engagement refers to the quality of the user experience that emphasizes the positive aspect of the interaction with an online service and, in particular, the phenomena associated with wanting to use that service longer and frequently [1]. User engagement is a key concept in the design of online services, as successful applications are not just used, but are engaged with. Users invest time, attention, and emotion with services they use [7]. How to measure user engagement and being able to drive it becomes a key element for evaluating the success of any online services, from news to e-commerce sites, as it informs on the understanding of user needs and expectations, system design and functionality.

User engagement is a multifaceted, complex phenomenon, and as such has given rise to a number of approaches for its measurement [7]. Common ways of measuring user engagement include: self-reporting, e.g., questionnaires; observational methods, e.g., desktop actions; and online analytics, which employ online behavior metrics that assess users' depth of engagement. These approaches represent various trade-offs between the scale of data analyzed and the depth of understanding. In this tutorial, we focus on the later, large-scale online analytics.

Within this approach, the most common way that engagement is measured is through various proxy measures of user engagement. Standard metrics include number of page views, number of unique users, dwell time, bounce rate, click-through rate, and return rate. We will review these metrics, and discuss what they measure, their advantages and drawbacks. We will provide extensive details on the appropriateness of these metrics to various types of online services. Finally, we will discuss how these measures have been used in three types of applications, news, search and e-commerce.

2 OUTLINE

The two presenters are experts in user engagement and have published widely on this topic. They have worked on products, focusing on understanding users to devise metrics to assess their depth of engagement, and influence the design of algorithms aiming at providing more engaging experience. The tutorial will be based around their work and other relevant works, focusing on large-scale measurement of online services. The tutorial will be organised around the following lines:

(1) We will start with an introduction to the tutorial, presenters and the scope of the tutorial. We motivate the tutorial by emphasizing that user engagement optimization is the key to successful modern data-driven products.
(2) We will provide an overview of a wide range of user engagement metrics, when to use them and why, their pros and cons. We will provide a taxonomy of metrics, for example, whether they reflect the during-the-moment interaction (e.g. dwell time) or popularity (e.g. number of sessions). We will also provide a classification of these metrics in terms of the types of services for which they are the most appropriate (e.g. dwell time on news portal).
(3) We will discuss the importance in understanding the relationship between short-term and long-term metrics, as the means to ensure we are measuring and optimising for the right thing. Long-term metrics are usually what we really want to be successfully measuring, like how frequently users come back to the service, how many monthly active users

WSDM 2018, February 5–9, 2018, Marina Del Rey, CA, USA

ACM ISBN 978-1-4503-5581-0/18/02.
https://doi.org/10.1145/3159652.3162010

a service would have and how much incremental revenue they could bring in for the service. However, they are hard to measure and difficult to directly optimize for. On the other hand, we may able to build machine learning models and algorithms that optimize for short-term engagement metrics (e.g. click-through rates or dwell time), but we need to be sure that by doing so actually leads to optimizing long-term engagement metrics.

(4) After generic discussions on user engagement metrics, we focus on user engagement optimization on three important online applications: news portals, search engines, and e-commerce sites. These three cover a large proportions of online services, and differ in the type of engagement they seek [8]; e.g. a successful experience with a search engine is one when the user enters his or her query, get the results fast, and is happy with them and as such is more likely to return to that search engine when he or she has another information need; whereas for a news portal, success means users spending time on the portal, and consuming many articles, every morning or during lunch time. Finally, a satisfied e-commerce user experience may contain both the ability to help users finding relevant products and completing their transactions, and to lead users to discover new interesting things they would not have considered in the first place. The presenters have also worked on these types of online services.

(5) We then briefly discuss how to incorporate user engagement metrics into machine learning models and algorithms by showing use cases from news recommendation [11] and mobile search applications [5]. We will also show how to design and carry out online experiments (e.g. so called A/B testing) to assess the impact of these machine learning approaches.

(6) We will end with some concluding remarks and future directions of research. We will highlight what are the main themes we believe we should be focussing on next, for example, metrics for mobile apps.

3 BIOGRAPHY

Mounia Lalmas has just joined Spotify, as Research Director, where she will build and lead a team of researchers working on engagement metrics. Before that, she was a Director of Research at Yahoo now Oath, where she led a team of researchers working on advertising quality for Gemini, Yahoo native advertising platform. She also worked with various teams at Yahoo on topics related to user engagement in the context of news, search, and user generated content. She also hold an Honorary Professorship at University College London. Prior to this, she held a Microsoft Research/RAEng Research Chair at the School of Computing Science, University of Glasgow. Before that, she was Professor of Information Retrieval at the Department of Computer Science at Queen Mary, University of London. Since 2011, her work has focused on studying user engagement [8] in areas such as native advertising [2], digital media [6], user generated content [9], and search [4]. She has given numerous talks and tutorials on these and related topics. She is regularly a senior programme committee member at conferences such as WSDM, WWW and SIGIR. She was co-programme chair for SIGIR 2015 and is this year co-programme chair for WWW. She is also the co-author of a book written as the outcome of her WWW 2013 tutorial [7].

Liangjie Hong is Head of Data Science at Etsy Inc., managing a group of data scientists to deliver cutting-edge scientific solutions for: Search and Discovery, Personalization & Recommendation and Computational Advertising. Previously, he was Senior Manager of Research at Yahoo Research, leading science efforts for Personalization and Search Sciences. Prior to Yahoo Research, he obtained his PhD in Computer Science from Lehigh University in 2013. Liangjie has given numerous technical talks at academic conferences as well as industrial meetings. He also co-founded User Engagement Optimization Workshop,[1] which has been held in conjunction with CIKM 2013 and KDD 2014. Liangjie has extensively published papers in optimizing user engagement in the context of personalization and recommendation systems, including designing metrics, developing machine learning methodologies as well as novel models (e.g., [3, 10–12]). He has served as program committee members on all major applied machine learning and data mining conferences including KDD, WSDM, WWW, SIGIR, EMNLP and ICML.

REFERENCES

[1] Simon Attfield, Gabriella Kazai, Mounia Lalmas, and Benjamin Piwowarski. 2011. Towards a science of user engagement. In *WSDM'11*. ACM.

[2] Nicola Barbieri, Fabrizio Silvestri, and Mounia Lalmas. 2016. Improving Post-Click User Engagement on Native Ads via Survival Analysis. In *Proceedings of the 25th International Conference on World Wide Web, WWW 2016, Montreal, Canada, April 11 - 15, 2016.* 761–770.

[3] Ting Chen, Yizhou Sun, Yue Shi, and Liangjie Hong. 2017. On Sampling Strategies for Neural Network-based Collaborative Filtering. In *Proceedings of the 23rd ACM SIGKDD International Conference on Knowledge Discovery and Data Mining (KDD '17)*. ACM, New York, NY, USA, 767–776. https://doi.org/10.1145/3097983.3098202

[4] Georges Dupret and Mounia Lalmas. 2013. Absence time and user engagement: evaluating ranking functions. In *Sixth ACM International Conference on Web Search and Data Mining, WSDM 2013, Rome, Italy, February 4-8, 2013.* 173–182.

[5] Liangjie Hong, Yue Shi, and Suju Rajan. 2016. Learning Optimal Card Ranking from Query Reformulation. *CoRR* abs/1606.06816 (2016). http://arxiv.org/abs/1606.06816

[6] Dmitry Lagun and Mounia Lalmas. 2016. Understanding User Attention and Engagement in Online News Reading. In *Proceedings of the Ninth ACM International Conference on Web Search and Data Mining, San Francisco, CA, USA, February 22-25, 2016.* 113–122.

[7] Mounia Lalmas, Heather O'Brien, and Elad Yom-Tov. 2014. *Measuring User Engagement.* Synthesis Lectures on Information Concepts, Retrieval, and Services, Morgan & Claypool Publishers.

[8] Janette Lehmann, Mounia Lalmas, Elad Yom-Tov, and Georges Dupret. 2012. Models of User Engagement. In *User Modeling, Adaptation, and Personalization - 20th International Conference, UMAP 2012, Montreal, Canada, July 16-20, 2012. Proceedings.* 164–175.

[9] Janette Lehmann, Claudia Müller-Birn, David Laniado, Mounia Lalmas, and Andreas Kaltenbrunner. 2014. Reader preferences and behavior on Wikipedia. In *25th ACM Conference on Hypertext and Social Media, HT '14, Santiago, Chile, September 1-4, 2014.* 88–97.

[10] Yue Ning, Yue Shi, Liangjie Hong, Huzefa Rangwala, and Naren Ramakrishnan. 2017. A Gradient-based Adaptive Learning Framework for Efficient Personal Recommendation. In *Proceedings of the Eleventh ACM Conference on Recommender Systems (RecSys '17)*. ACM, New York, NY, USA, 23–31. https://doi.org/10.1145/3109859.3109909

[11] Xing Yi, Liangjie Hong, Erheng Zhong, Nanthan Nan Liu, and Suju Rajan. 2014. Beyond Clicks: Dwell Time for Personalization. In *Proceedings of the 8th ACM Conference on Recommender Systems (RecSys '14)*. ACM, New York, NY, USA, 113–120. https://doi.org/10.1145/2645710.2645724

[12] Qian Zhao, Yue Shi, and Liangjie Hong. 2017. GB-CENT: Gradient Boosted Categorical Embedding and Numerical Trees. In *Proceedings of the 26th International Conference on World Wide Web (WWW '17)*. International World Wide Web Conferences Steering Committee, Republic and Canton of Geneva, Switzerland, 1311–1319. https://doi.org/10.1145/3038912.3052668

[1] http://www.ueo-workshop.com/

Network Science of Teams: Characterization, Prediction, and Optimization

Liangyue Li
Arizona State University
liangyue@asu.edu

Hanghang Tong
Arizona State University
hanghang.tong@asu.edu

KEYWORDS

Teamwork; network science

ACM Reference Format:
Liangyue Li and Hanghang Tong. 2018. Network Science of Teams: Characterization, Prediction, and Optimization. In *Proceedings of WSDM 2018: The Eleventh ACM International Conference on Web Search and Data Mining (WSDM 2018)*. ACM, New York, NY, USA, 2 pages. https://doi.org/10.1145/3159652.3162008

1 MOTIVATION

In defining the essence of professional teamwork, Hackman and Katz [4] stated that teams function as 'purposive social systems', defined as people who are readily identifiable to each other by role and position and who work interdependently to accomplish one or more collective objectives. Teams are increasingly indispensable to achievement in any organization. This is perhaps most evident in multinational organizations where communication technology has transformed the geographically dispersed teams and networks. Business operations in the large organizations now involve large, interactive, and layered networks of teams and personnel communicating across hierarchies and countries during the execution of complex and multifaceted international businesses. Despite the organizations' substantial dependency on teams, fundamental knowledge about the conduct of team-enabled operations is lacking, especially at the *social, cognitive* and *information* level in relation to team performance and network dynamics.

Generally speaking, the **team performance** can be viewed as the composite of the following three aspects, including (1) its users, (2) tasks that the team performs and (3) the networks that the team is embedded in or operates on. In this tutorial, we will provide a comprehensive review of the recent advances in *characterizing, predicting* and *optimizing* teams' performance in the context of composite networks (i.e., social-cognitive-information networks).

Research in sociology and psychology has long been trying to characterize the high-performing teams in organizations. The basics of team effectiveness were identified by J. Richard Hackman, who uncovered a groundbreaking insight: what matter most to collaboration are certain enabling conditions. Recent studies found that three of Hackman's conditions – a compelling direction, a strong structure, and a supportive context – continue to be particularly critical to team success [3]. We would comprehensively survey related literatures in sociology, psychology and computer science.

Understanding the dynamic mechanisms that drive the success of high-performing teams can provide the key insights into building the best teams and hence lifting the productivity and profitability of the organizations. For this purpose, we introduce some of the recent work on developing novel predictive models to forecast the long-term performance of teams (*point prediction*) as well as the pathway to impact (*trajectory prediction*).

From the practical perspective, it is important to form a good team in the context of networks for a given tasks. For an existing team, it is often desirable to optimize its performance through expanding the team by bringing a new team member with certain expertise, or finding a new candidate to replace a current under-performing team member. We would introduce recent advances in team performance optimization.

WSDM 2018, February 5–9, 2018, Marina Del Rey, CA, USA

ACM ISBN 978-1-4503-5581-0/18/02...$15.00
https://doi.org/10.1145/3159652.3162008

2 BRIEF OUTLINE OF THE TOPICS TO BE COVERED

- Introduction: why teams and research questions related to teams (10 minutes)
- Part I: Team Performance Characterization (20 minutes)
  - A comprehensive survey from sociology, psychology and computer science literatures
- Part II: Team Performance Prediction (1h)
  - Long-term performance prediction
  - Performance trajectory forecasting
  - team performance v.s. individual members' performance
- Part III: Team Performance Optimization (1h)
  - Team formation
  - Team member replacement
  - Team enhancement
  - Interactive visualization system
- Part IV: Future Research Directions (30 minutes)
  - Predictive optimization
  - Prediction explanation
  - Optimization explanation
  - From team optimization to network optimization

3 DESCRIPTION OF THE TOPICS TO BE COVERED

3.1 Part I: Team Performance Characterization

In this part, we aim to answer the question of what characterizations high-performing teams share. We will provide a comprehensive review of the existing discoveries for performance characterization from sociology, psychology and computer science literature. For example, Harvard Business Review conducted a 15 year long study into teams and groups in a variety of contemporary setting and found that a small number of factors have an outsized impact on their success in spite of the increasingly complicated set of challenges [3]. For research teams, Uzzi et al. [11] find that the highest-impact science work is primarily grounded in atypical combinations of prior ideas while embedding them in conventional knowledge frames. Google's project Aristotle went through intense data collections of its own teams and found that psychologically safe environment is crucial for success of teams [2].

3.2 Part II: Team Performance Prediction

In this part, we review the state-of-the-art techniques on modeling performance/impact of a variety of teams (e.g., research team, entertainment team, sports team, etc) for prediction purpose. We will categorize the team performance prediction algorithms according to the following two scenarios. (1) *The long-term performance prediction.* Some important work include a mechanistic model for the citation dynamics of research teamwork [12] and a network of predictive models [6]; and (2) *Performance trajectory prediction.* Representative work include a new predictive model tailored for scholarly entity impact pathway prediction [9]. We will also cover the latest work on a joint predictive model by exploring the relationship between team-level and individual-level performance for better prediction [10].

3.3 Part III: Team Performance Optimization

In this part, we will cover the recent advances in achieving the optimal configuration of a team in the context of networks for a given task. We will categorize the team performance optimization algorithms by the following two application scenarios. (1) *Team formation*, to assemble a team of people from scratch for a given task. To ensure success, the selected team members should possess the desired skills and have strong team cohesion, which is first studied in [5]. As follow-up work, Anagnostopoulos et al [1] studies forming teams to accommodate a sequence of tasks arriving in an online fashion. (2) *Team enhancement*, to enhance an existing team. For example, if a team member is leaving, how to find a good candidate to replace s/he (i.e., *team replacement* [7]). Other enhancement scenarios include *team expansion*, *team shrinkage*, and *team conflict resolution* [8].

3.4 Part IV: Future Research Directions

In this part, we will summarize several key open challenges and the future trends in this field, including (1) *predictive optimization*, to proactively recommend preventative actions should a stumbling performance is predicted, (2) *prediction explanation*, to provide explanation behind a performance prediction, (3) *optimization explanation*, to give reasons why the model recommendations are good candidates for certain enhancement scenarios, and (4) *network optimization*, to cultivate the optimal social network structure within an organization so that multiple teams can work synergistically.

4 LINKS TO RELATED RESOURCES

- Teamwork in Big Networks project page, including publications, presentations and prototype systems, is available a team-net-work.org
- Prof. Brian Uzzi's website: https://www.kellogg.northwester edu/faculty/uzzi/htm/
- Prof. Noshir Contractor's website: http://nosh.northwester edu/
- Prof. Evimaria Terzi's website: https://www.cs.bu.edu/~evim
- Prof. Divyakant Agrawal's website: https://www.cs.ucsb edu/~agrawal/
- AMiner datasets: https://aminer.org/data
- NBA dataset: http://www.databasebasketball.com/
- IMDb dataset: http://www.imdb.com/interfaces
- Microsoft Academic Graph: https://www.microsoft.com/en-research/project/microsoft-academic-graph/
- Stanford Large Network Dataset Collection: https://snap stanford.edu/data/

5 TYPE OF SUPPORT MATERIALS TO BE SUPPLIED TO ATTENDEES

- Tutorial slides will be made available at the presenters' web site

6 ACKNOWLEDGMENTS

This work is supported by National Science Foundation under Grant No. IIS-1651203, DTRA under the grant number HDTRA1-16-0017, Army Research Office under the contract number W911NF-16-1-0168, National Institutes of Health under the grant number R01LM011986, Region II University Transportation Center under the project number 49997-33 25, NSFC grant no. 61602306.

REFERENCES

[1] Aris Anagnostopoulos, Luca Becchetti, Carlos Castillo, Aristides Gionis, and Stefano Leonardi. 2012. Online team formation in social networks. In *WWW*. 839–848.
[2] Charles Duhigg. 2016. What Google Learned From Its Quest to Build the Perfect Team. https://www.nytimes.com/2016/02/28/magazine/what-google-learned-from-its-quest-to-build-the-perfect-team.html?mcubz=0&_r=0. (Feb. 2016). Accessed: 2017-09-22.
[3] Martine Haas and Mark Mortensen. 2016. The secrets of great teamwork. *Harvard business review* 94, 6 (2016), 70–6.
[4] J. R Hackman and N. Katz. 2010. *Group behavior and performance.* Wiley, New York, 1208–1251.
[5] Theodoros Lappas, Kun Liu, and Evimaria Terzi. 2009. Finding a team of experts in social networks. In *KDD*. 467–476.
[6] Liangyue Li and Hanghang Tong. 2015. The Child is Father of the Man: Foresee the Success at the Early Stage. In *KDD*. ACM, 655–664.
[7] Liangyue Li, Hanghang Tong, Nan Cao, Kate Ehrlich, Yu-Ru Lin, and Norbou Buchler. 2015. Replacing the Irreplaceable: Fast Algorithms for Team Member Recommendation. In *WWW*. ACM, 636–646.
[8] Liangyue Li, Hanghang Tong, Nan Cao, Kate Ehrlich, Yu-Ru Lin, and Norbou Buchler. 2017. Enhancing Team Composition in Professional Networks: Problem Definitions and Fast Solutions. *IEEE Trans. Knowl. Data Eng.* 29, 3 (2017), 613–626.
[9] Liangyue Li, Hanghang Tong, Jie Tang, and Wei Fan. 2016. *iPath:* Forecasting the Pathway to Impact. In *SDM*. SIAM, 468–476.
[10] Liangyue Li, Hanghang Tong, Yong Wang, Conglei Shi, Nan Cao, and Norbou Buchler. 2017. Is the Whole Greater Than the Sum of Its Parts?. In *KDD*. ACM 295–304.
[11] Brian Uzzi, Satyam Mukherjee, Michael Stringer, and Ben Jones. 2013. Atypical Combinations and Scientific Impact. *Science* 342, 6157 (2013), 468–472.
[12] Dashun Wang, Chaoming Song, and Albert-László Barabási. 2013. Quantifying long-term scientific impact. *Science* 342, 6154 (2013), 127–132.

A Critical Review of Online Social Data: Biases, Methodological Pitfalls, and Ethical Boundaries

Alexandra Olteanu
IBM T.J. Watson Research Center
Yorktown Heights, NY, US
alexandra.olteanu@ibm.com

Emre Kıcıman
Microsoft Research
Redmond, WA, US.
emrek@microsoft.com

Carlos Castillo
Universitat Pompeu Fabra
Barcelona, Spain
carlos.castillo@upf.edu

ABSTRACT

Online social data like user-generated content, expressed or implicit relations among people, and behavioral traces are at the core of many popular web applications and platforms, driving the research agenda of researchers in both academia and industry. The promises of social data are many, including the understanding of "what the world thinks" about a social issue, brand, product, celebrity, or other entity, as well as enabling better decision-making in a variety of fields including public policy, healthcare, and economics. However, many academics and practitioners are increasingly warning against the naïve usage of social data. They highlight that there are biases and inaccuracies occurring at the source of the data, but also introduced during data processing pipeline; there are methodological limitations and pitfalls, as well as ethical boundaries and unexpected outcomes that are often overlooked. Such an overlook can lead to wrong or inappropriate results that can be consequential.

This tutorial recognizes the rigor with which these issues are addressed by different researchers varies across a wide range, and aims to survey and categorize common classes of data biases and pitfalls that can occur both at the sources of social data as well as along the prototypical data processing pipeline.

CCS CONCEPTS

• **Human-centered computing** → **Collaborative and social computing**; • **Information systems** → **World Wide Web**; **Information systems applications**;

KEYWORDS

Data biases; behavioral data; social media; evaluation; ethics

ACM Reference Format:
Alexandra Olteanu, Emre Kıcıman, and Carlos Castillo. 2018. A Critical Review of Online Social Data: Biases, Methodological Pitfalls, and Ethical Boundaries. In *WSDM 2018: The Eleventh ACM International Conference on Web Search and Data Mining, February 5–9, 2018, Marina Del Rey, CA, USA.* ACM, New York, NY, USA, 2 pages. https://doi.org/10.1145/3159652.3162004

1 CONTEXT AND MOTIVATION

The proliferation of the Social Web—"a class of websites and applications in which user participation is the primary driver of value" [13], enables access to *social* traces at a scale and level of detail impractical with conventional data collection techniques. This access opens unprecedented opportunities to answer questions about society, policies, and health [4, 22, 35]. Yet, regardless of how large or varied such social data is, there are significant ethical and functional limitations to what can be discerned from it about real-world phenomena (online or offline), or even about media or application-specific phenomena—which have yet to be rigorously addressed [4, 31, 35].

As the insights derived from these data are increasingly used to drive policies, to shape products, and for automated decision making, it is becoming imperative to understand the limitations around their use; overlooking them can lead to wrong or inappropriate results [4, 20]. This tutorial offers a comprehensive overview of a variety of data biases and other issues that occur when working with social data, organized along the data analysis pipeline.

2 TUTORIAL OUTLINE

The tutorial is organized in 4 parts each covering a broad theme:
Context and applications: Why and how social data is used.

We begin the tutorial with a brief overview of various types of online social data (e.g., social interactions, social media posts, usage logs, location traces) and *applications* that use it to gain insights, to train models for various prediction or classification tasks, or to guide the design of tools. We then broadly overview the prototypical data processing and analysis pipeline, while providing examples of various pitfalls that may occur at different stages in the pipeline (e.g., data may under-represent a protected class, the relations extracted from the data may be spurious, the evaluation metrics may not reflect the application goals).

This part concludes with an overview of common classes of threats to the validity of research leveraging social data [17, 34]: *construct validity*—do data measurements actually capture the construct one aims to measure? *internal validity*—does the analysis correctly leads from the measurements to conclusions? or *external validity*—are the research findings generalizable to other situations?

Issues at the Data Source or Origin: General classes of social data biases such as population, behavioral, or temporal biases due to, e.g., platform specific norms or functionalities, or data decay.

In the second part, we scrutinize the representativeness of online social and behavioral data, covering major classes of social data biases such as population biases (distinct platforms are characterized by different demographic composition of users) [16, 24], or behavioral biases (users behave differently in different contexts) [23].

Further, the behaviors we observe in online social platforms can hardly be considered as "naturally occurring" [33]. Instead, they are determined by platform capabilities and engineered towards

ACM ISBN 978-1-4503-5581-0/18/02.
https://doi.org/10.1145/3159652.3162004

certain goals [11, 35]. To this end, we overview biases due to platform design and affordances (dubbed functional biases), or due to behavioral norms emerging on each platform (normative biases).

This part will also cover issues such as the incidence of non-humans (spammers, bots, organization accounts) along with "authentic" human users [4, 7]), temporal variations (e.g., the "swiss cheese" decay of social media datasets due to content deletions [2]), or content reliability (e.g., rumors). We will review both recent work raising concerns about what can be legitimately inferred from existing social datasets [31, 35], as well as research that tries to quantify the limits of such data [10, 14, 19, 27].

Issues Along the Data Analysis and Evaluation Pipelines: Data collection biases, use of opportunistic approaches, spurious associations, generalizability, disclaimers and negative results.

The third part covers challenges related to the design of data (processing and) analysis frameworks and tools to explain or predict various phenomena, to offer services, or for performance gains [5, 31]. In addition, we discuss existing solutions aiming at correcting or accounting for biased or innacurate datasets, and existing recommendations for adequately evaluate and validate methods and observations (including the need for disclaimers and standards [6, 8]), or to interpret results in context [28, 30].

Ethical Boundaries: Ethical concerns regarding the usage of social data, such as privacy risks and algorithmic discrimination.

In the last part, we will cover ethical caveats when leveraging social data such as discriminatory treatment as a result of algorithmic reinforcement of human prejudice [3], lack of explicit user consent [18, 37], user manipulation (see Facebook's contagion experiment [21]), identity disclosure [7], the risk of breaching users privacy [12] or of racial, socioeconomic or gender-based profiling (and possible consequences across application domains) [3].

The discussion about ethics is organized around three principles outlined in the Belmont report [32]: *autonomy*: experiments should show respect for individuals; *beneficence and non-maleficence*: experiments should minimize risk for research participants and maximize benefits for society; *justice*: the risks and benefits of experiments should be fairly distributed.

We end the tutorial with open questions and research directions on identifying or mitigating the issues we covered.

2.1 Resources

Our tutorial has a companion survey paper [26]. Other resources we recommend: books [29, 33], talks and tutorials [1, 9, 15, 36], and several overview papers [4, 25, 31, 35].

Slides availability. The slide decks are available at the Social Data Limits Tutorial Series website:
http://www.aolteanu.com/SocialDataLimitsTutorial/index.html.

Acknowledgements. We thank Fernando Diaz, who helped co-organizing earlier versions of this tutorial.

REFERENCES

[1] Ricardo Baeza-Yates. Data and algorithmic bias in the web. In *WebSci*, 2016.
[2] Mossaab Bagdouri and Douglas W Oard. On predicting deletions of microblog posts. In *Proc. of CIKM*, 2015.
[3] Solon Barocas and Andrew D Selbst. Big data's disparate impact. *SSRN*, 2014.
[4] danah boyd and Kate Crawford. Critical questions for big data: Provocations for a cultural, technological, and scholarly phenomenon. *Information, Communication & Society*, 15(5), 2012.
[5] Raviv Cohen and Derek Ruths. Classifying political orientation on Twitter: It' not easy! In *Proc. of ICWSM*, 2013.
[6] Scott Counts, Munmun De Choudhury, Jana Diesner, Eric Gilbert, Marta Gonzale Brian Keegan, Mor Naaman, and Hanna Wallach. Computational social scienc CSCW in the social media era. In *Proc. of CSCW Companion*, 2014.
[7] Kate Crawford and Megan Finn. The limits of crisis data: Analytical and ethica challenges of using social and mobile data to understand disasters. *GeoJourna* 2014.
[8] Fernando Diaz. Experimentation standards for crisis informatics. *SIGIR Forum* 48(2), 2014.
[9] Fernando Diaz. Worst practices for designing production information acces systems. In *ACM SIGIR Forum*, 2016.
[10] Fernando Diaz, Michael Gamon, Jake Hofman, Emre Kıcıman, and David Roth schild. Online and social media data as an imperfect continuous panel surve *PlosONE*, 11(1), 2016.
[11] Tarleton Gillespie. Platforms intervene. *Social Media+ Society*, 1(1), 2015.
[12] Daniel L Goroff. Balancing privacy versus accuracy in research protocols. *Science* 347, 2015.
[13] Tom Gruber. Collective knowledge systems: Where the social web meets the semantic web. *Web semantics: Science, services & agents on the WWW*, 6(1), 2008
[14] Pedro Calais Guerra, Wagner Meira Jr, and Claire Cardie. Sentiment analysis on evolving social streams: How self-report imbalances can help. In *WSDM*, 2014.
[15] Sara Hajian, Francesco Bonchi, and Carlos Castillo. Algorithmic bias: From discrimination discovery to fairness-aware data mining. In *Proc. of KDD*, 2016.
[16] Eszter Hargittai. Whose space? differences among users and non-users of social network sites. *Journal of Computer-Mediated Communication*, 13(1), 2007.
[17] James Howison, Andrea Wiggins, and Kevin Crowston. Validity issues in the use of social network analysis with digital trace data. *J. of Assoc. for IS*, 12(12), 2011
[18] Luke Hutton and Tristan Henderson. "I didn't sign up for this!": Informed consent in social network research. In *Proc. of ICWSM*, 2015.
[19] Emre Kıcıman. OMG, I have to tweet that! A study of factors that influence tweet rates. In *Proc. of ICWSM*, 2012.
[20] Emre Kıcıman, Scott Counts, Michael Gamon, Munmun De Choudhury, and Bo Thiesson. Discussion graphs: Putting social media analysis in context. In *Proc. of ICWSM*, 2014.
[21] Adam DI Kramer, Jamie E Guillory, and Jeffrey T Hancock. Experimental evidence of massive-scale emotional contagion through social networks. *National Academy of Sciences*, 111(24), 2014.
[22] David Lazer, Alex Sandy Pentland, Lada Adamic, Sinan Aral, Albert Laszlo Barabasi, Devon Brewer, Nicholas Christakis, Noshir Contractor, James Fowler, Myron Gutmann, et al. Life in the network: the coming age of computational social science. *Science*, 323(5915), 2009.
[23] Bang Hui Lim, Dongyuan Lu, Tao Chen, and Min-Yen Kan. # mytweet via Instagram: Exploring user behaviour across multiple social networks. In *Proc. of ASONAM*, 2015.
[24] Alan Mislove, Sune Lehmnan, Yong-Yeol Ahn Ahn, Jukka-Pekka Onnela, and J Niels Rosenquist. Understanding the demographics of twitter users. In *Proc. of ICWSM*, 2011.
[25] Dong Nguyen, A Seza Doğruöz, Carolyn P Rosé, and Franciska de Jong. Computational sociolinguistics: A survey. *arXiv preprint arXiv:1508.07544*, 2016.
[26] Alexandra Olteanu, Carlos Castillo, Fernando Diaz, and Emre Kiciman. Social data: Biases, methodological pitfalls, and ethical boundaries. *SSRN*, 2016.
[27] Alexandra Olteanu, Carlos Castillo, Fernando Diaz, and Sarah Vieweg. CrisisLex: A lexicon for collecting and filtering microblogged communications in crises. In *Proc. of ICWSM*, 2014.
[28] Alexandra Olteanu, Kartik Talamadupula, and Kush R Varshney. The limits of abstract evaluation metrics: The case of hate speech detection. In *WebSci*, 2017.
[29] Cathy O'Neil. *Weapons of Math Destruction: How Big Data Increases Inequality and Threatens Democracy.* Crown, 2016.
[30] Mattias Rost, Louise Barkhuus, Henriette Cramer, and Barry Brown. Representation and communication: Challenges in interpreting large social media datasets. In *Proc. of CSCW*, 2013.
[31] Derek Ruths and Jürgen Pfeffer. Social media for large studies of behavior. *Science*, 346, 2014.
[32] KJ Ryan, JV Brady, RE Cooke, DI Height, AR Jonsen, P King, K Lebacqz, DW Louisell, D Seldin, E Stellar, et al. *The Belmont report: Ethical principles and guidelines for the protection of human subjects of research.* Nat. Commission for the Protection of Hum. Subjects of Biomedical and Behavioral Research, 1978.
[33] Matthew J. Salganik. *Bit by Bit: Social Research in the Digital Age.* Princeton University Press, 2017.
[34] William M. Trochim. The research methods knowledge base, 2nd edition. October 20, 2006.
[35] Zeynep Tufekci. Big questions for social media big data: Representativeness, validity and other methodological pitfalls. In *Proc. of ICWSM*, 2014.
[36] H Wallach. Big data, machine learning, and the social sciences: Fairness, accountability, and transparency. In *NIPS Workshop on FAT/ML*, 2014.
[37] Michael Zimmer. "But the data is already public": on the ethics of research in Facebook. *Ethics and information technology*, 12(4), 2010.

Athlytics: Winning in Sports with Data

Konstantinos Pelechrinis
School of Computing & Information
University of Pittsburgh
kpele@pitt.edu

Evangelos Papalexakis
Department of Computer Science
University of California, Riverside
epapalex@cs.ucr.edu

ABSTRACT

Data and analytics have been part of the sports industry from as early as the 1870s, when the first boxscore in baseball was recorded. However, it is only recently that advanced data mining and machine learning techniques have been utilized for facilitating the operations of sports franchises. While part of the reason is related with the ability to collect more fine-grained data, an equally important factor for this turn to analytics is the huge success and competitive advantage that early adopters of investment in analytics enjoyed (popularized by the best-seller "Moneyball" that described the success that Oakland Athletics had with analytics). Draft selection, game-day decision making and player evaluation are just a few of the applications where sports analytics play a crucial role today. Apart from the sports clubs, other stakeholders in the industry (e.g., the leagues' offices, media, etc.) invest in analytics. The leagues increasingly rely on data in order to decide on potential rule changes. For instance, the most recent rule change in NFL, i.e., the kickoff touchback, was a result of thorough data analysis of concussion instances. In this tutorial we will review the literature in data mining and machine learning techniques for sports analytics. We will introduce the audience to the design and methodologies behind advanced metrics such as the adjusted plus/minus for evaluating basketball players, spatial metrics for evaluating the ability of a player to spread the defense in basketball, and the Player Efficiency Rating (PER). We will also go in depth in advanced data mining methods, and in particular tensor mining, that can analyze heterogeneous data similar to the ones available in today's sports world.

ACM Reference Format:
Konstantinos Pelechrinis and Evangelos Papalexakis. 2018. Athlytics: Winning in Sports with Data. In *Proceedings of WSDM 2018.* ACM, New York, NY, USA, 2 pages. https://doi.org//10.1145/3159652.3162005

1 WHY SPORTS ANALYTICS?

While statistics and data analysis have been a part of sports for almost as long as sports have existed for, the interest during the past few years has exponentially increased. The sports industry is a world-wide multi-billion dollar industry and franchises are turning to technology and data to gain any competitive advantage they can. This involves analyzing troves of data that go beyond the traditional boxscore information. Wearable sensors and optical technology has generated fine-grained spatio-temporal logs of games. For example, in NBA the locations of the players and the ball on the court are logged every 40msecs. Nevertheless, in order for this potential to come to fruition many challenges associated with spatio-temporal data need to be resolved. Furthermore, this spatio-temporal information is further combined with contextual information (e.g., shot clock, type of events, current score etc.) providing a rich data source that can be used to evaluate game aspects that it was not possible to do before. However, appropriate methods for analyzing heterogeneous, multidimensional data, are needed. Furthermore, efficiently storing and retrieving this information for assisting the coaching stuff is also a challenge. Leagues are interested in using these data for making rule changes that achieve an objective (e.g., reduce severe injuries and concussions). However, in order to do this causal links need to be established, something that is not possible with observational data. Therefore, appropriate quasi-experimental techniques need to be developed or adopted for similar tasks. Finally, even though not the focus of this tutorial, sports franchises and leagues are businesses. Therefore, they have turned to data and data mining techniques to understand their customers (i.e., clients) better and maximize their potential revenue.

The problems phased when analyzing modern sports data are very similar at a high level with those from other fields (e.g., transportation, network science, public policy, social computing, etc.). The added benefit of sports data is that they offer a controlled environment with rather *clean* information that eliminates many of the problems associated with datasets including missed or imputed information. Therefore, we believe that a tutorial on data mining for sports analytics will not only be beneficial for researchers and practitioners interested in sports, but also to other SDM attendees that work with similar data.

2 TUTORIAL OUTLINE

In what follows we outline the content to be included in the tutorial, organized in thematic modules.

2.1 Part A: Current Practises and State-of-the-Art

In this part of the tutorial we will present the status of analytics in operations of sports franchises ranging from the business side operations to game strategy and player development and evaluation. We will particularly focus on the different types of data that are possible to be collected today. These range from sensor biometric data to tracking data captured by wearables and/or computer vision technologies. We will also briefly describe novel applications of data mining in sports that have provided significant competitive advantage to the adopting entities.

WSDM 2018, February 5–9, 2018, Marina Del Rey, CA, USA.

ACM ISBN 978-1-4503-5581-0/18/02.
https://doi.org//10.1145/3159652.3162005

2.2 Part B: Advanced Statistics: Beyond the Boxscore

In this part of the tutorial we will describe in detail statistical frameworks that are fundamental in the field of sports analytics. In particular, we will present the Bradley-Terry regression model used for probabilistically predicting the outcome of a comparison, while we will also present literature on semi-supervised learning for ranking. Furthermore, we will elaborate on the fundamentals of statistical bootstrap, which is predominately used when simulating sports matchups. Finally, we will discuss the design and computation of advanced statistics and metrics that have revolutionized the way teams and players are being evaluated. In particular, we will describe in detail the Player Efficiency Rating (PER) as well as the regression models behind the adjusted plus/minus for basketball. We will also discuss the *Pythagorean theorem* in sports used to predict outcomes of games/seasons as well as the famous study of the "hot hand".

2.3 Part C: Spatio-temporal Analysis of Sports Trajectories

One of the most valuable type of sports data that have been made available during the past few years are spatio-temporal trajectories, i.e., detailed location information of players through the course of a game. This type of data have enabled a paradigm shift in sports analytics. In this part of the tutorial we will start by introducing the machine learning literature that facilitates automated tracking of players through computer vision, as well as, the application on analyzing spatio-temporal data of state-of-the-art frameworks (e.g., deep learning) that has made its way into sports analytics. We will then present the new possibilities opened by these data as well as the research in data mining and machine learning that tackles the associated challenges. For example, we will introduce spatial methods that quantify the spatial spreading of a defense at basketball as well as models for court realty based on the usage of space. We will also present how ideas from complex systems, and in particular fractal dimensionality, can also be used to analyze spatial sports data.

2.4 Part D: Network and Tensor Mining for Sports

In this last part of the tutorial we will discuss how network mining tools and methods have been used in a number of different sports to analyze exchanges between teammates (e.g., in basketball and soccer) in an effort to quantify measures such as the coherence of a team, ranking of players and teams etc. However, the main focus of this part of the tutorial is the introduction of the literature in tensor mining that can be used to analyze multiaspect data. Tensor analysis has been successfully used to analyze heterogenous and temporal networks. Many sports data include both a temporal dimension as well as heterogeneous relation types making tensor mining a very powerful tool. More specifically, we will present in detail literature on tensor decomposition and the different types of factorization available (e.g., PARAFAC, Tucker etc.). We will also present literature for scalable and efficient tensor decomposition as well as for model selection (i.e., choice of number of tensor factors to be kept). Finally, we will present specific examples on how tensor mining can facilitate tasks in the sports analytics area.

3 BRIEF BIOS

3.1 Konstantinos Pelechrinis

Dr. Pelechrinis is interested in all aspects of the information cycle (collection, transfer and analysis) and his ultimate goal is to deliver information-centric solutions in various fields. He is an associate professor at the School of Computing and Information at the University of Pittsburgh, where he is working on data and network science. He has experience in designing and delivering tutorials in major conferences (e.g., SIGKDD, WWW, ICWSM, SBP-BRiMS, etc.) in topics pertaining data mining. Relevant to this tutorial he has worked on the application of data mining techniques in sports analytics tasks including team rankings and player evaluation. His research on modeling American football has been featured in popular media outlets including Daily Mail, Yahoo! News and others. Konstantinos received his PhD from the Computer Science department of University of California, Riverside, in 2010. Previously he obtained his MSc degree from the Computer Science department of University of California, Riverside in 2008 and the diploma of Electrical and Computer Engineering from the National Technical University of Athens, Greece, in 2006. He has also held research intern positions at LANL, Thomson Research Labs Paris and MSR Cambridge. He was a visiting researcher at the University of Thessaly during Fall 2008. He is a recipient of the Army Research Office Young Investigator (2015) for his work on composite networks.

3.2 Evangelos Papalexakis

Dr. Papalexakis is an assistant professor of the CSE Dept. at University of California, Riverside. His research involves designing scalable algorithms for mining large multi-aspect datasets, with specific emphasis on tensor factorization models, and applying those algorithms to a variety of real world multi-aspect data problems, including sports. His work has appeared in KDD, ICDM, SDM, ECML-PKDD, WWW, PAKDD, ICDE, ICASSP, IEEE Transactions of Signal Processing, and ACM TKDD. He has also worked with co-tutor Pelechrinis on studies on modeling American football and basketball. He has also designed and delivered tutorials in major venues (e.g., SIGKDD, ICASSP etc.). He has a best student paper award at PAKDD'14, finalist best papers for SDM'14 and ASONAM'13 and he was a finalist for the Microsoft PhD Fellowship and the Facebook PhD Fellowship. Besides his academic experience at CMU, he has industrial research experience working at Microsoft Research Silicon Valley during the summers of 2013 and 2014 and Google Research during the summer of 2015. Prior to his current position he received his Ph.D from the Computer Science Department of Carnegie Mellon University, while he received his Electronic & Computer Engineering Diploma and M.Sc at the Technical University of Crete, Greece.

Mining Knowledge Graphs From Text

Jay Pujara
Information Sciences Institute
University of Southern California
jpujara@isi.edu

Sameer Singh
Computer Science Department
University of California, Irvine
sameer@uci.edu

ABSTRACT

Knowledge graphs have become an increasingly crucial component in machine intelligence systems, powering ubiquitous digital assistants and inspiring several large scale academic projects across the globe. Our tutorial explains why knowledge graphs are important, how knowledge graphs are constructed, and where new research opportunities exist for improving the state-of-the-art. In this tutorial, we cover the many sophisticated approaches that complete and correct knowledge graphs. We organize this exploration into two main classes of models. The first include probabilistic logical frameworks that use graphical models, random walks, or statistical rule mining to construct knowledge graphs. The second class of models includes latent space models such as matrix and tensor factorization and neural networks. We conclude the tutorial with a critical comparison of techniques and results. We will offer practical advice for novices to identify common empirical challenges and concrete data sets for initial experimentation. Finally, we will highlight promising areas of current and future work.

ACM Reference Format:
Jay Pujara and Sameer Singh. 2018. Mining Knowledge Graphs From Text. In *Proceedings of WSDM 2018: The Eleventh ACM International Conference on Web Search and Data Mining (WSDM 2018)*. ACM, New York, NY, USA, 2 pages. https://doi.org/10.1145/3159652.3162011

1 MOTIVATION

The task of extracting candidate facts from unstructured sources and producing a coherent knowledge graph has swiftly become a core challenge in machine learning. Applications that rely on structured knowledge representations include digital assistants (e.g., Siri, Alexa, Cortana, and Google Now), question answering, summarization, decision support, as well as many downstream autonomous decision-making tasks. As a result, nearly every major technology firm has an initiative to construct knowledge graphs. The topic has rallied researchers across many academic disciplines, spanning natural language processing, information extraction, information integration, databases, search, and machine learning.

WSDM 2018, February 5–9, 2018, Marina Del Rey, CA, USA

ACM ISBN 978-1-4503-5581-0/18/02.
https://doi.org/10.1145/3159652.3162011

The variety and complexity of the available scholarly work, however, makes it difficult for a newcomer to familiarize themselves with the field. Knowledge graph construction has been decomposed into a large number of inter-dependent and sometimes overlapping tasks, and the associated machine learning approaches have also been quite varied, ranging from classification/clustering, probabilistic graphical models, probabilistic logic formulations, matrix/tensor factorization-based approaches, and more recently, deep learning. Beyond the diversity in research approaches, there are also a plethora of existing systems that have been proposed, including from top universities such as Stanford (DeepDive), Carnegie Mellon (NELL), University of Washington (OpenIE), Mannheim (DBpedia), and the Max Planck Institut Informatik (YAGO, WebChild) among others. This diverse and fragmented literature poses a significant roadblock for newcomers to contribute to the field.

We have designed our tutorial to address this barrier. Our goal is to present an accessible and structured overview of the existing approaches to translating extractions from heterogeneous sources into a well-formed knowledge graph. Our approach includes identifying the common themes and challenges in the area, and comparing and contrasting the existing approaches on the basis of these aspects. We believe such a unifying framework will provide the necessary tools and perspectives to enable the newcomers to the field to explore, evaluate, and develop novel techniques for automated knowledge graph construction.

2 CONTENT AND OUTLINE

(1) Introduction (30 minutes)
  (a) What is a Knowledge Graph?
  (b) Why are Knowledge Graphs important?
  (c) Where do Knowledge Graphs come from?
  (d) Knowledge Representation Choices
  (e) Problem Overview
(2) Probabilistic Modeling Approaches (45 minutes)
  (a) The need for probabilistic approaches
  (b) Graphical Models
    (i) Markov Logic Networks [8]
    (ii) Probabilistic Soft Logic [7]
  (c) Random Walk Approaches
    (i) Path Ranking Algorithm (PRA[3]
    (ii) Probabilistic Proofs (ProPPR[10])
(3) Embedding and Neural Techniques (45 minutes)
  (a) Motivation and differentiation from probabilistic approaches
  (b) Relation extraction Techniques
    (i) Matrix factorization [9]

    (ii) Embedding entity pairs
  (c) Graph Completion Techniques
    (i) Tensor factorization (RESCAL[2], CNTF[6])
    (ii) Entity and relation embeddings (TransE[1], TransR [5], TransH[11], PTransE[4])
    (iii) Compositional models
(4) Conclusion (30 minutes)
  (a) Critical Summary
  (b) Success Stories
  (c) Practical Advice
  (d) Future Directions

3 RELATED TUTORIALS

3.1 Related Materials

We identify past tutorials by other presenters on similar topics that provide different perspectives than our proposed tutorial.

- SIGMOD 2017 Tutorial on "Building Structured Databases of Factual Knowledge from Massive Text Corpora" by Xiang Ren, Meng Jiang, Jingbo Shang, and Jiawei Han. http://xren7.web.engr.illinois.edu/sigmod17tutorial.html
- SIGIR 2016 tutorial on "Constructing and Mining Web-Scale Knowledge Graphs" by Evgeniny Gabrilovich and Nicolas Usunier. http://www.cs.technion.ac.il/~gabr/publications/papers/SIGIR-2016-KG-tutorial.pdf
- NAACL 2016 tutorial on "Statistical Relational Learning for NLP" by William Wang and William W. Cohen. http://www.cs.ucsb.edu/~william/software.html
- WWW 2015 tutorial on "Knowledge Bases for Web Content Analytics" presented by Johannes Hoffart, and Fabian M. Suchanek. http://resources.mpi-inf.mpg.de/yago-naga/www2015-tutorial/
- ACL 2015 tutorial on "Matrix and Tensor Factorization Methods for Natural Language Processing" by Bouchard et al. http://acl2015.org/tutorials-t5.html
- VLDB 2014 tutorial on "Knowledge Bases in the Age of Big Data Analytics" by Fabian M. Suchanek and Gerhard Weikum. http://resources.mpi-inf.mpg.de/yago-naga/vldb2014-tutorial/
- ISWC 2012 tutorial on "Machine Learning on Linked Data: Tensors and their Applications in Graph-Structured Domains Tutorial" by Maximilian Nickel and Volker Tresp. http://www.cip.ifi.lmu.de/~nickel/iswc2012-slides/

3.2 Additional Resources

Additional resources, including videos of recent presentations are also available:

- Jay Pujara: https://www.jaypujara.org/resources.html
- Sameer Singh: http://sameersingh.org/teaching.html

REFERENCES

[1] A. Bordes, N. Usunier, A. García-Durán, J. Weston, and O. Yakhnenko. Translating embeddings for modeling multi relational data. In *NIPS*, 2013.
[2] K.-W. Chang, W. tau Yih, B. Yang, and C. Meek. Typed tensor decomposition of knowledge bases for relation extraction. In *EMNLP*, 2014.
[3] N. Lao, T. M. Mitchell, and W. W. Cohen. Random walk inference and learning in a large scale knowledge base. In *EMNLP*, 2011.
[4] Y. Lin, Z. Liu, H.-B. Luan, M. Sun, S. Rao, and S. Liu. Modeling relation paths for representation learning of knowledge bases. In *EMNLP*, 2015.
[5] Y. Lin, Z. Liu, M. Sun, Y. Liu, and X. Zhu. Learning entity and relation embeddings for knowledge graph completion. In *AAAI* 2015.
[6] M. Nimishakavi, U. S. Saini, and P. Talukdar. Relation schema induction using tensor factorization with side information. *CoRR* abs/1605.04227, 2016.
[7] J. Pujara, H. Miao, L. Getoor, and W. W. Cohen. Knowledge graph identification. In *SEMWEB*, 2013.
[8] M. Richardson and P. M. Domingos. Markov logic networks *Machine Learning*, 62:107–136, 2006.
[9] S. Riedel, L. Yao, A. McCallum, and B. M. Marlin. Relation extraction with matrix factorization and universal schemas. In *NAACL*, 2013.
[10] W. Y. Wang, K. Mazaitis, and W. W. Cohen. Programming with personalized pagerank: a locally groundable first-order probabilistic logic. In *CIKM*, 2013.
[11] Z. Wang, J. Zhang, J. Feng, and Z. Chen. Knowledge graph embedding by translating on hyperplanes. In *AAAI*, 2014.

The 5th International Workshop on Social Web for Disaster Management (SWDM'18)

Collective Sensing, Trust, and Resilience in Global Crises

Yu-Ru Lin
School of Computing and Information, University of Pittsburgh, PA, USA
yurulin@pitt.edu

Carlos Castillo
Universitat Pompeu Fabra
Barcelona, Catalonia, Spain
chato@acm.org

Jie Yin
CSIRO
Epping, NSW, Australia
Jie.Yin@data61.csiro.au

ABSTRACT

During large-scale emergencies such as natural and man-made disasters, a massive amount of information is posted by the public in social media. Collecting, aggregating, and presenting this information to stakeholders can be extremely challenging, particularly if an understanding of the "big picture" is sought. This international workshop, the fifth in the series, is a key venue for researchers and practitioners to discuss research challenges and technical issues around the usage of social media in disaster management.

Workshop's website: https://sites.google.com/site/swdm2018/

CCS CONCEPTS

• **Information systems → Web mining;** • **Human-centered computing → Social networking sites;**

KEYWORDS

social media, emergency management, disaster response

ACM Reference Format:
Yu-Ru Lin, Carlos Castillo, and Jie Yin. 2018. The 5th International Workshop on Social Web for Disaster Management (SWDM'18): Collective Sensing, Trust, and Resilience in Global Crises. In *WSDM 2018: The Eleventh ACM International Conference on Web Search and Data Mining , February 5–9, 2018, Marina Del Rey, CA, USA.* ACM, New York, NY, USA, 2 pages. https://doi.org/10.1145/3159652.3160594

1 WORKSHOP OVERVIEW

The proliferation of social media platforms together with the wide adoption of smartphone devices has transformed how we communicate and share news. During large-scale emergencies, such as natural disasters or armed attacks, victims, responders, and volunteers increasingly use social media to post situation updates and to request and offer help. There are a number of challenges associated with near-real-time processing of vast volumes of information in a way that makes sense for people directly affected, for volunteer organizations, and for official emergency response agencies. As massive amount of relevant data are accumulated, there is a growing need for developing advanced techniques to harness this large-scale data to gain an understanding of the "big picture" of an emergency, and to detect and predict how a disaster could develop.

The Social Web for Disaster Management (SWDM) international workshop series, now in its fifth edition, is a key venue for computer scientists, government officials, emergency agencies, and other interested participants to discuss technical issues and research challenges in the understanding of digitally-mediated, social and technical systems during mass emergencies. The workshop theme for this year is "Collective Sensing, Trust, and Resilience in Global Crises," through which we aim to facilitate interdisciplinary discussion on a range of emergent challenges facing the world, from harnessing big data on the Web that facilitates disaster and risk management, to engaging citizen participation in disaster response, establishing trust in global and local communities, designing socio-technical systems, and building resilience to disasters through Internet of Things and ubiquitous intelligence.

2 RELEVANCE AND SIGNIFICANCE

Over the last decade, nearly 2.5 billion people have been affected by disasters, which claimed 1.3 million lives and costed US $2 trillion in economic losses. Large-scale emergencies including natural hazards and man-made disasters are an enormous threat to societies. There is an indisputably increasing need for building new data mining tools to strengthen disaster management and humanitarian response, by harnessing the data on the Web and the Social Web. The scope and focus of this workshop is well aligned with the theme of WSDM – which also emphasizes on "the practical and principled novel models of search and data mining on the Web and the Social Web." In particular, disaster-related data are big and noisy, and advanced algorithm design and analysis, and in-depth experimental analysis solutions are needed for a variety of applications in disaster scenarios.

Based on our prior successful experience in running related workshops in conjunction with conferences, this year we seek to deepen the research conversation from the aspects of knowledge management and discovery, and unstructured and spatiotemporal data mining, through engaging the researchers and practitioners from the WSDM community. Modern disaster management involves analysis of massive, noisy, and heterogeneous data sources, including urban sensors and various types of social media, which change very rapidly throughout a crisis. We would like to bring together WSDM participants who are interested in research challenges in crisis domains, such as stream processing of microtext and images,

WSDM 2018, February 5–9, 2018, Marina Del Rey, CA, USA

ACM ISBN 978-1-4503-5581-0/18/02.
https://doi.org/10.1145/3159652.3160594

situational information mining, dynamic network analysis, data quality assurance, and knowledge discovery applied to large-scale crisis data.

3 TARGET AUDIENCE

The target audience includes academic and industry researchers as well as government agencies. We welcome interested participants to discuss issues and challenges in the understanding of large-scale social media data during mass emergencies, especially researchers and practitioners who are interested in the area of disaster related data mining and machine learning approaches.

4 WORKSHOP FORMAT

The workshop will include four elements: keynotes, talks, demonstrations and panel discussion. As in previous editions, each session will be allocated with sufficient time for questions, interaction, and discussions. We plan to include two keynotes.

Keynote speaker: Dr. Carter T. Butts

"Attention, Amplification, Resilience, and Hazard Messaging at the Organizational/Public Interface"

Carter T. Butts is a Professor in the Departments of Sociology, Statistics, and Electrical Engineering and Computer Science at the University of California Irvine, where he directs the Center for Networks and Relational Analysis in the California Institute for Telecommunications and Information Technology. Professor Butts received his doctoral degree from Carnegie Mellon University, and his bachelor's degree from Duke University; he holds early career awards from the American Sociological Association and the International Network for Social Network Analysis, and is currently chair-elect of the ASA Section on Mathematical Sociology. Professor Butts's research involves the development and application of mathematical, computational, and statistical techniques to theoretical and methodological problems within the areas of social and biological network analysis, mathematical sociology, quantitative methodology, and human judgment and decision making. He has published extensively on communication in hazard response contexts, including work on emergent coordination in the World Trade Center Disaster, organizational collaboration in the aftermath of Hurricane Katrina, message passing following the Boston Marathon Bombing, and attentional dynamics during wildfires.

Keynote speaker: Dr. Paige Maas

"Leveraging Facebook Data for Disaster Response"

Paige Maas is a Data Scientist on the Core Data Science team at Facebook, where she has worked on understanding user experience and interactions and helping build tools to make that experience better. She earner her PhD in Biostatistics from Johns Hopkins University and did her dissertation research at the US National Cancer Institute, where she developed methods for synthesizing data sources to build risk prediction models for breast cancer. At Facebook, her current focus is on building data products that can be used by humanitarian organizations in disaster response.

5 WEBSITE

The workshop has a companion website where talk slides will be posted: https://sites.google.com/site/swdm2018/

6 ORGANIZERS

Yu-Ru Lin. (yurulin@pitt.edu) is an assistant professor at the School of Computing and Information, University of Pittsburgh. Her research interests include human mobility, social and political network dynamics, and computational social science. She has developed computational approaches for mining and visualizing large-scale, time-varying, heterogeneous, multi-relational, and semi-structured data. Her current research focuses on extracting system-level features from big data sets, including social media data, for studying social dynamics, particularly under exogenous events such as emergencies. Her work has appeared in prestigious scientific venues including WWW, SIGKDD, InfoVis, ACM TKDD, ACM TOMCCAP, IEEEP and PLoS ONE. She has served in program committees for international data and web mining conferences and has organized several workshops in data science including 2014 KDD Workshop on Learning about Emergencies from Social Information (KDD-LESI). She co-organized the SWDM 2016.

Carlos Castillo. (chato@acm.org) is a distinguished research professor at Universitat Pompeu Fabra. Carlos is an active researcher on web mining and search, with more than 75 papers in top-tier international conferences and journals, including a book on Big Crisis Data, a book on Information and Influence Propagation, and a monograph on Adversarial Web Search. Carlos received his Ph.D. from the University of Chile, and was senior scientist at Yahoo Research, principal scientist at the Qatar Computing Research Institute, and director of research for data science at Eurecat. He has served in the PC or SPC of all major conferences in his area (WWW, WSDM, KDD, SIGIR, CIKM) and is part of the editorial committee of ACM Transactions on the Web and Internet Research. He was Program Committee Co-Chair of ACM Digital Health 2016, and was Program Committee Co-chair of WSDM 2014, co-organized the Adversarial Information Retrieval Workshop and Web Spam Challenge in 2007 and 2008, the ECML/PKDD Discovery Challenge in 2010 and 2014, the Web Quality Workshop from 2011 to 2014, and the Social Web for Disaster Management Workshop in 2015 and 2016.

Jie Yin. (jie.yin@csiro.au) is a senior research scientist at CSIRO, Australia. Her main research interests include data mining, machine learning, and their applications to text mining, social media mining and pervasive computing. She received the Ph.D. degree in Computer Science from Hong Kong University of Science and Technology. Her research experience includes activity recognition from sensor data, text mining from social media and Web forums, active learning and transfer learning in social networks. Jie is an active researcher in data mining with more than 40 research papers published in top-tier international conferences (AAAI, IJCAI, CIKM, ICDM, etc.) and journals (TKDE, TPAMI, TOIS, TOSN, etc.). She has served as the PC of all major conferences in her area including ICDM, KDD, AAAI, CIKM, etc. She was co-organizer of the 3rd International Workshop on Social Web for Disaster Management (SWDM 2015).

First Workshop on Knowledge Base Construction, Mining and Reasoning

Xiang Ren, Craig Knoblock
Department of Computer Science
University of Southern California
xiangren@usc.edu,knoblock@isi.edu

William Wang, Yu Su
Department of Computer Science
University of California, Santa Barbara
william@cs.ucsb.edu,ysu@cs.ucsb.edu

ACM Reference format:
Xiang Ren, Craig Knoblock and William Wang, Yu Su. 2018. First Workshop on Knowledge Base Construction, Mining and Reasoning. In *Proceedings of 11th ACM International Conf. on Web Search and Data Mining, Marina Del Rey, CA, USA, February 5–9, 2018 (WSDM 2018),* 2 pages.
DOI: http://dx.doi.org/10.1145/3159652.3160596

1 WORKSHOP OVERVIEW

1. Motivation and Goals. The success of data mining and search technologies is largely attributed to the efficient and effective analysis of structured data. The construction of a well-structured, machine-actionable database from raw data sources is often the premise of consequent applications. Meanwhile, the ability of mining and reasoning over such constructed databases is at the core of powering various downstream applications on web and mobile devices. Recently, we have witnessed a significant amount of interests in building large-scale knowledge bases (KBs) from massive, unstructured data sources (*e.g.*, Wikipedia-based methods such as DBpedia [9], YAGO [19], Wikidata [22], automated systems like Snowball [1], KnowItAll [5], NELL [4] and DeepDive [15], and open-domain approaches like Open IE [2] and Universal Schema [14]); as well as mining and reasoning over such knowledge bases to empower a wide variety of intelligent services, including question answering [6], recommender systems [3] and semantic search [8].

Automated construction, mining and reasoning of the knowledge bases have become possible as research advances in many related areas such as information extraction, natural language processing, data mining, search, machine learning, databases and data integration. However, there are still substantial scientific and engineering challenges in advancing and integrating such relevant methodologies. The goal of this proposed workshop is to gather together leading experts from industry and academia to share their visions about the field, discuss latest research results, and exchange exciting ideas. With a focus on invited talks and position papers, the workshop aims to provide a vivid forum of discussion about knowledge base-related research.

2. Relevance to WSDM. Knowledge base construction, mining and reasoning is closely related to a wide variety of applications in WSDM, including web search, question answering, and recommender systems. Building a high-quality knowledge base from relevant web sources in an automatic way will largely benefit the development of these applications, in designing better hybrid approaches using both structured and unstructured data sources. At the heart of these intelligent systems, researchers want to understand and extract human knowledge from different data sources (*i.e.*, knowledge acquisition), represent such knowledge using effective forms (*i.e.*, knowledge representation) and apply such structured knowledge to power the services. In addition, many techniques studied by the WSDM community are critical for knowledge base construction, mining and reasoning. These include NLP for web mining, data cleaning and integration, information extraction and graph/network analysis. We believe WSDM is a perfect venue for such a workshop as the workshop would be related and interesting to WSDM's audience and it will also benefit from many recent advances in the WSDM community.

3. Duration and Schedule. The duration of the workshop is one day (9am to 5pm, including coffee and lunch breaks). The proposed workshop plans to include various forms of activities: invited talks, oral and poster presentations for accepted papers, and discussions.

4. Topics and Description. This workshop welcomes and covers a wide range of techniques developed for knowledge base construction, mining and reasoning. This includes three key issues:

(1) **Knowledge Base Construction**: information extraction; chunking, named entity recognition, relation extraction, entity resolution, synonym mining; ontology construction; information integration; schema alignment, ontology alignment; tools and systems for automated knowledge base construction; structured prediction methods on text, sequence labeling methods on text; distant supervision, weak supervision techniques for text; Human-in-the-loop techniques for KB construction.
(2) **Mining and Reasoning over Knowledge Bases**: structured search, KB querying, semantic search; representation learning on network/graph, knowledge graph embedding, knowledge base completion/population, link prediction; knowledge-based systems, probabilistic knowledge bases, graph databases.
(3) **Knowledge Base-related Applications**: KB-based QA, hybrid QA, QA with open-domain facts; Injecting rule/logic into recommendation systems, recommendation with knowledge bases; web search using knowledge bases, search by example; User study in KB-related applications, user interface.

5. Target audience and prerequisites. Researchers and practitioners in the field of data mining, web mining, search, information retrieval, natural language processing, semantic web and databases. While the audience with a good background in these areas would benefit most from this workshop, we believe the material to be

WSDM'18, February 5-9, 2018, Marina Del Rey, CA, USA

ISBN 978-1-4503-5581-0/18/02.
DOI: http://dx.doi.org/10.1145/3159652.3160596

presented would give general audience and newcomers an introductory pointer to the current work and important research topics in this field, and inspire them to explore more. Only preliminary knowledge about knowledge base, information extraction, data mining, algorithms and their applications are needed.

2 ORGANIZERS

• **Xiang Ren** (http://xren7.web.engr.illinois.edu/), Ph.D. candidate and Google Ph.D. Fellow, Department of Computer Science, Univ. of Illinois at Urbana-Champaign. He is currently a visiting scholar at Stanford University, Natural Language Processing Group. Starting in Spring 2018, he will join USC Computer Science Department as an assistant professor. Xiang's research focuses on developing automated and scalable techniques for turning massive text data into machine-actionable structures and applying structured knowledge to power intelligent services. Xiang's research has been recognized with several prestigious awards including a Google PhD Fellowship, a Yahoo!-DAIS Research Excellence Award, a Yelp Dataset Challenge award, a C. W. Gear Outstanding Graduate Student Award and a David J. Kuck Outstanding M.S. Thesis Award. His research results were presented in top conference tutorials and keynotes including KDD'16, WWW'17, ACL'15 and SIGMOD'17. Technologies he developed has been transferred to US Army Research Lab, National Institute of Health, Microsoft, Yelp and TripAdvisor.

• **Craig Knoblock** (http://usc-isi-i2.github.io/knoblock/), Research Professor in both Computer Science and Spatial Sciences at the University of Southern California (USC), Director of Information Integration at the Information Sciences Institute, and Associate Director of Informatics Program at USC. He received his Bachelor of Science degree from Syracuse University and his Masterfis and Ph.D. from Carnegie Mellon University in computer science. His research focuses on techniques related to information integration and the Semantic Web for describing, acquiring, and exploiting the semantics of data. He has published more than 250 journal articles and conference papers. Dr. Knoblock is a Fellow of the Association for the Advancement of Artificial Intelligence (AAAI), a Distinguished Scientist of the Association of Computing Machinery (ACM), a Senior Member of IEEE, past President and Trustee of the International Joint Conference on Artificial Intelligence (IJCAI), and winner of the 2014 Robert S. Engelmore Award.

• **William Wang** (https://www.cs.ucsb.edu/~william/), assistant professor, Department of Computer Science, University of California, Santa Barbara. He received his PhD from School of Computer Science, Carnegie Mellon University. He has broad interests in machine learning approaches to data science, including statistical relational learning, information extraction, computational social science, speech, and vision. He has published more than 30 papers at leading conferences and journals, and received best paper awards (or nominations) at ASRU 2013, CIKM 2013, and EMNLP 2015, a best reviewer award at NAACL 2015, and the Richard King Mellon Presidential Fellowship in 2011. He is an alumnus of Columbia University, and a former research intern of Yahoo! Labs, Microsoft Research Redmond, and University of Southern California.

• **Yu Su** (http://cs.ucsb.edu/~ysu/), PhD candidate, Department of Computer Science at the University of California, Santa Barbara. His research interests lie in data mining and natural language processing, with a focus on understanding the interplay of natural and formal languages to increase the accessibility of structured data (e.g., knowledge bases, web tables, and relational databases) and services (e.g., web APIs) to non-tech users. He has published his work on question answering, graph mining and querying, and crowdsourcing at leading conferences including SIGKDD, WWW and EMNLP. He has interned in IBM T.J. Watson Research Center, Microsoft Research Redmond, and U.S. Army Research Laboratory.

REFERENCES

[1] E. Agichtein and L. Gravano. Snowball: Extracting relations from large plain-text collections. In *ACM conference on Digital libraries*, 2000.

[2] M. Banko, M. J. Cafarella, S. Soderland, M. Broadhead, and O. Etzioni. Open information extraction from the web. In *IJCAI*, 2007.

[3] R. Burke. Hybrid recommender systems: Survey and experiments. *User modeling and user-adapted interaction*, 12(4):331–370, 2002.

[4] A. Carlson, J. Betteridge, B. Kisiel, B. Settles, E. R. Hruschka Jr, and T. M. Mitchell. Toward an architecture for never-ending language learning. In *AAAI*, 2010.

[5] O. Etzioni, M. Cafarella, D. Downey, S. Kok, A.-M. Popescu, T. Shaked, S. Soderland, D. S. Weld, and A. Yates. Web-scale information extraction in knowitall:(preliminary results). In *WWW*, 2004.

[6] A. Fader, L. Zettlemoyer, and O. Etzioni. Open question answering over curated and extracted knowledge bases. In *KDD*, pages 1156–1165, 2014.

[7] G. Gawriljuk, A. Harth, C. A. Knoblock, and P. Szekely. A scalable approach to incrementally building knowledge graphs. In *20th International Conference on Theory and Practice of Digital Libraries*, 2016.

[8] R. Guha, R. McCool, and E. Miller. Semantic search. In *WWW*, pages 700–709, 2003.

[9] J. Lehmann, R. Isele, M. Jakob, A. Jentzsch, D. Kontokostas, P. N. Mendes, S. Hellmann, M. Morsey, P. Van Kleef, S. Auer, et al. Dbpedia–a large-scale, multilingual knowledge base extracted from wikipedia. *Semantic Web*, 6(2):167–195, 2015.

[10] X. Ren, A. El-Kishky, C. Wang, F. Tao, C. R. Voss, and J. Han. Clustype: Effective entity recognition and typing by relation phrase-based clustering. In *SIGKDD*, 2015.

[11] X. Ren, W. He, M. Qu, L. Huang, H. Ji, and J. Han. Afet: Automatic fine-grained entity typing by hierarchical partial-label embedding. In *EMNLP*, 2016.

[12] X. Ren, W. He, M. Qu, C. R. Voss, H. Ji, and J. Han. Label noise reduction in entity typing by heterogeneous partial-label embedding. In *SIGKDD*, 2016.

[13] X. Ren, Z. Wu, W. He, M. Qu, C. R. Voss, H. Ji, T. F. Abdelzaher, and J. Han. CoType: Joint extraction of typed entities and relations with knowledge bases. In *WWW*, 2017.

[14] S. Riedel, L. Yao, A. McCallum, and B. M. Marlin. Relation extraction with matrix factorization and universal schemas. In *NAACL*, 2013.

[15] J. Shin, S. Wu, F. Wang, C. De Sa, C. Zhang, and C. Ré. Incremental knowledge base construction using deepdive. *VLDB*, 8(11):1310–1321, 2015.

[16] Y. Su, H. Sun, B. Sadler, M. Srivatsa, I. Gur, Z. Yan, and X. Yan. On generating characteristic-rich question sets for qa evaluation. In *EMNLP*, pages 562–572, 2016.

[17] Y. Su and X. Yan. Cross-domain semantic parsing via paraphrasing. In *EMNLP*, 2017.

[18] Y. Su, S. Yang, H. Sun, M. Srivatsa, S. Kase, M. Vanni, and X. Yan. Exploiting relevance feedback in knowledge graph search. In *SIGKDD*, pages 1135–1144, 2015.

[19] F. M. Suchanek, G. Kasneci, and G. Weikum. Yago: A large ontology from wikipedia and wordnet. *Web Semantics: Science, Services and Agents on the World Wide Web*, 6(3):203–217, 2008.

[20] M. Taheriyan, C. Knoblock, P. Szekely, and J. L. Ambite. Leveraging linked data to discover semantic relations within data sources. In *ISWC*, 2016.

[21] M. Taheriyan, C. A. Knoblock, P. Szekely, and J. L. Ambite. Learning the semantics of structured data sources. *Journal of Web Semantics*, 2016.

[22] D. Vrandečić and M. Krötzsch. Wikidata: a free collaborative knowledgebase. *Communications of the ACM*, 57(10):78–85, 2014.

[23] W. Y. Wang and W. W. Cohen. Joint information extraction and reasoning: A scalable statistical relational learning approach. In *ACL-IJCNLP*, 2015.

[24] W. Y. Wang and W. W. Cohen. Learning first-order logic embeddings via matrix factorization. In *IJCAI*, 2016.

[25] W. Y. Wang, K. Mazaitis, and W. W. Cohen. Programming with personalized pagerank: A locally groundable first-order probabilistic logic. *CIKM*, 2013.

[26] W. Y. Wang, K. Mazaitis, N. Lao, and W. W. Cohen. Efficient inference and learning in a large knowledge base. *Machine Learning*, pages 1–26, 2015.

[27] L. Zhu, M. Ghasemi-Gol, P. Szekely, A. Galstyan, and C. A. Knoblock. Unsupervised entity resolution on multi-type graphs. In *ISWC*, 2016.

HeteroNAM: International Workshop on Heterogeneous Networks Analysis and Mining

Shobeir Fakhraei [1], Yanen Li [2], Yizhou Sun [3], Tim Weninger [4]
fakhraei@usc.edu,yanen.li@snap.com,yzsun@cs.ucla.edu,tweninge@nd.edu
[1]Information Sciences Institute, University of Southern California
[2]Snap Research, Snap Inc.
[3]Computer Science Department, University of California Los Angeles
[4]Department of Computer Science and Engineering, University of Notre Dame

ABSTRACT

The first International Workshop on Heterogeneous Networks Analysis and Mining is held in Los Angeles, California, USA on February 9th, 2018 and is co-located with the 11th ACM International Conference on Web Search and Data Mining. The goal of this workshop is to bring together computing researchers and practitioners to address challenges in the mining and analysis of real-world heterogeneous networks. This workshop has an exciting program that spans a number of subareas including: graph mining, learning from structured data, statistical relational learning, and network science in general. The program includes six invited speakers, lively discussion on emerging topics, and presentations of several original research papers.

KEYWORDS

Graph Mining, Heterogeneous Information Networks, Multi-Relational Data, Signed Networks, Attributed Networks, Aligned Networks, Multigraphs, Multidimensional Networks, Multilayer Networks, Complex Networks, Multimodal Networks

ACM Reference Format:
Shobeir Fakhraei [1], Yanen Li [2], Yizhou Sun [3], Tim Weninger [4]. 2018. HeteroNAM: International Workshop on Heterogeneous Networks Analysis and Mining. In *WSDM 2018: WSDM 2018: The Eleventh ACM International Conference on Web Search and Data Mining , February 5–9, 2018, Marina Del Rey, CA, USA.* ACM, New York, NY, USA, Article 4, 2 pages. https://doi.org/10.1145/3159652.3160591

1 INTRODUCTION

Graphs naturally represent a host of processes, including interactions between people on social or communication networks, links between web-pages on the World Wide Web, protein interactions in biological networks, movement in transportation networks, electricity delivery in smart energy grids, relations in bibliographic data, and many others. In such scenarios, graphs that model real-world networks are typically heterogeneous, multi-modal, and multi-relational. In the era of big data, as more varieties of interconnected structured and semi-structured data are becoming available, the importance of leveraging this heterogeneous and multi-relational nature of networks in being able to effectively mine and learn this kind of data is becoming more evident. The objective of this workshop is to bring together researchers from a variety of related areas, and discuss commonalities and differences in challenges faced, survey some of the different approaches, and provide a forum to present and learn about some of the most cutting-edge research in this area. As an outcome, we expect participants to walk away with a better sense of the variety of different methods and tools available for heterogeneous network mining and analysis, and an appreciation for some of the interesting emerging applications, as well as the challenges that accompany these applications There are many challenges involved in effectively mining and learning from this kind of data, including:

- Understanding different techniques applicable, including heterogeneous graph mining algorithms, graphical models, latent variable models, matrix factorization methods and more.
- Representing and dealing with the heterogeneity of the data.
- The common need for information integration and alignment.
- Handling dynamic and changing data.
- Addressing each of these issues at scale.

Traditionally, a number of subareas have contributed to this space: communities in graph mining, learning from structured data, statistical relational learning, and, moving beyond sub-disciplines in computer science, social network analysis, and, more broadly network science.

2 OBJECTIVE AND TOPICS OF INTEREST

This workshop is a forum for exchanging ideas and methods for heterogeneous networks analysis and mining, developing new common understandings of the problems at hand, sharing of data sets where applicable, and leveraging existing knowledge from different disciplines. The goal is to bring together researchers from academia, industry, and government, to create a forum for discussing recent advances in this area. In doing so, we aim to better understand the overarching principles and the limitations of our current methods and to inspire research on new algorithms and techniques for heterogeneous networks analysis and mining.

To reflect the broad scope of work on heterogeneous networks analysis and mining, we encourage submissions that span the spectrum from theoretical analysis to algorithms and implementation, to applications and empirical studies is various domains. The need

WSDM 2018, February 5–9, 2018, Marina Del Rey, CA, USA

ACM ISBN 978-1-4503-5581-0/18/02…$15.00
https://doi.org/10.1145/3159652.3160591

for analysis and learning methods that go beyond mining simple graphs is emerging in many disciplines and are referred to with different names depending on the type of data augmenting the simple graph.

Topics of interest include, but are not limited to:

- Heterogeneous Information Networks
- Multi-Relational Data
- Signed Networks
- Attributed Networks
- Aligned Networks
- Multigraphs
- Multidimensional Networks
- Multilayer Networks
- Complex Networks
- Multimodal Networks

Heterogeneous networks are becoming the key component in many emerging applications and data-mining and graph-mining related tasks. Some of the related research areas and tasks related to heterogeneous networks include:

- Link and relationship strength prediction
- Clustering and community detection and formation modeling
- Learning to rank in information networks
- Similarity measures and relationship extraction
- Applications to modeling of weblogs, social media, social networks, medical networks, and the semantic web
- Statistical relational learning
- Tensor factorization
- Network-based classification
- Hybrid recommender systems
- Network embedding Information fusion
- Network evolution and dynamic networks

3 WORKSHOP ORGANIZATION AND PROGRAM

3.1 Organizers

Shobeir Fakhraei is a research (computer) scientist at Information Science Institute, University of Southern California. He received his Ph.D. from the Department of Computer Science, University of Maryland College Park (UMD). Shobeir's research interests include Machine Learning, Statistical Relational Learning, Multi-Relational Link Prediction and Graph Mining, Networked Data, Collective Classification, Recommender Systems, and Biomedical and Health Informatics. He has worked in several research groups including at Microsoft Research and Yahoo! Labs.

Yanen Li leads the Data Mining area at Snap Research. Yanen has led the effort in building the machine learning based personalized Discover Ranking platform, and has also built the relecance modeling library SnapRec, which is used throughout Snap Inc. He is also leading the personalized Lens Ranking that personalizes snapchatter.

Yizhou Sun is an assistant professor in the Department of Computer Science, University of California, Los Angeles. Her principal research interest is in mining information and social networks, and more generally in data mining, machine learning, and network science, with a focus on modeling novel problems and proposin scalable algorithms for large-scale, real-world applications. She is pioneer researcher in mining heterogeneous information network and has given many tutorials on this topic in several premier con ferences. She has received 2012 SIGKDD Best Student Paper Awar 2013 SIGKDD Doctoral Dissertation Award, 2013 Yahoo Academi Career Enhancement Award, 2015 NSF CAREER Award, and 201 CS@ILLINOIS Distinguished Educator Award.

Tim Weninger is an assistant professor at the University of Notr Dame. He has authored over 50 research publications in the area of data mining, machine learning and network science. The ke application of his research is to identify how humans generat curate and search for information in the pursuit of knowledge. H is a recipient of the NSF CAREER award, the Army Research Offic Young Faculty Award, and has received research grants from the Ai Force Office of Scientific Research, DARPA, and the John Templeto Foundation. He is an inaugural member of the ACM's Future o Computing Academy and serves on numerous scientific progran committees.

3.2 Contributed Papers and Reviews

We have received ten submissions. Each paper will receive review from at least three members of the program committee. Accepte papers will be presented at the workshop and be hosted on th workshop Website: http://www.heteronam.org/2018/

3.3 Program Committee

Nesreen Ahmed (Intel Research Labs), Yuxiao Dong (Microsoft Re search), Srijan Kumar (Stanford University), Julian McAuley (Uni versity of California, San Diego), Fred Morstatter (University o Southern California), Maximilian Nickel (Facebook AI Research) Evangelos Papalexakis (University of California Riverside), Ali Pina (Sandia National Laboratories), Arti Ramesh (Binghamton Univer sity), Neil Shah (Carnegie Mellon University), Chuan Shi (Beijin Uni. of Posts & Telecommunications), Jiliang Tang (Michigan Stat University), Elena Zheleva (University of Illinois at Chicago)

3.4 Invited Speakers

- Leman Akoglu, Assistant Professor at Carnegie Mellon Uni versity
- Nitesh Chawla, Professor at University of Notre Dame
- Jiawei Han, Professor at University of Illinois at Urbana Champaign
- Kristina Lerman, Associate Professor at Information Science Institute at University of Southern California
- Julian McAuley, Assistant Professor as University of Califor nia San Diego
- Jiliang Tang, Assistant Professor at Michigan State Univer sity

4 ACKNOWLEDGMENTS

The organizers would like to thank the program committee for thei service, as well as the invited speakers for sharing their research and perspective.

LearnIR: WSDM 2018 Workshop on Learning from User Interactions

Rishabh Mehrotra
Spotify Research
London, United Kingdom
rishabhm@spotify.com

Ahmed Hassan Awadallah
Microsoft Research
Redmond, WA
hassanam@microsoft.com

Emine Yilmaz
University College London
London, United Kingdom
emine.yilmaz@ucl.ac.uk

ACM Reference format:
Rishabh Mehrotra, Ahmed Hassan Awadallah, and Emine Yilmaz. 2018. LearnIR: WSDM 2018 Workshop on Learning from User Interactions. In *Proceedings of 11th ACM International Conference on Web Search and Data Mining, February 5–9,2018, Marina Del Rey, CA, USA, (WSDM 2018),* 2 pages.
DOI: https://doi.org/10.1145/3159652.3160598

Website: https://task-ir.github.io/wsdm2018-learnIR-workshop/

1 MOTIVATION

While users interact with online services (e.g. search engines, recommender systems, conversational agents), they leave behind fine grained traces of interaction patterns. The ability to understand user behavior, record and interpret user interaction signals, gauge user satisfaction and incorporate user feedback gives online systems a vast treasure trove of insights for improvement and experimentation. More generally, the ability to learn from user interactions promises pathways for solving a number of problems and improving user engagement and satisfaction.

Understanding and learning from user interactions involves a number of different aspects - from understanding user intent and tasks, to developing user models and personalization services. A user's understanding of their need and the overall task develop as they interact with the system. Supporting the various stages of the task involves many aspects of the system, e.g. interface features, presentation of information, retrieving and ranking. Often, online systems are not specifically designed to support users in successfully accomplishing the tasks which motivated them to interact with the system in the first place. Beyond understanding user needs, learning from user interactions involves developing the right metrics and experimentation systems, understanding user interaction processes, their usage context and designing interfaces capable of helping users.

Learning from user interactions becomes more important as new and novel ways of user interactions surface. There is a gradual shift towards searching and presenting the information in a conversational form. Chatbots, personal assistants in our phones and eyes-free devices are being used increasingly more for different purposes, including information retrieval and exploration. With improved speech recognition and information retrieval systems, more and more users are increasingly relying on such digital assistants to fulfill their information needs and complete their tasks. Such systems rely heavily on quickly learning from past interactions and incorporating implicit feedback signals into their models for rapid development.

WSDM 2018, February 5–9,2018, Marina Del Rey, CA, USA
 ISBN 978-1-4503-5581-0/18/02.
DOI: https://doi.org/10.1145/3159652.3160598

2 SCOPE

Learning from User Interactions will be a highly interactive full day workshop that will provide a forum for academic and industrial researchers working at the intersection of user understanding, search tasks, conversational IR and user interactions. The purpose is to provide an opportunity for people to present new work and early results, brainstorm different use cases, share best practices, and discuss the main challenges facing this line of research.

(1) **User Needs & Tasks Understanding:** User intent analysis/prediction; User goals & missions; Task identification; Task aware suggestions & recommendations
(2) **User Modeling & Personalization:** Short and Long-term User Modelling; Personalization; Diversification; Coherence
(3) **Metrics and Evaluation :** Metrics based on user interactions; User engagement metrics design; Evaluation mechanisms; User satisfaction prediction; Controlled laboratory study Online metrics Test collection
(4) **User Interaction Processes & Context :** User Journey Optimization; Evolution of search process; Stages of user interactions; User journey through the system; Leveraging contextual signals; Learning for user interaction optimization: algorithms; frameworks & system designs
(5) **Intelligent interface designs:** Adaptive personal digital assistants; Tailored decision support; Adaptive collaboration support
(6) **Applications:** Conversational search, chatbots, digital assistants; Contextual Advertising; E-commerce recommendations; Customer Support; Intelligent interfaces; Personal search; Case studies of real world implementations

3 EXPECTED OUTCOMES

This is a workshop proper where discussion is central, and all attendees are active participants. We intend to host a number of keynote and invited talks from experts in related fields to provide workshop participants with a crisp overview of work on tasks and other related domains. Given the apt industrial utility of the workshop topic, we intend to keep a balanced mix of speakers from industry and academia alike.

Contributed papers will either have a short presentation or be showcased in an interactive poster session during the coffee breaks.

Beyond traditional paper & poster presentations, we will organize breakout sessions with predefined themes to foster a more productive discussion on what we learned, concrete plans for the next year, and a roadmap for the longer term.

The results will be disseminated in various ways:

- A high quality, peer reviewed workshop proceedings, published in the CEUR workshop proceedings series.
- A report on the results of the workshop in the ACM SIGIR Forum.
- Depending on the outcome, we will consider a special issue in an appropriate journal.
- Last, but not least, the results can be fed into the running tracks at TREC, CLEF, and other evaluation campaigns.

4 RELATED WORKSHOPS

There have been several workshops focused on user interactions, user intents & task, including CHI 2012 workshop on End-user Interactions with Intelligent Systems [6], Larsen, Lioma and de Vries's Task-based and Aggregated Search Workshop [5] and the Second Strategic Workshop on Information Retrieval in Lorne (SWIRL) [1]. Task-based search was discussed within the context of several larger themes identified by SWIRL participants, and was also presented briefly as a mini-theme. A NII Shonan Meeting, which was held in Japan in October 2012, focused on whole-session evaluation of interactive information retrieval systems. Some of the organizers were involved in a closely related workshop on Supporting Complex Search Tasks [2, 4] at CHIIR 2017 and SIGIR 2011. The NSF Task-Based Information Search Systems Workshop [3] was an invite-only workshop which fostered initial discussions around task understanding. Also related are the recent TREC Tasks Track [7, 8].

5 LIST OF ORGANIZERS

The following organizers are involved in organizing the workshop:

Rishabh Mehrotra
Spotify Research
Rishabh Mehrotra is a Research Scientist at Spotify Research and recently finished his PhD at University College London partially supported by a Google Faculty Research Award. His PhD research focused on inference of search tasks from query logs and their applications. Beyond tasks, his research focuses on user modelling & personalization, counterfactual analysis and deep learning for modelling user satisfaction. Some of his recent work has been published at top conferences including WWW, SIGIR, NAACL, CIKM, RecSys and WSDM. He has given many guest and invited talks at various conferences, Machine Learning meetups, research group seminars and industrial research events. He has supervised over 10 Masters thesis and has served as a reviewer for top tier conferences and workshops. He is also a co-coordinator of the Tasks Track in TREC 2015, 2016 and 2017 and co-tutored tutorials at Search Solutions 2017 and CIKM 2017.

Ahmed Hassan Awadallah
Microsoft Research
Ahmed leads a team of scientists/engineers in Microsoft Research Technologies; a new R&D organization created to focus on large scale company technology initiatives. His work is focused on creating new technologies and experiences with end-to-end integration with current and future products in the areas of intelligence assistance, search and productivity improvement. A key part of his work involves using Machine Learning to model large scale text data and user behavior data with applications to user modeling, quality evaluation, ranking, recommendation, personalization and intelligent task completion assistance. In the past, Ahmed has organized a number of workshops including ACL workshop on Graph based methods (TexGraphs-7).

Emine Yilmaz
University College London
Emine Yilmaz is an associate professor in the Department of Computer Science University College London, a faculty fellow of the Alan Turing Institute on Data Science and a research consultant for Microsoft Research Cambridge. She is the recipient of the Karen Sparck Jones Award in 2015 and the Google Faculty Award in 2014/15. Her main interests are evaluating quality of retrieval systems, modelling user behaviour, learning to rank, and inferring user needs while using search engines. She has published research papers extensively at major information retrieval venues such as SIGIR, CIKM, WWW and WSDM. She has previously given keynote talks at various conferences & workshops including at ECIR 2016 along with several tutorials on various Information Retrieval topics at the CHIIR 2016, SIGIR 2015, SIGIR 2012 and SIGIR 2010 Conferences and at the RuSSIR/EDBT Summer School in 2011.She is also a co-coordinator of the Tasks Track in TREC 2015 and 2016.

Steering Committee

We're thankful to the members of our steering committee:

(1) Milad Shokouhi (Microsoft)
(2) Fernando Diaz (Spotify)
(3) Filip Radlinski (Google Research)
(4) Evangelos Kanoulas (University of Amsterdam)

REFERENCES

[1] James Allan, Bruce Croft, Alistair Moffat, and Mark Sanderson. 2012. Frontiers, challenges, and opportunities for information retrieval: Report from SWIRL 2012 the second strategic workshop on information retrieval in Lorne. In *ACM SIGIR Forum*, Vol. 46. ACM, 2–32.

[2] Nicholas J Belkin, Charles LA Clarke, Ning Gao, Jaap Kamps, and Jussi Karlgren. 2012. Report on the sigir workshop on entertain me: supporting complex search tasks. In *ACM SIGIR Forum*, Vol. 45. ACM, 51–59.

[3] Diane Kelly, Jaime Arguello, and Robert Capra. 2013. NSF workshop on task-based information search systems. In *ACM SIGIR Forum*, Vol. 47. ACM, 116–127.

[4] Marijn Koolen, Jaap Kamps, Toine Bogers, Nicholas J Belkin, Diane E Kelly, and Emine Yilmaz. 2017. Report on the Second Workshop on Supporting Complex Search Tasks. (2017).

[5] Birger Larsen, Christina Lioma, and Arjen de Vries. 2012. Report on TBAS 2012: workshop on task-based and aggregated search. In *ACM SIGIR Forum*, Vol. 46. ACM, 71–77.

[6] Simone Stumpf, Margaret Burnett, Volkmar Pipek, and Weng-Keen Wong. 2012. End-user interactions with intelligent and autonomous systems. In *CHI'12 Extended Abstracts on Human Factors in Computing Systems*. ACM, 2755–2758.

[7] Manisha Verma, Emine Yilmaz, Rishabh Mehrotra, Evangelos Kanoulas, Ben Carterette, Nick Craswell, and Peter Bailey. 2016. Overview of the TREC Tasks Track 2016.. In *TREC*.

[8] Emine Yilmaz, Manisha Verma, Rishabh Mehrotra, Evangelos Kanoulas, Ben Carterette, and Nick Craswell. 2015. Overview of the TREC 2015 Tasks Track.. In *TREC*.

MIS2: Misinformation and Misbehavior Mining on the Web

Srijan Kumar
Stanford University, USA
srijan@cs.stanford.edu

Meng Jiang
University of Notre Dame, USA
mjiang2@nd.edu

Taeho Jung
University of Notre Dame, USA
tjung@nd.edu

Roger Jie Luo
Snap Inc.
roger.luo@snap.com

Jure Leskovec
Stanford University, USA
jure@cs.stanford.edu

ABSTRACT

Misinformation and misbehavior mining on the web (MIS2) workshop is held in Los Angeles, California, USA on February 9, 2018, and co-located with the 11th ACM International Conference on Web Search and Data Mining (WSDM 2018). Web is a dynamic ecosystem that enables malicious users to create and spread deceptive information to a wide audience in a matter of minutes. These malicious actors work on a wide variety of platforms, such as social media, e-commerce, and more. The main object of MIS2 is to discuss new and upcoming research on modeling, discovery, detection, and mitigation methods of misbehavior and misinformation on the web. MIS2 is an interdisciplinary venue for leading researchers and practitioners from the areas of data mining, social network analysis, cybersecurity, communications, human-computer interaction, and natural language processing. The topics addressed in MIS2 are extremely timely and the research presented by refereed papers and invited keynote speakers will participants a full dose of emerging research.

ACM Reference Format:
Srijan Kumar, Meng Jiang, Taeho Jung, Roger Jie Luo, and Jure Leskovec. 2018. MIS2: Misinformation and Misbehavior Mining on the Web. In *Proceedings of WSDM 2018: The Eleventh ACM International Conference on Web Search and Data Mining (WSDM 2018).* ACM, New York, NY, USA, 2 pages. https://doi.org/10.1145/3159652.3160597

1 INTRODUCTION

Web is a space for all where people interact with each other and anyone can read, publish, and share content. While this has led to several groundbreaking innovations, it is also a breeding ground for misbehavior and misinformation [19, 26]. Anyone can reach thousands of people on the web instantaneously, say whatever they want, whenever they want, and yet be shielded by anonymity [4]. This has led to increase of misbehavior and misinformation, such as harrassment, scams, spread of propaganda, hate speech, fake reviews, and many more. Predicting misbehavior and misinformation online is strife with challenges primarily due to imbalance in data, lack of accurate labels, and deception on the part of perpetrators [36]. Study of this topic has become important among researchers across many subfields of the computational and social sciences, such as data mining, social network analysis, cybersecurity, communications, human-computer interaction, and natural language processing.

MIS2 is an interdisciplinary venue to present research on modeling, discovery, detection, and mitigation of misbehavior and misinformation on the web. The relevant platforms include social media, e-commerce platforms, collaborative and knowledge-based platforms (e.g., wikis and question-answer platforms like Quora, StackOverflow, etc.), computer mediated communications, both p2p (e.g., email, text chat, video chat, etc.) and broadcasting (e.g., notice boards, discussion boards, video broadcasts), online gaming platforms, online transactions platforms (e.g., credit card, cryptocurrency, etc.), crowdsourcing platforms, and more. MIS2 is home to novel research papers, demos, work-in-progress papers, and extended abstracts.

2 SCOPE

The areas of interest include:

- Misbehavior and threat on the web, such as trolling [2, 3, 27], bots [8, 35], fake followers and likes [18], coordinated attacks [1, 16, 17, 34], vandals [28], cyberbullying [6, 15], fake views [32], sockpuppets [11, 24, 38], crowdsourced manipulations [20, 21, 30], spam [12, 23, 37], propaganda and extremism [9, 31], hate speech [7, 39], and others.
- False information on the web: fake reviews [14, 25, 33, 40], fake news [5, 10, 13, 22, 41], fake articles [29], and others.

The topics of interest include:

- Empirical characterization of false information
- Measuring real world and online impact
- Deception in misinformation and misbehavior
- Reputation manipulation
- Multimodal data analysis for detection
- Measuring economic, ideological, and other rationale behind creation
- Rationale behind spread and success
- Targets or victims of misbehavior and misinformation
- Effect of echo chambers, personalization, confirmation bias, and other socio-psychological and technological phenomenon
- Detection methods using graphs, text, behavior, image, video, and audio analysis
- Adversarial analysis of misbehavior and misinformation
- Prevention and mitigation techniques, tools, and countermeasures

WSDM 2018, February 5–9, 2018, Marina Del Rey, CA, USA

ACM ISBN 978-1-4503-5581-0/18/02.
https://doi.org/10.1145/3159652.3160597

- Theoretical and/or empirical modeling of spread
- Visualizing spread of information
- Anonymity, security, and privacy aspects of data collection
- Usable security in misbehavior detection
- Ethics, privacy, fairness, and biases in current tools and techniques
- Case studies

ACKNOWLEDGMENTS

We would like to thank CreditX for sponsoring the best paper award. We are thankful to the speakers for their presentations and posters. We would like to acknowledge support from the following grants: NSF IIS-1149837, ARO MURI, ONR CEROSS, DARPA NGS2, and Stanford Data Science Initiative.

REFERENCES

[1] Alex Beutel, Wanhong Xu, Venkatesan Guruswami, Christopher Palow, and Christos Faloutsos. 2013. CopyCatch: stopping group attacks by spotting lockstep behavior in social networks. In *Proceedings of the 22rd International Conference on World Wide Web*. ACM.

[2] Justin Cheng, Michael Bernstein, Cristian Danescu-Niculescu-Mizil, and Jure Leskovec. 2017. Anyone can become a troll: Causes of trolling behavior in online discussions. *arXiv preprint arXiv:1702.01119* (2017).

[3] Justin Cheng, Cristian Danescu-Niculescu-Mizil, and Jure Leskovec. 2015. Antisocial Behavior in Online Discussion Communities.. In *Proceedings of the 9th International AAAI Conference on Web and Social Media*.

[4] Kimberly M Christopherson. 2007. The positive and negative implications of anonymity in Internet social interactions:âĂIJOn the Internet, Nobody Knows YouâĂŹre a DogâĂİ. *Computers in Human Behavior* 23, 6 (2007), 3038–3056.

[5] Niall J Conroy, Victoria L Rubin, and Yimin Chen. 2015. Automatic deception detection: Methods for finding fake news. *Proceedings of the Association for Information Science and Technology* 52, 1 (2015), 1–4.

[6] Maral Dadvar, Dolf Trieschnigg, Roeland Ordelman, and Franciska de Jong. 2013. Improving Cyberbullying Detection with User Context.. In *ECIR*. Springer, 693–696.

[7] Nemanja Djuric, Jing Zhou, Robin Morris, Mihajlo Grbovic, Vladan Radosavljevic, and Narayan Bhamidipati. 2015. Hate speech detection with comment embeddings. In *Proceedings of the 24th International Conference on World Wide Web*. ACM, 29–30.

[8] Emilio Ferrara, Onur Varol, Clayton Davis, Filippo Menczer, and Alessandro Flammini. 2016. The rise of social bots. *Commun. ACM* 59, 7 (2016), 96–104.

[9] Emilio Ferrara, Wen-Qiang Wang, Onur Varol, Alessandro Flammini, and Aram Galstyan. 2016. Predicting online extremism, content adopters, and interaction reciprocity. In *International Conference on Social Informatics*. Springer, 22–39.

[10] Adrien Friggeri, Lada A Adamic, Dean Eckles, and Justin Cheng. 2014. Rumor Cascades.. In *Proceedings of the 8th International AAAI Conference on Web and Social Media*.

[11] Neil Zhenqiang Gong, Mario Frank, and Prateek Mittal. 2014. Sybilbelief: A semi-supervised learning approach for structure-based sybil detection. *IEEE Transactions on Information Forensics and Security* 9, 6 (2014), 976–987.

[12] Thomas Green and Francesca Spezzano. 2017. Spam Users Identification in Wikipedia Via Editing Behavior.. In *ICWSM*. 532–535.

[13] Aditi Gupta, Hemank Lamba, Ponnurangam Kumaraguru, and Anupam Joshi. 2013. Faking sandy: characterizing and identifying fake images on twitter during hurricane sandy. In *Proceedings of the 22nd International Conference on World Wide Web*. ACM.

[14] Bryan Hooi, Hyun Ah Song, Alex Beutel, Neil Shah, Kijung Shin, and Christos Faloutsos. 2016. Fraudar: Bounding graph fraud in the face of camouflage. In *Proceedings of the 22nd ACM SIGKDD International Conference on Knowledge Discovery and Data Mining*. ACM.

[15] Homa Hosseinmardi, Amir Ghasemianlangroodi, Richard Han, Qin Lv, and Shivakant Mishra. 2014. Towards understanding cyberbullying behavior in a semi-anonymous social network. In *Advances in Social Networks Analysis and Mining (ASONAM), 2014 IEEE/ACM International Conference on*. IEEE, 244–252.

[16] Meng Jiang, Alex Beutel, Peng Cui, Bryan Hooi, Shiqiang Yang, and Christos Faloutsos. 2015. A general suspiciousness metric for dense blocks in multimodal data. In *Data Mining (ICDM), 2015 IEEE International Conference on*. IEEE, 781–786.

[17] Meng Jiang, Peng Cui, Alex Beutel, Christos Faloutsos, and Shiqiang Yang. 2014. CatchSync: catching synchronized behavior in large directed graphs. In *KDD*. ACM.

[18] Meng Jiang, Peng Cui, Alex Beutel, Christos Faloutsos, and Shiqiang Yang. 201 Detecting suspicious following behavior in multimillion-node social networ In *Proceedings of the 23rd International Conference on World Wide Web*. AC 305–306.

[19] Meng Jiang, Peng Cui, and Christos Faloutsos. 2016. Suspicious behavior dete tion: Current trends and future directions. *IEEE Intelligent Systems* 31, 1 (201 31–39.

[20] Parisa Kaghazgaran, James Caverlee, and Majid Alfifi. 2017. Behavioral Analys of Review Fraud: Linking Malicious Crowdsourcing to Amazon and Beyond. I *ICWSM*. 560–563.

[21] Parisa Kaghazgaran, James Caverlee, and Anna Squicciarini. 2018. Combatin Crowdsourced Review Manipulators: A Neighborhood-Based Approach. *Procee ings of the 11th ACM International Conference on Web Search and Data Minin* (2018).

[22] Jooyeon Kim, Behzad Tabibian, Alice Oh, Bernhard SchÃűlkopf, and Manu Gomez-Rodriguez. 2018. Leveraging the Crowd to Detect and Reduce the Sprea of Fake News and Misinformation. *Proceedings of the 11th ACM Internation Conference on Web Search and Data Mining* (2018).

[23] Vijay Krishnan and Rashmi Raj. 2006. Web spam detection with anti-trust ran In *AIRWeb*, Vol. 6. 37–40.

[24] Srijan Kumar, Justin Cheng, Jure Leskovec, and VS Subrahmanian. 2017. A army of me: Sockpuppets in online discussion communities. In *Proceedings of t 26th International Conference on World Wide Web*.

[25] Srijan Kumar, Bryan Hooi, Disha Makhija, Mohit Kumar, Christos Faloutsos, an VS Subrahamanian. 2018. REV2: Fraudulent User Prediction in Rating Platform *Proceedings of the 11th ACM International Conference on Web Search and Dat Mining* (2018).

[26] Srijan Kumar and Neil Shah. 2018. False information on web and social media: survey. *Social Media Analytics: Advances and Applications* (2018).

[27] Srijan Kumar, Francesca Spezzano, and VS Subrahmanian. 2014. Accuratel detecting trolls in slashdot zoo via decluttering. In *Advances in Social Network Analysis and Mining (ASONAM), 2014 IEEE/ACM International Conference o* IEEE, 188–195.

[28] Srijan Kumar, Francesca Spezzano, and VS Subrahmanian. 2015. Vews: wikipedia vandal early warning system. In *Proceedings of the 21th ACM SIGKD International Conference on Knowledge Discovery and Data Mining*. ACM.

[29] Srijan Kumar, Robert West, and Jure Leskovec. 2016. Disinformation on the we Impact, characteristics, and detection of wikipedia hoaxes. In *Proceedings of th 25th International Conference on World Wide Web*.

[30] Kyumin Lee, Prithivi Tamilarasan, and James Caverlee. 2013. Crowdturfers, Can paigns, and Social Media: Tracking and Revealing Crowdsourced Manipulatio of Social Media.. In *ICWSM*.

[31] Blake Andrew Phillip Miller. 2016. Automatic Detection of Comment Propagand in Chinese Media. *Available at SSRN* (2016).

[32] Neil Shah. 2017. FLOCK: Combating Astroturfing on Livestreaming Platform In *Proceedings of the 26th International Conference on World Wide Web*.

[33] Neil Shah, Alex Beutel, Bryan Hooi, Leman Akoglu, Stephan Gunnemann, Dish Makhija, Mohit Kumar, and Christos Faloutsos. 2016. EdgeCentric: Anomaly De tection in Edge-Attributed Networks. In *Proceedings of the 2016 IEEE Internationa Conference on Data Mining Workshops*.

[34] Neil Shah, Hemank Lamba, Alex Beutel, and Christos Faloutsos. 2017. The Man Faces of Link Fraud. In *Proceedings of the 2017 IEEE International Conference o Data Mining*.

[35] VS Subrahmanian, Amos Azaria, Skylar Durst, Vadim Kagan, Aram Galstyan Kristina Lerman, Linhong Zhu, Emilio Ferrara, Alessandro Flammini, and Filipp Menczer. 2016. The DARPA Twitter bot challenge. *IEEE Computer* 49, 6 (2016 38–46.

[36] VS Subrahmanian and Srijan Kumar. 2017. Predicting human behavior: The nex frontiers. *Science* 355, 6324 (2017), 489–489.

[37] Alex Hai Wang. 2010. Don't follow me: Spam detection in twitter. In *Securit and Cryptography (SECRYPT), Proceedings of the 2010 International Conference o* IEEE, 1–10.

[38] Gang Wang, Tristan Konolige, Christo Wilson, Xiao Wang, Haitao Zheng, and Ben Y Zhao. 2013. You Are How You Click: Clickstream Analysis for Sybi Detection.. In *USENIX Security Symposium*, Vol. 9. 1–008.

[39] Zeerak Waseem and Dirk Hovy. 2016. Hateful Symbols or Hateful People Predictive Features for Hate Speech Detection on Twitter.. In *SRW@ HLT-NAACL* 88–93.

[40] Yuanshun Yao, Bimal Viswanath, Jenna Cryan, Haitao Zheng, and Ben Zhao 2017. Automated Crowdturfing Attacks and Defenses in Online Review Systems In *Proceedings of the ACM Conference on Computer and Communications Security*.

[41] Arkaitz Zubiaga, Ahmet Aker, Kalina Bontcheva, Maria Liakata, and Rob Procter 2017. Detection and Resolution of Rumours in Social Media: A Survey. *arXi preprint arXiv:1704.00656* (2017).

Workshop on Two-sided Marketplace Optimization: Search, Pricing, Matching & Growth

Mihajlo Grbovic
Airbnb, Inc.
888 Brannan St
San Francisco, California 94103
mihajlo.grbovic@airbnb.com

Thanasis Noulas
Airbnb, Inc.
888 Brannan St
San Francisco, California 94103
thanasis.noulas@airbnb.com

ABSTRACT

The 1st International Workshop on Two-sided Marketplace Optimization: Search, Pricing, Matching & Growth (TSMO) will be held in Los Angeles, California, USA on February 9th, 2018, co-located with the 11th ACM International Conference on Web Search and Data Mining (WSDM). The main objective of the workshop is to address the challenges of two-sided marketplace optimization in web-scale settings. The workshop brings together interdisciplinary researchers in information retrieval, recommender systems, personalization, and related areas, to share, exchange, learn, and develop preliminary results, new concepts, ideas, principles, and methodologies on applying data mining technologies to marketplace optimization. We have constructed an exciting program papers and invited talks that will help us better understand the future of two-sided marketplaces

CCS CONCEPTS

• **Information systems** → *Web searching and information discovery*; *Web mining*; *Electronic commerce*; *Information retrieval*; • **Theory of computation** → *Computational pricing and auctions*; • **Computing methodologies** → *Machine learning*; • **Applied computing** → Forecasting;

KEYWORDS

Search Ranking; Smart Pricing; User Modeling; Personalization

ACM Reference format:
Mihajlo Grbovic and Thanasis Noulas. 2018. Workshop on Two-sided Marketplace Optimization: Search, Pricing, Matching & Growth. In *Proceedings of WSDM 2018: The Eleventh ACM International Conference on Web Search and Data Mining , Marina Del Rey, CA, USA, February 5–9, 2018 (WSDM 2018),* 2 pages.
https://doi.org/10.1145/3159652.3160593

ACM ISBN 978-1-4503-5581-0/18/02.
https://doi.org/10.1145/3159652.3160593

1 INTRODUCTION

In recent years two sided marketplaces have emerged as viable business models in many real world applications. In particular, we have moved from the social network paradigm to a network with two distinct types of participants representing supply and demand of a specific good. Examples industries include but are not limited to accommodation (Airbnb, Booking.com, HomeAway), video content (YouTube, Dailymotion), Ridesharing (Uber, Didi, Lyft), online shops (Etsy, Ebay), music (Soundcloud), app stores (Apple App Store, Google App Store) and job sites (LinkedIn).

The traditional research in most of these industries focused on satisfying the demand. OTAs would sell hotel accommodation, TV networks would broadcast their own content or taxi companies would own their own vehicle fleet. In modern examples like Airbnb, YouTube or Uber the platforms have customers on the supply side as well, and have to optimize their models taking into consideration host preferences, youtube producers and drivers.

2 OBJECTIVE

The objective of this workshop is to bring practitioners of two-sided marketplaces together and discuss the evolution of ranking, recommendation, matching and growth data mining to account for the dual nature of the problem.

3 TOPICS OF INTEREST

The TSMO workshop provides a forum for researchers from various areas to share information, challenges, and latest results from latest investigations into the diverse set of applications related to two-sided marketplaces. The topics of the workshop include, but are not limited to the following:

- Search in two-sided marketplaces
- Matching and Personalization in two-sided marketplaces
- Growth and Monetization for two-sided marketplaces
- Marketing Strategies
- Recommendation Systems
- Dynamic Pricing and Price Recommendations
- Fraud Detection
- Fake-content Detection
- Privacy-preserving
- Experience with deployed systems
- Learning to Rank
- Content Ranking in two-sided marketplaces
- User lifetime value modeling
- Churn prediction

4 ORGANIZERS

The TSMO workshop is organized by two researchers with several years of industry experience in the marketplace optimization field. The list of the organizers is presented below

- Mihajlo Grbovic (Airbnb Data Science Team, USA)
- Thanasis Noulas (Airbnb Data Science Team, USA)

5 WORKSHOP PROGRAM

The program will be presented in form of a full-day workshop, with paper presentation sessions and several invited talks from the leading researchers.

The list of confirmed speakers includes

- Bar Ifrach, Director of Data Science at Airbnb
- Liangjie Hong, Head of Data Science at Etsy
- Theofanis Karaletsos, Research Scientist Uber AI labs

ACKNOWLEDGEMENTS

Putting together TSMO 2018 was a team effort. We would like to thank the speakers and the authors for providing the content of this year's program. We are also very grateful to the members of the Program Committee, who worked diligently in reviewing papers and providing constructive feedback for the authors

GTA^3 2018: Workshop on Graph Techniques for Adversarial Activity Analytics

Summary Abstract

Jiejun Xu
HRL Laboratories, LLC
Malibu, California
jxu@hrl.com

Hanghang Tong
Arizona State University
Tempe, Arizona
hanghang.tong@asu.edu

Tsai-Ching Lu
HRL Laboratories, LLC
Malibu, California
tlu@hrl.com

Jingrui He
Arizona State University
Tempe, Arizona
jingrui.he@asu.edu

Nadya Bliss
Arizona State University
Tempe, Arizona
nadya.bliss@asu.edu

ABSTRACT

Networks are natural analytic tools in modeling adversarial activities (e.g., human trafficking, illicit drug production, terrorist financial transaction) using different intelligence data sources. However, such activities are often covert and embedded across multiple domains and contexts. They are generally not detectable and recognizable from the perspective of an isolated network, and only become apparent when multiple networks are analyzed in a joint manner. Thus, one of the main research topics in modeling adversarial activities is to develop effective techniques to align and fuse information from different networks into a unified representation for global analysis. Based on the combined network representation, an equally important research topic is on detecting and matching indicating patterns to recognize the underlining adversarial activities in the integrated network. Two key challenge problems involved in the modeling process include:

- Network alignment and merging: develop accurate and scalable methods for mapping of nodes across heterogeneous networks based on different associational and causal dependencies.
- Subgraph detection and matching: develop robust and efficient algorithms for richly attributed networks to support recognition of complex query patterns for networks.

The focus of this workshop is to gather together the researchers from all relevant fields to share their experience and opinions on graph mining techniques in the era of big data, with emphasis on two fundamental problems - "Connecting the dots" and "finding a needle in a haystack", in the context of graph-based adversarial activity analytics. A best paper will be selected and announced in our workshop based on the collective feedback from our reviewers.

This workshop (co-located with the 11th ACM Conference on Web Search and Data Mining) aims to bring together a cross-disciplinary audience of researchers from both academia and industry to share experience with techniques, resources and best practices, and to exchange perspectives and future directions. We expect the workshop to develop a community of interested researchers and facilitate their future collaborations.

Topics of Interest

- Data integration and alignment from multiple heterogeneous networks
- Novel algorithms for subgraph detection and matching in large networks
- Graph construction and modeling for different domains (e.g., financial fraud, human trafficking, DDoS attack)
- Complex anomaly (e.g., group anomaly) detection and interpretation
- Atypical behavior and rare event detection
- Limits of detectability and identifiability
- Evolution analysis and forecasting
- Game theoretic approach on anticipating opponent intents and actions
- Identification of novel datasets and/or evaluation metrics
- Multilayer and multiplex network analytics
- Clustering and ranking methods for composite networks
- Large-scaled link prediction and recommendation algorithms
- Community detection in big networks
- Information diffusion and influence maximization
- Interactive visualization for big graphs
- New methods and frontiers in spectral graph theory
- Analysis of network topologies (e.g., centrality and network motif analysis)
- Semi-supervised learning, Transductive inference, Active learning, and Transfer learning

ACM Reference Format:
Jiejun Xu, Hanghang Tong, Tsai-Ching Lu, Jingrui He, and Nadya Bliss. 2018. GTA^3 2018: Workshop on Graph Techniques for Adversarial Activity Analytics: Summary Abstract. In *WSDM 2018: WSDM 2018: The Eleventh ACM International Conference on Web Search and Data Mining , February 5–9, 2018, Marina Del Rey, CA, USA.* ACM, New York, NY, USA, Article 4, 1 page. https://doi.org/10.1145/3159652.3160595

WSDM 2018, February 5–9, 2018, Marina Del Rey, CA, USA

ACM ISBN 978-1-4503-5581-0/18/02.
https://doi.org/10.1145/3159652.3160595

IFUP: Workshop on Multi-dimensional Information Fusion for User Modeling and Personalization

Feida Zhu
School of Information Systems
Singapore Management University
fdzhu@smu.edu.sg

Yongfeng Zhang
Department of Computer Science
Rutgers University
zhangyf07@gmail.com

Neil Yorke-Smith
Delft University of Technology
American University of Beirut
nysmith@aub.edu.lb

Guibing Guo
Software College
Northeatern University
guogb@swc.neu.edu.cn

Xu Chen
School of Software
Tsinghua University
xu-ch14@mails.tsinghua.edu.cn

ABSTRACT

Recommendation system has became an important component in many real applications, ranging from e-commerce, music app to video-sharing site and on-line book store. The key of a successful recommendation system lies in the accurate user/item profiling. With the advent of web 2.0, quite a lot of multimodal information has been accumulated, which provides us with the opportunity to profile users in a more comprehensive manner. However, directly integrating multimodal information into recommendation system is not a trivial task, because they may be either homogenous or heterogeneous, which requires more advanced method for both fusion and alignment. This workshop aims to provide a platform for discussing the challenges and corresponding innovative approaches in fusing multi-dimensional information for user modeling and recommender systems. We hope more advanced technologies can be proposed or inspired, and also we hope that the direction of integrating different types of information can catch much more attention in both academic and industry.

KEYWORDS

Information Fusion; User Modeling; Multi-dimensional

ACM Reference Format:
Feida Zhu, Yongfeng Zhang, Neil Yorke-Smith, Guibing Guo, and Xu Chen. 2018. IFUP: Workshop on Multi-dimensional Information Fusion for User Modeling and Personalization. In *Proceedings of WSDM 2018: The Eleventh ACM International Conference on Web Search and Data Mining (WSDM 2018).* ACM, New York, NY, USA, 2 pages. https://doi.org/10.1145/3159652.3160592

1 INTRODUCTION

Real-world systems accumulate large-scale and various kinds of multimodal information rapidly, including but not limited to text, image, video, audio, social relations, meta data, etc. Such information has been incorporated in many recommendation models and systems to promote the performance and user experience, giving rise to some of the recent and/or classical topics in recommende[r] system, such as review-based recommendation, image-based recom[-]mendation, explainable recommendation, deep learning for recom[-]mendation, POI recommendation, video/music recommendatio[n] and many others.

Integrating multimodal side information is not a trivial task, be[-]cause information may be either homogeneous or heterogeneous which requires more advanced method for information fusion an[d] alignment. Besides, different information may play distinct roles fo[r] different domains, users, and tasks, and the availability of new infor[-]mation source may even lead to completely new recommendatio[n] research tasks. As a result, it needs significant efforts from both th[e] research community and industry to promote the recommendatio[n] system research and application in face of the various informatio[n] sources.

Based on this motivation, this workshop aims to provide a dedi[-]cated forum for discussing open problems, challenges and innova[-]tive research approaches in fusing multi-dimensional information for user modeling and recommender systems. The major goal of this workshop is to promote advanced recommendation solutions that can be easily and readily deployed to meet industrial demands for personalized recommendations. By this workshop, we hope more advanced technologies for user modeling can be proposed or inspired, and we also hope that the direction of integrating different types of information can catch much more attention both in academic and industry.

2 WORKSHOP RELEVANCE

The timing of WSDM 2018 is perfect for hosting the workshop with a concentration on recommendation system, with no potential conflict from other major conferences in this community. The location is also a good match for its convenience to attract researchers from over the world. This recommender system related workshop is also very much a good fit for the WSDM community, for its broad interest to researchers both from the IR community and the web mining community. Besides, multi-modal data analysis has recently been a very hot and important research topic for not only the recommender system researchers, but also researchers from other communities regarding intelligent information processing. As a result, we can well expect that a large amount of the WSDM participants will be interested in attending the workshop this year.

WSDM 2018, February 5–9, 2018, Marina Del Rey, CA, USA

ACM ISBN 978-1-4503-5581-0/18/02.
https://doi.org/10.1145/3159652.3160592

3 TARGET AUDIENCE

The target audience of this workshop includes but not limited to: Academic researchers (or people from industrial) who are interested in the fields related to recommendation system, information fusion or user behavior analysis. We plan this workshop as a half-day event, and it will consist of an invited talk and a series of presentations. The number of attendees is expected to be around 30.

4 THEME AND TOPICS

Papers should elaborate on theories and methods of information fusion for user modeling and personalization. The interesting topics include: (1) user modeling and user preference inference; (2) general recommender systems; (3) recommendation methods to fuse multi-dimensional information and (4) recommendation issues to be addressed. Topics of interest include but are not limited to:

- Text-based Recommendation: Sentiment Analysis for Recommendation, Topic Modeling Approaches to Recommendation, Deep Text Modeling for Recommendation, Natural Language Processing for Recommendation, Question Answering for Recommendation.

- Image-based Recommendation: Deep/Shallow Image Modeling for Recommendation, Image Recommendation in Social Media, Image-based Point of Interest Recommendation, Image Generation and Recommendation.

- Video/Audio-based Recommendation: Video Recommendation, Music Recommendation, Speech Proceeding for Recommendation.

- Social Recommendation: Heterogeneous Network Analysis for Recommendation, Friend Recommendation, Personalized News Feeding, Multimedia Recommendation in Social Networks.

- Multiple Information Fusion for Recommendation: Heterogeneous Information Analysis for Recommendation, Structured and Unstructured Data Analysis for Recommendation.

- Explainable Recommendation: Text-based Explainable Recommendation, Image-based Explainable Recommendation, Knowledge-base for Explainable Recommendation, Social Explainable Recommendation, Explainable Recommendation in Novel Applications.

- User Modeling with Multimodal Information: User modeling with heterogeneous data, User modeling based on social media, User modeling based on big data analytics, Preference inference based on explicit/implicit feedback.

- Exploiting Homogeneous/Heterogeneous Information: Multi-Criteria Ratings based Recommender Systems, Hierarchical Data Modeling for Item Recommendation, Integrating both Explicit and Implicit Feedback for Recommendations, Cross-domain Feedback Exploitation for recommendations, Multi-view Machine Learning for Recommendation.

- Addressing Special Issues in Recommender Systems: Resolving Cold-start and Data Sparsity with Auxiliary Information, Enhancing Recommendation Novelty and Explainability, Scalability when Integrating Multiple kinds of Auxiliary Information, Toolkits to Improve the Reproducibility of Recommendation Models.

- New Dataset and Applications: New Dataset Papers for Recommender Systems, New Recommendation Applications in Practice.

5 PARTICIPATION AND SELECTION PROCESS

For the authors of accepted papers, at least one of the paper authors must attend and present their paper at the workshop to ensure the paper appearance in the proceedings of the workshop. Papers will be subject to double blind peer review in which the reviewers do not know the author's identity. In order to make blind reviewing possible, authors must omit their names and affiliations from the paper. Selection criteria include originality of ideas, correctness, clarity, significance of results and quality of presentation. The workshop will have a two-tier program committee, with the program chairs and program committee members. The decision of the Program Committee will be final and cannot be appealed. All workshop submissions must be formatted according to ACM SIG Proceedings template, and the submissions can be made in either long (max 8 pages) or short (max 4 pages) format. Authors should submit original papers in PDF format through the Easychair system

6 ORGANISING/PROGRAM COMMITTEE

The organizers have a very broad background in the field of recommendation system and data mining, which will help to attract top researchers in this area and expand the influence of this workshop.

The following members form the program committee of the workshop:

- Paolo Cremonesi, Politecnico di Milano
- Xiangnan He, National University of Singapore
- Bin Li, NICTA, Australia
- Xin Liu, Institute for Infocomm Research, Singapore
- Weike Pan, Shenzhen University, China
- Alan Said, CWI
- Yue Shi, Yahoo
- Yao Wu, Twitter
- Fuzheng Zhang, Microsoft Research Asia
- Yong Zheng, DePaul University, USA

ACKNOWLEDGMENT

This work is supported by the National Natural Science Foundation for Young Scientists of China under Grant No. 61702084.

Author Index

www.ingramcontent.com/pod-product-compliance
Lightning Source LLC
LaVergne TN
LVHW080103011026
849160LV00013B/1024
* 9 7 8 1 4 5 0 3 5 8 6 9 9 *